Mark Wilson

Some say the real secrets of magic should never be revealed...

But I believe, if you are sincerely interested, you should have the finest, clearest instruction possible.

Over the years we have presented hundreds of television and stage shows. Now it's time to pass on what we have learned to you. That's why we created the **Mark Wilson Video Course in Magic.** I'll teach you hundreds of tricks and illusions, everything from simple close-up to the latest creations in the world of magic. Learning is easy and fast, just watch the video tapes.

Want to perform illusions?
If you like illusions, you should have the **Mark Wilson on Illusions** videos. Mark Wilson and the beautiful Nani Darnell teach you how to perform powerful illusions just as they did on television.

Want to see some great magic shows?

The Magic Land of Allakazam was the first network television magic series. Each half hour show features fast-paced openings, audience participation comedy magic, sleight of hand and at least one major illusion.

The Magic Circus television specials were the first prime-time full-color modern day magic shows. Mark, Nani and a glamorous cast perform 33 lavishly-produced illusions and many other powerful magic effects. Guest stars are the world's greatest magicians, Carl Ballantine, Shimada, Jay Marshall and Lefty and the Professor Dai Vernon.

We have more: **The Magic of Mark Wilson, The Magic of China,** and many others.

Need some magic props?
We also have a fine selection of **professional magic props**, as well as **classic memorabilia.**

To learn more and enter the wonderful World of Magic go to:
www.markwilsonmagic.com

**To order call: (800) 367-8749
e-mail: mark@markwilsonmagic.com
P.O. Box 801839 Santa Clarita, CA 91380**

**Web site design by Presto Productions
www.prestoproductions.com**

MARK WILSON'S COMPLETE COURSE IN MAGIC

ACKNOWLEDGMENTS

The contents of this course do not represent the efforts of only two, three, or a dozen individuals, but instead, of all those magicians of the past and the present who have labored so diligently to create, perfect, and present the art of magic.

Just as a stalagmite, buried unseen in a dark cave, builds from tiny drops into a towering structure, so has our art increased through the centuries, shrouded in a like darkness of secrecy, which remains a prerequisite to its growth.

With this course, you will join the ranks of those who have learned these inner secrets—and you must acknowledge and respect those whose contributions we enjoy. *Acknowledge* by being aware of the countless hours of study, work, and practice that have been expended by the magicians of the past to create our art. *Respect* the magicians of today, by never revealing any of these hard-earned secrets.

This, then, is the grateful acknowledgment of this course, *to the Magicians of all times and places*, for their countless contributions to the art of magic.
—M.W.

CREDITS

Course Coordinator . . . Larry Anderson
Assistant Course Coordinator . . . Don Wayne
Art Director . . . Julia Laughlin
Assistant Art Director . . . Manny Katz
Photographers . . . Terry S. Urie, Michael Wilson
Graphic Production . . . Susan Kennedy, Kathryn Capp
Digital Photography . . . Lincoln Bond

Contributing Writers (in alphabetical order)
Larry Anderson
Fr. Jim Blantz
Earl Nelson
Tom O'Lenick
Peter Pit
David Roth
Brick Tilley
Alan Wakeling

Special Contributing Author . . . U.F. Grant

Copyright © 1975, 1981, 1988, 2002 by Mark Wilson
Printed in the United States of America.

9   8   7   6   5   4   3   2   1

Digit on the right indicates the number of this printing

Library of Congress Control Number: 2002093018
ISBN 0-7624-1455-3 for paperback
ISBN 0-7624-1532-0 for hardcover
Front jacket photograph by Weaver Lilly
Revised edition edited by Michael Washburn

Original edition published by Ottenheimer Publishers, Inc. for Courage Books, an imprint of Running Press Book Publishers, 125 South Twenty-second Street, Philadelphia, Pennsylvania 19103

This book can be ordered by mail from the publisher.
But try your bookstore first!

Visit us on the web!
www.runningpress.com

CONTENTS

Dedication

Gratefully dedicated to two lovely and loving individuals without whom this would never have been written.My beautiful mother, Teta, for initially obvious reasons, but also for her continuing inspiration, and . . . My beautiful wife, Nani, who has given up so much . . . so that another prop could be purchased . . . another illusion built . . . another show successfully presented . . . another step taken in a journey toward some luminous, unknown goal . . . . . . and in the process has managed to raise our two fine sons, Mike and Greg, and make it all worthwhile.

If my magic were but real . . .

INTRODUCTION

Welcome to the wonderful world of magic! In the following pages I sincerely believe you will find the best illustrated, most easily understood, most completely developed method ever produced for learning the Art of Magic. All of the material was carefully selected, then written, rewritten, checked, and rewritten again. Over 50,000 photographs were shot—from these over 2,000 of the best were selected and then rendered as the line drawings which illustrate every move in the course. We have added a new section, "Reputation Makers," and sections on how best to use the magic you will learn in the course.

As you will see, most of the tricks have been divided into the following sections:

EFFECT—This is what the spectator sees—the mystery—the miracle—as performed by you, the magician.

SECRET AND PREPARATION—Describes the props that you will need, and the secret of how they work. Most of the items needed can be found around the house.

METHOD—This is the actual performance, explaining how you present the trick to the audience.

COMMENTS AND SUGGESTIONS—These are extra tips, suggestions, and ideas that will help you make each trick even more baffling and entertaining.

As you read and learn these great secrets, please remember and follow these four important rules:

(1) Never explain how a trick is done. If the audience knows the secret, then the mystery, the glamour, and the entertainment of the magic are lost.

(2) Never explain what you are going to do ahead of time. If the audience doesn't know what's going to happen, they won't know what to look for in advance and are much more likely to be baffled.

(3) Never repeat a trick for the same spectators. Once an audience has seen a trick performed, they have a much greater chance of "catching on."

(4) The most important rule of all: Always practice each trick before you present it.

Read the instructions. Practice with the props. When you can perform the effect smoothly and without hesitation, you are ready!

With the closely guarded secrets you will learn in this course, you can entertain your friends or a theater full of people, so there's an important point I must make. As a professional magician, I have promised never to reveal the inner secrets of magic except to those who are sincerely interested in learning our art. Before I open the door to these great mysteries for you, you must give me your word that, to the best of your ability, you will never reveal the secrets you learn to anyone.

You are not signing a legal document. It's a matter of honor and respect for the magicians who have gone before us. Maintaining these secrets is how we preserve the wonder and mystery of the art of magic, of which you will become a part.

Magic has taken my wife Nani and me around the world and helped us make friends everywhere. Now, with the complete course, you have taken the first steps on the road to the wonderful world of magic. With your pledge not to reveal these powerful secrets, I'm delighted to show you the way.

Happy Magic!

Mark Wilson

—Mark Wilson

A BRIEF BIOGRAPHY

Mark Wilson is not only a world-famous magician; he's also a producer, world traveler, teacher, author, businessman, creator of new approaches to sales and marketing, and the creative force behind an impressive display of television and stage attractions. Perhaps he's best known for his television appearances. *TV Guide* called him "the world's most televised magician," and it's easy to see why.

When James Mark Wilson was eight years old, he watched a magician perform and resolved then and there that the mystic art would be his own life calling. That ambition was furthered much sooner than he anticipated. Five years later, when he was a high school student in Dallas, Texas, where his family had settled, he took a part-time job at a magic shop called Douglas Magic Land and became the magic demonstrator.

A. Mark Wilson, fifteen years old and already an accomplished sleight-of-hand performer.

Billing himself as Mark Wilson, he gave his first professional show at the age of thirteen before a Rotary Club for a modest fee of five dollars, confident that such engagements would increase in number and financial return. Gone were the golden days of vaudeville and the full evening magic shows that heralded such names as Blackstone, Thurston, Houdini, and Kellar, playing theaters from coast to coast and even embarking on world tours.

With a definite goal in mind, Mark enrolled in Southern Methodist University's School of Business Administration to major in advertising and marketing. He was positive that he could use magic as a means of selling products and services as well as entertainment, combining his knowledge of the art with his business training. That was proven when Mark linked the old art of magic with the newest form of communication, television.

After graduating from S.M.U, Wilson met beautiful Nani

B. A twenty-year-old Mark, busy working his way through Southern Methodist University in Dallas, Texas.

C. In 1953, Mark won his first award—Most Outstanding Magician—at the Texas Association of Magicians Convention.

Darnell Arends, then a stewardess for American Airlines, who soon became his wife. With Nani's help, he was able to create, sell and present his first TV magic series, *Time For Magic,* sponsored by Dr. Pepper. The show debuted in February 1954 on WFAA-TV. It soon became the highest rated daytime show in Dallas.

Realizing, in 1958, that greater success could only be found with the major networks, Wilson began his efforts to sell the show as a network series. Success didn't come easily and he spent two years traveling around the country talking to every major advertising agency, kid-show sponsor and network executive he could corner.

After many months of meetings, phone calls, letters and presentations, sleepless nights and disheartening rejections, he received a call from the Kellogg Cereal Company who wanted to fully sponsor the show as part of the CBS Saturday morning lineup. Mark and Nani and their then six-year old son Mike left Dallas for Los Angeles to begin

production of *The Magic Land of Allakazam,* America's first network magic television series. The series began October 1, 1960 and aired for two years on the CBS network before being sold to the ABC network, where it ran for another three years. *Allakazam* was the first series ever aired on U.S. network television devoted exclusively to magic.

The Magic Land of Allakazam also set the standard for all future magic shows on television. Wilson always did his magic in front of a live audience, never used trick photography, and never allowed the camera to cut away during a trick, all to assure the home audience that magic was not accomplished through camera trickery … principles still used today on all major television magic shows.

In the 1970s, Mark Wilson produced and starred in six one-hour "Magic Circus" television specials, which were syndicated nationally by the Pillsbury Company. Later, in the 80s, he was host of *The Magic of Mark Wilson,* a half-hour, syndicated series co-starring wife Nani and the Wilsons' second son, 12-year-old Greg.

And when television and movie producers want magic, they know that Mark Wilson is the man to ask for. Once Mark and his creative staff have developed an appropriate concept, he turns to his vast warehouse, which houses the largest single collection of illusions (large magic props) under one roof in the entire world. In addition to his many "on camera" appearances, Mark has also often acted as magical creative consultant for many TV series and specials for all

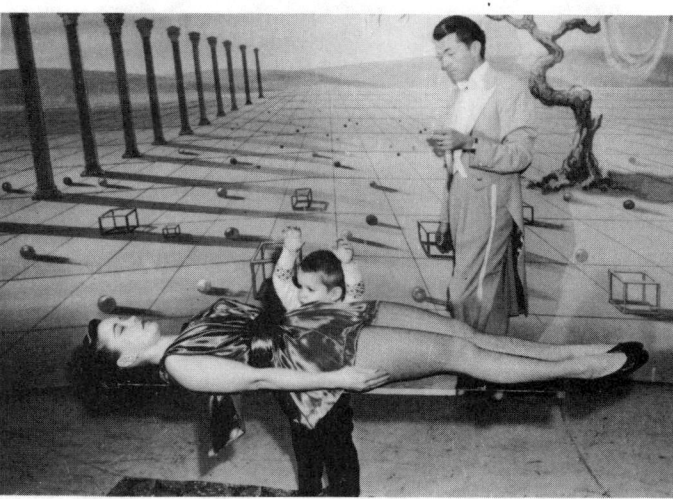

B

A

A. *Time for Magic,* Mark and Nani's first television series, made its debut in February, 1954.

B. A three-year-old Mike Wilson performs his first illusion.

C. Nani Darnell Wilson.

D. Mike, at four, picks up a few pointers from Dad.

C

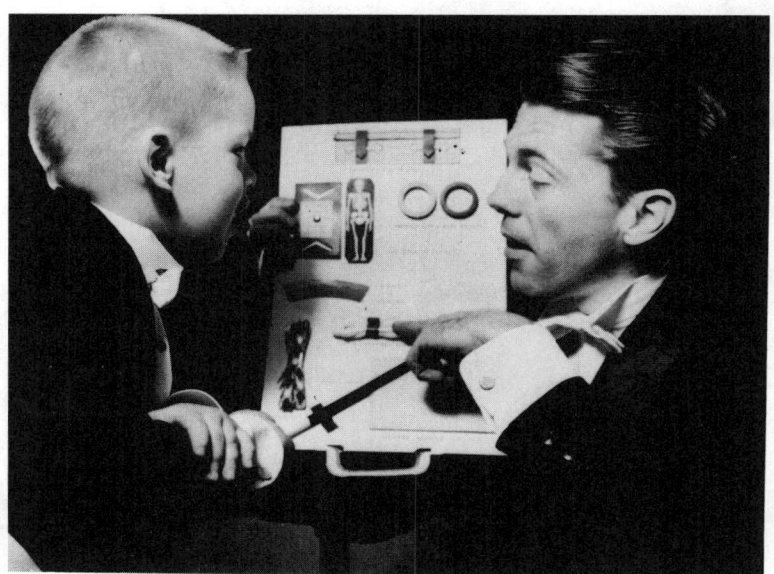

D

three television networks as well as most of the major motion picture studios.

Of particular note is *The Magician* television series for which Wilson provided all of the elaborate magic props, supplied story lines and script ideas and taught star Bill Bixby all of the magic for his role.

Mark has also instructed Hollywood's top stars in the performance of magic, working with such luminaries as Cary Grant, Tony Curtis, Peter Falk, Dick Van Dyke, John Denver,

Jackie Gleason, Cher, Johnny Carson, and Burt Reynolds.

In addition to his television appearances, Mark has toured extensively, producing and presenting magic shows throughout the world. In 1980, Mark Wilson received one of the greatest honors ever given to any performer when he was invited by the government of the People's Republic of China to be the first Western entertainer to perform in that awakening country. It was a landmark event when Mark and Nani Wilson, along with a company of 20 people, a television production crew, and over two and a half tons of props, performed throughout China.

For the Chinese people this was their first opportunity ever to see an American performance, since no Western performers had appeared in mainland China in the 32-year history of the People's Republic of China. They called him the "Magical Marco Polo," and in the packed theaters where they appeared, Mark and Nani introduced the Chinese people not only to Western magic, but also to Western dance,

A

B

A. Greg Wilson enjoys performing with Mom and Dad.

B. Cary Grant presents the Magician of the Year award.

C. The *Magic Circus* television specials were syndicated throughout the world.

D. *The Magic Land of Allakazam* was the first national magic show television series.

E. *Allakazam!* Rebo (Bev Bergeron), Mark, and Nani.

C

D

E

scenery, costuming, pacing, and showmanship.

So unique was this event that *Time* magazine carried both an article and photo coverage of Mark's advance visit to Beijing. China Central Television videotaped the show and aired it nationwide, another first for a Western performer. The government estimated that 200 million Chinese viewed *The Magic of Mark Wilson* television special, and the show has been rerun throughout China many times.

In addition, Mark reached out to the Chinese people by performing on location, another historic first. Mark entertained at agricultural communes and elementary schools, on trains, among workers tilling the fields, at the Children's Palace in Shanghai, in the Forbidden City and Tien An Mien Square in Beijing, in the courtyard of the Mausoleum of Sun Yat Sen in Nanking, and even on the ancient Great Wall. The tour produced three television specials, *The Magic of China* and *The Children of China,* and *The Adventures of a Young Magician* which aired on the CBS network and featured Greg Wilson co-starring with Bill Bixby.

Mark Wilson's work in China made him a celebrity there and, through the airing of his television series and specials in many countries, his fame has spread throughout the world. In 1983, he toured Southeast Asia, including Malaysia, Bangkok, Singapore, and Hong Kong, appearing in large theaters and giant arenas with an even larger cast and ten thousand pounds of equipment.

Mark Wilson authored *The Complete Course in Magic,* the highly-acclaimed volume which has been translated into Italian, French, Chinese and Russian. With more than three quarters of a million copies in print, it is the most popular book of magic instruction ever written.

Wilson has created and produced custom-designed magic productions for some of world's finest theme parks, world's fairs, and expositions, including: The Hall of Magic Pavilion at the New York World's Fair; ATT's Magic of the Telephone Pavilion at the Hemisfair; Disneyland; Disney World; Legoland; and all of the Busch Gardens Six Flags, and Kings Entertainment Parks.

Wilson's Magical Attractions are unique devices designed to attract, entertain and deliver commercial impact at trade shows. They include The Amazing Hand Machine, Man From Mars, Half Humanoid, Miniature Girl, Robot Girl, Miraculous Materializer, and Wilson's copyrighted Cinillusion©, which is the combination of a projected image of film or video, live action performers on stage and magic. Wilson has been issued five U.S. patents for these and other magical devices.

Mark Wilson and Nani Darnell's first son, Michael, born in 1954, graduated from the University of California, Berkeley with a Bachelor of Arts degree in 1977. In 1980, Michael was Road Show Manager for Mark Wilson's history-making tour of China, and became so fascinated by the Orient, he enrolled as a Chinese Language and International Business major in the graduate school of the University of Illinois, where he received the coveted Master of Business Administration degree. While studying for his degree, Michael attended the prestigious Peking University, living in Beijing for a year. Michael Wilson speaks fluent Mandarin, the official language of China, and now heads his own company, bringing international performers to the U.S. and

A

B

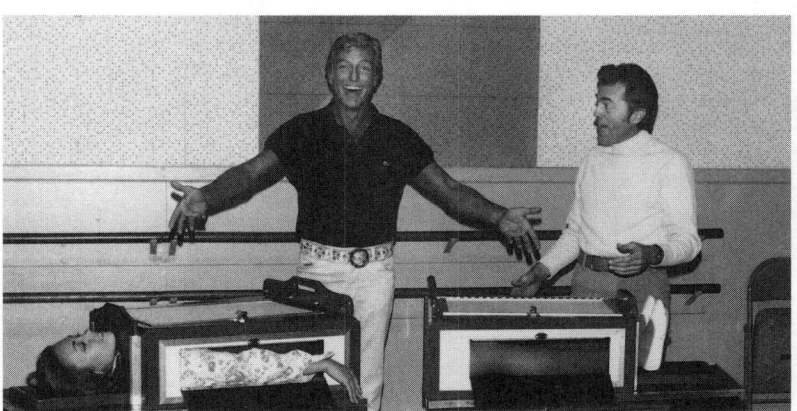

C

A. With Bill Bixby on "The Magician" set at Paramount Studios.

B. A giant billboard announces the appearance of the great American Magic Show in Bangkok.

C. Rehearsing with Dick Van Dyke.

booking U.S. entertainers overseas.

The Wilsons' younger son, Greg, was born in 1965, and he developed such an interest in magic that he became a skilled magician by the time he was eight years old, the very age at which his father, Mark, had first witnessed a magic show. In the early 1980s, Greg co-starred with his father and mother in *The Magic of Mark Wilson* series, which has delighted and baffled television viewers in many countries throughout the world. Greg is now an internationally recognized magician and illusionist carrying on the Wilson name.

In 1961, Mark Wilson brought a young college student, Johnny Gaughan, to Hollywood from Dallas where he had worked for Wilson. As John's great talent in design and woodworking became apparent, Mark made him supervisor of the Wilson workshop. John Gaughan now heads his own organization and is recognized as the leading expert in illusion design. John has built or supervised construction of almost all of the hundreds of illusions in Mark's warehouses, as well as for many other prominent magicians throughout the world.

Alan Wakeling, well known as a performing magician, joined Mark Wilson Productions in 1968 as Creative Director. Wilson credits Wakeling with the creation of many of his most effective and baffling magical presentations, including the Spiker, Excalibur, and Aquarian Illusions. After twenty-five years, Alan retired from Mark's company to pursue other endeavors including the building and restoring of exquisite automata.

Mark Wilson has become one of the world's most honored magicians. He is President Emeritus and former Chairman of the Board of the Academy of Magical Arts at the Magic Castle in Hollywood. Mark and Nani have received awards from major magic organizations throughout the world, including the Magician's Hall of Fame from the Society of American Magicians and Super Stars of Magic from the International Brotherhood of Magicians. Wilson was the first magician ever to receive two of the prestigious Magician of the Year awards from the Academy of Magical Arts, the magician's equivalent of winning two Oscars, and the Academy's top award, the Masters Fellowship. The readers of *Magic* magazine, America's leading independent publication for magicians, voted Mark Wilson one of the "Ten Most Influential Magicians of the 20th Century."

The eight-year-old boy who watched his first magic show with wide-eyed wonder has become the most well-known performer in the entire history of the ancient art of magic. But Wilson's world is not only one of magic, it encompasses the realm of producer, world traveler, teacher, author, businessman, creator of new approaches to sales and marketing, and the creative force behind a wide array of amusement park and stage attractions.

For a couple as diversified and talented as Mark Wilson and Nani Darnell Wilson, the greatest trick of all is finding the time to do everything.

A. Mark and his cast perform Robert Harbin's famous Zig Zag illusion on the Great Wall.

B. The "Magic Exchange." Magicians traveled from throughout China to exchange magic secerts with the magician from the west.

C. A Chinese boy is delighted by Mark's magic.

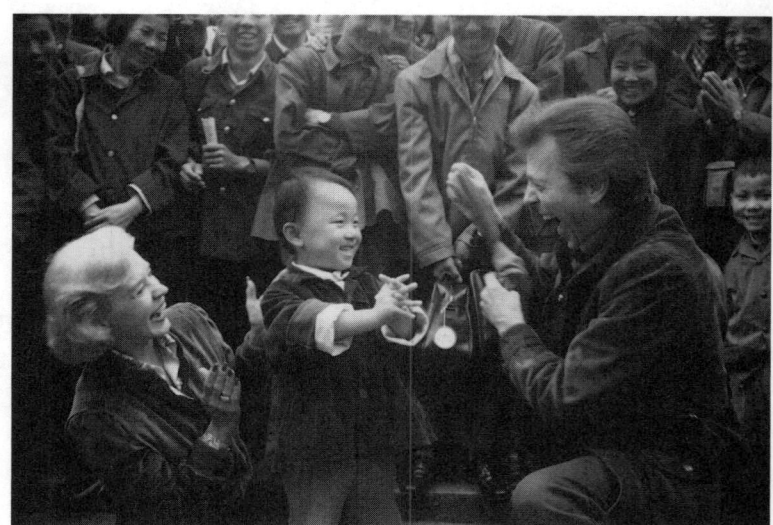

WALTER GIBSON (1897-1985): CO-AUTHOR

Walter Gibson was one of magic's most prolific journalists. As a young man, while working for the *Philadelphia Ledger*, he was commissioned to do a syndicated series of simple tricks, puzzles, and games. These caught the attention of Howard Thurston, who was then America's leading magician, and he engaged Gibson to prepare special booklets on magic to be sold at the Thurston show. Next, Gibson was working for Thurston on magical articles that were sold to popular magazines such as *The Saturday Evening Post* and *Boys' Life*.

Impressed with what he saw, Harry Houdini called on Gibson to prepare a series of three books to be published under Houdini's name. Only one had been completed at the time of Houdini's unfortunate death in 1926, but a few years later, the Houdini estate provided Gibson with all of Houdini's unpublished notes on magical methods. From those Gibson prepared two books under his own name—*Houdini's Escapes* and *Houdini's Magic*, which have become classics in the field.

Harry Blackstone, who had been one of Gibson's earliest magical friends and inspirations, contracted Gibson to write two books for him. Joseph Dunninger had Gibson pen books for him as well. Added to that, Gibson wrote innumerable magic books under his own name, and edited several different magic magazines throughout the course of his life.

Walter Gibson is probably best known as the creator of the character The Shadow, a hugely popular fictional crime fighter. Under the pen name Maxwell Grant, Gibson turned out 1,680,000 words of fiction during the year from March 1, 1932, to March 1, 1933, an all-time record for a year's wordage devoted to a single mystery character.

In 1966, a much younger mystifier was fast establishing himself as a master magician of the future. His name was Mark Wilson, and it was inevitable that he should later meet with Walter Gibson to discuss the shaping of magic in the years to come. When they did meet, their prime object of consideration was the comprehensive magic course that Mark Wilson was planning. They agreed that by combining the underlying principles of the past with the vast array of present methods currently available, future effects could be developed on a grand and lavish scale. Since then, they have cooperated to make the projected course the reality that it is today.

Walter Gibson's vast, highly respected literary output represents an immeasurable contribution to the art of magic.

U.F. "GEN." GRANT (1901-1978): CREATOR OF MAGIC

There is probably no other magician who has invented, devised, and improved more magic effects than U.F. "Gen." Grant. Practically every magician has performed at least a few (and often many) of Gen.'s creations. Certainly every modern magic catalog introduces some of Grant's remarkably marketable effects. Most assuredly this course owes a large debt to his fertile mind. As you progress in your knowledge of the principles of magic and their implementation, your respect and admiration will grow for this true master of magical invention—Mr. U.F. "Gen." Grant.

LARRY ANDERSON: COURSE COORDINATOR

By "magical" standards, Larry Anderson has attained a degree of pro in the art of magic, highly regarded by his peers. Larry first came to Wilson's attention at the age of nineteen, while still at the university in Minnesota. Mark required assistance with a large illusion show in the Twin Cities, and Larry's knowledge of magic, bearing, and hard work made him a stand out. Wilson was so pleased with his contribution, he flew Larry to California to be a full-time associate in his organization.

For this course, Larry, with the assistance of Don Wayne, coordinated the photography and artwork, and made valuable contributions in creative writing and rewriting, all essential to the result. Larry is now pursuing an acting and directing career, but still finds time to study, practice, and enjoy his first real love—magic.

HOW TO ADD MAGIC TO YOUR LIFE

I created the Complete Course in Magic because I believe that learning and performing really good magic can make your entire life better, just as it did mine. In the Course, you will find some of the most closely guarded secrets of the art of magic. In many ways, this book is similar to discovering a legendary volume of magical spells. Each trick is like an ancient incantation that will help you achieve some long wished for goal. (Watch out Harry Potter, here you come!)

Let me tell you a few of the things magic has done for me. As a youngster in school, I was shy … smaller than the other boys my age … not particularly good at any sport. Nobody hated me, but nobody seemed to like me very much either. I discovered I was not lucky enough to be inherently talented and certainly I was not an athlete. I was more of an introvert than a party animal, not particularly strong, and not as tall or well built as some of the other guys in my class. When they were picking a team for a ball game, I was not the first one chosen. I was all right scholastically, but my social life was lacking.

Then I saw a magic show. I was fascinated. I got books from the library. I studied everything I could find. Soon, I could do some simple tricks. I did some magic for a few kids at a class party … everybody gathered around … they liked my magic. More importantly, they liked me! The girls, as well as the guys, all seemed to like me more. I never expected this. The "magic" was working for me!

Then I figured out why it worked for me, and why it will work for you, too. When you show someone a really good magic trick, their first reaction is one of surprise and wonder …"How did you do that?"… followed by admiration and respect for you, the magician, "That was really good. Can you do something else?"

I began to be recognized as a magician. I began to stand out from the crowd. My confidence and feeling of self worth increased. I began to overcome my shyness. I was better able to deal with people. I became more successful in everything I did.

My life seemed to change, not immediately, but over time, as more people discovered what I could do. By the time I enrolled at Southern Methodist University, whenever I was invited to a party, I always had some magic in my pockets. I got invitations to a lot of parties. In fact, I was invited to so many parties, I couldn't attend them all.

Then I said to myself, "Wait a minute. They ask me to all those parties because I am a terrific guy. I don't need that "magic" anymore. They like me for who I am, not for my magic!" So, when I was beginning my sophomore year at the university, I took the tricks out of my pockets and stopped doing any magic at parties. I just went as myself. I didn't need that "magic!"

Sure enough, it worked! But not the way I thought it would. It worked in reverse. After a while, I was not invited to many parties. Then the invitations dwindled even more. That was not what I had expected. I had learned my lesson.

I put the magic back in my pockets. I did tricks for anyone who would watch. Sure enough, everything turned around. I was "popular" again. I was performing magic shows to help pay my way through college. I was asked to be the Master of Ceremonies for the annual homecoming show. My fraternity brothers elected me president of our chapter.

When I became a senior, in an attempt to gain more prestige for my fraternity, I ran for head cheerleader in the annual school election. I had never been any kind of cheerleader. I had no experience in leading thousands of people in "coordinated yelling." My opponent had a good track record as a cheerleader. I figured, "Okay, I won't win, but I will get some publicity for the fraternity." When the election was held, I won by the largest majority of votes of anyone running for any office that year.

The point of all this is, I'm sure none of these life shaping events would have ever happened if my fraternity brothers, the faculty members who produced that homecoming show, and my fellow students who voted for me in the election, had not known who I was. It wasn't, "Mark? Oh yeah, he's the short guy in my statistics class, I think." It was more like, "Mark Wilson. I remember him doing some magic at our sorority party last week. He might be a good head cheerleader. Maybe he could make the other football team disappear." … or whatever.

So, you see, it wasn't me, my athletic ability or my "wonderful" personality that gave me that recognition. It was because those people remembered who I was. And that was because of the magic.

I'm a lot older now. I have kept the magic in my pockets. I also have magic in my house, my office, and my warehouse. I have never left magic out of my life again. That's what magic did for me, and it will do the same for you.

Study this course, practice and rehearse the tricks, then try them on your friends. You will soon be recognized as a magician. Magicians make the impossible happen. There aren't many people who can make that claim. You will become a "special person" to your friends and to everyone you meet.

It really does happen. I've seen it hundreds of times. You will become more popular, your confidence will grow, your feelings of self-worth will increase. The magic will work for you. Here are a few of the many ways you can put the power of magic to work for you.

THE BENEFITS OF LEARNING MAGIC

You can meet people and make new friends. Your magic can help you "break the ice" and make new friends on a plane, in a restaurant, at the beach, just about anywhere. If there is someone you want to meet, perhaps he or she is across the room at any gathering, waiting near you in a line, or seated at another table in a restaurant, your magic will pave the way. Singles find it's an excellent way to meet members of the opposite sex.

You will be invited to many parties. As soon as your friends know you can perform magic, you'll be invited to every party. If you are not already known as a magician, do a trick or two for your host or hostess. They will ask you to do your magic for everyone at the party. You may just become the most popular person at the affair. The next time they see your name on a list of possible guests, someone will say, "Oh, yes, invite him. I still can't figure out how he did those amazing tricks at that last party."

You will be a sought-after dinner guest. With what you will learn in the course, you can do magic with objects found on any dinner table. Doing a few baffling tricks after dinner, along with the coffee, adds entertainment to the evening and assures your invitation to many more dinner affairs.

Sometimes, when dining in a restaurant, I do a few tricks for my friends at the table. Often the waiter will see what I am doing and ask if I will do a trick for him. When he is completely baffled, he will say, "Would you mind doing that for some of our other waiters?" When some waiters are gathered around, other dinner guests want to see what is going on and come over to our table to find out. So I warn you, if you are not careful, you can literally "take over" a small restaurant. I've had that happen many times.

You can be the family favorite. With just a few tricks, you can turn an ordinary family get-together into a special event. You'll find that magic has made you into a special person. A friend tells me his grandchildren are unanimous in saying, "I have two grandfathers. One does magic! And then there's that other guy."

Another example, is when mom says, with a great big smile, "Everybody climb into the car, we're going over to see grandma and grandpa." She doesn't want to hear, "Do I have to go, mom? We were just there last month." She's much happier when the response is, "Oh, goody, maybe grandpa will show me a new magic trick."

You can spread a bit of joy. Your magic can bring a few minutes of happiness to an orphanage, a children's hospital or a retirement home. You can be a great help at their next fund raiser. Church organization, civic clubs, underprivileged children's groups and many other charitable organizations are constantly looking for entertainment for their members. When you see that your magic brings smiles to those faces, it will be one of the greatest rewards you'll ever receive.

Your magic can help you set new sales records. Here's where your magic can really shine. If you call on clients at their offices or business establishments, a clever trick will brighten a receptionist's morning and give you an edge getting through to the boss. The right magic effect can emphasize your selling message and definitely add fun to a client's day. They'll be delighted to see you every time you call.

Or, if the customers come to your business, magic can help increase the selection of your establishment over your competition. "Let's go over to Joe's Place for our hamburgers. Maybe he will do one of those cool magic tricks for us." You'll find a whole section on applying magic to your sales later in this discourse.

You can make teaching interesting. Throughout the world, public interest in the art of magic has greatly increased, not only in watching magic, but also in learning how to perform it. With the knowledge you gain from this course, you may wish to become a magic instructor. There are many possibilities. The teaching of magic can be tailored to any group, selected and structured for their particular needs. As an example, check out what we suggest for summer campers in **Magic for Children.**

Many professional teachers have added magic to their course curriculums to entertainingly deliver educational material, emphasize particular learning points, maintain their students' attention in the classroom, or establish attendance-building, extra-curricular after-school activities.

You can make extra money in your spare time. There are many opportunities to make additional income with your magic. You don't have to be a full-time, professional magician to do it. You might want to become what we in the business call a "semi-pro." In your own neighborhood you can perform at birthday parties, bar mitzvahs, restaurants, retirement homes, anniversaries, sales meetings, office parties and all kinds of social affairs. There are many who have "worked their way through college" performing magic shows and many semi-pros who have magic as a secondary occupation, adding substantially to their income.

THE UNIVERSAL, INTERNATIONAL APPEAL OF MAGIC

Magic is a truly unique form of entertainment, appreciated by old and young alike. Magic knows no racial, geographic or language barriers. It is not even necessary to speak a country's language to perform magic and make friends in foreign lands. Presenting a few good magic tricks will make you welcome around the world.

Many times our personal experiences have illustrated to my wife Nani and me that the appeal of magic is truly universal and international. Universal because magic is equally appreciated by children in kindergarten, senior citizens in retirement homes, and every age in between. That appeal is also international, because magic works in any country in the world. Here's a perfect example of how the captivating power of magic is both universal and international.

In 1980, we were invited by the Chinese government to take our magic to mainland China. The invitation came from the Ministry of Culture, an agency of the People's Republic of China. At that time, they were in charge of all the performers in the country. China had been behind the "Bamboo Curtain" for 32 years, and the invitation came shortly after "joint recognition" between the U.S. and the P.R.C. Ancient China is the legendary home of magic.

We were the first "Western" entertainers allowed to perform for the people of China since the current government took control of the country in 1948. We had been preceded by a symphony orchestra and a ballet troupe, who performed one show in Beijing and another in Shanghai for government dignitaries and leading officials. We were to perform our illusion show in theaters in major cities and conduct the first ever "magic exchange" with Chinese magicians.

One part of the exchange was for us to teach the Chinese magicians the latest in western magic. That was easy for us. They hadn't seen any western magic for over three decades. (In a country of over a billion people, I was the only magician with a Zig Zag illusion!) The Chinese sorcerers would show us some of the classic Chinese wizardry handed down through the ages.

To us, the most important part of our visit was to see what "modern" China was like. We were going to a country that had been out of touch with the West for over thirty years. We spoke no Chinese. Their language, written in Chinese hieroglyphics, was totally unrecognizable to us as well. Our cultural backgrounds were entirely different. We were told different fairy tales as children and learned different nursery rhymes. Their music was cacophonous to us and ours equally strange to them. Almost all of the Chinese people we met and performed for had never seen anyone from the West. I'm sure our faces looked very strange to them. In the truest sense of the word, everything was as foreign to us as we were to the Chinese. And yet, our magic worked beautifully.

Because we wanted to meet as many of the people of China as possible, we performed not only in theaters, but also in communes, factories, schools, on trains, at national monuments, in parks, in Tiananmen Square, at the temple of Heaven, and on the Great Wall of China. The levitation of a young Chinese girl at the Great Wall was featured in *Time* magazine. Everywhere we went our magic got a warm welcome.

But it was in our appearances for smaller groups of Chinese that I could see their wonderful reactions. Several times I went alone to a public park and approached a group of old men, visiting in their retirement. I would say, *"Ne how,"* which is Chinese for hello, the only word of their language I knew. Then I would then show them a magic trick.

The initial puzzlement on their faces turned to smiles. They understood immediately that what they were seeing was "magic." They commented in pleasure to each other. After several more effects, I could tell they were glad I came to see them. I had a feeling they would be telling stories about that Western man they met in the park for years to come.

The most important part of that experience was I could feel the warmth and friendliness created by the magic. I had that same feeling during our visits to children in grade schools, family groups in communes and workers in the factories. The wonderful response to our magic was certainly universal and truly international in this foreign land. Check it out, you'll see. Magic works everywhere.

That's what magic did for me, and it will do the same for you. Study this course, practice and rehearse the tricks, then try them on your friends. You will soon be recognized as a magician. Magicians make the impossible happen. There aren't many people who can make that claim. You will become a "special person" to your friends and to everyone you meet. It really does happen. I've seen it hundreds of times. You will become more popular, your confidence will grow, your feelings of self-worth will increase. The magic will work for you.

CARD MAGIC

Tricks with cards form a branch of magic entirely on their own. In fact, there are some magicians who specialize in card tricks and nothing else, due to the wide range of opportunities offered by that field. This applies to everyone to some degree, because from the moment you start doing card tricks, you naturally acquire a manipulative ability. The mere act of cutting and shuffling a pack of cards, then dealing it, demands skill of a sort. When you spread the pack, inviting someone to "take a card," or run rapidly through the face-up pack while looking for cards needed for some special trick, you acquire further facility. Next you may find fancy cuts and flourishes to your liking; and if you do, you will be on the road to becoming a card expert almost before you realize it.

There are many tricks involved in the discovery of cards selected by members of the audience. These depend upon a variety of methods, which enable you to keep a "jump ahead" of keen-eyed and keen-witted spectators. Basically, there are three ways of discovering a chosen card: One is to "force" it on the spectator, so that you know the card beforehand and thereby can predict it, name it, or produce a duplicate from some unexpected place. Another way is to "locate" the card by its position in the pack, so you can find it by simply looking through the pack or studying the cards as you deal them. The third way is to "control" the chosen card, by shuffles, cuts and other manipulations that enable you to reveal it at any time.

All three ways are covered in this section and each has its own variations depending on different degrees of skill. So, by switching from one method to another, you can leave your audiences utterly nonplussed. Here, you will be further aided by special devices described or supplied with this course. One is the "Short" card, which you can find or control by the sense of touch alone. Another is the "Double-Backed" card which is responsible for several special effects, including those where a card reverses itself in the pack. Also, there is the "Double-Faced" card which enables you to apparently transform one card into another.

None of these devices is suspected by your audiences, yet all can be added to a standard pack, enabling you to accomplish remarkable feats that would be impossible with an ordinary pack alone. All this will add to your growing reputation as a card master while simplifying your work to a marked degree. By adding some of the more elaborate effects described in this section, you can soon round out a program of card magic that will stand as a complete act in itself.

CARD DEFINITIONS

The following is a list of definitions of words or terms used in Card Magic. You will find many of these used in the Course. Each is listed with either a brief definition or a reference to the page in the Course where that particular sleight or term is described.

FULL DECK:
52 cards consisting of four suits, Diamonds, Clubs, Hearts, and Spades with 13 cards per suit from Ace through King. . .with the Joker as an optional 53rd card.

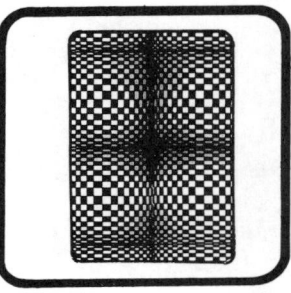

PATTERN BACK DECK:
Any deck with a *pattern* or *geometrical design* on its back.

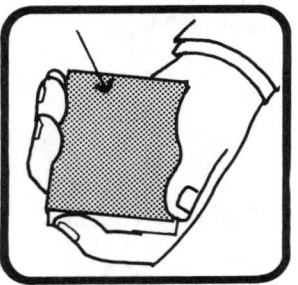

TOP OF DECK:
When the deck is face down, the *uppermost* card or portion of the deck.

PICTURE BACK DECK:
Any deck with a "picture" on its back. The picture may be of anything such as a dog, a cat, or the Grand Canyon. Since these are mostly "novelty" cards, they are usually not well suited for magic effects except in special instances such as card fans.

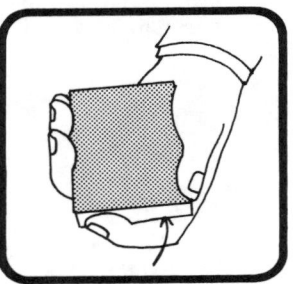

BOTTOM OF THE DECK:
The *lowermost* card or portion of the deck.

WHITE BORDERED BACK CARD:
Most "PATTERN BACKED" cards have a white border around the outer edge. (One notable exception is "Bee" brand decks.) A white border back is essential in the performance of many of the tricks described in this Course. This is because, when a card is reversed (turned *face up* in a *face-down* pack), it will not be noticeable because the white edges of the face are the *same* as the white border of the Pattern Back.

FACE:
The face of a card shows its value and suit.

SPOT CARDS:
Any card from Ace through Ten in any suit.

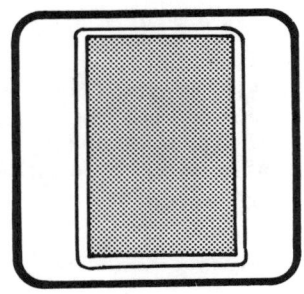

BACK:
The back of a card is the pattern or picture on the opposite side of the "face." The back design is repeated on all cards throughout the deck.

DEUCE:
Another name for a Two.

TREY:
Another name for a Three.

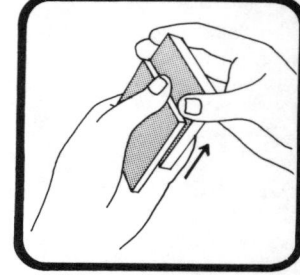

OVERHAND SHUFFLE:
See page 61

FACE CARDS, PICTURE CARDS, OR COURT CARDS:
All of the Jacks, Queens and Kings.

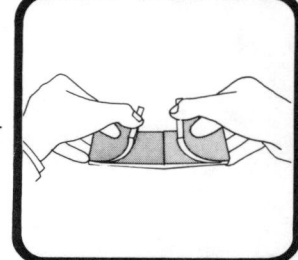

RIFFLE SHUFFLE OR DOVE-TAIL SHUFFLE:
See page 24

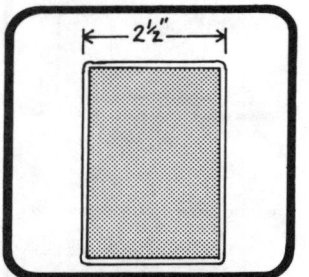

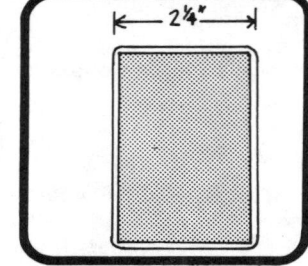

POKER-SIZE DECK:
This is a deck of "standard size" playing cards, measuring 2½" wide.

BRIDGE-SIZE DECK:
This is a deck of cards slightly smaller than a Poker Deck, measuring 2¼" wide. Bridge-size cards often give the magician an advantage in certain tricks because of their smaller width. Many magicians work with only Poker-Size while others prefer Bridge-Size because they find them easier to handle. Also, most "trick decks" are made in Bridge Size.

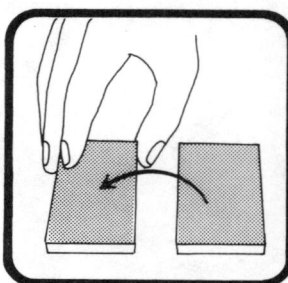

CUTTING THE DECK:
SINGLE CUT:
Removing a packet of cards from the top of the deck, placing it beside the lower portion and then "completing the cut" by placing the lower portion on *top* of the upper portion.

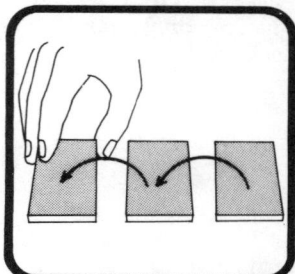

DOUBLE OR MULTIPLE CUT:
Dividing the deck into *more than two stacks* and then reassembling the deck.

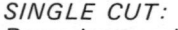

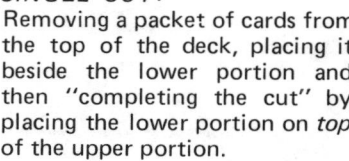

GIANT CARD:
An extra large card which is usually four times larger than a regular Poker-sized playing card.

FALSE CUT:
Any "cut" that leaves the deck *in the same order* as it was before the cut.

FALSE SHUFFLE:
Any shuffle which leaves the deck *in the same order* as it was before the shuffle.

MECHANICS' GRIP
A method used for holding the deck in the left hand for dealing. The left first finger extends around the *front* of the deck, the second, third, and little fingers around the right side, and the thumb on top (as shown). This is superior and more professional than the Standard Dealing Position in that the first finger keeps the cards "squared." The MECHANICS' GRIP should be used in almost all "dealing" tricks so that it becomes natural and easy. It is essential for more advanced sleights such as "Second" or "Bottom" dealing.

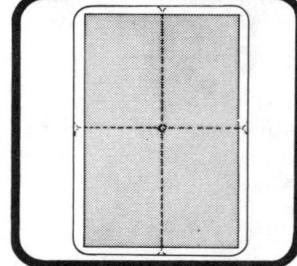
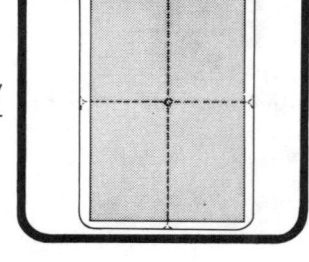

One-hand dealing

DEAL THE CARDS:
Removing cards from the pack, singly or in groups. Although this is usually done with two hands, it can also be done with one hand.

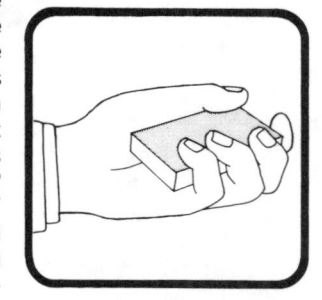

STANDARD DEALING POSITION:
The pack is held in the left hand resting on the palm, with the fingers extending around the right edge of the pack and the thumb on top. From this position, the thumb is ready to push off cards across the tips of the fingers, so that the right hand can draw, or "deal," each card away.

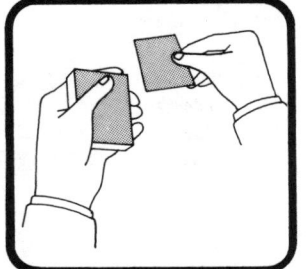

TWO-WAY FORCING DECK:
A deck in which the *top half* is composed of cards all of the same suit and value while the *bottom half* is composed of cards all the same but of a *different* suit and value. Used for "forcing" two different cards by spreading the cards so that the *first* spectator selects from the *top* half and the *second* spectator from the *bottom* half.

STANDARD DEAL:
Cards are drawn off, one at a time, face downward, and placed on the table, each card going on the card before it. This *reverses* the order of the cards.

THREE-WAY FORCE:
Same as Two-Way Force Deck except deck is divided into *three* similarly faced sections.

TURN-UP DEAL:
The cards are dealt singly from the top of the face-down deck but are *turned face up* as they are dealt. *This does not reverse the order of the deck.*

50/50 FORCING DECK:
A deck in which the top half is all the same (forcing) cards and the bottom half is differing (regular) cards. With this deck, the magician may turn the pack face up to show that the cards are all different, as long as *he does not spread past the lower half*. . .and then turn the deck back, face down, and "force" a card *by having it selected from the top half.*

ONE-WAY DECK:
This is usually a "PICTURE BACKED" deck in which the back patterns may all be arranged so that they face *one way*. This type of deck may be quickly made into a "trick deck" by arranging the Picture Backs so they are *all* facing one way. Have a card selected. . .then merely *turn the deck around* so that when the card is returned, ITS "PICTURE" IS FACING IN THE OPPOSITE DIRECTION. Then, by running through the pack and looking at the backs, you can easily find the selected card.

LOCATOR CARD:
Any card which can be used as a "key" to find some other card in the pack. Some examples of Locator Cards are:

Short Card, See page 125
Long Card, a card that is slightly longer than the rest of the pack. This card may be easily located because of its extra length.

FORCE:
Causing a spectator to select a particular card or cards *when he thinks he is making a FREE choice.*

See FORCES, Page 76

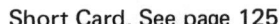

KEY CARD:
Any card that can be used as a "locator" card.

FORCING DECK:
A deck in which all of the cards are of the same value. (Usually the bottom or "face" card of the pack will be of a different value to mislead the spectators.)

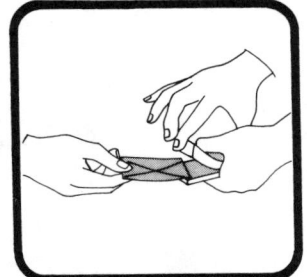

CARD LOCATION:
Any method that allows the magician to "find" or "locate" a selected card after it has been returned to the pack.

DOUBLE-FACED CARD:
A specially printed "trick" card with a FACE on *both* sides.

REVERSE COUNT:
See page 27

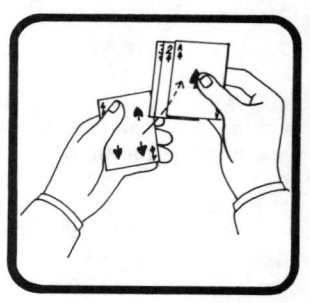

DOUBLE-BACKED CARD:
A specially printed "trick" card with a BACK on *both* sides.

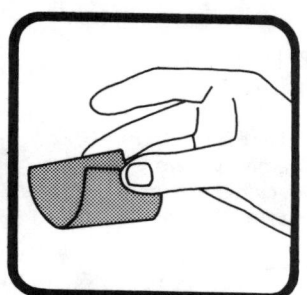

SLEIGHT:
A *"secret"* move done with the cards which is not known to the spectators. . .such as Double Lift, Glide, etc.

MOVE:
A "move" may be either *secret* in which case it is a Sleight, or some movement of the cards which the spectators can "see," such as Cutting the Pack.

SET-UP
Any preparation done before a show (or in many cases *during* a performance) which arranges the cards in a special order or location.

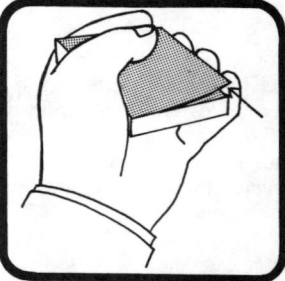

BREAK:
See page 83

PREARRANGED DECK:
A deck which has been "set up" or arranged in some special order before the performance.

DOUBLE LIFT:
See page 84

STOCK:
Any portion of the pack containing cards which have been "set up" in a special order.

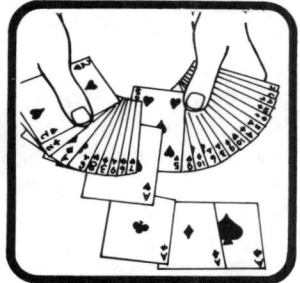

GLIDE:
See page 97

COUNTING THE CARDS:
See page 26

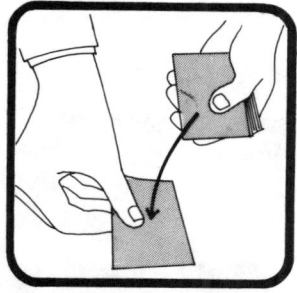

GLIMPSE:
Secretly noting a card while holding or shuffling the pack. See page 4 8

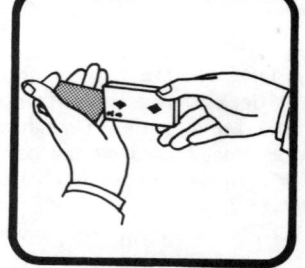

FLASH:
Allowing the spectator to "briefly see" the face of any card.

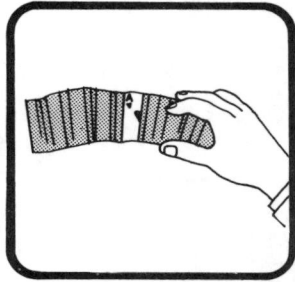

REVERSED CARD:
Any card which is *face up* in a *face-down* pack (or *face down* in a *face-up* pack).

CONTROL:
Any method (usually unknown to the audience) that allows the performer to know the location of a particular card or cards in the pack. This term is used extensively in the Course and in most every instance refers to the return to the pack of the selected card by the spectator and the magician's ability to "Control" the card to the top, bottom or some other location in the pack where the magician wants it.

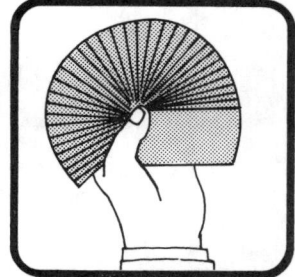

FLOURISH:
A display of skill with the cards. "Flourishes" are usually not tricks, although they can become important parts of some effects. Examples of flourishes are Fanning the Pack, Springing the Cards, the Ribbon Spread, One-Hand Cuts, etc.

GIMMICK:
Any *"secret"* device used to perform a trick. The audience is usually never aware of a "gimmick."

FAN OF CARDS:
A number of cards held in the hand in the shape of a fan.

CARD DISCOVERY:
The climax or end of many card tricks wherein the spectator's card is revealed or produced in a "magical" manner.

THE "MAGIC LOOP":
A very useful article in many magic effects is cellophane tape. Cellophane tape is manufactured in two ways. One is the conventional tape with the "sticky surface" on one side; the other has the "sticky surface" on both sides and is called Double Stick tape. As you will see, Double Stick tape is quite helpful for magical purposes, particularly if the audience is unaware of its presence. However, if you wish to do any of the tricks that call for Double Stick tape and do not have any on hand, you can easily make your own by forming a "Magic Loop." This is done by taking a piece of the regular single-sided tape and forming it into a loop, as shown, WITH THE STICKY SIDE OUT. Now, by placing this on whatever surface you wish to apply the tape to, and by pressing the loop flat, you will have, to all intents and purposes, formed a piece of *Double Stick tape.* At various places throughout this Course, you will find the Magic Loop referred to. Now, with this knowledge, you can form a piece of Double Stick tape and perform the many magical effects possible with it from standard cellophane tape.

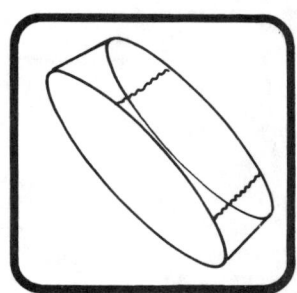

CARD HANDLING TECHNIQUES

Throughout all Card Magic, you will find that there are certain basic card handling techniques which are essential to your ability to perform card tricks. These include shuffling, counting, dealing, and spreading the pack. All of these techniques will not necessarily appear in each card trick, but there are very few tricks, for example, that do not require *at least* a shuffle. You probably already know one, but in Card Magic you will find that there are several kinds of shuffle. Most of them serve some special purpose, such as controlling the position of a card, and together they give you the opportunity to introduce *variety* into your card handling. Similarly, there are different techniques for dealing and counting which control card locations. The success of a trick frequently *depends* upon your skillful accomplishment of one of these manipulations. Therefore, you are urged to *practice ALL* of the following manipulations until you can do each one *smoothly, confidently,* and *without hesitation.*

Remember also, the mere appearance of skill and confidence in your handling of cards will add much to your audience's respect for your ability as a magician.

THE RIFFLE SHUFFLE

The RIFFLE SHUFFLE is probably the most widely used method of shuffling cards; and for that reason alone, you should be familiar with it. It is not difficult, but it will require some practice to perform it smoothly.

METHOD

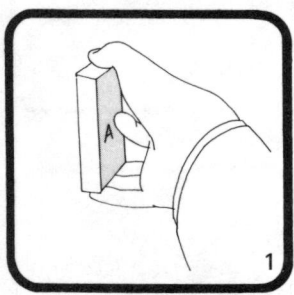 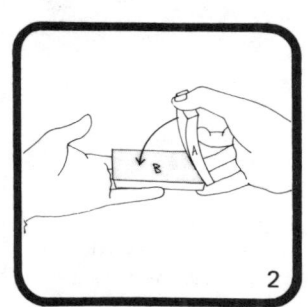  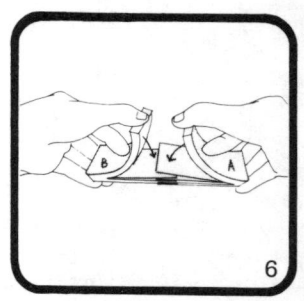

(1) Hold the pack in your right hand with your thumb at one end and your second, third, and fourth fingers at the other. The tip of your first finger should rest against the back of the top card of the pack. The pack should be held so that your right thumb is toward the ceiling with the face of the pack pointing to your left.
(2) Place the palm of your left hand on the bottom of the pack as shown. With your right hand, bend the pack outward and riffle about half of the pack with your right thumb, allowing the cards to fall forward onto the left fingers.

(5) Turn both packets face down and move the "thumb end" of each packet together. The backs of the second, third, and little fingers of both hands should rest on the top of the table.
(6) Slowly begin releasing (riffling) cards from *both* thumbs causing the cards to fall to the table and become <u>interlaced</u> at the inner ends. The ends of the cards should overlap about a half inch as they are "shuffled" together.

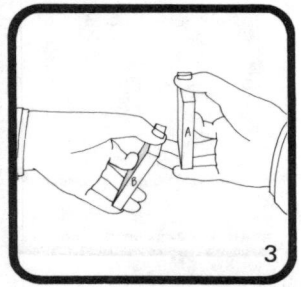 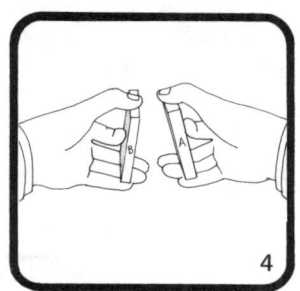 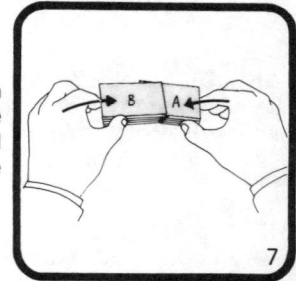

(3) Place the tip of your left thumb on the back of this new packet (B) and raise the lower end of Packet B *upward* until it clears Packet A in the right hand. As the end of Packet B comes clear, shift your left thumb to the right-hand end of Packet B.
(4) *The two packets should now be facing each other held with the same grip in each hand.* Your thumbs should be at one end of the packets, your first fingers resting against the backs of the packs and the remaining fingers at the opposite ends.

(7) When all the cards have been shuffled from both packets, push the two packets completely together and square the deck. This completes the RIFFLE SHUFFLE.

(8) Repeat Steps 1 through 7 in quick succession, executing the shuffle as many times as you wish, to thoroughly mix the cards.

THE TABLE SHUFFLE

This basic exercise is intended to show you how to shuffle a deck of cards in the proper manner. This is similar to, but considerably more "professional" than, the standard RIFFLE SHUFFLE. When working with cards, it is to your advantage to be able to mix the cards in a quick, graceful fashion and, since some of the best card tricks are performed while seated at a table, every magician should be familiar with the TABLE SHUFFLE. It gives your work an expert look, convincing your audience that even your simplest tricks are the result of great skill.

EFFECT

The magician divides the pack into two packets which he rests face down on the table. Lifting the *rear edges* of both packets, he begins to release the cards in succession causing their corners to interweave as they fall. He then pushes the two packets together and squares the pack, thoroughly mixing the pack.

METHOD

(1) Place the pack face down on the table in front of you and grasp the sides of the pack from above as shown. Using your thumbs, lift about half the pack from the top of the deck, near the middle.

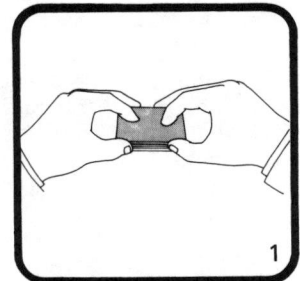

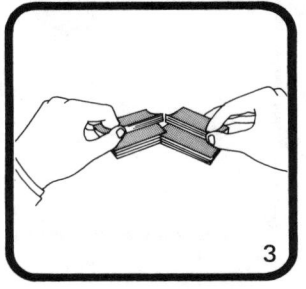

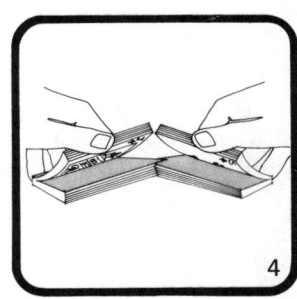

(3) Lift the inner edge of both packets with your thumbs and move the packets together so that the innermost corners will overlap slightly. Now, begin releasing the cards from your thumbs, allowing them to riffle downward onto the table so the inner corners of the cards weave together. (4) Here is a close-up view of the cards interweaving. The cards are released from your thumbs *interlacing at the corners only.*

(2) Now, separate the halves and place the packets on the table as shown. *The outer ends of both packets should be angled slightly toward you, to bring the innermost corners of the packets very close together.* Hold both packets with your *thumbs* along the *inner edge;* the *first finger* of each hand rests on the *top* of the packs, and your *remaining fingers* rest along the *outer edges.*

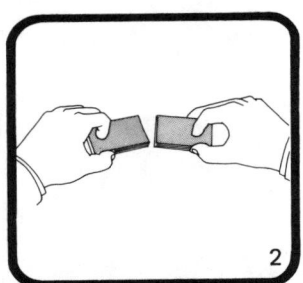

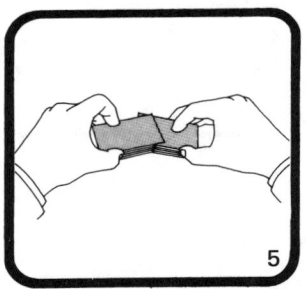

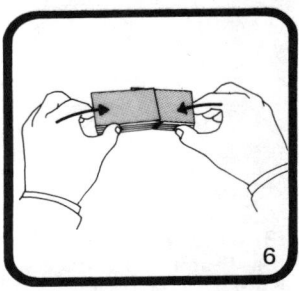

(5) Once all the cards have been released, . . . (6) . . . move your fingers to the extreme ends of both packets and push them together to form one complete "shuffled" pack.

(7) Repeat the shuffling process as many times as you like until all the cards in the pack have been completely mixed.

COMMENTS AND SUGGESTIONS

This type of shuffle, sometimes known as the "Dovetail Shuffle," is often used by gamblers or professional "dealers." Therefore, it is particularly effective when doing card tricks that have a gambling theme. Many gamblers, after completing the shuffle, will cut the pack by drawing out the *lower half* of the pack and placing it on *top* of the *upper packet.* As a magician, you can follow the same procedure, adding a natural and professional touch to your card work.

DEALING THE CARDS

Few actions are simpler than dealing cards from the top of a pack, but to do it smoothly, neatly and sometimes rapidly, the hands should work together, as described here.

METHOD

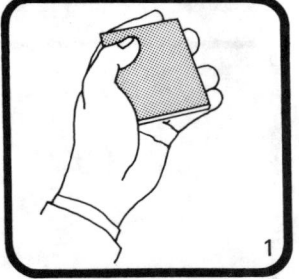

(1) Hold the deck in dealing position in your left hand, as shown in the illustration.

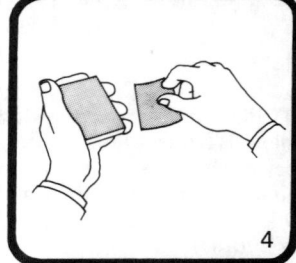

(4) . . . you relax the pressure of the left thumb on the top card allowing the right hand to carry it from the deck to the table.

(2) With your left thumb, push the top card forward and to the right about an inch, and at the same time move the right hand toward the pack in readiness to receive the card.

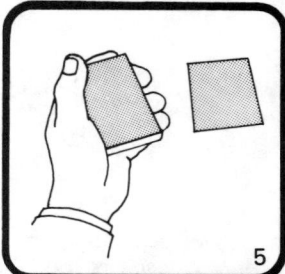

(5) The right hand then releases its grip on the card and leaves it on the table. The action can be repeated as often as necessary with each card desired.

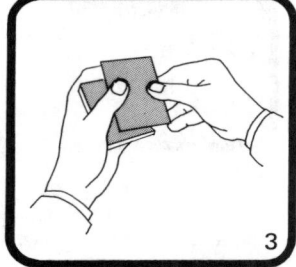

(3) Now, grasp the top card between the thumb and fingers of the right hand, as shown, as . . .

COMMENTS AND SUGGESTIONS

With some tricks, you may deal the cards in a single pile, with others, you may deal them in a row or in some special formation. When dealing cards in a pile, one on top of the other, you will REVERSE THE ORDER of the cards as you deal them. This is known as the "Reverse Deal" which is very important with certain tricks that will be described throughout the Course.

THE CARD COUNT — RETAIN ORDER

EFFECT

This is a method of counting cards from one hand to the other, RETAINING THE CARDS IN THEIR ORIGINAL ORDER, which is important in certain tricks. Moves are shown with just four cards, all face up, so that each card can be clearly followed.

METHOD

(1)   From the dealing position . . .

(5) Now, the left thumb pushes off card Number Three, again BENEATH the other two cards.

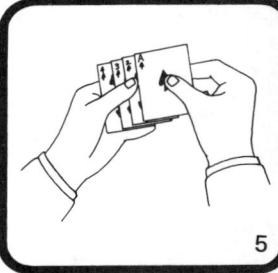

(2)   . . . the left thumb pushes one card from the pack into the fingers of the right hand, as you count, "one."

(6) The right fingers take this card along with the first two, lifting the three cards clear, counting out "three."

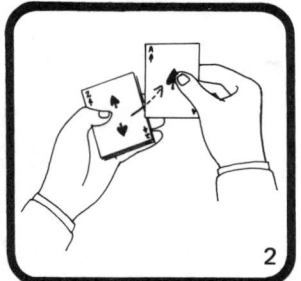

(3) The thumb then pushes off a second card in the same manner, so that it comes BENEATH the first card in the right hand.

(7) Finally, the last card in the left hand is placed BENEATH the other three cards in the right hand . . .

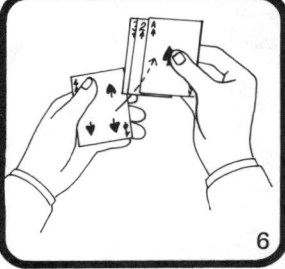

(4) The fingers of the right hand lift this card clear along with the first card, as you count, "two."

(8)   . . . as you finish the count with "four."

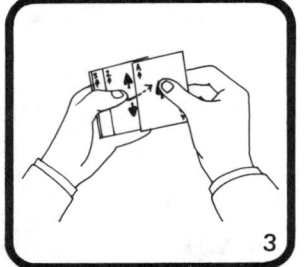

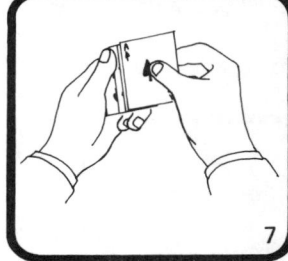

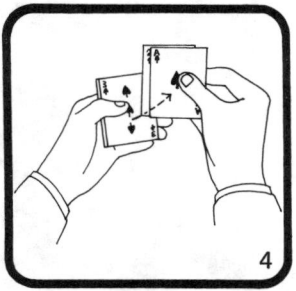

(9) NOTE: You have now counted the cards and are holding them as a separate group in your right hand — IN THEIR ORIGINAL 1-2-3-4 ORDER.

THE CARD COUNT — REVERSE ORDER

In all standard methods of counting, although you may not have thought of this before, the order of the cards is reversed. For instance, if you count cards one at a time from the top of the pack onto the table, the cards will be reversed. In other words, if you were to count through the whole deck, one at a time, the first card from the top, on the count of "one" would become the bottom card of the stack on the table. By the time you have counted all fifty-two cards onto the table, they would now be entirely *reversed in order* with the original BOTTOM card of the deck now the TOP card of the "counted" pack on the table. Also, when counting cards from one hand to the other, the cards will ordinarily be reversed in order. The following, using four face-up cards, explains the Standard Card Count Reverse Order.

METHOD

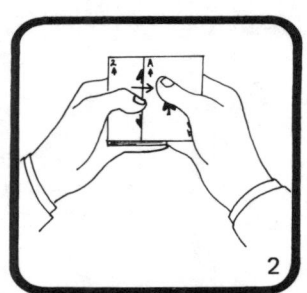

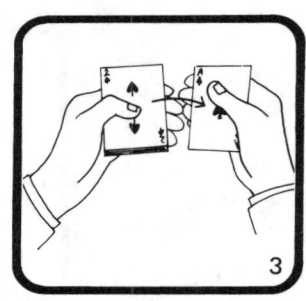

(1) With the pack in dealing position, (2) the left thumb pushes off one card, (3) which the right hand draws away as you count, "one."

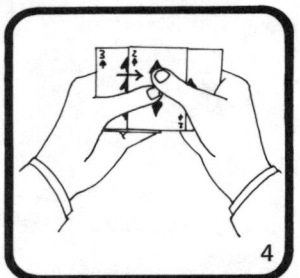

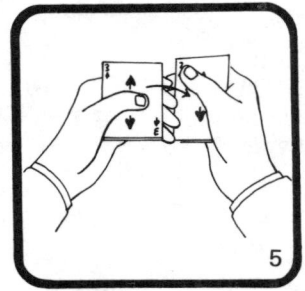

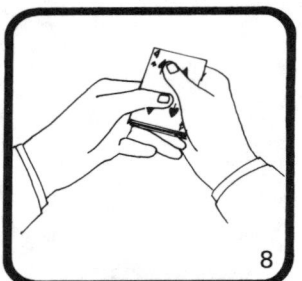

(4) Now, the left thumb pushes off card Number Two into the right hand **ABOVE THE FIRST CARD,** (5) as you draw them off together, counting out, "Two."

(8) The last card in the left hand is placed **ON TOP** of three cards in the right hand (9) as you finish the count with "Four."

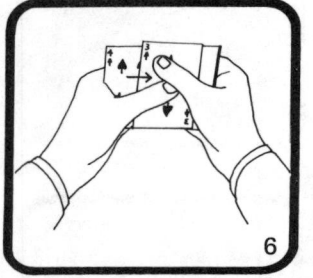

(6) Now, the left thumb pushes off card Number Three into the right hand **ABOVE THE FIRST TWO** cards. (7) You count out, "three."

(10) *NOTE: The right hand now holds the group of four cards in REVERSED ORDER 4-3-2-1 — instead of the original 1-2-3-4.*

SPREADING OR RUNNING THE PACK IN YOUR HANDS

This is a method of handling a pack of cards which will give your work a smooth professional touch. It is also a natural and effective way of having a spectator select a random card.

METHOD

(1) Hold the pack face down in your left hand with the fingers below and the thumb on top. The right hand waits alongside.

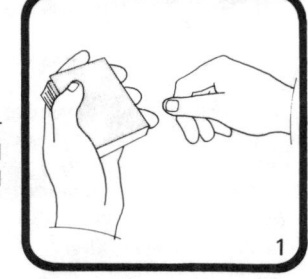

(2) With the left thumb, begin to push the cards from the top of the deck into the right hand.

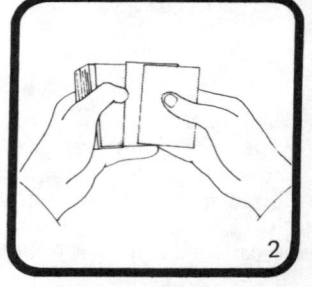

(3) Continue this action as the right thumb and fingers grasp the cards that are pushed over by the left thumb. *YOU ARE NOW "RUNNING" THE CARDS FROM YOUR LEFT HAND TO YOUR RIGHT HAND.* Proceed until the cards are about evenly distributed between both hands.

(5) From here, you can have the card returned to the pack, using any of the methods taught later in the course to "control or locate" the card. This spread should also be used when having someone draw cards for other purposes, as it thus becomes a natural procedure and helps you gain proficiency in your work.

(4) Offer the "spread" of cards to the spectator. Ask him to select a card and to remove it from the pack.

(6) Also, when looking for a particular card in the pack, you can see the spread with the cards face up, pushing the desired card (or cards) forward when you come to it.

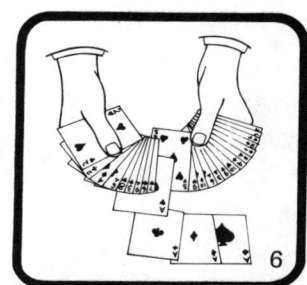

SELF-WORKING CARD TRICKS

There are many excellent card tricks that practically work themselves and are nearly fool-proof from the magician's viewpoint yet are real bafflers where the spectators are concerned.

In this section we have assembled some of the best of these self-working mysteries which are both deceptive and easy to perform. Therefore you can concentrate almost entirely upon presentation, without worrying about any special "moves" or "sleights." Often, when a smart spectator is watching for special moves, you can really flabbergast him with a self-working effect.

So, make it your policy to include a few self-workers when the occasion demands. You may discover that such effects will be regarded as highlights of your program.

Most importantly, never neglect practice with a self-working trick, even though it seems unnecessary. If you fumble or hesitate, the effect will lose its impact. Always remember that a trick is only as good as you make it look!

AUTOMATIC CARD DISCOVERY

EFFECT

Perhaps one of the most puzzling of all card effects is when a magician causes a selected card to reverse itself and appear face up a
the face-down cards in the deck. Here is one of the most basic and yet most effective means of accomplishing this feat.

SECRET AND PREPARATION

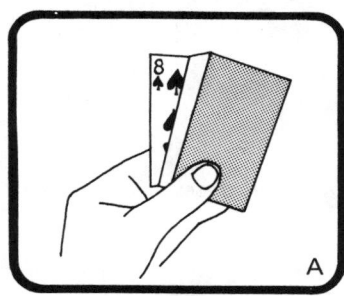
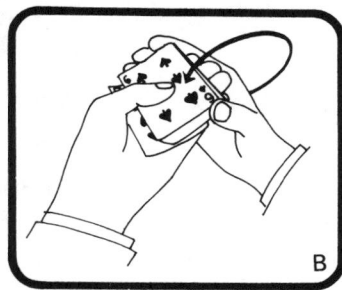
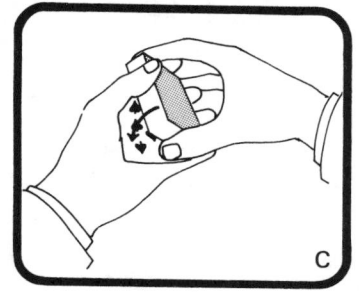

Simplicity is the answer here. The trick depends upon having the bottom card of the deck reversed from the start. (A) This can be set up
before hand with the deck in its box or it can be executed easily and quickly at a moment when the spectator's eyes leave your hands as
follows: (B) With the deck resting face up across the fingers of your left hand, your right thumb and fingers grip the ends of the pack
from below as shown. Now, slide the pack toward the tips of the left fingers , at the same time tilting or rotating the deck up on its left
edge. This leaves the lone card – in this case the Eight of Spades – still resting on the left fingers. (C) Continue the rotary motion until
the right hand has turned the pack face down upon the Eight of Spades, which thus becomes a face-up card at the bottom of the pack,
totally unsuspected by anyone. You are now ready to present the trick.

METHOD

(1) Spread the cards in your hands face down so that the spectator has an opportunity to freely select any card from the deck. Care must be taken here not to spread the cards too near the bottom of the deck, to avoid accidentally "flashing" the face up bottom card.

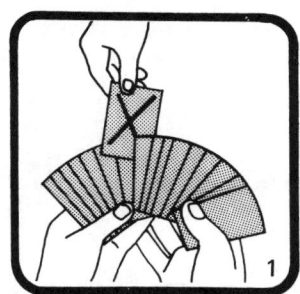

(4) Leave the deck sitting on the table as you tell the spectator to show the card to the other members of the audience.

(2) As soon as the card is selected by the spectator, square up the deck in the left hand and ask the spectator to look at his card.

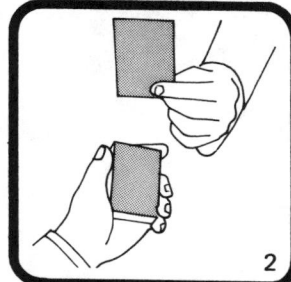

(5) When the spectator has shown his card, pick up the deck with the left hand, in its secretly reversed position. *Particular care must be taken here to keep the deck squared up so as not to "flash" the face up pack below the top single reversed card.*

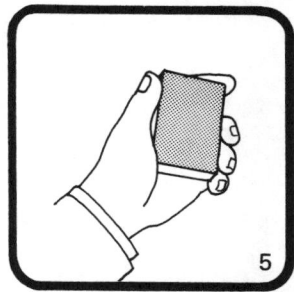

(3) *At the moment when the spectator's eyes are focusing on his card, the left hand TURNS COMPLETELY OVER and sets the deck of cards on the table. This action turns all of the cards in the deck face up, except for the "bottom" card which is now face down. Because of this single reversed card, it appears that the deck is still face down.*

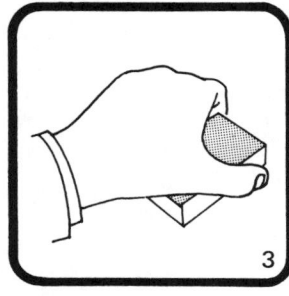

(6) Holding the deck firmly, ask the spectator to push his card face down anywhere into the deck. *Unknown to the spectator, he is really sliding his card face down into a face-up deck. (Except for the top card.)*

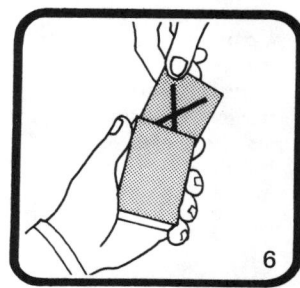

- Cont'd.

...has inserted his card into the deck, ...ur back and explain that since he ...the deck, that card will be a bit ...ards. State that, due to your highly ...will be able to find his card and ...vay.

(8) When you place the deck behind your back simply turn over the single reversed card and replace it FACE UP on the deck. *This places every card in the deck facing the same direction EXCEPT THE SPECTATOR'S CARD. It is the ONLY reversed card in the deck.*

SUPER AUTOMATIC CARD DISCOVERY

In performing the AUTOMATIC CARD DISCOVERY, here is another very easy and clever method for reversing the bottom card and secretly turning over the pack.

(1) It is not necessary to have the bottom card reversed before the start of the trick.

(2) After the spectator has selected his card from the deck, tell him to remember the card and that, after he replaces it in the deck, you are going to place the deck behind your back and locate his card in a very startling fashion....*at which time you DEMONSTRATE what you are going to do.*

(3) PLACE THE DECK BEHIND YOUR BACK. TURN THE BOTTOM CARD FACE UP. THEN TURN THE WHOLE PACK OVER SO THAT IT IS ALL FACE UP EXCEPT FOR THE ONE FACE-DOWN CARD ON TOP.

(4) Bring the deck out from behind your back. *You are now ready for the spectator to replace his card in the pack.*

COMMENTS AND SUGGESTIONS

With this method, you can perform the trick at any time with no previous "set-up." The spectator may even shuffle the deck himself before he freely selects a card. It only takes a moment to set up the pack behind your back as you "demonstrate" the first part of the startling way in which you are going to find the spectator's card. HOWEVER, WHEN YOU DO THIS "DEMONSTRATION," DO NOT TELL HIM THAT HIS CARD WILL LATER BE DISCOVERED FACE UP IN A FACE-DOWN PACK ... YOU MAY ALERT HIM TO YOUR SECRET SET-UP. This method not only allows you to reverse the bottom card, but also to turn the pack over for the replacement of the selected card without any tricky moves whatsoever. When you first place the deck behind your back, just do it naturally, as if you were illustrating what is going to happen next. You can now present a very puzzling, self-working card trick that appears to require great skill yet is practically automatic in every respect.

THE FANTASTIC FIVE

EFFECT

This is a clever self-working card discovery utilizing a set up deck in its simplest form. The trick finishes with a double twist that will leave the onlookers completely baffled. Adding one surprise onto another is always a good policy, especially with card tricks.

A card is freely selected by a spectator and returned to the pack, by placing the card on top and giving the pack a cut. The magician then spreads the pack on the table, revealing that one card is face up. It is a FIVE. He explains that the face-up card, the Five, is his "Magical Indicator Card." Then he counts down *five* cards in the deck below where the face-up card was located. Turning up the fifth card, it proves to be *the card chosen by the spectator!* If that were not enough, he now turns the four cards that were *between the face-up card and the spectator's card*....ALL FOUR ARE ACES!

SECRET AND PREPARATION

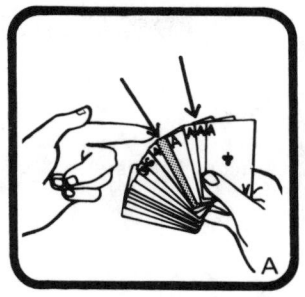 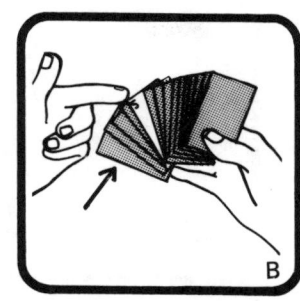

To prepare, run through the pack and remove the Four Aces and any Five-spot. This done, square up the pack and place the Five-spot *face up* on the bottom of the face-down pack and then place the four Aces *face down* below the Five. The first illustration shows the proper set-up with the pack held face up (A). The illustration (B) shows the pack held in its normal face-down position . Now, square up the pack and you're ready to begin.

METHOD

(1) Spread the pack and invite a spectator to select a card. Be sure not to spread the pack too near the bottom, accidentally exposing the face-up Five-spot.

(2) Tell the spectator to be sure and remember his card. Square up the deck and place it on the table.

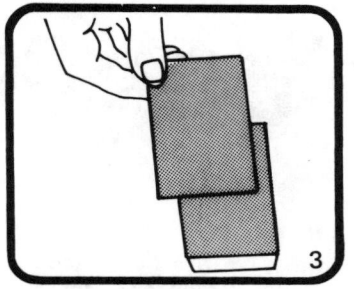 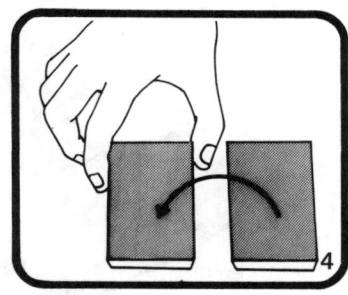 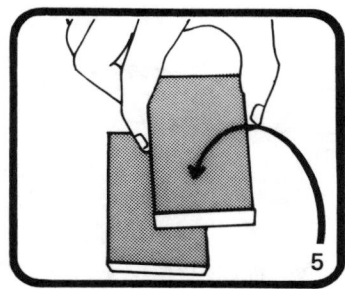

(3) Ask the spectator to place his card on top of the deck, **(4)** then to cut the deck, and **(5)** to complete the cut.

(6) *NOTE: Unknown to the spectator, when he cuts the deck, he places the four Aces and the face-up Five DIRECTLY ABOVE HIS SELECTED CARD.*

(8) Separate all the cards to the *right* of the face-up Five-spot.

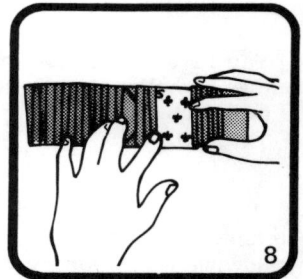

(7) Explain to the spectator that something magical is going to happen. At the same time, spread the deck, face down, on the table. Call attention to the *one face-up* card in the deck.

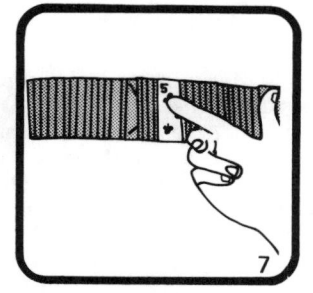

(9) Explain that the face-up card is your "Magical Indicator Card" and that it will help to locate the card the spectator selected. Since the card is a FIVE, that must be a "clue." Count down five cards in the deck.

(10) Push the Five-spot, the four face down Aces below it, and the next card (the spectator's card) all forward from the pack.

(11) Turn over the fifth card and show it to be the card that the spectator selected.

(12) The spectator will assume that the trick is over. Not content with this, you turn over the four remaining cards TO REVEAL THE FOUR ACES. This second added surprise, the appearance of the Aces, adds greatly to the effect. This is also a good lead-in to any four-Ace trick.

COMMENTS AND SUGGESTIONS

Here is another presentation idea. After the spectator has returned his selected card to the pack and completed the cut, pick up the deck and give it a snap *before* you spread it along the table. Say that this will cause a card to turn over somewhere in the deck. When the spread reveals the face-up Five, count down to the chosen card. Turn it over, revealing it to be the spectator's selected card. NOW FOR THE ADDED TOUCH....you then gather up the upper and lower portions of the pack, *placing the "Aces" half of the deck on TOP.* Say, "Whenever I snap the pack a second time, something good always turns up"...SNAP!...."like the four Aces!" Then deal the four Aces from the top of the deck, TURNING EACH ACE FACE UP AS YOU PLACE IT ON THE TABLE.

TURN OVER CARD

This surprising effect is performed with a pack of ordinary playing cards. It can be done with a borrowed deck and requires *no skill or practice.* The trick depends on the use of a "key card" which is one of the most basic and simple methods used in card magic to locate a selected card in a pack of cards.

THE EFFECT

You have a spectator shuffle a pack of cards and cut the cards anywhere he wishes. Next, you tell him to look at the card he cut to—then complete the cut, thus burying his card in the deck. Now you take the cards in your hands *for the first time* and proceed to find the selected card.

SECRET AND PREPARATION

The secret of the trick depends entirely upon the performer secretly learning the bottom card of the pack before it is placed on the table to begin the trick. This card is called a "key card" because it is to be your key to the location of the selected card. In the following description we will assume that your key card (the card on the bottom of the deck) is the Two of Clubs.

THE METHOD

(1) If you use a pack of cards that is already in its case at the start, you can glimpse the bottom card as you remove them from the case. Just lay the pack face down and go right into the trick without a shuffle.

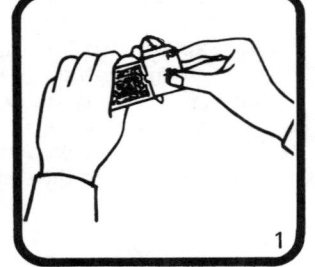

(2) Even better, if people want to shuffle the pack . . . let them. Often when a spectator is squaring up the pack after shuffling, he will "flash" the bottom card in your direction, not realizing it has anything to do with the trick.

(3) If you don't get a glimpse of the card during the shuffle, pick up the pack in your hands, turn it face-up, and begin running the cards from hand to hand, as shown.

Comment that the deck appears to be well shuffled and it would be impossible for you to know their order. Of course, here you see and remember your "key card". Now lay the pack face down on the table and you're ready to begin.

(4) With the pack lying face down on the table and the spectators satisfied that the cards are well mixed, ask someone to divide the pack into two parts.

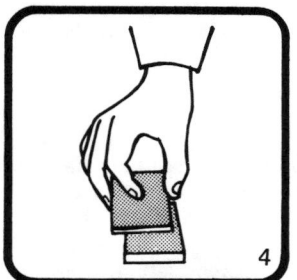

(5) Tell him he can cut anywhere in the deck he wishes and to place the upper portion on the table. *Note that the card which the spectator has cut to, which will be his selected card, we have marked with an "X" in the illustrations to make it easier for you to follow. Of course, when you perform the trick, there will be no "X" on the card.*

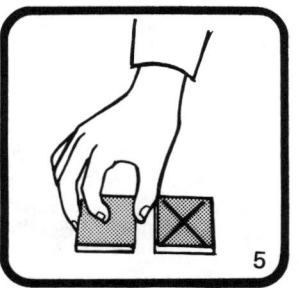

(6) After he has cut the cards tell him to remove the top card of the lower half, *look at it, and remember it* and then to place it on top of the other half of the pack. Let's assume that the card is the Five of Diamonds.

Spectator Looks At Card

(7) Point to the lower half and ask him to put those cards on top of his card so it will be buried somewhere in the pack.

NOTE: *In placing the lower half on top of the upper half, the spectator is also placing your "key card" directly above his chosen card.* Ask the spectator to give the pack another complete cut and then to let someone else cut it also.

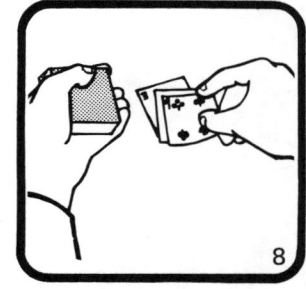

(8) When this is done, take the pack and begin dealing cards one by one on the table, turning each card face up. Tell the spectator that you are trying to get an impression of his card, *but he is not to say anything if he sees it,* or you will have to begin all over.

(9) As you deal cards one at a time from the pack, turning each face up, *watch for your key card,* the Two of Clubs. When it shows up, deal it on the table along with the others. You now know that the *next card* will be the spectator's card (the Five of Diamonds).

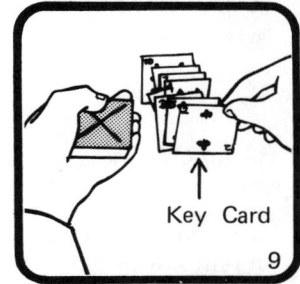

Key Card

(10) Deal the next card, the Five of Diamonds, but instead of stopping, just continue dealing as if you haven't reached the chosen card.

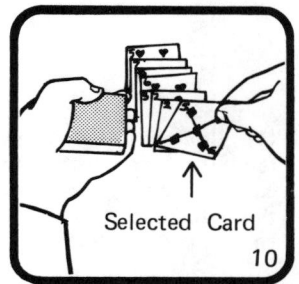

Selected Card

(11) After you have dealt a half-dozen or more cards, tell him you have received an impression and say: "The *next card I turn* over will be *your card.*" He will probably say you are wrong.

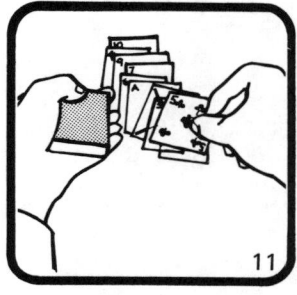

(12) But instead of dealing the next card off of the pack, reach among the face-up cards on the table and draw out the Five of Diamonds.

(13) Turn over the Five and lay it *face down* on the table and say: "I said the next card I *turned over* would be yours – and it is!"

Note: This trick is very effective because of its surprise ending! When the spectator sees you deal past his card he is sure that the trick has gone wrong. But when you actually do turn his card face down you really prove your "Magical" powers.

DOUBLE TURNOVER

In this card effect, the spectator plays such an active part that trickery seems impossible, yet the magical result is attained while the pack is practically in the spectator's hands. The secret is so simple – once you know it – you can fool an audience the first time you try.

EFFECT

The magician places a deck of cards on the table and invites a friend to remove the upper half of the pack for himself, while the magician takes the remaining lower half. Each puts his half behind his back and each removes a card at random. Each lays his half-pack on the table and looks at the card he selected. Then the magician and the spectator exchange their "selected cards" *without looking at each other's cards* and insert them face down into the respective half-packs — the MAGICIAN'S card in the SPECTATOR'S half-pack, and the SPECTATOR'S card in the MAGICIAN'S half. The full pack is immediately reassembled and both call out the names of the cards each has selected. The pack is spread face down on the table, and *both cards have magically turned FACE UP in the deck!*

METHOD

Glimpse bottom card

(1) Before the trick, give the pack a few cuts or a shuffle. In the process, casually spot the BOTTOM CARD of the deck, in this case the Five of Hearts, and *remember it.*

Magician

Cards held behind back

(4) Also remove any other card from your half. Turn it face down and bring it out from behind your back. To the spectators, this is *your* "selected" card.

Spectator takes top half

(2) Lay the pack on the table and tell your friend to cut off about half the pack and hold it behind his back. You do the same with the remaining lower half.

(5) *NOTE: The spectator does not suspect that your actions differ from his. In the illustration, your card, the Five of Hearts, is marked with an "M" ... the spectator's card, in this case the Two of Diamonds, is marked with an "X." The random card that YOU place on the table is marked with a "D" as it is a "decoy" that plays a special part, as you will see.*

Cards behind magician's back

(3) Instruct him to remove any card from his half, while you *supposedly* do the same. Actually you TURN YOUR HALF FACE UP. Then turn the card you glimpsed – the Five of Hearts – FACE DOWN *on top of the face-up packet.*

(6) Here you tell the spectator, "Look at the card you drew and remember it, while I do the same with my card." He looks at his card and notes that it is the Two of Diamonds. *You look at your card but it is not necessary to remember it ... just don't forget your "special" card, the Five of Hearts.*

(7) You continue, "Hold your card so I cannot see what it is, and lay your half of the pack face down on the table, just as I am doing. Do not tell me what card you selected. I also will keep my selected card a secret — FOR JUST A MOMENT."

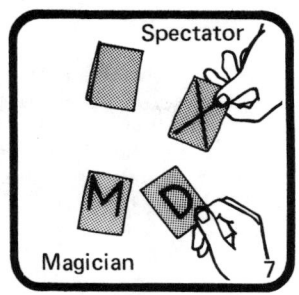

(8) Here you bring out your half of the pack from behind your back and set it on the table. Your half appears to be the same as the spectator's half. ACTUALLY, ALL OF THE CARDS IN YOUR HALF ARE FACE UP EXCEPT FOR THE FIVE OF HEARTS WHICH IS FACE DOWN AT THE TOP.

(9) *NOTE: Care must be taken to place the cards on the table squarely so as not to "flash" any of the face-up cards beneath the Five spot.*

(10) Then you add: "Give me your card and you take mine, but I won't look at the face of your card and you don't look at mine. That way, only we will know which cards we took."

(11) Now with your half of the pack resting on the table, insert the SPECTATOR'S card into YOUR half near the center, *keeping your half well squared with your left hand.* Tell the spectator to push YOUR card face down into HIS half of the pack.

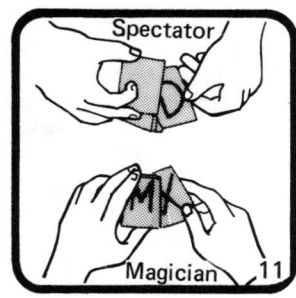

(12) *NOTE: At this point, your half of the pack has ALL its cards face up except for your face-down Five of Hearts ON TOP and his face-down Two of Diamonds NEAR THE MIDDLE.*

(13) Place your left hand over the top of your half in readiness to pick it up from the table, and at the same time, with your right hand, reach for the spectator's half-pack stating that you will add it to your own.

(14) At the exact moment your right hand picks up the spectator's packet, lift your packet from the table with your left hand and in the same motion, TURN YOUR HALF OVER. *Your half-pack now really is FACE DOWN except for the face-up Five of Hearts on the bottom.* This is the only "tricky" part of this effect. It does not require skill, merely the correct timing and should be well practiced before you present the trick.

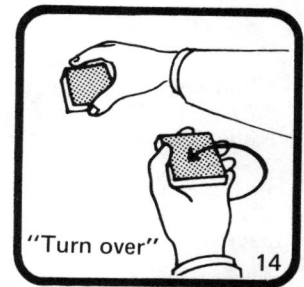

(15) Move your hands together and place the spectator's half on top of your half, squaring the halves together.

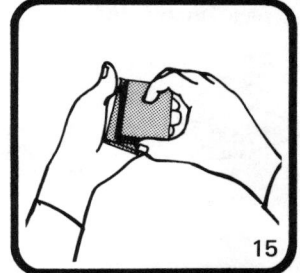

(16) *Now, the entire pack is face down, except for your Five of Hearts (on the bottom) and the spectator's Two of Diamonds, about a dozen cards above.*

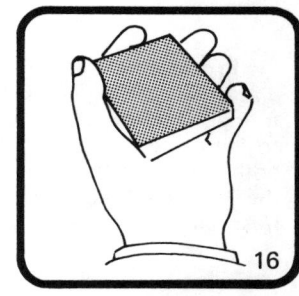

(17) Cut the pack about one third of the way down in the deck and place this packet on the table.

(18) Complete the cut by placing the remaining two thirds packet on top.

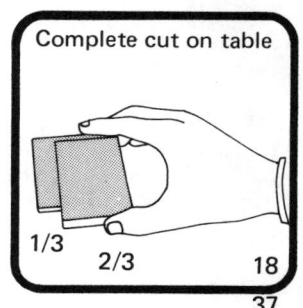

(19)   As you do, say to your friend, "My card was the Five of Hearts, what was yours?" He replies, "The Two of Diamonds." Square the pack and riffle the ends twice with your finger. Say, "Good!. . .Now I'll make both cards magically reveal themselves."

(20)   Ribbon Spread the pack along the table, face down, separating the cards rather widely. As you do, the two cards – the Five of Hearts and the Two of Diamonds – are seen to be FACE UP in the spread, for a startling climax.

COMMENTS AND SUGGESTIONS

When only a few spectators are present, it is not necessary to put the packs behind your back. Instead, you each can simply turn away, so that neither sees what card the other takes. This gives you an easy opportunity to note a card and place it face up on the bottom, while drawing out another card to serve as a decoy.

In either case, always use a pack with backs that have a WHITE MARGIN around the edges and be sure to keep the cards WELL SQUARED when handling your half-pack. Otherwise, a sharp-eyed spectator may notice the face-up cards in your supposedly face-down packet.

In turning your left hand over to bring your inverted half-pack to normal – as shown in Figs. 13 and 14 – you can cover the turnover by moving your left hand, with its packet, to the right. In this way you must reach *across* your left hand with your right hand in order to pick up the spectator's packet. That brings your right arm directly over your left hand, which does the dirty work under this cover.

THE DOUBLE X MYSTERY

EFFECT

Two spectators are invited to assist the magician. The magician gives the spectator on his left a pack of cards and a pen and asks him to place the pack behind his back and mark an X across the *face* of any card with the pen. The magician now gives the same deck and pen to the spectator on his right and asks him to mark the *back* of any card, also with the pack behind his back. The magician returns the deck to the person on his left and asks him to run through the deck and find the card with the X on the FACE, remove it, and hold it between both hands so that it is out of sight. This done, the spectator on the right is again given the deck and asked to find his card, the one with the X on the BACK. Upon searching through the deck, he finds that his card is missing. When the spectator on the left turns his card over, it is found to have an X on the back. It appears as if both spectators have chosen and marked the same card!

SECRET AND PREPARATION

The secret to this "coincidence" is so simple it's surprising. It all depends upon the unknown fact that the pen that the magician gives to the spectators just *doesn't work*. The best pen to use is of the felt tip variety. All that is required is to let it sit without the cap on until the tip is dried out. If a pencil is used, it is necessary to dip the tip of the pencil in clear varnish and allow it to dry overnight. This will prevent the pencil from making a mark on the cards although it appears to have a perfectly good "point." A drawback in using a pencil is that it does not make an easily visible mark on the card as does the felt tip pen. A ballpoint pen, which is out of ink, also works well but has the same "lack of visibility" as the pencil.

To prepare, remove any card from the pack and mark an X on both sides with a pen or pencil that really works and matches the special one you will use in the trick. The lines which form the X should appear irregular, as if the mark were made behind the back. Now replace the card back in the deck, and you're ready.

METHOD

(1)   With two spectators to assist you, give the deck face up to the spectator on your left. Ask him to place the deck behind his back, to run through the cards, and without looking at it, to bring any card to the top of the deck.

(2)   When he has done this, give him the prepared pen and instruct him to mark an X across the FACE of the card and then return the pen to you. Ask him to mix the cards behind his back so his card is lost somewhere in the deck. After he has done this, have him hand you the deck.

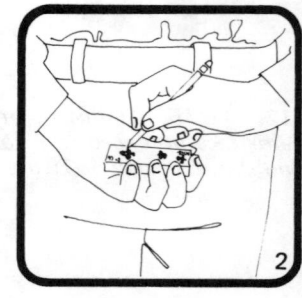

(3) Now turn the deck FACE DOWN and hand it to the spectator on your right. Instruct him just as you did the other spectator. But tell him to mark an X on the BACK of any card and mix the cards.

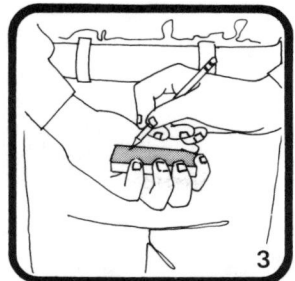

(4) When this has been done, take back the deck and put the pen away. Give the deck again to the spectator on your left, and ask him to look through the cards FACE UP and remove the card he marked from the deck. Have him hold this card between the palms of his hands so no one else can see the card. *Actually, the reason for doing this is so that no one sees the X on the back of this card.*

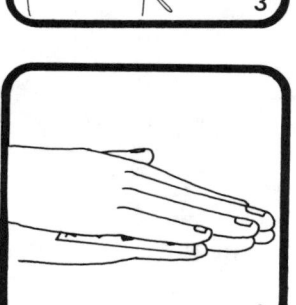

(5) *NOTE: Because of the prepared pen, neither spectator has made a mark on any card and both are unaware of the prepared X card in the deck.*

(6) This done, give the deck to the spectator on the right and ask him to do the same...."Please run through the deck and remove your card, the one with the X on the back." Of course, he will be unable to find his card.

(7) After several attempts, call attention to the fact that the only card missing from the deck is the one that the other spectator is holding between his hands. Tell the spectator on your left to look at the back of the card. It appears that the two spectators were some how able to freely select and mark the *very same card in the deck!*

COMMENTS AND SUGGESTIONS

It is a good idea at the start of the trick to run through the cards face up and show them to be an ordinary deck. In order to do this, it is necessary to have the secret X card close to the bottom of the deck. Then, run through the cards face up, supposedly to show that they are all different. Just be careful not to spread the cards near the position in the deck where the X card is located. The spectators will believe everything is on the up-and-up. You will be amazed at the effect that this trick has on an audience, as there appears to be no reasonable explanation for the astonishing results. Properly performed, no one will ever suspect the special pen as being the secret to the mystery.

THE SUPER DOUBLE X MYSTERY

One very subtle convincer, which can make this trick a COMPLETE baffler, is to introduce a duplicate pen (the one that REALLY made the X on the card), after the prepared pen has done the dirty work. Simply have the duplicate in your pocket and, after the second spectator has made his "mark," casually place the pen in the pocket with the duplicate. As the second spectator is looking for the card with the X, remove the unprepared pen and "help" him search by pointing to various parts of the deck with the "real" pen. Then just lay the pen somewhere in plain sight. Now *everything* can be examined.

SUPER ANYTIME DOUBLE X MYSTERY

With this method, you can perform the Double X Mystery at any time during your card routine....even though the deck has been used for a number of other tricks and even examined by the audience!

SECRET AND PREPARATION

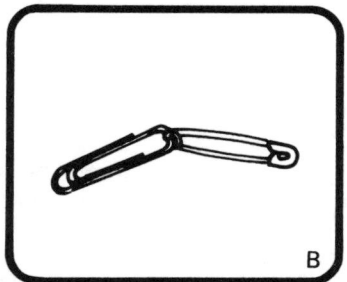
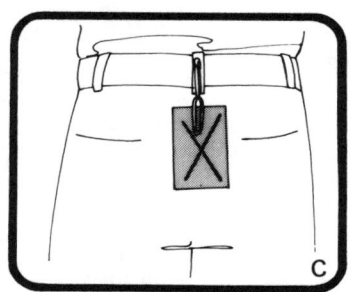

Before the show, place the X marked card either (A) under your belt behind your back or (B) in a "gimmick" card holder made from a safety pin and a paper clip. The special card is placed in the paper clip and the "holder" pinned inside the back of your coat (C) so that the card is just hidden by the bottom edge of your coat.

METHOD

(1) Have one of the spectators shuffle the deck. When he hands it back to you, place the deck behind your back to illustrate to your two assistants what they are to do....*it is now that you secretly remove the X card from beneath your coat and add it to the deck!*

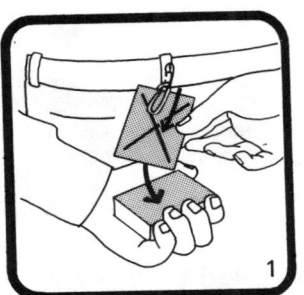

(2) Now you are ready to proceed with the Super Double X Mystery just as described.

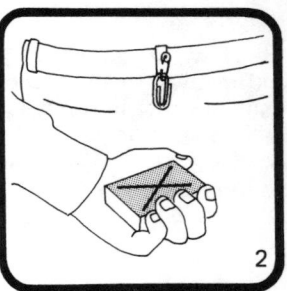

THE SIGNED CARD IN WALLET

Here is an effect which will cause spectators to give you credit for remarkable skill, yet no special moves or long practice is required. *Misdirection* is the main factor and even that becomes almost automatic, if you follow this timely, well-paced routine that has been carefully designed to baffle the sharpest spectators.

EFFECT

A card is selected by a spectator who signs his name on the back. The magician brings out his wallet which contains a "prediction" card which he has signed. When the "prediction" card is revealed, it is found to match the spectator's selection.

SECRET AND PREPARATION

For this trick you need a few simple props. First, an ordinary book-style wallet or checkbook. You will also need a pen, a small piece of either "double-faced" cellophane tape or regular cellophane tape made into a "Magic Loop" and a deck of cards. Also, you will need one duplicate card from another deck. It can be any card you choose, but for our explanation we will use an extra Four of Hearts. This card, known as the "prediction card," can be taken from a pack of a totally different design.

(1) Open the wallet or checkbook flat and place it on the table as shown. Next, sign your name across the back of the duplicate Four of Hearts and place it FACE DOWN on the LEFT SIDE of the wallet. *Now fold over the right side,* enclosing the card inside the wallet.

(3) With the taped side toward your body, insert the wallet in your left inside coat pocket.

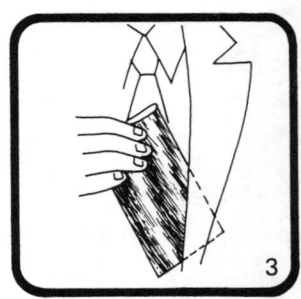

(2) Turn the entire wallet over and place a small (1½-inch) piece of double-faced cellophane tape or a "Magic Loop" of regular cellophane tape in the center of this side of the wallet. Then turn the wallet back over to its original position. Be careful not to stick the tape to the table. See MAGIC LOOP, page 23.

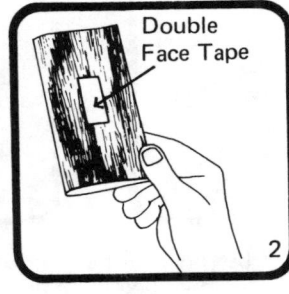

Double Face Tape

(4) Place the pen in the same pocket. Look through the deck until you locate the Four of Hearts. (This has been marked with an "X" in the illustrations.) Remove the Four and place it on top of the deck. You are ready to perform a truly fantastic trick.

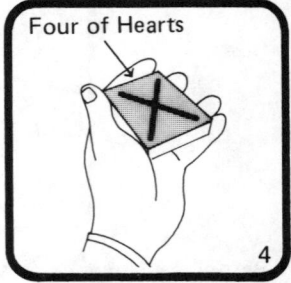

Four of Hearts

METHOD

(5) Spread the deck face down from hand to hand and ask a spectator to just TOUCH a card. *Emphasize that he has a completely free choice of ANY card.*

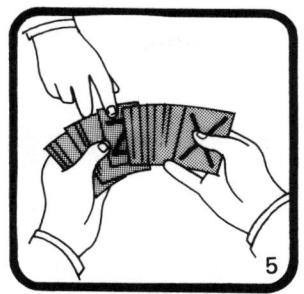

(6) When he does, separate the pack ABOVE the card (here marked with a "Z") that the spectator touched. Keep his "selected" card (Z) at the top of the left half of the pack.

(7) Deal this selected card (Z), *without looking* at it on top of the cards held in the right hand, explaining that you will move the chosen card to the top of the deck.

(8) Now, place the right-hand packet of cards on top of those in the left hand and square the cards up. *You should now have the selected card (Z) on top of the deck, with the Four of Hearts (X) directly below it.*

(9) Hold the deck in your left hand. With your right hand, bring the wallet from your inside coat pocket. Handle it in a casual manner, keeping the taped side toward you.

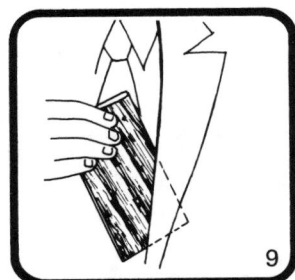

(10) Then, tilt the top (upper end) of the wallet toward your body, so the taped side is underneath....WITH YOUR RIGHT HAND, PLACE THE WALLET SQUARELY ON TOP OF THE PACK IN THE LEFT HAND.

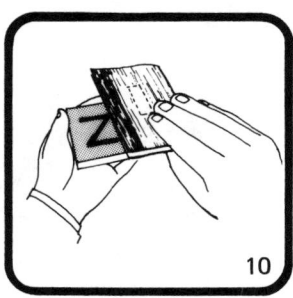

(11) Hold the wallet against the deck with your left thumb while your right hand moves back toward the pocket for the pen. WITH YOUR THUMB, PRESS FIRMLY ON THE WALLET CAUSING THE TOP CARD (Z) TO STICK TO THE TAPE ON THE UNDERSIDE OF THE WALLET.

(12) With your right hand, remove the pen from your pocket and hand it to the spectator.

(13) *NOTE: Reaching back into your pocket supplies a perfect reason for momentarily leaving the wallet on the deck as a resting place as you bring the pen out to give to the spectator.*

(14) With your right hand, remove the wallet from the top of the deck to the table, SECRETLY CARRYING AWAY THE SPECTATOR'S CARD (Z) WITH IT. *The spectator thinks his selected card is still on top of the deck, but really the Four of Hearts is in its place.*

(15) Deal the top card → NOW THE FOUR OF HEARTS, onto the table, face down, to the left of the wallet. State, "I'd like you to sign your name across the back of your card to clearly identify your selection."

(16) Have the spectator sign the back of the tabled card....(which only you know is the Four of Hearts). When he is finished, replace the pen in your coat pocket.

(17) Open the wallet to reveal your signed, face-down "prediction card." Remove the card from the wallet and place it, still face down, on the table next to the spectator's card.

Card with your name

(19) Before turning the two cards over, pause a moment to tell your audience about the "Mysteries of ESP," thus building up the suspense a little before you turn both signed cards face up. Of course, your "prediction" proves to be correct making the mystery complete!

(18) *Pick up the wallet and place it back in your coat pocket thus getting rid of any evidence beforehand. Be sure to handle the wallet so as not to reveal (or unstick) the card held on the underneath side.*

COMMENTS AND SUGGESTIONS

This is a VERY STRONG mental effect in which no manipulative skill is involved. It should be presented in your own personal style.

NOTE: Some coats have the inside pocket on the right side, not the left. In that case, after placing the "touched" card on the top of the pack, transfer the pack from your left hand to your right. Then remove the wallet with your left hand and place it on top of the pack in your right hand. The procedure is then exactly the same.

THE TORN AND RESTORED CARD

EFFECT

A card is selected and signed by the spectator. The card is torn into four quarters, which are wrapped in a handkerchief and given to the spectator to hold. When the handkerchief is opened, all the torn pieces have VANISHED except for one corner. The magician picks up the deck and riffles it. The selected card JUMPS OUT of the deck COMPLETELY RESTORED, except for the missing corner. The spectator matches the corner to the card and finds that it is a perfect fit!

SECRET AND PREPARATION

(A) Before the performance, tear off one index corner of an indifferent card. (You may discard this corner as you have no further need of it.) Place the torn card face down on top of the deck with the missing quarter at the lower left corner of the deck as shown. Place another card on top of the torn card to hide it. *(The torn corner card is now the second card from the top of the pack.)* Place a small rubber band in your right coat pocket.

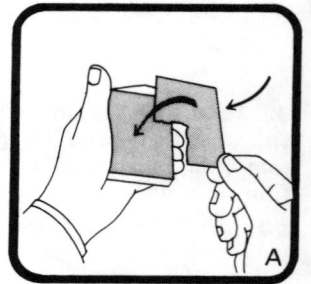

METHOD

(1) Remove the pack from its case and hold the deck face down in your left hand. Riffle the end of the deck with your right fingers to allow the spectator to select a card. After he has removed a card, immediately place the deck FACE UP on the table.

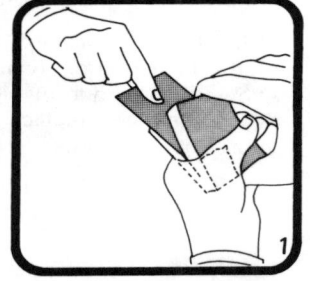

(2) As you do this, casually remove the card that is on the BOTTOM of the face up deck. (This is the card that was "hiding" the torn corner card.) Gesture with the card as you explain that the spectator could have selected *any* card. Return this card to the FACE of the deck.

(3) Take the spectator's card (X) and tear off one index corner. This should be approximately the same size as the quarter section already torn from the indifferent card.

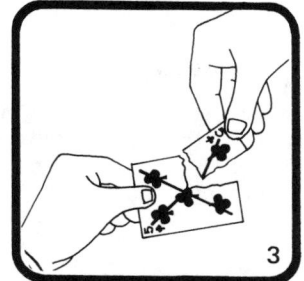

(4) Return the large portion of the chosen card to the spectator and have him sign the face of the card. When he has done this, take the card from him. Pick up the deck and hold it in your left hand with its face toward the spectators so that they cannot see the other torn corner card on top. Place the selected card (X) face down on the top of the deck on top of "your" torn card.

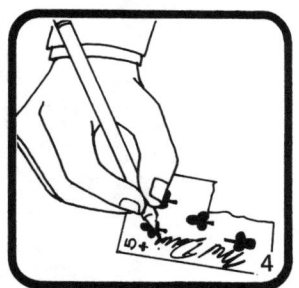

(5) *NOTE: The torn corner of the spectator's card is at the upper right-hand corner of the deck (the opposite corner from your previously torn card). The deck may not be lowered so the spectators can see the top.*

(6) Now, ask the spectator to sign the torn corner of the card also, merely using his initials if he wishes. In fact, any identifying mark will do.

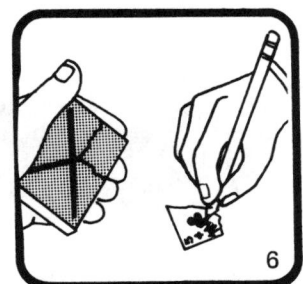

(7) While he is doing this, you apparently deal his card face down on the table. *Actually you press your right thumb upon the outer right corner of the pack and draw out the indifferent card from beneath the selected card.*

(8) THIS SWITCHES THE INDIFFERENT TORN CARD FOR THE SELECTED CARD, WHICH REMAINS ON TOP OF THE PACK. THE MOVE IS TERMED A "SECOND DEAL" AND THE MISSING CORNER OF THE SELECTED CARD MAKES THIS VERY EASY AND DECEPTIVE.

(9) As you deal the card onto the table, tilt the deck upward, toward your body, so the spectators cannot see the top.

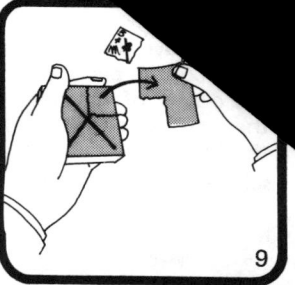

(10) With the deck in this position, give the deck one cut to place the selected card (X) in the center of the deck. Lay the deck face down on the table, as you did before.

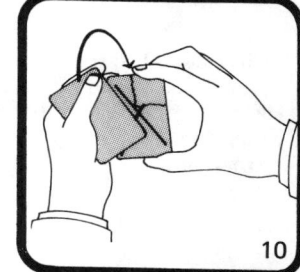

(11) Pick up the face-down indifferent card, *which the spectators think is their signed card,* and tear it into three pieces. Keep the pieces turned toward you so that no one can see the face of the card. The audience will suppose that you have torn the selected card into quarters.

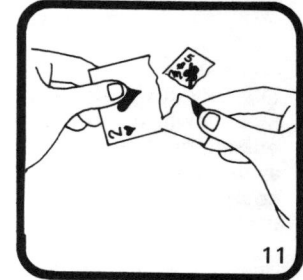

(12) Pick up the corner of the selected card (X) and place it on the face of the torn pieces. Hold all the pieces in your right hand. In this way you can exhibit the pieces, both front and back.

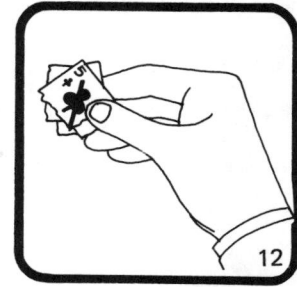

(13) Cover the torn pieces held in your right hand with an ordinary handkerchief. With your right thumb, push the corner of the selected card a little higher than the pieces of the indifferent card.

(14) With your left hand, grasp the corner (X) of the selected card through the fabric. Carry the rest of the torn pieces downward in your right hand, concealing them in the bend of your right fingers. Thrust your right hand into your coat pocket.

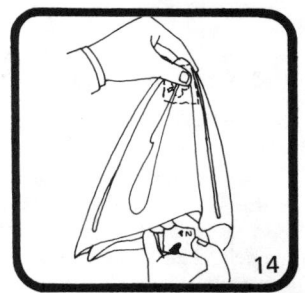

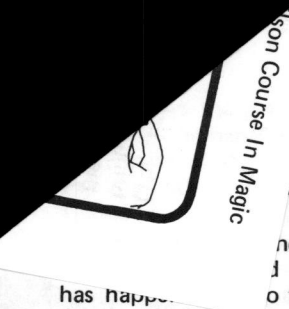

 - Cont'd.

...in your pocket, ...d place it around ...ndkerchief below ...that the audience ...quarters of the ...he handkerchief to ...d and restate what has happe... ...o this point....*Now, for the Magic!*

(18) Riffle the upper right corner of the deck with your right fingertips, keeping the pack tilted upward and forward, while the left hand retains its firm grip.

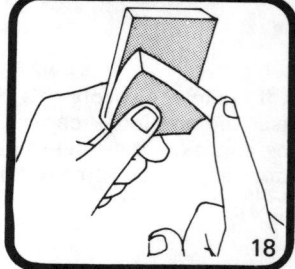

(16) Have the spectator remove the rubber band and spread the cloth. He will find *only* the torn corner, which he will recognize as the one he marked.

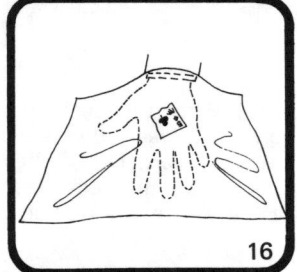

(19) The riffle action will cause the selected card (X) to jump half-way out of the deck. This is a very surprising effect, but only a prelude to the surprise that follows.

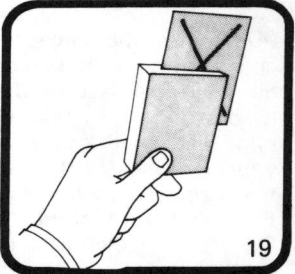

(17) Pick up the deck and hold it face down in such a way that the missing portion of the selected card is at the lower left. (The selected card, of course, is buried somewhere in the deck.)

Selected card in center of deck with torn corner here.

(20) Offer this card (X) to the spectator, letting him draw it from the deck himself. He will be amazed to find that the torn pieces of his own card have been magically restored!

(21) Have him match his torn corner to the card. It will be a perfect fit. THIS IS THE FINAL CONVINCER IN A TRULY GREAT CARD MYSTERY.

COMMENTS AND SUGGESTIONS

This feat of card magic was originated by the late Paul Le Paul and used for many years. It creates a startling effect, that is one of the best in magic. Give this the practice it deserves and you will have a card effect that will entertain and mystify all who witness it.

YOU DO AS I DO

As a "two person" trick, this is a real baffler. All you need are two ordinary decks of playing cards. It is a good idea to use packs with different colored backs, so that the audience can keep track of them as the trick proceeds.

EFFECT

Two packs of cards are thoroughly shuffled. . .one is shuffled by a spectator and the magician shuffles the other pack. The magician and the spectator then exchange packs and each selects a card, being sure that the other person does not see it. The cards are both replaced in their decks. The magician and the spectator exchange decks again and each finds the "duplicate" of the card he selected in the other pack. The spectator and the magician then place the cards that they have selected face down on the table. When the two cards are turned up, they prove to be identical!

SECRET AND PREPARATION

This is one of the finest self-working tricks in card magic. You need only two ordinary decks of cards, and the trick can be performed any time, anywhere, with no previous set-up. Let's assume that one deck has red backs and the other blue.

METHOD

(1) Place both decks on the table and ask the spectator to select either pack. *This is a free choice.* Let's assume that he takes the deck with the *red* backs. This leaves you with the *blue* backed deck.

(2) Tell the spectator that he is to please "Do As I Do"...and the first thing you will do is to shuffle your blue backed deck...so he should do the same with the red deck.

(3) As you complete the last shuffle, square up your deck as shown in the picture. As you do, turn the deck on its edge and "glimpse" the bottom card and remember it. Do not call attention to this, just remember the bottom card as it will serve as your "key card" for the rest of the trick. *NOTE: In the illustration, the Eight of Diamonds will be your "Key Card."*

Key Card

(4) Stress to the spectator that, to make sure that all is fair, you will trade decks with him so *you will be using a deck that he personally has shuffled.* Exchange decks with the spectator ... *UNKNOWN TO HIM, YOU KNOW THE BOTTOM CARD OF THE BLUE DECK HE NOW HOLDS.*

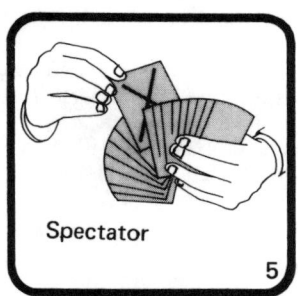

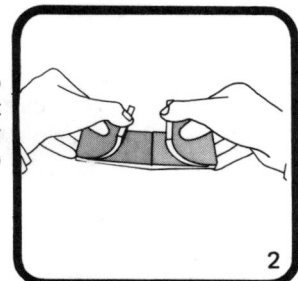

Magician 5

Spectator 5

(5) Instruct the spectator to spread the blue deck in his hands in front of him so that you cannot see the faces — just as you are doing with the red deck. He is to freely select any card from the deck and you will do likewise. Tell him it's best if he selects his "favorite card" and that you will do the same and select your "favorite card." *(To make the illustrations easy to follow, we have marked the spectator's card with an "X.")*

Magician 6

Spectator 6

(6) Explain to the spectator that he is to place the card he selected on the top of the deck (as shown in the picture) as you do the same with your card. It is not necessary for you to remember the card which you have selected at this point. *Just remember your "key card," the one that is on the bottom of the deck now held by the spectator — the Eight of Diamonds.*

Magician 7

Spectator 7

(7) Have the spectator square up his cards as you do the same. Then you each place your decks on the table.

(8) Tell the spectator to cut his deck, as you cut your deck, thus burying the selected cards somewhere in the middle of each pack. UNKNOWN TO HIM, THIS CUT PLACES THE BOTTOM CARD, WHICH IS YOUR "KEY CARD," THE EIGHT OF DIAMONDS, DIRECTLY ABOVE HIS SELECTED CARD.

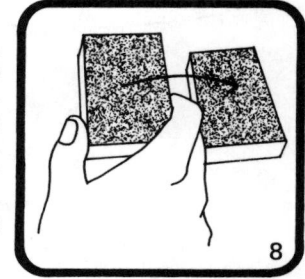

8

(9) Have him complete the cut and then ask him to cut two more times, as you do the same. *Be sure that each cut is a "single cut" and that the cut is completed each time. No matter how many times you cut the deck, as long as each cut is completed before the next cut is started, the "key card" will stay next to the selected card.*

(10) Stress the fact that there's no possible way that you could know where his "favorite card" is now located in the deck and likewise he could not know where your card is either.

(11) Now trade decks with the spectator once more. You now hold the one you originally shuffled, the blue deck with your "key card."

(14) Tell the spectator to remove his selected card without showing its face and you will do the same. *Actually, you remove the card which you now know to be the one the spectator selected, the TWO OF CLUBS.*

(12) Tell the spectator to look through that deck he now holds (the red deck) and to remove the card which matches his "favorite card" — and you will do the same with the blue deck.

(15) Have the spectator place his card on the table and you place yours beside it.

(13) While he does this, you spread your deck until you locate your "key card," the Eight of Diamonds. THE CARD IMMEDIATELY TO THE RIGHT OF THE "KEY CARD" WILL BE THE CARD THE SPECTATOR SELECTED.

Key Card   Spectator's Card

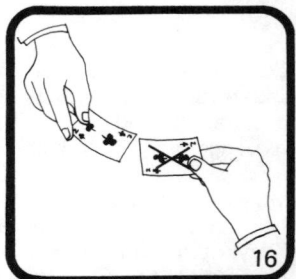

(16) Say, "It would be quite a coincidence if we *both* had the same favorite card, wouldn't it?" Stress the fact again that you each have been doing the same "You Do As I Do." Now you and the spectator turn your cards face up at the same time. HE WILL BE AMAZED TO SEE THAT THE CARDS MATCH!

THE HINDU SHUFFLE

The "Hindu Shuffle" is ideally suited to the needs of present-day magicians, and therefore, is a manipulation that all card workers should acquire. Various factors stand out strongly in its favor. It is easy to learn, it is a legitimate shuffle in its own right, and it is especially suited to card tricks.

As you become familiar with the Hindu Shuffle, you will also find that it can be readily adapted to important magical purposes, such as Forcing, Locating, or Controlling desired cards — and all without suspicion on the part of the spectators.

Because of its speed and precision, the Hindu Shuffle will give your audience the impression that you are an accomplished performer. That is an important aim when presenting Card Magic. SOME OF THE SIMPLEST TRICKS CAN BECOME UTTERLY BAFFLING WHEN THE SPECTATORS SUPPOSE THAT SKILLED MANIPULATION IS INVOLVED.

THE HINDU SHUFFLE

This type of shuffle supposedly gained its name from the fact that it was occasionally used by Hindu magicians who were unfamiliar with the usual shuffling methods. Whatever its origin, other magicians found that it gave them a great advantage when performing close-up card tricks, as the pack can be handled under the very eyes of the spectators in a deceptive manner without fear of detection. Hence it is recommended as the first and most important step toward acquiring skill as a card manipulator.

EFFECT

The magician holds a pack of cards in one hand and with the other hand proceeds to shuffle it by repeatedly drawing cards off the top -- *from the end of the pack* -- instead of drawing them *sideways* as with the Overhand Shuffle.

METHOD

(1) Hold the pack face down near one end with your right thumb and fingers at opposite sides of the pack.

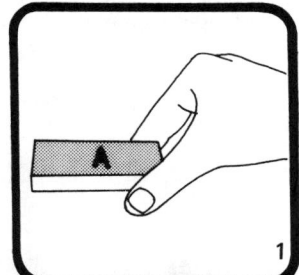

(2) Move the pack toward the left hand and grip the top portion of the deck between the tips of the left thumb and fingers. *NOTE: The first finger of the left hand is placed at the end of the pack as shown. This finger helps to keep the pack "squared" as you make the following movements.*

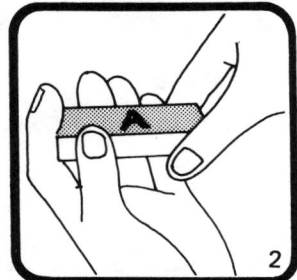

(3) With your right thumb and fingers, draw the bulk of the pack (B) out from beneath as you retain a small block of cards (A) with the fingers of your left hand.

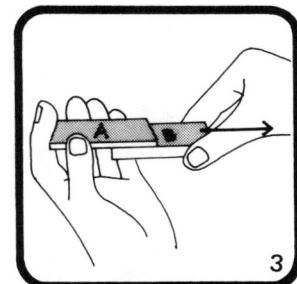

(4) As your right hand draws the bulk of the pack (B) clear, release the stack (A) in your left fingers, *so that it drops onto the palm of the left hand.*

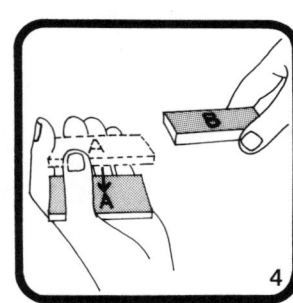

(5) Again, move the hands together and grip another small portion of cards from the top of the pack (B) between your left thumb and fingers.

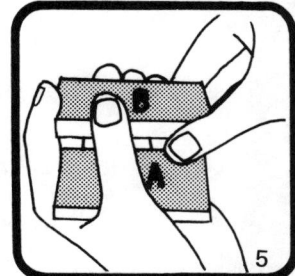

(6) Draw the bulk of the pack (C) from beneath the top stack (B). As soon as the pack is clear . . .

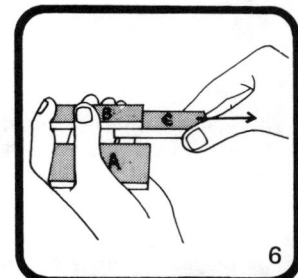

(7) . . .let the second stack (B) fall on the first stack (A) already lying in the left hand.

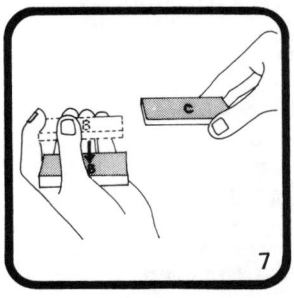

(8) Continue drawing off packets into the left hand until the right hand has only a small stack of its own (C), which you simply drop on the pack in the left hand.

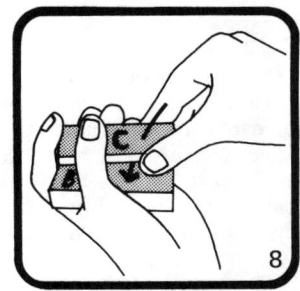

COMMENTS AND SUGGESTIONS

The shuffle should be executed at a moderately rapid pace, keeping the hands in continuous motion as you draw off the packets. This gives a polished and professional look. Because it is adaptable to various uses, the Hindu Shuffle is the basis for a whole series of clever but easy manipulations that will be described as we proceed. You will run into frequent mentions of the basic Hindu Shuffle and its more advanced forms throughout this series of lessons.

HOW TO USE THE HINDU SHUFFLE

Although the Hindu Shuffle *ACTUALLY MIXES* the pack, *it has many magical uses as well.* Once you have practiced and learned the regular Hindu Shuffle just described, you can use it to accomplish any of the three following purposes, which are indispensable in the presentation of good Card Magic.

(1)   LOCATING A SELECTED CARD . . . a card, freely selected from the pack is replaced wherever the chooser wishes . . . yet you can find the card in the "shuffled" deck. This uses a combination of a "key" card and the Hindu Shuffle. (Hindu Key Card Location and Short Card Location.)

(2)   "FORCING" A SPECIFIC CARD . . . a spectator has an apparently free choice of any card in the pack, but you "force" him to pick the one you want. (The Hindu Shuffle Flash Force.)

(3)   CONTROLLING THE LOCATION OF A CHOSEN CARD (OR CARDS) . . . after a card has been replaced in the pack, you can "control" it to the top or bottom of the deck while giving the deck an "honest" Hindu Shuffle. (The Hindu Shuffle Control.)

THE HINDU GLIMPSE

The Hindu Glimpse is a very useful and valuable move with the "Hindu Shuffle," enabling you to "sight" the bottom card of the deck secretly, in a natural manner that even the keenest observer will overlook.

EFFECT

The magician mixes the pack thoroughly, using the regular Hindu Shuffle. To keep the pack well-squared during this procedure, he taps the inner end of the left-hand packet with the right-hand pack pushing any protruding cards into place. This very action would seem to the spectators to eliminate the possibility of his seeing any cards in the pack, but actually it works to his advantage, enabling him to secretly note the bottom card of the right-hand packet.

METHOD

(1) Begin with the regular Hindu Shuffle, drawing off small blocks of cards from the top of the deck into the left hand.

(3) Then continue the shuffle pulling off small packets from the top of the right hand cards.

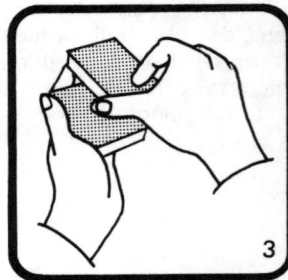

(2) As some point during the shuffle, when you hold about the same number of cards in each hand, turn the right hand packet at a slant, toward you, and tap the inner end of the left-hand packet in the pretense of "squaring up" the cards in that hand. This gives you the opportunity to sight the bottom card of the right hand packet ....the Two of Diamonds.

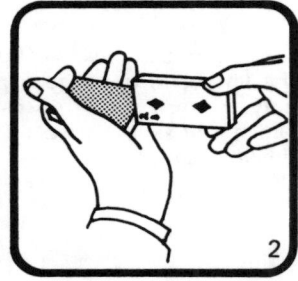

COMMENTS AND SUGGESTIONS

You only need a brief moment to glimpse the bottom card. Just make the move as a natural part of the shuffle. The Hindu Glimpse has many magical uses, as you will see.

THE HINDU KEY CARD LOCATION

Here is an example of a clever use of the Hindu Glimpse.

EFFECT

A spectator freely shuffles the deck as many times as he wishes and then has a free selection of any card. While the magician gives the deck a Hindu Shuffle, the spectator returns the card to the pack at any time that he wishes. The magician then shuffles the cards and gives them several cuts . . . yet he is still able to find and announce the spectator's selected card.

METHOD

(1) Let the spectator freely shuffle the deck as many times as he wishes so that you cannot know the location of any card.

(2) Ribbon Spread the cards on the table, or just spread them face down in your hands, so that the spectator may have a completely free selection . . . have him remove any card he wishes.

(3) Gather up the cards and begin the Hindu Shuffle. As you do the shuffle, glimpse and remember the bottom card of the packet in your right hand (THE HINDU GLIMPSE) . . . in this case the Two of Diamonds. This will be your "key" card in locating the spectator's card.

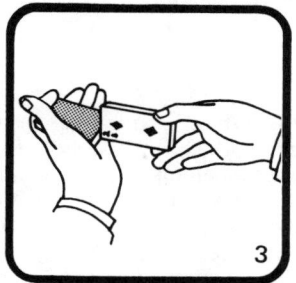

(4) Tell the spectator to look at his card (X) and remember it. Continue the shuffle and tell him to stop you when he would like to replace his card.

(5) When he says "Stop," have him return his card (X) to the top of the packet of cards in your left hand.

Spectator returns card here

"Key" card

5

(6) You immediately drop the cards in your right hand on top of the left hand packet burying his chosen card in the pack. THIS PLACES THE TWO OF DIAMONDS (YOUR "KEY" CARD) DIRECTLY ABOVE THE SPECTATOR'S CHOSEN CARD (X).

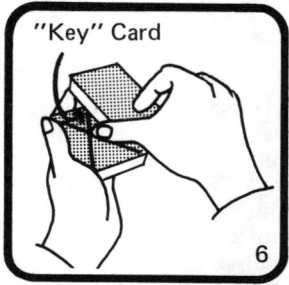

"Key" Card

6

(7) Then give the deck a few single cuts or let the spectator make the cuts. Turn the deck face up and spread it between your hands. Act as if you are concentrating on the spectator's face. When you sight your "key" card, the Two of Diamonds, *the selected card (X) will be immediately to its right.* After a suitable period of time, announce the name of the card.

7

IMPORTANT NOTE

In using the "Hindu Shuffle Key Card Location" system just described, you may sometimes encounter a hesitant spectator who does not wish to replace his chosen card until you are about to drop your last few cards on top. That means that you may have to complete the shuffle and begin all over, which is perfectly natural. However, if that happens, your "key" card becomes lost. Just start the shuffle again and glimpse and REMEMBER a NEW bottom "key" card.

COMMENTS AND SUGGESTIONS

This is an example of using the Hindu Glimpse to get your "key" card next to the spectator's selected card in a very clever way, even though he has first shuffled the deck himself.

SPELL-A-NAME

When you have practiced the Hindu Shuffle and the Hindu Glimpse enough to where you can execute them smoothly and at a moderately rapid pace, you are then ready to learn the following mystery. Spell-A-Name applies the *first* use of the Hindu Shuffle as defined under LOCATING A SELECTED CARD in the "How To Use The Hindu Shuffle" section described earlier. Like many tricks involving a selected card, it depends upon the use of a "key" card, with its climax producing a distinctly different touch.

EFFECT

A spectator is given a free selection of a card from an ordinary pack. After his card is replaced in the pack, you give the pack several cuts and then turn the deck face up and run through the cards to show that they are thoroughly mixed. Next, you hand the pack to the spectator face down and tell him to SPELL HIS OWN NAME, letter by letter, dealing a card from the top of the deck for each letter. After he comes to the final letter of his name, you tell him to turn the *next* card face up. IT PROVES TO BE HIS CHOSEN CARD!

SECRET AND PREPARATION

As mentioned above, this is a trick in which the bottom card of the pack is remembered and used as a "key" card. Also, you must know beforehand the name of the person whom you intend to have select the card. Assume that you are performing the trick for a friend named "Larry Jones."

METHOD

(1) Spread the pack so your friend can remove one card. Then begin a regular Hindu Shuffle asking him to call "Stop" at any time during the shuffle. As you shuffle, glimpse the bottom card of the pack (see Hindu Glimpse). This card (the Five of Diamonds in the illustration) will be your "key" in locating the spectator's card in the pack.

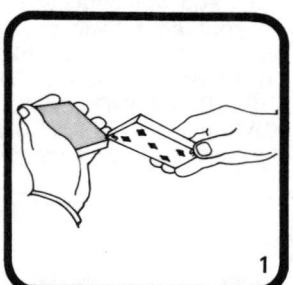

(2) When he says "Stop," have Larry put his card face down on the lower half of the pack (the card marked "X" represents the chosen card).

(3) When the card is replaced, drop the upper half of the pack on the lower so that your "key card" — the Five of Diamonds — comes directly over the chosen card (X).

(4) Now cut the pack several times to "lose" the card in the deck. Actually, as long as you give the deck only SINGLE CUTS, the selected card will not be separated from the key card. In fact, after you cut the deck — offer the pack to the spectator to cut as much as he likes. Make sure you specify he should make only SINGLE cuts.

(5) This done, turn the pack face up, remarking, "Your card is lost somewhere in the pack, so as I run through the deck, look for your card, but don't tell me when you see it!" With that, start "running" through the pack, thumbing cards from left to right, one at a time.

(6) When you come to your "key card" — the Five of Diamonds — start spelling your friend's name to yourself: "L-A-R-R-Y J-O-N-E-S" beginning with the letter "L" for the "key" card (the Five of Diamonds). *Continue spelling one letter of his name for each card you "run" from your left hand to your right.*

Key Card   Selected Card

(7) When you complete secretly spelling the name, separate the pack after the last letter ("S") in his name ("Jones") and ask the spectator if he has seen his card so far. *It is perfectly natural to gesture with your hands when asking this question, therefore, it should not arouse suspicion when you separate the pack at that point.*

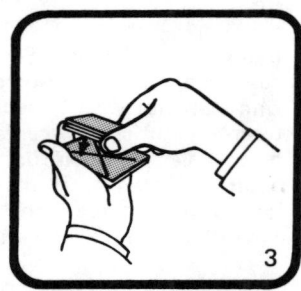

"S" Card

(8) When the spectator replies "Yes" to your question, reassemble the pack; *but instead of placing the halves together the way they were, place the left-hand packet ON TOP of the right-hand packet.*

(9) Square the pack, turn it face down and hand it to your friend. Tell him to "Deal the cards one by one, *spelling your own name,* card by card."

(10) This he does, finishing his "spell" on your key card. The next card (X) will be his chosen card, which you tell him to turn over. He will be amazed to find that HIS name has found HIS card!

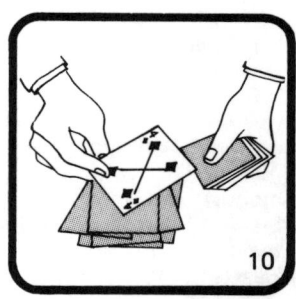

COMMENTS AND SUGGESTIONS

In this and in other similar "key" card tricks, when running through the pack, if you come to your "key" card before you are half way through the pack, "spell" the name and cut the rear portion of the front as usual. But instead of stopping there, run through the cards again before asking your friend if he has seen his card. When he says, "Yes," simply close the pack and hand it to him telling him to spell his name. The idea is to *let him see most of the cards in the pack BEFORE you put the question.* If he sees too few, the effect is weakened. Sometimes, in contrast, you may run through nearly all the cards before you come to your "key." This means you will not have enough remaining cards to spell your friend's name. In that case, simply close the pack and cut about a dozen cards from the face, to the back of the deck. Then start all over, running through the pack, in the usual fashion spelling your friend's name.

SPELL-A-CARD

EFFECT

This is an alternate version of "Spell-A-Name" which comes in very handy when you don't know the name of the person who selected the card. Rather than asking him his name and weakening the effect, you can switch to "Spell-A-Card."

METHOD

(1) Have a spectator select a card and return it to the pack; be sure to glimpse your "key card" in the usual fashion.

(2) Now, as you run face up through the pack, note the card JUST BEFORE THE "KEY" CARD. . .*this will be the spectator's card.* Let's suppose the spectator has selected the Five of Diamonds.

(3) As you run the cards from your left hand to your right hand,*secretly* spell the name of the spectator's card, letter by letter. . .F-I-V-E O-F D-I-A-M-O-N-D-S. . .passing one card for each letter BEGINNING WITH THE "KEY" CARD.

(4) This done, separate the pack at the proper location, just as you did in Spell a Name, as you ask, "Have you seen your card?"

(5) When he answers, "Yes," reassemble the pack, putting the left-hand packet on the top of the deck as before. *Thus you have secretly placed the selected card at the correct location to "spell out" its name.*

(6) Have the spectator spell the name of his card, letter by letter. When he turns up the next card, it will be his card. . .the FIVE OF DIAMONDS!

SPELL-A-CARD — OUTDONE

This version of SPELL-A-CARD offers an added feature which makes this a Double Mystery.

METHOD

(1) Follow the usual procedure for Spell-A-Card by having a spectator select a card (the Five of Diamonds in the illustrations) and return it to the pack below your secretly noted "key" card (the Eight of Clubs).

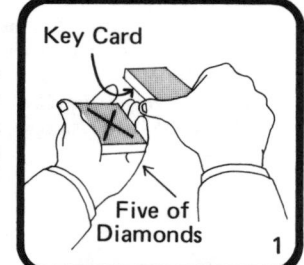

(2) After the pack has been cut several times, run through the cards from the left hand to the right hand *face up* telling the spectator to make sure that the deck is thoroughly mixed. As in Spell-A-Card, when you come to the card *just before the "key" card,* you know that it is the selected card. Begin spelling its name, F-I-V-E O-F D-I-A-M-O-N-D-S, as you run the cards from your left hand to your right hand.

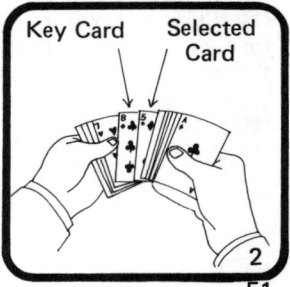

(3) Then, after spelling the Five of Diamonds, DO NOT CUT THE PACK AT THAT POINT as in the regular version. INSTEAD, note the NEXT card AFTER you have spelled the "selected" card, (the Five of Diamonds) and *secretly spell its name*, S-I-X O-F S-P-A-D-E-S, beginning with the next card above it (the Four of Hearts in the illustration).

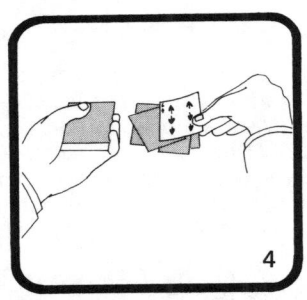

START New "Spell" Here   Next Card After "Spell"

3

(4) When you have finished secretly spelling this "new" card, cut the rear portion of the pack to the front and turn the pack face down as you state, "Here's something really magical. If I snap the end of the pack and spell out *any* card I have in mind, I find it. Take the Six of Spades for example." Here you deal cards, letter by letter -- spell S-I-X O-F S-P-A-D-E-S and turn up the next card, showing it to be the Six of Spades.

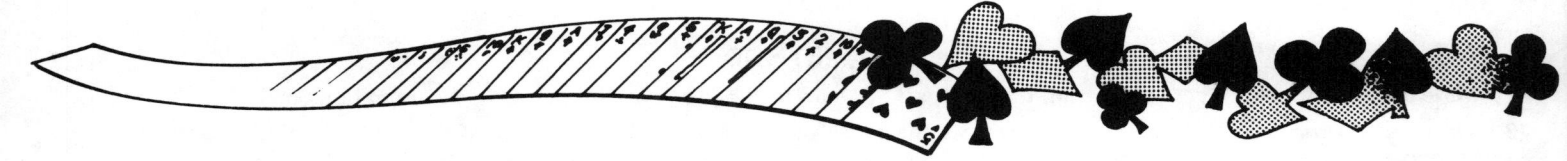

4

(5) Gather up the dealt cards, turn them face down and *put them on the bottom of the pack*. Now hand the spectator the deck and say "Here, try for yourself, spelling the name of the card you selected, whatever it happens to be. But don't forget to snap the end of the pack first, that's what works the magic".

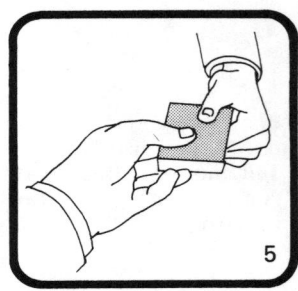

5

(6) The spectator spells his card, F-I-V-E O-F D-I-A-M-O-N-D-S, and it's right there, just as you said, to complete the double surprise! Nobody will suspect that you set up your "spell" by merely looking through the pack, and when the spectator finds his own card in the same way, the audience will be completely amazed.

COMMENTS AND SUGGESTIONS

One advantage of this "Double Speller" is that, when *you* spell a card first, it makes the process easy for the other person to follow. ALSO, SINCE THE PACK IS IN THE SPECTATOR'S OWN HANDS, IT APPARENTLY PUTS THE CARDS BEYOND YOUR CONTROL.

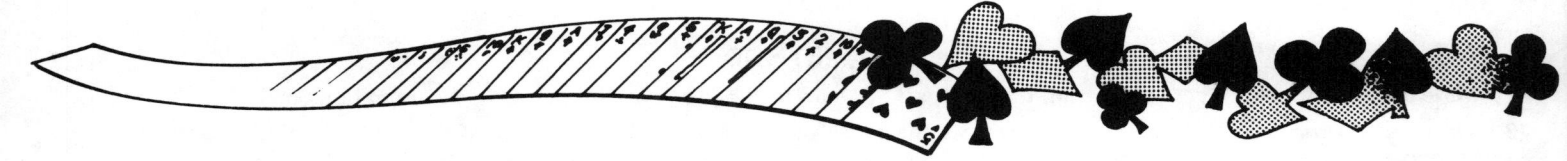

THE HINDU FLASH FORCE

There are many ways of "Forcing" a spectator to select a certain card without having him realize it – but to do this naturally and repeatedly was formerly somewhat difficult. It took the "Hindu Shuffle" to produce a sure-fire way of "Forcing" a card at a moment's notice. Try the method that follows and you will see why.

EFFECT

During the course of a Hindu Shuffle, at any time the spectator requests, the magician pauses long enough to give the spectator a "flash" of a card in the pack. Though the magician keeps his own head turned so that he cannot possibly see the card . . . the magician has actually "Forced" the spectator to select the very card that the magician wanted.

METHOD

(1) Suppose you want to "Force" the Five of Diamonds. Place the Five on the bottom of the pack. Start the usual Hindu Shuffle, telling the spectator to call "stop" at any time he wants.

Five of Diamonds "force card" on bottom

1

(2) Continue the shuffle at the usual speed, pulling packets from the TOP of the cards in the right hand. *This leaves the Five of Diamonds at the BOTTOM of the right-hand cards.*

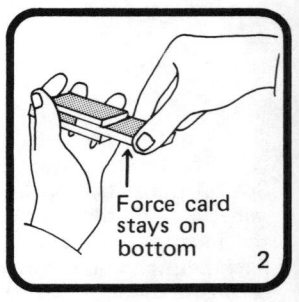

Force card stays on bottom

2

(3) When the spectator says "stop," slant the right-hand packet toward him, showing him the face of the card on the bottom. THIS IS THE ORIGINAL BOTTOM CARD OF THE PACK, THE FIVE OF DIAMONDS!

Five of Diamonds

(5) Drop the right-hand cards on the cards lying in your left hand to bury the card the spectator *thinks* he has freely chosen from the deck. Actually you already know the card. YOU HAVE "FORCED" HIM TO SELECT THE FIVE OF DIAMONDS JUST AS YOU HAD PLANNED!

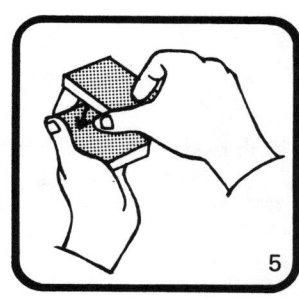

(4) *NOTE: Here is a view as the spectator sees it. Notice that the right hand is well forward toward the spectator to insure that the magician cannot see the card on the bottom. Tell the spectator to remember the card he has "selected."*

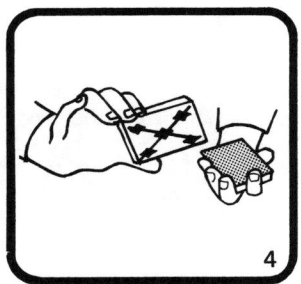

COMMENTS AND SUGGESTIONS

This is called a "Flash Force" because you simply "flash" the card before the spectator's eyes. But it is MORE THAN THAT. You can hold up the packet as long as you want. Just assure the spectator that you cannot see the card that he thinks is the result of HIS OWN FREE CHOICE, when he called "stop." When he is looking at the card, you should turn your head away to emphasize that you are the ONE PERSON who cannot possibly see that card. This is important, because it diverts the spectators' minds from the fact that you don't need to see it, BECAUSE YOU ALREADY KNOW IT. That is one use of "misdirection" – which you will learn to use more and more as you continue with the Course.

THE HINDU COLOR CHANGE

Here is a quick, baffling trick that makes a good opening number for a card routine. It depends upon the "Hindu Shuffle," so the skill that you have acquired in learning that important "move" can also be put to good use with this trick.

EFFECT

You take a red-backed pack of cards from its case and spread them FACE UP so that everyone can see that they are all different. Then, running through the face-up pack with a series of short cuts, you show the backs of the cards at frequent intervals. The spectators can see that all the cards have RED BACKS. Giving the face-up pack a "magic tap," you turn it face down and spread the cards along the table, and to everyone's astonishment, all the backs have turned from red to BLUE!

SECRET AND PREPARATION

All you need is a regular blue-backed pack and a *single red-backed card,* which you place on top of the pack before putting the deck in its box. You should use a RED CASE, as the pack is supposed to have RED BACKS at the start.

METHOD

(1) Open the box and bring out the pack face down, with the one red-backed card showing. Keep the cards well squared so you don't accidentally "flash" any of the blue cards beneath the top red card, as you remark, "Here is a pack of red-backed cards."

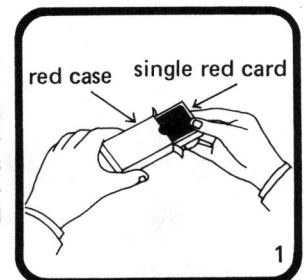

red case   single red card

(2) With that, you lay the box aside and turn the pack face up in your hands.

(3) Spread the pack *face up* in your hands showing the faces of the cards remarking: "As you can see, the cards are all different, as they should be . . ."

(4) Now square the pack *face up* in the left hand and begin a regular Hindu Shuffle, but with the deck *face up.*

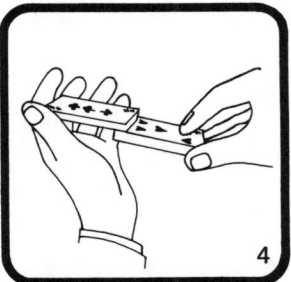

(5) At various intervals throughout the shuffle, swing the right-hand packet away from you and tilt the back of the packet toward the spectators showing them the single red-backed cards as you say, ". . . and the backs are the same, red, as they should be."

(6) *NOTE: Here you are simply combining the Hindu Shuffle with a REPEATED Flash Force while the pack is upside down. The audience thinks that you are cutting the pack at various places, showing a different red-backed card each time. Actually, you are always showing the SAME RED-BACKED CARD. Because of the "face-up" Hindu Shuffle, the red card remains on the bottom of the face-up right-hand packet. Do this deliberately and cleanly, keeping the pack well squared with each "flash" to prevent anyone from glimpsing a portion of a blue back during the process.*

(7) As you complete the series of "flashes," drop the last few cards face up on the pack. Or, the shuffle can even be carried *to the very last card,* thus placing the single red card at the top of the face-up deck.

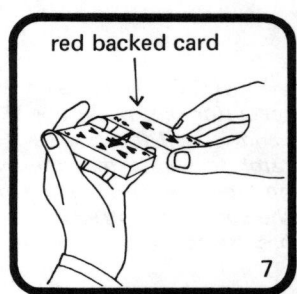

red backed card

(8) Square the face up pack and give it a sharp snap or riffle, saying you will change the backs from red to blue. With that, turn the pack face down (the single red-backed card is now face down at the bottom, or close to it) and spread or fan the pack *except for the last few bottom cards.* Apparently all the backs have magically changed from red to blue!

Single red back   All blue backs

COMMENTS AND SUGGESTIONS

(A) As already stated, the success of the effect depends upon keeping the upper packet well squared throughout the entire shuffle, so that the red-backed card can be shown repeatedly without exposing any blue card.

(B) To keep the packet square while shuffling you can tap it against the inner end of the pack, as described in the "Hindu Glimpse."

(C) When showing the blue backs at the finish, fan the cards from hand to hand, or spread them face down along the table....do just be careful NOT to spread the cards too close to the "secret" red-backed card. The simplest follow-up is to gather the pack and replace it in the case, which then goes in your pocket.

(D) As described later under A CLEVER COMBINATION, this makes a very good lead-in for DOUBLE THOUGHT....which also eliminates having to secretly get rid of the one red-backed card.

FINAL NOTE: By using a "short" red backed card (see "Short Card" section), after the color change, you can gather the out-spread pack, turn it face up and give it a Hindu Shuffle, this time flashing a blue backed card with each pause. Then turn the *back* of the pack *toward* the spectators and slowly riffle the cards, showing "all blue," as the short card will ride along unseen. Finally turn the pack face up in your left hand. With your right hand, riffle to the short card, and cut it to the face of the pack. Pick up the card case and dispose of the short red-backed card as described.

THE COLOR CHANGING DECKS
(Two-Deck Version)

In this modified version of the Hindu Color Change, you take the mystery one step further by adding a second pack of cards – of a different color – and convert the effect from a *color change* into a magical *transposition* of the two packs.

EFFECT

The magician removes a RED-BACKED pack of cards from its case and spreads them face up so that everyone can see that they are all different. Then, running through the face-up pack with a series of short cuts, he shows the *red* backs of the cards at frequent intervals, finally placing the pack face up on the table next to its *red box*. The performer then follows the exact same procedure with a BLUE-BACKED pack of cards, and places it face up on the table next to its *blue box*. The mystery begins when the magician removes one card from each pack. He places the one *red* card on the face of the *blue-backed* pack and the one *blue* card on the *red-backed* pack. Explaining that this causes the rest of the cards in both packs to "Follow the Leader," the magician turns over each pack and spreads it face down next to its correct colored box. The audience is amazed to discover that ALL THE BLUE-BACKED CARDS HAVE "MAGICALLY" CHANGED PLACES WITH ALL OF THE RED-BACKED CARDS!

SECRET AND PREPARATION

The only items required for this mystery are a red-backed pack of cards and its *red box* and a *blue*-backed deck and its *blue box* with a matching design. To prepare, remove a single *blue* card from the blue pack and place it face down on top of the *red deck*. Also, place a single *blue* card on top of the *red deck*. Now, place the red deck *(with the one blue card on top)* into the blue box; and place the blue deck *(with the one red card on top)* into the red box. You are ready to perform the COLOR CHANGING DECKS.

METHOD

(1) To begin, place both packs – in their boxes – on the table. Say, "I have two packs of cards, one red – and one blue."

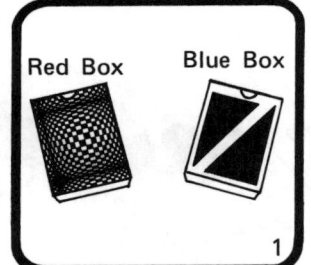

Red Box   Blue Box

(2) Pick up the BLUE BOX and remove the pack of cards face down.... SO THE SINGLE BLUE CARD, WHICH MATCHES THE COLOR OF THE BOX, IS SEEN BY THE SPECTATORS. They will assume it to be an all blue pack. *NOTE: As you remove the pack from the box, keep the cards well "squared" so you do not accidentally shift the top blue card exposing the red cards below.*

(3) Place the empty blue box on the table and turn the pack over (face up). Run through the pack showing the faces of the cards.... say, "As you can see, all the cards in the pack are different, as they should be."

(4) Now square the pack face up in your left hand and begin a regular Hindu Shuffle, WITH THE DECK FACE UP. At various intervals throughout the shuffle, execute the repeated "Flash Force" as described in the HINDU COLOR CHANGE. The audience believes you are cutting the pack at *various* places showing a *different* card each time. Remark, "And the backs are all blue, as they should be."

(5) IMPORTANT NOTE: In this trick, (unlike the HINDU COLOR CHANGE, the Hindu Shuffle, MUST BE CARRIED TO THE VERY LAST CARD. As you complete the Hindu Shuffle, the left fingers draw off all the remaining red cards leaving the single blue card in your right hand. Finish the shuffle by dropping the blue card *on top of the face-up deck.*

(6) This done, square up the pack and place it face up on the table *next to the empty blue box* from which you removed it.

(7) Now, pick up the *red box* and remove the *"red"* pack *(actually the blue pack with the single red card on top).*

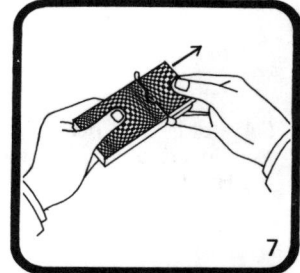

(8) Follow the same face-up Hindu Shuffle procedure using the repeated "Flash Force" showing the SINGLE RED card. Finish by shuffling the SINGLE RED CARD TO THE TOP OF THE FACE UP PACK. Square up this pack and place it face up on the table *next to the empty red box.*

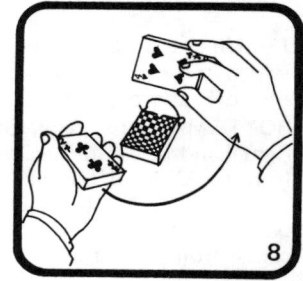

(9) With the packs resting face up next to their "own" colored boxes, (10) lift the two "odd" cards (the single red card and the single blue card) from the face of each pack and transpose them – (11) PLACING THE RED-BACKED CARD ON THE REAL RED PACK AND THE BLUE-BACKED CARD ON THE REAL BLUE PACK. As you do this say, "If I move just *one* card from each pack and place it on the pack of the opposite color, the rest of the cards in each pack will "Follow the Leader."

(12) Pick up both packs – one in each hand – and spread them face down on the table *next to the box you first removed it from*. The audience will be amazed to see that THE BLUE CARDS HAVE MAGICALLY CHANGED PLACES WITH THE RED CARDS – RIGHT BEFORE THEIR EYES!

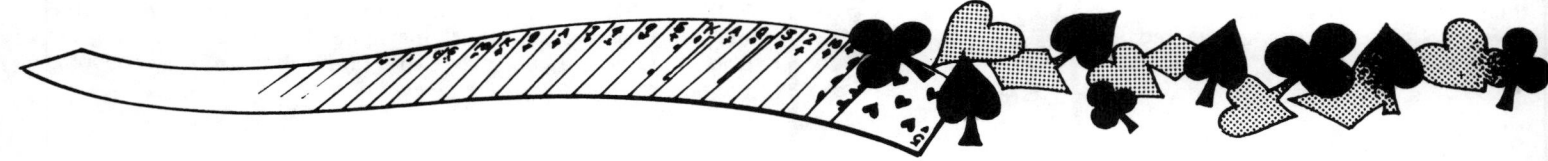

HINDU SHUFFLE — BOTTOM STOCK CONTROL

In certain card tricks, it is important that during a shuffle, the bottom card, or a group of cards already on the bottom, are retained there for some future purpose. Here is a way of accomplishing that with the aid of the Hindu Shuffle, making this an important utility sleight that every card worker should learn.

EFFECT

To all appearances, the magician gives the pack a regular Hindu Shuffle. Yet, in this modified version, the bottom stock of cards remains undisturbed or "unshuffled." Despite that important difference, the magician can switch from this form of the Hindu Shuffle to another without any chance of detection.

METHOD

(1) Hold the pack in the tips of the fingers of the left hand, ready for the Hindu Shuffle.

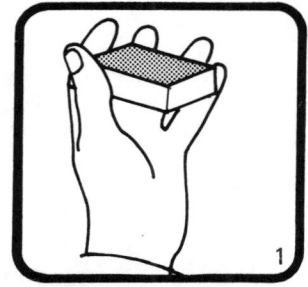

(2) Unlike a regular Hindu Shuffle, where the right hand begins by drawing off a group of cards from the BOTTOM of the pack, this time the right hand pulls out a section of cards from the CENTER, leaving the bottom group intact. The left hand retains the bottom stock *and* a small batch of cards from the top as in the usual Shuffle.

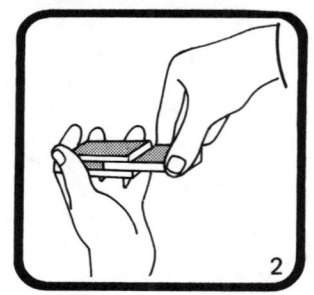

(3) Once the right hand has drawn the center packet of cards clear of the bottom and top packets, *the left hand allows the top packet to fall onto the bottom packet.*

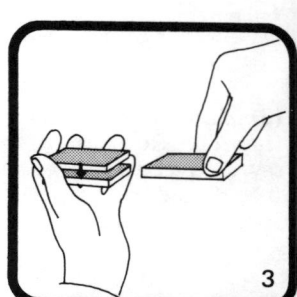

(4) Now, continue the regular Hindu Shuffle – repeatedly pulling off small batches of cards from the right-hand pack until the shuffle is complete.

(5) The pack has now been fairly shuffled EXCEPT FOR THE SMALL BATCH OF CARDS WHICH REMAINS UNDISTURBED. You are also now set to repeat the Hindu Shuffle — Bottom Stock Control as often as you like.

A FALSE CUT

EFFECT

Many very good card tricks depend upon your knowing the bottom card of the pack or bringing a chosen card to the top. At that point, a suspicious spectator may want to cut the pack. So to prove that all is fair, your best policy is to beat them to it by cutting the pack yourself. You can do that with the following "False Cut" that looks like the real thing, but actually leaves the pack just as it was.

METHOD

(1) Hold the deck in the left hand between the tips of the left fingers and thumb.

(2) With the thumb and fingers of your right hand, start to draw out about half the pack (B) from the lower part of the deck.

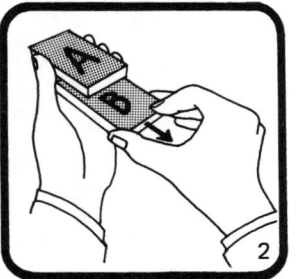

(3) As this lower stack (B) comes clear, sweep your right hand toward your body.

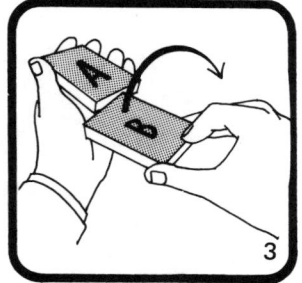

(4) Continue this sweep carrying the cards (B) in your right hand *up and over the top stack* (A) in your left hand.

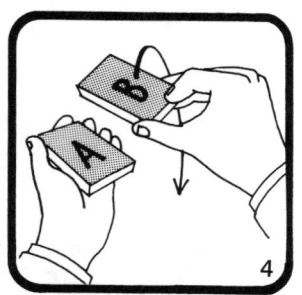

(5) Place the packet in your right hand (B) onto the table and leave it.

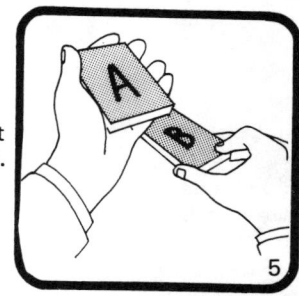

(6) Now with your right hand, take all of the cards (A) from the left hand and . . .

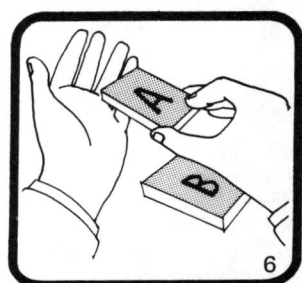

(7) . . . place them directly on top of the stack (B) on the table.

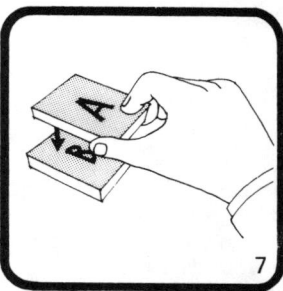

(8) It will appear as if the cards are fairly cut. Actually the order of the cards has not changed at all.

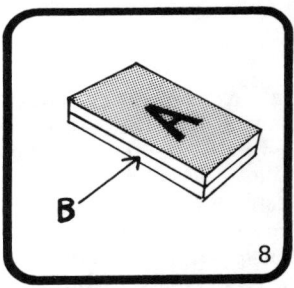

COMMENTS AND SUGGESTIONS

This False Cut should be performed at a moderate speed — not too slow and not too fast. Do not call special attention to it — *just do it as if you were cutting the cards in a normal manner.* Done correctly, no one will question it.

HINDU SHUFFLE PICK-UP CONTROL

This is one of the most deceptive and useful controls in all of Card Magic. If this sleight were the only one you used with the Hindu Shuffle, it would be well worth your time in learning it. The Pick-Up Control is not difficult to learn and, I am sure, you will be using it in many of your best card effects after you have mastered it.

EFFECT

A spectator returns a selected card to the pack while the magician is giving the deck a Hindu Shuffle. This apparently "loses" the card somewhere deep in the pack, yet the magician has secretly "controlled" the card to the top of the pack.

METHOD

(1) Ask a spectator to select a card freely from the pack, either as you spread the pack between your hands — or you can let him take a card by telling you to "stop" during the course of a Hindu Shuffle.

(2) While he is looking at his card, you square the pack and begin a new Hindu Shuffle, inviting him to replace his card any time he wants. You do the shuffle quite slowly, apparently to aid the replacement, *but actually to prepare for a simple but special move.*

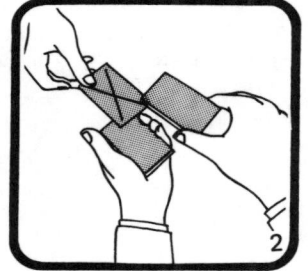

(3) After the spectator has replaced his card (X) on the left-hand section of the pack, move the bulk of the pack held in your right hand above the cards in your left hand as if to merely continue the shuffle.

(4) NOW THIS IS THE IMPORTANT MOVE. As the left fingers slide off another packet from the top of the bulk of the pack, the tips of your right thumb and second finger squeeze inward, grip the sides *and pick up a small packet of cards from the lower left-hand heap.* Now carry this small packet away on the bottom of the right-hand bulk of cards. Keep a "break" or "gap" between that small batch and the upper bulk of the pack in the right hand.

Pick up small packet with right fingers

(5) THE SELECTED CARD (X) IS THE TOP CARD OF THIS SMALL PACKET.

Selected card on top of small packet

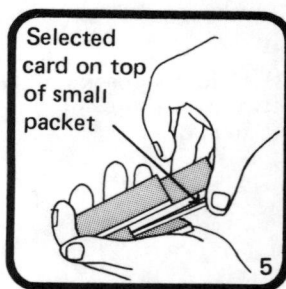

(6) Continue the shuffle, drawing off cards from the top of the right-hand packet, *still holding the small packet on the bottom of the right-hand bulk of cards, always maintaining the "gap" between the two portions.*

Selected card

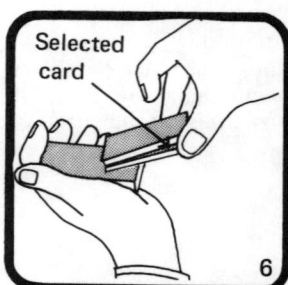

(7) As you finish the shuffle, *the left hand takes all the remaining cards ABOVE THE GAP . . .*

(8) . . .*while the right hand draws the little batch out from beneath . . .*

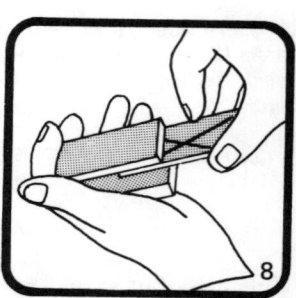

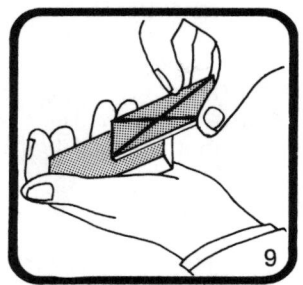

(9) . . .and drops it on the left-hand pack to complete the shuffle.

(10) Since the chosen card is the TOP CARD of that batch, it now becomes THE TOP CARD OF THE PACK. This means that YOU HAVE CONTROLLED THE CHOSEN CARD TO THE TOP OF THE PACK.

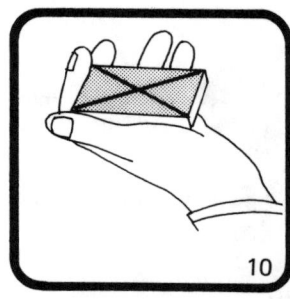

COMMENTS AND SUGGESTIONS

The Hindu Shuffle Control is one of the easiest and best ways to bring a selected card to the top of the pack. It also has many other uses . . . and is one of the most valuable sleights that you will learn from this Course. Please study the pictures carefully. The most important move and the "key" to this entire sleight is in Step 4. This is when you pick up the small batch of cards, with the selected card on top, with your right thumb and fingers from the top of the left-hand packet. At the same time that you do this, you pull off a small batch of cards from the TOP of the right-hand packet, *just as if you were continuing the regular Hindu Shuffle.* This completely covers your "secret" pick-up. You then continue the Hindu Shuffle in the normal fashion until you get to the last small batch of cards with the selected card on top. Just place that packet as the last "shuffle" on the top of the deck in the left hand. Thus, you have secretly brought the selected card to the top. I have repeated the description of this sleight in "COMMENTS AND SUGGESTIONS" BECAUSE OF ITS IMPORTANCE. Once you have mastered the Hindu Shuffle and the Hindu Shuffle Control, you have opened the door to hundreds of wonderful, baffling mysteries with cards. If you are interested in performing card tricks, please practice and learn this important sleight.

THE HINDU ACES

As its name implies, this routine utilizes the Hindu Shuffle, with the Hindu Card Pick-Up Control as its "secret weapon." The more you practice it, the more you will like it . . . and so will your audience!

EFFECT

The four Aces are removed from a pack of cards and given to a spectator to hold. As you shuffle the cards, Hindu style, he inserts the Aces at various intervals in the pack. When you finish the shuffle, you turn up the four top cards of the pack. All will be Aces!

METHOD

(1) From an ordinary pack of cards, run through the pack face up and remove the four Aces, placing them on the table. As you go through the deck, call attention to the fact that there are ONLY four Aces in the pack. Ask the spectator to pick up all four Aces and hold them face down in his hand.

(3) After the spectator has placed one Ace on top of the left-hand packet, continue the shuffle using the Hindu Pick-Up Control — secretly picking up a small batch from the top of the left-hand packet and maintaining a break between it and the bulk of the pack throughout the shuffle.

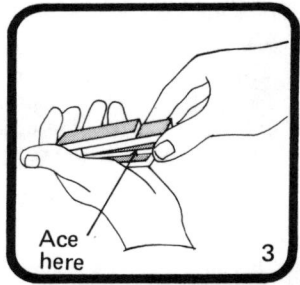

Ace here

(2) Begin a regular Hindu Shuffle, drawing small batches of cards from the bulk of the pack into the left hand until nearly half the pack has been shuffled, and then stop. Now, move the left hand packet toward the spectator telling him to place any one of the four Aces on top of the packet. (The Aces have been marked with number "One" through "Four" in the illustrations.)

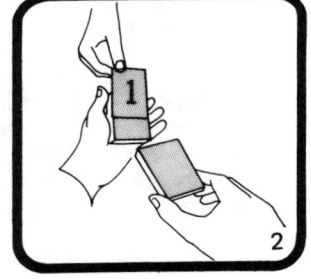

(4) When you have shuffled off all the cards above the break, the first Ace will have been secretly brought to the top of the deck with the cards in position to repeat the Hindu Shuffle.

(5) As you start the next Hindu Shuffle, draw about one-third of the deck (about 15 to 20 cards) from the top of the pack into the fingers of the left hand and STOP.

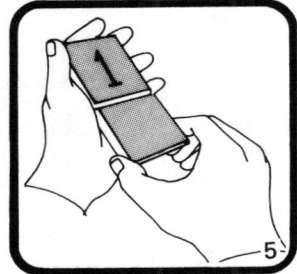

(7) This done, complete the Hindu Shuffle, using the Hindu Pick-Up Control, thus bringing both Aces to the top of the deck.

(6) Then, move your left hand toward the spectator and instruct him to place a second Ace on top of the packet in your left hand. *Unknown to the spectator, he will be placing this second Ace directly on top of the first Ace.*

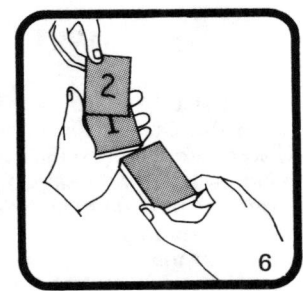

(8) Repeat the entire process with the third and fourth Aces until all four Aces have been secretly controlled to the top of the deck. You can then reveal them in any manner you wish, or simply deal them face down on to the table, and turn each card face up, one at a time, to bring the mystery to a startling finish.

COMMENTS AND SUGGESTIONS

Practice this effect until you can do it smoothly, but not too rapidly, as you may have to pause occasionally to square the pack. When performing for a group of people, you can vary the routine by first handing each Ace to a different person. You then move from one to another, giving you a chance to square the pack before each replacement of an Ace, which is helpful with the "pickup."

REVERSE ORDER COUNT TRICK

In this quick, surprising way of discovering a chosen card, the person who selected the card plays an important part, which adds greatly to its impact on your audience. Once you have convinced people that a chosen card is hopelessly lost in the pack, merely naming it is not enough to impress them with your magic powers. You must make the card show itself in some unexpected way, and this is one of those ways.

EFFECT

After a card has been selected and shuffled back into the pack, you ask someone to name a number, preferably below twenty, though he can go higher if he insists. You count that many cards – say fourteen – face down on the table; then give the packet to the spectator and ask him to verify the count. When he comes to the final number – fourteen – you tell him to look at that card. When he turns it face up, he finds that it is the very card that he selected!

METHOD

(1) Begin by having the spectator select a card from a thoroughly shuffled pack. Ask him to remember it and return it to the pack during the course of a Hindu Shuffle. Using the HINDU PICK-UP CONTROL, bring the spectator's selected card to the *top* of the pack. (The selected card is indicated by an "X.")

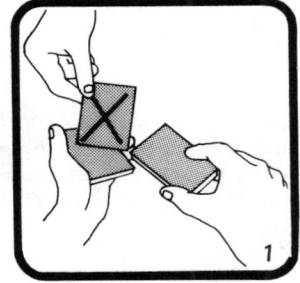

(2) With the pack held in dealing position in the left hand, ask the spectator to call out *any* number from one to twenty, explaining that you will count down that many cards in the pack. When the spectator names the number, begin dealing the cards, <u>one at a time</u> in a pile, from the top of the deck onto the table—beginning with the spectator's card.

(3) *NOTE: Dealing the cards in this fashion – one at a time on top of each other – reverses the order of the cards as you count them. As explained in the Course, this is known as a Reverse Order Count, which, as you will see, is used to your advantage.*

(6) Instruct him to recount the cards in the same manner you did, one at a time in a pile and to count aloud as he does so. As the spectator recounts the cards, he is again <u>reversing their order</u>, placing them in the same sequence as when you began your count – WITH THE SELECTED CARD AT THE TOP!

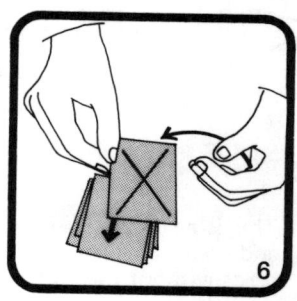

(4) Continue dealing and counting – one card for each number – until you have reached the number selected by the spectator.

(7) When the spectator completes the count and verifies that you counted correctly, ask him to name the card he selected. When he does, tell him to turn over the top card of the counted pile. He will be amazed to see his selected card at the very number he selected!

(5) This done, give the pile of "counted" cards, face down, to the spectator as you say, "I have counted out the exact number of cards which you selected. Please count them yourself to verify that I have counted correctly."

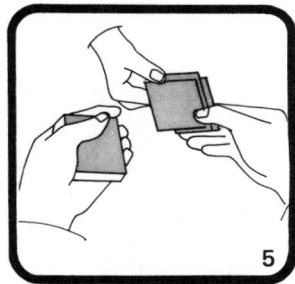

COMMENTS AND SUGGESTIONS

Since no one knows that the chosen card is on top of the pack to start, the fact that the spectator reverses your count *back* to where it was originally will not seem to have any apparent bearing on the result. In a sense, this is a *"double reverse,"* the only difference being that you did yours knowingly, while he did his unknowingly. Clever and bold secrets of this type give Card Magic much of its appeal and the more you vary your program with surprise discoveries of chosen cards, the better your audiences will like it.

OVERHAND SHUFFLE

The "Overhand Shuffle" is the most common of all shuffles. The very simplicity of the shuffle makes it easy to locate and control certain cards, bringing them to top or bottom of the pack and retaining them there. For that very reason, it should be practiced until it becomes second nature, so that the various subterfuges can be introduced without arousing suspicion. By using the Overhand Shuffle constantly in card tricks as well as in card games, merely handling the pack gives you the opportunity to practice.

Hundreds of excellent tricks can be developed directly from the Overhand Shuffle, many of which have been included in the Card Section of this Course.

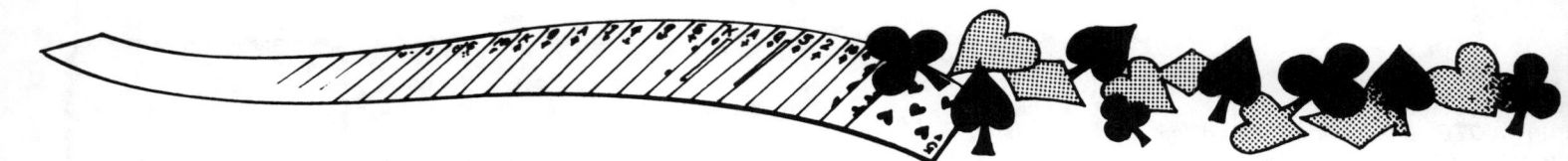

THE OVERHAND SHUFFLE

This is a simple, standard way of shuffling a pack of cards that you should use constantly when performing card tricks. It is both natural and convincing and is an honest shuffle. However, more importantly, it can be adapted to many special uses, such as "controlling" certain cards without the audience knowing it. These "controls," which will be taught later, are some of the most useful sleights in card magic.

METHOD

(1) Hold the deck with the thumb and fingers of your right hand.

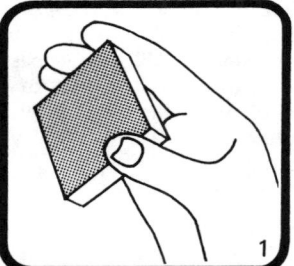

(2) Bring both your hands together. With your left thumb, from the top of the deck, pull off a block of several cards (indicated by the letter A), into your left hand, leaving the remainder of the deck (letter B) in the right hand.

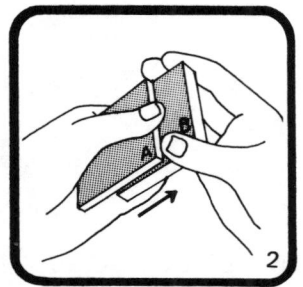

(3) Separate your hands completely. Hold the block of cards now in your left hand (A) firmly between the left thumb and fingers.

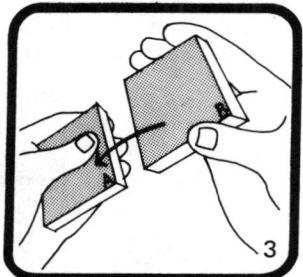

(4) Lift your left thumb enough to allow the packet in the right hand to be reinserted into the "pull-off position." With the left thumb, pull another block of several cards (B) into the left hand on top of the cards (A) already in the hand, leaving the remainder of the deck (C) in your right hand.

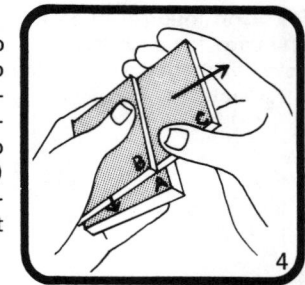

(5) Separate your hands, allowing the cards just removed (Block B) to fall on the cards already in the left hand (Block A).

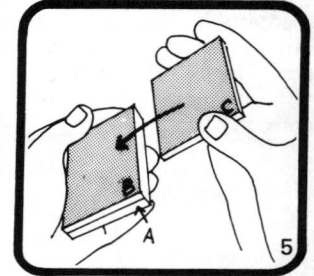

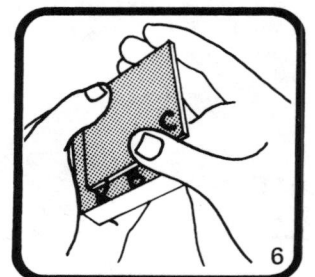

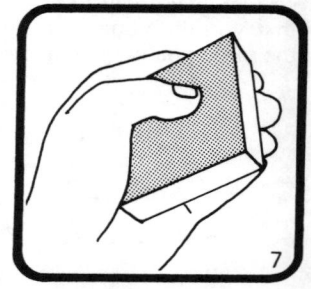

(6) Continue pulling off blocks of cards until all of the cards in the right hand (7) have been "shuffled off" into the left hand.

COMMENTS AND SUGGESTIONS

This is a natural way of shuffling a pack of cards and mixing it quite thoroughly . . . but it can also be easily diverted to magical uses . . . particularly in "controlling" cards on either the top or bottom of the pack or to a particular position in the deck. Therefore, easy as this shuffle is, you should practice it repeatedly until it can be executed without hesitation. This will enable you to perform the special variations as required.

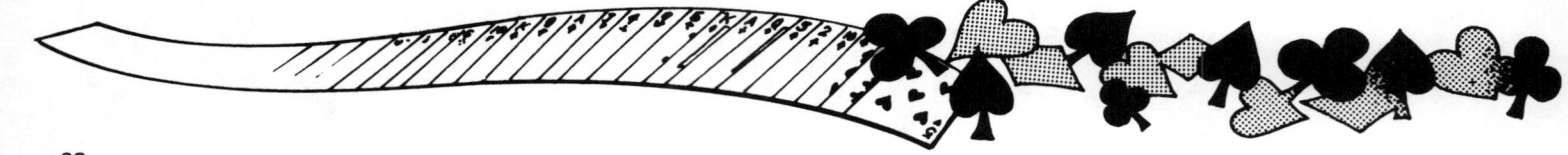

The Overhand Shuffle can also be done as a Reverse Shuffle. The movements are exactly the same as described in the Overhand Shuffle, except that the right hand holds the deck so that the faces of the cards are *outward* (with the back of the cards toward the right palm) instead of *inward* (with the faces of the cards toward the right palm). The operation of the Shuffle is the same. However, this Reverse has an important bearing on the "control" shuffles that follow.

THE OVERHAND IN-JOG CONTROL

EFFECT

This shuffle is very useful in controlling a selected card when the spectator returns the card to the pack. In addition, it can be used to bring a card to the top of the pack and also to keep it there. Yet all during the operation, the performer appears to be simply shuffling the pack in the normal Overhand fashion.

METHOD

(1) After a spectator has drawn a card from the pack and is looking at it, you start an Overhand Shuffle, drawing cards from the top of the pack with your left thumb. Tell the spectator to replace his card in the pack as you near the center.

(2) His card goes on the left-hand packet ... and, as you resume the shuffle, *bring your right hand slightly inward toward your body, a matter of a half an inch or so.* This is a simple action that might occur during any shuffle.

(3) With your left thumb, draw off a single card from the right-hand packet. Let this indifferent card fall upon the selected card, which is on the top of the left-hand packet. *The inward movement that you made in Step 2 will make this one card protrude slightly inward, toward your body, from the rest of the left-hand cards.*

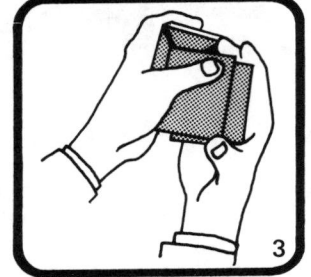

(4) This single, "off center" card is called an "IN-JOG." You can prevent anyone from noticing it by now simply moving your right hand forward to its normal position and continuing your Overhand Shuffle. The remainder of the cards go into their regular position, "evened up" with the first cards shuffled.

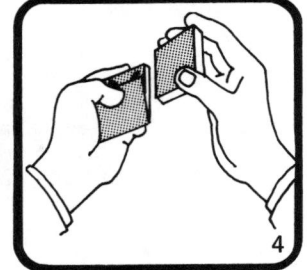

(5) As more cards cover the "Jogged" card, they help to hide it from view, *particularly if they are shuffled in a somewhat irregular manner.*

(6) As you continue "shuffling off" blocks of cards, be sure that the In-Jogged card is not pushed back into the deck.

(7) Continue shuffling until all the cards in the right hand are held in the left hand.

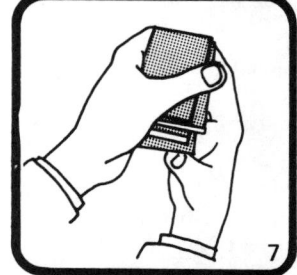

(8) After you have completed the shuffle, the deck should look like this with the Jogged card protruding toward you. *Of course, since this is a secret maneuver, you do not call the spectator's attention to it.*

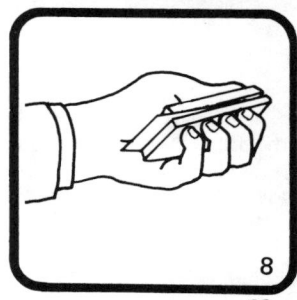

(9) You can now easily find the "Jogged" card *by pressing upward with your right thumb at the inner end of the pack.*

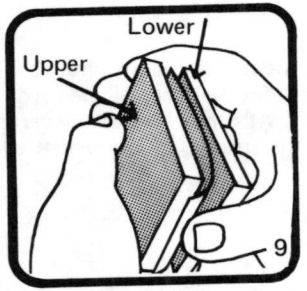

(12) Now, drop the packet in the right hand (with the selected card (X) on top) down in front of the cards held in the left hand. This is called a "throw" and to all appearances it adds a final and convincing touch to the shuffle.

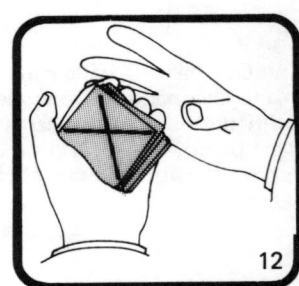

(10) This upward pressure causes the deck to divide at the Jogged card . . . by gripping the ends of the lower packet between your right thumb and fingers, you can lift the lower portion entirely clear of the rest of the deck.

(13) Actually, the "throw" brings the selected card to the top of the pack.

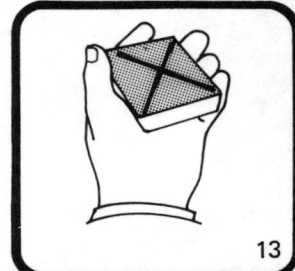

(11) With the right hand, carry the lower section completely over the upper section in the left hand.

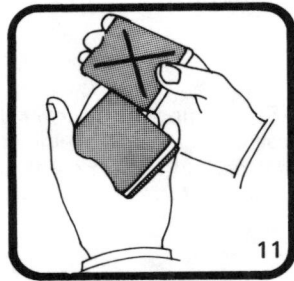

COMMENTS AND SUGGESTIONS

Treat the Jogged card much as you would any other "key" card. Never appear to pay any attention to its position, which should be easy, since you are depending on your sense of touch alone. Make the shuffle look natural, even sloppy if you wish, for if you do it too neatly, you may lose track of the Jogged card. Don't worry if you pull down an extra card or two when making the "Jog." A little group of Jogged cards will function just as effectively as a single card, for when you press the lowest card of the group upward, the others will go along with it, and you will still be able to cut to the selected card and "throw" the packet to the top of the deck.

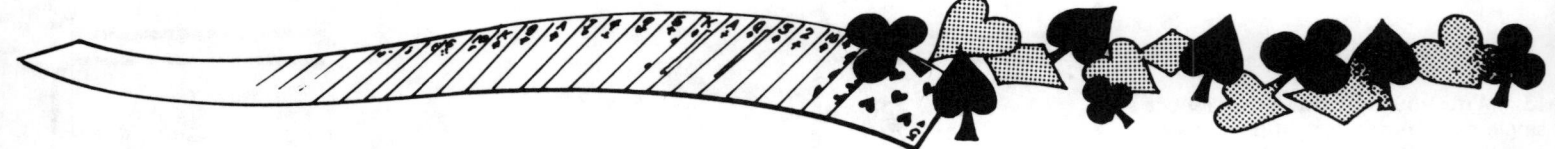

THE CARD CASE ESCAPE

Variety is an important factor in card tricks that end with the "discovery" of a card selected by a spectator. Many card discoveries, though clever, are too much alike to be presented on the same program, so it is a good procedure to inject something distinctly different. This effect falls into that category.

EFFECT

After a card has been selected by a spectator and shuffled back into the pack, the magician puts the entire pack into its box and closes the flap. Showing the box from all angles, he openly places it in his shirt pocket. Then, showing both hands empty, he reaches into his pocket. *He instantly removes the chosen card.* Immediately, he brings the card box from his pocket and gives it to the spectators, allowing them to open it for themselves and examine both box and pack. APPARENTLY, THE SELECTED CARD MANAGED TO PENETRATE THE CARD BOX UNDER ITS OWN POWER!

METHOD

(1) Remove a regular pack of cards from its box, shuffle it, and have a spectator select a card. Tell the spectator to remember the card and return it to the pack. As the card is returned to the pack, use your favorite method to control it to the top.

(2) Holding the pack in one hand, pick up the card box in the other. Replace the entire pack in the card box, making sure that the *top* of the pack (with the selected card on it) goes against the side of the box with the little "thumb slot" cut out. As you do this, say, "I will place the pack of cards into its card box, thus SEALING YOUR CARD INSIDE, SOMEWHERE IN THE DECK."

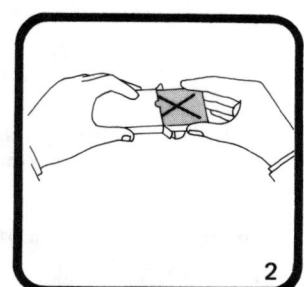

(3) Begin to close the lid of the box. As you do, *squeeze* the sides of the box containing the cards, as shown. This "squeezing" action will cause the top few cards of the pack to "bow" outwards against the top of the box, *making a small gap between each of the top few cards.*

(4) As you tuck the flap in, SLIDE IT BENEATH THE TOP CARD OF THE PACK (The spectator's card "X") as shown.

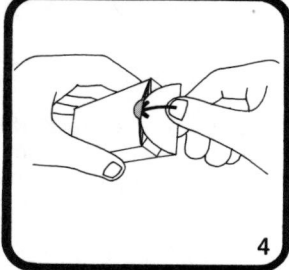

(5) Close the flap completely and transfer the box to your right hand.

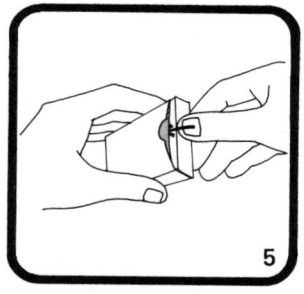

(6) As you hold the case, *make sure the fingers of your right hand COVER THE THUMB SLOT,* thus concealing the visible portion of the spectator's card from view. With the pack held in this manner, you can display it casually on both sides before you proceed to the next step.

(7) After briefly showing the box, place it into your shirt or coat breast pocket as you remark, "With the pack sealed in its box and hidden in my pocket, it would be very difficult for me to find your card."

(8) Show your hand empty and reach into your pocket. Use your fingers to work the end of the spectator's card out of the box by pulling it from the "thumb slot." As soon as you have a good grip on the card, *immediately withdraw it from your pocket.*

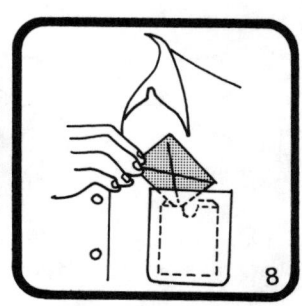

(9) The back of the card will be toward the spectator, therefore, he will not know what card you have in your hand. Ask the spectator to name the card he selected. When he replies, turn the card in your hand face up and show it to be his card. IMMEDIATELY REMOVE THE PACK FROM YOUR POCKET AND TOSS IT ON THE TABLE FOR ALL TO EXAMINE.

COMMENTS AND SUGGESTIONS

The proper type of card case for this trick is one with a flap that slides in easily and rather deeply. Some short flaps will not stay in place while you are extracting the chosen card, so be careful, as you draw the card from its box, that the flap remains closed. As soon as *one hand* removes the chosen card from the pocket, the *other hand* can bring out the case and offer it for examination.

OVERHAND SHUFFLE GLIMPSE

The Overhand Shuffle Glimpse is a very useful and valuable move enabling you to "sight" the bottom card of the deck secretly during the course of an Overhand Shuffle. It becomes especially valuable in tricks where it is necessary to use a "key" card as it supplies a direct, natural manner in which to note the bottom card without suspicion.

METHOD

(1) With the pack held firmly in the right hand, begin a regular Overhand Shuffle, drawing off small batches of cards from the bulk of the pack into the left hand.

(2) Then, at some point during the shuffle when the left hand has just drawn off a batch of cards and both hands are separated, *tilt the upper edge of the right hand packet away from you* just enough so you can see the bottom card of that packet.

(3) You only need a brief instant to glimpse the card, so make the move seem natural without pausing or breaking the flow of the shuffle.

SHUFFLE CONTROL WITH KEY CARD

Whenever you are using a "key" card to locate a chosen card, you must be careful NOT to let anyone shuffle the pack, as that may separate the two cards. However, you can do an actual shuffle of your own, as follows:

METHOD

(1) In Step 6 of the Hindu Key Card Location, after you have dropped the upper half of the pack on the lower, placing the "key" card next to the selected card, begin an Overhand Shuffle, drawing off little packets of cards from the top of the deck with your left thumb.

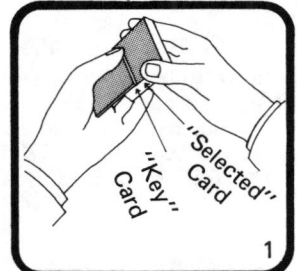

(3) Complete the shuffle by drawing off the lower cards in small packets again . . . then cut the pack as often as you want.

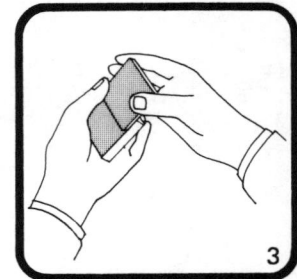

(2) WHEN YOU NEAR THE CENTER, DRAW OFF A LARGE BLOCK OF CARDS TOGETHER. *This section contains your two cards, the "key" card and the selected card. You draw off the large packet of cards so that they will not be separated.*

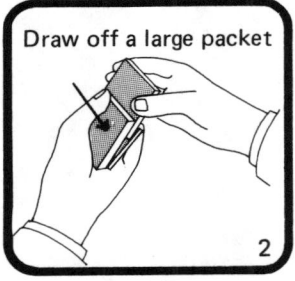

OVERHAND SHUFFLE CONTROL — TOP CARD TO BOTTOM

EFFECT

With the Overhand Shuffle, you can "control" the top card of the pack and bring it to the bottom of the pack while apparently giving the deck an honest shuffle.

METHOD

(1) Your control card is on the TOP of the deck. Hold the pack in your right hand.

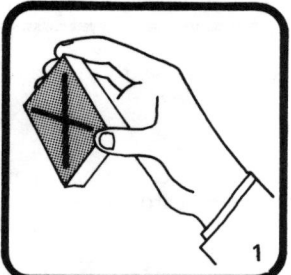

(3) Let it fall *alone* into the left hand.

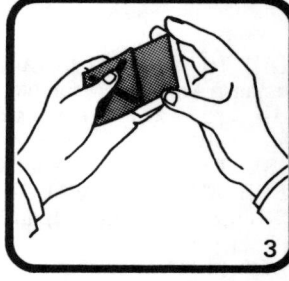

(2) Start by drawing off ONLY THE TOP CARD with the left thumb.

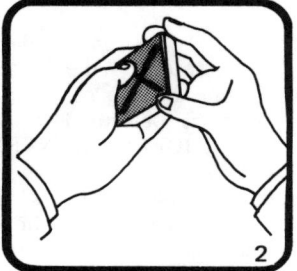

(4) Then continue the shuffle, pulling blocks of cards from the right hand with the left thumb on top of the "control" card, until all of the cards have been shuffled into the left hand. The "control" card will now be on the BOTTOM of the pack.

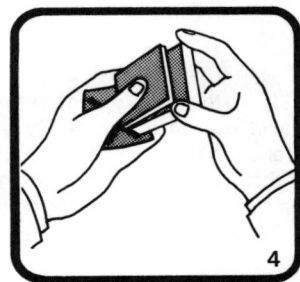

THE TRANSFERRED THOUGHT

Here is a card trick that will leave your audience believing in ESP, with the exception of one person, who will find himself "in the know," thanks to your choosing him as a helper. Actually, two spectators participate in the test, one as a "sender," the other as a "receiver," but the *sender* remains as baffled as the rest of the audience.

EFFECT

After a few remarks on Extra Sensory Perception (ESP), the magician invites two spectators to assist him in a test of thought transference. The magician tells *Spectator One* that he is the "Sender." He is to select any card from the pack and remember it, which he does. The Card is then returned to the pack, which is shuffled and put into its card case. The magician tells *Spectator Two* that he is to act as a "Receiver" by thinking of the pack and naming the *first* card that comes to his mind. After a brief period of concentration, *Spectator Two* announces the name of a card. To the surprise of everyone, especially *Spectator One*, that is the very card that was selected. The test can be repeated with the same remarkable result; and anyone who becomes suspicious of Spectator One is invited to serve as "Sender" himself. But no matter who tries it or how often it is repeated, *Spectator Two* always comes through with the correct card!

SECRET AND PREPARATION

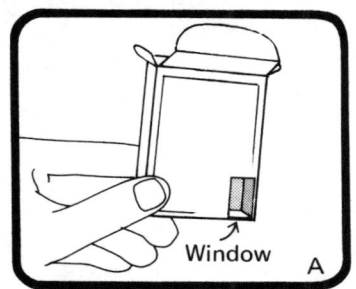

(A)   The secret of this trick depends upon the use of a specially prepared card box with a secret "window"! To make the *trick* box, with a sharp knife or razor blade, carefully cut a small rectangular opening or "window" in the lower right-hand corner of the <u>back</u> side of the card box. *This is the side which has the tuck flap attached to it.*

(B)   The "window" should be just large enough so, when the pack is inserted into the box, you are able to see the "index" with NUMBER AND SUIT VALUE of the <u>bottom</u> card of the pack. Place the box of cards in your coat pocket (or on your table with the "window" side down), and you are ready to begin.

METHOD

(1)   After a few brief remarks on ESP, invite two spectators to assist you in a test of Thought Transference. Have *Spectator One* stand at your extreme left and *Spectator Two* at your extreme right. Tell *Spectator One* that he will act as the "Sender" in this experiment and *Spectator Two* that he will be the "Receiver."

(2)   Take out the box of cards and remove the pack from the box. Then, place the box on the table with the WINDOW SIDE DOWN so it is concealed from view. *NOTE: In handling the box of cards, always be careful to keep the "window side" of the box facing down (toward the floor) so the audience cannot see that the box is specially prepared.*

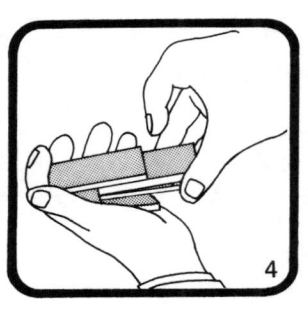

(3)   Run through the pack face down and invite Spectator One to select a card (X) from anywhere in the pack. Tell him to look at the card and remember it but not to show it to anyone else. (4)   Begin a regular Hindu Shuffle and have the spectator replace his card in the pack anywhere he wants. Then, using the HINDU PICK-UP CONTROL, bring the spectator's card to the top of the pack.

(5)   Now, begin a regular Overhand Shuffle, shuffling the spectator's card (X) from the <u>top</u> of the pack to the <u>bottom</u> as described in the OVERHAND SHUFFLE CONTROL — TOP CARD TO BOTTOM. As you shuffle off the remaining cards in the pack say, "Your card is now hopelessly lost in the pack."

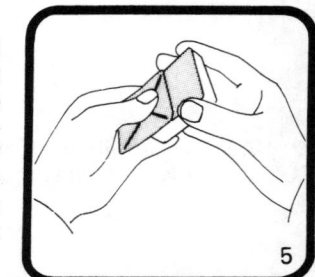

(6)   Holding the squared up pack face down in one hand, pick up the card box from the table ("window" side down) and insert the deck FACE DOWN into the box and tuck in the flap. *As you do this, the fingers of your left hand curl beneath the card box and cover the window from any possible view.*

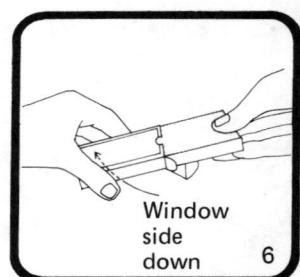

Window side down

(7)   By keeping the left thumb or fingers over the "window" in the corner, the box can now be shown casually on all sides. As you display the box, say to Spectator One, "I would like you to concentrate on the card you selected and try to 'send' a mental picture of that card to Spectator Two."

(8)   With that, turn your whole body to the right and face Spectator Two. As you do this, transfer the card box from your left hand to your right and hold it so the "window" faces him, enabling him to see the bottom card through the opening. Unknown to him, he is about to become your "confederate" in the trick. Now say, "I want you to concentrate as hard as you can and see if you can 'receive' a visual impression of the selected card. If so, what card do you see?" The illustration shows the spectator's view of the card box as you hold it in your right hand.

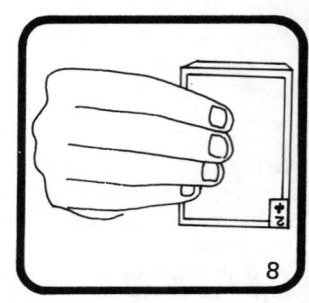

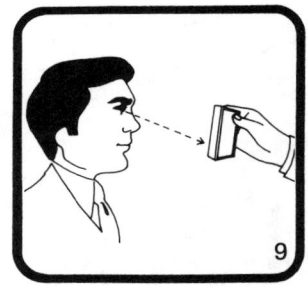

(9)   As you say this, look Spectator Two directly in the eyes and gesture with the card box <u>until you are sure he has seen the card in the "window."</u> If you play your part correctly, Spectator Two will "get the message" and will realize that <u>he</u> is now part of the deception. When he does, he will announce the name of the selected card! Once the test has succeeded, you will find Spectator Two more than happy to "receive" another image should you try the experiment again.

COMMENTS AND SUGGESTIONS

Repeating the trick will give Spectator Two another chance at "acting." Encourage him to play his part well. Once he realizes that he is "part of the act," he should cooperate in making the trick as mysterious as possible. If however, he becomes troublesome at any time during the trick, either choose another "receiver" or go on to the next trick. You can cover this easily by explaining to your audience that ESP experiments are never 100% sure and then move on to something else.

This trick is a good exercise in "controlling" the behavior of the spectator. Before beginning the trick, try to pick out someone who looks good-natured and cooperative. Treat this person with respect and kindness and he should help to make the trick a success.

If repeating the trick often, you can save time by simply handing the pack to a spectator — tell him to cut it anywhere and look at the bottom card. Have him turn the pack face down so you can place it into the card case without letting anyone see the bottom card other than Spectator One who chose it. You can even let the spectator push the pack in for himself, but your helper — Spectator Two — WILL NAME IT JUST THE SAME!

THE OVERHAND SLIP SHUFFLE
EFFECT

Once you are familiar with the standard "Overhand Shuffle," you can easily learn the "Slip Shuffle." The "Slip Shuffle" will enable you to retain the BOTTOM CARD ON THE BOTTOM OF THE PACK as the rest of the cards in the deck are being well mixed. To "control" the bottom card, proceed as follows:

METHOD

(1)   Hold the cards in your right hand in preparation for the standard Over-hand Shuffle.

(2)   As you begin the shuffle in the regular way by drawing off the top stack of cards, the fingers of your left hand naturally rest against the bottom card of the bulk of the pack . . . *this is the card (X) which you are going to control.* Press lightly against the face of the bottom card (X) with the left fingers. When you draw off the first stack from the top of the pack with the left thumb YOU ALSO DRAW OFF THE BOTTOM CARD (X) WITH THE LEFT FINGERS. Thus the "control" card (X) is added to the bottom of the packet being drawn off by the left thumb.

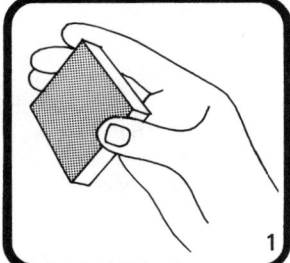

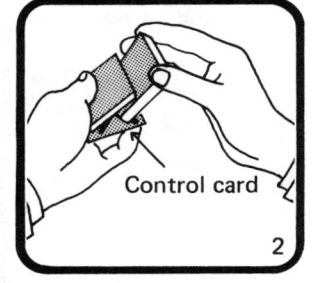

Control card

(3)   Here is a view from below of the left fingers "holding" the bottom card (X). *Note how the bottom card (X) is secretly being "slipped off" the bulk of the pack to retain its position at the bottom of the shuffled deck.*

(4)   From this point on you simply continue the regular Overhand Shuffle . . . Shuffling off small packets of cards from the bulk of the pack in the right hand onto the shuffled cards in the left hand. This "bottom control" can be repeated as often as necessary.

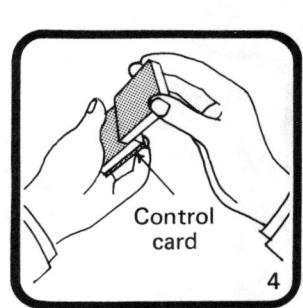

Control card

COMMENTS AND SUGGESTIONS

It is best to perform the Overhand Slip Shuffle with the left side of your body toward the audience. This keeps the faces of the cards away from the audience and prevents them from seeing that the bottom card *remains* on the bottom of the pack. Because this move is so natural and can be performed quite openly, there should be no suspicions aroused as the cards are being shuffled.

THE CARD THROUGH THE HANDKERCHIEF

Here is a classic of Card Magic that originally required considerable skill to perform. By eliminating the more difficult "moves," it has been reduced to a simple, direct presentation, without losing any of its masterful effect. Learn it now and you will still be using it, no matter how great a reputation you may gain as a card expert!

EFFECT

A card is selected and returned to the pack which is then thoroughly shuffled. The magician places it openly beneath the center of a fairly large handkerchief, proving that it would take x-ray vision to see through the cloth and find the selected card. Bringing the pack into view, the magician wraps it inside the handkerchief. Now, instead of trying to find the selected card, the wizard decides to let the card *reveal itself.* He starts to shake the handkerchief....amazingly, the chosen card *penetrates right through the cloth* and drops to the floor....while the balance of the deck remains wrapped in the handkerchief! The card and pack are then passed for examination along with the handkerchief, which is found to be intact.

METHOD

(1) Remove a regular pack of cards from its box, shuffle it, and have a spectator select any card. Tell him to remember the card and have him return it to the pack as you give it an Overhand Shuffle. When the card is returned to the pack, execute the OVERHAND SHUFFLE-IN JOG CONTROL, secretly bringing the selected card to the top of the pack.

(2) Hold the pack in dealing position in your left hand, with your thumb resting on top of the pack. (The selected card, the Two of Clubs, is on the top of the deck and has been marked with an "X" in the illustrations.)

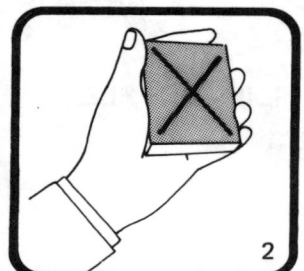

(6) Bring the pack from under the cloth into view, leaving the selected card hidden beneath the handkerchief, resting loosely in your partially open left hand.

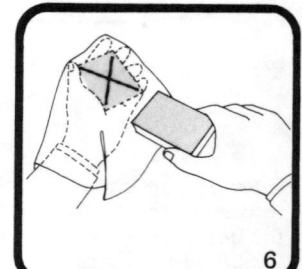

(3) With your right hand, drape the handkerchief over your left hand, so the pack is beneath the center of the handkerchief as you say, "It would be quite difficult for me to see through the handkerchief and find your card."

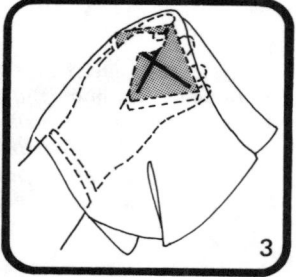

(7) Place the pack of cards in the center of the handkerchief, directly on top of the selected card. Then, square up the pack with your left thumb and fingers through the cloth even with the selected card hidden under the handkerchief.

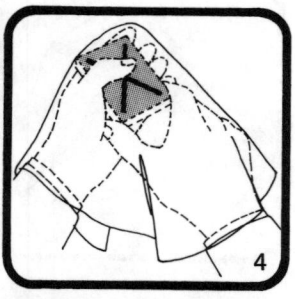

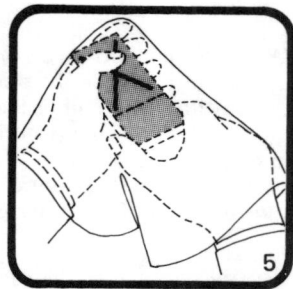

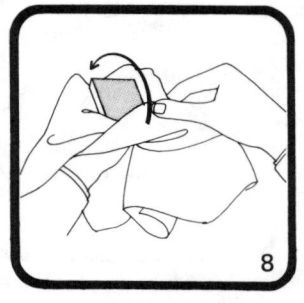

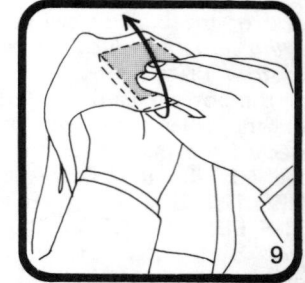

(4) Reach under the handkerchief with your right hand and grasp the inner end of the pack. (5) Now, pull all of the pack out from beneath the selected card. YOUR LEFT THUMB HOLDS THE SELECTED CARD IN PLACE, SECRETLY RETAINING IT IN YOUR LEFT HAND, UNDER THE HANDKERCHIEF.

(8) With your right hand, lift the edge of the handkerchief nearest you and fold this edge up and over the pack as shown.
(9) NOW, GRASP THE DECK AND THE HIDDEN CARD BETWEEN THE THUMB AND FINGERS OF YOUR RIGHT HAND — THUMB BELOW, FINGERS ABOVE.

(10) Raise your right hand upward and forward, bringing the selected card into view on your side of the handkerchief. KEEP THE SELECTED CARD COMPLETELY HIDDEN FROM THE AUDIENCE'S VIEW. This leaves two loose flaps of cloth hanging down at both sides of the handkerchief.

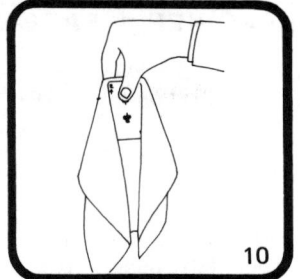

(15) Now, turn the whole affair completely over so the pack is "hanging" upside-down inside the handkerchief. Because of the firm grip your right hand has on the handkerchief, *the folds of the cloth retain the selected card in position (out of view) until you are ready for it to be revealed.*

Magician's view

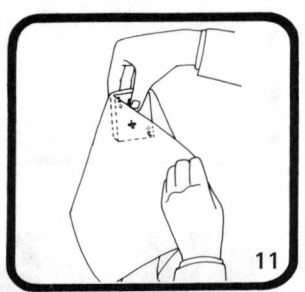

(11) With your left hand, grasp the left side of the handkerchief and fold it to the right, *across the pack, and the selected card, on your side of the handkerchief.* (12) Hold the fold in place with your left thumb. Then grip the entire pack with your left hand so your right hand can move away.

(16) Gently begin shaking the handkerchief up and down causing the hidden card to slowly start to slide from its hiding place.

Magician's view

(13) Now, with your right hand, fold both flaps of the handkerchief to the left, across the pack, THUS WRAPPING THE PACK INSIDE THE HANDKERCHIEF AND THE SELECTED CARD OUTSIDE THE HANDKERCHIEF, BENEATH THE FOLDS AS SHOWN.

(17) To the spectators it will appear as if the card is actually penetrating through the cloth. Continue to shake the handkerchief until the selected card falls to the floor, or you can draw it clear with your left hand, just as it is about to fall and give it to the person who selected it.

(18) To finish the trick, grip the pack through the outside of the cloth with your left hand. You may then give the still-wrapped pack to a spectator—or—release the ends of the handkerchief from your right hand, which then spreads open the handkerchief and removes the pack. In any event, the pack and the handkerchief are now given to the spectators for examination.

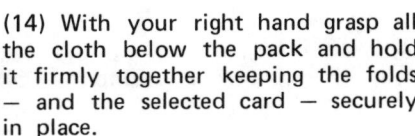

(14) With your right hand grasp all the cloth below the pack and hold it firmly together keeping the folds — and the selected card — securely in place.

COMMENTS AND SUGGESTIONS

Practice this effect until you can do it without fumbling or hesitation. Since everything is done "under cover," you can work deliberately without fear of detection, so it is wise to maintain a slow pace until you are fully sure of yourself. Don't rush when making the folds. Since everyone thinks that the chosen card is still deep in the deck, the more careful you are, the more impressed they will be.

THE CARD THROUGH HANDKERCHIEF — FACE-UP METHOD

In the Card Through the Handkerchief as just described, the spectator's card makes its appearance with the back of the card to the audience. Should you prefer that the face of the card be visible as the penetration takes place, the following adjustments must be made in handling the pack:

METHOD

(1) After the spectator's card has been controlled to the top of the pack, use the OVERHAND SHUFFLE — TOP TO BOTTOM CONTROL to bring the selected card to the bottom of the pack.

(2) Holding the pack face down in your left hand, start to drape the handkerchief over your left hand and in the same motion rotate the entire pack in your hand, turning it face up so the spectator's card is now on top of the face up pack. *Be sure that the pack is completely hidden by the handkerchief before turning it over.* From here, you proceed with the rest of the trick as described.

OVERHAND SHUFFLE CARD CONTROL — BOTTOM CARD TO TOP

EFFECT

In addition to controlling the top card to the bottom of the pack, the Overhand Shuffle Control can be worked in reverse to bring the bottom card to the top of the pack.

METHOD

(1) Hold the deck face outward as described in Overhand Reverse Shuffle. Your "control" card will be the Three of Diamonds, the BOTTOM card.

(3) *Draw off the front card by itself,* (the Three of Diamonds) with your left thumb.

(2) *NOTE: When working this method of the "top to bottom control," turn your body to the left so that the back of your right hand is toward the spectators. This keeps the bottom card from their sight.*

(4) Continue as already described, shuffling the rest of the deck on top of the Three. This will bring the bottom card to the TOP of the pack.

OVERHAND SHUFFLE
CONTROLLING BOTTOM CARD TO TOP — SECOND METHOD

With your LEFT side toward the spectators holding the deck in your right hand, begin the standard Overhand Shuffle. When you reach the last few cards in your right hand, pull off each card ONE AT A TIME with the left thumb. Thus, the BOTTOM card will be the last card remaining in your right hand and you just "shuffle" it on to the TOP of the pack.

COMMENTS AND SUGGESTIONS

This is superior in most cases to the first BOTTOM TO TOP CONTROL method described because you do not have to turn your other side (right side) of your body to the audience.

THE OVERHAND IN-JOG TOP CARD CONTROL

EFFECT

With this control, you perform what appears to be an ordinary Overhand Shuffle. Yet, when you finish, the top card of the deck is the same card as when you started.

METHOD

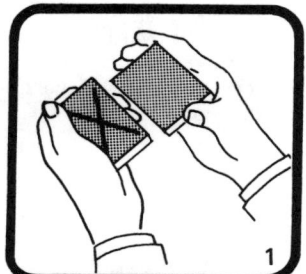

(1)   The card you will "control" is on the top of the deck. Start the shuffle by removing a block of cards from the top of the pack with the left hand. The "control" card is now the top card of this packet.

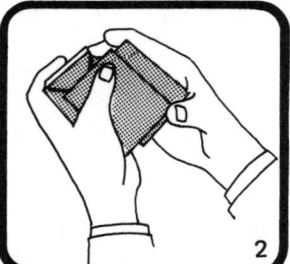

(2)   Immediately In-Jog the first card you shuffle off from the right-hand packet on top of the "control" card in the left-hand packet.

(3)   Then shuffle off the remainder of the deck in the regular manner, being sure not to disturb the "Jogged card." After all of the cards have been shuffled into the left hand, cut to the In-Jogged card as you did in Number 9 in the Overhand Shuffle In-Jog Control and throw the lower packet on top of the other cards in the left hand. The "control" card will now be back on the top of the pack.

THE MAGNETIZED CARD

There are many ways in which a magician can discover a card selected by a spectator, but those in which the card actually *reveals itself* are perhaps the most spectacular. One of the most impressive is the "Rising Card Trick," which has been shown in various forms over a period of many years. Usually, special preparation is needed, but here is a quick and simple impromptu version that can be performed as a close-up mystery with surprising effect!

EFFECT

A card is selected and returned to the pack which is shuffled by the magician in the usual fashion. Holding the pack upright in his left hand, with its face toward the audience, the magician rests the tip of his right first finger on the upper end of the pack. He states that he will "magnetize" the chosen card and cause it to "rise" from the pack of its own accord. As the magician lifts his finger, the card obeys, rising slowly and mysteriously until it is almost clear of the pack.

METHOD

(1)   From an ordinary pack of cards, invite a spectator to select any card, look at it and remember it. Using the HINDU PICK-UP CONTROL or the OVERHAND IN-JOG TOP CARD CONTROL, have the spectator return his card which you then control to the top of the pack.

(2)   Hold the pack upright in your left hand with the thumb at one side and the fingers of the other side. THE BOTTOM CARD OF THE PACK SHOULD FACE TOWARD THE PALM OF YOUR LEFT HAND, AND THE BACK OF YOUR LEFT HAND SHOULD FACE THE AUDIENCE.

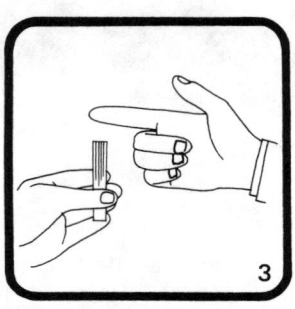

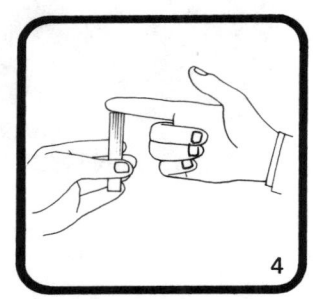

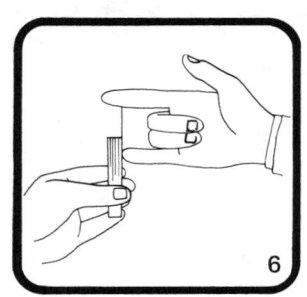

(3) With the pack held firmly in this position, extend the first finger of the right hand pointing it toward the audience. The remaining fingers should be curled into the palm of the hand. Hold your right hand about six inches above the top edge of the pack. (4) Then, slowly lower your right hand until the tip of the first finger rests on top of the pack as shown. Continue this up and down motion a few times as you say, "I will now attempt to magnetize the chosen card with my finger and cause it to rise from the pack on its own. Watch closely!"

(6) Without hesitation, slowly move the right hand upward *as you apply a slight pressure on the* <u>back</u> *of the spectator's card with the* <u>tip</u> *of the little finger*. This will cause the top card to slide "upward" and *appear* to be clinging to the tip of your right forefinger. (7) As the card slides upward, the tips of your <u>left</u> thumb and fingers serve as a "guide" or a "track" for the card during its rise.

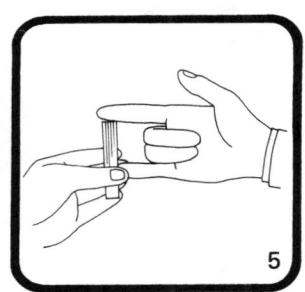

(5) With that, lower the right hand until the first finger touches the top of the pack. When it does, straighten out your little finger so it touches the back of the spectator's card as shown. Because the spectator sees the pack from the front, the extended little finger will not be seen as it is hidden by the pack.

(8) When the card has risen almost to the top of the pack, move your right hand away. Let the left thumb and fingers hold the card secure momentarily before removing it with your right hand and tossing it out for inspection.

COMMENTS AND SUGGESTIONS

The important factor in this trick is to guard against "bad angles." If your audience is spread out, stand well back so that everyone will have a <u>front view</u> of the deck and be unable to see your little finger extended behind the pack. For "close-up" work, when performing for just one person, you can hold the pack *right before the spectator's eyes* giving him no chance at all to see past the edges.

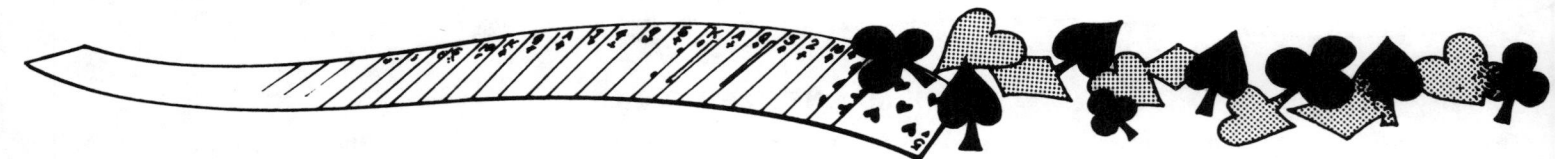

OVERHAND IN-JOG CONTROL — PLACING A CARD AT A SPECIFIC LOCATION IN THE DECK

EFFECT

This "control" is very useful in placing a selected card at any number of cards down in the pack that you wish. Let's assume that for the particular trick you need the card fourth from the top.

METHOD

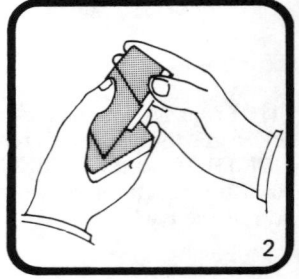

(1) With the selected card on top of the pack, begin a regular Overhand Shuffle drawing about half of the top of the pack into your left hand.

(2) Now, shuffle off *one at a time*, three cards on top of the selected card. DO NOT JOG THESE CARDS.

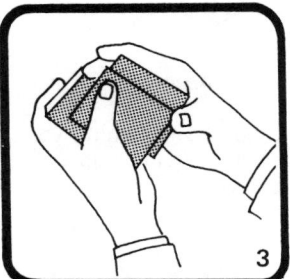

(3)   Then, In-Jog the FOURTH card and shuffle the rest of the cards on top of it into the left hand.

(4)   Cut the lower portion of the pack at the Jogged card and "throw" the lower block of cards to the top of the deck. The selected card will now be *fourth* from the top.

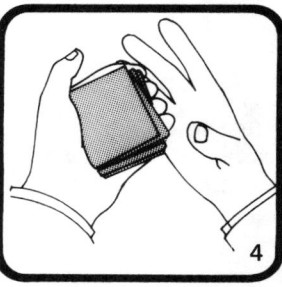

A SURPRISE APPEARANCE

This is a quick and clever card discovery using the Control just described.

EFFECT

The magician has the spectator select a card from the deck and then return it while he is doing an Overhand Shuffle. The magician states that he will bring the selected card to the top of the deck. After he fails three times, the selected card makes a surprise appearance.

METHOD

(1)   Have a card selected and then use the Overhand In-Jog Control to bring the selected card to the top. Then using the Overhand Shuffle Control To Any Location just described, control the spectator's card so that it is FOURTH from the top of the deck.

(2)   Give the deck a False Cut as previously described.

(3)   Hold the deck in your left hand and state, "I will now bring your card to the top of the deck." Slap the deck with your right hand and then show the spectator the top card.

(7)   NOTE: Each time you show a "wrong" card hold it with your right thumb and first finger and have your hand close to the top of the deck as shown.

(4)   When you remove the top card to show it, just slide the card over to the right with your left thumb and then grasp the outer right corner of the card with your right thumb underneath and right first finger on top. Turn the card over as shown, TOWARD THE SPECTATOR, so that it is face up.

(8)   As you show the third "wrong" card, push the top card of the pack, which is now the selected card (X), over slightly to the right.

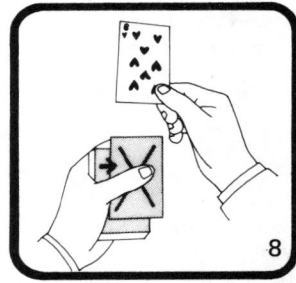

(5)   Ask him if this is the card he selected. Of course, his reply will be "No." Replace this card on the BOTTOM of the deck.

(6)   Slap the deck again and show him the next card. Again, you have failed to bring the selected card to the top. Replace this card on the BOTTOM of the deck as well.

(9)   As you display your third "mistake," grip the corner of the top card (X) between the tips of the third and little finger of your right hand.

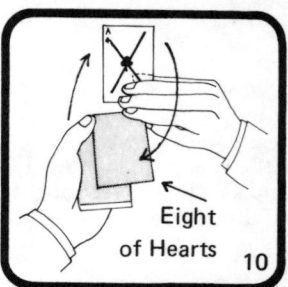

Eight
of Hearts

10

(10) Now, replace the third card on the TOP of the deck ... at the same time retaining your hold on the selected card (X) with your right third and little fingers. The selected card (X) will "pop up" unexpectedly facing the spectators ... held between your two fingers for a "Surprise Appearance."

FORCING A CARD

Forcing a card on an unsuspecting spectator is a sure way of bringing a trick to a successful conclusion. Since you already know what card will be chosen before you start, you can finish the trick almost any way you want — and the more surprising, the better. Try out the methods given in this section, and you will realize how effective they can be.

It is good policy to vary your forcing methods so that spectators will not become too familiar with your procedure. You will find additional forcing methods in the sections devoted to special types of cards, and these can be injected into your program whenever the opportunity arises, thus adding still more variety.

With most tricks, it is best to use a regular card location to reveal a chosen card, reserving the force for times when it is definitely needed. One such time is when a skeptical spectator wants to snatch the pack from your hands and shuffle it until you can't possibly find his card. If you force a card on such a customer, you won't have to worry about this shuffle.

There are many lesser forms of forcing applied to tricks involving the four Aces, the choice of different suits, or groups of cards. These are described in connection with the tricks to which they apply.

THE SLIP FORCE — FIRST METHOD

For a sure, deceptive FORCE, using any pack of cards, *this is one of the very best.* It depends upon a simple sleight known as the "SLIP," which can be learned quickly and performed almost automatically ... but it should be *practiced* until it becomes a smooth and natural move.

EFFECT

After shuffling a pack of cards, the magician holds it face down in his left hand. With his left thumb, he riffles the outer corner of the pack downwards. To a spectator, the magician says, "As I riffle the cards, please say 'Stop!'."

When the call comes, the magician grips the top portion of the pack in his right hand. Then, lifting that part of the pack upward, he extends the *bottom portion* in his left hand, so that the spectator can look at the top card of that packet ... the place where he called Stop! Apparently, this is a completely free selection, YET THE CARD HAS ACTUALLY BEEN "FORCED," thanks to the "SLIP"!

SECRET AND PREPARATION

The *top* card of the deck is the one which is "Forced" — therefore, it is necessary for you to know the top card beforehand. To do this, "glimpse" the *bottom* card using the OVERHAND SHUFFLE GLIMPSE or the HINDU SHUFFLE GLIMPSE. Then, shuffle the *bottom* card to the *top,* using either method of the OVERHAND SHUFFLE CONTROL — TOP TO BOTTOM. Once the top card is learned you are ready to begin. Also, in many tricks it is necessary to "Force" a particular card. In this case, position the card on top of the pack *before* you have the spectator make his "free" selection. (In the illustrations, the Force Card has been marked with an "X.")

METHOD

(1) Hold the deck in the MECHANIC'S GRIP dealing position in your *left hand.* Your left thumb is at one side of the pack, your first finger is at the front edge and the other three fingers are curled over the top of the pack at the right side.

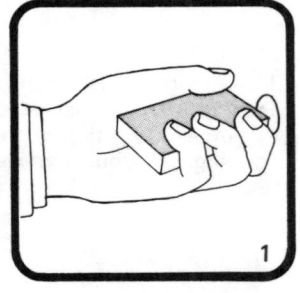

1

(2) With your left thumb, bend the outer left corner of the pack downwards. Slowly begin releasing cards from the tip of the thumb, allowing them to spring "upwards" as shown. This is called RIFFLING THE CARDS. As you do this, explain to the spectator that he should call "Stop" at any time during the "riffle" and that he will take the card at the point where he stops you.

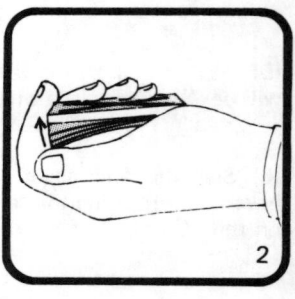

2

(3) Slowly begin riffling the cards and, when the call comes, you STOP. Without hesitation, move your right hand over the pack and grasp the *upper* packet of cards (above the point where you stopped) between your right thumb and fingers as shown. NOTE THAT YOUR *LEFT* FINGERS ARE CURLED *OVER THE TOP CARD OF THE PACK (X).*

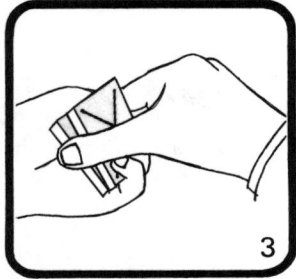

(6) The right hand *CONTINUES TO SLIDE OUT THE TOP PACKET* until it clears the edge of the "slipped" Force card (X), *WHICH FALLS ON TOP OF THE LEFT-HAND PACKET.*

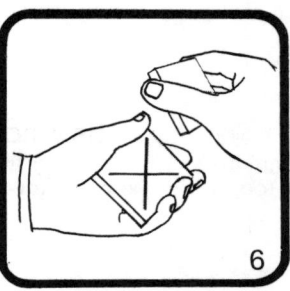

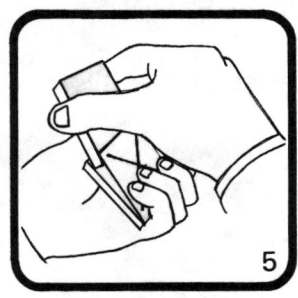

(7) Offer the left-hand packet to the spectator. Have him remove the top card, which is now the Force card (X), and look at it. You have now successfully "Forced" the card on the spectator using the SLIP FORCE. You can now reveal the name of the card in any manner you choose.

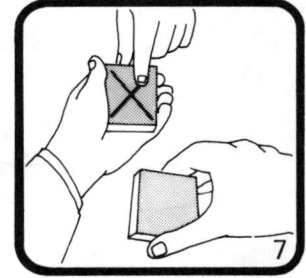

(4) Now, begin drawing the top packet upward. *The left fingers maintain a downward pressure on the top card (X).* (5) HOLD THE TOP CARD (THE "FORCE" CARD) *IN PLACE* WITH YOUR LEFT FINGERS AS YOUR RIGHT HAND SLIDES THE TOP PACKET *FROM BENEATH IT.*

COMMENTS AND SUGGESTIONS

The great feature of the "Slip Force" is that it is absolutely undetectable when properly handled. As long as the back of your right hand is toward the spectators, the slip will be completely hidden. The same applies when the left hand tilts the pack well upward, with the bottom turned toward the audience. (See Slip Force — Second Method.) That is the very reason why you should get it exactly right. In your regular cuts, handle the pack as though you were about to do the "Slip" . . . then there will be no suspicion when the time comes to actually execute the SLIP FORCE move.

THE SLIP FORCE — SECOND METHOD

The Slip Force is one of the most useful and deceptive methods of having a spectator select a "Forced" card. After you have learned the Basic Method just described, here is a variation which can make the trick even more effective.

METHOD

(1) As in the initial description of THE SLIP FORCE, the top card (indicated by an "X") is the card that will be forced. Follow Steps 1 through 5 just as described in THE SLIP FORCE.

(3) *NOTE: Turning the hands over as you make the "Slip" hides the move completely from the spectator's view, EVEN IF YOU ARE COMPLETELY SURROUNDED.*

(2) When you get to Step 6, the right hand is sliding out the top packet as the fingers of the left hand hold the top card of that packet which will fall on top of the left-hand packet. At the same time this action is being executed, both hands turn their packets face up. The hands rotate in opposite directions, as indicated by the arrows.

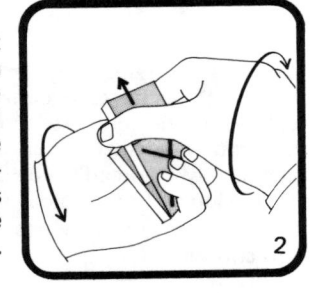

(4) At this point, the right-hand packet is face up and the left-hand packet is also face up WITH THE X CARD ON THE BOTTOM. Extend your left forefinger and point to the card on the face of the right-hand packet. Say, "I don't want you to take this card because I know what it is. . . ."

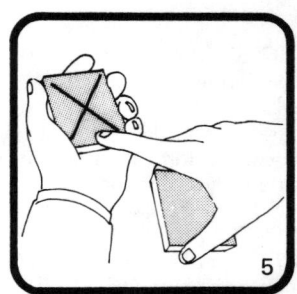

(5) With that, TURN BOTH HANDS OVER — BACK TO THEIR ORIGINAL POSITION. Extend your right forefinger pointing to the top card of the left-hand packet. Say, "Instead, take this one where you said 'Stop,' which no one knows."

COMMENTS AND SUGGESTIONS

As stated above, this variation should be learned <u>after</u> you master the "regular" Slip Force. When you can perform the regular "Slip" with ease, you can then add this "extra" touch which makes the SLIP FORCE *totally undetectable* under all conditions.

10—20 COUNT FORCE

EFFECT

The performer asks a spectator to call out *any* number between ten and twenty....stating that he will count that many cards from the pack onto the table. This done, the magician then *adds the two digits of the selected number* together to arrive at a total. He then counts *that many* cards from the top of the already dealt pile to arrive at a single card. The spectator is asked to look at that card and remember it. The performer automatically knows the name of this card which was really "Forced." The magician may now reveal the card in any manner he wishes.

SECRET AND PREPARATION

(A) Because of a simple but clever mathematical principle, this "Force" actually works itself. The only preparation necessary is that you know the TENTH *card from the top* of the deck beforehand. In the illustrations, this card is marked with an (X).

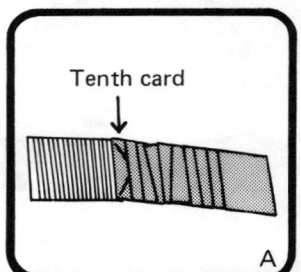
Tenth card

METHOD

(1) Hold the deck face down in dealing position in your left hand. Ask the spectator to name any number *between* 10 and 20. Suppose he says, "Thirteen." Count off thirteen cards, one at a time, face down in a pile on the table as shown. This dealing action *reverses* the order of the cards on the table. This places the "Force" Card FOURTH *from the top* in your new pile.

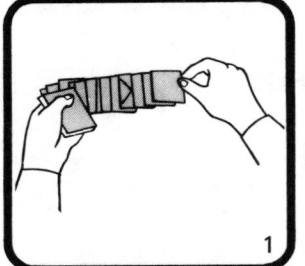

(2) Lay the pack aside and pick up the new pile of 13 cards in dealing position. State that you will add the figures of the chosen number...."13" ....(1 + 3 = 4) and count down *that many* in the pile.

(3) You do this with the following result: When you counted the original thirteen cards in a pile, you *reversed* their order as already stated. *Now, by counting four cards, one at a time, from that pile, you REVERSE THEM AGAIN. This system — which works with ANY NUMBER BETWEEN 10 AND 20 — causes the count to always end on the ORIGINAL TENTH CARD — your Force Card!*

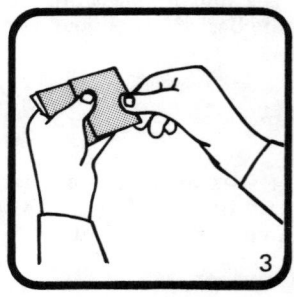

(4) Place the remaining cards with the rest of the deck and ask the spectator to look at the top card of the pile of four and remember it. You have now successfully "Forced" a card using the 10-20 Count Force. You may reveal the selected card in whatever manner you choose.

COMMENTS AND SUGGESTIONS

The subtle mathematical principle which causes this effect to work can be easily understood by sitting down with the pack and trying out the various number combinations a few times. No matter what number the spectator selects *(between 10 and 20),* the result is always the same. The original *tenth card* from the top of the deck, always ends up as the "selected" card.

THE ROLLOVER FORCE

Here is a sure-fire method of "Forcing" a card where the actual handling of the pack seems so haphazard and disorderly that it appears impossible for the magician to have control over the position of *any* card in the pack. This makes for a very convincing "Force" which is ideal for any card worker's program.

SECRET AND PREPARATION

For the ROLLOVER FORCE all you need is an ordinary pack of cards with the Force Card on top. (In the illustrations, the Force Card is marked with an "X.")

METHOD

(1) Hold the pack face down, in dealing position, in your left hand. State that you wish to have one card selected from the pack at random; to make sure that this choice is not influenced by you, the magician, you will let *the pack itself* determine which card will be selected.

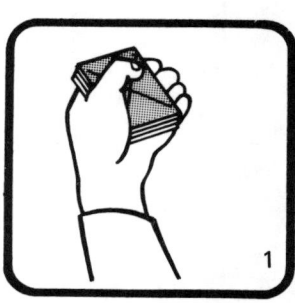

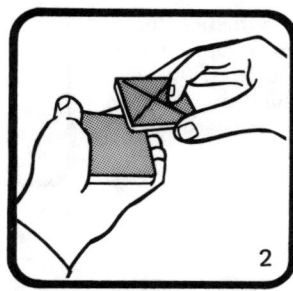
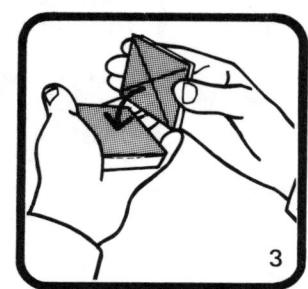

(2) With that, you lift off the upper fourth of the pack (about 10 to 15 cards), (3) turn them over (face up), and (4) replace them on top of the face-down pack as shown. As you turn the packet over say, "To completely *confuse* the order of the pack, I will not only mix the cards — I'll turn some face up and some face down."

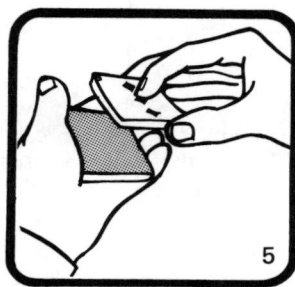
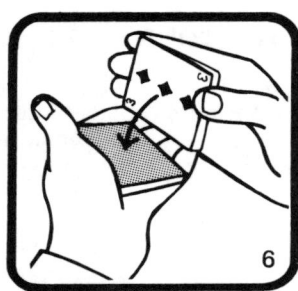
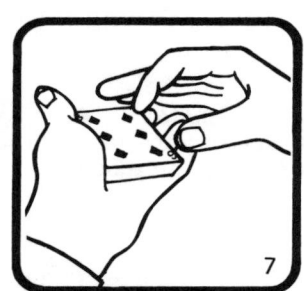

(5) Then, to make things *more confusing,* lift off nearly half the deck (20 to 25 cards), (6) turn these over as before, and (7) replace them on top of the rest of the pack.

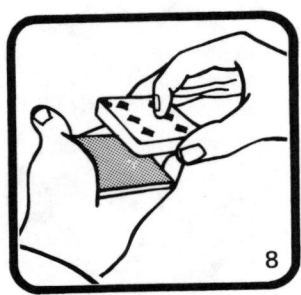
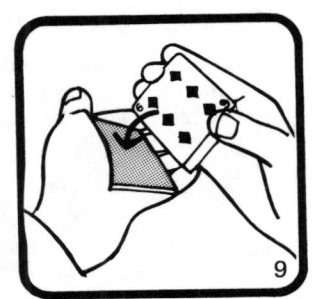
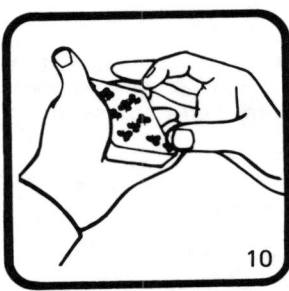

(8) To add to all this....lift off another stack of cards, this time cutting closer to the bottom (about ¾ of the deck) and (9) turn them over, (10) replacing them on top of the remaining cards.

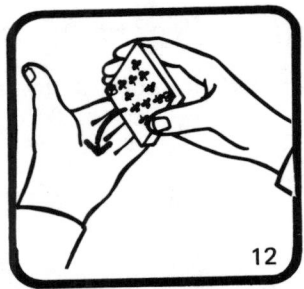
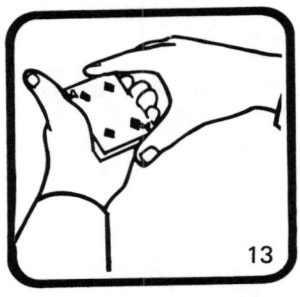

(11, 12, 13) You then state, "To confuse matters even further, I'll turn the whole pack over." — which you do.

(14) After turning the pack over say, "Now, we'll run through the pack and take the *first face-down card* that comes along." With that, you start to spread the pack, "running" the cards from your left hand to your right.

(15) The first face-down card you reach *will be the "Force" Card,* the Three of Clubs. The audience thinks it is just a random card. Have a spectator remove that card from the pack and look at it. When he does, you have successfully "Forced" the card....using the ROLLOVER FORCE.

THE COUNT FORCE

The more card tricks you perform, the more you must depend on subtle, unsuspected devices like the "Force," which enables you to know beforehand what card a spectator will select. As with all routines, people may become familiar with a "Force" if it is repeated too often, which means switching to another forcing system is in order. Here is a very natural "Force" that will serve that purpose perfectly.

EFFECT

After shuffling a pack of cards, the magician asks a spectator to think of a number between 1 and 52 (corresponding to the number of cards in the pack). Whatever the number, the magician demonstrates how the cards are to be counted one by one into a pile and then gives the entire pack to the spectator to count for himself. He does, and without realizing it, he picks the very card that the magician "Forced" him to choose!

SECRET AND PREPARATION

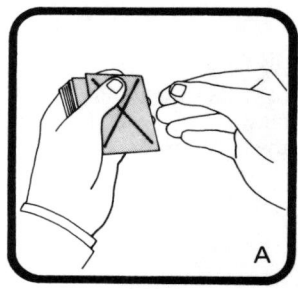

(A)   In this "Forcing" method the card to be "Forced" is the top card of the pack. This can be learned by first glimpsing the bottom card and then shuffling it to the top using either the Overhand Shuffle or Hindu Shuffle. Once the top card is learned by the magician, you are ready to begin the Count Force.

METHOD

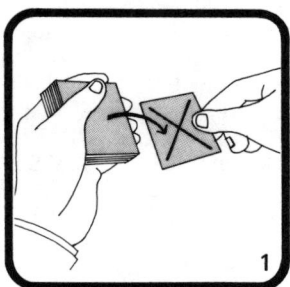

(1) Holding the pack in dealing position in your left hand, ask a spectator to call out any number from 1 to 52, thus limiting it to the number of cards in the pack. Assume that the number the spectator names is 7. Begin dealing the cards one at a time from the top of the deck into a pile on the table, starting with the "Force" card.

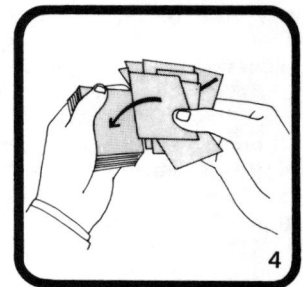

(4) Replace the seventh card back on top of the "counted" cards and then pick up the entire pile and place it on top of the bulk of the pack in the left hand. The Force card that was on top is now seventh down from the top of the pack because of the reverse order count. Now square up the pack and give it to the spectator to count for himself.

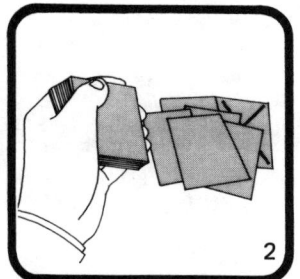

(2) As you deal, count each card aloud until you reach the spectator's number. By counting the cards one at a time in a pile, you reverse the order of the cards. You now have 7 cards in a pile on the table with the Force card at the bottom of the pile (seventh from the top).

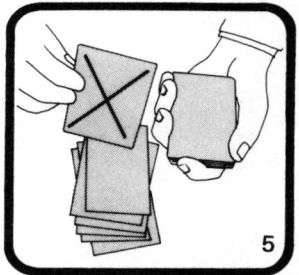

(5) After the spectator does the count and looks at your "Force" card, tell him to gather up all the cards and shuffle the pack. You have now successfully forced the original top card of the pack.

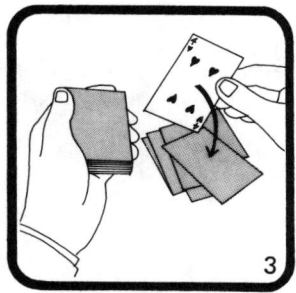

(3) State, as you deal, that you are merely demonstrating what you want the spectator to do. Explain that he should count down 7 cards as you have done and then pick up the seventh card — the last one dealt — look at it, and remember it. Demonstrate this by picking up the seventh indifferent card and looking at it. It is not necessary that you remember this indifferent card.

COMMENTS AND SUGGESTIONS

In the preceding explanation, we used the number 7 as the spectator's selected number. The Force will work with any number; however, it is best to keep his choice under 20. Remember, it is necessary for you to first count cards one at a time to the selected number. This can be time consuming if the spectator has called number 46, for example. Also, it may tend to arouse suspicion for you to give such a lengthy demonstration for a simple counting process. Therefore, when asking a spectator to pick a number from 1 to 52, you can modify it by saying, "Let's make it from 1 to 16, as a time-saver." If the spectator should insist on a higher number, do this: Instead of counting the cards as a demonstration of what the spectator is to do, count down to the spectator's number and then give the spectator the counted pile and ask him to recount the cards to verify that you have counted correctly. When he finishes recounting the cards, tell him to look at the *last* card he counted and remember it. This, of course, will be the Force card.

ROLL ANY NUMBER

By now, you can see that a vital part of many tricks is "Forcing." In other words, the spectator is allowed to make certain "free choices," believing that the end result is a product of his own decision – out of the magician's control. Yet, no matter what choice the spectator may make, he will always make the selection which the magician plans. The following "Force" illustrates how you can cleverly maneuver the spectator, completely without his knowledge.

METHOD

(1) This Force uses a single die from any pair of dice. It will work with any *four* objects. To aid in the explanation, we will assume that the object to be "Forced" is one of four piles in a single row. The pile to be "Forced" should be in the third position from your left. The four piles are numbered A through D in the illustrations. THE PILE TO BE "FORCED" IS THE "C" PILE.

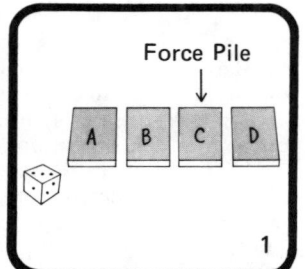

(2) Explain that the spectator should roll the die and that you will count its number along the row in order to choose a pile. This is done as follows:

(3) If the roll is "2," begin counting from the *right to the left.* Your count will end on the desired pile.

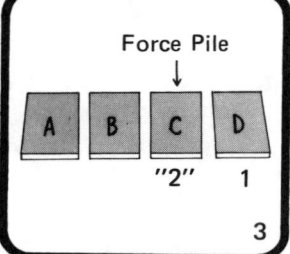

(4) If the roll is "3," begin counting from *left to right* to reach the correct pile.

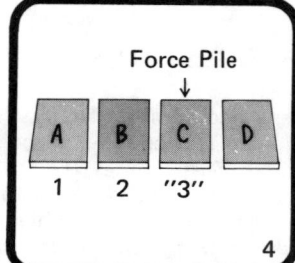

(5) If the spectator rolls a "5," count from *left to right.* When you reach the end of the row on "4," continue the count BACK, from *right to left,* to land on the proper pile (C). NOTE: DO NOT COUNT PILE (D) AS "5".... JUST IMMEDIATELY START YOUR COUNT BACK FROM "4" ON PILE (D) TO "5" ON PILE (C), YOUR FORCE PILE.

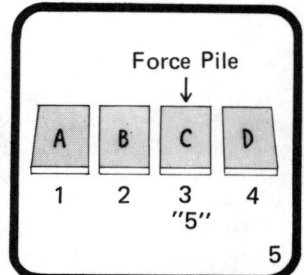

(6) If the roll is "6," count from *right to left* and then RETURN to the *right* to finish the count. NOTE: IN THIS CASE, YOU DO COUNT PILE (D) AS "4." THEN JUST CONTINUE AS IF STARTING FROM THE RIGHT, COUNTING PILE (D) AS "5" AND PILE (C) AS "6."

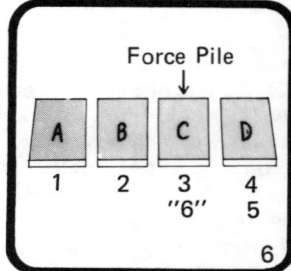

(7) The "Force" will not work with rolls of "1" or "4," *but such rolls make it all the better,* as they allow you to inject a clever twist that adds to the effect. If a "1" or a "4" turns up on the die, immediately say, "Good! We will use the 'hidden number,' the one that nobody knows!"

(8) With that, pick up the die, *turn it over,* and POINT TO THE BOTTOM NUMBER referring to this as the "Hidden Number." If "1" is rolled, the Hidden Number will be "6." If "4" is rolled, the Hidden Number will be "3." IN EITHER CASE, YOU END UP WITH A NUMBER THAT ENABLES YOU TO COUNT TO THE REQUIRED PILE.

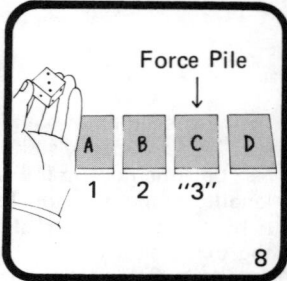

The following is a list of additional forces found elsewhere in the Course:

THE HINDU FLASH FORCE, see page 52

MAGICIAN'S CHOICE, see page 321

PERFECT CARD FORCE, see page 108

THE SHORT CARD FORCE, see page 129

THE TWO-CARD FORCE, see page 109

THE DOUBLE LIFT

Holding two cards together and exhibiting them as one is perhaps the oldest artifice in Card Magic. But it has attained new values in the comparatively modern sleight known as the "Double Lift." This maneuver is utterly deceptive in the hands of experts (many of whom have their own pet twists), but the basic principle is the same in all versions.

The Double Lift is one of the most effective and useful sleights in the realm of Card Magic, *providing it is not used too often or too boldly.* Originally intended simply to cause one card to "change" into another, newer and more subtle uses for the "Double Lift" were soon devised of which you will find a nice variety in this section. When worked in conjunction with other moves, the Double Lift is most effective, as results can be achieved that seem impossible — and all with an ordinary pack of cards.

THE LITTLE FINGER BREAK

This secret "move" is very important. The Little Finger Break has many uses....one of the most useful of which is to *prepare* for the DOUBLE LIFT....a simple sleight that is invaluable in the performance of MANY spectacular card tricks.

METHOD

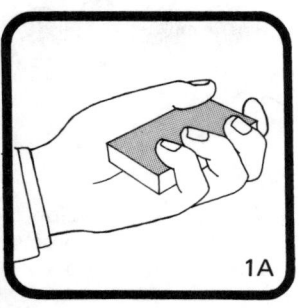

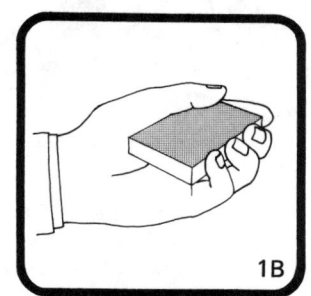

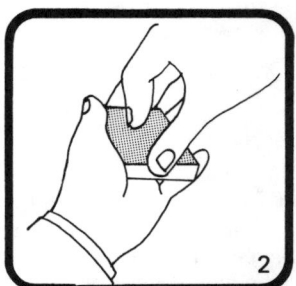

(2) Now, bring your *right hand* over the deck, right thumb at the inner end, your right first finger resting on top of the deck and your remaining fingers at the far end of the pack as shown.

(1) Hold the deck in dealing position in your left hand. However, unlike the regular dealing position (A) where the second and third and little fingers curl over the top of the deck (B), hold the deck so that just the *tips* of these three fingers extend above the right edge of the deck.

(3) With the ball of your right thumb, raise the inner end of the top card slightly off the top of the deck, then...

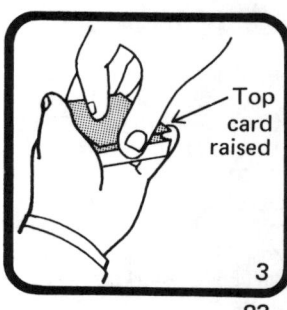

Top card raised

(4) . . .in the same motion, bend your right thumb inward *just enough to catch the edge of the second card* (the one just below the top card) and raise it also just slightly off the top of the deck as well.

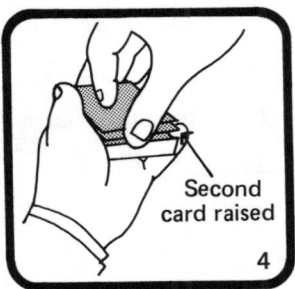

(7) Now relax your right thumb allowing the two lifted cards to come to rest together on the fleshy tip of your left little finger. You have now secured a "Little Finger Break" beneath the top two cards.

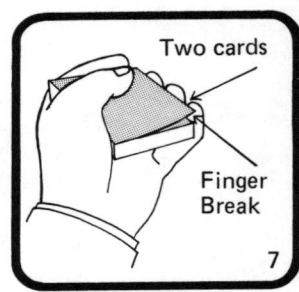

(5) *NOTE: The right first finger should apply a slight downward pressure on the top of the deck nearest the audience to assure that ONLY THE INNER ENDS OF THE CARDS ARE RAISED. From the audience view, it should appear that you are just holding the deck with both hands. ALL FINGER BREAKS ARE SECRET MOVES NOT KNOWN TO THE AUDIENCE.*

(8) Move the right hand away and, at the same time, move the left thumb so that it rests on top of the pack with your left first finger curled around the front of the pack. Keep the "audience end" of the top two cards flush with the deck. The pack, from the audience point of view, should look completely natural.

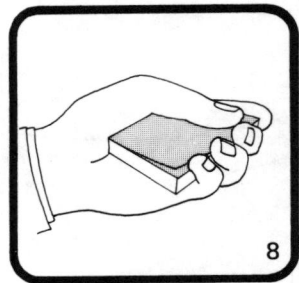

(6) When both cards are raised off the inner end of the deck, press lightly against the right side of the deck with your left little finger. This will cause the skin on the ball of the little finger to overlap the top edge of the deck just enough to hold a small "break" between the two "raised" cards and the rest of the cards in the deck.

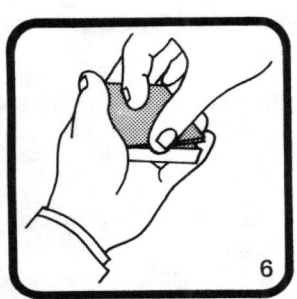

COMMENTS AND SUGGESTIONS

The entire procedure of securing the Little Finger Break should be done deliberately in the pretense of squaring up the deck as it is held in the left hand. *NOTE: It is also important, after you learn the sleight, NOT TO LOOK AT THE PACK as you "make the break." This is another example of MISDIRECTION as the audience will look where you look. So make some comment and LOOK AT THE SPECTATORS when you make the secret move.*

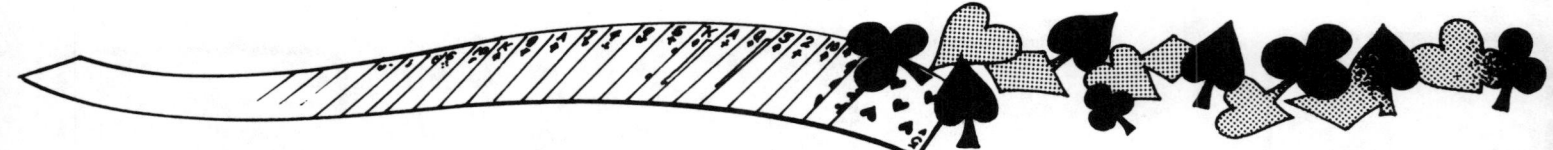

THE DOUBLE LIFT

Once you have mastered the LITTLE FINGER BREAK to the point where you can execute the "move" quickly and without suspicion, you are then ready to learn one of the most fundamental and useful sleights in Card Magic — the DOUBLE LIFT. This multi-purpose sleight is one of the most deceptive and practical moves in Card Magic and its uses are many. Learn it well, as it will soon become the basis for many of your most baffling card mysteries.

METHOD

(1) As mentioned earlier, you must first learn the LITTLE FINGER BREAK....before you learn the DOUBLE LIFT. To execute the DOUBLE LIFT, first secure a LITTLE FINGER BREAK beneath the *top two cards* of the pack. (These two cards have been marked "A" and "B" in the illustrations.)

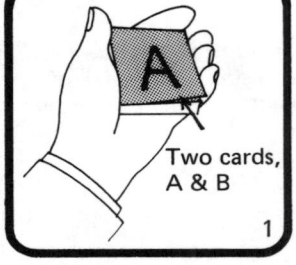

(2) Now, bring your right hand over the pack....with your *thumb* at the *inner end,* your *first finger* resting lightly on *top,* and your *other fingers* at the *outer end* of the pack as shown. This is the same position your right hand was in after securing the LITTLE FINGER BREAK.

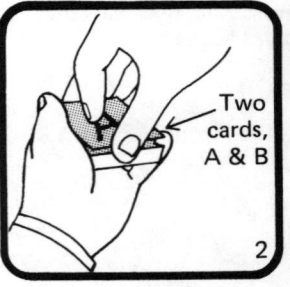

(3) With the ball of your right thumb, raise the inner end of two cards ("A" and "B") you hold above the "break." Now, with your right hand, *lift BOTH CARDS together (as one) completely off the top of the pack.* Your right first finger should press lightly against the back of the card(s). This keeps them from "bowing" apart and holds their edges "squared" so *THE TWO CARDS appear to be ONE CARD.*

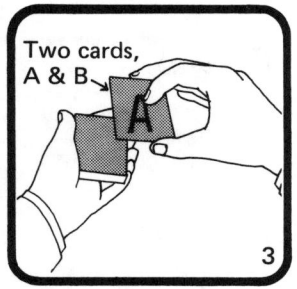

(6) With the left thumb, deal the *real* top card ("A") off the pack where it is taken by your right fingers.

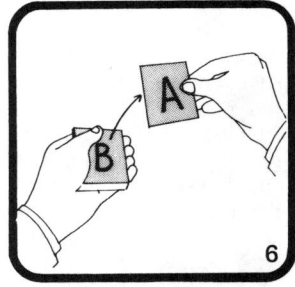

(4) Now, turn your right hand over, showing the face of the card(s). *NOTE: The audience believes you have simply picked up the top card of the pack and shown them the face of the card.* ACTUALLY, THE FACE OF THE CARD THEY SEE IS THAT OF THE SECOND CARD, THANKS TO THE DOUBLE LIFT.

(7) Set the pack on the table and turn this card face up, to show that the "top" card of the pack has magically changed to a different card....although we know better!

(5) Now, replace the card(s) back on top of the pack. Be sure that the two cards are "squared" even with the rest of the cards in the pack.

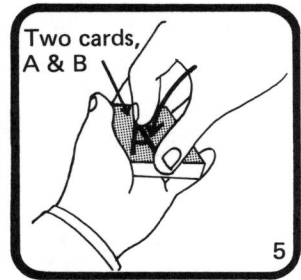

COMMENTS AND SUGGESTIONS

To review, the effect to the audience is that you remove the top card with your right hand, show them the face of the card, and then replace it on top of the deck. You then take this card face down with your right fingers — *where it "magically" changes to another card.* This is only one of the countless uses of the DOUBLE LIFT. In fact, one of the *dangers* of the DOUBLE LIFT is that it is so effective, once you have learned to present it well, you may use it *too much.* But don't worry about that right now — just PRACTICE and learn this sleight well. As you will see, it will be of tremendous value to you as you progress through the Course.

THE ELEVATOR CARD

Here is an effect that depends on the DOUBLE LIFT in its classical and most direct form. It provides the right amount of misdirection to catch the average spectator off guard, making it a good addition to any card worker's program.

EFFECT

After shuffling a pack of cards, the magician casually turns the top card of the pack — say the Three of Hearts — face up and shows it to the audience. He turns the card face down and replaces it on top of the pack. Explaining that the Three of Hearts has a peculiar ability to "rise" to the top of the pack on its own accord, he deliberately takes the card from the top of the pack and inserts it into the center of the pack. Without hesitation, he snaps his fingers and causes the Three of Hearts to "elevate" itself back to the top of the pack. Somehow the card, buried deep in the pack, has found its way to the top, giving it the title of the *"ELEVATOR CARD."*

METHOD

(1) After thoroughly shuffling the deck, secure a LITTLE FINGER BREAK beneath the top two cards of the pack in readiness to execute the DOUBLE LIFT. This done, grasp the two cards (as one) between the thumb and fingers of the right hand. Perform the Double Lift by turning them over and showing the face of what the audience believes to be the top card (Three of Hearts in the illustrations). Now, replace the card(s) face down on top of the pack.

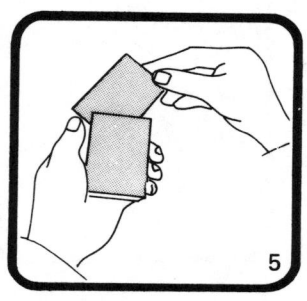

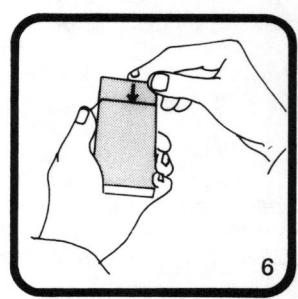

(5) Insert the *indifferent* card into the pack at the "break."
(6) Push the card all the way in until it is flush with the rest of the pack.

(2) Say, "An interesting characteristic of the Three of Hearts is that it has the peculiar ability to rise to the top of the pack by itself." Take the REAL TOP CARD from the top of the deck with your right hand as shown. *Be careful not to accidentally "flash" the face of this card exposing the fact that it is really an indifferent card.*

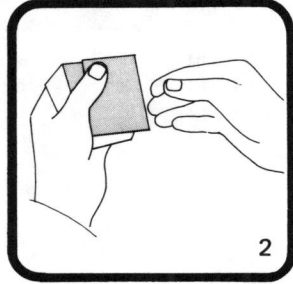

(7) Stating that the rest of the cards in the pack serve as an elevator for the Three of Hearts, snap your fingers and say, "The elevator card is now on top."

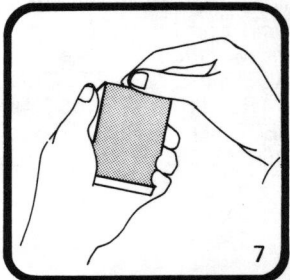

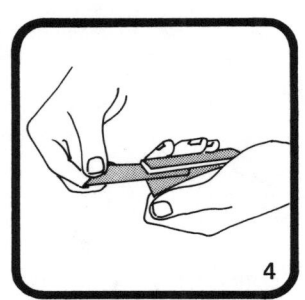

(8) Take just the top card of the pack (the Three of Hearts) in your right hand and turn it face up . . . to show that it has, in fact, *elevated* to the top of the pack!

(3) With the left thumb, riffle the outer corner of the pack downwards and stop somewhere near the center of the pack . . .
(4) . . .as you say, "Watch! I'll place the Three of Hearts here in the center and you'll see what I mean."

COMMENTS AND SUGGESTIONS

By adopting a casual manner when presenting this trick, you can be all "set" for the DOUBLE LIFT before anyone knows what to expect. While gathering cards or shuffling the pack after another trick, you are in an ideal situation to secure a LITTLE FINGER BREAK and move directly into the DOUBLE LIFT with any two cards that happen to be on top of the pack. As a neat bit of byplay, instead of snapping your fingers to bring the card to the top, you can *riffle* the outer corner of the pack slowly downward with your left thumb, saying, "This is the elevator going down. . . ." Then, after inserting the "top" card into the pack, you riffle the outer end upward with your right forefinger. Say, "And this is the elevator coming up!" Following that, you show the card back on top.

RIFFLE REVELATION

A very surprising "discovery" of a selected card, this is a basic application of the Double Lift already described, which can be presented at any time during your regular card routine.

EFFECT

A card is selected and shuffled back into the pack. The performer then shows that the selected card is not the bottom card or the top card, so it must be buried somewhere in the middle. He hands the chooser the top card, telling him to push it into the pack face down, while the pack is being riffled. Presumably, this card will "find" the chosen card...but it doesn't. The magician tries again and again fails. In desperation, the magician looks through the faces of the cards, wondering what could have possibly gone wrong. He asks the spectator what card he selected. When the spectator replies, the magician says, "Well that explains why we couldn't find your card in the deck.... it's the one you had in your hand all the time." To the spectator's surprise, the card he holds has magically changed into his selected card!

METHOD

(1) From an ordinary pack of cards have one card selected and returned to the deck. Using any of the methods you have learned, (the Hindu Shuffle Control, the Overhand Shuffle Control, etc.) bring the selected card (X) to the top of the pack.

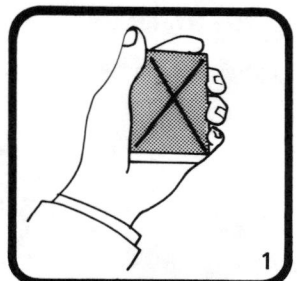

(6) Riffle the outer end of the pack with your right fingers as you explain that, as you riffle the deck, the spectator is to insert the end of his card into the pack anywhere he wants. Tell him that, when he does this, he will find the *exact spot* in the deck where his card lies.

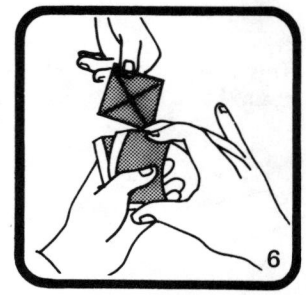

(2) With the chosen card (X) on the top, grip the deck between the right fingers and thumb and turn the entire pack face up, calling the spectator's attention to the card at the bottom of the deck....as you say, "There's only a small chance that your card would be the bottom card of the pack, is this it?" Of course, the spectator will answer "No."

(7) Here is a side view as the spectator inserts the supposedly indifferent top card (really his selected card) into the deck as you riffle. Be careful not to let the spectator see the face of the card he holds and tell him NOT TO RELEASE IT — "Just hold it firmly."

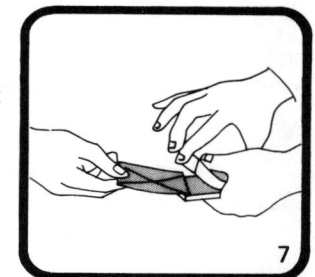

(3) Turn the pack over and hold it in your left hand in position to execute a Double Lift. However, before letting go of the cards with the right hand, secure a Little Finger Break beneath the top two cards of the deck.

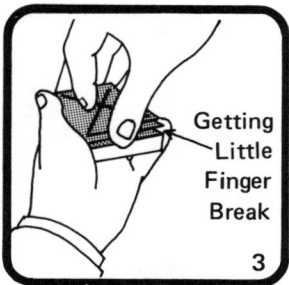

Getting Little Finger Break

(8) After you have riffled the end of the pack and the spectator has inserted the card he holds into the deck, lift all the cards *above* his inserted card and turn this packet face up in your right hand to show the card at that point. Inform the spectator that the card on the face of the right hand packet should be his selected card.

(4) *Now Double Lift the top two cards as one card* with the right hand. Turn the card(s) face up calling attention to what the spectator believes to be the top card of the deck....as you ask, "And is this your card at the top of the deck?" Again, the spectator will answer "No."

(9) *NOTE: Be sure the spectator maintains his hold at all times on what he believes to be the indifferent card in his hand....when actually the card he holds is his own selected card.*

(5) REPLACE THE TWO CARDS ON TOP OF THE PACK. Then, with your right hand, take the top (selected) card (X) and hand it, *face down,* to the spectator....as you say, "With the aid of the top card, we will find the exact location of *your* card in the deck."

(10) Here you reassemble the deck and riffle the cards again, explaining that you will give *him* a second try at finding his card. When you are wrong again, act as if the trick has failed and you don't know why. Turn the cards face up and run through them as if trying to find his card.

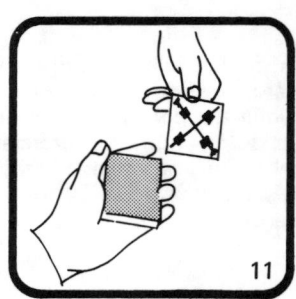

(11) Again, still puzzled at your failure, and without looking up from the cards, ask him, "What card did you take?"....when he replies, say, "Well that explains it, you were holding the card all the time." Of course, when the spectator looks, he will be surprised that the card has changed in his own hand, while he had control of it all along!

COMMENTS AND SUGGESTIONS

This is a good trick to use in which a chosen card is actually "found" by inserting another in the pack. When people want to "see it again," you can use the other instead.

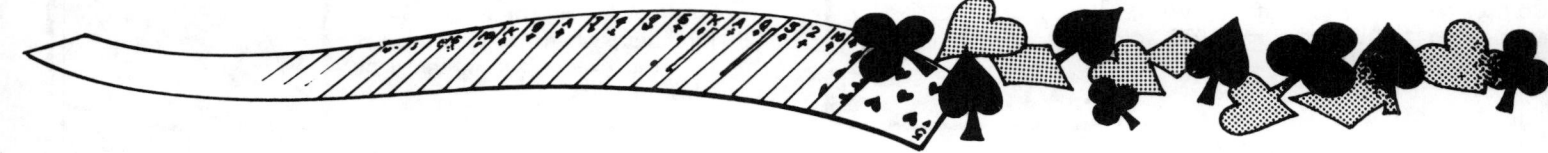

SNAP-IT!

This quick way of "magically" changing one card into an entirely different card will create a real suprise when injected into a regular card routine and is guaranteed to keep people wondering what will happen next.

EFFECT

The magician removes the top card of the pack and shows it to be the Eight of Hearts. Turning the card face down, he gives it a "snap" with his finger. When the card is turned over, it is seen to have MAGICALLY CHANGED TO AN ENTIRELY DIFFERENT CARD!

METHOD

This is a classic utilization of the Double Lift.

(1) Hold the deck face down in dealing position in the left hand and with the help of the right hand, secure a Little Finger Break beneath the top two cards of the pack.

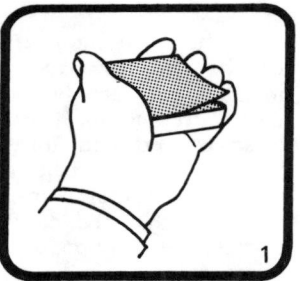

(2) With the right hand, execute the Double Lift *by picking up the top TWO cards as ONE CARD.*

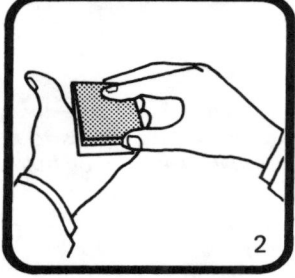

(3) Turn the card(s) over showing the face of what the spectators believe to be the top card of the pack (the Eight of Hearts). As you display the card(s), say, "You will notice a peculiar characteristic of these playing cards."

(4) Replace the two cards on top of the packet and . . .

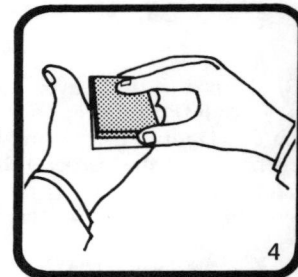

(5) . . . deal the REAL top card off the deck into the right fingers.

(6) Place the rest of the deck aside as you continue, "If I take the top card of the pack, in this case the Eight of Hearts, and give it a snap . . ."

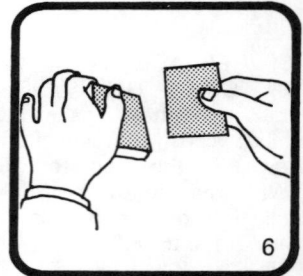

(7) Holding the card firmly in the right hand, give the back of the face down card a sharp "snap" by hitting it with your left fingers.

(9) ... THE CARD HAS CHANGED FROM THE EIGHT OF HEARTS TO THE FOUR OF CLUBS!

(8) Say, "... it causes the card to change like this!" Turn the card face up to show that ...

(10) Toss the card on to the table, just in case a suspicious spectator should want to examine it — and chances are he will!

COMMENTS AND SUGGESTIONS

Instead of the change as just described, you can add a clever twist by secretly placing two cards of the same suit on the pack with the lesser value card on top. For example: the Four of Diamonds on *top* of the pack, with the Five of Diamonds *just below*. Execute the Double Lift, replace the card(s) on the deck and remove the single top card and hold it in your right hand. PRETEND TO "KNOCK" ONE OF THE SPOTS OFF THE CARD BY SNAPPING IT. This can also be done with *any* two cards of the same suit, just remember to "knock-off" enough spots to correspond with the difference in the values of the two cards. If you're working standing up and have no place to lay the deck aside, simply strike the single card against the pack to "knock-off" the spots.

COLOR CHANGING ACES NO. 1

This is a novel and baffling version of the ever-popular "Four Aces" that can be presented in a quick, effective form, ending with a real surprise. In many Four Ace routines, extra cards are used....but here, *only* the Four Aces are involved making the entire trick clean, simple and most startling.

EFFECT

The magician displays the Four Aces. Then, holding them in his left hand, he deals the two red Aces, one at a time, face down on the table. To avoid any confusion, the magician openly shows the face of each red Ace *before* dealing it. This automatically leaves him holding the two black Aces. At the wizard's command, the Aces instantly change places. The spectators can even turn over the cards themselves, to find that the black Aces are now the two cards on the table, and that the magician holds the pair of red Aces!

METHOD

The only sleight necessary for this trick is the DOUBLE LIFT.

(1) From an ordinary pack of cards, remove the four Aces and place the rest of the pack aside. Display the four Aces to the spectators.

(2) Arrange the Aces in the following order: One black Ace on top of the packet (Ace of Clubs), the two red Aces in the middle (Ace of Hearts and Ace of Diamonds), and the other black Ace (Ace of Spades), at the bottom of the pile. *This should be done casually without calling attention to the fact that the cards are in any specific order.* (In the illustrations, the Aces have been numbered 1 through 4 to make them easier to follow.)

(3) Now, with the cards in their proper sequence, with your right hand place the fanned packet into your left hand...and, as you close the fan, *secure a Little Finger Break beneath the top two Aces* (the Ace of Clubs and the Ace of Hearts).

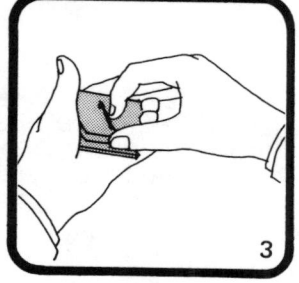

(4) You are now ready for the Double Lift.

(5) Lift the two cards as one (Double Lift) off the packet and show the face of what the spectators believe to be the top card — the Ace of Hearts — as you say, "Here is the Ace of Hearts — a red card — on top."

(6) Replace the two cards on the packet and then deal the REAL top card — the Ace of Clubs — from the top of the packet to the table as you state, "I will place the first red Ace on the table."

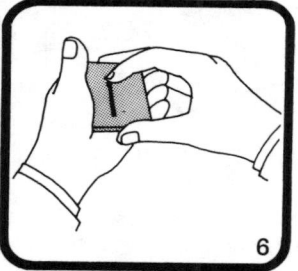

(7) *This next step is very important.* REVERSE COUNT the remaining three Aces, one at a time, from the left hand into the right hand as you say, "That leaves one, two, three remaining Aces."

(8) The reverse count moves the two red Aces to the bottom of the packet and the remaining black Ace (the Ace of Spades) to the top.

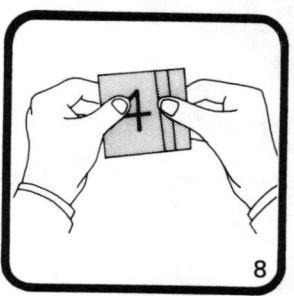

(9) Now place the packet face down in the left hand as before and, as you square the cards, *secure a Little Finger Break beneath the top two cards* (the Ace of Spades and the Ace of Diamonds).

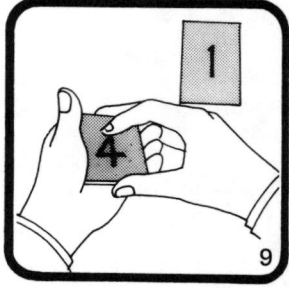

(10) Lift these two cards as one (Double Lift) off the packet and show the face of what the spectators believe to be the top card — the Ace of Diamonds as you say, "Here is the Ace of Diamonds....the other red card."

(11) Replace the two cards on the packet and deal the REAL top card — the Ace of Spades — from the top of the packet next to the Ace of Clubs already on the table as you say, "The second red Ace goes on the table with the first."

(12) The rest of the trick is just presentation. After a little byplay, turn over the red Aces in your hand and invite a spectator to turn over the black Aces on the table to prove that the Aces have actually changed places!

COMMENTS AND SUGGESTIONS

By handling the cards in an apparently casual manner, this trick can be built into an extremely deceptive mystery. Here is another clever procedure you can use when you do make the "set-up": After you have opened and removed the Aces from the pack and displayed them to the audience, hold them so that only you can see the faces as you arrange the Aces in their proper order. Say, "I'll put the black Aces in the middle and the reds on the top and bottom....although *actually the REDS go in the middle.* After showing the first red Ace and placing it (really the black Ace) on the table, when you reverse count the three Aces one at a time from the left hand to the right, you can call each card by its supposed color, i.e., "Black, Black, Red."

SPECIAL NOTE: In many cases, you can place the two "red" (really black) Aces DIRECTLY ONTO THE SPECTATOR'S OUT-STRETCHED PALM. After you deal each card to him, have him place his other hand flat on top of the cards. Apparently this is so that you can not do anything "tricky"....BUT IN REALITY THIS KEEPS HIM FROM LOOKING AT THE FACES OF THE CARDS. With this form of presentation, the Aces apparently change places while held tightly in the spectator's own hands!

REVERSED CARD IN DECK

Magically speaking, a "reversed card" effect is one in which a card mysteriously reverses itself by turning *face up* in a *face-down* pack. There are various ways of accomplishing this, all dependent on different methods. The one about to be described is particularly useful as it can be done with a borrowed pack.

EFFECT

A spectator is allowed to select a card at random from an ordinary pack. It is returned to the pack, which the magician shuffles. He then shows both the top card and the bottom card, asking if the spectator selected either. The reply is "no" in both cases, so the wizard exerts some magic power and causes the selected card to turn face up in the middle of the pack!

SECRET AND PREPARATION

Two basic sleights, already described, are combined to accomplish this result: The Hindu Shuffle Control and the Double Lift. The first is used to bring the selected card to the top of the pack; the second enables you to show two cards as one. If you have already mastered those sleights, you can easily perform this effect.

METHOD

(1) The spectator freely selects a card, which we will assume to be the Two of Spades. Have it returned and bring it to the top of the pack by the Hindu Shuffle Control.

(2) Under the selected card (indicated by an "X" in the illustration) is a second card (indicated by a "Z"). AS YET, YOU DO NOT KNOW THE IDENTITY OF EITHER CARD. *NOTE: The illustration with Step 1 shows the location of the "Z" card and is not part of the routine.*

(3) *Get and hold a Little Finger Break under the two top cards in preparation for a Double Lift.* Tell the spectator to concentrate on his card, so that you can gain a mental impression. This distracts attention from the pack during your preparatory action.

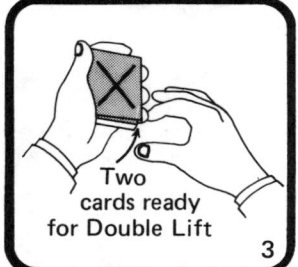

Two cards ready for Double Lift

(4) Finally shake your head and say, "Your mental impressions are too weak. I want you to look at the top card and tell me if it is yours." With that, you remove the top cards, using the Double Lift to turn them face up and show them *as one*. The spectator sees the *second card* (Z) which in this case is the Four of Diamonds. He says, "No." That is not his card.

Two cards held as one

(5) *Place the two cards FACE UP on top of the pack, keeping them squared as a single card.* Hold the pack firmly in your left hand. Say, "So that isn't your card?" At the same time, point to the Four of Diamonds with your right first finger.

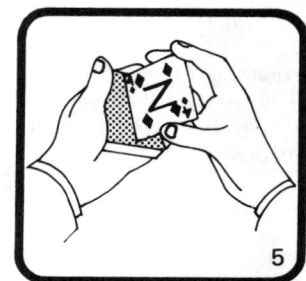

(6) Hold the two top cards — Z and X — firmly in position, as you say, "Well, let's look at the bottom card of the pack and see if that is yours."

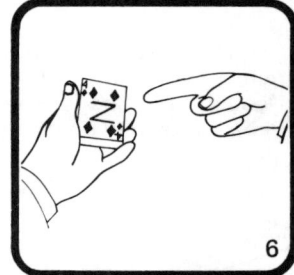

(7) Here, you turn the entire pack, face up, showing the bottom card — which we will assume is the Ten of Hearts. When you ask, "Is that yours?" the spectator again responds, "No." *At this point, you have all the cards face up except the two cards that you originally showed as the top card. They are FACE DOWN beneath the FACE-UP pack.*

Turn deck face up

(8) You next say, "Then neither the *top* nor the *bottom* card is the one you selected." As you are making this statement, with your right fingers, slide out the face down Four of Diamonds (Z) from beneath the pack.

(9) Turn the Four face up and display it beside the Ten. *This leaves the chosen card (X) FACE DOWN on the BOTTOM of the FACE-UP PACK.*

(12) Give the pack a complete cut, keeping both halves squared, as a slip here might allow a fleeting glimpse of the face up chosen card. Once the cut is made, THE SPECTATOR'S CARD WILL BE FACE UP IN THE MIDDLE OF THE PACK.

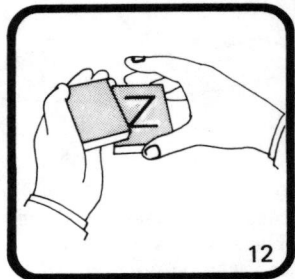

(10) Now, replace the Four of Diamonds (Z) *FACE UP on the bottom of the face-up pack. Thus, the Four goes back next to the still face-down chosen card.* As you do this, remark that, since the spectator's card is neither at the top or the bottom, it must be completely lost in the pack.

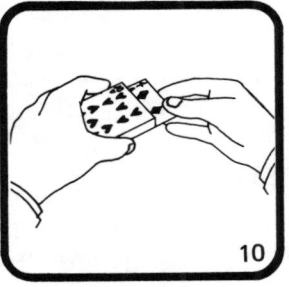

(13) So you promptly add, "It would be really magical if I could make your card *SHOW ITSELF* in the pack!" Spread the cards along the table and there is the chosen Two of Spades (X) face up among all the face down cards!

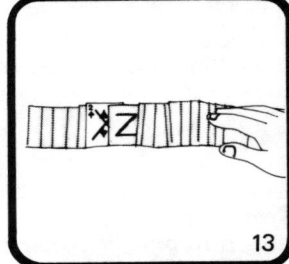

(11) Turn the pack over, face down, squaring the deck neatly, as you do. *The top card is now the Four (Z) while the chosen card (X) is FACE UP just below it.*

Turn deck face down

COMMENTS AND SUGGESTIONS

Actually, you do not know the chosen card before it reveals itself as described; but there is no reason why you have to know it, for if you follow the routine just as explained, the card will come up automatically. The only actual sleights — the Hindu Shuffle Control and the Double Lift — are executed at the very outset. From then on, it is only a matter of precision and close attention to detail. This gives you a chance to build up the effect as you proceed to the climax.

SANDWICHED ACES

Here is a baffling "Four-Ace" routine that people will talk about and want to see again. Once you have mastered it, you will probably keep it as a highlight in your program. Best of all, only a few special "moves" are required; and they fit into the routine so neatly that there is little chance that anyone will begin to suspect them.

EFFECT

The magician openly deals the TWO <u>BLACK</u> ACES face down on the table. The spectator then freely selects any card from the pack — say the Five of Diamonds. The Five is turned <u>face up</u> and "sandwiched" between the two <u>face-down</u> BLACK ACES. The three cards are then turned over as a group and placed on top of the pack.

Without hesitation, the magician spreads the top two cards showing that the Five of Diamonds has *vanished* from between the Black Aces. He deals the Black Aces onto the table and . . . immediately spreads the pack face down along the table — revealing the <u>TWO RED ACES</u> FACE UP IN THE CENTER, WITH A <u>SINGLE</u> FACE-DOWN CARD BETWEEN THEM. "I knew your card was sandwiched between two Aces," the magician declares. When a spectator turns over the face-down card, <u>it proves to be the missing Five of Diamonds</u>!

SECRET AND PREPARATION

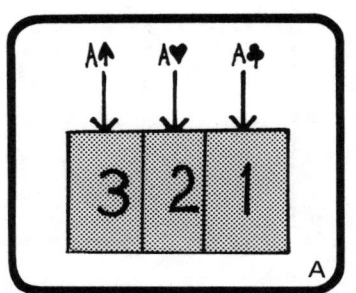
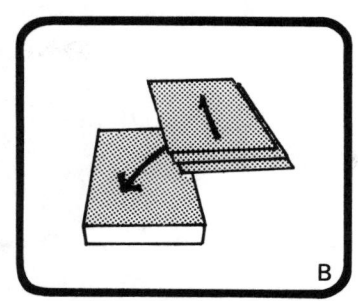

The success of this trick depends upon the proper set-up of the Four Aces in the deck before the trick begins. From a regular pack of cards, remove the Aces and arrange them in the following positions:

(A) Place the two <u>Black</u> Aces (Ace of Clubs and Ace of Spades) face down together and <u>one</u> of the Red Aces (the Ace of Hearts, in the illustrations) face down between them.

(B) Now, place this group of three cards on <u>top</u> of the face-down pack.

(C) Place the remaining <u>Red</u> Ace (Ace of Diamonds) <u>FACE UP</u> on the <u>BOTTOM</u> of the pack and you're ready. [In the illustrations, the Aces have been numbered 1 through 4 to make them easier to follow . . . (1) Ace of Clubs, (2) Ace of Hearts, (3) Ace of Spades and (4) Ace of Diamonds. The selected card is indicated by an "X."]

METHOD

(1) With the pack held in dealing position in the left hand, grasp the top card of the pack [the Ace of Clubs (1)] between the thumb and fingers of your right hand in the same grip as if executing the DOUBLE LIFT.

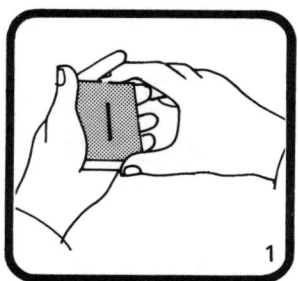

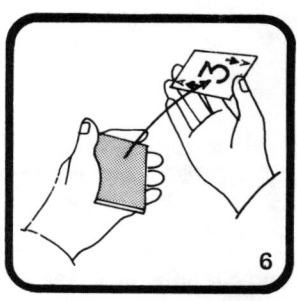

(2) <u>DO NOT DO THE DOUBLE LIFT</u>, just pick up the Ace of Clubs and turn it face up . . . showing it to the audience. Say, "The top card of the pack is the Ace of Clubs. . . ."

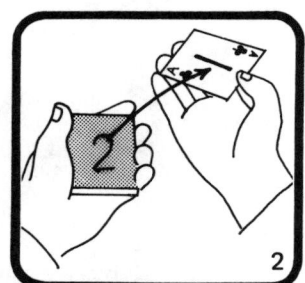

(5) Now, SECURE A <u>LITTLE FINGER BREAK</u> BETWEEN THE NEXT TWO CARDS ON TOP OF THE PACK [the Ace of Hearts (2) and the Ace of Spades (3)]. (6) <u>Execute a DOUBLE LIFT</u>, lifting both cards (as one) from the top of the pack. Turn them over showing the face of what the spectators believe to be the top card — the Ace of Spades (3). As you display the Ace, remark, "Here is the next card, the Ace of Spades. . . ."

(7) Replace the two cards back on the top of the pack and. . .
(8) . . .immediately take the REAL <u>TOP</u> CARD [the Ace of Hearts (2)] from the top of the pack and place it face down next to the Ace of Clubs (1) on the table. Say, ". . .which I will place here next to the Ace of Clubs."

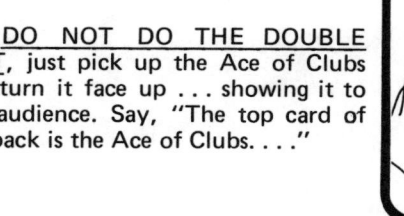
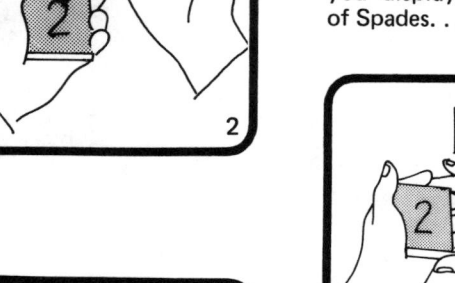

(3) Replace the Ace on top of the pack and, without hesitation,
(4) . . .take it with your right fingers and place it face down on the table. Say, "I will place it here on the table."

(9) NOTE: As it stands now, you have <u>one RED</u> Ace and <u>one BLACK</u> Ace face down on the table, <u>which the spectators believe are the two Black Aces.</u> The other Black Ace is really on top of the pack and the last Red Ace is <u>face up</u> on the <u>bottom</u> of the pack.

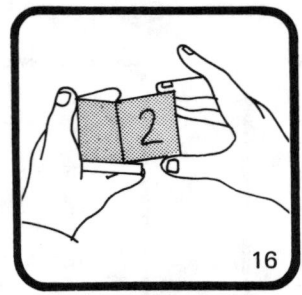

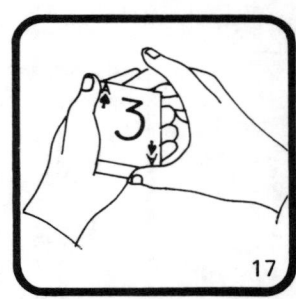

(10) Run through the pack face down and invite the spectator to select any card. When he does, square the pack and hold it in dealing position in the left hand. **(11)** Instruct the spectator to turn his card face up and slide it between the two "Black Aces" on the table, thus "sandwiching" his card between them.

(12) *NOTE: Be sure the spectator understands your instructions and does not pick up the Aces on the table. If you're not sure of the spectator, hold the two Aces face down in your hand and tell him to slip his card face up between them.*

(13) Now, secure a LITTLE FINGER BREAK under only the top card of the pack [the Ace of Spades (3)]. Because the attention of the audience is focused on what the spectator is doing, obtaining the Little Finger Break will go completely unnoticed.

(14) Next, pick up the three cards on the table and **(15)** ... place them on top of the pack — ADDING THEM TO THE ACE OF SPADES — AND SQUARE ALL FOUR CARDS TOGETHER ABOVE THE BREAK.

(16) Without hesitation, turn over all four cards (as three) face up on the pack as shown. **(17)** *The two Black Aces will now be face up on top of the pack ... the spectator's card will be face down below the Aces ... and below that will be the face-up Ace of Hearts.*

(18) As soon as the four cards have been turned over, carefully take the two Black Aces [(1) and (3)] with your right hand and place them face up on the table. Remark, "Your card seems to have disappeared from between the two Black Aces." *Be sure when you deal the two Black Aces off the pack that you do not shift the face-down card below them accidentally exposing the face-up Ace of Hearts.*

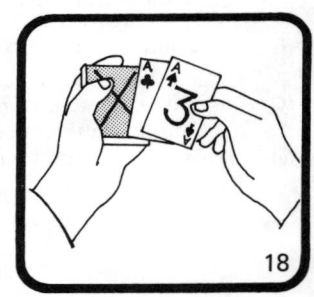

(19) HOLDING THE PACK IN YOUR HANDS, GIVE THE DECK A SINGLE CUT. THIS PLACES THE FACE-UP ACE OF DIAMONDS (THE BOTTOM CARD) DIRECTLY ON TOP OF THE SELECTED CARD AND THE FACE-UP ACE OF HEARTS BELOW IT. YOU HAVE AUTOMATICALLY "SANDWICHED" THE SELECTED CARD BETWEEN THE TWO FACE-UP RED ACES.

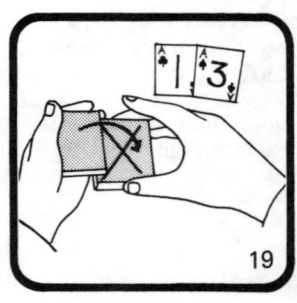

(20) All that remains is to spread the pack face down on the table revealing the two Red Aces and the face-down card between them. When the spectator turns over the "sandwiched" card, he will be amazed to see that his card has mysteriously appeared between the two RED ACES, the Ace of Hearts and the Ace of Diamonds!

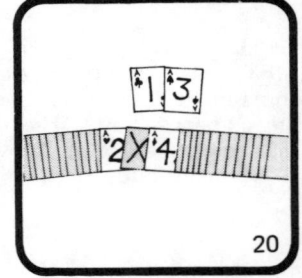

COMMENTS AND SUGGESTIONS

Precision, more than skill, is the main factor in this mystery, so PRACTICE can make it perfect. In showing the *first* Black Ace, display it just as if you were doing a "Double Lift," replacing it on the pack and dealing it face down as a single card. Now, when you show and deal the Ace of Spades, your action is identical — so the "DOUBLE LIFT" will never be suspected.

DOUBLE THOUGHT PROJECTION

This is an exceptionally fine mental effect using only two ordinary packs of cards with contrasting backs....such as one red-backed deck and one with blue backs....and requires only one easily learned sleight which you have already been taught.

EFFECT

The magician runs through a deck of cards face up and asks a spectator to freely name any card in the pack. Assume that he selects the Seven of Diamonds. The wizard removes this card from the pack and turns it face down showing that it has a BLUE BACK. With that, he spreads the rest of the pack face down on the table revealing that every card in the deck EXCEPT the Seven of Diamonds has a RED BACK! Then, to take the mystery one step further, he spreads the BLUE-backed deck face down on the table to reveal a SINGLE RED-BACKED CARD right in the middle of the pack. When this card is turned face up, it is found to be the Seven of Diamonds FROM THE RED-BACKED DECK!

SECRET AND PREPARATION

The only sleight used in this amazing mystery is the DOUBLE LIFT.

You will need two "matching" decks of cards with different colored backs, say one red and one blue. Beforehand, remove a card from the blue-backed deck and place it on the bottom of the red-backed deck. In the illustrations this card is shown as the Four of Clubs, however, any card may be used. Then replace the red pack *with the one blue card,* in its case and have the blue-backed pack lying openly on the table. In fact, you can use the blue pack for a few preliminary tricks if you wish, as the absence of a single card (the blue-backed Four of Clubs) will not be noticed.

METHOD

(1) Bring out the case containing the red-backed pack and announce that you will *mentally* project the name of one card to the spectator. Fan or spread the cards FACE UP in your hands and ask the spectator to name any card of his choice. *Stress the fact that he has an absolutely free selection of any card.*

(4) Reassemble the halves of the pack, placing the right-hand packet on top of the left-hand packet. *This leaves the spectator's card on the face of the deck with the blue-backed Four just below it.*

(2) When the spectator names a card, in this case the Seven of Diamonds, divide the pack into two sections at the place in the deck where his card is located. Keep the selected card at the top of the packet in your left hand. *NOTE: The Four of Clubs, THE SECRET BLUE-BACKED CARD is at the face of the right-hand packet.*

(5) At this point, get ready for the DOUBLE LIFT by securing a *Little Finger Break* beneath the Seven of Diamonds AND the blue-backed Four of Clubs under it.

(3) As you comment about the fact that his was a completely free selection, deal the Seven of Diamonds from the top of the left-hand packet *directly on top of the blue-backed Four of Clubs in the right-hand packet.*

(6) As you remark that the spectator could have selected any card in the pack, execute the DOUBLE LIFT and turn the two cards over *as one,* displaying the blue back of what the spectator believes to be his card, the Seven of Diamonds. ACTUALLY THE BLUE BACK HE SEES BELONGS TO THE FOUR OF CLUBS.

(7) Now to prove that you knew which card the spectator would choose all along, turn over the pack you are holding in your left hand and spread the deck face down on the table, showing them all to be red backed cards. *Be sure to keep the two cards in your right hand, WHICH THE AUDIENCE THINKS IS A SINGLE CARD, held firmly as shown.*

(11) Cut the deck burying the Seven of Diamonds somewhere near the center.

(8) Immediately pick up the blue backed pack (which has been sitting on the table all along) in your left hand and turn it face up.

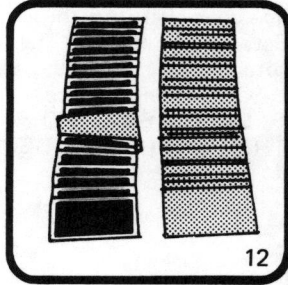

(12) The final proof of your Miraculous Powers comes when you now spread the blue backed deck face down to reveal one RED-BACKED card in the center of the deck.

(9) Place the DOUBLE CARD face up on the face of the blue-backed pack as you remark that the blue back Seven of Diamonds really belongs in the blue deck.

(13) Remove the card and turn it face up to reveal it is the Seven of Diamonds . . . THE ONLY RED-BACKED CARD IN THE BLUE DECK.

(10) *NOTE: What the spectator does not know is that the Seven of Diamonds you have just placed on the blue-backed deck is really a red-backed card, thanks to your secret Four of Clubs! You are now set up perfectly to add a DOUBLE BARRELED impact to this mystery.*

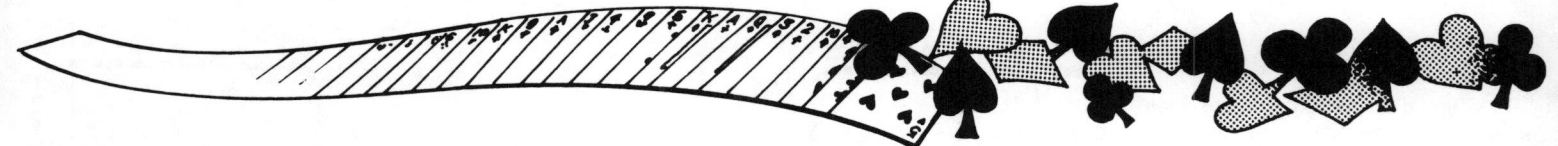

A CLEVER COMBINATION

Here is a possibility for combining two very powerful card tricks into an excellent opening routine. The first is the HINDU COLOR CHANGE followed by DOUBLE THOUGHT PROJECTION. The routine goes like this.

EFFECT

FIRST EFFECT — The magician places two decks of cards on the table, both in their cases, one case is red and the other is blue. He opens the *blue*-backed case and takes out the pack of cards, showing that the faces are all different as they should be. But when he shows the backs to the audience, they are *red.* The magician explains that he obviously made a mistake after his last show and put the red-backed deck back into the blue box and the blue deck back in the red box. He further explains that there are two things he can do....ONE, he can remove the cards from both cases and replace them in their proper colored boxes OR,....and at this point he "taps" the red deck.... *he can change all of the red cards to blue and all of the blue cards to red.* He now spreads the "red" deck face down on the table. To the audience's surprise they see that ALL OF THE RED CARDS HAVE INDEED CHANGED TO BLUE. The magician then opens the red case and, sure enough, there is a red deck just as it should be.

SECOND EFFECT — The magician then proceeds to have a spectator touch any of the cards in the now blue-backed deck as he runs them from hand to hand face up. When he turns the selected card over, it is found to have a *red* back. THE SPECTATOR HAS SELECTED THE ONLY RED CARD IN THE BLUE-BACKED DECK. The red-backed deck is then spread and is found to contain *one blue-backed card,* and that card matches the very same card that the spectator touched in the blue-backed deck!

SECRET AND PREPARATION

As mentioned above, this is a combination of the HINDU COLOR CHANGE and DOUBLE THOUGHT PROJECTION. It makes an ideal combination because you already have the "extra" red card in the blue deck at the start of the routine. Just make sure that when you finish the last Hindu Shuffle before the deck "color change," that the *single* red card ends up on the *face* of the deck. This automatically gives you the "set-up" for Double Thought Projection. Complete the First Effect by removing the red deck from its case where it has been all along. You can then perform DOUBLE THOUGHT PROJECTION just as described. At the end of DOUBLE THOUGHT PROJECTION after the duplicate blue card is found in the red deck, the blue card can be returned ot its correct colored pack and *you have two perfectly ordinary decks ready for whatever additional tricks you wish to perform.*

COMMENTS AND SUGGESTIONS

Remember, at the start of the routine, the apparently red-backed deck, (really the blue deck with one red-backed card) is in the *blue* case. The remainder of the red cards (all except for the one red card in the blue case) are placed, as they should be, in the *red* case. This second "color change" of the *blue* deck in the *red* case is another good example of "misdirection," as the audience has never actually seen the color of the deck in the red box until you remove it to show that it has changed colors!

THE GLIDE

For directness, efficiency, and complete concealment, the "Glide" rates high among card sleights. Simple though it is, it does require practice to be done properly and convincingly. The Glide is an effective sleight, especially suited to beginners but equally valuable to all card workers, as it enables you to show a card and undetectably switch it for another. It is a most important move, and there are some excellent routines for it described in this section.

THE GLIDE

One of the simplest of card sleights, The Glide is also one of the most useful. With it, you can practically duplicate the work of some of the greatest card experts, without any chance of detection, as the vital move is entirely concealed from view. Some of the most deceptive card effects depend on the "Glide," so you can regard this sleight as a major step along the road to card magic.

EFFECT

You hold a pack of cards face up in your left hand, and call attention to the bottom card — say the Two of Clubs. Turning the pack face down, you draw out the bottom card with the tips of your right fingers and place it, still face down, on the table. When the card is turned over by a spectator, *the Two of Clubs has changed into a totally different card!*

METHOD

(1) Hold the pack *face up* in your left hand with the thumb at one side, and the fingers at the other. The tips of the second, third, and little fingers should curl over the top of the pack and rest gently, as shown, against the face of the bottom card (the Two of Clubs).

(2) *NOTE: YOUR FIRST FINGER REMAINS ON THE SIDE OF THE DECK AND DOES NOT TOUCH THE FACE OF THE BOTTOM CARD.*

(3) Turn the left hand over, toward yourself, rotating your hand at the wrist.

(9) Place the card on the table.

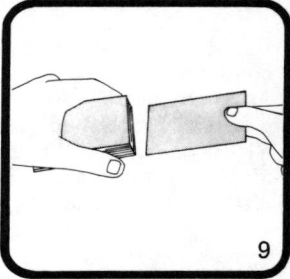

(4) As soon as the pack is face down, with the tips of your *left* second, third and little fingers, *slide the bottom card back,* so that it extends beyond the inner end of the pack about a half an inch. From underneath, the deck now looks like this.

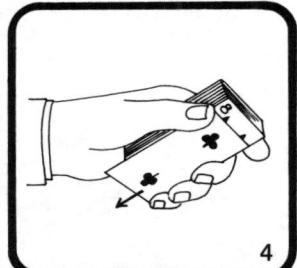

(10) *NOTE: The audience believes you have just pulled the bottom card (the Two of Clubs) from the deck....really, you have removed the second card (the Eight of Spades).*

(5) From above, the pack should appear to be *completely natural,* with the back of your hand hiding the protruding bottom card.

(11) As the right hand places its card on the table, use the left fingers to return the "Glided" bottom card back to its original position flush with the rest of the pack. (See optional move described in Note 13.)

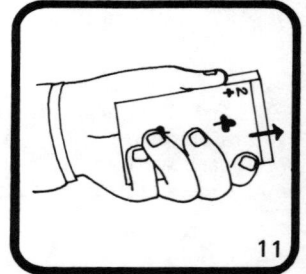

(6) Now, with your right hand, reach beneath the pack and press the tips of your *right* first and second fingers against the face of the now exposed SECOND CARD FROM THE BOTTOM (the Eight of Spades).

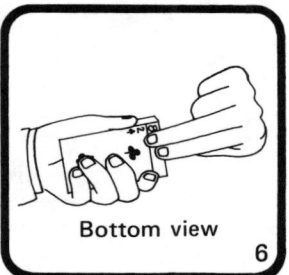

Bottom view

(12) The card on the table can now be turned over to show that it has magically changed to a different card.

(7) Begin to slide this card (the Eight) out from beneath the pack with the tips of your right fingers. When it is far enough out, place your right thumb on top of the card and draw it clear of the pack.

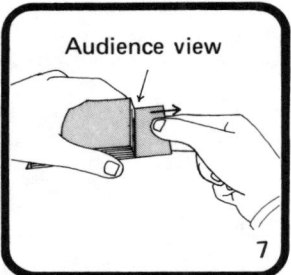

Audience view

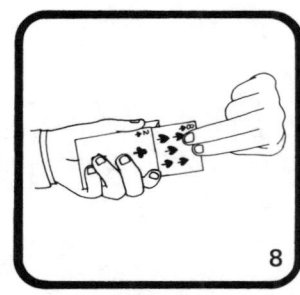

(8) This is the view of the pack from the bottom.

(13) NOTE: As mentioned above in Step 11, if you find it difficult to return the Glided card to its original position using only the second, third, and little fingers of the left hand, you may wish to use this optional move: After the card has been removed by the right hand and is clear of the deck, extend your left first finger over the front of the deck. Then by a combination of pushing *back* with the left first finger and *forward* with the second, third, and little fingers, you will find that you can return the bottom card to its squared-up position on the bottom of the deck quite easily.

COMMENTS AND SUGGESTIONS

The "Glide" may be performed with only a few cards, rather than the entire pack, and still be equally deceptive. As you practice, you will find that only a very light pressure from your left fingers is required to "Glide" the bottom card back. Practice so that you can draw back *only* the bottom card, neatly and secretly, without having other cards tag along. Sometimes, you need a little more pressure, but always be careful never to apply too much. Also, many beginners, when learning the "Glide," hold the deck too tightly in the left hand. The pack should be held so that the back of the pack does not touch the palm of the left hand. Hold the deck so that just enough of your second, third and little fingers extend around the bottom of the pack to touch the face of the card to be "Glided." When working with a new or borrowed pack, test the "Glide" before using it, to get the "feel" of the cards. If necessary, the right fingers can actually take over the whole operation, by simply pushing back the bottom card and then pulling out the next, but this slows the action and should only be used in an emergency.

THE GLIDE — ALTERNATE METHOD

(A) After you have learned the basic Glide, you may wish to add this extra touch. When you begin turning your hand over, as in Step 3 in the Glide, begin *at the same time* to draw back the bottom card with the tips of the left second and third fingers. If *both* the turning of the pack face down *and* the Glide are executed SIMULTANEOUSLY, the movement of your left fingers becomes even more undetectable.

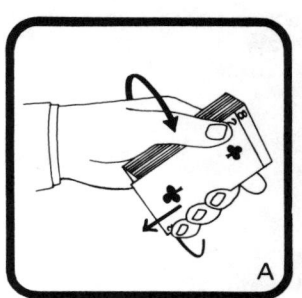

COLOR CHANGING ACES NO. 2 — (Double Lift and Glide)

One good trick deserves another; and that rule applies to the second version of the "Color Changing Aces," which is very similar to the method already given. However, this version depends upon the "Glide" as its second move instead of another "Double Lift."

EFFECT

From the audience's view, the effect is identical with Color Changing Aces No. 1. The magician displays the four Aces. Holding them face down in a packet, he shows the face of both red Aces as he deals them on to the table. Holding the two black Aces in his hand, he commands the Aces to change places. When the cards are turned over, the black Aces are on the table and the magician is holding the red Aces!

METHOD

For this trick, you must do THE GLIDE and THE DOUBLE LIFT.

(1) From a regular pack of cards, remove the four Aces and place the rest of the deck aside. *(In the illustrations, the Aces have been numbered 1 through 4 to make them easier to follow.)* As you display the Aces, gather them into a packet and casually arrange them so that the Aces *alternate* in color — starting with a black Ace at the top of the face-down packet.

(2) As you place the packet face down in dealing position in the left hand, . . .

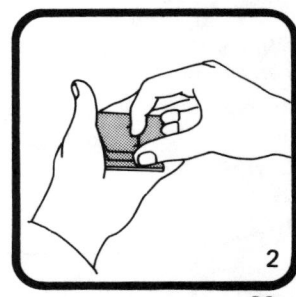

(3) ... obtain a Little Finger Break beneath the top two cards of the packet (Ace of Clubs and Ace of Hearts).

(8) Instead of doing a reverse count and another Double Lift, turn the packet face up in the left hand, in position to execute the Glide. As you do this, point to the bottom card of the packet (the Ace of Diamonds) saying, "And here is the Ace of Diamonds — the other red Ace."

(4) Now lift these two cards as one (DOUBLE LIFT) off the top of the packet and show the face of what the spectators believe to be the top card — the Ace of Hearts — as you say, "Here is the Ace of Hearts — the top card of the pack."

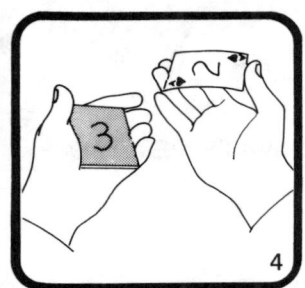

(9) With this, turn the packet face down and *execute the Glide* — DRAWING OUT THE CARD SECOND FROM THE BOTTOM (the Ace of Spades) instead of the "real" bottom card, the Ace of Diamonds.

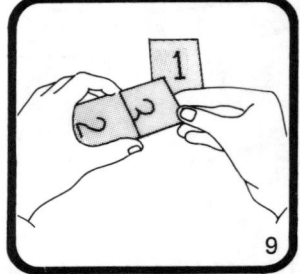

(5) With that, replace the two cards on top of the packet and ...

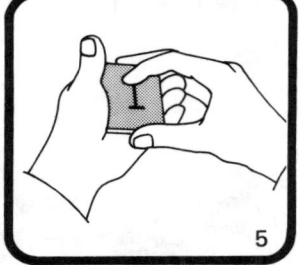

(10) Place the card on the table as you say, "I'll put the Ace of Diamonds on the table along with the Ace of Hearts."

(6) ... deal the REAL top card — the Ace of Clubs — from the top of the packet to the table as you say, "I'll place the first *red* Ace here on the table."

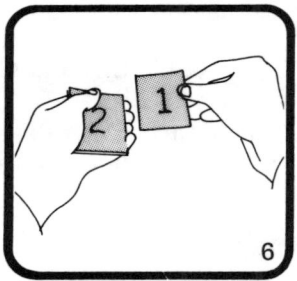

(11) At this point, the trick is really over; all that's left is presentation. After a little byplay, turn over the two red Aces in your hand to show that they have changed from black to red and invite a spectator to do the same with the black Aces on the table!

(7) NOTE: So far, this follows exactly the Color Changing Aces No. 1 routine (except for the color "set-up." Now comes the special added twist.

COMMENTS AND SUGGESTIONS

As you arrange the Aces in order: Clubs, Hearts, Spades, Diamonds, you can miscall their position by remarking: "Blacks in the middle; reds on top and bottom." Then, using the "Double Lift," you apparently deal one red Ace from the TOP. Then, *immediately* turn the packet face up and supposedly deal the other red Ace from the BOTTOM.

When "Changing the Aces," one good presentation is to hold one pair face down in each hand and slap their free ends together, with an up and down action. Then deliberately turn both pairs face up to show that they have "magically" changed places.

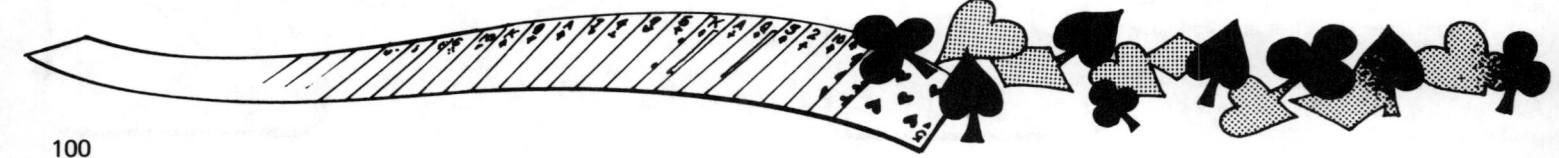

OIL AND WATER

"Dealing" tricks form a definite departure from other forms of card magic because they usually require only a small group of cards rather than a full pack. Also, they generally get away from the usual procedure of having a spectator select a card from the pack. As a result, "Dealing" tricks are very helpful toward making up a varied program. This applies particularly to this fine effect.

EFFECT

Six cards, three red and three black, numbering from Ace through Six, are arranged in alternating colors and number values. After displaying the cards in that manner, the magician turns them face down in his left hand and draws them out one at a time from the bottom and transfers them to the top, calling their colors, "Red — Black —" and so on. At intervals, individual cards are shown face up to prove that they are still in their alternating color order. The climax comes when the entire packet is turned face up and fanned. Amazingly, the cards have rearranged themselves in two separate groups; one composed of three black cards, the other of three red cards all in perfect number order from Ace to Six!

SECRET AND PREPARATION

THE ONLY SLEIGHT USED IN THIS TRICK IS <u>THE GLIDE</u>

(A) From a regular pack of cards, remove the Ace, Deuce, and Three of Diamonds, and the Four, Five, and Six of Spades. Now arrange the six cards so they appear in the exact order as shown. This done, you are ready to begin.

METHOD

(1) Fan the six cards face up and call attention to the fact that their number values are mixed and the cards alternate in color. Square up the packet of cards and hold them face up in your left hand in position for the Glide. Explain that, "Like Oil and Water, Red cards and Black cards just don't mix." *NOTE: Make sure that the spectator understands that the cards in your hand ALTERNATE in color.*

(2) As you display the Red Ace at the face of the pack, call out the word "RED." Then, turn the left hand over so that the cards are face down. Remove the card from the bottom, the Ace of Diamonds, with your right fingers.

(3) Place it on top of the packet. DO NOT DO THE GLIDE, simply remove the Ace from the bottom and move it to the top.

(4) With the left hand still face down remove the next card, the Five of Spades, from the bottom in your right fingers. To assure the spectator that this card is, in fact, a black card, with your right hand TURN THE FIVE OVER TO SHOW ITS FACE. As you do this, say, "BLACK." Turn the card back over and place it face down on top of the packet.

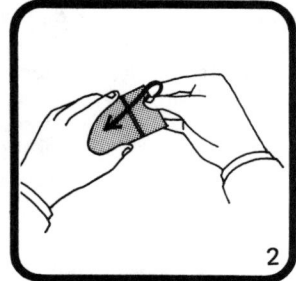

(5) Again turn the left hand over to show the face of the bottom card (Three of Diamonds) to the spectator, as you call out the word "RED." Immediately turn the packet face down and THIS TIME, EXECUTE THE GLIDE, actually drawing out the card SECOND from the bottom, the Four of Spades. Once the card has been removed from the "bottom," place it face down on top of the pack of cards.

(6) Still holding the cards face down in the left hand, draw out the bottom card of the pack, the Three of Diamonds, and hold it face down in your right hand. Pause for a moment as you call out the word "BLACK." DO NOT TURN THIS CARD FACE UP. Instead, place the card face down on top of the packet.

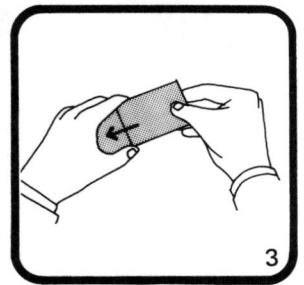

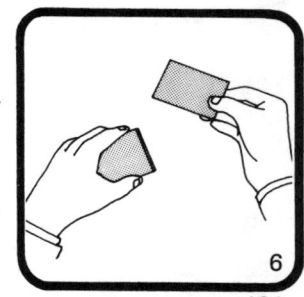

(7) With the packet still face down, remove the bottom card of the pack, the Two of Diamonds, and TURN IT FACE UP IN THE RIGHT HAND. Pause for a moment and call out the word, "RED." Then place this card face down on top of the packet.

(9) NOTE: Apparently you have just shown each card in the packet one at a time without disturbing their alternating color order or number order. Of course, you know different!

(8) Finally, turn the packet face up, in position for the Glide, and display the face of the Six of Spades as you say, "BLACK." Then turn the pack face down and ONCE AGAIN EXECUTE THE GLIDE, actually removing the card SECOND from the bottom, the Ace of Diamonds. Place this card on top of the rest of the cards of the packet.

(10) All that remains is to fan the packet face up displaying that the cards have arranged themselves in numerical order and that, like Oil and Water, playing cards just don't mix.

COMMENTS AND SUGGESTIONS

Practice with the six cards until you memorize the routine as given and this trick becomes virtually self-working. Its only move, the "Glide," should be done smoothly and at exactly the same pace as when you are "really" removing the bottom card. The total routine has been carefully designed so that each time you display a RED or BLACK card, either on the bottom of the packet or in your right hand, you are psychologically convincing the spectators of the "honesty" of moving each card from the bottom to the top and away from the real secret.

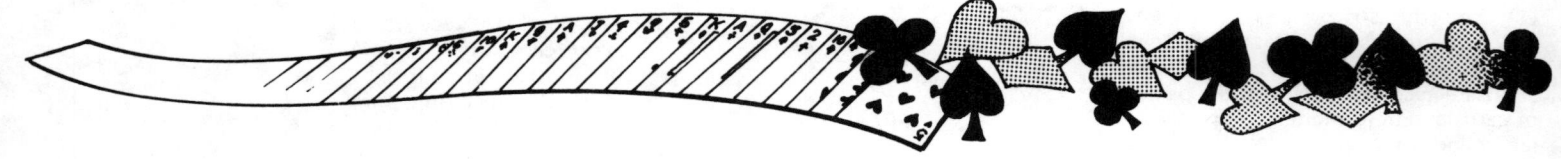

DO AS I DO OIL AND WATER

This is a version of the "Oil and Water" effect involving audience participation. The working is the same, but you have a spectator follow your moves with a packet of cards arranged in the red, black alternating order exactly like your own. Although the spectator duplicates your moves exactly, your cards magically arrange themselves in separate groups, while the spectator's stay in alternate order, just as they started.

When done in that manner, this trick makes an excellent follow-up to the "You Can't Do As I Do," in which some face-down cards turn themselves face up during a similar type of deal. It can also be used instead of "You Can't Do As I Do," when you are performing for a group of people who have seen the five-card effect before. Actually, the two effects depend upon totally different principles, but to most observers, they appear to be practically the same. That serves as an excellent "throw off" to lead the audience away from the real secret.

You can enlarge the "Do As I Do" routine to include two or more spectators, giving each a group of six cards, half red and half black, so they can all go wrong together while trying to duplicate your magical procedure.

BIRDS OF A FEATHER

This is a modernized version of a card classic known as "Follow the Leader." Here, all difficult sleights have been eliminated, reducing the routine to a single, simple sleight — the "GLIDE" — with everything else working almost automatically.

EFFECT

From an ordinary pack, the magician removes five red cards, the Ace through Five of Diamonds, and five black cards, the Ace through Five of Clubs. Placing the Ace of Diamonds and the Ace of Clubs face up on the table to serve as "leaders," he deals the four remaining red cards face down on the red Ace and all the four remaining black cards face down on the black Ace. He then openly "transposes" the face-up Aces — and at his command, the two "Deuces" invisibly "jump" to the pile of the opposite color — each next to the Ace of its own suit. Next, the face-down piles are transposed and yet another pair of cards — this time, the "Threes" — follows suit in the same mysterious fashion, "magically" moving to their matching colored Aces. This is continued — transposing the piles in every possible combination. Yet each time two cards are turned up, *they prove to be a matching pair,* having "magically" changed places to appear next to the Aces of their own suits!

SECRET AND PREPARATION

From an ordinary pack, remove two groups of five cards — one group of red cards numbering Ace through Five, and one group of black cards of the same values. In the illustrations, all Clubs (black) and Diamonds (red) have been used. Place the two Aces face up on the table and casually arrange the remaining eight cards in a fan from left to right in the following sequence: Five of Clubs, Four of Clubs, Three of Clubs, Two of Clubs, Three of Diamonds, Four of Diamonds, Five of Diamonds, and Two of Diamonds. (See illustration for Step 1.) With the cards arranged in this order, you are ready to begin.

METHOD

(1) Display the eight cards in a face-up fan, pointing out that the cards are separated into two groups, RED and BLACK. Do not call attention to the numerical sequence of the cards. Shown casually, *they will not appear to be in any special order.*

(2) Close the fan and turn all the cards face down. Hold the packet in your left hand in position for the GLIDE. Now, *execute the Glide,* apparently dealing the bottom red card (really the second from the bottom) onto the table next to the Ace of Diamonds. Say, "I will deal the RED cards here on the table next to their leader, the RED Ace of Diamonds."

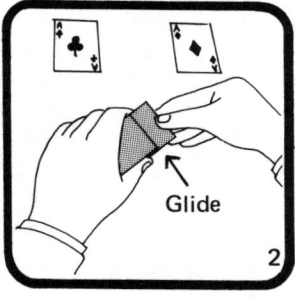

Glide

(3) After dealing the second card from the bottom, *do not return the bottom "Glided" card back to its former position.* Instead, hold the card in its "Glided" position and *deal three more cards,* one at a time, apparently from the bottom of the pack onto the first card.

Deal from bottom

(4) Stop dealing after you have the four cards face down in a pile next to the red Ace. Because of the "Glide," *the last card dealt on the "red" packet is really a black card.*

(5) Square up the packet in your left hand (secretly bringing the "Glided" card even with the rest of the packet) and deal the remaining cards *from the TOP of the packet,* one at a time, onto the table next to the black Ace. As you deal these cards say, "All the BLACK cards go next to their leader, the BLACK Ace."

Deal from top

(6) NOTE: As shown in the illustration for Step 6, unknown to the audience, you now have one RED card on top of the BLACK pile and one BLACK card on top of the RED pile, thanks to the Glide! If you have executed the Glide and the dealing correctly as described in Steps 1 through 5, the rest of the trick will work automatically.

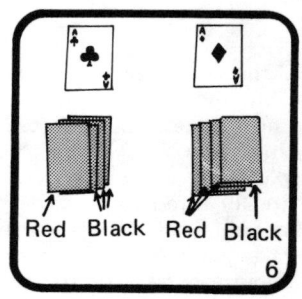

Red Black Red Black

(7) Now exchange the positions of the two "leader" Aces. Say, "No matter how I change the Aces, the rest of the cards will 'Follow the Leader' and turn up in matching pairs."

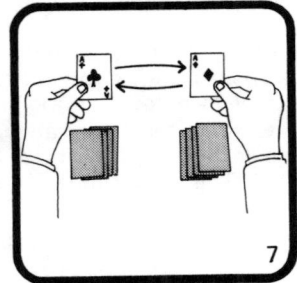

(11) Now exchange either pile of face-up cards with the face-down pile of cards *diagonally across from it* as shown.

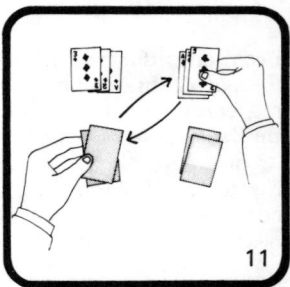

(8) With that, *turn over the top cards of both face-down packets.* These two cards will be the "Deuces" (twos) *which match in suit and color their new "leader" Aces.* Place the "Deuces" face up on top of their correct color "leader" Aces and continue.

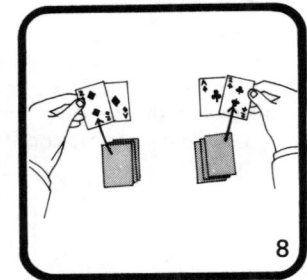

(12) Turn over the top two cards from the face-down piles to show the matching "Fours" and place them on their respective "leader" packets.

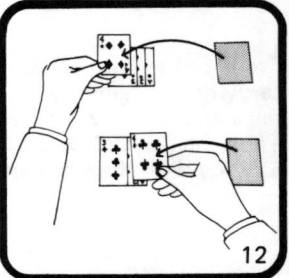

(9) Next, *exchange the positions of the two face-down piles.* Say, "Even if I switch the *piles,* it always works out the same."

(13) Now exchange the *other pile* of face-up cards with the single face-down card *diagonally across* from it as shown.

(10) Turn over the top card of each pile, revealing the "Threes," as they too follow *their* "leaders."

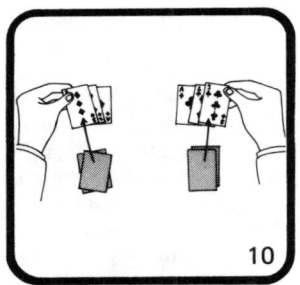

(14) Turn over the remaining two face-down cards. These will be the "Fives" which also match in suit and color to their "leader" packets!

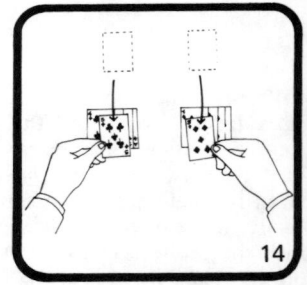

COMMENTS AND SUGGESTIONS

After practicing this trick until you can present it smoothly and without hesitation, you can add the following touch: Instead of starting with the cards in a pre-arranged sequence, begin by openly shuffling the four red cards and place them face down on the table; then shuffle the four black cards and place them face down on the red cards. Since no one knows the bottom card, you can "Glide" it back and *show the faces of the first three red cards* as you deal them to the table. *The fourth card (really a black card) you deal on top of the red cards without showing it.* Now, deal the first three black cards in the same manner — showing their faces — dealing the last card (really a red card) *face down without showing it.* Those two final cards are the first to follow the leader. The rest of the cards travel automatically as already described. The one *disadvantage* to this method is when you turn over each set of cards to show that they have changed piles to match the color of their leaders, *the cards will not be matching pairs.* In the FIRST method, however, if you were to show the faces of the cards before you dealt them, someone might notice that the first red card you deal from the "bottom of the packet" is *not* the card they saw on the bottom when you showed the fan at the start.

DOUBLE-BACKED CARD

Many surprising effects are possible with the use of a Double-Backed Card which has been added to a regular pack without the knowledge of the spectators.

Most of the tricks you can perform with a Double-Backer would be impossible without it. Others would require difficult sleights to accomplish the same result. Those are two good reasons for including the Double-Backed Card effects in your program. None of the following mysteries requires any special skill, and each can be mastered with just a little practice.

After you have mastered these mysteries, add a little creative thinking of your own, and you may discover many new and amazing card effects which incorporate the Double-Backer as their "secret weapon."

THE STUBBORN CARD

This is an example of an easy "quick trick" involving a DOUBLE-BACKED card that can be used as a prelude to a more impressive effect, or even as a follow up to another trick. Such forms of byplay introduce a surprise element that will leave your audience wondering what can happen next.

EFFECT

A spectator is given a card and asked to place it *face down* into a deck held *face up* by the magician. Riffling the deck, the magician commands the card to turn face down of its own accord. Upon spreading the pack, the magician shows that all of the cards are face down. He can even count the cards separately onto the table to prove there is not a single face-up card among them.

SECRET AND PREPARATION

(A) Place a Double-Backed card on top of the pack and return the deck to its box. You are now ready to present the Stubborn Card as the opening number in your card routine. *NOTE: In this illustration and the others that follow, the Double-Backed card is indicated with the letter "D."*

METHOD

(1) Remove the pack from the box and spread the cards face down between your hands as you remark that all the cards in the deck are face down and that there are no "reversed" (face-up) cards anywhere in the pack.

(3) With that, turn the pack face up and spread it between your hands, asking him to insert his *face-down* card anywhere in the *face-up* pack. As he does, spread the cards still wider, proving that *every card is face up except his.*

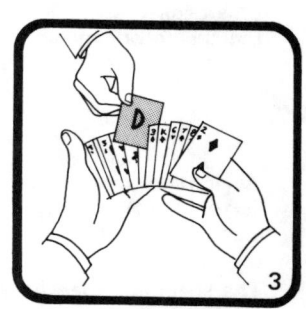

(2) Square the deck in your left hand and deal off the top card of the pack. Hand this card *(really the Double Backer)* to the spectator, telling him to keep it face down, so you can show him how stubborn *any* card can be.

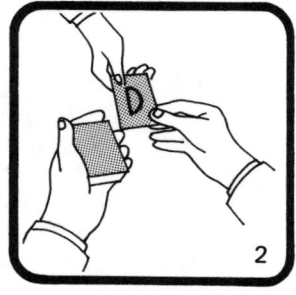

(4) After he has inserted the card, square the pack and turn it over, so that the pack is again face down. Here, you remark that no card likes to be face up in a face-down pack, and that his card is probably as stubborn as the rest. With that, riffle the end of the pack and then spread the cards between your hands telling him to watch for his *face-up* card.

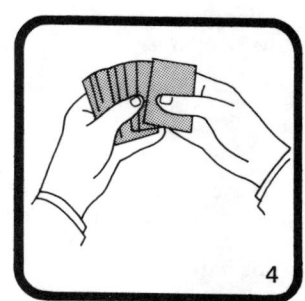

(5) No matter how closely he watches, he won't see his card because THE "DOUBLE BACKER" APPEARS TO BE A REGULAR FACE DOWN CARD LIKE THE REST OF THE CARDS IN THE DECK.

(7) Reassemble the two halves of the pack so the Double-Backed card will again be on top, just as it was at the start.

(6) To conclude the trick, turn the pack face up and start spreading through the cards saying, "There's no way of finding the Stubborn Card, since all the cards are face up and we don't even know what card it is!" As you spread the pack from left to right, tilt it toward yourself, so that you alone can see the Double-Backed card when you come to it.

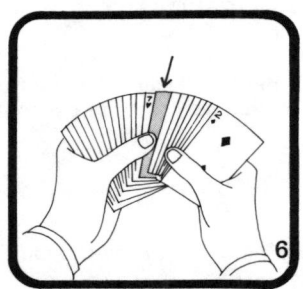

COMMENTS AND SUGGESTIONS

You can now go into almost any other trick requiring a Double-Backed card, since it is handy on the top of the pack. The five-card "You Can't Do As I Do" is particularly effective as a follow-up to the Stubborn Card. You do not even have to cut the Double Backer to the top of the pack. Instead, you draw four random cards from the pack, casually showing their faces as you place them face down on the table. Finally, you add the Double-Backed card WITHOUT showing its "face" as you lay it down. You are then free to hand the pack to the spectator and tell him to remove any five cards he likes, just as you did.

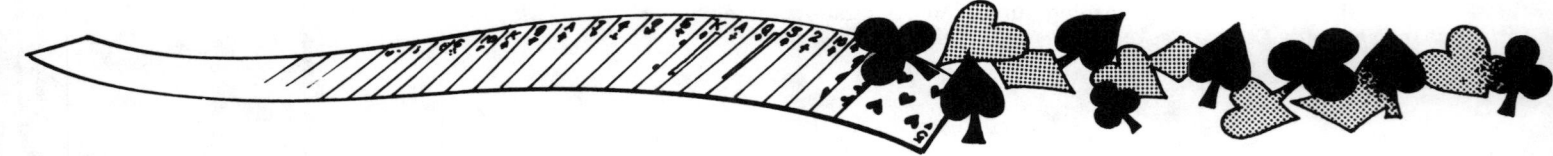

SATAN BEHIND YOU

This begins as a "Do As I Do" effect and then develops into a "Do It Yourself" procedure on the spectator's part. Under your guidance, the spectator "magically" discovers a card that he previously selected, yet finds he cannot duplicate the trick on his own. As a mystery involving audience participation with a surprise payoff, this will add zest to any program of Card Magic.

EFFECT

Dividing a pack of cards, the magician gives one half to a spectator and keeps the other half for himself. He explains that the spectator is to "Do As I Do." The magician places his half behind his back, removes any card and looks at it. He then puts the card behind his back again and places it on *top* of his packet.

The spectator then does the same with his half. The magician then reassembles the pack, putting his half on top, burying the spectator's card in the middle. Now, the magician instructs the spectator to place the *entire* pack behind his back. The spectator is to remove the magician's card from the top, turn it face up, and insert it somewhere in the pack. The spectator then hands the deck back to the magician who *immediately* spreads it face down on the table. Near the center of the spread is the magician's face-up card which he removes *along with the face-down card just below it.* When the magician turns over the face-down card, *the spectator acknowledges it to be the very card he selected.*

SECRET AND PREPARATION

The only items required for this mystery are a regular pack of cards and one DOUBLE-BACKED CARD which matches the back of the pack being used. To prepare, place the DOUBLE-BACKED CARD on top of the pack and place the pack in its box. (The Double-Backed Card has been marked with a "D" and the spectator's card with an "X" in the illustrations.)

METHOD

(1) Remove the deck from its box and divide it into two fairly equal packets. Give the <u>lower half</u> of the pack to the spectator. Keep the <u>upper half</u> for yourself . . . it has the DOUBLE-BACKED CARD on <u>top</u>.

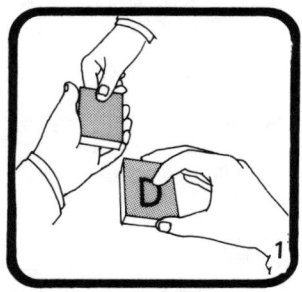

(2) Place your half behind your pack and withdraw any card from your packet. Tell the spectator to do the same. Instruct him to bring his card out from behind his back and look at it and remember it. . . . *He is to be sure you cannot see the face of his card.* As you say this, you also bring your card into view. Look at it and remember it (in this case your card is the Ace of Clubs). *Be sure the <u>face</u> of your card is toward you when you bring it out from behind your back.*

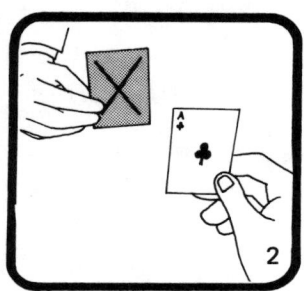

(3) When you have each looked at your cards, tell the spectator to return his card behind his back and place it on top of his packet. You *pretend* to do the same. Actually, when you replace your card, SECRETLY <u>TURN IT OVER</u> AND PLACE IT <u>FACE UP</u> ON THE <u>BOTTOM</u> OF YOUR PACKET.

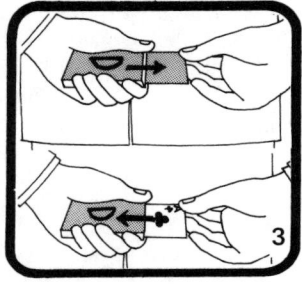

(4) Now, you both bring your packets back to the front. *Be careful not to "flash" the bottom of your packet, exposing the reversed card.* PLACE YOUR PACKET ON TOP OF THE SPECTATOR'S PACKET. Say, "If I place my packet on top of yours, your card will be buried in the middle of the pack." *Unknown to the spectator, this places <u>your face-up card</u> directly above his card.* The Double Backer still remains <u>on top</u> of the pack.

(5) Give the deck to the spectator. Instruct him to place the entire pack behind his back. He is to remove the top card *(which he <u>thinks</u> is your card . . . but is really the <u>Double-Backer</u>).*

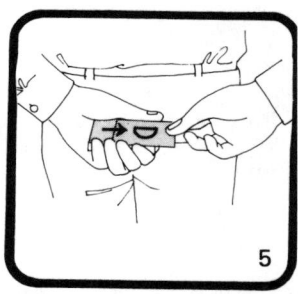

(6) He is to turn your card (really the Double Backer) "face up" and (7) . . .insert it anywhere in the pack.

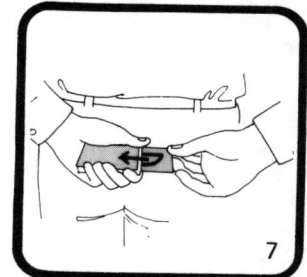

(8) This done, tell him to bring the pack forward and give it to you. Without hesitation, spread the cards face down on the table as you say, "My card was the Ace of Clubs — here it is <u>face up</u> in the pack where <u>you</u> placed it. What was your card?"

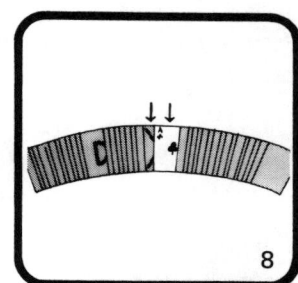

(9) Whatever the reply, remove the face-up card from the spread *along with the card directly beneath it* and turn that card face up! The spectator will be amazed to see that he has mysteriously managed to "locate" his card in the deck . . . ALL BEHIND HIS OWN BACK!

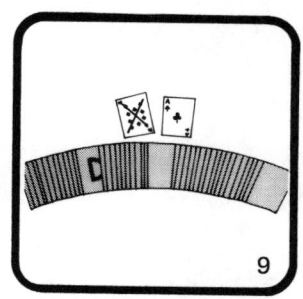

COMMENTS AND SUGGESTIONS

If you like, before you spread the pack on the table, you can <u>both</u> name your cards aloud. In fact, you can show your card to some other spectator before putting it behind your back; have the "participating" spectator do the same with his card. *Just be sure no one sees you place your card <u>face up</u> on the bottom of your packet.*

There is a slight chance that the spectator may happen to insert the Double Backer just below the face-up card, thus separating your card from his. So, as you remove the two cards from the spread, tilt them slightly so that you can "glimpse" the face of the lower card before removing it from the spread. If it happens to be the Double Backer, also remove the <u>next</u> card below it (which is the spectator's card). Then, remove the Double Backer from between the two cards and drop it on the pack, saying, "And here we have a 'mystery card,' with <u>my</u> card face up <u>above</u> it — and <u>your</u> card face down <u>below</u> it!"

THE PERFECT CARD FORCE

This can be termed as a "perfect" force, because if done deliberately and handled carefully, it defies detection. This is due to the presence of a "DOUBLE-BACKED" card which you secretly add to the pack beforehand, enabling you to accomplish what would otherwise be impossible. Hence it is a good method to have in reserve for some very special trick that *depends* on a successful force.

EFFECT

The magician asks a spectator to cut off a packet of cards — from a face-down pack. The magician takes the "cut" portion and turns it face up, placing it squarely on the rest of the face-down pack. He then gives the pack to the spectator and instructs him to run through the face-up cards until he comes to the *first* face-down card, where the spectator divided the pack. The spectator is asked to look at that card and remember it. ALTHOUGH THE SPECTATOR WAS FREE TO CUT WHEREVER HE WANTED, THE MAGICIAN ALREADY KNOWS THE CARD!

SECRET AND PREPARATION

The only items required for this force are a regular pack of playing cards and one DOUBLE BACKED card that matches the back design of the cards in the pack.

(A) To prepare, place the card to be "Forced" FACE UP on top of the face-down pack. (In the illustrations the Eight of Spades is the "Force" card and is marked with an "F.") Directly above this, place the Double-Backed card. (The Double-Backed card is marked with a "D.") The face-up Eight of Spades is now *second* from the top *hidden by the Double Backer.* Square up the pack, and you are ready to begin.

METHOD

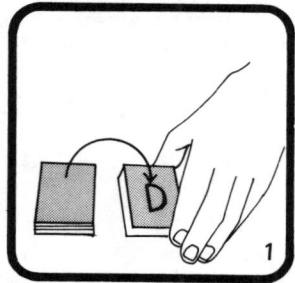

(1) Place the pack face down on the table and ask the spectator to divide the pack into two parts. Tell him that he can cut *anywhere* in the deck he wishes — and to then place the upper portion on the table. *Stress the fact that the spectator is cutting the pack at a location of his own free choice.*

(2) *NOTE: IT IS VERY IMPORTANT HERE THAT THE SPECTATOR CUT THE CARDS NEATLY SO AS NOT TO ACCIDENTALLY SHIFT THE DOUBLE BACKER EXPOSING THE FACE-UP FORCE CARD BENEATH IT. FOR THIS REASON, IT IS WISE FOR YOU TO DEMONSTRATE BEFOREHAND HOW THE SPECTATOR SHOULD DIVIDE THE PACK INTO TWO "NEAT PILES."*

(3) This done, pick up the packet the spectator cut off the deck. CAREFULLY TURN THE PACKET OVER, AND REPLACE IT FACE UP ON TOP OF THE REST OF THE PACK. Say, "By placing these cards face up on top of the face-down cards, we will mark the location where you divided the pack."

(4) *NOTE: This automatically reverses the Double-Backed card and the secret face-up Eight of Spades and makes them the first two cards of the face-down portion of the pack.*

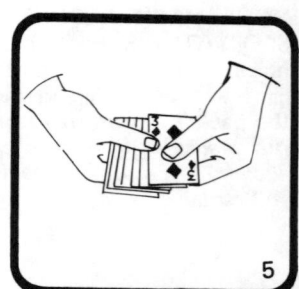

(5) Pick up the pack from the table and hand it to the spectator. Tell him to run through the pack until he reaches THE FIRST FACE-DOWN CARD — WHERE HE DIVIDED THE PACK.

(6) He is to remove that card from the pack.

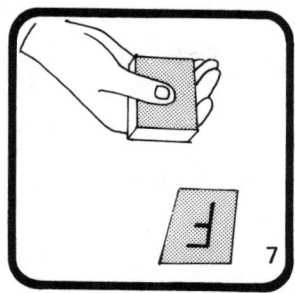

(7) The <u>first face-down card</u> he *arrived at was your "Force" card, the Eight of Spades.* After he removes the card, tell him to reassemble the pack and give it to you. YOU HAVE NOW SUCCESSFULLY EXECUTED THE PERFECT CARD FORCE.

COMMENTS AND SUGGESTIONS

The "Force" can be ruined if the spectator handles the cards too carelessly and the top (Double-Backed) card slides from the pack, exposing the face-up "Force" card beneath. *Therefore, if you are not sure of the spectator, you will do better to handle the pack yourself.* Simply riffle the outer end slowly and let the spectator insert his forefinger; or have him lift up a portion of the pack at the outer end as *you* hold the cards. Either way, *you* then divide the pack at the point he selected and carefully turn the whole group face up on the pack. Then immediately square the deck with your hands. You are then ready to let the spectator run through the cards until he comes to the one that he thinks is his "free" selection.

THE TWO-CARD FORCE

While this can be classified as a "Force" involving a Double-Backed card, its effect is so strong that it can be presented as a prediction trick in its own right. No skill whatever is required, yet the performer will be given credit for a near miracle. This trick alone makes it worthwhile to include "Double-Backed" card effects in your program.

EFFECT

The magician gives a sealed envelope to a spectator and says that it contains a "Double Prediction." He then takes a pack of cards from its case, and handing the top card face down to another spectator, he explains that this card is to be used as an "indicator." *Turning the squared pack face up,* he tells the spectator to insert the indicator card *face down* ANYWHERE he wishes in the pack. This done, the magician turns the pack back over and runs through the now face-down deck. When he comes to the *face-up* "indicator" card. The spectator is asked to remove the two cards on both sides of the indicator and looks at them. When the envelope is opened, IT CONTAINS A SLIP OF PAPER WITH THE NAMES OF THOSE TWO CARDS!

SECRET AND PREPARATION

The only requirements for this mystery are a regular pack of cards and a single Double-Backed card which matches the back design of the cards in the pack. To prepare, write the names of any two cards on a slip of paper. These will be your "Force" cards. Seal the piece of paper in an envelope and place it in your pocket. This done, run through the pack of cards and find the two "Force Cards" and place them together, face down, somewhere near the center of the face-down pack. NOW REMOVE ANY INDIFFERENT CARD AND PLACE IT FACE UP BETWEEN THE TWO FACE-DOWN FORCE CARDS. Finally, place the Double-Backed card on *top* of the pack and you're ready. (In the illustrations, the Double Back card is indicated by a "D" and the two "Force" cards by "F.")

METHOD

(1) Begin the presentation by removing from your pocket the sealed envelope. Say, "In this envelope is a slip of paper with a double prediction." Place the envelope on the table or hand it to a spectator to hold and pick up the pack of cards.

(2) Holding the pack face down in dealing position in the left hand, deal the top card (the Double Backer) from the top of the pack into your right fingers. Give this card to the spectator, asking him to hold it face down — without looking at it — as it will be used simply as an "indicator" card.

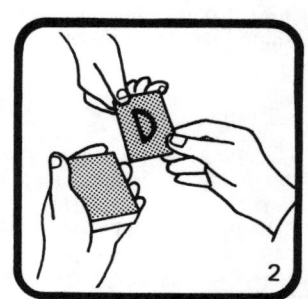

(3) Now TURN THE PACK FACE UP and tell the spectator to insert the indicator card FACE DOWN *anywhere* he wishes in the pack.

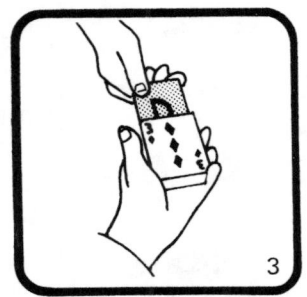

(6) Run through the face-down pack until you come to the face up Six of Clubs in the center as you say, ". . . and here is your face-up indicator card, the Six of Clubs."

(4) *NOTE: The spectator will believe that when this card is replaced "face down" in the "face-up" pack, it will be the ONLY reversed card in the pack. What he doesn't know is that the card he holds is a Double Backed card....and that you have previously reversed one card (the Six of Clubs) in the pack beforehand.*

(7) Ask the spectator to remove *the two cards on either side of the face up indicator card.* THESE ARE YOUR TWO "FORCE" CARDS WHICH MATCH THE PREDICTION ON THE SLIP OF PAPER IN THE ENVELOPE.

(5) After the spectator has inserted the indicator card (the Double Backer) into the pack, TURN THE PACK OVER (FACE DOWN). Say, "When I turn the pack over, your indicator card will become the only face-up card in the pack, right?"

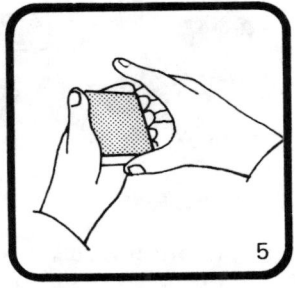

(8) Tell the spectator to turn the two cards face up. Then, to complete the mystery, ask another spectator to open the envelope and read the "Double Prediction"!

COMMENTS AND SUGGESTIONS

Another way of handling the insertion of the indicator card is to give the entire pack, face down to the spectator and tell him to put the pack behind his back. Then tell him to remove the top card with his right hand, *turn it face up,* and insert it anywhere into the pack. This done, you can even let *him* spread the pack along the table to find the face up indicator. In this modified version, *he* actually turns over the Double-Backed card, but since it is behind his back, no one can see that it is a Double Backer.

ADDED NOTE: You can also use this method to force a single card. Simply state that you will use whatever card happens to show up face to face with the indicator card. When you come to the face-up card you set up beforehand, remove it with the card above and let the spectator look at that card without showing it to you. YOU WON'T HAVE TO SEE IT, BECAUSE YOU ALREADY KNOW IT!

INSTO—TRANSPO

Three elements are combined to produce this super mystery: A Double-Backed card, a Double Lift and a simple but deceptive turnover that provides a final touch. Each element strengthens the others and the mystery itself is built around an element of "misdirection" designed to aid all three.

EFFECT

The magician gives a spectator a free choice of any card in the pack. The spectator signs his name on the face of the card and gives it to the magician, who places it *face down* on the table. Now, the *spectator* runs the pack from hand to hand and the *magician* selects one card from the pack. The magician signs the face of his selected card and *lays it face down beside the card signed by the spectator.* FROM THAT MOMENT ON, THE MAGICIAN NEVER TOUCHES THE CARDS. The magician, commands the two cards to change places. When the spectator turns both cards over, HE HAS THE MAGICIAN'S SIGNED CARD, WHILE THE SPECTATOR'S SIGNED CARD IS WHERE THE MAGICIAN'S CARD SHOULD BE!

SECRET AND PREPARATION

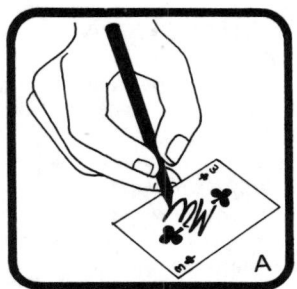

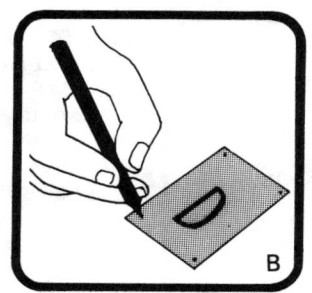

All that is required for this baffling mystery is a regular pack of cards and a matching Double-Backed card. *To prepare,* (A) Remove any spot card (for the illustrations we will use the Three of Clubs), from the pack and sign your name or initials across the face of the card with a marking pen. (B) Next, make a small pencil mark in each of the four corners *on both sides* of the Double-Backed card. The marks should be just dark enough so you can see which card is the Double Backer as the cards are run from hand to hand. (C) To set up, place the initialed card (the Three of Clubs) FACE UP on top of the face-down pack. On top of this, place the Double-Backed card (in the illustrations the Double-Backed card is marked with a "D"). Now square up the deck and you are ready to begin.

METHOD

(1) Run the cards from hand to hand and ask the spectator to select a card. Be careful not to separate the cards too near the top and expose the *face-up* card second from the top.

(2) After the spectator freely selects a card (the Four of Diamonds in the illustration), square up the pack and ask him to sign the face of his card with your marking pen.

IMPORTANT NOTE: The following Steps, 3, 4, and 5, are very important and are the real secret to the mystery. Follow them carefully.

(3) While the spectator is signing his card, with the help of your right hand, OBTAIN A LITTLE FINGER BREAK BELOW THE TOP TWO CARDS OF THE PACK (THE DOUBLE BACKER AND YOUR *FACE-UP* INITIALED CARD BELOW IT).

(4) When the spectator has signed his card, place it *face up* on top of the deck, *adding it to the two cards above the Break,* and square all three cards together.

(5) *Almost immediately turn over all three cards (as one) face down on top of the deck.* Turning the three cards as one is called a "Triple Lift." WHEN THE THREE CARDS ARE TURNED OVER, BECAUSE YOUR CARD (THE THREE OF CLUBS) WAS FACE UP, IT WILL APPEAR TO BE THE BACK OF THE SPECTATOR'S SIGNED CARD.

Three cards turned as one

(6) *NOTE: The spectator's Four of Diamonds is now third from the top, the Double-Backed card is second, and your initialed Three of Clubs is on top.*

(7) Now deal the top card (really your initialed card), face down on the table as you say, "I'll place *your* card on the table in front of you where you can keep close watch on it all the time."

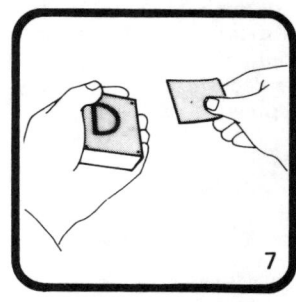

(8) This done, give the pack one complete cut — cutting as close to the CENTER as possible. This buries the Double-Backed card and the spectator's initialed card near the middle of the pack.

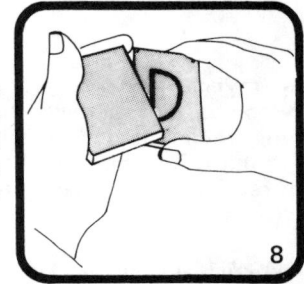

(9) GIVE THE PACK TO THE SPEC-TATOR and ask *him* to run the cards from hand to hand, as you did, so that *you* may select a card FROM THE CENTER OF THE PACK.

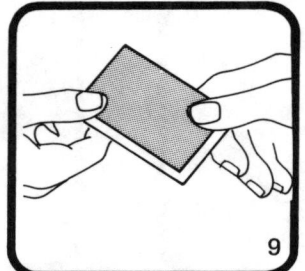

(12) DO NOT LET THE SPECTA-TOR SEE THE FACE OF THIS CARD. Pick up the marking pen and *pretend* to sign your name or initials on the face of the card. *The spectator will believe this card was a random selection and that you are simply signing your own name on the card.* After you have supposedly signed the card, place it face down on the table in front of you.

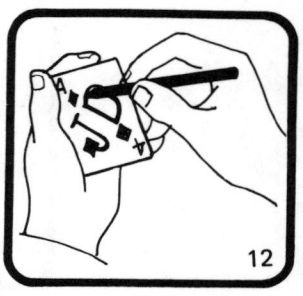

(10) As the spectator does this, *watch closely for the small pencil dots on the Double-Backed card.* The Double Backer is your "Key" card in locating the spectator's signed card in the pack.

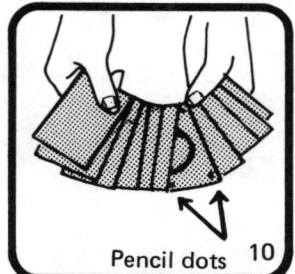

Pencil dots 10

(13) The trick is now over. The rest is just presentation. State that you will command the two cards to change places. Then, after a little byplay, turn over your card to show that it has changed places with the spectator's signed card. Of course, when the spectator follows suit, his card will bear your signature thus completing THE IMPOSSIBLE TRANSPOSITION!

(11) When you spot the "Double Backer," REMOVE THE CARD DIRECTLY BELOW IT. *This is the spectator's original selected card with his initials on the face!*

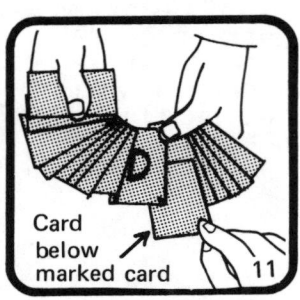

Card below marked card 11

COMMENTS AND SUGGESTIONS

The real secret of this trick comes very early, before anyone suspects it; namely, while the spectator is signing his chosen card. Since the pack is not involved at that moment, you have ample time to "set" the two top cards with a Little Finger Break in readiness for the replacement of the spectator's card. Then you can easily do the "Triple Lift" when you turn over the top three cards AS ONE CARD.

In preparing the Double-Backed card, make the pencil marks rather light, so that they will not be noticed unless you are looking for them. As mentioned, it is a good idea to put the dots *on both sides* of the Double Backer; otherwise, you will have trouble if you put the Double Backer wrong side up. Afterward, you can erase the pencil marks. Some Double-Backed cards may not exactly match the color of the deck that you are using. With such a card, you may not need the pencil marks, as you can spot it by its off-color shade when the pack is spread.

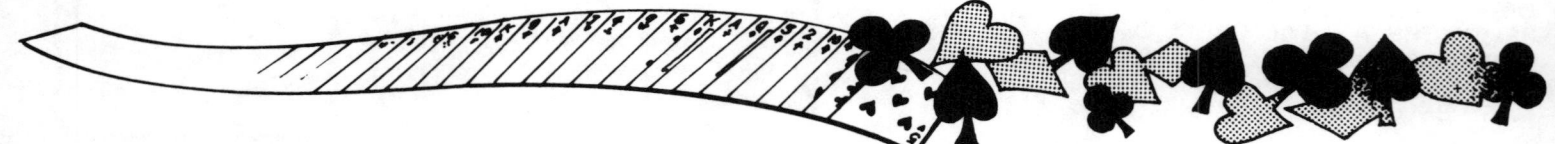

THE PERFECT CARD LOCATION

EFFECT

The magician hands a spectator a deck of cards. While the magician's back is turned, the spectator cuts anywhere in the deck. He is told to look at the card to which he cut and remember it. The spectator then loses the card in the pack by cutting it again. When the magician turns around, he immediately spreads the deck face up on the table. One card is found turned over in the deck. The magician explains that this card is his special "Finder" card, which always manages to locate a selected card. Sure enough, the selected card is found to be the one card directly beneath the "Finder" card.

SECRET AND PREPARATION

This trick actually works itself. The only preparation needed is to have a matching "Double Backed" card on the top of the deck before the trick. The deck is then placed in the box and you are ready to perform. *NOTE: In the illustration, the Double-Backed card is marked with a "D."*

METHOD

(1) Remove the deck from its box and casually spread the cards face down on the table. This subtly shows that there are no face-up cards in the pack, *but do not call attention to this now.* Explain to the spectator that this is a very "special" card trick in which *he* will do all of the work but that *you* will still get all of the credit.

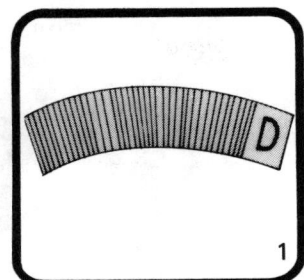

(2) Gather up the cards and hand the deck *face down* to the spectator. Explain that you will now turn your back and give him instructions which he is to follow.

(3) With your back to the spectator, tell him to cut off as many cards as he wishes from the top of the deck.

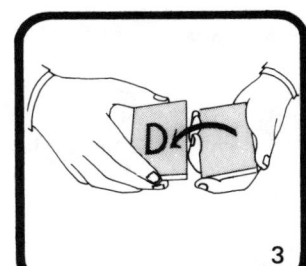

(4) He should *turn these cards over* (face up) and replace them on the deck, *on TOP of the remaining face-down cards.*

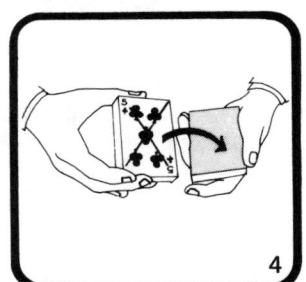

(5) Tell him to look at and remember the card he cut to ... the card which is now *face up* on top of the deck. *(In the illustrations, this card is the Five of Clubs and is marked with an "X.")*

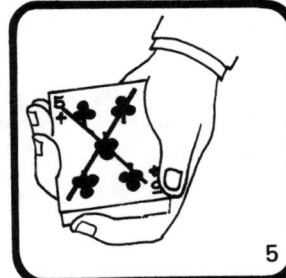

(6) Now, instruct the spectator to run through the deck UNTIL HE LOCATES THE POINT AT WHICH THE FACE-UP CARDS MEET THE FACE-DOWN CARDS. Have him separate the cards at this point.

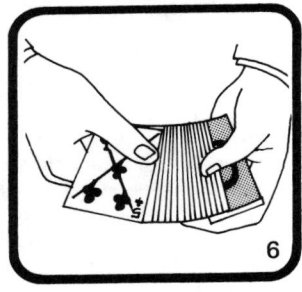

(7) *NOTE: Unknown to the spectator, when he separates the cards, the Double-Backed card now becomes the top card of the face-down portion.*

(8) Tell him to turn over the face-up cards so that they are ALL FACE DOWN and to replace them ON TOP of the other face-down cards. This apparently returns the deck to its original "all face down" condition. *However, this actually places his selected card, the Five of Clubs, directly above the Double-Backed card.* All of this is done while your back is to the spectator.

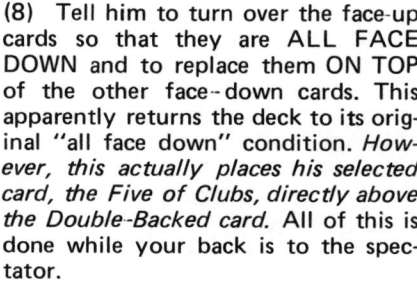

Five of Clubs

(9) Instruct the spectator to give the cards several complete cuts, thus mixing the cards thoroughly. *Be sure that these are "single" cuts and that they are each completed before he cuts the deck again.* When he has cut the deck as much as he wishes, turn and face the spectator. EMPHASIZE THAT, SINCE THE VERY START OF THE TRICK, THE SPECTATOR HAS HAD THE CARDS IN HIS OWN HANDS AND YOUR BACK HAS BEEN TURNED ... YOU COULD NOT HAVE SEEN ANYTHING HE HAS DONE.

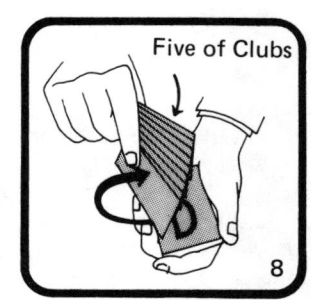

(10) Immediately spread the pack FACE UP on the table. One card will appear to be reversed in the deck (actually the Double-Backed card). Call attention to the reversed card, and explain that in every deck of cards you always have one special "Finder" card.

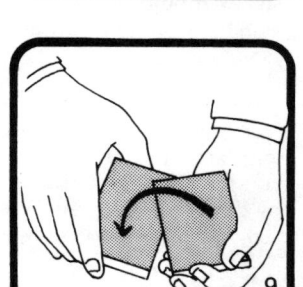

Selected Card

(11) As you talk, draw out the card directly *beneath* the "Finder" card. THIS IS THE SPECTATOR'S CARD and the mystery is complete.

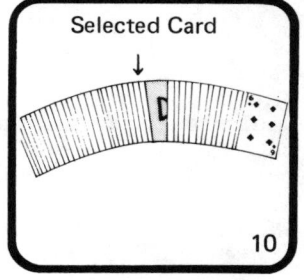

COMMENTS AND SUGGESTIONS

The audience will be especially puzzled at this one because AT NO TIME DURING THE TRICK DO YOU HANDLE THE DECK after you hand it to the spectator... Until you spread the pack on the table and show the reversed "Finder" card RIGHT NEXT TO THE CARD THAT HE FREELY SELECTED.

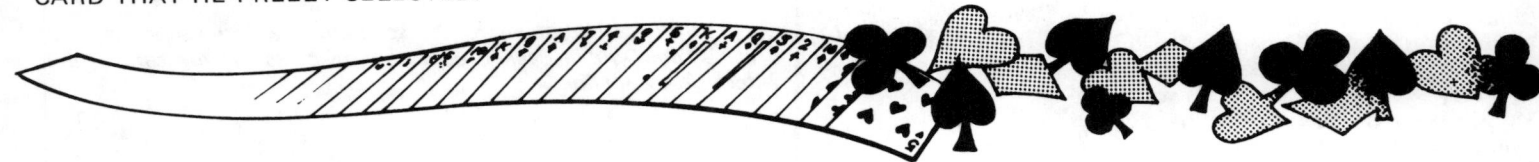

YOU CAN'T DO AS I DO

(FIVE CARDS)

Audience participation is an important phase of today's magic and it reaches a peak where tricks of the "You Do As I Do" category are involved. For that reason, this five-card fooler should prove ideal.

EFFECT

The magician deals five cards to a spectator and five cards to himself, each group being dealt face down. The magician then moves cards from the top of his packet to the bottom, turning some face up and keeping others face down, while the spectator does each move exactly the same with the cards in his packet. The magician then spreads his cards, showing ALL FIVE FACE DOWN, saying that the spectator's packet should be the same. But when the spectator spreads his cards, he finds ONE FACE UP! This happens every time the routine is repeated, no matter how closely the spectator follows the magician's pattern.

SECRET AND PREPARATION

This trick practically works itself. It all depends on the use of ONE DOUBLED-BACKED CARD among the magician's five cards. To set up, place the Double-Backed card in the deck, ninth from the top. With the Double-Backed card in this position, all that is necessary is to deal the top five cards to the spectator and then five to yourself, one at a time, on the table. This will automatically reverse the order of the cards and place the Double-Backed card *just below the top of your five cards.* Therefore, with the card in the ninth position, place the deck in its box and you are ready to begin.

METHOD

(1) Deal the cards out as described above so the spectator holds five regular cards face down and you hold five cards with the Double-Backed card in the second position from the top. Fan the cards open and tell the spectator to be sure that his cards are all FACE DOWN like yours. (In the illustration, the Double-Backed card is marked with a "D.")

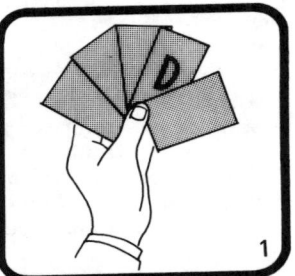

(2) Explain to the spectator that he is to move each of his cards EXACTLY AS YOU DO, one by one. Your first move is to turn the top card of your stack face up and place it on the bottom of your stack. *NOTE: Be sure that the spectator moves each of his cards just as you do on this and all the following steps.*

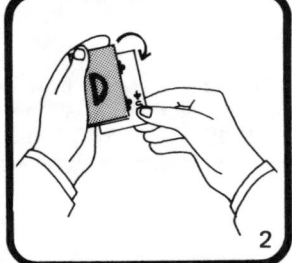

(3) Second, take the next card off the top and place it on the bottom, this time without turning it over. *Unknown to the spectator, this card in your stack is the Double-Backed card.*

(4) Third, remove the top card, turn it face up, and place it on the bottom.

(5) Fourth, move the next card from the top to the bottom without turning it face up.

(6) At this point, you stop to make sure that the spectator has followed your moves correctly. Fan your cards open and tell the spectator to do the same. Your cards should appear with the two face-up cards sandwiched between the face-down cards. *The spectator does not know that you have the Double-Backed card in the center.* When the spectator fans his cards, they will appear in the same sequence as yours.

Magician's cards

(7) Now close your fan of cards and instruct the spectator to follow your next moves exactly. First you turn the top card over and leave it face up on top of the stack.

(10) This is the point in the trick where you reach the pay off. When you fan your cards, all five cards will be face down.

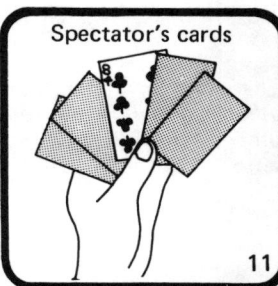

Spectator's cards

(8) Now turn the ENTIRE STACK OF FIVE CARDS over in your hand.

(11) However, when the spectator does the same, one card will appear face up in the center of the face-down cards....leaving no possible explanation for this mysterious occurance.

(9) For the final move, turn the top face-up card face down on the stack.

NOTE: When the trick is over, it can be immediately repeated merely by shifting the top card of your stack to the bottom, thus placing the Double-Backed card in the proper starting position for the effect.

COMMENTS AND SUGGESTIONS

Often, the routine can be ended exactly as described; in that case, you can compliment the spectator for having made such a good try; then gather the cards and go on with something else. Or, another trick involving a Double-Backed card can very well be introduced, since you already have one in the pack. Another possibility is to invite other spectators to try along with your original victim, dealing them five cards each and turning the trick into a form of "group participation." When they all find they can't do it, the laugh is on everybody instead of just your one original spectator. You conclude the operations by gathering their packets along with your own.

DOUBLE-FACED CARD

The legendary Burling Hull introduced some revolutionary principles which were unique to Card Magic when he developed the "Double" card. These principles are used to a great extent today because they enable magicians to perform "miracles" without the long hours of practice required to accomplish the same result through Sleight-of-Hand.

The Double-Faced Card is a great aid to the card worker because it can be added to almost any borrowed pack to produce effects that could not be duplicated without it. To change one card into another, or cause a card to turn face up in the pack become simple matters when a Double-Facer is secretly put to work.

TWO CARD MONTE

Tricks involving special cards are extremely baffling when injected into a series of effects performed with an ordinary pack. When a touch of skill is added, you can sometimes gain seemingly impossible results; and that rule applies to the following trick.

EFFECT

From a pack, the magician removes two contrasting cards; one red card and one black card which he places back to back. After turning them over several times, showing both sides, the performer takes the face-up red card in one hand and puts it behind his back, keeping the face-down black card in his other hand. When he asks which card he put behind his back and the spectator replies, "The red card," the magician brings it into view only to find it has changed to the black card. This is repeated, several times, always with the same result: Whichever face up card he puts behind his back invariably changes places with the face-down card in his other hand, unless the magician deliberately decides to keep them as they were. Always, both cards are under his magical control!

SECRET AND PREPARATION

The secret to this mystery is in the cards, themselves, as *both* cards used in the effect are special cards. *One is a Double-Faced card; the other is a Double-Backed card.* The Double Facer shows a black card on one side (Five of Clubs in the illustrations) and a red card on the other (Ace of Hearts). First you must learn the very important "secret" move which is the basis of the entire trick. This move will be referred to as the MASTER MOVE and it is executed as follows:

METHOD

(1) Hold the two cards together partially fanned in your right hand with your thumb on top and your first and second fingers beneath as shown in the illustration.

(2) With the cards held in this position, slide the top card (the Double Backer) to the *left* with your thumb and *in the same motion,* slide the bottom card (the Double Facer) to the *right* with the first and second fingers. THIS REVERSES THE POSITIONS OF THE TWO CARDS IN THE FAN.

(3) At the same time this sliding action is executed, the right hand turns completely over — so the back of the hand is up — as if to show the face of the other card. To the spectators it will appear to be the face of the other card, thanks to the secret sliding action which transposes the positions of the two cards. NOTE: The sliding motion of the two cards will go undetected due to the more extreme motion of the right hand as it turns over.

(4) Now, reverse the process exactly turning your hand back over, and the cards will again appear as they did when you started.

(5) Now that you have learned the MASTER MOVE, you are ready to actually perform the Two-Card Monte as a trick. Begin by placing the two cards together with the Double Backer on top of the Double Facer in position to execute the MASTER MOVE.

(6) Show the two cards on both sides, using the MASTER MOVE as you say, "For this trick, we use two cards, one black card and one red card, such as the Five of Clubs and the Ace of Hearts."

(7) Now, grasp the Double Facer in your left hand and place it behind your back. *Be careful not to accidentally "flash" the other side of the Double Facer as you handle the card.*

(8) Ask the spectator to name the card which remains in your *right* hand. Of course, he will answer "The Ace of Hearts." Before bringing the card from behind your back, *secretly turn it over so the Ace of Hearts side is face up.*

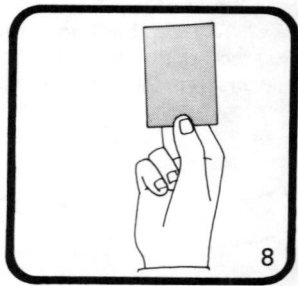

(9) Bring it into view as you say, "No, I'm sorry, I have the Ace of Hearts behind my back. You must not be watching closely enough."

(10) With that, place the Double Facer *beneath* the Double Backer in position for the MASTER MOVE. You are now ready to repeat the Two-Card Monte again, as often as you like.

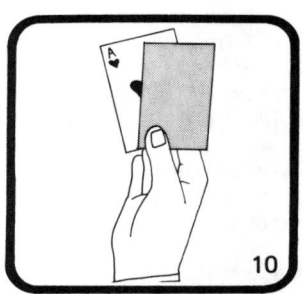

COMMENTS AND SUGGESTIONS

A neat way to begin the Monte trick is to have the Double Backer on top of a pack of cards and the Double Facer on the bottom. Remove the pack from its case and deal a row of three face-down cards from the top; THEN TURN OVER THE PACK and deal three cards face up from the bottom. Place two of the ORDINARY cards face to face and turn them over a few times; then do the same with the other ordinary pair. Finally, settle on the "third" pair — the Double Backer and Double Facer — and replace the others back in the pack. This will help avert any suspicion of the two trick cards, as they look just like the ordinary pairs.

NEW CARD MONTE

EFFECT

Two cards are removed from an ordinary pack and shown front and back. Both cards are then placed inside the card box. The performer openly removes one of the cards and places it in his shirt pocket. Now, to the amazement of the spectators, the two cards magically change places. From his pocket, the performer brings the card that was in the card box....a spectator opens the card case and finds the card that the performer put into his pocket! Everything can then be examined.

SECRET AND PREPARATION

(A) For this trick, you use one of the specially printed DOUBLE-FACED cards described earlier. In the illustrations, the Double-Faced card has the Seven of Hearts on one side and the Ten of Spades on the other side.

(B) Before beginning the trick, place the "Double Facer" in your shirt pocket *and remember which side of the card is toward the audience* (in this case the Seven of Hearts in the illustrations). You are now ready to begin.

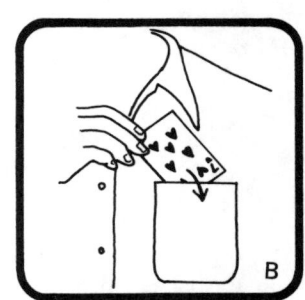

METHOD

PHASE I - THE SET-UP

(1) Remove an ordinary pack of cards from its box. Leave the box open and lay it on the table with the flap *facing up.* Now run through the cards face up and find the two cards which match those printed on your Double-Faced card (Seven of Hearts and Ten of Spades). Casually remark, "For this we need two cards. Any two will do — let's use the Seven of Hearts and the Ten of Spades."

(2) Remove the two cards from the pack and set the rest of the deck aside. Now place the Seven and the Ten *back to back* with the Seven of Hearts facing up as shown.

(3) Insert the two cards into the card box *with the lid facing up* as shown – close the lid, and place the box on the table. Now tell the audience: "If I openly remove one card from the box, and place it in my pocket, it would be easy for you to tell me which card remains in the box, right?"

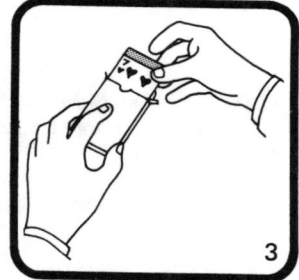

(4) As you say this, open the lid and remove the Seven of Hearts from the box and place it in your shirt pocket with the face of the Seven toward the audience. Be sure to place this card BEHIND THE SECRET DOUBLE FACER which is already in your pocket.

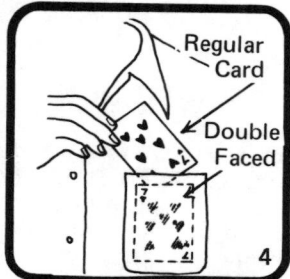

(5) Ask the audience to name the card which remains in the box. Of course, the answer will be the Ten of Spades. With this, REMOVE THE DOUBLE FACER WITH THE SEVEN SIDE SHOWING from your pocket and place it on the table next to the box as you remark, "That's right. I can see that you are watching me closely."

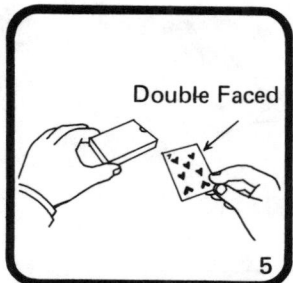

(6) *NOTE: Because the Seven of Hearts side of the Double-Faced card was toward the audience, they will believe this is the same card which you just placed in your pocket. Be careful not to "flash" the other side of the Double Facer as you remove it from your pocket.*

(7) As soon as the Double Facer is on the table, open the lid of the box and remove the Ten of Spades. Turn it face up as you remark: "That was easy. Now I'll make it just a little more difficult."

PHASE II - THE TRANSPOSITION

(8) Repeat the same actions as in Steps 2 and 3, apparently placing the two cards back to back – except this time TURN THE TEN OF SPADES FACE DOWN AND PLACE THE DOUBLE-FACED CARD WITH THE SEVEN SIDE "UP" ON TOP OF THE TEN. Place the two cards in the box and close the flap.

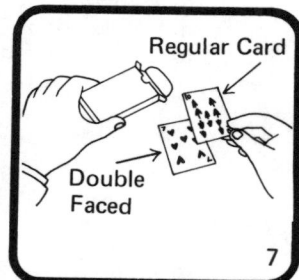

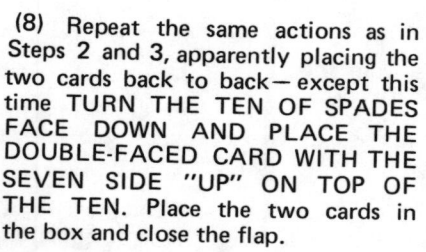

(9) *NOTE: You have apparently just repeated the same action of placing the two cards back to back and putting them in the box.*

(10) *This next step is an important part of the trick.* After you have placed the cards in the box, pick the box up off the table as you close the lid. Then, as you place the box back on the table, casually TURN IT OVER so that *the flap is now facing down.* This turns the regular Ten of Spades face up in the box with the "Ten" side of the Double-Faced card *face up beneath it.*

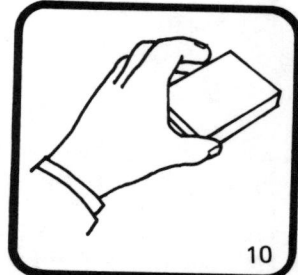

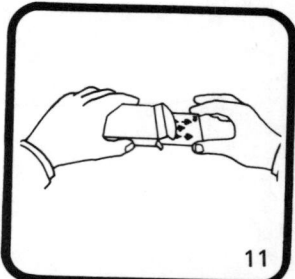

(11) Tell the audience that you will remove one of the cards from the box and place it in your pocket – and, as before, they are to remember the position of both cards. Open the lid of the box and remove the *bottom card* – THE DOUBLE FACER WITH THE TEN SIDE SHOWING. To the audience it will look as if you are removing the regular Ten of Spades, leaving the Seven of Hearts in the box.

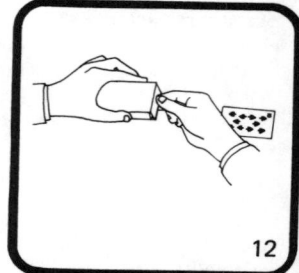

(12) As soon as the Double-Faced card is out of the box, lay the card on the table and *immediately close the lid of the box so that the audience will not see the regular Ten of Spades inside.*

(13) Pick up the Double-Faced card and place it in your shirt pocket BEHIND THE REGULAR SEVEN OF HEARTS that was left in your pocket. Do this openly as you say, "Keep close watch on the position of both cards — and don't let me fool you."

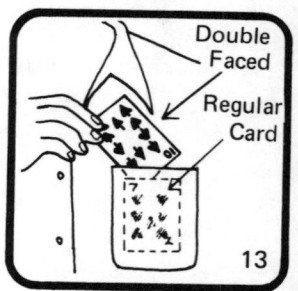

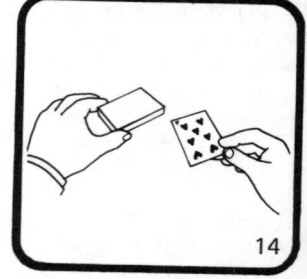

(14) After the Double-Faced card is in your pocket, lift the box slightly off the table in the tips of your left fingers and shake it lightly back and forth, remarking "If I do this, do you think it could have any effect on the position of the two cards?" No matter what the answer, reach into your shirt pocket and REMOVE THE FRONT CARD — THE REAL SEVEN OF HEARTS. Place it on the table next to the box.

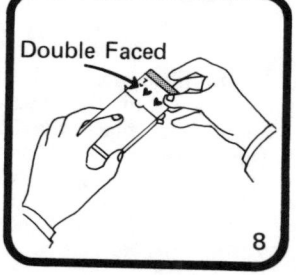

(15) Then, immediately open the lid of the box and remove the real Ten of Spades — or better yet, have the spectator do it himself, thus, completing the impossible transposition!

COMMENTS AND SUGGESTIONS

If you start by taking the pack from the card case, you can already have the two matching cards — the Seven of Hearts and Ten of Spades — together at the face of the pack. It would then be quite natural for you to take them as the first two cards in hand. In Step 8, after you place the real Ten of Spades back to back with the Double-Faced Seven of Hearts, if you keep the two cards squared together, you can turn them over to show the face of the Ten of Spades. Then, when you turn them over again with the Seven of Hearts face up, you can casually spread the cards to let the audience see the back of the Ten of Spades.

NOTE: If the card may be seen through the material of your shirt pocket because it is too "transparent," you may use your inside coat pocket or your pants pocket instead. If you use your pants pocket, be sure to remove the Double-Faced card before you sit down as you might crease it.

IMPORTANT POINT — Another very strong feature of this effect is that the Double-Faced card is NOT in the deck at the START or at the CONCLUSION of the trick. Thus, everything can be handed for examination!

FORCED CARDS REVERSE

For a double-barreled mystery, this must be given top rating. It fulfills our old saying that "One good trick deserves another," by repeating itself under conditions that would normally be impossible without the secret presence of a "special card." Read the effect closely, and you will appreciate its impact on the average audience. Then try it yourself and prove it!

EFFECT

A spectator selects two cards by cutting anywhere in the pack. As the magician shuffles the pack, he asks the spectator to replace *both* cards face down in the pack. This done, the magician *immediately* Ribbon Spreads the pack face down across the table. There, staring face up in the middle of the pack is THE FIRST CARD THE SPECTATOR LOOKED AT AND REPLACED FACE DOWN!

All this is done very openly, leaving the audience quite amazed. The performer removes this revealed card and replaces it in the pack face down. The magician then asks the spectator if he would like to see the miracle again. When the spectator says, "Yes," the magician again *immediately* spreads the pack of cards face down on the table displaying THE SECOND SELECTED CARD, FACE UP, IN THE MIDDLE OF THE SPREAD!

SECRET AND PREPARATION

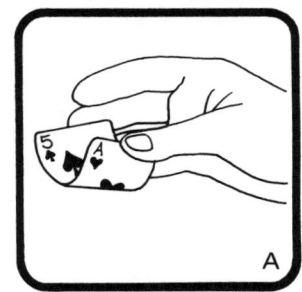

(A) For this trick, you need an ordinary pack of cards and one DOUBLE-FACED card. In the illustrations, the Double Facer has the Ace of Hearts on one side and the Five of Spades on the other. To prepare, run through the pack and remove the two regular cards that match those shown on the Double-Faced card.

(B) Place one of these regular cards (the Ace of Hearts in the illustration) on *top* of the deck and the other regular card (the Five of Spades) on the *bottom* of the pack. *The Double-Faced card goes second from the bottom* with the "Five" side facing the same direction as the rest of the cards in the pack. The illustration shows this clearly. Now, place the deck in its box and you are ready.

(1) To begin the presentation, remove the pack of cards from its box and place it face down on the table in front of the spectator.

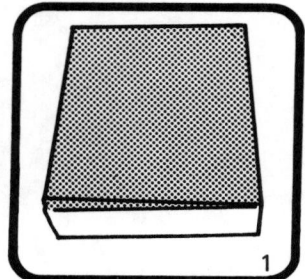

(2) Ask him to divide the deck into two parts. Tell him he can cut *anywhere* in the deck he wishes and to place the upper portion on the table. *Stress the fact that the spectator is cutting the pack AT A LOCATION OF HIS OWN FREE CHOICE.*

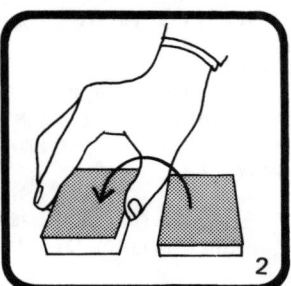

(3) Now, *you* pick up the LOWER packet of cards from the table and place it *cross-wise* on top of what was originally the UPPER packet.

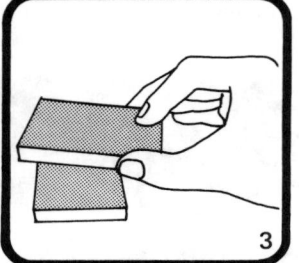

(4) THIS PLACES THE ORIGINAL TOP AND BOTTOM CARDS (ACE OF HEARTS AND FIVE OF SPADES) TOGETHER IN THE CENTER OF THE PACK WHERE THE TWO HALVES CROSS. *The spectator believes they are two random cards which he cut to in the middle of the pack.*

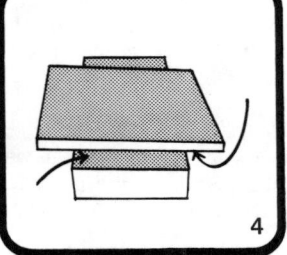

(5) Stall for a few seconds with a statement such as, "Rarely are two randomly selected cards of the same suit. Let's check yours." Then lift the crosswise portion of the pack and remove the bottom card of that pile (Five of Spades) and . . .

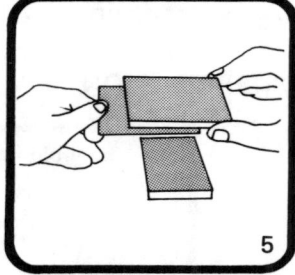

(6) . . .place it face down on the table. *At the same time, place the cross-wise portion of the pack on the table next to the rest of the pack.*

(7) Next, remove the *top* card (Ace of Hearts) from the other packet and place it next to the Five already on the table.

(8) YOU HAVE NOW "FORCED" THESE TWO CARDS. Ask the spectator to look at the two cards he "selected" and to remember them. Reassemble the pack, making sure to place the original *lower* portion of the pack BENEATH the original *upper* portion, THUS RETAINING THE DOUBLE FACER ON THE BOTTOM OF THE PACK.

(9) When the pack is reassembled, begin a regular Hindu Shuffle. Instruct the spectator to call "Stop" any time he wishes to replace one of the two "selected" cards back in the pack.

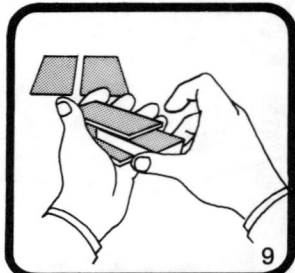

(10) When he says, "Stop," extend the left-hand packet toward the spectator and instruct him to place either one of the two selected cards on top of that packet.

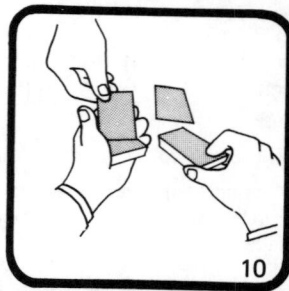

(11) This done, continue the shuffle and instruct the spectator to call "Stop" when he would like to replace the second card. When the call comes, stop the shuffle and have the spectator replace the second "selected" card.

(12) *NOTE: Just do a regular Hindu Shuffle as it does not matter where the spectator replaces the cards.*

(13) After the second card is re-placed, reassemble the pack *by placing the right-hand packet on TOP of the left-hand packet* and square up the pack.

(16) With the pack *face up* in your left hand, insert the Double Facer – *Ace of Hearts side up* – into the center of the deck as shown. The spectator thinks you are merely replacing the card "correctly" back in the pack.

(14) Riffle the ends of the pack a couple of times as you say, "The easy part of the trick is to make the *first card* turn face up in the deck, LIKE THIS!" Spread the pack face down on the table to reveal the first card (REALLY THE DOUBLE-FACED ACE OF HEARTS) *face up* in the face-down spread.

(17) Say, "But the difficult part is to find the SECOND CARD." Now turn the pack face down and once again spread the cards on the table – *revealing the face-up Five of Spades* (REALLY THE FIVE OF SPADES SIDE OF THE DOUBLE-FACED CARD).

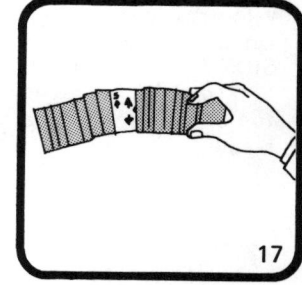

(15) Remove the Double Facer from the spread. Gather up the rest of the pack and *turn the deck face up.* Be *careful not to accidentally "flash" the other side of the Double-Faced Ace as you handle it.*

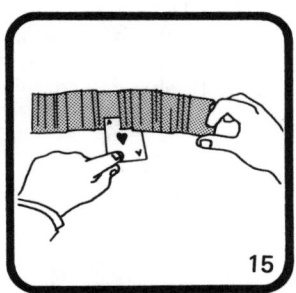

(18) Both cards have instantly and magically reversed themselves in the pack without any false or suspicious moves of any kind. The spectator will be left speechless.

COMMENTS AND SUGGESTIONS

Since no moves or sleights are required other than the regular HINDU SHUFFLE, your only concern is the handling of the DOUBLE-FACED card. Let the spectator cut the pack at the start, but be sure to *complete the cut yourself,* keeping the pack well squared to prevent the Double-Faced card from showing at the wrong time. If you intend to continue on with other tricks, you must dispose of the Double-Faced card. One easy way is, with the Double Facer on the face of the pack, start to put the pack in your coat pocket as if you were finished. With your thumb, push the Double-Faced card off the face of the pack into your pocket.... Then, "remembering" another trick, bring out the pack and continue with your routine.

IMPOSSIBLE PREDICTION

Any effect involving a *Prediction* should be treated strongly from the spectator's angle. Instead of trying to outwit the audience, the magician is dealing with a fixed result that "nothing can change." So, giving the spectator a chance to change it, only to find that he can't, becomes a real convincer, as you will see in the effect that follows.

EFFECT

The magician displays a small, sealed envelope, which he places upon the table. He brings out a pack of cards and allows a spectator to divide the pack into two piles so that *either of two cards* can be taken from the point at which the pack was cut. THE SPECTATOR IS ALLOWED FREE CHOICE OF EITHER CARD. After the spectator makes his decision, the magician opens the envelope and removes a *single* face-up card. When the spectator's card is turned over, IT PROVES TO BE THE SAME SUIT AND VALUE AS THE PREDICTION CARD. The envelope may be immediately examined to prove that it contains no other card and the pack may be inspected to show that it has no duplicate cards.

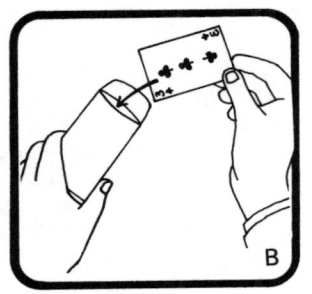

For this effect, in addition to a regular pack of cards, you will need (A) one Double-Faced card (the Three of Clubs on one side and the Eight of Diamonds on the other in the illustrations) and an envelope large enough to contain the Double Faced card. This can be any envelope as long as it is opaque. Small "coin envelopes", which are available in stationery stores, work well for this effect. (B) Place the Double Faced card in the envelope. BE SURE TO REMEMBER WHICH SIDE OF THE DOUBLE FACED CARD FACES THE FLAP SIDE OF THE ENVELOPE (THE THREE OF CLUBS). (C) Seal the envelope and place it in your pocket. (D) Next, remove from the deck the two regular cards that match your Double Face card, the Eight of Diamonds and the Three of Clubs. Place one of the cards on top of the deck (Three of Clubs) and the other on the bottom (Eight of Diamonds). Square up the pack, place it in its box, and you're ready.

METHOD

(1) Explain that, for this effect, you will enter into the realm of *mentalism,* rather than magic. Remove the envelope from your pocket as you say, "I have sealed a prediction in this envelope". Hand the envelope to a spectator to hold or place it on the table so everyone can see it.

(5) After a few seconds, pick up the crosswise portion of the pack and remove the *bottom* card of that pile (Eight of Diamonds) and . . .

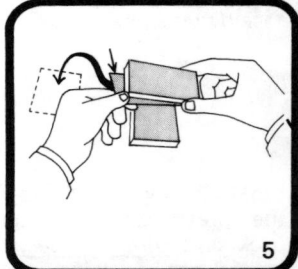

(2) Remove the pack from its box and place it face down on the table. Ask someone to divide the pack into two parts; telling him he may cut anywhere in the pack he wishes. He is to place the "upper" packet that he cuts off, beside the "lower" packet which remains on the table. Stress the fact that the spectator is cutting the pack at a location of his OWN FREE CHOICE.

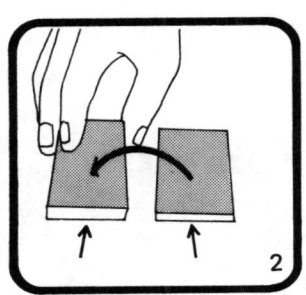

(6) . . . place it face down on the table.

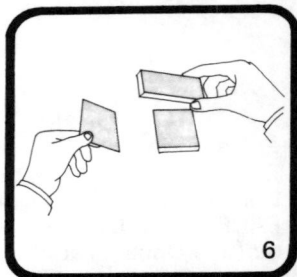

(3) Now you pick up the LOWER packet of cards from the table and place it crosswise *on top* of what was originally the UPPER packet.

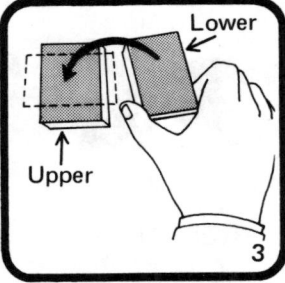

(7) Next, remove the *top* card (Three of Clubs) from the other packet and . . .

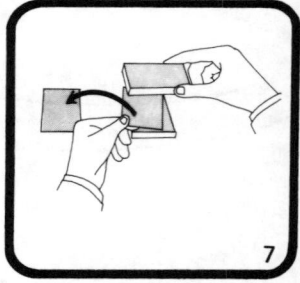

(4) THIS PLACES THE ORIGINAL TOP AND BOTTOM CARDS (EIGHT OF DIAMONDS AND THREE OF CLUBS) TOGETHER IN THE CENTER OF THE PACK WHERE THE TWO HALVES CROSS. *The spectator believes they are two random cards which he cut to in the middle of the pack.*

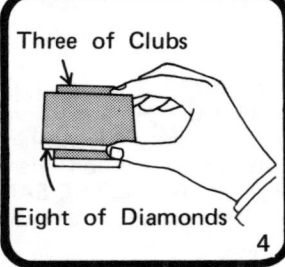

(8) . . . place it next to the Eight already on the table.

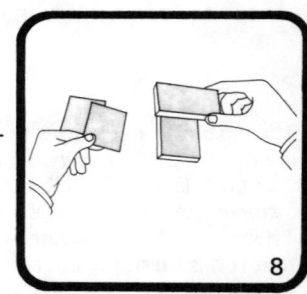

(9) Reassemble the pack and explain to the spectator he has a FREE CHOICE of *either* of the two cards he cut to. Ask him to choose one of the two cards and give him every opportunity to change his mind.

(12) Now ask the spectator to turn his card over so that everyone can see, FOR THE FIRST TIME, the card he freely selected from the pack. Pick up the prediction envelope and tear off the end.

(10) When the spectator is satisfied with his selection, (let's assume he takes the Eight of Diamonds), SHOW HIM THE FACE OF THE CARD HE DID NOT SELECT and replace it in the pack. Pick up the prediction envelope saying, "I hold in my hand the prediction envelope which has been on the table (or held by a spectator) all along."

(13) Then, holding it slightly above the table, tilt your hand enough so the Double Facer slides out of the envelope onto the table. Your prediction card will match the spectator's card exactly!

(11) Using the flap on the envelope as your "key," lay the envelope on the table next to the spectator's card so that the side of the Double Facer that corresponds with the spectator's selection is *face up* in the envelope.

(14) Immediately hand the envelope for examination proving that there are no other cards inside. While the spectator's attention is on the envelope, pick up the Double Facer and place it in your pocket and hand out the deck for examination.

COMMENTS AND SUGGESTIONS

From the very start, this effect offers a series of options that you can introduce as you see fit. It is a good plan to vary these, so you can stress a different factor when working for people who may have seen the effect before, thus giving it something of a "new" look. For instance, one idea is to have someone sign their name on the envelope before you bring out the pack. This keeps the envelope identified throughout the effect and eliminates the possibility of your "switching" it for another. As another neat touch, when the spectator cuts the pack into two separate piles side by side, *lay the envelope on top of the upper pile* and tell the spectator to "complete the cut." The spectator is then to choose either of the cards above and below the envelope. This is quite deceptive, giving the impression that you inserted the envelope somewhere near the middle of the pack, instead of between the top and bottom halves. At the finish of the routine, you can open the envelope and remove your prediction card BEFORE the spectator turns over his card and hand the envelope out for inspection right away. Or you can just leave the envelope on the table, bring out another pack of cards, and add the Double Facer to that pack as though it belonged there. Later, some suspicious spectator may snatch up the envelope, only to find it empty.

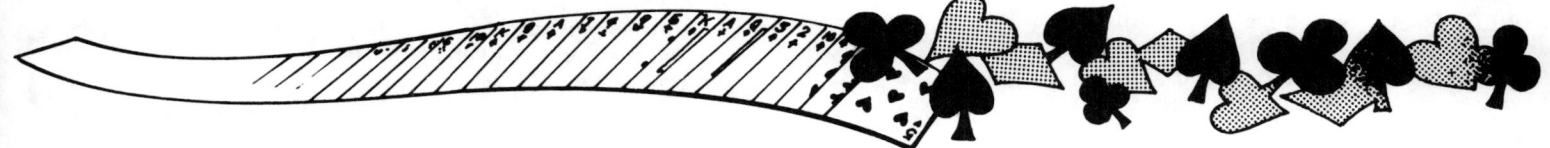

THE FOUR-CARD ASSEMBLY

This is a classic card effect and a favorite with many of the great card workers. The method given here is one of the best and has the added advantage of requiring absolutely no skill, so you can perform it immediately after reading the instructions.

EFFECT

From a pack of cards, you take four cards of the same value — for example, the four Aces — and lay them in a face up row. You now deal three cards face down on each of the four Aces, giving you four piles of four cards each. One pile — is chosen and placed in front of a spectator on the table. The other three piles are gathered together and returned to the pack, which is cut a few times and turned face up. Now, you give the deck three snaps or riffles and, when you run through the pack, the three Aces are gone! To the spectator's amazement, he finds that the three missing Aces have joined the one Ace in his pile giving him all four Aces.

SECRET AND PREPARATION

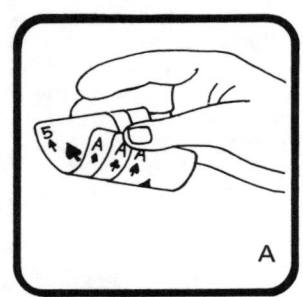

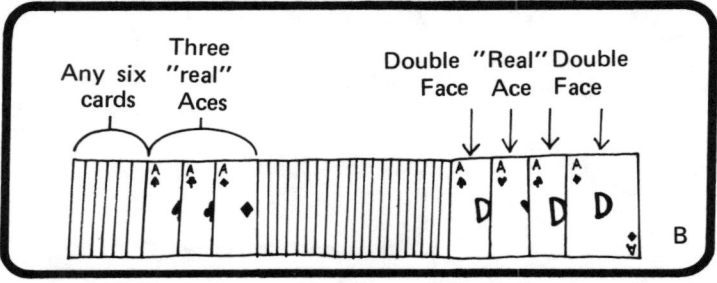

(A) The trick depends upon three Double-Faced cards, each showing an Ace of a different suit on one side and an indifferent card on the other. (For convenience, in the illustrations, we are supposing that one side of each of the Double-Faced cards are: Ace of Diamonds, Ace of Clubs, Ace of Spades.) (B) Beforehand, arrange the pack as shown. The three Double-Faced cards are at the bottom of the pack in the *first, second,* and *fourth* positions with the regular Ace of Hearts in the *third* position. On the top of the pack, place any six indifferent cards above the three remaining regular Aces. Thus, the other three "real" Aces are in the *seventh, eighth,* and *ninth* positions from the top of the pack. Now square up the deck and place it in its box and you are ready to begin. (C) *NOTE: In the illustrations, the Double-Faced cards are marked with a "D."*

METHOD

(1) Bring out the pack and remove it from its box saying, "For my next surprise, I need four cards all of the *same value.* Let's use the four Aces. I'll deal them face up in a row on the table." Turn the deck face up and deal the four Aces on the bottom of the deck (really three Double-Faced cards and one regular card) face up on the table from left to right. *This places the regular Ace (the Ace of Hearts) in the third position from your left.*

(2) Now turn the pack face down and deal three indifferent cards *from the top of the pack* onto the "Ace" at the left end of the row (the Double-Faced Ace of Diamonds). Then deal three more cards on the next "Ace" (the Double-Faced Ace of Clubs). Deal the next three cards on the real Ace (Ace of Hearts). THE THREE CARDS YOU JUST DEALT ONTO THE "REAL" ACE OF HEARTS (NUMBER 8, 9, 10) ARE THE OTHER THREE "REAL" ACES, THUS BRINGING ALL FOUR REGULAR ACES TOGETHER IN THIS PILE. Finally deal three more cards on the last "Ace" (the Double-Faced Ace of Spades) at the right end of the row.

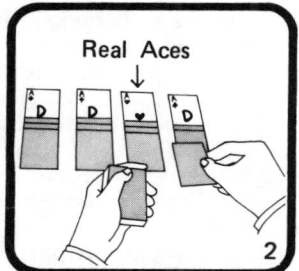

(3) This done, it becomes necessary to "force" the spectator to choose the pile of cards containing all the regular Aces. Use any of the appropriate "Forces" described in the Course. (The "Magician's Choice" or "Roll Any Number" are particularly good here.)

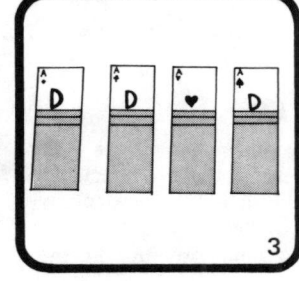

(4) Once you have "forced" the pile of regular Aces, gather the three remaining piles on top of one another and add them to the top of the face-down pack just as they are. The fact that the "Aces" are face up, while the other cards are face down, does not matter, as you will see.

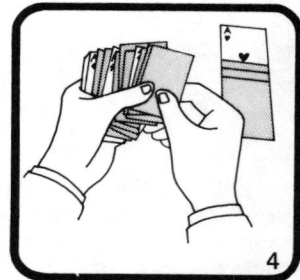

(5) Square the three piles on top of the pack and give the pack several cuts. Then *turn the pack face up* and give it a few more cuts. Finish by giving the pack three fast riffles or snaps as you say, "One snap (or riffle) for each Ace in the pack."

(6) With that, spread the pack *face up* on the table, or run the cards from hand to hand to show that the Aces have vanished from the pack. By now the repeated cuts (face up and face down) will have your audience too confused to suspect that they are seeing the "backs" of the Double-Faced vanished Aces!

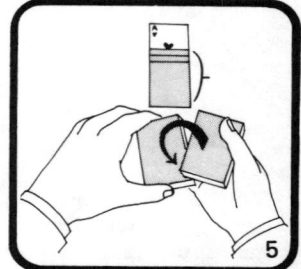

(7) Now turn over the remaining three face-down cards to reveal that all four Aces have amazingly assembled in one pile! This, of course, applies to whatever value cards you may be using instead of Aces.

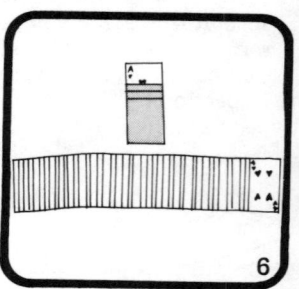

COMMENTS AND SUGGESTIONS

Beforehand, remove from the pack the three regular cards that appear on the "other sides" of the Double Facers. Then, when the pack is spread face up on the table to show the "Aces" have vanished, none of the spectators can spot any "duplicate" cards in the pack.

THE SHORT CARD

HOW TO MAKE A SHORT CARD

The "SHORT CARD" is one of the most useful devices ever designed for Card Magic. It can be used for "Locating," "Forcing," or even "Vanishing" a card, yet it will pass totally unsuspected by even the keenest observers. As its name implies, it is a card which is "shorter" than those in the rest of the pack and can be simply and easily prepared with any deck.

METHOD

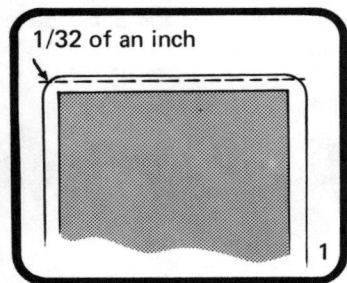 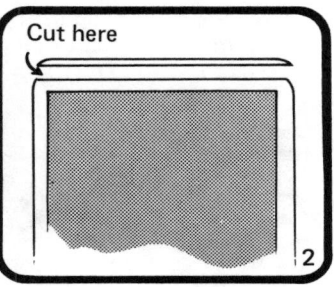 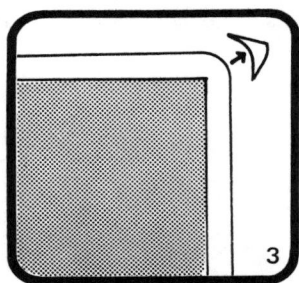 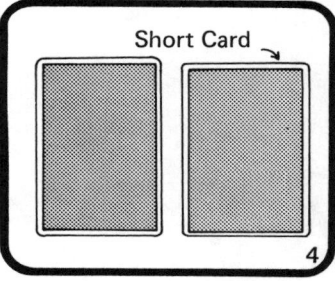

(1)   To make a SHORT CARD, first draw a ruled line one-thirty-second of an inch from *both ends* of a standard playing card.
(2)   Then, with a pair of good, sharp scissors, carefully trim off the ends using the ruled line as a guide.

(3)   Next, "round" all four of the cut corners so they will match the corners of the "regular" cards in the pack. *NOTE: For "rounding" the corners, a pair of curved manicure scissors is helpful, but ordinary scissors will also work. Just cut the corners very carefully.* (4)   This illustration compares a Short Card with a regular card from the same pack. As you can see, it would be difficult for anyone to detect the Short Card mixed among the regular cards in a pack.

(5)   Some magicians carry a pair of small "fold-away" scissors with them, to use with a *borrowed deck.* All you have to do is to secretly pocket a card from the borrowed deck. Then work some trick — such as a "mental" effect — in which you *leave the room.* While outside, you cut the end from the card and round the corners. You can then return the card to the pack later. The pack can still be used by its owner in regular card games, without the players ever realizing that one of the cards has been "shortened."

COMMENTS AND SUGGESTIONS

For purposes of practice, you can make your first Short Card from the Joker (or the Extra Joker, if the pack has one). In this way, you can then either add the Joker when you wish to do a Short Card trick — or you can later "shorten" any other regular card after you have learned how to use your "practice" Short Card.

HOW TO "RIFFLE" THE SHORT CARD TO TOP

No matter where the Short Card may be in the pack, you can find it almost instantly *by sense of touch alone* in a number of ways. (In all of the following illustrations, the Short Card is indicated by an "S.")

METHOD

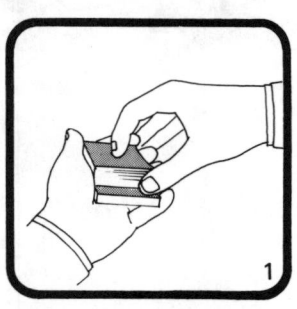 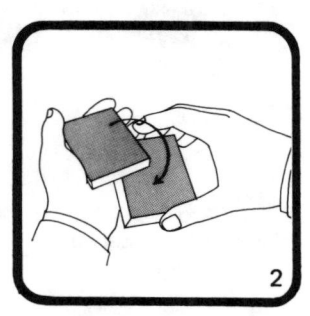 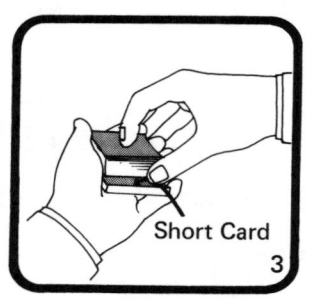 

Short Card

(1) Square the shuffled pack and hold it in "dealing position" in your left hand. Cut the pack a few times by "riffling" the inner end of the deck with your right thumb. (2) Stop your "riffle" about half-way through the pack and transfer the remaining upper half to the bottom of the pack to complete the cut.

(3) On your *last cut,* when you "riffle" the inner end of the pack upward with your thumb, if you *listen* and *feel* with your thumb, you will notice a slight "SNAP" when you reach the Short Card. When this happens, STOP YOUR RIFFLE. Then, make your cut, lifting off all of the cards *above* the Short Card. (4) Complete the cut by placing this upper packet beneath the lower, as shown. *This puts the Short Card on top of the pack.*

SHORT CARD TO BOTTOM

In some tricks it may be necessary to control the Short Card to the *bottom* of the pack instead of to the top. This can be done in several ways:

FIRST METHOD

Bring the Short Card to the *top* of the pack as just described in SHORT CARD TO TOP. Then, using the OVERHAND SHUFFLE — TOP TO BOTTOM CONTROL, *shuffle* the *top* card (Short Card) to the *bottom* of the deck. Now you have not only placed the Short Card where you want it, on the bottom of the pack, at the same time you have convinced the spectators that all the cards in the pack are well mixed.

SECOND METHOD

A second method of bringing the Short Card to the bottom of the pack is simplicity itself. After your "riffle" which places the Short Card on top, simply turn the pack *face up* in your left hand. Then proceed with the instructions for SHORT CARD TO TOP as described. This brings the Short Card to the *top* of the *face-up* pack — and — *if you turn the pack over,* the Short Card will be at the *bottom!*

THIRD METHOD

Of the three methods described, this is the cleanest and quickest method of getting the Short Card to the bottom of the deck, although it will require a bit more practice. In Method No. 1, you have to riffle the card to the *top* and then *shuffle* it to the *bottom.* In the Second Method, the deck must be held face up, in which case the Short Card may be noticed — particularly if you are doing a number of tricks in which the same Short Card is used. This Third Method avoids both of the "shortcomings" (pardon the pun) of the previous two methods.

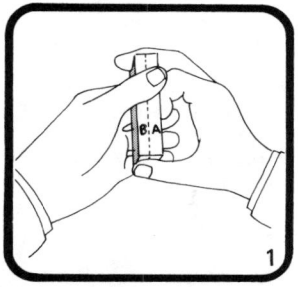 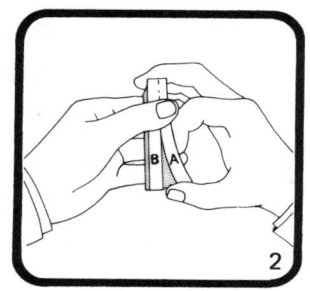 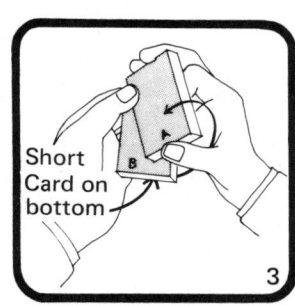

Short Card on bottom

(1) Hold the deck in your left hand as if you were starting to perform an Overhand Shuffle. Your right hand grasps the deck with the first finger on the face of the pack, your other three fingers cover the outside end, and your thumb is at the end nearest you as shown. (2) Now, riffle the deck *downward* — starting with the top card — with your right thumb. When you get to the Short Card and hear and/or feel the "Snap," STOP YOUR RIFFLE. (3) Then, either cut the bottom portion to the top of the pack or Overhand Shuffle the bottom portion to the top of the pack, *leaving the Short Card on the bottom.*

THE SHORT CARD AS A "LOCATOR"

Once you have controlled the Short Card to the top of the pack, you can use it effectively as a "Locator" for finding other cards as well. This is highly baffling to those spectators who think they have followed a trick up to a certain point, only to find that it goes completely beyond their idea of "how it's done." This is a combination consisting of the Short Card and the Hindu Shuffle, which is always effective, as each helps the other to gain results which neither could gain alone.

EFFECT

A card is freely chosen from the pack. The spectator who took it is allowed to replace it wherever he wants. The magician gives the pack a thorough, genuine shuffle; then causes the card to appear on top of the pack; or finds it in some other unaccountable way. In brief, this method can be used as a very baffling "card control" in many standard tricks.

METHOD

(1) A Short Card is already in the pack and is brought to the bottom by the riffle method described under the "Short Card." From then on, the trick is handled in conjunction with the Hindu Shuffle and standard riffle shuffles.

(3) This gives you ample time to square the pack in readiness for the Hindu Shuffle. Don't actually begin the shuffle until the spectator is about ready to return his card to the pack; otherwise, you may have to go through the shuffle more than once, which is apt to slow the action.

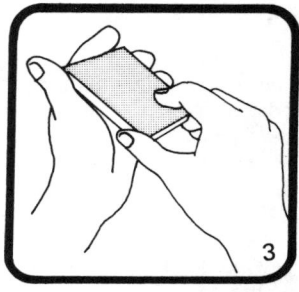

(2) With the Short Card on the bottom of the pack, spread the cards and let the spectator take any one he wants. Tell him that he can show the card to the audience before returning it to the pack.

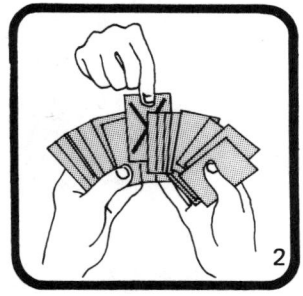

(4) Proceed with the regular Hindu Shuffle, drawing back the lower portion of the pack with your right hand. *Keep the Short Card on the bottom of the packet in your right hand as you draw off small batches of cards with the fingers of your left hand.* Tell the spectator to say "stop" at any time during the shuffle.

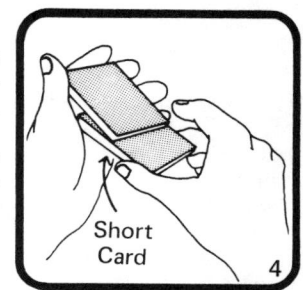

Short Card

(5) Let the spectator return his card (X) on the portion of the pack resting in your left hand. Then drop the right-hand packet on the left-hand cards, as with the Hindu Shuffle Location. In this case, the Short Card becomes the "key" card, as it is placed directly upon the selected card (X).

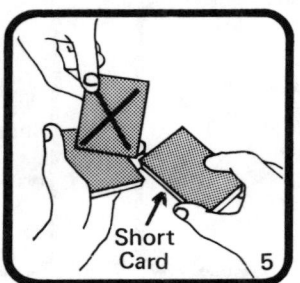

(6) Now square the pack, cut it, and give it a regular riffle shuffle, riffling the ends of the two halves of the pack together. This can be repeated and it *will not* separate the two cards, as the Short Card (S) will ride along with the longer selected card (X).

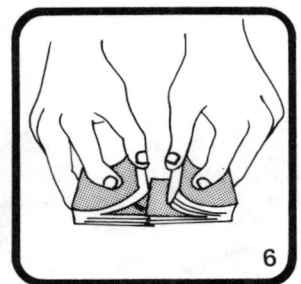

(7) *NOTE: You should try this shuffle a few times to see how well it works. Be sure to tap the end of the pack on the table, to make sure that the Short Card is "down" in the pack.*

(8) After each shuffle, square and tap the pack. Finally riffle the inner end *upward* with your right thumb. You will note the *click* when you come to the Short Card. Cut the pack at that point. The Short Card (S) will stay on top of the lower packet.

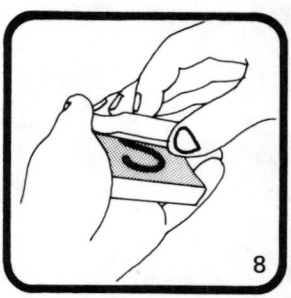

(9) In cutting, place the right-hand packet beneath the left-hand packet, which will automatically bring the Short Card (S) to the top, with the selected card (X) just beneath it. Thus, you have used your "key" card to bring a chosen card to the top *without* looking through the pack; and you have legitimately shuffled the pack as well!

(10) Since you now know the position of the selected card in the pack you may proceed with any "discovery" that you wish.

COMMENTS AND SUGGESTIONS

The Short Card as a Locator can be used in any trick where you must first bring a chosen card to the top of the pack. In Step 10, the selected card (X) is actually *second* from the top, but you can handle that quite easily. One way is to turn up the top card, asking if it was the card the spectator took. He says, "No," so you push the Short Card face down into the middle of the pack, saying that you will find his card in a most mysterious way, *which you are now prepared to do!*

THE SURPRISE DISCOVERY
Using the Short Card as a Locator

(1) For an immediate and effective "discovery" of the chosen card, you can proceed as follows: Take the Short Card (S) from the pack, removing it face down with your right hand. Tap the Short Card on top of the pack, and tell the spectator that this will cause his card to "rise to the top of the pack."

(2) Since the selected card (X) is already there, the trick is really done; but for added effect, you should thumb the top card (X) onto the table; then casually replace the Short Card (S) on top of the pack, as though it had played no real part in the trick.

(3) Now have the spectator turn up the tabled card (X). To his surprise, it will be the very card he took! Or, if you prefer, you can have him name his card and let someone else turn it up. This will dumbfound all the spectators, particularly those who did not see the spectator's card when he removed it from the pack.

A WEIGHTY PROBLEM
Using the Short Card as a Locator

Here is another good effect using the Short Card as a Locator. When the selected card is second from the top, directly under the Short Card, cut a dozen or more cards from the bottom of the pack to the top. Then start dealing the cards *face up* from the top of the pack, one at a time, stating that, "Since the spectator is concentrating on the particular card that he selected, it will add an infinitesimal amount of weight to the card. Through long study and practice, I can tell which card he took just by this small bit of increased weight." Deal the cards one at a time pretending to "weigh" each card on the fingertips of your right hand before you turn it face up. You don't actually know the chosen card, but when you turn up the Short Card, you know that the spectator's card will be next — so you will have no trouble "weighing" it, and then announcing that, "This is the card you selected." *Only then* do you turn the card over to show the sensitivity of your magical fingers — as you comment that the spectator certainly is a "heavy thinker."

QUICK RIFFLE LOCATION

This form of the "Short Card Location" is very effective when done briskly and convincingly. It forms a nice variation from the usual "location."

METHOD

Have the Short Card either on the bottom or on the top to start. While the spectator is looking at his card, cut the Short Card to the center of the pack. Then, riffle the pack for the card's return — *but stop at the Short Card.* The spectator's card is replaced in the pack where you stopped — *on top of the Short Card.* You can then locate the Card by riffling the Short Card to the top of the pack. This automatically brings the spectator's card to the bottom where you can reveal it in any manner you wish.

THE SHORT CARD FORCE

As stated before, the "Forcing" of a card on an unsuspecting spectator is essential in many tricks. This means that not only must you have several methods at your disposal; you should also take advantage of any "special" device that can render forcing more effective. The "SHORT CARD" meets both of these qualifications, as it can be forced on a spectator almost automatically, leaving him totally unaware that the Force took place.

EFFECT

The magician gives a pack of cards a thorough shuffle and even hands it to a spectator so he can do the same. Then, gripping the pack firmly in his left hand, the magician riffles the outer end of the pack with his right fingers, telling the spectator to call "Stop!" while the riffle is in progress. Cutting the pack at that point, the magician extends the lower portion to the spectator, telling him to look at the card where he called "Stop." *When he does, the spectator will be looking at a card that was just "Forced" on him without him even realizing it!*

SECRET AND PREPARATION

The only requirements for this Force are an ordinary pack of cards and one SHORT CARD which matches the rest of the cards of the pack.

METHOD

(1) To prepare, place the Short Card somewhere near the center of the pack. (In the illustrations the Short Card is indicated by an "S.") Square up the deck and you are ready to begin.

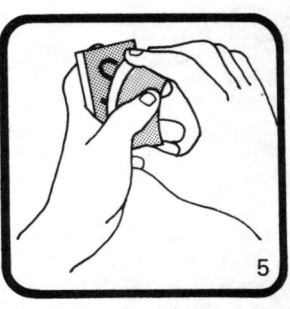

(5) When the spectator understands what he is to do, slowly start to riffle the end of the pack. TRY TO TIME THE RIFFLE SO YOU NEARLY REACH THE SHORT CARD JUST WHEN THE SPECTATOR IS ABOUT TO CALL "STOP."

(2) Hold the pack face down firmly in your left hand with the outer end of the pack extending half-way out of your hand.

(6) When the "Stop" call comes, *allow the Short Card AND ANY REMAINING CARDS BELOW IT to quickly riffle onto the lower packet of cards.* This should be done deliberately as if a few extra cards "just happened" to riffle after the spectator said "Stop."

(3) Move your right hand over the pack and grip it between your thumb— at the inner end — and your first and second fingers at the outer end towards the spectator.

(7) Divide the pack at this point and extend the *lower* packet toward the spectator. Instruct him to remove the top card and look at it. YOU HAVE NOW SUCCESSFULLY EXECUTED THE <u>SHORT CARD FORCE</u>. The "Forced" card can now be shuffled back into the pack and revealed in any manner that you wish.

(4) Explain that, as you riffle the end of the pack, the spectator is to call "Stop" at any time during the "riffle." Demonstrate this by riffling the end of the pack a few times.

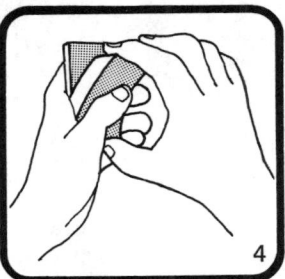

COMMENTS AND SUGGESTIONS

Since you already know what card the spectator will take, you can use the "Force" for a prediction effect. Simply write the name of the Short Card on a slip of paper, fold it, and give it to someone beforehand, to be opened after the Force. You can also "reveal" the card by pretending to read the spectator's mind, or by producing a *duplicate* of the Forced card from some unexpected place.

Another way is to "discover" the card by bringing it to the top of the deck *after the cards have been thoroughly shuffled by the spectator.* Simply riffle the Short Card to the top of the deck and turn it over, showing it to be the spectator's card. Or, since you have the chosen card on top, you can reveal it in a variety of ways, described in other areas of the Course.

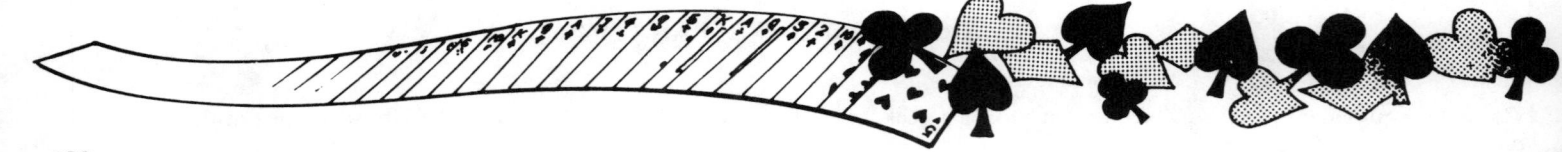

THE MYSTIC COUNTDOWN

Here is another baffling effect using the SHORT CARD. The result is gained so smoothly that you will have your audience puzzled from start to finish . . . and the routine can be repeated with equal impact. Try it a few times and you will probably make it a regular feature in your program.

EFFECT

After shuffling a pack of cards, the magician hands the deck to a spectator. The wizard tells him to start dealing cards, one at a time, from the top of the pack onto the table into a face-down pile. The spectator is to stop dealing wherever he wants, look at that card, replace it face down on the pile, and drop the rest of the pack on top. The magician then squares the pack and gives it a few cuts. He then uses the top card to flip over the card just below it — WHICH PROVES TO BE THE SPECTATOR'S CARD.

SECRET AND PREPARATION

The only items required for this mystery are an ordinary pack of cards with one SHORT CARD. To prepare, place the SHORT CARD on the bottom of the pack and place the deck in its box. (In the illustrations the SHORT CARD has been marked with an "S" and the selected card with an "X.") You are ready to begin.

METHOD

(1) Remove the pack from its box and shuffle the cards. Use the OVERHAND SLIP SHUFFLE to retain the SHORT CARD on the bottom of the pack.

(2) NOTE: As an alternate method *you can even have the spectator shuffle the cards himself.* After taking the pack back, riffle the SHORT CARD to the top of the pack. Then bring it to the bottom by executing the OVERHAND SHUFFLE — TOP CARD TO BOTTOM.

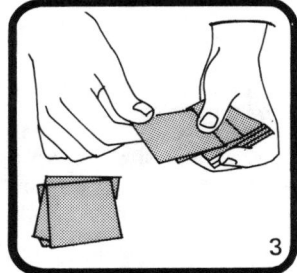

(3) With the SHORT CARD on the bottom of the pack, give the pack to a spectator. Instruct him to start dealing cards, one at a time, from the top of the deck in a pile on the table.

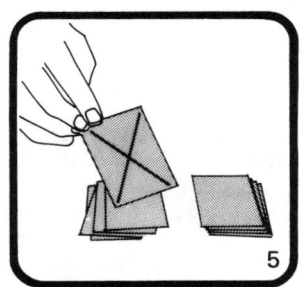

(4) Explain that he can stop dealing wherever he wants. (5) He is then to look at the top card of the "dealt" pile and remember it.

(6) After he looks at and remembers the card, tell him to return it to the top of the "dealt" pile and place the rest of the pack on top of the dealt cards, burying his card into the deck. UNKNOWN TO THE SPECTATOR, THIS PLACES THE BOTTOM CARD OF THE PACK (THE SHORT CARD) DIRECTLY ABOVE THE SELECTED CARD (X).

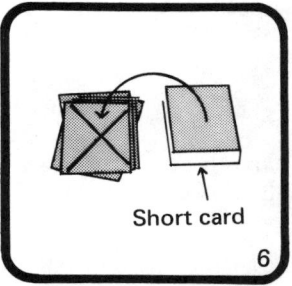

Short card

(7) After he has reassembled the pack, instruct him to give the pack as many single cuts as he wishes. *It is important that the spectator give the pack only single cuts so as not to separate the SHORT CARD and the selected card in the pack.*

(8) When the spectator is satisfied that the pack is thoroughly mixed, take the deck and give it a few more single cuts. Say, "Using my extra fine sense of touch, I can find your card merely by cutting the pack. Watch!" Suiting your action to your words, riffle the SHORT CARD to the top of the deck. THIS PLACES THE SELECTED CARD (X), WHICH IS DIRECTLY BENEATH THE SHORT CARD, SECOND FROM THE TOP.

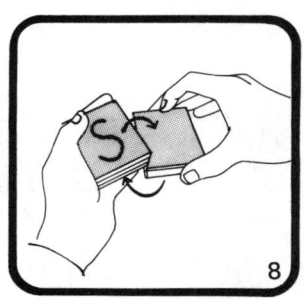

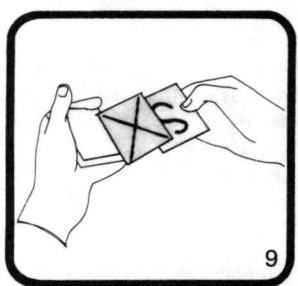

(9) Now, take the SHORT CARD from the top of the pack in your right hand. Then, using the SHORT CARD as a lever, turn over the second card which is the selected card (X), face up on top of the pack — as you say, "Here is your card."

COMMENTS AND SUGGESTIONS

Instead of placing the SHORT CARD on the bottom of the pack beforehand, you can easily get it there at any time during a series of card effects by cutting it to the top and shuffling it to the bottom using the OVERHAND SHUFFLE CONTROL — TOP CARD TO BOTTOM. You can keep it there with a "Table Shuffle" by simply releasing the bottom few cards first, as you riffle the ends of the two halves together. For a repeat, this trick is set up perfectly, truly a magician's dream! After flipping the chosen card face up on the pack, you are still holding the SHORT CARD. Simply slide it underneath the pack, where it becomes the bottom card . . . ready for a repeat of the "Mystic Countdown."

CUTTING THE ACES

People are always impressed by card tricks involving the four Aces, particularly when a performer shows his ability at finding an Ace in a pack that has been shuffled and cut. This ranks with the fabled feats of famous gamblers, yet you can accomplish the same effect with very little skill.

EFFECT

Without looking at the faces of the cards, you shuffle the pack and cut it repeatedly. In the course of the shuffling and cutting, you turn up an Ace and place it on the table. Continuing, as you shuffle and cut the cards, you find the three remaining Aces in the same baffling fashion.

SECRET AND PREPARATION

This is a perfect example of a trick demonstrating your ability to control the location of cards in a deck while it is being shuffled. *The success of this trick depends upon the use of a SHORT CARD.*

(A) To prepare, place the Four Aces on top of the pack with the Short Card just above them, making the Short Card the top card of the pack. Now, place the pack back in the box and you're ready to begin. (In the illustrations, the Aces have been marked "1, 2, 3, and 4" and the Short Card is indicated by an "S.")

METHOD

(1) Remove the pack from the box and start by giving it a regular Overhand Shuffle. *Be sure that the first batch of cards you shuffle from the deck consists of a dozen cards or more to retain your five card "set-up" in its original order.* Once this first batch of cards has been "shuffled off," continue shuffling the rest of the cards in the pack upon it.

(2) After the pack has been shuffled, cut about one third of the pack from the top of the deck to the bottom. You have now fairly shuffled and cut the pack leaving your set-up — the Four Aces and the Short Card — somewhere near the center of the pack in their original order.

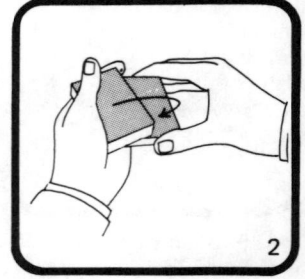

(3) Square up the pack in your left hand. With your right thumb at the rear end of the pack, riffle the end of the pack from bottom to top until you "feel" the Short Card.

(7) Now with the left thumb, push the first Ace from the top of the pack face onto the table and replace the Short Card face down on top of the deck. (*This places the Short Card back on top of the three remaining Aces.*)

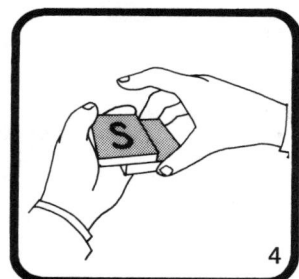

(4) Here you cut all the cards above the Short Card to the bottom of the pack, thus bringing your set up to the top.

(8) Square the pack and do the Overhand Shuffle, again making sure that the first batch you pull off contains the Short Card and the three Aces. Cut and riffle as you did before bringing the Short Card to the top and use it again to turn up the second Ace.

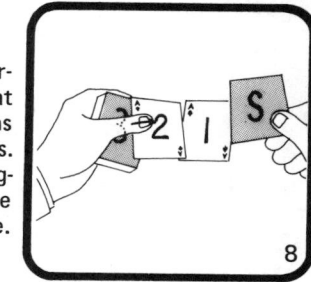

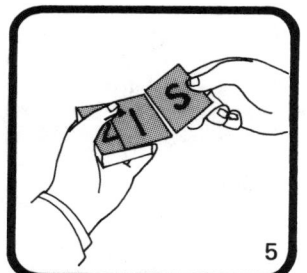

(5) Take the Short Card from the top of the deck with your right hand. Now with your left thumb, push the first Ace (1) a little to the right so that it protrudes about an inch off the right side of the pack.

(9) After dealing the second Ace face up on the table, replace the Short Card on the pack and repeat the same "shuffle, cut and riffle" routine, bringing up the third Ace.

(6) Using the Short Card as a lever, raise the right side of the first Ace, causing the Ace to hinge on its left edge. Continue rotating the Ace on edge with the Short Card until the first Ace is turned completely over (face up) on top of the deck.

(10) As the suspense increases, repeat the procedure with the fourth Ace and deal it on the table along side the other Aces and the effect is complete. You have cut all the Aces to the top of the pack!!!

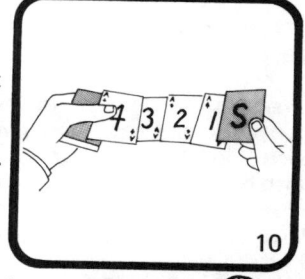

GIANT CARDS

Giant Cards represent a comparatively new type of magic that has come into popularity. Since the cards are *four times* as large as ordinary playing cards, they have little in common where manipulation is concerned, and their added thickness makes the giants still more cumbersome to handle. However, they can be dealt face down or face up and shown fanwise like smaller cards, which makes them adaptable to certain tricks.

Giant Cards can also be identified by suit and value, so that the discovery of chosen cards in *giant* size can be worked in conjunction with cards from ordinary packs. Such tricks will be found in this section along with other effects of a more varied nature.

Most important is the use of Giant Cards when performing for larger audiences where smaller card effects would be less effective and those of the "card table" type would be lost entirely. The bigger the audience, the bigger the cards is the rule in this case, just as with any other magical appliances.

When working before smaller audiences, you can reserve a Giant Card trick for a "smash" ending to a regular card routine. Always, people are impressed by a climax that tells them that the show is over, and a Giant Card finish will fill that purpose perfectly.

THE BIGGER CARD TRICK

A bit of comedy usually adds spice to a mystery and this trick stands as a good example. By having it ready, you can inject it at a timely moment, dependent on the mood of your audience. It can also serve as a prelude to a more ambitious effect.

EFFECT

A card is selected and returned to the pack, which the magician shuffles and places in a paper bag. Showing his right hand empty, he thrusts it into the bag, announcing that he will find the chosen card by his "magic touch." He brings out a card, such as the Three of Clubs, and shows it triumphantly, only to have the chooser say it is the wrong card. The magician asks the spectator if his card was a "bigger" card, to which he replies, "Yes." The Wizard tries and fails again — the card is still not "big" enough. This third time the magician is successful and brings out the chosen card, the Nine of Hearts, which is not only "bigger" in value, but proves to be FOUR TIMES BIGGER in size, for it emerges in the form of a Giant Card!

SECRET AND PREPARATION

(A) All that is required for this effect is a regular pack of cards, an ordinary paper bag, and one Giant Card. The Giant Card should be a Seven or higher in value.

(B) Place the Giant Card (the Nine of Hearts in the illustrations) inside the paper bag.

(C) Then fold the bag flat and place it aside. Find the Nine of Hearts in the regular pack and place it in position in the pack ready for one of the card "forces" you have learned.

METHOD

(1) Begin by "forcing" the Nine of Hearts by any method you have learned. After the audience has seen the card, have it returned to the pack and have the pack thoroughly shuffled by a spectator. When he returns the deck to you, thumb through the deck and say something like "Well you have mixed them well....so thoroughly that I certainly couldn't find your card just by looking. *So I'll find it without looking at all!*" AS YOU RUN THROUGH THE DECK, PICK ANY TWO "SMALLER" VALUE CARDS AND PLACE THEM ON THE TOP OF THE PACK.

(4) Actually, grasp the top card of the deck (the Three of Clubs in the illustration). After a few seconds, remove the Three and show it to the audience triumphantly as you remark, "Here is your card." Of course, the answer will be that it is not. Act puzzled for a moment and then ask, "Was yours a bigger card?" The spectator will, of course, reply "Yes."

(2) Now pick up the folded bag and shake it open. Be careful to keep the Giant Card inside the bag as you do so. Place the deck into the bag. Do not disturb the cards as you put them in so that you will be able to find the two "small" cards on top of the deck.

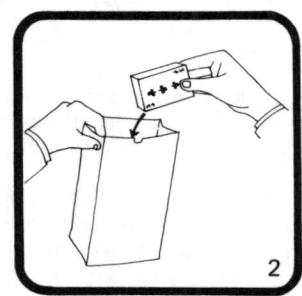

(5) Place the Three aside and repeat the procedure, again removing the "smaller" second card from the top of the pack.

(6) Now even more puzzled, reach into the bag as you say "Even bigger?" Then remove the GIANT Nine of Hearts and ask, "Well, is this big enough?" The audience will not only be surprised that you have found the correct card, but also that it has grown to four times its normal size!

(3) Once the cards are in the bag, announce that you will attempt to find the selected card by your magic touch alone. With this, reach in the bag and pretend to grope around as if searching for the spectator's card.

COMMENTS AND SUGGESTIONS

Handle the paper bag casually as though it had nothing really important to do with the trick. Also, if you present the effect in a serious vein, as if you were honestly attempting to find the spectator's card through your sense of touch, it will turn the climax into a real comedy surprise when you produce the much "bigger" card.

SYMPATHETIC CARDS

Here is a really "magical" effect performed with any standard pack of cards and a "GIANT CARD." No special skill is required — *proper timing* is the important factor. Therefore, the trick should be carefully rehearsed until you are familiar with the entire procedure. After that, the presentation will become almost automatic. You, yourself, may be amazed by the way it will mystify your audiences — even at the closest range — for the trick depends upon a subtle principle that truly deceives the eye.

EFFECT

The magician displays an ordinary deck and asks a spectator to shuffle it until the cards are well mixed. Holding the pack face down in one hand and a Giant Card face down in the other hand, the wizard begins dealing cards, *one at a time,* onto the back of the Giant Card. He then, in turn, tosses the cards, *one at a time,* into a pile on the table.

This is continued, card by card, as the magician tells the spectator that he should give the order to "Stop!" *at any card he wishes.* When he does, the magician remarks what a "magical coincidence" it would be if *both* the Giant Card *and* the card from the pack at which the spectator stopped were *identical.* The magician then turns both cards face up — REVEALING THEM TO BE EXACTLY THE SAME!

SECRET AND PREPARATION

The only items needed for this effect are a GIANT CARD and an ordinary pack from which the "duplicate" of the GIANT CARD is removed in advance. To prepare, place the Giant Card face down *on top* of the regular-size "duplicate" card. Hold both cards in your right hand — with your fingers beneath holding the "duplicate" small card and your thumb on top of the Giant Card. (In the illustrations, the Giant Card and its "duplicate" are the *Ace of Hearts*. The "duplicate" regular-size Ace of Hearts is indicated with an "X.") You are now ready to begin.

METHOD

(1) Hand the pack to a spectator to shuffle. Pick up the Giant Card *and (secretly)* the "duplicate" regular card in your right hand. Hold the two cards face down above the table, as shown. Be careful not to show the face(s) of the card(s). *NOTE: For a clever method of pre-setting the Giant Card and its "duplicate" before the show — which makes the "pickup" of the two cards quite easy — please see COMMENTS AND SUGGESTIONS at the end of this trick.*

(2) After the spectator is satisfied that the cards are well mixed *and* you have the GIANT CARD and its "secret" smaller duplicate held firmly in your right hand, pick up the shuffled deck in your left hand. Hold the pack in "dealing position" as shown in Step 1. *NOTE: You may find it easier to position the shuffled pack in your left hand first — then pick up the Giant Card and its secret "duplicate." In that case, just reverse Steps 1 and 2. In any event, you should now be in "dealing position" ready for the next step.*

(3) Tell the audience that you are *not* going to show the face of the Giant Card. Explain that you are doing this for a special reason, since the object of the mystery is for the spectator to magically determine the *suit* and *value* of the Giant Card *without knowing it.*

 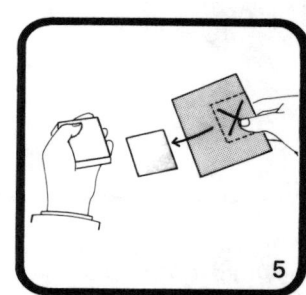

(4) Deal the top card from the pack in your left hand, face down, onto the back of the Giant Card as shown. (Just push the card from the top of the pack onto the back of the Giant Card with your left thumb.) (5) Pause a moment — and then *tilt* the Giant Card, allowing the smaller card to slide off the Giant Card and drop, *face down,* on the table.

(6) With your left hand, deal the next (top) card from the pack onto the back of the Giant Card *in exactly the same way.* After a brief pause, your right hand tilts the Giant Card, letting the smaller card slide off on top of the first card already on the table. Continue thumbing off cards, one by one, onto the back of the Giant Card, then let them slide onto the pile of cards on the table.

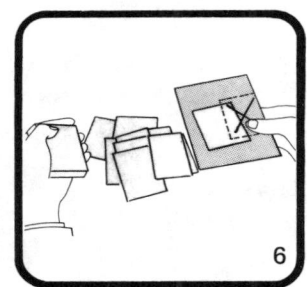

(7) Explain to the spectator that he is to say, "Stop!" *at any time as* you deal through the deck. *NOTE: Be careful that none of the regular cards turns face up as you slide them from the Giant Card onto the pile of cards on the table.*

(8) When the call comes — STOP! If you are in the middle of a "deal," or if you are sliding one of the regular cards onto the pile on the table, ask the spectator *which card* he is selecting — thereby indicating that you are giving him *every opportunity to make a "free choice."* Whatever his final decision, see that the "selected" card is positioned on the back of the Giant Card as shown in Step 6.

(9) *NOTE: Here is the situation at this point: The GIANT CARD is held in your right hand. It acts as a "tray" for the spectator's freely selected card which rests on the Giant Card's back. Unknown to the audience, with your right fingers, you are holding, UNDERNEATH the Giant Card, the secret "duplicate" regular card which matches the Giant Card.*

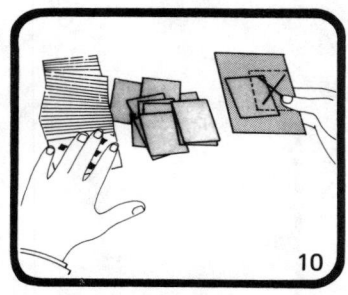

(10) Now spread the remainder of the cards which you are holding *in your left hand* FACE UP on the table with your left hand. As you spread the left-hand packet face up, remind the spectator that he could have selected *any of those cards.* (11) Now, pick up the pile of cards *already dealt,* and turn *them all* FACE UP. Casually spread them on the table as shown. State, "If the spectator had 'stopped' me sooner, he would have gotten *one of those.*"

(12) As you make the statement about the "already dealt" cards in Step 11, your left hand moves its fingers *beneath* the Giant Card. With your left fingers, hold the regular "duplicate" card against the bottom of the Giant Card. Your left thumb holds the spectator's "selected card" above. *This allows your right hand to release its grip on the Giant Card and the secret "duplicate" card.*

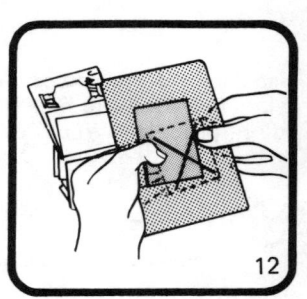

(13) Now, with the first finger of your right hand, point to the "selected" card lying *on top* of the Giant Card. Say, "Out of *all* the different cards in the pack, *this* is the card you chose." *NOTE: In transferring the Giant Card from your right hand to your left hand, you have subtly convinced the audience that all is "fair" — as both hands are obviously quite empty.*

(14) THE FOLLOWING THREE STEPS (14, 15, and 16) ARE THE MOST IMPORTANT AND DECEPTIVE PART OF THE ROUTINE — STUDY THEM CAREFULLY. Your right hand now returns to its former position so that the *fingers of your right hand* also hold the "duplicate" card under the Giant Card. Your left fingers now *release* their hold on the "duplicate" card — *but your left thumb continues to press against the spectator's "selected" card on top of the Giant Card as shown in Step 12.*

(15) You now begin THREE actions that take place *simultaneously:* FIRST, *both hands* begin tilting the *audience end* of the Giant Card upward; SECOND, at the same time, your *right fingers* begin to draw the secret "duplicate" card to the right, *off the face of the Giant Card;* THIRD, with your *left thumb,* retain the spectator's "selected" card *on top* of the Giant Card.

(16) Continue rotating the Giant Card so that the face of the Giant Card is toward the audience. *You secretly retain* the spectator's "selected" card *on top* of the Giant Card with your *left thumb. With your right fingers, draw the hidden "duplicate" card, face up, fully into view.* YOU HAVE NOW UNDETECTIBLY SWITCHED THE "SELECTED" CARD FOR THE SECRET "DUPLICATE" CARD. To the spectator, it will appear that you are merely turning his card *and* the Giant Card face up at the same time. *This is a very deceptive and totally convincing move.*

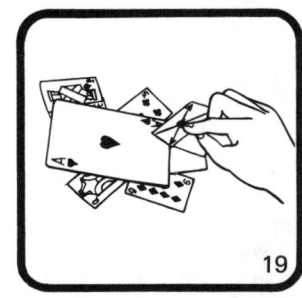

(17) *NOTE: At this point, the spectator's "freely selected" card is hidden UNDER the face-up Giant Card. The "duplicate" regular card, which matches the Giant Card, is face up in your right hand. TO YOUR AUDIENCE, IT WILL APPEAR AS THOUGH THE "DUPLICATE" CARD CAME OFF THE <u>BACK</u> OF THE GIANT CARD INSTEAD OF FROM <u>BELOW</u>.*

(18) Now, casually place the Giant Card *face up on the face-up pile of cards on the table.* THE HIDDEN "SELECTED" CARD FALLS UNNOTICED BENEATH THE GIANT CARD AND BECOMES ANOTHER OF THE MISCELLANEOUS FACE-UP CARDS IN THE PILE OF CARDS ON THE TABLE.

(19) Drop the "duplicate" regular card face up on the Giant Card — PROVING THAT THE SPECTATOR HAS MIRACULOUSLY PICKED THE EXACT DUPLICATE OF THE GIANT CARD FROM THE PACK!

(20) The trick is now over. However, at this point you can add a subtle touch by picking up the Giant Card and its "duplicate" from the table and handing them to the spectator. As you hand them to him, *turn both cards over,* showing the backs to be unprepared. The original "selected" card lies forgotten in the mass of cards on the table.

IMPORTANT NOTE: This entire, very clever effect hinges upon the "Secret Move" (Steps 14, 15, and 16). This is when you secretly "switch" the spectator's freely "selected" card for the "duplicate" card under the Giant Card. Here is the sequence *as seen by the spectators:*

(21) As described in Step 14, your right hand moves to the Giant Card and your right fingers grasp the secret "duplicate" card and press it against the bottom of the Giant Card. Then, both hands start to rotate the Giant Card face up *toward the spectator.*   (22) Your right fingers begin to slide the "duplicate" card off the face of the Giant Card. Your left thumb maintains its pressure on the selected card on top of the Giant Card.   (23) The selected card is now hidden by the Giant Card as your right hand continues sliding the "duplicate" card to your right.   (24) Your left hand drops the Giant Card and the selected card face up on the pile of face-up cards already on the table. Your right hand displays the "duplicate" small card *as if it were the freely "selected" card.*

COMMENTS AND SUGGESTIONS

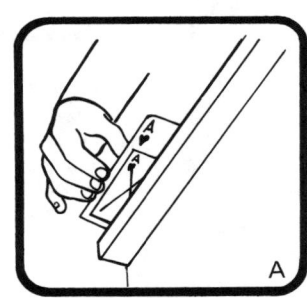

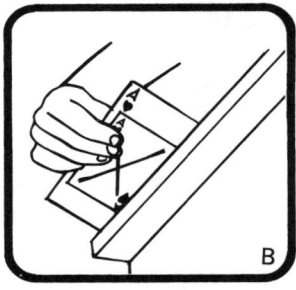

If you wish to perform this effect *during* your card routine, rather than at the start, you can use the following clever set-up: (A) Place the GIANT CARD *and* its regular "duplicate" on the edge of the table so that they *both* overlap the edge. You may then present any card effects which do not involve the "duplicate" card. When you are ready to present the SYMPATHETIC CARDS . . . (B) . . . reach over with your right hand and pick up the Giant Card *and the secret "duplicate"* card as shown. You are now all set to present this extremely clever close-up mystery. If more convenient, you may also place the Giant Card and the secret "duplicate" card on a book, ashtray, or some other handy object that is already on the table, rather than placing the two cards on the edge of the table. Just be sure that *both* the Giant Card *and* the secret "duplicate" can be easily picked up at the same time.

IMPORTANT NOTE: In the "switch" of the "duplicate" for the spectator's card, *timing is the key factor.* For best results, you should *practice in front of a mirror.* The "draw-off" should begin as the edge of the Giant Card is level with the eyes of the spectators. That is the time when the *ends* of ALL THREE CARDS are toward the spectators. At that instant, the spectators lose sight of the BACKS *before* they see the FACES. When your right hand draws the card to the right, as it comes into view, LOOK AT IT. *All of the eyes of the audience will follow* — never suspecting that the card they are watching came from the FRONT and not the BACK of the Giant Card. This is another excellent example of *MISDIRECTION.*

THE APPLAUSE CARD

This is a surprise ending for a card routine in which a clever trick is followed by a comedy gag. Audiences appreciate such touches and, even if you have patterned your program along serious lines, it is often good to conclude your show with a "magical" comedy closing effect such as this one.

EFFECT

A spectator selects a card and returns it to the pack, which is thoroughly shuffled. The magician announces that he intends to produce the chosen card by using his "sense of touch" alone, as he places the pack in his inside coat pocket. After several "wrong" cards are removed, the magician reaches into his pocket and brings out the spectator's card, but it is now a giant size! When the audience applauds, a banner drops from beneath the big card saying, "THANK YOU."

SECRET AND PREPARATION

(A) The props needed for this effect are a deck of cards, a jumbo card and a piece of light colored paper approximately two feet long and three inches wide. With a heavy marking pen, print the words THANK YOU or some other appropriate phrase such as GOOD BYE, or APPLAUSE, down the length of the paper, allowing enough blank space (about half the length of the jumbo card) at the top of the piece of paper before beginning your lettering. Then, pleat the strip of paper, "accordian fashion" as shown.

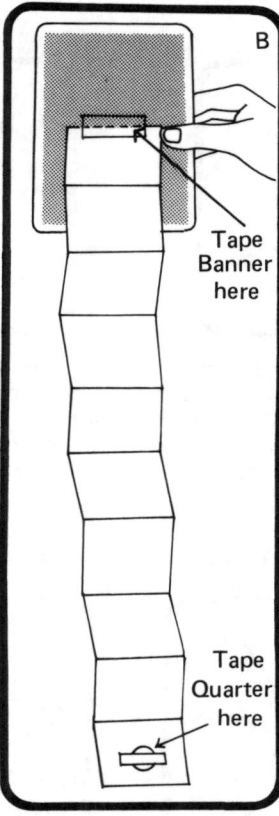

Tape Banner here

Tape Quarter here

(B) Attach the top of the banner to the center of the back of a giant card, in this case the Four of Diamonds, with a piece of tape as shown. Also, tape a quarter to the "unlettered" side of the banner near the very bottom. This will act as a weight and cause the banner to open quickly.

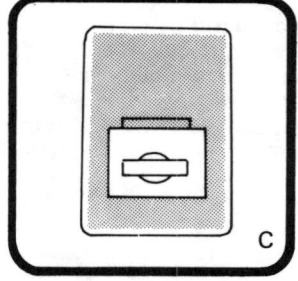

(C) This done, fold the banner and hold the pleated banner against the back of the giant card. Place the giant card in your inside coat pocket with the face side of the card toward the audience. You are now ready.

METHOD

(1) From a regular size pack of cards, force the Four of Diamonds on the spectator using any of the forcing methods previously explained. After the card is noted by the spectator and shown to the rest of the audience (but, of course, not to you), let him replace the card anywhere in the deck and have any member of the audience thoroughly shuffle the pack.

(2) Ask the spectator if he is satisfied that his card is lost in the shuffled deck and you could not possibly know where it is (as, indeed you do not!). If he wishes, he may even shuffle the deck again. When he is completely satisfied, state that your "super sensitive" fingers will now find his card while the deck is completely hidden from view in your pocket. Place the deck in the same inside coat pocket that contains the giant card.

(3) NOTE: When you take the shuffled deck back from the spectator, casually look at the first two cards on the face of deck to make sure that neither is the Four of Diamonds. If either of them is the Four, just remove the cards from the top of the deck instead of the face of the deck in Step 4.

(4) Reach into your pocket and remove one of the regular cards that you know is NOT the Four of Diamonds. Display the card triumphantly and ask him if you are correct. The spectator will reply, "No." Say that this is an extremely difficult trick and you will try again. Remove the second card, and, with a bit less confidence, ask the spectator if this is the one. Again the response is "No."

(5) You now become even more embarassed....you might say something like, "I hope none of you have any place you were planning to be soon as we have fifty cards left to go." Then, ask the spectator to help by concentrating on his card. "Just make a BIG mental picture of it." Reach into your pocket and get ready to remove the GIANT CARD. Be sure to hold the pleated banner with your thumb so that it does not unfold.

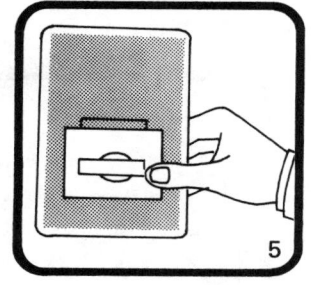

(6) Ask him to name his card out loud and AT THE SAME TIME remove the giant card.

(7) As you show the huge Four of Diamonds and the spectator acknowledges that you have at last found his card, say something like, "Well, I see you really did make a BIG mental picture!"

(8) The unexpected appearance of the giant card will always get a laugh and applause. As the spectators react to this first surprise, draw back your right thumb and allow the banner to unfold to reveal your, "THANK YOU" message. This is sure to get an even greater response from your audience.

COMMENTS AND SUGGESTIONS

This particular card trick can be seen by a large group of a hundred or more people, particularly if you leave the stage and go into the audience to have the card selected. Then have the spectator show the card to the rest of the audience while your back is turned. Have him replace the card in the deck and return to the stage. If more convenient, you may also have a spectator join you on the stage for the selection of the card and the follow-up comedy "discovery." This is a very clever comedy effect as well as good magic and makes an excellent closing number for your show.

DOUBLE APPLAUSE CARD

It is possible to tape two or more pleated banners on the same Giant Card for a repeated comedy effect. For instance, the first banner can say "THANK YOU" and the second "BOTH OF YOU" — or for a birthday party, "THANK YOU" and then "HAPPY BIRTHDAY MARY," etc. After the first banner falls, simply tear it off and set it aside still keeping the second banner in place with your thumb. Then move your thumb allowing the second banner to fall for the double-barreled impact. When using more than one banner, tape them directly above one another so you are able to hold them both in position with your thumb and release them one at a time. You can also print the second message on the back of the banner. Then just turn the card around after the audience reads the "front side" of the banner. In this case make the banner "double" to hide the quarter you are using as a weight. Audiences always enjoy clever bits of comedy along with their magic and the Applause Card is excellent for this type of effect.

A GIANT MISTAKE — FIRST VERSION

Comedy effects add a light touch to a card routine, so it is always wise to have a few ready for the right occasion. Here is one that should bring a "big" laugh as it takes a "big" card to do it.

EFFECT

This is similar to the "Applause Card" trick except that it has a different comedy ending. A spectator selects a card, remembers it, and returns it to the pack. The magician states that he will find the selected card by his "sense of touch" alone and places the deck in his inside coat pocket. The wizard reaches into his pocket and draws out several "wrong" cards (just as in the "Applause Card" trick). In desperation, he asks the spectator to "form a BIG picture of the card in your mind"....the magician then reaches into his pocket and starts to draw out a "giant" Seven of Spades! Pausing with just the top half of the large card in view, the magician asks, "Was this your card?" The spectator replies "No," stating that he took the FIVE of Spades. The magician responds, "Then this IS your card" and draws the Seven completely from his pocket, showing it to be only a *part* of the jumbo Seven of Spades, bearing ONLY FIVE SPOTS!

SECRET AND PREPARATION

The only requirements for this effect are a regular pack of cards and one Giant Card.

To prepare, cut off a portion of the Giant Card, reducing its value from that shown on the card to the "spot" value of the card you will later "Force" on the spectator. In the illustrations, the Seven of Spades has been cut to show FIVE spots instead of SEVEN. Other combinations that make an effective change are: A SIX-spot changed to a FOUR-spot, a NINE changed to a SEVEN, a TEN changed to a FIVE, a THREE changed to a TWO, etc. No matter what combination you choose, remove from the regular pack of cards the card that matches the "lowered" value of your prepared Giant Card. Place this card in the position in the deck for your favorite "Force." Put the "cut" Giant Card in your inside coat pocket and you're ready.

METHOD

The working of the trick is exactly the same as the "Applause Card" trick....except that you use the comedy "cut" card instead of the Applause Card.

COMMENTS AND SUGGESTIONS

When you first start to show the "top" part of the Giant Card coming from your pocket, hold the card as shown in Illustration A. Then when you remove the card completely from your coat, cover the index number of the card with the tips of your fingers as in Illustration B so that only the spots on the face of the card are visible. Then, point to the spots on the card and count them out loud, proving that you have humorously "discovered" the spectator's card!

A GIANT MISTAKE — SECOND VERSION

Here is another clever method of presenting this effect.

METHOD

From the regular pack of cards, "Force" the card that matches the prepared jumbo card using your favorite method. Ask the spectator to show the card to all the members of the audience and then to return the card to the pack....then have him thoroughly shuffle the cards so that there is no chance for you to know the location of his card in the pack. Now, (instead of placing the deck in your pocket) explain that you will attempt to find the spectator's card by EXTRA-SENSORY PERCEPTION, as he concentrates upon it. As you say this, start running through the pack face up as if looking for the spectator's selection. Then, after several wrong guesses, confess that you seem to be having some trouble reading the spectator's mind. Explain that whenever this happens, you always have "THE MAGICIAN'S SPECIAL *WHAT-TO-DO-IF-A-TRICK-GOES-WRONG* TRICK." With that, reach into your inside coat pocket and triumphantly start to remove the jumbo Seven from your coat — but withdraw the card so that only *half* of the card is visible.

Ask, "Is THIS the card on which you are concentrating?" Of course, the answer will be "No." Ask the spectator what the card was that he selected and, when the answer comes, remove the jumbo card completely from your coat pocket as you say, "Then this IS your card."

COMMENTS AND SUGGESTIONS

You can also do a clever impromptu version of this comedy effect on a small scale by simply carrying the cut portion of a normal sized card taken from an old pack. In this version, the "half card" can be brought from your shirt pocket, the outside pocket of your coat or even your wallet.

A GIANT MYSTERY

Here is a mystery that goes well beyond the scope of many card effects; therefore, you may wish to use it as a *special feature,* possibly the finale of your routine. You could also use it as an encore, on the theory that when people are eager for you to shown them "one more trick," it should not only be something *different,* but also something *big.* This striking effect meets both those qualifications.

EFFECT

Starting in a conventional manner, the magician has a spectator select a card from the pack, remember it, and return it. After the pack is thoroughly shuffled, the magician decides to make the card reveal itself in a very unusual way. For this purpose, he uses two large pieces of stiff cardboard. He shows the boards on both sides, finally placing them together and resting them on the table. The magician explains that he will make the chosen card appear *between* the panels. After some byplay, he separates the two panels only to find that the card has failed to materialize. So, again he shows the two boards and places them together for another try. This time, he succeeds "in a big way" — for when the boards are separated, a GIANT CARD, a duplicate of the very card the spectator selected, is found between them!

SECRET AND PREPARATION

Required for this effect are a regular deck of cards; two pieces of stiff cardboard or artist's construction board, approximately eight inches by ten inches; and a Giant Card.

(A) On one of the cardboard squares, attach a Giant Card with glue, Double Stick tape, or a "Magic Loop." For clarity, *the prepared board is a DARKER color than the unprepared board in the illustrations.* We will call the side of the prepared board that has the Giant Card attached to it, the "face" of the prepared board.

(B) To set up, place the regular board on top of the "face-up" prepared board with the Giant Card side of the prepared board "face up." The regular board should be "angled" slightly to the right so that the four corners of the prepared board show beneath it. Now place the two boards on your table in this position.

(C) From a regular pack of cards, remove the card that matches the Giant Card (in this case the Ten of Hearts) and place it at the position in the deck ready for your favorite "Force." Now place the deck in its box, and you are ready to begin.

METHOD

(1)   Remove the pack of cards from its box and "force" the Ten of Hearts on a spectator using any of the methods you have learned. Tell the spectator to remember the card, and after he has returned it to the pack, he is to shuffle the deck until the cards are thoroughly mixed.

(7)   Your left fingers grip the prepared board as both hands begin to pull the boards apart as shown.

(2)   Place the pack aside and pick up the two cardboard panels in your left hand, thumb on top, fingers beneath, saying, "I have here two pieces of cardboard."

(8)   When the two boards are completely apart . . .

(3)   As you say this, grasp the two boards in your right hand — fingers on top, thumb beneath — and *turn both cards over,* toward the audience.

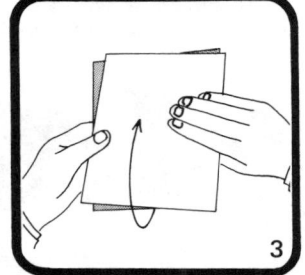

(9)   . . . TURN   THE   REGULAR BOARD (IN YOUR RIGHT HAND) OVER — toward yourself — to show the other side of the board saying, "As you can see, they are the same on both sides."

(4)   THE   PREPARED   BOARD   IS NOW ON TOP "FACE DOWN."

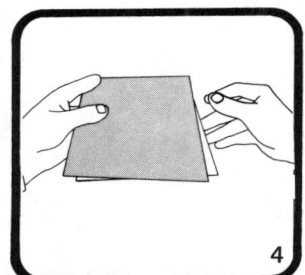

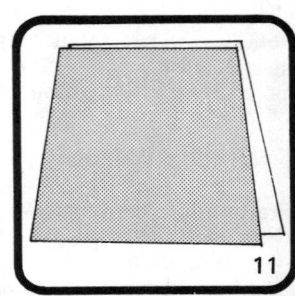

(10) With that, TURN THE RIGHT HAND "REGULAR" BOARD BACK TO ITS ORIGINAL POSITION. SLIDE THE TWO BOARDS TOGETHER PLACING THE PREPARED BOARD ON TOP OF THE REGULAR BOARD and (11) put the boards on the table.

(5)   Without hesitation, pull the two boards apart, *keeping the top prepared board in your right hand and the regular board in your left hand.*

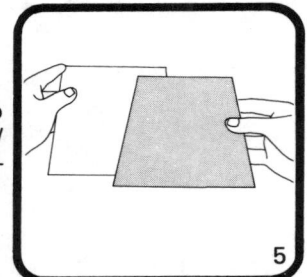

(12) *NOTE: As you execute this series of movements, the audience will believe they have seen all sides of both panels of cardboard and will be convinced that everything is on the level.*

(6)   As soon as the two boards are apart, *place the regular board on top of the prepared board and SLIDE IT TO THE RIGHT COMPLETELY ACROSS THE TOP OF THE PREPARED BOARD into the tips of your right fingers.*

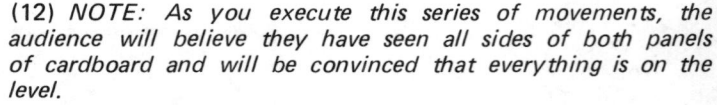

(13) Pick up the pack of cards and state that you will attempt to make the chosen card appear between the two boards. Toss the pack face down on top of the boards as if to cause the selected card to "penetrate" between them.

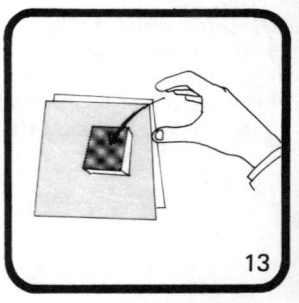

(14) Place the deck aside and pick up both boards. Separate them so that the *regular* board is in your left hand and the *prepared* board is in your right. Since no card is found between the boards, tell your audience that you must have made a "minor" error, so you will attempt the feat once more.

(18) This time, however, instead of immediately placing them on the table, grasp the boards in your right hand, fingers on top and thumb below, and TURN BOTH BOARDS OVER. THIS PLACES THE PREPARED BOARD ON THE BOTTOM WITH THE REGULAR BOARD ON TOP HIDING THE NOW "FACE-UP" TEN OF HEARTS.

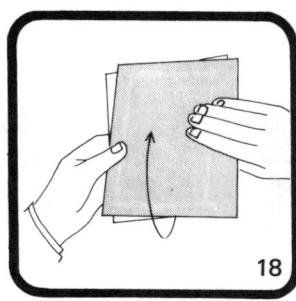

(15) As you make this remark, TURN THE LEFT-HAND PANEL OVER TOWARD YOURSELF showing the other side of the regular board as if hoping to find the selected card there.

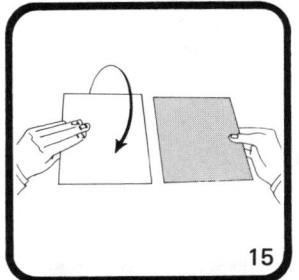

(19) Place both boards on the table and pick up the deck. Explain that you expect the trick to "work" this time as you toss the cards onto the boards.

(20) Place the pack aside, and pick up the boards. Separate them to reveal the Giant Ten of Hearts as you say something like, "When this trick works – it works in a big way!"

(16) Turn the left-hand panel back over to its original position.
(17) NOW, SLIDE THE TWO BOARDS TOGETHER. PLACE THE PREPARED BOARD ON TOP OF THE REGULAR BOARD.

COMMENTS AND SUGGESTIONS

The beauty of this effect lies in its certainty. This is another reason why it is a good effect to use as a *finish* or an *encore*. IT CANNOT FAIL IF YOU REHEARSE IT TO THE POINT WHERE EVERY MOVE IS SECOND NATURE. The smoother the routine, the more deceptive it becomes. Simply follow the steps as described and the big climax will take care of itself automatically.

SPECIAL CARD TRICKS

Certain card tricks can be classified as "special" because they depend on methods or procedures that are somewhat unusual. Since they belong in no other category, they deserve one of their own and the term "Special" most adequately defines it.

In a sense, these are advanced card tricks — not necessarily because they are difficult to perform — but because they are the type that a performer is apt to add to his program *after* he has mastered tricks of a more general nature. So test these "specials" by incorporating them into your regular program, one by one, and see for yourself how effective they are in enhancing the overall variety of your card mysteries.

SELF-REVERSING PACK

EFFECT

The magician shows an ordinary pack and begins to demonstrate various ways used to shuffle cards. Finally, taking the pack in both hands, he gives it a peculiar shuffle by repeatedly mixing batches of *face-up* cards with *face-down* cards until the whole pack is a hopeless jumble. Then, giving the pack a single tap, he spreads the cards on the table and shows that the entire pack has regained its normal order with every card in the deck in its original face-down position.

METHOD

(1) Begin by demonstrating various different shuffles used with a pack of cards, such as Overhand Shuffle, Hindu Shuffle, Riffle Shuffle, etc.

(2) Square the pack and hold it face down in your right hand with your thumb on top. Slide a small batch of cards from the top of the deck into your left fingers, which grip them as shown.

(3) Now turn your left hand over, so that its cards are face up. Then your right thumb slides another batch of face-down cards from the TOP of the pack BENEATH the face-up cards in the left hand.

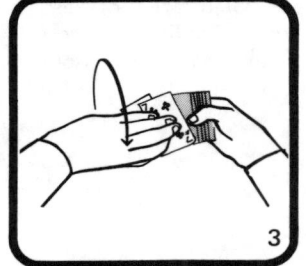

(4) The left hand turns over again *retaining its grip on both of the packets that have been slid off.* The right thumb then pushes more cards from the TOP of the deck to the left, so that the left hand (now thumb upward) can use its fingers to take these along BENEATH its group.

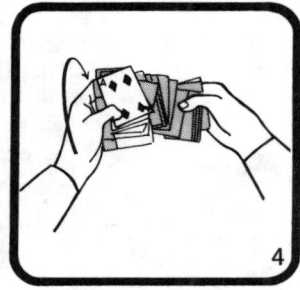

(5) This process of sliding batches of cards from the TOP of the pack to the left BENEATH the cards held in the left hand continues as the left hand alternately turns over to receive some face up and some face down. This is repeated until all the cards in the right hand have been transferred to the left.

(6) *NOTE: Actually, instead of mixing the pack, YOU ARE DIVIDING IT INTO TWO SECTIONS, BACK TO BACK. The face-up cards are never really intermingled with the face-down cards, although to the spectators it appears that is the case.*

(7) Square the pack, remarking something like "The cards are now hopelessly mixed, with batches of face-down cards among the face-up cards." To further demonstrate the "mixed up" nature of the deck, cut DEEP in the pack and turn your right hand palm upward stating: "Here you see some cards back to face–" as you show the *face* of the card on the right-hand packet and the *back* of the card on the left-hand packet.

(8) Now reassemble the two halves and cut the pack again; but this time you cut NEAR THE TOP of the pack. Turn the right hand palm upward adding, "And here are cards that happen to be face to back." Show as in Step 7, but since you now are in the top half of the pack, the right-hand packet will show a *back* while the left packet will show a *face*.

(9) Again reassemble the pack and cut it once more. This time cutting at the spot WHERE THE TWO GROUPS MEET BACK TO BACK. You will find this easy to do. Because of the natural bend in a deck of cards, when a portion of the deck is reversed on itself, it leaves a definite "break" between the two sections....making it very simple to find. When you locate the spot where the halves meet, separate the two sections and TURN THE RIGHT HAND PALM UPWARD, saying, "And here are some others that are back to back."

(10) *Now, instead of turning the right hand palm downward to replace the packet the way it was, REASSEMBLE THE PACK LEAVING THE RIGHT-HAND PACKET PALM UPWARD. Just slide the right-hand packet on top of the left-hand packet. By this maneuver you have turned the upper half (the face-up cards) face down on the rest of the face-down pack. ALL OF THE CARDS ARE NOW FACE DOWN.*

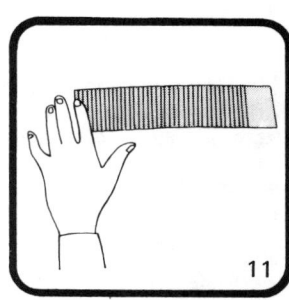

(11) Holding the pack in your left hand say, "Now for some real magic; One little tap" – tap the pack with your right forefinger – "and all those mixed up cards turn *face down,* as they were originally–" Spread the pack face down on the table to show ALL BACKS; your "magic tap" worked!

COMMENTS AND SUGGESTIONS

No real skill is required for this effect, as the "sloppier" the shuffle looks, the better. You should practice it, though, in order to do it rapidly, thus convincing the audience that you have really mixed face-up cards with face-down cards all through the pack. Also, your rapid action will be hard to follow, so if a spectator tries to duplicate your shuffle, he will get the cards really mixed.

SELF-REVERSING PACK — OUTDONE

EFFECT

A card is selected, noted and returned to the pack which is then shuffled by the magician in an apparently ordinary manner. Then, holding the deck in both hands, the magician gives the pack a very peculiar "slip-slop" shuffle, carelessly mixing *face-up* cards with *face-down* cards in a hopeless jumble. Then, with the aid of a single "magic" tap, the pack is spread on the table showing that all the cards in the deck have turned face down, with one exception....THE CHOSEN CARD IS FACE UP IN THE CENTER OF THE PACK!

METHOD

(1) Using methods you have learned, have the selected card (in the illustration, the Five of Hearts) returned to the deck and control it to the bottom of the pack. This can be done effectively by bringing the card to the top of the pack using the "Hindu Shuffle Pick-Up Control." From there it can be brought to the bottom by the "Overhand Shuffle, Top Card to Bottom."

(2) Another neat way is to have the card returned to the pack in the course of the "Hindu Shuffle." As the card is replaced, you "glimpse" the bottom card (Hindu Glimpse) which then becomes your "key." Give the pack a few single cuts, apparently "losing" the card completely. Now look through the pack and say you will try to find the chosen card . . . which you *actually do,* thanks to the *"key."*

(3) Run through the deck, holding the cards so that only you can see their faces. When you come to the chosen card, shake your hand and say that you just can't find it—so you will do another trick instead. Tell the spectator to remember his card anyway, as you may be able to locate it later on. With that, you cut the pack, bringing his Five of Hearts to the top of the face-up pack. Now turn the pack over so it is the bottom card of the face-down pack.

(4) *NOTE: Whichever method you use, be careful when you turn the pack face down, so that no one sees that the chosen card (the Five of Hearts) is on the bottom; you are ready to proceed with the "Self-Reversal."*

(5) With the chosen card at the bottom of the pack, begin the "slip-slop" shuffle, repeatedly sliding off batches of cards (some face up, some face down) from the left hand into the right hand, as already described in the Self-Reversing Pack.

(6) The slip-slop shuffle is continued until only a few cards remain in your right hand. Then, when the LEFT HAND is in its THUMB DOWNWARD position, the right thumb pushes THE CARDS REMAINING IN THE RIGHT HAND onto the bottom of the pack EXCEPT THE BOTTOM "SELECTED" CARD (indicated by the "X"), which is still held in the right hand.

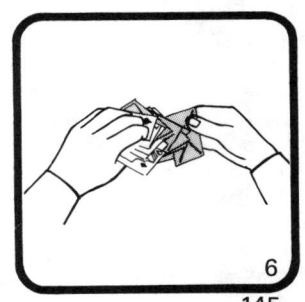

(7) After the left hand turns over (thumb upward) *the right hand places its single card (the chosen "X" card) ON TOP OF THE PACK* — beneath the left thumb, as though to complete the hit-or-miss shuffle, which now looks "sloppy" indeed.

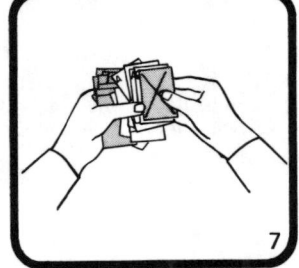

(9) Then, with the last cut, repeat the procedure where you divide the pack between the back-to-back sections and reassemble the deck. *All the cards in the pack will now be face down except for the chosen Five of Hearts (X), which is face up in the center of the pack.*

(8) Square the deck, remarking that the cards are hopelessly mixed, as you proceed to cut the pack (once near the top and once near the bottom) to show how some cards are "face to back" and some "back to face," as described in the Self Reversing Pack.

(10) Immediately spread the pack face down on the table, showing all backs except for the single face-up Five of Hearts in the middle!

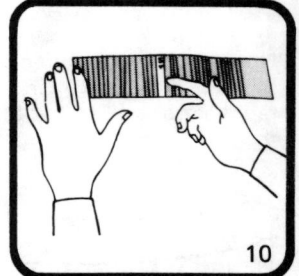

GRANT'S SUPERIOR CARD TRICK

Here is a triple mystery created by "Gen" Grant, whose ingenious card effects are becoming classics in their own right. In this particular effect, the magician starts by pretending to show the spectators how a trick is done, which is an excellent way of misleading them from the *real* secret. From there, the trick builds to the *TRIPLE CLIMAX.* This trick should usually be reserved for a spectator who has some small knowledge of magic, and perhaps is aware of the "key" card principle. In this case, "a little knowledge" turns out to be a very "baffling" thing.

EFFECT

The magician has a spectator select a card and replace it in the pack. The magician then shows the audience how easily a "selected" card can be found by simply noting the card above it and watching for that card to appear when the pack is dealt. Proceeding along that line, the magician deals the *chosen* card face down to the spectator, then deals an *indifferent* card to another person, and keeps the *"key"* card for himself. But when the faces of the three cards are shown, ALL HAVE MAGICALLY CHANGED PLACES!

SECRET AND PREPARATION

(A) The only special item needed is an extra card with the same back design as the pack that you intend to use. This extra card is a DUPLICATE of a card already in the pack with the same color back and back design. Assuming that the *duplicate* card is a Four of Diamonds, remove the *regular* Four of Diamonds from the self-pack and place *both* cards on the bottom of the deck. In the illustrations, we will call the bottom Four "A" and the next Four "B."

(B) Also remove *any* indifferent card from the deck. (For the illustrations we will use the Ace of Hearts.) Place it *in your shirt pocket,* WITH ITS BACK TOWARD THE AUDIENCE. You do not even have to know the name of this odd card.

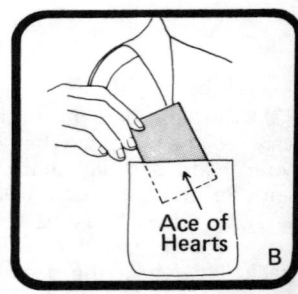

Ace of Hearts

METHOD

(1) To begin, spread the pack face down and ask a spectator to take a card, telling him that you will "teach" him how to do a trick. (In the illustrations, the selected card is marked with an "X," and we will assume that it is the Six of Spades.)

(2) While the spectator is looking at his card, square the pack and begin a regular HINDU SHUFFLE by drawing off half the pack in your left hand. Tell the spectator to replace his card (X) on that half of the pack.

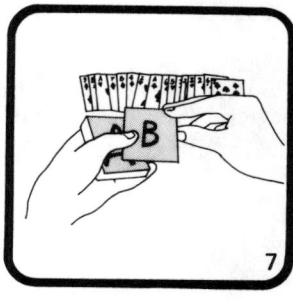

(3) Now, deliberately turn the right hand packet *face up,* SHOWING THE FOUR OF DIAMONDS (A) on the bottom of that packet. Say, "All you have to do in order to find any selected card is secretly note the bottom card of the upper packet before you place it on top of the selected card (X). The Four of Diamonds will be my secret "locator" card in this trick."

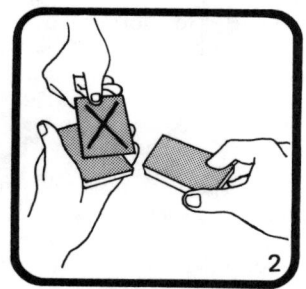

(4) Place the right-hand packet face down upon the left-hand packet. Call to the audience's attention that this places the "locator" card (A) next to the "spectator's" card (X). Remind the viewers that your "locator" card is the Four of Diamonds and tell them to watch for it as you deal the cards.

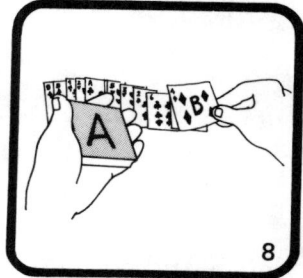

(5) Holding the pack in your left hand, begin dealing cards one at a time, (6) face up on the table, placing each card on the one before. You can do this rapidly at first . . .

(7) . . . then, *slow down as you near the center of the pack,* and continue dealing until you reach the FIRST Four of Diamonds (B). The other DUPLICATE Four (A) is just below it, *the top card of the packet you hold in your left hand.*

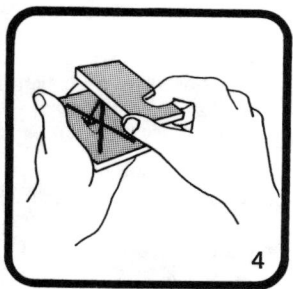

(8) When you turn over the FIRST Four of Diamonds (B), deal it on the row of face up cards, saying, "That's *my* locator card, the Four of Diamonds, which means *your* card is next."

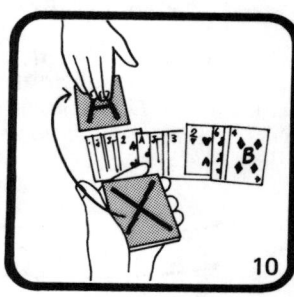

(9) *NOTE: UNKNOWN TO THE SPECTATOR, THE "NEXT" CARD IS THE DUPLICATE FOUR OF DIAMONDS (A), WHICH HE NATURALLY ASSUMES TO BE HIS CHOSEN CARD (X), SINCE HE SAW YOU PLACE THE FOUR OF DIAMONDS JUST ABOVE IT.*

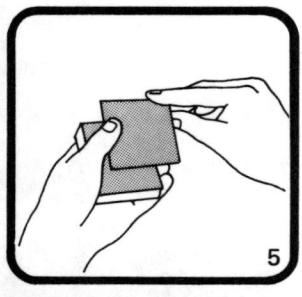

(10) Deal the top card (A) on the table in front of the spectator saying, "There is *your* card, just below the Four of Diamonds, so I want you to keep *your* hand on it." *HE DOES, NEVER SUSPECTING THAT INSTEAD OF HIS CARD (X) HE HAS THE DUPLICATE FOUR OF DIAMONDS (A).*

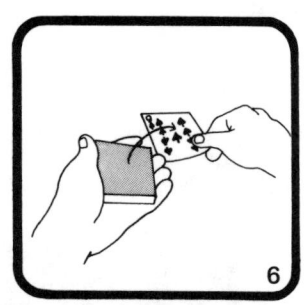

(11) Now, turn to *another* person and deal the *next card* (X) face down on the table in front of him. Tell him to put his hand on it. State that since NO ONE knows what this card is, you will call it the *"mystery card."* ACTUALLY, IT IS THE CARD CHOSEN BY THE FIRST SPECTATOR, THE SIX OF SPADES (X).

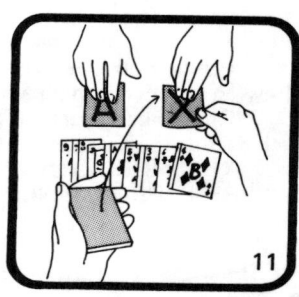

(12) Say to the first spectator, "You now have YOUR CARD, which YOU ALONE know." Turn to the second person and add, "And you have the MYSTERY CARD, which NOBODY KNOWS." Then, pick up the face-up Four of Diamonds (B) from the row saying, "Since EVERYBODY knows MY CARD, I'll put it in my pocket."

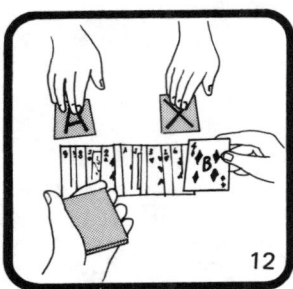

(15) "Wait! This isn't my card!" Turn to the first spectator and add, "It must be your card!" With that, turn the card face up, showing it to be an *indifferent card* – (as in the illustrations) the Ace of Hearts.

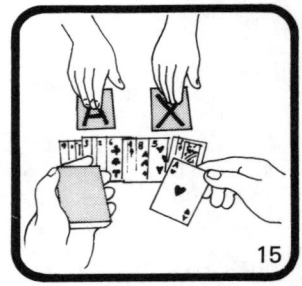

(13) With that, turn the back of *your* Four toward the spectators and slide it into your shirt pocket with your right hand.

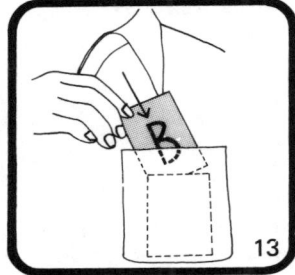

(16) Then have the spectator turn over his card. He finds, to his amazement, that instead of HIS chosen card (X) the Six of Spades, he has YOUR "locator" card, the Four of Diamonds (A). Say, "Why, that's my card! What was your card?"

(14) IN THE SAME MOVE, grip the indifferent card that you placed there beforehand and bring it out IMMEDIATELY. Glance at it with a puzzled frown and say,

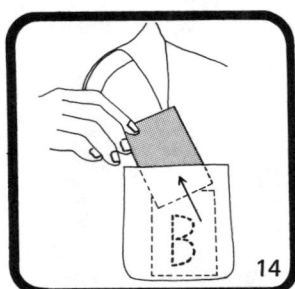

(17) The spectator will answer, "The Six of Spades." With that, turn to the *second* person and say, "Let's see your MYSTERY card that NOBODY knows!" He turns it over, revealing the *first* spectator's chosen card, the Six of Spades (X). THIS IS THE CARD WHOSE NAME THE FIRST SPECTATOR HAS JUST REVEALED FOR THE FIRST TIME ... WHICH, SO FAR AS HE KNEW, WAS KNOWN ONLY TO HIM ... and the climax is complete.

COMMENTS AND SUGGESTIONS

This is not *really* a three-way change, because only *two* cards, the one chosen by the first spectator and the card you showed as your "locator," *actually change places.* The fact that the second person's *"mystery card"* is missing and you come up with the *odd* card is sufficient to make it look like a magical "round robin."

Revealing the indifferent card IMMEDIATELY is very important because *before suspicion can be aroused,* you spring the twin surprises of the "locator" card *and* the selected card, both showing up where they don't belong. The cleverest part is that your duplicate "locator" (B), Four of Diamonds, is now safely hidden in your shirt pocket, leaving only a complete pack which can be examined by the spectators, enabling you to proceed with whatever other tricks you wish.

FLOURISHES

Fancy flourishes with cards date far back to the self-styled "Kard Kings" of the vaudeville era. Houdini himself had lithographs showing him performing a myriad of masterful card flourishes.

One thing is certain, card flourishes are sure to impress your audience. Whatever practice you give to such manipulations is time well spent. Your audience will recognize your skill and respect it.

THE MORE YOU PRACTICE THEM, THE MORE YOUR CARD WORK WILL IMPROVE IN GENERAL, MAKING YOUR ENTIRE PERFORMANCE MORE EFFECTIVE.

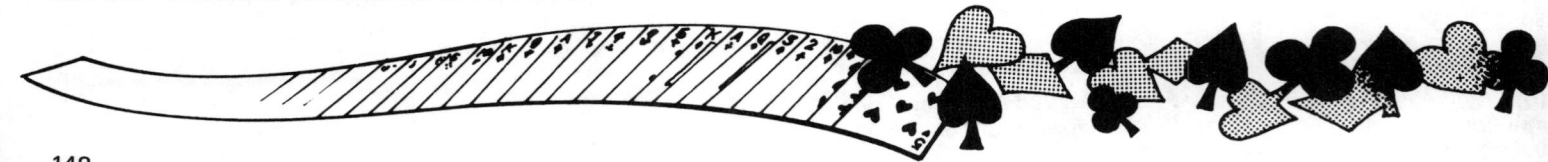

ONE-HAND CUT — BASIC METHOD

To many people, sign of a real card expert is the ability to "cut" a pack of cards using only one hand. It appears difficult, but it's really much easier than it looks. Try it and you'll see!

METHOD

(1) Hold the pack between the tips of your thumb and fingers as shown. Your first finger and little finger are at the opposite ends of the pack. Your other fingers and thumb are at the sides as shown. Be sure your thumb and fingers point *almost straight up.* Also, hold the deck at the *tips* of your fingers to form a deep "well" between the deck and the palm of your hand.

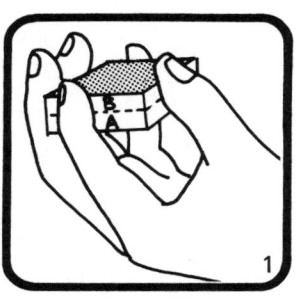

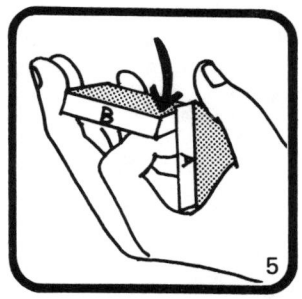

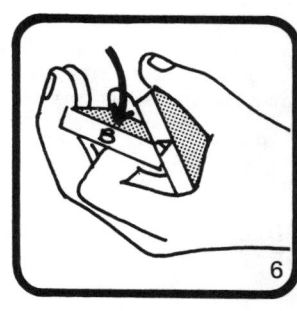

(2) To begin, bend your thumb just enough to let the *lower half* (which we will call Packet A) of the deck drop into the palm of your cupped hand. The upper half remains held between the tips of your thumb and your two middle fingers. (We will call this Packet B.) Your little finger will help to keep the cards from sliding out of your hand.

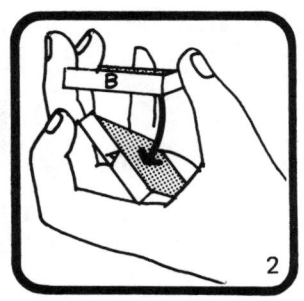

(5) Now, gently extend your fingers just enough to allow the edges of the two halves to clear so that your thumb releases Packet B which drops on top of your curled first finger. (6) By curling your first finger lower into your hand, Packet B will come down with it. *Packet B now becomes the lower half.*

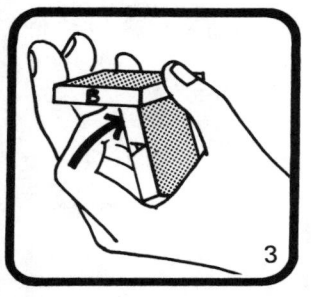

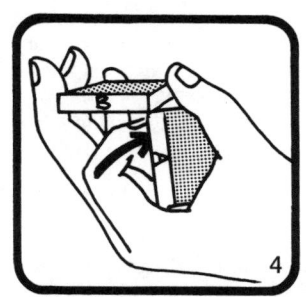

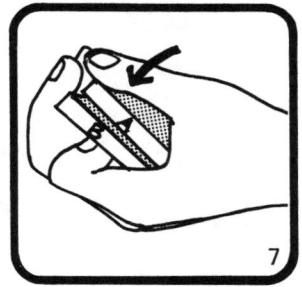

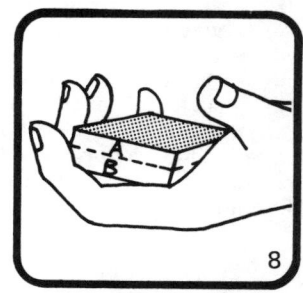

(3) Bring your first finger below the lower half, Packet A, and push the packet upward, sliding it along the bottom card of the upper half, Packet B. (4) Continue pushing the edge of the lower half, Packet A, *all the way up* to your thumb as shown.

(7) Slowly begin closing up your hand — bringing both halves together — with Packet A *on top* of Packet B. (8) Extend your first finger around the end of the pack, squaring the halves into place. YOU HAVE JUST DONE A ONE-HAND CUT!

ALL OF THE ILLUSTRATIONS ARE FROM THE AUDIENCE POINT OF VIEW WITH THE DECK HELD IN THE LEFT HAND.

COMMENTS AND SUGGESTIONS

Although this "Flourish" appears quite difficult, once you take the deck in your hand and follow the steps as shown in the pictures, you will find the ONE-HAND CUT quite easy to do. It is best, particularly when first learning, to use the narrow, Bridge-size cards rather than the wider Poker-size. After you have mastered the sleight, you may wish to try it with the larger cards. You can also then begin to practice the variations that follow.

ONE-HAND CUT — FIRST VARIATION

This is the first of two variations of the "ONE-HAND CUT — BASIC METHOD" enabling you to display your dexterity while also serving as a step toward other card manipulations involving the same basic sleight.

EFFECT

Holding a pack of cards in one hand, the magician starts a simple ONE-HAND CUT, but pauses during the early stage to turn it into a "three-way" cut. Steadily, he transposes the bottom, center, and top portions of the pack. This makes an impressive ornamental flourish when the three sections drop neatly into place.

METHOD

NOTE: In all ONE-HAND CUTS, you may hold the deck in either your right or your left hand, whichever is easier for you. ALL OF THE ILLUSTRATIONS ARE FROM THE SPECTATORS' VIEW WITH THE DECK HELD IN THE LEFT HAND.

(1) Begin by holding the pack in the same position as you did for the regular ONE-HAND CUT. Your first finger and little finger are at opposite ends of the pack; your two middle fingers and thumb are at the sides. Be sure that your fingers and thumb point "up" or slightly to the "right" if this is easier for you. Also be certain, as before, that you have formed a deep "well" between the deck and the palm of your hand.

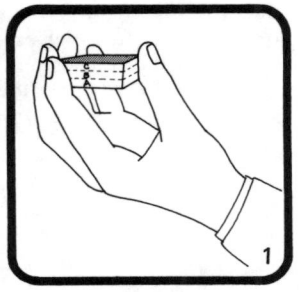

(2) Unlike the regular ONE-HAND CUT — where the pack is cut into two *equal* sections — in this modified version, begin by bending your thumb just enough to let the *lower third* (Packet A) of the deck drop into your cupped hand. Your little finger will help to keep the cards from sliding out of your hand.

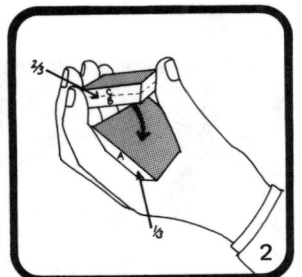

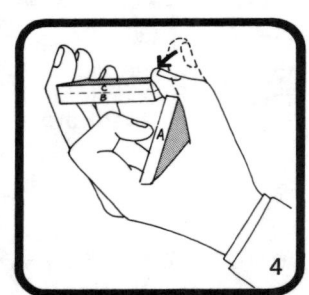

(3) Bring your first finger *below* Packet A and begin pushing its edge *upward* toward your thumb as shown. (4) Continue pushing Packet A all the way up to your left thumb. The top edge of Packet A will contact your thumb near the "bend" of the first joint of the thumb.

(5) *NOTE: Your hand now holds the bulk of the deck (the remaining two-thirds) between the tip of the thumb and your fingers — while the bottom third of the deck (Packet A) is held between the "bend" of your thumb and the palm of your hand as shown in Step 4.*

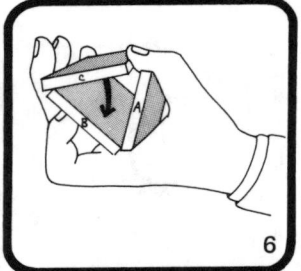

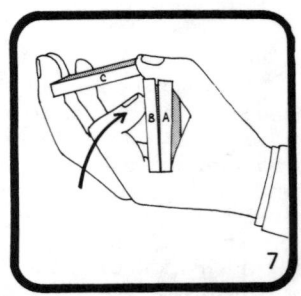

(6) With the cards held firmly in this position, relax the tip of your left thumb allowing *another third of the deck,* Packet B (the middle third), to *drop* from the bulk of the pack *into your cupped hand.* (7) Once again, bring your first finger below Packet B and push it upwards toward your thumb until it is all the way *up against the bottom of Packet A.* The remaining third of the deck, Packet C, is still being held by the tips of your thumb and fingers as shown.

(8) Now, release your thumb tip from Packet C and allow its top to clear the top edge of Packets A and B. *You can help the packets to clear by pushing the bottom of Packet B with your first finger.* Packet C will come down with it into your palm. *Packet C now becomes the LOWER THIRD of the pack.*

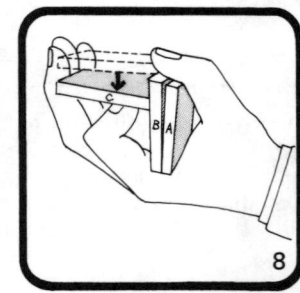

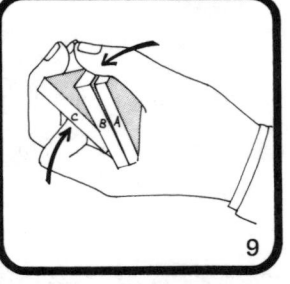

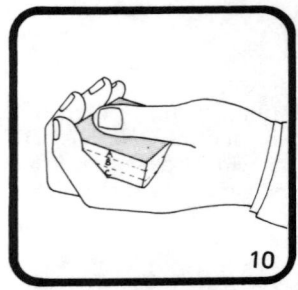

(9) Now, slowly begin closing up your hand, bringing all three sections together to complete the cut. (10) Finally, extend your first finger around the end of the pack and square the deck as the sections settle into place. You have just executed the ONE-HAND CUT — FIRST VARIATION.

COMMENTS AND SUGGESTIONS

Practice this flourish with a narrow, Bridge-sized pack, as it is much easier to handle than the wider "Poker" deck. Later, you can switch to the wider size if your fingers are long enough to handle it easily. *The dropping of the center section, Packet B, is the vital point,* because your thumb must hold both Packets A and C in place until your first finger releases Packet B. If Packet A should accidentally drop during that maneuver, that's OK — just let it fall on top of Packet B and complete what would then be a slightly different "cut" than you had originally planned.

THE ONE-HAND CUT — SECOND VARIATION

This is another variation of the ONE-HAND CUT that can be used interchangeably with the one already described. The two cuts can also be worked in combination, starting with one, and ending with the other, all in the same sequence.

EFFECT

In this triple cut, the magician divides the lower section into two packets and lets the upper third drop in between. This can be repeated several times, either in slow motion, or at a rapid speed once the knack is acquired. Either way, it increases the audience's admiration of the magician's skill.

METHOD

(1) In the usual One-Hand Cut style, hold the pack between the tips of the thumb and fingers of either hand. The first finger and little finger are at opposite ends of the pack, the other fingers and thumb are at the sides. Be sure the fingers point straight up (or nearly straight up if this is easier for you). Just be sure to form a deep well between the deck and the palm of your hand.

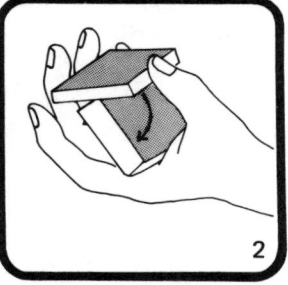

(4) *Here your left thumb retains hold of HALF of the bulk of the pack* as you begin to open your first finger, *allowing the other half to DROP BACK DOWN into your hand.*

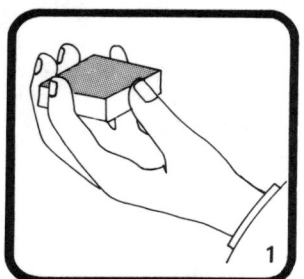

(2) To begin, bend the thumb just enough to let the lower *two-thirds* of the pack drop into the cupped hand. The little finger will help to keep the cards from sliding out of your hand.

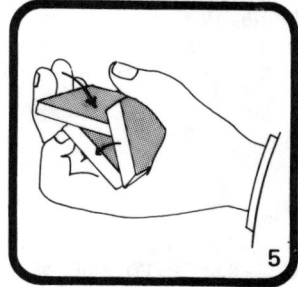

(5) As the packet falls into your hand, relax the grip of the tip of your thumb on the top third of the pack, and *allow it to fall into the hand BETWEEN the two packets already formed.*

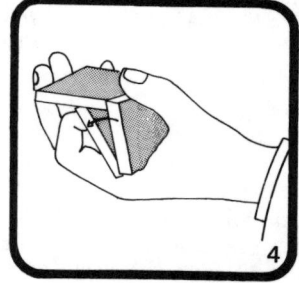

(3) Bring your first finger *below* the bulk of the pack and push its edge upward, *sliding it along the bottom of the upper third of the pack.* Continue pushing the lower section all the way up to the ball of the thumb as shown.

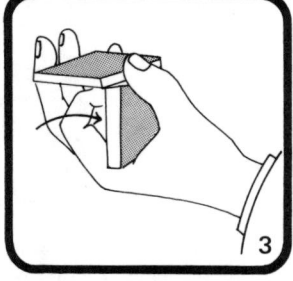

(6) Slowly begin closing up your hand *bringing all three packets* together to complete the cut. Finally, extend your first finger around the end of the pack and square the pack as the three packets settle into place. You have just done the ONE-HAND CUT, SECOND VARIATION.

COMMENTS AND SUGGESTIONS

Along with serving as an ornamental flourish, this variation of the ONE-HAND CUT fulfills a useful purpose. With it, you can "bury" the top card of the pack somewhere in the middle of the deck. Then, as you call attention to that fact, the audience doesn't realize that the bottom card remains the same and can, therefore, be used as a "key" in a trick that follows.

THE ONE-HAND CUT — SECOND METHOD

In this "ONE-HAND CUT," the technique is somewhat different from those already given, as the pack is held in an entirely new position to start. This forms an interesting contrast to the previous methods, which, in itself, is a good reason why you should include it among your "Flourishes."

EFFECT

Holding the pack upright in the crook of his thumb, the magician cuts the lower third into the tips of his fingers, bringing both sections upright with a wide space between. He then cuts another section of the pack from his left thumb and "folds" the lower third between it and the top packet. This completes a very neat *triple* cut in which all three sections of the pack go into action almost simultaneously, having a very strong effect upon the observers.

METHOD

(1) The pack is held upright in the left hand. One edge of the pack is held by the *ball and first joint of your left thumb* and the other edge is *wedged deeply into the palm* at the very base of the thumb. NOTE: STEPS 1 AND 2 ARE SHOWN FROM THE SPECTATORS' VIEWPOINT.

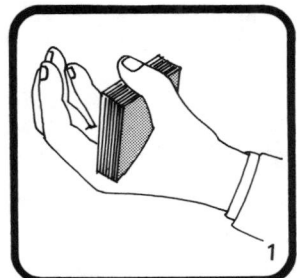

(2) With the pack held firmly in this position, curl the left fingers up against the face of the pack, *except for the second finger which is brought OVER the top edge of the deck next to the thumb.* With the second finger in this position, draw away the *lower third* of the pack as shown.

(3) HERE IS THE SAME ACTION AS SEEN FROM YOUR VIEWPOINT. Note that, as the second finger draws its packet away from the bulk of the pack, the other fingers are curled against the face of the pack. We will call this Packet A.

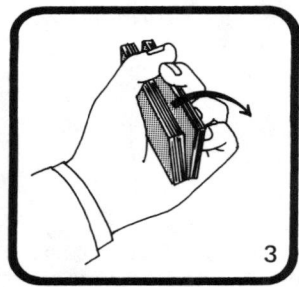

(4) Pull Packet A all the way down against the curled fingers and then . . .

(5) . . .GRIP PACKET A BETWEEN THE SECOND FINGER ON TOP AND THE FIRST AND THIRD FINGERS UNDERNEATH. Slowly begin to straighten out the left fingers, lifting Packet A upwards, swinging it out from beneath the bulk of the pack. This is a view of the completed action from your viewpoint. *Packet A is now held firmly between the second finger and the first and third fingers. Meanwhile, the bulk of the pack is still held tightly in position by the left thumb.*

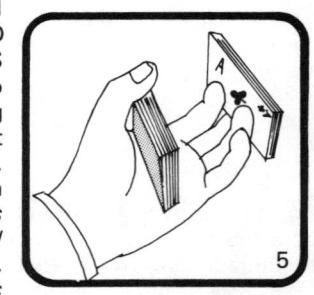

(6) Now relax the left thumb enough to allow *half* of the pack it holds (Packet B) *to fall into your hand* as shown. THE ILLUSTRATION IS FROM YOUR POINT OF VIEW.

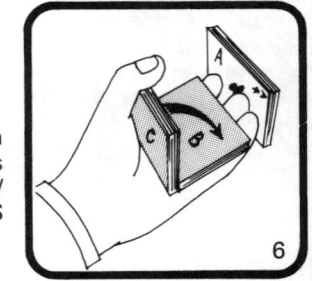

(7) Curl the left fingers inwards, placing Packet A on top of Packet B.

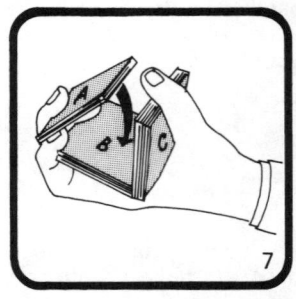

(8) Now begin to close up your hand. *Bring the cards held by the thumb (Packet C) down onto the rest of Packet A . . .*

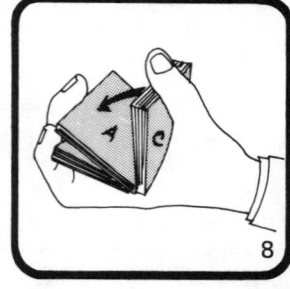

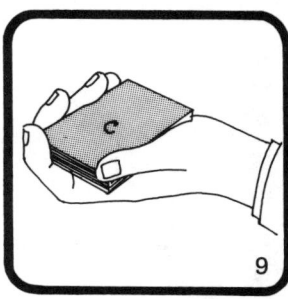

(9) ... at the same time, extend the fingers of your left hand allowing the three packets to settle into one place. You have just completed ONE-HAND CUT — SECOND METHOD.

COMMENTS AND SUGGESTIONS

A BRIDGE-SIZE PACK is highly helpful for this cut, as the thumb has a "long stretch" to hold the pack upright in the crook of the thumb. The narrow Bridge-size pack is also helpful in supplying the space needed *between* the first two packets (A and B) when they are levered apart. In this form of the One-Hand Cut the *bottom* card is buried into the pack, while the *top* card remains in place. In this way, it differs from the previous version where the *bottom* card remains in place.

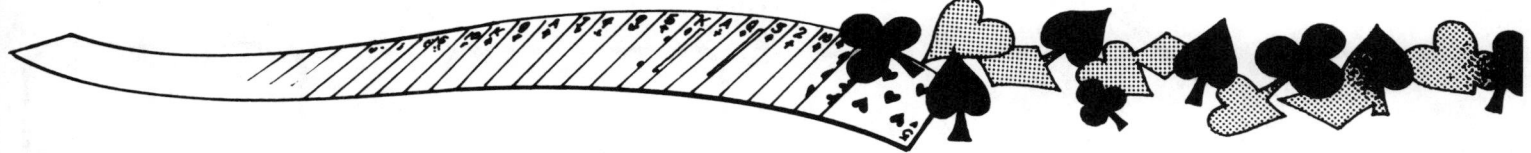

SPREADING THE CARDS — THE RIBBON SPREAD

EFFECT

In the performance of card tricks, it is often necessary to spread the entire pack of cards across the table so all of their backs or faces are visible to the spectators. The following describes the method for executing a "Ribbon Spread" which looks very nice and demonstrates your ability to handle cards skillfully.

METHOD

NOTE: The Ribbon Spread is difficult to do on a slick or hard surface. However, it is quite easy on a soft, textured surface such as a felt top table, a rug, a heavy table cloth or the magician's "Close Up Mat."

(1) Place the deck on the table face down slightly bevelled at the side of the deck as shown.

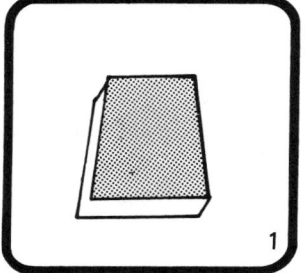

(3) Now with a slight downward pressure of the hand, move your arm and hand to the right. The cards will begin to spread apart evenly FROM THE BOTTOM OF THE PACK as you slide the bulk of the pack along the table.

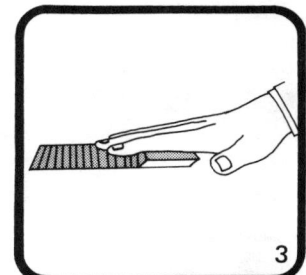

(2) Lay all four fingers of your right hand across the top of the pack, with the tips of the fingers extending over the bevelled edge.

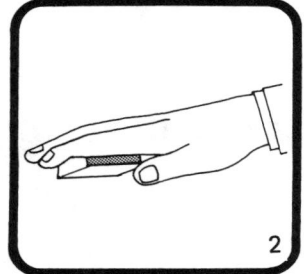

(4) Continue this sliding motion releasing cards from the bottom of the pack until all of the cards are evenly spread in a "ribbon pattern" along the table.

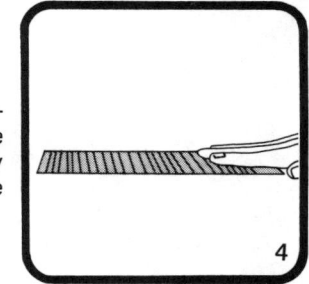

COMMENTS AND SUGGESTIONS

In practicing the Ribbon Spread, be sure you have a soft surface and remember that the sliding motion of the hand must be smooth and unbroken in order to achieve even spacing between the individual cards. The motion should not be done too slowly either. A moderately fast movement is most effective for the best results. As always, *PRACTICE* is the key to success.

RIBBON SPREAD TURNOVER

This is an ideal flourish to use when doing card tricks at a table. Though easily learned, it gives the impression that you are displaying great skill. Always take advantage of such opportunities . . . they create a lasting impression on the audience regarding your work. It's all part of the game called MAGIC.

EFFECT

The magician takes an ordinary pack of cards and spreads them in an even row *face down* along the table. Then, by *tilting up* one end of the spread, HE CAUSES THE ENTIRE ROW OF CARDS TO TURN *face up!*

METHOD

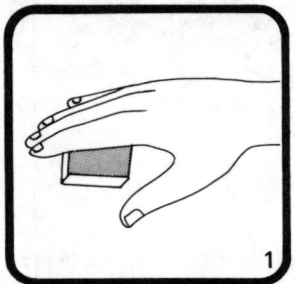 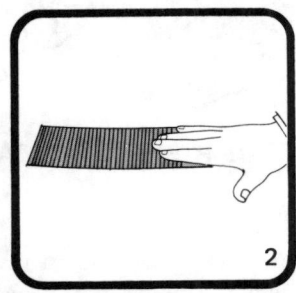  

(1) Set the pack *face down* on the table in preparation for the RIBBON SPREAD. (2) RIBBON SPREAD the pack from left to right as described earlier. *The cards in the spread must be evenly spaced. . . . Any "gaps" or "breaks" in the spread will disrupt the TURNOVER.*

(5) Rotate the card on its edge until it turns over (face up) *causing all of the cards above it to "follow the leader" as they begin to TURN OVER in sequence.* (6) The TURNOVER will progress throughout the spread until *all of the cards* are FACE UP, as shown.

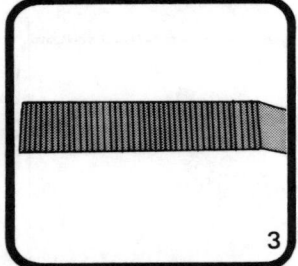 

(3) The completed spread should look like this . . . *until the TURNOVER.* (4) Now, with your left fingers, raise the *outer edge* of the card on the *left end* of the spread . . . tilting it "up" on its edge as shown.

COMMENTS AND SUGGESTIONS

This is the "basic" TURNOVER. A rather easy and most impressive flourish. To add even more to your display of skill, you can incorporate the two following variations.

REVERSE TURNOVER

After completing the TABLE SPREAD TURNOVER, you may immediately reverse the procedure as follows:

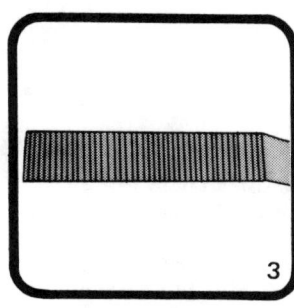

(1) With your *right hand,* lift the card at the far *right end* of the now face-up spread. Using this card as the "pusher" card, pivot it on its edge... (2) ...causing the cards to repeat the TURNOVER... (3) ...this time back to their original *face-down* position.

COMMENTS AND SUGGESTIONS

By placing your left hand at the left end of the spread and your right hand at the right end of the spread, you can "flip-flop" the cards back and forth as they TURN OVER in rotation — first, *face up* — then, *face down* — making not only a remarkable display of skill, but also a very pretty picture.

TURNOVER CONTROL

This is another even more intriguing use of the TURNOVER, which is particularly good when used *between* effects in your card routine. This is also a most spectacular way of showing that the deck is "ordinary" . . . composed of "all different" cards.

METHOD

(1) First remove any card from the deck and place it on the table. Then perform Steps 1 through 5 in the RIBBON SPREAD TURNOVER. When the cards have "turned" to approximately the middle of the spread, pick up the card you removed and hold it, as shown, in your right hand. This card will be used to "control" the sequence of the TURNOVER in the following manner:

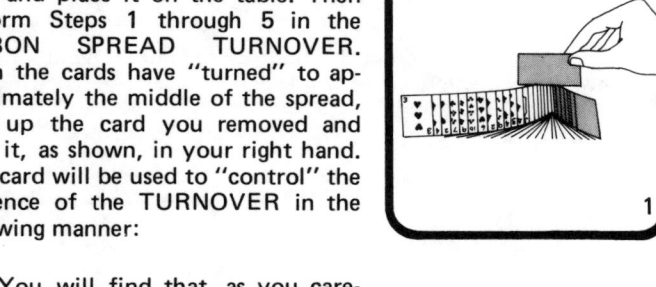

(2) You will find that, as you carefully touch the *edge* of the single card in your right hand to the "peak" of the TURNOVER, you can very easily "control" the sequence and direction of the TURNOVER. For instance, you can now *reverse* the TURNOVER by moving the single card *back to the left* as shown. *As you move the card to the left, keep the edge of the card touching the new, constantly changing "peak."* This can be done back and forth as often as you wish, as long as the cards remain evenly spread on the table.

(3) The single card is then used to "control" the TURNOVER all the way over to the *right end* of the spread . . . where the cards will fall *face up* . . . as they did at the conclusion of the regular RIBBON SPREAD TURNOVER.

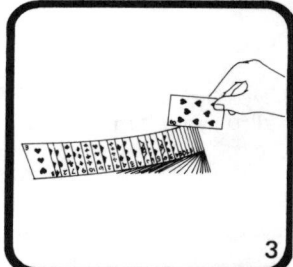

TURNOVER PICK-UP

A *spectacular conclusion* to the TURNOVER can be accomplished by using the single card that you have used to "control" the rotation of the cards as follows:

METHOD

(1) As you control the TURNOVER to the right end of the spread with the single card, just before the last card in the spread "flops" to the table, quickly insert the "control" card *between* the falling spread and the table as shown.

(2) Then, *use the card as a "scoop,"* along with the fingers of your right hand to *gather up all of the cards in the spread* as shown. At the conclusion of this "pick-up," the entire deck will be face up in your right hand. A fitting conclusion to a spectacular series of flourishes!

COMMENTS AND SUGGESTIONS

As mentioned, all of the four TURNOVER flourishes depend upon the initial table spread of the cards being *evenly spaced,* without any breaks or gaps. Thus, you must first learn to do the RIBBON SPREAD well before adding these very effective extra touches. The combination of the RIBBON SPREAD . . . the RIBBON SPREAD TURNOVER . . . the REVERSE TURNOVER . . . the TURNOVER CONTROL . . . and concluding with the TURNOVER PICK-UP, is easily learned with a relatively small amount of practice. It is quite spectacular and can be used to attract attention, as well as to display your skill as a card manipulator. One final word: As emphasized in the RIBBON SPREAD, the surface on which the SPREAD TURNOVER is best presented is one which is *soft* and has a "texture," such as a tablecloth, felt table top, a blanket, or, ideally, a Magician's Close-Up Mat. This type of surface enables you to spread the cards evenly. It also keeps the cards in place so they will not slip as they rotate "over" during the TURNOVER.

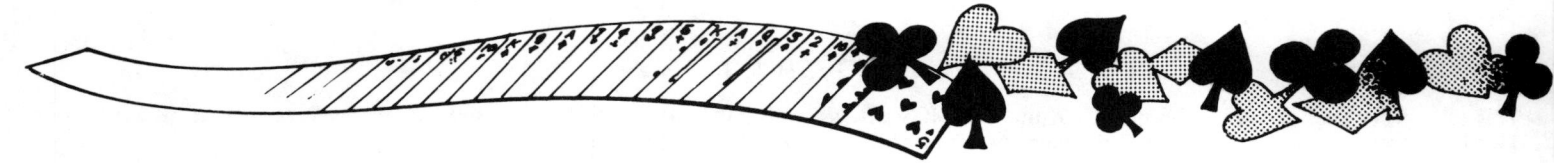

PRESSURE FAN

Giving your performance a professional look should be a primary aim when taking up card magic. Shuffles and cuts should all be done smoothly and neatly, as a prelude to fancier moves. This applies specifically to the PRESSURE FAN, which follows.

EFFECT

Holding the pack squared in one hand, the magician deftly spreads it in a circular fashion across the fingers of his other hand — finally displaying it in a broad "fan" — with the index corners of the cards showing evenly throughout its colorful span.

METHOD

(1) Hold the pack by the ends between the tips of the right thumb and fingers. Your thumb is at the center of the lower end and your first, second and third fingers are across the upper end as shown. Your little finger rests lightly on the side of the deck.

(3) To begin the fan, squeeze the fingers of your right hand downward, BENDING THE CARDS OVER THE LEFT FOREFINGER.

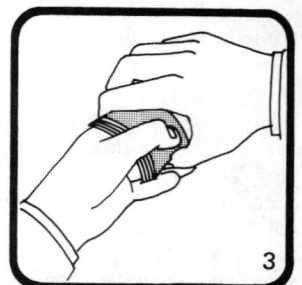

(2) With the cards HELD FIRMLY IN THE RIGHT HAND, place the pack *against the fingers of the left hand* in the position shown. The ball of the left thumb rests at the middle of the lower end of the pack. *NOTE: The right hand is* <u>not</u> *shown in the drawing in order to show more clearly the exact position in which the pack is* HELD AGAINST THE LEFT HAND BY THE RIGHT HAND.

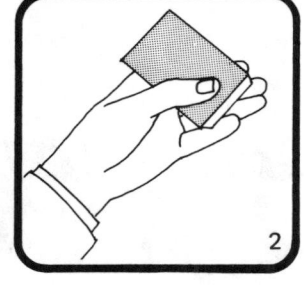

(4) This is the spectator's view as you begin the fan.

(5) Then IN ONE CONTINUOUS MOTION – allow the cards to start "springing" from the right fingertips as the right hand begins to rotate the pack to the right. The left thumb acts as a pivot point holding the lower left corner of the pack.

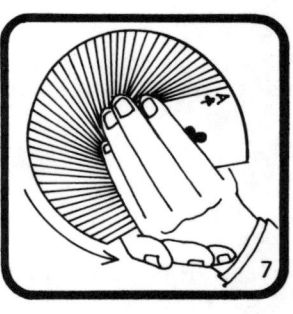

(7) . . . as you continue to "spring release" cards in succession until the fan is complete. This action is shown from the point of view of the audience.

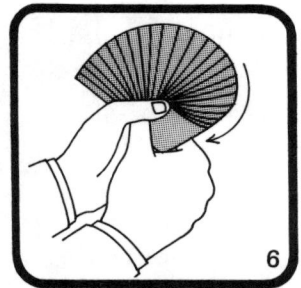

(6) Continue the CIRCULAR MOTION of the right hand *around* the tips of the left fingers and *down* the side of the left hand. . .

(8) There is only one secret in making a good Pressure Fan, and that is – PRACTICE. First attempts at making the Fan may be very discouraging – the cards may "bunch up" and not spread far enough or evenly, or they may even "spring" completely out of your hands! But, little by little, you will eventually get the knack of making an evenly spaced, beautiful fan. Most importantly, remember that a good Pressure Fan is accomplished by a *rapid, unbroken, sweeping* motion of the right hand – and PRACTICE is the answer!

COMMENTS AND SUGGESTIONS

The amount of pressure necessary to make the fan depends considerably upon the pack you are using. A brand new, high-quality pack can be fanned with a light touch but will need more "bending" pressure by the right thumb and fingers. With a new, "clean" deck, the cards are smooth enough to spread evenly and stiff enough to resist pressure. The more a pack is shuffled and used, the more flexible it becomes, and the pressure must be *decreased* proportionately. Also, as the deck is "soiled," it becomes more and more difficult to get the cards evenly spaced.

CLOSING THE FAN – TWO-HAND METHOD

All of the illustrations are from the spectators' viewpoint.

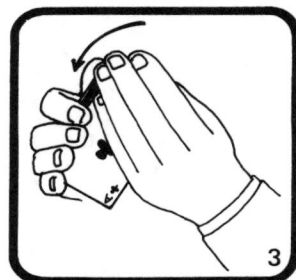

(1) To close the fan, curl the tips of your right fingers around the extreme left edge of the fan as shown. (2) Then, in one continuous motion, sweep your right hand in an arc around the left fingers causing the cards to start to collect against the fingers of your right hand. (3) Continue to sweep the fan closed until all the cards have gathered together into a single packet, thus completing the procedure.

CLOSING THE FAN — ONE-HAND METHOD

The simple action of closing the PRESSURE FAN can be as impressive as the fan itself — particularly when executed *without the aid of the other hand,* as described below.

METHOD

(1) Begin by forming a Pressure Fan as described earlier. The four fingers should be flat against the face of the pack with the thumb pressing inwards at the pivot point on the back of the fan.

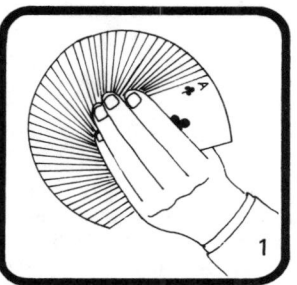

(3) With a slight amount of pressure from your left first finger on the face card of the deck, begin to push your finger in a circular motion . . . upwards and to the right . . . as you slowly begin to close the fan.

(2) To close the fan, shift your left first finger so that its fingertip rests on the face of the first card AS CLOSE TO THE OUTER EDGE OF THE FAN AS POSSIBLE.

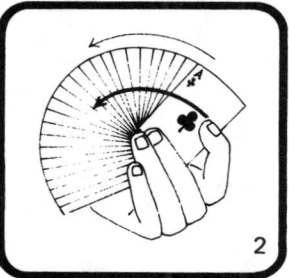

(4) Continue pushing the fan closed and open the remaining fingers of the left hand when necessary, allowing the first finger to sweep the cards downward as they collect in succession against the heel of the hand until the fan is closed.

THE ONE-HAND FAN

Though basically a Card "Flourish," this is also a useful move in connection with various tricks. That makes two good reasons why you should practice it, as each will add a professional touch to your work.

EFFECT

Holding a pack of cards face front between the thumb and fingers of the right hand, the magician, with one deft move, instantly spreads the pack in a broad fan, showing the index corners of the cards in colorful fashion. Closing the fan and turning the pack over, he fans them again, showing the backs spread evenly, allowing a spectator to select a card — an excellent opening move for many card effects.

METHOD

(1) Hold the pack in your right hand with your thumb on the face of the pack and your fingers flat against the back. Position your thumb at the lower right-hand corner of the pack as shown.

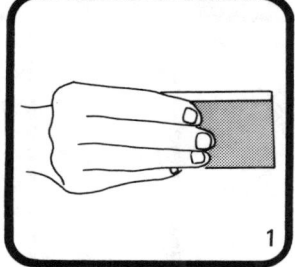

(3) Now in one smooth, continuous motion, start to *slide your thumb upwards. AT THE SAME TIME, curl your fingers inwards and downwards,* as the pack begins to spread out in the form of a fan.

(2) Here is a view of the pack from the other side. Notice that your fingers only cover half of the length of the pack.

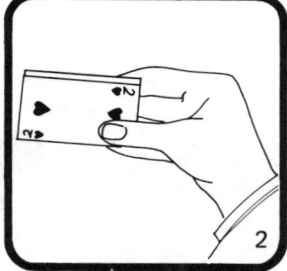

(4) Continue sliding your thumb upwards as the fingers continue pushing the cards in a sort of "smearing" motion down the heel of the hand until they curl into the palm....almost forming a fist with the cards held tightly between. When your thumb and fingers have reached this position, the fan should be fully formed as shown.

(5) NOTE: Your *fingers* are responsible for forming the *lower half* of the fan and the *thumb* is responsible for forming the *upper half*. DO NOT BE DISAPPOINTED IF YOU CANNOT MASTER THE ONE-HAND FAN IMMEDIATELY. Careful practice will teach you exactly how much pressure to exert with the thumb and fingers in order for the cards to distribute properly from the top and bottom of the pack, forming an evenly spaced fan.

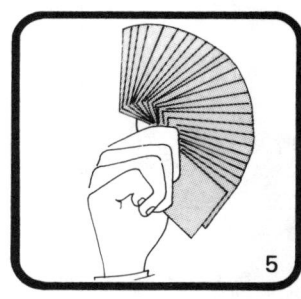

(6) Here is a view of the completed fan from the other side. Notice the right fingers have curled into the palm of the hand to form a fist.

COMMENTS AND SUGGESTIONS

In tricks where you are using half a pack or less, fanning is just as effective as with a full pack, as all the cards in the half-packet can be spread out evenly and more of each card will show. Even when doing a trick with only a few cards — such as the Four Aces — using a ONE-HAND FAN to show their faces has a striking effect and adds to your style as a performer. You may also wish to learn the fan with both hands. Then, by splitting the deck and holding half in each hand, the *two* fans will form a truly spectacular display.

SPRINGING THE CARDS

This fancy flourish is the basis for many other flourishes with a pack of cards. It is one that should be practiced first on a limited scale (springing the cards only a short distance) with a pack that can be handled easily and comfortably. Then, you can gradually increase the scope of this manipulation.

EFFECT

The magician holds a pack of cards lengthwise between his thumb and fingers. By applying steady pressure on the pack, he causes all the cards in the pack to "spring" in succession from one hand to the other — in mid-air! This has a very impressive effect upon the audience, as the cards form a colorful cascade that can cover a surprising distance.

METHOD

(1) Hold the pack lengthwise in your right hand . . . with your thumb at the lower end and your first, second, and third fingers at the upper end. The pack should be held close to the tips of the fingers as shown.

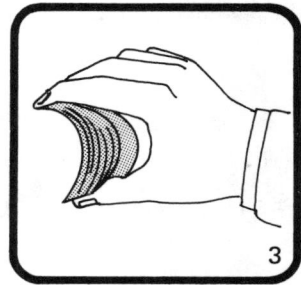

(3) With the pack held firmly in your right hand, squeeze your thumb and fingers together, bending the cards inwards toward the palm of your hand and move the right hand about three inches above the "cupped" left hand.

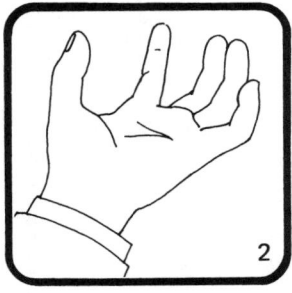

(2) Your left hand is held palm up with the fingers spread wide — pointing upward. This forms a sort of "trap" to catch the cards as they cascade from the right hand into the left.

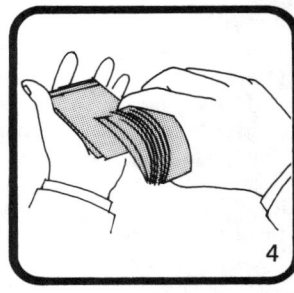

(4) Continue to squeeze the pack inwards as you begin to RELEASE THE CARDS FROM THE TIPS OF YOUR RIGHT FINGERS sending them springing, one by one, from the right hand into the awaiting left hand.

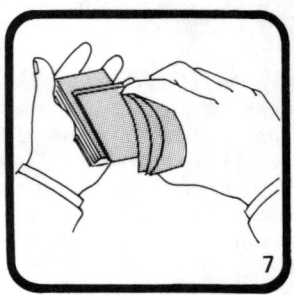

(5) *NOTE: The left hand should be positioned so that, as the cards arrive in the hand, the outer ends of the cards hit the* <u>*left first fingers*</u> *... which prevents them from shooting out of the hand onto the floor.*

(7) When the bulk of the pack has arrived in the left hand and only a few cards remain in the right, move your right hand toward your left hand, gathering all the cards in between to conclude the flourish.

(6) As the cards start to "spring" from one hand to the other, GRADUALLY BEGIN DRAWING YOUR RIGHT HAND FARTHER AWAY — a few inches at first — then more and more. No matter what distance you will eventually achieve, ALWAYS BEGIN WITH THE TWO HANDS CLOSE TOGETHER. Then, draw the right hand away as the cards "spring" into your left hand.

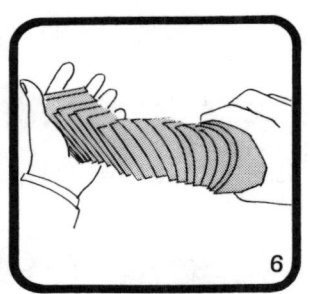

COMMENTS AND SUGGESTIONS

In first practicing the "spring," place your left hand just below your right hand and spring the pack for a distance of only a few inches. Your purpose is to gain the knack of springing the cards smoothly and evenly without losing any of them. Once you learn to release the cards in an even stream, <u>with practice</u> you can then spread your hands a foot or so apart. When you first practice, it is best to use <u>soft, flexible cards</u> ... an "old" used deck works well.

It is also a good idea to practice over a bed, as a certain amount of failure is inevitable at first. One final suggestion: If you swing your body from left to right during the "spring," the distance effect between your hands is further exaggerated, *creating the illusion* that the cards cover a distance of eighteen inches to two feet.

ARM SPREAD CATCH

One of the most spectacular of card flourishes, this also appears to be one of the most difficult. Proper technique, attention to detail, and a reasonable amount of practice combine toward impressive results in this special branch of magic that blends juggling with wizardry.

EFFECT

The magician spreads a pack of cards lengthwise along his left arm from the base of his fingers to his elbow. With the cards neatly set in place, he gives his arm an upward toss and *at the same time,* makes a long, inward sweep with his right hand, "SCOOPING UP" THE ENTIRE PACK OF CARDS IN MID-AIR WITHOUT DROPPING A SINGLE CARD.

METHOD

(1) Hold the pack in your right hand, with the thumb at one end and the fingers at the other. Extend your left arm, palm up, and hold the pack slightly above the fingers of the left hand. Bend the entire pack inwards toward the right palm (this is the same "bending" by the right hand as in "SPRINGING THE CARDS").

(2) Slowly begin to release the cards from the *tips* of the right fingers onto the left hand ... and, AT THE SAME TIME, move your right hand down the length of your left arm. The cards should begin forming an even spread along the left arm.

Arm Spread Catch - Cont'd.

(3) Continue releasing the cards from the fingertips along the left arm until *all* the cards have been spread. With practice you can attain a spread which extends from the tips of the left fingers to the elbow.

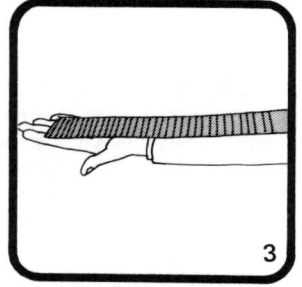

(6) With an upward lifting and tossing motion of the left arm, *gently throw the entire spread of cards into the air* as shown.

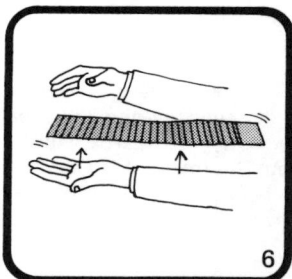

(4) *NOTE: After the cards are spread along the arm, it is necessary to keep the arm VERY STILL to keep the cards from falling.*

(7) WITHOUT HESITATION, and in ONE CONTINUOUS MOVEMENT, swing your entire body to the left and, with a long sweeping motion of the right hand, begin gathering or "scooping up" the cards *in mid-air* from one end of the spread to the other.

(5) With the cards neatly set in place, position your "cupped" right hand near the left fingertips, at the beginning of the spread, in readiness to catch the cards.

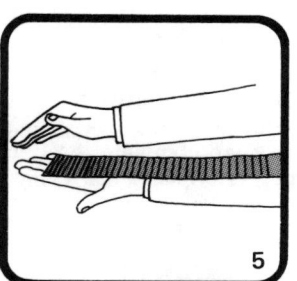

(8) With practice you should be able to catch the entire pack without any cards falling to the floor. At first, practice the Arm Spread Catch using a half-pack and a shorter arm spread. Then, gradually add more cards until you can perform the flourish with a full pack, spread from the tips of the fingers to the elbow.

COMMENTS AND SUGGESTIONS

In early trials, as you practice "springing" the cards along the arm, the spread may prove too irregular for an "effective catch." In that case, simply lower the left arm rapidly and let the pack slide down into the cupped left hand. This is a neat manipulation in itself, so you can use it as a preliminary "warm-up" before the catch.

THE WATERFALL

EFFECT

The magician grasps the entire pack in his right hand with his left hand cupped beneath it. Skillfully, he begins to release the cards in rapid succession, causing them to cascade downward, one at a time like a "Waterfall" into his waiting left hand. The flourish reaches its conclusion after the entire pack has made its impressive journey through the air into the magician's left hand.

METHOD

(1) Grasp and hold the deck lengthwise in your right hand with your thumb at one end of the pack and your four fingers at the other end. Your right fingers and thumb should be straight with only the edges of the top card touching your right hand.

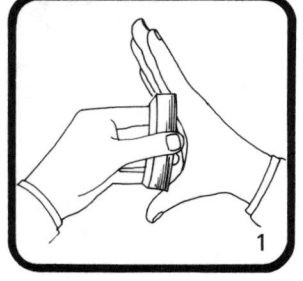

(2) *Keeping your fingers and thumb straight,* slowly squeeze them together so that the cards bend *inward* toward your right palm. This action is very similar to Springing the Cards except here, the object is to get a small amount of space between each and every card as you hold the pack.

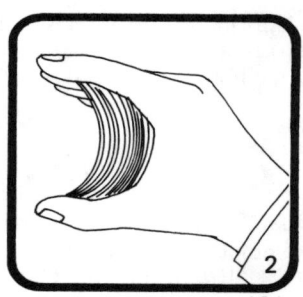

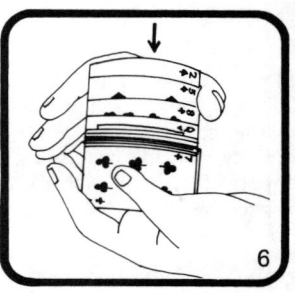

(3) The special grip described here allows the ends of the cards to "spread" *along the length* of your thumb and fingers. Done correctly, the cards should "fill up" all the open space between your thumb and fingers. Careful practice will teach you just how to bend the pack to secure this small gap between the individual cards.

(6) At the same time, move your left hand *downward* as the cards continue to fall from your right hand. If you release the cards in an even flow, they will resemble a Waterfall as they cascade from one hand to the other.

(4) With the cards held in this manner, you are ready to begin the Waterfall. Position your cupped left hand directly below your right hand in readiness to receive the cards as they fall. The illustration shows the proper position of both hands at the beginning of the flourish. *This and all the following steps are shown from the audience point of view.*

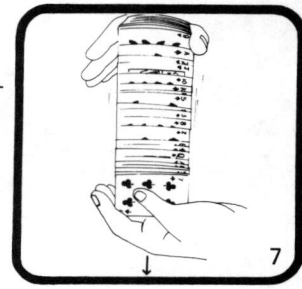

(7) *To achieve maximum distance between your hands, move your right hand up a few inches at the same time you move your left hand down. With practice you can attain a Waterfall of eight to twelve inches — or even longer.*

(5) Slowly begin to spread open your right thumb and fingers — releasing the cards in succession *from the face of the pack.* This action causes the cards to fall into the left hand in an even flow.

(8) When nearly all cards have been released from your right hand, quickly move your hands back together, squaring up the cards, to complete the flourish. You are now prepared to repeat the Waterfall as many times as you wish. Your audience will be more than convinced that you possess great skill as a card manipulator.

COMMENTS AND SUGGESTIONS

The real secret of the Waterfall is *your intial grip on the pack* shown in Step 1 and Step 2. The cards must be spread evenly along your thumb and fingers. At the start, practice the flourish with your hands very close together. Then, as you begin to acquire the "knack" necessary to release the cards in an even stream, move your hands farther apart. When selecting cards to use for this flourish, it is a good idea to experiment with different decks. Choose cards which bend easily enough for you to space them evenly in your hand. If you practice this flourish with a deck that suits you well, you will be pleased at the progress you will make in achieving a perfect "Waterfall" effect.

THROWING A CARD

Many famous magicians, most notably Herrmann, Thurston, and Raymond, have intrigued audiences throughout the world with their ability at "Scaling" cards to the highest balconies of the largest theaters. How far you can go toward achieving a similar result will depend upon how much practice you are willing to devote to this very impressive flourish.

EFFECT

Upon concluding his card routine, the magician offers several cards for examination by "Scaling" them across the room to different members of the audience. This is done in a smooth, graceful manner, sending the cards skimming into the air while the audience watches in amazement as they whiz by.

METHOD

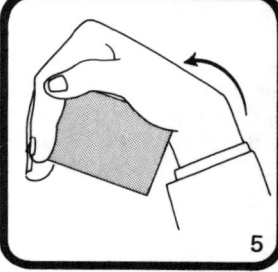

(1) Holding the card in the proper "throwing position" is essential in attaining effective results. There are two "correct" positions and you should try them both to see which works best for you. (The other "optional" holding position will be described in the next effect.)

(4) Start by bending *all four fingers inward,* until the lower right edge of the card touches the heel of your hand. This is shown from above.

(2) To place the card in the first position, clip the very end of the card between the first and second fingers of your right hand as shown. Do not allow the card to "droop," but hold it firmly so that it is level with the fingers at all times.

(5) In the same movement, *bend your wrist inward,* toward yourself, as far as it will go.

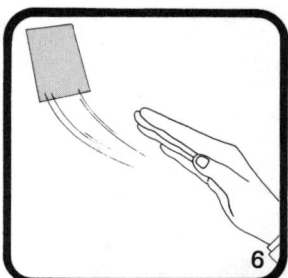

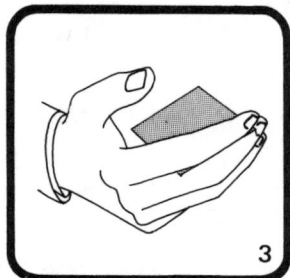

(3) Here is the card held in proper "throwing position" as seen from the spectator's point of view.

(6) Now, to make the actual throw, snap your wrist "open" AS HARD AS YOU CAN. AT THE SAME TIME, *straighten out your fingers* and release the card to send it spinning out of your hand.

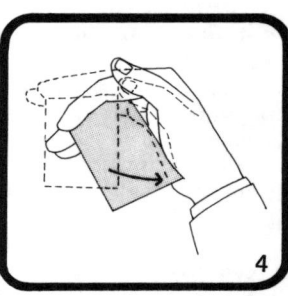

COMMENTS AND SUGGESTIONS

Keeping the card level with the fingers and maintaining a consistent wrist action are essential factors in developing the "throw," which can cover a long range once the knack is acquired. When aiming for higher levels, the hand must be kept "on target" and the force of throw increased. Along with accuracy, the practiced performer can propel the cards an impressive distance by combining a *throwing motion of the arm* with the action of the wrist as a means of gaining still greater distance.

THE BOOMERANG CARD

After demonstrating his skill by throwing playing cards great distances into the audience, the magician begins throwing cards toward the ceiling only to have them sail out into the air and return to his hand, much the same as a Boomerang.

METHOD

(1) In order to achieve the "Boomerang" effect, the card should be held either in the position described in THROWING A CARD or in this new position as follows: Hold the card at one end between the tips of the right thumb and fingers as shown. Grip the card near the outer right corner between your right thumb and second finger. Your first finger rests against the left corner of the card to serve as a pivot point to start the "spinning" action of the card as it leaves the hand.

(2) With the card held in this position, it can be sent spinning out of the hand using the same arm and wrist action as described in THROWING A CARD.

(3) To achieve the BOOMERANG effect, hold the card in either "throwing" position. Then, instead of throwing the card out of the hand on a level plane, throw it at an upward angle of 45 degrees or more, *with just enough force to send it only a few yards away from you.* In throwing the card, concentrate on obtaining as much spin as possible. This is done by "snapping" your hand back *toward your body just before you release the card.* Your first finger on the outer right corner acts as the pivot point to aid in starting the card in its spin as it leaves your right hand.

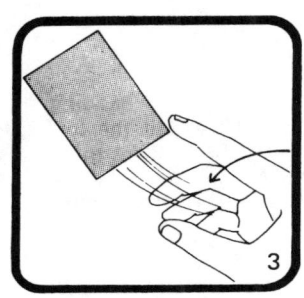

(4) Once the card has reached its maximum distance in the air and begins its downward fall, it will return to you instead of falling straight down to the floor. This is due to the 45-degree angle of the card in the air. With practice you will be able to cause the card to return directly to your hand where you can catch it between your thumb and fingers.

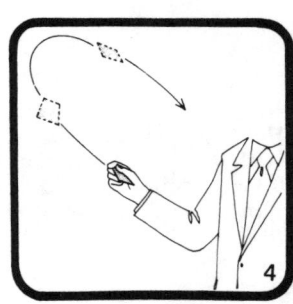

COMMENTS AND SUGGESTIONS

Practice the BOOMERANG CARD until it can be done with neatness and precision. Performed properly, it creates an impression of great skill and dexterity. A certain amount of failure is inevitable at first, but once you develop the knack of THROWING A CARD, the BOOMERANG should come quickly and easily.

GENII CARDS

In contrast to tricks with regulation playing cards, the "Genii" tricks require a special type of card.   Since the Genii Cards are handled somewhat like playing cards, they have been included in this section.

While several tricks may be performed with the "Genii Cards," all depend upon the same simple, but deceptive, move. Although this move is excellent, you should not perform more than one Genii trick at any performance. It is better to keep a few Genii tricks in reserve, so that on your next show you can switch to another.

This keeps people wondering just what to expect, which is an important factor in all magic. If you wish, you can use the Genii Cards for an introductory trick, or inject them as an interlude during a program of effects with playing cards, and you will always be on the safe side.

The Genii Cards and their routines were specially devised for use with this magic course, which means that they will be entirely new to many people who see them. This gives you, as the performer, a real advantage over your audiences from the start — so make the most of it!

You may have the Genii Cards and the special half-cards printed on business card-sized stock at a local printer. Because spectators will be asked to write on the full-sized Genii cards in most of the following routines, we suggest a number of these be printed. Approximately 20 of the half-cards will last a long time.

THE GENII OF THE LAMP

In this very basic form of the Genii, the only "props" needed are the cards themselves. The effect is that a Genii mysteriously appears thanks to the magic of Aladdin's Lamp.

EFFECT

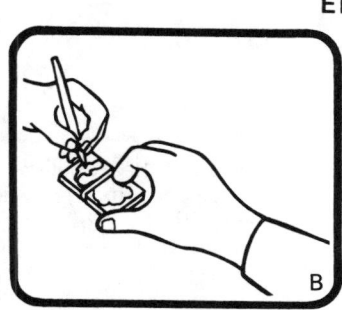 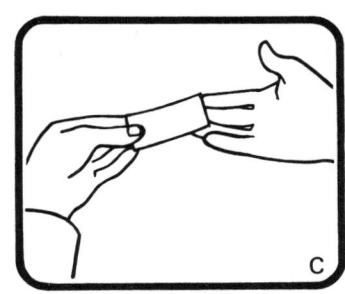 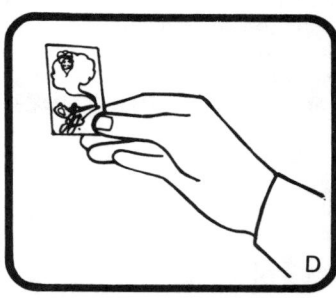

(A) You show a stack of cards with a rubber band around it. The top card shows a magic lamp giving off a cloud of smoke, but no Genii. (B) Remarking that this represents Aladdin's wonderful lamp, you invite a spectator to write his initials in the lamp. You then remove the card and state that whenever Aladdin rubbed the lamp, his Genii appeared. (C) Holding the card face down in one hand, you rub the lamp with the fingers of your other hand. (D) After a few rubs, you turn the card over showing that the Genii himself has "magically" appeared in the cloud of smoke and the spectator's initials are still in the lamp!

SECRET AND PREPARATION

This basic trick, and all other tricks with the Genii cards, depend on a simple, natural movement which secretly switches one card for another. We call this the "Master Move". Here is the explanation of the trick and how the "Master Move" makes this a real mystery.

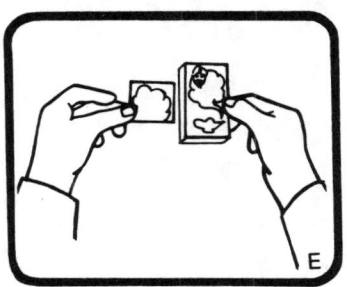 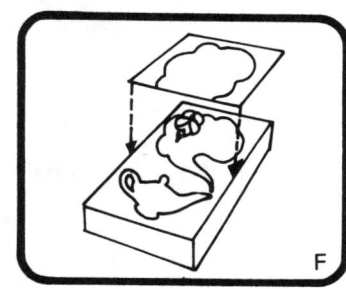 

(E) A special half-card showing only an empty cloud is used, shown here next to the packet of regular full-sized cards. Approximately ten full-sized cards should be used to make up the packet. (F) Before the trick, one half-card is placed on the packet so that it covers the cloud portion of the top card with the Genii in it. (G) Now, put the rubber band around the cards so that the half-card is held firmly in place and its bottom edge is completely hidden by the rubber band. Once the half-card is in position and held there by the rubber band, the top card of the packet looks like a full-sized card showing a lamp, a cloud, and nothing else. Use only one half-card when you set up the packet for the trick. Save the others for spares.

METHOD AND MASTER MOVE

(1) You show the packet to a spectator, and ask him to write his initials in the lamp of the top card.

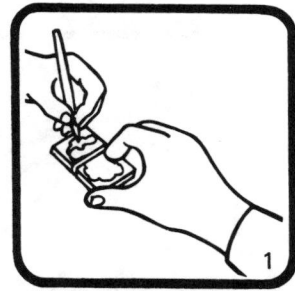

(3) Now, your left hand starts to turn the packet over as you begin to pull out the Genii card with your right fingers.

(2) Now for the Master Move: Holding the packet in your left hand as shown, you lift up the lamp end of the initialed card with your right finger.

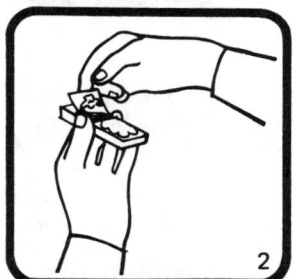

(4) Here is the action as seen from below. The spectators see the back of the packet instead of the face. Everyone is sure you are drawing out the initialed card.

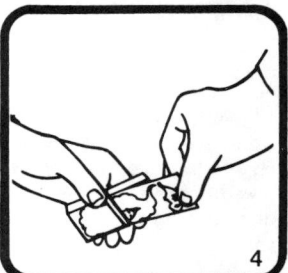

(5) As the card comes clear, both the packet and the card have been turned all the way over so that no one can see their faces. Although you *have* actually drawn out the initialed card, the secret half-card remains on the packet. Place the packet face down somewhere out of reach, or drop in your pocket, so that no one will learn about the half-card.

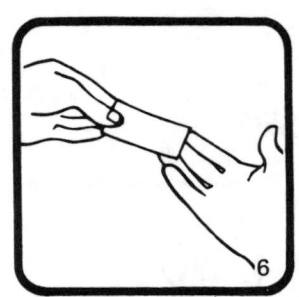

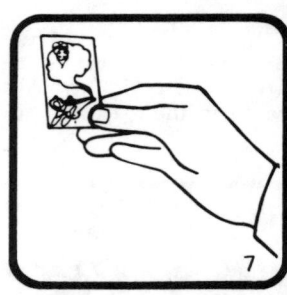

(6) Hold the initialed card face down in your left hand. Place your right fingers under the card and rub the lamp a few times. (7) When you turn the card over, the Genii is found to have "magically" appeared in the cloud of smoke!

COMMENTS AND SUGGESTIONS

Through this Master Move, you have secretly switched what the spectators thought was the original Genii card for another; yet the change seems impossible because the person who wrote his initials on the card will find that they are still there. This is something of a miracle in its own right, and when used in association with other effects, it becomes even more sensational. These added details will be covered in the Genii tricks that follow, all using the Master Move just described.

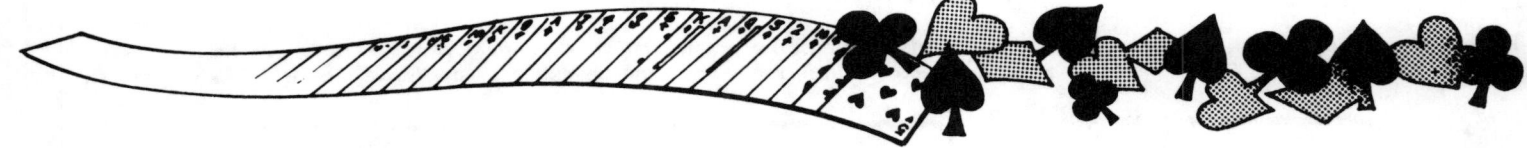

THE GENII'S NUMBER

In this trick, the Genii does magical mathematics and predicts a chosen number. And he does it very well, as you will see.

SECRET AND PREPARATION

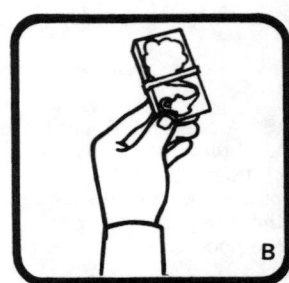

(A) Before the trick, write the number "1089" in the cloud of the top Genii card; (B) then cover it with the empty half-card and place a rubber band around the packet.

METHOD

(1) Have a spectator write his initials in the lamp as you did in the Genii of the Lamp trick.

(2) Remove the initialed card using the Master Move (actually removing the "1089" card) and place it face down on the table.

(3) Lay a pad and pencil beside it.

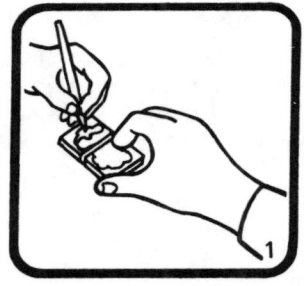

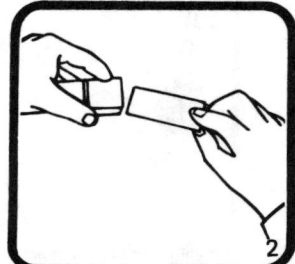

(4) Now tell the spectator: "I want you to write a number of *three different figures,* any number between one hundred and one thousand, without letting me see it." Let's say that he writes "318."

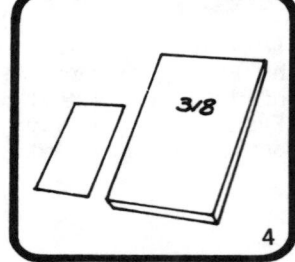

(5) You continue: "Now reverse that number and subtract the smaller number from the larger." *NOTE: Here you tell him if the answer is less than a hundred to leave a zero in front of it so he will still have a number with three figures.*

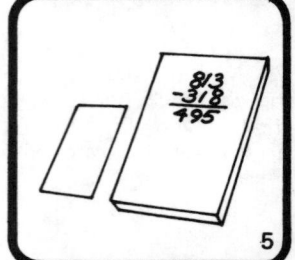

(6) As soon as he has done the subtraction, you state: "Now reverse your answer and write it just below." When he does this, tell him: "I want you to add those two numbers so you will get a *grand total.*"

(8) Explain that you will call upon your invisible Genii to check the spectator's arithmetic. Pick up the Genii card and place it face down on top of the pad. Then, pretend to catch the Genii out of the air and slip him between the pad and Genii card.

(7) You then tell him to circle the grand total, and lay the pad down beside the Genii card.

(9) After a few moments, ask the spectator to turn over the card. He does, and to his amazement, the Genii has appeared *showing* the same number as his slip: 1089.

COMMENTS AND SUGGESTIONS

Whatever the original three-figure number, the grand total will always be 1089, unless the original figures are all alike, as 333 or 555. That is why you tell him that he is to write a number with *three different figures.* When subtracted, they will always produce numbers that, when reversed, and added, will total *1089.* In some cases, like 463 minus 364, the subtraction gives him 99. That is why you tell the spectator to put a zero in front of anything under 100, so if he makes it 099 and reverses it to form 990, the two will add up to the usual 1089. If he should get some other total, simply check his figures for him and he will find that the Genii was right all along!

THE GENII PREDICTS

In this Genii trick, along with the packet of Genii cards, you need an ordinary pack of playing cards, which may be borrowed for this effect.

EFFECT

The magician shows the Genii Packet with the rubber band around it. The top card shows a magic lamp giving off a cloud of smoke, but no Genii. A spectator writes his initials in the lamp of the top card of the Genii Packet, which is then removed from the packet and placed face down on the table. A card is chosen by the spectator from the pack, and placed on the table beside the Genii card. The magician then picks up the Genii card. Keeping the Genii card face down, the performer reaches beneath and, with his finger, "rubs" the lamp a few times. When the card is turned over, both the Genii and the words "Three of Clubs" have mysteriously appeared in the cloud. When the "chosen" card is turned over, it is the Three of Clubs....PROVING THE GENII'S PREDICTION TO BE CORRECT!

SECRET AND PREPARATION

Before the performance, write the name of any card, say the "Three of Clubs" in the cloud section of the top card of the Genii Packet. Cover this top card with the half-card and place the rubber band around the packet. Then, go through the pack of playing cards, find the Three of Clubs and move it to the position in the pack ready for your favorite force. The ROLLOVER FORCE or SLIP FORCE described in the Card Section of the Course both work well for this effect. (In the illustrations, the Three of Clubs has been marked with an "X" to make it easy to follow.) Place the pack in its card box or simply have it lying handy on the table and you're ready to begin.

METHOD

(1) Lay the Genii Packet face up on the table and place the pack of playing cards face down beside it.

(2) Pick up the Genii Packet and point out the empty cloud on the top card stating that "The Genii, who usually lives in the lamp, apparently isn't home today." Then, ask a spectator to write his initials in the lamp.

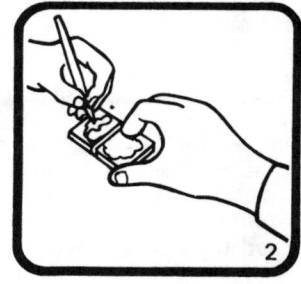

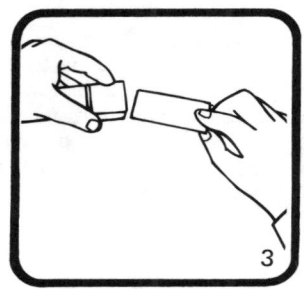

(3) That done, you remove the initialed card from the packet *(actually the prediction card)* using the MASTER MOVE, and place it face down on the table.

(5) Tell the spectator to turn over the Genii Card and see if the Genii has anything to say. When he does, he will see that the Genii has appeared and has written "Three of Clubs" in the cloud.

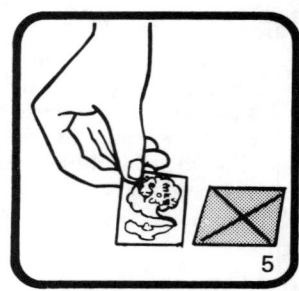

(4) Put away the rest of the Genii Packet and pick up the pack of playing cards. State that you wish to have one card selected at random from the pack. With that, force the Three of Clubs on the spectator, using whichever method you have decided upon. Have the spectator place his "chosen card" face down on the table next to the Genii Card.

(6) When the spectator turns over the playing card, the Genii's prediction proves correct!

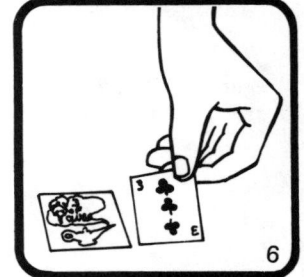

COMMENTS AND SUGGESTIONS

In this Genii routine, *after* you have drawn out the Genii Card and placed it on the table, you can let the spectators see the packet of Genii Cards face up. Since the half-card is still in place and has no writing in the cloud, it will be mistaken for the second Genii Card. Just make sure that the rubber band is still in proper position *hiding the edge* of the half-card. If the half-card has slipped from place, put the packet away without turning it face up. A quick glance will tell you which to do. *Also, if you use a pencil to write the Genii Prediction, you can later erase it and use the Genii Card over again.*

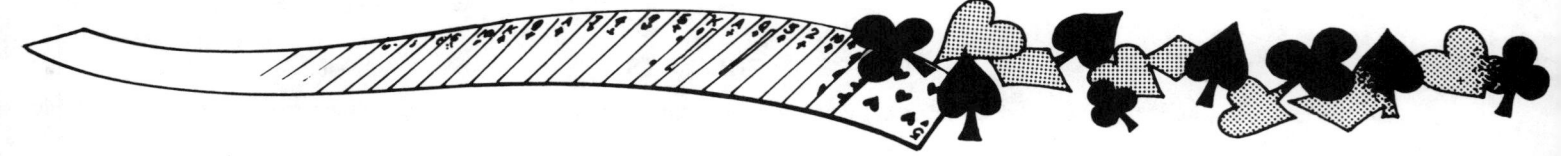

THE SANDWICHED GENII

EFFECT

This is similar to the "Genii Predicts." In this trick after the spectator has initialed the lamp he places the Genii card in the center of a deck of playing cards. When the deck is spread the spectator finds that the Genii has not only mysteriously appeared, but he has also "magically" written the names of two playing cards in the cloud of smoke—and when the spectator looks, he finds that *these are the two playing cards that are next to the Genii card in the deck!*

SECRET AND PREPARATION

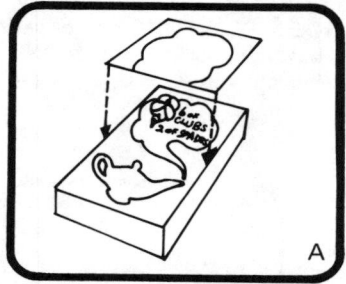   

In addition to the Genii cards, you will need a regular deck of playing cards. (A) Before you perform the trick, with a pencil write the names of any two playing cards in the cloud of smoke on the top card of the Genii card packet. Let's suppose that you write the "Six of Clubs" and the "Two of Spades." This is now your *Genii prediction card.* (B) Then cover your "prediction" card with one of the "empty cloud" half-cards and put the rubber band around the packet. Now, from the deck of playing cards, remove the Two of Spades and the Six of Clubs. (C) Put the Six of Clubs on the top and (D) the Two of Spades on the bottom of the deck of playing cards and place the deck back in the box. Now you are ready to perform the trick. *NOTE: In the illustrations we have marked the Six of Clubs with the letter "A" and the Two of Spades with the letter "B" to make them easier to follow.*

METHOD

(1) To begin the presentation lay the Genii packet face up on the table with a pencil and the box of playing cards. Remark that the Genii who *usually* lives in the lamp must not be home, so ask a spectator to write his initials in the lamp of the top card.

(2) Remove the initialed card using the Master Move (actually removing the prediction card) and lay it face down on the table. Put the rest of the Genii cards in your pocket or just lay them aside.

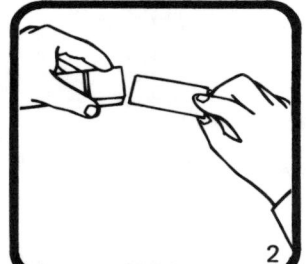

(3) Tell the spectator to write his name on the back of the Genii card. While he is writing, pick up the deck of playing cards, remove it from the box and set it on the table next to the Genii card.

(4) Now, ask the spectator to divide the deck into two parts. Tell him he can cut anywhere in the deck he wishes, and place the upper portion on the table on the other side of the Genii card.

(5) *NOTE: Stress the fact that the spectator is cutting the pack at a location in the deck of his own free choice!*

(6) Then, tell him to place his Genii card face down on top of this new pile (which places it on top of the Six of Clubs).

(7) Now tell him to place the lower half of the deck on top of the Genii card, thus burying it in the deck. (This now places the Two of Spades which was on the bottom of the deck — directly above the Genii card.)

(8) *NOTE: At this point, the Genii card has been "sandwiched" between the Six of Clubs and Two of Spades, while the spectator thinks he has merely placed the Genii card in the deck at the spot to which he has freely cut.*

(9) Now say that you will have to call upon the Genii to help with this trick. Explaining that the Genii is always invisible when he's not at home, pretend to spot him in the air and reach out and catch him in your hand. Then pretend to slip the Genii into the pack of cards on the table.

(10) Pick up the pencil and lay it on the end of the pack and say: "This Genii is very intelligent. He can even write if he has a pencil." Move the pencil forward, sliding it completely across the top of the pack; then lay the pencil aside.

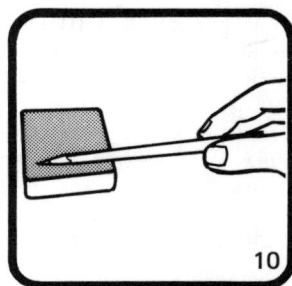

(11) "That gave the Genii time to write a message. Let's find him and see if he did." With that, you spread the pack along the table.

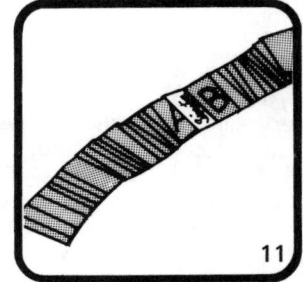

(12) Push the Genii card out of the deck along with the card just below it (A) and the card just above it (B) as shown.

(13) "I'll just turn over the Genii card, and we'll see what the Genii knows." When the signed Genii card is turned over, the names of the two playing cards are seen in the cloud with the spectator's initials still in the lamp.

(14) You then turn over cards A and B showing the Six of Clubs and the Two of Spades, which makes the amazement complete.

COMMENTS AND SUGGESTIONS

As in the previous trick, once you have drawn out the previously prepared Genii prediction card, you may allow the spectators to see the face of the packet of Genii cards. As long as the half-card is still in place and securely bound by the rubber band, they will think they are seeing the second Genii card in the packet. Be sure to glance at the face of the packet, though, to be sure the rubber band is still hiding the edge of the half-card.

THE GENII SAVES THE DAY!

EFFECT

In this GENII CARD effect, the magician makes a prediction, writing it in the Genii's cloud. When the prediction goes wrong, the Genii magically "fixes" it, producing a *double surprise*. Again, the MASTER MOVE is used along with the "Force" of a card from a regular pack of playing cards.

SECRET AND PREPARATION

To prepare, before the show, write the name of a playing card — say "Three of Clubs" in the cloud section of the top Genii card. Cover this with one of the "blank" half-cards and place the rubber band around the packet. From an ordinary pack of cards, remove the Three of Clubs and place it at the correct position in the pack ready for any of the "Forces" you have learned.

METHOD

(1) State that you are going to make a "prediction" — you will predict the very same card that a spectator will later select from an ordinary deck of playing cards! So, you OPENLY write the name of some other card — say the Five of Hearts — in the Genii's cloud, stating that this is your prediction.

(3) Now, go through the Master Move, laying the Genii card (actually the Three of Clubs prediction card) face down on the table and place a coin or other small object on top of it. The half-card with your "Five of Hearts" prediction remains on the Genii packet.

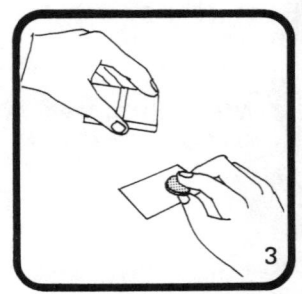

(2) *Actually, your prediction is written on the half-card which no one knows about.* You then have the spectator put his initials in the lamp to identify the "prediction" card.

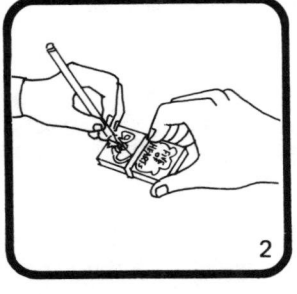

(4) *NOTE: Placing a coin or other small object on the Genii card is important as it discourages anyone from turning the card over until you're ready.*

(5) Drop the Genii packet in your pocket and bring out the pack of playing cards. Remove the pack from its box and "Force" the Three of Clubs on the spectator using the force you are set up for.

(6) Ask the spectator to look at the card he selected and see if your prediction is correct. When he does, he sees that you are <u>wrong</u>, since he saw you write "<u>Five of Hearts</u>" on the Genii card and the card he selected is the <u>Three of Clubs</u>.

(7) That's when you call on the invisible Genii for help — *and the Genii does help.* Remove the coin and ask the spectator to turn over the prediction card. He will find that the Genii has "magically appeared" AND has changed your prediction to the "Three of Clubs," THE SAME CARD HE SELECTED! *HOORAY FOR THE GENII!*

COMMENTS AND SUGGESTIONS

This effect is "super" for three reasons. *One,* it fulfills a prediction; *two,* it mysteriously changes one prediction into another; and *three,* it proves you are <u>right</u> when the spectator thinks that you are <u>wrong</u>. All these combined will have your audience trying to figure out <u>three things at once</u>, which is sure to leave them totally baffled.

One word of caution. You must keep the packet of Genii cards <u>FACE DOWN</u> after the Master Move so that no one will see the "false" prediction on the half-card. Just drop the packet in your pocket and you will find that by the end of the trick, the spectators will have forgotten the packet completely.

GENII'S LIBRARY

EFFECT

The magician has a spectator write his initials in the lamp on the face card of a packet of Genii cards. The picture on the card shows a magic lamp giving off a cloud of smoke — *but no Genii.* This done, he removes the initialed Genii card from the stack and places it face down on the table.

The magician then displays an ordinary paperback book and "riffles" through its pages inviting the spectator to call "Stop" at any time during the riffle. When the call comes, the magician inserts an envelope into the book to mark the exact page selected by the spectator. The spectator is then asked to note the word in the text located in the upper right corner of the selected page.

In an attempt to locate the Genii *and* learn the selected word, the Genii card is partially inserted into the book for only a brief moment. When the card is removed and turned face up, it shows that *both* the Genii and the exact word which was selected from the text have "magically" appeared — with the word written in the Genii's cloud of smoke!

SECRET AND PREPARATION

(A) Carefully cut one page from the center of the paperback book you plan to use and place it on your table, with the *front* of the page (that is, the odd-numbered side of the page that was originally facing the front of the book) <u>facing up</u>. This done, apply a very thin strip of rubber cement along the "binding" edge of the page *and* on the top edge of the envelope as shown.

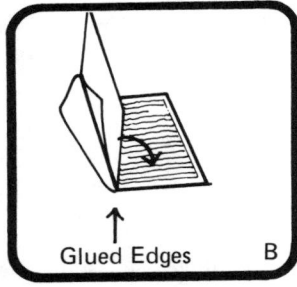

(B) Allow the cement to dry on both surfaces and then attach the glued edge of the page to the glued edge of the envelope. Be sure that the edges of the page are *exactly even* with the left side and lower edges of the envelope. Although this is difficult to describe in written form, it is really quite simple to make. Just study the pictures and you will see exactly how to make this "special" envelope prop which is the key to the entire trick.

(C) NOTE: The envelope should be *longer* and *wider* than the book page, so that when it is turned over, the page will be completely hidden from view beneath the envelope.

(D) After the glue has set, insert the prepared envelope into the book so that the "secret" page is lined up with the rest of the pages in the book. If this is done correctly, everything should appear natural from all angles. It will look like a book with an envelope stuck in its pages.

(E) Next, write the prediction word from the "force" page (the page you have glued to the envelope) in the cloud of the top card of the Genii packet. Then, cover this with the half-card and place the rubber band around the entire stack.

(1) To begin, place the packet of Genii cards on the table and bring the book into view, casually showing it on both sides. Then, turn the book "face up" and remove the envelope with your right hand. *Make sure not to flash the attached page as you do this.*

(7) Immediately lay the book on the table and pick up the initialed Genii card.

(2) Pick up and display the packet of Genii cards. Have a spectator write his initials in the lamp of the top Genii card as usual. Remove the initialed card using the Master Move (actually removing the prediction card). Place the card face down on the table.

(8) *NOTE: Picking up the Genii card at this time is actually a clever ruse to let you set down the book with the "special" envelope inserted into it. If you did not use the Genii card here, then there would be no reason for you not to show the spectator the page he selected.*

(3) Pick up the book in your left hand and riffle through the pages with your left thumb. Explain to the spectator that he may say "Stop" at *any time* during the riffle.

(9) Slide the Genii card *face down* through the pages of the book. Say, "I will now attempt to locate the Magic Genii within the pages of this book — where he frequently visits on vacation. If we're lucky, perhaps he will also reveal to us the word that you selected." After this bit of byplay, replace the prediction card *face down* on the table.

(4) When the call comes, stop riffling and (5) insert the envelope into the book where the spectator called stop. Be sure to insert the envelope so that the "bottom" of the envelope is lined up evenly with the bottom edge of the book. Also, insert the envelope *all the way* into the book <u>so that the glued edge of the envelope</u> and the secret prediction page are wedged securely into the binding of the book.

(10) *NOW HERE IS THE MOST IMPORTANT MOVE IN THE TRICK.* Pick up the book and open it (11) so that the book hinges open <u>between</u> the envelope and the secretly attached page. The envelope should cover the left-hand portion of the book, exposing the front side of the attached "force" page. Point out to the spectator the *last word* in the *top line* of this page (actually the "force" word) and ask him to <u>remember that word</u>.

(6) Without hesitation, gently tap the bottom edge of the book on the table. This squares up the envelope (and the hidden page) with the rest of the pages of the book.

(12) *NOTE: Do not look at the page or the word as you do this. Hold the book away from you so that it faces the spectator and you obviously cannot see the "freely selected" page. Unknown to the spectator, you have now "forced" him to choose a word which he thinks is the result of his random selection.*

(13) Close the book and *remove the envelope,* bringing along the secret page. Immediately place the envelope aside, or better yet, into your coat pocket, *making sure not to expose the secret page as you do.*

(14) To bring the mystery to its close, ask the spectator to call out the word he selected. When he does, turn over the Genii card revealing *both* the Genii *and* the word written in the cloud that *exactly matches* the word "selected" from the text of the book!

COMMENTS AND SUGGESTIONS

Be sure and use a book which *does not open out flat* for this trick. A "paperback" book is best. This is because, if the book opened wide, the spectators might notice that the page he "freely selected" is *actually glued to the envelope.*

Do not call any unnecessary attention to the envelope during the presentation. Handle it as if its *only purpose* is to mark the selected page in the book. Then, after it has done its work, place it in your pocket and continue. By the end of the trick, the audience will most likely forget that you ever used any additional "props" other than the book.

SPECIAL NOTE: Since all of the Genii tricks use the same magical principle, the half-card and the Master Move, you should present only one of the Genii tricks at any one performance. This is an example of Rule 3. . .*NEVER* repeat a trick for the same spectators.

MONEY MAGIC

Tricks with coins date back almost to the beginning of magic, and they are as popular as ever today. Coins are always handy if you want to borrow some for impromptu work. If you carry a supply of your own, you will be equipped for feats of really surprising wizardry. Tricks of both types are covered in abundance in this section.

Some good coin tricks are quite simple, others require a great deal of practice while of the best depend on basic moves that are quite easy to learn and a number of them will be described in detail in this section. Your knowledge of such sleights will enable you to build up highly effective coin routines without going into more difficult manipulations which have created the impression that coin work is for "experts" only. Even some coin flourishes come easily with reasonable practice and those, too, have been included in this section.

By putting coin effects into your general programs, you can learn as you go, expanding your coin routines until they become all-inclusive. Even before then, you should become sufficiently "money minded" to go in for tricks with folding currency. So some of those have been included in this same section, to be used as required. The same rule applies both to coins and bills: When performing either type of money magic, stress the fact that you use ordinary means-in some cases, borrowing them, thus proving that skill, not trickery, is the great factor in your work. The more you have them believing that, the more wonderful your money magic will appear.

THE COIN FOLD

The magician borrows a coin from a member of the audience and has it marked by its owner for later identification. A small sheet of paper is then folded around the coin so it is completely enclosed within the paper. This little package can even be tapped on the table so the audience can hear that the coin is actually inside. At all times the folded paper remains in view of the spectators — yet the magician causes the coin to vanish from within the paper — which he tears into pieces. He then reproduces the coin from his pocket, the spectator's lapel, or anywhere he wishes.

SECRET AND PREPARATION

No special items are required for this effect. The coin, however, which can be borrowed, should be large enough for an effective vanish. A half-dollar or dollar-sized coin works well and is easily visible even at some distance. The piece of paper used should measure approximately 4 x 6 inches.

METHOD

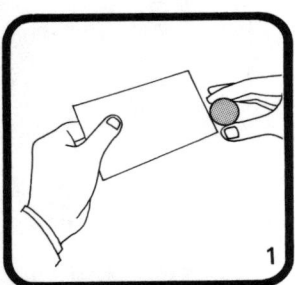

(1) Borrow a coin from a member of the audience and have the spectator mark the coin with a permanent ink marking pen for later identification. This done, hold the paper in your left hand and display the coin openly at your right fingertips. You remark, "I will seal the borrowed coin within the folds of this piece of paper." (2) Place the coin in the center of the paper and hold it there with your left thumb and fingers as shown.

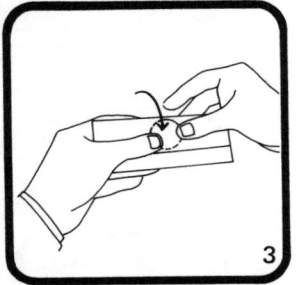

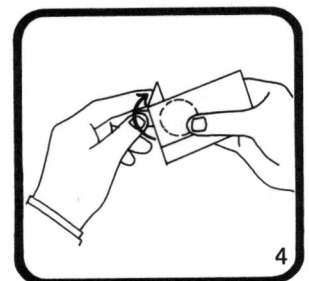

(3) With the right fingers, fold the upper half of the paper *toward you* as shown — completely over the coin — so that no part of the coin is visible to you or the spectators. (4) Next, fold the left side of the paper — *away from you* — against the back of the coin. This seals the coin in the paper at the *left side.* Do not fold the paper tightly against the edge of the coin. Instead, leave about a quarter inch of "play" between the fold and the left edge of the coin.

(5) Now fold the right side of the paper — *away from you* — against the back of the coin so it overlaps the left-hand fold. This seals the coin in the paper from the *right side.* Again, leave another quarter inch of "play" between the crease of the right fold and the right edge of the coin.

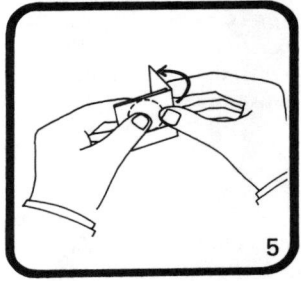

(6) *NOTE: At this point, the coin is sealed in from all sides except for the bottom edge of the paper, which remains open. In making the folds, be sure to maintain enough pressure on the coin through the paper to keep it inside, so it won't slide out the open bottom edge.*

(7) The last fold is the most important. If you folded the bottom edge upward — *toward you* — it would seal the coin inside. Instead, the last fold is made upward — *but toward the audience* — leaving the bottom edge of the package open. This provides a means of escape for the coin.

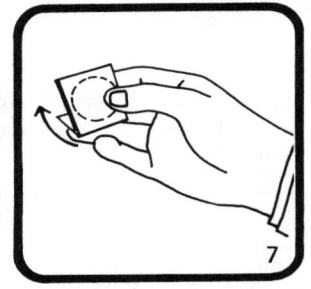

(8) When the last fold has been made, press the paper firmly around the edge of the coin *leaving a distinct impression of the coin outlined on the surface of the paper.* This impression is important. It will later convince the audience that the coin is still wrapped securely within the folded package.

(9) Hold the small package with the tips of your right fingers. Tap the edge of the folded paper on the table allowing the spectators to "hear" the coin inside. Say, "The coin is now securely sealed within the folded paper. If you listen, you can even hear it."

(13) *NOTE: As the folded package is transferred from the right to the left hand, if you wish, instead of leaving the coin in the right hand, you can place your hand casually in your right pants or coat pocket where you leave the coin to be reproduced later. In this way, the right hand will be empty as you move on to the next step.*

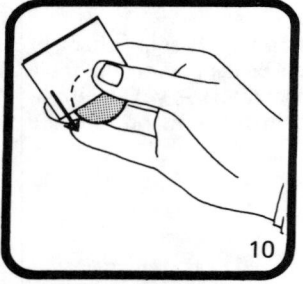
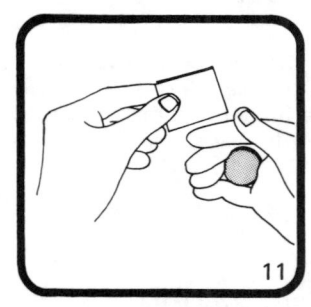

(10) To make the coin "vanish," you do the following moves: Hold the folded paper with the "opening" pointing downward toward the base of the fingers. Relax the pressure of your right thumb and fingers and the coin will slide out of the bottom of the paper into your right hand — where it remains hidden in your curled fingers. (11) After the coin drops into your hand, take the package with your left fingers. Your right hand falls casually to your side with the coin held secretly in the Finger Palm position as shown.

(12) With your left hand, casually display the folded package to the spectators, who believe that the coin is still wrapped inside. *This is where the outlined impression of the coin becomes so valuable.* As you display the paper, casually show both sides, *allowing the spectators to see the impression made by the coin,* thus proving the presence of the coin.

(14) Bring both hands together in front of you and tear the paper in half. (The illustration shows how to hold the coin in the Finger Palm position as you tear the paper.) Toss the pieces onto the table. You can even tear the paper into many pieces to prove, without a doubt, that the coin has truly "vanished." The coin can then be reproduced from your pocket — or, if you still hold the coin in the Finger Palm position, you can produce it from the spectator's coat lapel, tie, or anywhere you desire.

COMMENTS AND SUGGESTIONS

The Coin Fold is a standard method for vanishing a coin and can be used in conjunction with many coin routines where the vanish of a coin is necessary.

COIN THROUGH HANDKERCHIEF

Here is a clever effect using a pocket handkerchief and a coin (a half-dollar is a good size to use).

EFFECT

The magician displays the coin at the tips of his right thumb and fingers. He then drapes the handkerchief over the coin so that the coin seems to penetrate the fabric of the handkerchief, without leaving a trace of a tear or a hole. The magician can then hand both the coin and the handkerchief for examination.

METHOD

(1) For this effect you may use your own handkerchief, but the trick is stronger if you utilize a borrowed one. In either case, first display the coin by holding it at the tips of your right thumb and first two fingers. Your fingers and thumb are pointing *up* with one side of the coin facing the audience.

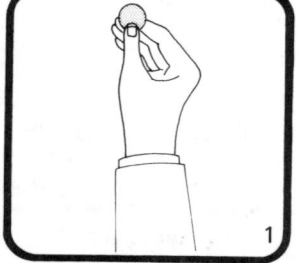

(2) With your left hand, drape the handkerchief over the coin *and over your right hand.* The coin should be under the center of the handkerchief.

(3) With your left hand adjust the handkerchief around the coin. At the same time, underneath the handkerchief, secretly lift a small bit of cloth behind the coin with your right thumb and fold it around your left thumb as shown.

(9) With the left hand, grasp the coin through the now doubled over fabric and remove your right hand as shown. It will appear to the audience as if the handkerchief is draped completely around the coin.

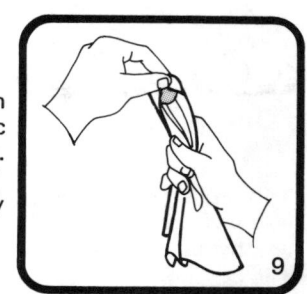

(4) Remove your left hand, leaving the small bit of handkerchief "nipped" between your right thumb and the back of the coin. This places two layers of fabric between the right thumb and the coin.

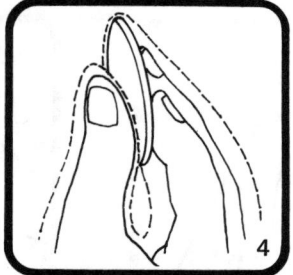

(10) With your now free right hand twist the lower part of the handkerchief around the coin.

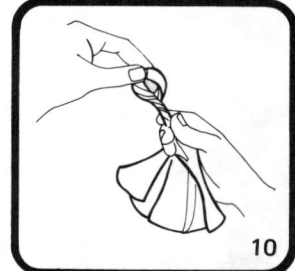

(5) Now, grasp the front edge of the handkerchief with your left hand, lifting it up, back and completely over the coin. This action will expose the coin to the spectators, supposedly to assure them that the coin is still in its original position.

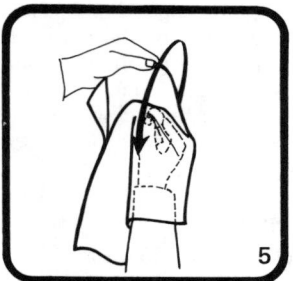

(11) As you twist the handkerchief, the shape of the coin will become visible under the fabric.

(6) THE FOLLOWING MOVE IS THE REAL SECRET OF THE TRICK: With your left hand, grasp BOTH EDGES of the handkerchief and lift them both up and over the coin as shown.

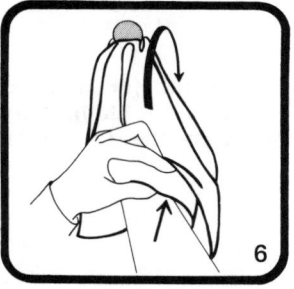

(12) You may also adjust the cloth over the exposed "Back" of the coin and show the handkerchief on all sides, if you wish.

(7) The effect on the spectators will be that you simply exposed the coin for them to show that it was still there and then re-covered it with the handkerchief as before.

(13) Now, slowly push the coin upwards in the handkerchief as your left hand comes over to take the edge of the coin as it "penetrates" the handkerchief.

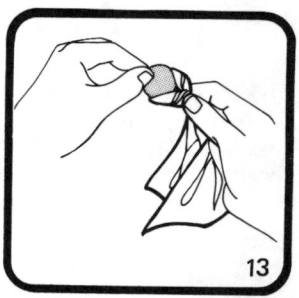

(8) *In actuality you are now holding the coin OUTSIDE the back of the handkerchief.*

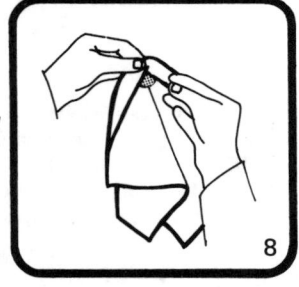

(14) You may now hand both the handkerchief and the coin for examination.

COIN THROUGH HANDKERCHIEF — SECOND VERSION

This effect will appear exactly the same to your audience as the first COIN THROUGH HANDKERCHIEF, yet *the METHOD is entirely different*. But because it is so direct and bold, it will fool anyone who might know the first method just described. This is another example of an ingenious mystery devised by "Gen" Grant.

EFFECT

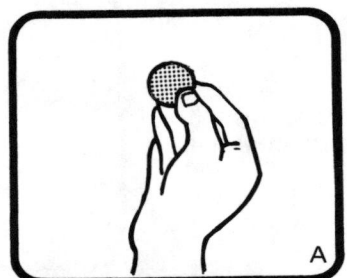

The magician displays a Half-Dollar between the tips of the fingers of his right hand. The left hand holds a handkerchief which he drapes over both the coin *and* his right hand. Then, with his left hand, he grips the coin through the cloth from the outside, holding it there while his right hand is withdrawn from beneath. The right hand again grasps the coin — this time *through* the material. Now he moves his left hand down and grasps the "hanging" corners of the handkerchief while his right continues to hold the coin. The magician gives a sharp downward jerk to the handkerchief — and the coin "penetrates" completely through the cloth, leaving no trace of a hole.

METHOD
ALL OF THE FOLLOWING ILLUSTRATIONS ARE AS SEEN BY THE MAGICIAN.

(1)   Hold the coin by the tips of your right finger and thumb as shown. Pick up the handkerchief with your left hand.

(4)   Your left hand then grips the coin through the cloth, *from the outside,* between the thumb and fingers as shown.

(2)   As you display the coin, begin to cover it with the handkerchief. Notice that your left hand holds the edge of the handkerchief by the *side,* not by the *corner.*

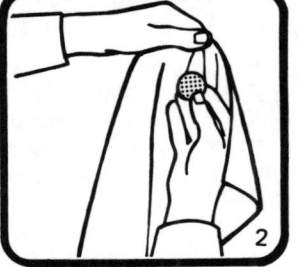

(5)   Now, as you withdraw your right hand from beneath the handkerchief, you really *keep the coin in your right hand* and *secretly* bring it down below the rear edge of the handkerchief. Your left hand holds the handkerchief at the center, AS IF IT WERE STILL HOLDING THE COIN THROUGH THE CLOTH.

(3)   When the coin is completely covered, the *front* edge of the cloth (the edge toward the spectators) drapes a little *lower* than the *back* edge. *This leaves the handkerchief a bit shorter in back than in front.*

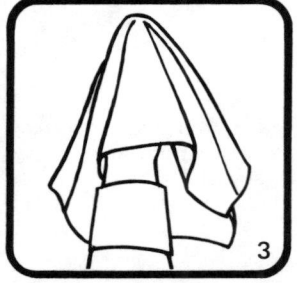

(6)   With your right hand, bring the coin up *behind the handkerchief* and SLIDE IT UNDER YOUR LEFT THUMB — "clipping" the coin *behind* the cloth, out of the spectators' view.

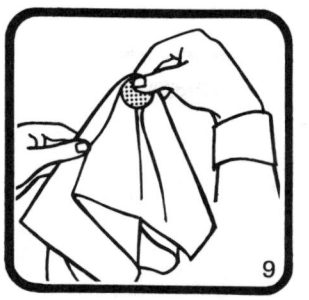

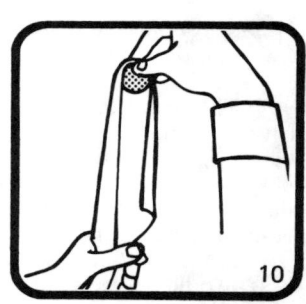

(7) With the right fingers, *pretend* to adjust the folds of the *right* side of the handkerchief by sliding your fingers down along the cloth.

(9) Then, with your left fingers, *pretend* to adjust the *left* side of the handkerchief, sliding the fingers down the cloth as before.
(10) Now gather all four corners of the handkerchief into your left hand. Your right hand still holds the coin *behind* the cloth.

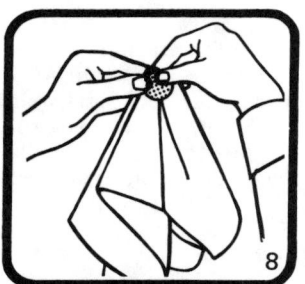

(8) Bring your right hand back up to the center (top) of the handkerchief and *transfer BOTH the coin AND the handkerchief from your left fingers to your right fingers, still keeping the coin hidden behind the cloth.*

(11) Hold the corners tightly in your left hand. Then "jerk" the handkerchief **sharp**ly downward — *out of your right hand. Pull the handkerchief AWAY from the coin — WHICH REMAINS HELD BY YOUR RIGHT FINGERTIPS.* The coin has apparently penetrated the center of the handkerchief! The handkerchief and the coin can then be tossed to the spectators for examination.

COMMENTS AND SUGGESTIONS

As bold as this may seem, performed correctly, every movement is natural and, therefore, accepted by even the sharpest observers, who are looking for quick or suspicious movements. Rehearse it first by *actually leaving the coin under the handkerchief* and going through the rest of the "Steps" just as described. Then repeat *the very same action,* following the "magical penetration" routine given here. *When both look the same,* you will be ready to present this second version of the COIN THROUGH HANDKERCHIEF.

MAGICALLY MULTIPLY YOUR MONEY

For a neat, close-up effect, this is ideal, as it can be set up in a moment and performed almost anywhere — provided the spectators are close enough to appreciate it fully. As a result, it makes an excellent "close-up" trick — but it also can be worked quite as readily while standing.

EFFECT

The magician displays a "Nickel" between the tips of his right thumb and first finger. The other fingers of his right hand are *open wide.* Everyone can see his hand is quite empty except for the Nickel.

Showing his left hand to be equally empty, the magician slowly grasps the Nickel with his left thumb and first finger. For a brief moment, both hands hold the coin at the fingertips — then the hands draw apart in a slow, outward motion. The audience is amazed to see *two Half-Dollars* emerging instead of the Nickel. When both hands are separated, each unmistakably holds a real Half-Dollar, proving that his money has multiplied *twenty times over.* THAT'S MAGIC!

SECRET AND PREPARATION

The entire effect depends upon an artful form of concealment, which is simplicity itself, yet so deceptive that no one will suspect it. Skill is reduced to a minimum. So just follow instructions and see for yourself — which you can do quite nicely by testing the routine before a mirror.

To prepare, hold the two Half-Dollars *edgewise* (horizontally) near the tips of your right thumb and forefinger, keeping the two coins together. Now, place the Nickel *upright* (vertically) between the tips of the same thumb and forefinger. Center the Nickel against the outer edge of the Halves. With the coins held firmly in this position, you are ready to begin.

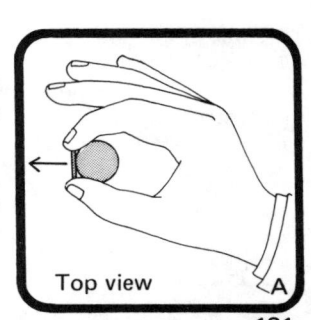

Top view

METHOD

(1) As you face the spectator, position your right hand full front before him, showing him the Nickel *at his eye level*. The spectator will not see the Halves hiding edgewise behind the Nickel if, *and only if,* your hand is held so the Halves are parallel to his line of vision — hidden "edgewise" behind the much smaller Nickel. Illustration A shows the starting position as it would be seen *from slightly above*. Note how the Nickel masks the Half-Dollars since the edges of the Halves are at the *exact center* of the Nickel.

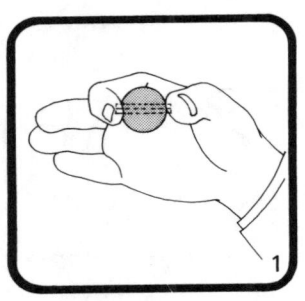

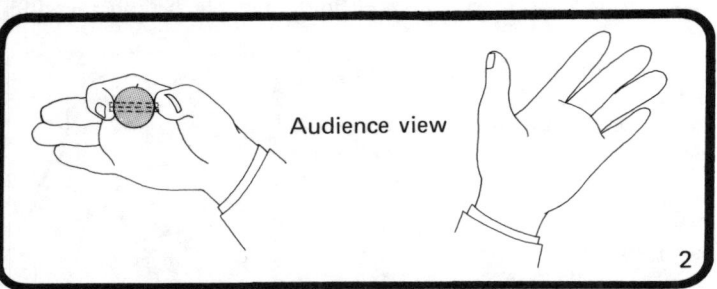

(2) From the spectator's view, your right hand is so obviously empty (except for the Nickel) that any suspicion would be directed toward your left hand — which you now show just as empty — front and back.

(3) Slowly and deliberately, bring your hands together, with the thumbs and forefingers of *both hands* pointing toward each other. The remaining fingers of both hands should be slightly opened to give the spectator a clear view of your "empty" hands. *NOTE: Keep your hand "level" with the spectator's eyes so that he does not see the concealed Halves as you turn your hand.*

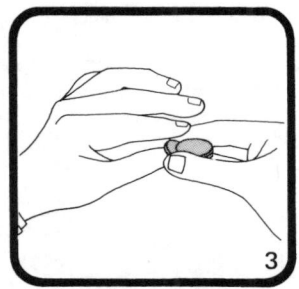

(4) As your hands move closer together, your left thumb comes *beneath* the coins, pushing the lower edge of the Nickel inwards, *rotating the Nickel up against the bottom Half-Dollar* — ALL THREE COINS ARE NOW HORIZONTAL. This is the *one moment* when the coin(s) are out of the spectator's direct view.

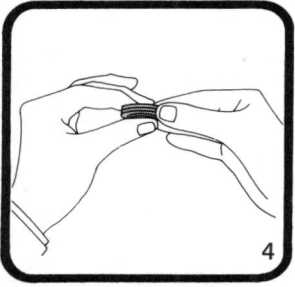

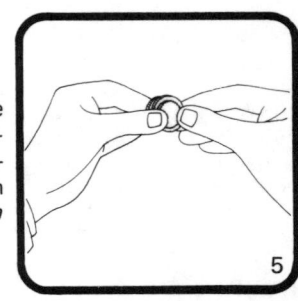

(5) All in the same action, "tip" the three coins upright *toward the spectator* with your left thumb and first finger. The coins are all held together in a stack, *with the Nickel "hidden" in back.*

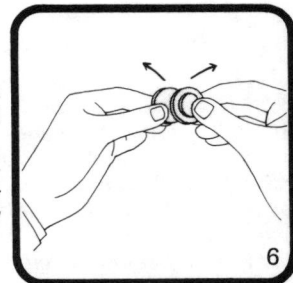

(6) Without stopping, grip the stack between your thumbs and fingers and begin drawing the two Halves apart. Your *left* hand draws the *front* Half-Dollar to the left while your *right* hand draws the *rear* Half-Dollar *and the Nickel* to the right.

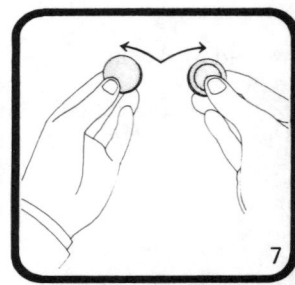

(7) Your right thumb keeps the Nickel hidden behind the rear Half-Dollar — retaining it there as you separate the two Halves. To the audience, the Nickel will appear to have "magically" *enlarged* AND *doubled* before their eyes — in an instant!

(8) The coins are then drawn completely apart and shown as two Half-Dollars at the fingertips of each hand. Be careful not to accidentally "flash" the hidden Nickel when displaying the two Halves to the audience.

COMMENTS AND SUGGESTIONS

This is a brief but baffling effect. The only question left concerns the disposal of the Nickel, which would spoil the mystery if seen. When seated at a table, after displaying the Half-Dollars, bring both hands near the edge of the table and dip your right hand a little behind your left hand. This hides your right hand momentarily. At that moment, your right thumb releases the Nickel, letting it fall into your lap. *NOTE: This is one method of LAPPING.* Both hands then come forward and toss their coins on the table. The hands can be shown completely empty, proving that the Nickel is no longer there. If you are standing, just place the "right-hand" Half in your pocket (along with its "secret" Nickel) and proceed with any effect using the other, "left-hand," Half.

FOUR-COIN ASSEMBLY

This highly effective table trick is performed with the simplest of objects: four coins, either half-dollars or quarters; two pieces of cardboard about 3 x 5 inches ("index" cards work nicely); and a napkin or fairly thick handkerchief.

EFFECT

A handkerchief is spread on the table and four coins are placed near the corners, with the two cards lying along with them. Picking up the cards, the magician shows various ways in which they can be used to cover any two of the coins. After deciding on diagonal corners, he takes the uncovered coins, one at a time, under the handkerchief and causes each coin to mysteriously penetrate the cloth under the card at the Corner A. At the end of the trick, *all four coins appear under the card* — including the coin at Corner D — WHICH THE MAGICIAN APPARENTLY NEVER TOUCHED DURING THE ENTIRE PERFORMANCE.

METHOD

The presentation depends upon a well-designed routine that directs the spectator's attention away from the few simple moves required. By following it with the actual items, all the details can be easily learned and mastered:

(1) Begin by laying out four coins, one on each corner of the cloth, as shown. The cards are tossed on the handkerchief as you say, "Here are *four* coins, *two* cards and *one* handkerchief."

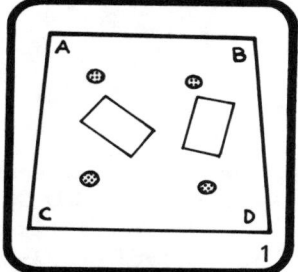

(2) Pick up a card in each hand, thumb on top, fingers below, and cover the two coins at Corners C and D. Say, "I can use these cards to cover the two coins in this row."

(3) Lift the cards and move them to cover the coins at Corners A and B. Say, "Or I can cover the coins in this row."

(4) Next, your right hand again moves to cover the coin at D, while your left hand moves its card from A across to B. State, "Also, I can cover two coins at the sides."

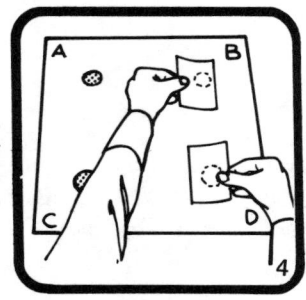

(5) Here, as you cover the coin at D, YOUR RIGHT THUMB PRESSES DOWN ON THE LEFT EDGE OF THE COIN SO THAT THE FINGERS OF YOUR RIGHT HAND CAN SLIDE UNDER THE COIN AND SECRETLY PICK IT UP AND HOLD IT AGAINST THE CARD.

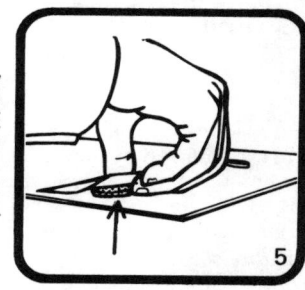

(6) *NOTE: When you "secretly" pick up the coin, it is important that your right fingers make as little motion as possible. Your right hand should look completely natural with no suspicious movements that might give you away. ALSO, YOU WILL FIND THE "PICK-UP" MUCH EASIER TO DO IF YOU ARE PERFORMING ON A SOFT SURFACE, SUCH AS A CLOSE-UP MAT.*

(7) Your left hand draws its card toward you, SLIDING IT OVER THE RIGHT-HAND CARD, as if to cover the coin at Corner D.

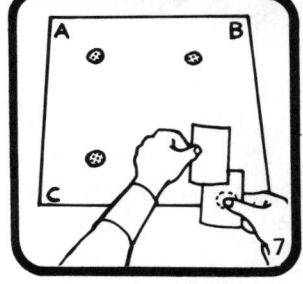

(8) Then, your right hand draws its card toward you, HOLDING THE COIN UNDER IT AS SHOWN IN THIS VIEW FROM BELOW. Your left hand leaves its card at D *over the exact spot where the "stolen" coin was located.*

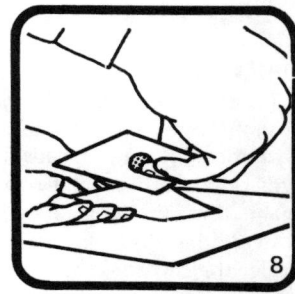

(9) Your right hand then places its card over the coin at Corner A, LEAVING WITH IT THE COIN THAT IT SECRETLY BROUGHT FROM D. Leave the cards at A and D as you comment, "Or I can cover two coins, 'criss-cross,' like this."

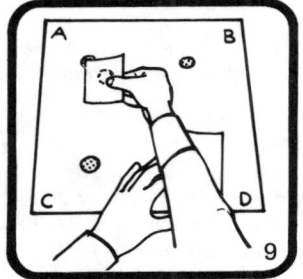

(10) *Note the "build-up" and timing up to this point. By covering C-D, then A-B, then B-D, you "condition" the observers to expect another simple placement of cards. The fact that the left hand is moved first, showing the coin at B, will cause people to think they also saw the coin at D before the left-hand card covered it.*

(11) Remark that you have now covered coins at the diagonal corners (A and D). *Pick up the coin from C with your right hand and lift that corner of the cloth with your left hand as shown.* State that you will now magically "push" the coin up through the cloth, causing it to join the coin under the card at Corner A.

(12) Here you make another secret move — AS YOU MOVE YOUR RIGHT HAND UNDER THE CLOTH, SECRETLY CLIP THE COIN BETWEEN THE TIPS OF THE FINGERS OF YOUR LEFT HAND. Your right hand should continue its forward motion under the cloth to Corner A without pausing, as you secretly transfer the coin from your right to your left hand.

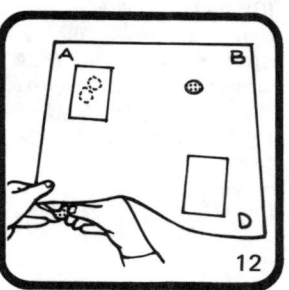

(13) Here, the "secret transfer" of the coin is shown from a different view.

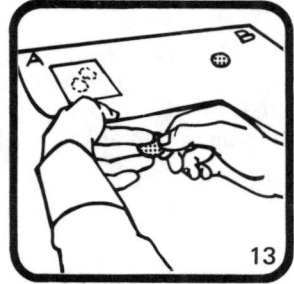

(14) When the now empty right hand is under the coin(s) at Corner A, make a slight upward "flicking" movement with the right fingers, causing the coins under the card to clink together. Explain that the coin has just "penetrated" the cloth and joined the coin under the card.

(15) The right hand is now removed from under the cloth and casually shown empty as it reaches to turn over the card at Corner A. THE LEFT FINGERS STILL HOLD THE CLIPPED COIN, BUT KEEP IT HIDDEN BENEATH THE HANDKERCHIEF.

(16) The right hand now turns over the card at Corner A, and, in the same motion, moves the card toward your left hand *bringing it directly over Corner C.*

(17) In one continuous motion, YOUR RIGHT HAND SLIDES THE CARD UNDER YOUR LEFT THUMB ....AS THE LEFT HAND DRAWS THE CLIPPED COIN FROM UNDER THE CLOTH, PRESSING IT UP AGAINST THE CARD.

(18) Then, the left hand places the card over the two coins at Corner A, SECRETLY ADDING THE COIN IT HOLDS UNDER THE CARD.

(19) Your left hand returns to Corner C and lifts the cloth while your right hand picks up the coin at Corner B. Announce that you will push another coin up through the cloth.

(20) Place your right hand under the cloth the same as before, WITH YOUR LEFT FINGERS CLIPPING THE COIN AND STEALING IT AWAY, AS YOUR RIGHT HAND GOES BENEATH THE CLOTH.

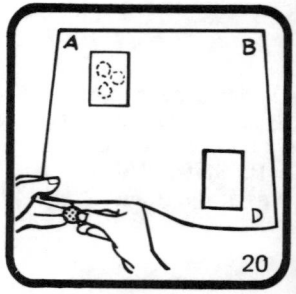

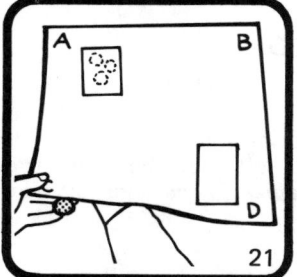

(21) The right hand then pretends to push the coin up through the cloth under the card at Corner A (also with a clink).

(24) As before, the right hand transfers the card to the left hand, which secretly carries the coin away beneath the card. Place the card over the three coins at Corner A, just as before, secretly adding the fourth coin. *(NOTE: Be careful not to let the "secret" coin clink against the other coins as you lay the card down.)*

(22) Remove your right hand from beneath the cloth, then lift the card at Corner A.

(25) With no more coins in view, you remind the audience that one coin is still under the other card at Corner D. So you command it to join the other three. When you lift the card at Corner D, the spectators see, to their amazement, that the coin has really gone!

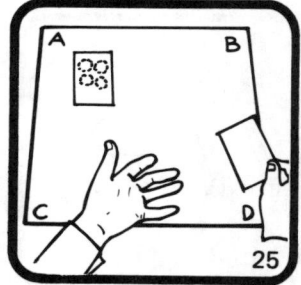

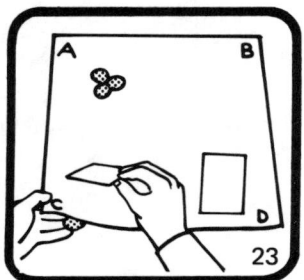

(23) As you reveal the *three* coins, turn the card over toward your left hand, which has the clipped coin ready. Remark, "And another coin has come up through!"

(26) Use your left hand to lift the card at Corner A, showing all four coins there, making the mystery complete!

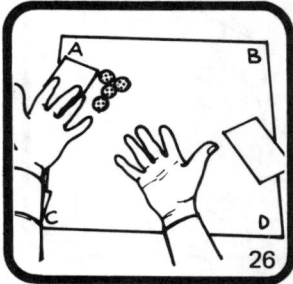

COMMENTS AND SUGGESTIONS

The entire routine should be practiced until it can be done smoothly, and without hesitation where the "secret moves" are concerned. You may experiment with other patterns of covering the coins that work well in directing attention away from the right hand when it secretly picks up the coin at Corner D. For example: Cover the coins at A and B, then bring the right-hand card down to D, so that A and D are covered. Now the left hand moves its card from A to B, while your right fingers secretly pick up the coin at D — *all attention is naturally centered on the left-hand card.* From there simply proceed with the usual routine. Keep alert for audience reactions whenever you present this excellent close-up mystery, and other ideas will suggest themselves.

SLEIGHTS WITH COINS

The following four effects are "pure" *sleight-of-hand* and are all done with an ordinary object that you almost always have with you — a *coin.* After you have mastered them, you will not only have acquired several great effects that can be presented anywhere and anytime, but also you will have opened the door to a multitude of additional, truly sensational Magical Mysteries. Most important of all, you are beginning to learn two of the basic prerequisites to becoming an expert magician — *Dexterity and Misdirection.*

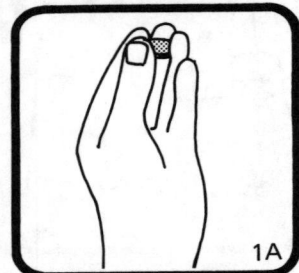

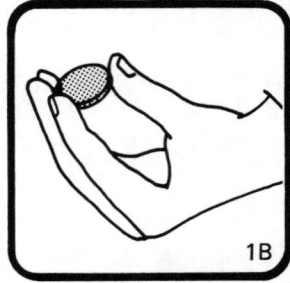

(1) Hold the coin level between the tips of your left thumb and fingers. All four fingers and the thumb of your left hand should point *upward.* Your fingers should be held *close together* so the audience cannot see between them.

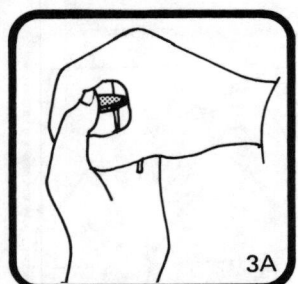

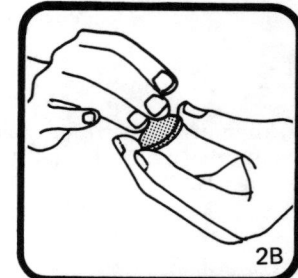

(2) Your right hand approaches from behind to apparently take the coin by sliding your right thumb beneath and your right fingers above the coin. Your left hand should be held as shown from the "Spectators' View" (right side of page), so the coin can still be seen.

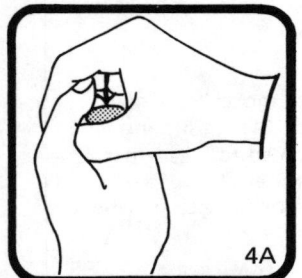

(3) Now the fingers of your right hand close over the coin — covering the coin as shown.

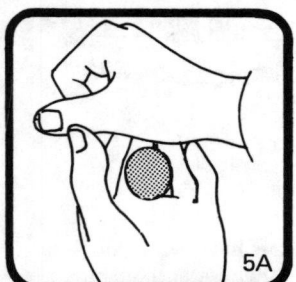

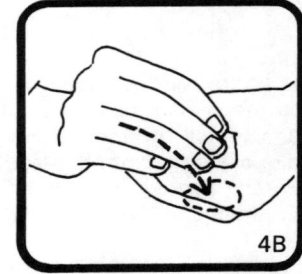

(4) As your right hand pauses momentarily, your left thumb *releases the coin* so that it "secretly" *drops* into the bend of your left fingers.

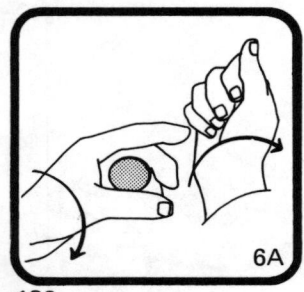

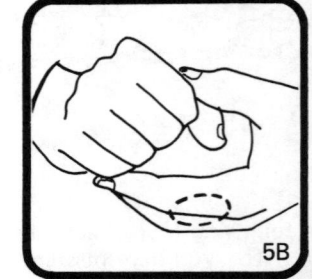

(5) Without hesitation, your right hand closes into a fist *as if taking the coin* from your left fingers.

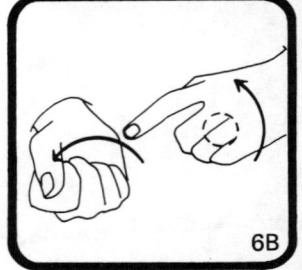

(6) Then, in one continuous motion, *turn both hands over* (see arrows) — as you turn your body to the right. (Just twist your left hand inward, toward your body, so the coin stays hidden from view, and *at the same time,* turn your right hand so that its *closed fingers* face the audience.) As you rotate your hands, your left first finger casually points toward your right hand. *Follow your RIGHT HAND with your eyes* — IT IS SUPPOSED TO CONTAIN THE COIN.

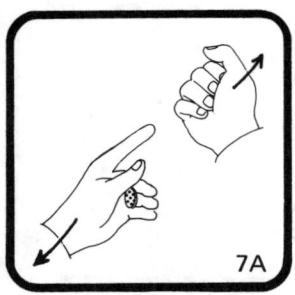

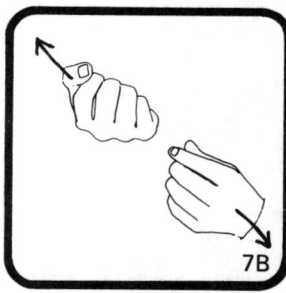

(7) As your right hand moves away, casually let your left hand fall to your side with the coin held secretly in its curled fingers. *Your eyes should remain fixed on your right hand at all times. This is MISDIRECTION.*

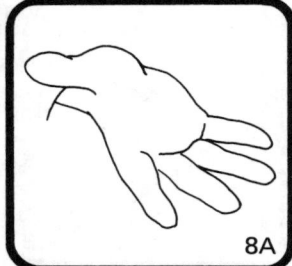

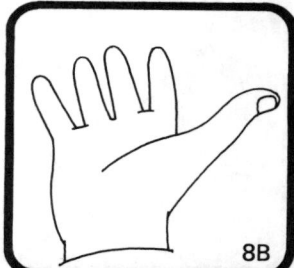

(8) Slowly begin to make a "rubbing" motion with your right fingers, as if to rub the coin away. Then, open your hand to show the coin has "vanished."

THE FINGER PALM VANISH

EFFECT

In this vanish, the coin is actually retained *in the same spot in your left hand* from start to finish. This allows you to perform the sleight either swiftly or slowly, as you prefer. The instruction is given with TWO sets of illustrations. . . . Those at the *left* show how it appears to you, the *performer;* those at the *right* represent the *spectators'* view.

METHOD

MAGICIAN'S VIEW

SPECTATORS' VIEW

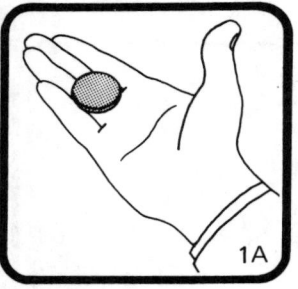

(1) Display a coin lying on the finger of your right hand, as shown.

(2) Your left hand is held palm up, about waist high, with your left fingers pointing just to the right of the center of your audience. Your right little finger rests across the tips of your left fingers.

MAGICIAN'S VIEW

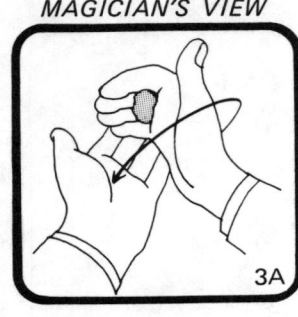

3A

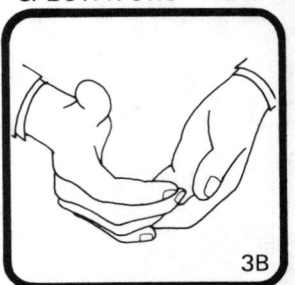

3B

(3) The right hand starts to turn over toward you. *At the same time, curl your right fingers inward just enough to hold the coin securely in the right fingers,* as shown. The coin is now in the FINGER PALM position.

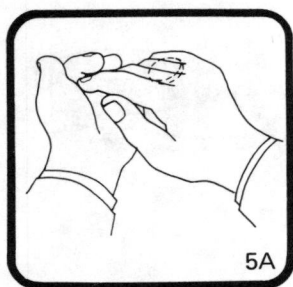

4A

4B

(4) Tip your right hand over even more, as shown . . . right now is the moment when the coin "should" be falling into your left hand. *Actually, the right hand secretly retains the coin in the FINGER PALMED position.*

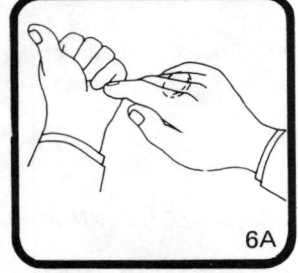

5A

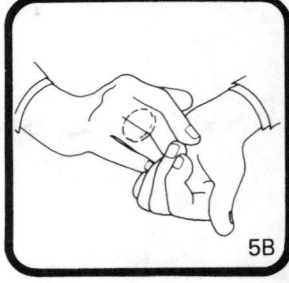

5B

(5) Your left fingers close, *as if they contained the coin.* Your right hand begins to move away from your left hand with the coin secretly FINGER PALMED.

6A

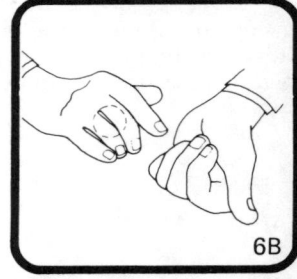

6B

(6) As your left hand closes into a loose fist, your right hand pauses briefly, pointing the first finger toward the closed left hand, which carries attention by moving away to the left.

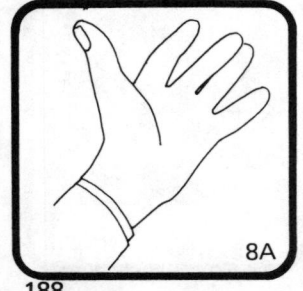

7A

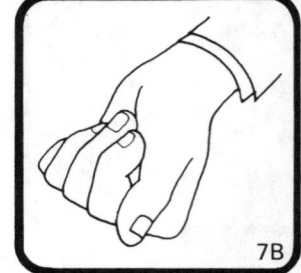

7B

(7) Lower your right hand casually to your side . . . *as your eyes follow your left hand.* . . . THIS IS MISDIRECTION.

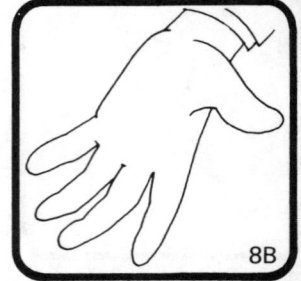

8A

8B

(8) The left hand is now "on its own." It apparently squeezes the coin into "nothing" and opens to show that the coin has "vanished."

THE PINCH OR DROP VANISH

METHOD

MAGICIAN'S VIEW

SPECTATORS' VIEW

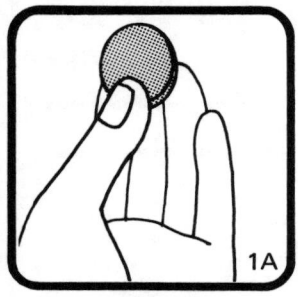

(1) Hold a coin at the tips of your left thumb and first three fingers so it projects straight upward. Keep your fingers *close together* so that the viewers cannot see between them. The palm of your hand faces you.

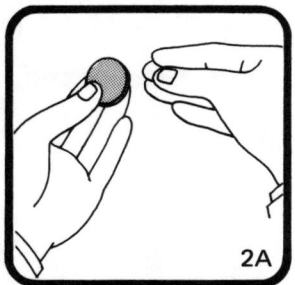

(2) Your right hand approaches your left hand as if to grasp the coin.

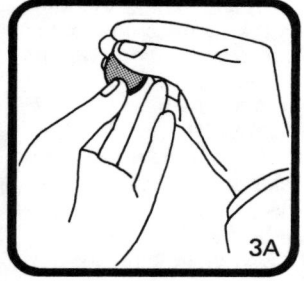

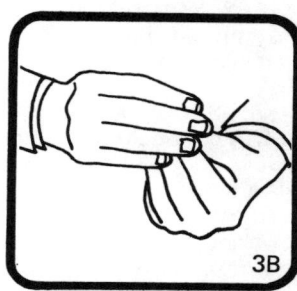

(3) The right hand continues to move until it *completely covers the coin* as if to remove it from between your left thumb and fingers.

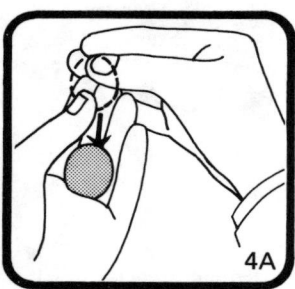

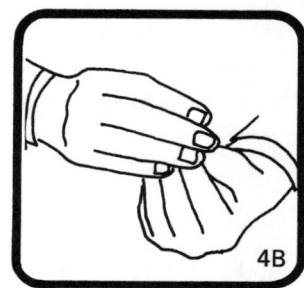

(4) As soon as the coin is concealed by the right fingers, your left thumb releases its "pinching" grip, *allowing the coin to slide secretly down to the base of the left fingers.*

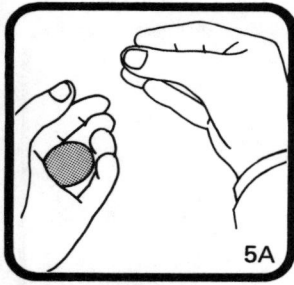

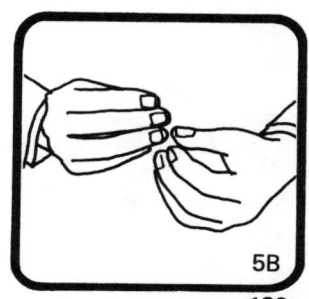

(5) The coin remains concealed in your left hand, held in the FINGER PALM position. Your right hand moves away, *apparently taking the coin with it.* As you move your right hand away, *keep your eyes "fixed" on your right hand,* as if it really contained the coin. *The audience's attention will follow your right hand* — while you casually drop your left hand to your side with the coin secretly held in its fingers.

MAGICIAN'S VIEW   *SPECTATORS' VIEW*

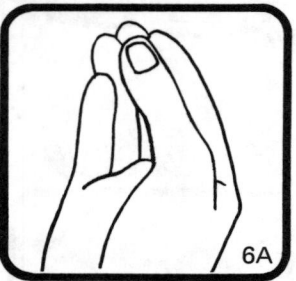

(6) With the back of the right hand still toward the audience, "rub" your thumb and fingers together as if to "dissolve" the coin in your fingertips.

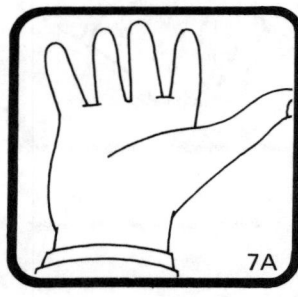

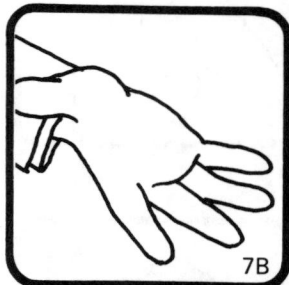

(7) Finally, open your hand and show it empty to complete the "vanish."

NOTE: In Steps 6 and 7 of this "vanish," your right hand *does not* close into a fist. It appears to "take" the coin from your left hand and then "pretends" to display it — before grinding it into "nothing."

COMMENTS AND SUGGESTIONS

In Steps 5, 6, and 7 and in all other Sleight-of-Hand vanishes where the coin is *apparently* transferred from one hand to the other, it is *ESSENTIAL that your eyes follow the hand which apparently contains the coin.* This is one of the most basic and important examples of *"MISDIRECTION."* In fact, in this case, where you *look* is as important as the *sleight* itself. THE AUDIENCE WILL LOOK WHERE YOU LOOK. Therefore, when you practice this or any other similar sleight, you should first practice *really* taking the coin away in your right hand. This will accomplish two things: FIRST, you want the audience to believe that you are taking the coin in your right hand when you are really concealing it in your left. Therefore, the more *natural* this move looks, the more your audience will "believe." Thus, *by really taking the coin,* you will discover for yourself exactly how the move should look *when you perform the sleight.* SECOND, and of equal importance, you will see that, if you *really* take the coin in your right hand, *that is where you will look.* You would *not* take the coin in your *right* hand and *look* at your *left.* All of the moves in the PINCH VANISH are fully illustrated. Stand in front of a mirror — hold the coin at the tips of your left fingers — *then, really take the coin in your right hand.* Do this a number of times. Make your actions correspond to the pictures on the right-hand side of the page. Just make the "pickup" motion in an easy and natural way. THEN, still standing in front of the mirror, try the *sleight.* As you "pretend" to take the coin, let it slide down into your left hand, as shown on the *left* side of the page. By using the mirror and the two sets of illustrations, you can see exactly how this sleight will appear to you *and* to your audience. And always remember your *MISDIRECTION* — ALWAYS LOOK AT THE HAND THAT *SUPPOSEDLY* CONTAINS THE COIN!

THE CLASSIC PALM

Using a Coin

This is probably the oldest and most basic of all coin sleights used to conceal a coin in the hand in a natural manner. It is also one of the most difficult to master....but, once learned it will be of great value to you — not only with coins, but with other objects as well.

METHOD

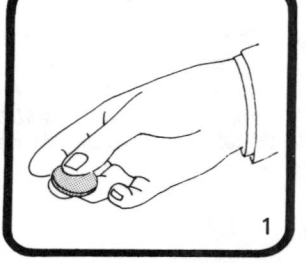

(1) Place a coin on the tips of your two middle fingers and hold it there with the tip of your thumb.

(2) Remove the thumb and bend your fingertips inward, sliding the coin along the underside of your thumb until it reaches your palm. As you slide the coin into the palm, *stretch your hand* open so the muscles at the base of your thumb and little finger are fully expanded.

(3) Press the coin *firmly into the palm* and *contract the muscles* of your hand inward – thus gaining a grip on the edges of the coin. Draw your thumb inward only as far as needed to retain the coin comfortably. Too much "grip" will make your hand appear cramped and tense.

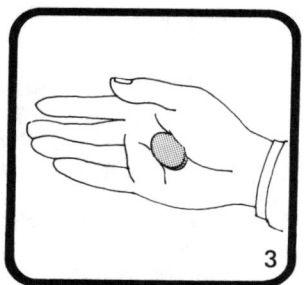

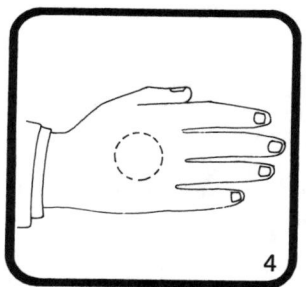

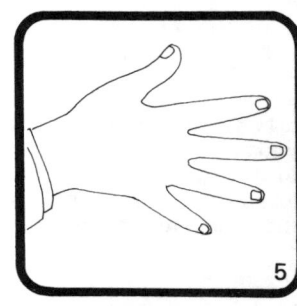

(4) Seen from the back, the hand should look relaxed and natural, with the fingers close together. (5) Avoid the common fault of holding the coin too tightly and spreading the thumb and fingers wide, as shown here. This will only give away the fact that you are "hiding" something. Only when the hand looks natural will you be above suspicion and thus have mastered the Classic Palm.

COMMENTS AND SUGGESTIONS

The basic magical term "Palm" comes from this method of concealment, as the coin is actually gripped in the *palm* of the hand. Keep practicing it until you can place the coin in just the right position. It will then become "second nature" and will prove extremely useful. Once the knack is acquired, coins of various sizes can be retained. It is a good idea to use the hand containing the palmed coin for various gestures such as snapping the fingers, pulling back the sleeve, or picking up articles from the table. These natural actions will direct attention *away* from the hand as people will automatically assume that it is empty. NOTE: The object being "Palmed" must be placed in the CLASSIC PALM position with the aid of only the finger and thumb of the hand doing the "Palming" – with no help from your "other" hand. You should also practice this important sleight so that you can "Palm" objects in *either hand* with equal ease.

MASTER COIN MYSTERIES

Now that you have learned four basic coin sleights — The French Drop; The Finger Palm Vanish; The Pinch Vanish, and The Classic Palm — you are ready to move ahead to the outstanding *Master Coin Mysteries* that follow.

THE COIN-VANISHING HANDKERCHIEF

EFFECT

The magician borrows a coin from a spectator and has it marked for future identification. The magician places the coin under a pocket handkerchief and gives it to a spectator to hold. Under these conditions, *even though the volunteer can feel the coin through the fabric of the handkerchief and the audience can plainly see its shape,* the performer causes the marked coin to *VANISH right from under the spectator's fingertips!*

SECRET AND PREPARATION

The following method for the vanish of a coin or any other small object has many uses, as you will find later in the Course.

(A) For this you need an inexpensive pocket handkerchief. Place the handkerchief flat on a table. Place a coin of the same size as the one which you will later borrow from the spectator on the lower right hand corner of the handkerchief.

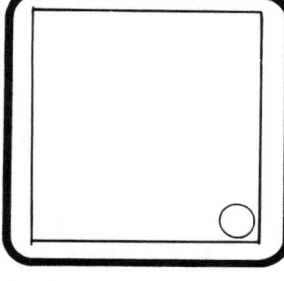

(B) Now cover the coin with a small square piece of matching fabric (a piece cut from a duplicate handkerchief is perfect). Sew the four edges of the small square of cloth to the handkerchief. THE COIN IS NOW HIDDEN INSIDE A SECRET POCKET YOU HAVE MADE IN THE CORNER OF THE HANDKERCHIEF.

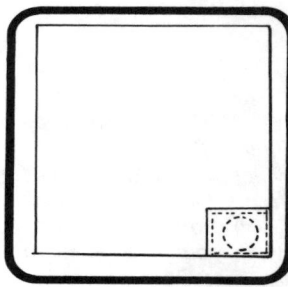

(1) Put the prepared handkerchief into your pocket or lay it on your table. If you can do so, it's a nice touch to wear it as a part of your wardrobe. If worn in your top coat pocket, as an example, it subtly influences your audience into assuming that the handkerchief is not a "magical prop."

(2) Borrow a coin from a spectator which duplicates the coin hidden in your handkerchief. Bring him up on the platform with you and have him mark the coin for identification. Stand your volunteer to your left and remove your pocket handkerchief.

(3) Hold the borrowed coin between your left thumb and first fingers, with your fingers and thumb pointing "up" and one side of the coin toward the audience. With your right hand cover the coin *and* your left hand with the prepared handkerchief. THE CORNER WITH THE SECRET POCKET SHOULD BE ON THE SIDE OF THE HANDKERCHIEF *THAT IS TO-WARD YOU,* AS SHOWN.

(4) Grasp the hidden coin with the right thumb and fingers and, *with your right hand, lift the corner with the concealed duplicate coin up under the handkerchief.* POSITION IT <u>NEXT</u> TO THE BORROWED COIN.

(5) At this point, you substitute the hidden coin for the marked coin BY FINGER PALMING THE MARKED COIN IN YOUR LEFT HAND. Withdraw your left hand holding the borrowed coin as shown.

(6) *NOTE: Either your right or your left hand can be used for Finger Palming and removing the borrowed coin — just use whichever hand is easier for you and whichever works best for the "reproduction" of the coin that you have set up. In the illustrations, your left hand is shown palming the spectator's coin while your right hand holds the handkerchief and the "secret" duplicate coin.*

(7) Now grasp the "secret" coin through the fabric of the handkerchief with your left hand. Remove your right hand from beneath the handkerchief as you hold the coin with your left thumb and fingers. Then, with your right hand, twist the cloth around *below* the coin. *Make sure that the spectators don't get a "flash" of the marked coin that is Finger Palmed in your left hand.*

(8) Grasp the handkerchief beneath the coin with your right hand and offer the cloth-covered coin to a spectator to hold. Just act natural and remember that the audience's attention is on the duplicate coin which is now under the handkerchief. Ask the spectator to hold *his* coin through the fabric of the handkerchief as you (a) either casually drop the coin into your pocket or (b) place the coin in position for its mysterious reappearance — (as in THE COIN IN THE BALL OF WOOL).

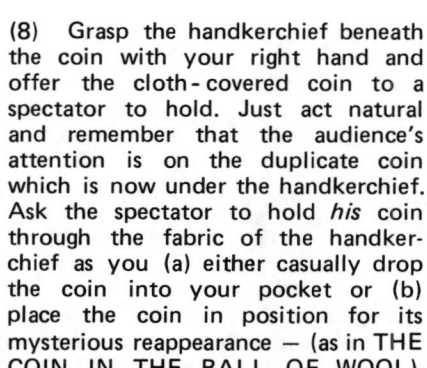

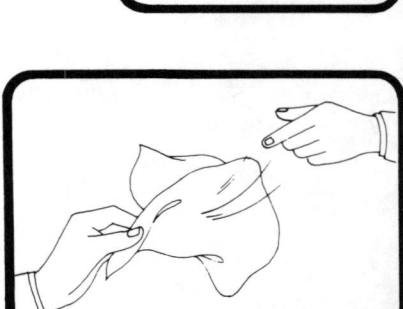

(9) When you are ready for the "vanish," ask the spectator if he can still feel his coin under the handkerchief. He will reply, "Yes."

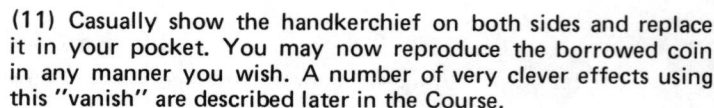

(10) GRASP ONE CORNER of the handkerchief and "jerk" the handkerchief and the coin away from the spectator's grasp. *It will appear as if the coin has "vanished" from the spectator's fingertips.*

(11) Casually show the handkerchief on both sides and replace it in your pocket. You may now reproduce the borrowed coin in any manner you wish. A number of very clever effects using this "vanish" are described later in the Course.

THE COIN-VANISHING HANDKERCHIEF — SECOND VARIATION

EFFECT

The effect is the same as the COIN-VANISHING HANDKERCHIEF, except that in this case, the borrowed coin is further "secured" in the handkerchief before the Vanish by a rubber band.

SECRET AND PREPARATION

In addition to the specially prepared COIN-VANISHING HANDKERCHIEF, you will need a small rubber band which you place in your left coat pocket.

METHOD

(1) Proceed as in the Coin-Vanishing Handkerchief through Step 9.

(2) As the left hand leaves with the Finger Palmed marked coin, reach into your coat pocket and remove the rubber band, *leaving the coin in your pocket.*

(3) Place the rubber band around the handkerchief *below* the coin as shown.

(4) *NOTE: The reason for the rubber band is twofold. First, it permits a natural way in which to dispose of the marked coin in your pocket temporarily. Second, it prevents the spectator from visually inspecting the contents of the handkerchief while he is holding the coin.*

(5) When you are ready for the Vanish, ask the spectator if he still has the coin in his grasp. After he answers "Yes," *remove the rubber band.* Then, quickly snap the handkerchief out of his hand as usual.

COMMENTS AND SUGGESTIONS

The addition of the rubber band can come in handy to cover what might otherwise be a "suspicious" move when you pocket the borrowed coin. The rubber band could also be placed in the location where the marked coin is going to be reproduced, say in the box holding the COIN IN THE BALL OF WOOL. This would give you a natural reason for going to the box and inserting the coin in the slide before the audience is aware of trickery of any kind.

GRANT'S SUPER COIN-VANISHING HANDKERCHIEF

"GEN" GRANT

Here is a clever variation for the specially prepared COIN-VANISHING HANDKERCHIEF. The construction of this handkerchief is different in that the "secret" coin, which is concealed in the corner of the handkerchief, is *removable.* The handkerchief can therefore be adapted to *many different tricks* requiring the vanish of various sized coins or other small objects.

METHOD

(1) Purchase two identical pocket handkerchiefs. Open one of them flat on your table as shown. (2) Cut a 2" square from the corner of the second handkerchief and place it over the matching corner of the first handkerchief.

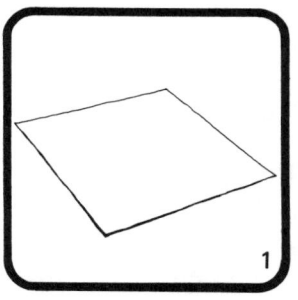

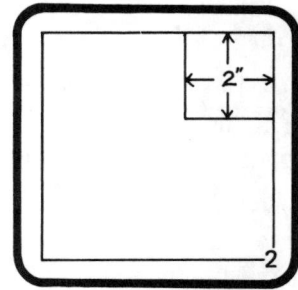

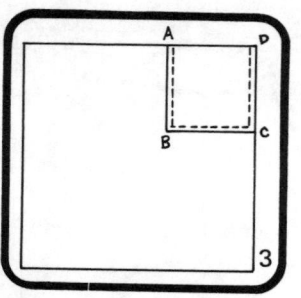

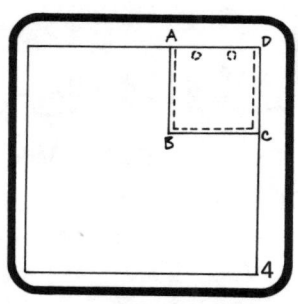

(5) IMPORTANT NOTE: The most important value of this specially prepared handkerchief is that you can now insert *any coin or small object* into the secret pocket. A ring, coin, or folded up dollar bill are just a few examples of the small items which can be vanished by this versatile and inexpensive piece of magical apparatus.

(3) Sew *three* of the edges of the small square of cloth (indicated by dotted lines in the illustration) to the first handkerchief. Leave the outside seam, A to D, *open. NOTE: The unhemmed edges of the corner patch, A to B and B to C, should be turned under before sewing to prevent the cut edges from fraying.*
(4) This done, sew two small dress snaps on the inside hem of the "open" seam (A to D), as indicated. You now have a secret pocket in the corner of the handkerchief which will safely conceal a coin or other small object inside.

SUPER DOOPER VERSATILE VANISHER

Here is an even more versatile and deceptive "Vanishing" Handkerchief. It combines all of the best features of the previous special handkerchiefs and adds another improvement as well.

EFFECT

The effect is the same as the COIN-VANISHING HANDKERCHIEF.

SECRET AND PREPARATION

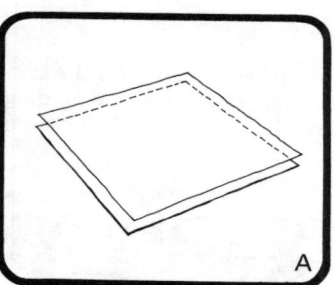

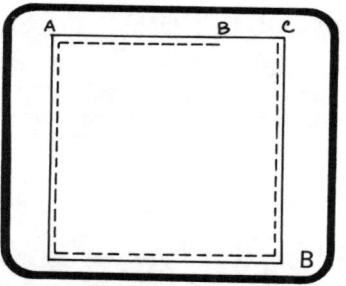

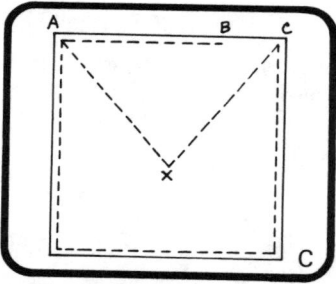

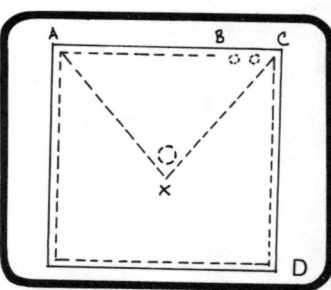

(A) Purchase two identical pocket handkerchiefs that are made with a colorful pattern or design. (A common "bandana" works well.) Place one on top of the other as shown. (B) Sew the two handkerchiefs together along the four sides and leave the top hem open at one corner. This opening is between Points B and C in the illustration. The opening should be about two inches wide or slightly larger than the object you intend to vanish. (C) Also, sew the handkerchiefs together as indicated by the dotted line in Illustration C. The stitching from A to X to C forms a "V-shaped" pocket *inside the handkerchief.* Point X should be slightly below the exact center of the handkerchief. (D) Sew two small dress snaps inside the open hem between B and C as shown. Any size coin (or any other small object) may then be inserted into the opening and sealed inside with the snaps. In the following description, you will be "vanishing" a coin, so place a coin that matches the one that you wish to vanish inside the secret pocket and you are ready to begin.

METHOD

(1) To vanish the coin, grasp the handkerchief in both hands at Corners A and C and snap it open. The "hidden" coin will automatically position itself *in the center of the double handkerchief.*
(2) Drape the handkerchief over your left hand so the hidden coin rests on your open left palm. Place the borrowed coin *directly on top* of the hidden coin as shown.

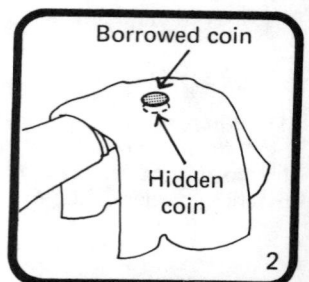

Borrowed coin

Hidden coin

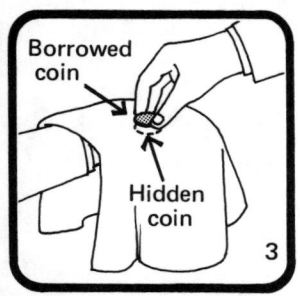

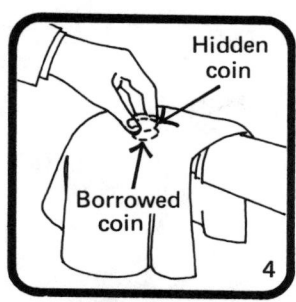

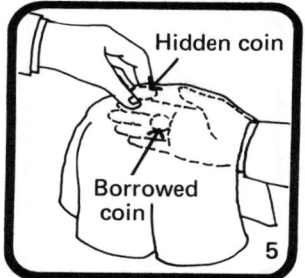

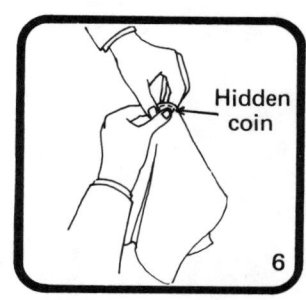

(3) With the fingers of the right hand, hold the borrowed coin and the secret duplicate in place. (4) Turn the entire affair upside down so that the handkerchief falls over your right hand and the coin(s).

(5) Now with your left hand, grasp the *duplicate coin* through the fabric. At the same time, your right hand allows the spectator's coin to fall into the Finger Palm position as shown. (6) Casually withdraw your right hand (and the spectator's coin) from beneath the handkerchief, as you ask the spectator to grasp "his" coin (really the duplicate) through the fabric of the handkerchief. At this point, your right hand, which secretly holds the borrowed coin concealed in the curled fingers, can be casually placed in your right pocket where it leaves the coin to be reproduced later.

(7) When you are ready to "vanish" the coin, grasp the bottom corner of the handkerchief and give it a sharp downward tug — pulling it from the spectator's grip. The duplicate coin is retained within the double handkerchief giving the impression that the borrowed coin vanished from between the fingertips of the volunteer.

COMMENTS AND SUGGESTIONS

There are three advantages to this type of "vanishing" handkerchief: First, you may insert any small object into the secret pocket to be "vanished." Second, because the duplicate is located in the center, the placement of the object under the handkerchief as described in Steps 3 and 4 is very natural. Third, the "V" type pocket is so constructed that a somewhat larger or bulkier object may be used and will still not show after the vanish because of the size of the "secret" pocket and the location of the object *in the center of the handkerchief* after the vanish.

COIN THROUGH LEG

EFFECT

The magician apparently causes a half-dollar to magically pass completely through his right leg.

METHOD

All that is required are an unprepared half-dollar and mastery of the FINGER PALM.

(1) Display a half-dollar to your audience. The coin is held between the thumb and fingers of the right hand. Now lower the coin to your right side, next to your right trouser leg and slightly above your right knee.

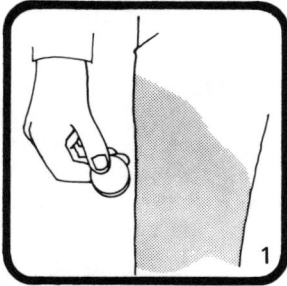

(3) Bring your left hand over beside the coin. With the fingers of *both* the right and left hands, lift a portion of the trouser fabric *up and under* the coin.

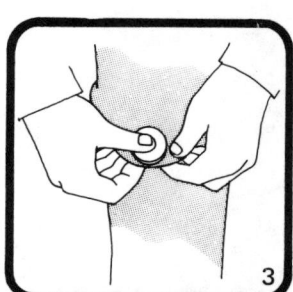

(2) Place the coin on your leg as shown. Your right thumb holds the coin *against* your trouser leg just above the knee.

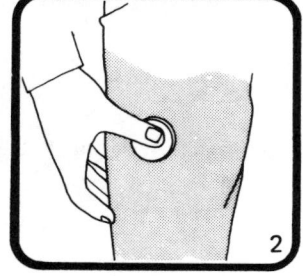

(4) Now, *fold the cloth that you have just pulled under the coin UP AND OVER THE COIN.* The left thumb holds the fold of cloth in place.

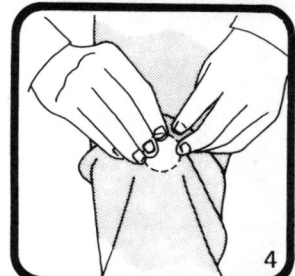

195

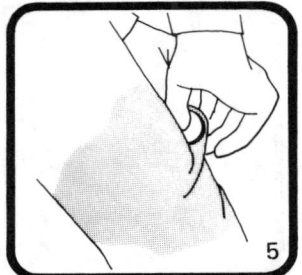

(5) This is how the coin and folded cloth should look to you.

(8) *NOTE: The right hand will appear to be empty, while the left hand is apparently still holding the coin behind the fold of cloth in your trouser leg.*

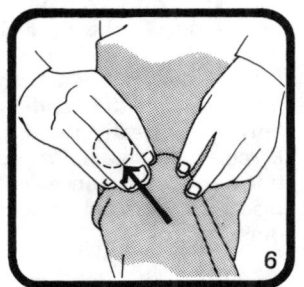

(6) As soon as the coin is covered by the fold in the trouser leg, THE THUMB OF YOUR RIGHT HAND SECRETLY PULLS THE COIN UP BEHIND YOUR RIGHT FINGERS.

(9) NOW FOR THE "VANISH." The left hand releases the fold of cloth in the trouser leg. The fabric will drop revealing the "vanish" of the coin. Turn your left hand over to show the audience that it is empty.

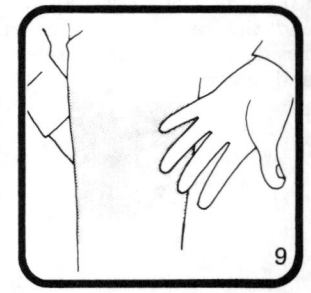

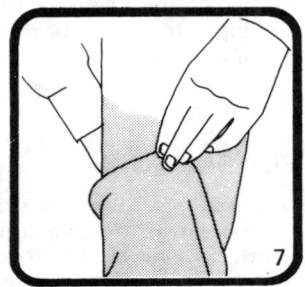

(7) You now FINGER PALM the coin in your right hand. Move your right hand away and, slowly and deliberately, place it behind your right leg.

(10) With your right hand, slowly withdraw the coin from behind your right knee. Apparently, the coin has gone "magically" right through your leg!

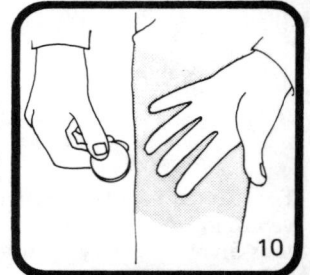

COMMENTS AND SUGGESTIONS

This is a very clever and easily learned "sleight" which can be used as a trick in itself as just described . . . or for the *Vanish* of a coin, as explained in the next effect, which can be useful in other coin routines.

CHALLENGE COIN VANISH

EFFECT

The magician displays a coin and places it in a fold of cloth on the leg of his trousers. A member of the audience is allowed to feel the coin to see if it is still there. Yet, under these seemingly impossible circumstances, the coin vanishes completely.

SECRET AND PREPARATION

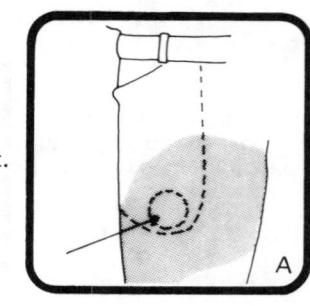

(A) Place a "duplicate" of the coin you intend to vanish in your right trouser pocket.

METHOD

Proceed exactly as in the COIN THROUGH LEG, through Step 5.

(1) However, when you place the coin which will vanish on your leg in Step 1 this time position it *directly above* the "secret" duplicate coin in your right pants pocket. *NOTE: Because of the location of the duplicate coin in your pocket, it will be necessary to place the "vanishing" coin slightly higher on your pants leg than in the COIN THROUGH LEG.*

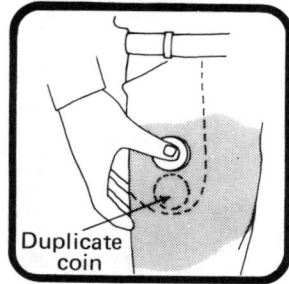

(4) Now proceed to "steal" the coin away in the FINGER PALM position as explained in Step 6 in COIN THROUGH LEG.

(2) Now, when you fold the cloth up around the coin, make sure that the duplicate coin is in the fold of cloth ON TOP OF THE COIN WHICH WILL VANISH.

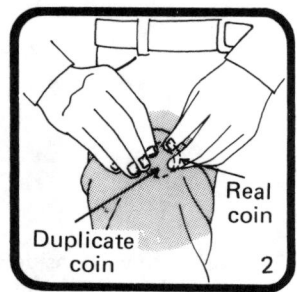

(5) Ask the spectator to feel and see if the coin is still there. *When he does, he will feel the duplicate coin which is in your pocket.* THIS GIVES YOU IDEAL "MISDIRECTION" TO SECRETLY DROP THE FINGER PALMED COIN INTO YOUR RIGHT COAT POCKET.

(3) *NOTE: You now have the real coin, the one that the audience knows about, under the duplicate coin, which is really in your right trouser pocket.*

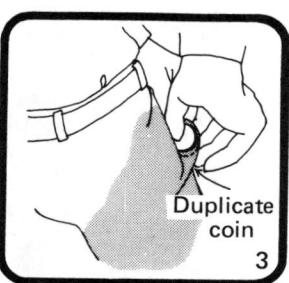

(6) After the spectator is satisfied that the coin is still there, merely let the fold of cloth drop as before. You may then show both hands to be completely empty. The coin has vanished.

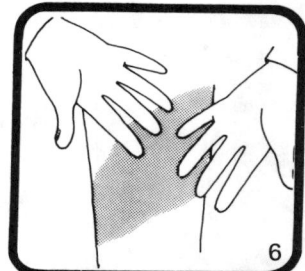

COIN-A-GO-GO

EFFECT

The magician borrows a half dollar from a member of the audience. The spectator is handed a black grease pencil with which to mark the coin. Working at very close range, the performer causes the coin to vanish right before the spectator's eyes, utilizing the pencil as an impromptu wand. The magician shows both hands to be unmistakably empty, and even hands the pencil to the spectator to examine. Then, to bring the mystery to a happy conclusion, the magician simply taps the back of his left hand with the pencil and magically reproduces the marked coin.

SECRET AND PREPARATION

This is a very good impromptu trick. Carry a grease pencil, marking pen, ballpoint pen, or just a regular lead pencil in your left inside coat pocket, and you are always ready to perform. To insure the proper working of the effect, do not use a coin smaller than a quarter. Only one sleight is used, the "Finger Palm" which you have already learned. After you have mastered this move, this routine will become an excellent addition to your impromptu program.

METHOD

(1) Borrow a half-dollar from a spectator and have him mark it with the pen or pencil. Let's suppose you are using a pencil. After the spectator is satisfied that he will be able to identify the coin later, replace the pencil into your left-hand inside coat pocket.

(5) . . . finally ending up with the half-dollar enclosed in the left hand.

(2) Place the coin on the palm of your right hand.

(6) Reach into your inside coat pocket with your right hand and retrieve the pencil.

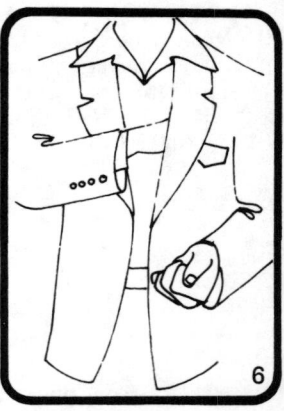

(3) Now toss the coin from hand . . .

(7) Point the pencil at your left hand and ask the spectator to call "heads or tails."

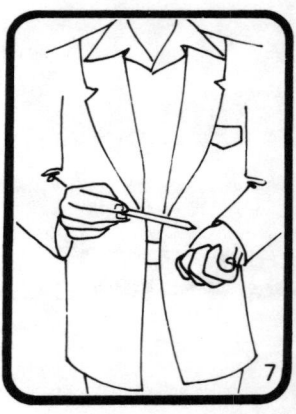

(4) . . . to hand . . .

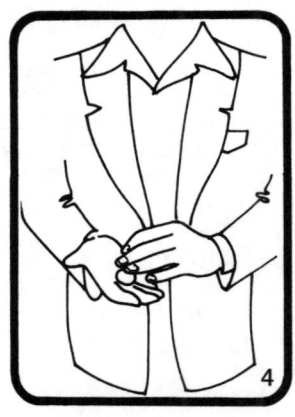

(8) After the spectator makes his choice, open your left hand and allow him to verify whether or not he was correct. *NOTE: All of the preceeding has nothing to do with the actual working of the trick but adds greatly to the "misdirection," as you will see.*

(9) In any event, you tell the spectator that you would like to try it again. Replace the pencil in your pocket and once again toss the coin back and forth from hand to hand. However, on the last "toss," when you apparently throw the coin into the left hand, execute the Finger Palm with your right hand. *Secretly retain the coin in your right hand as your left hand apparently closes over the coin.*

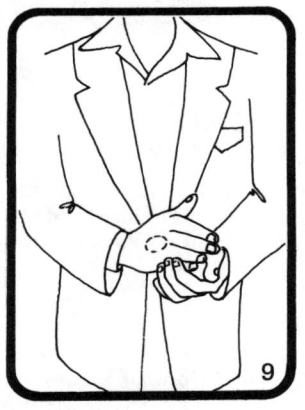

(10) Now the effect should be exactly the same as before as far as the spectator is concerned. With the coin concealed in your right hand, reach into your coat for the pencil. THIS TIME, HOWEVER, DROP THE COIN DOWN THE TOP OF YOUR LEFT SLEEVE AT THE INSIDE ARMHOLE OF YOUR COAT. The coin will fall down your sleeve to your left elbow and will remain there as long as you keep your left arm bent as shown.

(11) The above move should be accomplished smoothly. As you remove your right hand from your jacket, bring the pencil into view and once again use it to point to the left hand. Ask the spectator to call heads or tails. Since every move you have just made duplicates the first run through, the spectator will have absolutely no reason for doubting the presence of the coin in your left hand.

(12) After the spectator has made his choice, slowly open the hand and reveal the startling vanish of the coin. HAND THE PENCIL TO THE SPECTATOR AND SHOW BOTH HANDS TO BE COMPLETELY EMPTY.

(13) Lower your left arm to your side as you ask the spectator to return the pencil.

(14) The spectator's eyes will be diverted by the pencil as the marked coin falls silently into your left palm. Take back the pencil from the spectator as you close your left hand around the coin.

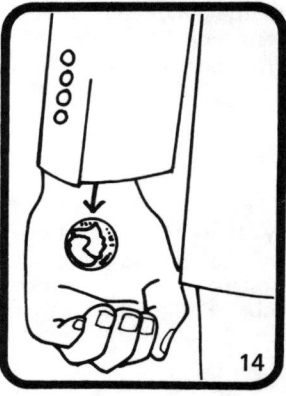

(15) Raise your left hand to waist level and tap it with the pencil.

(16) Slowly open your hand revealing the magical reappearance of the coin. Have the spectator identify the half dollar as being the original borrowed coin and thank him for his assistance.

CONTINUOUS COINS

Catching coins from the air and dropping them in a high hat was long a classic among old-time magicians. Coins are still with us, and to produce them magically in endless fashion is even more wonderful when done at close range. In this modern version, you either borrow a handkerchief or use one of your own and begin to extract countless coins from its folds to the amazement of your audience.

EFFECT

The magician's hands are unmistakably empty as he removes a handkerchief from his breast pocket. This handkerchief is draped over his right hand. The left hand is shown to be empty as the handkerchief is transferred from his right hand to his left. The audience is surprised to see a large silver coin has "magically" appeared in the folds of the handkerchief! Removing the coin, the magician places it into his right side trouser pocket. He now transfers the handkerchief back to his right hand. Another coin is seen to materialize from the center of the handkerchief. After pocketing this second coin, the magician increases his pace — producing coin after coin in an apparently unlimited supply. Finally, the performer sets his handkerchief aside and removes the coins from his pockets. The spectators see them shower from both of his hands into a container on the table.

SECRET AND PREPARATION

The only sleight needed for this clever bit of skullduggery is the "Finger Palm" and some practice so that you present the routine smoothly. It will be necessary for you to perform the Finger Palm with both your left hand and your right hand, which you should find quite easy to learn as you practice. The items needed to present this effective mystery are: An ordinary pocket handkerchief, twelve coins (half-dollars are recommended for visibility — even silver dollars if you have large hands), and a glass or metal bowl which you place on your table. Put the handkerchief in your coat pocket or simply have it already on the table. Place six of the coins in your left trouser pocket and the other six in your right trouser pocket. Now you are ready.

METHOD

(1) Remove the handkerchief and display it on both sides. SHOW CLEARLY THAT YOU ARE NOT CONCEALING ANYTHING IN EITHER OF YOUR HANDS OR IN THE HANDKERCHIEF.

(4) Show your left hand to be empty, then grasp the center of the handkerchief with your left fingertips as shown.

(2) Now, position your right hand as shown — all of your fingers and thumb should touch at the tips and all are pointed "up."

(5) The object of the next move is to reverse the positions of your hands. That is, to cover your left hand with the handkerchief and to free your right hand. With the left fingers grasping the center of the handkerchief as shown in Step 4, THE RIGHT HAND THROWS THE HANDKERCHIEF OVER THE LEFT HAND. The left hand turns over, assuming the same position previously held by the right. The left hand is now covered by the handkerchief.

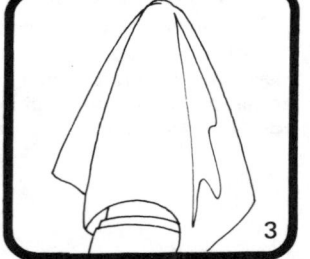

(3) *With your left hand, drape the handkerchief over your right hand.* Make sure that your right fingertips are near the center of the handkerchief.

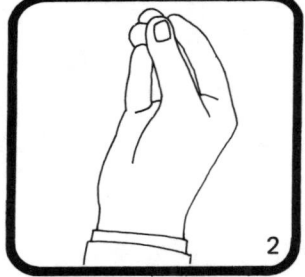

(6) You then "pretend" to see something protruding from the center of the handkerchief. Your right fingers grasp the phantom object. *By keeping the back of your hand to the audience, they will assume that you are holding some item that they cannot see.*

(7) Without hesitation, place the imaginary object into your right hand trouser pocket. YOU NOW SECRETLY FINGER PALM ONE OF THE SIX COINS IN YOUR POCKET IN YOUR RIGHT HAND.

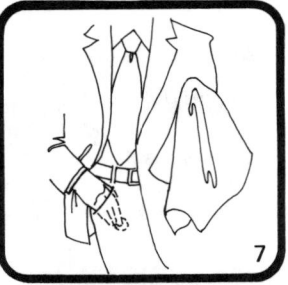

(8) *NOTE: The total action here must be timed so that you give the impression of putting something INTO your pocket not REMOVING something.*

(9) Now bring your hand out of your pocket. *Keep the back of your hand toward the audience which will effectively conceal the Finger Palmed coin.* Grasp the center of the handkerchief with the right fingertips as shown.

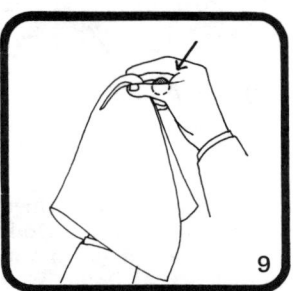

(10) Once again, you are going to "reverse" hand positions – this time covering your right hand, *which contains the hidden coin,* with the handkerchief. The left hand throws the handkerchief over the right hand as the right hand turns over assuming its original position.

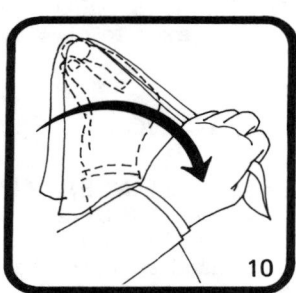

(11) *NOTE: The audience is unaware of the coin now palmed in your right hand. At this point you have successfully "loaded" your first coin into the handkerchief.*

(12) Once again, you pretend to see something protruding from the center of the handkerchief. But this time, the *left* fingers grasp the phantom object.

(13) You promptly thrust this newly found item into your left trouser pocket as in Step 7. While your hand is in your left pocket, FINGER PALM ONE OF THE SIX COINS LOCATED THERE IN YOUR LEFT HAND AND REMOVE YOUR HAND. Then, with the coin secretly held in the Finger Palm, reach for the center of the handkerchief with your left fingertips.

(14) *This next move is important.* WITH YOUR LEFT FINGERS AND THUMB GRASP THE HANDKERCHIEF IN THE CENTER AND ALSO GRASP THE HIDDEN COIN THROUGH THE CLOTH, THE COIN THAT IS UNDER THE HANDKERCHIEF IN YOUR RIGHT HAND.

(15) *NOTE: Make sure not to "flash" the Finger Palmed coin in your left hand during this action. It must look as if you are only grasping the handkerchief, when in reality you are also lifting the hidden coin out of your right hand.*

(16) Now repeat the moves described in Step 5. However, this time the result will be the SUDDEN APPEARANCE OF A HALF-DOLLAR IN THE CENTER OF THE HANDKERCHIEF! *The "appearing" coin is held through the cloth by the left fingers.*

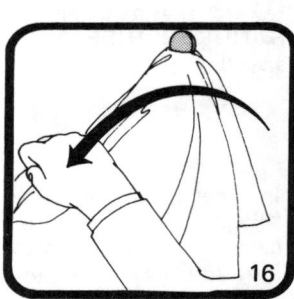

(17) Grasp the coin and display it between the right thumb and fingers as shown. Then place the coin into your right-hand pocket. ACTUALLY, AS SOON AS YOUR RIGHT HAND IS INSIDE YOUR POCKET, FINGER PALM THE COIN. Then withdraw your hand with the secretly Finger Palmed coin. *The effect is that you left the coin in your pocket since your hand will appear to be empty when you bring it out.*

(18) NOW, WITH YOUR RIGHT FINGERS AND THUMB GRASP THE CENTER OF THE HANDKERCHIEF AND THE COIN HIDDEN UNDERNEATH IN YOUR LEFT HAND. Repeat Step 14 for the *left-handed* production of the next coin.

(19) These moves are repeated between the right and left hands until you have apparently produced a dozen coins.

(20) Finally, discard the handkerchief, reach into both trouser pockets and grasp all of the coins. Remove your hands and allow the coins to shower from your palms into the receptacle on your table. At this point, your audience will be completely convinced that you actually produced *all* of the coins from your empty hands and the equally empty handkerchief, *when in reality you accomplished the effect using ONLY TWO COINS.*

COMMENTS AND SUGGESTIONS

The usual way to conclude this effect is simply to spread the handkerchief and give it back to its owner, telling him you hope that he can get the same results later on. If it is your own handkerchief, put it in your pocket and then go on with your next trick, letting the audience wonder where the coins could have come from.

A clever effect is to have coins of different values and sizes in each pocket. Then, after producing and pocketing several half-dollars, you can switch to a dollar sized coin in your right pocket and begin producing those. Your left hand could then switch to a large copper coin — such as an old English penny. You can finish by switching to a dime or a nickel giving you an excuse for ending the production, since the coins are dwindling in size, indicating that the magic must be running out.

COPPER-SILVER PENETRATION

EFFECT

The magician requests the assistance of a spectator and asks that he stand to his (the performer's) left. The magician removes two coins from his trouser pocket. One of the coins is an English Penny, the other an American Half-Dollar. Both of these coins are the same size, but the copper Penny contrasts attractively against the silver Half. The coins are handed to a spectator for examination. The performer then displays an empty pocket handkerchief and wraps the silver Half in it. The Half-Dollar, wrapped in the handkerchief, is given to the spectator to hold. The magician calls the audience's attention to the English Penny. The magician then "invisibly" throws the Penny toward the handkerchief. To everyone's surprise, THE VANISHED PENNY IS HEARD TO MAGICALLY PENETRATE THE HANDKERCHIEF AND FALL ALONGSIDE THE HALF! The spectator is asked to open out the handkerchief to verify the coin's arrival.

SECRET AND PREPARATION

In order to present this effect, it will be necessary for you to have mastered the FINGER PALM and the FRENCH DROP or any other "sleight-of-hand" vanish of a coin. You will also need two English Pennies, one Half-Dollar and a Pocket Handerchief. *(If you do not have two English Pennies, see COMMENTS AND SUGGESTIONS at the end of this trick.)* Fold the pocket handkerchief and place it into your inside coat pocket. Place one of the English Pennies next to the handkerchief so that you will be able to grasp it easily. Then, put the Half-Dollar and the "duplicate" English Penny into your right trouser pocket.

METHOD

(1) Ask for the assistance of a volunteer from the audience and have him stand to your left. (This will give you the most protection from "accidental exposure" during the presentation.)

(2) Remove the Penny and the Half from your right trouser pocket and give them to the spectator for examination.

(3) While he is busy examining the coins, reach into your inside coat pocket with your left hand and secretly *Finger Palm the duplicate Penny.* As soon as the coin is securely palmed, grasp the handkerchief and bring it into view. *Make sure the spectators do not catch a glimpse of the hidden coin as you display the handkerchief.*

(4) After showing the handkerchief, hold it in your left hand . . . *this disguises the fact that you are also concealing a coin in that hand as well.*

(5) Ask the spectator for the Half-Dollar. Hold the coin by your *right* fingertips and display it to the audience. Now, transfer the Half so that it is held by your *left* fingertips. YOUR LEFT HAND IS NOW HOLDING THE HALF-DOLLAR IN PLAIN VIEW, THE DUPLICATE COPPER PENNY IN A FINGER PALM, <u>AND</u> A CORNER OF THE HANDKERCHIEF. The illustration shows the positions of the three objects.

(6) Your right hand now grasps the bottom corner of the handkerchief and "snaps" it free of your left hand. Then cover your left hand and the coin(s) with the handkerchief. *NOTE: Position the handkerchief so that the Half-Dollar is near the center of the handkerchief.*

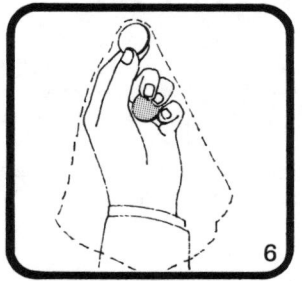

(7) With your *right fingers,* grasp the Half-Dollar *through the fabric* and lift the coin out of your left fingers.

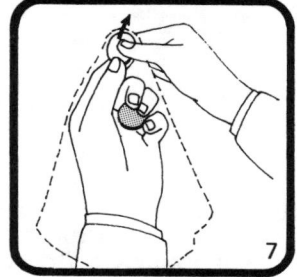

(8) *Now, under cover of the handkerchief, with your left hand, secretly place the Finger Palmed Penny into the palm of your right hand. THE ENGLISH PENNY STAYS UNDER THE HANDKERCHIEF as your right fingers curl around the handkerchief AND the Penny and HOLD THE PENNY THROUGH THE FABRIC UNDER THE HANDKERCHIEF AS SHOWN.*

(9) Have the spectator grasp the Half-Dollar *through* the fabric of the handkerchief. As he does this, *slide the Penny down, inside the handkerchief,* as you continue to hold the Penny with your right fingers.

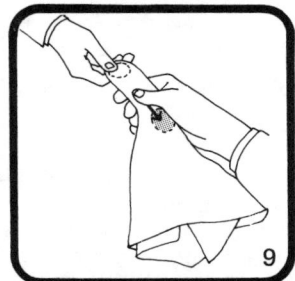

(10) *Turn the handkerchief parallel to the floor. . . .* Then slide your right hand to the right end (where the corners are) of the handkerchief. As you slide your hand, LEAVE THE PENNY IN THE MIDDLE AREA as shown. . . . The Penny is now in the handkerchief between *your* right hand and the *spectator's* hand holding the Half-Dollar.

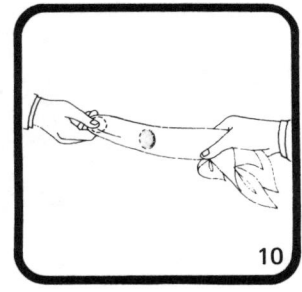

(11) *Immediately reach up with your left hand and HOLD THE PENNY IN PLACE* by grasping the handkerchief *in the middle* as shown.

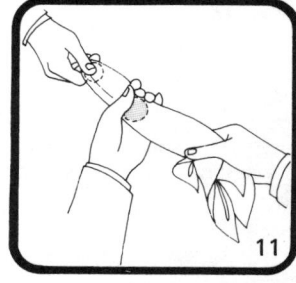

(12) Ask the spectator to hold the handkerchief with his free hand somewhere between your right and left hands as shown. *NOTE: Since the duplicate Penny is being held by your left hand, he cannot accidentally feel the Penny.*

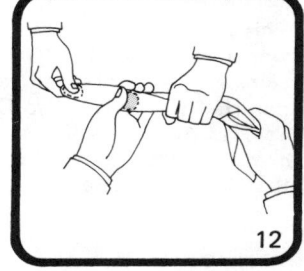

(13) You can now remove your hands from the handkerchief. *As long as the spectator holds his hands apart and the handkerchief level with the floor, the hidden Penny will stay "in place."* Pick up the other "visible" Penny and display it in your left hand.

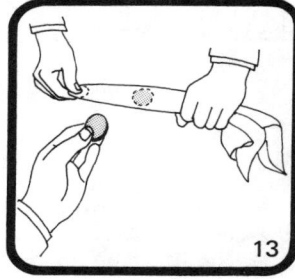

(14) Reach over with your right hand and execute the FRENCH DROP. As you know, this move will lead the audience to believe that the Penny is in your closed right hand . . . *when actually it is "secretly" being held in your left hand.* (NOTE: If you prefer, any other "vanishing" sleight may be used here.)

(15) Move your right hand, supposedly containing the Penny, above the handkerchief being held by the spectator. You are about to "slap" the handkerchief free of his right hand. To accomplish this correctly, be sure to strike the handkerchief *as close to the Half-Dollar as possible.* Make a sharp downward motion with your right hand. *Open your hand just before it hits the handkerchief.*

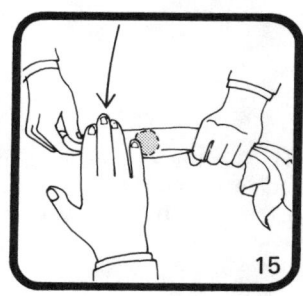

(16) The handkerchief will fall free of the spectator's *right hand,* CAUSING THE HIDDEN COPPER COIN TO FALL INTO THE CENTER OF THE HANDKERCHIEF AND STRIKE THE HALF-DOLLAR. To the spectator and to the audience, it appears that the Penny penetrated the handkerchief and joined the Half-Dollar.

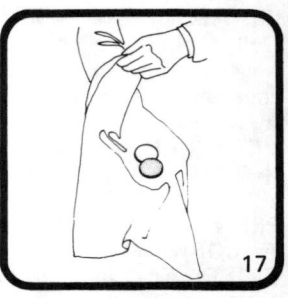

(17) The spectator is told to unfold the handkerchief. He will discover *both* coins in its center. While he is examining the coins, secretly drop the duplicate Penny into your pocket.

COMMENTS AND SUGGESTIONS

This is an excellent Sleight-of-Hand trick. Although it requires a bit of practice to get all of the moves and the timing correct, it is well worth the effort. IF YOU DO NOT HAVE TWO ENGLISH PENNIES, YOU MAY SUBSTITUTE ANY TWO HEAVY COINS. Foreign coins are best since you can get more "contrast" between the coins. However, two American coins may be used as well . . . for instance, one Half-Dollar and two Quarters, or one Silver Dollar and two Half-Dollars. In this case, it is better to use the smaller as the "duplicate" coin, as these are the two that are involved in all of the "Palming." The different sizes will not matter since the spectator "feels" only *one* coin (the larger coin) when he holds the coin under the handkerchief. Thus, the difference in size will not be noticed. Just be sure that the "duplicate" coin is heavy enough to fall within the handkerchief when it makes its mysterious appearance with the other coin.

THE SHRINKING COIN

EFFECT

The magician borrows a finger ring from one spectator and a half-dollar from another. He also requests that these two members of the audience assist him on stage as he presents his next mystery. He has the spectators stand beside him . . . one spectator on his left side, the other on his right. The magician now removes a handkerchief from his pocket. The borrowed half-dollar is wrapped securely in the center of the handkerchief and one of the spectators threads the four corners of the handkerchief *through* the finger ring . . . *imprisoning the coin in the handkerchief.* Each of the spectators is asked to hold two of the corners of the handkerchief (one in each hand) and to stretch the handkerchief out between them so that it is parallel to the floor. The magician reaches underneath the handkerchief and grasps the ring and the imprisoned coin. He then asks the spectators to gently pull on the corners of the handkerchief. To the amazement of all, *the coin slowly penetrates UP THROUGH THE RING.* The ring is now free and is removed from under the handkerchief by the magician . . . and the coin lies on the handkerchief held between the two spectators. All of the items can be examined . . . the ring and coin are returned to the spectators, along with the magician's thanks for their assistance.

SECRET AND PREPARATION

All that is required for this effect is a pocket handkerchief, a half-dollar, and a finger ring, all of which are quite ordinary. You must also be able to perform the COIN THROUGH HANDKERCHIEF trick. No preparation is necessary as THIS IS A COMPLETELY IMPROMPTU MYSTERY.

METHOD

(1) Borrow a half-dollar and a finger ring from members of the audience. You will also need the assistance of two spectators. If they are the same ones who lent you the borrowed articles, so much the better.

(2) Remove your pocket handkerchief and display the borrowed half-dollar. Now, WRAP THE COIN IN THE CENTER OF THE HANDKERCHIEF AS DESCRIBED IN THE COIN THROUGH HANDKERCHIEF TRICK (Page 178). *As you know, the "special" way in which you wrap the coin leaves the coin on the OUTSIDE of the handkerchief. To the audience, it appears as though the coin is securely held INSIDE the handkerchief.* Follow the COIN THROUGH HANDKERCHIEF routine only through Step 10, then STOP. *Do not perform the "penetration" of the coin through the handkerchief.*

(3) Now hold the handkerchief and coin with both hands as shown. *Be sure the side of the handkerchief that was toward you in the COIN THROUGH HANDKERCHIEF, Steps 8 and 9, where a portion of the coin might be visible, is resting next to your left fingers, so the spectators cannot see that the coin is not REALLY inside the handkerchief.*

(4) Now have the spectator thread the four corners of the handkerchief *through* his finger ring as shown. As he does this, retain your grip on the coin with your left hand. *Also, hold the handkerchief ABOVE the coin with your right hand, as shown, so the handkerchief does not "untwist" revealing the coin.*

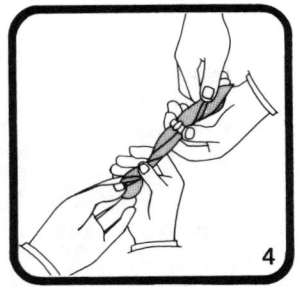

(5) After the spectator has threaded the ends through the ring, tell him to slide the ring down the handkerchief until it rests tightly against the wrapped coin. *This will lock the coin into position and KEEP THE HANDKERCHIEF FROM UNWRAPPING.*

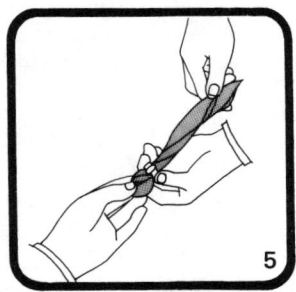

(6) Ask the spectators to hold the four corners of the handkerchief as shown. The handkerchief should be level with the floor. The coin and ring are hanging underneath the handkerchief.

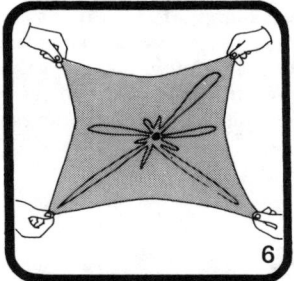

(7) *NOTE: To the spectators, it appears that you have placed the borrowed coin underneath the handkerchief. Then a spectator has threaded his own ring over the corners of the handkerchief imprisoning the coin in the center of the handkerchief. Since the coin is much LARGER than the INSIDE of the ring, there is apparently no way for the coin to escape.*

(8) Now, using both hands, reach underneath the outstretched handkerchief. Grasp the ring with the thumb and first finger of your left hand. Work the ring slightly *upward* so that you gain a bit of slack in the handkerchief. With the right hand you can now slip the coin free of the handkerchief as shown.

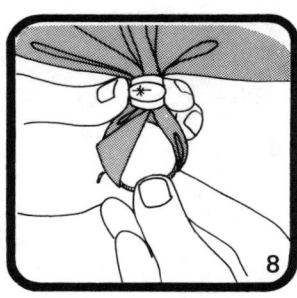

(9) IMPORTANT NOTE: FROM NOW ON, UNTIL THE COIN "PENETRATES" THE RING (Step 17), HOLD THE CENTER OF THE HANDKERCHIEF WITH YOUR LEFT HAND SO THAT THE SPECTATORS ARE NOT AWARE THAT YOU HAVE REMOVED THE COIN.

(10) *Under the handkerchief, secretly FINGER PALM the coin in your right hand.* Then, as your right second and third fingers hold the coin FINGER PALMED, your right first finger and thumb pull the ring off the handkerchief and place it in your left hand . . . so that the ring may be held by your left third and fourth fingers as shown

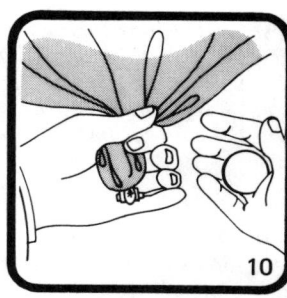

(11) *NOTE: As pointed out in Step 9, BE SURE TO MAINTAIN YOUR GRIP ON THE FABRIC WITH YOUR LEFT THUMB AND FIRST FINGER so that the spectators are unaware that either the coin or the ring has been removed.*

(12) Bring your right hand *with the secretly FINGER PALMED coin,* out from beneath the handkerchief. MOVE YOUR RIGHT HAND DIRECTLY OVER THE CENTER OF THE HANDKERCHIEF AS SHOWN.

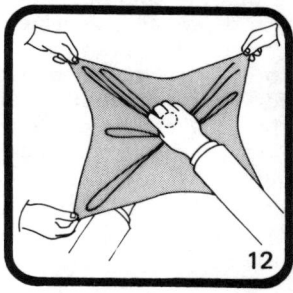

(13) *The following step is most important.* YOUR RIGHT HAND NOW SECRETLY DROPS THE COIN INTO THE "WELL" IN THE CENTER OF THE HANDKERCHIEF (which the audience *thinks* is made by the ring and coin). Under the handkerchief your left fingers open momentarily to let the coin into the "well."

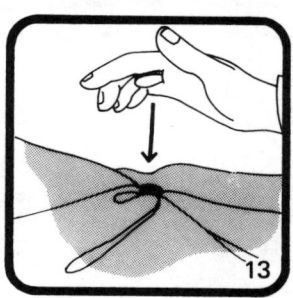

(14) The drawing in Step 13 shows the right hand held "high" above the handkerchief. This is only TO ILLUSTRATE THE "MOVE." When you are ACTUALLY PERFORMING THE TRICK, your hand should be resting DIRECTLY ON TOP of the fabric when the "drop" is made.

(15) When the coin is "dropped" into the well, the left fingers open to receive it and then close around the coin and the fabric. To the audience, the handkerchief appears just as it did before. Your right hand continues to move over the handkerchief, apparently smoothing out its folds. This "smoothing" move is used before and after the "drop" as MISDIRECTION for what you are really doing, which is secretly bringing the coin from beneath the handkerchief and dropping it into the "well."

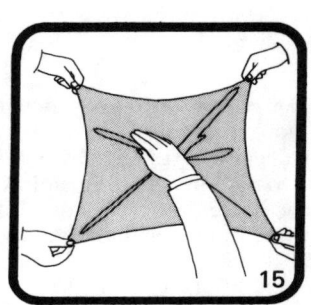

(16) *NOTE: At this point, the spectator's borrowed ring is held by your left third and fourth fingers UNDER the handkerchief. The coin is now ON TOP of the handkerchief in the "well." Your left thumb and first finger hold the handkerchief closed over the coin so that all appears as it did at the start.*

(17) As your left hand continues its hold on the ring and coin, have the spectators gently pull on the four corners of the handkerchief. With your left fingers, *let the coin slowly appear from the well* as it works its way up through your left fingers. *TO THE AUDIENCE, IT WILL APPEAR THAT THE COIN IS PASSING THROUGH THE RING,* WHICH IS MUCH SMALLER THAN THE COIN.

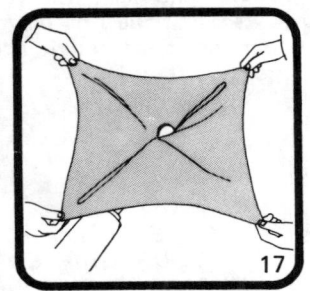

(18) When the coin is completely on top of the handkerchief, and the handkerchief is stretched "flat" between the two spectators, with your left hand slowly and dramatically bring the ring from under the handkerchief. Drop it next to the coin on the outstretched cloth. The effect is two-fold. The coin has passed *through* the much smaller ring, which also *releases* the ring from the handkerchief. You may now pass all of the articles, the ring, the coin, and the handkerchief, for examination . . . as you thank the spectators for their assistance.

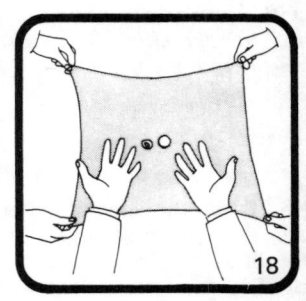

COMMENTS AND SUGGESTIONS

This is a very clever adaptation of the Coin Through Handkerchief move. It is particularly misleading for the spectators since the "effect" is that the coin does not *penetrate* the handkerchief but passes *through* the ring instead. The outstretched handkerchief forms a perfect "cover" when you secretly palm the coin and slip the ring off the handkerchief. This makes an ideal close-up effect since it may be performed at any time and uses small borrowed articles, all of which may be examined. The effect works particularly well if performed so that the handkerchief is held over a low table (such as a coffee table) at which you and the other participants are seated. If performing for a larger group, have the spectators who are holding the handkerchief "tilt" the side nearest the audience slightly downward so that the handkerchief is "angled" toward the spectators. This will allow you all of the cover necessary and also keep anyone from seeing under the handkerchief as you perform this Miniature Miraculous Mystery.

COINS ACROSS

EFFECT

The magician is seated at a table. From his pocket he removes six coins and places them on the table, arranging them in *two* rows of *three* coins each. The performer gathers three coins into each hand and — "magically" causes THE THREE COINS FROM HIS RIGHT HAND TO TRAVEL ONE AT A TIME INTO HIS LEFT HAND.

SECRET AND PREPARATION

In order to present this classic Sleight-Of-Hand effect, you must first have learned the CLASSIC PALM. Since this mystery is presented as a *close-up* trick, you should practice until you can perform the "Palm" easily. You also will need seven *identical* coins. Be sure to pick a coin of the size that is the easiest for you to palm. (Either quarters, half-dollars, or silver dollars, depending upon the size of your hands.) Place the seven coins in your right pocket.

METHOD

(1) Reach into your pocket and remove the coins. As you do, secretly CENTER PALM ONE OF THE COINS. Arrange the six remaining coins on the table into two rows of three as shown. In the illustrations, we have lettered the six coins on the table "A," "B," "C," "D," "E," and "F," and the seventh, palmed, coin "G."

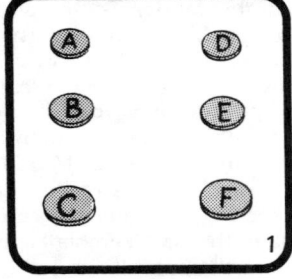

(2) With your right hand concealing the seventh coin, G, reach across the table and pick up the *first* coin from the *left* row (A).

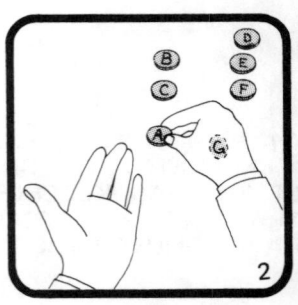

(3) If the "angles" permit (if the audience is located in front of you), you may now display Coin A at the tips of your thumb and fingers of the right hand while still concealing the palmed coin, G, as shown here. The fingers and thumb of the right hand *point up* and the palmed coin is concealed from the audience. If, on the other hand, you are surrounded by spectators, then just keep your right hand with your palm toward the table as you place the coins into your left hand.

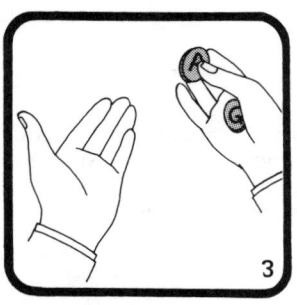

(8) This time, when you throw the third coin into your left hand, SIMULTANEOUSLY RELEASE THE PALMED COIN, G, SO THAT BOTH THE THIRD COIN, C, AND THE PALMED COIN, G, GO INTO YOUR OPEN LEFT HAND TOGETHER.

(4) Throw this first coin, A, into your open left hand.

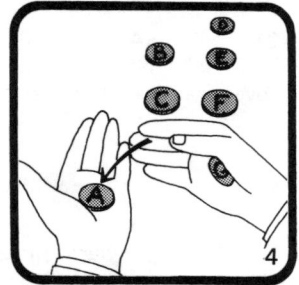

(9) Close your left hand IMMEDIATELY around the four coins and turn your hand over. AT THIS POINT, THE AUDIENCE BELIEVES THAT YOU HAVE SIMPLY COUNTED THREE COINS INTO YOUR LEFT HAND.

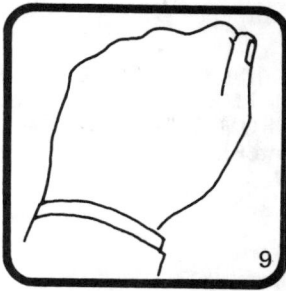

(5) With your right hand still concealing Coin G, reach across the table and pick up the *second* coin, B, from the left-hand row.

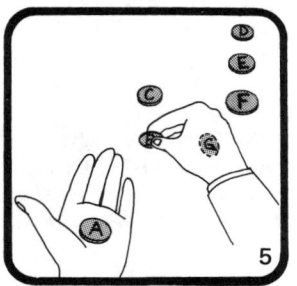

(10) *NOTE: Although the illustration in Step 8 shows Coin C on top of Coin G, this is not necessarily the way the coins will land. Just drop both coins as one and immediately close your hand.*

(6) Throw Coin B into your open left hand alongside Coin A.

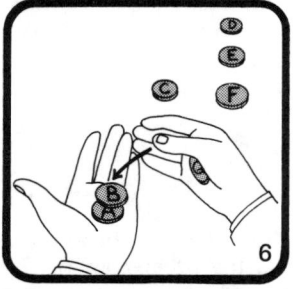

(11) With your left hand apparently holding the three coins from the left row (really four coins), the right hand starts picking up the three coins (D, E, and F) still on the table.

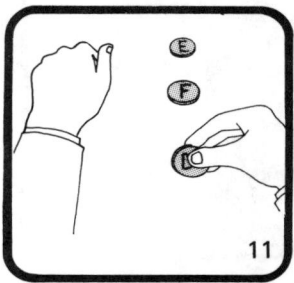

(7) The right hand picks up the *third* and last coin, C, in the left-hand row. Coin G is still hidden in your right palm. *NOTE: Watch your "angles" to be sure that you do not FLASH the palmed coin, G, during any of Steps 1 through 7.*

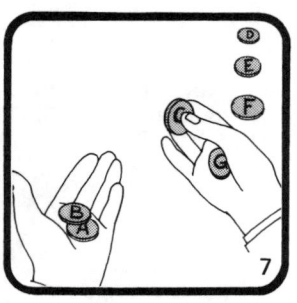

(12) Pick up the first coin, D, and display it in your right hand. AS YOU DO, POSITION THE COIN IN YOUR HAND IN READINESS FOR THE CLASSIC PALM.

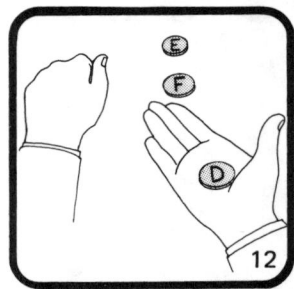

(13) Now, close your right hand and turn it over. USE YOUR FINGERS TO PUSH COIN D INTO THE CLASSIC PALM. Pick up the two remaining coins (E and F) with your thumb and fingers. Then close your right fingers around all of the coins.

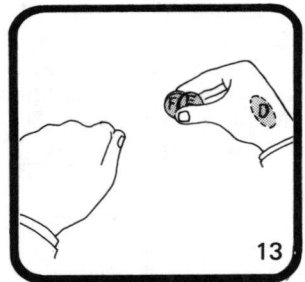

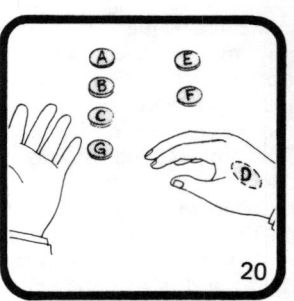

(20) Casually show your left hand empty — but be sure the spectators are not aware of Coin D hidden in your right hand.

(14) MAKE SURE TO KEEP THE PALMED COIN D SEPARATED FROM THE LAST TWO COINS (E and F).

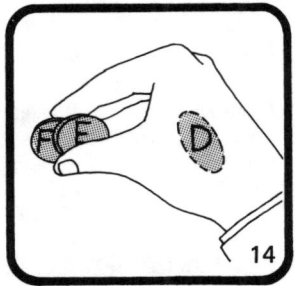

NOTE: At this point, the spectator will believe that each hand contains three coins.

(21) YOU HAVE JUST LEARNED THE BASIC SEQUENCES IN CREATING THIS EFFECT. From this point on the basic moves are repeated starting from Step 2 through Step 9.

(22) The right hand picks up the four coins from the left row one at a time and throws them into your open left hand. AS YOU THROW THE LAST COIN, G, THE CLASSIC-PALMED COIN D IS ADDED TO THE OTHER FOUR COINS IN THE LEFT HAND.

(15) Now make a slight "throwing" motion with your right hand in the direction of your left hand. Loosen your left fingers so that the coins in your left hand will "clank" together. Tell the spectators that one of the coins has "magically" traveled to your left hand.

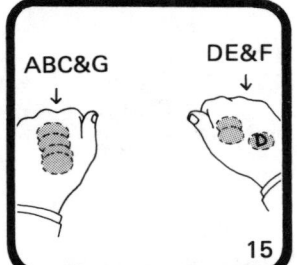

(23) Then the right hand picks up the two remaining coins on the table. THE FIRST, COIN E, IS PLACED IN THE CLASSIC PALM. *Be sure to keep the second, Coin F, separated from the first, Coin E, as in Steps 13 and 14.*

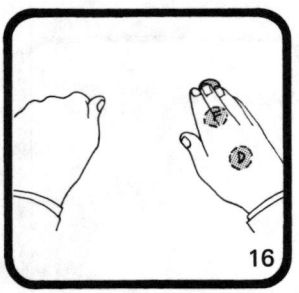

(24) Make the "throwing" motion with your right hand. "Clink" the coins in your left hand to signal the mysterious arrival of the fifth coin.

(16) The right hand, WHILE RETAINING COIN D IN THE THE CLASSIC PALM (17) places the other two coins (E and F) on the table.

(25) The right hand places only one coin (E) on the table, keeping the other coin (F) in the Classic Palm. The left hand then spreads the five coins on the table.

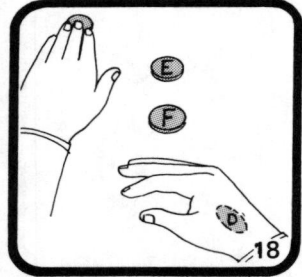

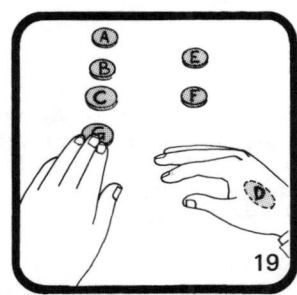

(26) Now, repeat Steps 2 through 9 as you place the five coins into your left hand. SECRETLY ADD THE PALMED COIN E FROM YOUR RIGHT HAND ON THE FIFTH "THROW."

(18) The left hand immediately spreads the four coins on the table. (19) The effect is that one coin traveled "magically" from your right hand to your left hand.

(27) At this point you will be left with *one* coin on the table. For this you use a special method of Lapping called the "Pull Off" Method. Steps 28, 29, and 30 describe this method of Lapping.

LAPPING — PULL-OFF METHOD

EFFECT

The magician picks a coin up from the table and it *vanishes completely* from his hand!

SECRET AND PREPARATION

The following "Vanish" describes how this useful sleight is used for the magical transposition of the last coin in COINS ACROSS.

METHOD

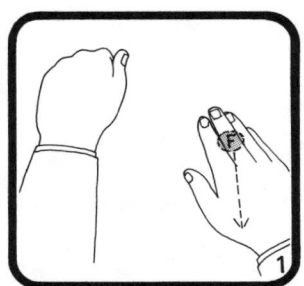
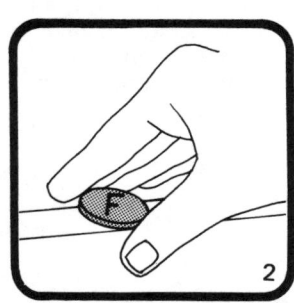
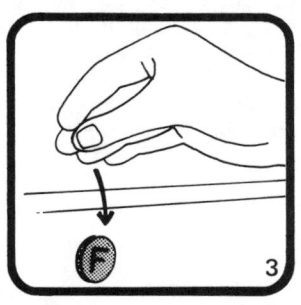

(1) Cover the last coin with your right-hand fingers and slide it toward yourself as if you were going to "scoop" it up into your hand.
(2) *Instead of actually picking up the coin,* (3) ALLOW THE COIN TO FALL UNSEEN OFF THE BACK EDGE OF THE TABLE ONTO YOUR LAP — as your right hand continues the "scooping" motion with the fingers apparently closing around the coin.

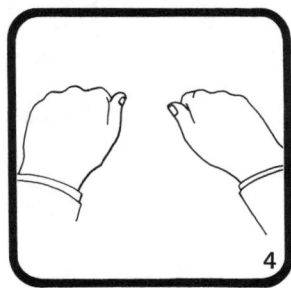

(4) Now hold both hands closed on the table in front of you. (5) Lift your right hand above your left and apparently "rub" the coin *through* the back of your left hand. Then show your right hand empty. (6) Now dramatically spread the six coins onto the table.

(7) While the spectators are examining the six coins, casually retrieve the extra coin from your lap. Add this coin to the six on the table as you gather them up to put them away, or secretly drop it in your coat pocket as you continue your "close-up" routine.

THE COIN IN THE BALL OF WOOL

The following effect is one of those classic tricks that deserves your very best effort.

EFFECT

The magician borrows a quarter from a spectator in the audience and asks him to mark the coin so that he can identify it at a later time. (A black grease pencil carried in the performer's pocket is good for this purpose.) The magician removes his pocket handkerchief and wraps the coin in its folds. The volunteer is given the folded package to hold. He can and does confirm the presence of the coin by feeling it through the fabric.

EFFECT Cont'd.

A ball of wool is freely shown to the audience and dropped into a clear glass. (In the illustrations and the written instructions, we will use a brandy snifter; however, any glass of the correct size will do.) A second spectator is asked to hold the glass containing the yarn ball high enough so that all can see. Returning to the first spectator, the magician causes the borrowed coin to vanish from the handkerchief. The performer explains that, since the first volunteer has apparently lost the borrowed coin, the magician must give him a chance to recover it. The performer grasps the loose end of the yarn ball and passes it to the first spectator. As the volunteer pulls on the yarn, the ball unwinds, spinning merrily in the brandy snifter held by the second spectator. A matchbox bound with rubber bands is found in the center of the wool ball. The second spectator is asked to remove the box from the snifter and open it. The spectator's marked quarter is found inside the box!

SECRET AND PREPARATION

(A) In order to present this effect, you will need the following items: 1) a ball of wool (heavy knitting or rug yarn is good for this), 2) a common "penny" matchbox or some other small box, 3) a brandy snifter or other transparent container large enough to contain the yarn ball, 4) a "Vanishing Handkerchief" of any of the types already described (in this case a quarter is placed in the "secret" corner), 5) four small rubber bands, and 6) a special coin "slide" which may be constructed as follows:

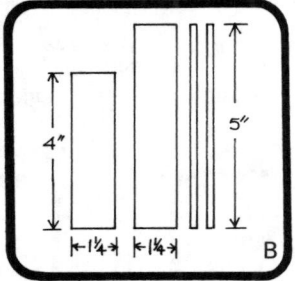

(B) Cut four pieces of heavy cardboard (1/16" thick is about right) as shown. The two narrow strips and one of the wide strips should measure approximately 5 inches in length. The shorter piece should be cut about 1 inch shorter.

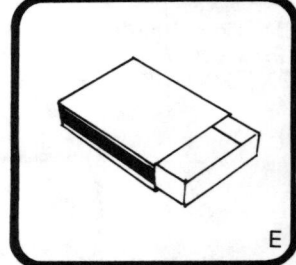

(E) Open the drawer of the empty matchbox and . . .

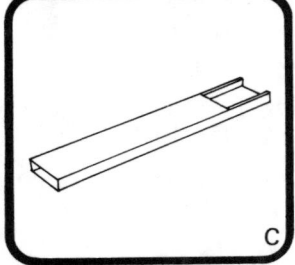

(C) Now glue the four pieces together to form a tube. When finished, the slide must be large enough to allow a quarter to pass completely through it without binding.

(F) . . . insert the blunt end of the slide into the open drawer.

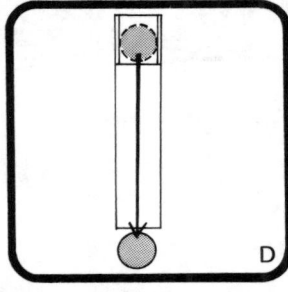

(D) The short side of the tube makes it a simple matter to insert the coin into the tube.

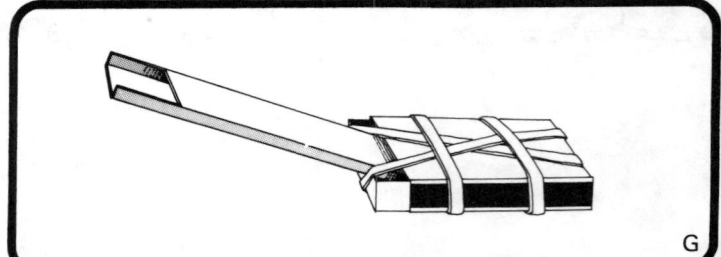

(G) Wrap the four rubber bands around the box as shown. *NOTE: The rubber bands serve two purposes. The first is to hold the slide in position in the matchbox, and the second is to close the box after the slide has been removed.*

(H) Wrap the matchbox with the yarn until you have formed a ball with the matchbox hidden in the center. This must be done loosely in order not to create a bind in the tube or prevent its easy removal.

(I) Attach the yarn ball and tube to the rear edge of your table or on the back of a chair. The important thing to look out for here is that the ball must not be visible to the spectators. If necessary, throw an attractive drape over the table top prior to attaching the prepared ball to its rear edge. In the event a chair is used, be sure the back is solid. In any event, no one should get a glimpse of the coin slide.

(J) Put the brandy snifter on top of your table or on the seat of the chair (depending on the method you have chosen) and pocket the "special" Vanishing Handkerchief. You are now ready to present a very startling mystery.

METHOD

(1) Borrow a quarter from a spectator and have him mark the coin for future identification. While this is being done, remove the special handkerchief from your pocket and spread it over your left hand. The coin previously concealed in the handkerchief should now be in the rear right-hand corner of the special handkerchief as previously explained.

(2) Take the now "marked" coin from the spectator and place it in the handkerchief. *Really retain the marked coin secretly in your right hand as you bring up the duplicate quarter to take its place.*

(3) Allow the spectator to hold the handkerchief containing the duplicate coin. The spectator's marked quarter is Finger Palmed in your right hand.

(4) *NOTE: See Vanishing Handkerchief, Pages 191 to 195.*

(5) Ask for the assistance of a second member of the audience. At this point the first volunteer holding the wrapped coin should be standing to your left. Have the second spectator stand to your right.

(6) With the left hand, reach for the brandy snifter. During this move the right hand grasps the rear edge of the table as if to steady it. *When the left hand lifts the snifter into the air, the right hand secretly drops the marked coin into the tube at the rear of the table.* Immediately hand the snifter to the spectator standing to your right.

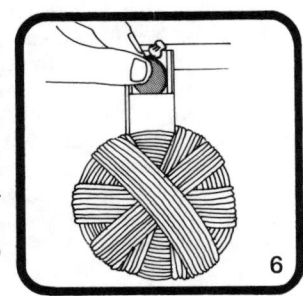

(7) Go back to your table, reach behind it and grasp the ball of wool and *pull it down and off of the slide.*

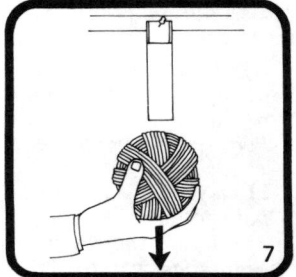

(8) Display the ball to the audience and drop it into the empty brandy snifter, hand the glass to the second spectator.

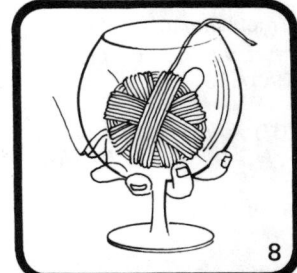

(9) Return and ask the first spectator if he is still holding his coin through the handkerchief. After he agrees, jerk the handkerchief from his grasp and show that the coin has vanished. Display both sides of the handkerchief.

(10) As the second spectator holds the brandy glass, grasp the loose end of the ball of yarn and hand it to the first spectator. Instruct him to unravel the ball. As he pulls on the brandy snifter will spin in a very attractive manner.

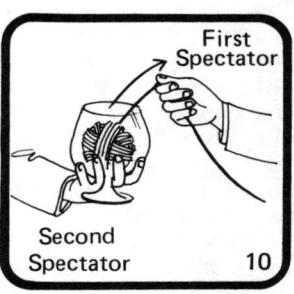

(11) When the wool has been exhausted, the matchbox will be left inside the brandy snifter. Take the brandy snifter from the second spectator and pour the box into his hand.

11

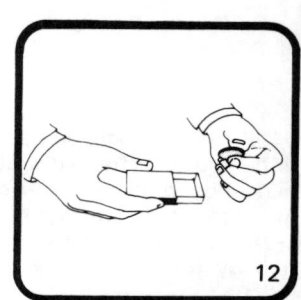

(12) Instruct the spectator to remove the rubber bands and open the box. He discovers the marked coin inside. Have him return the coin to the lender for positive identification.

12

COMMENTS AND SUGGESTIONS

Properly presented, this is one of the finest tricks in magic. Here are some additional important points:

(A) *The audience is never aware of the "slide."*

(B) *The slide can be made from cardboard as described or, if you are handy with tools, from a thin sheet of metal which can be cut with tin snips and bent into the correct shape. The slide, matchbox and ball of yarn, can also be purchased if you do not wish to make them yourself.*

(C) *The small box can either be a matchbox or a small box with a hinged top. Either will be automatically closed by the rubber bands when the slide is removed.*

(D) *In Steps 6 and 7, if you are working surrounded or if it is more convenient, you may have the ball of yarn with the slide in place inside a box or even in a paper bag which is sitting on your table. In this case, after the first spectator is apparently holding the coin under the handkerchief, just put both of your hands, one of which contains the palmed quarter, into the box or bag. Drop the coin down the slide and remove the slide from the ball of yarn. Then bring out the ball cupped in both hands.*

(E) *If you use a "grease pencil" to have the spectator mark the quarter, be sure that you do not rub off the mark while carrying the "palmed" coin in your hand or inserting it into the slide — because if you do, NO ONE will ever believe that the coin inside the ball of yarn, inside the sealed matchbox is the SAME quarter that you borrowed from the spectator. You may wish to have the coin marked by having the spectator "scratch" it with some sharp object like a knife.*

(F) *When the first spectator is pulling on the end of the yarn, as the second spectator holds the brandy snifter, have them move several feet apart as the yarn unravels. This presents a very interesting and dramatic picture to the audience.*

(G) *AFTER the ball of yarn is in the brandy snifter and BEFORE the coin has "vanished" from beneath the handkerchief, emphasize that THE SPECTATOR IS HOLDING HIS MARKED COIN AND THAT YOU WILL NOT TOUCH OR GO NEAR THE BRANDY SNIFTER OR THE BALL OF WOOL UNTIL THE CONCLUSION OF THE TRICK — AND BE SURE THAT YOU DO JUST THAT.*

(H) *Allow the spectator to remove the rubber bands from the matchbox, DO NOT TOUCH THE BOX AT ANY TIME UNTIL AFTER THE MARKED COIN HAS BEEN REMOVED AND IDENTIFIED.*

Follow the above rules and you will have, not just another magic trick, but one of the classic miracles of our art.

THE EXPANDED SHELL HALF-DOLLAR

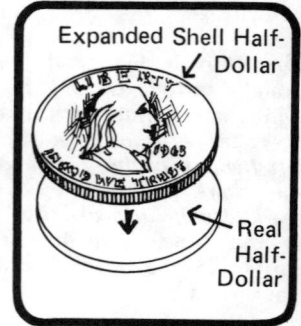

This is a special "gimmicked" Half-Dollar which has been hollowed out until all that remains is the mere "shell" of the original coin. Then the edges of the Shell Half are "stretched open" just enough so that it will fit perfectly over any "regular" Half-Dollar. Thus, a "real" Half-Dollar can slip in or out of the shell easily, without binding. When the Expanded Shell Half is over a "real" Half, they appear to be only one coin. NOTE: The Expanded Shell Half-Dollar is an improvement over the gimmicked coin that was originally made and which is still available, called a "Shell Half-Dollar." In this instance, the hollowed out coin *has not been expanded* so that it is impossible to fit a "real" Half inside it. Although Regular Shell Halves are available, in most instances everything that can be done with a Regular Shell Half can be done with an Expanded Shell Half. In addition, there are many other tricks that can *only* be done with an Expanded Shell. Thus we recommend that, if you are going to purchase one of these special coins, you make the extra investment and obtain an Expanded Shell Half.

TWO HALVES AND TWO QUARTERS

This clever coin sequence uses the EXPANDED SHELL HALF-DOLLAR. As you will see, some very mystifying coin tricks can be done with a Shell Coin. Here is one of the best.

EFFECT

The magician shows *two* half-dollars, held at his fingertips. He begins to slide the coins over and under each other. During this action, one of the half-dollars *visibly* changes into TWO QUARTERS. The magician is left holding *one* half-dollar and *two* quarters, which he displays freely.

SECRET AND PREPARATION

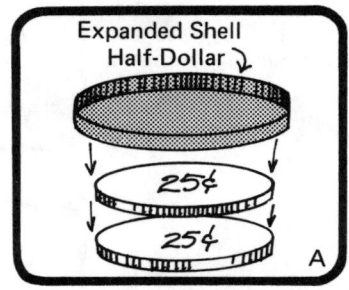

(A) Place two quarters inside the Expanded Shell Half.

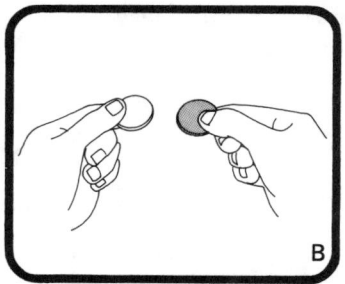

(B) Hold both halves as shown, with the Shell Half in your right hand. (In the illustrations, the Shell Half is a darker color so that you can follow it in the routine.) Your right first finger holds the Shell from beneath and prevents the quarters from falling out, and your right thumb holds the Shell from above. The left hand holds the "regular" coin in the same way. Both hands are held at waist level, with the coins parallel to the floor. Now you are ready.

METHOD

(1) Place the right-hand coin (Shell) on top of the left-hand coin.

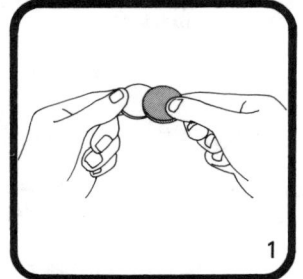

(3) Separate your hands. The coins are held as they were at the beginning, but now *the left hand holds the Shell with the quarters inside, and the right hand holds the regular half-dollar.*

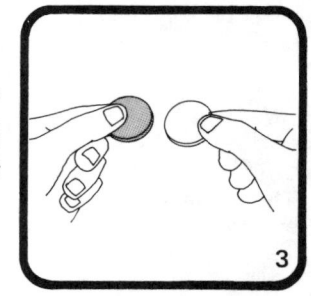

(2) With the right thumb, push or slide the Shell coin to the left. Use the left fingers to push the lower coin into the right fingers. *You have now "reversed" the positions of the coins.*

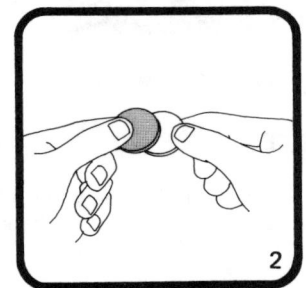

(4) Place the right-hand unprepared coin on top of the gimmicked coin.

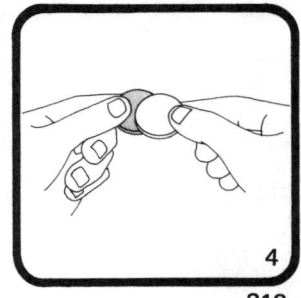

(5) Repeat the "sliding" over and under motion described in Step 2. *This brings the Shell Half back into the right fingers, and the regular half back into the left hand.*

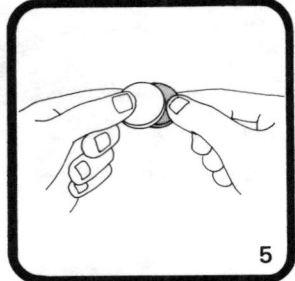

(9) SLIDE THE REGULAR HALF-DOLLAR INTO THE SHELL. THIS WILL AUTOMATICALLY DISPLACE THE TWO QUARTERS. Again, this is shown from underneath.

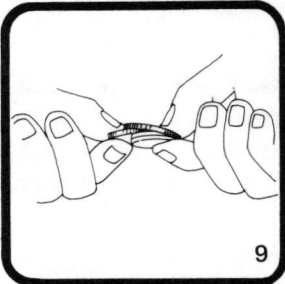

(6) Separate your hands. The coins should be in the same position they were in at the start of the trick. NOW FOR THE MAGIC!

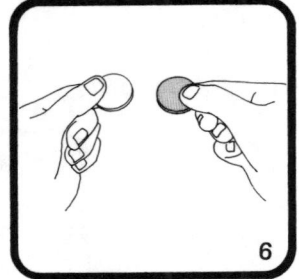

(10) Press the regular half-dollar UP INSIDE THE SHELL with your left thumb and first finger. Grasp the two quarters between your right thumb and first fingers.

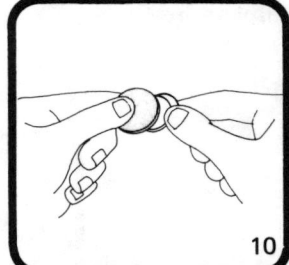

(7) Again, place the Shell coin on top of the regular half so that it overlaps slightly. HOWEVER, THIS TIME YOU SECRETLY INSERT THE REGULAR HALF DOLLAR BETWEEN THE SHELL AND THE TWO QUARTERS.

(11) Separate your hands. *You now hold the regular half-dollar, covered with the Shell in your left hand. The right fingers hold the two quarters.*

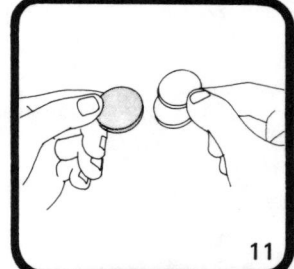

(8) Here is how this action looks from underneath. Note that the quarters are *under* the "regular" coin.

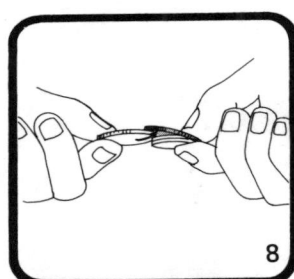

(12) Turn your hands over to show the opposite side of the coins. The Shell-covered half-dollar will appear as *one coin* in your left hand. To the audience it appears you have "magically" *changed* one of the half-dollars into two quarters.

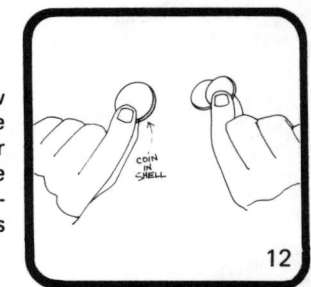

COMMENTS AND SUGGESTIONS

The entire sequence takes only a few seconds and the change of coins should appear *INSTANTANEOUS*. The change is quite visual and startling because you apparently do not use any extra coins and because the handling is so clean.

TWO HALVES AND A "HALF" DOLLAR

EFFECT

This is a clever variation of the TWO HALVES AND TWO QUARTERS routine. The only difference in this routine is that you substitute "half" OF A PAPER DOLLAR BILL for the two quarters. Instead of going from *two* halves to *one* half-dollar and *two* quarters . . . you "magically" change one of the halves to one "half-dollar" . . . meaning *half of a paper dollar bill*. This works well as a startling comedy effect.

SECRET AND PREPARATION

Expanded Shell Half-Dollar

Dollar bill torn in half and folded.

A

(A) Tear a dollar bill in half, fold it, and place it inside the Shell just as you did with the two quarters in the effect first described.

METHOD

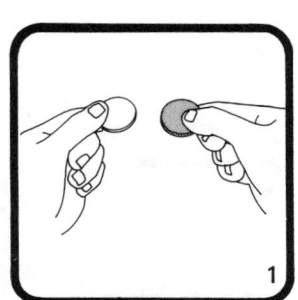

1

(1) Display the coins as in the previous routine. The gimmicked coin is held in your right hand.

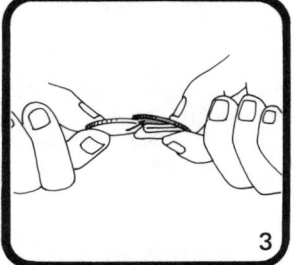

5

(5) Use your right fingers to grasp the bill and bring it out from beneath the nested Shell and coin. The left thumb and first finger hold the Shell and coin firmly together.

(2) Execute Steps 2 through 7, as in the previous routine. *You will find it considerably easier to hold the bill inside the Shell than it was to hold the two quarters.*

6

(6) Your right fingers open out the torn bill. You can use the left second and third fingers to help.

(3) NOW INSERT THE UNPREPARED COIN INTO THE SHELL <u>BETWEEN</u> THE SHELL AND THE FOLDED BILL. This shows the action from underneath.

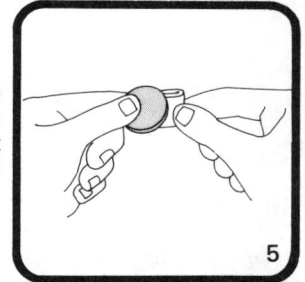

3

(7) Once the half-bill is unfolded, turn both hands over as you did in Step 12 of the previous effect. The sequence is finished. The clever and impossible climax can make this into a fine "comedy" effect to add to your coin routine.

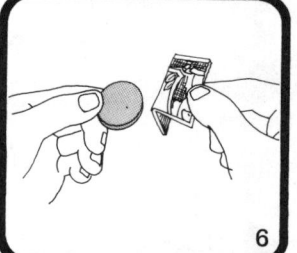

4

(4) The unprepared coin will slide into place inside the Shell and will force the folded bill out of the Shell.

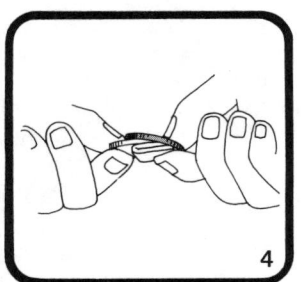

7

COIN IN SHELL

COINS THROUGH THE TABLE

EFFECT

The magician, who is seated at a table, shows four Half-Dollars. He places them on the table with each coin slightly overlapping the next. He then scoops up all four coins in his right hand and taps the edge of the stack on the table. Immediately, the coins are spread to reveal only *three* coins left in what was a stack of four. Showing his other hand empty, the magician reaches beneath the table and brings the missing coin into view — it has apparently "magically" *penetrated through the top of the table!* This feat is repeated with the remaining coins, one at a time, until all four coins have passed through the table.

SECRET AND PREPARATION

This routine utilizes an Expanded Shell Half-Dollar. *NOTE: In the illustrations, the Shell is darker in color so you can follow its moves during the routine.*

METHOD

FIRST PENETRATION

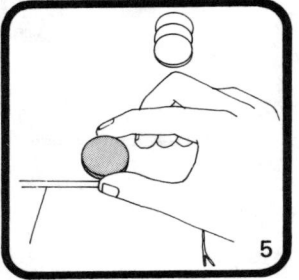

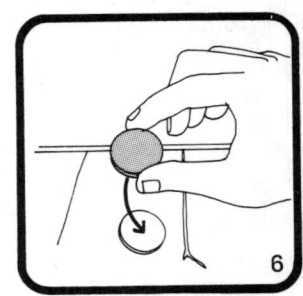

(1) You will need four regular Half-Dollars and one Expanded Shell Half. Place the four regular coins in a row near the edge of the table in front of you. Unknown to the viewers, the coin on the left is the Shell-covered coin.

(5) Now, grip the last coin (the one with the Shell over it) in the same manner, by the edges between your right thumb and first finger, *just as you did the first three.* (6) However, this time, when you slide the coin(s) off the edge of the table, LET THE REGULAR COIN SECRETLY FALL OUT OF THE SHELL INTO YOUR LAP, where it remains held between your legs.

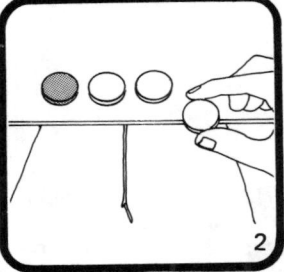

(2) With your right thumb and first finger, grasp the coin at the far right by the edges as shown. Then, slide the coin toward you *until it clears the edge of the table.*

(7) Without pausing, place the Shell with the other coins so that it overlaps the uppermost coin in the row. *The audience believes the Shell is an ordinary coin like the others.*

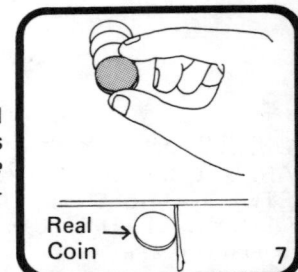

(3) Now, move the coin forward and <u>place</u> it near the center of the table. Be sure to place the coin — do not <u>drop</u> it — on the table.

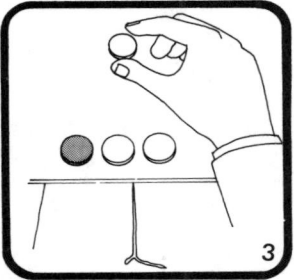

(8) Call attention to the four coins on the table as you casually show both hands empty. NOW FOR THE MAGIC!

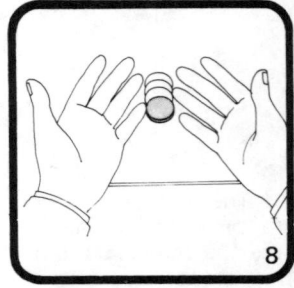

(4) Repeat this action with the next two coins, sliding each coin off the edge of the table and then <u>placing</u> it on the first coin so that its outer edge *overlaps the coin beneath it.* Repeat the *placing* and *overlapping* with the third coin.

(9) Place your left arm beneath the table as if reaching to the spot *directly below the coins.* What you <u>really</u> do is to *secretly pick up the coin from your lap* as your hand travels under the table. Explain to the audience that the reason you are placing your hand underneath is to "catch" the first coin as it falls through the table.

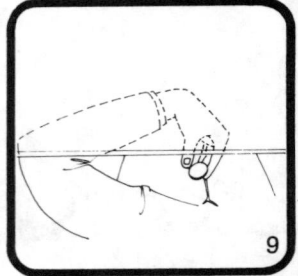

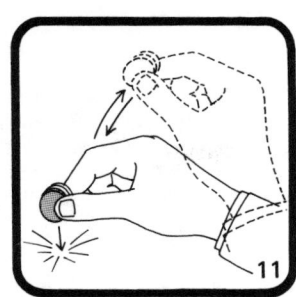

(10) With your right finger, square the row of coins on the table into a single stack. *This causes the Shell to drop down over the top coin in the row.* (11) Pick up the coins by tilting the stack on its edge and grasping the coins firmly with the fingers of your right hand. Without hesitation, raise your right hand. Then, with a downward motion, *gently* (so you do not bend the edge of the Shell) tap the edge of the stack on the table. Say, "Watch as I send one of the coins *right through the table!"*

(16) Spread the stack on the table to reveal only *two* coins. Bring your left hand into view with the "lapped" coin. Having completed the penetration, PLACE THIS SECOND COIN ASIDE WITH THE FIRST.

THIRD PENETRATION

(17) You are now left with two coins (and the Shell) on the table. Position both coins near the edge of the table with the Shell-covered coin at the left end of the row as in Step 1.

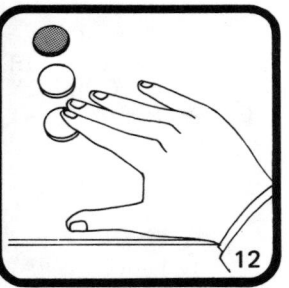

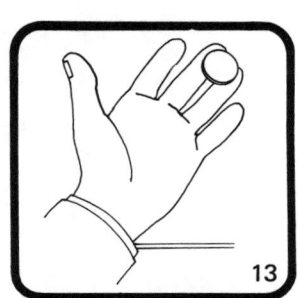

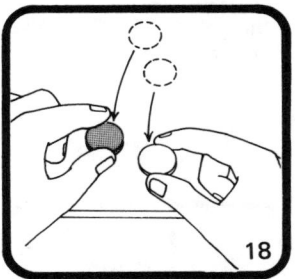

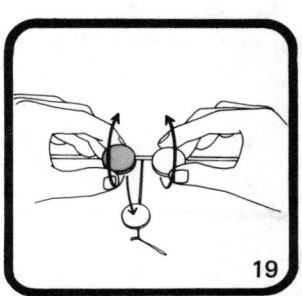

(12) Immediately spread the stack on the table to show that only three coins remain. *Be careful not to accidentally separate the Shell from the regular coin it now covers as you spread them on the table.* Practice will teach you how to handle the Shell correctly. (13) Now, bring your left hand from beneath the table *with the coin you picked up from your lap.* Display it and say, "That makes *one* coin that has passed through the solid table." PLACE THIS COIN ASIDE and go on to the next step.

(18) Holding one coin in each hand, move *both* coins back to the table edge at the same time. (19) When the Shell coin reaches the edge, *let the regular coin drop into your lap.*

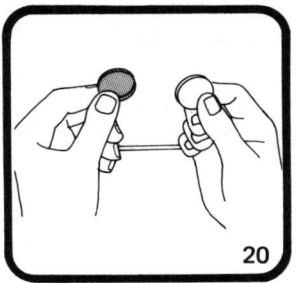

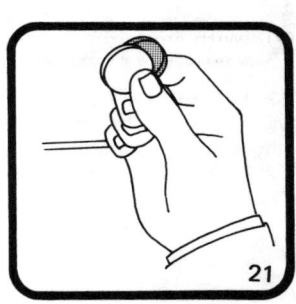

SECOND PENETRATION

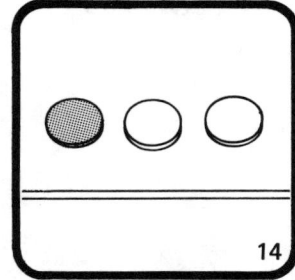

(14) Position the remaining three coins (and the Shell) in a row near the edge of the table just as you did in Step 1. The Shell-covered coin should be at the left end of the row as shown.

(20) Display the two coins (really one coin and the Shell) one in each hand. (21) Transfer the left-hand coin to your right hand so that the two coins overlap, *with the Shell in front* as shown.

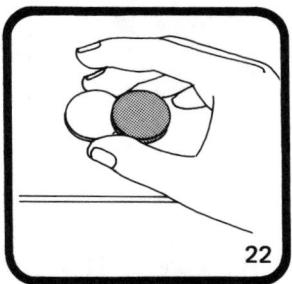

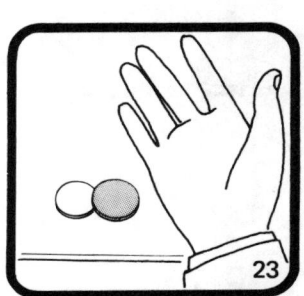

(15) Now, follow the same moves as you did in Steps 2 through 12. However, this time you are performing the sequence with *three* coins instead of four. Here is a recap of the moves:

The three coins are slid, one at a time, from the table and then placed in an overlapping row. On the last "pick-up," secretly drop the Shell-covered coin into your lap. Your left hand goes under the table again and picks up the "lapped" coin, as your right hand squares the three coins (two and the Shell) into a stack. You then "tap" the stack on its edge, to "magically" make the second coin penetrate the table — just like the first.

(22) Place both coins on the table. *Do not let the Shell fall over the "real" coin.* (23) Now rest your right hand on its edge near the coin and Shell as shown in the illustration. Your right hand should be about an inch or so away from the *right edge* of the Shell coin.

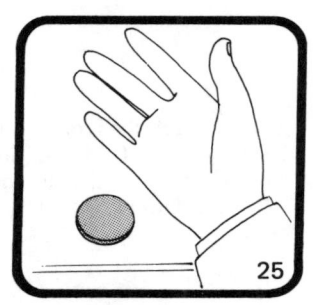

(24) Now, lower your right hand, palm downward, on top of the coins. Then, shift your hand slightly to the left, *causing the Shell half to fall over the regular coin.* At the same time, make a "rubbing" motion as if causing the coin to penetrate the table.

(25) As soon as you feel the two coins nest together, rotate your right hand upward — back to its former position — to reveal only *one* coin remaining on the table.

(26) Bring your left hand from beneath the table with the "lapped" coin as if it has penetrated the table. PLACE THIS THIRD COIN ASIDE and continue with the next step.

FOURTH PENETRATION

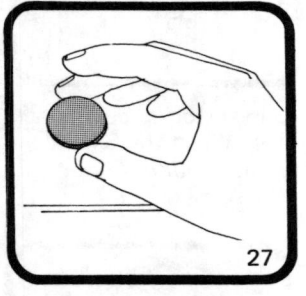

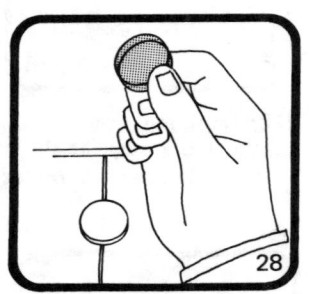

(27) You now have one coin covered by the Shell on the table. With your right thumb and first finger, grasp the coin by the edges and slide it toward you until it clears the edge of the table.

(28) As usual, *the regular coin will drop unnoticed into your lap.*

(29) Now, instead of placing the last coin on the table, hold the coin (really the Shell) in your right hand in position ready for the FINGER PALM VANISH. As you hold the coin in your hand say, "This is the only coin left." *Be careful not to expose the "inside" of the Shell coin as you display it to the audience.*

(30) Execute the FINGER PALM VANISH by apparently taking the Shell coin from your right hand into your left hand. Really the coin is retained in your curled right fingers. *Direct the attention of the audience toward your left hand,* which supposedly holds the coin. *This is MISDIRECTION.* Say, "Follow the last coin closely and see if you can spot the moment when it actually penetrates the table."

(31) As you say this, reach your RIGHT arm beneath the table as if to catch the coin when it falls through. ACTUALLY, YOUR RIGHT HAND SECRETLY PLACES THE SHELL COIN ON YOUR LAP AND PICKS UP THE REGULAR COIN THAT IS ALREADY THERE.

(32) In a sharp, deliberate motion, slam your left hand down onto the table as if to <u>force</u> the coin through the table top. Immediately raise your left hand to show that the coin is no longer there.

(33) Without hesitation, bring your right hand into view with the regular coin as if it were the coin that penetrated the table. Place this coin on the table with the three others, and the mystery is complete. All can now be examined *as the Shell Half remains in your lap for you to secretly dispose of later.*

COMMENTS AND SUGGESTIONS

This is a brilliant piece of coin manipulation and is well worth the practice it takes to perform it smoothly. Remember to always <u>place</u>, never <u>drop</u> the Shell on the other coins, since the Shell does not "sound" like a real coin if it is dropped.

COINS THROUGH THE TABLE
FOURTH PENETRATION — ALTERNATE METHOD

DAVID ROTH

Here is an alternate method for making the last coin (really the Shell) penetrate the table. This can also be used as a very clever trick by itself with a single coin and an Expanded Shell.

METHOD

(1) After you have completed Steps 27 and 28 of the Coins Through the Table — with the real coin secretly on your lap and the Shell coin held by your right hand — <u>place</u> the Shell coin on the table near the edge in front of you.

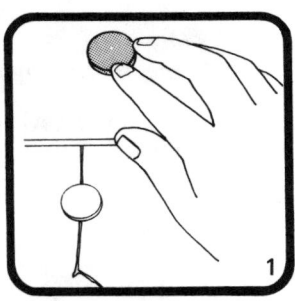

(4) Spread your right fingers to show that the last coin has vanished. *Without moving your right hand,* bring your left hand, which has retrieved the coin from your lap, from beneath the table. The fourth coin has apparently penetrated the table.

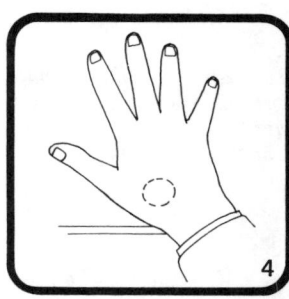

(2) Now, with your right hand, appear to push the Shell coin forward on the table. Actually, *you do not move the coin at all* — you leave it in its original position near the edge of the table. The fingers of your right hand are held close together as if they cover the coin.

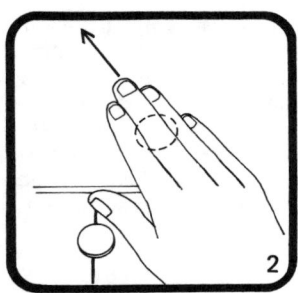

(5) Place the coin in your left hand on the table. *At the same time,* slide your right hand back over the rear edge of the table. As you do this, press gently down on the Shell with the heel of your hand. This will cause the Shell to slide over the edge of the table and fall, unnoticed, into your lap.

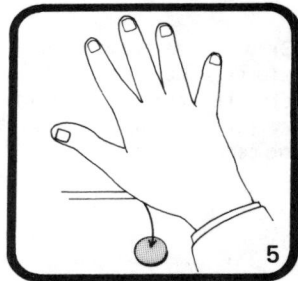

(3) Your right hand moves forward as if pushing the coin along, really leaving the coin in its original position. The Shell is now under your hand near the wrist. *The audience thinks that the coin is under your fingertips.*

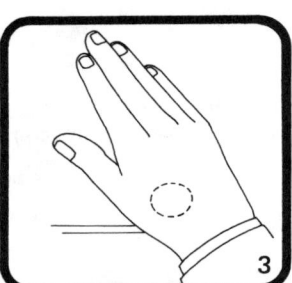

(6) Once the Shell is hidden in your lap, you may show both hands empty, and all may be examined.

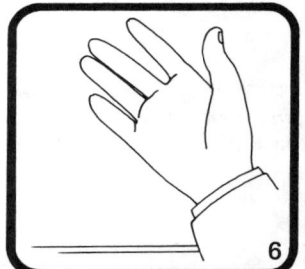

THE COIN ROLL

Though this is strictly an ornamental flourish and not a magical effect, it belongs in every coin manipulator's program. When you are doing coin tricks, it is always wise to impress your audience with your skill causing them to believe that the simplest of your routines must depend upon your remarkable dexterity.

EFFECT

The performer demonstrates his dexterity as a magician by causing a half-dollar to roll from finger to finger across the back of his hand. When it has finished this surprising run, it drops from sight beneath his little finger and pops up again between his thumb and first finger, only to repeat its remarkable roll. He does this repeatedly, so that the coin really seems to come alive, rolling of its own accord. When the magician performs the COIN ROLL deftly, it will surely dress up his coin routine giving the appearance of great professional dexterity.

METHOD

NOTE: So that you can follow the coin as it "rolls" over the fingers, we have added the letters "A" and "B" to the opposite edges of the coin.

(1) Hold the coin by Edge A in your right hand between your thumb and first finger as shown.

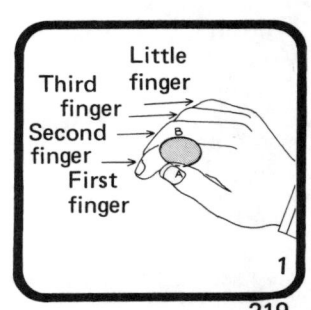

(2) *Push the coin up and release the thumb,* allowing the coin to "roll over" the back of the first finger near the knuckles.

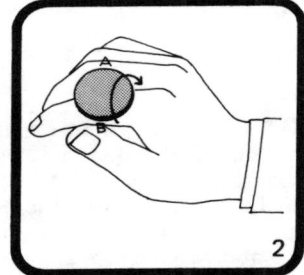

(3) *Lift the second finger* and allow it to clip the right-hand Edge B of the coin. The coin will assume a temporary position clipped between the first and second fingers.

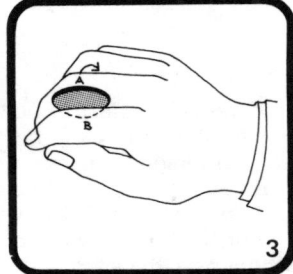

(4) Without stopping, *raise the first finger* which pushes the coin on to the back of the second finger.

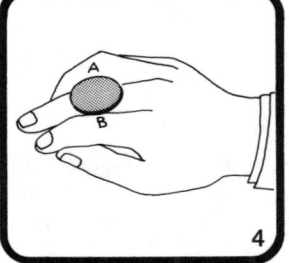

(5) *Lift the third finger* and grip Edge A which allows the coin to roll over the second finger. The coin will again assume a temporary "clipped" position between the second and third fingers.

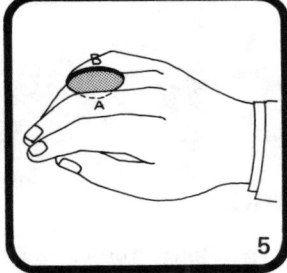

(6) Without stopping, and by tilting the hand, the coin is allowed to fall onto the back of the third finger.

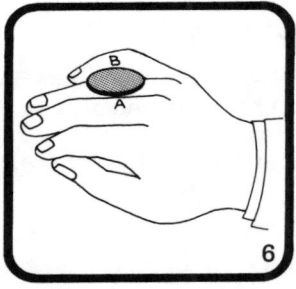

(7) *Lift the fourth finger* and clip Edge B of the coin. The coin will now be temporarily held between the third and fourth fingers.

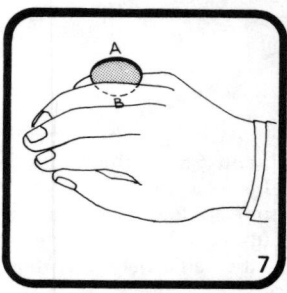

(8) Move your little finger up and allow the coin to drop or be pulled down by the little finger through the opening between the third and little fingers. The majority of the coin is now protruding from the palm side of the hand — clipped between the third and little fingers.

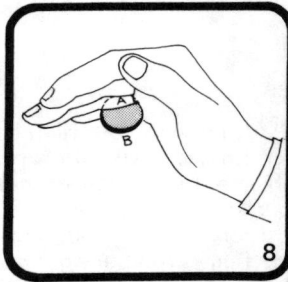

(9) Move your right thumb to a position beneath the coin.

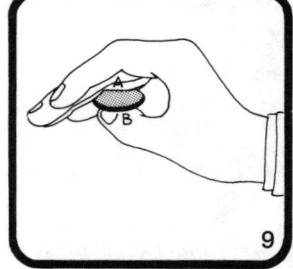

(10) Release the coin and balance it on the ball of your right thumb.

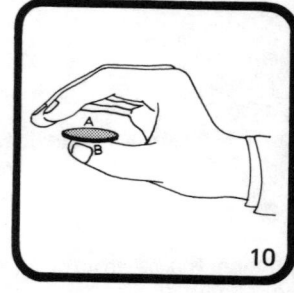

(11) Move your thumb under your fingers and transfer the coin back to the original starting point at the base of the first finger.

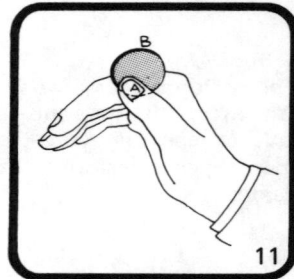

(12) Now you can push the coin up over the knuckle of the first finger and begin the entire sequence again. You may repeat the same set of moves as many times as you wish.

COMMENTS AND SUGGESTIONS

Along with its value as a flourish, the COIN ROLL is highly helpful toward developing skill in sleight-of-hand, as it limbers your fingers so they can execute difficult moves with speed and precision.

It will require considerable practice on your part in order to master the COIN ROLL. Depending upon the size of your hand, you may wish to use either a quarter or a silver dollar instead of the half-dollar. Also, although all of the "moves" are described in detail above, you may develop a slightly different technique that is better for your hand. Some performers, through a great deal of practice, are able to roll more than one coin on the same hand — or to roll one coin on the left hand and another on the right hand at the same time. But don't expect to master either of these variations quickly. One great advantage of this type of flourish, however, is that although it requires a great deal of practice, you may practice it while you are doing something else — watching television, listening to the radio, traveling — at any time when your hands are free and you will not disturb anyone if you drop the coin — *which you surely will as you learn this flourish.* Once learned, it is a great "attention getter" as you idly *sit rolling a coin back, up and around your fingers!*

THE ROLL DOWN

EFFECT

The performer, during a coin routine, displays a stack of four coins. Suddenly, the coins "roll down" his fingers until each coin is held *separately* <u>between</u> the fingers of the magician's hand.

The ROLL DOWN might be classified as a *MASTER FLOURISH*. Once learned, it can truly demonstrate your skill as a manipulator. We recommend the use of half-dollars (or silver dollars if you can manage them) for two reasons. The flourish with larger coins appears to be more difficult (in truth it is easier) and visually, a larger audience can see the effect.

METHOD

(1) Begin by placing four stacked coins in your right hand, holding them between your thumb and first finger. The palm of your right hand should be up, as shown.

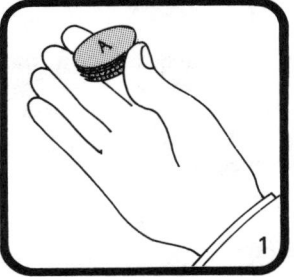

(4) *NOTE: It is important that you master Steps 1, 2, and 3, before moving on to Step 4. <u>The security with which Coins A & B are held between the third and fourth fingers will determine the success or failure of the next steps.</u>*

(2) Now bend your second finger into your palm and tilt your hand slightly to the left.

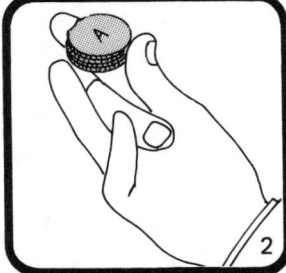

(5) With Coins A & B held between your third and fourth fingers, lift your second finger and grip the edges of Coin B and Coin C. Your thumb applies pressure to Coin D.

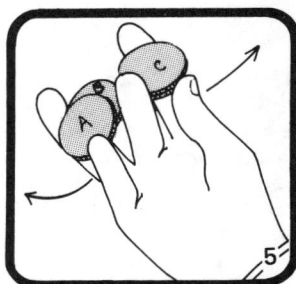

(3) The object at this point is to allow the top two coins (A & B) of the stack to slide (or be rotated by the little finger) to the left and wedge themselves between the third and little fingers.

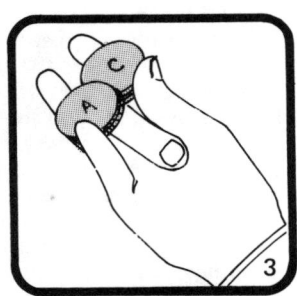

(6) Slowly straighten out your fingers. Your thumb pivots Coin D to the *right* as your little finger pivots Coin A to the *left*. The second finger rolls in between Coins B and C holding their edges.

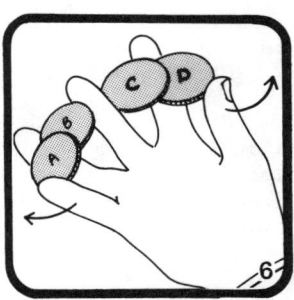

(7) The coins are now in position . . . DRAMATICALLY DISPLAYED BETWEEN YOUR FINGERS.

COMMENTS AND SUGGESTIONS

If you have followed each of the above steps with the four coins in your hand, you will have discovered that this is *not* an easy flourish to learn. But, <u>with practice, it can be mastered</u>. The obvious display of skill will be instantly recognized and appreciated by any audience.

MONEY MAGIC
BILLS

ROLL THE BILLS

For a close-up mystery, this is a real puzzler. It's a good one to perform when someone asks you to "Do A Trick" and you're not really prepared.

EFFECT

The magician lays two bills on the table — say a One-Dollar bill and a Five-Dollar bill — so they form a "V." With the One on top, he calls the audience's attention to the fact that the One-Dollar bill is on *top* of the Five. The magician then begins "rolling" the two bills together, starting at the point of the "V." While he is rolling the bills, the magician asks the spectator to place one of his fingers on the corner of the One-Dollar bill and another finger on the corner of the Five. The spectator now has both bills *pinned to the table*. So far, so good — with no chance for deception. But now, when the magician unrolls the bills, *the FIVE is on top of the ONE*, yet the spectator still has his fingers on both bills. AND THAT'S IMPOSSIBLE!

METHOD

(1) Lay the two bills on the table with the One *on top* of the Five as shown. *Notice that the One is a bit further forward (toward the spectator) than the Five.* This illustration is from the *MAGICIAN'S VIEWPOINT.*

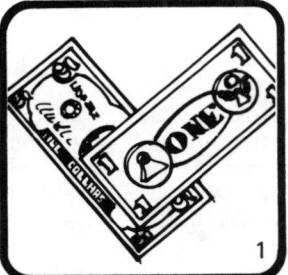

(2) With the first fingers of both hands, start rolling the bills together beginning at the point of the "V." NOTE: In this step and all of the following steps, all of the illustrations are from the *SPECTATOR'S VIEWPOINT.*

(3) Continue rolling the two bills until just a small part of the corner of the Five remains in view — then STOP. As shown, *more of the corner of the One shows* because it was placed further forward in the initial layout (Step 1).

(4) STEPS 4 AND 5 ARE THE SECRET MOVE. As you continue to roll the bills forward, open the fingers of your left hand over the corner of the Five. Apparently you are merely holding the bills as you roll them, but actually you are *hiding the corner* of the Five from the spectator's view as shown. At the same time, point to the corner of the One with your right hand. Ask the spectator to place his left finger on that corner to hold it in place.

(5) As he does this, place your right finger on the *center* of the roll of bills and roll them slightly forward. The corner of the Five, which is hidden by your left fingers, *flops over.* In other words, this corner goes beneath the rolled bills and does a *forward flipover* back to its original position on the table. *This is unknown to the spectators,* as it is hidden by your left hand.

(8) Ask the spectator to place his *right finger* on the corner of the Five. *Emphasize that he is pinning the corners of both bills to the table.*

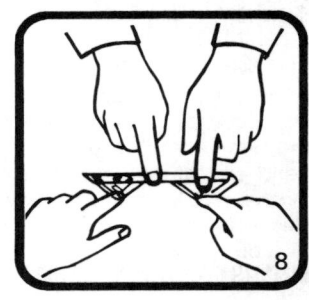

(6) This is a view of the action as shown *from the side.* Notice how your left fingers cover the "secret" *flipover* of the corner of the Five.

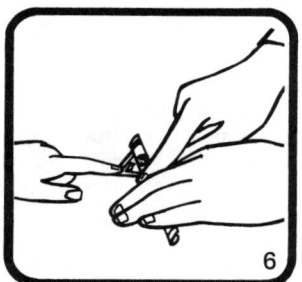

(9) All that is left now is for you to unroll the bills as shown. As a result of the "secret" flipover of the corner of the Five, the position of the bills will be reversed — with the Five-Dollar bill now *on top* of the One-Dollar bill!

(7) Now, still holding the roll of bills with your right finger, lift your left hand and point to the corner of the Five.

COMMENTS AND SUGGESTIONS

It is not necessary to use bills of different values in order to perform ROLL THE BILLS. If the two bills are the same, simply turn one of them over and you have bills of different colors (one black and one green). So that the trick will be easily followed by the spectator, be sure to point out which color is on top *before you start* rolling the bills. For that matter, it is not even necessary to use bills at all — different colored slips of paper will work just as well.

BILLS FROM NOWHERE — First Version

The following effect makes an excellent opening number for your act. The magician enters and walks briskly down stage center. He shows his hands to be unmistakably empty. Then, holding his hands together, a quantity of One-Dollar bills "magically" appears from out of the magician's empty palms!

SECRET AND PREPARATION

  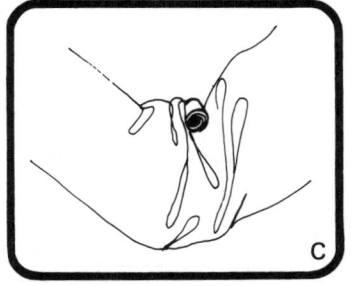 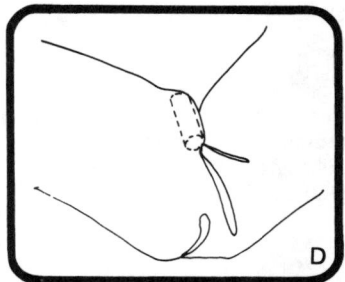

You must be wearing a suit or sport coat in order to present this effect properly (A) Make a stack of 5 or 6 one-dollar bills. . . (B). . . and roll them into as "tight" a roll as you can. (C) Place the roll of bills into the crook of your LEFT elbow. (D) Then, pull the fabric of the coat sleeve up and over the bills. *Keep your arm slightly bent in order to hold the roll of bills in place.*

(1) With the bills "loaded" as described, make your entrance and face the audience. As you make your opening remarks, reach over with your *left* hand and grasp your *right* coat sleeve at the crook of your elbow. Pull the sleeve back, clear of your right wrist as you show your RIGHT HAND IS UNMISTAKABLY EMPTY.

(2) Now reach across with the *right* hand and grasp your *left* coat sleeve at the crook of the elbow and pull that sleeve back and clear of the left wrist as you show your LEFT HAND EMPTY.

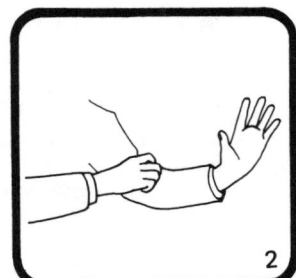

(3) DURING THIS MOVE, IT IS VERY NATURAL FOR YOUR <u>RIGHT FINGERS</u> TO <u>SECRETLY "STEAL" THE CONCEALED BILLS FROM THE FOLD IN YOUR JACKET</u>.

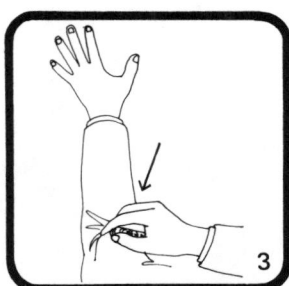

(4) The roll is held in your right hand between your fingers and palm as shown.

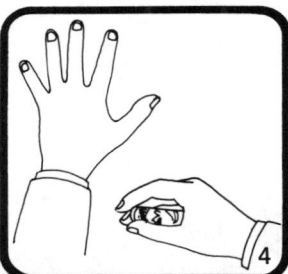

(5) Now hold both of your hands in front of you at shoulder height with your left hand in front of your right hand. *This position will give you maximum coverage for the next move.*

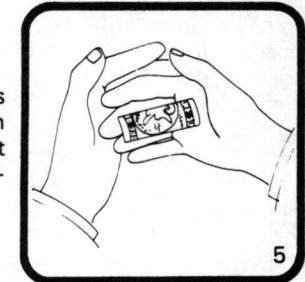

(6) Using the thumb and fingers of *both* hands, unroll the bills so that they begin to appear at the top of your fingers.

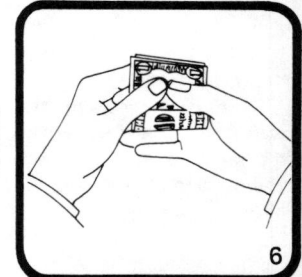

(7) After unrolling the bills halfway, suddenly pull the left hand down so that the thumb of the left hand unrolls the bills the rest of the way from the bottom . . . leaving the open bills in the right hand. Fan the bills and display them to the audience.

BILLS FROM NOWHERE — VERSION NO. 2

EFFECT

The magician reaches into his pocket and removes his wallet. Opening the wallet, the performer removes a <u>single</u> one-dollar bill. After replacing the wallet, the magician clearly demonstrates that, other than the *one* bill, his hands are absolutely empty. By suddenly slapping the bill against the palm of one hand, THE SINGLE BILL MAGICALLY MULTIPLIES INTO A QUANTITY OF NEW ONE-DOLLAR BILLS!

SECRET AND PREPARATION

Place a single bill into a "secretarial" wallet or check book and put the wallet into your inside coat pocket. Prepare a stack of bills as described in Steps A, B, C, and D in BILLS FROM NOWHERE, Version 1.

METHOD

(1) With the bills loaded into the crook of your left arm, reach into your coat pocket and remove your wallet. Take out the single bill and display it to the audience. Clearly show your hands to be empty except for the one bill.

(4) Without hesitation, grasp your right sleeve at the crook of the elbow and pull this sleeve back until you bare your right wrist.

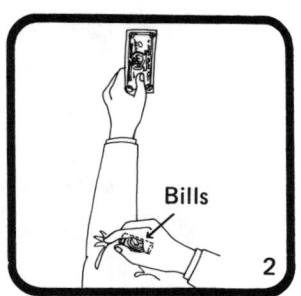

(2) Now, with the bill in your left hand, reach over with your right hand and grasp your left coat sleeve at the crook in the elbow. Pull the sleeve back until your left wrist is bare. AS YOU PULL BACK YOUR SLEEVE, SECRETLY STEAL THE HIDDEN BILLS INTO YOUR RIGHT HAND (as in Step 3 of the First Version).

(5) *NOTE: The spectator will have seen BOTH of your hands empty except for the single bill, which has constantly been in view.*

(6) Now, *behind the visible bill,* unroll the hidden bills.

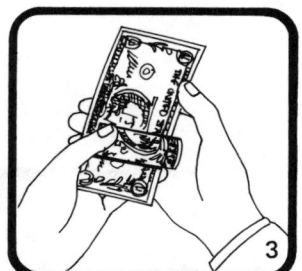

(3) With the roll of bills hidden in your right hand, transfer the single bill from your left hand to your right fingers. Place the single bill in front of the roll. The "secret" roll of bills will be effectively hidden behind the single bill as shown.

(7) As you fan these "new" bills from behind the single bill, the effect will be the instant multiplication of a SINGLE bill into MANY! ... *AN EFFECT SURE TO CAPTIVATE ANY AUDIENCE'S IMAGINATION.*

THE TORN AND RESTORED DOLLAR BILL

EFFECT

The magician displays a One-Dollar Bill front and back ... and then proceeds to tear the bill into two parts. Not satisfied with just the halves, the performer puts the two parts together and tears through them both. He now has four separate pieces of a once-whole bill. He folds the torn pieces neatly into a small square package. Then he makes a magical gesture over the small green bundle.... When he opens it, the audience is amazed to see that all of the pieces have mysteriously joined together to restore themselves into a completely undamaged bill.

SECRET AND PREPARATION

You will certainly want to practice this trick using "stage money" or "play money." Or, you may merely cut some pieces of paper to the correct "dollar bill" size for practice purposes. When performing for an audience, you may prefer to use real bills. This certainly strengthens the effect.

(A) Take one of the bills and place it flat on a table. Now, "accordian pleat" the bill into seven equal parts as shown. *NOTE: On a "real" dollar bill, the FACE of the bill is printed in black while the BACK is printed in green. To make the rest of the steps clear, they will be described using a "real" bill.*

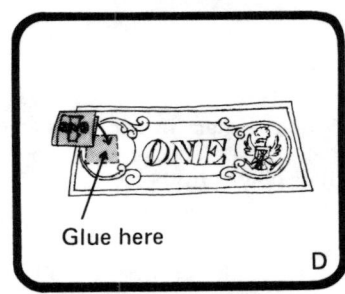

Glue here

(B) With your bundle now folded into seven pleats, *one* of the outside surfaces of the packet will show part of the bill's *face* (dark side) while the *other* surface will show part of the bill's *back* (green side). Place the folded bill with the *back* (green side) next to the table. The *face* (dark side) is on top. Now fold over one-third of the left side of the bill to the center as shown.

(C) Now fold the other end (right side) of the bill over as shown. This last fold should bring the corner of the back (green side) of the bill to the top of the folded package. The complete folded package should appear as shown.

(D) If the preceding three steps have been done correctly, you should have a small flat package approximately three-quarters of an inch square. Now glue this packet to the back of a duplicate bill. NOTE: If you use rubber cement, the bills can be easily separated after the show. Position the bills as shown here. *The glue is applied to the third of the bill that was NEXT TO THE TABLE when you folded the bill in Step C.*

METHOD

In the illustrations, to make the two bills easy to follow, the secret bundle has been colored darker than the open bill that you first display to the audience.

(1) Display the dollar bill to your audience, holding the bill opened out between the thumbs and fingers of both hands. Your left thumb serves two purposes: *First,* it keeps the duplicate folded bill from opening, and *second,* it conceals the folded bill from being seen by any spectators located on the sides.

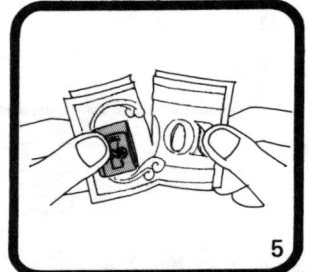

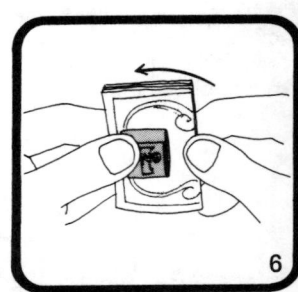

(5) Grip the two halves between the thumb and fingers of both hands and tear <u>both</u> halves as shown. (6) Again, place the torn pieces in the right hand, IN FRONT of the pieces in the left hand . . . and square the packet. To you, the torn pieces and the "secret" duplicate bills should appear as shown here.

(2) *NOTE: You may wish to start the routine by holding the bill in your right hand with your right fingers on the side of the duplicate bill . . . COMPLETELY HIDING IT FROM SIGHT. In this way, you may show the bill on BOTH sides. Then, turn the face of the bill to the audience and transfer your grip on the duplicate bill from the fingers of the right hand to the thumb of the left hand.*

(7) *NOTE: A neat touch here can be added by first placing the torn pieces in the right hand to the rear of the packet held in the left hand. The four pieces can then be spread in a small fan and shown on both sides. The pieces at the rear will conceal the folded duplicate bill. Then, in squaring up the packet, you replace the rear pieces to the front and continue as follows.*

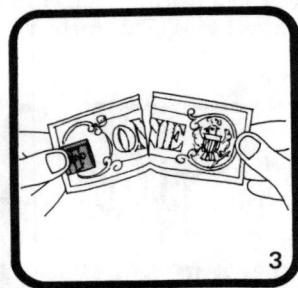

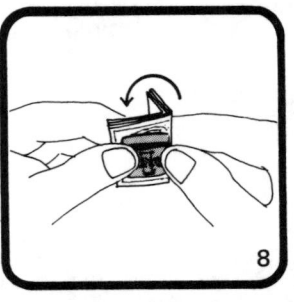

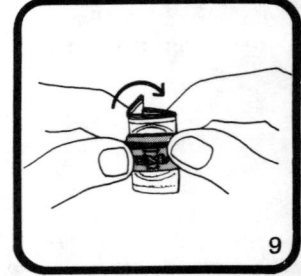

(3) Now tear the bill down the center line into two equal parts as shown. (4) Place the *right-hand half* of the bill IN FRONT of the *left-hand half*.

(8) Fold the *right*-hand edges of the torn pieces *forward* so that they are even with the right side of the secret folded bill as shown. (9) This done, fold the *left*-hand edges of the torn pieces *forward,* even with the left edge of the secret bill.

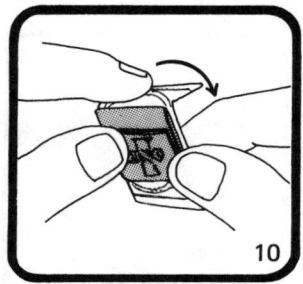 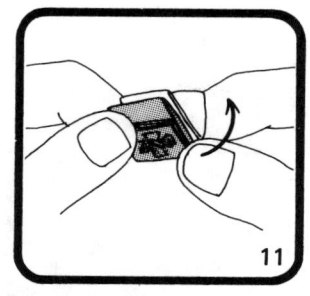

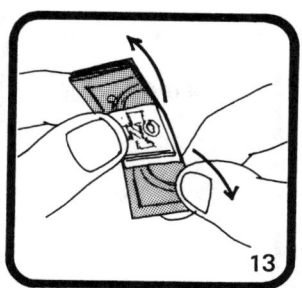 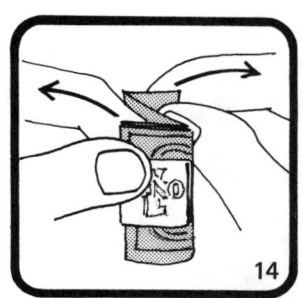

(10) Now fold *down* the *top edges* of the *torn pieces* even with the *top edge* of the *secret bill*.   (11) Lastly, do the same with the *bottom edges,* folding them *upwards* even with the *bottom edge* of the secret bill. *NOTE: You have now created a folded package of the torn pieces that matches exactly in size and shape the duplicate "whole" bill behind it.*

(13) Make a *magical gesture* or say an appropriate *magic word* and begin unfolding the top and bottom thirds of the *whole bill* as shown.   (14) When these portions have been unfolded, grasp the right-hand edge of the pleated bill with your right thumb and first finger. YOUR LEFT THUMB HOLDS THE FOLDED TORN PACKET AGAINST THE BACK OF THE BILL AS SHOWN.

(12) Folded in this way, the *total package* gives the impression of being *only* the folded pieces of the original bill. This makes it easy to casually *turn the package over* showing both sides of the torn bill. WHEN YOU FINISH SHOWING BOTH SIDES, BE SURE THAT YOU END WITH THE DUPLICATE "WHOLE" BILL IN FRONT AND THE FOLDED TORN PIECES TO THE REAR.

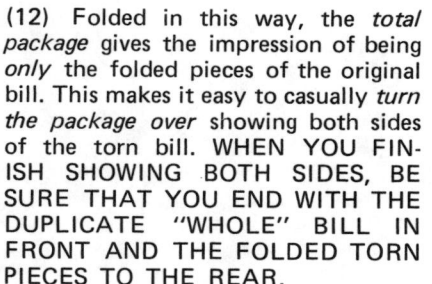 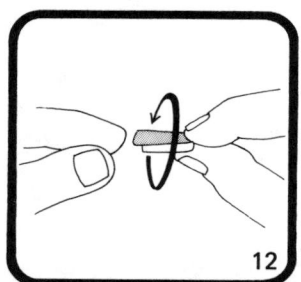

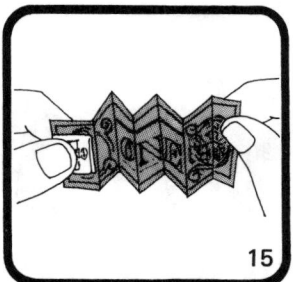 

(15) Now, by pulling your hands apart, the duplicate bill unfolds so quickly it will seem to the spectators as if the torn pieces are instantly restored.   (16) Briefly display the restored bill. Then fold it in half back over the torn pieces . . . thus eliminating the possibility of accidentally exposing the torn packet as you return the "restored" bill to your pocket.

INFLATION
PETER PIT

Here is a baffling "Cut and Restored" routine that is particularly effective when performed with "real" Dollar Bills. You can use play money, stage money, blank checks, or any form of printed paper about the size of regular currency.

EFFECT

The magician openly displays two Dollar Bills and places them back to back. He then cuts through the center of both bills with a pair of scissors — unmistakably cutting the two bills into four "halves." Without any suspicious moves, the *magician instantly restores both bills to their original condition right before the eyes of the astonished spectators!*

SECRET AND PREPARATION

  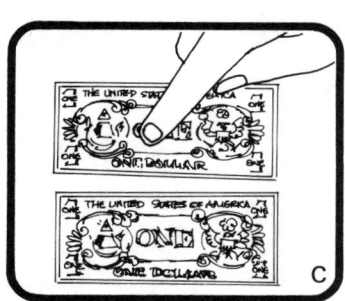

(A) Place two new or nearly new Dollar Bills face down on a table with the "green" side up.   (B) Apply a thin layer of *rubber cement,* about a half-inch wide, down the center of the back (the "green" side) of each bill. When this is dry, add a *second coat* of cement and allow it to dry also.   (C) Next, sprinkle a little talcum powder on the "cement covered" area on each bill. Spread the powder over the entire surface of the cement with your finger, or better yet, a soft brush. You will notice that now the "treated" areas of both bills *will not stick to each other* because of the powdered surface. Put the bills in your wallet or on your table and you are ready to perform this very clever close-up mystery.

METHOD

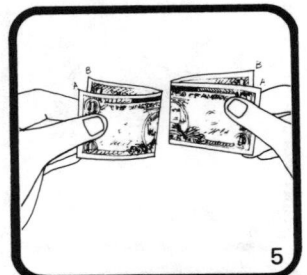

(1) Begin by removing the two prepared bills from your wallet and casually showing both sides of the bills. Place them *back to back* as shown. (We will call the bill nearest you "Bill A," and the one nearest the spectators "Bill B.") (2) Square up both bills. *Be sure that the cemented areas are touching each other.*

(5) With the thumb and fingers of both hands, separate the "halves" of the bills and . . . (6) . . . shake them open. Because of the rubber cement, *the halves in each hand will stick together at the cut edges* giving the illusion that the four "half" bills have "fused" together — TO FORM TWO COMPLETE BILLS!

(3) Hold *both bills* with the thumb and fingers of your left hand as shown. With your right hand holding the scissors, carefully cut through the center of both bills. *Make sure that you cut within the areas covered by the cement strips.* Done openly and deliberately, there will be no question in the audience's mind that both bills have actually been cut in half — *which they have.*
(4) Place the scissors aside. Grasp the halves on the right sides of the cut in your right hand (one-half of Bill A and one-half of Bill B) and the left side's two halves (the other two halves of Bill A and Bill B) in your left hand.

COMMENTS AND SUGGESTIONS

Done well, this "quickie" is a real eyepopper. First practice with stage money or with newspaper cut to the size of Dollar Bills. In this way you will find out just how much rubber cement and talcum powder to apply. Then, if you wish, you can try it with "real" bills. These should be new and crisp and fit together neatly for Steps 2 and 3. Don't worry about losing money when using real bills, as the halves can be mended with transparent tape, just as with any torn bills.

THE SIX-BILL REPEAT

If you can throw away your money and still keep it, that would be *REAL MAGIC* . . . like "having your cake and eating it too." That is exactly what you do with the "Six-Bill Repeat" — or it is at least what you appear to do. The best part of this effect is that the surprise increases with each repeat, which is quite unusual as most tricks lose their impact after they have been performed once. This makes the "Bill Trick" an outstanding number in any program, as you will find out for yourself when you perform it.

EFFECT

The magician removes his wallet from his inside coat pocket and takes out a number of one dollar bills. Counting them one-by-one for the audience, they see that he has *six* dollars. Dealing *three* of the bills on the table, the performer calls to the spectator's attention that simple mathematics would dictate that he has just *three* bills left in his hand. After all, three from six leaves three, doesn't it? Well, not in this case, for when the magician recounts the money, he finds he still has *six* one dollar bills. The performer keeps discarding three bills — only to find that each time he is "magically" left with six. This continues until a sizable amount of money is displayed on the table.

SECRET AND PREPARATION

We will assume that you will be using stage money for this effect, although real bills can be prepared in the same way.

(A) The secret lies in four special "envelope" type bills which you must construct. The first step is to cut the corner off of four bills as per Fig. A.

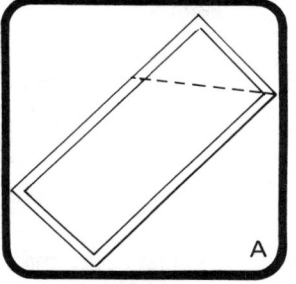

(E) Insert three unprepared bills into the "envelope" bill. Be sure that the unprepared bills all face in the proper direction and are correctly aligned so they match the printing of the "envelope" bill.

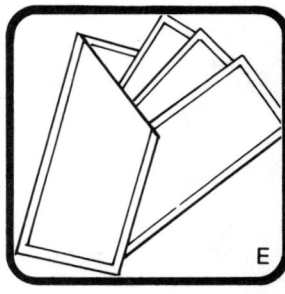

(B) Place the long edge of one of the cut bills next to an unprepared bill as in Fig. B. Be sure that the unprepared bill is *face down* and the the cut bill is *face up.*

(F) Make up three more "envelope" bills and insert three regular bills inside.

(C) With a strip of cellophane tape, tape the edges of the bills together.

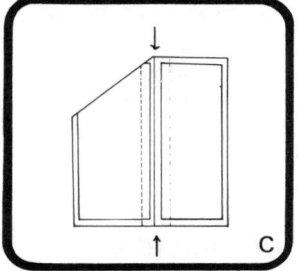

(G) Arrange the four *loaded* envelope bills and add two unprepared bills to the front of the final stack.

(D) Fold the cut bill down on top of the unprepared bill. Now, by taping the narrow edges at the left end of the bills, you have created an "envelope." *NOTE: To hide the tape on the narrow edges, first, fold the tape with the sticky side out and tape the narrow edges INSIDE the bills.*

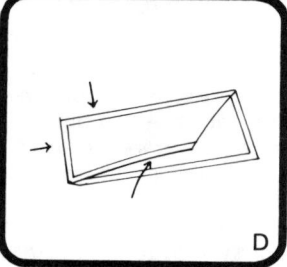

(H) Square up the stack so that the diagonal cuts of the prepared bills are at the top and facing in your direction. Place the bills in a "secretary" type wallet (or a business letter size envelope) and you are ready to perform.

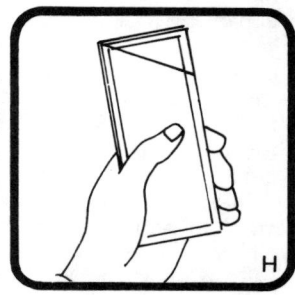

METHOD

(1) Remove the bills from your wallet and hold the stack in your left hand. Slowly and deliberately count the bills into your right hand, *making sure not to disturb their original order.*

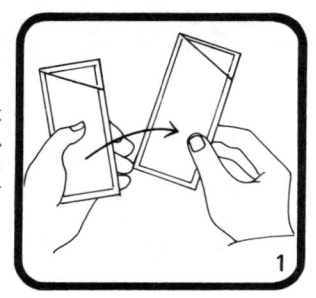

(2) At the completion of the count, all six bills should be in your right hand with the four prepared envelope bills still facing you.

(3) Square up the stack and transfer all to your left hand.

(6) Then slowly count the bills as before (Step 1), demonstrating the "magical" restoration to six bills.

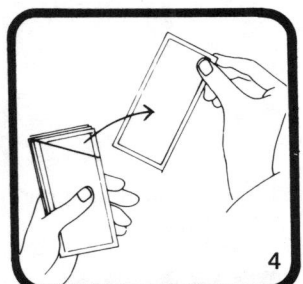

(4) Now count off three unprepared bills, *pulling them out of the top envelope bill one at a time.* Count them aloud, "One, Two, Three," as you place them on the table.

(7) It is important that during the "counts" you maintain the order of the two regular bills and the four envelope bills. In other words, from your point of view you should now have in your right hand, starting from the side nearest you, three "loaded" envelope bills, two regular bills and one empty envelope bill. In the illustration the bills have been purposely fanned open to show more clearly their position at this point in the routine.

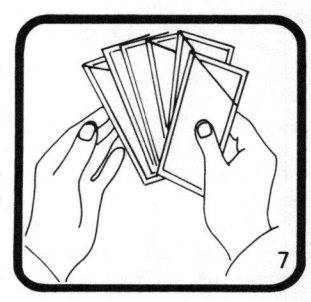

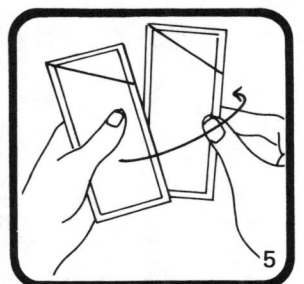

(5) You are now left with an empty envelope bill at the rear of the stack. MOVE THIS ENVELOPE TO THE FRONT OF THE STACK *(audience side)* and give the remaining three bills a deliberate snap with your fingers. As you do this, remark, "By placing the *back* bill in the *front* and giving the packet a *magic tap,* it magically doubles the amount of money left in my hand."

(8) This process continues until all of the loaded envelopes have been emptied. All in all, twelve "new" dollar bills make their magical appearance. The effectiveness of this illusion is enhanced by repetition, which does not normally hold true in presenting a trick. But in this case, the audience becomes more and more involved as the effect progresses.

COMMENTS AND SUGGESTIONS

This trick is quite effective and the props can be made quite inexpensively, and it can be seen by a large audience. The entertainment value of the trick lies in the "patter" story that you devise to accompany it. Here is an example:

"I saw an ad in a magazine for the Mark Wilson Course In Magic. The ad said that one of the tricks I would learn if I studied the course is how to count, one-two-three-four-five-six dollar bills — and then remove one-two-three - - and I would still have one-two-three-four-five-six dollar bills left. So I ordered the Course and while I was waiting for it to come, I wondered how you could possibly have one-two-three-four-five-six dollar bills, remove one-two-three and have one-two-three-four-five-six dollar bills left. When I received the Mark Wilson Course, sure enough, after I practiced the trick I learned how to count one-two-three-four-five-six dollar bills, remove one-two-three and still have one-two-three-four-five-six dollar bills left." You have now emptied three of the envelope bills, you have one "loaded" envelope left. Your patter continues: "And now I am going to tell you the secret. Instead of starting with one-two-three-four-five-six dollar bills, you really have one-two-three-four-five-six-SEVEN-EIGHT-NINE bills to start with. AND THAT'S HOW THE TRICK WORKS." The last count of nine — the comedy explanation -- is performed by counting the first three bills from the last envelope bill and *then counting the envelope bills as well* onto the table.

NOTE: When you count the bills in the final "nine count," be sure to place the envelope bills on the table so that the "cut side" of the bills is face down so they will not be seen by the audience.

THE BILL IN LEMON

The BILL IN LEMON is one of the great "classics" of modern magic. That claim is supported by the fact that several famous magicians have featured it as the highlight of their individual programs. There are several different versions of this mystery. In the clever method described here, no special skill is required, which makes it ideal for new students of magic as well as advanced practitioners.

EFFECT

From a bowl containing three lemons, a spectator is given a free choice of whichever one he wants. The selected lemon is then placed in an ordinary paper or plastic bag and the spectator holds the lemon throughout the entire presentation. _After the lemon has been selected and is securely held by the first spectator,_ the magician borrows a dollar bill and writes its serial number on the back of a small envelope. He then inserts the bill into the envelope, seals it, and gives it to a second spectator to hold. He then recaps exactly what has happened up to this point. Then, the spectator holding the envelope is told to tear it open and remove the borrowed bill. When he does, _instead of the bill,_ he finds an I.O.U. for one dollar, _signed by the magician._ The first spectator is given a knife and asked to cut open the selected lemon, _which has remained in his custody at all times._ Inside the lemon, he finds a tightly rolled dollar bill. When the bill is opened, its serial number is found to be exactly the same as the number written on the envelope, proving that the _borrowed bill_ has magically travelled _from the envelope to the inside of the freely selected lemon._

SECRET AND PREPARATION

For this amazing effect, you will need the following items: a stack of a dozen or more envelopes (small "pay" envelopes are best, however, any small opaque envelope can be used), three lemons, a bowl, a dollar bill, your handwritten I.O.U. which is the same size as a dollar bill, a rubber band, some glue and a small paper or plastic bag. (A transparent plastic bag is best.)

HOW TO PREPARE THE ENVELOPES

(A) To begin, write the serial number of _your_ dollar bill on the back of one of the envelopes near the lower end as shown. For future reference, this envelope has been marked with an "O" in the illustrations.

(F) Then place Envelope X (the one with the flap cut off) directly on top of Envelope O, concealing the serial number from view.

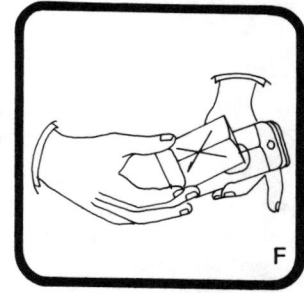

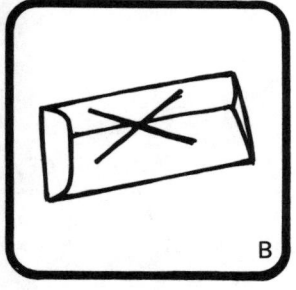

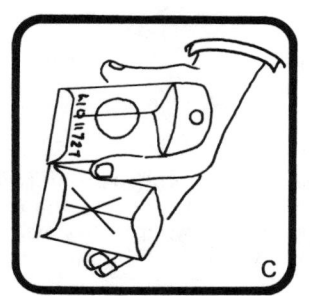

(B) Then, _carefully cut off the gummed flap from another envelope._ This envelope is identified with an "X" in the illustrations. (C) This is how Envelopes X and O should look at this point.

(G) Now, square up the envelopes and place the rubber band around the entire stack. _Done properly, the gummed flap of Envelope O will appear to be the flap belonging to Envelope X._

HOW TO PREPARE THE "SPECIAL" LEMON

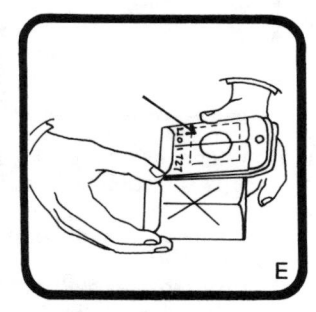

(H) First, _carefully_ remove the "pip" from one of the lemons with the point of a knife. _Do not throw the pip away as you will need it later._

(D) Fold the I.O.U. and insert it into Envelope O. (E) Place Envelope O on top of the stack of regular envelopes so that the written serial number is facing up as shown.

(I) Then, using a smooth, round stick (like the kind used for candied apples), or any similarly shaped slim long object, carefully make a hole in the center of the lemon as shown. This will *expand the inner core area of the lemon* and make the necessary space to accommodate a rolled bill. *Be careful not to go too far and puncture the skin at the other end of the lemon with the stick.*

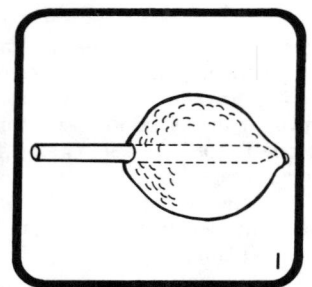

(L) Push the rolled bill *completely into the lemon.* Use a small dab of glue to fix the pip back on the lemon (model airplane glue works well). *Be sure that you have written down the serial number of the bill before you insert it into the lemon.* When you glue the pip back in place, adjust it so that it hides the small hole in the end of the lemon.

(J) *NOTE: If a wooden stick of this type is not available, certain kinds of ball point pens and some pencils are* <u>thin enough</u> *to make the correct sized hole in the lemon. The important point here is that whatever object you are using be thin enough so that it does not puncture the inside "juicy" portion of the lemon when it is inserted.*

(M) Finally, place the prepared lemon (marked "X" in the illustrations) in a bowl with two "ordinary" lemons. *Be certain that you are able to distinguish the "prepared" lemon ("X") from the other two at a glance.*

(K) Now roll the dollar bill into a tight, compact cylinder.

(N) NOTE: There may be some special "blemish" on the prepared lemon that you can remember — or you can make a small mark with a black pen or pencil on the lemon that will not be noticed by the audience.

(O) Place the bowl of lemons, the stack of envelopes, the pencil, the knife, and the small bag on your table. YOU ARE NOW READY TO PRESENT THIS CLASSIC MYSTERY.

METHOD

(1) *FIRST, THE "FREE" CHOICE OF THE "SPECIAL" LEMON:* This is accomplished by "forcing," using the MAGICIAN'S CHOICE, which is described in detail on Page 321 of the Course. In this force, the spectator *believes* he is given a free choice of any of the three lemons, when *actually* you cleverly maneuver him to select the special Lemon X. After he has made his "selection," pick up the small bag from your table. Hold the bag open and have the spectator drop the lemon inside. Tell him to hold the bag tightly so that the lemon *he selected* cannot get away!

(2) *NOW FOR THE BILL AND THE ENVELOPE* — Borrow a dollar bill from some member of the audience. Explain that you will write its serial number on the top of the stack (Envelope X). As you "pretend" to copy the number from the borrowed bill, you *actually write any number you wish on the envelope,* as it will automatically be "switched" for the correct serial number which is now hidden on the second in the stack, Envelope O. (It is best if you remember the <u>first letter</u> of the serial number of *your* bill as this is the most obvious thing that the audience might see and remember.) Just casually copy the number (with *your* first letter) of the <u>borrowed bill.</u> Remember, the audience, at this time, does not know what trick you are going to perform — so they will not pay particular attention to the serial number now <u>if you do not call special attention to it.</u> (3) This done, fold the borrowed bill to about the same size as your I.O.U. Then openly insert it *into the flapless Envelope X.* Be sure that everyone sees that the bill is definitely going into the <u>top envelope of the stack.</u> Be careful not to expose that Envelope X <u>does not have a flap.</u>

(4) *NOTE: Inserting the bill into Envelope X requires some practice in the handling of the envelopes so that you can do it smoothly and not arouse suspicion. It may be helpful to remove the rubber band before attempting to insert the bill into the top envelope. This depends on how tight the rubber band holds the packet of envelopes.*

(10) Immediately place the rest of the envelopes in your pocket, eliminating the possibility of anyone discovering that a switch was made. Now, seal Envelope O and give it to a spectator to hold.

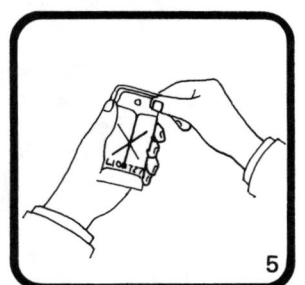

(5) Once the bill has been inserted into Envelope X on the top of the stack, grip the <u>uppermost flap</u> (actually the flap of Envelope O) between your right thumb and fingers — and <u>draw this envelope from the rest of the stack.</u>

(11) This done, ask the person holding the sealed envelope to raise it toward the light *so he can see that the bill is really there.* Of course, what he <u>actually</u> sees is the outline of your I.O.U.

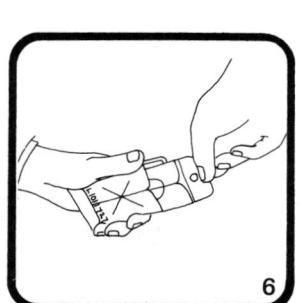

(6) What you are really doing is drawing out Envelope O instead of Envelope X, but you hide that move from the spectators BY TURNING THE STACK <u>COMPLETELY OVER AS YOU DRAW THE ENVELOPE CLEAR.</u>

(12) Now ask the first spectator if he is still holding the bag with the lemon inside. When he says he is, ask him if there is any way *anything* could have gotten inside the bag with the lemon. After he replies, recap what has happened up to this point. Explain that <u>first</u> you had *one* of three lemons selected and that *that lemon* has been securely held by a member of the audience *at all times.* Now take the two remaining lemons from the bowl and <u>toss them to other members of the audience.</u> This will strengthen the effect later after the borrowed bill is found inside the selected lemon. The spectators may even cut open these "ungimmicked" lemons which will only increase the mystery.

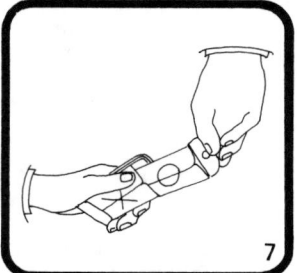

(7) This makes a *perfect switch* of Envelope X, the one containing the borrowed bill, for Envelope O, the one that contains your I.O.U.

(13) Now, emphasize that you *then* borrowed a dollar bill from someone in the audience — <u>AFTER</u> THE SELECTED LEMON WAS SAFELY IN THE BAG HELD BY THE SPECTATOR. The serial number of the bill was recorded on the outside of an envelope and the bill sealed inside. Emphasize again that THE ENVELOPE, <u>WITH THE BILL STILL SEALED INSIDE,</u> IS NOW HELD BY THE SECOND SPECTATOR.

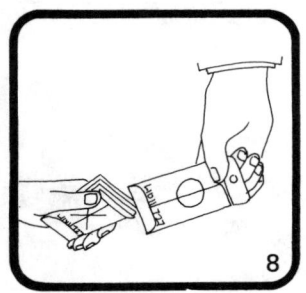

(8) Once Envelope O is entirely clear of the rest of the stack, . . .
(9) turn it "flap side up" so that the serial number that you previously wrote on Envelope O is clearly visible to the spectators. The audience will be convinced that *it is the same envelope* and that everything is aboveboard.

(14) NOW FOR THE MAGIC! *Really the trick is already done, but the audience doesn't know it!* Ask the second spectator to tear open the envelope and remove the bill. (15) When he does, *he finds your I.O.U. instead.*

(16) Next, give the knife to the person holding the bag with the lemon inside. Tell him to remove the lemon from the bag. <u>After</u> he removes the lemon, *take the bag from him and hold it in your hand.* With your other hand, give him the knife and ask him to cut the lemon open. (It's even better if he uses a pocket knife borrowed from someone in the audience!) As he cuts the lemon, instruct him to "rotate" the lemon around the knifeblade as if it had an inner "core" which he did not wish to cut.

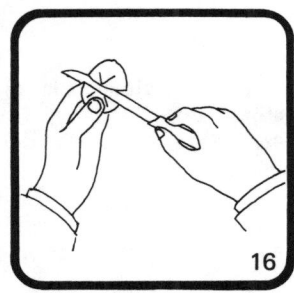

(19) <u>After</u> *the bill is removed from the lemon by the spectator,* take the lemon "halves" from him and *drop them into the bag.* Put the bag on your table or casually toss it off stage. (This subtly gets rid of the "gimmicked" half of the lemon so that it is not lying about where someone might pick it up and examine it later on.) Then, have the spectator compare the serial number on the bill he found in the lemon with that of the now "vanished" borrowed bill which was written on the envelope. HE WILL FIND THAT THE NUMBERS ARE IDENTICAL — proving that the borrowed bill has "magically" gone from the sealed envelope into the freely selected lemon — A MAGICAL MIRACLE! Take back your I.O.U. in exchange for the borrowed bill and thank the spectators for their assistance.

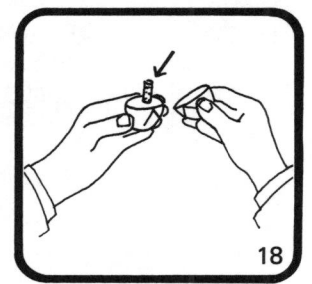

(17) When the spectator draws the halves of the lemon apart, . . .
(18) he finds the bill imbedded in the center! EMPHASIZE THAT <u>YOU HAVE NEVER TOUCHED THE LEMON</u> SINCE IT WAS SELECTED FROM THE BOWL.

COMMENTS AND SUGGESTIONS

Be sure to write down the serial number of *your* bill <u>before</u> you load it into the lemon. Also, have the first letter of the serial number written somewhere handy for quick reference in case you forget it. You can strengthen the effect even more by really writing the *complete serial number* of your "loaded" bill on Envelope X. To help you remember it, you may write the number *very lightly* so that no one can notice it on the back of Envelope X before the show. Another subterfuge for "remembering" the number is to have the number already written near the center of the envelope and then cover it with a wide rubber band. You can then shift or remove the rubber band as you "pretend" to copy the number from the borrowed bill. If you use this method, be sure to keep the stack of envelopes turned toward you as you write. Then, after the number is written, since it *matches identically* the previously written number on Envelope O underneath, *you may display the stack freely to the audience.* As for the rubber band, its main purpose is to keep the envelopes neatly in place during the early handling of the stack. It does not have to be removed from the stack during the performance as it may prove helpful for the "switch," *if it is not too tight.*

Another suggestion is to use an *orange* instead of a lemon. As an orange is somewhat larger, it is easier to load, and you can easily withdraw the "pip" from the orange before inserting the bill.

It is a good plan to get *several* people to offer you a bill for the trick so *you can pick the one that <u>most closely resembles</u> the age and "wear" of the bill already in the lemon.* Also, don't give the owner time to note the serial number, as you are going to give him back *your* bill instead of the one you borrowed from him.

As you can see, this is one of the truly great tricks in magic. You can build your reputation on this one trick alone — <u>so *study* it and *practice* it before you *perform* it</u>. Add your own touches — emphasize the "impossible" nature of what the audience is seeing — and always protect the truly marvelous secret of THE BILL IN LEMON.

ROPE MAGIC

Here is a highly popular branch of modern wizardry that has grown by leaps and bounds, for a very good reason. Simple tricks with rope can be done any time, anywhere, in an impromptu fashion, making them ideal for beginners who can later graduate into more elaborate "rope work" suitable for platform or stage. With ropes, once you have learned a good trick, it invariably paves the way to another, gradually enabling you to build a reputation as well as a program.

Originally, rope magic was confined chiefly to "Trick Knots" that puzzled spectators but did not actually mystify them. A new era arrived with the "Cut and Restored Rope," which soon became popular with stage magicians, although for a long time it was the only rope trick on their programs. However, various methods were soon devised, so that audiences were continually deceived by new versions with unexpected twists. This led to improvements that were baffling even to magicians who depended on the old-time routines; and that rule prevails today.

Now, instead of merely cutting a rope in half, a magician can cut it into several pieces before restoring it. Short ropes can be tied together with knots that disappear, leaving one long rope. Stretching short ropes to various lengths is another specialty, and knots can be made to come and go in amazing fashion. Though every rope has an end, there seems to be no end to rope tricks, and that is why you will find this section of very special value. It will teach you rope magic as it stands today, so that your program will represent a long step toward the rope magic of tomorrow!

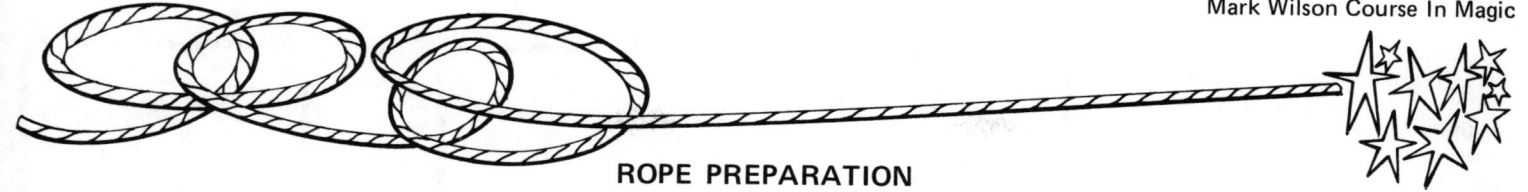

ROPE PREPARATION

In performing Rope Magic, there are several "tips" you should know about the preparation of the rope to achieve the most effective results in practice and presentation.

CORING: In certain tricks it is important that the rope be extremely flexible — even more so than it already is. In that case, you can do what is known as "Coring" with many types of rope — especially the soft cotton rope used by magicians. If you look at the end of some types of rope, you will notice that the rope is constructed of a woven outer "shell" which contains an inner "core." This core is made up of a number of individual cotton strands running the entire length of the rope. To remove the core, first, cut off a piece of rope and spread open the threads of the outer "shell" at one end. With your fingers, firmly grasp the strands of cord which make up the core. Now with your other hand, get a firm hold on the outer shell near the same end and start pulling the core from within the rope's outer shell. As you pull the "core" and slide the outer "shell," you will find that the shell tends to "bunch up" and then bind, making it difficult to pull out the inner core. When this happens, grasp the rope just below the "bunched up" shell and pull the shell *down along the length of the remaining core* until the shell is "straight" again — with the empty shell extending from the other end of the "core." Then pull another length of core out from within the outer shell until it "binds" again. Continue this process of pulling and "unbunching" until the core has been completely removed from within the shell of the rope. Discard the core. This leaves you with the soft, flexible outer shell of the Rope. To the audience, however, *the rope will appear just the same as before you removed the core.*

FIXING THE ENDS: Another suggestion which will aid in maintaining the appearance of your rope, particularly if it has been "Cored," is to permanently "fix" the ends of the rope so that they will not fray (come apart). This can be done in several ways.

(1)   A particularly good method is to dip the end of the rope into a small amount of *white glue* and allow it to dry over night. This will permanently bond all the loose fibers together and prevent them from unraveling.

(2)   Another substance which works well for this purpose is *wax* or *paraffin*. The wax is melted and the ends of the rope dipped into the liquid wax and allowed to dry. This method has the advantage that wax requires only a short period of time to dry and your ropes can be prepared only minutes before a performance.

(3)   Another method which works well is to "tie off" the ends of the rope with regular *white sewing thread* after the rope has been cut to the desired length. Simply wrap the thread around the ends of the rope and tie the ends tightly to keep the rope from unwinding.

(4)   One final method is to wrap a small piece of white *adhesive tape* or *transparent cellophane tape* around the ends of the rope. Because tape is more easily visible, however, it may draw undue attention to the ends of the rope and distract from the effect being presented. The "tape method" is a good, fast way to get your "rehearsal" ropes ready.

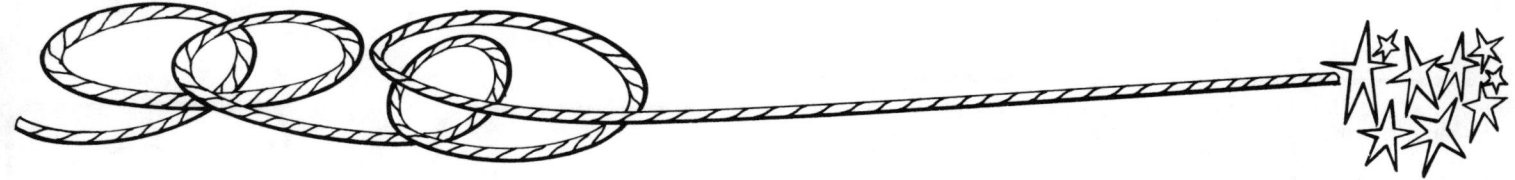

CUT AND RESTORED ROPE — FIRST METHOD

This effect has become a magical "classic" in its own right and is one with which every magician should be familiar. Most all versions of the CUT AND RESTORED ROPE are based upon the same simple method. Once you have learned it well, you can continue with other forms of the trick described later in the Course.

EFFECT

The magician displays a six-foot length of rope. He then forms the center of the rope into a loop in his hand and cuts it there — explaining that the rope must first be divided into *two equal* sections. However, it becomes immediately evident — first to the audience and then to the magician — that the two resulting lengths of rope are not the same length, much to the dismay of the performer. Somewhat frustrated, the magician ties the cut ends together with a simple knot — and then winds the rope around his hand. After a little "magic," the performer unwinds the rope to show that the knot has "dissolved" — leaving the rope COMPLETELY RESTORED!

SECRET AND PREPARATION

The only items required for this effect are a length of rope, a coin (or some other small object), and a pair of sharp scissors. To prepare, place the coin in your right trouser or jacket pocket. Have the scissors on a table nearby. This done, you are ready to begin.

(1) Display the rope to your audience, holding the ends between the thumb and fingers of your left hand, so that the center of the rope hangs down as shown. NOTE: There are *two key locations* on the rope that will help greatly in explaining the secret of the CUT AND RESTORED ROPE. The *first* is a point about four inches from the end of the rope. We will call this "Point A." The *second* is the *true center* of the rope — this we will call "Point B."

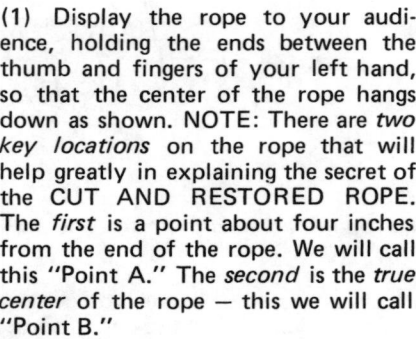

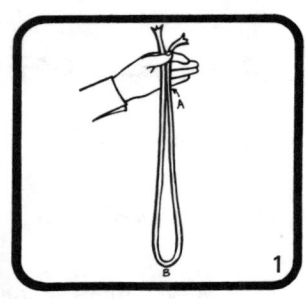

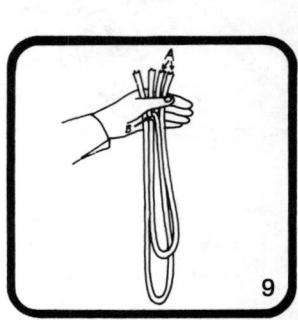

(8) With the scissors, cut the rope at Point A. Say, "I'll cut the rope at the *center,* which makes *two ropes exactly equal* in length." (9) After the cut the audience will see *four ends* projecting above your left hand. Point A has now been cut into *two parts* as shown.

(2) Insert your right thumb and first finger through the center loop, Point B, from the *audience side* of the rope as shown. *NOTE: Your right thumb and first finger are pointing upward and slightly back toward you as you insert them into the loop.* (3) With your right hand, bring the rope up toward your left hand, keeping the loop, Point B, draped loosely over your right thumb and first finger.

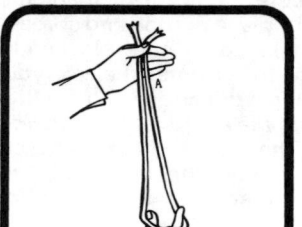

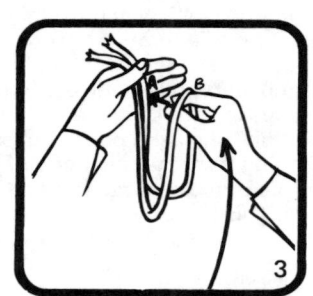

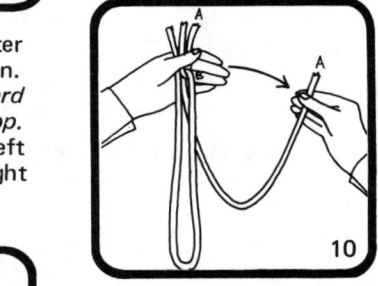

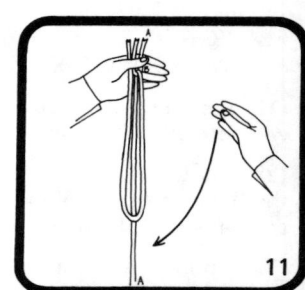

(4) As your hands come together, your right thumb and first finger grasp the rope *at Point A* as shown. (5) HERE COMES THE "SECRET MOVE" WHICH MAKES THE TRICK WORK. Now, pull Point A upward so that it forms a small loop of its own, which you hold between your right thumb and first finger. At the same time that you pick up Point A, tilt your right fingers downward so that Point B — *the real center of the rope* — slides off your right fingers into the cradle of rope formed when you lifted Point A into a loop. STUDY THE ILLUSTRATION FOR STEPS 4 AND 5. *NOTE: Steps 4 and 5 must be hidden from the spectators by your left hand.*

(10) With your right hand, draw the end at the *far right* away from your left hand and (11) drop it. As you do this say, "That is *one* rope . . ."

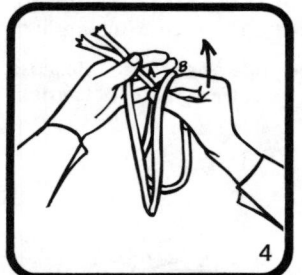

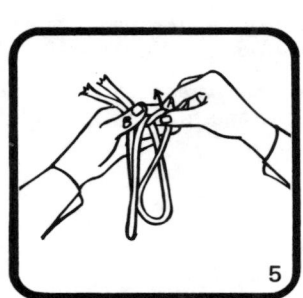

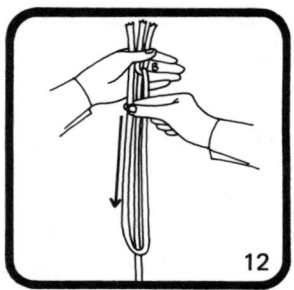

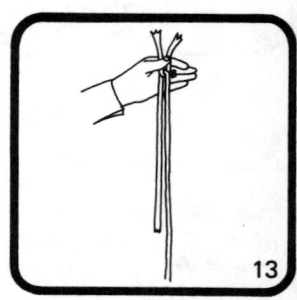

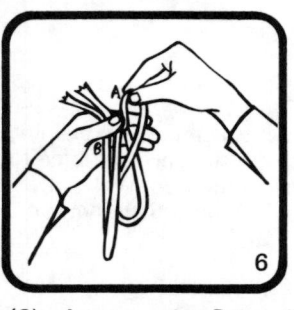

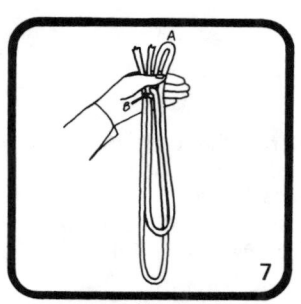

(6) As you raise Point A upward to form the new loop, your left thumb keeps the real center, Point B, down in your left hand, out of view of the spectators. (7) This new loop, Point A, takes the place of what the audience still believes is *the real center of the rope,* Point B — since your left hand concealed the "secret" switch.

(12) Grasp the end of the rope at the *far left* and (13) let it fall next to the first as you say, ". . . and here is the *second* rope." At this point it will become obvious to the audience that the "two" ropes did not come out equal in length as you had intended. Pretend to be puzzled and somewhat frustrated at the results; as you say, "Something seems to have gone wrong; the rope must be cut into two equal pieces." *NOTE: The two ends of the short piece of rope that project above your left hand look like the ends of two separate long ropes. The real center of the rope (Point B) is looped over the short piece of rope.*

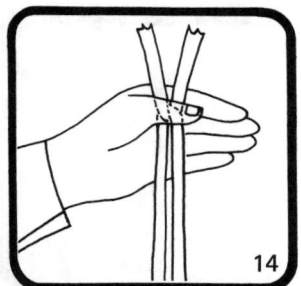

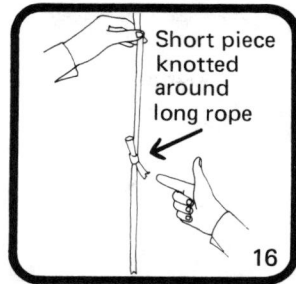

(14) As an optional "convincer," you can add the following move to prove that you actually have "two separate pieces" of rope. Cover the interlocking loops at Point B with your left thumb. Then swing your left arm out to your left side so that the palm of your left hand is facing the audience. This lets you casually show *both sides* of the cut ropes — while your left thumb hides the fact that the upper ends are really the ends of a short loop — not the ends of two long ropes. Then swing your arm back to its former position in front of your body and continue with the next step. (15). While your hands conceal the true condition of the ropes, *tie the ends of the short rope around the center of the long piece of rope at Point B.* Be careful not to reveal that you really have <u>one long rope</u> and <u>one short rope</u> while tying the knot.

(16) This done, you can now openly display the rope to the audience, as you call attention to the knot which is tied slightly "off center." (17) Then, starting at either end, begin to wind the rope around your left hand. What you really do, however, is *slide the knot along the rope* with your right hand as you continue the winding process. Keep the knot hidden in your right hand as you slide it along.

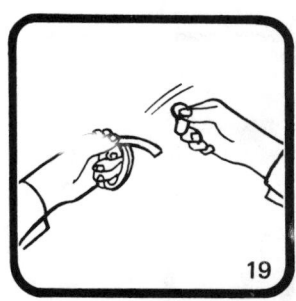

(18) As you complete the winding, *slide the knot off the end of the rope.* Hold the knot secretly in your curled right fingers. Without pausing, dip your right hand into your pocket, remarking, "I will now need my magic coin" (or whatever small object you are using). With that, *leave the knot in your pocket* and bring out the coin. Wave it over the rope as you make some remark about the "Magic Coin." (19) Now, release the coin in your pocket and uncoil the rope — showing that the knot has vanished and the rope is COMPLETELY RESTORED! The rope can then be tossed to the audience for examination.

COMMENTS AND SUGGESTIONS

The length of the rope used in this trick can vary from three to eight feet. It is a good plan to start with a *long* rope, as with each performance the rope loses several inches. When it finally becomes too short to be effective, discard it and use another long rope or save it for some other trick in which a "short" rope is used.

CUT AND RESTORED ROPE — SECOND METHOD

EFFECT

The performer draws a long piece of rope through his hand and asks a member of the audience to call "Stop" to select a point anywhere along the length of the rope. When the call comes, the magician cuts the rope at the spot indicated by the spectator. After displaying the two pieces of rope, the performer decides that the rope served a more useful purpose as one long piece. As if by magic, the performer *instantly restores the rope back to its original condition!* The presentation can end at this point, or be used as a lead-in to a series of other rope effects.

SECRET AND PREPARATION

As in the First Method, the rope is unprepared. Again, the only items required are a sharp pair of scissors and a piece of soft rope about five or six feet in length.

METHOD

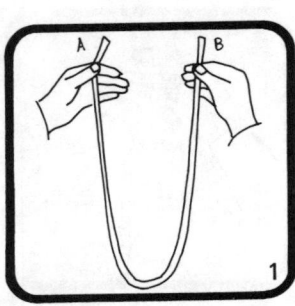

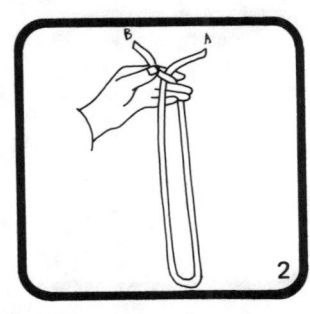

(1) Display the length of rope, holding it by the ends as shown. We will call the ends of the ropes A and B in the illustrations. End A is held in your left hand, and End B in your right.

(2) With your right hand, place End B into your left hand between your first and second fingers. End B is positioned as shown, overlapping End A. Hold End B in place with your left thumb as shown.

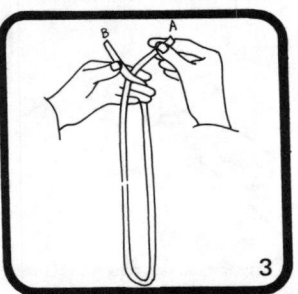

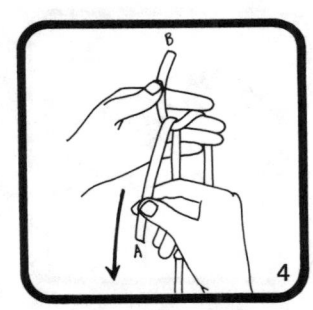

(3) Grasp End A with your right hand. (4) With End B held tightly by your left thumb, your right hand pulls End A down (toward yourself) as shown. As you pull the rope down, ask the spectator to tell you when to "stop" pulling.

(5) As you pull End A, the loop in the rope will get smaller and smaller. The illusion created by this move is that the spectator is given a "free choice" as to where the rope will be cut. As you will see, *it makes no difference where he stops you.*

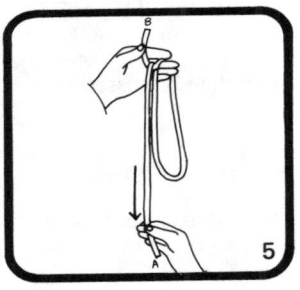

(6) When the spectator calls "Stop," release End A and *grasp the side of the loop closest to End B* (Point X in the illustration) as shown. Ask the spectator to cut the rope you hold between your hands (at Point X). If you study the illustration, you will see that THE SPECTATOR IS ACTUALLY CUTTING OFF ONLY A SMALL PIECE OF ROPE CLOSE TO END B — *not near the center of the rope as he thinks.*

(7) As soon as the spectator makes the cut, release your right hand. This allows the "new" end, which we will call X2, to fall next to End A. You now hold one *short* piece and one *long* piece of rope looped together in your left hand.

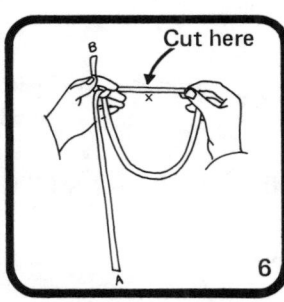

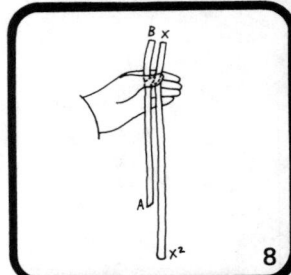

(8) Adjust End X up next to End B and hold them with your left thumb and fingers. *To the audience, it will appear that you hold two separate long lengths of rope.*

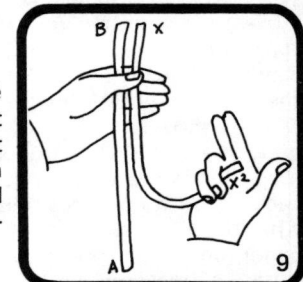

(9) At this point, comment to the audience that the two ropes have not come out equal and you are a bit embarrassed by your "mistake." With that, grasp End X2 in your right hand as shown, keeping the end well within the hand.

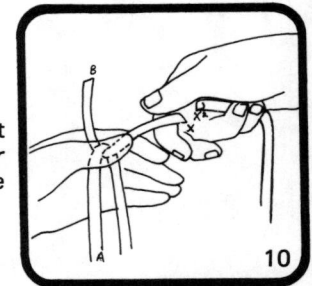

(10) Bring End X2 up to meet End X1 and grasp *both ends together* in your right hand, as shown in the illustration.

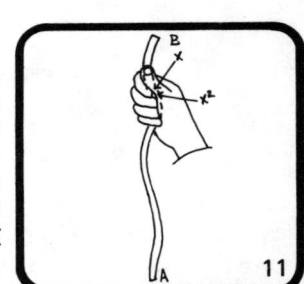

(11) As soon as you have both ends held firmly together within your right fingers, release your left hand and shake the rope open, holding it with your right hand so that it *appears* to be one long rope restored into a single length. *The effect is __instant restoration__.*

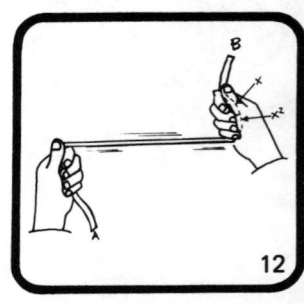

(12) Comment that "It wasn't a very good trick anyway," as you tug on the now "restored" rope.

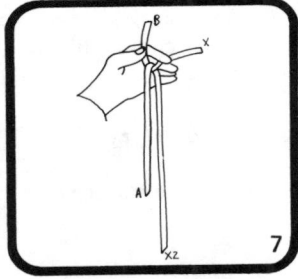

(13) With the "secret" joint still concealed by your right hand, coil the rope and place it in your pocket.

COMMENTS AND SUGGESTIONS

In both methods of the CUT AND RESTORED ROPE, after you apparently cut the rope into two pieces (Step 13 in the First Method, Step 8 in the Second Method), you are actually holding *a long piece of rope which is secretly looped with a short piece.* To the audience, it appears that you hold two separate long pieces of rope. At this point in the trick, because your left fingers conceal the interlocking loops, you may conclude the effect using <u>either version</u> of restoring the rope back to one long piece, as they are interchangeable.

If you restore the rope as described in the Second Method and you wish to continue with other rope tricks, you will need to dispose of the short end which extends from your right hand. A natural way to do this is to reach into your pocket to remove some object and simply carry the end of the "restored" rope and the short piece along. Then, when you remove your hand with the object, leave the short piece behind. The audience will not notice that the long rope has now become a bit "shorter" than before. If you use a pocket knife to cut the rope, this makes a logical item to remove from your pocket. You could also remove some small prop which you plan to use in your next trick, such as a ring, coin, or handkerchief. Another suggestion is to reach for some object on your table, carrying along the end of the rope and the short piece. When you pick up the object, you can leave the short piece on the table behind (or in) some prop that is already there.

Both methods of the CUT AND RESTORED ROPE are <u>true classics of magic</u>. Although quite simple, once learned they will become a permanent addition to your repertoire. Also, this is one of the few tricks that are just as effective when performed for a small intimate crowd as they are for large audiences. THIS IS A VALUABLE AND MUCH USED PRINCIPLE OF MAGIC. PRACTICE IT WELL BEFORE YOU PRESENT IT, AND — ABOVE ALL — DO NOT REVEAL ITS SECRET.

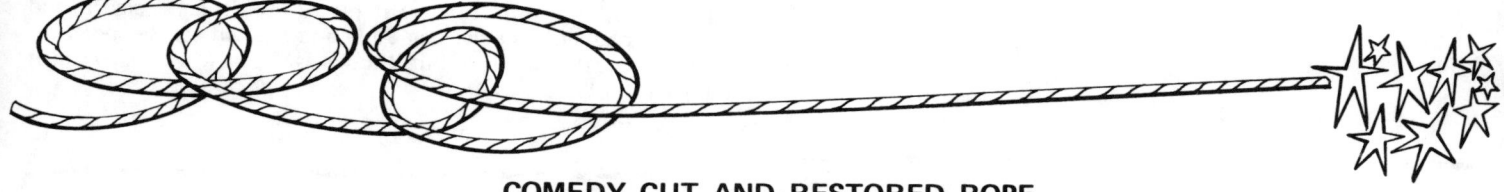

COMEDY CUT AND RESTORED ROPE

EFFECT

The performer gives a member of his audience a piece of rope approximately three feet in length and has the spectator cut the rope into two equal parts. After viewing the result, the magician decides to have the spectator cut the two pieces again, making four equal parts. Taking the four pieces of rope, the performer drops them one by one into an empty paper bag. Next, he closes the top of the bag and shakes it vigorously. The magician tells the spectator that, by waving the scissors over the bag, the rope will "mysteriously" restore itself to one piece. Upon opening the bag, the audience sees that the rope has restored itself, *but not in the way the magician intended.* Instead of *one* piece, the rope has "magically" *tied itself together* with *three* equally spaced knots. The bag is shown to be empty and is tossed aside. In order to solve this new problem, the magician simply gives the end of the "tied" rope a sharp pull. THE THREE KNOTS FLY OFF THE ROPE LEAVING IT COMPLETELY RESTORED!

SECRET AND PREPARATION

(A) Cut *two* 3-foot lengths of soft rope and *three* short pieces of rope about 3½ inches long. These short lengths will be used to form fake knots, which later "pop" off the rope. Stretch out one of the 3-foot lengths of rope and mark it lightly with a pencil in quarters as shown. These marks show you where to attach the fake knots which *apparently* divide the rope into four equal parts.

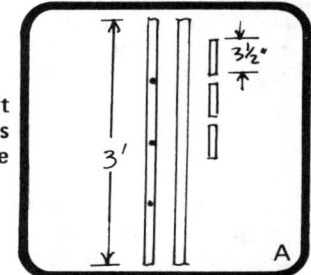

  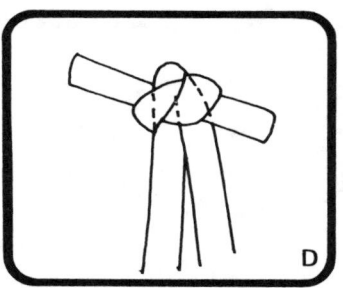 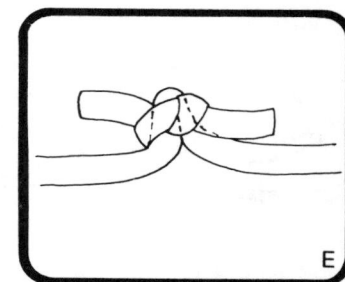

(B) First, to tie the fake knots, fold the long rope at one of the three pencil marks. (C) Then, tie one of the short pieces of rope . . . (D) . . . *around* the folded rope as shown. (E) When you straighten the long rope, the knot will appear like this. If you pull on the rope, the knot will "pop" off.

(F) Tie the other two short pieces around the other two marked spots on the long rope. You now appear to have one long piece of rope made up of three short pieces knotted together.

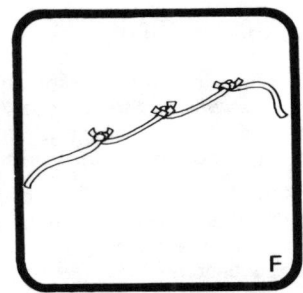

(G) You will also need a DOUBLE-WALLED BAG (see Page 357). Open the bag and place the prepared rope into the *main compartment* as shown. DO NOT PLACE IT INTO THE "SECRET" POCKET, *as this area will be used to conceal the cut pieces later in the routine.* Fold the bag flat and put it on your table.

METHOD

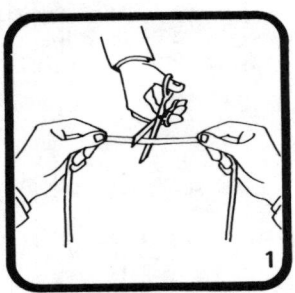

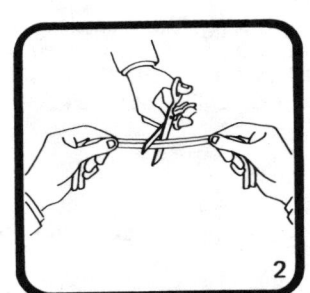

(1) Invite a spectator to join you on stage so that you may teach him how to present a trick. Hand him the scissors and display the 3-foot length of rope to the audience. Turn to your volunteer and instruct him to cut the rope — first in half . . . (2) . . . and then into four equal parts.

(3) Pick up the paper bag and open it. *Be careful not to show the inside of the bag or you will expose the presence of the prepared rope.* Drop the four pieces of rope, one at a time, INTO THE SECRET COMPARTMENT OF THE BAG.

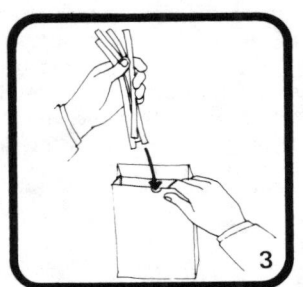

(4) Close the top of the bag and shake it so that the spectator can hear the rope inside. Tell him to wave the scissors over the bag, and the rope will restore itself — "as if by magic."

(5) Then, reach into the *main compartment* of the bag and remove *the prepared rope* (the one with the fake knots). Be sure to keep the secret pocket closed while you do this.

(6) Place the knotted rope aside and tear open the front of the bag to show it empty. (The cut pieces remain concealed in the "secret" pocket.) Set the bag aside and explain to the spectator that he almost made it — but it looks as if you will have to finish the trick for him.

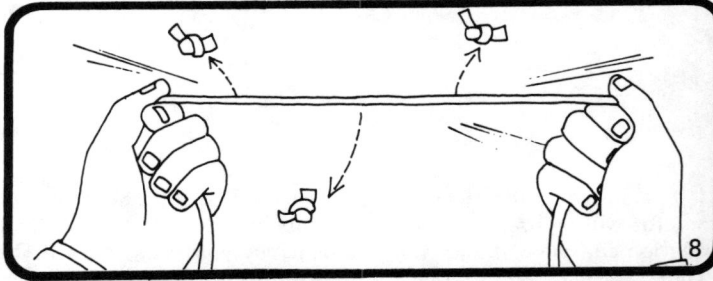

(7) Hold both ends of the prepared rope between your hands as shown.

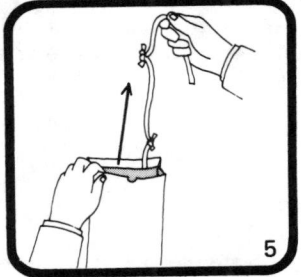

(8) Now, pull sharply on the ends of the rope, *causing the fake knots to fly off the rope into the air.* The rope has become instantly restored! Give the rope to the spectator so he can "practice" at home and thank him for his assistance.

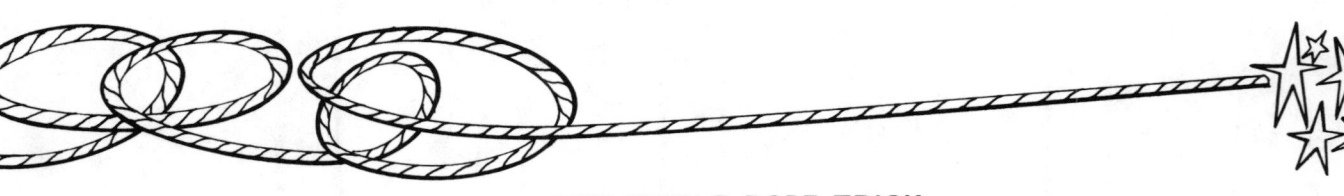

THE TRIPLE ROPE TRICK

This differs from a CUT AND RESTORED ROPE because no actual *cutting* is done. Instead, you start with *three* short lengths of rope and magically form them into one *single* long rope. One particular advantage to this mystery is that no scissors are needed; so you can carry the ropes in your pocket and work it anytime, anywhere.

EFFECT

The magician shows three pieces of rope that are about equal in length, pointing out that all three are knotted together at both ends. He unties one group of three knotted ends and then reties two of the ropes together again. Next, he unties the other group of three knotted ends, and reties two of these ropes together. This leaves the three ropes tied end to end, forming one long rope — *except for the knots!* The performer then coils the rope around one hand and removes a half-dollar from his coat pocket, which he waves over the rope. When the rope is uncoiled, *the knots have vanished* and the three short ropes have amazingly turned into one single length — which can be tossed to the spectators for examination.

SECRET AND PREPARATION

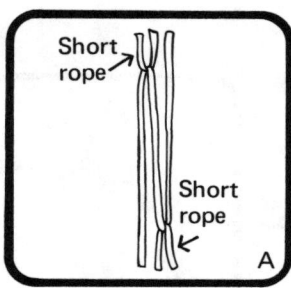 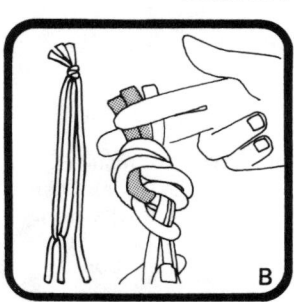 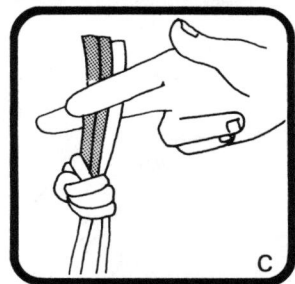 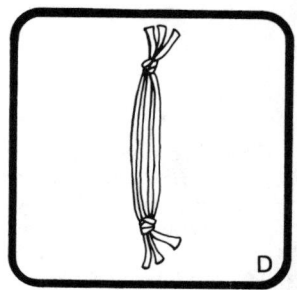

Actually, *one long rope* is used and *two short pieces*. The long rope is about three feet in length; the short pieces are each about four inches long. *(NOTE: The short pieces can be the leftover "ends" from the CUT AND RESTORED ROPE.)* The preparation for this trick is as follows:

(A) Lay out the long rope in three sections. Then loop a short piece of rope in the two "bends" of the long piece as shown. (B) Tie the three upper ends (one end of the long rope and two ends of the short rope) into ONE SINGLE KNOT as shown. To the audience, these appear to be the ends of *three single ropes.* Only *you* know that *two* of the ends are from the *short rope* and the third is *one* end of the *long rope.* (C) This is how the knot looks when pulled tight. (D) Now, tie the other three "ends" together IN EXACTLY THE SAME WAY. This is all prepared before the performance. To your audience it appears that you have "three lengths of rope" — with their ends tied together. You are now ready for a real "fooler."

METHOD

 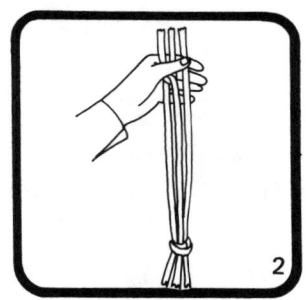

(5) Tie the short rope in a single knot around the long rope. Say, "I will tie two of the ropes together." Be sure to keep the small loop hidden by your fingers until the knot is tied. After that, it can be freely shown.

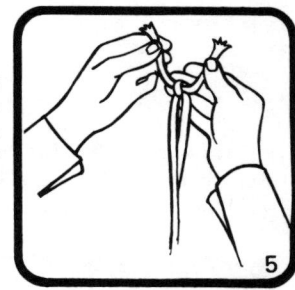

(1) Display the "three ropes" to the audience. Then, with both hands, UNTIE THE LARGE KNOT AT ONE END. *Make sure not to reveal that two of the ends are from the short piece of rope.* (2) This done, hold the ropes in your left hand between your thumb and fingers as shown. Your left thumb clips the short loop above where the long rope loops over the short rope, concealing it from view with your left fingers.

(6) Grasp the remaining large knot and repeat Steps 1 through 5. Say, "Now I will tie these two pieces of rope together as well."

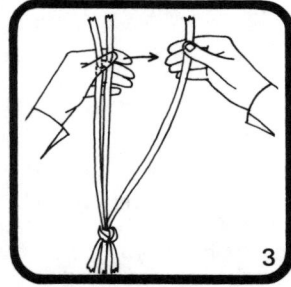 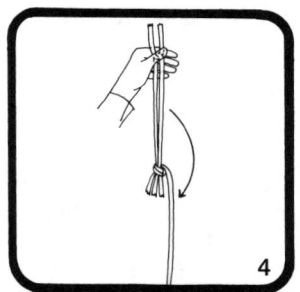

(7) You now show what appears to be three short ropes knotted to form a single long one. *Actually, it is <u>one long rope</u> with two short ropes tied to look like "connecting" knots.*

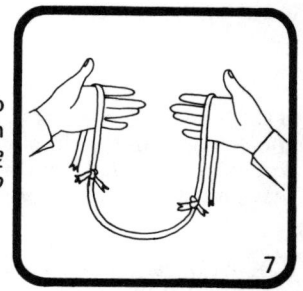

(3) Let the end of the long rope drop, so that you are holding only the two ends of the short piece and the "looped over" part of the long rope. (4) After you drop the "long end," the rope should look like this.

(8) Hold one end of the rope in your left hand and begin coiling the rope around your left hand with your right hand. As you "wrap" it around, the rope naturally SLIDES THROUGH YOUR RIGHT HAND. When you come to the first knot, *keep it in your right hand,* secretly "slipping" it along the rope.

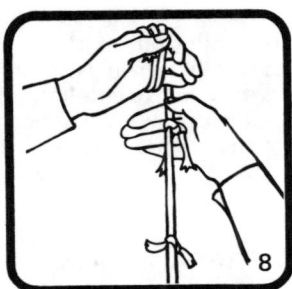

(9) When you come to the second knot, your right hand *slides it along in the same way.* THE AUDIENCE WILL THINK THAT THE KNOTS ARE STILL ON THE ROPE COILED AROUND YOUR LEFT HAND.

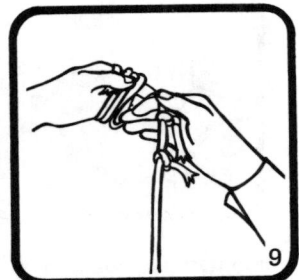

(10) As you complete the coiling, secretly *slide both knots off the end of the rope.*

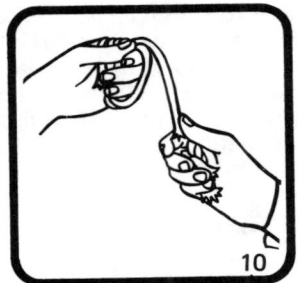

(11) Remark that you will now use your "Magic Coin." Your right hand then goes into your right pocket — *where you leave the knots and bring out the half-dollar.*

(12) Make a "magical" wave of the coin over the rope. Then replace the coin in your pocket and unwind the rope from your hand, *showing the knots completely gone!*

(13) The three short ropes have been "magically" transformed into one single, long rope — much to the amazement of your audience!

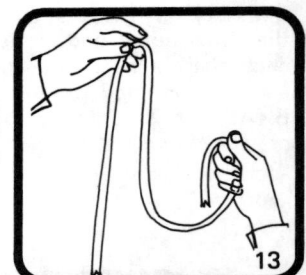

COMMENTS AND SUGGESTIONS

The strong point of this clever mystery is that the "trick" is actually done *before you begin.* Therefore, you should stress that you have three single ropes at the start. If the audience wants you to repeat the TRIPLE ROPE, you can follow with the DOUBLE RESTORATION in which you actually cut a long rope into three short ones and then restore it.

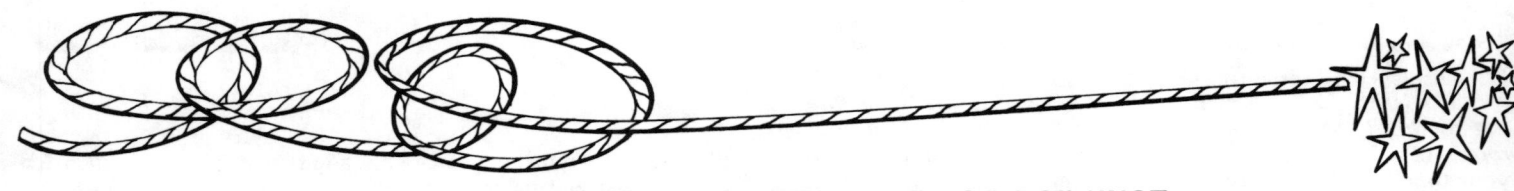

TRIPLE ROPE — MULTIPLE "DO AS I DO" KNOT

With a receptive audience, you can amplify this effect by giving out three sets of knotted ropes letting *two* spectators follow along with you. Again, *your* ropes come out as one long piece and *theirs* do not. That is why you call it "Do As I Do" Knot.

METHOD

(1) In using three sets — one special and two regular — the selection procedure is simple and neat. If each spectator takes an ordinary set, you keep the special and proceed with your routine, having them both copy your moves.

(2) However, if Joe happens to take the special set, say, "You can see that your three ropes are knotted together at both ends." Then, take your set and give it to Joe, saying, "Now take my ropes and give yours to Tom . . ." As Joe gives the special set to Tom, take the ordinary set that Tom is holding, as you continue, ". . . so Tom can give his ropes to me."

(3) Briefly look at the set you just took from Tom; then give it to Joe, saying, "Now take Tom's ropes and give him mine." As Joe does that, take the special set that Tom has saying, "And Tom, give me yours." Then, speaking to both, you say, "Now that we have each checked *all three sets of ropes* to see that they are exactly alike, I want each of you to do exactly as I do."

COMMENTS AND SUGGESTIONS

In winding the coils around your left hand, be sure to tell your helpers to coil each knot inside the left hand, just as you do. Then go through the motion of bringing "Invisible Magic Dust" from your pocket and tell them to do the same. The only difference is that your powder works, while theirs doesn't. This is proven when you each uncoil your rope and you have one long, single length, free of knots, while theirs haven't changed at all. An optional ending is when you explain that your Magic Powder is "truly invisible," whereas theirs is "purely imaginary."

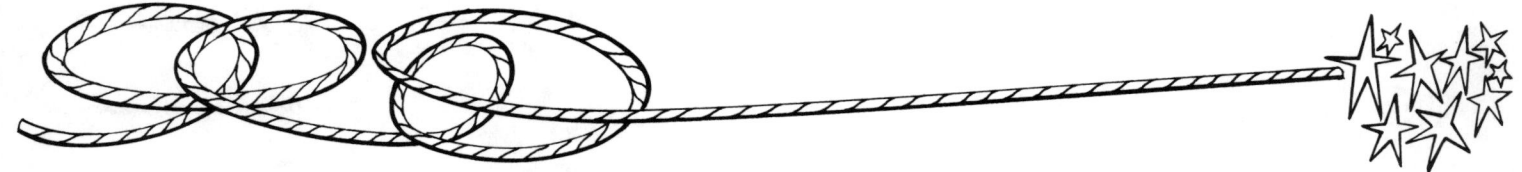

TRIPLE ROPE — "TIMES TWO"

This is a special form of presentation for the TRIPLE ROPE trick, especially suited for small or intimate audiences. It falls into the category of a Do As I Do effect, making it an ideal addition to the "audience participation" portion of your program.

SECRET AND PREPARATION

This time start with two sets of knotted ropes. One is the "special" type already described: _One long rope,_ with _two_ short loops, each looped to a portion of the long rope and knotted there to show three "ends." The second set consists of _three separate ropes,_ about the same length. These are actually knotted at both ends, so they look exactly the same as your faked set. You can identify the special set by making a small ink or pencil mark on one of the knots. The mark should be just large enough for you to notice. You then proceed as follows:

METHOD

(1) Bring out both sets of knotted ropes, remarking that each consists of _three short ropes_ knotted at both ends. Explain that _you_ intend to use one set in this mystery and the _spectator_ is to use the other. Tell the spectator that since both are exactly alike, he may choose either set.

(2) If he takes the _ordinary set,_ you keep the special set and tell him, "I want you to do exactly as I do. Untie your ropes like this." With that, you proceed step by step as already described with the "Three in One" effect.

(3) If he takes the _special set,_ the one that you should have, you can handle the situation quite easily. Say, "Good, now I want you to do just as I do. Give me your three ropes, so I can untie their ends, while I give you my three ropes, so you can untie them." Thus the exchange of ropes becomes the first step in the "Do As I Do" procedure and you simply carry on from there.

(4) Now proceed with the step-by-step process moving slowly and deliberately, so the spectator can copy your moves exactly. Since everyone sees that he has three separate ropes, they will assume that yours are the same.

(5) On the last step, you wrap the rope around your hand and then reach into your pocket to remove some "Invisible Magic Dust." The spectator, who has been duplicating your every move, will have to admit that he has no "Magic Dust" with him at the moment. Tell him to "pretend" that he has a pocketful and have him remove and "sprinkle" it on his rope as you do the same. (It is at this point that you leave the two knots in your pocket.) Your rope now comes out all in one piece while his is still in three pieces — proving that there is no substitute for "real" Invisible Magic Dust. Give the spectator a handful from your pocket along with the unrestored rope and tell him to take it all home and practice!

DOUBLE RESTORATION

As stated before, cutting and restoring a length of ordinary rope has become a classic feat of modern magic. Here is a method as simple as it is deceptive. What's more, this version enables you to "go one better" than the standard CUT AND RESTORED ROPE, because here you cut the rope twice — making three lengths instead of two — and then restore both cuts simultaneously.

EFFECT

The magician shows an ordinary rope about six feet in length, which he measures into three equal sections. He then ties both ends firmly around the center of the rope. When the rope is stretched between his hands, it is in three equal sections with the knots as dividing markers. The performer then cuts the rope near each knot so that the knots now connect the three pieces of rope. The magician then coils the rope loosely around one hand. With a little "Magic," the rope is uncoiled to reveal the knots have vanished — the three pieces of rope are completely restored to one long rope!

SECRET AND PREPARATION

(A)   The secret of this effect is quite subtle, and — after you practice and learn it — the working is almost automatic. Beforehand, use a pen or pencil to make a small mark about **6 inches** from each end of the rope. Make the marks just large enough so you can see them when you look for them. This done, you are ready to begin.

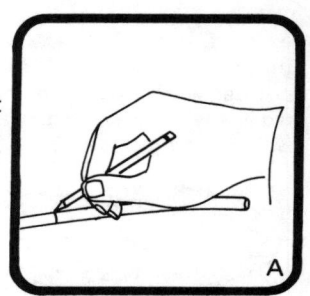

METHOD

(1)   Display the rope to your audience by grasping one of the ends in your hand, allowing the rope to hang full length in front of your body as shown. Now, step on the loose end with your foot and give the rope a sharp upward pull to prove to the audience that the rope is genuine. From this point on, we will refer to the ends of the rope as A and B.

(6)   Now, *turn the rope over* so that End B and the center of the lower loop (Point Y) are on top as shown and then tie End B around Point Y in another single overhand knot. *At this point, both of your "secret" marks should be visible to you as indicated by the arrows in this illustration.*

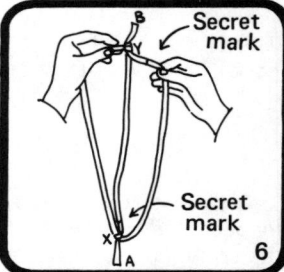

(2)   Hold End A firmly in your left hand. Then loop End B over the top of your left fingers and pull End B down to the center of the lower loop as shown. This "measures" the rope into *three equal sections* as illustrated. The centers of the upper and lower loops are indicated as X and Y in the illustrations.

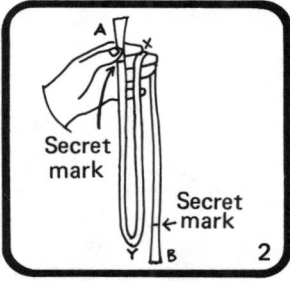

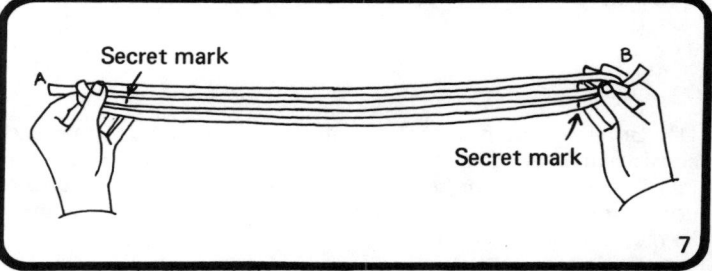

(3)   Now, tie End A *around the bend in the loop* at Point X, using a single overhand knot as shown. Notice that the knot is in the center of the short section marked at the end of the rope.

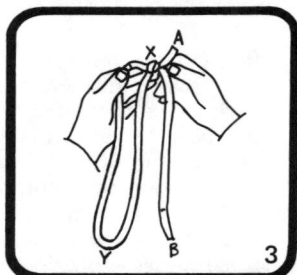

(7)   When the rope is stretched between the thumbs and fingers of each hand, it can be shown in three distinct sections with the knots as dividing markers.

(4)   Here is a close-up view of the knot.

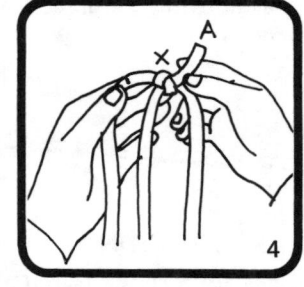

(8)   With a pair of scissors, cut the rope at one of your secret marks near the knot. The spectators think you are cutting the main section of the rope. Actually, you have only cut off a short piece at one end. This creates the perfect illusion that you have a separate piece of rope hanging from the loop as illustrated.

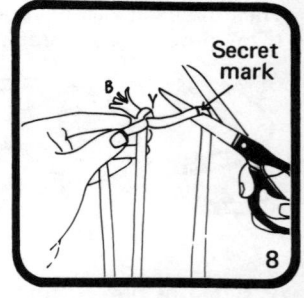

(5)   Holding the knot in one hand, display the rope with the free end dangling next to the loop, showing the loop and the "free" end to be about equal in length.

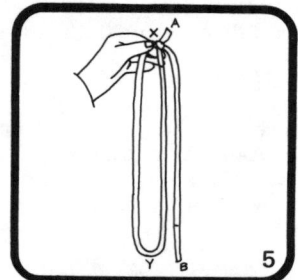

(9)   Now, turn the loop over so that the other knot is on top.

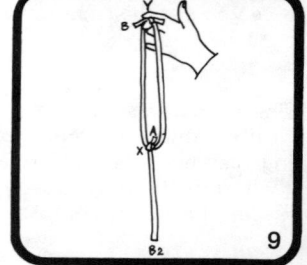

(10) Cut the rope at the other mark, stating that you have now cut the rope into *three* equal pieces.

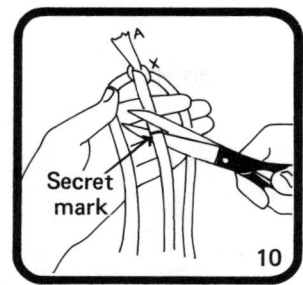

(13) Now, begin to coil the rope around your left hand. When you come to the knots, pretend to wind them into the left hand. Actually, your right hand secretly retains the knots in the bend of the fingers and draws them along the rope completely off the end.

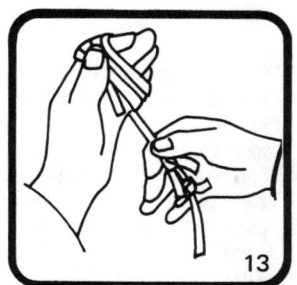

(11) The rope will now appear as shown here. It appears to the audience as if you actually cut the rope into three equal parts and tied them together. Unknown to your audience, the "twice cut" rope *is really already restored* — since the "knots" are just short ends tied around a single length of rope!

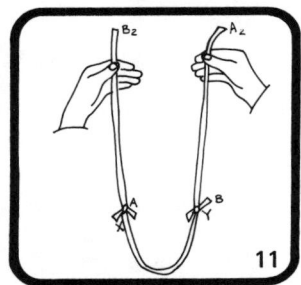

(14) With the knots concealed in your right hand, reach into your coat pocket for your "magic" coin. As soon as your hand is out of sight, exchange the knots for the coin. Immediately bring the coin into view, *leaving the knots behind in your pocket.* Wave the coin over the coiled rope as shown.

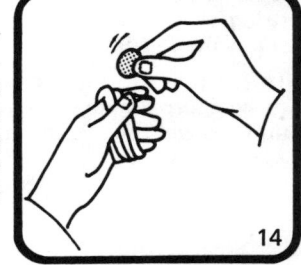

(12) Once again, allow the rope to fall full length in front of you and step on the lower end with your foot. Pull sharply on the rope as if to tighten the knots even more.

(15) Drop the coin back into your pocket and allow the rope to unwind from around your left fingers. Demonstrate the complete restoration of the rope by again testing it for strength.

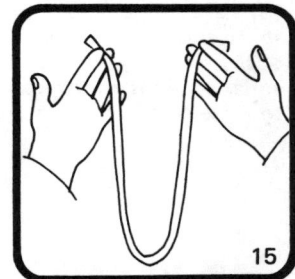

COMMENTS AND SUGGESTIONS

At the finish of the trick, the rope will be a bit shorter than it was to start. No one will realize this as it is nearly impossible to estimate the length of a piece of rope without a frame of reference. Once the rope has been cut and knotted, you can purposely call attention to the length of the rope *as it will remain the same length from that point on,* thus adding to the deception. Each time you do the trick, the rope becomes about eight inches shorter (allowing four inches to be cut from each end) so, if you present the trick with a six-foot rope, it should be good for about four performances.

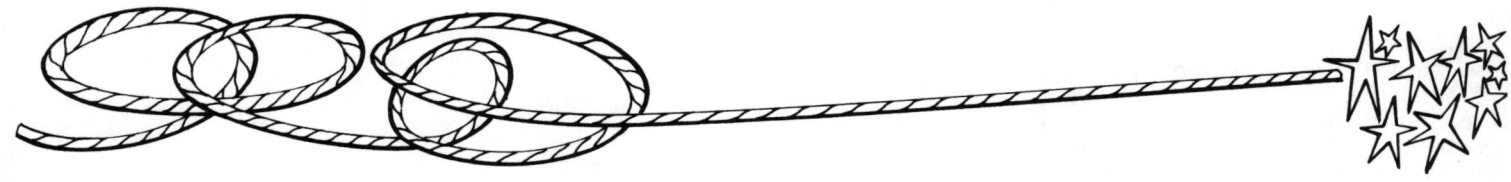

CUT AND RESTORED STRING

The following is one of those clever effects that can be presented anywhere and always leaves the spectators completely baffled. It might well be classified as a *close-up* version of the more familiar CUT AND RESTORED ROPE. However, the *method* for this effect is quite different, which makes the mystery all the more puzzling.

EFFECT

The magician calls attention to a single length of string which he proceeds to cut into two equal parts. He then gives one end of each of the "cut" strings to a spectator to hold. With everything in full view, the spectator instantly restores the twine to its original condition right before his own eyes. The stunned volunteer is then given the piece of string as a souvenir.

SECRET AND PREPARATION

(A) The secret of this trick depends on a *very clever principle* based on the properties of a certain type of common string which is *so obvious,* that it goes totally unsuspected by anyone. The string is the type which is composed of *many individual strands of twine* twisted together to form a multi-stranded string. This is sometimes referred to as "butcher's twine." It is usually thicker than ordinary string (like "kite" string) and is soft and white in color.

To perform this mystery, all you need is a length of this type of string approximately 18 inches long. For the purpose of explanation, we will refer to the ends of the string as X and Y.

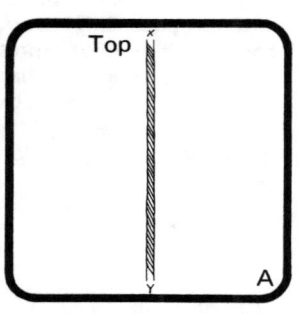

(B) Locate the *center* of the piece of string and *spread the individual strands open,* dividing the string into two equal sections of twine. We will refer to *these sections* as A and B.

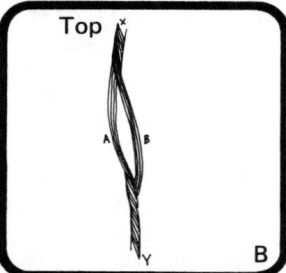

(C) Pull Sections A and B about five inches apart as shown. Then, slowly roll each section between your fingers so that they twist together to form *two new false ends.*

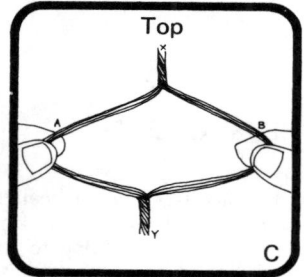

(D) This done, adjust the entire affair so that the "two" newly formed string "ends" (AX and BY) run so close together at the place where they connect (letter "Z") that the secret connection between them is nearly impossible to detect.

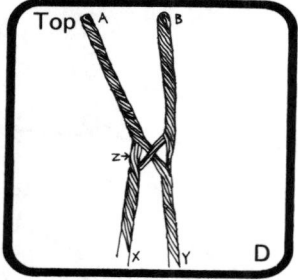

(E) NOTE: At this point, A and B form two "fake" ends of string, and X and Y (the real ones) the other ends. It appears that you have two separate strings. But, you're not through yet.

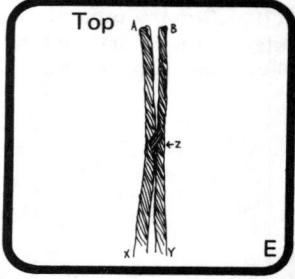

(F) Apply a very small dab of rubber cement to Ends X and Y and allow them to become nearly dry. Then, *attach the two ends* (X and Y) *together* — roll them between your fingers until they are joined.

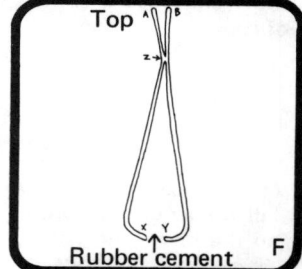

(G) The resulting product should look like *one continuous length of string as shown.* If done correctly, the "string" can be handled quite casually as you display it during the presentation.

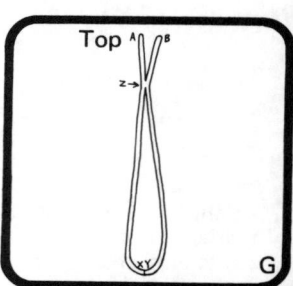

METHOD

(1) To begin, display the prepared string casually calling attention to the fact that you hold *only one piece of string.* Then, as you prepare to cut the string, adjust your grip so that you hold it between the tips of your left fingers as shown here. Your thumb and first finger should cover the secret connection (Z).

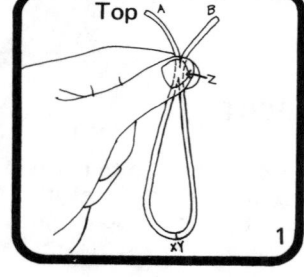

(2) With scissors cut the string (both pieces) near the bottom of the hanging loop *just above* Point XY. Let the glued joint (XY) drop to the floor leaving you two *new* "unglued" X and Y ends. *NOTE: This automatically removes the only gimmicked, non-examinable part of the string for the astonishing conclusion of the trick.*

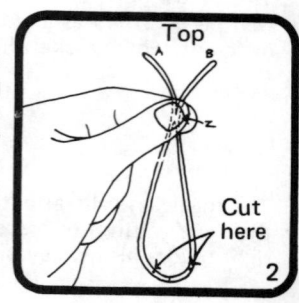

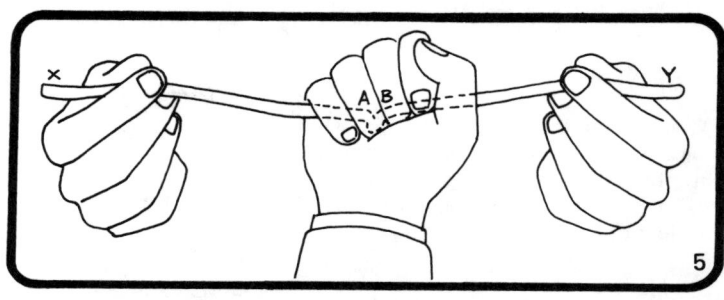

(3) Call attention to the *absolute fairness* of every move you make. The audience will be convinced that you have merely cut a single length of twine into two equal parts.

(5) Now, ask a spectator to grasp Ends X and Y. When he does you hold Ends A and B (and the secret connection Z) in your closed fist as shown.

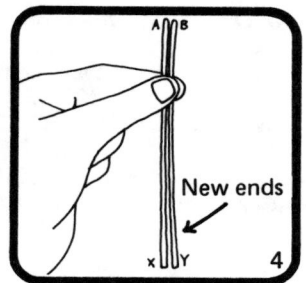

(4) Place the scissors aside and display the two "separate" pieces of string. Be sure to handle the string(s) in a casual manner so as not to give the impression that you are concealing something from the audience — *but keep the strings together at the secret connection (Z).*

(6) Then tell him to *pull sharply* on the ends in opposite directions. When he does, release your grip on the string. Allow the secret connection to "untwist" and thus restore itself to its *original form* — the center of the string! The spectator will be astonished to see the strings "weld" themselves together as he pulls on their ends.

COMMENTS AND SUGGESTIONS

Stress the fact that the string actually "restores" itself while the *spectator holds both ends.* The beautiful thing here is that there are no secret "gimmicks" or extra pieces of string to get rid of. As you can see, this is another outstanding close-up mystery. Build it up properly, and you will be credited with performing a small miracle.

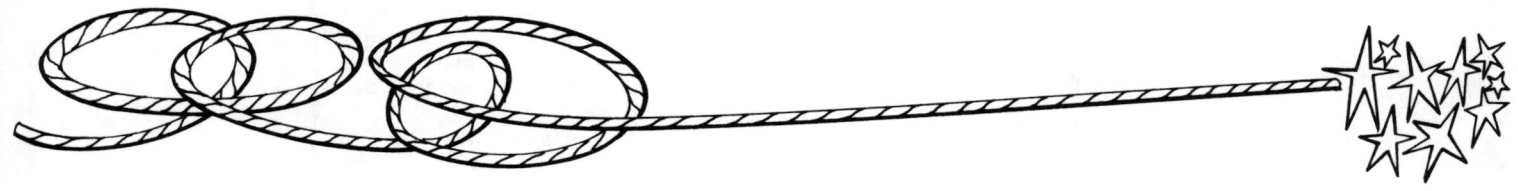

THREADING THE NEEDLE

EFFECT

The magician calls the audiences' attention to an ordinary piece of soft rope approximately three feet in length. He explains that even under the most adverse circumstances it is easy to *magically* "thread" a needle, IF you know the secret. To demonstrate, the magician forms a small loop from one end of the rope to represent the eye of a needle — the other end will substitute for the thread. The performer, with the loop in the left hand and the "thread" end of the rope in his right, makes a quick thrust at the loop. In spite of his speed and even though he may not even come near the loop, the needle has been magically threaded!

METHOD

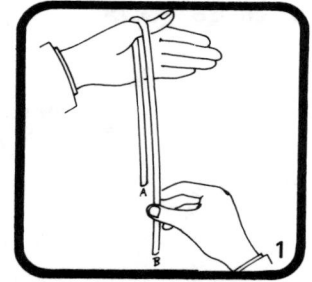

(1) After displaying the rope to your audience, lay the rope over your left thumb so that Length A will measure approximately 12 inches and Length B will measure about 24 inches.

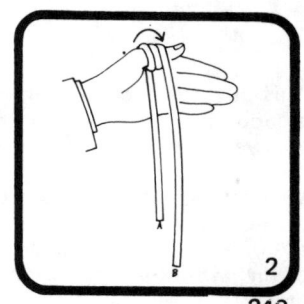

(2) Grasp Length B with your right hand and wrap the rope around your left thumb twice. BE SURE YOU WRAP THE ROPE AROUND YOUR THUMB IN THE DIRECTION SHOWN IN THE PICTURE.

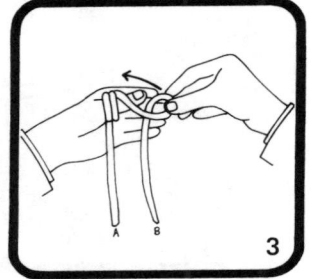

(3) With your right hand, grasp Length B and twist the rope to form a loop about two inches high, as shown. This loop is lifted and placed between your left thumb and forefinger.

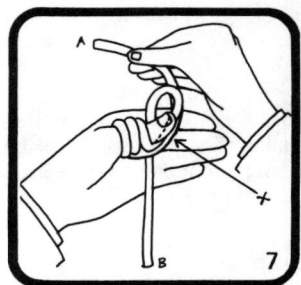

(7) As Length A passes between the left thumb and the left fingers, loosen your grip slightly by relaxing the left thumb as you pull Length A up sharply with the right hand.

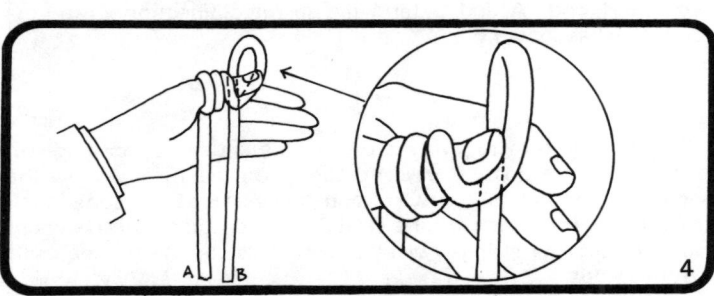

(4) Grip the loop between your left thumb and forefinger so that it protrudes over the top of the thumb. This loop now represents the "eye" of the needle. *NOTE: End B of the rope must be the side of the loop CLOSEST TO THE PALM OF YOUR LEFT HAND as shown by the dotted lines in 4.*

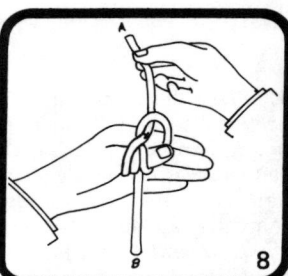

(8) The "X" part of Length A will now be through the loop and it will appear as if you have "threaded" the eye without even coming close with the thread. NOTE: THERE IS NOW ONE LESS TURN OF ROPE AROUND YOUR LEFT THUMB. YOU LOSE ONE OF THESE TURNS EACH TIME YOU "THREAD" THE NEEDLE.

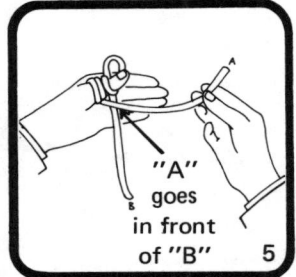

(5) End A will now become the thread. Grasp A with your right thumb and fingers about one inch from the end. Then lift A *in front of* B and hold as shown.

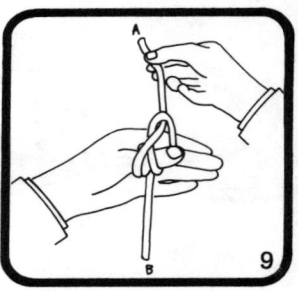

(9) If you "unthread" the needle by really pulling End A back through the loop, you can immediately "magically" thread it again. When you do, the rope around your thumb will look like this. (Notice again that there is one less "turn" around your left thumb.)

(6) *Steps 6 and 7 are the actual "threading."* With End A in your right hand, move that hand forward MISSING THE LOOP WITH THE END but allow the lower part of A (marked with an "X" in the illustration) to pass BETWEEN the left thumb and left fingers.

COMMENTS AND SUGGESTIONS

This effect is excellent when used in combination with other rope tricks to create an entertaining rope routine. On its own, it also makes a good "challenge" at a party, for no matter how hard anyone tries to duplicate your movements, he will find it impossible to "thread the eye of the needle."

When using the effect as a spectator challenge, be sure that he attempts the threading using Length B as the "thread." By substituting B for A, the trick becomes impossible to duplicate. You will also find, during practice, that you will be able to move your right hand as fast as you wish and still thread the needle — *as the end of the thread never actually passes through the needle anyway.* I have had a great deal of fun with this little trick over the years, and I am sure that you will too.

—MW

ONE HAND KNOT

EFFECT

The magician displays a 3-foot length of soft rope. Casually tossing the rope into the air, a genuine knot appears magically in its center.

METHOD

(1) Display a length of rope (a piece about 3 feet is best). Then drape it over your right hand with End A hanging between the third and fourth fingers and End B between your thumb and first finger. Although End A may be any length, End B *must not fall more than about one foot below your hand.*

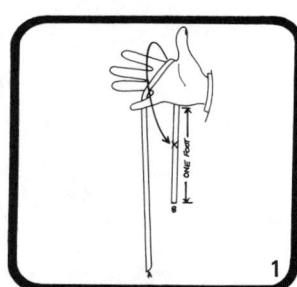

(2) Now turn your right hand over and grasp Length B between the first and second fingers at "X" as shown.

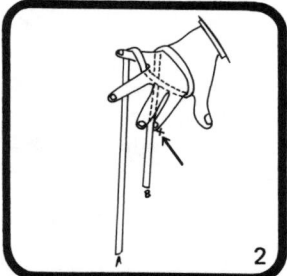

(3) Now rotate your hand back up as shown holding B firmly between the first and second fingers.

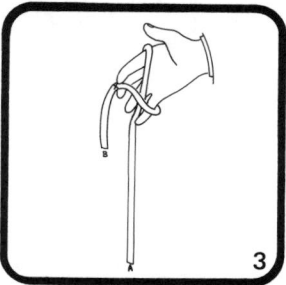

(4) Simply allow the loop that has been formed around your right hand to fall off your hand.

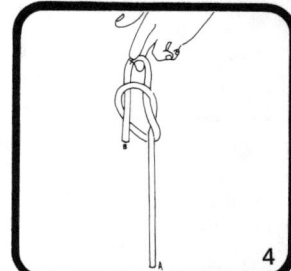

(5) The end of B will be drawn through this loop forming a knot in the rope. You may also "snap" the rope off your hand rather than letting it fall.

COMMENTS AND SUGGESTIONS

In order to disguise what is actually happening, practice the following movement: After grasping Length B firmly with the first and second fingers of the right hand (Fig. 2) throw the rope straight up into the air letting go of Length B *after* it has passed through the loop. The effect will be that the knot was tied *in the air.*

NOTE: The softer the rope, the easier this trick is to do. It will also work equally well with a soft handkerchief (silk is best) of the proper size.

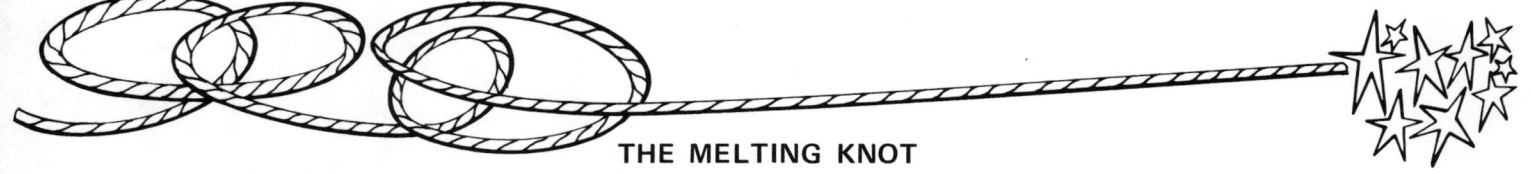

THE MELTING KNOT

EFFECT

The performer slowly and deliberately ties a knot in the center of a three-foot piece of rope. The audience watches as the magician gradually tightens the knot by pulling on both ends of the rope. The knot becomes smaller until, just before "cinching up" tight, it *melts away* into nothingness!

SECRET AND PREPARATION

Once again you will have use for that 3-foot length of soft rope. This mystery, combined with "Threading the Needle" and other such effects, makes an entertaining routine with just this short length of rope.

METHOD

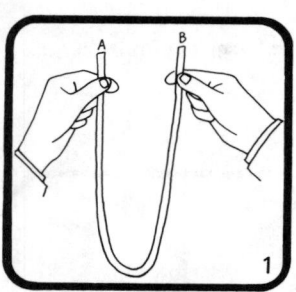

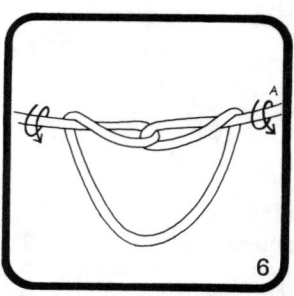

(1)   Display the rope to the audience. (In the illustrations we will call the end in your left hand End A and the one in your right End B.) (2)   With your right hand, bring End B around *behind* your left hand and *over the top* of End A. Place End B *between* your left first and second fingers and release your right hand. You should now be holding the rope as shown.

(5)   You have now formed a "false" knot. In order to keep the knot from dissolving prematurely, you must "roll" the rope *with the thumb and first finger of each hand.* Roll or twist the rope *in the direction shown by the arrows* (toward yourself). (6)   You can see the reasons for twisting the rope clearly here. The "rolling" action of the ends forces the false knot to ride *up* and *over* itself, thus maintaining its "knot" shape.

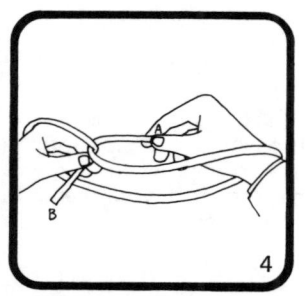

(7)   When the knot is just about to tighten up, blow on it as you pull the ends. The knot seems to "dissolve" into thin air. Properly performed, the illusion is so perfect that you may immediately repeat the trick without fear of discovery.

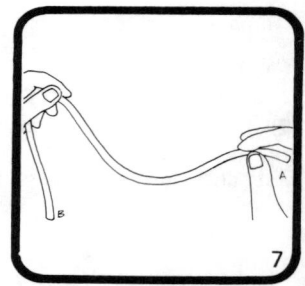

(3)   Pass your right hand *through the loop of rope* and grasp End A between your right thumb and first finger. (4)   Now pull Ends A and B apart. Hold End B with your left thumb and fingers. As you do this, pull End A *through the loop* and slowly separate your hands.

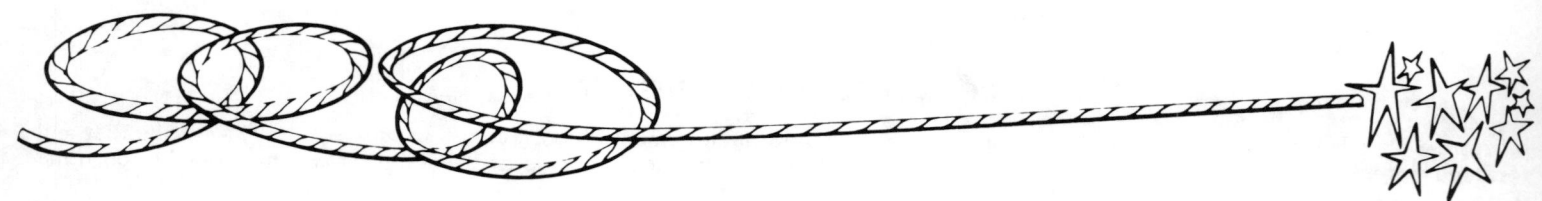

SHOELACE ROPE TIE

EFFECT

The magician displays a three-foot length of soft rope to his audience. Holding it between both hands, he skillfully ties a "bow knot" in the rope. The performer then threads the ends of the rope *through* the loops of the bows — and then pulls the ends so that a hopeless knot is formed in the center of the rope. The audience understands the magician's problem, for they have probably had this happen with their shoelaces many times. However, as if to defy the laws of nature, the magician causes the cumbersome knot to "dissolve" before the eyes of the audience!

METHOD

All you need for this clever effect is a length of soft rope approximately three feet in length.

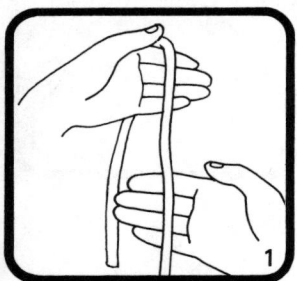 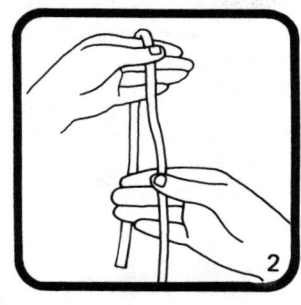 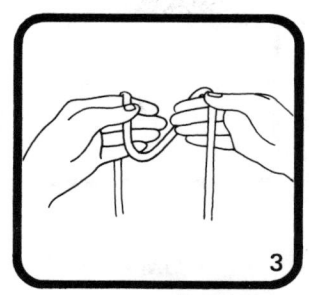 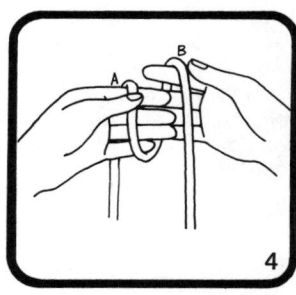

(1) Display the rope to your audience and then lay it across the fingers of your right and left hands as shown. Your left hand is above your right hand, your palms face you and the backs of your hands are toward the audience. (2) Hold the rope in position by pressing your thumbs against the rope. (3) Now, move your right hand next to your left hand, allowing the rope to hook *underneath* the left fingers and *over the top* of the right fingers. (4) Then, move your right hand *behind your left hand* as shown in this illustration.

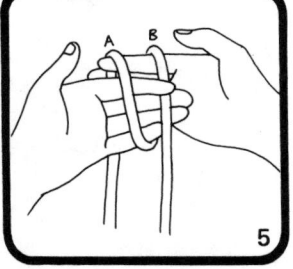

(5) Now, clip the rope at Point A between the tips of your *right* first and second fingers. At the same time, grasp the rope at Point B with your *left* first and second fingers. (Study the drawing carefully.)

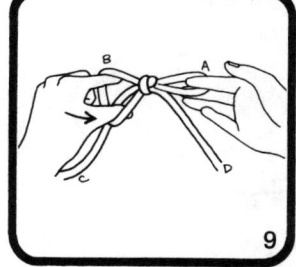

(9) Then, with your *left* thumb and first finger, reach *through* the left bow (B), grasp the left end of the rope (C) . . .

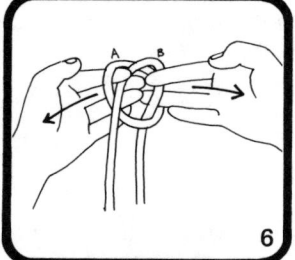

(6) Hold the two points (A and B) tightly between the fingers of each hand and *begin to draw your hands apart.*

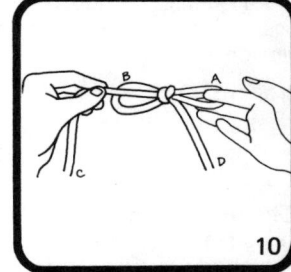

(10) . . . and pull the left end of the rope (C) *back through the loop.*

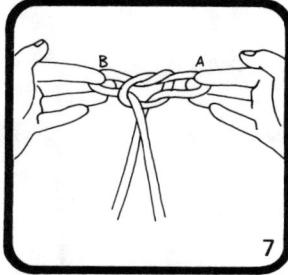

(7) Continue to pull your hands apart, and a bow knot will begin to form in the middle of the rope.

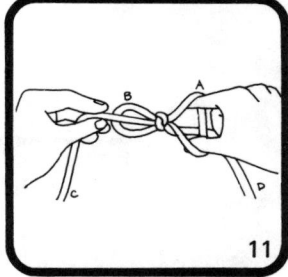

(11) With your *right* thumb and first finger, reach *through* the right-hand bow (A), grasp the right-hand end of the rope (D) . . .

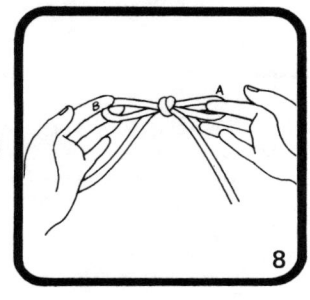

(8) Now, gently pull the completed "bow knot" taut as shown.

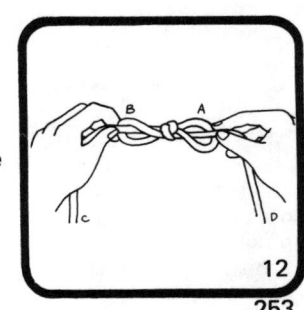

(12) . . . and pull that end of the rope (D) *back through the loop* (A).

(13) Release the bow and gently pull on the ends of the rope causing the bow to "cinch up" and form a large knot in the center of the rope. *If you have followed the steps correctly, this knot will actually be a slip-knot or "dissolving" knot as magicians often call it.* Do not pull too hard on the ends or you will dissolve the knot too soon!

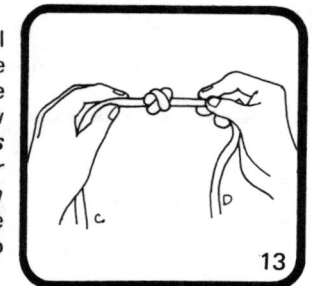

(14) Instead, display the "knot" to the audience as you comment about how bothersome a situation like this can be when it happens in everyday life. You might remark, "Being a magician comes in handy when this happens because all you have to do is to use the old 'knot-vanishing move' to get out of trouble." (As you say this, pull on the ends of the rope, and the knot will magically vanish.)

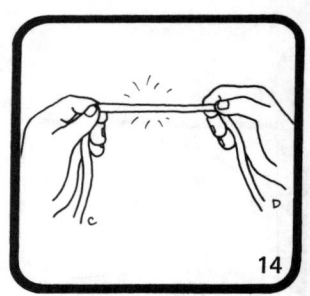

COMMENTS AND SUGGESTIONS

At first, when you start learning this clever effect, it may seem complicated and difficult to follow. Follow the pictures carefully. The tying of the bow and the pulling of the ends through the loops will be perfectly natural and easy and can be accompanied by a clever patter story — perhaps about how you became interested in magic as a child when you found that, in tying your shoes, the ends of the laces would slip through the bows, and you always ended up with a knot. But then *you began to study magic.* You discovered that by merely pulling on the ends of the laces and blowing on the knot at the same time (or saying the "magic words"), the knot would dissolve itself *as if by magic!*

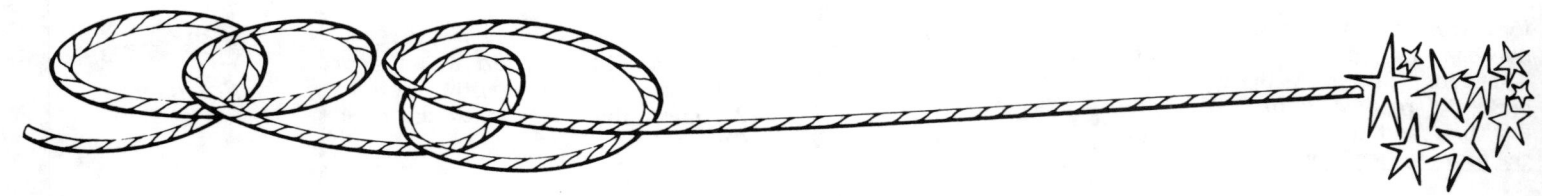

THE RIGID ROPE

The legendary Hindu Rope Trick, wherein the fakir would throw a coil of rope into the air and cause it to remain suspended, has long been a mystery to which the exact method still remains questionable to this day. The following trick might well be considered a smaller version of this great mystery. It has the advantage that it can be performed anywhere — before small groups or larger audiences as well.

EFFECT

The magician displays a length of rope about 3 to 4 feet long. It appears to be normal in every respect and yet, upon his command, it becomes rigid and stands straight up from his fingertips. The performer passes his other hand around the rope on all sides, proving to the audience that the rope is unmistakably free from any threads or other hidden attachments. Then, with a mere wave of his hand, the magician causes the rope to gradually fall and return to its natural "flexible" state, right before the eyes of the spectators!

SECRET AND PREPARATION

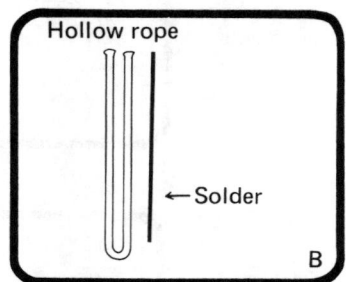

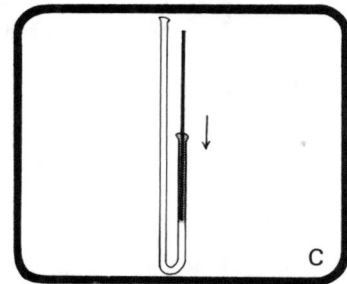

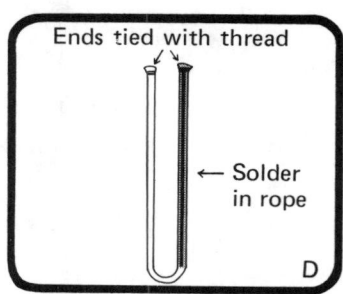

(A) To present this trick, it is necessary to construct a "special" rope. First, remove the inner core from a piece of rope approximately 4 feet long. (See "Coring" at the beginning of this section.) This leaves just the woven outer shell, which now forms a small hollow "tube" 4 feet long. (B) Next, cut a piece of solder wire (the kind of wire that is melted with a soldering iron to make electrical connections) so that it is <u>slightly shorter</u> than *half* the length of the rope. The solder should be about 1/16" to 1/8" in diameter and should be as straight as possible. (C) Now insert the piece of solder carefully *into* the hollow length of rope. (D) Tie off both ends of the rope with white thread. This will prevent the solder from falling out of the rope during the presentation.

METHOD

(1)   Hold the prepared rope with one end in each hand as you display it to your audience. The end containing the solder is held in your left hand; the hollow end in your right. *Be sure to allow enough slack at the bottom of the rope so that it will curve naturally.*

(2)   Release the *hollow end* of the rope from your right fingers and let it hang freely as shown in the illustration. This subtly conveys to the audience that the rope is flexible.

(3)   Now grasp the rope with your right fingers slightly above the center of the rope. You will be able to feel the solder through the woven shell of the rope. At this point, your left hand *still retains its grip* on the "top" end of the rope.

(4)   Now, *relax the pressure on the solder* with your right fingers and allow the wire to secretly *slide down* into the bottom half of the rope.

(5)   Release the upper end of the rope from your left fingers — it falls limp over your right hand. *At this point, the audience has seen that the entire length* of rope is flexible.

(6)   Reach down and grasp the *hollow end* with your left hand and raise it upward.

(7)   Release the *center* of the rope from your right fingers and allow the rope to hang *full length* from your left hand.

(8)   Now, grip the center of the rope once again between your right thumb and forefinger, but this time turn your right hand palm up so that your right thumb grips the rope from the audience side.

(9) With your right hand still holding the center of the rope, release the hollow top end of the rope from your left hand and let it fall.

(12) Now, slowly and dramatically, remove your left hand from the top of the rope. Hold the bottom of the solder in the top half firmly with your right hand. To the amazement of the viewers, the rope stays straight up — rigid! As the rope stands "unsupported" from your right hand, pass your left hand over the top and around all sides of the rope to prove that there are no outside connections responsible for this mystery.

(10) Then grasp the bottom end *with the solder in it* with your left hand palm up.

(13) To restore the rope back to its flexible state, *gradually* relax your grip on the solder with your right fingers. Allow the solder to *slowly* slide into the bottom half of the rope. *The effect will be that the rope gradually "wilts."* Gesture with your left hand as if the rope is always under your control as it loses its power to remain rigid.

(11) HERE IS THE KEY MOVE IN THE TRICK. As you keep the *solder end* of the rope pulled taut between your hands, with your left hand swing *the solder end up* to the top and, at the same time, rotate the right wrist as shown. By the pressure of the fingers of both hands, keep the solder in the "top" half.

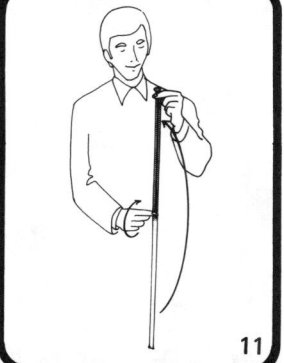

(14) When the rope falls completely limp, grasp the hollow end of the rope with your left hand. With your right hand still retaining its hold on the rope, begin to coil the hollow half of the rope around your left fist. When you reach the solder half of the rope, *continue to wind the rope and the solder around your left fist.* Due to the softness of the solder, the rope, with the solder inside, will coil around your hand. Place the coiled rope in your pocket or on your table and take your bows.

EQUAL-UNEQUAL ROPES
"GEN" GRANT
EFFECT

The performer displays four lengths of rope by holding two ropes in each hand. Each pair is tied together in the center so that they form two sets of two ropes each. One of these sets consists of one long piece of rope and one short piece, while the other set contains two ropes exactly the same length. The magician asks for two volunteers to come up on the stage. Each is then given one set of ropes. The spectator on the right, who holds the long and the short pair of ropes, is asked to turn his back to the audience. The magician then pins one short and one long piece of ribbon to the back of his jacket to identify which set he holds. The volunteer on the left, who holds the two "equal" ropes, is marked by attaching two equal pieces of ribbon to the back of his coat. The magician points out that the two volunteers are marked so that the audience can easily identify the location of each set of ropes, even when the backs of the spectators are facing them. The performer then has both spectators face the audience as he explains that he will cause something "magical" to happen. With that, the performer asks the volunteers to again turn their backs to the audience and to then untie their pairs of ropes. This done, the volunteers are asked to turn around and face the audience to show the ropes which they now hold. To the surprise of the audience, as well as the two volunteers, the two equal lengths of rope have "magically" exchanged positions with the two unequal pieces of rope!

SECRET AND PREPARATION

This clever mystery can most certainly be classified as a "self-working" trick, as the entire trick takes place in the hands of the spectators. The secret lies in the clever manner in which you have knotted the ropes before the show. For the trick, all you need are three pieces of soft rope about five feet in length and *one* piece of rope exactly half that long.

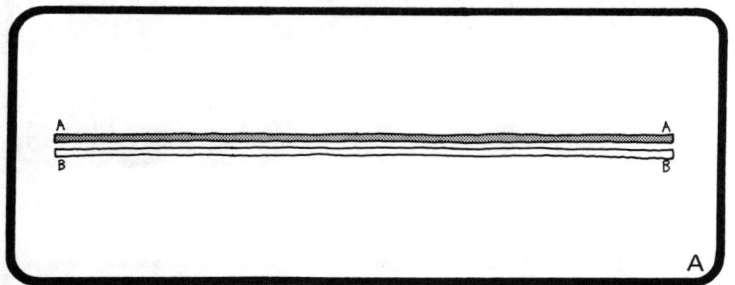

(A) To prepare, place two of the five-foot lengths side by side as shown. For the purpose of explanation, the ropes have been labeled A and B and, *for clarity only,* are shown in different colors. When performing the trick, __all__ of the ropes must be the *same color.*

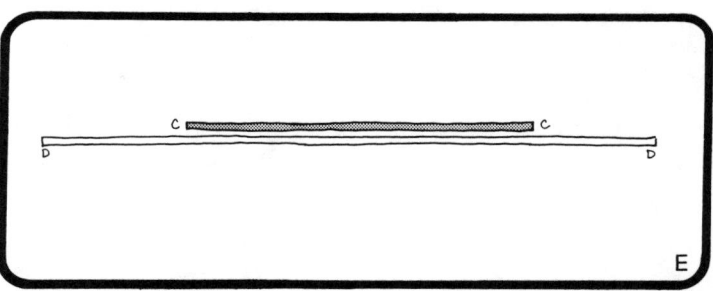

(E) The next step is to tie the two *unequal lengths* of rope together so that they look as if they are *equal* in length. To do this, place the short piece (C) next to the long piece (D). The short rope (C) must be *centered* between the ends of the long rope (D).

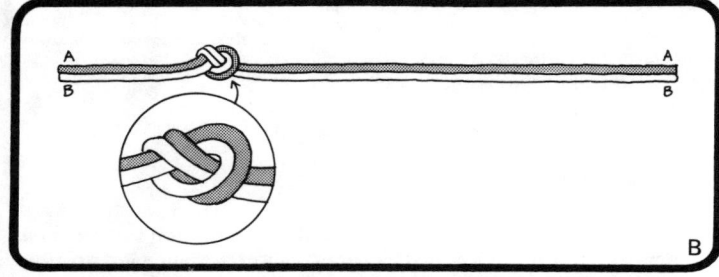

(B) Tie the two ropes together with a *single overhand knot* at a point approximately one third from the end as illustrated.

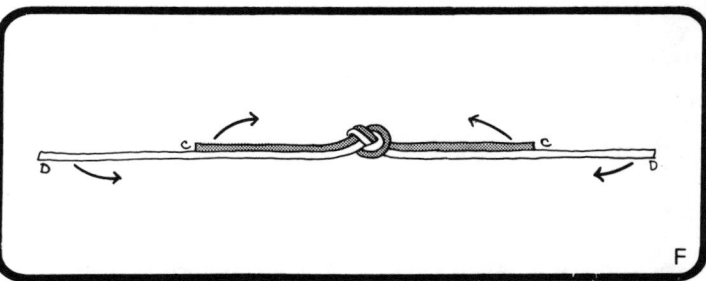

(F) Tie the ropes together in the center using a single overhand knot as shown.

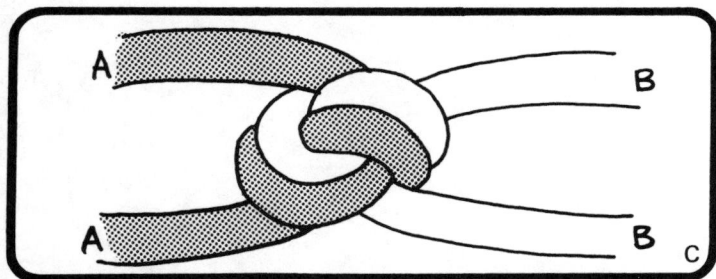

(C) Now, fold both ends of Rope B together, so that they run *side by side in the same direction.* Do the same with the ends of Rope A as shown in this illustration.

(G) Now, bring both ends of the short rope (C) together so they run *side by side,* and do the same with the ends of the long rope (D). Secure the ends in place with another overhand knot — the result will appear to be two *equal* pieces of rope tied together at their centers.

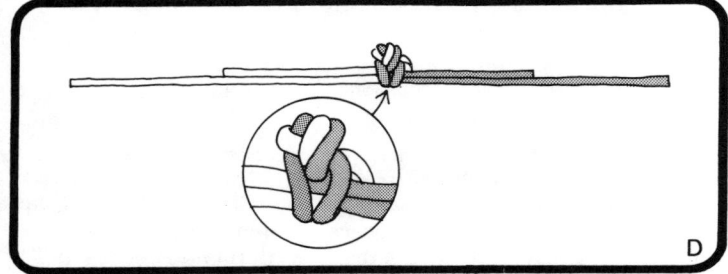

(D) Now, tie another overhand knot *on top of the first knot* to further confuse the spectators. *The result will appear to be* one long and one short *piece of rope tied together at the center.*

(H) Finally, you will need three pieces of colorful ribbon about two feet long, and a fourth piece about one foot long. Attach a small pin to the end of each ribbon and you are ready to present the EQUAL-UNEQUAL ROPES.

METHOD

(1)   To begin, display the two sets of ropes as you ask for the assistance of two volunteers from the audience.

(3)   Have both assistants turn their backs to the audience and attach the corresponding lengths of ribbon to their coats. Have them turn back to face the audience as you explain that the ribbons will serve to identify which spectator holds which set of ropes.

(4)   Instruct the spectators to again turn their backs to the audience and then to untie their ropes. If you wish, you can now state that something "magical" is going to happen. With that, instruct your volunteers to turn and face the audience — holding *one rope in each hand.* Sure enough, when they turn, the spectator on the left, instead of having two ropes of the same length, now has *one short* and *one long* rope — and the spectator on the right now has two ropes of the *same length.* The two sets of ropes have magically exchanged positions *while in the hands of the volunteers!*

(2)   Give the spectator to your *right* the set of ropes that <u>appears</u> to be the *unequal* lengths (actually the <u>equal</u> ropes), and to the volunteer on your *left,* give the set which appears to be two *equal lengths.*

COMMENTS AND SUGGESTIONS

This is a very clever "novelty" trick which always brings a laugh. Performed correctly, your two assistants themselves will not even get wise to the trick. With this type of knot, strange as it seems, when the spectators untie the knots, the ropes seem to change length <u>right in their hands</u> — and they will not be able to understand how it happened! Of course, *if you were to immediately repeat the trick,* they would watch the ends and no doubt figure it out. But the <u>first</u> time you work this, if you follow the instructions carefully, it will leave the volunteers as mystified as your audience — which, of course, enhances the total effect.

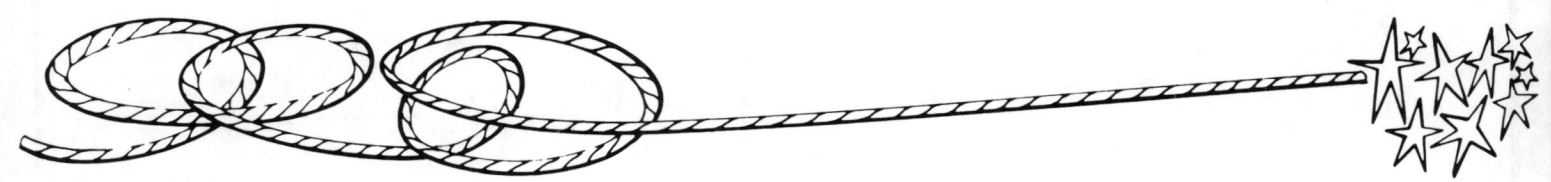

THE GREAT COAT ESCAPE

Audience participation is the theme of this mystery, since you work directly with one spectator and call upon another for further assistance. The GREAT COAT ESCAPE is an excellent trick for a small group and also can be presented just as effectively before a large audience, as part of your stage show.

EFFECT

The magician asks for the assistance of two gentlemen from the audience and requests that one of them remove his coat. The performer then displays two 8-foot lengths of rope which he proceeds to thread through the sleeves of the borrowed coat. The spectator is asked to put his jacket back on while holding the ends of the ropes in his hands. This leaves the spectator with the two ropes running through his sleeves and the ends of the ropes protruding from both cuffs. Two of the ropes, one from each sleeve, are then tied together in a single overhand knot in front of the volunteer. The knot is tightened. This draws the spectator's wrists together, thus imprisoning him — and the ropes — securely within his own jacket. However, when the ends of the ropes are pulled sharply by the magician and the other volunteer, the ropes seem to *penetrate* the spectator's body *visibly,* leaving him and his coat *entirely free of the ropes!*

SECRET AND PREPARATION

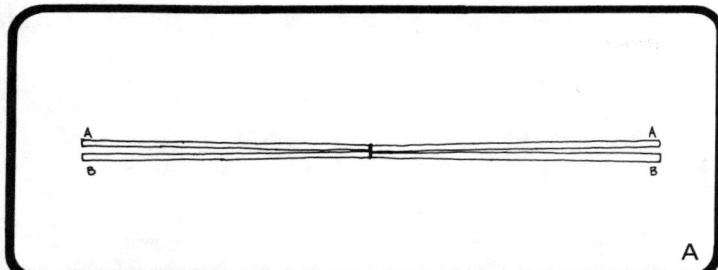

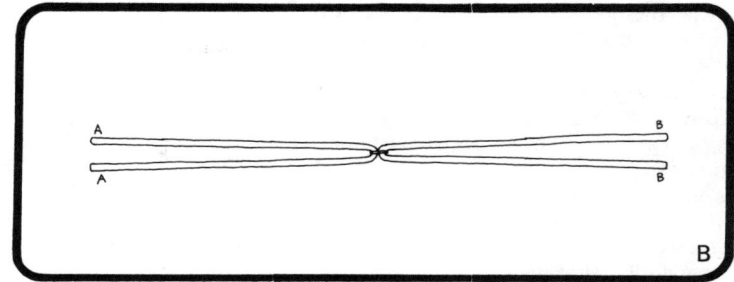

(A)   The only items required to present this seemingly impossible mystery are two 8-foot lengths of soft rope and a small amount of ordinary white sewing thread. To prepare, lay the two lengths of rope *side by side* with their *ends <u>even</u>.* For the purpose of explanation, the two ropes have been labeled "A" and "B" in the illustrations. At the center of the ropes, tie a short piece of white thread *around both ropes,* forming a tight link that secretly holds them together.

(B)   *NOTE: This "secret link" later will enable you to "double back" the ends of the ropes as shown here giving the appearance that the ropes are still running full length, side by side, as you will see.* You are now ready to proceed with THE GREAT COAT ESCAPE.

METHOD

(1)   Pick up the two ropes and casually display them together with the secretly "linked" centers resting across the open fingers as shown.

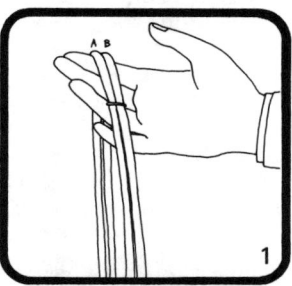

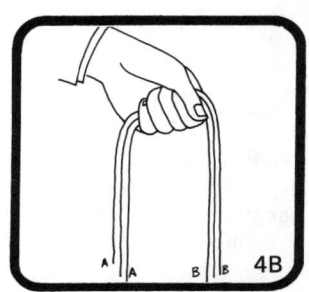

(4)   *NOTE: In Illustration 4A, the fingers are purposely lowered to show the "secret link." Actually, the fingers should be closed around the centers of the ropes as shown in 4B so that the link is never seen.*

(2)   Ask the spectator to remove his coat, and while he is doing so, transfer the ropes to your left hand, swinging them carelessly back and forth, while you reach for the coat with your right hand.

(5)   With your right hand, take the spectator's coat and lift it so that your left hand can grip the coat by the collar, along with the "doubled back" centers of the ropes as shown. *The back of your left hand is toward the audience during this action and in Step 6 which follows.*

(3)   During that action, slide your left fingers between the ropes of both sides of the "secret link," *doubling back the centers of the ropes* as shown. This brings *both ends* of Rope A <u>together</u> at one side of the center link, and *both ends* of Rope B <u>together</u> at the other side. The "doubled" centers remain concealed in the bend of your left fingers. To the spectators, everything seems normal, as you still hold the ropes at the center with the four ends dangling from your left hand.

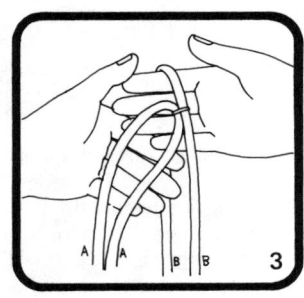

(6)   Ask the spectator who lent you the coat to grasp the ends of one set of ropes (A) in his right hand and insert his right arm into the coat sleeve, *carrying the ends of the rope (A) along.* Note that your left hand still firmly holds and conceals the "doubled" centers of the ropes.

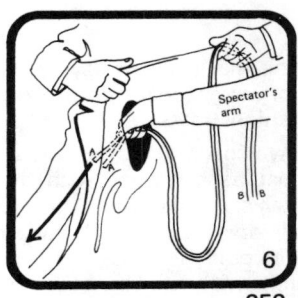

(7) As the spectator's right hand emerges from the sleeve, tell him to let go of the ends of the ropes so that they dangle from the sleeve. Then, bring your right hand up to your left and _transfer the centers of the ropes, along with the coat collar, into your right hand._ This frees your left hand, so it can open the left side of the coat as you ask the spectator to grasp the other ends (B) and carry them down his left sleeve. Then have him release those ends (B) as well.

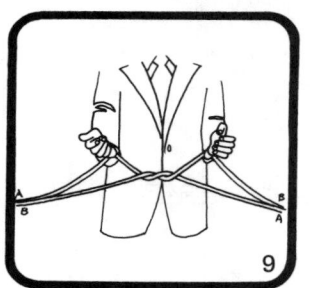

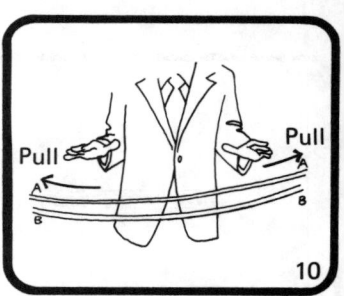

(8) As you adjust the spectator's jacket, _push the doubled centers (and the "secret link") inside his coat down below his coat collar between his coat and his shirt,_ where they are hidden beneath his coat behind his back.

(9) Then, take _one end (A)_ that protrudes from the spectator's _right_ sleeve and _one end (B)_ from his _left_ sleeve. Tie them together in a _single overhand knot_ in front of the spectator's body. _You must now have one End A and one End B paired up on each side of the volunteer._ By doing this, you have "cancelled out" the secret link in the center of the ropes. As soon as you have tied the single ropes together (one from each sleeve), give the left-hand pair of ropes (one End A and one End B) to the assisting spectator, and grasp the right-hand pair (the other End A and End B) in your own hands. This will position the bound volunteer between you and the other spectator. (10) Upon your command, you and the spectator holding the other ends both pull your ropes sharply in opposite directions. _This breaks the hidden thread,_ disposing of the secret link in the process. The two ropes will slide from the "bound" spectator's coat sleeves _completely releasing him from the rope!_ Your volunteers will be as mystified as your audience as to how you just accomplished an "impossible penetration."

COMMENTS AND SUGGESTIONS

Be sure that the two pieces of rope you use are soft. If the rope is too stiff, the centers will not "double" properly. For that reason, it is a good idea to "core" the ropes as described elsewhere in the Rope Section. Each rope should be approximately six to eight feet in length to allow for the crossing of the two ends that are tied. Extra length does not matter, as you and the other spectator can stand farther apart before you both pull the ropes.

Use a _fairly strong_ thread (or wrap a lightweight thread around several times) to tie the centers. This will assure that it will not break _before_ the ropes are pulled.

Keep a firm grip on the centers when you are holding them along with the coat collar, _particularly while the spectator is pulling the ropes down his sleeves._ Be sure to tell him not to release the ends until the ropes are completely through, so there will be no extra strain on them.

This is an excellent effect that uses a proven, practical, basic and very baffling magic principle. You can have great fun with THE GREAT COAT ESCAPE.

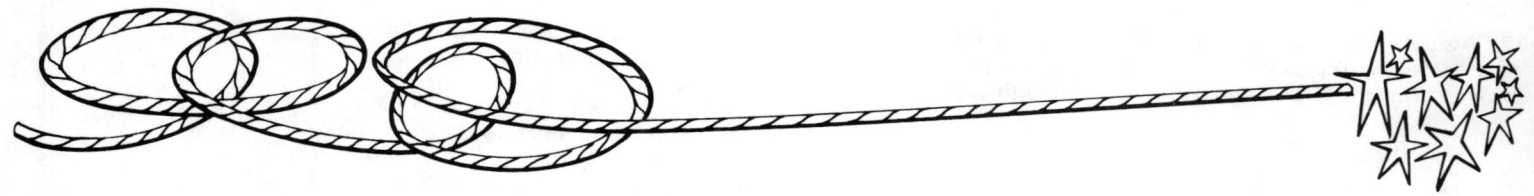

ROPE AND COAT RELEASE

EFFECT

The magician displays a wooden coat hanger, pointing out to his audience that the hanger supports two lengths of rope and thus is a convenient way for a magician to store his props. However, this so-called "convenience" has its problems, one of which the performer demonstrates.

Two spectators are invited to join the magician on stage. Borrowing one of the volunteers' jackets, the magician hangs it neatly on the coat hanger along with the two lengths of rope. The ends of both ropes are threaded through the sleeves of the borrowed coat. The magician takes _one rope from each sleeve_ and ties them together, imprisoning the jacket on the hanger. The magician then hands a pair of rope ends to each volunteer as he supports the coat and hanger with his other hand. Then, upon the magician's command, the spectators pull the ropes in opposite directions. Magically, the ropes penetrate the hanger and the coat! The jacket is returned to the spectator unharmed and all of the equipment may be examined by the audience.

SECRET AND PREPARATION

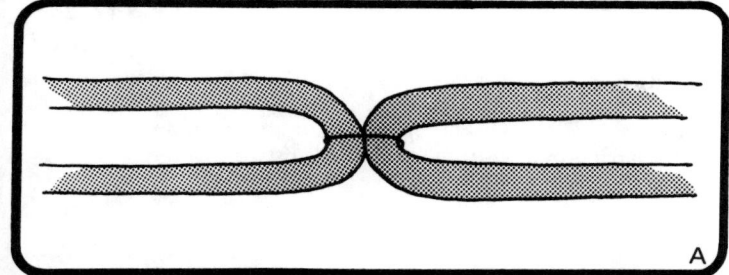

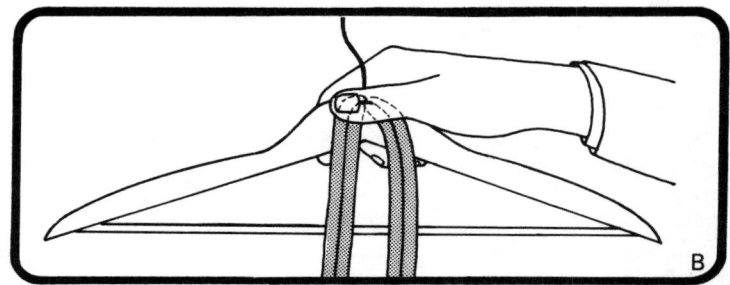

(A)   Cut two pieces of soft rope approximately six feet in length. Now, fold each piece in the middle and tie them together with a *lightweight* piece of white thread as shown.

(B)   It is best to use a wooden coat hanger with a wide shoulder support. You may already have one — if not, most clothing stores use this type for displaying men's suits. There are two important reasons for choosing this type of hanger: First, maximum protection for the spectator's jacket; and second, better concealment of the prepared ropes. Place the ropes around the coat hanger. Cover the "join" in the ropes (where the ropes are held together by the thread) with the thumb and fingers of your right hand as shown.

METHOD

(1)   Ask for the assistance of two spectators, one of whom must be wearing a suitable coat. Borrow his jacket and place it on the coat hanger. *Keep the thread-connected loops to the rear of the hanger.*

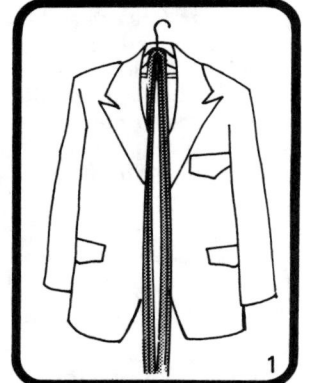

(4)   With the back of the jacket facing the audience, pick up any *one* of the two ends from *each* sleeve and tie them in a *single overhand knot* as shown.

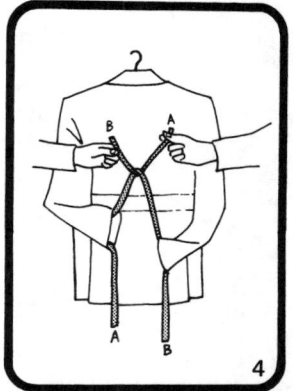

(2)   Have one of the volunteers hold the hanger, and drop the pairs of rope ends down the corresponding sleeves of the jacket as shown.

(5)   THIS   IS   AN   IMPORTANT POINT IN THE TRICK. When you tie the ends, you automatically *reverse their sides.* This means that the single end that is tied from the *left* sleeve is handed to the spectator on the *right,* and the single end from the *right* sleeve is given to the spectator on the *left.* Be sure "not" to recross the tied pair and defeat your purpose.

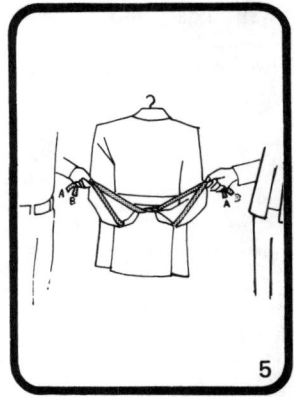

(3)   Now turn the coat around and hand it back to the spectator to hold by the hook on the hanger. The secret thread "join" will now be concealed by the back of the jacket.

(6)   Stand behind the coat and hold the hanger — making sure that the spectators are standing one on each side holding their ends of the ropes. Now, instruct the spectators to pull on their ropes. *This will cause the secret thread to break.* The two lengths of rope will appear to penetrate the hanger *and* the jacket! You now return the jacket to your volunteer and allow the audience to examine the ropes and the hanger.

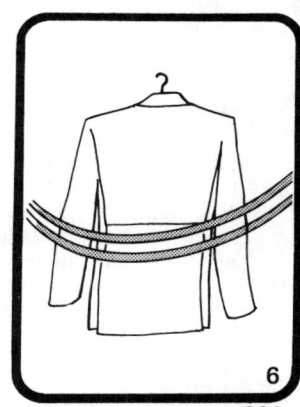

RING OFF ROPE

There are various tricks involving "rings" and "ropes," and this is one of the best. RING OFF ROPE has the impact of an impromptu effect when done at close range — yet it can also be performed before a fairly large group, with the assistance of two spectators from the audience, making it an equally good item for your stage show.

EFFECT

The magician borrows a finger ring from a member of the audience. He asks the spectator to thread it on a rope about three feet in length. Two spectators now hold the rope — one at each end — yet the performer causes the ring to magically "penetrate" right through the center of the rope! The ring is immediately returned to its owner. The ring can be thoroughly examined, along with the length of rope.

METHOD

(1) Hand one of the spectators a piece of rope about three feet long for examination as you ask to borrow a finger ring from any gentleman in the audience. Retrieve the now examined rope from the audience and invite a spectator to thread the borrowed ring on the rope.

(6) With the ring and rope held in this position, reach your left hand *across your right forearm* and grasp the dangling rope where it emerges from your right hand. Slide your left hand along the rope and give the right end of the rope to the spectator on that side. Ask him to hold that end. *NOTE: The illustration is from the spectator's viewpoint.*

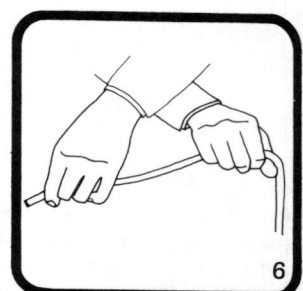

(2) Lay the "threaded" ring and rope across your upturned right hand. The ring should rest near the base of your first finger, and the ends of the rope should hang down from both sides of your hand as shown.

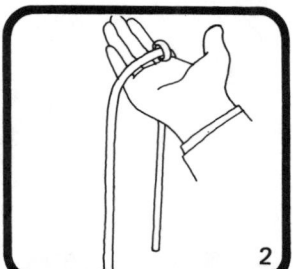

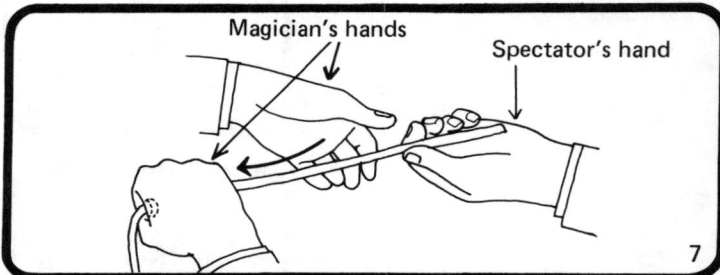

Magician's hands — Spectator's hand

(7) After the spectator grasps the right end of the rope, slide your half-cupped left hand along the rope *bringing it beneath your right fist.*

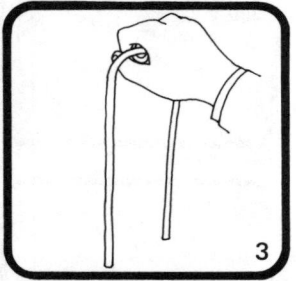

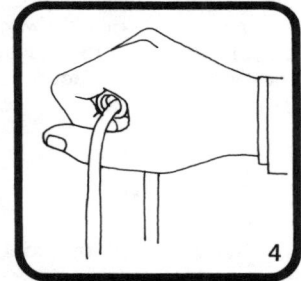

(3) As you display the rope in this manner, remark that it would be impossible to remove the ring from the rope without sliding it off one of the ends. With that, close your fingers over the ring and turn your hand completely over so that the back of your hand is up. The ring should be held loosely by your first finger *near the very edge of your hand as shown.* (4) This illustration is a close-up view of how the ring should be held in your hand.

(5) *NOTE: To conceal the ring from the view of the spectators on your left, you can move your right thumb upward to fill in the open space where the ring might be seen in your hand.*

(8) <u>At the very moment your left hand arrives below your fist</u>, tilt your right hand slightly to the left and relax your right first finger. *Allow the ring to secretly drop from your right fist <u>into your left fingers</u>.* NOTE: This "drop" should be done smoothly and without hesitation. If your left hand pauses for even the slightest moment, you will "tip" the audience that something suspicious is happening. *THIS IS THE KEY "MOVE" FOR THIS TRICK.*

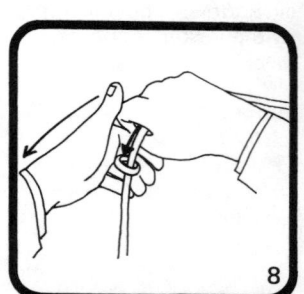

(9) *After* your left hand catches the ring, *raise your right hand upward.* Look directly into the eyes of the spectator *on your right* and say, "Hold your end a little higher."

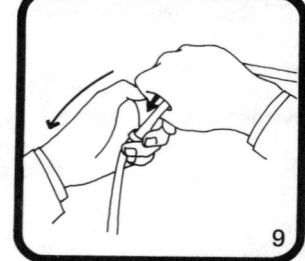

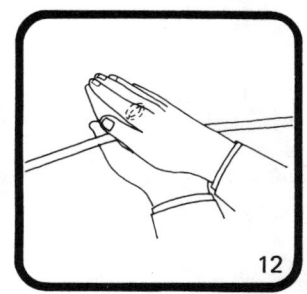

(10) NOTE: This is a good example of the use of "Misdirection" while the vital move of the trick takes place. By *looking* at the spectator and *directing a comment toward him,* you take his attention *off the rope* just long enough to make the secret "steal." Also, by raising your right hand upward, the attention of the audience *will follow that hand,* instead of your left hand, which secretly contains the ring.

(12) Bring your left hand up beneath your right fist. Quickly open both hands, placing your palms together so that the rope and the now "free" ring are trapped between them. Start to roll your hands back and forth as if to cause the ring to "dissolve" through the center of the rope.

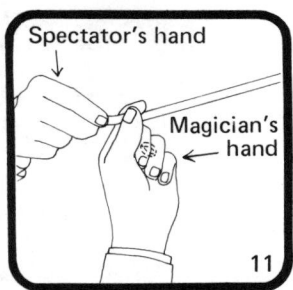

(11) As you raise your right hand upward, your left hand (and the ring) slides down along the rope and secretly carries the ring *completely off the end of the rope.* Without hesitation, as you secretly hold the ring in the Finger Palm position, lift this end and give it to the spectator on your left. Tell him to hold the end firmly in his hand.

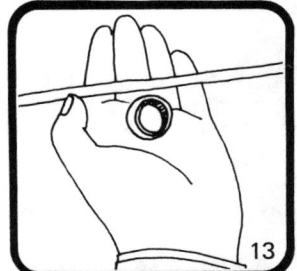

(13) Lift your right hand to reveal the ring resting on your left hand next to the rope. Return the ring to its owner and pass the rope for examination.

COMMENTS AND SUGGESTIONS

Although using a borrowed ring is best, the routine is just as effective with your own finger ring, or even a small curtain ring or a metal washer. At the finish, everything can be examined, just as with the borrowed ring, so the effect on the audience is the same. The vital point is to *make your presentation natural,* so that no one will suspect the "secret move." As you practice, and by working slowly and deliberately, you will find that the "steal" becomes easier and all the more deceptive. To "condition" the audience to the "naturalness" of your actions, you can introduce the following before actually performing the trick. Hold the threaded ring in your open right palm as in Step 2. Say to the spectator on your right, "I am going to give you *this end* of the rope." With that, reach over with your left hand and *start* to give him the right end but let it drop. Then say to the spectator on the left, "And I will give you *this* end," as you bring your left hand over and lift the left end of the rope and then let it drop. Then say, "And all the while, I will keep the ring tightly in my right hand." With that, you now, *for the first time,* turn your right fist downward. You are now all set to proceed, using *almost the same moves* with the ends of the rope, making the routine *entirely natural throughout.*

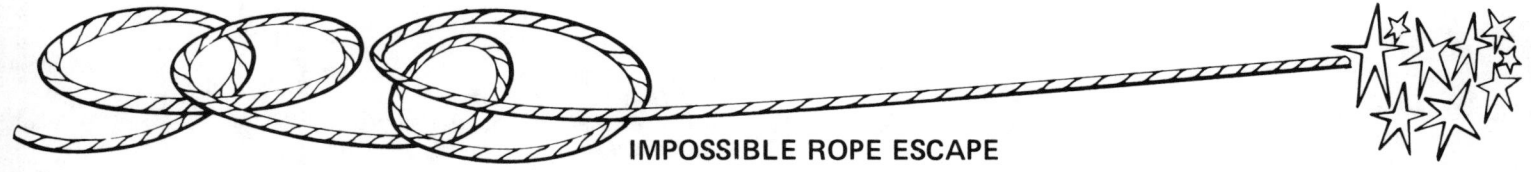

IMPOSSIBLE ROPE ESCAPE

DON WAYNE

EFFECT

The magician calls the audience's attention to two 5-foot lengths of unprepared rope. The performer then asks for the assistance of two spectators. Each spectator is handed one of the ropes for examination. While the spectators are busy with the ropes, the magician places a chair in the center of the stage. After the spectators have confirmed the unprepared nature of the ropes, the magician sits in the chair and allows the two volunteers to tie his knees and wrists together. When the spectators are satisfied that the performer is securely bound, they cover his wrists with a large cloth. *INSTANTLY,* one of the magician's hands is free—but before the spectators are able to remove the cloth, the performer plunges his hand back beneath the cloth. When the cloth is removed, the audience can see that the magician is *STILL BOUND AS TIGHTLY AS BEFORE.* The surprised spectators are asked to tie still another knot in the ropes above the magician's wrist. They then replace the cloth over his arms. Once more the performer escapes. But this time, upon lifting the cloth, *HE IS COMPLETELY FREE*—the ropes have apparently penetrated the magician's arms and legs as well!

SECRET AND PREPARATION

All you need for this excellent effect are two lengths of rope approximately 5 feet long, an opaque piece of cloth approximately 4 feet square and a chair.

METHOD

(1) Invite two members of your audience to join you on stage. Hand each of them one of the lengths of rope for their examination. While the two volunteers examine the ropes, place the folding chair at stage center.

(2) Take the rope back from the spectator on your right and drape it over the right hand as shown. We will call this Rope A. The middle of Rope A should rest on top of the first finger of the right hand near the thumb. Now, with the left hand, take the other rope from the spectator on your left. We will call this Rope B. Place the center of B between the first and second fingers of the right hand near the finger tips. Ropes A and B should now appear as shown.

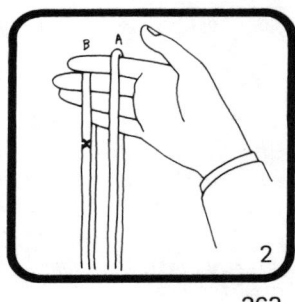

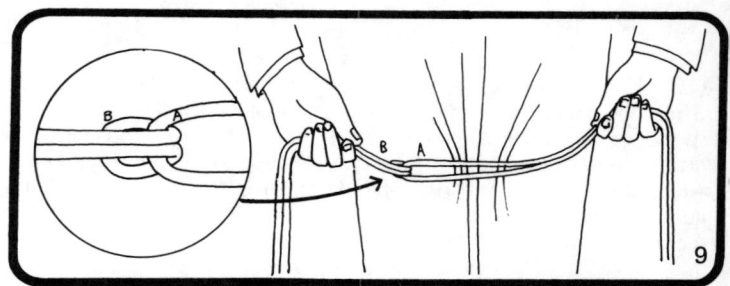

(3) The following series of moves will be made as you transfer the ropes from your right hand to your left. During this transfer you will be inviting the spectator on your left to cross in front of you so that he, and the other spectator, can "examine" the chair.

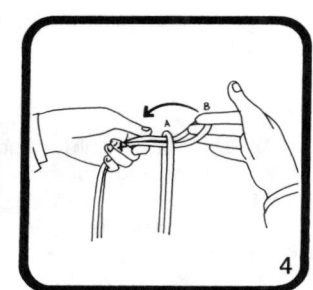

(4) With your left hand, grasp Rope B at a point about 6 inches down from the loop of the rope, which is shown as Point X, and allow Rope A to slide off your right first finger onto the loop formed by B, as shown.

(9) Now reach behind your legs with your right hand and grasp both ends of Rope B. *Be sure to hold the "hooked" loops securely in your left hand.* Bring the ends of both A and B around your legs with the "hooked" loops behind your left knee as in the illustration. Now sit down and, at the same time, place the loops in the bend behind your left knee.

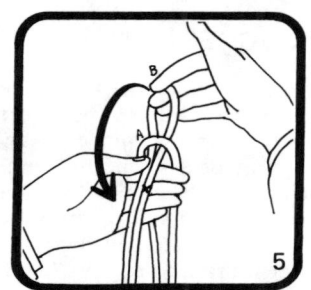

(5) With your right hand, pull Rope B up and over Rope A and down into the left hand to Point X.

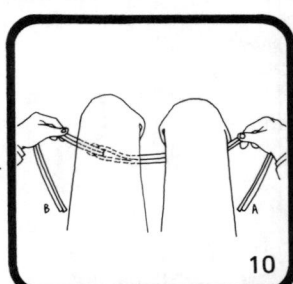

(10) THE HOOKED LOOPS MUST BE POSITIONED DIRECTLY BEHIND YOUR LEFT KNEE SO THAT, AS YOU SIT DOWN, <u>THE LOOPS WILL BE HELD FIRMLY IN PLACE BY THE BEND IN YOUR LEG.</u> Slide your *left hand out* along the ropes to your left.

(11) *ALSO NOTE: By holding the ropes as shown in Step 10 it appears to the audience that the two separate ropes pass directly under your legs.*

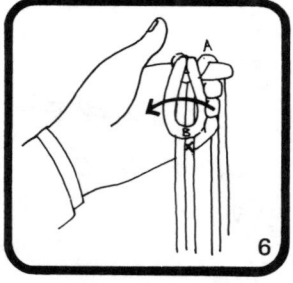

(6) Close the left fingers around the two "hooked" loops.

(12) Now cross the two pairs of ends up and over your knees. *Be sure that the left-hand Pair B crosses to the REAR of the right-hand Pair A as shown. Pull the ropes tightly in opposite directions. This action apparently binds the knees together.*

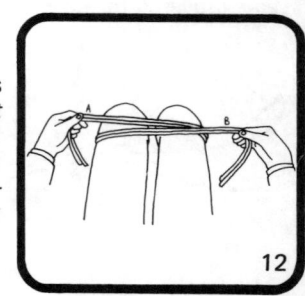

(7) To the audience the ropes will appear as if they *both pass straight through your left hand.*

(13) Then position your wrists on top of the ropes. STILL HOLD THE LOOPS FIRMLY WITH THE BEND IN YOUR LEFT KNEE.

(8) The two spectators will have examined the chair by now, so position yourself in front of the chair. Have the spectators stand, one on each side, beside you.

(14) Ask the spectator on your left to tie your wrists tightly using as many knots as he wishes.

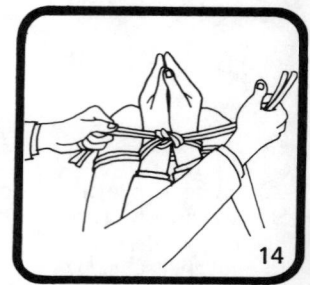

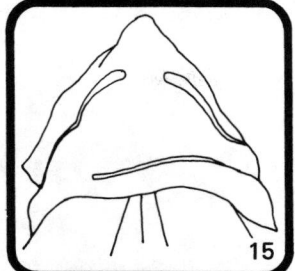

(15) Ask the spectator on your right to cover your hands and knees with the cloth.

(16) Under cover of the cloth, *twist your wrists to the RIGHT.* You will find that your left hand will easily come free of the rope. Bring your left hand into view and adjust the cloth. This action will bring a laugh from the audience. Quickly place your hand back under the cloth *and into the ropes.* Twist your hands to the left to retighten the ropes.

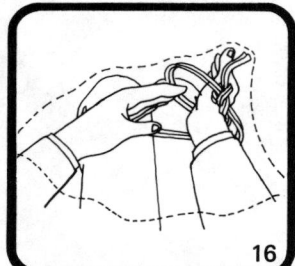

(17) The spectator to your right is asked to remove the cloth. THE AUDIENCE WILL SEE THAT YOU ARE STILL SECURELY TIED. To make sure that you cannot escape, the spectator on your left is asked to tie another knot *on top of those already there.*

(18) After the new knot is tied, have the spectator on your right re-cover your hands with the cloth. As soon as you are covered, twist both hands to the right as in Step 16. This time release *both* your hands from the loop and bring them both into view on top of this cloth. During the laughter, grasp the ropes through the cloth and lift sharply, *as you relax your hold on the loops with your left knee.* The ropes will come completely loose—apparently having penetrated both legs.

(19) Stand up and drop the cloth containing the ropes on the chair seat. Thank your volunteers and congratulate them on tying you so well as they leave the stage.

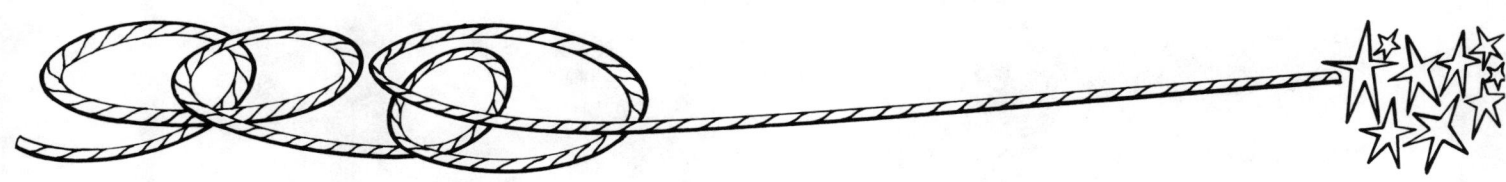

SILK AND HANDKERCHIEF MAGIC

Tricks with handkerchiefs form quite a large category of magic and perhaps the most unusual. While it is possible to put card tricks, coin tricks, and even stage illusions in categories of their own, it is often difficult to classify a handkerchief trick exactly. Besides, there are distinctly different types of handkerchief magic, as will be seen.

Besides openly playing a major role in certain tricks, a handkerchief often serves as an important adjunct in other effects where its purpose is totally unsuspected. The broken and restored match is a typical example of this, wherein the secret depends on the handkerchief that is unobtrusively introduced into the routine.

The type of handkerchief to be used in certain tricks is also of importance. With effects involving knots, larger handkerchiefs are better. Houdini used huge handkerchiefs throughout his knot-tying routines that were a feature of his big show.

In other effects, cotton handkerchiefs are excellent—bandana type, polka dots or other designs aid concealment of small objects in their folds. For effects where the handkerchief seems totally unimportant, a plain white hankie is often best. At times you may borrow such handkerchiefs, so if you happen to bring but one of your own, nobody will suspect trickery.

In stage work before large audiences, some magicians go in for elaborate effects with colored silk handkerchiefs requiring special apparatus. Such handkerchiefs are popularly termed "silks" and should be made from thin silk with a very narrow hem. Being compressible, they are excellent for production effects in which very large silks with colorful ornamental designs may be used. For less elaborate effects, such as bare hand productions, vanishes, color changes, and the like, small silks are preferable. Silk effects really form a separate category of their own, and there's no question on that score. Hermann and Kellar both featured silk routines in their performances, and in later years, other magicians developed elaborate silk acts that helped them pave their roads to fame.

HYPNOTIZED HANDKERCHIEF

EFFECT

The magician displays a pocket handkerchief and twirls it between his hands in a "rope-like" fashion. Always under the performer's control, the handkerchief stands erect, bows to the audience, and moves back and forth in a very puzzling manner. He then attaches an "invisible" thread to the upper corner of the handkerchief and causes the handkerchief to follow his lead by pulling on the "magical" leash. Even after crushing the handkerchief down with his other hand, the magician cannot seem to discourage the persistant performance of the HYPNOTIZED HANDKERCHIEF.

METHOD

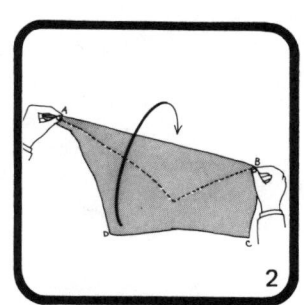

(1) Borrow a spectator's handkerchief (or use your own), and spread it open on the table. Now hold the left-hand corner (A) securely between your left thumb and fingers and grasp the *hem* at the *center of the right side* (B) with your right hand as shown. (2) Pick up the handkerchief and hold it in front of you.

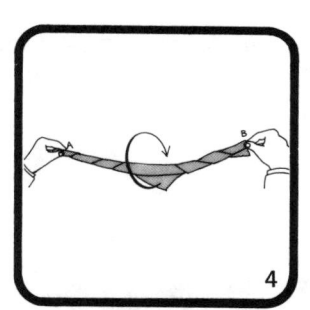

(3) Twirl the handkerchief between your hands ... (4) ... until the entire handkerchief is rolled in a tightly twisted rope-like configuration.

(5) As you continue to hold the "twisted" handkerchief, move your right hand *above* your left hand so that the right end (B) is directly above the left end (A) as shown.

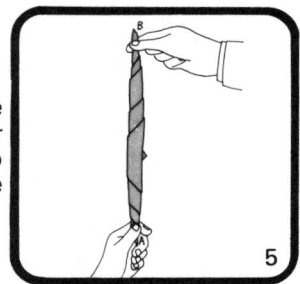

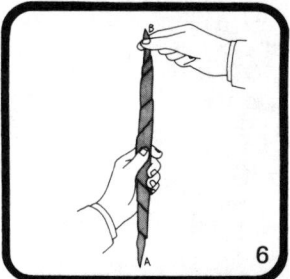

(6) Now, move your left hand up so that it can grasp the rolled handkerchief near the center. *Do not allow the twists in the handkerchief to "unroll" as you change the position of your left hand.* Your right hand maintains its grip on the *top* end (B).

(7) Pull the handkerchief "tight" between your hand ... then, slowly release the handkerchief from your right fingers. *It will stand erect as if "hypnotized."* (In reality, the natural rigidity given to the material by the many twists is what causes the handkerchief to maintain its upright position.)

(8) Pretend to pluck an imaginary strand of hair from your head and go through the motions of tying it to the upper end of the handkerchief (B). Holding the "free" end of this fictitious hair in your hand, slowly pull it towards your body. At the same time, draw your left thumb gently downward against your left fingers. The downward motion of your thumb will cause the handkerchief to obediently lean in your direction. NOTE: Practice will teach you how to synchronize the handkerchief's "leaning" movement with the pulling motion of the "invisible" hair in your right hand.

(9) Now move your right hand *and* the invisible hair forward, toward the spectators. To make the handkerchief lean away from you and follow the invisible tug, simply slide your left thumb up and forward on the center of the handkerchief.

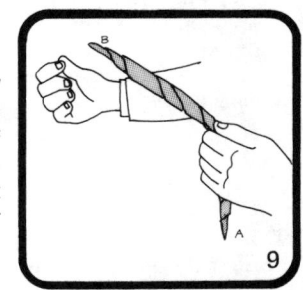

(10) Here is a more detailed illustration of the move required for Step 8. This shows how the left thumb pulls *down* on the center of the handkerchief to lean toward you.

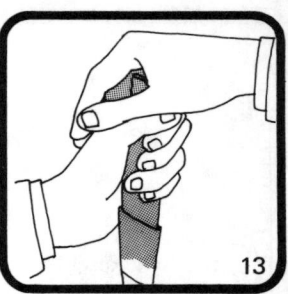

(13) Now, in one swift downward motion, bring your right hand down on top of the handkerchief . . . crushing it between your right palm and the top of your left fist.

(11) And here is the action as your left thumb pushes *up and forward* on the center of the handkerchief, causing the handkerchief to lean away from you for Step 9.

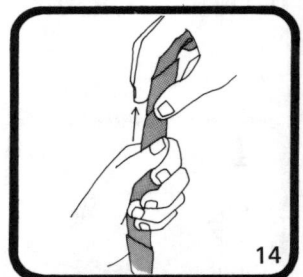

(14) Quickly raise your right hand back up. As you do, secretly use your right fingers and thumb to straighten the handkerchief and . . .

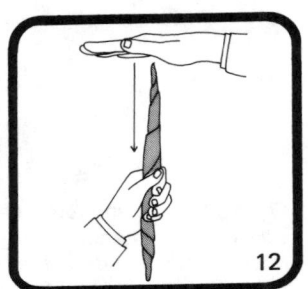

(12) After repeating this back and forth pulling movement with the "invisible" hair several times, bring the handkerchief back to its original upright position. Then hold your right hand above the hypnotized handkerchief as shown.

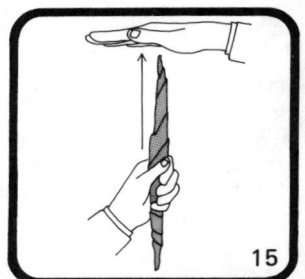

(15) . . . bring the handkerchief back to its original "hypnotized" upright position. With practice you will learn to execute this upward movement so swiftly and smoothly that the handkerchief will appear to "bounce back" into shape on its own accord.

(16) To conclude the effect, snap the handkerchief open and offer it to the spectators for examination.

FATIMA, THE DANCER

EFFECT

As an interlude between effects, the magician tells the story of an exotic dancer named Fatima. Although she lived and danced many years ago, her exotic movements and high kicks have never been forgotten. To illustrate, the performer ties a knot in his pocket handkerchief — and then, with a twist and a twirl, he turns it into a doll-like replica of the famous dancer. To the accompaniment of a short poem, the magician seems to make the cloth figure come alive, dancing about between his hands, finishing in grand style with a *high, spinning kick!*

SECRET AND PREPARATION

This clever bit of business never fails to create interest and laughter. Since the handkerchief is completely unprepared, you are able to present this effect any time, with any handkerchief!

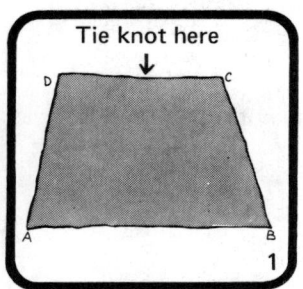

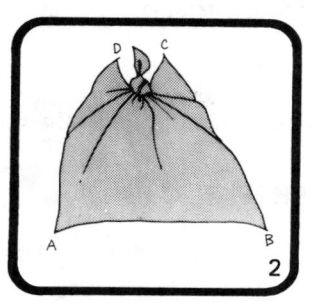

(1) Spread the handkerchief open and (2) tie a knot in the *center of one side* of the hem as shown. This knot represents the head of Fatima. Be sure that a small portion of the hem protrudes from the completed knot, forming a sort of "tail," which you can use to hold the handkerchief later.

(3) *NOTE: Be sure you do <u>not</u> tie the knot in one of the corners of the handkerchief, or the effect will not work. Tie the knot in the center of one of the side edges of the handkerchief as shown.*

(4) Grasp the two corners (A and B) on the *side opposite the knot* between the thumb and forefingers of both hands as shown.

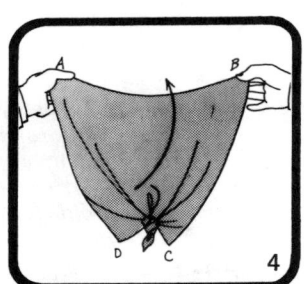

(5) Now, "twirl" the handkerchief away from you, causing the knotted portion of the handkerchief to spin around Ends A and B that you are holding. *Be sure to twirl the handkerchief as <u>tightly</u> as possible until it will no longer accept any additional twists in the material.*

(6) Now, bring Corners A and B together and grasp them *both* in your <u>right</u> hand as shown. With your <u>left</u> hand, grasp the "tail" of the knot (Fatima's head) between your left thumb and first finger.

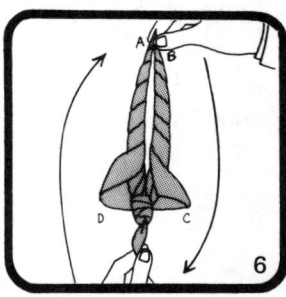

(7) Now, turn the entire affair *completely over.* This brings Corners A and B to the <u>bottom</u> and the knot to the top. If you use your imagination, you can see the form of a dancer created by the handkerchief.

(8) By moving your hands back and forth, Fatima will dance about and swing her hips as if to keep time with the music. You can recite the following poem suiting the action to the words:

> *FATIMA was a dancer gay.*
> *For fifty cents she'd dance this way,*
> (Shake the figure)
> *But if a dollar you would pay,*
> (Release one leg)
> *She'd do "Ta Ra Ra Boom De Aye."*

NOTE: The high kick could also be done at the word "aye."

(9) On the last line of the poem, to bring the dance to its grand finale, pull your left hand <u>up</u> and your right hand <u>down</u>. *At the same time,* release <u>one</u> of the bottom corners of the handkerchief (either A or B) from your right hand. The result will be a *high kick* and a *dramatic spin* — performed by Fatima at the peak of her career!

COMMENTS AND SUGGESTIONS

The clever poem was written by that excellent magician, showman, writer, and lawyer, William Larsen, Sr. and is still a favorite of his son, Bill Larsen, President of the Academy of Magical Arts in Hollywood.

THE DISSOLVING KNOT

EFFECT

During a routine with a silk handkerchief, the magician casually ties a knot in the center of the scarf. Then the knot simply "melts" away.

SECRET AND PREPARATION

You will require a handkerchief (silk is best) at least 18" square in order to present this trick effectively.

METHOD

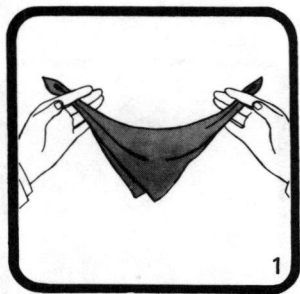

(1) Grasp the diagonal corners of the handkerchief between the first and second fingers of each hand. (2) Now twirl the handkerchief into a loose "rope-like" configuration. We will call the end pinched between the first and second fingers of your left hand *End A,* and the end in your right hand *End B.*

(7) THIS IS THE KEY MOVE. Now pull End A through the loop with your right hand. End B is held firmly by the thumb and first finger of your left hand. The third and fourth fingers of your left hand release their grip around the silk *as your left second finger hooks and pulls the lower portion of End B through the loop.* STUDY THE ILLUSTRATION CAREFULLY.

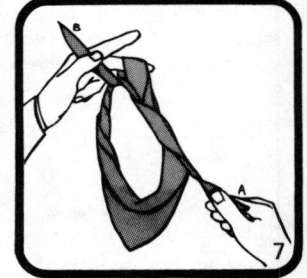

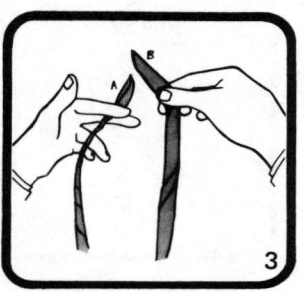

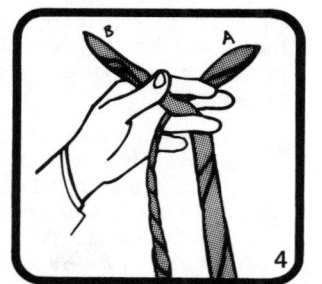

(3) Bring End B over toward your left and open the second and third fingers of your left hand as shown. (4) Lay End B *over* End A . . . passing End B *between* the second and third fingers of your left hand.

(8) As you continue pulling on End A, a knot will form *around the loop* held by the second finger of your left hand as shown. *When this knot is tight enough to hold its shape, remove your left second finger from inside the loop.*

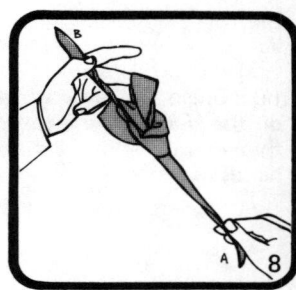

(5) Your right hand now reaches *through* the loop and grasps End A as shown. The third and fourth fingers of your left hand curl around the twisted silk below End A.

(9) NOTE: You now have apparently tied a "real" knot in the handkerchief. Really you have cleverly (and secretly) tied a "slip" knot. If you were to pull on the ends of the handkerchief now the knot would "dissolve."

(6) After the third and fourth fingers of the left hand are closed around the handkerchief, *the second finger of your left hand "hooks" the silk just below where the two ends cross . . . below End B as shown.*

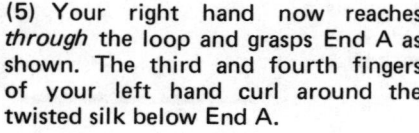

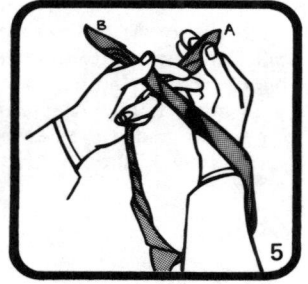

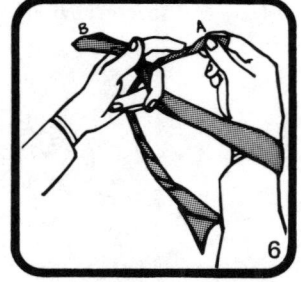

(10) Allow the handkerchief to hang freely from the thumb and first finger of your left hand.

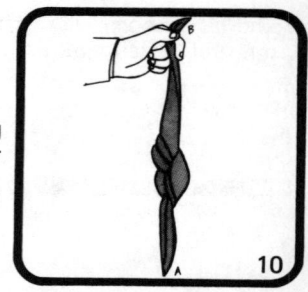

(11) Now grasp End A lightly with the thumb and first finger of your right hand. Hold the handkerchief horizontally in front of you and gently blow on the knot. At the same time, pull on the ends of the handkerchief and the knot will "dissolve" away!

COMMENTS AND SUGGESTIONS

The Dissolving Knot is one of the basic, classic effects in magic. It is important that you practice until you can tie the "Dissolving Knot" just as easily and quickly as you would a "real" knot. The ability to tie this trick knot will then become the basis for many other baffling effects. Two of these stunners are the tricks that follow.

THE KNOT THROUGH THE ARM

EFFECT

The magician displays an ordinary handkerchief. A spectator stands to the performer's left and is asked to extend his left arm about waist high. Grasping the diagonal corners of the handkerchief, the magician spins the scarf into a loose rope-like configuration. The handkerchief is now tied around the volunteer's wrist. With a sudden jerk, the handkerchief seems to visibly penetrate the spectator's arm leaving the magician with the undamaged handkerchief and the knot still intact!

SECRET AND PREPARATION

This effect is one of those beautiful little gems that can be done anywhere at any time. All that is needed is a large pocket handkerchief, a silk scarf, or an 18- or 24-inch square "magician's" silk handkerchief.

This trick is based on THE DISSOLVING KNOT, which you must learn first.

METHOD

(1) Grasp the diagonal corners of the handkerchief and spin it into a loose "rope-like" configuration. In the illustration we have marked the two ends "A" and "B." Hold the handkerchief as shown.

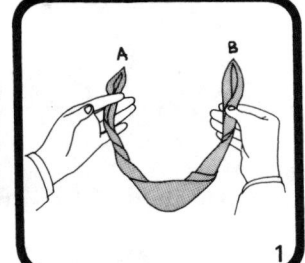

(2) Now, place the handkerchief around the spectator's left wrist and grasp both ends of the handkerchief in your left hand in preparation for the Dissolving Knot.

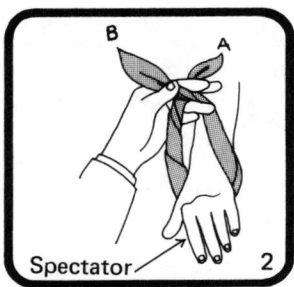

(3) With the spectator's wrist still in position, insert your right hand through the loop and grasp End A. Pull this end back through the loop and tie the Dissolving Knot.

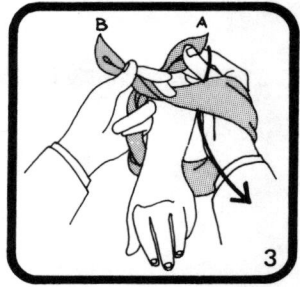

(4) *NOTE: As you pull the ends in opposite directions (End B to your right), be sure to retain the small loop in End A with the second finger of the left hand as described in the Dissolving Knot.* This small loop will fall under End A between the handkerchief and the spectator's wrist. You can now pull on the ends to tie the handkerchief <u>firmly</u> around the spectator's wrist AS LONG AS YOU KEEP YOUR LEFT SECOND FINGER IN PLACE HOLDING THE SMALL LOOP. When the handkerchief is tightly around the spectator's wrist, remove your left second finger.

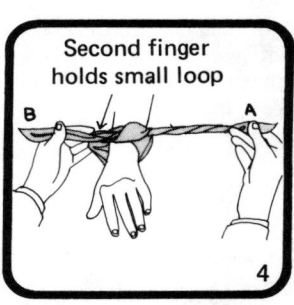

(5) Now with your right hand, swing End A to the left *around the spectator's wrist.* Continue to hold End A with your left hand. BE SURE THAT END B GOES <u>IN FRONT</u> OF END A as shown.

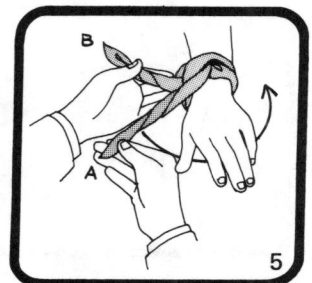

(8) Holding one end in each hand, pull up and out on *both ends* of the handkerchief. This "dissolves" the false knot around the wrist, creating a perfect illusion of the handkerchief penetrating the spectator's arm. The last (legitimate) knot is left in the handkerchief as a final convincer.

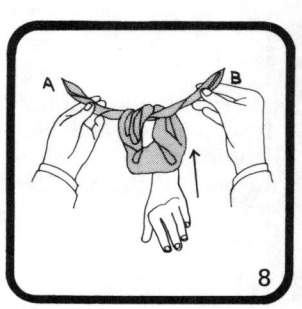

(6) After you have wrapped End B around the spectator's wrist, the entire affair should look like this.

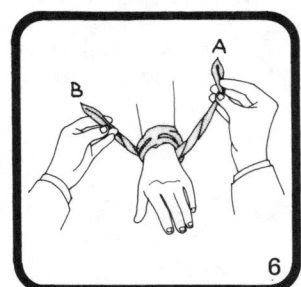

(9) *NOTE: After you have tied BOTH knots, have the spectator grasp his hands together. In this way, you strengthen the mystery by making it impossible for the handkerchief to have been slipped over the end of the spectator's left hand when you perform the "penetration." Also, when tying the Dissolving Knot in Step 3, try to make it a bit off center so that End A is longer than End B as shown in Step 4. This is so you will have plenty of handkerchief left to wrap End A around the spectator's wrist the second time in Step 5.*

(7) Now tie a *single legitimate knot* on top of the Dissolving Knot. This will put End A in your <u>left</u> hand and End B in your <u>right</u>.

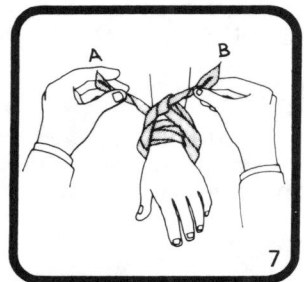

COMMENTS AND SUGGESTIONS

This is an excellent impromptu trick which can be performed for one person or, on stage, for a large audience. I have used it for many years, and it is well worth the small amount of practice necessary to learn it.

—MW

HANDKERCHIEF THROUGH HANDKERCHIEF

EFFECT

The magician displays two silk handkerchiefs. He twists one into a rope-like configuration and gives it to a spectator to hold outstretched between his hands. He then twists the second handkerchief in the same manner and ties it *around* the first handkerchief held by the spectator. The spectator is then asked to tie a knot in his handkerchief so that both handkerchiefs are securely bonded together. Under these impossible conditions, the magicians causes the handkerchiefs to seemingly "melt" apart — leaving their knots intact.

SECRET AND PREPARATION

In order to perform this trick, you must first have mastered THE DISSOLVING KNOT.

This illusion is an effective variation of the KNOT THROUGH ARM. You will require two large silk handkerchiefs. They should be at least 18" square and preferably of contrasting colors. In the illustrations, one of the handkerchiefs is light-colored and the other is dark-colored to make the description easier to follow.

METHOD

(1) Grasp the light-colored handkerchief by two diagonal corners and "twirl" it between your hands into a "loose rope." Hand it to a spectator and request that he hold it outstretched by those same corners as shown.

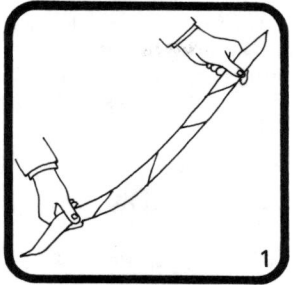

(5) With the fake knot cinched up tightly against the light-colored handkerchief, loop the dark handkerchief around the light handkerchief *a second time* and tie *one legitimate knot* just as you did in Steps 5, 6, and 7 in the "Handkerchief through the Wrist."

(2) Now twirl the dark-colored handkerchief in the same manner. Holding it by the ends, position it under the handkerchief being held by the spectator as shown.

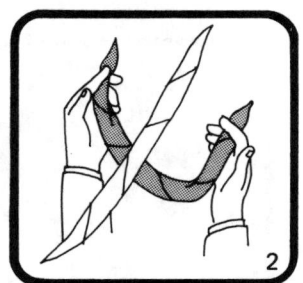

(6) Now ask the spectator to tie a knot in his handkerchief. As he does, you may find it necessary to hold the dark-colored handkerchief by its knot. There are two reasons why this may be necessary: First, to protect the fake knot from being pulled loose, and second, to prevent the spectator from tying his knot too tightly around your handkerchief. You can avoid this possibility by tying both knots yourself, but the effectiveness of the illusion is enhanced if the spectator ties the real knot in the light-colored handkerchief.

(3) *NOTE: In the illustration for Step 2, the* spectator's hands *that are holding the light-colored handkerchief have been omitted for clarity.* You can also see from this illustration the similarity between this effect and the "Handkerchief through the Wrist." In this version, you are substituting the light-colored *handkerchief* for the volunteer's *wrist.*

(7) Have the spectator hold the corners of the light handkerchief as you hold the corners of the dark handkerchief. With a gentle shaking motion, pull on the ends of your handkerchief and instruct the spectator to do the same. Your knot will "dissolve" and the two handkerchiefs will "magically" separate from each other. Because of the <u>second</u> "real" knot that you tied and the "real" knot that the spectator tied, you are both left with knots in your handkerchiefs! Done correctly, this is a beautiful and baffling mystery.

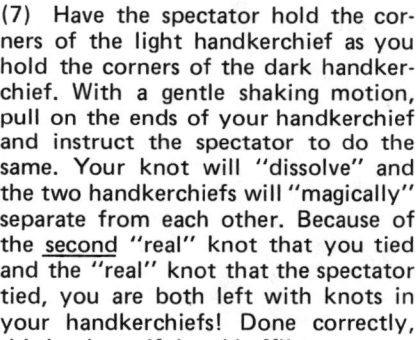

(4) Utilizing the "Dissolving Knot" as described in Steps 3 and 4 in the "Handkerchief through the Wrist," tie the dark handkerchief around the light handkerchief.

THE PENETRATING HANDKERCHIEF

Here is a simple but effective mystery involving objects easily found around the house. All you need is an ordinary drinking glass, two handkerchiefs, and a rubber band. This is another of those little "gems" from the inventive mind of "Gen" Grant.

EFFECT

The magician displays a drinking glass, holding it mouth up with the tips of his fingers. He then places a handkerchief into the glass and covers both this handkerchief and the glass with a *second* handkerchief. Next, he places a rubber band over the second handkerchief *and* the glass, thus sealing the first handkerchief inside the glass. Now, holding the glass from the outside, he reaches under the handkerchief for a brief moment and instantly withdraws the first handkerchief — the one that was sealed inside the glass! The outside handkerchief is removed and all may now be examined. AN IMPOSSIBLE PENETRATION!

SECRET AND PREPARATION

This trick depends entirely upon a simple "move" which involves secretly turning the glass upside down while it is being covered by the second handkerchief. *All of the illustrations are from the magician's point of view.*

METHOD

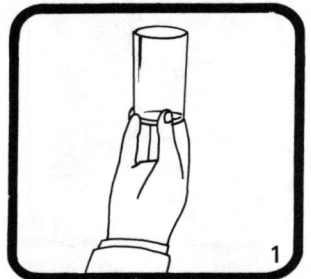  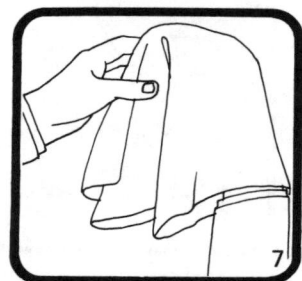 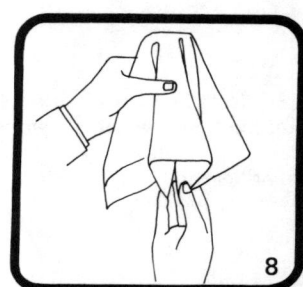

(1) Begin by holding the drinking glass, mouth up, at the tips of the fingers and thumb of your right hand as shown.   (2) Display a handkerchief — this is the one that will later "penetrate" the glass. With your left hand, push it into the glass.

(7) As the glass turns over, your left hand finishes covering *both* the right hand and the glass.   (8) After the glass is covered, grip the glass *through* the cloth with your left hand as shown.

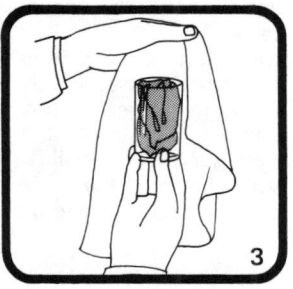

(3) Pick up the second handkerchief with your left hand. Bring it up in front of the glass, *momentarily hiding the glass from the spectators' view.*

(9) Remove your right hand, casually showing it empty, and pick up the rubber band from the table. Spread the rubber band with your right fingers and place it around the handkerchief and the "top" of the glass (really the *bottom,* unknown to the spectators).

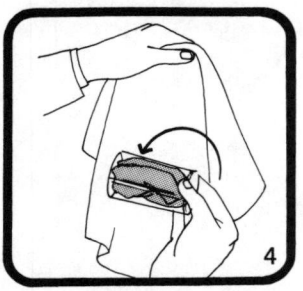 

(10) With the empty right hand, reach underneath the covering handkerchief and grasp the first handkerchief — the one that is inside the glass. Pull it straight down into view. *To the audience it appears that the handkerchief has "magically" penetrated through the bottom of the glass!*

(4) NOW HERE COMES THE SECRET "MOVE." As you begin to cover the glass with the handkerchief, *your right hand slightly relaxes its grip on the bottom of the glass, allowing the glass to pivot between your thumb and fingers* (5) *until the glass has TURNED COMPLETELY UPSIDE DOWN.*

(6) *NOTE: The handkerchief inside the glass should be large enough so that it will not fall out when you turn the glass upside down.*

(11) Now with your right hand, reach under the covering handkerchief and grip the glass *in position to make the secret turn-over once again* — this time with the mouth of the glass (which is at the *bottom* because the glass is upside down) between the tips of your right thumb and fingers.

(12) With your left hand, grip the outer (second) handkerchief between the tips of the fingers at the very "top" of the covered glass (actually the "real" bottom) and pull the cloth *just enough to release the rubber band from around the glass* — and then *STOP*. Now, pause for a moment, *just long enough to allow the glass to PIVOT in the fingers BACK TO ITS ORIGINAL MOUTH-UP POSITION.*

(13) As soon as the glass is mouth up, draw the handkerchief away from the glass and all can be examined.

THE MAGICAL PRODUCTION OF A HANDKERCHIEF

EFFECT

The following effects comprise an entire routine for the "production" and "vanish" of a silk handkerchief. You will first learn how to fold the handkerchief so that you can produce it from the air. Then you will learn how to construct a "vanisher" to cause the handkerchief to disappear from your hands leaving them completely empty.

SECRET AND PREPARATION

To perform the production, it is best to use a handkerchief made of pure silk (the type sold by magic supply houses is best — these are called "silks"). A silk handkerchief can be easily folded in the special manner described here and it will spring open when it is produced. Also, a "magician's silk" can be more easily compressed so that it makes a smaller "package" . . . thus it can be more easily concealed for any production or vanish.

(A) Begin by placing the handkerchief flat on the table in front of you.

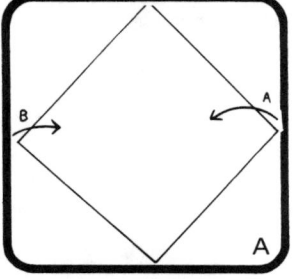

(B) Fold corners A and B into the center of the handkerchief. The corners A and B should just touch in the center of the handkerchief as shown.

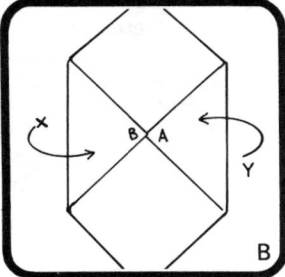

(C) Now grasp the handkerchief at points X and Y. Fold these two edges of the handkerchief into the center so that points X and Y touch. You'll notice that the handkerchief is getting thinner in width with each fold.

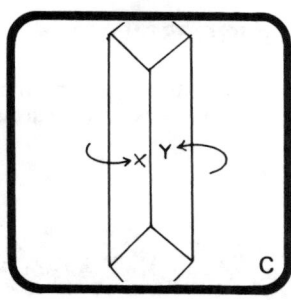

(D) Repeat the folding actions as you did in Steps B and C. Then, continue folding the edges of the handkerchief into the center until the folded handkerchief is about 3" wide.

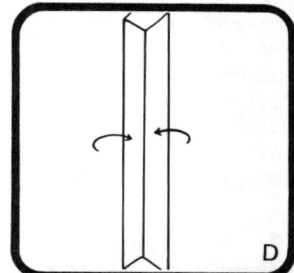

(E) Now fold the right-hand half of the handkerchief over *on top of the left-hand half*. The handkerchief should now be about 1½" wide.

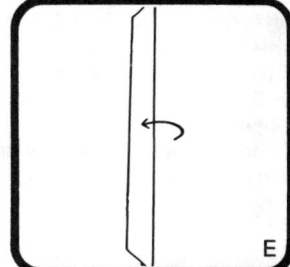

(F) Fold the bottom end of the handkerchief about an inch towards your right as shown. This forms a "tab" like protrusion which is labeled "T" in the illustration.

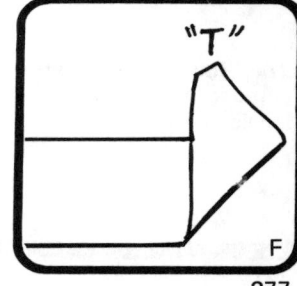

(G) Beginning at the bottom of the handkerchief, roll it up tightly so that the tab (T) protrudes from the bundle. Roll up the entire length of the handkerchief until it forms a tight little package.

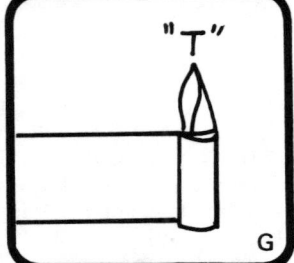

(I) With the handkerchief now properly rolled, it forms a tight little bundle which will not unroll until time for the production.

(H) The handkerchief should now look like this. Tuck the top "free" end of the handkerchief into the left-hand side of the rolled hank. (This is the side opposite the "tab.") You may use a blunt stick or other object to tuck this end down between the folds if you wish.

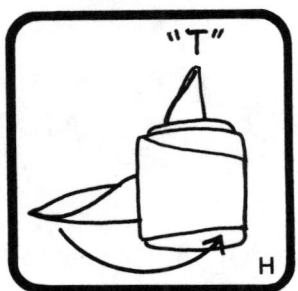

METHOD

(1) With the handkerchief folded and rolled into this compact bundle you are now ready for the production. Secretly obtain the bundle in your hand. (A good idea is to have the bundle hidden behind some prop on your table and then pick it up as you set down some other prop used in the preceeding trick in your show.) When you pick up the bundle, grasp the protruding tab (T) and hold it firmly in the crook of your thumb. Relax your hand so that it appears normal to the audience. Keep the back of your hand to the spectators so that no one can see the hidden bundle.

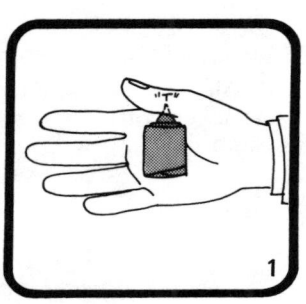

(3) Quickly bend your right fingers inward and grasp the end of the handkerchief between your first and second fingers as shown.

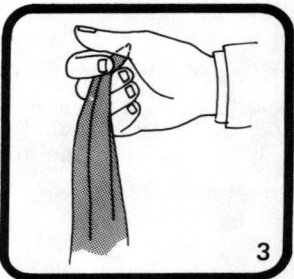

(2) To produce the handkerchief, if it is held in your right hand, turn your *right side* toward the audience. Make a "grabbing" motion in the air to your left with your right hand. As you do this, straighten out your fingers and snap your wrist sharply. This action will cause the bundle to unroll and open out quickly. You now have the handkerchief held at one corner by the crook of your right thumb.

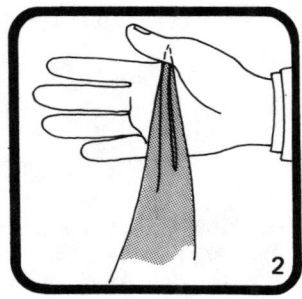

(4) Straighten out the fingers of your hand as you turn the hand palm up. The handkerchief is seen by the audience held at one end between the first and second fingers of your right hand. This completes the production sequence.

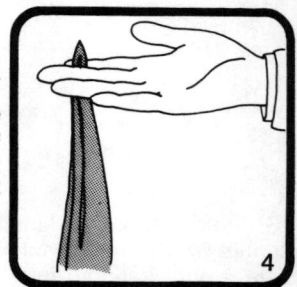

COMMENTS AND SUGGESTIONS

The "folding" and rolling of the silk handkerchief described here is a basic method used by magicians for making a handkerchief into a compact "self-contained" bundle. It has many other applications that you will use as you progress to more advanced effects in the Art of Magic.

THE VANISH OF THE HANDKERCHIEF

In order to vanish the handkerchief, you must first construct a *pull*. A "pull" is a clever device used by magicians that will enable you to cause the handkerchief to completely "disappear" in a startling manner.

SECRET AND PREPARATION

For the body of the "pull," you can use either a hollow rubber ball or a small plastic bottle.

(A) For the "ball pull," you must obtain a hollow ball that is small enough to be concealed in your hand, yet large enough to contain the handkerchief. Cut a small hole about 1" wide in the ball. This hole must be large enough for you to easily stuff the handkerchief into the ball. Then attach a length of strong, black round elastic on the other side of the ball — directly opposite the hole. Fasten a safety pin securely to the free end of the elastic.

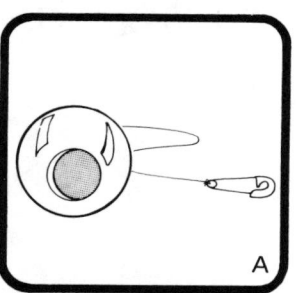

(C) *NOTE: You may construct either pull you wish, or you may find some other suitable container, such as the small metal cans which come with certain types of film, etc. In any event, the pull must be small enough so that it can be comfortably held in your fist. Just remember that if the pull is too large for your hand, your audience will see it, and the trick will be spoiled.*

(B) For the "bottle pull," obtain a small plastic bottle which will easily hold the handkerchief. (The best bottle is the kind with a snap-on or twist-on cap in which the bottom is as large as the top. These are often used as containers for pills. If you don't have one around the house, you can buy it from the pharmacist at your local drug store.) Make a small hole in the bottom of the bottle. Tie a large knot in one end of the elastic. Then, thread the other end through the mouth of the bottle and out the hole on the bottom. The knot will keep the end of the elastic from going through the hole, thus attaching it to the bottle. Tie a safety pin to the free end of the elastic.

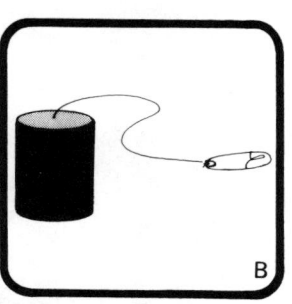

(D) After you have completed making the pull, fasten the safety pin to one of the rear belt loops of your trousers. Allow the elastic to run *beneath* the next two or three belt loops so that the pull will hang on your *left side near the seam of your trousers*. When performing the vanish, you must wear a coat or jacket so that the pull will be hidden from view.

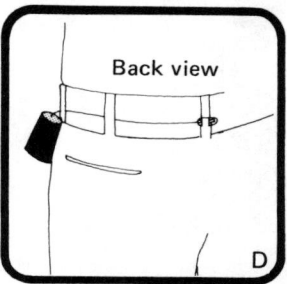

Back view

METHOD

(1) Assume that you are wearing the pull on your left side and have just produced the handkerchief from the air as described in the preceding trick. You are now prepared to vanish the handkerchief. Notice in the illustration that, as you produce the handkerchief, your left hand is momentarily hidden from the audience's view by your body.

Audience view

(2) As you produce the handkerchief with your right hand, *secretly grasp the pull with your left hand.*

Back view

Audience view   3

(3) *NOTE: At this point you should be giving your full attention to the handkerchief that is held in your right hand. At no time do you ever call attention to the hand containing the pull.*

Audience view   4

(4) Now turn your left side toward the audience as your left hand stretches the elastic attached to the pull. Your left hand should now be about six to ten inches away from your body.

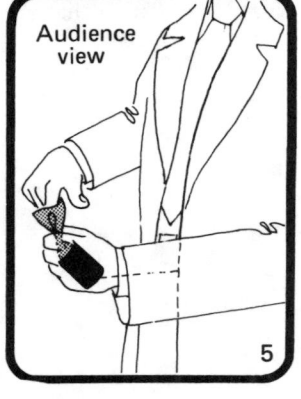

Audience view   5

(5) Place the handkerchief, which you are holding in your right hand, on top of your closed left fist. Use your right fingers to push the handkerchief into your closed left fist. Unknown to the audience, *you are pushing the handkerchief into the pull as well.*

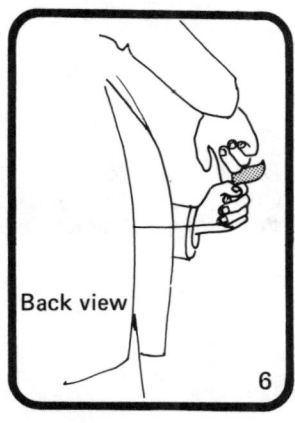

Back view   6

(6) Here is a view of the action from the rear. The right fingers are pushing the handkerchief into the pull. Notice how the elastic runs from within your closed left fist, behind your left arm, and back inside your coat.

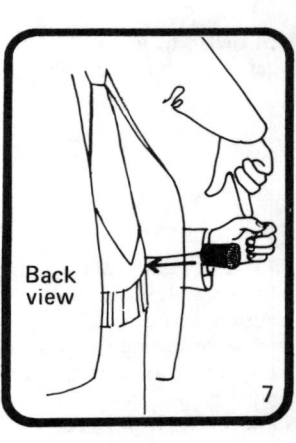

Back view   7

(7) When the entire handkerchief has been pushed into the pull, relax the left-hand grip slightly. *The pull will fly secretly out of your hand and be carried inside your coat.*

(8) *NOTE: You will have to experiment a little in order to get the elastic to the proper length to insure the maximum effect. The stretched elastic, when released, should cause the pull to go instantly inside the coat, while your left hand is held as if it still contained the handkerchief. During this action, your right index finger continues to pantomime the action of pushing the handkerchief into your closed left fist.*

Audience view   9

(9) Continue the action, pretending to pack the handkerchief into your left fist with your right index finger. As you do this, *turn full front and extend both arms slightly away from your body* without any jerking or unnatural motions. The audience is led to believe that *the handkerchief is still held inside your left fist.*

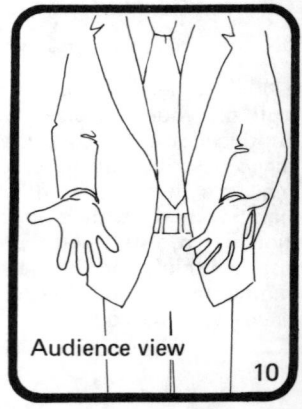

Audience view   10

(10) You may now open your left hand to show that the handkerchief has vanished without a trace. This should catch your audience totally by surprise. You may wish to pull up both your coat sleeves to prove that the handkerchief has not gone "up your sleeve."

COMMENTS AND SUGGESTIONS

It is important to remember when you release the pull, to do it in a natural manner so as not to arouse any suspicion. If the release is accompanied by any jerking of the hands, the audience may suspect "when" the dirty work was done. Remember to keep your left hand motionless when you let go of the pull. Don't worry about it; the elastic will do the work. Now that you know the moves, you can begin to practice the whole routine until the actions blend together to form a smooth, relaxed sequence.

The "pull" and the variations of the principle on which it is based are all derived from a basic magic concept with many important applications. Now that you know the important secret, you can devise many other ways to use this method of "vanishing" an object.

THE UNIVERSAL VANISHER

If you wish, you can construct a special UNIVERSAL PULL. This pull can be used to vanish a coin, button, ring, or practically any other small object as well as a handkerchief.

SECRET AND PREPARATION

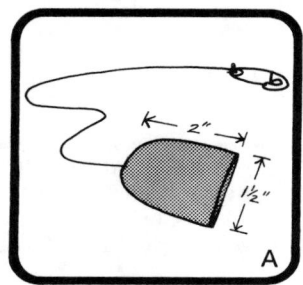

(A) Make a small bag about 1½" by 2" out of black cloth as shown.

(B) Sew two stiff plastic shirt collar stays (or cut two strips from a sheet of stiff plastic) inside the hem around the mouth of the bag. This is done so that you can open and close the bag by squeezing it between your left thumb and fingers. Attach a length of black elastic to the bottom of the bag. Fasten a safety pin to the free end of the elastic.

(C) Arrange this special pull on your body exactly as you did for the handkerchief vanish pull just described.

METHOD

(1) For the most part, the vanish using the Universal Pull is handled just like the previous model. Stand with your right side toward the audience. Secretly obtain the cloth bag from your left side as your right hand picks up the item to be vanished from your table. Once you have a firm grip on the bag, turn your left side toward the audience. As you do this action, stretch out the length of elastic attached to the pull.

(2) Squeeze the bag with your left hand until the mouth opens wide enough to allow the object to be inserted inside. With your right hand, put the object into your closed left fist. *Unknown to the audience, you place the object into the cloth bag.*

(3) Once the object is "in the bag," relax your left fingers slightly so that the mouth of the bag will close up.

(4) You may then vanish the object just as you did the handkerchief, or you may use this other optional method. Extend your left arm in a throwing motion as you release the bag. The bag will fly, unnoticed, inside your coat. You can now turn full front and show both your hands to be completely empty.

THE SERPENTINE SILK

EFFECT

The magician displays a colorful silk handkerchief which he twirls into a loose rope-like configuration and then he ties a knot in its center. Holding the handkerchief at one end, the performer causes the handkerchief to *visibly* untie itself right before the unbelieving eyes of the spectators

SECRET AND PREPARATION

(A)   You will need a silk scarf or magicians' silk handkerchief approximately 18" to 36" square and a spool of fine black nylon or silk thread. To prepare, attach one end of a six-foot length of thread to one corner of the silk handkerchief. In the illustrations that follow, this corner has been labeled A and the free end of the handkerchief is marked B. The other end of the thread must be securely fastened to the top of your table (a small thumb tack works well). Now, fold the handkerchief and place it on your table making sure that the thread is coiled next to the handkerchief as shown in the illustration. You are now ready to present this classic mystery.

METHOD

(1)   Pick up the folded handkerchief and stand approximately three feet in front of the table edge. Then, grasp Corner A in your right fingers and allow the silk to unfold in front of you. The thread should now be hanging at your right side *below your right arm.* Reach down and grasp the bottom of the handkerchief, Corner B, in your left hand and twirl the handkerchief into a loose rope-like configuration as shown. *The thread now runs across the top of your right thumb and under your right arm to the table top.*

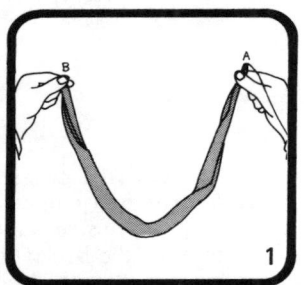

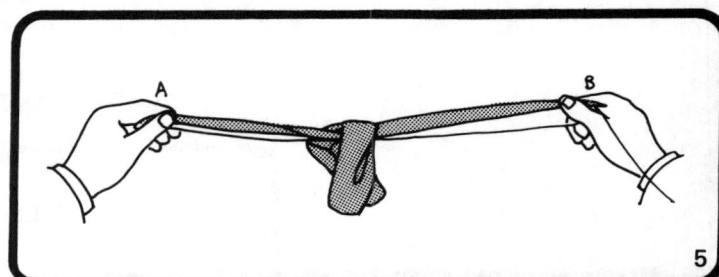

(5)   Slowly and steadily draw your hands apart, forming a loose knot in the middle of the handkerchief. The thread sewn to Corner A will be drawn *through the knot* and should now run *over* your right thumb as shown.

(2)   Now bring End A *across and over* End B as shown. As you do this, move your right hand so that the thread is being held in position *under* your right thumb.

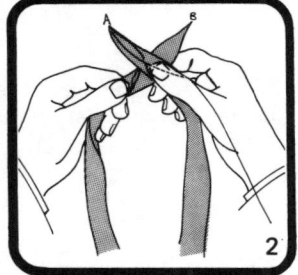

(6)   Release Corner A and allow the handkerchief to hang from your right hand. If you have performed all the steps correctly, the situation will be as follows: The thread, which is attached to Corner A, runs up and through the knot in the handkerchief.

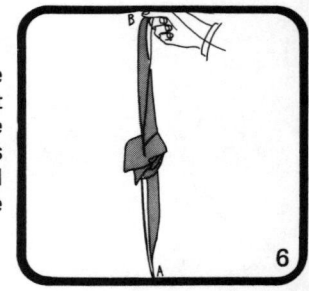

(3)   With your left hand reach through the loop formed by the handkerchief and . . .

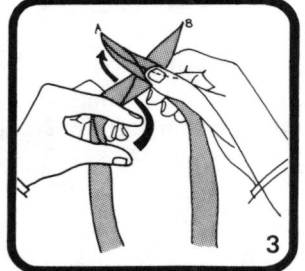

(7)   From there, it travels *up* and *over* your right thumb and then *under* your right arm to the table.

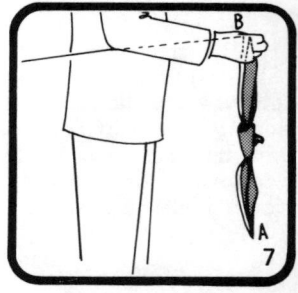

(4)   . . . grasp End A (and the thread) with the tips of your left fingers. Then pull End A back through the loop.

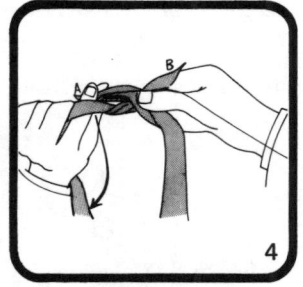

(8)   Hold the handkerchief close to your body and move forward just enough to remove any remaining slack in the thread. Now, *by extending your right arm,* the thread will begin to pull End A upward as shown.

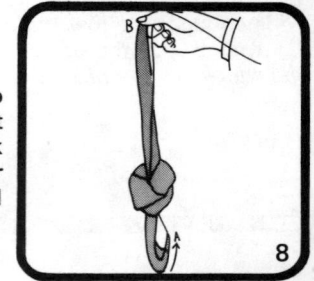

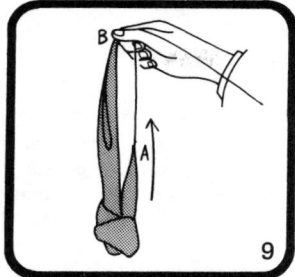

(9) As you move your arm farther from the table, End A will be drawn *into and completely through the knot* as shown.

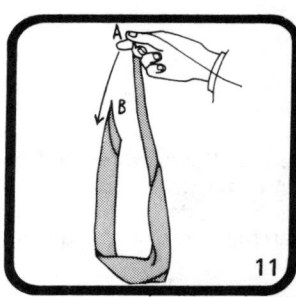

(11) ...*immediately release Corner B, let it fall from your hand, and grasp Corner A.*

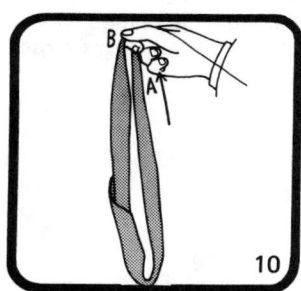

(10) Now, by moving your body slightly forward, the thread will pull the rest of the End A portion of the handkerchief through the knot, causing it to *visibly dissolve.* As soon as Corner A reaches your right fingers . . .

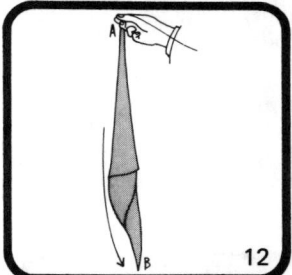

(12) You now hold the "untied" handkerchief by Corner A with Corner B hanging below as shown.

COMMENTS AND SUGGESTIONS

It will appear to the audience that the handkerchief has a life of its own and has wiggled out of its own knot. The position of the handkerchief at the end of the sequence leaves you all set to repeat the effect. This happens to be one of the rare cases in magic where repetition will help to build the mystery — but it is best to repeat the effect only once. At the conclusion, simply crumple the handkerchief and drop it on your table.

THE SERPENTINE SILK — SECOND VERSION

You may wish to try the SERPENTINE SILK by this alternate method. Use a shorter length of thread with a small plastic bead tied to the free end. The end with the thread does not run to the table as in the previous method. In this method, after the knot is tied, the bead is secretly held under your right foot. The tying of the knot is the same as before, as is the action of the untying of the knot except that this time you *lift your arm* instead of moving it forward. The benefit of this method is that you do not have to rely on a hookup to your table. With the bead-under-the-foot method, you can work the trick anywhere without fear of spoiling your set-up. You will, however, need a bit more distance from your audience as the thread is more visible since it is not hidden by your body.

THE PHANTOM

EFFECT

The magician removes his pocket handkerchief and spreads it open on the table in front of him. He then carefully folds over the four corners of the handkerchief creating a small, temporary pocket or "ghost trap" as the performer calls it. Grasping an obviously empty handful of air, the magician tells the audience that he has actually captured a *small phantom ghost*. Pretending to place his mysterious little friend inside the miniature trap, the "ghost" takes on a solid lifelike form which is clearly seen and heard through the fabric of the handkerchief. Yet, when the magician opens the handkerchief, the invisible phantom has escaped — leaving the handkerchief quite empty!

SECRET AND PREPARATION

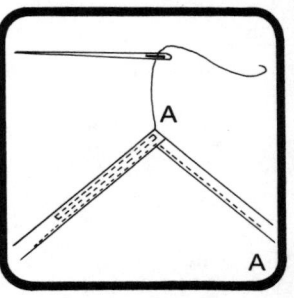

In this effect, as in THE BROKEN AND RESTORED MATCH, you need a gentleman's pocket handkerchief with a wide hem. To prepare, cut a length of coat hanger wire (or any similar thin, stiff wire) approximately 2½" long. Carefully insert the wire into the hem of the handkerchief at one corner (Corner A in the illustrations). Now sew the wire into place with a needle and thread. Fold the handkerchief and put it in your pocket. You will also need a common metal spoon. You are now ready to perform this excellent close-up mystery.

METHOD

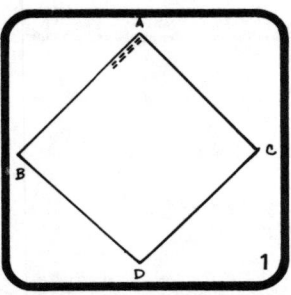

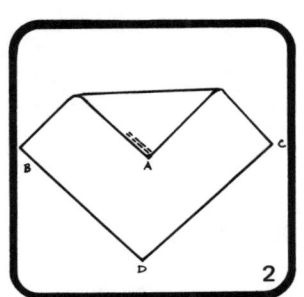

(1) To begin the presentation, remove the prepared handkerchief from your pocket and spread it open on the table in front of you. Corner D should be nearest you, pointing in your direction. Corner A, which contains the short length of wire, should be closest to the spectators. (2) With your right hand, grasp Corner A and fold it up and over to the center of the handkerchief as shown.

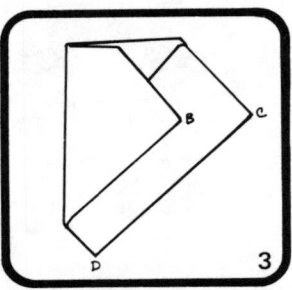

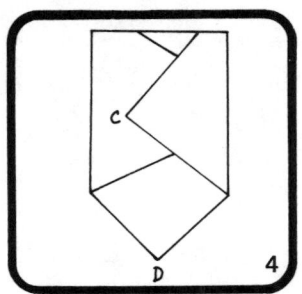

(3) Grasp Corner B in your left hand and fold it *over* Corner A as shown. (4) Now, grasp Corner C in your right hand and fold it over *both* Corners A and B so that it is even with the left edge of the handkerchief as shown. You will notice that the three folded Corners A, B, and C form a sort of "pocket" with the opening of the pocket facing you at Corner D.

(5) With your right hand, reach out and *pretend* to grasp something from the air. State that you have just caught a small "invisible ghost." Be sure your audience realizes that your hand is *quite empty* and that you are merely *pretending* to hold something in your hand.

(6) With your left hand, slightly raise the three folded corners (A, B and C), opening the "pocket" just enough to insert your right hand as if to give the illusive spirit a place to hide. Now, while your hand is inside the pocket, *grasp the secret wire that is sewn in Corner A and stand the wire upright, on its end.*

(7) As soon as the wire is secure in this position, remove your right hand from inside the pocket and release your hold on the handkerchief with your left hand. The wire will stand on its own accord due to the weight of the fabric. This creates the illusion of "something" within the folds of the handkerchief. With your left hand, lift Corner D and fold it up and over the opening of the pocket, thus imprisoning the "ghost" inside.

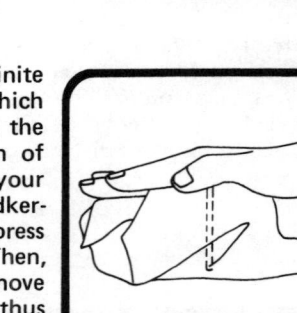

(8) The spectators will see a definite form inside the handkerchief, which you claim to be your little friend, the ghost. To further convince them of his presence, place the palm of your hand directly on top of the handkerchief, allowing the secret wire to press against the middle of your palm. Then, with a slight downward pressure, move your hand in a circular motion, thus creating the very eerie illusion of a *solid, round object* inside the handkerchief.

(9) The real convincer comes with this next move: Hold a spoon in your right hand — *then hit the end of the secret wire several times with the back of the spoon.* The noise created by the spoon against the hidden wire will convince the spectators — not only *visually*, but *audibly* as well — that you have really "captured" the small phantom.

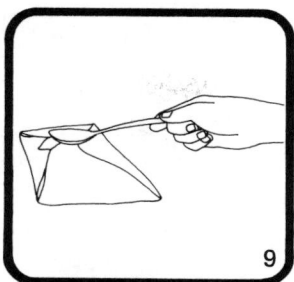

(10) To bring the mystery to its conclusion, set the spoon aside and quickly snap the handkerchief open, allowing the ghost to make his escape. Immediately show your hands and the handkerchief completely empty. Casually put the handkerchief in your pocket, leaving your audience totally baffled!

THE BROKEN AND RESTORED MATCH

EFFECT

The magician displays a wooden kitchen match and gives it to a spectator for examination. The performer then spreads out his pocket handkerchief on the table and places the match on the handkerchief near the center. He now folds the four corners of the handkerchief over the match so it is hidden from view. The magician asks the spectator to grip the match in both hands, through the folds of cloth, and break it into a number of pieces. Without any suspicious moves, the performer unfolds the handkerchief revealing the match *completely unharmed* — fully restored to its original condition!

SECRET AND PREPARATION

The secret to this mystery depends on the use of a certain type of handkerchief. It must be the kind which has a *wide hem* around the sides. This enables you to secretly conceal a duplicate match inside the hem. The audience is never aware of the duplicate match. NOTE: *Toothpicks* may also be used quite effectively in this trick instead of matches.

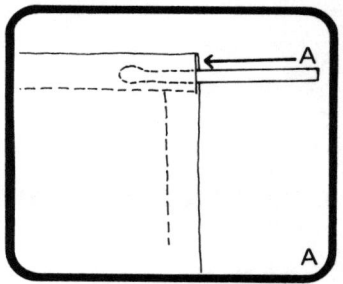

(A) To prepare, carefully insert the match into the open end of the hem of the handkerchief. Push it just far enough inside so that it is completely hidden from view. In the illustrations, the corners of the handkerchief have been labeled A, B, C, and D with the match inside the hem at Corner A. Fold the handkerchief and place it in your pocket and have a box of duplicate matches handy for the presentation.

METHOD

(1) Display the box of matches and open it, requesting that a spectator select one match to use in the trick. This done, remove your handkerchief (with the secret match hidden in the hem) and spread it on the table in front of you. Place the handkerchief so that the hidden match is in the *lower right-hand corner* (A) nearest you. Now, take the match from the spectator and place it in the center of the handkerchief as shown. Note that both matches are running parallel to one another at the start.

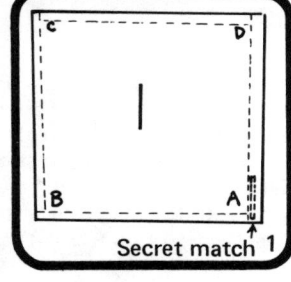

Secret match 1

(2) Now, fold Corner A up and over the center of the handkerchief placing the secret match by the selected match. Notice that the *selected* match and the *secret* match are now perpendicular to each other. This way, it will be easy for you to distinguish which match is which *without having to see them.* Now you can rely upon your sense of touch to tell them apart.

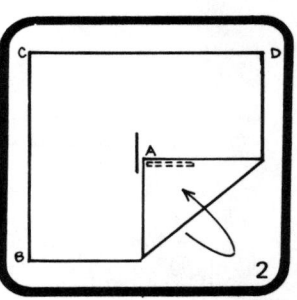

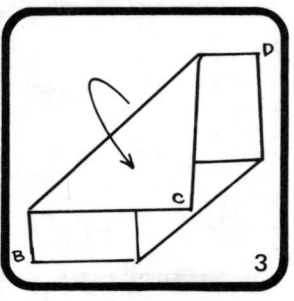

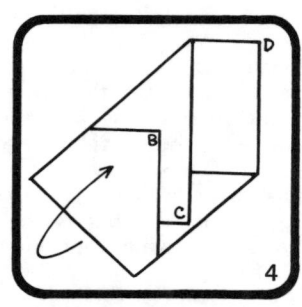

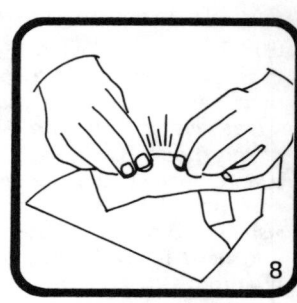

(3) Next, fold the top left Corner C over the selected match and over Corner A as shown. (4) Then fold Corner B over Corners A and C as in the illustration.

(7) Now, hand the match to the spectator and (8) instruct him to break it several times through the fabric of the handkerchief. *He believes he is breaking the same match which he just selected and watched you fold inside the handkerchief.*

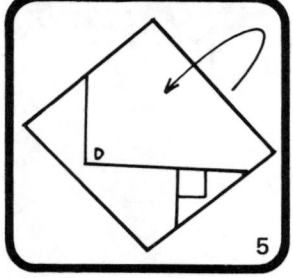

(5) Finally, bring Corner D over Corners A, B, and C as shown.
(6) Now, openly and deliberately grasp the *secret match* through the folds of the handkerchief and hold it between the thumb and fingers of both hands. You can be sure to grasp the secret match easily by simply "feeling" for the match that runs parallel to the edge of the table nearest you. *NOTE: The <u>selected match</u> remains within the handkerchief.*

(9) When the spectator is quite satisfied that the match has been completely destroyed, slowly and deliberately unfold each corner of the handkerchief one at a time.

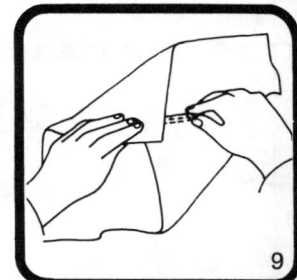

(10) As you unfold Corner C with your left hand, keep your right hand over Corner A to conceal any possible bulge or disconfiguration of the hem, due to the broken shape of the secret match. When you have completely opened the handkerchief, the audience will be amazed to see that the broken match is now completely restored.

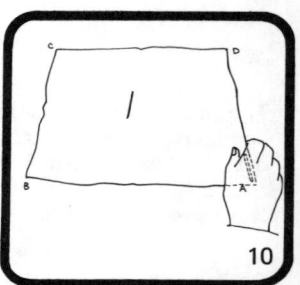

(11) Immediately give the match to the spectator for examination. Hold up the handkerchief, shake it, and show it on both sides so that all can see that it is completely empty before you casually replace it in your pocket.

EGGS FROM NOWHERE

EFFECT

The magician calls attention to a woven basket and a folded handkerchief resting on his table. Picking up the handkerchief, he unfolds it and shows it to be quite ordinary by displaying both sides. Folding the handkerchief in half to form a sort of "pocket," the magician causes an egg to make its magical appearance inside and "allows" it to fall from within the folds of the handkerchief into the basket. Repeating the same procedure, *another* egg appears and is dropped into the basket. This production continues, egg after egg, until the audience is sure that the basket is *nearly full.* Setting the handkerchief aside, the magician removes one of the eggs from the basket and breaks it into a glass to prove that it is genuine. Then, picking up the basket, the magician throws the contents into the air *directly over the audience.* To their surprise — and relief — the eggs have magically transformed into a SHOWER OF CONFETTI!

SECRET AND PREPARATION

(A) The items necessary for this effect are an opaque handkerchief (a bandana is ideal), a medium-sized basket, a gentleman's hat or a similar sized box, and a plastic egg. This type of egg can be purchased from a novelty or "dime" store and is especially easy to find during the Easter season. The basket, hat, or box should be opaque, so that the spectators cannot see through, and deep enough to conceal a quantity of confetti and one *real* egg. You will also need some confetti (or just tear some paper into small pieces), a glass, and some fine sewing thread *which closely matches the color of the handkerchief.*

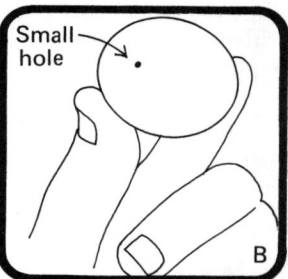

(B) To prepare, drill a small hole in one end of the hollow plastic egg as shown. Also cut a piece of thread about 12" long (the length of the thread will depend upon the size of the handkerchief and the basket).

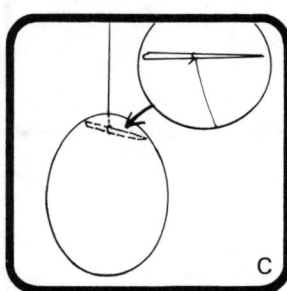 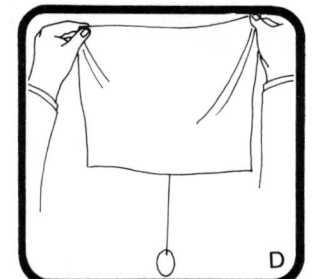 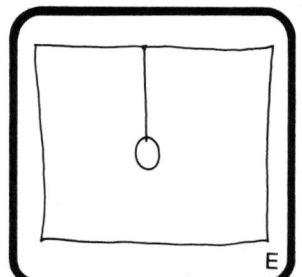 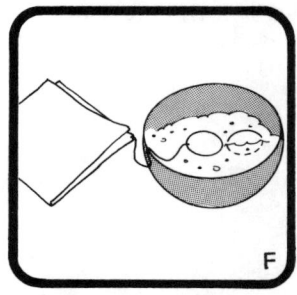

(C) Tie a short piece of toothpick to one end fo the thread. Push the toothpick through the hole in the egg, and the thread will be secured to the egg as shown. (You can also use transparent tape to secure the thread to the egg.) (D) Now, sew the other end of the thread to the *middle* of the hem of the handkerchief as shown. (E) As shown here, the length of the thread should be long enough to allow the egg to hang just below the center of the handkerchief. (F) Fold the handkerchief and place it on the table next to the basket. The thread should run *from* the handkerchief *into* the basket with the egg lying in the basket as shown. The basket should also contain a quantity of confetti and one real egg. *(NOTE: The real egg should be down in the confetti to protect it from the plastic egg when it falls into the basket.)*

METHOD

(1) To begin the presentation, pick up the handkerchief by the lower two corners (C and D) and display it on both sides as shown. The egg remains concealed in the basket.

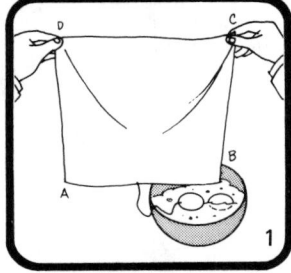

(2) Now lay the handkerchief partially over the basket with the top hem (the hem with the attached thread) draped across the opening of the basket. The center of this hem, where the thread is attached, should be *directly above* the plastic egg in the basket.

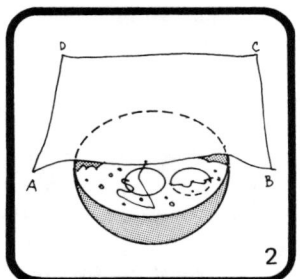

(3) Show your hands empty and grasp the handkerchief at Corners A and B as shown.

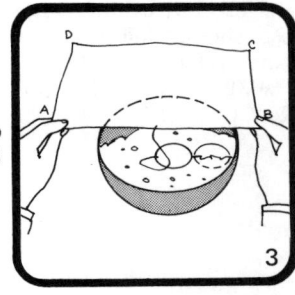

(4) Keep the top hem *stretched tightly between both hands* as you lift the handkerchief upward, away from the table and the basket. The thread will secretly draw the plastic egg *out* of the basket *behind* the handkerchief as shown. Keep the handkerchief stretched tightly so that you do not allow the weight of the egg to pull down the top hem of the handkerchief.

(5) Now, place the top corners (A and B) together in your left hand, hiding the plastic egg completely within the folds of the handkerchief. Hold both corners (A and B) with your left hand as you . . .

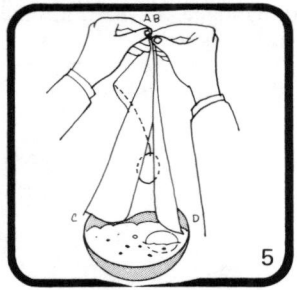

(10) Now, grasp the right Corner B in your right hand while continuing to hold the other Corner A in your left and draw your two hands apart as shown. *Be sure the entire bottom edge of the handkerchief (C and D) is resting in front of the bowl as you stretch the handkerchief open.*

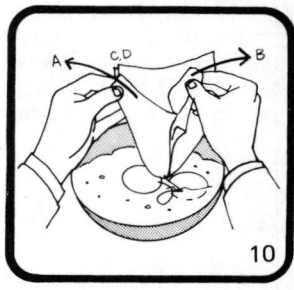

(6) . . . reach down with your right hand and grasp the two lower corners (C and D). (Be sure you have folded the handkerchief *around* the hanging egg.)

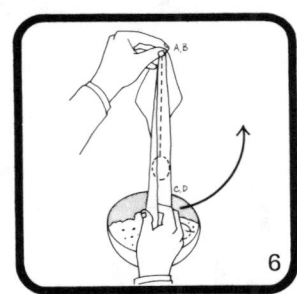

(11) As you draw your hands apart, raise the top corners (A and B), *again secretly drawing the plastic egg out of the basket behind the handkerchief,* ready to make its magical reappearance.

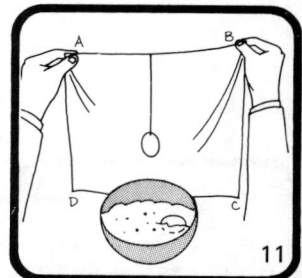

(7) Then swing those corners (C and D) upward — to your right — as shown.

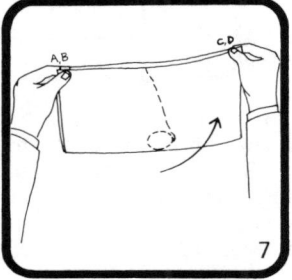

(12) Repeat Steps 5 through 7 to fold the egg inside the handkerchief as you did the first time. Tilt the handkerchief, and a "second" egg (really the same egg) falls out.

(8) The folded handkerchief should now be broadside to the audience. Raise the right hand corners (C and D) slightly upward and gently shake the egg out of the handkerchief. The egg should fall into the basket and land safely on the confetti. YOU HAVE JUST "MAGICALLY" PRODUCED AN EGG FROM AN EMPTY HANDKERCHIEF!

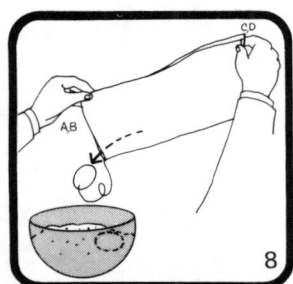

(13) Follow the sequences as described from Step 9 through Step 12 for each egg you want to "produce." When you wish to conclude the production portion of the trick, repeat the procedure only through Step 11. At this point simply gather the handkerchief and place it aside, *with the plastic egg concealed inside its folds.*

(9) After the egg lands in the basket, toss the right hand corners (C and D) of the folded handkerchief on the table in front of the bowl leaving the two top corners (A and B) in your left hand.

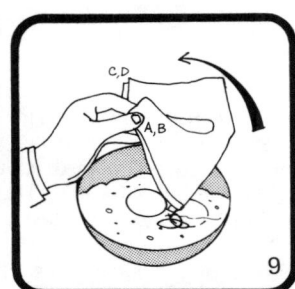

(14) Now, remove the *real egg* from the basket and display it as you pick up the glass in your other hand. Then, deliberately break the egg in the glass, proving it to be genuine.

(15) For a conclusion, pick up the basket from your table and carry it toward the audience. They believe it is full of *real eggs.* Suddenly, toss the contents of the basket into the air above the audience *showering them with confetti!* If you have followed all of the steps correctly and practiced the trick well before you present it, you will now have a very surprised and very bewildered audience.

THE VANISHING GLASS

EFFECT

The magician openly exhibits an ordinary drinking glass. Covering the glass with a handkerchief, the performer lifts the glass into the air. The audience can plainly see that the glass is under the handkerchief. Suddenly, the magician throws the bundle high above his head. Instantly, the glass *vanishes* . . . allowing the empty handkerchief to flutter into the magician's hands.

SECRET AND PREPARATION

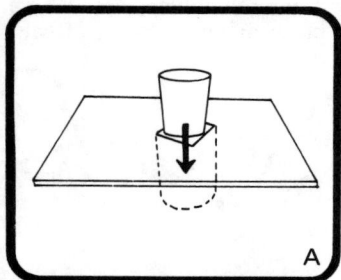

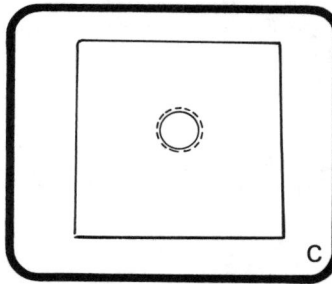
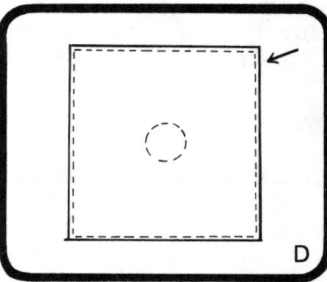

(A)   To present this effect, you must have a magician's table with a "well," like the one described elsewhere in the Course. You will also need an ordinary drinking glass. The glass must fit comfortably into the "well" in your table.

(B)   Cut a disc of plastic or cardboard just slightly larger than the mouth of the glass.

(C)   You will also need two matching handkerchiefs. (If possible, the handkerchiefs should have some kind of pattern or design on them.) Sew the disc to the center of one of the handkerchiefs.

(D)   Now cover the handkerchief and its attached disc with the duplicate handkerchief. Carefully sew the two handkerchiefs together around the edges with the disc sandwiched in between. Put the glass on your table with the folded handkerchief next to it and you are ready to perform.

METHOD

(1)   Pick up the glass and display it. Put the glass back on your table just in front of the "well." Now pick up the handkerchief. Snap it open so that the audience can see that it is apparently unprepared. Hold the handkerchief with the thumb and first fingers of each hand and position it behind the glass as shown.

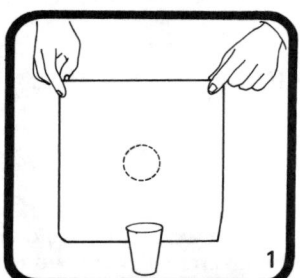
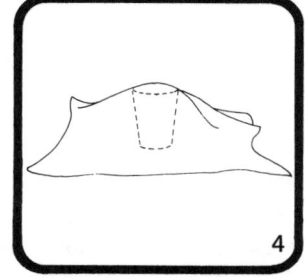
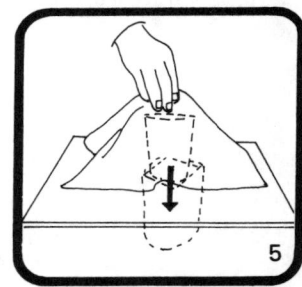

(4)   With the glass completely covered and the disc over the mouth of the glass, grasp the disc *and* the glass through the fabric of the handkerchief. *Without lifting the glass, slide it backward until it is directly over the "well" in your table.*   (5)   Now, while still holding onto the disc, LET THE GLASS SLIDE INTO THE WELL. *The disc will maintain the shape of the glass under the handkerchief.*

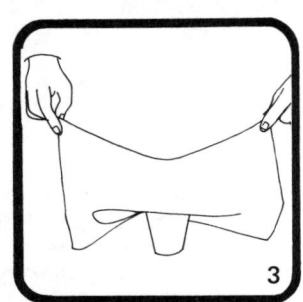

(2)   The next move is critical. As you place the handkerchief over the glass,   (3)   . . .be sure that the hidden disc *goes over the mouth of the glass.*

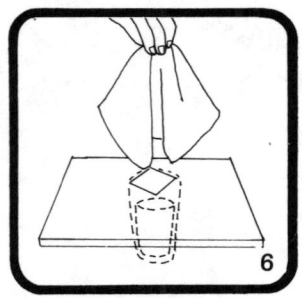

(6) Lift the handkerchief clear of the table and walk forward. The disc should be held lightly with your thumb and fingers *so that it appears that the glass is still under the handkerchief.*

(7) Throw the handkerchief high into the air. The effect upon an audience is that the glass *vanishes* into thin air. Crumple the handkerchief and drop it on your table.

COMMENTS AND SUGGESTIONS

Apparently having an object under a handkerchief or cloth after it has actually "gone" is an important basic principle of magic. This effect is a classic example of the use of this principle. The "secret disc" concealed in the handkerchief leads the audience to believe that the glass is still there long after it has gone. This subtle method will be of great value to you in the performance of many effects. There is even an "impromptu" version of the Vanishing Glass, which is described in the following.

THE VANISHING GLASS — IMPROMPTU VERSION

EFFECT

While seated at a table, the magician covers an empty glass with his pocket handkerchief. He raises the covered glass from the table and then throws the handkerchief in the air . . . *the glass has vanished.* The magician reaches under the table, directly below the spot where the handkerchief landed, and reproduces the glass. The glass has apparently penetrated the table!

SECRET AND PREPARATION

You will need the same special handkerchief with the disc sewn in it as described in The Vanishing Glass. You will also need a glass with the mouth approximately the same size as the disc. The effect is even better when this trick is performed in an impromptu manner . . . using an empty glass that is already on the table . . . for instance, after dinner or when you are seated with friends at a party.

METHOD

(1) The presentation of this effect is exactly the same as in Steps 1 to 4 of the VANISHING GLASS except, instead of dropping the glass into the well on your table, you merely move the handkerchief back past the edge of the table and drop the glass into your lap!

(3) Now, as you hold the glass and handkerchief with your right hand, hold your left hand up, palm towards the spectators. Say, "As you can see, there is nothing in my left hand."

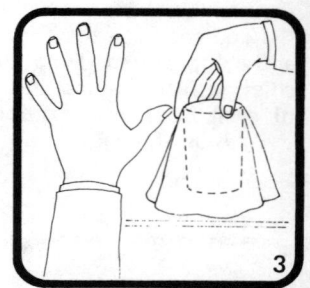

(2) This can be done quite effectively in the following manner. Cover the glass with the handkerchief, being sure that the disc is properly positioned over the mouth of the glass. Pick the glass and the handkerchief up in your right hand as shown.

(4) *As you show your left hand, move the handkerchief and the glass back over the edge of the table so that the edge of the handkerchief is still touching the top of the table.* As you display your empty left hand, DROP THE GLASS INTO YOUR LAP.

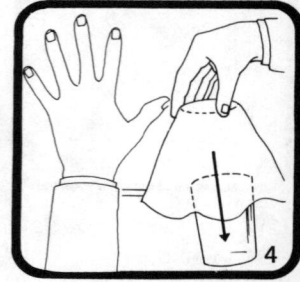

(5) Holding the "secret" disc by the edges in your right hand, move the now "empty" handkerchief (as if it still covered the glass) back over the table.

(6) Say, "And, there is nothing under the handkerchief!" As you say this, at the same time, throw the handkerchief up into the air. Catch it as it comes down and show the handkerchief on both sides. Then drop it onto the table in front of you.

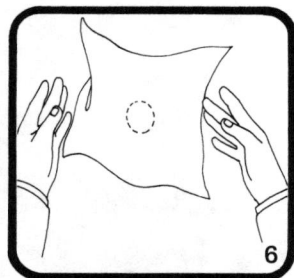

(7) Show both hands empty and reach under the table. As you do, say, "The reason that you don't see the glass any more is because it has gone right through the table . . . like this." As your hands go under the table, with your right hand pick up the glass from your lap and carry it under the table to a spot directly beneath the crumpled handkerchief. With a "pulling motion" apparently "extract" the glass from the table. Bring the glass out and set it on the table and put the handkerchief back in your pocket.

IMPROMPTU MAGIC

Here are some "quick tricks" that you can do anywhere at any time. Some are puzzles rather than tricks, others are more in the nature of stunts, but the majority are quite deceptive and all will arouse interest among people who see them. In fact, that is the great purpose of this branch of magic, for once you have gained people's interest with something trivial and find that they want to see more, you can go into your regular routine with confidence, since you know you already have a receptive audience.

Certain of these impromptu tricks are sometimes termed "ice-breakers" because when people seem cold or aloof, particularly at a party where very few know one another, they will often "thaw" quite rapidly when you show them a few bafflers. Also, some of these tricks, particularly the puzzle type, are expendable, in the sense that as a part of the presentation, you can explain them to your audience and they can use them to "puzzle" their friends as well.

This is quite important when you are doing magic for your friends, as they are very apt to ask you how some tricks are done and at times, you may find it difficult to refuse them. So, to keep from reaching the point where you have to choose between losing a good trick or a good friend, you can come up with one of these "quickies" to divert attention from something more important.

At the same time, as always, never explain any of the real "magic" bafflers. Keep these impromptu effects for yourself—because, as you advance in magic, you will find that some of the keenest spectators, when describing later what you did are apt to magnify trifling perplexities into near-miracles. When that happens, it is up to you, as a magician, to turn it to your own advantage.

THE JUMPING RUBBER BAND

EFFECT

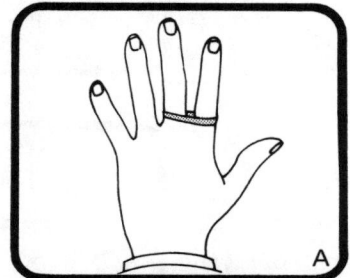 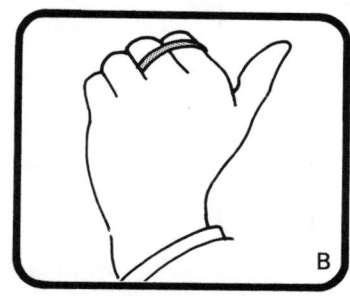 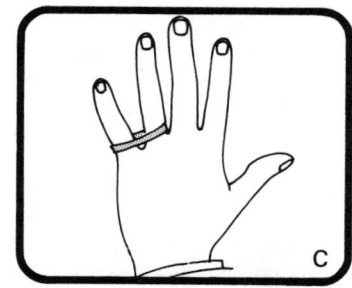

(A) The magician places a rubber band around his first and second fingers. (B) He closes his hand into a fist. (C) When he opens his hand, the band "magically" jumps to his third and fourth fingers. (A, B, and C show the spectator's viewpoint. In all the illustrations the magician's fingers are pointing "up.")

METHOD

(All illustrations are as the magician sees the trick.)

(1) Place the rubber band around the base of your first and second fingers on your left hand. If the band is too loose, you may put it around twice. Experiment with whatever rubber band you're using, so that you get the proper tension on the band. Your hand is toward the audience — and your palm faces you.

(3) This is how your hand now looks to you. (To the audience, your hand will appear as in (B).

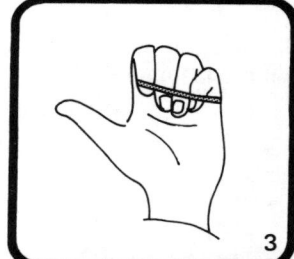

(2) Close your left hand into a fist by bending your fingers into your palm. At the same time, secretly use the first finger of your right hand to stretch the rubber band so that the tips of all four left fingers can be inserted into the rubber band.

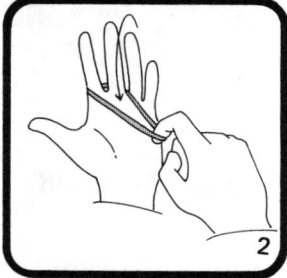

(4) Now straighten out your fingers and the band will automatically jump to a new position around your left third and fourth fingers.

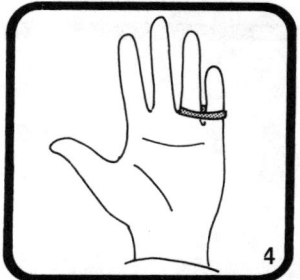

REVERSE JUMPING RUBBER BAND

EFFECT

The magician makes the rubber band jump *back* from his third and fourth fingers to his first and second fingers.

METHOD

(1) Simply reverse the procedure used for the first jump.

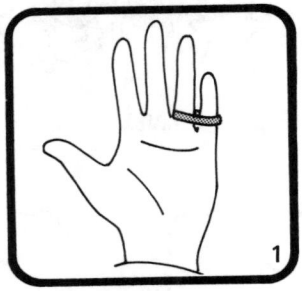

(4) Then, when you close your left hand, secretly insert the tips of all four left fingers as you did before.

(2) After the band has "jumped" to your third and fourth fingers, fold your hand into a fist again. As you do, use the first finger of your right hand to stretch the rubber band.

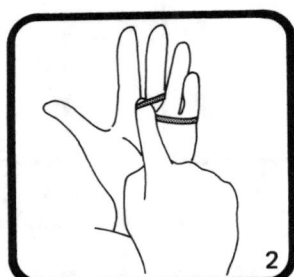

(5) When you straighten out your fingers, the band will jump *back* to your first and second fingers.

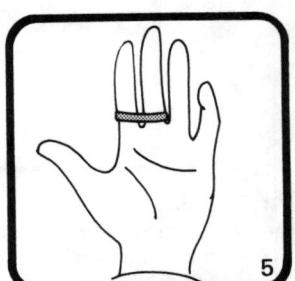

(3) Another way is to use your left thumb to stretch the band.

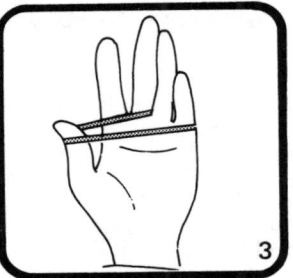

THE DOUBLE JUMPING RUBBER BAND
VERSION I

EFFECT

You can double the mystery of this trick by magically making two rubber bands change places.

METHOD

(1) Place *one* rubber band (a white one, for instance) around your left first and second fingers. Place a *second,* different colored rubber band (say a blue one) around your left third and fourth fingers.

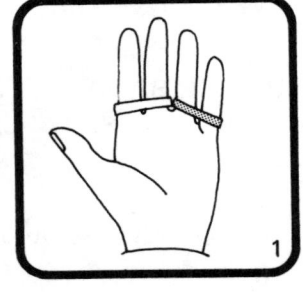

(2) Before you close your hand into a fist, reach over with your left thumb and stretch the rubber band that is around the third and fourth fingers as shown.

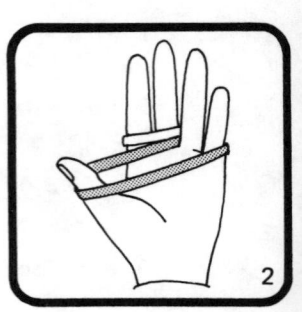

(3) Then, use your right first finger to pull the band that is around the first and second fingers of your left hand as shown.

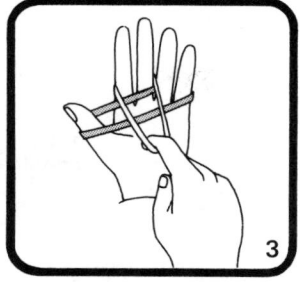

(6) Call to the spectator's attention that the *white* band is around your first and second fingers, and the *blue* band is around your third and fourth fingers. To the audience, it looks like this.

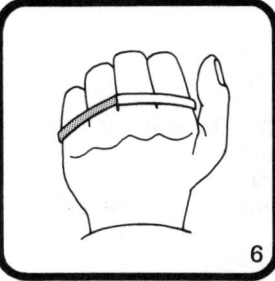

(4) Now, secretly place the tips of all four fingers into BOTH rubber bands as you close your hand. The fingers of the left hand go into the opening indicated by the arrow.

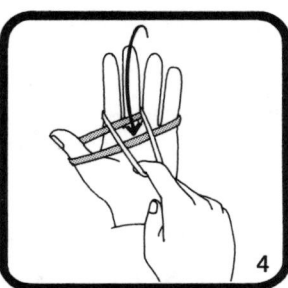

(7) Now, just straighten out your fingers. THE BANDS WILL JUMP TO THE OPPOSITE FINGERS.

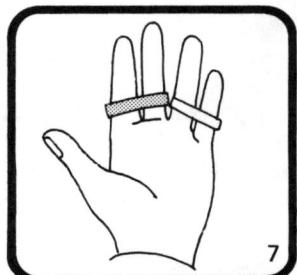

(5) At the same time that you insert the fingers of the left hand into the bands, release both the bands from your left thumb and from the first finger of the right hand. Your hand will look like this to you.

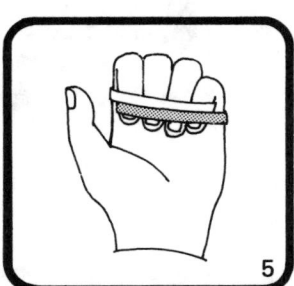

THE DOUBLE JUMPING RUBBER BAND
SECOND VERSION

EFFECT

The effect is the same as in the DOUBLE JUMPING RUBBER BAND described above; however, the "secret" method is slightly different.

METHOD

(1) Place the two rubber bands on your fingers as before.

(2) With the *first finger* of the right hand, secretly nip each of the bands.

(3) Then insert the *second finger* of the right hand into the loops formed by the right first finger and spread the loops open, using both right fingers.

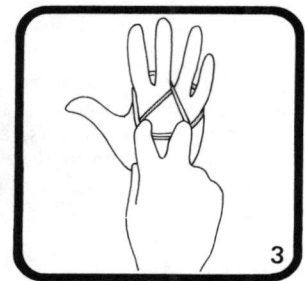

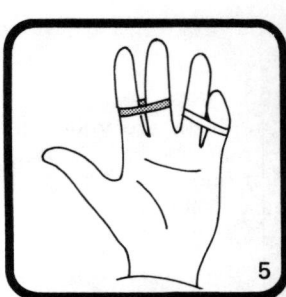

(5) Just straighten out your fingers in the usual way and the bands will change places.

(4) Fold your left hand into a fist and insert the tips of the left fingers into the opening formed by the right fingers. To you, your hand looks like this.

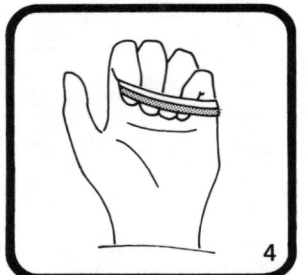

THE CHALLENGE JUMPING RUBBER BAND

EFFECT

This can be used as a follow-up for either the Regular or Double Jumping Rubber Bands. You explain that to make it *impossible* for the band to jump, you will encircle the tips of all of the fingers of your left hand individually with another rubber band.

METHOD

(1) Place an additional rubber band around the tips of the fingers of your left hand, as shown in the picture.

(2) Then proceed in exactly the same way as you did before: fold your hand into a fist, inserting the tips of the fingers into the band which is to jump. Straighten out your fingers, and behold — another minor miracle — the band jumped just as before!

The adding of the extra band to "lock in" the jumper is a clever touch which makes a simple trick into a very strong effect.

LINKING PAPER CLIPS

This is a most entertaining combination magic trick and puzzle. After you perform it, everyone will want to try it . . . and if someone should figure it out, don't worry — they'll have as much fun with it as you.

EFFECT

You show two paper clips and a dollar bill. Then you give the bill a three-way fold and use the clips to fasten the folds in place. As you pull the ends of the pleated bill, slowly but steadily the clips come closer together. You finish the pull with a sharp snap as the clips fly from the bill and land on the table . . . *linked together!*

The trick is almost automatic. It depends entirely upon proper placement of the clips. Practice the setup until you can place the clips in position quickly and neatly, so observers will be unable to follow, and therefore find it difficult to duplicate the trick.

(1) Start by holding the bill open between both hands.

(2) Fold one-third of the length of the bill over to the right as shown.

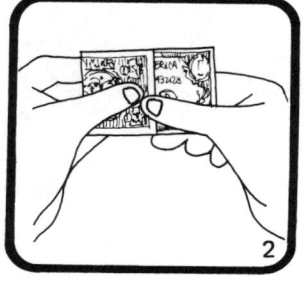

(3) Place one of the paper clips over this fold to hold it in place, and push it down so it is snug against the top edge of the bill.

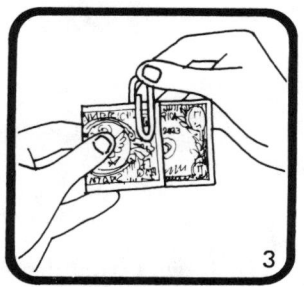

(4) The clip should be positioned near the end of the folded portion of the bill directly over the number that shows its value.

(5) Now turn the bill completely *around* so you are looking at the other side. *Do not* turn the bill "upside down" in the process . . . the clip should still be at the top as shown.

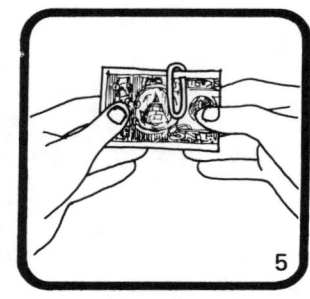

(6) Fold the left end of the bill over to the right as shown in the illustration.

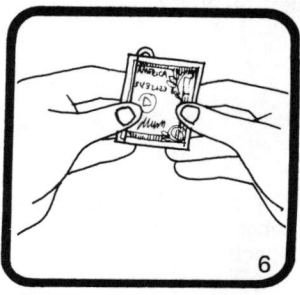

(7) Put the other paper clip on the bill from the top, thus holding this end in place, too. Clip together *just the two front folds*—those that are *toward you.*

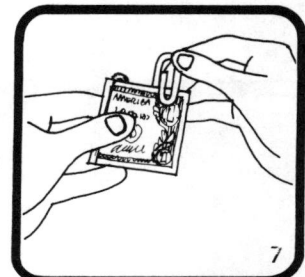

(8) Again, the clip should be positioned near the end of the bill over its number value, as shown here.

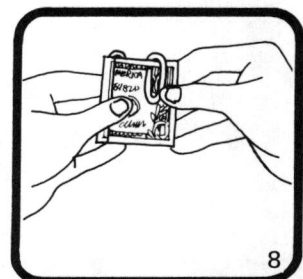

(9) *NOTE: If both clips have been properly placed the bill should look as shown in this view.*

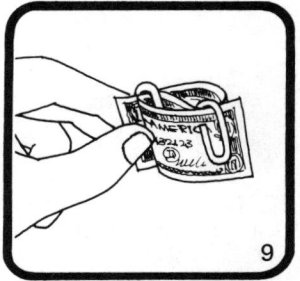

(10) Now firmly grip both ends of the bill near the top and start to pull them apart. As the bill unfolds, the clips will start moving together still pinned to the bill.

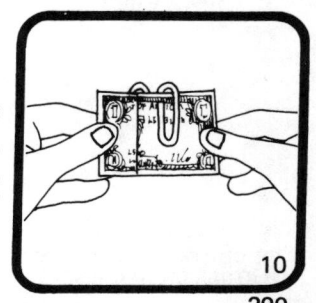

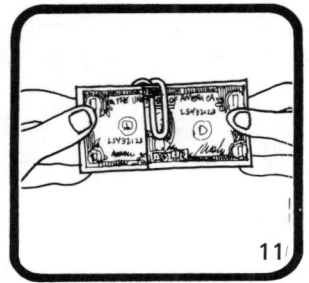

11

12

(11) When you reach the point where the clips are practically on top of each other, give the ends of the bill a sharp tug.

(12) The bill will open out and send the paper clips sailing across the table, linking them as they go!

COMMENTS AND SUGGESTIONS

The trick is particularly effective with "jumbo" clips, which are longer and wider so the linking can be followed easily. With ordinary paper clips, only a slight tug is needed; otherwise they may fly clear across the table as they link — and if they go off the edge, the effect will be weakened.

With practice, placing the clips in position becomes a simple and rapid process. If using small clips, you can put two on the top edge and another pair on the bottom edge. The tug will shoot them in opposite directions and each pair will be found linked.

LINKING PAPER CLIPS WITH RUBBER BAND

EFFECT

Here is a clever addition to the LINKING PAPER CLIP where the two clips mysteriously link themselves — but also link to a rubber band which was previously looped around the bill. This little twist not only takes the effect one step further, but also creates a very puzzling finish for the Linking Paper Clips.

METHOD

(1) Follow Steps 1 through 4 as already described in the Linking Paper Clips placing the first clip over the folded portion of the bill as shown.

(3) Fold back the right end of the bill and attach the second paper clip as you did in the original routine. If both clips and the rubber band have been properly placed, the bill should look like this.

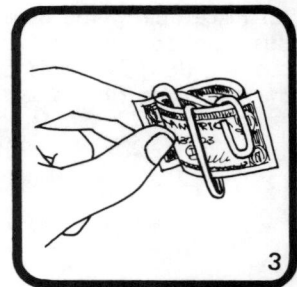

3

(2) Now, loop a rubber band of the size shown around the *right end of the bill.* The rubber band should be slightly longer than the width of the bill so that a portion of the band hangs below the bottom edge of the bill.

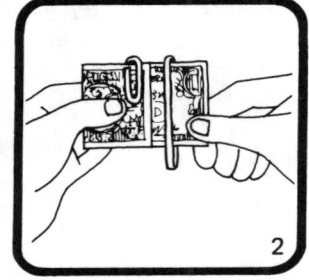

2

(4) Now, firmly grip both ends of the bill and pull them apart. The rubber band will remain looped around the bill with the paper clips linked to it in a chain as shown.

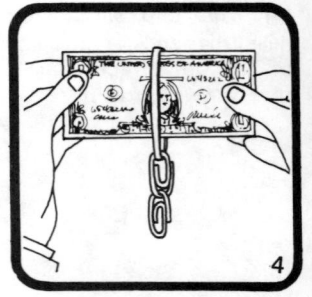

4

COMMENTS AND SUGGESTIONS

It is a good idea to practice this a few times until you understand "why" it works as it does. Once you understand the working, concentrate on placing the paper clips and the rubber band in *exactly the same position* every time you perform the trick. You can then succeed in baffling your audience without fear of any "mistake" in the handling of the props.

BAG TAG ESCAPE

EFFECT

The performer displays a typical paper tag and gives it to the nearest spectator to examine. A second spectator is given a length of string to examine. The tag and the string prove to be normal in every respect. The magician then proceeds to thread the string through the small hole in the tag. He then gives one end of the string to each spectator to hold. With the tag hanging in the center of the string, the magician covers the string and the tag with his pocket handkerchief. Reaching beneath the handkerchief, the performer "magically" removes the tag from the center of the string *without damage to either!* The spectators are left holding the now empty string suspended between them with no explanation for the mystery they have just witnessed.

SECRET AND PREPARATION

(A) For this trick you will need to construct some small tags from cardboard. (Filing card stock is best.) The tags should be cut so that they measure approximately 3" x 1½" in size. Shape the tags by cutting off the two top corners at a 45-degree angle and then punch a hole in the center of the top edge of each of the tags as shown. The result will be a tag which closely resembles a standard baggage tag in every respect *except one.* Most standard tags are <u>heavily reinforced</u> around the small hole so that they will not tear when fastened to some object. This slight difference is what makes the entire effect possible. You will also need a piece of string about two feet long which you place on the table along with *one* of the tags. Place an ordinary handkerchief in your left pocket and a *duplicate tag* in your <u>right coat sleeve</u> so that it is out of view of the audience.

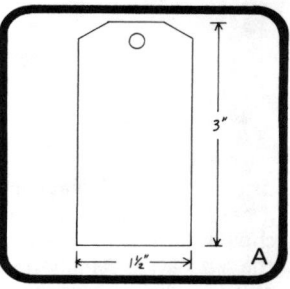

METHOD

(1) To begin the presentation, ask for the assistance of two spectators. Hand one of the spectators the tag for examination and the other spectator the length of string. When they are satisfied that everything is unprepared, thread the string through the small hole at the top of the tag as shown in the illustration.

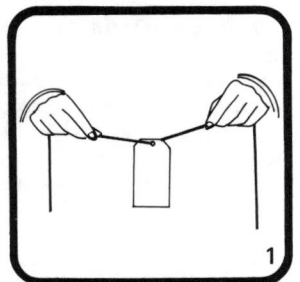

(4) Carefully TEAR THROUGH THE TAG to the hole. Then remove the torn tag from the string.

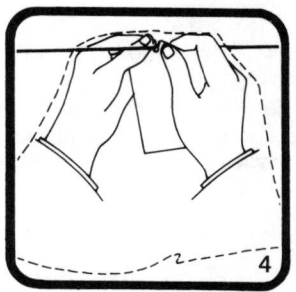

(2) Now, give one end of the string to each spectator, leaving the suspended tag imprisoned on the string.

(5) *NOTE: You may find it helpful to raise both hands slightly upward, thus lifting the handkerchief away from the tag. This will prevent the spectators from "seeing" the motion of what is actually taking place.*

(3) Remove your handkerchief from your pocket, show it to be completely empty, and cover the tag *and* the center of the string as shown. Be sure the handkerchief is spread open enough to provide the "cover" necessary to conceal your hands beneath it. This done, reach under the handkerchief with both hands and grasp the tag near the hole at the top.

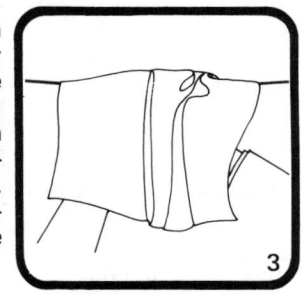

(6) With the fingers of your right hand, secretly insert the <u>torn</u> tag *into your left coat sleeve.*

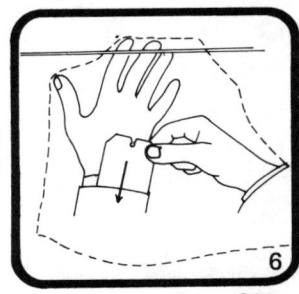

(7) Now exchange hand positions so that your left hand can withdraw the <u>duplicate</u> tag from your right sleeve as shown.

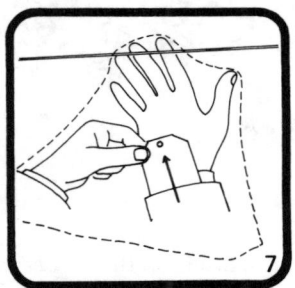

(8) NOW FOR THE STARTLING CLIMAX. Bring both hands into view along with the <u>duplicate</u> tag. Ask the spectators to look beneath the handkerchief to see if you actually removed the tag from the string as it appears. You may then offer the tag, the string, and the handkerchief for examination.

LIFESAVERS* ON THE LOOSE!

EFFECT

The magician displays an ordinary shoelace and hands it to a spectator for examination. Reaching into his pocket, the performer removes a new package of Lifesavers candy mints and gives it to another spectator to open. A number of the Lifesavers are then threaded onto the shoelace, and the ends of the lace are handed to two spectators to hold. Removing the handkerchief from his pocket, the magician covers the Lifesavers dangling in the middle of the lace, concealing them from view. Reaching under the handkerchief, the performer magically removes the imprisoned Lifesavers, leaving the now empty shoelace suspended between the two volunteers.

METHOD

(1) The only items required for this effect are an ordinary shoelace or a length of string and a package of Lifesavers or some similar candy with a hole in the center. To begin the presentation, hand the shoelace for examination as you introduce the package of Lifesavers and give them to another spectator to open.

(4) Now give both ends of the shoelace to a spectator to hold between his hands; or, give one end of the lace to one spectator and the other end to another spectator to hold. Either way, have the spectator(s) hold the ends far apart to allow enough space to drape your handkerchief over the suspended Lifesavers.

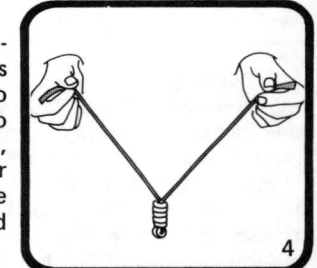

(2) Now pick up one of the Lifesavers and thread it on the shoelace as shown.

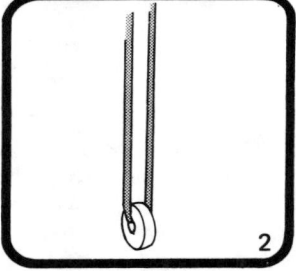

(5) Remove your handkerchief and cover the Lifesavers as shown. Be sure to spread open the handkerchief along the shoelace to provide enough "cover" for your hands when you place them underneath.

(3) With the candy suspended from the center of the lace, thread the remaining Lifesavers on the shoelace by running both ends of the lace through the holes in the candy as shown.

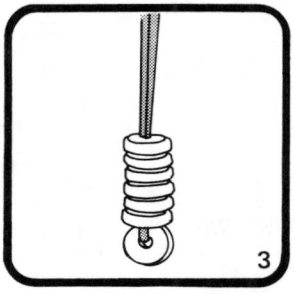

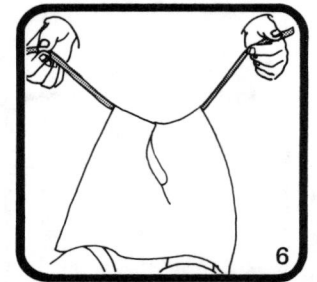

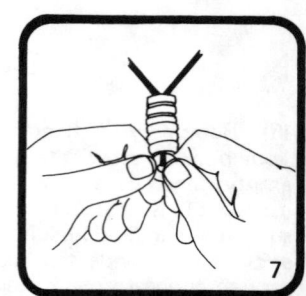

(6) Reach under the handkerchief with both hands and, (7) as soon as they are out of view, grasp the bottom Lifesaver between both hands and <u>break it</u> in half as shown.

(8) *NOTE: Try not to break it into little pieces as these can be difficult to conceal in your hand and may also fall to the floor during the presentation and spoil the trick.*

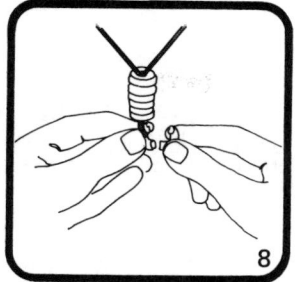

(10) Now, with your right hand (still concealing the broken pieces), lift the handkerchief away from the shoelace revealing the loose Lifesavers* in your left hand.

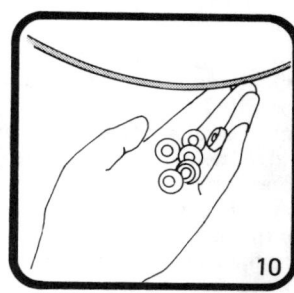

(9) Hold the broken pieces so that they are concealed in your curled right fingers. Allow the loose candy to slide from the shoelace into your left hand.

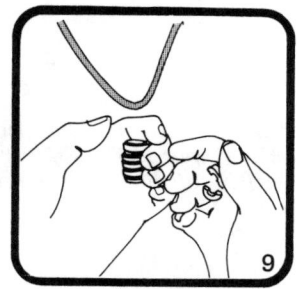

(11) Now, place the handkerchief back into your pocket *along with the broken pieces* and the mystery is complete.

COMMENTS AND SUGGESTIONS

This is truly an ideal "impromptu" mystery. All of the items are ordinary and easily obtainable. Just be sure to thread enough Lifesavers on the string, and no one will miss the broken one — which is the real secret of this clever mystery.

CORDS OF FANTASIA

EFFECT

The magician borrows two finger rings from members of the audience. Handing one of the spectators a pencil, the performer then displays two shoelaces. These laces are securely tied around the pencil. Both rings are threaded onto the shoelaces and held in place with an overhand knot. Under these conditions, even with the spectator holding onto the ends of the laces, the magician causes the rings to magically "melt" through the cords, leaving the rings, pencil and laces intact!

SECRET AND PREPARATION

All you require are a pencil, a pair of shoelaces and the two finger rings. All of the "props" are quite unprepared, and this clever effect can be presented "impromptu" at any time and any place that these common items can be obtained.

METHOD

(1) First, borrow two finger rings from members of the audience. Then have a spectator hold the pencil by the ends, between his hands. Now drape the two shoelaces over the pencil as illustrated. From this point on, we will refer to these as Lace A and Lace B.

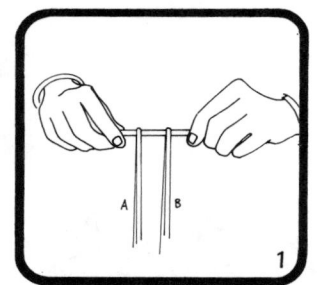

(2) While the spectator holds the pencil, grasp both strands of Lace A in your left hand and both strands of Lace B in your right. Now tie a *single overhand knot* as shown.

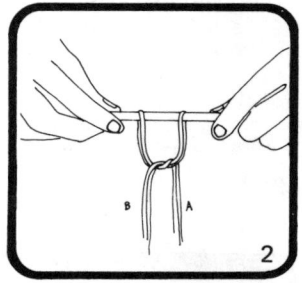

(3) Pull the knot up tight and ask the spectator to release his grip on the pencil. Turn the laces so that they are now parallel to the floor and the pencil is held by the laces in an upright position. Pull the laces tight on the pencil so that the pencil does not slide out. Now, hand the ends of the laces to the spectator.

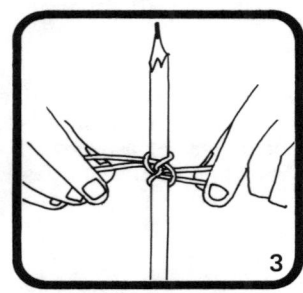

(8) With your right hand <u>firmly holding onto the knot</u>, with your left hand, pull the pencil out of the laces.

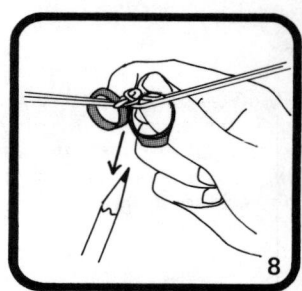

(4) Call attention to the two borrowed finger rings and thread them onto the laces. Thread one ring on each side of the pencil as shown. To do this, be sure to put *both* strands of Lace A through one ring and *both* strands of Lace B through the other.

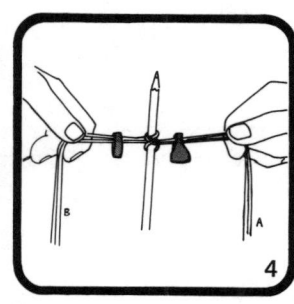

(9) Now thread the pencil *through* the rings. *NOTE: The right hand, which still holds the knot firmly, has been eliminated from this illustration for clarity.*

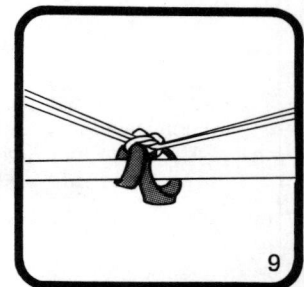

(5) You are now about to tie the rings in place. To do this, take *one* of the B ends and *one* of the A ends. *Then tie those ends in a <u>single overhand knot</u>* as shown. You will notice that when you tie this knot, you are *crossing* an A end with a B end. It makes no difference which of the two A ends or which of the two B ends you have chosen to tie. *Just be sure that you end up with one A end and one B end <u>paired on each side of the pencil</u> as shown.*

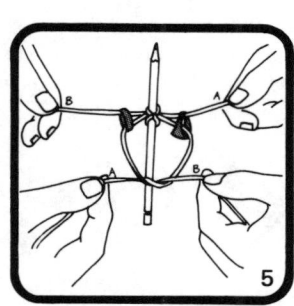

(10) Ask the spectator to pull on the ends of the laces. *At the same time, <u>release</u>* your grip on the knot held by your right hand. The illusion is perfect The rings seem to "melt" *right through the laces!*

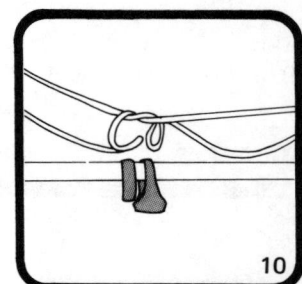

(6) Pull this new knot up tight. The rings will be jammed against the pencil. Now hand the ends back to the spectator so that he is now holding the entire affair as shown.

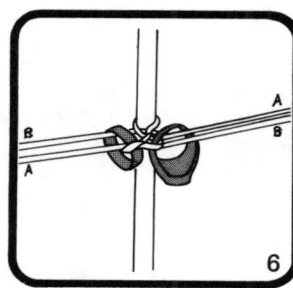

(11) The spectator is left holding only the two laces — the rings are on the pencil. Immediately allow the spectators to examine everything and return the rings to their owners with your thanks.

(7) Now with your right hand, *grasp the knot on the pencil as shown.* With your left hand, hold the pencil near the bottom and prepare to slip it free of the knot.

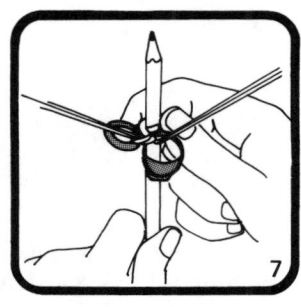

THE SUCKER TORN AND RESTORED NAPKIN

EFFECT

The magician announces that he is going to "teach" the audience how to perform a trick as he displays two paper napkins. One napkin he crumples into a ball and shows how he secretly "palms" it in his left hand. He explains that this is a "secret" napkin which no one in the audience is supposed to know about. The performer then tears the other napkin into a number of pieces. NOW FOR THE SECRET. The magician demonstrates exactly how he cleverly *switches* the torn napkin for the secret napkin. He even opens up the "secret" napkin to show how the torn pieces have supposedly been restored. The spectators, believing that they know how the trick is done, are warned by the magician that, if they should ever perform the trick, never to let anyone see the torn pieces in their hand. The performer explains that *if that should ever happen,* they would need to restore those pieces by "magic." With that, the magician opens the torn pieces revealing that *they too have been restored into a whole napkin!* It is then that the audience realizes *they have been taken in by the magician all along.*

SECRET AND PREPARATION

(A) To perform this highly entertaining effect, you will need three identical paper napkins. In this illusion, the napkins are numbered 1, 2, and 3. To prepare, spread open two of the napkins (1 and 2) and place one napkin (2) on top of the other napkin (1). Now, crumple the third napkin (3) into a ball and place it at the bottom center edge of the open napkins as shown.

(B) Starting at the top edge, roll the two open napkins down into a "tube" around the third napkin. This done, you are now ready to present the TORN AND RESTORED NAPKIN.

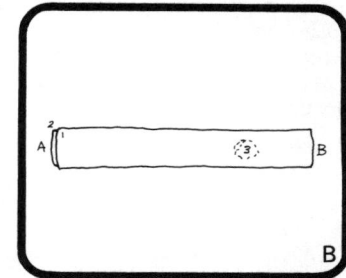

METHOD

(1) To begin, pick up the "tube" in your right hand near the center. Hold the tube so that End B is on top, and hold *the third napkin (3) through the other two napkins (1 and 2).* With your left hand, grasp the edges of the tube and start to unroll the open napkins (1 and 2) with your right hand. You should be able to feel the third napkin (3) inside as you unroll the tube. When the napkins are completely opened, secretly roll the inner crumpled napkin (3) into your right fingers so that it is hidden from the spectators.

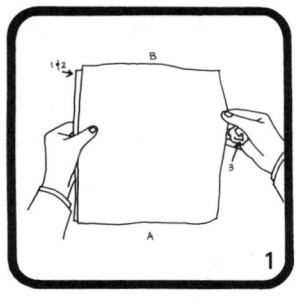

(2) Separate the two open napkins, taking one napkin (1) in your left hand and the other napkin (2) in your right. Announce to the audience that you are going to "teach them how to perform a trick."

(3) Explain that one of the two napkins (1) is a "secret" napkin and must be concealed in the magician's left hand until the proper moment. As you say this, with your left hand, crumple the left-hand napkin (1) into a ball. Then hold it in the curled fingers of your left hand (the same as the third napkin (3) in your right hand *of which the audience is totally unaware*). Explain to the audience that this "secret" napkin must be secretly "palmed" in the magician's left hand at all times as he performs the trick.

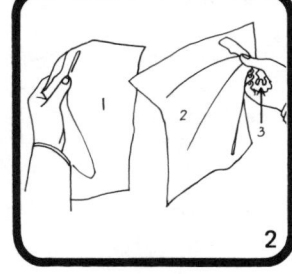

(4) Now, explain that the trick begins when the magician tears the whole napkin (2) into a number of pieces — which you proceed to do. Then, roll these torn pieces into a *small* ball.

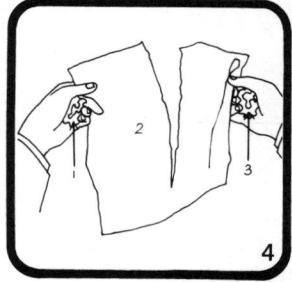

(5) Here's how your hands should look from your point of view. The napkin (2) between the tips of your thumbs and fingers is the torn one, the napkin (1) in your left hand is the "secret" napkin *which the audience knows about,* and the napkin (3) in your right hand is the one *only you know about.*

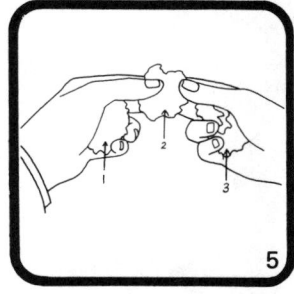

(6) As you are finishing, roll the torn pieces (2) into a ball and secretly add to them the whole napkin (3) in your right hand.

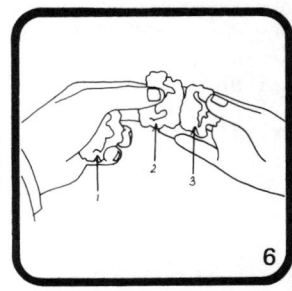

(7) You can now show *both napkins (2 and 3) together* as if they were *just the torn pieces.* As you display the supposedly torn pieces — really the torn pieces (2) and the third whole napkin (3) — turn your right hand so the audience can see that it is *quite empty.* THIS IS A VERY IMPORTANT PART OF THE TRICK. It convinces the audience that everything is "on the level" so that they will not suspect there is a *third* napkin.

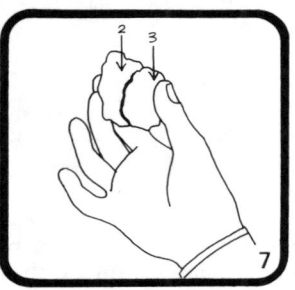

(8) Now, pretend to roll these "pieces" (Napkins 2 and 3) into a smaller ball. As you do, *secretly draw the torn pieces (2) downward behind your right fingers with your right thumb.* This leaves only the "whole" napkin (3) at the tips of your right fingers.

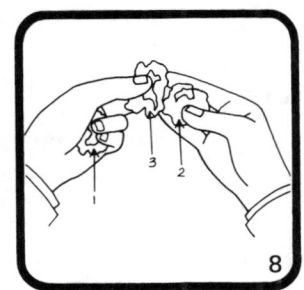

(9) Now, transfer *only* the "whole" ball (3) to the tips of your left fingers *as if it were the torn pieces.*

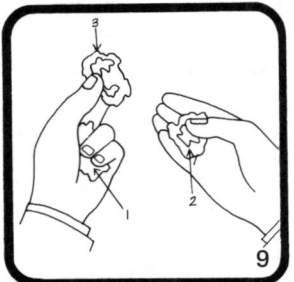

(10) *NOTE: The spectators think that you have merely placed the torn pieces — which they just saw you crumple into a ball — into your left fingers. Here is the audience view of this action.*

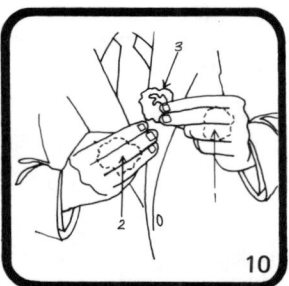

(11) Explain that when they (the spectators) perform the trick for their friends, they should have a coin in their right pocket to use as a sort of "magic wand." With your right hand reach into your right pocket and bring out the coin. When you do, LEAVE THE TORN PIECES (2) IN YOUR POCKET.

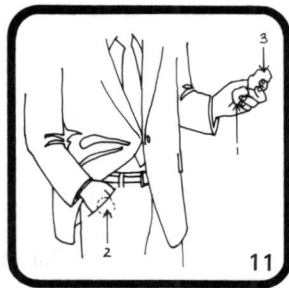

(12) *NOTE: The audience will not suspect anything because you have offered a* <u>logical reason</u> *for placing your hand in your pocket. This is a very important lesson to be learned by all magicians.* <u>There must be a reason for every move you make.</u> *Otherwise, you will arouse suspicion and, more than likely, spoil the entire effect.*

(13) At this point, the audience still believes that the torn pieces are held at the tips of your left fingers and the "secret" whole napkin is hidden in the curled fingers of the same hand. *Actually,* both of these napkins (1 and 3) are <u>whole</u>.

(14) Tell the spectators that the <u>real</u> reason for getting the coin is to direct the audience's attention <u>away</u> from the magician's left hand *so he can execute the "switch."* Explain that when your right hand reaches into your pocket, the spectators' eyes follow it, leaving your *left hand free to do the "dirty work."*

(15) Openly demonstrate this "dirty work" (the "switch") in the following manner: Slowly draw your left thumb and fingers down into your left hand (16) bringing the supposedly "torn pieces" (3) along.

(17) Now, move your thumb over to the "secret" napkin (1).
(18) Then, with the aid of your third and little fingers, raise this napkin (1) up to the tips of the fingers. Execute this series of moves slowly and deliberately *with the palm of your left hand toward the audience* to show them exactly how the "switch" is made.

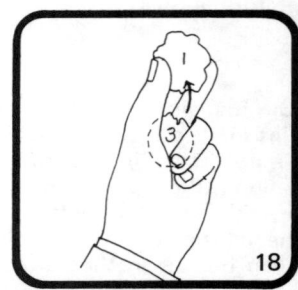

(19) Explain to the audience that *at exactly the same time* the "switch" is being made in the left hand, the magician removes the coin from his pocket with his right hand. Then wave the coin over the napkin(s) and replace it in your pocket.

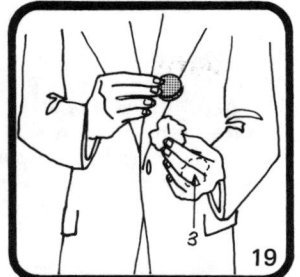

(21) Caution the spectators that they must always be very careful not to accidentally show the torn pieces concealed in their hand as they unfold the napkin — as that would be "very embarrassing." There is *one thing,* however, they can do to save themselves IF THAT SHOULD EVER HAPPEN.

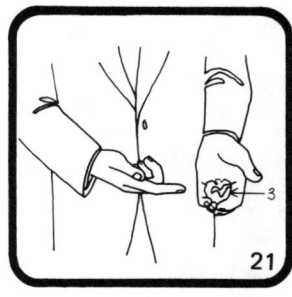

(20) State that all that remains is to open the "secret" napkin and show it restored — as you do just that.

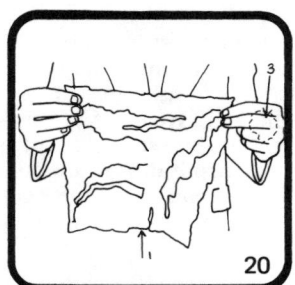

(22) The only thing a magician can do in that case is to *restore the torn pieces.* As you say this, open up the napkin (3) which the audience believes to be the torn pieces and *show it to be completely restored!* It is then that the spectators will realize *you have baffled them once again!*

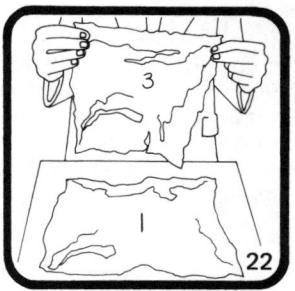

(23) Pick up both napkins (1 and 3) and hold one in each hand. Show both of your hands to be unmistakably empty as you toss the completely restored napkins to the audience.

RING ON WAND

EFFECT

The magician asks to borrow an ordinary finger ring from a member of the audience. For safe keeping, the ring is wrapped in a pocket handkerchief and given to another spectator to hold. The performer then displays an empty paper bag which he pierces on both sides with a pencil. The exposed ends of the pencil are then given to another volunteer to hold. This done, the performer asks the first spectator if he still feels the borrowed ring within the folds of the handkerchief. When the spectator replies, "Yes," the magician jerks the handkerchief from his hands only to find that the ring has vanished! The second spectator is instructed to hold the ends of the pencil tightly. The magician tears away the paper bag, *revealing the borrowed ring threaded on the pencil!* All of the props are handed for immediate examination as the ring is returned to its owner.

SECRET AND PREPARATION

The secret is in the use of a *second* finger ring and a previously prepared handkerchief. Purchase an average-sized, inexpensive ring. Avoid large costume jewelry. Also, you will need two identical pocket handkerchiefs. Prepare the handkerchiefs as described in THE SUPER DOOPER VERSATILE VANISHER. This "special" handkerchief can be shown as apparently unprepared, yet it actually contains the second finger ring in the secret pocket. Place the handkerchief in your top pocket or on your table along with a small ("lunch" size) paper bag and a pencil.

METHOD

(1) From a member of the audience, borrow a finger ring that most resembles the duplicate ring concealed in the secret pocket of the prepared handkerchief. Display the borrowed ring so that the audience can identify it later. Pick up the prepared handkerchief and spread it over the palm of your left hand. The concealed ring should be located in the right-hand corner, nearest you.

(2) Now, apparently wrap the borrowed ring within the handkerchief, as described in THE SUPER DOOPER VERSATILE VANISHER. Actually retain the *borrowed* ring in the Finger Palm position as you wrap the *duplicate* ring in the center of the handkerchief.

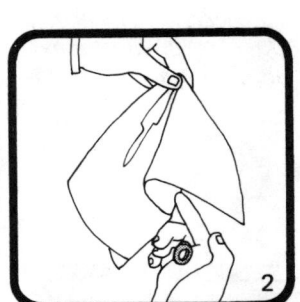

(3) Now, ask a spectator to grasp the (duplicate) ring through the folds of the handkerchief and hold it securely. The spectator believes he is holding the borrowed ring, so *do not* give the handkerchief to the owner of the ring as he might "feel" the ring and be able to tell that the ring inside is not his own.

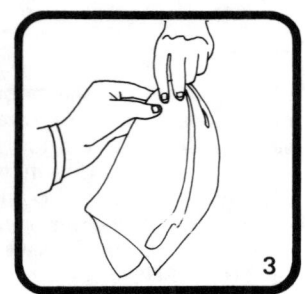

(8) Immediately remove your right hand and close the top of the bag. Then hand the whole affair to another spectator (the person you borrowed the ring from is best). Have him hold the pencil by the ends as shown.

(4) With the borrowed ring held secretly in your curled right fingers, place your right fingers (and the ring) inside the bag. Hold the open mouth of the bag toward the audience and show it to be empty and unprepared. *Be careful not to "flash" the borrowed ring as you handle the paper bag.*

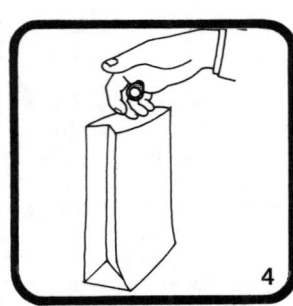

(9) From this point on it is just a matter of presentation. Check with the spectator who is holding the handkerchief and ask him if he is still holding the ring. When he assures you that he is, take one corner of the handkerchief and snap it downward out of his grasp. To the audience the effect will be that the ring has apparently vanished from between the spectator's fingertips!

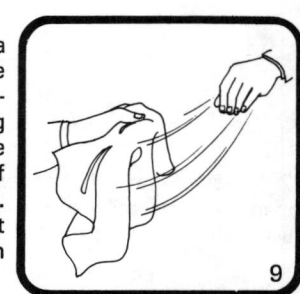

(5) Now, pick up the pencil from the table as you continue to hold the bag at the top edge — fingers inside and thumb outside — *with the borrowed ring pressed against the inner wall of the bag by your right fingers.*

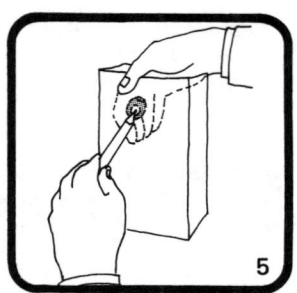

(10) Quickly turn to the other spectator. Grasp the bottom of the paper bag firmly in your right hand and give it a sharp downward pull, tearing the bag away from the pencil.

(6) Now pierce the point of the pencil through the side of the bag and *also through the ring inside.* <u>The ring is now threaded on the pencil</u> as shown. Without pausing, push the pencil on through the other side of the bag. *The ring is now secretly on the pencil — <u>inside the bag</u>.*

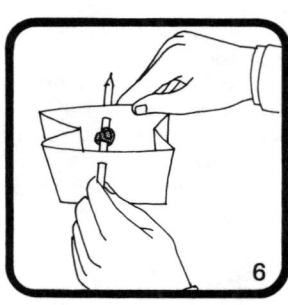

(11) The missing ring will be spinning on the pencil which the second spectator has been holding at both ends *even before the ring ever vanished* (or so they think)!

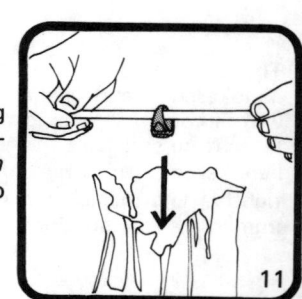

(7) *NOTE: The action of pushing the pencil through the bag (Step 6) should be executed quickly and smoothly so as not to alert the audience to any suspicious handling of the items.*

(12) Replace the handkerchief in your pocket as you ask the second spectator to return the borrowed ring to its lender. (Or have him verify that the ring on the pencil is his if he has been the "second" spectator.) The pencil, bag, and ring can then be examined by all.

THE JUMPING MATCH

EFFECT

The magician, during a casual encounter with a group of friends, announces that he has discovered a surefire method for checking his own pulse. After removing two ordinary wooden kitchen matches from his pocket, the performer places one across the palm of his left hand. He explains that his match will serve as the "counter." The second match is slipped under the first—for this demonstration it will serve as the "transmitter." As the spectators watch the counter, it is seen to bounce rhythmically as if counting out the heartbeats of the magician. Suddenly it stops, then beats erratically, creating a humorous finish to this puzzling feat. The spectators are handed the matches for examination and are challenged to try and duplicate the test. Of course, they can't, and the two matches will keep them busy for days in vain attempts to make the experiment work.

SECRET AND PREPARATION

Use large wooden kitchen matches for this effect. They are not prepared in any way and therefore can be borrowed. The secret to this experiment lies in your unseen manipulation of the "transmitter match."

METHOD

(1) Place the first or "counter" match across your left palm, as shown. Position the *end* of this match so that it is resting against the side of your first finger with the *head* of the match pointed toward you.

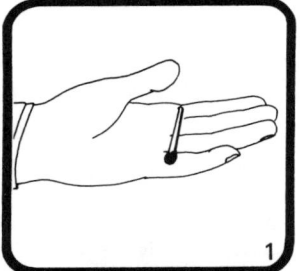

(3) If you now exert pressure against the match with the nail of the second finger, and slowly and imperceptively slide the match across the nail, the match will create the necessary unseen "pulses."

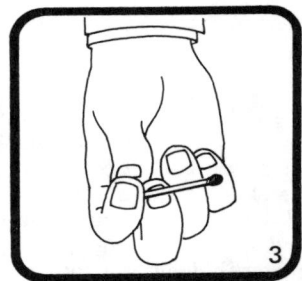

(2) The second or "transmitter" match is held between the thumb and first finger of your right hand. Your second finger *presses its nail against the back side of the match* as shown.

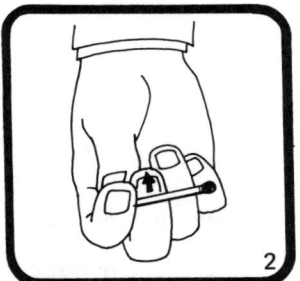

(4) Position the "transmitter" match under the "counter" match as shown. Then secretly slide your right second fingernail across the match as described in Step 3. The right-hand transmitter match will cause the left-hand counter match to jump in a rhythmic beat.

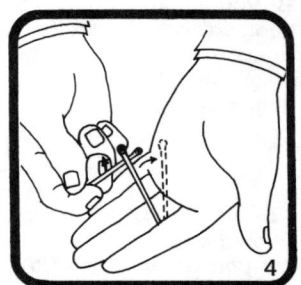

COMMENTS AND SUGGESTIONS

This fine pocket trick is completely impromptu, and can be very mystifying if done well. Large wooden kitchen matches are best since they show up better and make the "secret move" easier to perform. Remember that the counter match won't jump unless your right second fingernail is pressing firmly against its match when you slide it across.

Another patter theme for this effect is to explain that you have learned how to magically magnetize matches. Then rub the first (transmitter) match several times on your sleeve or the tablecloth. Sure enough, when you hold the "magnetized" first match up against the second (counter) match, it vibrates and shakes as if it really were impelled by some strange new power!

THE FLYING MATCH

EFFECT

The magician shows an ordinary book of paper matches. The book is opened and the matches, *all still attached to the book,* are counted for all to see. One match is removed from the book and the matchbook cover closed. The performer lights the match by striking it on the book and then blows the match out. He then makes the burnt match "vanish" as he throws it toward the matchbook. When the matchbook is opened by a spectator, *the burnt match is found inside, <u>attached</u> to the matchbook like the rest of the matches!* As an added convincer, the matches are counted and the number is found to be <u>the same as at the start of the effect.</u>

SECRET AND PREPARATION

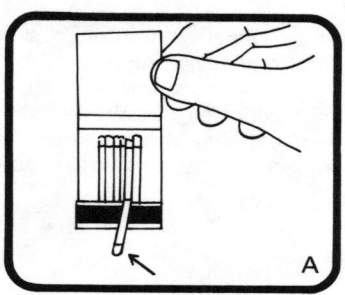
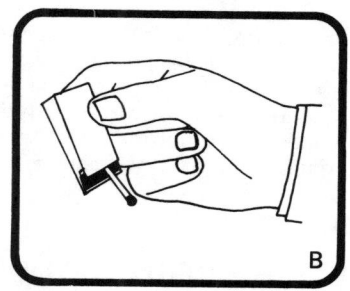
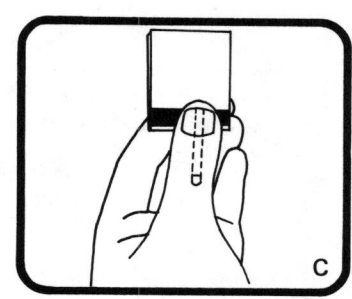

(A)   Before you perform this clever trick, you open the matchbook and bend one match in the first row "down" at the base as shown.
(B)   Now close the matchbook cover. The cover can't be tucked in because of the bent match, but don't worry about that yet. Take a *second* "lose" match, strike it, and set the head of the "bent" match on fire. Then quickly blow out both matches.   (C)   Now you must "hide" the burnt match that is still attached to the book. Place your left thumb on top of the matchbook so that it completely covers the bent match. The illustration shows how to conceal the match with your left thumb and hold the matchbook closed at the same time. With this "secret" preparation completed, you are now ready to perform.

METHOD

(1)   With the "bent" match concealed by your left thumb, open the cover of the matchbook with your right hand and ask a spectator to watch closely as you count the matches in the book. Be sure to keep the bent match hidden, and don't let the spectator take the matchbook from you as you count. Just hold the matchbook so that it's easy for the spectator to see the matches — then bend each match slightly forward with your right fingers as you count them.

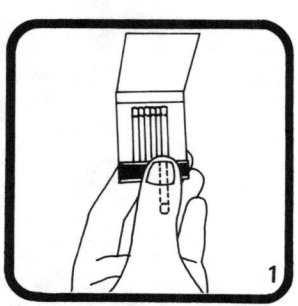

(2)   *NOTE: It is best to have only 10 to 12 matches remaining in the book when you perform the trick. This gives fewer matches for you to count, and there is less chance for the spectator to see the "bent" match during the counting. Also, the smaller number of matches makes the reappearance of the burnt match even more startling.*

(3)   Now, with your right fingers, remove one match from the first row. This must be a match that is located *next to the hidden bent match.* Put this match on the table and close the matchbook cover.

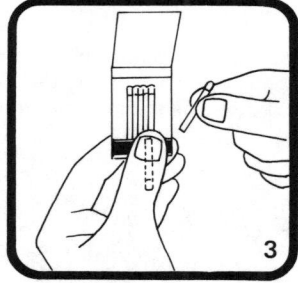

(4)   As you close the cover, hold the book up in front of you so that the *back* of the book is toward the audience.

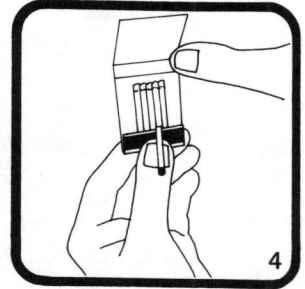

(5)   As your right fingers close the cover, your left thumb slips *under* the bent match and levers it upward *into the matchbook.*

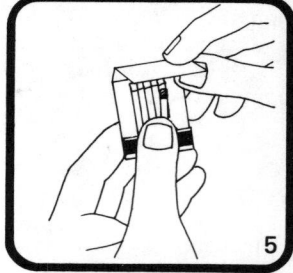

(6)   Immediately close the matchbook and tuck in the cover. The entire sequence takes but a few seconds and is hidden from the spectators, who see only the back of the matchbook.

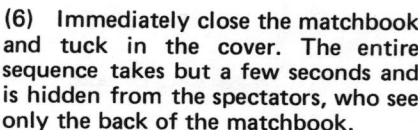

(7)   Pick up the match you placed on the table (the one you just removed) and strike it on the matchbook. Let only the <u>head</u> of the match burn and then blow it out. Put the matchbook near the center of the table. *NOW FOR THE MAGIC!*

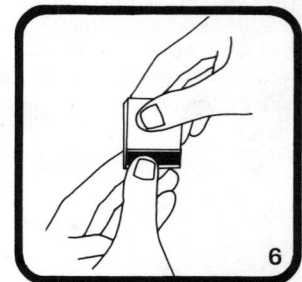

(8)   Pretend to pick up the match on the table with your right hand. Your right fingers really only *cover* the match and, as you slide your right hand back toward yourself . . .

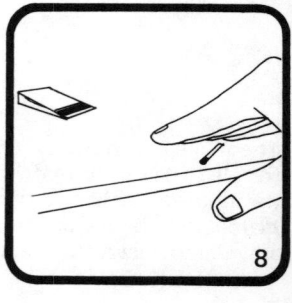

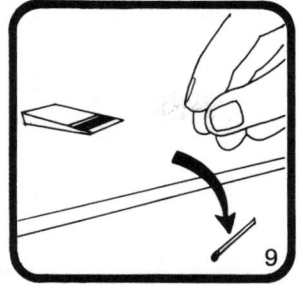

(9) . . . the match is secretly swept *off the table* and falls into your lap.

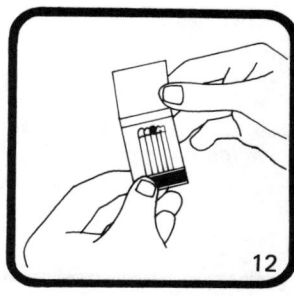

(12) . . . have *the spectator pick up the matchbook and open it.* Inside he will find what he thinks is the "original" match, now burnt and <u>firmly attached</u> with the rest of the matches to the matchbook.

(10) Hold up your right fingers *as if they contain the match.* Done correctly, the illusion of picking up the match is perfect.

(13) As a final convincer, *have the spectator count the matches.* He will find the number of matches to be the same as at the start of the trick!

(11) Apparently "throw" the burnt match (from your really empty hand) toward the closed matchbook. Show your right hand empty and . . .

COMMENTS AND SUGGESTIONS

The vanish of the match, its reappearance in the matchbook, <u>and</u> the fact that the match is <u>burnt and attached to the matchbook</u> all add up to an outstanding close-up mystery.

DOTS MAGIC
(The Paddle Move)

After you become known as a magician, many times you will be asked to perform while you are seated at a table. The following effect teaches you a sleight (the Paddle Move) which is a magical "classic" that is ideal to be used under these very conditions.

EFFECT

The magician displays a clean table knife. After polishing both sides of the blade with his napkin, he attaches three red dots, one at a time, to the top surface of the blade. As he attaches each dot, three identical dots appear on the opposite side of the knife, one at a time, as if in sympathy with the first three dots. The magician hands the knife to a spectator seated near him and asks that he verify the existence of the duplicate set of dots. Upon retrieving the knife, the performer removes the top three dots from the blade and, magically, the bottom three dots vanish in sympathy. Suddenly all six dots reappear, three on each side of the knife blade. The magician now removes the dots one at a time from the top of the blade. As he removes each dot, the corresponding dot on the bottom vanishes in perfect synchronization. With the table knife now as clean as it was in the beginning, it is again handed to a spectator for examination.

SECRET AND PREPARATION

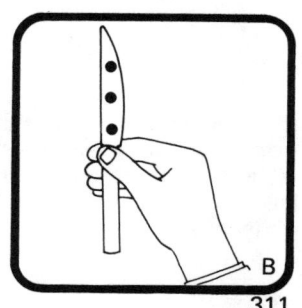

(A) The small circular "dots" needed for this effect are available at your local stationery store. They are "self-adhering" and come in several colors. Red has a high visibility and is therefore recommended for the trick, but any color will do. (If you wish, you can even cut dots out of gummed paper, but the "pressure sensitive" commercial dots can be much more easily attached and removed for this particular routine.) The dots selected should measure about ¼" in diameter.

(B) For practice purposes, prepare the table knife by placing three of the dots on one side of the blade as in Figure B. Then, turn the blade over so that the "blank" side is face up.

(C)   NOTE: This next step is the classic *turn* entitled the "Paddle Move." After you have learned it, you will be able to show the blank side of the blade *twice* as you turn the knife over in your hand, *apparently showing both sides.* This will leave the spectators with the impression that they actually saw both sides of the blade. *This is the one sleight used in this entire routine. It is one of the most valuable principles in close-up magic.*

THE PADDLE MOVE

 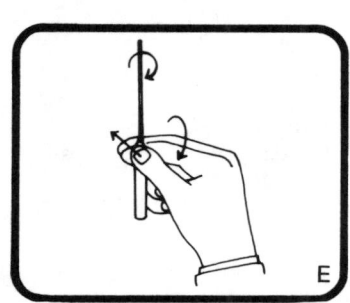 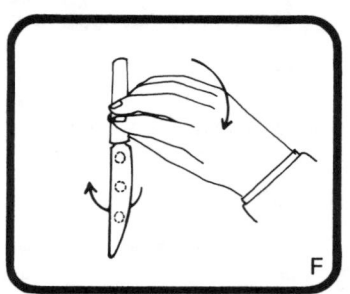 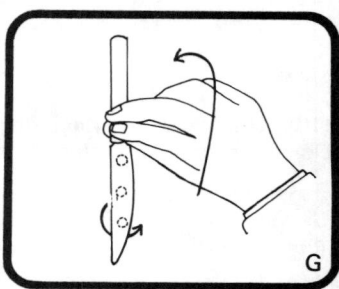

(D)   To perform the Paddle Move, pick up the knife between the thumb and first two fingers of your right hand by the handle as shown. The blank side of the blade should be facing up. You will notice that the blade is facing away from you (pointing toward the spectators) and should be held at about waist level. You are about to turn the knife over so that the blade points toward you. In order to prevent the dots fastened on the bottom of the blade from being exposed, *you must simultaneously revolve the knife between your thumb and first two fingers as you turn the knife over.* (E)   What happens is that your right thumb "rolls" the knife handle with your thumb and fingers *one-half turn to your left* (Illustrations E and F) . . .   (F)   . . . as you rotate the blade over so that it points toward you (Illustration F). (G)   Then rotate the blade back toward the spectators. At the same time, execute Steps E and F *in reverse* and "roll" the knife back (to your right) with your thumb and fingers so that the blank side is still up. This is the Paddle Move. Practice in front of a mirror until you can execute the move smoothly. When properly done, the blade will appear to be blank on both sides. When you have mastered the Paddle Move, you will be ready to present this most clever and entertaining effect.

(H)   Before the performance, place six of the dots in your wallet (or an envelope). After you are seated at the dinner table and have the opportunity, secretly attach three of the dots to the underside of the blade of your knife. You are now ready to perform a Minor Miracle.

The pictures describing the Paddle Move above as well as those in the Method which follows are from a point of view looking down on the magician's hand with the knife held horizontally over the surface of the table.

METHOD

(1)   Stand up and display the knife to the spectators. By executing the "Paddle Move," show both sides of the blade to be empty. (Really, there are three dots on one side.) Now, wipe both sides of the blade, one at a time (really the same side twice, thanks to the Paddle Move), with your napkin to further create the illusion of a "clean" knife.

(3)   Display the dot and execute the Paddle Move to apparently show the opposite side of the blade. To the audience it will appear that a duplicate dot has "magically appeared" on the other side of the blade.

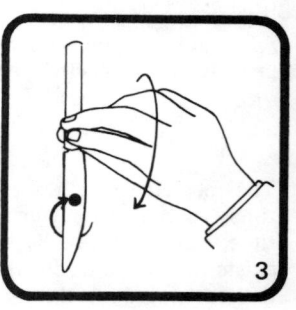

(2)   Remove the three remaining dots from your wallet and set them on the table. Now place one of these on the blank side of the blade directly in the center as shown.

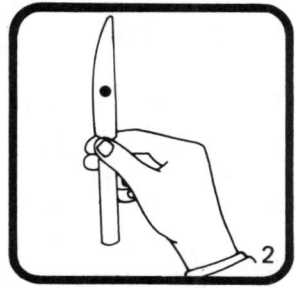

(4)   Now return the knife to its original position and attach the second dot near the end of the blade as shown.

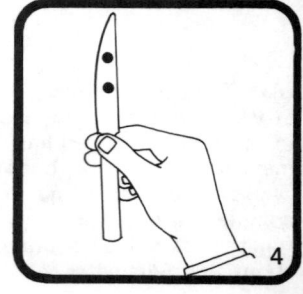

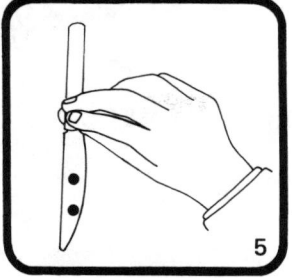

(5) Once again, execute the Paddle Move and apparently show the arrival of the second dot on the back of the blade.

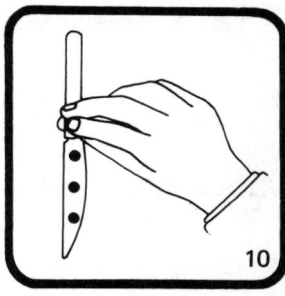

(10) Now, by executing the Paddle Move, you can show that the dots have not only magically returned, not only to the top of the blade, *but to the back as well.*

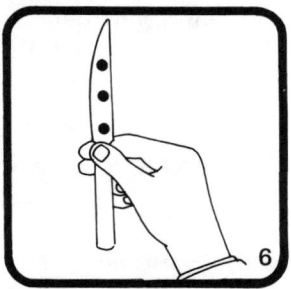

(6) Repeat Step 3 with the third and last dot again showing the knife on both sides. The spectators will now be convinced that the blade of your knife has three dots on both sides. At this point, *it actually does have three dots on both sides* because of the three "secret" dots you previously attached. You can now hand the knife to a spectator for examination.

(11) *NOTE: At this point, you are set up for the sympathetic VANISH of the dots <u>one at a time</u> since the blade now has three red dots on the top surface only. Just repeat Steps 2 through 6 IN REVERSE.*

(7) As soon as the knife is returned to you, openly remove the three dots from the top of the blade and put them into your pocket.

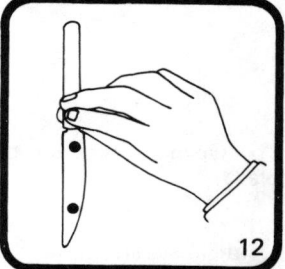

(12) Begin by removing the center dot and executing the Paddle Move. It will appear as if the center dot vanished from the back of the knife as well.

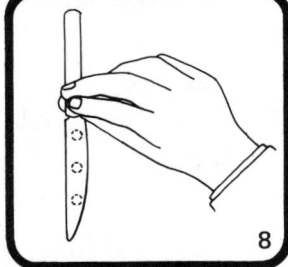

(8) Execute the Paddle Move and show that the three dots on the back of the blade have sympathetically "vanished" as well.

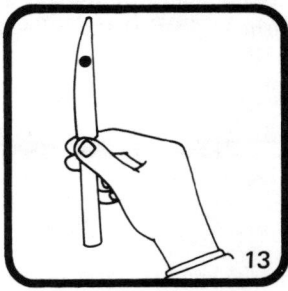

(13) Now remove the dot closest to the handle and apparently show both sides as before. This will leave you with apparently one dot on the tip of both sides of the blade.

(9) Pick up your napkin and apparenly wipe the blade clean. Under cover of this wiping action, turn the blade over. *The audience will be surprised to see that the three dots have reappeared on the knife!*

(14) Remove the last dot and slowly show both sides of the knife. The blade will be clean of spots and may now be handed to the spectator for examination.

COMMENTS AND SUGGESTION

As mentioned earlier, the Paddle Move is a classic sleight with many important uses in magic. Study the illustrations and practice the move until you can do it smoothly and almost without thinking. You will have learned an extremely valuable sleight that you will perform in many different effects as you progress through the wonderful world of Magic.

DOTS MAGIC — IMPROMPTU VERSION

DOTS MAGIC, as just described, can also be performed in a completely impromptu situation when you do not have the "commercial" dots with you.

EFFECT

The effect is the same as in DOTS MAGIC except that instead of dots, you cut or tear small squares of paper (a paper napkin works well) for use in the trick. The squares are attached to the knife by moistening them slightly using the tip of your finger to obtain a drop of water from your water glass and applying it to each square. The slightly dampened squares will now adhere to the blade of the knife.

SECRET AND PREPARATION

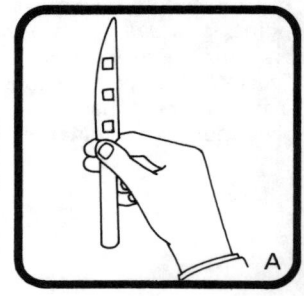

(A) If you have an opportunity to apply the three "secret" squares before the performance, you may utilize the same routine as described in DOTS MAGIC. If you do not have the time or opportunity to tear, moisten and apply the three extra squares, just start the routine from Step 10, using a total of three squares for the trick.

METHOD

(1) Openly attach the three squares to one side of the examined blade.

(2) Using the Paddle Move, you then show that three more identical squares have "magically" appeared on the opposite side of the blade.

(3) Now turn the blade over to show the spots to have vanished. Then use the Paddle Move to show the other side blank.

(4) After showing both sides of the blade blank (through the courtesy of the Paddle Move), the three squares reappear.

(5) Now proceed with Steps 12, 13, and 14, as the squares are openly removed from the top side of the blade and "sympathetically vanish" from the bottom side.

GLASS THROUGH THE TABLE

EFFECT

The magician states that he will cause a solid object to penetrate through the top of the table. With that, he places a coin on the table and covers it with a glass, mouth down. He then *covers the glass* with two paper napkins, which conceal both the glass and coin from view. The magician explains that, by mere concentration, he will cause the coin to "melt" through the top of the table. After several unsuccessful attempts, he explains that the reason for failure is that he forgot one of the most important parts of the experiment. He must first strike the top of the glass, giving the coin the momentum to penetrate the table. Suddenly, with a sharp downward motion of his hand, the performer smashes the glass and the napkins *flat on the table*. When the napkins are lifted, the coin is still there but THE GLASS IS GONE! Immediately, the magician reaches beneath the table and reproduces the same glass.

SECRET AND PREPARATION

The secret of this trick is based on a very clever principle. Due to the natural stiffness of the paper napkins, they will retain the form or shape of the glass *even if the glass is not within them*. This creates a very convincing illusion which makes this mystery possible. The glass should be smooth-sided so it slides easily from within the napkins. It should also be slightly smaller at the *base* than at the *mouth*. A glass which is approximately four or five inches tall works well. Also you need a coin (a half-dollar is a good size) and two ordinary paper napkins.

METHOD

(1) *You must be SEATED AT A CARD TABLE OR DINING TABLE to perform this close-up mystery.* Also, it is better if the spectators are also seated at the same table. With the glass, napkins, and coin lying on the table, tell the spectators that you will attempt to cause a solid object to pass through the top of the table.

(2) With that, place the coin directly in front of you, about 12 inches from the edge of the table. Then, cover the coin with the glass, *mouth downward.* Point out that the glass completely encloses the coin so that it is impossible for you to touch it.

(3) Next, open out both napkins, lay them on top of each other, and then over the glass as shown. Explain that the coin must be kept "in the dark" — so, you will cover the glass with the napkins.

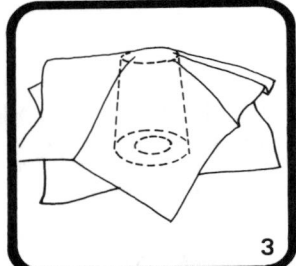

(4) With both hands, pull the napkins downward around the glass. This makes the form of the glass clearly outlined through the napkins.

(5) With one hand, grip the top of the glass through the napkins and place your other hand around the mouth of the glass. Then, twist the glass as shown, *drawing the napkins tightly against the sides of the glass.* This helps to form the shape of the glass even more distinctly inside the paper napkins.

(6) This done, lift both the glass and the napkin together — to reassure the audience that the coin is still on the table.

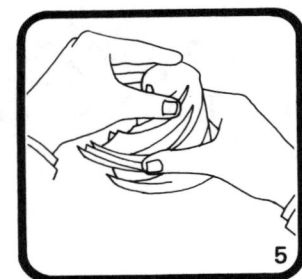

(7) Once again, cover the coin with the glass and explain that through "deep concentration" you can cause the coin to penetrate through the table. All eyes will be fixed on the napkin-covered glass, waiting to see if the coin actually does as you say.

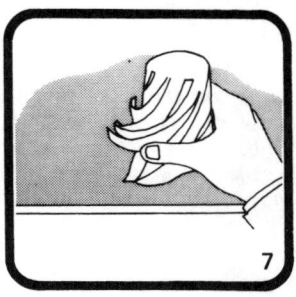

(8) Pretend to concentrate for a few seconds. Then announce that you think the coin has done its work. With your *right hand,* lift the napkins and glass revealing that the coin is still on the table. Act surprised, as if you actually expected the coin to be gone.

(9) Pick up the coin in your *left hand* as you remark that something seems to be wrong. *At the same time,* your right hand — holding the napkins and the glass — MOVES TO THE EDGE OF THE TABLE as shown. This motion of your right hand is completely natural, as it must move away to make room for your left hand, which picks up the coin. Your eyes, your gestures, *your total attention* should ALL BE DIRECTED AT THE COIN. This is MISDIRECTION!

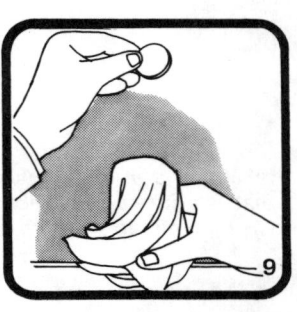

(10) Here is a *side view* of the right hand holding the napkin-covered glass at the edge of the table. *Notice that the hand is actually resting on the table.*

(11) IT IS AT THIS TIME THAT THE "SECRET MOVE" TAKES PLACE. While the attention of the spectators is on the coin, the fingers of your right hand relax their grip on the glass through the napkin. *The weight of the glass will cause it to slide from within the napkins* INTO YOUR LAP.

(12) *The napkins retain the shape of the glass,* creating the illusion that the glass is still there.

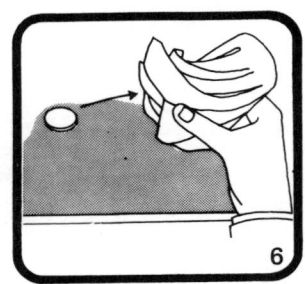

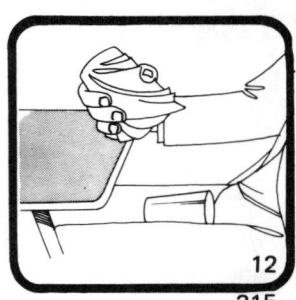

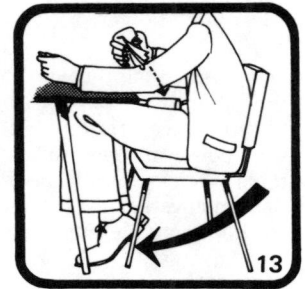

(13) As the glass falls into your lap, raise your heels enough to bring your knees a bit higher than your lap. *This keeps the glass in your lap so it does not roll onto the floor.*

(17) SMASH THE NAPKINS FLAT ON THE TABLE WITH YOUR LEFT HAND. When this is done *fast* and *hard,* the reaction from the spectators will be one of complete astonishment.

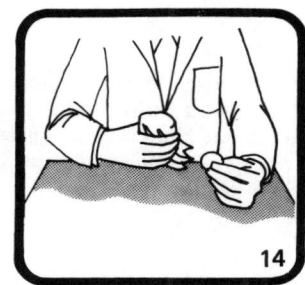

(14) Here is the *audience view* of the performer as the "secret drop" takes place. *Notice how the left hand is forward,* FOCUSING ATTENTION ON THE COIN.

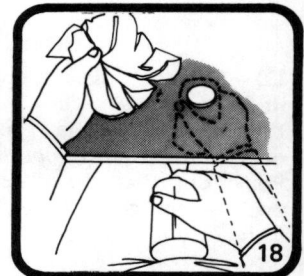

(18) Act puzzled for a moment. Then lift the napkins with your *left hand,* revealing the coin on the table. At the same time, your *right hand* grasps the glass in your lap and *carries it beneath the table,* as if reaching below the spot where you "smashed" the glass. Then bring your hand into view from beneath the table *with the glass.*

(15) *NOTE: The action of dropping the glass in your lap should take only a moment. As soon as the glass falls from the napkins, that is your cue to place the coin back on the table and cover it with the napkins (which apparently still contain the glass).*

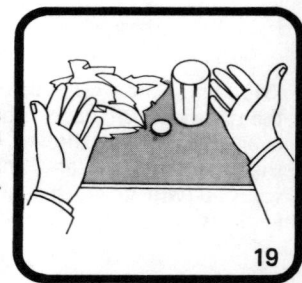

(19) Place the glass on the table as you say, *"Now I remember* how the trick is done! It's the glass that is supposed to penetrate the table, *not* the coin."

(16) Explain that the trick failed because you forgot to strike the top of the glass. As you say this, raise your left hand above the glass and . . .

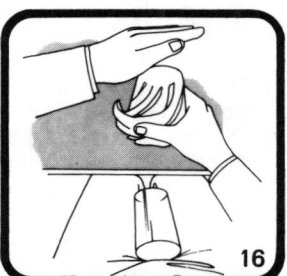

MENTAL MAGIC

This type of magic is unique because it depends on the effect created on the audience rather than the objects used. Instead of making things vanish and reappear or cutting them up and restoring them, you use them in special tests whereby you presumably "read people's minds." Since this goes along with modern talk of ESP, or Extra Sensory Perception, this type of magic has become so popular that some performers prefer to call themselves "mental-ists" rather than magicians, as if they really were endowed with some super-normal power.

For practical purposes, however, it is better to inject a few mental effects at different parts of your performance and watch for audience reactions. If those prove favorable, add others to your program or play them up more strongly, until you strike the right balance. That, however, often depends upon the mood of your audience. Some people take mental magic so seriously that they don't care for anything else. If you run into people like that, you may just as well do a complete mental routine and forget your other tricks for the time being.

Most mental effects depend upon some secret that spectators are apt to overlook, so it is your job to see that they do exactly that. Never refer to a mental effect as a "trick." Call it a "test" or an "experiment" and in most cases, treat it rather seriously. If you run into complications or find that some-body is watching you too closely, don't try to work your way out of it as you would with other types of magic. Just put the blame on other people. Say that they are not "projecting" the right thoughts, or that you find it impossible to pick up the "impressions" that you need. That makes it look all the more genuine and gives you a chance to switch to another test.

THREE-WAY TEST

Reading a person's mind is surely a most effective way of demonstrating your magical powers. In this ESP experiment, using a small pad and pencil, you show your ability to predict and control the minds of three spectators. This effect requires a little closer study than most "magic" tricks, but it is well worth the sensational impact of your "magical mindreading."

THE EFFECT

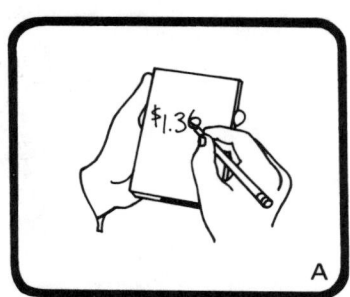

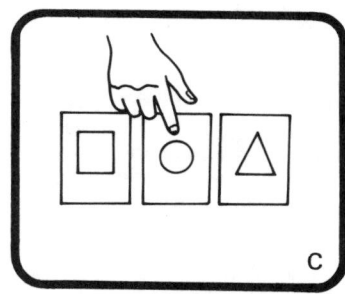

(A)   In this mental effect, you demonstrate three different experiments in extrasensory perception. In the first experiment, you correctly determine the exact amount of change that a spectator has in his pockets.   (B)   In the second test, you receive a mental impression of an object that a spectator is thinking of before he picks it up in his hand.   (C)   And in the last experiment, you correctly predict which of three figure drawings a spectator will select from the table. With a small pad and pencil on your table, you are ready to begin.

THE METHOD

First explain that you are going to demonstrate three different forms of ESP, and to do this, you need three spectators to assist you — one person for each test. Then ask the members of the audience to assemble four or more small objects from around the room and place them on the table in front of one of the volunteers.

(1) These can be any objects, as long as they are all different. Let's assume that the four items gathered are: ashtray, pen, matchbook and paper clip.

(4)   You are now ready to begin the actual experiments. Explain that the first experiment is a test in *clairvoyance,* which is the ability to see hidden objects.

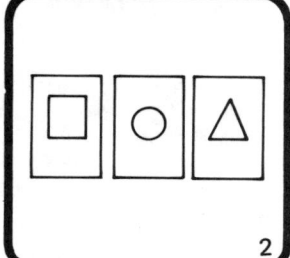

(2) Next pick up the pad of paper and tear off three of the blank sheets. On one sheet of paper draw a circle; on the second, draw a square; and on the third, draw a triangle. Place these slips face up in a row in front of one of the other volunteers.

(5) Pick up the pad and pencil and hold it so no one can see what you write. To the "money" spectator, say: "I am now going to write down my impression of the amount of change in your hand. "Obviously, you can't write this amount, because you don't know it yet! *Instead, draw a circle on the slip of paper.*

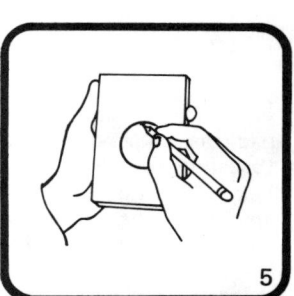

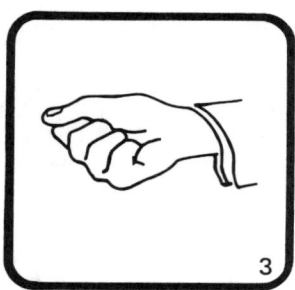

(3) Ask the third spectator to reach in his pocket or purse and bring out all of the small change he has there. Tell him *not to count it* but to keep it held tightly in his closed fist.

(6)   Now tear off the slip and fold it without letting anyone see what you have written. Say that you will call this first test "Test A" and that you will write the letter A on the outside of the slip. *Instead, you really mark it with the letter C.*

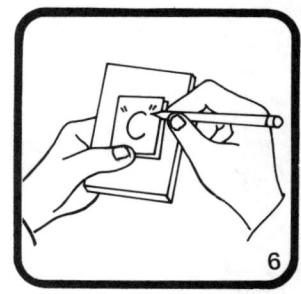

(7) After you have marked the slip, place it where it will be out of view of the spectators. (Be careful not to let anyone see the letter C on the slip of paper.) A drinking glass or coffee cup works well if it is the type you *can't see through.*

(8) Another suggestion would be to turn an ashtray or saucer upside down on the table and place the slips under it. It's not important where you place the slips *as long as the letters written on the outside cannot be seen by the spectators.* Let's assume you place the slips in a coffee mug.

(9) After the folded slip is in the mug, tell Person A to count his money out onto the table and leave it there for everyone to see. Let's say it comes to exactly $1.36.

(10) Now you turn to the second person and say, "I'm going to try a test in *telepathy* with you. This means that I can mentally pick up an impression that you *already* have in your mind. To do this, I want you to concentrate on one of the four objects on the table — the object *you are going to pick up in your hand.* Tell me when you have decided on the one you want, but *don't tell me* which object, and don't pick it up until *after* I have written down my impression."

(11) Then, instead of writing on the pad the name of one of the objects (because you don't know which one he's thinking of), *you write the amount of change that has been counted on the table from Test A — $1.36.*

(12) NOTE: *Learning information from one test and secretly using it in the next test is called the ONE-AHEAD PRINCIPLE.*

(13) Now tear off this sheet and fold it. Tell him that this is Test B and you will mark his slip with the letter B. But *instead of writing B, you mark it with the letter A.*

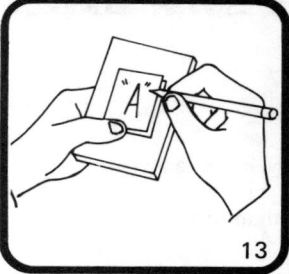

(14) Put this slip into the mug along with the other one.

(15) Now tell the spectator to pick up the object he was thinking of. Let's say he picks up the match book.

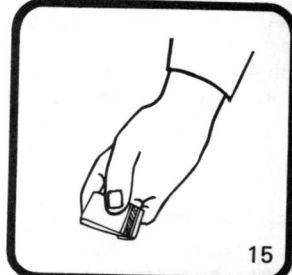

(16) Tell the third volunteer that you will do an experiment in *precognition.* This means you will *predict* a certain result before he knows what he is going to do.

(17) Pretend to write a prediction on the pad, but *really* write down the object that Person B is holding in his hand — the match book. NOTE: Again you are using the ONE-AHEAD PRINCIPLE.

(18) Now tear off the slip, fold it and say you'll call this Test C. Instead of marking the slip with the letter C, you mark it with the letter B as shown.

(19) Place this slip into the mug along with the other two.

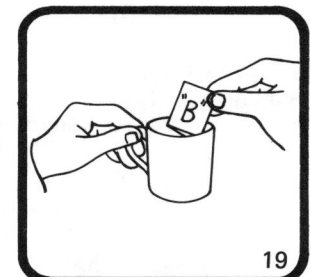

(25) "Fine, I'll tear this one up and that leaves only two."

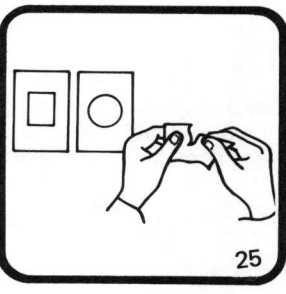

(20) Now you must maneuver the spectator into selecting the slip of paper with the circle on it. This is called "Forcing," although the spectator believes he is getting a free choice. The "Force" you will learn here is called the MAGICIAN'S CHOICE.

(26) Then ask him to *pick up* either one of the remaining slips of paper. Either one of two things will now happen.

(27) If he picks up the paper with the *circle* on it . . .

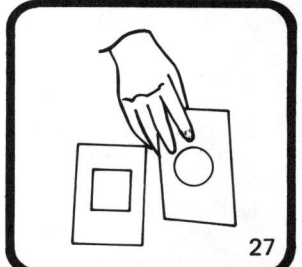

(21) Point out to the volunteer that you have drawn a different figure on each of the three papers on the table. Ask him to *point* to any one of the three slips. Now, one of several situations will arise:

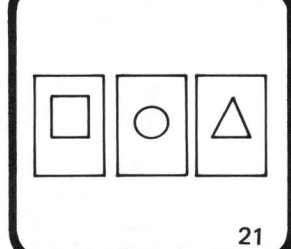

(28) . . . then you pick up the one remaining on the table and tear it up saying, "OK, the circle is the one you selected, so we won't need this one either."

(22) *First Situation:*
If he points to the *circle,* say: "Would you pick up the slip that you have selected and hold it in your hand."

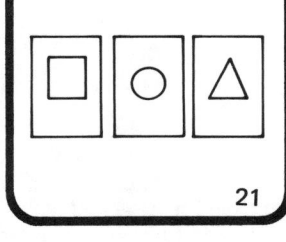

(29) If he picks up the paper *without the circle* on it, say:

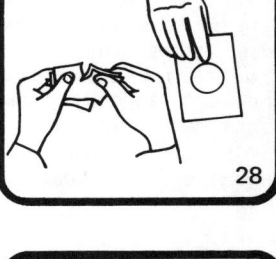

(23) When he does this, you pick up the other two slips and tear them up, saying: "We will not need these, so I'll tear them up."

(30) "OK, *you* tear up that slip, which leaves just the one on the table" (the circle).

(24) *Second Situation:*
If the spectator points to the *square* or the *triangle,* you pick up the one he points to and say:

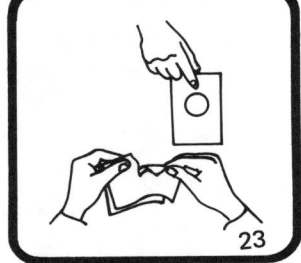

(31) Now that you have successfully "Forced" the circle, you are ready for the "payoff." Pick up the mug and dump the slips onto the table. Ask each spectator to take the slip that has his letter on it and open it. When each slip is opened, all three of your tests prove to be correct!

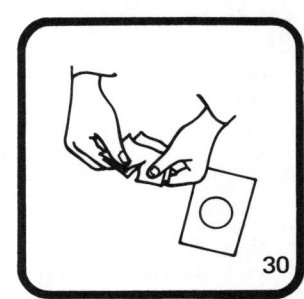

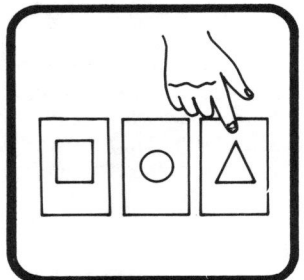

COMMENTS AND SUGGESTIONS

This is a very strong trick. It can be performed anywhere; all you need are a pencil and some pieces of paper. There is no "sleight of hand" or special skill needed. But it is a trick that must be studied thoroughly and practiced until you can remember easily which part comes next — which letter to write on each slip, etc. After you have mastered it, you will be able to baffle your friends with one of the finest "mindreading" mysteries in the entire Art of Magic.

THE MAGAZINE TEST

Among mental mysteries, those in which a spectator does all the work can be rated among the best, for this apparently makes it impossible for the performer to inject any element of trickery. In fact, there are cases in which the magician does not even figure as a performer except to guide the spectator's actions. THE MAGAZINE TEST falls into that special category. You will find, however, that the effect does involve a small bit of work on your part, but this is mostly done beforehand. Hence, no one even knows about it, which makes it all the better for you.

EFFECT

The magician displays a sealed envelope and a current issue of a well known magazine. The performer explains to the audience that, prior to his appearance, he wrote one word on a white card and sealed it in an envelope. It is this envelope that he now hands to one of the spectators in the audience. A second spectator is asked to join the magician on stage and assist in a demonstration of the wizard's ability to "see into the future." The magician hands the magazine to the spectator along with a pencil or felt-tipped pen. In order not to influence the spectator's choice of a word from the magazine, the volunteer is asked to hold the magazine behind his back and mark a page at random with a bold X. Retrieving the now-closed magazine, the magician asks the first spectator to tear open the envelope he has held from the very start and read to the audience the predicted word. The magazine is then opened to the marked page. The spectators are surprised to see that the intersecting lines of the X *are directly through the identical word.*

SECRET AND PREPARATION

(A) Select a current issue of a magazine. Turn to any right-hand page located near the center of the magazine and draw a large X on the page. Make the mark so that the two lines of the X "cross" over a single word as shown. From this point on, we will refer to this word, "news," as the "Force Word."

(C) Now print the Force Word across the face of a white card and seal the "prediction" in an opaque envelope.

(B) NOTE: You should try marking the magazine page behind your own back before doing "The Magazine Test." In fact, several such trials are advisable in order to see just what a pair of crossed lines will look like when a spectator goes through the same procedure. Then, when you are ready to prepare the magazine that you intend to use in the test, you can copy one of your previous attempts, giving the lines slight curves or an irregular appearance to make them look authentic. Never have them cross exactly in the center of the "Forced" word. Hit near one end, or just above or below, yet close enough so everyone will agree upon that word.

(D) The final step is to prepare a pen or pencil in the same manner (so that it will not write) as for the "Double X Mystery" found elsewhere in the Course. *This prevents the spectator from actually making a mark on the magazine.* Be sure that this pen or pencil matches the one you used to mark the page.

METHOD

(1) Display the sealed envelope with the Force Word written on the card inside. Have a member of the audience hold the envelope. Pick up the magazine and demonstrate for the audience how you would like a spectator to mark the magazine page. Tell the spectator that you would like him to thumb through the magazine while holding it behind his back. Once he has selected a page, show him how he is to fold the *left-hand* pages of the magazine to the rear. This insures that the spectator will mark on a *right-hand* page of the magazine. (NOTE: Do not call them "left-hand" or "right-hand" pages. Just demonstrate what the spectator is to do so that, when he does "make his mark," it will be on the right-hand pages.

(2) When you are sure that the spectator understands the proper procedure for marking the magazine, give him the *prepared* pen or pencil. (This is a good place for the "pencil switch" described in the "Super Double X Mystery.") Have him hold the magazine behind his back, select any (right-hand) page, fold the other (left-hand) pages out of the way, and mark the page with a large X. *The prepared pen or pencil will insure that no mark is made by the spectator.*

(3) Have him close the magazine before bringing it out from behind his back. Take the pen or pencil and the magazine from the spectator. *Put the pen or pencil away in your pocket as soon as you have finished this phase of the trick.* (You are now ready to later remove the ungimmicked pencil if you wish.)

(4) Call attention to the sealed envelope which is being held by a member of the audience. Emphasize that the envelope was given to the spectator before the magazine was marked! Have the person holding the envelope tear it open and call out the word written on the card inside.

(5) Give the magazine back to the spectator who marked the page and have him look through the pages until he locates the page he marked (or so he thinks!) with an X. When he has found it, have him call out the word which is indicated by that mark. *It will match the Force Word which was written on the prediction card!*

THE CURIOUS COINCIDENCE

When performing mental marvels, always remember that your main purpose is to create an effect in the minds of your audience, not to display skill or spring some quick surprise. In short, *method* is a secondary factor in any mental test and should be played down to such degree that no one will suspect that trickery is under way. That is the case with the effect that follows. Though the procedure is extremely bold, it will be free from suspicion if you adopt a matter-of-fact delivery.

EFFECT

Four identical pairs of papers bearing the names of past famous magicians are shown, along with two ordinary paper bags. One complete set of papers is put in a bag and given to a spectator. The other identical set of papers is placed in the remaining bag and held by the performer. The spectator and the performer each remove one of the folded papers from the bags and exchange their choices with one another. When the papers are opened and read aloud, they are found to match. This is repeated three more times with amazing results. The papers match perfectly each time.

SECRET AND PREPARATION

(A)   For this amazing trick you will need two ordinary paper bags and two matching sets of papers bearing the names of famous magicians. (Any names or words may be used, such as famous singers or actors, presidents, cities — just use whatever best suits your act.) Make up two identical sets of papers. Write the names of the four magicians on the papers before folding each of them into quarters. Secretly prepare one set of papers as shown: The Dunninger paper is left unprepared. The Thurston paper has one corner folded up. The Houdini paper has two corners folded, and the Kellar paper has three folded corners. With the papers secretly prepared in this manner, you can tell at a glance which paper bears what name. This is your "key" to the trick; these prepared papers are the ones you will handle during the trick.

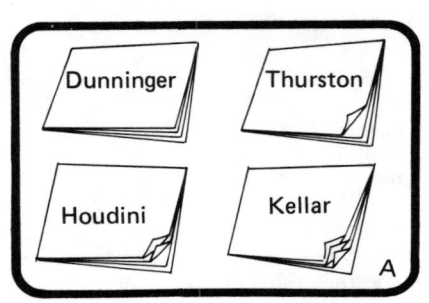

METHOD

(1)   To perform the effect, place the unprepared set of papers into one bag and give it to the spectator to hold. Place the prepared set of papers in the other bag and hold it in your left hand.

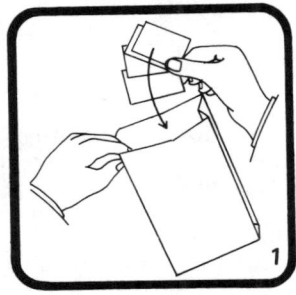

(2)   Instruct the spectator to remove one of the folded papers from his bag. You do likewise. As soon as you remove your paper, you will be able to tell at a glance which name is written inside because of the folded "key" corner(s). In the illustration, the paper with two folded corners — the "Houdini" paper — has been removed.

(3)   Once you have removed a folded paper from your bag, place the paper in full view on the table.

(4)   By now, the spectator has had time to remove a paper from his bag. Caution the spectator that he is not to open his paper yet.

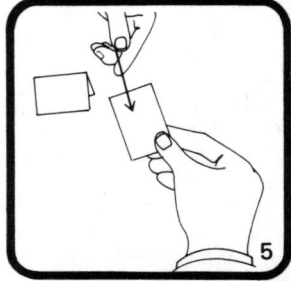

(5)   Take the spectator's folded paper from him. Instruct him to pick up your paper from the table and open it.

(6)   While the spectator is unfolding the paper, you open the paper which you took from him. Because of your "key" corner-fold system, you already know what name appears on the paper held by the spectator. If you are not holding the matching paper, then you miscall the paper you hold. This means that if the paper you hold says "Kellar," as in the illustration, you say, "Houdini." The spectator will be amazed because he will believe that he holds the matching paper. After you have "miscalled" the paper you hold, fold it back up and place it aside on the table.

(7)   Repeat the entire process with the three remaining pairs of papers. If by chance, the two of you remove identical papers, then you have an actual miracle. If not, simply miscall each paper as described in Step 6. The effect will work perfectly due to your corner-fold "key" papers. A little practice will show you how clever an effect you can make of this simple secret principle.

COMMENTS AND SUGGESTIONS

It is important that the slips not be examined or compared until *after* the effect is over. Keep the used slips in a confused pile on the table so that the spectators can't mentally pair up the slips at the trick's conclusion and discover one of your miscalls. Try this one a few times and you will be amazed at the startling effect it has on the spectators.

MILLION TO ONE

EFFECT

The magician shows the audience ten small cards with a large spot printed on the face of each card. These cards are placed on the table in a long straight row so that they alternate face up and face down. In this arrangement, the spectator can see five of the red spots and five of the red backs. The performer now asks one of the spectators to think of the color <u>blue</u>. As soon as the volunteer acknowledges, the magician asks him to call out a number between one and ten. With the number selected, the performer quickly points to the card that corresponds to the spectator's choice. To the complete surprise of the audience, this card proves to be the only blue card in the row.

SECRET AND PREPARATION

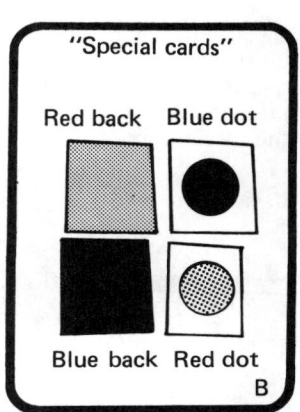

"Special cards"

Red back   Blue dot

Blue back   Red dot

B

(A) The cards may be made from "index cards" or any type of stiff white cardboard. Use crayons or marking pens to color each card. Eight of the ten cards are alike. They all have a red spot on the face, and the backs are also colored red.

(B) <u>The two remaining cards are pre-pared differently</u>. One card has a *red* spot on the <u>face</u> but the <u>back</u> is colored *blue*. The other special card has a *red* <u>back</u> and a *blue* spot on the <u>face</u>.

(C) Arrange the ten cards in a stack in this manner: The top (uppermost) card is a regular card, <u>face up</u>. The second card from the top is also regular, <u>face down</u>. The third card is the *special* <u>blue-backed</u> card, face up. The fourth card is the other *special* card with the <u>blue dot</u>, face down. The fifth card is regular, face up. The sixth card is regular, face down. The seventh card is regular, face up. The eighth card is regular, face down. The ninth card is regular, face up. The last and tenth card is regular, face down.

METHOD

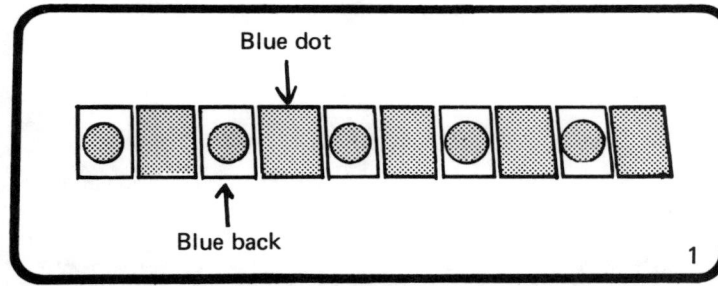

Blue dot

Blue back

1

(1) Hold the cards in the prearranged order in your left hand. Now, with your right hand, deal the ten cards, starting at the top of the packet, onto the table from left to right. This means that the cards *alternate* face up and face down and that the two *special* cards will be in the <u>third and fourth positions from your left</u>.

(2) After you have placed the cards on the table, ask a spectator to concentrate on the color "blue." Then have him call out any number between one and ten. You now proceed to *Force* one of the two specially prepared (blue) cards on the spectator.

(3) After hearing the spectator's number, count the cards as follows. Here is a procedure for <u>whatever number the spectator calls</u>:

    NUMBER ONE — Begin with the card at the <u>left</u> end and *spell* "O-N-E," arriving at the third (blue-backed) card.

    NUMBER TWO — Begin at the <u>left</u> end and *spell* "T-W-O," arriving at the third (blue-backed) card.

    NUMBER THREE — *Count* "One, Two, Three" from the <u>left</u> arriving at the third (blue-backed) card.

    NUMBER FOUR — *Count* "One, Two, Three, Four" from the left, arriving at the fourth (blue-spotted) card.

    NUMBER FIVE — Begin at the left and *spell* out "F-I-V-E," arriving at the fourth (blue-spotted) card.

    NUMBER SIX — Begin at the left and *spell* "S-I-X," arriving at the third (blue-backed) card.

    NUMBER SEVEN — Have the <u>spectator</u> count from the <u>right</u> end of the row, and he will arrive at the fourth (blue-spotted) card.

    NUMBER EIGHT — Have the <u>spectator</u> count from the <u>right</u> end until he arrives at the eighth special (blue-backed) card.

    NUMBER NINE — Begin at your <u>left</u> end and *spell* "N-I-N-E," arriving at the fourth (blue-spotted) card.

    NUMBER TEN — Begin at your <u>left</u> end and *spell* "T-E-N," arriving at the third (blue-backed) card.

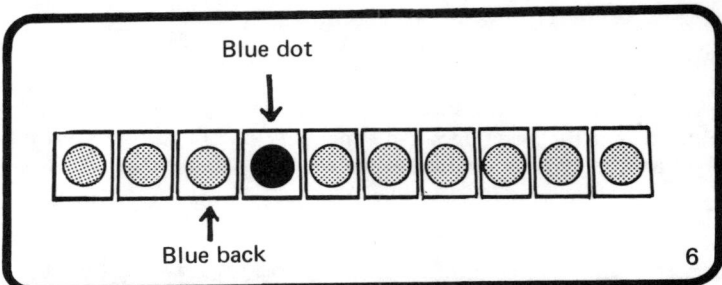

(4) After you have finished the spelling or counting, emphasize the fact that the spectator was given a <u>free</u> choice of any card. (Or so he thinks!) Now turn the chosen (Force) card over to show that the opposite side is <u>blue</u>.

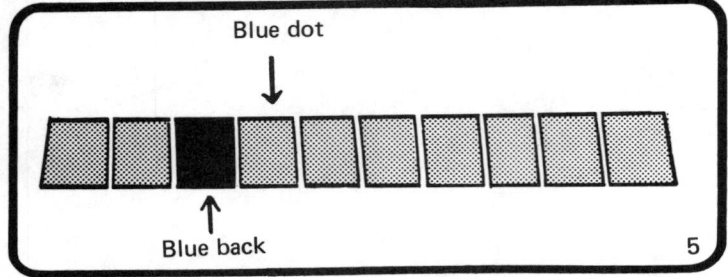

(5) If the selected card is the *blue-backed* (third) card, turn all the cards which are face-up cards <u>face down</u> to show that all have <u>red</u> backs <u>except his chosen card</u>.

(6) If the selected card is the *blue-spotted* (fourth) card, turn all the cards that are face down <u>face up</u> to show that all have red spots <u>except his chosen card</u>.

(7) This final turning of the cards serves to convince the spectators that the cards are all identical *except* for the one card which he selected and conceals the fact that you are using one more specially prepared card. After this turn-over, gather up all the cards, being careful not to expose the remaining special (blue) card among the rest.

COMMENTS AND SUGGESTIONS

Carry the ten cards in their prearranged stack in a separate pocket so that you can remove the cards and place them on the table in a smooth, unhurried fashion. Practice placing the cards on the table until you can do it in a natural, relaxed manner. This effect can be presented either as a demonstration of ESP or as a magic trick. Never repeat this trick, or you will give away the principle used to force the special card.

THE GYPSY MINDREADER
(PSYCHOMETRY)

The subject of "psychometry" is based on the theory that objects belonging to a person, particularly those that he carries with him, can be identified as belonging to the person even when they are removed from the owner. For years, this was an old gypsy custom, depending on guesswork or trickery. Today, many people — including some professors — regard psychometry as a form of Extra-Sensory Perception (ESP). As such, it belongs in a program of mental magic, and the test about to be described is one of the best of that type.

EFFECT

Five plain white envelopes are distributed among the audience. Each recipient is asked to place a small article into his envelope and seal it. A volunteer gathers up the envelopes and thoroughly mixes them before handing them back to the performer. The magician openly places the envelopes into a clear glass bowl and explains to his audience that the little-explored subject of "psychometry" is based on the theory that, by handling articles belonging to a person, it is possible to gain a mental impression of the actual person, even though the articles are sealed in an envelope. In order to demonstrate the validity of this theory, the magician picks up one of the envelopes and holds it to his forehead. Without hesitation, he announces that the article inside the sealed envelope belongs to a young lady. The performer opens the envelope and allows the article to fall into his open palm. He closes his hand around the item and, apparently from the vibrations received from the article, proceeds to describe the owner in minute detail. Finally, the magician walks among the spectators and is mysteriously led to the surprised girl.

This demonstration is repeated using the four remaining envelopes and the objects they contain with the same unfailing accuracy.

NOTE: Properly performed, the above effect is one of the strongest mental feats available. Some professional magicians have built their entire reputation based on the above presentation. Again, it is important that you present this effect as entertainment, assuring your audience that it is merely a magician's demonstration of the phenomenon of psychometry.

SECRET AND PREPARATION

(A) You will need a number of plain white envelopes — "Letter" size, measuring approximately 3½" x 6½", are perfect for this effect. Four of the five envelopes are prepared by placing a small pencil dot in a *different corner* of each of the envelopes. The dots are put on the flap side of the envelope — one in each of the four corners. *They are made in pencil, lightly, so as not to be noticed by the spectators.*

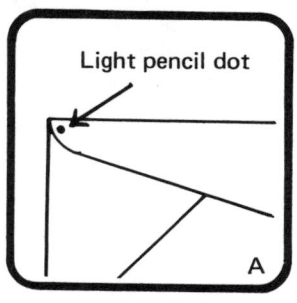

(B) Each of the four corner dots represents a different spectator. The fifth envelope is left unmarked. Stack the five envelopes so that the spectator number dots are arranged, clockwise from top to bottom, running one through five as shown.

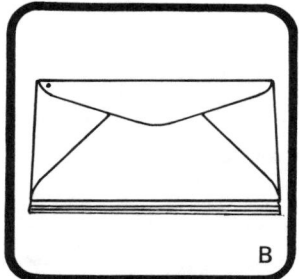

METHOD

(1) Holding the envelopes in this prearranged stack, pass them out to the spectators, moving from left to right through the audience. *All you have to do is remember who gets each envelope.*

(2) After returning to the stage, instruct the five spectators to place a small object into their envelopes, seal them, and pass them to another spectator. This volunteer is asked to mix up the envelopes to his satisfaction and hand them back to you.

(3) Drop the envelopes into a clear glass container. As you remove the first envelope, turn it flap side up and locate the coded dot. You now know to whom this envelope belongs.

(4) Hold the envelope to your forehead and slowly reveal whether the object belongs to a man or a woman. An example might be as follows: "I'm getting a very strong vibration from this envelope. Yes, the article inside must belong to a gentleman in his late twenties or early thirties."

(5) At this point, tear open the envelope and allow the article to fall into your hand. After discarding the envelope, close your fingers around the item and begin to reveal details regarding this person's appearance (which you can see from the stage or, better yet, which you remember from when you handed out the envelopes).

(6) During this reading, start moving down into the audience and, as if being led by the vibrating force of the object in your hand, dramatically locate the owner.

(7) Repeat the demonstration with the four remaining objects. When you have finished, the audience will be left with a profound mystery that is quite different from any other effect on your program.

THE CENTER TEAR

This is without a doubt one of the simplest yet cleverest of all methods for learning the contents of a short message, a word or a number written by a spectator. Properly performed, it is so deceptive that your audience will have no idea that trickery is involved — with the result that many may be ready to accept it as a display of actual mindreading. Naturally, you should disclaim such power, yet at the same time keep the secret to yourself, thus adding to a very perplexing mystery.

EFFECT

The magician gives a spectator a square slip of paper and a pencil, telling him to write a name, a number, or even a brief message in the center. This is done while the magician's back is turned. Then the spectator folds the paper in half and then in quarters, so that the performer cannot possibly see the writing. The magician tears up the folded slip, and its pieces are openly dropped into an ashtray and burned. Yet the magician learns the spectator's message and reveals it!

SECRET AND PREPARATION

(A) To prepare for this trick, you will need to place a book of matches in your left trouser or coat pocket and you will need to have an ashtray handy.

(B) Cut out a small slip of paper approximately three inches square. *Draw a circle about 1¼ inches wide in the center of one side of the paper as shown.*

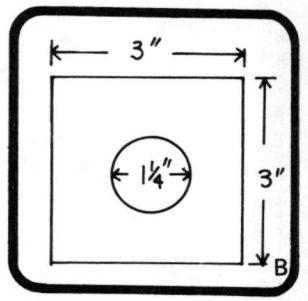

METHOD

(1) Give the paper to a spectator and instruct him to write a word or a short message within the "magic circle." Make sure that the spectator understands that you are not to see what he writes on the paper.

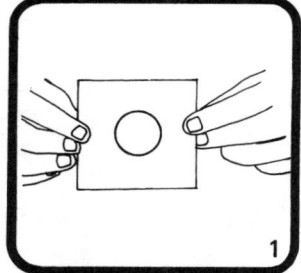

(2) When the message is complete, instruct the spectator to fold the paper in half so that his writing is within the fold.

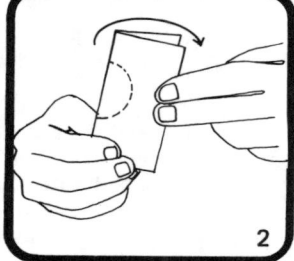

(3) Then have him fold the paper once again, so that it is in quarters.

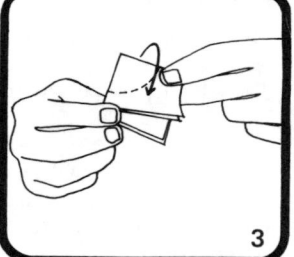

(4) Take the folded slip from the spectator. You can look at the packet and easily see which corner is actually the center "magic circle" of the piece of paper. *NOTE: Practice folding the paper yourself, and it will help you to instantly spot the desired corner.*

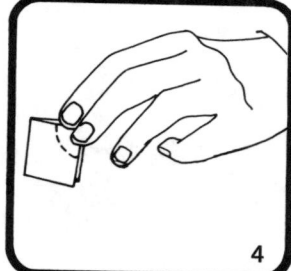

(5) When you have located the center corner of the paper, hold the folded packet so that the "magic circle" is in the upper right-hand corner facing you. With the packet held in this manner, tear it in half. This tear should leave the "magic circle" undamaged.

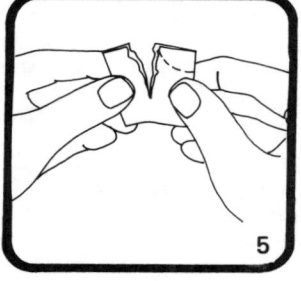

(6) Once you have torn the packet in half, place the left-hand pieces of paper behind the right-hand pieces. Hold all the pieces in your left hand. The "magic circle" should be at the top of the packet, and it should be nearest your body.

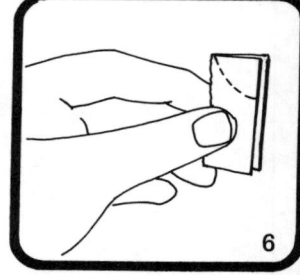

(7) Now rotate the packet a quarter-turn to the right and grasp it between both hands. The "magic circle" is still facing you, held by your right thumb and first finger. Holding the packet in this position, tear it in half once more.

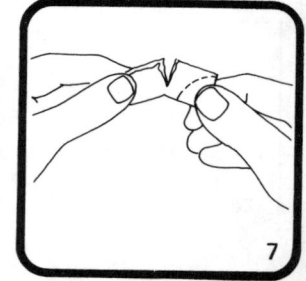

(8) Again, place the left-hand pieces behind the right-hand pieces. Then take all the pieces in your right finger-tips. The "magic circle" is still facing you and is directly under your right thumb.

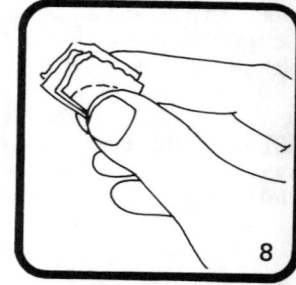

(9) Hold all the pieces in your right hand, between your thumb and fingers. Now position your right hand over the ashtray. Drop all of the pieces of paper except the "magic circle" which is held directly under your thumb, into the ashtray. As you release the pieces, use your thumb to slide the piece of paper containing the "magic circle" back toward the middle joints of your fingers.

(10) You now secretly hold the "magic circle" concealed in your right fingers. The rest of the pieces of paper have fallen into the ashtray. The audience is unaware that you hold this paper (which contains the message) in your hand.

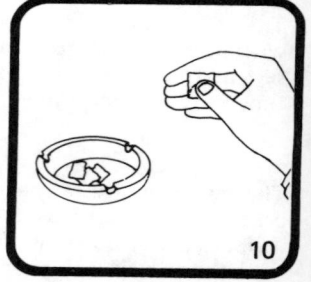

(11) With the "magic circle" safely hidden in your right hand, use your left hand to reach into your trouser pocket and take out the book of matches. Then use both hands to remove a match, strike it, and set fire to the piece of paper in the ashtray. Place the matchbook on the table with your right hand and use your left hand to hold the lighted match.

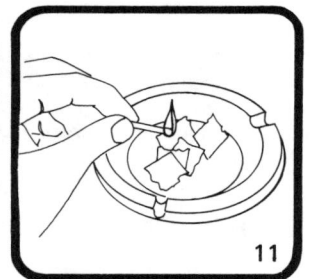

(12) While the spectators are concentrating on the burning pieces of paper, drop your right hand below the table and use your right thumb to secretly open up the "magic circle" hidden in your right fingers. As soon as you have read the message, quietly crumple up or refold the paper. As the paper continues to burn, pick up the packet of matches and place them *and the "magic circle"* in your right pocket. Concentrate deeply on the rising smoke before you reveal the words of the message!

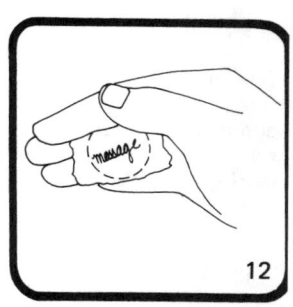

COMMENTS AND SUGGESTIONS

The most important thing to remember is that your right hand, while it secretly holds the center portion of the paper, must be held completely relaxed and natural. Then, when you drop your right hand below the table to open up the paper and read the message, ask the spectators to focus their attention on the burning pieces of paper and the smoke as you casually glance at the message.

This is another "classic" method that is used not only by magicians, but also by fraudulent spirit mediums and psychics. Its great strength lies in that it uses only ordinary objects. With the proper "build-up," this simple effect can be made into a real miracle!

THE CENTER TEAR

"Standing" Variation

When working away from a table, as you occasionally may have to do, you can use the following subterfuge.

METHOD

(1) Light the match with your left hand, placing the match pack in your right hand, hiding the torn center.

(2) As you start to set fire to the pieces in the ashtray, place the matchbook on the table.

(3) Then purposely let the match go out, *while your right thumb is secretly opening the torn center.*

(4) Your right hand now picks up the match pack in order to strike another match. Both hands are needed for that action, particularly if the left hand dawdles while lighting the pieces in the ashtray, giving you an opportunity to read the message.

(5) Finally, the right hand can slide the match pack over the torn center, hiding it. You dispose of the torn center *by simply dropping it in your right pocket along with the match pack.*

SPECTRUM PREDICTION

PREDICTION effects form an important phase of Mentalism and therefore should be included on nearly every program. Moreover, where predictions are concerned, one good test definitely calls for another, because the more predictions you fulfill, the less chance there is that luck has anything to do with it. Any good prediction may puzzle your audience, but if you follow one with another, or even hit three in a row, people will really be bewildered. However, simply repeating the same prediction time after time is not the right policy. Some spectators lose interest when the same trick is repeated; others are apt to watch for a weak point and may be just sharp enough to spot it. So the answer is to have some special type of divination in reserve, differing from the rest in regard to objects used, as well as method. The SPECTRUM PREDICTION meets both those qualifications.

EFFECT

The magician displays eight brightly colored squares of cardboard and spreads them out on the table so that everyone can see that each square is a different color. The performer then writes a "prediction" on a piece of paper which he folds and gives to a member of the audience to hold. The colored chips are gathered together by a spectator and wrapped in the magician's opaque handkerchief. This same spectator is then asked to reach into the folds of the handkerchief and withdraw a single chip. This done, the prediction is unfolded and read aloud. The performer proves to be correct!

SECRET AND PREPARATION

(A) From a stationery or art supply store, obtain eight different colors of cardboard, or you may use colored "construction" paper, or even white cardboard which you color with paint, crayons, or ink. The colors you use are unimportant, but use easily recognizable colors such as: yellow, blue, green, red, orange, purple, black and white. In any event, make eight one-inch squares, all of a different color. You also need to cut eight more squares which *are all the same color*. For the purpose of explanation, let's assume that these additional squares are all red. *You, therefore, have eight different colored squares and eight squares which are all red.*

(B) You will also need two identical pocket handkerchiefs. Handkerchiefs made with a colored pattern work best. (Bandanas are good.) Now place one upon the other and sew them together exactly as shown by the dotted lines.

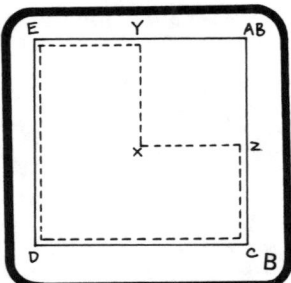

(C) You will notice that point "X" is the center of the handkerchief. The stitching along lines "XY" and "XZ" form a "hidden pocket" which can be opened at "AB." Now sew two small beads at the "A" and "B" corners. These beads will enable you to find the pocket opening quickly. (The beads are optional, but they do help greatly in locating the secret pocket at the proper time.)

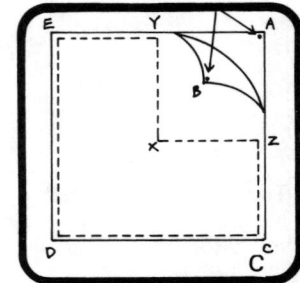

(D) *Place the eight red squares into the hidden pocket.* Grasp corners A and B and shake out the handkerchief. Place the prepared handkerchief into your inside coat pocket with corners A and B on top where you can grasp them easily so that the extra "secret" squares will not fall out when you remove the handkerchief.

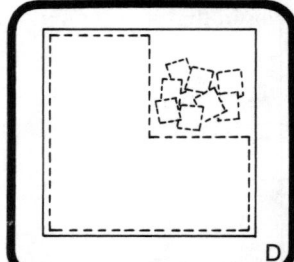

(E) Along with the eight squares of different colors, place a small pad of paper and a pencil on the table.

METHOD

(1) Call the spectator's attention to the colored squares. Pick up the pad and, without letting the spectators see what you are writing, write, "You will select the color red." Tear the "prediction" from the pad and fold it so that it cannot be read by the spectators. Hand the folded slip to one of the spectators to hold.

(2) With your right hand, reach into your inside coat pocket and grasp the prepared handkerchief by the small beads which are sewn into the Corners A and B. Withdraw the handkerchief, show it on both sides, and then gather all of the corners together forming a "bag" as shown.

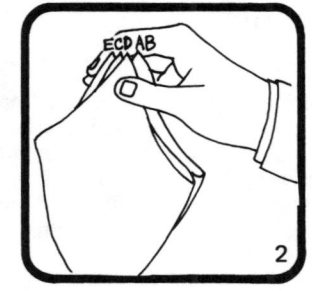

(3) Have the spectator pick up the colored squares from the table. You are holding the handkerchief by the corners in your right hand. With your left thumb and first finger, hinge down Corner D and allow the spectator to drop the squares into the handkerchief. *These squares do not go into the secret pocket.*

(4) Shake the impromptu bag, mixing the colored squares inside. *Now hinge Corner A down and allow the spectator to reach inside and remove a single square.* He will be reaching inside the hidden pocket which contains only red squares. *Be sure he removes only one of the squares.*

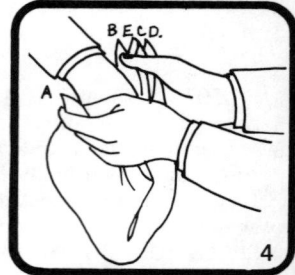

(5) Once the spectator has the red square in his hand, simply bunch up the handkerchief and put it back into your pocket, squares and all.

(6) Ask the spectator to unfold the slip of paper . . . again you have proven your "Magical Powers" . . . your prediction proves to be exactly correct!

COMMENTS AND SUGGESTIONS

The success of this trick depends upon handling the handkerchief in a natural, casual manner, so as to avoid suspicion. Since the handkerchief is a common article, it seems nothing more than a mere adjunct to the prediction, hence it is comparatively easy to focus attention on the colored squares at the outset and the prediction slip at the finish, leaving the spectator with one red square and the prediction.

If you have an *ordinary handkerchief* resembling the special double handkerchief, you can use it in some previous effect in which it plays an innocent part; then place it in your pocket afterward. When you bring out the *double handkerchief* for the SPECTRUM PREDICTION, everyone will suppose it to be the same one that you used before, so any suspicion will be lulled from the start. It is also a good plan to have eight extra squares of some color other than red, so that if you perform the prediction for the same group of people on another occasion, you can "Force" a different color.

SPECTRUM PREDICTION
"Number" Variation

A clever and simple variation of the SPECTRUM PREDICTION is the use of the numbers One through Eight written on separate slips of paper rather than the colored squares of cardboard used in the first version.

EFFECT

The magician displays a pad of paper and openly writes the numbers One through Eight on individual sheets of paper from the pad. After all of the papers have been numbered, each is folded, first in half and then into quarters, and the entire lot is placed into a makeshift bag constructed from the magician's handkerchief. The magician then writes an additional "prediction" number, which he does not let the audience see, on one more slip of paper. This is folded and handed to one of the spectators to hold. A second spectator is asked to select one of the eight slips from the handkerchief. After the slip is selected, the magician opens the handkerchief to show that only seven slips remain. The two spectators then open their papers. The slip containing the prediction is found to match exactly the "freely selected" number on the paper held by the second spectator.

SECRET AND PREPARATION

The secret of this trick is exactly the same as the SPECTRUM PREDICTION; however, it does have certain advantages and one disadvantage as well. The disadvantage is that the colored slips are perhaps more spectacular and can certainly be seen from a greater distance if you are performing for a large group. The number variation, however, has the advantage of the "look" of a totally impromptu mystery in that all of the props are ordinary objects as opposed to the specially colored squares. Also, in the following method, the handkerchief may be opened so that the remaining slips fall out after the second spectator has made his selection.

Before the show, on eight slips of paper write the same number — let's assume the number is *Five.* Fold all of the slips and place them in the secret pocket of the Double Handkerchief just as you did in Step D of the SPECTRUM PREDICTION. Then place the handkerchief in your pocket.

METHOD

(1) Display a pad of paper (this must be the same paper as the previously written and folded slips) and <u>openly</u> write the numbers One through Eight individually on different sheets from the pad. Write the number "1," tear that sheet off, fold it in half and then into quarters, and place it on the table. Then write the number "2," tear it off and fold it, and place it on the table with the first. Continue until you have eight separate slips with different numbers.

(2) Now, just as you did in Step 2 of the Spectrum Prediction, remove the handkerchief from your pocket and, as in Step 3, form the handkerchief into a bag by holding it by the four corners. Then place all eight slips into the main body of the handkerchief. *Do not put the slips in the secret pocket.*

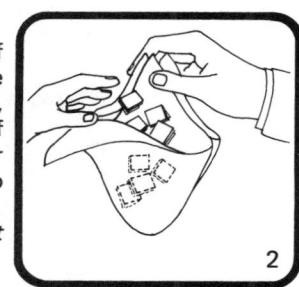

(3) Now explain to the spectator what he is to do. Tell him that he is to reach into the handkerchief and remove *one* of the slips. He is to hold the slip tightly in his hand so that no one can see what number is written on it until the conclusion of the effect. As you explain to him what he is to do, *you demonstrate his actions at the same time.* Reach into the "bag" (be sure you reach into the main body of the handkerchief, <u>not</u> the secret compartment) and remove one of the regular slips. After explaining that he is to hold the slip tightly, put your hand back into the handkerchief <u>apparently</u> replacing the slip. *Really, you secretly hold the slip in the Finger Palm position and remove your hand as if it were empty.*

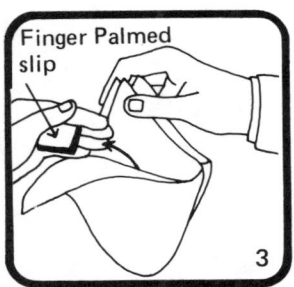

Finger Palmed slip

(4) *NOTE: You will find this quite easy to do as the spectators are not expecting trickery of any kind at this point.*

(5) Reach into your pocket and remove the pencil. *At the same time, leave the extra slip, which you have just palmed, in your pocket.* Gaze intently at the spectator who will select the slip as if to gain a "mental impression" of his future actions. Then pick up the pad with your other hand and write the prediction (the number "Five") on the pad. Tear off the slip, fold it, and hand it to some other spectator to hold.

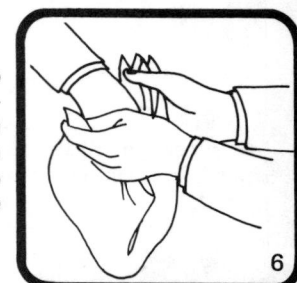

(6) Now ask the first spectator to reach into the handkerchief and remove <u>one</u> of the slips. Be sure that you open the handkerchief as you did in Step 4 of the Spectrum Prediction so that he will remove one of the Force papers.

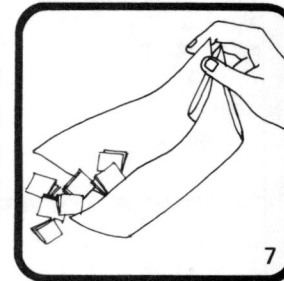

(7) Now open up the handkerchief holding Corners A and B gathered in your right hand (so that the "secret" Force slips do not fall out) and let the seven remaining slips in the main portion of the handkerchief fall on the table.

(8) Place the handkerchief in your pocket (along with the Force slips). Then, with your right hand, pick the slips up one at a time and count them, <u>without unfolding them</u>, from the table into your left hand. Indicate to the spectator that he could have had a free selection of any of the eight slips as you openly place the seven pieces of paper in your pocket.

(9) Have the second spectator open the prediction slip and read the number aloud. Emphasize again the free selection that the first spectator had. Have him open his slip for the first time and read his "freely selected" number. The two numbers match! You have just presented what appears to be another completely impromptu Mental Miracle.

PING PONG PRESTIDIGITATION

Here is a comedy trick in which you let everyone in the audience in on the secret of the effect except for one person — a volunteer from the audience who assists you on stage. He is the only person who is deceived by your magical methods, creating a situation that develops into good fun for everyone.

EFFECT

The magician displays three pairs of different colored ping pong balls. One pair is white, one pair red, and one pair blue. The performer drops all six balls into a paper bag and invites two spectators on stage to assist in the effect. The spectator on the magician's left is asked to reach into the bag — without looking — and to remove any ball. No matter which ball he withdraws, the other spectator is always able to reach into the bag and remove the matching ball without looking inside the bag. The selected balls are replaced, and the trick is repeated over and over again with the same impossible results.

SECRET AND PREPARATION

What the first spectator doesn't know is that the entire audience and the other spectator on stage can see the colored balls all along through a secret "window" in the side of the bag! Because of the secret window, everyone sees how the trick works *except* for the spectator on the left who is unaware throughout the presentation that the bag is cleverly "gimmicked."

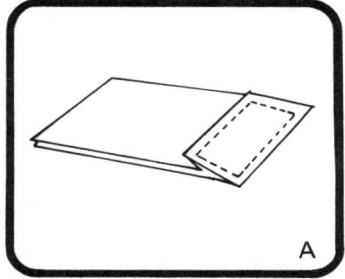
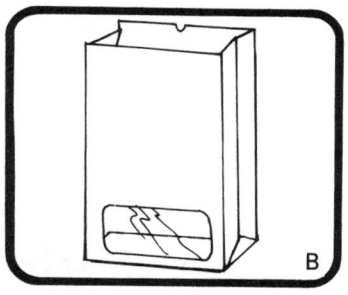
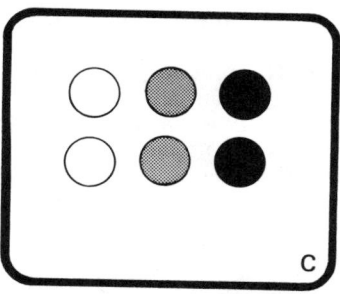

(A) To prepare, obtain an ordinary brown paper bag, about the size of a standard "lunch bag," and cut a hole in the side of the bag as shown. The position of the hole should be such that it is completely hidden from view by the bottom portion of the bag when the bag is folded flat. This way the bag can be freely shown on both sides and handled quite casually before it is opened to begin the effect. (B) This done, glue or tape a piece of transparent kitchen wrap (clear plastic) over the hole so that the balls will not fall out of the bag during the presentation. The construction of the bag is complete. As you can see, you formed a sort of "window" in the bag which allows you to see into the bag quite easily. (C) The next step is to purchase six ordinary ping pong balls. Prepare the three pairs of balls by painting or dyeing them in three brightly contrasting colors. Permanent ink marking pens also work well for coloring the balls and can be purchased at most stationery stores.

Instead of ping pong balls, you can use lightweight plastic or rubber balls which can be obtained at department or toy stores. Be sure they are all the same size and are made of the same material so that it is impossible to distinguish one color from another without looking at them. The construction of the props is now complete and you are ready to perform this clever comedy mystery.

METHOD

(1) Invite two spectators on stage and position yourself between them, facing the audience. Display the balls and call attention to the fact that there are three pairs of different colored balls. Then pick up the bag and display it — folded flat — so that everyone (especially the spectator on the left) can see that it is quite "ordinary." Now, open the bag *so that the window faces the audience* (and not the spectator on your left) and openly drop the six balls into the bag. The audience will immediately see that the bag is gimmicked and will begin to see "why" as you continue.

(2) Speaking to the spectator on your left, instruct him to reach into the bag — without looking — and remove *one* ball. *Tell him to keep it concealed in his closed hand so that only he knows its color.* Be sure to hold the bag so that the window is facing away from him so he cannot see that the bag is prepared.

(3) After he removes the ball, swing your body to the right and explain to the other spectator that he is to concentrate very hard and then reach into the bag and try to remove the matching colored ball. *Be sure to hold the bag so that the window faces him.* He will "catch on" immediately once he sees the window in the bag. It is a simple matter for the volunteer to remove the correct ball, *as it will be the only ball inside the bag without a matching color.*

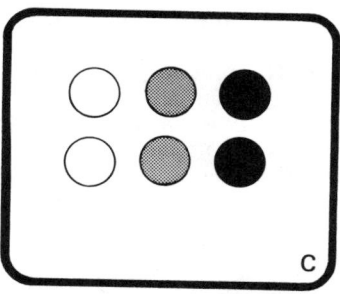

(4) Once the second spectator has removed the ball, have both spectators openly display the two selected balls to the audience. Since the volunteer on your right has removed the correct ball, the two balls will match in color.

(5) Now have, both spectators replace the balls in the bag and perform the effect a few more times. Each time the trick is successful, the reaction of the spectator on your left will become more and more humorous. Because he is unaware of the secret window, he will not be able to explain this seemingly impossible series of "coincidences."

COMMENTS AND SUGGESTIONS

At the end of the trick, you should humorously reveal the secret of the trick to the puzzled spectator by "accidentally" turning the window side of the bag toward him as you reach out to shake his hand. Then thank both of your volunteers for being such good sports as they return to the audience.

This is a good trick to work at a party when you are waiting for more people to arrive before you begin your regular show. After Mr. Left has been utterly baffled, you tell him that next time, he can play the part of Mr. Right. After some newcomers arrive, you repeat the trick, inviting one of them to serve as Mr. Left. Your former victim, now Mr. Right, then has the pleasure of seeing how nicely he was fooled the time before. This procedure can be repeated with other new arrivals, making an excellent prelude for your show.

NOTE: You must be careful in presenting tricks of this nature that you don't offend or insult the intelligence of the volunteer who is unaware of the working of the effect. Present the trick in a warm, humorous style so that the spectator does not get annoyed at the fact that he "can't see how it's done."

THE ENVELOPE STAND

With mental tests, it is always a good plan to use some simple props only if they make the presentation more direct and therefore more effective. When such devices actually aid in the deception without the audience realizing it, the effect is all the better. This applies strongly with THE ENVELOPE STAND, which is so named because it has much to do with the effect that follows.

EFFECT

The magician displays an attractive pasteboard stand with five numbered envelopes arranged on it. The performer announces that <u>one</u> of the sealed envelopes contains a *dollar bill* and the <u>rest</u> are *empty*. A spectator is given a free choice of any envelope. When the chosen envelope is opened, it is found to contain the dollar bill. It appears as if the magician has been able to influence the decision of the spectator.

SECRET AND PREPARATION

(A) Actually, all five envelopes are empty. The stand is constructed in such a way as to deliver the bill into any selected envelope. Construct the stand as shown. Use a piece of cardboard about 10" x 15" (depending upon the size of the envelopes). Cut out a hole in the center of the back of the stand. Then tape the lower portion of an envelope that you have cut in half to the back of the cardboard just below the opening.

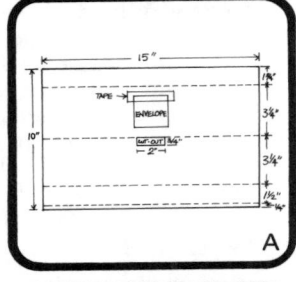

(B) Fold the cardboard as shown by the dotted lines so that the half-envelope is hidden inside the triangular body of the stand.

(C) This illustration shows the completed stand. Notice the turned up "lip" located on the front edge of the stand. This ledge prevents the envelopes from slipping off the stand.

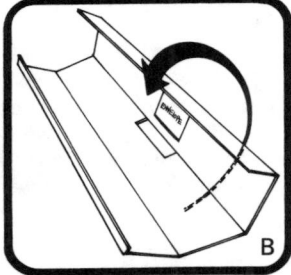

(D) Arrange five numbered envelopes on the face of the stand. *Secretly place a folded dollar bill out of sight in the half-envelope.*

(E) This is a view from the rear. Notice how the dollar bill protrudes slightly from the hole behind the center envelope. The top edge of the bill extends a quarter inch or so from the hole *and cannot be seen from the front side of the stand.*

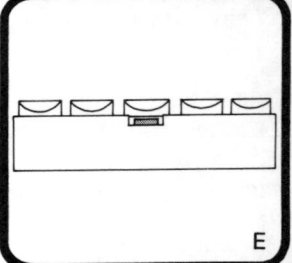

METHOD

(1) To perform the trick, display the stand and call attention to the five numbered envelopes displayed on the stand. (Small "coin" or "pay" envelopes work best.) Announce that you have placed a dollar bill in only *one* of the envelopes prior to the trick. Predict that the dollar envelope will be chosen at random by a spectator. Select a spectator and allow him to choose any envelope. Give him the opportunity to change his mind if he wishes.

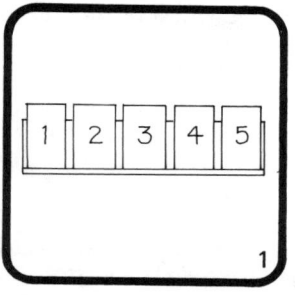

(5) Remove the selected envelope from the stand with the thumb and fingers of your right hand and, as you do, secretly grasp the upper end of the hidden bill with your right fingers. Hold it firmly behind the selected envelope as you remove the envelope from the stand, being sure not to expose the bill hidden behind it.

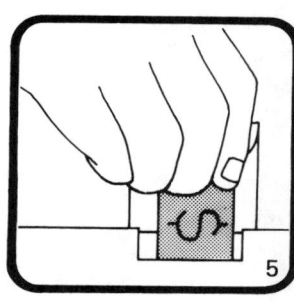

(2) Then remove all envelopes not chosen from the stand.

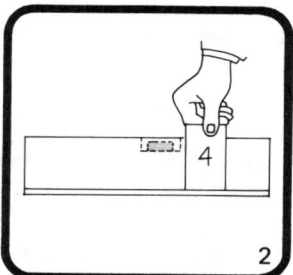

(6) Now casually transfer the envelope (and the hidden bill) to your left hand. The left thumb now holds the bill against the back of the envelope. This move gives the spectators a chance to see that both of your hands are empty. With your free right hand, tear off one end of the sealed envelope. Be sure not to prematurely expose the bill.

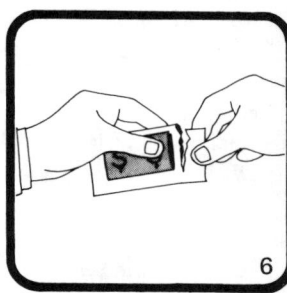

(3) *Place the selected envelope, in this case Number FOUR, directly in front of the secret hole in the stand.*

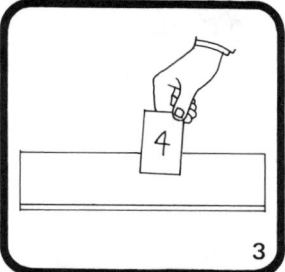

(7) Insert your right first and second fingers into the envelope and appear to remove the bill from inside. *Actually, you pull the bill out from behind the envelope using your right thumb.* Display the folded bill, held between the thumb and fingers of your right hand.

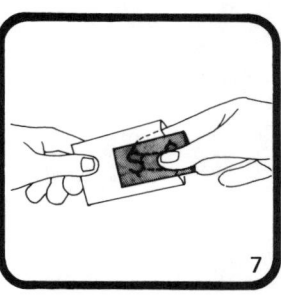

(4) Here is the rear view of the stand at this point in the routine. Notice how the bill in the half-envelope protrudes slightly from the hole in the stand.

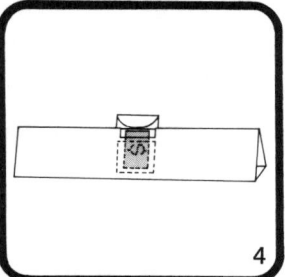

(8) Unfold the bill and show it to be authentic before you pick up the other four envelopes. Tear these envelopes in half to show that they are all empty — or better yet, have the spectators open and examine them. You may reward your spectator with the dollar as a souvenir if you wish. In any event, hand the remains of all of the envelopes out to your audience for inspection.

THE ENVELOPE STAND
"Bank Night" Variation

EFFECT

An effective comedy variation of this mystery can be worked with *four* spectators. The audience is informed that only one of the envelopes contains a real bill — the rest have only blank slips of paper. Each spectator will be allowed to choose any envelope, and they may change their minds as often as they wish. The performer states that *whoever picks the envelope with the dollar bill can keep it* and that he will keep only the final envelope for himself. Thus, the spectators do all of the "choosing." When each spectator opens his envelope, he finds a blank piece of paper the size of a dollar bill. The magician then opens his envelope and removes the "real" dollar bill!

SECRET AND PREPARATION

The trick works exactly the same as THE ENVELOPE STAND except that you must be sure that all the envelopes are opaque since the spectators will have an opportunity to handle them and change their minds, and thus perhaps "see through" an envelope made of light-weight paper. Cut <u>five</u> blank pieces of paper the same size as a dollar bill and place one in each of the five numbered envelopes. Conceal the dollar bill in the envelope stand as before.

METHOD

(1)   Explain that only <u>one</u> envelope contains a dollar bill and that the lucky spectator who selects it <u>will get to keep it</u>.

(2)   Have each spectator *call out the number of the envelope he wants.* When each makes his choice, <u>you hand the envelope to the spectator.</u> *(In this way, the spectators never have a chance to come near the Stand and discover its secret.)*

(3)   After each has decided which envelope he wants, position the remaining envelope in the center of the stand — <u>directly in front of the hidden bill</u>.

(4)   Emphasize the fairness of the selection and then have each spectator open his envelope — *one at a time.* <u>Now the suspense builds as the odds grow shorter</u> as the contents of each envelope are revealed.

(5)   *Just as the last spectator removes the blank paper, pick up <u>your</u> envelope and <u>steal the bill from the stand</u>.* All eyes will be on the spectator at this time, which will aid in the <u>misdirection</u> as you remove the remaining envelope *and* the bill.

(6)   Now open your envelope and remove (from behind) the "real" dollar.

(7)   Thank the spectators as you crumple up your envelope (with the last blank paper inside). Casually place the envelope on your table (or toss it off stage) as you display the dollar to the audience!

"BETCHAS"

In magical parlance, the term "Betcha" is short for "I'll bet you!"—which means that you, as the magician, would be willing to bet a spectator that you can do something that he can't. Of course, you don't have to make a bet to prove your point. You can go right ahead and do it, just for the fun of it. People appreciate that because, if they get fun out of watching magic, they want to see more. That works to your advantage as much as theirs.

Actually, a "Betcha" is more of a puzzle than a trick. If you lay a row of coins on a table and state that in three moves you can bring all the heads together and all the tails together, people may not believe you until you have done it. But once you have done it, you have shown them how to do it for themselves. With a full-fledged trick, it is different. You accomplish a seeming impossibility without disclosing the secret.

"Betchas," however, can prove both useful and effective, so it is wise to have them available. Practically every "Betcha" has some neat twist which gives it audience appeal, and some, if done smoothly and fairly rapidly, may even become tricks in their own right. Although you show people exactly what they are supposed to do, the moves may be too complex for them to follow. So instead of learning "how it's done," they only become all the more puzzled.

There are some other good reasons why "Betcha" should be cultivated. When performing before small groups, some people may want you to start before the rest are ready to watch. This can upset your routine, and it is also likely to interrupt a good trick at a crucial moment, spoiling the effect entirely. Even worse, you may have to do some of your tricks over to please people who weren't there to see them the first time, which can really detract from your performance and also give those who see them twice an opportunity to discover the secret.

So the best plan is to "warm up" with a few "Betcha"—getting people to try some trifling tricks for themselves, which will put them in a mood to appreciate the real magic that you show them later, when the group is fully assembled.

There are also times when you are starting an impromptu performance that somebody may come up with some trick of the "Betcha" type and try to steal some of your thunder. Even if you are familiar with this trick, it won't do any good to say so once your would-be rival has put it across. So the answer here is to come back with a few "Betchas" of your own, picking those that are so intriguing that you friends will forget the one they saw at the start.

Finally, "Betchas" are the real answer to the question that some friend is sure to ask—"Say! How about showing me how some of your tricks are done? Maybe just one trick that I could do myself . . ." Naturally, you won't want to lose a good trick by telling how it's done, but you won't want to lose a good friend either. So show him a few "Betchas." They're expendable!

THE IMPOSSIBLE PENETRATION

EFFECT

The magician displays two rolled up Dollar Bills. He places a bill in the crook of each of his thumbs, one bill in each hand. By grasping the ends of the bills with the *thumbs* and *second fingers* of the opposite hands, he is able to separate his hands — causing the bills to apparently pass "magically" through one another. The real mystery is that the spectators are unable to duplicate the feat.

METHOD

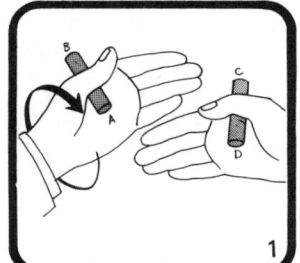

(1) Roll two Dollar Bills into tight cylinders and hold the bills in the crooks of the thumbs as shown.

(4) Rotate your hands in opposite directions as you pull your hands apart.

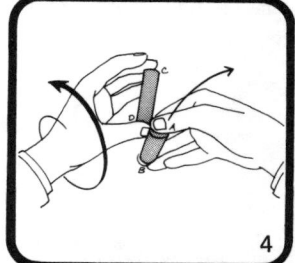

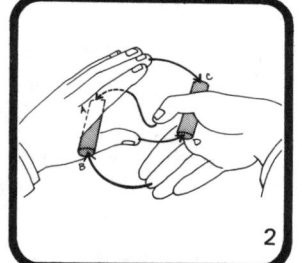

(2) Rotate your hands in opposite directions so that you can take the *left-hand* bill with the *right thumb* at A and the *right second finger* at B. At the same time, your left hand grasps the *right-hand* bill with the *left thumb* at D and the *left second finger* at C.

(5) The bills will free themselves and appear to "magically" pass through each other.

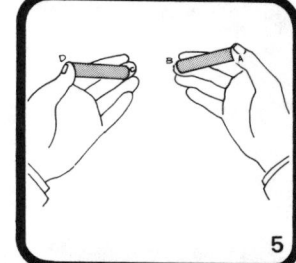

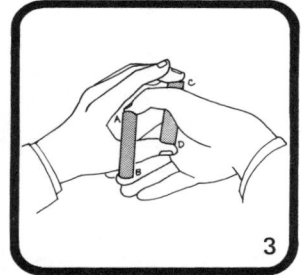

(3) Held correctly, your hands should look like this. To the audience, the illusion of the "linking" of your fingers and the bills is perfect.

COMMENTS AND SUGGESTIONS

This effect can also be done with two corks, short pencils, or any small objects of the correct shape and size. Whatever you use, it's a very deceptive "quickie." Or it may be done as a "puzzle." In this case, you repeat the trick over and over as the spectators try to duplicate it. Each time do the "penetration" a little slower. Finally, someone will "get it" and start to fool the other participants. Present it this way at the next party you attend and see how much fun you will have!

THE IMPOSSIBLE KNOT

Tricks of the "Do As I Do" type are always effective, and this is one of the best. All you need are two ropes, each about three feet in length; one for yourself, the other for a spectator. With a little practice and one simple, secret move, you can baffle your audience time after time — to the point where they will actually fool themselves!

EFFECT

The magician holds a length of rope with one end in each hand. He invites a spectator to do the same with another piece of rope. Stating that it would be impossible to tie a knot in a rope without letting go of at least one end, the wizard proceeds to drape the rope over his arms, forming a series of simple loops and twists. This is done slowly, without letting go of the ends, so the spectator can copy *every move the magician makes* with his rope. Still holding both ends, the magician shakes the rope from his arms and — a knot appears "magically" in the center. No knot is formed in the spectator's rope, even though he is sure he has copied the magician's every move exactly.

METHOD

(1) Hold the rope near the ends between the thumb and first finger of each hand with the rope hanging below as shown.

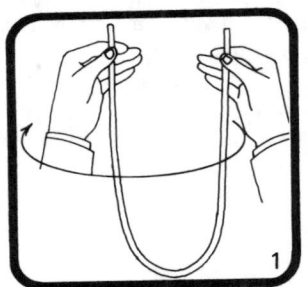

(2) Bring your right hand inwards (toward you) and drape the rope over your left wrist as shown.

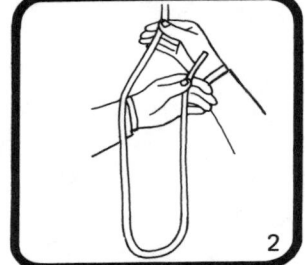

(3) Draw the right end of the rope downward and beneath the hanging loop. This divides the hanging loop into two sections, left and right.

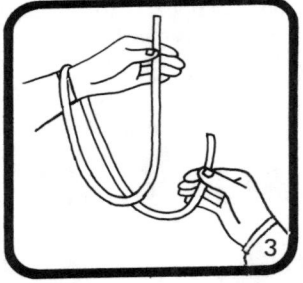

(4) Insert your right hand (still holding the right end) through the *left* section of the loop; and, in the same continuous action, bring your hand back through the *right* section of the loop *nipping the rope at Point A* as shown.

(5) Without releasing either hand, move your right hand back to the right, bringing the "nipped" rope with it. Point A is now resting on the back of your right wrist. (NOTE: This is the only part of this excellent magical puzzle that is difficult to illustrate. Just try it with the rope in your hands until you hold the rope as shown in Step 5. Another way to describe Step 4 is that your right hand, still holding its end, goes into the loop and "picks up" Point A on the back of your right wrist. Point A is then pulled *out through the loop* to form the set-up shown in Step 5.)

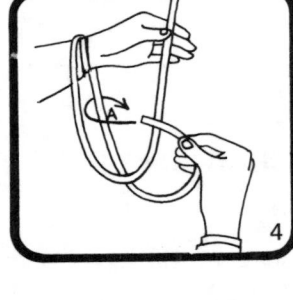

(6) Move your right hand level with your left and pull the rope taut so it forms the "criss-cross" pattern between your wrists as shown. *Note that in the illustration a new spot is indicated on the rope, Point B. Point B is just below the end held by your right hand.* Now, relax the tension on the rope and tilt both hands forward and downward, so the *outside loops*, which are pressed against your wrists, begin to slide over the tops of your hands.

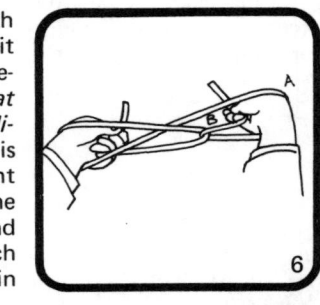

(7) YOU ARE NOW READY FOR THE SECRET MOVE. As the rope begins to fall off your wrists, your right hand prepares to *secretly release its end and grasp the rope at Point B* as described in Step 8.

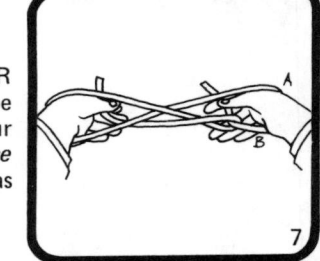

(8) As the loops slide completely over and off of your hands, draw your hands apart. At the same time, *release the right end of the rope with your thumb and first finger, and secretly grasp Point B with your other three fingers.* Because of the "tossing" movement of the loops as they fall off your wrists, the audience is completely unaware of this small "move" which is the *whole secret of the trick.*

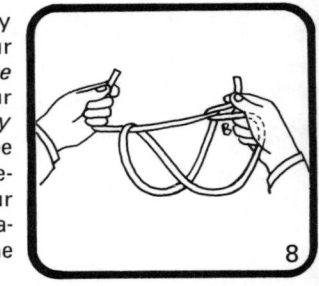

(9) As you draw your hands apart, the right end of the rope will automatically pull through the little loop forming a knot in the center of the rope.

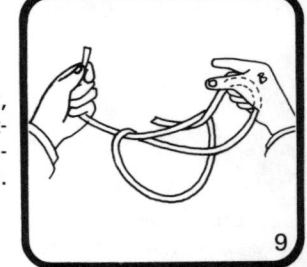

(10) Your right thumb and first finger immediately regain their original grip on the end of the rope so all looks the same — as the knot is formed.

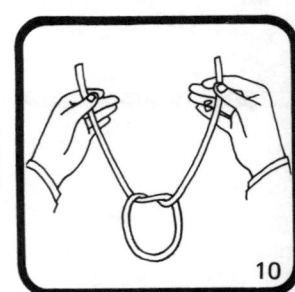

COMMENTS AND SUGGESTIONS

All through the routine, you should emphasize that you *never release the ends of the rope.* Yet a knot still appears in the rope. That makes this an "Impossible Knot." Practice the moves until they become smooth and natural. When you present the effect, do each move *very slowly, step by step,* so the spectators can follow them easily. Your purpose is to show the audience exactly how to do it — *except for the final "toss"* where you "secretly" release the right end of the rope — enabling *you* to produce a knot where *everyone else* fails. Although they copy your moves with ropes of their own, they will always miss at the vital point — making the trick more baffling each time it is repeated. And then, to top off the IMPOSSIBLE KNOT, you can follow with . . . .

THE "DO IT YOURSELF" KNOT

To show the baffled spectators how "easy" the IMPOSSIBLE KNOT really is, the magician forms the preliminary loops with his own rope. He then hands the ends to the spectator *before* he "tosses" the rope from around his hands. When the spectator takes the rope from the performer's hands, he still finds that a knot has mysteriously appeared!

METHOD

(1) Simply go through all of the preliminary Steps 1 through 5 to the point where you have the two ends projecting from each hand, with the "loops" still around your wrists.

(2) Now, extend your hands and invite the spectator to take the ends of the rope, one end in each of his hands, and draw them apart himself. When he does, the knot will make its puzzling appearance!

COMMENTS AND SUGGESTIONS

The neat feature here is that the "Secret Move" is not necessary. The mere transfer of the ends to the spectator *before* you toss the rope off, sets up the formation of the knot. You can further emphasize that the ends of the rope *are never released,* just as with the IMPOSSIBLE KNOT.

Having shown the spectator "how easy it is," you can revert back to the original "Impossible Knot" routine. He will again find he cannot form a knot on his own.

Here, you can offer further help by having *him* go through the preliminary moves with his own rope. You then say to him, "I think you've got it!" Now *you* take the ends and take the rope from his hands to show the knot. Give him back the rope, and tell him to start again *now that he has found he can do it.* But when he tries, he fails as usual! This is a great "party" trick. Just have a number of ropes handy as everyone will want to try it!

TURNED-UP GLASSES

EFFECT

The magician places three glasses in a row on the table and announces that he will turn over two glasses at a time — and in three "moves" he will have them all facing *mouth upward.* Without hesitation he proceeds to do just as he said. At the end of the third move all three glasses are mouth up. This seems easy enough to accomplish, yet every time the spectators try to duplicate the performer's actions, something goes wrong. They always finish with the three glasses mouth down! No matter how often you repeat the effect, the spectators are unable to arrive at the same result as the magician and are left totally puzzled as to the reason why!

METHOD

(1) Arrange the three glasses *in the position shown here.* Cups A and C are mouth down at both ends of the row, and Cup B is mouth up between them. With the cups in this position, the stunt is really quite easy to accomplish. What the spectators do not realize is that *when you let them try it, the three glasses are not in this same starting position,* although it seems that they are.

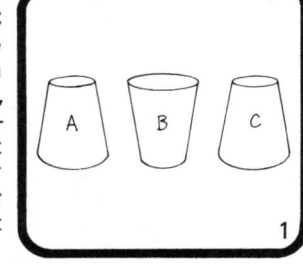

(2) To perform the feat, turn your hands thumbs down and grasp the two glasses at your right (B and C) and turn them over as shown.

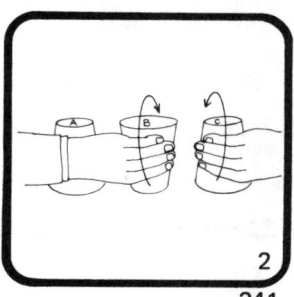

(3) The arrangement of the glasses should now appear as shown in the illustration. This completes move Number One.

(7) This completes move Number Three. *All three glasses are now mouth upward.* You have performed the stunt, as you said you would, in only three moves.

(4) Again, start thumbs down and grasp the two glasses at both ends of the row (Cups A and C) and turn them over as well.

(8) Now for the "dirty work." To position the cups for the *spectator* to try, simply turn over the *center* glass as shown. Remember, when *you* performed the stunt you started with *one up* and *two down* — AND THAT WILL WORK. But *one down* and *two up* WILL NOT! Therefore, with the cups arranged as shown here, the spectator never will be able to perform the feat with the same results as you.

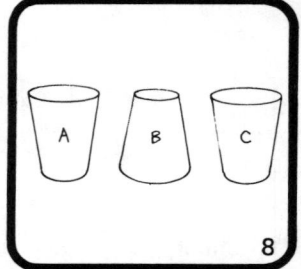

(5) Now the cups should be positioned as shown here. This completes move Number Two.

(9) If the spectator follows the series of moves *exactly as you did,* he will be left with the three glasses facing bottoms-up as shown here.

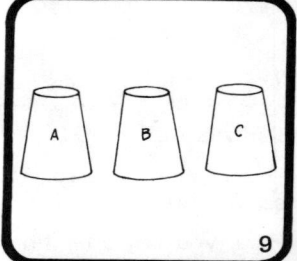

(10) By turning over the center glass when all three are in this position, you regain your original position and your moves are ready-made.

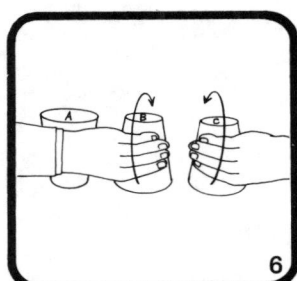

(6) Lastly, grasp the two glasses at the right (B and C) and turn them over, just as you did in move Number One.

(11) Then turn down the center glass, leaving the end ones up, and he is doomed to failure once again.

COMMENTS AND SUGGESTIONS

If you perform the stunt too many times, it is possible that your spectators will begin to "catch on" to the fact that you are changing the arrangement of the cups. It is usually best to do it just once; then let others try and fail. Give another quick demonstration later, but let others worry meantime. So use discretion in determining how many times to perform it for the same audience. You can vary your moves, starting with the two at the left instead of the right, if you wish, but speed is the factor that counts. People are then less likely to note the "difference" at the start, thanks to your casual turnover of the middle glass.

RUBBER BAND RELEASE

Here is another stunt which the magician is able to perform quite easily yet no one else is able to duplicate.

EFFECT

The magician displays an ordinary rubber band, twirling it between the first fingers of each hand. He then proceeds to touch the tips of his right thumb and first finger to the tips of his left thumb and first finger. Even though the tips of the performer's fingers remain touching, the rubber band instantly drops to the table. Yet, when the spectator tries to duplicate the stunt, the rubber band remains trapped between his thumbs and forefingers. No matter how many times the magician repeats the feat, no one else is able to perform it.

METHOD

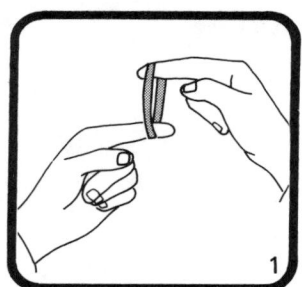

(1) Begin by displaying the rubber band looped over the tips of your two first fingers as shown.

(5) NOTE: This quarter turn move, as you <u>continue</u> to hold the band between your fingers, is the whole secret of the mystery. Later, when the spectator tries to duplicate your moves, he will neglect <u>to hold the finger and thumb of each hand together</u> and to execute the <u>quarter turn</u>. He will probably just touch both thumbs together and both first fingers together instead. Or, even if he touches the first fingers of each hand with the thumbs of the other hand, the trick is still impossible unless he <u>holds the band in place</u> as shown in Step 4.

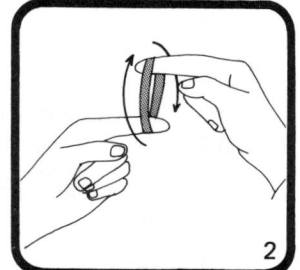

(2) Then rotate your fingers *around each other* as shown by the arrows — always keeping the rubber band lightly stretched between your fingers.

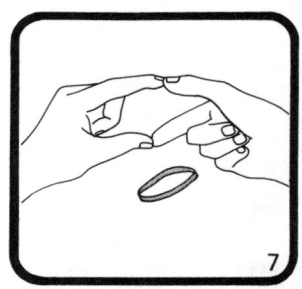

(6) To release the band, spread your thumbs and first fingers apart as shown. (7) The band will drop free to the table.

(3) Stop twirling the band and move both <u>thumbs</u> so that they touch the tips of the <u>first fingers</u> of the *same* hand. The band is now held between both hands as shown.

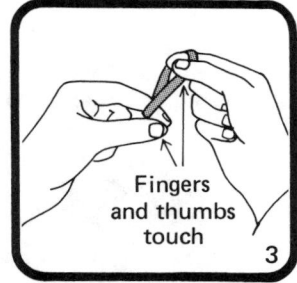

Fingers and thumbs touch

(8) This very puzzling stunt is quite difficult to figure out without being shown the proper procedure. Give the band to a spectator and encourage him to attempt to duplicate your moves. He will most surely be unable to do so as he will fail to touch the proper fingers together and make the correct moves in order to release the band from his fingers.

(4) HERE IS THE KEY MOVE. Rotate both hands a quarter turn in opposite directions so that you are able to touch the tip of your *left first finger* to your *right thumb* and the tip of your *right first finger* to your *left thumb* as shown. As you do this, <u>continue to hold the tips of the fingers of each hand together</u> as shown in Step 3.

COMMENTS AND SUGGESTIONS

Experiment with the rubber band until you fully understand the *release positions* of the fingers. When you can perform the routine smoothly and without hesitation, you will be ready to present the stunt. This deceptive little maneuver will cause a stir among your friends and keep them busy for some time.

KNOT IN HANDKERCHIEF

EFFECT

Here is a quick and easy challenge which can be performed anywhere with any handkerchief. The magician wagers that he can tie a knot in a handkerchief *without letting go of either end* in the process. With that, he offers the handkerchief to anyone who wishes to try their luck before he attempts the seemingly impossible task himself. It soon becomes quite apparent that no one is able to perform the feat under those conditions. When all have tried and failed, the magician cleverly performs the stunt with ease and grace.

METHOD

(1) Hold the handkerchief at opposite corners and twirl it in a rope-like fashion between your hands. Then, place it on the table directly in front of you.

(3) Now, lean forward until you can grasp *one end* of the handkerchief in *each hand.*

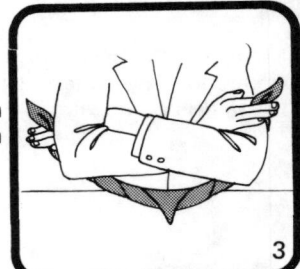

(2) In order to meet the terms of the challenge, before you pick up the handkerchief, *cross your arms as shown.*

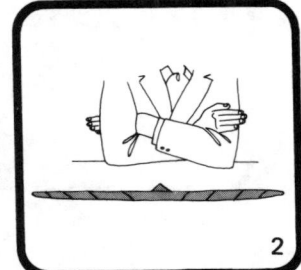

(4) With one end of the handkerchief held tightly in each hand, simply *uncross your arms.* As you do, the ends of the handkerchief will be drawn through your arms, creating a single knot in the center of the handkerchief — *without releasing the ends!*

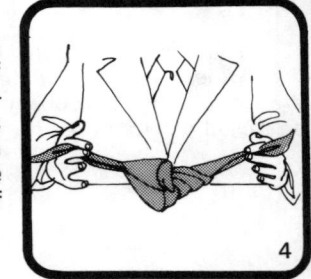

(5) Immediately toss the handkerchief to your spectators as they will, no doubt, want to try the stunt themselves and later perform this "Betcha" for *their* friends.

MAKE AT-
HOME MAGIC

When a magician speaks of "building an act," he may mean two different things. Usually, he means that he intends to choose certain effects or routines that can be "built" (combined) into a complete program. For instance, he might "build" a routine composed entirely of card tricks, or impromptu magic involving common objects such as coins, rings, string and handkerchiefs; or it could refer to a combination of larger and more elaborate effects. So, in this instance, "building an act" means that the magician is selecting which tricks to use for a particular performance.

The other definition of "building an act" means the actual construction of the magic apparatus to be used in a show. Here, instead of selecting the tricks he intends to do, the magician goes to his workshop and builds them. Every magician needs a "workshop," even if it is only a desk drawer containing old playing cards, envelopes, and sheets of construction paper along with scissors to cut them and colored pencils to mark them. But for more ambitious projects, you will require a well-equipped home workshop—either your own or one belonging to a friend who is mechanically minded.

Such "build-it-yourself" projects are covered in this section, which includes simple working plans and the magical effects that can be presented with the apparatus after it has been constructed. They have all been chosen because they are easy to build and effective when performed. If you feel that you require very special work, you can have the props built to order or buy them ready-made.

So, if you intend to "build an act," in both senses of the phrase, delve deeply into this section, and you will find it made to your order!

VASE OF ALLAH

EFFECT

The performer displays an attractive vase and a length of rope. The diameter of the rope is only about half the width of the mouth of the vase. The magician calls this to the audience's attention by inserting the end of the rope into the vase and then easily removing it. He then reinserts one end of the rope into the vase and *turns the whole affair upside down.* Yet, when the performer releases the rope, it remains suspended, hanging from the vase as if held there by some mysterious force. The performer then grasps the lower end of the rope and turns the vase right side up. Then, by holding *only* the end of the rope, he is able to swing the vase back and forth as if it were some sort of magical pendulum. The full weight of the vase will not break this strange power which now holds the vase to rope. Finally, the magician causes the rope to "lose its power" and *withdraws it effortlessly* from the neck of the vase. *Both the rope and the vase are immediately handed to the spectators for examination.*

SECRET AND PREPARATION

You will find that the items necessary to present this classic effect are very easy to acquire. First, you will need a long-necked flower vase (a "bud" vase is ideal) or a correctly shaped bottle. It must be opaque so that anything inside the vase will not be seen by the audience. The neck of the vase (or bottle) should be about twice the diameter of the rope which is used.

NOTE: Some salad dressing bottles work well for this effect. When you find one the proper size, you can paint it to make it opaque and also decorate it with "magical symbols" to suit your "patter" presentation.

You must also have a piece of rope about 2 feet long. (This is one of the few tricks in the Course in which hard or stiff rope works *better* than the soft magician's rope.) Lastly, you need a special item which is the secret of the trick. This is simply a *small cork or rubber ball* which is a little larger than half the diameter of the neck of the vase and will roll easily into the vase, where it remains throughout the presentation. Small rubber or cork balls can be purchased at many variety, drug or department stores, or you may carve a ball of the proper size from an ordinary bottle cork.

METHOD

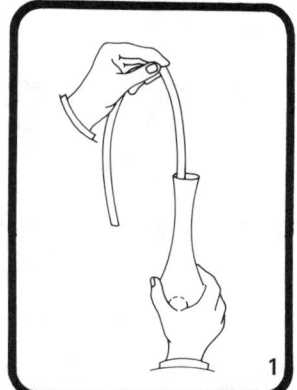

(1) Start with the "secret" ball inside the bottle as you casually display the vase and the rope to your audience. You will find that you can turn the vase in many directions without revealing the secret ball. Just be sure not to tip the bottle too far so that the ball does not roll out of the vase.

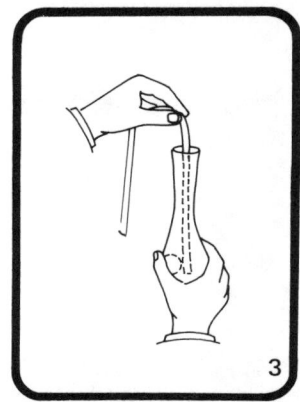

(3) As you demonstrate how the rope slides easily in and out of the vase, when you insert the rope for the last time, slide it into the vase until its end rests near the bottom of the vase as shown.

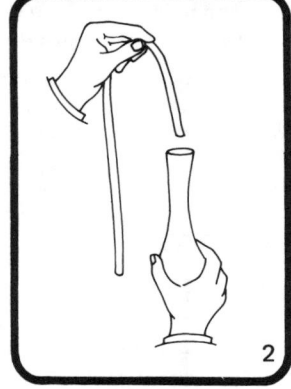

(2) Now, demonstrate how the rope fits loosely into the neck of the bottle. (This subtly shows the audience that it would be difficult to "jam" the rope into the vase without it being obvious to everyone watching.)

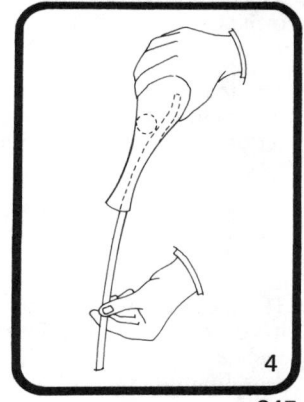

(4) Now, with the rope in this position, slowly invert the rope *and* the vase so that the vase is upside down. Hold the vase in one hand and the free end of the rope in the other hand. When you do this, the "secret" ball will roll *between* the rope and inner wall of the neck of the vase as shown.

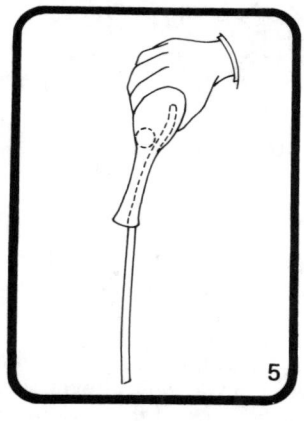

(5) Slowly release your grip on the rope and it will seem to be held in place by a magical force (really by the secret ball). To assure that the rope remains in place, give it a slight pull on the end of the rope before you release it. This causes the ball to "wedge" securely in place.

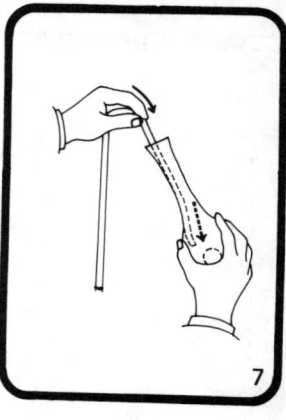

(7) To release the "mysterious force," grasp the vase in your hand and push the rope slightly into the vase — *just enough to cause the secret ball to fall down to the bottom of the vase and free the rope.*

(6) Again, grasp the free end of the rope and turn the whole affair back over so that the vase is right side up. Then, hold the end of the rope in one hand and *release your grip on the vase.* You can now swing the vase back and forth while it remains suspended from the end of the rope!

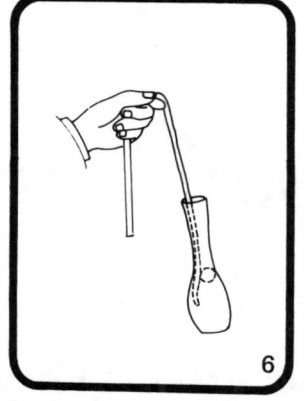

(8) Now, if you are performing close to the audience, *allow a spectator to pull the rope from the bottle.* (If not, just pull it out yourself.) As soon as he has the rope in his possession, *turn the bottle over* as if to show the bottom and *allow the secret ball to roll unseen into your curled fingers.* Then, hand the vase for examination as well.

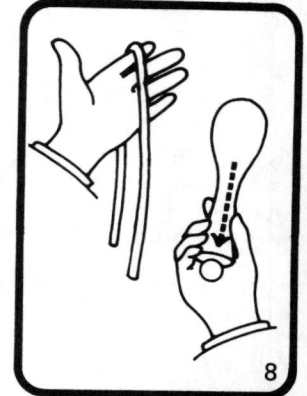

COMMENTS AND SUGGESTIONS

Experiment with different sized balls until the trick works most effectively. Once you have determined the size that works best with your bottle and rope, make up several in case you lose one.

THE AFGHAN BANDS

EFFECT

The magician shows the audience a wide strip of cloth material that has been glued end to end to form a continuous loop of fabric. By tearing the loop lengthwise twice, the performer divides the circle into three separate rings of cloth. One of these rings is handed to a spectator, another is set aside, and the third ring the performer proceeds to again tear lengthwise down the middle. As he does this, the magician instructs the spectator to tear his ring of cloth in the same manner. As one would expect, the *magician* ends up with two *separate* rings of cloth. The *spectator,* however, manages somehow to create a *linked* chain of two rings.

The magician offers to give the spectator another chance and hands him the remaining single loop of cloth. As the spectator tears it down the middle, the audience anticipates that the circle will again become two linked rings. The final surprise, however, comes when the loop suddenly transforms into *one large, continuous circle of cloth* — <u>twice</u> *the size that it was at the start!*

SECRET AND PREPARATION

The cloth chosen for this effect must be a type that will tear easily. All *woven* fabrics tear in a straight line, but *knits* must be cut; so if you must purchase fabric, be sure it is a woven one. A lightweight cotton such as percale will tear the easiest, will be the least expensive to buy, and is available in many attractive colors and patterns. An excellent choice that will cost you nothing is to use strips cut from the remnants of worn bedsheets, which are usually made from percale.

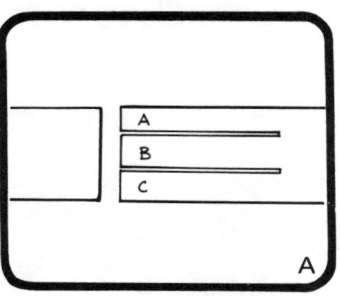

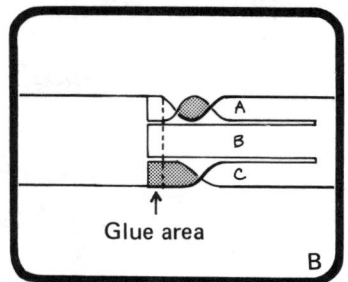

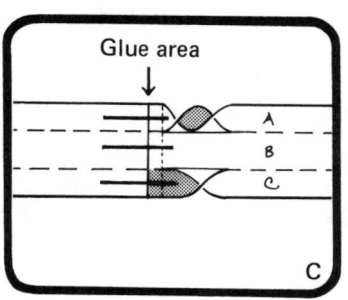

(A)   After you have found a material that works well, cut a strip of the cloth 36″ long by 6″ wide. At one end, cut two slits about 2½″ long, dividing the end of the strip into three 2″ wide bands. We will refer to these new bands as A, B, and C.   (B)   Give Band A a <u>full twist</u> (360 degrees) and glue it to the opposite end of the cloth strip as shown. Be sure to allow about ½″ overlap of gluing surface. Next, glue Band B <u>directly</u> to the other end of the strip <u>without twisting it</u>, as shown. Finally, give Band C just <u>one-half twist</u> (180 degrees) before gluing it to the opposite end of the loop.   (C)   The next step is to cut several slits about two inches long in the <u>exact center</u> of each band. <u>This slit must pass through the glue joint.</u> Study the illustrations for the correct location of these three slits. You are now ready to present THE AFGHAN BANDS. Special glues for fabrics are available where you buy the fabric. Or the ends of the strips may be sewn together.

METHOD

(1)   Holding the glued joints and the twists concealed in your right hand, display the loop of cloth to your audience. Call attention to the fact that the fabric is formed into one *continuous loop.*

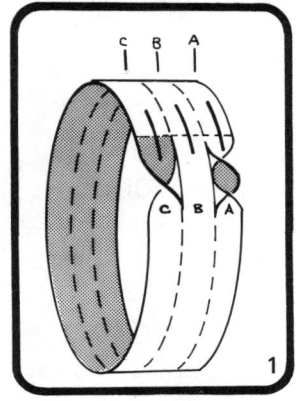

(4)   Band B, being an unprepared section, will result in two *equal* and *separate* rings after the tear is completed as shown.

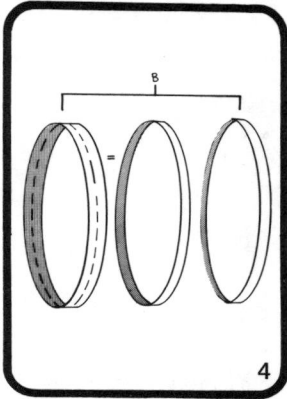

(2)   Now, tear Band C away from the main loop (the dotted lines in the illustration show the path of the tear) and drape it over your right arm, *concealing the twist in the crook of your elbow.*

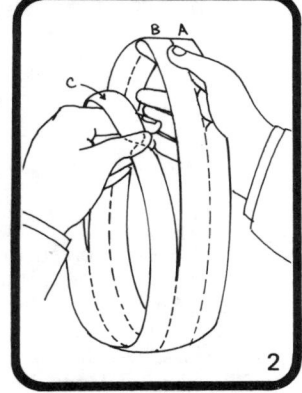

(5)   As the spectator completes the tearing of his Band A, the audience will expect the same result which you achieved. It comes as quite a surprise when the spectator ends up with two *linked* loops as shown.

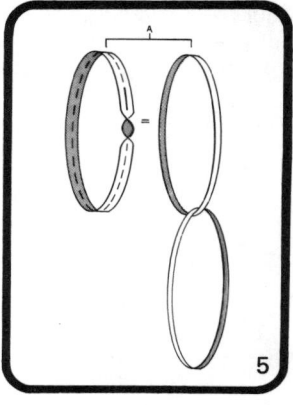

(3)   Now, tear the main loop again, separating Bands A and B as shown. Give Band A to the spectator and keep Band B for yourself. Call attention to the narrow slit in the middle of both bands and instruct the spectator to tear his Band A lengthwise into two parts while you do the same with your Band B.

(6)   Explain to the volunteer that, since there is still one loop remaining, you will give him another chance. Remove Loop C from your right arm and instruct him to tear it down the middle as before. The climax comes when Loop C transforms into *one large loop* right in the spectator's own hands!

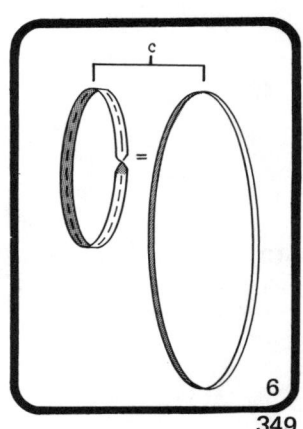

COMMENTS AND SUGGESTIONS

The AFGHAN BANDS can also be performed using strips of paper instead of cloth. The preparation is identical except that, instead of *tearing* the loops, you must *cut* them with a pair of scissors.

THE UTILITY CONE

Here is a clever utility prop which you can construct out of paper. (Construction paper and newspaper both work well, depending upon what "props" you will be using in the cone. If you use construction paper, you may wish to decorate it with a suitable design to help conceal the glued edges of the secret pocket.) When you have completed the construction of THE UTILITY CONE, you will have a very useful device which you can use to vanish things like a handkerchief, a card, stamps, and many other flat or comparable items.

EFFECT

The magician displays a sheet of newspaper. He folds the paper into the shape of a cone and then places a silk handkerchief (or other item) in the cone. Immediately the cone is opened up and shown on both sides. The handkerchief has completely vanished.

Here is the method for constructing a UTILITY CONE out of newspaper.

SECRET AND PREPARATION

(A) Obtain two *identical* pages of newspaper. Square the two pages together and place them so the identical sides are showing and the <u>long edges</u> of one side of the sheets is nearest you.

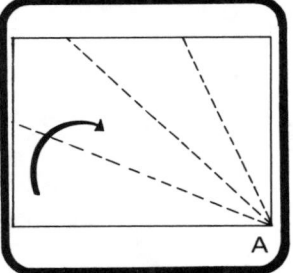

(D) Then make the third fold in the papers following the dotted line as shown. The cone, folded with both papers, should look something like this.

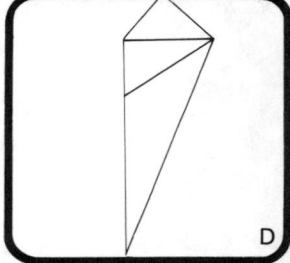

(B) Make the *first* fold in *both* of the papers as shown.

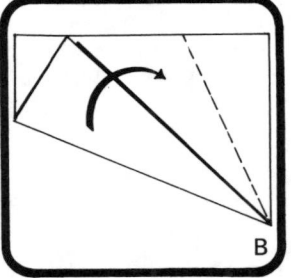

(E) Now, carefully unfold the two pieces of paper. Spread the papers out on the table in exactly the same position as in Step A. Pick up the top sheet of paper and carefully cut out Section X (indicated by the dark shading in the illustration) from this sheet. Once this is done, *discard the rest of this page.*

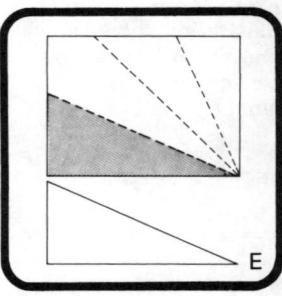

(C) Now make the second fold in the papers following the dotted line as shown.

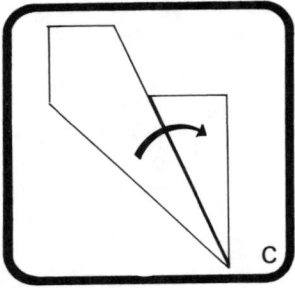

(F) You now have one complete sheet of paper and one extra piece, Section X, which matches a portion of the complete sheet. Glue this matching extra, triangular Section X on top of its identical portion of the side of the full-size page. Glue it along the *two long edges only* as shown. You now have created a "secret hidden pocket" in the newspaper page. If you place an object into the open top of the pocket, it will be hidden inside.

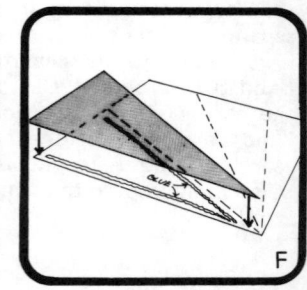

METHOD

(1) To perform the vanish, pick up the specially prepared newspaper page from your table. Hold the page with both hands so that the secret pocket faces the audience. Your right hand is positioned over the mouth of the secret pocket holding it closed, as shown. Use both hands to refold the paper *along the original fold lines.* When you have completed the folding, the opening to the secret pocket should be located at the mouth of the cone on the very inside fold of the paper. Position the cone so that the secret pocket is on the side of the cone *nearest you.*

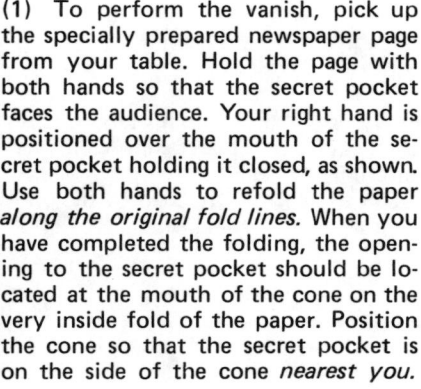

(2) Hold the body of the cone in your left hand. Insert your right fingers into the mouth of the cone and *open the secret pocket.* Do this in a casual manner, as if you are merely straightening up the cone a bit.

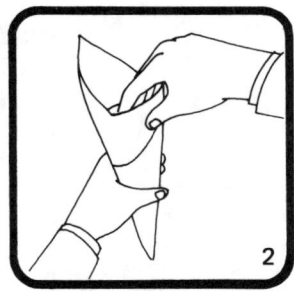

(3) After you have opened the secret pocket, remove your right hand from within the cone. Then, with your right hand, pick up the handkerchief from your table. Use your right fingers to push the handkerchief all the way down *into the secret pocket.*

(4) Once the handkerchief is securely inside the secret pocket, close the top opening of the pocket and hold it shut, pinching the top edges together between your right thumb and fingers. NOTE: Position your right hand with the fingers <u>inside</u> the cone and your thumb on the <u>outside</u>.

(5) <u>Without removing your right hand from this fixed position</u>, use your left hand to open out the piece of paper.

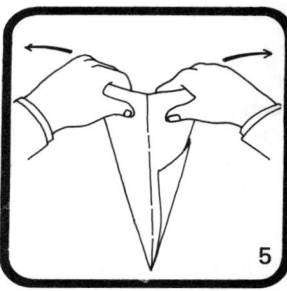

(6) Once this is done, you should be holding the open sheet of paper with both hands by the two upper corners. *Your right hand continues to hold the top of the secret pocket closed after the paper has been fully opened out.* It will appear as if the handkerchief has vanished.

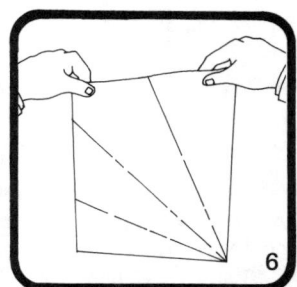

(7) You may now release the left hand and show the paper on both sides with your right hand. When doing this, be sure that you have a firm grasp on the mouth of the secret pocket. You do not want to risk dropping the paper on the floor.

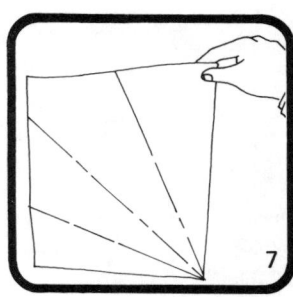

COMMENTS AND SUGGESTIONS

If you wish, you may crush the paper into a ball before you casually toss it aside. This action serves to convince your audience that the paper is unprepared. *Pay very little attention to the paper once the "vanish" has been done.* Always handle the page of newspaper as if it were *totally* unprepared. There are many uses for THE UTILITY CONE. It makes an ideal magic "prop" because it appears to be so "ordinary" — just a sheet of paper!

THE SORCERER'S STAMP ALBUM
(SVENGALI BOOK)

EFFECT

The magician riffles through the blank pages of a stamp album showing it to be quite empty. He then places the album on his table where it remains *in full view of the spectators* throughout the presentation. The performer then displays a collection of loose stamps, which he pours into an empty paper cone. Immediately, the cone is snapped open. Instead of the stamps scattering all over the stage, they *vanish* in mid air! Without hesitation, the magician picks up the empty stamp album and slowly flips through the pages. Attached to the previously blank pages are the missing stamps — pasted in neat rows *completely filling the book.*

SECRET AND PREPARATION

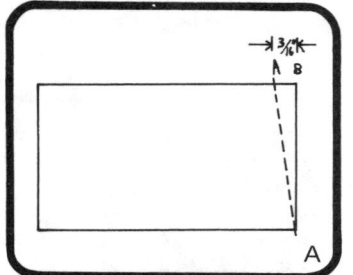 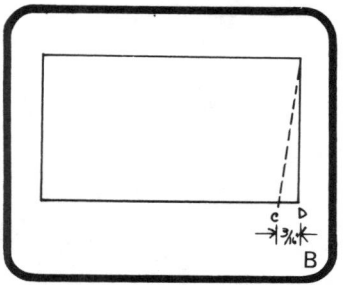 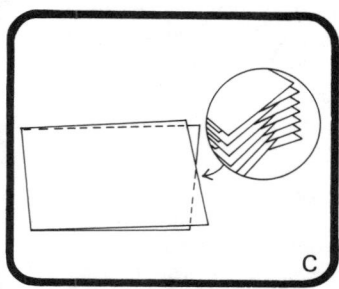

(A)   You will need to purchase enough black construction paper to make 20 sheets of paper approximately 8½ x 11 inches in size. Divide the pages into two equal piles of 10 pages each. Now, cut *all the pages* in one of these piles on a diagonal as shown in Fig. A. The angle of the cut is exaggerated in the illustration for clarity. The actual distance between A and B should be approximately 3/16''.   (B)   Next, cut the remaining 10 pages in the other pile as shown in Fig. B. Again, the distance between Points C and D should be about 3/16''. (C)   Restack the prepared sheets *alternating* them so that every other sheet in the resulting stack is cut on the opposing diagonal as shown.

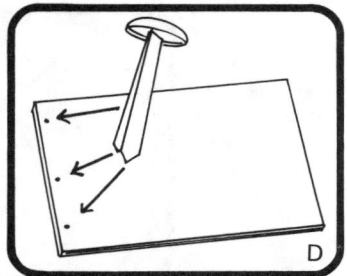 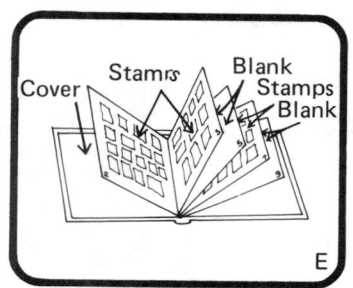 

(D)   Without disturbing the arrangement of the sheets, punch three holes through the pages as illustrated and then bind the end of the ''album'' together with brass brads. A nice touch would be to cut two additional pages of contrasting color and use them as the front and back covers for your album.   (E)   Your next step is to purchase several inexpensive packages of loose stamps. These can be found in hobby and department stores and, of course, stamp shops. Starting with the *back* side of the *first* sheet in the book (Page 2), paste the stamps in neat rows on this page and on the page directly across from it (Page 3). Leave the next pair of adjacent pages *blank* (4 and 5). Then, paste stamps on the *two adjacent pages* after those (6 and 7). Continue pasting stamps on *alternate pairs of adjacent pages* until you reach the end of the book. If you have done this correctly, the pages numbered 2 and 3, 6 and 7, 10 and 11, 14 and 15, and 18 and 19 *should contain stamps.* Pages 1, 4 and 5, 8 and 9, 12 and 13, 16 and 17, and 20 *should be blank.*   (F)   You can now test your work by grasping the spine of the prepared volume in your left hand. Then, riffle through the pages with your right thumb — at the lower corner of the book. If all is well, the book will appear *empty.* Due to the diagonal cuts in the sheets, your thumb will only touch the blank pages as you riffle through the volume. The stamp-filled pages will automatically follow the blank pages as they flip unnoticed, two pages at a time, from one side of the book to the other.

 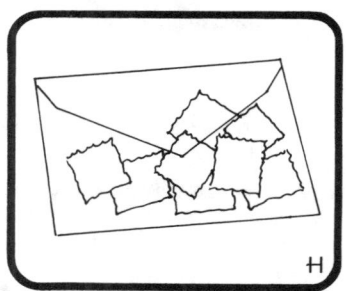 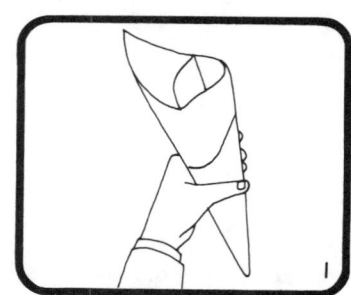

(G)   Now close the book and repeat the procedure, this time with your thumb riffling the book *at the upper corner.* The result should be that the entire book appears *completely filled with stamps.*   (H)   You will also need a number of other duplicate loose stamps which you do not glue into the album. Place these into a transparent cellophane envelope or clear plastic bag. (A glass will also work well.)   (I)   Finally, you will need to construct a ''Utility Cone'' which is explained in detail elsewhere in the Course.   (J)   At the start, the prepared album and the Utility Cone should be on your table and the package of loose postage stamps in your coat pocket (or on your table). You are now ready to perform THE SORCERER'S STAMP ALBUM.

METHOD

(1) Pick up the album from your table and display it to the audience. Then, riffle through the pages by their lower corners allowing the spectators to clearly see that the album is "empty."

(4) Now, make a magical gesture at the cone and then at the album. Immediately snap the cone open to show that the stamps have completely vanished! *Be sure to hold the secret pocket closed during this action.*

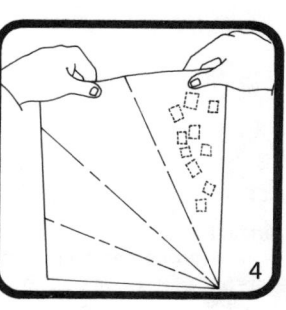

(2) Place the album in full view on the table. A good idea is to lean the album against something that is already on the table. The important part is that your audience *never loses sight of the book at any time during the presentation.*

(5) Pick up the album and flip through the pages by their upper corners. The effect will be that the stamps have "magically" appeared" pasted to the previously empty pages of the stamp album!

(3) Display the package of loose stamps to the audience. Then pick up the Utility Cone from the table and openly pour all of the loose stamps from the package into the *secret pocket* of the cone.

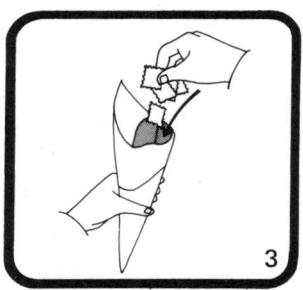

COMMENTS AND SUGGESTIONS

Instead of constructing the stamp album yourself, you can purchase an inexpensive *photo album* from a stationery or department store. The kind with black pages is ideal. Also, be sure the album contains at least 20 sheets. The pages of most photo albums can be easily removed from the cover and then can be prepared in the same manner as described.

THE COMEDY CUT AND RESTORED PAPER
(CLIPPO)

EFFECT

The magician displays a single column cut from the classified section of a newspaper. Folding the paper strip in half, the performer cuts away the folded center leaving him with two separate strips of paper. When he "unfolds" the two individual strips, the performer finds that the news column has mysteriously restored itself back to one piece! It seems as though the ends of the strips have magically "healed" together. Somewhat puzzled at this strange occurrence, the magician repeats the cutting process, this time cutting the center fold at an angle. To everyone's surprise, when the paper is unfolded it is again found restored — *with a sharp bend in the center of the column!* Finally, the paper strip is cut for the last time, and is once again restored to its original form.

SECRET AND PREPARATION

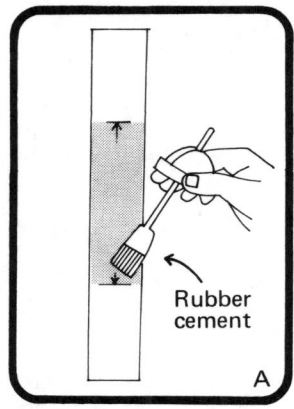

(A) This clever "cut and restored" effect works on the same principle as Inflation as described on Page 227. To prepare, with a pair of sharp scissors cut a single ad column from the classified section of a newspaper. The column should be about 24 inches in length or longer if possible.

(B) Now, place the strip of paper on the table and apply a thin coat of *rubber cement* all along the center section of one side as shown and allow it to dry. Next, sprinkle a little talcum powder on the treated (rubber cement) area. Spread the powder over the entire surface with a tissue or soft brush. (The powder will prevent the treated surfaces from sticking together when the strip is folded in half.) This done, you are now ready to present this clever mystery.

METHOD

(1) Begin by displaying the paper strip as you make some comment about the large variety of items that you can find advertised in the newspaper. This is a good opportunity to inject comedy into the routine by pretending to read some humorous ads. These are really ads which you have memorized and should be as crazy and absurd as you can make them. As an example: "For Sale: Used tombstone — great buy for someone named Murphy!"

(4) Now, carefully open out the paper strip revealing it restored to one piece! Because of the rubber cement, the paper strips will stick together at the cut edges giving the illusion that the news column has restored itself. Even at a slight distance, no one will notice that the strip is secretly "joined" at the center.

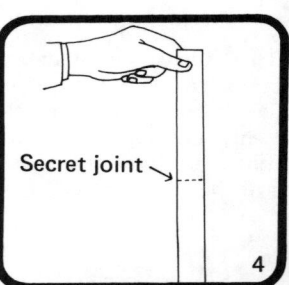

(2) After apparently reading the first ad from the center of the column, fold the news strip in half so the treated surfaces of the paper are together.

(5) Pretend to read another crazy ad and then fold the strip again and snip off another section from the center. This time, instead of cutting straight across, cut the paper at an *angle* to the right as shown.

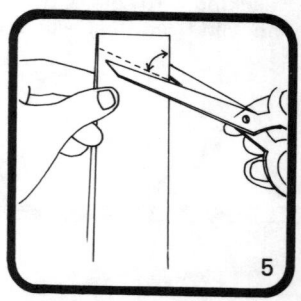

(3) Then, using the scissors, snip off the fold in the *center of the strip* making sure to cut *straight across* the paper. Make this cut in the pretense of cutting away the advertisement which you just read. The section which you cut away should be no more than a half-inch wide. *Make sure that the cemented areas are touching each other before making the cut.* Done openly and deliberately, there will be no question in the audience's mind that the strip has actually been cut into two pieces . . . which it has.

(6) When you open out the paper strip, the rubber cement will again restore the two pieces, *but the upper half of the paper will veer off to the right at a sharp angle!*

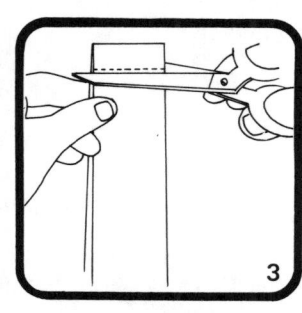

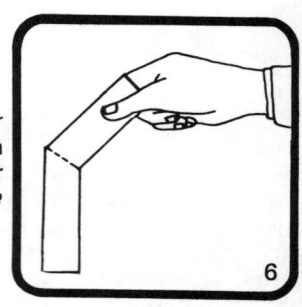

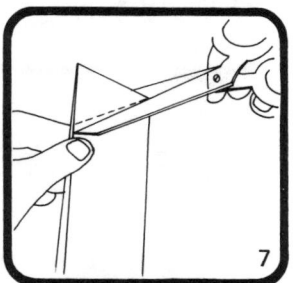

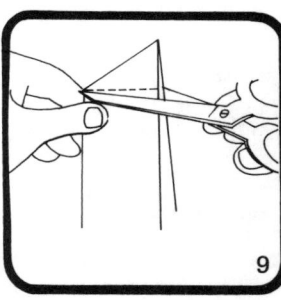

(7) Repeat the cutting process again. This time cut the strip at an angle to the left.

(9) Finally, fold the paper in half again and cut it for the last time — *straight across* — as in Step 3.

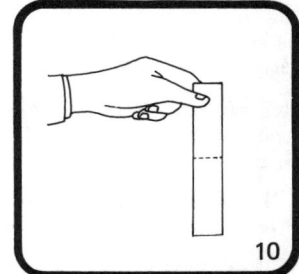

(8) When the paper is opened out, the upper half will veer off to the left as shown.

(10) When you open the paper strip, it will appear to be restored to its original condition in a straight column.

(11) To conclude, fold or crumple the piece of newspaper and place it aside, out of reach of the spectators.

COMMENTS AND SUGGESTIONS

You can also play the cutting of the paper for laughs by appearing to be confused every time you cut away a section of the paper. Each time you make a "mistake" you try to solve the problem by cutting a little more of the paper away. An audience is always amused when they think that the magician has made a mistake, so ham it up a bit, and your audience will enjoy the trick even more.

THE MAGIC CARD FRAME

EFFECT

The magician displays an empty picture frame. Covering the frame with a cloth, the performer picks up a deck of playing cards. The magician asks a spectator to select a card from the deck. The spectator is then requested to reveal the name of the chosen card. Turning to the covered frame, the magician lifts away the cloth. The audience sees that an oversized card has magically appeared imprisoned behind the glass in the previously empty frame. The Giant Card exactly matches the card selected by the spectator!

SECRET AND PREPARATION

(A) You will need an ordinary picture frame which you will change into a "Magic Card Frame." The frame should be of the size that holds an 8" by 10" picture. The type of frame you use should have a cardboard back, indicated by the letter "B" in the illustrations, and a glass front, indicated by the letter "D." You will need to turn the frame so that the "open" end will be at the *top*. This will require that you remove the "stand" that is attached to the back (B) that is used to hold the frame up and turn the stand around so that it matches the now "reversed" frame back (B). The stand now holds up the whole affair as it was originally intended to do. (For ideas for obtaining a frame, see Comments and Suggestions.)

(B) Now cut a square of black opaque cloth (felt is good) the width of the cardboard back of the frame (B). The cloth should be approximately one or two inches *longer* than the back (B). This piece of cloth is called the "flap" and is indicated by the letter "C" in the illustrations.

(C) Either glue a piece of cloth that *matches the flap* (C) onto the cardboard (B) which forms the back of the frame or paint it black.

(D) Next, attach a Giant playing card to the center of the cardboard back (B) so that it will face the audience.

(E) Assemble the frame as shown. The black cardboard back (B) with the Giant Card on it is slid into the frame (A). Carefully place the black flap (C) over the black cardboard back. Then slide the glass (D) into the frame *in front* of the flap. Leave enough of the flap cloth protruding from the top of the frame so that you can grasp it and pull it out of the frame later, as you will see.

(F) Viewing the frame from the front, it appears that the frame is empty, thanks to the black cloth flap that is in front of the Giant Card.

(G) Set this frame on your table, making sure that the part of the flap that extends from the top is folded out of sight behind the frame.

(H) You will also need an attractive cloth, a large handkerchief, or a square scarf. This must be large enough to completely cover the frame. Set the folded cloth and a regular deck of cards next to the frame on your table.

(I) You should have the <u>duplicate card</u> in the correct location in the deck for the "Force" which you will perform in Step 1 of the Method which follows. You are now ready to present this spectacular effect.

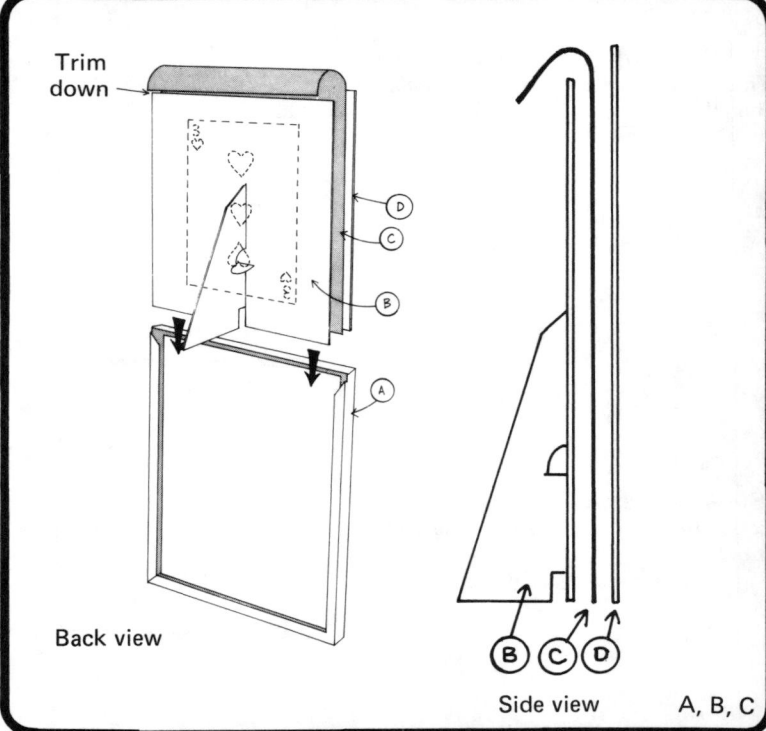

Trim down

D
C
B

A

Back view

Side view   A, B, C
B C D

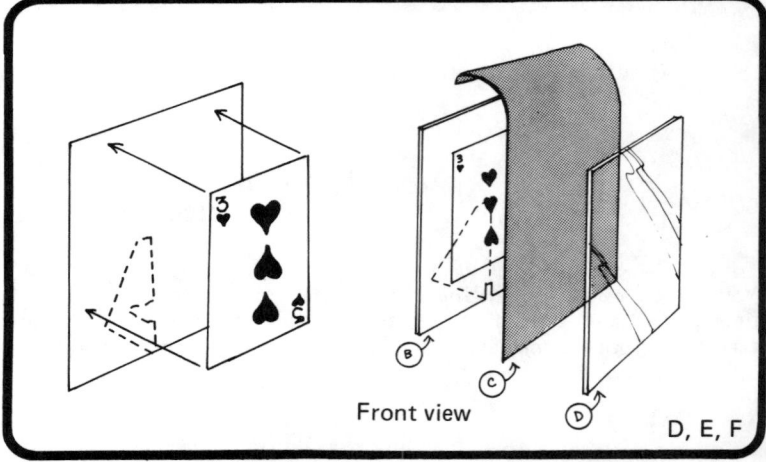

Front view

B
C
D

D, E, F

METHOD

(1) Pick up the deck and ask a spectator to select a card. *You must now "Force" the <u>duplicate</u> of the Giant Card hidden in the frame.* Use any of the methods of forcing a card that are explained in the Course.

(2) After the duplicate card has been "selected" (really <u>Forced</u>), replace the remaining cards in their case. Ask the spectator to put his card in his pocket (or somewhere out of sight) so that there will be no possibility of your catching a glimpse of his selection.

(3) Now direct the audience's attention to the apparently empty frame on the table and cover it with the cloth.

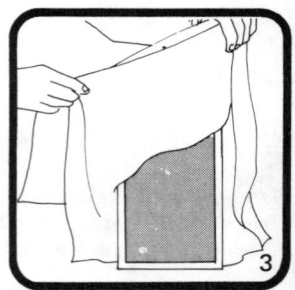

3

(4) Ask the spectator to remove the card from his pocket and reveal its value to you and to the audience *for the first time.*

(5) Now, lift the cloth from the frame. As you do, *grasp the top edge of the black cloth "flap" through the fabric of the covering cloth and simultaneously* <u>pull the flap from the frame</u> *as you remove the covering cloth.* The flap will be concealed inside the cloth. The audience will be surprised to see the "magical" appearance of the Giant Card inside the frame. Casually discard the covering cloth with the secret flap inside. Have the spectator remove the selected card from his pocket to further confirm that the Giant Card matches the one he "freely selected" from the deck!

COMMENTS AND SUGGESTIONS

If you do not already have a suitable frame with which to make the trick, you can almost always find them for sale in local variety or department stores. They are called "Picture" or "Diploma" frames. The frame itself is made of metal and is complete with a glass front and a cardboard back. The bottom of the frame is open so that the glass and back can be removed. Just invert the frame and follow Steps A through G to make your MAGIC CARD FRAME.

THE DOUBLE-WALLED BAG

As the title of this next item might suggest, this is not a trick in itself, but rather a "magical" prop which will be very useful to you as a utility piece of equipment for switching one item for another or when used as a complete "vanish" for small objects. The strong point of this special bag is that it can be torn open after completing an effect to show it empty.

SECRET AND PREPARATION

(A) Acquire two identical paper bags. The brown "lunch bag" size available at any grocery is perfect. Cut one of the bags along the dotted line as illustrated. Save Part B and discard Part A.

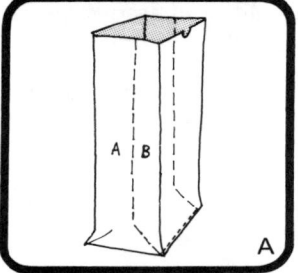

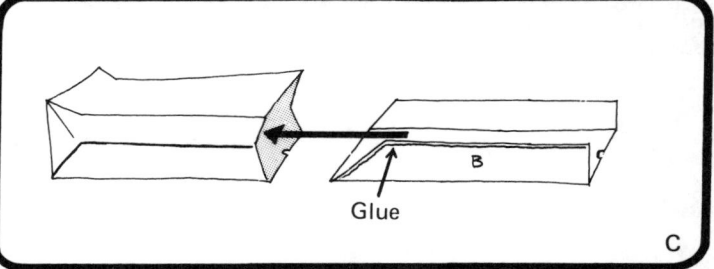

(C) Carefully slide Part B *into* the unprepared bag and align the top edges of both bags. Now press the glued edges of Part B to the bottom and sides of the unprepared bag. The edges of Part B are glued to the same "matching" parts of the inside of the unprepared bag.

(B) Spread Part B flat on the table and apply glue along the three edges as shown.

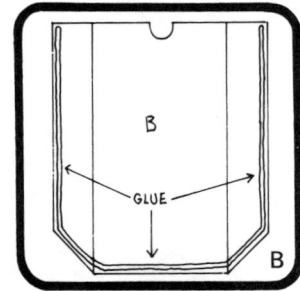

(D) You now have an ordinary looking paper bag as far as the audience is concerned — but you have added an undetectable "secret pocket."

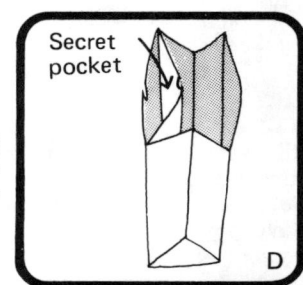

(E)   Before its use in a trick, the bag should be folded flat. When you are ready to use it, just pick up the flat bag and open it. This helps give the audience the impression that it is just an ordinary paper bag. At the conclusion of the effect, you can tear away the *unprepared side* so that the spectators can see clearly into the bag. Make sure to keep the prepared side closed by holding it at the top edge with your hand. Some of the many uses of the bag will be explained in the following effects.

THE DOUBLE-WALLED BAG — VANISH

EFFECT

If you have constructed the Double-Walled Bag properly, you should have no trouble in causing an item to vanish from within the bag.

METHOD

(1)   Let's suppose you are going to vanish a dollar bill. To do this, pick up the bag from your table and open it, *with the secret pocket side toward you.* Hold the bag with your left hand. Your left thumb should be located on the outside of the bag, while your left first finger is inside the "secret pocket" and your other three fingers are in the main compartment of the bag. This means that the mouth of the secret pocket is open. Keep the open bag tilted slightly away from the audience so that they do not see the double wall.

Secret pocket

(5)   *NOTE: When you pick up the bag, your left fingers grasp* both *the rear side of the bag* and *the extra flap of the secret pocket. You now hold the secret pocket closed between your left thumb and fingers.*

(2)   Pick up the dollar bill with your right hand. Place the bill *in the secret pocket* of the bag.

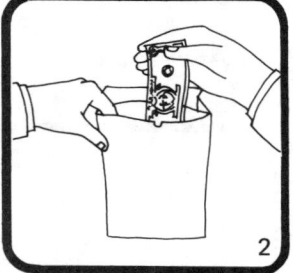

(6)   Make a magical gesture to "make the bill vanish" and then grasp the front, <u>unprepared</u> edge of the bag with your right hand. Pull down with your right hand, tearing the unprepared side of the bag open down the center, exposing the empty interior. The dollar bill you placed inside the bag has "vanished."

(3)   With your left hand, place the bag on your table in full view and position the bag *so that the secret pocket is toward the rear.*

(7)   After showing the empty bag, crumple it up and place it aside on the shelf behind your magic table or just toss it off stage. Handle the bag naturally, but be careful not to expose the bill which is hidden inside the secret pocket.

(4)   When you are ready to make the bill vanish, pick up the bag, grasping the rear (secret pocket) side with your left hand so that the secret pocket is held <u>closed</u>.

THE DOUBLE-WALLED BAG — TRANSFORMATION

EFFECT

In addition to being able to *vanish* an object from within the special bag, you can also *transform* one object into a completely different one. The handling of the bag in both routines is practically identical.

SECRET AND PREPARATION

Secret pocket

(A) For explanation purposes, assume that you wish to transform a silk handkerchief into a playing card. Place the playing card into the *main body* of the bag. Fold the bag flat and lay it on your table.

METHOD

(1) Pick up the bag, open it, and hold it with your left hand at the top just as you did in Step 1 of the "Vanish" so that the secret pocket is to the back. *NOTE: The secret pocket is open and is toward your body.*

(4) When you are ready for the transformation, pick up the bag with your left hand, *closing the secret pocket as you do* with your left thumb and fingers. This is exactly as in Step 4 of the "Vanish" routine.

(2) With your right hand, pick up the silk from your table and place it *into the secret pocket* of the bag.

(5) Reach into the bag with your right hand and remove the card secretly placed inside earlier. Show the card to the audience and place it on your table.

(3) Place the bag on your table so that the secret pocket is still to the back, exactly as you did for the "Vanish" sequence.

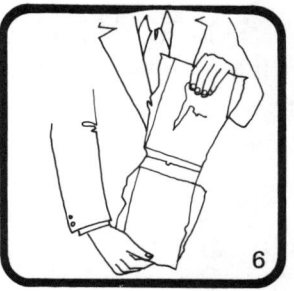

(6) Now grasp the front edge of the bag with your right hand and tear the bag open just as you did for Step 6 in the "Vanish." The bag appears to be empty — the silk handkerchief has "magically" turned into a playing card!

COMMENTS AND SUGGESTIONS

If the item which is preset in the main body of the bag is flat, such as a playing card, fold the bag flat prior to the performance. If the object is a *bulky item,* such as an orange, you will have to leave the bag standing open on your table. If you use a *heavy object* inside the bag, it is best that you perform the routine with the bag sitting on your table until <u>after</u> this object has been removed from the bag in Step 5. You can then pick up the bag and proceed to tear it open to show the interior.

THE SUN AND MOON

Here is a mystery which is sure to please any audience. It is a "comedy" effect, and centers around the apparent destruction of two sheets of tissue paper. One sheet is white, the other is any other contrasting color. Let's suppose that the other color is *red*.

EFFECT

Two sheets of tissue are shown front and back. The magician folds them into quarters and tears out the "centers". The torn sheets, along with their centers, are placed in a paper bag for their "magical" restoration. The wizard makes a "magical" gesture at the bag and, when the papers are removed, they are restored *except that the center portions are transposed!* Undaunted, the magician places the "mismade" tissues back into the bag. This time he holds the bag very still as he "MAKES THE MAGIC." The sheets of tissue are removed *again* from within the bag and opened out. This time they are completely restored to their original state. The bag is torn open to show it to be empty and the papers may be passed for examination.

SECRET AND PREPARATION

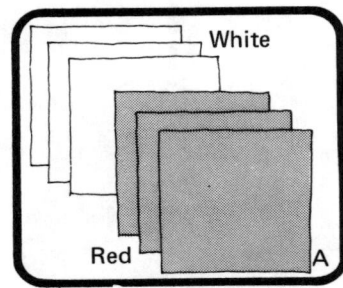
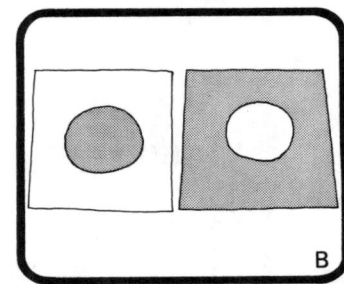
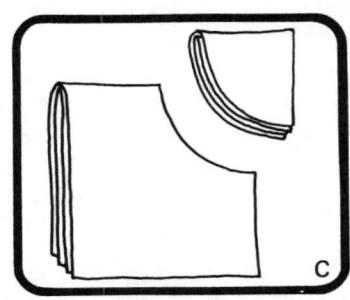

(A) You will need six sheets of tissue, three white and three red—about one foot square is a good size. The first pair of papers, consisting of *one white sheet* and *one red sheet* are unprepared. (B) The second "mismade" pair of tissues (one white, one red) have circles of the *opposite* color tissue pasted on them in the center on *both* sides. (C) To prepare the "mismade" tissues, carefully tear or cut *four* circles of the same size (two red and two white) out of other "matching" pieces of tissue. (D) Glue these circles, one on each side, in the center of the sheet of the *opposite* color. (E) The third pair of tissues, like the first pair, are unprepared.

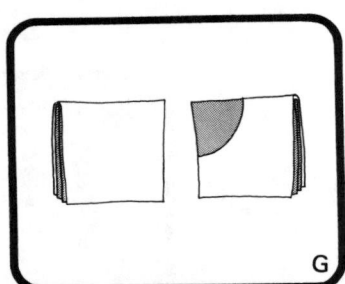

(F) The paper bag is really the special DOUBLE-WALLED BAG which you have already learned to construct. Make the bag of a size which will easily accomodate *two sets* of the folded tissue papers in the "secret" compartment. (G) Fold the first pair of unprepared tissues into quarters. Do the same also with the second, "mismade" pair of tissues. (H) Put both these folded separate packets together and place them into the Double-Walled Bag. *Do not put these papers into the secret pocket.* PLACE THEM INTO THE LARGER SECTION OF THE BAG. (I) Fold the bag flat. This will conceal the presence of the papers which are secretly hidden inside. Fold the bag and place it on your table. Put the remaining (ungimmicked) pair of tissues on the table beside the paper bag.

METHOD

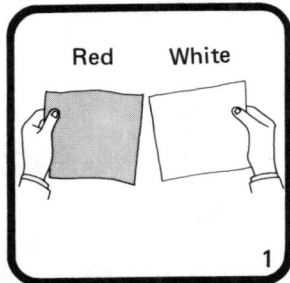

Red White

(1) Pick up the two papers, holding one in each hand. Say, "Here are two sheets of tissue. One is white, one is red."

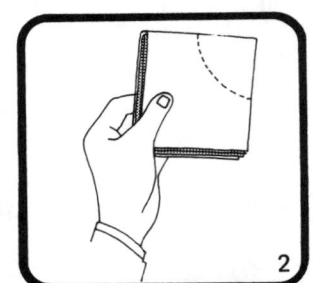

(2) "I shall place the tissues together, fold them into quarters, and tear out the center portions." (3) As you say this, tear the "center corner" out of the tissues in a quarter circle as shown.

(4) *NOTE: When tearing the circles, try to make the torn "centers" approximately the same size as the center portions you pasted on the second "mismade" pair of tissues. You may have to practice tearing the tissues a few times before you can do this action automatically.*

(9) Act surprised as you look at the papers, wondering what went wrong. Place the tissues together and refold them into quarters. Hold the folded papers as shown in the illustration.

(5) Once you have removed the centers, open out the tissues and the centers. Display them to the audience.

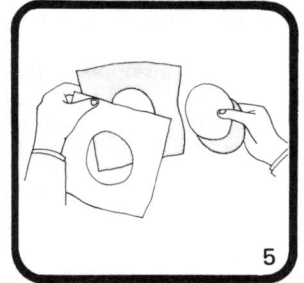

(10) "It seems I have made a terrible mistake. Wait a moment! Perhaps I can correct the situation." As you say this, *tear the centers out of the mismade tissues as shown.*

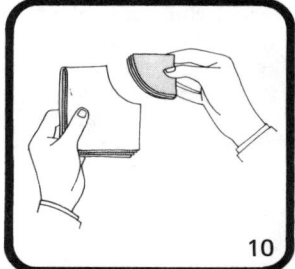

(6) Refold the tissues into quarters and put them, along with the center portions, into the bag. As you do this, PLACE THEM ALL INTO THE SECRET POCKET. Close the bag and shake it. Announce that, by making a *"MAGIC GESTURE"* and by "shaking" the bag, you will cause the tissues to restore themselves.

(11) Pick up the bag and place the torn tissues, *and their centers,* INTO THE SECRET POCKET. Say, "I know what happened, I *shook* the bag when the MAGIC was happening and the papers got a little mixed up."

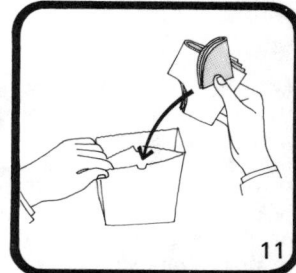

(7) Reach inside and REMOVE THE "MISMADE" PAIR OF TISSUES FROM THE BAG. Place the bag on the table *with the interior facing away from your audience.*

(12) Holding the bag very still, make a magical gesture at the bag. Then, TEAR OPEN THE BAG TO REVEAL THE REMAINING PAIR OF UNTORN TISSUES. *Be careful not to expose the extra tissues hidden in the secret pocket.*

(8) Open the "mismade" tissues to show your *mistake.* The papers are restored – BUT THE CENTERS ARE SWITCHED AROUND!

(13) Toss the torn bag aside before you unfold the two tissues. Now unfold the two papers, as you say, "Things seem to have worked out for the best." You can now hand both tissues for examination if you wish.

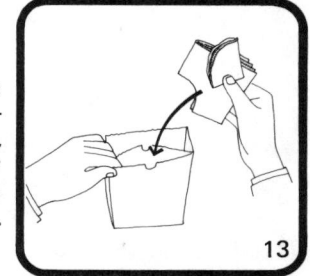

COMMENTS AND SUGGESTIONS

This trick will be very well received if you play it in a "tongue-in-cheek" fashion. The only thing you have to worry about is when you tear open the bag — be careful not to expose the "secret" pocket or its contents. This classic "comedy" effect gives you an opportunity to add as much "acting" as you wish to emphasize your "mistake" when you display the *mismade* tissues.

THE CUT AND RESTORED NECKTIE

EFFECT

The magician requests the assistance of a volunteer from the audience. Once on stage, the spectator is given a piece of rope to examine. After confirming that the rope is unprepared, the performer temporarily drapes the rope around the gentleman's neck so that the spectator may examine a very sharp pair of scissors. In order to demonstrate the efficiency of the scissors, the performer grasps both ends of the rope and, in one quick cut, he severs the rope in two places. Unfortunately, in his haste, *he also cuts through the spectator's tie —* which flutters to the floor. With a chagrinned look on his face, the magician sheepishly picks up the cut ends of the tie and hurriedly stuffs them into a paper bag along with the remaining portion of the tie which he has had the spectator remove. The embarrassed magician suggests that the volunteer take it to a seamstress for repair as the magician attempts to get *another* volunteer for the trick! Needless to say, his search for a new "volunteer" is remarkably unsuccessful. This leaves the magician only one recourse — that is to promptly restore the spectator's tie to its original condition. When the performer withdraws the once severed tie from the paper bag, it is found completely restored — leaving the bag absolutely empty — much to the relief of the spectator, the audience, *and* the magician!

SECRET AND PREPARATION

(A) You will need to purchase two *duplicate* neckties. It is not necessary to purchase expensive ties; in fact, this would hinder the effect. Expensive ties are generally <u>lined</u> and are more difficult to cut. A pair of sharp scissors is also essential to the working of this presentation, as any problems in cutting the tie *quickly* and *smoothly* spoils the comedy effect. In addition, you will also need to make one of the special Double-Walled Paper Bags as explained in the Course. The last item is a piece of soft rope approximately five feet long. If possible, the rope should have its "inner core" removed ("Coring") to make the cutting process easier. Now place *one* of the duplicate ties in the *main compartment* of the Double-Walled Bag along with the rope and scissors. The *secret pocket* in the bag is left *empty*.

Before the performance, discreetly choose a member of the audience who appears to have an out-going personality to be your "partner" in this effect. Take him aside where the other spectators cannot see and have him put on the other duplicate tie. Explain to him exactly what will happen on stage and instruct him to volunteer to assist you when the time comes to present this effect. (Or arrange to "select" him yourself from the audience.) Tell him to act somewhat annoyed when he discovers that you have ruined his tie. He is to "play along" with the situation as it progresses to produce as much laughter and audience response as possible. Have your volunteer take a seat that is easily accessible to the stage and you are ready.

METHOD

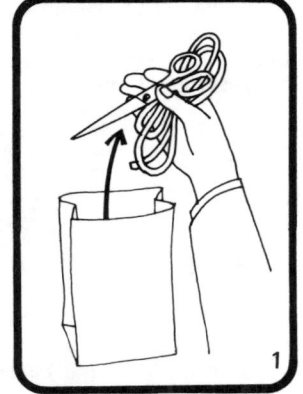

(1) To begin the presentation, ask for the assistance of a member of the audience. As your pre-arranged "volunteer" arrives on stage, remove the length of rope and the scissors from the bag and place the bag aside. Ask the spectator to stand to your right and hand him the length of rope to examine.

(2) After he has confirmed that the rope is unprepared, drape it around his neck. The ends of the rope should extend below the edge of the tie as shown.

(3) Now give the scissors to the spectator and ask him to verify their "sharp" condition. While he is looking at the shears, gather both ends of the rope in your left hand. As he hands the scissors back to you, explain to the audience how it will only take *one* cut to divide the rope into *three* parts. As you say this, open the scissors and pass the back blade behind the ends of the rope — *and the volunteer's tie* as shown.

(6) After the comedy byplay with your volunteer, discard the rope and pick up the end of the severed tie from the floor. Ask the volunteer to remove what is left of his tie. Then place all the pieces of the tie into the *secret pocket* of the paper bag as shown.

(4) With one quick cut, sever the rope *and* the tie, leaving you with two pieces of rope in your left hand *as the end of the spectator's tie flutters to the floor.*

(7) Offer the bag to the spectator suggesting that he have the tie mended by his wife or a local seamstress — as you quickly attempt to get another volunteer so you can repeat the trick! When the "tieless" spectator protests, explain that the only apparent solution to the dilemma is for you to use "a little more magic." Make a magical gesture at the bag, then reach into the bag and remove the whole duplicate tie from the *main compartment* of the bag.

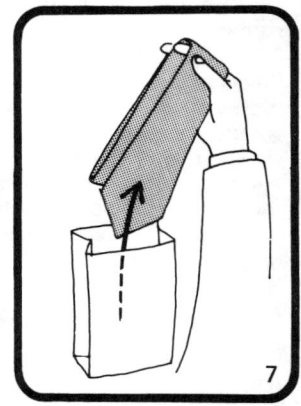

(5) NOTE: Now is the time when the acting ability of you and the spectator comes into play. You will, no doubt, get an immediate response when the audience realizes the terrible mistake you have made. You can then carry the humor of this misfortune as far as you wish. This is a wonderful opportunity to build the presentation into a complete "comedy of errors." One suggestion would be to *continue* cutting the tie into more pieces in an attempt to "make the trick work." You might even cut the remaining portion of the tie so it falls off the spectator, eliminating the need to have him remove it himself. (Be careful not to cut the spectator.)

(8) Return the necktie to your assistant and tear the bag open to prove it is empty. *Be careful not to expose the pieces of the cut tie in the secret compartment.* Thanks to the Double-Walled Paper Bag and a more than helpful "volunteer," the audience will be again convinced of your remarkable abilities as a magical mystery worker!

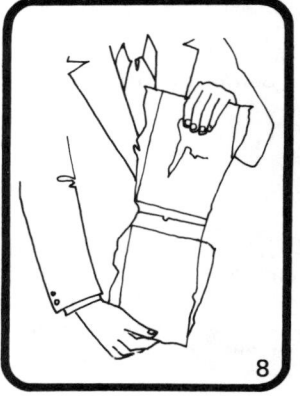

WINE GLASS PRODUCTION

EFFECT

This is excellent as an OPENING EFFECT. The performer freely displays both sides of an attractive handkerchief, showing it to be quite empty. He drapes the handkerchief over his open palm, and suddenly, a form is seen to appear under the fabric. When he lifts the handkerchief away, the spectators are astonished to see that a wine glass — *full of liquid* — has magically appeared and is resting upright on the magician's outstretched hand!

SECRET AND PREPARATION

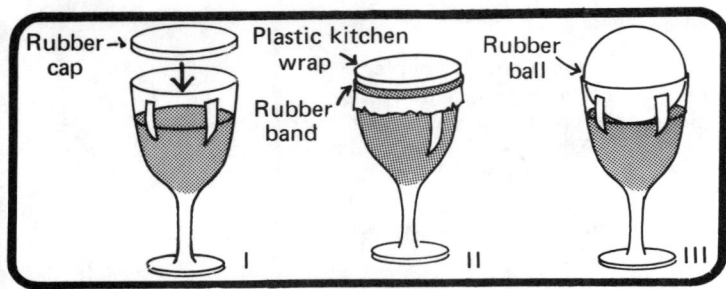

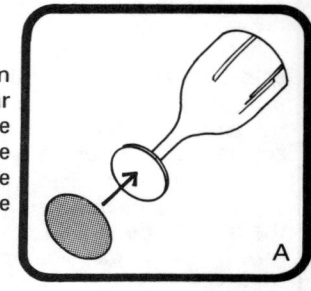

In order to present this startling effect, you will need the following items: A long-stemmed wine glass, an opaque handkerchief, about 24" square, a piece of material that *closely matches* the coat you will wear during your performance, and a soft plastic or rubber cover that fits snugly over the mouth of the wine glass. This cover serves to hold the liquid inside the glass before its "magical" appearance. Most camera stores carry various sizes of rubber *lens caps* which will fit tightly over the mouth of many standard size wine glasses. In place of the lens cap, you can use a sheet of *plastic kitchen wrap* held in place with a rubber band. Another excellent suggestion is to wedge a *rubber ball* into the mouth of the glass. In this case, in order to make an effective seal, you will have to experiment with different sized rubber balls until you find one that works well for retaining the liquid in the glass, yet can be quickly and easily removed without giving you any trouble.

(A) The first step in the preparation of the wine glass is to cut a circular patch of cloth the same size as the bottom of the wine glass from the material that matches your coat. Glue the cloth circle to the bottom of the glass as shown.

(B) Next, fill the glass approximately three-quarters full of colored liquid and fasten the rubber cap (or whatever method you are using) in place, sealing the liquid inside.

(C) Now, position the prepared glass under your left arm just below the shoulder with the *bottom* of the glass *facing the audience* as shown. (You can see why the fabric on the bottom of the glass must closely resemble your coat. Also, because you hold the glass under your arm, this must be the *opening effect* in your performance.) Place the handkerchief in your breast pocket and prepare to make your entrance.

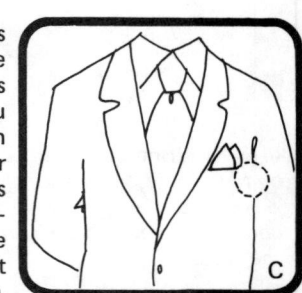

METHOD

(1) As soon as you arrive center stage, remove the handkerchief from your breast pocket and display it, holding it between both hands as shown in this audience view.

(2) Your thumbs should grip the handkerchief *over* the *top hem* with the rest of your fingers positioned behind the scarf as illustrated here from your viewpoint.

(3) Keeping the handkerchief tightly stretched between your hands, cross your arms as shown. Your right hand moves inward behind your left arm, as your left hand swings out toward the audience to its new position in *front* of your right elbow. As you display the handkerchief in this position, your right fingers curl under the stem of the wine glass *secretly securing it between your right first and second fingers*. As soon as your fingers are around the stem of the glass, relax the pressure of your left arm. This allows the mouth of the glass to pivot downward *behind the right corner of the handkerchief* where it remains held by your right fingers concealed from the audience. Your left elbow also aids in concealing this action as you display the handkerchief.

(4) Now, uncross your arms and bring the handkerchief back to its original position. This action secretly carries the glass, in its inverted position in your right hand, behind the right-hand corner of the handkerchief.

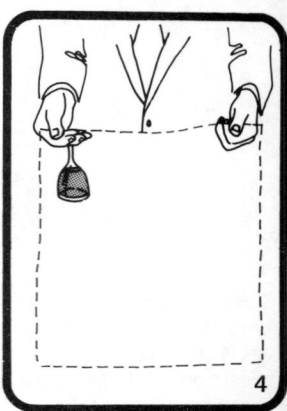

(5) The entire procedure of showing both sides of the handkerchief (Steps 1 through 4) must be performed in *one continuous flowing movement,* without directing any undue attention toward your right hand. Practice the "steal" before a mirror until you are exactly sure what "angles" are working against you. If the glass is "flashing" at any point during the steal, adjust your actions to correct the problem. Then, practice the steal over and over until you are able to execute the entire procedure smoothly and naturally.

(8) Repeat this move, but this time, as you lift the handkerchief, *bring the glass to an upright position* by curling the right fingers into your palm as shown. Now release the handkerchief as you did before; only this time, it falls over the upright glass *revealing the shape of the glass under the handkerchief.* This instant appearance is quite astonishing when performed correctly.

(6) Once you have executed the "steal," the glass should be hanging in its inverted position behind the right-hand corner of the handkerchief. Now, release your grip on the handkerchief with your right thumb (continue to hold the other corner with your left hand) and quickly slide your right hand forward to the center of the handkerchief, allowing the fabric to drape over your open hand and the glass as shown. Because the glass extends *downward* from your right hand, the effect to the audience is that the handkerchief is now covering your *empty* palm.

(9) With your left hand, grasp the rubber cap (or whatever you are using) *through the fabric of the handkerchief* and pull it from the mouth of the glass as you begin to lift away the handkerchief. Keep the rubber cap concealed within the folds of the material. Just as the handkerchief clears the glass, uncurl the fingers of your right hand allowing the glass to rest on your left palm as though it has just "magically" appeared in that position. Place the handkerchief aside (along with the rubber cap) and toast your audience as you drink the liquid to prove that it is genuine.

(7) Now, grasp the handkerchief at its center with your left fingers and lift it straight upward forming a sort of "tent" in the material of the handkerchief. Pause for just a moment and then <u>drop</u> the handkerchief, allowing it to <u>fall flat</u> against your palm once again. *Keep the glass hanging upside down from your right hand during this move.*

THE TAKE-APART VANISH

EFFECT

The performer displays a dove or small rabbit and openly places the animal into an attractive wooden box. Instantly, the box is taken apart — piece by piece — allowing the spectators to view all sides of the now dismantled container. Impossible as it seems, the animal has mysteriously vanished from within the box without a trace.

SECRET AND PREPARATION

To perform this astonishing vanish, you will need to construct a specially gimmicked wooden box. This box works on the same principle as a number of large stage illusions. The quality of the finished product will depend upon your ability as a craftsman. If you take your time in the construction of the prop, however, you will probably be using this vanish in your act for many years.

CONSTRUCTION

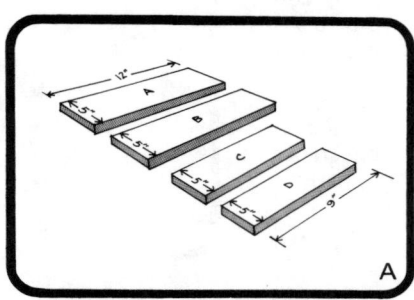

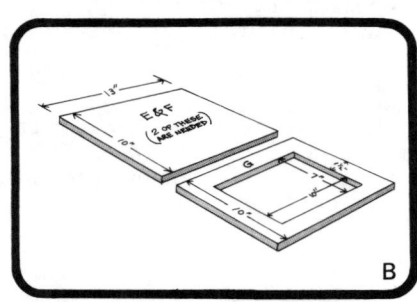

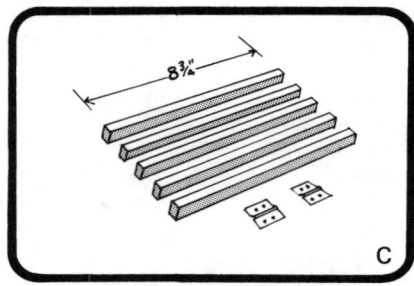

(A)   From a sheet of ½" plywood, cut two pieces which measure 5" x 12" (labeled A and B in the illustrations) and two more pieces 5" x 9" (labeled C and D).   (B)   You will also need three 10" x 13" pieces of ½" plywood labeled E, F, and G. One of these pieces (G) has a 7" x 10" opening cut in the center leaving a 1½" border around the opening.   (C)   Next cut 5 strips of ¼" square soft pine 8¾" long. This type of wood can be purchased at most arts and crafts shops or obtained at any lumber yard. You will also need two 1½" butt hinges which can be purchased inexpensively at any hardware store. (The illustration shows this type of hinge.)

ASSEMBLY

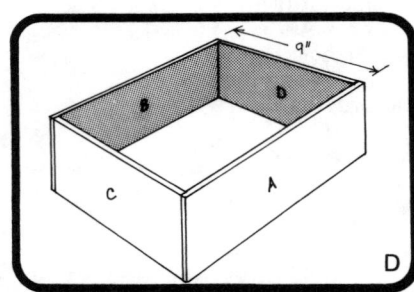

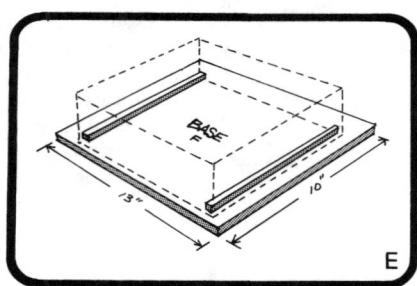

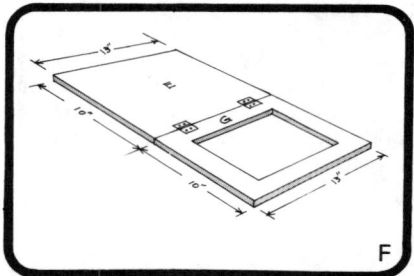

The assembly of the apparatus is quite simple. Take care, however, in fitting the parts together to guarantee the proper working of the equipment and to insure the overall attractiveness of the prop.

(D)   Begin by constructing the rectangular frame of the box as illustrated, using Parts A, B, C, and D. Be sure that A and B overlap the ends of C and D so that the inside width of the frame is 9".   (E)   Next, attach two of the ¼" strips to the top surface of Part F, which serves as the removable bottom for the rectangular frame constructed in Step D. To insure exact alignment, center the frame on top of the board (F) and position the two strips along the inner walls of the frame as illustrated. Then, fasten these strips to the baseboard with wood glue and finishing nails. If done correctly, the frame should fit easily over the baseboard with the two strips serving to hold the frame in position during the presentation.   (F)   To construct the lid of the box, butt the long ends of E and G together and attach the two hinges as illustrated here. When E is hinged over — on top of G — the two boards should align evenly on all sides.

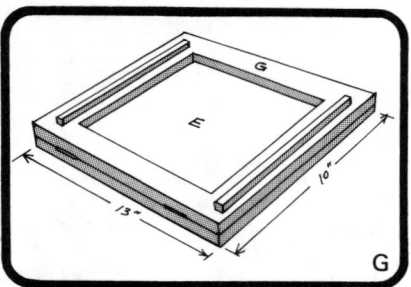

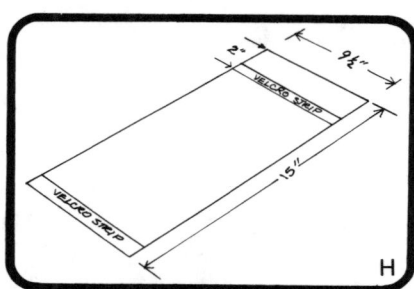

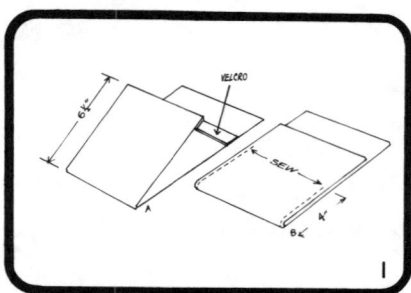

(G)   Now, turn the unit over and attach two ¼" strips to the underside of Part G as shown here. To insure their exact alignment, follow the same procedure outlined in Step E.   (H)   The basic construction is now complete except for the addition of a secret cloth bag which is attached to the lid of the box. The bag should be constructed from a strip of strong, black material approximately 15" long by 9½" wide. Cut a strip of Velcro to fit across the full width of the cloth. (Or you may use snaps or a zipper.) Velcro can be obtained in the sewing notions section of department or yard goods stores. You will notice that the Velcro strip consists of two pieces of ribbon with fuzzy nylon loops which stick together. Each half of the Velcro strip has a different texture. Sew one side of the strip of Velcro across the width of the cloth approximately 2" from one end. Then sew the corresponding side of the Velcro strip (the one with the different texture) even with the edge of the opposite end of the cloth as shown.   (I)   Now fold the cloth over as shown and press the Velcro strips together. This fold will form a bag approximately 6½" deep and 9½" wide. Now, sew the two layers of material together along the sides of the bag — *but only sew about 4" up from the fold which forms the bottom of the bag.*

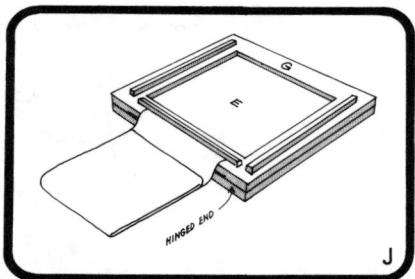
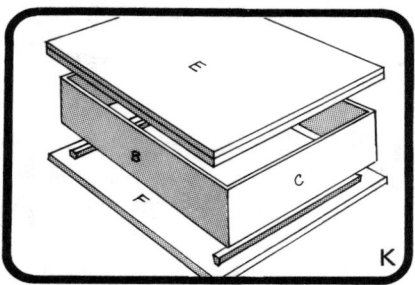
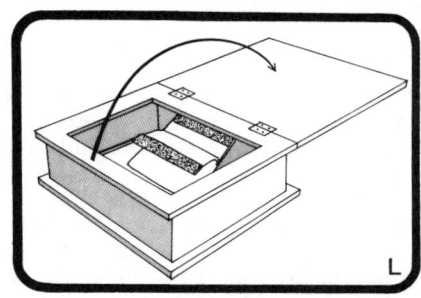

(J) Next, place the lid of the box on the table — bottom side up — *so that Part G of the lid is facing up.* Position the bag so that its upper edge lies over the *hinged side* of G as shown. Place the remaining ¼" strip of wood on top of the edge of the bag and secure the wood strip <u>and the bag</u> to Part G with glue and finishing nails as shown here. This strip must be properly positioned to insure the centering of the lid on the rectangular frame. The *construction* of the box is now complete, and you are ready to assemble the components into the finished product. (K) Place the baseboard F on your table with the ¼" strips facing up. Next, set the open frame on top of the baseboard; then, place the lid E on top of the frame. (L) Be sure that the bag hangs inside the frame and the hinges are nearest to the audience as shown. (M) If everything fits together well, paint the equipment in a decorative manner, and you are ready to present this most baffling vanish.

METHOD

(1) As you display the rabbit (or other small animal or object) to the audience, step to your table and open the lid of the box. The lid should open *away* from you *in the direction of the audience* as shown in Step L. Carefully place the rabbit into the black bag and press the Velcro strips together. This done, close the lid as if to prevent the rabbit from escaping.

(2) You are now ready to "vanish" the rabbit by showing all the sides of the box as you take it apart. Although this procedure can be executed by the magician alone, *the handling of the apparatus is easier and much less risky if you utilize the aid of an assistant.* With your assistant standing at your left, open the lid, Part E, completely so that the audience can see its top surface. Then grasp Part G by the *back edge* with your left hand and lift the entire lid assembly off the frame as shown. This will pull the bag — and the animal — out of the frame, *concealing it behind Part E. The spectators have now seen <u>both sides</u> of the lid — which you give to your assistant to hold.* Be sure not to let the audience catch a glimpse of the hidden bag as you hand the lid to your assistant.

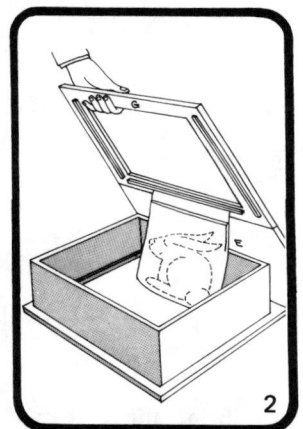

(3) Now direct your attention to the rectangular frame. *Lift it slowly from the baseboard <u>as though it contained the rabbit</u>.* Slowly move forward and then suddenly spin the frame between your hands showing it empty. Hang the empty frame over your assistant's free arm and once again direct your attention back to the table. Pick up the baseboard by tilting it toward the audience and hold it as though you were concealing something behind it. Take a few steps forward and then slowly turn the board over with a smile. The *total vanish* of the rabbit will leave the audience contemplating this mystery for a long time to come.

CONFETTI TO CANDY — FIRST VERSION

EFFECT

The magician displays a large bowl full of confetti and sets it on his table. (It can also be held by his assistant.) He calls his audience's attention to an empty paper cup. Plunging the cup into the bowl of loose confetti, the performer lifts the now full cup into the air and allows the confetti to shower back into the bowl. Once again the magician fills the empty cup with confetti, but this time, instead of pouring it back into the bowl, he covers the brimming cup with a handkerchief. Upon removing the handkerchief from the cup, the audience is surprised to see that the confetti has magically changed into candy! The candy is then passed out to the children in the audience.

SECRET AND PREPARATION

(A) In order to perform the effect, you will need the following:
1. Two medium-sized paper cups.
2. One cardboard lid that will fit into the mouth of one of the cups.
3. Several bags of confetti.
4. One large opaque bowl. This bowl must be large enough so that it will conceal one of the paper cups with enough room to spare for the confetti and the second cup.
5. An unprepared pocket handkerchief.
6. A bag of individually wrapped candies.

(C) Be sure that the tab or fishing line loop is protruding from the cup as shown.

(B) Your first project is to construct a "special" cup. Take the cardboard lid and glue a quantity of confetti to its upper surface. Most lids of this type have a small tab located on their outer rims. If yours does not have this tab, simply make a tab with cellophane tape or substitute with a loop of strong black fishing line. Now fill the cup with candy and press the confetti-covered lid into place as in the illustration. *NOTE: From this point on, we will refer to this prepared cup as Cup B and the unprepared cup as Cup A.*

(D) Fill the large bowl about half full of confetti. Then nestle Cup B deep enough into the bowl so that the audience cannot see the cup over the bowl's edge. (E) Place the bowl on your table with the empty cup (A) sitting beside it. Put the handkerchief into your left inside coat pocket (or on the table) and you will be ready to magically turn CONFETTI into CANDY!

METHOD

(1) Display the bowl and replace it on your table. Pick up Cup A, show it to be empty, and then, with a "scooping" motion, place it into the bowl and fill it with confetti. *Make sure that you don't accidentally expose Cup B during this maneuver.*

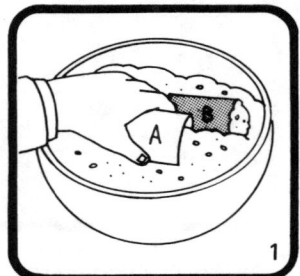

(4) *This time, leave Cup A under the confetti and, as you make the "scoop," grasp Cup B.*

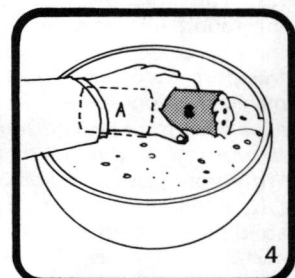

(2) Now pour the confetti back into the bowl from a sufficient height to dramatize the unprepared nature of the equipment.

(5) Bring the prepared Cup B into view with the excess confetti spilling from its lid. *NOTE: This action must be made in one flowing motion. If done properly, the audience will not be aware of the "switch" of the cups.*

STEPS 3, 4, and 5 ARE THE IMPORT-ANT MOVES IN THIS TRICK.

(3) Dip Cup A once again into the bowl as if to fill it with confetti.

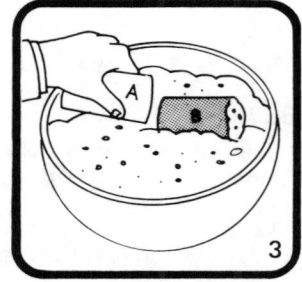

(6) Brush off the excess leaving only the confetti that you previously glued to the lid. Hold the apparently confetti-filled cup up for all to see.

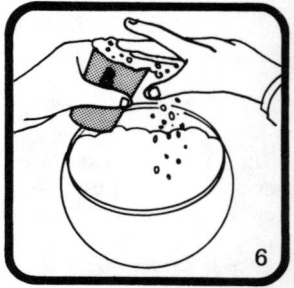

(7)   Reach into your coat pocket and remove the handkerchief. Then, drape the handkerchief over the cup. Make a "magical gesture" toward the cup with your free hand or say a "magical word" to accomplish the small miracle.

(9)   Lift the handkerchief *and the confetti-covered lid* off and away from the cup. Keep the lid concealed in the handkerchief as you drop them both into the bowl. All that is left is to reveal the "magical" change of the confetti to candy and pass it out among the children in the audience.

(8)   Now grip the handkerchief *and* the tab underneath with the thumb and fingers of your right hand.

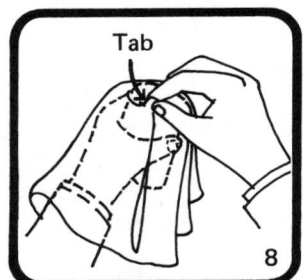

CONFETTI TO CANDY — SECOND VERSION

EFFECT

The effect in this version is identical to the First Version except that a box with a *transparent front* is used instead of an opaque bowl.

SECRET AND PREPARATION

(A)   The cups are prepared in the same manner as described in the first version. In this variation, however, instead of the bowl, you must build a rectangular box approximately 12" long by 6" wide and 8" deep. The front of the box is open, and a piece of glass or clear plastic forms this side.

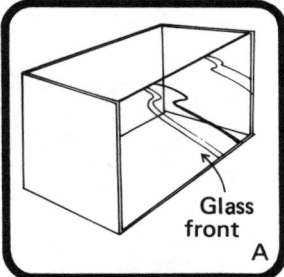

(D)   Now place enough confetti in the rear compartment to fill it about half way.

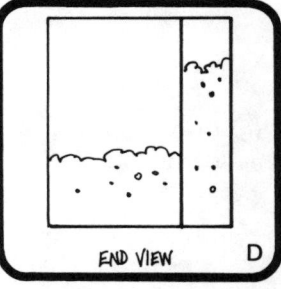

(B)   A second piece of glass or plastic is set into grooves 2" back from the front.

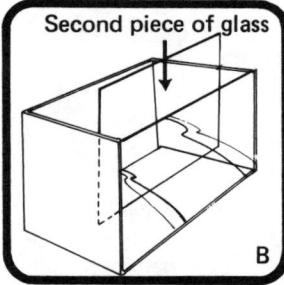

(E)   Place the prepared Cup B in this back compartment. *Position it near the left side with its mouth facing left as shown.* The confetti in the front compartment conceals this cup (B) from view.

(C)   Pour loose confetti into this front compartment until it is 3/4 full.

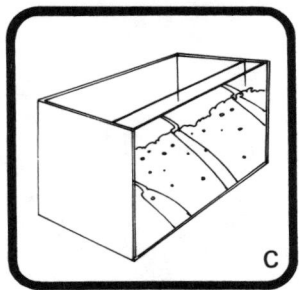

METHOD

The presentation is the same as in the First Version with the added advantage that the audience can actually see you dip up the confetti through the clear front in the box. At the same time, it gives you the ability to boldly make the "switch" of the cups right in front of them without being detected.

CONFETTI TO CANDY — THIRD VERSION

EFFECT

The effect to the audience is the same as in the previous two versions. You may use either the *bowl* or the *box with the clear front* for this method.

SECRET AND PREPARATION

(A) You will need to construct a special set of *nesting* paper cups for this variation. You will need two identical paper cups and one cardboard lid. Glue the confetti to the lid as before, but this time, cut the top rim off Cup B as shown.

(C) When the lid is in position on Cup B and B is nested into Cup A, it will look as if you have only *one single cup full of confetti.*

(B) This will enable Cup B to be nested into Cup A.

(D) Place the prepared Cup B into the container of your choice — hidden from view. Be sure it is positioned to your left so that there will be enough room for your hand and Cup A when they scoop up the loose confetti on the first pass.

METHOD

(1) Hold Cup A in your right hand. Show it empty and then scoop it up full of loose confetti as before. Pour the confetti back into the bowl.

(2) On the second "scoop," instead of exchanging the cups, simply scoop the loaded cup (B) into the empty cup (A) and lift the nested cups into view.

COMMENTS AND SUGGESTIONS

The advantage of this method is the elimination of any possible hesitation in the second scooping action. The combination of the glass-front box (Second Version) and the nested cups (Third Version) makes this clever effect even more baffling and foolproof. Performed correctly, it is well worth the small amount of time necessary to construct the various parts.

THANK YOU BANNER — FIRST METHOD

EFFECT

The magician displays a large square of velvet cloth and shows the audience that both sides are blank. He then gives the banner a sudden shake. As if by magic, the words "THANK YOU" magically appear on the previously blank surface of the material.

SECRET AND PREPARATION

(A) You will need to purchase 2½ yards of black velvet or velveteen and cut a piece to measure 28" wide by 84" long. These dimensions give you a strip of cloth whose *length* is three times longer than its *width.* In the illustrations, the letters A, B, and C represent the three "sides" of the banner, each of which are 28" square.

(B) To make the banner, first spread the material out on the table or floor with the nap (the velvet surface) facing down. Then fold it across the width with the nap outside forming three equal square areas of cloth (Sides A, B, and C) that all hinge at a common point (X). If you have folded the fabric correctly, it should appear as illustrated in Step B. Study the picture and then pin the "sides" in place to see if you have folded the cloth as shown.

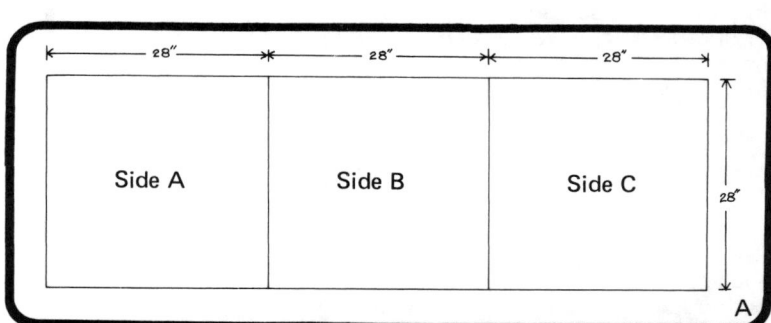

You will notice that the bottom half of Side A forms a sort of "flap" which, when folded up reveals Side B. When this "flap" is folded down, it *covers* Side B and *reveals* Side A again. (Side C is the blank "back" of the banner and does not change.) Insert a weight (Comments and Suggestions) between the layers of fabric in each bottom corner of the "flap" as shown and sew them in place with strong thread. These "weights" will cause the flap to drop smoothly and quickly when you make the "magical appearance" of the THANK YOU. They also help to pull the cloth downward so that Side A of the "flap" hangs straight as you display the banner to the audience after the "appearance." Now sew the banner together around the outside edges. *NOTE: Leave the hem open at the top edge of the banner where Side A and Side C come back to back. This leaves a sort of "secret pocket" between the two layers of material which you will use in the THANK YOU BANNER — SECOND METHOD described immediately after this effect.*

Then sew completely through the entire width of the banner at Point X where the three sides meet in the center. The line formed by sewing through the banner from X to X should be *exactly in the center of all three sides*, A, B, and C. Thus there should be precisely 14" between Line X-X and the ends of each of the individual sides. If not, make the necessary adjustments before sewing the banner together.

You will also need two pieces of black felt material that measure approximately two feet long and one foot wide. It is on these pieces of felt that the greeting or message (the "THANK YOU") that you wish to convey is written. One spectacular and attractive way of writing the words of the message across the felt is with an artists brush dipped in white glue. This done, sprinkle the glued surface with glitter and allow it to dry. Another method is to cut the individual letters of the message from a piece of brightly colored material and glue them to the black felt. With a little experimenting, you will discover other easy and practical ways of achieving the decorative results that will make an attractive-looking message on your banner.

Now, sew the felt to the top and bottom halves of Side A. As you see, the word "THANK" is positioned in the center of the top half of Side A and the word "YOU" on the bottom half. Be sure not to stitch through both layers of the banner when you sew on the felt pieces; *sew only through the material that makes up Side A.* Also, use only as many stitches as necessary to secure the felt pieces to the banner. This way they can be easily removed and replaced with other pieces that convey a different message. The construction of the banner is complete. You are now ready to present the THANK YOU BANNER.

METHOD

(1) Place the banner on a flat surface and fold the "flap" so that it covers Side A. Where the two weighted corners of the "flap" meet the upper half of Side A is now the "top" of the banner. When you are ready to present the trick, pick up one pair of these corners in your right hand and the other pair in your left hand and display Side B of the banner to your audience. *Be sure that Side B of the "flap" is closest to the audience.* Otherwise, your magical message will result in the appearance of the THANK YOU written upside-down across the banner — which is most embarrassing!

(2) Now cross your arms showing the audience the other side of the "blank" banner (Side C). *Be sure to keep the upper edges of both layers stretched tightly between your hands so the audience is not aware that you hold two separate layers of material together "as one."*

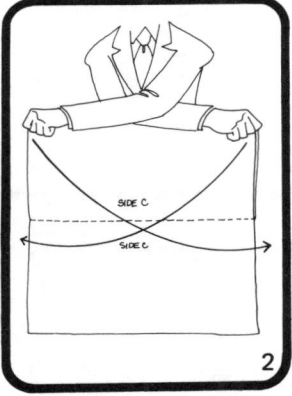

(3) Now, uncross your arms and bring the banner back to its former position as shown in Figure 1.

(4) All that remains is to give the banner a sharp SHAKE. At the same time, release your hold on the corners of the "flap."

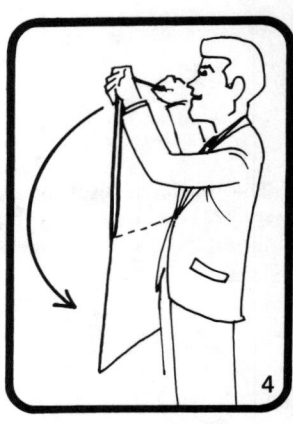

(5) Retain a firm grip on the *upper corners* of Side A. The weights in the corners of the "flap" will cause it to drop with a snap, revealing the magical "THANK YOU" spelled out across the face of the now-exposed Side A.

COMMENTS AND SUGGESTIONS

When you are in the store to purchase the velvet or velveteen, ask for drapery weights. These are flat lead weights, usually square, with a cut-out in the center providing a bar by which they may be sewn to the fabric. If the fabric store does not have them, the curtain and drapery department of a large department store will. You could also use flat metal washers about 1" in diameter from any good hardware store, but they will be harder to sew on.

THANK YOU BANNER — SECOND METHOD

EFFECT

The magician displays a large, square cloth banner, showing the audience that both sides are blank. He then folds the banner in half and his assistant lowers two coils of rope into the folds of the material. With a snap, the performer flips the banner open. As if by magic, the rope mysteriously clings to the previously blank surface of the cloth, spelling out the words "THANK YOU" as a fitting close to the magician's performance.

SECRET AND PREPARATION

This is a clever variation of the THANK YOU BANNER. Instead of using glitter or cloth letters, however, sew or glue a length of soft rope to the black felt, spelling out whatever message or greeting you wish to convey. (Or you may sew the ropes directly to Side A of the banner.) Now, attach the felt pieces to the banner in their proper positions and you are ready to perform.

METHOD

(1) Hold the banner in the same starting position described in Step 1 of the THANK YOU BANNER, with Side A folded up concealing the message. Again, be sure that Side B of the "flap" is closest to the audience as you display the blank banner stretched between your hands. Now, display both sides of the apparently blank material to the audience to prove that it is "unprepared" as in Step 2.

(4) Now your assistant displays the two pieces of rope and apparently drops them into the folded banner. Actually, she places them into the "secret pocket" between the layers of material in the open hem where Sides A and C come together back to back.

(2) Have your assistant reach down and grasp the bottom corners of the banner (Side B) in both hands and fold the lower portion upward so that you can grasp these corners from your assistant — one in each hand.

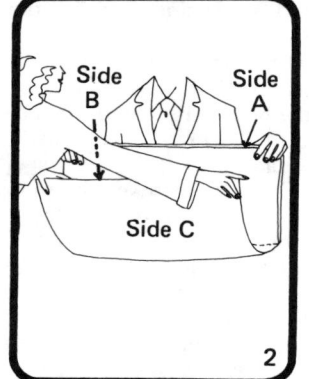

(5) All that remains is to give the banner a fast shake at the same time releasing your grip on the lower half of Sides B and C. Make sure, however, to retain a firm grip on the upper corners of Side A. The weights in the corners of the "flap" will cause the banner to open out with a snap, revealing the magical message spelled out across the face of the exposed surface.

(3) You now hold all three corners of Sides A, B, and C together in both hands. As you hold the folded banner, insert your first fingers between the faces of Side A (the side containing the message) in preparation for the flip when the message will be revealed.

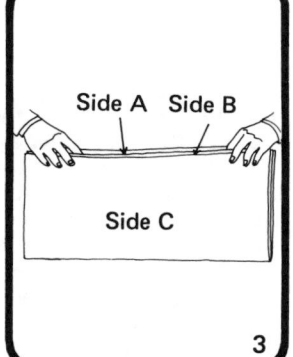

(6) To the audience, the loose rope will appear to have magically arranged itself to form the words "THANK YOU." Actually, the loose rope is safely hidden within the secret pocket.

THANK YOU BANNER — THIRD METHOD

Instead of using a length of rope to form the magical greeting, you can purchase a quantity of glittering rhinestones at an Arts and Crafts shop or costume jewelry store and attach them to the black felt to spell out your message. The glittering stones create a brilliant display under the lights and can be seen clearly by everyone in the audience. To perform, simply fill a small brandy glass with the rhinestones. Then, after folding the banner in half as described above, your assistant pours the stones into the "secret pocket" at the open hem. When the banner flies open, the audience will see that the loose stones have magically attached themselves to the surface of the banner spelling out the words "THANK YOU."

VANISHING BOWL OF WATER

One of the most spectacular liquid tricks involves the vanish of a large bowl filled with water. The following is a simple, direct and very mystifying method for accomplishing this feat. It appears as if the bowl of water disappears right *under the noses of the spectators!*

EFFECT

The magician's assistant enters carrying a large bowl resting on a thin tray. The magician picks up a pitcher filled with water and pours the liquid into the bowl. The performer covers the bowl with an attractive cloth. He then picks up the covered bowl and walks forward into the audience. The cloth is snapped out into the air and the bowl of water has *vanished without a trace!*

SECRET AND PREPARATION

TO ACCOMPLISH THIS FEAT, YOU WILL NEED TO PREPARE THE BOWL, THE TRAY, AND THE CLOTH AS FOLLOWS: (A) THE BOWL: It is a good idea to use a lightweight metal, wooden or plastic bowl. The bowl must have a thin sheet of plastic glued over *half of the mouth of the bowl* as shown. The plastic will prevent the liquid from escaping when the bowl is tipped on its side. Position the plastic piece inside the rim of the bowl and use epoxy or waterproof cement to glue it in place. Also, obtain a strong metal "hook and bracket" combination from a hardware store. Mount the <u>hook</u> on the outside of the bottom of the bowl near the edge using epoxy or other strong cement as shown. (You may also use small nuts and bolts to secure the hook to the bowl. Just be sure to "waterproof" the holes with glue.) The bowl is now prepared for performance. (B) THE TRAY: The tray may be cut from 3/8-inch plywood and decorated to match the rest of your props (or buy an attractive metal, wooden or plastic tray). Mount the <u>bracket</u> on one side of the tray using short wood screws, epoxy or nuts and bolts. Paint the bracket the same color as the tray. The bracket and hook must be positioned so that you can hook the bowl secretly to the tray. Once this is done, you will be able to tip the tray "up," perpendicular to the floor, so that the bowl will be hidden from the audience. NOTE: When the tray is tipped in this fashion, the plastic piece in the top half of the bowl should be <u>lowermost</u>. *This will cause the liquid to remain trapped inside the bowl.* (C) THE CLOTH: The cloth is really two cloths, sewn together at the edges and has a cardboard or plastic disc *the same size as the mouth of the bowl* sewn into the center of the fabric, hidden between the two thicknesses of cloth.

METHOD

(1) Have the bowl, the folded special cloth and a pitcher of liquid on your table. Your assistant enters at the proper time, carrying the tray. Place the bowl on the tray *secretly hooking it to the tray.* Pick up the pitcher and pour the liquid into the bowl. *NOTE: At this point, the <u>open half</u> of the mouth of the bowl is <u>toward</u> the audience.*

(2) Pick up the cloth from your table and unfold it. Handle the cloth so that you do not expose the "secret" disc sewn inside it.

(3) Use both hands to spread the cloth over the bowl and tray. Place the cloth over the bowl so that the disc is located *directly over the mouth of the bowl.*

(4) For this phase of the trick, TIMING IS CRITICAL. With both hands, grasp the *disc* as if you were picking up the *bowl.* Lift the disc upward as you turn to face the audience. At the same time that you lift the cloth (and the secret disc), your assistant tips the <u>front</u> edge of the tray upwards and takes one step back.

(5) This shows how the bowl, attached to the tray, swings to a position hidden by the bottom of the tray. *The piece of plastic glued in the mouth of the bowl prevents the liquid from escaping.*

(6) Step forward as you hold what *appears* to be the bowl of liquid under the cloth (really just the disc). <u>The audience's attention will be entirely on you.</u> *This gives your assistant the opportunity to exit, secretly carrying the bowl of liquid hidden on the rear side of the tray.*

(7) Continue to walk forward until you are well into the audience (or near the front edge of the stage). You may wish to "stumble" slightly for effect as you near some members of the audience. This bit of comic action serves to reinforce to the rest of the audience that you are performing the delicate task of holding the bowl of liquid through the cloth. Suddenly, release your grasp on the disc and toss the cloth upward. As it descends toward the floor, catch one corner (or two corners if you wish) and snap the cloth back up into the air. *Show both sides of the cloth and toss it to your assistant.* Your audience will gasp in amazement at the apparant vanish of the bowl and the liquid in mid air!

COMMENTS AND SUGGESTIONS

If you have a FOO CAN (described elsewhere in the Course), you may wish to present it just prior to the BOWL VANISH. After openly filling the can with liquid, you proceed to show it to be empty — the water has vanished. At this point, your assistant enters with the bowl and tray. You then make the water "reappear" as you pour it from the FOO CAN into the bowl. Then proceed with the BOWL VANISH. Performed in this fashion, the two effects blend together in a smooth sequence which builds to a logical "magical" climax.

THE BUNNY BOX

EFFECT

This is a clever variation of the VANISHING BOWL OF WATER. In this adaptation, however, you vanish an attractive *box* which contains a rabbit (or other livestock) instead of the *bowl* of liquid. The method used for the vanish of the box is the same as for the bowl. You will find THE BUNNY BOX an excellent effect to perform for children as they are always delighted to see tricks with livestock.

SECRET AND PREPARATION

(A) Construct the box out of 1/4" pine or plywood to a size which suits the rabbit you wish to vanish. You will need to add some hardware to the box so that the lid can be locked shut. Then mount two metal hooks on the underneath side of the box. Position the two corresponding brackets on the plywood tray so that the hooks on the bottom of the box fit into them exactly. The box may now be hooked to the tray just like the bowl was in the previous "vanish." Drill a few air holes in the ends of the box so that your livestock can get plenty of air. Paint the box one color and the tray another, but select colors that match the rest of your props, so that the entire affair will blend in nicely with your other props.

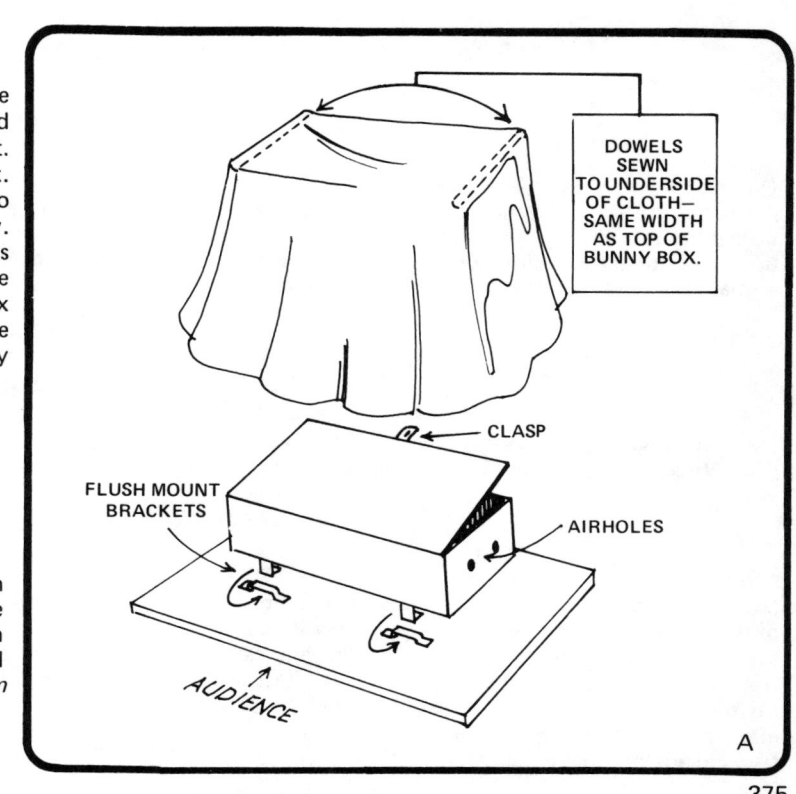

DOWELS SEWN TO UNDERSIDE OF CLOTH— SAME WIDTH AS TOP OF BUNNY BOX.

CLASP

FLUSH MOUNT BRACKETS

AIRHOLES

AUDIENCE

A

(B) Prepare the double cloth by sewing two dowels between the double cloth. (In the vanish, the *dowels* are used just as the *disc* was in the bowl vanish.) The dowels must correspond with the top outside edges of the box. By grasping the dowels, and stretching them tightly between your hands, you retain the *form* of the livestock box beneath the cloth.

METHOD

(1) Show the box and place it on the tray held by your assistant so that the hooks attach firmly to the brackets. Now gently place the bunny into the box. *Close the lid and fasten it securely before covering the box with the prepared cloth.*

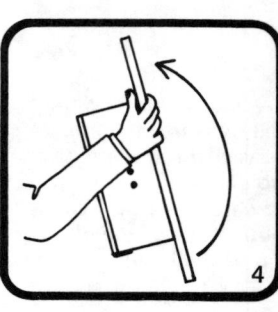

(4) The timing of the tipping of the tray is the same as with the Vanishing Bowl of Water. At the proper moment, your assistant tips the tray before leaving with it. The box is secretly hidden on the rear side of the tray.

(2) Execute Steps 3 through 6 as explained in The Vanishing Bowl of Water.

(3) Grasp the two dowels through the cloth. Hold one dowel in each hand and stretch the cloth between the dowels as shown to retain the form of the box.

(5) Step toward the audience holding the cloth with the box apparently underneath. Toss the cloth into the air to cause the box *and* the bunny to vanish!

COMMENTS AND SUGGESTIONS

When you "vanish" the box and the bunny, grasp the cloth by one corner as it falls and snap it out sharply. You may now drape the cloth over one arm as you take your bow. This small addition of business is not always possible with the bowl vanish due to the large size of the disc sewn into the cloth. It can be done, however, with the livestock vanish because of the flexibility of the cloth containing the dowels. To see the magician drape the cloth over one arm before taking his bow not only creates an attractive picture, but also serves to convince the audience that the cloth is unprepared.

PRODUCTION BOX

EFFECT

On the magician's table rests what appears to be an ordinary shoe box. The performer picks up the box and shows it inside and out, proving it to be quite empty. Replacing the box on his table, the magician picks up the lid and allows the spectators to clearly see it on both sides as well. It is just what it appears to be — an ordinary cardboard lid to a shoe box. Placing the lid on the box, the magician picks up the container and displays it to his audience. Upon lifting the lid, the performer reaches into the previously empty box and removes a small live animal or any other similar sized item, much to the delight of the astonished spectators.

SECRET AND PREPARATION

The following is a simple but effective method to produce a live dove or other small animal. The items you will need for this effect are: a shoe box complete with lid, some black felt, a table, and, of course, the animal (let's assume it's a dove) to be produced.

(A) The first step in construction of the "production box" is to sew together a cloth bag made of strong black felt. Let's assume you will be using a standard shoe box with a lid that measures 12" x 6" x ¾". (The size of the lid determines the size of the bag you will make.) In this case, the bag should measure approximately 8" x 4". Cut an 8" square piece of felt and fold it in half. Now, sew up the *ends* of the folded square to form an 8" x 4" bag or pouch that is open at the top and large enough to contain the live dove. Sew a small dress snap in the center of the opening at the top of the bag, as shown in the illustration.

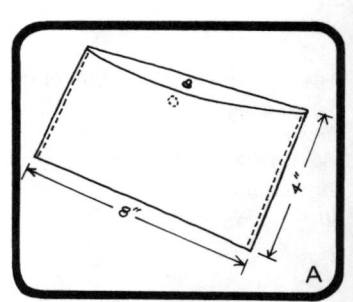

(B) Next, cut a length of strong clear mono-filament fishing line or heavy thread. This line should be threaded through the lip of the lid and then sewn to the top corners of the bag as in the illustration.

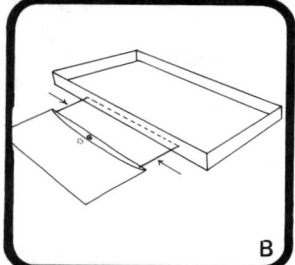

(D) This done, carefully load the dove into the bag and close the snap to prevent it from escaping. Then rest the lid of the box near the back edge of your table with the <u>inside</u> of the lid *facing up.* The bag containing the dove should be suspended *below the table top* as shown. Position the empty shoe box in front of the lid, and you are ready.

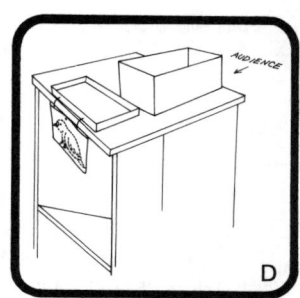

(C) The exact length of the line must be determined through experimentation. The end result, however, should center the load bag on the back of the lid as shown.

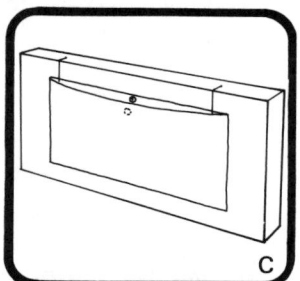

METHOD

(1) Begin by picking up the empty shoe box and displaying it on all sides. Make sure to give the audience a clear view of the inside of the box.

(4) Release your grip on the lid and show your hands empty. Then lift the lid <u>just enough</u> so you can *rotate the lid completely over* and place it on the box. *Be careful not to raise the lid too high when you rotate it as that would lift the load bag out of the box where it would be seen by the audience.*

(2) Replace the box on your table and pick up the lid. This is done by *tilting the lid forward <u>before</u> lifting it clear of the table.* The load bag will be lifted *unseen* into position <u>behind</u> the lid as shown.

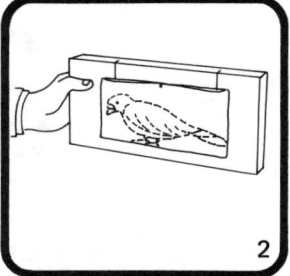

(5) Now pick up the covered box and display it freely on all sides. Then, place the box back on your table and raise the back of the lid with your left hand as shown. With your right hand reach into the box, open the snap, and remove the dove from the bag.

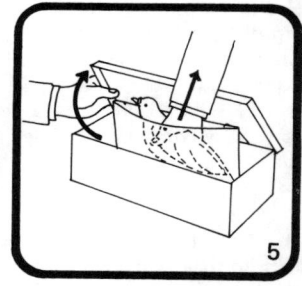

(3) Keeping the inside of the lid facing the audience, lower the lid directly in front of the shoe box *allowing the load bag to secretly slip inside the box.* Now, stand the lid on its edge using the shoe box as a support.

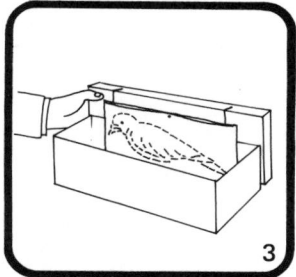

(6) To conclude the production, bring the dove into view and then close the lid of the box and take your bow.

COMMENTS AND SUGGESTIONS

The above principle may be applied to any size box. Simply adjust the dimensions of the load bag to fit the concealment area behind the lid.

It is a good idea to practice this production before a mirror and watch your angles. You will find that by *reversing* the procedure, a very effective <u>vanish</u> can also be presented with the same equipment.

THE SQUARE CIRCLE

EFFECT

The magician introduces his audience to an empty rectangular tube, one side of which is cut into an open grillwork or filigree pattern. A cylinder is next displayed and is also proven to be empty. The rectangular tube (the Square) and the cylinder (the Circle) are nested and placed on a small elevated stand. The spectators never lose sight of the cylinder, as its contrasting color can be clearly seen through the openings in the side of the rectangular cover. In spite of these impossible conditions, the performer succeeds in magically producing yards and yards of silk streamers and brightly colored scarves. The magician again proves both the Square and the Circle to be empty. After replacing the tubes, the magician produces a small bowl — complete with water and goldfish — which provides an effective climax to the SQUARE CIRCLE.

SECRET AND PREPARATION

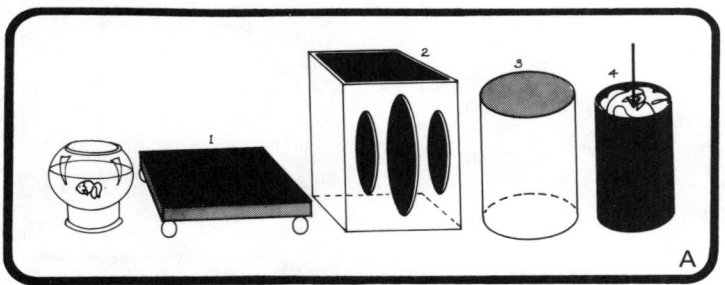

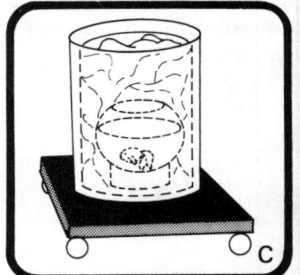

(A) The equipment necessary to present this effect is illustrated in Figure A. The apparatus is divided into four parts. Item 1 is a small elevated stand, 2 is a rectangular tube with one side cut out in an attractive pattern, 3 is a cylinder of the appropriate size to fit inside the rectangle, and 4 is a smaller tube that will comfortably rest within the larger cylinder. From this point on, we will refer to the rectangular tube (Item 2) as the "Square" and the larger of the two cylinders (Item 3) as the "Circle." The small cylinder (Item 4) is never seen by the audience. Its function is to conceal the production articles, and we will refer to this piece as the "Load Chamber." The top surface of the small stand (Item 1), all of the inside walls of the Square except for the front "cut out" pattern, and the outside surface of the Load Chamber are covered with black velvet. The outside of the Square should be painted some bright color such as blue, green, or red. The Circle should be decorated in a contrasting color such as yellow, orange, or silver in order to be in direct contrast with the Square.

(C) Place the black velvet-covered Load Chamber over the bowl. The silk handkerchiefs, streamers, or other production articles are packed inside the Load Chamber around (and carefully over) the fish bowl as illustrated.

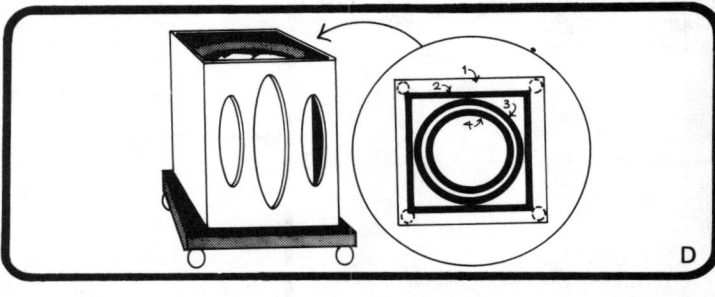

(D) Now set the Square over the Load Chamber. You will see an amazing illusion. By viewing the set-up through the openings in the Square, the Square looks *quite empty*. Herein lies the secret to this effect. Now drop the Circle over the Load Chamber. Be sure the cut out front of the Square is facing your audience, and the entire arrangement will look as illustrated in Figure D. You are now ready to present THE SQUARE CIRCLE.

(B) Let us assume that you will be finishing the trick with the production of the small fish bowl as described. Obtain a bowl that will just fit into the Load Chamber. Place it on the platform as shown. Fill the bowl approximately half full of water and then add several goldfish to complete the picture.

METHOD

(1) Call the audience's attention to the equipment on your table. Lift the Square and show it freely to the spectators.

(2) Drop the Square back on the Stand around the Circle. *Be sure the cut-outs are to the front.*

(3) Now lift the Circle from inside Square, *leaving the Load Chamber in place.* Thanks to the black velvet, *the Square appears to be empty.* Then make sure that the audience has a clear view through the empty Circle. AT THIS POINT, BOTH THE CIRCLE AND THE SQUARE APPEAR TO BE EMPTY.

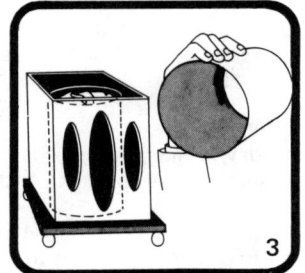

(4) Replace the Circle in the Square. The contrasting color of the Circle can be clearly seen by the audience as it is lowered into the Square. *Unknown to the spectators, you are covering the Load Chamber at the same time.*

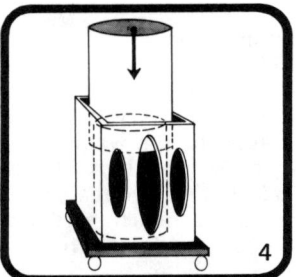

(6) After all of these smaller items have been produced, show the Square and the Circle empty again by repeating Steps 1, 2, 3, and 4. After the audience is convinced that there is nothing left to produce, lift the Square and set it on its side as shown. This will leave only the Circle resting on the small base.

(7) Grasp the top edges of the Circle *and* the Load Chamber. *Now, lift them both together, as one unit, off the base.* The goldfish bowl will be revealed for the first time to a greatly surprised audience.

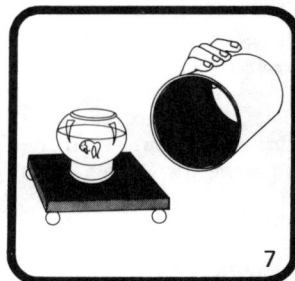

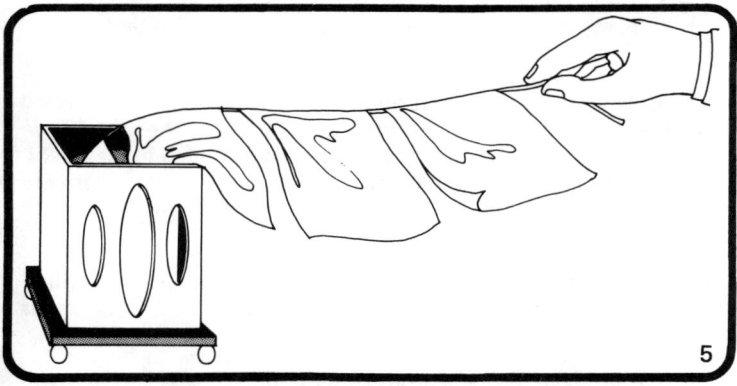

(5) Reach into the top of the Circle and "magically" produce the streamers, silk handkerchiefs, etc.

COMMENTS AND SUGGESTIONS

THE SQUARE CIRCLE is a tried and true classic magic prop. It can be made or purchased in many forms, designs, and sizes. In fact, you can easily even build one out of heavy cardboard that is big enough to produce a person! Be sure, as with all the other tricks you learn from the Course, to protect and never reveal the secret of THE SQUARE CIRCLE.

THE ALLAKAZAM HAT

INTRODUCTION

When I first succeeded in selling the *Magic Land of Allakazam* television series, the original contract was for a thirty-minute show to be aired every Saturday morning over the full CBS Television Network for 26 weeks. Although Nani and I had sold, produced, and performed in many of our own local television series and one syndicated series that was seen in a number of major cities throughout the United States, this was not only my first network series, but also the first time I had ever appeared on any network at all, even as a guest. At that time, unless you were a well established star with a proven show, the longest initial contract any show was likely to receive was 13 weeks. Therefore, we were quite lucky in being given 26 weeks to prove the entertainment value of the first network television magic series.

Nani and I assembled our first creative staff which consisted of a number of very talented people. Although our creative group enlarged and changed throughout the succeeding five-year run of the series (two years on the CBS network and three years on the ABC network), these magical talents remained with us throughout the entire period.

In order to present thirty minutes of magic every week, we not only had to devise many variations on standard tricks, but also create numerous original effects as well. One of the most practical and certainly the most used prop of the entire series was the ALLAKAZAM HAT.

The Allakazam Hat was created to fill a specific need. The show required a connective device which could produce, vanish or change objects; have a "magical" appearance; and be attractive, yet unique enough in design to fit into the overall concept and decor of the show. The Square Circle had the necessary "magical" properties, but the standard Square Circle design looked like nothing other than a magic prop — there was nothing that corresponded to it in "real life."

It was during one of our many extensive creative sessions that we decided that a unique "magician's hat" would be the ideal device — now how to do it? The Square Circle *principle* was an obvious "magical" answer, but it had one major drawback, *the rim of the hat!*

The problem caused by the rim was this: If the rim of the Hat (the Circle) were very large and the Hat were placed mouth upward inside the Square, then the Square could not be lifted off of the Hat because the rim would block it. We discussed the possibility of not showing the Square empty at all, merely lifting out the Hat and letting the viewers look into the Square through the grillwork in front to justify the "emptiness" of that portion of the apparatus. This was rejected for two reasons. First, merely *seeing* into the blackness of the Square without actually *showing* the Square empty would not be deceptive enough, particularly for a prop which we intended to use in many shows. Second, since television is two-dimensional and has no "depth" for the home viewer, this weakness would be doubly amplified.

As with most problems that you will come up against in magic, the answer was quite simple — *once you discover it!* We merely hinged the Square at the back, as you see illustrated in the explanation that follows. In this way, the Square could be removed from the back of the Hat rather than lifted over the top, *thereby eliminating the problem of the brim!*

As it turned out, this made the trick even stronger, and the Allakazam Hat became a regular effect on many of the Allakazam episodes that were seen by many millions of viewers every week. As a matter of fact, the Allakazam Hat became the "on camera" home of *Basil the Baffling Bunny,* the live rabbit who appeared in so many of our episodes, and was also on occasion the domicile of some of Basil's friends, such as *Doris the Daring Dove, Gertrude the Glamorous Guinea Pig, Harriet the Harmonious Hamster* and *Charles the Charming Chicken.* It was not, however, quite large enough to contain one of our most popular characters, our giant rabbit, *Bernard the Biggest Bunny in the Business!*

I feel sure that, at the end of the five-year run of the Allakazam series, because of the vast audiences available through the medium of television, the Allakazam Hat was the one magic prop that had been seen by more people throughout the world than any other magic prop in history.

If you should decide to make an ALLAKAZAM HAT for yourself, I hope that you will have great pleasure in presenting it and perhaps recall a bit of its history as you do. Of even more importance, I hope that this example of a "magical problem" and the technique we used to resolve it will help you to find solutions for some of the obstacles that you may encounter as you develop your own style and effects in the Art of Magic.

So here for the very first time is a complete description of how you can make and use an ALLAKAZAM HAT. Good Luck!

—MW

THE ALLAKAZAM HAT

EFFECT

The ALLAKAZAM HAT is a stylized, improved version of the SQUARE CIRCLE, which has been previously described. Since the secret is a refinement of principles you have already learned and you are also now familiar with the workings of the original trick, we will only discuss the *variations* involved in this particular form of equipment. NOTE: With the ALLAKAZAM HAT all of the parts should be made *larger* than a standard Square Circle, so that a sizable production of items is possible.

SECRET AND PREPARATION

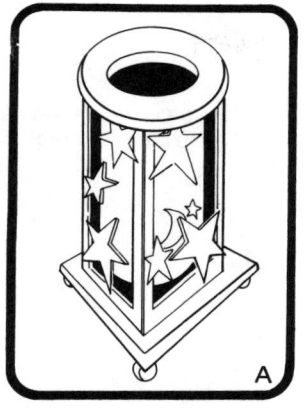

(A) In the ALLAKAZAM HAT, the "Circle" has been designed to look like a *magical hat* with its brim extending beyond the top edges of the "Square." The Square has been modified by cutting the open filigree into *two* adjacent sides. The corner between the cut out areas becomes the front of the Square, which gives a wide open view of the Hat inside.

(B) The load chamber is resting inside the Hat (Circle), as before; but the Square is made to *hinge* from the back corner as shown. In this way, the Square can be opened and removed from around the Hat, since the brim of the Hat prevents you from *lifting* the Square as in the original Square Circle routine.

METHOD

(1) To show the Square to your audience, simply hinge it open and lift it *back and away* from the Hat. You can then openly display it as shown.

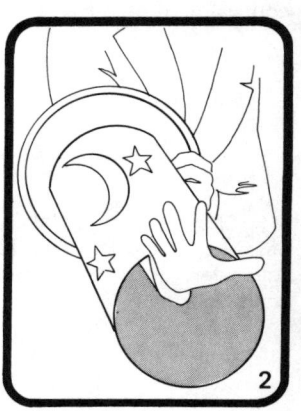

(2) Replace the Square around the Hat. Then grasp the brim of the Hat with both hands. Lift the Hat up and out of the Square and show it empty. (The load chamber stays inside the Square as usual.)

(3) After replacing the Hat inside the Square, make your production as previously described. NOTE: The small amount of extra work involved in the construction of this "special version" of the Square Circle will not only result in a professional looking piece of equipment with maximum production space and deceptive values — but also allows you to present what is probably the most famous magic trick of all ... *PRODUCING A RABBIT FROM A TOP HAT!*

THE ALLAKAZAM HAT — A VARIATION

Because of the unique construction of the ALLAKAZAM HAT there is a special "move" that can be easily added to the routine that will fool even those who know the secret of the regular Square Circle.

METHOD

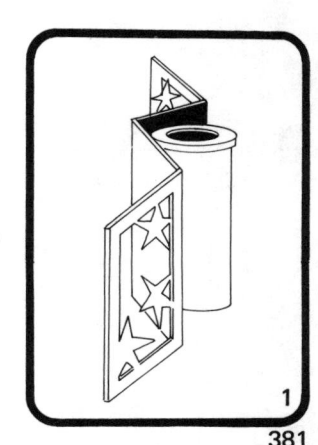

(1) After you have removed the Square and shown it empty as in Step 1 of the previous routine, do not replace the Square around the Hat. *Instead, set the Square, still folded open, in front of the Hat as shown.*

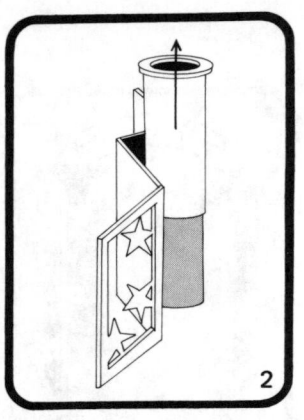

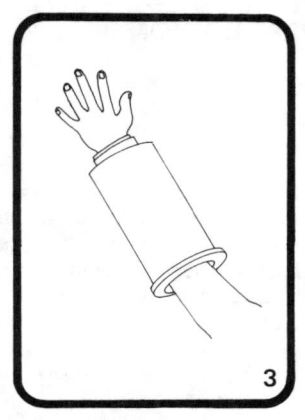

(2) Now pick up the Hat, *leaving the load chamber behind the solid sides of the open Square.* (3) These sides form a natural hiding place for the load chamber. Also, because of the "V" shaped area created by the solid sides, the "line of sight" for concealment of the load is also quite good.

(5) Now pick up the Square, show it briefly again and then replace it around the Hat.

(6) You have now shown *both* the Square *and* the Hat empty at *the same time* . . . thanks to the special Allakazam Hat move!

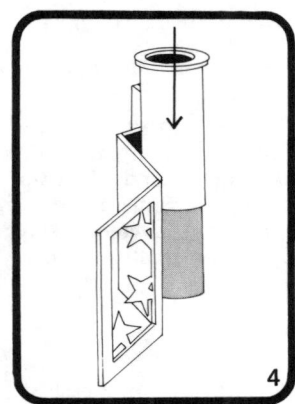

(4) Show that the Hat is completely empty . . . and then replace it behind the open Square . . . over the load chamber.

(7) Begin to make the production from the Hat. Then, after about half of the articles have been produced, pick up the Hat from inside the Square and show it empty again. Replace the Hat and continue with the rest of the "production." In this way you have now used the original Square Circle principle to add further to the deception.

MAGIC TABLE

If you intend to perform on a stage or for larger groups, you should have a "Magic Table." The following plans explain how you can easily and inexpensively build your own table in a style that is ideal for this purpose. It is attractive, simple to build and folds flat for travelling or storage between shows.

CONSTRUCTION

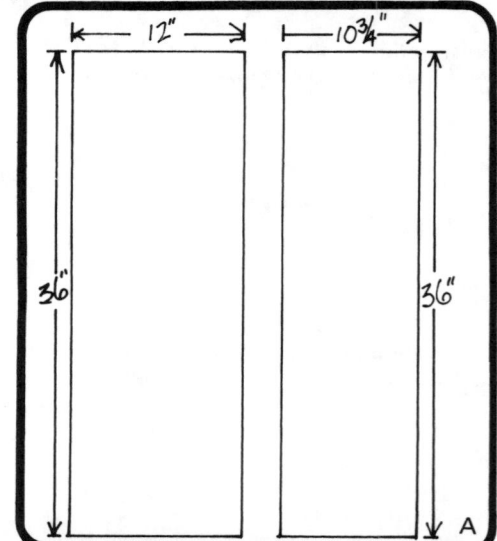

(A) The entire table is constructed from thick plywood and 1" x 2" clear pine stiffeners. Begin by cutting one piece of plywood 36" x 12" and another 36" x 10¾".

(B) Now take the 12″ width and add the 1″ x 2″ pine stiffeners as shown here. Attach the long stiffener "A," flush with the right side of the panel. Be sure to set the wooden stiffener marked "B," ½″ *below* the top edge of the panel as illustrated. Position the stiffener marked "C" 12″ below stiffener B. Stiffener D should be flush with the bottom edge of the panel. The next step is to install the stiffeners on the 10¾″ width. Stiffener A is attached to the left side of the panel. Stiffeners B, C, and D are attached as they were on the first panel. When finished, sand the panels smooth in preparation for painting.

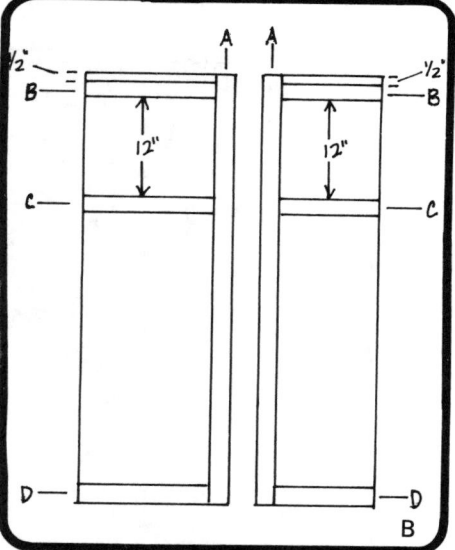

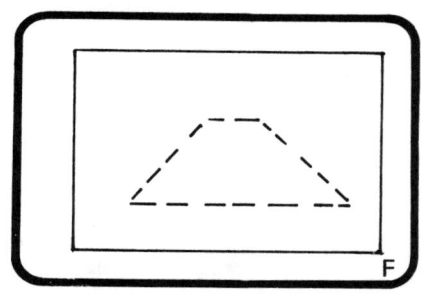

(F) The second triangular section must be glued to the underside of the table top as illustrated in Figure F. This will insure the proper positioning of the top into the screen-like uprights. Now sand these parts thoroughly, and you will be ready for the final assembly.

(C) Butt the end of the 10¾″ panel next to the outer back edge of the 12″ panel . . .

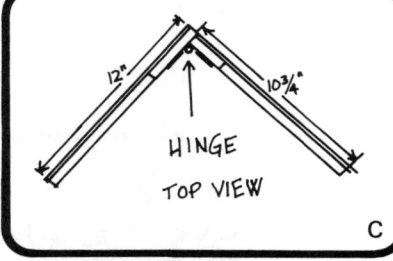

(D) . . . and attach two hinges to the stiffeners as indicated. You will notice that both sides of the screen-like table base will now measure 12″. This hinging arrangement provides an automatic stop when opening the panels but allows them to be folded flat for storage.

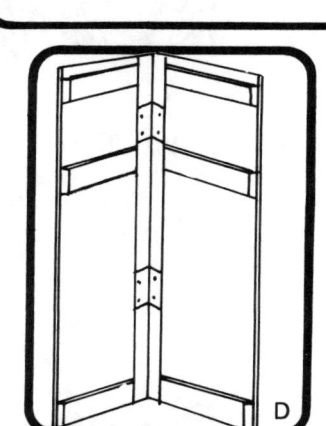

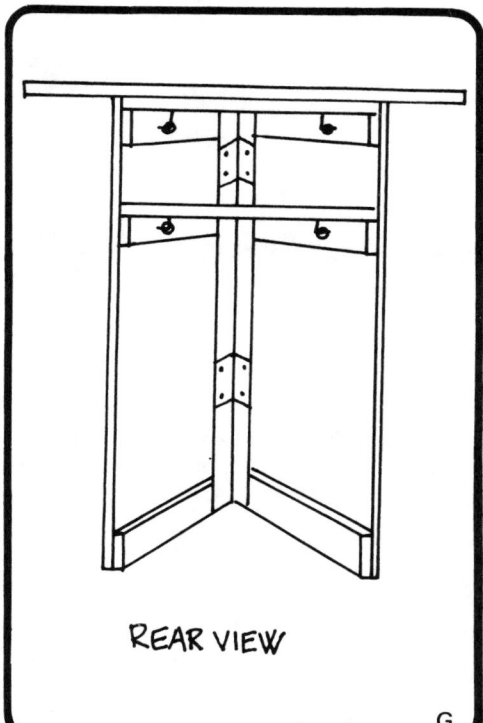

(G) You will need 4 small "screen door" fasteners to hook the entire arrangement together. Two of these are mounted to the table top with the eyes positioned in the uppermost stiffener, A, as illustrated. As you can see from this diagram, these fasteners hold the top to the panels. The triangular piece fastened to the underside of the top prevents the panels from closing unexpectedly.

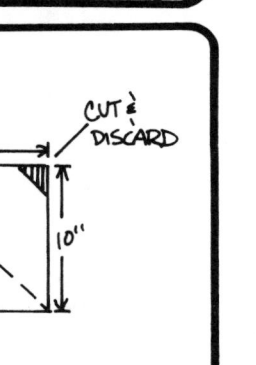

(E) In order to build the top and storage shelf, you will need to cut a piece of ½″ thick plywood 18″ long by 12″ wide and an additional piece 10″ square as in Figure E. The larger of the two pieces is utilized as the top of your table. The 10″ square must now be cut diagonally in order to form two triangular sections. One of these will serve as the *rear shelf* and rests on top of the C stiffeners.

(H) This hook and eye arrangement is also used to secure the triangular shelf into position on top of the B stiffeners as shown in Step G.

(I) After you have positioned the fasteners and are satisfied with the rigidity of the equipment, you can begin to decorate the table. The first step is to paint the back side of the screen, the underside of the top, and the small triangular shelf "flat black." When these parts are dry, cover the *top* surface of your table with black felt and trim the *edges* with silver (or some other bright color) braid. The front surfaces of the screen can be decorated in any motif that you feel is attractive and suitable to your style of performance.

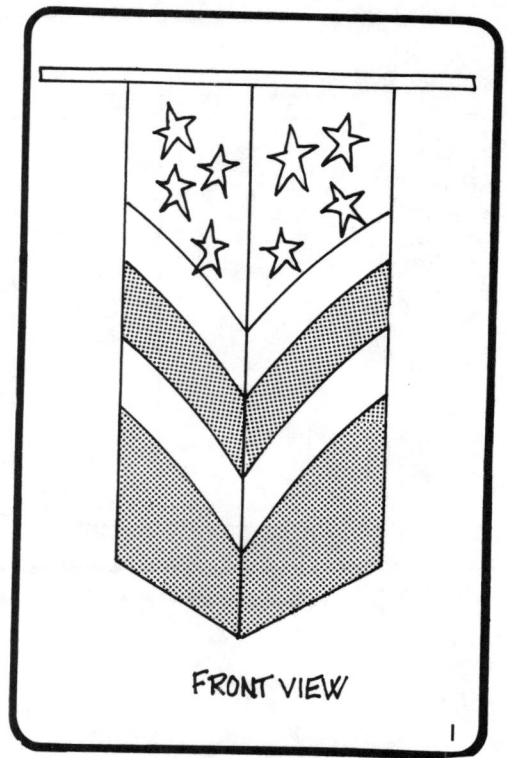

FRONT VIEW

THE BLACK ART WELL

The above title graphically describes a very useful addition to your magic table. Simply stated, a BLACK ART WELL is an "invisible hole" in the top of your table which enables you to vanish an object. The VANISHING GLASS described elsewhere in this Course can utilize a "well" of this nature.

CONSTRUCTION

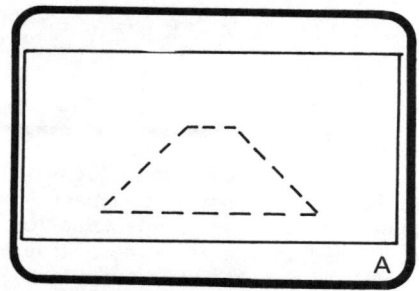

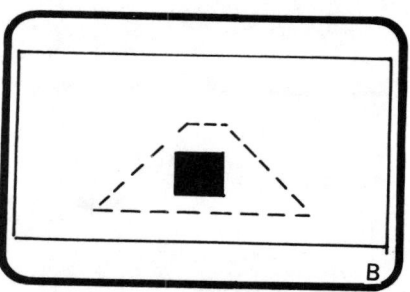

(A) Cut a piece of ½" thick plywood into a rectangular shape measuring 12" x 18". Now add a triangular section measuring 10" on each of the right-angled sides to the bottom of this new top in the same manner as you did with the regular top in Step F of the MAGIC TABLE.

(B) Now, cut a 3" square hole through *both layers* of your new top as illustrated.

(C) Sand the top smooth on all sides and then paint the entire unit flat black.

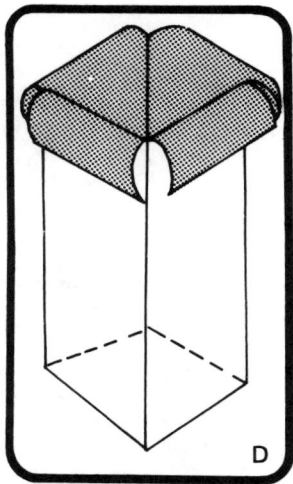

(D) You will need to sew up a square black velvet bag. This bag should measure 3" square and at least 7" deep as shown. Also, be sure that the soft (napped) side of the velvet is on the *inside surface* of the bag.

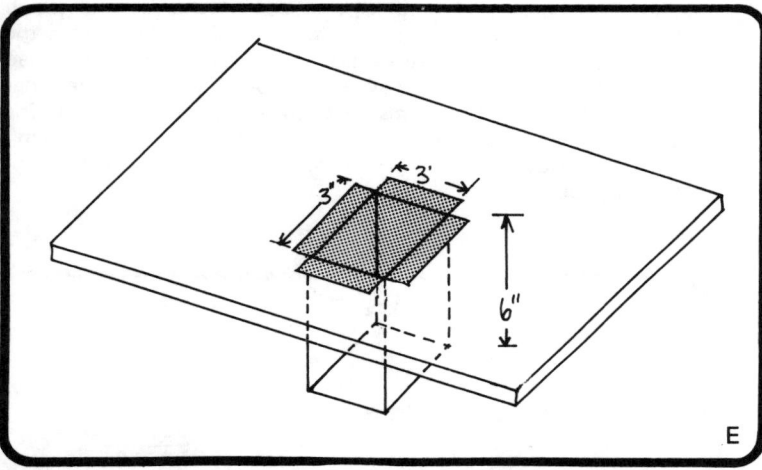

(E) Pull the bag up through the hole in your table top and staple it into position as illustrated. At this point, the well should measure 6" deep.

(F) It is now necessary to cover the entire table top with a piece of matching velvet measuring 12" x 18". This is best accomplished by gluing the fabric directly to the plywood top.

(G) Allow the adhesive to dry thoroughly and then *carefully cut out the excess material above the well with a sharp razor blade.*

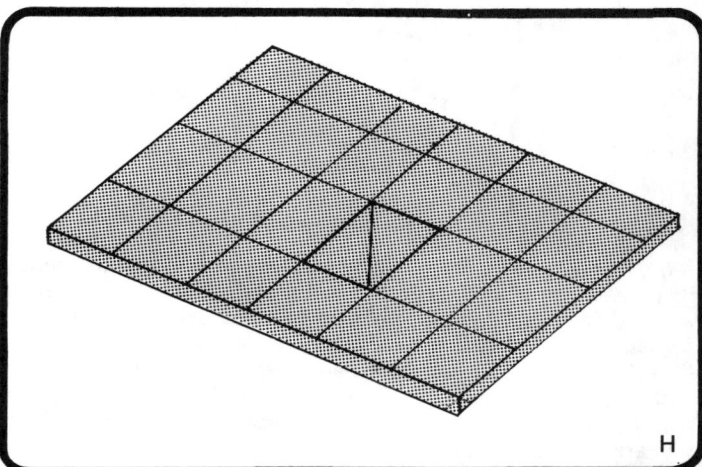

(H) In order to conceal the edges around the well, stretch bright colored braid across the top as shown here. You can attach this braid to the edges of the table by using small carpet tacks or staples. When you have completed the above, trim the edge of the top with a strip of matching braid.

(I) All that is left is to mount the two hooks to the underside of the completed top as described in the MAGIC TABLE.

MECHANICAL MAGIC

Although the following three tricks would be difficult to "Make At Home" — unless you are a skilled craftsman with a variety of tools — they have been included in this section for two reasons. First, they depend upon the *clever construction* of the prop, rather than on sleight-of-hand or misdirection, for their magical effect; and second, they incorporate *basic magic principles* which you should know and understand to aid your progress and help you to build a firm foundation in the Art of Magic.

THE DOVE PAN

If you are building your first magic act, here is an excellent, all-purpose utility prop which is very easy to use and which can be of great value to you. This trick, because of the huge magical "production" which is possible, makes a good closing (or opening) effect for any magical performance.

EFFECT

The magician displays an empty metal pan. A bit of tissue is placed in the pan and set on fire. The pan's cover is quickly clamped on the pan to smother the flames. When the cover is removed, the pan is seen to have become "magically" filled to the brim with candy, handkerchiefs, a dove, or a young rabbit — in fact, any item that would fit within the pan!

SECRET AND PREPARATION

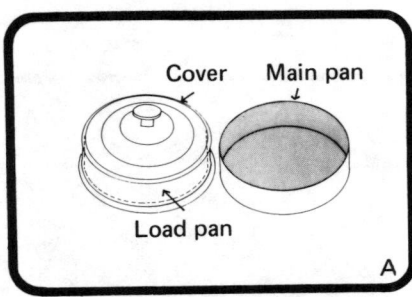

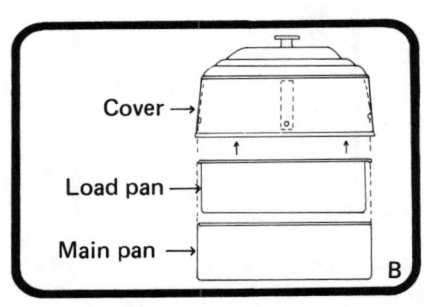

(A)   This is an extremely practical piece of magic equipment as it may be employed to make a variety of items "magically" appear. The "load" (the item(s) to be produced) is hidden *inside the cover of the pan*. When the cover is set over the pan, the "load" secretly goes into the pan. You can fill the "load pan" with anything from a duckling to a string of flags. Thus, this piece of magical apparatus is very useful because of the large "load" you are able to produce.

(B)   Here is an "exploded" view of the parts of the pan. As you see, there are three parts: (1) the "pan" which you display to the audience, (2) the cover, and (3) the secret "load pan" of which the audience is never aware. The load pan fits exactly into the "main" pan or can be secretly hidden inside the cover. The load pan is held inside the cover by metal stops located on the inner sides of the cover. The items to be produced are placed inside the "load pan" before the trick begins and then the "load pan" is inserted inside the cover. The cover and the main pan are both placed on your table.

METHOD

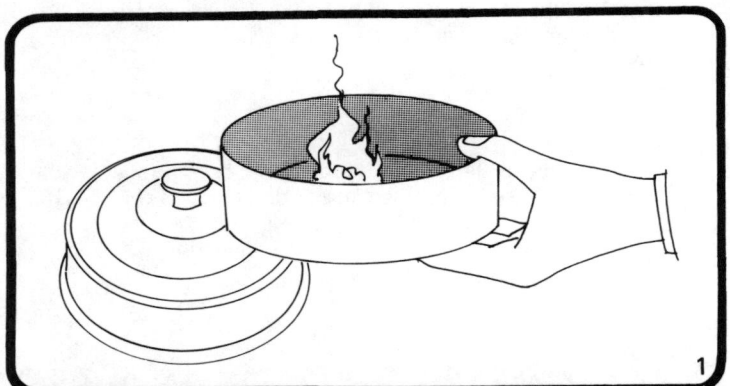

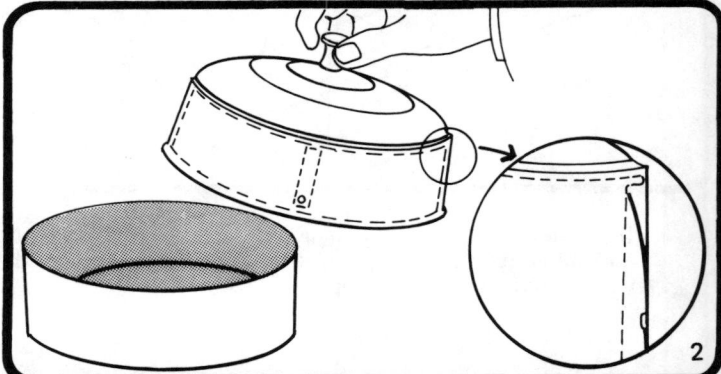

(1)   Pick up the main pan from your table. Show it to be empty and then place a small piece of crumpled tissue paper inside. Use a match to set the tissue afire. As the flames begin to rise, pick up the cover and quickly clamp it *over the main pan.*

(2)   When you put the cover on the main pan, the top edge releases the "load pan" from its secret position inside the cover. The "load pan" drops down *inside* the main pan — so that, when you remove the cover, the pan appears to have filled itself with the "load" items.

COMMENTS AND SUGGESTIONS

This clever piece of apparatus lends itself to almost any magical performance. You can use your imagination in determining what type of "load" is best suited for you. One inexpensive production can be to fill the pan with popcorn. This piece of equipment has long been a favorite with children and is very practical for the working magician.

THE FOO CAN

The vanish of a quantity of liquid has always been a favorite with audiences. Here is one of the simplest yet one of the most effective methods of accomplishing the feat.

EFFECT

The magician displays a tall metal canister. The canister is filled with water and immediately turned upside-down. The water appears to *vanish instantly* from within the can. The magician rights the container and then utters the proper magic words. As if by magic, the water *reappears* and is poured freely from the can.

METHOD

(1) This effect works with the aid of a specially constructed container called the Foo Can. The can is made with a double wall on one side so that the water can be trapped within a secret compartment. The dotted line in the illustration represents the "double wall" within the body of the can. Thus, if the can is rotated in the proper direction when it is turned upside-down, the water will be trapped inside.

(5) As you turn the can over, all of the liquid is trapped within the secret compartment. The can may then be turned all the way upside-down, giving the appearance that the liquid has completely vanished.

(2) The can may be shown empty before the liquid is poured into the mouth of the can. You will have to experiment with the amount of liquid which can be held within the secret compartment. Be careful not to pour *too much* water into the can as the secret double-walled compartment is designed to hold only a certain amount of liquid.

(6) Now tip the can back until it assumes its original upright position. This allows the liquid to flow *out* of the secret compartment and *back* into the main body of the can.

(3) After the water is poured in, make a few "magical" passes over the can and perhaps tap it with your wand. Then pick up the can, holding it by the neck.

(7) If the can is now tipped to the side *away* from the double wall, the liquid will flow freely out of the mouth of the can — having "magically" reappeared!

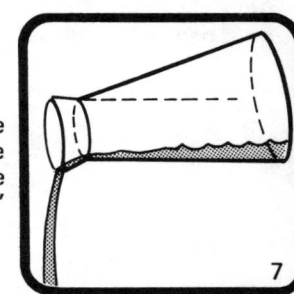

(4) Using both hands, tip the can *toward* the side with the double wall. This causes the liquid to begin to run *into the secret compartment.*

COMMENTS AND SUGGESTIONS

This is one of the oldest and most effective methods for vanishing a quantity of liquid. When the can is upside-down, demonstrating that it is empty (Step 5), you may wish to insert a wand (a pencil or any other suitable object will do) into the can. With the wand in this position, you may casually, *but carefully,* spin the "empty" can on the wand. This effective bit of business will convince your audience even more that the liquid has "vanished."

You may use this useful prop in conjunction with many other effects. For instance, you could perform the Foo Can effect first, followed by the VANISHING BOWL OF WATER. Follow the Foo Can routine until the water reappears in the container — then pour it directly into the "vanishing" bowl. After putting the Foo Can aside, you can proceed to vanish the bowl filled with water.

THE LOTA BOWL

EFFECT

A large attractive bowl already filled to the top with water is displayed by the magician. He then proceeds to empty *all* the water out of the bowl. Yet, a number of times during the performance, the magician picks up the bowl and empties <u>more</u> water out of the "empty" bowl. The effect created is that the bowl "magically" <u>fills itself</u> — *over and over again.* In the end, the magician has apparently poured more water from the bowl than it could possibly hold!

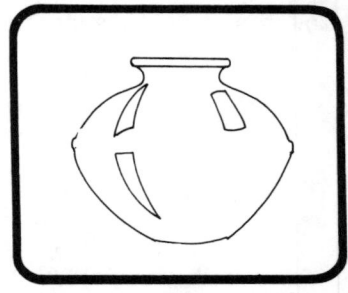

SECRET AND PREPARATION

(A) This is an excellent "running gag" which can be easily added to any of your magical performances — particularly when you are appearing for large groups on a stage. (There are also "miniature" versions of the Lota Bowl for "close-up" shows.) The secret lies in the special construction of the bowl. It has a "double wall" built inside it which, because of the deceptive shape of the bowl, allows a great quantity of water to be hidden in a large secret compartment. A small hole (a) on the *outside* neck of the bowl controls the filling action of the water. Another small hole (b) *inside* at the bottom of the bowl allows the flow of the liquid *from* the secret compartment *into* the main body of the bowl.

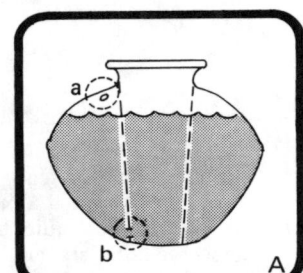

(B) To fill the bowl with water, you can hold it totally immersed in a bucket or sink *with both holes open.* Once this is done, wipe off the excess water from the outside of the bowl. Another more convenient but slower method of filling the bowl is to merely pour water *into the top* of the bowl from another container. When the bowl is "brim full," you must wait until a portion of water runs down into the secret compartment through the inside hole. Then you repeatedly fill the bowl back to the top as the water runs down seeking its own level. After repeated fillings, both the main body *and* the secret compartment will be full.

(C) Place the bowl on your table in preparation for performance. You must also have another container handy in which to pour the liquid from the bowl.

METHOD

(1) When you are ready to perform Lota Bowl, pick up the bowl from the table. *Place your thumb <u>over the</u> outside hole in the neck and pour "all" of the liquid from the bowl. This allows only the liquid <u>from the main body</u> to flow out of the bowl.*

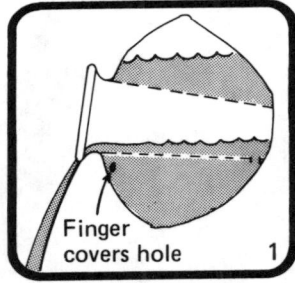

Finger covers hole

(3) The water will rise in the main body until it reaches the level of the liquid remaining in the secret compartment.

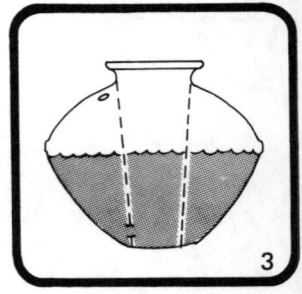

(2) Turn the "empty" bowl upright and place it back on your table. Because of the double-walled construction, the water from the secret compartment will run through the small hole *inside* the bowl into the main body.

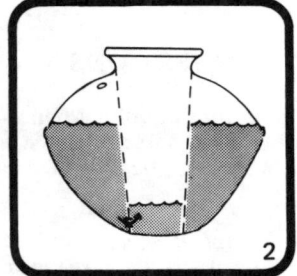

(4) As soon as the main body of the bowl has "refilled" itself with liquid, you may pour out water again — *but be sure to cover the <u>outside hole</u> as you do.*

(5) The bowl will refill itself over and over again until almost all the water is exhausted from the secret compartment.

(6) *NOTE: Always place your thumb over the outside hole located in the neck <u>before</u> you pour out any liquid. This assures that <u>only</u> the water from the <u>main body</u> of the bowl is poured.*

COMMENTS AND SUGGESTIONS

As a container for holding the water that you pour out, a large FOO CAN is ideal. Now you can perform a double mystery. When all the liquid has been poured from the bowl into the FOO CAN, you then cause the liquid to *vanish completely* from the can!

SPONGE BALL MAGIC

Tricks with sponge balls represent a type of magic distinctively its own. With other articles such as cards, coins, thimbles, cigarettes, matches, and matchboxes, ways were designed to "palm" or manipulate such items purely because they were used in everyday life and were therefore natural objects to carry or borrow for magical purposes. Even the so-called magicians' "billiard balls" used in manipulative magic can be classed as something ordinary—for although they are smaller than the standard size, such balls are actually used on miniature pool tables. Sometimes they are even disguised as golf balls, being just about the right size.

But nobody ever heard of "sponge balls." That is, until magicians began carving them out of rubber sponges—simply because they were compressible and therefore could be handled in a special way. As the variety of different weights, textures, and compressibility of synthetic sponges increased, magicians found an ever-widening selection, and the "sponge balls" of today are much finer and easier to manipulate than their predecessors. "Magical" sponges today have a fairly solid look. This causes the average person to overlook the fact that they are remarkably compressible—which, of course, is the magician's reason for using them.

"Square" sponges are popular with many performers. These are actually cubical in shape and are handled the same as sponge balls. Since sponge ball routines are usually performed at a table, the square type has the advantage of never rolling off. Thus they are easier to use and to learn with. Square sponges are called sponge cubes, and are easily made by cutting soft foam rubber into one-inch cubes. Later you may wish to change to some other shape such as sponge balls which you can make yourself from soft sponge or buy from a magic supply house.

Whatever type you choose, you'll find the following routine well worth the effort required to learn it. Once you have seen the delighted response of your audience, chances are the sponges will become a permanent part of your act.

SPONGE SORCERY

EFFECT

The performer magically causes three sponges to appear, multiply, and vanish in an entertaining and amusing manner — they even seem to multiply in the hands of the spectator.

SECRET AND PREPARATION

Before the performance, place three of the sponge cubes in your right pants pocket and one sponge in your left pants pocket.

METHOD

Sponge balls are used in the following illustrations. To practice and present your routine, just use your sponge cubes in place of the balls as shown.

"A SPONGE APPEARS"

(1) With the four sponges located in your pants pockets as described, casually place your hand in your right pants pocket. Grasp one of the sponges in the Finger Palm Position and remove your hand, holding the sponge secretly. Then, reach into the air and "produce" it at the tips of your right fingers. You can also produce the sponge from the spectator's coat lapel, from behind his ear, or any other appropriate place.

(2) As you display the first sponge in your right hand, position it in readiness for the Finger Palm by placing it on your open hand at the base of the second and third fingers as shown. The left hand lies casually, palm down, on the table.

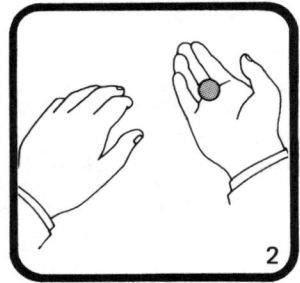

(3) Now, in one smooth, flowing movement, bring both hands together turning them over as you do. This is done in the pretense of gently tossing the sponge from your right hand into your left hand. But, instead of actually *tossing* the sponge in the left hand, it is *secretly retained* in the second and third fingers of the right hand — in the Finger Palm Position.

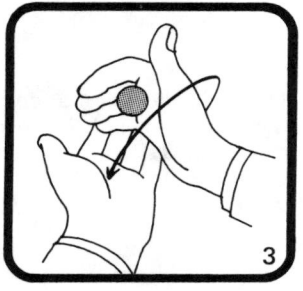

(4) Move your right hand away (with the sponge) as you close your left hand into a loose fist. The first finger of your right hand should casually point toward your left fist as shown in the illustration.

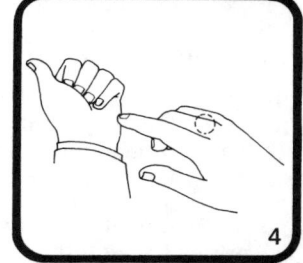

(5) Pause for a moment and then make a crumbling motion with your left fingers as if to cause the sponge to "dissolve" in your hand. Then, open your left hand to show that the sponge has vanished.

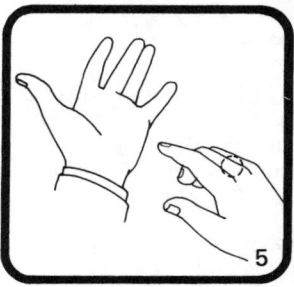

(6) *NOTE: What you have just done is the Basic Finger Palm Vanish with a sponge. Practice it with the sponge until it becomes smooth and convincing. When done correctly, the spectators should not suspect that you really retain the sponge in your right hand. The Finger Palm Vanish is described in detail in the Coin Section of the Course. The proper performance of this move is essential as it is used several times throughout the Sponge Sorcery routine. See Page 187 for the Finger Palm Vanish.*

"THE FLIGHT TO THE POCKET"

(7) Explain to the audience that often, when a sponge vanishes, it manages to reappear in your *right pocket*. Reach into your right pants pocket (being careful not to flash the "vanished" sponge that is now concealed in your right fingers) and grasp one of the two sponges that are left in that pocket.

(8) Openly remove this sponge — still keeping the first sponge Finger Palmed — from your pocket and display it in your right fingertips. *Again, be careful not to let the audience see the sponge Finger Palmed in your right hand as you display the other sponge.* The effect is that you vanished a sponge from your left hand and caused it to reappear in your pants pocket.

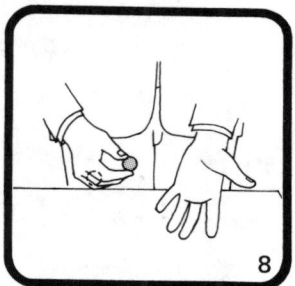

"GUESS WHICH HAND"

(9) Upon completing "The Flight to the Pocket," you now hold one sponge at your right fingertips and one sponge secretly in the Finger Palm position of the same hand. Openly place the sponge from your right fingertips into the palm of your left hand as shown.

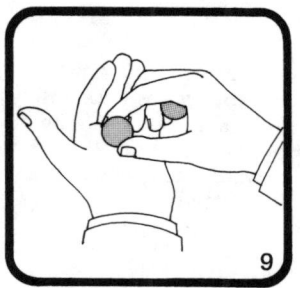

(10) Close your left hand into a fist and hold it *palm up* in front of you as shown. Then, close your right hand and hold it *palm down* next to your left fist. *The audience still believes that only one sponge is being used and that it is in your left hand.*

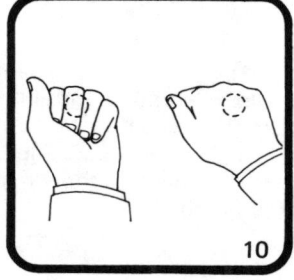

(11) Now, strike both fists together several times and hold your hands "crossed" at the wrist as shown. Explain how this seems to have a "strange effect" upon the location of the mischievous sponge. With that, ask the spectator which hand he thinks the sponge is in.

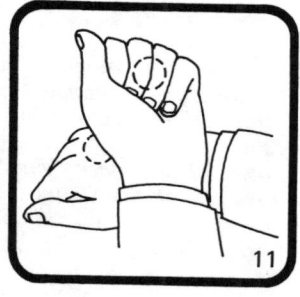

(12) The answer will probably be, "In your left hand." *No matter which hand the spectator says,* uncross your hands and open your left hand — revealing the sponge still there.

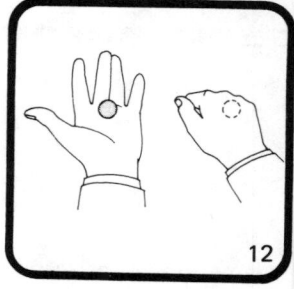

(13) Tell the spectator that it really didn't matter which hand he chose; he would have been correct in either case. With that, turn your right hand palm up and open the fingers revealing the other sponge. *It appears that this "strange effect" you spoke about has caused one sponge to multiply into two!*

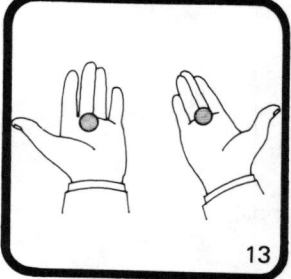

"SPECTATOR'S DOUBLES"

(14) Place the *left*-hand sponge on the table and hold the *right*-hand sponge in position for the Finger Palm Vanish.

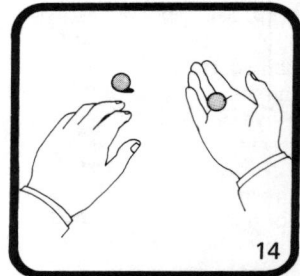

(15) Now, you pretend to place the sponge in your left hand. Actually you execute the Finger Palm Vanish, secretly retaining the sponge in your right hand. *Remember that each time you perform this vanish, your left hand should be closed in a loose fist as if it actually contained the sponge.*

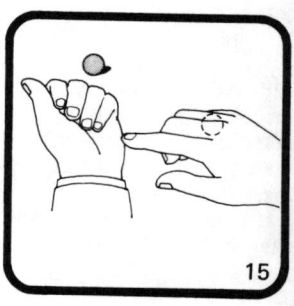

(16) Without hesitation, move your right hand toward the sponge lying on the table. *Be careful not to expose the sponge Finger Palmed in your right hand.*

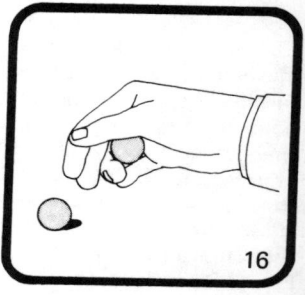

(17) As your right hand arrives above the sponge on the table, secretly place the Finger Palmed sponge directly *on top* of the sponge on the table.

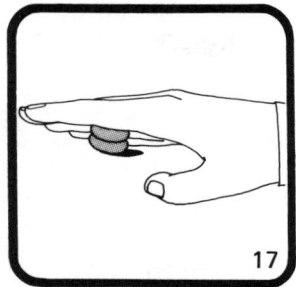

(18) Now, by drawing your right hand along the table, the sponges will roll toward the tips of your right fingers, where they can be picked up together <u>as one sponge</u>. Because of the soft texture of the sponges, when they are pinched together slightly, this will appear to be just *one* sponge.

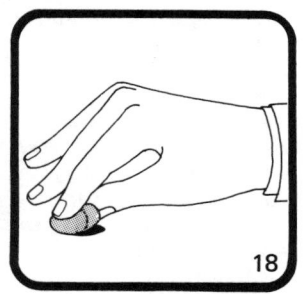

(19) As you display the two sponges (<u>as one</u>) at the tips of your right fingers, ask the spectator to open his right hand and hold it palm up above the table.

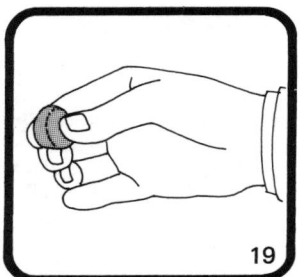

(20) Now, place the sponge(s) in the spectator's hand as you state, "Here, *you* hold this sponge in your hand while I hold the other." At this point, the spectator *thinks that you still hold one sponge in your left hand* and that you are merely giving him the other sponge to hold, *when actually you are giving him <u>both</u> sponges.*

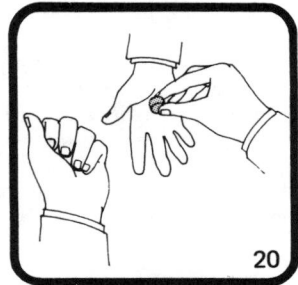

(21) Now, instruct him to close his fingers around the sponge and squeeze it tightly so it would be impossible for you to remove it without his knowledge. *Be sure you maintain a firm grip on the two sponges <u>until the spectator's fingers are completely closed around them</u>.* Then, and only then, should you remove your fingers from his fist.

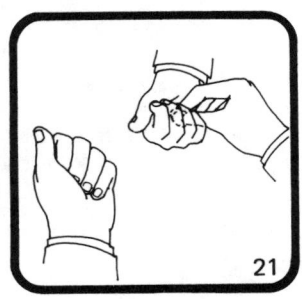

(22) Tell the spectator that you intend to cause the sponge which you are holding to travel *invisibly* from your hand into his closed fist.

(23) Again, make a crumbling motion with your left fingers and open your hand to show it empty. Ask the spectator if he felt anything happen in his hand. Whatever his answer, tell him to open his hand <u>revealing the two sponges</u>.

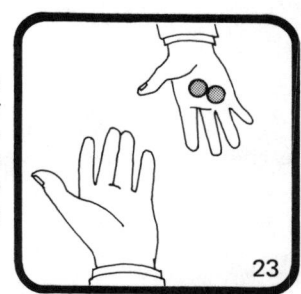

"TRANSPOSITION IN YOUR HANDS"

(24) Take both sponges from the spectator and place them on the table in front of you about 12 inches apart. Then, turn your hands palm up and openly place the <u>back</u> of your hands on top of the sponges as shown. This is the *starting position* for the next series of moves.

THE FOLLOWING STEPS (25 through 36) ARE A CLEVER SEQUENCE OF MOVES DESIGNED TO CONFUSE AND AMAZE THE SPECTATORS.

(25) First, raise your <u>right</u> hand, turn it over, and pick up the sponge that was beneath it with the tips of your <u>right</u> thumb and finger.

(26) Second, *without lifting your left hand from the table,* rest the sponge in the palm of your <u>left</u> hand. Then, close your hand into a fist over your right fingers *and* the sponge. As you do this say, "The *right* sponge goes in the *left* hand . . ." Then, withdraw your right fingers actually *leaving the sponge in your closed left hand.*

(27) Third, raise your <u>left</u> fist off the table and pick up the sponge that was beneath it with the tips of the <u>right</u> fingers. Then, close your <u>right</u> fingers into a fist around the sponge. Hold your right fist next to your left fist as you say, ". . . and the *left* sponge goes in the *right* hand."

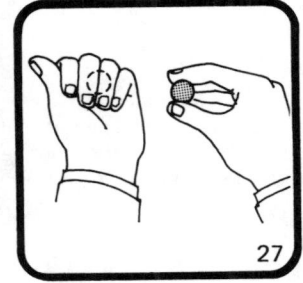

(28) You now hold one sponge in each hand as shown in the illustration.

(29) Now open both hands together revealing the two sponges, one in each hand. So far, NO "MAGIC" HAS HAPPENED! State that you will now do the *same thing again*. Unknown to the audience, this "trial run" is a very important part of the mystery that is about to take place. By first executing this series of moves *without any magic*, you *condition* the spectators to expect the same results next time.

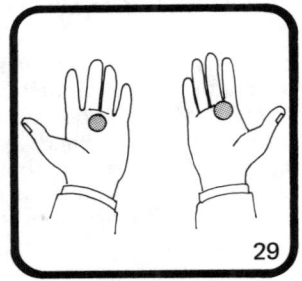

(30) Again, place both hands on top of the two sponges in starting position for the same series of moves.

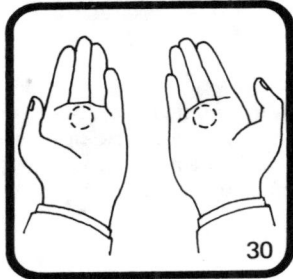

(31) Again, raise your <u>right</u> hand, turn it over and pick up the sponge beneath it in the tips of the <u>right</u> fingers (just as you did in Step 25).

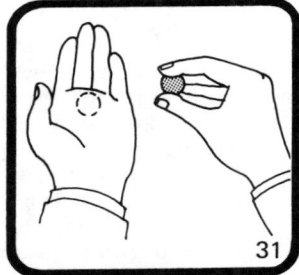

(32) Rest the sponge in the palm of the <u>left</u> hand and close your left fingers over your right fingers and the sponge. Again you say, "The *right* sponge goes in the *left* fist . . ." This time, however, *instead of leaving the sponge in your left fist, as you withdraw your right hand, <u>secretly retain the sponge between your right thumb and fingers</u>.* Be sure to keep your right fingers together so the audience cannot see the sponge between them.

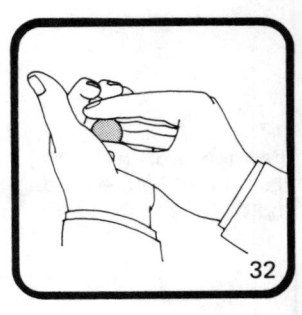

(33) Immediately move your right hand away from your closed left hand, <u>secretly carrying the sponge in your right hand as shown</u>. *Direct your complete attention toward your left hand as if it really contained the sponge.* As your right hand moves away, draw your right thumb inward moving the sponge slightly deeper into your hand where it will not be seen by the spectators.

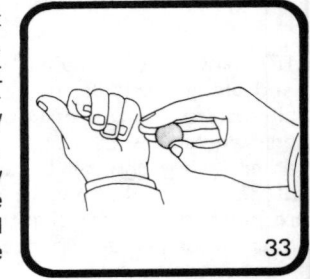

(34) Now, raise your left hand and, with your right fingers, pick up the sponge which lay beneath it. When you pick up the "left-hand" sponge, secretly add the palmed "right-hand" sponge to it (just as you did in Step 18).

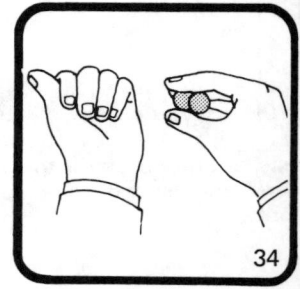

(35) Now, close your <u>right</u> hand into a fist around the *two* sponges. Hold your right fist next to your left fist as shown. To the audience you have apparently just repeated Steps 24 through 28, and they think that you now hold one sponge in each hand.

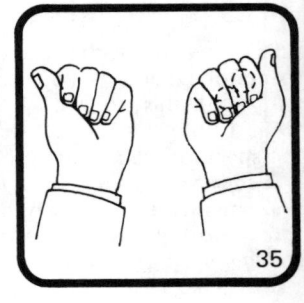

(36) Make a crumbling motion with your left fingers — open your left hand to show that the sponge has *vanished*. Then, slowly open your right hand — revealing *both* sponges! *It appears as though one sponge has jumped "invisibly" from your left hand into your right hand!*

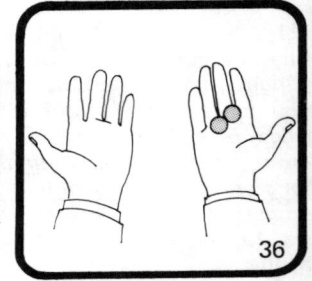

"IMPOSSIBLE PENETRATION"

NOTE: IF YOU HAVE BEEN <u>SITTING</u> AT A TABLE AS YOU PERFORM THE TRICK, YOU MUST NOW <u>STAND UP</u> FOR THE NEXT PORTION OF THE ROUTINE. Steps 36 through 44 are all shown from the <u>SPECTATOR'S VIEW</u>POINT.

(41) With that, move your right hand (which secretly holds the other sponge) in front of your left pants pocket. *Your left hand is still inside your pocket.* Now, with your right hand, press the sponge against your pants leg next to where your left hand is inside your pocket.

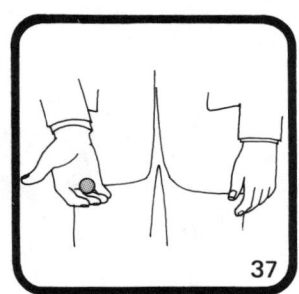

(37) After the "Transposition in Your Hands," place one sponge on the table and keep the other sponge in your right hand in position ready for the Finger Palm Vanish.

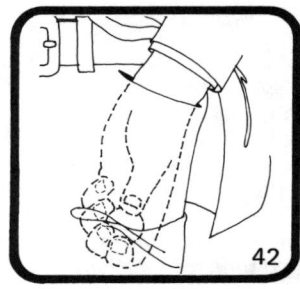

(42) Inside your pocket, your left thumb and fingers *grasp the sponge through the fabric* and hold it between the folds of the cloth so that it is *concealed from view by the material.* As soon as the sponge is in position, move your right hand away from in front of your pant leg. The "pinched" section of the fabric will look like a fold in the cloth.

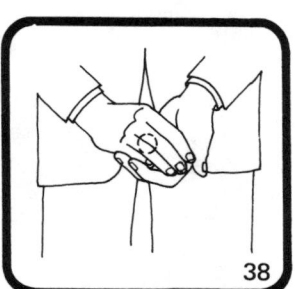

(38) Execute the Finger Palm Vanish, pretending to place the sponge in your left hand but actually retaining it Finger Palmed in your right hand.

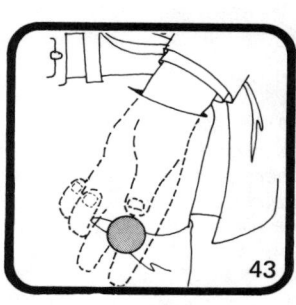

(43) Immediately begin a "back and forth" rubbing motion with your left fingers. At the same time, relax your grip on the sponge through the fabric. This will cause the sponge to slowly emerge into view <u>as though it were penetrating right through the cloth.</u> *NOTE: This illusion is very effective — don't worry if the sponge is not completely hidden in the folds of the fabric before you remove your right hand. It will just appear that the "penetration" of the cloth started when you first placed your right hand on your pants leg.*

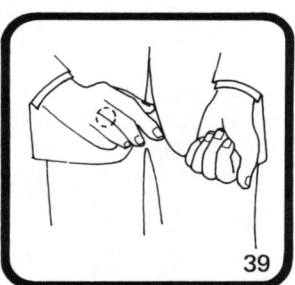

(39) Hold your closed left hand in a loose fist as if it actually contained the sponge and casually move your right hand (with the Finger Palmed sponge) away. *Again, be sure to direct your <u>complete attention</u> toward your left fist.*

(44) When the sponge emerges almost totally into view, grasp it in your right hand and pull it away from the pocket. At the same time, *your left hand secretly secures the sponge already in that pocket in the Finger Palm position.* While all the attention is on the sponge in your right hand, remove your left hand from your pocket with the new "secret" sponge.

"THE SPECTATOR'S HAND REVISITED"

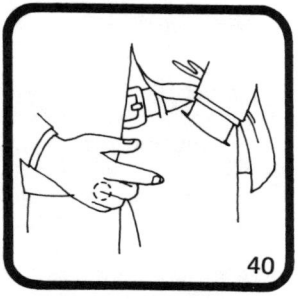

(40) Place your left hand (which supposedly contains the sponge) into your left pants pocket as you explain that your clothes are made of a "special material."

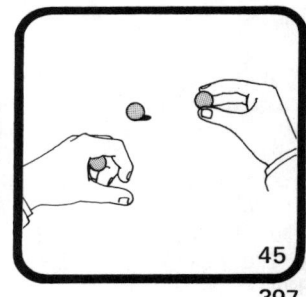

(45) There are now *three* sponges in play, although the audience is aware of only *two.* One sponge is on the table, another is held at the tips of your right fingers, and the "secret" sponge is Finger Palmed in your left hand.

(46) Call attention to the sponge in your right hand. While the audience is looking at it, with your left hand pick up the sponge on the table and add the "secret" sponge to it.

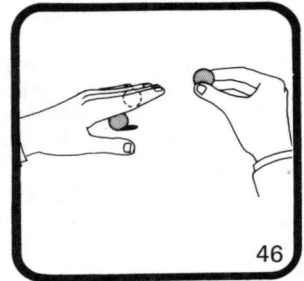

(47) With your left hand, you now display the sponge which was on the table *and* the secret sponge as *one*, holding them with your left thumb and fingers. At this point you actually hold three sponges (one in your right hand and two in your left). *To the audience it appears that you hold only* <u>*one*</u> *sponge in each hand.*

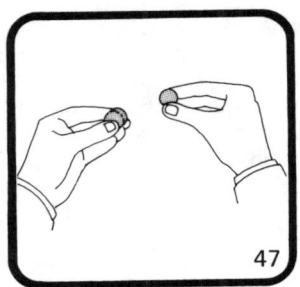

(48) Transfer the two sponges in your left hand to your right hand, *placing them directly on top of the sponge in your right fingers.* Say, "Now I would like you to hold these two sponges."

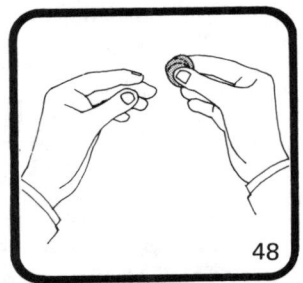

(49) Move your right hand (which now holds the three sponges) toward the spectator and ask him to open his hand so that he may take the sponges from you.

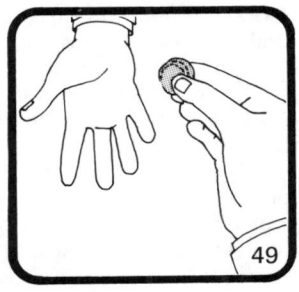

(50) Place *all three sponges* in the spectator's hand. Instruct him to close his fingers around them. Tell him to squeeze his fist tightly to make sure that you cannot remove them. *Again, remember to wait until the spectator's hand is <u>completely closed</u> before releasing your grip on the sponges.*

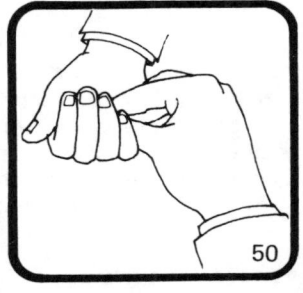

(51) Once the spectator has a firm grip on the sponges, reach into your right pants pocket and remove the *fourth sponge* from your pocket. Openly display the sponge as you say, "You may be wondering how all this is happening. Well the secret is that I have a *third* sponge which nobody knows about."

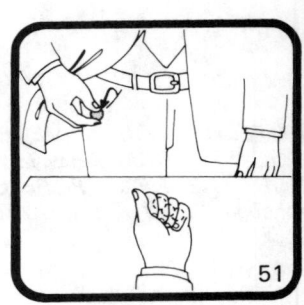

(52) With that, execute the Finger Palm Vanish, pretending to place the sponge into your left hand but actually retaining it in the Finger Palm position in your right hand.

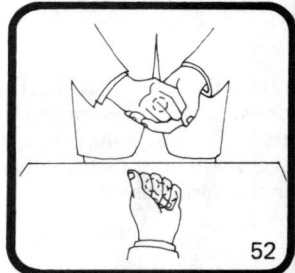

(53) Casually drop your right hand to the table and move your closed left fist next to the spectator's hand.

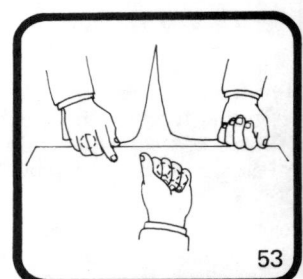

(54) Make the crumbling motion with your left fingers and open your hand to show it empty. Instruct the spectator to open his hand revealing *all three sponges*. It appears that the third sponge has flown invisibly from your fingers into the spectator's hand.

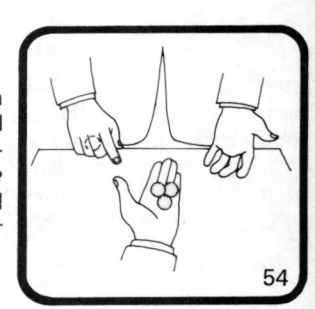

"TWO IN THE HAND, ONE IN THE POCKET — PHASE ONE"

(55) After "The Spectator's Hand Revisited," there are *four* sponges in use, although the audience is only aware of *three*. The next sequence begins with the three sponges in a horizontal row in front of you and the fourth sponge held secretly in your curled right fingers.

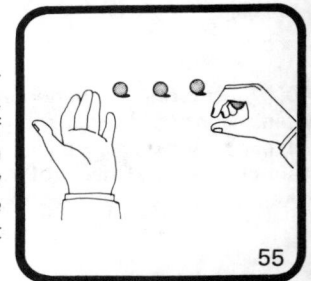

(56) With your right hand pick up the sponge at the right end of the row, and execute the "two-as-one" pick-up (Step 17). In your right hand you now hold two sponges together (as one).

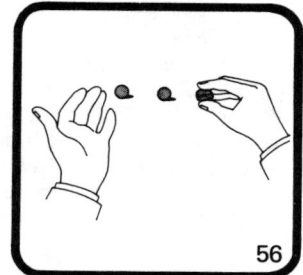

(61) Openly place the last sponge into your right pants pocket. Say, "And one in the pocket." As your hand reaches in your right trouser pocket, *do not leave the sponge in your pocket*. Instead, hold it in the Finger Palm Position and *remove your hand from your pocket* <u>*secretly carrying the sponge along*</u>. The audience will believe that you merely placed the sponge in your pocket.

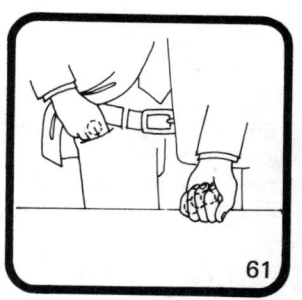

(57) Place the two sponges in the palm of your left hand and close your left fingers around them as you say, "<u>One</u> in the hand."

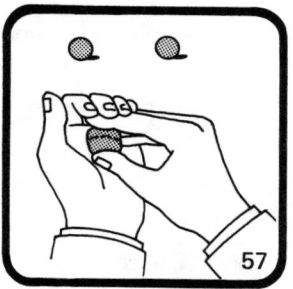

(62) Now, ask the spectator, "How many sponges are in my hand?" The answer will be, "Two." With that, open your left hand revealing *three* sponges — as you remark, "Maybe I went too fast. I'll do that again."

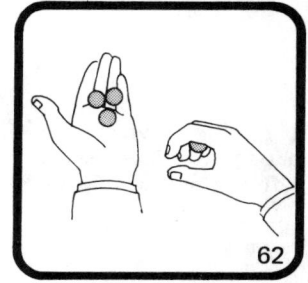

(58) Withdraw your right hand from your left fist. Then pick up another of the sponges on the table with your right hand as shown.

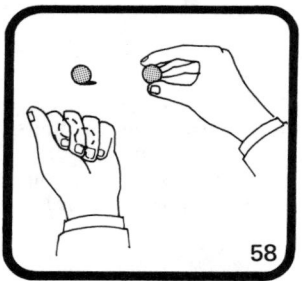

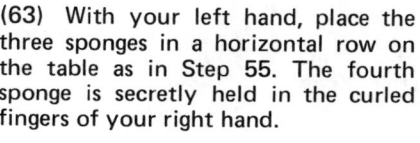

"TWO IN THE HAND, ONE IN THE POCKET — PHASE TWO"

(63) With your left hand, place the three sponges in a horizontal row on the table as in Step 55. The fourth sponge is secretly held in the curled fingers of your right hand.

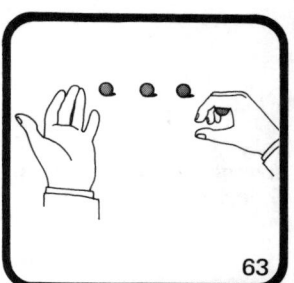

(59) Move your right hand toward your left fist. Open your left fingers *just enough* to place the sponge in your left hand. Say, "<u>Two</u> in the hand." Close your left fingers around the *three* sponges and withdraw your right hand from your left fist.

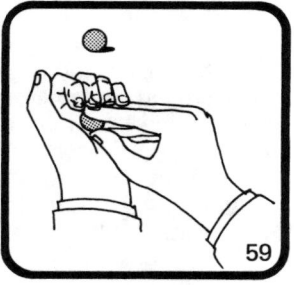

(64) As before, execute the "two-as-one" pick-up with the sponge on the right as in Step 56.

(60) Pick up the remaining sponge in your right hand.

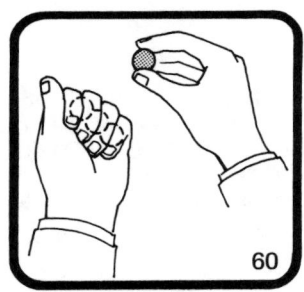

(65) Place the two sponges (as one) in your left hand and close your left fingers into a fist around them (as in Step 57). Say, "<u>One</u> in the hand."

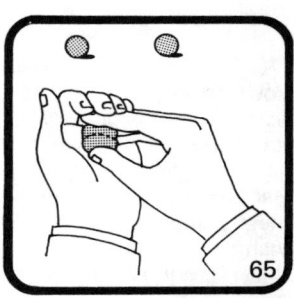

(66) Withdraw your right fingers from your left fist and pick up another sponge with your right hand (as in Step 58).

(71) As you gesture ask, "How many in the hand?" The answer will probably be "Two." The spectators are so baffled by this time, however, that there is no predicting what they will say! In any event, open your left hand revealing all three sponges. Now say, "Let's try just once more."

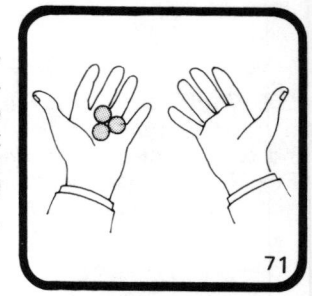

(67) Open your left fingers just enough to place the sponge into your left fist as you did in Step 59. Say, "Two in the hand."

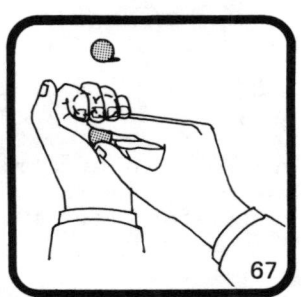

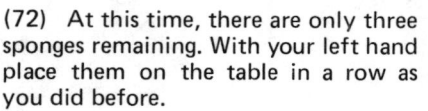

"THE TOTAL VANISH"
NOW FOR A "SMASHING" CLIMAX TO THE ROUTINE.

(72) At this time, there are only three sponges remaining. With your left hand place them on the table in a row as you did before.

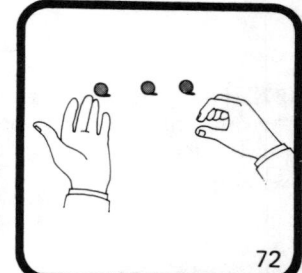

(68) Now pick up the remaining sponge in your right fingertips (as in Step 60).

(73) Begin again, just as you did before, by picking up the sponge on the far right with your right thumb and fingers. Rest this sponge on the palm of your open left hand as shown.

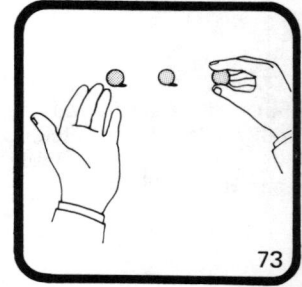

(69) Say, "And one in the pocket." Openly place this sponge into your right pants pocket, the same as in Step 61 — BUT THIS TIME, LEAVE THE SPONGE IN YOUR POCKET.

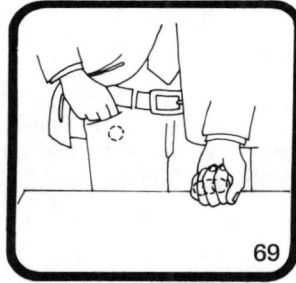

(74) Now close the fingers of the left hand around the sponge *and* the fingers of your right hand. *Your right fingers retain their grip on the sponge.* "One in the hand." Your right fingers continue to hold the sponge inside your closed left hand.

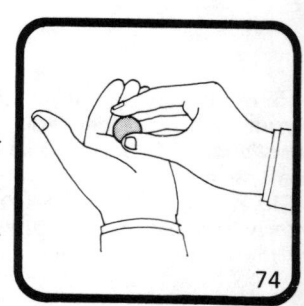

(70) Withdraw your right hand from your pocket and gesture toward your fist. *Make the gesture in a way that the audience can see that your right hand is quite empty. Do not call special attention to your right hand —* merely show it in an open and casual manner so that there is no question that it is empty.

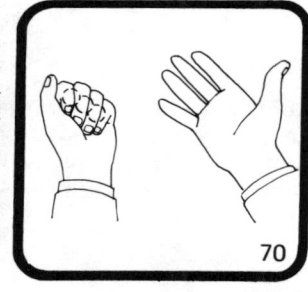

(75) Now, *instead of leaving the sponge in your left hand,* SECRETLY RETAIN THE SPONGE IN YOUR RIGHT FINGERS AS YOU WITH-DRAW YOUR RIGHT HAND FROM YOUR LEFT FIST.

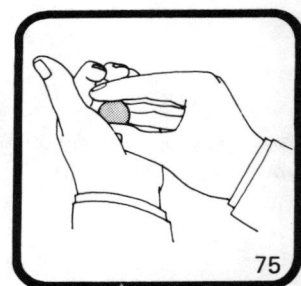

(76) To keep the sponge concealed from view during this procedure, as you withdraw your hand, move your right thumb slightly inward, rolling the sponge behind your right fingers out of sight.

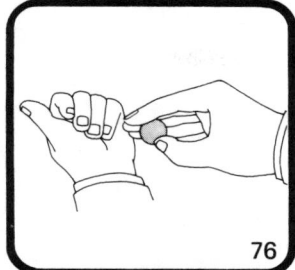

(80) <u>Without pausing</u>, pick up the remaining sponge in your right hand. Do <u>not</u> execute the "two-as-one" pick-up — just keep the two "palmed" sponges behind your fingers and openly pick up the third sponge, holding it at the fingertips of your right hand.

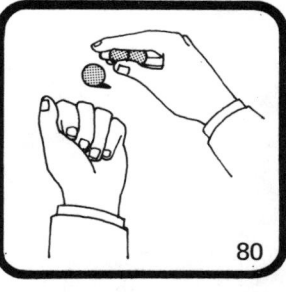

(77) Without hesitation, move your right hand toward the next sponge and *execute the "two-as-one" pick-up.*

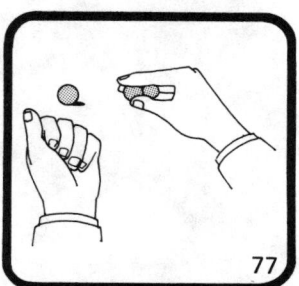

(81) <u>Immediately</u>, place your right hand into your right pants pocket. Say, "And the <u>last</u> sponge goes in the pocket." Now *leave <u>all three sponges</u>* in your pocket as you . . .

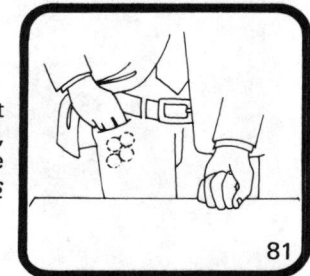

(78) With the two sponges held together (as one) in your right hand, open your left fist *just enough to place your right fingers into your hand.* Say, "<u>Two</u> in the hand." Once again, your thumb secretly draws *both sponges* behind your right fingers out of view . . .

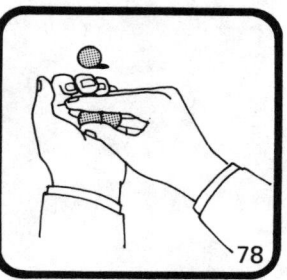

(82) . . . remove your right hand from your pocket. With your right hand, gesture toward your left fist *so the audience can see that your right hand is <u>quite empty</u>.*

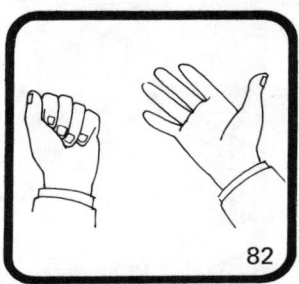

(79) . . . as you withdraw your right fingers from your left hand and close your left hand into a loose fist.

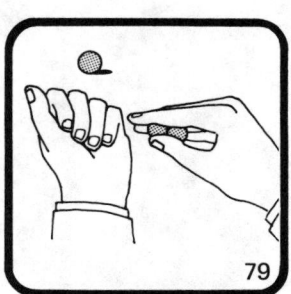

(83) Ask, "How many in my hand?" By now, the audience will probably answer "Three," thinking that they know what is going to happen. Whatever the number given say, "No, actually they are all gone — because <u>that was the end of the trick</u>." With that, open your left hand to show that all three sponges have *vanished,* bringing the routine to a startling climax!

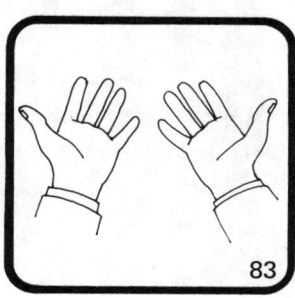

COMMENTS AND SUGGESTIONS

It is generally good policy to avoid handling sponges either too boldly or too cautiously. A quick thrust of the hand excites suspicion, and so does a tight squeeze of the sponge itself when the performer is actually giving the spectator two as one. A casual in-between course is best, particularly when done in an unhurried manner. In fact, the correct preliminary procedure will do much toward dispelling suspicion on the part of the spectators.

If a sponge is held lightly at the fingertips, with absolutely no pressure, no one is apt to regard it as compressible; and later, when two are shown as one, correct pressure of the thumb and fingers can give the "double" ball a distinctively "single" appearance. While a natural, unhurried motion of the hand is sufficient to cover the deception, larger loads depend upon fuller compression for complete concealment.

It is a good idea when practicing, to break the routine down into smaller units. Then, learn each phase before you go on to the next. The "Sponges" is undoubtedly one of the finest close-up tricks in magic. Each effect in this routine can be performed separately — and, as you will see when you perform it for your friends, the entire routine is constructed in a logical progression, building to a perfect climax — truly a masterpiece of magic!

BILLIARD BALL MAGIC

Very few magicians have performed tricks with full-sized balls, as they are too large and too heavy to handle except with oversized hands and a powerful grip. However, modern pool tables that come in less than standard sizes are supplied with numbered balls that are proportionally smaller and therefore, can be manipulated effectively, but magicians prefer to work with lighter balls made of wood, plastic or rubber.

These run in sizes from larger golf balls down to marbles; but generally speaking, the medium sizes are easier to handle. This may sound odd, but if you try out the various sizes, you will soon realize why. The medium-size ball has a more gradual curvature than its smaller counterpart—making it easier to grip by the basic palming methods described in this section. That is from the magician's viewpoint; while from the spectators' viewpoint, a similar situation applies. The larger the ball, the greater the effect, as it is more surprising to see a magician "vanish" a golf ball than a marble.

The answer to this is twofold: If you are planning a billiard ball routine in which you have the choice of sizes, pick the largest you can handle comfortable and go right ahead. Making that decision is easy enough when you are familiar both with the necessary moves and the effect that the audience expects. Such factors are covered in individual descriptors that follow.

THE CLASSIC PALM
Using a Ball

If you wish to learn Billiard Ball manipulation, you must first learn to "palm" a ball properly. To *palm* is to hold a ball (or any object) secretly in your hand so that the audience does not know it is there. As you practice, you will probably find it is easier to palm a ball than to palm, for instance, a coin. The curved surface of the ball gives you an opportunity for a much better grip, and since the entire surface of a ball is the same, spherical, it is not necessary to hold it by any particular side. You should also develop the skill required to palm a ball with *either* hand.

Probably the oldest method of "palming," and certainly one of the most useful, is known as the CLASSIC PALM.

METHOD

1) Hold the ball in the center of your palm by a slight contraction of your thumb and little finger. This causes the two masses of flesh on the opposite sides of the palm to exert a slight pressure on the ball — enough to hold it firmly in place while the hand is moved about.

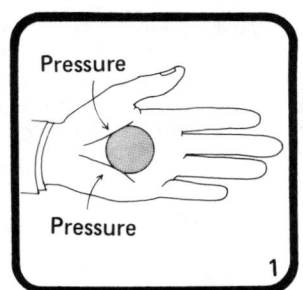

(2) If this seems a bit difficult at first, you should experiment with different-sized balls until you find the one best suited to your hands. Here is how your hand should look from the audience's view. You must avoid holding your hand with the thumb and fingers *stiff* or *abnormally separated*. The most important point of all is that the hand palming the ball *must always look RELAXED and COMPLETELY NATURAL.*

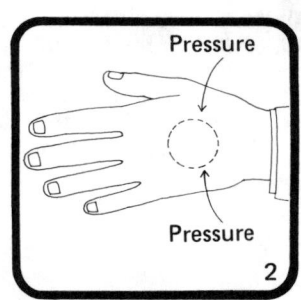

COMMENTS AND SUGGESTIONS

If the ball is properly palmed, you should be able to make a variety of gestures with your hand, move your fingers, and so on, without arousing suspicion. Most of the time when using the CLASSIC PALM, you will find it advisable to keep the hand that is holding the ball close to your body *and always keep the back of your hand* to the audience — for any "flash" of the ball will ruin the illusion. You should practice and learn the CLASSIC PALM as it is one of the most basic and versatile sleights in magic.

LET ME EMPHASIZE AGAIN, THE MOST IMPORTANT POINT OF ALL — THE HAND CONTAINING THE BALL (OR WHATEVER ELSE YOU ARE PALMING) MUST ALWAYS LOOK RELAXED AND COMPLETELY NATURAL. THAT IS THE TRUE SECRET, NOT ONLY OF THE CLASSIC PALM, BUT OF PALMING OF EVERY KIND.

THE CLASSIC PALM VANISH

EFFECT

This is a basic sleight for causing a ball (or any small object) to "disappear" from your hand. It utilizes the CLASSIC PALM and should be practiced until it can be performed smoothly with almost no conscious effort.

METHOD

(1) Stand facing the spectators with both hands at about waist level. Hold the ball in the palm of your right hand as shown. Your left hand is also held palm up, ready to receive the ball.

(2) Rotate your right hand over so that your right fingers point to the left and . . .

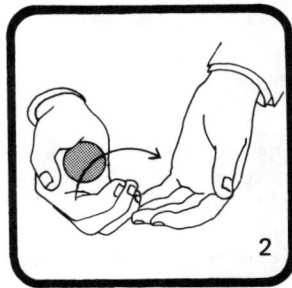

(3) . . . let the ball drop (or roll) into your left hand. Your left fingers should be pointing toward the audience when you drop the ball into your left hand as shown.

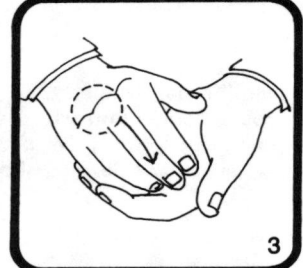

(7) Again, *with the very same movement as in Steps 2 and 3,* the right hand turns until the back of the hand is toward the audience. As the right hand turns, *the ball is secretly retained in the right hand in the Classic Palm.* Your left fingers bend slightly, as if receiving the ball.

Ball retained in Classic Palm

(4) Now repeat the exact same procedure but from *left to right.* Hold both hands palm up, then rotate your *left* hand and drop the ball back into your *right* hand. Do this "back and forth" tossing motion several times.

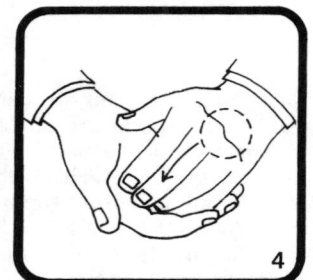

(8) Move your right hand up and from your left hand, retaining the ball in the Classic Palm. Your left hand quickly closes into a loose fist, *as if the left hand is holding the ball.*

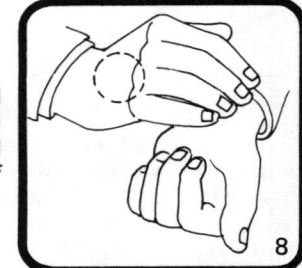

(5) NOW FOR THE VANISH. Hold the ball on the palm of your right hand just as before, but be sure it is in position so that you may retain it easily in the Classic Palm. As usual, the left hand is held open waiting to receive the ball.

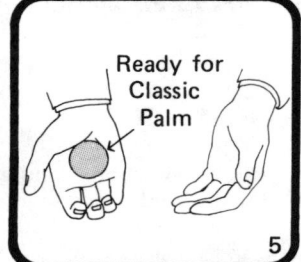

Ready for Classic Palm

(9) Your right hand assumes a relaxed position and casually points to the left fist. The fingers of the left hand make a "crumbling" motion, as if you were slowly crushing the ball.

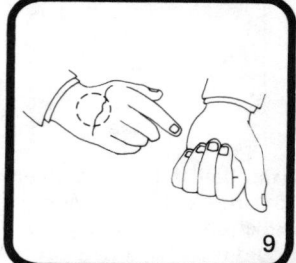

(6) Turn your right hand at the wrist as if you were going to drop the ball into your left hand.

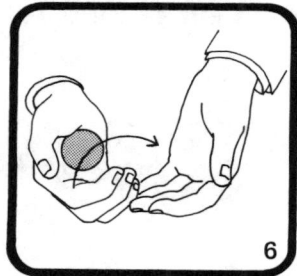

(10) Your right hand drops to the side of your body in a casual manner as you *concentrate all of your attention on your left hand.* Slowly open your left hand to reveal the ball has "vanished."

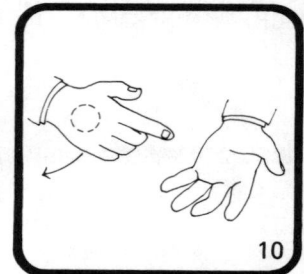

(11) Your right hand can now reproduce the ball from behind your right knee, from under your left elbow, or any appropriate place you may wish.

COMMENTS AND SUGGESTIONS

The CLASSIC PALM VANISH is a very versatile and deceptive sleight that can be performed with almost any small object. Practice the moves so that they can be done in an easy, natural manner — as if you are merely tossing the ball back and forth between your hands — finally ending with the ball in your closed left fist (really it is secretly held in the Classic Palm in your right). The tossing *conditions* the audience to believe that the ball is contained in the left hand. Your concentration on your closed left hand furnishes the *misdirection.* Combine these two deceptive elements with *practice* and you will have a truly "magical" vanish.

THE FRENCH DROP
Using a Ball

This is one of the most deceptive of all vanishes. Along with the Classic Palm, it surely ranks among the most practical and widely used sleight-of-hand moves.

EFFECT

The magician holds a ball in the left hand. He takes the ball in his right hand — makes a crumbling motion — and causes the ball to vanish!

METHOD

THE ILLUSTRATIONS ON THE *LEFT* SHOW THE <u>MAGICIAN'S</u> VIEW AND THOSE ON THE *RIGHT* SHOW THE <u>VERY SAME MOVE</u> FROM THE <u>SPECTATOR'S</u> VIEWPOINT.

MAGICIAN'S VIEW   *SPECTATORS' VIEW*

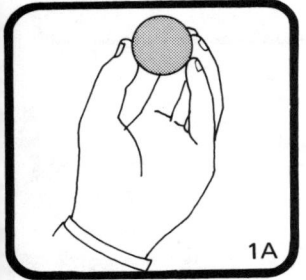

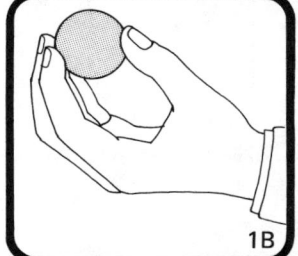

(1) Hold the ball between your left thumb and fingertips as shown. Your hand is held palm upward and your thumb and fingers point up. Display the ball to your audience.

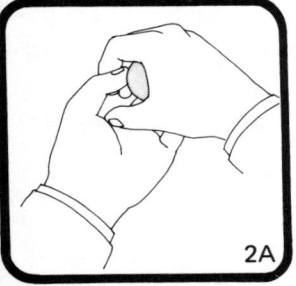

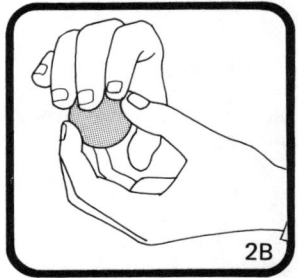

(2) Bring your hands together. Your left hand continues holding the ball as in Step 1 as your right hand approaches and then covers the ball as shown. Tuck your right <u>thumb</u> *under* the ball as your <u>fingers</u> *encircle* the ball over the top.

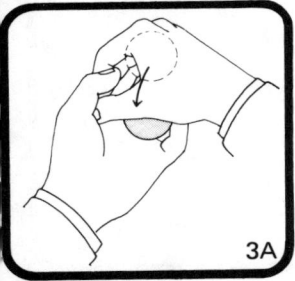

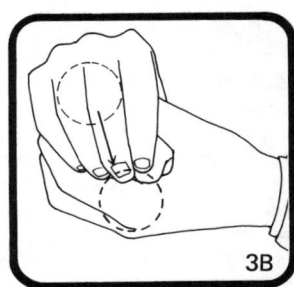

(3) Apparently close your right fingers around the ball — this momentarily conceals the ball from the audience's view. At that very moment, release the ball from your left thumb and fingers and allow it to drop secretly into your left hand. If your left hand is held correctly, the ball will fall into the Finger Palm position. When it does, curl your left fingers loosely around the ball. *Close your right hand around the space between your left thumb and fingers where the ball was before you secretly dropped it AS IF TO TAKE THE BALL.*

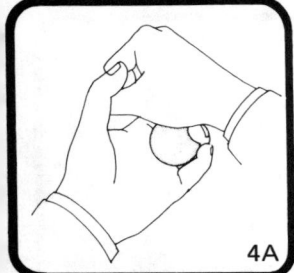

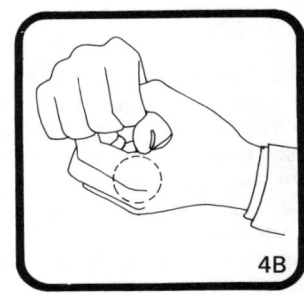

(4) Turn your *right* side toward the audience as you *appear to take the ball away in your right hand*. Keep your left hand with its palm toward you as you continue to hold the ball secretly in the Finger Palm position. Your right hand moves to the right, closed into a loose fist *as if it contained the ball.*

MAGICIAN'S VIEW

SPECTATORS' VIEW

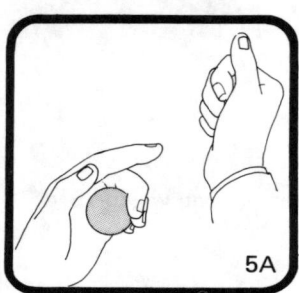

(5) The first finger of your left hand points at your closed right hand *as you direct all of your attention to your right hand.* Make a "crumbling" motion with your right hand as if the ball were turning to dust.

5A

5B

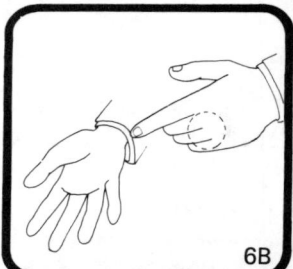

(6) Continue pointing with your left hand as you open your right hand to show that the ball has completely "vanished." (The ball is still secretly Finger Palmed in your left hand.) You can now reproduce the palmed ball with your left hand in any way that you wish.

6A

6B

FIST VANISH

This is another basic sleight which will enable you to vanish a ball or other small object in a very deceptive manner.

EFFECT

The magician places a ball on top of his left fist, and then takes it away with his right hand. When the hand is opened, the ball has vanished.

METHOD

(1) Stand with your *left side* toward the spectators. Hold your left hand in a loose fist with the *back* of your hand toward the audience. Place the ball on top of the fist with your right hand. Display the ball atop your left fist, then start to move your right hand toward the ball. Rotate your right hand so that the back of your hand is toward the audience as shown.

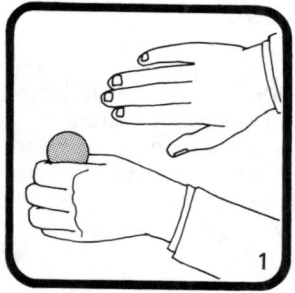

1

(3) <u>Without moving your left fingers,</u> move your <u>left thumb</u> just enough to allow the ball to drop secretly into your left hand, which holds the ball in the curled fingers. *Close your right hand as if it were grasping the ball.*

3

(2) Bring your open right hand against the top of your left fist so that your right first finger is resting on your left first finger and your right thumb touches your left thumb. Begin to curl your right fingers around the ball. The ball should now be out of the sight of the audience, hidden by the right hand.

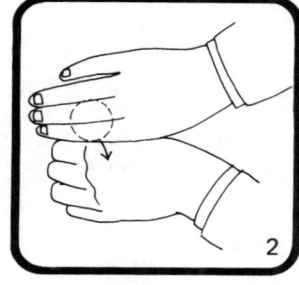

2

(4) Move your right hand, *which pretends to hold the ball,* up and away from your left fist. Your left hand secretly holds the ball in the Finger Palm position. Extend the first finger of your left hand and point to your right hand. *Follow your right hand with your eyes.*

4

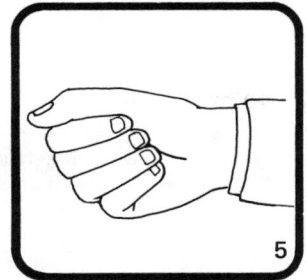

5) Turn your closed right hand, which apparently holds the ball, so that its palm and closed fingers are acing the audience.

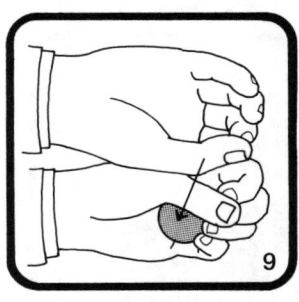

(9) Your right fingers curl around the ball, pretending to take it, as in Step 3. At the same time, your left thumb relaxes a bit, *allowing the ball to drop secretly into your left fist.*

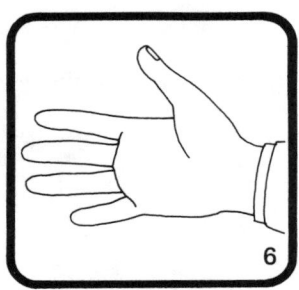

6) Slowly open your right hand and eveal that the ball has vanished.

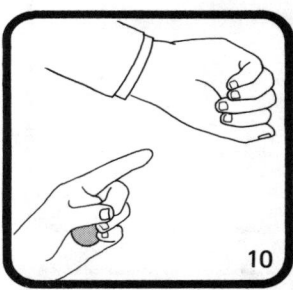

(10) As in Step 4, your right hand moves away as if it holds the ball. Be sure *your eyes follow your right hand* as your left first finger casually points to your right fist.

7) To conclude the trick, you can move the left hand, which ontains the Finger Palmed ball, down behind your leg and repro-uce the ball from behind the left knee.

(11) Slowly open your right hand to reveal the disappearance of the ball as described in Steps 5 and 6.

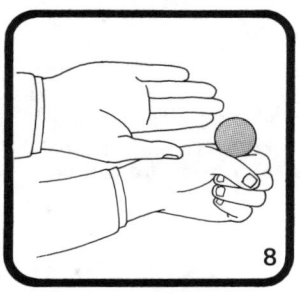

8) The following are illustrations of teps 1, 3, and 4 *as seen from the magician's viewpoint.* The ball is on op of your left fist as your right hand pproaches the ball as in Step 1.

(12) Now reproduce the ball from behind your left knee as explained in Step 7.

COMMENTS AND SUGGESTIONS

This is a very basic and useful sleight. Practice it and you will find that it can be done with almost any small object.

CHANGE-OVER PALM

This is a very useful sleight that can be used *before* the production or *after* the vanish of a ball.

EFFECT

The magician shows both hands to be empty — yet he has a ball palmed secretly in one hand.

MAGICIAN'S VIEW

METHOD

SPECTATORS' VIEW

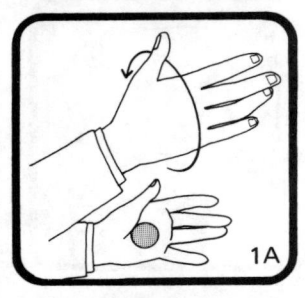

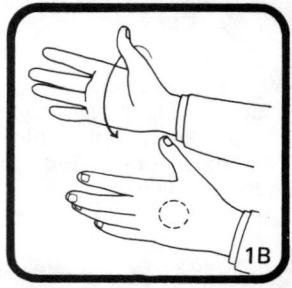

(1) Stand with your left side toward the audience. The ball is held secretly in the Classic Palm in your *left* hand. Show your *right* hand empty. Rotate your hand so that the audience may see both sides.

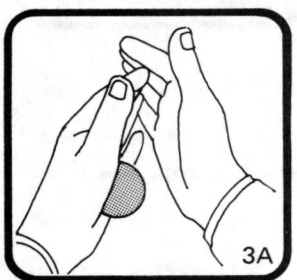

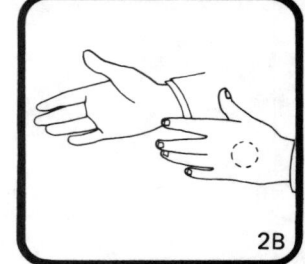

(2) After showing your right hand empty, place your left first finger on the base of your right palm at the wrist as shown.

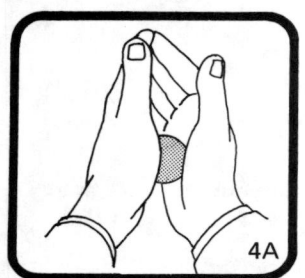

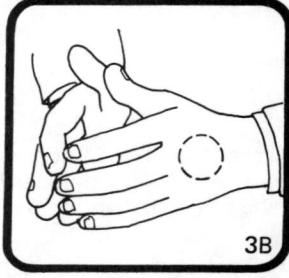

(3) Now turn your body to the *left* so that your <u>right side faces the audience</u>. As you turn, your hands will naturally come together in front of your body.

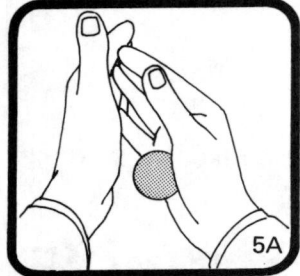

(4) Your left palm, which contains the ball, will be facing your right palm when you are half way through the turn. At that moment the tips of the fingers of both hands are pointing toward the audience. Be sure to keep the tips of the fingers of both hands *together* (the right fingertips touch the left fingertips) to prevent anyone from seeing a "flash" of the palmed ball as you turn your body from right to left.

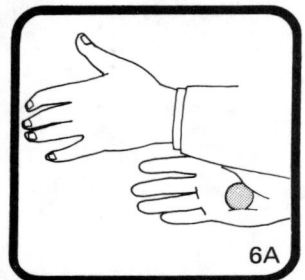

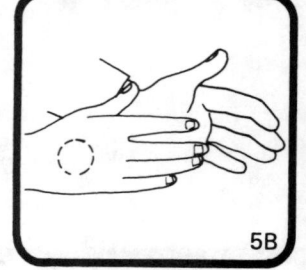

(5) As you turn, when the palms of your hands are together, <u>secretly transfer</u> the ball from the Classic Palm in your left hand to the Classic Palm in your right hand.

(6) Once the ball is held in the Classic Palm in your right hand *and* your right side is toward the audience, move your right hand back toward your body. Your hands are now *reversed* from the position they were in in Step 1. The ball is palmed in your *right* hand as the *left* hand is now shown empty on both sides.

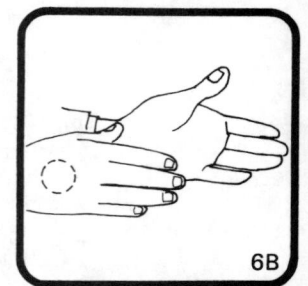

(7) You have now shown *both hands empty* — yet you have a ball (or any other small object) secretly palmed in your right hand!

THE FINGER ROLL FLOURISH

EFFECT

This is a beautiful "flourish" to add to your Billiard Ball repertoire. The ball rolls rapidly from finger to finger convincing your audience that you possess great skill as a manipulator. This feat requires practice — so be prepared to devote considerable time to it so that your hands become accustomed to the ball and to the series of finger positions. After you once work out the basic moves, you will find that it becomes easier and easier to do. Practice it well and you will have a bit of manipulative magic of which you can be justly proud.

METHOD

(1) Begin the "roll" with the ball held between your right thumb and first finger with the back of your hand toward the audience. Swing your second finger under the ball (it does not touch the ball) toward the right until it reaches your thumb.

(2) Now hold the ball *between your first and second fingers,* and *release* your thumbs' grasp on the ball.

(3) The ball is now held between your first and second fingers. Move your second finger to the left "rolling" the ball on your first finger. At the same time, your third finger moves to the right to meet the first finger. *Your third finger has not yet touched the ball.*

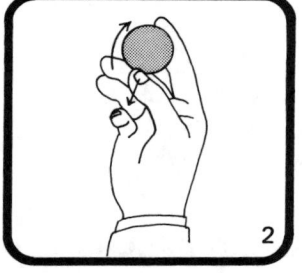

(4) Swing your first finger to the left rolling the ball until it touches your third fingertip. You now hold the ball between your second and third fingers. Remove your first finger from the ball.

(5) As you hold the ball between your second and third fingers, swing your second finger to the left as you did with the first finger in Step 4. At the same time, bring your little finger to the right and under but not touching the ball yet.

(6) Continue to swing your second finger to the left until its tip touches your little finger. Clip the ball between your third and fourth fingers, and release your second finger's hold on the ball.

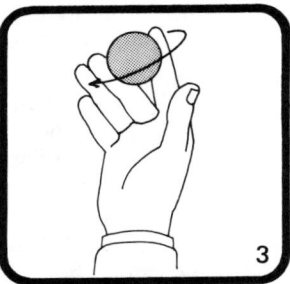

(7) You now hold the ball clipped between your third and little fingers. Now pivot your little finger *around behind* your third finger. This rolls the ball to the *back* of your third finger.

(8) Continue to move the little finger around *behind* the third finger. Move your second finger *behind* your third finger *and* the ball until you can clip the ball between the third and second finger — with the ball resting on the *back* of your third finger. As soon as the ball is held between the second and third fingers, release the little finger's grip on the ball.

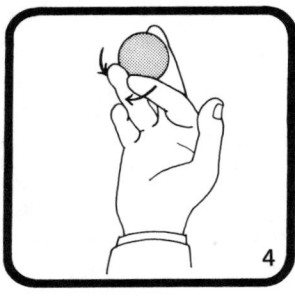

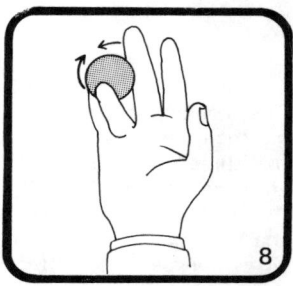

(9) The ball is now held between your second and third fingers *on the back of your hand.* Swing your third finger in an arc to the right rolling the ball around *behind* your second finger. Your first finger moves left *behind* the ball *and* your second finger, *but does not touch the ball.*

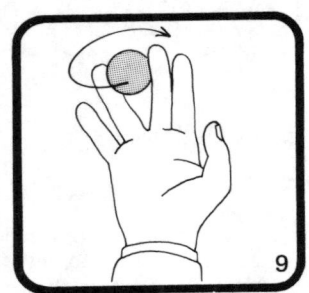

(10) Continue with the third finger rolling the ball around behind the second finger until the tips of the third and first finger touch. Then, clip the ball between the tips of your first and second fingers and remove your third finger from the ball.

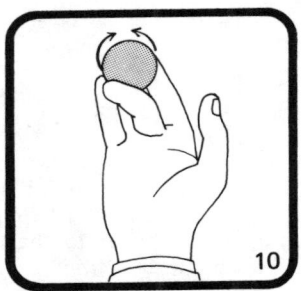

(11) You now hold the ball between the tips of your first and second fingers. You have executed the complete Finger Roll. The ball was rolled down the *front* of your hand, *around* your third finger, and then rolled on the *back* of your hand to the position it now occupies.

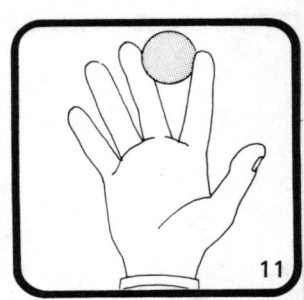

(12) Now repeat Steps 3 through 10 in quick succession a few more times to further display this spectacular flourish.

(13) *NOTE: After Step 11, DO NOT USE YOUR THUMB. The ball is pivoted between your first and second fingers (around your second finger) for its repeat journey.*

COMMENTS AND SUGGESTIONS

This flourish may seem difficult, if not impossible, at first. Do not become discouraged. Experiment with balls of different sizes until you find the right size for your hands. (Rubber balls are easier and sponge balls are the easiest of all.) Carry a ball with you and practice whenever you can — I'll bet that sooner than you think, you will be able to perform the FINGER ROLL FLOURISH like a professional.

THE MARK WILSON BILLIARD BALL ROUTINE

This is an entire BILLIARD BALL ROUTINE made up of a number of vanishes, productions, and multiplications. The routine is described exactly as I have presented it for many years, and thus has been well tried and tested. I have performed it on all of the major television networks, on hundreds of local television shows, in thousands of "live" appearances, and in many countries throughout the world. It is extremely practical and, although it requires practice, it is not nearly as difficult as you may assume when you first read it, and it certainly is not as difficult as it appears to the audience.

For the routine, you will require a standard set of Magicians' Billiard Balls. This consists of three *solid* balls and one *"shell."* A *shell* is actually a hollow half-ball into which one of the solid balls may be secretly inserted. When the solid ball is inside the shell, the two appear to be only one ball. This is the basic secret of the BILLIARD BALLS and, as you will see, is used in a number of different ways throughout the routine.

Rather than teach you the sleights that go to make up the routine individually, I have described them all in sequence as they occur in the presentation (with the exception of the CHANGE-OVER and the FIST VANISH, which are standard ball sleights, and the CLASSIC PALM, all of which have been previously described). In this way, you can see how each sleight fits in context into the routine and how each move blends with the next to create a truly outstanding sleight-of-hand presentation. In learning the routine, you should practice one phase at a time — learn it — and then move on to the next sequence.

—MW

EFFECT

The magician shows both hands empty and states, "I would like to show you a trick in which I reach out into the air and produce a ball." He then does just that — he produces a solid ball from the air. The performer explains that he will now make the ball *vanish* on the count of "three." He tosses the ball into the air as he counts "one" — and then catches the ball between his hands as it descends. He tosses it again and counts "two." On the count of "three," the magician *apparently* tosses the ball into the air with his right hand, whereupon it "vanishes." His hand, however, suspiciously strikes his right back pocket as he makes this third upward throw. The audience assumes that instead of "vanishing" the ball, the magician has cleverly slipped the ball into his back pocket. Rather jokingly, the performer confirms the spectators' suspicions by removing the ball from that very pocket.

The magician, however, quickly re-establishes his ability by rapidly producing *two more* solid balls from the air, giving him a total of three.

Pretending to hear someone in the audience question whether the balls are solid, the magician, who now holds the three balls between the fingers of his right hand, takes one of the balls in his left hand and apparently "throws" it to a member of the audience. Actually, when he makes the throwing motion, the audience is surprised to find that his left hand is empty — the ball has vanished!

Continuing as if nothing out of the ordinary has happened, the magician requests that the spectator to whom he tossed the "invisible ball" examine it and then toss it back to him. When the spectator throws the imaginary ball back to the magician, he "catches" it out of the air — back in its solid, *visible* form.

Replacing the ball between the other two held in his right fingers, the wizard explains that he will demonstrate something that his viewers should never do. Taking one of the balls from his right hand with his left, he apparently places the ball in his mouth — whereupon he swallows it! Then, showing his left hand empty, the performer reaches down into the waistband of his trousers — where his shirt meets the top of his belt — and openly removes the apparently swallowed ball!

The magician goes on to explain that what he "really wanted to do" was to produce a ball from the air. The magician then reaches out into the air with his left hand and produces yet a *fourth* ball from the air. This is placed in the last remaining space between the fingers of his right hand. *STARTING WITH ONLY HIS EMPTY HANDS, THE MAGICIAN HAS NOW MAGICALLY PRODUCED FOUR BALLS FROM THE AIR!*

Now for the second half of the routine. First the magician removes one of the balls from between the fingers of his right hand with his left. Then, by merely squeezing it. "dissolves" it completely away.

Then with a slight wave of the right hand, one of the three remaining balls vanishes. Reaching behind his left knee with his left hand, he reproduces the vanished ball. This ball he openly places in his left coat pocket (or in a bowl, hat, or some other container on his table).

The magician is now left with two balls in the right hand. After rearranging them so that they are held side by side, one of them visibly vanishes and is reproduced, this time not from behind his knee, but from the magician's right elbow.

Now for a little "magical" byplay. The magician displays the two balls in his right hand as he swings both arms down so that his hands are beside his knees. With a wave of his right hand, one of the two balls disappears and is reproduced from behind his left knee. This is repeated several times. As soon as the ball is replaced by the left hand into the right, one of the balls in the right vanishes and is reproduced behind the magician's left knee.

After several unsuccessful attempts to keep the two spheres in his right hand, the magician places one of the balls into his pocket. He now explains that he will be unable to perform the trick that he had planned to do with this last ball because he does not have on his "special coat." Yet, despite the magician's explanation as to why he cannot present this last mystery, he proceeds to do exactly what he said ' couldn't — which brings the routine to a clever, happy, and inexplicable conclusion.

SECRET AND PREPARATION

As stated above, you will need one set of multiplying Billiard Balls. First, place one of the balls *and* the shell (with the ball *inside* the shell) in your right back trouser pocket. One of the two remaining solid balls is placed inside the waistband of your pants, between your pants and shirt. (This will be directly behind where your belt buckle is located if you are wearing a belt.) The remaining solid ball is either placed in your left coat pocket or in a location on your table so that it is hidden by some other prop and where it may be easily obtained when necessary.

METHOD

IN ALL OF THE ILLUSTRATIONS FOR THIS ROUTINE, THE SHELL IS A DARKER COLOR THAN THE BALLS SO THAT YOU CAN KEEP TRACK OF ITS POSITION DURING THE PRESENTATION.

PHASE ONE

(1) Secretly obtain the ball from your left coat pocket (or from behind the object on your table) and hold it in the Classic Palm in your left hand as your left arm hangs casually at your side.

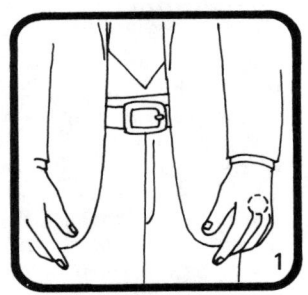

(2) NOTE: There are any number of clever ways of obtaining the ball without the audience's knowledge. For instance, you may replace some small object used in a previous trick in your left coat pocket and secretly palm the ball before you remove your hand. The same holds true if you are replacing an object on the table, which gives you a similar opportunity to secretly obtain the ball. If you are using the routine as an opening effect, for which it is quite well suited by the way, then enter from the left side of the stage with the ball *already palmed* in your left hand.

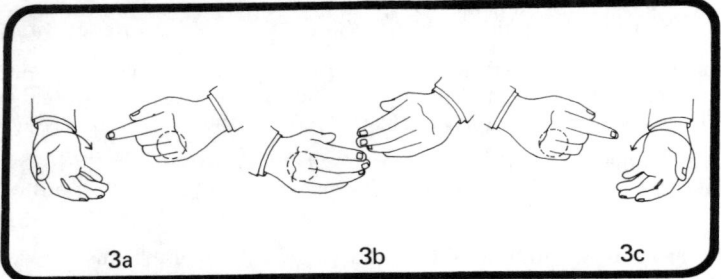

3a   3b   3c

(3a) In any event, with the ball secretly palmed in your left hand, show both hands "empty" using the Change-Over Palm already described in the Billiard Ball Section of the Course. In this case, start with your <u>left</u> side toward the audience. Point to your right hand with your left first finger as you turn your right hand over showing both sides. It is undoubtedly empty! Then rotate your whole body so that your <u>right</u> side is toward the audience. (b) During the "turning" movement, it is quite natural that your hands approach each other, palm to palm, as you secretly execute the Change-Over. (c) Now you can show your left hand on both sides — it too is "empty" (since the ball is now palmed in your <u>right</u> hand). Point at your left hand with your right first finger to further direct (and "misdirect") the audience's attention.

(4) Explain to the audience, "I would like to show you a trick in which I reach out into the air and get a ball — like this!" With your right side still to the audience, reach out with your right hand and produce the ball "from the air."

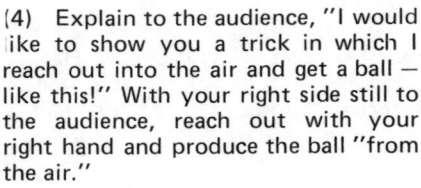

(5) NOTE: It is important that this, and all of the following "productions" be presented so that you apparently do "pluck" the ball from the air (as opposed to merely "seeing" it in your hand). To do this, the fingers and thumb of your right hand reach down and obtain the ball from the Classic Palm as your hand begins its motion away from your body to your left. As your hand moves, *look at the exact spot in the air where the ball is going to come from, <u>as if you already see it there.</u>* It is important, as your hand reaches the top of its swing for the "grasp," that the ball "appear" at the tips of your fingers *just as your hand starts its downward motion.* <u>In this way, you apparently "pluck" the ball from the air.</u> (Just imagine that you were going to "pick" an apple from a tree. <u>First</u> your eyes would see the apple. <u>Then,</u> your hand would reach for it. *Your eyes would remain on the apple — not on your hand —* until your hand reached the apple and "picked" it from the tree. <u>Then</u> your eyes would follow the apple.)

PHASE TWO

(6) Now explain that you will make the ball *vanish* when you count to "three." Turn your left side to the audience and hold the ball in your right hand. The left hand is held waist high with its back to the spectators. Toss the ball two or three feet in the air with your right hand. Then catch the ball with *both* hands, <u>being sure to keep the back of your left hand to the audience.</u>

(7) Immediately toss the ball in the air again as you count "two." Again catch the ball exactly as you did before with both hands.

(8) Now you apparently toss the ball in the air for the third and last time. *What you actually do, however, is to retain the ball in your left hand in the Classic Palm.* Your right hand, apparently containing the ball, makes an exaggerated sweep, first downward behind your body, and then up into the air as if to toss the ball. However, your right hand strikes your pants in the area of your right back pocket as it passes behind you. The right hand then continues its motion of tossing the ball up in the air. You count "three."

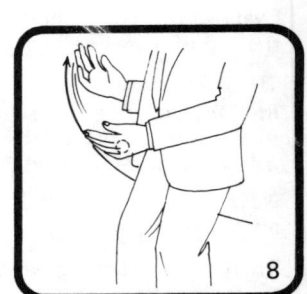

(9) Make this third toss an obviously suspicious move (and thus quite different from the first two "tosses") because you want the audience to believe that you cleverly placed the ball in your right back pocket.

(10) Smile and say, "I see — you think the ball went into my back pocket. Well you are right!" Reach into your back pocket and remove *the ball <u>and</u> the shell* and . . .

(11) . . . display them as *one ball* between your right first finger and thumb. (At this point, you have one ball palmed in your left hand and the ball and shell displayed as one ball in your right hand.)

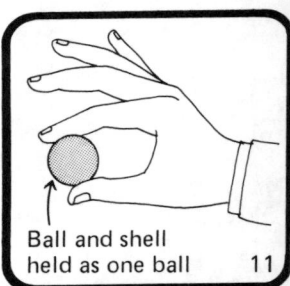

Ball and shell held as one ball

PHASE THREE

(12) Keep the left side of your body toward the audience. Say, "Actually that <u>isn't</u> the trick that I <u>wanted to do.</u> The trick I <u>wanted to do</u> is the one where I reach into the air and produce a ball!" As you say this, with your left hand (which has a ball secretly retained in the Classic Palm) reach out and produce the ball from the air on your right side.

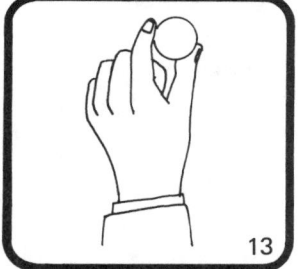

PHASE FOUR

(13) Display this "new" ball (really the <u>first</u> ball) and . . .

(14) . . . then place it between your right <u>first</u> and <u>second</u> fingers.

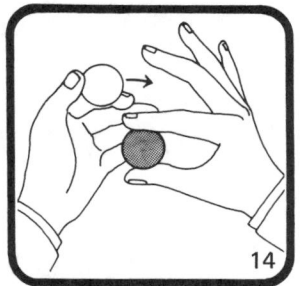

(15) As you <u>openly</u> place the ball between your right first and second fingers, <u>secretly steal the ball out of the shell</u> with the second, third, and fourth fingers of your left hand. Then, use the fingers of your left hand to press the ball into the Classic Palm position.

(16) NOTE: THE PRECEDING "STEAL" (STEP 15) IS ONE OF THE KEY MOVES IN THE BILLIARD BALL ROUTINE.

(17) Here is a side view of this important move. This is how <u>you</u> see the "steal" as you hold your hands about shoulder high on your right side.

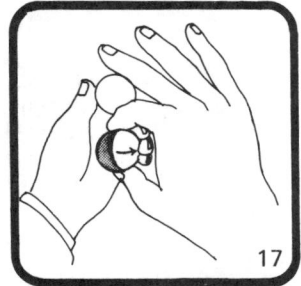

(18) Separate your hands so that your left hand is positioned about waist high as your right hand holds what appears to be two solid balls (actually only one ball and the shell. The left hand secretly holds the other solid ball in the Classic Palm).

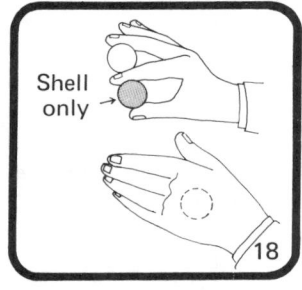

(19) NOTE: Be sure to keep the <u>back</u> of your left hand toward the audience. Also be sure that you keep the <u>full front</u> of the <u>shell</u> facing the audience at all times, <u>particularly when it does not contain a solid ball</u>, so that the audience cannot see that it is merely a half ball.

(20) Here is a <u>rear</u> view of the situation at this point. The <u>shell</u> is held between your right thumb and first finger and the <u>solid ball</u> is gripped between your right first and second fingers. Another solid ball is secretly held in the Classic Palm in your left hand.

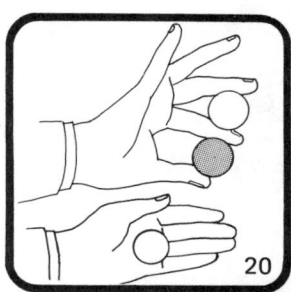

(21) Repeat the line you just said before with the following variation. "If you didn't see that — I will do it again. The trick I <u>really</u> wanted to do is the one where I reach out into the air and produce a ball like this!" As you say the above, reach out with your left hand and "produce" the palmed ball.

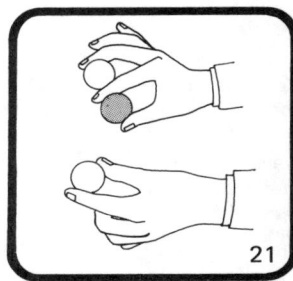

PHASE FIVE

(22) Display the ball and then place it between your right <u>second</u> and <u>third</u> fingers as shown.

(23) You now appear to be holding three solid balls in your right hand. Actually, you hold two balls and one shell.

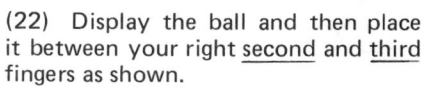
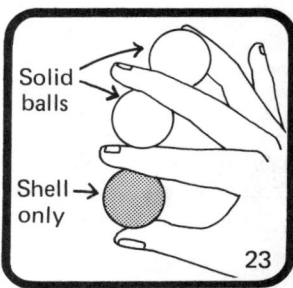

(24) <i>You are now apparently going to "throw one of the balls to a member of the audience."</i> <u>Actually</u> you will make the ball "vanish" and throw an "invisible" ball to the startled spectator. During this entire sequence it is important to remember that the left side of your body is toward the audience.

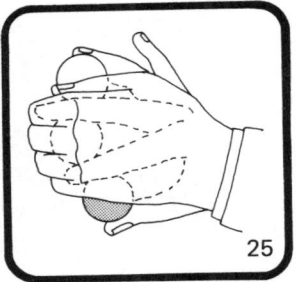

(25) *Here is what you really do.* Move your left hand to a position so that it covers the two lowermost balls held in the right hand (actually the shell and one ball). You now *appear* to take the ball from between your right first and second fingers with your left hand.

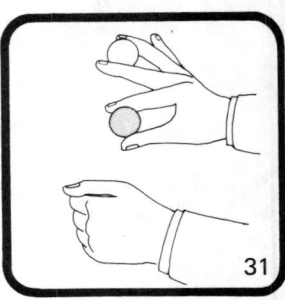

(31) Move your closed left hand down and away, *held as if it contained a ball.*

(26) *NOTE: In Steps 27, 28, and 29, the left hand has been removed from the illustration so that you can better understand the action of the right hand.*

(32) *NOTE: THE PRECEDING (STEPS 27, 28, 29, AND 30) IS A KEY MOVE IN THE BILLIARD BALL ROUTINE.*

(27) What you really do is the following important secret move. Your right second finger rotates downward (toward the floor) and lowers the solid ball held between your right first and second fingers *into the shell.*

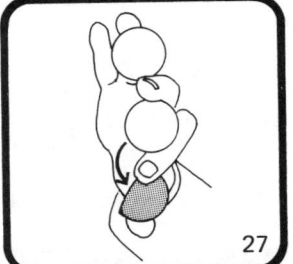

(33) Keep your right hand motionless, held about shoulder high directly to your right side. Continue to swing your left hand down so that it is held about waist high with the left fingers pointing up as if you are about to toss the ball to the audience. Say, "I can see that some of you think that the balls are not solid. Here — catch!"

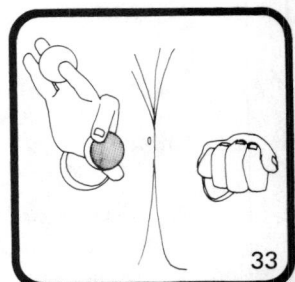

(28) Once the ball has been pivoted *all the way into the shell,* the ball is held inside the shell by your right thumb and first finger as shown.

(34) Pretend to toss the ball to one particular spectator. He, and the rest of the audience, will see as you make the throwing motion that there is *nothing in your left hand.* The ball has either "vanished" or become "invisible." Make no comment about this but, addressing yourself to the person in the audience to whom you apparently "threw" the ball, say, "Now when you are through examining it, please throw the ball back."

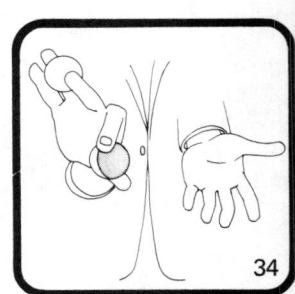

(29) As soon as the ball is inside the shell, *bring your right second finger back up to the position where it was before.* Remember, all of this action is covered by your left hand which . . .

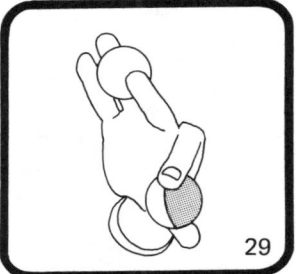

PHASE SIX

(35) As if to occupy your time while the spectator "examines" the ball, bring your left hand back up to your right hand. Take the ball from between your right second and third fingers and transfer it down one notch so that it is held between your right first and second fingers.

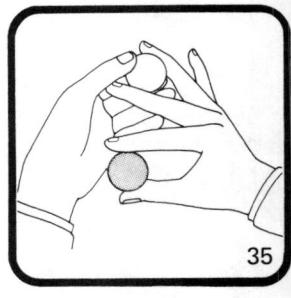

(30) . . . has apparently removed the ball from between your right first and second fingers. *Actually,* your left hand is empty.

Solid ball →

Ball and shell

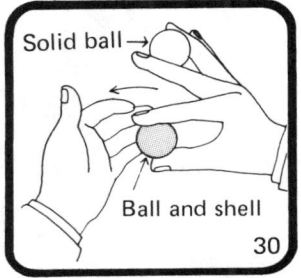

(36) As you do this, *steal the ball out of the shell with your left fingers as you did in Step 15.*

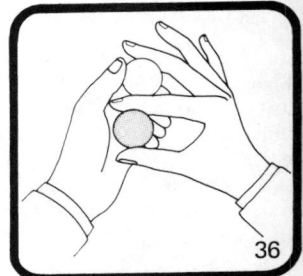

(37) Now, keeping the back of your left hand to the audience, bring your left hand (which secretly contains the just stolen ball in the Classic Palm) down to about the level of your waist.

(38) Addressing the spectator to whom you threw the "invisible" ball say, "Are you through with the ball? Then would you please toss it back." The spectator may "play along" and pretend to throw the invisible ball to you (usually this is the case) or he may just sit there! In any event, reach out in the air with your left hand and *pretend to catch the ball,* really "producing" it as you did before at the tips of your left fingers. Say, "Thank you," to the spectator as you display the ball at your left fingertips.

PHASE SEVEN

(39) Now, reach up and place this ball between your right <u>second</u> and <u>third</u> fingers. You apparently have three solid balls held in your right hand. (Actually, you hold <u>two</u> balls and the <u>shell</u>.)

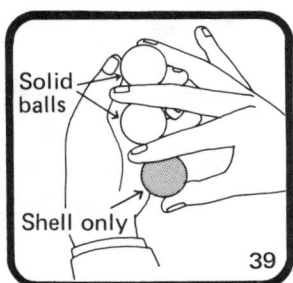

(40) Now move your left hand in front of your right hand just as you did before and perform Steps 27, 28, 29, and 30, *apparently* taking the ball from between your right first and second fingers into your left hand. *You actually pivot that ball down into the shell as you did before.*

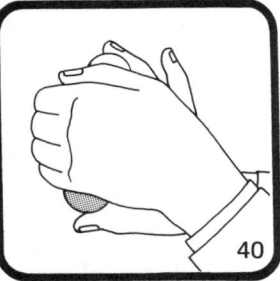

(41) You now have two balls showing in your right hand. (Really <u>one</u> of the balls is the shell with a solid ball inside.) Your left hand appears to be holding one ball, but it is really empty.

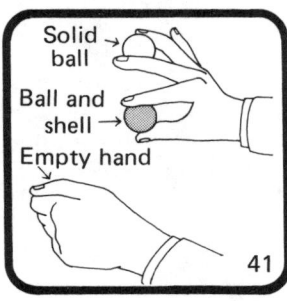

(42) Keeping the back of your left hand to the audience, bring your closed left fist up to your mouth. Now pantomime the action of placing the ball from your left hand into your mouth. As soon as you do this, turn the palm of your left hand toward the audience — showing it to be empty — as you apparently hold the ball in your closed mouth.

(43) *NOTE: As shown in the illustration for Step 42, you should bring your right hand down and hold it <u>in front of your body</u>. This "pivoting" move with your right hand is fully explained in Step 53.*

(44) Now with your tongue, push out your left cheek as if it contained the ball. Then repeat the same motion with your tongue on the inside of your right cheek. Now make a very obvious "swallowing" motion — just as if you have swallowed the ball!

(45) Look a bit dismayed. Then, with your empty left hand, reach down and remove the ball from the waistband of your trousers. (This is the ball which you preset and has been there from the start of the routine.) Your audience will think you were extracting the "swallowed" ball from your stomach.

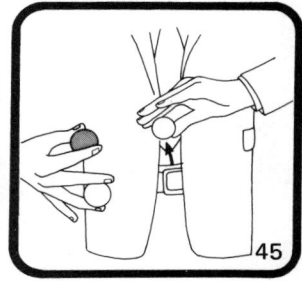

PHASE EIGHT

(46) Display the ball and place it between your right first and second fingers.

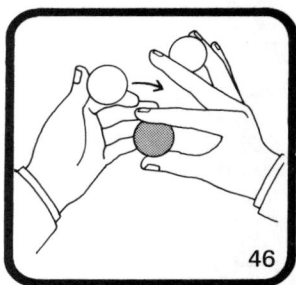

(47) As you do this, *steal the ball out of the shell with your left hand* as in Step 15.

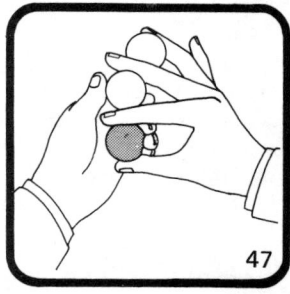

(48) You now appear to be holding three solid balls in your right hand. (You really hold two balls and the shell. Your left hand secretly holds one ball in the Classic Palm.)

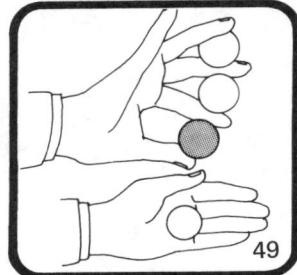

(49) Here is the view from the <u>rear</u> with the palmed ball hidden in your left hand.

(55) You are now in an ideal position to make a slight bow toward the audience as you hold the four balls in front of your body. If you have performed the routine correctly up to this point, you are sure to get applause (which, by the way, you certainly deserve!).

NOW FOR THE SECOND HALF OF THE ROUTINE.

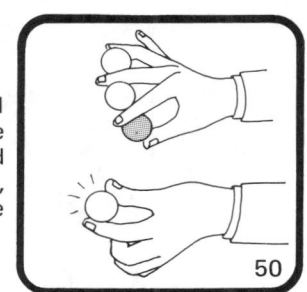

(50) Say, "However, the trick that I <u>really</u> wanted to show you is the one in which I reach out into the air and produce a ball." With your left hand, reach into the air and produce the fourth ball.

(56) Pivot your right hand back out so that the four balls are held as before on the right side of your body about shoulder high.

PHASE NINE

(51) Then place the ball between the third and little fingers of your right hand.

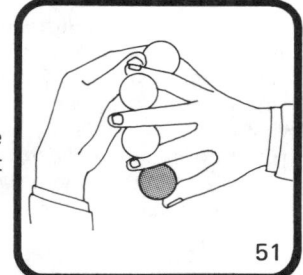

(57) Reach up with your left hand and cover the two lowermost balls. Execute Steps 27, 28, 29, and 30 as you *apparently* take the ball from between your right first and second fingers into your left hand. *(Actually, you pivot the ball down into the shell.)*

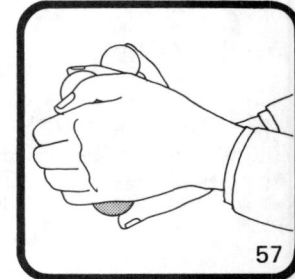

(52) You have now magically produced four balls "from the air" (really three balls and the shell).

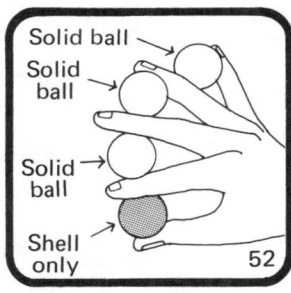

Solid ball

Solid ball

Solid ball

Shell only

(58) Move your left hand down and away as if it contained the ball . . .

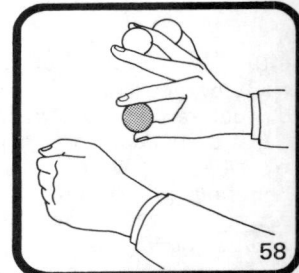

(53) You are now going to give the audience <u>a direct applause cue</u>. To do this, pivot your right hand down and around so that it is held in front of your body. *You must make this move without exposing the "half-ball" shell. Just swing your right hand down and then back up in a half-circle as shown in the illustration. Be sure to keep the <u>front</u> of the shell toward the audience at all times.*

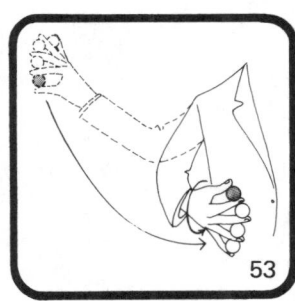

(59) . . . until your left hand is in front of your body. Hold your left hand just as you did before you tossed the "invisible" ball into the audience. This time, however, make a "squeezing" motion with the left hand as if grinding the ball to dust.

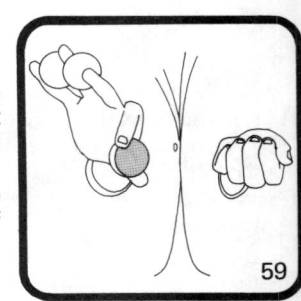

(54) After you "pivot" your hand down, it will appear as shown here.

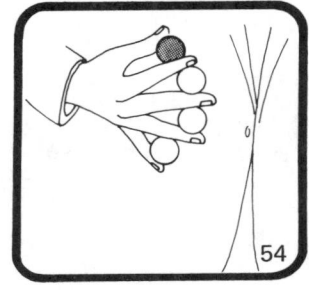

(60) Then slowly open your left hand to show that the ball has vanished.

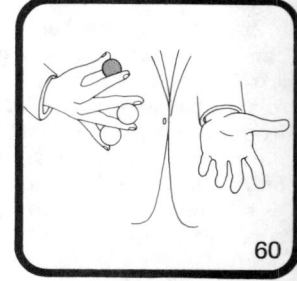

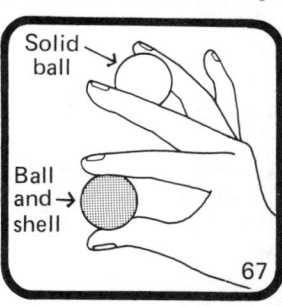

(61) *NOTE: In Steps 59 and 60, you may either leave your right hand held out to your right as shown in Step 59 or pivot it down in front of you as shown in Step 60.*

(67) . . . down into the shell. *It will appear as if the ball held between your right first and second fingers* <u>*visibly*</u> <u>*vanishes.*</u>

(62) After the audience sees that your left hand is completely empty, move your left hand back up to your right and grasp the ball that is located between your right <u>third</u> and <u>little</u> fingers.

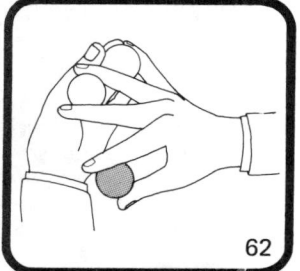

(68) This "visible" variation on Steps 27, 28, and 29 is another key move in the Billiard Ball Routine.

(63) Move this ball down to the position between your right first and second fingers. As you do this, *steal the ball from the shell as you did in Step 15 and hold it in the Classic Palm.*

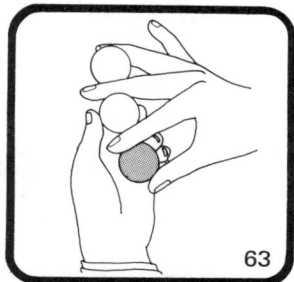

(69) With your left hand, reach down behind your left knee and produce the palmed ball. Apparently this is the ball that has "vanished" from your right hand and has now "reappeared" from behind your left knee.

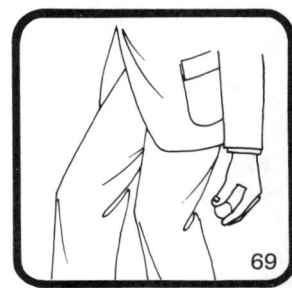

(64) Display what appears to be three balls in your right hand. (Actually, you hold two balls and the shell. Your left hand has one ball held secretly in the Classic Palm.)

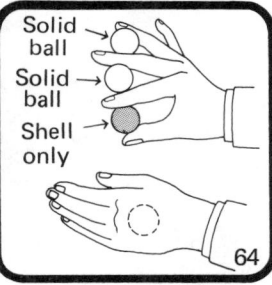

PHASE TWELVE

(70) Display this ball in your left hand and then drop it into your left coat pocket (or place it in some receptacle such as a bowl or a hat on your table).

(65) Now wave your right hand up and down as you perform the *same move* that you did in Steps 27, 28, and 29 — *except this time you do it WITHOUT THE COVERING OF YOUR LEFT HAND.*

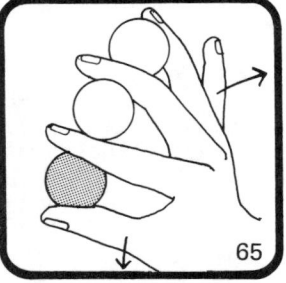

(71) Now move your left hand up to your right hand and take the ball that is located between your right second and third fingers and move it down one notch so that it is held between your right first and second fingers *in readiness for the same* <u>*visible vanish*</u> *that you just performed in Steps 65, 66, and 67.*

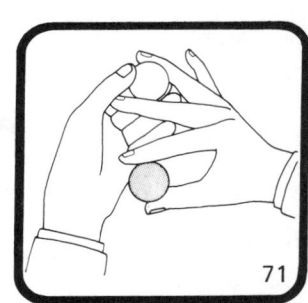

(66) Just as you did in Step 28, with your right second finger roll the ball that is held immediately above the shell . . .

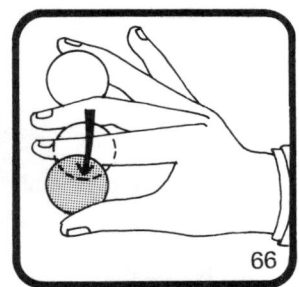

(72) At the same time that you place the ball between your first and second fingers, *secretly steal the ball from the shell as you did in Step 15.*

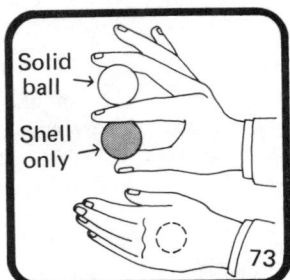

(73) Exhibit the two visible balls in your right hand. (*Actually*, you hold one ball and the shell. Unknown to the audience, you have one ball secretly held in the Classic Palm in your left hand.)

(74) Wave your right hand up and down as you did in Step 65 and execute Steps 66 and 67.

(75) Here is a <u>side view</u> as you roll the ball held between the first and second fingers down into the shell.

(76) Here is a <u>side view</u> at the completion of the move. Again, you have apparently caused a ball to "visibly" vanish at the tips of your right fingers.

(77) With your left hand, reach behind your <u>right</u> elbow and "reproduce" the ball (really the ball you were holding in the Classic Palm in your left hand).

PHASE THIRTEEN

(78) Now for a bit of "magical fun" with the Billiard Balls. Display the solid ball you now hold in your <u>left</u> hand and then place it between the first and second fingers of your right hand. *At the same time, steal the ball from the shell as you did in Step 15.*

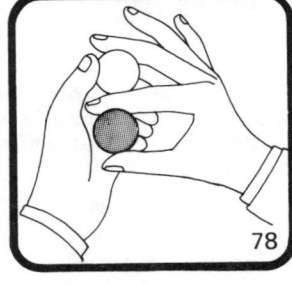

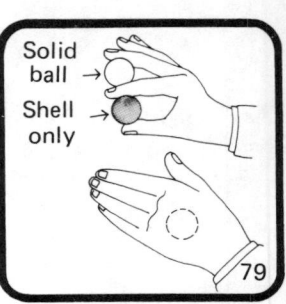

(79) You now apparently hold two balls in your right hand. (Actually you hold one ball and the shell. Another ball is held secretly in the Classic Palm in your left hand.)

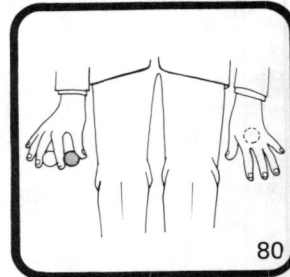

(80) Now pivot your right hand down so that it is beside your right knee. Your left hand also swings down so that it is on the other side of your body beside your left knee.

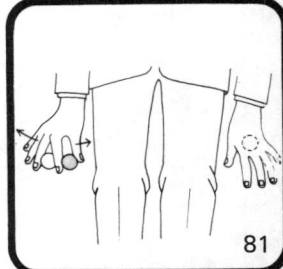

(81) Move the right hand away from your right knee and make a slight "tossing" motion toward your left.

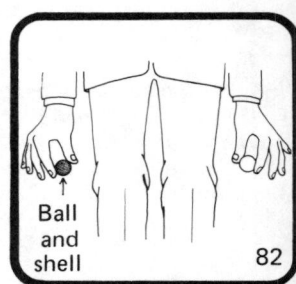

(82) As you do this "toss," pivot the ball that is held between the right first and second fingers into the shell. (This is the "visible" vanish again as in Steps 66 and 67.) Immediately, reach behind your left knee with your left hand and apparently reproduce the ball.

PHASE FOURTEEN

(83) You may now repeat this same effect by placing the ball held in your left hand back between your right first and second fingers. (The hands can remain down by your legs during this procedure. It is not necessary to return the right hand to its shoulder height position.) When you place the ball between the first and second fingers of your right hand, repeat Step 78 and steal the other ball from the shell. You are now set for the "Ball through the Knees" effect again.

(84) Make the "tossing" motion with your right hand beside your right knee. At the same time, pivot the ball between your right first and second fingers into the shell and reproduce the palmed ball from behind your left knee with your left hand.

(85) *NOTE: Here is an opportunity to add comedy to the act if you wish. This can be presented as a "perplexing situation" during which you apparently cannot control the balls — as one continues to vanish from your right hand and reappear behind your left knee. Or you may wish to make this appear to be a "magical transposition" which is under your control at all times. The choice is yours and should be made to fit the style of your presentation.*

(86) After several repetitions of the "Ball through the Knee," stop when you have one ball in each hand. (Really you have the ball and shell in your right and a solid ball in your left.) Place the *ball and shell,* as one, into your right coat pocket (or into the receptacle).

PHASE FIFTEEN

(87) You are now left with one ordinary ball which you display in your left hand. Say to the audience, "I am sorry that I will not be able to perform the last trick that I wanted to do for you with this ball — but you see, I don't have on my 'special coat.' If I had on my special coat, you wouldn't know it — but it would have a tube that runs *down* my right sleeve, *across* my back, and then *down* my left sleeve . . .

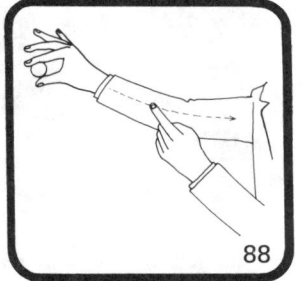

(88) . . . like this." As you make this statement, openly transfer the ball to your right hand and hold it at your right fingertips. Then use your left first finger to trace the path of the nonexistent "tube" down your right sleeve and across your back. Then extend your left arm as if to display where the tube would be if you had on your "special coat."

(89) Continue by saying, "You see, if I had on my special coat, I could take the ball in my right hand like this. It would travel *down* the tube and come out here." As you say this, perform the following action. Close your left hand into a fist. Place the ball, which is being held at the right fingertips, on top of your left fist. Then with the right hand, apparently grasp the ball, really performing the Fist Vanish that is described earlier in this section of the Course.

(90) Extend your right arm so that it is held as shown, with your right hand apparently containing the ball. Your left fingers should be extended and the ball held secretly in the Classic Palm. Swing your left hand down as shown so that it is extended to your left completing the "tube." *Be sure to keep the back of your left hand to the audience so as not to expose the palmed ball.*

(91) Squeeze your right fingers together and then turn your right-hand palm toward the audience to show that it is empty. Then the left hand apparently "receives" the ball that has traveled down the nonexistent tube.

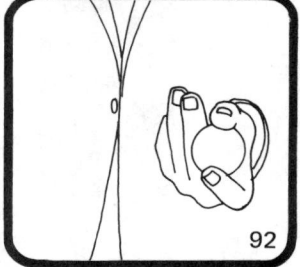

(92) Still holding your left hand extended, turn it around so that your left palm is to the audience and display the ball at the left fingertips.

(93) Bring both hands in front of your body and say, "I am sorry that I do not have on the special coat, so *I can't do that one for you today — but maybe next time!"*

(94) Then drop the ball in your pocket or the receptacle for the conclusion of an extremely clever sleight-of-hand routine with the classic Billiard Balls.

COMMENTS AND SUGGESTIONS

Along with the CUPS AND BALLS, the BILLIARD BALLS is another true Classic of Magic. Before you attempt to present the routine, be sure that you have practiced it well. As you can see, there are a number of sleights that are repeated several times. However, the entire routine has been designed so that each move is natural and there do not appear to be any unnecessary motions or suspicious moves.

In selecting your Billiard Balls, you should try to obtain a set which fits your hands well, as they are available in different sizes. The criterion here is that you must be able to comfortably hold the four balls (really the *three* balls and the *shell*) individually between your right fingers as shown in Step 52 of the routine.

Routines with Billiard Balls are literally endless. I am sure you will think of many variations and devise your own routine as you practice and progress with this classic effect.

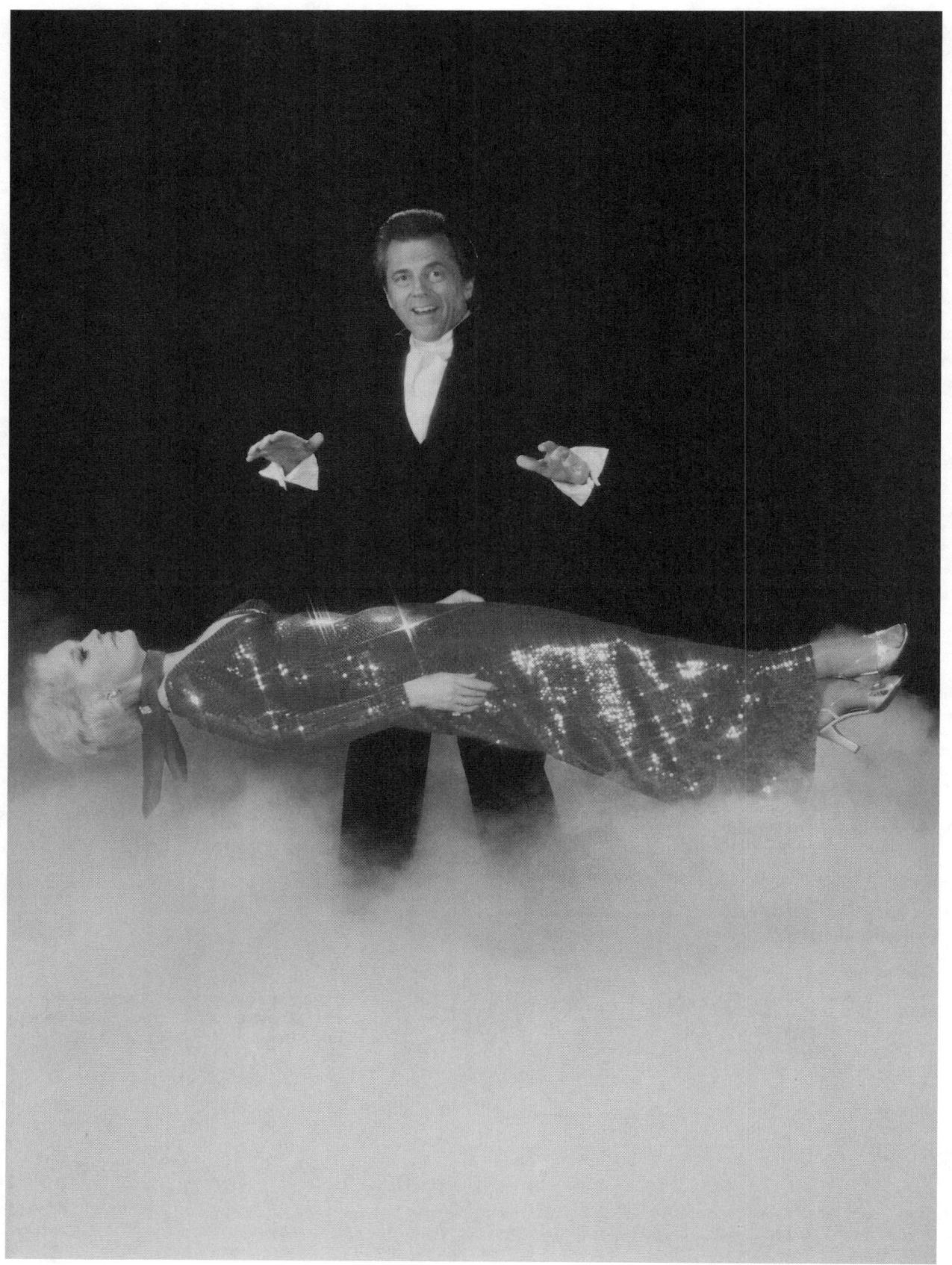

CUPS
AND BALLS

We must delve far back into antiquity to learn the origins of magic. There, perhaps, to our surprise, we will learn that the mysteries known to the ancients were the largest and the smallest, with virtually none in between. The reason for this was that they did not class them all as "magic." The larger effects were regarded as miracles because they were seen only in the pagan temples where doors opened with a sound resembling a peal of thunder and life-sized statues poured water on a fire when it was kindled on an altar. These were the equivalent of our modern stage illusions, and their purpose was to excite the awe of the populace.

So much for the large effects. The small were feats performed by jugglers who claimed no supernatural powers but merely embellished their usual juggling routines with feats of sleight-of-hand, the commonest being to put a pebble under one cup and have it disappear from there only to be found beneath another. This was practiced by the ancient Egyptians, later by the Greeks, and by Roman times, such deceptions were known as *acetabularii*. The name is derived from the cups they used which were called *acetabula*. Times had changes by the Middle Ages, though not too greatly. Jesters and minstrels were performing their share of magic along with jugglers, and in many instances, cups and balls had become their mainstay. Numerous old prints dating from around the year 1500 and continuing onward show performers at tables manipulating conically shaped cups with small balls made of cork, which was the one great improvement over the pebbles used in ancient times. The cork balls were light, and therefore easy to manipulate, much to the amazement of the onlookers. And the trick itself was so good that it underwent practically no improvement during the next 400 years.

Professor Hoffman, in his famous book *Modern Magic* which appeared in 1878, devoted an entire chapter to the cups and balls, classing the trick as "the groundwork of legerdemain," and "the very earliest form in which sleight-of-hand was exhibited." He recommends the use of tin cups and cork balls of various sizes and describes a series of passes for the secret transfer of the balls from cup to cup that follow the pattern of the past four centuries.

Improvements have been made, however, since Hoffman's time. Nickel- and chromium-plated cups have replaced the old tin variety along with those of other materials that make handling easier. Balls of soft rubber have supplanted the old cork type, also with good results. Routines have been simplified and modernized to suit the needs of today's close-up workers so the descriptions that appear in the following section might prove amazing, even to Professor Hoffman as well as to his predecessors of the centuries before.

This classic of magic deserves a top rating, for although it dates back to ancient times, it has still maintained its popularity throughout the centuries. Even though it is among the oldest of magical effects, it always seems new. The following routine gives the appearance of requiring great skill, yet actually the basic moves are comparatively simple. This is due largely to the fact that the CUPS AND BALLS combines *misdirection* with the element of *surprise* so that the spectators never know what to expect next.

EFFECT

On the table before the magician are three empty cups and three small colored balls. The performer positions the three balls in a horizontal row and places a cup, mouth down, behind each ball. He then places one of the balls on top of the center cup and stacks the remaining two cups on top of the first, imprisoning the ball between them. Upon lifting the stack of cups as a group, the ball is found to have mysteriously penetrated *through* the center cup and now rests on the table. This baffling process is repeated with the two remaining balls until all three balls have magically gathered beneath the stack of cups. The magician then varies his procedure by causing a single ball to vanish from his hand and appear beneath the center cup on the table.

Next he places a ball beneath each cup. He then mysteriously causes the ball under the center cup to vanish and join the ball under the right-hand cup. From there, it vanishes once again, and reappears with the ball under the left-hand cup. The performer then places the three balls in his pocket — one at a time — only to find that they have once again appeared beneath the cups on the table. This procedure is repeated once more, when suddenly the performer reveals the surprise appearance of three full-size lemons — one beneath each cup.

SECRET AND PREPARATION

(A) You will need to acquire the proper type of cups in order to perform this routine effectively. These cups should nest within each other easily and leave enough space between each cup to permit the concealment of a ball between them. (See Comments and Suggestions.) You will also need four small identical balls of the appropriate size to be used with the cups. The only other props you need are three ordinary lemons (or a lemon, a small potato and an onion, or three small rubber balls, etc.) The primary requirement for these props is that each can fit easily inside one of the cups.

(C) Now turn the entire stack mouth up and drop the three remaining balls into the top cup of the stack. Throughout the presentation, the audience should only be aware of three balls. A primary secret to the entire routine is the hidden "fourth" ball.

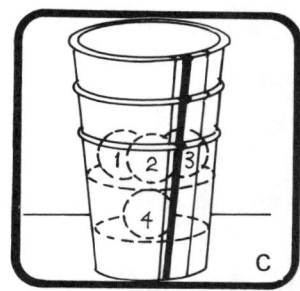

(B) To set up the apparatus for the start of the routine, place one of the cups mouth down on your table and put a ball on top of it. Now nest the other two cups on over the first, concealing the ball between the first and second cups.

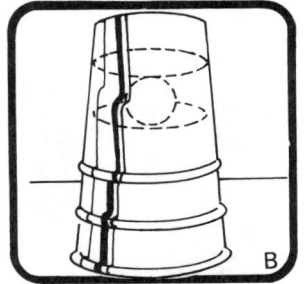

(D) At the start, have the three lemons in your right jacket pocket, and you are ready. The lemons are not used until the final phase of the routine, but it is a good idea to practice with them in position so that you become used to their presence as you practice.

NOTE: TO MAKE CUPS AND BALLS EASY TO LEARN, THE ROUTINE HAS BEEN BROKEN DOWN INTO SEPARATE PHASES. LEARN EACH PHASE BEFORE PROCEEDING TO THE NEXT, AND THEN PRACTICE THE ENTIRE ROUTINE FROM THE START TO FINISH UNTIL EACH PORTION BECOMES SMOOTH AND NATURAL.

METHOD

PHASE 1 — "PENETRATION"

All of the illustrations in this phase are from the audience's viewpoint.

(1) Stand at the table with the spectators across from you. Pick up the cups with your left hand and tip the three balls from the top cup of the stack onto the table. With your right hand arrange the balls in a horizontal row. The stack of nested cups is held in your left hand so that the bottom of the cups slants toward the table and the mouth of the cups tilts slightly up toward you as shown. *This angle is important in order to prevent the audience from seeing into the cups during the performance of the following steps.*

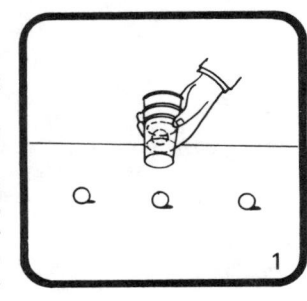

(2) With your right hand, draw the *bottom* cup from the stack downward as shown.

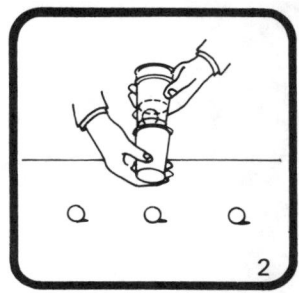

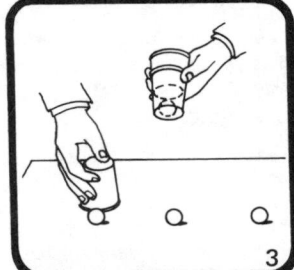

(3) *In one continuous flowing motion,* turn the cup *mouth down* and place it on the table behind the ball at the *right* end of the row.

(9) NOTE: It is important that the placement of the individual cups on the table be executed at the *same exact pace* so as not to attract undue attention to the center cup.

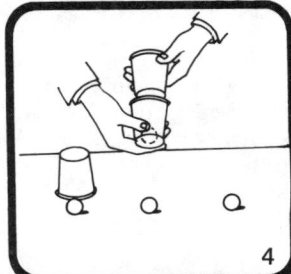

(4) Now remove the *second* cup from the stack in the same manner and . . .

(10) The three cups are now mouth down on the table with the extra ball secretly under the center cup. The three visible balls are positioned in front of the cups as shown.

(5) . . . place it *mouth down* on the table behind the *center* ball.

(11) You are now ready to execute the first trick — the Penetration. Pick up the *right-hand ball* and place it on top of the *center* cup.

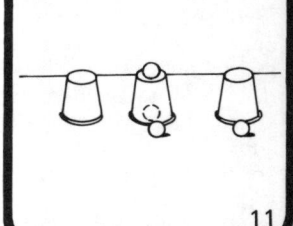

(6) *NOTE: You can now see why the cups must be tilted slightly toward you, since this cup is concealing the fourth "secret" ball. If this step is executed in a smooth, unbroken motion, the secret ball will be secretly carried along inside the cup to the table unnoticed by the spectators.*

(12) Then, lift the *right-hand cup* and nest it over the *center* cup imprisoning the ball between the two cups as shown.

(7) Next grasp the last cup in your right hand and . . .

(13) Now pick up the *left-hand cup* and add it to the stack.

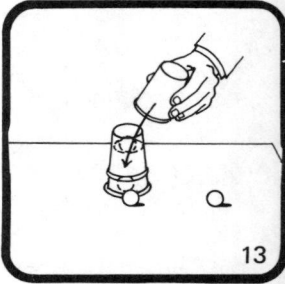

(8) . . . place it *mouth down* behind the ball at the *left* end of the row.

(14) With your right first finger, tap the top cup of the stack and say, "I'll make the first ball penetrate the cup."

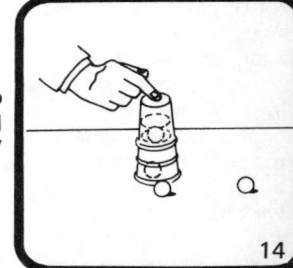

(15) Without hesitation, lift the *entire stack* of cups with your left hand, revealing the ball on the table beneath them. *To the spectators, it will look as if the ball you placed on the center cup "penetrated" the solid bottom of the cup and landed on the table!*

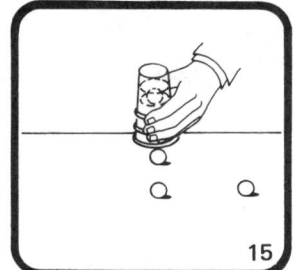

(16) Holding the three cups together in your left hand, turn your left hand palm up so that the cups are positioned just as they were in Step 1.

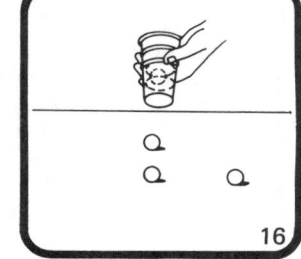

(17) *You are now going to repeat the same series of moves that you used in Steps 2 through 8.* Remove the bottom cup and place it mouth down on the table to your right. Then remove the second cup (which now contains the secret ball) and set it mouth down over the ball that just penetrated the cup in the previous sequence. *Unknown to the audience there are now two balls under this cup instead of one.* Then, place the last cup mouth down behind the left-hand ball. The situation should be as shown here.

(18) You are now ready to execute the *second* penetration. Pick up the ball in front of the center cup and place it on top of the center cup.

(19) Now, nest the other two cups, one at a time, over the center cup — and the ball — just as you did in Steps 12 and 13.

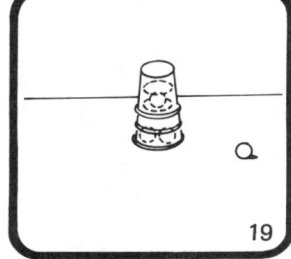

(20) Tap the top cup once with your right finger and say, "Now I'll make the *second* ball penetrate the cup."

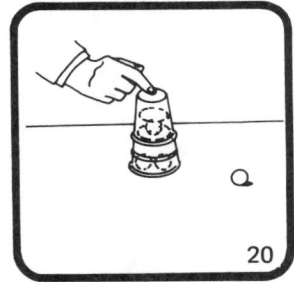

(21) Immediately lift the stack of three cups revealing the two balls beneath them. To the audience, it appears as if the ball on the second cup penetrated through the cup to join the other ball beneath it.

(22) Once again turn your left hand palm up, holding the cups in the basic starting position as in Step 1.

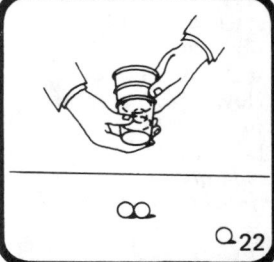

(23) Now repeat the same sequence again (Steps 2 through 8), placing the cups — one at a time — mouth down on the table. *Be sure to place the second cup containing the secret ball over the two balls which have already "penetrated" through the cup.*

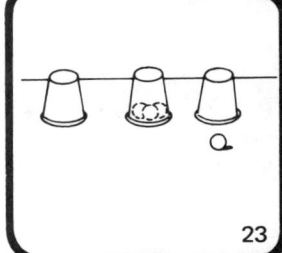

(24) You now repeat the same series of moves (Steps 9 through 15) to "penetrate" the last ball. Pick up the ball and place it on top of the center cup.

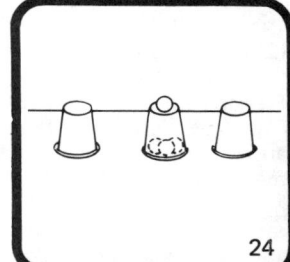

(25) Then, nest the other two cups over the ball and tap the top cup to make the ball "magically penetrate" the cup.

(26) Lift the stack to reveal all three balls on the table, beneath the center cup!

NOTE: BEFORE CONTINUING, BE SURE YOU HAVE MASTERED THE FIRST PHASE OF THE ROUTINE. WHEN YOU CAN PERFORM IT SMOOTHLY AND WITH CONFIDENCE FROM START TO FINISH, THEN YOU ARE READY TO MOVE ON TO THE SECOND PHASE.

PHASE 2 – "INVISIBLE FLIGHT"

All of the illustrations in Phase 2 are from the audience's viewpoint!

(27) With the left hand holding the stack of cups in the basic starting position, arrange the three balls on the table in a horizontal row before you. Now place the three cups, one at a time, mouth down behind the three balls as shown here. *The secret ball will once again be carried along, unnoticed, inside the center cup to the table.*

(28) With your right hand, pick up the ball in front of the center cup and display it briefly on your right fingers in readiness for the Finger Palm Vanish.

(29) Now apparently transfer the ball to your left hand. Really execute the Finger Palm Vanish as described in the Coin Section (See Page 187.) The audience will believe that you have merely placed the ball into your left hand. *Actually, the ball is secretly retained in the fingers of your right hand.*

(30) Casually lower your right hand and make a tossing motion with your left hand as if to throw the ball invisibly from your left fist into the center cup.

(31) With your left hand, lift the center cup and roll the ball slightly forward to reveal its "magical" arrival.

(32) Then, set the center cup on the table, mouth down, behind the center ball. *This is a very important phase of the routine as it allows you to get the secret ball out of the cups and into your hand where you can use it to execute the next series of "impossibilities" described in Phase Three.*

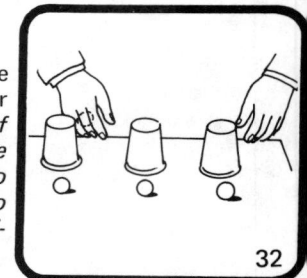

(33) Still holding the secret ball in the Finger Palm position in your right hand, pick up the ball in front of the cup on the right with the tips of your right thumb and fingers as shown.

PHASE 3 – "ANY CUP CALLED FOR"

In Phase 3, the illustrations are both from the audience's and the magician's viewpoint as indicated.

(34) Here is a view of this action from your point of view. Notice how the *visible* ball is held between the thumb and first finger while the *secret* ball is still concealed in the curled fingers. As you pick up the ball, your left hand grasps the right cup near the mouth as shown.

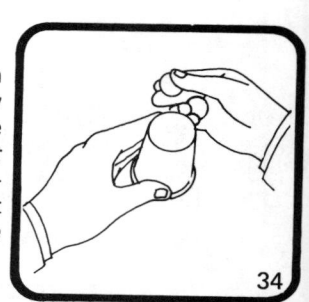

(35) Now, tilt the cup back toward you *leaving the rear edge of the cup resting on the table.* At the same time, allow the visible ball to roll alongside the secret ball in your curled fingers.

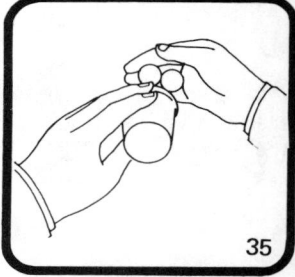

(36) Without hesitation, slip *both balls* well under the front edge of the cup as shown.

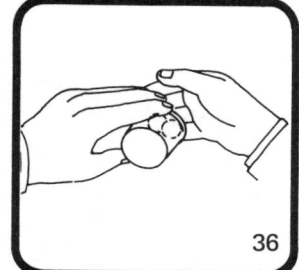

(42) As soon as your fingers are well beneath the cup, remove your thumb from the ball and hold the ball with your right fingers as shown. Withdraw your hand secretly carrying the ball along. *As you withdraw your hand from beneath the cup, be sure to tilt the back of your hand toward the audience so no one will see that you still hold the ball in your fingers instead of leaving it under the cup.*

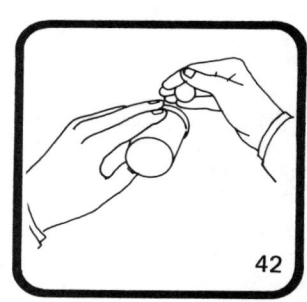

(37) Here is a view of this action from the spectators' point of view. *The audience will believe that you are placing only one ball under the cup.*

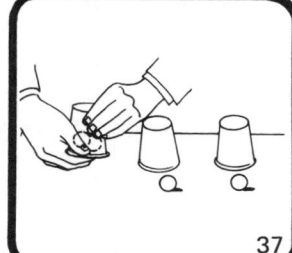

(43) Immediately lower the front edge of the cup to the table as you remove your fingers — and the ball — from beneath the cup. *The audience believes that you merely placed the second ball under the center cup.*

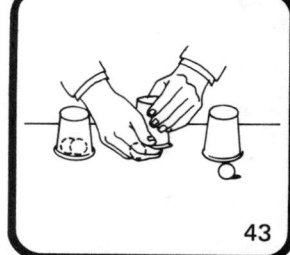

(38) As you hold the balls under the cup, tilt the cup down and withdraw your fingers *leaving both balls beneath the cup.*

(44) Without hesitation, move your right hand (still concealing the ball) to the last visible ball which you pick up with your right thumb and fingers (just as you did in Step 33) as your left hand grasps the cup.

(39) Without pausing, pick up the ball in front of the center cup with the tips of your right thumb and fingers, just as you did the first ball in Step 33. At the same time, grasp the center cup in position to apparently repeat the previous series of moves as when you placed the ball(s) under the right cup.

(45) You are now going to repeat Steps 34 through 38 with the third cup. With your left hand, tip the third cup back on its edge and place *both balls* under the cup, "as one," as shown in this illustration from your point of view.

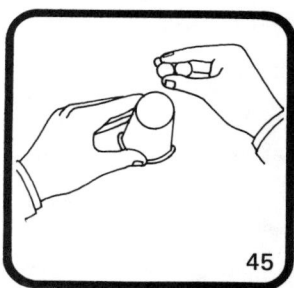

(40) Here is the situation as seen from your point of view. Notice how the ball is held against the second and third fingers with your thumb.

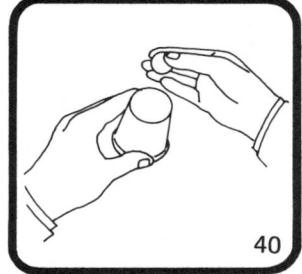

(46) Here is the same action as seen from the audience point of view. *To the spectators, it should appear as if you are merely placing a single ball under the third cup, just as you did with the other cups.*

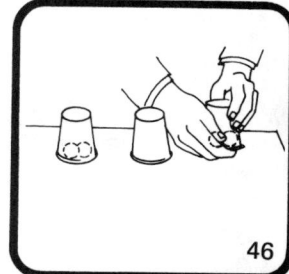

(41) Now, tip the center cup back on its edge and move your right fingers and the ball under the front edge of the cup as shown.

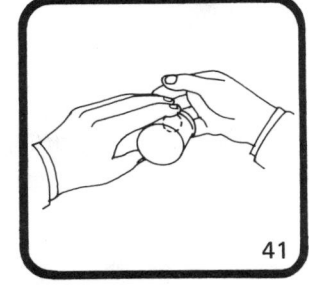

(47) Now, lower the front edge of the cup allowing it to drag *both balls* from your fingers as you withdraw your hand.

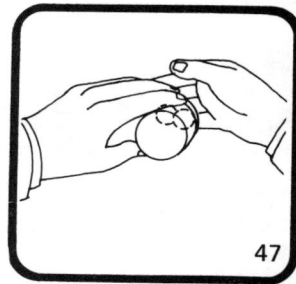

(48) As soon as your fingers clear the front edge of the cup, set the mouth of the cup down flush with the top of the table.

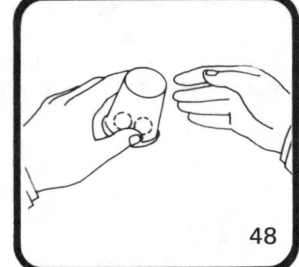

(49) *NOTE: At this point, the audience believes that you have simply placed one ball under each of the three cups. Actually, you have two balls under both end cups and nothing under the center cup.*

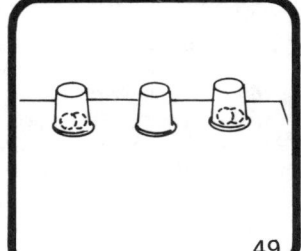

(50) State that you will cause the ball under the *center* cup to vanish and appear beneath *whichever end cup the spectator wishes.* Assuming the spectator chooses the right-hand cup, slowly tip over the center cup allowing your audience to see that the ball which you placed under that cup has vanished. *Leave the center cup on its side on the table as shown.*

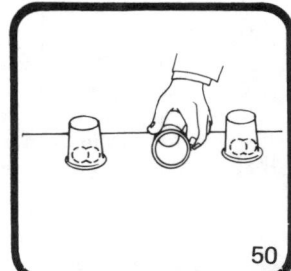

(51) Then, tip over the selected cup (in this case the right-hand cup) to reveal the mysterious arrival of the missing ball, *apparently joining the ball already under that cup.*

(52) With your right hand, pick up one of the two balls and display it at the base of your curled fingers in readiness for the Finger Palm Vanish. As you display the ball, make some comment about how difficult it is to keep track of that particular ball.

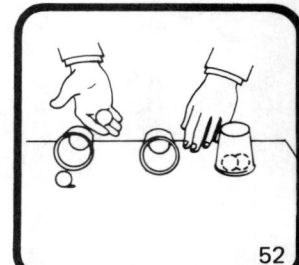

(53) With that, apparently transfer the ball into your left hand, executing the Finger Palm Vanish. *Actually, the ball is secretly retained in your right fingers as shown.*

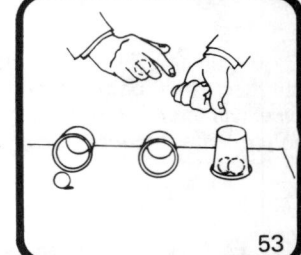

(54) Your left hand (which the spectators believe contains the ball) makes a tossing motion toward the left cup. As you "toss" the ball, open your left hand showing that the ball has vanished. At the same time, your right hand drops casually to your right side, carrying the secret ball with it.

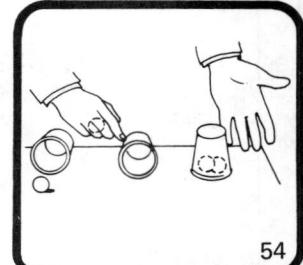

(55) With your empty left hand, tip the left cup over revealing the missing ball to complete the sequence.

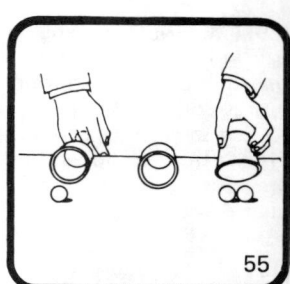

NOTE: AFTER MASTERING THIS PHASE, COMBINE THESE THREE PHASES INTO A SMOOTH ROUTINE. WHEN YOU HAVE ACCOMPLISHED THIS AND FEEL CONFIDENT OF ALL OF THE MOVES, YOU WILL BE READY TO LEARN PHASE FOUR.

PHASE 4 — "THE REPEAT PRODUCTION"

In Phase 4, all of the illustrations are from the audience's viewpoint.

(56) After the conclusion of Phase 3, rearrange the three visible balls in a horizontal row and place one cup mouth down over each ball as shown. *The secret ball is still concealed in the curled fingers of your right hand.*

(57) With your *left* hand, lift the cup on the *right.*

(58) Without pausing, turn the cup *mouth up* and transfer it to your *right* hand which contains the secret ball.

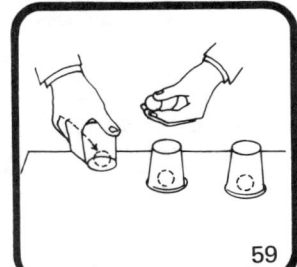

(59) Without hesitation, pick up the ball that was under the cup with your left fingers. *At the same time, release your grip on the palmed ball in your right hand and allow it to roll secretly into the cup as shown.*

(60) In a smooth, unbroken motion with your right hand, turn the cup mouth down and place it on the table in its former position. If the action of setting the cup down is done properly, *the ball will remain hidden in the cup as the mouth of the cup comes to rest on the table.*

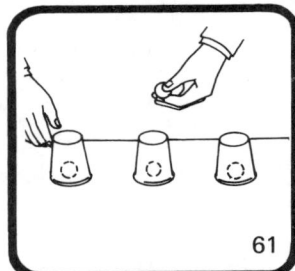

(61) At this point, you have apparently lifted the right-hand cup, picked up the ball that was under it, and replaced the cup on the table. *Really you have secretly "loaded" the fourth ball into the cup.*

(62) Once the cup is on the table, openly transfer the ball from your left hand to your right hand.

(63) Now place your right hand into your coat pocket, apparently leaving the ball there. *Actually, you secretly retain the ball in the Finger Palm position and remove your right hand from your pocket with the ball concealed in your right fingers.*

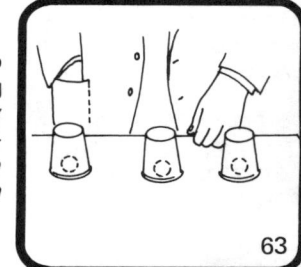

(64) NOTE: Steps 57 through 63 are the key moves in Phase 4. *The audience will be convinced that the first cup is empty and the ball is now in your pocket.*

(65) Now, repeat this same sequence of moves (Steps 57 through 63) with the *center* cup, secretly loading the extra ball into the cup as you apparently place the visible ball in your pocket.

(66) Once again repeat the same sequence (Steps 57 through 63) with the last (left) cup *up to the point where your hand is in your coat pocket apparently leaving the last ball there.*

(67) The situation at this point should look as shown in this illustration. *Unknown to the audience, there is one ball under each cup and the extra ball is in your coat pocket with the three lemons.*

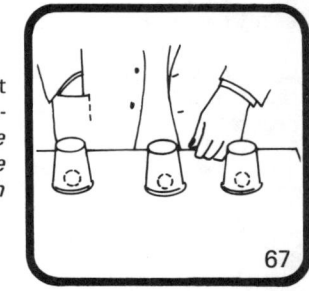

The audience thinks you have placed all three balls, one at a time, in your right coat pocket. Really, you have secretly loaded the balls back under the three cups. If you wished, you could stop now by merely revealing the "return" of the three balls. However, you don't make that revelation quite yet, as you continue to Phase Five.

NOTE: THE NEXT SERIES OF MOVES IS BASED ON THE SAME SECRET "LOADING" PROCESS WHICH YOU HAVE JUST LEARNED. PRACTICE THEM THOROUGHLY UNTIL YOU CAN LOAD EACH CUP QUICKLY AND SMOOTHLY WITHOUT UNDUE ATTENTION TO YOUR RIGHT HAND.

PHASE 5 — "THE LEMON SURPRISE"

(68) When your right hand is in your pocket in Step 67, *release* the ball and *grasp* one of the three lemons, curling your fingers around it as far as possible. Now, remove your hand from your pocket, secretly holding the lemon, and let your hand fall casually to your side. *Be sure to use a lemon (or any other suitable small object) which can be totally concealed from view as you hold it in your hand as shown.*

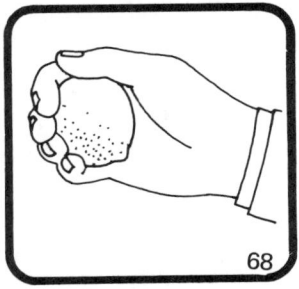

(69) As your right hand secretly holds the lemon, grasp the cup on the *right* with your *left* hand in readiness to lift it from the table. Then, as you lift the cup to reveal the ball beneath it, bring your right hand up from your side, making sure to keep the back of your hand to the audience. *The surprise appearance of the ball under this cup will draw the eyes of the audience to the table.*

(70) In the same motion, your left hand *turns the cup mouth upward* and places it into your right hand as shown here from your viewpoint. Be sure the fingers and the back of your right hand completely cover the top of the cup so that the audience cannot see *between* your hand and the mouth of the cup.

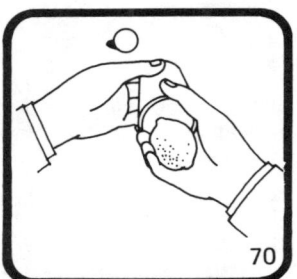

(71) This shows the action from the spectators' point of view. *IT IS VERY IMPORTANT THAT YOU PRACTICE THESE CRITICAL MOVES BEFORE A MIRROR IN ORDER TO OBSERVE THE AUDIENCE'S VIEW OF THE PRESENTATION AS WELL AS YOUR OWN.*

(72) *As soon as you transfer the cup to your right hand, move your left hand to the table and pick up the now visible ball. At the same time, allow the lemon to drop unseen into the cup.*

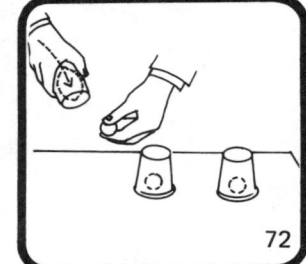

(73) From your point of view, this "loading" action looks like this. *Be sure to keep the mouth of the cup tilted toward you during this procedure.*

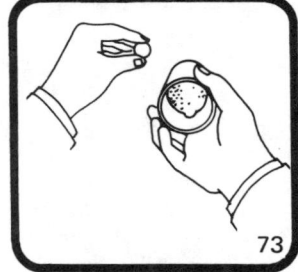

(74) As you lift the ball from the table with your left hand, "swing" the cup mouth down and place it on the table with your right hand as shown here. The important point here is to execute this movement *smoothly* and *quickly,* keeping the lemon well within the cup and out of sight of the audience.

(75) Now, openly transfer the ball from your left hand to your right hand and place it in your right coat pocket. While your hand is in the pocket, *grasp another lemon* in readiness to "load" the next cup.

(76) Now, repeat the exact same sequence (Steps 68 through 75) with the center cup. Just go back to Step 68 and repeat all of the steps through Step 75 with the second cup, *ending with a lemon secretly loaded under the cup* and your right hand in your pocket grasping the third lemon.

(77) Now repeat Steps 68 through 75 with the third (left) cup, *ending with a lemon secretly loaded under it as well.*

(78) When the last ball is placed in your pocket, leave it there and remove your empty right hand. The three mouth-down cups now each conceal a lemon beneath them. *The audience believes that you merely placed the three balls back into your pocket and that the cups are now empty.*

(79) To bring the routine to its startling and spectacular conclusion, ask a spectator if he thinks there is a ball under *any* of the cups. No matter what his answer, lift the cup he points to, *revealing the lemon beneath it!* The appearance of the first lemon will catch your spectators completely off guard.

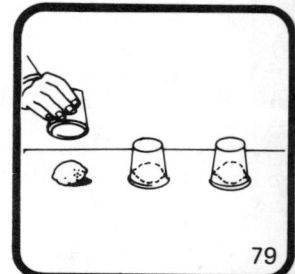

(80) Then, without hesitation, quickly lift the other two cups, one at a time, *revealing the other two lemons.*

COMMENTS AND SUGGESTIONS

The CUPS AND BALLS is probably the oldest and certainly one of the most popular tricks in magic. The necessary props (three cups and four balls) may be purchased at any good magic supply company. For practice purposes, and even for your first performances, a very practical set of "cups" may be made from paper cups. The heavy paper kind are best — the type used for coffee or other hot beverages. They are strong, usually have a slightly recessed bottom, and often have "fold out" handles, which you leave "folded in." The cups can be decorated by painting them an attractive color if you wish.

The balls of a professional set may be made of cork, hard rubber, or often are a knitted or crocheted cover over a cork ball. You may also make your first set of these as well. Balls made from sponge rubber are excellent for practice. They are quite easy to make and equally easy to handle during the presentation.

Though the basic moves are relatively simple, they should be practiced until they become almost automatic in order to blend into a convincing routine. Any hesitation on your part may detract from the effect, as the whole purpose is to keep just enough ahead of the spectator so that he is constantly wondering what will happen next. In placing the balls beneath the cups, or pretending to do so, the moves must be *natural* and *identical* to one another. Once your actions become automatic, the vital moves will begin to feel more casual and less conspicuous and therefore less likely to arouse suspicion. Another reason for continued practice is that of gaining self-confidence. When first performing the CUPS AND BALLS, you yourself may wonder just why the routine deceives people. This is particularly true when you "load" the lemons at the finish. Having watched the small balls jump from cup to cup, spectators become so caught up with the action of the balls on the table they are never ready for the unexpected appearance of the lemons.

The CUPS AND BALLS is especially suited for performance when seated at a table but, it can be worked just as well when standing at a table. Any points of individuality that you may add to the routine will most likely prove helpful. Some performers like to vary it by using either hand to turn over a cup, even though the hand may have a ball palmed at the time. Just think of the CUPS AND BALLS as *your* trick, to be done the way you like it most. Once you have mastered the CUPS AND BALLS, you will be able to present one of the finest and most respected effects in the Art of Magic.

MAGICAL ILLUSIONS

★ ★ ★

In magical terms, an "illusion" is any trick or effect involving a human being, most notably an appearance, vanish or transformation. The term has been extended to include large animals and sizeable objects as well, while many unique effects, such as levitation, where a girl is floated in mid-air, or a "spook" cabinet, in which ghostly phenomena occur, also fall into this category. Formerly such effects were called "stage illusions," but today, some are presented in night clubs and outdoor shows or under almost any circumstances, hence "Magical Illusions" is a better way to define them.

From your standpoint, as a magician, the introduction of illusions can always be considered if they are in keeping with your act or suited to the circumstances under which you perform. If your specialty is impromptu magic, you naturally can't jump into illusions as part of your regular act. But an impromptu worker who is going to a large party, or putting on a children's show will often take alone some showy tricks, such as a box for the production of colorful silk handkerchiefs or the vanish of a rabbit.

Once such a step is taken, it can lead to more, and when audiences like tricks with small or middle-sized apparatus, it is a foregone conclusion that they will like illusions as well. If you can set up your act to produce an assistant as an opening number or early in the show, you may find it highly effective. If working on a platform or a stage where you have the benefit of a curtain, you can "close in" and work in front of the curtain with smaller magic. In the meantime, your assistant—or assistants—can be setting up your next illusion.

Two factors are important when considering the inclusion of illusions in a show: One is expense; the other, portability. It is unwise to spend times as well as money building illusions unless you feel sure you can use them often enough to make it worthwhile. Similarly, it is a mistake to make an act too big for the places you expect to play, or to run up extra costs for transporting you equipment. Such points have been considered in designing the illusions that appear in this section. All are inexpensive to construct and light to carry, so, if you plan to perform before large audiences, you can't go wrong on either count!

THE ARABIAN TENT ILLUSION
"GEN" GRANT

This is a very effective illusion which, once again, comes from the mind of that outstanding magical inventor, Gen. Grant.

EFFECT

The magician calls the audience's attention to a stack of heavy cardboard sheets. The performer displays each part and begins to fit them together one at a time. The spectators soon realize that the magician is building a small tent. With the four walls standing intact, the performer positions the roof, which completes the structure. Almost instantly, the magician lifts the roof *revealing the magical appearance of a lovely young lady from within the tent!*

SECRET AND PREPARATION

A very inexpensive and practical way to build this illusion is out of heavy cardboard. If you decide, after presenting the effect, to incorporate the illusion as a permanent part of your show, you can rebuild the equipment using wooden frames made of 1" x 2" pine covered with colorful lightweight canvas.

(A) If you plan to use cardboard as your building material, it must be strong and sturdy. You can buy *new* cardboard at wholesale paper supply houses or from companies that manufacture large cardboard cartons. A local printer is an excellent person to help you find a source of supply for for the cardboard sheets you will need. Also, moving and storage companies usually have large cardboard boxes for sale. On the other hand, you may wish to build your first illusion from materials that cost little or nothing. In this case, obtain a large cardboard box or shipping carton such as the kind in which stoves, refrigerators, furniture, and other large items are shipped.

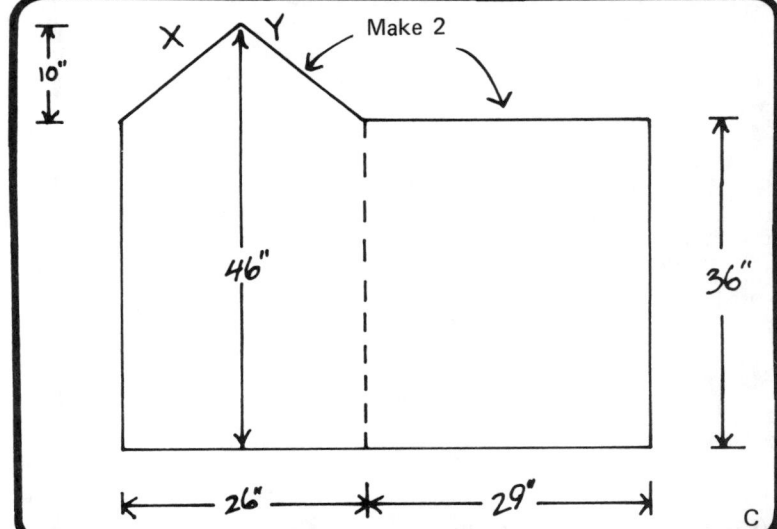

(B) The only other items you will need for this illusion are some strong paper or cloth tape with which to make the "hinges" that hold the various parts together and, if you wish, some paint and brushes to decorate the final prop.

(C) After you have obtained your materials, from the cardboard cut out *two* identical pieces as shown here. If your cardboard is not exactly the dimensions shown here, don't worry. The parts just need to be large enough to hide your assistant as you perform the routine as outlined under *METHOD.*

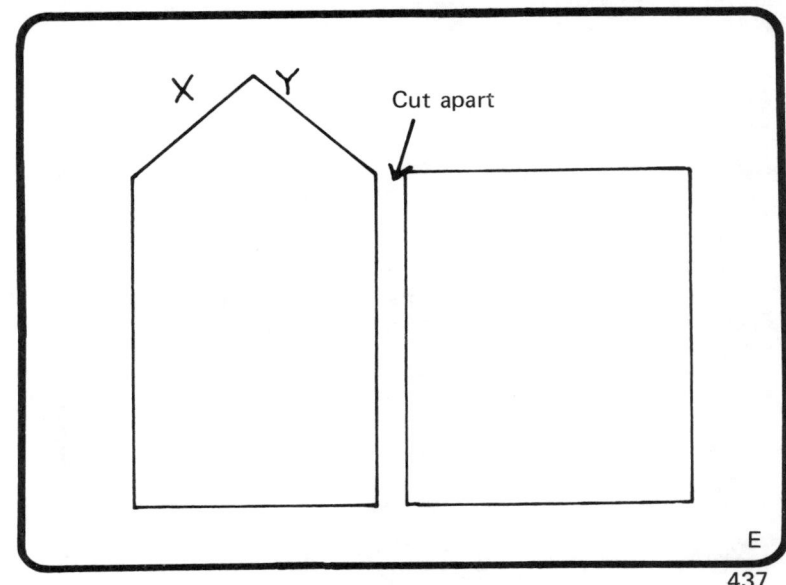

(D) Fold the two parts where indicated by the dotted line in Figure C.

(E) If you find that the board is too stiff to make a clean fold, it may be necessary to cut the piece in two as shown in Figure E . . .

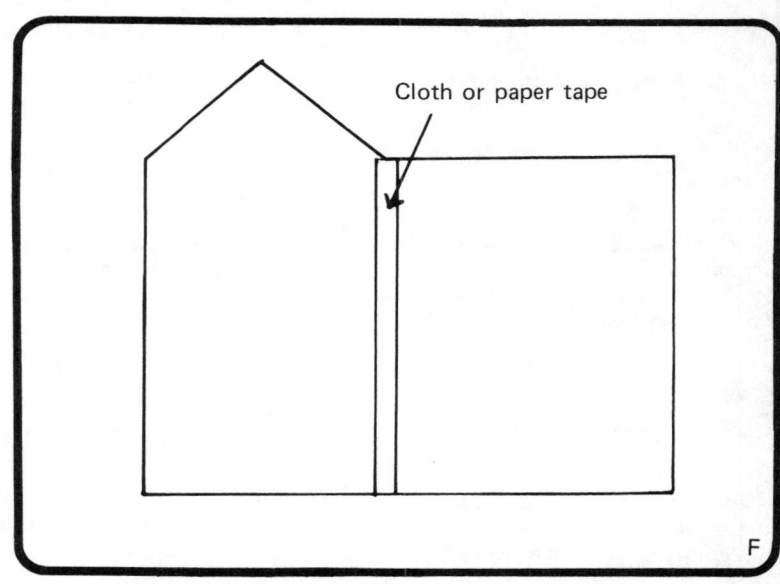

(F) ... and then "hinge" them back together with a wide band of paper or cloth tape. When you have them completed, these parts make up the four *walls* of your tent.

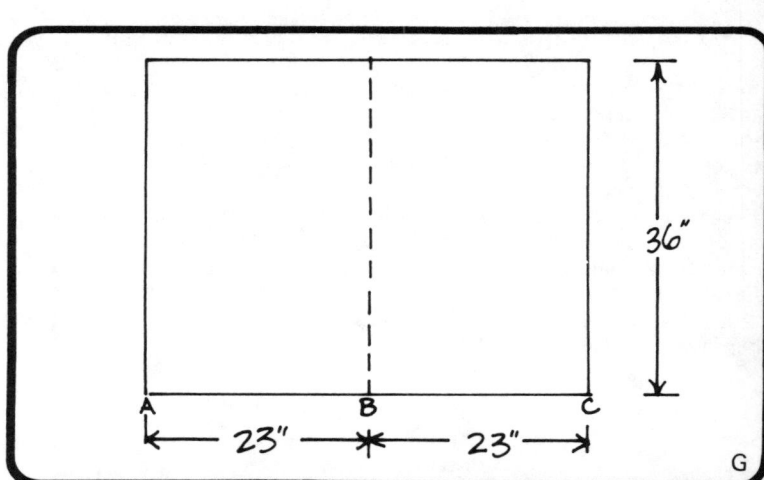

(G) Next cut out one piece of board as shown here. This is the *roof* of the tent. It must also be folded as indicated by the dotted line. If necessary, cut and hinge the two parts with tape as suggested in Steps E and F.

(H) *NOTE: Be sure that the two sides of the roof (A to B and B to C) are the same size and that they are each approximately 2" longer than the top of the tent's walls (X and Y) on which the roof will rest after you have assembled the tent.*

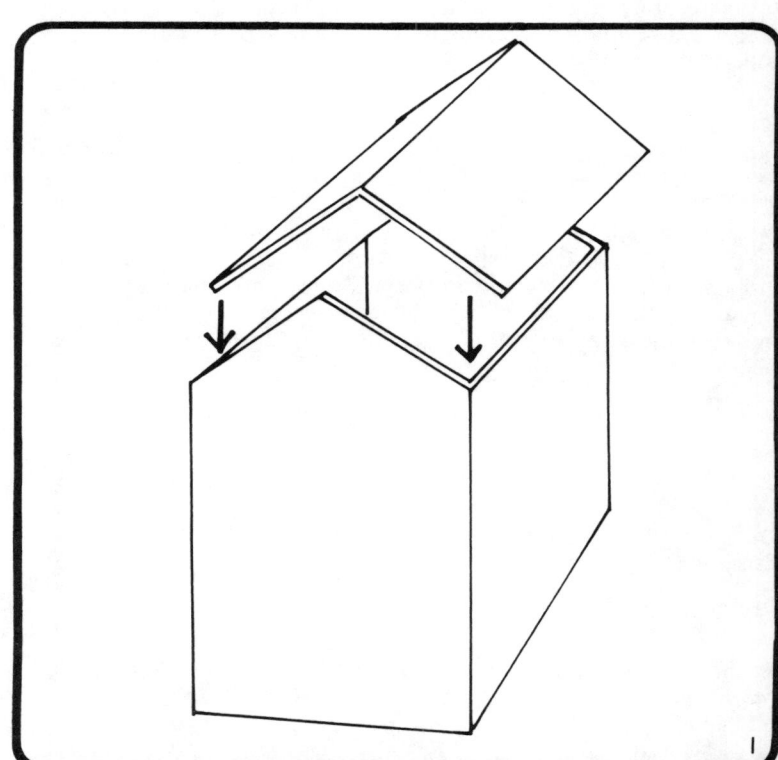

(I) Check to see that all parts fit well to make up the completed tent. Then decorate the tent to fit the patter theme that you will use for the trick (Circus Tent, Haunted House, Doll House etc.).

(J) *NOTE: This type of cardboard will take paint very well so don't hesitate to use it. Any slight warping that may occur can be cured by bending the part in the opposite direction to the warp. However, if you paint both sides of the board, the possibility of warping is minimized. You can also use "contact paper" or colored paper to decorate this illusion.*

(K) After your construction and decoration are completed, stand the roof on end like a two-fold screen. Fold the two side pieces flat and lean them against the left side of the roof as shown. The girl must be secretly positioned behind the roof section as illustrated by the circle in the "overhead" view shown in Figure K.

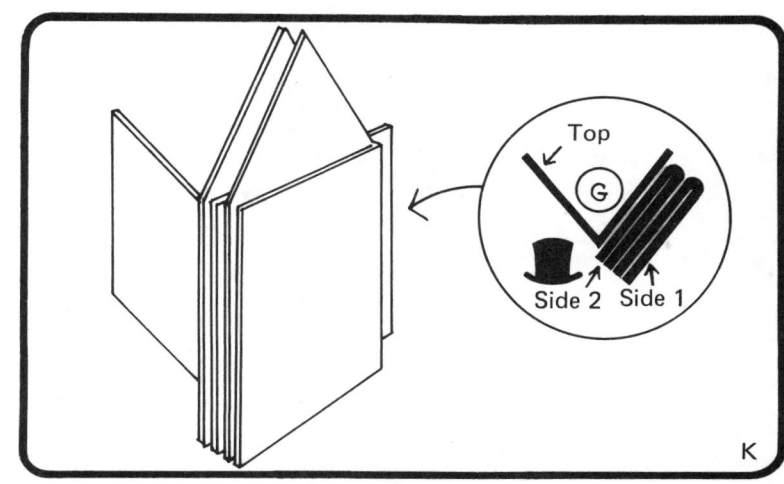

NOTE: IN THESE PICTURES, AND IN ALL THOSE THAT FOLLOW, THE LOCATION OF THE MAGICIAN IS INDICATED BY THE TOP HAT AND YOUR BEAUTIFUL GIRL ASSISTANT BY THE LETTER "G."

METHOD

(1) After the curtain opens, explain that you are going to do a little "Magical Construction." Take the first folded part (one of the sides of the tent), open it out and allow the spectators to see it on all sides. Position this piece as illustrated in the circular insert picture.

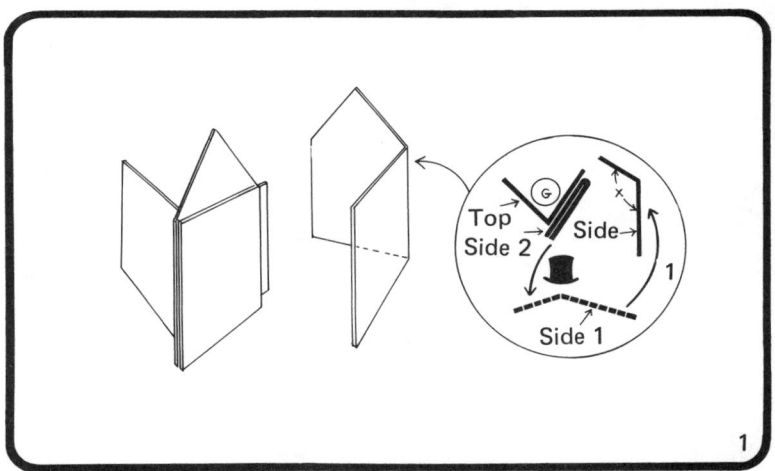

(2) *NOTE: The piece shown by the DASHES in the picture is the SIDE when you are showing it to the audience during the MIDDLE of Step 1. Also, when you study the insert drawing, you will see that the back of this side is left "open" when you place it in position on the floor. There is a very important reason for this, as you will see. Also note that the longer side of Side 2 is pointing directly at the audience.*

(3) *Immediately* pick up the second folded section (the other "side") and display it to the audience. Turn, and position it exactly as illustrated here.

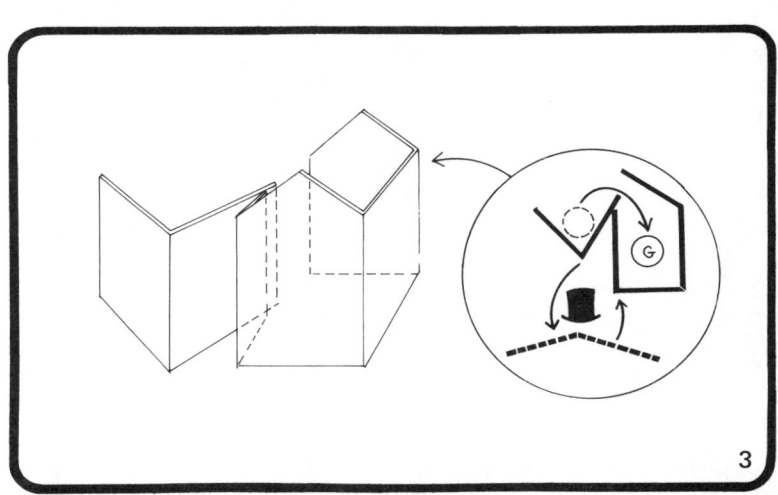

(4) It is at this precise moment that the girl moves secretly from *behind* the roof *into* the "tent" as shown in the insert drawing. This move is masked from the audience by the arrangement of the top and the two sides as you can see from the encircled diagram in Step 3.

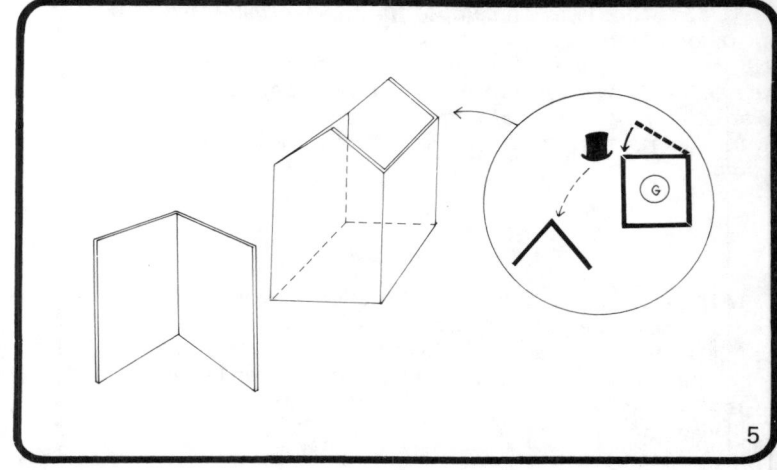

(5) Now quickly walk around the tent circling to your left. As you do, openly close the gap in the rear panel as you pass as if merely straightening the sides. Cross on the right of the tent and then pick up the roof section and display it.

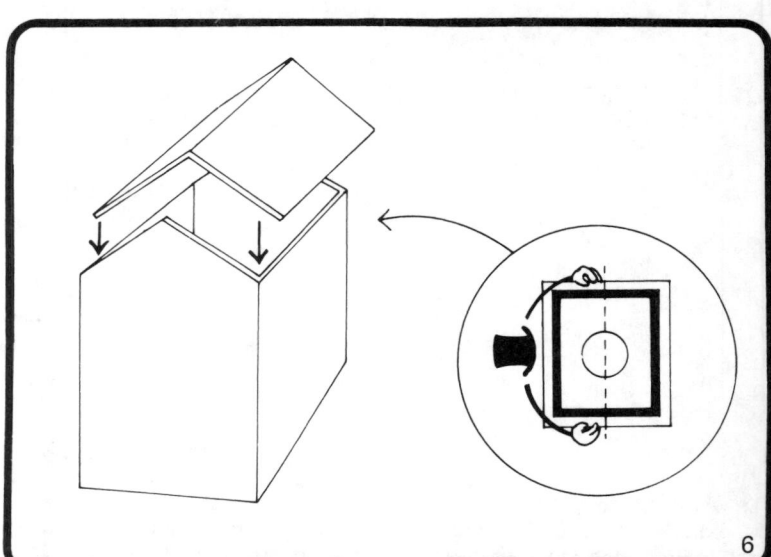

(6) After showing the roof to the audience, set it in place on top of the tent. (Be careful not to move the sides and expose the presence of the girl inside.)

(7) Make a magical gesture toward the tent and then suddenly lift the roof section. At the same time, have the girl stand erect. *She has just magically appeared!*

(8) During the applause, hinge open the front panel and allow the girl to step forward for a bow.

THE HAUNTED HOUSE

MARK WILSON

EFFECT

The magician calls attention to the stacked sections of a miniature house with weird decorations and hooded figures peering from windows with broken shutters. He states that this is a replica of a haunted house that is waiting for a ghost to rent it, so that strange manifestations can take place within its musty walls and beneath its ramshackle roof. The magician decides to play the part of a ghost by putting on a sheet. Thus attired, he sets up the walls and finally picks up the roof and puts it in place. Continuing his ghostly act, he walks around the house, then makes weird gestures and suddenly raises the roof. To the audience's amazement, who pops up but the magician himself! Then, stepping from the house, he grabs the ghost before it can get away. When the sheet is whisked clear, the "ghost" proves to be a beautiful young lady, who takes a bow along with the magician.

SECRET AND PREPARATION

(A) The equipment for this startling effect is the same as used in the ARABIAN TENT ILLUSION which has been previously described. The only change required will be in the decoration of the parts.

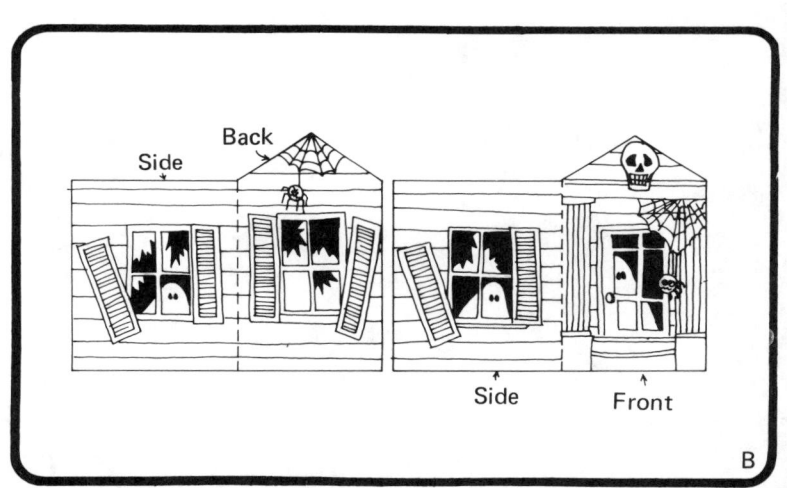

(B) This is an appropriate design for the "walls" of the House.

(C) The roof should be painted to look like worn shingles as shown here.

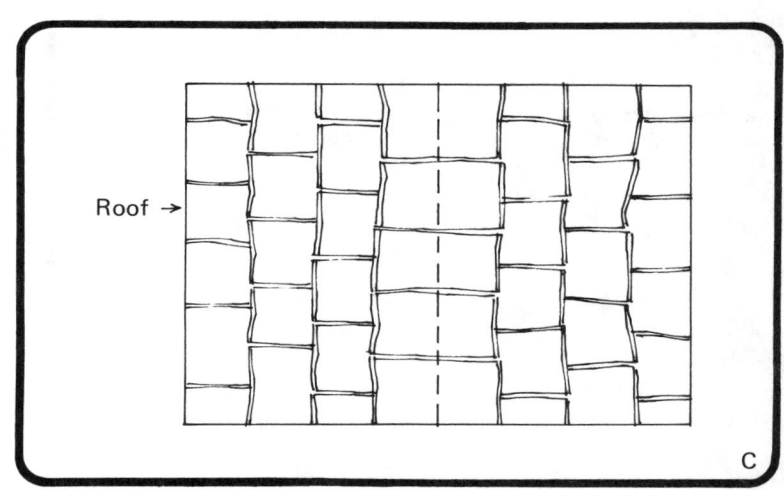

(D) You will need *two identical* white sheets. The size of the sheets is determined by your and the assistant's heights. *Be sure to make the ghost costumes long enough to touch the stage floor so that your feet do not show.* The eye holes should be cut as shown. You should also pin the sides of the sheets together and sew the material so that it forms make-shift "sleeves" as well.

(E) The parts of the Ghost House should be arranged exactly the same as in the ARABIAN TENT ILLUSION at the start. The girl should be wearing her "ghost" sheet and be positioned behind the roof as before. Now drape the duplicate sheet over your arm and make your entrance.

NOTE: WE WILL ASSUME THAT YOU ARE FAMILIAR WITH THE METHODS USED TO PRODUCE THE GIRL IN THE ARABIAN TENT ILLUSION SO THE FOLLOWING WILL EXPLAIN ONLY THIS STARTLING VARIATION.

METHOD

(1) Call attention to the vertical stack of parts on stage. Unfold the sheet and cover yourself completely. Make sure the eye holes line up properly. Then lift the first section (the back and left side of the House) from the stack as in Step 1 of the Tent.

(2) Now display and position the second side (the front and right side of the House) just as in Step 2.

(3) The illustration here gives you a back view of the situation at this point in the presentation.

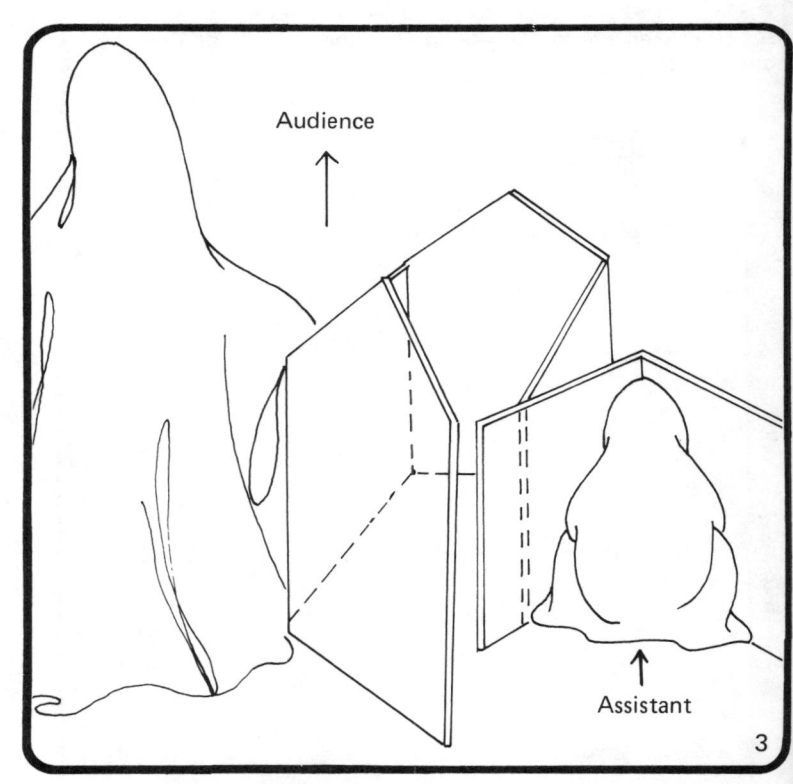

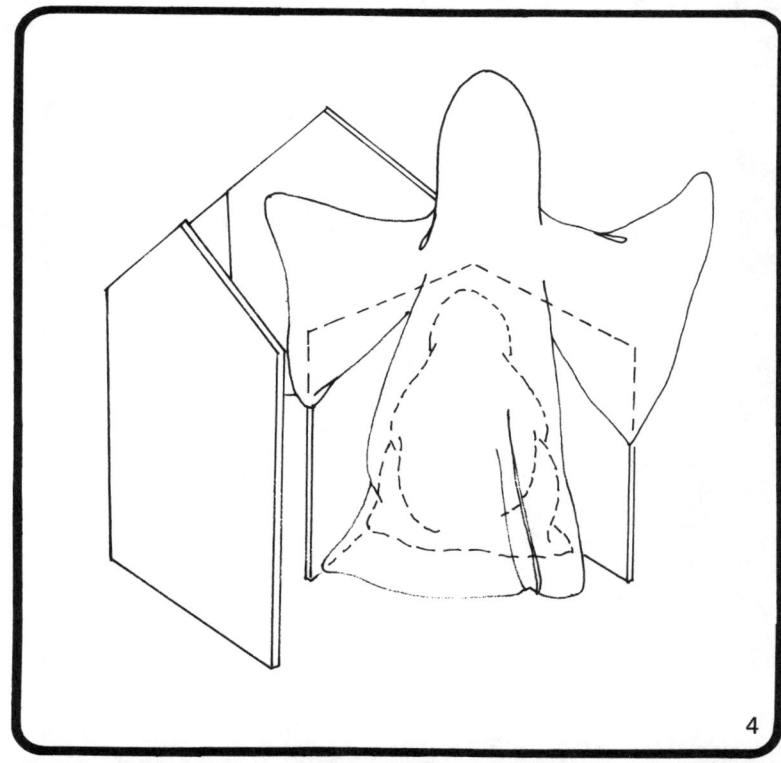

(4) After the second side is in place, circle the illusion to your left and end up standing *directly behind the concealed girl assistant.*

(5) *NOTE: It is very important at this point in the illusion that you don't look down and give away the presence of the girl to the audience. YOU ARE ABOUT TO MAKE THE MOST CRITICAL MOVE IN THIS PRESENTA-TION — and any hesitation will mean failure.*

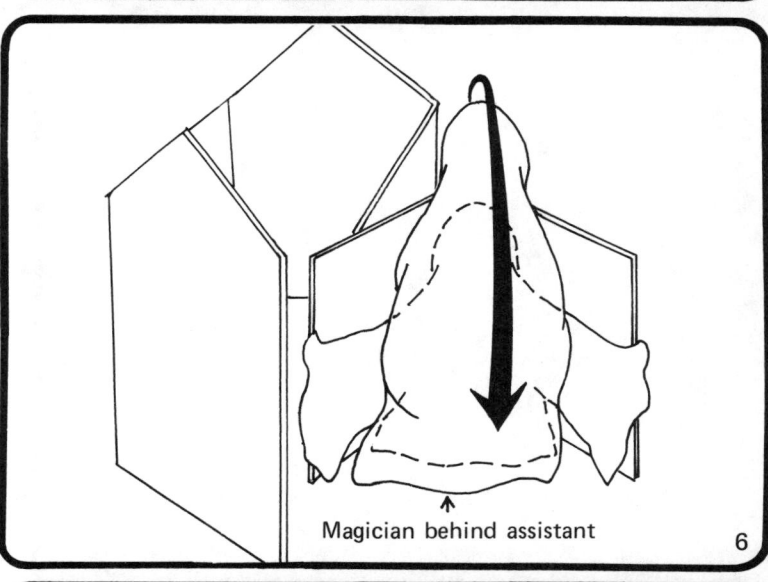

Magician behind assistant

(6) Stoop down behind your assistant *and* the folded roof as shown. Keep your arms to your sides, for as soon as you are out of sight, *the girl assistant grasps the outer edges of the roof as illustrated.* The audience will believe that these are *your hands,* since they are completely unaware of the concealed "duplicate" ghost.

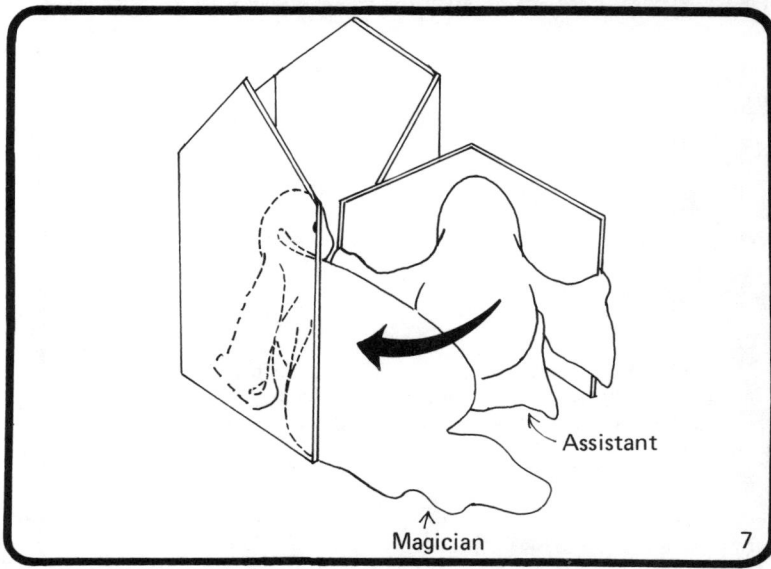

Assistant

Magician

(7) Quickly crawl into the "House" as shown here. (This is the same secret move the girl made in the "Tent.")

(8) *As soon as you are inside the House, your assistant immediately stands up, picking up the roof as shown here.*

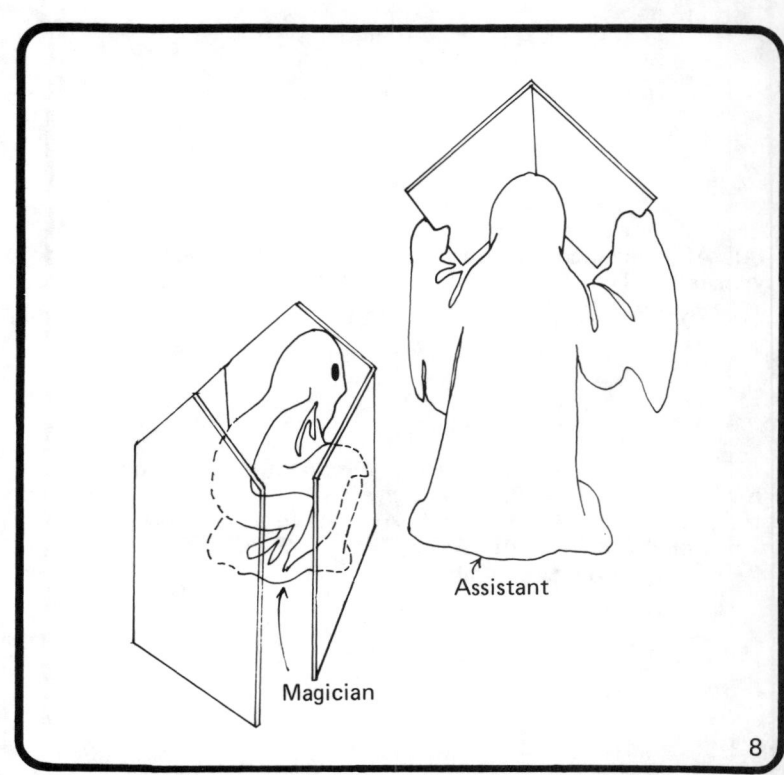

(9) *NOTE: YOU AND THE GIRL MUST PRACTICE THIS MANEUVER UNTIL IT BLENDS INTO <u>ONE FLOWING MOTION</u>. THIS MOVE IS SO DECEPTIVE THAT, IF DONE CORRECTLY, THE AUDIENCE WILL BELIEVE THAT <u>YOU NEVER LEFT THEIR SIGHT</u>.*

(10) The ghost (really the girl) now displays the roof *as if she were you.*

(11) She then sets the roof back down on the floor (slightly away from the House). Circling to her left, she closes the rear gap in the back wall of the House.

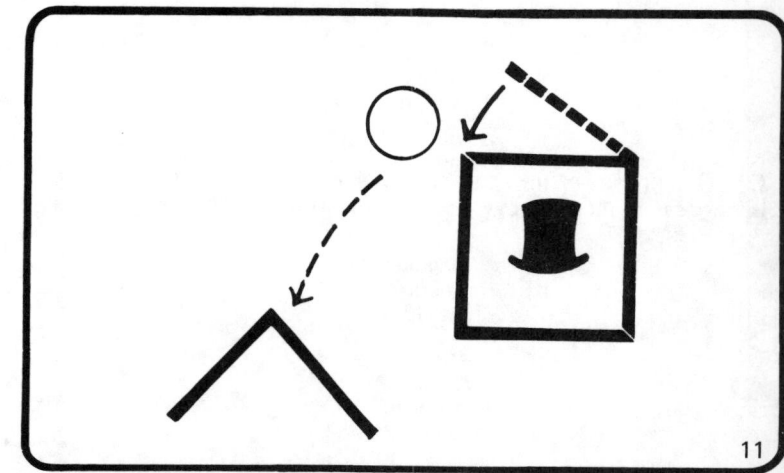

(12)   Next she places the roof into position on the House.

(13)   *NOTE: Steps 10, 11, and 12 of this routine are a slightly different sequence from their counterpart in the "Tent" routine.*

(14)   Making one more circle around the "Haunted Mansion," she prepares to lift the roof. During the time it takes her to complete this circle, *you carefully remove your ghost costume.* (Don't hit the sides of the House.)

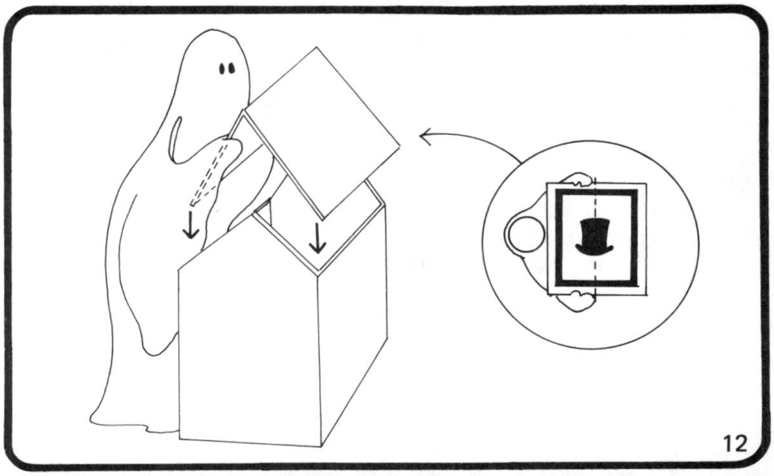

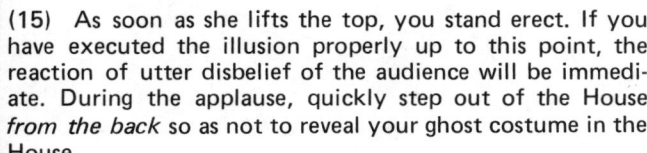

12

(15)   As soon as she lifts the top, you stand erect. If you have executed the illusion properly up to this point, the reaction of utter disbelief of the audience will be immediate. During the applause, quickly step out of the House *from the back* so as not to reveal your ghost costume in the House.

15

(16)   Now unveil the girl! This *second* surprise will boost the reaction so that you may both take the bows.

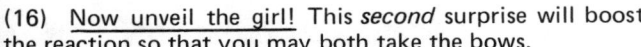

16

COMMENTS AND SUGGESTIONS

Much depends on how the magician plays his part as the "ghost" when presenting this striking illusion. By having the sheet handy at the start, he can put it on immediately and begin a weird pantomime. But another way is to have the sheet hanging over the second wall, so the magician can put the first side of the House in position *before* he comes to the sheet and decides to play the "ghost."

Also, the girl must copy the magician's gestures *exactly,* once she appears in his place, so the audience will be held in suspense until the climax. By taking her time in parading around the assembled House, she can give the magician ample opportunity to dispose of his ghost costume. There is definitely no need to hurry, for, if spectators suspect that somebody is due to appear from the House, the one person they *won't* expect is the *magician* — so the longer the suspense, the stronger the climax.

THE VICTORY CARTONS ILLUSION

"GEN" GRANT

For a quick and surprising way to produce a girl from nowhere, this is ideal, both from the standpoint of its surprising magical effect, its portability, and its inexpensive cost. In addition, it can be set up in a matter of moments and worked on any stage or platform where your audience is located in front, making it a valuable feature for your magical program.

EFFECT

The magician displays two large cardboard boxes. Both boxes are folded flat and held upright by the magician's assistant. The tops and bottoms of the boxes have been removed so that actually the boxes are rectangular tubes which fold along their seams. The magician takes the first box from his assistant and opens it out into a square. Obviously, nothing of any size could be concealed inside since the box has been folded "flat" from the beginning. The second box is then also opened. To prove even more convincingly that it too is completely empty, the magician and his assistant show the audience a clear view through the ends of the box. The second box, being slightly larger than the other, is then placed over the first box. The two "nested" boxes are now revolved to show the audience all sides. It seems impossible that anything could be concealed within the cardboard containers. Yet, upon the magician's command, a beautiful young lady makes her appearance from within the boxes!

SECRET AND PREPARATION

(A) All you need are two large cardboard boxes of the size shown and the proper amount of rehearsal with your assistants. As you can see from the dimensions on the illustration, one of the boxes must be slightly larger so that one will fit over the other box. We will call the inner or smaller box No. 1 and the larger box No. 2.

From corrugated paperboard or any lightweight material, make two boxes as described. The sides are held together with heavy paper or cloth tape. The boxes are both 36 inches high. The smaller box is 28 inches square, and the larger 30 inches as shown. Neither box has a top or bottom — so actually they are large rectangular tubes. The smaller box has an opening cut in one side. The opening is 24 inches high by 20 inches wide with a 3-inch "lip!" around the sides and bottom and a 9-inch lip at the top. The audience is *never aware* of this opening. The boxes must fold "flat" as shown.

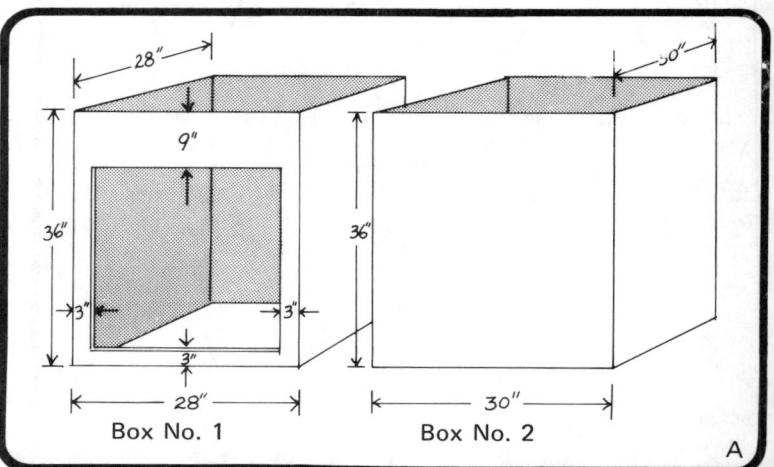

Box No. 1   Box No. 2

METHOD

(1) Fold both boxes flat and stand them on end with the prepared box (No. 1) nearest the audience. The "secret" opening in Box No. 1 must face to the rear. Box No. 2 is directly behind it. Your assistant should stand at the right side of the cartons supporting them in their vertical position. Step 1 shows the "backstage" view with the proper position of the two containers at the start. Unknown to the audience, the girl is crouched behind the two cartons as shown.

1

(2) To begin the presentation, call attention to the two flattened containers. Lift the front box (No. 1) and open it out into a square as shown. *Be sure to keep the "secret" opening to the back so that the audience cannot see it.*

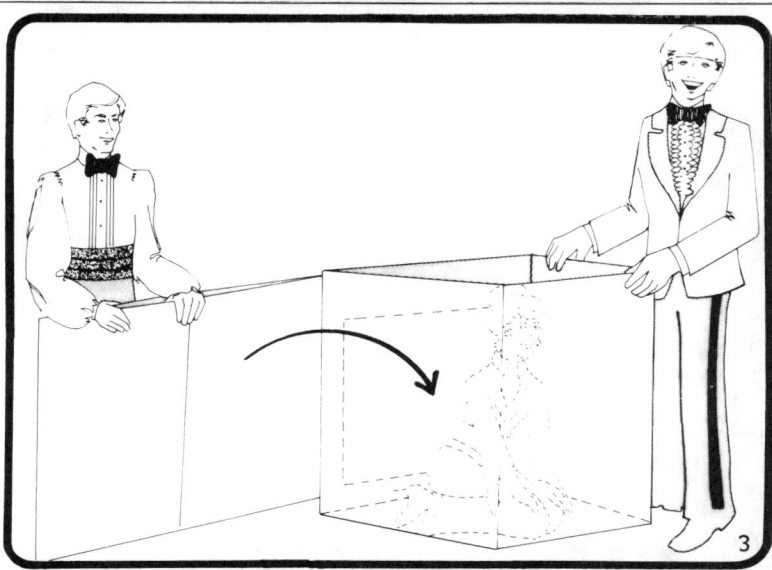

(3) Place the box (No. 1) in the position illustrated, *so that it overlaps the left edge of the other box (No. 2)* which is still held by your assistant. As soon as Box No. 1 is open and on the floor, *the girl crawls from behind the other, still "flat" box (No. 2) through the "secret" opening into the "open" Box No. 1.* Because the boxes overlap, the movement of the girl from behind the closed box (No. 2) into the open box (No. 1) will not be seen by the audience. Your position at the left of the open box (No. 1) will also help to hide the girl's movement from any spectators watching from that side. Your assistant's body helps hide the girl's movement from the right side.

(4) After the girl enters the open box (No. 1), your assistant immediately lifts the other box (No. 2) and hands it to you. *This action must be done smoothly — with perfect coordination between you and your assistant.* With the help of your assistant, open Box No. 2 and tilt it on its side — allowing the audience to see completely through the box. Now, slide Box No. 2 over the prepared box (No. 1) which now conceals the girl.

(5) With the aid of your assistant, revolve the nested cartons one complete turn to show the audience all sides of the cardboard containers. Since the outer container conceals the cut out portion of the inner box, everything appears quite normal. *Be sure to keep the bottoms of the boxes on the floor as you turn them so that you do not expose the girl's feet.*

(6) Upon your command, the young lady quickly stands up — apparently having "magically appeared" inside the two empty boxes! You and your assistant now help the young lady out of the box by holding her beneath the arms as she "jumps" out of the box. (See Comments and Suggestions.) Your male assistant can now carry the equipment safely off stage as the audience applauds this startling illusion.

COMMENTS AND SUGGESTIONS

Although the construction and the presentation are comparatively simple, this illusion must be carefully rehearsed until you can perform it in a brisk, straightforward manner. *Coordination* and *timing* on the part of the magician and both of his assistants is the vital factor. Any *hesitation* at the wrong moment may arouse audience suspicion that could otherwise be avoided, and the same applies to too much *haste.* As an example of proper timing, the girl should begin to enter the smaller box (No. 1) while you are adjusting it to its proper position overlapping the other, still flat box (No. 2). In this way, if the girl hits Box No. 1 as she enters through the opening, the motion will be attributed to your handling of the box. The quicker the girl enters the open smaller Box No. 1, the better. Your male assistant can then *immediately* pick up the larger box, with less chance that anyone will guess its real purpose — which was to conceal the girl behind it. You can then slow down the pace while showing the large box (No. 2) *as the real work is now done.* Revolving the boxes is very effective because, when the spectators think back later, they will be sure that each box was shown "clear through" and "all around" at the start.

THE MYSTERY OF THE MAGICAL MUMMY

EFFECT

The performer unfolds an attractive piece of cloth measuring approximately 6 x 8 feet in size. A male assistant, standing to the magician's left picks up the left top corner of the loose material and stretches it tightly between the performer and himself. Upon the magician's command, the assistant "rolls" himself into the cloth and then turns his body so that the material is wrapped tightly around him. The performer walks quickly around the "mummy-like" figure and then grasps the loose end of the cloth. With a broad flourish, the fabric is unrolled from the body within. When the cloth falls free, the audience is surprised to see a beautiful young lady standing in place of the male assistant!

SECRET AND PREPARATION

(A)   The only prop you will need is a 6- x 8-foot piece of cloth. If you are presenting this illusion in your home, you can use a blanket or a sheet. For stage use, however, an attractive, opaque piece of fabric is far better.

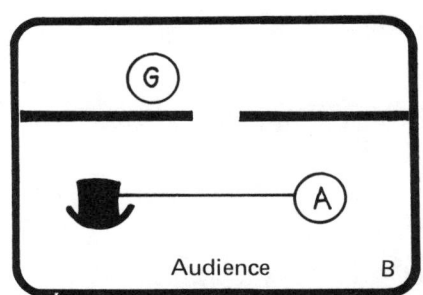

(B)   This *first version* of the MUMMY is the method for presenting the effect in your home. Select a room in the house where there is a door or archway located approximately in the center of a wall as shown here. The girl should be hidden behind this wall and to the right of the door as illustrated. Your male assistant, who, by the way, should be close to the same height as the girl, is standing to your left with the folded cloth over his arm. The spectators must be located in front of you, so that the door is obscured by the cloth when you and the assistant hold it up between you as shown in Step 1 that follows.

METHOD

IN THE CIRCULAR INSERTS, IN ADDITION TO THE LOCATIONS OF YOU (TOP HAT) AND YOUR BEAUTIFUL GIRL ASSISTANT (G), YOUR MALE ASSISTANT IS SHOWN AS "A."

(1)   Take the cloth and open to your left. Your male assistant (A) grasps the fabric by the top left corner and stretches it between you both as shown. This action must place the archway *directly behind the cloth* as illustrated in Step B above. *Also, be sure that the bottom edge of the fabric is touching the floor.*

(2)   As soon as the cloth is in position, the girl (G) leaves her hiding place and positions herself *directly behind the cloth.*

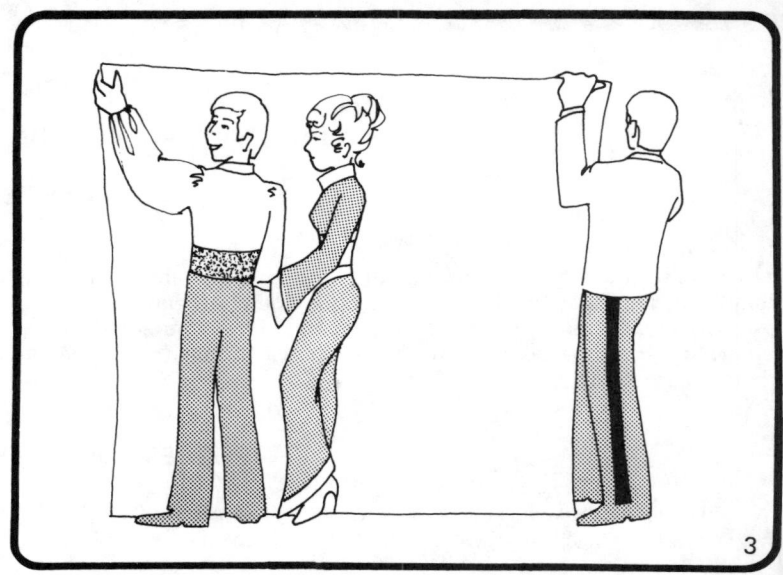

(3) STEPS 3 AND 4 ARE THE IMPORTANT SECRET MOVES IN THIS ILLUSION. On your command, the male assistant openly steps around the left edge of the cloth and stands behind the fabric as shown. *You and he must keep the cloth tightly stretched while he moves.*

(4) As your male assistant moves out of sight behind the cloth, the girl takes a new position *between* the male assistant and the cloth, as shown here. The male assistant has allowed her room in this area by extending his left arm and taking an unseen step backward. The girl, in the meantime, grasps the side of the cloth with her right hand at Point X as shown in the illustration. The assistant's left hand should curl the top corner of the cloth inward *just prior to the girl's move* in order to conceal his own hand from the audience's view.

(5) *NOTE: All of the above (Steps 3 and 4) take only a second or two and must be executed without hesitation. The flow of action should continue smoothly into the following steps.*

(6) As soon as the girl (G) takes hold of the cloth, the male assistant (A) quickly and secretly exits through the arch.

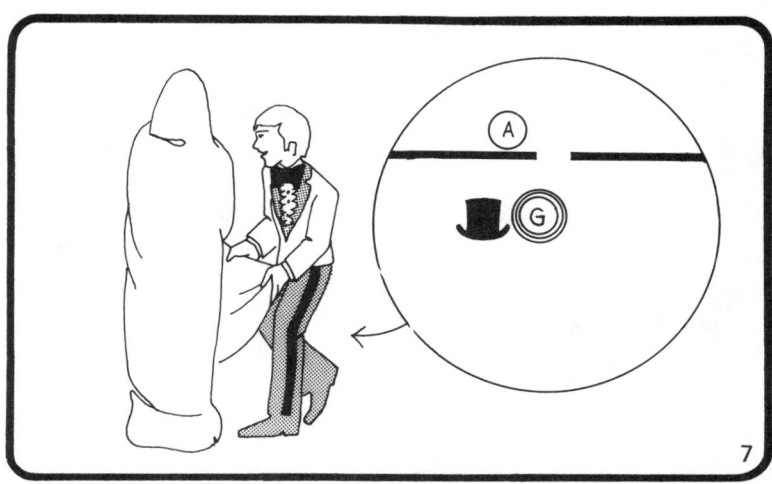

(7) Simultaneously, *the moment the assistant is out of sight through the door,* the girl begins to wrap herself into the cloth until she is standing next to you.

(8) *NOTE: The effect to the audience at this point is that the male assistant simply stepped behind his edge of the fabric and immediately wrapped himself in the cloth.*

(9) Now walk around the "mummy" and grasp the loose end of the cloth. *At this point in the presentation the audience does not anticipate the final result, so you should play it up to the fullest.*

(10) Start to unwrap the figure, slowly at first, then gradually increase your tempo until the concealed girl is about to be revealed. With a flourish, whip the remaining cloth away and dramatically point up the magical appearance of the young lady.

COMMENTS AND SUGGESTIONS

For an added climax, the male assistant can do a "run around" and make a surprise appearance in the audience. A "run around" means that as soon as the assistant is out of sight through the doorway, he literally runs through (or outside) the house by some route that the spectators cannot see and secretly enters at the back of the audience. If the physical set-up of the house is right, the assistant may have time to actually *sit down in the audience.* The viewers are concentrating on the action "on stage" and will not notice this new arrival. Then the assistant can loudly *lead the applause* until he is discovered by the now doubly amazed spectators!

THE MYSTERY OF THE MAGICAL MUMMY
Second Version

EFFECT

The effect in this variation is identical to that of the first version; however, this is the presentation as designed for use *on stage* in a theater. Therefore the placement of assistants and the "sightline" controls must be changed. We will assume that you are now completely familiar with the first version and move directly into the description of this new method.

SECRET AND PREPARATION

This on-stage version of the "Mummy" must be performed in a theater with vertical legs (side curtains) as shown in the illustrations. The right center "leg" will serve as a replacement for the doorway used in the first method. The girl is hidden behind this leg as shown.

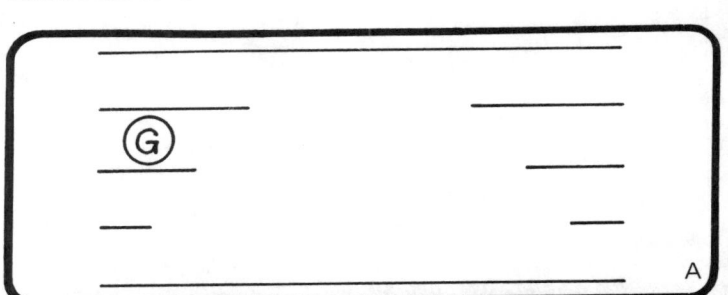

METHOD

NOTE: ALL ILLUSTRATIONS ARE FROM THE OVERHEAD POINT OF VIEW IN ORDER TO DIAGRAM THE MOVES MORE CLEARLY.

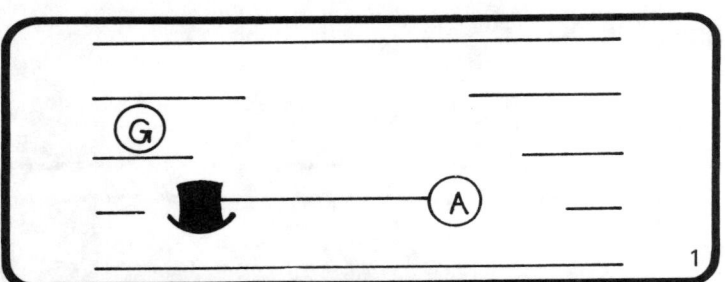

(1) Stretch the cloth between you and your male assistant (A). It is important that *you* are standing so that your body and the cloth *mask the on-stage edge of the right center leg as illustrated.* This will protect the girl's unseen entrance from the curtain to her new position behind the cloth in Step 2.

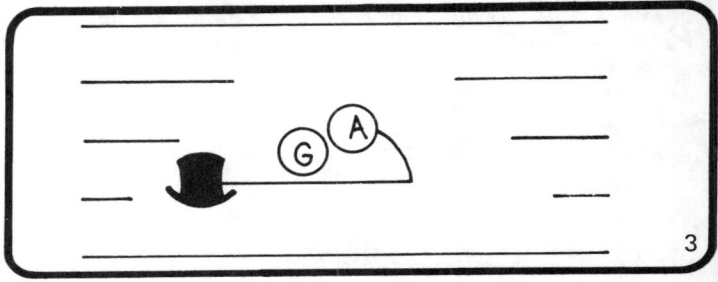

(3) At this point, upon your command, the assistant steps behind the cloth in the same manner as in the first version.

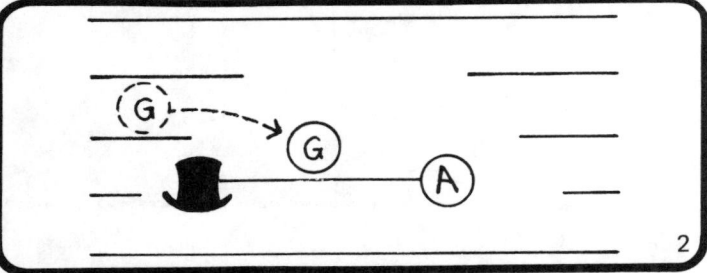

(2) As soon as the cloth is stretched, *with its bottom edge resting on the stage floor,* the girl secretly moves into position behind the cloth.

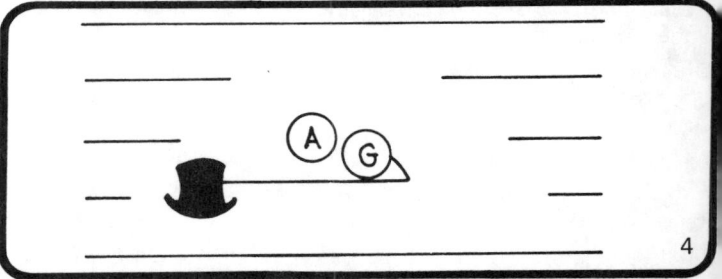

(4) The girl immediately takes her position *between* the assistant and the cloth as shown and substitutes her own grip on the top corner of the cloth for that of the assistant as before.

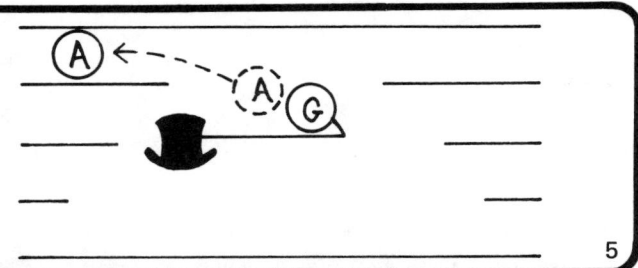

(5) The assistant makes his quick exit *into the wings* as illustrated.

(6) *Simultaneously with the assistant's unseen exit,* the girl starts to wrap herself into the cloth. In the meantime, the male assistant is making a rapid (but hidden) journey around the outside of the theater (or through a hallway, etc.) so that he will be ready for his "magical reappearance" from behind the audience

(7) When the girl has utilized approximately one-half of the material, you carry the right end of the cloth in and around the girl as shown. *This serves the purpose of positioning you away from the wings.*

(8) Now unwrap the figure until the girl has been magically revealed.

(9) During the audience's surprise reaction, point dramatically to the rear of the theater as your vanished assistant makes his unexpected appearance by running down the aisle among the members of the unbelieving audience!

THE CURIOUS CABINET CAPER
EFFECT

A tall, slender, attractive cabinet is revealed in the center of the stage. The magician and his male assistant spin the equipment so that the audience can see it on all sides. The performer opens the front and then the back doors which allows the spectators a clear view through the cabinet. The magician even walks through the empty cabinet and then he and the assistant close the doors. Instantly the front door bursts open, revealing the magical appearance of a beautiful girl!

SECRET AND PREPARATION

A) This effective production is quite easy to build. The illusion's dimensions and materials are as follows: The cabinet should measure approximately 2½ feet square by 6 feet tall and rest upon a castered platform about 5 feet square. The doors hinge open from *diagonal corners* as illustrated. In order to save weight, the cabinet may be made of ¼-inch thick plywood framed in 1" x 2" pine. The base should be made of ½-inch thick plywood with vertical framing underneath to prevent sagging with the girl's weight.

B) After the construction is complete, decorate the cabinet in a style that blends with the theme of your presentation.

METHOD

For simplicity and clarity the male assistant is not shown in the illustrations. All of his actions can be clearly followed from the written description.

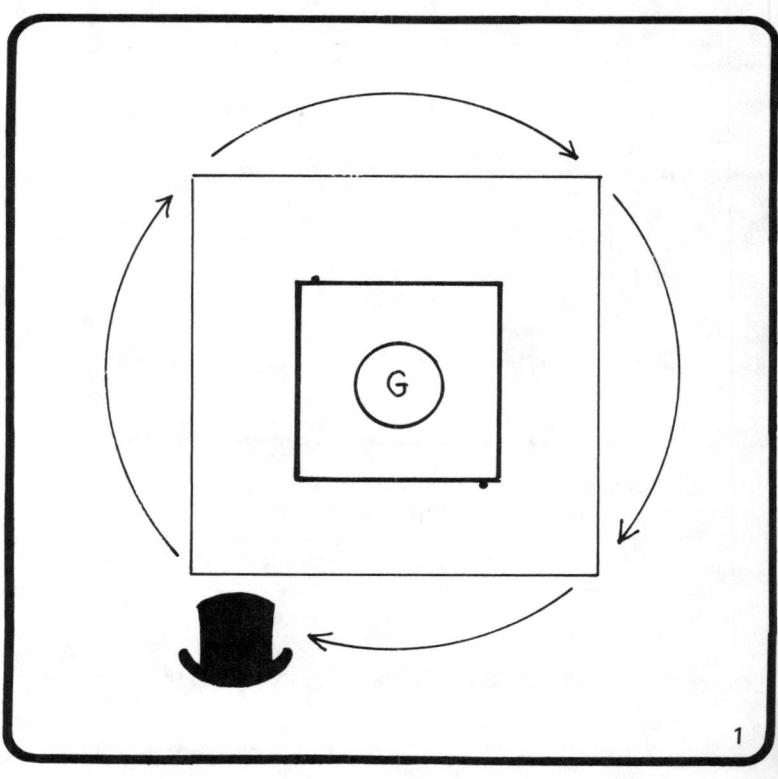

(1) The girl is loaded into the cabinet off stage. On your cue, the illusion is wheeled rapidly to the center of the stage. You and your assistant then spin the cabinet — showing all sides.

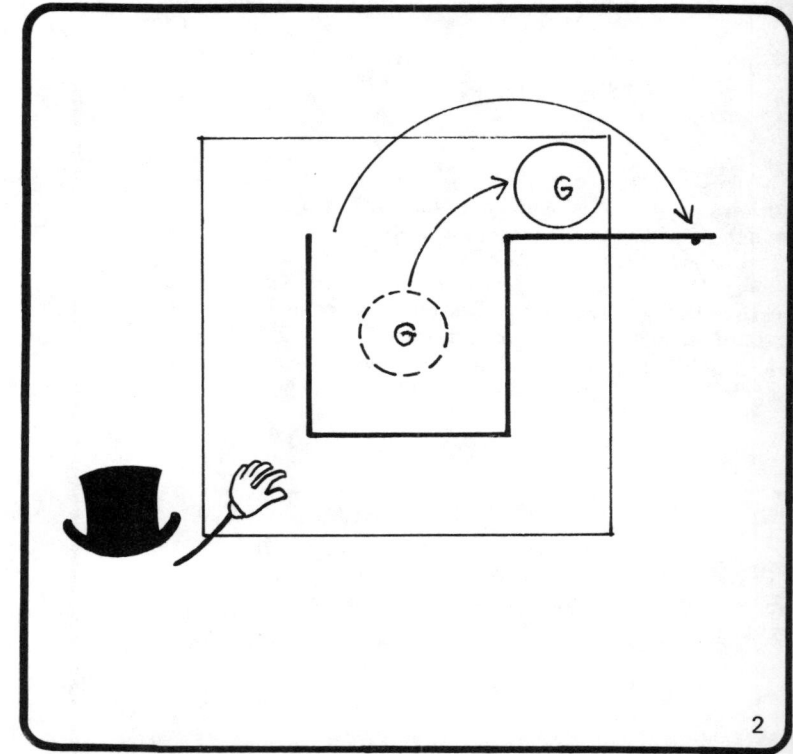

(2) The assistant opens the back door. Immediately the girl moves secretly from inside the cabinet to a new position *behind* this door as shown.

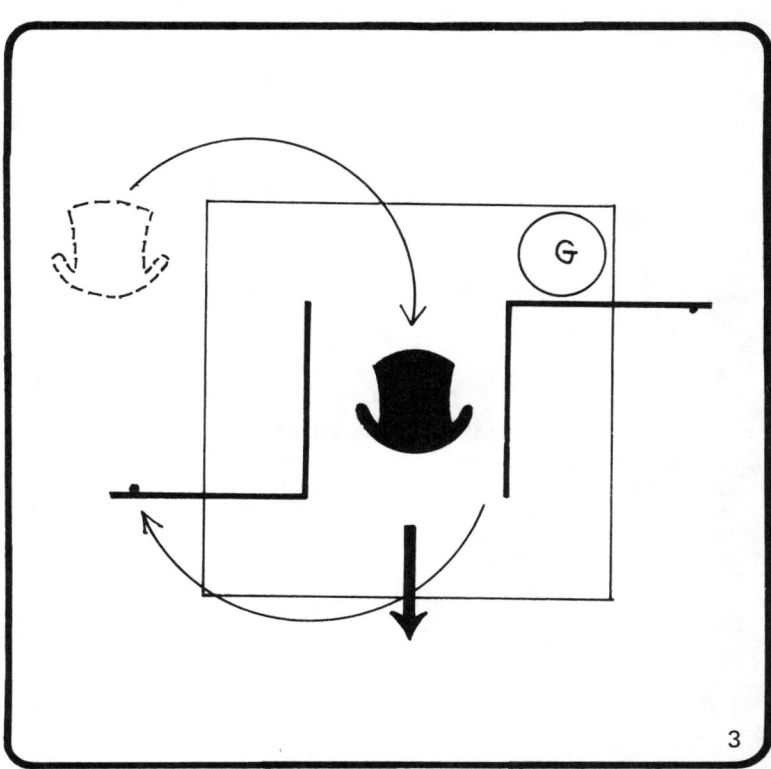

(3) Almost simultaneously, you walk around to the back of the illusion and quickly step through the cabinet *pushing the front door open toward the audience as you exit.*

(4) Your male assistant has moved forward and is now standing at attention to the left of the front door.

(5) You are standing to the right and pointing out the empty interior of the illusion. The girl is hidden behind the open back door.

(6) THIS NEXT STEP IS IMPORTANT. Since both you and your assistant are standing to the front of the illusion, the proper timing in closing the doors is essential. You close the front door first — as your assistant moves to close the back door. *The time it takes for your assistant to get into position will create the fraction of a second necessary for the girl to step back into the cabinet.* If these moves are properly timed, the effect will be that both doors are closed simultaneously.

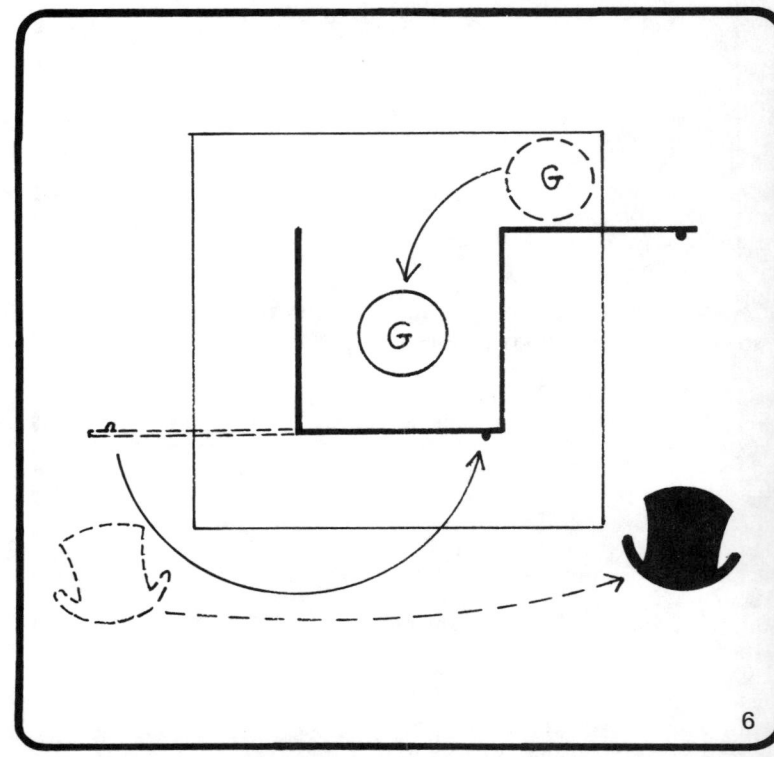

(7) You and your assistant step away from the cabinet. The girl flings open the front door, making her magical appearance!

MUMMY'S CASKET

EFFECT

A tall, slender cabinet decorated to resemble an Egyptian Mummy Casket, is wheeled on stage by the magician's assistant. All sides of the equipment are shown to the audience prior to opening front and back doors. As you might expect, the casket contains a cloth-wrapped mummy covered with the dust of ages past. The assistant carefully removes this relic as the magician steps through the cabinet brushing away the imaginary cobwebs. The audience can see completely through the casket as the performer walks through it. Together, the magician and his aid reposition the mummy inside the casket and close the doors. Once again, they revolve the equipment to prove to the audience that the mummy is safely sealed inside its tomb. Suddenly the doors are opened revealing the startling transformation of the mummy into a beautiful young girl dressed in the ancient style of an Egyptian princess.

SECRET AND PREPARATION

(A) The equipment and the method are basically the same as in the CURIOUS CABINET CAPER. The only difference is in the decoration of the equipment and the additional task of constructing a replica of an Egyptian mummy. There are several ways in which to construct the "mummy." The best method, but unfortunately the most difficult, is to build a wire form in the shape of a person approximately 5' 3" tall and then completely wrap the finished form in wide surgical gauze. The second method is to sew up a cloth dummy of the same height as the girl and stuff this large doll with lightweight foam rubber. Wrap the dummy figure with gauze as before. The last, but least desirable method is to simply cut out an outline of the figure in ¼" thick plywood. Wrap this silhouette with gauze as in the first two descriptions. Remember, whichever method you choose, to keep the figure as light as possible. Also, lightly spray the completed figure with black or gray paint to "age" it. Now attach a thin piece of wire to the top of the mummy's head as shown.

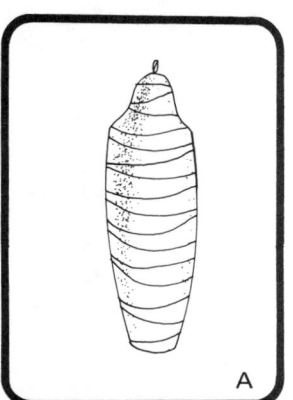

A

(B) This wire should be of the proper length to suspend the figure from a hook fastened to the inside top of the casket as shown in Step 3 of Method.

(C) A metal ring should now be sewn to the *back* of the mummy in the position diagrammed.

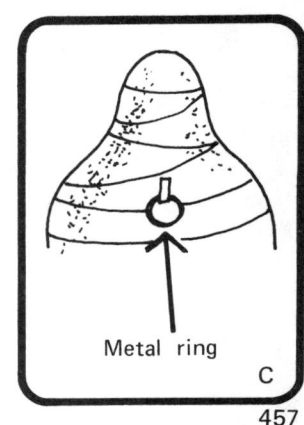

Metal ring

C

(D) This ring will enable the figure to be hung on the back door from a hook screwed into the panel as shown here.

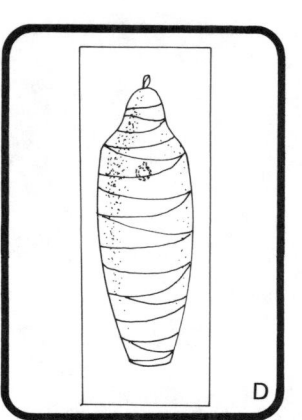

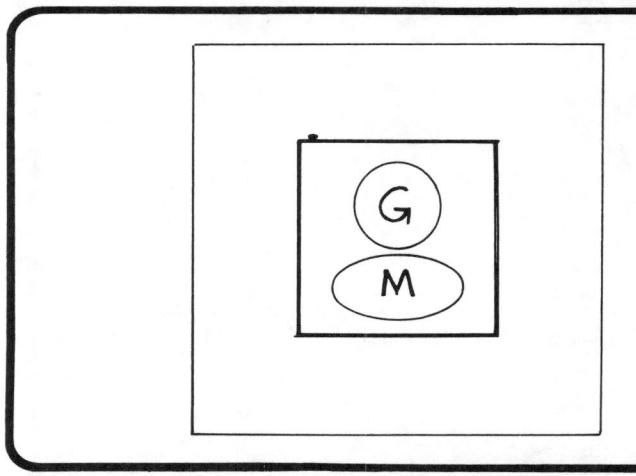

(E) To present the illusion, first, hang the mummy from the top of his head inside the casket. Place the girl in the cabinet so that she stands behind the suspended figure as shown in this diagram. Then close both doors and have your assistant wait for your cue.

METHOD

(1) After you have verbally introduced the illusion to your audience, the assistant wheels the equipment on stage so that it stands to your left. Together you revolve the cabinet. Your assistant steps back and opens the *rear* door. The girl shifts to her new position behind this door as shown.

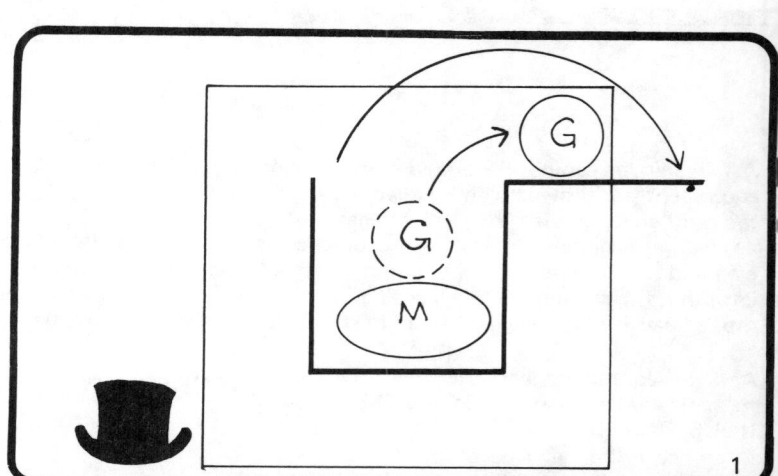

(2) *As soon as the back door is open,* your assistant moves back into position near the front of the equipment. Simultaneously with his forward movement, you open the front door.

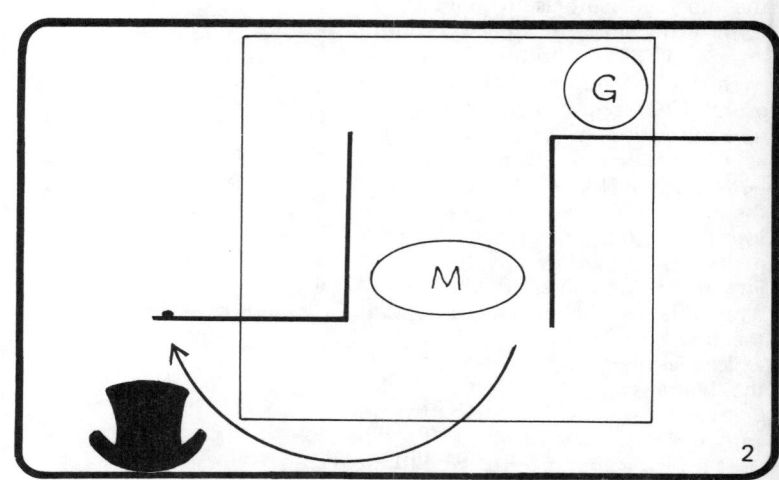

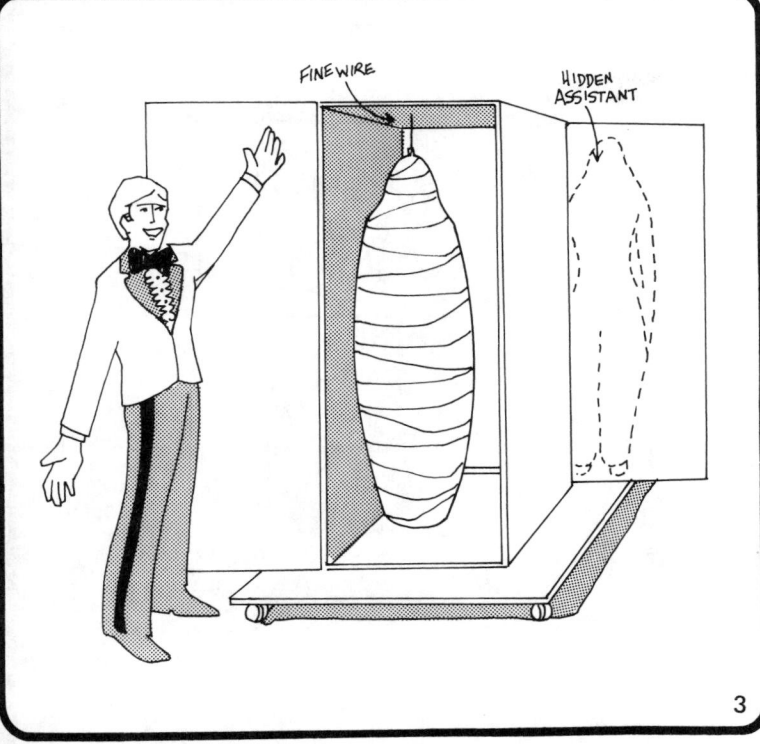

(3) Here is the audience's view at this point in the presentation.

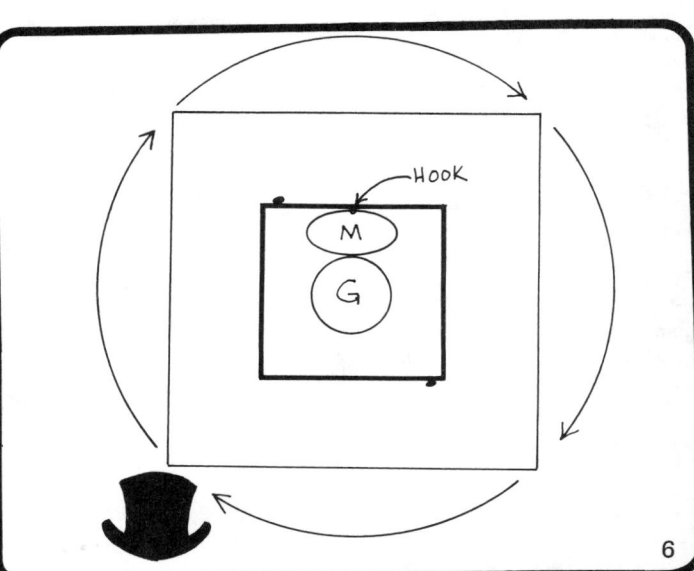

(6) Now revolve the cabinet in order to assure your audience that the mummy is still inside. During this rotation, *the girl unhooks the mummy from the top and fastens it by the ring on the back door* as illustrated.

(4) Your assistant reaches into the cabinet and removes the wrapped figure. This clears the way for you to walk into and through the empty cabinet as you did in Step 3 of the Curious Cabinet Caper.

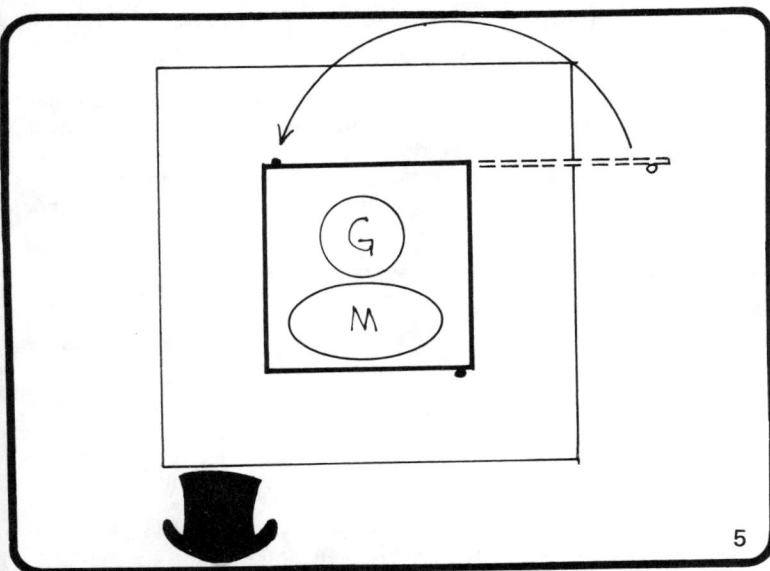

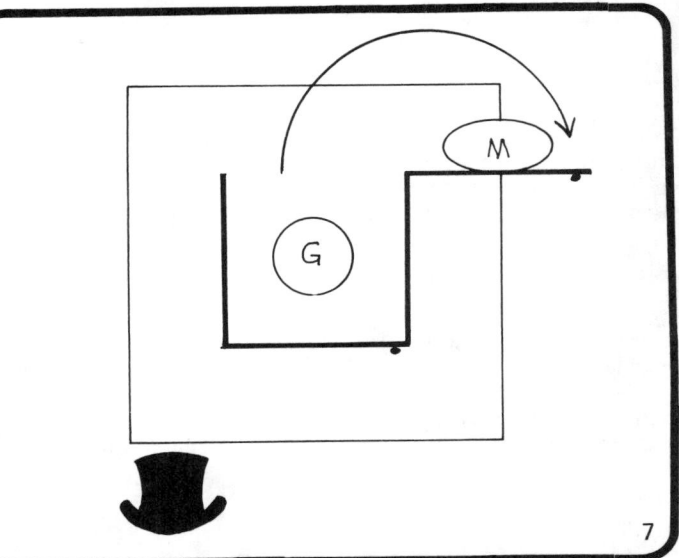

(7) Your assistant moves to the rear and opens the back door as before. This time, however, the *mummy* swings into concealment behind the back door.

(5) As you exit from the front, turn and help your assistant in repositioning the mummy in the casket. As soon as the figure is secure, close the front door. Your assistant moves directly to the rear. The girl has already moved back into the casket by the time your assistant can close the back door.

(8) As soon as your assistant has opened the back door completely, you immediately swing the front door wide open — the transformation of the mummy into the beautifully alive girl will shock the audience into real applause.

WHO'S THERE

This is the modern equivalent of one of the popular cabinet illusions featured in big-time magic shows that worked on full-size stages in large theaters. It usually required several assistants to move a cabinet around so that the magician could open the door and show it empty. Here, the illusion has been reduced to simply a *door,* a *frame,* and a *curtain* — making it easy to do and light to handle. The effect is nearly the same, but it is enhanced by the simplicity of the equipment itself.

EFFECT

Standing on stage is a full-sized door mounted in a thin door frame. The magician's attractive assistant opens the door revealing a curtain hanging across the threshold. Drawing the drape aside, the girl walks through the door and around its skeleton framework. The audience can see that the doorway is quite normal and totally unprepared. Without hesitation, the assistant redraws the curtain and closes the door so that everything is exactly as it was originally. Immediately a loud knocking sound is heard coming from the other side of the door. The assistant swings the door open and there stands the magician — making his first appearance onstage in a startling and amazing manner.

SECRET AND PREPARATION

(A) The equipment necessary to present this illusion is quite simple and easily constructed. As you can see from the illustrations, the door is mounted in a simple frame, which in turn is, anchored securely to a thin platform for sturdiness. An opaque curtain is hung from a rod at the top of the frame where it will not interfere with opening and closing the action of the door. *The curtain must be long enough so that it touches the surface of the platform.* This will prevent the spectators from seeing behind or under the curtain when the door is open.

(B) Here is a "backstage" view of the doorway. The angle brackets serve to support the apparatus in its upright position and keep the framework from moving about when the door is open.

METHOD

(1) At the start, the door should be in its closed position with the curtain drawn closed also. You (the magician) should be standing on the back edge of the platform behind the center fo the curtain as shown from this top view.

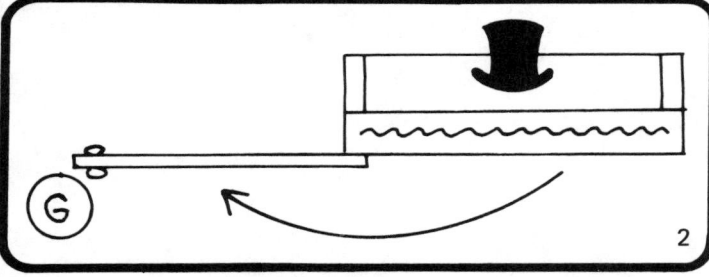

(2) To present the illusion, the girl (G) steps to the front of the framework and opens the door to its maximum capacity as shown. You should still be concealed by the closed curtain at this point in the presentation.

(3) Here is the audience's view of the situation at this point. You can now see why it is important that the curtain is long enough to touch the platform.

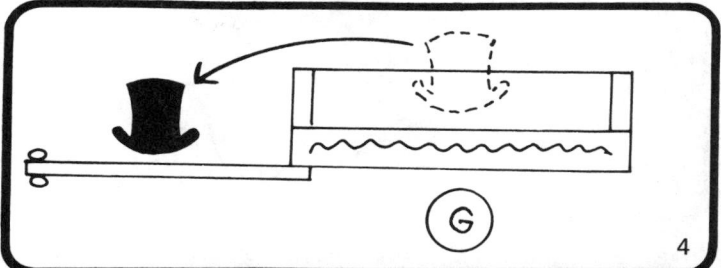

(4) As soon as the door is completely open, quickly and quietly move to a new position behind the open door as shown. *At the same time,* your assistant crosses in front of the framework to a position in front of the closed curtain. Practice exact timing with your assistant so that *both* moves are perfectly synchronized, thus eliminating any hesitation in the presentation.

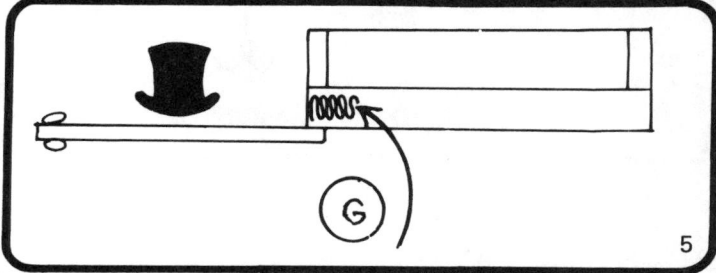

(5) *Immediately* your assistant draws the curtain open as illustrated.

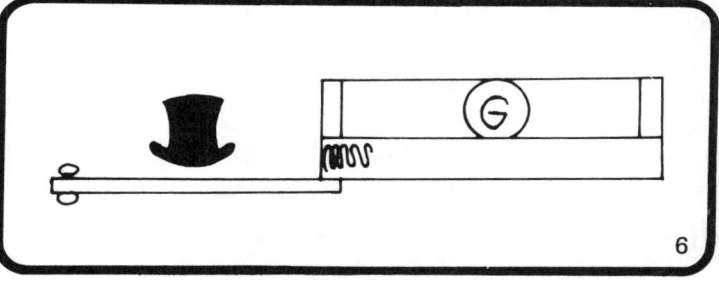

(6) From the spectators' point of view, the doorway appears to be quite empty. Your assistant immediately walks through the open doorway and turns to face the audience proving that everything is just as it appears. Be sure that she does not glance in your direction. After a brief pause, she walks back through the threshold and closes the curtain.

(7) At this point, you return quickly to your former position behind the curtain.

(8) During your move, your assistant walks from in front of the curtain to the edge of the open door and closes it. As soon as you hear the door click shut, pull the curtain open and begin to knock loudly on the back of the door.

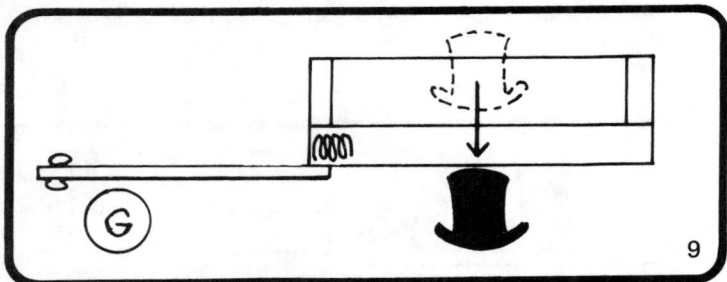

(9) With this as her cue, your assistant swings the door open.

(10) You immediately step through the doorway in a grand gesture making your magical appearance on the stage.

TIP-OVER TRUNK

EFFECT

An attractive trunk is shown and revolved by the magician and his assistant. All sides are displayed to the audience. The trunk is even tilted on its side, permitting a clear view of the top. In this position, the lid is raised, giving the spectators an opportunity to view the trunk's empty interior. Closing the lid, the magician and his assistant return the trunk to its original upright position. Immediately the top of the trunk bursts open, revealing the magical appearance of an attractive young lady!

SECRET AND PREPARATION

(A) The dimensions of the trunk shown here are for instructive purposes only. You will notice that two hinges, indicated by the letter "C," hold the trunk to the platform by its bottom front edge. This allows the performer and his assistant to "tip" the trunk over (hence the name) on the base and, at the same time, keep the trunk in place on the platform. The two handles mounted on the front edge of the lid make it convenient for the magician to open the lid while the trunk is "tipped" on its side. The casters fastened to the four corners of the base permit the easy rotation of the trunk during the performance.

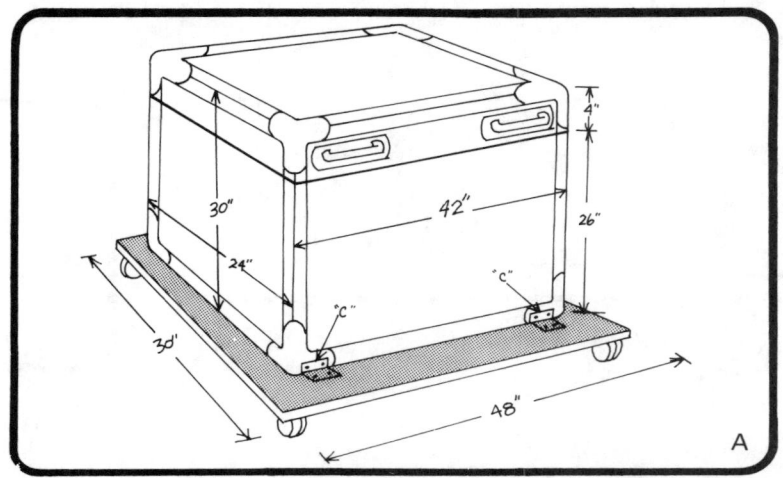

(B) In this illustration you can see that the trunk actually has no bottom. The shaded area represents the top surface of the platform. The upright panel marked "A" is mounted permanently to the top surface of the platform and held in this position by Sections B1 and B2 which are also permanently attached to the platform and to Panel A. These end pieces (B1 and B2) are cut into a pie wedge shape in order to allow the bottom back edge of the trunk to pass over them during the "tipping" action. A length of webbing (or lightweight chain) is attached to the lid as illustrated to prevent the lid from falling too far back and shearing the hinges when the lid is open.

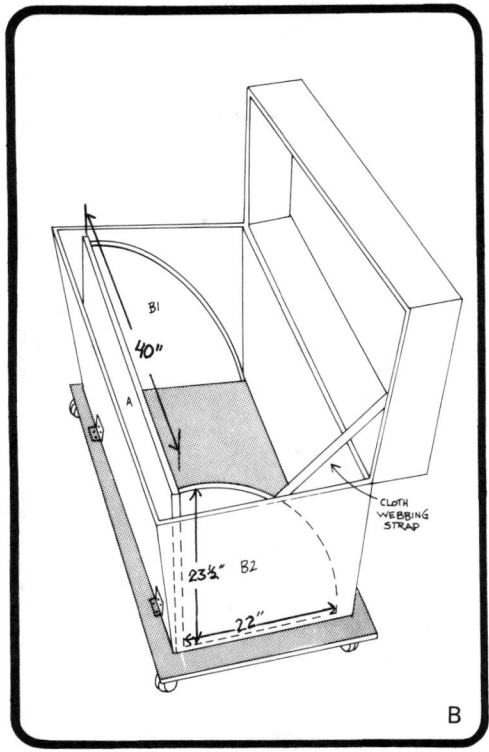

(C) When the trunk has been tipped over on its side as in Figure 3, *the upright Panel A becomes the bottom of the trunk.* The magician is then free to lift the lid as illustrated and allow the audience a clear view into the trunk's empty interior.

METHOD

(1) With the girl concealed in the trunk, the entire affair is rolled on stage so that it stands between you and your assistant. The two of you now revolve the trunk, showing all sides.

(2) With the front now facing the audience, with the aid of your assistant, grasp the handles at the back and tip the trunk forward on its base. *Be sure to keep the lid closed as you tip the trunk or the audience will see the false bottom swinging into position.* When the trunk is on its side, swing the lid open and allow the audience to see that the inside of the trunk is empty.

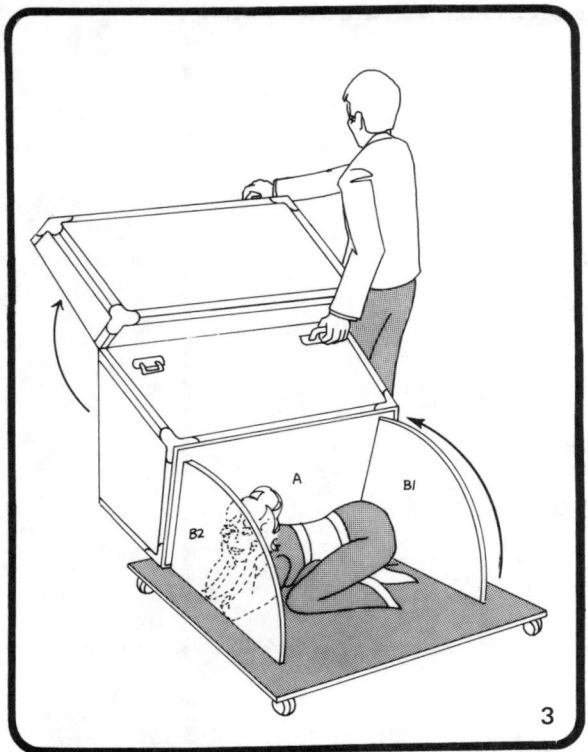

(3)   This is a backstage view and shows how the girl is hidden behind the false bottom (A). Depending upon the "line of sight" of your audience, you and your assistant should stand next to the open trunk, one on each side, to hide the two end supports (B1 and B2) which also conceal the girl.

(4)   Now close the lid and set the trunk upright on its base. Step in front of the trunk, turn and clap your hands. On this cue, the girl stands erect, pushing open the lid, which flies back into the hands of your waiting assistant.

(5)   NOTE: In order to give the girl a graceful exit from the trunk, it will be necessary for you and your assistant to vault her out in a strong, sweeping motion so that she lands on both feet to conclude her dramatic "magical" appearance.

An interesting term used by professional illusionists that is appropriate here is *"Box Jumpers."* A Box Jumper is the assistant, who helps the magician by conveniently appearing, vanishing, being divided into two or more parts and then becoming "magically" restored, and so on during the illusion show. You can see from the "exit" the girl makes from the TIP-OVER TRUNK after she appears just how these talented ladies acquired that unusual nickname.

THE FARMER AND THE WITCH

"GEN" GRANT

EFFECT

From the large crowd of eager volunteers, the magician selects one boy and two girls to participate in the next mystery. On a small table to the performer's right, place two costumes. One represents a *witch,* the other an old *farmer.* The girl is selected by the magician to play the part of the witch. She is sent back stage with the appropriate cloak and mask, in the company of the other girl, whose job is to act as *wardrobe mistress.* While the girl is backstage slipping on her costume, the magician gives the farmer's costume to the boy who will be playing the part of the farmer in the story the magician is about to tell. The old witch enters and the boy exits to allow the wardrobe mistress to dress him as the farmer. After a bit of funny by-play, all three children are standing around the magician, the farmer smoking his pipe, the witch brandishing her broom and the wardrobe mistress observing all their antics. Suddenly, the witch waves her broom at the farmer. Upon removing the farmer's costume, the audience is surprised to see the *girl,* who moments before had been the witch. The second surprise comes when it is discovered that the witch's costume now covers the *boy,* who had been the farmer. Through all the applause and laughter, the children are thanked for their participation and excused from the stage.

SECRET AND PREPARATION

(A)   This highly entertaining and portable illusion is made up of the following elements: one broom, *two identical* witches' costumes complete with hooded masks and one farmer's outfit with mask to match.

NOTE: All of the costumes should be made so that they can be quickly slipped on over the children's clothes.

(C)   The farmer's mask may be purchased from a novelty store. Be sure that the mask is opaque except for the eye, nose, and mouth openings. Fashion a hood of the same blue material and stitch it around the edges of the mask. The addition of a bandana around the neck is a nice touch. Just be sure that the entire mask assembly can pass freely over a child's head.

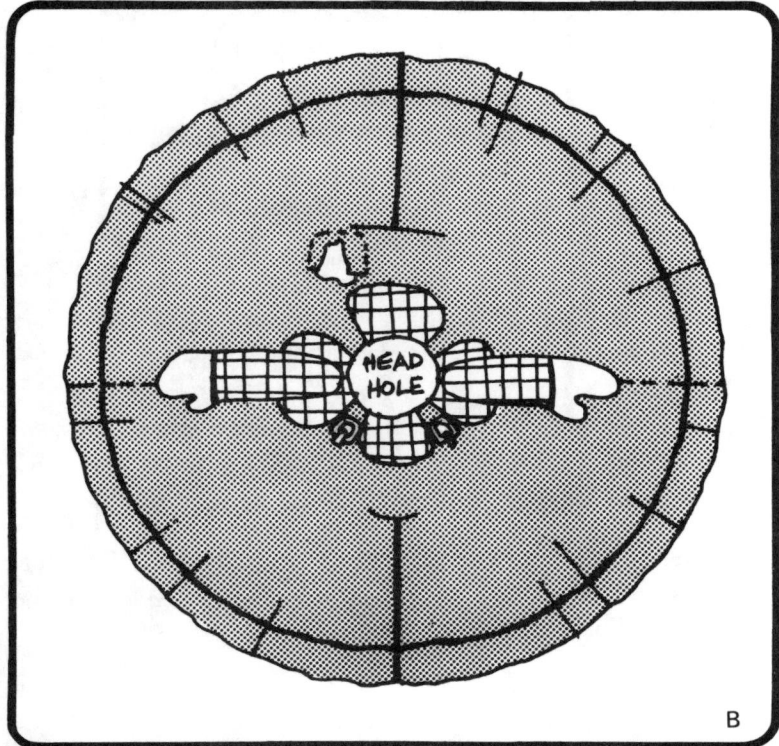

(B)   To create the farmer's costume, you will need to purchase a quantity of blue cotton material and sew it into a large circle as shown. The hole in the center is passed over the child's head and allows the material to fall around his shoulders and hang to the floor. For a more charming look, you can add the shirt and hands as illustrated. The shirt can be made of a red and white checkered material and appliqued to the blue cape. NOTE: The arms and hands are not real, but merely designs made from the material.

(D)   The completed costume, when worn, should look like this.

(E) The *two* identical witches' costumes are made in the same manner as just described, except that in this case, select a black material for the background color to accentuate the patches as illustrated.

(G) The completed costume will look like this. The broom is held *through the fabric of the cape* as shown.

(F) The mask should look like a witch and be completed with a black hood. You will notice that all the hoods (the farmer and the two witches) extend well below the neck in order to cover any possibility of seeing the child through the hole in the center of the cape.

(H) Now place *one* of the witch's costumes and the farmer's costume on your table. The *second* witch costume and the broom are stationed back stage on your left with an assistant.

METHOD

All of the following illustrations are diagrammed from an overhead view. In this way, you can more clearly visualize the sequence of events as it takes place. The boy is represented by the "B," the girl who is to play the witch by the "G," the girl who is to play the wardrobe mistress by the "W," and your assistant by the "A."

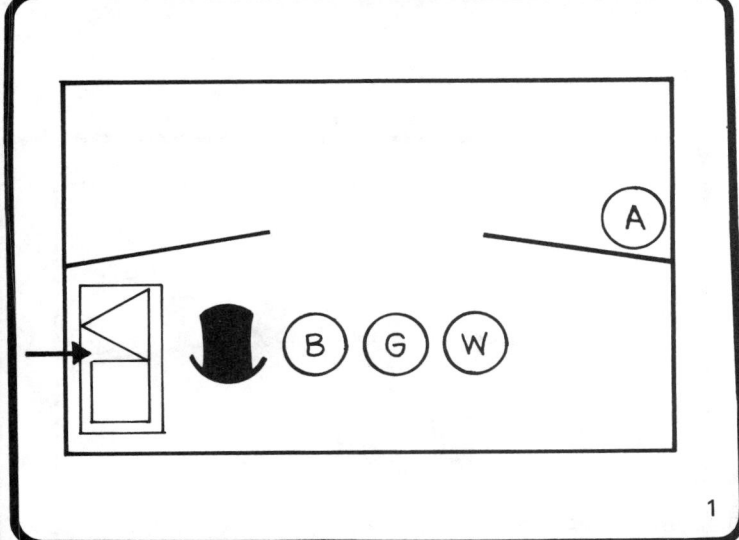

(1) Request the assistance of two girls and a boy from your audience. At this point you will usually be mobbed with volunteers. Select three that are very close to the same height — thank and excuse the rest. The table containing the costumes is to your right. The three children should be standing on your left.

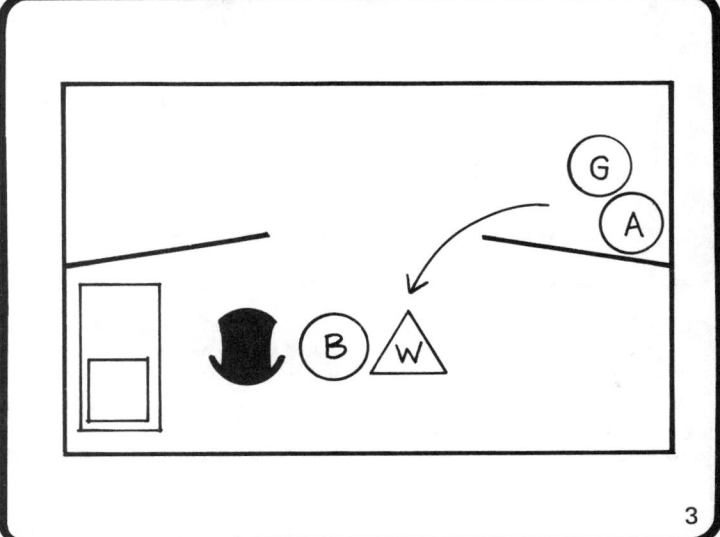

(2) Hand the witch's costume and mask to the girl chosen to act as wardrobe mistress and send her *with the second girl, who is to play the witch,* back stage to change.

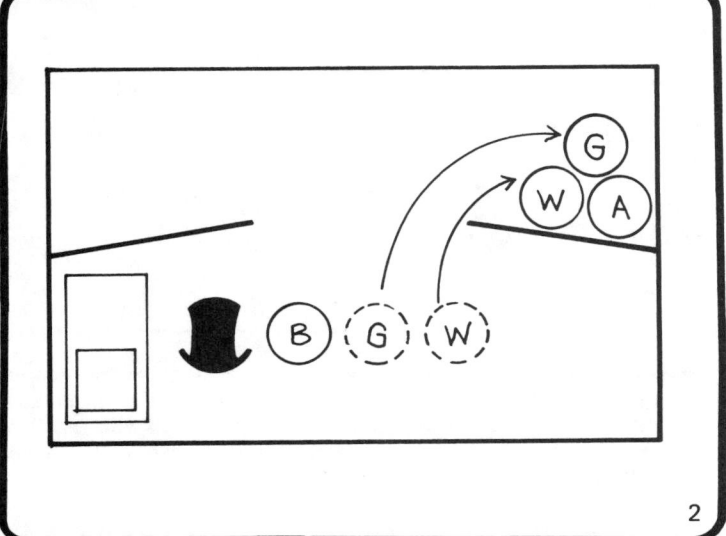

(3) What *actually* takes place is that your assistant costumes the wardrobe mistress in the *witch's* outfit and sends her back on stage as diagrammed here. (The "triangle" represents one of the *witch's* costumes.)

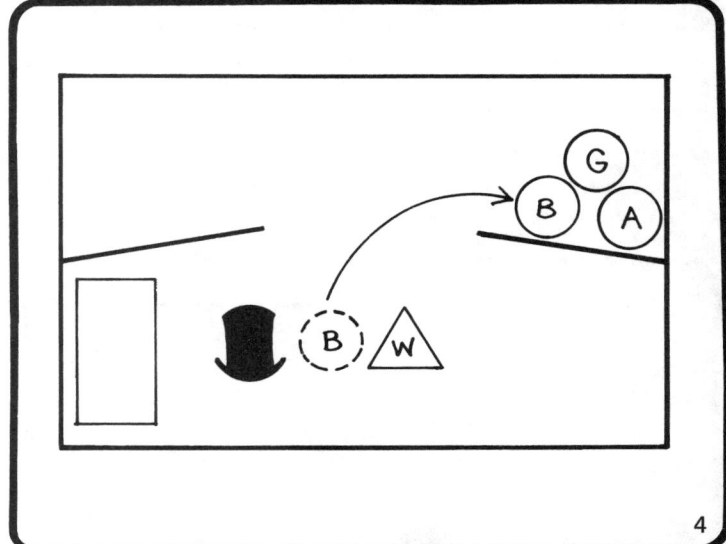

(4) As soon as the "witch" (really the wardrobe mistress) appears on stage, the boy is sent back with the farmer's costume so that he can be quickly dressed.

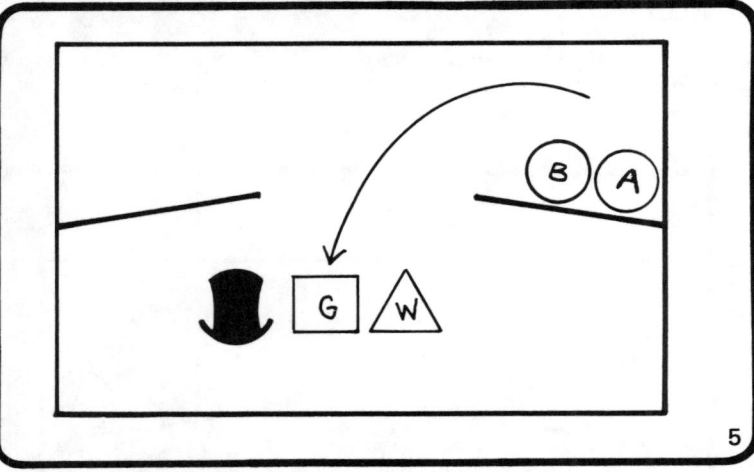

(5)   *Instead of dressing the boy,* the off-stage assistant puts the *farmer's* outfit on the *girl* and sends her on stage *as the farmer.* The diagram illustrates the situation at this point in the presentation. (The "square" represents the farmer's costume.)

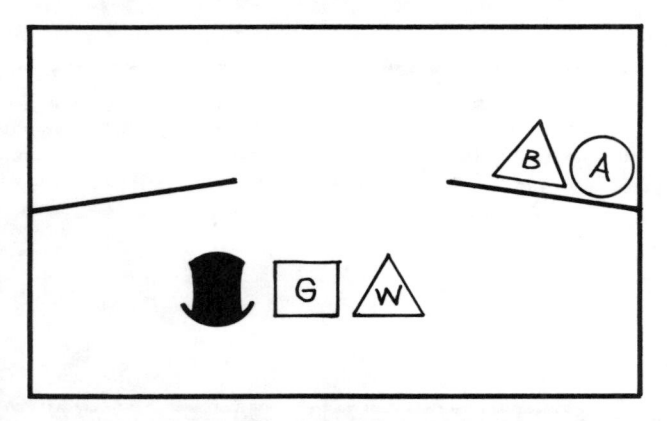

(6)   During the "farmer's" entrance, the assistant costumes the *boy* in the *duplicate witch's* outfit, gives him the broom and keeps him back stage as shown here.

(7)   *NOTE: On stage, the magician now has a farmer and a witch standing next to him. Unknown to the audience, the farmer is really the leading lady in our skit (the girl, G, and the witch is the wardrobe mistress, W.*

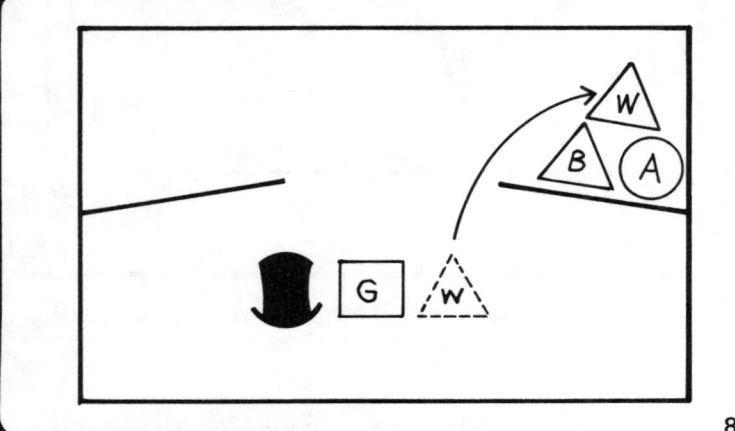

(8)   The performer turns to the witch telling her that she has forgotten her broom and sends her back stage to get it, as shown here.

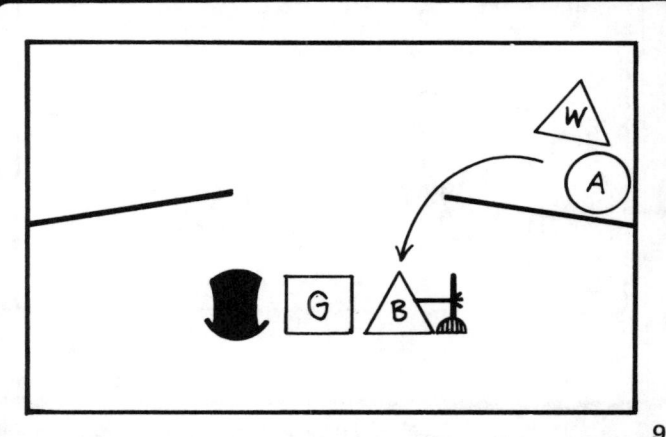

(9)   As soon as the witch disappears back stage, the assistant sends out the *boy* in the *duplicate witch's costume* carrying the broom — and immediately *removes* the costume from the wardrobe mistress.

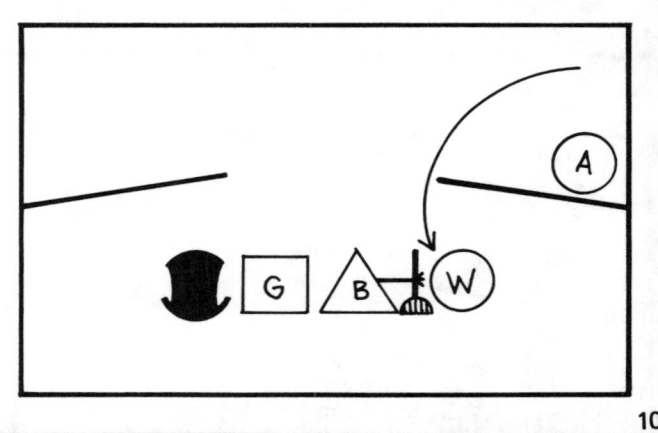

(10)   As the witch arrives with the broom, the magician calls for the return of the wardrobe mistress. She makes her entrance, and the performer compliments her on the help she has given in preparing the cast.

(11)   Under the direction of the magician, the witch waves her broom at the farmer. The performer removes the farmer's costume from around the child. The audience will burst into laughter at the surprising transformation of the boy into the girl. More applause will come upon revealing the boy, who now wears the witch's cape.

COMMENTS AND SUGGESTIONS

This exchange is a real puzzler. Its principle has been used by magicians for many years — and it has been presented in glamorous variations by some of the great showmen in our industry. Gen Grant's version is a classic, mystifying, and practical use of this clever concept in a very colorful and entertaining presentation.

THE SUSPENSION ILLUSION

For centuries, tales were told of Hindu fakirs who could levitate themselves and remain suspended in mid-air for hours or even days. Such exaggerated reports caused the magicians of Europe and America to devise their own methods of presenting this fanciful effect, but in its ultimate form, the illusion was costly, difficult to transport, and could only be presented on a fully equipped stage in a large theater. In contrast, the version about to be described is inexpensive, portable, easy to set up, and can be presented on practically any stage that has drapes and on which the "angles" (line of sight) are those normally found in a theater.

EFFECT

The magician calls the audience's attention to a thin board resting on two small, sawhorse-like supports. These supports are positioned at the ends of the board and elevate it to a height of approximately 3 feet. This equipment is standing in the middle of the stage, and the audience can see the basic simplicity of the arrangement. An attractive young lady makes her entrance and sits comfortably on the board. With the aid of the magician, the girl turns and positions herself horizontally on the board. Walking behind the girl and leaning over her body, the performer apparently hypnotizes the girl. Her arm falls limply over the side of the board as her eyes close. Carefully placing her arm next to her body, the magician moves to the girl's feet and slowly removes the sawhorse from beneath this end of the board. Magically, and with only the support of the single sawhorse, the girl remains suspended as if being held in balance by an unseen force. Passing his hands under the suspended girl, the magician carefully removes the last sawhorse. The audience is stunned to see that the sleeping girl is now "floating on air" with no other support than the magician's will!

Again, the performer passes his hands under and over the young lady's suspended figure, proving to the audience that she is truly "levitated." Quickly replacing the supports beneath the board, the magician snaps his fingers and awakens the young lady. She stands and bows to the applauding spectators.

SECRET AND PREPARATION

NOTE: Since this is one of the true classics of magic, it is important that you construct this illusion with care. Any skimping or make-do arrangements will only spoil a great effect.

(A) Figure A tells the whole story. Except for the 12" x 54" x ¾" plywood board, the entire structure is made up of hardened steel 2" wide by ¼" to ½" thick. The board is fastened to the top extension arm by two heavy angle brackets (A and B) as illustrated. After construction, paint the entire unit flat black, then cover the board with a good quality black felt. Trim the edge of the board with a 5-inch fringe as illustrated. This fringe conceals the steel support directly under the board. You will also require an attractive carpet that can be thrown over the floor supports of the apparatus and two lightweight sawhorses that are the correct height to *apparently* support the board. In fact, the board is *always* supported by the secret device located behind the curtain. Paint these supports white (or leave them their natural light color of unfinished wood) in order to create the contrast necessary to help divert the spectators' eyes from the board. If the black felt-covered board is also trimmed with black fringe, the audience, many times, will leave the theater with the impression that the girl was only supported by the two white sawhorses.

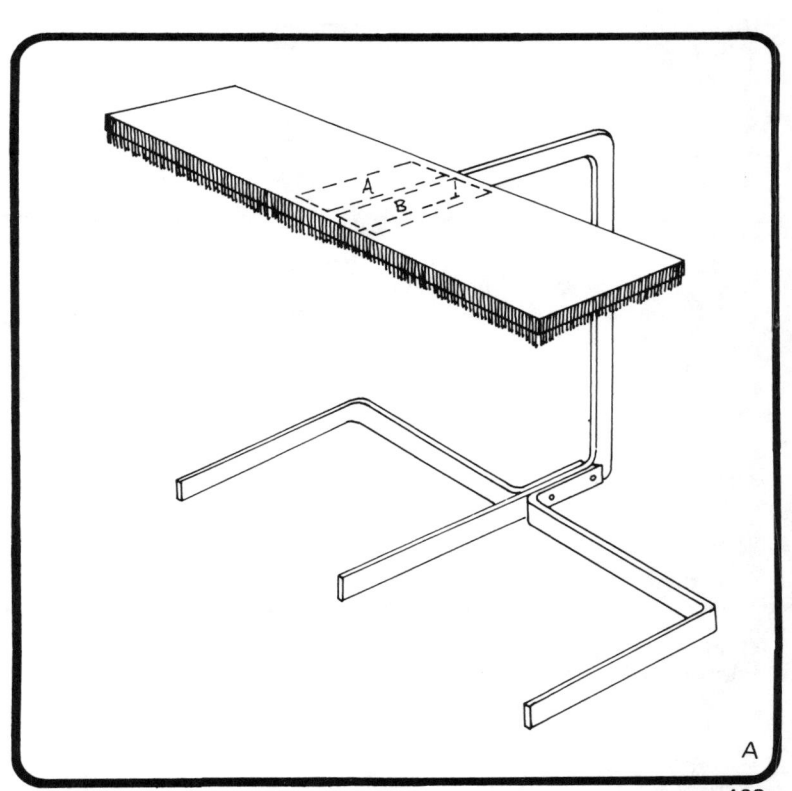

A

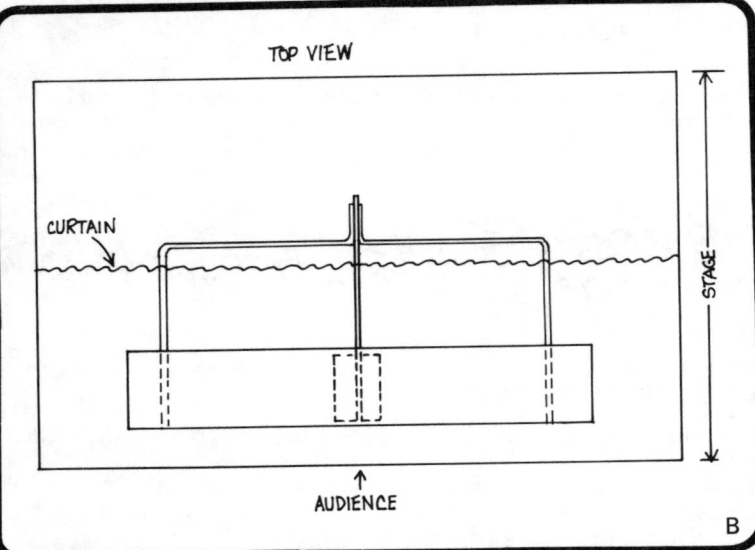

(B) You will also require a curtain directly behind the illusion as shown in the top view. The support arm for the board must extend through the curtain as shown. The brighter the color of this curtain, the better. The object here is to create a brilliant area behind the girl giving the audience the impression of a clean separation.

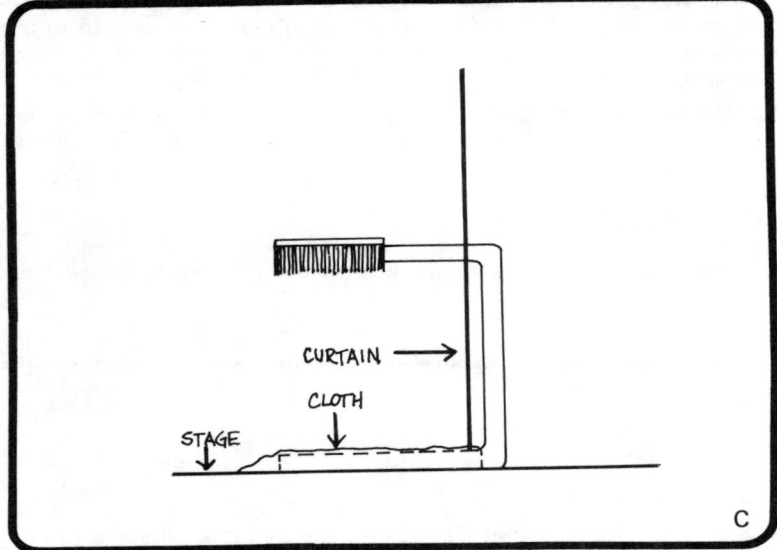

(C) The equipment is positioned on stage as shown in this side view. You will notice that the support arm extends through the center slit in the backdrop. The floor supports extend under the bottom edge of the curtain and are disguised with the small carpet.

(D) Now place the two sawhorses under the ends of the board as in Figure D. The effect will be as illustrated.

METHOD

(1) Introduce the girl to your audience and have her sit on the center of the board. Take hold of her ankles and help her in positioning her feet near the left end support.

(2) Walk around the front side of the equipment and assist the girl in leaning back until she is resting flat on the board with her neck just above the sawhorse support at that end.

(3) Now move around the head end of the board until you are standing *behind* the girl and the board. The hidden arm of the equipment will be next to your left wrist.

(4) The following move will help establish separation between the girl and the curtain. Lean over the young lady and apparently hypnotize her. As she closes her eyes, have her drop her right arm limply off the board. This diversion gives you an excuse for moving back to the *front* of the girl in order to replace her arm next to her side.

(5) After repositioning the girl's arm, move to the end of the board supporting her head. Reach under it, remove the sawhorse, and set it aside.

(6) Step around *behind* the girl at the head end of the board and pass your hands over and under the suspended figure.

(7) Now move back around to the *front* and cross over to the foot end of the equipment. Gently slide the last sawhorse from beneath the board, *leaving the girl apparently suspended in the air!*

(8) Pass your hands over and under the suspended figure.

(9) Quickly replace the foot support. Then cross over to the other side and slide the second sawhorse under her head. Snap your fingers as if to awaken the girl and then help her to her feet as you take your bows.

REPUTATION MAKERS

★ ★ ★

REPUTATION MAKERS

You will find magic can help you in many ways. With what you learn in this course, you can entertain almost anybody, any time, in any country in the world. The following pages teach you a number of excellent tricks not previously covered in the course. I call them "Reputation Makers." But, even more importantly, you'll learn how magic can be useful in different situations, for different people, of different ages, to help you achieve your goals.

Let me give you an example. Performing a bit of magic has gotten me tables in restaurants that were "fully booked," rooms in hotels that had "no vacancies," and seats on trains and airplanes where there were "none available." Magic worked for me, not just in places where I may have been known before as a magician, but in foreign countries where they had no idea who I was. It wasn't me, it was the magic.

Now I would like to pass on to you how you can use your magic in different situations. This is knowledge gained from researching and studying literally thousands of tricks and illusions, and then presenting the best of these under many varying conditions. Here's how the need for so many different tricks came about.

In the past, great magicians traveled from city to city, showing the same magic to new audiences, year after year. That was wonderful for them. The more you perform any magic effect, the better you become at presenting it. Every time you do a trick for an audience of any size you learn something: what works … what doesn't work … what gets a laugh … what just lays there and dies. It is performing experience that teaches you how to better present that trick next time.

On the other hand, when you perform on a television series, you must present new material every week. We were constantly revising old or creating new magical effects week after week for the entertainment of repeat television audiences. I was always happy when we concluded a television show on which everything seemed to go well. But that nice feeling left quickly when I realized we had to do it all over again the following week, with all new material.

When we moved from our local television series to the CBS network for *The Magic Land of Allakazam,* we had a fine creative staff. It consisted of Bev Bergeron, known to millions as "Rebo the Clown," John Gaughan, Leo Behnke, Bob Towner, and Bob Fenton. Although the group enlarged and changed during the five-year run of the show, these fine magical talents remained for the entire series.

Our creative group, drawing from our background of magical knowledge, perusing books and working with new and existing props and illusions, was able to devise, develop, and construct a steady succession of baffling mysteries. Almost every one of the illusions featured Nani Darnell. (In magic terminology, an illusion is a large magic effect that utilizes someone in addition to the magician, like Floating a Lady in the Air.) Fortunately, Nani is a beautiful and versatile performer who was a professional entertainer and nationally recognized dancer before becoming my wife. With the constant creation and testing of new illusions and their performance, some only once for television, Nani Darnell Wilson set a new record for having been in and out of more different illusions than anyone in history.

Although I did not realize it at the time, we were ushering in a new era in the history of magic. Because *Allakazam* was the first network magic television series, we were bringing modernized versions of classic magic, and new effects as well, to people in their own homes every week. It was estimated that in one week, more viewers watched our show than the total number of people who saw Houdini during his entire lifetime.

It was after we completed the five-year run of *The Magic Land of Allakazam,* that our magic business really expanded. Our "Hall of Magic" at the New York World's Fair, was seen by more than two million people. The "Magic of the Telephone" for A.T.T. at the Hemisfair in San Antonio, Texas, debuted our patented Cinillusion process. We supplied major productions for corporate sales meetings and feature attractions for trade shows, fairs and exhibitions, along with continuing magical revues for some of America's leading amusement parks. We produced the first, full-color, magic television specials, *The Magic Circus,* and a series of five-minute/half-hour television shows, *The Magic of Mark Wilson.* I had offices in Los Angeles, New York and Chicago.

The point of all this is, I had learned that "magic" can be much more than just good entertainment. Although performance of magic was the end result of our efforts, it was *sales magic* that greatly helped in getting those contracts in the first place. Now I would like to show you how to put that kind of magic to work for you. Let me explain.

I think the best way to convey this knowledge is with some specific examples. **Magic for Children** covers the three ways you can present your magic for youngsters. **After Dinner Magic** is another special category and **Party Magic** explains what works for a number of different kinds of affairs. In **Sales Magic Secrets,** you'll see how magic can improve your sales meetings, group presentations, networking and trade shows. Magic can help you in all of these various situations. Here's a good example, **The Challenge Coin Vanish.**

THE CHALLENGE COIN VANISH

This is one of the easiest of tricks in this course. Yet, properly presented, it appears to be one of the most amazing and difficult feats of magic, comparable to those professional magicians practice for years to perfect. It illustrates three major principles in the performance of magic. One is *presentation.* "It's not what you do, but the way that you do it," as someone said long ago. The second is the clever *secret*. The third, an important component of many tricks, is *misdirection.*

EFFECT:

"I will now demonstrate one of the most baffling feats of prestidigitation ever attempted, I will perform it under the strictest test conditions. You all will be the judges. You will remember and tell your grandchildren about what you are about to witness. You will see it, but you won't believe it."

You continue, "This silver coin is a half a dollar." (This will work with any coin, a poker chip, a small ball, a crumpled up dollar bill ... any small object.) You hand the coin to a spectator. "Would you please examine the coin."

"This is an ordinary pocket handkerchief." You display a handkerchief on both sides. "Please examine the handkerchief. You will find it is perfectly normal. There are no trapdoors, mirrors, ducks or elephants concealed inside."

"To eliminate any of the usual skullduggery, I am removing my coat and rolling up one sleeve of my shirt to isolate this hand from all outside contact." With your sleeve now rolled up, you hold out your left hand and show it on both sides. "You'll see why in just a moment."

"Have you thoroughly inspected the coin? Is it exactly what it appears to be, a regular coin, is that correct?" The man replies, "Yes, it is." "And you madam, do you find that to be a run of the mill pocket handkerchief?" The lady confirms that is exactly what it is.

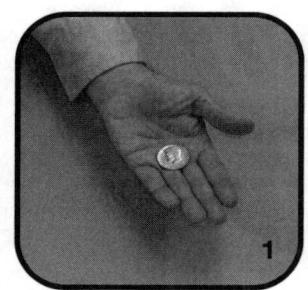 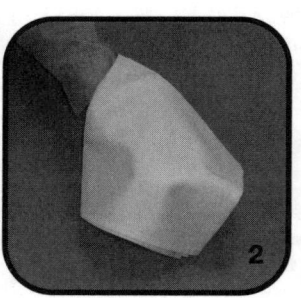

"Now, I want you to watch this very closely. Would you please place the coin on my left hand." You extend your open hand, palm up. The spectator places the coin on your palm. (Image 1)

"You can all see the coin is truly there, on my hand. Now, would you, oh beautiful lady, drape the handkerchief over my hand and, thus, over the coin as well." The lady does this. (Image 2)

"It is important that you watch me closely. You all saw the coin on the palm of my hand, but I want your confirmation that it is still there."

"Would you, young lady, please feel and see that the coin is still in my hand. You could just feel the coin through the cloth of the handkerchief, but I want you to be absolutely sure it is still there by feeling under the handkerchief to confirm the coin's continued presence in my hand."

The lady reaches under the hank and states that the coin is still there. (Image 3)

You have two more spectators substantiate her statement by reaching under the cloth and feeling the coin.

You continue, "I have now proven, without a question of a doubt, the coin is resting on my hand. Watch even more closely than before, because ladies and gentlemen, I will now make that coin disappear!"

Your right hand has never been near your left hand since the coin was placed by a spectator on the palm of your left hand. You make a magical gesture or say some ancient "magic word." "And now, the coin is totally gone. It has disappeared into thin air. I can see, you may not believe me."

You go back to the lady who placed the handkerchief over your hand. "Would you please, slowly, remove the handkerchief!" She removes the handkerchief. Sure enough your hand is totally empty!

"As you see, the coin has completely vanished." You now show both your hands on both sides. "There is no possible explanation. The coin is gone. It must be magic."

"However, there are some rules those of us with great magical ability must obey. When we make something vanish, the cardinal discipline is we must bring that very same item back! You can see that if any object, no matter how small, were to be permanently eliminated from this dimension, it could cause the whole universe to go out of balance. We wizards know and live by this principle. Therefore, of necessity, I must make that very same coin reappear. Let's retrace our steps."

You extend your empty hand, palm up, toward the woman holding the handkerchief. "Would you check to see there is absolutely nothing hidden in the handkerchief, and nothing in my hand." She confirms your statement. "Now, please cover my hand, just as you did before," which she does.

"I know you may not believe what you have seen. You must confirm the emptiness of my hand, before I conclude this extraordinary demonstration." You approach those spectators who felt the coin in your hand before. "Please check under the handkerchief, as you did before. Is my hand completely empty?" All three confirm your hand is empty, there is nothing there.

"Now for the unbelievable ending. To you this has appeared to be a bizarre experiment. To me it is but a simple demonstration of the inherent magical powers within us all. Watch closely as I will now make that coin reappear."

You say the "magic word" again. (Perhaps this time you say it backwards. After all, this is to make the coin reappear.) Addressing any spectator you say, "Please remove the handkerchief." Sure enough, there, on the palm of your hand, is the coin!

"As you can see, the coin has now returned from the atmosphere to the hand of its master. As I told you when we started, you would see it but you would not believe it!"

You bow and say, "I thank you for all your attention." You can end by saying, "next show at five o'clock," or whatever, which will give a happy ending to your magical extravaganza.

SECRET:

As I told you, this is a very simple trick and quite easy to perform. What really happens is, unknown to the audience, one of the spectators acts as your secret accomplice. The last person who feels under the handkerchief and states that they feel the object in your hand is your collaborator. What they really do, when they reach under the handkerchief, is take the coin away in their hand. They keep the coin until it's time for you to make it "reappear." Your unknown protege is the last person to confirm your hand is "empty." What they actually do, when they reach under the handkerchief, is replace the coin on your palm.

Basically, that's it. That's the secret. As you see, it is quite simple and very easy to do. However, the success of the secret depends on your *presentation*, and a little *misdirection*.

THE PRESENTATION

It is the eloquence of your narration that first misleads the audience and elevates this effect to a small miracle. Your overly-elaborate phrasing intentionally leads viewers down the wrong track. Rolling back your sleeve adds to the mystery. Frankly, the true secret is so elemental, and the answer so compounded by your elaborate presentation, most people never arrive at the very simple solution.

Your presentation is in the same genre as those delivered by the wonderful wizard in *The Wizard of Oz*. As you may recall, Dorothy, the lion, tin man and scarecrow discovered that the wizard didn't have any real magical powers, but maintained his position as Exalted Ruler of Oz with his grandiose statements and (questionable) magical demonstrations. Actually, rulers, charlatans, mountebanks and magicians have been using these mythical presentations for centuries. And now it's your turn!

I have performed this effect many times. Let's suppose you are at a party. You can usually "set up" the person who will secretly help you, even when you don't know anyone at the party before you arrive. Of course, your accomplice can always be your host or the person who has invited you to the party. You can even explain everything on the phone beforehand, if you wish.

However, I have found it is usually better to recruit someone you haven't met before. If your "secret help" comes from someone you (apparently) don't even know, this becomes an even more sensational feat of magic. If you have the opportunity, explain your need to someone at the party discreetly. Everyone I have ever given this opportunity has accepted. Your new undercover associate doesn't even need any actual rehearsal. Just explain exactly what you want him or her to do.

THE MISDIRECTION

Here's where the misdirection comes in. As you perform this effect, be careful to always keep your right hand away from your left hand after it is covered by the handkerchief. This seemingly adds to the impossibility of the vanish and reappearance of the coin. Actually, it gives you the opportunity to perform the two important misdirections.

FIRST MISDIRECTION

When your unknown accomplice places her hand under the handkerchief to "feel" the coin in your left hand, you raise your right hand. You say, "As you have seen, my right hand has not even touched the hand covered by the handkerchief." As you say this, look at your right hand. As with all misdirection, *the audience will look where you look.*

That is when your confidential cohort secretly takes the coin out of your hand.

Your secret assistant does not need to "palm" the coin. Just hold the coin in their hand when they take their hand out from under the handkerchief. (Image 4)

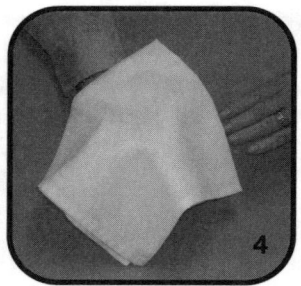 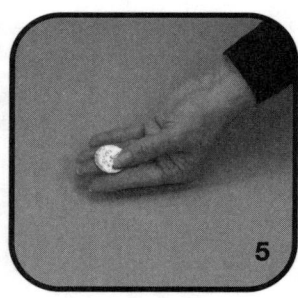

This is a picture of your secret assistant's hand from underneath. (Image 5)

When your secret assistant says, "Yes, I feel the coin," it's the *third* confirmation that you are still holding the coin. Their action and their statement are almost redundant. Their removal of the coin will never be noticed.

SECOND MISDIRECTION

You use the same kind of misdirection for the reappearance of the coin. As your secret assistant is reaching under the handkerchief, secretly replacing the coin in your hand, raise your right hand in the air again. Flex your fingers several times and say, "Notice that my right hand is also empty. I do not wish for you to assume this is a mere sleight-of-hand trick." Be sure to look at your right hand when you say this. The misdirection is perfect. Now anyone can remove the handkerchief and all will see the coin has returned!

USING THE CHALLENGE COIN VANISH

There are many excellent opportunities to present this trick. Not only will you have a lot of fun doing it, even the selection of your secret collaborator can be beneficial.

For instance, let's say you are on a sales call. Your confederate can be the boss's secretary. You may have a unique opportunity to arrange everything with her as you wait in the outer office for your appointment. Depending upon the situation and the personalities of the people involved, this may work very well.

Or, better yet, your accomplice can be the boss himself. Assume you've made your business card appear by magic and perhaps done another magic effect or two during your meeting. The boss may ask if you would perform some of your magic for his office staff. Of course, you will be happy to fulfill his request. Ask him if he will be your clandestine confidant when you do the magic for his associates and quickly explain to him his part in **The Challenge Coin Vanish**. I have always found the executive is delighted to help. He will enjoy himself even more as he secretly participates in the mystery.

This can lead to another way this sneaky deception can improve your relationship with the company even more. After you (and the boss) perform the trick for his employees, you offer to teach the trick to everyone, so they can do that magic for their friends and family. You ask the boss if it is all right with him if you reveal the secret. He will always say "yes." When you think about it, what else is he going to say? He can't really say "no," his employees would not understand why he kept this unique opportunity from them.

When you explain that your "secret helper" was the boss, everyone will laugh. You will cement your relationship, not only with the executive who helped you, but with all of his employees as well. Many of them will do the trick for their family and friends. When they do, they will remember who taught it to them. You'll get a wonderful reception the next time you visit that company.

Please understand, one of the most important rules of magic is to never reveal any of the secrets. Maintaining the mystery of the magic is one of the most important principles of our art. You may well ask, why is it all right to teach **The Challenge Coin Vanish**? Good question.

It's because this effect is basically a "magic gag," It depends upon having an unknown accomplice who tells a fib about feeling the coin. When they say, "Yes, the coin is there," they are lying and secretly taking the coin out of your hand.

Throughout the ages, magicians have often used audience members as "stooges," "plants," "sticks," or whatever the current name is at that time, as confederates. Quite possibly, ancient priests used this type of bogus testimony to prove their god given powers to the masses. Charlatans and con men often employ unknown confederates.

Frankly, I don't like magic that depends upon someone telling a lie about some amazing effect I have just presented. If I show a playing card and say, "Is this the card you selected?" If that spectator lies and says "yes" to any card I display, that is not my kind of magic.

On the other hand, after performing **The Challenge Coin Vanish,** when you explain to the spectators exactly what happened, you can add, "The moral of what you have just seen is, *don't trust anybody.*" You will not only get a good laugh, but might actually be helping some in your audience analyze a future real life situation.

As an example, the principle of "not telling the truth," on which this trick is based, creates the kind of conflicting courtroom testimony judges must evaluate every day to reach just decisions. Law schools can use the trick to illustrate how witnesses can be misled in their "Eye Witness Testimony" classes. In mystery stories a key person not telling the truth is often used to explain what appeared to be an inexplicable event, such as the strange disappearance of the crown jewels from the sealed safe, or how the victim was murdered while alone in a "locked room."

If you are teaching magic to a class which consists of students of any age, be they in grade school, high school or college, or if they are Ph.D.'s, professors, or corporate executives, **The Challenge Coin Vanish** is an excellent way to start. You begin your teaching by explaining that presenting "magic" is quite different from that of any other form of entertainment. Then you vanish the coin and make it reappear under "challenge" conditions.

The class will be totally bamboozled (except for your secret assistant). Your explanation reveals that the students were baffled, not by your great magical skill, learned through years of practice, or by some complicated or expensive magic prop. The magic they witnessed was based entirely upon the "secret." If they had known that secret in advance, there would have been no magic. This is an excellent way to begin any magic instruction class, which visually illustrates the importance of the "secret" in magic.

MAGIC FOR CHILDREN

Let's say you want to perform your magic to make children happy. There are three ways you may channel your wonders. *Entertain* them with magic … *Teach* them the magic … *Learn* the magic together. The age of the children and your goals for them determines which of these avenues will work best for you.

1. *Entertain children with magic.* Magicians have always been primarily known as entertainers. With your wizardry you can fascinate one or two children or an assemblage of youngsters. The most basic trick for a single child or two is when an adult vanishes a coin and finds it behind a child's ear. Fathers, grandfathers and favorite uncles have been doing that for centuries. An easy method for accomplishing this is **The French Drop** (Page 186). There are other sleights which accomplish this same thing, such as **The Pinch and Drop Vanish** (Page 189) and **The Finger Palm Vanish** (Page 187). Some other tricks with coins for a single child or small group are **The Coin Through Leg** (Page 195), **Coin-A-Go-Go** (Page 197) and **Continuous Coins** (Page 200). Of course, almost any effect in this course can be performed to a single child. As with all of the other magic, it's up to you to decide what will work best for your small viewers.

If you are appearing for a larger group of children, say, at a birthday party, there are many tricks that will work beautifully. Every trick in this course can be entertaining, but some work particularly well for younger folks. There is: **Fatima the Dancer** (Page 270) in which you make a little dancing doll from an ordinary handkerchief. When you perform **The Sorcerer's Stamp Album** (page 352), you magically transfer postage stamps from a paper cone into a previously empty stamp album. Any of the versions of **Confetti to Candy** (Pages 367 through 371) are enjoyed by youngsters. All of these effects are, in a way, the fulfillment of children's dreams.

2. *Teach children magic.* Over the years, I have often been told something like this, "I know only one trick. My grandfather used to do it. I still remember how happy I was when he taught it to me. Now I do it for my kids."

When you have learned and practiced the magic this course, you might like to teach some magic to children. You can deliver your instruction to an individual child or to a classroom full of youngsters. What you teach is determined, primarily, by the age of the students.

The Cut and Restored String (Page 247) is an excellent effect, easily understood by students. Because the only prop is a piece of string (and some glue) it's easy for the children to take home and show their family what they learned today. Another good "teaching" trick is **Magically Multiply Your Money** (Page 181), a basic sleight-of-hand effect. The first magic trick I ever learned, which was taught to me by my great, great aunt when I was a small boy, was **The Broken and Restored Match** (Page 285). I'm still doing it and teaching it as well.

There is one effect I have found that can be easily taught to children of all ages of (and it works well for adults, too). It is **The Jumping Rubber Band** (Page 293). There are three follow up effects, **Reverse Jumping Rubber Bands** (Page 295), **Double Jumping Rubber Bands** (Page 297), and **The Challenge Jumping Rubber Band** (Page 298). These are all simple, easily-taught tricks, which only require a few rubber bands. Children are delighted to learn these effects and show them to their friends. Perhaps, a few generations from now, they will teach magic with rubber bands to their children.

Another method of "teaching" is for you to act as the child's co-star as you both perform the magic together for family and friends. Or the child can become the magician and you assume the roll of the magician's assistant. Your choice of either of these approaches depends upon the age, physical ability, and psychological orientation of the child. The major advantage here is when an adult and a child are presenting the magic together, whether the grown-up is the co-star or the magician's assistant, the adult can assure that everything is done correctly to make the magic work.

Let me give you an example. In the presentation of the hypnotized handkerchief (page 269), the handkerchief can be held by the child, who then does all of the "magic." If the child is not old enough, or for some other reason has a problem performing the trick, the handkerchief can be held by the adult as the co-star or as the assistant. The child, with appropriate gestures, hypnotizes the handkerchief. The handkerchief then magically "moves" (in the adult's hand) under the spell cast by the child, with the "handling" really done by the adult.

Another example, the props in **The Sorcerer's Stamp Album** (page 352) can be easily made and shared in the presentation between both the child and the adult as co-stars. Or, the child plays the part of the magician and the props are all handled entirely by the adult, acting as the assistant. Either way, you are assured everything will be presented correctly. When the spectators give their applause, it can give some sorely needed recognition to the young magician … something the child might need and will always remember.

3. *Learn magic together.* Often it is good to have a partner in any learning situation. If you are going on a diet, lifting weights or learning Latin, having a partner can help. When I first became interested in magic, after baffling my parents with a few simple tricks, I teamed up with my best friend, Malcolm Ogden to learn more magic. We studied together and practiced what we had learned on each other. We criticized the other guy's magic and had a lot of laughs while we were doing it. When we thought we were good enough to start doing shows, we appeared together as "Malcolm and Mark" (He got first billing because he was bigger than I!)

Learning magic together is an excellent way to create bonding between an adult and a child. This course works well for that. Both the child and the adult not only learn *how* to perform the tricks, they also learn the *secrets* together. They have pledged, to each other, not to reveal those secrets to anyone, which strengthens the bonding even more.

Let's say a child's home is divided by divorce. Father has custody one day a week, usually on weekends. He and the child have gone to all the amusement parks and seen most of the suitable movies. A better relationship might be developed if some of that valuable time was spent studying magic together. In addition to strengthening the bonding between them, what they learn together will be pleasantly remembered as the child matures.

Of course, any of the tricks in this course can be learned with another person. Some particularly good ones for that are **Threading the Needle** (Page 249), **One Hand Knot** (Page 251), **The Melting Knot** (Page 251) and **The Shoe Lace Rope Trick** (Page 252). For these effects you need only two pieces of rope, each about three feet long. The pictures in course show exactly how to do everything. The two pieces of rope allow both the parent and child to learn at the same time. Sometimes the adult will achieve success first. But, more often than not, it will be the child who figures everything out. When one "teaches" the other exactly how it works, it strengthens the bonding between them even more.

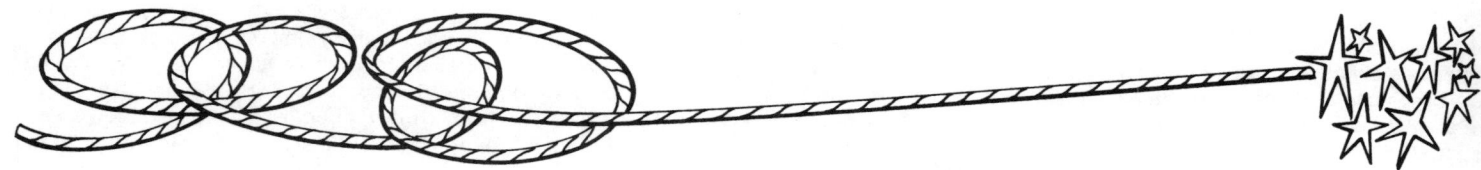

THE COWBOY ROPE TRICK

Of course, some tricks can be presented almost anywhere. **The Cowboy Rope Trick** can be performed for an individual child or a theater full of children. It can be adapted to fit any of the categories listed above. All you need is a piece of rope and a pair of scissors. It's incredibly easy to do. Its appeal is based on the story you deliver, which adds significantly to the magic.

EFFECT:

"Let me show you something very interesting with a piece of rope." You display a six-foot length of rope. "How many of you have seen a cowboy on television? Good." (In the following description, to each of the children's responses to your questions, you give an appropriate reply). "Now, cowboys always carry ropes, but the don't call them ropes. Do you remember what they do call them?" The children will respond. "That's right, (or whatever …) they call them lariats or lassos. Now a lariat or a lasso is a rope that has a loop in the end like this." You tie one end of the rope to the middle of the rope, forming a loop.

"The cowboys twirl the lasso or the lariat around like this and what do they catch with it?" Again the children respond with many different answers. Often they will say, "people" or "another cowboy." "Well, yes, sometimes, if they're not careful, they may catch another cowboy, but usually they catch cows. That's why we call them cowboys. If they caught rabbits, we would call them rabbitboys."

"The cow doesn't like getting caught by the cowboy and always tries to get away. That makes the rope tight around the cow's neck. The cow really doesn't like that. So, the cowboy takes a pair of scissors and cuts the cow loose, like this." You cut the rope in two where the loop is tied. You now have what appears to be two pieces of rope tied together in the middle. "That makes the cow happy because she's loose, but the cowboy is unhappy because his lasso is in two pieces."

"You know what the cowboys do? They bring the rope to me. I wrap the rope round my hand like this. Then I reach in my pocket and I get a pinch of magic dust. I always carry some magic dust for problems like this."

You reach into your pocket for the imaginary magic dust, which you show to the children between your pinched fingers. "Do you see the magic dust?" You will either hear "yes" or "no," or usually both. Either way you go on to explain, "That's right, because the magic dust is invisible. I just sprinkle it on the rope like this." You pretend to sprinkle the dust on the rope around your closed hand.

"Then I ask the cowboy to hold on to the end of the rope. Would you hold this for me please?" The youngster you have selected holds on to the end of the rope, which is still wrapped around your hand. This is a good opportunity to use the birthday child, or the person for whom the party is being held. As he or she hold on to the end of the rope, you let it unroll it from your hand. Everyone can see that the rope has been restored to one long piece!

"You see, it's the magic dust that makes the rope come out all in one piece. That means cowboys don't have to use as many ropes, which cuts down on the price of beef, and that's why you can have hamburgers for supper!"

SECRET:

The Cowboy Rope Trick is very easy to do. The rope should be about six feet long. (Image 1)

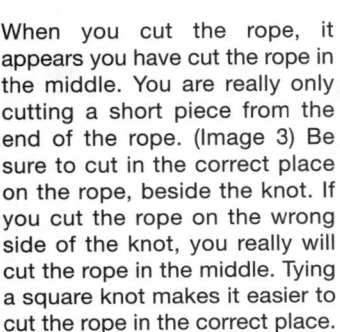

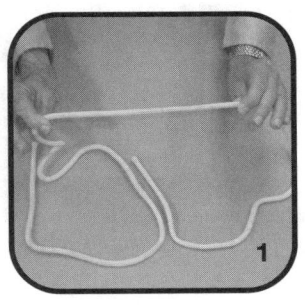

When you tell the story and make the loop, you tie one end of the rope to the middle of the rope. Just be sure to tie a square knot. In the picture, we have used two different colored ropes to make the square knot, so you can see exactly how it looks. (Image 2)

When you cut the rope, it appears you have cut the rope in the middle. You are really only cutting a short piece from the end of the rope. (Image 3) Be sure to cut in the correct place on the rope, beside the knot. If you cut the rope on the wrong side of the knot, you really will cut the rope in the middle. Tying a square knot makes it easier to cut the rope in the correct place.

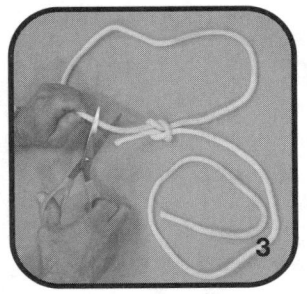

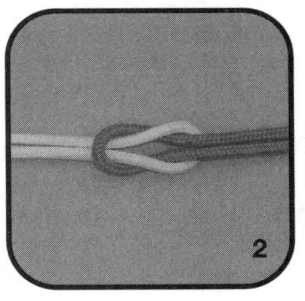

Display the "cut" rope to the audience (Image 4).

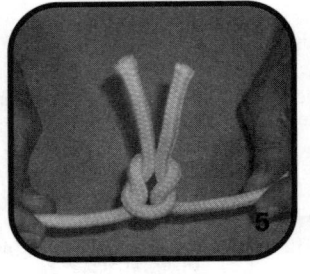

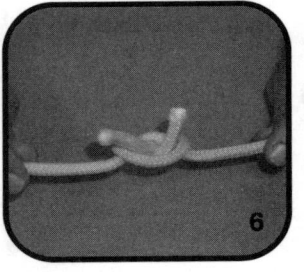

Then pull on the rope (Image 5) . . .

. . . which "upsets" the square knot and makes it into a slip knot (Image 6). Now you can easily slide the knot along the rope.

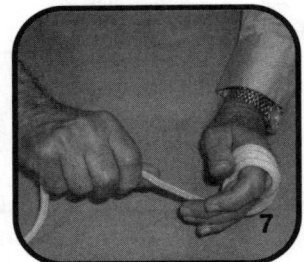

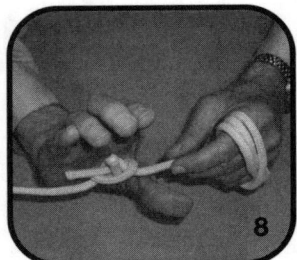

With your right hand, begin to wrap the rope around your left hand. (Image 7)

As you pull the rope through your right hand, secretly slide the knot along the rope. (Image 8) Keep the knot hidden in your right hand as you slide it along. (Image 8) (I have raised my fingers in the picture to show you the knot.)

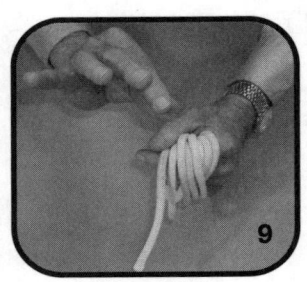

As you complete the winding, slide the knot off the end of the rope secretly in your right hand. Without pausing, reach your into your right pocket and say, "I need some magic dust." Leave the knot in your pocket and bring out the (imaginary) magic dust. Pretend to sprinkle it on the rope. (Image 9) Have someone hold the end of the rope as you uncoil it from your left hand. The children will see the knot has vanished and the rope is completely restored! The rope can then be tossed to the audience for examination.

Another way to be sure you cut the rope at the right place is also explained in **The Double Knot Restoration.** (page 245)

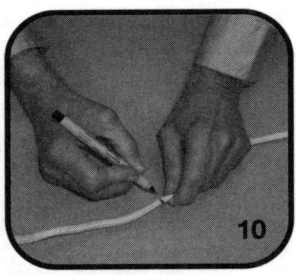

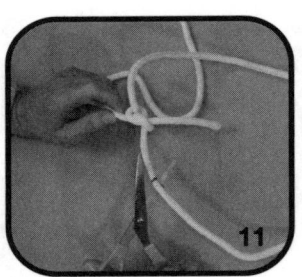

For this method, before the show, make a small mark about 5 inches from one end of the rope. (Image 10) That is the end that you tie to the middle of the rope to make the "loop."

After you tie the knot, cut the rope at the secret mark. (Image 11) This will assure you only cut off the short end piece.

In **The Double Rope Restoration** on page 247, pictures 13, 14, and 15 show wrapping the rope around your hand to secretly slide the knot off of the rope.

Here is an example of how magic can be added to a wide area of interest to children, teenagers and adults, utilizing all of the three methods outlined above. That is magic specifically selected for summer camps.

MAGIC FOR CAMPERS

Every year, there are thousands of summer camps attended by millions of children and teenagers. Investigating some of possibilities for the instruction of magic to campers, I conducted a number of teaching seminars for camp owners, executives and camp directors. I taught them magic tricks that I thought were suitable for campers and they gave me insight into how that magic could be of help to them for their particular needs and goals. Here are some of the conclusions the camping people reached and conveyed to me at the end of the seminars.

"Magic can be inexpensively incorporated into camping programs."

"It was easy to understand, so campers can learn easily and take magic skills home and show their friends."

"Learning magic can help increase a camper's social skills and self-confidence."

"Magic can help counselors 'bring out' a shy kid or a homesick scout."

"Magic can be used to gain the attention of staff members and/or campers to emphasis important points."

Most of the magic I taught in the seminars was easy-to-do and could be performed with inexpensive items such as rubber bands, paper clips, paper cups, rope, etc.—all items easily found by campers when they returned home. In this way, the campers can show their friends and family the magic they learned at camp, which helps create lasting memories of their camping experience. There are many such tricks in the course.

Some of the magic taught in the seminar required a bit more preparation or larger props. All of these tricks could be easily learned and then performed by the camp directors for their staff or by the staff members for campers. Each effect could be used to emphasize an important point such as fire safety, teamwork, rewards for effort, etc. Such effects as **The Comedy Cut and Restored Rope** (page 241), **The Comedy Cut and Restored Paper** (page 353) and **The Rope and Coat Release** (page 260) worked well for this. Another example is **The Magic Card Frame** (page 355) which does not have to be as small as shown in the picture, but can be made in any size from an appropriately-sized picture frame, which can then magically produce any graphic to highlight a specific goal. The opportunities to use magic to emphasize particular points are many.

Also included were some illusions which could be inexpensively made from cardboard boxes, corrugated board, bed sheets, etc. Then the camp could put on their own magic show. The show could be performed by the camp staff, or the councelors could teach the magic to campers so the youngsters would become the "magicians." The end result would be a magic show performed for other campers or for the camper's parents, who come on the last day to pick up their children.

Such illusions as **The Arabian Tent** (Page 437) and **The Haunted House** (Page 441) can be made inexpensively from corrugated board or foam core. A bit more elaborate is **The Mummy's Casket** (Page 449) which can be made quite inexpensively by the counselors or the campers. For **The Victory Cartons Illusion** (page 446) all that is needed are two large corrugated boxes which can be easily found. **The Mystery of the Magical Mummy** (page 449) requires only a large bedspread or sheet. The conclusion of that illusion is explained on page 451. The person the audience thought was wrapped inside the cloth turns out to be somebody else. Then, when that person comes running from behind the watching campers or makes some other miraculous appearance, it lends a terrific finale to the show.

Now here's a trick that will work well at any camp, and most any other place as well.

TIC TAC TOE PREDICTION

Here is an excellent effect that very few people have ever seen, and even fewer know how to perform. It can be presented in almost any conditions for any size audience.

EFFECT:

You offer to play a game of tic-tac-toe with a spectator. The spectator will have complete freedom of choice, making his or her mark in any of the squares. You state you have made a prediction of exactly how that game will be played, where each X and each O will be on the board. You hold up an envelope which contains your prediction and give it to someone in the audience to hold.

Then, you play a standard game of tic-tac-toe with any spectator. And yet, when your prediction is removed from the envelope, it proves to be entirely correct!

SECRET:

You can write up the prediction at home or somewhere out of sight of the spectators before you present the trick. Now, all you have to do is make sure the tic-tac-toe game you play with the spectator ends up looking just like your prediction … and it will! Here's what you do.

METHOD:

To begin, you explain, as in any game of tic-tac-toe, the first player to get three X's or three O's in a row wins. The spectator must play the game as if they are trying to be the winner and to stop you from winning. Then, you make the first mark, an X, in the center square (Image 1)

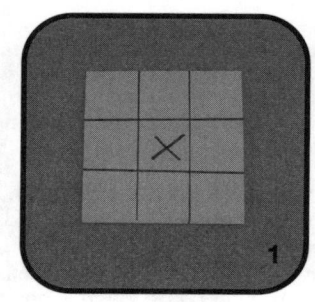

The spectator can then make their O mark in any square. There are really only two possibilities. The O will be in one of the corner squares (Image 2) . . .

. . . or in one of the inner squares (Image 3)

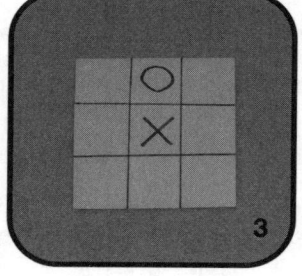

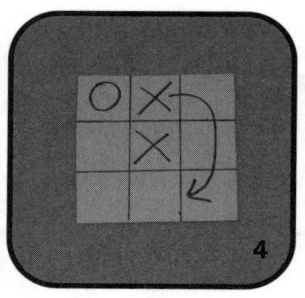

This is what you must remember. If the O is in a corner square, every X you make for the rest of the game will be in the first open square moving clockwise. (Image 4)

If the O is an inside square, every X you make for the rest of the game is made in the first open square moving counter-clock-wise. (Image 5)

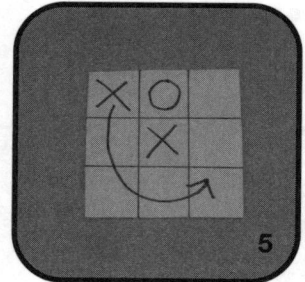

As you play the game, the spectator always has a free choice of any open square. Just remember to make all of your X marks in a clockwise square or a counter clockwise square, determined by the location of the spectator's first O mark. The completed game will always match your prediction. (Image 13)

To practice, play both sides of the game and you will see it always comes out exactly the same. Here is the progression on a game in which the spectator's first mark is in the corner square. Then, all of the X's are made in a clockwise square. (Images 6 through 12)

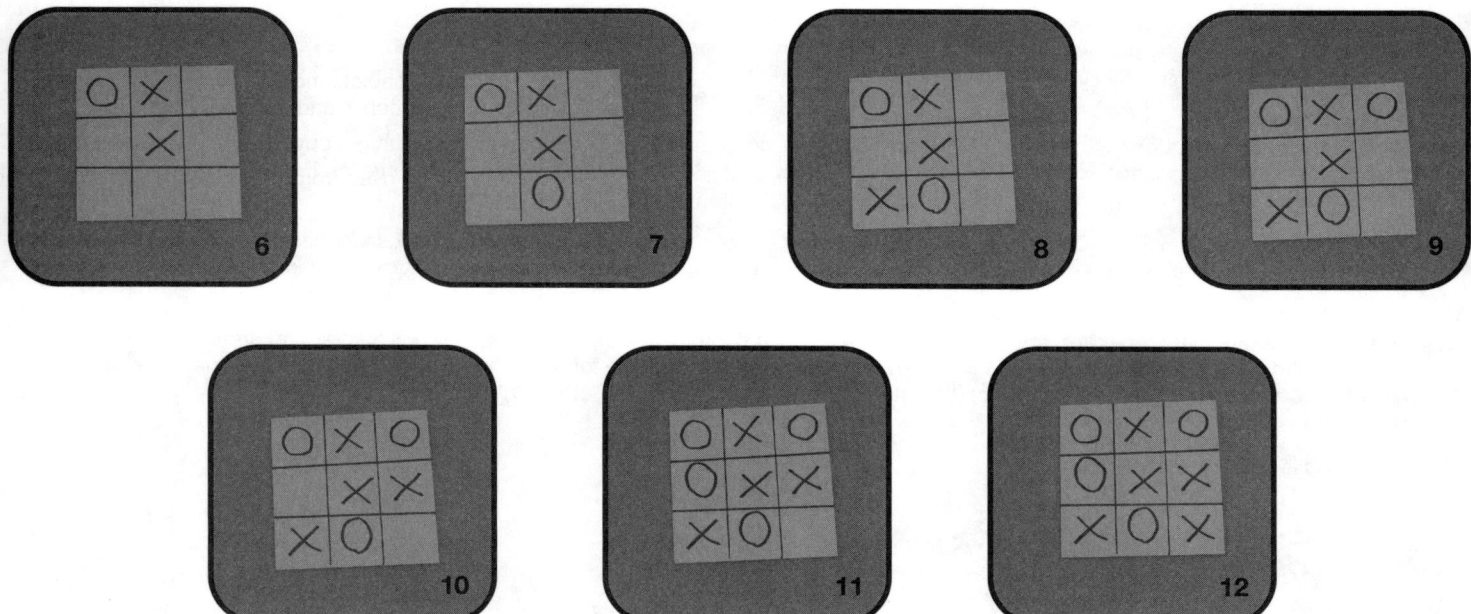

There is one more thing you can do to make your prediction even more impressive. You can sign your name on the bottom of the prediction. Still, the game you play with the spectator will match your prediction exactly, The reason is, there is no special "top" or "bottom" to a game of Tic Tac Toe. The game is "square", so any of the sides can be the top or the bottom. You must remember that, in your prediction, the three top squares are O/X/O. When you have finished playing with the spectator, before you reveal your prediction, turn the spectator's game so that O/X/O is the top. Then that game will match your prediction perfectly.

AFTER DINNER MAGIC

Performing a few baffling magic tricks as you sit at the dinner table is a natural. I've called this section **After Dinner Magic,** because that's the time your magic usually works best. When you are dining in a home, everyone, particularly mom if it's a family affair or your host if it's not, will be more interested in seeing that the food on the table is warm, rather than being distracted by your wizardry. After the meal, things are different. The dishes are cleared. You've had dessert (if you're lucky). Now is time for your magic.

In a restaurant, the timing can be different. There's a period between when the order is placed, until it is served. Sometimes this bit of time works well for magic. If the dining is preceded by a social get-together, that can be a good place to start. However, the safest time may be "after" dinner in a restaurant as well. Homes, restaurants, picnics, buffet-type affairs and banquets all have varying schedules, so it's up to you to select the most appropriate time, as well as the best possible magic for the occasion.

What you do is wide open, as well. There are several unique advantages in being seated at the dinner table when you fascinate the folks with your sorcery. For one thing, the table is right in front of you. You don't have to move the furniture or redo the landscape. That table is the perfect place for your "close-up" miracles. The viewers are seated there, so they can see everything very well. They are relaxing after a good meal. They are ready to be entertained.

Another advantage, there is a secret move many magicians use in their close-up performance called "lapping." Lapping is when you secretly drop some small object into you lap, or secretly pick-up something from your lap. You must be seated at a table to do any kind of lapping. Since that's exactly where you are, there is no suspicion, so performance of this particular ploy works wonderfully at the dinner table.

As an example, **The Glass Through Table** (page 314) is a true classic of magic. It's in the **Impromptu Magic** section of the course, because everything you need, the glass, a couple of paper napkins and any coin are all readily available. Images 11 and 12 in **The Glass Through Table** description show the lapping of the glass. In images 17 and 18, you see how you secretly pick up the glass from your lap to show everyone it has (apparently) penetrated the table.

There are many other tricks in the course that can be done with items usually found on or near the table. **The Turned Up Glasses** (page 341) uses only three regular drinking glasses and **The Knot in Handkerchief** (page 344) can be done with a cloth napkin. These are two of the many "Betcha" possibilities. **Roll the Bills** (page 222) is another excellent choice. Then there's **Dots Magic** (page 311) and **Dots Magic Impromptu Version** (page 314) where all of your magic is done with a dinner table knife and a few small pieces of paper.

If you just happen to have a deck of cards in your pocket or purse, some of your excellent card tricks can occupy the entire evening. Another good selection are tricks with **Sponge Balls**. In **Sponge Ball Magic** (page 391) you learn many powerful effects. Each of those tricks can stand alone or be presented as part of a routine. Then your magic can be made to fit the time available.

The Cords of Fantasia (page 303) works beautifully at the dinner table. You can usually borrow the necessary finger rings and have the guest on each side of you hold the cords, as you perform the magic. It's great entertainment based on a century-old principle of magic.

The Flying Match (page 309) should be performed only by adults because it involves the use of matches. It is one of the best after dinner magic effects. If you are in a restaurant, they will almost always have personalized match books. Do the "secret preparation" before dinner or excuse yourself from the table for a moment to set it up. The table is a perfect place for the effect, which uses lapping to make the match vanish. When that burnt match reappears, attached to the matchbook with all of the other unburnt matches, you will have made a powerful impression with your magical powers.

The following is ideal for performing after dinner.

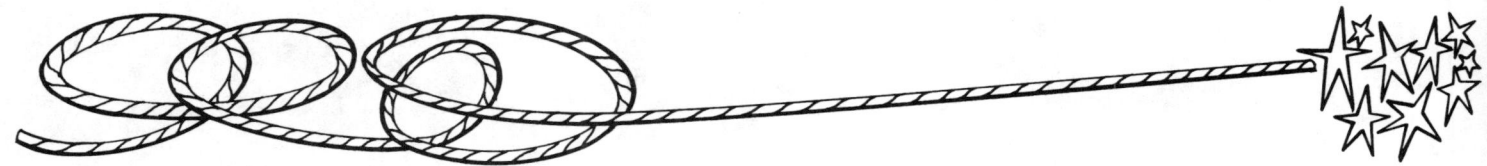

THE RING ON THE ROPE

Now you will learn one of the most baffling close-up magic tricks I have ever had the privilege of performing. I learned it first when I was thirteen years old and worked as the "magic demonstrator" in Douglas Magicland, the magic shop in my home town, Dallas, Texas. I have been puzzling audiences with this trick ever since. I'm sure you'll find it a valuable magical asset.

One of the great advantages of the Ring on Rope is you do it with four ordinary articles that you can find anywhere. They are a piece of rope about 2 feet long (you can use a shoe lace or a ribbon), a large safety pin, a handkerchief or cloth napkin, and a ring about the size of a finger ring, to as large as a curtain ring or harness ring. Everything can be examined before and after the trick, because they are exactly what they appear to be, just four ordinary objects.

EFFECT:

You tell the viewers that they are going to see a visual impossibility, so they should watch very closely. You show the four items and suggest the spectators examine everything. Ask if you may borrow someone's finger ring (A man's wedding ring works very well for this, but it will work with any ring).

You place all of the items on the table in front of you. (Image 1)

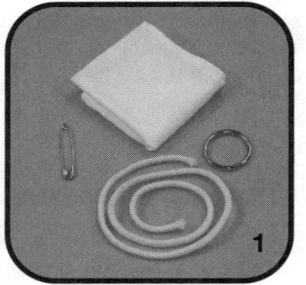

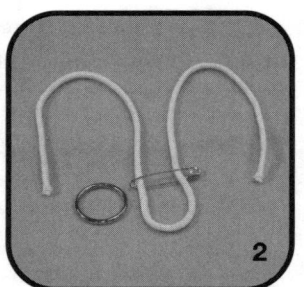

You put the safety pin (It's good to use a large safety pin for this) through the rope twice, making a loop as shown in the picture. Place the ring beside the loop. (Image 2)

Call to the spectator's attention, the ring is not on the rope. Also, emphasize that the ends of the rope will always be visible as you perform this seeming miracle.

Show the handkerchief on both sides and place it over the rope and the ring As you do this, it is most important that the spectator always sees both ends of the rope at all times.

The handkerchief now covers the rope and the ring. The ends of the rope are not covered by the handkerchief. You reach under the handkerchief with both hands. (Image 3) The viewers can see your hands are moving under the handkerchief. You explain you are now doing the "magic."

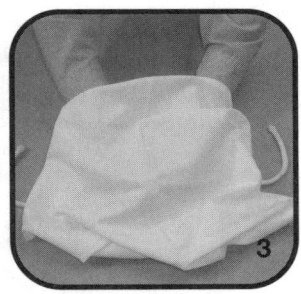

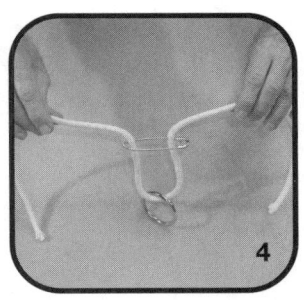

After thirty seconds or so, you say, "I have completed the magic." Ask the spectator, "Have the ends of the rope have been completely visible at all times?" The answer is, "Yes." "And yet, the ring is now on the rope." You pull the rope out from under the handkerchief. Sure enough, the impossible has happened, the ring is on the rope. (Image 4)

SECRET:

Before I explain the secret, let me assure you, at the conclusion of the trick, the ring is really on the rope. These are all ordinary objects, there are no "duplicates." All these items can be borrowed, if you wish. There are no suspicious moves. The secret is so subtle and so rational, "the Ring on the Rope" is really is one of the masterpieces of the art of magic.

METHOD:

Here is the closely guarded secret to this unbelievable trick. Everything the spectators see is exactly as described in the Effect. When you place both of your hands beneath the handkerchief, here's what you do.

First, slip the ring over the top of the loop of rope. (Image 5)

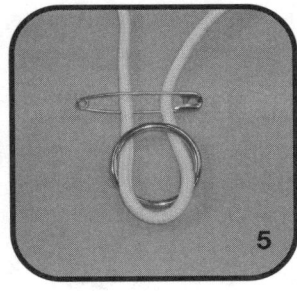

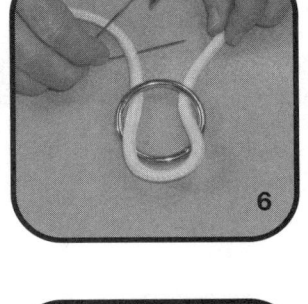

Open the safety pin and remove it from one side of the rope. (Image 6)

Slide the ring a short distance down the rope, past the place on the rope where you removed the pin. (Image 7)

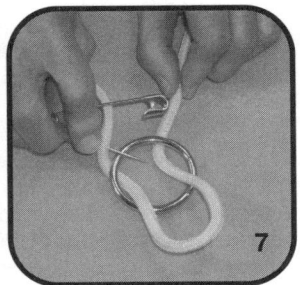

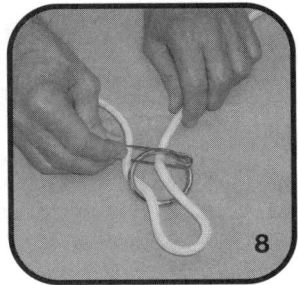

Place the pin back through the rope in the same place it was before. *Do not put the pin through the ring.* Fasten the pin closed. (Image 8)

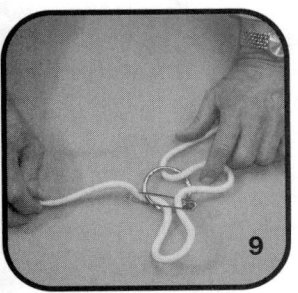

Both of your hands are still under the handkerchief. Pull a bit of the rope through the ring and insert the first finger of your left hand just above the place where you refastened the pin as shown in the picture. (Image 9) As you see, your finger is between the pin and the ring and the rope runs around it. *Study the picture so you will put your finger in the correct place.* Press the tip of that left finger down on the table. You should learn to do this by "feeling" what you are doing, so you do not need to look under the handkerchief.

You now state, "Although the ends of the rope have been visible at all times, impossible as it seems, the ring is now on the rope." (Actually, the ring is not on the rope, but *you want the spectators to believe you have already performed the "magic."*)

To show everyone that the ring is on the rope, you pull the rope out from under the handkerchief. To do this, remove your right hand from under the handkerchief, pick up the end of the rope on the right side and pull the rope out from under the handkerchief.

When you pull the rope out, *the left end of the rope is out of view of the audience for a fraction of a second,* as that end goes under the handkerchief. (Image 10)

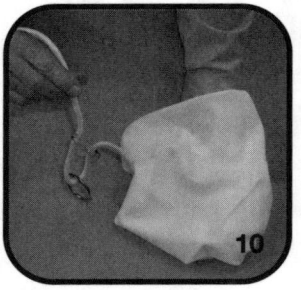

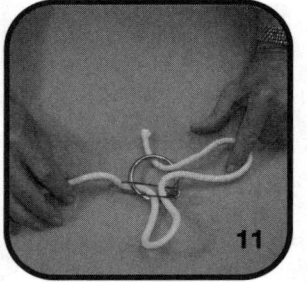

Because of the placement of your left first finger on the table, when you pull the rope out, *the left end of the rope secretly travels through the ring.* (Image 11)

(Image 12) These pictures show what is happening under the handkerchief as you pull the rope out.

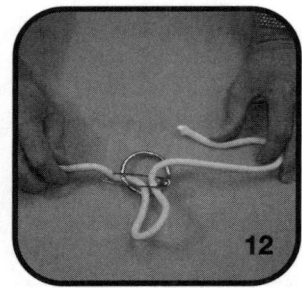

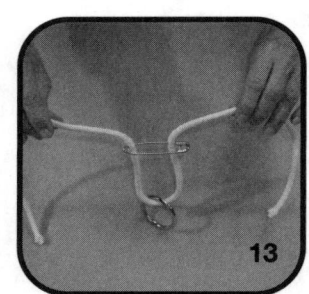

You give the impression that you merely pull the rope out to show the spectators that the ring is on the rope, but that's when the "real" magic happens. When you have pulled the rope all the way out from under the handkerchief, the audience can see, the solid ring is really on the equally solid rope. (Image 13)

Before you perform "the Ring on the Rope" for anyone, I would sincerely appreciate your learning and practicing this trick thoroughly. That way we will all protect the secret to this astonishing effect.

PARTY MAGIC

Parties can be ideal for your magic. There are many different types of parties and just as many different kinds of magic. The magic you do at any get-together is determined by three criteria. One is the age of your audience… young, old, all around the same age, or spanning many generations. The second is the type of occasion… birthday party, bar mitzvah, retirement celebration, church affair, or grand extravaganza. The third is the performing conditions… intimate gathering, walk around, stage setting, indoor or outdoor. Whatever these criteria are, they establish what magic will work best for you at that particular party.

Let's assume you are attending a gathering that would really appreciate a good card trick. You've got lots of them. There are many excellent effects in the chapter in this course.

The Fantastic Five (page 32) is a good start for your initial card routine. This can be followed by **Turn Over Card** (page 34) during which you have apparently made a mistake, but are saved by the magic. **You Do As I Do** (page 44) was one of the first card tricks I ever learned. It takes two decks of cards. If you wish, both decks can be borrowed from the host at the party. In any event, the effect is outstanding. There are many other terrific self-working card tricks.

Here is a self-working card trick with an exceptionally powerful effect and many endings, one after another. The final climax provides a super conclusion. Properly presented, this effect, alone, can make you the hit of the party.

FURTHER THAN THAT

This is an excellent trick you can do with any deck of cards. It has not just one, but a whole series of magical endings. You'll see why it really deserves the name "Further Than That."

EFFECT:

Holding a deck of cards, you say, "Perhaps the oldest card tricks is one in which the magician has you freely select any card from the deck, and then tells you what card you selected. But the trick I'll show you now *goes further than that*."

While saying this you spread the cards from hand to hand, as if you were going to have one selected by the spectator. (Image 1) But don't have one chosen, just keep the deck in your hands.

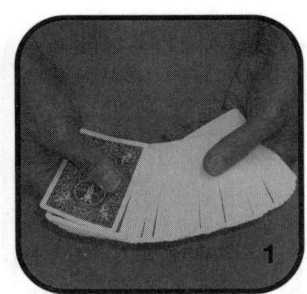

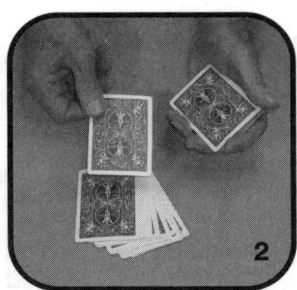

"Please name a small number." Pause for just a brief moment as if you are making up your mind. "Why don't you select a number between 10 and 20. What is the number? I'll count that number of cards from the deck." Let's assume the spectator says "Fifteen." You count off 15 cards, one at a time, from the top of the deck, placing them in a stack on the table. (Image 2)

Say each card's number as you count them, "1,2,3, etc." Set the deck down and point to the top card of the stack. "This could be the card you selected, but *this trick goes further than that*." "To make this a truly random selection, we'll add together the two digits that make up the number 15. That would be a one and a five. When you add those numbers together it totals 6."

Pick up the packet of 15 cards and count off six cards, one at a time, to the table. Say the number of each card as you deal them, "1, 2, 3, 4, 5, 6." (Image 3)

Keep the balance of the packet in your left hand. Show the top card of the six cards on the table and say, "This is the card you selected. I will not look at the card. Remember it ... it is very important that you remember it." (Image 4)

Show the "selected" card, the Ace of Spades, to the spectator. You know it is the ace of spades, but hold the card so you cannot see its face. Replace the selected card on top of the stack on the table.

Place the cards in your hand on top of the stack of cards on the table. (Image 5)

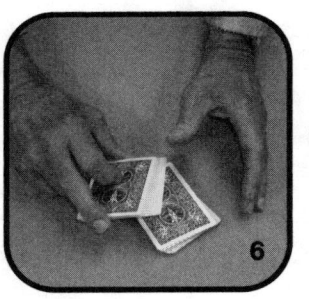

Pick up the stack of cards from the table and place it on top of the deck. (Image 6)

"If I were to tell you now which card you freely selected, that would be a good trick. But *this trick goes further than that*." "Your card is somewhere in the deck. I don't know what card you selected. But let me show you something I have learned as I studied magic." Hold the deck beside your ear and riffle the corner of the deck with your thumb. "I'll let the deck tell me the name of your card."

Now hold the deck in front of you and speak to the deck, "Yes deck, I hear you." To the spectator, you say, "The deck tells me you selected the Ace of Spades, is that right?" When the spectator says, "Yes," you say, "Now that would be an excellent conclusion to this trick. But *this trick goes further than that*."

"I will now find your card by magic. I'll just spell the name of your card. It was an ace ... A ... C ... E ..."

From the top of the deck, count off one card for each letter. When you say, "A," you count one card to the table in a pile slightly to your right. Say "C" and place the second card on top of the "A" card. The "E" card goes on top of the other two. (Image 7)

"And the suit was spades. I'll spell spades." From the top of the deck, count one card for each letter, into a pile slightly to the left, "S ... P ... A ... D ... E ... S ..." (Image 8)

"Having spelled its name, we find your selected card is right here on top of the deck!" Turn over the top card, it is the Ace of Spades. (Image 9) Place the ace on the table between the two stacks of cards "And that would be a great ending. Except *this trick goes further than that*."

"Look, these cards are the other three aces." Turn the three ace cards in the right side stack face up. (Image 10) "Locating all four aces would be a wonderful ending! *But this trick goes further than that*."

"The suit of your card was spades. And look, these cards are, all spades!" Turn over the stack of cards on your left to show they are all spades. (Image 11) "That would be a really tremendous ending, *but this trick goes further than that*."

"If I deal the next four cards from the deck and combine them with the Ace of Spades, like this ..."From the top of the deck, deal the next four cards face down in front of the Ace of Spades on the table. (Image 12)

"Then we would have," turn the cards face up, (Image 13) "a royal flush, which always wins, *and you can't go any further than that!*"

SECRET:

As you see, with **Further Than That,** you apparently reach the end of the trick several times. Each false conclusion builds to a really grand climax. You might think, because of its powerful effect on the audience, this trick may be very difficult to do, requiring a great deal of practice. Actually, this is one of the very best self-working card tricks. Just follow the directions and it performs itself! This effect was originally devised by the creator of many clever and ingenious tricks, Stewart James.

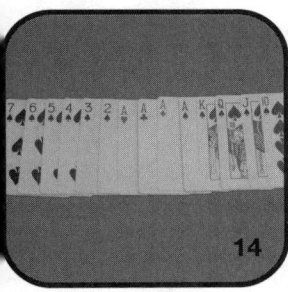

Unknown to the audience, before you perform the trick, you arrange (stack) the top cards of the deck like this:

Top card 7S, 6S, 5S, 4S, 3S, 2S, AH, AC, AD, AS, KS, QS, JS, 10S. Bottom card (Image 14)

Your audience must not be aware that the deck is "stacked." If you wish, you can just take the stacked deck out of the card case, as you begin the presentation.

The only magic in the routine is that the Ace of Spades is "forced" on the spectator, which is automatic in the routine. It uses The 10-20 Count Force, which is fully explained on page 78. The spectator is free to name any number between 10 and 20. You count that many cards from the deck, one at a time, to the table. Then you total the two digits of the selected number and count that number of cards from those you just counted to the table. This will automatically force the tenth card, the Ace of Spades.

To learn this trick, all you need to do is stack the deck as shown and follow the directions. Everything happens automatically. This trick has a terrific built-in presentation, which always gets laughs and has a powerful ending. It will be a real "reputation maker" for you.

After you learn a few card sleights, the number of possibilities is increased even more. An easily learned sleight is **The Hindu Shuffle.** (page 46). You can control a selected card with **The Hindu Key Card Location** (page 49) or a group of cards using **The Hindu Shuffle—Bottom Stock Control** (page 56). You can "force" a card with **The Hindu Flash Force** (page 52), and magically make a red-backed deck change into a blue backed deck employing **The Hindu Color Change** (page 53). You can even make two different colored decks change places by learning **The Color Changing Decks—Two Deck Version** (page 55). All of these, and a lot more, can be performed using only this one sleight.

Of course, it's not just card tricks, there are many other magic effects in the course that work beautifully at parties. An excellent choice is **The Sucker Torn and Restored Napkin** (page 305), which you can perform with whatever paper napkins are available at the affair. **The Three Way Test** (page 318) is a great baffler which can be done with just pieces of paper, predicting three items to be selected by the party goers. One of the strongest effects at any party can be **The Cut and Restored Neck Tie** (page 362). Although it does take a bit of preparation and some cooperation from your "victim," the effect is really hilarious and has a great pay off.

RANDOM NUMBER SELECTOR MYSTERY

EFFECT:

This baffling prediction can be terrific at parties. You write a prediction on a piece of paper, fold the paper and hand it to a spectator to hold. Then five different numbers between 1 and 25 are selected, at random, by members of the audience. These numbers are added together to reach an even more random total. Your prediction, which has been in the spectator's position since long before any of the numbers were chosen, is revealed to the audience. They are amazed to see that your prediction is entirely correct!

PRESENTATION:

For selection of the numbers, you use the Random Number Selector chart, which is a display of the numbers 1 through 25 arranged in 5 horizontal rows with 5 numbers in each row. (Image 1) The chart can be printed on a postcard-sized card, on a large display board, or displayed in any size in between, just so it is large enough to be seen by the people in your audience.

Ask a spectator to call out any number from 1 to 25. You circle that number on the Random Number Selector chart. (Image 2)

Then you cross out all of the numbers in the row, (going across the chart) and all of the numbers in the column (going up and down the chart) of the selected number. (Image 3)

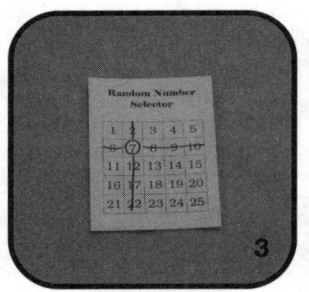

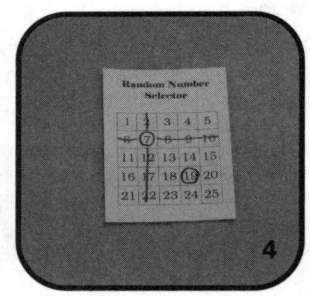

You ask another spectator to select any other number that has not been marked off of the chart. You circle the selected number (Image 4) . . .

. . . and mark off all the other numbers in the row and column of that number. (Image 5)

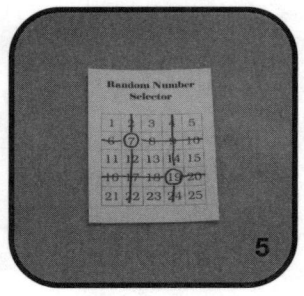

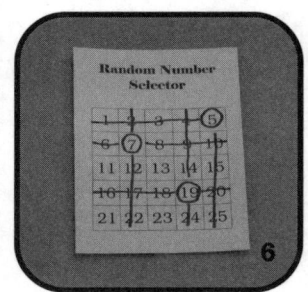

You ask a third audience member to select any number that has not been eliminated. You circle that number and mark off its appropriate row and column. (Image 6)

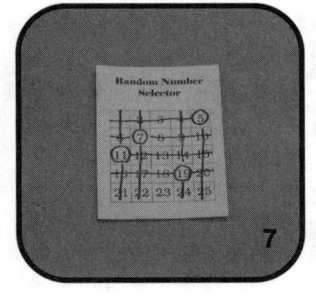

You do the same with a fourth spectator, marking off the selected numbers in the row and column. (Image 7)

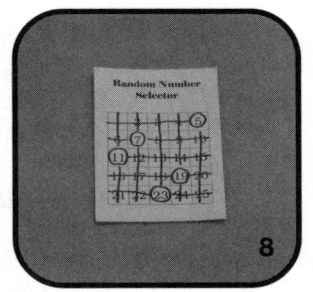

The last number, which would be the fifth choice, is actually the only remaining open number on the chart. You circle that number. (Image 8)

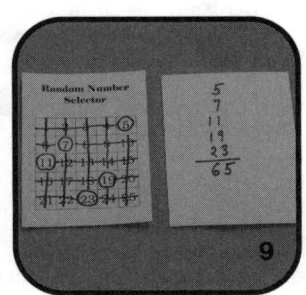

You now make a list of the five numbers that have been "select-ed." Then you add those numbers together for a total. (Image 9)

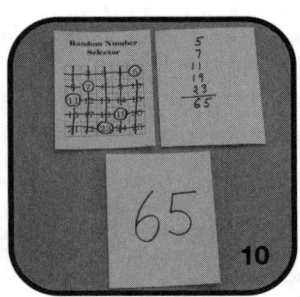

Sure enough, that total is exactly what you have written as your prediction! (Image 10)

SECRET:

This effect is based on a little known mathematical principle. The working of the trick is totally automatic. Each spectator has a free choice of any number from 1 to 25. Then any other number that has not been crossed out can be selected by a spectator. As the numbers are chosen, you eliminate all of the other numbers in the row and the column of each selected number. Interestingly, when those five "selected" numbers are added together, the total will always be 65.

If you are performing this for only one person, she or he can make all of the number selections. Or, this magical mystery can be performed in a giant auditorium, an arena or a coliseum. For a larger group, I recommend you have different audience members select each number, which strengthens the effect. Just be sure the display chart of the 25 numbers is visible to everyone.

If the numbers are on a small card or drawing pad, you can hand the Random Number Selector chart to the audience for marking. If the spectators follow your directions as they select the five numbers, and mark out the rows and columns correctly, you don't even need to know what numbers they have selected. The total will always total 65. This makes a very strong presentation.

The main problem I have found in handing the chart to the spectators for marking is that the audience members must be correct in crossing out both the rows and the columns of the numbers they select. If someone doesn't get that part right, it throws the whole effect out of whack, and your prediction will be wrong. So, I feel it is better if you do the marking. The choice of all the numbers is done by the audience. You do the marking, so the rows and columns are marked off correctly.

You can make Random Number Selector charts on a copy machine. Or, you can scan the chart into your computer and print out copies. For business or promotional purposes, let's say you are using a bingo-sized card for the chart. Then you can have your name printed on the top or bottom of the card. You can put more information, your address, or any other promotional material you wish on the back of the card. You can leave the card with your host, the birthday party celebrant, the person who booked the show, etc.

You can do the trick even if you don't have any cards printed. On a sheet of paper, draw the lines and put in the numbers. It will take you a few minutes, but this is an excellent trick.

Actually, every trick in this course can be adapted and performed at various get-togethers. It's up to you to choose what will work best for you. The magic you present at parties will not only add to your social life, as your ability to present the magic increases, these affairs can also be consistent income producers for you, if you wish.

SALES MAGIC SECRETS

Everybody sells something and everybody wants to sell more of it. You may sell a product or a service. If you are not directly involved in sales, you are selling your wonderful personality or the excellent work you do for the company. The response you get from the other kids, your team-mates, your family, your fellow workers in the production line, or your peers at the university … whoever it is that you work with and for … is important to your life. In other words, no matter what kind of work you do, whether it's white collar at the office, blue collar at the factory or no collar at all at the swimming pool, there are people you want to please. You want those people to appreciate what you do. They should recognize you as an individual, not just part of the operation.

Magic can help you do that. You see, now you are on your way to being a "special" person. Those "amazing" things you do will gain you that recognition, which can be a unique advantage over your competition, whatever that competition is.

Of course, you must decide what magic is best to help you achieve your goals in the conditions in which you find yourself. As an example, let's say you are a salesman and you need to get in to see the purchasing agent at a major corporation, someone you have never met before. You are in the waiting room with several other people who would like to do that very same thing.

Just suppose, between those incoming phone calls the receptionist is taking, you show her a simple trick, like **The Linking Paper Clips** (Page 298). The effect requires only one dollar bill and two paper clips. You can supply the dollar bill. She will have the paper clips. When you snap those paper clips off of the dollar bill and they are "magically" linked together, she is intrigued! You do it again, and this time you add a rubber band to the bill. When the clips are magically linked, they are also attached to the rubber band! See Page 300.

Now here's where your magic can really help: You volunteer to teach her exactly how to magically link those paper clips, so she can show it to her family when she gets home tonight. She's happy because you brought a little joy to her day. You've just gained a definite advantage over all those other people waiting to get in.

This is a large company you are calling on and making this sale is important. Many are still waiting, but you're on your way down the hall to meet that purchasing agent. While you're walking to his office, he gets a call from an even higher executive of the company. They'll talk while you wait with his secretary, outside his office. The secretary thought he was going to be meeting with you and has nothing particular to do at the moment. You have another opportunity.

You could tell her a joke, but you're not sure she would laugh at it. You could sing her a song. (With my voice, that would be a really dumb idea. She might call security and then I'd never get in to see anybody in that company again.) Or you could do a simple magic trick, something like **Sponge Ball Magic** (Page 391).

That trick is actually a series of effects made into a routine. You can stop the magic at any time, when her boss is ready to see you. If you do those tricks well, there's a very good chance, when she ushers you into see him, she will make a favorable comment about what she has just seen. You begin your relationship with this gentleman on a very pleasant note … and that's good.

So you've finally gotten in to see the purchasing agent. Now it's time to present your products, your competitive advantages, and the excellence of the company you represent. If appropriate, there are many points you can illustrate or emphasize "by magic." For a starter, you can magically imprint your business card for him.

At the end of this section I'll teach you how to "magically" print your business card. It's easy to do, you can present it in less than one minute, it immediately establishes your "magical powers" and adds to the possibility that the potential customer will keep your business card, not throw it away.

When the person with whom you are meeting sees your magic, quite often they will call some of their associates into their office, or take you where there are a number of company employees, and ask you to do your magic for them.

An excellent series of magic effects I have used in this kind of situation are **The Dissolving Knot** (page 272), next **The Knot Through Arm** (Page 273), followed by **The Coin Through Handkerchief** (page 178), concluding with **The Hypnotized Handkerchief** (Page 269). These can be combined into one fast moving routine. I do the magic with my pocket handkerchief and a half dollar, both of which I always have with me. I have performed these tricks in business meetings around the world.

YOUR MAGIC WILL OPEN MANY DOORS

Many times, when I'm seeing a doctor or a dentist, and I present a bit of magic, they will call in their nurses and technicians. An auto shop foreman will assemble his mechanics. In my initial meeting with Frito Lay, I had to come back very early the next morning to perform a few tricks at the Morning Meeting. At a giant silk mill in China, I was asked to perform on the dusty factory floor for the production workers. At the conclusion of the International Air Show in Paris, Martin-Marretta Company held a reception in the large mezzanine ballroom of the Eiffel Tower. I was asked to perform some of my magic for the many different small groups of guests, all speaking many different languages, gathered for the huge affair. Remember, the more people you entertain with your magic, the better impression you will make on the client and the more they will like you and the product or services you are selling.

SPEECHES AND PRESENTATIONS

Here's another effective way to apply magic. Let's say you are the new Chief Executive Officer of the company, making an important speech to the company employees concerning the exciting future their company now has with the new operational procedures you have installed. You've been preparing this presentation for weeks. It's important that it be a success, not just for the bright future you are predicting, but, perhaps even more importantly, so your associates will see you as a person, not just the new boss.

Near the beginning of your presentation you display three short pieces of rope. You explain that each rope represents one of the three major divisions of the company: Sales, Production, and Management. You show that the three ropes are exactly the same length. Each rope is two feet long.

You explain how each of the three divisions must work closely with the other two for any company to achieve maximum success. "In the best of all worlds, Sales must not outstrip Production. Production must keep up with Sales. The positive interaction between Sales and Production must be optimized by Management."

You expound on the important role of each division of their company. Nearing the conclusion of your presentation, you say, "Under our reorganization, these three divisions are combined, integrated, and coordinated as never before, into one dynamic, seamless organization."

To demonstrate how effective these changes will be, you, amazingly, turn those three short pieces of rope into one strong, six-foot long rope. This graphically illustrates the importance of what you have brought to the company. You've smoothed out the rough spots and added continuity and strength to the organization. You've also shown your own personality to the employees in a very positive way. (**Triple Rope Trick,** Page 242)

You can do the triple rope trick with two ropes or four ropes, if that better illustrates your theme. It is quite easy to do and the ending is powerful. You can perform it for one person or for a large audience. When the three short ropes become one long rope, if you're doing it for an individual, you can leave the rope as a souvenir. In a corporate meeting, you can hand the rope to the next speaker on the bill, or toss it out to the audience. It is a powerful effect.

IF YOUR CUSTOMERS COME TO YOUR BUSINESS

Let's say you are not the new CEO. Perhaps you are a barber, work in a restaurant or own a shoe store. Your customers come to you. That's where magic can give you a definite competitive advantage over that other company down the street, your competition.

Many previous customers that you've done a bit of magic for will come back to your business because they would like to see another trick. "Let's go get our ice cream sundae from that guy who has the shop on the corner. I'm gonna ask him if he can make those three short ropes into one long rope, like he did last time. Remember, he gave me the long rope. When I got home, I cut it up but it didn't go back together. Or maybe he'll show us a new trick. Come on, let's go." This is an example of how that same bit of magic that worked well to illustrate a speech can be adapted to other situations. Every trick in this course can do that. Just use your imagination.

Perhaps you'd like to be the most popular baby sitter in town. "We need a babysitter for Saturday night. Let's ask Julie. Last time she taught Sally and Johnny how to make rubber bands jump around on their fingers. They've done it now for all their friends and for Grandma and Grandpa when they came over to visit last week. Let's get her again. Maybe she will teach the kids another trick." **The Jumping Rubber Band,** page 295, can easily be taught to someone else and particularly fits the need in this instance.

The following could be a recorded message on a phone answering machine. "Hi Ed, it's Joe. I'm calling you from the car. I'm on my way from my office to meet you for dinner. Let's meet at the ABC Bar & Grill, you know where it is. I was there last week and that guy Frank, the bartender, did the darndest card trick. He and I each selected the very same card from two different deck of cards. I want you to see it. I'll meet you there at eight." When Ed meets Joe, Frank will perform **You Do As I Do** (Page 44). It's really a great trick and it's what is bringing Joe and Ed in tonight.

TRADE SHOWS AND NETWORKING

Magic can be used to great advantage in trade shows and networking events, helping you to attract more potential customers and to deliver your sales message more effectively.

Let's say you're standing in your company's booth at a trade show. Several conventioneers are looking at your product. You introduce yourself and shake hands. Then, unmistakably showing both of your hands empty, you reach into the air and produce a number of dollar bills. You explain that, "If you use our company's product, which is on display right here in our booth, you will get the same results."

You have just performed, **Bills From Nowhere** (Page 223). You loaded the rolled up bills in the fold of your left arm when you saw those customers coming. You're free to shake hands, show both of your hands empty and produce those bills from the air. You don't ordinarily see someone pulling money out of thin air at a trade show, or anywhere else for that matter. Those folks will remember you and your product … and that's why you are there.

There are many tricks in the course you can use for trade events and networking. Any of the cut and restored rope effects, beginning on page 237, can be used to illustrate many sales points, marketing plans or corporate promotions. If you have a little more time available, **Roll the Bills** (Page 222) is an excellent "betcha." You then explain it to the visitors, who will roll the bills for their friends. When they do this, they'll remember they learned that "betcha" from you.

MAGIC BUSINESS CARD PRINTING

EFFECT:

Whether you go to your customers, or they come to you, they will all remember you and your business. You know why they remember you? Because they've all kept your business card. You printed the card, by magic, right in their own hand. They're still talking about it. Your magic is working for you.

"Let me give you my business card." You remove three blank business cards from your pocket or business card case. "Oh, that's right, the printer forgot to print the cards. Let me just double check."

"Let's see. One, Two, Three cards." You count the cards, one at a time, and (apparently) show the three cards are all blank on both sides.

"They're blank all right. I have an idea. Would you hold out your hand for me please." You place one of the cards on the spectator's outstretched palm. "Please place your other hand on top, like this." "Now, turn both of your hands over." You indicate what you want. "I'll add a little magic." You make a magical gesture, or say a magic word. "Let's see what happened. Please take your top hand away." The spectator is greatly surprised to discover the formerly blank card is now your printed business card! As the spectator looks with amazement at your business card, you say, "It's a good thing I know some magic!"

SECRET:

To do this trick, all you need is one of your regular business cards and two blank business cards to match. There are several ways to obtain blank business cards.

You can ask the company that printed your business cards to send you some blank cards or include some blank cards with your next order of business cards.

You can create blank cards from your existing business cards. All you do is glue two of your business cards together, face to face. When you glue together the printed sides of two of your business cards, they appear to be one blank card. You can use any kind of glue, rubber cement, paste, etc. Make two of the "blank" cards, add one of your regular business cards and that's all you need.

An excellent way to make your own business cards is to use blank business card stock and print them on your computer printer. You can buy blank business card stock at any office supply store. Use an unprinted sheet for the blank cards. Usually, each sheet carries ten cards. From one printed sheet and two unprinted sheets, you can make ten sets of the three cards.

A few requirements for the cards ...

The paper stock on which the cards are printed must be thick enough so, when you look at the printed card from the back, you cannot see through the card and tell that it is printed on the other side.

The blank cards must look the same on both sides. Some business cards are glossy on one side and dull on the other. Or, the color or the finish of the stock may vary from one side to the other. Because of the way you show the three cards "blank" on both sides, the sides must all appear to be the same.

The design (printing) on your card should not extend to the edge of the card. That's because the requirement for your business cards for this trick is the same as for playing cards. As stated in Card Definitions under "White Bordered Back Cards" on page 19. "A white bordered back is essential in the performance of many of the tricks described in this course. This is because, when a card is reversed (turned face-up in a face-down pack), it will not be noticeable because the white edges of the face are the same as the white border of the pattern back." The same is true of the business cards used for Magic Business Cards printing.

METHOD:

For these instructions, we have put an "X" on the blank side of the printed card. (Image 1)

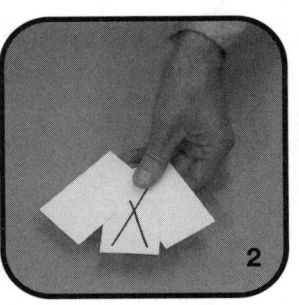

Before you present the effect, place your printed business card face down, between the blank cards. (Image 2)

I often carry my business cards in a leather or plastic business card case. That is not needed for the trick, but it is a convenient way of carrying your cards. Or, the cards can just be in your pocket.

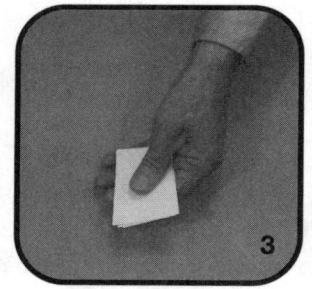

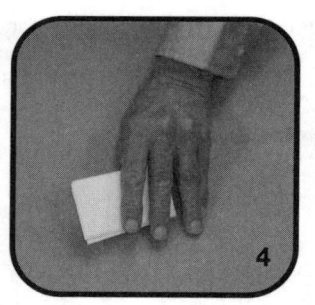

When you remove the three cards from your business card case or pocket, they are stacked one on top of the other. (Image 3)

You can show the stack on both sides, because the printed card is concealed between the two blank cards. (Image 4)

You talk about the printer having delivered blank cards, as you show the stack on both sides.

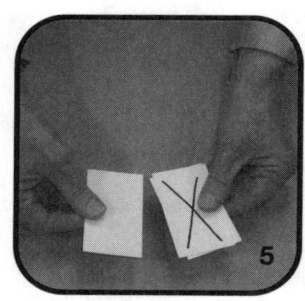

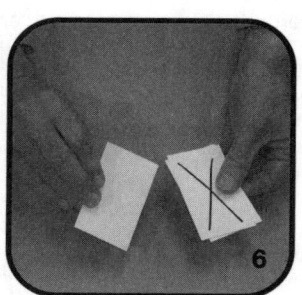

Here's how you display, individually, that the three cards are all blank. "Let me double check." Hold the stack of three cards in your left hand, with the printed card face down between the other two. Say, "One" and push off the top card of the stack of three with your left thumb and take it with your right thumb on top and fingers underneath. (Image 5)

Show the card in your right hand on both sides by turning your hand over. (Image 6)

Turn your hand back as it was before. You have shown the card blank on both sides.

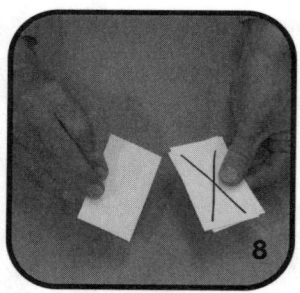

Now comes the only "move" in the routine. Count "Two," and place the top card of the two in your left hand, (that's the card with the printing on it), on top of the card in your right hand. (Image 7) The printing is now face down on the top card of the two in your right hand.

Then turn your right hand over, as you did before, showing the blank back of the business cards you hold in that hand. (Image 8) *To the spectators it appears you have shown both of the cards blank on both sides. What you're actually showing is the back of the first card you put in your right hand, again.* You have now, apparently, shown the two cards in your right hand are blank.

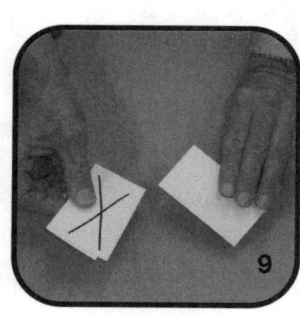

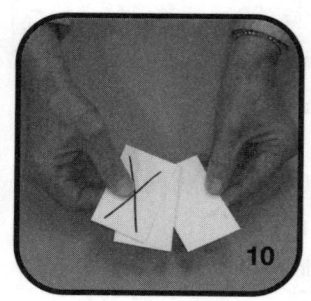

Say, "Three," but *do not* place the card in your left hand into your right hand. When you say, "Three," *turn your left hand over* to show the other side of that card, which is also blank. (Image 9) *To the spectators, you have shown all three cards blank on both sides!*

Place the card in your left hand, *under* the two held in your right hand. (Image 10) To the spectator say, "Would you please hold out your hand like this." Show what you want the spectator to do by holding out your left hand, palm up. The spectator holds out his or her hand.

With your left hand, remove the two bottom cards from the stack of three in your right hand and casually show those two cards blank on both sides. (Image 11) Put them away in your pocket, or just drop them on the table. *Everything* the spectator has seen so far are *blank cards.*

Place the printed card face down on the spectator's palm. (Image 12)

"Please place your other hand on top like this." (Image 13) You demonstrate what you want with your hands.

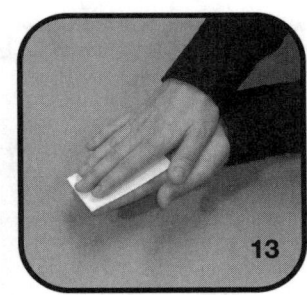

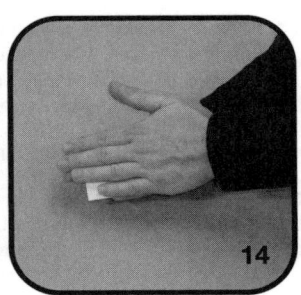

"Just turn both hands over like this," Again you demonstrate with your hands. The printed card is now face up in the spectator's hand. (Image 14)

"I'll use a little magic." Make a magic gesture, say a magic word, your company's name or whatever is appropriate for the occasion. "Please remove your top hand."

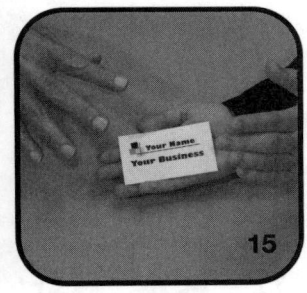

When the spectator removes their hand, they are always greatly surprised to see they are holding your imprinted business card. (Image 15) The effect is that the blank card was printed while in their own hands. With a little practice, this entire affect can be done in less than one minute. It's really a terrific trick.

I perform this effect often, because it is an excellent way to give out my business card. I have refined the method several times. Originally, I started with a more difficult sleight using several more blank cards. Then I incorporated the "Olram subtlety" move. ("Olram" is Marlo spelled backwards, named after its inventor, Edward Marlo, who is legendary in the creation of many excellent sleights and tricks primarily with playing cards.)

Showing the three cards totally blank is quite easy. Just follow the directions. This trick is so strong, often you will be asked, by the person in whose hands the card was "printed," "Would you do that for my boss?" Because you are always happy to oblige, it is good to have several sets of three cards with you, ready to go. I always carry 4 or 5 sets in my pocket or business card case.

Magically "printing" your blank business card, right on the customer's hand, serves a number of purposes.

Delivering your business card magically is much better than just handing your card to a client.

Printing your business card is entertaining, memorable and impressive, because the "magic" seems to happen as the spectator holds the blank card.

The magic happens quickly. You can do the effect in less than one minute.

It immediately proves your magical powers.

Because the magic is with your business card, which they receive and keep, the customer is less likely to throw it away. "How did you do that? It must be some kind of special invisible ink. I'll keep it and see if it fades out." And, that's good!

THE MAGICAL BOTTOM LINE

In addition to helping you achieve specific sales goals, your magic will help you in another, more subtle way. "People do business with people they like," is certainly true. If they like you, they are more likely to buy your product. If they don't like you, you'll have a hard time making any sale.

Here's an example. Many times I have gone to a restaurant where the food was excellent, but the waiter was so rude I never went back to that establishment again. And the reverse is true as well. In some restaurants, the food may not be wonderful, but, if your waiter is very personable and efficient, you feel as if you've really selected the right place for that dinner. You'll be back.

It's that same way with your customers. Your magic has made you a special person. You've entertained them. You've made their day a bit better. They like you. And remember, when they like you, they are more likely to buy your product. It has always been that way.

The bottom line is, because of the magic you do, your customers will remember you and your product. They will be delighted to see you the next time you call. They will probably say, "What are you going to do for me this time?" ... Study this course; practice the tricks; learn the magic; add your own presentation ... and you will be ready. And that's good!

THE LAST TRICK IN THE BOOK

I have saved this trick for last. It is ideal for just about any occasion. You can present it in Carlsbad Caverns, on a cruise ship in the middle of any ocean or on a jet plane thirty thousand feet high in the air. It works with foreign currency as well as U.S. dollars. You can do it anywhere, anytime, for just about anyone. It is truly a reputation maker.

THE CHAPSTICK CAPER

What you will learn now is one of the finest magic tricks I know. I have created this routine over the years, which I first did with a whole borrowed bill appearing in a lemon. This is a greatly improved version which uses only two ordinary objects, a dollar bill, and, of all things, a tube of Chapstick. The spectators see no "magic" props. (I have included an optional vanish for the dollar bill which uses a "trick" handkerchief.) You can easily carry the effect with you anywhere and perform it for only a few people or, with the proper staging, present it in a large theater. When you tear the borrowed bill in half, it is very funny for everyone except the lender. What happens after that is impossible. Frankly, I thought for a long time before I decided to include this in the course. It does require some practice, but it is truly sensational magic. Let me tell you the effect, and you'll see why.

EFFECT:

"Let me show you a magic trick that I'm just learning. To do it I need my magic wand." You feel in your pockets (a lady can look in her purse). "I don't seem to have my magic wand with me today, but I do want to show you this trick ..." As if the thought is just occurring to you, "Tell you what, let's use this Chapstick as the magic wand." You remove a Chapstick from your pocket and hand it to a spectator. A standard Chapstick is black with a white tip, the same color scheme as most magic wands. "Please hold this for me for a moment. It's smaller than my regular magic wand, but I think it will work. Now, I'll show you what I've learned."

"I'd like to borrow a dollar bill. I could do the magic with a larger denomination bill, but since I'm just learning, I guess I'd better stick to a dollar." Someone will volunteer a dollar, which can be pretty funny in itself.

"Thank you … oh, I'm sorry, I forgot your receipt." To the surprise of everyone, particularly the person who just lent you the bill, you visibly tear the bill in half. "Here's your receipt. I hope I'm remembering correctly what I'm supposed to do." You hand half of the now torn bill to the startled spectator. "I'll use these halves of the bill for the magic."

"Please crumple your half into a small ball. I'll do the same with mine." As you say this you have been crumpling the half bill into a very small ball. "Now hold your half tightly in your closed hands. I'll hold the other half." You hold the crumpled bill tightly in your closed left hand as the spectator does the same with their half.

"Now folks, here comes that wonderful magic I was telling you about. You have one half of the bill in your hand, and I have the other half in mine. Believe it or not, I'm going to make my half travel, invisibly, to your half and then reunite both halves into one bill. Everyone watch closely."

You point to the person holding the Chapstick and say, "Please wave the magic wand over both of our hands." That person waves the Chapstick as requested. This will always get a laugh.

"Here comes the first part of the magic." You open your left hand and they see that it is empty. To emphasize the effect, you show your right hand is empty, too. "As you see, my half has vanished."

Obviously elated by your success in making half of the dollar vanish, you continue, "Now, ladies and gentlemen, you may have seen a lot of magic in your lives. You've seen some good tricks and you've seen some bad tricks, but I'm going to show, the greatest miracle you have ever seen! If you open your hand, you will see the bill is completely restored! Unfold the bill and raise it high over your head so we can all see this wonder." During your soliloquy, the person holding the half bill has opened it. Sure enough, what he is holding is exactly the same as he had before, it's still only half a bill.

You say sheepishly, "Whoops, it didn't work." You pause for a moment and deliver a line that has been getting me laughs for many years, "I think it would work better with a larger bill. Does anyone have a twenty dollar bill I can borrow?"

Everyone will laugh. No one will volunteer another bill. You will, however, hear a lot of interesting comments from the spectators. Whatever they say, you respond, "Yes, I see what you mean. No one wants to lend me any more money. I better try to do that trick again. Crumple the half bill up in your hand as we try this one more time."

To the Chapstick-holding spectator you say, "Please wave that small magic wand over my friend's hand THREE times." In desperation you add, "And say any magic word you can think of." Whatever the person says gets a laugh, even if they say nothing. "Now, look and see what has happened. Three's the charm …" As the spectator unfolds the bill and finds he's still holding only half a bill, you add "… but not this time."

"This is pretty embarrassing. In his magic course, Mark Wilson told me this would work. I better try some of my own magic. Perhaps this will help. Would you please open the Chapstick." Your volunteer takes off the top of the Chapstick. Inside is not the usual contents of the tube, but something with a greenish color that may be paper. "Let's see what that is. Please remove the contents, I don't want to touch it." To strengthen the magic, it is important that you not touch the small rolled-up piece of paper the spectator is taking out of the Chapstick. "Now would you please open that little package." The person unrolls the paper. It is one half of a dollar bill.

"Now we must check to see if that just happens to match the other half of the bill." Speaking to the now much happier spectator from whom you borrowed the bill. "I don't see how they could match, because I handed this person the magic wand, I mean the Chapstick, before I borrowed the bill from you." This statement emphasizes the impossibility of the magic everyone is seeing.

"There are two ways to see if those halves match. One is by checking the serial numbers. There is a serial number on both halves. Do you see it on yours? It 's on the gray side of the bill, right above the green seal. The other serial number is just below the black seal on your half. Now, most serial numbers start with a letter. Is there a letter? And is there one on yours? Very good. Now, would you both say the letter and then read the numbers off, both of you at the same time. And the letter is …"

At this point both spectators will say the same letter and continue with the same numbers. As they read the numbers together, everyone now knows the numbers on both half bills are exactly the same.

"And the other way to check is to put the two halves together and see if they match." The half found in the Chapstick is returned to the person who lent you the bill. Everyone can see that the halves match perfectly. Then you say to the person who lent you the bill, "Thank you. I couldn't have done this without your help. You are going to get all of my borrowing business from now on."

Remember, the Chapstick is handed to the spectator before the dollar bill is borrowed and never leaves the spectator's hand until he removes the half bill. At the conclusion, the two halves of the bill match perfectly. Correctly performed, this is one of the strongest effects in the world of magic, a real "Reputation Maker."

CHAPSTICK CAPER EXPLANATION

To perform this caper, you must do only two sleights. (If you use the trick handkerchief to make the bill vanish, only one sleight.) They are both easy to do, and do not requiring any great finger dexterity. Both sleights are primarily based on timing. With a little practice, you will get them exactly right.

SECRET:

Before the show, you must really tear a dollar bill in half. Use a bill that is slightly aged so it will match the bill you borrow, even if it is a new or an old bill. Put the right torn half of that bill in your right coat or pants pocket. The left torn half of the bill you place inside an empty tube of Chapstick. (You do not have to use Chapstick. You can use any container for the "magical" reappearance of the "vanished" half of the torn bill. It could be an aspirin box, a sealed envelope, or any suitable object. I think the Chapstick is particularly good because of its small, round design, which is like a little magic wand. Also, they are found in the pants pockets or purses of many people.)

PREPARATION:

If you use a Chapstick, you must first remove the lip balm from the tube. You can use a small knife, a stick, a pair of tweezers or even a strong tooth pick, anything small enough to reach inside the Chapstick. The bottom of the lip balm is in a small round base that rests within the tube. After you remove all of the lip balm use a paper towel or tissue to clean the inside and outside of the tube.

You are going to put the left half of the bill into the Chapstick. But, before you insert it, crumple the half bill into a small ball. The reason you crumple the half bill before you put it in the Chapstick, is it then appears to be the same crumpled half bill that vanishes from your hand and "reappears" in the Chapstick. Unroll the crumpled half bill, fold and roll it into the round shape required to insert it into the empty Chapstick. The half bill must fit far enough down in the Chapstick so you can replace the top of the tube. Put the "loaded" Chapstick in your left side pants pocket. Do not crumple the right half bill that you put in your right pocket. The spectator will crumple that half into a small ball during the routine.

An advantage of crumpling both halves of the bill during the routine is, at the conclusion of the trick, it greatly disguises the age of the bill, so they appear to be the two halves of the bill you borrowed from the spectator.

ROUTINE:

You borrow a dollar bill from someone in the audience. Display the bill between your right and left hand with the picture of George Washington facing the audience. (Image 2) You apparently tear the bill in half. You have really not torn the bill at all.

THE MAGIC TEAR

Here's what you really do. Let's assume you are right handed. Face the audience and hold the bill a little below your eye level (Image 2). You appear to tear the bill apart in the middle with a downward motion of your right hand.

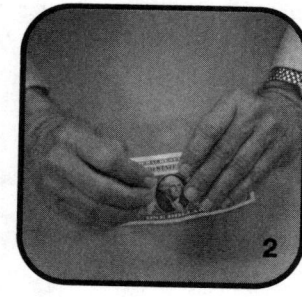

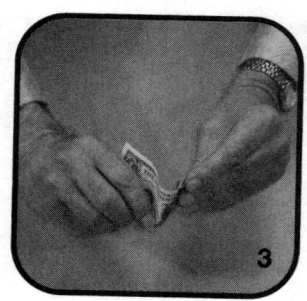

Your left hand remains in place. Move your right hand down and slightly toward you as you (apparently) tear the bill into two parts. (Image 3)

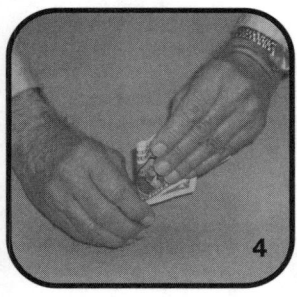

As you make the "tearing" motion, what you actually do is slide your right hand down the bill, and fold the bill in half. The half in your right hand folds towards you and behind the other half held in your left hand. (Image 4) Your left thumb holds the now folded bill in place in your left hand.

When you make the phony tear, hold the bill tightly enough so your right thumb makes a scraping noise rubbing on the bill as your right hand slides down. It sounds exactly as if the bill is being torn into two parts.

Let me emphasize, all of this is much more difficult to explain than it is to do. Practice with a real bill. Learn the movements of your hands from the pictures. Practice the move slowly at first, then learn to do it quickly. The entire tearing action takes about one second. Because of the visual effect of the "tearing" movement you make with your hands and the sound your thumb makes moving down the bill, the spectators see and hear everything, just as if you were actually tearing the bill in half.

You should learn the "tearing" move before you learn the rest of the trick. As you practice, you may, accidentally, really tear a bill in half. I certainly did that several times as I was learning. Put that bill back together with clear Scotch tape and practice with another bill!

There is one additional thing you must do. That is to hold the half of the bill you tore before the show in your right hand when you do the fake tearing move. Here's how you do it.

When you receive the borrowed bill from the spectator, take it from them with your left hand. As you do this, place your right hand into your right side pocket and grasp the half bill you put there before the show. (Image 5)

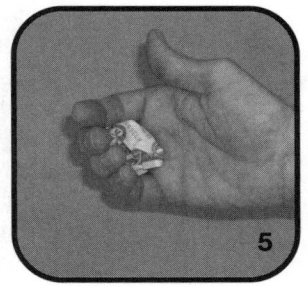

Your right hand holds the half bill in your fingers as you do the tearing with the borrowed bill. (Image 6) After the fake tear, you will have the folded whole bill in your left hand and that half bill in your right hand.

Don't let holding the half bill in your right hand when you make the tear scare you. Just hold the bill with your fingers as you make the "tear." (Image 7)

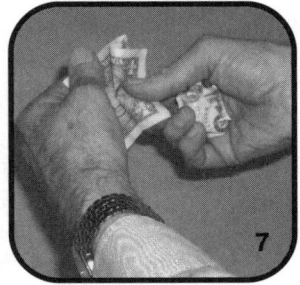

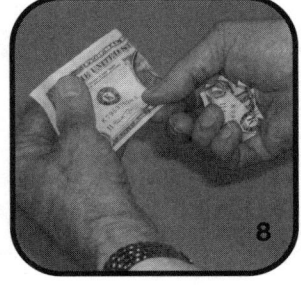

After the tear is completed, you can now show there is a "half bill" in each of your hands. (Image 8)

Your right hand shows the torn half bill. Your left hand reveals a part of the folded whole bill. (Image 9)

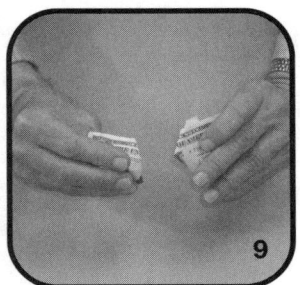

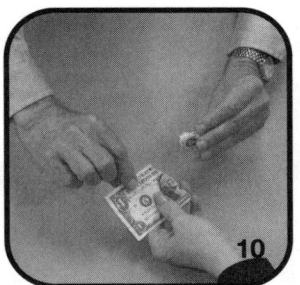

Hand the half bill in your right hand, as the "receipt," to the lender. (Image 10)

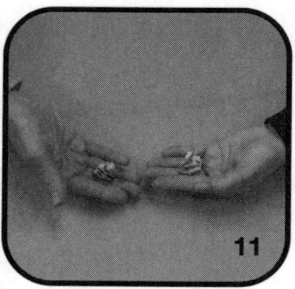

Now you must vanish the borrowed bill held in your left hand. Explain that you will now crumple up your half of the borrowed bill, and ask the spectator to do the same with theirs. As you crumple it, do not let the spectators see you have a whole bill. As you will see when you try it, you can crumple the bill into such a small ball, the spectators think it is only half a bill. Place the crumpled bill on your open right hand. Have the spectator place their crumpled bill on their open hand. (Image 11)

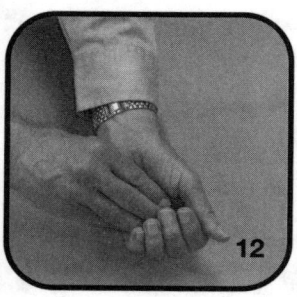

Say to the lender, "Please hold your half tightly in your closed hand, and I'll hold the other half." As you say this, you (apparently) place the bill held in your right hand into your left hand, which you close into a fist. Actually, you perform **The Finger Palm Vanish,** page 187 and secretly retain the bill in your right hand. This should be done casually, not as if you are performing any "sleight of hand." The move looks like this, (Image 12) as you (apparently) put the small rolled up ball of a bill into your left hand, but really keep the bill in your right hand in the finger palm position. (Image 13)

Immediately reach your right hand into your right coat or pants pocket, as if you are looking for the magic wand. Leave the bill in your pocket as you say, "Oh, that's right, you have my magic wand," as you remove your now-empty hand from your pocket. This is a very clever excuse for reaching into your pocket, which works beautifully in this routine.

If you would prefer not to do the finger palm vanish to make the bill disappear, you can use **The Coin Vanishing Handkerchief** (page 191). Instead of a coin, you sew a folded piece of paper the size of a dollar bill into the corner of the handkerchief. At this point, the spectators think you have one half of the bill in your closed left hand (which is really empty), and the other half is held by the lender. Actually, you have already done all the magic. What's left is the spectacular reveal.

You announce the great magical miracle they are all about to see. You ask the person with the Chapstick to wave it over the lender's hand and then over yours. Slowly open your left hand. It is empty! To emphasize the vanish, you show your right hand is also empty. To the viewers, the half bill has vanished!

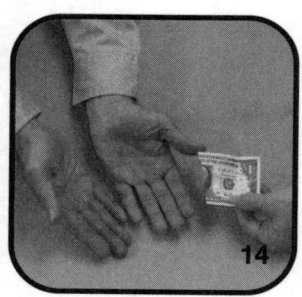

Ask the spectator to show everyone the bill is now restored. The lender unfolds the bill and finds it is still only half a bill! (Image 13)

You appear to have made a terrible mistake. Say you will try it one more time. Have the lender hold the half bill tightly again. Ask the wand holder to wave the Chapstick three times over the lender's hand. Again, the trick doesn't work. It is still only half a bill. Apparently, you are in big trouble.

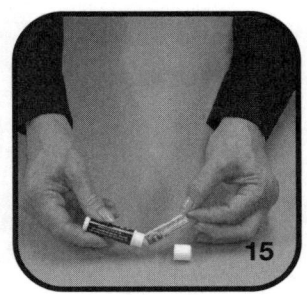

You ask the person holding the Chapstick to look inside the tube. They find the half bill. (Image 14)

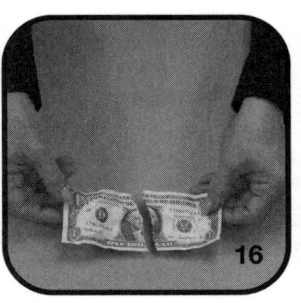

When everyone sees that the halves match perfectly, they will know you have just performed a real miracle! (Image 15)

Please study and practice this amazing trick before you present it. When you do, it will be one of your best "Reputation Makers."

YOUR FUTURE IN MAGIC

In looking toward your future in magic, you may find that magic itself can shape it for you. That rule has held true for many years, and numerous instances could be cited to prove it: How men who intended to be doctors, lawyers, or scientists turned to magic as a profession. In contrast, there have been magicians who abandoned the stage to become doctors, lawyers, ministers, or professors. The reasons for this are that the study and practice of magic can develop versatility, the ability to handle emergencies while under pressure and to recognize coming trends, and perhaps most importantly, how to appear before and speak to groups of people, both large and small, which can be a definite asset in almost any career you may choose.

Interest in magic has expanded so rapidly that it has become an adjunct not only to professions, but, most certainly, to social life as well. Salesmen, executives, and educators can use it to advantage. Anyone versed in magic will find it helpful in making contacts in almost any line. Moreover, the demand for magic has increased so greatly that it can be turned to profit as a sideline.

First, you must learn to do magic. The fact that you are studying this course shows that you have already made progress in that direction. You should learn it in a comprehensive way, for two reasons: One, many phases of magic, particularly misdirection and showmanship, apply to small tricks as well as large, so anything you learn from one will be helpful toward the other. Two, only by trying your hand at different types or styles of magic can you find the one to which you are best suited, for audience reaction to your work is what counts. Get people talking about you and the way you do your magic rather than about the tricks you perform. That will enable you to find your place in magic according to your own individuality.

Harry Houdini originally billed himself as the "King of Cards" but dropped it when he found that his Escape Act created a sensation. T. Nelson Downs was so successful as the "King of Coins" that he retired early with a fair-sized fortune. Then, in later years, he took up card work and became one of the best in the business.

Where you go from there will be largely up to you. Once you have a working pattern and style, you can decide whether to regard magic simply as a fascinating hobby, a form of social contact and enjoyment, a paying sideline, or an outright profession. New fields are constantly developing within the realm of magic. The demand for new tricks has attracted inventors, stimulated the manufacture of special apparatus, and magic dealers are increasing steadily. So if you have talents in any of those fields, they may be worthy of consideration.

The choice is yours, so make the most of it!

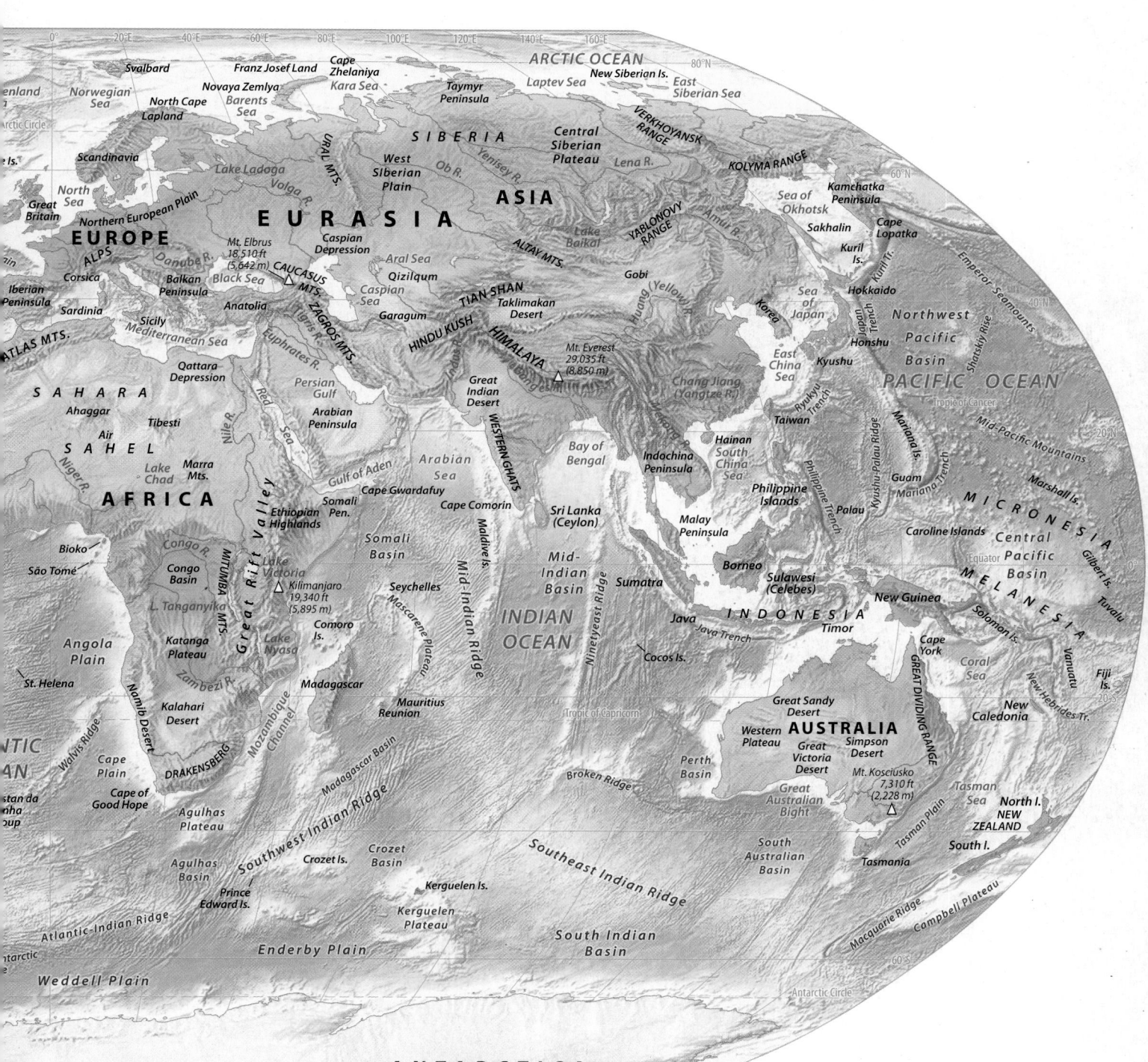

ARCTIC OCEAN

Svalbard
Franz Josef Land
Cape Zhelaniya
New Siberian Is.
80°N

Norwegian Sea
Novaya Zemlya
Kara Sea
Taymyr Peninsula
Laptev Sea
East Siberian Sea

North Cape
Lapland
Barents Sea
SIBERIA
Central Siberian Plateau
VERKHOYANSK RANGE

Scandinavia
Lake Ladoga
West Siberian Plain
Ob R.
Yenisey R.
Lena R.
KOLYMA RANGE
60°N

Great Britain
North Sea
EURASIA
Volga R.
ASIA
Lake Baikal
YABLONOVY RANGE
Amur R.
Sea of Okhotsk
Kamchatka Peninsula
Cape Lopatka

EUROPE
ALPS
Mt. Elbrus 18,510 ft (5,642 m)
Caspian Depression
Aral Sea
ALTAY MTS.
Gobi
Sakhalin
Kuril Is.

Corsica
Danube R.
CAUCASUS MTS.
Qizilqum
TIAN SHAN
Huang (Yellow) R.
Korea
Sea of Japan
Hokkaido

Iberian Peninsula
Balkan Peninsula
Black Sea
Caspian Sea
Garagum
Taklimakan Desert
Sea of Japan
Honshu
Northwest Pacific Basin

Sardinia
Sicily
Anatolia
ZAGROS MTS.
HINDU KUSH
HIMALAYA
East China Sea
Kyushu
Ryukyu Trench

ATLAS MTS.
Mediterranean Sea
Euphrates R.
Persian Gulf
Mt. Everest 29,035 ft (8,850 m)
Chang Jiang (Yangtze R.)
Taiwan
PACIFIC OCEAN

Qattara Depression
Nile R.
Arabian Peninsula
Great Indian Desert
Hainan
South China Sea
Mariana Is.
Mid-Pacific Mountains

SAHARA
Ahaggar
Tibesti
Air
Red Sea
WESTERN GHATS
Bay of Bengal
Indochina Peninsula
Philippine Islands
Guam

SAHEL
Marra Mts.
Lake Chad
Arabian Sea
Cape Gwardafuy
Cape Comorin
Sri Lanka (Ceylon)
Malay Peninsula

AFRICA
Niger R.
Gulf of Aden
Somali Pen.
Maldive Is.
Mid-Indian Basin

Bioko
Ethiopian Highlands
Somali Basin
Mid-Indian Ridge
Borneo
Sulawesi (Celebes)

São Tomé
Congo R.
MITUMBA MTS.
Lake Victoria
Kilimanjaro 19,340 ft (5,895 m)
Seychelles
Mascarene Plateau
INDONESIA
Timor
New Guinea

Angola Plain
Congo Basin
Katanga Plateau
L. Tanganyika
Comoro Is.
Java
Java Trench

St. Helena
Zambezi R.
Lake Nyasa
Kalahari Desert
Madagascar
Mauritius
Reunion

Namib Desert
DRAKENSBERG
Mozambique Channel
INDIAN OCEAN

Cape Plain
Agulhas Plateau
Southwest Indian Ridge
Crozet Is.
Crozet Basin
Mid-Indian Ridge

Agulhas Basin
Prince Edward Is.
Kerguelen Is.
Kerguelen Plateau
South Indian Basin

Atlantic-Indian Ridge
Enderby Plain

Weddell Plain

ANTARCTICA

MCKNIGHT'S

THIRD CALIFORNIA EDITION

Physical Geography

Taken from:

McKnight's Physical Geography: A Landscape Appreciation

Eleventh Edition

By **DARREL HESS**

City College of San Francisco

Illustrated by **DENNIS TASA**

Pearson Learning Solutions, 501 Boylston Street, Suite 900, Boston, MA 02116
A Pearson Education Company
www.pearsoned.com

Printed in the United States of America

1 2 3 4 5 6 7 8 9 10 V011 17 16 15 14 13

000200010271719604

RM/LC

ISBN 10: 1-269-14437-5
ISBN 13: 978-1-269-14437-7

INTRODUCTION TO THE THIRD CALIFORNIA EDITION

It would be difficult to find another part of the world where the physical geography is as varied and interesting as here in California. Our state contains an astonishing range of environments that include coastal beaches, high mountain peaks, wet temperate forests, and the driest of deserts.

Inside the Third California Edition

In this *Third California Edition* of *McKnight's Physical Geography: A Landscape Appreciation*, 11th edition, by Darrel Hess, you will find the textbook in its entirety, plus a collection of 13 Field Guides that introduce the diverse physical geography of the state.

New to this edition is a Field Guide for *The Central Valley* of California, along with updates to the 12 Field Guides from the previous edition. Two of the earlier Field Guides—*Mono Lake* and *Redwood Forests*—have been enlarged to include additional Field Guide stops, and *Yosemite Valley* and *Death Valley* contain expanded material on identifying plant life.

Each Field Guide now has a QR ("quick reference") code box that can be read by most smartphones (you may need to download QR scanning software for your phone before using these codes). Each QR code will immediately link your phone to a short video—such as to a Google Earth™ virtual tour of Field Guide stops, or to a weather satellite movie.

How to Use the California Edition

Throughout the textbook you will see California map icons directing you to specific Field Guides,(FG1, FG2, and so on). Each Field Guide includes information exclusively about California, along with locator maps, photographs, textbook references, key terms, additional reading, and recommended Web sites. Eleven of the 13 Field Guides feature detailed road logs for self-guided field trips to locations around the state—including in many of our most popular National Parks.

The Field Guides are designed for use both in the classroom and in the field—enabling armchair travelers and outdoor adventurers alike to better understand the physical geography of California. The pages of these guides are perforated so that they may be separated from the textbook and taken on a field trip.

The latitudes and longitudes of Field Guide stops are provided to aid in navigating to these locations using GPS, and so that these locations can be studied remotely using Google Earth™ or the U.S. Geological Survey *National Map*. Links to the KMZ files of the Google Earth™ virtual tours of Field Guide locations, along with many other resources to help you succeed in your physical geography class, appear in the MasteringGeography™ course that accompanies this California Edition.

Resources for Field Study

The *Additional Resources* section of each Field Guide directs you to books and Web sites to help you learn more about the physical geography of different regions in California. Out in the field, you may find a general natural history guide helpful when learning to identify the plants and animals you may encounter. Of the many good natural history guides available, if you are looking for a modest-priced, comprehensive field identification guide for the entire state, consider the *National Audubon Society Field Guide to California* by Peter Alden (New York: Alfred A. Knopf, 1998)—it is very compact, easy to use, and surprisingly complete. For the Sierra Nevada specifically, *The Laws Field Guide to the Sierra Nevada* by John Muir Laws (Berkeley, CA: Heyday Books, 2007) is a good choice.

If you plan to visit a number of National Parks during the year, consider purchasing a *National Parks & Federal Recreational Lands Interagency Annual Pass* (http://www.nps.gov/findapark/passes.htm). The pass is good for 12 months and covers entrance fees to all National Parks and many other Federal lands—such as the South Tufa Area at Mono Lake (Field Guide #6), the *Forest Adventure Pass* (Field Guides #3 and #12), and the Sacramento National Wildlife Refuge (Field Guide #13).

Traveling Safely

Many of the locations described in the Field Guides are reached by way of narrow, often winding mountain roads. Do not try to sightsee and drive at the same time; pull over and park if you see something of interest. Also, it is a good idea to check the weather forecast before heading into remote locations—especially in the mountains, weather can change with little warning.

Although the locator maps in the Field Guides show major roads, you should bring a larger, detailed road map with you. If you are using GPS to navigate to Field Guide stops, keep in mind that the base maps loaded in many GPS units sometimes show roads that may be impassible—particularly in remote areas such as Death Valley. Always check with local park or forest service personnel before venturing off well-marked paved roads.

For the Teacher

You will find the Field Guides useful when assigning independent field work projects for students—even for areas of California not mentioned specifically in the road logs. For example, the background information in the *Sierra Nevada via Tioga Pass* and *Yosemite Valley* Field Guides can be the foundation for student field projects in other parts of the Sierra. The KMZ files for the Google Earth™ virtual tours of Field Guide sites can also be used as the starting point for student projects. Assignable Field Guide reading questions are found within the MasteringGeography™ course which accompanies the California edition, and also may be obtained by contacting your Pearson Representative. If you wish to adopt MasteringGeography™ for this California edition, please contact your local Pearson representative for instructions on obtaining access to this course.

To place an order for the discounted text package containing the MasteringGeography Student Access code, please order the following ISBN:

10 Digit ISBN—1256993956—Physical Geography 3rd CA Edition with MasteringGeography Access Code PKG

13 Digit ISBN—9781256993957—Physical Geography 3rd CA Edition with MasteringGeography Access Code PKG

Acknowledgements

I extend my special thanks to Professors Edward Aguado, Patricia Deen, Barbara Holzman and Les Rowntree—their enthusiasm and knowledge of California is clearly revealed in their contributions to this Field Guide collection. Thanks also to Professors Chris Lewis of City College of San Francisco and Anne Saxe of Saddleback College for their suggestions on both textbook and Field Guide content.

Thanks to all at Pearson Education who made this edition possible, especially to Geography Editor Christian Botting, Development Editor Ruth Moore, Project Manager Carrie Wagner, and Media Producers Ziki Dekel and Tim Hainley. Most of all, I offer my great appreciation to Assistant Vice President of Pearson Learning Solutions, Elizabeth Kaster, for her vision and steadfast support of this California edition.

All of us hope that these Field Guides help you appreciate and enjoy the physical geography of the Golden State.

Darrel Hess
Earth Sciences Department
City College of San Francisco
50 Phelan Avenue
San Francisco, CA 94112
dhess@ccsf.edu

FIELD GUIDES IN THE THIRD CALIFORNIA EDITION

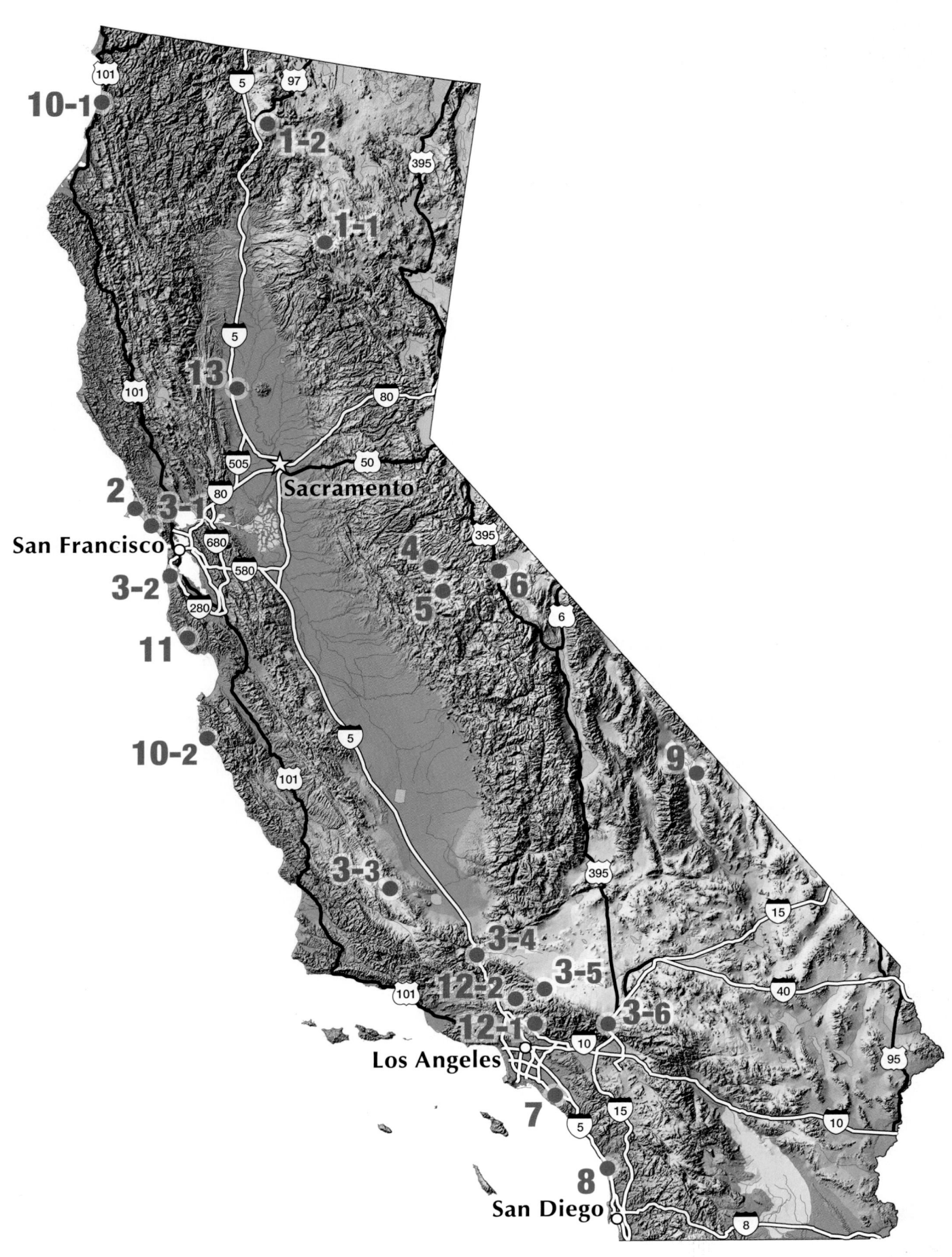

BRIEF CONTENTS

GEOSCIENCE ANIMATION LIBRARY

Animation
Convection and
Plate Tectonics

Covering the most difficult-to-visualize topics in physical geography, the Geoscience Animations can be accessed by students with mobile devices through Quick Response Codes in the book, or through the MasteringGeography™ Study Area. Teachers can assign these media with assessments in MasteringGeography™.

VIDEOS

Video
Hurricane
Sandy

Videos providing engaging visualizations and real world examples of physical geography concepts can be accessed by students with mobile devices through Quick Response Codes in the book, or through the MasteringGeography™ Study Area. Teachers can assign these media with assessments in MasteringGeography™.

Field Guide Videos for the Third California Edition

CONTENTS

1 Introduction to Earth 2

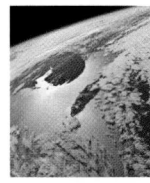

2 Portraying Earth 30

3 Introduction to the Atmosphere 54

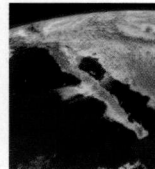

4 Insolation and Temperature 76

5 Atmospheric Pressure and Wind 108

6 Atmospheric Moisture 140

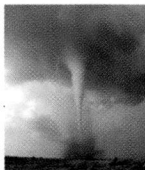

7 Atmospheric Disturbances 176

8 Climate and Climate Change 206

9 The Hydrosphere 252

15 Preliminaries to Erosion: Weathering and Mass Wasting 446

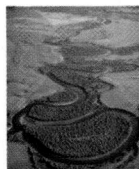

16 Fluvial Processes 466

17 Karst and Hydrothermal Processes 498

18 The Topography of Arid Lands 514

19 Glacial Modification of Terrain 540

20 Coastal Processes and Terrain 572

PREFACE

McKnight's Physical Geography: A Landscape Appreciation presents the concepts of physical geography in a clear, readable way to help students comprehend Earth's physical landscape. The 11th edition of the book has undergone a thorough revision, while maintaining the time-proven approach to physical geography first presented by Tom McKnight nearly 30 years ago.

NEW TO THE 11TH EDITION

Users of earlier editions will see that the overall sequence of chapters and topics remains the same, with material added or updated in several key areas. Changes to the new edition include the following:

- The entire art program has continued its thorough revision and updating by illustrator Dennis Tasa. Dozens of new diagrams, maps, and photographs are found throughout.
- Each chapter includes a new learning path, beginning with a series of new *Key Questions* to help students prioritize key issues and concepts.
- Chapters now open with new *Seeing Geographically* features that ask students observational questions about the chapter's opening image, and are revisited in the end-of-chapter *Learning Review*.
- Throughout each chapter, new *Learning Check* questions periodically confirm a student's understanding of the material.
- An expanded end-of-chapter *Learning Review* now includes new basic **quantitative** Exercises.
- The series of boxed essays called *Energy for the 21st Century* has been expanded from the 10th edition (where it was called *Renewable Energy*). The boxes have been updated and are now more closely tied to the main text. Contributed by professors from across the country, the essay topics include *Our Continuing Dependence on Fossil Fuels; Solar Energy; Wind Energy; Strategies for Reducing Greenhouse Gas Emissions; Fracking for Natural Gas; Geothermal Energy; Biofuels; Hydropower;* and *Tidal Power.*
- In Chapter 1, information on *Earth's Environmental Spheres* and *Earth Systems* has been greatly expanded.
- In Chapter 2, material on *contour lines* and *portraying the three-dimensional landscape* has been reorganized.
- Material on the *development of Earth's modern atmosphere* has been added to Chapter 3.
- In Chapter 3, the section on the *Coriolis effect* has been revised and reorganized to clarify the concept for students, and examples have been added of topics in later chapters for which understanding of the Coriolis effect is important.

- In Chapter 4, the material on *energy, heat,* and *temperature* has been revised and expanded.
- New diagrams in Chapter 5 illustrate the *Pacific Decadal Oscillation.*
- Chapter 8, *Climate and Climate Change,* has been thoroughly updated and revised with the latest data and applications, and more detailed explanations of *oxygen isotope analysis* and *radiocarbon dating.*
- The material on *rocks* has been expanded in Chapter 13, as has the discussion of *geologic time.*
- Material on *differential weathering* is now incorporated into Chapter 15.
- Chapter 18 on *desert landscapes* and Chapter 20 on *coastal processes and landforms* have been thoroughly reorganized for clarity.
- Some key material previously found in Focus Boxes has been integrated directly into the text. Updated and revised Focus Boxes include *The UV Index; Monitoring Earth's Radiation Budget; Forecasting El Niño; GOES Weather Satellites; Global Dimming; Lessons of Hurricane Katrina; The Great Pacific Garbage Patch; Bark Beetles Killing Forests in Western North America; Signs of Climate Change in the Arctic; Climate Change Affects Bird Populations; Rainforest Loss in Brazil; The La Conchita Landslides; The Changing Mississippi River Delta; Disintegration of Antarctic Ice Shelves; Shrinking Glaciers;* and *Imperiled Coral Reefs.*
- New Focus Boxes include *Using Remote Sensing Images to Study a Landscape; The Conveyor Belt Model of Midlatitude Cyclones; Weather Radar; The Devastating Tornadoes of 2011; Monitoring Groundwater Resources from Space; The 2010 Deepwater Horizon Oil Spill; Using Soil Profiles to Decipher Past Environmental Changes; The 2010 Haiti Earthquake; Earthquake Prediction; Desertification;* and *The 2011 Japan Earthquake and Tsunami.*
- Quick Response (QR) Codes are integrated throughout the book to enable students with mobile devices to access mobile-ready versions of the *Geoscience Animations* and new *videos* as they read, for just in time visualization and conceptual reinforcement. These media are also available in the Student Study Area of MasteringGeography, and many can also be assigned by teachers for credit and grading.
- The 11th edition is now supported by **MasteringGeography™,** the most widely used and effective online homework, tutorial, and assessment system for the sciences. Assignable media and activities include: Geoscience Animations, Videos, *Encounter Physical Geography* Google Earth™ Explorations, MapMaster™ interactive maps, coaching activities on the toughest topics in physical geography, end-of-chapter questions and exercises, reading quizzes, and Test Bank questions.

TO THE STUDENT

Welcome to *McKnight's Physical Geography: A Landscape Appreciation*. Take a minute to skim through this book to see some of the features that will help you learn the material in your physical geography course:

- You'll notice that the book includes many diagrams, maps, and photographs. Physical geography is a visual discipline, so studying the figures and their captions is just as important as reading through the text itself.
- Many photographs have "locator maps" to help you learn the locations of the many places we mention in the book.
- A reference map of physical features of the world is found inside the front cover of the book, and a reference map of the countries of the world is found inside the back cover.
- Each chapter begins with a quick overview of the material, as well as series of questions—think about these questions as you study the material in that chapter.
- Look at the photograph that begins each chapter. The *Seeing Geographically* questions for this photograph will get you thinking about the material in the chapter, and about the kinds of things that geographers can learn by looking at a landscape.
- As you read through each chapter, you'll come across short *Learning Check* questions. These quick questions are designed to check your understanding of key information in the text section you've just read. Answers to the Learning Check questions are found in the back of the book.
- Each chapter concludes with a *Learning Review*. Begin with the *Key Terms and Concepts* questions—these will check your understanding of basic factual information and key terms (key terms are printed in **bold type** throughout the text). Then, answer the *Study Questions*—these will confirm your understanding of major concepts presented in the chapter. Finally, you can try the *Exercises*—for these problems you'll interpret maps or diagrams and use basic math to reinforce your understanding of the material you've studied.
- Finish the chapter by answering the *Seeing Geographically* questions at the end of the Learning Review. To answer these questions, you'll put to use things you've learned in the chapter. As you progress through the book, you begin to recognize how much more you can "see" in a landscape after studying physical geography.
- The alphabetical glossary at the end of the book provides definitions for all of the key terms.
- Most chapters include QR codes/icons that direct you to online animations and videos that you can access with your mobile device. The animations help explain important concepts in physical geography and include a written and an audio narration. The animations and videos can also be accessed through the Student Study Area in MasteringGeography, and animations can also be assigned for credit by teachers.

THE TEACHING AND LEARNING PACKAGE

The author and publisher have been pleased to work with a number of talented people to produce an excellent instructional package.

FOR TEACHERS AND STUDENTS

MasteringGeography™ with Pearson eText

The **Mastering** platform is the most widely used and effective online homework, tutorial, and assessment system for the sciences. It delivers self-paced tutorials that provide individualized coaching, focus on course objectives, and are responsive to each student's progress. The Mastering system helps teachers maximize class time with customizable, easy-to-assign, and automatically graded assessments that motivate students to learn outside of class and arrive prepared for lecture.

MasteringGeography offers:

- **Assignable activities** that include Geoscience Animation activities, *Encounter Physical Geography* Google Earth Explorations, Video activities, MapMaster™ Interactive Map activities, Map Projection activities, coaching activities on the toughest topics in physical geography, end-of-chapter questions and exercises, reading quizzes, Test Bank questions, and more.
- **Student Study Area** with Geoscience Animations, Videos, MapMaster™ interactive maps, web links, glossary flashcards, "In the News" RSS feeds, chapter quizzes, an optional Pearson eText (including versions for iPad and Android devices), and more.

Pearson eText gives students access to the text whenever and wherever they can access the Internet. The eText pages look exactly like the printed text, and include powerful interactive and customization functions, including links to the multimedia.

Geoscience Animation Library on DVD 5th edition (0321716841) This resource offers over 100 animations covering the most difficult-to-visualize topics in physical geography, physical geology, oceanography, meteorology, and Earth science. The animations are provided as Flash files and preloaded into PowerPoint slides for both Windows and Mac. This library was created through a unique collaboration among Pearson's leading geoscience authors—including Darrel Hess, Robert Christopherson, Frederick Lutgens, Aurora Pun, Gary Smith, Edward Tarbuck, and Alan Trujillo.

Television for the Environment *Earth Report* Videos on DVD (0321662989) This three-DVD set helps students visualize how human decisions and behavior have affected the environment, and how individuals are taking steps toward recovery. With topics ranging from the poor land management promoting the devastation of river systems in Central America to the struggles for electricity in China and Africa, these 13 videos from Television for the Environment's global *Earth Report* series recognize the efforts of individuals around the world to unite and protect the planet.

Practicing Geography: Careers for Enhancing Society and the Environment by Association of American Geographers (0321811151) This book examines career opportunities for geographers and geospatial professionals in business, government, nonprofit, and educational sectors. A diverse group of academic and industry professionals share insights on career planning, networking, transitioning between employment sectors, and balancing work and home life. The book illustrates the value of geographic expertise and technologies through engaging profiles and case studies of geographers at work.

Teaching College Geography: A Practical Guide for Graduate Students and Early Career Faculty by Association of American Geographers (0136054471) This two-part resource provides a starting point for becoming an effective geography teacher from the very first day of class. Part One addresses "nuts-and-bolts" teaching issues. Part Two explores being an effective teacher in the field, supporting critical thinking with GIS and mapping technologies, engaging learners in large geography classes, and promoting awareness of international perspectives and geographic issues.

Aspiring Academics: A Resource Book for Graduate Students and Early Career Faculty by Association of American Geographers (0136048919) Drawing on several years of research, this set of essays is designed to help graduate students and early career faculty start their careers in geography and related social and environmental sciences. *Aspiring Academics* stresses the interdependence of teaching, research, and service—and the importance of achieving a healthy balance of professional and personal life—while doing faculty work. Each chapter provides accessible, forward-looking advice on topics that often cause the most stress in the first years of a college or university appointment.

FOR THE TEACHER

- ***Instructor Resource Manual*** (032186400X) Available for download, this resource for both new and experienced teachers includes learning objectives, detailed chapter outlines, icebreakers to initiate classroom discussions, answers to end-of-chapter questions and a sample syllabus.

- ***TestGen/Test Bank®*** (0321863992) TestGen is a computerized test generator that lets teachers view and edit *Test Bank* questions, transfer questions to tests,

and print the test in a variety of customized formats. This *Test Bank* includes over 3000 multiple-choice, true/false, and short-answer/essay questions. Questions are correlated against learning outcomes as well as U.S. National Geography Standards and Bloom's Taxonomy to help teachers to better map the assessments against both broad and specific teaching and learning objectives. The *Test Bank* is also available in Microsoft Word©, and is importable into Blackboard and WebCT.

- ***Instructor Resource DVD*** (0321863909) Everything teachers need, where they want it. The *Instructor Resource DVD* helps make teachers more effective by saving them time and effort. All digital resources can be found in one well-organized, easy-to-access place, and include:

  Figures—All textbook images as JPGs, PDFs, and PowerPoint Slides

  Lecture Outline PowerPoint Presentations, which outline the concepts of each chapter with embedded art and can be customized to fit teachers' lecture requirements

  CRS "Clicker" Questions in PowerPoint format correlated against U.S. National Geography Standards, chapter specific learning outcomes, and Bloom's Taxonomy

  TestGen—The TestGen software, questions, and answers for both MACs and PCs

  Electronic Files of the *Instructor Resource Manual* and *Test Bank*

  This Instructor Resource content is also available completely online via the Instructor Resources section of www.pearsonhighered.com/irc.

- ***Answer Key to Laboratory Manual*** (0321864026) Available for download, the answer key provides answers to problem sets presented in the Laboratory Manual: www.pearsonhighered.com/irc.

- ***AAG Community Portal for Aspiring Academics and Teaching College Geography:*** This website is intended to support community-based professional development in geography and related disciplines. Here you will find activities providing extended treatment of the topics covered in both books. The activities can be used in workshops, graduate seminars, brown bags, and mentoring programs offered on campus or within an academic department. You can also use the discussion boards and contributions tool to share advice and materials with others: www.pearsonhighered.com/aag/.

- ***Course Management:*** Pearson is proud to partner with many of the leading course management system providers on the market today. These partnerships enable us to provide our testing materials already formatted for easy importation into the powerful Blackboard course management system. Please contact your local Pearson representative for details: www.pearsonhighered.com/elearning/.

FOR THE STUDENT

- **Physical Geography Laboratory Manual, 11th edition** by Darrel Hess (0321863968) This lab manual offers a comprehensive set of more than 45 lab exercises to accompany any physical geography class. The first half covers topics such as basic meteorological processes, the interpretation of weather maps, weather satellite images, and climate data. The second half focuses on understanding the development of landforms and the interpretation of topographic maps and aerial imagery. Many exercises have problems that use Google Earth™, and the lab manual website contains maps, images, photographs, satellite movie loops, and Google Earth™ KMZ files. The 11th edition of the lab manual includes both new and revised exercises, new maps, and expanded use of Google Earth™. www.mygeoscienceplace.com

- **Goode's World Atlas** (0321652002) *Goode's World Atlas* has been the world's premiere educational atlas since 1923, and for good reason. It features over 250 pages of maps, from definitive physical and political maps to important thematic maps that illustrate the spatial aspects of many important topics. The 22nd edition includes 160 pages of new, digitally produced reference maps, as well as new thematic maps on global climate change, sea level rise, CO_2 emissions, polar ice fluctuations, deforestation, extreme weather events, infectious diseases, water resources, and energy production.

- **Dire Predictions** by Michael Mann and Lee Kump (0136044352) Periodic reports from the Intergovernmental Panel on Climate Change (IPCC) evaluate the risk of climate change brought on by humans. But the sheer volume of scientific data remains inscrutable to the general public, particularly to those who may still question the validity of climate change. In just over 200 pages, this practical text presents and expands upon the essential findings in a visually stunning and undeniably powerful way to the lay reader. Scientific findings that provide validity to the implications of climate change are presented in clear-cut graphic elements, striking images, and understandable analogies.

PEARSON'S ENCOUNTER SERIES

Pearson's Encounter series provides rich, interactive explorations of geoscience concepts through Google Earth™ activities, exploring a range of topics in regional, human, and physical geography. For those who do not use MasteringGeography, all chapter explorations are available in print workbooks as well as in online quizzes, at www.mygeoscienceplace.com, accommodating different classroom needs. Each exploration consists of a worksheet, online quizzes, and a corresponding Google Earth™ KMZ file:

- **Encounter Physical Geography** Workbook and Website by Jess C. Porter and Stephen O'Connell (0321672526)

- **Encounter Geosystems** Workbook and Website by Charlie Thomsen (0321636996)
- **Encounter Earth** Workbook and Website by Steve Kluge (0321581296)
- **Encounter Human Geography** Workbook and Website by Jess C. Porter (0321682203)
- **Encounter World Regional Geography** Workbook and Website by Jess C. Porter (0321681754)

ACKNOWLEDGMENTS

I offer my great appreciation to illustrator Dennis Tasa. Now in our second edition working together, my admiration for his ability to take my ideas and sketches and turn them into effective and impressive illustrations has only grown.

Over the years, scores of colleagues, students, and friends have helped me and the founding author of this book, Tom McKnight, update and improve this textbook. Their assistance has been gratefully acknowledged previously. Here we acknowledge those who have provided assistance in recent years by acting as reviewers of the text and animations that accompany it, or by providing helpful critiques and suggestions:

Victoria Alapo, *Metropolitan Community College*
Casey Allen, *Weber State University*
Sergei Andronikov, *Austin Peay State University*
Greg Bierly, *Indiana State University*
Mark Binkley, *Mississippi State University*
Peter Blanken, *University of Colorado*
Margaret Boorstein, *Long Island University*
James Brey, *University of Wisconsin Fox Valley*
David Butler, *Texas State University*
Karl Byrand, *University of Wisconsin*
Sean Cannon, *Brigham Young University—Idaho*
Wing Cheung, *Palomar College*
Jongnam Choi, *Western Illinois University*
Glen Conner, *Western Kentucky University*
Carlos E. Cordova, *Oklahoma State University*
Richard A. Crooker, *Kutztown University of Pennsylvania*
Mike DeVivo, *Grand Rapids Community College*
Bryan Dorsey, *Weber State University*
Don W. Duckson, Jr., *Frostburg State University*
Tracy Edwards, *Frostburg State University*
Steve Emerick, *Glendale Community College*
Doug Foster, *Clackamas Community College*
Basil Gomez, *Indiana State University*
Jerry Green, *Miami University—Oxford*
Michael Grossman, *Southern Illinois University—Edwardsville*
Perry J. Hardin, *Brigham Young University*
Ann Harris, *Eastern Kentucky University*

Miriam Helen Hill, *Jacksonville State University*

Barbara Holzman, *San Francisco State University*

Robert M. Hordon, *Rutgers University*

Paul Hudson, *University of Texas*

Catherine Jain, *Palomar College*

Steven Jennings, *University of Colorado at Colorado Springs*

Dorleen B. Jenson, *Salt Lake Community College*

Kris Jones, *Saddleback College*

Ryan Kelly, *Lexington Community College*

Rob Kremer, *Metropolitan State College of Denver*

Kara Kuvakas, *Hartnell College*

Steve LaDochy, *California State University*

Michael Madsen, *Brigham Young University—Idaho*

Kenneth Martis, *West Virginia University*

William (Bill) Monfredo, *University of Oklahoma*

Mandy Munro-Stasiuk, *Kent State University*

Paul O'Farrell, *Middle Tennessee State University*

Thomas Orf, *Las Positas College*

Michael C. Pease, *University of New Mexico*

Stephen Podewell, *Western Michigan University*

Nick Polizzi, *Cypress College*

Robert Rohli, *Louisiana State University*

Anne Saxe, *Saddleback College*

Randall Schaetzl, *Michigan State University*

Jeffrey Schaffer, *Napa Valley College*

John H. Scheufler, *Mesa College*

Robert A. Sirk, *Austin Peay State University*

Dale Splinter, *University of Wisconsin—Whitewater*

Stephen Stadler, *Oklahoma State University*

Herschel Stern, *Mira Costa College*

Jane Thorngren, *San Diego State University*

Timothy Warner, *West Virginia University*

Shawn Willsey, *College of Southern Idaho*

My thanks go out to contributors of new and revised short boxed essays included in this edition: Ted Eckmann of Bowling Green State University, Matt Huber of Syracuse University, Ryan Jensen of Brigham Young University, Michael C. Pease of Central Washington University, Nancy Wilkinson of San Francisco State University, Jennifer Rahn, Samford University, Birmingham, Alabama, Valerie Sloan, University of Colorado at Boulder, and Kenneth Zweibel of George Washington University. Thanks also to Randall Schaetzl of Michigan State University, who contributed a new boxed essay, as well as a detailed review of the material on soils and geomorphology.

Special thanks go to Karl Byrand of the University of Wisconsin Colleges and Stephen Stadler of Oklahoma State University. In addition to contributing essays to this edition, both have long shared their expertise by providing student- and teacher-support materials for this textbook series. I would also like to thank Jess Porter of University of Arkansas at Little Rock, Stephen O'Connell of the University of Central Arkansas, Jason Allard of Valdosta State University, Richard Crooker of Kutztown University, Chris Sutton of Western Illinois University, and Andrew Mercer of Mississippi State University for their contributions to MasteringGeography and other supporting material.

Many of my colleagues at City College of San Francisco offered valuable suggestions on sections of the previous and current edition of the book: Carla Grandy, Dack Lee, Joyce Lucas-Clark, Robert Manlove, Kathryn Pinna, Todd Rigg-Carriero, Carole Toebe, and Katryn Wiese. I especially want to thank Chris Lewis, who reviewed large sections of this book for clarity and accuracy. I also extend my appreciation to my many students over the years—their curiosity, thoughtful questions, and cheerful acceptance of my enthusiasm for geography have helped me as a teacher and as a textbook author.

Textbooks of this scope cannot be created without a production team that is as dedicated to quality as the authors. First of all, my thanks go to Pearson Geography Editor Christian Botting, who provided skillful leadership and assembled the outstanding group of professionals with whom I worked. My thanks and admiration go to Senior Project Editor Crissy Dudonis, who cheerfully kept me on track throughout the entire production process. Many thanks also to Project Manager Anton Yakovlev, Senior Project Manager Katy Gabel, Production Project Liaison Ed Thomas, Photo Researcher Kristin Piljay, Art Development Editor Jay McElroy, Senior Project Manager Kevin Lear, Assistant Editor Kristen Sanchez, Editorial Assistant Bethany Sexton, Senior Marketing Manager Maureen McLaughlin, Marketing Assistant Nicola Houston, Copyeditor Nicole Schlutt, and Media Producers Tim Hainley and Ziki Dekel. Special thanks go to Marcia Youngman, who has worked as copyeditor or proofreader with me on so many books that I can't imagine sending a book to press before she's looked at it. I offer my greatest appreciation to Executive Development Editor Jonathan Cheney, who provided me with unwavering support and sound advice on every aspect of this book.

Finally, I wish to express my appreciation for my wife, Nora. Her help, understanding, and support have once again seen me through the long hours and many months of work that went into this book.

Darrel Hess
Earth Sciences Department
City College of San Francisco
50 Phelan Avenue
San Francisco, CA 94112
dhess@ccsf.edu

DEDICATION

For my wife, Nora

D.H.

ABOUT OUR SUSTAINABILITY INITIATIVES

Pearson recognizes the environmental challenges facing this planet, as well as acknowledges our responsibility in making a difference. This book is carefully crafted to minimize environmental impact. The binding, cover, and paper come from facilities that minimize waste, energy consumption, and the use of harmful chemicals. Pearson closes the loop by recycling every out-of-date text returned to our warehouse.

Along with developing and exploring digital solutions to our market's needs, Pearson has a strong commitment to achieving carbon-neutrality. As of 2009, Pearson became the first carbon- and climateneutral publishing company. Since then, Pearson remains strongly committed to measuring, reducing, and offsetting our carbon footprint.

The future holds great promise for reducing our impact on Earth's environment, and Pearson is proud to be leading the way. We strive to publish the best books with the most up-to-date and accurate content, and to do so in ways that minimize our impact on Earth. To learn more about our initiatives, please visit www.pearson.com/responsibility.

PEARSON

Darrel Hess began teaching geography at City College of San Francisco in 1990 and served as chair of the Earth Sciences Department from 1995 to 2009. After earning his bachelor's degree in geography at the University of California, Berkeley, in 1978, he served for two years as a teacher in the Peace Corps on the Korean island of Jeju-do (see Figure 2-24). Upon returning to the United States, he worked as a writer, photographer, and audiovisual producer. His association with Tom McKnight began as a graduate student at UCLA, where he served as one of Tom's teaching assistants. Their professional collaboration developed after Darrel graduated from UCLA with a master's degree in geography in 1990. He first wrote the *Study Guide* that accompanied the fourth edition of *Physical Geography: A Landscape Appreciation*, and then the *Laboratory Manual* that accompanied the fifth edition. Darrel has been authoring both works ever since. In 1999 Tom asked Darrel to join him as coauthor of the textbook. As did Tom, Darrel greatly enjoys the outdoor world. Darrel and his wife, Nora, are avid hikers, campers, and scuba divers.

Tom L. McKnight taught geography at UCLA from 1956 to 1993. He received his bachelor's degree in geology from Southern Methodist University in 1949, his master's degree in geography from the University of Colorado in 1951, and his Ph.D. in geography and meteorology from the University of Wisconsin in 1955. During his long academic career, Tom served as chair of the UCLA Department of Geography from 1978 to 1983, and was director of the University of California Education Abroad Program in Australia from 1984 to 1985. Passionate about furthering the discipline of geography, he helped establish the UCLA/Community College Geography Alliance and generously funded awards for both undergraduate and graduate geography students. His many honors include the California Geographical Society's Outstanding Educator Award in 1988, and the honorary rank of Professor Emeritus upon his retirement from UCLA. In addition to *Physical Geography: A Landscape Appreciation*, his other college textbooks include *The Regional Geography of the United States and Canada*; *Oceania: The Geography of Australia, New Zealand, and the Pacific Islands*; and *Introduction to Geography*, with Edward F. Bergman. Tom passed away in 2004—the geographic community misses him enormously.

A Learning Path Guides Students

Each chapter's learning tools form a path that gives students a consistent framework to learn about the processes and patterns that create our planet's landscape.

NEW! Seeing Geographically questions at the beginning and end of each chapter ask students to perform visual analysis and critical thinking to check their understanding of key chapter concepts and overcome any misconceptions.

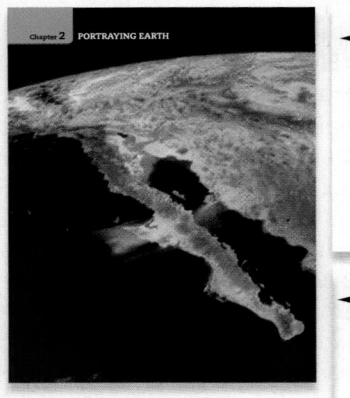

Chapter 2 PORTRAYING EARTH

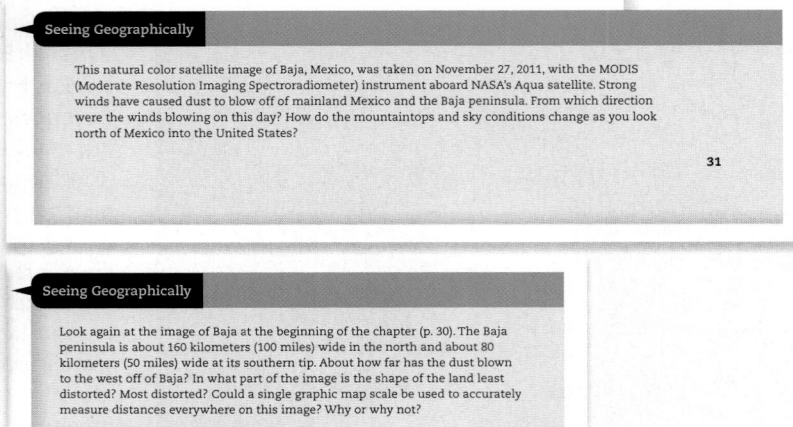

Seeing Geographically

This natural color satellite image of Baja, Mexico, was taken on November 27, 2011, with the MODIS (Moderate Resolution Imaging Spectroradiometer) instrument aboard NASA's Aqua satellite. Strong winds have caused dust to blow off of mainland Mexico and the Baja peninsula. From which direction were the winds blowing on this day? How do the mountaintops and sky conditions change as you look north of Mexico into the United States?

31

Seeing Geographically

Look again at the image of Baja at the beginning of the chapter (p. 30). The Baja peninsula is about 160 kilometers (100 miles) wide in the north and about 80 kilometers (50 miles) wide at its southern tip. About how far has the dust blown to the west off of Baja? In what part of the image is the shape of the land least distorted? Most distorted? Could a single graphic map scale be used to accurately measure distances everywhere on this image? Why or why not?

NEW! Key Questions work as chapter-specific learning outcomes in the chapter opening pages, which connect to Learning Checks, End of Chapter Questions, and the Learning Outcomes in MasteringGeography.™

NEW! Learning Checks integrate review questions at the end of chapter sections, helping students check comprehension.

Learning Check 2-5 Would a Mercator projection be a good choice for a map used to study the loss of forest cover around the world? Why or why not?

Learning Check 3-6 Is photochemical smog considered a *primary pollutant* or a *secondary pollutant* in the atmosphere? Why?

Learning Check 9-7 What are some of the consequences of thawing permafrost around the Arctic?

Review and Study questions appear at the end of every chapter, giving students the practice they need to learn and master the material. There are three exercise types.

- **Questions on Key Terms & Concepts** ensure students have a firm grasp of the essential vocabulary.
- **Study Questions** reinforce the main concepts in the chapter.
- **NEW! Exercises** offer optional mathematical treatments of chapter concepts, and are also available in MasteringGeography.

KEY TERMS AND CONCEPTS

The Nature of Water: Commonplace but Unique (p. 142)

1. Briefly describe how water moves through the **hydrologic cycle**.
2. What is a **hydrogen bond** between water molecules?
3. Describe what happens to the density of water as it freezes.
4. What is meant by **surface tension** of water?
5. What is **capillarity**?

STUDY QUESTIONS

1. Why does ice float on liquid water?
2. Why is evaporation a "cooling" process and condensation a "warming" process?
3. What happens to the relative humidity of an unsaturated parcel of air when the temperature decreases? Why?
4. What happens to the relative humidity of an unsaturated parcel of air when the temperature increases? Why?
5. Why does a rising parcel of unsaturated air cool at a greater rate than a rising parcel of saturated air (in which condensation is taking place)?

EXERCISES

1. Calculate the relative humidity for the following parcels of air:
   a. If the specific humidity is 5 g/kg and the capacity is 20 g/kg: _____ %
   b. If the specific humidity if 35 g/kg and the capacity is 40 g/kg: _____ %
2. Use Figure 6-8 to estimate the water vapor capacity (the saturation specific humidity in g/kg) of air at the following temperatures:
   a. 0°C (32°F): _____ g/kg
   b. 30°C (86°F): _____ g/kg
3. Using your answers for Exercise Problem 2 above, calculate the relative humidity of the following parcels of air at the temperature given:
   a. If the specific humidity is 3 g/kg at a temperature of 0°C: _____ %

Current, Compelling Applications Boost Comprehension

Expert contributors author many of the special Focus, People and the Environment, and Energy for the 21st Century features, sharing a variety of expertise and experience with students.

NEW! Energy for the 21st Century feature boxes provide balanced coverage of both renewable and non-renewable energy resources authored by expert contributors, including a new feature on *Our Continuing Dependence on Fossil Fuels* (Chapter 3) and *Fracking for Natural Gas* (Chapter 13).

People and the Environment boxes discuss the effects of human activity on the environment. New topics in the Eleventh Edition include *The Record Breaking Tornadoes of 2011* (Chapter 7) and the *2010 Haiti Earthquake* (Chapter 14).

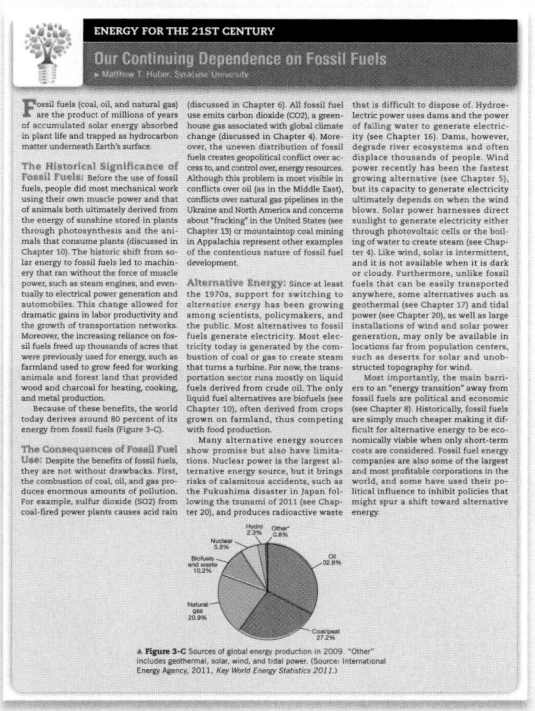

Focus features present in-depth case studies of special topics in physical geography. New topics in the Eleventh Edition include *Using Remote Sensing Images to Study a Landscape* (Chapter 2), *The Conveyor Belt Model of Midlatitude Cyclones* (Chapter 7), and *Monitoring Groundwater Resources from Space* (Chapter 9).

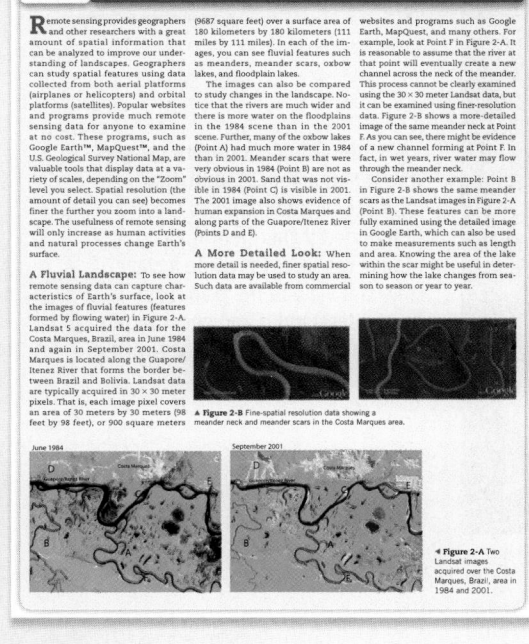

Dynamic Media to Engage Students

Multimedia resources are linked throughout the text and eText, bringing the concepts to life.

Animation
Convection and
Plate Tectonics

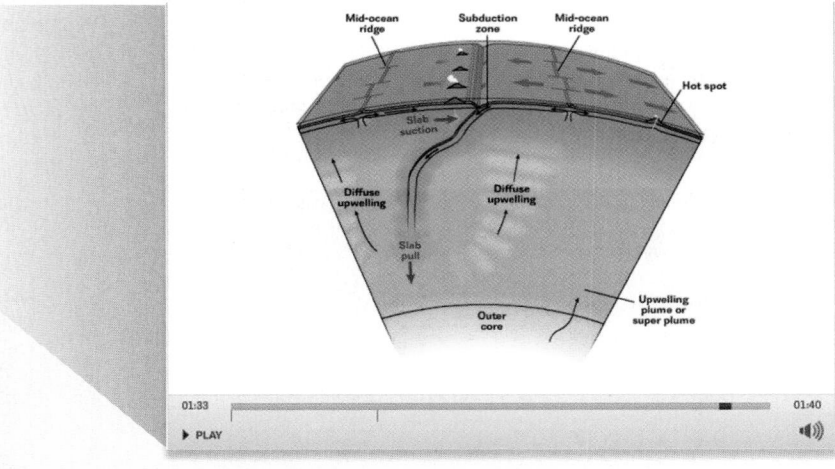

NEW! Quick Response (QR) Codes within the pages of the book link to a variety of animations and videos, providing students with just-in-time access to media resources tied to the book's concepts. Media are automatically linked in the eText and also available in the MasteringGeography™ study area.

Video
Hurricane
Hot Towers

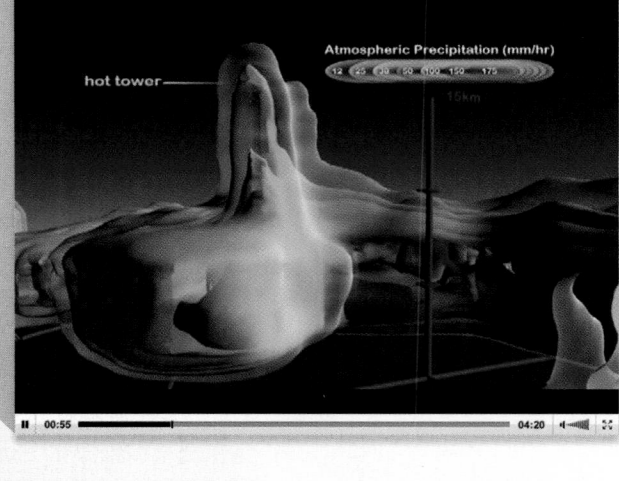

NEW! Additional satellite images, the latest science, statistics, and associated graphics are integrated throughout the text. These resources provide a clear, relevant view of the planet as we understand it and encourage students to explore on their own.

▲ **Figure 3-24** The wind pattern within storms such as hurricanes is influenced by the deflection of the Coriolis effect. This image shows Tropical Storm Beryl in May 2012, just before making landfall.

Stunning Graphics Visualize Earth's Landscape

The excellent cartographic and illustration program by renowned geoscience illustrator Dennis Tasa helps students visualize and understand the concepts covered in this text.

(a) High-resolution orthoimagery

(b) Topographic map

(c) Geologic map

(d) Google map

▲ **Figure 2-1** Different types of maps convey different kinds of information about the landscape, as shown in these four maps of a region near Salem, Massachusetts. (a) High-resolution orthophoto imagery (original scale 1:24,000). (b) Topographic map with elevation contour lines (original scale 1:24,000). (c) Geologic map showing rock types: orange = coarse glacial deposits; blue = glaciomarine deposits; green = glacial till; lavender = swamp deposits (original scale 1:50,000). (d) Google™ Map showing streets and highways.

Hundreds of maps include shaded relief where appropriate.

Major photos paired with locator maps to enhance geographic literacy.

"Bathtub ring" from higher reservoir level

Hoover Dam

▲ **Figure 9-24** Hoover Dam and Lake Mead on the Colorado River. The "bathtub ring" around the margin of the reservoir marks the water level when Lake Mead is at full capacity.

Transform fault

(a) Transform plate boundary

Continental crust

Midocean ridge

Oceanic crust

Seafloor spreading

Lithosphere

Asthenosphere

(b) Divergent plate boundary

Oceanic trench

Oceanic crust

Oceanic crust

Continental crust

Lithosphere

Lithosphere

Subducting plate

Asthenosphere

(c) Convergent plate boundary (oceanic–oceanic subduction)

Oceanic trench

Oceanic crust

Lithosphere

Continental crust

Lithosphere

Subducting plate

Asthenosphere

(d) Convergent plate boundary (oceanic–continental subduction)

▲ **Figure 14-12** Three kinds of plate boundaries. The edges of lithospheric plates slide past each other along transform boundaries such as the San Andreas Fault system in California (a); move apart at divergent boundaries such as continental rift valleys and midocean ridges (b); and come together at convergent boundaries such as oceanic-oceanic plate subduction zones (c), oceanic-continental plate subduction zones (d), and continental collision zones.

Line art with numerous multi-part photorealistic illustrations capture sequence and evolution to help students understand various processes.

MasteringGeography™

MasteringGeography delivers engaging, dynamic learning opportunities—focusing on course objectives and responsive to each student's progress—that are proven to help students absorb physical geoscience course material and understand difficult geographic concepts.

Give students a sense of place and an understanding of physical concepts

Encounter Activities provide rich, interactive explorations of geography concepts using the dynamic features of **Google Earth™** to visualize and explore Earth's physical landscape. Dynamic assessment includes multiple-choice and short-answer questions related to core physical geography concepts. All Explorations include corresponding Google Earth KMZ media files, and questions include hints and specific wrong-answer feedback to help coach students towards mastery of the concepts.

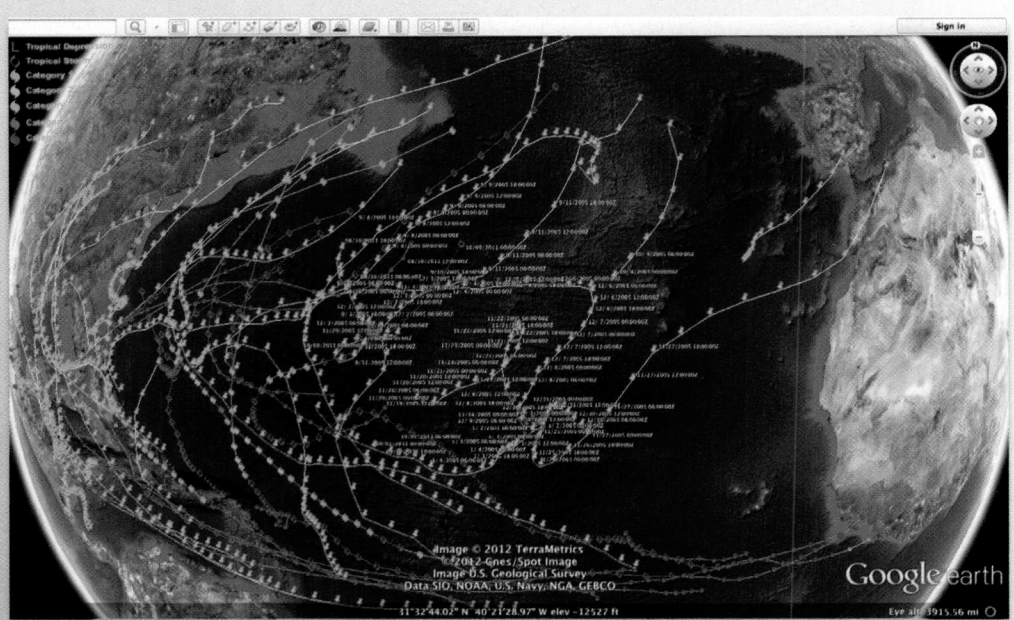

Geoscience Animations illuminate the most difficult-to-visualize topics from across the physical geosciences, such as solar system formation, hydrologic cycle, plate tectonics, glacial advance and retreat, global warming, etc. Animations include audio narration, a text transcript, and assignable multiple-choice quizzes with specific wrong-answer feedback to help guide students towards mastery of these core physical process concepts.

NEW! Quick Response Codes link to video and animation resources as a means to provide students with just-in-time access to visualization or indicate to students when they can login to the Study Area of MasteringGeography to access these media.

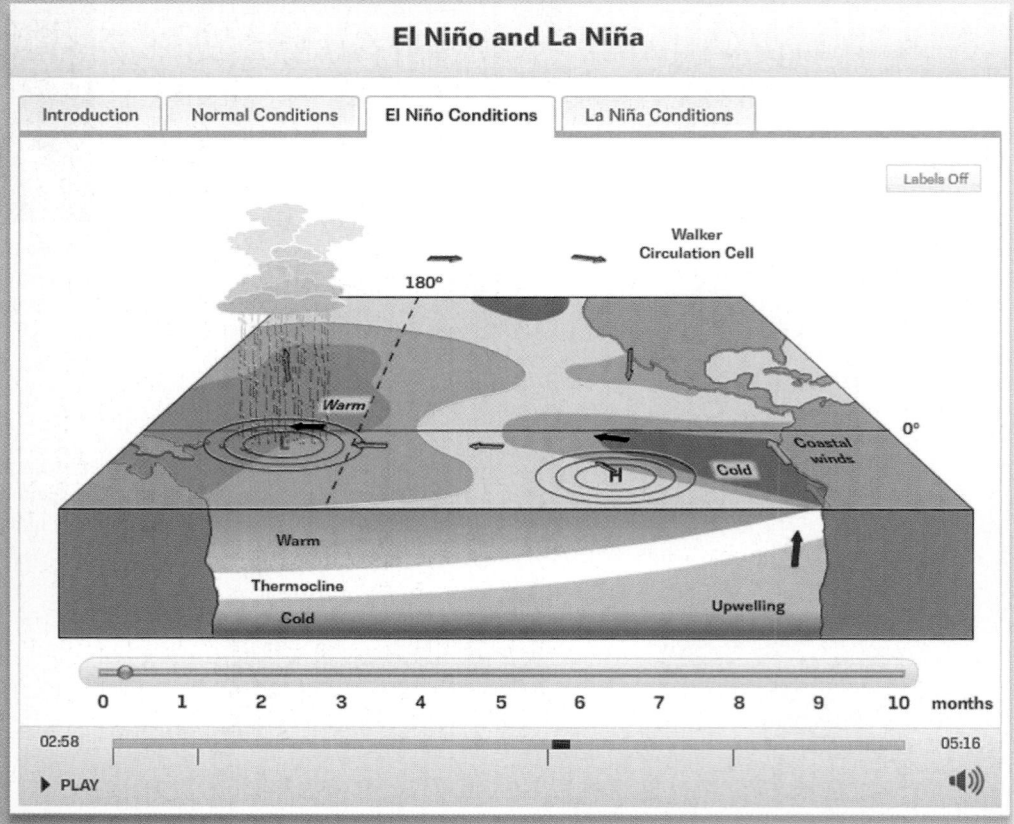

Improve critical thinking and geographic literacy while exploring Earth's physical landscape

MapMaster is a powerful tool that presents assignable layered thematic and place name interactive maps at world and regional scales for students to test their geographic literacy and spatial reasoning skills, and explore the modern geographer's tools.

MapMaster Layered Thematic Interactive Map Activities act as a mini-GIS tool, allowing students to layer various thematic maps to analyze spatial patterns and data at regional and global scales. Multiple-choice and short-answer questions are organized around the textbook topics and concepts.

NEW! MapMaster has been updated to include:

- 90 new map layers
- Zoom and annotation functionalities
- Current U.S. Census, United Nations, and Population Reference Bureau Data

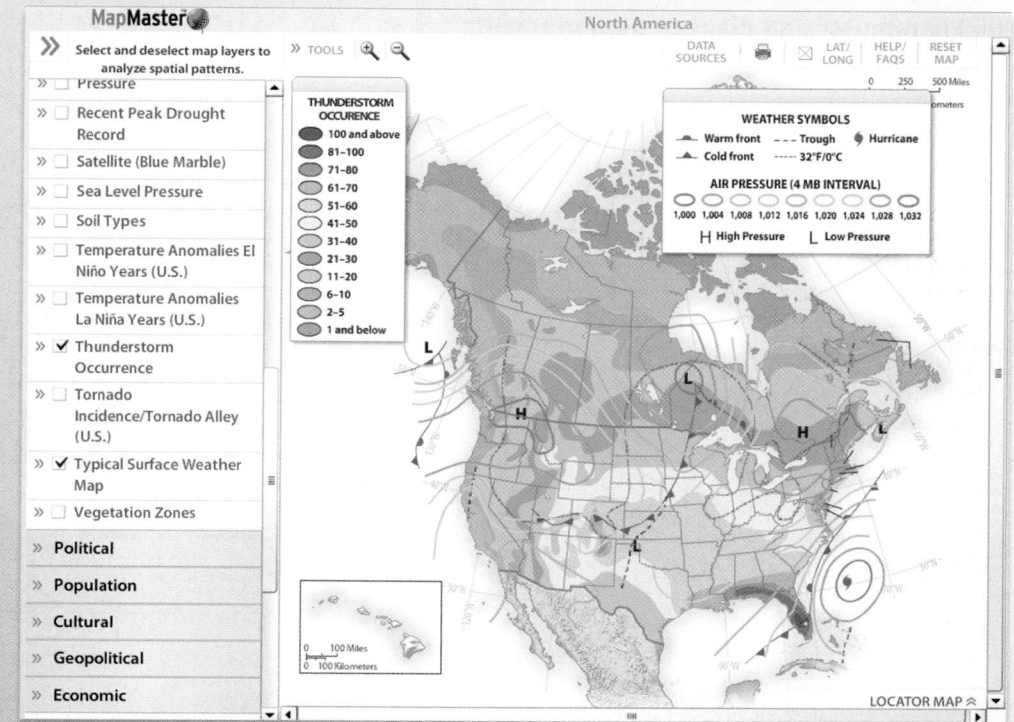

NEW! Coaching Activities are built around the toughest topics in physical geography.

Geography videos provide students a sense of place and allow them to explore a range of locations and topics related to physical geography. A variety of video clips cover diverse locations and physical geoscience concepts, with quiz questions to make these assignable and assessable. These video activities allow instructors to test students' understanding and application of concepts, and offer hints and wrong-answer feedback to guide students towards mastering the concepts.

Student Resources in MasteringGeography

- Geoscience Animations
- MapMaster™ interactive maps
- Practice quizzes
- Geography videos
- "In the News" RSS feeds
- Glossary flashcards
- Optional Pearson eText and more

Callouts to MasteringGeography appear at the end of each chapter to direct students to extend their learning beyond the textbook.

MasteringGeography™

www.masteringgeography.com

With the Mastering gradebook and diagnostics, you'll be better informed about your students' progress than ever before. Mastering captures the step-by-step work of every student—including wrong answers submitted, hints requested, and time taken at every step of every problem—all providing unique insight into the most common misconceptions of your class.

Quickly monitor and display student results

The **Gradebook** records all scores for automatically graded assignments. Shades of red highlight struggling students and challenging assignments.

Diagnostics provide unique insight into class and student performance. With a single click, charts summarize the most difficult questions, vulnerable students, grade distribution, and score improvement over the duration of the course.

With a single click, **Individual Student Performance Data** provides at-a-glance statistics into each individual student's performance, including time spent on the question, number of hints opened, and number of wrong and correct answers submitted.

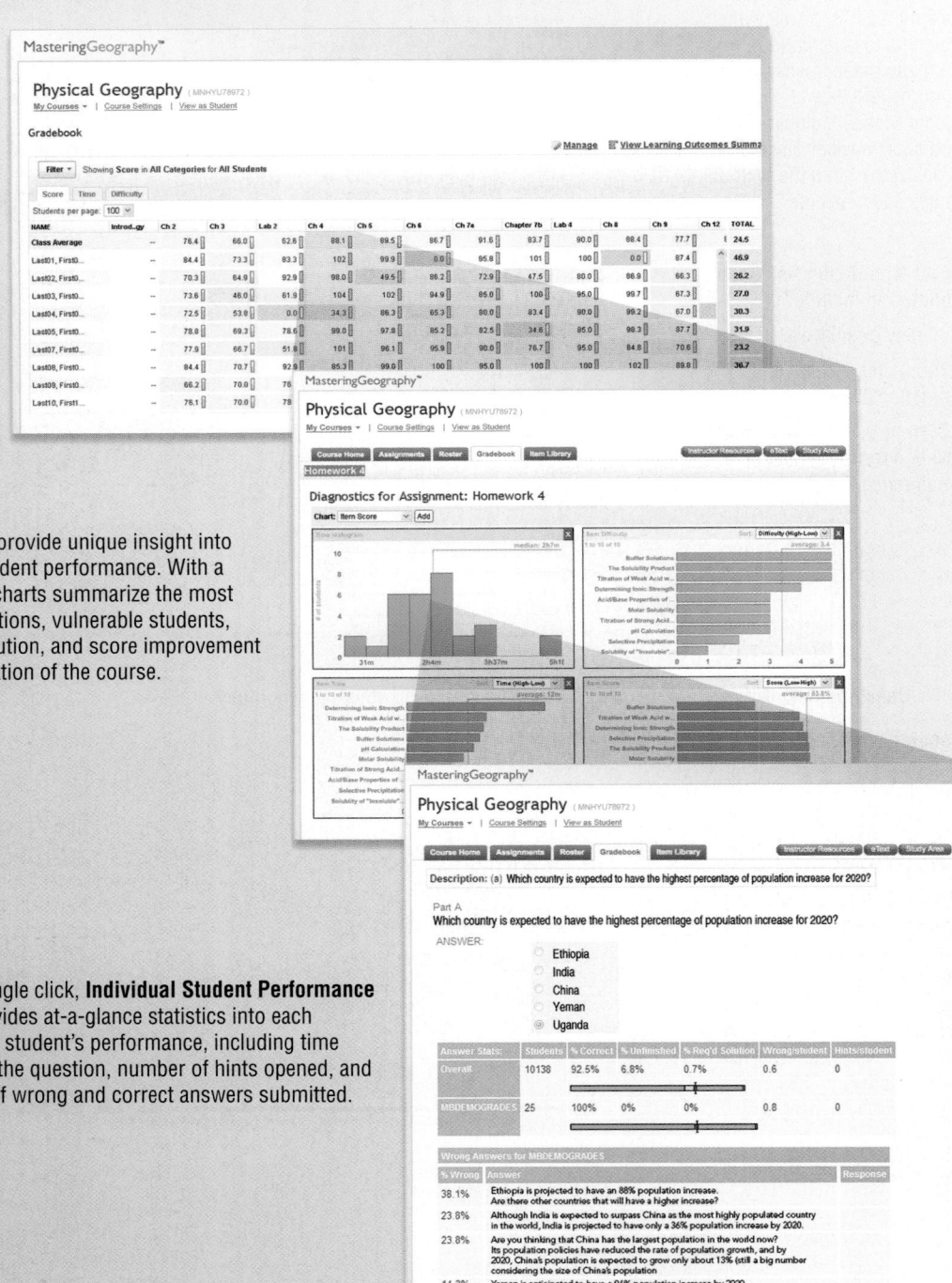

Easily measure student performance against your Learning Outcomes

Learning Outcomes

MasteringGeography provides quick and easy access to information on student performance against your learning outcomes and makes it easy to share those results.

- Quickly add your own learning outcomes, or use publisher-provided ones, to track student performance and report it to your administration.

- View class and individual student performance against specific learning outcomes.

- Effortlessly export results to a spreadsheet that you can further customize and/or share with your chair, dean, administrator, and/or accreditation board.

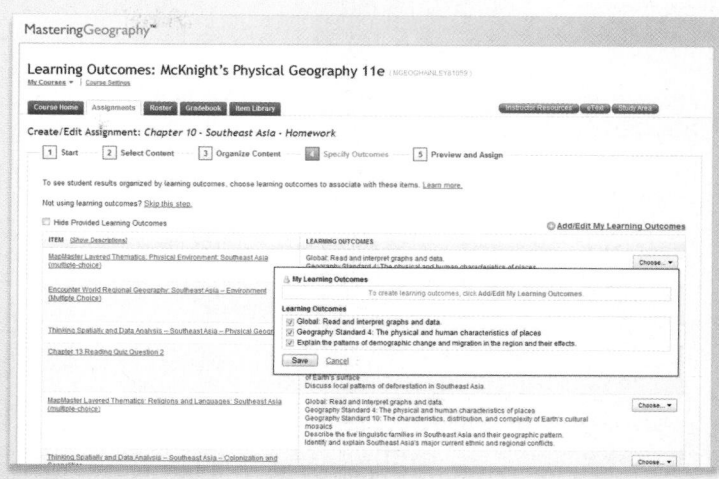

Easy to customize

Customize publisher-provided items or quickly add your own. MasteringGeography makes it easy to edit any questions or answers, import your own questions, and quickly add images, links, and files to further enhance the student experience.

Upload your own video and audio files from your hard drive to share with students, as well as record video from your computer's webcam directly into MasteringGeography—no plug-ins required. Students can download video and audio files to their local computer or launch them in Mastering to view the content.

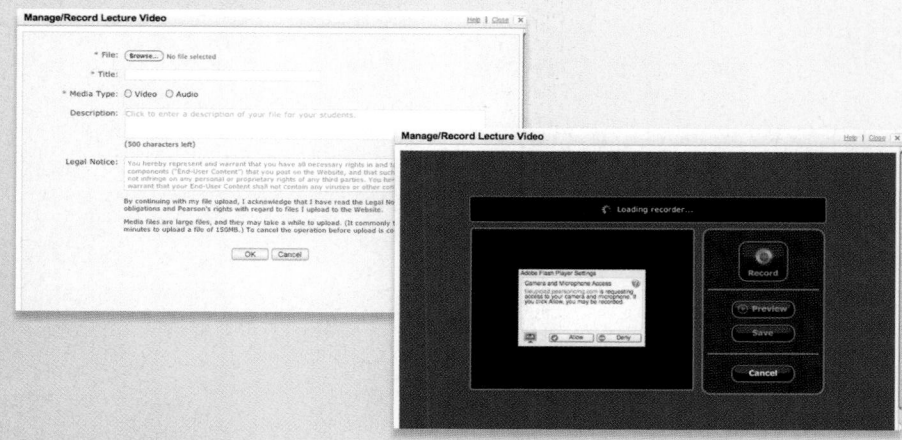

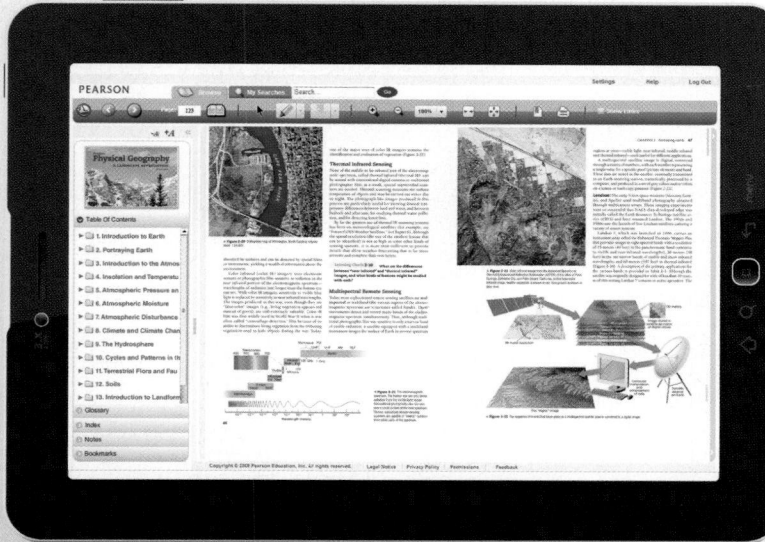

Pearson eText gives students access to *McKnight's Physical Geography: A Landscape Approach,* **Eleventh Edition** whenever and wherever they can access the Internet. The eText pages look exactly like the printed text, and include powerful interactive and customization functions. Users can create notes, highlight text in different colors, create bookmarks, zoom, click hyperlinked words and phrases to view definitions, and view as a single page or as two pages. Pearson eText also links students to associated media files, enabling them to view an animation as they read the text, and offers a full-text search and the ability to save and export notes. The Pearson eText also includes embedded URLs in the chapter text with active links to the Internet.

NEW! The Pearson eText app is a great companion to Pearson's eText browser-based book reader. It allows existing subscribers who view their Pearson eText titles on a Mac or PC to additionally access their titles in a bookshelf on the iPad and Android devices either online or via download.

IF YOU OPENED THIS BOOK EXPECTING THAT THE STUDY OF

geography was going to be memorizing names and places on maps, you'll be surprised to find that geography is much more than that. Geographers study the location and distribution of things—tangible things such as rainfall, mountains, and trees, as well as less tangible things such as language, migration, and voting patterns. In short, geographers look for and explain patterns in the physical and human landscape.

In this book you'll learn about fundamental processes and patterns in the natural world—the kinds of things you can see whenever you walk outside: clouds in the sky, mountains, streams and valleys, and the plants and animals that inhabit the landscape. You'll also learn about human interactions with the natural environment—how events such as hurricanes, earthquakes, and floods affect our lives and the world around us, as well as how human activities are increasingly altering our environment. By the time you finish this book you'll understand—in other words you'll appreciate—the landscape in new ways.

This opening chapter sets the stage for your study of physical geography. Here we introduce concepts and terms used throughout the book.

As you study this chapter, think about these key questions:

- **How do geographers study the world and use science to explain and understand the natural environment?**
- **What are the overlapping environmental "spheres" of Earth, and how does the concept of Earth systems help us understand the interrelationships of these spheres?**
- **How does Earth fit in with the solar system, and how does the size of Earth compare with the size of its surface features?**
- **How does the system of latitude and longitude describe location on Earth?**
- **What causes the annual change of seasons, and how do patterns of sunlight around Earth change during the year?**
- **How is the system of time zones used to establish times and dates around the world?**

GEOGRAPHY AND SCIENCE

The word *geography* comes from the Greek words meaning "Earth description." Several thousand years ago many scholars were indeed "Earth describers," and therefore geographers, more than anything else. Nonetheless, over the centuries there was a trend away from generalized Earth description toward more specialized disciplines—such as geology, meteorology, economics, and biology—and so geography as a field of study was somewhat overshadowed. Over the last few hundred years, however, geography reaffirmed its place in the academic world, and today geography is an expanding and flourishing field of study.

Seeing Geographically

This is a natural color, composite satellite image of Earth created by NASA. In the image can you see any indications of human presence? What might explain the differences in the color of land areas? What might explain the differences in the color of ocean areas?

Elements of Geography

Physical Geography   ## Cultural Geography

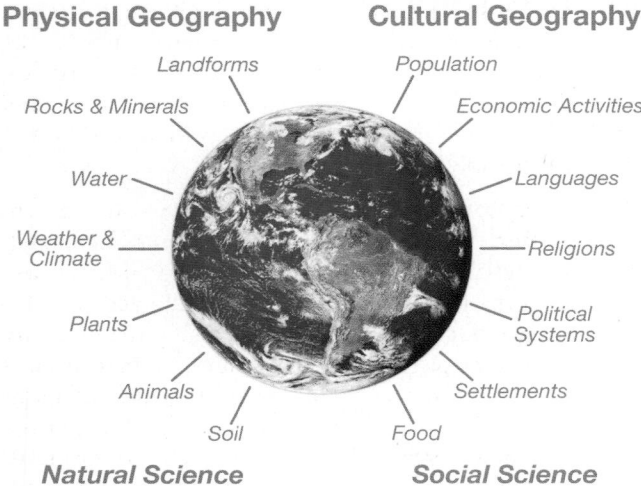

Landforms

Rocks & Minerals

Water

Weather & Climate

Plants

Animals

Soil

Natural Science

Population

Economic Activities

Languages

Religions

Political Systems

Settlements

Food

Social Science

▲ **Figure 1-1** The elements of geography can be grouped into two broad categories. Physical geography primarily involves the study of natural science, whereas cultural geography primarily entails the study of social science.

Studying the World Geographically

Geographers study how things differ from place to place—the distributional and locational relationships of things around the world (what is sometimes called the "spatial" aspect of things). Figure 1-1 shows the kinds of "things" geographers study, divided into two groups representing the two principal branches of geography. The elements of **physical geography** are natural in origin, and for this reason physical geography is sometimes called *environmental geography*. The elements of **cultural geography** are those of human endeavor, so this branch is sometimes referred to as *human geography*. The almost unlimited possible combinations of these various elements create the physical and cultural landscapes of the world that geographers study.

All of the items shown in Figure 1-1 are familiar to us, and this familiarity highlights a basic characteristic of geography as a field of learning: Geography doesn't have its own body of facts or objects that only geographers study. The focus of geology is rocks, the attention of economics is economic systems, demography examines human population, and so on. Geography, on the other hand, is much broader in scope than most other disciplines, "borrowing" its objects of study from related fields. Geographers, too, are interested in rocks and economic systems and population—especially in describing and understanding their location and distribution. We sometimes say that geography asks the fundamental question, "Why what is where and so what?"

Learning Check 1-1   **What are the differences between physical geography and cultural geography? (Answer on p. AK-1)**

Another basic characteristic of geography is its interest in interrelationships. One cannot understand the distribution of soils, for example, without knowing something about the rocks from which the soils were derived, the slopes on which the soils developed, and the climate and vegetation under which they developed. Similarly, it is impossible to comprehend the distribution of agriculture without an understanding of climate, topography, soil, drainage, population, economic conditions, technology, historical development, and many other factors, both physical and cultural. Because of its wide scope, geography bridges the academic gap between natural science and social science, studying all of the elements in Figure 1-1 in an intricate web of geographic interrelationships.

In our study of physical geography, our emphasis is on understanding the surface environment of Earth and the ways in which humans utilize and alter this environmental home. The habitable environment for humans exists over almost the entire land surface of Earth (Figure 1-2). It is only in the most extremely dry, cold, and rugged places

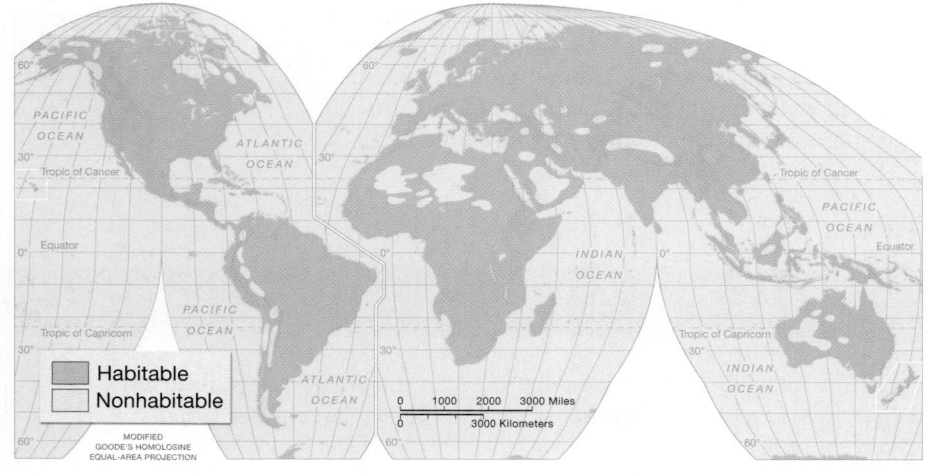

◄ **Figure 1-2** Most of Earth's land surface is habitable. The uninhabitable areas are too hot, too cold, too wet, too dry, or too rugged to support much human life—such as parts of the Arctic, most of Greenland, Antarctica, various mountainous regions, and several deserts.

Habitable
Nonhabitable

that humans rarely venture, and even in such locations, other forms of life may be found. Earth's "life zone," encompassing oceanic, terrestrial, and atmospheric life, extends from the bottom of the deepest oceanic trench to the atmosphere above the highest mountain peaks—a zone perhaps 30 kilometers (20 miles) deep. It is primarily within this shallow life zone that geographers focus their interests and do their work.

In this book we concentrate on the physical elements of the landscape, the processes involved in their development, their distribution, and their basic interrelationships. As we proceed from chapter to chapter, this notion of landscape development by natural processes and landscape modification by humans serves as a central focus. We will pay attention to elements of cultural geography only when they help to explain the development or patterns of the physical elements—especially the ways in which humans influence or alter the physical environment.

Global Environmental Change:
Several broad geographic themes run through this book. One of these themes is *global environmental change*—both the human-caused and natural processes that are currently altering the landscapes of the world. Some of these changes can take place over a period of just a few years, whereas others require many decades or even thousands of years (Figure 1-3). We pay special attention to the accelerating impact of human activities on the global environment: In the chapters on the atmosphere we discuss such issues as human-caused climate change, ozone depletion, and acid rain, whereas in later chapters we look at issues such as rainforest removal and coastal erosion.

Rather than treat global environmental change as a separate topic, we integrate this theme throughout the book. To help with this integration, we supplement the main text with short boxed essays, such as those entitled "People and the Environment" that focus on specific cases of human interaction with the natural environment, as well as boxes entitled "Energy for the 21st Century" that

focus on the challenge of supplementing—and perhaps eventually replacing—fossil fuels with renewable sources of energy. These essays serve to illustrate the connections between many aspects of the environment, such as the relationships between changing global temperatures, changing sea level, changing quantities of polar ice, and the changing distribution of plant and animal species, and the global economy and human society.

Globalization:
A related but less obvious theme running through this book is *globalization*. In the broadest terms, globalization refers to the processes and consequences of an increasingly interconnected world—connections between the economies, cultures, and political systems of the world. Although globalization is most commonly associated with the cultural and economic realms of world, it is important to recognize the environmental components of globalization as well. For example, the loss of tropical rainforest for timber or commercial agriculture in some regions of the world is driven in part by growing demand for commodities in countries far away from the tropics (Figure 1-4). Similarly, rapid economic growth in newly industrialized countries is contributing to the already high atmospheric greenhouse gas emissions of industrialized countries—the interconnected economies of the world are thus interconnected in their influence on the natural environment.

Because of geography's global perspective and its interest in both the natural and human landscape, geographers are able to offer insights into many of the world's most pressing problems—problems too complex to address from a narrower perspective. For example, the detrimental consequences of climate change cannot be addressed if we ignore the economic, social, historical, and political aspects of the issue. Similarly, global inequities of wealth and political power cannot be addressed if we ignore environmental and resource issues.

Just about everything in the world is in one way or another connected with everything else! Geography helps us understand these connections.

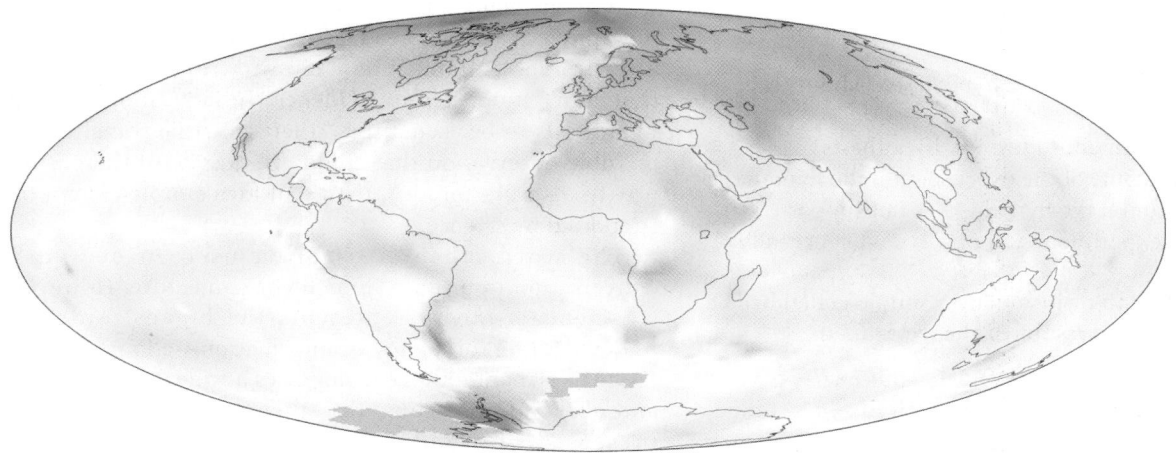

◀ **Figure 1-3**
Earth's climate is changing. This image shows the difference in temperature (the *temperature anomaly* in °C) during the period 2000 to 2009 compared with the average temperatures for the baseline period 1951 to 1980. *(NASA)*

Temperature Anomaly (°C)

−2.5 −1.5 −0.5   0   +0.5 +1.5 +2.5

▲ **Figure 1-4** Deforestation in some parts of the tropics is influenced by consumer demand in other parts of the world. This logging operation is in Perak, Malaysia.

Learning Check 1-2 **Why are physical geographers interested in globalization?**

The Process of Science

Because physical geography is concerned with processes and patterns in the natural world, knowledge in physical geography is advanced primarily through the study of science, and so it is useful for us to say a few words about science in general.

Science is often described—although somewhat simplistically—as a process that follows the *scientific method*:

1. Observe phenomena that stimulate a question or problem.
2. Offer an educated guess—a *hypothesis*—about the answer.
3. Design an experiment to test the hypothesis.
4. Predict the outcome of the experiment if the hypothesis is supported, and if the hypothesis is not supported.
5. Conduct the experiment and observe what actually happens.
6. Draw a conclusion or formulate a simple generalized "rule" based on the results of the experiment.

In practice, however, science doesn't always work through experimentation; in many fields of science, data collection through observation of a phenomenon is the basis of knowledge. In some regards science is best thought of as a process—or perhaps even as an attitude—for gaining knowledge. The scientific approach is based on observation, experimentation, logical reasoning, skepticism of unsupported conclusions, and the willingness to modify or even reject long-held ideas when new evidence contradicts them. For example, up until the 1950s most Earth scientists thought it impossible that the positions of continents could change over time; however, as we'll see in Chapter 14, by the late 1960s enough new evidence had been gathered to convince them that their earlier ideas were wrong—the configuration of continents has changed, and continues to change!

Although the term "scientific proof" is sometimes used by the general public, strictly speaking, science does not "prove" ideas. Instead, science works by eliminating alternative explanations—eliminating explanations that aren't supported by evidence. In fact, in order for a hypothesis to be "scientific," there must be some test or possible observation that could *disprove* it—if there is no way to disprove an idea, then that idea simply cannot be supported by science.

The word "theory" is often used in everyday conversation to mean a "hunch" or conjecture. However, in science a *theory* represents the highest order of understanding for a body of information—a logical, well-tested explanation that encompasses a wide variety of facts and observations. Thus, the "theory of plate tectonics" presented in Chapter 14 represents an empirically supported, broadly accepted, overarching framework for understanding processes operating within Earth.

The acceptance of scientific ideas and theories is based on a preponderance of evidence, not on "belief" and not on the pronouncements of "authorities." New observations and new evidence often cause scientists to revise their conclusions and theories or those of others. Much of this self-correcting process for refining scientific knowledge takes place through peer-reviewed journal articles. Peers—that is, fellow scientists—scrutinize a scientific report for sound reasoning, appropriate data collection, and solid evidence before it is published; reviewers need not agree with the author's conclusions, but they strive to ensure that the research meets rigorous standards of scholarship before publication.

Because new evidence may prompt scientists to change their ideas, good science tends to be somewhat cautious in the conclusions that are drawn. For this reason, the findings of many scientific studies are prefaced by phrases such as "the evidence suggests," or "the results most likely show." In some cases, different scientists interpret the same data quite differently and so disagree in their conclusions. Frequently, studies find that "more research is needed." The kind of uncertainty sometimes inherent in science may lead the general public to question the conclusions of scientific studies—especially when presented with a simple, and perhaps comforting nonscientific alternative. It is, however, this very uncertainty that often compels scientists to push forward in the quest for knowledge and understanding!

In this book we present the fundamentals of physical geography as it is supported by scientific research and evidence. In some cases, we will describe how our current understanding of a phenomenon developed over time; in other cases we will point out where uncertainty remains, where scientists still disagree, or where intriguing questions still remain.

Learning Check 1-3 **Why is the phrase "scientific proof" somewhat misleading?**

Numbers and Measurement Systems

Because so much of science is based on observation and measurable data, any thorough study of physical geography entails the use of mathematics. Although this book introduces physical geography primarily in a conceptual way without the extensive use of mathematical formulas, numbers and measurement systems are nonetheless important for us. Throughout the book, we use numbers and simple formulas to help illustrate concepts—the most obvious of which are numbers used to describe distance, size, weight, and temperature.

Two quite different systems of measurement are used around the world today. In the United States much of the general public is most familiar with the so-called *English System* of measurement—using measurements such as miles, pounds, and degrees Fahrenheit. However, most of the rest of the world—and the entire scientific community—uses the **International System** of measurement (abbreviated **S.I.** from the French *Système*

TABLE 1-1	Unit Conversions—Quick Approximations	
	S.I. to English Units	**English to S.I. Units**
Distance:	1 centimeter = a little less than ½ inch	1 inch = about 2½ centimeters
	1 meter = a little more than 3 feet	1 foot = about ⅓ meters
	1 kilometer = about ⅔ mile	1 yard = about 1 meter
		1 mile = about 1½ kilometers
Volume:	1 liter = about 1 quart	1 quart = about 1 liter
		1 gallon = about 4 liters
Mass:	1 gram = about ¹⁄₃₀ ounce	1 ounce = about 30 grams
	1 kilogram = about 2 pounds	1 pound = about ½ kilogram
Temperature:	1°C change = 1.8°F change	1°F change = about 0.6°C change

For exact conversion formulas, see Appendix I.

International; also sometimes called the "metric system")—using measurements such as kilometers, kilograms, and degrees Celsius.

You will notice that this book gives measurements in both S.I. and English units. If you are not familiar with both systems, Table 1-1 provides some quick approximations to help you learn the basic equivalents in each; detailed tables of conversion formulas between English and S.I. units appear in Appendix I.

ENVIRONMENTAL SPHERES AND EARTH SYSTEMS

From the standpoint of physical geography, the surface of Earth is a complex interface where four principal components of the environment meet and to some degree overlap and interact (Figure 1-5). These four components are often referred to as Earth's *environmental spheres.*

Earth's Environmental Spheres

The solid, inorganic portion of Earth is sometimes called the **lithosphere**[1] (*litho* is Greek for "stone"), comprising the rocks of Earth's crust as well as the unconsolidated particles of mineral matter that overlie the solid bedrock. The lithosphere's surface is shaped into an almost infinite variety of landforms, both on the seafloors and on the surfaces of the continents and islands.

---

[1]As we will see in Chapter 13, in the context of *plate tectonics* and our study of landforms, the term "lithosphere" is used specifically to refer to large "plates" consisting of Earth's crustal and upper mantle rock.

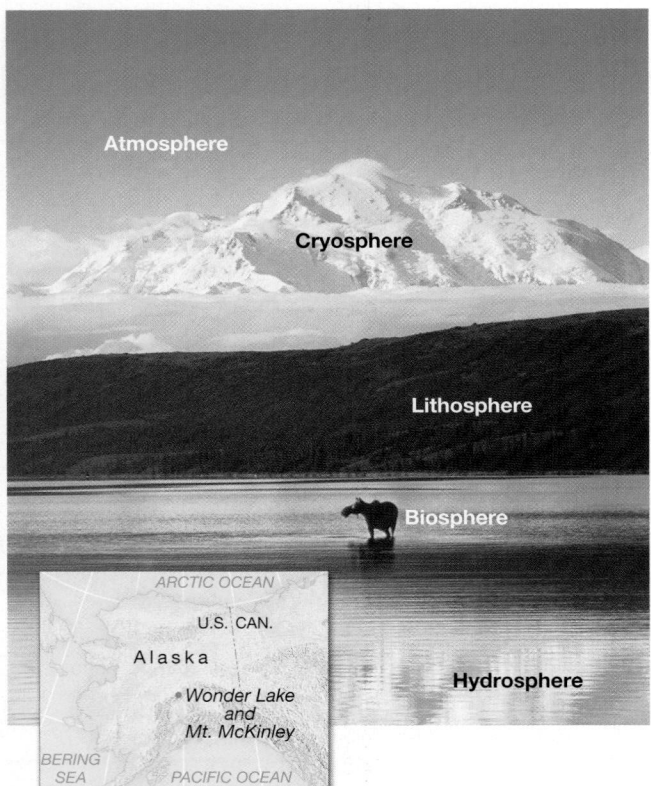

▲ **Figure 1-5** The physical landscape of Earth is composed of four overlapping and interacting systems called "spheres." The atmosphere is the air we breathe. The hydrosphere is the water of rivers, lakes, and oceans, the moisture in soil and air, as well as the snow and ice of the cryosphere. The biosphere is the habitat of all earthly life, as well as the life forms themselves. The lithosphere is the soil and bedrock that cover Earth's surface. This scene shows Wonder Lake and Mt. McKinley (Denali) in Denali National Park, Alaska.

The gaseous envelope of air that surrounds Earth is the **atmosphere** (*atmo* is Greek for "air"). It contains the complex mixture of gases needed to sustain life. Most of the atmosphere is close to Earth's surface, being densest at sea level and rapidly thinning with increased altitude. It is a very dynamic sphere, kept in almost constant motion by solar energy and Earth's rotation.

The **hydrosphere** (*hydro* is Greek for "water") comprises water in all its forms. The oceans contain the vast majority of the water found on Earth and are the moisture source for most precipitation. A subcomponent of the hydrosphere is known as the **cryosphere** (*cry* comes from the Greek word for "cold")—water frozen as snow and ice.

The **biosphere** (*bio* is Greek for "life") encompasses all the parts of Earth where living organisms can exist; in its broadest and loosest sense, the term also includes the vast variety of earthly life forms (properly referred to as *biota*).

These "spheres" are not discrete and separated entities but rather are considerably interconnected. This intermingling is readily apparent when considering an ocean—a body that is clearly a major component of the

hydrosphere and yet may contain a vast quantity of fish and other organic life that are part of the biosphere. An even better example is soil, which is composed largely of bits of mineral matter (lithosphere) but also contains life forms (biosphere), along with air (atmosphere), soil moisture (hydrosphere), and perhaps frozen water (cryosphere) in its pore spaces.

The environmental spheres can serve to broadly organize concepts for the systematic study of Earth's physical geography and are used that way in this book.

> **Learning Check 1-4** **Briefly define the lithosphere, atmosphere, hydrosphere, cryosphere, and biosphere.**

Earth Systems

Earth's environmental spheres operate and interact through a complex of *Earth systems*. By "system" we mean a collection of things and processes connected together and operating as a whole. In the human realm, for example, we talk of a global "financial system" that encompasses the exchange of money between institutions and individuals, or of a "transportation system" that involves the movement of people and commodities. In the natural world, systems entail the interconnected flows and storage of energy and matter.

Closed Systems: Some systems are effectively self-contained and therefore isolated from influences outside that system—and so are called *closed systems*. It is rare to find closed systems in nature. Earth as a whole is essentially a closed system with regard to matter—currently there is no significant increase or decrease in the amount of matter (the "stuff") of Earth, although relatively small but measurable amounts of meteoric debris arrives from space, and tiny amounts of gas are lost to space from the atmosphere. Energy, on the other hand, does enter and exit the Earth system constantly.

Open Systems: Most Earth systems are *open systems*—both energy and matter are exchanged across the system boundary. Matter and energy that enter the system are called *inputs*, and losses from the system to its surroundings are called *outputs*. For example, as we'll see in Chapter 19, a glacier behaves as an open system (Figure 1-6). The material inputs to a glacier include water in the form of snow and ice, along with rocks and other materials picked up by the moving ice; the material outputs of a glacier include the meltwater and water vapor lost to the atmosphere, as well as the rock transported and eventually deposited by the ice. The most obvious energy input into a glacial system is solar radiation that melts the ice by warming the surrounding air and by direct absorption into the ice itself. But also at work are less obvious exchanges of energy that involve *latent heat*—energy stored by water during melting and evaporation, and released during freezing and condensation (latent heat is discussed in detail in Chapter 6).

Equilibrium: When inputs and outputs are in balance over time, the conditions within a system remain the same; such a system can be described as being in *equilibrium*. For

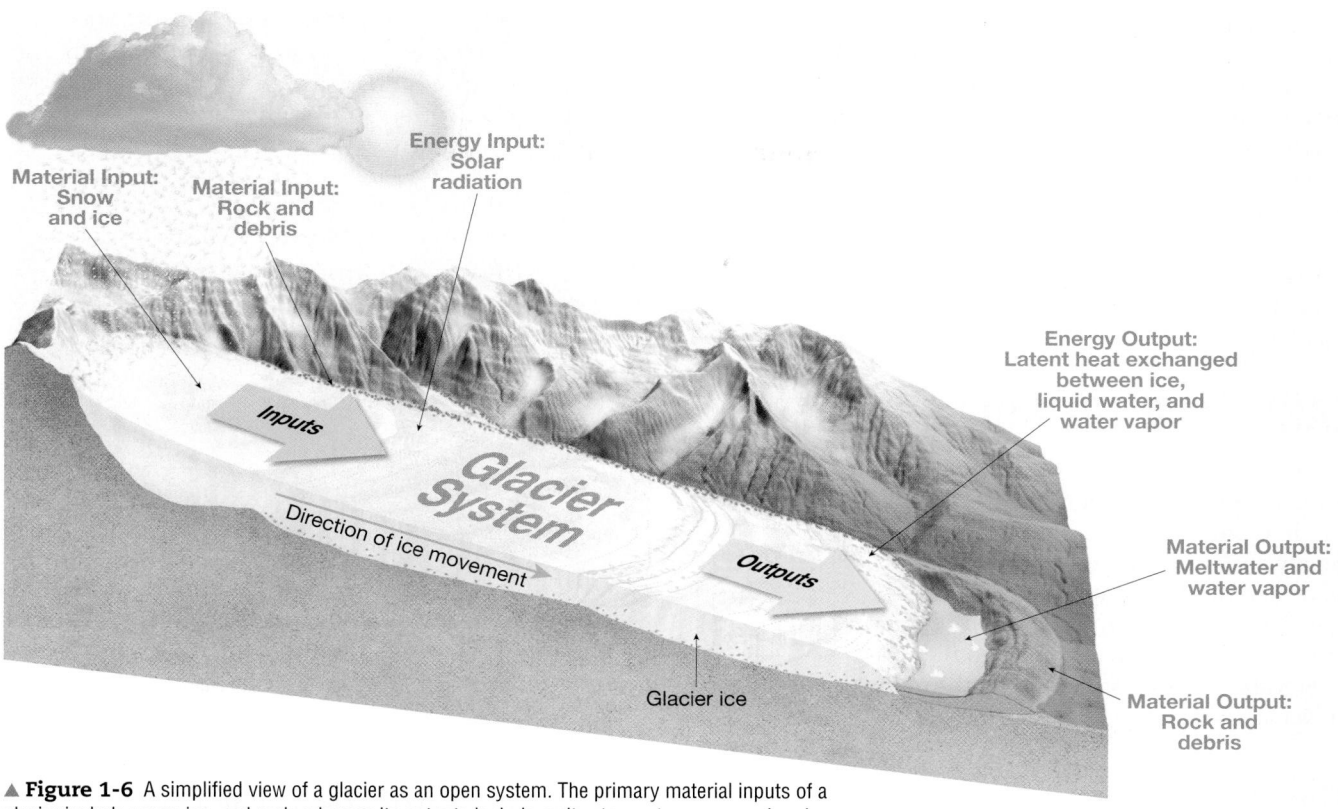

Material Input: Snow and ice

Material Input: Rock and debris

Energy Input: Solar radiation

Inputs

Glacier System

Direction of ice movement

Outputs

Glacier ice

Energy Output: Latent heat exchanged between ice, liquid water, and water vapor

Material Output: Meltwater and water vapor

Material Output: Rock and debris

▲ **Figure 1-6** A simplified view of a glacier as an open system. The primary material inputs of a glacier include snow, ice, and rock, whereas its outputs include meltwater, water vapor, and rock transported by the flowing ice. The energy interchange includes incoming solar radiation and the exchange of latent heat between ice, liquid water, and water vapor.

instance, a glacier will remain the same size over many years if its inputs of snow and ice are balanced by the loss of an equivalent amount of ice through melting. If, however, the balance between inputs and outputs changes, equilibrium will be disrupted—increasing snowfall for several years, for example, can cause a glacier to grow until a new equilibrium size is reached.

Interconnected Systems: In physical geography we study the myriad of interconnections between Earth's systems and subsystems. Continuing with our example of a glacier: The system of an individual glacier is interconnected with many other Earth systems, including Earth's solar radiation budget (discussed in Chapter 4), wind and pressure patterns (discussed in Chapter 5), and the hydrologic cycle (discussed in Chapter 6)—if inputs or outputs in those systems change, a glacier may also change. For instance, if air temperature increases through a change in Earth's solar radiation budget, both the amount of water vapor available to precipitate as snow and the rate of melting of that snow, may change, causing an adjustment in the size of the glacier.

> **Learning Check 1-5**   **What does it mean when we say a system is in equilibrium?**

Feedback Loops: Some systems produce outputs that "feedback" into that system, reinforcing change. As we'll see in Chapter 8, over the last few decades increasing

temperatures in the Arctic have reduced the amount of highly reflective, summer sea ice. As the area of sea ice has diminished, the darker, less reflective ocean has absorbed more solar radiation, contributing to the temperature increase—which in turn has reduced the amount of sea ice even more, further reducing reflectance and increasing absorption. Were Arctic temperatures to decrease, an expanding cover of reflective sea ice would reduce absorption of solar radiation and so reinforce a cooling trend. These are examples of *positive feedback loops*—change within a system continuing in one direction.

Conversely, *negative feedback loops* tend to inhibit a system from changing—in this case increasing a system input tends to *decrease* further change, keeping the system in equilibrium. For example, an increase in air temperature may increase the amount of water vapor in the air; this greater amount of water vapor may in turn condense and increase the cloud cover—which can reflect incoming solar radiation and so prevent a further temperature increase.

Although systems may resist change through negative feedback loops, at some point a system may reach a *tipping point* or *threshold* beyond which the system becomes unstable and changes abruptly until it reaches a new equilibrium. For instance, as we'll see in Chapter 9, it is possible that the increasing freshwater runoff from melting glaciers in the Arctic could disrupt the energy transfer of the slow, deep ocean *thermohaline circulation* in the Atlantic Ocean, triggering a sudden change in climate.

The preceding examples are not intended to confuse you, but rather to illustrate the great complexity of Earth's interconnected systems! Because of this complexity, in this book we often first describe one process or Earth system in isolation before presenting its interconnections with other systems.

Learning Check 1-6   **What is the difference between a positive feedback loop and a negative feedback loop?**

EARTH AND THE SOLAR SYSTEM

Earth is part of a larger *solar system*—an open system with which Earth interacts. Earth is an extensive rotating mass of mostly solid material that orbits the enormous ball of superheated gases we call the Sun. The geographer's concern with spatial relationships properly begins with the relative location of this "spaceship Earth" in the universe.

Animation
Solar System
Formation

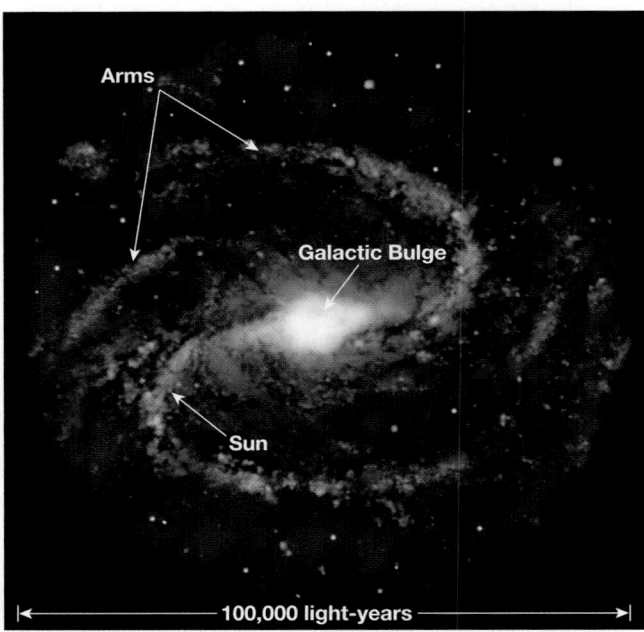

▲ **Figure 1-7** The structure of the Milky Way Galaxy showing the approximate location of our Sun on one of the spiral arms.

The Solar System

Earth is one of eight planets of our solar system, which also contains more than 160 natural satellites or "moons" revolving around the planets, an uncertain number of smaller *dwarf planets* such as Pluto, scores of comets (bodies composed of frozen liquid and gases together with small pieces of rock and metallic minerals), more than 500,000 asteroids (small, rocky, and sometimes icy objects, mostly less than a few kilometers in diameter), and millions of meteoroids (most of them the size of sand grains).

The medium-massed star we call the Sun is the central body of the solar system and makes up more than 99.8 percent of its total mass. The solar system is part of the Milky Way Galaxy, which consists of at least 200,000,000,000 stars arranged in a disk-shaped bared-spiral that is about 100,000 light-years in diameter (1 light-year equals about 9.5 trillion kilometers—the distance a beam of light travels over a period of one year) and 10,000 light-years thick at the center (Figure 1-7). The Milky Way Galaxy is only one of hundreds of billions of galaxies in the universe.

To begin to develop an understanding for astronomical distances, we might consider a reduced-scale model of the universe: if the distance between Earth and the Sun, which is about 150,000,000 kilometers (93,000,000 miles), is taken to be 2.5 centimeters (1 inch), then the distance from Earth to the nearest star would be 7.2 kilometers (4.5 miles), and the distance from Earth to the next similar-sized galaxy beyond the Milky Way would be about 240,000 kilometers (150,000 miles)!

Origins: The origin of Earth, and indeed of the universe, is incompletely understood. It is generally accepted that the universe began with a cosmic event called the *big bang*. The most

widely held view is that the big bang took place some 13.7 billion years ago—similar to the age of the oldest known stars. The big bang began in a fraction of a second as an infinitely dense and infinitesimally small bundle of energy containing all of space and time started to expand away in all directions at extraordinary speeds, pushing out the fabric of space and filling the universe with the energy and matter we see today.

Our solar system originated between 4.5 and 5 billion years ago when a *nebula*—a huge, cold, diffuse cloud of gas and dust—began to contract inward, owing to its own gravitational collapse, forming a hot, dense *protostar* (Figure 1-8). This hot center—our Sun—was surrounded by a cold, revolving disk of gas and dust that eventually condensed and coalesced to form the planets.

All of the planets revolve around the Sun in elliptical orbits, with the Sun located at one focus (looking "down" on the solar system from a vantage point high above the North Pole of Earth, the planets appear to orbit in a counterclockwise direction around the Sun). All the planetary orbits are in nearly the same plane (Figure 1-9), perhaps revealing their relationship to the original spinning direction of the nebular disk. The Sun rotates on its axis from west to east. Moreover, most of the planets rotate from west to east on their own axes (Uranus rotates "sideways" with its rotational axis almost parallel to its orbital plane; Venus rotates from east to west). The planets revolve more slowly and generally have a lower temperature as their distance from the Sun increases.

The Planets: The four inner *terrestrial planets*—Mercury, Venus, Earth, and Mars—are generally smaller, denser, and less oblate (more nearly spherical), and they rotate more slowly on their axes than the four outer

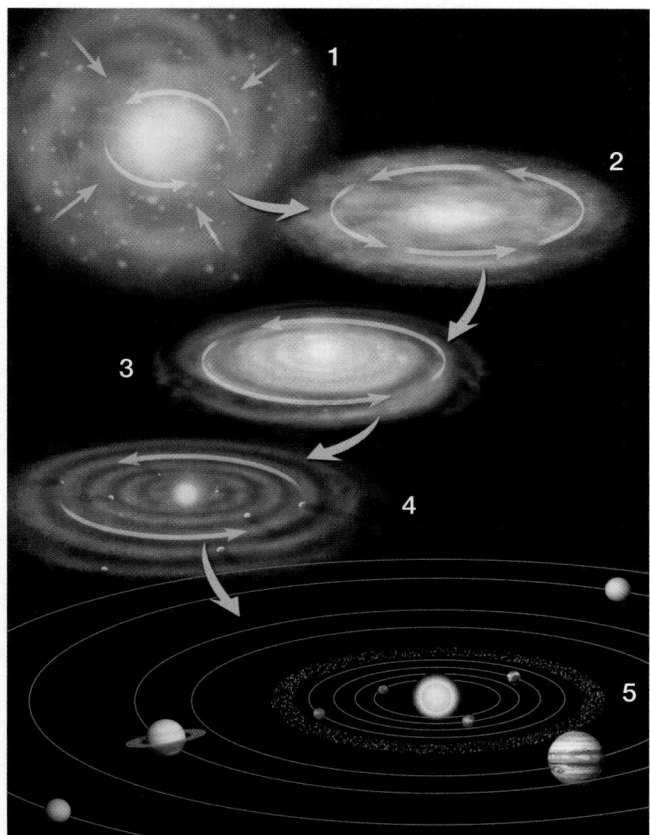

▲ **Figure 1-8** The birth of the solar system. (1) Diffuse gas cloud, or nebula, begins to contract inward. (2) Cloud flattens into nebular disk as it spins faster around a central axis. (3) Particles in the outer parts of the disk collide with each other to form protoplanets. (4) Protoplanets coalesce into planets and settle into orbits around the hot center. (5) The final product: a central Sun surrounded by eight orbiting planets (solar system not shown in correct scale). The original nebular disk was much larger than our final solar system.

Jovian planets—Jupiter, Saturn, Uranus, and Neptune. Also, the inner planets are composed principally of mineral matter and, except for airless Mercury, have diverse but relatively shallow atmospheres.

By contrast, the four Jovian planets tend to be much larger, more massive (although they are less dense), and much more oblate (less perfectly spherical) because they rotate more rapidly. The Jovian planets are mostly composed of elements such as hydrogen and helium—liquid near the surface, but frozen toward the interior—as well as ices of compounds such as methane and ammonia. The Jovian planets generally have atmospheres that are dense, turbulent, and relatively deep.

It was long thought that tiny Pluto was the ninth and outermost planet in the solar system. In recent years, however, astronomers have discovered other icy bodies, such as distant Eris, Makemake, and Haumea that are similar to Pluto and orbiting the Sun beyond Neptune in what is referred to as the *Kuiper Belt* or *trans-Neptunian region*. In June 2008 the International Astronomical Union reclassified Pluto as a special type of dwarf planet known as a *plutoid*. Some astronomers speculate that there may be several dozen yet-to-be-discovered plutoids and other dwarf planets in the outer reaches of the solar system.

> **Learning Check 1-7** **Contrast the characteristics of the terrestrial and Jovian planets in our solar system.**

The Size and Shape of Earth

Is Earth large or small? The answer to this question depends on one's frame of reference. If the frame of reference is the universe, Earth is almost infinitely small. The diameter of our planet is only about 13,000 kilometers (7900 miles), a tiny distance at the scale of the universe—for instance, the Moon is 385,000 kilometers (239,000 miles) from Earth, the Sun is 150,000,000 kilometers (93,000,000 miles) away, and the nearest star is 40,000,000,000,000 kilometers (25,000,000,000,000 miles) distant.

The Size of Earth: In a human frame of reference, however, Earth is impressive in size. Its surface varies in elevation from the highest mountain peak, Mount Everest, at 8850 meters (29,035 feet) above sea level, to the deepest oceanic trench, the Mariana Trench of the Pacific Ocean, at

▲ **Figure 1-9** The solar system (not drawn to correct scale). The Sun is not exactly at the center of the solar system—the planets revolve around the Sun in elliptical orbits. The Kuiper Belt, which includes dwarf planets such as Pluto, begins beyond Neptune.

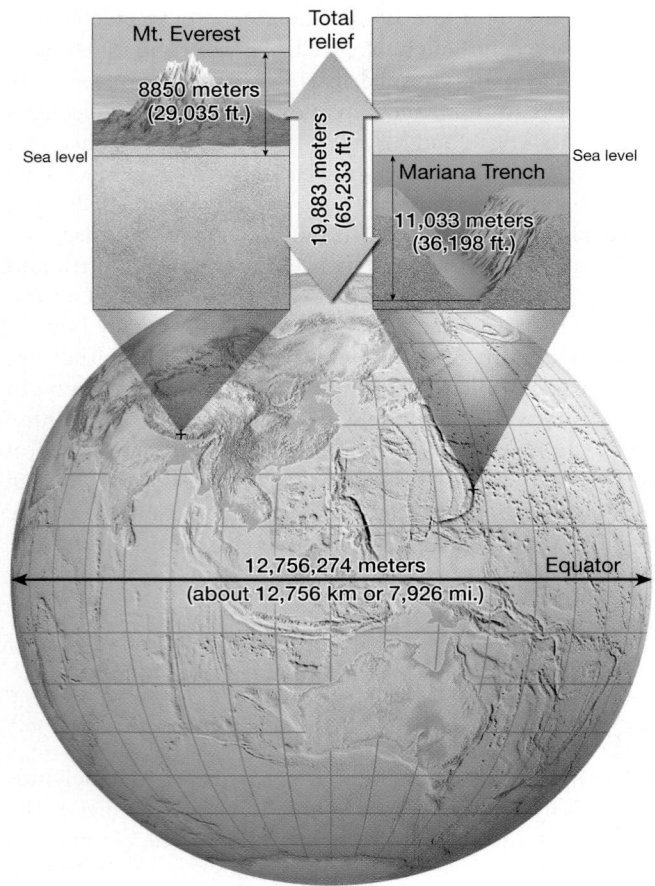

▲ **Figure 1-10** Earth is large relative to the size of its surface features. Earth's maximum relief (the difference in elevation between the highest and lowest points) is 19,883 meters (65,233 feet) or about 20 kilometers (12 miles) from the top of Mount Everest to the bottom of the Mariana Trench in the Pacific Ocean.

11,033 meters (36,198 feet) below sea level, a total difference in elevation of 19,883 meters (65,233 feet).

Although prominent on a human scale of perception, this difference is minor on a planetary scale, as Figure 1-10 illustrates. If Earth were the size of a basketball, Mount Everest would be an imperceptible pimple no greater than 0.17 millimeter (about 7 thousandths of an inch) high. Similarly, the Mariana Trench would be a tiny crease only 0.21 millimeter (about 8 thousandths of an inch) deep—this represents a depression smaller than the thickness of a sheet of paper.

Our perception of the relative size of topographic irregularities on Earth is often distorted by three-dimensional wall maps and globes that emphasize such landforms. To portray any noticeable appearance of topographic variation, the vertical distances on such maps are usually exaggerated 8 to 20 times their actual proportional dimensions—as are many diagrams used in this book. Further, many diagrams illustrating features of the atmosphere also exaggerate relative sizes to convey important concepts.

More than 2600 years ago Greek scholars correctly reasoned Earth to have a spherical shape. About 2200 years ago, Eratosthenes, the director of the Greek library at Alexandria, calculated the circumference of Earth

trigonometrically. He determined the angle of the noon Sun rays at Alexandria and at the city of Syene, 960 kilometers (600 miles) away. From these angular and linear distances he was able to estimate an Earth circumference of almost 43,000 kilometers (26,700 miles) which is reasonably close to the actual figure of 40,000 kilometers (24,900 miles).

The Shape of Earth: Earth is almost, but not quite, spherical. The cross section revealed by a cut through the equator would be circular, but a similar cut from pole to pole would be an ellipse rather than a circle (Figure 1-11). Any rotating body has a tendency to bulge around its equator and flatten at the polar ends of its rotational axis. Although the rocks of Earth may seem quite rigid and immovable to us, they are sufficiently pliable to allow Earth to develop a bulge around its middle. The slightly flattened polar diameter of Earth is 12,714 kilometers (7900 miles), whereas the slightly bulging equatorial diameter is 12,756 kilometers (7926 miles), a difference of only about 0.3 percent. Thus, our planet is properly described as an *oblate spheroid* rather than a true sphere. However, because this variation from true sphericity is exceedingly small, in most cases in this book we will treat Earth as if it were a perfect sphere.

Learning Check 1-8 What are Earth's highest and lowest points, and what is the approximate elevation difference between them?

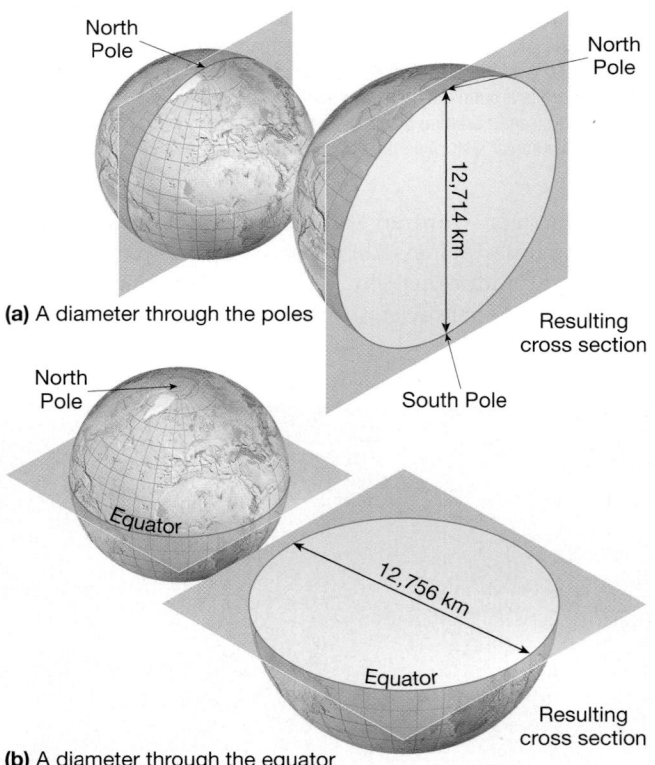

▲ **Figure 1-11** Earth is not quite a perfect sphere. Its surface flattens slightly at the North Pole and the South Pole and bulges out slightly around the equator. Thus, a cross section through the poles, shown in (a), has a diameter slightly less than the diameter of a cross section through the equator, shown in (b).

THE GEOGRAPHIC GRID— LATITUDE AND LONGITUDE

Any understanding of the distribution of geographic features over Earth's surface requires some system of accurate location. The simplest technique for achieving this is a grid system consisting of two sets of lines that intersect at right angles, allowing the location of any point on the surface to be described by the appropriate intersection, as shown in Figure 1-12. Such a rectangular grid system has been reconfigured for Earth's spherical surface.

If our planet were a nonrotating body, the problem of describing surface locations would be more difficult than it is: imagine trying to describe the location of a particular point on a perfectly round, perfectly clean Ping-Pong ball. Because Earth does rotate, we can use its rotation axis as a starting point to describe locations.

Earth's rotation axis is an imaginary line passing through Earth that connects the points on the surface called the **North Pole** and the **South Pole** (Figure 1-13). Further, if we visualize an imaginary plane passing through Earth halfway between the poles and perpendicular to the axis of rotation, we have another valuable reference feature: the *plane of the equator*. Where this plane intersects Earth's surface is the imaginary midline of Earth, called simply the **equator**. We use the North Pole, South Pole, rotational axis, and equatorial plane as natural reference features for measuring and describing locations on Earth's surface.

Great Circles: Any plane that is passed through the center of a sphere bisects that sphere (divides it into two equal halves) and creates what is called a **great circle** where

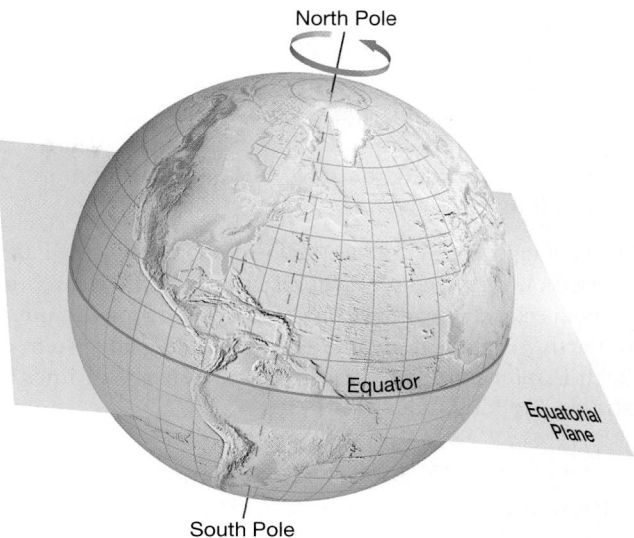

▲ **Figure 1-13** Earth spins around its rotation axis, an imaginary line that passes through the North Pole and the South Pole. An imaginary plane bisecting Earth midway between the two poles defines the equator.

it intersects the surface of the sphere (Figure 1-14a). The equator is such a great circle. Planes passing through any other part of the sphere produce what are called *small circles* where they intersect the surface (Figure 1-14b). Great circles have two properties of special interest for us:

1. A great circle is the largest circle that can be drawn on a sphere; it represents the circumference of that sphere and divides its surface into two equal halves or *hemispheres*. As we'll see later in this chapter, the

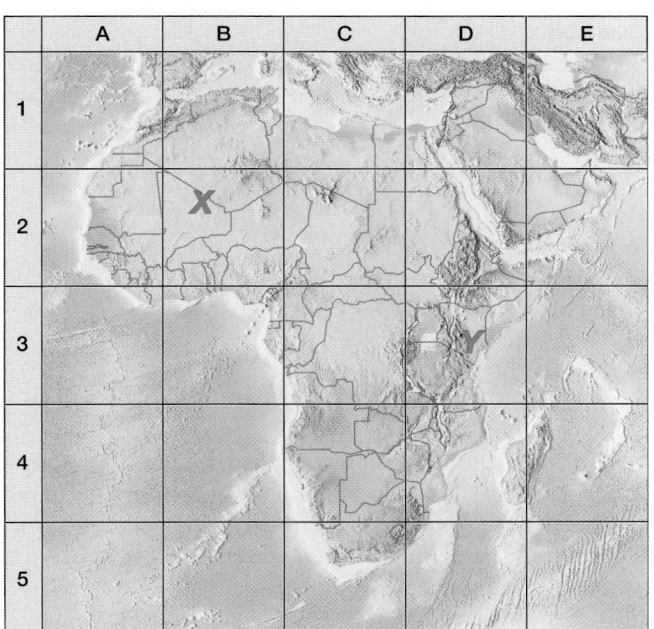

▲ **Figure 1-12** An example of a grid system. The location of point X can be described as 2B or as B2; the location of Y is 3D or D3.

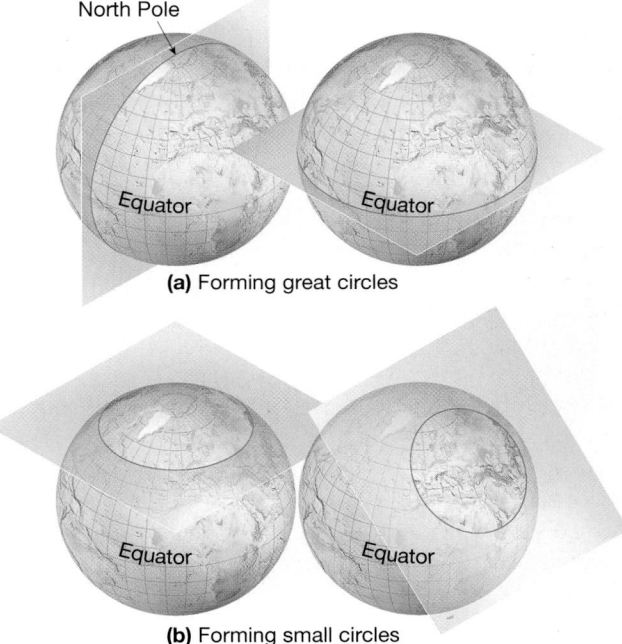

(a) Forming great circles

(b) Forming small circles

▲ **Figure 1-14** Comparison of great and small circles. (a) A great circle results from the intersection of Earth's surface with any plane that passes through Earth's center. (b) A small circle results from the intersection of Earth's surface with any plane that does not pass through Earth's center.

dividing line between the daytime and nighttime halves of Earth is a great circle.

2. A path between two points along the arc of a great circle is always the shortest route between those points. Such routes on Earth are known as *great circle routes* (great circle routes will be discussed in more detail in Chapter 2).

The geographic grid used as the locational system for Earth is based on the principles just discussed. Furthermore, the system is closely linked with the various positions assumed by Earth in its orbit around the Sun. The grid system of Earth is referred to as a *graticule* and consists of lines of latitude and longitude.

Learning Check 1-9 What is a great circle? Provide one example of a great circle.

Latitude

Latitude is a description of location expressed as an angle north or south of the equator. As shown in Figure 1-15, we can project a line from any location on Earth's surface to the center of Earth. The angle between this line and the equatorial plane is the latitude of that location.

Latitude is expressed in degrees, minutes, and seconds. There are 360 degrees (°) in a circle, 60 minutes (') in one degree, and 60 seconds (″) in one minute. With the advent of GPS navigation (discussed in Chapter 2), it is increasingly common to see latitude and longitude designated using decimal notation, for example, 38°22′47″ N can be written 38°22.78′ N or even 38.3797° N.

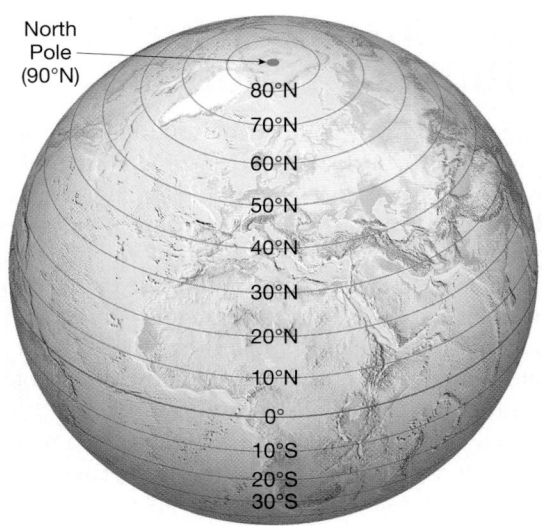

▲ **Figure 1-16** Lines of latitude indicate north-south location. They are called *parallels* because they are always parallel to each other.

Latitude varies from 0° at the equator to 90° north at the North Pole and 90° south at the South Pole. Any position north of the equator is north latitude, and any position south of the equator is south latitude (the equator itself is simply referred to as having a latitude of 0°).

A line connecting all points of the same latitude is called a **parallel**—because it is parallel to all other lines of latitude (Figure 1-16). The equator is the parallel of 0° latitude, and it, alone of all parallels, constitutes a great circle. All other parallels are small circles—all aligned in true east–west directions on Earth's surface. Because latitude is expressed as an angle, it can be infinitely subdivided—parallels can be constructed for every degree of latitude, or even for fractions of a degree of latitude.

Although it is possible to either construct or visualize an unlimited number of parallels, seven latitudes are of particular significance in a general study of Earth (Figure 1-17):

1. Equator, 0°
2. Tropic of Cancer, 23.5° N
3. Tropic of Capricorn, 23.5° S (Figure 1-18)
4. Arctic Circle, 66.5° N
5. Antarctic Circle, 66.5° S
6. North Pole, 90° N
7. South Pole, 90° S

The North Pole and South Pole are of course points rather than lines, but can be thought of as infinitely small parallels. The significance of these seven parallels will be explained later in this chapter when we discuss the seasons.

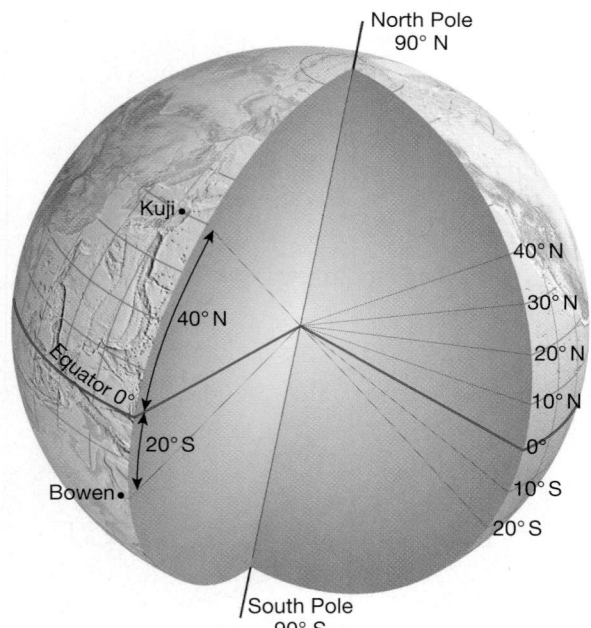

▲ **Figure 1-15** Measuring latitude. An imaginary line from Kuji, Japan, to Earth's center makes an angle of 40° with the equator. Therefore, Kuji's latitude is 40° N. An imaginary line from Bowen, Australia, to Earth's center makes an angle of 20°, giving this city a latitude of 20° S.

Learning Check 1-10 Why are lines of latitude called parallels?

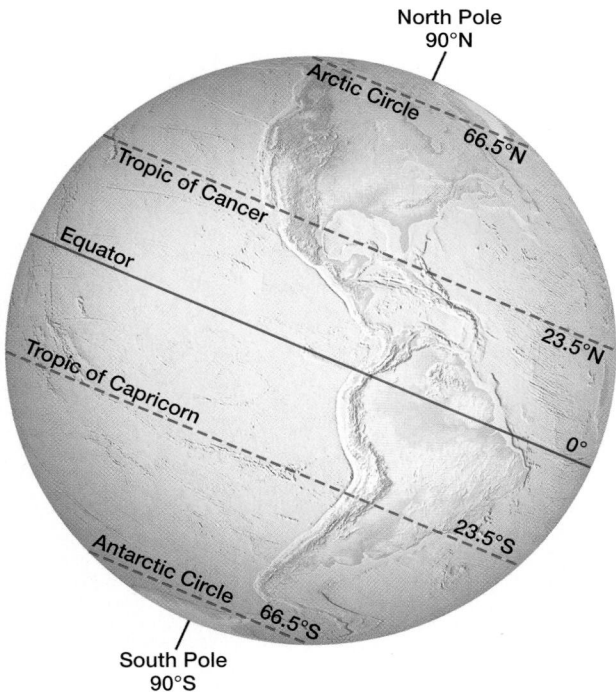

▲ Figure 1-17 Seven important parallels. As we will see when we discuss the seasons, these latitudes represent special locations where rays from the Sun strike Earth's surface on certain days of the year.

▲ Figure 1-18 The Tropic of Capricorn; like all other parallels of latitude, is an imaginary line. As a significant parallel, however, its location is often commemorated by a sign. This scene is near Alice Springs in the center of Australia.

Descriptive Zones of Latitude: Regions on Earth are sometimes described as falling within general bands or zones of latitude. The following common terms associated with latitude are used throughout this book (note that there is some overlap between several of these terms):

- *Low latitude*—generally between the equator and 30° N and S
- *Midlatitude*—between about 30° and 60° N and S
- *High latitude*—latitudes greater than about 60° N and S
- *Equatorial*—within a few degrees of the equator
- *Tropical*—within the tropics (between 23.5° N and 23.5° S)
- *Subtropical*—slightly poleward of the tropics, generally around 25–30° N and S
- *Polar*—within a few degrees of the North or South Pole

Nautical Miles: Each degree of latitude on the surface of Earth covers a north–south distance of about 111 kilometers (69 miles). The distance varies slightly with latitude because of the flattening of Earth at the poles. The distance measurement of a *nautical mile*—and the description of speed known as a *knot* (one nautical mile per hour)—is defined by the distance covered by one minute of latitude (1′), the equivalent of about 1.15 statute ("ordinary") miles or about 1.85 kilometers.

Longitude

Latitude comprises the north–south component of Earth's grid system. The other half is **longitude**—an angular description of east–west location, also measured in degrees, minutes, and seconds.

Longitude is represented by imaginary lines extending from pole to pole and crossing all parallels at right angles. These lines, called **meridians**, are not parallel to one another except where they cross the equator. Any pair of meridians is farthest apart at the equator, becoming increasingly close together northward and southward and finally converging at the poles (Figure 1-19).

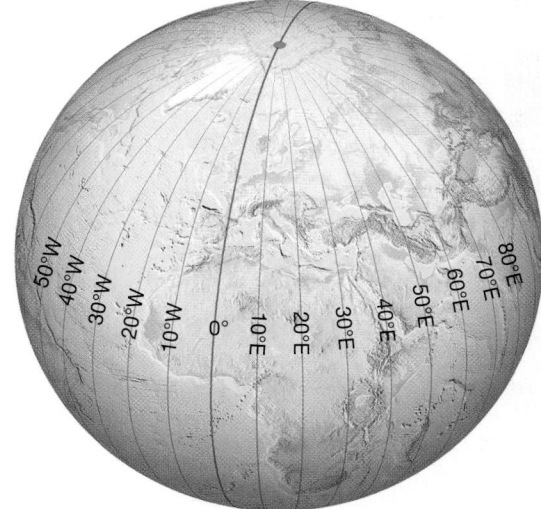

▲ Figure 1-19 Lines of longitude, or *meridians*, indicate east–west location and all converge at the poles.

Establishing the Prime Meridian: The equator is a natural baseline from which to measure latitude, but no such natural reference line exists for longitude. Consequently, for most of recorded history, there was no accepted longitudinal baseline; each country would select its own "prime meridian" as the reference line for east–west measurement. Thus, the French measured from the meridian of Paris, the Italians from the meridian of Rome, and so forth. At least 13 prime meridians were in use in the 1880s. Not until the late 1800s was standardization finally achieved.

United States and Canadian railway executives adopted a standard time system for all North American railroads in 1883, and the following year an international conference was convened in Washington, D.C., to achieve the same goal on a global scale and to agree upon a single prime meridian. After weeks of debate, the delegates chose the meridian passing through the Royal Observatory at Greenwich, England, just east of London, as the **prime meridian** for all longitudinal measurement (Figure 1-20). The principal argument for adopting the Greenwich meridian as the prime meridian was a practical one: more than two-thirds of the world's shipping lines already used the Greenwich meridian as a navigational base.

Thus, an imaginary north–south plane passing through Greenwich and through Earth's axis of rotation represents the plane of the prime meridian. The angle between this plane and a plane passed through any other point and the

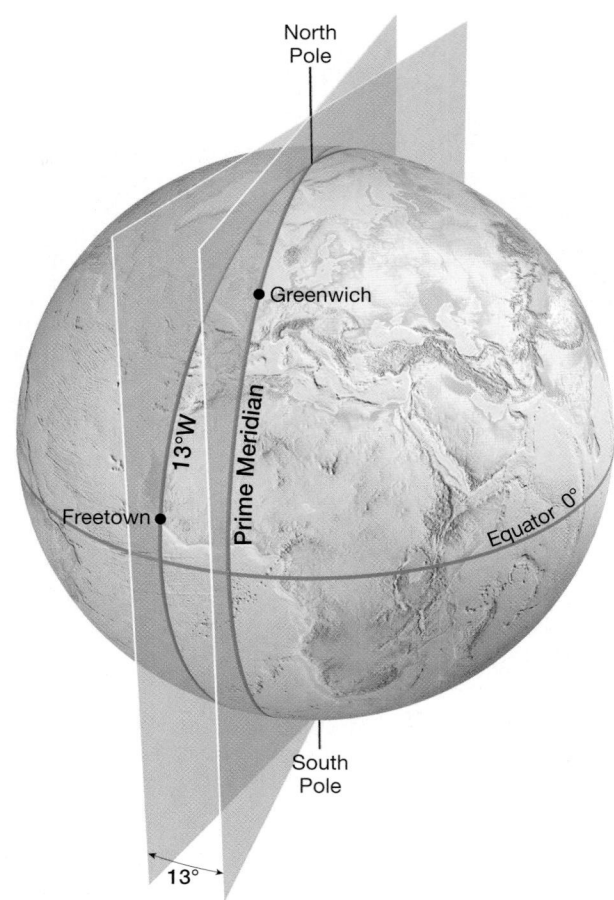

▲ **Figure 1-21** The meridians that mark longitude are defined by intersecting imaginary planes passing through the poles. Shown here are the planes for the prime meridian through Greenwich, England, and the meridian through Freetown, Sierra Leone, at 13° west longitude.

axis of Earth is a measure of longitude. For example, the angle between the Greenwich plane and a plane passing through the center of the city of Freetown (in the western African country of Sierra Leone) is 13 degrees, 15 minutes, and 12 seconds. Because the angle is formed west of the prime meridian, the longitude of Freetown is written 13°15′12″ W (Figure 1-21).

Measuring Longitude: Longitude is measured both east and west of the prime meridian to a maximum of 180° in each direction. Exactly halfway around the globe from the prime meridian, in the middle of the Pacific Ocean, is the 180° meridian (Figure 1-22). All places on Earth, then, have a location that is either east longitude or west longitude, except for points exactly on the prime meridian (described simply as 0° longitude) or exactly on the 180th meridian (described as 180° longitude).

The distance between any two meridians varies predictably. At the equator, the surface length of one degree of longitude is about the same as that of one degree of latitude. However, because meridians converge at the poles, the distance covered by one degree of longitude decreases poleward (Figure 1-23), diminishing to zero at the poles where all meridians meet at a point.

▲ **Figure 1-20** The prime meridian of the world, longitude 0°0′0″ at Greenwich, England, which is about 8 km (5 miles) from the heart of London.

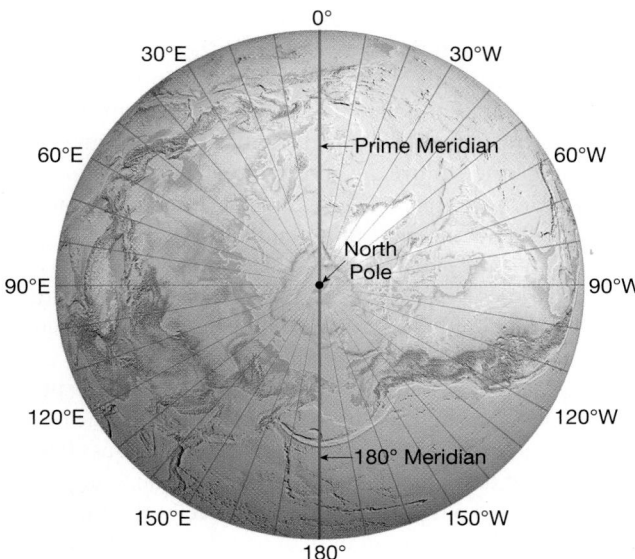

0°
30°E   30°W
60°E   Prime Meridian   60°W
90°E   North Pole   90°W
120°E   120°W
150°E   180° Meridian   150°W
180°

▲ **Figure 1-22** A polar view of meridians radiating from the North Pole. Think of each line as the top edge of an imaginary plane passing through both poles. All the planes are perpendicular to the plane of the page.

Locating Points on the Geographic Grid

The network of intersecting parallels and meridians creates a geographic grid over the entire surface of Earth (see Figure 1-23). The location of any place on Earth's surface can be described with great precision by reference to detailed latitude and longitude data. For example, at the 1964 World's Fair in New York City, a time capsule (a container filled with records and memorabilia of contemporary life) was buried. For reference purposes, the U.S. Coast and Geodetic Survey determined that the capsule was located at 40°28′34.089″ north latitude and 73°43′16.412″ west longitude. At some time in the future, if a hole were to be dug at the spot indicated by those coordinates, it would be within 15 centimeters (6 inches) of the capsule.

Learning Check 1-11 **Are locations in North America described by east longitude or west longitude?**

EARTH–SUN RELATIONS AND THE SEASONS

Nearly all life on Earth depends on solar energy; therefore, the relationship between Earth and the Sun is of vital importance. Because of the perpetual motions of Earth, this relationship does not remain the same throughout the year. We begin with a description of Earth movements and the relationship of Earth's axis to the Sun, and then we offer an explanation of the change of seasons.

Animation Earth–Sun Relations

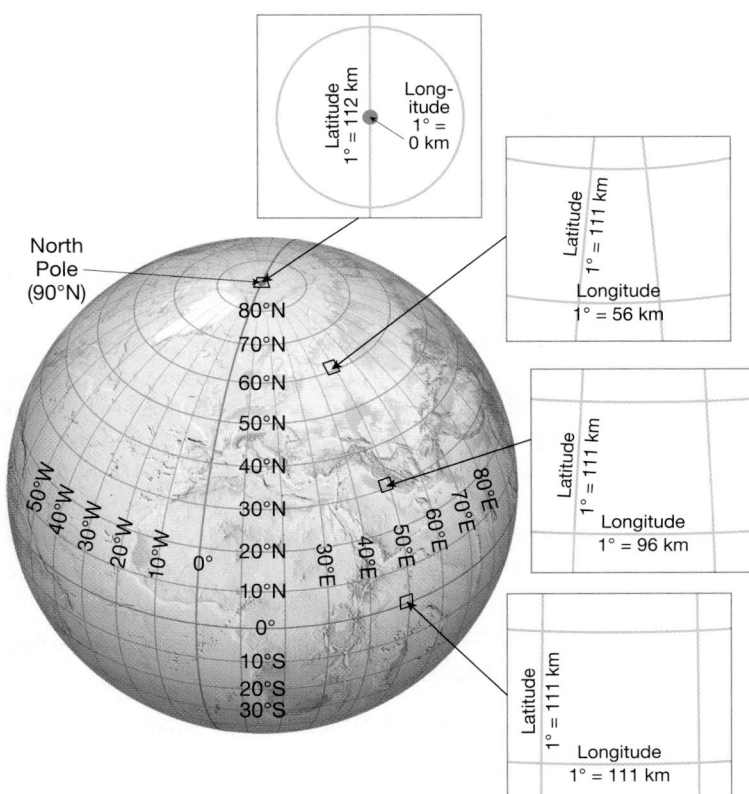

◀ **Figure 1-23** The complete grid system of latitude and longitude—the *graticule*. Because the meridians converge at the poles, the distance of 1° of longitude is greatest at the equator and diminishes to zero at the poles, whereas the distance of 1° of latitude varies only slightly (due to the slight flattening of Earth at the poles).

Earth Movements

Two basic Earth movements—its daily rotation on its axis and its annual revolution around the Sun—along with the inclination and "polarity" of Earth's rotation axis, combine to change Earth's orientation to the Sun—and therefore produce the change of seasons.

Earth's Rotation on Its Axis: Earth rotates from west to east on its axis (Figure 1-24), a complete **rotation** requiring 24 hours (from the vantage point of looking down at the North Pole from space, Earth is rotating in a counterclockwise direction). The Sun, the Moon, and the stars appear to rise in the east and set in the west—this is, of course, an illusion created by the steady eastward spin of Earth.

Rotation causes all parts of Earth's surface except the poles to move in a circle around Earth's axis. Although the speed of rotation varies by latitude (see Figure 1-24), it is constant at any given place on Earth and so we experience no sense of motion. This is the same reason that we have little sense of motion on a smooth jet airplane flight at cruising speed—only when speed changes, such as during takeoff and landing, does motion become apparent.

Rotation has several important effects on the physical characteristics of Earth's surface:

1. Earth's constant rotation causes an apparent deflection in the paths of both wind and ocean currents—to the right in the Northern Hemisphere and to the left in the Southern Hemisphere. This phenomenon is called the *Coriolis effect* and is discussed in detail in Chapter 3.

2. The rotation of Earth brings any point on the surface through the increasing and then decreasing gravitational pull of the Moon and the Sun. Although the land areas of Earth are too rigid to be significantly moved by these oscillating gravitational attractions, oceanic waters move onshore and then recede in a rhythmic pattern of *tides*, discussed further in Chapter 9.

3. Undoubtedly the most important effect of earthly rotation is the *diurnal* (daily) alternation of daylight and darkness, as portions of Earth's surface are turned first toward and then away from the Sun. This variation in exposure to sunlight greatly influences local temperature, humidity, and wind movements. Except for the organisms that live either in caves or in the ocean deeps, all forms of life have adapted to this sequential pattern of daylight and darkness. We human beings fare poorly when our *circadian* (24-hour cycle) rhythms are misaligned as the result of high-speed air travel that significantly interrupts the normal sequence of daylight and darkness. We are left with a sense of fatigue known as "jet lag," which can include unpleasant changes in our usual patterns of appetite and sleep.

Earth's Revolution around the Sun: Another significant Earth motion is its **revolution** or orbit around the Sun. Each revolution takes 365 days, 5 hours, 48 minutes, and 46 seconds, or 365.242199 days. This is known officially as the *tropical year* and for practical purposes is usually simplified to 365.25 days. (Astronomers define the year in other ways as well, but the duration is very close to that of the tropical year and need not concern us here.)

The path followed by Earth in its journey around the Sun is not a true circle but an ellipse (Figure 1-25). Because of this elliptical orbit, the Earth–Sun distance is not constant; rather, it varies from approximately 147,100,000 kilometers (91,400,000 miles) at the closest or **perihelion** position (*peri* is from the Greek and means "around" and *helios* means "Sun") on about January 3, to approximately 152,100,000 kilometers (94,500,000 miles) at the farthest or **aphelion** position (*ap* is from the Greek and means "away from") on about July 4. The average Earth–Sun distance is defined as one *astronomical unit* (1 AU) and is about 149,597,871 kilometers (92,960,117 miles). Earth is 3.3 percent closer to the Sun during the Northern Hemisphere winter than during the Northern Hemisphere summer, an indication that variations in the distance between Earth and the Sun do not cause the change of seasons; instead, two additional factors in the relationship of Earth to the Sun—inclination and polarity—work together with rotation and revolution to produce the change of seasons.

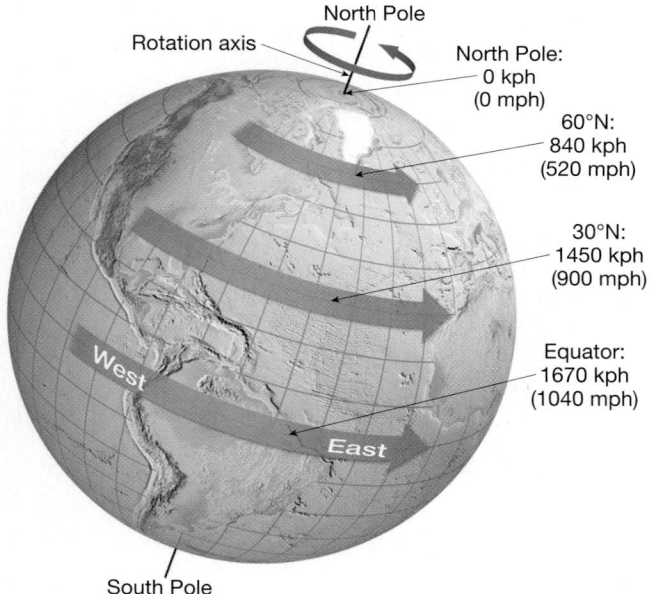

▲ **Figure 1-24** Earth rotates from west to east. Looking down at the North Pole from above, Earth appears to rotate in a counterclockwise direction. The speed of Earth's rotation is constant but it varies by latitude, being greatest at the equator, and effectively diminishing to zero at the poles. The speed of rotation at different latitudes is shown in kilometers per hour (kph) and miles per hour (mph).

Labels in figure:
North Pole
Rotation axis
North Pole: 0 kph (0 mph)
60°N: 840 kph (520 mph)
30°N: 1450 kph (900 mph)
Equator: 1670 kph (1040 mph)
West
East
South Pole

Learning Check 1-12 **Distinguish between Earth's rotation and its revolution.**

Inclination of Earth's Axis: The imaginary plane defined by the orbital path of Earth around the Sun is called the **plane of the ecliptic** (see Figure 1-25). However,

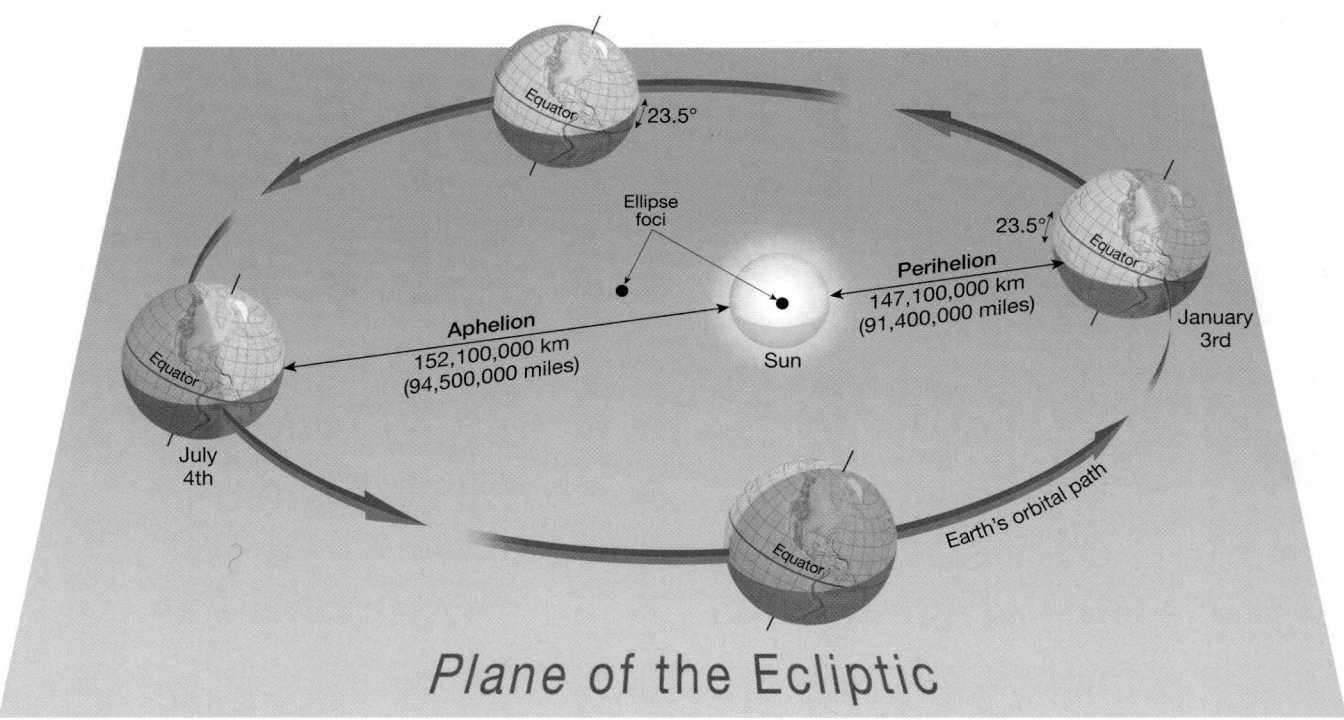

▲ **Figure 1-25** The plane of the ecliptic is the orbital plane of Earth. Because Earth's rotation axis is tilted, the plane of the ecliptic and the equatorial plane do not coincide. The path Earth follows in its revolution around the Sun is an ellipse with the Sun at one focus. Earth reaches perihelion (its closest point to the Sun) on about January 3rd and aphelion (its farthest point from the Sun) on about July 4th. (In this diagram the elliptical shape of Earth's orbit is greatly exaggerated.)

Earth's rotation axis is not perpendicular to the plane of the ecliptic. Rather, the axis is tilted about 23.5° from the perpendicular (Figure 1-26) and maintains this tilt throughout the year. This tilt is referred to as the **inclination of Earth's axis.**

Polarity of Earth's Axis: Not only is Earth's rotation axis inclined relative to its orbital path, no matter where Earth is in its orbit around the Sun the axis always points in the same direction relative to the stars—toward the North Star, Polaris (Figure 1-27). In other words, at any time during the year, Earth's rotation axis is parallel to its orientation at all other times. This characteristic is called the **polarity of Earth's axis** (or **parallelism**).

The combined effects of rotation, revolution, inclination, and polarity result in the seasonal patterns experienced on Earth. Notice in Figure 1-27 that at one point in Earth's orbit, around June 21, the North Pole is oriented most directly toward the Sun, whereas six months later, around December 21, the North Pole is oriented most directly away from the Sun—this is the most fundamental feature of the annual march of the seasons.

Learning Check 1-13   **Does the North Pole lean toward the Sun throughout the year? If not, how does the North Pole's orientation change during the year?**

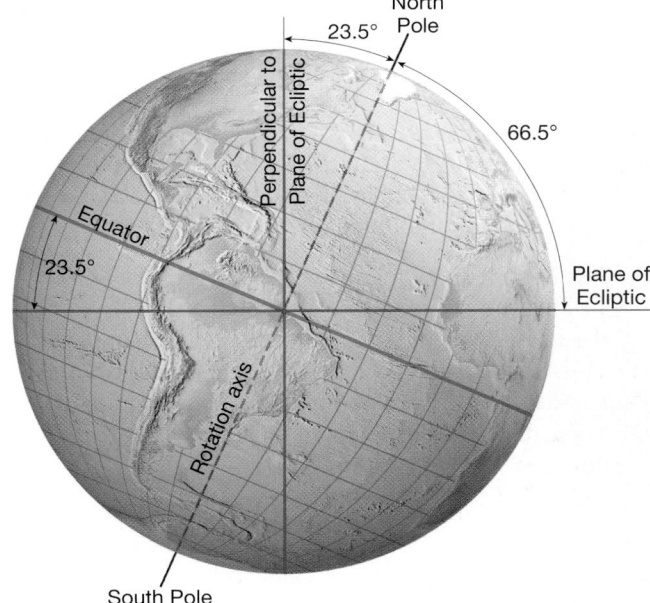

▲ **Figure 1-26** Earth's rotation axis is inclined 23.5° from a line perpendicular to the plane of the ecliptic.

The Annual March of the Seasons

During a year, the changing relationship of Earth to the Sun results in variations in day length and in the angle at which the Sun's rays strike the surface of Earth. These changes are

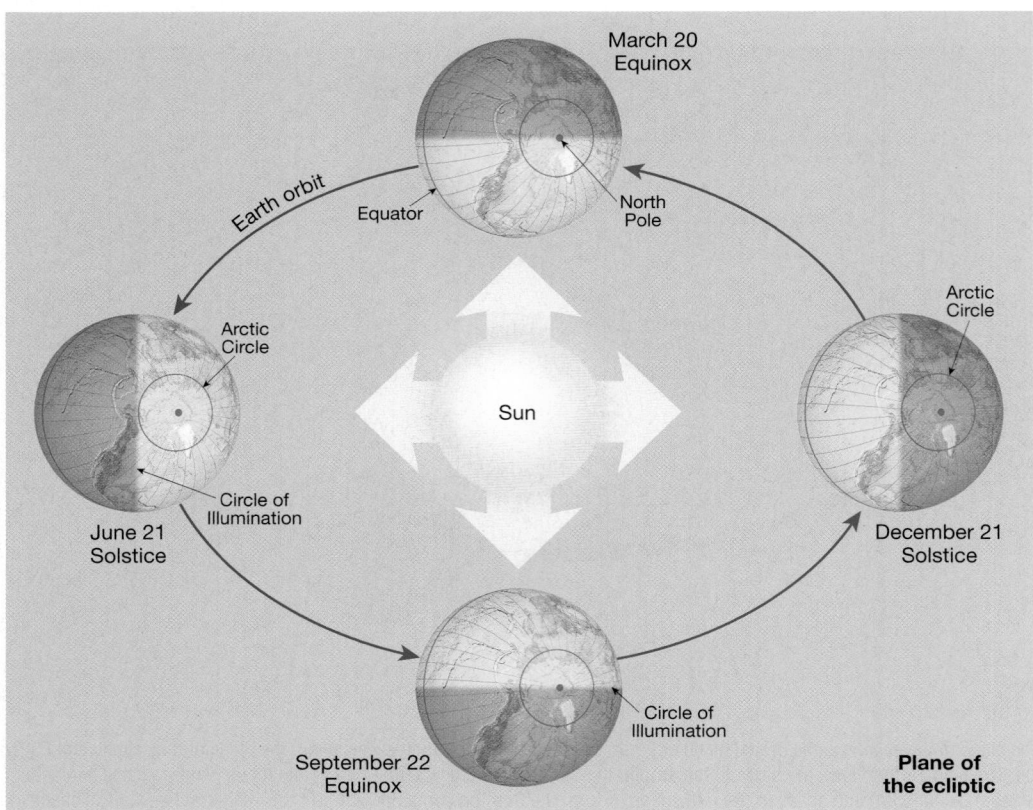

▲ **Figure 1-27** A "top view" of the march of the seasons. Earth's rotational axis maintains polarity (points in the same direction) throughout the year, so on the June solstice the North Pole leans most directly toward the Sun, whereas on the December solstice the North Pole leans most directly away from the Sun (the dates shown are approximate). One-half of Earth is illuminated at all times during the year. The line between the two halves is called the *circle of illumination*.

most obvious in the mid- and high latitudes, but important variations take place within the tropics as well.

As we discuss the annual march of the seasons, we will pay special attention to three conditions:

1. The latitude receiving the vertical rays of the Sun (rays striking the surface at a right angle), also referred to as the *subsolar point* or the *declination of the Sun*.
2. The **solar altitude** (the height of the Sun above the horizon) at different latitudes.
3. The length of day (number of daylight hours) at different latitudes.

Initially, we emphasize the conditions on four special days of the year: The March equinox, the June solstice, the September equinox, and the December solstice (Figure 1-28). As we describe the change of seasons, the significance of the "seven important parallels" discussed earlier in this chapter will become clear. We begin with the June solstice.

June Solstice: On the **June solstice**, which occurs on or about June 21 (the exact date varies slightly from year to year), the Earth reaches the position in its orbit where the North Pole is oriented most directly toward the Sun. On this day, the vertical rays of the Sun at noon are

striking the **Tropic of Cancer**, 23.5° north of the equator (Figure 1-28b). Were you at the Tropic of Cancer on this day, the Sun would be directly overhead in the sky at noon (in other words, the solar altitude would be 90°). The Tropic of Cancer marks the northernmost location reached by the vertical rays of the Sun during the year.

The dividing line between the daylight half of Earth and nighttime half of Earth is a great circle called the **circle of illumination**. On the June solstice, the circle of illumination bisects ("cuts in half") the equator (Figure 1-28b), so on this day the equator receives equal day and night—12 hours of daylight and 12 hours of darkness. However, as we move north of the equator, the portion of each parallel in daylight increases—in other words, as we move north of the equator, day length increases. Conversely, day length decreases as we move south of the equator.

Notice in Figure 1-28b that on the June solstice, the circle of illumination reaches 23.5° *beyond* the North Pole to a latitude of 66.5° N. As Earth rotates, all locations north of 66.5° remain continuously in daylight and so on this day experience 24 hours of daylight. By contrast, all points south of 66.5° S are always outside the circle of illumination and so have 24 continuous hours of darkness. These special parallels defining the equatorward limit of 24 hours of light

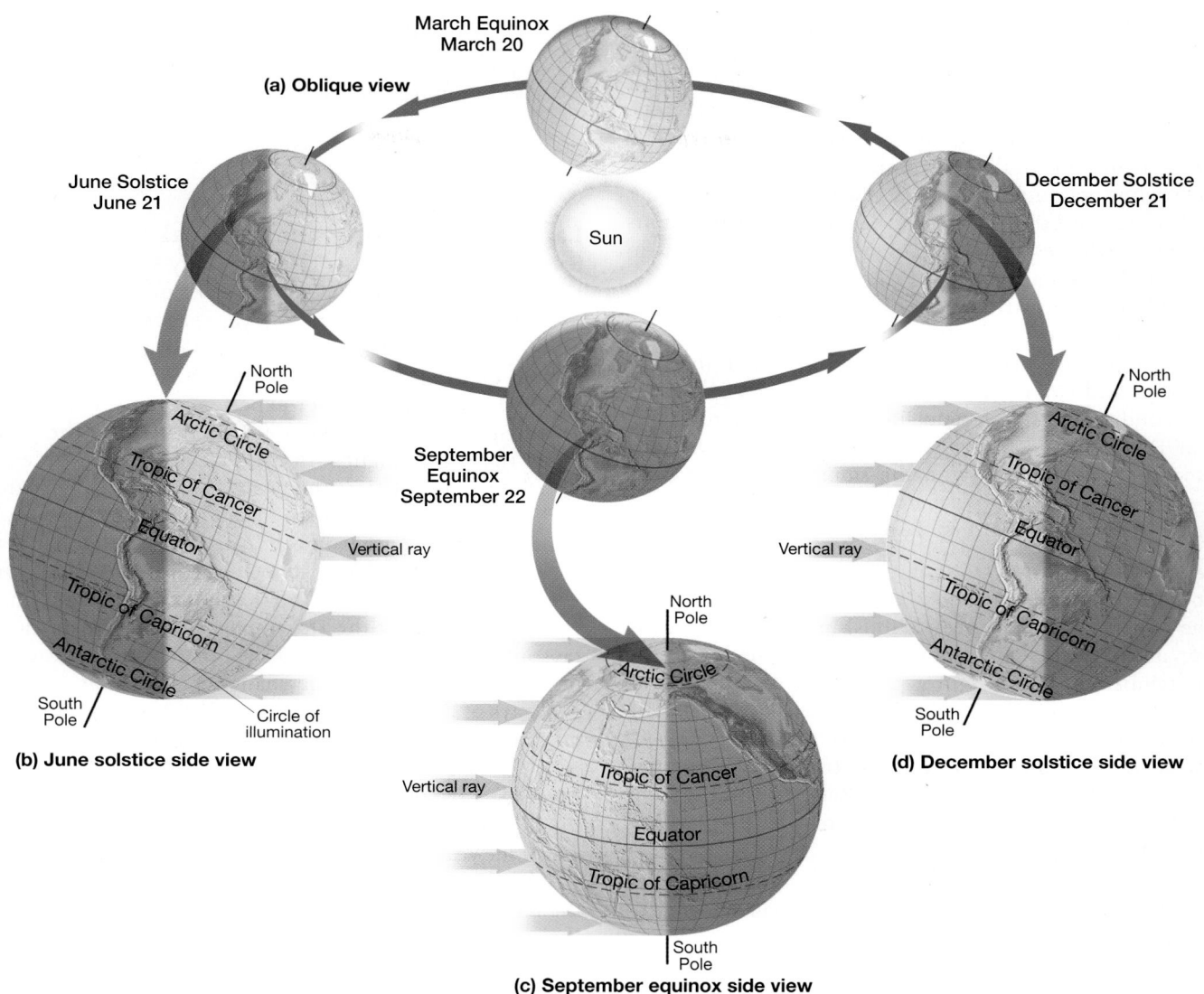

▲ **Figure 1-28** (a) The annual march of the seasons showing Earth–Sun relations on the June solstice, September equinox, December solstice, and March equinox (the dates shown are approximate). The circle of illumination is the dividing line between the daylight and nighttime halves of Earth. (b) On the June solstice the vertical rays of the noon Sun strike 23.5° N latitude. (c) On the March equinox and September equinox, the vertical rays of the noon Sun strike the equator. (d) On the December solstice, the vertical rays of the noon Sun strike 23.5° S latitude.

and dark on the solstice dates are called the *polar circles*. The northern polar circle, at 66.5° N, is the **Arctic Circle**; the southern polar circle, at 66.5° S, is the **Antarctic Circle.**

The June solstice is called the *summer solstice* in the Northern Hemisphere and the *winter solstice* in the Southern Hemisphere (what are commonly called the "first day of summer" and the "first day of winter" in their respective hemispheres).

Learning Check **1-14**   **What is the latitude of the vertical rays of the Sun on the June solstice?**

September Equinox: Three months after the June solstice, on approximately September 22 (as with solstice dates, this date also varies slightly from year to year), Earth

experiences the **September equinox**. Notice in Figure 1-28c that the vertical rays of the Sun are striking the equator. Notice also that the circle of illumination just touches both poles, bisecting all other parallels—on this day all locations on Earth experience 12 hours of daylight and 12 hours of darkness (the word "equinox" comes from the Latin, meaning "the time of equal days and equal nights"). At the equator—and only at the equator—every day of the year has virtually 12 hours of daylight and 12 hours of darkness; all other locations have equal day and night only on an equinox.

The September equinox is called the *autumnal equinox* in the Northern Hemisphere and the *vernal equinox* in the Southern Hemisphere (and what are commonly called the "first day of fall" and the "first day of spring" in their respective hemispheres).

December Solstice: On the **December solstice**, which occurs on or about December 21, the Earth reaches the position in its orbit where the North Pole is oriented most directly away from the Sun; the vertical rays of the Sun now strike 23.5° S, the **Tropic of Capricorn** (Figure 1-28d). Once again, the circle of illumination reaches to the far side of one pole and falls short on the near side of the other pole—areas north of the Arctic Circle are in continuous darkness, whereas areas south of the Antarctic Circle are in daylight for 24 hours.

Although the latitude receiving the vertical rays of the Sun has shifted 47° from June 21 to December 21, the relationships between Earth and the Sun on the June solstice and the December solstice are very similar—the conditions in each hemisphere are simply reversed. The December solstice is called the *winter solstice* in the Northern Hemisphere and the *summer solstice* in the Southern Hemisphere (what are commonly called the "first day of winter" and the "first day of summer," respectively).

March Equinox: Three months after the December solstice, on approximately March 20, Earth experiences the **March equinox**. The relationships of Earth and the Sun are virtually identical on the March equinox and the September equinox (Figure 1-28c). The March equinox is called the *vernal equinox* in the Northern Hemisphere and the *autumnal equinox* in the Southern Hemisphere (what are commonly called the "first day of spring" and the "first day of fall," respectively). Table 1-2 summarizes the conditions present during the solstices and equinoxes.

> **Learning Check 1-15** **How much does day length at the equator change during the year?**

Seasonal Transitions

In the preceding discussion of the solstices and equinoxes, we mainly emphasized the conditions on just four special days of the year. It is important to understand the transitions in day length and Sun angle that take place between those days as well.

Latitude Receiving the Vertical Rays of the Sun: The vertical rays of the Sun only strike Earth between the Tropic of Cancer and the Tropic of Capricorn. After the March equinox, the vertical rays of the Sun migrate north from the equator, striking the Tropic of Cancer on the June solstice (although latitudes north of the Tropic of Cancer never experience the vertical rays of the Sun, the June solstice marks the day of the year when the Sun is highest in the sky in those latitudes). After the June solstice, the vertical rays migrate south, striking the equator again on the September equinox and finally to their southernmost latitude on the December solstice (the December solstice marks the day of the year when the Sun is lowest in the sky in the Northern Hemisphere). Following the December solstice, the vertical rays migrate northward, reaching the equator once again on the March equinox. The changing latitude of the vertical rays of the Sun during the year is shown graphically on a chart known as the *analemma* (Figure 1-29).

Day Length: Only at the equator is day length constant throughout the year—virtually 12 hours of daylight every day of the year.

For all regions in the Northern Hemisphere up to the latitude of the Arctic Circle, after the shortest day of the year on the December solstice, the number of hours

TABLE 1-2 · Conditions on Equinoxes and Solstices

	March Equinox	June Solstice	September Equinox	December Solstice
Latitude of Vertical Rays of Sun	0°	23.5° N	0°	23.5° S
Day length at Equator	12 hours	12 hours	12 hours	12 hours
Day length in midlatitudes of Northern Hemisphere	12 hours	Day length becomes longer with increasing latitude north of equator	12 hours	Day length becomes shorter with increasing latitude north of equator
Day length in midlatitudes of Southern Hemisphere	12 hours	Day length becomes shorter with increasing latitude south of equator	12 hours	Day length becomes longer with increasing latitude south of equator
24 hours of daylight	Nowhere	From Arctic Circle to North Pole	Nowhere	From Antarctic Circle to South Pole
24 hours of darkness	Nowhere	From Antarctic Circle to South Pole	Nowhere	From Arctic Circle to North Pole
Season in Northern Hemisphere	Spring	Summer	Autumn	Winter
Season in Southern Hemisphere	Autumn	Winter	Spring	Summer

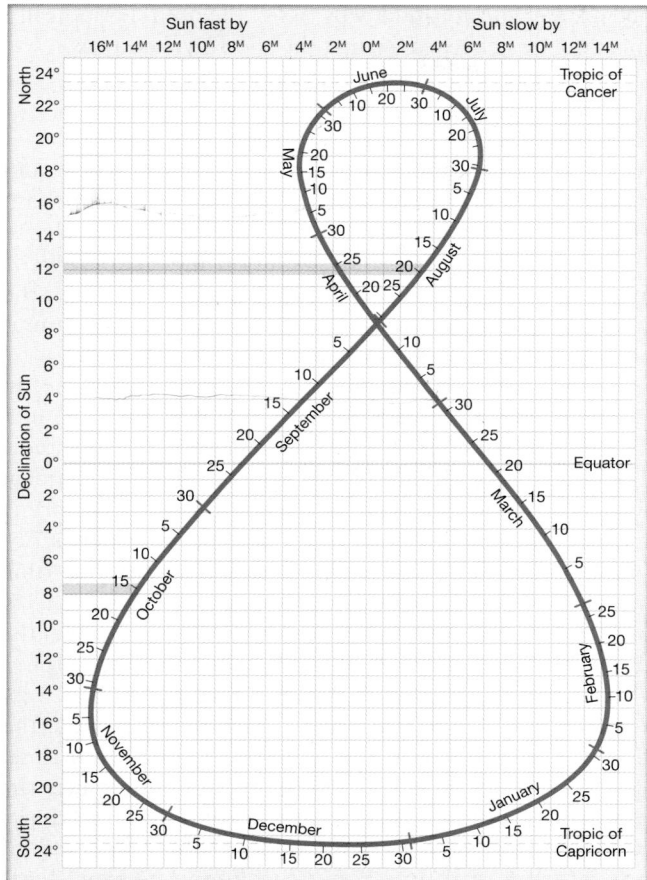

▲ **Figure 1-29** The analemma shows the latitude of the vertical rays of the noon Sun (the *declination of the Sun*) throughout the year. For example, on August 20 the vertical rays of the Sun are striking 12° N, whereas on October 15 they are striking 8° S. The values across the top of the analemma show the *equation of time*—the number of minutes that solar noon is fast or slow compared with mean (average) time.

TABLE 1-3	Day Length at Time of June Solstice	
Latitude	**Day Length**	**Noon Sun Angle (degrees above horizon)**
90° N	24 h	23.5
60° N	18 h 53 min	53.5
30° N	14 h 05 min	83.5
0°	12 h 07 min	66.5
30° S	10 h 12 min	36.5
60° S	05 h 52 min	6.5
90° S	0	0

Source: After Robert J. List, *Smithsonian Meteorological Tables*, 6th rev. ed. Washington, D.C.: Smithsonian Institution, 1963, Table 171.

of daylight gradually increases, reaching 12 hours of daylight on the March equinox. After the equinox, day length continues to increase until the longest day of the year on the June solstice. (During this period, day length is diminishing in the Southern Hemisphere.)

Following the longest day of the year in the Northern Hemisphere on the June solstice, the pattern is reversed, with the days getting shorter in the Northern Hemisphere—reaching 12 hours on the September equinox, and then diminishing until the shortest day of the year on the December solstice. (During this period, day length is increasing in the Southern Hemisphere.)

Overall, the annual variation in day length is the least in the tropics and greatest in the high latitudes (Table 1-3).

> **Learning Check 1-16**   **On which days of the year do the vertical rays of the Sun strike the equator?**

Day Length in the Arctic and Antarctic: The patterns of day and night in the Arctic and Antarctic deserve special mention. For an observer exactly at the North Pole,

the Sun rises on the March equinox and is above the horizon continuously for the next six months—circling the horizon higher and higher each day until the June solstice, after which it circles lower and lower until setting on the September equinox.

Week by week after the March equinox, the region experiencing 24 hours of daylight grows, extending from the North Pole until the June solstice—when the entire region from the Arctic Circle to the North Pole experiences 24 hours of daylight. Following the June solstice, the region in the Arctic experiencing 24 hours of daylight diminishes week by week until the September equinox—when the Sun sets at the North Pole and remains below the horizon continuously for the next six months.

Week by week following the September equinox, the region experiencing 24 hours of darkness extends from the North Pole until the December solstice—when the entire region from the Arctic Circle to the North Pole experiences 24 hours of darkness. Following the December solstice, the region experiencing 24 hours of darkness diminishes week by week until the March equinox—when the Sun again rises at the North Pole.

In the Antarctic region of the Southern Hemisphere, these seasonal patterns are simply reversed.

Significance of Seasonal Patterns

Both day length and the angle at which the Sun's rays strike Earth determine the amount of solar energy received at any particular latitude. As a generalization, the higher the Sun is in the sky, the more effective is the warming. Day length influences patterns of solar energy receipt on Earth as well. For example, short periods of daylight in winter and long periods of daylight in summer contribute to seasonal differences in temperature in the mid- and high latitude regions of Earth.

Thus, the tropical latitudes are generally always warm because they always have high Sun angles and consistent day lengths that are close to 12 hours long. Conversely, the polar regions are consistently cold because they always have low Sun angles—even the 24-hour days in summer do not compensate for the low angle of incidence of sunlight. Seasonal temperature differences are large in the midlatitudes because of sizable seasonal variations in Sun angles and length of day. This topic will be explored further in Chapter 4.

Learning Check 1-17   **For how many months of the year does the North Pole go without sunlight?**

TELLING TIME

Comprehending time around the world depends on an understanding of both the geographic grid of latitude and longitude, and of Earth–Sun relations. As Malcolm Thomson, a Canadian authority on the physics of time has noted, there are really only three natural units of time: the *tropical year*, marked by the return of the seasons; the *lunar month*, marked by the return of the new moon; and the *day*, marked by passage of the Sun. All other units of time measurement—such as a second, an hour, or a century—are human-made to meet the needs of society.

In prehistoric times, the rising and setting of the Sun were probably the principal means of telling time. As civilizations developed, however, more precise timekeeping was required. Early agricultural civilizations in Egypt, Mesopotamia, India, China, and England, as well as the Aztec and Mayan civilizations in the Western Hemisphere, observed the Sun and the stars to tell time and keep accurate calendars.

Local *solar noon* can be determined by watching for the moment when objects cast their shortest shadows. The Romans used sundials to tell time (Figure 1-30) and gave great importance to the noon position, which they called the *meridian*—the Sun's highest (*meri*) point of the day (*diem*). Our use of A.M. (*ante meridian*: "before noon") and P.M. (*post meridian*: "after noon") was derived from the Roman world.

When nearly all transportation was by foot, horse, or sailing vessel, it was difficult to compare time at different localities. In those days, each community set its own time by correcting its clocks to high noon at the moment of the shortest shadow. A central public building, such as a temple in India or a county courthouse in Kansas, usually had a large clock or loud bells to toll the hour. Periodically, this time was checked against the shortest shadow.

Standard Time

As the telegraph and railroad began to speed words and passengers between cities, the use of local solar time created increasing problems. A cross-country rail traveler in the United States in the 1870s might have experienced as many as 24 different local time standards between the Atlantic and Pacific coasts. Eventually, the railroads stimulated the development of a standardized time system.

At the 1884 International Prime Meridian Conference in Washington, D.C., countries agreed to divide the world into 24 standard **time zones**, each extending over 15° of longitude. The mean local solar time of the Greenwich (prime) meridian was chosen as the standard for the entire system. The prime meridian became the center of a time zone that extends 7.5° of longitude to the west and 7.5° to the east of the prime meridian. Similarly, the meridians that are multiples of 15° both east and west of the prime meridian, were set as the *central meridians* for the 23 other time zones (Figure 1-31).

Although **Greenwich Mean Time (GMT)** is now referred to as **Universal Time Coordinated (UTC)**, the prime meridian is still the reference for standard time. Because it is always the same number of minutes after the hour in all standard time zones (keeping in mind that a few countries, such as India, do not adhere to standard one-hour-interval time zones), to know the exact local time, we usually need to know only how many hours later or earlier our local time zone is compared to the time in Greenwich. Figure 1-31 shows the number of hours later or earlier than UTC it is in each time zone of the world.

Most of the countries of the world are sufficiently small in their east–west direction so as to lie totally within a single time zone. However, large countries may encompass several zones: Russia occupies nine time zones; including Alaska and Hawai'i, the United States spreads over six (Figure 1-32); Canada, six; and Australia, three. In international waters, time zones are defined to be exactly 7°30′ to the east and 7°30′ to the west of the central meridians. Over land areas, however, zone boundaries vary to coincide with appropriate political and economic boundaries. For example, continental Europe from Portugal to Poland shares one time zone, although longitudinally covering about 30°. At the extreme, China extends across four 15° zones, but the entire nation, at least officially, observes the time of the 120° east meridian, which is the one closest to Beijing.

In each time zone, the central meridian marks the location where clock time is the same as mean Sun time

◀ **Figure 1-30** A typical sundial. The edge of the vertical *gnomon* slants upward from the dial face at an angle equal to the latitude of the sundial, pointing toward the North Pole in the Northern Hemisphere and the South Pole in the Southern Hemisphere. As the Sun appears to move across the sky during the course of a day, the position of the shadow cast by the gnomon changes. The time shown in this photograph of a sundial in Cornwall, United Kingdom, is about 11:00 A.M.

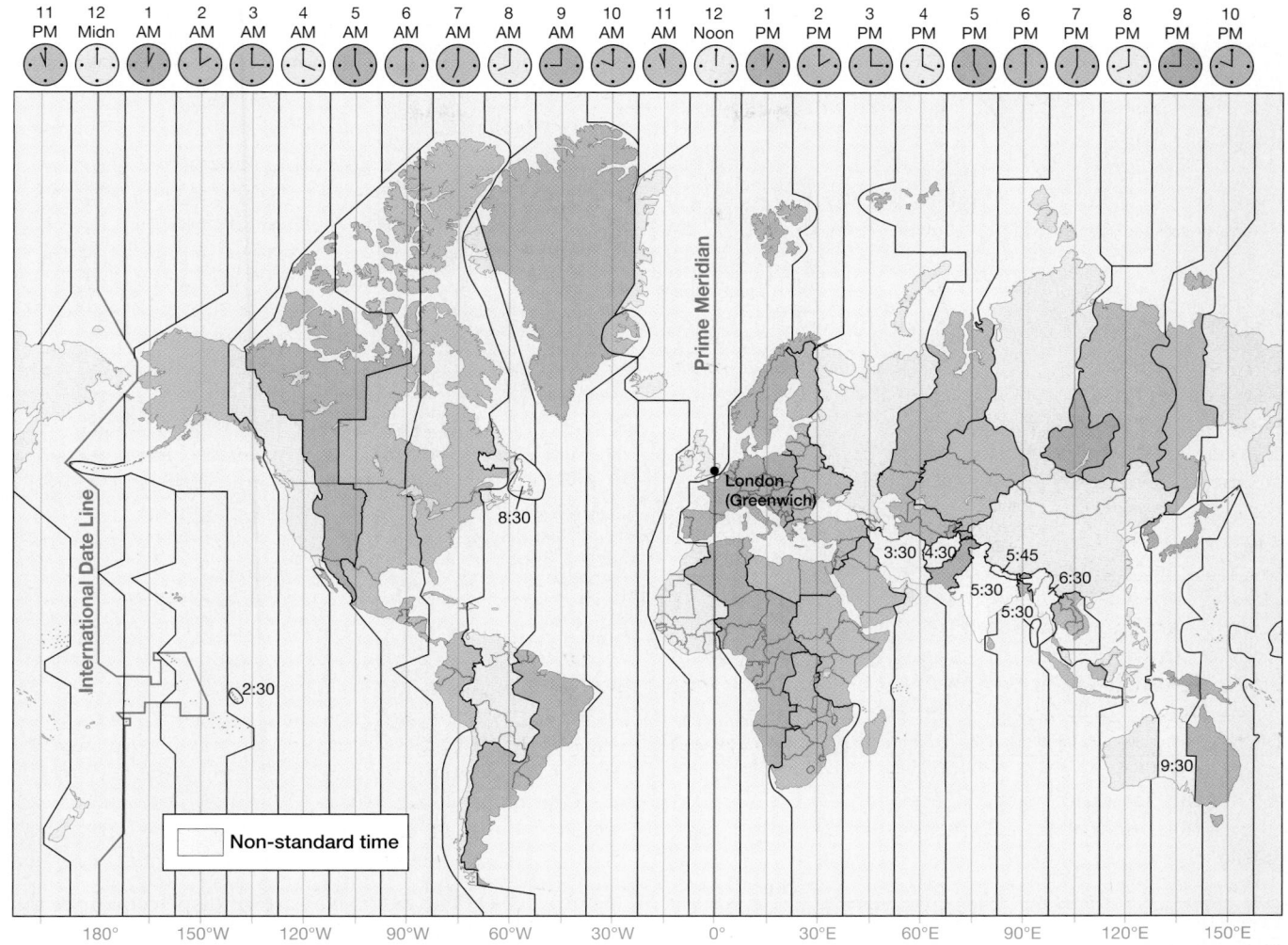

▲ **Figure 1-31** The 24 time zones of the world, each based on central meridians spaced 15° apart. Especially over land areas, these boundaries have been significantly adjusted.

(i.e., the Sun reaches its highest point in the sky at 12:00 noon). On either side of that meridian, of course, clock time does not coincide with Sun time. The deviation between the two is shown for one U.S. zone in Figure 1-33.

From the map of time zones of the United States (Figure 1-32), we can recognize a great deal of manipulation of the time zone boundaries for economic and political convenience. For example, the Central Standard Time Zone, centered on 90° W extends all the way to 105° W (which is the central meridian of the Mountain Standard Time Zone) in Texas to keep most of that state within the same zone. By contrast, El Paso, Texas, is officially within the Mountain Standard Time Zone in accord with its role as a major market center for southern New Mexico, which observes Mountain Standard Time. In the same vein, northwestern Indiana is in the Central Standard Time Zone with Chicago.

Learning Check 1-18   **What happens to the hour when crossing from one time zone to the next going from west to east?**

International Date Line

In 1519, Ferdinand Magellan set out westward from Spain, sailing for East Asia with 241 men in five ships. Three years later, the remnants of his crew (18 men in one ship) successfully completed the first circumnavigation of the globe. Although a careful log had been kept, the crew found that their calendar was one day short of the correct date. This was the first human experience with time change on a global scale, the realization of which eventually led to the establishment of the **International Date Line**.

One advantage of establishing the Greenwich meridian as the prime meridian is that its opposite arc is in the Pacific Ocean. The 180th meridian, transiting the sparsely populated mid-Pacific, was chosen as the meridian at which new days begin and old days exit from the surface of Earth. The International Date Line deviates from the 180th meridian in the Bering Sea to include all of the Aleutian Islands of Alaska within the same day and again in the South Pacific to keep islands of the same group (Fiji, Tonga) within the same day

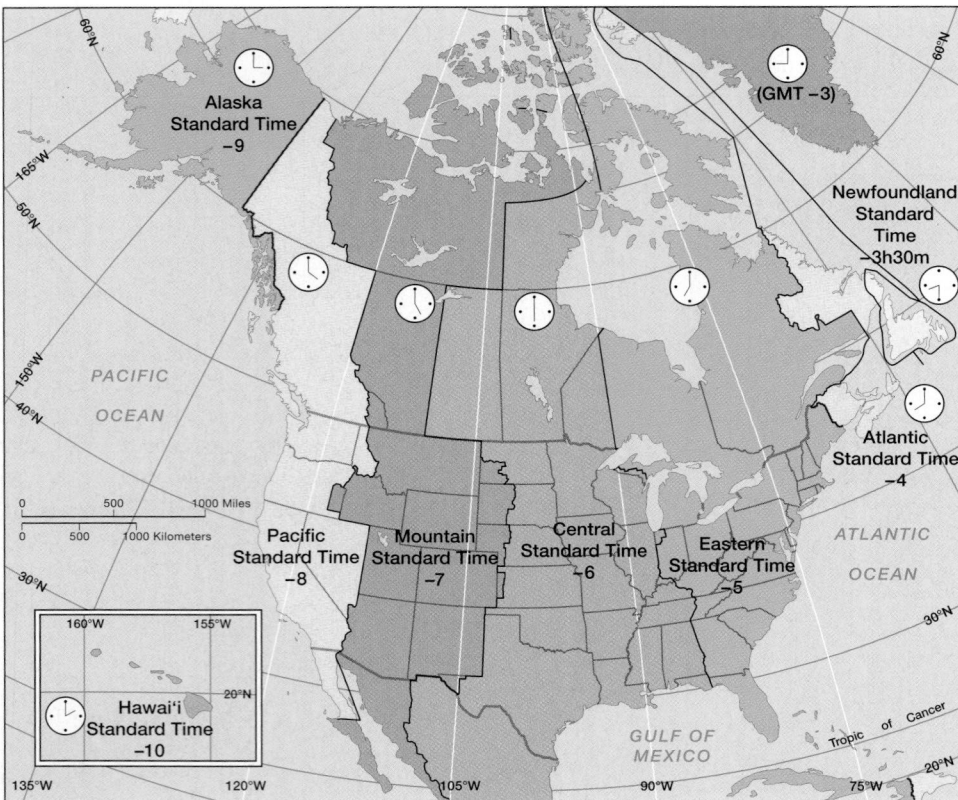

◄ **Figure 1-32** Times zones for Canada, the United States, and northern Mexico. The number in each time zone refers to the number of hours earlier than UTC (GMT).

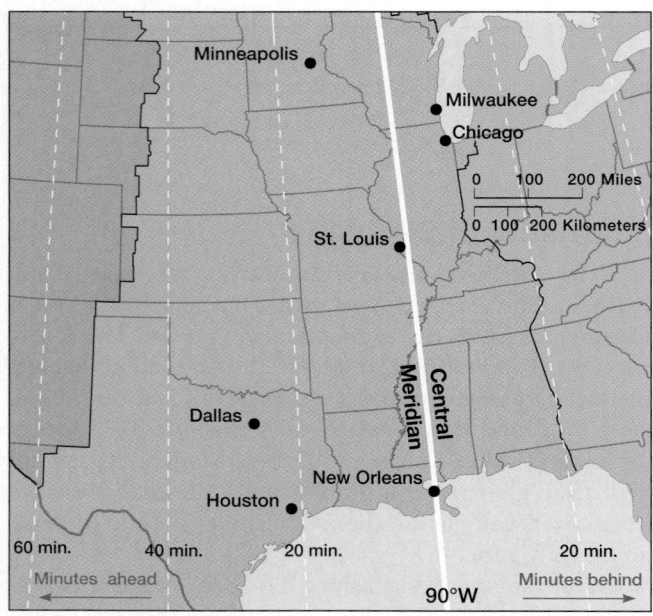

▲ **Figure 1-33** Standard clock time versus Sun time. The Sun reaches its highest point in the sky at 12:00 noon in St. Louis and New Orleans because these two cities lie on the central meridian. For places east of the central meridian, the Sun is highest in the sky a few minutes before standard time noon; for locations west, local solar noon is a few minutes after. In Chicago, for instance, the Sun is highest in the sky at 11:50 A.M. and in Dallas it is highest in the sky at 12:28 P.M.

(Figure 1-34). The extensive eastern displacement of the date line in the central Pacific is due to the widely scattered locations of the many islands of the country of Kiribati.

The International Date Line is in the middle of the time zone defined by the 180° meridian. Consequently, there is no time (i.e., hourly) change when crossing the International Date Line—only the calendar changes, not the clock. When you cross the International Date Line going from west to east, it becomes one day earlier (e.g., from January 2 to January 1); when you move across the line from east to west, it becomes one day later (e.g., from January 1 to January 2).

> **Learning Check 1-19** **What happens to the day when crossing the International Date Line going from west to east?**

Daylight-Saving Time

To conserve energy during World War I, Germany ordered all clocks set forward by an hour. This practice allowed the citizenry to "save" an hour of daylight by shifting the daylight period into the usual evening hours, thus reducing the consumption of electricity for lighting. The United States began a similar policy in 1918, but

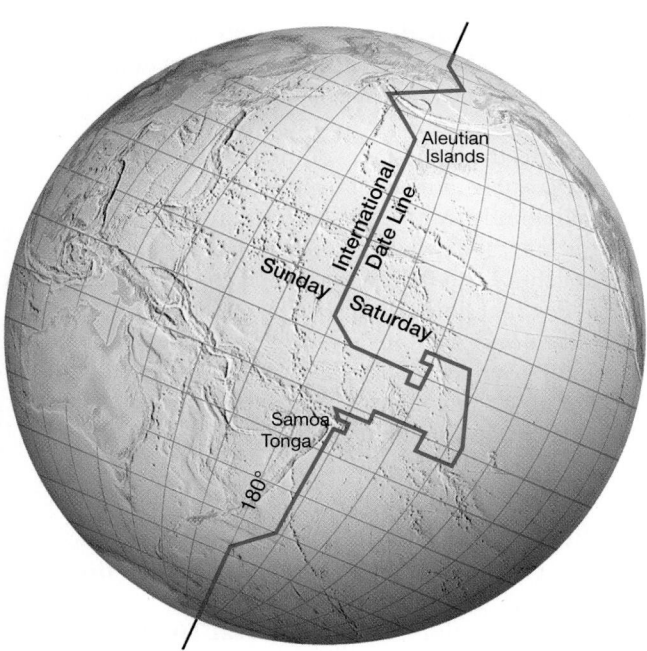

▲ **Figure 1-34** The International Date Line generally follows the 180th meridian, but it deviates around various island groups, most notably Kiribati.

many localities declined to observe "summer time" until the Uniform Time Act made the practice mandatory in all states that had not deliberately exempted themselves. Hawai'i, and parts of Indiana and Arizona, have exempted themselves from observance of **daylight-saving time** under this act.

Russia has adopted permanent daylight-saving time (and double daylight-saving time—two hours ahead of Sun time—in the summer). In recent years, Canada, Australia, New Zealand, and most of the nations of western Europe have also adopted daylight-saving time. In the Northern Hemisphere, many nations, like the United States, begin daylight-saving time on the second Sunday in March (in the spring we "spring forward" one hour) and resume standard time on the first Sunday in November (in the fall we "fall back" one hour). In the tropics, the lengths of day and night change little seasonally, and there is not much twilight. Consequently, daylight-saving time would offer little or no savings for tropical areas.

| Chapter **1** | **LEARNING REVIEW** |

After studying this chapter, you should be able to answer the following questions. Key terms from each text section are shown in **bold type**. Definitions for key terms are also found in the glossary at the back of the book.

KEY TERMS AND CONCEPTS

Geography and Science (*p. 3*)

1. Contrast **physical geography** and **cultural geography**.
2. If an idea cannot be disproven by some possible observation or test, can such an idea be supported by science? Explain.
3. What is the approximate *English System* of measurement equivalent of one kilometer in the **International System (S.I.)**?

Environmental Spheres and Earth Systems (*p. 7*)

4. Briefly describe the environmental "spheres": **atmosphere**, **hydrosphere**, **cryosphere**, **biosphere**, and **lithosphere**.
5. Contrast *closed systems* and *open systems*.
6. What does it mean when a system is in *equilibrium*?
7. How does a *positive feedback loop* differ from a *negative feedback loop*?

Earth and the Solar System (*p. 10*)

8. In what ways do the inner and outer planets (the terrestrial and Jovian planets) of our solar system differ from each other?
9. Compare the size of Earth to that of its surface features and atmosphere.
10. Is Earth perfectly spherical? Explain.

The Geographic Grid—Latitude and Longitude (*p. 13*)

11. Define the following terms: **latitude**, **longitude**, **parallel**, **meridian**, and **prime meridian**.
12. Latitude ranges from _____° to _____° north and south, whereas longitude ranges from _____° to _____° east and west.
13. State the latitude (in degrees) for the following "special" parallels: **equator**, **North Pole**, **South Pole**, **Tropic of Cancer**, **Tropic of Capricorn**, **Arctic Circle**, and **Antarctic Circle**.

14. What is a **great circle**? A small circle? Provide examples of both.

Earth–Sun Relations and the Seasons (*p. 17*)

15. Describe and explain the four factors in Earth–Sun relations associated with the change of seasons: **rotation**, **revolution** around the Sun, **inclination of Earth's axis**, and **polarity (parallelism) of Earth's axis**.
16. Does the **plane of the ecliptic** coincide with the plane of the equator? Explain.
17. On which day of the year is Earth closest to the Sun **(perihelion)**? Farthest from the Sun **(aphelion)**?
18. Provide the approximate date for the following special days of the year: **March equinox, June solstice, September equinox,** and **December solstice**.
19. What is the **circle of illumination**?
20. What is meant by the **solar altitude**?
21. Briefly describe Earth's orientation to the Sun during the Northern Hemisphere summer and the Northern Hemisphere winter.
22. Beginning with the March equinox, describe the changing latitude of the vertical rays of the noon Sun during the year.
23. In the midlatitudes of the Northern Hemisphere, on which day of the year is the Sun highest in the sky? Lowest in the sky?

24. For the equator, describe the approximate number of daylight hours on the following days of the year: *March equinox, June solstice, September equinox,* and *December solstice.*
25. What is the longest day of the year (the day with the greatest number of daylight hours) in the midlatitudes of the Northern Hemisphere? What is the longest day in the Southern Hemisphere?
26. For the North Pole, describe the approximate number of daylight hours on the following days of the year: March equinox, June solstice, September equinox, and December solstice.
27. For how many months of the year does the North Pole have no sunlight at all?

Telling Time (*p. 24*)

28. What happens to the hour when crossing a **time zone** boundary moving from west to east?
29. What is meant by **UTC (Universal Time Coordinated)** and **Greenwich Mean Time (GMT)**?
30. What happens to the day when crossing the **International Date Line** moving from east to west?
31. When **daylight-saving time** begins in the spring, you would adjust your clock from 2:00 A.M. to _____.

STUDY QUESTIONS

1. Why are physical geographers interested in globalization of the economy?
2. Why is a distance covered by 1° of longitude at the equator different from the distance covered by 1° of longitude at a latitude of 45° N?
3. What is the significance of *aphelion* and *perihelion* in Earth's seasons?
4. In terms of the change of seasons, explain the significance of the Tropic of Cancer, the Tropic of Capricorn, the Arctic Circle, and the Antarctic Circle.
5. Is the noon Sun ever directly overhead in Madison, Wisconsin (43° N)? If not, on which day of the year is the noon Sun *highest* in the sky there, and on which day is it lowest?

6. What would be the effect on the annual march of the seasons if Earth's axis was *not* inclined relative to the plane of the ecliptic?
7. What would be the effect on the annual march of the seasons if the North Pole was always leaning toward the Sun?
8. If Earth's axis was tilted only 20° from perpendicular, what would the latitudes of the Tropic of Cancer and Arctic Circle become?
9. Why are standard time zones 15° of longitude wide?
10. Most weather satellite images are "time-stamped" using UTC or "Zulu" time (UTC expressed using 24-hour or military time) instead of the local time of the region below. Why?

EXERCISES

1. Using formulas found in Appendix I (p. A-1), make the following conversions between the International System (S.I.) and English systems of measurements:
   a. 12 centimeters   = _____ inches
   b. 140 kilometers   = _____ miles
   c. 12,000 feet   = _____ meters
   d. 3 quarts   = _____ liters
   e. 5 kilograms   = _____ pounds
   f. 10°C   = _____ °F

2. Using a world map or globe, estimate the latitude and longitude of both New York City and Sydney, Australia. Be sure to specify if these locations are north or south latitude, and east or west longitude.

3. The solar altitude (the angle of the noon Sun above the horizon) can be calculated for any latitude on Earth for any day of the year, by using the formula: SA = 90° − AD, where SA is the "solar altitude" and AD is the "arc distance" (the difference in latitude between the declination of the Sun and the latitude in question). Use the analemma (Figure 1-29) to determine the declination of the Sun, and then calculate the solar altitude at the following locations on the day given:
   a. Beijing, China (40° N) on November 25th
   b. Nairobi, Kenya (1° S) on September 25th
   c. Fairbanks, Alaska (65° N) on July 10th

4. Using the map of North American time zones (Figure 1-32) for reference, if it is 5:00 P.M. standard time on Thursday in New York City (41° N, 74° W), what is the day and time in Los Angeles (34° N, 118° W)?

5. Using the map of world time zones (Figure 1-31) for reference, if it is 11:00 A.M. UTC (Universal Time Coordinated or Greenwich Mean Time), what is the standard time in Seattle (48° N, 122° W)?

Seeing Geographically

Look again at the image of Earth at the beginning of the chapter (p. 2). What evidence can you see of each of Earth's "spheres" in this image? What is the approximate latitude and longitude of the center of the image? Based on the position of the circle of illumination, is it early morning or late afternoon in Beijing, China? Generally, how do the clouds look different in the tropics compared with the clouds in higher latitudes?

MasteringGeography™

Looking for additional review and test prep materials? Visit the Study Area in MasteringGeography™ to enhance your geographic literacy, spatial reasoning skills, and understanding of this chapter's content by accessing a variety of resources, including geoscience animations, MapMaster interactive maps, videos, RSS feeds, flashcards, web links, self-study quizzes, and an eText version of *McKnight's Physical Geography: A Landscape Appreciation*.

Chapter 2 PORTRAYING EARTH

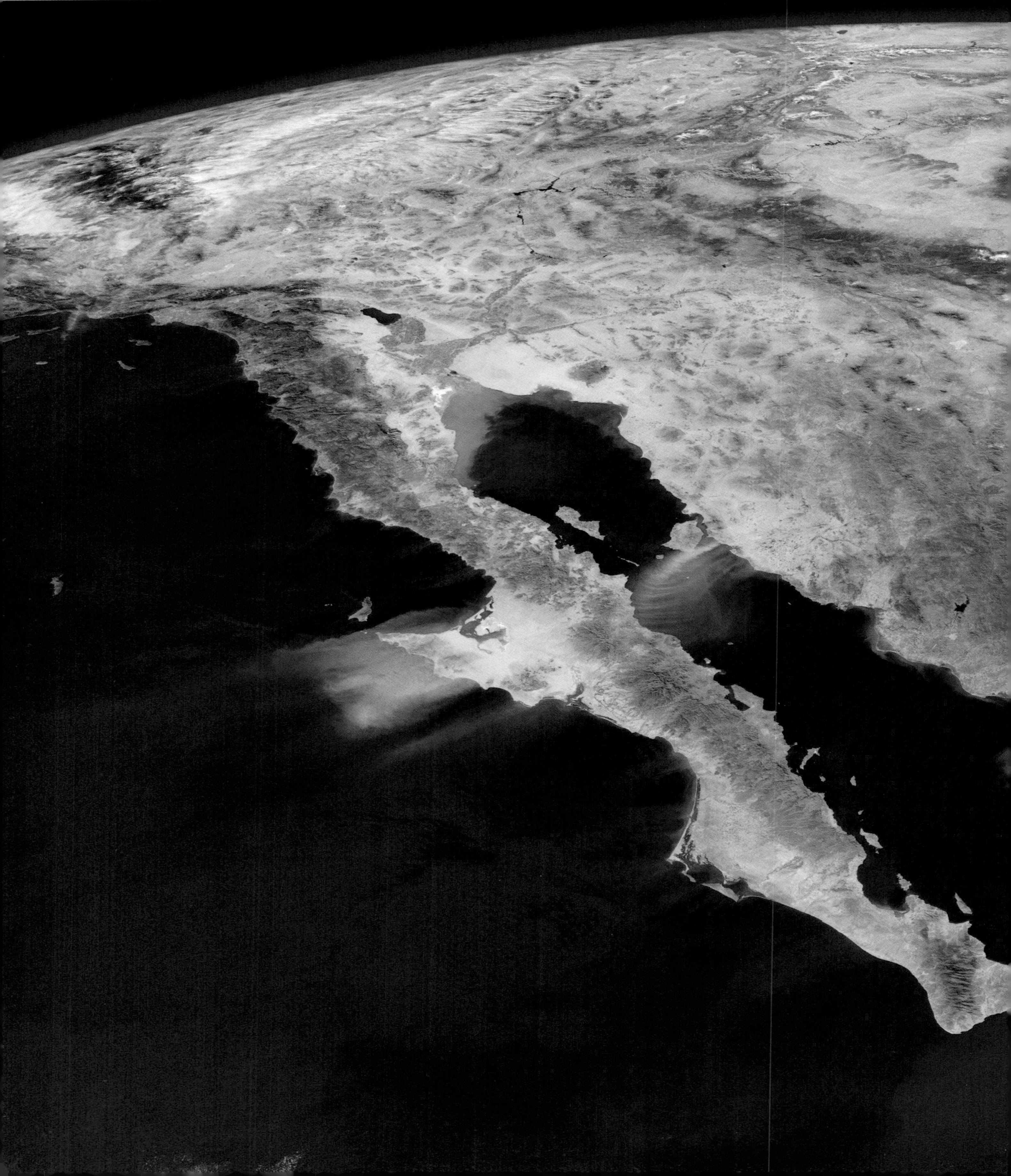

THE SURFACE OF EARTH IS THE FOCUS OF THE GEOGRAPHER'S

interest. The enormity and complexity of this surface would be difficult to comprehend and analyze without tools to systematically organize the varied data.

Although many kinds of tools are used in geographic studies, the most important are maps. The mapping of a geographic feature is often an essential first step toward understanding the spatial distributions and relationships of that feature. This book is a case in point—it contains numerous maps of various kinds, each included to further your understanding of some concept, fact, or relationship.

The purpose of this chapter is twofold: (1) To describe the basic characteristics of maps, including their capabilities and limitations; and (2) to describe the various ways a landscape can be portrayed—through maps, globes, photographs, and remotely sensed imagery (Figure 2-1).

As you study this chapter, think about these key questions:

- **Why can no map of the world be as accurate as a globe?**
- **What is meant by the *scale* of a map, and what are the different ways that map scale is described?**
- **What are the differences between *equivalent* ("equal area") maps and *conformal* maps, and when are these properties most important in geographic studies?**
- **How do the four major families of map projections differ from each other, and what are some of the best uses for maps in each of these families of projections?**
- **How are *isolines* used to convey information on a map?**
- **How does a GPS unit know where we are, and what are some common uses of GPS?**
- **What is *remote sensing*, and what kinds of information can be gathered in this way?**
- **How does GIS help in the analysis of geographic data?**

MAPS AND GLOBES

For portraying the geographic features of Earth as a whole, there is no substitute for a globe (Figure 2-2). Not only does a well-made globe accurately convey the spherical shape of Earth, it can show, essentially without distortion, the spatial relationships of Earth's surface, maintaining correct size, shape, distance, and direction relationships of features around the planet.

A globe, of course, has limitations. Most importantly, almost all globes are constructed at a very small scale, which means that they cannot show much detail. In order for a globe to show as much detail as the maps in Figure 2-1, it would need to be about 500 meters (1600 feet) in diameter! Because maps are much more portable and versatile than globes, there are literally billions of maps in use over the world, whereas globes are extremely limited both in number and variety.

Seeing Geographically

This natural color satellite image of Baja, Mexico, was taken on November 27, 2011, with the MODIS (Moderate Resolution Imaging Spectroradiometer) instrument aboard NASA's Aqua satellite. Strong winds have caused dust to blow off of mainland Mexico and the Baja peninsula. From which direction were the winds blowing on this day? How do the mountaintops and sky conditions change as you look north of Mexico into the United States?

(a) High-resolution orthoimagery

(b) Topographic map

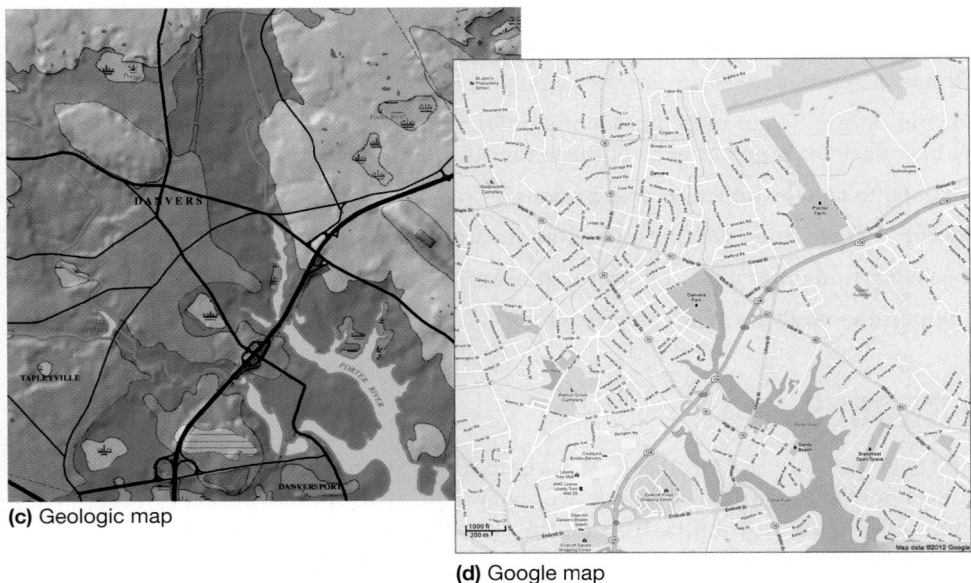

(c) Geologic map

(d) Google map

▲ **Figure 2-1** Different types of maps convey different kinds of information about the landscape, as shown in these four maps of a region near Salem, Massachusetts. (a) High-resolution orthophoto imagery (original scale 1:24,000). (b) Topographic map with elevation contour lines (original scale 1:24,000). (c) Geologic map showing rock types: orange = coarse glacial deposits; blue = glaciomarine deposits; green = glacial till; lavender = swamp deposits (original scale 1:50,000). (d) Google™ Map showing streets and highways.

Maps

In the simplest terms, a **map** is a flat representation of Earth, shown reduced in size with only selected features or data showing. A map serves as a surrogate (a substitute) for any surface we wish to portray or study. Although any kind of surface can be mapped—the lunar surface, for instance, or that of Mars—all the maps in this book portray portions of Earth's surface.

The basic attribute of maps is their ability to show distance, direction, size, and shape in their horizontal (that is to say, two-dimensional) spatial relationships. In addition to these fundamental graphic data, most maps

show other kinds of information as well. Most maps have a special purpose, and that purpose is usually to show the distribution of one or more phenomena (see Figure 2-1). Such *thematic maps* may be designed to show street patterns, the distribution of Tasmanians, the ratio of sunshine to cloud, the number of earthworms per cubic meter of soil, or any of an infinite number of other facts or combinations of facts. Because they depict graphically "what is where" and because they are often helpful in providing clues as to "why" such a distribution occurs, maps are indispensable tools for geographers. Even so, it is important to realize that maps have limitations.

▲ **Figure 2-2** A model globe provides a splendid broad representation of Earth at a very small scale, but few details can be portrayed.

Map Distortions: Although most people understand that not everything we may read in a book, in a newspaper, or on the Internet is necessarily correct (thus the somewhat cynical adage, "Don't believe everything you read"), these same people may uncritically accept all information portrayed on a map as being correct. However, no map can be perfectly accurate because it is impossible to portray the curved surface of Earth on a flat map without distortion. Imagine trying to flatten an orange peel—in order to do this, you must either stretch or tear the peel; effectively, the same thing must happen to Earth when we flatten its surface onto a map.

The extent to which the geometric impossibility of flattening a sphere without distortion becomes a problem on a map depends on two related variables. First: how much of Earth is being shown on the map—for example, these distortions are always significant on a world map, but less so on a map showing a very limited region of Earth. Second: the *scale* of the map—the topic to which we turn next.

Learning Check **2-1** **Why can't a map represent Earth's surface as perfectly as a globe? (Answer on p. AK-1)**

MAP SCALE

Because a map is smaller than the portion of Earth's surface it represents, in order to understand the geographic relationships (distances or relative sizes, for example) depicted on that map, we must know how to use a **map scale**. The scale of a map describes the relationship between distance measured on the map and the actual distance that represents on Earth's surface. Knowing the scale of a map makes

it possible to measure distance, determine area, and compare sizes.

Because Earth's surface is curved and a map's surface is flat, scale can never be perfectly correct over an entire map. In practice, if the map is of a small area a single scale can be used across the entire map. However, if the map is showing a large portion of Earth's surface (such as a world map), there may be significant scale differences from one part of the map to the next—such a map, for example, might need to list different scales for different latitudes.

Scale Types

Three ways of portraying map scale are widely used: the graphic scale, the fractional scale, and the verbal scale (Figure 2-3).

Graphic Map Scales: A **graphic map scale** uses a line marked off in distances to represent actual distance on Earth's surface. To use a graphic map scale, we measure off the distance between two points on the map (such as by making two pencil marks along the edge of a piece of paper), and then compare that measured distance to the graphic map scale—the graphic scale gives you a direct reading of the actual distance. The advantage of a graphic scale is its simplicity: you determine approximate distances on the surface of Earth by measuring them directly on the map (such as a motorist can do to estimate travel distances on a road map). Moreover, a graphic scale remains correct when a map is enlarged or reduced in size because the length of the graphic scale line is also changed as the map size is changed.

Fractional Map Scales: A **fractional map scale** conveys the relationship between distance measured on a map and the actual distance that represents on Earth with a fraction or ratio called a *representative fraction*. For example,

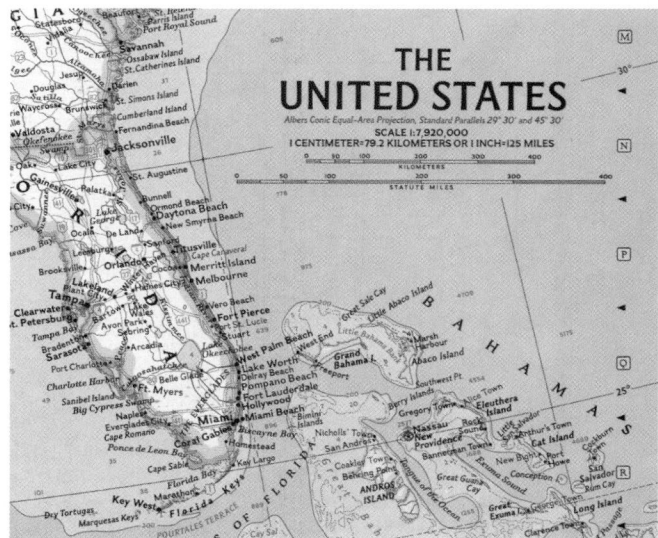

▲ **Figure 2-3** All three types of scale are shown on this map. Included are a fractional scale, a verbal scale, and a graphic (shown in both miles and kilometers).

a common fractional scale uses the representative fraction 1/63,360 (often expressed as the ratio 1:63,360): this notation means that 1 unit of measure on the map represents an actual distance of 63,360 units of measure on Earth. The "units of measure" are the same on both sides of the fraction, so 1 millimeter measured on the map represents an actual distance of 63,360 millimeters on Earth's surface, whereas 1 inch measured on the map represents an actual distance of 63,360 inches on Earth's surface, and so forth.

Verbal Map Scales: A verbal map scale (or *word scale*) states in words the relationship between the distance on the map and the actual distance on Earth's surface, such as "one centimeter to ten kilometers" or "one inch equals five miles." A verbal scale is simply a mathematical manipulation of the fractional scale. For instance, there are 63,360 inches in 1 mile, so on a map with a fractional scale of 1:63,360 we can say that "1 inch represents 1 mile."

Learning Check 2-2 **On a map with a fractional scale of 1:10,000, one centimeter measured on the map represents what actual distance on Earth's surface?**

Large and Small Scale Maps

The adjectives large and small are comparative rather than absolute. In other words, scales are "large" or "small" only in comparison with other scales (Figure 2-4). A **large-scale map** is one that has a relatively large representative fraction, which means that the denominator is small. Thus, 1/10,000 is a larger value than, say, 1/1,000,000, and so a scale of 1:10,000 is large in comparison with one of 1:1,000,000; consequently, a map at a scale of 1:10,000 is called a large-scale map—such a map portrays only a small portion of Earth's surface but portrays it in considerable detail. For example, if

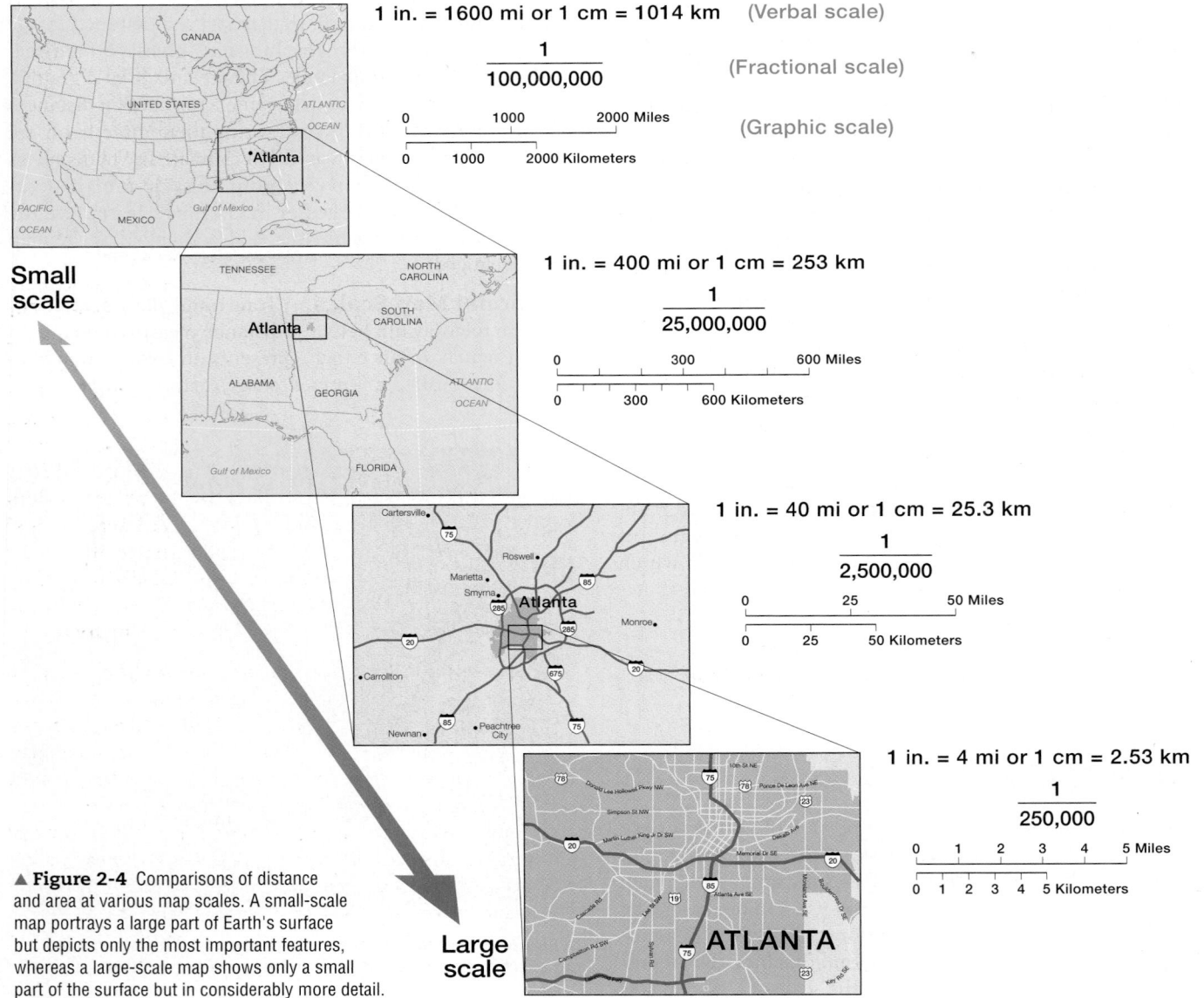

1 in. = 1600 mi or 1 cm = 1014 km   (Verbal scale)

$$\frac{1}{100,000,000}$$ (Fractional scale)

0   1000   2000 Miles
0   1000   2000 Kilometers   (Graphic scale)

Small scale

1 in. = 400 mi or 1 cm = 253 km

$$\frac{1}{25,000,000}$$

0   300   600 Miles
0   300   600 Kilometers

1 in. = 40 mi or 1 cm = 25.3 km

$$\frac{1}{2,500,000}$$

0   25   50 Miles
0   25   50 Kilometers

1 in. = 4 mi or 1 cm = 2.53 km

$$\frac{1}{250,000}$$

0 1 2 3 4 5 Miles
0 1 2 3 4 5 Kilometers

▲ Figure 2-4 Comparisons of distance and area at various map scales. A small-scale map portrays a large part of Earth's surface but depicts only the most important features, whereas a large-scale map shows only a small part of the surface but in considerably more detail.

Large scale

ATLANTA

this page were covered with a map having a scale of 1:10,000, the map would be able to show just a small part of a single city, but that area would be rendered in great detail.

A **small-scale map** has a small representative fraction—in other words, one having a large denominator. A map having a scale of 1:10,000,000 is classified as a small-scale map. If it were covered with a map of that scale, this page would be able to portray about one-third of the United States, but only in limited detail.

MAP PROJECTIONS AND PROPERTIES

The challenge to the cartographer (map-maker) is to try to combine the geometric exactness of a globe with the convenience of a flat map. This melding has been attempted for many centuries, and further refinements continue to be made. The fundamental problem is always the same: to transfer data from a spherical surface to a flat map with a minimum of distortion. This transfer is accomplished with a *map projection.*

Animation
Map Projections

Map Projections

A **map projection** is a system in which the spherical surface of Earth is transformed for display on a flat surface. The basic principle of a map projection is simple. Imagine a transparent globe on which are drawn meridians, parallels, and continental boundaries; also imagine a lightbulb in the center of this globe. A piece of paper, either held flat or rolled into some shape such as a cylinder or cone, is placed over the globe as in Figure 2-5. When the bulb is lighted, all the lines on the globe are projected outward onto the paper. These lines are then sketched on the paper.

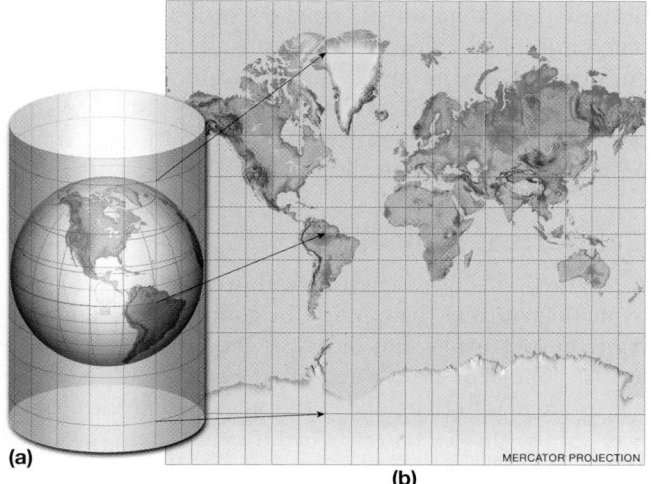

(a)

(b)

MERCATOR PROJECTION

▲ **Figure 2-5** The concept of map projection. A cylinder is wrapped around a globe with a light in its center (a), and the features of the globe are projected onto the adjacent cylinder. (b) The resulting map is called a cylindrical projection.

When the paper is laid out flat, a map projection has been produced. Few map projections have been made by actual "optical" projection from a globe onto a piece of paper; instead, map projections are derived by mathematically transferring the features of a sphere onto a flat surface.

Because a flat surface cannot be closely fitted to a sphere without wrinkling or tearing, no matter how a map projection is made, data from a globe (parallels, meridians, continental boundaries, and so forth) cannot be transferred to a map without distortion of shape, relative area, distance, and/or direction. However, the cartographer can choose to control or reduce one or more of these distortions—although all distortions cannot be eliminated on a single map.

Learning Check 2-3   **What is a map projection?**

Map Properties

Cartographers often strive to maintain accuracy either of size or of shape—map properties known as *equivalence* and *conformality*, respectively (Figure 2-6).

Equivalence: In an **equivalent map projection** (also called an **equal area map projection**) the correct size ratio of area on the map to the corresponding actual area on Earth's surface is maintained over the entire map. For example, on an equivalent world map, if you were to place four dimes at different places (perhaps one on Brazil, one on Australia, one on Siberia, and one on South Africa), the area on Earth covered by each coin would be the same.

Equivalent projections are very desirable because, with them, misleading impressions of size are avoided. The world maps in this book are mostly equivalent projections because they are so useful in portraying distributions of the various geographic features we will be studying.

There are trade-offs, of course, with equivalent maps. Equivalence is difficult to achieve on small-scale maps because correct shapes must be sacrificed in order to maintain proper area relationships. Most equivalent world maps (which are necessarily small-scale maps) show distorted shapes of landmasses—especially in the high latitudes. For example, as Figure 2-6b shows, on equivalent maps the shapes of Greenland and Alaska are usually shown as more "squatty" than they actually are.

Conformality: A **conformal map projection** is one in which proper angular relationships are maintained across the entire map so that the shapes of features such as coastlines are the same as on Earth. It is impossible to depict true shapes for large areas such as a continent, but they can be approximated, and in practice for small areas we can say that conformal maps show correct shapes. All conformal projections have meridians and parallels crossing each other at right angles, just as they do on a globe.

The main problem with conformal projections is that the size of an area must often be considerably distorted to depict the proper shape. Thus, the scale necessarily changes from one region to another. For example, a

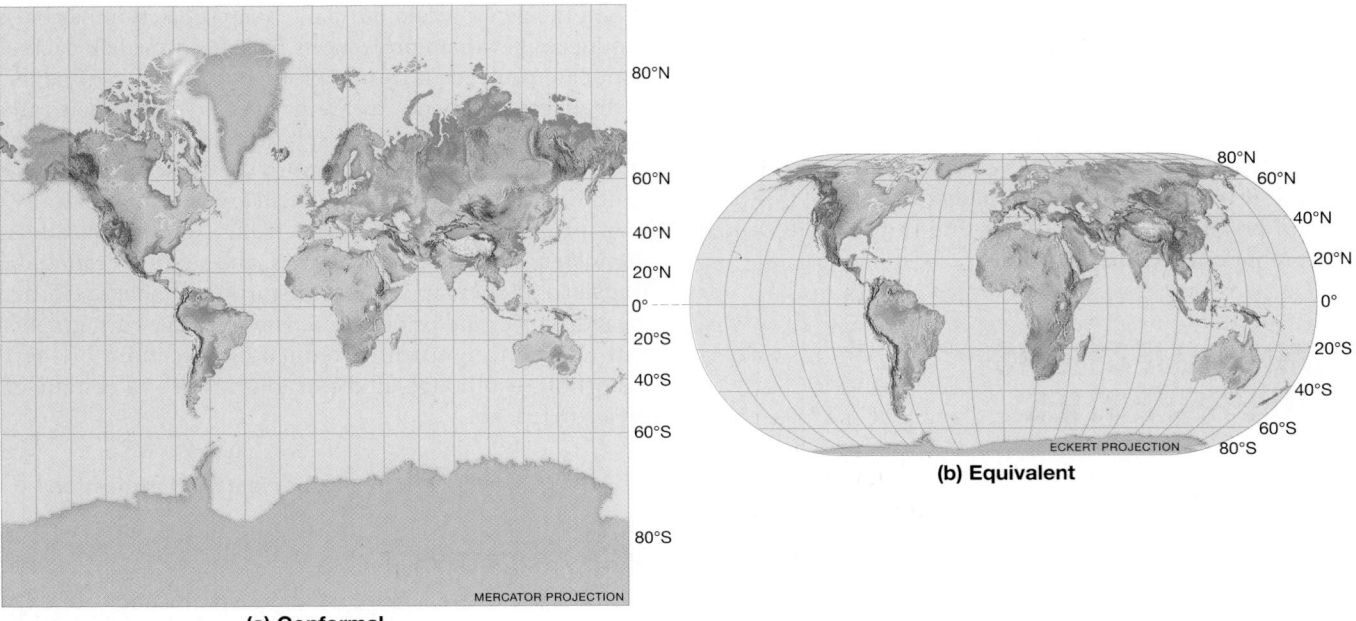

(a) Conformal

(b) Equivalent

▲ **Figure 2-6** Conformal and equivalent maps. (a) A conformal projection (the Mercator) depicts accurate shapes, but the sizes are severely exaggerated in high latitudes. (b) An equivalent (equal area) projection (the Eckert) is accurate with regard to size, but shapes are badly distorted in high latitudes. It is impossible to portray both correct size and correct shape on a world map. Compare the sizes and shapes of Antarctica, Alaska, and Greenland in these examples.

conformal map of the world normally greatly enlarges sizes in the high latitudes. Figure 2-6a shows the conformal projection known as a Mercator projection (discussed in greater detail later in this chapter)—notice the exaggerated apparent sizes of landmasses toward the poles.

Compromise Projections: Except for maps of very small areas (in other words, large-scale maps), where both properties can be closely approximated, conformality and equivalence cannot be maintained on the same projection, and thus the art of mapmaking, like politics, is often an art of compromise. For example, Figure 2-7 shows a Robinson projection—a **compromise map projection**; it is neither equivalent nor conformal, but instead balances reasonably accurate shapes with reasonably accurate areas. The Robinson projection is a popular choice as a general-purpose classroom map.

As a rule of thumb, it can be stated that some map projections are purely conformal, some are purely equivalent, none are both conformal and equivalent, and many are neither, but are instead a compromise between the two.

Learning Check 2-4 What is the difference between an equivalent map and a conformal map?

FAMILIES OF MAP PROJECTIONS

Because there is no way to avoid distortion completely, no map projection is ideal for all uses. So, hundreds of different map projections have been devised for one purpose or another. Most of them can be grouped into just a few families. Projections in the same family generally have similar properties and related distortion characteristics.

Cylindrical Projections

As Figure 2-5 shows, a **cylindrical projection** is obtained by mathematically "wrapping" the globe with a cylinder of paper in such a way that the paper touches the globe only at the globe's equator. We say that paper positioned this way is tangent to the globe at the equator, and the equator is called the *circle of tangency* (some cylindrical projections choose a circle of tangency other than the equator). The curved parallels and meridians of the globe then form a perfectly rectangular grid on the map. Having the equator as the tangency line produces a right-angled grid (meridians and parallels meet at right angles) on a rectangular

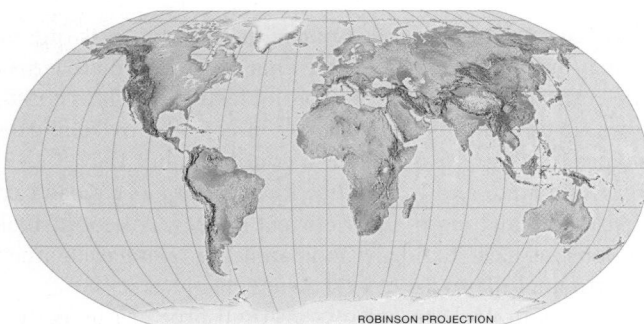

▲ **Figure 2-7** Many world maps are neither purely conformal nor purely equivalent, but a compromise between the two. One of the most popular compromises is the Robinson projection shown here.

map. There is no size distortion at the circle of tangency, but size distortion increases progressively with increasing distance from this circle, a characteristic clearly exemplified by the *Mercator projection*.

Mercator: The Most Famous Projection: Although some map projections were devised centuries ago, projection techniques have improved right up to the present day. Thus, it is remarkable that the most famous of all map projections, the **Mercator projection,** originated in 1569 by a Flemish geographer and cartographer, is still in common usage today without significant modification (see Figure 2-6a).

Gerhardus Mercator produced some of the best maps and globes of his time. His place in history, however, is based largely on the fact that he developed a special-purpose projection that became inordinately popular for general-purpose use.

The Mercator projection is a conformal map projection designed to facilitate oceanic navigation. The prime advantage of a Mercator map is that it shows *loxodromes* as straight lines. A **loxodrome,** also called a *rhumb line,* is a curve on the surface of a sphere that crosses all meridians at the same angle and represents a line of constant compass direction. A navigator first plots the shortest distance between origin and destination on a map projection in which great circles are shown as straight lines, such as the gnomonic projection shown in Figure 2-8a (great circle routes are discussed in Chapter 1), and then transfers that route to a Mercator projection with straight-line loxodromes. This procedure allows the navigator to generally take the shorter path of a great circle route by simply making periodic changes in the compass course of the airplane or ship. Today, of course, these calculations are all done by computer.

A Mercator map is relatively undistorted in the low latitudes. However, because the meridians do not converge at the poles but instead remain parallel to each other, size distortion increases rapidly in the mid- and high latitudes. Further, to maintain conformality and the map's navigational virtues, Mercator compensated for the east–west stretching by spacing the parallels of latitude increasingly farther apart so that north–south stretching occurs at the same rate. This procedure allowed shapes to be approximated with reasonable accuracy, but at great expense to proper size relationships. Area is distorted by 4 times at the 60th parallel of latitude and by 36 times at the 80th parallel. If the North Pole could be shown on a Mercator projection, it would be a line as long as the equator rather than a single point!

The Mercator projection was a major leap forward in cartography when it was devised, and it remains an excellent choice for large-scale navigation maps and other uses where conformality is important. Unfortunately, by the early twentieth century, Mercator projections were widely used in American classrooms and atlases. Indeed, several generations of American students have passed through school with their principal view of the

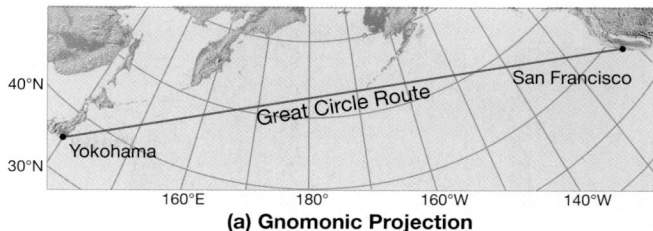

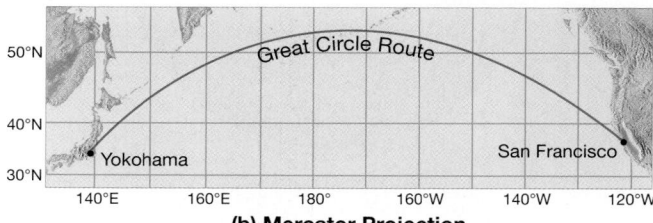

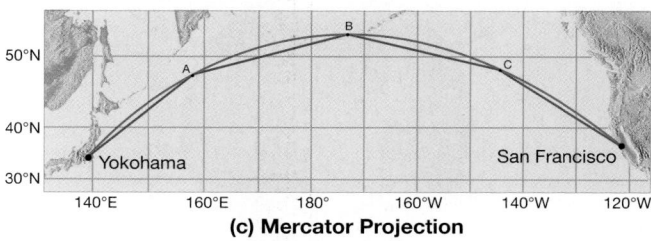

▲ **Figure 2-8** The prime virtue of the Mercator projection is its usefulness for straight-line navigation. (a) The shortest distance between two locations—here San Francisco and Yokohama—can be plotted on a *gnomonic* projection (on which great circles are shown as straight lines). (b) The great circle route can be transferred to a Mercator projection. (c) On the Mercator projection, straight-line loxodromes can then be substituted for the curved great circle. The loxodromes allow the navigator to maintain constant compass headings over small distances while still approximating the curve of the great circle.

world provided by a Mercator map. This has created many misconceptions, not the least of which is confusion about the relative sizes of high-latitude landmasses: on a Mercator projection, the island of Greenland appears to be as large as or larger than Africa, Australia, and South America. Actually, however, Africa is actually 14 times larger than Greenland, South America is 9 times larger, and Australia is 3.5 times larger.

The Mercator projection was devised several centuries ago for a specific purpose, and it still serves that purpose well. Its fame, however, is significantly due to its misuse.

Learning Check 2-5 **Would a Mercator projection be a good choice for a map used to study the loss of forest cover around the world? Why or why not?**

Planar Projections

A **planar projection** (also called a *plane, azimuthal,* or *zenithal projection*) is obtained by projecting the markings of a center-lit globe onto a flat piece of paper that is tangent to the globe at one point (Figure 2-9)—usually the North or South Pole, or some point on the equator. There

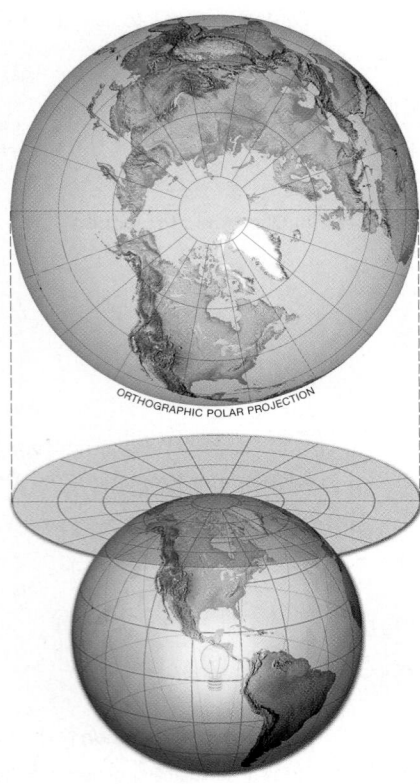

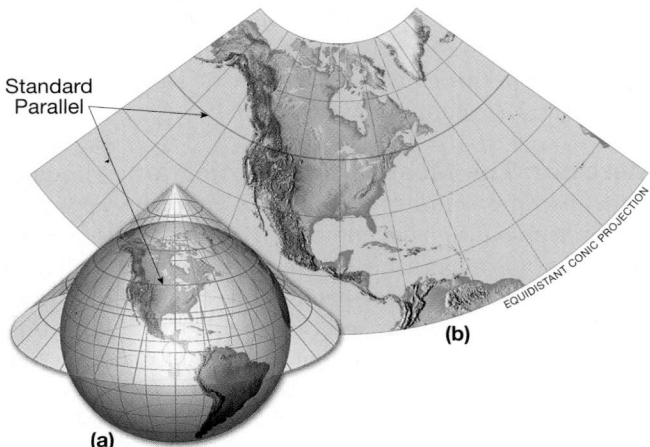

▲ **Figure 2-11** The origin of a conic projection, as illustrated by a globe with a light in its center (a), projecting images onto a cone. (b) The resulting map is called a conic projection.

▲ **Figure 2-9** The origin of a planar projection, as illustrated by a globe with a light in its center, projecting images onto an adjacent plane. The resulting map goes by various names: azimuthal projection, plane projection, or zenithal projection.

is no distortion immediately around the point of tangency, but distortion increases progressively away from this point.

Typically, planar projections show only one hemisphere, and some types can provide a perspective of Earth similar to the view one gets when looking at a globe or that of an astronaut looking at Earth from space (Figure 2-10). This half-view-only characteristic can be a drawback, of course,

▲ **Figure 2-10** An orthographic planar projection showing Earth as it would appear from space.

just as it is with a globe, although planar projections can be useful for focusing attention on a specific region, and they are common projections when mapping the Arctic and Antarctic regions.

Conic Projections

A **conic projection** is obtained by projecting the markings of a center-lit globe onto a cone wrapped tangent to, or intersecting, a portion of the globe (Figure 2-11). Normally the apex of the cone is positioned above a pole, which means that the circle of tangency coincides with a parallel. This parallel then becomes the *standard parallel* of the projection; distortion is least in its vicinity and increases progressively as one moves away from it. Consequently, conic projections are best suited for regions of east–west orientation in the midlatitudes, being particularly useful for maps of the United States, Europe, or China.

It is impractical to use conic projections for more than one-fourth of Earth's surface (a semihemisphere), but they are particularly well adapted for mapping relatively small areas, such as a state or county.

Pseudocylindrical Projections

A **pseudocylindrical projection** (also called an *elliptical* or *oval projection*) is a roughly football-shaped map, usually of the entire world (see the Eckert in Figure 2-6b and the Robinson in Figure 2-7), although sometimes only the central section of a pseudocylindrical projection is used for maps of lesser areas. Mathematically, a pseudocylindrical projection wraps around the equator like an ordinary cylindrical projection, but then further "curves in" toward the poles, effectively conveying some of the curvature of Earth.

In most pseudocylindrical projections, a central parallel (usually the equator) and a central meridian (often the prime meridian) cross at right angles in the middle of the map, which is a point of no distortion; distortion in size and/or shape normally increases progressively as one moves

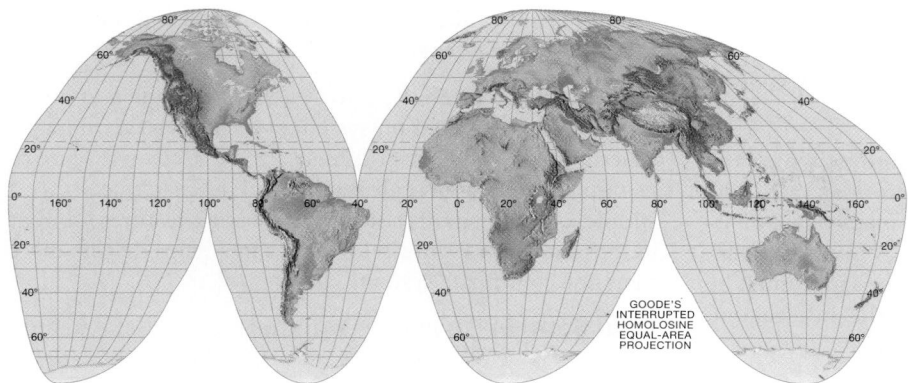

◀ **Figure 2-12** An interrupted projection of the world. The purpose of the interruptions is to portray certain areas (usually continents) more accurately, at the expense of portions of the map (usually oceans) that are not important to the map's theme. The map shown here is a *Goode's interrupted homolosine equal-area projection*. A variation of this projection is used for many maps in this book.

away from this point in any direction. All of the parallels are drawn parallel to each other, whereas all meridians, except the central meridian, are shown as curved lines.

Interrupted Projections: One technique used with pseudocylindrical projections to minimize distortion of the continents is to "interrupt" oceanic regions—*Goode's interrupted homolosine equal-area projection* (Figure 2-12) is a popular example of this. Goode's projection is equivalent, and, although it is impossible for this map to be conformal, the shapes of continental coastlines are very well maintained even in high latitudes.

When global distributions are mapped, the continents are often more important than the oceans, and yet the oceans occupy most of the map space in a typical projection. A projection can be interrupted ("torn apart") in the Pacific, Atlantic, and Indian Oceans and then based on central meridians that pass through each major landmass—with no land area far from a central meridian, shape and size distortion is greatly decreased. For world maps that emphasize ocean areas, continents can be interrupted instead of ocean basins. You'll see that many of the maps used in this book employ variations of Goode's interrupted projection.

Learning Check 2-6 **What are the advantages of an "interrupted" projection, such as the Goode's projection?**

CONVEYING INFORMATION ON MAPS

Now that we have described the fundamentals of map scale, properties and projections, let's think about some of the ways that information is presented on maps. We begin with basic features of all maps.

Map Essentials

Maps come in an infinite variety of sizes and styles and serve a limitless diversity of purposes. Regardless of type, however, every map should contain a few basic components to facilitate its use (Figure 2-13). Omission of any of these essential components decreases the clarity of the map and may make it more difficult to interpret.

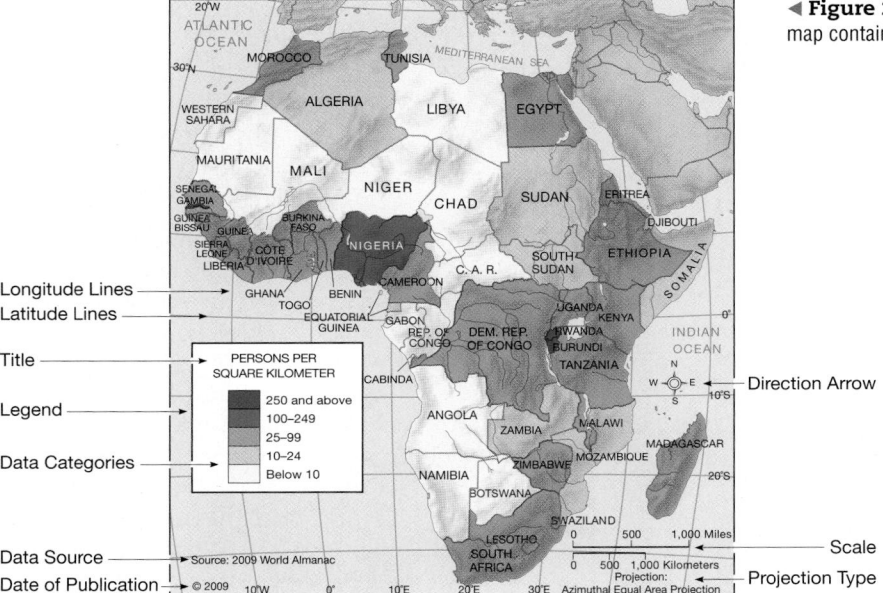

◀ **Figure 2-13** A typical thematic map containing all of the essentials.

Title: This should be a brief summary of the map's content or purpose. It should identify the area covered and provide some indication of content, such as "Road Map of Kenya," or "River Discharge in Northern Europe."

Date: This should indicate the time span over which the information was collected. In addition, some maps also give the date of publication of the map. Most maps depict conditions or patterns that are temporary or even momentary. For a map to be meaningful, therefore, the reader must be informed when the data were gathered, as this information indicates how timely or out of date the map is.

Legend: Most maps use symbols, colors, shadings, or other devices to represent features or the amount, degree, or proportion of some quantity. Some symbols are self-explanatory, but it is usually necessary to include a legend box in a corner of the map to explain the symbolization.

Scale: Any map that serves as more than a pictogram must be drawn to scale, at least approximately. A graphic, verbal, or fractional scale is, therefore, necessary.

Direction: Direction is normally shown on a map by means of the geographic grid of parallels and meridians. If no grid is shown, direction may be indicated by a straight arrow pointing northward, which is called a *north arrow*.

A north arrow is aligned with the meridians and thus points toward the north geographic pole.

Location: Although the grid system of latitude and longitude is the most common system of location seen on maps, other types of reference grids may also be used on maps. For example, some large-scale maps (such as road maps) use a simple x- and y-coordinate grid to locating features (similar to that shown in Figure 1-11), and some maps display more than one coordinate system.

Data Source: For most thematic maps, it is useful to indicate the source of the data.

Projection Type: On many maps, particularly small-scale ones, the type of map projection is indicated to help the user assess the kinds of distortions on the map.

Isolines

Maps can display data in a number of different ways. One of the most widespread techniques for portraying the geographic distribution of some phenomenon is the *isoline* (from the Greek *isos*, meaning "equal"). **Isoline** is a generic term that refers to any line that joins points of equal value of something.

Some isolines represent tangible surfaces, such as the **elevation contour lines** on a topographic map (Figure 2-14). Most, however, signify such intangible features as

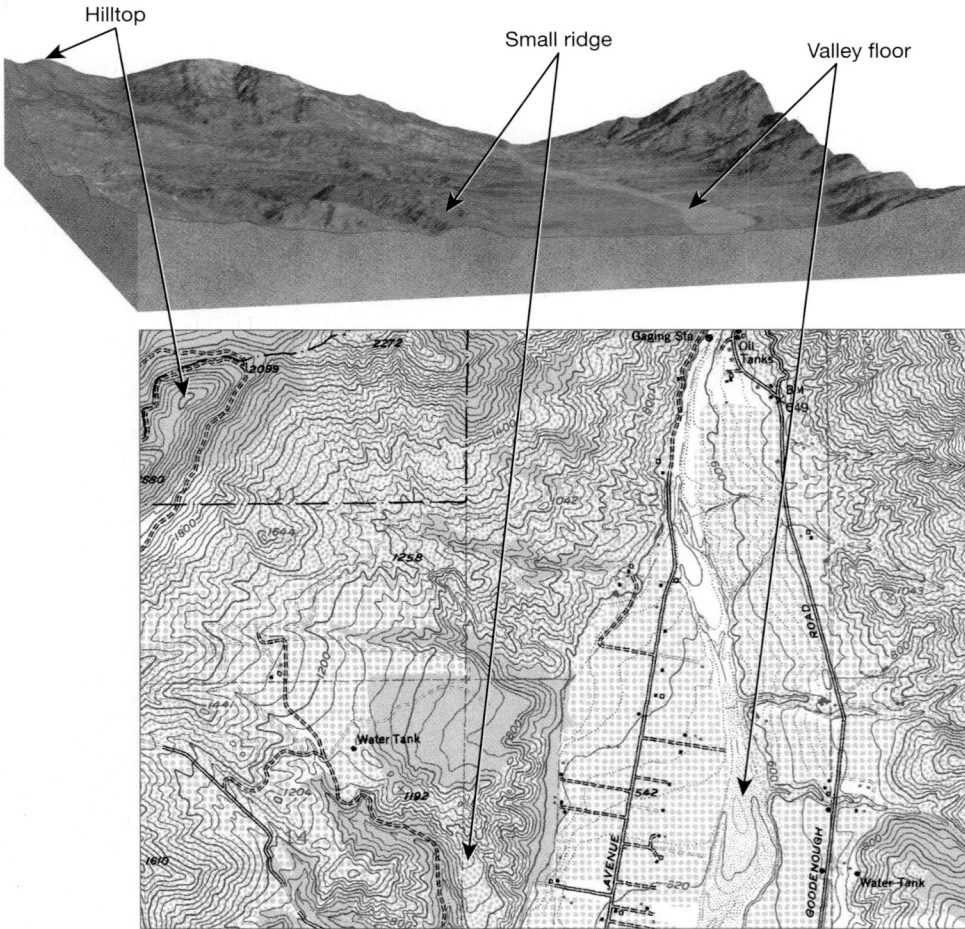

▶ **Figure 2-14** This portion of a typical United States Geological Survey topographic map quadrangle illustrates the use of contour lines, shown here with a matching landscape diagram and labeled features. This is a section of the Fillmore, California, quadrangle. The original map scale was 1:24,000; the contour interval is 40 feet (12 meters).

temperature and precipitation, and some express relative values such as ratios or proportions (Figure 2-15). More than 100 kinds of isolines have been identified by name, ranging from *isoamplitude* (used to describe radio waves) to *isovapor* (water vapor content of the air), but only a few types are important in an introductory physical geography course:

- *Elevation contour line*—a line joining points of equal elevation (see Appendix II for a description of U.S. Geological Survey topographic maps)
- *Isotherm*—a line joining points of equal temperature
- *Isobar*—a line joining points of equal atmospheric pressure
- *Isohyet*—a line joining points of equal quantities of precipitation (*hyeto* is from the Greek, meaning "rain")
- *Isogonic line*—a line joining points of equal magnetic declination

Drawing Isolines: To draw an isoline on a map, it is often necessary to estimate values that are not available. As a simple example, Figure 2-16 illustrates the basic steps in constructing an isoline map—in this case, an **elevation contour line** map. Each dot in Figure 2-16a represents a data collection location, and the number next to each dot is the elevation above sea level in meters.

We begin by drawing the 115-meter elevation contour: the 115-meter contour line passes between 114 and 116, and between 113 and 116 (Figure 2-16b). In Figure 2-16c this estimation process is repeated for other elevation contours, and in Figure 2-16d shading is added to clarify the pattern.

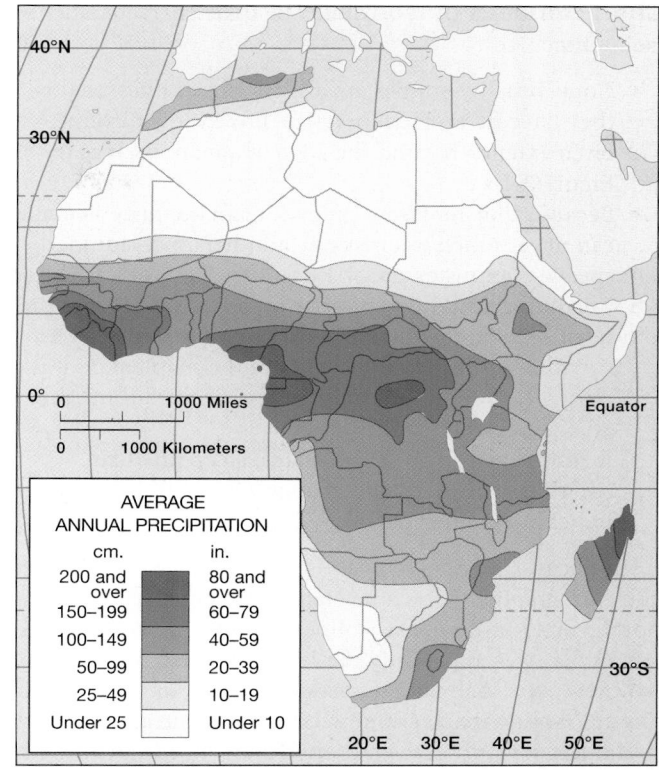

▲ **Figure 2-15** Isolines can be used to show the spatial variation of even intangible features, such as in this map that shows average annual precipitation for the continent of Africa (on this map the areas between isolines have been shaded to clarify the pattern).

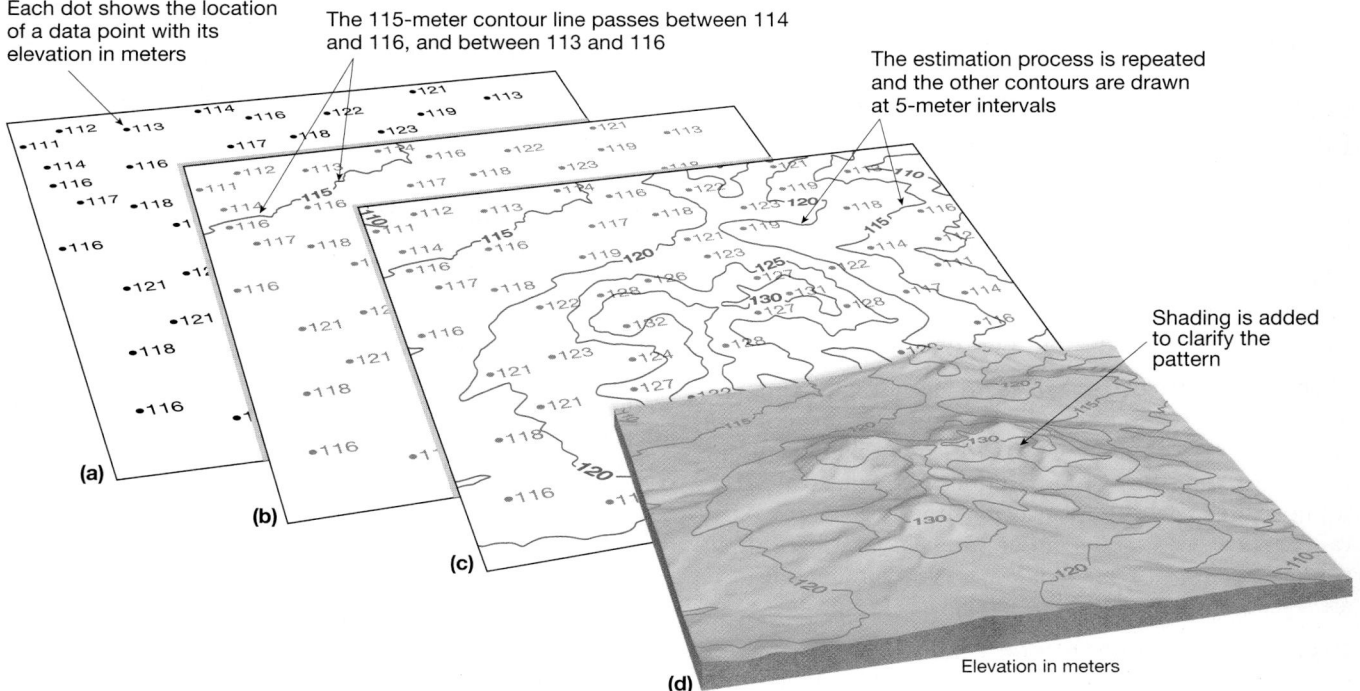

▲ **Figure 2-16** Drawing isolines. (a) Each dot represents an elevation above sea level in meters. (b) The 115-meter elevation contour is drawn. (c) The other contour lines at 5-meter intervals are drawn. (d) Shading is added for clarity.

Characteristics of Isolines: The basic characteristics of isolines include:

- Conceptually, isolines are always closed lines; that is, they have no ends. In practice, however, an isoline often extends beyond the edge of a map, such as in Figure 2-16.
- Because they represent gradations in quantity, isolines can never touch or cross one another, except under special circumstances.
- The numerical difference between one isoline and the next is called the *interval*. Although intervals can be varied according to the wishes of the mapmaker, it is normally more useful to maintain a constant interval all over a given map.
- Isolines close together indicate a steep gradient (in other words, a rapid change); isolines far apart indicate a gentle gradient.

Edmund Halley (1656–1742), an English astronomer and cartographer (for whom Halley's Comet is named), was not the first person to use isolines, but in 1700 he produced a map that was apparently the first published map to have isolines. This map showed isogonic lines in the Atlantic Ocean. Isoline maps are now commonplace and are very useful to geographers even though an isoline is an artificial construct—that is, it does not occur in nature. For instance, an isoline map can reveal spatial relationships that might otherwise go undetected. Patterns that are too large, too abstract, or too detailed for ordinary comprehension are often significantly clarified by the use of isolines.

> **Learning Check 2-7**   **Define "isoline" and give one example of a kind of distribution pattern that can be mapped with isolines.**

Portraying the Three-Dimensional Landscape

Although many maps are simply flat representations of Earth, in physical geography the vertical aspect of the landscape is often an important component of study. In addition to actual raised-relief models of landforms, many other methods can be used to convey the three-dimensional aspect of the landscape on a two-dimensional map.

Elevation Contours: For many decades, topographic maps using elevation contour lines were a workhorse of landform study (see Figure 2-14)—and remain so today even as we transition from traditional paper maps to electronic maps such as those available from the U.S. Geological Survey (USGS) on its online *National Map* site (http://nationalmap.gov/). Topographic maps and contour line rules are discussed in detail in Appendix II.

Digital Elevation Models: A remarkable recent advance in cartography has been the use of **digital elevation models (DEM)** to convey topography. The starting point for creating a DEM image is a detailed database of precise elevations. For example, the USGS maintains such a

▲ **Figure 2-17** An oblique shaded-relief digital elevation model of post-1980 eruption Mount St. Helens.

database for the United States at several different spatial resolutions—a 30-meter grid being one of the most commonly used (meaning that elevation data are available at distance intervals of 30 meters, both north–south and east–west, across the entire country). Similar digital elevation data are increasingly available for the entire world.

From digital elevation data, a computer can generate a shaded-relief image of the landscape by portraying the landscape as if it were illuminated from the northwest by the Sun (Figure 2-17). Although shaded relief maps have been drafted by hand in the past, one of the great virtues of a DEM is that the parameters of the image—such as its orientation, scale, and vertical exaggeration of the topography—can be readily manipulated. Further, various kinds of information or images can be overlain on the topography to create maps that were once impossible to conceive (for example, see Figure 2-29).

> **Learning Check 2-8**   **How does a digital elevation model convey the topography of Earth's surface?**

GPS—THE GLOBAL POSITIONING SYSTEM

In recent decades, new electronic technologies have transformed map making. One such technology provides precise locational data for points on Earth's surface. The **Global Positioning System,** or simply **GPS,** is a global navigation satellite system for determining accurate positions on or near Earth's surface. It was developed in the 1970s and 1980s by the U.S. Department of Defense to aid in navigating aircraft, guiding missiles, and controlling ground troops. The first receivers were the size of a file cabinet, but continued technological improvement has reduced them to the size of a cell phone (Figure 2-18). In fact, increasingly devices such as portable computers, digital cameras, and cell phones contain built-in GPS receivers—revolutionizing both the way that data from field observations are gathered for use on maps and the way that data from maps can be retrieved in the field.

▲ **Figure 2-18** A handheld GPS receiver. It receives signals sent by the network of Global Positioning System satellites, calculating its position anywhere in the world to within 10 meters (33 feet).

▲ **Figure 2-19** Global Positioning System (GPS) satellites circling 17,700 kilometers (11,000 miles) above Earth broadcast signals that are picked up by the receiver in an ambulance and used to pinpoint the location of the ambulance at any moment. A transmitter in the ambulance then sends this location information to a dispatch center. Knowing the location of all ambulances at any given moment, the dispatcher is able to route the closest available vehicle to each emergency and then direct that vehicle to the nearest appropriate health facility.

The GPS system (formally called NAVSTAR GPS [Navigation Signal Timing and Ranging Global Positioning System]) is based on a constellation of at least 24 high-altitude satellites configured so that a minimum of four—and preferably six—are in view of any position on Earth (currently there are 31 active satellites, with several older satellites still in orbit as backups). Each satellite continuously transmits both identification and positioning information that can be picked up by receivers on Earth (Figure 2-19). The distance between a given receiver and each member in a group of four or more satellites is calculated by comparing clocks stored in both units, and then the three-dimensional coordinates of the receiver's position are calculated through triangulation. The greater the number of channels in a GPS unit (even inexpensive units now have 12), the greater the number of satellites that can be tracked, and so the better the accuracy. The system already has accuracy greater than that of the best base maps. Even the simplest GPS units determine position to within 15 meters (49 feet).

Wide Area Augmentation System (WAAS):

Increased GPS accuracy is gained when the *Wide Area Augmentation System* (*WAAS*) is employed. Originally developed in cooperation with the Federal Aviation Administration (FAA) and the U.S. Department of Transportation, WAAS was implemented to increase the accuracy of instrument-based flight approaches for airplanes. Several dozen ground-based stations across North America monitor GPS signals from the satellites and then generate a correction message that is transmitted to GPS units. With WAAS, GPS units achieve a position accuracy of 3 meters (about 10 feet) about 95 percent of the time. WAAS capability is built into virtually all new GPS receivers today. WAAS service is not yet available around the world, although similar systems are being implemented in Asia (Japan's Multi-Functional Satellite Augmentation System) and Europe (the Euro Geostationary Navigation Overlay Service).

Continuously Operating GPS Reference Stations (CORS):

The National Oceanic and Atmospheric Administration (NOAA) manages a system of permanently installed GPS receiving stations known as *Continuously Operating GPS Reference Stations* (*CORS*). These highly accurate units are capable of detecting location differences of less than 1 centimeter of latitude, longitude, and elevation. They are used, for example, for the long-term monitoring of slight changes in the ground surface caused by lithospheric plate movement or the bulging of magma below a volcano.

GPS Modernization Program:

The United States has an ongoing modernization program for its GPS system. The upgrades already underway include replacing older satellites with newer ones that broadcast a *second civilian GPS signal* (known as "L2C") that allows ionospheric correction to provide greater accuracy. Further improvements for civilian, aviation, and military use are also being implemented.

GPS Applications: Since 1983, when access to GPS was made free to the public, astounding commercial growth has resulted. It is anticipated that eventually practically everything that moves in our society—airplane, truck, train, car, bus, ship, cell phone—will be equipped with a GPS receiver. Meanwhile, GPS has been employed in earthquake forecasting, ocean floor mapping, volcano monitoring, and a variety of mapping projects. For example, recognizing that GPS is a relatively inexpensive way of collecting data, the Federal Emergency Management Agency (FEMA) has used the system for damage assessment following such natural disasters as floods and hurricanes. GPS was used by workers to catalog items found in the enormous heaps of rubble at Ground Zero following the World Trade Center disaster of September 11, 2001.

Commercial applications now far outnumber military uses of the system. The sale of GPS services is now a multibillion dollar a year industry in the United States. What was born as a military system has become a national economic resource.

Because of the growing importance of GPS applications, other global navigation satellite systems are being implemented around the world. Russia's GLONASS system is operational as of this writing, and Europe's *Galileo* and China's *BeiDou* ("Compass") systems are under development.

Decimal Form of Latitude & Longitude: In part because of the great accuracy of even inexpensive GPS units, latitude and longitude are increasingly being reported in decimal form, such as 94°45.5′ W or even 94.7583° W rather than in its traditional form of 94°45′30″ W. Even the simplest handheld GPS units can provide location coordinates with a resolution of 0.01′ (1/100th minute) or even 0.001′ (1/1000th minute) of latitude and longitude (for reference, a difference in latitude of 0.001′ represents a distance of less than 2 meters [about 6 feet]).

Learning Check 2-9   **How does GPS determine locations on Earth?**

REMOTE SENSING

Throughout most of history, maps were the only tools available to depict anything more than a tiny portion of Earth's surface with any degree of accuracy. However, sophisticated technology developed in recent years permits precision recording instruments to operate from high-altitude vantage points, providing a remarkable new set of tools for the study of Earth. **Remote sensing** refers to any measurement or acquisition of information by a recording device that is not in physical contact with the object under study—in this case, Earth's surface.

Originally utilizing only airplanes, the use of satellites revolutionized remote sensing. We now have hundreds of satellites from dozens of countries perched high in the atmosphere where they either are circling Earth in a "low" orbit (an altitude of 20,000 kilometers [12,400 miles] or less) or in a lofty *geosynchronous orbit* (usually about 36,000 kilometers [22,400 miles] high) that allows a satellite to remain over the same spot on Earth at all times. These satellites gather data and produce images that provide communications, global positioning, weather data, and a variety of other information for a wide range of commercial and scientific applications—for example, see the box, "Focus: Using Remote Sensing Images to Study a Landscape."

Aerial Photographs

Aerial photography was almost the only form of remote sensing used for geographic purposes until the 1960s. The earliest *aerial photographs* were taken from balloons in France in 1858 and in the United States in 1860. During World War I (1914–1918), systematic aerial photographic coverage from airplanes was possible. In World War II (1939–1945) color aerial photographs became important, and by this time *photogrammetry*—the science of obtaining reliable measurements and mapping from aerial photographs—had developed.

Although satellite imagery has taken over the role of aerial photography for some applications, aerial photographs—now available in digital form from agencies such as the USGS—remain an important source of large-scale geographic imagery.

Orthophoto Maps: *Orthophoto maps* are multicolored, distortion-free photographic maps prepared from aerial photographs or digital images. Displacements caused by camera tilt or differences in terrain elevations have been removed, which gives the orthophoto the geometric characteristics of a map (Figure 2-20). Thus, an orthophoto can show the landscape in much greater detail than a conventional map, but retains the map characteristic of a common scale that allows precise measurement of distances. Orthophoto maps are particularly useful in flat-lying coastal areas because they can show subtle topographic detail in areas of very low relief, such as marshlands.

Visible Light and Infrared Sensing

One of the most important advancements in remote sensing came when wavelengths of radiation other than visible light were first utilized. As we will see in Chapter 4, *electromagnetic radiation* includes a wide range of wavelengths of energy emitted by the Sun and other objects (Figure 2-21). The human eye (and conventional photographic film) is only sensitive to the narrow portion of the electromagnetic spectrum known as *visible light*—the colors seen in a rainbow. However, a wide range of other wavelengths of energy—such as *X-rays*, *ultraviolet radiation*, *infrared radiation*, and *radio waves*—are emitted, reflected, or

Using Remote Sensing Images to Study a Landscape

▶ Ryan Jensen, Brigham Young University

Remote sensing provides geographers and other researchers with a great amount of spatial information that can be analyzed to improve our understanding of landscapes. Geographers can study spatial features using data collected from both aerial platforms (airplanes or helicopters) and orbital platforms (satellites). Popular websites and programs provide much remote sensing data for anyone to examine at no cost. These programs, such as Google Earth™, MapQuest™, and the U.S. Geological Survey National Map, are valuable tools that display data at a variety of scales, depending on the "Zoom" level you select. Spatial resolution (the amount of detail you can see) becomes finer the further you zoom into a landscape. The usefulness of remote sensing will only increase as human activities and natural processes change Earth's surface.

A Fluvial Landscape: To see how remote sensing data can capture characteristics of Earth's surface, look at the images of fluvial features (features formed by flowing water) in Figure 2-A. Landsat 5 acquired the data for the Costa Marques, Brazil, area in June 1984 and again in September 2001. Costa Marques is located along the Guapore/Itenez River that forms the border between Brazil and Bolivia. Landsat data are typically acquired in 30 × 30 meter pixels. That is, each image pixel covers an area of 30 meters by 30 meters (98 feet by 98 feet), or 900 square meters

(9687 square feet) over a surface area of 180 kilometers by 180 kilometers (111 miles by 111 miles). In each of the images, you can see fluvial features such as meanders, meander scars, oxbow lakes, and floodplain lakes.

The images can also be compared to study changes in the landscape. Notice that the rivers are much wider and there is more water on the floodplains in the 1984 scene than in the 2001 scene. Further, many of the oxbow lakes (Point A) had much more water in 1984 than in 2001. Meander scars that were very obvious in 1984 (Point B) are not as obvious in 2001. Sand that was not visible in 1984 (Point C) is visible in 2001. The 2001 image also shows evidence of human expansion in Costa Marques and along parts of the Guapore/Itenez River (Points D and E).

A More Detailed Look: When more detail is needed, finer spatial resolution data may be used to study an area. Such data are available from commercial

websites and programs such as Google Earth, MapQuest, and many others. For example, look at Point F in Figure 2-A. It is reasonable to assume that the river at that point will eventually create a new channel across the neck of the meander. This process cannot be clearly examined using the 30 × 30 meter Landsat data, but it can be examined using finer-resolution data. Figure 2-B shows a more-detailed image of the same meander neck at Point F. As you can see, there might be evidence of a new channel forming at Point F. In fact, in wet years, river water may flow through the meander neck.

Consider another example: Point B in Figure 2-B shows the same meander scars as the Landsat images in Figure 2-A (Point B). These features can be more fully examined using the detailed image in Google Earth, which can also be used to make measurements such as length and area. Knowing the area of the lake within the scar might be useful in determining how the lake changes from season to season or year to year.

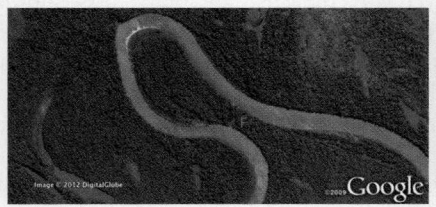
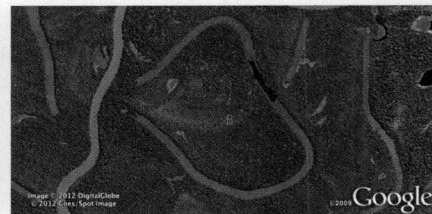

▲ **Figure 2-B** Fine-spatial resolution data showing a meander neck and meander scars in the Costa Marques area.

June 1984

September 2001

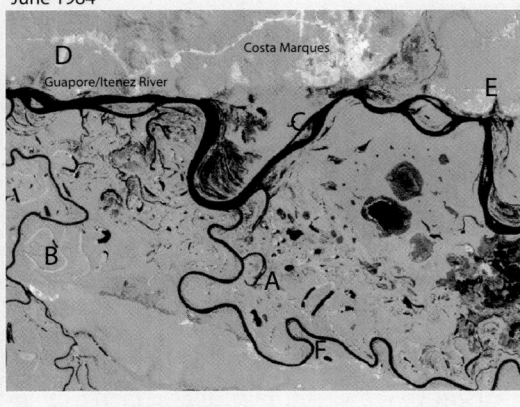
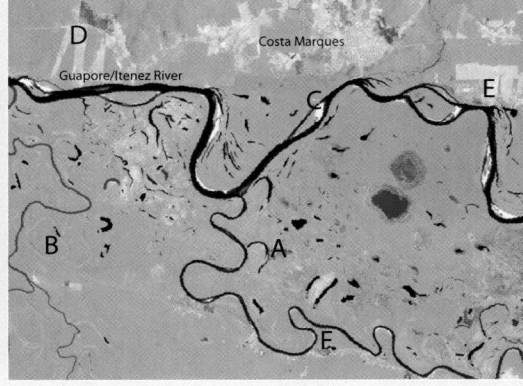

◀ **Figure 2-A** Two Landsat images acquired over the Costa Marques, Brazil, area in 1984 and 2001.

▲ **Figure 2-20** Orthophoto map of Wilmington, North Carolina; original scale: 1:24,000.

absorbed by surfaces and can be detected by special films or instruments, yielding a wealth of information about the environment.

Color infrared (color IR) imagery uses electronic sensors or photographic film sensitive to radiation in the *near infrared* portion of the electromagnetic spectrum—wavelengths of radiation just longer than the human eye can see. With color IR imagery, sensitivity to visible blue light is replaced by sensitivity to near infrared wavelengths. The images produced in this way, even though they are "false-color" images (e.g., living vegetation appears red instead of green), are still extremely valuable. Color IR film was first widely used in World War II when it was often called "camouflage-detection" film because of its ability to discriminate living vegetation from the withering vegetation used to hide objects during the war. Today,

one of the major uses of color IR imagery remains the identification and evaluation of vegetation (Figure 2-22).

Thermal Infrared Sensing

None of the middle or far infrared part of the electromagnetic spectrum, called *thermal infrared* (thermal IR), can be sensed with conventional digital cameras or traditional photographic film; as a result, special supercooled scanners are needed. Thermal scanning measures the radiant temperature of objects and may be carried out either day or night. The photograph-like images produced in this process are particularly useful for showing diurnal temperature differences between land and water, and between bedrock and alluvium, for studying thermal water pollution, and for detecting forest fires.

By far the greatest use of thermal IR scanning systems has been on meteorological satellites (for example, see "Focus: GOES Weather Satellites," in Chapter 6). Although the spatial resolution (the size of the smallest feature that can be identified) is not as high as some other kinds of sensing systems, it is more than sufficient to provide details that allow weather forecasting that is far more accurate and complete than ever before.

Learning Check 2-10 **What are the differences between "near infrared" and "thermal infrared" images, and what kinds of features might be studied with each?**

Multispectral Remote Sensing

Today, most sophisticated remote sensing satellites are **multispectral** or *multiband* (the various regions of the electromagnetic spectrum are sometimes called *bands*). These instruments detect and record many bands of the electromagnetic spectrum simultaneously. Thus, although traditional photographic film was sensitive to only a narrow band of visible radiation, a satellite equipped with a multiband instrument images the surface of Earth in several spectrum

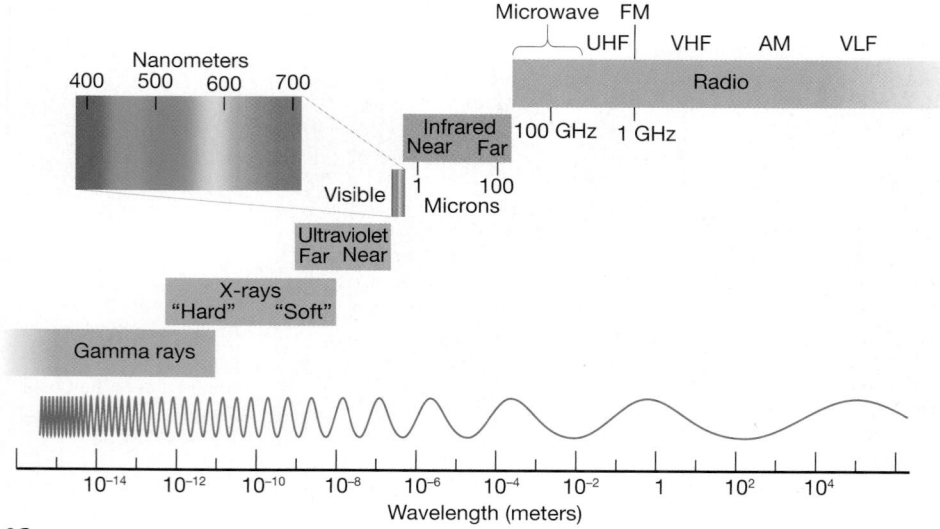

◄ **Figure 2-21** The electromagnetic spectrum. The human eye can only sense radiation from the visible-light region. Conventional photography also can use only a small portion of the total spectrum. Various specialized remote-sensing scanners are capable of "seeing" radiation from other parts of the spectrum.

▲ **Figure 2-22** Color infrared image from the Advanced Spaceborne Thermal Emission and Reflection Radiometer (ASTER) of the cities of Palm Springs, Cathedral City, and Palm Desert, California. In this false-color infrared image, healthy vegetation is shown in red; bare ground is shown in gray-blue.

regions at once—visible light, near infrared, middle infrared and thermal infrared—each useful for different applications.

A multispectral satellite image is digital, conveyed through a matrix of numbers, with each number representing a single value for a specific *pixel* (picture element) and band. These data are stored in the satellite, eventually transmitted to an Earth receiving station, numerically processed by a computer, and produced as a set of gray values and/or colors on a screen or hard-copy printout (Figure 2-23).

Landsat: The early NASA space missions (Mercury, Gemini, and Apollo) used multiband photography obtained through multicamera arrays. These imaging experiments were so successful that NASA then developed what was initially called the *Earth Resources Technology Satellite series* (*ERTS*) and later renamed *Landsat*. The 1970s and 1980s saw the launch of five Landsat satellites carrying a variety of sensor systems.

Landsat 7, which was launched in 1999, carries an instrument array called the Enhanced Thematic Mapper Plus that provides images in eight spectral bands with a resolution of 15 meters (49 feet) in the panchromatic band (sensitive to visible and near infrared wavelengths), 30 meters (98 feet) in the six narrow bands of visible and short infrared wavelengths, and 60 meters (197 feet) in thermal infrared (Figure 2-24). A description of the primary applications for the various bands is provided in Table 2-1. Although the satellite was originally designed for a life of less than 10 years, as of this writing Landsat 7 remains in active operation. The

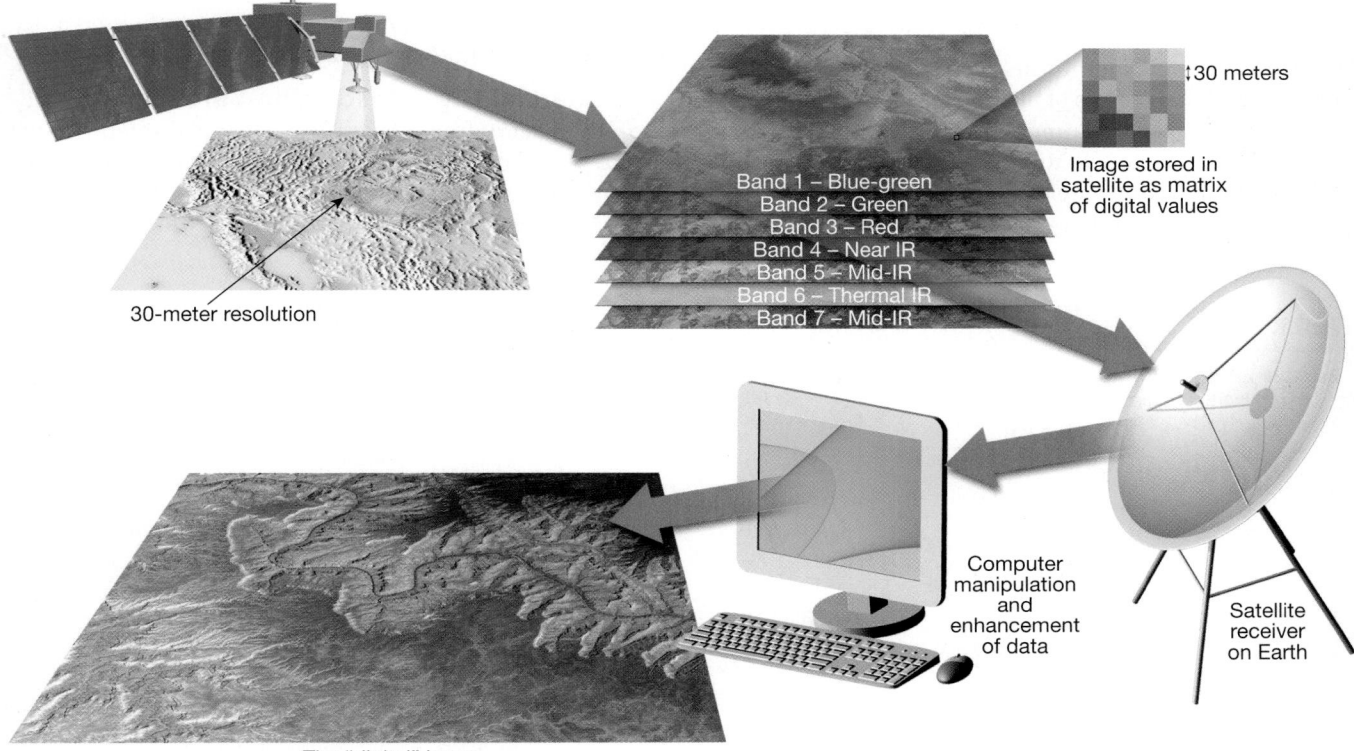

30-meter resolution

Band 1 – Blue-green
Band 2 – Green
Band 3 – Red
Band 4 – Near IR
Band 5 – Mid-IR
Band 6 – Thermal IR
Band 7 – Mid-IR

30 meters

Image stored in satellite as matrix of digital values

Computer manipulation and enhancement of data

Satellite receiver on Earth

The "digital" image

▲ **Figure 2-23** The sequence of events that takes place as a multispectral satellite scan is converted to a digital image.

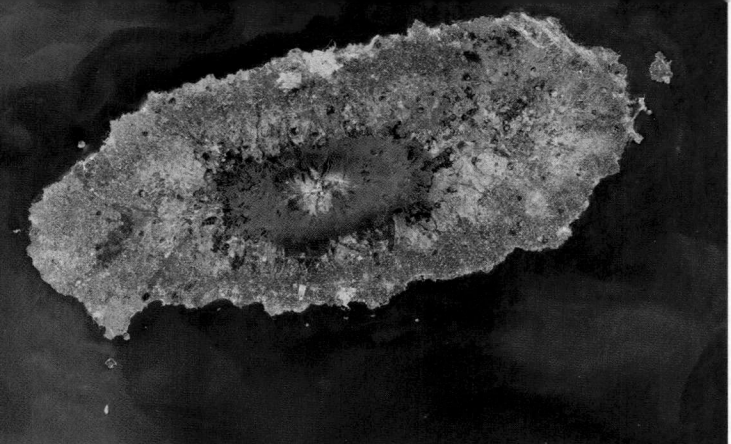

▲ **Figure 2-24** Landsat 7 satellite image of the island of Jeju-do, South Korea, taken with the Enhanced Thematic Mapper Plus in April 2000. The central shield volcano of Mount Halla rises to an elevation of 1950 meters (6398 ft). The provincial capital city of Jeju City is the gray patch along the northern shore. Note the subtle differences in the color of the water around the island.

▲ **Figure 2-25** Natural color satellite image showing the northeastern United States after an early season heavy snowstorm. This image was taken on October 30, 2011, with the MODIS (Moderate Resolution Imaging Spectroradiometer) instrument aboard NASA's Terra satellite.

next-generation Landsat satellite, known as the *Landsat Data Continuity Mission*, is scheduled for launch in 2013.

Earth Observing System Satellites: In 1999 NASA launched the first of its *Earth Observing System* (*EOS*) satellites known as *Terra*. The key instrument of these satellites is the Moderate Resolution Imaging Spectroradiometer (MODIS), which gathers data in 36 spectral bands (Figure 2-25) and provides images covering the entire planet every one to two days. Other devices onboard Terra include the Clouds and the Earth's Radiant Energy System (CERES) instruments for monitoring the energy balance of Earth, and the Multiangle Image Spectroradiometer (MISR) capable of distinguishing various types of atmospheric particulates, land surfaces, and cloud forms—with special processing, three-dimensional models of image data are possible.

The more recently launched EOS satellite, *Aqua*, is designed to enhance our understanding of Earth's water cycle by monitoring water vapor, clouds, precipitation, glaciers, and soil wetness. In addition to instruments such as MODIS, Aqua includes the Atmospheric Infrared Sounder (AIRS), designed to permit very accurate temperature measurements throughout the atmosphere.

In June 2011, NASA launched an Argentine-built satellite that included an instrument called *Aquarius* that enables scientists to monitor concentrations of dissolved salts near the surface of the ocean (see Figure 9-6)—improving our understanding of the effects of long-term climate change and short-term phenomena such as *El Niño* (discussed in Chapter 5).

Many satellite images are now easily available for viewing and downloading via the Internet from NASA and NOAA. For example, you can visit http://earthobservatory.nasa.gov/ and http://www.goes.noaa.gov/.

Commercial High-Resolution Satellites: In addition to imagery from government-operated satellites that is often available either free of charge or for a nominal fee (such as the GOES satellites, Landsat, and the EOS satellites), a number of satellites now offer very high-resolution

TABLE 2-1	Bands of the Landsat 7 Enhanced Thematic Mapper Plus			
Band Number	**Bandwidth (micrometers)**	**Spectral Region**	**Resolution (meters)**	**Applications**
1	0.45–0.52	Blue	30	Water penetration and vegetation analysis
2	0.52–0.60	Green	30	Vegetation analysis
3	0.63–0.69	Red	30	Vegetation analysis
4	0.77–0.90	Near IR	30	Biomass and soil analysis
5	1.55–1.75	Middle IR	30	Soil moisture and hydrologic analysis
6	10.4–12.5	Thermal	60	Geothermal resources and vegetation stress
7	2.08–2.35	Middle IR	30	Geologic features
8	0.52–0.90	Panchromatic	15	High-resolution images

imagery (up to 50- to 60-centimeter [20 to 24 in.] resolution) for commercial applications, including SPOT (*Satellite Pour l'Observation de la Terre*), *GeoEye-1*, *QuickBird*, and *WorldView*. The market for these images seems to be growing remarkably.

> **Learning Check 2-11**   **What is "multispectral" remote sensing?**

Radar and Sonar Sensing: All the systems mentioned so far work by sensing the natural radiation emitted by or reflected from an object and are therefore characterized as *passive systems*. Another type of system, called an *active system*, has its own source of electromagnetic radiation. The most important active sensing system used in the Earth sciences is **radar**, the acronym for *radio detection and ranging*. Radar senses wavelengths longer than 1 millimeter, using the principle that the time it takes for an emitted signal to reach a target and then return to the sender can be converted to distance information.

Initially, radar images were viewed only on a screen, but they are now available in photograph-like form (Figure 2-26). In common with some other sensors, radar is capable of operating by day or night, but it is unique in its ability to penetrate atmospheric moisture. Thus, some wet tropical areas that could never be sensed by other systems have now been imaged by radar. Radar imagery is particularly useful for terrain analysis in places of frequent cloud cover or thick vegetation, and for meteorology—especially in the real-time study and mapping of rainfall and severe weather (the use of specialized Doppler radar in meteorology is discussed in Chapter 7).

Another active remote sensing system, **sonar** (*sound navigation and ranging*), permits underwater imaging so that scientists can determine the form of that part of Earth's crust hidden by the world ocean.

GEOGRAPHIC INFORMATION SYSTEMS (GIS)

Cartographers have been at work since the days of the early Egyptians, but it was only with the introduction of computers in the 1950s that their technology has advanced beyond manual drawing on a piece of paper. Computers have provided incredible improvements in speed and image handling ability—as one example, all of the maps in this textbook were made with desktop computers. Of all the technological advances in cartography over the last few decades, however, one of the most revolutionary has been *geographic information systems*.

Geographic Information Systems (GIS): Geographic **information systems**—commonly called simply **GIS**—are computer systems designed to analyze and display spatial data. GIS involves specialized hardware and software that allow users to collect, store, retrieve, reorganize, analyze, and map geographic data from the real world (Figure 2-27).

Geographic information systems originally developed out of computer science, geography, and cartography, and they found their greatest early uses in surveying, photogrammetry, spatial statistics, and remote sensing. So commonly are they now used in geographical analysis that GIS has become a science of spatial analysis by itself, known as *geographic information science*, and the software has spun off a multibillion-dollar industry in spatial data and spatial information.

Geographic information systems are libraries of information that use maps to organize, store, view, and analyze information in an intuitive, visual manner. Just as an ordinary computer database management system can manipulate rows and columns of data in tabular form, a GIS allows data management using the link between data and a map. This means that the map and data are encoded, usually as numbers representing coordinates of locations at points on a grid covering the mapped area. Once the data and the map are inside the GIS, the user can organize or search the data using the map, or the map using the data. An important attribute is the capability of GIS data from different maps and sources, such as field data, map data, and remotely sensed images, to be registered together at the correct geographic location within a common

▼ **Figure 2-26** Radar image showing the topography of the island of Ireland. The data were gathered from the Shuttle Radar Topography Mission using synthetic aperture radar aboard Space Shuttle Endeavour in 2000. The data were processed with elevations represented by different colors, ranging from green for lowlands to white for high mountaintops. Shaded relief was added to highlight the topography.

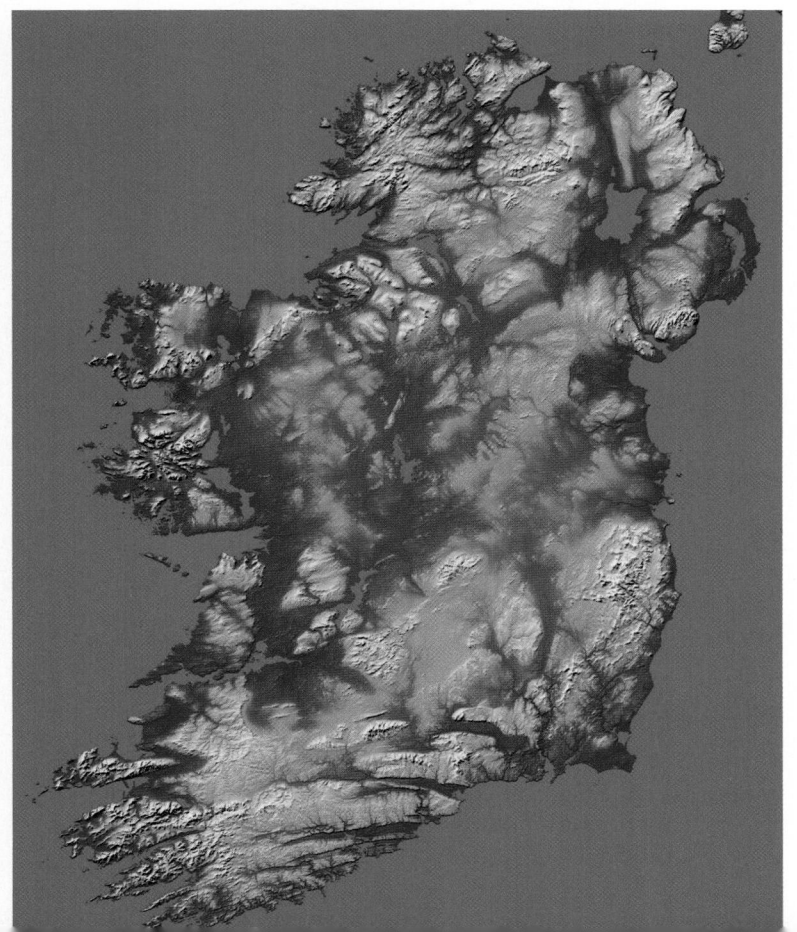

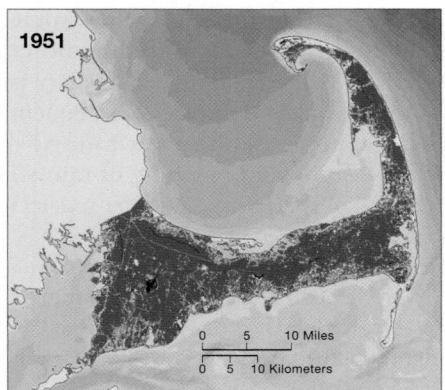
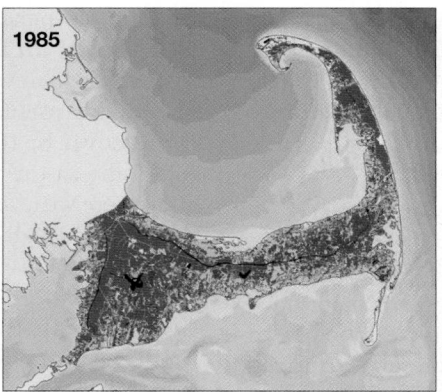
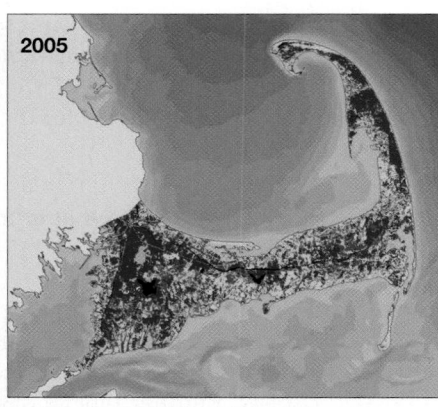

▲ **Figure 2-27** Land use changes on Cape Cod from 1951 to 2005, showing the expansion of residential housing and the accompanying loss of forest. Dark green shows areas of forest, yellow shows areas of residential housing, and red shows areas of commercial and industrial development.

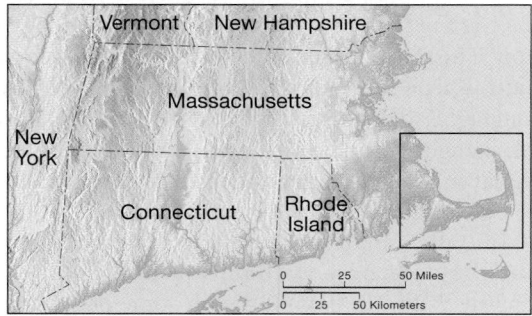

database, with a common map scale and map projection. In this way, one map layer, such as the locations of rivers, can then be cross-referenced to another, such as geology, soils, or slope.

Overlay Analysis: GIS is frequently used in overlay analysis, where two or more layers of data are superimposed or integrated. GIS treats each spatially distributed variable as a particular layer in a sequence of overlays. As shown in Figure 2-28, input layers bring together such diverse elements as topography, vegetation, land use, land ownership, and land survey. Details of these various components are converted to digital data and are synthesized onto a reference map or data set. Particularly useful images for the study of physical geography can be developed with GIS when data or satellite images are overlain on topography generated with a digital elevation model, offering oblique views of the landscape previously impossible to obtain (Figure 2-29).

Geographic information systems are used today in a diverse array of applications concerned with geographic location. Because they provide impressive output maps and a powerful methodology for analytical studies, GIS can bring a new and more complete perspective to resource management, environmental monitoring, natural hazards assessment—and a host of other fields. The growth of GIS is so rapid today that there are few fields of academic study, sectors of the economy, and divisions of government not using these powerful tools.

▲ **Figure 2-28** Much GIS work involves layers of spatial data superimposed upon one another.

Tools of the Geographer

As we have just seen, a vast array of maps, remotely sensed imagery, satellite data, and GIS applications are now available, making the tools of the geographer more widely used than ever before. The effective use of these tools, however,

Learning Check 2-12   **How is GIS different from GPS?**

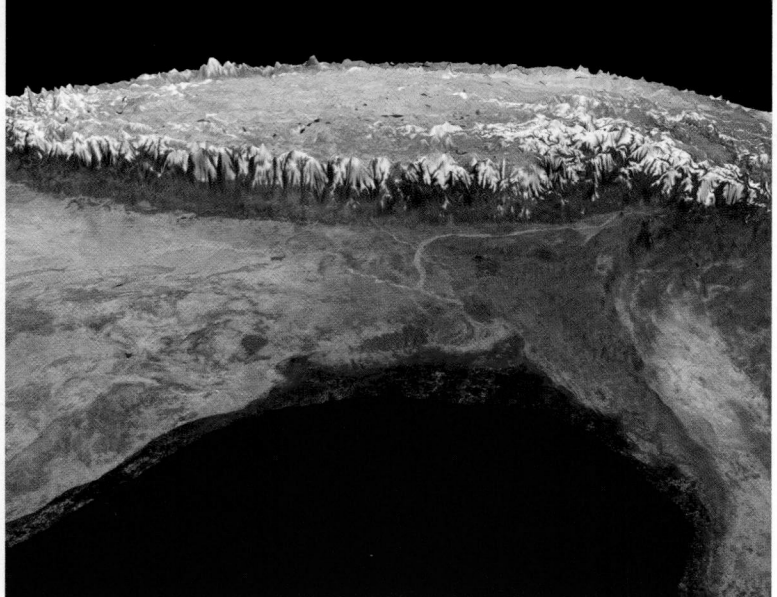

▲ **Figure 2-29** This oblique view of Bangladesh and the Himalayas was created by configuring MODIS images from the Terra satellite over a 50-times vertically exaggerated digital elevation model of the topography.

still entails thoughtful consideration. Although it is easy to download a satellite image or quickly print a handsome-looking map from the Internet, those images and maps may or may not be useful for analysis—and might actually be deceptive—unless care is taken to choose an appropriate map projection, an appropriate scale, and an appropriate selection of data to depict.

Choosing Effective Maps and Imagery: Certain types of imagery are useful for particular purposes.

For example, when studying major features of the lithosphere, high-altitude space imagery is especially valuable (Figure 2-30), although this type of imagery might have limited use in detailed local terrain studies where large-scale oblique aerial photographs or topographic maps might be more appropriate. For studying the hydrosphere, multiband satellite images of an entire hemisphere can tell us much about the water content in clouds, air masses, glaciers, and snowfields at a given time, although detailed conventional color images might be better for discriminating complicated shoreline features.

Vegetation patterns in the biosphere are often best appreciated with color infrared imagery—overall vegetation patterns on small-scale satellite images and detailed aerial photographs for crop and forest inventory studies. Features of human creation are generally not evident on very high-altitude imagery, but they become increasingly clear as one approaches Earth, and so survey patterns, transportation lines, rural settlements, and cities are best interpreted on imagery of intermediate or large scale. And in all cases, GIS may be used to uncover or highlight geographic relationships that may not be obvious when employing any single source of data or kind of imagery.

In using these tools, the geographer should never lose sight of our major objective: to better understand Earth. Such understanding does not come simply through the application of technology, however. Understanding comes from a carefully designed investigation, often using technology, but frequently supported by such traditional sources of information as field study and observation.

◀ **Figure 2-30** Natural color satellite image of the Yukon River Delta, Alaska, taken with the Enhanced Thematic Mapper Plus on Landsat 7.

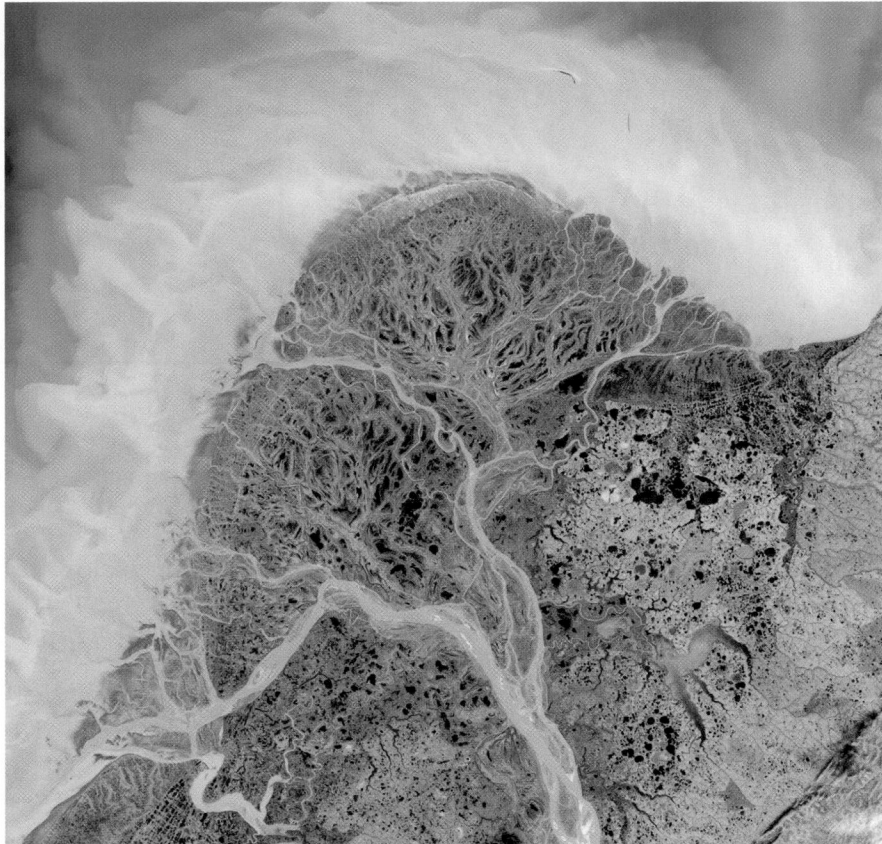

After studying this chapter, you should be able to answer the following questions. Key terms from each text section are shown in **bold type**. Definitions for key terms are also found in the glossary at the back of the book.

KEY TERMS AND CONCEPTS

Maps and Globes *(p. 31)*

1. How is a **map** different from a globe?
2. Why is it impossible for a map of the world to portray Earth as accurately as can be done with a globe?

Map Scale *(p. 33)*

3. Describe and explain the concept of **map scale**.
4. Contrast **graphic map scales**, **fractional map scales**, and **verbal map scales**.
5. What is meant by a map scale with a representative fraction of 1/100,000 (also written 1:100,000)?
6. Explain the difference between **large-scale maps** and **small-scale maps**.

Map Projections and Map Properties *(p. 35)*

7. What is meant by a **map projection**?
8. Explain the differences between an **equivalent** (equal area) **map projection** and a **conformal map projection**.
9. Is it possible for a map to be both conformal and equivalent?
10. What is a **compromise map projection**?

Families of Map Projections *(p. 36)*

11. Briefly describe the four major families of map projections: **cylindrical projections**, **planar projections**, **conic projections**, and **pseudocylindrical projections**.
12. Why is a **Mercator projection** useful as a navigation map? Why is it not ideal for use as a general purpose map?

13. What is a **loxodrome** (rhumb line)?

Conveying Information on Maps *(p. 39)*

14. Explain the concept of **isolines**.
15. What characteristics on maps are shown by *isotherms*, *isobars*, and **elevation contour lines**?
16. How does a **digital elevation model** (DEM) depict the landscape?

GPS—The Global Positioning System *(p. 42)*

17. Briefly explain how the **Global Positioning System** (**GPS**) works.

Remote Sensing *(p. 44)*

18. What is **remote sensing**?
19. Briefly define the following terms: *aerial photograph*, *photogrammetry*, *orthophoto map*.
20. What are some of the applications of color infrared imagery?
21. What are some of the applications of thermal infrared imagery?
22. Describe **multispectral** remote sensing.
23. Compare and contrast **radar** and **sonar**?

Geographic Information Systems (GIS) *(p. 49)*

24. Distinguish between GPS and GIS (geographic information systems).

STUDY QUESTIONS

1. Why are there so many types of map projections?
2. What kind of map projection would be best for studying changes in the amount of permafrost in the Arctic? Why? Consider both the general family of projection, and its properties such as equivalence and conformality.
3. Look at Figure 1-31, the world map of time zones shown in Chapter 1:
   a. Is this map an equivalent, conformal, or compromise projection? How can you tell?
   b. In which of the four families of map projections does it belong? How can you tell?

4. Isolines never just start or stop on a map—every isoline must close on itself, either on or off the map. Why?
5. A GPS receiver in your car simply calculates your current latitude and longitude. How can it use this basic locational data to determine your *speed* and *direction* of travel?
6. Describe one kind of application where radar imagery may be useful for geographical analysis. Explain the advantages of radar over other kinds of remote sensing in your example.

EXERCISES

1. On a map with a fractional scale of 1:24,000
   a. One inch represents how many feet? _____
   b. One centimeter represents how many meters?

      _____

   c. If the map is 18 inches wide and 22 inches tall, how many square miles are shown on the map?

      _____

2. If we construct a globe at a scale of 1:1,000,000, what will be its diameter? (You may give your answer in either feet or meters.)

3. Convert the following latitude and longitude coordinates presented in decimal form (as might be shown on a GPS unit) into their conventional form of degrees/minutes/seconds:

   42.6700° N = _____° _____′ _____″ N
   105.2250° W = _____° _____′ _____″ W

4. Convert the following latitude and longitude coordinates from their conventional form of degrees/minutes/seconds into decimal form:

   22°20′15″ N = _____° N
   137°30′45″ E = _____° E

Seeing Geographically

Look again at the image of Baja at the beginning of the chapter (p. 30). The Baja peninsula is about 160 kilometers (100 miles) wide in the north and about 80 kilometers (50 miles) wide at its southern tip. About how far has the dust blown to the west off of Baja? In what part of the image is the shape of the land least distorted? Most distorted? Could a single graphic map scale be used to accurately measure distances everywhere on this image? Why or why not?

MasteringGeography™

Looking for additional review and test prep materials? Visit the Study Area in MasteringGeography™ to enhance your geographic literacy, spatial reasoning skills, and understanding of this chapter's content by accessing a variety of resources, including geoscience animations, MapMaster interactive maps, videos, RSS feeds, flashcards, web links, self-study quizzes, and an eText version of *McKnight's Physical Geography: A Landscape Appreciation.*

EARTH IS DIFFERENT FROM ALL OTHER KNOWN PLANETS IN A

variety of ways. One of the most notable differences is the presence around our planet of an atmosphere distinctive from other planetary atmospheres. It is our atmosphere that makes life possible on Earth. The atmosphere supplies most of the oxygen that animals must have to survive, as well as the carbon dioxide needed by plants. It helps maintain a water supply, which is essential to all living things. It insulates Earth's surface against temperature extremes and thus provides a livable environment over most of the planet. It also shields Earth from much of the Sun's ultraviolet radiation, which otherwise would be damaging to most life forms.

The atmosphere is a complex and dynamic system. This chapter provides a foundation for understanding the atmosphere and the patterns and processes of weather and climate. Here we describe the composition and structure of the atmosphere, the basic elements or "ingredients" of weather and climate, and the most important "controls" or influences of weather and climate.

As you study this chapter, think about these key questions:

- **What major gases are found in the atmosphere, and what roles do small concentrations of variable gases and impurities play in weather and climate?**

- **What are the characteristics and significance of the various layers of the atmosphere, especially the troposphere?**

- **In what ways have humans altered the composition of the atmosphere, such as by releasing chemicals that deplete the ozone layer or by releasing other types of air pollution?**

- **What is the difference between "weather" and "climate," and what are the four elements of weather and climate and the seven most important controls of weather and climate?**

SIZE AND COMPOSITION OF THE ATMOSPHERE

Air—generally used as a synonym for atmosphere—is not a specific gas, but rather a mixture of gases, mainly nitrogen and oxygen. It often contains small quantities of tiny solid and liquid particles held in suspension in the air, as well as varying amounts of gaseous impurities.

Pure air is odorless, tasteless, and invisible. Gaseous impurities, on the other hand, can often be smelled, and the air may even become visible if enough microscopic solid and liquid impurities coalesce (stick together) to form particles large enough to either reflect or scatter sunlight. Clouds, by far the most conspicuous visible features of the atmosphere, represent the coalescing of water droplets or ice crystals around microscopic particles that act as condensation nuclei.

Seeing Geographically

This view looking west over the Gulf of St. Lawrence toward the Gaspé Peninsula in Canada was taken from the International Space Station. How thick does the visible part of the atmosphere appear in relation to the size of Earth itself? Where does the layer of clouds appear to be in relation to the overall thickness of the atmosphere?

Size of Earth's Atmosphere

The atmosphere completely surrounds Earth and can be thought of as a vast ocean of air, with Earth at its bottom (Figure 3-1). It is held to Earth by gravitational attraction and therefore accompanies our planet in all its celestial motions. The attachment of Earth and atmosphere is a loose one, however, and the atmosphere can therefore move on its own, doing things that the solid Earth cannot do.

Density Decrease with Altitude: Although the atmosphere extends outward at least 10,000 kilometers (6000 miles), most of its mass is concentrated at very low altitudes. More than half of the mass of the atmosphere lies below the summit of North America's highest peak, Mount McKinley (Denali) in Alaska, which reaches an elevation of 6.2 kilometers (3.8 miles), and more than 98 percent of it lies within 26 kilometers (16 miles) of sea level (Figure 3-2). Therefore, relative to Earth's diameter of about 13,000 kilometers (8000 miles), the "ocean of air" we live in is a very shallow one.

In addition to reaching upward above Earth's surface, the atmosphere also extends slightly downward. Because air expands to fill empty spaces, it penetrates into caves and crevices in rocks and soil. Moreover, it is dissolved in the waters of Earth and in the bloodstreams of organisms.

The atmosphere interacts with other components of Earth's environment, and it is instrumental in providing a hospitable setting for life. Whereas we often speak of human beings as creatures of Earth, it is perhaps more accurate to consider ourselves creatures of the atmosphere. As surely as a crab crawling on the sea bottom is a resident of the ocean, a person living at the bottom of the ocean of air is a resident of the atmosphere.

▼ **Figure 3-1** The atmosphere completely surrounds Earth in this composite satellite image; beyond the narrow blue band of the atmosphere is the blackness of outer space.

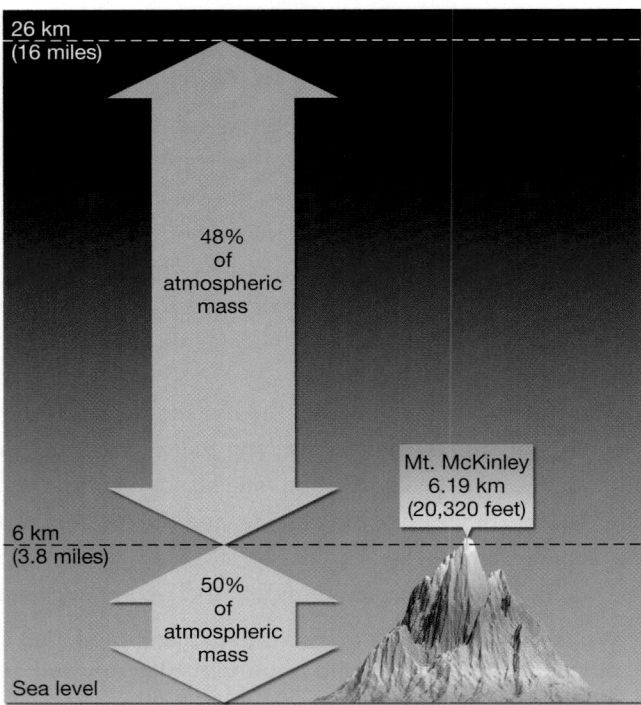

▲ **Figure 3-2** Most of the atmospheric mass is close to Earth's surface. More than half of the mass is below the highest point of Mount McKinley (Denali), North America's highest peak.

Learning Check 3-1 **What generally happens to the density of the atmosphere with increasing altitude? (Answer on p. AK-1)**

Development of Earth's Modern Atmosphere

The atmosphere today is very different from what it was during the early history of Earth. Shortly after Earth formed about 4.6 billion years ago, the atmosphere probably consisted mostly of light elements such as hydrogen and helium. By perhaps 4 billion years ago, this ancient atmosphere was changing as those light gases were being lost and as outgassing from volcanic eruptions added large amounts of carbon dioxide and water vapor, along with small amounts of other gases such as nitrogen. It is likely that arriving comets also contributed water to Earth's atmosphere. As ancient Earth cooled, most of the water vapor condensed out of the atmosphere, forming the world ocean.

By about 3.5 billion years ago, early forms of life—such as bacteria that could survive without oxygen—were beginning to remove carbon dioxide and release oxygen into the atmosphere. Over time, oceanic and terrestrial plants continued the transformation from a carbon dioxide-rich to an oxygen-rich atmosphere through the process of *photosynthesis* (photosynthesis is discussed in Chapter 10). Our modern atmosphere, therefore, was significantly influenced by life on Earth.

Composition of the Modern Atmosphere

The chemical composition of pure, dry air at lower altitudes (altitudes lower than about 80 kilometers or 50 miles) is simple and uniform, and the concentrations of the major components—the *permanent gases*—are essentially unvarying over time. However, certain minor gases and nongaseous particles—the *variable gases* and *particulates*—vary markedly from place to place or from time to time, as does the amount of moisture in the air.

Permanent Gases

Nitrogen and Oxygen: The two most abundant gases in the atmosphere are nitrogen and oxygen (Figure 3-3). Nitrogen makes up more than 78 percent of the total, and oxygen makes up nearly 21 percent. Nitrogen is added to the air by the decay and burning of organic matter, volcanic eruptions, and the chemical breakdown of certain rocks, and it is removed by certain biological processes and by being washed out of the atmosphere in rain or snow. Overall, the addition and removal of nitrogen gas are balanced, and consequently the quantity present in the air remains constant over time. Oxygen is produced by vegetation and is removed by a variety of organic and inorganic processes; its total quantity also apparently remains stable.

The remaining 1 percent of the atmosphere's volume consists mostly of the inert gas argon. These three principal atmospheric gases—nitrogen, oxygen, argon—have a minimal effect on weather and climate and therefore need no further consideration here. The trace gases—neon, helium, krypton, and hydrogen—also have little effect on weather and climate.

Variable Gases

Several other gases occur in sparse but highly variable quantities in the atmosphere, but their influence on weather and climate is significant.

Water Vapor: Water in the form of a gas is known as **water vapor**. Water vapor is invisible—the visible forms of water in the atmosphere, such as clouds and precipitation, consist of water in its liquid or solid form (ice). Water vapor is most abundant in air overlying warm, moist surface areas such as tropical oceans, where water vapor may amount to as much as 4 percent of total volume. Over deserts and in polar regions, the amount of water vapor is but a tiny fraction of 1 percent.

In the atmosphere as a whole, the total amount of water vapor remains nearly constant. Thus, its listing as a "variable gas" in Figure 3-3 means variable in location. Water vapor has a significant effect on weather and climate: it is

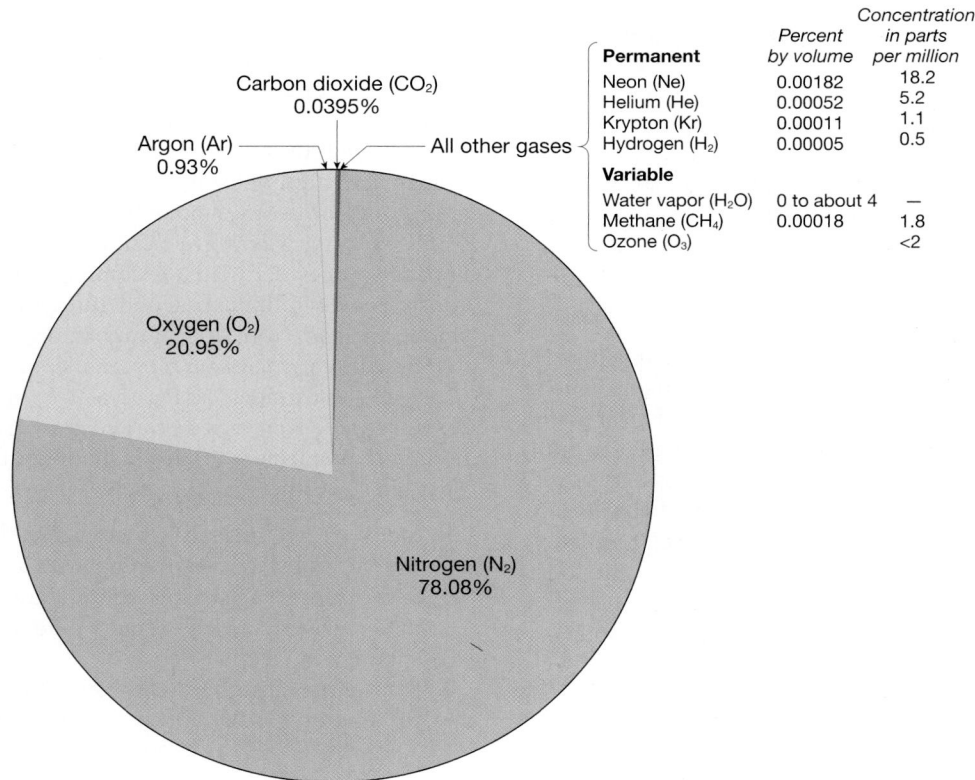

▲ **Figure 3-3** Proportional volume of the gases in the atmosphere. Nitrogen and oxygen are the dominant components. Although found in tiny amounts, some variable gases play important roles in atmospheric processes.

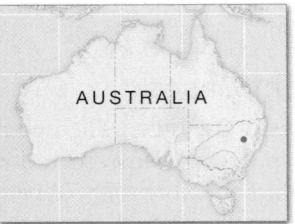

AUSTRALIA

◀ **Figure 3-4** Dust particles sometimes cloud the sky for a short time over a limited part of Earth's surface. On some occasions, as in this scene from the central part of New South Wales, Australia, the term "dust storm" is very appropriate, and the visual effect is imposing, if not menacing.

the source of all clouds and precipitation, and also plays important roles in a number of warming and cooling processes in the atmosphere.

Carbon Dioxide: Another important atmospheric component is **carbon dioxide** (CO_2). Like water vapor, carbon dioxide also has a significant influence on climate, primarily because of its ability to absorb thermal infrared radiation and thereby help warm the lower atmosphere. Carbon dioxide is distributed fairly uniformly in the lower layers of the atmosphere, although its concentration has been increasing steadily for the last century or so because of the increased burning of fossil fuels. The proportion of carbon dioxide in the atmosphere has been increasing at a rate of more than 0.0002 percent (2 parts per million) per year and at present is about 396 parts per million. Most atmospheric scientists conclude that the increased levels of CO_2 are causing the lower atmosphere to warm up enough to produce significant, although still somewhat unpredictable, global climatic changes (the topic of "global warming" will be presented in greater detail in Chapter 4).

Ozone: Another minor but vital gas in the atmosphere is **ozone**, which is a molecule made up of three oxygen atoms (O_3) instead of the more common two oxygen atoms (O_2). For the most part, ozone is concentrated in a layer of the atmosphere called the *ozone layer,* which lies between 15 and 48 kilometers (9 and 30 miles) above Earth's surface. Ozone is an excellent absorber of ultraviolet solar radiation; it filters out enough of this radiation to protect life forms from potentially deadly effects (a discussion of the recent thinning of the ozone layer follows later in this chapter).

Other Variable Gases: Methane (CH_4), introduced into the atmosphere both naturally and through human activity, absorbs certain wavelengths of radiation and so plays a role in regulating the temperature of the atmosphere. Tiny amounts of other variable gases—carbon monoxide, sulfur dioxide, nitrogen oxides, and various hydrocarbons—are also increasingly being introduced into the atmosphere by emission from

factories and automobiles. All of them can be hazardous to life and may possibly have some effect on climate.

Particulates (Aerosols)

The larger nongaseous particles in the atmosphere are mainly liquid water and ice, that form clouds, rain, snow, sleet, and hail. There are also dust particles large enough to be visible, which are sometimes kept aloft in the turbulent atmosphere in sufficient quantity to cloud the sky (Figure 3-4), but they are too heavy to remain long in the air. Smaller particles, invisible to the naked eye, may remain suspended in the atmosphere for months or even years.

The solid and liquid particles found in the atmosphere are collectively called **particulates** or **aerosols**. They have innumerable sources: some natural and some the result of human activities. Volcanic ash, windblown soil and pollen grains, meteor debris, smoke from wildfires, and salt spray from breaking waves are examples of particulates from natural sources. Particulates coming from human sources consist mostly of industrial and automotive emissions and smoke and soot from fires of human origin.

These tiny particles are most numerous near their places of origin—above cities, seacoasts, active volcanoes, and some desert regions. They may be carried great distances, however, both horizontally and vertically by the restless atmosphere. They affect weather and climate in two major ways:

1. Many are *hygroscopic* (which means they absorb water), and water vapor condenses around such *condensation nuclei*. This accumulation of water molecules is a critical step in cloud formation, as we shall see in Chapter 6.
2. Some either absorb or reflect sunlight, thus decreasing the amount of solar energy that reaches Earth's surface.

Learning Check 3-2 **What is the most abundant gas in the atmosphere? Does this gas play an important role in processes of weather and climate?**

VERTICAL STRUCTURE OF THE ATMOSPHERE

The next five chapters of this book deal with atmospheric processes and their influence on climatic patterns. Our attention in these chapters will be devoted primarily to the lower portion of the atmosphere, which is the zone in which most weather phenomena occur. Even though the upper layers of the atmosphere usually affect the environment of Earth's surface only minimally, it is still useful to have some understanding of the total atmosphere.

A given layer (altitude zone) of the atmosphere has different names, depending on the characteristic or feature under discussion. We begin with the layers of the atmosphere largely defined by temperature characteristics; later we introduce other overlapping layers defined by different characteristics.

Thermal Layers

Most of us have had some personal experience with temperature differences associated with altitude. As we climb a mountain, for instance, we notice a decrease in temperature. Until about a century ago, it was generally assumed that temperature decreased with increasing altitude throughout the whole atmosphere, but now we know that such is not the case.

As shown in Figure 3-5, the vertical pattern of temperature is complex, consisting of a series of layers in which temperature alternately decreases and increases. From the surface of Earth up, these thermal layers are called the *troposphere, stratosphere, mesosphere, thermosphere,* and *exosphere*. In addition to these five principal names, we also have special names for the top of the first three layers: *tropopause, stratopause,* and *mesopause*. We use the *–sphere* name when talking about an entire layer and the *–pause* name when our interest is either in the upper portion of a layer or in the boundary between two layers.

Troposphere: The lowest layer of the atmosphere—and the one in contact with Earth's surface—is known as the **troposphere**. The names *troposphere* and *tropopause* (the top of the troposphere) are derived from the Greek word *tropos* ("turn") and imply an overturning of the air in this zone as a result of vertical mixing and turbulence. The depth of the troposphere varies in both time and place (Figure 3-6). It is deepest over tropical regions and shallowest over the poles, deeper in summer than in winter, and varies with the passage of warm and cold air masses. On the average, the top of the troposphere (including the tropopause) is about 18 kilometers (11 miles) above sea level at the equator and about 8 kilometers (5 miles) above sea level over the poles.

Stratosphere: The names **stratosphere** and *stratopause* come from the Latin *stratum* ("a cover"), implying a layered or stratified condition without vertical mixing. If we describe the air in the troposphere as being "turbulent," we can describe the air in the stratosphere as being "stagnant." The

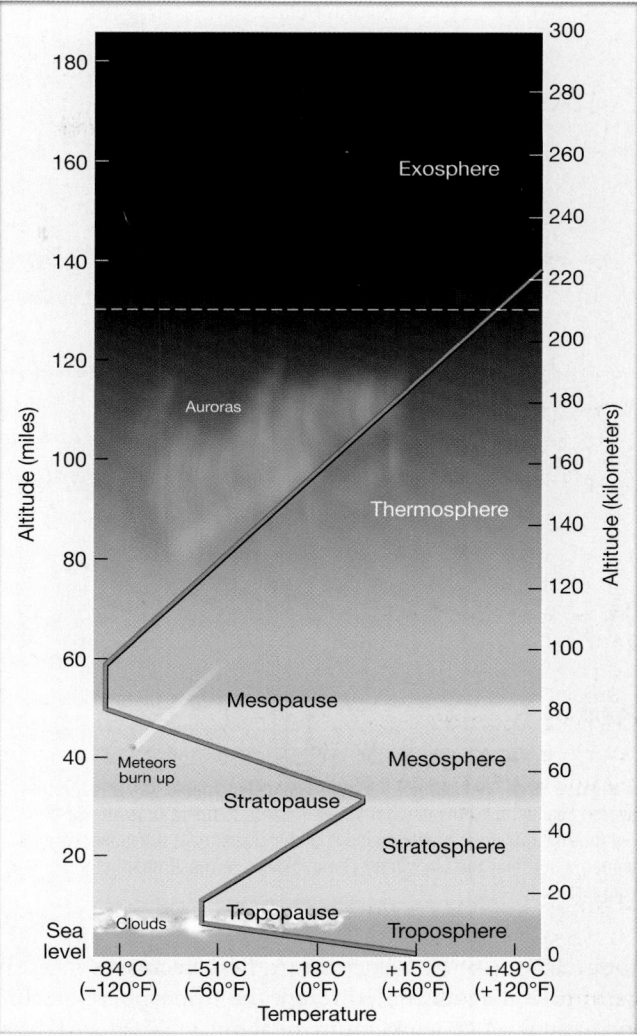

▲ **Figure 3-5** Thermal structure of the atmosphere. Air temperature (shown with the red line) decreases with increasing altitude in the troposphere and mesosphere and increases with increasing altitude in the stratosphere and thermosphere.

stratosphere extends from an altitude of about 18 kilometers (11 miles) above sea level to about 48 kilometers (30 miles).

Upper Thermal Layers: The names *mesosphere* and *mesopause* are from the Greek *meso* ("middle"). The mesosphere begins at 48 kilometers (30 miles) and extends to about 80 kilometers (50 miles) above sea level. Above the mesopause is the *thermosphere* (from the Greek *therm*, meaning "heat"), which begins at an altitude of 80 kilometers (50 miles) above sea level and has no definite top. Instead it merges gradually into the region called the *exosphere*, which in turn blends into interplanetary space. Traces of atmosphere extend for literally thousands of kilometers higher. Therefore, "top of the atmosphere" is a theoretical concept rather than a reality, with no true boundary between atmosphere and outer space.

Temperature Patterns in the Atmosphere: Air temperature changes with altitude (see Figure 3-5). Beginning at sea level, where the average global temperature is

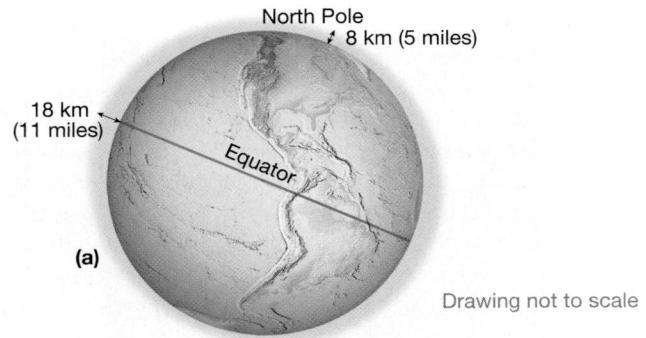

(a)

North Pole
8 km (5 miles)

18 km (11 miles)

Equator

Drawing not to scale

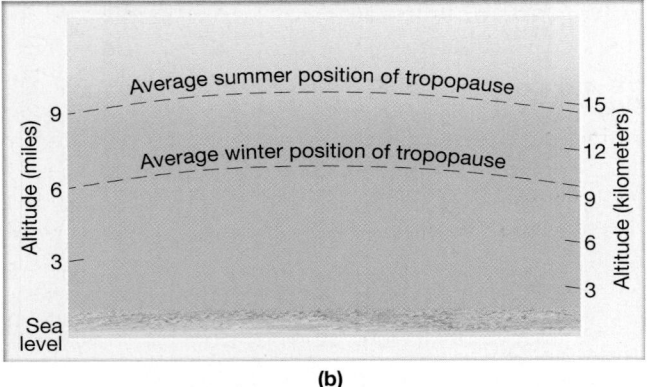

Average summer position of tropopause

Average winter position of tropopause

(b)

▲ **Figure 3-6** The depth of the troposphere is variable. (a) This thermal layer is deepest over the equator where surface temperatures are warm and thermal mixing is greatest, and it is shallowest over the poles. (b) It is deeper in summer than in winter. The thickness of the atmosphere is greatly exaggerated in (a).

about 15°C (59°F), temperature first decreases steadily with increasing altitude through the troposphere, declining to an average temperature of about −57°C (−71°F) at the tropopause. Temperature remains constant through the tropopause and for some distance into the stratosphere. At an altitude of about 20 kilometers (12 miles), air temperature begins increasing with increasing altitude, reaching a maximum at 48 kilometers (30 miles) at the bottom of the mesosphere, where the temperature is about −2°C (28°F). Then, the temperature decreases with increasing altitude all through the mesosphere, reaching a minimum at the top of that layer at an altitude of 80 kilometers (50 miles). Temperature remains constant for several kilometers into the thermosphere and then begins to increase until, at an altitude of 200 kilometers (125 miles), it is higher than the maximum temperature in the troposphere. In the exosphere, the normal concept of temperature no longer applies.

Each "warm zone" in this temperature gradient has a specific source of heat. In the lower troposphere, the heat source is the surface of Earth itself—solar energy warms the surface of Earth, and this energy is in turn transferred through a number of different processes to the troposphere immediately above. The warm zone at the stratopause is near the top of the ozone layer, where ozone is absorbing the ultraviolet energy from the Sun and thereby warming the atmosphere. In the thermosphere, various atoms and molecules also absorb ultraviolet energy from the Sun and

are thus split and heated. The "cold zones" that separate these warm zones are cold simply because they lack such sources of warmth.

Although the stratosphere, mesosphere, thermosphere, and exosphere have many interesting physical relationships, our attention in this book is directed almost entirely to the troposphere because storms and essentially all the other phenomena we call "weather" occur here. Occasionally, however, we must consider atmospheric conditions above the troposphere—especially the ozone layer.

Learning Check 3-3 What generally happens to the temperature of the atmosphere from the surface of Earth to the tropopause? What happens to temperature above the tropopause in the stratosphere?

Pressure

Atmospheric pressure can be thought of, for simplicity's sake, as the "weight" of the overlying air. (In Chapter 5, we explore the concept of pressure in much greater detail.) The taller the "column of air" above an object, the greater the air pressure exerted on that object, as Figure 3-7 shows. Because air is highly compressible, the lower layers of the atmosphere are compressed by the air above, and this compression increases both the pressure exerted by the lower layers and the density of these layers. Air in the upper layers is subjected to less compression and therefore has a lower density and exerts a lower pressure.

Air pressure is normally highest at sea level and decreases rapidly with increasing altitude. The change of pressure with altitude is not constant, however. As a generalization, pressure decreases upward at a decreasing rate, as Figure 3-8 shows.

At an altitude of 5.6 kilometers (3.5 miles), atmospheric pressure has decreased to 50 percent of its sea-level value. In other words, one-half of all the gas molecules making up the atmosphere lie below 5.6 kilometers, whereas 90 percent of them are concentrated in the first 16 kilometers (10 miles) above sea level (a typical altitude of the tropopause over the

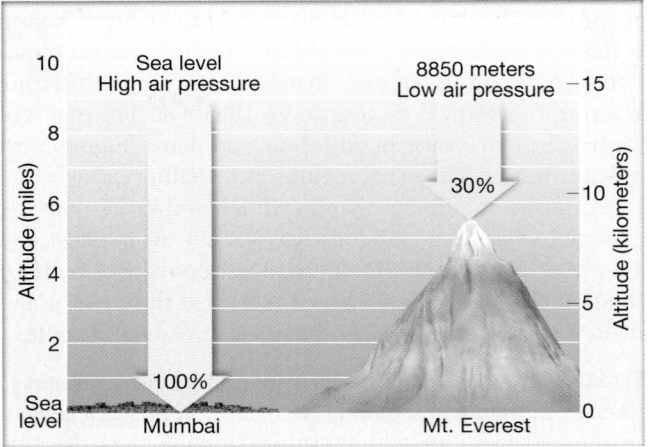

Sea level
High air pressure

8850 meters
Low air pressure

30%

100%

Mumbai

Mt. Everest

▲ **Figure 3-7** Atmospheric pressure is highest at sea level and diminishes rapidly with increasing altitude.

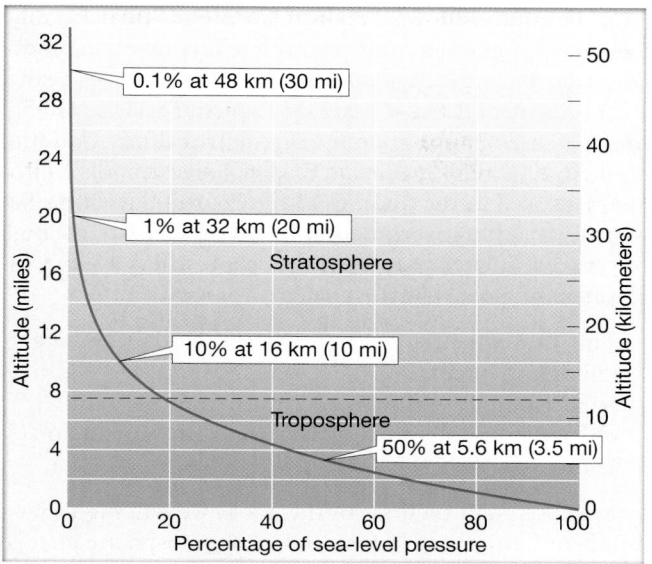

▲ **Figure 3-8** Air pressure decreases with increasing altitude, but not at a constant rate. Pressure decreases to 50 percent of sea level by an altitude of 5.6 kilometers (3.5 miles), and to just 1 percent of sea level at an altitude of 32 kilometers (20 miles).

tropics). Pressure becomes so slight in the upper layers that, above about 80 kilometers (50 miles), there is not enough to register on an ordinary barometer, the instrument used to measure air pressure. Above this level, atmospheric molecules are so scarce that air pressure is less than that in the most perfect laboratory vacuum at sea level.

Composition

The principal gases of the atmosphere have a remarkably uniform vertical distribution throughout the lowest 80 kilometers (50 miles) or so of the atmosphere. This zone of homogenous composition is referred to as the *homosphere* (Figure 3-9). The sparser atmosphere above this zone does not display such uniformity; rather, the gases are layered in accordance with their molecular or atomic weights—molecular nitrogen (N_2) below, with atomic oxygen (O), helium (He), and hydrogen (H) successively above. This higher zone is called the *heterosphere*.

Distribution of Water Vapor: Water vapor also varies in its vertical distribution. Most is found near Earth's surface, and generally diminishes with increasing altitude. Over 16 kilometers (10 miles) above sea level, the temperature is so low that any moisture formerly present in the air has already frozen into ice. At these altitudes, therefore, there is rarely enough moisture to provide the raw material to make even a wisp of a cloud. If you have done any flying, you may recall the remarkable sight of a cloudless sky overhead once the plane breaks through the top of a solid cloud layer below.

Two other vertical compositional patterns are worthy of mention here.

Ozone Layer: The **ozone layer**, which, as stated above, lies between 15 and 48 kilometers (9 and 30 miles) up, is sometimes called the *ozonosphere*. Despite its name, the ozone layer is not composed primarily of ozone. It gets its name because

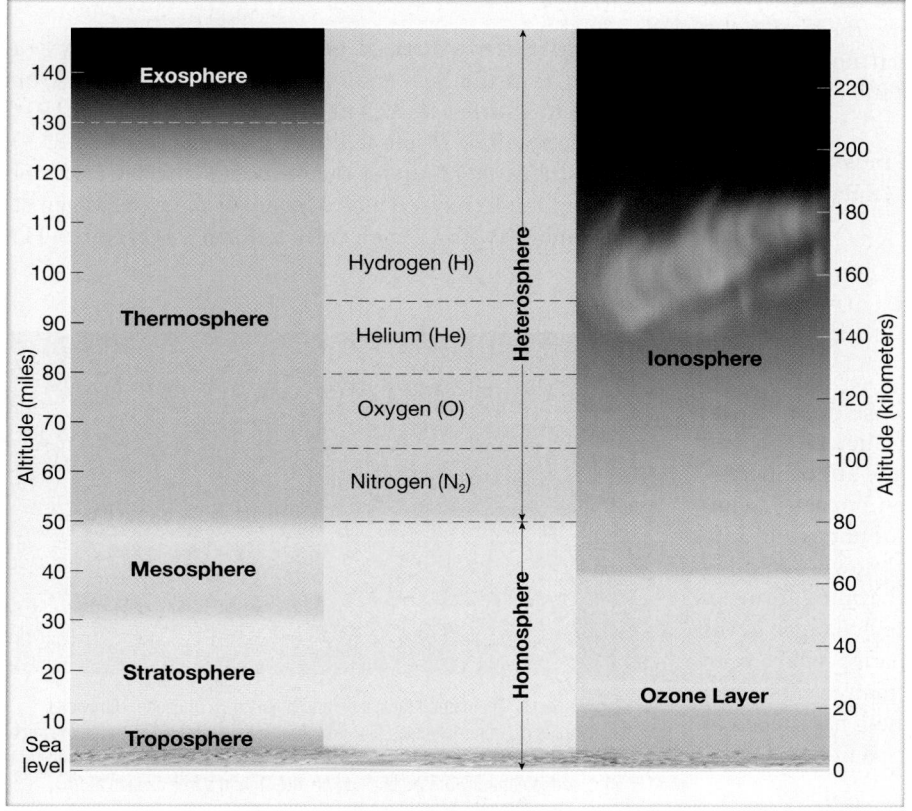

◄ **Figure 3-9** Relationships among the layers of the atmosphere. The *homosphere* is a zone of uniform vertical distribution of gases; in the *heterosphere* above, however, gases are distributed according to molecular or atomic weight, heavier below and lighter above. The ozone layer contains significant concentrations of ozone; the ionosphere is a deep layer of ions, which are electrically charged molecules and atoms.

▲ **Figure 3-10** The Aurora Borealis (Northern Lights) in the ionosphere, as seen from Bear Lake, Alaska.

that is where the concentration of ozone relative to other gases is at its maximum. Even in the section of the ozone layer where the ozone attains its greatest concentration, at about 25 kilometers (15 miles) above sea level, this gas only accounts for no more than about 15 parts per million of the atmosphere.

Ionosphere: The *ionosphere* is a deep layer of electrically charged molecules and atoms (which are called *ions*) in the middle and upper mesosphere and the lower thermosphere, between about 60 and 400 kilometers (40 and 250 miles). The ionosphere is significant because it aids long-distance communication by reflecting radio waves back to Earth. It is also known for its auroral displays, such as the "northern lights" (Figure 3-10) that develop when charged atomic particles from the Sun are trapped by the magnetic field of Earth near the poles. In the ionosphere, these particles "excite" the nitrogen molecules and oxygen atoms, causing them to emit light, not unlike a neon lightbulb.

Learning Check 3-4 **Is ozone the most abundant gas in the stratospheric ozone layer? Explain.**

HUMAN-INDUCED ATMOSPHERIC CHANGE

As the world population grows and the use of industrial technology intensifies, human activity has increasingly had unintended and uncontrolled effects on the atmosphere— effects seen around the globe. This human impact, in simplest terms, consists of the introduction of impurities into the atmosphere at a pace previously unknown—impurities capable of altering global climate or harming forms of life. The consequences of human-produced changes in the atmosphere—especially global climate change—have been a concern for atmospheric scientists for many years. Over the last decade, however, those consequences have received international attention not only from the scientific community but from the general public as well.

In February 2012, the United States Global Change Research Program, a joint scientific effort involving more than a dozen federal agencies and the White House, issued a report entitled *Our Changing Planet: The U.S. Global Change Research Program for Fiscal Year 2012*. Building on their 2009 report, *Climate Change Impacts in the United States*, as well as the findings of the *Fourth Assessment Report* of the Intergovernmental Panel on Climate Change (discussed in later chapters), the report offers a blunt assessment of global climate change:

> This fundamental research has shown that climate change is occurring, and that these changes can be attributed to human activities, and that climate change poses significant risks for both human and natural systems.

In subsequent sections of the book, we will highlight a number of aspects of human-induced atmospheric change and some of the steps that can be—and are being—taken to ameliorate them. The first major topic of global environmental change we spotlight is the depletion of the ozone layer.

Depletion of the Ozone Layer

As we saw earlier, ozone is naturally produced in the stratosphere. It is a form of oxygen molecule consisting of three atoms of oxygen (O_3) rather than the more common two atoms (O_2). Ozone is created in the upper atmosphere by the action of ultraviolet solar radiation on *diatomic oxygen* (O_2) molecules.

Animation
Ozone
Depletion

Natural Formation of Ozone: Ultraviolet (UV) radiation from the Sun is divided into three bands (from longest to shortest wavelengths): *UV-A*, *UV-B*, and *UV-C* (radiation will be discussed in more detail in Chapter 4). In the stratosphere, under the influence of UV-C, O_2 molecules split into oxygen atoms; some of the free oxygen atoms combine with O_2 molecules to form O_2 (Figure 3-11).

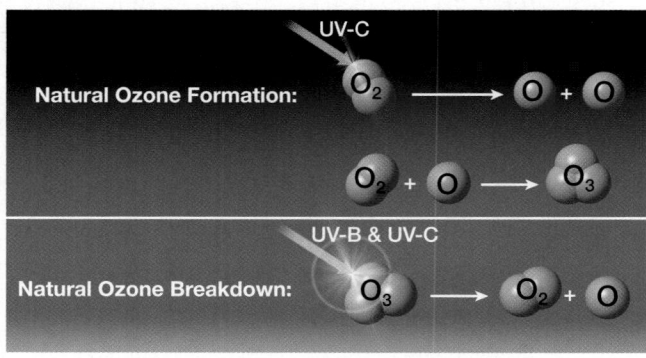

▲ **Figure 3-11** The natural formation and breakdown of ozone. Ultraviolet radiation splits oxygen molecules (O_2) into free oxygen atoms (O), some of which combine with other O_2 molecules to form ozone (O_3); also under the influence of UV light, ozone naturally breaks back down into O_2 and a free oxygen atom.

The natural breakdown of ozone in the stratosphere occurs when, under the influence of UV-B and UV-C, ozone breaks down into O_2 and a free oxygen atom. Through this ongoing natural process of ozone formation and breakdown, nearly all of UV-C and much of UV-B radiation is absorbed by the ozone layer. The absorption of UV radiation in this photochemical process also serves to warm the stratosphere.

About 90 percent of all atmospheric ozone is found in the stratosphere where it forms a fragile "shield" by absorbing most of the potentially dangerous ultraviolet radiation from the Sun. Ultraviolet radiation can be biologically harmful in many ways. Prolonged exposure to UV radiation is linked to skin cancer—both the generally curable nonmelanoma varieties as well as much more serious melanoma; it is also linked to increased risk for cataracts; it can suppress the human immune system, diminish the yield of many crops, disrupt the aquatic food chain by killing microorganisms such as phytoplankton on the ocean surface, and may have other negative effects still undiscovered.

Ozone is also produced near Earth's surface in the troposphere through human activities, forming one of the components of photochemical smog (discussed later in this chapter). However, it was a thinning of the stratospheric ozone layer first observed in the 1970s that triggered extensive research and monitoring.

The "Hole" in the Ozone Layer:

Video
Ozone Hole

Although natural factors can alter the ozone layer, the consensus among atmospheric scientists today is that the dramatic thinning of the ozone layer observed since the 1970s is due primarily (if not entirely) to the release of human-produced chemicals. Pioneering research by atmospheric scientists Sherwood Rowland and Mario Molina in the 1970s showed that the most problematic of these chemicals are **chlorofluorocarbons (CFCs)**, but other ozone-depleting substances include halons (used in some kinds of fire extinguishers), methyl bromide (a pesticide), and nitrous oxide. (In 1995, Rowland, Molina, and fellow scientist Paul Crutzen received the Nobel Prize for Chemistry for their research on ozone depletion.)

CFCs are odorless, nonflammable, noncorrosive, and generally nonreactive. For this reason, scientists originally believed CFCs could not have any effect on the environment. They were widely used in refrigeration and air-conditioning (the cooling liquid Freon™ is a CFC), in foam and plastic manufacturing, and in aerosol sprays.

Although extremely stable and inert in the lower atmosphere, CFCs are broken down by ultraviolet radiation once they reach the ozonosphere. Under the influence of UV radiation, a chlorine atom is released from a CFC molecule (Figure 3-12); the chlorine atom then reacts with ozone, breaking it apart to form one chlorine monoxide (ClO) molecule and one O_2 molecule. The chlorine monoxide molecule can then react with a free atom of oxygen, forming a diatomic oxygen molecule while freeing the

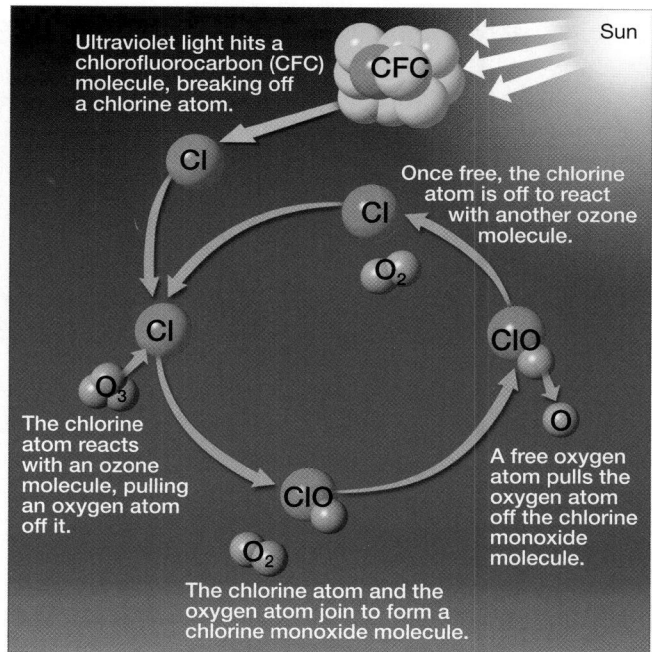

▲ **Figure 3-12** The destruction of ozone in the stratosphere by chlorine atoms derived from the breakdown of CFCs in the atmosphere. Chlorine atoms are unchanged by the reaction and can repeat the process. Thus, a single chlorine atom can destroy tens of thousands of ozone molecules.

chlorine atom to react with another ozone molecule. As many as 100,000 ozone molecules can be destroyed for every chlorine atom released.

Not only is the ozone layer thinning, in some places it has temporarily disappeared almost entirely. Monitored by a satellite instrument called *TOMS* (Total Ozone Mapping Spectrometer), the annual ebb and flow of the ozone layer has been continuously mapped since 1979 with a "hole" developing and persisting over Antarctica longer and longer each year (Figure 3-13). By the late 1980s, an ozone hole was found over the Arctic as well.

Antarctic Polar Vortex: Why is ozone depletion more severe over the polar regions, particularly Antarctica? In part because of the extreme cooling of Antarctica during the winter, a whirling wind pattern known as the *polar vortex* develops, effectively isolating the polar air from the atmosphere in lower latitudes. Within the stratosphere, ice crystals form thin *polar stratospheric clouds* (PSC). The presence of these clouds can dramatically accelerate the process of ozone destruction. The ice crystals in PSCs provide surfaces on which a number of reactions can take place, including the accumulation of chlorine-based molecules. With the return of sunlight in the polar spring (September in the Southern Hemisphere), UV radiation triggers the catalytic reaction, and ozone depletion begins.

The thinning of ozone over the Arctic has been generally less severe than over the Antarctic because over the North Pole, comparable atmospheric conditions to those in Antarctica are less well developed.

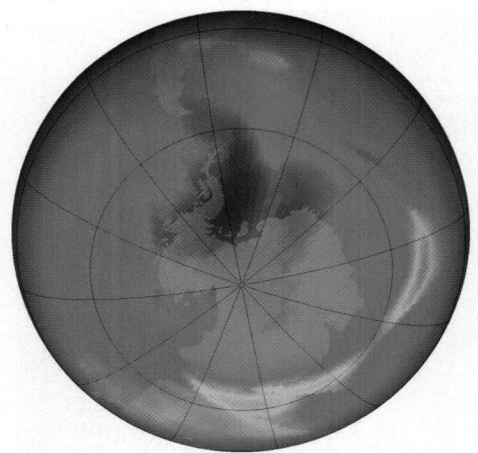 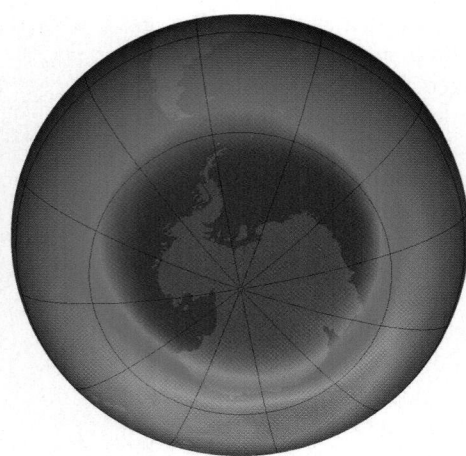

◀ **Figure 3-13** The Antarctic ozone hole in 1979 and 2012. The area over Antarctica, shown in dark blue and purple, has the lowest concentration of ozone. As a result of international efforts to limit the production of ozone-depleting chemicals, after growing in size since the 1970s, the Antarctic ozone hole seems to be stabilizing.

September 1979   September 2012

The UV Index: Stratospheric ozone depletion has been correlated with increased levels of ultraviolet radiation reaching ground level in Antarctica, Australia, mountainous regions of Europe, central Canada, and New Zealand. In part because of the increased health risks posed by higher levels of UV radiation reaching the surface, a *UV Index* has been established to provide the public with information about the intensity of UV radiation in an area (see the box, "People and the Environment: The UV Index").

The Montreal Protocol: These discoveries were sufficiently alarming that a number of countries including the United States banned the use of CFCs in aerosol sprays in 1978. A major international treaty—the Montreal Protocol on Substances That Deplete the Ozone Layer—was negotiated in 1987 to set timetables for phasing out the production of the major ozone-depleting substances. More than 189 countries, including all major producers of ozone-depleting substances, have ratified the proposal. Following stipulations of the treaty and its more recent amendments, the industrialized countries of the world banned CFC production by 1996. Moreover, the protocol signatories pledged a fund of more than $700 million to help developing countries implement alternatives to CFCs and end their production by 2010.

Even with the Montreal Protocol fully implemented, the ozone layer will not recover immediately because the reservoir of CFCs in the atmosphere may persist for 50 or 100 years—and because levels of human activity–released nitrous oxide remain high. The largest measurable Antarctic ozone hole was observed in 2006, and since then it appears that ozone loss is stabilizing. However, some studies suggest that it may be 2050 before recovery is well under way.

Addressing the depletion of the ozone layer is considered by many scientists to be an example of an environmental success story: a human-produced problem was identified, and a global strategy was implemented to counteract it. In 2009, an international team of scientists used computer models to predict what would have happened if CFC use had *not* been curtailed by the Montreal Protocol. Their study suggested that

without the ban on CFC use, by the year 2100 ozone levels over the tropics would have collapsed to levels found today only in the Arctic and Antarctic, exposing large populations in summertime to UV radiation levels more than three times greater than what is considered "very high" today.

Learning Check 3-5 **What is the explanation for the thinning of the ozone layer that has been observed since the 1970s?**

Air Pollution

In addition to diminishing stratospheric ozone, humans have altered the composition of the atmosphere in other ways as well, most obviously in the form of photochemical smog and other forms of air pollution.

The atmosphere has never been without pollutants. Many natural sources of contaminants are found in the atmosphere: smoke from wildfires, ash from volcanic eruptions, windblown dust, pollen from plants, and salt particles from breaking waves. Humans, however, have dramatically increased both the frequency and the magnitude of pollutants released into the atmosphere. By far the greatest problems are associated with cities because of the concentration of people and activities, and particularly from internal combustion engines and industry. The presence of pollutants in the air is most obviously manifest by reduced visibility due to fine particulate matter and associated water droplets. More critical, however, is the health hazard imposed by increasing concentrations of chemical impurities in the air.

With the advent of the Industrial Revolution in the 1700s, pollution became more widespread and intense, and by the twentieth century it was recognized as a major societal problem. Air-pollution "episodes" have often been death-dealing: 63 people killed over a five-day period in Belgium's Meuse Valley in 1930; 6000 illnesses and 20 deaths in Donora, Pennsylvania, during a week in 1948; 4000 deaths in London during a five-day ordeal in 1952. In addition to these isolated episodes, however, is the general increase in foul air over most large urban areas of the world.

The UV Index

In the United States, skin cancer is the most commonly diagnosed form of cancer. Unprotected exposure to ultraviolet (UV) radiation—whether it comes from the Sun or from tanning beds—is considered the most preventable risk factor for skin cancer. Skin damage from exposure to ultraviolet radiation is cumulative. It is especially important that young children—of all skin types—be protected from excessive Sun exposure through the use of sunscreens of SPF (Sun Protection Factor) 15 or greater and by taking other measures such as wearing hats and protective clothing.

The UV Index, or UVI, was developed in the 1990s by the Environmental Protection Agency (EPA) and National Weather Service of the United States to inform the public about levels of harmful ultraviolet radiation reaching the surface. The index was revised in 2004 to conform to international reporting standards coordinated by the World Health Organization.

UV Index Forecasts: UVI forecasts describe the expected level of ultraviolet radiation one day in advance using a scale of 1 to 11+, with 1 representing relatively low UV exposure risk and levels of 8 or greater representing relatively high UV exposure risk. Each risk category of the UVI is accompanied by recommended precautions that should be taken by people exposed to outside sunlight (Table 3-A).

The UV Index forecast for a city or region is based on concentrations of ozone in the atmosphere (measured by satellites), as well as the amount of cloud cover and the elevation of the location (Figure 3-A). In general, the lower the concentration of stratospheric ozone and the clearer the skies, the greater the level of harmful UV radiation that will reach the surface (Figure 3-B).

To find the UVI forecast for your location, go to http://www.epa.gov/sunwise/uvindex.html.

TABLE 3-A	UV Index Scale	
UVI Range	**Exposure Risk**	**Recommendations**
Less than 2	Low	If you burn easily or are exposed to reflections off snow or water, take precautions, such as wearing sunglasses and applying sunscreen.
3–5	Moderate	Protect yourself while outside by wearing protective clothing, hats, and sunglasses. Limit midday Sun exposure.
6–7	High	Apply sunscreen of SPF 15 or greater. Use sunglasses and wide-brim hat. Reduce midday Sun exposure.
8–10	Very High	Take extra precautions. Use SPF 15+ sunscreen liberally. Minimize Sun exposure between 10 A.M. and 4 P.M.
11 or greater	Extreme	Take all precautions. Avoid midday Sun exposure between 10 A.M. and 4 P.M. Reapply SPF 15+ sunscreen liberally every two hours.

Source: U.S. Environmental Protection Agency, SunWise Program.

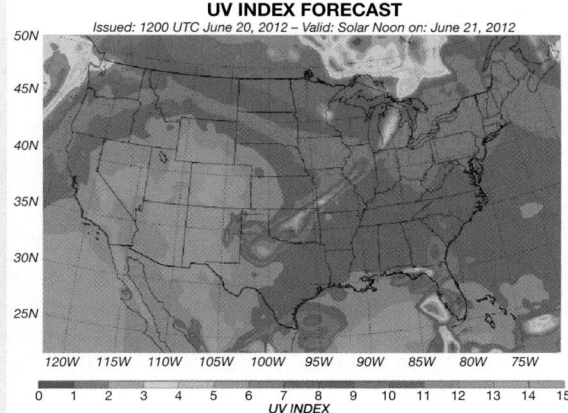

▲ **Figure 3-A** UV Index forecast map.

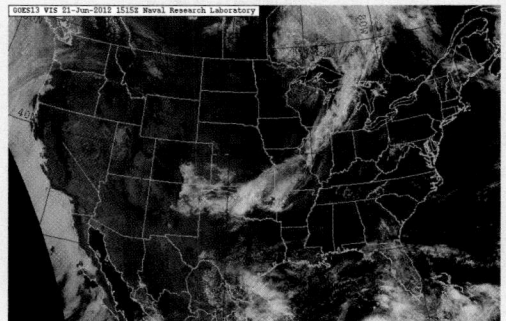

▲ **Figure 3-B** Visible light satellite image showing the location of cloud cover over the United States at the time of the UVI forecast in Figure 3-A. The areas of cloudiness were generally forecast to have lower amounts of UV radiation reaching the surface than areas with clearer skies.

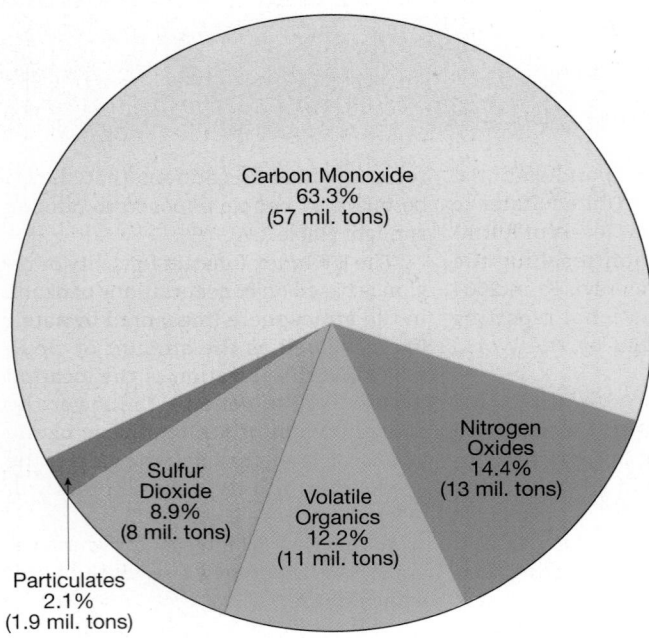

▲ **Figure 3-14** The emissions of primary atmospheric pollutants by the United States in 2010. Values given represent the percentage of the total weight of pollutants emitted, estimated at 90 million tons in 2010.

Primary and Secondary Pollutants: Two general categories of air pollutants can be identified. **Primary pollutants** are contaminants released directly into the air, such as particulates, sulfur compounds, nitrogen compounds, carbon oxides, and hydrocarbons. In the United States alone, about 90 million tons of primary pollutants were released in 2010 (Figure 3-14). **Secondary pollutants**, such as photochemical smog, are not released directly into the air but instead form as a consequence of chemical reactions or other processes in the atmosphere.

Carbon Monoxide: Carbon monoxide (CO) is the most plentiful primary pollutant, formed by the incomplete combustion of carbon-based fuels, especially by motor vehicles. Because this gas is odorless and colorless, people exposed to carbon monoxide in confined spaces can be quickly overcome after CO enters the bloodstream and decreases the amount of oxygen available to their brain and other organs.

Nitrogen Compounds: Nitric oxide (NO) is a gas that can form in water and soil as a natural by-product of biological processes; it generally breaks down quite quickly. However, NO may also form through combustion that takes place at high temperatures and pressures—such as in an automobile engine. Nitric oxide reacts in the atmosphere to form nitrogen dioxide (NO$_2$) a corrosive gas that gives some polluted air its yellow and reddish-brown color. Although NO$_2$ itself tends to break down quickly, it may in turn react under the influence of sunlight to form several different components of smog.

Sulfur Compounds: A large portion of the sulfur compounds found in the atmosphere are of natural origin,

released from volcanoes or hydrothermal vents such as those in Yellowstone National Park—hydrogen sulfide (H$_2$S) with its familiar "rotten egg" smell is one example of this. However, especially over the last century, human activity has increased the release of sulfur compounds into the atmosphere, primarily through the burning of fossil fuels such as coal and petroleum. Sulfur is one of the minor impurities in coal and oil; when those fuels are burned, sulfur compounds such as sulfur dioxide SO$_2$ are released. Sulfur dioxide itself is a lung irritant and corrosive, but it also may react in the atmosphere to produce secondary pollutants such as sulfur trioxide (SO$_3$) and sulfuric acid (H$_2$SO$_4$)—one of the contributors to acid rain (discussed in Chapter 6).

Particulates: Particulates (or aerosols) are tiny solid particles or liquid droplets suspended in the air. Primary sources of particulates from human activities include smoke from combustion and dust emitted from industrial activities. The concentration of particulates may also increase through secondary processes, such as when small particles coalesce to form larger particles, or when liquid droplets develop around condensation nuclei. It appears that many of the health hazards associated with particulates are greatest when the particles are less than 2.5 micrometers (<2.5 millionths of a meter) in diameter. In 1997, the U.S. Environmental Protection Agency revised its regulations to take into account the harmful effects of such fine particulates, known as PM$_{2.5}$, although recent research indicates that still smaller particulates may also pose a significant hazard.

Photochemical Smog: A number of gases react to ultraviolet radiation in strong sunlight to produce secondary pollutants, making up what is known as **photochemical smog** (Figure 3-15). (The word "smog" was originally derived from the combination of the words *smoke* and *fog*; photochemical smog usually includes neither.) Nitrogen

▼ **Figure 3-15** Photochemical smog over the city of Santiago, Chile. The top of the temperature inversion layer trapping the smog is seen just below the peaks of the nearby mountains.

Top of temperature inversion

dioxide and hydrocarbons (also known as *volatile organic compounds* or *VOC*)—both of which can result from the incomplete burning of fuels such as gasoline—are major contributors to photochemical smog. Nitrogen dioxide breaks down under ultraviolet radiation to form nitric oxide, which may then react with VOC to form peroxyacetyl nitrate (PAN), which has become a significant cause of crop and forest damage in some areas.

The breakdown of NO_2 into NO also frees an oxygen atom that can react with O_2 molecules to form ozone—the main component of photochemical smog. Ozone has an acrid, biting odor that is distinctive of photochemical smog, causing damage to vegetation, corroding building materials (such as paint, rubber, plastics), and damaging sensitive tissues in humans (eyes, lungs, noses).

The state of the atmosphere is also an important determinant of the level of air pollution, especially photochemical smog. If there is considerable air movement, the pollutants can be quickly and widely dispersed. On the other hand, stagnant air allows for a rapid accumulation of pollutants. Thus, air pollution is particularly notable when high-pressure conditions prevail, when there is little surface wind flow and air subsiding from above. If the air is particularly stable, *temperature inversions* (cooler air below warmer) develop, functioning as "stability lids" that inhibit updrafts and general air movement (temperature inversions are discussed in Chapter 4). Almost all the cities that are persistently among the smoggiest in the world, such as Mexico City and Los Angeles, are characterized by a high frequency of temperature inversions (see Figure 3-15).

Consequences of Anthropogenic Air Pollution: Although the effects of atmospheric pollutants vary, in general all forms of air pollution adversely affect lung function. Carbon monoxide, sulfur dioxide, and particulates can contribute to cardiovascular disease, while prolonged exposure to some particulates may promote lung cancer. Nitrogen oxides and sulfur dioxide are the principal contributors to acid rain. Tropospheric ozone damages crops and trees, and it is now the most widespread air pollutant and continues on a rising trend. The Environmental Protection Agency (EPA) reports that perhaps one-fifth of all hospital cases involving respiratory illness in the summer are a consequence of ozone exposure.

In the last few decades in the United States, there has been a downward trend in the emission of nearly all pollutants except ozone, largely as a result of increasingly stringent emission standards imposed by the EPA. Although significant steps are now being taken to reverse the growth of atmospheric pollution, as global population expands, the pollutant load expands with it, and an ongoing effort on the part of all countries will be required to curtail the problem.

Learning Check 3-6 **Is photochemical smog considered a *primary pollutant* or a *secondary pollutant* in the atmosphere? Why?**

Energy Production and the Environment

Although the release of many air pollutants has decreased in recent years, the release of the carbon dioxide through the burning of fossil fuels is still on the rise. The full significance of this increase will be explored in subsequent chapters, but here we begin our look at a topic that underlies this and many of the environmental and economic challenges faced by the world today: our growing demand for energy to power our homes, automobiles, and industries.

In the chapters that follow, we will explore a number of the methods used to generate power—from our long-standing use of fossil fuels such as coal and oil, to renewable methods such as wind and tides—describing the technology, as well as the virtues and drawbacks of each. There is no simple solution to our demand for energy. However, understanding how energy production fits in with physical geography and Earth's interconnected systems can help us assess the long-term consequences of our decisions.

We begin with the box, "Energy for the 21st Century: Our Continuing Dependence on Fossil Fuels," on page 68.

WEATHER AND CLIMATE

Now that we have described the composition and structure of the atmosphere, we turn more specifically to the broad set of processes operating within this ocean of air.

Weather: The vast and invisible atmospheric envelope is energized by solar radiation, stimulated by earthly motions, and affected by contact with Earth's surface. The atmosphere reacts by producing an infinite variety of conditions and phenomena known collectively as *weather*—the study of weather is known as *meteorology*. The term **weather** refers to short-run atmospheric conditions that exist for a given time in a specific area. It is the sum of temperature, humidity, cloudiness, precipitation, pressure, winds, storms, and other atmospheric variables for a short period of time. Thus, we speak of the weather of the moment, the week, the season, or perhaps even of the year or the decade.

Climate: Weather is in an almost constant state of change, sometimes in seemingly erratic fashion, yet in the long view, it is possible to generalize the variations into a composite pattern that is termed *climate*. **Climate** is the aggregate of day-to-day weather conditions over a long period of time. It encompasses not only the average characteristics, but also the variations and extremes of weather. To describe the climate of an area requires weather information over an extended period, normally at least three decades.

Weather and climate, then, are related but not synonymous terms. The distinction between them is the difference between immediate specifics and protracted generalities. As a whimsical country philosopher once said, "Climate is what you expect; weather is what you get." Stated more sarcastically, "It is the climate that attracts people to a location, and the weather that makes them leave."

Weather and climate have direct and obvious influences on agriculture, transportation, and human life in general.

Our Continuing Dependence on Fossil Fuels

▶ Matthew T. Huber, Syracuse University

Fossil fuels (coal, oil, and natural gas) are the product of millions of years of accumulated solar energy absorbed in plant life and trapped as hydrocarbon matter underneath Earth's surface.

The Historical Significance of Fossil Fuels:

Before the use of fossil fuels, people did most mechanical work using their own muscle power and that of animals both ultimately derived from the energy of sunshine stored in plants through photosynthesis and the animals that consume plants (discussed in Chapter 10). The historic shift from solar energy to fossil fuels led to machinery that ran without the force of muscle power, such as steam engines, and eventually to electrical power generation and automobiles. This change allowed for dramatic gains in labor productivity and the growth of transportation networks. Moreover, the increasing reliance on fossil fuels freed up thousands of acres that were previously used for energy, such as farmland used to grow feed for working animals and forest land that provided wood and charcoal for heating, cooking, and metal production.

Because of these benefits, the world today derives around 80 percent of its energy from fossil fuels (Figure 3-C).

The Consequences of Fossil Fuel Use:

Despite the benefits of fossil fuels, they are not without drawbacks. First, the combustion of coal, oil, and gas produces enormous amounts of pollution. For example, sulfur dioxide (SO_2) from coal-fired power plants causes acid rain (discussed in Chapter 6). All fossil fuel use emits carbon dioxide (CO_2), a greenhouse gas associated with global climate change (discussed in Chapter 4). Moreover, the uneven distribution of fossil fuels creates geopolitical conflict over access to, and control over, energy resources. Although this problem is most visible in conflicts over oil (as in the Middle East), conflicts over natural gas pipelines in the Ukraine and North America and concerns about "fracking" in the United States (see Chapter 13) or mountaintop coal mining in Appalachia represent other examples of the contentious nature of fossil fuel development.

Alternative Energy:

Since at least the 1970s, support for switching to *alternative energy* has been growing among scientists, policymakers, and the public. Most alternatives to fossil fuels generate electricity. Most electricity today is generated by the combustion of coal or gas to create steam that turns a turbine. For now, the transportation sector runs mostly on liquid fuels derived from crude oil. The only liquid fuel alternatives are biofuels (see Chapter 10), often derived from crops grown on farmland, thus competing with food production.

Many alternative energy sources show promise but also have limitations. Nuclear power is the largest alternative energy source, but it brings risks of calamitous accidents, such as the Fukushima disaster in Japan following the tsunami of 2011 (see Chapter 20), and produces radioactive waste that is difficult to dispose of. Hydroelectric power uses dams and the power of falling water to generate electricity (see Chapter 16). Dams, however, degrade river ecosystems and often displace thousands of people. Wind power recently has been the fastest growing alternative (see Chapter 5), but its capacity to generate electricity ultimately depends on when the wind blows. Solar power harnesses direct sunlight to generate electricity either through photovoltaic cells or the boiling of water to create steam (see Chapter 4). Like wind, solar is intermittent, and it is not available when it is dark or cloudy. Furthermore, unlike fossil fuels that can be easily transported anywhere, some alternatives such as geothermal (see Chapter 17) and tidal power (see Chapter 20), as well as large installations of wind and solar power generation, may only be available in locations far from population centers, such as deserts for solar and unobstructed topography for wind.

Most importantly, the main barriers to an "energy transition" away from fossil fuels are political and economic (see Chapter 8). Historically, fossil fuels are simply much cheaper making it difficult for alternative energy to be economically viable when only short-term costs are considered. Fossil fuel energy companies are also some of the largest and most profitable corporations in the world, and some have used their political influence to inhibit policies that might spur a shift toward alternative energy.

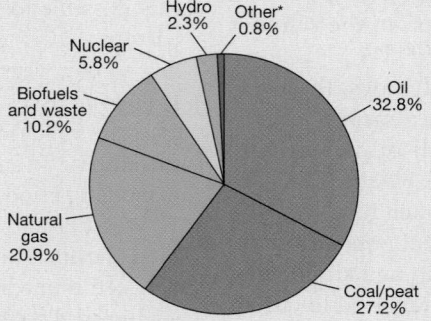

▲ **Figure 3-C** Sources of global energy production in 2009. "Other" includes geothermal, solar, wind, and tidal power. (Source: International Energy Agency, 2011, *Key World Energy Statistics 2011*.)

Moreover, climate is a significant factor in the development of all major aspects of the physical landscape—soils, vegetation, animal life, hydrography, and topography.

Because and weather are generated in the atmosphere, our goal in studying the atmosphere is to understand the distribution and characteristics of climatic types over Earth. To achieve this understanding, we must consider in detail many of the processes that take place in the atmosphere. Although our ultimate goal is an understanding of long-run atmospheric conditions (climate), we will spend the next four chapters gaining an appreciation for the dynamics involved in the momentary state of the atmosphere (weather).

> **Learning Check 3-7** **What is the difference between *weather* and *climate*?**

The Elements of Weather and Climate

The atmosphere is a complex medium, and its mechanisms and processes are sometimes very complicated. Its nature, however, is generally expressed in terms of only a few measurable variables.

These variables can be thought of as the **elements of weather and climate**. The most important are (1) temperature, (2) moisture content, (3) pressure, and (4) wind (Table 3-1). These are the basic ingredients of weather and climate—the ones you hear about on weather reports. Measuring how they vary in time and space makes it possible to decipher at least partly the complexities of weather dynamics and climatic patterns.

The Controls of Weather and Climate

Variations in the climatic elements are frequent, if not continuous, over Earth. Such variations are caused, or at least strongly influenced, by certain semipermanent attributes of our planet, that are often referred to as the **controls of weather and climate** (Table 3-1). The principal controls

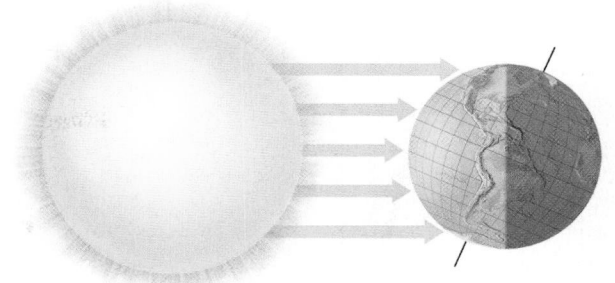

▲ **Figure 3-16** Solar energy coming to Earth. As we will see in Chapter 4, the amount of solar energy received at Earth's surface varies by latitude.

are briefly described in the paragraphs that follow and are explained in more detail in later chapters. Although they are discussed individually here, it should be emphasized that there often is overlap and interaction among them, with widely varying effects.

Latitude: We noted in Chapter 1 that the continuously changing seasonal relationship between the Sun and Earth brings continuously changing amounts of sunlight, and therefore of radiant energy, to different parts of Earth's surface. Thus, the basic distribution of solar energy over Earth is first and foremost a function of latitude, as indicated in Figure 3-16. In terms of elements and controls, we say that the control latitude strongly influences the element temperature. Overall, latitude is the most fundamental control of climate.

Distribution of Land and Water: Probably the most fundamental distinction concerning the geography of climate is the distinction between continental climates and maritime (oceanic) climates. Oceans warm and cool more slowly and to a lesser degree than do landmasses. This means that maritime areas experience milder temperatures than continental areas in both summer and winter. For example, Seattle, Washington, and Fargo, North Dakota, are at approximately the same latitude (47° N), with Seattle on the western coast of the United States and Fargo deep in the interior (Figure 3-17). Seattle has an average January temperature of 6°C (42°F), whereas the January average in Fargo is −14°C (7°F). In the opposite season, Seattle has a July average temperature of 19°C (66°F), whereas in Fargo the July average is 22°C (71°F).

Oceans are also a much more abundant source of atmospheric moisture than land. Thus, maritime climates are normally more humid than continental climates. The uneven distribution of continents and oceans over the world, then, is a prominent control of the elements moisture content and temperature.

General Circulation of the Atmosphere: The atmosphere is in constant motion, with flows that range from temporary local breezes to vast regional wind regimes. At the planetary scale, a semipermanent pattern of major wind and pressure systems dominates the troposphere and greatly influences most elements of weather

TABLE 3-1	The Elements and Controls of Weather and Climate
Elements of Weather and Climate	**Controls of Weather and Climate**
Temperature	Latitude
Pressure	Distribution of land and water
Wind	General circulation of the atmosphere
Moisture content	General circulation of the oceans
	Altitude
	Topographic barriers
	Storms

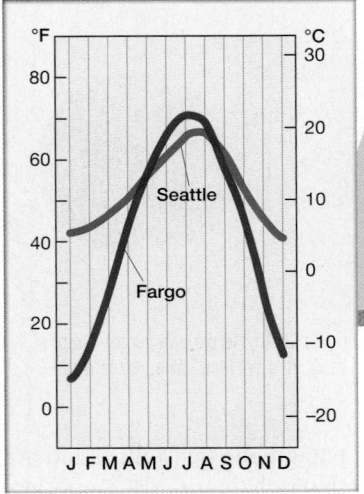

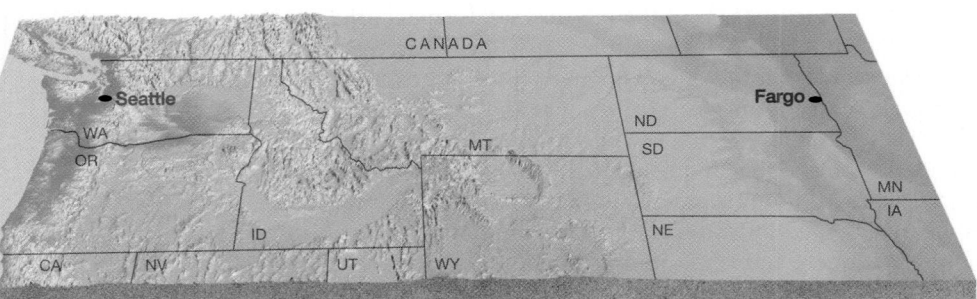

▲ **Figure 3-17** Land–water contrasts. The inland city of Fargo, North Dakota, experiences both hotter summers and colder winters than the coastal city of Seattle, Washington.

and climate. As a simple example, in the tropics, most surface winds come from the east, whereas the middle latitudes are characterized by flows that are mostly from the west, as Figure 3-18 shows.

General Circulation of the Oceans: Somewhat analogous to atmospheric movements are the motions of the oceans (Figure 3-19). Like the atmosphere, the oceans have many minor motions, but they also have a broad general pattern of currents. These currents assist in heat transfer by moving warm water poleward and cool water equatorward. Although the influence of currents on climate is much less than that of atmospheric circulation, ocean currents are not inconsequential. For example, warm currents are found off

the eastern coasts of continents, and cool currents occur off western coasts—a distinction that has a profound effect on coastal climates.

Altitude: We have already noted that three of the four weather elements—temperature, pressure, and moisture content—generally decrease upward in the troposphere and are therefore under the influence of the control altitude. This simple relationship between the three elements and the control has significant ramifications for many climatic characteristics, particularly in mountainous regions (Figure 3-20).

Topographic Barriers: Mountains and large hills sometimes have prominent effects on one or more elements of climate by diverting wind flow (Figure 3-21). The side of a mountain range facing the wind (the "windward" side), for

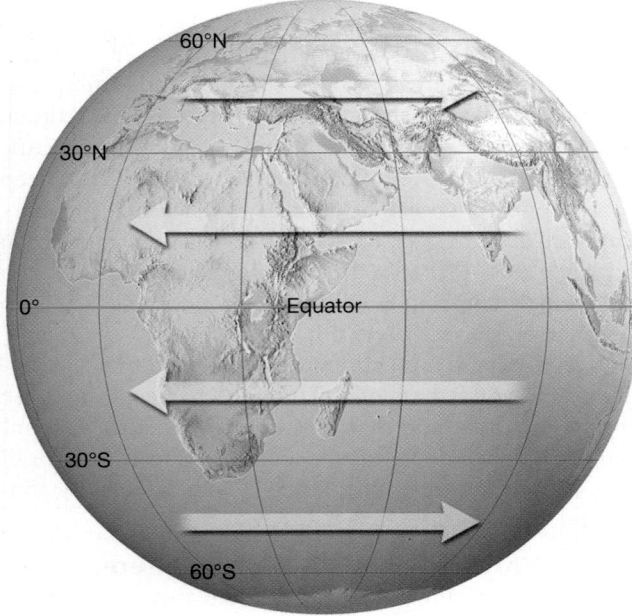

▲ **Figure 3-18** The general circulation of the atmosphere is an important climatic control. This highly simplified diagram shows that surface wind generally blows from the east in the tropics, and from the west in the midlatitudes; the complete patterns of atmospheric wind and pressure are discussed in Chapter 5.

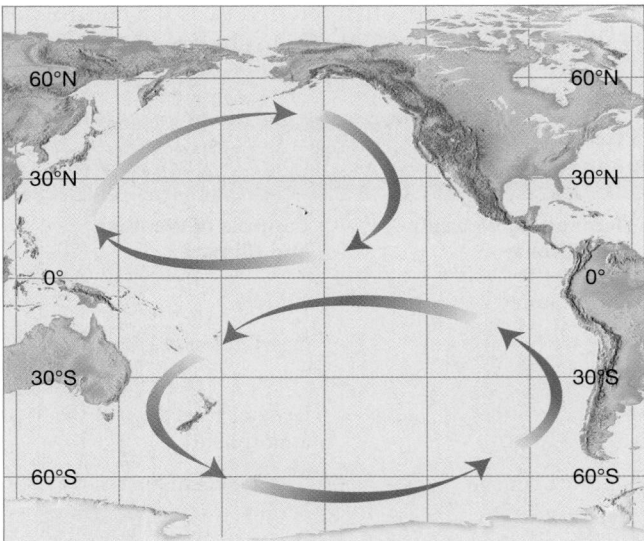

▲ **Figure 3-19** The general circulation of the oceans involves the movement of large amounts of warm water (red arrows) and cool water (blue arrows). These surface ocean currents have a significant climatic effect on neighboring landmasses.

▲ **Figure 3-20** Increasing altitude affects many components of the environment, as indicated by the variety of natural vegetation patterns on the slopes of Blanca Peak in south-central Colorado.

example, is likely to have a climate vastly different from that of the sheltered ("leeward") side.

Storms: Various kinds of storms occur over the world; some have very widespread distribution, whereas others are localized (Figure 3-22). Although they often result from interactions among other climate controls, all storms create specialized weather circumstances and so are considered to be a control. Indeed, some storms are prominent and frequent enough to affect not only weather but climate as well.

Before we move on to Chapter 4 to discuss temperature, the first of the elements of weather and climate, we need to

▲ **Figure 3-22** A prominent midlatitude cyclone storm system over the British Isles is counterpointed by localized thunderstorms over North Africa, Sicily, Italy, and Greece.

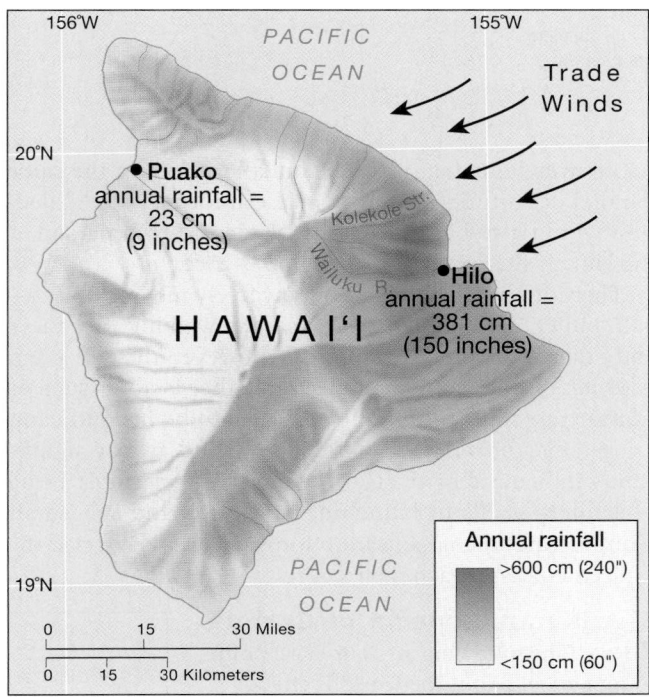

▲ **Figure 3-21** A topographic barrier as a control of climate. The difference in average annual rainfall in these two locations on the island of Hawai'i is caused by the mountain range separating them. Moisture-laden trade winds coming in from the northeast drop their moisture when forced to rise by the eastern face of the mountains. The result is a very wet eastern side of the island and a very dry western side.

consider one additional control of weather and climate— or perhaps more correctly, a control of some of the controls of weather and climate—the rotation of Earth.

Learning Check 3-8 What is the relationship of the "controls" of weather and climate to the "elements" of weather and climate?

The Coriolis Effect

Everyone is familiar with the unremitting force of gravity—its powerful pull toward the center of Earth influences all vertical motion that takes place near Earth's surface. Much less well known, however, because of its inconspicuous nature, is a pervasive influence on the direction of objects moving horizontally around Earth—a phenomenon known as the **Coriolis effect.**

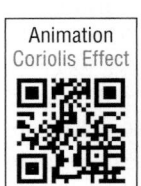

Animation
Coriolis Effect

Cause of the Coriolis Effect: Due to the Coriolis effect, all things moving over the surface of Earth or in Earth's atmosphere appear to drift sideways as a result of Earth's rotation beneath them. Stated in the simplest terms: As a result of the rotation of Earth, the path of any free-moving object appears to deflect to the right in the Northern Hemisphere, and to the left in the Southern Hemisphere.

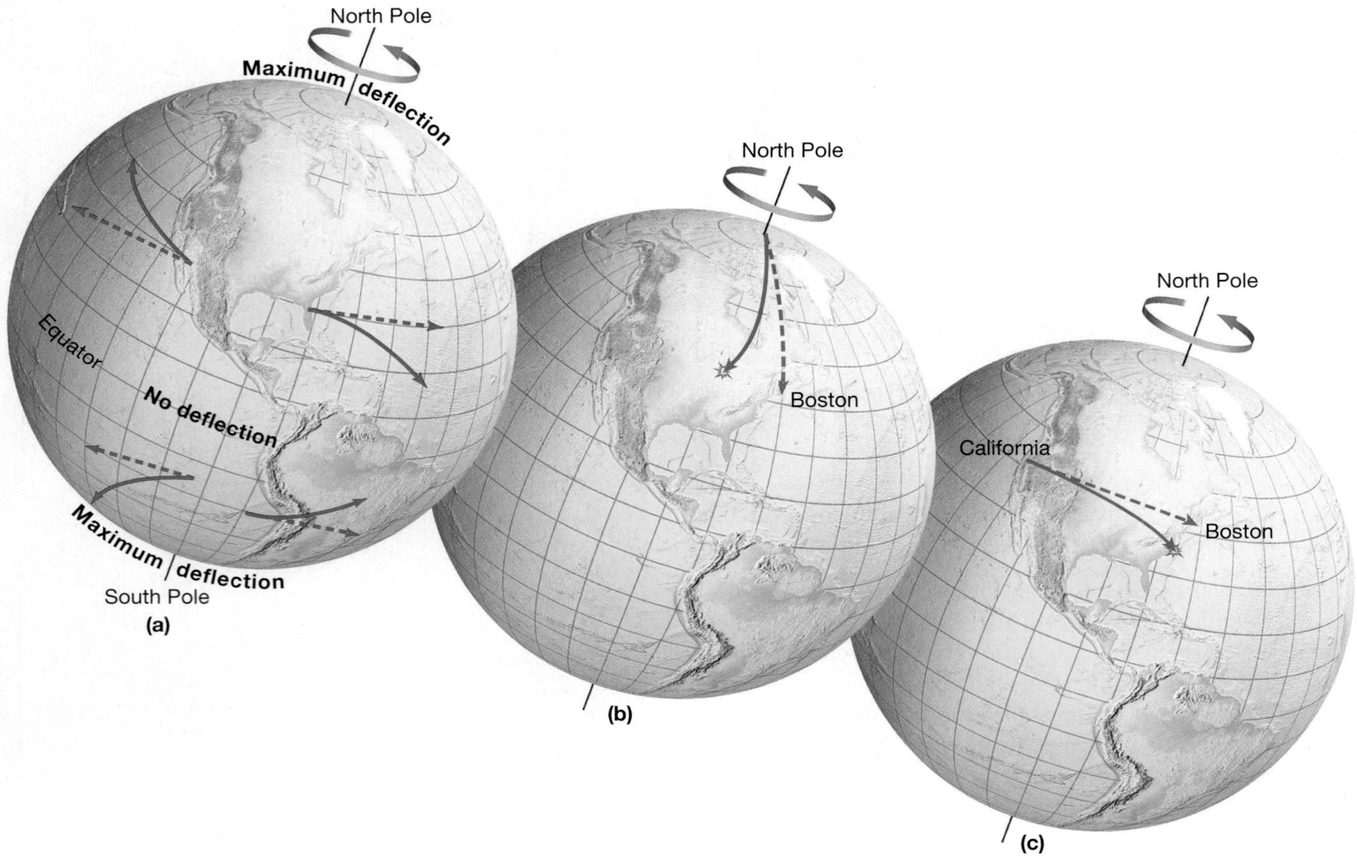

▲ **Figure 3-23** (a) The deflection caused by the Coriolis effect is to the right in the Northern Hemisphere and to the left in the Southern Hemisphere. The dashed lines represent the planned route, and the solid lines represent actual movement. (b) A rocket launched from the North Pole toward Boston lands to the west of the target if the Coriolis effect is not considered when the flight path is computed. (c) A rocket fired toward Boston from a point at the same latitude in California also appears to curve to the right because of the Coriolis effect deflection.

George Hadley described this apparent deflection in the 1730s, but it was not explained quantitatively until Gaspard G. Coriolis (1792–1843), a French civil engineer and mathematician, did so a century later. The phenomenon is called the Coriolis effect in his honor (Figure 3-23a). The Coriolis effect is frequently, and correctly, referred to as the "Coriolis force," especially when mathematically calculating its consequences. In this book we retain the more general term *Coriolis effect* when referring to this phenomenon.

The nature of the deflection due to the Coriolis effect can be demonstrated by imagining a rocket fired toward Boston from the North Pole. During the few minutes that the rocket is in the air, earthly rotation will have moved the target some kilometers to the east because the planet rotates from west to east. If the Coriolis effect was not included in the calculation of the trajectory, the rocket would pass some distance to the west of Boston (Figure 3-23b). To a person standing at the launch point and looking south, the uncorrected flight path appears to deflect to the right.

Although the Coriolis effect deflection is easier to envision when an object is moving north–south, the deflection occurs no matter which direction an object moves. If a rocket were aimed at Boston from a location on the same parallel of latitude—say, northern California—the deflection would also be to the right, as viewed by a person at the launch site looking east (Figure 3-23c).

The Coriolis effect influences any freely moving object— ball, bullet, automobile, even a person walking. For these and other short-range movements, however, the deflection is so minor and counterbalanced by other factors (such as friction, air resistance, and inertia) as to be insignificant. Long-range movements, on the other hand, can be significantly influenced by the Coriolis effect. The accurate firing of artillery shells or launching of rockets and spacecraft requires careful compensation for the Coriolis effect if the projectiles are to reach their targets.

Significant Aspects of Coriolis Effect: The following are four basic points to remember about the Coriolis effect:

Video
Coriolis Effect
Merry-Go-Round

1. Regardless of the initial direction of motion, any freely moving object appears to deflect to the right in the Northern Hemisphere and to the left in the Southern Hemisphere.

◀ **Figure 3-24** The wind pattern within storms such as hurricanes is influenced by the deflection of the Coriolis effect. This image shows Tropical Storm Beryl in May 2012, just before making landfall.

2. The apparent deflection is strongest at the poles and decreases progressively toward the equator, where the deflection is zero.
3. The Coriolis effect is proportional to the speed of the object, and so a fast-moving object is deflected more than a slower one.
4. The Coriolis effect influences direction of movement only; it does not change the speed of an object.

Learning Check 3-9 **Describe the Coriolis effect and its cause.**

Important Consequences of Coriolis Effect: Strictly speaking, the Coriolis effect is an apparent deflection caused by Earth rotating beneath a moving object; however, the consequences of the Coriolis effect are very real. As we will see in Chapter 4, Northern Hemisphere ocean currents trend to the right and Southern Hemisphere currents to the left. Furthermore, as we will see in Chapter 5, wind patterns and the circulation of wind within storms such as hurricanes are influenced by the Coriolis effect (Figure 3-24). The Coriolis effect is also a factor associated with the *upwelling* of cold water that takes place in subtropical latitudes where cool currents veer away from continental coastlines. The surface water that moves away from the shore is replaced by cold water rising from below.

One phenomenon that the Coriolis effect does not appear to influence is the circulation pattern of water that drains out of a sink or bathtub. A folk tale claims that Northern Hemisphere sinks drain clockwise and Southern Hemisphere sinks counterclockwise. The time involved is so short and the speed of the water so slow, however, that the Coriolis effect cannot be offered to explain these movements—the characteristics of the plumbing system, the shape of the washbowl, and pure chance are more likely to determine the flow patterns. A reader can test this hypothesis, of course, by filling and emptying several sinks and recording the results. Geographer and founding author of this textbook, Tom McKnight, spent 5 months in Australia in 1992–1993 and tested 100 sinks. The results: 34 that emptied clockwise, 39 that emptied counterclockwise, and 27 that simply gushed down without a swirl in either pattern.

Chapter 3	LEARNING REVIEW

After studying this chapter, you should be able to answer the following questions. Key terms from each text section are shown in **bold type**. Definitions for key terms are also found in the glossary at the back of the book.

KEY TERMS AND CONCEPTS

Size and Composition of the Atmosphere (*p. 55*)

1. What is meant by the terms *constant gases* and *variable gases* in the atmosphere?
2. Describe the most important constant gases of the atmosphere.
3. Briefly describe some of the roles that **water vapor, carbon dioxide, ozone,** and **particulates (aerosols)** play in atmospheric processes.
4. Describe both the vertical distribution of water vapor in the atmosphere and its horizontal (geographic) distribution near Earth's surface.

Vertical Structure of the Atmosphere (*p. 59*)

5. Discuss the size and general temperature characteristics of the **troposphere** and **stratosphere**.
6. Describe how atmospheric pressure changes with increasing altitude.
7. What is the **ozone layer,** and where is it located?

Human-Induced Atmospheric Change (*p. 62*)

8. How is ozone formed and why is it important in the atmosphere?
9. What is meant by the "hole" in the ozone layer, and what role have **chlorofluorocarbons (CFCs)** played in this?
10. Describe and contrast **primary pollutants** and **secondary pollutants** in the atmosphere.
11. Describe and explain the causes of **photochemical smog**.

Weather and Climate (*p. 67*)

12. What is the difference between **weather** and **climate**?
13. What are the four **elements of weather and climate**?
14. Briefly describe the seven dominant **controls of weather and climate.**
15. Describe the **Coriolis effect** and its cause.

STUDY QUESTIONS

1. What prevents the atmosphere from "escaping" into space?
2. Why is the question "How deep is the atmosphere?" difficult to answer?
3. In what ways was life on Earth responsible for the composition of our modern atmosphere?
4. Why are you likely to get out of breath more easily when hiking in the mountains than at sea level?
5. Why does the altitude of the tropopause vary from summer to winter and from equator to the poles?
6. Why should humans be concerned about the depletion of the ozone layer?
7. Why is it inappropriate to talk about a change in climate from last year to this year?
8. In our study of physical geography, why do we concentrate primarily on the troposphere rather than on other zones of the atmosphere?
9. Why does the Coriolis effect influence the direction of ocean currents but not the direction of water draining down in a kitchen sink?

EXERCISES

1. Using Table 3-1 for reference:
   a. How much more nitrogen is in the atmosphere than oxygen?
   b. How much more oxygen is in the atmosphere than carbon dioxide?
2. Using Figure 3-8 for reference:
   a. If you are on top of Pikes Peak in Colorado at an altitude of 4.3 kilometers (2.7 mi.; 14,110 ft.), what is the approximate percentage of surface atmospheric pressure?
   b. If you were in an unpressurized balloon at an altitude of 10 kilometers (6.2 mi.; 33,000 ft.), what is the approximate percentage of surface atmospheric pressure?

Seeing Geographically

Look again at the photograph of the Gaspé Peninsula at the beginning of the chapter (p. 54). Within which layer of the atmosphere are the clouds in this photograph likely found? If so, what would be the maximum altitude of the tops of the clouds you see here? Are these clouds above or below the densest part of the ozone layer?

MasteringGeography™

Looking for additional review and test prep materials? Visit the Study Area in MasteringGeography™ to enhance your geographic literacy, spatial reasoning skills, and understanding of this chapter's content by accessing a variety of resources, including geoscience animations, MapMaster interactive maps, videos, RSS feeds, flashcards, web links, self-study quizzes, and an eText version of *McKnight's Physical Geography: A Landscape Appreciation*.

WE NOW BEGIN OUR LOOK AT THE FIRST ELEMENT OF

weather and climate—temperature—and introduce one of the most fundamental of all Earth systems: the warming of Earth's atmosphere and surface by solar energy, and the subsequent loss of this energy back into space.

Many of the geographic patterns discussed in chapters that follow—including atmospheric pressure and wind, the distribution of precipitation, the characteristics of storms, the distribution of plants and animals, and the development of soils—are in part related to the arrival of solar energy, the warming and cooling that takes place on Earth's surface and in the atmosphere, and the transfer of this energy from one part of the planet to another.

As you study this chapter, think about these key questions:

- **How are the concepts of *energy, heat,* and *temperature* related?**
- **How is *shortwave radiation* from the Sun different from *longwave radiation* emitted by Earth's surface and atmosphere?**
- **What processes are involved in warming and cooling Earth's surface and atmosphere?**
- **How is the atmosphere warmed indirectly by the Sun?**
- **Why does the amount of solar energy received by Earth vary by latitude?**
- **Why do landmasses warm and cool faster and to a greater extent than do ocean areas?**
- **How is energy transferred from low latitudes to high latitudes?**
- **Why and how do temperatures vary with increasing altitude in the troposphere?**
- **What factors explain global patterns of temperature?**
- **How is human activity likely changing global climate?**

The Impact of Temperature on the Landscape

Global temperature patterns leave a prominent mark on the landscapes of Earth. Many physical features of the landscape are affected by local temperature conditions. For example, temperature fluctuations are one cause of the breakdown of exposed bedrock and the rate of chemical processes associated with soil development (Figure 4-1). Further, long-term temperature patterns influence the presence of many agents of erosion and deposition, such as streams and glaciers.

All organisms have temperature tolerances, and most are harmed by wide fluctuations in temperature. Both animals and plants often evolve in response to hot or cold climates, and so the types of flora and fauna in any area of temperature extremes are influenced by the capability of the various species to withstand the long-term temperature conditions. Thus, when the weather becomes particularly hot or cold, mobile organisms are likely to search for shelter, and their apparent presence in the landscape may be diminished. Humans also seek haven from temperature extremes, although they have other options such as specialized clothing and buildings that allow them to survive in both extremely hot and extremely cold environments.

Sun setting behind the San Juan Islands in Washington State. What is the dominant color of the light coming from the Sun in this photograph? Does it appear that the Sun has warmed this region enough to generate strong local winds? Explain why you say this.

ENERGY, HEAT, AND TEMPERATURE

In the most basic sense, the universe is made up of just two kinds of "things": *matter* and *energy*. The concept of matter is fairly easy to comprehend. Matter is the "stuff" of the universe: the solids, liquids, gases—and their atomic particles—from which all things are made. Matter has mass and volume; we can easily see and feel many kinds of matter. The concept of energy, on the other hand, may be more difficult to grasp.

Energy

Energy is what makes "stuff" move. For example, it takes energy to cause something to move faster, or to change direction, or to break apart. The transfer of energy from one form to another causes changes to the condition of matter—whether that matter is a single molecule in the atmosphere or the entire volume of water in Earth's oceans.

There are many forms of energy: *kinetic energy*, *chemical energy*, *gravitational potential energy*, and *radiant energy*, among many others. Although energy can neither be created nor destroyed, it can—and frequently does—change from one form to another. In our discussion of the warming of the atmosphere, we will look at just a few forms of energy and the transformations between these forms.

Work: Energy is commonly defined as the "ability to do work." *Work* refers to *force acting over distance*. So, when a force is involved in moving matter around, energy has been transferred from one form to another. The International System (S.I.) unit of energy is called the *joule* (J). Two examples may help you visualize how much energy a joule represents:

- Lifting up a 1 kilogram (2.2 pound) mass a distance of 1 meter (about 3 feet) increases the *gravitational potential energy* of that mass (the energy that object possesses because of its position in Earth's gravitational field) by about 10 joules.
- Perhaps you are familiar with the energy unit of the *calorie*: 1 calorie is the amount of energy needed to increase the temperature of 1 gram of water by 1°C (at 15°C). For comparison, it takes 4.184 joules of energy to increase the temperature of 1 gram of water by 1°C. So, 1 calorie = about 4.184 joules, and 1 joule = about 0.239 calories. We'll say much more about temperature shortly.

Power: Another way to look at energy is to measure how much energy is being *transferred per unit of time*. For example, later in this chapter we will describe how much energy is delivered by the Sun to Earth. Energy per unit of time is defined as *power*. The S.I. unit of power is called the *watt* (W): 1 watt is equal to 1 joule per second (in other words, 1 W = 0.239 calories per second). You've probably seen that the power consumption of lightbulbs and electrical appliances is commonly described in watts.

Internal Energy: To understand the warming of the atmosphere—or anything else—we first need to consider what is happening at the atomic or molecular level—a scale that we do not readily comprehend in our everyday lives. A greatly simplified model of reality can help clarify one of the relationships between matter and energy: all substances are composed of extraordinarily tiny, constantly "jiggling" *atoms*, commonly bonded together into combinations of atoms called *molecules*. The state of those substances—whether they are solid, liquid, or gas, (or plasma, which is an ionized gas)—depends in part on how vigorously the molecules are jiggling back and forth in place. Because of this constant movement, the molecules in all substances possess energy. This kind of *internal energy* is a form of **kinetic energy**—the energy of movement.

The average amount of kinetic energy possessed by the molecules in a substance is closely associated with a physical property that we can readily sense in our everyday lives: how hot or cold something is. When a substance becomes warmer, it indicates that the average kinetic energy of the molecules in that substance has increased. In other words, energy has been added that has caused the molecules to jiggle back and forth more vigorously. So this brings us to several important definitions.

Temperature and Heat

Temperature is a description of the average kinetic energy of the molecules in a substance (strictly speaking, the average "back and forth" or *translational kinetic energy* of the molecules). The more vigorous the jiggling of the molecules is—and therefore the greater the internal kinetic energy—the higher the temperature of a substance.

Heat refers to energy that transfers from one object or substance to another because of a *difference* in temperature. Sometimes the term *thermal energy* is used interchangeably with the term heat. A substance doesn't really "store" heat or "contain" heat—heat is simply the energy that is transferred from an object with a higher temperature to an object with a lower temperature, thereby increasing the internal energy of the cooler object and decreasing the internal energy of the hotter object.

In addition to heat transfer, the total internal energy of an object can be changed in other ways. For instance, the internal energy of an object can be changed by *work* (as we saw above, work is force applied to an object over some distance). For example, striking a piece of metal with a hammer increases the internal energy of the molecules in the metal, and so the metal is warmed. As with heat, an object doesn't "contain" work, but its internal energy can be changed by doing work or having work done on it.

> **Learning Check 4-1** **What is the difference between *temperature* and *heat*? (Answer on p. AK-1)**

Measuring Temperature

Instruments used to measure temperature are called *thermometers*. The temperature of an object is relative to one of three temperature scales that are in concurrent use (Figure 4-2). Each permits a precise measurement, but the existence of three scales creates an unfortunate degree of confusion.

Fahrenheit Scale: The temperature scale most widely understood by the general public in the United States is the Fahrenheit scale (named after Gabriel Daniel Fahrenheit, the eighteenth-century German physicist who devised it). Public weather reports from the National Weather Service in the United States and the news media usually state temperatures in degrees Fahrenheit. Reference points on this scale include the sea-level freezing and boiling points of pure water, which are 32° and 212°, respectively. The

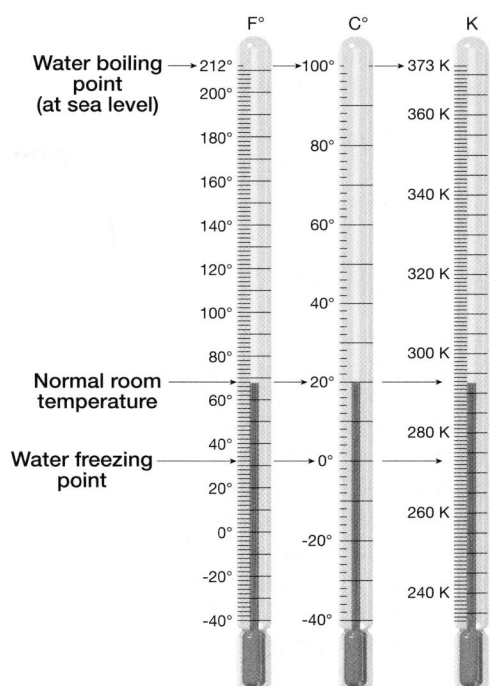

▲ **Figure 4-2** The Fahrenheit, Celsius, and Kelvin temperature scales.

United States is one of only a few countries that still use the Fahrenheit scale.

Celsius Scale: In most other countries the Celsius scale (named for Anders Celsius, the eighteenth-century Swedish astronomer who devised it) is used either exclusively or predominantly. It is an accepted component of the International System of measurement (S.I.) because it is a decimal scale with 100 units (degrees) between the freezing and boiling points of water. The Celsius scale has long been used for scientific work in the United States and is now slowly being established to supersede the Fahrenheit scale in all usages in this country.

For converting from degrees Celsius to degrees Fahrenheit, the following formula is used:

degrees Fahrenheit = (degrees Celsius × 1.8)+32°

For converting from degrees Fahrenheit to degrees Celsius, the following formula is used:

degrees Celsius = (degrees Fahrenheit−32°)÷1.8

Kelvin Scale: For many scientific purposes, the Kelvin scale (named for the nineteenth-century British physicist William Thomson, also known as Lord Kelvin) has long been used because it measures what are called *absolute temperatures*, which means that the scale begins at *absolute zero* (0 K or "zero kelvin"), the lowest possible temperature.[1] The scale maintains a 100-unit range between the boiling and freezing points of water. There are no negative values. Because this scale is not normally used by climatologists and meteorologists, we ignore it in this

---

[1]In classical physics, *absolute zero* is the temperature at which molecules have their *zero-point energy*—have no kinetic energy that can be given up.

book except to compare it to the Fahrenheit and Celsius scales. On the Celsius scale, absolute zero is at about −273° and so the conversion is simple:

$$\text{degrees Celsius} = \text{kelvin} - 273$$
$$\text{kelvins} = \text{degrees Celsius} + 273$$

SOLAR ENERGY

The Sun is the only significant source of energy for Earth's atmosphere. Millions of other stars radiate energy, but they are too far away to affect Earth. Energy is also released from inside Earth, primarily from radioactive decay of elements such as uranium (^{238}U), thorium (^{232}Th), and potassium (^{40}K). This energy can be transferred through Earth to be eventually released at the surface. For example, energy is released on the ocean floor through hydrothermal vents, although probably not enough to influence the atmosphere significantly.

The Sun supplies essentially all of the energy that drives most of the atmospheric processes. Further, we will see that it is the *unequal* warming of Earth by the Sun that ultimately puts the atmosphere in motion and is responsible for the most fundamental patterns of weather and climate.

The Sun is a star of average size and average temperature, but its proximity to Earth gives it a far greater influence on our planet than that exerted by all other celestial bodies combined. The Sun is a prodigious generator of energy. In a single second, it produces more energy than the amount used by humankind since civilization began. The Sun functions as an enormous thermonuclear reactor, producing energy through *nuclear fusion*—under extremely high temperatures and pressures, nuclei of hydrogen are fused together to form helium—a process that utilizes only a very small portion of the Sun's mass but provides an immense and continuous flow of energy that is dispersed in all directions.

Electromagnetic Radiation

The Sun gives off energy in the form of **electromagnetic radiation**—sometimes referred to as **radiant energy**. (The Sun also gives off energy as streams of ionized particles called the *solar wind*, but we can ignore that kind of energy in our discussion here because its effect on weather is minimal.) We experience different kinds of electromagnetic radiation every day: visible light, microwaves, X-rays, and radio waves are all forms of electromagnetic radiation.

Electromagnetic radiation entails the flow of energy in the form of waves. These waves of energy move through space by way of rapidly oscillating electromagnetic fields. These electromagnetic fields are oscillating at the same frequency as the vibrations of the electrical charges that form them—for example, it is the oscillation of electrons within an atom that can generate visible light. Electromagnetic radiation does not require a medium (the presence of matter) to pass through. The electromagnetic waves traverse the great voids of space in unchanging form. The waves travel outward from the Sun in straight lines at the speed of light—300,000 kilometers (186,000 miles) per second.

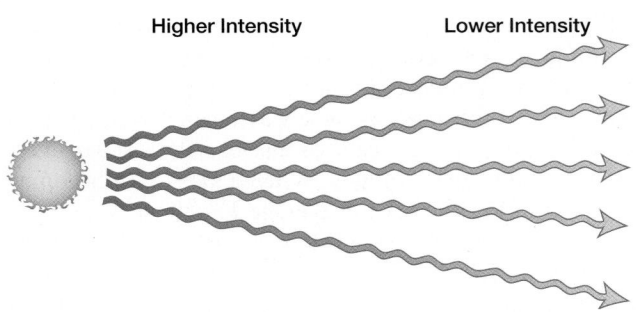

Higher Intensity   **Lower Intensity**

▲ **Figure 4-3** Electromagnetic waves from the Sun spread out as they move outward, and thus their intensity decreases as they get farther and farther from the Sun.

Only a tiny fraction of the Sun's total energy output is intercepted by Earth. The waves travel through space without loss of energy, but because they are diverging from a spherical body their intensity continuously diminishes with increased distance from the Sun (Figure 4-3)—the energy actually decreases following the *inverse square law*, so energy intensity decreases with the *square* of the distance, so twice the distance means only one-fourth (2^2) the intensity. As a result of this intensity decrease and the distance separating Earth from the Sun, less than one two-billionth of total solar output reaches the outer limit of Earth's atmosphere, having traveled 150,000,000 kilometers (93,000,000 miles) in just over 8 minutes. Although it consists of only a minuscule portion of total solar output, in absolute terms the amount of solar energy Earth receives is enormous: the amount received in 1 second is approximately equivalent to all the electric energy generated on Earth in a week.

Because of the enormous amount of energy Earth receives from the Sun, solar energy is increasingly viewed as an important source of renewable energy that can be used to generate electricity, as explained in the box, "Energy for the 21st Century: Solar Power."

The Electromagnetic Spectrum: Electromagnetic radiation can be classified on the basis of wavelength—the distance between the crest of one wave and the crest of the next (Figure 4-4). Collectively, electromagnetic radiation of all wavelengths comprises what is called the **electromagnetic spectrum** (Figure 4-5). Electromagnetic radiation varies enormously in wavelength—ranging from

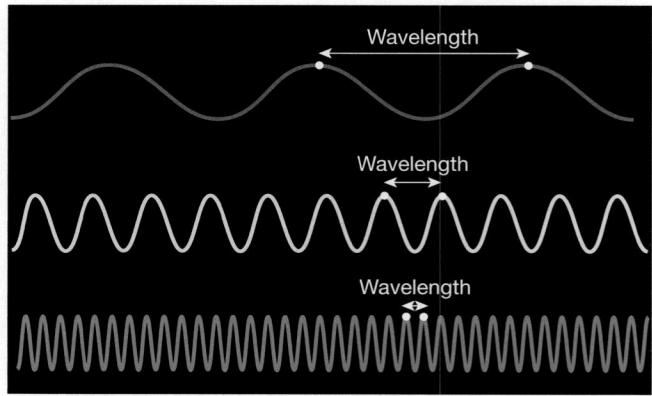

Wavelength

Wavelength

Wavelength

▲ **Figure 4-4** Electromagnetic waves can be of almost any length. The distance from one crest to the next is called the *wavelength*.

Solar Power

▶ Karl Byrand, University of Wisconsin Colleges

During a 24-hour day, an average of 164 watts per square meter shines on Earth's surface, providing more than enough energy to meet the electrical generation needs of the entire planet. Yet humans make little use of this clean and relatively cheap form of energy. Although solar power provides only a fraction of a percent of global energy, the world's photovoltaic capacity has increased from 15 gigawatts (GW; 1 billion watts) in 2008 to approximately 69 GW in 2011.

How Photovoltaic Cells Work:
Photovoltaic (PV) cells are constructed of inorganic materials such as silicon. However, silicon is a poor electrical conductor, so minute amounts of other elements are added to increase the silicon's conductivity and to determine polarity. Alternate layers of positive and negative polarity are stacked and contacts are added to form a "silicon sandwich" that comprises a complete electrical circuit. When photons (particles of light) strike the cell's surface, some of the electrons are displaced from the circuit's negative layer and are forced to flow into the cell's positive layer (Figure 4-A). This electron flow creates an electrical current that can then be used as a power source.

Although the electrical output of one PV cell is small, many cells may be wired together to form a module, and many modules can be connected to form an array. Depending on the array's size, the cumulative output can be quite large.

Advantages and Drawbacks of Solar Energy:
Using photovoltaics for electrical generation offers several advantages. Compared to coal and nuclear power plants, a PV power plant has a low capital cost and, once installed, requires little maintenance. Likewise, no fuel is required! Perhaps one of the largest advantages is photovoltaic's potential to create decentralized electrical generation: A solar array does not have to be wired into a grid but instead can generate its own energy (Figure 4-B).

Despite these advantages, photovoltaic cells must overcome several challenges if they are going to replace other forms of electrical generation. One is efficiency. Today's PV cells can only capture a limited portion of the solar spectrum, while much of the captured photon energy is lost as heat. An individual cell can attain 15 to 25 percent efficiency. However, wiring cells together into modules, and modules into arrays, further reduces efficiency. In addition, because photovoltaics generate only limited power under cloudy and hazy conditions and generate none when it is dark, storage batteries must provide power during down hours.

The Geography of Solar Capacity:
Solar capacity varies regionally, with climate and latitude being the most significant limiting factors. Climates with more annual cloud cover limit the amount of energy a solar array will receive. They are not optimal locations for photovoltaic technology. Solar capacity also decreases as latitude increases because, as distance from the equator increases, Earth's curved surface causes incoming solar radiation to be spread out over a larger area, thus diminishing beam intensity. For example, during the equinoxes, the equator receives a direct beam (that is, 90°), whereas at both 45° North and South latitudes, the Sun's rays strike at an angle of only 45°. This reduction in Sun angle translates to nearly a 71 percent reduction in energy on those days. Therefore, high-latitude regions are at a disadvantage in developing their solar potential.

Some countries that experience lower levels of solar radiation have increased their solar capacity by adopting policies that favor alternative energy development. For example, Germany and Italy greatly increased their solar energy output in 2011. Germany currently leads the world in photovoltaic solar capacity, with a 24,700 megawatt peak (MWp)—about 3 percent of Germany's total electricity. The United States, however, only has a 4200 MWp capacity, despite a population nearly four times as large as Germany's.

The Future of Photovoltaic Technology:
Continual improvements in solar technology may help to widen solar energy adoption. For instance, simply by using mirrors and lenses to better focus the Sun's rays onto photovoltaic arrays, researchers have boosted PV output. However, because these concentration devices must continually track the Sun, they are more costly and less maintenance-free than their static counterparts. Other research is underway to develop multispectral PV cells that can capture more of the electromagnetic spectrum—including infrared energy—and to incorporate organic elements that will integrate photovoltaic capability into thin, flexible, and, in some instances, even transparent materials. Such light-sensitive materials have the potential to allow everyday objects, such as paint, windows, curtains, and even clothing, to generate electricity.

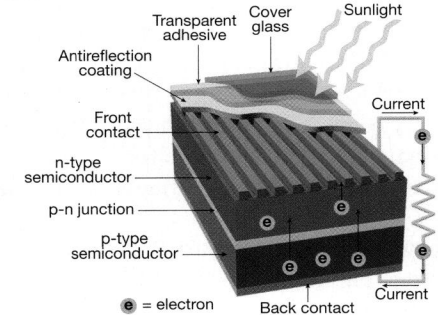

▲ **Figure 4-A** When sunlight strikes a photovoltaic cell, some electrons are displaced from the negative layer to the positive layer, generating an electrical current.

▲ **Figure 4-B** Photovoltaic panels installed on the roof of a house.

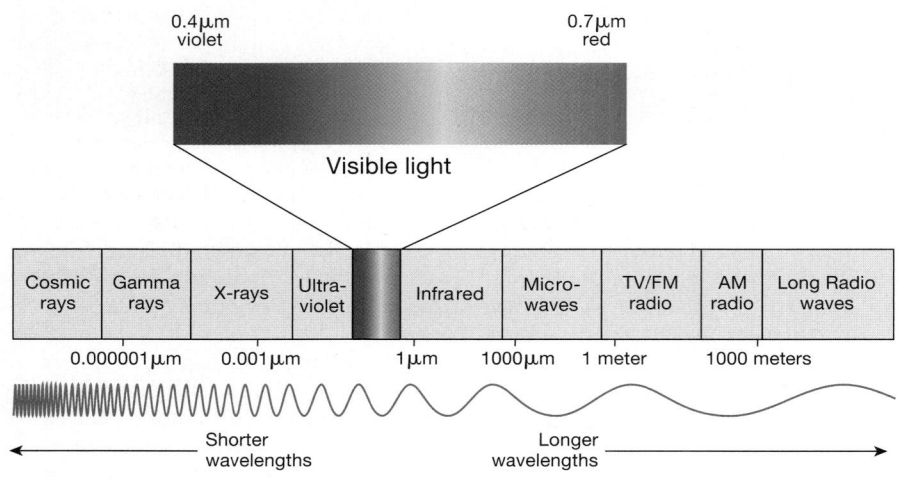

◀ **Figure 4-5** The electromagnetic spectrum.

the exceedingly short wavelengths of gamma rays and X-rays (with some wavelengths less than one-billionth of a meter), to the exceedingly long wavelengths of television and radio waves (with some wavelengths measured in kilometers). For the physical geographer, however, only three areas or "bands" of the spectrum are of importance:

1. **Visible light:** Wavelengths of radiation to which the human eye is sensitive make up a fairly narrow band of the electromagnetic spectrum known as **visible light**, and include wavelengths between about 0.4 and 0.7 micrometers (μm; 1 micrometer equals one-millionth of a meter). Visible light ranges from the shortest wavelength of radiation the human eye can sense—violet—through the progressively longer wavelengths of blue, green, yellow, orange, and finally red, the longest wavelength of radiation

the human eye can see. This sequence of color is the same as you see in a rainbow, from inner to outer (Figure 4-6). Although visible light makes up a narrow band on the electromagnetic spectrum, the peak intensity of electromagnetic radiation arriving from the Sun is in the visible portion of the spectrum, and approximately 47 percent of the total energy coming from the Sun arrives at Earth as visible light.

2. **Ultraviolet Radiation:** Wavelengths of radiation just shorter than the human eye can sense, with wavelengths from about 0.01 to 0.4 micrometers, make up the **ultraviolet (UV)** portion of the electromagnetic spectrum. The Sun is a prominent natural source of ultraviolet rays, and solar radiation reaching the top of our atmosphere contains a considerable amount (approximately 8 percent of the total energy coming from the Sun). However, as we saw in Chapter 3, much of the UV radiation from the Sun is absorbed by the ozone layer, and so the shortest ultraviolet wavelengths do not reach Earth's surface, where they could cause considerable damage to most living organisms.

3. **Infrared Radiation:** Wavelengths of radiation just longer than the human eye can sense make up the **infrared (IR)** portion of the electromagnetic spectrum, with wavelengths between 0.7 and about 1000 micrometers (1 millimeter). Infrared radiation ranges from the short or *near infrared* wavelengths emitted by the Sun to much longer wavelengths sometimes called **thermal infrared**. (Infrared "heat lamps" are designed to emit thermal infrared energy.) A large portion of solar energy comes to Earth as short infrared radiation (approximately 45 percent of the total), whereas radiation emitted by Earth is entirely thermal infrared.

Shortwave versus Longwave Radiation: Solar radiation is almost completely in the form of visible light,

◀ **Figure 4-6** The sequence of colors in a rainbow is determined by wavelength: from the shortest wavelengths of visible light—violet—through the progressively longer wavelengths of blue, green, yellow, orange, and finally the longest wavelengths, red.

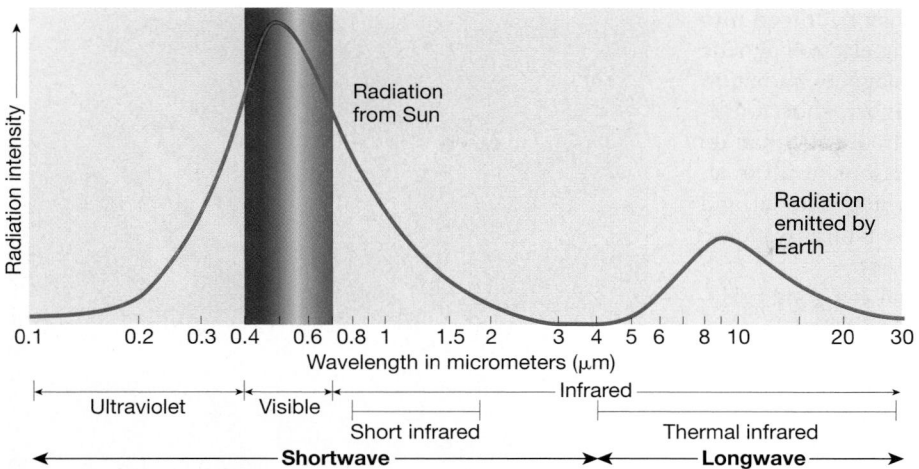

◄ **Figure 4-7** Comparison of solar and terrestrial radiation. Shortwave radiation from the Sun consists of ultraviolet wavelengths (about 8 percent of total solar energy), visible light (about 47 percent of total solar energy), and short infrared wavelengths (about 45 percent of total solar energy). Longwave radiation emitted by Earth consists entirely of thermal infrared wavelengths. The wavelength scale (shown here in micrometers [μm]) is logarithmic—it compresses the scale dramatically as wavelengths increase to the right; if a linear wavelength scale had been used, the peak of radiation emitted by Earth would be 20 inches off the page!

ultraviolet and short infrared radiation, which as a group is referred to as **shortwave radiation** (Figure 4-7). Radiation emitted by Earth—or **terrestrial radiation**—is entirely in the thermal infrared portion of the spectrum and is referred to as **longwave radiation**. A wavelength of about 4 micrometers is considered the boundary on the spectrum separating longwave radiation from shortwave radiation. Thus, all terrestrial radiation is longwave radiation, whereas virtually all solar radiation is shortwave radiation.

> **Learning Check 4-2**   **Contrast *shortwave radiation* with *longwave radiation.***

Insolation

The total **insolation** (*inco*ming *sol*ar rad*iation*) received at the top of the atmosphere is believed to be constant when averaged over a year, although it may vary slightly over long periods of time with fluctuations in the Sun's temperature. This constant amount of incoming energy—referred to as the *solar constant*—is about 1372 watts per square meter (W/m²; recall that 1 watt is equal to 1 joule per second).

The entrance of insolation into the upper atmosphere is just the beginning of a complex series of events in the atmosphere and at Earth's surface. Some of the insolation is reflected off the atmosphere back out into space, where it is lost. The remaining insolation may pass through the atmosphere, where it can be transformed either before or after reaching Earth's surface. This reception of solar energy—and the resulting energy cascade that ultimately warms Earth's surface and atmosphere—is discussed after we define a set of important concepts.

BASIC WARMING AND COOLING PROCESSES IN THE ATMOSPHERE

Before looking at the events that occur after energy travels from the Sun to Earth, we first need to examine the physical processes involved in the transfer of energy. Our goal is to provide practical explanations of the most important processes associated with the warming and cooling of the atmosphere. As such, in some cases we limit our discussion of a process to the aspects of direct importance to meteorology.

Radiation

Radiation—or **emission**—is the process by which electromagnetic energy is emitted from an object. So the term "radiation" refers to both the emission and the flow of electromagnetic energy. All objects emit electromagnetic energy, but hotter objects are more intense radiators than cooler objects. In general, the hotter the object, the more intense its radiation. (Radiation *intensity* is commonly described in W/m²—the amount of energy emitted or received in a given period of time in a given area.) Because the Sun is much hotter than Earth, it emits about two billion times more energy than Earth. In addition, the hotter the object, the shorter the wavelengths of that radiation. Hot bodies radiate mostly short wavelengths of radiation, whereas cooler bodies radiate mostly long wavelengths.

The Sun is the ultimate "hot" body of our solar system, and so nearly all of its radiation is in the shortwave portion of the electromagnetic spectrum. Earth, on the other hand, is cooler than the Sun, so Earth emits longer wavelengths of radiant energy (thermal infrared).

Temperature, however, is not the only control of radiation intensity. Objects at the same temperature may vary considerably in their radiating efficiency. A body that emits the maximum possible amount of radiation at all wavelengths is called a *blackbody radiator*. Both the Sun and Earth function very nearly as blackbodies, that is, as perfect radiators. They radiate with almost 100 percent efficiency for their respective temperatures. The atmosphere, on the other hand, is not as efficient a radiator as either the Sun or Earth's surface.

Absorption

Electromagnetic waves striking an object may be assimilated by that object—this process is called **absorption**. Different materials have different absorptive capabilities, with the variations depending in part on the wavelength of radiation involved. Although it is a great simplification, when electromagnetic waves strike a material, the electrons in atoms or even whole molecules in that material may be forced into vibration by the frequency of the incoming electromagnetic waves. (Since all wavelengths of electromagnetic radiation travel at the same speed [the speed of light], short wavelengths of radiation arrive with a higher frequency than do longer wavelengths.) The increased vibrations result in an increase in the internal energy of the absorbing material, and that leads to an increase in temperature—a typical response to the absorption of electromagnetic radiation.

As a basic generalization, an object that is a good radiator is also a good absorber, and a poor radiator is a poor absorber. Mineral materials (rock, soil) are generally excellent absorbers; snow and ice are poor absorbers; water surfaces vary in their absorbing efficiency. One important distinction concerns color. Dark-colored surfaces are much more efficient absorbers of radiation in the visible portion of the spectrum than light-colored surfaces (as exemplified by the skier wearing dark clothing in Figure 4-8).

As we will see, though, both water vapor and carbon dioxide are efficient absorbers of longwave radiation emitted by Earth's surface, whereas nitrogen, the most abundant gas in the atmosphere, is not.

Reflection

If incoming solar radiation is not absorbed, it may be reflected. **Reflection** is the ability of an object to repel ("bounce back") electromagnetic waves that strike it. When insolation is reflected by the atmosphere or the surface of Earth, it is deflected back to space at the same angle and initial wavelength with which it arrived. A mirror, for example, is designed to be highly efficient in reflecting visible light—reflecting 90 percent or more of the incoming light.

In our context, reflection is the opposite of absorption. If the wave is reflected, it cannot be absorbed. Hence, an object that is a good absorber is a poor reflector, and vice versa (see Figure 4-8). A simple example of this principle

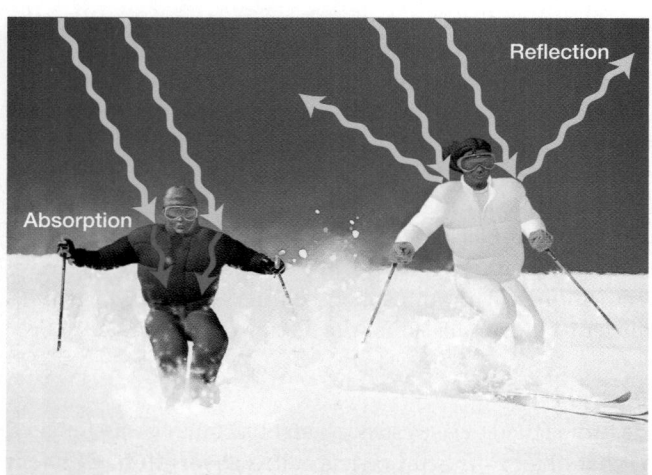

▲ **Figure 4-8** Most solar radiation that reaches Earth's surface is either absorbed or reflected. In this example, the white clothes of one skier reflect much of the solar energy, keeping her cool, whereas the dark clothes of the other skier absorb energy, thereby raising his temperature.

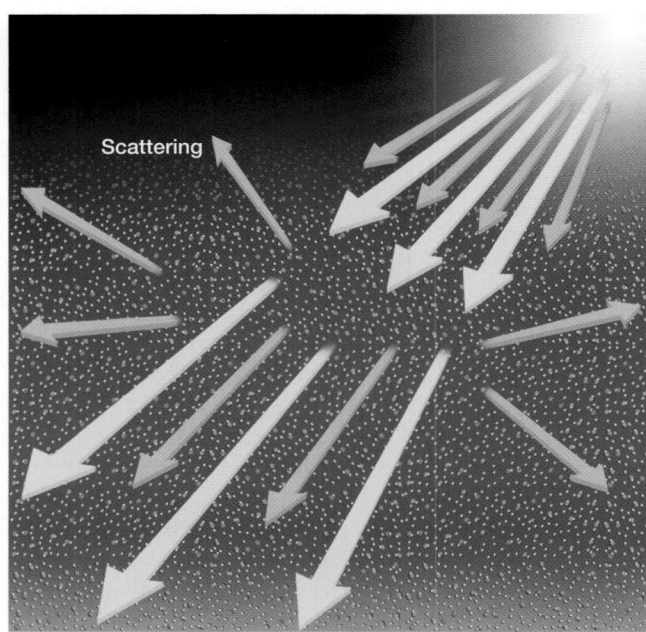

▲ **Figure 4-9** Gas molecules and impurities in the atmosphere scatter and redirect light waves. Some waves are scattered into space and therefore lost to Earth; others are scattered but continue through the atmosphere in altered directions. There is greater scattering of blue light than the longer wavelengths of visible light, resulting in a blue sky.

is the existence of unmelted snow on a sunny day. Although the air temperature may be well above freezing, the snow does not melt rapidly because its white surface reflects rather than absorbs a large share of the solar energy that strikes it.

The term **albedo** refers to the overall reflectivity of an object or surface, usually described as a percentage—the higher the albedo, the greater the amount of radiation reflected. Snow, for example, has a very high albedo (as much as 95 percent), whereas a dark surface, such as dense forest cover, can have an albedo as low as 14 percent.

Learning Check **4-3**   **Compare the processes of** *radiation*, *absorption*, **and** *reflection*.

Scattering

Gas molecules and particulate matter in the air can deflect light waves and redirect them in a type of reflection known as **scattering** (Figure 4-9). This deflection involves a change in the direction of the light wave, but no change in wavelength. Some of the waves are back-scattered into space and thus are lost to Earth, but many of them continue through the atmosphere in altered but random directions, eventually striking the surface as *diffuse radiation*.

The amount of scattering that takes place depends on the wavelength of the light as well as on the size, shape, and composition of the molecule or particulate. In general, shorter wavelengths are more readily scattered than longer wavelengths by the gases in the atmosphere. One prominent kind of scat-

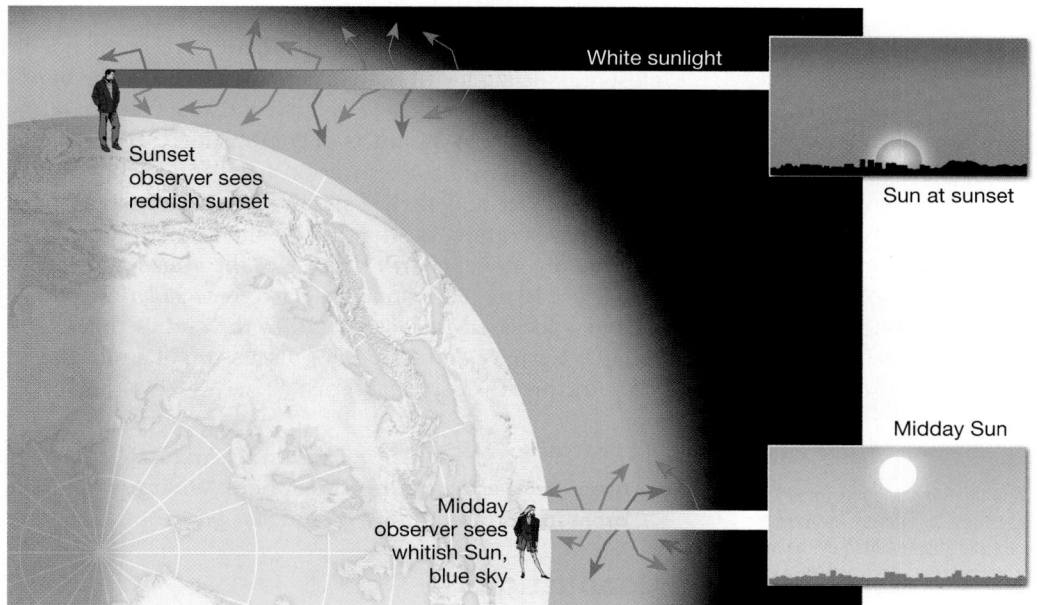

◄ **Figure 4-10** Short wavelengths of visible light (blue and violet) are scattered more easily than longer wavelengths. Consequently, when the Sun is overhead on a clear day, one can see blue sky in all directions because blue light was selectively scattered. At sunrise or sunset, however, the path that light must take through the atmosphere is much longer, with the result that most of the blue light is scattered out before the light waves reach Earth's surface. Thus, the Sun appears reddish in color.

tering, known as *Rayleigh scattering*, takes place when the shortest wavelengths of visible light—violet and blue—are scattered more easily in all directions by the gas molecules in the atmosphere than are the longer wavelengths of visible light—orange and red. This is why on a clear day the sky is blue. The sky is blue and not violet because of the greater prevalence of blue wavelengths in solar radiation and because our eyes are less sensitive to violet light. Were blue light not scattered by the atmosphere, the sky would appear black. When the Sun is low in the sky, the light has passed through so much atmosphere that nearly all of the blue wavelengths have been scattered away, leaving only the longest wavelengths of visible light, orange and red—the dominant colors of light we see at sunrise and sunset (Figure 4-10).

When the atmosphere contains large quantities of larger particles, such as suspended aerosols, all wavelengths of visible light are more equally scattered (a process known as *Mie scattering*), leaving the sky looking gray rather than blue.

In terms of atmospheric warming, one of the consequences of scattering—especially Rayleigh scattering—is that the intensity of solar radiation striking the surface of Earth is diminished because scattering redirects a portion of the insolation back out to space (Figure 4-11).

Transmission

If incoming solar radiation is neither absorbed nor reflected, it may instead pass through a surface or object. **Transmission** is the process whereby electromagnetic waves pass completely through a medium, as when light waves are transmitted through a pane of clear, colorless glass. Obviously mediums vary considerably in their capacity to transmit electromagnetic waves. Earth materials,

for example, are typically opaque and therefore very poor transmitters of insolation; sunlight is absorbed at the surface of rock or soil and does not penetrate at all. Water, on the other hand, transmits sunlight well: even in very murky water, light penetrates some distance below the surface, and in clear water, sunlight may illuminate to considerable depths.

The transmission ability of a medium generally depends on the wavelength of radiation. For example, glass has high transmissivity for shortwave radiation but not for longwave radiation. Temperature increases inside a closed automobile left parked in the Sun in part because shortwave radiation transmits through the window glass where it is absorbed by the upholstery, thereby increasing its temperature. The longwave radiation then emitted

▼ **Figure 4-11** The predominant colors of a sunset are orange and red, due to the scattering away of blue light, as in this scene of the Sun setting behind the Golden Gate Bridge in San Francisco.

▲ **Figure 4-12** Shortwave radiation from the Sun transmits through the glass of the car windows and is absorbed by the car interior. Because the glass does not easily transmit the longwave radiation emitted by the heated upholstery, the temperature inside the car increases. This is known as the greenhouse effect.

by the interior of the car does not readily transmit back through the glass, causing the inside of the car to warm up (Figure 4-12). This is commonly called the *greenhouse effect*.

The Greenhouse Effect: The **greenhouse effect** is at work in the atmosphere[2]. A number of gases in the atmosphere, known as **greenhouse gases**, readily transmit incoming shortwave radiation from the Sun but do not easily transmit outgoing longwave terrestrial radiation (Figure 4-13). The most important greenhouse gas is water vapor, followed by carbon dioxide. Many other trace gases such as methane also play a role, as do some kinds of clouds.

In the simplest terms, incoming shortwave solar radiation transmits through the atmosphere to Earth's surface, where this energy is absorbed, increasing the temperature of the surface. However, the longwave radiation emitted by Earth's surface is inhibited from transmitting back through the atmosphere by the greenhouse gases. Much of this outgoing terrestrial radiation is absorbed by greenhouse gases and clouds, and then reradiated back toward the surface, hence delaying this energy loss to space.

The greenhouse effect is one of the most important warming processes in the troposphere. The greenhouse effect keeps Earth's surface and lower troposphere much warmer than would be the case if there were no atmosphere—without the greenhouse effect, the average temperature of Earth would be about –15°C (5°F) rather than the present average of 15°C (59°F).

Although the ongoing, natural greenhouse effect in the atmosphere makes life as we know it possible, over the last century or so a significant increase in greenhouse

gas concentration—especially carbon dioxide—has been measured. This increase in atmospheric carbon dioxide is closely associated with human activity, especially the burning of fossil fuels such as petroleum and coal (carbon dioxide is one of the by-products of combustion). The increase in greenhouse gas concentration has been accompanied by a slight, yet nonetheless significant, increase in average global temperature, raising the likelihood that humans are altering the global energy balance of the atmosphere. This important issue, commonly referred to as *global warming*, will be addressed in more detail at the end of this chapter after we have concluded our discussion of atmospheric warming processes and patterns.

Learning Check 4-4 **Explain the natural** *greenhouse effect* **in the atmosphere. What are the two most important natural** *greenhouse gases?*

Conduction

The transfer of heat from one molecule to another without changes in their relative positions is called **conduction**. This process enables energy to be transferred from one part of a stationary body to another, or from one object to a second object when the two are in contact.

Conduction occurs through molecular collision, as the blown-up view in Figure 4-14 illustrates. A "cool" molecule becomes increasingly agitated as a "hotter" molecule collides with it and so transfers some kinetic energy to it. In this manner, the energy is passed from one place to another. When two molecules of unequal temperature are in contact with one another, energy transfers from the hotter to the cooler until they attain the same temperature.

The ability of different substances to conduct heat is quite variable. For example, most metals are excellent conductors, as can be demonstrated by pouring hot coffee into a metal cup and then touching your lips to the edge of the cup. The

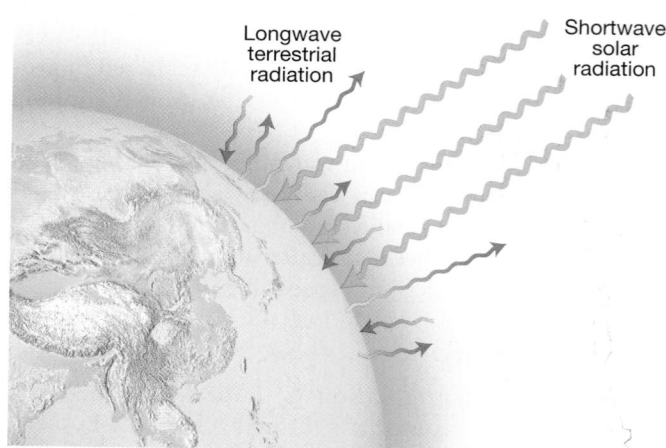

▲ **Figure 4-13** The atmosphere easily transmits incoming shortwave radiation from the Sun but is a poor transmitter of outgoing longwave radiation emitted by Earth's surface. This differential transmission of shortwave and longwave radiation causes the greenhouse effect in the atmosphere.

Longwave terrestrial radiation   Shortwave solar radiation

[2]As it turns out, actual greenhouses are not warmed simply by the greenhouse effect—the lack of mixing of warm inside air with cooler outside air also plays a role. Nonetheless, the term *greenhouse effect* is still used to describe the warming of the lower atmosphere caused by the differential transmission of shortwave and longwave radiation.

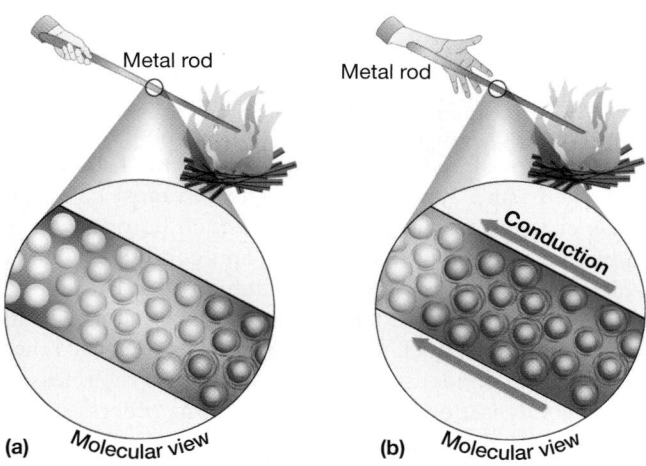

▲ **Figure 4-14** Energy is conducted from one place to another by molecular agitation. (a) One end of the metal rod is in the flame and so becomes hot. (b) This energy is then conducted the length of the rod and will burn the hand of the rod-holder.

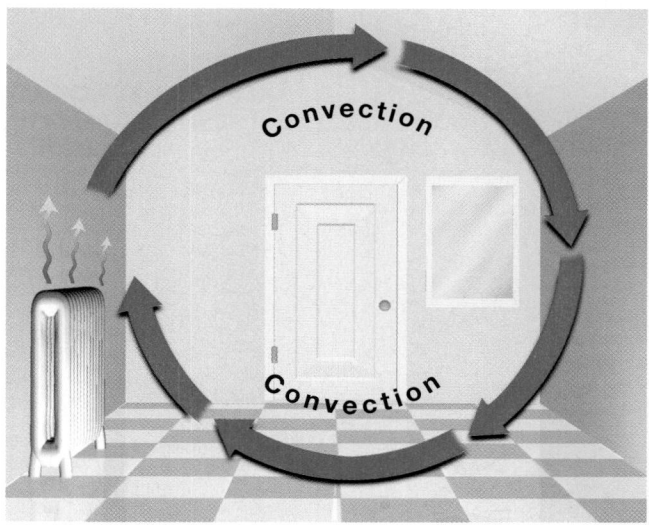

▲ **Figure 4-15** A "radiator" in a closed room sets up a convective circulation system. Air warmed by the radiator rises, and cooler air flows toward the radiator to replace the warmed air that has risen.

warmth of the coffee is quickly conducted throughout the metal and burns the lips of the drinker. In contrast, hot coffee poured into a ceramic cup warms the cup very slowly because such earthy material is a poor conductor.

Earth's land surface warms rapidly during the day because it is a good absorber of incoming shortwave radiation, and some of that warmth is transferred away from the surface by conduction. A small part is conducted deeper underground, but not much, because Earth materials are not good conductors. Another portion of this absorbed energy is transferred to the lowest portion of the atmosphere by conduction from the ground surface. Air, however, is a poor conductor, and so only the air layer touching the ground is warmed very much (perhaps a layer just a few millimeters thick); physical movement of the air is required to spread the warmth around. In contrast, when the ground surface is very cold, heat can transfer from the air to the ground through conduction, chilling the air above.

Moist air is a slightly more efficient conductor than dry air. If you are outdoors on a winter day, you will stay warmer if there is little moisture in the air to conduct heat away from your body.

Convection

In the process of **convection**, energy is transferred from one point to another by the predominately vertical circulation of a fluid, such as air or water. Convection involves movement of the warmed molecules from one place to another. (Do not confuse the movement of molecules from one place to another in the process of *convection* with the back-and-forth vibratory movement and molecular collisions associated with *conduction*—in convection, the molecules physically move away from the heat source; in conduction, they do not.)

If your room is heated by a "radiator" (Figure 4-15), you have taken advantage of convection. The air immediately above the radiator rises because warming has caused it to expand and therefore become less dense than the

nearby air. Surrounding air then moves in to fill the void left by the rising warm air. In turn, cooler air from above descends to replace that which has moved in from the side, and a cellular circulation is established—up, out, down, and in.

A similar convective pattern frequently develops in the atmosphere. Unequal warming (for a variety of reasons) may cause a parcel of surface air to become warmer than the surrounding air, and thus the warm air will rise. The warm air expands and moves upward in the direction of lower pressure. The cooler surrounding air then moves in from the sides, and air from above sinks down to replace it, thus establishing a convective circulation system, also called a **convection cell**. The prominent elements of the system are an updraft of warm air and a downdraft of air after it has cooled. Convection is common in each hemisphere during its summer and throughout the year in the tropics.

Advection

When the dominant direction of energy transfer in a moving fluid is horizontal (sideways), the term **advection** is applied. In the atmosphere, wind may transfer warm or cool air horizontally from one place to another through the process of advection. As we will see in the following chapter, some wind systems develop as part of large atmospheric convection cells: the horizontal component of air movement within such a convection cell is properly called *advection*.

> **Learning Check 4-5** **Contrast the energy transfer processes of *conduction* and *convection*.**

Adiabatic Cooling and Warming

Whenever air ascends or descends, its temperature changes. This invariable result of vertical air movement is due to the change in pressure. When air rises, it expands because

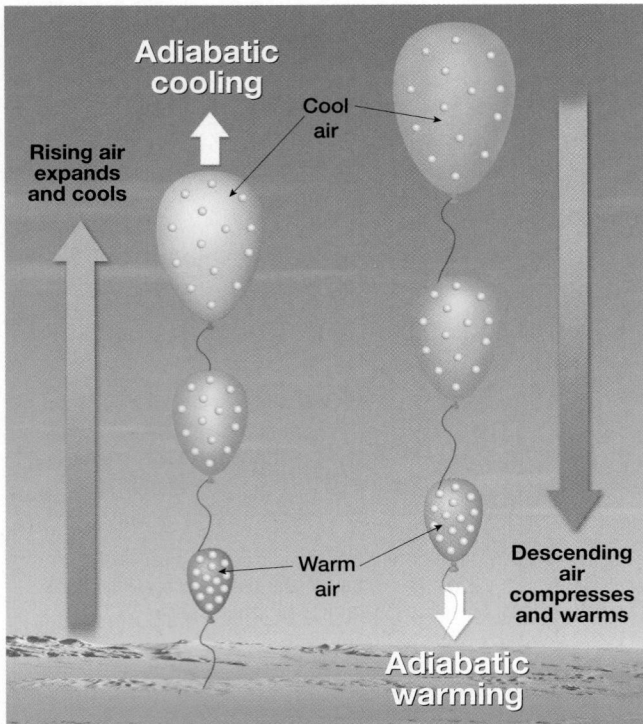

▲ **Figure 4-16** Rising air (represented by a balloon) expands and cools adiabatically, whereas descending air compresses and warms adiabatically. No actual transfer of energy is involved in either process.

there is less air above it, and so less pressure is exerted on it (Figure 4-16). When air descends, it is compressed because there is more air above it, and so more pressure is exerted on it.

Expansion—Adiabatic Cooling: The expansion that occurs in rising air is a cooling process even though no energy is lost. As air rises and expands, the molecules spread through a greater volume of space—the "work" done by the molecules during expansion reduces their average kinetic energy and so the temperature decreases. This is called **adiabatic cooling**—cooling by expansion (*adiabatic* means without the gain or loss of energy). In the atmosphere, any time air rises, it cools adiabatically.

Compression—Adiabatic Warming: Conversely, when air descends, it becomes warmer. The descent causes compression as the air comes under increasing pressure—the work done on the molecules by compression increases their average kinetic energy and so the temperature increases even though no energy was added from external sources. This is called **adiabatic warming**—warming by compression. In the atmosphere, any time air descends, it warms adiabatically.

As we will see in Chapter 6, adiabatic cooling of rising air is one of the most important processes involved in cloud development and precipitation, whereas the adiabatic warming of descending air has just the opposite effect.

Learning Check 4-6 **What happens to the temperature of air as it rises, and what happens to the temperature of air as it descends? Why?**

Latent Heat

The physical state of water in the atmosphere frequently changes—ice changes to liquid water, liquid water changes to water vapor, and so forth. Any phase change involves an exchange of energy known as **latent heat** (*latent* is from the Latin, "lying hidden"). The two most common phase changes are **evaporation**, in which liquid water is converted to gaseous water vapor, and **condensation**, in which water vapor is converted to liquid water. During the process of evaporation, latent heat energy is "stored" and so evaporation is, in effect, a cooling process. On the other hand, during condensation, latent heat energy is released and so condensation is, in effect, a warming process.

As we will explore more fully in Chapters 6 and 7, a great deal of energy is transferred from one place to another in the atmosphere through the movement and phase changes of water vapor. Energy that is stored in one location through evaporation can be released in another location far away. We will also see that many storms, such as hurricanes, are fueled by the release of latent heat during condensation.

EARTH'S SOLAR RADIATION BUDGET

We now turn to the specifics of atmospheric warming. What happens to solar radiation when it enters Earth's atmosphere? How is it received and distributed? How does electromagnetic radiation warm the atmosphere? We begin by discussing Earth's solar radiation "budget"—the balance of incoming and outgoing radiation.

Animation
Atmospheric
Energy Balance

Long-Term Energy Balance

In the long run, there is a balance between the total amount of energy received by Earth and its atmosphere as insolation on one hand, and the total amount of energy returned to space on the other (Figure 4-17). (As we suggested earlier, humans are likely altering the energy balance of the atmosphere through greenhouse gas emissions—for the

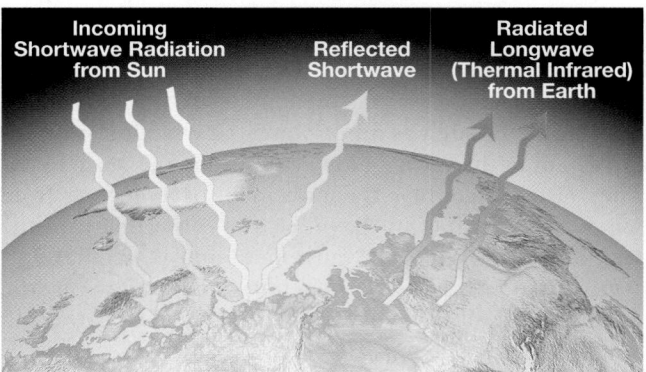

▲ **Figure 4-17** The big picture: Earth's energy budget in simplified form. Incoming shortwave radiation and outgoing longwave radiation are in a long-term balance.

purposes of understanding atmospheric warming processes, we will ignore that possibility for the moment.) Although there is an overall long-term balance between incoming and outgoing radiation, the details of the energy exchanges between Earth's surface and atmosphere are important for understanding basic weather processes.

Earth's Energy Budget

The annual balance between incoming and outgoing radiation is the *global energy budget*, which can be illustrated by using 100 "units" of energy to represent total insolation (100 percent of insolation) received at the outer edge of the atmosphere and tracing its dispersal (Figure 4-18). Keep in mind that the values shown here are approximate annual averages for the entire globe and do not apply to any specific location.

Radiation Loss from Reflection: Most of the incoming solar radiation that arrives at the upper atmosphere does not warm it directly. About 31 units of total insolation are reflected (or scattered) back into space by the atmosphere and the surface. The *albedo* of Earth, therefore, is about 31 percent.

Direct Absorption of Solar Radiation: Only 24 units of incoming solar radiation warm the atmosphere directly. About 3 units of radiation (in the ultraviolet portion of the spectrum) are absorbed by ozone and so warm the ozone layer. Another 21 units are absorbed by gases and clouds as incoming radiation passes through the rest of the atmosphere.

Surface-to-Atmosphere Energy Transfer: About 45 units of insolation—nearly half of the total—simply transmit through the atmosphere to Earth's surface where it is absorbed, warming the surface. The warmed surface of Earth then in turn transfers energy to the atmosphere above in a number of ways.

About 4 units of energy are conducted from Earth's surface back into the atmosphere, where it is dispersed by convection. Energy is also transferred from the surface to the atmosphere through the transport of latent heat in water vapor. About three-fourths of all sunshine falls on a water surface when it reaches Earth. Much of this energy is utilized in evaporating water from oceans, lakes, and other bodies of water. About 19 units of energy pass into the

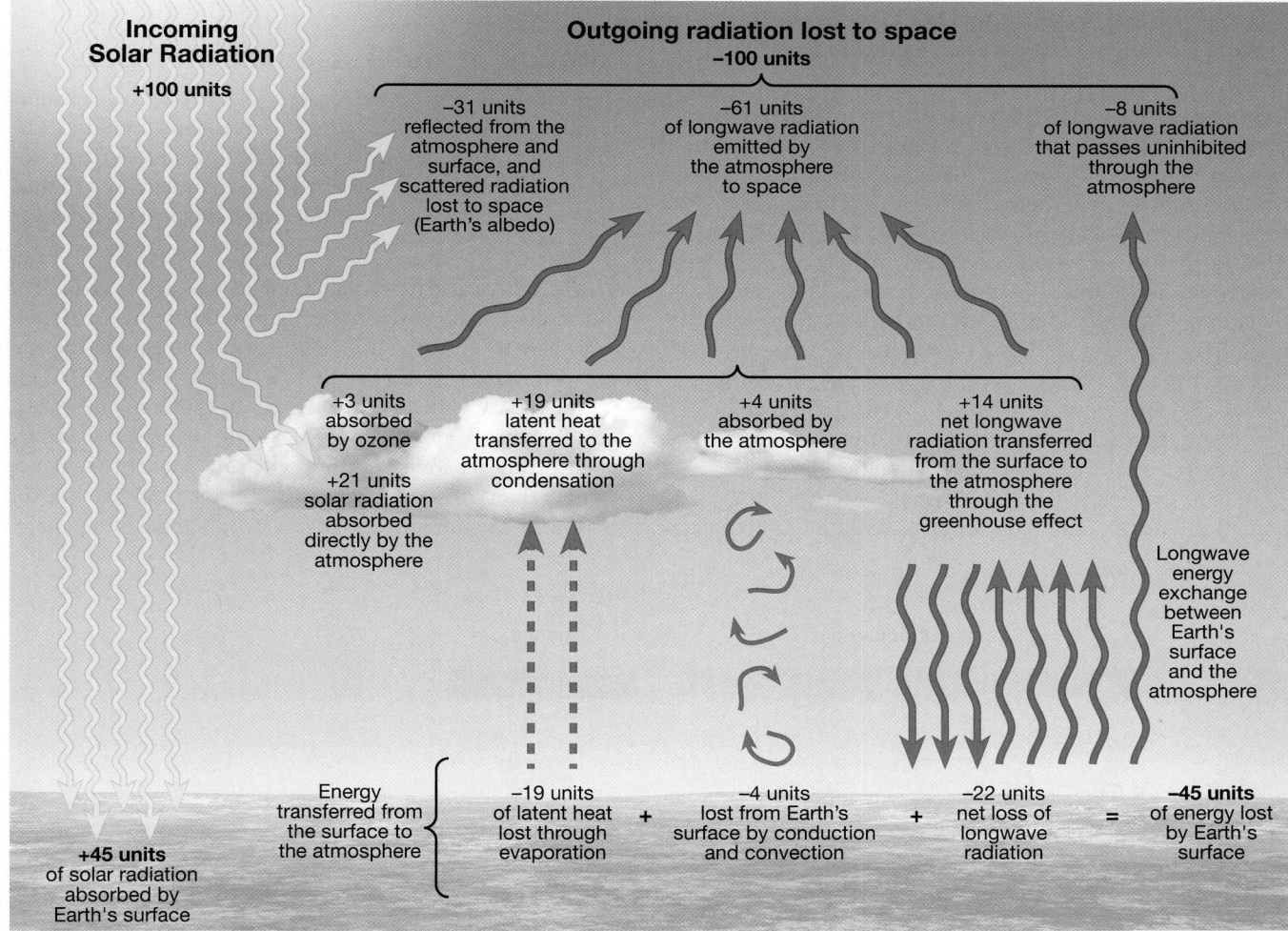

▲ **Figure 4-18** The generalized energy budget of Earth and its atmosphere, shown here with 100 "units" of energy arriving from the Sun balanced by 100 units of energy eventually lost to space. Notice that about one-third of incoming shortwave radiation is reflected and scattered away, and that nearly half of incoming radiation simply transmits through the atmosphere and is absorbed by the surface—the surface then warms the atmosphere above.

atmosphere as latent heat stored in water vapor, eventually released when condensation takes place.

Greenhouse gases absorb large amounts of longwave radiation emitted by the surface, and in turn radiate much of this energy back to the surface where it may be absorbed—and then reemitted as longwave radiation again. Through the absorption of terrestrial radiation by greenhouse gases, the atmosphere receives a net gain of 14 units of energy.

A portion of the longwave radiation emitted by Earth's surface, however, is transmitted directly through the atmosphere without being absorbed by the greenhouse gases. Approximately 8 units of energy—in the form of longwave radiation with wavelengths between about 8 and 12 micrometers—transmit through what is called the *atmospheric window*, a range of wavelengths of infrared radiation that is not strongly absorbed by any atmospheric component.

For the most part, then, the atmosphere is warmed indirectly by the Sun: the Sun warms the surface, and the surface, in turn, warms the air above.

> **Learning Check 4-7**   **In what ways does the surface of Earth warm the troposphere above?**

Consequences of Indirect Warming of Atmosphere: This complicated sequence of atmospheric warming has many ramifications. Because the atmosphere is warmed mostly from below rather than from above, the result is a troposphere in which cold air overlies warm air. This "unstable" situation (explored further in Chapter 6) creates an environment of almost constant convective activity and vertical mixing. If the atmosphere were warmed directly by the Sun, resulting in warm air at the top of the atmosphere and cold air near Earth's surface, the situation would be stable, essentially without vertical air movements. The result would be a troposphere that is largely motionless, apart from the effects of Earth's rotation.

As you can see in the box, "Focus: Monitoring Earth's Radiation Budget," satellites are used to gather global data on insolation and on the absorption and emission of radiation by the atmosphere and surface. These data are one key to understanding both human-caused and natural changes in Earth's radiation budget.

VARIATIONS IN INSOLATION BY LATITUDE AND SEASON FG9

The energy budget we just discussed is broadly generalized. Many latitudinal and vertical imbalances are in this budget, and these are among the most fundamental causes of weather and climate variations.

In essence, we can trace a causal continuum wherein insolation absorption differences lead to temperature differences that lead to air-density differences that lead to pressure differences that lead to wind differences that often lead to moisture differences. It has already been noted that world weather and climate differences are fundamentally caused by the unequal heating of Earth and its atmosphere. This unequal heating is the result of latitudinal and seasonal variations in insolation.

Latitudinal and Seasonal Differences

There are only a few basic reasons for the unequal warming of different latitudinal zones. These reasons include variations in the angle at which solar radiation strikes Earth, the influence of the atmosphere itself on the intensity of radiation transmitted to Earth's surface, and seasonal variations in day length.

Angle of Incidence: The angle at which rays from the Sun strike Earth's surface is called the **angle of incidence**. This angle is measured from a line drawn tangent to the surface, as Figure 4-19 shows. By this definition, a ray striking Earth's surface vertically, when the Sun is directly overhead, has an angle of incidence of 90°, a ray striking the surface when the Sun is lower in the sky has an angle of incidence smaller than 90°, and a ray striking Earth tangent to the surface (as at sunrise and sunset) has an angle of incidence

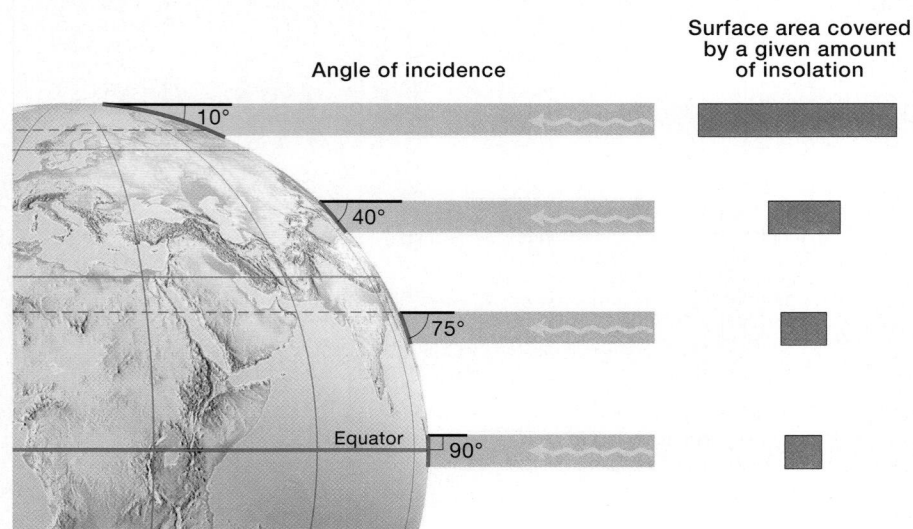

◀ **Figure 4-19** The angle at which solar rays hit Earth's surface varies with latitude. The higher the angle, the more concentrated the energy and therefore the more effective the warming. The day shown in this diagram is the March/September equinox.

Monitoring Earth's Radiation Budget

Earth's radiation budget is monitored on an ongoing basis by several satellites operated by the National Oceanic and Atmospheric Administration (NOAA). Sensors onboard the satellites detect both reflected shortwave radiation and emitted longwave radiation in several wavelength bands to gather information about Earth's surface and atmosphere.

Earth's radiation budget is monitored day and night using an instrument called the Advanced Very High Resolution Radiometer (AVHRR/3), such as is aboard the NOAA-19 satellite. First operational in 2009, NOAA-19 is one of several Polar Orbiting Environmental Satellites (POES) operated by NOAA. Polar orbits allow these satellites to provide complete global coverage four times each day. Data gathered from the POES is used to monitor weather and ocean conditions, as well as to provide a database for climate change research.

Available Solar Energy: Total incoming shortwave radiation—known as available solar energy—is measured at the top of the atmosphere in watts per square meter (W/m^2; Figure 4-C). The total amount of incoming solar radiation in any given location is a consequence of the angle of the Sun and the number of hours of daylight. Notice in this image, taken in July 2012, that the highest average daily insolation occurs over the Arctic—the Sun's angle of incidence is quite low, but 24 hours of daylight result in a very high daily average.

Absorbed Solar Energy: The total amount of shortwave energy absorbed by the atmosphere and surface is referred to as absorbed solar energy—this is the difference between the total shortwave radiation striking the top of the atmosphere and the total shortwave radiation reflected back to space. In Figure 4-D notice the high absorption in subtropical latitudes where the Sun is highest in the sky.

Nighttime Longwave Emissions: Figure 4-E shows outgoing longwave radiation at night. Notice the very high emission of longwave radiation from the subtropical and midlatitude desert regions in the southwestern United States, northern Africa, and east-central Eurasia. The clear nighttime skies and the generally low water vapor content of the air permit significant transmission of longwave radiation away from the surface into space.

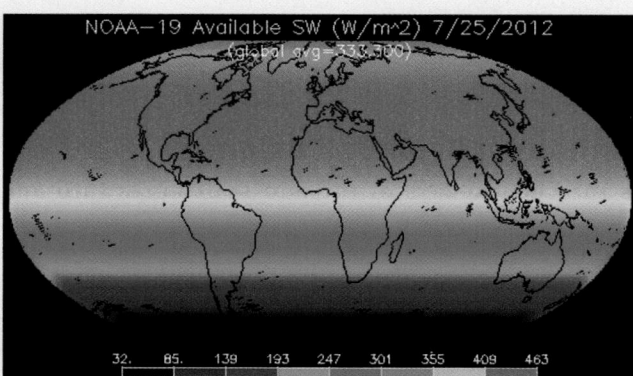

▲ **Figure 4-C** Available solar energy at the top of the atmosphere in W/m^2, taken by the NOAA-19 satellite. Notice that the most solar energy (red and orange areas) is available in the Northern Hemisphere, where it is summer.

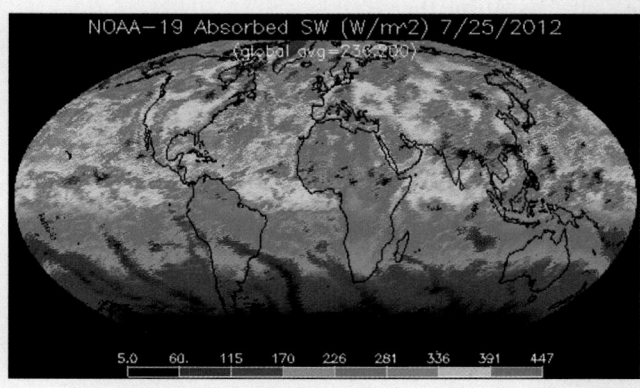

▲ **Figure 4-D** Absorbed solar radiation in W/m^2 on the same day as Figure 4-C, taken by the NOAA-19. Energy absorbed and surface characteristics (for example, land or water) determine the patterns of radiation absorption.

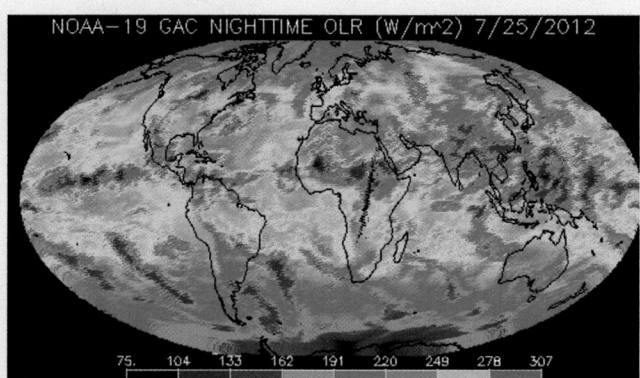

◄ **Figure 4-E** Nighttime emission of outgoing longwave radiation in W/m^2, taken by the NOAA-19 satellite image on the same day as Figures 4-C and 4-D. Surface characteristics, as well as energy previously absorbed, determine the patterns of radiation emission.

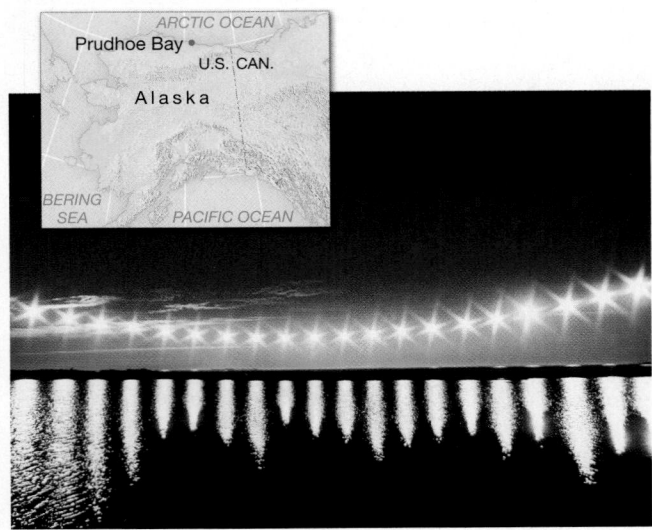

▲ **Figure 4-20** The Sun is low in the sky even during the summer in high latitudes. This time-lapse photograph shows the "midnight Sun" on the June solstice at Prudhoe Bay, Alaska (70° N).

of 0°. Because Earth's surface is curved and because the relationship between Earth and the Sun changes with the seasons, the angle of incidence for any given location on Earth also changes during the year.

The angle of incidence is the primary determinant of the intensity of solar radiation received at any spot on Earth. If a ray strikes Earth's surface vertically, the energy is concentrated in a small area; if the ray strikes Earth obliquely, the energy is spread out over a larger portion of the surface. The more nearly perpendicular the ray (in other words, the closer to 90° the angle of incidence), the smaller the surface area warmed by a given amount of insolation and the more effective the heating. Averaged over the year as a whole, the insolation received by high-latitude regions is much less intense than that received by tropical areas (Figure 4-20).

Atmospheric Obstruction: Insolation does not travel through the atmosphere unimpeded—it encounters various obstructions in the atmosphere. We have already noted that clouds, particulate matter, and gas molecules in the atmosphere may absorb, reflect, or scatter incoming solar radiation. The result of these obstructions is a reduction in the intensity of this energy by the time it reaches Earth's surface. On average, sunlight received at Earth's surface is only about half as strong as it is at the top of Earth's atmosphere.

The attenuation (weakening) of radiation that passes through the atmosphere varies from time to time and from place to place depending on two factors: the amount of atmosphere through which the radiation has to pass and the transparency of the air. The distance a ray of sunlight travels through the atmosphere (commonly referred to as *path length*) is determined by the angle of incidence (Figure 4-21). A high-angle ray traverses a shorter course through the atmosphere than a low-angle one. A tangent ray (one having an incidence angle of 0°) must pass through nearly 20 times as much atmosphere as a vertical ray (one striking Earth at an angle of 90°).

The effect of atmospheric obstruction tends to reinforce the pattern of solar energy distribution at Earth's surface established by the angle of incidence. For example, in high latitudes the Sun has a lower angle of incidence and a greater path length through the atmosphere than in the tropics. Thus, there are smaller losses of energy in the tropical atmosphere than in the polar atmosphere; however, as we will see, this general pattern is complicated by patterns of cloud cover.

Day Length: The duration of sunlight is another important factor in explaining latitudinal inequalities in warming. Longer days allow more insolation to be received and thus more solar energy to be absorbed. In tropical regions, this factor is relatively unimportant because the number of hours between sunrise and sunset does not vary significantly from one month to another; at the equator, of course, daylight and darkness are equal in length (12 hours each) every day of the year. In middle and high latitudes, however, there are pronounced seasonal variations in day length. The conspicuous buildup of warmth in summer in these regions is largely a consequence of the long hours of daylight, and the winter cold is a manifestation of limited insolation being received because of the short days.

> **Learning Check 4-8**   **Why does more solar energy reach the surface when the Sun is high in the sky than when it is low in the sky?**

Latitudinal Radiation Balance

As the vertical rays of the Sun shift northward and southward across the equator during the course of the year, the belt of maximum solar energy swings back and forth through the tropics. Thus, in the low latitudes,

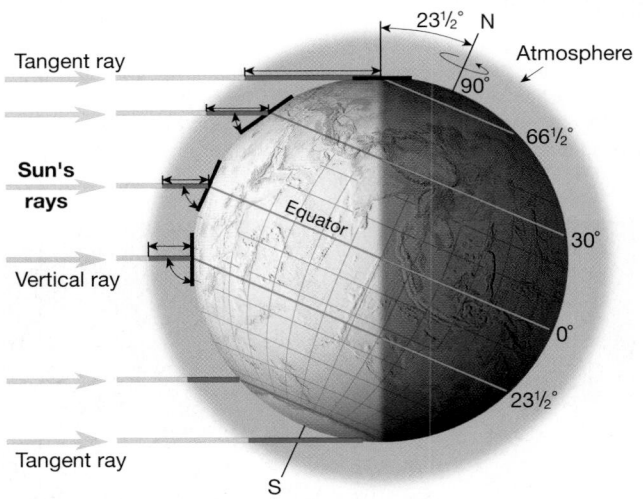

▲ **Figure 4-21** Atmospheric obstruction of sunlight. Low-angle rays (such as in the high latitudes) must pass through more atmosphere than high-angle rays; the greater the length of travel through the atmosphere, the more the intensity of radiation is reduced through reflection, scattering, and absorption. The day shown in this diagram is the December solstice.

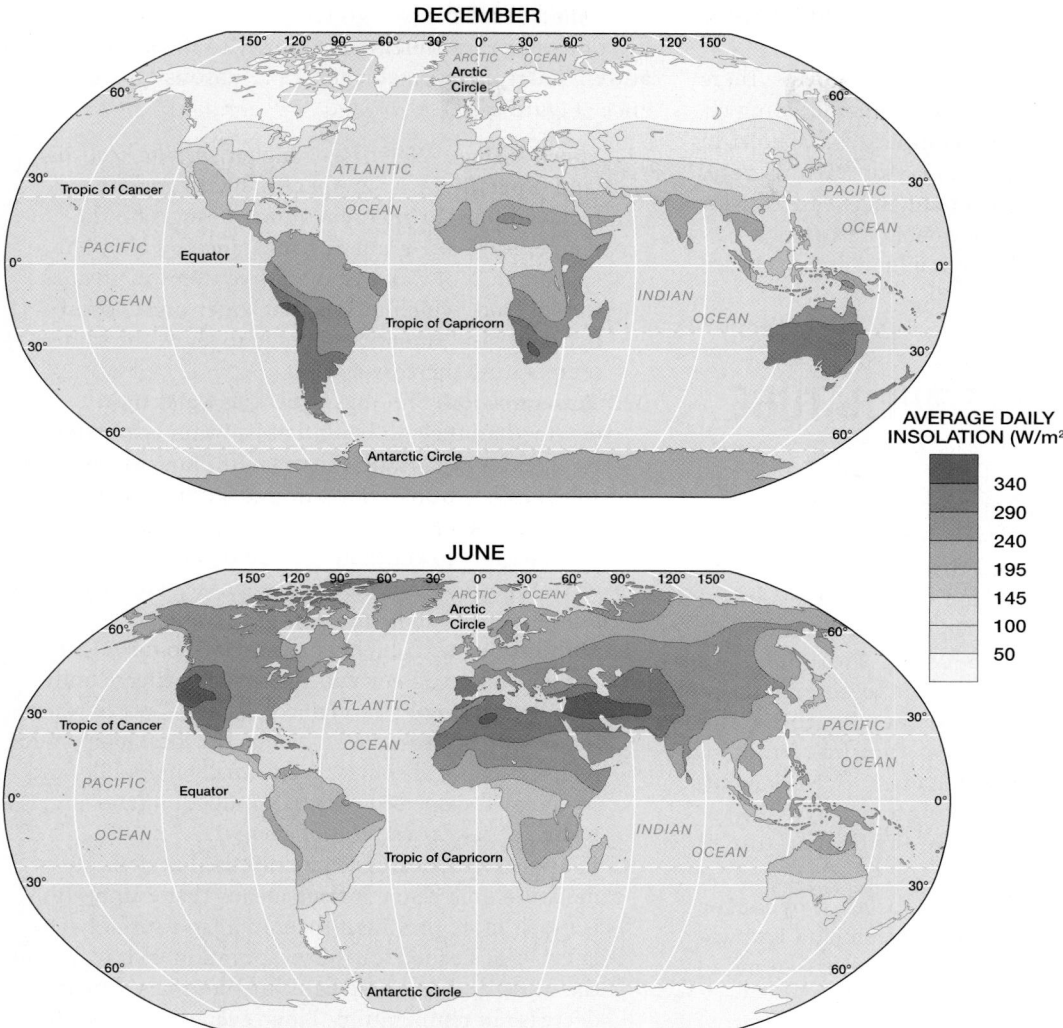

DECEMBER

JUNE

AVERAGE DAILY
INSOLATION (W/m²)

340
290
240
195
145
100
50

◀ **Figure 4-22** World distribution of average daily insolation for December and June in watts per square meter. The pattern is determined mainly by latitude (note the low December levels in northern areas) and amount of cloudiness (note the high June levels in such cloud-free desert areas as the southwestern United States and southern Eurasia).

between about 38° N and 38° S, there is an energy surplus, with more incoming than outgoing radiation. In the latitudes north and south of these two parallels, there is an energy deficit, with more radiant loss than gain. The surplus of energy in low latitudes is directly related to the consistently high angle of incidence, and the energy deficit in high latitudes is associated with low angles.

Figure 4-22 shows the distribution of average daily insolation at the surface around the world for December and June, and Figure 4-23 shows the annual average daily insolation for the United States and parts of Canada and Mexico. The maps show the average daily insolation received in watts per square meter (W/m²; 1 watt = joule per second). The variations are largely latitudinal, as is to be expected. The principal interruptions to the simple latitudinal pattern are based on the presence or absence of frequent cloud cover, where insolation is reflected, diffused, and scattered. In Figure 4-23, for example, notice that insolation is greatest in the southwestern United States, where clouds are consistently sparse, and is least in the

Video
Seasonal
Radiation
Patterns

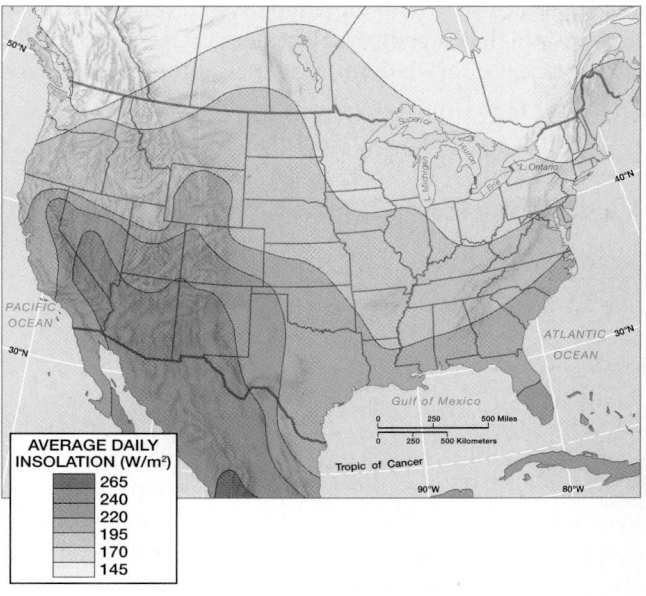

AVERAGE DAILY
INSOLATION (W/m²)

265
240
220
195
170
145

▲ **Figure 4-23** Average annual daily insolation in watts per square meter received in the 48 conterminous states and adjacent parts of Canada and Mexico. The sunny southwestern areas receive the most radiation; the cloudy northeastern and northwestern areas receive the least.

northwestern and northeastern corners of the country, where cloud cover is frequent.

Despite the variable pattern shown on the maps, there is a long-term balance between incoming and outgoing radiation for the Earth–atmosphere complex as a whole; in other words, the net radiation balance for Earth is zero. The mechanisms for exchanging energy between the surplus and deficit regions involve the general circulation patterns of the atmosphere and oceans, which are discussed later in the book.

LAND AND WATER TEMPERATURE CONTRASTS

As we've seen, the atmosphere is warmed mainly by energy reradiated and transferred from Earth's surface rather than by energy received directly from the Sun. So the warming of Earth's surface is a primary control of the warming of the air above it. To understand variations in air temperatures, it is useful to understand how different kinds of surfaces react to solar energy. There is considerable variation in the absorbing and reflecting capabilities of the almost limitless kinds of surfaces found on Earth—soil, water, grass, trees, cement, rooftops, and so forth. Their varying receptivity to insolation in turn causes differences in the temperature of the overlying air.

Although Earth has many kinds of surfaces, by far the most significant contrasts are those between land and water. As a generalization: land warms and cools faster and to a greater extent than water.

Warming of Land and Water

A land surface warms up more rapidly and reaches a higher temperature than a comparable water surface receiving the same amount of insolation. In essence, a thin layer of land is warmed to relatively high temperatures, whereas a thick layer of water is warmed more slowly to moderate temperatures. There are several significant reasons for this difference (Figure 4-24).

1. **Specific Heat:** Water has a higher *specific heat* than land. **Specific heat** (or **specific heat capacity**) is the amount of energy required to increase the temperature of 1 gram of a substance by 1°C. The specific heat of water is about five times as great as that of land, which means that water must absorb five times the amount of energy to show the same temperature increase as land.

2. **Transmission:** Sun rays penetrate water more deeply than they do land; that is, water is a better transmitter of radiation than land. Thus, in water solar energy is absorbed through a much greater volume of matter, and maximum temperatures remain considerably lower than they do on land, where the warming is concentrated at the surface and maximum temperatures can be much higher.

3. **Mobility:** Water is highly mobile, and so turbulent mixing and ocean currents disperse the energy both broadly and deeply through convection—warm water mixes with cooler water, reducing the local temperature increase. Land, of course, is essentially immobile, and so energy is dispersed only by conduction (and land is a relatively poor conductor of energy).

4. **Evaporative Cooling:** The unlimited availability of moisture on a water surface means that evaporation is much more prevalent than on a land surface. The latent heat needed for this evaporation is drawn from the water and its immediate surroundings, causing a decrease in temperature. Thus, evaporative cooling counteracts some of the warming of a water surface.

Learning Check 4-9 **How does the high *specific heat* of water influence how quickly it warms?**

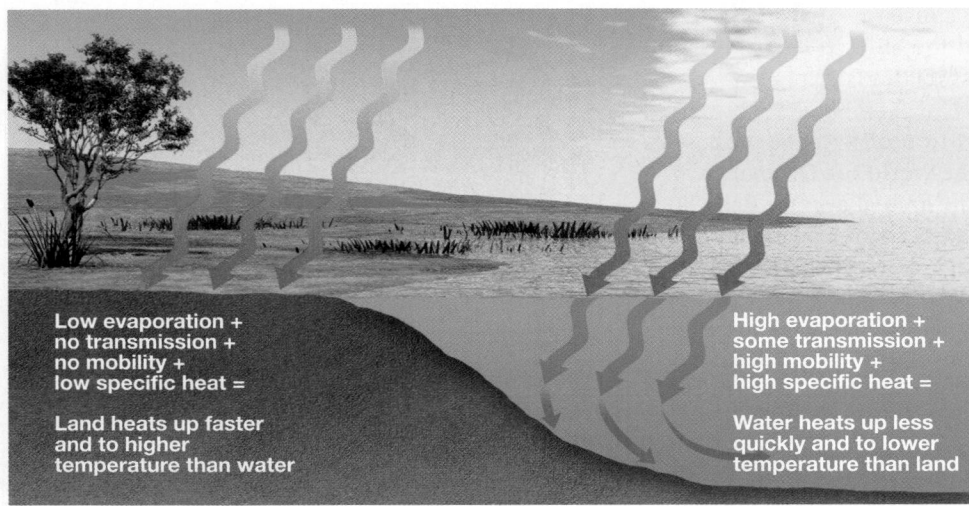

Low evaporation +
no transmission +
no mobility +
low specific heat =

Land heats up faster
and to higher
temperature than water

High evaporation +
some transmission +
high mobility +
high specific heat =

Water heats up less
quickly and to lower
temperature than land

◄ **Figure 4-24** Some contrasting characteristics of the warming of land and water—in general, land warms faster and to a greater extent than water.

Cooling of Land and Water

Land cools more rapidly and to a lower temperature than a water surface for many of the same reasons it warms more rapidly. For example, during winter, the shallow, warmed layer of land radiates its energy away quickly. Water loses its warmth more gradually because of its high specific heat and because the energy has been stored deeply and is brought only slowly to the surface for radiation. As the surface water cools, it sinks and is replaced by warmer water from below. The entire water body must be cooled before the surface temperatures decrease significantly.

Implications

The significance of these contrasts between land and water warming and cooling rates is that both the hottest and coldest areas of Earth are found in the interiors of continents, distant from the influence of oceans. In the study of the atmosphere, probably no single geographic relationship is more important than the distinction between continental and maritime climates. A continental climate experiences greater seasonal extremes of temperature—hotter in summer, colder in winter—than a maritime climate.

These differences are shown in Figure 4-25, which portrays average monthly temperatures for San Diego and Dallas. These two cities are at approximately the same latitude and experience almost identical lengths of day and angles of incidence. Although their annual average temperatures are

Latitude	Northern Hemisphere	Southern Hemisphere
0	0	0
15	3	4
30	13	7
45	23	6
60	30	11
75	32	26
90	40	31

TABLE 4-1 Average Annual Temperature Range by Latitude, in Degrees Celsius

Source: From Frederick K. Lutgens and Edward J. Tarbuck, *The Atmosphere: An Introduction to Meteorology*, 9th ed., Upper Saddle River, NJ: Pearson-Prentice Hall, 2004, p. 71. Used by permission of Prentice Hall.

almost the same, the monthly averages vary significantly. Dallas, in the interior of the continent, experiences notably warmer summers and cooler winters than San Diego, which enjoys the moderating influence of an adjacent ocean.

The oceans, in a sense, act as great reservoirs of energy. In summer they absorb solar energy and store it. In winter they release some of this energy and warm the air. Thus, they function as a sort of global thermostat, moderating temperature extremes.

Differences Between Hemispheres: The ameliorating influence of the oceans can also be demonstrated, on a totally different scale, by comparing latitudinal temperature variations in the Northern Hemisphere with those in the Southern Hemisphere. The Northern Hemisphere is often thought of as a "land hemisphere," because 39 percent of its area is land surface; the Southern Hemisphere is a "water hemisphere," with only 19 percent of its area as land. Table 4-1 shows the average *annual temperature range* (difference in average temperature of the coldest and warmest months) for comparable parallels in each hemisphere. It is obvious that the land hemisphere has greater extremes.

Learning Check 4-10 Which midlatitude location will typically experience higher summer temperatures: a coastal area, or a location deep in the interior of a continent? Why?

MECHANISMS OF GLOBAL ENERGY TRANSFER

As we've seen, during the year more total solar energy arrives in the tropics than at the poles, and this is the basis for the broad difference in temperature observed between low latitudes and high latitudes. However, were it not for mechanisms of energy transfer, the tropics would be warmer than they actually are, and the poles would be colder.

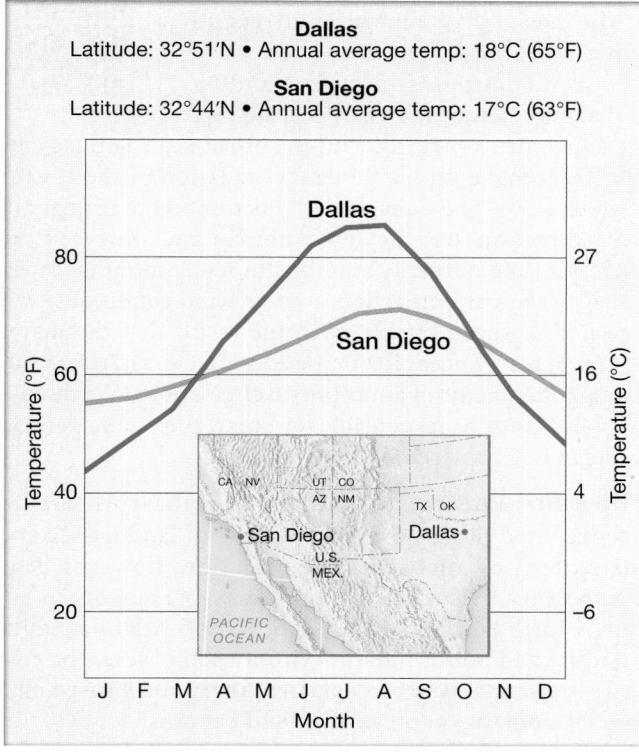

▲ **Figure 4-25** Annual temperature curves for San Diego, California, and Dallas, Texas. Although both have similar average annual temperatures, they have very different annual temperature regimes. In both summer and winter, San Diego, situated on the coast, experiences milder temperatures than inland Dallas.

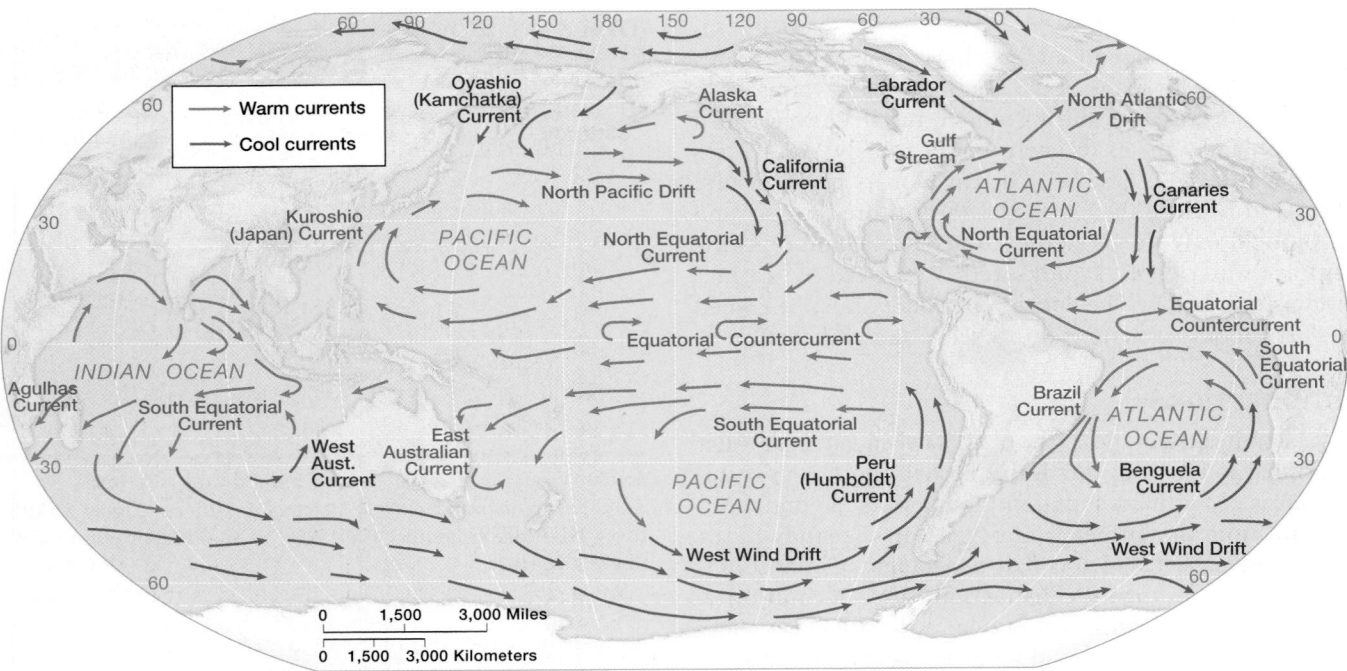

▲ **Figure 4-26** The major surface ocean currents. Warm currents are shown with red arrows and cool currents with blue arrows. Notice that in the midlatitudes, warm currents are flowing along the eastern coasts of continents, while cool currents are flowing along the western coasts.

Two important mechanisms of energy transfer—circulation patterns in the atmosphere and in the oceans—shift some of the warmth of the low latitudes toward the high latitudes, and so moderate both the warmth of low latitudes and the cold of the high latitudes. Both the atmosphere and oceans act as enormous thermal engines, with their latitudinal imbalance of energy driving the currents of air and water, which in turn transfer energy and somewhat modify the imbalance.

Atmospheric Circulation

Of the two mechanisms of global energy transfer, by far the more important is the general circulation of the atmosphere. Air moves in an almost infinite number of ways, but there is a broad planetary circulation pattern that serves as a general framework for moving warm air poleward and cool air equatorward. Some 75 to 80 percent of all horizontal energy transfer is accomplished by atmospheric circulation.

Our discussion of atmospheric circulation is withheld until Chapter 5, following consideration of some fundamentals concerning pressure and wind.

FG11

Oceanic Circulation

Winds disturb the surface of the ocean with swells and waves. Wind can also propel the surface of the water to move forward in the form of a *current.* Surface ocean currents can flow at about 1 to 2 percent of wind speed, meaning that water in a surface current might travel some tens or even hundreds of kilometers in a day.

A close relationship exists between the general circulation patterns of the atmosphere and oceans. It is wind blowing over the surface of the water that is the principal force driving the major surface ocean currents. However, the influence works both ways: energy stored in the oceans has important effects on patterns of atmospheric circulation.

For our purposes in understanding global energy transfer by the oceans, we are concerned primarily with the broad-scale surface currents that make up the general circulation of the oceans (Figure 4-26). These major currents respond to changes in wind direction, but they are so broad and slow that the response time normally amounts to many months. In essence, ocean currents reflect average wind conditions over a period of several years, with the result that the major components of oceanic circulation are closely related to major components of atmospheric circulation. (We discuss the wind patterns responsible for ocean current movement in detail in Chapter 5.)

The Basic Pattern: All the oceans of the world are interconnected. Because of the location of landmasses and the pattern of atmospheric circulation, however, it is convenient to visualize five relatively separate ocean basins—North Pacific, South Pacific, North Atlantic, South Atlantic, and South Indian. Within each of these basins, there is a similar pattern of surface current flow based on a general similarity of prevailing wind patterns.

Despite variations based on the size and shape of the various ocean basins and on the season of the year, a single simple pattern of surface currents is characteristic of all the basins. It consists of a series of enormous elliptical loops elongated east–west and centered approximately at 30° of

Animation
Ocean Circulation
Patterns–
Subtropical Gyres

latitude (except in the Indian Ocean, where it is centered closer to the equator). These loops, called **subtropical gyres**, flow clockwise in the Northern Hemisphere and counterclockwise in the Southern Hemisphere (see Figure 4-26).

On the equatorward side of each subtropical gyre is an *Equatorial Current*, which moves steadily from east to west. The equatorial currents have an average position 5° to 10° north or south of the equator and, as we'll see in Chapter 5, are propelled by the dominant wind system of the tropics: the east-to-west blowing *trade winds*.

Near the western margin of each ocean basin, the general current curves poleward. As these currents approach the poleward margins of the ocean basins, they curve back to the east—here propelled by the west-to-east blowing *westerly winds*. As the currents reach the eastern edges of the basins they curve back toward the equator, producing an incompletely closed loop in each basin.

The movement of these currents, although impelled by the wind, is also influenced by the deflective force of Earth's rotation—the Coriolis effect (discussed in Chapter 3). The Coriolis effect dictates that the ocean currents are deflected to the right in the Northern Hemisphere and to the left in the Southern Hemisphere. A glance at the basic pattern shows that the current movement around the gyres responds precisely to the Coriolis effect.

Equatorial Countercurrents: Notice in Figure 4-26 that the Northern and Southern Hemisphere equatorial currents are separated by an *Equatorial Countercurrent*—a west-to-east moving flow approximately along the equator in each ocean. The equatorial currents feed the Equatorial Countercurrent near its western margin in each basin. Water from the Equatorial Countercurrent in turn drifts poleward to feed the Equatorial Current near the eastern end of its path.

Northern and Southern Variations: In the two Northern Hemisphere basins—North Pacific and North Atlantic—the bordering continents lie so close together at the northern basin margin that the bulk of the current flow is prevented from entering the Arctic Ocean. This effect is more pronounced in the Pacific than in the Atlantic. The North Pacific has very limited flow northward between Asia and North America, whereas in the North Atlantic a larger proportion of the flow escapes northward between Greenland and Europe.

In the Southern Hemisphere, the continents are far apart. Thus, the southern segments of the gyres in the South Pacific, South Atlantic, and South Indian Oceans are connected as one continuous flow in the uninterrupted belt of ocean that extends around the world in the vicinity of latitude 60° S. This circumpolar flow is called the *West Wind Drift*.

Current Temperatures: Of utmost importance to our understanding of latitudinal energy transfer are the temperatures of the various ocean currents. Each major current is classified as either *warm* or *cool* relative to the surrounding water at that latitude. Each "leg" of the subtropical gyres has its own general temperature characteristics:

- Low-latitude currents (Equatorial Current and Equatorial Countercurrent) have relatively warm water.
- Poleward-moving currents on the western sides of ocean basins (off the east coast of continents) carry relatively warm water toward higher latitudes, such as the Gulf Stream off the east coast of North America (Figure 4-27).
- The high-latitude currents in the Northern Hemisphere gyres carry relatively warm water to the east, while the high-latitude currents in the Southern Hemisphere gyres (generally combined into the West Wind Drift) carry relatively cool water to the east.
- Equatorward-moving currents on the eastern sides of ocean basins (off the west coasts of continents) carry relatively cool water toward the equator.

In summary—from the perspective of the margins of the continents—the general circulation of the oceans is a poleward flow of warm, tropical water along the east coasts of continents and an equatorward movement of cool, high-latitude water along the west coasts of continents.

Learning Check 4-11   **What is the relative temperature of the ocean current flowing along the west coast of a midlatitude continent? Along the east coast?**

Western Intensification: In addition to differences in temperature, the poleward-moving warm currents off the east coast of continents tend to be narrower, deeper, and

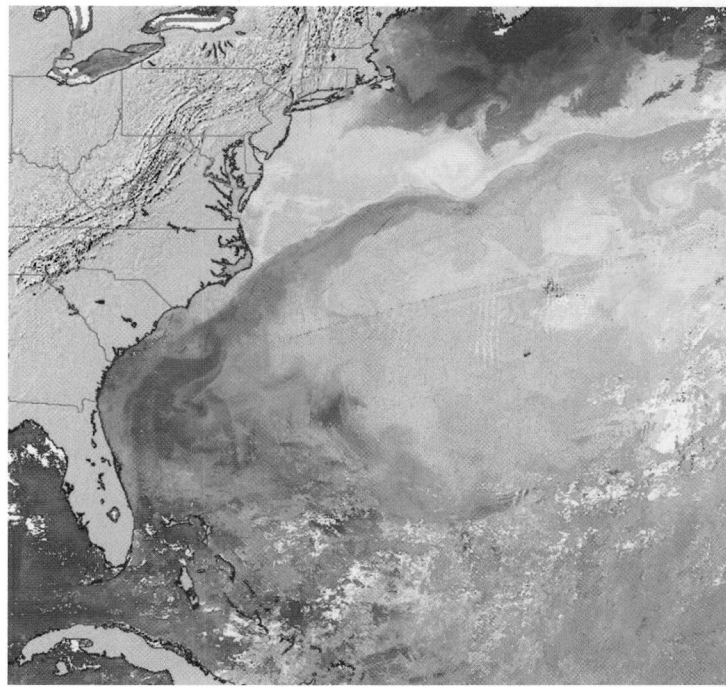

▲ **Figure 4-27** Multi-pass satellite image showing the Gulf Stream off the east coast of North America. Red represents relatively high water temperature while blue represents relatively low water temperatures. Several vertical and horizontal bands are not actual temperature features but are caused by incomplete satellite data.

faster than the equatorward-moving cool currents flowing off the west coast of continents. This phenomenon is called *western intensification* because it occurs on the western side of the subtropical gyres (in other words, it occurs in the currents flowing poleward off the east coasts of continents in the midlatitudes).

This intensification of poleward moving warm currents arises for a number of reasons, including the Coriolis effect. Recall from Chapter 3 that the Coriolis effect is greater in higher latitudes, and so the eastward moving high-latitude current flow is deflected back toward the equator more strongly than the westward moving equatorial current flow is deflected toward the poles. This means that cool water is slowly flowing back toward the equator across much of the eastward-moving high-latitude currents, whereas the poleward-flowing warm currents are confined to a fairly narrow zone off the east coasts of continents.

Rounding out the Pattern: Three other aspects of oceanic circulation are influential in energy transfer:

1. The northwestern portions of Northern Hemisphere ocean basins receive an influx of cool water from the Arctic Ocean. For example, the Labrador Current is a prominent cool current flowing southward from the Arctic Ocean between Greenland and the Canadian coast (see Figure 4-26). A smaller flow of cold water issues from the Bering Sea southward along the coast of Siberia to Japan.
2. Wherever an equatorward-flowing cool current pulls away from a subtropical western coast, a pronounced and persistent **upwelling** of cold water occurs. For example, if winds along the west coast of a Northern Hemisphere continent are blowing from the north or northwest, the Coriolis effect will deflect some of the surface water to the right, away from the coast.

As surface water pulls away from the coast, it will be replaced with water from deeper below. Upwelling brings nutrient-rich water to the surface, making west-coast marine ecosystems highly productive. The upwelling also brings colder water to the surface, generally decreasing the surface temperature of the already cool currents off the western coast of continents (Figure 4-28). Upwelling is most striking off South America but is also notable off North America, northwestern Africa, and southwestern Africa. It is much less developed off the coast of western Australia.

3. In addition to the surface ocean currents we have just described, there is a deep ocean circulation pattern—sometimes called the *global conveyor belt circulation*—that influences global climate in subtle, but nonetheless important ways. The deep ocean conveyor belt circulation is discussed in greater detail in Chapter 9.

VERTICAL TEMPERATURE PATTERNS

As we study the geography of weather and climate most of our attention is directed to the horizontal dimension; in other words, we are concerned with the geographic distribution of atmospheric phenomena around the surface of Earth. However, to fully understand these distributional patterns, we must also pay attention to a number of important vertical patterns in the atmosphere. One such vertical pattern involves variations in temperature with increasing altitude in the troposphere.

Environmental Lapse Rate

Temperature change with increasing altitude within the troposphere is relatively predictable. As we learned in Chapter 3, throughout the troposphere, under typical conditions, a general decrease in temperature occurs with increasing altitude (Figure 4-29a). However, there are many exceptions to this general statement. Indeed, the rate of vertical temperature decline can vary according to season, time of day, amount of cloud cover, and a host of other factors. In some cases, there is even an opposite trend, with the temperature increasing upward for a limited distance.

The observed trend of vertical temperature change in the atmosphere is called the **environmental lapse rate**. Determining the lapse rate of a "column" of air involves measuring air temperature at various altitudes. Then a graph of temperature as a function of height is drawn to produce a temperature profile of that air column. When measuring such a lapse-rate temperature change, only the thermometer is moved; the air is at rest. If the air is moving vertically, expansion or compression will cause an adiabatic temperature change—such adiabatic lapse rates are explored more fully in Chapter 6.

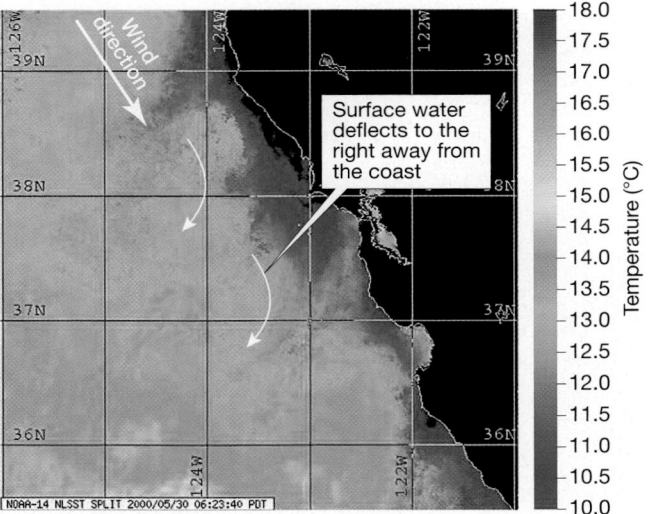

▲ **Figure 4-28** Upwelling of cold water (shown in violet and blue colors) along the West Coast of North America near San Francisco. As wind blows over the surface of the ocean, the surface water is deflected to the right by the Coriolis effect; as the surface water veers away from the coast, it is replaced by cold water from below.

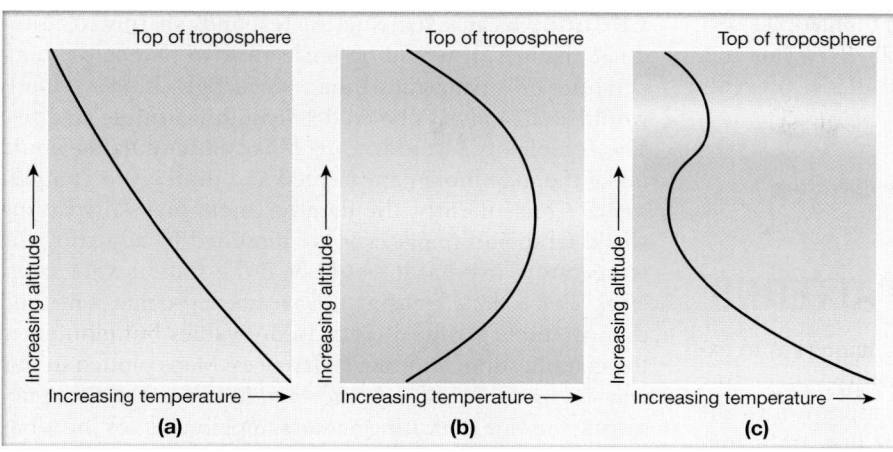

◀ **Figure 4-29** A comparison of normal and inverted lapse rates. (a) Tropospheric temperature normally decreases with increasing altitude. (b) In a surface inversion, temperature increases with increasing altitude from ground level to some distance above the ground. (c) In an upper-air inversion, temperature first decreases with increasing altitude as in a normal lapse rate, but then at some altitude well below the tropopause begins to increase with increasing altitude.

Average Lapse Rate

Although the environmental lapse rate varies from place to place and from time to time, particularly in the lowest few hundred meters of the troposphere, the average rate of temperature change is about 6.5°C per 1000 meters (3.6°F 1000 feet). This is called the **average lapse rate**, or *average vertical temperature gradient* within the troposphere. The average lapse rate tells us that if a thermometer measures the temperature 1000 meters above a previous measurement, the reading will be, on average, 6.5°C cooler. Conversely, if a second measurement is made 1000 meters lower than the first, the temperature will be about 6.5°C warmer.

Temperature Inversions

The most prominent exception to an average lapse-rate condition is a **temperature inversion**, a situation in which temperature in the troposphere *increases*, rather than decreases, with increasing altitude. Inversions are relatively common in the troposphere but are usually of brief duration and restricted depth. They can occur near Earth's surface, as in Figure 4-29b, or at higher levels, as in Figure 4-29c.

Inversions influence weather and climate. As we shall see in Chapter 6, an inversion inhibits vertical air movements and greatly diminishes the possibility of precipitation. Inversions also contribute significantly to increased air pollution because they create stagnant air conditions that greatly limit the natural upward dispersal of urban-industrial pollutants (Figure 4-30).

Surface Inversions: The most readily recognizable inversions are those found at ground level. These are often *radiation inversions* that can develop on a long, cold winter night when a land surface rapidly emits longwave radiation into a clear, calm sky. The cold ground then cools the air above by conduction. In a relatively short time, the lowest few hundred meters of the troposphere become colder than the air above and a temperature inversion is in effect. Radiational inversions are primarily winter phenomena because there is only a short daylight period for incoming solar heating and a long night for radiational

cooling. They are therefore much more prevalent in high latitudes than elsewhere.

Advectional inversions develop where there is a horizontal inflow of cold air into an area. This condition commonly is produced by cool maritime air blowing into a coastal locale. Advectional inversions are usually short-lived (typically overnight) and shallow. They may occur at any time of year, depending on the location of the relatively cold surface and on wind movement.

Another type of surface inversion results when cooler air slides down a slope into a valley, thereby displacing slightly warmer air. This fairly common occurrence during winter in some midlatitude regions is called a *cold-air-drainage inversion.*

Upper-Air Inversions: Temperature inversions well above the ground surface nearly always are the result of air descending from above. These *subsidence inversions* are usually associated with high-pressure conditions, which are particularly characteristic of subtropical latitudes throughout the year and of Northern Hemisphere continents in winter.

▼ **Figure 4-30** Downtown Los Angeles on a "mild" smog day. The top of the inversion is visible where the mountains rise above the smog layer.

A subsidence inversion can be fairly deep (sometimes several thousand meters), and its base is usually a few hundred meters above the ground, as low-level turbulence prevents the warmer air from sinking lower.

Learning Check **4-12** **What is a *temperature inversion*?**

GLOBAL TEMPERATURE PATTERNS

The goal of this and the four succeeding chapters is to examine the global pattern of climate. With the preceding pages as background, we now turn our attention to the worldwide distribution of temperature, the first of the four elements of weather and climate.

Maps of global temperature patterns usually show seasonal extremes rather than annual averages. January and July are the months of lowest and highest temperatures for most places on Earth, and so maps portraying the average temperatures of these two months provide a simple but meaningful expression of temperature conditions in winter and summer (Figure 4-31 and Figure 4-32). Temperature distribution is shown by means of **isotherms**, lines joining points of equal temperature. Temperature maps are based on monthly averages, which are based on daily averages; the maps do not show the maximum daytime heating or the maximum nighttime cooling. Although the maps are on a very small scale, they permit a broad understanding of temperature patterns for the world.

Prominent Controls of Temperature

Patterns of temperature are controlled largely by four factors—altitude, latitude, land–water contrasts, and ocean currents.

Altitude: Because temperature responds sharply to altitudinal changes, it would be misleading to plot actual temperatures on a temperature map, since high-altitude stations would almost always be colder than low-altitude stations. The complexity introduced by hills and mountains would make the map more complicated and difficult to comprehend. Consequently, the data for most maps displaying world temperature patterns are modified by adjusting the temperature to what it would be if the station were at sea level. This is done by using the average lapse rate, a method that produces artificial temperature values but eliminates the complication of terrain differences. Maps plotted in this way are useful in showing world patterns, but they are not satisfactory for indicating actual temperatures for locations that are not close to sea level.

Latitude: Clearly the most conspicuous feature of any world temperature map is the general east–west trend of the isotherms, roughly following the parallels of latitude. If Earth had a uniform surface without ocean currents and wind systems, the isotherms would probably coincide exactly with parallels, showing a progressive decrease of temperature poleward from the equator. However, temperature variations between land and water, and the circulation of ocean currents around the margins of ocean basins, complicates the actual temperature pattern significantly. Nonetheless, the fundamental cause of temperature variation around the world is insolation variation, which is governed primarily by latitude, and so general global temperature patterns reflect this latitudinal control.

Land-Water Contrasts: The different warming and cooling characteristics of land and water are also reflected conspicuously on a temperature map. Summer temperatures

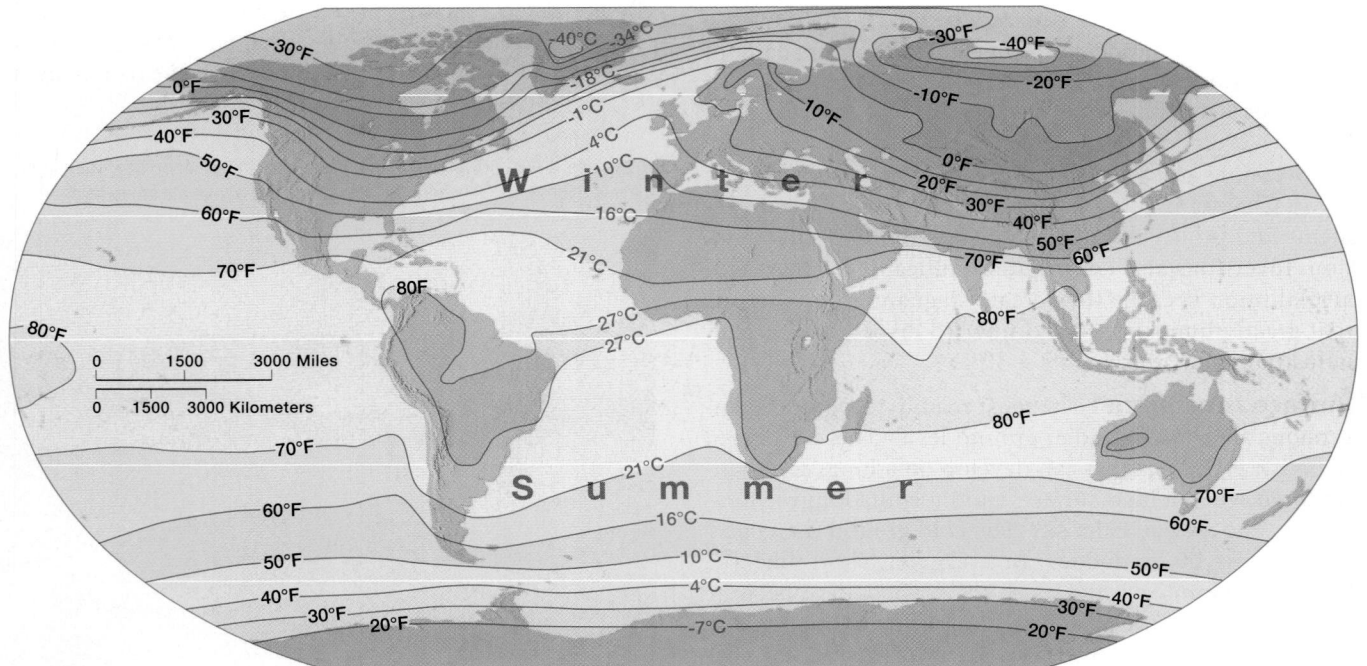

▲ **Figure 4-31** Average January sea-level temperatures.

are higher over the continents than over the oceans, as shown by the poleward curvature of the isotherms over continents in the respective hemispheres (July in the Northern Hemisphere, January in the Southern Hemisphere). Winter temperatures are lower over the continents than over the oceans; the isotherms bend equatorward over continents in this season (January in the Northern Hemisphere, July in the Southern Hemisphere). Thus, in both seasons, isotherms make greater north–south shifts over land than over water.

Another manifestation of the land–water contrast is the regularity of the isotherm pattern in the midlatitudes of the Southern Hemisphere, in contrast to the situation in the Northern Hemisphere. There is very little land in these Southern Hemisphere latitudes, and so contrasting surface characteristics are absent.

Ocean Currents: Some of the most obvious bends in the isotherms occur in near-coastal areas of the oceans, where prominent warm or cool currents reinforce the isothermal curves caused by land–water contrasts. Cool currents deflect isotherms equatorward, whereas warm currents deflect them poleward. Cool currents produce the greatest isothermal bends in the warm season: note the January situation off the western coast of South America and the southwestern coast of Africa, or the July conditions off the western coast of North America. Warm currents have their most prominent effects in the cool season: witness the isothermal pattern in the North Atlantic Ocean in January.

> **Learning Check 4-13**   **What generally happens to global temperatures going from the equator toward the poles? Why?**

Seasonal Patterns

Video
Seasonal
Changes in
Temperature

Apart from the general east–west trend of the isotherms, probably the most conspicuous feature of Figure 4-31 and Figure 4-32 is the latitudinal shift of the isotherms from one map to the other. The isotherms follow the changing balance of insolation during the course of the year, moving northward from January to July and returning southward from July to January. Note, for example, the 10°C (50°F) isotherm in southernmost South America: in January (midsummer), it is positioned at the southern tip of the continent, whereas in July (midwinter), it is shifted considerably to the north.

This isotherm shift is much more pronounced in high latitudes than in low and also much more pronounced over the continents than over the oceans. Thus, tropical areas, particularly tropical oceans, show relatively small displacement of the isotherms from January to July, whereas over middle- and high-latitude landmasses, an isotherm may migrate northward or southward more than 4000 kilometers (2500 miles)—some 14° of latitude—as illustrated in Figure 4-33.

Isotherms are also more tightly "packed" in winter. This close line spacing indicates that the temperature gradient (rate of temperature change with horizontal distance) is steeper in winter than in summer, which in turn reflects the greater contrast in radiation balance in winter. The temperature gradient is also steeper over continents than over oceans.

Coldest Winter Locations: The coldest places on Earth are over landmasses in the higher latitudes. During July, the polar region of Antarctica is the dominant area of coldness. In January, the coldest temperatures occur many hundreds

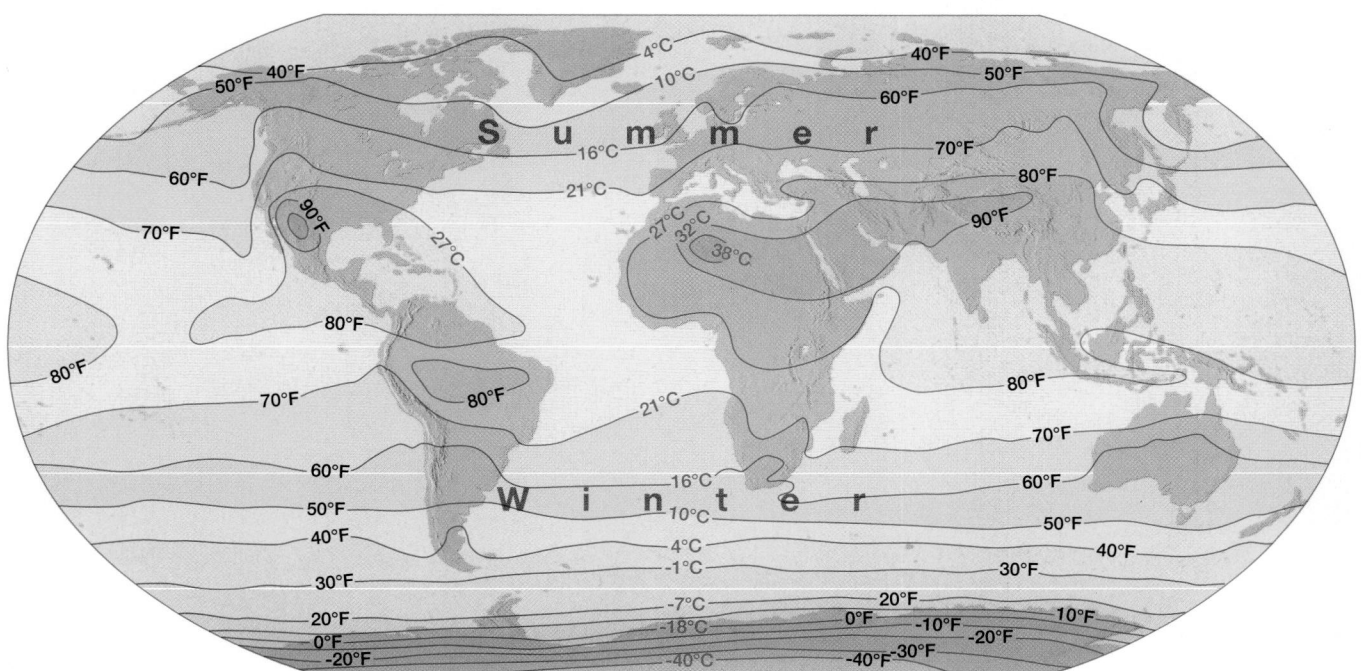

▲ **Figure 4-32** Average July sea-level temperatures.

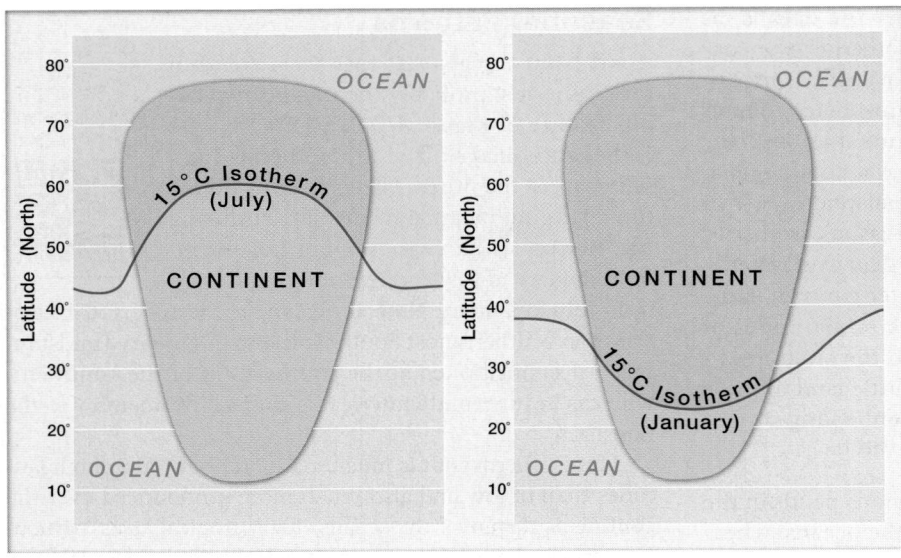

◀ **Figure 4-33** Idealized seasonal migration of the 15°C (59°F) isotherm over a hypothetical Northern Hemisphere continent. The latitudinal shift is greatest over the interior of the continent and least over the adjacent oceans. For example, over the western ocean, the isotherm moves only from latitude 38° N in January to 42° N in July, but over the continent the change is from 22° N in January all the way to 60° N in July.

of kilometers south of the North Pole, in subarctic portions of Siberia, Canada, and Greenland. The principle of greater cooling of land than water is clearly demonstrated.

Hottest Summer Locations: The highest temperatures also are found over the continents. The locations of the warmest areas in summer, however, are not equatorial. Rather, they are in subtropical latitudes, where descending air maintains clear skies most of the time, allowing for almost uninterrupted insolation. Frequent cloudiness prevents such a condition in the equatorial zone. Thus, the highest July temperatures occur in northern Africa and in the southwestern portions of Asia and North America, whereas the principal areas of January warmth

are in subtropical parts of Australia, southern Africa, and South America.

Average annual temperatures are highest in equatorial regions, however, because these regions experience so little winter cooling. Subtropical locations cool substantially on winter nights, and so their annual average temperatures are lower. The ice-covered portions of Earth—Antarctica and Greenland—remain quite cold throughout the year.

Annual Temperature Range

Another map useful in understanding the global pattern of air temperature is one that portrays the average annual

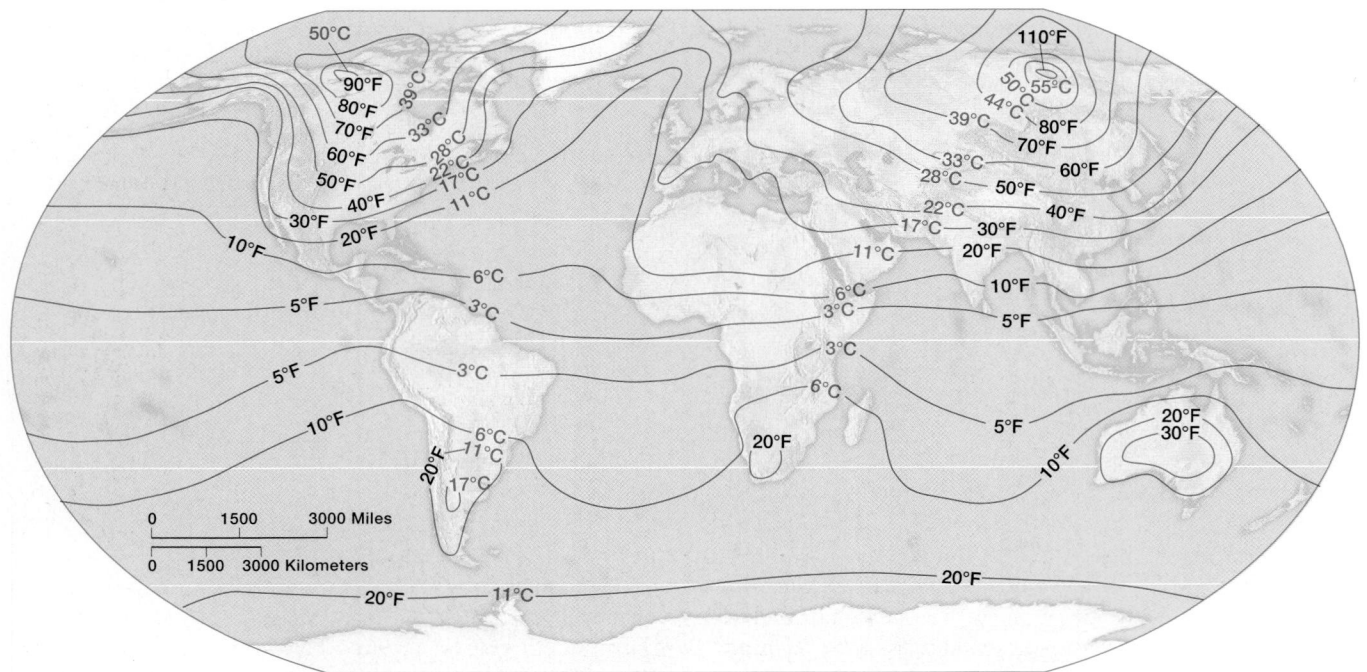

▲ **Figure 4-34** The world pattern of average annual temperature range. The largest ranges occur in the interior of high-latitude landmasses.

range of temperatures (Figure 4-34). **Average annual temperature range** for a location is the difference between the average temperature of the warmest month and the average temperature of the coldest month—normally July and January. Enormous seasonal variations in temperature occur in the interiors of high-latitude continents, and continental areas in general experience much greater ranges than do equivalent oceanic latitudes. At the other extreme, the average temperature fluctuates only slightly from season to season in the tropics, particularly over tropical oceans.

> **Learning Check 4-14** **What kinds of locations around the world have a very small *average annual temperature range*, and what kinds of locations have a very large annual temperature range?**

Measuring Earth's Surface Temperature by Satellite

Before the advent of remote sensing, scientists relied on ships, buoys, and land-based instruments to gather temperature data, leaving large gaps in coverage, especially over ocean areas. In recent years, scientists have used the Moderate Resolution Imaging Spectroradiometer (MODIS) on NASA's Aqua and Terra satellites to gather surface temperature data around the globe. By using computer algorithms to compensate for factors such as absorption and scattering in the atmosphere, the "skin" temperature of ocean and land surfaces can be estimated by measuring emitted thermal infrared radiation.

Sea Surface Temperature: Sea surface temperature (SST; Figure 4-35a) influences not only the temperature of air masses that originate over ocean areas (and so the weather of continental areas over which these air masses may pass), but also the intensity of storms such as hurricanes (discussed in Chapter 7). Regular monitoring of SST also helps scientists anticipate the onset of El Niño events (discussed in Chapter 5) and provides important information about long-term changes to Earth's environment.

Land Temperature: Satellite-derived day and night land temperatures (Figures 4-35b and 4-35c) measure the temperature of the surface itself, not the temperature of the air above. In these images, yellow represents the highest land temperatures and blue represents the lowest. Notice the high daytime surface temperatures in the Northern Hemisphere subtropical and midlatitude deserts—a consequence of high Sun and sparse cloud cover. These same areas cool off significantly at night, as do high mountain areas, such as the Himalayas, where the thinner atmosphere allows rapid heat loss at night.

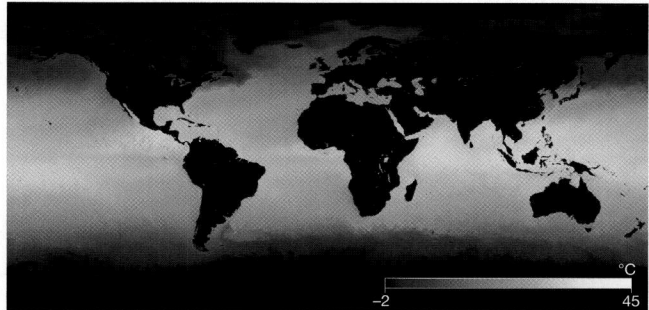

(a) Sea Surface Temperature, May 2012

(b) Daytime Land Surface Temperature, May 2012

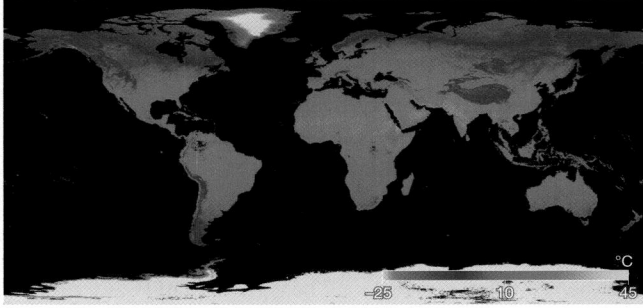

(c) Nighttime Land Surface Temperature, May 2012

▲ **Figure 4-35** Global temperatures in May 2012 derived from the MODIS instruments on NASA's Aqua and Terra satellites. (a) Sea surface temperature. Dark blue represents the coldest surface water (–2°C) while white (not seen on this image) represents the warmest (45°C). (b) Daytime land surface temperature. Light blue represents the coldest land surface temperature (–25°C), whereas bright yellow represents the warmest (45°C). (c) Nighttime land surface temperature.

CLIMATE CHANGE AND "GLOBAL WARMING"

As we described earlier in this chapter, the "natural" greenhouse effect has been part of the basis of life on Earth since the early atmosphere formed. Without it, our planet would be a frozen mass, perhaps 30°C (54°F) colder than it is today. Over the last three decades, human-produced changes to the greenhouse effect have been brought to the attention of the media and the general public by the scientific community. Data gathered from surface weather stations, ships, buoys, balloons, satellites, ice cores, and other paleoclimatological sources indicate that the climate of Earth is becoming warmer. This warming trend became known to the public

Animation
Global Warming

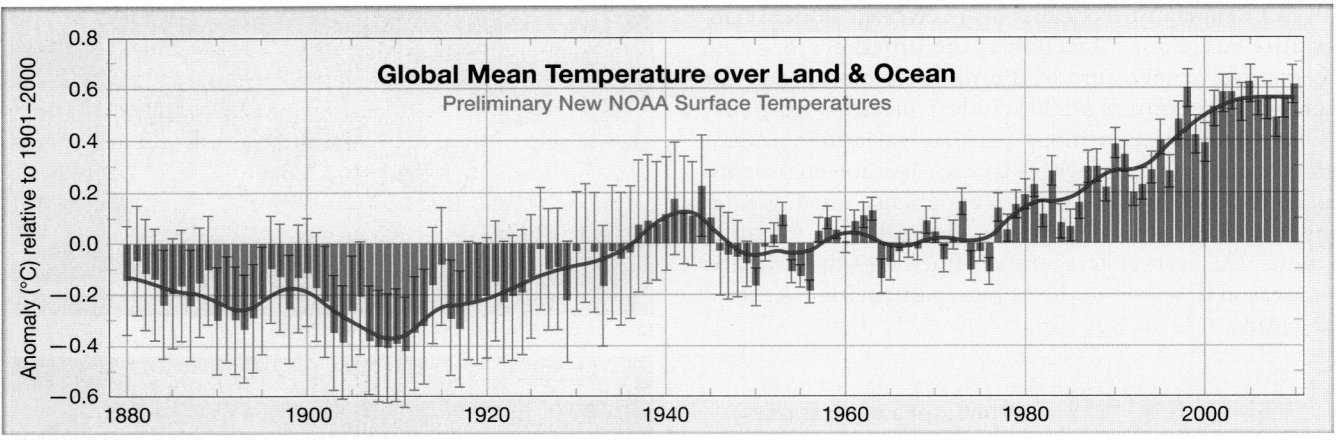

▲ **Figure 4-36** Global Mean Temperature over Land and Ocean, 1880–2011. The scale on the left shows the temperature difference relative to the 1901–2000 average. The blue line shows the smoothed temperature trend, and the vertical green bars show the estimated range of error.

as **global warming**, although many climate scientists prefer the more general term *climate change* because it encompasses the many effects of warming, such as changes in precipitation patterns.

Temperature Change During Twentieth Century

Over the twentieth century, average global temperatures increased by more than 0.7°C (1.3°F)—in the last quarter of the twentieth century alone temperatures increased 0.2–0.3°C (0.4°F; Figure 4-36). This temperature increase over the last 100 years is apparently greater than that of any other century in at least the last 1000 years, and the rate of temperature increase over the last three decades may be greater than at any time in the last 800,000 years. Overall, global temperatures are higher today than they have been in at least 100,000 years, and the last two decades have been the hottest since widespread instrument readings began about 140 years ago—9 of the 10 hottest years on record have occurred since the year 2000, and 2010 was tied with 2005 as the hottest year in the instrument record. Although the year 2011 was the second *coolest* year of the twenty-first century, its average annual temperature was the same as 1997—the second *warmest* year of the twentieth century!

Because direct instrument measurements of Earth's temperature only go back a few centuries, past temperature patterns are calculated using "proxy" measures—such as data deciphered from polar ice cores, oceanic sediments, and pollen analysis. Although there is a margin of error in these figures, evidence clearly points to warming.

Increasing Greenhouse Gas Concentrations

The cause of global climate change appears to be *human-enhanced greenhouse effect*. Since the industrial era began in the mid-1700s, human activities have increased the concentrations of greenhouse gases—such as carbon dioxide, methane, tropospheric ozone, and chlorofluorocarbons in the atmosphere. As greenhouse gas concentrations in the atmosphere increase, more terrestrial radiation is retained in the lower atmosphere, thereby increasing global temperatures.

Carbon dioxide (CO_2) is thought to be responsible for at least 60 percent of the human-enhanced greenhouse effect. CO_2 concentrations have been rising steadily since the Industrial Revolution began in the mid-1700s (Figure 4-37). Carbon dioxide is a principal by-product of combustion of anything containing carbon, such as coal and petroleum.

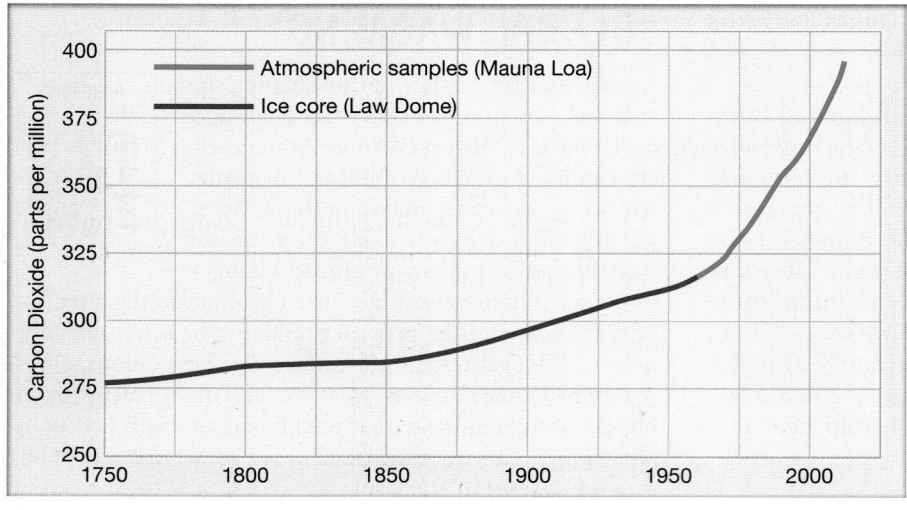

◀ **Figure 4-37** Change in atmospheric carbon dioxide concentration from 1750–2012. The dark blue line shows values derived from ice cores at Law Dome, Antarctica; the light blue line shows measured values from Mauna Loa, Hawai'i.

Since 1750—when estimates show the concentration of CO_2 in the atmosphere was about 280 parts per million (ppm)—carbon dioxide levels in the atmosphere have increased by more than 40 percent. The latest paleoclimatological data indicates that the current (May 2012) concentration of CO_2 in the atmosphere of about 396 ppm is greater than at any time in the last 800,000 years.

Many other greenhouse gases have been added to the atmosphere by human activity. Methane—produced by grazing livestock and rice paddies and as a by-product of the combustion of wood, natural gas, coal, and oil—has more than doubled since 1750 and is about 25 times more potent as a greenhouse gas than CO_2. Nitrous oxide—which comes from chemical fertilizers and automobile emissions—has increased by about 18 percent since 1750. Chlorofluorocarbons (CFCs) are synthetic chemicals that were widely used as refrigerants and as propellants in spray cans until quite recently (see Chapter 3 for a discussion of another consequence of CFCs and nitrous oxide in the atmosphere—ozone depletion). Many of these gases, and others, are being released into the atmosphere at accelerating rates.

The increase in greenhouse gas concentrations, especially carbon dioxide, correlates well with the observed increase in global temperature: as CO_2 has increased, so have average global temperatures.

Intergovernmental Panel on Climate Change (IPCC)

It is well known that climate undergoes frequent natural fluctuations, becoming warmer or colder regardless of human activities. There is, however, an increasing body of evidence that indicates that *anthropogenic* (human-induced) factors are largely, if not wholly, responsible for the recent temperature increase. The Intergovernmental Panel on Climate Change (IPCC) is the most important international organization of atmospheric scientists and policy analysts assessing global climate change. In 2007, in recognition of their many years of work on climate change, the IPCC was the corecipient of the Nobel Peace Prize. The *Fourth Assessment Report* of the IPCC released in 2007 concluded bluntly:

> Warming of the climate system is unequivocal, as is now evident from observations of increases in global average air and ocean temperatures, widespread melting of snow and ice, and rising global average sea level.

With regard to the causes of this climate change, the IPCC concluded:

> Most of the observed increase in globally averaged temperatures since the mid-20th century is very likely [greater than 90% probability] due to the observed increase in anthropogenic greenhouse gas emissions.

Because both the causes and implications of climate change are so complicated—due especially to the many feedback loops involved in climate systems—the preceding description of global warming serves only as our introduction to the topic. In subsequent chapters, after increasing our understanding of processes of weather and climate, we will further explore both the natural and anthropogenic aspects of global environmental change, including global warming, in much greater detail.

Learning Check 4-15 **How has human activity likely caused a slight increase in global temperature over the last century?**

Chapter 4 LEARNING REVIEW

After studying this chapter, you should be able to answer the following questions. Key terms from each text section are shown in **bold type**. Definitions for key terms are also found in the glossary at the back of the book.

KEY TERMS AND CONCEPTS

Energy, Heat, and Temperature (*p. 78*)

1. What is the difference between **heat** (thermal energy) and **temperature**?
2. What is the relationship between the internal **kinetic energy** of a substance and its temperature?

Solar Energy (*p. 80*)

3. Briefly describe the following bands of **electromagnetic radiation (radiant energy)**: **visible light**, **ultraviolet (UV)**, **infrared**, **thermal infrared**.

4. Describe and contrast the portions of the **electromagnetic spectrum** referred to as **shortwave radiation** and **longwave radiation (terrestrial radiation)**.
5. What is **insolation**?

Basic Warming and Cooling Processes in the Atmosphere (*p. 83*)

6. Describe and contrast the following processes associated with electromagnetic energy: **radiation (emission)**, **absorption**, **reflection**, and **transmission**.

7. What generally happens to the temperature of an object as a response to the absorption of electromagnetic radiation?
8. What is **albedo**?
9. How is **scattering** different from reflection?
10. Describe and explain the **greenhouse effect** in the atmosphere, noting the two most important natural greenhouse gases.
11. What is the difference between **conduction** and **convection**?
12. How and why does conduction influence the temperature of air above a warm surface? Above a cold surface?
13. Describe the pattern of air movement within a **convection cell**.
14. Briefly describe the process of **advection** in the atmosphere.
15. How does expansion lead to **adiabatic cooling**, and compression to **adiabatic warming**?
16. What happens to the temperature of rising air? Of descending air? Why?
17. What is **latent heat**?

Earth's Solar Radiation Budget (*p. 88*)

18. Approximately what percentage of incoming solar radiation is reflected and scattered away from Earth?
19. Approximately what percentage of incoming solar radiation is transmitted through the atmosphere and is absorbed by the surface?
20. Briefly describe how the troposphere is warmed by the Sun.

Variations in Insolation by Latitude and Season (*p. 90*)

21. What is meant by the **angle of incidence** of the Sun's rays?
22. Explain the reasons for the unequal warming (by latitude) of Earth by the Sun.

Land and Water Temperature Contrasts (*p. 94*)

23. How does the **specific heat** of a substance influence its rate of warming?

24. Explain why land warms faster and to a greater extent than water.
25. Explain why land cools faster and to a greater extent than water.

Mechanisms of Global Energy Transfer (*p. 95*)

26. What are the two dominant mechanisms of energy transfer around the world?
27. What is the relative temperature of the ocean current flowing along the west coast of a continent in the midlatitudes? Along the east coast of a continent?
28. Describe the basic pattern of ocean currents (the **subtropical gyres**) around the margins of a major ocean basin (including the relative temperature of each current—either "cool" or "warm"). You should be able to sketch the direction of movement and note the relative temperature of major ocean currents on a blank map of an ocean basin.
29. Describe **upwelling** and its cause.

Vertical Temperature Patterns (*p. 98*)

30. What is meant by the **environmental lapse rate**?
31. What is the **average lapse rate** in the troposphere?
32. What is a **temperature inversion**?
33. What is the difference between a radiational inversion and an advectional inversion?

Global Temperature Patterns (*p. 100*)

34. What is an **isotherm**?
35. Where in the world do we find the greatest **average annual temperature ranges** and where do we find the smallest average annual temperature ranges? Why?

Climate Change and "Global Warming" (*p. 103*)

36. What is meant by the term **global warming**?
37. How might humans be enhancing the natural greenhouse effect?

STUDY QUESTIONS

1. Why is the sky blue? Why are sunsets orange and red?
2. Why do we say that **evaporation** is a cooling process and **condensation** is a warming process?
3. Why does temperature generally decrease with increasing altitude in the troposphere?
4. "The atmosphere is mostly warmed by Earth's surface rather than directly by the Sun." Comment on the validity of this statement.
5. If the concentration of greenhouse gases were to *decrease*, what would likely happen to global temperatures? Why?
6. Why are seasonal temperature differences greater in the high latitudes than in the tropics?
7. Why are the hottest and coldest places on Earth over land and not over water?

8. How would global temperature patterns be different without the transfer of energy by the circulation of the atmosphere and ocean currents?
9. Using the isotherm maps of average January and July sea level temperature (Figure 4-31 and Figure 4-32), explain the influence of latitude, season, land-water contrasts, and ocean currents on global temperature patterns. For example, explain why the following isotherms vary in latitude across the maps:

- January –1°C (30°F) isotherm in the Northern Hemisphere
- July 21°C (70°F) isotherm in the Northern Hemisphere

EXERCISES

1. Make the following conversions between the Celsius and Fahrenheit temperature scales:
   a. 10°C = _____ °F
   b. –20°C = _____ °F
   c. 100°F = _____ °C
   d. 5°F = _____ °C
2. If the temperature of the air is 25°C at sea level, use the average lapse rate to calculate the expected temperature at the top of a 5000-meter-high mountain: _____ °C

3. If the air temperature outside a jet air plane flying at 34,000 feet is –40°F, use the average lapse rate to estimate the temperature at sea level below: _____ °F
4. One gram of water and 1 gram of soil ("land") are at a temperature of 20°C (68°F). If 5 calories of heat are added to each, what will be the temperature of the water and what will be the approximate temperature of the soil?

Seeing Geographically

Look again at the photograph of the sunset behind the San Juan Islands at the beginning of the chapter (p. 76). Explain why the color of the sky around the Sun appears orange in this photograph. How would the color of the sky likely be different if the Sun was high in the sky? Which likely warmed more during this day: the islands or the water surrounding them? Why?

MasteringGeography™

Looking for additional review and test prep materials? Visit the Study Area in MasteringGeography™ to enhance your geographic literacy, spatial reasoning skills, and understanding of this chapter's content by accessing a variety of resources, including geoscience animations, MapMaster® interactive maps, videos, RSS feeds, flashcards, web links, self-study quizzes, and an eText version of *McKnight's Physical Geography: A Landscape Appreciation*.

TO THE LAYPERSON, ATMOSPHERIC PRESSURE IS THE MOST

difficult element of weather and climate to comprehend. The other three—temperature, wind, and moisture—are more readily understood because our bodies are much more sensitive to them. We can feel warmth, air movement, and moisture, and we are quick to recognize variations in these elements. Pressure, on the other hand, is a phenomenon of which we are usually unaware—our bodies cannot sense the relatively small changes in atmospheric pressure that can be responsible for significant changes in the atmosphere. We're usually only aware of pressure changes when we experience rapid vertical movement, as in an elevator or an airplane, when the difference in pressure inside and outside our ears causes them to "pop."

Despite its inconspicuousness, pressure is an important feature of the atmosphere. It is tied closely to the other weather elements, acting on them and responding to them. Pressure has an intimate relationship with wind: spatial variations in pressure are responsible for air movements. Hence, pressure and wind are often discussed together, as is done in this chapter.

The general circulation pattern of global wind and pressure discussed here is a component of several major Earth systems. For example, the movement of the atmosphere is not only a consequence of the receipt of solar energy, it is one of the key mechanisms of energy transfer itself. Further, patterns of wind and pressure are key aspects of the hydrologic cycle—the systematic movement of water around the planet.

As you study this chapter, think about these key questions:

- **What influences the development of high pressure cells and low pressure cells near Earth's surface?**
- **How and why are wind patterns different near the surface and in the upper atmosphere?**
- **What is the pattern of wind and vertical air movement within cyclones and anticyclones?**
- **How do the Hadley cells fit in with the general circulation patterns of wind and pressure around the world?**
- **What causes seasonal shifts of global wind and pressure systems, and the development of monsoons?**
- **How can differences in temperature lead to local winds such as land and sea breezes?**
- **What happens in the ocean and atmosphere during El Niño?**
- **How do long-term atmospheric and oceanic cycles such as the Pacific Decadal Oscillation influence regional weather conditions?**

Seeing Geographically

Hurricane Frances strikes the Florida coast near Fort Pierce with 145 kilometer per hour (90 mile per hour) winds. Describe how the wind appears to be affecting the waves coming on shore. What characteristics of palm trees that you can see helps explain why they can survive hurricanes?

The Impact of Pressure and Wind on the Landscape

The influence of atmospheric pressure on the landscape is significant but indirect. This influence is manifested mostly by wind, which responds to pressure changes. Wind has the energy to transport solid particles in the air and thus has a visible component to its activity. Vegetation may bend in the wind and loose material such as dust or sand may be shifted from one place to another. The results are nearly always short-run and temporary, however, and usually have no lasting effect on the landscape except at the time of a severe storm. Nevertheless, pressure and wind are major elements of weather and climate, and their interaction with other atmospheric components and processes cannot be overestimated.

THE NATURE OF ATMOSPHERIC PRESSURE

Gas molecules, unlike those of a solid or liquid, are not strongly bound to one another. Instead, they are in continuous motion, colliding frequently with one another and with any surfaces to which they are exposed. Consider a container in which a gas is confined, as in Figure 5-1. The molecules of the gas zoom around inside the container and collide again and again with the walls. The pressure of the gas is the force the gas exerts on the container walls.

The atmosphere is made up of gases that have mass, and so the atmosphere has *weight* because this mass is pulled toward Earth by gravity. **Atmospheric pressure** is the force exerted by the weight of these gas molecules on a unit of area of Earth's surface or on any other body—including yours! At sea level, the pressure (the "weight") exerted by the atmosphere is about 14.7 pounds per square inch, or in S.I. units, about 10 newtons (N) per square centimeter

▲ **Figure 5-2** The empty plastic bottle on the left was opened and then sealed tightly at an elevation of 3030 meters (9945 feet); when the bottle is brought down to sea level, the surrounding higher atmospheric pressure partially collapses the bottle. The bottle on the right contains air at sea-level pressure.

(1 newton is the force required to accelerate a 1-kilogram mass 1 meter per second per second).[1] This value decreases with increasing altitude because the farther away you get from Earth and its gravitational pull, the fewer gas molecules are present in the atmosphere.

The atmosphere exerts pressure on every surface it touches. The pressure is exerted equally in all directions—up, down, sideways, and obliquely. This means that every square centimeter of any exposed surface—animal, vegetable, or mineral—at sea level is subjected to atmospheric pressure (Figure 5-2). We are not sensitive to this ever-present burden of pressure because our bodies contain solids and liquids that are not significantly compressed and air spaces that are at the same pressure as the surrounding atmosphere; in other words, outward pressure and inward pressure balance exactly.

Learning Check 5-1 **Explain why *atmospheric pressure* decreases with altitude. (Answer on p. AK-2)**

Factors Influencing Atmospheric Pressure

The pressure, temperature, and density of a gas are all related to each other—if one of those variables changes, it can cause changes in the other two.

The Ideal Gas Law: The relationship between pressure, temperature, and density can be summarized by an equation called the *ideal gas law*:

$$P = \rho RT$$

where P is pressure, ρ ("rho") is density, R is the constant of proportionality, and T is temperature. Explained with words, this equation says that pressure (P) will increase if

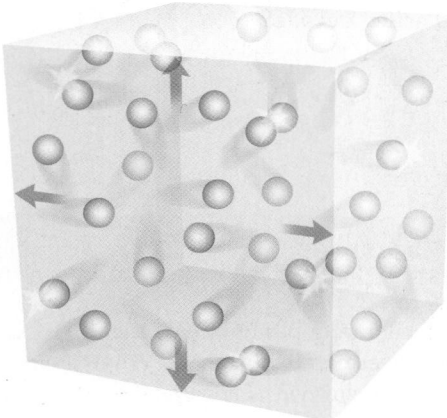

▲ **Figure 5-1** Gas molecules are always in motion. In this closed container, they bounce around, colliding with one another and with the walls of the container. These collisions give rise to the pressure exerted by the gas.

---

[1]In the definition of a newton, the term "per second per second" may seem strange. However, a newton describes the force required to *accelerate* a mass: in other words, the force required to change its speed or direction. Thus, the newton describes a rate of change, not a speed.

density remains constant but temperature (T) increases, and that pressure will increase if temperature remains constant but density (ρ) increases.

In a closed container (a sealed jar, for example), the relationship between pressure, temperature, and density is straightforward. However, the atmosphere is not a closed container in which any of these variables can be easily held constant and so the cause-and-effect relationships are actually quite complex. It may be useful, however, to examine some of the possibilities one at a time, looking at how pressure varies with density, with temperature, and with the vertical movement of air.

Density and Pressure Relationships: Density is the mass of matter in a unit volume. For example, if you have a 10-kilogram cube of material with edge lengths of 1 meter, the density of that material is 10 kilograms per cubic meter (10 kg/m³). The density of solid material is the same on Earth or the moon or in space; that of liquids varies very slightly from one place to another, but that of gases varies greatly with location. Gas density changes easily because a gas is free to expand as far as the environmental pressure will allow.

For example, if you have 10 kg of gas in a container that has a volume of 1 cubic meter, the gas density is 10 kg/m³. If you were to transfer all the gas to a container having twice the volume (2 cubic meters), the gas expands to fill the larger volume. The same number of gas molecules are now spread through a volume twice as large, and so the gas density is half what it was before, or 5 kg/m³ (10 kg divided by 2 cubic meters).

The pressure exerted by a gas is proportional to its density. The denser the gas, the greater the pressure it exerts. The atmosphere is held to Earth by the force of gravity which prevents the gas molecules from escaping into space. At lower altitudes, the gas molecules of the atmosphere are packed more densely together (Figure 5-3). Because the density is higher, there are more molecular collisions and therefore higher pressure at lower altitudes. At higher altitudes, the air is less dense and there is a corresponding decrease in pressure.

Temperature and Pressure Relationships: If air is warmed, as we noted in the preceding chapter, the molecules become more agitated and their speed increases. This increase in speed produces a greater force to their collisions and results in higher pressure. Therefore, if other conditions remain the same (in particular, if volume is held constant), an increase in the temperature of a gas produces an increase in pressure, and a decrease in temperature produces a decrease in pressure.

Knowing this, you might conclude that the air pressure will be high on warm days and low on cold days. Such is not usually the case, however; warm air is generally associated with low atmospheric pressure and cool air with high atmospheric pressure. Although this seems contradictory, recall that we made the qualifying statement "if other conditions remain the same" in describing how temperature and pressure are related. When air is warmed in the atmosphere, it will expand, which decreases its density. Thus, the increase

▲ **Figure 5-3** In the upper atmosphere, gas molecules are far apart and collide with each other infrequently, a condition that produces relatively low pressure. In the lower atmosphere, the molecules are closer together, and there are many more collisions, a condition that produces high pressure.

in temperature may be accompanied by a decrease in pressure caused by the decrease in density.

Dynamic Influences on Air Pressure: Surface air pressure may also be influenced by "dynamic" factors. In other words, air pressure may be influenced by the movement of the air—especially the vertical movement of air associated with different rates of air convergence and divergence at the surface and in the upper troposphere. As a generalization, descending air tends to be associated with relatively high pressure at the surface, whereas rising air tends to be associated with relatively low pressure at the surface.

In short, atmospheric pressure is affected by differences in air density, air temperature, and air movement. It is important for us to be alert to these linkages, but it is often difficult to predict how a change in one variable will influence the others in a specific instance. Nevertheless, some useful generalizations about the factors associated with areas of high pressure and low pressure near the surface can be made:

- Strongly descending air is usually associated with high pressure at the surface—a **dynamic high**.

- Very cold surface conditions are often associated with high pressure at the surface—a **thermal high**.
- Strongly rising air is usually associated with low pressure at the surface—a **dynamic low**.
- Very warm surface conditions are often associated with relatively low pressure at the surface—a **thermal low**.

Surface pressure conditions usually can be traced to one of these factors being dominant.

Learning Check 5-2 Is descending air more likely to be associated with high or low atmospheric pressure at the surface? Rising air?

Mapping Pressure with Isobars

Atmospheric pressure is measured with instruments called **barometers**. The first liquid-filled barometers date back to the 1600s, and measurement scales based on the height of a column of mercury are still in use (average sea-level pressure using a mercury barometer is 760 millimeters or 29.92 inches). For meteorologists in the United States, however, the most common unit of measure for atmospheric pressure is the **millibar**. The millibar (mb) is an expression of force per surface area. One millibar is defined as 1000 dynes per square centimeter (1 dyne is the force required to accelerate 1 gram of a mass 1 centimeter per second per second). Average sea-level pressure is 1013.25 millibars. The S.I. unit used to describe pressure is the *pascal* (Pa; 1 Pa = newton/m²) and in some countries the *kilopascal* is used in meteorology (kPa; 1 kPa = 10 mb).

Highs and Lows: Once pressure in millibars is plotted on a weather map, it is then possible to draw isolines of equal pressure called **isobars**, as shown in Figure 5-4. The pattern of the isobars reveals the horizontal distribution of pressure in the region under consideration. Prominent on such maps are roughly circular or oval areas characterized as being either "high pressure" or "low pressure." These **highs** and **lows** represent relative conditions—pressure that

TABLE 5-1	Atmospheric Pressure Variation with Altitude	
Altitude Kilometers	**Miles**	**Pressure (millibars)**
18	11	76
16	10	104
14	8.7	142
12	7.4	194
10	6.2	265
8	5.0	356
6	3.7	472
4	2.5	617
2	1.2	795
0	0	1013

is higher or lower than that of the surrounding areas. In a similar way, a **ridge** is an elongated area of relatively high pressure, whereas a **trough** is an elongated area of relatively low pressure. It is important to keep the relative nature of pressure centers in mind. For example, a pressure reading of 1005 millibars could be either "high" or "low," depending on the pressure of the surrounding areas.

Pressure Decrease with Altitude: On most maps of air pressure, actual pressure readings are adjusted to represent pressures at a common elevation, usually sea level. This is done because, as we first saw in Chapter 3, with only minor localized exceptions, pressure decreases rapidly with increasing altitude (Table 5-1); consequently significant variations in pressure readings are likely at different weather stations simply because of differences in elevation. This pressure change is most rapid at lower altitudes, and the rate of decrease diminishes significantly above about 3 kilometers (10,000 feet).

As with other types of isolines, the relative closeness of isobars indicates the horizontal rate of pressure change, or **pressure gradient**. The pressure gradient can be thought of as representing the "steepness" of the pressure "slope" (or more correctly, the abruptness of the pressure change over a distance), a characteristic that has a direct influence on wind, the topic to which we turn next.

THE NATURE OF WIND

The atmosphere is virtually always in motion. Air is free to move in any direction, its specific movements being shaped by a variety of factors. Some airflow is weak and brief; some is strong and persistent. Atmospheric motions often involve both horizontal and vertical movement.

Animation
Development of
Wind Patterns

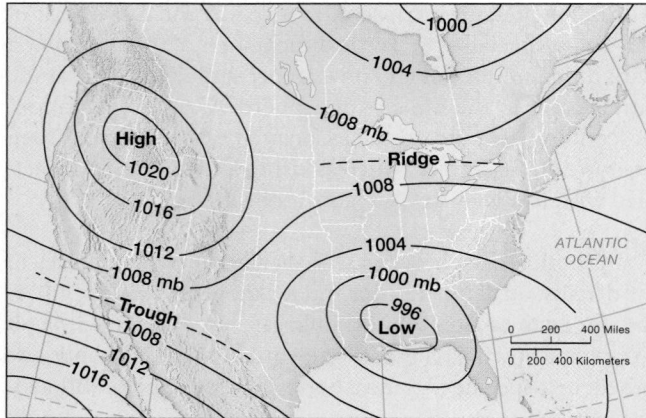

▲ **Figure 5-4** Isobars are lines connecting points of equal atmospheric pressure. When they have been drawn on a weather map, it is easy to determine the location of high-pressure and low-pressure centers. This simplified weather map shows pressure in millibars.

Wind refers to horizontal air movement; it has been described whimsically as "air in a hurry." Instead of being called wind, small-scale vertical motions are normally referred to as *updrafts* and *downdrafts*; large-scale vertical motions are *ascents* and *subsidences*. The term *wind* is applied only to horizontal movements. Although both vertical and horizontal motions are important in the atmosphere, much more air is involved in horizontal movements than in vertical.

Direction of Movement

Insolation is the ultimate cause of wind because all winds originate from the same basic sequence of events: unequal heating of different parts of Earth's surface brings about temperature gradients that generate pressure gradients, and these pressure gradients set air into motion. Wind represents nature's attempt to even out the uneven distribution of air pressure across Earth's surface.

Air generally begins to flow from areas of higher pressure toward areas of lower pressure. If Earth did not rotate and if friction did not exist, that is precisely what would happen—a direct movement of air from a high-pressure region to a low-pressure region. However, rotation and friction both exist, and so this general statement is usually not completely accurate. The direction of wind movement is determined principally by the interaction of three factors: the pressure gradient, the Coriolis effect, and friction.

Pressure Gradient: If there is higher pressure in one area than in another, air will begin to move from the higher pressure toward the lower pressure in response to the *pressure gradient force*, as shown in Figure 5-5. If you visualize a high-pressure area as a pressure "hill" and a low-pressure area as a pressure "valley," it is not difficult to imagine air flowing "down" the pressure gradient in the same manner that water flows down a hill (keep in mind that these terms are metaphorical—air is not necessarily actually flowing downhill).

The pressure-gradient force acts at right angles to the isobars in the direction of the lower pressure. If there were no other factors to consider, that is the way the air would move, crossing the isobars at 90° (Figure 5-6a). However, such a flow rarely occurs in the atmosphere.

The Coriolis Effect: Because Earth rotates, any object moving freely near Earth's surface appears to deflect to the right in the Northern Hemisphere and to the left in the Southern Hemisphere. Recall from Chapter 3 the significant aspects of the Coriolis effect:

- Regardless of the initial direction of motion, any freely moving object appears to deflect to the right in the Northern Hemisphere and to the left in the Southern Hemisphere.
- The apparent deflection is strongest at the poles and decreases progressively toward the equator, where deflection is zero.
- The Coriolis effect is proportional to the speed of the object, and so a fast-moving object is deflected more than a slower one.

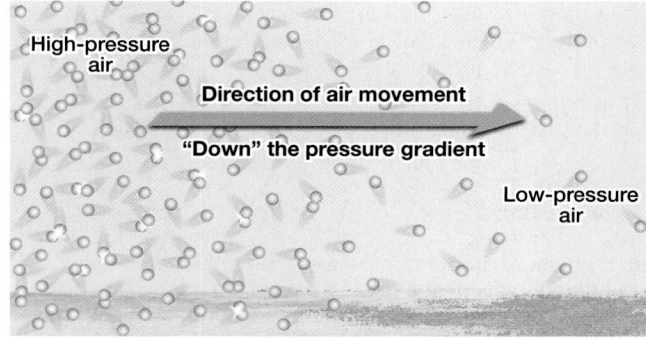

(a) Side view

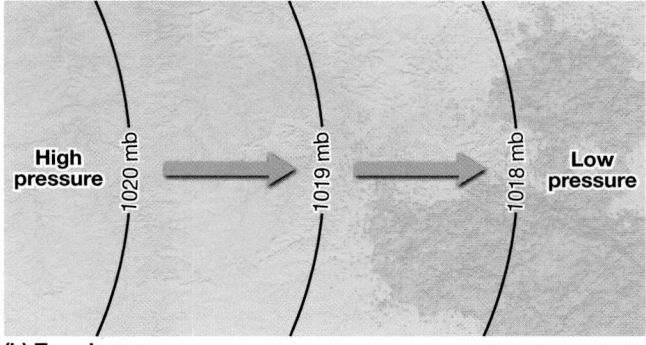

(b) Top view

▲ **Figure 5-5** (a) Air tends to move from areas of higher pressure toward areas of lower pressure. We say this movement is "down the pressure gradient." (b) If pressure gradient were the only force involved, air would flow perpendicular to the isobars (would cross the isobars at 90°).

- The Coriolis effect influences direction of movement only; it does not change the speed of an object.

The Coriolis effect has an important influence on the direction of wind flow. The Coriolis effect deflection acts at 90° from the direction of movement—to the right in the Northern Hemisphere and to the left in the Southern Hemisphere. There is an eternal battle, then, between the pressure-gradient force moving air from high toward low pressure and the deflection of the Coriolis effect 90° from its pressure-gradient path: the Coriolis effect keeps the wind from flowing directly down a pressure gradient, whereas the pressure gradient force prevents the Coriolis effect from turning the wind back "up" the pressure slope. Where these two factors are in balance—as is usually the case in the upper atmosphere—wind moves parallel to the isobars and is called a **geostrophic wind**[2] (Figure 5-6b).

Most winds in the atmosphere are geostrophic or nearly geostrophic in that they flow nearly parallel to the isobars. Only near the surface is another factor significant—friction—to further complicate the situation.

Friction: In the lowest portions of the troposphere, a third force influences wind direction—*friction*. The frictional drag of Earth's surface slows wind movement and so the influence

---

[2]Strictly speaking, geostrophic wind is only found in areas where the isobars are parallel and straight; the term *gradient wind* is a more general term used to describe wind flowing parallel to the isobars. In this book we use the term *geostrophic* to mean all wind blowing parallel to the isobars.

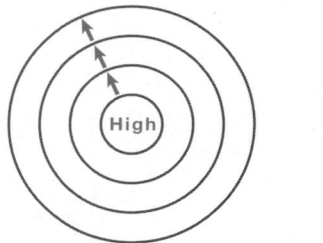 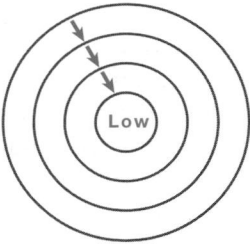

(a) If pressure gradient force were the only factor, wind would blow "down" the pressure gradient away from high pressure and toward low pressure, crossing the isobars at an angle of 90°.

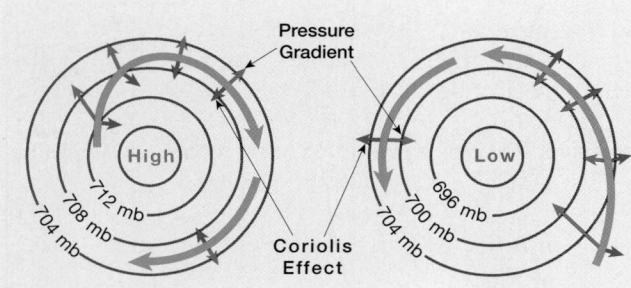

(b) In the upper atmosphere the balance between the pressure gradient force and the Coriolis effect results in geostrophic wind blowing parallel to the isobars.

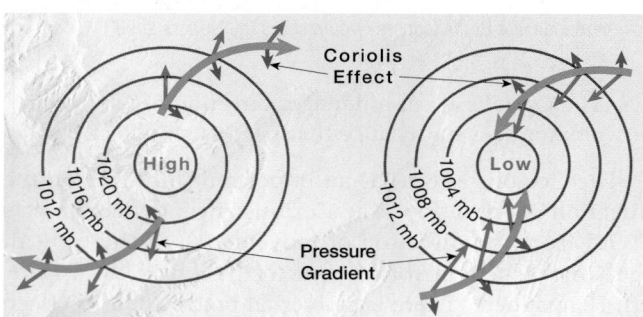

(c) In the lower atmosphere, friction slows the wind (which results in less Coriolis effect deflection) and so wind diverges clockwise out of a high and converges counterclockwise into a low in the Northern Hemisphere.

▲ **Figure 5-6** The direction of wind flow is influenced by a combination of three factors: pressure gradient force, Coriolis effect, and friction. (a) Hypothetical pattern if pressure gradient force was the only factor. (b) In the upper atmosphere (above about 1000 m/3300 ft.), a balance develops between the pressure gradient force and the Coriolis effect, resulting in geostrophic wind blowing parallel to the isobars. (c) In the lower atmosphere, friction slows the wind (which results in less Coriolis effect deflection) and so wind diverges out of a high and converges into a low.

of the Coriolis effect is reduced (recall that rapidly moving objects are deflected more by the Coriolis effect than are slowly moving objects). Instead of blowing perpendicular to the isobars (in response to the pressure gradient) or parallel to them (where pressure gradient force and the Coriolis effect are in balance), the wind takes an intermediate course between the two and crosses the isobars at angles between

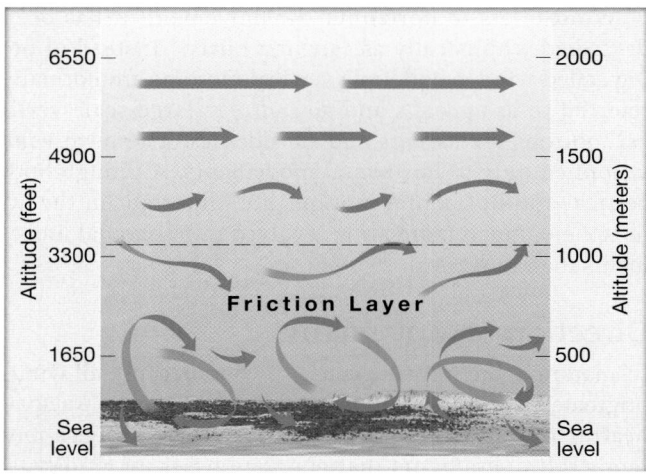

▲ **Figure 5-7** Near Earth's surface friction causes wind flow to be turbulent and irregular. Above the friction layer (altitudes higher than about 1000 m/3300 ft.), the wind flow is generally smoother and faster.

0° and 90° (Figure 5-6c). In essence, friction reduces wind speed, which in turn reduces the Coriolis effect deflection—thus, although the Coriolis effect does introduce a deflection to the right (in the Northern Hemisphere), the pressure gradient "wins the battle" and air flows into an area of low pressure and away from an area of high pressure.

As a general rule, the frictional influence is greatest near Earth's surface and diminishes progressively upward (Figure 5-7). Thus, the angle of wind flow across the isobars is greatest (closest to 90°) at low altitudes and becomes smaller at increasing elevations. The **friction layer** of the atmosphere extends to only about 1000 meters (approximately 3300 feet) above the surface. Higher than that, most winds follow a geostrophic or near-geostrophic course.

Learning Check 5-3   **How does friction influence the direction of wind flow?**

Wind Speed

Thus far, we have been considering the direction of wind movement and paying little attention to speed. Although some complications are introduced by factors such as *inertia* (the tendency of an object to resist changes in its motion), it is accurate to say that the speed of wind flow is determined primarily by the pressure gradient. If the gradient is steep, the air accelerates swiftly; if the gradient is gentle, acceleration is slow. This relationship can be portrayed in the simple diagram of Figure 5-8. The closeness of the isobars indicates the steepness of the pressure gradient.

Describing Wind Speed: In meteorology, wind speed is frequently described in terms of *knots* (nautical miles per hour). Recall from Chapter 1 that a nautical mile is a bit longer than a "statute" mile, so one knot is equivalent to 1.15 statute miles per hour, or 1.85 kilometers per hour. You may have noticed that when speeds are given for ships and airplanes, knots is also the most common unit of measurement.

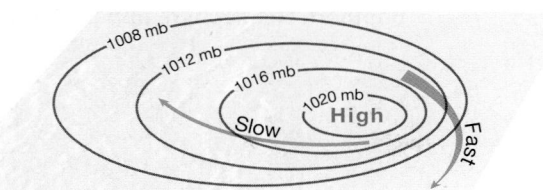

▲ **Figure 5-8** Wind speed is determined by the pressure gradient, which is indicated by the spacing of isobars. Where isobars are close together, the pressure gradient is "steep" and wind speed is high; where isobars are far apart, the pressure gradient is "gentle" and wind speed is low.

Global Variations in Wind Speed: Over most of the world most of the time, surface winds are relatively gentle. As Figure 5-9 shows, for instance, annual average wind speed in North America is generally between 6 and 12 knots. Cape Dennison in Antarctica holds the dubious distinction of being the windiest place on Earth, with an annual average wind speed of 38 knots. The most persistent winds are usually in coastal areas or high mountains. Locations with persistent winds are often suitable for facilities that generate electricity using wind power—see the box, "Energy for the 21st Century: Wind Power."

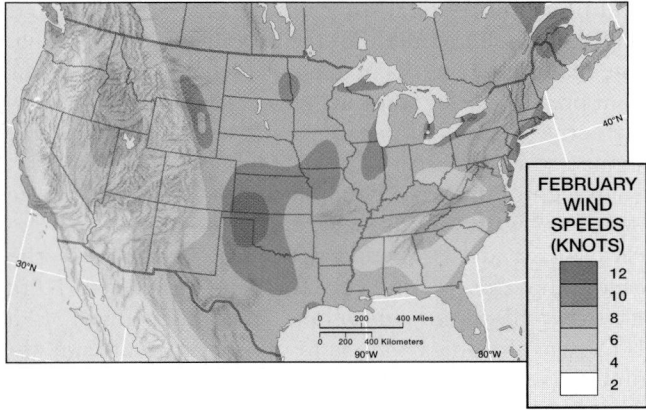

FEBRUARY WIND SPEEDS (KNOTS)
12
10
8
6
4
2

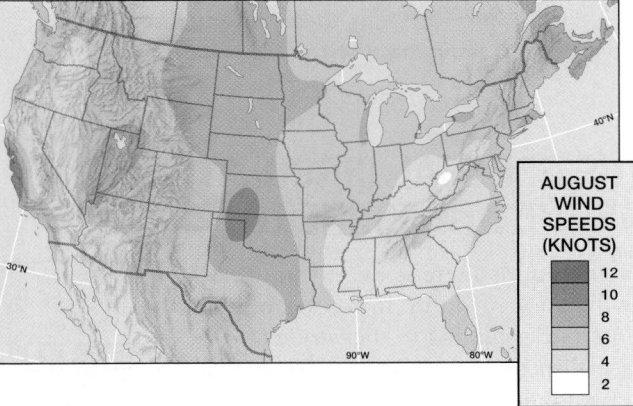

AUGUST WIND SPEEDS (KNOTS)
12
10
8
6
4
2

▲ **Figure 5-9** Average North American wind speeds in February and August. Wind speed tends to be higher in winter than in summer due to greater temperature contrasts and more frequent storms. The Great Plains tend to have the highest speed winds in all seasons; the strong summer winds in California result from heating in the interior Central Valley (such sea breezes are discussed later in this chapter).

Wind speed is quite variable from one altitude to another and from time to time, usually increasing with height. Winds tend to move faster above the friction layer. As we shall see in subsequent sections, the very strongest tropospheric winds are usually found at intermediate levels in what are called *jet streams* or in violent storms near Earth's surface.

CYCLONES AND ANTICYCLONES

Animation
Cyclones and Anticyclones

Distinct and predictable wind-flow patterns develop around all high-pressure and low-pressure centers—patterns determined by the pressure gradient, Coriolis effect, and friction. A total of eight circulation patterns are possible: four in the Northern Hemisphere and four in the Southern Hemisphere. Within each hemisphere, two patterns are associated with high-pressure centers and two patterns associated with low-pressure centers, as shown in Figure 5-10.

High-Pressure Wind Patterns: A high-pressure center is known as an **anticyclone**, and the flow of air associated with it is described as being *anticyclonic*. The four patterns of anticyclonic circulation are shown in Figure 5-10:

1. In the upper atmosphere of the Northern Hemisphere, the winds move clockwise in a geostrophic manner parallel to the isobars.
2. In the friction layer (lower altitudes) of the Northern Hemisphere, there is a divergent clockwise flow, with the air spiraling out away from the center of the anticyclone.
3. In the upper atmosphere of the Southern Hemisphere, there is a counterclockwise, geostrophic flow parallel to the isobars.
4. In the friction layer of the Southern Hemisphere, the pattern is a mirror image of the Northern Hemisphere, with air diverging in a counterclockwise pattern.

Low-Pressure Wind Patterns: Low-pressure centers are called **cyclones**, and the associated wind movement is said to be *cyclonic*. As with anticyclones, Northern Hemisphere cyclonic circulations are mirror images of their Southern Hemisphere counterparts:

5. In the upper atmosphere of the Northern Hemisphere, air moves counterclockwise in a geostrophic pattern parallel to the isobars.
6. In the friction layer of the Northern Hemisphere, a converging counterclockwise flow exists.
7. In the upper atmosphere of the Southern Hemisphere, a clockwise, geostrophic flow occurs paralleling the isobars.
8. In the friction layer of the Southern Hemisphere, the winds converge in a clockwise spiral.

Northern Hemisphere upper-air pattern

Anticyclonic geostrophic
clockwise flow

Cyclonic geostrophic
counterclockwise flow

Southern Hemisphere upper-air pattern

Anticyclonic geostrophic
counterclockwise flow

Cyclonic geostrophic
clockwise flow

Northern Hemisphere friction-layer pattern

Anticyclonic divergent
clockwise flow

Cyclonic convergent
counterclockwise flow

Southern Hemisphere friction-layer pattern

Anticyclonic divergent
counterclockwise flow

Cyclonic convergent
clockwise flow

▲ **Figure 5-10** The eight basic patterns of air circulation around pressure cells in the upper atmosphere (above the friction layer) and in lower atmosphere of the Northern and Southern Hemispheres. Upper-atmosphere winds are geostrophic, blowing parallel to the isobars, whereas near the surface, wind diverges from highs and converges into lows.

Cyclonic patterns in the lower troposphere may at first glance appear to be puzzling because the arrows seem to defy the Coriolis effect: in the Northern Hemisphere, the arrows seem to "bend" to the left, whereas we know that the Coriolis deflection is to the right. Remember, however, that wind patterns are the balance of several different forces acting in different directions: as air begins to flow down the pressure gradient into a low, the Coriolis effect does indeed deflect wind to the right—and this introduces the counterclockwise flow in the Northern Hemisphere (see Figure 5-6c).

Learning Check 5-4 **What is the pattern of wind circulation associated with a surface *cyclone* in the Northern Hemisphere?**

Vertical Movement within Cyclones and Anticyclones: A prominent vertical component of air movement is also associated with cyclones and anticyclones. As Figure 5-11 shows, air descends in anticyclones and rises

in cyclones. Such motions are particularly notable in the lower troposphere. The anticyclonic pattern can be visualized as upper air sinking down into the center of the high and then diverging near the ground surface. Opposite conditions prevail in a low-pressure center, with the air converging horizontally into the cyclone and then rising. Note that these patterns match our earlier generalizations about pressure: descending air is associated with high pressure at the surface and that rising air is associated with low pressure at the surface.

Notice in Figure 5-11 that cyclones and rising air are associated with clouds, whereas anticyclones and descending air are associated with clear conditions—the reasons for this will be explained in Chapter 6. Note also that well-developed cyclones and anticyclones often "lean" with height, which is to say that they are not absolutely vertical in orientation.

Learning Check 5-5 **Describe the direction of vertical air movement within an *anticyclone*.**

THE GENERAL CIRCULATION OF THE ATMOSPHERE

Earth's atmosphere is an extraordinarily dynamic medium. It is constantly in motion, responding to the various forces described previously as well as to a variety of more localized conditions. Some atmospheric motions are broadscale and sweeping; others are minute and momentary. Most important to an understanding of geography is the general pattern of circulation, which involves major semipermanent conditions of both

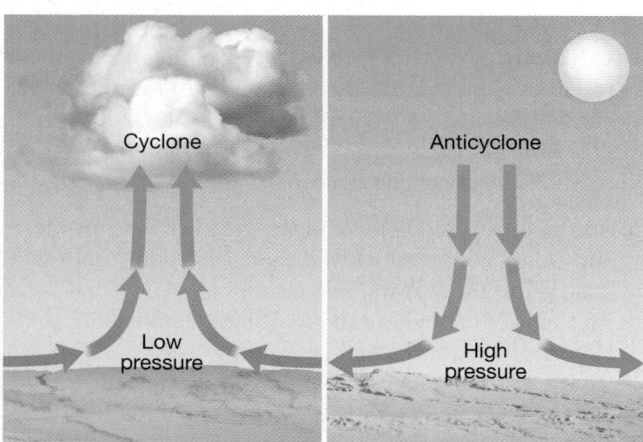

▲ **Figure 5-11** In a cyclone (low-pressure cell), air converges and rises. In an anticyclone (high-pressure cell), air descends and diverges.

Animation
Global Atmospheric
Circulation

Wind Power
▶ Stephen Stadler, Oklahoma State University

Wind has been used as a mechanical power source for thousands of years. Ships have used sails for at least 6000 years and wind-powered mills have ground grain and pumped water for more than a millennium. Wind has generated electricity since 1888, but it was in the latter part of the twentieth century that it became a significant power source.

Rather than being an energy fad, wind is the world's fastest-growing source of electrical power generation because of long-term concerns with the supply of fossil fuels and their environmental consequences (Figure 5-A). Wind power generates more than 3 percent of the world's electricity, and that amount is expected to increase significantly in the coming decades.

turbines can be cost-competitive even in areas of moderate winds. Some windy places have little installed wind power because there are other, inexpensive sources of energy such as hydropower.

Wind Turbines: Today's utility-scale turbines are massive machines costing millions of dollars per unit. Figure 5-B illustrates the major parts of a large turbine. Turbines are placed on tall towers because wind availability increases dramatically with elevation above the surface. A large turbine has three blades mounted 50 meters (164 feet) or more from the surface. The blades may be more than 35 meters (115 feet) long and are made from light but strong carbon-fiber composites. The blades turn 12 to 15 revolutions per

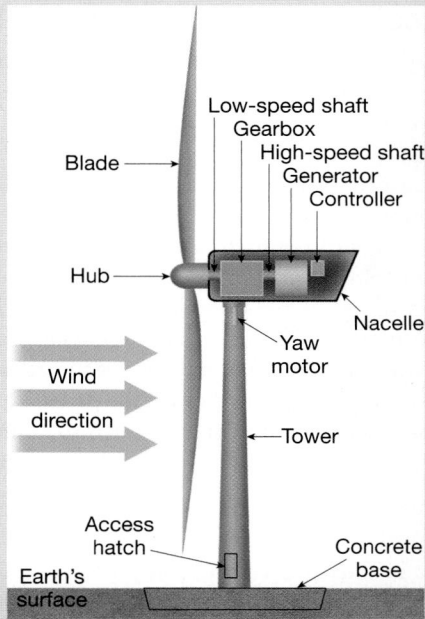

▲ **Figure 5-B** Schematic of modern wind turbine with distance between blade tip and ground not to scale. (After Michael Larson, Oklahoma State University Cartography Service.)

▲ **Figure 5-A** Wind turbines at the port of Copenhagen, Denmark. The Danes now generate more than 20 percent of their electricity from wind and are aiming at 50 percent by 2025.

Wind Geography: In wind power generation, it can be said that geography is everything. Physical geography is directly relevant because windier climates can help turbines generate more electricity. The most advantageous turbine placements are on high ground away from trees and other obstructions. This increases wind velocity by minimizing friction with Earth's surface. Human geography also plays a large role in the siting of turbines. Some windy places are not exploited because of distance from significant populations. Where electrical power from fossil fuels is expensive, wind

minute (rpm) and power a low-speed shaft attached to the hub. In a gearbox, low rpms are converted to high rpms on a shaft turning an electrical turbine. Most turbines in the United States commonly generate over 1.5 megawatts, enough to power a couple of thousand homes. Typically, the electricity from large turbines goes directly to the power grid—battery storage is very expensive.

Advantages of Wind Power: Electricity from wind power has some notable advantages. First, "fuel" is the wind and is always free. Second, wind power has

no "carbon footprint" because no fuel is burned. Third, wind power is now economically competitive with fossil fuel costs at windy sites. Fourth, wind generation holds much promise for the developing world where smaller turbines can serve rural populations not well-connected to regional power transmission grids.

Disadvantages of Wind Power: Wind power's biggest drawback is that wind is not constant, even in the windiest areas. If an uninterrupted power supply is necessary, then wind generation must be mixed with other power sources. The windiest places (such as the Great Plains of the United States and Canada) are seldom densely populated, so wind-generated electricity must sometimes be transported over long distances to population centers via expensive transmission lines. It is possible that the blades are a hazard to birds or bats, although the towering heights of modern turbines and the ready visibility of the large blades has minimized this problem. Finally, there is an aesthetic perspective: although the machines appear graceful and useful to some, they are noisy and ugly to others.

wind and pressure. This circulation is the principal mechanism for both latitudinal and longitudinal heat transfer and is exceeded only by the global pattern of insolation as a control of world climate patterns.

Idealized Circulation Patterns

Hypothetical Pattern of Nonrotating Earth: If Earth were a nonrotating sphere with a uniform surface, we could expect a very simple global atmospheric circulation pattern (Figure 5-12). The greater amount of solar warming in the equatorial region would produce a band of low pressure around the world, and radiational cooling at the poles would develop a cap of high pressure in those areas. Surface winds in the Northern Hemisphere would flow directly "down the pressure gradient" from north to south, whereas those in the Southern Hemisphere would follow a similar gradient from south to north. Air would rise at the equator in a large convection cell and flow toward the poles (south to north in the Northern Hemisphere and north to south in the Southern Hemisphere), where it would subside into the polar highs.

The Hadley Cells: Earth does rotate, however, and in addition has an extremely varied surface. Consequently, the broadscale circulation pattern of the atmosphere is much more complex than that shown in Figure 5-12. Apparently only the tropical regions have a complete vertical convective circulation cell. Similar cells have been postulated for the middle and high latitudes, but observations indicate that the midlatitude and high-latitude cells either do not exist or are weakly and sporadically developed.

The low-latitude cells—one north and one south of the equator—are gigantic convection systems (Figure 5-13).

These two prominent tropical convection cells are called **Hadley cells**, after George Hadley (1685–1768), an English meteorologist who first conceived the idea of enormous convective circulation cells in 1735.

Around the world in equatorial latitudes, warm air rises, producing a region of relative low pressure at the surface. This air ascends to great heights, mostly in thunderstorm updrafts. By the time this air reaches the upper troposphere at elevations of about 15 kilometers (50,000 feet), it has cooled. The air then spreads north and south and moves poleward, eventually descending at latitudes of about 30° N and S, where it forms bands of high pressure at the surface (Figure 5-14). One portion of the air diverging from these surface high-pressure zones flows toward the poles, whereas another portion flows back toward the equator—where the Northern and Southern Hemisphere components converge and the warm air rises again.

Learning Check 5-6 **Describe the pattern of air movement within the *Hadley cells.***

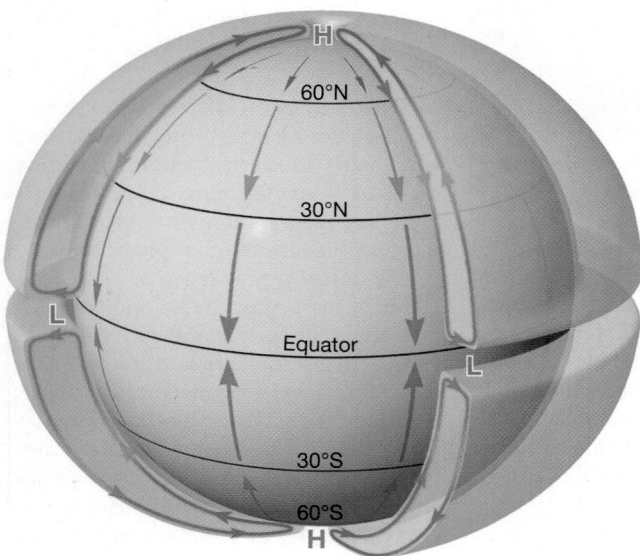

▲ **Figure 5-12** Wind circulation patterns would be simple if Earth's surface were uniform (no distinction between continents and oceans) and if the planet did not rotate. High pressure at the poles and low pressure at the equator would produce northerly surface winds in the Northern Hemisphere and southerly surface winds in the Southern Hemisphere.

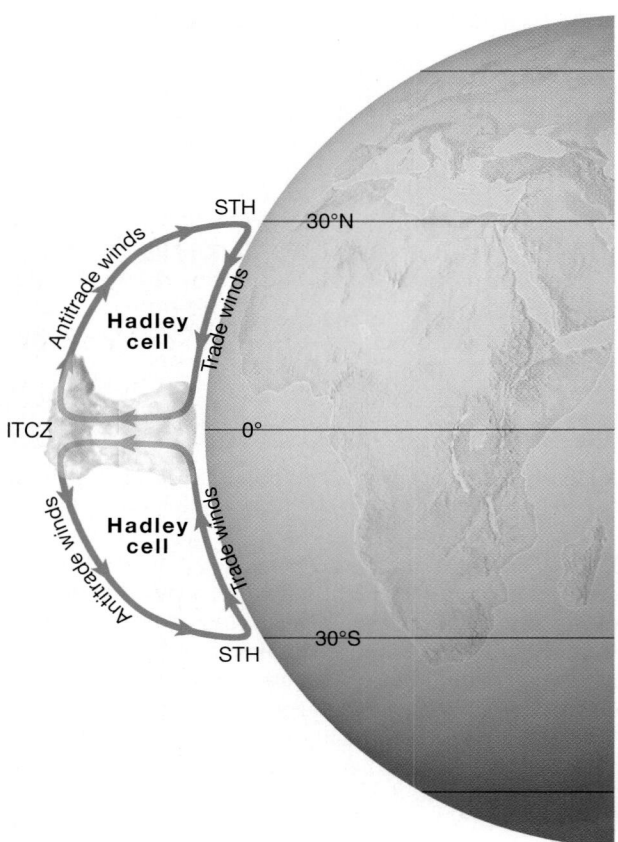

▲ **Figure 5-13** Distinct cells of vertical circulation occur in tropical latitudes; they are called Hadley cells. The equatorial air rises to some 12 to 15 kilometers (40,000 to 50,000 feet) in the intertropical convergence zone (ITCZ) before spreading poleward. This air descends at about 30° N and S into subtropical high-pressure (STH) cells. The vertical dimension of the Hadley cells is considerably exaggerated in this idealized diagram.

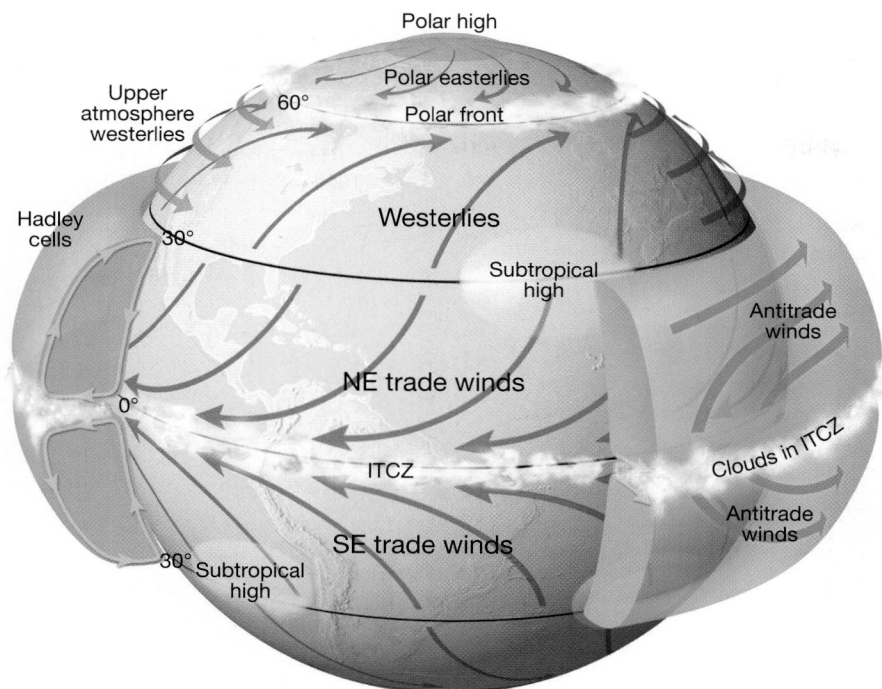

◀ **Figure 5-14** Idealized global circulation. Rising air of the ITCZ in the Hadley cell is deflected aloft and forms westerly antitrade winds, while surface winds diverging from the STH form easterly trade winds and the westerlies. The upper atmosphere flow of the westerlies is shown with faint blue arrows. (Vertical dimension exaggerated considerably.)

Seven Components of the General Circulation

Although the Hadley cell model is a simplification of reality, it is a useful starting point for understanding the main components of the general circulation of the atmosphere. The basic pattern has seven surface components of pressure and wind, intimately linked together. The Northern Hemisphere and Southern Hemisphere patterns are mirror images of each other. From the equator to the poles, the seven components are

1. Intertropical convergence zone (ITCZ)
2. Trade winds
3. Subtropical highs
4. Westerlies
5. Polar front (Subpolar lows)
6. Polar easterlies
7. Polar highs

The pattern general circulation within the troposphere is essentially a closed system, with neither a beginning nor an end, and so we could begin describing it almost anywhere. Rather than start at the equator or the poles, however, it is helpful to begin our discussion of the general circulation in the subtropical latitudes of the five major ocean basins—where the descending air of the Hadley cells becomes the "source" of the major surface winds of the planet.

Subtropical Highs

Each ocean basin has a large semipermanent high-pressure cell centered at about 30° of latitude called a **subtropical high (STH)** (Figure 5-15). These gigantic anticyclones, with an average diameter of perhaps 3200 kilometers (2000

miles), develop from the descending air of the Hadley cells. They are usually elongated east–west and tend to be centered in the eastern portions of an ocean basin (in other words, just off the west coasts of continents). Their latitudinal positions vary from time to time, shifting a few degrees poleward in summer and a few degrees equatorward in winter.

The STHs are so persistent that some have been given a proper name, such as the *Azores High* in the North Atlantic and the *Hawaiian High* in the North Pacific (Figure 5-16). From a global standpoint, the STHs represent intensified cells of high pressure (and subsiding air) in two general ridges of high pressure that extend around the world in these latitudes, one in each hemisphere. The high-pressure ridges are significantly broken up over the continents, especially in summer when inland temperatures produce lower air pressure, but the STHs normally persist over the ocean basins throughout the year because temperatures and pressures there remain nearly constant.

Associated with these high-pressure cells is a general subsidence of air from higher altitudes in the form of a broadscale, gentle downdraft. A permanent feature of the STHs is a subsidence temperature inversion that covers wide areas in the subtropics.

Weather of the Subtropical Highs: Within an STH, the weather is nearly always clear, warm, and calm. We shall see in the next chapter that subsiding air is not conducive to the development of clouds or the production of rain. Instead, these areas are characterized by warm, subtropical sunshine. Thus, it comes as no surprise that these anticyclonic, subsiding-air regions coincide with many of the world's major deserts.

Subtropical highs are also characterized by an absence of wind: in the center of an STH air is primarily subsiding;

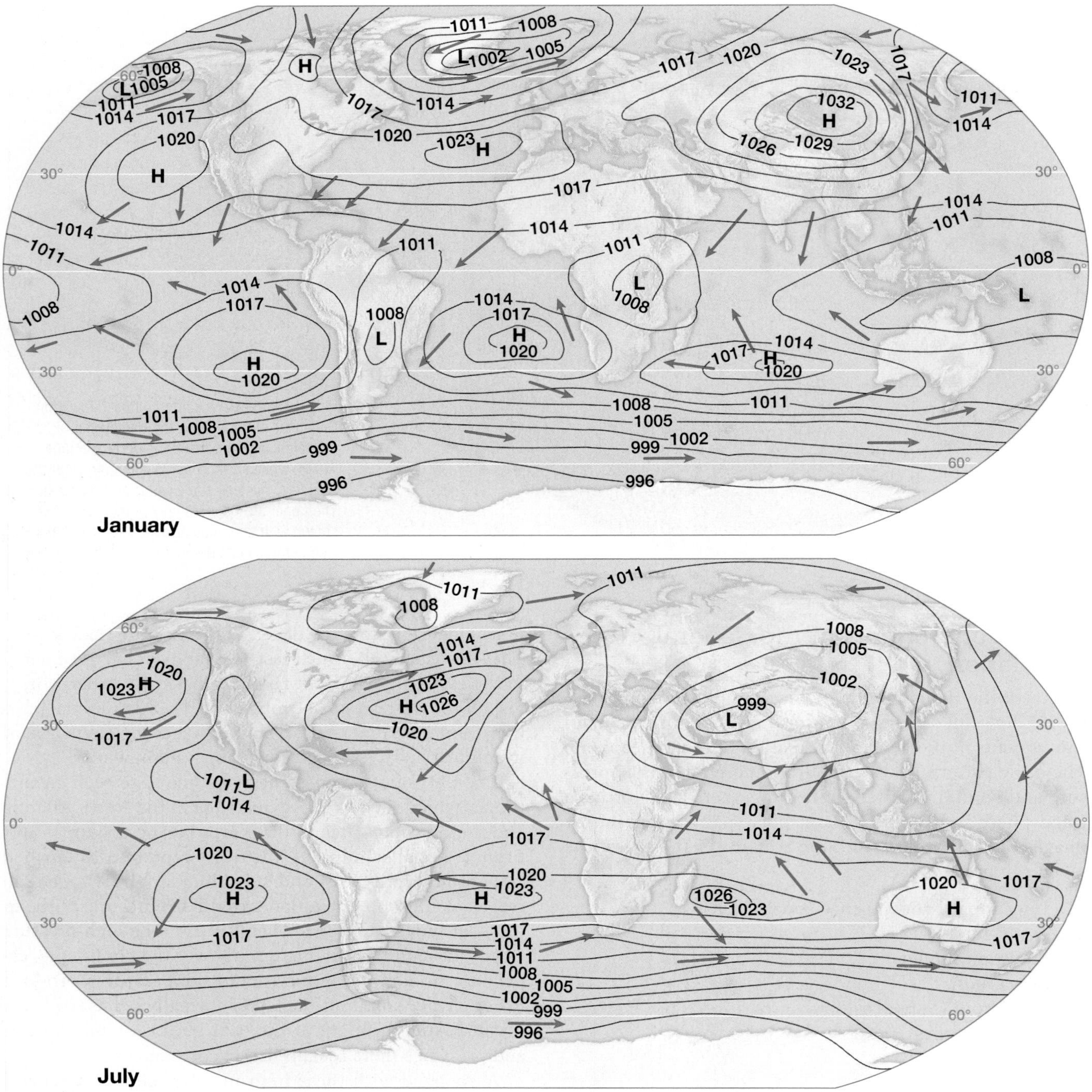

January

July

▲ **Figure 5-15** Average atmospheric pressure and wind direction in January and July. Pressure is reduced to sea-level values and shown in millibars. Arrows indicate generalized surface wind movements.

horizontal air movement and divergence begin toward the edges. These regions are sometimes called the **horse latitudes**, presumably because sixteenth- and seventeenth-century sailing ships were sometimes becalmed there and their cargos of horses were thrown overboard to conserve drinking water.

The air circulation pattern around an STH is anticyclonic: diverging clockwise in the Northern Hemisphere

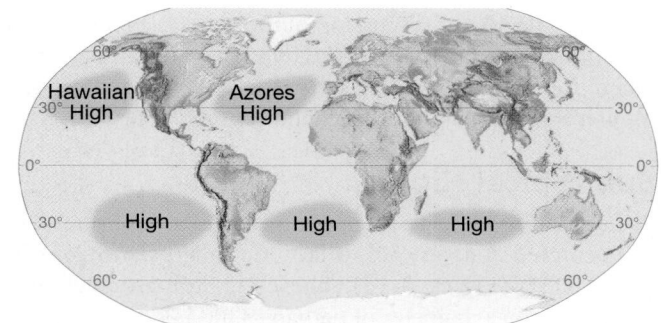

▶ **Figure 5-16** The subtropical highs are generally located over ocean basins at latitudes of about 30° N and S; also called the horse latitudes.

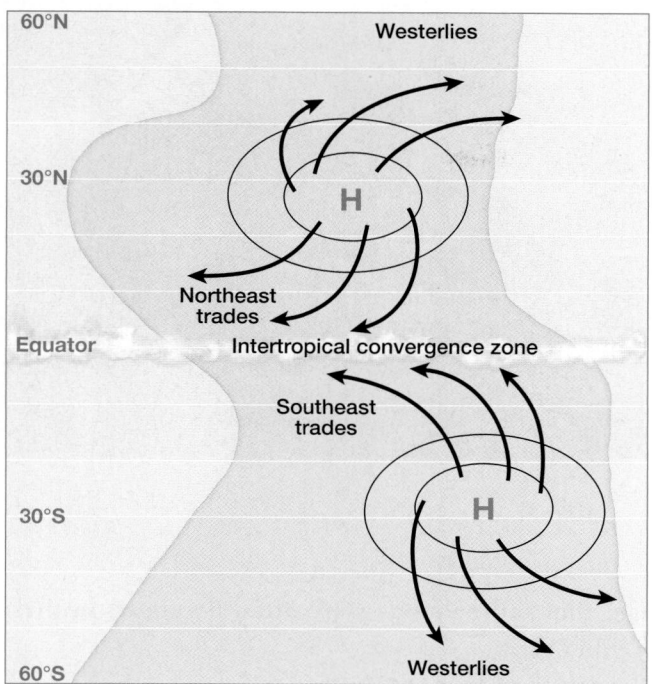

▲ **Figure 5-17** The air that descends and diverges out of the subtropical highs is the source of the surface trade winds and westerlies. This map shows the generalized location of the intertropical convergence zone, trade winds, subtropical highs, and westerlies in hypothetical Northern and Southern Hemisphere ocean basins.

and counterclockwise in the Southern Hemisphere. In essence, the STHs can be thought of as gigantic "wind wheels" whirling in the lower troposphere, fed with air sinking down from above and spinning off winds horizontally in all directions (Figure 5-17). The winds are not dispersed uniformly around an STH, however; instead, they are concentrated on the northern and southern sides.

Although the global flow of air is essentially a closed circulation from a viewpoint at Earth's surface, the STHs can be thought of as the source of two of the world's three major surface wind systems: the *trade winds* and the *westerlies*.

> **Learning Check 5-7** **Describe the general locations and the kind of weather associated with the *subtropical highs*.**

Trade Winds

Diverging from the equatorward sides of the subtropical highs is the major wind system of the tropics—the **trade winds**. These winds cover most of Earth between about latitude 25° N and latitude 25° S (see Figure 5-17). They are particularly prominent over oceans but tend to be significantly interrupted and modified over landmasses. Because of the vastness of Earth in tropical latitudes and because most of this expanse is oceanic, the trade winds dominate more of the globe than any other wind system.

The trade winds are predominantly "easterly" winds—that is, they generally blow from east to west. In meteorology winds are named for the direction *from which they blow*: an easterly wind blows from east to west, a westerly wind blows from the west, and so forth.

In the Northern Hemisphere, the trade winds usually blow from the northeast (and are sometimes called the *northeast trades*); south of the equator, they are from the southeast (the *southeast trades*). There are exceptions to this general pattern, especially over the Indian Ocean, where westerly winds sometimes prevail, but for the most part the flow is easterly over the tropical oceans.

Consistency of Trade Winds: The trade winds are by far the most "reliable" of all winds. They are extremely consistent in both direction and speed, as Figure 5-18 shows. They blow most of the time in the same direction at the same speed, day and night, summer and winter (Figure 5-19). This steadiness is reflected in their name: trade winds really means "winds of commerce." Mariners of the sixteenth century recognized early that the quickest and most reliable route for their sailing vessels from Europe to the Americas lay in the belt of northeasterly winds of the southern part of the North Atlantic Ocean. Similarly, the trade winds were used by Spanish galleons in the Pacific Ocean, and the name became applied generally to these tropical easterly winds.

The trades originate as warming, drying winds capable of holding an enormous amount of moisture. As they blow across the tropical oceans, they evaporate vast quantities of moisture and therefore have a tremendous potential for storminess and precipitation. They do

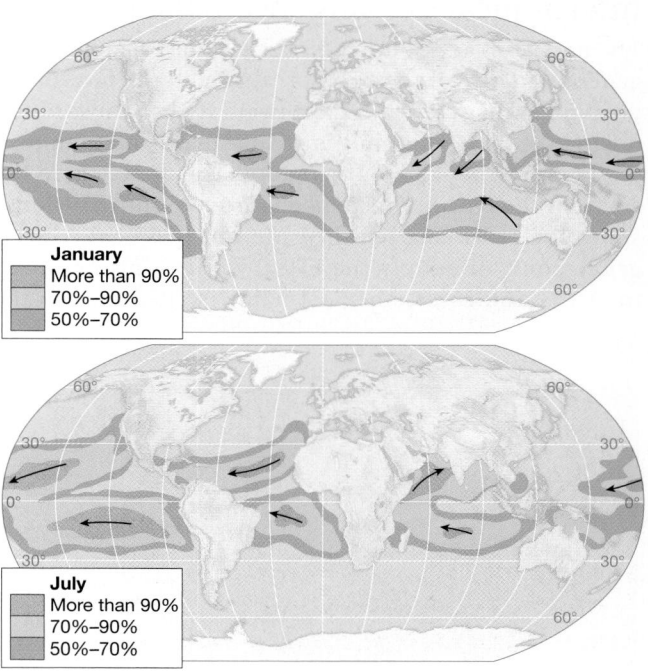

▲ **Figure 5-18** The trade winds are the most consistent of the major wind systems. These maps show their frequency of consistency for the midseason months of January and July. In the orange areas, for instance, the wind blows in the indicated direction more than 90 percent of the time. Note the monsoon wind reversal in southern Asia during July (discussed later in this chapter).

▶ **Figure 5-19** Tropical coastal areas often experience the ceaseless movement of the trade winds. This breezy scene is at Cairns on the northeastern coast of Queensland, Australia.

not release the moisture, however, unless forced to do so by being uplifted by a topographic barrier or some sort of pressure disturbance (the reasons for this will be explained in Chapter 6). Low-lying islands in the trade-wind zone are often desert islands because the moisture-laden winds pass over them without dropping any rain. If there is even a slight topographic irregularity, however, the air that is forced to rise may release abundant precipitation (Figure 5-20). Some of the wettest places in the world are windward slopes in the trade winds, such as in Hawai'i (see Figure 3-21).

Intertropical Convergence Zone (ITCZ)

The northeast and southeast trades come together in the general vicinity of the equator, although the latitudinal position shifts seasonally northward and southward following the Sun. This shift is greater over land than over sea because the land warms more. The zone where the air from the Northern Hemisphere and Southern Hemisphere meet is usually called the **intertropical convergence zone**, or simply the **ITCZ**, but it is also referred to as the **doldrums** (this last name is attributed to the

fact that sailing ships were often becalmed in these latitudes).

Weather of the ITCZ: The ITCZ is a zone of convergence and weak horizontal airflow characterized by feeble and erratic winds. It is a globe-girdling zone of warm surface conditions, low pressure associated with high rainfall, instability, and rising air in the Hadley cells (see Figure 5-14). It is not a region of continuously ascending air, however. Almost all the rising air of the tropics ascends in the updrafts that occur in thunderstorms in the ITCZ, and these updrafts pump an enormous amount of sensible heat and latent heat of condensation into the upper troposphere, where much of it spreads poleward.

The ITCZ often appears as a well-defined, relatively narrow cloud band over the oceans near the equator (Figure 5-21). Over continents, however, it is likely to be more diffused and indistinct, although thunderstorm activity is common.

Learning Check 5-8 Describe the general location and kind of weather associated with the ITCZ.

The Westerlies

The fourth component of the general atmospheric circulation is the great wind system of the midlatitudes, commonly called the **westerlies**, represented by the arrows that issue from the poleward sides of the STHs in Figure 5-17. These winds flow basically from west to east around the world in the latitudinal zone between about 30° and 60° both north and south of the equator. Because the circumference of Earth is smaller at these latitudes than in the tropics, the westerlies are less extensive than the trades; nevertheless, they cover much of Earth.

Animation
The Jet Stream and Rossby Waves

▲ **Figure 5-20** Trade winds are usually heavily laden with moisture, but usually do not produce clouds and rain unless forced to rise. Thus, they may blow across a low-lying island with little or no visible effect. An island of greater elevation, however, causes the air to rise up the side of the mountain, and the result is usually a heavy rain.

Wind direction

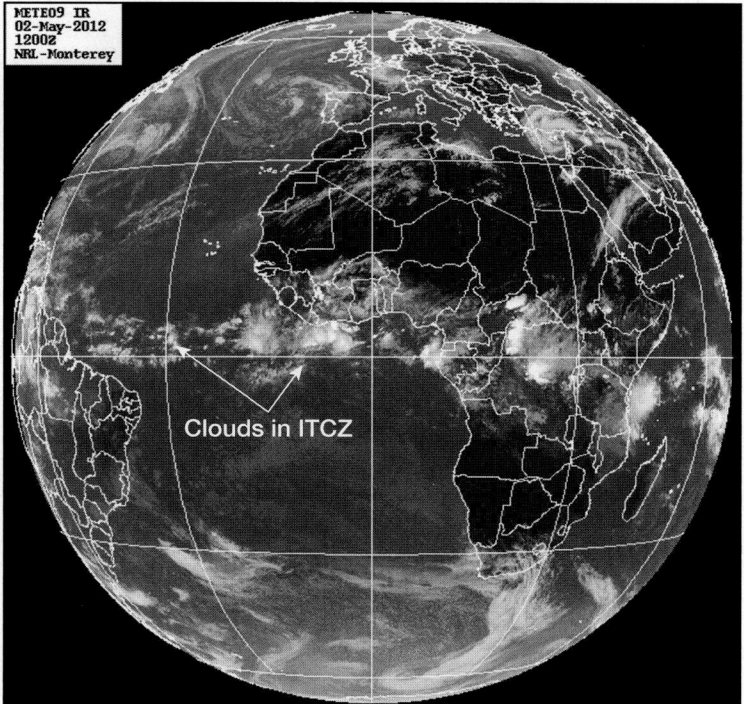

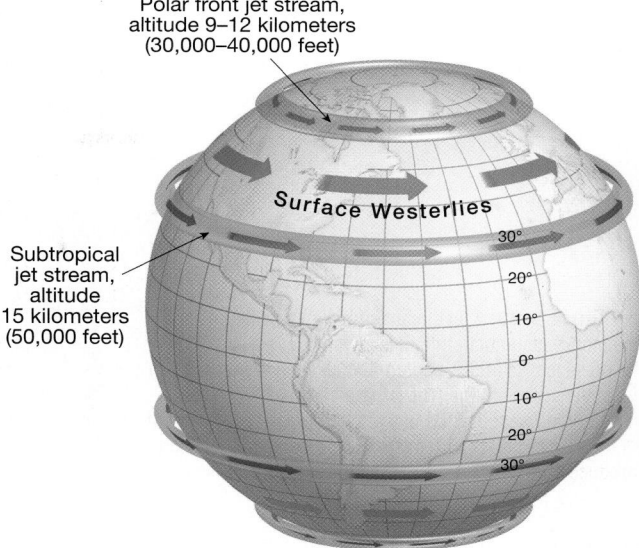

▲ **Figure 5-22** Neither jet stream is centered in the band of the westerlies. The polar front jet stream is closer to the poleward boundary, and the subtropical jet stream is closer to the equatorward boundary of this wind system. The two jet streams are not at the same altitude; the subtropical jet stream is at a higher altitude than the polar front jet stream.

▲ **Figure 5-21** A well-defined band of clouds marks the ITCZ over equatorial Africa in this infrared satellite image (darker shades of gray indicate warmer surface temperatures). This image was taken during the Northern Hemisphere summer, so the ITCZ has shifted slightly north of the equator. Note the generally clear skies off the west coasts of northern and southern Africa, corresponding to the areas of the subtropical highs, and the cloudiness and storms in the band of westerlies in the midlatitudes.

The surface westerlies are much less constant and persistent than the trades, which is to say that in the midlatitudes surface winds do not always flow from the west but may come from almost any point of the compass. Near the surface there are interruptions and modifications of the westerly flow, which can be likened to eddies and countercurrents in a river. These interruptions are caused by surface friction, by topographic barriers, and especially by migratory pressure systems, which produce airflow that is not westerly.

> **Learning Check 5-9** **What is the relationship of the subtropical highs to the *trade winds* and the *westerlies*?**

Jet Streams: Although the surface westerlies are somewhat variable, the geostrophic winds aloft, however, blow very prominently from the west. Moreover, there are two remarkable "cores" of high-speed winds in each hemisphere called **jet streams**: one called the *polar front jet stream* (or simply the *polar jet stream*) and the other called the *subtropical jet stream*, at high altitudes in the westerlies (Figure 5-22). The belt of the westerlies can therefore be thought of as a meandering river of air moving generally from west to east around the world in the midlatitudes, with the jet streams as its fast-moving cores.

The polar front jet stream, which usually occupies a position 9 to 12 kilometers (30,000 to 40,000 feet) high, is not centered in the band of the westerlies; it is displaced poleward, as Figure 5-22 shows (the name comes from its location near the polar front). This jet stream is a feature of the

upper troposphere located over the area of greatest horizontal temperature gradient—that is, cold just poleward and warm just equatorward.

A jet stream is not always the sharply defined narrow ribbon of wind, as often portrayed on weather maps; rather it is a zone of strong winds within the upper troposphere westerly flow. Jet stream speed is variable. Sixty knots is generally considered as the minimum speed required for recognition as a jet stream, but wind speeds five times that fast have been recorded (Figure 5-23).

Commercial air travel can be significantly influenced by the high-speed flow of upper tropospheric winds. The cruising altitude of commercial jetliners is usually 9 to 12 kilometers (30,000 to 40,000 feet)—a typical elevation for the polar front jet stream. It generally takes longer to fly from east to west across North America than it does to fly from west to east. When one is traveling from the east, a "headwind" is likely to impede progress, whereas when traveling from the west, a "tailwind" may reduce travel time.

Rossby Waves: The polar front jet stream shifts its latitudinal position with some frequency, and this change has considerable influence on the path of the westerlies. Although the basic direction of movement is west to east, frequently sweeping undulations develop in the westerlies and produce a meandering jet stream path that wanders widely north and south (Figure 5-24). These curves are very large and are generally referred to as *long waves* or **Rossby waves** (after the Chicago meteorologist C. G. Rossby, who first explained their nature).

At any given time, there are usually from three to six Rossby waves in the westerlies of each hemisphere. These waves can be thought of as separating cold polar air from warmer tropical air. When the polar front jet stream path is more directly west–east, there is a *zonal flow* pattern in

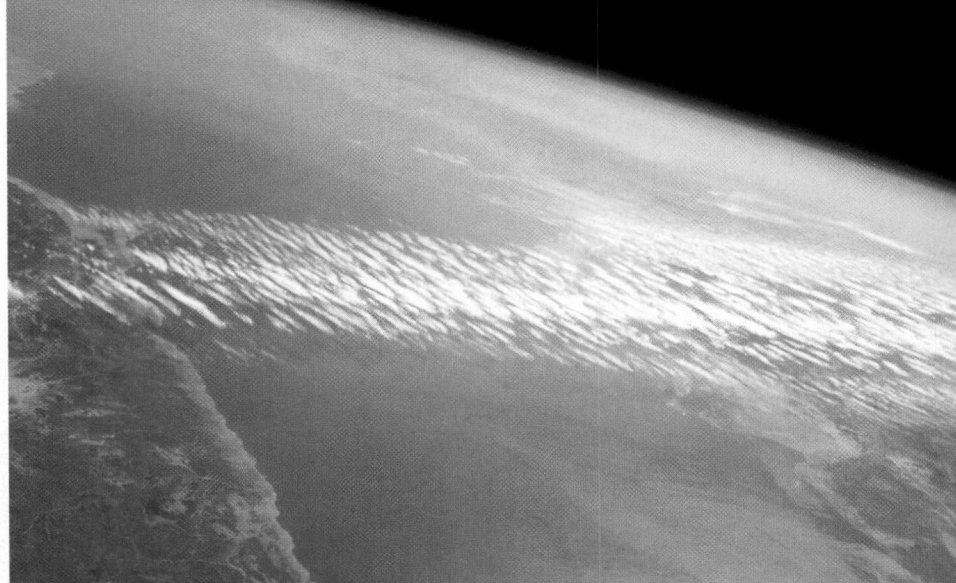

▶ **Figure 5-23** A jet stream sometimes generates a distinctive cloud pattern that is conspicuous evidence of its presence, as in this photograph taken over the Red Sea from the space shuttle. The jet stream was flowing from left to right (west to east) in this photograph. Equatorward of the axis of the jet air tends to rise, a condition that can produce thin clouds. Poleward of the axis, the air is clear.

the weather, with cold air poleward of warm air. However, when the jet stream begins to oscillate and the Rossby waves develop significant amplitude (which means a prominent north–south component of movement) there is a *meridional flow*: cold air is brought equatorward and warm air moves poleward, bringing frequent and severe weather changes to the midlatitudes.

The subtropical jet stream is usually located at high altitudes—just below the tropopause, as Figure 5-25a shows—over the poleward margin of the subsiding air of the STH. It has less influence on surface weather patterns because there is less temperature contrast in the associated air streams. Sometimes, however, the polar front jet and the subtropical jet merge, as shown in Figure 5-25b, to produce a broad belt of high-speed winds in the upper troposphere—a condition that can intensify the weather conditions associated with either zonal or meridional flow of the Rossby waves.

All things considered, no other portion of Earth experiences such short-run variability of weather as the midlatitudes.

Learning Check 5-10   What are *jet streams* and where they are usually found?

Polar Highs

Situated over both polar regions are high-pressure cells called **polar highs** (see Figure 5-14). The Antarctic high, which forms over an extensive, high-elevation, very cold continent, is strong, persistent, and almost a permanent feature above the Antarctic continent. The Arctic high is much less pronounced and more transitory, particularly in winter. It tends to form over northern continental areas rather than over the Arctic Ocean. Air movement associated with these cells is typically anticyclonic. Air from above sinks down into the high and diverges horizontally near the surface, clockwise in the Northern Hemisphere and counterclockwise in the Southern Hemisphere, forming the third of the world's wind systems, the polar easterlies.

▶ **Figure 5-24** Rossby waves as part of the general flow (particularly the upper-airflow) of the westerlies. (a) When there are few waves and their amplitude (north–south component of movement) is small, cold air usually remains poleward of warm air. (b) This distribution pattern begins to change as the Rossby waves grow. (c) When the waves have great amplitude, cold air pushes equatorward and warm air moves poleward.

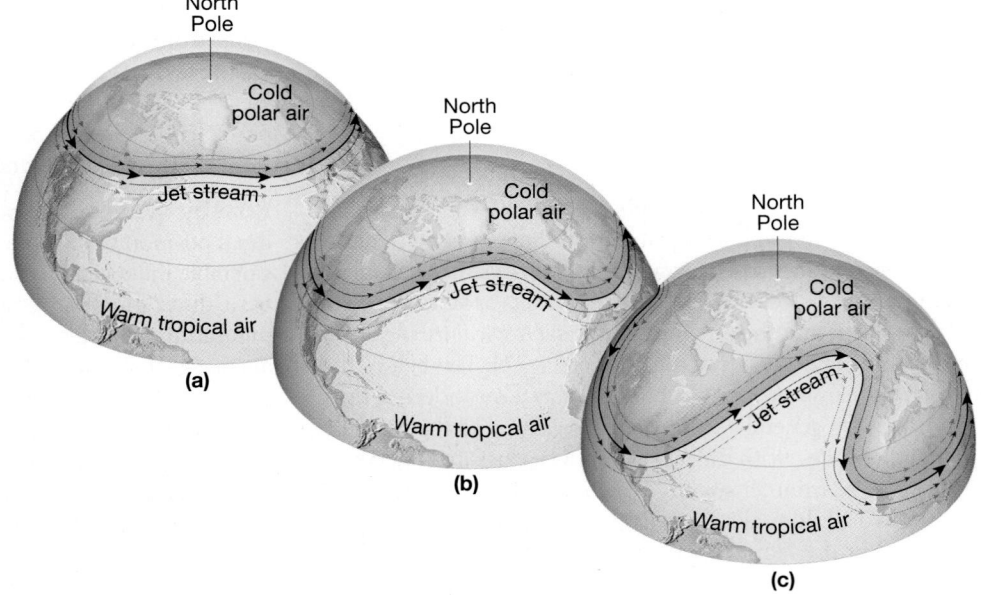

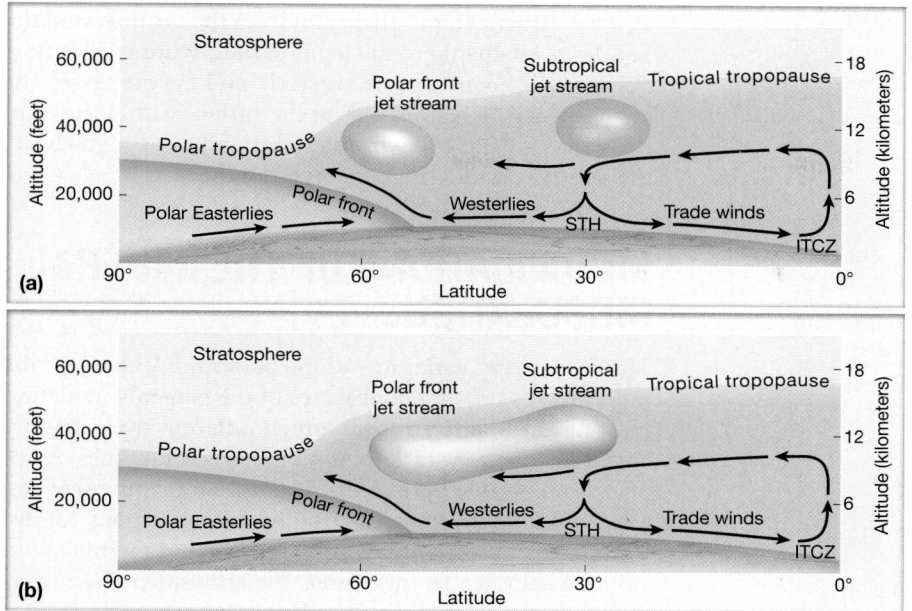

◄ **Figure 5-25** (a) A vertical cross section of the atmosphere from the equator to the poles showing the usual relative positions of the two jet streams. (b) The two jet streams sometimes merge, and the result is intensified weather conditions.

Polar Easterlies

The third broad-scale global wind system occupies most of the area between the polar highs and about 60° of latitude (Figure 5-26). The winds move generally from east to west and are called the **polar easterlies**. They are typically cold and dry but quite variable.

Polar Front

The final surface component of the general pattern of atmospheric circulation is a zone of low pressure at about 50° to 60° of latitude in both Northern and Southern Hemispheres. The zone is commonly called the **polar front**, although it is sometimes most clearly visible by the presence of semipermanent zones of low pressure called the **subpolar lows**.

The polar front is a meeting ground and zone of conflict between the cold winds of the polar easterlies and the relatively warmer westerlies. The subpolar low of the Southern Hemisphere is nearly continuous over the uniform ocean surface of the cold seas surrounding Antarctica. In the Northern Hemisphere, however, the low-pressure zone is discontinuous, being interrupted by the continents. It is much more prominent in winter than in summer and is best developed over the northernmost reaches of the Pacific and Atlantic Oceans, forming the *Aleutian Low* and the *Icelandic Low*, respectively.

The polar front area is characterized by rising air, widespread cloudiness, precipitation, and generally unsettled or stormy weather conditions (Figure 5-27). Many of the migratory storms that travel with the westerlies have their origin in the conflict zone of the polar front.

Vertical Patterns of the General Circulation

As we have seen, over tropical regions, between the equator and 20° to 25° of latitude, surface winds generally blow from the east. In the midlatitudes, the surface winds are

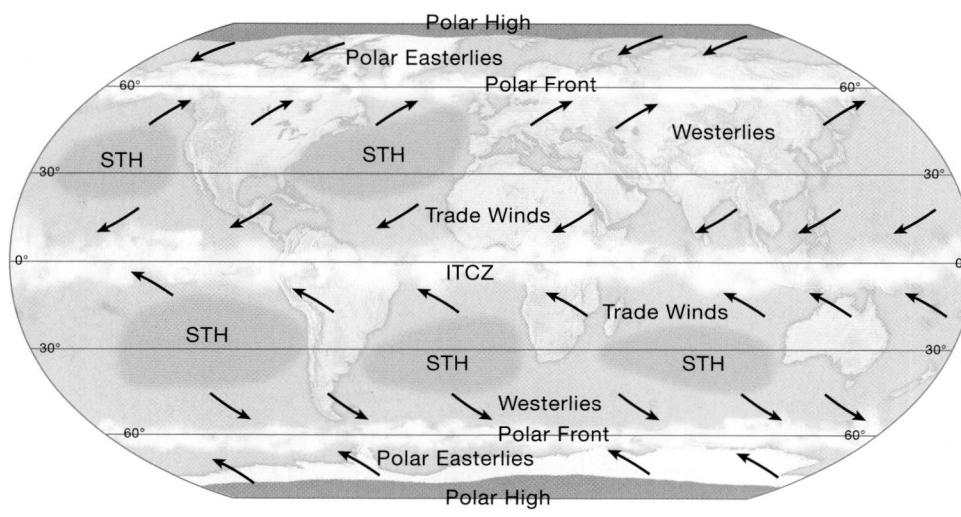

◄ **Figure 5-26** Map showing the generalized locations of the seven components of the general circulation patterns of the atmosphere. (In this map projection, the areal extent of the high-latitude components—polar high, polar easterlies, polar front—is considerably exaggerated.)

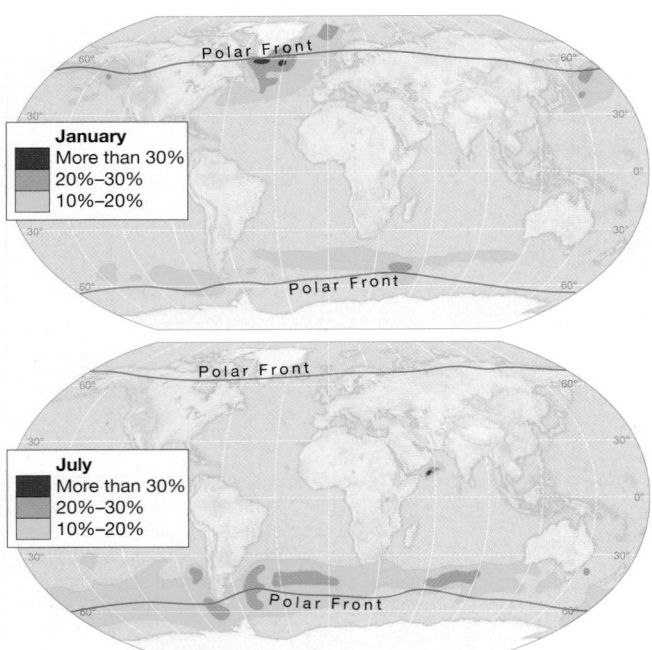

▲ **Figure 5-27** Frequency of gale-force (34 knot) winds over the oceans in January and July. It is clear from this map that the strongest oceanic winds are associated with activities along the polar front (subpolar lows).

generally westerly, whereas in the highest latitudes, surface winds are again easterly. In the upper altitudes of the troposphere, however, the wind patterns are somewhat different from the surface winds (Figure 5-28).

The most dramatic difference is seen over the tropics. After equatorial air has risen in the ITCZ, the high-elevation poleward flow of air in the Hadley cell is deflected by the Coriolis effect (see Figure 5-14). This results in upper-elevation winds blowing from the southwest

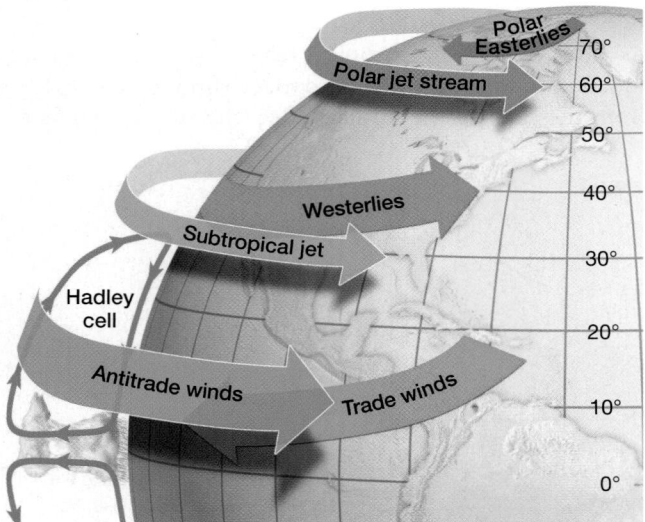

▲ **Figure 5-28** A generalized cross section through the troposphere, showing the dominant wind directions at different latitudes near the surface and in the upper troposphere. Surface winds in the tropics are generally easterly, but high above, the antitrade winds are blowing from the west, as are the upper troposphere jet streams of the westerlies.

in the Northern Hemisphere and from the northwest in the Southern Hemisphere in the **antitrade winds**. This flow eventually becomes more westerly and encompasses the subtropical jet stream. Thus, at the surface within the tropics, winds are generally from the east, whereas high above, the antitrade winds are blowing from the west.

MODIFICATIONS OF THE GENERAL CIRCULATION

There are many variations to the pattern discussed on the preceding pages, and all features of the general circulation may appear in altered form, much different from the idealized description. Indeed, components sometimes disappear from sizable parts of the atmosphere where they are expected to exist. Even the tropopause sometimes "disappears" (for example, during a high-latitude winter with very cold surface temperatures, the atmospheric temperature may steadily increase with height into the stratosphere; in such cases the tropopause cannot be identified).

Nevertheless, the generalized pattern of global wind and pressure systems comprises the seven components described above. To understand how real-world weather and climate differ from this general picture, it is necessary to discuss two important modifications of the generalized scheme.

Seasonal Variations in Location

FG11

Animation
Seasonal Pressure and Precipitation Patterns

The seven surface components of the general circulation shift latitudinally with the changing seasons. When sunlight, and therefore surface warming, is concentrated in the Northern Hemisphere (Northern Hemisphere summer), all components are displaced northward; during the opposite season (Southern Hemisphere summer), everything is shifted southward. The displacement is greatest in the low latitudes and least in the polar regions. The ITCZ, for example, can be found as much as 25° north of the equator in July and 20° south of the equator in January (Figure 5-29), while the polar highs experience little or no latitudinal displacement from season to season.

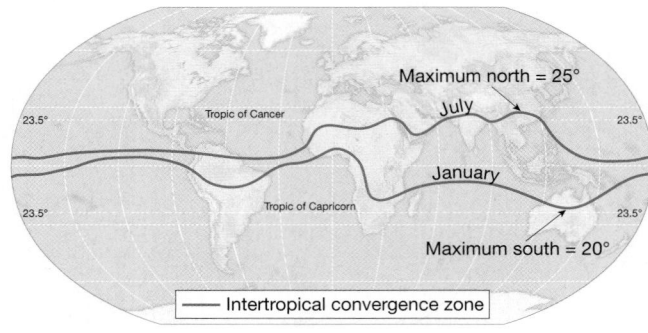

▲ **Figure 5-29** Typical maximum poleward positions of the intertropical convergence zone at its seasonal extremes. The greatest variation in location is associated with monsoon activity in Eurasia and Australia.

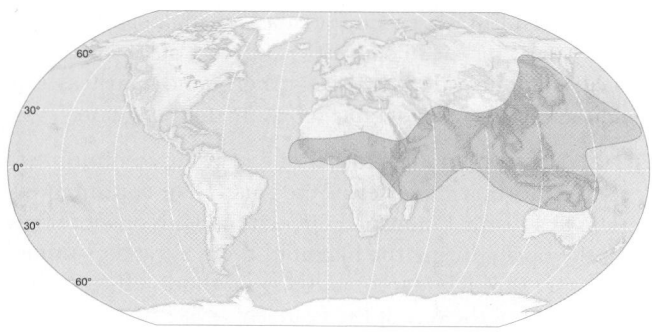

▲ **Figure 5-30** The principal monsoon areas of the world.

Weather is affected by shifts in the general circulation components only minimally in polar regions, but the effects can be quite significant in the tropics and midlatitudes. For example, as we will see in Chapter 8, regions of *mediterranean climate* found along the west coasts of continents at about 35° N and S latitude, have warm, rainless summers while under the influence of the STH; in winter, however, the belt of the westerlies shifts equatorward, bringing changeable and frequently stormy weather to these regions (see Figure 5-15). Also, as we will see, the shift of the ITCZ is closely tied to seasonal rainfall patterns in large areas within the tropics.

Learning Check 5-11 Why does the location of the ITCZ shift north during the Northern Hemisphere summer?

Monsoons

By far the most significant deviation from the pattern of general circulation is the development of **monsoons** in certain parts of the world, particularly southern and eastern Eurasia (Figure 5-30). The word *monsoon* is derived from the Arabic *mawsim* (meaning "season") and has come to mean a seasonal reversal of winds, a general sea-to-land movement—called *onshore flow*—in summer and a general land-to-sea movement—called *offshore flow*—in winter. Associated with the monsoon wind pattern is a distinctive seasonal precipitation regime—heavy summer rains derived from the moist maritime air of the onshore flow and a pronounced winter dry season when continental air moving seaward dominates the circulation.

Causes of Monsoons: It would be convenient to explain monsoon circulation simply on the basis of the unequal warming of continents and oceans. A strong thermal (warm surface) low-pressure cell generated over a continental landmass in summer attracts oceanic air onshore; similarly, a prominent thermal anticyclone in winter over a continent produces an offshore circulation. It is clear that these thermally induced pressure differences contribute to monsoon development (see Figure 5-15), but they are not the whole story.

Monsoon winds essentially represent unusually large latitudinal migrations of the trade winds associated with the large seasonal shifts of the ITCZ over southeastern Eurasia. The Himalayas evidently also play a role—this significant topographic barrier allows greater winter temperature contrasts between South Asia and the interior of the continent to the north, and this in turn may influence the location and persistence of the subtropical jet stream in this region.

Significance of Monsoons: It is difficult to overestimate the importance of monsoon circulation to humankind. More than half of the world's population inhabits the regions in which climates are largely controlled by monsoons. Moreover, these are generally regions in which the majority of the populace depends on agriculture for its livelihood. Their lives are intricately bound up with the reality of monsoon rains, that are essential for both food production and cash crops (Figure 5-31). The failure, or even late arrival,

▶ **Figure 5-31** Flooding caused by summer monsoon rains in the central business district of Dhaka, Bangladesh.

of monsoon moisture inevitably causes widespread hunger and economic disaster.

Although the causes are complex, the characteristics of monsoons are well known, and it is possible to describe the monsoon patterns with some precision. There are two major monsoon systems (one in South Asia and the other in East Asia), two minor systems (in Australia and West Africa), and several other regions where monsoon patterns develop (especially in Central America and the southwest United States).

South Asian Monsoon: The most notable environmental event each year in South Asia is the annual burst of the summer monsoon, illustrated in Figure 5-32a. In this first of the two major monsoon systems, prominent onshore winds spiral in from the Indian Ocean, bringing life-giving rains to the parched subcontinent. In winter, South Asia is dominated by outblowing dry air diverging generally from the northeast. This flow is not very different from normal northeast trades except for its low moisture content.

East Asian Monsoon: Turning to the second of the two major monsoon systems, we see that winter is the more prominent season in the East Asian monsoon system, which primarily affects China, Korea, and Japan and is illustrated in Figure 5-32b. A strong outflow of dry continental air, largely from the northwest, is associated with anticyclonic circulation around the massive thermal high-pressure cell over western Eurasia called the Siberian High. The onshore flow of maritime air in summer is not as notable as that in South Asia, but it does bring southerly and southeasterly winds, as well as considerable moisture, to the region.

Other Monsoon Areas: In one of the two minor systems, the northern quarter of the Australian continent experiences a distinct monsoon circulation, with onshore flow from the north during the height of the Australian summer (December through March) and dry, southerly, offshore flow during most of the rest of the year. This system is illustrated in Figure 5-33a.

The south-facing coast of West Africa is dominated within about 650 kilometers (400 miles) of the coast by the second minor monsoonal circulation. This system is shown in Figure 5-33b. Moist oceanic air flows onshore from the south and southwest during summer, and dry, northerly, continental flow prevails in the opposite season.

The so-called "Arizona Monsoon" of the southwestern United States is actually part of a broader minor monsoon pattern called the North American Monsoon. These onshore winds in summer carry moisture from the Gulf of California and the Gulf of Mexico into New Mexico, Arizona, and northwestern Mexico, bringing bursts of thunderstorm activity.

Learning Check 5-12 **How does wind direction in South Asia different from summer to winter?**

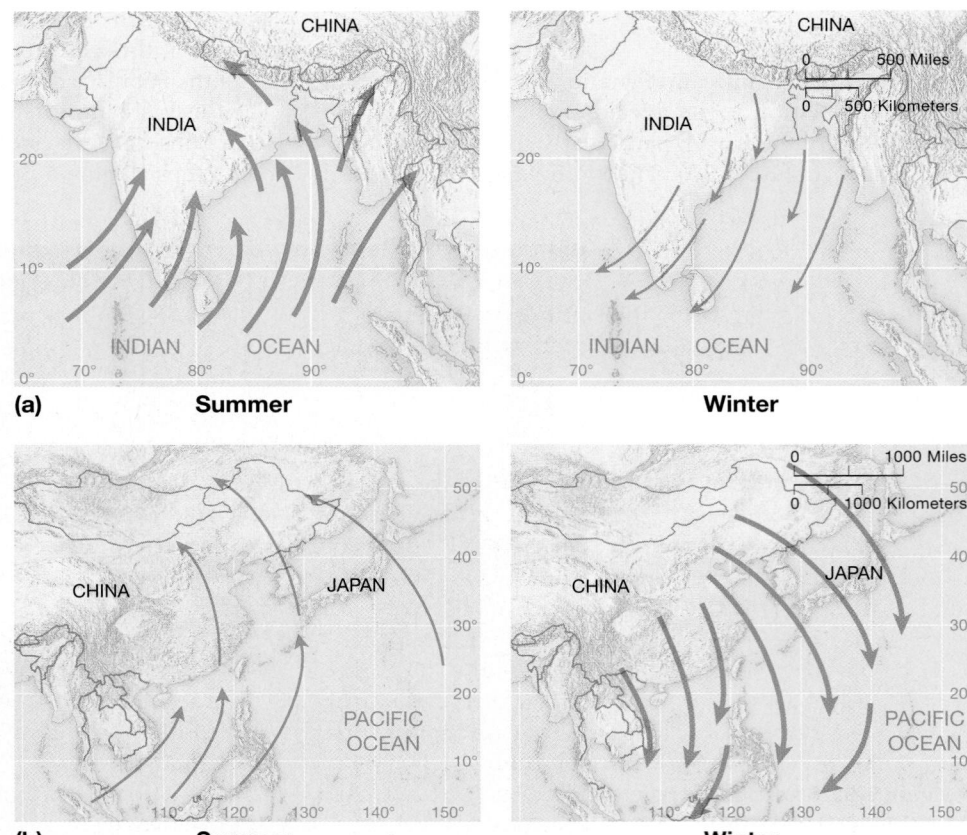

▶ **Figure 5-32** The two major monsoon systems. (a) The South Asian monsoon is characterized by a strong onshore flow in summer (rainy season) and a somewhat less pronounced offshore flow in winter (dry season). (b) In East Asia, the outblowing winter monsoon is stronger than the inblowing summer monsoon.

(a) **Summer**

Winter

(b) **Summer**

Winter

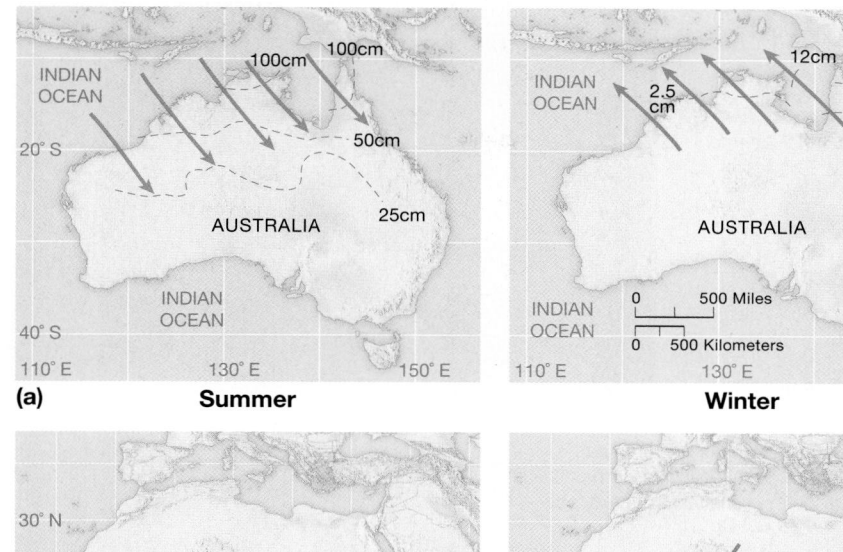

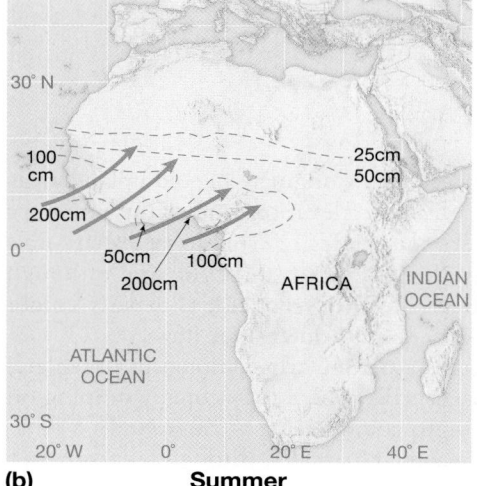

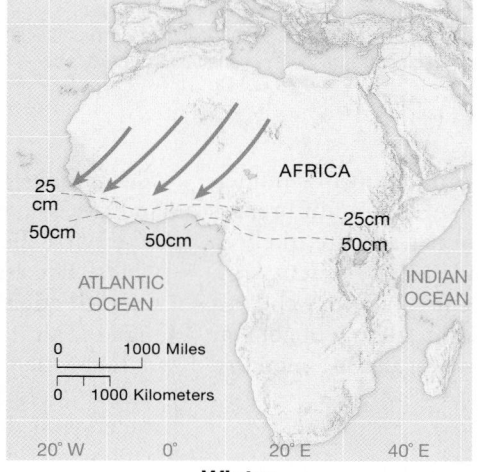

◀ **Figure 5-33** The two minor monsoon systems, showing 3-month seasonal rainfall isohyets (lines of equal rainfall). (a) In Australia, northwesterly summer winds bring the wet season to northern Australia; dry southeasterly flow dominates in winter. (b) In West Africa, summer winds are from the southwest and winter winds are from the northeast.

LOCALIZED WIND SYSTEMS

The preceding sections have dealt with only the broadscale wind systems that make up the global circulation and influence the climatic pattern of the world. Many kinds of lesser winds, however, are of considerable significance to weather and climate at a more localized scale. Such winds are the result of local pressure gradients that develop in response to topographic configurations in the immediate area, sometimes in conjunction with wider circulation conditions.

Sea and Land Breezes FG7

A common local wind system along tropical coastlines and to a lesser extent during the summer in midlatitude coastal areas is the cycle of **sea breezes** during the day and **land breezes** at night (Figure 5-34). (As is usual with winds, the name tells the direction from which the wind comes: a sea breeze blows from sea to land, and a land breeze blows from land to sea.) This is essentially a convectional circulation caused by the differential warming of land and water surfaces. The land warms up rapidly during the day, warming the air above by conduction and reradiation. This warming causes the air to expand and rise, creating low pressure that attracts surface breezes from over the adjacent water body. Because the onshore flow is

relatively cool and moist, it holds down daytime temperatures in the coastal zone and provides moisture for afternoon showers. Sea breezes are sometimes strong, but they rarely are influential for more than 15 to 30 kilometers (10 to 20 miles) inland.

The reverse flow at night is normally considerably weaker than the daytime wind. The land and the air above it cool more quickly than the adjacent water body, producing relatively higher pressure over land. Thus, air flows offshore in a land breeze.

Valley and Mountain Breezes

Another notable daily cycle of airflow is characteristic of many hill and mountain areas. During the day, conduction and reradiation from the land surface cause air near the mountain slopes to warm more than air over the valley floor (Figure 5-35). The warmed air rises, creating a low-pressure area, and then cooler air from the valley floor flows upslope from the high-pressure area to the low-pressure area. This upslope flow is called a **valley breeze**. The rising air often causes clouds to form around the peaks, and afternoon showers are common in the high country as a result. After dark, the pattern is reversed. The mountain slopes lose warmth rapidly through radiation, which chills the adjacent air, causing it to slip downslope as a **mountain breeze**.

▲ **Figure 5-34** In a typical sea–land breeze cycle, daytime warming over the land produces relatively low pressure there, and this low-pressure center attracts an onshore flow of air from the sea. Later, nighttime cooling over the land causes high pressure there, a condition that creates an offshore flow of air.

Valley breezes are particularly prominent in summer, when solar warming is most intense. Mountain breezes are often weakly developed in summer and are likely to be more prominent in winter. Indeed, a frequent winter phenomenon in areas of even gentle slope is cold air drainage, which is simply the nighttime sliding of cold air downslope to collect in the lowest spots; this is a modified form of mountain breeze.

Learning Check 5-13 *How do sea breezes form?*

Katabatic Winds

Related to simple air drainage is the more general and powerful spilling of air downslope in the form of **katabatic winds** (from the Greek *katabatik*, which means "descending"). These winds originate in cold upland areas and cascade toward lower elevations under the influence of gravity; they are sometimes referred to as *gravity-flow winds*. The air in them is dense and cold, and although warmed adiabatically as it descends, it is usually colder than the air it displaces in its downslope flow.

Katabatic winds are particularly common in Greenland and Antarctica, especially where they come whipping off the edge of the high, cold ice sheets. Sometimes a katabatic wind will become channeled through a narrow valley where it may develop high speed and considerable destructive power. An infamous example of this phenomenon is the *mistral*, which sometimes surges down France's Rhône Valley from the Alps to the Mediterranean Sea. Similar winds are called *bora* in the Adriatic region and *taku* in southeastern Alaska.

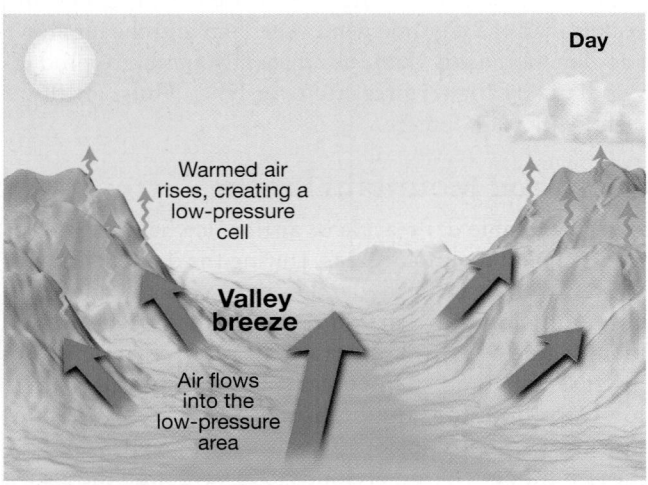 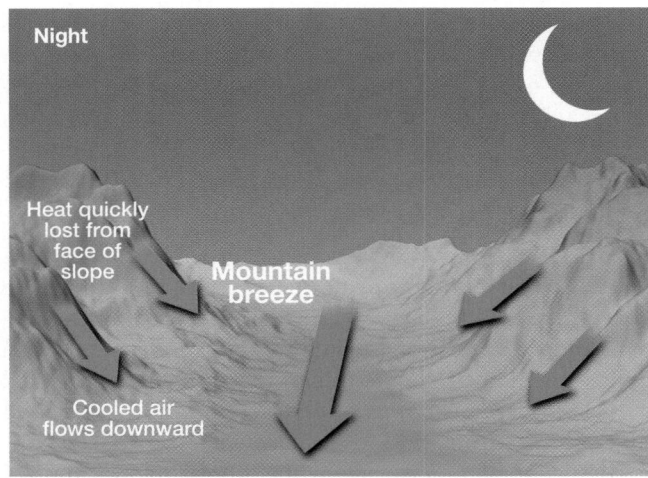

▲ **Figure 5-35** Daytime warming of the mountain slopes causes the air above the slopes to warm and rise, creating lower air pressure than over the valley. Cooler valley air then flows along the pressure gradient (in other words, up the mountain slope) in what is called a valley breeze. At night, the slopes radiate their warmth away and as a result the air just above them cools. This cooler, denser air flows down into the valley in what is called a mountain breeze.

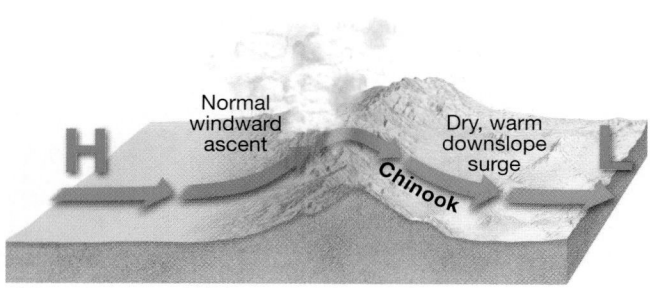

▲ **Figure 5-36** A chinook is a rapid downslope movement of relatively warm air. It is caused by a pressure gradient on the two faces of a mountain.

Foehn and Chinook Winds

Another downslope wind is called a **foehn** (pronounced as in fern but with a silent "r") in the Alps, and a **chinook** in the Rocky Mountains. It originates only when a steep pressure gradient develops with high pressure on the windward side of a mountain and a low-pressure trough on the leeward side. Air moves down the pressure gradient, which means from the windward side to the leeward side, as shown in Figure 5-36.

The downflowing air on the leeward side is dry and relatively warm: it has lost its moisture through precipitation on the windward side, and it is warm relative to the air on the windward side because it contains all the latent heat of condensation given up by the condensing of the snow or rain that fell at the peak. As the wind blows down the leeward slope, it is further warmed adiabatically, and so it arrives at the base of the range as a warming, drying wind. It can produce a remarkable rise of temperature leeward of the mountains in just a few minutes. It is known along the Rocky Mountains front as a "snow-eater" because it not only melts the snow rapidly but also quickly dries the resulting mud.

Santa Ana Winds

FG7

Similar drying winds in California, known as **Santa Ana winds**, develop when a cell of high pressure persists over the interior of the western United States for several days. The wind diverges clockwise out of the high, bringing dry, warm northerly or easterly winds to the coast (instead of the more typical cool, moist air off the ocean from the westerlies). The Santa Anas are noted for high speed, high temperature, and extreme dryness. Their presence provides ideal conditions for wildfires. Virtually every year they make headlines by fanning large brush fires that destroy dozens of homes in late summer and fall and occasionally in spring.

EL NIÑO–SOUTHERN OSCILLATION

One of the basic tenets of physical geography is the interrelatedness of the various elements of the environment. So far in our look at weather and climate, we have introduced patterns of temperature, ocean circulation, wind, and pressure without fully

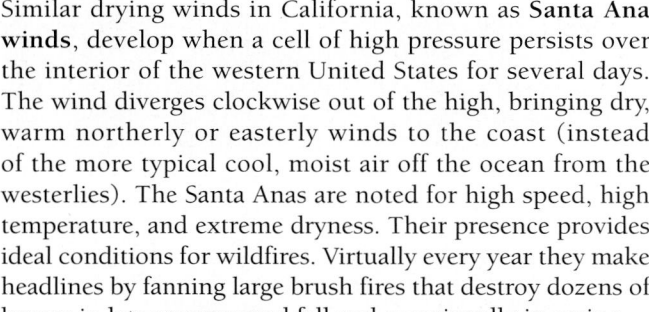

Animation
El Niño

exploring important feedback mechanisms that are a part of such interactions. Nor have we explored the complexity introduced by cyclical variations in oceanic and atmospheric patterns, occurring over periods of years or even decades.

A prize example of this interrelatedness and complexity is **El Niño**, an episodic atmospheric and oceanic phenomenon of the equatorial Pacific Ocean, particularly prominent along the west coast of South America.

Effects of El Niño

During an El Niño event, abnormally warm water appears at the surface of the ocean off the west coast of South America, replacing the cold, nutrient-rich water that usually prevails. Once thought to be a local phenomenon, we now know that El Niño is associated with changes in pressure, wind, precipitation, and ocean conditions over large regions of Earth. During a strong El Niño event, productive Pacific fisheries off South America are disrupted and heavy rains come to some regions of the world while drought comes to others.

A slight periodic warming of Pacific coastal waters has been noticed by South American fishermen for many generations. It typically occurs around Christmastime—hence the name *El Niño* (Spanish for "the boy" in reference to the Christ child). Every three to seven years, however, the warming of the ocean is much greater, and fishing is likely to be much poorer. Historical records have documented the effects of El Niño for several hundred years, with archeological and paleoclimatological evidence pushing the record back several thousand years.

It was not until the major 1982–1983 event, however, that El Niño received worldwide attention (Figure 5-37). Over a period of several months, there were crippling droughts in Australia, India, Indonesia, the Philippines, Mexico, Central America, and southern Africa; devastating floods in the western and southeastern United States, Cuba, and northwestern South America; destructive tropical cyclones in parts of the Pacific (such as in Tahiti and Hawai'i) where they are normally rare; and a vast sweep of ocean water as much as 8°C (14°F) warmer than normal stretched over 13,000 kilometers (8000 miles) of the equatorial Pacific, causing massive die-offs of fish, seabirds, and coral. Directly attributable to these events were more than 1500 human deaths, damage estimated at nearly $9 billion, and vast ecological changes.

In 1997–1998, another strong El Niño cycle took place. This time worldwide property damage exceeded $30 billion, at least 2100 people died, and tens of thousands of people were displaced. There were severe blizzards in the Midwest, devastating tornadoes in the southeastern United States, and much higher than average rainfall in California.

So what happens during El Niño that correlates with such widespread changes in the weather?

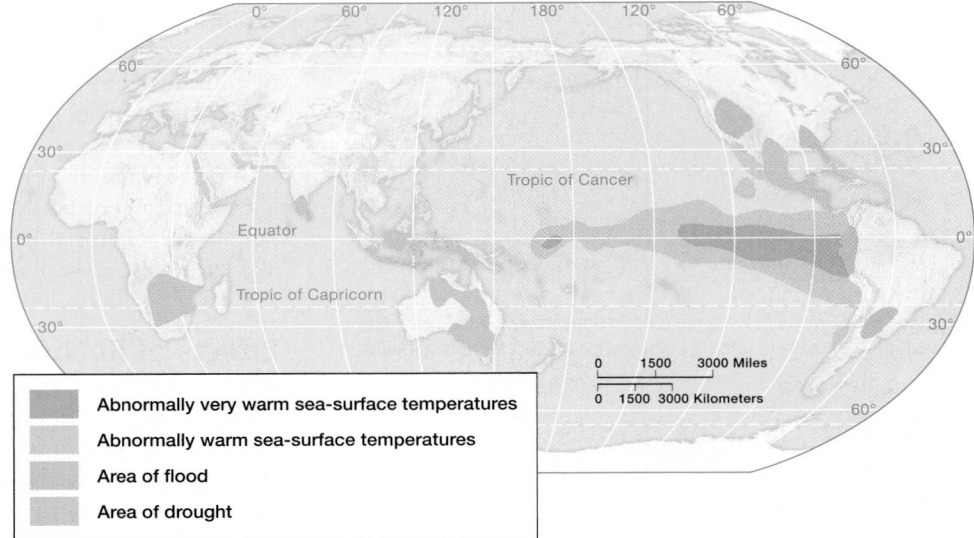

▶ **Figure 5-37** The ocean and atmospheric conditions associated with a major El Niño event, here generalized after the 1982–1983 event. Abnormally warm ocean water in the eastern equatorial Pacific is the most readily recognizable characteristic.

	Abnormally very warm sea-surface temperatures
	Abnormally warm sea-surface temperatures
	Area of flood
	Area of drought

Normal Pattern

To understand El Niño, we begin with a description of the normal conditions in the Pacific Ocean basin (Figure 5-38a). As we saw in Chapter 4, usually the waters off the west coast of South America are cool. The wind and pressure patterns in this region are dominated by the persistent subtropical high (STH) associated with the subsiding air of the Hadley cell circulation (see Figure 5-17).

Cool Water off West Coast: As the trade winds diverge from the STH, they flow from east to west across the Pacific—this tropical airflow drags surface ocean water westward across the Pacific basin in the warm Equatorial

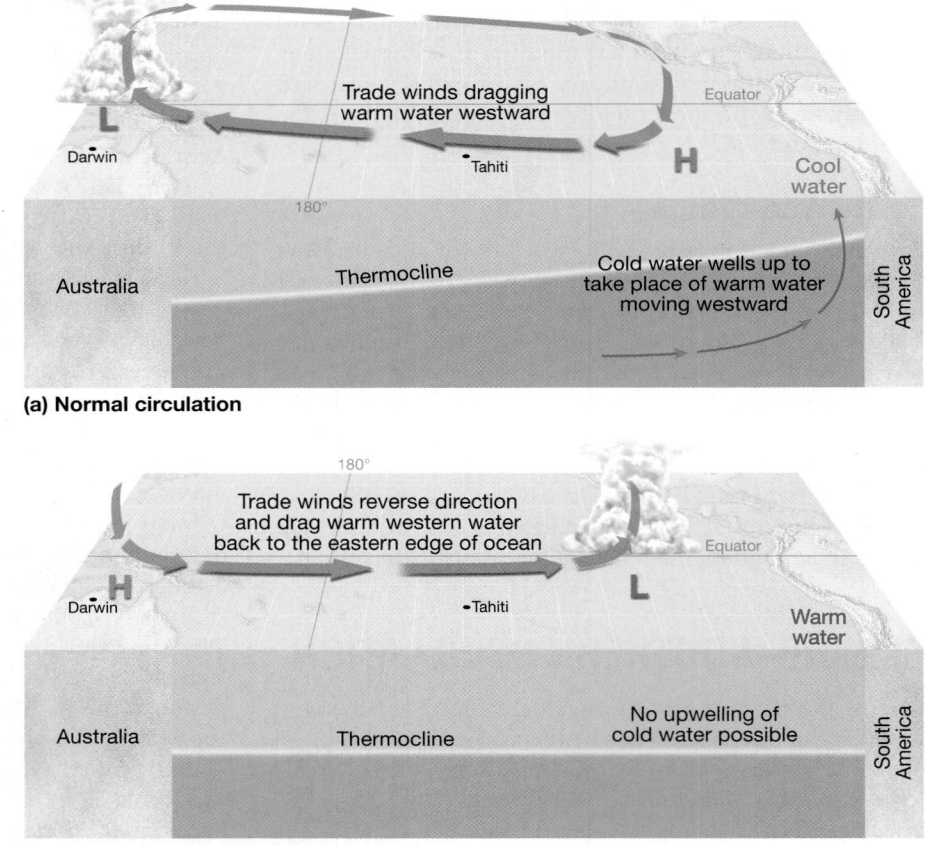

▶ **Figure 5-38** (a) Normal conditions in the South Pacific. The trade winds carry warm equatorial water across the Pacific from east to west. (b) These conditions either weaken or reverse during an El Niño event. The upwelling of cold water off of South America diminishes, the thermocline boundary between near-surface and cold deep water lowers, and much warmer water than usual is present there.

Current (introduced in Chapter 4; see Figure 4-26). As surface water pulls away from the coast of South America, an upwelling of cold, nutrient-rich ocean water rises into the already cool Peru current. This combination of cool water and high pressure result in relatively dry conditions along much of the west coast of South America.

In contrast to the cold water and high pressure near South America, in a normal year on the other side of the Pacific Ocean near Indonesia things are quite different. The trade winds and the Equatorial Current pile up warm water, raising sea level in the Indonesian region as much as 60 centimeters (about 2 feet) higher than near South America, turning the tropical western Pacific into an immense storehouse of energy and moisture.

The Walker Circulation: Warm water and persistent low pressure prevail around northern Australia and Indonesia; local convective thunderstorms develop in the intertropical convergence zone (ITCZ), producing high annual rainfall in this region of the world. After this air rises in the ITCZ, it begins to flow poleward but is deflected by the Coriolis effect into the upper-atmosphere westerly *antitrade* winds; some of this airflow aloft eventually subsides into the STH on the other side of the Pacific (see Figure 5-14). This general circuit of airflow is called the **Walker Circulation**, after the British meteorologist Gilbert Walker (1868–1958) who first described these circumstances. (Although Figure 5-38a shows the Walker Circulation as a closed convection cell, recent studies suggest that this is probably too simplistic—although the upper atmosphere is generally flowing from west to east, a closed "loop" of airflow probably does not exist.)

El Niño Pattern

Every few years, the normal pressure patterns in the Pacific change (Figure 5-38b). High pressure develops over northern Australia and low pressure develops to the east near Tahiti. This "seesaw" of pressure is known as the **Southern Oscillation**.

Video El Niño

It was first recognized by Gilbert Walker in the first decade of the twentieth century.

Walker had become director of the Meteorological Service in colonial India in 1903, where a search was underway for a method to predict the monsoon—when the life-giving South Asian monsoon failed to develop, drought and famine ravaged India. In the global meteorological records, Walker thought that he saw a pattern: in most years pressure is low over northern Australia (specifically, Darwin, Australia) and high over Tahiti, and in these years, the monsoon usually comes as expected.

However, in some years pressure is high in Darwin and low in Tahiti, and in these years the monsoon would often—but not always—fail. As it turned out, Walker's observed correlation between the monsoons in India and the Southern Oscillation of pressure was not reliable enough to predict the monsoons. However, by the 1960s meteorologists recognized a connection between Walker's Southern Oscillation and the occurrence of strong El Niño warming near South America. This overall coupled ocean-atmosphere pattern is now known as the **El Niño-Southern Oscillation** or simply **ENSO**.

Learning Check 5-14 **How do the trade winds differ during an El Niño event compared with the normal pattern?**

Onset of El Niño Event: Although no two ENSO events are exactly alike, we can describe a typical El Niño cycle. For many months before the onset of an El Niño, the trade winds pile up warm water in the western Pacific near Indonesia. A bulge of warm equatorial water perhaps 25 centimeters (10 inches) high then begins to move to the east across the Pacific toward South America. Such slowly moving bulges of warm water are known as *Kelvin waves*. A Kelvin wave might take two or three months to arrive off the coast of South America (Figure 5-39). The bulge of warm water in a Kelvin wave spreads out little as it moves across the ocean since the Coriolis effect effectively funnels the eastward-moving water toward the equator in both hemispheres.

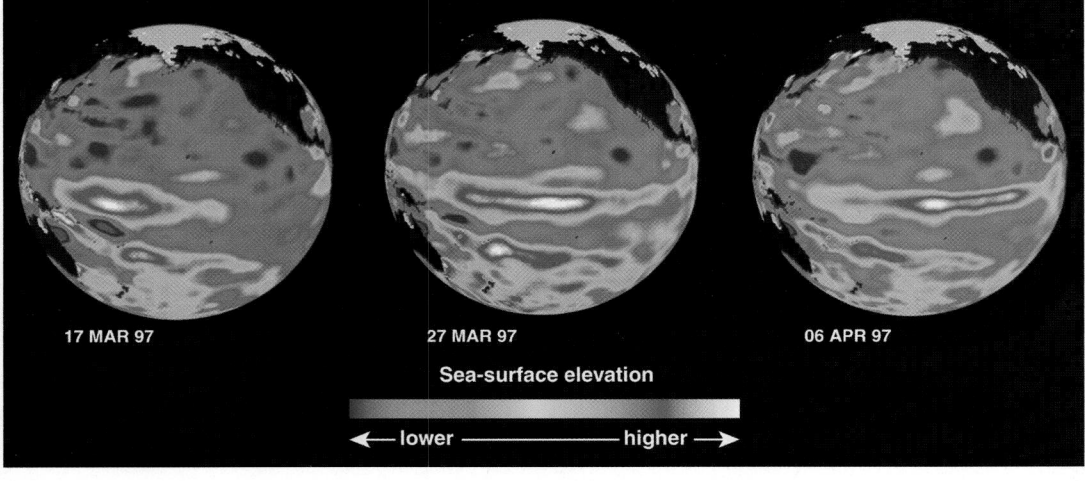

17 MAR 97   27 MAR 97   06 APR 97

Sea-surface elevation

← lower ———— higher →

◄ **Figure 5-39** Progress of a Kelvin wave during the 1997–1998 El Niño. These satellite images from the California Institute of Technology, Jet Propulsion Laboratory, show the bulge of warm water in a Kelvin wave slowly moving across the equatorial Pacific Ocean.

Arrival of El Niño Conditions: When the Kelvin wave arrives at South America, sea level rises as the warm water pools. The usual high pressure in the subtropics has weakened; upwelling no longer brings cold water to the surface, so ocean temperature increases still further—an El Niño is under way. By this time, the trade winds have weakened or even reversed directions and started to flow from the west—blowing moist air into the deserts of coastal Peru. The thermocline boundary between near-surface and cold deep ocean waters lowers. Pressure increases over Indonesia and the most active portion of the ITCZ in the Pacific shifts from the now-cooler western Pacific, toward the now-warmer central and eastern Pacific basin. Drought strikes northern Australia and Indonesia; the South Asian monsoon may fail or develop weakly. The subtropical jet stream over the eastern Pacific shifts its path, guiding winter storms into the southwestern United States—California and Arizona experience more powerful winter storms than usual, resulting in high precipitation and flooding.

La Niña

Adding to the complexity is a more recently recognized component of the ENSO cycle, **La Niña**. In some ways, La Niña is simply the opposite of El Niño: the waters off South America become unusually cool (Figure 5-40); the trade winds are stronger than usual; the waters off Indonesia are unusually warm; the southwestern United States is drier than usual while Southeast Asia and northern Australia are wetter.

Video
La Niña

Because El Niño and La Niña conditions are generally identified by sea-surface temperature trends, sometimes El Niño is referred to as the "warm" phase of ENSO while La Niña is referred to as the "cold" phase.

Causes of ENSO

So which comes first with the onset of an El Niño event—the change in ocean temperature or the change in pressure and wind? The "trigger" of an ENSO event is not clear

since atmospheric pressure and wind patterns are tied together with the ocean in a complex feedback loop with no clear starting point: if atmospheric pressure changes, wind changes; when wind changes, ocean currents and ocean temperature may change; when ocean temperature changes, atmospheric pressure changes—and that in turn may change wind patterns still more. In short, the causes of ENSO are not fully understood.

Not only are the causes of ENSO elusive, even the effects are not completely predictable. For example, while a strong El Niño generally brings high precipitation to the southwestern United States, a mild or moderate El Niño could bring either drought or floods. Further, although we can generalize that during a strong El Niño high rainfall is more likely in California than in La Niña years, very wet winters can occur in any year no matter what ENSO is doing. In other words, El Niño might "open the storm door" every few years, but there is no guarantee that the storms will actually come.

Teleconnections

As more has been learned about ENSO over the last few decades, its connections with oceanic and atmospheric conditions inside and outside the Pacific basin are increasingly being recognized (Figure 5-41). Drought in Brazil; cold winters in the southeastern United States; high temperatures in the Sahel; a weak monsoon in India; tornadoes in Florida; fewer hurricanes in the North Atlantic—all seem to correlate quite well with a strong El Niño event. Such coupling of weather and oceanic events in one part of the world with those in another are termed **teleconnections**. Adding to the complexity of these teleconnections is growing evidence that long-term ENSO patterns may be influenced by other ocean-atmosphere cycles, such as the *Pacific Decadal Oscillation* (discussed below).

Over the last century, El Niño events have occurred on average once every two to seven years. It appears that El Niños have been becoming more frequent and progressively warmer in recent decades—the 1997–1998 event was probably the strongest El Niño of the last 200 years, and it developed more rapidly than any in the last 50 years—although the reasons for this are not yet clear. A much weaker El Niño took place in 2002–2003, and a mild El Niño occurred in 2009–2010. Some scientists speculate that global warming may be influencing the intensity of the El Niño cycle, but a clear connection has not yet been found.

Over the last 30 years, great strides have been taken toward forecasting El Niño events months in advance—largely because of better satellite monitoring of ocean conditions and the establishment of the TAO/TRITON array of oceanic buoys in the tropical Pacific (see the box, "People and the Environment: Forecasting El Niño"). Although much remains to be learned, a clearer understanding of cause and effect, of countercause and countereffect of ENSO, is gradually emerging.

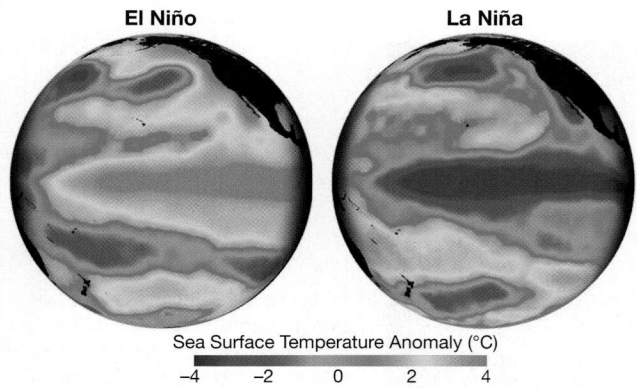

El Niño   **La Niña**

Sea Surface Temperature Anomaly (°C)

-4   -2   0   2   4

▲ **Figure 5-40** In contrast to the warm ocean conditions in the equatorial eastern Pacific during an El Niño event, ocean conditions are much cooler during a La Niña. These images show the temperature anomalies, or differences from average, during major El Niño and La Niña events.

Learning Check **5-15**   **What is a *teleconnection?* Describe one example of a teleconnection.**

Forecasting El Niño

After the powerful El Niño of 1982–1983 caught large populations unprepared, a concerted multinational effort was undertaken to understand El Niño and its teleconnections. Part of this effort included anchoring some 70 instrument buoys in the tropical Pacific Ocean. Beginning in 1985, the initial installations were part of the Tropical Atmosphere Ocean Array (TOA) administered by the National Oceanic and Atmospheric Administration (NOAA), but the array was soon expanded to include the Triangle Trans Ocean Buoy Network (TRITON) maintained by Japan. The combined TAO/TRITON array monitors ocean and atmospheric conditions—especially sea-surface temperature and wind direction—across the tropical Pacific Ocean (Figure 5-C).

By 1994, sufficient data had been gathered to develop computer models to predict the onset of an El Niño event several months in advance. These efforts were rewarded in 1997: by that spring, the TAO/TRITON buoys were recording a surge of warm water moving to the east across the equatorial Pacific (Figure 5-D). Months in advance of its arrival, the onset of the strong 1997–1998 El Niño was announced by

NOAA's Climate Prediction Center, and preparations were made for the series of powerful storms that eventually struck southwestern North America that winter. Because of this early success, the TAO/TRITON network was expanded to include the Research Moored Array for African-Asian-Australian Monsoon Analysis (RAMA) in the Indian Ocean, and the Prediction and Research Moored Array in the Atlantic (PIRATA), forming a complete Global Tropical Moored Buoy Array (see Figure 5-C).

Changing El Niño Patterns: Using data gathered by the TAO/TRITON array, by the late 1990s scientists were noticing a different kind of El Niño pattern than

in previous decades; during some El Niño events, the warmest water is found in the central Pacific Ocean rather than the usual location in the eastern Pacific. For example, the 2009–2010 El Niño was very warm in the central Pacific, but only modestly so in the eastern Pacific (Figure 5-E). One hypothesis explaining this change is that climate change may be shifting the region of warmest water during an El Niño. If this is the case, forecasting the effects of El Niño may become more difficult until this new pattern is understood. The data supplied by the TAO/TRITON array will be indispensable in this quest to fully understand El Niño, as well as to understand the atmospheric and oceanic conditions in the tropical Pacific in general.

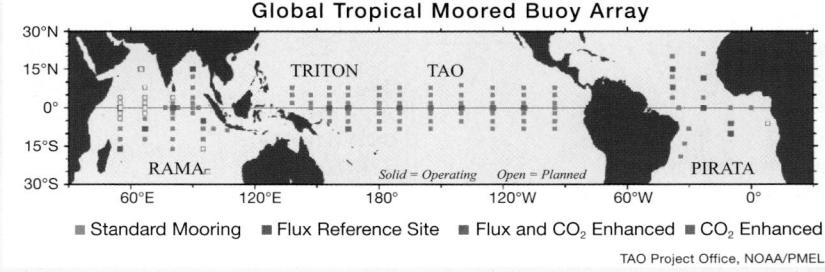

▲ **Figure 5-C** The TAO/TRITON Array of instrument buoys in the tropical Pacific Ocean is part of a Global Tropical Moored Buoy Array.

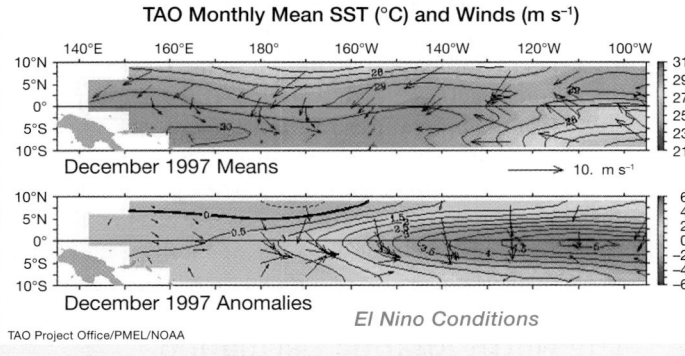

▲ **Figure 5-D** El Niño conditions in the tropical Pacific Ocean in December 1997; sea-surface temperature and wind measured by the TAO/TRITON Array. Orange areas represent warmer surface water temperatures.

▲ **Figure 5-E** Sea-surface temperature anomaly at the peak of the 2009–2010 El Niño. The greatest warming was in the central Pacific Ocean rather than the eastern Pacific.

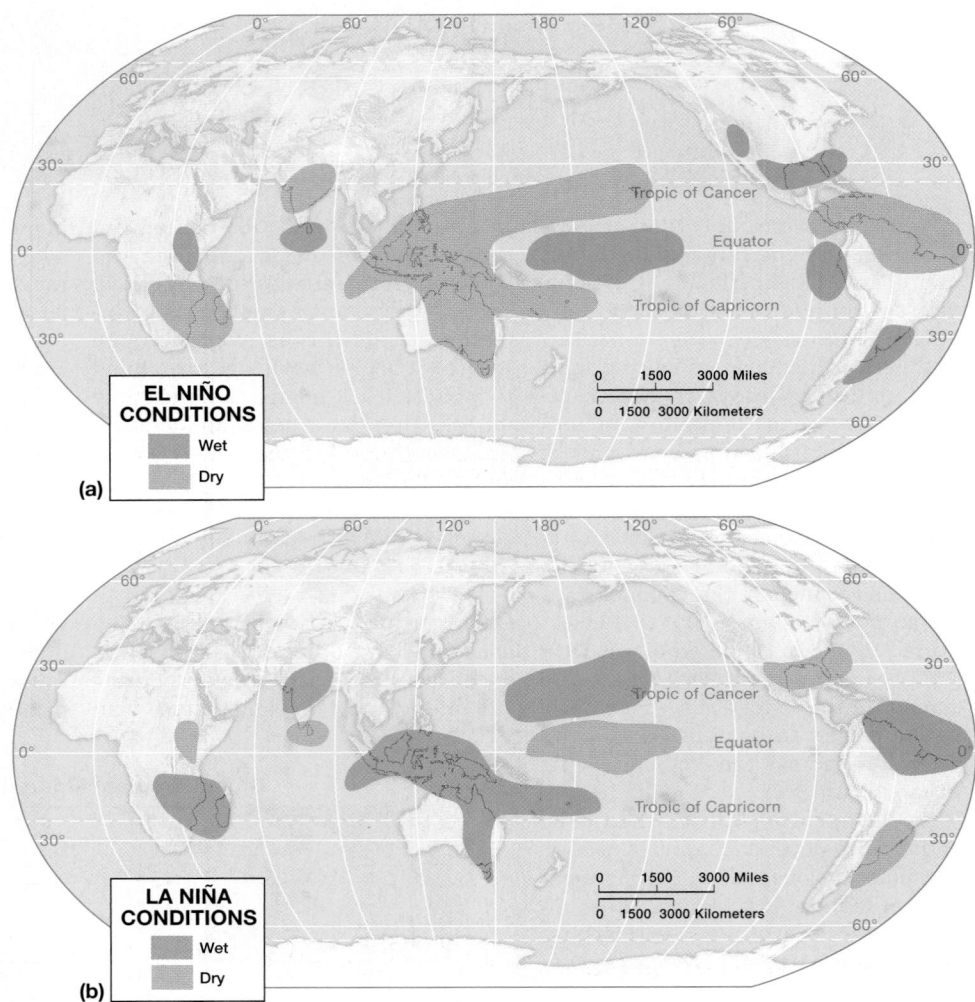

▶ **Figure 5-41** Generalized precipitation patterns during (a) El Niño conditions and (b) La Niña conditions.

OTHER MULTIYEAR ATMOSPHERIC AND OCEANIC CYCLES

El Niño is the best known multiyear atmospheric/oceanic cycle, although a number of other cyclical patterns have now been recognized.

Pacific Decadal Oscillation

The *Pacific Decadal Oscillation (PDO)* is a long-term pattern of sea surface temperature change between the northern/west tropical and eastern tropical Pacific Ocean. Approximately every 20 to 30 years the sea-surface temperatures in these zones abruptly shift. From the late 1940s to late 1970s, the northern/west tropical Pacific was relatively warm and the eastern tropical Pacific was relatively cool (the PDO "negative" or "cool" phase); from the late 1970s through the mid-1990s, this pattern switched, with cooler sea-surface temperatures in the northern/west tropical Pacific and warmer conditions in the east tropical Pacific (the PDO "positive" or "warm" phase; Figure 5-42). In the late 1990s a switch back to the negative phase had taken place,

but at present it is not clear if this negative phase is going to be short-lived.

Although the causes of the PDO are not well understood, the pattern of relatively warm and relatively cool ocean water seems to influence the location of the jet stream, and so storm tracks across North America. During a warm phase of the PDO, temperatures in Alaska are often warmer than average, whereas during a cool phase, they are cooler.

The PDO can also influence the intensity of El Niño events. For example, when the PDO is in a positive phase with warmer water in the eastern tropical Pacific, the influence of El Niño on regional weather patterns appears to be more significant.

The North Atlantic Oscillation and the Arctic Oscillation

In the North Atlantic Ocean basin two related but somewhat irregular multiyear cycles of pressure, wind patterns, and temperature exist: the North Atlantic Oscillation and the Arctic Oscillation.

North Atlantic Oscillation: The *North Atlantic Oscillation (NAO)* is an irregular "seesaw" of pressure differences

Pacific Decadal Oscillation

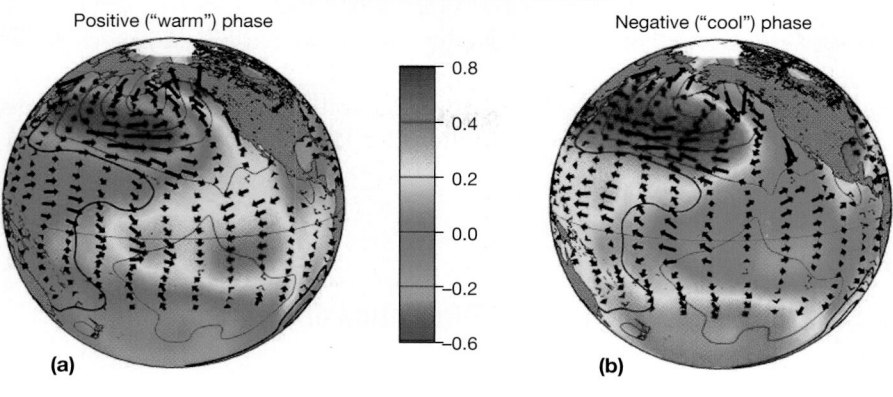

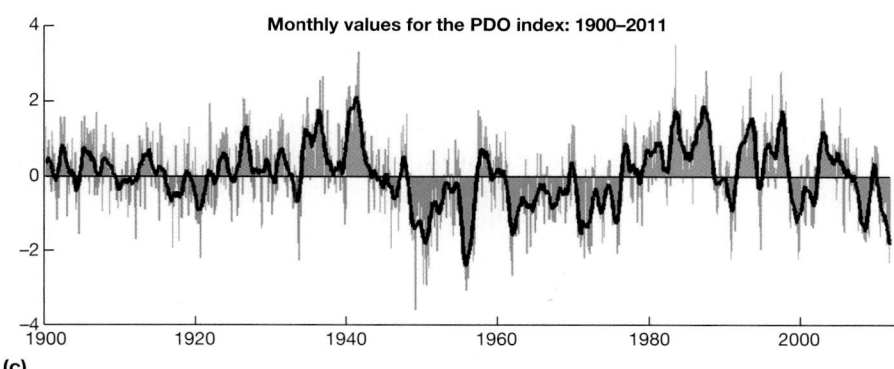

(c)

◀ **Figure 5-42** The Pacific decadal oscillation (PDO). (a) Positive values indicate warm water in the eastern tropical Pacific, (b) whereas negative values indicate relatively cool water in the same area. (c) The PDO index from 1900 to 2011.

between two regional components of the general atmospheric circulation in the North Atlantic Ocean basin: the Icelandic Low and the Azores High (the STH in the North Atlantic; see Figures 5-15 and 5-16). In the "positive" phase of the NAO, a greater pressure gradient exists between the Icelandic Low and the Azores High (in other words, the low exhibits lower-than-usual pressure, and the high exhibits higher-than-usual pressure). During such a positive phase, winter storms tend to take a more northerly track across the Atlantic, bringing mild, wet winters to Europe and the eastern United States, but colder, drier conditions in Greenland.

In the "negative" phase of the NAO, both the Icelandic Low and the Azores High are weaker. During such a negative phase, winter storms tend to bring higher-than-average precipitation to the Mediterranean and colder winters in northern Europe and the eastern United States, whereas Greenland experiences milder conditions.

Arctic Oscillation: The *Arctic Oscillation* alternates between warm and cold phases that are closely associated with the NAO. During the Arctic Oscillation "warm" phase (associated with the NAO positive phase), the polar high is weaker, so cold air masses do not move as far south and sea-surface temperatures tend to be warmer in Arctic waters—although Greenland tends to be colder than usual. During the Arctic Oscillation "cold" phase (associated with the NAO negative phase), the polar high is strengthened, bringing cold air masses farther south and leaving Arctic waters colder—although Greenland tends to be warmer than usual (Figure 5-43).

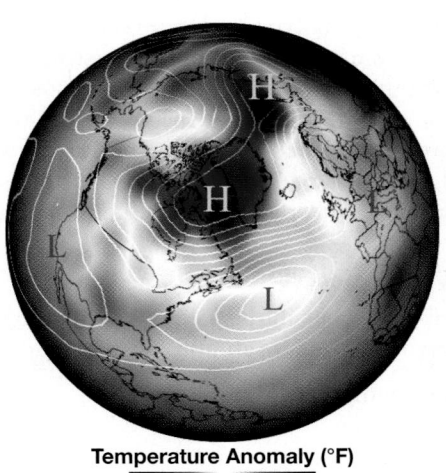

Temperature Anomaly (°F)
−31   31

▲ **Figure 5-43** The "cold" phase of the Arctic Oscillation in February 2010, showing temperature anomalies compared with the average temperatures from 1971 to 2000. The polar high was stronger than usual and the midlatitudes were generally colder than usual, although Greenland was warmer.

As with El Niño and the Pacific Decadal Oscillation, the causes of the North Atlantic Oscillation and the Arctic Oscillation are not well understood. Nor are all of the possible teleconnections between atmospheric and oceanic cycles in the North Atlantic and other parts of the world.

After studying this chapter, you should be able to answer the following questions. Key terms from each text section are shown in **bold type**. Definitions for key terms are also found in the glossary at the back of the book.

KEY TERMS AND CONCEPTS

The Nature of Atmospheric Pressure (p. 110)

1. What generally happens to **atmospheric pressure** with increasing altitude?
2. Explain how atmospheric pressure is related to air density and air temperature.
3. What causes a **thermal high** near the surface? A **thermal low**?
4. What causes a **dynamic high** near the surface? A **dynamic low**?
5. Define the following terms: **barometer**, **millibar**, **isobar**.
6. When referring to air pressure, what is a **high**, a **low**, a **ridge**, and a **trough**?
7. What is meant by a **pressure gradient**?

The Nature of Wind (p. 112)

8. What three factors influence the direction of **wind** flow?
9. How and why are **friction layer** (surface) winds different from upper-atmosphere **geostrophic winds**?
10. Describe the relationship between the "steepness" of a pressure gradient and the speed of the wind along that pressure gradient. Describe the general wind speed associated with a gentle (gradual) pressure gradient and a steep (abrupt) pressure gradient.

Cyclones and Anticyclones (p. 115)

11. Describe and explain the pattern of wind flow in the Northern Hemisphere around:

    • a surface high
    • a surface low
    • an upper atmosphere high
    • an upper atmosphere low

    (You should be able to sketch in wind direction on isobar maps of highs and lows near the surface and in the upper atmosphere for both the Northern and Southern Hemispheres.)

12. What is the reason for the difference in wind flow patterns in the Northern Hemisphere and the Southern Hemisphere?
13. What is a **cyclone**? An **anticyclone**?
14. Describe the pattern of vertical air movement within a cyclone and within an anticyclone.

The General Circulation of the Atmosphere (p. 116)

15. What are the **Hadley cells**, and what generally causes them?
16. Describe the general location and characteristics of the following atmospheric circulation components:

    • **intertropical convergence zone (ITCZ)**
    • **trade winds**
    • **subtropical highs**
    • **westerlies**

    (You should be able to sketch in the location of these four components on a blank map of an ocean basin.)

17. Discuss the characteristic weather associated with the ITCZ and the characteristic weather associated with subtropical highs.
18. What are meant by the **horse latitudes** and the **doldrums**?
19. Describe the general location and characteristics of the **jet streams** of the westerlies.
20. What are **Rossby waves**?
21. Briefly describe the location and general characteristics of the high-latitude components of the general circulation patterns of the atmosphere:

    • **polar front (subpolar lows)**
    • **polar easterlies**
    • **polar highs**

22. Differentiate between trade winds and **antitrade winds**.

Modifications of the General Circulation (p. 126)

23. Describe and explain the seasonal shifts of the general circulation patterns; especially note the significance of the seasonal shifts of the ITCZ and the subtropical highs.
24. Describe and explain the South Asian **monsoon**.

Localized Wind Systems (p. 129)

25. Explain the origin of **sea breezes** and **land breezes**.
26. In what ways are sea breezes and land breezes similar to **valley breezes** and **mountain breezes**?
27. What is a **katabatic wind** and where are such winds commonly found?

28. In what ways are **Santa Ana winds** similar to **foehn** and **chinook** winds?

El Niño–Southern Oscillation (*p. 131*)

29. What is the **Walker Circulation**?
30. Why is **El Niño** commonly referred to as **El Niño-Southern Oscillation (ENSO)**?
31. Contrast the oceanic and atmospheric conditions in the tropical Pacific Ocean basin during an El Niño event with those of a normal pattern.

32. Contrast the oceanic and atmospheric conditions during an El Niño event with those of a **La Niña** event.
33. What is meant by **teleconnections**?

Other Multiyear Atmospheric and Oceanic Cycles (*p. 136*)

34. What are the conditions and weather effects of the "warm" phase and the "cool" phase of the Pacific Decadal Oscillation?

STUDY QUESTIONS

1. Why does atmospheric pressure decrease with height?
2. Why is it misleading to describe atmospheric pressure as simply the weight of the air only pressing down on a surface?
3. When moving over any significant distance, why doesn't wind simply flow straight "down" a pressure gradient?
4. Why are upper-atmosphere winds usually faster than surface winds?
5. Why do the trade winds cover such a large part of the globe?

6. Why are the subtropical highs and the ITCZ characterized by little wind?
7. Explain why the trade winds and the antitrade winds blow in opposite directions?
8. Why does the ITCZ generally shift north of the equator in the Northern Hemisphere summer, and south of the equator in winter?
9. How can the Pacific Decadal Oscillation serve to "intensify" an El Niño event?

EXERCISES

1. Using Table 5-1 for reference:
   a. Estimate the altitude where atmospheric pressure has decreased to about half its surface value: _____ kilometers
   b. Estimate the atmospheric pressure at the cruising altitude of a jet airliner (about 34,000 feet): _____ mb

2. When the winds in a hurricane are blowing at 150 knots, what is the wind speed in
   a. Miles per hour: _____
   b. Kilometers per hour: _____
3. If the atmospheric pressure is 1010 millibars, what is the equivalent pressure in kilopascals? _____ kPa
4. If the atmospheric pressure is 99 kilopascals, what is the equivalent pressure in millibars? _____ mb

Seeing Geographically

Look again at the photograph of the hurricane-strength winds striking Florida at the beginning of the chapter (p. 108). Based on its latitude (between about 25° and 27° N), which global wind system frequently blows over this part of southern Florida? What explains a hurricane's high wind speeds? What will likely happen to the speed of the hurricane's winds as they come off the water onto land? Why?

MasteringGeography™

Looking for additional review and test prep materials? Visit the Study Area in MasteringGeography™ to enhance your geographic literacy, spatial reasoning skills, and understanding of this chapter's content by accessing a variety of resources, including geoscience animations, MapMaster interactive maps, videos, RSS feeds, flashcards, web links, self-study quizzes, and an eText version of *McKnight's Physical Geography: A Landscape Appreciation.*

THE FOURTH ELEMENT OF WEATHER AND CLIMATE IS

moisture. Although it might seem that we all are familiar with water, most atmospheric moisture occurs not as liquid water but rather as the gas water vapor—which is much less conspicuous and much less familiar.

One of the most distinctive attributes of water is that it occurs in the atmosphere in three physical states: solid (snow, hail, sleet, ice), liquid (rain, water droplets in clouds), and gas (water vapor). Of the three states, the gaseous state is the most important insofar as the dynamics of the atmosphere are concerned—and it is water vapor that we spend the most time discussing in this chapter, especially the relationships between water vapor, relative humidity, adiabatic temperature changes, and condensation.

The movement of water vapor is a component of several key Earth systems. Most obviously, the movement of water vapor is part of the hydrologic cycle—a key to understanding weather and climate, the biosphere, and many processes shaping Earth's surface. Also, the evaporation of water, the transport of water vapor from one location to the next, and the eventual condensation of water vapor to form clouds and precipitation is a key component of Earth's energy cycle.

In this chapter we limit our focus to the role of water in weather processes in Earth's atmosphere. In chapters that follow, we will broaden our discussion of water to include the dynamics of the oceans, lakes, streams, and underground water.

As you study this chapter, think about these key questions:

- **Which key properties of water influence its effects in the atmosphere?**
- **Why is evaporation a cooling process and condensation a warming process in the atmosphere?**
- **Under what conditions does evaporation occur rapidly, and when does it occur slowly?**
- **What is relative humidity, and what circumstances cause it to change?**
- **Under what conditions does condensation take place?**
- **How does the temperature and relative humidity of air change as it rises or descends?**
- **What are the different kinds of clouds?**
- **What makes air stable or unstable, and how does this influence cloud formation and precipitation?**
- **What conditions lead to precipitation?**
- **What are the ways that air is lifted enough to make clouds and precipitation?**
- **Which factors influence the global patterns of precipitation?**
- **What are the causes and effects of acid rain?**

A late afternoon rainstorm in Nevada. Does the rain in this area appear to be widespread? What do you see in the photograph that supports your answer? What do you see in the landscape that indicates the general kind of climate of this region?

The Impact of Atmospheric Moisture on the Landscape

When the atmosphere contains enough moisture, water vapor may condense to form haze, fog, clouds, rain, sleet, hail, or snow, producing a skyscape that is both visible and tangible. Especially through precipitation, water can produce dramatic short-run changes in the landscape whenever rain puddles form, streams and rivers flood, or snow and ice blanket the ground.

The long-term effect of atmospheric moisture is even more fundamental. Water vapor stores energy that can incite the atmosphere into action. Rainfall and snowmelt in soil and rock are an integral part of weathering and erosion. In addition, the presence or absence of precipitation is critical to the survival of almost all forms of terrestrial vegetation.

THE NATURE OF WATER: COMMONPLACE BUT UNIQUE

Water is the most widespread substance on Earth's surface, occupying more than 70 percent of the surface area of the planet. Water is also perhaps the most distinctive substance found on Earth: pure water has no color, no taste, and no smell. It turns to a solid at 0°C (32°F) and boils at sea level at 100°C (212°F). The density of liquid water at 4°C is 1 gram per cubic centimeter (1 g/cm³), but the density of ice is only 0.92 g/cm³—meaning that ice

Animation
Hydrologic
Cycle

floats in liquid water. Water has a very high heat capacity and is an extremely good solvent. It has the ability to move upward in narrow openings. Water set the stage for the evolution of life and is still an essential ingredient of all life today. In order to understand the significance of these properties and others, we begin with an introduction to water at two different scales: the hydrologic cycle and the water molecule.

The Hydrologic Cycle

Video
Hydrologic
Cycle

The widespread distribution of water vapor in the atmosphere reflects the ease with which moisture can change from one state to another at the pressures and temperatures found in the lower troposphere.

Moisture can leave Earth's surface as a gas and return as a liquid or solid. Indeed, there is a continuous interchange of moisture between Earth and the atmosphere (Figure 6-1). This unending circulation of our planet's water supply is referred to as the **hydrologic cycle**, and its essential feature is that liquid water (primarily from the oceans) evaporates into the air, condenses to the liquid (or solid) state, and returns to Earth as some form of precipitation.

The movement of moisture through the cycle is intricately related to many atmospheric phenomena and is an important determinant of climate because of its role in rainfall distribution and temperature modification. We will discuss the complete hydrologic cycle in greater detail in Chapter 9, but in the present chapter we begin with the basic dynamics of water transfer to and from the atmosphere.

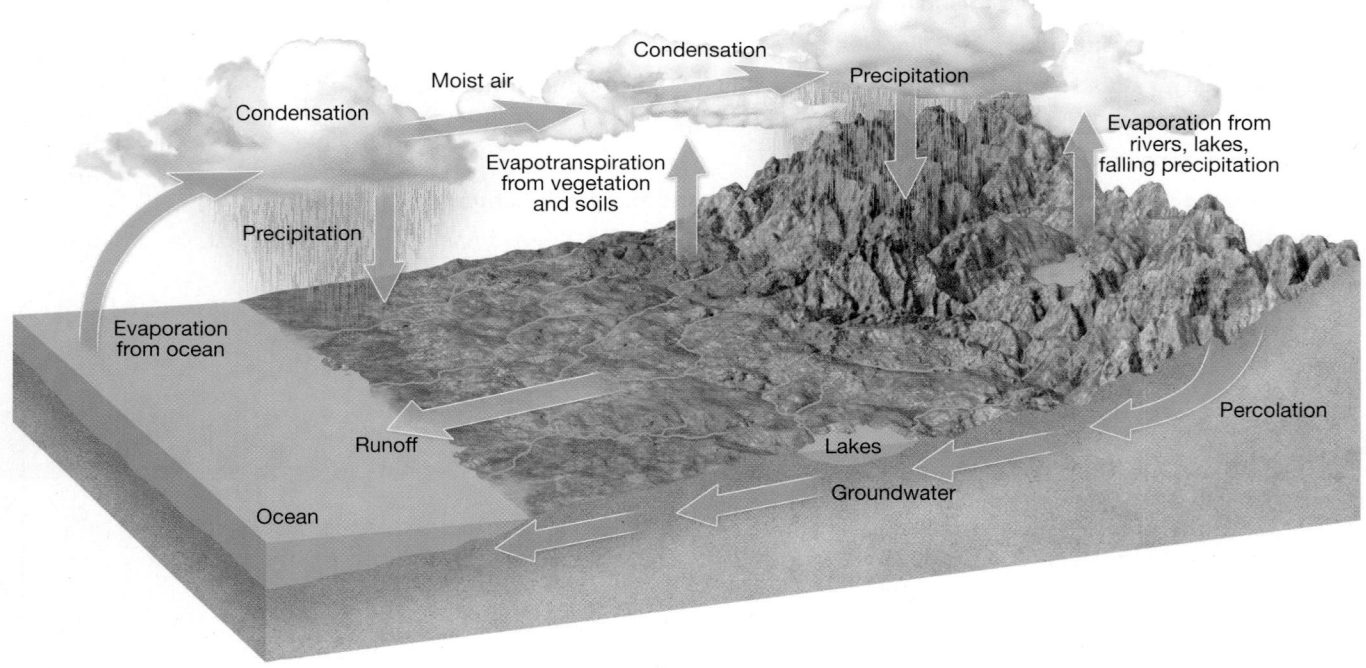

▲ **Figure 6-1** The hydrologic cycle is a continuous interchange of moisture between the atmosphere and Earth.

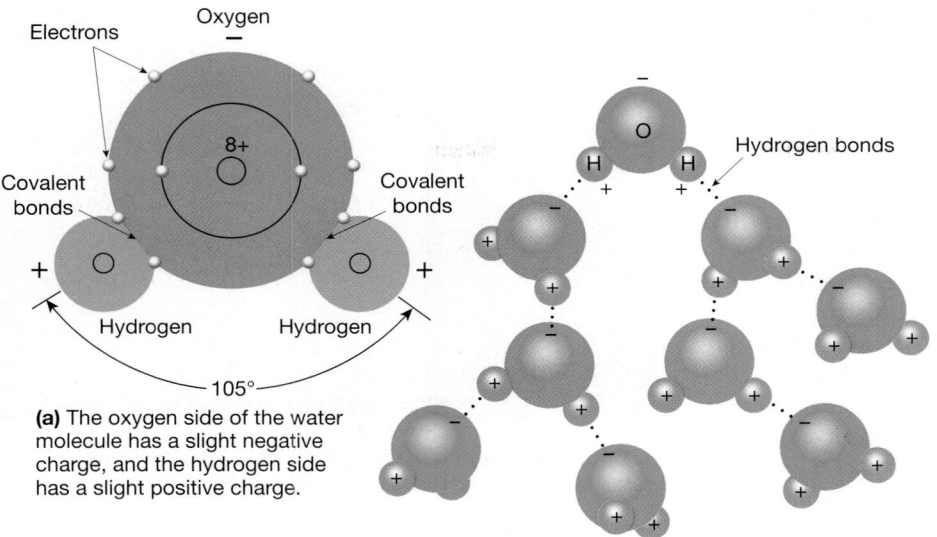

(a) The oxygen side of the water molecule has a slight negative charge, and the hydrogen side has a slight positive charge.

(b) Hydrogen bonds form between water molecules because the negatively charged oxygen side of one molecule is attracted to the positively charged hydrogen side of another molecule.

◀ **Figure 6-2** (a) A water molecule is made up of two hydrogen atoms and one oxygen atom. (b) Hydrogen bonds form between water molecules because the negatively charged oxygen side of one molecule is attracted to the positively charged hydrogen side of another molecule.

The Water Molecule

Before we look specifically at the role of water in weather and climate, we must look at the water molecule itself, because the characteristics of the water molecule help explain many of water's unique properties. What we learn about the nature of water over the next few pages will help us understand many processes discussed in the remaining chapters of the book.

As we discussed in earlier chapters, the fundamental building blocks of matter are *atoms*. Atoms are almost incomprehensibly small—there are about 100,000,000,000,000,000,000,000 atoms in a thimble filled with 1 gram of water! Atoms are composed of still smaller *subatomic particles*: positively charged *protons* and neutrally charged *neutrons* in the nucleus of the atom, surrounded by negatively charged *electrons*.[1]

The whirling electrons are held by electrical attraction to the protons in "shells" surrounding the nucleus of the atom. In many atoms the number of electrons, protons, and neutrons are normally equal—for example, an atom of the element oxygen typically has eight protons and eight electrons, along with eight electrically neutral neutrons. The number of neutrons in an element's individual atoms can vary without affecting the chemical behavior of the atom—an atom in which the number of neutrons is different from the number of protons is called an *isotope*. Similarly, if the number of electrons in an atom is different from the number of protons, the neutral atom becomes an electrically charged *ion*.

Hydrogen Bonds: Two or more atoms can be held together to form a *molecule* by "bonding." Many different types of bonds are found in nature. Inside the water molecule two atoms of hydrogen and one atom of oxygen (H_2O) are held together by *covalent bonds*, in which the oxygen and hydrogen atoms share electrons (some of the electrons move between energy shells of both atoms; Figure 6-2a). Because of the shape of the electron shells around the oxygen, the resulting structure of a water molecule is such that the hydrogen atoms are not opposite one another, but rather are on the same side of the molecule (separated by an angle of 105°). As a consequence of this geometry, a water molecule has electrical *polarity*: the oxygen side of the molecule has a slight negative charge, whereas the hydrogen side has a slight positive charge (Figure 6-2b).

It is the weak electrical polarity of the molecules that gives water many of its interesting properties. For example, water molecules tend to orient themselves toward each other so that the negatively charged oxygen side of one molecule is next to the positively charged hydrogen side of another molecule. This attraction forms a **hydrogen bond** between adjacent water molecules (see Figure 6-2b). Although hydrogen bonds are relatively weak (compared with the covalent bonds that hold together the atoms in an individual water molecule), it does mean that water molecules tend to "stick" to each other (when molecules of the same substance stick together it is called *cohesion*).

Learning Check 6-1   **What is a *hydrogen bond*?**
(Answer on p. AK-2)

Important Properties of Water

Water has a number of properties that are important in our study of physical geography.

---

[1]Although it was once thought that the smallest particles of matter were electrons, protons, and neutrons, we know now that some subatomic particles are made of still smaller particles such as *quarks*.

Liquidity: One of the most striking properties of water is that it is liquid at the temperatures found at most places on Earth's surface. The liquidity of water greatly enhances its versatility as an active agent in the atmosphere, lithosphere, and biosphere.

Ice Expansion: Most substances contract as they get colder no matter what the change in temperature. When freshwater becomes colder, however, it contracts only until it reaches 4°C (39°F) and then expands (as much as 9 percent) as it cools from 4°C to its freezing point of 0°C (32°F). As water is cooled from 4°C to its freezing point, water molecules begin to form hexagonal structures, held together by hydrogen bonding. When frozen, water is made entirely of these structures—hexagonal snowflakes reflect the internal structure of these ice crystals. As we will see in Chapter 15, this expansion of ice can break apart rocks and so is an important process of *weathering* (the disintegration of rock exposed to the atmosphere).

Because water expands as it approaches freezing, ice is less dense than liquid water. As a result, ice floats on and near the surface of water. If it were denser than water, ice would sink to the bottom of lakes and oceans, where melting would be virtually impossible, and eventually many water bodies would become ice choked. In fact, because freshwater becomes less dense as it approaches its freezing point, water that is ready to freeze rises to the tops of lakes, and hence all lakes freeze from the top down. (Note: the expansion of liquid water is not a factor for ocean water because the high salinity prevents the hexagonal structures from forming until the water is completely frozen.)

Surface Tension: Because of its electrical polarity, liquid water molecules tend to stick together (*cohesion*), giving water extremely high **surface tension**—a thin "skin" of molecules forms on the surface of liquid water, causing it to "bead." Some insects use the stickiness of water to stride atop the surface of a body of water—the weight of the insect spread over the surface area of the water is less than the force of the hydrogen bonds sticking the water together (Figure 6-3). Later in this chapter we'll see that surface tension influences the way that water droplets grow within a cloud.

> **Learning Check 6-2**   **What happens to the volume of water when it freezes?**

Capillarity: Water molecules also "stick" easily to many other substances—a characteristic known as *adhesion*. Surface tension combined with adhesion allows water to climb upward in narrow openings. Confined in this way, water can sometimes climb upward for many centimeters or even meters, in an action called **capillarity**. Capillarity enables water to circulate upward through rock cracks, soil, and the roots and stems of plants.

Solvent Ability: Water can dissolve almost any substance and it is sometimes referred to as the "universal solvent."

▲ **Figure 6-3** Weight of this raft spider (*Dolomedes fimbriatus*) is supported by the surface tension of the water surface.

Because of the polarity of water molecules, they not only are attracted to each other but also to other "polar" chemical compounds as well. Water molecules attach themselves quickly to the ions that constitute the outer layers of solid materials and in some cases can overcome the strength of those bonds, tearing the ions out of the solid and eventually dissolving the material. As a result, water in nature is nearly always impure, meaning that it contains various other chemicals in addition to its hydrogen and oxygen atoms. As water moves through the atmosphere, on the surface of Earth, and in soil, rocks, plants, and animals, it carries with it a remarkable diversity of dissolved minerals and nutrients as well as tiny solid particles in suspension.

Specific Heat: Another environmentally important characteristic of water is its great heat capacity. As we saw in Chapter 4, *specific heat* (or *specific heat capacity*) is defined as the amount of energy required to raise the temperature of 1 gram of a substance (at 15°C) by 1 degree Celsius. When water is warmed, it can absorb an enormous amount of energy with only a small increase in temperature. Water's specific heat (1 calorie/gram or about 4190 joules/kg) is exceeded by no other common substance except ammonia, and is about five times greater than that of materials such as soil and rock—in other words, it takes five times as much energy to increase the temperature of water by 1°C as it does to increase the temperature of soil or rock by the same amount.

The high specific heat of water is a consequence of the relatively large amount of kinetic energy required to overcome the hydrogen bonds between water molecules. The practical result, as we saw in Chapter 4, is that bodies of water are very slow to warm up during the day or in summer, and very slow to cool off during the night or in winter. Thus, water bodies have a moderating effect on the temperature of the overlying atmosphere by serving as reservoirs of warmth during winter and having a cooling influence in summer.

> **Learning Check 6-3**   **How does the *specific heat* of water influence how rapidly it warms during the summer?**

PHASE CHANGES OF WATER

Earth's water is found naturally in three states: as a liquid, as a solid, and as a gas. The great majority of the world's moisture is in the form of liquid water, which can be converted to the gaseous form (water vapor) by **evaporation** or to the solid form (ice) by *freezing*. Water vapor can be converted to liquid water by **condensation** or directly to ice by *sublimation*.

Animation
Phase Changes
of Water

Sublimation is the process whereby a substance converts either from the gaseous state directly to the solid state, or from the solid state directly to the gaseous state without ever passing through the liquid state (the term *deposition* is sometimes used to describe the phase change from a gaseous state directly to a solid state). Ice can be converted to liquid water by melting or to water vapor by sublimation.

In each of these phase changes, there is an exchange of *latent heat* energy, a concept we first introduced in Chapter 4 (Figure 6-4). An understanding of phase changes and latent heat are central to understanding several atmospheric processes we will describe later in this chapter.

Latent Heat

If you insert a thermometer into a pan of cool water on your stove and then warm the water by turning on the burner, you will notice an interesting pattern of temperature change: at first, the temperature of the water will increase, as you might expect. However, once the water begins to boil, the temperature of the water will not increase above 100°C (212°F; at sea level)—even if you turn up the flame on your stove! This result is just one of several important observations we can make about water as it changes states.

Figure 6-5 is a temperature chart showing the amount of energy (in calories) required to melt a 1-gram block of ice and then convert it to water vapor. Recall that 1 calorie is the amount of heat required to increase the temperature of 1 gram of liquid water by 1°C—about 4.184 joules (J).

In this example, we begin with our block of ice at a temperature of –40°C. As energy is added, the temperature of the ice increases quickly; only 20 calories (84 J) of energy are needed to increase the temperature of the ice to its melting point of 0°C. Once the ice begins to melt, it absorbs 80 calories (335 J) of energy per gram, but the temperature does not increase above 0°C until all of the ice has melted.

We then add another 100 calories (418 J) of energy to increase the temperature of the liquid water from 0°C to 100°C, its boiling point at sea level. Once the water is boiling, it absorbs 540 calories (2260 J) per gram, but once again, the temperature does not increase above 100°C until all of the liquid water is converted to water vapor.

Notice that even as energy was added, the temperature of the water did not increase while it was undergoing a *phase change*. Here's why: in order for ice to melt, energy must be added to "agitate" water molecules enough to break some of the hydrogen bonds that are holding these molecules together as ice crystals—the energy added does not increase the temperature of the ice, but it does increase

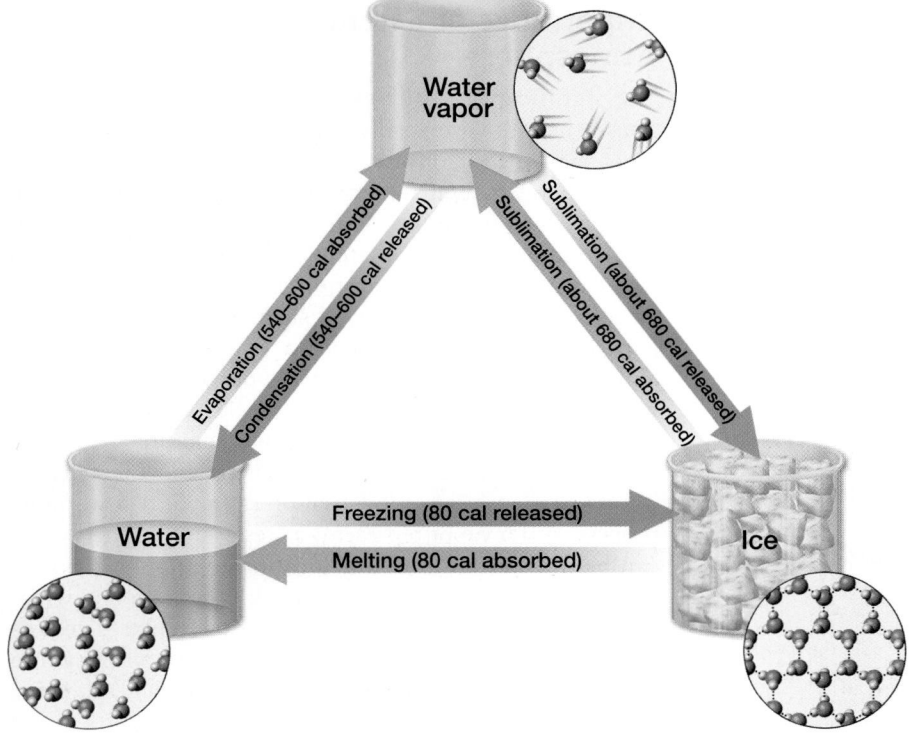

◄ **Figure 6-4** Phase changes of water are accompanied by the exchange of latent heat. The red arrows indicate that latent heat is absorbed; the blue arrows indicate that latent heat is released. The values given for heat absorbed or released during evaporation, condensation, and sublimation are for 1 gram of water.

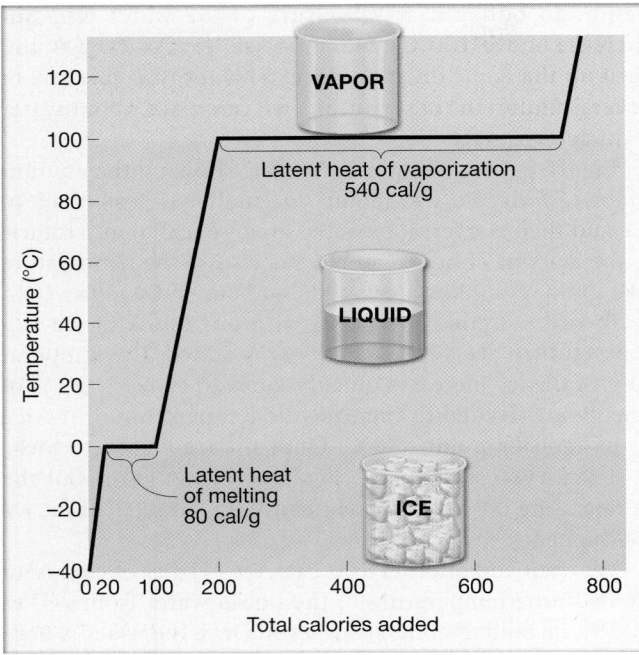

▲ **Figure 6-5** The energy input (in calories) and the associated temperature changes as 1 gram of ice starting at a temperature of –40°C is melted and then converted to water vapor. The latent heat of vaporization is much greater than the latent heat of melting.

the *internal structural energy* of the water molecules so that they can break free to become liquid.[2]

As we saw in Chapter 4, the energy exchanged during a phase change is called **latent heat**. Although the terms sound similar, *latent heat* is different from *specific heat* (also discussed in Chapter 4). It may be helpful to think of *latent heat* as the energy used to break or form the bonds (the rearrangement of the structure between two phases), whereas *specific heat* is the energy used to raise the temperature (the "speed" of the molecules in one phase).

Melting and Freezing: The energy required to melt ice is called the *latent heat of melting*. The opposite is also true: When water freezes, the liquid water molecules must give up some of their internal structural energy in order to revert to a less agitated condition in which ice can form. The energy released as water freezes is called the *latent heat of fusion*. For each gram of ice, 80 calories (335 J) of energy are absorbed when ice melts, and 80 calories of energy are released when water freezes.

Evaporation and Condensation: In a similar way, energy must be added to agitate liquid water molecules enough for them to escape into the surrounding air as water vapor—the energy added does not increase the temperature of the liquid water, but instead increases the internal

structural energy of water molecules so that they can break free to become vapor.

The energy required to convert liquid water to water vapor is called the *latent heat of vaporization*. And, once again, the opposite is also true: when water vapor condenses back to liquid water, the highly agitated water vapor molecules must give up some of their internal structural energy in order to revert to a less agitated liquid state. The energy released during condensation is called the **latent heat of condensation**. For each gram of liquid water at a temperature of 100°C, 540 calories (2260 J) of energy are absorbed as water vaporizes, and 540 calories of energy are released when water vapor condenses.

The value for the latent heat of vaporization given above refers to circumstances in which water is boiling. *Boiling* occurs when vaporization takes place beneath the surface of the liquid water—not just at the surface. In nature, however, most water vapor is added to the atmosphere through simple *evaporation* off the surface of water bodies at temperatures below 100°C. In this case, the energy required for vaporization is greater than it is for boiling water. The **latent heat of evaporation** ranges from 540 calories to about 600 calories, depending on the temperature of the water (it is approximately 585 calories [2450 J] when the liquid water is at a temperature of 20°C [68°F]).

Notice in Figures 6-4 and 6-5 that about seven times more energy is needed to evaporate 1 gram of liquid water than is needed to melt 1 gram of ice. Notice also that when sublimation takes place, the latent heat exchange is simply the total of the solid–liquid and liquid–gas exchanges.

> **Learning Check 6-4**   **Why doesn't the temperature of a block of ice increase while it is melting?**

Importance of Latent Heat in the Atmosphere

The significance of the exchange of latent heat during phase changes—especially between liquid water and water vapor—is straightforward. Whenever evaporation takes place, energy is removed from the liquid to vaporize some of the water, and so the temperature of the remaining liquid is reduced. Because latent heat energy is "stored" in water vapor during evaporation, evaporation is, in effect, a cooling process. The effect of such evaporative cooling is experienced when a swimmer leaves a swimming pool on a dry, warm day. The dripping wet body immediately loses moisture through evaporation to the surrounding air, and the skin feels the resulting drop in temperature.

Conversely, because latent heat energy must be released during condensation, condensation is, in effect, a warming process. Water vapor represents a "reservoir" of energy that can be transferred from one location to another through the movement of air masses by wind. Whenever and wherever condensation of that water vapor takes place, this energy is added back to the atmosphere. As we will begin to see later in this chapter, the release of latent heat during condensation plays important roles in the stability of the atmosphere and in the power of many storms.

---

[2]The *internal structural energy* of water molecules includes the *translational kinetic energy* associated with temperature (the "jiggling" of molecules), as well as from energy associated with the rotation and vibration of the molecules and the *potential energy* associated with forces between molecules such as bonds.

WATER VAPOR AND EVAPORATION

Although the vast majority of water on Earth is in liquid form—and although the ultimate goal of this chapter is to understand the development of clouds and precipitation—for the moment we will direct our attention to water vapor, the source of moisture for clouds and precipitation.

Water vapor is a colorless, odorless, tasteless, invisible gas that mixes freely with the other gases of the atmosphere. We are only likely to become aware of water vapor when humidity is high because the air feels sticky, clothes feel damp, and our skin feels clammy, or when humidity is low because our lips chap and our hair will not behave. Water vapor is a minor constituent of the atmosphere, with the amount present being quite variable from place to place and from time to time. It is virtually absent in some places but constitutes as much as 4 percent of the total atmospheric volume in others. Essentially, water vapor is restricted to the lower troposphere. More than half of all water vapor is found within 1.5 kilometers (about 1 mile) of Earth's surface, and only a tiny fraction exists above 6 kilometers (about 4 miles).

Now we turn specifically to the process that puts water vapor into the atmosphere: evaporation.

Evaporation and Rates of Evaporation

In our previous description of the phase changes of water, we simplified things a bit. As it turns out, both evaporation and condensation may be taking place at the same time. Strictly speaking, water vapor is added to the air when the rate of evaporation exceeds the rate of condensation; in other words, when there is *net evaporation* (Figure 6-6).

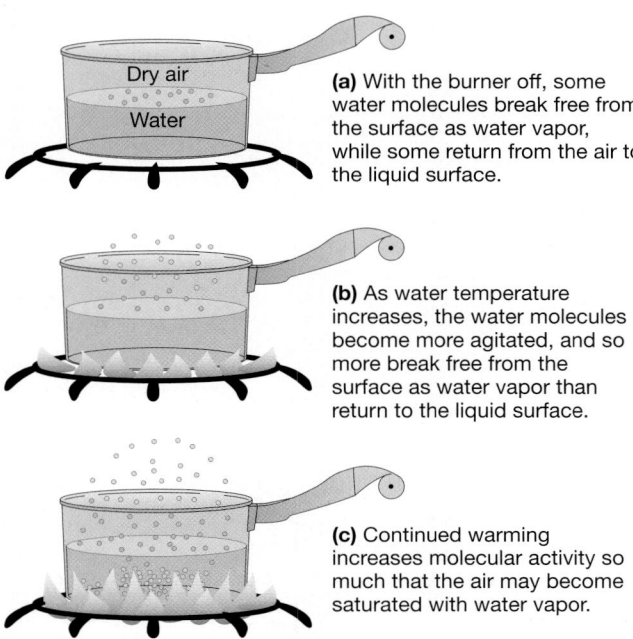

(a) With the burner off, some water molecules break free from the surface as water vapor, while some return from the air to the liquid surface.

(b) As water temperature increases, the water molecules become more agitated, and so more break free from the surface as water vapor than return to the liquid surface.

(c) Continued warming increases molecular activity so much that the air may become saturated with water vapor.

▲ **Figure 6-6** Evaporation involves the escape of water molecules from a liquid surface into the air as water vapor. It can take place at any temperature, but high temperatures increase the energy of the molecules in the liquid and therefore increase the rate of evaporation.

The rate of evaporation from a water surface, and therefore net evaporation, depends on several factors: the temperature (of both air and water), the amount of water vapor already in the air, and whether the air is still or moving.

Temperature: The water molecules in warm water are more "agitated" than those in cool water; thus there tends to be more evaporation from warm water than from cold. Warm air also promotes evaporation. Just as high water temperature produces more agitation in the molecules of liquid water, high air temperature produces more agitation in the molecules of all the gases making up the air. The more "energetic" gas molecules in warm air may collide with the liquid water surface and impart enough kinetic energy for some of the liquid water molecules to break their hydrogen bonds and enter the air above as vapor.

Water Vapor Content of Air: Water molecules cannot keep vaporizing and entering the air without limit, however. As we learned in Chapter 5, each gas in the atmosphere exerts pressure. Total atmospheric pressure is simply the sum of the pressures exerted by all of the individual gases in the atmosphere. The pressure exerted by water vapor is called the **vapor pressure**.

At any given temperature, there is a maximum vapor pressure that water molecules can exert. The higher the temperature, the higher the maximum vapor pressure; in other words, there can be more water vapor in warm air than in cold air. When water molecules in the air are exerting the maximum possible vapor pressure at a given temperature, the air is "saturated" with water vapor—at this point, the rate of evaporation and the rate of condensation are the same. If this maximum vapor pressure is exceeded, more water vapor molecules will leave the air through condensation than are added to the air through evaporation—*net condensation* will take place until the rates of evaporation and condensation are again matched and the air again has its maximum vapor pressure. In practice, this means that evaporation tends to take place more rapidly when relatively little water vapor is in the air, and that the rate of evaporation drops off as the air gets closer to saturation.

Wind: If the air overlying a water surface is almost saturated with water vapor, the rate of evaporation is about the same as the rate of condensation, and so very little further evaporation can take place. If the air remains calm and the temperature does not change, there is no net evaporation. If the air is in motion, however, through wind and/or turbulence, the water vapor molecules in it are dispersed more widely. This dispersing of water vapor molecules originally in the air at the air–water interface means that air is now further from saturation and so the rate of evaporation increases.

Learning Check 6-5 **What happens to the rate of evaporation as air approaches saturation?**

Evapotranspiration

Although most of the water that evaporates into the air comes from bodies of water, a relatively small amount comes from the land. This evaporation from land has two sources: (1) soil and other inanimate surfaces and (2) plants. The amount of moisture that evaporates from soil is relatively minor, and thus most of the land-derived moisture present in the air comes from plants. The process whereby plants give up moisture through their leaves is called *transpiration*, and so the combined process of water vapor entering the air from land sources is called **evapotranspiration** (see Figure 6-1). Thus, water vapor in the atmosphere is added through evaporation from bodies of water and evapotranspiration from sources on land.

Potential Evapotranspiration: Whether a given land location is wet or dry depends on the rates of evapotranspiration and precipitation. To analyze these rates, we need to know about a concept called *potential evapotranspiration*. This is the amount of evapotranspiration that would occur if the ground at the location in question were sopping wet all the time. To determine a value for the potential evapotranspiration at any location, data on temperature, vegetation, and soil characteristics at that location are added to the actual evapotranspiration value in a formula that results in an estimate of the maximum evapotranspiration that could result under local environmental conditions if the moisture were available.

In locations where the precipitation rate exceeds the potential evapotranspiration rate, a water surplus accumulates in the ground. In many parts of the world, however, there is no groundwater surplus, except locally and/or temporarily, because the potential evapotranspiration rate is higher than the precipitation rate. Where annual potential evapotranspiration exceeds actual precipitation, there is no water available for storage in soil and in plants; dry soil and sparse vegetation are the result.

MEASURES OF HUMIDITY

The amount of water vapor in the air is referred to as the *humidity*. However, humidity can be measured and expressed in a number of ways, each useful for certain purposes.

Actual Water Vapor Content

The actual amount of water vapor in the air can be described in several different ways.

Absolute Humidity: One direct measure of the water vapor content of air is **absolute humidity**—the mass of water vapor in a given volume of air. Absolute humidity is usually expressed in grams of water vapor per cubic meter of air (g/m³; 1 gram is approximately 0.035 ounces, and 1 cubic meter is about 35 cubic feet). For example, if a cubic meter of air contains 12 grams of water vapor, the absolute humidity

would be 12 g/m³. The maximum possible absolute humidity—the *water vapor capacity*—for a parcel of air is limited by the temperature: cold air has a small maximum absolute humidity and warm air has a great maximum absolute humidity (Figure 6-7).

If the volume of air changes (as happens when air expands or compresses as it moves vertically), the value of the absolute humidity also changes even though the total amount of water vapor remains unchanged. For this reason, absolute humidity is generally not used to describe moisture in air that is rising or descending.

Specific Humidity: The mass of water vapor in a given mass of air is called the **specific humidity** and is usually expressed in grams of water vapor per kilogram of air (g/kg; for comparison 1 cubic meter of air at sea level has a mass of about 1.4 kg at room temperature). For example, if 1 kilogram of air contains 15 grams of water vapor, the specific humidity is 15 g/kg.

Specific humidity changes only as the quantity of water vapor varies; it is not affected by variations in air volume as is absolute humidity. Specific humidity is particularly useful in studying the characteristics and movements of air masses (discussed in Chapter 7).

Vapor Pressure: As we saw earlier, the contribution of water vapor to the total pressure of the atmosphere is called the *vapor pressure*. Vapor pressure can be expressed in the same way as total atmospheric pressure, in millibars (mb) or kilopascals (kPa). The maximum possible vapor pressure (the water vapor capacity) at a given temperature is called the **saturation vapor pressure**. Notice in Figure 6-8 that at

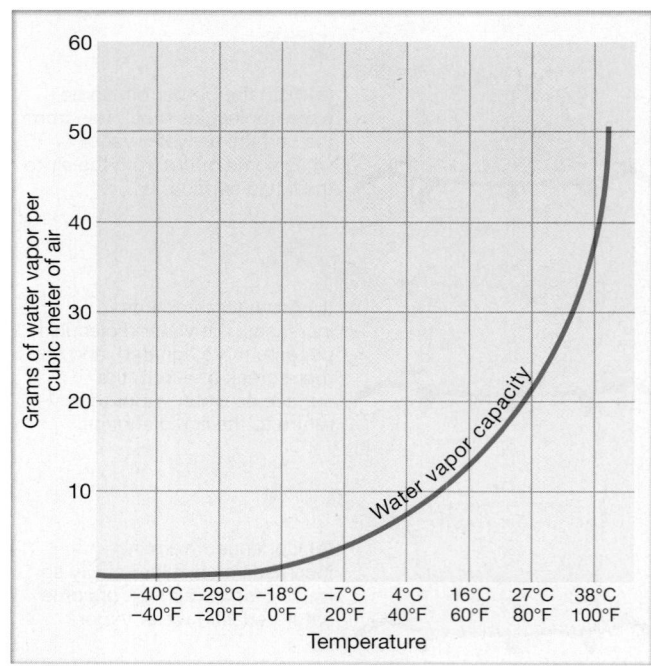

▲ **Figure 6-7** Water vapor capacity (the maximum amount of water vapor that can be in the air) increases as temperature increases. This chart shows the saturation absolute humidity in g/m³.

a temperature of 10°C (50°F) the saturation vapor pressure is a little over 10 mb, whereas at 30°C (86°F) the saturation vapor pressure is about 40 mb—illustrating again that warm air has the potential to contain much more water vapor than cold air.

Absolute humidity, specific humidity, and vapor pressure are all ways of expressing the actual amount of water vapor in the air—and as such, are indications of the quantity of water that could be extracted by condensation and precipitation. However, before we discuss condensation and precipitation, we need to introduce the important concept of *relative humidity*.

Learning Check 6-6 **What does it mean when the absolute humidity of the air is 10 g/m³?**

 FG7

Relative Humidity

The most familiar of humidity measures is **relative humidity**. Unlike absolute humidity, specific humidity, and vapor pressure, however, relative humidity does not describe the actual water vapor content of the air. Rather, relative humidity describes how close the air is to saturation with water vapor. Relative humidity is a ratio (expressed as a percentage) that compares the actual amount of water vapor in the air to the water vapor capacity of the air.

Water Vapor Capacity: Water vapor **capacity** is the maximum amount of water vapor that can be in the air at a given temperature. Depending on the measure of actual water vapor content being used, capacity may also be called the *saturation absolute humidity*, *saturation specific humidity*, or *saturation vapor pressure*.

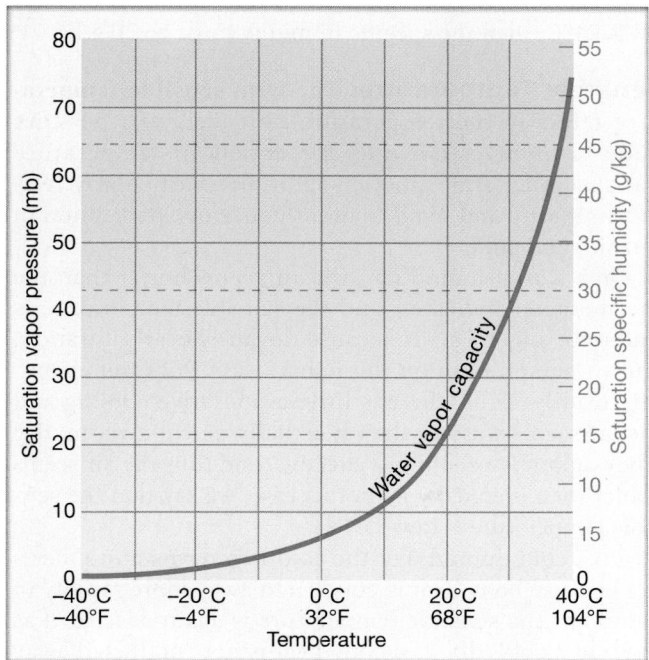

▲ **Figure 6-8** Saturation vapor pressure (in millibars) and saturation specific humidity (in g/kg). As temperature increases, the water vapor capacity of the air increases.

As we have seen in Figures 6-7 and 6-8, cold air has a low water vapor capacity, and warm air has a high water vapor capacity. In popular terms, it is sometimes said that warm air can "hold" more water vapor than cold air, but this is somewhat misleading. The air does not actually hold water vapor as if it were in a sponge. Water vapor is simply one of the gaseous components of the atmosphere. The water vapor capacity of the air is determined by the temperature, which determines the rate of vaporization of water.

Relative humidity is calculated with a simple formula:

$$\text{Relative humidity} = \frac{\text{Actual water vapor in air}}{\text{Capacity}} \times 100$$

For example, suppose that 1 kilogram of air contains 10 grams of water vapor (in other words, the specific humidity is 10 g/kg). If the temperature is 24°C (75.2°F), the capacity of the air is about 20 g/kg (see Figure 6-8; note that the g/kg scale is on the right side of chart), and so the relative humidity is

$$\frac{10 \text{ g}}{20 \text{ g}} \times 100 = 50\%$$

A relative humidity of 50 percent means that the air contains half of the maximum possible water vapor at that temperature. In other words, the air is 50 percent of the way to saturation.

Learning Check 6-7 **If the water vapor content of air is 5 g/kg and the capacity is 20 g/kg, what is the relative humidity?**

Factors Changing Relative Humidity: Relative humidity changes if either the water vapor content of the air changes or if the water vapor capacity of the air changes. If, in our example above, 5 grams of water vapor are added to the air through evaporation while the temperature remains constant (so keeping the capacity unchanged), relative humidity will increase:

$$\frac{15 \text{ g}}{20 \text{ g}} \times 100 = 75\%$$

Conversely, if water vapor is removed from the air by condensation or dispersal, the relative humidity can decrease.

Relative humidity will also change when the temperature changes—*even if the actual amount of water vapor in the air remains the same*. Again, beginning with our initial example above, if the temperature increases from 24°C to 32°C (89.6°F), the water vapor capacity increases from 20 to 30 grams, and so relative humidity decreases:

$$\text{at } 24°C \,(75.2°F): \frac{10 \text{ g}}{20 \text{ g}} \times 100 = 50\%$$

$$\text{at } 32°C \,(89.6°F): \frac{10 \text{ g}}{30 \text{ g}} \times 100 = 33\%$$

On the other hand, if the temperature decreases from 24°C to 15°C (59.0°F), the capacity decreases from 20 to 10 grams, and so relative humidity increases:

$$\text{at } 24°C\ (75.2°F): \frac{10\text{ g}}{20\text{ g}} \times 100 = 50\%$$

$$\text{at } 20°C\ (68.0°F): \frac{10\text{ g}}{15\text{ g}} \times 100 = 67\%$$

$$\text{at } 15°C\ (59.0°F): \frac{10\text{ g}}{10\text{ g}} \times 100 = 100\%$$

Notice that the air can be brought to saturation (100 percent relative humidity) simply through a decrease in temperature—no water vapor has been added. As we will see, the most common way that air is brought to the point of saturation and condensation is through cooling. It is unusual for air to reach saturation through an increase in water vapor content via evaporation—remember, when air already contains a lot of water vapor, the rate of evaporation decreases.

Temperature–Relative Humidity Relationship: The relationship between temperature and relative humidity is one of the most important in all of meteorology: as temperature increases, relative humidity decreases; as temperature decreases, relative humidity increases (at least until condensation begins).

This inverse relationship is portrayed in Figure 6-9, which demonstrates the fluctuation in temperature and relative humidity during a typical day (assuming no variation in the amount of water vapor in the air). In the early morning, the temperature is low and the relative humidity is high because the air's water vapor capacity is low. As the air warms up during the day, the relative humidity declines because the warm air has a higher water vapor capacity than cool air. With the approach of evening, air temperature decreases,

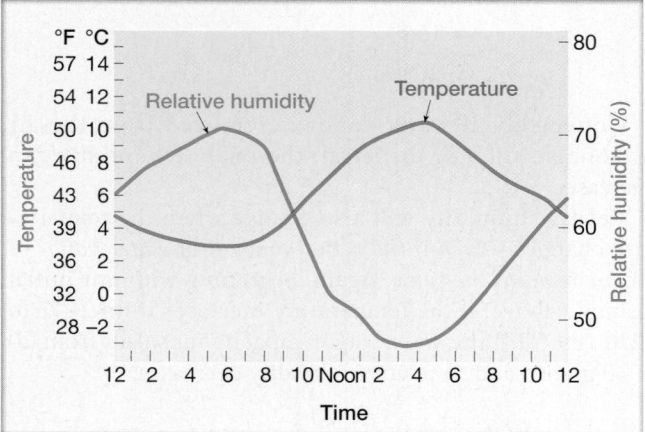

▲ **Figure 6-9** Typically there is an inverse relationship between temperature and relative humidity on any given day. As the temperature increases, the relative humidity decreases. Thus, relative humidity tends to be lowest in midafternoon and highest just before dawn.

the air's water vapor capacity diminishes, and relative humidity increases.

See Appendix III for a description of how relative humidity can be determined using a simple instrument known as a psychrometer.

Learning Check 6-8 **What happens to the relative humidity of unsaturated air if the temperature decreases? Why?**

Related Humidity Concepts

Two other concepts related to relative humidity are useful in a study of physical geography: *dew point temperature* and *sensible temperature*.

Dew Point Temperature: As we have seen, when air is cooled the water vapor capacity decreases and relative humidity increases. Cooling can bring formerly unsaturated air to the saturation point. The temperature at which saturation is reached is called the **dew point temperature**, or simply the **dew point**. The dew point temperature varies with the moisture content of the air. In our example above, we saw that air containing 10 grams of water vapor per kilogram of air reaches its dew point when chilled to about 15°C (59.0°F); air containing 20 grams of water vapor per kilogram of air reaches its dew point at about 24°C (75.2°F).

Although dew point is expressed as a temperature, in practice it becomes one of the most useful ways of describing the actual water vapor content of a parcel of air. For example, as shown above, if a parcel of air has a dew point temperature of 15°C, then we know that the specific humidity of the parcel is 10 g/kg; if the dew point of the parcel is 24°C, then the specific humidity must be 20 g/kg.

Sensible Temperature: The term **sensible temperature** refers to the temperature as it feels to a person's body. It involves not only the actual air temperature but also other atmospheric conditions, particularly relative humidity and wind, that influence our perception of warmth and cold.

On a warm, humid day, the air seems hotter than the thermometer indicates, and the sensible temperature is said to be high. This is because the air is near saturation, and so perspiration on the human skin does not evaporate readily. Thus, there is little evaporative cooling and the air seems warmer than it actually is. On a warm, dry day, evaporative cooling is effective, and thus the air seems cooler than it actually is; in this case, we say that the sensible temperature is low.

On a cold, humid day, the coldness seems more piercing because body heat is conducted away more rapidly in damp air; the sensible temperature is again described as low. On a cold, dry day, body heat is not conducted away as fast. The temperature seems warmer than it actually is, and we say that the sensible temperature is relatively high.

The amount of wind movement also affects sensible temperature, primarily by its influence on evaporation and the convection of heat away from the body. This is especially true when the air temperature is below the freezing point of water—on windy cold days, the wind may lower the apparent temperature significantly. See Appendix III for a description of the *heat index* and *wind chill*.

CONDENSATION

Condensation is the opposite of evaporation. It is the process whereby water vapor is converted to liquid water. In other words, it is a change in state from gas to liquid. In order for condensation to take place, the air must be saturated. In theory, this saturated state can come about through the addition of water vapor to the air, but in practice it is usually the result of the air being cooled to a temperature below the dew point.

The Condensation Process

Saturation alone is not enough to cause condensation, however. Surface tension makes it virtually impossible to grow liquid droplets of pure water from a vapor phase. Because surface tension inhibits an increase in surface area, it is very difficult for additional water molecules to enter or form a droplet. (On the other hand, molecules can easily leave a small droplet by evaporation, thereby decreasing its area.) Thus, it is necessary to have a surface on which condensation can take place. If no such surface is available, no condensation occurs. In such a situation, the air becomes **supersaturated** (has a relative humidity greater than 100 percent) if cooling continues.

Condensation Nuclei: Normally, plenty of surfaces are available for condensation. At ground level, availability of a surface is obviously no problem. In the air above the ground, there is also usually an abundance of "surfaces," as represented by tiny particles of dust, smoke, salt, pollen, bacteria, and other compounds. Most of these various particles are microscopic and therefore invisible to the naked eye (Figure 6-10). They are most concentrated over cities, seacoasts, and volcanoes, which are the source of much particulate matter, but they are present in lesser amounts throughout the troposphere. They are referred to as *hygroscopic particles* or **condensation nuclei**, and they serve as collection centers for water molecules during condensation.

As soon as the air temperature cools to the dew point, water vapor molecules begin to condense around condensation nuclei. The droplets grow rapidly as more and more water vapor molecules stick to them, and as they become larger, they bump into one another and coalesce as the colliding droplets stick together. Continued growth can make them large enough to be visible, forming haze or cloud particles. The diminutive size of these particles can be appreciated by realizing that a single raindrop may contain a million or more condensation nuclei plus all their associated moisture.

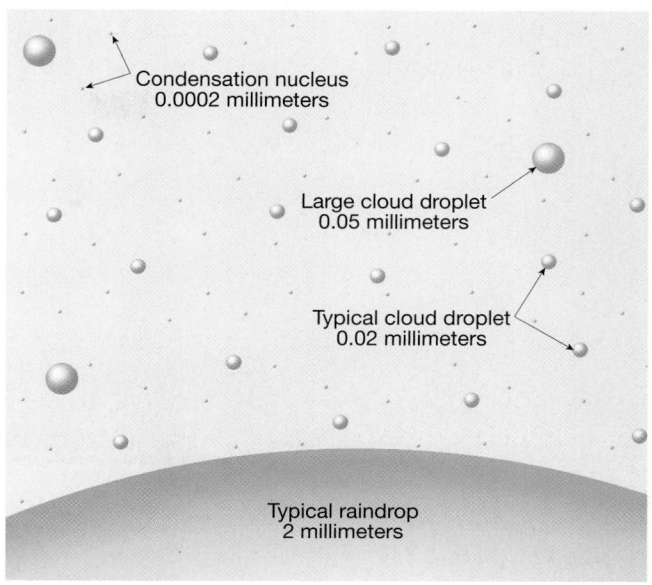

▲ **Figure 6-10** Comparative sizes of condensation nuclei and condensation particles. Condensation nuclei can be particles of dust, smoke, salt, pollen, bacteria, or any other microscopic matter found in the air.

Learning Check 6-9 **Name the two conditions necessary for *condensation* to occur.**

Supercooled Water: Clouds often may be composed of liquid water droplets even when their temperature is below freezing. Although water in large quantity freezes at 0°C (32°F), if it is dispersed as fine droplets, it can remain in liquid form at temperatures as cold as –40°C (–40°F). Water that persists in liquid form at temperatures below freezing is said to be "supercooled." **Supercooled water** droplets are important to condensation because they promote the growth of ice particles in cold clouds by freezing around the particles or by evaporating into vapor from which water molecules are readily added to the ice crystals.

ADIABATIC PROCESSES FG7

One of the most significant facts in physical geography is that the only way in which large masses of air can be cooled to the dew point temperature is by expansion as the air masses rise. Thus, the only prominent mechanism for the development of clouds and the production of rain is *adiabatic cooling*. As we noted in Chapter 4, when air rises, its pressure decreases, and so it expands and cools adiabatically.

Animation
Adiabatic
Processes and
Atmospheric
Stability

Dry and Saturated Adiabatic Rates

Dry Adiabatic Rate: As a parcel of unsaturated air rises, it cools at the relatively steady rate of 10°C per 1000 meters

▲ Figure 6-11 The flat bottom of this cumulus cloud represents the lifting condensation level.

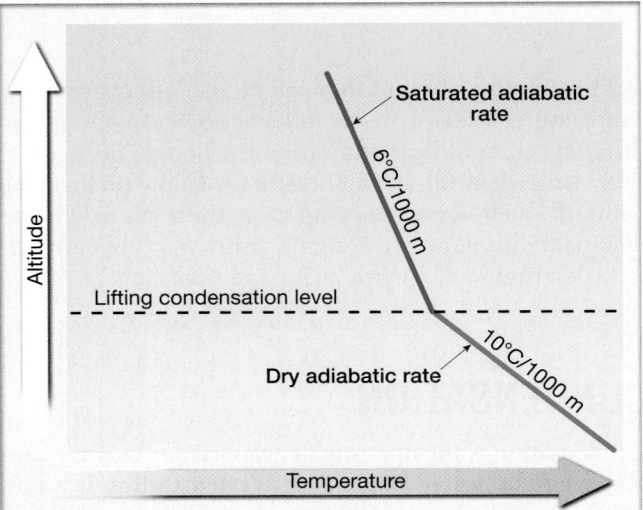

▲ Figure 6-12 Unsaturated rising air cools at the dry adiabatic rate. Above the lifting condensation level, rising saturated air cools at the saturated adiabatic rate.

(5.5°F per 1000 feet). This is known as the **dry adiabatic rate** (also called the *dry adiabatic lapse rate*). This term is a misnomer: the air is not necessarily "dry"; it is simply unsaturated (relative humidity less than 100%).

If the air mass rises high enough, it cools to the dew point temperature, the air saturates, condensation begins, and clouds form. The altitude at which this occurs is known as the **lifting condensation level (LCL)**. Under many circumstances, the LCL is clearly visible as the often flat base of the clouds that form (Figure 6-11).

Saturated Adiabatic Rate: As soon as condensation begins, latent heat is released (this energy was absorbed originally as the latent heat of evaporation). If the air continues, to rise, cooling due to expansion continues, but release of the latent heat during condensation counteracts some of the adiabatic cooling and lessens the rate of cooling. This diminished rate of cooling is called the **saturated adiabatic rate** (also called the *wet* or *saturated adiabatic lapse rate,* or the *moist adiabatic rate*) (Figure 6-12) and depends on temperature and pressure, but it averages about 6°C per 1000 meters (3.3°F per 1000 feet).

Adiabatic Warming of Descending Air: Adiabatic warming occurs when air descends. Typically, descending air will warm at the dry adiabatic rate of 10°C/1000 meters (5.5°F/1000 feet).[3] The increasing temperature

---

[3]Although descending air typically warms following the dry adiabatic rate, there is a circumstance when this may not be the case. If air descends through a cloud, some water droplets may evaporate and the evaporative cooling will counteract some of the adiabatic warming. As a result, such descending air can warm at a rate close to the saturated adiabatic rate. As soon as evaporation of water droplets ceases, this descending air will warm following the dry adiabatic rate.

of descending air increases the water vapor capacity of the air and thus causes saturated air to become unsaturated. In short, this is why descending air does not make clouds.

Adiabatic Rates versus Environmental Lapse Rate: In any consideration of adiabatic temperature changes, remember that we are dealing with air that is rising or descending. The adiabatic rates are not to be confused with the *environmental lapse rate* or the *average lapse rate* discussed in Chapter 4, that describe the temperature of the still air at different altitudes in the atmosphere (Figure 6-13).

▼ Figure 6-13 A hypothetical comparison of lapse rates. The column of temperatures on the left represents the vertical temperature gradient (the environmental lapse rate in °C) of the surrounding air through which a parcel of air is rising and cooling adiabatically. The rising parcel of air first cools at the dry adiabatic rate (DAR = 10°C per 1000 meters). As the parcel of air rises above the lifting condensation level, the release of latent heat lessens the rate of cooling and so the parcel cools at the saturated adiabatic rate (SAR = 6°C per 1000 meters).

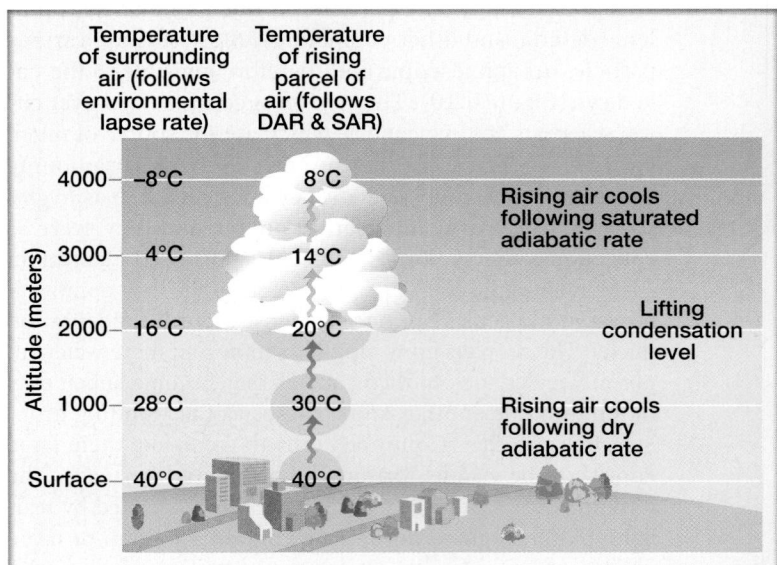

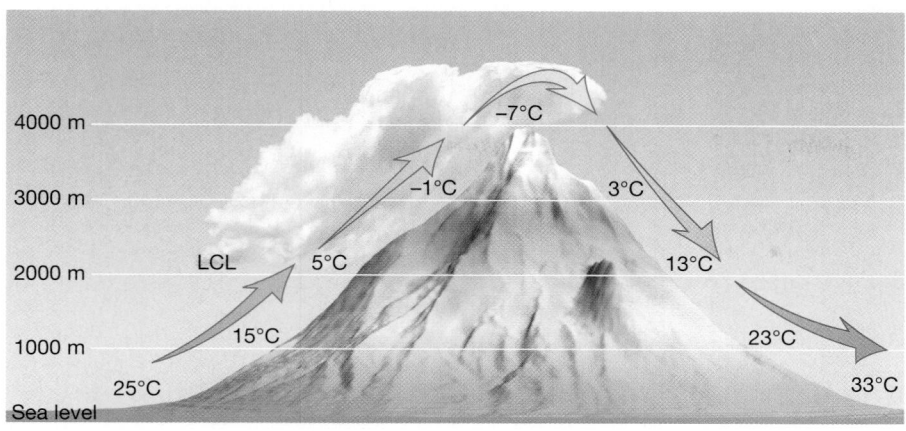

◄ **Figure 6-14** Temperature changes in a hypothetical parcel of air passing over a 4000 meter (13,100 ft) high mountain. The lifting condensation level of the parcel is 2000 meters, the dry adiabatic rate is 10°C/1000 m, and the saturated adiabatic rate is 6°C/1000 m. Notice that because of the release of latent heat during condensation on the windward side of the mountain, by the time the air has descended back down to sea level on the leeward side, it is warmer than before it started up the windward side. (This example assumes that no evaporation takes place as the air descends.)

Learning Check 6-10   **Why does air rising above the *lifting condensation level* cool at a lesser rate than air rising below the lifting condensation level?**

Significance of Adiabatic Temperature Changes

Some of the implications of adiabatic temperature changes can be seen in Figure 6-14, showing the temperature changes associated with a hypothetical parcel of air moving up and over a mountain range.

The parcel is unsaturated when it begins to rise over the mountain, so it cools at the dry adiabatic rate. Once the lifting condensation level is reached, the air continues to rise and cool at the saturated adiabatic rate as condensation forms a cloud. Once the air reaches the summit, it begins to descend down the lee side of the mountain. The descending air warms at the dry adiabatic rate, so by the time the air has reached sea level again, it is significantly warmer and significantly drier—in both relative and absolute terms—than when it started. In this hypothetical example, we assume that moisture condensed out of the rising air is left as precipitation or clouds on the windward side of the mountain, and that no evaporation takes place as the air descends—in most cases essentially the same thing happens in the real world. We will see that this circumstance is one way in which deserts are formed.

CLOUDS

Clouds are collections of minute droplets of liquid water or tiny crystals of ice. They are the visible expression of condensation and provide perceptible evidence of other things happening in the atmosphere. They provide at a glance some understanding of the present weather and are often harbingers of things to come. At any given time, about 50 percent of Earth is covered by clouds, the basic importance of which is that they are the source of precipitation. Not all clouds precipitate, but all precipitation comes from clouds.

Classifying Clouds

Although clouds occur in an almost infinite variety of shapes and sizes, certain general forms recur commonly. Moreover, the various cloud forms are normally found only at certain generalized altitudes, and it is on the basis of these two factors—form and altitude—that clouds are classified (Table 6-1).

Cloud Form: The international classification scheme for clouds recognizes three forms (Figure 6-15):

1. *Cirriform* clouds (Latin *cirrus*, "a lock of hair") are thin and wispy and composed of ice crystals rather than water droplets.
2. *Stratiform* clouds (Latin *stratus*, "spread out") appear as grayish sheets that cover most or all of the sky, rarely broken up into individual cloud units.
3. *Cumuliform* clouds (Latin *cumulus*, "mass" or "pile") are massive and rounded, usually with a flat base and limited horizontal extent but often billowing upward to great heights.

TABLE 6-1	The International Classification Scheme for Clouds			
Family	Type	Abbre-viation	Form	Characteristics
High	Cirrus	Ci	Cirriform	
	Cirrocumulus	Cc	Cirriform	Thin, white, icy
	Cirrostratus	Cs	Cirriform	
Middle	Altocumulus	Ac	Cumuliform	Layered or puffy; made of liquid water
	Altostratus	As	Stratiform	
Low	Stratus	St	Stratiform	
	Stratocumulus	Sc	Stratiform	General overcast
	Nimbostratus	Ns	Stratiform	
Vertical	Cumulus	Cu	Cumuliform	Tall, narrow, puffy
	Cumulonimbus	Cb	Cumuliform	

▲ **Figure 6-15** (a) The classic cirrus clouds referred to as "mares' tails" because of their shape. (b) Low stratus clouds over the Arctic Ocean. (c) Cumulus clouds. (d) Cirrostratus clouds have characteristics of both cirrus and stratus clouds. (e) Altocumulus clouds. (f) Nimbostratus clouds often bring widespread precipitation.

These three cloud forms are subclassified into 10 types based on shape (Figure 6-16). The types overlap, and cloud development frequently is in a state of change, so that one type may evolve into another. Three of the 10 types are purely of one form, and these are called **cirrus clouds**, **stratus clouds**, and **cumulus clouds**. The other seven types may be combinations of these three. Cirrocumulus clouds, for example, have the wispiness of cirrus clouds and the puffiness of cumulus clouds.

Precipitation comes from clouds that have "nimb" in their name, specifically *nimbostratus* or *cumulonimbus*. Normally these types develop from other types; that is, cumulonimbus clouds develop from cumulus clouds, and nimbostratus clouds develop from stratus clouds.

Cloud Families: As the final detail of the international classification scheme, the 10 cloud types are divided into four families on the basis of altitude.

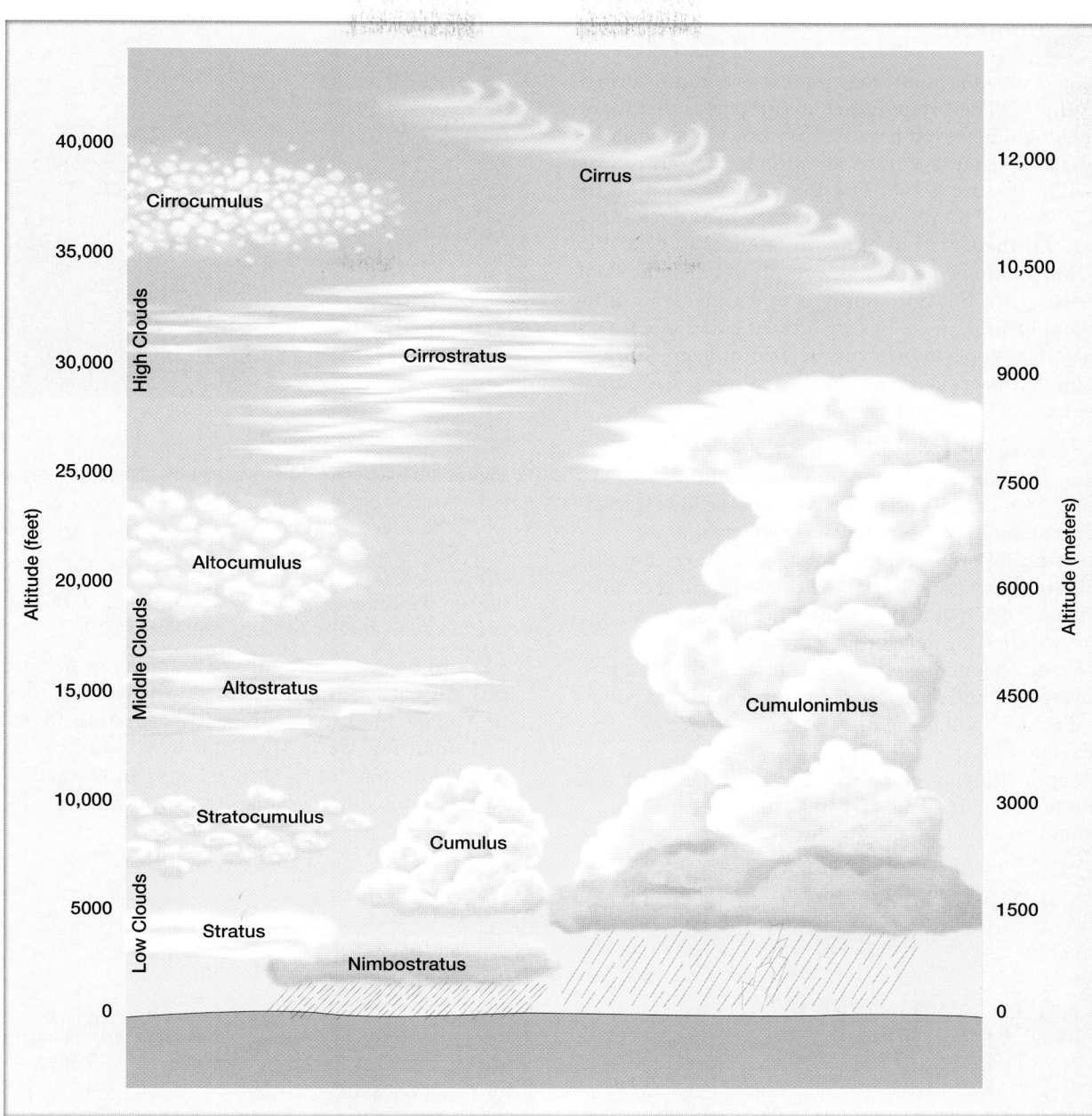

▲ **Figure 6-16** Typical shapes and altitudes of the 10 principal cloud types.

1. *High clouds* are generally found above 6 kilometers (20,000 feet). Because of the small amount of water vapor and low temperature at such altitudes, these clouds are thin, white, and composed of ice crystals. Included in this family are *cirrus, cirrocumulus,* and *cirrostratus.* These high clouds often are harbingers of an approaching weather system or storm.

2. *Middle clouds* normally occur between about 2 and 6 kilometers (6500 and 20,000 feet). They may be either stratiform or cumuliform and are composed of liquid water. Included types are altocumulus and altostratus. The puffy *altocumulus* clouds usually indicate settled weather conditions, whereas the lengthy *altostratus* are often associated with changing weather.

3. *Low clouds* usually are below 2 kilometers (6500 feet). They sometimes occur as individual clouds

but more often appear as a general overcast. Low cloud types include *stratus, stratocumulus,* and *nimbostratus.* These low clouds often are widespread and are associated with somber skies and drizzly rain.

4. A fourth family, *clouds of vertical development,* grows upward from low bases to heights of as much as 15 kilometers (60,000 feet). Their horizontal spread is usually very restricted. They indicate very active vertical movements in the air. The relevant types are *cumulus,* which usually indicate fair weather, and **cumulonimbus,** which are storm clouds.

Learning Check **6-11**   **Name the three main forms by which clouds are classified.**

Fog   FG10, FG11

From a global standpoint, fogs represent a minor form of condensation. Their importance to humans is disproportionately high, however, because they can hinder visibility enough to make surface transportation hazardous or even impossible (Figure 6-17). **Fog** is simply a cloud on the ground. There is no physical difference between a cloud and fog, but there are important differences in how each forms. Most clouds develop as a result of adiabatic cooling in rising air, but only rarely is uplift involved in fog formation. Instead, most fogs are formed either when air at Earth's surface cools to below its dew point temperature or when enough water vapor is added to the air to saturate it.

Four types of fog are generally recognized (Figure 6-18):

1. A *radiation fog* results when the ground loses heat through radiation, usually at night. The heat radiated away from the ground passes through the lowest layer of air and into higher areas. The air closest to the ground cools as heat flows conductively from it to the relatively cool ground, and fog condenses in the cooled air at the dew point, often collecting in low areas.
2. An *advection fog* develops when warm, moist air moves horizontally over a cold surface, such as snow-covered ground or a cold ocean current. Air moving from sea to land is the most common source of advection fogs.
3. An *upslope fog*, or *orographic fog* (from the Greek *oro*, "mountain"), is created by adiabatic cooling when humid air climbs a topographic slope.

▲ **Figure 6-17** Advection fog enveloping the harbor at Ketchikan, Alaska.

4. An *evaporation fog* results when water vapor is added to cold air that is already near saturation.

As can be seen in Figure 6-19, areas of heavy fog in North America are mostly coastal. The western-mountain and Appalachian fogs are mostly radiation fogs. Areas of minimal fog are in the Southwest, Mexico, and the Great Plains in both the United States and Canada, where available atmospheric moisture is limited and winds are strong.

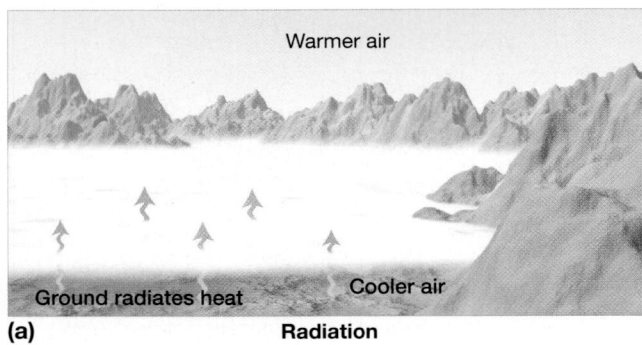

(a)   **Radiation**

(b)   **Advection**

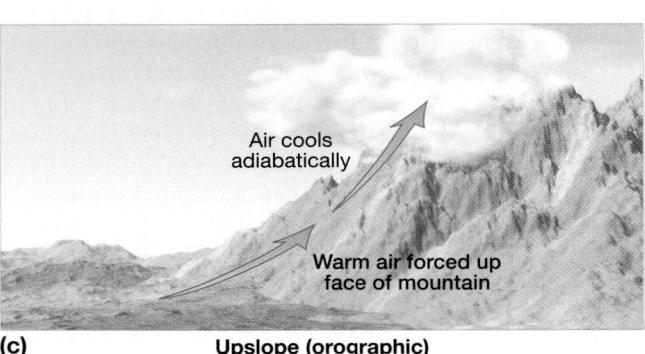

(c)   **Upslope (orographic)**

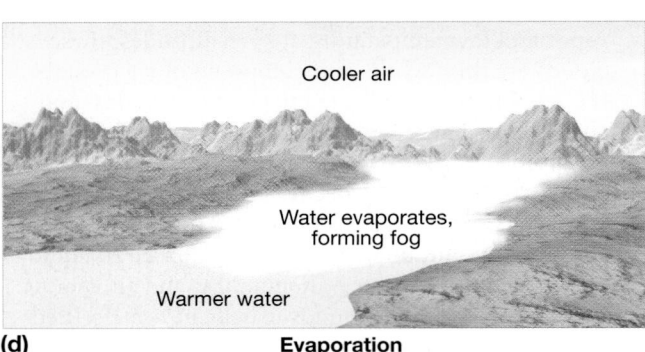

(d)   **Evaporation**

▲ **Figure 6-18** The four principal types of fog: (a) radiation, (b) advection, (c) upslope (orographic), (d) evaporation.

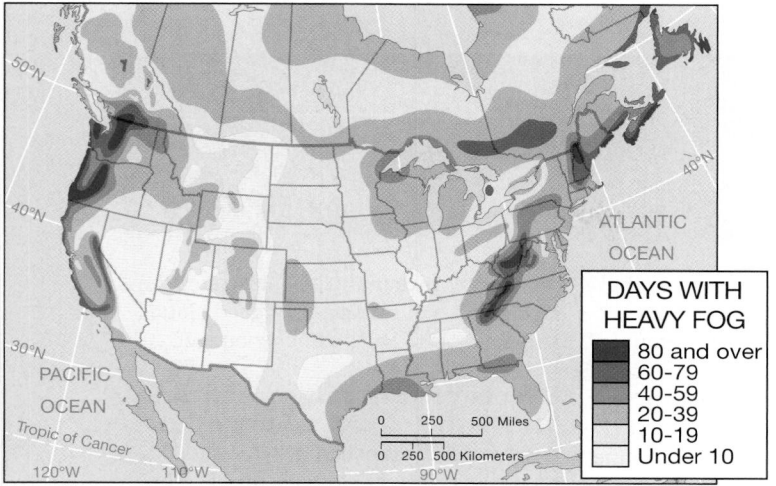

▲ **Figure 6-19** Distribution of fog in the United States and southern Canada.

Dew

Dew usually originates from terrestrial radiation. Nighttime radiation cools objects (grass, pavement, automobiles, or whatever) at Earth's surface, and the adjacent air is in turn cooled by conduction. If the air is cooled enough to reach saturation, tiny beads of water collect on the cold surface of the object. If the temperature is below freezing, ice crystals (*white frost*) rather than water droplets are formed (Figure 6-20).

Clouds and Climate Change

In addition to their obvious role in precipitation, clouds are important because of their influence on radiant energy. They receive both insolation from above and terrestrial radiation from below, and then they may absorb, reflect, scatter, or reradiate this energy. Thus understanding the

function of clouds in the global energy budget is important, and clouds must be taken into account when trying to anticipate the causes or consequences of climate change—see the box, "People and the Environment: Global Dimming."

ATMOSPHERIC STABILITY

Because most condensation and precipitation are the result of rising air, conditions that promote or hinder upward movements in the troposphere are obviously of great importance to weather and climate. Depending on how "buoyant" it is, air rises more freely and extensively under some circumstances than under others. Therefore, the topic of atmospheric stability is one of the most significant in physical geography.

Buoyancy

The tendency of any object to rise or sink in a fluid under the influence of gravity is called the *buoyancy* of that object. In general, the following is true:

- If an object is less dense than the surrounding fluid, it will float or rise.
- If it is denser than the surrounding fluid, it will sink.
- If it is the same density as the fluid, it will neither rise nor sink.

The Stability of Air

In the case of our discussion of air, imagine a parcel of air— a volume of air with boundaries, such as a balloon—as being an "object" and the surrounding air as being the fluid.

(a)

(b)

▲ **Figure 6-20** (a) Dewdrops on a wild daisy. (b) White frost emphasizes the delicate lacework of a spider web in Yellowstone Park's Hayden Valley.

Global Dimming

Atmospheric aerosols are a long recognized influence on weather and climate. As early as 1783, Benjamin Franklin proposed that the massive volcanic eruption of Laki fissure in Iceland was responsible for months of unusually frigid weather in Europe. By the 1980s, ice cores in Greenland suggested that in years following the release of ash and sulfuric acid from large volcanic eruptions, global temperatures were lower. This was confirmed when sulfate aerosols released by the 1991 eruption of Mount Pinatubo in the Philippines lowered global temperatures by approximately 0.5°C (0.9°F) for about one year.

Effects of Anthropogenic Aerosols:
Human-released aerosols can also influence weather. In the late 1980s, satellite images showed clouds persisting over oceanic shipping lanes: the sulfate aerosols from ship smokestacks were in effect "seeding" clouds. In the 1990s, research showed that the plume of sulfates, smoke particles, and other anthropogenic aerosols blowing over the Indian Ocean was blocking sunlight and promoting cloud formation, effectively reducing the amount of sunlight reaching the surface by about 10 percent.

In short, it appears that anthropogenic aerosols may directly block sunlight, absorb solar energy high in the atmosphere, and create more reflective clouds—all of which can act to cool the surface and lower troposphere. This phenomenon is known as "global dimming."

Airplane Contrails:
Atmospheric scientists had long suspected that the "contrails" (condensation trails) from jet airliners might locally alter the atmospheric energy budget slightly (Figure 6-A). Condensation trails develop when water vapor in jet exhaust cools in the cold air of the upper troposphere. These human-made clouds can reflect radiation when they are thick (acting much like a reflective cover of stratus clouds), but after some time they may turn into a wispier cover of cirrus-like clouds that absorb outgoing longwave radiation and so act as "warming" clouds.

Until September 11, 2001, there were few opportunities to study the atmosphere when contrails are absent. The grounding of all commercial airline traffic over the United States in the three days following 9/11 showed that in the absence of contrails, the daily temperature range across the country increased sharply by more than 1°C (2°F). Without contrails on those three days to absorb longwave radiation at night (and so keep conditions warmer) or reflect incoming radiation during the day (and so keep conditions cooler), the days were hotter and the nights were colder than usual.

Although contrails are not seen by most atmospheric scientists to be a major contributor to global dimming, their measurable effect on local temperatures dramatically illustrates the significance of human-produced clouds and aerosols to Earth's energy budget.

Effects of "Dimming" Aerosols on Earth's Energy Budget:
The Aqua satellite launched by NASA in 2002 carries instruments to measure the consequences of human-released "dimming" pollutants on Earth's energy budget. Early results suggested that perhaps as much as one-third to one-half of the warming caused by human greenhouse gas emissions has been counteracted by cooling from human aerosol pollution. A 2007 NASA study found that the overall "optical thickness" of aerosols in the atmosphere declined steadily between about 1991 and 2005—by as much as 20 percent from previous decades—largely because of reduced emissions from industrialized countries (Figure 6-B). This decline in aerosols helps explain the slight increase in sunlight striking Earth's surface after about 1990.

However, more recent research using instruments such as NASA's *Cloud Aerosol Lidar and Infrared Pathfinder Satellite Observation* (CALIPSO) spacecraft documented an increase in stratospheric aerosols over the last decade that likely continues to suppress warming. This raises a paradoxical concern for atmospheric scientists: if human-produced global dimming has been masking some of the effects of global warming, if we continue to reduce "dimming pollutants" we will face higher temperatures from global warming.

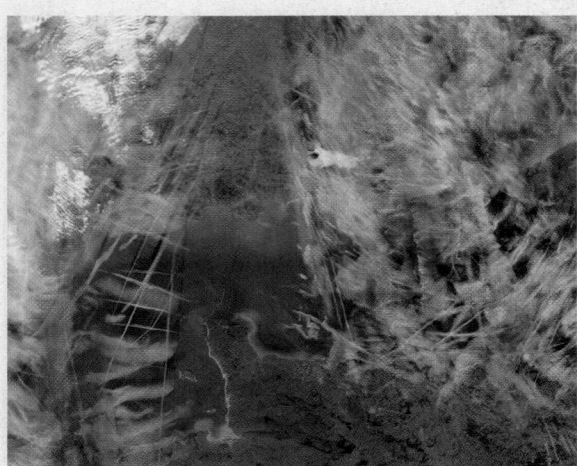

▲ **Figure 6-A** Airplane contrails over the English Channel are shown in this MODIS satellite image.

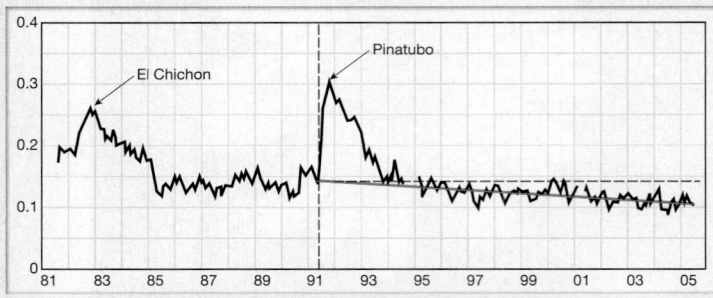

▲ **Figure 6-B** Overall, atmospheric aerosols declined between 1991 and 2005, although stratospheric aerosols may be increasing. The two large spikes in aerosols were produced by the 1982 eruption of El Chichón in Mexico and the 1991 eruption of Mount Pinatubo in the Philippines.

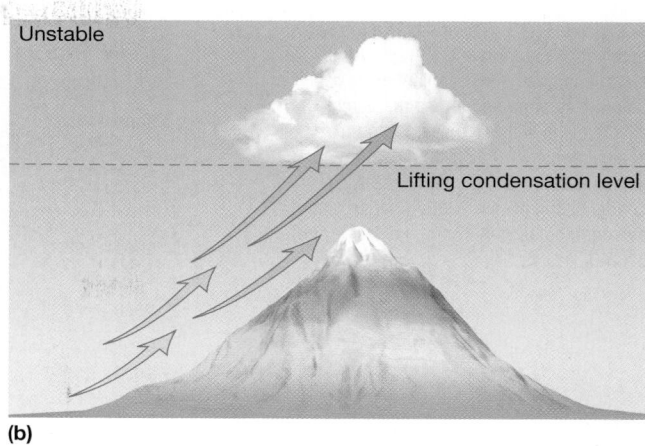

▲ **Figure 6-21** (a) As stable air blows over a mountain, it rises only as long as it is forced to do so by the mountain slope. On the leeward side, it moves downslope. (b) When unstable air is forced up a mountain slope, it is likely to continue rising of its own accord until it reaches surrounding air of similar temperature and density; if it rises to the lifting condensation level, clouds form.

As with other gases (and liquids, too), an air parcel tends to seek its equilibrium level. This means that a parcel of air moves up or down until it reaches an altitude at which the surrounding air is of equal density. Said another way, if a parcel of air is warmer, and thus less dense, than the surrounding air, it tends to rise. If a parcel is cooler, and therefore denser, than the surrounding air, it tends either to sink or at least resist uplift. Thus, we say that warm air is more buoyant than cool air.[4]

Stable Air: If a parcel of air resists uplift, it is said to be **stable** (Figure 6-21). If stable air is forced to rise, perhaps by wind forcing it up a mountain slope, it does so only as long as the force is applied. Once the force is removed, the air sinks back to its former position. In other words, stable air is nonbuoyant. When unstable air comes up against the same mountain, it continues to rise once it has passed the peak.

In the atmosphere, high stability is promoted when cold air is beneath warm air, a condition most frequently observed during a *temperature inversion* (discussed in Chapter 4). With colder, denser air below warmer, lighter air,

upward movement is unlikely. A cold winter night is typically a highly stable situation, although high stability can also occur in the daytime. Because it does not rise, and therefore stays at an essentially constant pressure and volume, highly stable air obviously provides little opportunity for adiabatic cooling unless there is some sort of forced uplift. Highly stable air is normally not associated with cloud formation and precipitation.

Unstable Air: Air is said to be **unstable** if it either rises without any external force other than the buoyant force, or if it continues to rise after such an external force has ceased to function. In other words, unstable air is buoyant. When a mass of air is warmer than the surrounding air, it becomes unstable. This is a typical condition on a warm summer afternoon (Figure 6-22). The unstable air rises until it reaches an altitude where the surrounding air has similar temperature and density, which is referred to as the *equilibrium level*. While ascending, it will be cooled adiabatically. In this situation, clouds are likely to form.

Latent Heat and Instability: Between stability and instability is an intermediate condition, sometimes called *conditional instability*. Near the surface, such a parcel of air is the same temperature or cooler than the surrounding air and so is stable. If forced to rise above the lifting condensation level, however, the release of latent heat during condensation may warm the air enough to make the parcel unstable. It will then rise until it reaches an altitude where

---

[4]Water vapor content may also slightly influence air buoyancy. Because water vapor molecules have a lower molecular weight than nitrogen molecules (N_2) or oxygen molecules (O_2), when air has a high water vapor content, heavier N_2 and O_2 molecules have been displaced by lighter H_2O molecules and so such moist air is just slightly "lighter" than dry air. Overall, however, air temperature is by far the most important determinant of air buoyancy.

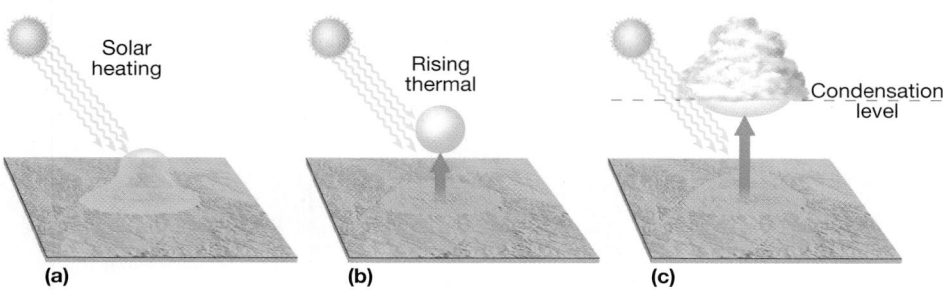

◄ **Figure 6-22** (a) Localized heating of Earth's surface warms a parcel of air. (b) Because this parcel of air is warmer than the surrounding air, it is unstable and so begins to rise. (c) If this "thermal" rises high enough it may reach the lifting condensation level, forming a cloud.

▶ **Figure 6-23** Rising stable air is shown here with a diagram and a graph. At all elevations, the rising parcel of air is cooler than the surrounding air, so the parcel is stable and will rise only if forced. (Dry adiabatic rate = 10°C/1000 m; saturated adiabatic rate = 6°C/1000 m; lifting condensation level = 2000 m; lapse rate of surrounding air [environmental lapse rate] = 5°C/1000 m.)

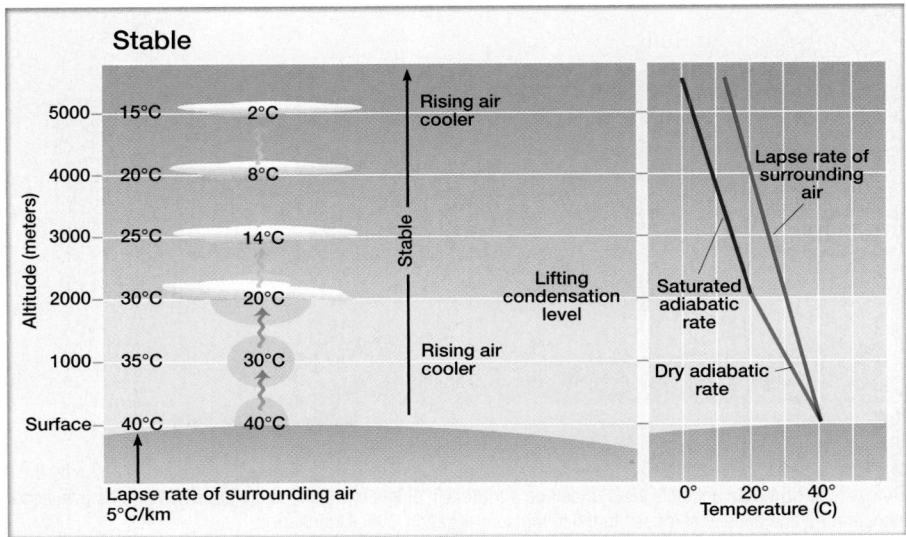

the surrounding air has density and temperature similar to its own.

Learning Check 6-12 **What makes a parcel of air unstable?**

Determining Atmospheric Stability

An accurate determination of the stability of any mass of air generally depends on temperature measurements.

Temperature, Lapse Rate, and Stability: The temperature of a parcel of rising air can be compared with the temperature of surrounding (nonrising) air by a series of thermometer readings at different elevations. The rising air cools (at least initially) at the dry adiabatic rate of 10°C per 1000 meters (5.5°F per 1000 feet). The *environmental lapse rate* of the surrounding (nonrising) air depends on many things and may be different from the dry adiabatic rate.

For example, if the environmental lapse rate of the surrounding air is less than the dry adiabatic rate of the rising air, as in Figure 6-23, at every elevation the rising air is cooler than the surrounding air and therefore stable. Under such conditions, the air rises only when forced to do

so. Once the lifting force is removed, the air ceases to rise and will actually sink.

On the other hand, if the environmental lapse rate of the surrounding air is greater than the dry adiabatic rate of the rising air, at every elevation the rising air is warmer than the surrounding air and so it is unstable. The unstable air rises until it reaches an elevation where the surrounding air is of similar temperature and density (Figure 6-24).

In another situation, after rising stable air is cooled to its dew point temperature at the lifting condensation level, condensation begins and latent heat is released. This situation, in which the air is conditionally unstable, the release of latent heat increases the tendency toward instability and reinforces the rising trend (Figure 6-25).

Visual Determination of Stability: The cloud pattern in the sky is often indicative of air stability. Unstable air is associated with distinct updrafts, which are likely to produce vertical clouds (Figure 6-26). Thus, the presence of cumulus clouds suggests instability, and a towering cumulonimbus cloud is an indicator of pronounced instability. Horizontally developed clouds, most notably stratiform, are characteristic of stable air that has been forced to rise, and a cloudless sky may be an indicator of stable air that is immobile.

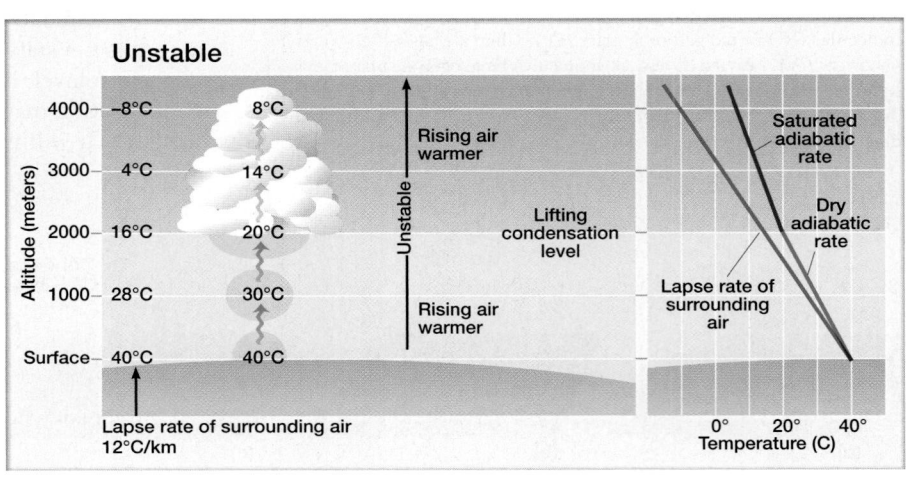

▶ **Figure 6-24** Rising unstable air. At all elevations, the rising parcel of air is warmer than the surrounding air, so the parcel is unstable and will rise because of its buoyancy. (Dry adiabatic rate = 10°C/1000 m; saturated adiabatic rate = 6°C/1000 m; lifting condensation level = 2000 m; lapse rate of surrounding air = 12°C/1000 m.)

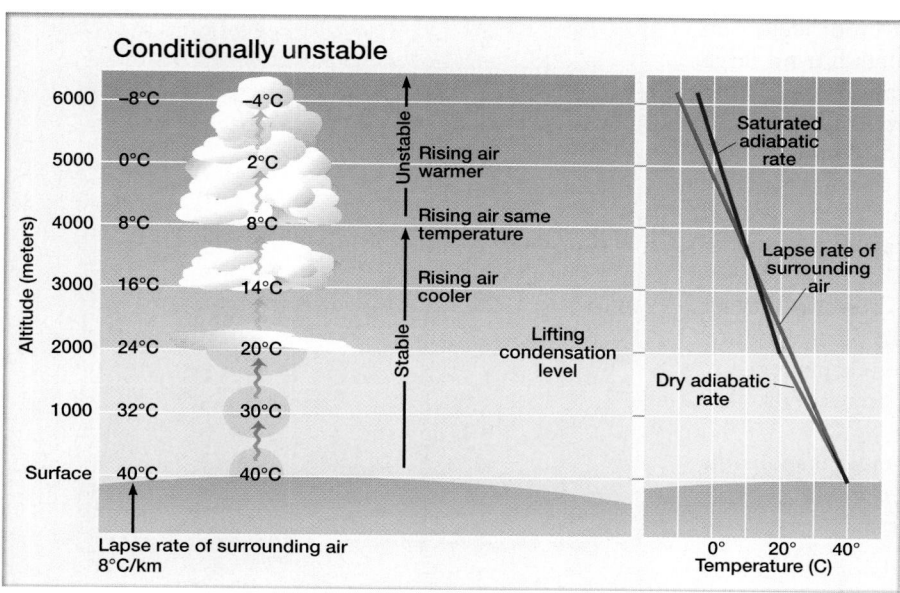

◀ **Figure 6-25** Conditionally unstable air. In this case, the rising parcel of air is cooler than the surrounding air and so is stable up to an elevation of 4000 meters. However, above that elevation, the release of latent heat during condensation warms the rising air enough to make it unstable—thus the rising air is conditionally unstable. (Dry adiabatic rate = 10°C/1000 m; saturated adiabatic rate = 6°C/1000 m; lifting condensation level = 2000 m; lapse rate of surrounding air = 8°C/1000 m.)

Regardless of stability conditions, no clouds form unless the air is cooled to the dew point temperature—unstable rising air will not produce any clouds if the dew point of the rising air is not reached. Thus the mere absence of clouds is not certain evidence of stability; it is only an indication. The general features of stable and unstable air are summarized in Table 6-2.

PRECIPITATION

All **precipitation** originates in clouds, but most clouds do not yield precipitation. Exhaustive experiments have demonstrated that condensation alone is insufficient to produce raindrops. The tiny water droplets that make up clouds cannot fall to the ground as rain because their size makes them very buoyant and the normal turbulence of

▼ **Figure 6-26** A large cumulonimbus cloud as seen from an airplane cockpit window. The anvil-shaped top is characteristic of cumulonimbus clouds.

the atmosphere keeps them aloft. Even in still air, their fall would be so slow that it would take many days for them to reach the ground from even a low cloud. Besides that, most droplets would evaporate in the drier air below the cloud before they made a good start downward.

Despite these difficulties, rain and other forms of precipitation are commonplace in the troposphere. What is it, then, that produces precipitation in its various forms?

The Processes

An average-sized raindrop contains several million times as much water as the average-sized water droplet found in any cloud. Consequently, great multitudes of droplets must join together to form a drop large enough to overcome both turbulence and evaporation and thus be able to fall to Earth under the influence of gravity.

Two mechanisms are believed to be principally responsible for producing precipitation particles: (1) collision and coalescence of water droplets, and (2) ice-crystal formation.

Collision/Coalescence: In many cases, particularly in the tropics, cloud temperatures are greater than 0°C (32°F); these are known as *warm clouds*. In such clouds, rain is produced by the collision and coalescing (merging)

TABLE 6-2	Characteristics of Stable and Unstable Air	
Stable Air	**Unstable Air**	
Nonbuoyant; remains immobile unless forced to rise	Buoyant; rises without outside force	
If clouds develop, tend to be stratiform or cirriform	If clouds develop, tend to be cumuliform	
If precipitation occurs, tends to be drizzly	If precipitation occurs, tends to be showery	

of water droplets. Condensation alone cannot yield rain because it produces lots of small droplets but no large drops. Thus, tiny condensation droplets must coalesce into drops large enough to fall as precipitation. Different-sized water droplets fall through a cloud at different speeds. Larger ones fall faster, overtaking and often coalescing with smaller ones, which are swept along in the descent (Figure 6-27). This sequence of events favors the continued growth of the larger particles.

Not all collisions result in coalescence, however. The air displaced around a falling large drop can push very tiny droplets out of its path. In addition, there is evidence to suggest that differences in the electrical charges of droplets may influence coalescence as well.

Collision/coalescence is the process most responsible for precipitation in the tropics, and it also produces some of the precipitation in the middle latitudes.

Ice-Crystal Formation: Many clouds or portions of clouds extend high enough to have temperatures well below the freezing point of liquid water (these are known as *cold* or *cool clouds*). In this situation, ice crystals and supercooled water droplets often coexist in the cloud. These two types of particles are in direct "competition" for the water vapor that is not yet condensed.

Saturation vapor pressure is lower around the ice crystals than around liquid water droplets—this means that if the air around a liquid water droplet is saturated (100 percent relative humidity), that same air is *supersaturated* around an ice crystal. Thus, the ice crystals attract most of the water vapor, and the liquid water droplets, in turn, evaporate to replenish the diminishing supply of vapor, as shown in Figure 6-28. Therefore, the ice crystals grow at the expense of the water droplets until the crystals are large enough to fall. As they descend through the lower, warmer portions of the cloud, they pick up more moisture and become still larger. They may then either precipitate from the cloud as snowflakes or melt and precipitate as raindrops.

Precipitation by ice-crystal formation was first proposed by the Swedish meteorologist Tor Bergeron more than half a century ago. It is now known as the *Bergeron process* and is believed to account for the majority of precipitation outside of tropical regions.

Forms of Precipitation

Several forms of precipitation can result from the processes just described depending on air temperature and turbulence.

Rain: By far the most common and widespread form of precipitation is **rain**, which consists of drops of liquid water. Most rain is the result of condensation and precipitation in ascending air that has a temperature above freezing, but some results from the melting of ice crystals as they descend through warmer air (Figure 6-29).

Meteorologists often make a distinction among "rain," which goes on for a relatively long time; *showers*, which are relatively brief and involve large drops; and *drizzle*, which consists of very small drops and usually lasts for some time.

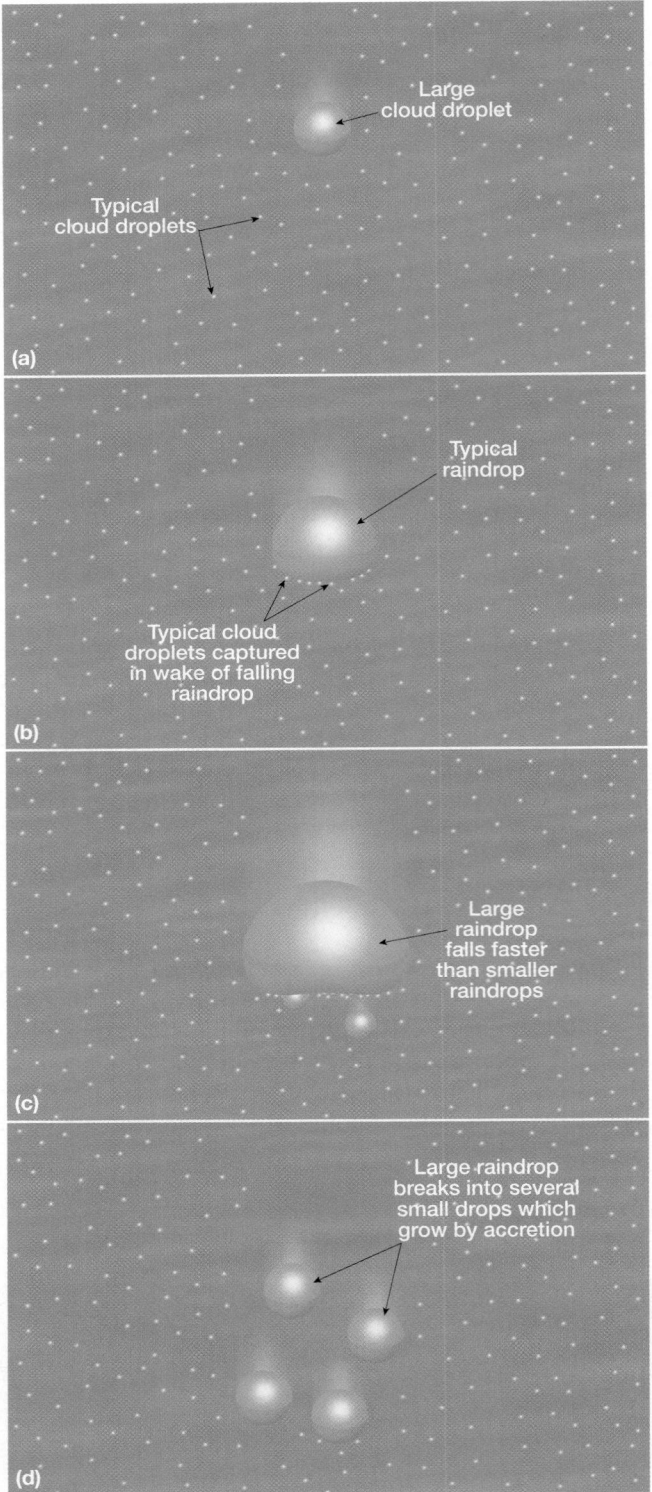

▲ **Figure 6-27** Raindrops forming by collision and coalescence. (a) Large droplets fall more rapidly than small ones, (b) coalescing with some and sweeping others along in their descending path (c). As droplets become larger during descent, they sometimes break apart (d). (Cloud droplets and raindrops are not drawn at same scale.)

Snow: The general name given to solid precipitation in the form of ice crystals, small pellets, or flakes is **snow**. It is formed when water vapor is converted directly to ice through sublimation without an intermediate liquid stage.

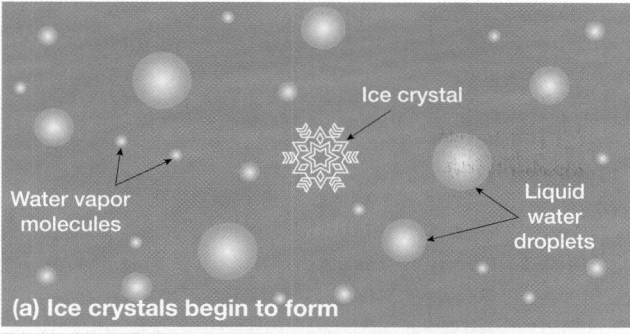

▲ **Figure 6-28** Precipitation by means of ice-crystal formation in clouds (the Bergeron process). (a) Ice crystals grow by attracting water vapor to themselves, (b) causing the liquid water droplets that make up the cloud to evaporate to replenish the water vapor supply. (c) The process of growing ice crystals and shrinking cloud droplets may continue until the ice crystals are large and heavy enough to fall. (Particle sizes are greatly exaggerated.)

However, the water vapor may have evaporated from super-cooled liquid cloud droplets inside cold clouds.

Sleet: In the United States, *sleet* refers to small raindrops that freeze during descent and reach the ground as small pellets of ice. In other countries, the term is often applied to a mixture of rain and snow.

Glaze: *Glaze* (or *freezing rain*) is rain that turns to ice the instant it collides with a solid object. Raindrops fall through a shallow layer of subfreezing air near the ground. Although the drops do not freeze in the air (in other words, they do not turn to sleet), they become supercooled while in this cold layer and are instantly converted to an icy surface when they land. The result can be a thick coating of ice that makes both pedestrian and

▲ **Figure 6-29** A towering cumulonimbus cloud produces a small but intense thunderstorm over the desert of northern Arizona near Third Mesa.

vehicular travel hazardous as well as breaks tree limbs and transmission lines.

Hail: The precipitation form with the most complex origin is **hail**, which consists of either small pellets or larger lumps of ice (Figure 6-30). Hailstones are usually composed of roughly concentric layers of clear and cloudy ice. The cloudy portions contain numerous tiny air bubbles among small crystals of ice, whereas the clear parts are made up of large ice crystals.

▲ **Figure 6-30** The largest documented hailstone, shown here, fell in Vivian, South Dakota, on July 23, 2010. It weighed 879 g (1.94 lbs.).

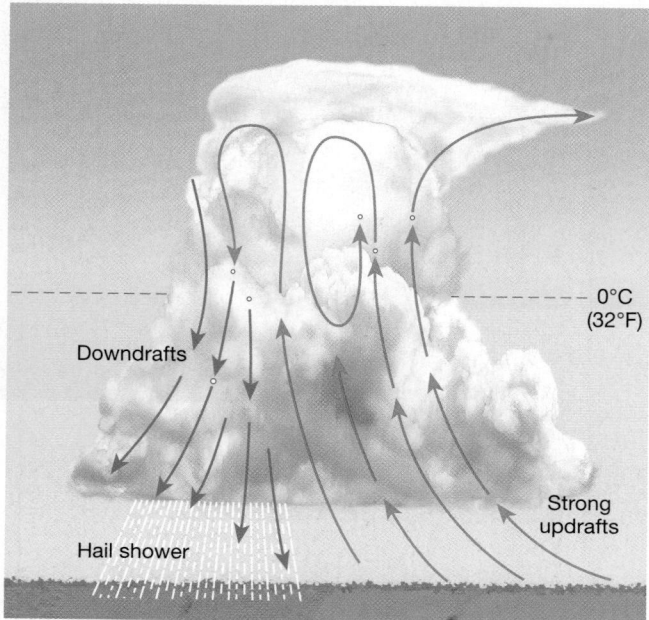

▲ **Figure 6-31** Hail is produced in cumulonimbus clouds with strong updrafts that are partly at a temperature above the freezing point of water and partly at a temperature below the freezing point of water. The curved and spiral arrows indicate paths a hailstone takes as it is forming.

Hail is produced in cumulonimbus clouds as a result of great instability and strong vertical air currents (updrafts and downdrafts) (Figure 6-31). Because highly unstable air is needed for it to form, hail tends to be more common in summer than in the middle of winter. For hail to form from a cloud, the cloud must have a lower part that is warmer than the freezing point of 0°C (32°F) and an upper part that is colder than this. Updrafts carry water from the above-freezing layer or small ice particles from the lowest part of the below-freezing layer upward, where they grow by collecting moisture from supercooled cloud droplets. When the particles become too large to be supported in the air, they fall, gathering more moisture on the way down. If they encounter a sufficiently strong updraft, they may be carried skyward again, only to fall another time. This sequence may be repeated several times, as indicated by the spiral path in Figure 6-31.

A hailstone normally continues to grow whether it is rising or falling in the below-freezing layer, providing it passes through portions of the cloud that contain supercooled droplets. If considerable supercooled moisture is available, the hailstone, which is ice, becomes surrounded by a wet layer that freezes relatively slowly, producing large ice crystals and forcing the air out of the water. The result is clear-ice rings. If the supply of supercooled droplets is more limited, the water may freeze almost instantly around the hailstone. This fast freezing produces small crystals with tiny air bubbles trapped among them, forming opaque rings of ice.

The eventual size of a hailstone depends on the amount of supercooled water in the cloud, the strength of the updrafts, and the total length (up, down, and sideways) of the path taken by the stone through the cloud. The largest

documented hailstone fell in South Dakota on July 23, 2010 (see Figure 6-30), and was 20 centimeters (8 inches) in diameter and weighed 879 grams (1.9375 pounds).

Learning Check 6-13 **Why is hail associated with highly unstable air?**

Virga: If the relative humidity of the air below a precipitating cloud is quite low, falling precipitation may evaporate before reaching the surface. The streaks of rain that disappear before hitting the ground under these circumstances are called *virga*.

Among the most important tools for meteorologists studying precipitation today are weather satellites. By providing such information as the moisture content of air masses, temperature profiles of the atmosphere, and the location and characteristics of clouds, weather satellites help forecasters predict rain, cloud cover, and other weather events. For example, see the box, "Focus: GOES Weather Satellites."

ATMOSPHERIC LIFTING AND PRECIPITATION

The role of rising air and adiabatic cooling has been stressed in this chapter. Only through these events can any significant amount of precipitation originate. It remains for us to consider the causes of rising air. There are four principal types of atmospheric lifting. One type is spontaneous, and the other three require the presence of some external force. More often than not, however, the various types operate in conjunction.

Convective Lifting

Because of unequal heating of different surface areas, a parcel of air near the ground may be warmed by conduction more than the air around it. The density of the warmed air is reduced as the air expands, and so the parcel rises toward a lower-density layer, in a typical **convective lifting** situation, as shown in Figure 6-32a. The pressure of the unstable air decreases as the air rises, and so it cools adiabatically to the dew point temperature. Condensation begins and a cumulus cloud forms. With the proper humidity, temperature, and stability conditions, the cloud is likely to grow into a towering cumulonimbus thunderhead, with a downpour of showery raindrops and/or hailstones accompanied sometimes by lightning and thunder (see Figure 6-29).

An individual convective cell is likely to cover only a small horizontal area, although sometimes multiple cells are formed very close to each other, close enough to form a much larger cell. *Convective precipitation* is typically showery, with large raindrops falling fast and furiously but only for a short duration. It is particularly associated with the warm parts of the world and warm seasons.

GOES Weather Satellites

The satellite images commonly seen on television and Internet weather reports in North America come from a pair of satellites known as GOES, or *Geostationary Operational Environmental Satellites*. The satellites are operated by the National Oceanic and Atmospheric Administration (NOAA) and are essential tools for weather forecasting.

The GOES satellites are geostationary, orbiting at a distance of 35,800 kilometers (22,300 miles) in fixed locations above the surface of Earth below. GOES-East (GOES-13) orbits above the equator in South America (75° W), where it can see the conterminous United States, as well as much of the North and South Atlantic Ocean. GOES-West (GOES-15) orbits above the equator in the Pacific (135° W), where it can see most of the Pacific Ocean from Alaska to New Zealand. Similar weather satellites are maintained by other countries, providing complete global coverage.

▲ **Figure 6-C** Visible light satellite image taken by NOAA's GOES-West satellite. The cold front of a midlatitude cyclone is over the central Pacific Ocean, and a band of large thunderstorms cuts across the continent from northern Mexico to the midwestern United States.

The GOES satellites have instruments to measure vertical temperature and moisture variations within the atmosphere, ozone distribution, and sensors to detect both reflected and radiated electromagnetic energy in several different wavelength bands—images in each wavelength band provide different kinds of information about Earth's surface and atmosphere. The GOES satellites send back several images each hour, allowing time-lapse satellite "movie" loops to be produced.

Visible Light Images: Visible light ("VIS") satellite images show sunlight that has been reflected off the surface of Earth or by clouds in the atmosphere (Figure 6-C). The brightness of a surface depends both on its *albedo* (reflectance) and the angle of the light striking it. The brightest surfaces in visible light are typically the tops of clouds, and snow or ice-covered surfaces. The darkest surfaces are typically land areas (especially unvegetated land surfaces), and the oceans—which are usually the darkest surfaces seen on visible light satellite images.

Infrared Images: The infrared ("IR") images of Earth and its atmosphere are produced day and night and are among the most widely used in meteorology. Infrared images show the longwave ("thermal infrared") radiation emitted by the surface of Earth or

by clouds in the atmosphere (Figure 6-D). Warm objects emit more longwave radiation than cold objects, and so infrared images show us, in effect, differences in temperature. On grayscale ("black-and-white") IR images, cooler surfaces are shown in white, whereas warmer surfaces are shown in black. The tops of high clouds, such as massive cumulonimbus clouds, are much colder than low clouds and fog, and so will appear brighter (white) on infrared images, whereas low clouds are warmer and so appear nearly the same shade of gray as the surface below.

Water Vapor Images: By measuring the wavelengths of longwave infrared radiation strongly absorbed and reemitted by water vapor (specifically at wavelengths of 6.7 μm and 7.3 μm), scientists have a way to estimate the quantity of water vapor in the atmosphere. Regions with high emission of infrared radiation at 6.7 μm and 7.3 μm contain relatively large amounts of water vapor, whereas regions with low emission of those wavelengths contain relatively small amounts of water vapor. Satellite water vapor ("WV") images show regions of dry air and moist air in the atmosphere—even if these areas are cloud free and so will not show clearly on conventional visible light or infrared weather satellite images (Figure 6-E).

Viewing GOES Images: Up-to-date GOES satellite images are readily available to the public through many Internet sites, such as http://www.goes.noaa.gov and http://www.nrlmry.navy.mil/sat_products .html.

▲ **Figure 6-E** Water vapor satellite image taken at the same time as Figures 6-C and 6-D. Note the relatively dry area (shown in dark blue) from southern California to Hawai'i, and the moist areas (yellow and orange) of the cold front and the thunderstorms.

▲ **Figure 6-D** Infrared satellite image taken at the same time as Figure 6-C.

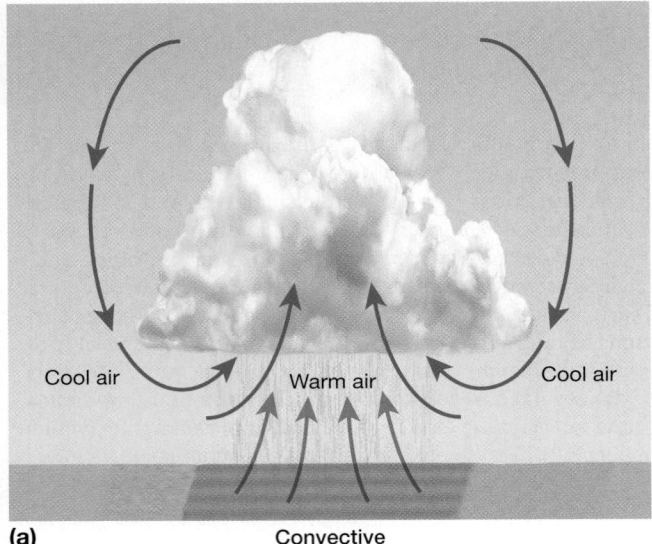

(a) Convective

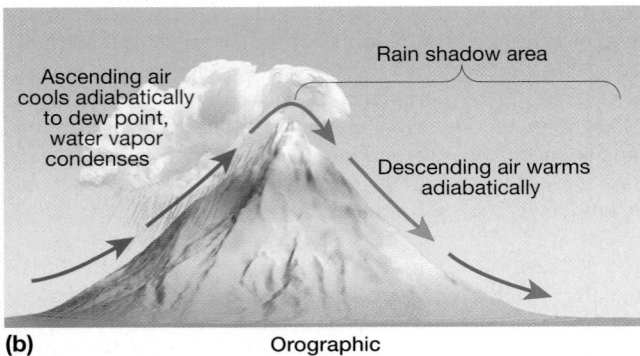

(b) Orographic

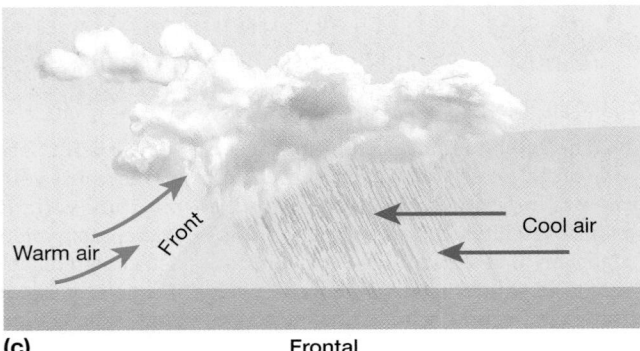

(c) Frontal

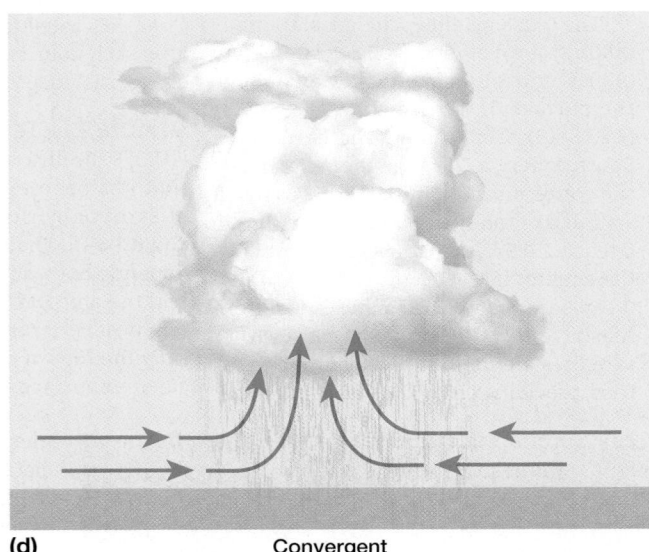

(d) Convergent

▲ **Figure 6-32** The four basic types of atmospheric lifting and precipitation: (a) convective, (b) orographic, (c) frontal, (d) convergent.

In addition to the spontaneous uplift just described, various kinds of forced uplift, such as air moving over a mountain range, can trigger formation of a convective cell if the air tends toward instability. Thus convective uplift often accompanies other kinds of uplift.

Orographic Lifting  FG6, FG9

Topographic barriers that block the path of horizontal air movements are likely to cause large masses of air to travel upslope, as Figure 6-32b shows. This kind of forced ascent from **orographic lifting** can produce *orographic precipitation* if the ascending air is cooled to the dew point. As we learned, if significant instability has been triggered by the upslope motion, the air keeps rising when it reaches the top of the slope and the precipitation continues. More often, however, the air descends the leeward side of the barrier. As soon as it begins to move downslope, adiabatic cooling is replaced by adiabatic warming and condensation and precipitation cease. Thus the windward slope of the barrier is the wet side, the leeward slope is the dry side, and the term **rain shadow** is applied to both the leeward slope and the area beyond as far as the drying influence extends (Figure 6-33).

Orographic precipitation can occur at any latitude, any season, any time of day. The only requisite conditions are a topographic barrier and moist air to move over it. Orographic precipitation is likely to be prolonged because there is a relatively steady upslope flow of air.

Frontal Lifting

When unlike air masses meet, they do not mix. Rather, a zone of discontinuity called a *front* is established between them, and the warmer air rises over the cooler air, as shown in Figure 6-32c. As the warmer air is forced to rise, it may be cooled to the dew point with resulting clouds and precipitation. Precipitation that results from such **frontal lifting** is referred to as *frontal precipitation*. We shall discuss frontal precipitation in greater detail in the next chapter. It tends to be widespread and protracted, but it is also frequently associated with convective showers.

Frontal activity is most characteristic of the midlatitudes, and so frontal precipitation is particularly notable in those regions, which are meeting grounds of cold polar air and warm tropical air. It is less significant in the high latitudes and rare in the tropics because those regions contain air masses that tend to be like one another.

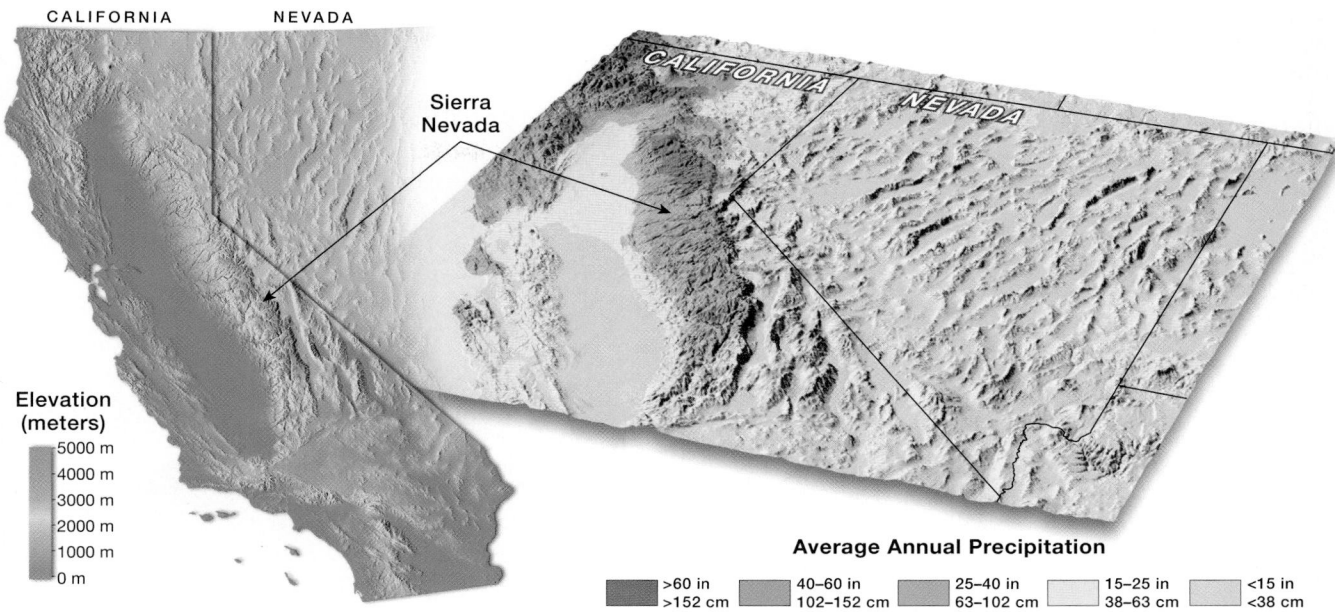

Elevation
(meters)

5000 m
4000 m
3000 m
2000 m
1000 m
0 m

Average Annual Precipitation

>60 in   40–60 in   25–40 in   15–25 in   <15 in
>152 cm   102–152 cm 63–102 cm   38–63 cm   <38 cm

▲ **Figure 6-33** Nevada is in the rain shadow of the Sierra Nevada Mountains of California. The west slope of the Sierra has high rainfall because of the orographic lifting of the moist westerly winds coming from the Pacific Ocean. East of the Sierra, the climate is arid.

Convergent Lifting

Less common than the other three types, but nevertheless significant in some situations, is **convergent lifting** and the accompanying *convergent precipitation*, illustrated in Figure 6-32d. Whenever air converges, the result is a general uplift because of the crowding. This forced uplift enhances instability and is likely to produce showery precipitation. It is frequently associated with cyclonic storm systems and is particularly characteristic of the low latitudes. It is common, for example, in the intertropical convergence zone (ITCZ; discussed in Chapter 5) and is notable in such tropical disturbances as hurricanes and easterly waves.

> **Learning Check 6-14**   **What causes a *rain shadow*?**

GLOBAL DISTRIBUTION OF PRECIPITATION

The most important geographic aspect of atmospheric moisture is the spatial distribution of precipitation. The broadscale zonal pattern is based on latitude, but many other factors are involved and the overall pattern is complex. This section of the chapter focuses on a series of maps that illustrate worldwide and U.S. precipitation distribution. A major cartographic device used on these maps is the **isohyet**, a line joining points of equal quantities of precipitation.

Animation
Seasonal
Pressure and
Precipitation
Patterns

The amount of precipitation on any part of Earth's surface is determined by the nature of the air mass involved and the degree to which that air is uplifted. The moisture content, temperature, and stability of the air mass are mostly dependent on where the air originated (over land or water, in high or low latitudes) and on the trajectory it has followed. The amount of uplift of that air mass is determined largely by zonal pressure patterns, topographic barriers, storms, and other atmospheric disturbances. The combination of these factors produces the annual distribution of precipitation shown in Figure 6-34.

Regions of High Annual Precipitation

High annual precipitation is generally found in three types of locations.

Region of the ITCZ and Trade Wind Uplift: The most conspicuous feature of the worldwide annual precipitation pattern is that the tropical latitudes contain most of the wettest areas. The warm easterly trade winds are capable of carrying enormous amounts of moisture, and where they are forced to rise, very heavy rainfall is usually produced. Equatorial regions particularly reflect these conditions where warm ocean water easily vaporizes and warm, moist, unstable air is uplifted in the ITCZ.

Considerable precipitation also results where trade winds are forced to rise by topographic obstacles. As the trades are easterly winds, it is the eastern coasts of tropical landmasses—for example, the east coast of Central America, northeastern South America, and Madagascar—where this orographic effect is most pronounced.

Tropical Monsoon Regions: Where the normal trade-wind pattern is modified by monsoons, the onshore

▶ **Figure 6-34** Average annual precipitation over the land areas of the world.

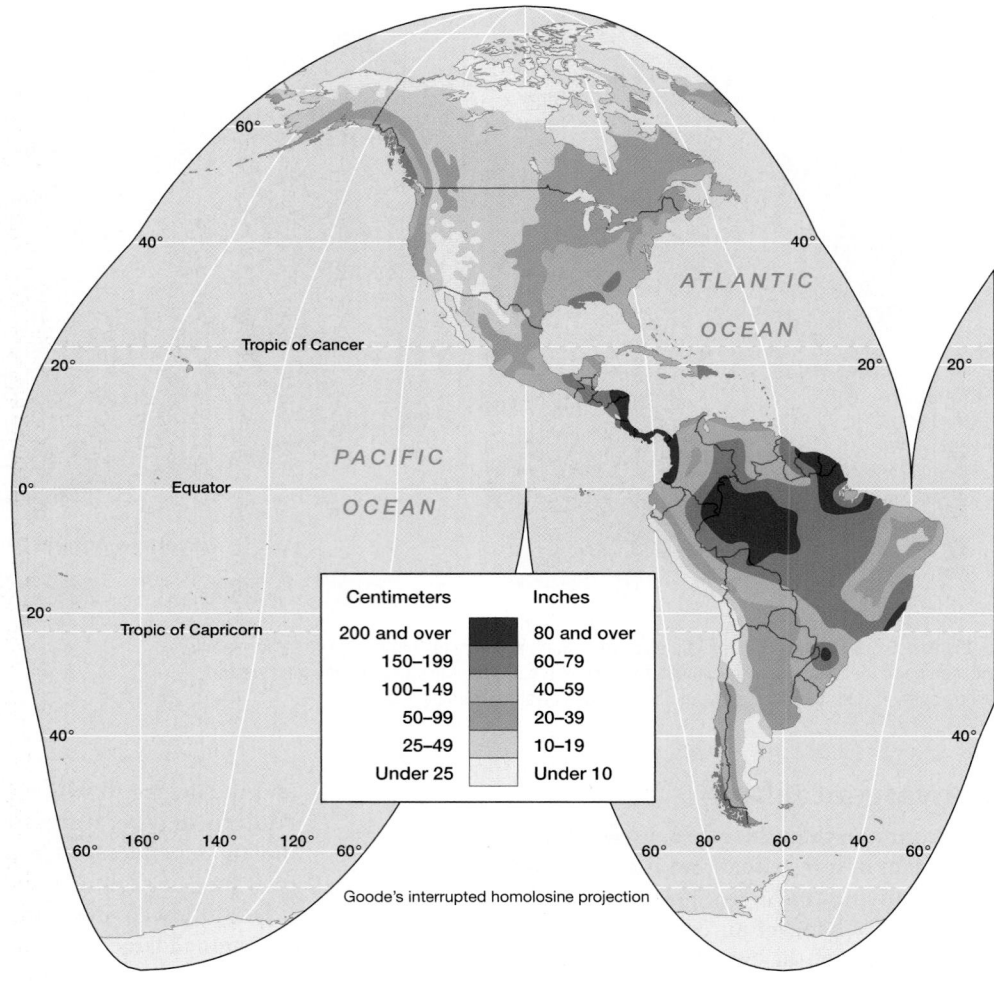

Goode's interrupted homolosine projection

trade-wind flow may occur on the western coasts of tropical landmasses. Thus, the wet areas on the western coast of southeastern Asia, India, and what is called the Guinea Coast of West Africa are caused by the onshore flow of southwesterly winds that are nothing more than trade winds diverted from a "normal" pattern by the South Asian and West African monsoons.

Coastal Areas in Westerlies: The only other regions of high annual precipitation shown on the world map are narrow zones along the western coasts of North and South America between 40° and 60° of latitude. These areas reflect a combination of frequent onshore westerly airflow, considerable storminess, and mountain barriers running perpendicular to the direction of the prevailing westerly winds. The presence of these north–south mountain ranges near the coast restricts the precipitation to a relatively small area and creates a pronounced rain shadow effect to the east of the ranges.

Learning Check 6-15 **Why do equatorial regions generally have high annual precipitation?**

Regions of Low Annual Precipitation

The principal regions of sparse annual precipitation on the world map are found in three types of locations.

Areas of Subtropical Highs: Dry lands are most prominent on the western sides of continents in subtropical latitudes (centered at 25° to 30°). High-pressure conditions dominate at these latitudes, particularly on the western sides of continents, which are closer to the normal positions of the subtropical high-pressure cells. High pressure means sinking air, which is not conducive to condensation and precipitation.

The presence of cool ocean currents also contributes to the atmospheric stability and dryness of these regions. These dry zones are most extensive in North Africa and Australia primarily because of the blocking effect of landmasses or highlands to the east. (The presence of such landmasses prevents moisture from coming in from the east.)

Interiors of Continents: Dry regions in the midlatitudes are most extensive in central Eurasia, but they also occur in western North America and southeastern South America. In each case, the dryness is due to lack of access for moist air masses. In the Eurasian situation, this lack of access is essentially a function of distance from any ocean where onshore airflow might occur. In North and South America, there are rain shadow situations in regions of predominantly westerly airflow.

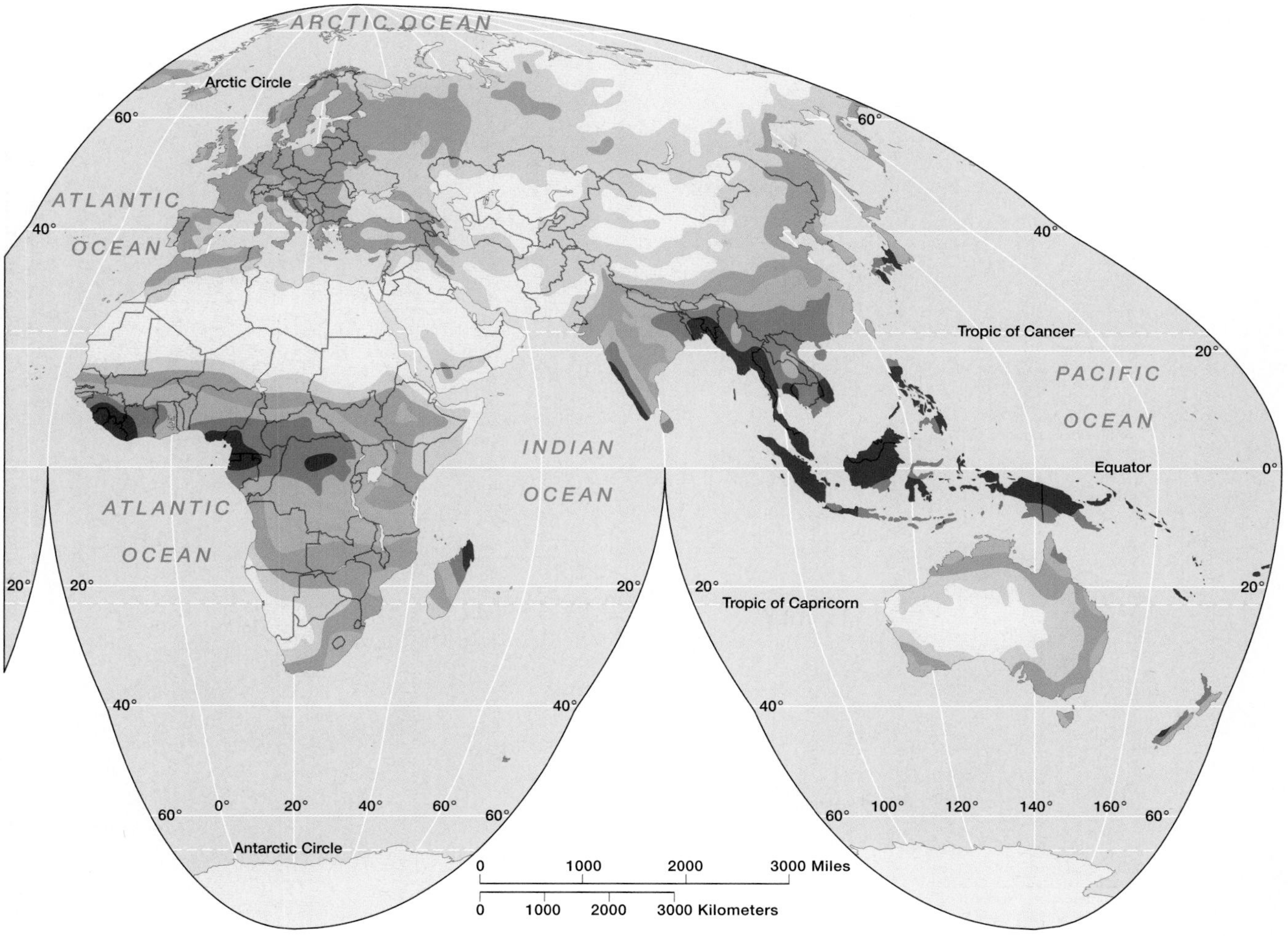

High-Latitude Regions: In the very high latitudes, there is not much precipitation anywhere. Water surfaces are scarce and cold, and so little opportunity exists for moisture to evaporate into the air. As a result, polar air masses have low absolute humidities and precipitation is slight. These regions are referred to accurately as cold deserts.

> **Learning Check 6-16** **Why do west coast locations at about 25° to 30° N and S typically have low annual precipitation?**

Seasonal Precipitation Patterns

A geographic understanding of climate requires knowledge of seasonal as well as annual precipitation patterns. Over most of the globe, the amount of precipitation received in summer is considerably different from the amount received in winter. This variation is most pronounced over continental interiors, where strong summer warming at the surface induces greater instability and the potential for greater convective activity. Thus, in interior areas, most of the year's precipitation occurs during summer months, and winter is generally a time of anticyclonic conditions with diverging airflow. Coastal areas often have a more balanced seasonal precipitation regime, which is again a reflection of their nearness to moisture sources.

Video
Global
Precipitation

Maps of average January and July precipitation show the contrasts between winter and summer rain–snow conditions around the world (Figure 6-35). Several seasonal patterns are important to note:

ITCZ Shifts: The seasonal shifting of major pressure and wind systems, a shifting that follows the Sun (north by July and south by January), is mirrored in the displacement of wet and dry zones. This is seen most clearly in tropical

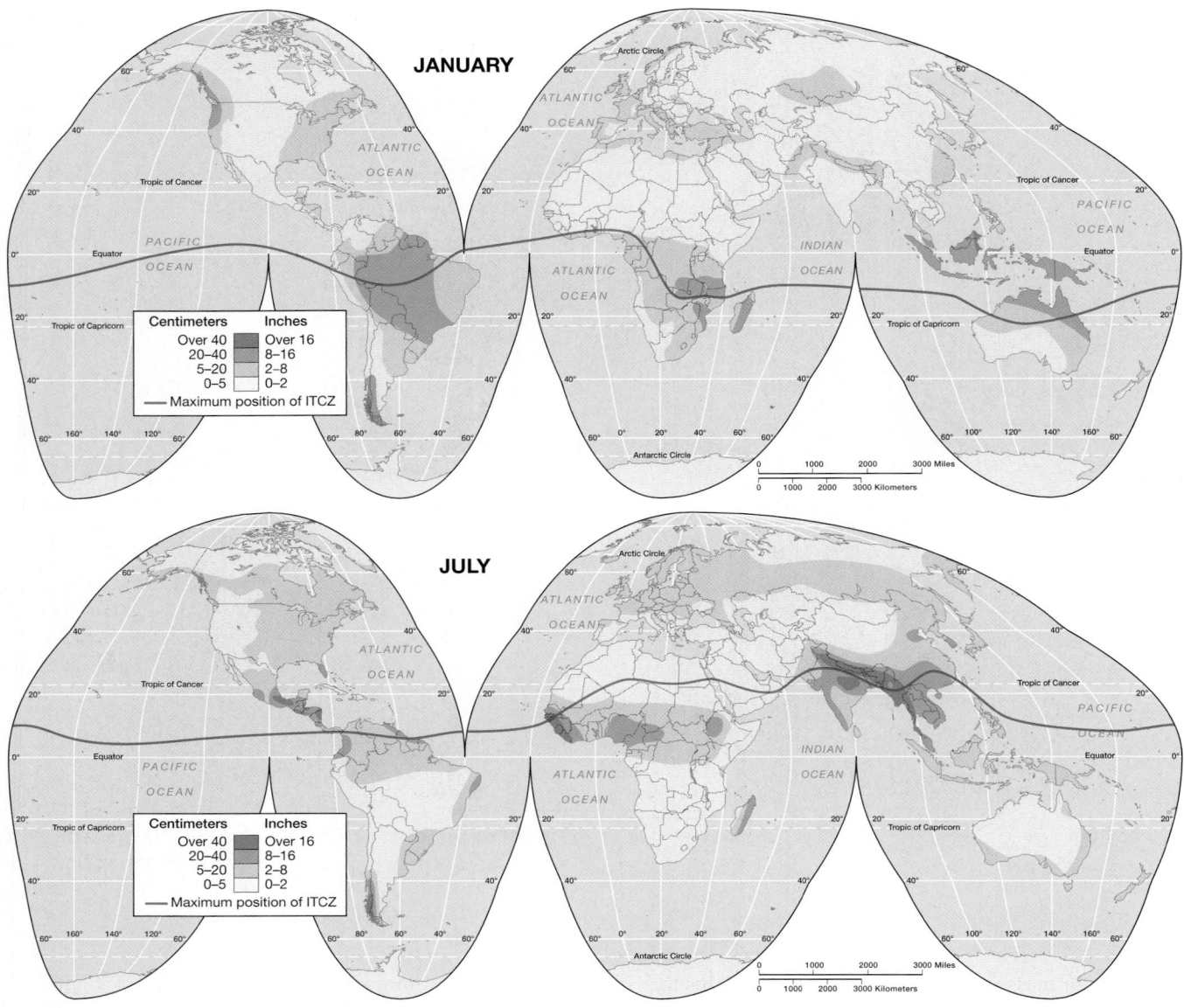

▲ **Figure 6-35** Average January and July precipitation over the land areas of the world. The red line marks the typical maximum poleward position of the intertropical convergence zone (ITCZ).

regions, where the heavy rainfall belt of the ITCZ clearly migrates north and south in different seasons.

Subtropical High Shifts: Summer is the time of maximum precipitation over most of the world. Northern Hemisphere regions experience heaviest rainfall in July, and Southern Hemisphere locations receive most precipitation in January. The only important exceptions to this generalization occur in relatively narrow zones along western coasts between about 35° and 50° of latitude, as illustrated for the United States in Figure 6-36. The same abnormal trend occurs in South America, New Zealand, and southernmost Australia. These regions experience the summer dryness associated with the seasonal shift of the subtropical highs.

Monsoon Regions: The most conspicuous variation in seasonal precipitation is found, predictably, in tropical

monsoon regions (principally southern and eastern Asia, northern Australia, and West Africa), where summer tends to be very wet and winter is generally dry.

Precipitation Variability

The maps considered thus far all portray average conditions. The data on which they are based were gathered over decades, and thus the maps represent abstraction rather than reality. In any given year or any given season, the amount of precipitation may or may not be similar to the long-term average.

Precipitation variability is the expected departure from average precipitation in any given year, expressed as a percentage above or below average. For example, a precipitation variability of 20 percent means that a location expects to

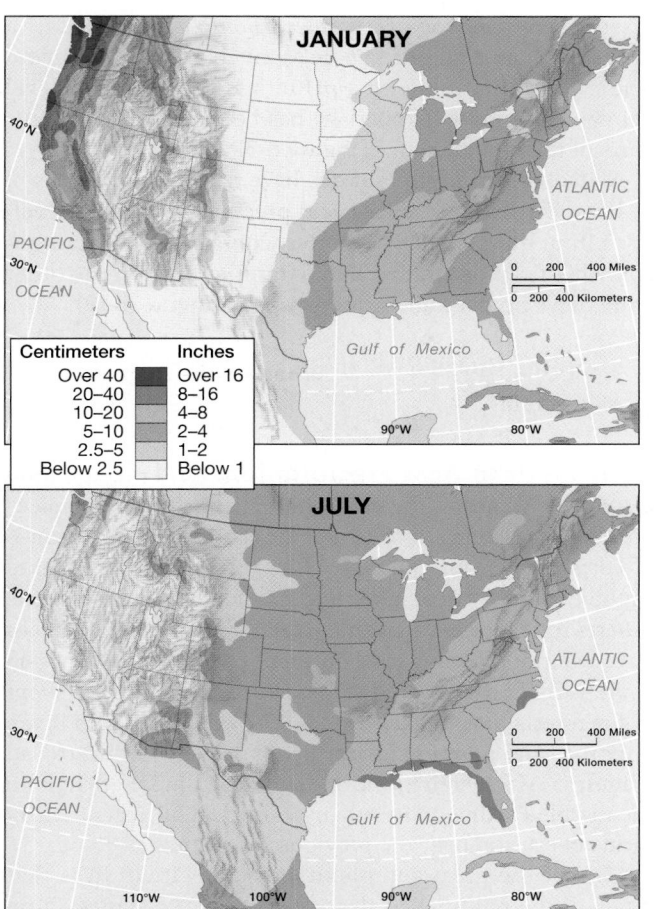

▲ **Figure 6-36** Average January and July precipitation in southern Canada, the conterminous United States, and northern Mexico. Winter precipitation is heaviest in the Pacific Northwest; summer rainfall is greatest in the Southeast.

receive either 20 percent more or 20 percent less precipitation than average in any given year. If a location has a long-term average annual precipitation of 50 cm (20 in.) and has a precipitation variability of 20 percent, the "normal" rainfall for a year would be either 40 cm (16 in.) or 60 cm (24 in.)—in the long run, the average comes out to 50 cm.

Figure 6-37 reveals that regions of normally heavy precipitation experience the least variability and normally dry regions experience the most. Said another way, dry regions experience great fluctuations in precipitation from one year to the next.

Learning Check 6-17   **Is a desert likely to have high precipitation variability or low precipitation variability?**

ACID RAIN

One of the most troublesome environmental problems since the latter part of the twentieth century is **acid rain**—more generally called *acid precipitation* or *acid deposition*. This term refers to the deposition of either wet or dry acidic materials from the atmosphere on Earth's surface. Although most conspicuously associated with rainfall, the pollutants may fall to Earth with snow, sleet, hail, or fog or in the dry form of gases or particulate matter.

Sources of Acid Precipitation

Sulfuric and nitric acids are the principal culprits recognized thus far. Evidence indicates that the principal human-induced sources are sulfur dioxide (SO_2) emissions from smokestacks (particularly electric utility companies in the

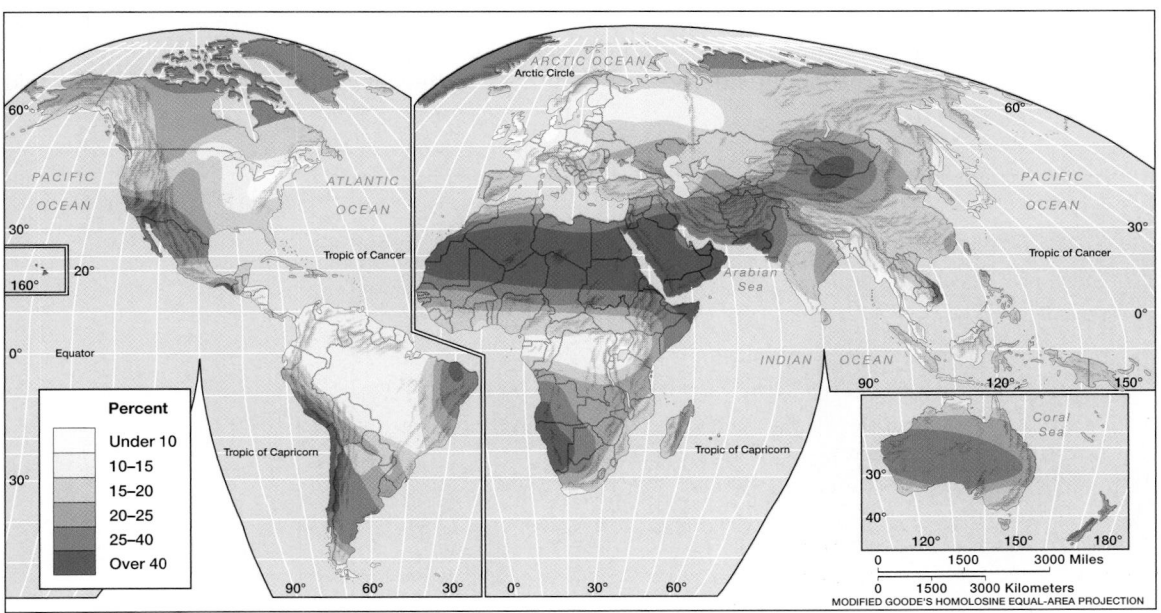

▲ **Figure 6-37** Precipitation variability is the expected departure from average precipitation in any given year, expressed as a percentage above or below average. Dry regions (such as northern Africa, the Arabian peninsula, southwestern Africa, central Asia, and much of Australia) experience greater variability than humid areas (such as the eastern United States, northern South America, central Africa, and western Europe).

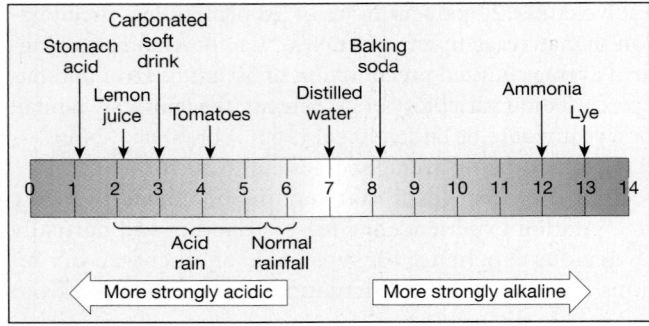

▲ **Figure 6-38** The pH scale. Rainfall in clean air has a pH of about 5.6 (slightly acidic). Acid rain can have a pH as low as 2.0.

United States, the smelting of metal ores in Canada), and nitrogen oxides (NO_x) from motor vehicle exhaust. These and other emissions of sulfur and nitrogen compounds are expelled into the air, where they may drift hundreds or even thousands of kilometers by winds. During this time they may mix with atmospheric moisture to form the sulfuric and nitric acids that are precipitated sooner or later.

Measuring Acidity: Acidity is measured on a *pH scale* based on the relative concentration of hydrogen ions (H^+) (Figure 6-38). The scale ranges from 0 to 14, where the lower end represents extreme *acidity* (battery acid has a pH of 1) and the upper end extreme *alkalinity*. Alkalinity is the opposite of acidity; a substance that is very acidic can also be characterized as being of very low alkalinity, and a highly alkaline substance has very low acidity. The alkaline chemical lye, for instance, has a pH of 13. The pH scale is a logarithmic scale, which means that a difference of one whole number on the scale reflects a 10-fold change in absolute values.

Rainfall in clean, dust-free air has a pH of about 5.6. Thus any precipitation that has a pH value of less than 5.6 is considered to be acid precipitation. Normal rain is slightly acidic (because slight amounts of carbon dioxide

dissolve in raindrops to form *carbonic acid* [H_2CO_3], a mild acid), but acid rain can be as much as 100 times more acidic. Precipitation with a pH of less than 4.5 (the level below which most fish perish) has been recorded in some parts of the United States (Figure 6-39).

Many parts of Earth's surface have naturally alkaline soil or bedrock that neutralizes acid precipitation. Soils developed from limestone, for example, contain calcium carbonate, which can neutralize acid. Granitic soils, on the other hand, have no neutralizing component (Figure 6-40).

Learning Check 6-18 **What are the main sources of acid rain?**

Damage from Acid Precipitation: Acid precipitation is a major hazard to the environment. The most conspicuous damage is being done to aquatic ecosystems. Thousands of lakes and streams are now acidic, and hundreds of lakes in the eastern United States and Canada became biological deserts in recent decades due to acid rain. Forest diebacks have been noted on every continent except Antarctica—in some parts of eastern and central Europe, 30 to 50 percent of the forests have been affected or killed by acid rain. Even buildings and monuments are being damaged or destroyed (Figure 6-41); acid deposition has caused more erosion on the marble Parthenon in Athens in the last 30 years than all forms of erosion over the previous 30 centuries.

One of the great complexities of the situation is that much of the pollution is deposited at great distances from its source. Downwind locations receive unwanted acid deposition from upwind origins. Thus Scandinavians and Germans complain about British pollution; Canadians blame U.S. sources; New Englanders accuse the Midwest.

One of the thorniest issues in North American international relations during the 1980s was Canadian dissatisfaction with U.S. government efforts to mitigate acid rain. Acid

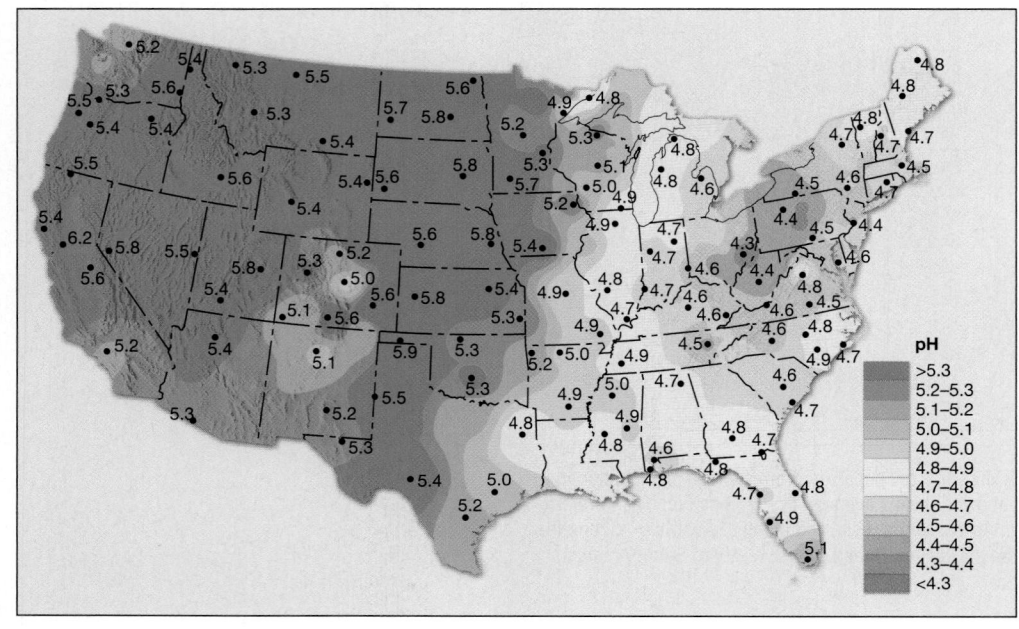

◄ **Figure 6-39** Map showing acidity of rain in the conterminous United States in 2006.

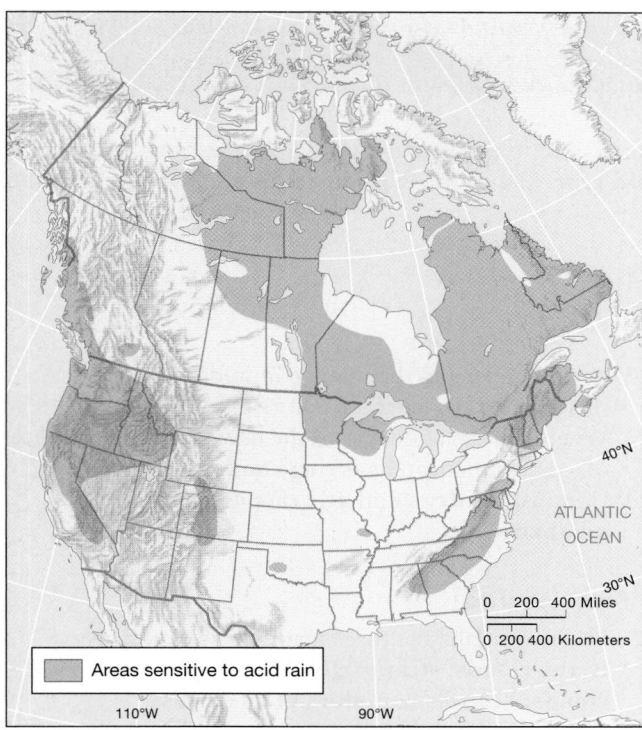

▲ **Figure 6-40** Areas in the United States and Canada particularly sensitive to acid rain because of a scarcity of natural buffers.

rain was viewed by Canadians as a grave environmental concern, and at the time perhaps half the acid rain falling on Canada came from U.S. sources, particularly older coal-burning power plants in the Ohio and Tennessee River valleys.

Action to Reduce Acid Precipitation: In the United States, significant progress toward reducing emissions that cause acid rain has been made since Title IV of the 1990 Clean Air Act Amendments was implemented, creating the Acid Rain Program monitored by the Environmental Protection Agency (EPA). The program requires major reductions in SO_2 and NO_x especially from coal-burning electricity-generating plants that annually produce about 70 percent of SO_2 emissions and 20 percent of NO_x emissions in the United States.

In 1991, Canada and the United States signed the bilateral Air Quality Agreement that addressed the issue of acid rain and transboundary air pollution. In 2000, the United States and Canada signed Annex 3 to the Agreement, with the goal of reducing emission of both NO_x and volatile organic compounds (VOC); in the years that followed, initiatives also addressed reducing particulate matter as well.

These programs have been quite successful: the EPA reports that by 2010, SO_2 emissions in the United States had been reduced to 67 percent of 1990 levels, and NO_x emissions had been reduced by two-thirds. Such reductions in emissions are central to the sustained effort needed to reduce the effects of acid rain.

▶ **Figure 6-41** Damage from acid rain to a statue at Lichfield Cathedral, England.

Chapter **6**	**LEARNING REVIEW**

After studying this chapter, you should be able to answer the following questions. Key terms from each text section are shown in **bold type**. Definitions for key terms are also found in the glossary at the back of the book.

KEY TERMS AND CONCEPTS

The Nature of Water: Commonplace but Unique (*p. 142*)

1. Briefly describe how water moves through the **hydrologic cycle**.
2. What is a **hydrogen bond** between water molecules?
3. Describe what happens to the density of water as it freezes.
4. What is meant by **surface tension** of water?
5. What is **capillarity**?

Phase Changes of Water (*p. 145*)

6. Briefly define the following terms: **evaporation**, **condensation**, **sublimation**.
7. How do phase changes of water entail the exchange of energy? (In other words, explain **latent heat**.)
8. What is meant by the **latent heat of condensation**? **Latent heat of evaporation**?

Water Vapor and Evaporation (*p. 147*)

9. Describe the conditions associated with relatively high rates of evaporation, and the conditions associated with relatively low rates of evaporation.
10. What is meant by the **vapor pressure** of water in the atmosphere?
11. What is **evapotranspiration**?

Measures of Humidity (*p. 148*)

12. What is **absolute humidity**? **Specific humidity**?
13. What is meant by **saturation vapor pressure**?
14. What determines the water vapor **capacity** of air?
15. Describe and explain what is meant when we say that the **relative humidity** of the air is 50 percent.
16. What is the **dew point temperature**?
17. Explain **sensible temperature**.

Condensation (*p. 151*)

18. Under what circumstances can air become **supersaturated**?
19. Explain the role of **condensation nuclei** to the condensation process.
20. What are **supercooled water** droplets?

Adiabatic Processes (*p. 151*)

21. Which cooling process in the atmosphere is responsible for the formation of most clouds (and nearly all clouds that produce precipitation)?

22. What happens to the relative humidity of an unsaturated parcel of air as it rises? Why?
23. What is the relationship of the dew point temperature of a parcel of air to its **lifting condensation level**?
24. Contrast the **dry adiabatic rate** and a **saturated adiabatic rate**.

Clouds (*p. 153*)

25. Briefly describe the three main forms of **clouds**: **cirrus clouds**, **stratus clouds**, and **cumulus clouds**; describe **cumulonimbus** clouds.
26. Identify the four families of clouds.
27. Describe the four principal types of **fog**.
28. How and where does **dew** form?

Atmospheric Stability (*p. 157*)

29. What is the difference between **stable** air and **unstable** air?
30. What conditions make a parcel of air unstable?
31. Are stratus clouds associated with stable or unstable air? Are cumulus clouds associated with stable or unstable air?

Precipitation (*p. 161*)

32. Briefly describe the following kinds of **precipitation**: **rain**, **snow**, **hail**.
33. How is hail related to atmospheric instability?

Atmospheric Lifting and Precipitation (*p. 164*)

34. Describe the four main lifting mechanisms of air: **convective**, **orographic**, **frontal**, and **convergent**.
35. What is a **rain shadow**?

Global Distribution of Precipitation (*p. 167*)

36. What is an **isohyet**?
37. What is meant by the term **precipitation variability**?
38. What is the general relationship of precipitation variability to average annual precipitation?

Acid Rain (*p. 171*)

39. What are some of the circumstances that cause **acid rain**?

STUDY QUESTIONS

1. Why does ice float on liquid water?
2. Why is evaporation a "cooling" process and condensation a "warming" process?
3. What happens to the relative humidity of an unsaturated parcel of air when the temperature decreases? Why?
4. What happens to the relative humidity of an unsaturated parcel of air when the temperature increases? Why?
5. Why does a rising parcel of unsaturated air cool at a greater rate than a rising parcel of saturated air (in which condensation is taking place)?
6. Why can't descending air form clouds?
7. Why does the dew point temperature of an air parcel indicate its actual water vapor content?
8. How can rising stable air become unstable above the lifting condensation level?
9. Explain the role of adiabatic temperature changes, as well as changes in both the relative humidity and the actual water vapor content of the air, in the formation of rain shadows.
10. Using the global map of average annual precipitation (Figure 6-34), explain the causes of
   a. Wet regions within the tropics
   b. Wet regions along the west coasts of continents in the midlatitudes (between about 40 and 60° N and S)
   c. Dry regions along the west coasts of continents in the subtropics (at about 20 to 30° N and S)
   d. Dry areas within the midlatitudes
11. Using the maps of average January and July precipitation (Figure 6-35) contrast and explain the seasonal rainfall patterns in central Africa.

EXERCISES

1. Calculate the relative humidity for the following parcels of air:
   a. If the specific humidity is 5 g/kg and the capacity is 20 g/kg: _____ %
   b. If the specific humidity if 35 g/kg and the capacity is 40 g/kg: _____ %
2. Use Figure 6-8 to estimate the water vapor capacity (the saturation specific humidity in g/kg) of air at the following temperatures:
   a. 0°C (32°F): _____ g/kg
   b. 30°C (86°F): _____ g/kg
3. Using your answers for Exercise Problem 2 above, calculate the relative humidity of the following parcels of air at the temperature given:
   a. If the specific humidity is 3 g/kg at a temperature of 0°C: _____%
   b. If the specific humidity is 3 g/kg at a temperature of 30°C: _____%
4. Assume that a parcel of unsaturated air is at a temperature of 20°C at sea level before it rises up a mountain slope, and that the lifting condensation level of this parcel is 3000 meters:
   a. What is the temperature of this parcel after it has risen to 2000 meters? _____ °C
   b. What is the temperature of this parcel after it has risen to 5000 meters? _____ °C
5. Assume that 1 gram of liquid water is at a temperature of 20°C. How many calories (or joules) of energy must be added for the water to warm to 40°C? _____ calories or _____ joules

Seeing Geographically

Look again at the photograph of the Nevada rainstorm at the beginning of the chapter (p. 140). What kinds of clouds are seen in the distance beyond the mountains? What do the clouds you see and the nature of the rainfall suggest about the most likely lifting mechanism for this rain? How long would you expect this kind of rain to last?

MasteringGeography™

Looking for additional review and test prep materials? Visit the Study Area in MasteringGeography™ to enhance your geographic literacy, spatial reasoning skills, and understanding of this chapter's content by accessing a variety of resources, including geoscience animations, MapMaster interactive maps, videos, *In the News* RSS feeds, flashcards, web links, self-study quizzes, and an eText version of *McKnight's Physical Geography: A Landscape Appreciation* at www.masteringgeography.com.

IN THE PREVIOUS THREE CHAPTERS WE EXPLORED THE

global atmospheric patterns of temperature, pressure, wind, and precipitation. Now we sharpen our focus a bit.

Over most of Earth, particularly in the midlatitudes, day-to-day weather conditions are accompanied by events that are smaller in scale and shorter lived than in the general circulation. These more limited events include air masses, and fronts, as well as a variety of disturbances usually referred to as *storms*. Such disturbances are secondary features of the general circulation of the atmosphere. They move with the general circulation, persisting for a relatively short time before dissipating. Although air masses, fronts, and storms are migrating and temporary, in some parts of the world they are so frequent and dominating that their interactions are major determinants of weather and, to a lesser extent, climate.

As you study this chapter, think about these key questions:

- **What are air masses, and where and how do they develop?**
- **How do fronts form and what happens as they move?**
- **What are midlatitude cyclones and what explains the weather associated with them?**
- **What are midlatitude anticyclones?**
- **What is an easterly wave?**
- **How do hurricanes form, move, and cause damage?**
- **How do thunderstorms and tornadoes form?**

The Impact of Storms on the Landscape

Storms are usually very dramatic atmospheric events. The combination of expansive clouds, swirling winds, and abundant precipitation—often accompanied by thunder and lightning—that characterizes many storms makes us acutely aware of the power usually hidden in the atmosphere we inhabit.

The landscape may be quickly and significantly transformed by a storm—flooded streets, windblown trees, and darkened skies are prominent examples of the changes that occur. The long-run impact of storms on the landscape is often equally notable. Damage varies with the intensity of the disturbance, but such things as uprooted trees, accelerated erosion, flooded valleys, destroyed buildings, and decimated crops can result. Most storms also have a positive long-term effect on the landscape, however, as they promote diversity in the vegetative cover, increase the size of lakes and ponds, and stimulate plant growth through the moisture they add to the ground.

This tornado in Ellis County, Oklahoma, was one of several that touched down in the area on May 4, 2007. Look carefully at the tornado extending down from the cloud base. Describe what you see. Does the composition of the tornado appear to be the same from the cloud base all of the way down to the ground?

AIR MASSES

Although the troposphere is a continuous body of mixed gases that surrounds the planet, it is by no means a uniform blanket of air. Instead, it is composed of many large parcels of air that are distinct from one another. Such large parcels are referred to as **air masses**.

Characteristics

To be recognized as a distinct air mass, a parcel of air must meet three requirements:

1. It must be large. A typical air mass is more than 1600 kilometers (1000 miles) across and several kilometers deep (from Earth's surface to the top of the air mass).
2. It must have uniform properties in the horizontal dimension. This means that at any given altitude in the air mass, its physical characteristics—primarily temperature, humidity, and stability—are relatively homogeneous.
3. It must travel as a unit. It must be distinct from the surrounding air, and when it moves it must retain its original characteristics and not be torn apart by differences in airflow.

Origin

An air mass develops its characteristics when it stagnates or remains over a uniform land or sea surface long enough to acquire the temperature/humidity/stability characteristics of the surface below. This stagnation needs to last for only a few days if the underlying surface has prominent temperature and moisture characteristics. Stable air is more likely to remain stagnant for a few days than unstable air, so regions with anticyclonic (high pressure) conditions commonly form air masses.

Source Regions: The formation of air masses is usually associated with what are called *source regions*: regions of Earth's surface that are particularly well suited to generate air masses. Such regions must be extensive, physically uniform, and associated with air that is stationary or anticyclonic. Ideal source regions are ocean surfaces and extensive flat land areas that have a uniform covering of snow, forest, or desert. Air masses rarely form over the irregular terrain of mountain ranges.

Figure 7-1 portrays the principal recognized source regions for air masses that affect North America. Warm air masses can form in any season over the waters of the southern North Atlantic, the Gulf of Mexico/Caribbean Sea, and the southern North Pacific, and in summer, they can form over the deserts of the southwestern United States and northwestern Mexico. Cold air masses develop over the northern portions of the Atlantic and Pacific Oceans and over the snow-covered lands of north-central Canada.

It may well be that the concept of source regions is of more theoretical value than actual value. A broader view, one subscribed to by many atmospheric scientists, holds that air masses can originate almost anywhere in the low or high latitudes but rarely in the midlatitudes due to the

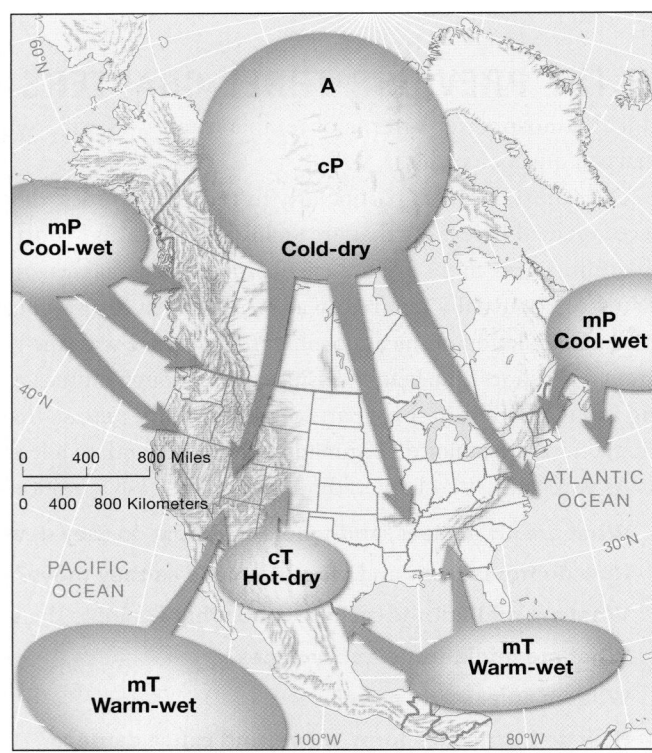

▲ **Figure 7-1** Major air masses that affect North America and their generalized paths. The tropics and subtropics are important source regions as are the high latitudes. Air masses do not originate in the middle latitudes except under unusual circumstances. (For an explanation of the air-mass codes A, cP, mP, cT, and mT, see Table 7-1.)

prevailing westerlies where persistent wind would prevent air mass formation.

Classification

Air masses are classified on the basis of source region. The latitude of the source region correlates directly with the temperature of the air mass, and the nature of the surface strongly influences the humidity content of the air mass. Thus, a low-latitude air mass is warm or hot; a high-latitude one is cool or cold. If the air mass develops over a continental surface, it is likely to be dry; if it originates over an ocean, it is usually moist.

A one- or two-letter code is generally used to identify air masses. Although some authorities recognize other categories, the basic classification is sixfold, as shown in Table 7-1.

> **Learning Check 7-1** **How do air masses form?**
> (Answer on p. AK-2)

Movement and Modification

Some air masses remain in their source region for long periods, even indefinitely. In such cases, the weather associated with the air mass persists with little variation. Our interest, however, is in masses that leave their source region and move into other regions, particularly into the midlatitudes.

When an air mass departs from its source region, its structure begins to change. This change is due in part to thermal modification (warming or cooling from below), in

TABLE 7-1	Simplified Classification of Air Masses		
Type	**Code**	**Source Regions**	**Source Region Properties**
Arctic/Antarctic	A	Antarctica, Arctic Ocean and fringes, and Greenland	Very cold, very dry, very stable
Continental polar	cP	High-latitude plains of Eurasia and North America	Cold, dry, very stable
Maritime polar	mP	Oceans in vicinity of 50°–60° N and S latitude	Cold, moist, relatively unstable
Continental tropical	cT	Low-latitude deserts	Hot, very dry, unstable
Maritime tropical	mT	Tropical and subtropical oceans	Warm, moist, of variable stability
Equatorial	E	Oceans near the equator	Warm, very moist, unstable

part to dynamic modification (uplift, subsidence, convergence, turbulence), and perhaps also in part to addition or subtraction of moisture.

Once it leaves its source area, an air mass modifies the weather of the regions into which it moves: it takes source-region characteristics into other regions. A classic example of this modification is displayed in Figure 7-2, which diagrams a situation that may occur one or more times every winter. A midwinter outburst of continental polar (cP) air from northern Canada sweeps down across the central part of North America. With a source-region temperature of –46°C (–50°F) around Great Slave Lake, the air mass has warmed to –34°C (–30°F) by the time it reaches Winnipeg, Manitoba, and it continues to warm as it moves southward. Throughout its southward course, the air mass becomes warmer, but it also brings some of the coldest weather that each of these places will receive all

winter. Thus, the air mass is modified, but it also modifies the weather in all regions it passes through.

Temperature, of course, is only one of the characteristics modified by a moving air mass. There are also modifications in humidity and stability.

North American Air Masses

The North American continent is a prominent area of air mass interaction. The lack of mountains trending east to west permits polar air to sweep southward and tropical air to flow northward unhindered by terrain, particularly over the eastern two-thirds of the continent (see Figure 7-1). In the western part of the continent, though, air masses moving off the Pacific are impeded by the prominent north–south trending mountain ranges.

Continental polar (cP) air masses develop in central and northern Canada, and *Arctic* (A) air masses originate farther north and so are colder and drier than cP air masses—both are dominant features in winter with their cold, dry, stable nature.

Maritime polar (mP) air from the Pacific in winter can bring cloudiness and heavy precipitation to the mountainous west coastal regions. In summer, cool Pacific mP air produces fog and low stratus clouds along the coast. North Atlantic mP air masses are also cool, moist, and unstable, but except for occasional incursions into the mid-Atlantic coastal region, Atlantic mP air does not affect North America because the prevailing circulation of the atmosphere is westerly.

Maritime tropical (mT) air from the Atlantic/Caribbean/Gulf of Mexico is warm, moist, and unstable. It strongly influences weather and climate east of the Rockies in the United States, southern Canada, and much of Mexico, serving as the principal precipitation source in this broad region. It is more prevalent in summer than in winter, bringing periods of uncomfortable humid heat.

Pacific mT air originates over water in areas of anticyclonic subsidence, and so it tends to be cooler, drier, and more stable than Atlantic mT air; it is felt only in the southwestern United States and northwestern Mexico, where it may produce coastal fog and moderate orographic rainfall where forced to ascend mountain slopes. It is also the source of some summer rains in the southwestern interior.

Continental tropical (cT) air is relatively unimportant in North America because its source region is not extensive. In summer, hot, very dry, unstable cT air surges into

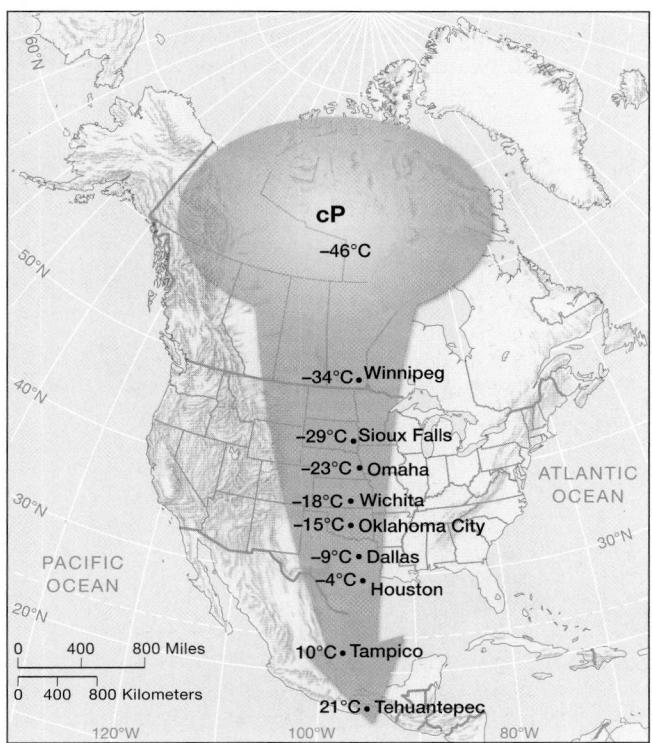

▲ **Figure 7-2** An example of temperatures resulting from a strong midwinter outburst of cP air from Canada. All temperatures are in degrees Celsius.

the southern Great Plains area on occasion, bringing heat waves and dry conditions.

Equatorial (E) air affects North America only in association with hurricanes. It is similar to mT air except that E air provides an even more copious source of rain than does mT air because of high humidity and instability.

> **Learning Check 7-2** **Describe and explain the temperature and moisture characteristics of a maritime polar (mP) air mass.**

FRONTS

When unlike air masses meet, they do not mix readily; instead, a boundary zone called a **front** develops between them. A front is not a simple two-dimensional boundary. A typical front is a narrow three-dimensional transition zone several kilometers or even tens of kilometers wide. Within this zone, the properties of the air change rapidly.

The frontal concept was developed by Norwegian meteorologists during World War I, and the term *front* was coined because these scientists considered the clash between unlike air masses to be analogous to a confrontation between opposing armies along a battle front. As the more "aggressive" air mass advances at the expense of the other, some mixing of the two occurs within the frontal zone, but for the most part the air masses retain their separate identities as one is displaced by the other.

Types of Fronts: The most conspicuous difference between air masses is usually temperature. A **cold front** forms where an advancing cold air mass meets and displaces warmer air (Figure 7-3), whereas a **warm front** forms where an advancing warm air mass meets colder air (Figure 7-4). In both cases, there is warm air on one side of the front and cool air on the

other, with a fairly abrupt temperature gradient between. Air masses may also have different densities, humidity levels, wind patterns, and stability, and so these factors can have a steep gradient through the front as well.

In some cases, a front may remain stationary for a few hours or even a few days. More commonly, however, a front is in more or less constant motion. Usually one air mass is displacing the other; thus, the front advances in the direction dictated by the movement of the more active air mass.

Regardless of which air mass is advancing, it is always the warmer air that rises over the cooler. The warmer, lighter air is inevitably forced aloft, and the cooler, denser air mass functions as a wedge over which the lifting occurs. As you can see in Figures 7-3 and 7-4, fronts "lean" or slope upward from the surface, and it is along this slope that the warmer air rises and cools adiabatically to form clouds and often precipitation. Indeed, fronts lean so much that they are much closer to horizontal features than vertical ones. The slope of a typical front averages about 1:150, meaning that 150 kilometers away from the surface position of the front, the height of the front is only 1 kilometer above the ground. Because of this very low angle of slope (less than 1°), the steepness shown in most diagrams of fronts is greatly exaggerated.

Notice that the "leading edge" of a cold front precedes its higher altitude "trailing edge," whereas a warm front leans "forward" so that the higher altitude part of the front is ahead of its lower altitude "trailing edge."

Cold Fronts

Because of friction with the ground, the advance of the lower portion of a cold air mass is slowed relative to the upper portion. As a result, a cold front tends to become steeper as it moves forward and usually develops a

Animation
Cold Fronts

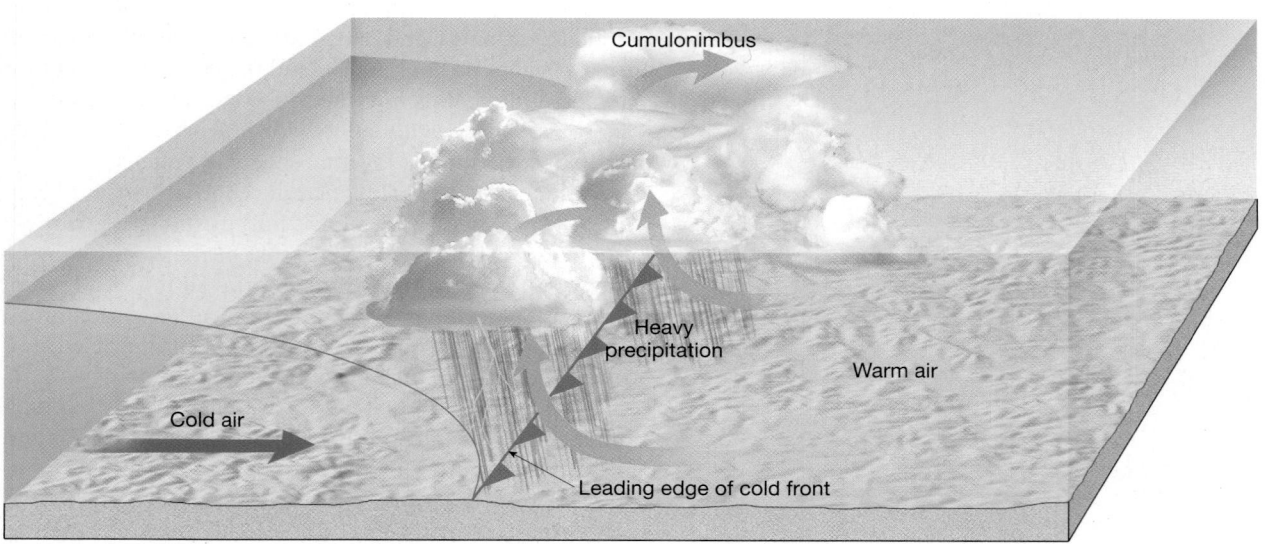

▲ **Figure 7-3** A cold front forms when a cold air mass is actively underriding a warm air mass. As a cold front advances, the warm air ahead of it is forced upward. This displacement often creates cloudiness and relatively heavy precipitation along and immediately behind the ground-level position of the front. (In this diagram, the vertical scale has been exaggerated.)

Cumulonimbus

Heavy precipitation

Warm air

Cold air

Leading edge of cold front

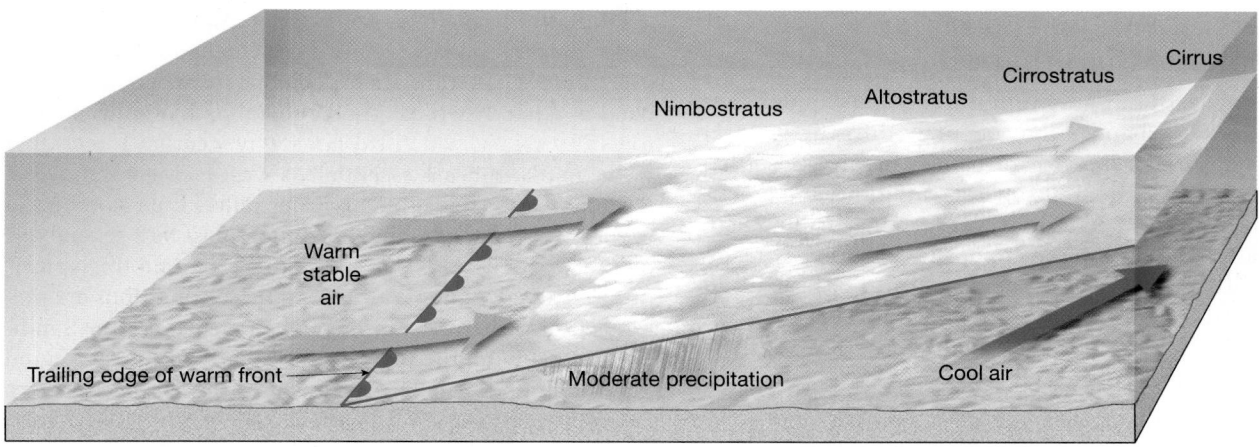

▲ **Figure 7-4** A warm front forms when a warm air mass is actively overriding a cold air mass. As warm air rises above cooler air, widespread cloudiness and precipitation develop along and in advance of the ground-level position of the front. Higher and less dense clouds are often dozens or hundreds of kilometers ahead of the ground-level position of the front. (In this diagram, the vertical scale has been exaggerated.)

protruding "nose" a few hundred meters above the ground (see Figure 7-3). The average cold front is twice as steep as the average warm front. Moreover, cold fronts normally move faster than warm fronts because the dense, cold air mass easily displaces the lighter, warm air.

This combination of steeper slope and faster advance leads to rapid lifting and adiabatic cooling of the warm air ahead of the cold front. The rapid lifting often makes the warm air very unstable, and the result is blustery and violent weather along the cold front. Vertically developed clouds, such as cumulonimbus clouds, are common, with considerable turbulence and showery precipitation. Both clouds and precipitation tend to be concentrated along and immediately behind the ground-level position of the front. Precipitation is usually of higher intensity but shorter duration than that associated with a warm front.

On a weather map, the ground-level position of a cold front is shown either by a blue line or a solid line studded at intervals with solid triangles that extend in the direction toward which the front is moving (Figure 7-5).

Warm Fronts

The slope of a typical warm front is more gentle than that of a cold front, averaging about 1:200 (see Figure 7-4). As the warm air pushes against and rises over the retreating cold air, it cools adiabatically, usually resulting in clouds and precipitation. Because

Animation
Warm Fronts

the frontal uplift is very gradual, clouds form slowly and turbulence is limited. High-flying cirrus clouds may signal the approaching front many hours before it arrives. As the front comes closer, the clouds become lower, thicker, and more extensive, typically developing into altocumulus or altostratus. Precipitation usually occurs broadly; it is likely to be protracted and gentle, without much convective activity. If the rising air is inherently unstable, however, precipitation can be showery and even violent. Most precipitation falls ahead of the ground-level position of the moving front.

The ground-level position of a warm front is portrayed on a weather map either by a red line or by a solid line along which solid semicircles are located at regular intervals, with the semicircles extending in the direction toward which the front is moving (see Figure 7-5).

Learning Check 7-3   **What is the difference between a cold front and a warm front?**

Stationary Fronts

When neither air mass displaces the other—or if a cold front or warm front "stalls"—their common boundary is called a **stationary front**. It is difficult to generalize about the weather along such a front, but often gently rising warm air produces limited precipitation similar to that along a warm front. As Figure 7-5 shows, stationary fronts are portrayed on a weather map by a combination of warm and cold front symbols, alternating on opposite sides of the line—cold air is opposite the triangles, and warm air opposite the half circles.

Occluded Fronts

A fourth type of front, called an *occluded front*, is formed when a cold front overtakes a warm front. Occluded fronts are shown on a weather map by a combination of warm and cold front symbols, alternating on the same side of the line. The development of occluded fronts is discussed later in this chapter.

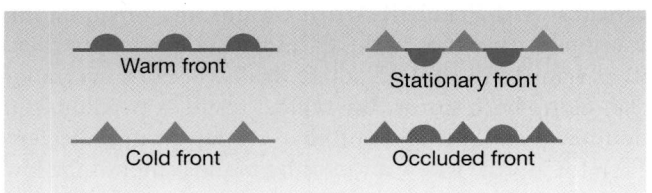

Warm front

Stationary front

Cold front

Occluded front

▲ **Figure 7-5** Weather map symbols for fronts.

Air Masses, Fronts, and Major Atmospheric Disturbances

We will now turn our attention to the major kinds of atmospheric disturbances that occur within the general circulation. Most of these disturbances involve unsettled and sometimes violent atmospheric conditions and are referred to as *storms*. Some, however, produce calm, clear, quiet weather that is quite the opposite of stormy. Some of these disturbances involve air mass contrasts or fronts, and many are associated with migrating pressure cells.

The following are common characteristics of atmospheric disturbances in general:

- They are smaller than the components of the general circulation, although they are extremely variable in size.
- They are migratory.
- They have a relatively brief duration, persisting for only a few minutes, a few hours, or a few days.
- They produce characteristic and relatively predictable weather conditions.

Midlatitude Disturbances: The midlatitudes are the principal "battleground" of tropospheric phenomena: where polar and tropical air masses meet, where most fronts occur, and where weather is most dynamic and changeable from season to season and from day to day. Many kinds of atmospheric disturbances are associated with the midlatitudes, but two of these—*midlatitude cyclones* and *midlatitude anticyclones*—are much more important than the others because of their size and prevalence.

Tropical Disturbances: The low latitudes are characterized by monotony—the same weather day after day, week after week, month after month. Almost the only breaks are provided by transient atmospheric disturbances, of which by far the most significant are *tropical cyclones* (locally known as *hurricanes* when they intensify), but also less dramatic disturbances known as *easterly waves*.

Localized Severe Weather: Other localized atmospheric disturbances occur in many parts of the world. Short-lived but sometimes severe atmospheric disturbances such as *thunderstorms* and *tornadoes* often develop in conjunction with other kinds of storms.

MIDLATITUDE CYCLONES

Probably most significant of all atmospheric disturbances are **midlatitude cyclones**. Throughout the midlatitudes, they dominate weather maps, are basically responsible for most day-to-day weather changes, and bring precipitation to much of the populated portions of the planet. Consisting of large, migratory low-pressure cells, they are usually called *depressions* in Europe and *lows* or *low pressure systems*, *wave cyclones*, *extratropical cyclones*, or even simply (although not very precisely) as "storms" in the United States.

Midlatitude cyclones are associated primarily with air-mass convergence in regions between about 30° and 70° of latitude. Thus, they are found almost entirely within the band of westerly winds. Their general path of movement is toward the east, which explains why weather forecasting in the midlatitudes is essentially a west-facing vocation.

Because each midlatitude cyclone differs from all others in greater or lesser detail, any description must be a general one only. The discussions that follow, then, pertain to "typical" or idealized conditions. Moreover, these conditions are presented as Northern Hemisphere phenomena. For the Southern Hemisphere, the patterns of isobars, fronts, and wind flow should be visualized as mirror images of the Northern Hemisphere patterns (see Figure 7-13).

Characteristics

A typical mature midlatitude cyclone has a diameter of 1600 kilometers (1000 miles) or so. It is essentially a vast cell of low-pressure air, with ground-level pressure in the center typically between 990 and 1000 millibars. The system (shown by closed isobars on a weather map, as in Figure 7-6a) usually tends toward an oval shape, with the long axis trending northeast–southwest. Usually a clear-cut pressure trough extends southwesterly from the center.

Formation of Fronts: Midlatitude cyclones have a converging counterclockwise circulation pattern in the Northern Hemisphere. This wind flow pattern brings together cool air from the north and warm air from the south. The convergence of these unlike air masses characteristically creates two fronts: a cold front that extends to the southwest from the center of the cyclone and runs along the pressure trough extending from the center of the storm, and a warm front extending eastward from the center and running along another, usually weaker, pressure trough.

Sectors: The two fronts divide the cyclone into a *cool sector* north and west of the center where the cold air mass is in contact with the ground, and a *warm sector* to the south and east where the warm air mass is in contact with the ground. At the surface, the cool sector is the larger of the two, but aloft the warm sector is more extensive. This size relationship exists because both fronts "lean" over the cool air. Thus, the cold front slopes upward toward the northwest and the warm front slopes upward toward the northeast, as Figure 7-6b shows.

Learning Check 7-4 What causes fronts to develop within a midlatitude cyclone?

Clouds and Precipitation: Clouds and precipitation develop in the zones within a midlatitude cyclone where air is rising and cooling adiabatically. Because warm air rises along both fronts, the typical result is two zones of cloudiness and precipitation that overlap around the center of the storm (where air is rising in the center of the low pressure cell) and extend outward in the general direction of the fronts.

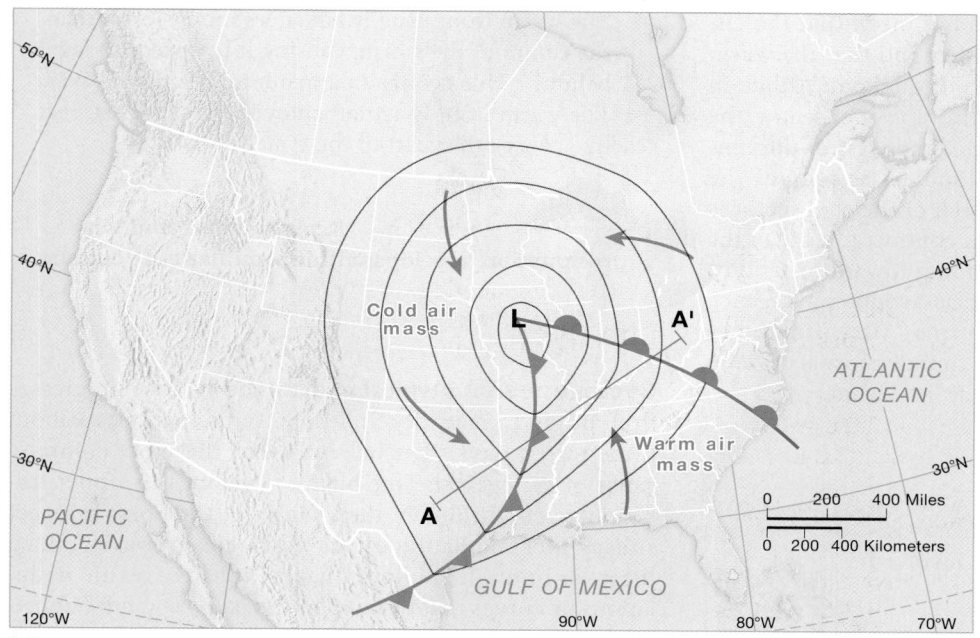

(a)

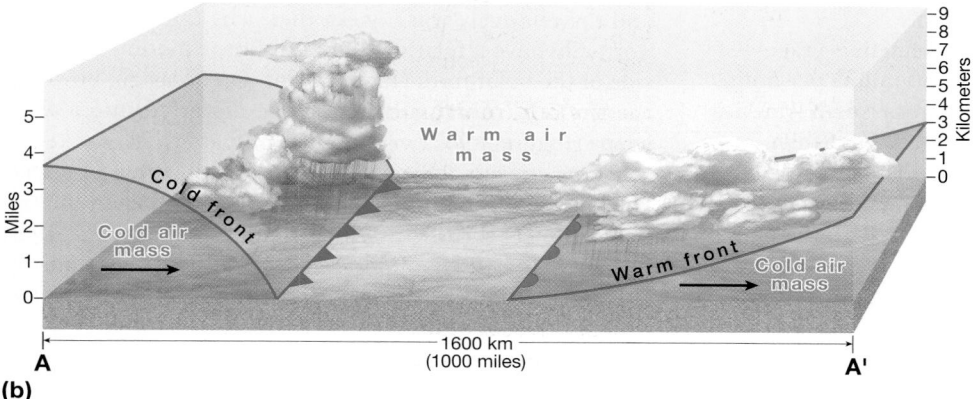

(b)

◀ **Figure 7-6** A map (a) and a cross section (b) of a typical mature midlatitude cyclone. In the Northern Hemisphere, there is usually a cold front trailing to the southwest and a warm front extending toward the east. A well-developed trough of low pressure usually accompanies the surface position of the cold front. Arrows in (b) indicate the direction of frontal movement.

Along and immediately behind the ground-level position of the cold front (the steeper of the two fronts), a band of cumuliform clouds usually yields showery precipitation. The air rising more gently along the more gradual slope of the warm front produces a more extensive expanse of horizontally developed clouds, perhaps with widespread, protracted, low-intensity precipitation (Figure 7-7). In both cases, most of the precipitation originates in the warm air rising above the fronts and falls down through the front to reach the ground in the cool sector.

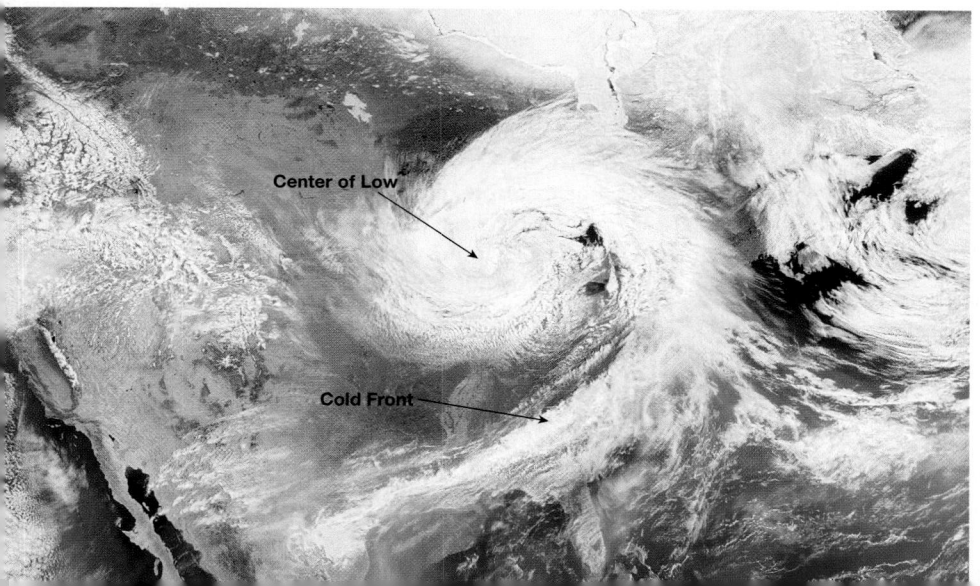

◀ **Figure 7-7** A large midlatitude cyclone centered near Lake Michigan. The band of clouds extending down across the southern states to the west marks the cold front.

This precipitation pattern does not mean that the entire cool sector has unsettled weather and that the warm sector experiences clear conditions throughout. Although most frontal precipitation falls within the cool sector, the general area to the north, northwest, and west of the center of the cyclone is frequently cloudless as soon as the cold front has moved on. Thus, much of the cool sector is typified by clear, cold, stable air. In contrast, the air of the warm sector is often moist and tending toward instability, and so thermal convection and surface-wind convergence may produce sporadic thunderstorms. Also, sometimes one or more *squall lines* of intense thunderstorms develop in the warm sector in advance of the cold front.

Movements

Midlatitude cyclones are essentially transient features, on the move throughout their existence. Four kinds of movement are involved (Figure 7-8):

1. The whole storm moves as a major disturbance in the westerlies, traversing the midlatitudes generally from west to east. The rate of movement averages 30 to 45 kilometers (about 20 to 30 miles) per hour, which means that the storm can cross North America in three to four days (often faster in winter than in summer). The route of a cyclone is likely to be undulating and erratic, although it moves generally from west to east, often in association with the path of the jet stream.
2. The system has a cyclonic wind circulation, with wind generally converging counterclockwise (in the Northern Hemisphere) into the center of the storm from all sides.
3. The cold front usually advances faster than the center of the storm (the advancing dense, cold air easily displaces the lighter, warm air ahead of the front).

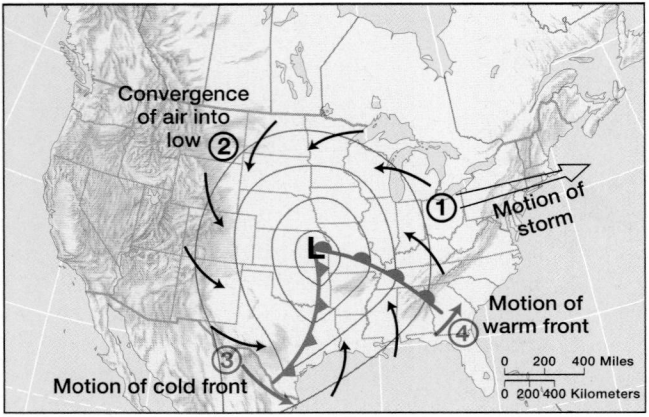

▲ **Figure 7-8** Four components of movement occur in a typical midlatitude cyclone: (1) The entire storm moves west to east in the general flow of the westerlies; (2) airflow is cyclonic converging counterclockwise; (3) the cold front advances; (4) the warm front advances.

4. The warm front usually advances more slowly than the center of the storm, causing it to appear to lag behind. (This is only an apparent motion, however. The warm front is actually moving west to east, just like every other part of the system.)

Learning Check 7-5 **Explain where and why precipitation develops within a midlatitude cyclone.**

Life Cycle

Cyclogenesis: A typical midlatitude cyclone progresses from origin to maturity, and then to dissipation, in about three to ten days. It is believed that the most common cause of *cyclogenesis* (the birth of cyclones) is upper troposphere conditions in the vicinity of the polar front jet stream. Most midlatitude cyclones begin as "waves" along the polar front. Recall from Chapter 5 that waves are undulations or curves that develop in the paths taken by upper-level winds such as a jet stream, and that the polar front is the contact zone between the relatively cold polar easterlies and the relatively warm westerlies. The opposing airflows normally have a relatively smooth linear motion on either side of the polar front (Figure 7-9a). On occasion, however, the smooth frontal surface may be distorted into a wave shape (Figure 7-9b).

There appears to be a close relationship between upper-level airflow and ground-level disturbances. When the upper airflow is *zonal*—by which we mean relatively straight from west to east—ground-level cyclonic activity is unlikely. When winds aloft begin to meander north to south in a *meridional airflow* (Figure 7-10), large waves of alternating pressure troughs and ridges are formed and cyclonic activity at ground level is intensified. Most midlatitude cyclones are centered below the polar front jet stream axis and downstream from an upper-level pressure trough.

A cyclone is unlikely to develop at ground level unless there is divergence above it. In other words, the convergence of air near the ground must be supported by divergence aloft. Such divergence can be related to changes in either speed or direction of the wind flow, but it nearly always involves broad north-to-south meanders in the Rossby waves and the jet stream.

Various ground factors—such as topographic irregularities, temperature contrasts between sea and land, or the influence of ocean currents—can apparently initiate a wave along the front. For example, cyclogenesis also occurs on the leeward side of mountains. A low-pressure area drifting with the westerlies becomes weaker when it crosses a mountain range. As it ascends the range, the column of air compresses and spreads, slowing down its counterclockwise spin. When descending the leeward side, the air column stretches vertically and contracts horizontally. This change in shape causes it to spin faster and may initiate cyclonic development even if it were not a full-fledged cyclone before.

This chain of events happens with some frequency in winter on the eastern flanks of the Rocky Mountains,

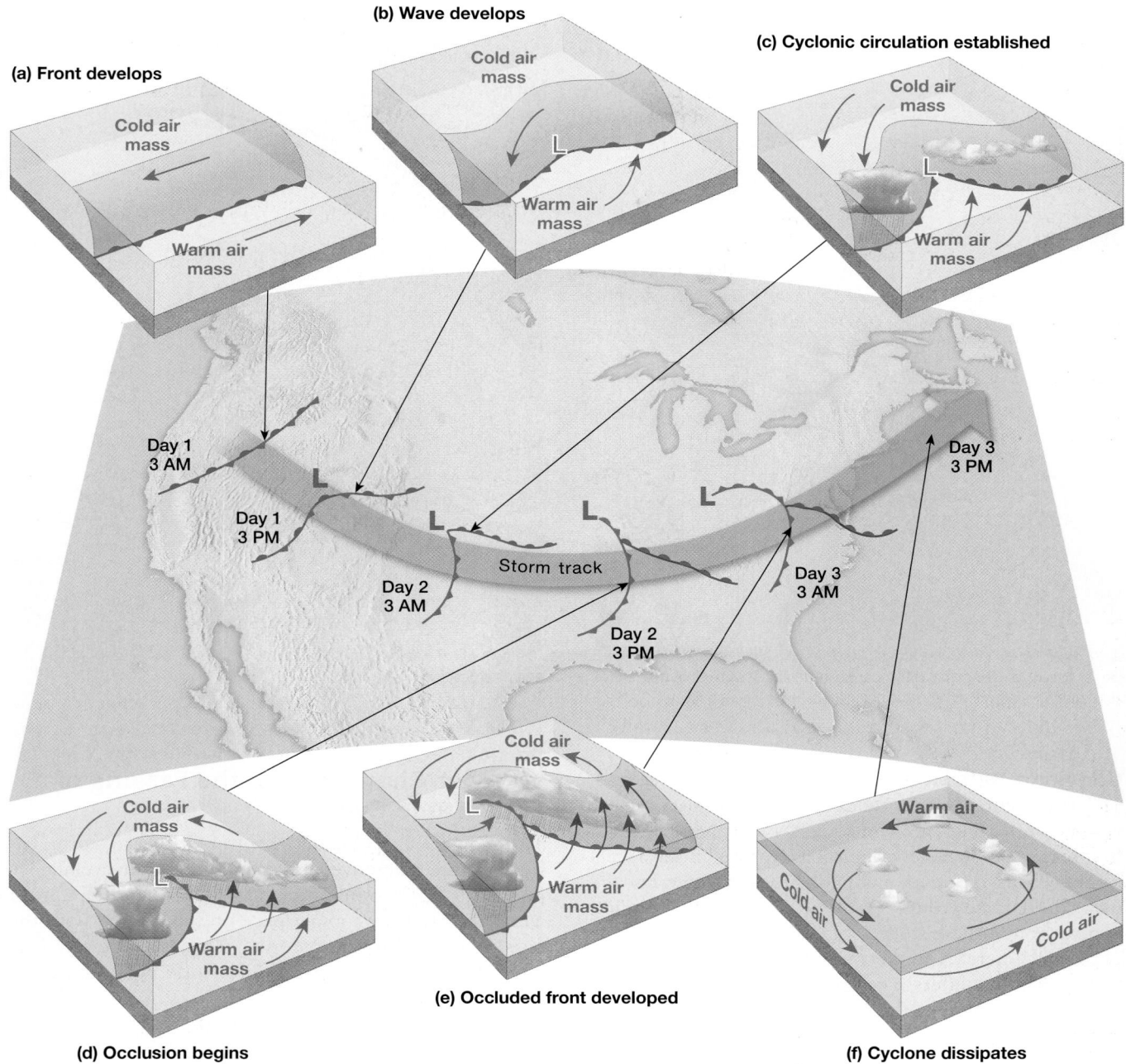

(a) Front develops

Cold air mass

Warm air mass

(b) Wave develops

Cold air mass

L

Warm air mass

(c) Cyclonic circulation established

Cold air mass

L

Warm air mass

Day 1
3 AM

L

Day 1
3 PM

L

Day 2
3 AM

Storm track

L

Day 2
3 PM

L

Day 3
3 AM

Day 3
3 PM

(d) Occlusion begins

Cold air mass

L

Warm air mass

(e) Occluded front developed

Cold air mass

L

Warm air mass

(f) Cyclone dissipates

Warm air

Cold air

Cold air

▲ **Figure 7-9** Schematic representation of the life cycle of a midlatitude cyclone passing over North America during a three-day period. (a) Front develops between unlike air masses. (b) Wave appears along front. (c) Cyclonic circulation is well developed around a low. (d) Occlusion begins. (e) Occluded front is fully developed. (f) Cyclone dissipates after all warm surface air has been lifted and cooled.

particularly in Colorado, and with lesser frequency on the eastern side of the Appalachian Mountains, in North Carolina and Virginia. Cyclones formed in this way typically move toward the east and northeast and often bring heavy rain or snowstorms to the northeastern United States and southeastern Canada.

Occlusion: Ultimately, the storm dissipates because the cold front overtakes the warm front. As the two fronts come closer and closer together (Figure 7-9c–e), the warm sector at the ground is increasingly displaced, forcing more and

more warm air aloft. When the cold front catches up with the warm front, warm air is no longer in contact with Earth's surface and an **occluded front** is formed (Figure 7-11).

This **occlusion** process usually results in a short period of intensified precipitation and wind until eventually all the warm sector is forced aloft and the ground-level low-pressure center is surrounded on all sides by cool air, a stable condition. This sequence of events weakens the pressure gradient and shuts off the storm's energy and air lifting mechanism—and so its cloud-producing mechanism—and the storm dies out (Figure 7-9f).

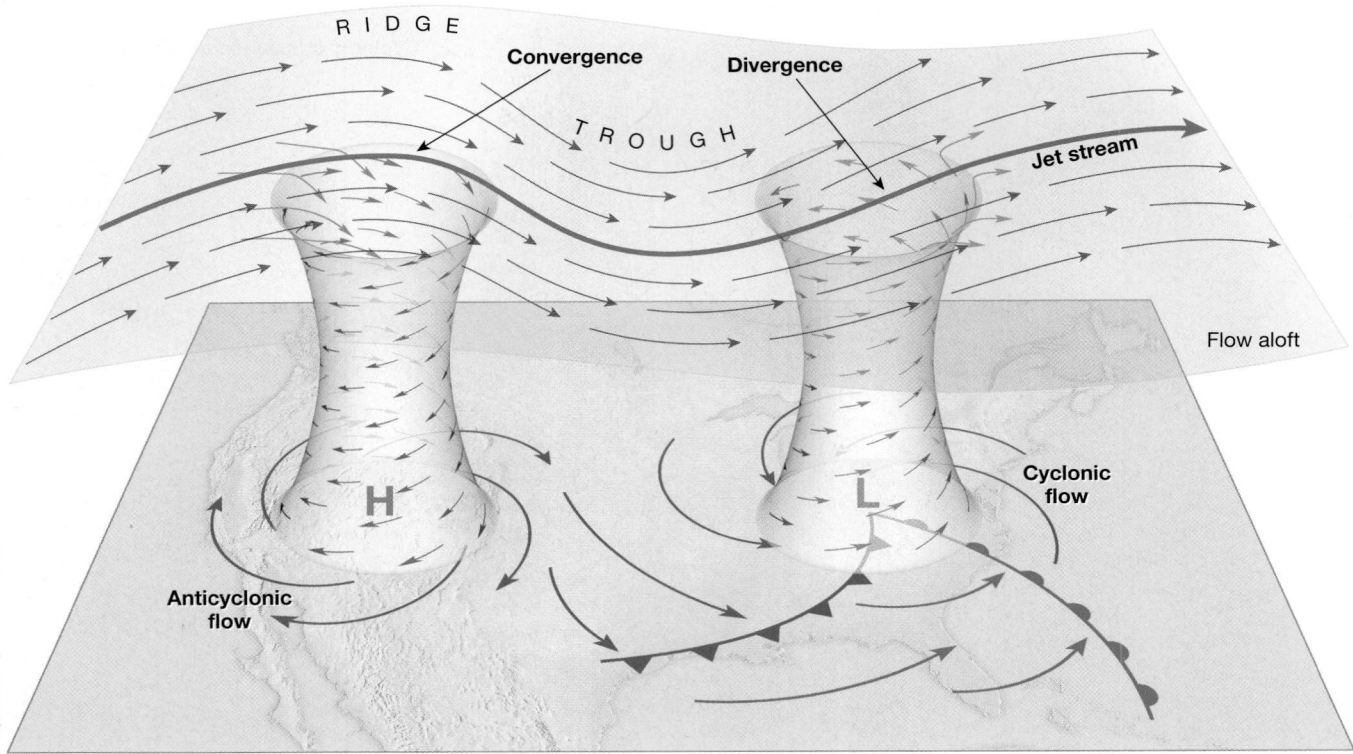

▲ **Figure 7-10** A typical winter situation in which the upper-level airflow, such as the path of the jet stream, is meridional (meandering north and south). Note how convergence and divergence aloft support anticyclonic and cyclonic circulation at ground level.

Conveyor Belt Model of Midlatitude Cyclones: The description of midlatitude cyclones we've just provided is sometimes called the "Norwegian" model because it was first presented by meteorologists in Norway in the 1920s. Although this explanation of midlatitude cyclones remains useful today, new data has provided a more complete explanation of these storms, especially air flow in the upper troposphere. A modern model, called the *conveyor belt model*, now offers a better explanation of the three-dimensional aspects of these storms—see the box, "Focus: Conveyor Belt Model of Midlatitude Cyclones."

> **Learning Check 7-6**   **Describe the process that forms an occluded front.**

Weather Changes with the Passing of a Midlatitude Cyclone

Although the exact details vary from storm to storm, basic structure and movements of a midlatitude cyclone we just described can help us understand the often abrupt weather changes we experience on the ground with the passing of one of these storms. This is especially true when the cold front of a midlatitude cyclone passes through in winter.

For example, imagine we're in the warm sector of a midlatitude cyclone—the situation just before the cold front moves through (see Figure 7-6). Remember, the whole storm is moving from west to east and so the cold front is moving closer to us hour by hour. When the

▶ **Figure 7-11** An occluded front develops when the leading edge of a cold front catches up with the trailing edge of a warm front, lifting all of the warm air off the ground. Once lifted, the warm air is much cooler than before.

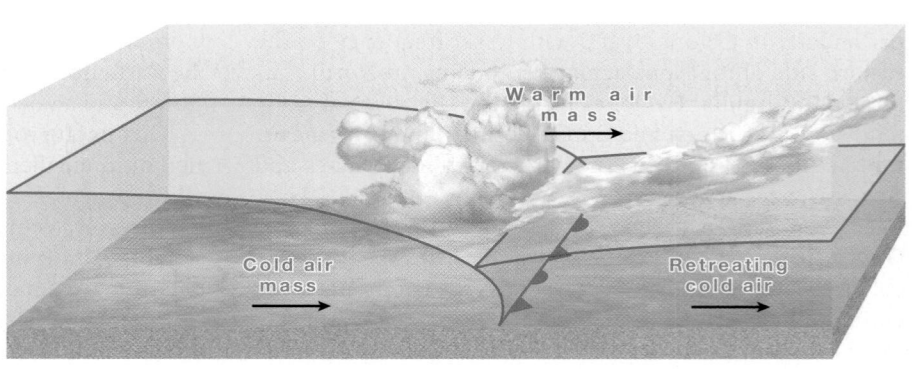

Conveyor Belt Model of Midlatitude Cyclones

▶ Ted Eckmann, Bowling Green State University

Satellite and weather balloon measurements have revealed that midlatitude cyclones involve more than just surface fronts and a low-pressure center; they also tend to include several well-defined channels of air called "conveyor belts" (Figure 7-A). Our discussion uses examples from the Northern Hemisphere, but the conveyor belt model fits many midlatitude cyclones in the Southern Hemisphere as well. The conveyor belt model has improved understanding of midlatitude cyclones and forecasting of their effects by explaining interactions between surface and upper-level winds.

The Warm Conveyor Belt: The midlatitude cyclone's surface low draws air northward from the southeastern portion of the cyclone. The air to the southeast tends to be warm and moist because those are characteristics of the air mass where it originates. A *warm conveyor belt* develops from this air, which starts at the surface, but eventually rises up and over the cooler air to the north of the warm front, because air in the warm conveyor belt is less dense. As the warm conveyor belt reaches higher altitudes, it can turn eastward by joining the prevailing westerly winds of the upper troposphere, as shown in Figure 7-A.

North of the warm front, the warm conveyor belt produces mostly stratus-type clouds because the air is only rising gradually. These stratus-type clouds tend to produce light but steady precipitation over a large area. However, the warm conveyor belt also delivers plenty of moisture to the area just ahead of the cold front. The cold front then lifts this air rapidly to form convective clouds like cumulonimbus. These clouds produce showers that are more intense, but also more sporadic, than those from the stratus-type clouds north of the warm front.

The Cold Conveyor Belt: Just north of the warm front, cooler, drier surface air moves westward towards the cyclone's central low, forming the *cold conveyor belt*. Like the warm conveyor belt, some of this cold air can rise to merge with the general westerly flow at upper levels, as shown in Figure 7-A. However, the cold conveyor belt can also split, with the rest of the air turning cyclonically and rising as it moves

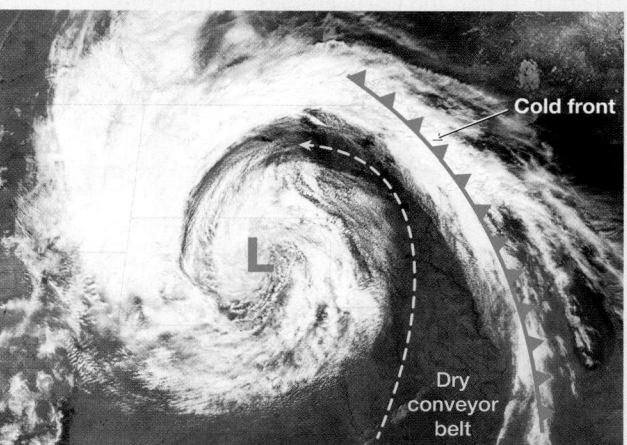

▲ **Figure 7-B** As the dry conveyor belt spirals towards the low-pressure center of this midlatitude cyclone, it produces a dry slot behind the cold front that has significantly less cloud cover than the adjacent areas where the other two conveyor belts are producing thick clouds and precipitation.

toward the low-pressure center. In winter, this often produces the midlatitude cyclone's heaviest snowfall just northwest of the low because it delivers two key ingredients for intense snow: cold air at the surface with rising air above. While the cold conveyor belt starts out relatively dry, it can gain moisture as precipitation falls into it from the warm conveyor belt above, and thus be moist enough to support significant snow by the time it reaches the area northwest of the low.

The Dry Conveyor Belt: On the western side of a typical midlatitude cyclone, convergence in the upper troposphere produces descending air, some of which swirls counterclockwise into the cyclone's low, forming the *dry conveyor belt*. This air from the upper troposphere is much drier than the air in the other conveyor belts because it is farther from the surface and thus farther from sources of moisture. Few clouds, if any, can form in this dry air, which often produces a "dry slot" of air just behind the cold front that is lacking in clouds compared to other areas nearby (see Figure 7-B). The dry conveyor belt thus gives the cyclone a "comma" shape by separating clouds defining the comma's head, formed primarily by the cold conveyor belt, from clouds defining the comma's tail, formed primarily by the warm conveyor belt.

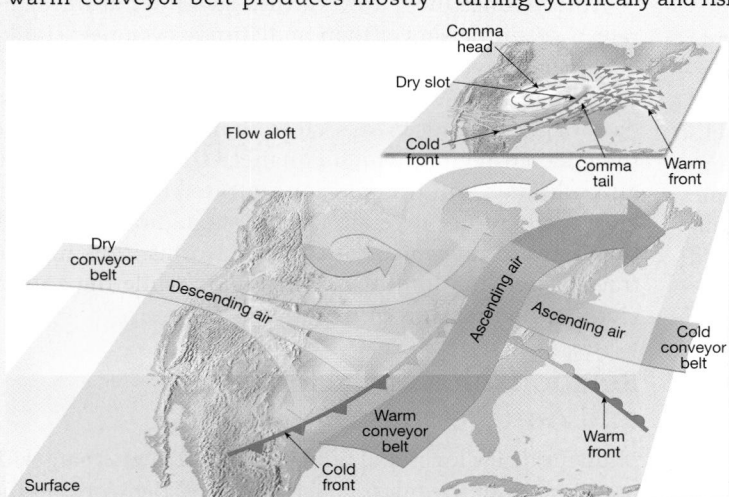

▲ **Figure 7-A** A typical midlatitude cyclone in the Northern Hemisphere with the warm conveyor belt in red, the cold conveyor belt in blue, and the dry conveyor belt in yellow. The inset shows the typical cloud coverage produced by a midlatitude cyclone such as this.

cold front passes, all four elements of weather will likely change:

Temperature: As the cold front passes, temperature drops abruptly because the cold front is the boundary between the cold air mass and the warm air mass of the storm.

Pressure: Because the cold front is associated with a trough (a linear band of low pressure) extending south from the heart of the storm, as the front approaches, pressure will be falling, reaching its lowest point at the front. Then, as the cold front passes and the trough moves away, pressure will begin to rise steadily.

Wind: Because of the overall converging counterclockwise wind pattern (in the Northern Hemisphere), winds in the warm sector come from the south (the situation before the cold front). Once the front passes, wind will tend to shift and come from the west or northwest.

Clouds and Precipitation: The generally clear skies ahead of the cold front are replaced by cloudiness and precipitation at the front—generated by the adiabatic cooling of the warm air as it is lifted along the front—to be replaced again some hours later by clear skies in the cold air mass behind the cold front.

Similar changes, although of lesser magnitude, occur with the passage of a warm front.

Learning Check 7-7 Why is pressure falling as a cold front approaches, and rising as a cold front moves away?

Occurrence and Distribution

At any given time, from 5 to 15 midlatitude cyclones exist in the Northern Hemisphere midlatitudes, and an equal number in the Southern Hemisphere. They occur at scattered but irregular intervals throughout the zone of the westerlies.

In part because temperature contrasts are greater during the winter, these migratory disturbances are more numerous, better developed, and faster moving in winter than in summer. They also follow much more equatorward tracks in winter. In the Southern Hemisphere, the Antarctic continent provides a prominent year-round source of cold air, and so vigorous cyclones are almost as numerous in summer as in winter. The summer storms are farther poleward than their winter cousins, however, and are mostly over the Southern Ocean. Thus, they have little effect on land areas.

MIDLATITUDE ANTICYCLONES

Another major disturbance in the general flow of the westerlies is the **midlatitude anticyclone**, frequently referred to simply as a "high" (H). This is an extensive, migratory high-pressure cell of the midlatitudes (Figure 7-12). Typically it is larger than a midlatitude cyclone and generally moves west to east with the westerlies.

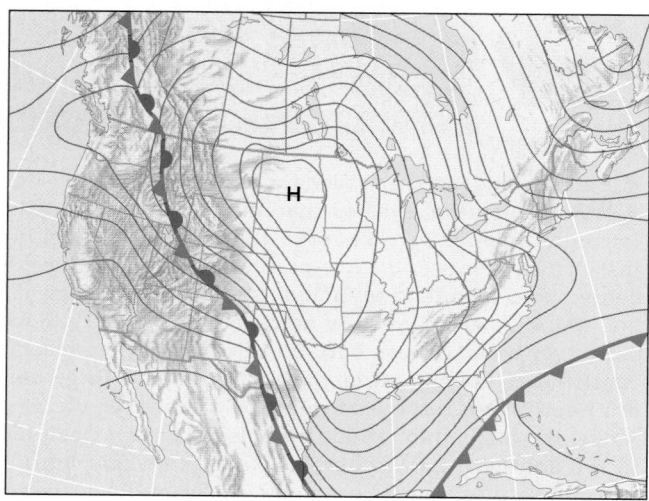

▲ **Figure 7-12** A typical well-developed midlatitude anticyclone centered over the Dakotas. Both fronts shown here are outside the high-pressure system.

Characteristics

As with any other high-pressure center, a midlatitude anticyclone has air converging into it from above, subsiding, and diverging at the surface, clockwise in the Northern Hemisphere and counterclockwise in the Southern Hemisphere. No air-mass conflict or surface convergence is involved, and so anticyclones contain no fronts (the fronts shown in Figure 7-12 are outside the high-pressure system). The weather is clear and dry with little or no opportunity for cloud formation. Wind movement is very limited near the center of an anticyclone but increases progressively outward. Particularly along the eastern margin (the leading edge) of the system, there may be strong winds. In winter, anticyclones are characterized by very low temperatures (recall that high pressure cells may be associated with cold surface conditions).

Anticyclones move toward the east either at the same rate as or a little slower than midlatitude cyclones. Unlike cyclones, however, anticyclones are occasionally prone to stagnate and remain over the same region for several days. This stalling brings clear, stable, dry weather to the affected region, which enhances the likelihood that air pollutants will become concentrated under a subsidence temperature inversion. Such stagnation may block the eastward movement of cyclonic storms, causing protracted precipitation in another region while the anticyclonic region remains dry.

Relationships of Cyclones and Anticyclones

Midlatitude cyclones and anticyclones often alternate with one another in irregular sequence around the world in the midlatitudes (Figure 7-13). Each can occur independently of the other, but there is often a functional relationship between them. This relationship can be seen when an anticyclone closely follows a cyclone, as diagrammed in Figure 7-14. The winds diverging from the eastern margin of the high fit into

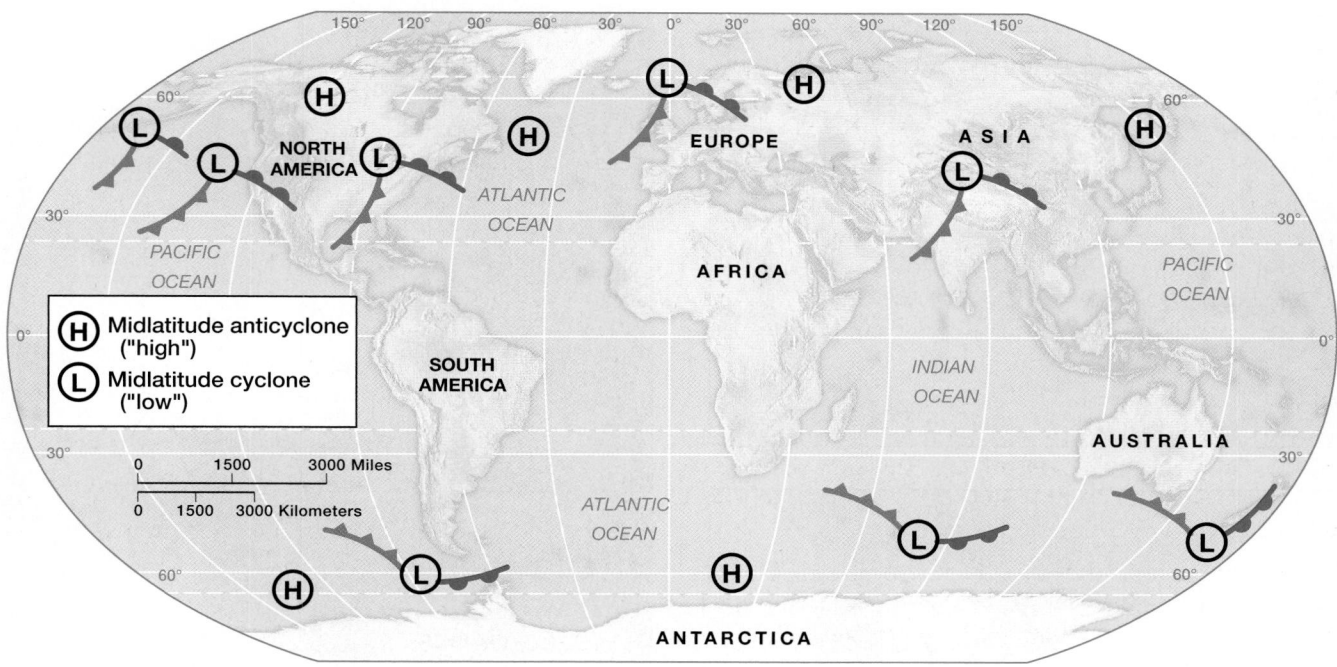

▲ **Figure 7-13** At any given time, the midlatitudes are dotted with midlatitude cyclones and anticyclones. This map depicts a hypothetical situation in January that shows only mature midlatitude cyclones. Note the orientation of fronts in the Southern Hemisphere storms.

the flow of air converging into the western side of the low. It is easy to visualize the anticyclone as a polar air mass having the cold front of the cyclone as its leading edge.

Learning Check 7-8 **Why are midlatitude anticyclones associated with dry weather?**

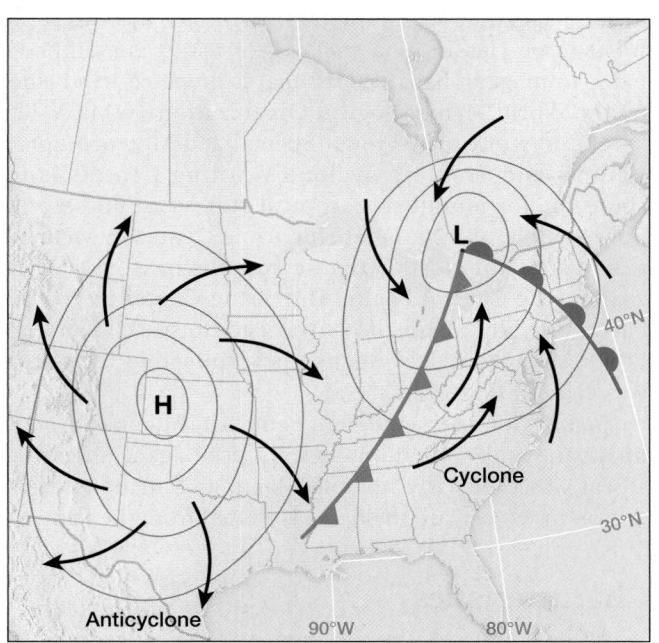

▲ **Figure 7-14** Midlatitude cyclones and anticyclones often occur in juxtaposition in the midlatitudes, with the anticyclone pumping cold air into the cyclone.

EASTERLY WAVES

In the tropics, not all migrating atmospheric disturbances are associated with well-developed cyclones or anticyclones. For example, an **easterly wave** is a long but weak migratory, low-pressure system that may occur almost anywhere between 5° and 30° of latitude (Figure 7-15).

Characteristics

Easterly waves are a common kind of tropical disturbance, usually consisting of a band of small thunderstorms with little or no cyclonic rotation. Easterly waves are usually several hundred kilometers long and nearly always oriented north–south. They drift slowly westward in the flow of the trade winds, bringing characteristic weather with them: Ahead of the wave is fair weather with divergent airflow. Behind the wave, convergent conditions prevail, with moist air being uplifted to yield convective thunderstorms and sometimes widespread cloudiness. There is little or no temperature change with the passage of easterly waves.

Origin

Most of the easterly waves that move across the North Atlantic originate over North Africa and then move out over the Atlantic in the trade winds. The vast majority of easterly waves weaken and die out over the ocean, but a small percentage intensify into more powerful tropical cyclones—our next topic.

Learning Check 7-9 **Describe the characteristics of an easterly wave.**

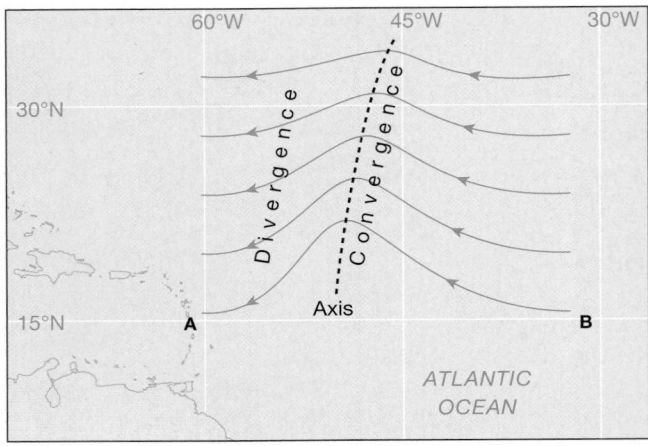

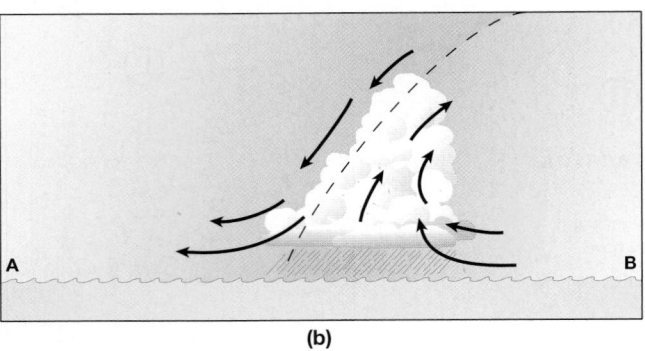

▲ **Figure 7-15** Diagrammatic map view (a) and cross section (b) of an easterly wave. The arrows indicate general direction of airflow.

TROPICAL CYCLONES: HURRICANES

Tropical cyclones are intense, low-pressure disturbances that develop in the tropics and occasionally move poleward into the midlatitudes. Tropical cyclones are considerably smaller than midlatitude cyclones, typically having a diameter of between 160 and 1000 kilometers (100 and 600 miles; Figure 7-16).

Categories of Tropical Disturbances

Intense tropical cyclones are known by different names in different parts of the world: *hurricanes* in North and Central America, *typhoons* in the western North Pacific, *baguios* in the Philippines, and simply *cyclones* in the Indian Ocean and Australia.

Tropical cyclones develop from minor low-pressure perturbations in trade-wind flow (such as easterly waves), that are generally called *tropical disturbances* by the U.S. National Weather Service. About 100 of these are identified each year over the tropical North Atlantic, but only a few strengthen into hurricanes. Three categories of tropical disturbances are recognized on the basis of wind speed:

1. A **tropical depression** has wind speeds up to 62 kilometers per hour (38 mph; 33 knots), but has developed a closed wind circulation pattern.

▲ **Figure 7-16** Hurricane Irene approaching The Bahamas on August 24, 2011. This image was captured by the Moderate Resolution Imaging Spectroradiometer (MODIS) on NASA's Aqua satellite.

2. A **tropical storm** has winds between 63 and 118 kilometers per hour (39–73 mph; 34–63 knots).
3. A **hurricane** has winds that reach or exceed 119 kilometers per hour (74 mph; 64 knots).

Named Storms: When a tropical depression's winds reach a speed of 63 kilometers per hour (the threshold for it to be classed as a *tropical storm*), it is assigned a name from an alphabetical list that is prepared in advance by the World Meteorological Organization (WMO). The WMO network of Regional Specialized Meteorological Centers and Tropical Cyclone Warning Centers is responsible for monitoring tropical storms around world. For example, the National Hurricane Center in Miami is responsible for North Atlantic and northeastern Pacific storms, the Central Pacific Hurricane Center in Hawai'i is responsible for north-central Pacific storms, and the Japan Meteorological Agency is responsible for northwestern Pacific storms.

Each region uses a different name list. After a few years, hurricane and typhoon names are used again unless the storm was especially notable—such as Katrina and Andrew—in which case the name is retired from the list.

Characteristics

Hurricanes (as we generally refer to tropical cyclones in this chapter) consist of prominent low-pressure centers that are essentially circular, with a steep pressure gradient

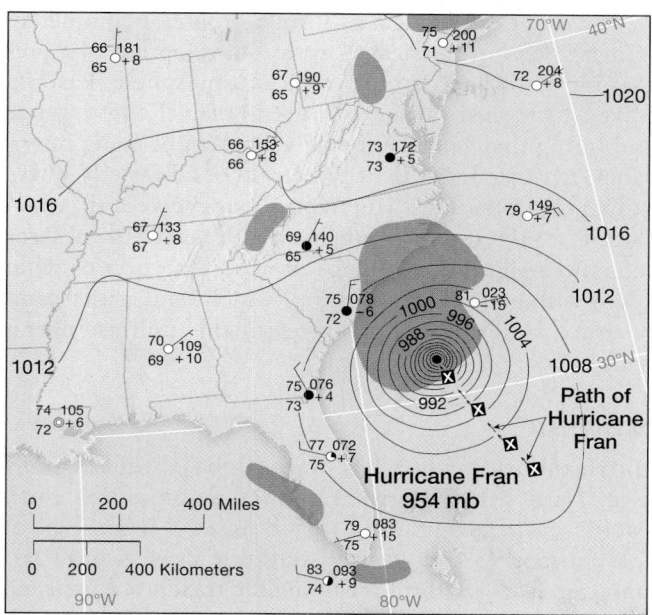

▲ **Figure 7-17** Weather map of Hurricane Fran on September 5, 1996. The isobars show a very steep gradient around the low-pressure center. The chain of black boxes shows the position of Fran at 6-hour intervals.

outward from the center (Figure 7-17). As a result, strong winds spiral inward. Winds must reach a speed of 119 kilometers per hour (74 mph; 64 knots) for the storm to be officially classified as a hurricane, although winds in a well-developed hurricane often double that speed and occasionally triple it.

Animation
Hurricanes

The converging cyclonic wind pattern of a hurricane pulls in warm, moist air—the "fuel" that powers the storm. As warm, water vapor–laden air spirals into the storm, it

rises in intense updrafts within towering cumulonimbus clouds. As the air rises it cools adiabatically, bringing the air to saturation; condensation releases vast amounts of liquid water that builds up the huge clouds and feeds the heavy rain. Condensation also releases latent heat. It is the release of latent heat that powers and strengthens a storm by increasing the instability of the air: in a short period of time and in a relatively small area, a hurricane releases an enormous amount of energy into the atmosphere. An average mature hurricane releases in one day approximately as much energy as generated by all electric utility plants in the United States in one year.

Hurricanes are not characterized by fronts as are midlatitude cyclones: all of the air associated with hurricanes is warm and moist, and so dissimilar air masses are not pulled together as in the midlatitudes.

Learning Check 7-10 **Why is warm, moist air the "fuel" for a hurricane?**

Eye of a Hurricane: A remarkable feature of a well-developed hurricane is the nonstormy **eye** in the center of the storm (Figure 7-18). The winds do not converge to a central point, but rather reach their highest speed at the *eye wall,* which is the edge of the eye. The eye has a diameter of from 16 to 40 kilometers (10 to 25 miles) and is a singular area of calmness in the maelstrom that whirls around it.

The weather pattern within a hurricane is relatively symmetrical around the eye. Bands of dense cumulus and cumulonimbus clouds (called *spiral rain bands*) curve in from the edge of the storm to the eye wall, producing heavy rain that generally increases in intensity inward.

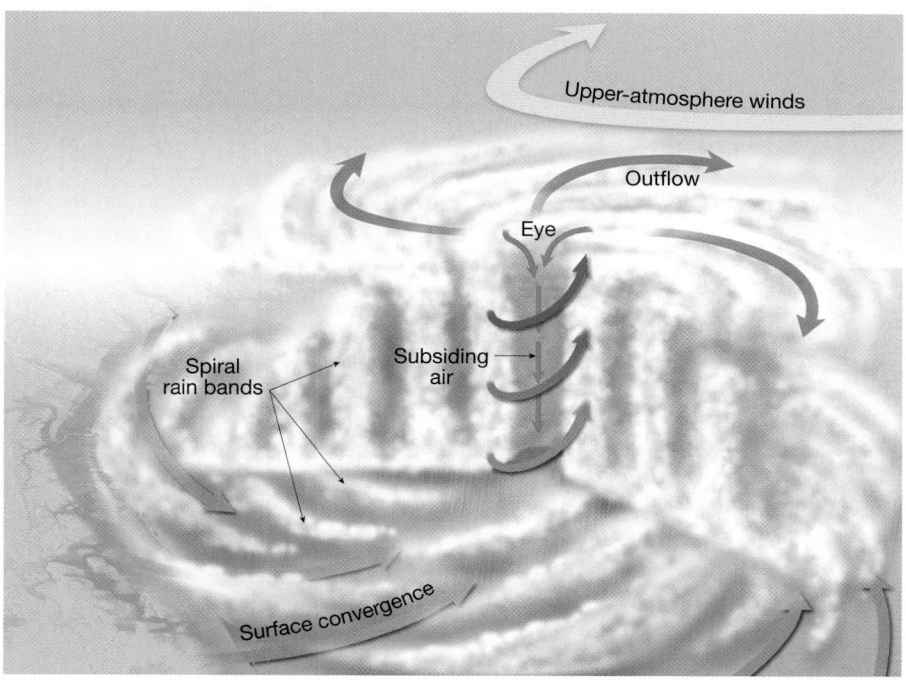

◀ **Figure 7-18** An idealized cross section through a well-developed hurricane. Air spirals into the storm horizontally and rises rapidly to produce towering cumulus and cumulonimbus clouds that yield torrential rainfall. In the center of the storm is the eye, where air movement is downward.

Updrafts are common throughout the hurricane, becoming most prominent around the eye wall. However, within the eye itself a downdraft is found. Near the top of the storm, air diverges clockwise out into the upper troposphere.

The clouds of the eye wall tower to heights that may exceed 16 kilometers (10 miles). Within the eye, there is no rain and almost no low clouds—here adiabatic warming of descending air inhibits cloud formation. In the eye, scattered high clouds may part to let in intermittent sunlight. The wall of thunderstorms circling the eye is sometimes surrounded by a new wall of thunderstorms. The inner wall disintegrates and is replaced by the outer wall. The process, called *eye-wall replacement*, usually lasts less than 24 hours and tends to weaken the storm.

Origin

Video
Hurricane Hot
Towers

Hurricanes form only over warm oceans in the tropics and at least a few degrees north or south of the equator (Figure 7-19). The ocean water temperature generally needs to be at least 26.5°C (80°F) to a depth of 50 meters (160 feet) or more. Because the Coriolis effect is so minimal near the equator, no hurricane has ever been observed to form within 3° of it, no hurricane has ever been known to cross it, and the appearance of hurricanes closer than some 8° or 10° of the equator is very rare. More than 80 percent originate in or just on the poleward side of the intertropical convergence zone.

The exact mechanism of formation is not completely understood, but hurricanes always develop out of a pre-existing disturbance in the tropical troposphere. Easterly waves, discussed earlier, provide low-level convergence and lifting that catalyze the development of many hurricanes. Even so, fewer than 10 percent of all easterly waves grow into hurricanes. Hurricanes can evolve only when there is no significant **wind shear** with height (*wind shear* refers to a significant change in wind direction or wind speed with increasing elevation), which implies that temperatures at low altitudes are reasonably uniform over a wide area.

Movement

Hurricanes occur in a half-dozen low-latitude regions (see Figure 7-19). They are most common in the North Pacific basin, originating largely in two areas: east of the Philippines and west of southern Mexico and Central America. The third most notable region of hurricane development is in the west-central portion of the North Atlantic basin, extending into the Caribbean Sea and Gulf of Mexico. These ferocious storms are also found in the western portion of the South Pacific and all across the South Indian Ocean, as well as in the North Indian Ocean both east and west of the Indian peninsula. They are very rare in the South Atlantic and in the southeastern part of the Pacific, apparently because the water is too cold and because high pressure dominates. The strongest and largest hurricanes are typically those of the western Pacific Ocean. Only a few storms in other parts of the world

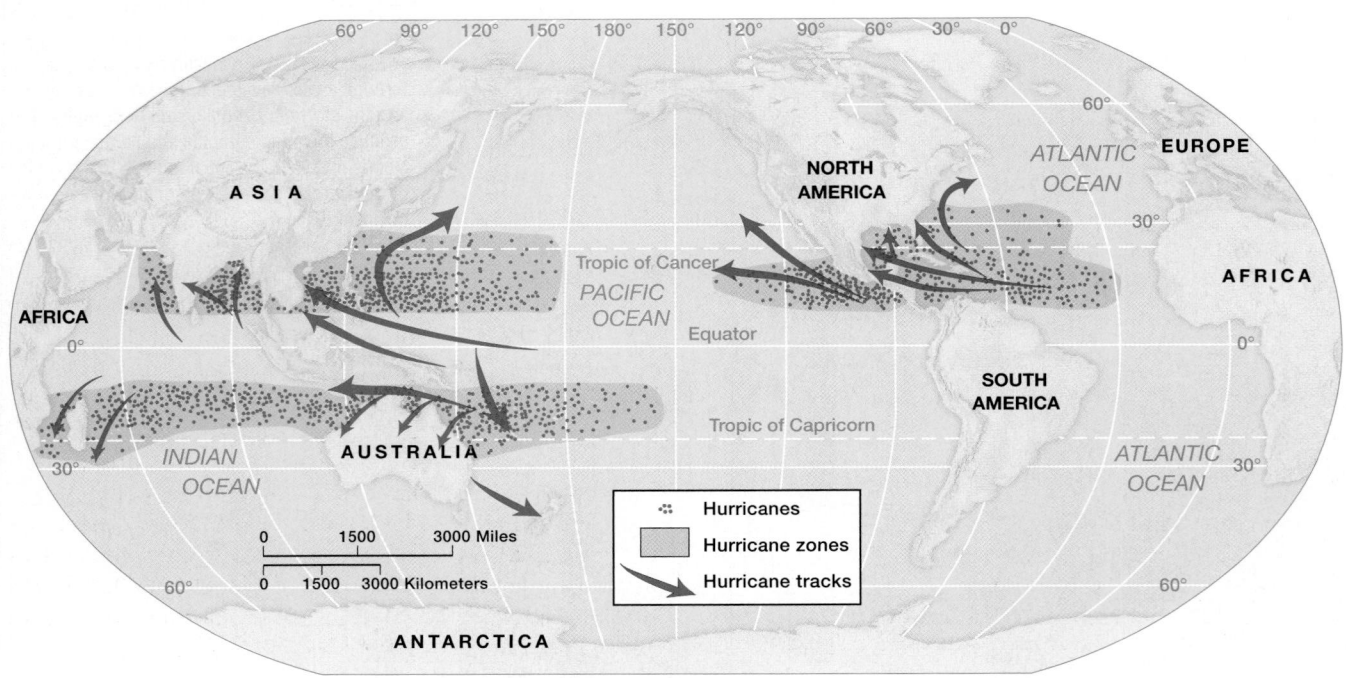

▲ **Figure 7-19** Major generalized hurricane tracks and location of origin points of hurricanes over a 19-year period.

have attained the size and intensity of the large East Asian "super" typhoons.

Hurricane Tracks: Once formed, hurricanes follow irregular tracks within the general flow of the trade winds. A specific path is very difficult to predict many days in advance, but the general pattern of movement is highly predictable. Roughly one-third of all hurricanes travel east to west without much latitudinal change. The rest, however, begin on an east–west path and then curve prominently poleward, where they either dissipate over the adjacent continent or become enmeshed in the general flow of the midlatitude westerlies (Figure 7-20).

Video
2005 Hurricane
Season

Hurricanes sometimes survive (with diminished intensity) off the east coasts of continents in the midlatitudes because of the warm ocean currents there; hurricanes do not survive in the midlatitudes off the west coasts of continents because of the cool ocean currents there.

In one region—the southwestern Pacific Ocean north and northeast of New Zealand—there is a marked variation from this general flow pattern. Hurricanes in this part of the Pacific usually move erratically from northwest to southeast. Therefore, when they strike an island such as Fiji or Tonga, they approach from the west, a situation not replicated anywhere else in the world at such a low latitude. These seemingly aberrant tracks apparently result from the simple fact that the tropospheric westerlies extend quite far equatorward in the Southwest Pacific, and hurricanes there are basically steered by the general circulation pattern.

Learning Check 7-11 **Why can hurricanes move up into the midlatitudes along the east coast of North America, but not along the west coast?**

Life Span: Whatever their trajectory, hurricanes do not last long. The average hurricane exists for only about a week, with four weeks as the maximum duration. The

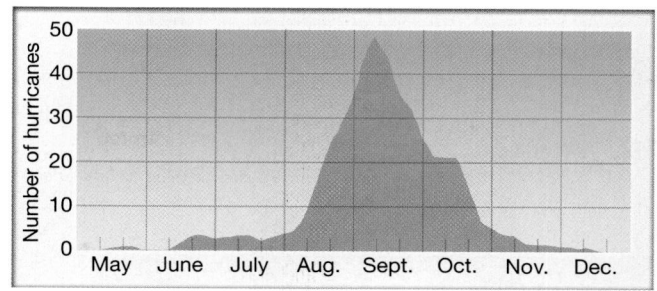

▲ **Figure 7-21** Seasonality of North Atlantic–Caribbean hurricanes over a nine-year period. Hurricane season reaches its peak in the autumn, with a prominent maximum in September.

longer-lived hurricanes are those that remain over tropical oceans. As soon as a hurricane leaves the ocean and moves over land, it begins to die because its energy source (warm, moist air) is cut off. If it stays over the ocean but moves into the midlatitudes, it dies as it penetrates the cooler environment. It is not unusual for a tropical hurricane that moves into the midlatitudes to diminish in intensity but grow in areal size until it develops into a midlatitude cyclone that travels with the westerlies.

In most regions, there is a marked seasonality to hurricanes (Figure 7-21). They are largely restricted to late summer and fall, presumably because this is the time that ocean temperatures are highest and the intertropical convergence zone is shifted farthest poleward.

Damage and Destruction

Hurricanes are known for their destructive capabilities. Some of the destruction comes from high winds and torrential rain, and in some cases, tornadoes are spawned by a hurricane. However, the overwhelming cause of damage and loss of life is the flooding brought by high seas.

Storm Surges: The low pressure in the center of the storm allows the ocean surface to bulge up as much as 1 meter (3 feet). Wind driven waves increase water height even more, producing a **storm surge** of water as much as 7.5 meters (25 feet) above normal tide level when the hurricane pounds into a shoreline. Thus, a low-lying coastal area can be severely inundated, and 90 percent of hurricane-related deaths are drownings (Figure 7-22).

The greatest hurricane disaster in U.S. history occurred in 1900 when Galveston Island, Texas, was overwhelmed by a 6-meter (20-foot) storm surge that killed as many as 8000 people, nearly one-sixth of Galveston's population. In other regions, hurricane devastation has been much greater. The flat deltas of the Ganges and Brahmaputra rivers in Bangladesh have been subjected to enormous losses of human life from Indian Ocean cyclones: 300,000 deaths in 1737, another 300,000 in 1876, another 500,000 in 1970, and 175,000 in 1991. In 2008, flooding from Cyclone Nargis in Myanmar (Burma) killed at least 130,000 people (Figure 7-23). Most of the damage along the Gulf coast of the United States in August 2005 from Hurricane

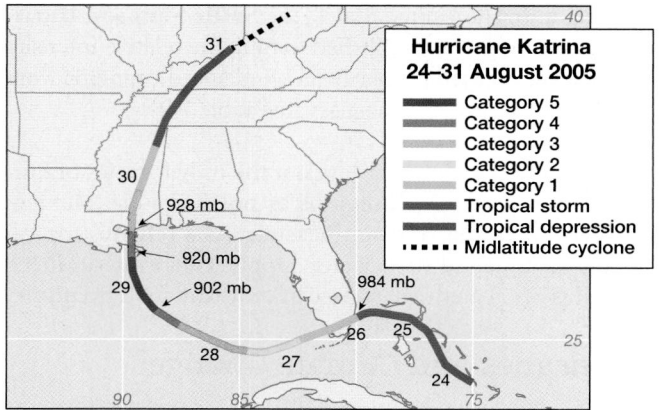

Hurricane Katrina
24–31 August 2005

■ Category 5
■ Category 4
■ Category 3
■ Category 2
■ Category 1
■ Tropical storm
■ Tropical depression
∙∙∙∙∙ Midlatitude cyclone

928 mb
920 mb
902 mb
984 mb

▲ **Figure 7-20** Path of Hurricane Katrina from August 24 to August 31, 2005. Notice that storm strength increased as it passed over the warm water in the Gulf of Mexico, but diminished quickly after the storm moved over land.

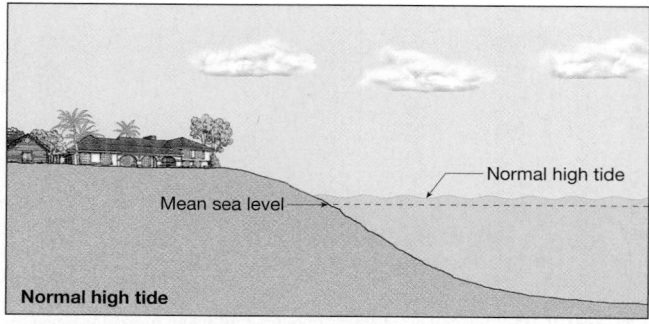

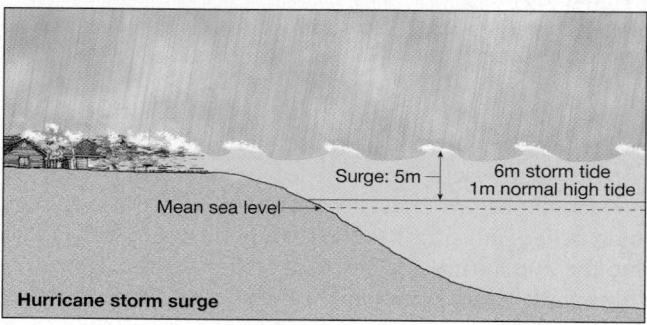

▲ **Figure 7-22** When a hurricane storm surge accompanies a normal high tide, flooding can overwhelm a coastal area.

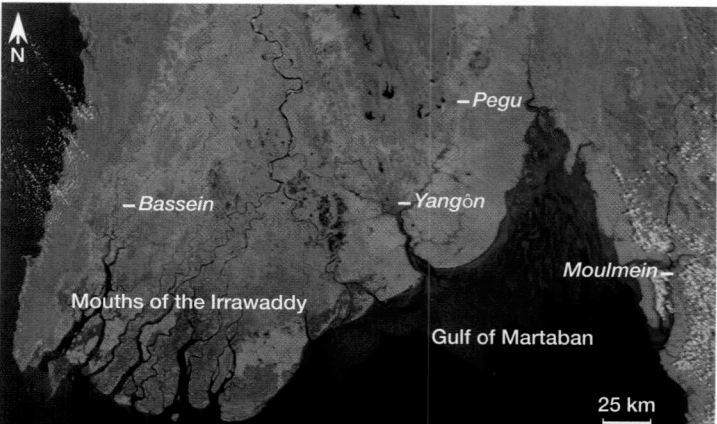

April 15, 2008

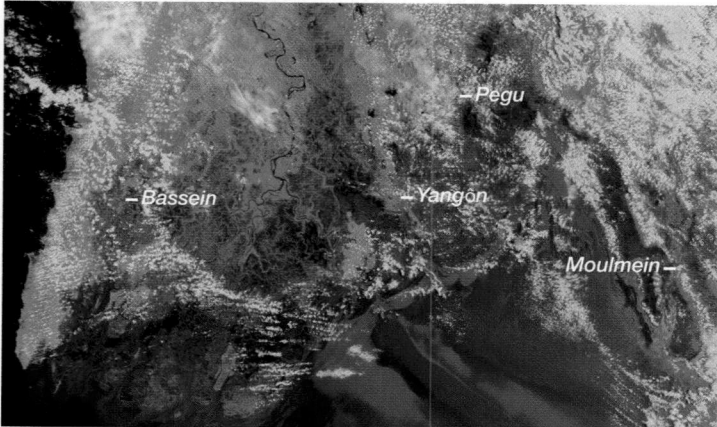

May 5, 2008

▲ **Figure 7-23** In 2008 Cyclone Nargis flooded more than 14,000 square kilometers (5500 square miles) of the low-lying Irrawaddy River delta in Myanmar (Burma), killing more than 130,000 people. The top satellite image was taken on April 15 before the storm hit; the bottom image was taken on May 5 after the storm came ashore.

Katrina was caused by an eight-meter high (26 foot) storm surge (Figure 7-24)—see the box, "People and the Environment: Lessons of Hurricane Katrina."

Heavy Rain and Flooding: Strong hurricanes can inflict heavy damage from flooding even after they weaken and move inland. For example, in August 2011 Hurricane Irene brought extensive flooding to many parts of the northeastern United States and southeastern Canada.

Video
Hurricane
Sandy

After passing over Puerto Rico on August 21 and the Bahamas on the 25th, Irene made landfall at North Carolina on August 27 where it dumped as much as 400 mm (15.74 inches) of rain. Irene had weakened to tropical storm strength on August 28 when it made another landfall in New York City. From there, the remnants of the storm moved north into Connecticut, Massachusetts, and Vermont—the state hardest hit by flooding from the storm; Irene left over 175 mm (7 inches) of rain in parts of Vermont, where the ground was already saturated from earlier rainfall (Figure 7-25).

More recently, Hurricane Sandy brought unprecedented flooding to coastal New Jersey and New York City when it came ashore on October 29, 2012. Blocked by a cold air mass in the west and high-pressure cell in the north, Sandy transformed into a rare post-tropical cyclone "super storm" that generated record storm surges, heavy rain, and early season blizzards. Flooding closed New York's subways, left millions without power, devastated coastal communities (Figure 7-26), and caused more than $50 billion in damage. In all, Sandy killed at least 160 people in the Caribbean, the United States and Canada.

Learning Check 7-12 What causes a hurricane's storm surge?

Hurricane Strength: Although the amount of damage caused by a hurricane depends in part on the physical configuration of the landscape and the population size and density of the affected area, storm strength is the most important factor. In the United States, the **Saffir-Simpson Hurricane Scale** has been established to rank the relative intensity of hurricanes (based primarily on wind speed), ranging from 1 to 5, with 5 being the most severe (Table 7-2).

Destruction and tragedy are not the only legacies of hurricanes, however. Such regions as northwestern Mexico, northern Australia, and southeastern Asia rely on tropical storms for much of their water supply. Hurricane-induced rainfall is often a critical source of moisture for agriculture.

Hurricanes and Climate Change

The 2005 hurricane season in the North Atlantic was the most active on record, with 28 named storms. Three of the most powerful hurricanes ever measured in terms of minimum atmospheric pressure in the eye occurred that year: Katrina,

Lessons of Hurricane Katrina

On August 23, 2005, the 12th tropical depression of the season developed in the southeastern Bahamas. By the next day, the depression had strengthened and was named Tropical Storm Katrina. Within a week, Katrina was to create one of the greatest natural disasters in United States history.

Katrina Strengthens: The storm moved slowly to the northwest, strengthening into a Category 1 hurricane just a few hours before making landfall in south Florida on August 25. Weakened by its passage over land, Katrina quickly intensified again as it moved out over the warm waters of the Gulf of Mexico (Figure 7-C), becoming a Category 5 storm on the 28th with winds of more than 275 kph (170 mph; 150 knots), and a central pressure of 902 mb (the sixth lowest of any recorded Atlantic storm; the lowest on record was Hurricane Wilma two months later that year, with a pressure of 882 mb).

Katrina Makes Landfall: By the time Katrina made its second landfall on the Gulf Coast just southeast of New Orleans on the morning of August 29, it had weakened slightly to a strong Category 3 storm (see Figure 7-20). Sustained wind speeds at landfall in southeastern Louisiana were more than 200 kph (125 mph; 108 knots); wind gusts of more than 160 kph (100 mph; 87 knots) were recorded in New Orleans. Rainfall storm totals exceeded 25 centimeters (10 inches) along much of Katrina's path, with a maximum of nearly 38 centimeters (15 inches) recorded in Big Branch, Louisiana. Sixty-two tornadoes were spawned by Katrina.

The Storm Surge: The greatest devastation came from Katrina's storm surge and flooding from heavy rain. Mobile, Alabama, and large areas of Gulfport and Biloxi, Mississippi, were inundated by Katrina's 8.0 to 8.5 meter (26 to 28 foot) high storm surge. New Orleans, although spared from a direct hit by the storm (the eye passed just east of the city), was first flooded beginning at about 7:00 A.M. A 3.0 to 3.6 meter (10 to 12 foot) storm surge rolled up the Intercoastal Waterway from the Gulf into the city's Industrial Canal, overtopping and scouring levees and flooding the eastern parts of the city. About 3 hours later—after some news agencies had reported that New Orleans had luckily escaped the worst destruction of Katrina—a second flood hit the city when the London Avenue and 17th Street canals failed, sending water pouring into the central parts of the city from Lake Pontchartrain. By August 31, 80 percent of New Orleans was underwater—in some places 6 meters (20 feet) deep (Figure 7-D).

For the next few days, the world watched events in New Orleans on television and the Internet while government officials seemed unable to coordinate the rescue effort needed to help the thousands of people trapped in the flooded city. The loss of life from Hurricane Katrina may never be known with certainty, but is likely to have been more than 1200.

Explaining the Disaster: So why was New Orleans so devastated by this storm? Many factors contributed to this disaster. New Orleans sits in a shallow "bowl" alongside the Mississippi River. Draining this once swampy area over the last few hundred years has led to soil compaction and subsidence that has left parts of the city below sea level, protected only by a series of levees and pumps. The wetlands of the Mississippi River delta once offered some protection by slowing and absorbing the punch from hurricane storm surges, but flood control efforts upstream have changed the sediment load of the river and over the last few decades these protective marshlands on the lower delta have been sinking and eroding away, now offering little protection from storms. Finally, the levees themselves were inadequate, not being designed to handle such an enormous surge of water.

Preparing for the Next One: Some scientists had warned about such a potential disaster for years, and local authorities were pressing for financial help to strengthen the levees. Following Katrina, a vast effort was undertaken to strengthen New Orleans' defenses. By the 2012 hurricane season, about 14.5 billion dollars had been spent repairing and reinforcing more than 210 kilometers (130 miles) of levees and floodwalls, constructing huge new floodgates to close off the city from Lake Pontchartrain, nearby Lake Borgne, and from storm surges moving up the canals, and by "storm-proofing" the network of high-capacity pumping stations.

In 2012, the new defenses worked well for New Orleans when Hurricane Isaac, a weak Category 1 hurricane, struck the city. Extensive flooding took place around New Orleans, however, and some scientists and local officials still wonder what will happen when the next great storm arrives.

▲ **Figure 7-C** Satellite image of Hurricane Katrina at 9:15 A.M. Eastern time on August 29, 2005.

▲ **Figure 7-D** New Orleans after Hurricane Katrina on August 30, 2005.

▲ **Figure 7-24** Large casino barges washed across Highway 90 in Biloxi, Mississippi, by the storm surge of Hurricane Katrina in August 2005.

	TABLE 7-2	**Saffir-Simpson Hurricane Scale**			
		Wind Speed			
Category	km/hr	mph	knots	Damage	
1	119–153	74–95	64–82	Very dangerous winds will produce some damage.	
2	154–177	96–110	83–95	Extremely dangerous winds will cause extensive damage.	
3	178–208	111–129	96–112	Devastating damage will occur.	
4	209–251	130–156	113–136	Catastrophic damage will occur.	
5	>252	>157	>137	Catastrophic damage will occur.	

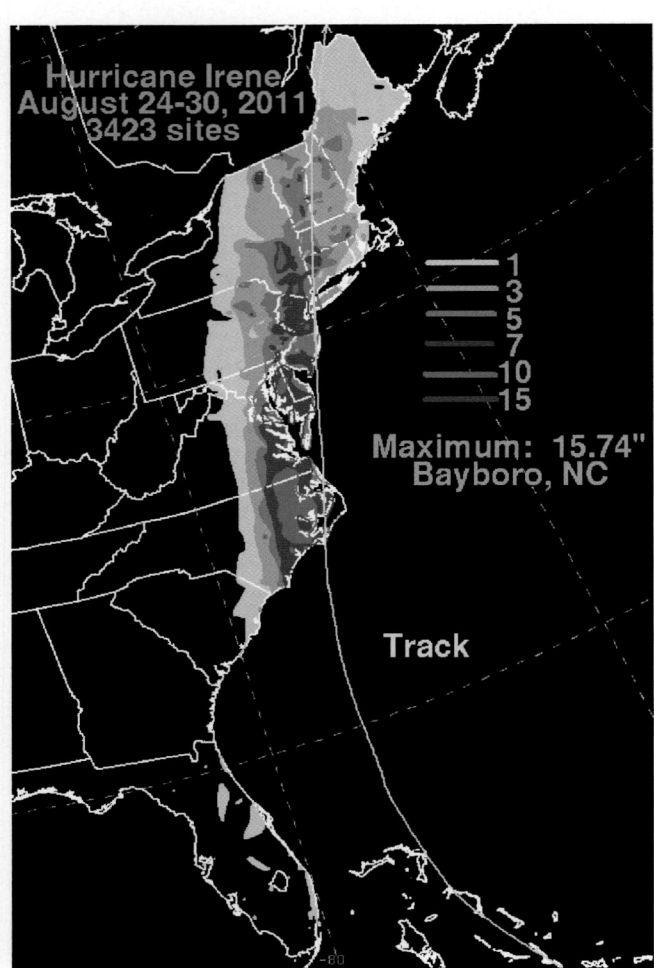

▲ **Figure 7-25** Rainfall totals (in inches) from Hurricane Irene after making landfall along the East Coast of the United States in August 2011. Some locations received over 380 mm (15 inches) of rain from the storm.

Rita, and Wilma (Table 7-3). The 2011 season was another very active year, tied with 1887, 1995, and 2010 for third over-all with 19 named storms (the annual average is 11). Given the connection between high ocean temperature and hurricane formation in general—as well as evidence that global warming is slightly increasing sea–surface temperatures—an obvious question to ask is whether the recent increase in hurricane activity (either the number of storms or their intensity) is tied to global warming.

Number of Hurricanes: Over the last 20 years or so, the annual number of hurricanes in the North Atlantic has generally increased. However, many meteorologists think that this increase in frequency is simply part of a multidecadal cycle of hurricane activity that has been well documented since the early 1900s. Known as the *Atlantic Multi-Decadal Signal*, the pattern includes such factors as higher sea–surface temperatures (SST), lower vertical wind shear, and an expanded upper-level westward flow of the atmosphere off North Africa. Although the underlying causes of all the components of the Atlantic Multi-Decadal Signal are not completely understood, the recent upswing in hurricane frequency can likely be explained without tying it to global warming. Meteorologists at NOAA's Climate Prediction Center have generally been forecasting a higher-than-average number of North Atlantic tropical storms since the early 2000s.

Intensity of Hurricanes: On the other hand, recent studies based on the computer modeling of a number of greenhouse gas emissions scenarios suggest that it is likely (greater than 66 percent probability) that we will observe an increase in the average *intensity* of tropical cyclones during this century—increasing by up to 10 percent in one projection. Studies further suggest that although the total

▲ **Figure 7-26** Damage from Hurricane Sandy along the New Jersey shoreline on October 30, 2012.

number of hurricanes is more likely to remain the same or even decrease by the end of the century, the number of very intense hurricanes in some ocean basins may increase—there is, however, great uncertainty in those projections. In addition, studies also point to a 20 percent increase in the amount of near-storm rainfall from hurricanes over this century.

LOCALIZED SEVERE WEATHER

Several kinds of smaller atmospheric disturbances are common in various parts of the world. Some are locally of great significance, and some are destructive. All occur at a much more localized scale than do tropical cyclones and midlatitude cyclones, although thunderstorms and tornadoes may be associated with both kinds of larger storms.

TABLE 7-3	Ten Most Intense Hurricanes (based on lowest central pressure) in the North Atlantic Basin from 1851 to 2011		
	Hurricane	**Year**	**Minimum Pressure**
1	Hurricane Wilma	2005	882 mb
2	Hurricane Gilbert	1988	888 mb
3	1935 Labor Day Hurricane	1935	892 mb
4	Hurricane Rita	2005	895 mb
5	Hurricane Allen	1980	899 mb
6	Hurricane Katrina	2005	902 mb
7	Hurricane Camille	1969	905 mb
	Hurricane Mitch	1998	905 mb
	Hurricane Dean	2007	905 mb
10	1924 Cuba Hurricane	1924	910 mb*
	Hurricane Ivan	2004	910 mb

*The strength of the 1924 Cuba Hurricane was recently reevaluated by meteorologists; its minimum central pressure is estimated to have been 910 mb.
(Data source: U.S. Department of Commerce/NOAA.)

Thunderstorms

FG9

A **thunderstorm**, defined as a violent convective storm accompanied by thunder and lightning, is usually localized and short-lived. It is always associated with vertical air motion, considerable humidity, and instability—a combination that produces a towering cumulonimbus cloud and (nearly always) showery precipitation.

Thunderstorms sometimes occur as individual clouds, produced by nothing more complicated than thermal convection; such developments are commonplace in the tropics and during summer in much of the midlatitudes. Thunderstorms are also frequently found in conjunction with other kinds of storms, however, or are associated with other mechanisms that can trigger unstable uplift. Thus thunderstorms often accompany hurricanes, tornadoes, fronts (especially cold fronts) in midlatitude cyclones, and orographic lifting that may produce instability.

Development: The uplift, by whatever mechanism, of warm, moist air must release enough latent heat of condensation to sustain the continued rise of the air. In the early stage of thunderstorm formation (Figure 7-27), called the *cumulus stage*, updrafts prevail and the cloud grows. Above the freezing level, supercooled water droplets and ice crystals coalesce: when they become too large to be supported by the updrafts, they fall. These falling particles drag air with them, initiating a downdraft. When the downdraft with its accompanying precipitation leaves the bottom of the cloud, the thunderstorm enters the *mature stage*, in which updrafts and downdrafts coexist as the cloud continues to enlarge. The mature stage is the most active time, with heavy rain often accompanied by hail, blustery winds, lightning, thunder, and the growth of an "anvil" top composed of ice crystals on the massive cumulonimbus cloud (see Figure 6-26). Eventually downdrafts dominate and the *dissipating stage* is reached, with light rain ending and turbulence ceasing.

Thunderstorms are most common where there are high temperatures, high humidity, and high instability, a combination typical of the intertropical convergence zone. Thunderstorm frequency generally decreases away from the equator, and they are virtually unknown poleward of 60° of latitude (Figure 7-28). There is much greater frequency of thunderstorms over land than water because summer

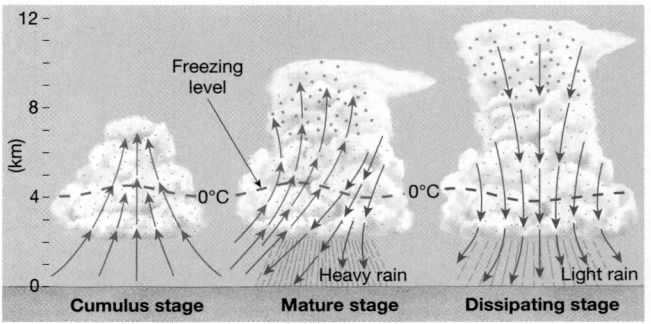

▲ **Figure 7-27** Sequential development of a thunderstorm cell. Red arrows show updrafts and blue arrows show downdrafts.

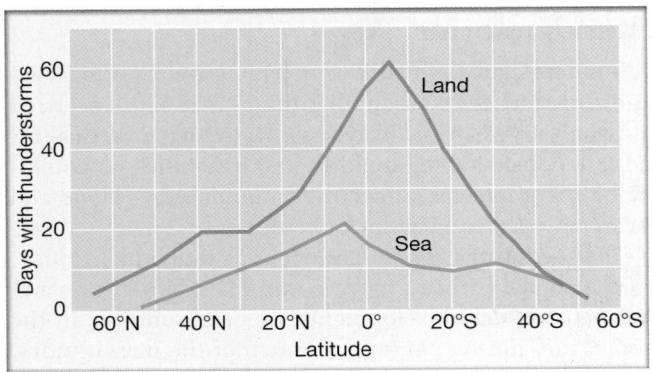

▲ **Figure 7-28** Average number of days per year with thunderstorms, as generalized by latitude. Most thunderstorms are in the tropics. Land areas experience many more thunderstorms than ocean areas because land warms up much more in summer.

temperatures are higher over land and most thunderstorms occur in the summer. In the United States, the greatest annual thunderstorm activity occurs in Florida and the Gulf Coast, where moist, unstable air often prevails in spring and summer (Figure 7-29), whereas the fewest thunderstorms occur along the Pacific coast, where cool water and subsidence from the subtropical high lead to stable conditions.

Learning Check 7-13 **Describe the sequence of development and dissipation of a typical thunderstorm.**

Lightning: At any given moment some 2000 thunderstorms exist over Earth. These storms produce about 6000 flashes of **lightning** every minute, or more than 8.5 million lightning bolts daily. A lightning flash heats the air along its path to as much as 10,000°C (18,000°F), and can develop 100,000 times the amperage used in household electricity (Figure 7-30).

With such frequency and power, lightning clearly poses a significant potential danger for humanity. In the United States, on average about 65 deaths are blamed on lightning

annually. The most dangerous places to be during a lightning storm are under a tree, in a boat, on a tractor, and playing golf. However, two out of three people struck by lightning in this country are not killed. It is a massive but brief shock, and quick first aid (mouth-to-mouth resuscitation and cardiopulmonary resuscitation) can save most victims.

The sequence of events that leads to lightning discharge is known, but the exact mechanism of electrification is not completely understood. Development of a large cumulonimbus cloud causes a separation of electrical charges. Updrafts carrying positively charged water droplets or crystals rise in the icy upper layers of the cloud while falling ice pellets gather negative charges and transport them downward (Figure 7-31). The growing negative charge in the lower part of the cloud attracts a growing positive charge on the Earth's surface immediately below. The contrast between the two (cloud base and ground surface) builds to tens of millions of volts before the insulating barrier of air that separates the charges is overcome.

Finally, a finger of negative current flicks down from the cloud and meets a positive charge darting upward from the ground. This makes an electrical connection of ionized air from cloud to ground, and a surge of electrical power strikes downward as the first lightning flash. Other flashes may follow in relatively quick succession, until all or most of the negative charges have been drained out of the cloud base.

In addition to such ground-to-cloud discharges, less spectacular but more frequent lightning is exchanged between adjacent clouds or between the upper and lower portions of the same cloud.

Thunder: The abrupt heating caused by a lightning bolt produces instantaneous expansion of the air, which creates a shock wave that becomes a sound wave that we hear as **thunder**. The lightning and thunder occur simultaneously, but we perceive them at different times. Lightning is seen at essentially the instant it occurs because its image travels at the speed of light. Thunder, however, travels at the much slower speed of sound. Thus, it is possible

◀ **Figure 7-29** Average number of days per year with thunderstorms in the conterminous United States.

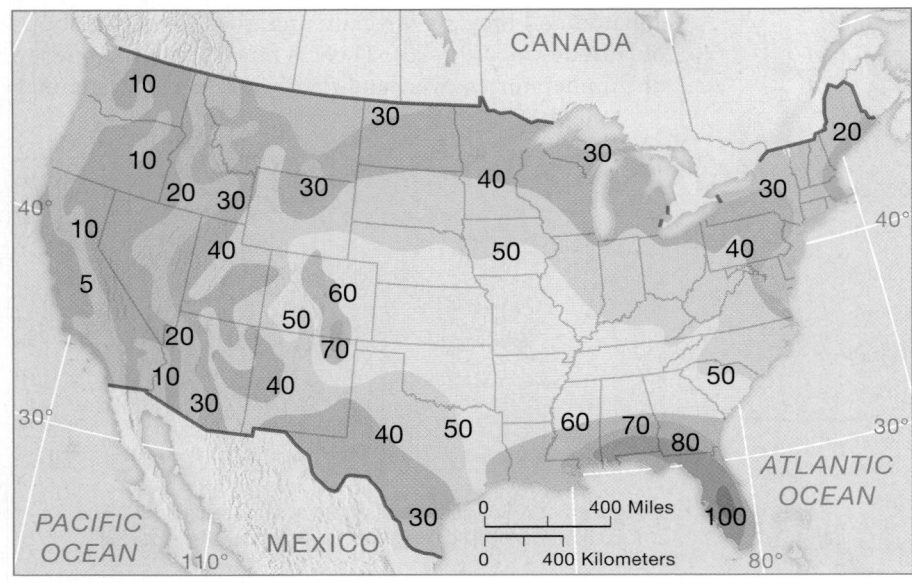

▲ **Figure 7-30** Lightning over Tucson, Arizona.

to estimate the distance of a lightning bolt by timing the interval between sight and sound: a 3-second delay means the lightning strike was about 1 kilometer away; a 5-second interval indicates that the lightning flash was about 1 mile away. Rumbling thunder is indicative of a long lightning trace some distance away, with one portion being nearer than another to the hearer. If no thunder can be heard, the lightning is far away—probably more than 20 kilometers (a dozen miles).

Tornadoes

Although very small and localized, the **tornado** is one of the most destructive of all atmospheric disturbances. It is the most intense vortex in nature: a deep low-pressure cell surrounded by a violently whirling cylinder of wind (Figure 7-32). These are tiny storms, generally less than 400 meters (a quarter of a mile) in diameter, but they have the most extreme pressure

▼ **Figure 7-31** Typical arrangement of electrical charges in a thunderstorm cloud. Positively charged particles are mostly high in the cloud, whereas negatively charged particles tend to be concentrated near the base.

gradients known—as much as a 100-millibar difference from the center of the tornado to the air immediately outside the funnel. This extreme pressure difference produces winds of extraordinary speed. Maximum wind speed estimates range up to 480 kilometers (300 miles) per hour, and air sucked into the vortex also rises at an inordinately fast rate. These storms are of such incredible power, it is no wonder that one was invoked by author Frank Baum, and later Hollywood, to transport a little girl to the Land of Oz.

Funnel Clouds: Tornadoes usually originate a few hundred meters above the ground, the rotating vortex becoming visible when upswept water vapor condenses into a **funnel cloud**. The tornado advances along an irregular track that generally extends from southwest to northeast in the United States. Sometimes the funnel sweeps along the ground, devastating everything in its path, but its trajectory is usually twisting and dodging and may include frequent intervals in which the funnel lifts completely off the ground and then touches down again nearby. Most tornadoes have damage paths 50 meters (about 150 feet) wide, move at about 48 kilometers (30 miles) per hour, and last for only a few minutes. Extremely destructive ones may be more than 1.5 kilometers (1 mile) wide, travel at 95 kilometers (60 miles) per hour, and may be on the ground for more than an hour, with maximum longevity recorded at about 8 hours.

▼ **Figure 7-32** This EF-3 tornado in Mulvane, Kansas, on June 12, 2004, severely damaged the barn behind this farmhouse.

The dark, twisting funnel of a tornado contains not only cloud but also sucked-in dust and debris. Damage is caused largely by the strong winds, flying debris, and swirling updraft. The old advice of opening a window when faced with an approaching tornado (supposedly to reduce an abrupt drop in pressure when the center of the storm passes over a closed building) is no longer given—and in fact opening a window may *increase* the chance of injury from flying debris.

Tornado Formation: As with many other storms, the exact mechanism of tornado formation is not well understood. They may develop in the warm, moist, unstable air associated with a midlatitude cyclone, such as along a squall line that precedes a rapidly advancing cold front or along the cold front itself. Virtually all tornadoes are generated by severe thunderstorms. The basic requirement is vertical wind shear—a significant change in wind speed or direction from the bottom to the top of the storm.

Animation
Tornadoes

On a tornado day, low-level winds are southerly and jet stream winds are southwesterly, and this difference in direction causes turbulence on the boundary between the two systems. The conventional updrafts that become thunderstorms reach several kilometers up into the atmosphere, and the wind shear can cause air to roll along a horizontal axis (Figure 7-33). Strong updrafts in such a rapidly maturing *supercell* thunderstorm may then tilt this rotating air vertically, developing into a **mesocyclone**, with a diameter of 3 to 10 kilometers (2 to 6 miles). About half of all mesocyclones formed result in a tornado.

Spring and early summer are favorable for tornado development because of the considerable air-mass contrast present in the midlatitudes at that time; a tornado can form in any month, however (Figure 7-34). Most occur in midafternoon, at the time of maximum heating. Spring 2011 was an especially destructive tornado season in the United States—see the box, "People and the Environment: The Devastating Tornadoes of 2011."

Tornadoes do occur in the midlatitudes and subtropics, but more than 90 percent are reported in the United States, where about 1000 are sighted each year (Figure 7-35). Such concentration in a single area presumably reflects optimum environmental conditions, with the relatively flat terrain of the central and southeastern United States providing an unhindered zone of interaction between prolific source regions for Canadian cP and Gulf mT air masses. Although between 800 and 1200 tornadoes are recorded annually in the United States, the actual total may be considerably higher than that because many small tornadoes that occur briefly in uninhabited areas are not reported.

Learning Check 7-14 Explain the sequence of formation of a typical tornado associated with a mesocyclone.

Strength: The strength of a tornado is commonly described using the **Enhanced Fujita Scale (EF Scale; Table 7-4)**, named after the late University of Chicago meteorologist, Theodore Fujita. The EF Scale is based on estimates of 3-second gust wind speeds as determined by observed damage after a tornado. About 69 percent of all tornadoes

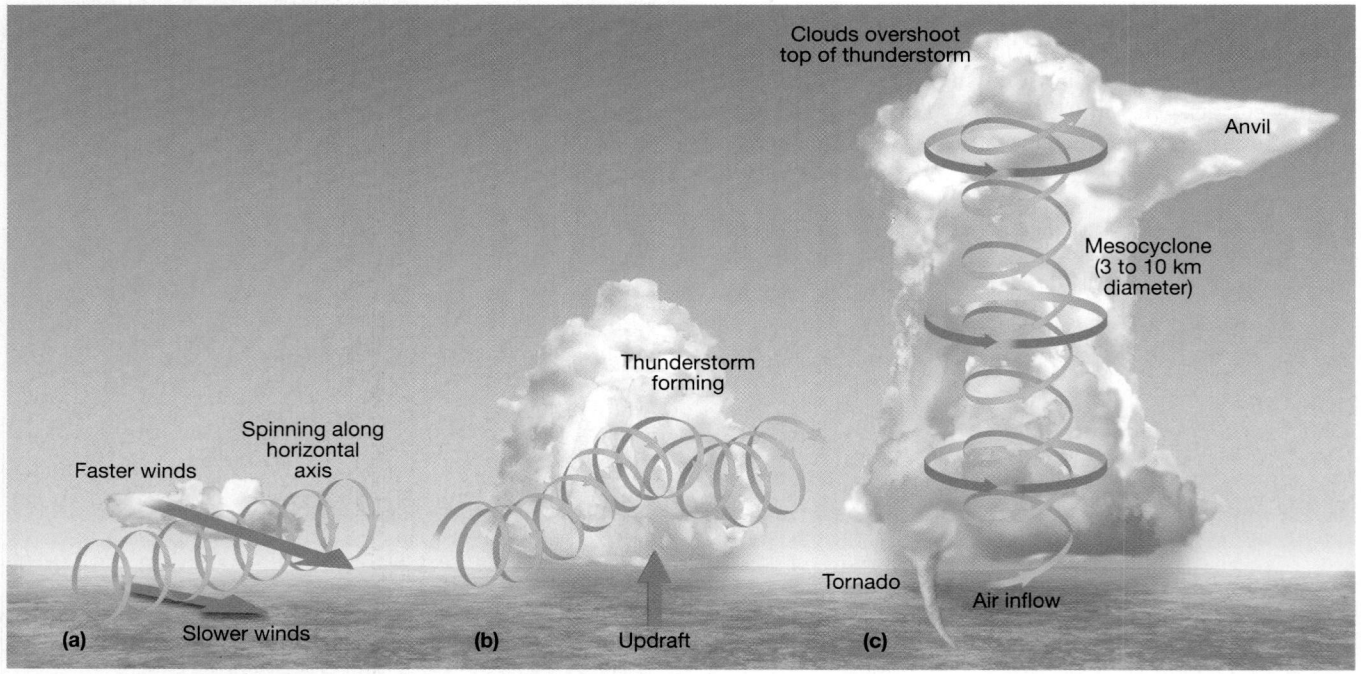

▲ **Figure 7-33** The formation of a mesocyclone often precedes tornado formation. (a) Winds are stronger aloft than at the surface (called *speed wind shear*), producing a rolling motion around a horizontal axis. (b) Strong thunderstorm updrafts tilt the horizontally rotating air to a nearly vertical alignment. (c) The mesocyclone, a vertical cylinder of rotating air, is established. If a tornado develops it will descend from a slowly rotating wall cloud in the lower portion of the mesocyclone.

The Devastating Tornadoes of 2011
▶ Ted Eckmann, Bowling Green State University

The tornadoes of 2011 shattered many long-standing records and demonstrated that despite advances in detection and warning technology, tornadoes still pose major threats. Prior to 2011, the record for the largest number of tornadoes in a single month stood at 542, but April 2011 surpassed this in dramatic fashion with 758 tornadoes reported across the United States. The most active part of the month was from April 25 to April 28, and it included the deadliest tornado outbreak since modern recordkeeping began. This outbreak produced 343 confirmed tornadoes and killed 321 people (Figure 7-E). Damage likely exceeded 10 billion dollars. Four of these tornadoes produced damage up to the EF-5 category—the first EF-5 tornadoes anywhere on Earth since 2008. However, these storms would not be the last tornadoes to reach EF-5 strength in this record-breaking year.

EF-5 Tornadoes: Although EF-5 is the rarest ranking for a tornado, EF-5s produce a disproportionately large share of overall tornado fatalities because they can destroy even well-built structures. Thus, even people in shelters who would be adequately protected from weaker tornadoes sometimes die in EF-5 strength winds, which can be the fastest on Earth. All four of the EF-5 tornadoes in Figure 7-E occurred on the same day—April 27, 2011—that set a new record for the largest number of confirmed tornadoes in a 24-hour period: 199. The largest of the EF-5 tornadoes from April 27 remained on the ground for almost 2 hours, producing a damage path 172 kilometers (107 miles) long and up to 2 kilometers (1.25 miles) wide.

Joplin Tornado: Less than one month later, on May 22, another EF-5 tornado occurred, this time in Joplin, Missouri (Figure 7-F). In comparison to many of the tornadoes from the April outbreak, the EF-5 in Joplin was relatively compact, with a path length of

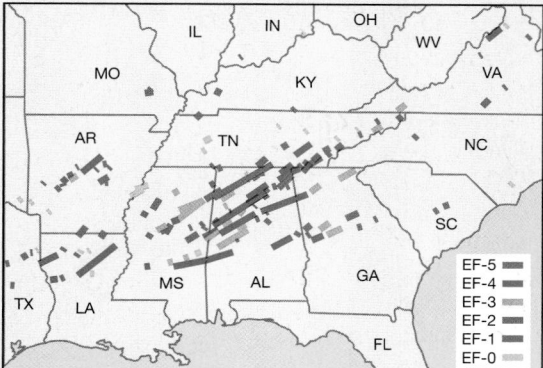

▲ **Figure 7-E** Approximate paths of tornadoes from April 25 to 28, 2011, color-coded by maximum intensity reached along the path.

only 36 kilometers (22 miles). However, the Joplin tornado reached its peak strength in a densely populated city of around 50,000 residents. Most of the areas affected in the April outbreak had substantially lower population densities, and although parts of urban areas like Tuscaloosa and Birmingham, Alabama, did experience EF-4 level damage, the EF-5 tornadoes in the April outbreak mostly occurred outside large cities.

The Joplin tornado's combination of EF-5 strength with a densely populated area produced catastrophic results. It killed 158 people and caused three billion dollars of damage, making it the most destructive and most deadly tornado since modern recordkeeping began. Tornadoes occurred in seven other states on the same day as the Joplin tornado, but the Joplin tornado was the day's only EF-5, and the totals for destruction and fatalities from that day remained well below the records set in the April outbreak a few weeks earlier.

Lessons Learned: By the end of 2011, tornadoes had killed 551 people in the United States—the largest annual total in 62 years of modern records. Even though weather forecasting and warning technologies have improved dramatically over the last 62 years, population densities have also increased, and studies have found that some people may even be taking tornadoes less seriously than they did in the past—education and communication about tornado hazards remain important components of public safety during severe storms.

▲ **Figure 7-F** Damage in Joplin, Missouri, two days after an EF-5 tornado devastated the city.

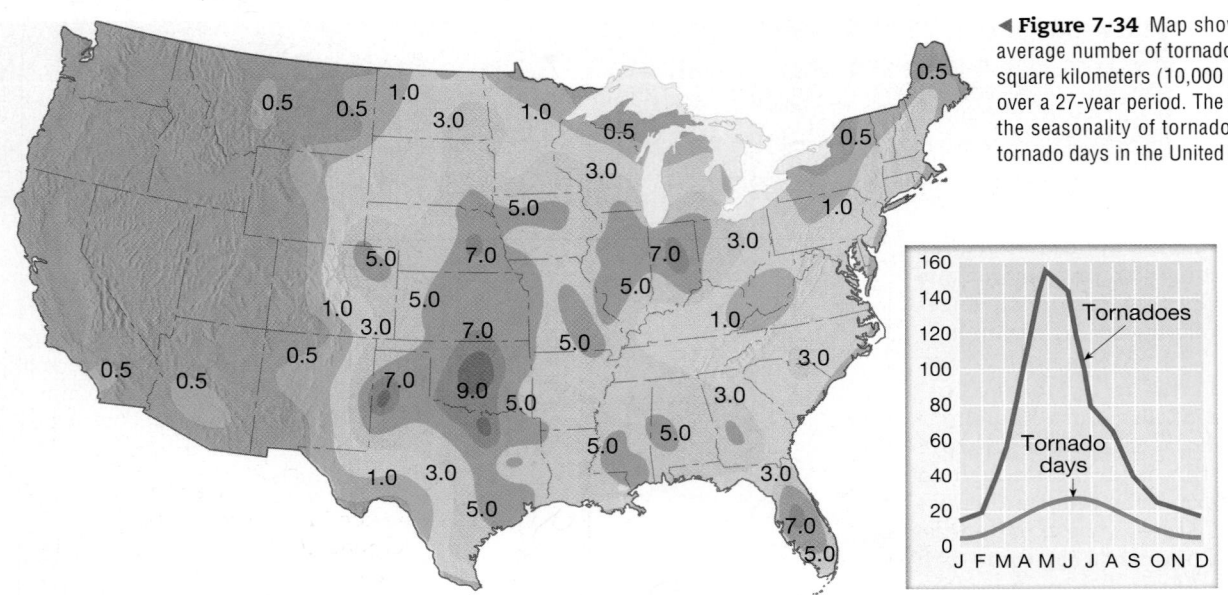

◀ **Figure 7-34** Map showing the average number of tornadoes per 26,000 square kilometers (10,000 square miles) over a 27-year period. The chart shows the seasonality of tornadoes and tornado days in the United States.

in the United States are classified as *light* or *moderate* (EF-0 or EF-1), about 29 percent are classified as *strong* or *severe* (EF-2 or EF-3), and 2 percent are classified as *devastating* or *incredible* (EF-4 or EF-5). The average annual death toll from violent tornadoes in the United States has declined over the last 50 years, primarily due to better forecasting and emergency broadcasts—the 551 deaths in 2011 were a tragic exception.

Waterspouts

True tornadoes are apparently restricted to land areas. Similar-appearing funnels over the ocean, called **waterspouts**, have a lesser pressure gradient, gentler winds, and reduced destructive capability.

Severe Storm Watches and Warnings

Forecasting severe thunderstorms and tornadoes has improved remarkably over the last few decades, largely due to a better understanding of these events and more sophisticated technology—see the box, "Focus: Weather Radar."

The U.S. National Weather Service provides two types of advisories when severe weather such as a strong thunderstorm or tornado is likely: *watches* and *warnings*.

A severe **storm watch** is an advisory issued for a region (perhaps the area of one or more counties) where over the next 4 to 6 hours the conditions are favorable for the development of severe weather. A watch only means that the conditions are right for severe weather, not that such weather has developed or is even impending.

In contrast, a severe **storm warning** is issued by a local weather forecasting office when a severe thunderstorm or tornado has actually been observed—such warnings are often accompanied by civil defense sirens and emergency broadcasts on radio and television. When a warning is given, the public is directed to take immediate action, such as seeking safety in a storm shelter.

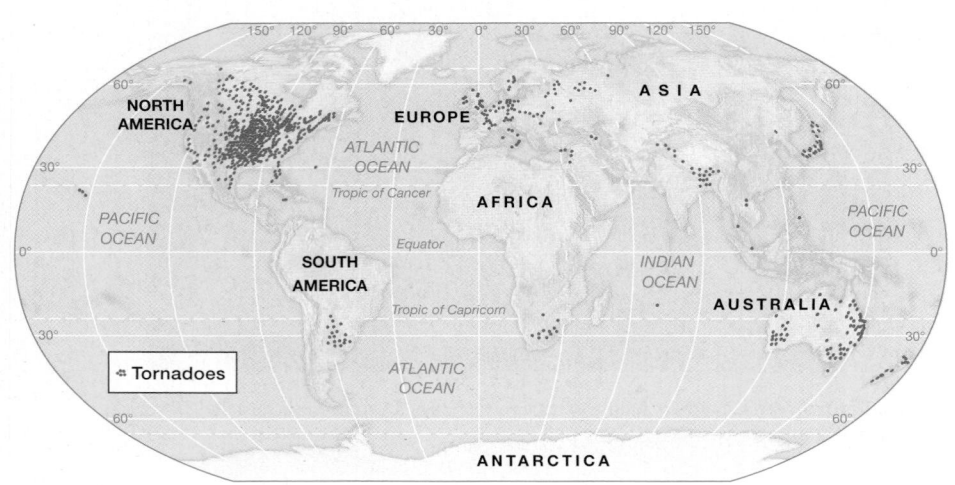

◀ **Figure 7-35** Anticipated distribution of tornadoes over the world in any given five-year period. The Great Plains of North America is clearly a favored area of development.

Weather Radar

▶ Steve Stadler, Oklahoma State University

For more than a half century, radar has enabled meteorologists to observe weather and produce timely warnings that have saved many lives. NEXRAD (an abbreviation of NEXt-generation RADar) is the system of weather radars installed at over 150 locations in the United States.

Weather radar's operating principle is the *Doppler effect*, familiar to anyone who has ever stopped at a railroad track as a speeding train passes. As the train approaches, the pitch of its whistle seems to get higher and higher. After the train passes, the whistle's pitch seems to get lower and lower as the train moves away. In reality, the pitch does not change. The apparent change depends on whether the sound source is approaching or receding from the listener.

NEXRAD: NEXRAD transmits microwave pulses through the atmosphere (Figure 7-G). Water—cloud droplets, raindrops, ice crystals, and hail—reflects some of the microwaves back to the NEXRAD site. The strength of the reflected signal provides an estimate of the intensity of the storm. NEXRAD uses the Doppler effect to sense motion toward and away from the radar site in order to determine the internal structure of the storm. If the pulses received back at the radar site are of shorter wavelengths

▲ **Figure 7-G** Tower and radar dome of a NEXRAD site.

than the transmitted wavelengths, that part of the storm is moving toward the radar. If the pulses are of longer wavelengths, that part of the storm is moving away from the radar.

Starting in 2011, NEXRAD radars underwent upgrades of hardware and software to incorporate *dual polarization*. The upgraded system simultaneously emits pulses of horizontally oriented and vertically oriented microwaves that are reflected in a manner analogous to the radar pulses. Based on the reflected microwave data, the software identifies

the forms of precipitation present and the precipitation rate.

One important use of NEXRAD is in detecting tornadoes. Figures 7-H and 7-I show a huge thunderstorm containing an EF-5 tornado as it passed over Joplin in southwestern Missouri (see the box, "The Devastating Tornadoes of 2011"). Figure 7-H is a NEXRAD reflectivity scan from Springfield, Missouri, in the eastern part of the image. Units in the legend are dbz (decibels), with more intense colors representing higher reflectivity from very large raindrops and hail.

Tornado funnels are usually only a few hundred meters across, and it is rare that NEXRAD can detect them using reflectivity alone. However, NEXRAD can detect motion to within 0.9 meters per second (2 mph). Figure 7-I shows the same storm as Figure 7-H, but using NEXRAD's motion-detection capability. Greens indicate movement away from the radar, and reds indicate movement toward the radar. In this case, reds and greens are nearby each other, implying a strong counterclockwise rotation. This large area of rotation is a mesocyclone, a part of the thunderstorm that might produce a tornado. Based on this display, a radar operator would issue a tornado warning.

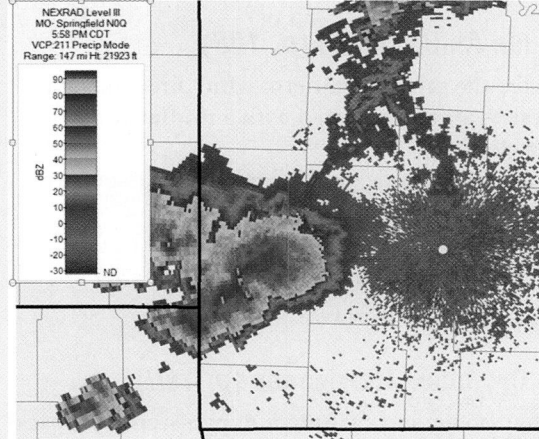

▲ **Figure 7-H** NEXRAD reflectivity image of May 2011 Joplin tornadic storm. Visualization software courtesy of the Oklahoma Mesonetwork.

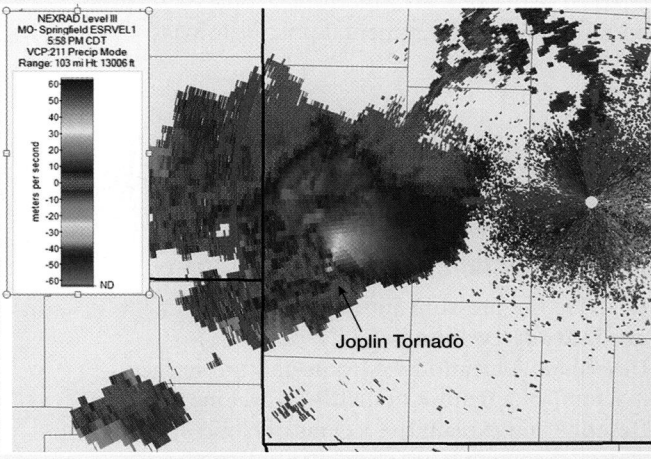

▲ **Figure 7-I** NEXRAD storm relative velocity image of May 2011 Joplin tornadic storm. Visualization software courtesy of the Oklahoma Mesonetwork.

TABLE 7-4	Enhanced Fujita Scale (EF Scale) for Tornadoes

EF Scale	Enhanced F Scale 3-second gust km/hr	3-second gust mph	Expected Level of Damage
0	105–137	65–85	Light: Broken tree branches; uprooted small trees; billboards and chimneys damaged.
1	138–177	86–110	Moderate: Roof surfaces peeled off; mobile homes overturned or pushed off their foundations.
2	178–217	111–135	Strong: Mobile homes destroyed; roofs blown off wooden-frame houses; uprooted large trees; light objects become "missiles."
3	218–266	136–165	Severe: Trains derailed or overturned; walls and roofs torn from well-constructed houses; heavy cars thrown off ground.
4	267–322	166–200	Devastating: Structures with weak foundations blown for some distance; well-built houses destroyed; large objects become missiles.
5	Over 322	Over 200	Incredible: Well-built houses lifted off foundations and carried considerable distance before complete destruction; tree bark removed; automobile-sized missiles carried more than 100 meters.

Chapter 7   LEARNING REVIEW

After studying this chapter, you should be able to answer the following questions. Key terms from each text section are shown in **bold type**. Definitions for key terms are also found in the glossary at the back of the book.

KEY TERMS AND CONCEPTS

Air Masses (*p. 178*)

1. What is an **air mass**, and what conditions are necessary for one to form?
2. What regions of Earth are least likely to produce air masses? Why?
3. Contrast and explain the moisture and temperature characteristics of a mT (maritime tropical) air mass with that of a cP (continental polar) air mass.

Fronts (*p. 180*)

4. What is the relationship of air masses to a **front**?
5. What is a **cold front**? What is a **warm front**?
6. What is a **stationary front**?

Midlatitude Cyclones (*p. 182*)

7. Describe the pressure and wind patterns of a **midlatitude cyclone**.
8. Describe the locations of fronts and the surface "sectors" of a mature midlatitude cyclone.
9. Describe and explain the regions of cloud development and precipitation within a midlatitude cyclone.
10. Discuss the four components of movement of a midlatitude cyclone.
11. Explain the process of **occlusion**.
12. Why does an **occluded front** usually indicate the "death" of a midlatitude cyclone?

13. Discuss the origin of midlatitude cyclones. What is the relationship between upper-level airflow and the formation of surface disturbances in the midlatitudes?
14. Describe and explain the changes in wind direction, atmospheric pressure, sky conditions (such as clouds and precipitation), and temperature with the passing of a cold front of a midlatitude cyclone.

Midlatitude Anticyclones (*p. 188*)

15. Describe the pressure pattern, wind direction, and general weather associated with a **midlatitude anticyclone**.
16. How are midlatitude anticyclones often associated with midlatitude cyclones?

Easterly Waves (*p. 189*)

17. What is an **easterly wave**?

Tropical Cyclones: Hurricanes (*p. 190*)

18. Distinguish among a **tropical depression**, a **tropical storm**, and a **hurricane**.
19. Describe and explain the pressure and wind patterns of a **tropical cyclone (hurricane)**.
20. Discuss the characteristics of the **eye** of a hurricane.
21. What is **wind shear**?
22. Discuss the conditions necessary for a hurricane to form.

23. Describe and explain the typical paths taken by hurricanes in the North Atlantic Ocean basin.
24. Why do hurricanes weaken when they move over land?
25. What is a hurricane **storm surge**, and what causes one?
26. Briefly explain the **Saffir-Simpson Hurricane Scale**.
27. Do hurricanes have any beneficial effects? Explain.

Localized Severe Weather *(p. 197)*

28. Discuss the general sequence of **thunderstorm** development and dissipation.

29. What is the relationship of **thunder** to **lightning**?
30. Describe the wind and pressure characteristics of a **tornado**.
31. What is a **funnel cloud**?
32. Discuss the general formation of a tornado from a supercell thunderstorm and **mesocyclone**.
33. Briefly explain the **Enhanced Fujita Scale (EF Scale)** for tornadoes.
34. What is the difference between a tornado and a **waterspout**?
35. What is the difference between a **storm watch** and a **storm warning**?

STUDY QUESTIONS

1. Why is an air mass unlikely to form over the Rocky Mountains of North America?
2. Why are maritime polar air (mP) masses from the Atlantic Ocean less important to the United States than mP air masses from the Pacific Ocean?
3. Explain why clouds develop along cold fronts and warm fronts.
4. Why do midlatitude cyclones develop in the midlatitudes but not in the tropics?

5. Why are there no fronts in a midlatitude anticyclone?
6. Why are there no fronts in a hurricane?
7. Why are tropical cyclones common along the east coasts of continents in the midlatitudes, but not along the west coasts?
8. Why are thunderstorms more common over land than over water?
9. Why are thunderstorms sometimes called "convective storms"?

EXERCISES

1. If you see a flash of lightning and you hear thunder 15 seconds later, how far away are you from the lightning in the thunderstorm? _____ miles
2. Four minutes after the first flash of lightning, you see another flash from the same storm, but the thunder arrives in only 10 seconds. How fast is

the thunderstorm moving toward you? _____ miles per hour
3. Look at the map of thunderstorm activity in the United States (Figure 7-29). Explain why the west coast of California has so little thunderstorm activity, while Florida has so much.

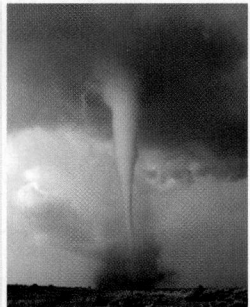

Seeing Geographically

Look again at the photograph of the tornado at the beginning of the chapter (p. 176). Explain why the funnel cloud doesn't look the same all of the way down from the cloud base to the ground. Why was a tornado outbreak such as this much more likely to occur in spring than any other time of year? How might topography of the Great Plains influence the prevalence of tornadoes?

MasteringGeography™

Looking for additional review and test prep materials? Visit the Study Area in MasteringGeography™ to enhance your geographic literacy, spatial reasoning skills, and understanding of this chapter's content by accessing a variety of resources, including geoscience animations, MapMaster interactive maps, videos, RSS feeds, flashcards, web links, self-study quizzes, and an eText version of *McKnight's Physical Geography: A Landscape Appreciation.*

THIS CHAPTER IS THE CULMINATION OF OUR STUDY OF THE

atmosphere. Our goal here is to recognize and understand basic patterns of climate around the world.

Describing the geographic distribution of many things—such as population density, voting patterns, or a host of other concrete entities or simple relationships—is relatively easy. Climate, however, is the product of a number of elements that are, for the most part, continuously and independently variable—making the task of describing climate distribution quite complex.

Temperature, for instance, is one of the simplest climatic elements to describe, and yet in this book more than 40 maps and diagrams are used to convey various temperature patterns around the world: daily, monthly, and annual averages, as well as temperature ranges and extremes. Climate involves almost continuous variation from place to place, not only of temperature but also many other factors.

Adding to the complexity of understanding climate distribution is that climate can change over time. The geologic record reveals times in both the distant and recent past when Earth's climate was markedly different from today—such as the great ice ages of the Pleistocene Epoch that ended about 10,000 years ago (the Pleistocene is discussed in Chapter 19). More important for us today, however, are the indications of climate change that seem to be under way as a result of human activity.

In this chapter we begin by describing the classification and distribution of global climate types—discussing climate largely as it has been over the last few thousands of years. We conclude the chapter with a discussion of climate change: recognizing, explaining, and anticipating the consequences of a climate system that seems to be in a state of flux.

As you study this chapter, think about these key questions:

- **How is the *Köppen system* used to classify climate?**
- **What factors explain the seasonal rainfall patterns of *tropical humid climates*?**
- **What are the main controls responsible for the dryness of *desert climates*?**
- **Why do *mediterranean climates* have dry summers, whereas the other *mild midlatitude climates* do not?**
- **What explains the cold winters of the *severe midlatitude climates*?**
- **Why are *polar climates* both so cold and so dry?**
- **How do we know what climate was like in the past?**
- **What are some causes of long-term climate change?**
- **What is the evidence for—and possible consequences of—present-day climate change?**

Seeing Geographically

Aerial view of glaciers in the mountains of southeastern Greenland. Other than the glaciers, what do you see in the photograph that suggests that this is an extremely cold environment? How does the topography here influence where snow and ice are likely to remain throughout the year?

CLIMATE CLASSIFICATION

To cope with the great diversity of information encompassed by the study of global climate distribution, we need a classification scheme to simplify, organize, and generalize a vast array of data.

As an illustration of how a classification system can help us understand global climate patterns, suppose that a geography student in Atlanta, Georgia, is asked to describe the climate of southeastern China. A world map portraying the distribution of climate types (such as the map in Figure 8-3 on p. 210) shows that southeastern China has the same climate as the southeastern United States. So, the student's familiarity with the home climate in Georgia provides a basis for understanding the general characteristics of the climate of southeastern China.

Early Classification Schemes

The earliest known climatic classification scheme originated with the ancient Greeks, perhaps 2200 years ago. Although the "known world" was very small at that time, Greek scholars were aware of the shape and approximate size of Earth. They knew that at the southern limit of their world, along the Nile River and the southern coast of the Mediterranean, the climate was much hotter and drier than on the islands and northern coast of that sea. At the other end of the world known to the Greeks, along the Danube River and the northern coast of the Black Sea, things were much colder, especially in winter. So the Greeks spoke of three climatic zones: the *Temperate Zone* of the midlatitudes, in which they lived (Athens is at 38° N); the *Torrid Zone* of the tropics to the south; and the *Frigid Zone* to the north. Because they knew that Earth is a sphere, they suggested that the Southern Hemisphere has similar Temperate and Frigid Zones, making five in all.

For many centuries, this classification scheme was handed down from scholar to scholar. Gradually these five climatic zones were confused with, and eventually their climates ascribed to, the five astronomical zones of the Earth, bounded by the Tropics of Cancer and Capricorn and the Arctic and Antarctic Circles (Figure 8-1). This revision put the equatorial rainy zone in with the hot arid region in the Torrid Zone, extended the Temperate Zone to include much of what the Greeks had called Frigid, and moved the Frigid Zone poleward to the polar circles. This simplistic but unrealistic classification scheme persisted for more than a thousand years and was finally discarded only in the twentieth century.

The Köppen Climate Classification System

The **Köppen climate classification system** is by far the most widely used modern climate classification system. Wladimir Köppen (1846–1940; pronounced like "kur-pin" with a silent r) was a Russian-born German climatologist who was also an amateur botanist. The first version of his

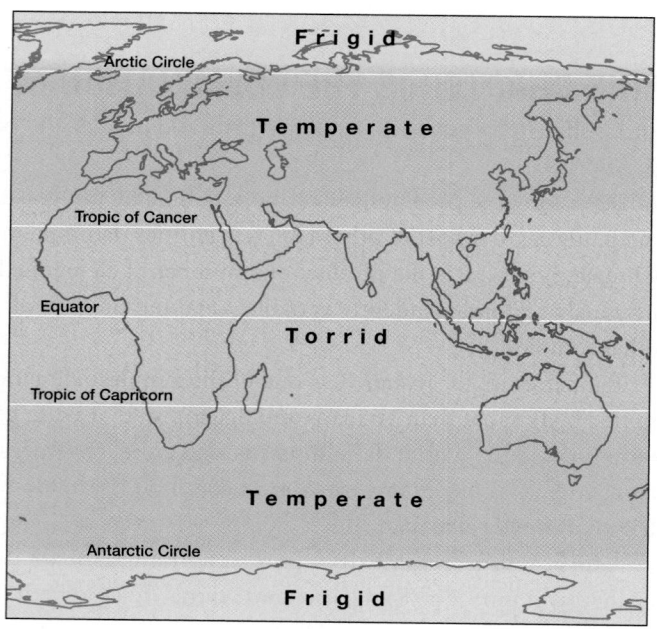

▲ **Figure 8-1** The original Greek climate classification scheme was expanded and correlated with Earth's five astronomical zones to depict a world comprising five climate zones.

climate classification scheme appeared in 1918, and he continued to modify and refine it for the rest of his life, the last version being published in 1936.

The system uses as a database only the average annual and average monthly values of temperature and precipitation, combined and compared in a variety of ways. Consequently, the necessary statistics are commonly tabulated and easily acquired. Data for any location (called a *station*) on Earth can be used to determine the precise classification of that place, and the geographical extent of any recognized climatic type can be determined and mapped. This means that the classification system is functional at both the local and the global scale.

Köppen defined four of his five major climatic groups primarily by temperature characteristics, the fifth (the B group) on the basis of moisture. He then subdivided each group into climate types according to various temperature and precipitation relationships.

Köppen was unsatisfied with his last version and did not consider it a finished product. Thus, many geographers and climatologists have used the Köppen system as a springboard to devise systems of their own or to modify Köppen's classifications. The system of climate classification used in this book is properly called the *modified Köppen system*. It encompasses the basic design of the Köppen system but with a variety of minor modifications. Some of these modifications follow the lead of Glen Trewartha, who was a geographer and climatologist at the University of Wisconsin.

The modified Köppen system describes five major climate groups (groups A, B, C, D, and E) which are subdivided into a total of 14 individual climate types, along with the special category of highland (H) climate. In this book, no attempt is made to distinguish between pure Köppen and modified Köppen system definitions: our goal is to comprehend the general pattern of world climate, not to learn a specific system or to nitpick about boundaries.

> **Learning Check 8-1** What kinds of data are used to classify climates in the Köppen system? (Answer on p. AK-2)

Köppen Letter Code System: In the modified Köppen system, each climate type is designated by a descriptive name and by a series of letters defined by specific temperature and/or precipitation values (Figure 8-2). The first letter designates the major climate group, the second letter usually describes precipitation patterns, and the third letter (if any) describes temperature patterns. Figure 8-3 (on the following page) is a map showing the global distribution of all these climates and provides a general description of the meaning of the letters. (See Appendix V for the exact definitions used for classification.)

Although the letter code system seems complicated at first, it provides a shorthand method for summarizing key characteristics of each climate. For example, if we look for the definitions of the letters in *Csa*, one of the letter code combinations for a *mediterranean climate*, we see that:

C = mild midlatitude climate
s = summer dry season
a = hot summers

As we will see later in this chapter, that is a very good synopsis of the distinctive characteristics of this climate type.

Climographs

Probably the most useful tool in a general study of world climatic classification is a simple graphic representation of monthly temperature and precipitation for a specific weather station. Such a graph is called a **climograph** (or

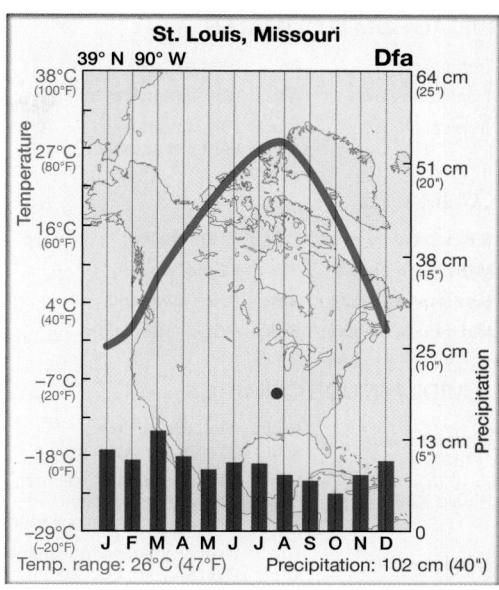

▲ **Figure 8-4** A typical climograph. Average monthly temperature is shown with a solid red line (scale along left side), and average monthly precipitation is shown with blue bars extending from the bottom (scale along the right side).

climatic diagram); a typical one is shown in Figure 8-4. The customary climograph has 12 columns, one for each month, with a temperature scale on the left side and a precipitation scale on the right. Average monthly temperatures are connected by a curved line in the upper portion of the diagram, and average monthly precipitation is represented by bars extending upward from the bottom.

The value of a climograph is twofold: (1) it displays precise details of important aspects of the climate of a specific place, and (2) it can be used to recognize and classify the climate of that place.

> **Learning Check 8-2** What information is conveyed on a *climograph?*

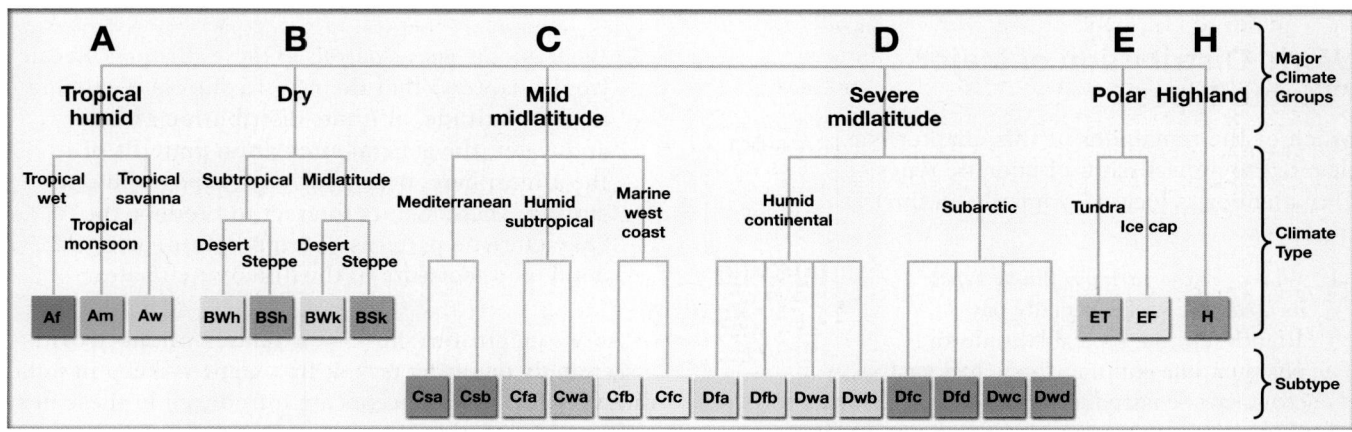

▲ **Figure 8-2** The modified Köppen climatic classification. There are 5 major climate groups (and the special category of Highland) and 15 individual climate types.

A TROPICAL HUMID CLIMATES

	Tropical wet	**Af**	(Wet all year)
	Tropical savanna	**Aw**	(Dry winter; wet summer)
	Tropical monsoon	**Am**	(Dry winter; very wet summer)

B DRY CLIMATES

	Subtropical desert	**BWh**	("Hot" desert)
	Midlatitude desert	**BWk**	("Cold" desert)
	Subtropical steppe	**BSh**	("Hot" semiarid)
	Midlatitude steppe	**BSk**	("Cold" semiarid)

C MILD MIDLATITUDE CLIMATES

	Mediterranean	**Csa** **Csb**	(Hot, dry summer) (Warm, dry summer)
	Humid subtropical	**Cfa** **Cwa** **Cwb**	(Wet all year; hot summer) (Dry winter; hot summer) (Dry winter; warm summer)
	Marine west coast	**Cfb** **Cfc**	(Wet all year; warm summer) (Wet all year; cool summer)

D SEVERE MIDLATITUDE CLIMATES

	Humid continental	**Dfa**	(Cold winter; wet all year; hot summer)
		Dfb	(Cold winter; wet all year; warm summer)
		Dwa	(Cold, dry winter; hot summer)
		Dwb	(Cold, dry winter; warm summer)
	Subarctic	**Dfc**	(Cold winter; no dry season; cool summer)
		Dfd	(Very cold winter; no dry season)
		Dwc	(Cold, dry winter; cool summer)
		Dwd	(Very cold, dry winter)

E POLAR CLIMATES

	Tundra	**ET**	(Polar tundra; no true summer)
	Ice cap	**EF**	(Polar ice cap)

H HIGHLAND CLIMATES

		H	(High elevation climates)

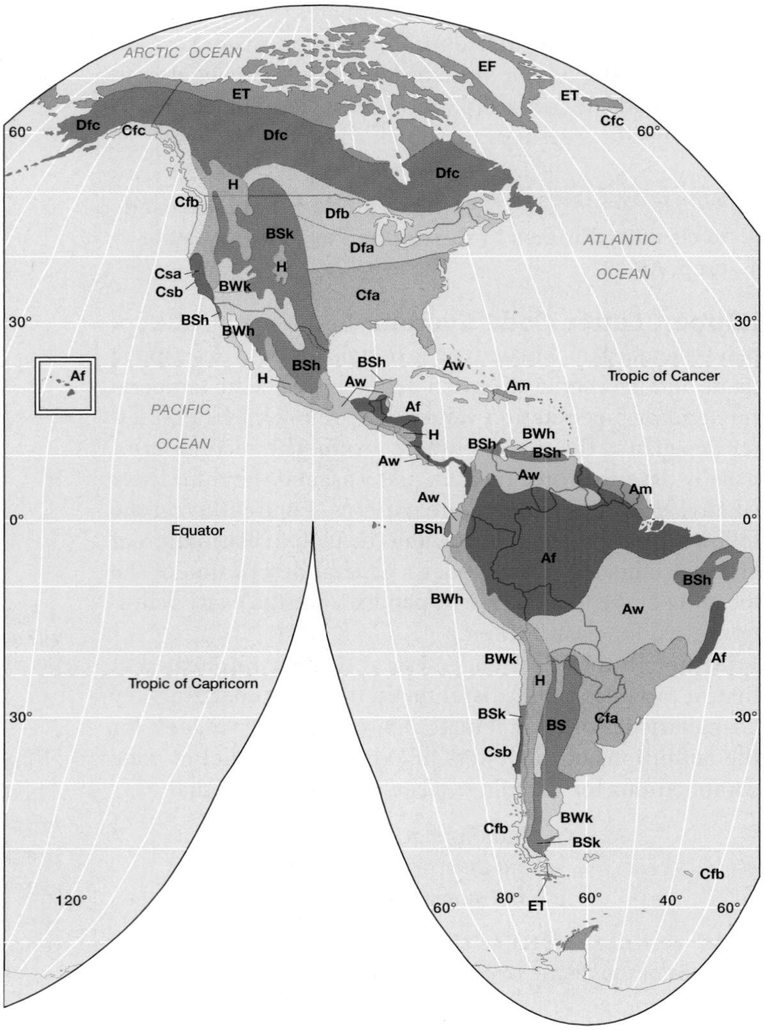

▲ **Figure 8-3** Climatic regions over land areas (modified Köppen system).

World Distribution of Major Climate Types

Much of the remainder of this chapter is devoted to a discussion of climatic types. Our attention is focused primarily on three questions:

Animation
Seasonal
Pressure and
Precipitation
Patterns

1. *Where are the various climate types located?* We will especially pay attention to the typical latitude and position on a continent—such as east coast, west coast, or interior—of each climate.

2. *What are the characteristics of each climate?* We are especially interested in the annual and seasonal temperature and precipitation patterns of each climate.

3. *What are the main controls of these climates?* Recall from Chapter 3 that the major controls of climate include latitude, altitude, distribution of land and water, the general circulation patterns of the atmosphere, ocean currents, topography, and storms. These factors interact to produce the characteristic patterns of temperature, pressure, wind, and moisture of the different climates.

As we begin our look at climates of the world—a seemingly daunting task at first glance—keep in mind that very few new concepts are introduced in these next sections. Rather, this discussion of climate distribution lets us systematically organize what we have *already* learned about weather and climate in previous chapters.

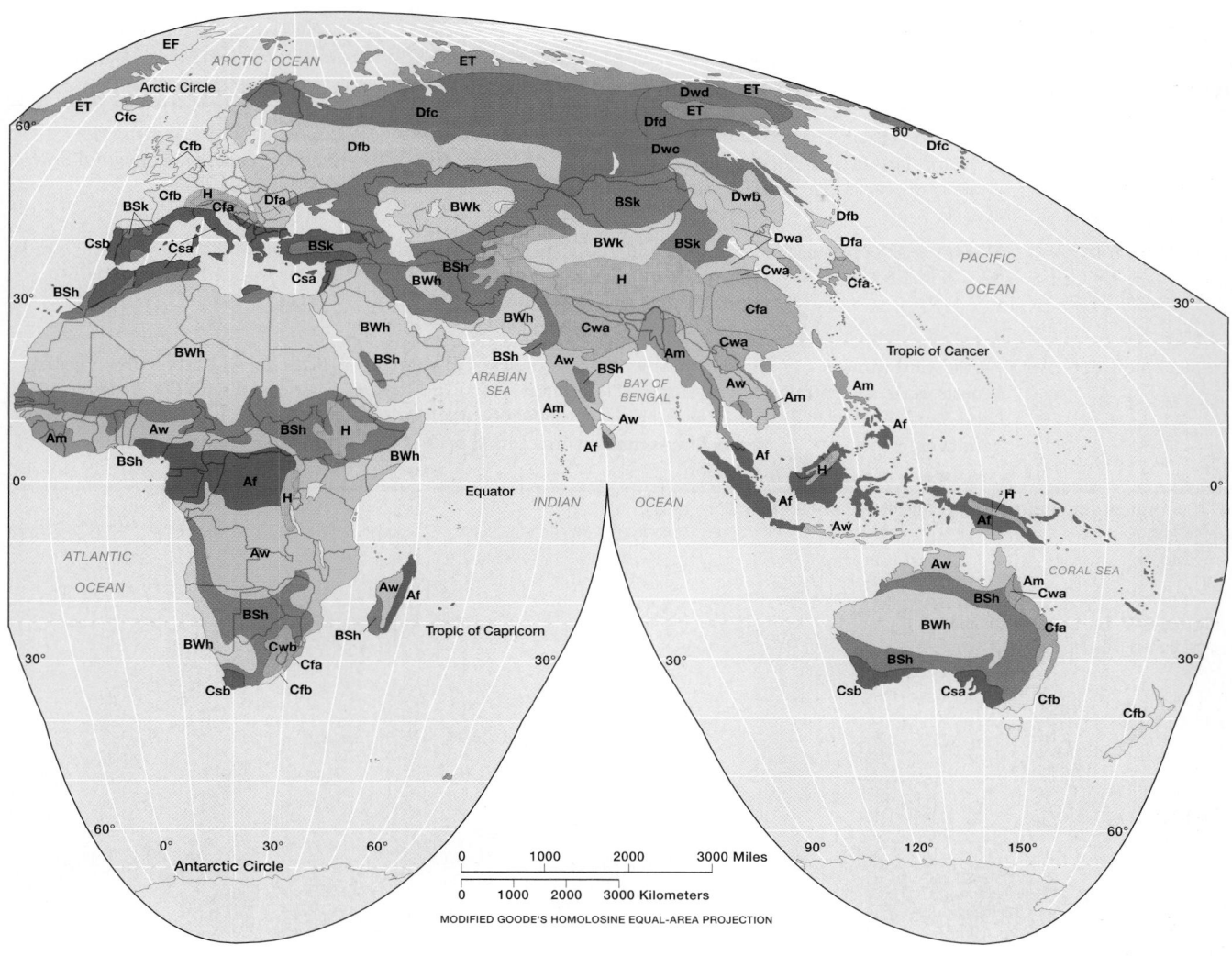

Also, take advantage of the climate "summary" tables for each major climate group (such as Table 8-1 on p. 212). This series of tables concisely describes the general location, temperature and precipitation characteristics, and dominant controls for each climate in the Köppen system.

TROPICAL HUMID CLIMATES (GROUP A)

The *tropical humid climates* (Group A) occupy almost all the land area of Earth within the tropics (Figure 8-5), interrupted only here and there by mountains or small regions of aridity. The A climates are noted not so much for warmth as for lack of coldness. Interestingly though, they do not experience the world's highest temperatures for reasons we shall see later.

These are the only truly winterless climates of the world. However, the terms *winter* and *summer* are sometimes used in discussing tropical climates, as in the "winter monsoon" and the "summer monsoon"—in this context, these adjectives mean the time of the year when mid- and high-latitude locations are indeed cold or hot. Alternately, we can refer to the "high-Sun season" (summer) and the "low-Sun season" (winter), where *high* and *low* are strictly relative terms.

The second typifying characteristic of the tropical humid climates is the prevalence of moisture. Although not universally rainy, much of the tropical humid zone is among the wettest in the world, influenced at least part of the year by the thermal convection and onshore winds associated with the intertropical convergence zone (ITCZ), and regionally from monsoon wind patterns.

The tropical humid climates are classified into three types on the basis of annual rainfall. The *tropical wet* has abundant rainfall every month of the year. The *tropical savanna* is characterized by a low-Sun dry season and a prominent but not extraordinary high-Sun wet season. The *tropical monsoon* has a dry season and a distinct very rainy high-Sun wet season (Table 8-1).

TABLE 8-1	Summary of A Climates: Tropical Humid			
Type	**Location**	**Temperature**	**Precipitation**	**Dominant Controls of Climate**
Tropical wet (Af)	Within 5–10° of equator; farther poleward on eastern coasts	Warm all year; very small ATR; small DTR; high sensible temperature	No dry season; 150–250 cm (60–100 in.) annually; many thunderstorms	Latitude; ITCZ; trade wind convergence; onshore wind flow
Tropical savanna (Aw)	Fringing Af between 25° N and S	Warm to hot all year; moderate ATR and DTR	Distinct summer wet and winter dry seasons; 90–180 cm (35–70 in.) annually	Seasonal shifting of tropical wind and pressure belts, especially ITCZ
Tropical monsoon (Am)	Windward tropical coasts of Asia, Central and South America, and west Africa	Similar to Af with slightly larger ATR; hottest weather just before summer monsoon	Very heavy in summer; short winter dry season; 250–500 cm (100–200 in.) annually	Seasonal wind direction reversal associated with ITCZ movement; jet stream fluctuation; continental pressure changes

ATR = annual temperature range; DTR = daily temperature range.

▶ **Figure 8-5** The global distribution of tropical humid (A) climates.

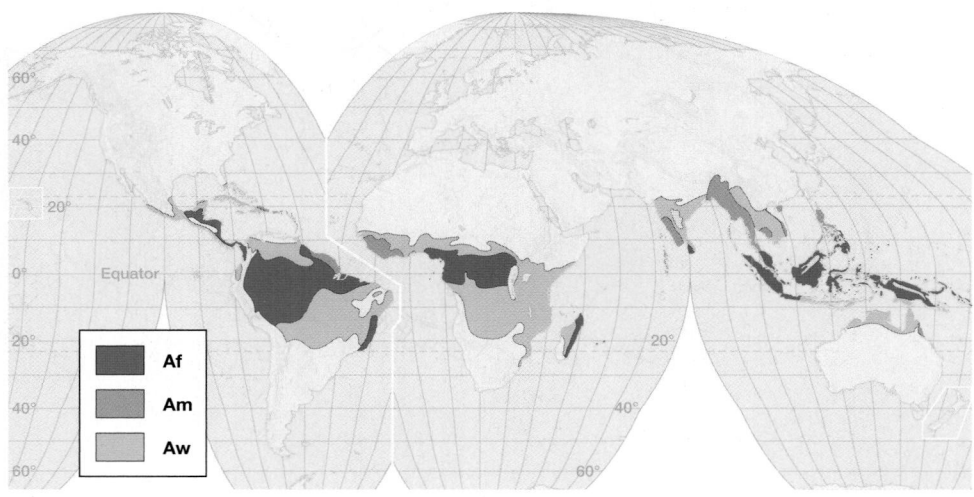

Tropical Wet Climate (Af)

The **tropical wet climate** is predominantly equatorial, found in an east-west sprawl astride the equator—typically extending to about 10° N and S (see Figure 8-5), but in a few east–coast locations as much as 25° poleward of the equator. The largest areas of Af climate occur in the upper Amazon basin of South America, the northern Congo basin of Africa, and the islands of Southeast Asia.

Characteristics of Af: The single most descriptive word that can be applied to the tropical wet climate is "monotonous." This is a seasonless climate, with endless repetition of the same weather day after day after day. Warmth prevails, with every month having an average temperature close to 27°C (80°F)—as Figure 8-6 shows, and an average annual temperature range that is typically only 1 to 2°C (2 to 4°F)—by far the smallest annual temperature range of any climatic type.

This seasonless condition in Af regions gives rise to the saying, "Night is the winter of the tropics"—this is one of the few climates in which the *average daily temperature range* (the difference in temperature between day and night) is greater than the *average annual temperature range* (the difference in temperature between summer and winter; Figure 8-7a). Daytime highs climb into the low 30s°C (high 80s°F) but only fall into the low 20s°C (low 70s°F) just before dawn.

Regardless of the thermometer reading, however, the weather feels warm in this climate because high humidity makes for high sensible temperatures. Both absolute and relative humidity are high, and rain can be expected just about every day—sometimes twice or three times a day (Figure 8-7b). Rainfall typically comes from convective thunderstorms that yield heavy rain for a short time.

A typical morning dawns bright and clear. Cumulus clouds build up in the late morning and develop into

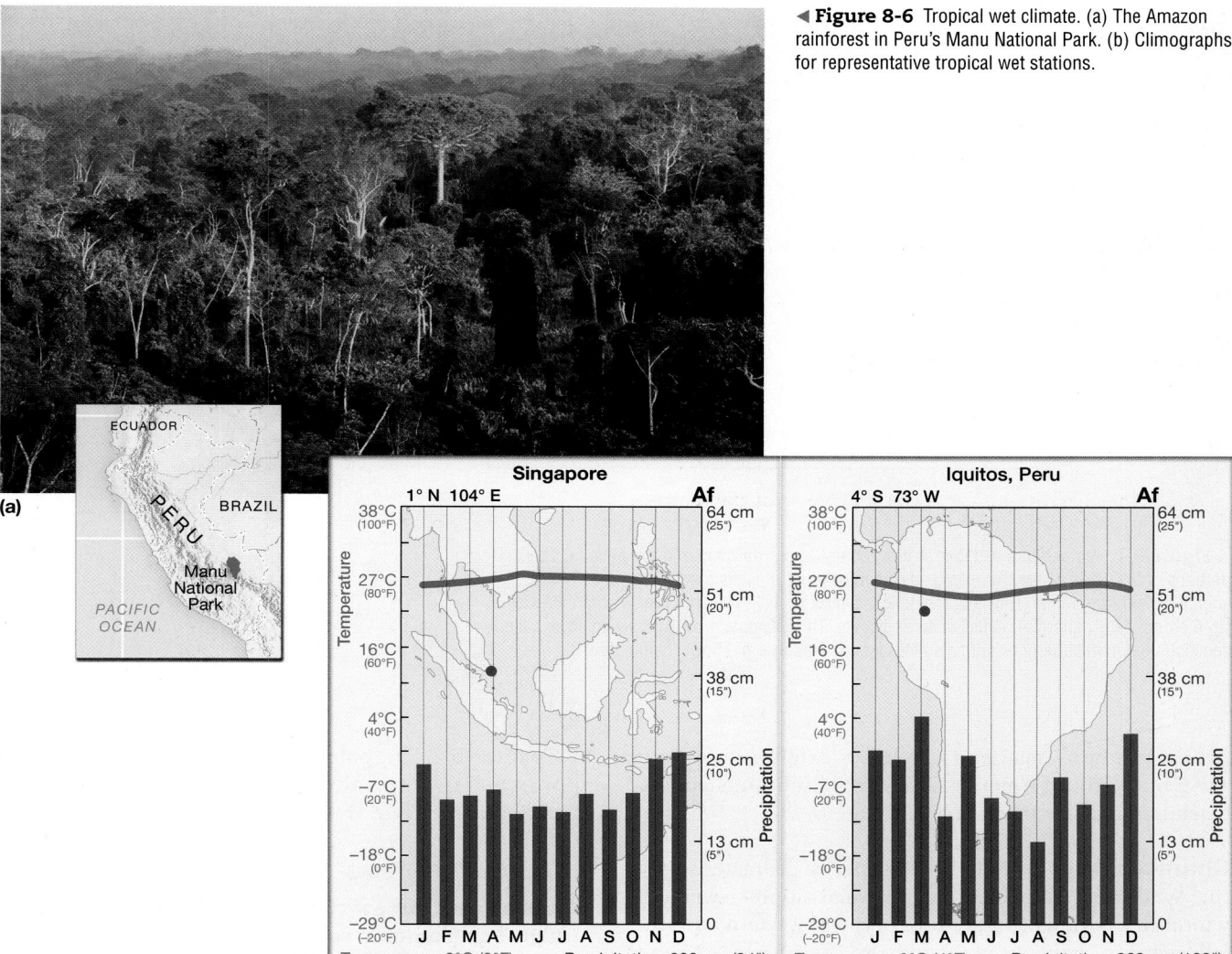

◀ **Figure 8-6** Tropical wet climate. (a) The Amazon rainforest in Peru's Manu National Park. (b) Climographs for representative tropical wet stations.

cumulonimbus thunderheads, producing a furious convectional rainstorm in early afternoon. Then the clouds usually disperse so that by late afternoon there is a partly cloudy sky and a glorious sunset. The clouds often recur at night to create a nocturnal thunderstorm, followed by dispersal once again. The next day dawns bright and clear, and the sequence repeats.

As you can see in Figure 8-6b, each month receives at least moderate precipitation, with annual totals typically between 150 and 250 centimeters (60 and 100 inches), although in some locations it is considerably greater. Yearly rainfall in the Af climate is exceeded by that of only one other type of climate—*tropical monsoon*.

Controls of Af: Why these climatic conditions occur where they do is relatively straightforward. The principal climatic control is latitude. The Sun high in the sky throughout the year and little or no variation in day length make for relatively uniform insolation, and so

there is little opportunity for seasonal temperature variation. This extensive warming produces considerable thermal convection, which accounts for a portion of the raininess. More important, the influence of the ITCZ for most or all of the year leads to widespread uplift of warm, humid, unstable air. Persistent onshore winds along trade-wind (east-facing) coasts provide a consistent source of moisture and add another mechanism for precipitation—orographic uplift. Interior areas, however, typically lack a great deal of wind—a consequence of the persistent influence of the ITCZ and its ongoing convective updrafts (you will recall that the latitudes around the equator are sometimes referred to as the "doldrums" because of the lack of horizontal air movement).

Tropical Savanna Climate (Aw)

The most extensive of the A climates, the **tropical savanna climate**, generally lies both to the north and south of Af climates (Figure 8-5). It occurs broadly in South America,

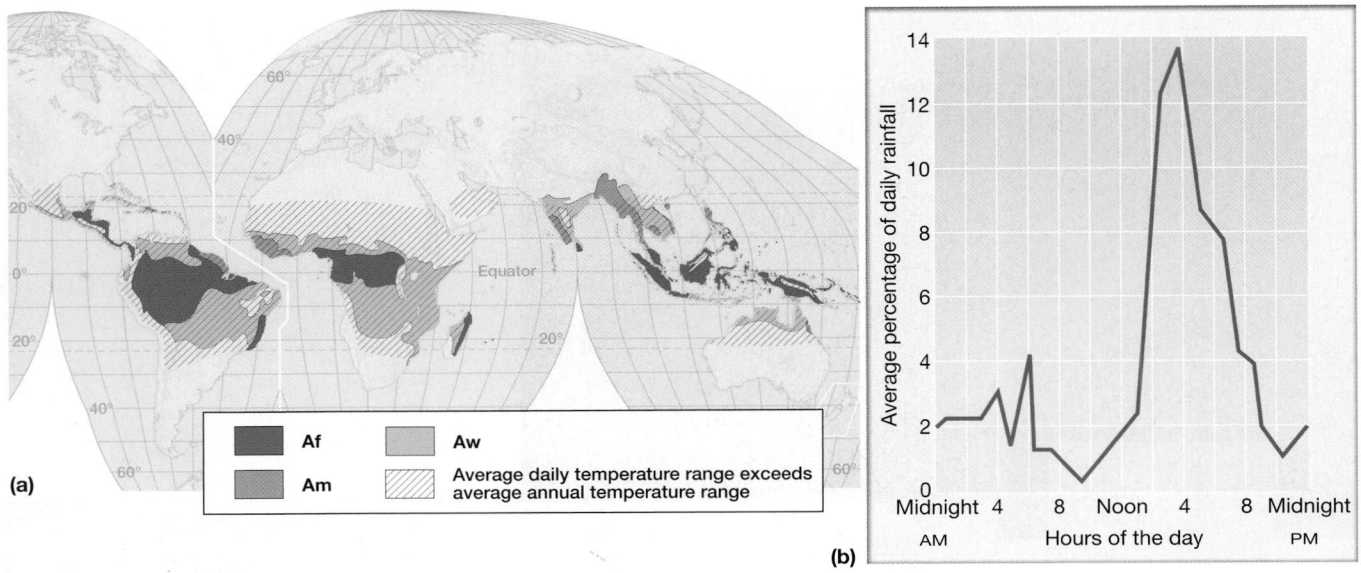

▲ **Figure 8-7** Temperature and rainfall characteristics of tropical humid climates. (a) Land portions of the world where the average daily temperature range is greater than the average annual temperature range. This characteristic is typical of A climates but rare in other climates. (b) A typical daily pattern of rainfall in an Af climate. This example, from Malaysia, shows a heavy concentration in midafternoon with a small secondary peak at or shortly before dawn.

Africa, southern Asia, and to a lesser extent in northern Australia, Central America, and the Caribbean islands—extending in a few places to 25° N and S.

Characteristics of Aw: The distinctive characteristic of the Aw climate is its clear-cut seasonal summer-wet and winter-dry periods (Figure 8-8). Typical Aw annual rainfall averages are between 90 and 180 centimeters (35 and 70 inches)—almost all coming during the months of the high-Sun season.

The average annual temperature range in Aw regions is typically slightly greater than that of Af regions (3 to 8°C [5 to 15°F]), with the higher annual variations occurring in locations farther from the equator. The hottest time of the year is likely to be in late spring just before the onset of the summer rains.

Controls of Aw: The rainfall characteristic of the Aw climates is explained by their location between the unstable, converging air of the ITCZ (which dominates the Af climates all year) on their equatorial side and stable, subsiding air of the subtropical high on their poleward side.

During the low-Sun season (winter) when pressure belts shift equatorward, savanna regions are dominated by the dry conditions and clear skies associated with the subtropical highs. In summer, the pressure systems "follow the Sun," shifting poleward and bringing the thunderstorms and convective rain of the ITCZ into the Aw region (these seasonal precipitation patterns are clearly seen in Figure 6-35

in Chapter 6). The poleward limits of Aw climate are approximately equivalent to the poleward maximum migration of the ITCZ (Figure 8-9).

Learning Check 8-3 Why do Af climates have rain all year, but Aw climates have rain only in the high-Sun (summer) season?

Tropical Monsoon Climate (Am)

The **tropical monsoon climate** is found in tropical regions with a prominent monsoon wind pattern. It is most extensive on the windward (west-facing) coasts of southeastern Asia (primarily India, Bangladesh, Myanmar [formerly Burma], and Thailand), but it also occurs in more restricted coastal regions of western Africa, northeastern South America, the Philippines, and northeastern Australia (see Figure 8-5).

Characteristics of Am: The distinctiveness of the Am climate is primarily its rainfall pattern (Figure 8-10). During the high-Sun season, an enormous amount of rain falls in association with the "summer" monsoon. It is not unusual to have more than 75 centimeters (30 inches) of rain in each of two or three months. The annual total for a typical Am station is between 250 and 500 centimeters (100 and 200 inches). An extreme example is Cherrapunji (in the Khasi hills of Assam in eastern India), which has an annual average of 1065 centimeters (425 inches). Cherrapunji has been inundated with 210 centimeters (84 inches)

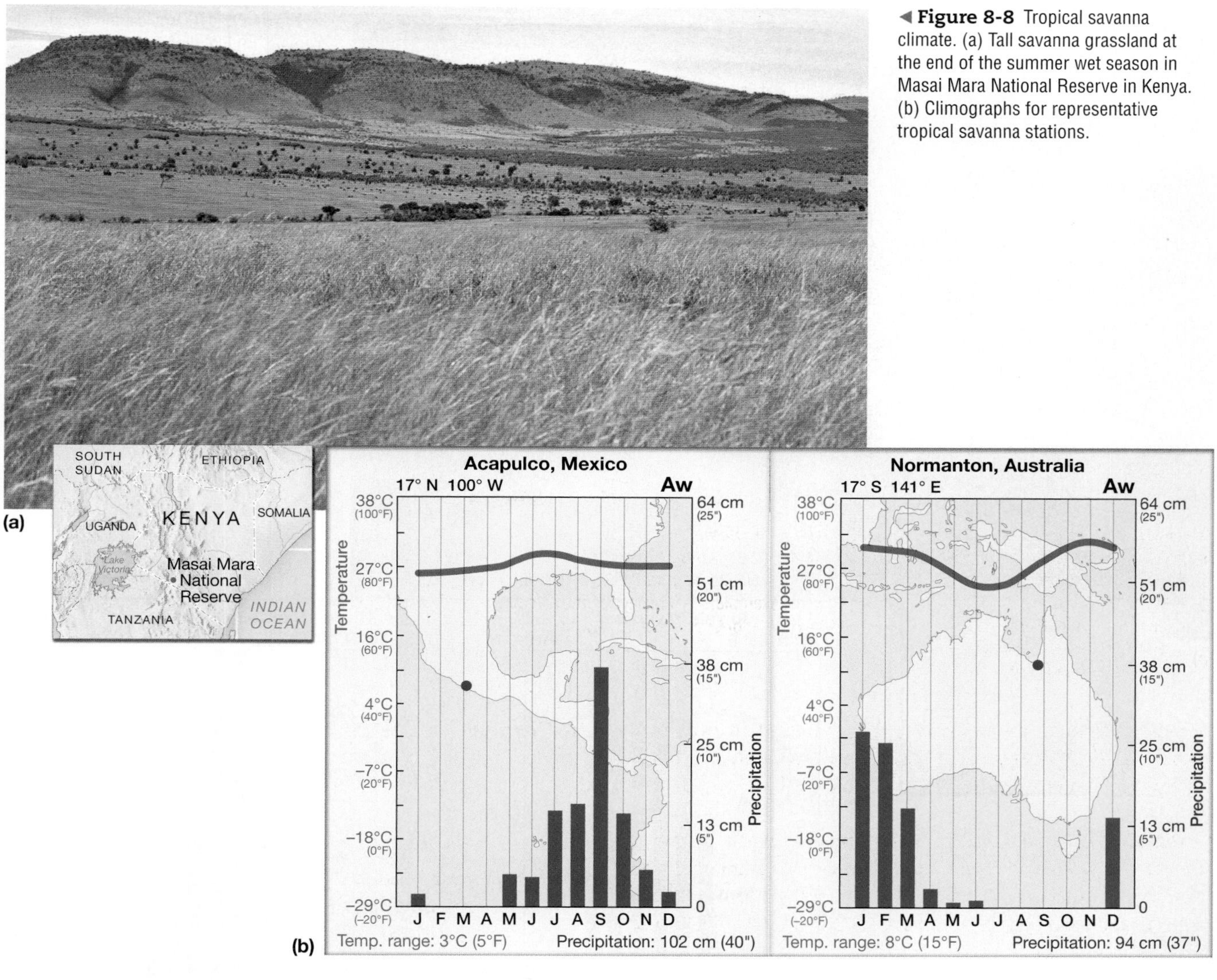

◀ **Figure 8-8** Tropical savanna climate. (a) Tall savanna grassland at the end of the summer wet season in Masai Mara National Reserve in Kenya. (b) Climographs for representative tropical savanna stations.

(a)

(b)

Acapulco, Mexico	Normanton, Australia
17° N 100° W Aw	17° S 141° E Aw
Temp. range: 3°C (5°F) Precipitation: 102 cm (40")	Temp. range: 8°C (15°F) Precipitation: 94 cm (37")

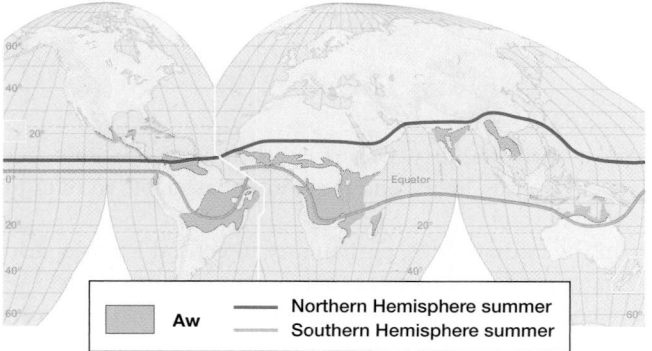

▲ **Figure 8-9** The intertropical convergence zone (ITCZ) migrates widely during the year. The red line shows its typical northern boundary in the Northern Hemisphere summer, and the orange line indicates its southern boundary in the Southern Hemisphere summer. These lines coincide approximately with the poleward limits of Aw climate.

Aw — Northern Hemisphere summer / Southern Hemisphere summer

in three days, with 930 centimeters (366 inches) in one month, and with a memorable 2647 centimeters (1042 inches) in its record year (Figure 8-11).

A lesser distinction of the Am climate is its annual temperature curve. Although the annual temperature range may be only slightly greater than in a tropical wet climate, the highest Am temperatures normally occur in late spring prior to the onset of the summer monsoon. The heavy cloud cover of the wet monsoon period shields out some of the insolation, resulting in slightly lower temperatures in summer than in spring.

Controls of Am: The extremely wet high-Sun season of the Am climate is explained by the onset of the summer monsoon that brings moist onshore winds and thunderstorms. During the low-Sun season, Am climates are dominated by offshore winds—the "winter" monsoon during this season produces little precipitation, and one or two months may be rainless.

◀ **Figure 8-10** Tropical monsoon climate. (a) Flooding from monsoon rains in Cuttack, Orissa state, India, in 2008. (b) Climographs for representative tropical monsoon stations.

(a)

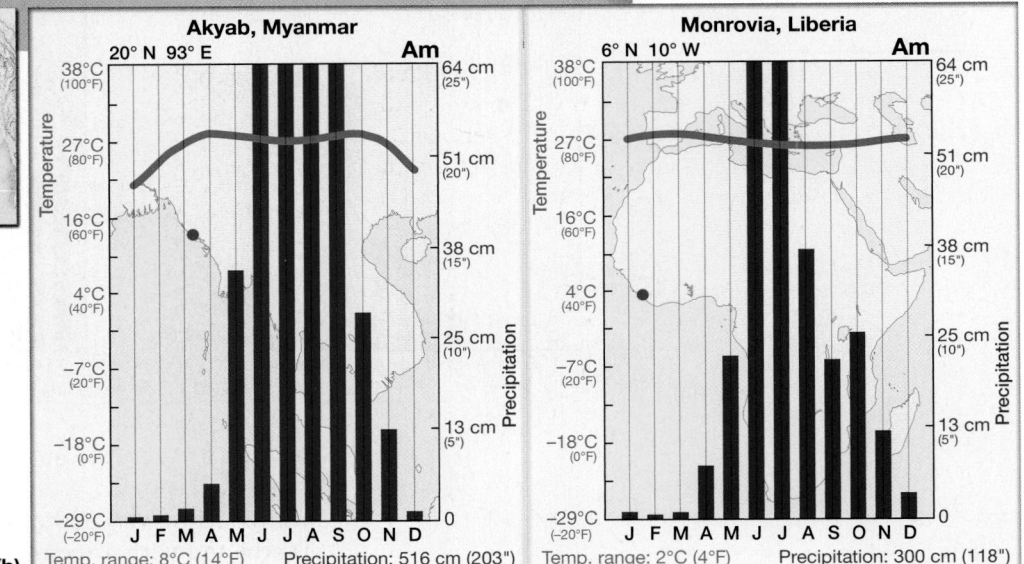

(b)

DRY CLIMATES (GROUP B) FG9

The *dry climates* cover about 30 percent of the land area of the world (Figure 8-12)—more than any other climatic group. Although at first glance their distribution pattern appears erratic and complex, it actually has a considerable degree of predictability: arid regions of the world develop either as (1) a result of the lack of air uplift necessary for cloud formation or (2) from the lack of moisture in the air—in some cases, both.

The largest expanses of dry areas are in subtropical latitudes, especially in the western and central portions of continents where subsidence associated with the subtropical highs and cool ocean currents serve to increase

atmospheric stability. Desert conditions also occur over extensive ocean areas, and it is quite reasonable to refer to marine deserts.

In the midlatitudes, particularly in central Eurasia, arid climates are found in areas that are cut off from sources of surface moisture either by great distances or by their position in the rain shadow of mountain ranges.

The concept of a dry climate is a complex one because it involves the balance between precipitation and evapotranspiration, and so depends not only on rainfall but also on temperature. Generally, higher temperature engenders greater potential evapotranspiration, and so hot regions can receive more precipitation than cool regions and yet be classified as dry.

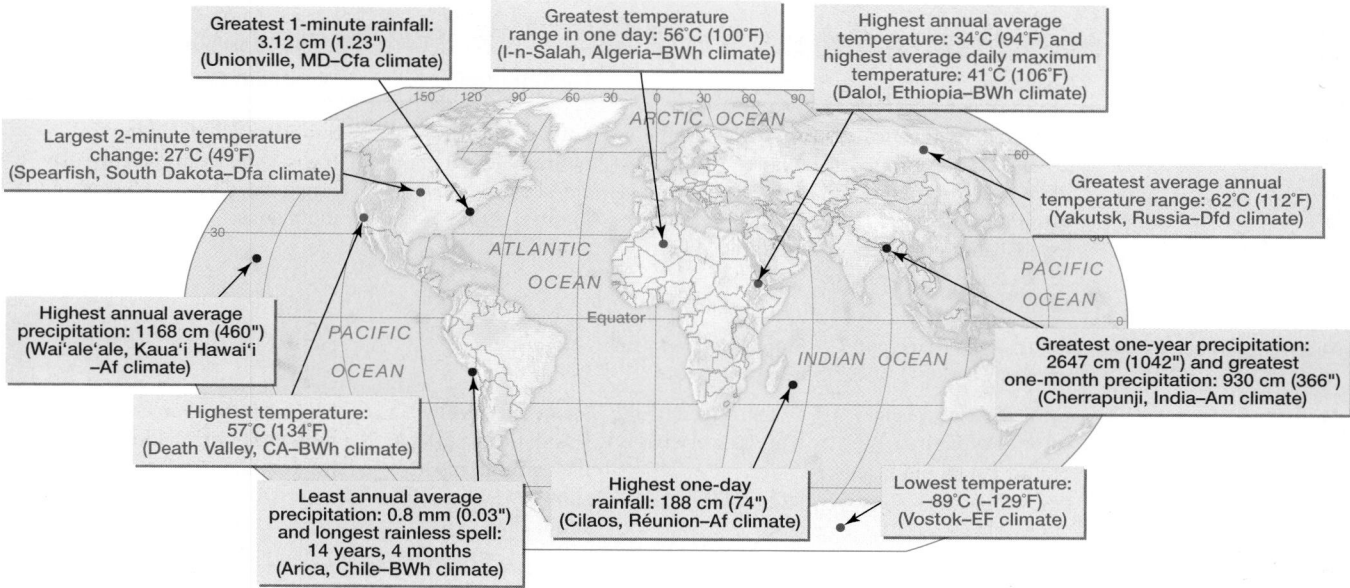

▲ **Figure 8-11** Locations of some extreme weather records.

As Figure 8-3 shows, the two main categories of B climates are *desert* and *steppe*. Deserts are extremely arid, whereas steppes are semiarid. Normally the deserts of the world are large core areas of aridity surrounded by a transitional fringe of steppe that is slightly less dry. The two B climates are further classified based on temperature into "hot" *subtropical desert* and *subtropical steppe*, and "cold" *midlatitude desert* and *midlatitude steppe*. Our discussion here focuses on the deserts because they represent the epitome of dry conditions—the arid extreme. Most of what is stated about deserts applies to steppes but in modified intensity. Table 8-2 gives an overview of all the B climates.

Learning Check 8-4   **Explain the two main causes of dry climates.**

Subtropical Desert Climate (BWh)

In both the Northern and Southern Hemispheres, **subtropical desert climates** lie either in or very near the band of the subtropical highs (Figure 8-13), centered between 25° and 30° N and S latitude, especially along the west coasts of continents. Climographs for two typical BWh locations are shown in Figure 8-14.

The enormous expanse of BWh climate in North Africa (the Sahara) and southwestern Eurasia (the Arabian Desert) represents more desert area than is found in the rest of the world combined—here, the adjacency of Eurasia makes Africa a continent without an eastern coast north of 10° N, and so this region lacks maritime moisture sources from the east. Subtropical desert climate is also expansive in Australia (50 percent of the continental area) because the mountains that parallel the continent's east

◀ **Figure 8-12** The global distribution of dry (B) climates.

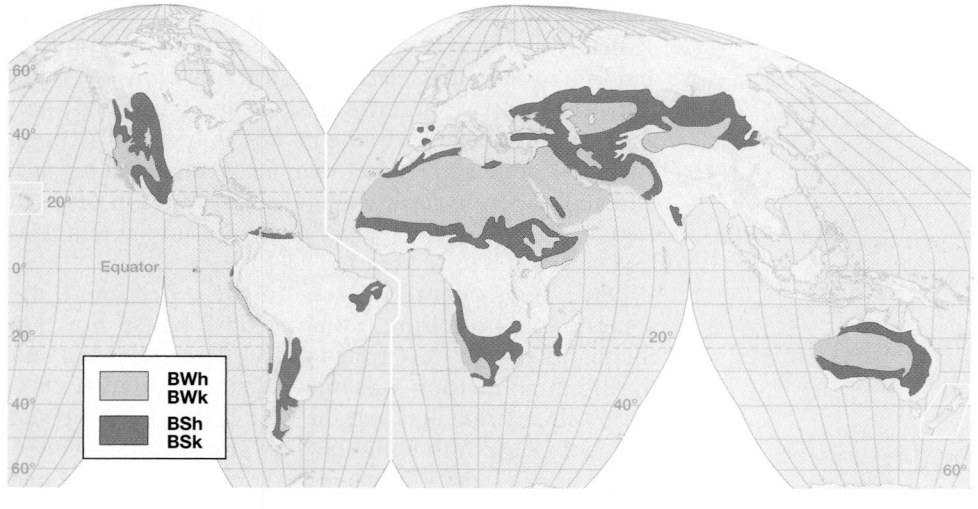

TABLE 8-2	Summary of B Climates: Dry			
Type	**Location**	**Temperature**	**Precipitation**	**Dominant Controls of Climate**
Subtropical desert (BWh)	Centered at latitudes 25–30° on western sides of continents, extending into interiors; most extensive in northern Africa and southwestern Eurasia	Very hot summers, relatively mild winters; enormous DTR, moderate ATR	Rainfall scarce, typically less than 30 cm (12 in.); unreliable; intense; little cloudiness	Subsidence from subtropical highs; cool ocean currents; may be extended by rain shadow of mountains
Subtropical steppe (BSh)	Fringing BWh except on west	Similar to BWh but more moderate	Semiarid	Similar to BWh
Midlatitude desert (BWk)	Central Asia; western interior of United States; Patagonia	Hot summers, cold winters; very large ATR, large DTR	Meager: typically less than 25 cm (10 in.); erratic, mostly showery; some winter snow	Distant from sources of moisture; rain shadow of mountains
Midlatitude steppe (BSk)	Peripheral to BWk; transitional to more humid climates	Similar to BWk but slightly more moderate	Semiarid; some winter snow	Similar to BWk

ATR = annual temperature range; DTR = daily temperature range.

coast are just high enough to prevent Pacific winds from penetrating.

Characteristics of BWh: The distinctive climatic characteristic of deserts is lack of moisture, and three adjectives are particularly applicable to precipitation conditions in subtropical deserts: scarce, unreliable, and intense.

1. *Scarce*—Subtropical deserts are among the most nearly rainless regions on Earth. According to unofficial records, some have experienced several consecutive years without a single drop of moisture falling from the sky. Most BWh regions, however, are not totally without precipitation. Annual totals of between 5 and 20 centimeters (2 and 8 inches) are characteristic, and some places receive as much as 38 centimeters (15 inches).

2. *Unreliable*—An important climatic axiom is that the lower the average annual precipitation, the greater its variability (see Figure 6-37 in Chapter 6). The very concept of an "average" yearly rainfall in a BWh location is misleading because of year-to-year fluctuations. Yuma, Arizona, for example, has a long-term average rainfall of 8.4 centimeters (3.30 inches), but over the last two decades it has received as little as 0.4 centimeters (0.15 inches) and as much as 18.8 centimeters (7.39 inches) in a given year.

3. *Intense*—Most precipitation in these regions falls in vigorous convective showers that are localized and of short duration. Thus, the rare rains may bring brief floods to regions that have been deprived of surface moisture for months.

Temperatures in BWh regions are also distinctive. The combination of low-latitude location (so that the vertical or near-vertical rays of the Sun are striking in summer) and lack of cloudiness permits a great deal of insolation to reach the surface. Summers are long and blisteringly hot, with monthly averages in the middle to high 30s°C (high 90s°F)—significantly hotter than most equatorial regions. Midwinter months have average temperatures in the high teens °C (60s°F), which gives moderate annual temperature ranges of 8 to 14°C (15 to 25°F).

Daily temperature ranges, on the other hand, are sometimes astounding. Summer days are so hot that the nights do not have time to cool off significantly, but during the transition seasons of spring and fall, a 28°C (50°F) fluctuation between the heat of the afternoon and the cool of the following dawn is not unusual—generally clear skies and low water vapor content permit rapid

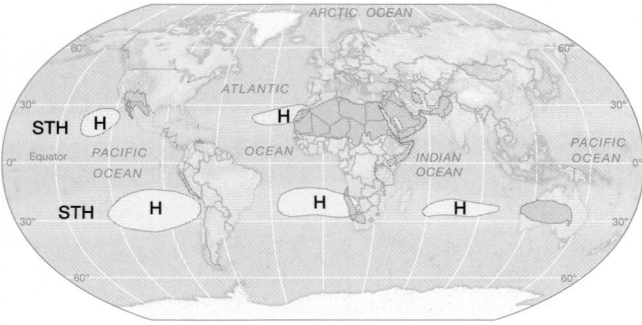

▲ **Figure 8-13** The coincidence of the subtropical high-pressure zones and BWh climates is striking.

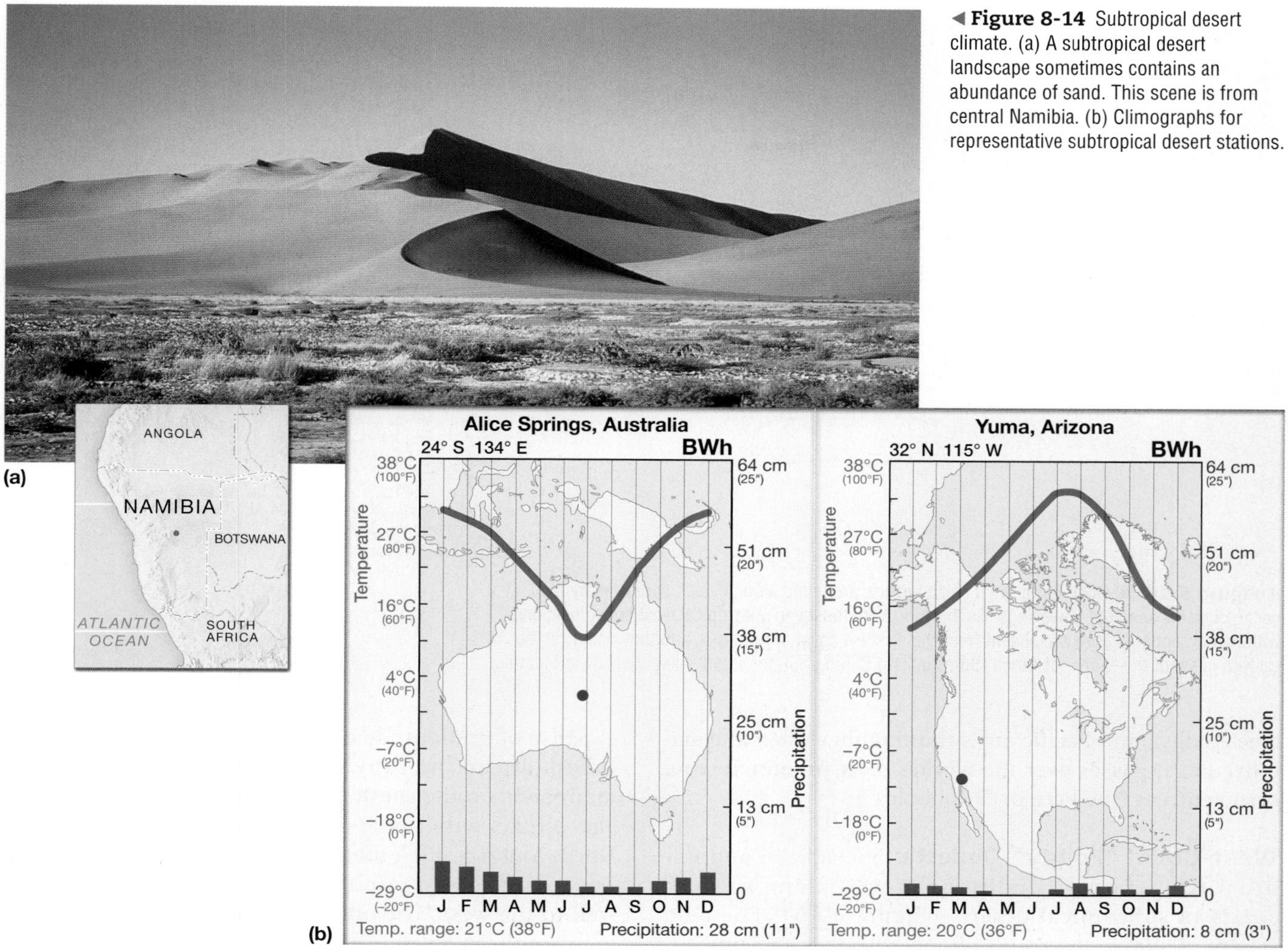

◀ **Figure 8-14** Subtropical desert climate. (a) A subtropical desert landscape sometimes contains an abundance of sand. This scene is from central Namibia. (b) Climographs for representative subtropical desert stations.

(a)

Alice Springs, Australia
24° S 134° E   **BWh**

Temp. range: 21°C (38°F)   Precipitation: 28 cm (11")

Yuma, Arizona
32° N 115° W   **BWh**

Temp. range: 20°C (36°F)   Precipitation: 8 cm (3")

(b)

nighttime cooling because there is unimpeded longwave radiation transmission through the atmosphere (less local "greenhouse effect").

Subtropical deserts often experience considerable windiness during daylight, but the air is usually calm at night. The daytime winds are apparently related to rapid daytime warming and strong convective activity, which accelerates surface currents. The persistent winds are largely unimpeded by soil and vegetation, with the result that a great deal of dust and sand is frequently carried along.

Controls of BWh: Subtropical deserts extend inland from the west coasts of continents in the subtropics where subsidence from the STH is stronger and where cool ocean currents provide added stability.

Subtropical deserts are restricted to coastal regions in southwest Africa, South America, and North America. The greatest north–south elongation occurs along the western side of South America, where the Atacama Desert is not only the "longest" but also the driest of the dry lands. The Atacama is sandwiched in a "double" rain shadow position (Figure 8-15): moist winds from the east are kept out of this region by one of the world's great mountain ranges

▲ **Figure 8-15** The Atacama Desert is in a "double" rain shadow: the Andes Mountains to the east block the movement of moist air from the Atlantic, and the cold Peru (Humboldt) Current to the west stabilizes the moist Pacific air, inhibiting uplift.

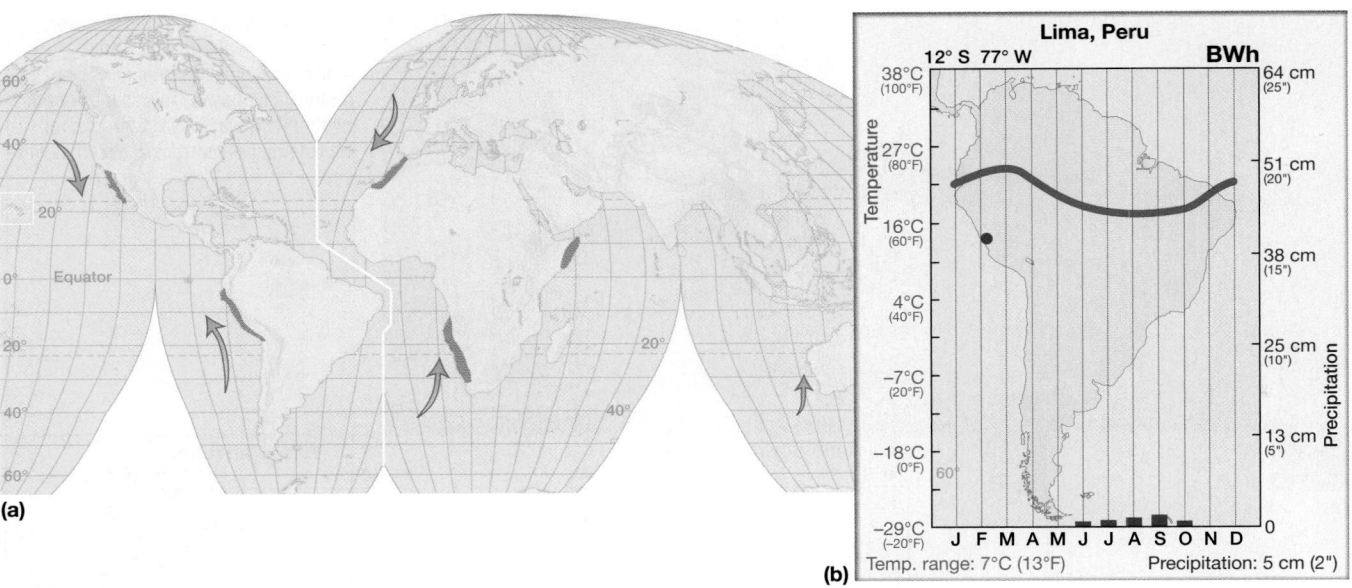

(a)

(b)

▲ **Figure 8-16** (a) Cool, foggy west coast deserts are found along coasts paralleled by cool ocean currents and cold upwellings. Such deserts are mostly in subtropical west coast locations, with two exceptions: They are absent from the western coast of Australia, and they occur on the eastern coast of the "horn" of Africa (Somalia). (b) Climograph for a cool west coast desert station.

(the Andes), and Pacific air is thoroughly chilled and stabilized as it passes over the world's most prominent cool ocean current (the Peru or "Humboldt").

West-Coast "Foggy" Deserts: Specialized and unusual temperature conditions prevail along western coasts in subtropical deserts (Figure 8-16). The cold waters offshore (the result of cool currents and upwelling of cold deeper ocean water) chill any air that moves across them. This cooling produces high relative humidity as well as frequent fog and low stratus clouds. Precipitation almost never results from this advective cooling, however, and the influence normally extends only a few kilometers inland. The immediate coastal region, however, is characterized by such abnormal desert conditions as relatively low summer temperatures (typical summer averages in the low 20s°C or low 70s°F), continuously high relative humidity, and greatly reduced annual and daily temperature ranges, as indicated by a comparison of Figures 8-14b and 8-16b.

Subtropical Steppe Climate (BSh): The *subtropical steppe climates* characteristically surround the BWh climates (except on the western side where desert extends to the ocean), separating the deserts from the more humid climates. Temperature and precipitation conditions are not significantly unlike those just described for BWh regions, except that the extremes are more muted in the steppes (Figure 8-17).

Midlatitude Desert Climate (BWk)

The **midlatitude desert climates** occur primarily in the deep interiors of continents (see Figure 8-3). The largest

expanse of midlatitude dry climates, in central Eurasia, is both distant from any ocean and protected by massive mountains on the south (especially the Himalayas) from any contact with the South Asian summer monsoon. In North America, high mountains closely parallel the western coast and as a result, the dry climates are displaced well to the west. The only other significant BWk region is in southern South America, where the desert reaches all the way to the eastern coast of Patagonia (southern Argentina). Climographs for two typical BWk locations are shown in Figure 8-18.

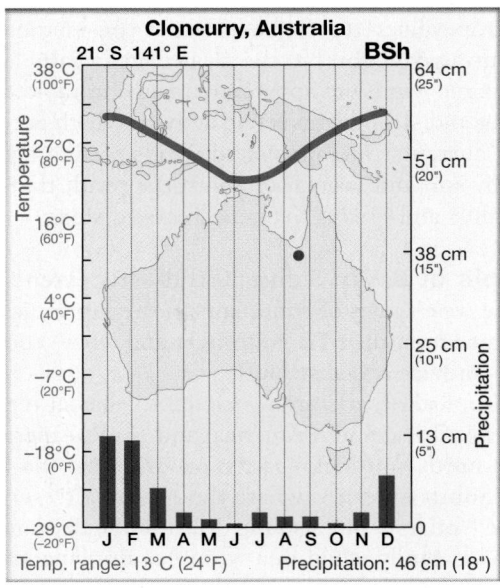

▲ **Figure 8-17** Climograph for representative subtropical steppe station.

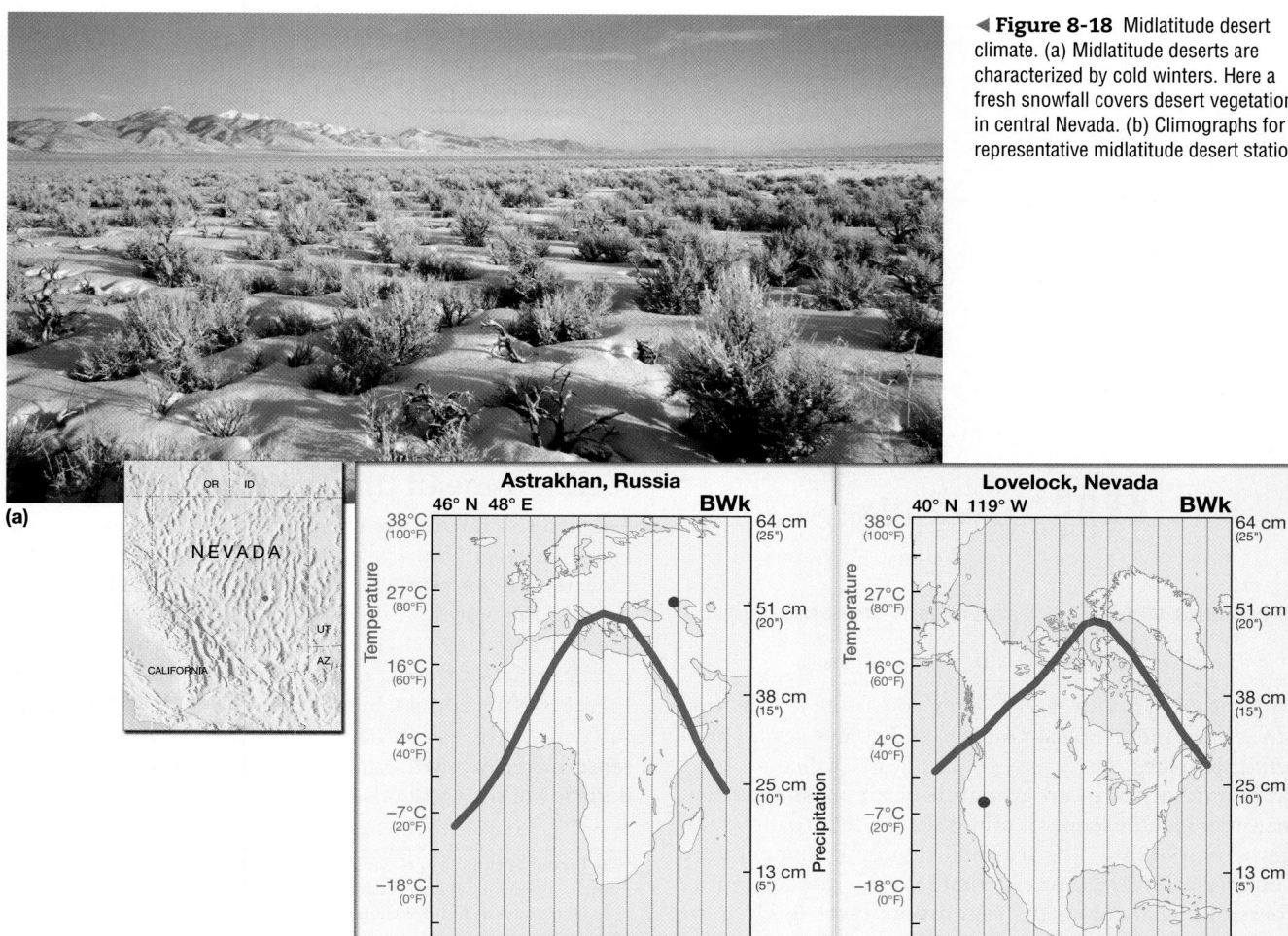

◀ **Figure 8-18** Midlatitude desert climate. (a) Midlatitude deserts are characterized by cold winters. Here a fresh snowfall covers desert vegetation in central Nevada. (b) Climographs for representative midlatitude desert stations.

Characteristics of BWk: Precipitation in midlatitude (BWk) deserts is much like that of subtropical (BWh) deserts—meager and erratic. Differences lie in two aspects: seasonality and intensity. Most BWk regions receive the bulk of their precipitation in summer, when continental warming and instability are common. Winter is usually dominated by low temperatures and anticyclonic conditions—and when precipitations falls, it may come as snow.

The principal climatic differences between midlatitude and subtropical deserts are in temperature, especially winter temperature (see Figure 8-18), with BWk regions having severely cold winters. The average cold-month temperature is normally below freezing (some BWk stations have 6 months with below-freezing averages), producing much lower average annual temperatures than in BWh regions but much greater average annual temperature ranges—some BWk locations have a 30°C (54°F) difference between winter and summer months.

Controls of BWk: Midlatitude deserts develop in the band of the westerlies in locations either far removed geographically or blocked from oceanic influence by mountain

ranges. The low winter temperature and large annual temperature reflect these midlatitude, continental locations.

Learning Check 8-5 **Explain the differences in temperature patterns of the BWh and BWk climates.**

Midlatitude Steppe Climate (BSk): As in the subtropics, *midlatitude steppe climates* generally occupy transitional positions between deserts and humid climates. Typically midlatitude steppes have more precipitation than midlatitude deserts and lesser temperature extremes (Figure 8-19). In western North America, the steppe climate is broadly found, and only in the interior southwest of the United States is the climate sufficiently arid to be classified as desert.

MILD MIDLATITUDE CLIMATES (GROUP C)

The *mild midlatitude climates* (Group C climates) occupy the equatorward margin of the midlatitudes, extending farther poleward along the west coasts of continents than

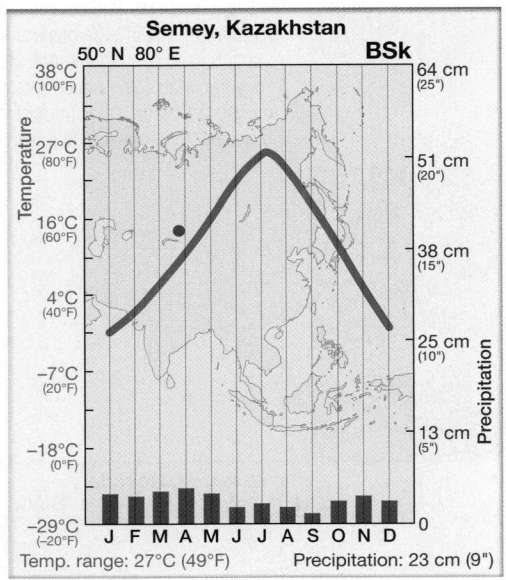

▲ **Figure 8-19** Climograph for representative midlatitude steppe station.

along the east (Figure 8-20). They constitute a transition between warmer tropical climates and colder severe midlatitude climates.

The midlatitudes are a region of air mass contrast, creating a kaleidoscope of atmospheric disturbances and weather variability. The seasonal rhythm of temperature is usually more prominent than that of precipitation. Whereas in the tropics the seasons are more likely to be

characterized as "wet" and "dry," in the midlatitudes they are clearly "summer" and "winter."

Summers in the C climates are long and sometimes hot; winters are short and relatively mild. These zones, in contrast to the A climate zones, experience occasional winter frosts and therefore do not have a year-round growing season. Precipitation is highly variable in the C climates with regard to both total amount and seasonal distribution.

The C climates are subdivided into three types primarily on the basis of precipitation seasonality and secondarily on the basis of summer temperatures: *mediterranean*, *humid subtropical*, and *marine west coast*. Table 8-3 presents an overview.

Mediterranean Climate (Csa, Csb)

FG5, FG7

The two Cs climates are sometimes referred to as *dry summer subtropical*, but the more widely used designation is **mediterranean climate**.[1] Cs climates are found in five parts of the world on the western side of continents centered at about 35° N and 35° S. Cs regions are restricted to the coasts in central and southern California (see Figure 8-20), central Chile, the southern tip of Africa, and the two southwestern "corners" of Australia; the only extensive area of mediterranean climate is around the borderlands of the Mediterranean Sea.

[1]The proper terminology is without capitalization because it is a generic term for a type of climate; Mediterranean with the capital M refers to a specific region around the Mediterranean Sea.

TABLE 8-3	Summary of C Climates: Mild Midlatitude			
Type	**Location**	**Temperature**	**Precipitation**	**Dominant Controls of Climate**
Mediterranean (Csa, Csb)	Centered at 35° latitude on western sides of continents; limited east–west extent except in Mediterranean Sea area	Warm/hot summers; mild winters; year-round mildness in coastal areas	Summer dry season; moderate rain: 38–64 cm (15–25 in.) annually, nearly all in winter; much sunshine, some coastal fog	Subtropical high subsidence and stability in summer; westerly winds and cyclonic storms in winter
Humid subtropical (Cfa, Cwa, Cwb)	Centered at 30° latitude on eastern sides of continents; considerable east–west extent	Summers warm/hot, sultry; winters mild to cold	Abundant: 100–165 cm (40–65 in.) annually, mostly rain; summer maxima but no true dry season	Westerly winds and storms in winter; moist onshore flow in summer; monsoons in Asia
Marine west coast (Cfb, Cfc)	Latitudes 40°–60° on western sides of continents; limited inland extent except in Europe	Very mild winters for the latitude; generally mild summers; moderate ATR	No dry season; moderate to abundant: 75–125 cm (30–50 in.) mostly in winter; many days with rain; much cloudiness	Westerly flow and oceanic influence year-round

ATR = annual temperature range.

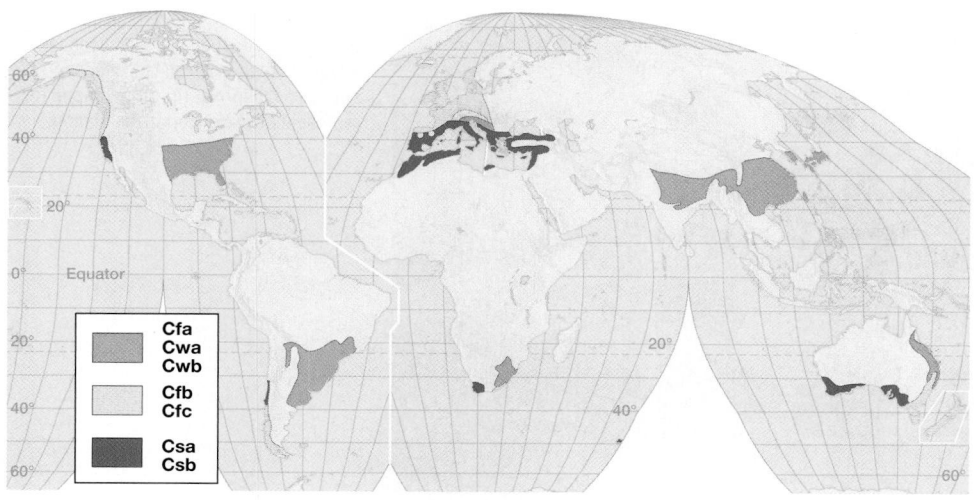

◄ **Figure 8-20** The global distribution of mild midlatitude (C) climates.

Characteristics of Cs: Cs climates have three distinctive characteristics:

1. The modest annual precipitation falls in winter, summers being virtually rainless.
2. Winter temperatures are unusually mild for the midlatitudes, and summers vary from warm to hot.
3. Clear skies and abundant sunshine are typical, especially in summer.

Two representative climographs are shown in Figure 8-21. Average annual precipitation is modest, ranging from about 38 to 64 centimeters (15 to 25 inches), with midwinter rainfall of 8 to 13 centimeters (3 to 5 inches) per month, and the two or three midsummer months are totally dry. Only one other climatic type, *marine west coast*, has such a concentration of precipitation in winter.

Most mediterranean climate is classified as Csa, which means that summers are hot, with midsummer monthly averages between 24 and 29°C (75 and 85°F) and frequent high temperatures above 38°C (100°F). Coastal mediterranean areas (Csb) have much milder summers than inland mediterranean areas as a result of sea breezes and frequent coastal advection fog (Figure 8-22), with midsummer month temperature averages of 16 to 21°C (60 to 70°F). Csb winters are slightly milder than Csa winters, with midwinter month averages of about 13°C (55°F), and only rarely temperatures falling below freezing.

Controls of Cs: The origin of mediterranean climates is clear-cut: in summer, these regions are dominated by dry, stable, subsiding air from the eastern portions of subtropical highs; in winter, the wind and pressure belts shift equatorward, and mediterranean regions come under the influence of the westerlies with their migratory midlatitude cyclones and associated fronts. Almost all precipitation comes from these cyclonic storms.

Humid Subtropical Climate (Cfa, Cwa, Cwb)

Whereas mediterranean climates are found on the western side of continents, **humid subtropical climates** are found on the eastern side of continents centered at about the same latitude. However, humid subtropical climates extend farther inland and over a greater range of latitude than do mediterranean climates—especially in North America, South America, and Eurasia (Figure 8-23).

Characteristics of Cfa: The humid subtropical climates differ from mediterranean climates in several important respects:

1. Summer temperatures in humid subtropical regions are generally warm to hot—similar to mediterranean climates—but with high humidity, so sensible temperatures are higher. Cfa days tend to be hot and sultry, and often night brings little relief.
2. Precipitation in humid subtropical regions tends to have a summer maximum, associated with onshore flow and frequent convection. Winter is a time of diminished precipitation, but it is not really a dry season (except in China, where dry winter monsoon conditions dominate). In the North American and Asian coastal areas, a late summer–autumn bulge in the precipitation curve is due to rainfall from tropical cyclones. Annual precipitation is generally abundant, averaging 100 to 165 centimeters (40 to 65 inches), with a general decrease inland.
3. Winter temperatures in Cfa regions are mild, but typically 6°C (10°F) cooler than in mediterranean regions. Winter is punctuated by cold waves that

(a)

◄ **Figure 8-21** Mediterranean climate. (a) An open oak woodland is a typical mediterranean landscape in southern California. (b) Climographs for representative mediterranean stations.

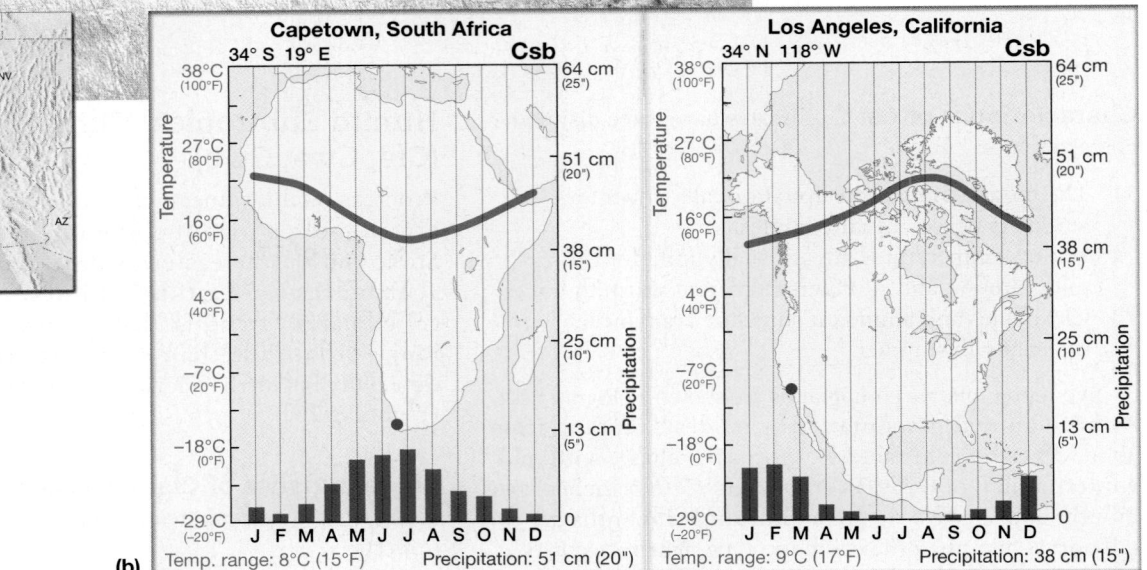

(b)

can bring severe weather and killing frosts for a few days at a time—this is one reason that frost-sensitive citrus production can extend farther north in California than it can in the southeastern United States.

Controls of Cfa: To understand the controls of humid subtropical climates, it is again useful to make a comparison with mediterranean regions since both generally lie in the same latitude. During winter, westerly winds bring midlatitude cyclones and precipitation to both regions. In summer, however, in mediterranean regions along west coasts, the poleward migration of the subtropical high and relatively cool ocean water stabilizes the atmosphere, bringing dry weather, while on the eastern side of continents, where humid subtropical climates are found, no

such stability exists—summer rain comes from the on-shore flow of maritime air and frequent convective uplift, as well as the influence of tropical cyclones.

Learning Check 8-6 **Why do Cs climates have dry summers, but Cfa climates have precipitation all year?**

Marine West Coast Climate (Cfb, Cfc)

As the name implies, **marine west coast climates** are situated on the western side of continents between about 40° and 60°; this is a windward location in the band of the westerlies.

The most extensive area of marine west coast climate is in western and central Europe. The North American region is much more restricted by the presence of mountain

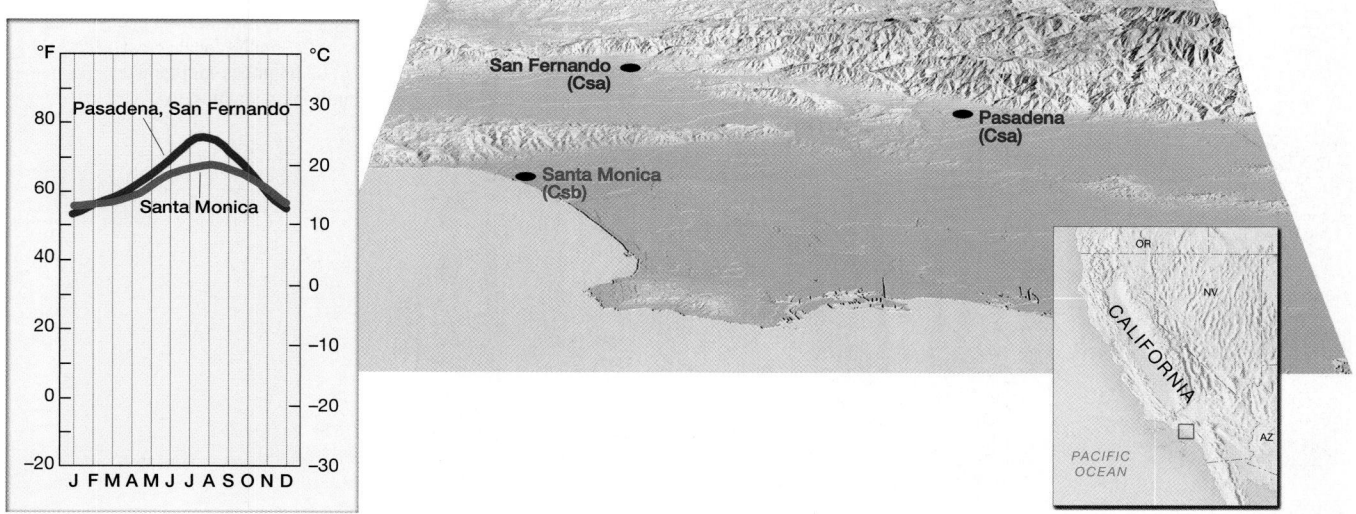

▲ **Figure 8-22** There are often significant temperature differences between coastal and inland mediterranean areas. This climograph shows the annual temperature curves for three stations in Southern California: Santa Monica (a coastal station; Csb climate), and Pasadena and San Fernando (inland stations having exactly the same average temperature for each month; Csa climate). The physiographic map shows the topographic and coastal relationships of the three stations.

ranges that run perpendicular to the direction of onshore flow. Only in the Southern Hemisphere, where landmasses are small in these latitudes (New Zealand, southeast Australia, and southernmost South America), does this oceanic climate extend across to eastern coasts (Figure 8-24).

Characteristics of Cfb: The oceanic influence moderates temperatures most of the time. Average summer month temperatures are generally between 16 and 21°C (60 and 70°F), with winter months averaging between 2 and 7°C (35 and 45°F). There are occasionally very hot days, but prolonged heat waves are rare. Similarly, very cold days occur on occasion, but frosts are relatively infrequent. There is also an abnormally long growing season for the latitude; around Seattle, for instance, the growing season is a month longer than that around Atlanta, a city lying 14° of latitude closer to the equator.

Marine west coast climates are among the wettest of the midlatitudes. Annual totals of between 75 and 125 centimeters (30 and 50 inches) are typical, with much higher totals recorded on exposed mountain slopes. Drizzly frontal precipitation and much cloudiness are characteristic. Snow is uncommon in the lowlands, but higher, west-facing slopes receive some of the heaviest snowfalls in the world.

Perhaps more important to an understanding of the character of the marine west coast climate than total precipitation is precipitation frequency. Seattle, for example, receives only 43 percent of the total possible sunshine each year, in contrast to 70 percent in Los Angeles; London has experienced as many as 72 consecutive days with rain (is it any wonder that the umbrella is that city's civic symbol?). Indeed, some places on the western coast of New Zealand's South Island have recorded 325 rainy days in a single year!

Controls of Cfb: The dominant climate control for these regions is straightforward: the year-round cool maritime influence brought by the onshore flow of the westerlies leads to frequent cloudiness and high proportions of days with some precipitation, as well as an extraordinarily temperate climate considering the latitude. In contrast, mediterranean climates equatorward of Cfb regions come under greater influence of the subtropical high in summer, bringing clear, dry conditions during that time of year. Two typical Cfb climographs are shown in Figure 8-24b.

SEVERE MIDLATITUDE CLIMATES (GROUP D)

The *severe midlatitude climates* occur only in the Northern Hemisphere (Figure 8-25) because the Southern Hemisphere has limited landmasses at the appropriate latitudes—between 40° and 70°. This climatic group extends broadly across North America and Eurasia.

Continentality, by which is meant remoteness from oceans, is a keynote in the D climates. Landmasses are broader at these latitudes than anywhere else in the world. Even though these climates extend to the eastern coasts of the two continents, they experience little maritime influence because the general flow of the westerlies brings air from the interior of the continents to the east coasts.

These climates have four clearly recognizable seasons: a long, cold winter, a relatively short summer that varies from warm to hot, and transition periods in spring and fall. Annual temperature ranges are very large, particularly

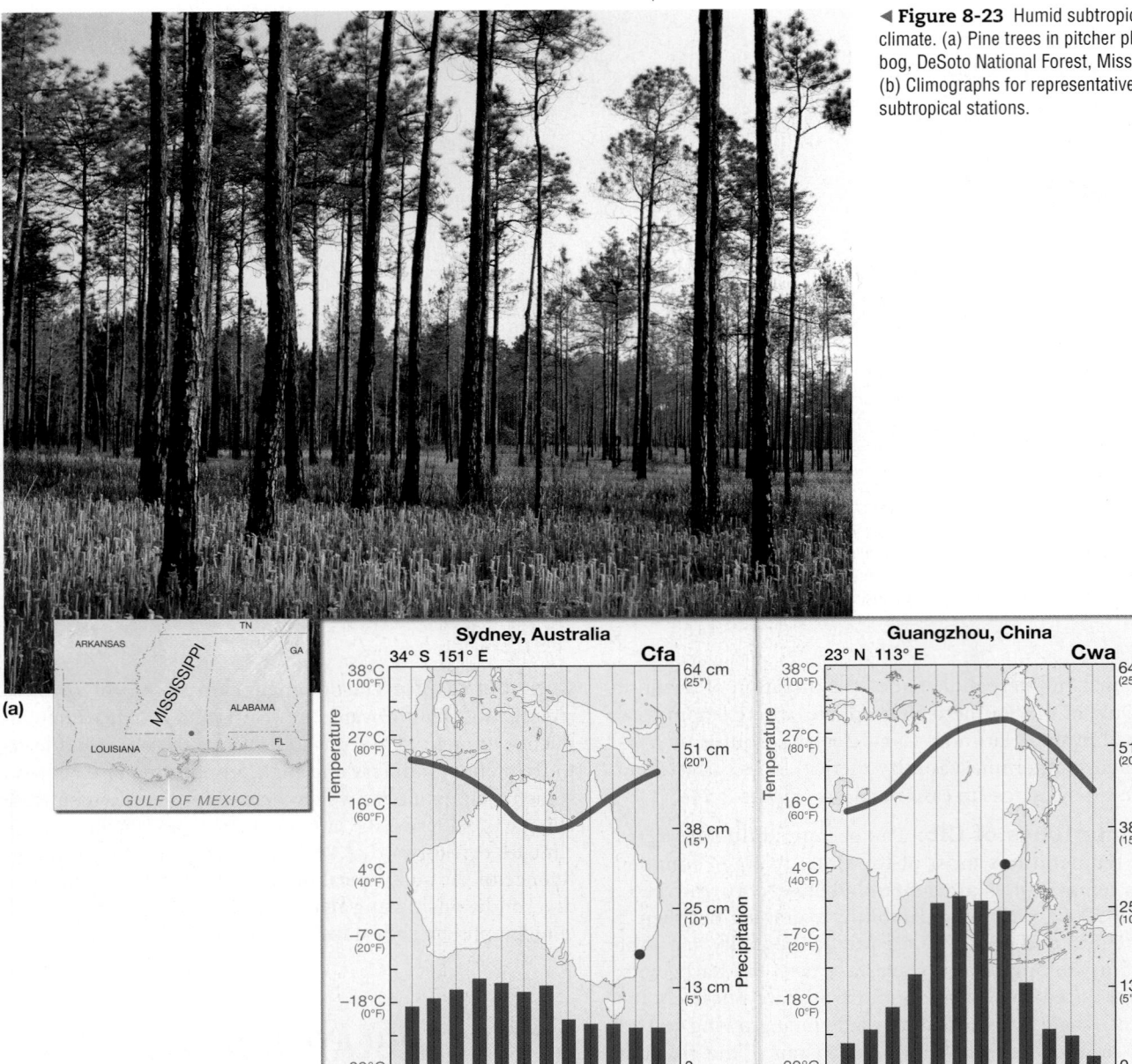

◀ **Figure 8-23** Humid subtropical climate. (a) Pine trees in pitcher plant bog, DeSoto National Forest, Mississippi. (b) Climographs for representative humid subtropical stations.

(a)

Sydney, Australia

34° S 151° E   **Cfa**

Temp. range: 19°C (35°F)   Precipitation: 119 cm (47")

Guangzhou, China

23° N 113° E   **Cwa**

Temp. range: 16°C (28°F)   Precipitation: 165 cm (65")

(b)

at more northerly locations where winters are most severe. Summer is the time of precipitation maximum, but winter is by no means completely dry, and snow cover lasts for many weeks or months.

The severe midlatitude climates are subdivided into two types on the basis of temperature. The *humid continental* type has long, warm summers, while the *subarctic* type is characterized by short summers and very cold winters. Table 8-4 summarizes the D climates.

Humid Continental Climate (Dfa, Dfb, Dwa, Dwb)

The **humid continental climate** (Figure 8-26) is found over a large area of east-central North America and

northern and northeastern Eurasia, between 35° and 55° N.

Characteristics of Dfa: Day-to-day variability and dramatic changes are prominent features of the weather pattern of humid continental climates. These are regions of cold waves, heat waves, blizzards, thunderstorms, tornadoes, and other dynamic atmospheric phenomena.

Summer temperatures are warm, generally averaging in the mid-20s°C (mid-70s°F), and so are comparable although shorter than those of the humid subtropical climate to the south. On the other hand, the average winter month temperature is usually between –12°C and –4°C (10 and 25°F), with from 1 to 5 months averaging below freezing. Winter temperatures decrease rapidly northward in the humid

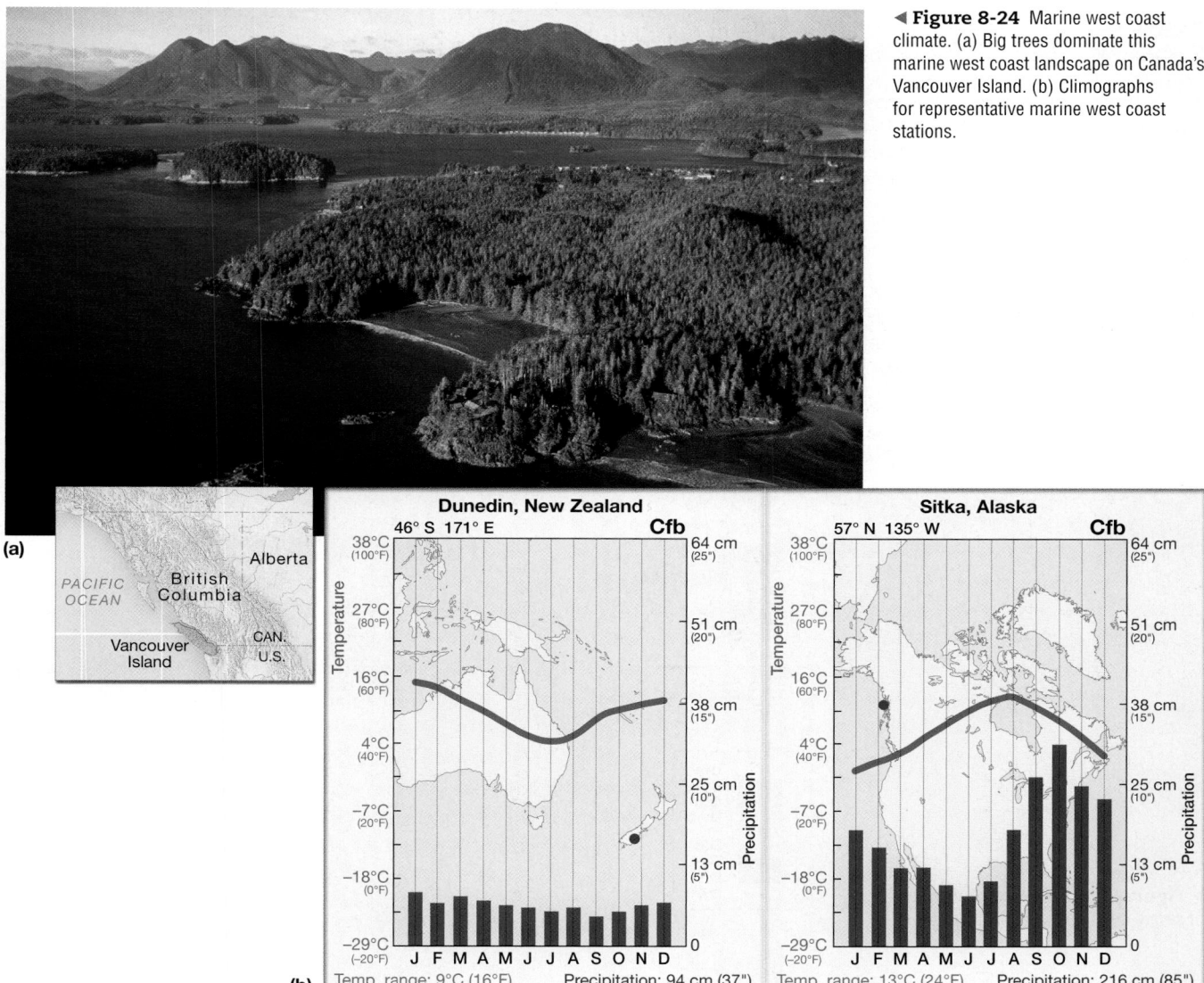

◀ **Figure 8-24** Marine west coast climate. (a) Big trees dominate this marine west coast landscape on Canada's Vancouver Island. (b) Climographs for representative marine west coast stations.

(a)

(b)

continental climates, as Figure 8-27 shows, and the growing season diminishes from about 200 days on the southern margin to about 100 days on the northern edge.

Despite their name, precipitation is not high in humid continental climates. Annual totals average between 50 and 100 centimeters (20 and 40 inches), with the highest values on the coast and a general decrease inland, and from south to north (see Figure 6-36 in Chapter 6). Both of these trends reflect increasing distance from warm, moist air masses. Summer is distinctly the wetter time of the year, but winter is not totally dry, and in coastal areas the seasonal variation is muted.

Controls of Dfa: This climatic type is dominated by the westerlies throughout the year, resulting in frequent weather changes associated with the passage of migratory pressure systems, especially in winter. Although large areas of humid continental climate are located along the coastlines of eastern North America and Eurasia—at much the same latitude as marine west coast climates—the temperature pattern is continental. The explanation for this is simple: while westerly winds bring maritime influence to marine west coast locations throughout the year, westerly winds bring continental air to the east coast locations of humid continental climates—especially cold continental air masses during winter.

Summer rain is mostly convective or monsoonal in origin. Winter precipitation is associated with midlatitude cyclones, and much of it falls as snow. During a typical winter, snow covers the ground for only 2 or 3 weeks in the southern part of these regions, but for as long as 8 months in the northern portions.

Learning Check 8-7   **Why do coastal Dfa climates—such as in New York City and Boston—have such cold winters?**

TABLE 8-4	Summary of D Climates: Severe Midlatitude			
Type	**Location**	**Temperature**	**Precipitation**	**Dominant Controls of Climate**
Humid continental (Dfa, Dfb, Dwa, Dwb)	Northern Hemisphere only; latitudes 35–55° on eastern sides of continents	Warm/hot summers; cold winters; much day-to-day variation; large ATR	Moderate to abundant: 50–100 cm (20–40 in.) annually with summer maxima; diminishes interiorward and poleward	Westerly winds, storms, and continental air masses, especially in winter; monsoons in Asia
Subarctic (Dfc, Dfd, Dwc, Dwd)	Northern Hemisphere only, latitudes 50–70° across North America and Eurasia	Long, dark, very cold winters; brief, mild summers; enormous ATR	Meager: 13–50 cm (5–20 in.) annually with summer maxima; light snow in winter but little melting	Pronounced continentality; westerlies and cyclonic storms alternating with prominent anticyclonic conditions

ATR = annual temperature range.

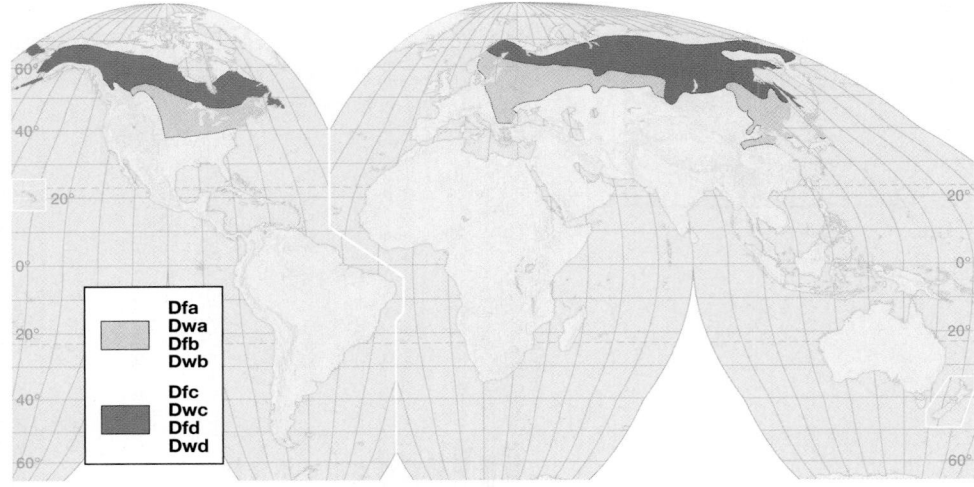

► **Figure 8-25** The global distribution of severe midlatitude (D) climates.

Subarctic Climate (Dfc, Dfd, Dwc, Dwd)

The **subarctic climate** occupies the higher midlatitudes generally between 50° and 70° N. As Figure 8-3 shows, this climate occurs as two vast, uninterrupted expanses across the broad northern landmasses: from western Alaska across Canada, and across Eurasia from Scandinavia to easternmost Siberia. The name *boreal* (which means "northern" and comes from *Boreas*, mythological Greek god of the north wind) is sometimes applied to this climatic type in Canada; in Eurasia it is often called *taiga*, after the Russian name for the forest in the region where this climate occurs. Figure 8-28 shows some typical climographs.

Characteristics of Dfc: The keyword in the subarctic climate is "winter," which is long, dark, and bitterly cold. Summers are short, and fall and spring slip by rapidly. In most places, ice begins to form on the lakes in September or October and doesn't thaw until May or later. For 6 or 7 months, the average temperature is below freezing, and the coldest months

have averages below −38°C (−36°F). The world's coldest temperatures, apart from the Antarctic and Greenland ice caps, are found in the subarctic climate; the records are −68°C (−90°F) in Siberia and −62°C (−82°F) in Alaska.

Summer warms up remarkably despite its short duration—although the intensity of the sunlight is low (because of the small angle of incidence), summer days are very long and nights are too short to permit much radiational cooling. Average summer temperatures are typically in the midteens °C (high 50s°F), but frosts may occur in any month.

Annual temperature ranges in this climate are the largest in the world. Variations from average summer month to average winter month temperatures frequently exceed 45°C (80°F). The *absolute annual temperature variation* (the difference in temperature from the very coldest to the very hottest ever recorded) sometimes reaches unbelievable magnitude—especially in deep inland locations; the world record is −68°C to +37°C (−90°F to +98°F), a range of 105°C (188°F) in Verkhoyansk, Russia!

◀ **Figure 8-26** Humid continental climate. (a) The barren look of winter in a humid continental climate. This open woodland of deciduous trees is near Detroit in southern Michigan. (b) Climographs for representative humid continental stations.

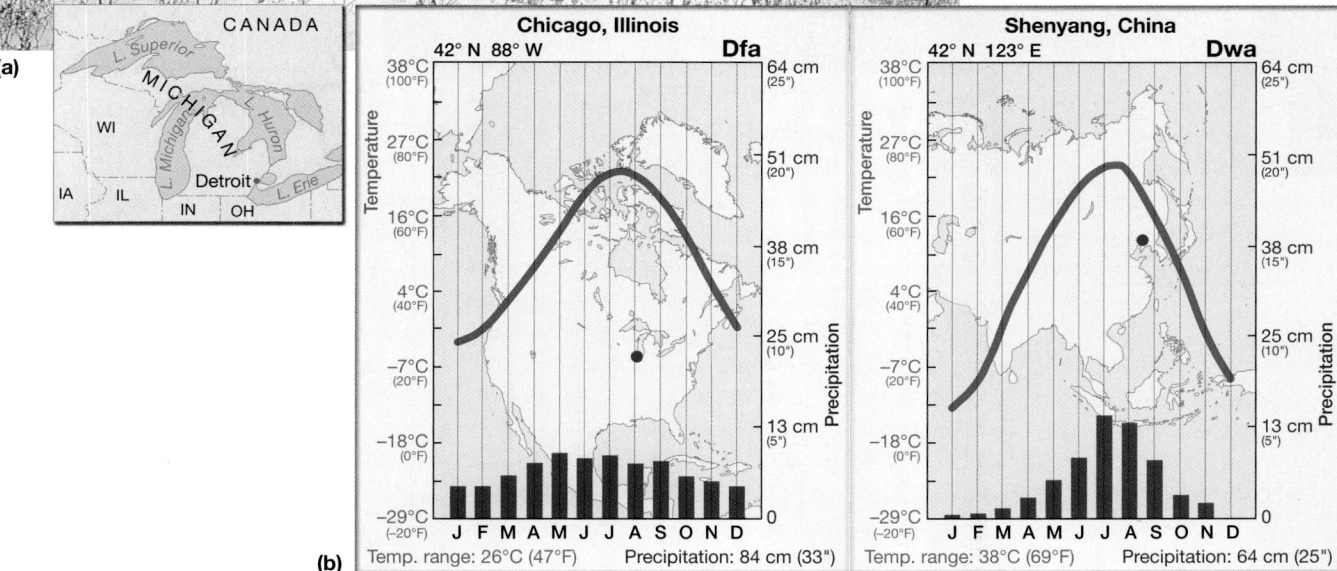

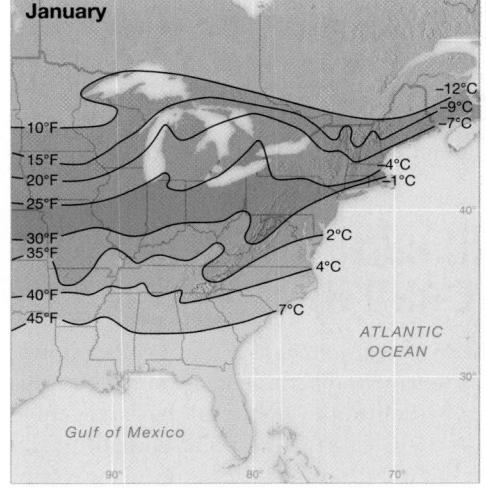
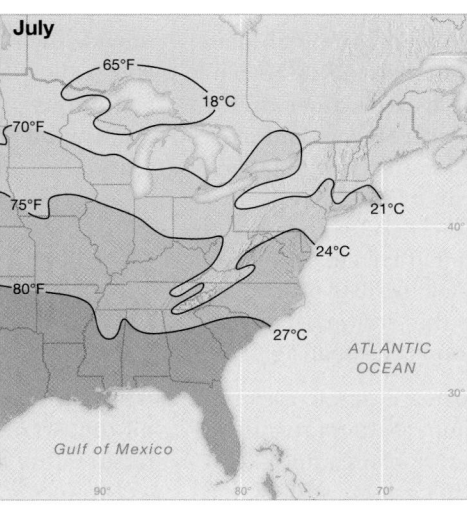

◀ **Figure 8-27** North–south temperature variation in the midlatitudes is much sharper in winter than in summer. These maps of the eastern United States show a very steep north–south average temperature gradient in January (left), with a more gradual gradient in July (right).

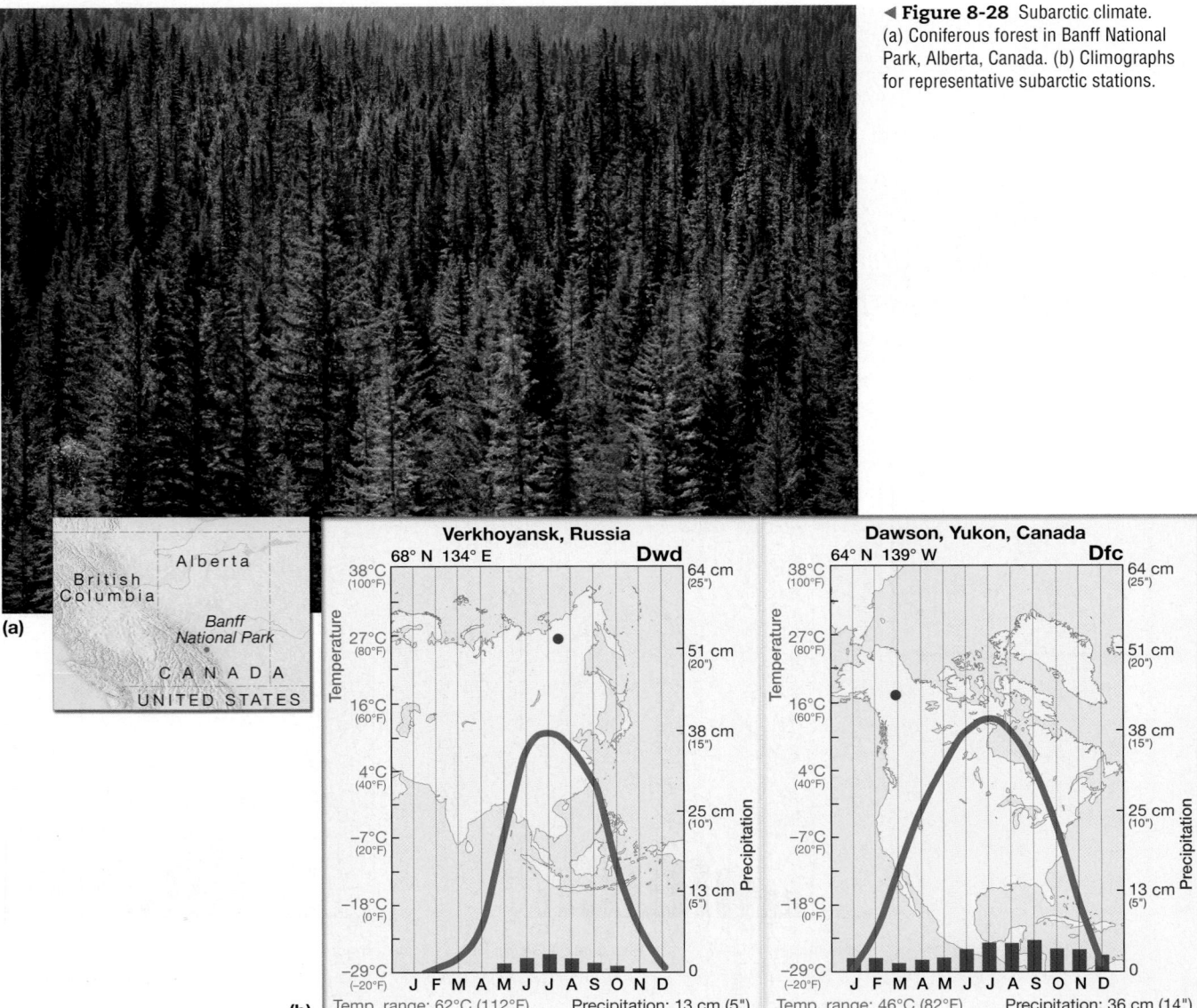

◀ **Figure 8-28** Subarctic climate. (a) Coniferous forest in Banff National Park, Alberta, Canada. (b) Climographs for representative subarctic stations.

Precipitation is usually low in the subarctic climate with annual averages ranging from perhaps 13 to 50 centimeters (5 to 20 inches), with the higher values occurring in coastal areas. Summer is the wet season, and most precipitation comes from scattered convective showers. Winter experiences only modest snowfalls (except near the coasts), perhaps accumulating to depths of 60 to 90 centimeters (2 or 3 feet). The snow that falls in October is likely to still be on the ground in May because little melts over the winter. Thus, a continuous thin snow cover exists for many months despite the sparseness of actual snowfall.

Controls of Dfc: Subarctic climates are largely the consequence of their continental location, that removes them from both the moisture and temperature-moderating effects of the ocean. The westerlies bring in cyclonic storms that

provide their meager precipitation. The low winter temperatures allow for little moisture in the air, and anticyclonic conditions predominate. Despite these sparse totals, the evaporation rate is low and the soil is frozen for much of the year so that enough moisture is present to support a forest.

POLAR AND HIGHLAND CLIMATES (GROUPS E AND H)

Being farthest from the equator, as Figure 8-29 shows, the *polar climates* receive too little insolation for any significant warming. By definition, no month has an average temperature above 10°C (50°F) in a polar climate. If the wet tropics represent conditions of monotonous warmth,

TABLE 8-5 Summary of E Climates: Polar

Type	Location	Temperature	Precipitation	Dominant Controls of Climate
Tundra (ET)	Fringes of Arctic Ocean; small coastal areas in Antarctica	Long, cold, dark winters; brief, cool summers; large ATR, small DTR	Sparse: less than 25 cm (10 in.) annually, mostly snow	Latitude; distance from sources of warmth and moisture; extreme seasonal contrasts in sunlight and darkness
Ice cap (EF)	Antarctica and Greenland	Long, dark, windy, bitterly cold winters; cold, windy summers; no monthly average above 0°C (32°F); large ATR, small DTR	Very sparse: less than 13 cm (5 in.) annually, all snow	Latitude; distance from sources of heat and moisture; extreme seasonal contrasts in sunlight and darkness; polar anticyclones

ATR = annual temperature range; DTR = daily temperature range.

◄ **Figure 8-29** The global distribution of polar (E) climates.

the polar climates are known for their enduring cold. They have the coldest summers and the lowest annual and absolute temperatures in the world. They are also extraordinarily dry, but evaporation is so minuscule that the group as a whole is classified as nonarid in the Köppen system. There are indications that high-latitude climates are changing more rapidly than midlatitude and tropical areas—see the box, "Focus: Signs of Climate Change in the Arctic."

The two types of polar climates are distinguished by summer temperature. The *tundra* climate has at least one month with an average temperature exceeding the freezing point; the *ice cap* climate does not. Table 8-5 summarizes the E climates.

Tundra Climate (ET)

The name *tundra* originally referred to the low, ground-hugging vegetation of high-latitude and high-altitude regions, but the term has been adopted to refer to the climate of the high-latitude regions as well. The generally accepted equatorward edge of the **tundra climate** is the 10°C (50°F) isotherm for the average temperature of the warmest month. This same isotherm corresponds approximately

with the poleward limit of trees so that the boundary between D and E is the "treeline."

At the poleward margin, the ET climate is bounded by the isotherm of 0°C (32°F) for the warmest month, which approximately coincides with the extreme limit for growth of *any* plant cover. More than for any other climatic type, the delimitation of the tundra climate demonstrates Köppen's contention that climate is best delimited in terms of plant communities (Figure 8-30).

Characteristics of ET: Long, cold, dark winters and brief, cool summers characterize the tundra. Only one to four months experience average temperatures above freezing, and the average summer temperature is between 4 and 10°C (in the 40s°F). Freezing temperatures can occur any time of year, and frosts are likely every night except in midsummer. Although an ET winter is bitterly cold—winter months might average –18°C (0°F) in coastal areas and –35°C (–30°F) in interior regions—it may not be as severe as in the more-continental subarctic climate just equatorward. Annual temperature ranges are fairly large, commonly more than 30°C (54°F).

Annual total precipitation is generally less than 25 centimeters (10 inches). Generally, more precipitation falls in

Although signs of climate change are observed in many parts of the world, among the most dramatic come from the polar regions. During the last 50 years, average temperatures in the Arctic have been increasing at about twice the rate as in lower latitudes. In western Canada and Alaska, winter temperatures are about 3°C (5°F) higher today than they were just 50 years ago.

Declining Summer Sea Ice: Since 1979, the winter maximum extent of sea ice decreased by about 1 million square kilometers (386,000 square miles). The decline of summer sea ice—known as *perennial sea ice*—is even greater: the summer retreat of sea ice by August 26, 2012, was the greatest ever measured since regular satellite monitoring of the ice pack was started in 1979—and this minimum was reached with several more weeks of further melting likely (Figure 8-A). The extent of perennial sea ice is about 40 percent lower than the 1979–2000 average, and by some estimates 50 percent lower than the 1950s–1970s long-term average.

The retreat of the Arctic sea ice leads to a feedback loop in the climate system: as the cover of sea ice diminishes, there is less reflectance and more absorption by the relatively dark ocean surface now exposed to sunlight—which leads to higher ocean temperatures and so greater melting of the ice pack. Some computer models suggest that with projected temperature increases associated with some greenhouse gas emission scenarios, it is possible that the summer Arctic sea ice cover could actually disappear within two or three decades.

Greenland Ice Sheet: The Greenland Ice Sheet covers nearly all of Greenland. As temperatures have increased over the last few decades, the extent of the seasonal melting of the ice sheet has expanded significantly. The area of the ice sheet exhibiting summer surface melting and *melt pond* formation was 60 percent greater in 2007 than it was in 1998 (the second greatest year on record). More recently, for several days in mid-July 2012, 97 percent of the ice sheet showed signs of surface melting—more than ever observed in 30 years of satellite monitoring (Figure 8-B). Although scientists acknowledge that the extreme melting of the surface of Greenland ice sheet in 2012 represented an unusual event (the ice core record indicates that the last such event took place in 1889), data clearly point toward an ongoing loss of ice mass—and the rate of loss appears to be accelerating.

The surface meltwater ponds not only signal the loss of ice, but the darker surface lowers albedo, thereby increasing the absorption of solar radiation and causing even greater melting (2011 recorded the lowest albedo in the 12 years of satellite monitoring). Further, as meltwater seeps down into the ice sheet through openings called *moulins*, it can increase the melting of ice and accelerate movement of the glacier over the bedrock below. In addition, the increase in freshwater entering the ocean reduces salinity and can potentially alter the deep ocean global conveyer-belt circulation (discussed in more detail in Chapter 9)—which could alter the exchange of heat between the tropics and polar latitudes.

Habitat Change: Concern about habitat change in the Arctic is growing among scientists. Satellite images show land areas are becoming "greener" as warmer conditions increase the vegetation cover—parts of the North Slope of Alaska are now changing from tundra to shrub.

The greater extent of open water in the Arctic Ocean because of sea ice reduction appears to be causing increases in marine *net primary productivity* (the net amount of carbon fixed by photosynthesis). Data show that primary production from phytoplankton has increased about 20 percent over the last three decades. How such changes in phytoplankton will influence organisms higher up in the often-short Arctic food chain is unclear.

As the extent of sea ice diminishes, changes are now being observed in both marine and terrestrial mammal populations. For example, over the last few years, thousands of Pacific walruses have hauled out on land along the northwest coast of Alaska during the summer—this behavior, rarely observed in the past, appears to be associated with the loss of summer sea ice. In addition, polar bears regularly hunt for seal pups and other prey on the sea ice during the summer, but because the sea ice is breaking up earlier than in the past, polar bears face the potential loss of access to prey.

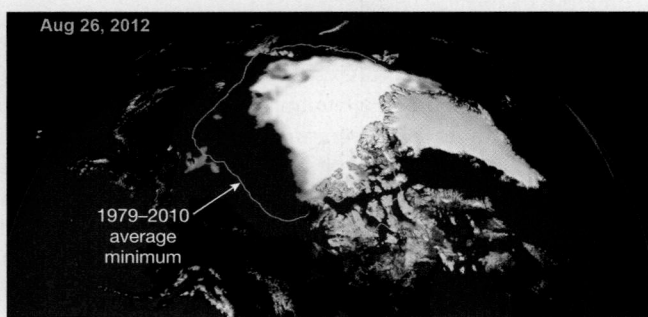

▲ **Figure 8-A** Summer sea ice on August 26, 2012—the lowest extent ever measured until surpassed the following month.

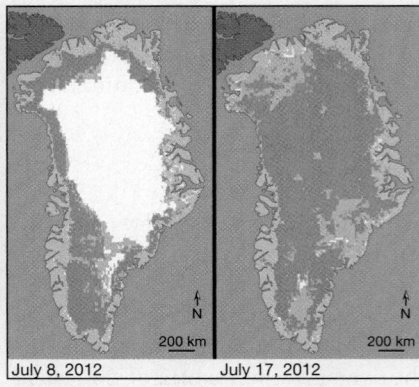

◀ **Figure 8-B** Surface melting of the Greenland ice sheet in July 2012. Surface melting (dark red) suddenly increased from about 40 percent on July 8th, to 97 percent on July 12—caused when the surface air temperature rose just above freezing for a few hours.

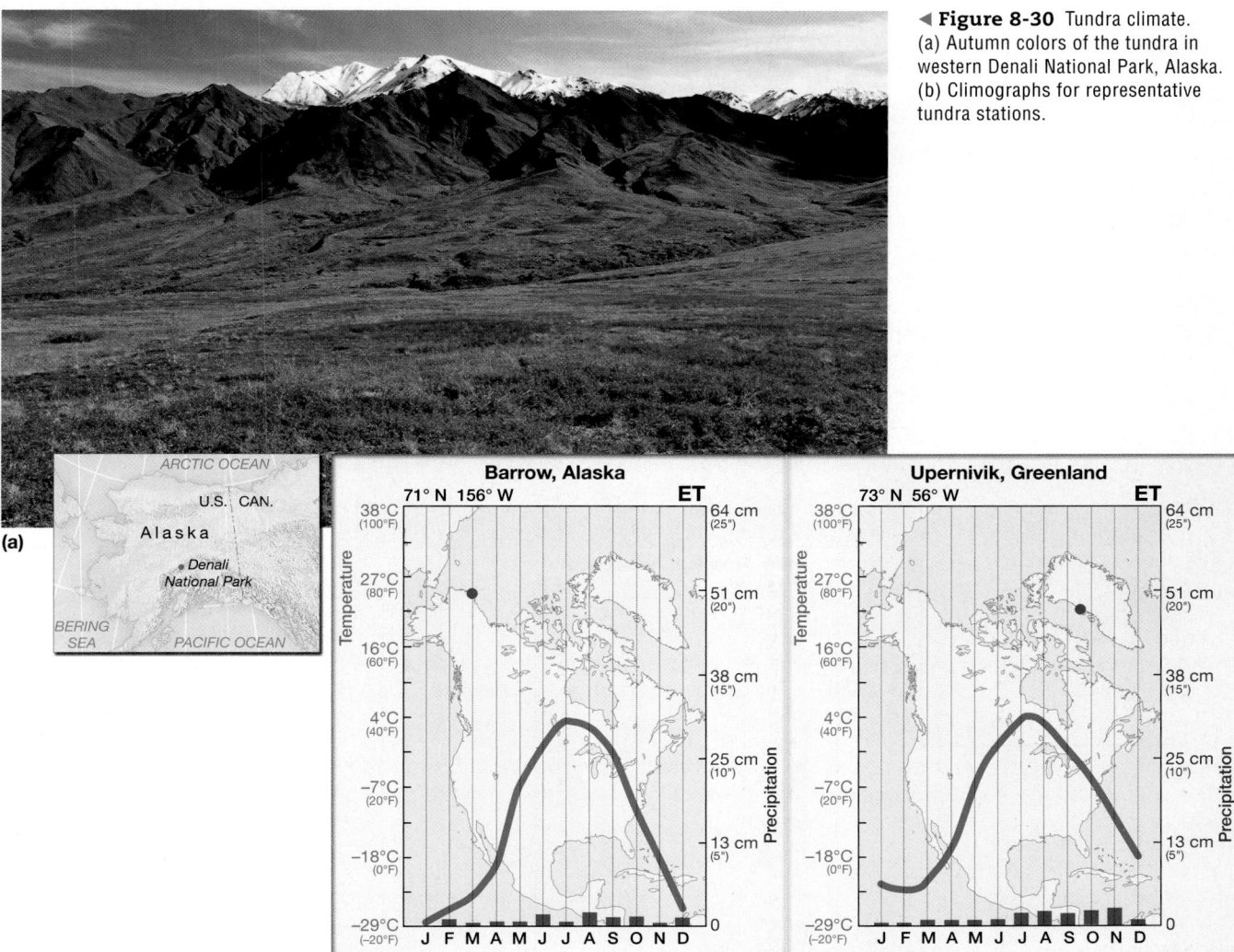

◀ **Figure 8-30** Tundra climate. (a) Autumn colors of the tundra in western Denali National Park, Alaska. (b) Climographs for representative tundra stations.

the warm season than in winter, although the total amount in any month is small, and the month-to-month variation is minor. Winter snow is often dry and granular; it appears to be more than it actually is because there is no melting and because winds swirl it horizontally even when no snow is falling. Radiation fogs are fairly common throughout ET regions, and sea fogs are sometimes prevalent for days along the coast.

Controls of ET: Daily temperature ranges are small because the Sun is above the horizon for most of the time in summer and below the horizon for most of the time in winter; thus nocturnal cooling is limited in summer, and daytime warming is almost nonexistent in winter. Moisture availability is very restricted in ET regions despite the proximity of an ocean—the air is simply too cold to contain much water vapor, and so the absolute humidity is almost always very low. Moreover, anticyclonic conditions are common, with little uplift to encourage condensation.

Ice Cap Climate (EF)

The most severe of Earth's climates, **ice cap climate**, is restricted to Greenland (all but the coastal fringe) and most of Antarctica, the combined extent of these two regions amounting to more than 9 percent of the world's land area (Figure 8-31).

Characteristics of EF: The EF climate is one of perpetual frost where vegetation cannot grow, and the landscape consists of a permanent cover of ice and snow. The extraordinary severity of EF temperatures is increased because both Antarctica and Greenland are ice plateaus, so that relatively high altitude is added to high latitude as a thermal factor. All months have average temperatures below freezing, and in the most extreme locations the average temperature of even the warmest month is below –18°C (0°F). Winter temperatures average between –34 and –51°C (–30°F and –60°F) and extremes well below

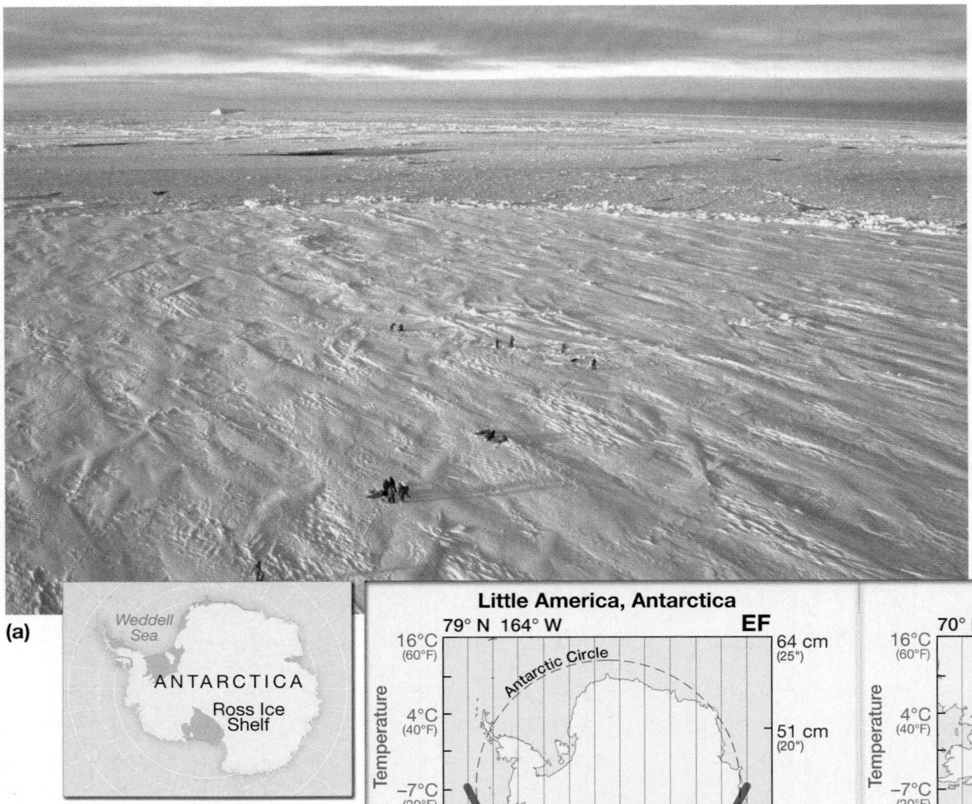

◀ **Figure 8-31** Ice cap climate.
(a) The infinite bleakness of an ice
cap can be imagined in this view of
scientists at work on the Ross Ice
Shelf of Antarctica. (b) Climographs for
representative ice cap stations. Notice
that Little America, Antarctica, receives
almost no measurable precipitation in a
typical year. (Note that the temperature
scales are different from those of the
other climographs in the chapter; note
also that the climograph for Eismitte,
Greenland, is based on less than 30 years
of data.)

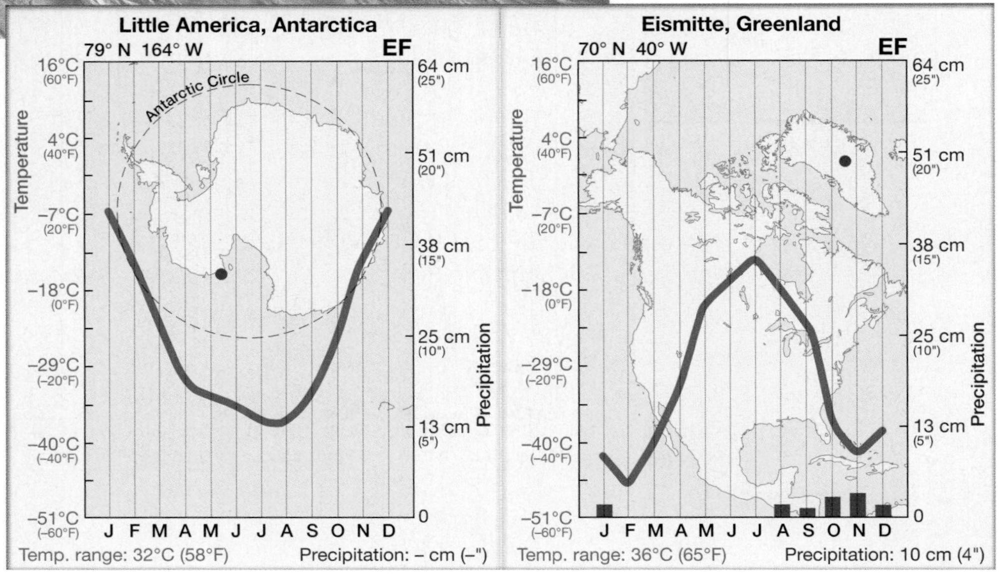

(a)

Little America, Antarctica
79° N 164° W   **EF**

Temp. range: 32°C (58°F)   Precipitation: – cm (–")

Eismitte, Greenland
70° N 40° W   **EF**

Temp. range: 36°C (65°F)   Precipitation: 10 cm (4")

(b)

–73°C (–100°F) have been recorded at interior Antarctic weather stations.

The air is chilled so intensely from the underlying ice that strong surface temperature inversions prevail most of the time. Heavy, cold air often flows downslope as a vigorous *katabatic wind* (discussed in Chapter 5), and characteristics of the ice cap climate, particularly in Antarctica, are strong winds and blowing snow.

Precipitation is very limited. These regions are essentially polar deserts; most places receive less than 13 centimeters (5 inches) of moisture annually.

Controls of EF: The cold of EF climates is due to their extremely high latitude—even when the Sun is above the

horizon, it is so low in the sky that little warming is possible. The extreme dryness of these areas is largely due to the low temperatures: the extremely cold air has almost no water vapor capacity, and the cold conditions result in stable conditions with too little likelihood of uplift to permit much precipitation.

Learning Check 8-8   **Why are polar climates so dry?**

Highland Climate (Group H)    FG1, FG4

Highland climate is not defined in the same sense as all the others we have just studied. Climatic conditions in mountainous areas have almost infinite variations from

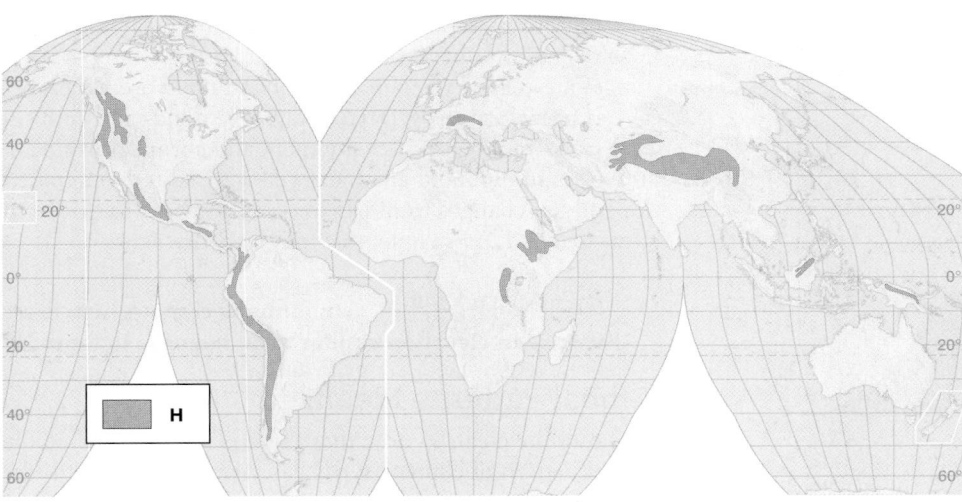

◀ **Figure 8-32** The global distribution of highland (H) climate.

place to place, and many of the differences extend over very limited horizontal distances. Köppen did not recognize highland climate as a separate group, but most of the researchers who have modified his system have added such a category. Highland climates are delimited in this book to identify relatively high uplands (mountains and plateaus) having complex local climate variation in small areas (Figure 8-32). The climate of any highland location is usually closely related to that of the adjacent lowland, particularly with regard to seasonality of precipitation.

Characteristics and Controls of H Climates:

Altitude variations influence all four elements of weather and climate. As we learned in Chapters 4, 5, and 6, with increasing altitude, temperature and pressure generally decrease; wind is less predictable but tends to be brisk and abrupt with many local wind systems. Because of orographic

lifting, precipitation is characteristically heavier in highlands than in surrounding lowlands, so that the mountains usually stand out as moist islands on a rainfall map (Figure 8-33).

Altitude is more significant than latitude in determining climate in highland areas. Steep vertical gradients of climatic change are expressed as horizontal bands along the slopes. An increase of a few hundred meters in elevation may be equivalent to a journey of several hundred kilometers poleward insofar as temperature and related environmental characteristics are concerned. Such *vertical zonation* is particularly prominent in tropical highlands (Figure 8-34); we will explore this topic again in Chapter 11 when we discuss patterns in *biogeography*.

Exposure—whether a slope, peak, or valley faces windward or leeward—has a profound influence on climate. Ascending air on a windward face brings a strong likelihood of heavy precipitation, whereas a leeward location is

◀ **Figure 8-33** Climate of a lowland station (Sacramento) and two nearby highland localities (Placerville and Twin Lakes) at about the same latitude in California (approximately 38°40′ N). With increasing elevation, we see the expected decrease in temperature and increase in precipitation, although all three exhibit the characteristic summer-dry regime of the lowland mediterranean (Cs) climate.

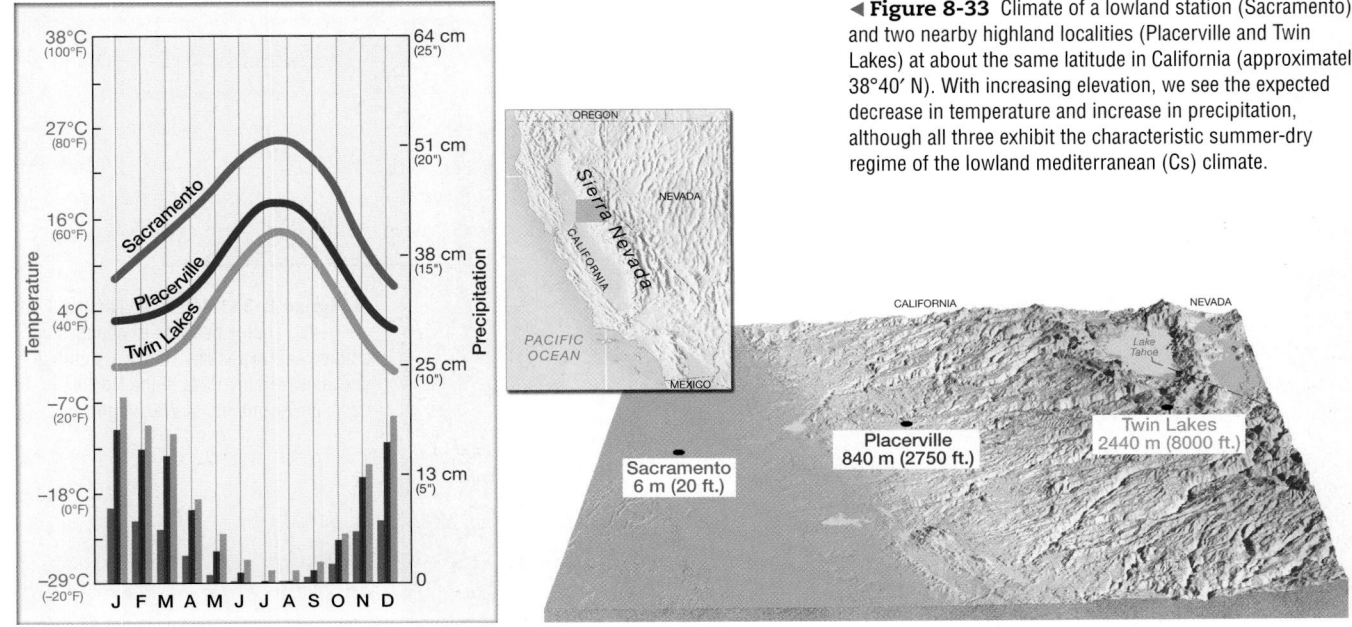

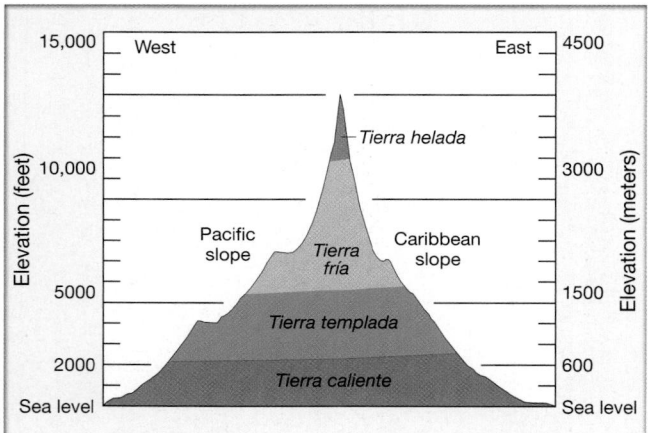

▲ **Figure 8-34** Vertical climate zonation is particularly noticeable in tropical mountainous areas. This diagram idealizes the situation at about 15° N in Guatemala and southern Mexico. *Tierra caliente* ("hot land") is a zone of high temperatures, dense vegetation, and tropical agriculture. *Tierra templada* ("temperate land") is an intermediate zone of slopes and plateaus and temperatures most persons would find comfortable. *Tierra fria* ("cold land") is characterized by warm days and cold nights, and its agriculture is limited to hardy crops. *Tierra helada* ("frozen land") is a zone of cold weather throughout the year.

sheltered from moisture or has predominantly downslope wind movement with limited opportunity for precipitation. The angle of exposure to sunlight is also a significant factor in determining climate, especially outside the tropics. Slopes that face equatorward receive direct sunlight, which makes them warm and dry; adjacent slopes facing poleward may be much cooler and moister simply because of a smaller angle of solar incidence and more shading.

Changeability is perhaps the single most conspicuous characteristic of highland climate (Figure 8-35). The thin, dry air permits rapid influx of insolation by day and rapid loss of radiant energy at night, and so daily temperature ranges are very large, with frequent and rapid oscillation between freeze and thaw. Daytime upslope winds and convection cause rapid cloud development and abrupt storminess. Travelers in highland areas are well advised to be prepared for sudden changes from hot to cold, from wet to dry, from clear to cloudy, from quiet to windy, and vice versa.

Learning Check 8-9 In terms of climate, how is an increase in elevation similar to an increase in latitude?

Global Patterns Idealized

It should be clear by now that there is a fairly predictable global pattern of climatic types based primarily on latitude, position on a continent, and the general circulation of the atmosphere and oceans. Figure 8-36 summarizes the idealized distribution of the mild (A, B, and C) climates along the west coasts of continents, where the distribution pattern is slightly more regular than along the east coasts. Notice especially the relationship of climate types to the seasonal shifts of the intertropical convergence zone and the subtropical highs.

A more general model of the climate distribution on a *hypothetical continent* is shown in Figure 8-37. The model portrays the idealized distribution of five of the six groups and most of the types and subtypes; highland climate is not included because its location is determined solely by topography. Groups A, C, D, and E are defined by temperature, which means that their boundaries are strongly latitudinal because they are determined by insolation. The B group is defined by moisture conditions, and its distribution cuts across those of the thermally defined groups. Such a model is a predictive tool. One can state, with some degree of assurance, that at a particular latitude and a general location

◀ **Figure 8-35** Mountain climates are quite variable because of changes in altitude and exposure. This is a summer scene near Rainy Pass in the North Cascade Mountains of Washington.

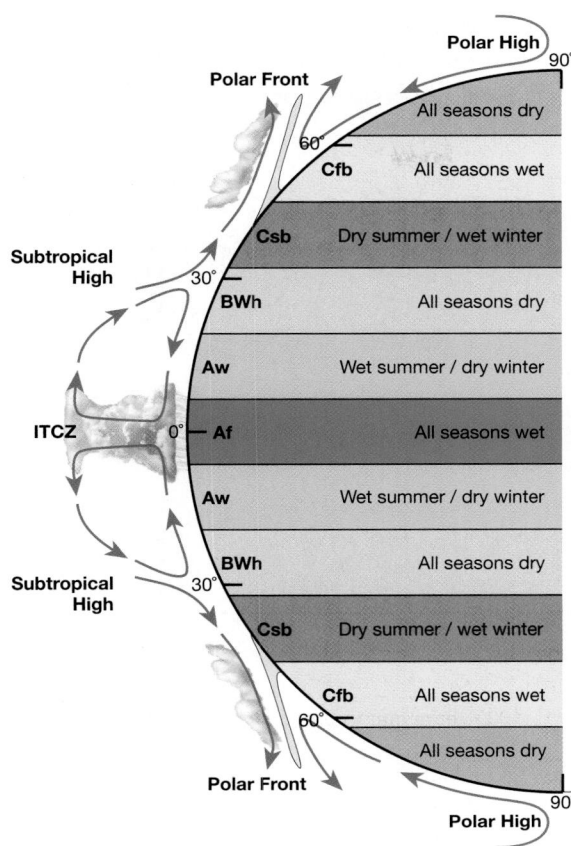

▲ **Figure 8-36** Idealized seasonal precipitation patterns and climates along the west coast of continents. Note that the progressions north and south of the equator are mirror images. Much of this pattern is due to the seasonal shifts of the ITCZ and the subtropical highs.

on a continent, a certain climate is likely to occur. Moreover, the locations of the climatic types relative to one another can be understood more clearly when they are all shown together this way.

GLOBAL CLIMATE CHANGE

So far in this chapter we have discussed the complexity of global climate patterns as we observe them in the present day. Although it is important for us to learn the fundamentals of weather and climate by first studying such "stable" circumstances, a thorough understanding of the atmosphere requires us now to explore how patterns can change over time.

For the remainder of this chapter, we look more specifically at climate change. We especially want to address questions first raised in Chapter 4: Is human activity causing global climate change, and if so, what are the likely long-term consequences? In providing a thoughtful answer to these questions, we will look at how past climate is inferred, how climate change is recognized, what kinds of factors may lead to climate change, and what evidence indicates that climate is currently changing.

As we first saw in Chapter 3, within any climate system there is expected fluctuation in weather from year to year. The random variation in weather from year to year can be thought

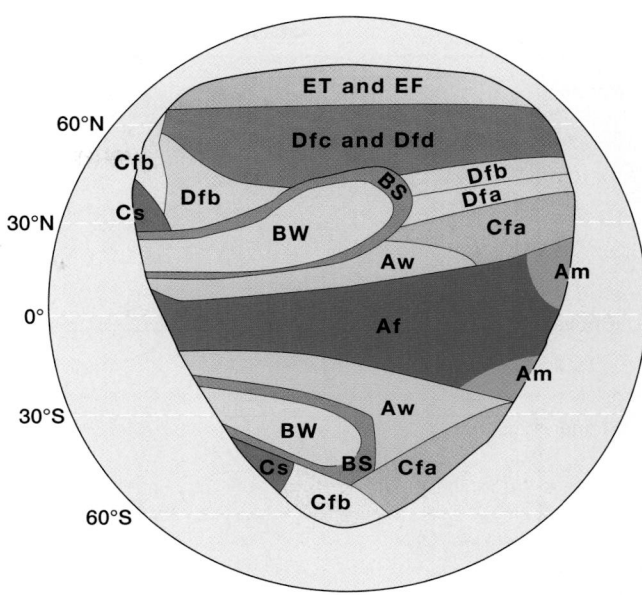

▲ **Figure 8-37** The presumed arrangement of Köppen climatic types on a large hypothetical continent.

of as the background "noise" in the long-term climate record. Within the climate record, however, other kinds of variation may be present: episodic events and natural cycles of change with periods ranging from a few years to many decades (El Niño and the Pacific Decadal Oscillation discussed in Chapter 5 are examples of this), as well as long-term global climate change (which can also exhibit cycles of its own).

Time Scales of Climate Change: The time scale of observations influences which kinds of patterns stand out in the climate record. For example, in the case of global temperature:

- Over the last 70 million years, a clear global cooling trend is visible (Figure 8-38a).
- Over the last 150,000 years, temperature fluctuated significantly until about 10,000 years ago when temperature increased sharply; temperature has remained warm and fairly steady since (Figure 8-38b).
- Over the last 150 years a warming trend appears underway—a clear departure from the previous 850 years (Figure 8-38c).

These trends are actually even more complicated than might first appear: these temperature changes weren't necessarily uniform around the world.

Determining Climates of the Past

Before we can assess the possibility of climate change today, we must have some understanding of past climates and the causes of past climate change, a field of study known as **paleoclimatology**.

Detailed instrument records of weather go back only a few hundred years, so it is necessary to use *proxy* ("substitute") measures of climate

Animation
End of the Last
Ice Age

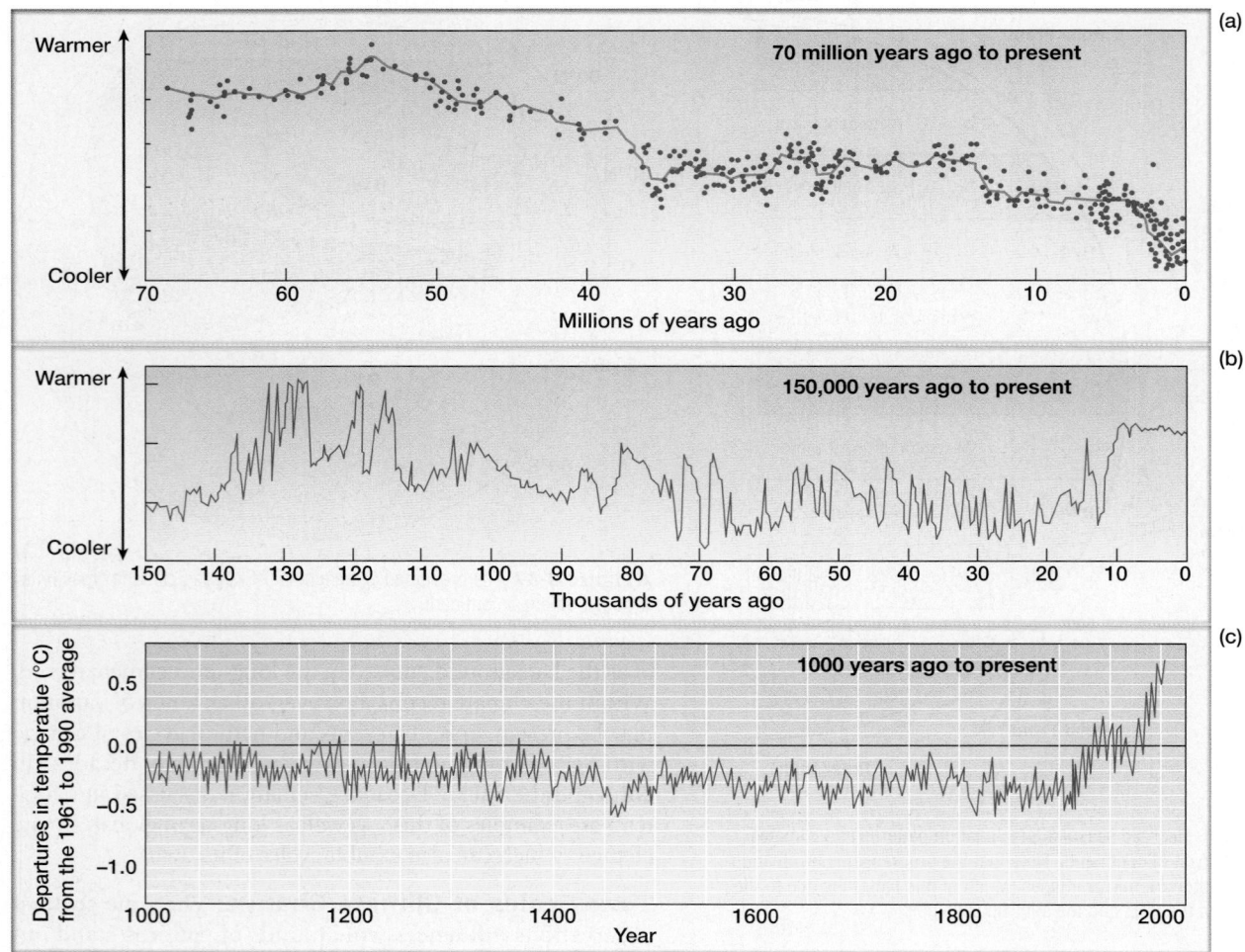

GENERALIZED GLOBAL TEMPERATURE TRENDS

▲ **Figure 8-38** Generalized global temperature trends at three time scales. (a) 70 million years ago to present. (b) 150,000 years ago to present. (c) 1000 years ago to present. The curve in (a) was generalized from ice volume and ocean temperature proxy measures; the curve in (b) was derived from North Atlantic Ocean proxy measures; the curve in (c) was derived from proxy measures and the historical record after 1900.

to reconstruct conditions in the past. Information about past climate can come from many different sources: tree rings, ice cores, oceanic sediments, coral reefs, relic soils, and pollen, among others. No single method for determining past climate conditions is ideal—each has its own strengths and weaknesses. However, by correlating the results achieved with one method with those from another, paleoclimatologists are able to construct a detailed history of Earth's climate.

Dendrochronology

Most trees growing in temperate areas increase trunk diameter by adding one concentric *tree ring* for each year of growth. By counting the number of rings, the age of a tree may be determined. Tree rings also provide information about climate: during years when the growing conditions are favorable (such as mild temperatures and/or ample precipitation), tree rings tend to be wider than in years when the growing conditions are harsher (Figure 8-39).

Both living and dead trees can be used in **dendrochronology** (the study of dating past events through the analysis of tree rings). Small cores are taken so that living trees are not harmed, and fallen trees, buried trunks, and timber from archeological sites all may be used to extend tree ring chronology. By comparing and correlating the tree ring patterns of many trees in an area, dendrochronologists can not only determine the age of the trees, but can establish dates for catastrophic events such as floods and fires that have killed trees, as well as identify periods of drought and lower or higher temperatures.

Oxygen Isotope Analysis

In the nucleus of many atoms, the number of protons and neutrons is the same. For example, most oxygen atoms have 8 protons and 8 neutrons, giving them an atomic weight of 16 (^{16}O or "oxygen 16"). However, a small number of oxygen atoms have 2 extra neutrons, giving these atoms an atomic weight of 18 (^{18}O). ^{16}O and ^{18}O are known

▲ **Figure 8-39** Dendrochronology uses tree rings to identify past climate. Each ring represents one growing season; wider rings often indicate favorable growing conditions, whereas narrow rings indicate harsher conditions.

as *isotopes* of oxygen. Both isotopes of oxygen can be found in common molecules such as water (H_2O) and calcium carbonate ($CaCO_3$).

Through **oxygen isotope analysis**, the ratio of $^{18}O/^{16}O$ in the molecules of substances such as water and calcium carbonate can tell us something about the environment in which those molecules formed. Because they contain the lighter oxygen isotope, water molecules with ^{16}O evaporate more easily than those with ^{18}O, and so precipitation such as rain and snow tends to be relatively rich in ^{16}O. During an ice age, great quantities of ^{16}O are locked up in glacial ice on the continents, leaving a greater concentration of ^{18}O in the oceans; during a warmer, interglacial period, the glacial ice melts, returning ^{16}O to the oceans.

Oceanic Sediments: Ocean floor sediments provide a record of the changing $^{18}O/^{16}O$ ratio in seawater over periods of thousands of years. A number of common marine microorganisms, such as *foraminifera*, excrete shells or exoskeletons of calcium carbonate, and the remains of these organisms build up layer upon layer on the ocean floor (see Figure 9-7 on p. 258). By comparing the $^{18}O/^{16}O$ ratio of the calcium carbonate in these layers of sediment, scientists can determine when periods of glaciation took place. If the $^{18}O/^{16}O$ ratio in the calcium carbonate is high (in other words, relatively high amounts of ^{18}O are present), we can infer those organisms were living during a glacial period; if the $^{18}O/^{16}O$ ratio is low, we can infer those organisms were living during an interglacial period.

Coral Reefs: Coral reefs are built up in tropical ocean areas by massive colonies of tiny coral polyps that excrete calcium carbonate exoskeletons (coral is discussed in more detail in

Chapter 20). Because this $CaCO_3$ was extracted from the seawater, the $^{18}O/^{16}O$ ratio of the coral provides information about the climate at the time the reef was forming. Further, because coral reefs develop in shallow water, the relative height of old reefs may help us determine past fluctuations in sea level.

Learning Check 8-10 How can oxygen isotope analysis tell us about temperature in the past?

Ice Cores

The analysis of ice cores can also give us information about past climate. By drilling down into glaciers, a record of snowfall going back hundreds of thousands of years may be obtained in some locations (Figure 8-40). Such ice cores offer several kinds of information about past conditions. A greater number of water molecules with ^{18}O evaporate from the oceans when temperatures are high than when temperatures are low, thus the $^{18}O/^{16}O$ ratio found in a layer of ice serves as a "thermometer" for the climate at the time that snow fell. Oxygen isotope analysis of ice cores has become one of the most important ways scientists have been able to construct a record of past global temperature.

Ice cores also provide direct information about the composition of the atmosphere in the past. As snow accumulates and is compacted into glacial ice, air bubbles from the atmosphere become frozen into the ice. These tiny air bubbles deep in glaciers are preserved samples of the ancient atmosphere, allowing direct measurements of the

▲ **Figure 8-40** Scientists in Antarctica drilling an ice core as part of the EPICA project (European Project for Ice Coring in Antarctica).

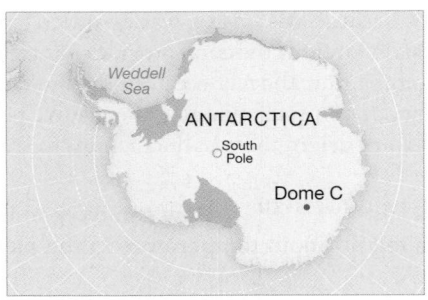

▲ **Figure 8-41** Map of Antarctica showing the location of EPICA Dome C.

concentration of CO_2 and other gases to be made. In addition, particulates in the ice can offer information about past cataclysmic events such as major volcanic eruptions.

Dome C in Antarctica: Of all the locations where ice cores have been extracted from glaciers, the most significant is probably Dome C in Antarctica. Dome C is located about 1750 kilometers (1090 miles) from the South Pole at a latitude of 75° S and a longitude 123° E—this is where the Antarctic ice cap is at its thickest (Figure 8-41). The coring has been undertaken by the European Project for Ice Coring in Antarctica (EPICA). A multinational team of scientists has extracted a continuous 10 centimeter (4 inch) diameter ice core record to a depth of more than 3 kilometers (2 miles). The analysis has provided climate and atmospheric composition data back 800,000 years—far longer than any other ice core—providing climate information on eight complete glacial/interglacial cycles (Figure 8-42).

The findings at Dome C closely match the proxy climate record derived from the nearby Vostok, Antarctica, ice core, as well as oxygen isotope analysis of the calcium carbonate in foraminifera found in oceanic sediments, adding to the scientists' confidence in the soundness of the Dome C data.

The Dome C climate record shows that the present concentration of CO_2 in the atmosphere is greater than at any time in the last 800,000 years, and that increases and

decreases in global temperature are closely correlated with changes in greenhouse gas concentration (especially carbon dioxide and methane): lower concentrations of greenhouse gases are present during glacial episodes, whereas higher concentrations of greenhouses gases are present during interglacial warm periods. However, research shows that it is usually several hundred years after an interglacial temperature increase begins before atmospheric CO_2 concentrations increase. This suggests that the increase in greenhouse gas concentration was not the trigger for the interglacial temperature increase; increasing CO_2 levels may have simply amplified the warming climate. Today, however, an increase in temperature is closely following an increase in greenhouse gases, indicating that the temperature increase has been caused by the increase in greenhouse gases.

Learning Check 8-11 How can ice cores give us information about past concentrations of greenhouse gases in the atmosphere?

Pollen Analysis

Another important method used for determining past climates comes from the field of *palynology*, or *pollen analysis*. Airborne pollen from trees and other plants can be preserved in sediment layers on lake bottoms and in bogs. Cores of these sediment layers are taken and analyzed.

Video
20,000 years of
Pine Pollen

Radiocarbon dating of material in each layer provides an estimate of the age of organic material younger than about 50,000 years. Radiocarbon dating works by comparing the ratio of two isotopes of carbon found in organic material: radioactive ^{14}C decays over time at a known rate into ^{14}N, a stable isotope of nitrogen. The more common stable isotope of carbon, ^{12}C, remains constant no matter how old the sample is. So the $^{14}C/^{12}C$ ratio serves as indication of how long ago the plant or animal material was alive. With

▶ **Figure 8-42** Temperature record over the last 800,000 years from EPICA Dome C ice core, and the corresponding CO_2 record derived from Dome C and other locations. Temperature scale is relative to average temperature over the last 1000 years.

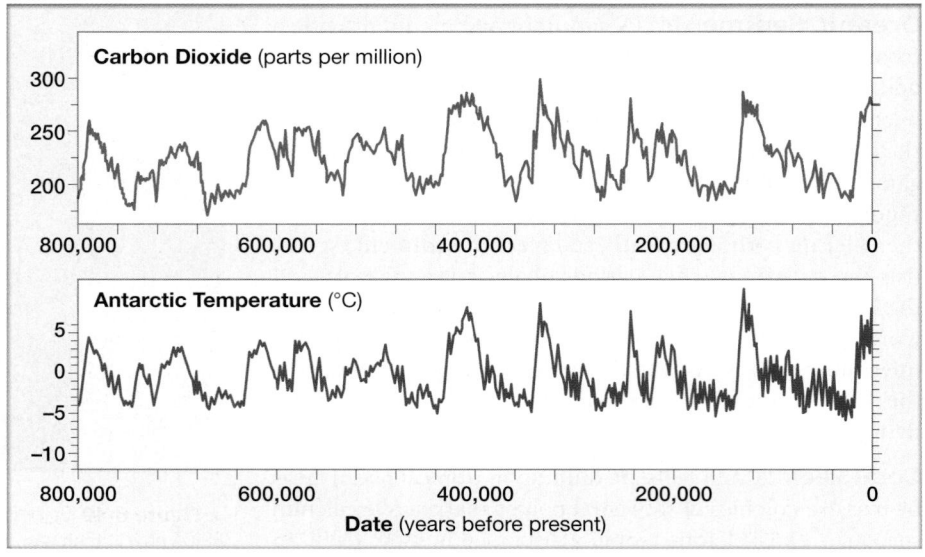

the age of a sediment layer known, palynologists look at the types of pollen present to determine which plants and trees were living at the time that layer was forming. Since plant species change as the environment changes—some species are better adapted for colder conditions, for example—the prevalence of one plant community over another acts as a proxy for the climate of the time.

Urban Heat Islands

When using the instrument record to discern climate change over the last century, an interesting factor comes into play: urban areas tend to be warmer than rural areas. This often-observed increase in temperature associated with cities is known as the **urban heat island (UHI) effect**. The UHI effect is thought to be caused mostly from reduced nighttime cooling because buildings inhibit the loss of longwave radiation to space and reduce the mixing of warmer surface air with cooler air above. Lower reflectance (and so greater absorption of insolation) in urban areas may also play a role.

The United States Environmental Protection Agency (EPA) estimates that temperatures within a city of one million people are typically 1 to 3°C (1.8 to 5.4°F) warmer than nearby rural areas, with nighttime temperature differences much greater than this. However, some recent research suggests that the UHI effect may be smaller than previously thought—perhaps as little as a 0.9°C (1.6°F) difference between cities and the surrounding rural areas. Even so, this factor must be accounted for when using historic data from weather stations in areas that have urbanized significantly.

In addition to temperature, precipitation in urban areas (and downwind of urban areas) may be affected by the higher concentrations of aerosols released by industries or other human activity.

CAUSES OF LONG-TERM CLIMATE CHANGE

A quick glance back to Chapter 4 and the diagram showing Earth's solar radiation budget (Figure 4-18) will remind you of the many variables that influence patterns of temperature: the quantity of incoming solar radiation, the albedo of the atmosphere and surface, the concentration of greenhouse gases, the transfer of energy through oceanic and atmospheric circulation, and many others. A change in any one of those variables has the potential to change temperature, wind, pressure, and moisture patterns.

Not surprisingly then, a number of mechanisms are likely to have had a role in past climate change and may be operating in the present day as well. Although by no means a comprehensive description, in the following sections we describe several kinds of mechanisms of climate change.

Atmospheric Aerosols

Large quantities of particulates ejected into the atmosphere by volcanic eruptions can alter global temperatures

(Figure 8-43). Fine volcanic ash and other aerosols can reach the stratosphere, where they may circle the globe for years, blocking incoming solar radiation and lowering temperature. For example, the 1991 eruption of Mount Pinatubo in the Philippines increased aerosol concentrations (especially sulfur dioxide) in the atmosphere enough to lower global temperatures by about 0.5°C (0.9°F) for the next year.

Large asteroid impacts also can eject enough dust into the atmosphere to significantly alter global climate. It is widely accepted by scientists that the impact of a 10-kilometer wide asteroid 65 million years ago was one factor that contributed to the extinction of the dinosaurs—environmental change associated with massive *flood basalt* eruptions occurring at the same time is likely to have been a more significant factor (flood basalt is discussed in Chapter 14).

As we saw in Chapter 6 ("People and the Environment: Global Dimming"), anthropogenic aerosols may influence climate—especially sulfates and black carbon. Sulfates released by the burning of fossil fuels tend to scatter incoming solar radiation and so have a net cooling effect. On the other hand, black carbon emissions from the burning of

▲ **Figure 8-43** Eruption of Mt. Shinmoe, Japan, on January 27, 2011. The plume of ash reached an altitude of more than 2500 meters (8200 feet).

diesel and biofuels tend to absorb solar radiation and so lead to warming.

Over the last 35 years stricter environmental regulations in industrialized countries have cut sulfate emissions in half, while over the same time period, emissions of black carbon from industrializing countries in the Northern Hemisphere—especially in Asia—have risen. A 2009 NASA study suggested that much of the warming in the Arctic since 1976 may be linked to changes in aerosols—less cooling from sulfates combined with more warming from black carbon.

Fluctuations in Solar Output

A link between past climates and variations in the energy output of the Sun has been pursued for many decades. For example, researchers have looked for a connection between climate and sunspot activity. *Sunspots* appear as dark spots on the surface of the Sun. They are slightly cooler regions of the Sun's *photosphere* and are associated with intense magnetic storms on the surface of the Sun, as well as the ejection of charged particles (some of the charged particles reach Earth as part of the *solar wind* where they produce auroral displays in the upper atmosphere; see Figure 3-10).

Some scientists have noted that several past climate events, such as the *Little Ice Age*—a period of unusually cold weather from about 1400 to 1850—corresponded with a period of greatly reduced sunspot activity between 1645 and 1715 (known as the *Maunder Minimum*). Recent satellite measurements show that the energy striking Earth's upper atmosphere, or *total solar irradiance* (TSI), varies by about 0.1 percent over the well-documented 11-year cycle of sunspot activity—with less energy received during periods of low sunspot activity. Ultraviolet radiation seems to vary much more than this, and so fluctuations in TSI may affect the ozone layer and perhaps other aspects of energy flow through the atmosphere.

Although some of the relationships between sunspot cycles and climate appear at first to be strong statistically, many scientists remain unconvinced—in part because not all episodes of unusual sunspot activity correlate with changes in climate. Further, although variation in TSI may well play a role in climate change, the measured fluctuations do not seem to be nearly enough to account for the global warming trend observed over the last century.

Learning Check 8-12 **How can differences in atmospheric aerosols influence climate?**

Variations in Earth–Sun Relations

Animation
Orbital Variations and Climate Change

As we saw in Chapter 1, the change of seasons is largely a consequence of the changing orientation of Earth's rotational axis to the Sun during the year (see Figure 1-28). You will recall that we said that Earth's axis maintains an inclination of 23.5° at all times, that Earth's axis always points toward the North Star Polaris, and that Earth is closest to the Sun on January 3rd. As it turns out, all of those aspects of Earth–Sun relations change over periods of thousands of years in a series of predictable, well-documented cycles (Figure 8-44).

Eccentricity of Orbit: The "shape" of Earth's elliptical orbit, or *eccentricity*, varies in a series of cycles lasting about 100,000 years. Sometimes Earth's orbit is nearly circular, whereas at other times the orbit is much more elliptical, thus influencing the distance between the Sun and Earth. The present difference in distance between the Sun and Earth at aphelion and perihelion is about 3 percent

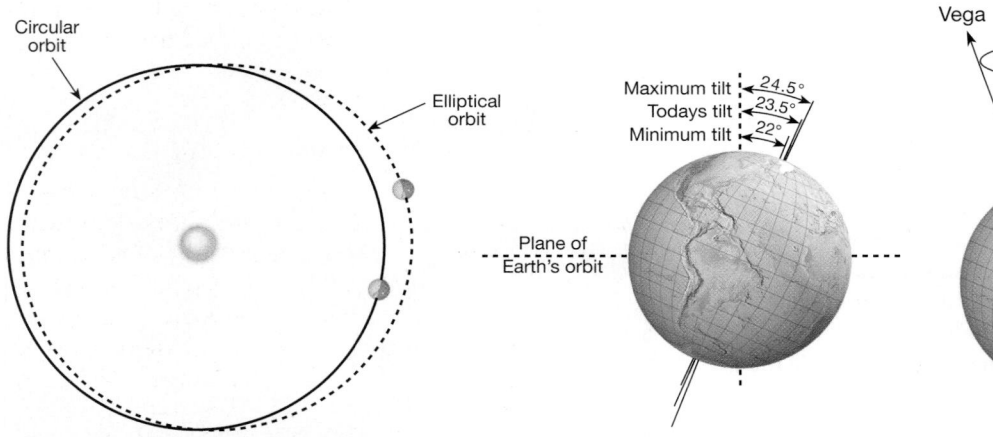

(a) The shape of Earth's elliptical orbit, or *eccentricity*, varies in a cycle lasting about 100,000 years.

(b) The inclination of Earth's axis, or *obliquity*, varies in a cycle lasting 41,000 years.

(c) The orientation of Earth's axis varies in the 25,800-year cycle of *precession*.

▲ **Figure 8-44** Orbital variation cycles in Earth–Sun relations. (a) The shape of Earth's elliptical orbit, or eccentricity, varies in a cycle lasting about 100,000 years. (b) The inclination of Earth's axis, or obliquity, varies in a cycle lasting 41,000 years. (c) The orientation of Earth's axis varies in the 25,800-year cycle of precession.

(about a 5,000,000 kilometer difference), but over the last 600,000 years or so, the difference has varied from 1 percent to 11 percent. The greater the difference in distance, the greater the difference in insolation at various points in Earth's orbit.

Obliquity of Rotational Axis: The inclination of Earth's axis, or *obliquity*, varies from 22.1° to 24.5° in a cycle lasting about 41,000 years. When there is greater inclination, seasonal variation between the low latitudes and high latitudes tends to be greater; when there is less inclination, seasonal contrasts are less significant.

Precession: Earth's axis "wobbles" like a spinning top, and so over time it points in different directions relative to the stars in a 25,800-year cycle called *precession*. Precession alters the timing of the seasons relative to Earth's position in its orbit around the Sun.

As these long-term cycles "overlap" there are periods of time when significantly less radiation reaches Earth's surface (especially in the high latitudes), and periods of time when there are greater or lesser seasonal contrasts. For example, during periods when there is less "seasonality"—in other words, when there are smaller contrasts between winter and summer—more snow can accumulate in high latitudes due to greater snowfall from milder winters and less melting will take place due to lower summer temperatures.

These cycles are known as **Milankovitch cycles**, after Milutin Milankovitch, an early twentieth-century Yugoslavian astronomer. Milankovitch looked at the combined effects of these cycles and concluded that they were responsible for an approximately 100,000-year cycle of insolation variation that has taken Earth into and out of periods of glaciation over the last few millions of years. Although his ideas were mostly rejected by other scientists during his lifetime, recent paleoclimatological work has shown that cyclical variation in Earth–Sun relations is one key to the timing of glacial and interglacial events.

However, these astronomical cycles present some problems as well—for example, the effects of precession that produce cooler conditions in one hemisphere should produce warmer conditions in the other, but this does not appear to be the case. Other factors certainly play a part in the onset and end of glacial periods.

> **Learning Check 8-13**   What are *Milankovitch cycles?*

Greenhouse Gases Concentration

As we first saw in Chapter 4, greenhouse gases, such as water vapor, carbon dioxide, and methane, play an important role in regulating the temperature of the troposphere. It is also well known—most notably through ice-core analysis—that past fluctuations in global temperature have been accompanied by fluctuations in greenhouse gas concentration: warmer periods in the past are generally associated with higher concentrations of gases such as CO_2,

while cooler periods are associated with lower concentrations of CO_2.

The well-documented increase in atmospheric CO_2 that was underway by the early twentieth century (see Figure 4-37), is thought by most atmospheric scientists to be the main cause of contemporary global warming. But how do we know if this increase in CO_2 is the result of human activity or if it is the result of natural processes? Several lines of evidence support the conclusion that human activity is responsible for this CO_2 increase, such as

- The increase in atmospheric CO_2 correlates well with fossil fuel use since the industrial revolution—although only about half of the human-released CO_2 seems to have remained in the atmosphere; the balance was either absorbed by the oceans or fixed by plants through photosynthesis.
- The radioactive isotope ^{14}C forms naturally in the upper atmosphere and exists along with the stable ^{12}C isotope. Measurements of the $^{14}C/^{12}C$ ratio derived from tree cores show that the relative level of the radioactive isotope ^{14}C in the atmosphere has been decreasing since the industrial revolution. This indicates that the additional CO_2 in the atmosphere was released from old "dead" sources of carbon, such as coal and petroleum—formed so long ago that most of the radioactive ^{14}C has decayed, leaving relatively more of the stable ^{12}C isotope.

A complication in trying to understand the role of greenhouse gases in climate change is that both the relative potency and the residence time of these gases varies greatly. For example, methane is a much more "efficient" greenhouse gas than carbon dioxide, but it has a shorter "lifetime" in the atmosphere—in other words, the effects of methane in the short term may not be the same as in the long term.

Further, adding to the complexity of the relationship between greenhouse gas concentrations and global temperatures are a number of important *feedback mechanisms* (feedback mechanisms were first described in Chapter 1 where we introduced Earth systems).

Feedback Mechanisms

Sea ice and continental ice sheets have high *albedos*—in other words, these surfaces reflect much of the shortwave radiation that strikes them (Figure 8-45). If global climate were to cool, ice would expand and this would in turn reflect more incoming radiation, which would lead to more cooling—which in turn would lead to greater expansion of ice; a *positive feedback mechanism*. On the other hand, if climate were to warm, this would reduce the ice cover, which would reduce the albedo and therefore increase absorption by the surface, which would lead to higher temperatures and therefore still less ice cover—another positive feedback mechanism.

One of the most complicated series of feedback mechanisms associated with climate change has to do with water vapor. As climate warms, evaporation increases—thereby increasing the concentration of water vapor in the atmosphere. As we have learned, water vapor is one of the key greenhouse gases, so as warming increases evaporation, the greater concentrations of water vapor in the atmosphere will lead to still more warming—another positive feedback mechanism. However, here is where things become complicated.

An increase in water vapor would also likely lead to increased cloud cover. Clouds can act as efficient reflectors of solar radiation (so leading to cooling), as well as efficient absorbers of terrestrial radiation (and so contributing to warming). In other words, increased cloud cover can lead to both cooling and warming!

The net effect—cooling or warming—evidently depends on the type of clouds that form. For example, a deep layer of cumulus clouds does not increase albedo as much as it increases absorption of longwave radiation from the surface—thus leading to warming. On the other hand, the expansion of stratus cloud cover increases albedo more than it increases longwave absorption—thus leading to cooling. The effects of clouds remain one of the great complications when modeling future climate change.

Learning Check 8-14 How can rising temperature lead to a feedback mechanism that further increases global temperature?

▲ **Figure 8-45** Sea ice off the east coast of Greenland during the summer thaw.

The Roles of the Ocean

Many important variables in climate change involve the oceans. The oceans absorb a great deal of CO_2 from the atmosphere—some estimates suggest that the oceans have absorbed one-third to one-half of the carbon that human activities have released into the atmosphere since the industrial revolution. Once in the ocean, marine plants and animals remove carbon from the ocean water through photosynthesis and the extraction of calcium carbonate to form shells and exoskeletons. Much of this carbon is eventually deposited in sediment layers on the ocean floor.

In addition, vast quantities of carbon in the form of *methane hydrates* (a kind of ice made from methane and water) are found in some oceanic sediments. Should these methane hydrates be destabilized by higher temperatures and the trapped methane (a greenhouse gas) released into the atmosphere, a sudden increase in atmospheric temperature could result (some evidence suggests that this actually happened about 55 million years ago, resulting in a prominent warming period in Earth's history).

Finally, the oceans obviously play an important role in transferring energy from low latitudes to high latitudes. Should patterns of ocean circulation change, climate can be significantly altered (this possibility is considered in Chapter 9).

ANTHROPOGENIC CLIMATE CHANGE

The paleoclimatological record provides the backdrop with which we can compare both the rate and the magnitude of climate change over the last century. We're especially interested in knowing if human activity is responsible for climate change—what is sometimes called *anthropogenic forcing*.

Evidence of Current Climate Change FG1

As we saw in Chapter 4, the Intergovernmental Panel on Climate Change (IPCC) is the most authoritative international body providing information about climate change to global leaders. In evaluating evidence of climate change over the last century, the *Fourth Assessment Report* of the IPCC released in 2007 concluded that the warming of global climate is "unequivocal."

The *Fifth Assessment Report* of the IPCC is due out beginning in 2013, and the findings it will present are expected to reinforce and clarify the findings of the *Fourth Assessment Report* (AR4). Findings of the AR4 along with updates from recent research include:

Changes in Air Temperature:

- Between 1906 and 2005 global average temperature increased by 0.74°C (1.33°F), with estimates ranging from 0.57 to 0.95°C (1.03 to 1.71°F). Figure 8-46 shows the global *temperature anomalies*, or departure from average, from 1880 to 2011.

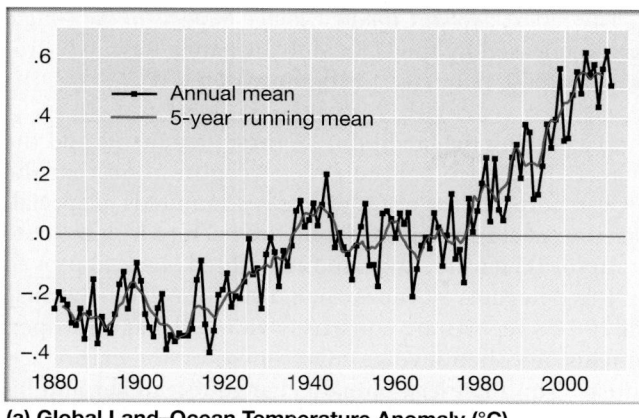

(a) Global Land–Ocean Temperature Anomaly (°C)

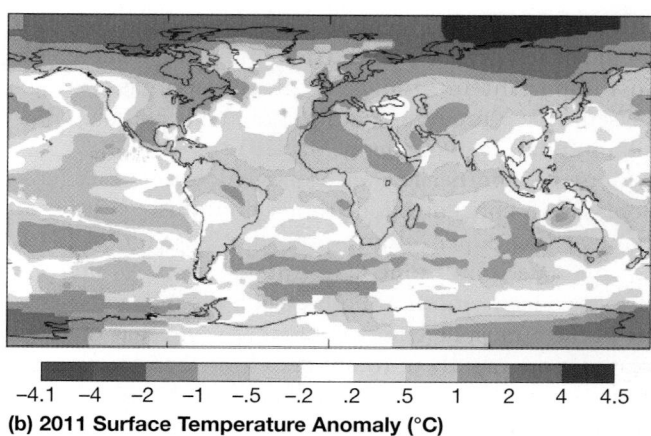

(b) 2011 Surface Temperature Anomaly (°C)

▲ **Figure 8-46** (a) Temperature anomalies of global air temperature from 1880 to 2011. (b) 2011 temperature anomalies; notice that the greatest increase was generally in the high latitudes of the Northern Hemisphere.

- Based on instrument data of temperature since 1880, 9 of the 10 warmest years on record have occurred since 2000 (1998 is the only year in the twentieth century that is in the "top ten"). The year 2011 ranked ninth overall, 0.51°C (0.92°F) warmer than the mid-twentieth century baseline and, as of this writing, 2012 was on track to be one of the warmest years on record.
- Over the last 50 years average global temperature has been increasing at a rate of about 0.13°C (0.23°F) per decade, almost twice the rate of the twentieth century as a whole. Average temperatures in the Northern Hemisphere during this time period are likely (greater than 66 percent probability) to be higher than at any time in at least 1300 years.

Changes in the Oceans:

- Data since 1961 shows that global ocean temperature has increased to depths of at least 3000 meters (9800 feet), and that 80 percent of the energy added to the global climate system has been absorbed by the oceans.
- In part because of thermal expansion of seawater, global sea level has been rising. During the twentieth century, the estimated total global sea level rise was 0.17 meters (6.7 inches). The average rate of global sea level rise between 1961 and 2003 was about 1.8 mm (0.07 inches) per year, although since 1993 the rate has increased to about 3.27 mm (0.128 inches) per year.

Changes in Polar Regions:

- In the Arctic, over the last 100 years average temperatures have been increasing at almost twice the global rate, although in this region there is high observed variability from decade to decade.
- Between 1978 and 2007, data from satellites shows that average extent of summer sea ice in the Arctic

was decreasing at a rate of about 7.4 percent per decade (by 2011, the rate had increased to 12 percent per decade). By the end of the summer in 2007 the extent of Arctic sea ice was the smallest measured since regular satellite monitoring of the ice pack began in 1979 (a new record low was set in 2012). Sea ice around Antarctica has shown great annual variation and local changes, but no statistically significant average trend was noted by the IPCC.
- Ice caps and glaciers decreased in both hemispheres, contributing to sea level rise; the flow speed of some Greenland and Antarctic outlet glaciers has increased.
- Since 1980, temperatures at the top of the permafrost layer have increased by as much as 3°C (5.4°F), and since 1900 the extent of seasonally frozen ground has been reduced by about 7 percent.

Changes in Weather Patterns:

- Observations indicate that there may have been an increase in the number of intense tropical cyclones in the North Atlantic Ocean basin since 1970, and this is correlated with an increase in sea-surface temperatures in the tropics.
- The average amount of water vapor in the atmosphere over both land and ocean areas has increased since the 1980s, consistent with the higher water vapor capacity of warmer air.
- Between 1900 and 2005 statistically significant increases in average precipitation were observed in parts of North America, South America, Central and Northern Asia, and Northern Europe, whereas decreases in average precipitation were observed in Southern Africa, South Asia, around the Mediterranean, and in the Sahel; since the 1970s, longer and more intense droughts have been observed over wide areas.

These observed increases in global temperature and the secondary effects of this warming correlate very closely with an increase in greenhouse gas concentrations tied to human activity. Carbon dioxide in the atmosphere, the most important anthropogenic greenhouse gas, had increased from a preindustrial level of about 280 parts per million (ppm) to 396 ppm by May 2012.

Methane, another key anthropogenic greenhouse gas, increased in concentration from a preindustrial level of about 715 parts per billion (ppb) to 1799 ppb by 2010. Ice-core data from Dome C in Antarctica shows that the current concentrations of both carbon dioxide and methane in the atmosphere are now higher—and that they increased more rapidly in recent decades—than at any time in the past 800,000 years. It is likely that this increase in greenhouse gases would have caused more warming than that observed if not offset by slight cooling from anthropogenic and volcanic aerosols.

> **Learning Check 8-15**   What are temperature anomalies? Describe the trend in land–ocean temperature anomalies over the last century.

Natural or Anthropogenic Climate Change?

So, is it possible that the changes in climate observed over the last century have natural causes and are not the result of anthropogenic increases in greenhouses gases? Although scientists must always leave open that possibility, the current consensus of atmospheric scientists is that the observed changes in global climate over the last century cannot be explained through natural causes alone.

It may be instructive to provide several examples of the findings of the scientific community about global climate change. In 2007 the American Geophysical Union (AGU), an international organization of research scientists, concluded:

> The Earth's climate is now clearly out of balance and is warming. Many components of the climate system—including the temperatures of the atmosphere, land and ocean, the extent of sea ice and mountain glaciers, the sea level, the distribution of precipitation, and the length of seasons—are now changing at rates and in patterns that are not natural and are best explained by the increased atmospheric abundances of greenhouse gases and aerosols generated by human activity during the 20th century.
>
> (*Source: American Geophysical Union*, AGU Position Statement: Human Impacts on Climate, *adopted by AGU Council December 2003, revised and reaffirmed December 2007.*)

As we first saw in Chapter 4, the *Fourth Assessment Report* of the IPCC released in 2007 concluded:

> Most of the observed increase in globally averaged temperatures since the mid-20th century is very likely [greater than 90 percent probability] due to the observed increase in anthropogenic greenhouse gas concentrations. . . . Discernible human influences now extend to other aspects of climate, including ocean warming, continental-average temperatures, temperature extremes and wind patterns.

The report *Global Climate Change Impacts in the United States*, released by the U.S. Global Change Research Program in 2009, reiterated the findings of the IPCC.

In assessing the credibility of these statements and the quality of science behind them, keep in mind that the IPCC reports are the result of work of hundreds of specialists; the conclusions of the report are refereed by a separate group of reviewers, and the final edited work approved by the delegates of more than 100 countries. Because the IPCC's reports are consensus views, the agreed-upon conclusions often involve compromise on the part of scientists. Tim Flannery, climate change researcher and biologist, has described the IPCC report conclusions as "lowest-common-denominator science" and that the conclusions "carry great weight . . . precisely because they represent a consensus view."[2]

Using Models to Predict Future Climate

Even though the consensus of atmospheric scientists is that human activity is indeed altering global climate, predicting the extent of future climate change and its consequences are less certain. So, how do atmospheric scientists predict what climate will be like in the decades ahead? Such projections of future temperature and precipitation patterns are mostly the product of sophisticated computer simulations known as *general circulation models (GCMs)*. In short, a GCM is a mathematical model of Earth's climate system. In such a computer-simulated world, assumptions are made about many parameters: the amount of radiation striking the surface, the extent of cloud cover, variations in ocean temperature, changes in wind and pressure patterns, changes in greenhouse gas concentration, variations in surface albedo, as well as many others.

Testing Climate Models with Past Climates: Before trying to predict future climates, a GCM must pass several "tests." First, the GCM must be able to simulate present atmospheric processes and climate—in other words, it must reliably replicate processes and patterns in the present-day atmosphere. Next, the GCM must be able to simulate past climate change, so data on past climate conditions are input into the program and the simulation is run "forward" to the present day. If the model cannot "predict" what has actually happened to climate, adjustments must be made to the program. The model can then be run forward to make projections about future climate.

Because of the enormous complexities in the atmosphere, different GCMs use different assumptions about how the atmosphere works, and so each GCM will come up with slightly different projections about climate in the future. Among the most important uses of GCMs today

[2]Flannery, Tim, *The Weather Makers: How Man Is Changing the Climate and What It Means for Life on Earth*, New York: Atlantic Monthly Press, 2005, p. 246.

is to anticipate how climate will change in the future given various scenarios of greenhouse gas increase in the atmosphere.

Projections of Future Climate

Video
Temperature
and Agriculture

The IPCC's *Fourth Assessment Report* concluded that global climate "sensitivity" to a doubling of preindustrial carbon dioxide levels is likely [a greater than 66 percent probability] to be a temperature increase of 2.0 to 4.5°C (3.6 to 8.1°F), with a best estimate of about 3.0°C (5.4°F).

However, projections of the temperature increase expected by the middle or end of this century are more complicated to calculate: In addition to the great complexity of the global climate system is uncertainty about how levels of greenhouse gases will actually change in coming decades. Six different *emission scenarios* were modeled by the IPCC. The various scenarios were based on different rates of global population increase, different rates of fossil fuel use, different rates of per capita economic growth around the world, among other factors (Figure 8-47a).

The projections of the IPCC in the *Fourth Assessment Report* include

Temperature Change Projections:

- Over the next two decades climate will warm at a rate of about 0.2°C (0.4°F) per decade.
- If greenhouse gas emissions continue at or above the present rates, the changes in global climate during this century will very likely be (greater than 90 percent probability) greater than the observed changes during the twentieth century.
- The best estimates of the global temperature increase by the year 2099 for the six emissions scenarios studied for the *Fourth Assessment Report* range from a low of 1.8°C (3.3°F) to a high of 4.0°C (7.2°F).

Sea-Level Change Projections:

- The accompanying rise in sea level from thermal expansion and increased rates of ice flow from Antarctica and Greenland under these scenarios ranges from about 0.18 meters (7.1 inches) to 0.59 meters (23.2 inches) by the end of this century.

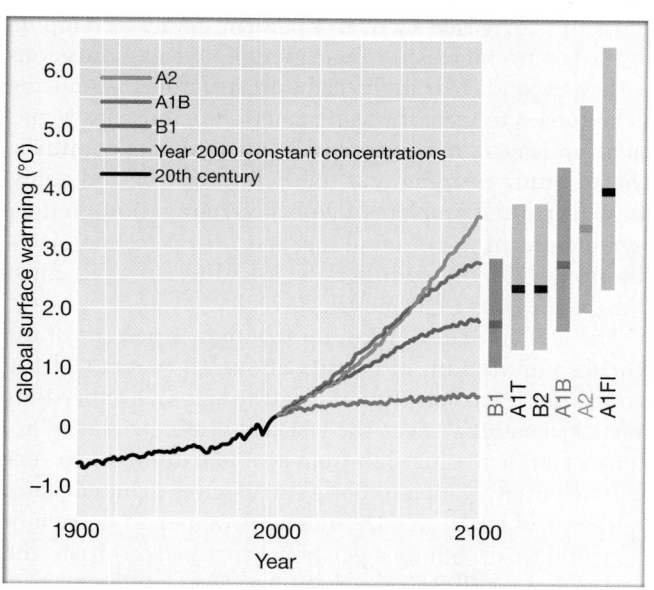

(a) Projected temperature changes from 2000 to 2100 under different IPCC emission scenarios.

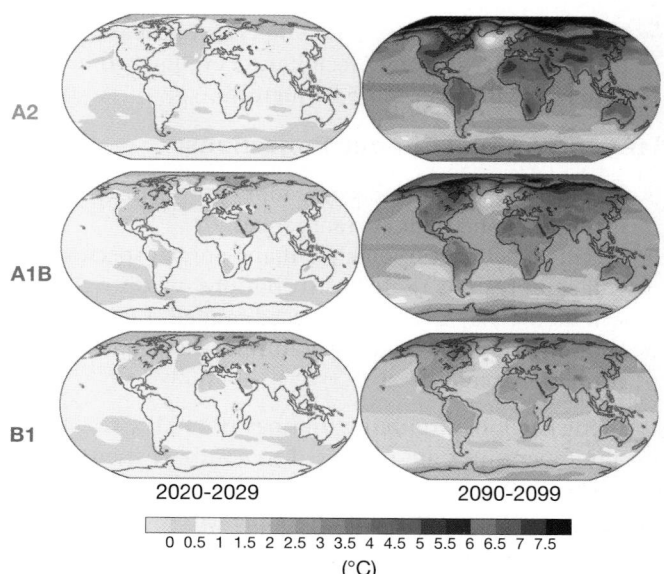

(b) Projected global surface temperature changes for the years 2020 to 2029 and 2090 to 2099 under different IPCC emission scenarios.

A2 and A1FI: greenhouse gas emissions continue to rise through the end of the century.
B1: greenhouse gas emissions begin to decline after reaching midcentury peak.
Pink line shows the projected temperature increase if greenhouse gas concentration did not rise above its level in the year 2000 (an impossibility).

▲ **Figure 8-47** (a) Projected temperature changes from 2000 to 2100 under different emission scenarios presented in the Fourth Assessment Report of the IPCC. The vertical bars show the range of temperature estimates by century's end. (b) Maps showing projected global surface temperature changes for the years 2020–2029 and 2090–2099 under three different emission scenarios.

(More recent studies have taken into account a better understanding of ice sheet flows and predict greater sea-level increases than the IPCC: from about 0.69 to 1.4 meters [27 to 55 inches] by the end of this century.) Even a modest increase in sea level, however, will cause widespread retreat of shorelines, inundating many heavily populated coastal areas and increasing vulnerability to storms such as hurricanes.

Polar Region Change Projections:

- Warming is expected to be greatest over land and in high northern latitudes, and least over the Southern Ocean; snow cover on land is expected to diminish (Figure 8-47b).
- Sea ice is projected to diminish in the Arctic and Antarctic in all emission scenarios, with summer sea ice disappearing in the Arctic by the end of this century in some scenarios.

Weather Pattern Change Projections:

- It is likely that tropical cyclones will become more intense in association with projected increases in sea-surface temperatures; the storm tracks of midlatitude cyclones are projected to move poleward.
- Precipitation is very likely to increase in high latitudes and likely to decrease in most subtropical areas over land.
- It is very likely (greater than 90 percent probability) that heat waves, heavy precipitation events, and hot extremes will occur more frequently.

Plant and Animal Change Projections:

- Tropical diseases may become more prevalent in regions beyond their current ranges.
- As climate changes, some plant and animal species will exhibit shifts in their distributions; wildfire risk will increase in areas of decreased rainfall.
- With increased global temperatures, risk of species extinction may increase.

Among the most troubling findings of the IPCC is that global temperatures are projected to continue increasing and sea level to continue rising even if the concentrations of greenhouse gases are stabilized immediately.

Learning Check 8-16 **Describe and explain at least one possible change in global climate projected by the IPCC to occur during this century.**

Addressing Climate Change

The vast majority of atmospheric scientists accept the conclusions of the IPCC: that global climate is warming and that human activity is very likely the cause of most of this climate change. It is primarily in the arena of politics, economics, and public policy that strong disagreement about global warming remains. This disagreement centers especially on

what should be done to address global warming—see the box, "Energy for the 21st Century: Strategies for Reducing Greenhouse Gas Emissions."

The Kyoto Protocol: One of the first important steps taken at the global level to cut back on carbon emissions was the Kyoto Protocol. The participants in the *Kyoto Protocol* to the *United Nations Framework Convention on Climate Change* in 1997 agreed that all emitters of carbon dioxide (the top six are China, the United States, Russia, Japan, Germany, and India) would cut greenhouse gas emissions by an average of 5 percent below 1990 levels by the year 2012. As of this writing in 2012, 191 countries (as well as European Union as a regional economic organization) have ratified the agreement, but the United States has not.

By even the most optimistic accounts, however, the modest greenhouse gas reductions of the Kyoto Protocol would at best curtail global warming slightly. Nonetheless, the agreement is an historic first step. The first commitment period of the Kyoto Protocol expired in 2012, but parties to negotiations in Durban, South Africa, in December 2011 agreed to a second commitment period that will last either 5 or 8 years (the period had not been decided at the time of this writing). New international negotiations aimed at much steeper cuts in greenhouse gas emissions are set to be under way by fall 2012.

Newly Industrialized Countries: In 2011, global CO_2 emissions increased by over 3 percent. Many developing countries are increasing their greenhouse gas emissions as they expand their industrial infrastructures. Requiring all countries to meet the same emission reductions seems unfair to leaders in some newly industrializing countries. These countries argue that the rich industrialized countries created the problem of global warming through their own unfettered use of fossil fuel and "dirty" technology—should developing countries be asked to cut back emissions as much as rich countries?

The United States makes up less than 5 percent of the world's population, but emits about 19 percent of the world's total carbon dioxide—although CO_2 emissions started to stabilize over the last few years, primarily because of an increasing shift from coal to natural gas to generate electricity. China recently surpassed the United States as the world leader in CO_2 emissions (about 23 percent of the world total), but on a per capita (per person) basis, the United States still far exceeds China. Clearly, all countries of the world will need to participate in greenhouse gas reductions, but just how the economic needs of all countries can be balanced is not yet clear.

Mitigating and Adapting

Because of the long residence time of some greenhouse gases in the atmosphere, even if the goals of carbon dioxide reduction specified under the Kyoto Protocol—or even more ambitious goals proposed for new negotiations—are achieved, we can expect global temperatures to continue

Strategies for Reducing Greenhouse Gas Emissions

It is likely that many different strategies will be needed to address the energy needs of the world in a way that addresses global climate change. Just a few of the possibilities for reducing greenhouse gas emissions are described below.

Conservation: Perhaps the simplest and most immediate strategy that can be used to reduce greenhouse gas emissions is to burn less fossil fuel. Electrical power generation and transportation are responsible for almost 40 percent of all greenhouse gas emissions worldwide and so conservation in these areas is an obvious goal. Seemingly small steps can add up: driving less, taking public transportation, using energy-efficient lighting, improving home insulation, and simply turning off lights and low-drain electronic devices when not in use.

Being aware of our own resource use can be a helpful first step toward conservation. You can calculate your "carbon footprint" by going to one of several Internet sites, such as http://atmospheres.gsfc.nasa.gov/iglo/.

Cap-and-Trade versus Carbon Tax: For the most part, reluctance on the part of the United States and some other industrialized countries to immediately and significantly cut back on greenhouse gas emissions centers on issues of short-term cost. For that reason, many economists argue that any pragmatic approach to reducing carbon emissions must involve market incentives. There are two main approaches to this. One, a *cap-and-trade* system, places declining limits (a "cap") on carbon emissions from industries, but allows one emitter to sell or trade its excess carbon allotments to another emitter. In other words, industries that emit less than their carbon allotment can sell their remainder to industries still emitting too much—this provides financial incentives to innovate and conserve, while offering more time for industries making a slower transition to cleaner energy technology.

The second method, a *carbon tax*, on the other hand, simply penalizes industries that emit more than an established emissions cap. To a certain extent, a carbon tax acts as a financial "stick" to reduce emissions, while a cap-and-trade system offers somewhat of a "carrot." There are advocates for both systems, but in either case the key to greenhouse gas reductions is setting meaningful emissions caps and timetables.

Progress on reducing carbon emissions in the United States has been slow. After years of delay, in June 2009 the Environmental Protection Agency gave the State of California permission to enforce its tougher mileage and emissions standards for new automobiles—aimed at reducing greenhouse gas emissions by 30 percent by the year 2016. Other states followed with similar stricter standards. In June 2012 the U.S. Court of Appeals for the District of Columbia upheld the EPA's authority to regulate greenhouse gases. Further, in the spring of 2012, the State of California and the Canadian province of Quebec moved closer to establishing a cross-border carbon trading system, although the likelihood of such a cap-and-trade system expanding quickly appears limited.

"No Regrets" Opportunities: The IPCC highlights a number of "no regrets" opportunities—practices that reduce greenhouse gas emissions while having a net cost saving for society and therefore need not be postponed for reasons of cost. In other words, the cost of implementing these policies is offset by the cost savings through direct or indirect benefits to individuals or society. A few examples of these opportunities include cost savings from lower energy bills as energy-efficient lighting, building insulation, and heating are adopted; cost savings in health care as air pollution is reduced; cost and time savings for commuters as carpooling and expanded public transportation lessen traffic congestion (Figure 8-C).

The Clean Energy Economy: A final set of economic arguments is also beginning to receive serious attention. As the world slowly but inevitably moves toward less dependence on fossil fuel for its energy needs, an important question remains unanswered: Which companies and which countries will lead the way by developing the cost-effective technology and infrastructure to deliver so-called green energy? Many economists argue that those who have the foresight to invest in clean energy technology today may reap enormous financial benefits in the future.

▲ **Figure 8-C** Much of the traffic congestion in American cities during commuting times comes from automobiles with single occupants.

rising for some time into the future. A 2009 study led by the National Oceanic and Atmospheric Administration (NOAA) concluded that temperature increases, sea-level increases, and rainfall changes are essentially irreversible for perhaps several centuries after CO_2 emissions are stabilized.

So this raises the question: In addition to efforts to prevent greater global warming, what should be done to adapt to the consequences of climate change? For example, should coastal dikes or seawalls be raised to compensate for higher sea level and storm surge potential? Or should drinking water storage reservoirs be expanded to compensate for reductions in winter snow pack? The costs and environmental consequences of these and many other strategies will need to be thoughtfully weighed.

The findings of the IPCC point to a related problem: the consequences of global climate change may not be shared equally around the world. Many of the populations most vulnerable to sea-level rise, changes in precipitation for agriculture and drinking water, and the expanding ranges of insect pests and disease, are found in the poorest parts of the world—populations with the least financial means to adapt. So an appropriate question to ask is: What can and should the richest countries of the world do to assist the poorest to adapt to climate change?

It remains to be seen how the people of the world—as individuals and as countries—will choose to address global climate change, a problem without quick or easy solutions.

Chapter 8   LEARNING REVIEW

After studying this chapter, you should be able to answer the following questions. Key terms from each text section are shown in **bold type**. Definitions for key terms are also found in the glossary at the back of the book.

KEY TERMS AND CONCEPTS

Climate Classification (p. 208)

1. Explain the basic concept of the **Köppen climate classification system.**
2. In the Köppen climate classification letter code system, what information is given by the first letter, the second letter, and the third letter?
3. Briefly describe the major climate groups of the modified Köppen climate classification system: A, B, C, D, E, and H.
4. What information is conveyed in a **climograph**?

Tropical Humid Climates (Group A) (p. 211)

5. Describe the general location, temperature characteristics, precipitation characteristics, and main controls of the following climates. You should be able to recognize these climates from a climograph:
   - Af **Tropical wet**
   - Aw **Tropical savanna**
   - Am **Tropical monsoon**
6. Why do Af (tropical wet) climates receive rain all year, whereas Aw (tropical savanna) climates receive rain only in the summer (the high-Sun season)?

Dry Climates (Group B) (p. 216)

7. Describe the general location, temperature characteristics, precipitation characteristics, and main controls of the following climates. You should be able to recognize these climates from a climograph:
   - BWh **Subtropical desert**
   - BWk **Midlatitude desert**
8. What is the general difference between a desert climate and a steppe climate?
9. What are the main differences in controls of BWh (subtropical desert) and BWk (midlatitude desert) climates?

Mild Midlatitude Climates (Group C) (p. 221)

10. Describe the general location, temperature characteristics, precipitation characteristics, and main controls of the following climates. You should be able to recognize these climates from a climograph:
    - Cs **Mediterranean**
    - Cfa **Humid subtropical**
    - Cfb **Marine west coast**
11. Why do Cs (mediterranean) climates have dry summers and wet winters?
12. What causes the relatively mild temperatures of marine west coast climates?

Severe Midlatitude Climates (Group D) (p. 225)

13. Describe the general location, temperature characteristics, precipitation characteristics, and main controls of the following climates. You should be able to recognize these climates from a climograph:
    - Dfa **Humid continental**
    - Dfc **Subarctic**
14. What is meant by the phrase "continentality is a keynote in D climates"?
15. Why do subarctic (Dfc) climates have such a wide annual temperature range?

Polar and Highland Climates (Groups E and H) (p. 230)

16. What general temperature characteristic distinguishes **tundra climate** from **ice cap climate**?
17. Why are polar climates so dry?
18. In what ways is altitude more important in determining a **highland climate** than latitude?

Global Climate Change (*p. 237*)

19. What is meant by **paleoclimatology**?
20. How is **dendrochronology** used in studies of past climate?
21. How does the **oxygen isotope analysis** of ocean floor sediments and glacial ice tell us about past temperatures?
22. How can ice-core analysis provide information about the gas composition of the atmosphere in the past?
23. What is the **urban heat island effect**?

Causes of Long-Term Climate Change (*p. 241*)

24. What are **Milankovitch cycles** and in what ways might they help explain past climate change?

25. Describe and explain at least one feedback mechanism that would further increase global temperatures once a warming trend has started.
26. What kinds of clouds tend to cool the surface of Earth, and what kinds of clouds tend to warm it?
27. What roles do the oceans play in influencing the carbon dioxide concentrations in the atmosphere?

Anthropogenic Climate Change (*p. 244*)

28. What is the overall trend in global temperature since 1880?
29. What is the current consensus among atmospheric scientists as to the causes of the observed changes in climate over the last century?
30. What is the Kyoto Protocol?

STUDY QUESTIONS

1. Why are subtropical desert (BWh) climates generally hotter in summer than tropical humid (A) climates?
2. Why are subtropical desert (BWh) climates usually displaced toward the western sides of continents?
3. Why are dry climates much more extensive in North Africa than in any other subtropical location?
4. Although both cities are coastal, New York City has a continental climate, whereas Seattle, Washington, has a maritime climate. Why?

5. What is the annual temperature pattern likely to be in a high elevation location on the equator?
6. What explains the alternating bands of wet and dry seasons in Figure 8-36?
7. What explains the differences between the climate zones on the east and west sides of the hypothetical continent in Figure 8-37?

EXERCISES

1. Estimate the average monthly precipitation in Singapore using the climograph in Figure 8-6b (p. 213): _____ centimeters (inches)
2. Estimate the average monthly precipitation in Alice Springs, Australia, using the climograph in Figure 8-14b (p. 219): _____ centimeters (inches)
3. Carbon-14 (^{14}C) is a radioactive isotope of carbon with a half-life of 5730 years—meaning that half of

the ^{14}C in a sample decays into ^{14}N during that time. Suppose a scientist analyzes a sample of ancient plant material from a bog and finds that it contains 1/8th as much ^{14}C as when it formed. Roughly how old is the sample? _____ years

Seeing Geographically

Look again at the photograph of southeastern Greenland at the beginning of the chapter (p. 206). What do the sky conditions suggest about the stability of the atmosphere on this day? Would these conditions be unusual here? Why? Based on its location, which climate type is likely found here? Would you expect this region to receive relatively large amounts of precipitation or relatively small amounts? Why?

MasteringGeography™

Looking for additional review and test prep materials? Visit the Study Area in MasteringGeography™ to enhance your geographic literacy, spatial reasoning skills, and understanding of this chapter's content by accessing a variety of resources, including geoscience animations, MapMaster interactive maps, videos, RSS feeds, flashcards, web links, self-study quizzes, and an eText version of *McKnight's Physical Geography: A Landscape Appreciation*.

THE HYDROSPHERE IS AT ONCE THE MOST PERVASIVE AND

the least well defined of the four "spheres" of Earth's physical environment. It includes the surface water in oceans, lakes, rivers, and swamps; all underground water; frozen water in the form of ice, snow, and high-cloud crystals; water vapor in the atmosphere; and the moisture temporarily stored in plants and animals.

The hydrosphere overlaps significantly with the other three spheres. Liquid water, ice, and even water vapor occur in the soil and rocks of the lithosphere. Water vapor and cloud particles composed of liquid water and ice are important constituents of the lower portion of the atmosphere, and water is a critical component of every living organism of the biosphere. Life is impossible without water; every living thing depends on it. Watery solutions in living organisms dissolve or disperse nutrients for nourishment. Most waste products are carried away in solutions. Indeed, the total mass of every living thing is more than half water, the proportion ranging from about 60 percent for some animals to more than 95 percent for some plants.

It is through water, then, that the interrelationships of the four spheres are most conspicuous and pervasive. In Chapter 6 we introduced many of the physical properties of water and the roles of water in weather and climate. In this chapter, we examine the geography of water more broadly and explore one of the most important of all Earth systems.

As you study this chapter, think about these key questions:

- **How does the *hydrologic cycle* involve movement of water between the four "spheres" of Earth?**
- **What are the four oceans of Earth, and what factors influence characteristics of ocean water, such as salinity?**
- **How are the causes of tides different from the causes of surface ocean currents?**
- **What are the main components of the *cryosphere*?**
- **How and why do natural lakes and human made reservoirs change over time?**
- **What factors influence the quantity and availability of *groundwater*?**

THE HYDROLOGIC CYCLE

We begin this chapter with a more detailed look at the movement of water—in all its forms—through the hydrosphere. Water, essential to life and finite in amount, is distributed very unevenly on, in, and above Earth. The great bulk of all moisture, more than 99 percent, is in "storage"—in oceans, lakes, and streams, locked up as glacial ice, or held in rocks below Earth's surface (Figure 9-1). Water frozen as ice in glaciers and continental ice sheets represents about three-fourths of all of the freshwater on the planet.

Animation
Hydrologic Cycle

Seeing Geographically

Goðafoss, or "waterfall of the gods," along the river Skjlfandafljt, in north central Iceland. What different forms of water can you see in this image? How are these forms of water connected through Earth's systems?

253

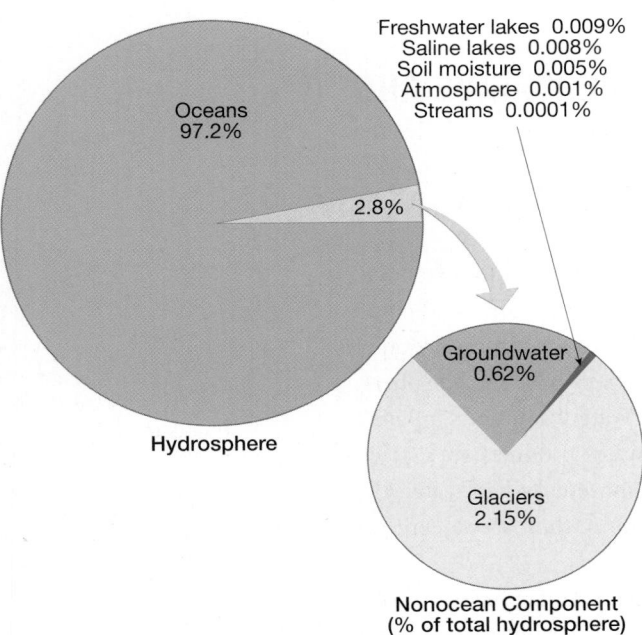

Freshwater lakes 0.009%
Saline lakes 0.008%
Soil moisture 0.005%
Atmosphere 0.001%
Streams 0.0001%

Oceans
97.2%

2.8%

Hydrosphere

Groundwater
0.62%

Glaciers
2.15%

Nonocean Component
(% of total hydrosphere)

▲ **Figure 9-1** Moisture inventory of Earth. More than 97 percent of all water is contained in the oceans.

The proportional amount of moisture in these various storage reservoirs is relatively constant over thousands of years. Only during an ice age is there a notable change in these components: as we will see in Chapter 19 during periods of glaciation, the volume of the oceans becomes smaller as the ice sheets grow and the level of atmospheric water vapor diminishes; then during deglaciation, the ice melts, the volume of the oceans increases as the meltwater

Video
Hydrologic
Cycle

flows into them, and there is an increase in atmospheric water vapor.

The remaining small fraction—less than 1 percent—of Earth's total moisture is involved in an almost continuous sequence of movement and change, the effects of which are absolutely critical to life on this planet. This tiny portion of Earth's water supply moves from one storage area to another—from ocean to air, from air to ground, and so on—in the **hydrologic cycle**. We first introduced the hydrologic cycle in Chapter 6. In this chapter, we examine the complexities of this cycle in detail.

The hydrologic cycle can be viewed as a series of storage areas interconnected by various transfer processes, in which there is a ceaseless interchange of moisture in terms of both its geographic location and its physical state (Figure 9-2). Liquid water on Earth's surface evaporates to become water vapor in the atmosphere. That vapor then condenses and precipitates, either as liquid water or as ice, back onto the surface. This precipitated water then runs off into storage areas and later evaporates into the atmosphere once again. Because this is a closed, circular system, we can begin the discussion at any point. It is perhaps clearest to start with the movement of moisture from Earth's surface into the atmosphere.

Surface-to-Air Water Movement

Most of the moisture that enters the atmosphere from Earth's surface does so through *evaporation* (transpiration from plants is the source of the remainder). The oceans, of course, are the principal source of water for evaporation. They occupy 71 percent of Earth's surface, have unlimited moisture available for evaporation, and are extensive in low latitudes, where considerable

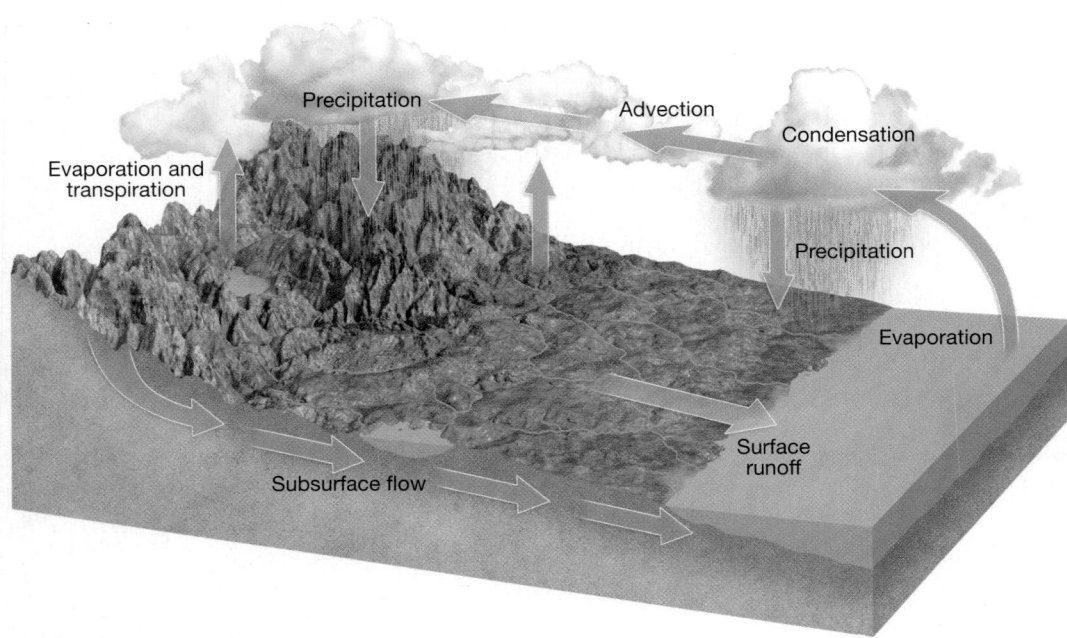

◀ **Figure 9-2** The hydrologic cycle. The two major components are evaporation from surface to air and precipitation from air to surface. Other important elements of the cycle include transpiration of moisture from vegetation to atmosphere, surface runoff and subsurface flow of water from land to sea, condensation of water vapor to form clouds from which precipitation may fall, and advection of moisture from one place to another.

Precipitation — Advection — Condensation — Precipitation — Evaporation and transpiration — Evaporation — Subsurface flow — Surface runoff

TABLE 9-1	Moisture Balance of Continents and Oceans		
	Total of World Surface Area	Total of World Precipitation Received	Total of World Water Vapor From Surface
Oceans	71%	78%	86%
Continents	29%	22%	14%

warmth and wind movement facilitate evaporation. As a result, an estimated 86 percent of all evaporated moisture is derived from ocean surfaces (Table 9-1). The 14 percent that comes from land surfaces includes the twin processes of evaporation and transpiration, referred to as *evapotranspiration*.

Water vapor from evaporation remains in the atmosphere a relatively short time—usually only a few hours or days. During that interval, however, it may move a considerable distance, either vertically through convection or horizontally through advection driven by wind.

Air-to-Surface Water Movement

Sooner or later, water vapor in the atmosphere condenses to liquid water or sublimates to ice to form cloud particles. As we saw in Chapter 6, under the proper circumstances clouds may drop precipitation in the form of rain, snow, sleet, or hail. As Table 9-1 shows, 78 percent of this precipitation falls into the oceans and 22 percent falls onto land.

Over several years, total worldwide precipitation is approximately equal to total worldwide evaporation/transpiration. Although precipitation and evaporation/transpiration balance in time, they do not balance in place: evaporation exceeds precipitation over the oceans, whereas the opposite is true over the continents. This imbalance is explained by the advection of moist maritime air onto land areas, so that there is less moisture available for precipitation over the ocean. Except for coastal spray and storm waves, the only route by which moisture moves from sea to land is via the atmosphere.

Movement On and Beneath Earth's Surface

Looking at Table 9-1, you see 8 percent more water is leaving the ocean than precipitating back into it. The "surplus" precipitation over the continents is effectively returned to the ocean through surface **runoff**, water draining off the land and back into the sea in streams.

The 78 percent of total global precipitation that falls on the ocean is simply incorporated immediately into the water already there; the 22 percent that falls on land goes through a more complicated series of events. Rain falling on a land surface collects in lakes, runs off if the surface is a slope, or infiltrates the ground. Any water that pools on the surface eventually either evaporates or sinks into

the ground, runoff water eventually ends up in the ocean, and infiltrated water is either stored temporarily as soil moisture or percolates farther down to become part of the underground water supply.

Much of the soil moisture eventually evaporates or transpires back into the atmosphere, and much of the underground water eventually reappears at the surface via springs. Then sooner or later, and in one way or another, most of the water that reaches the surface evaporates again, and the rest is incorporated into streams and rivers and becomes runoff flowing into the oceans. This runoff water from continents to oceans amounts to 8 percent of all moisture circulating in the global hydrologic cycle. It is this runoff that balances the excess of precipitation over evaporation taking place on the continents and that keeps the oceans from drying up and the land from flooding.

Learning Check 9-1   **Is the amount of precipitation and evapotranspiration over the continents the same? Explain. (Answer on p. AK-3)**

Residence Times

Although the hydrologic cycle is a closed system with an essentially finite total capacity, there is enormous variation in *residence times* for individual molecules of water as they move through different parts of the cycle. For example, a particular molecule of water may be stored in oceans and deep lakes, or as glacial ice, for thousands of years without moving through the cycle, and one trapped in rocks buried deep beneath Earth's surface may be excluded from the cycle for thousands or even millions of years.

However, whatever water is moving through the cycle is in almost continuous motion (Figure 9-3). Runoff water can

◄ **Figure 9-3** Oregon's Mount Hood and Lake Trillium with morning fog. Moisture constantly moves through the hydrologic cycle through evaporation, condensation, precipitation, and runoff.

travel hundreds of kilometers to the sea in only a few days, and moisture evaporated into the atmosphere may remain there for only a few minutes or hours before it is precipitated back to Earth. Indeed, at any given moment, the atmosphere contains only a few days' potential precipitation.

Energy Transfer in the Hydrologic Cycle

As we've seen, the hydrologic cycle is powered by the Sun. Recall from our discussion of Earth's energy cycle in Chapters 4 and 6 that water vapor represents not only a reservoir of moisture for precipitation, but a reservoir of energy as well. The latent heat "stored" in water vapor is released during condensation—acting as the fuel of storms such as hurricanes—and serving as one way that energy is transferred from the tropics toward the poles.

THE OCEANS

Despite the facts that most of Earth's surface is oceanic and that the vast majority of all water is in the oceans (see Figure 9-1), our knowledge of the seas was fairly limited until recently. Only within the last six decades or so has sophisticated equipment been available to catalog and measure details of the maritime environment.

How Many Oceans?

From the broadest viewpoint, there is but one interconnected ocean. This "world ocean" has a surface area of 360 million square kilometers (139 million square miles) and contains 1.32 billion cubic kilometers (317 million cubic miles) of saltwater. It spreads over almost three-fourths of Earth's surface, interrupted here and there by continents and islands. Although tens of thousands of bits

of land protrude above the blue waters, the world ocean is so vast that half a dozen continent-sized portions of it are totally devoid of islands, without a single piece of land breaking the surface of the water. It is one or more of these large expanses of water we are usually referring to when we use the term *ocean*.

In generally accepted usage, the world ocean is divided into four principal parts—the Pacific, Atlantic, Indian, and Arctic Oceans (Figure 9-4). Some people refer to the waters around Antarctica as the *Antarctic Ocean* or the *Great Southern Ocean*, but this distinction is not universally accepted. The boundaries of the four oceans are not everywhere precise, and around some of their margins are partly landlocked smaller bodies of water called *seas*, *gulfs*, *bays*, and other related terms. Most of these smaller bodies can be considered as portions of one of the major oceans, although a few are so narrowly connected (Black Sea, Mediterranean Sea, Hudson Bay) to a named ocean as to deserve separate consideration, as Figure 9-4 shows. This nomenclature is further clouded by the term *sea*, which is used sometimes synonymously with *ocean*, sometimes to denote a specific smaller body of water around the edge of an ocean, and occasionally to denote an inland body of water.

- The *Pacific Ocean* (Figure 9-5a) is twice as large as any other body of water on Earth. It occupies about one-third of the total area of Earth, more than all the world's land surfaces combined. It contains the greatest average depth of any ocean as well as the deepest known oceanic trenches. Although the Pacific extends almost to the Arctic Circle in the north and a few degrees beyond the Antarctic Circle in the south, it is largely a tropical ocean. Almost one-half of the 38,500-kilometer (24,000-mile) length of the equator is in the Pacific. The character of this ocean often

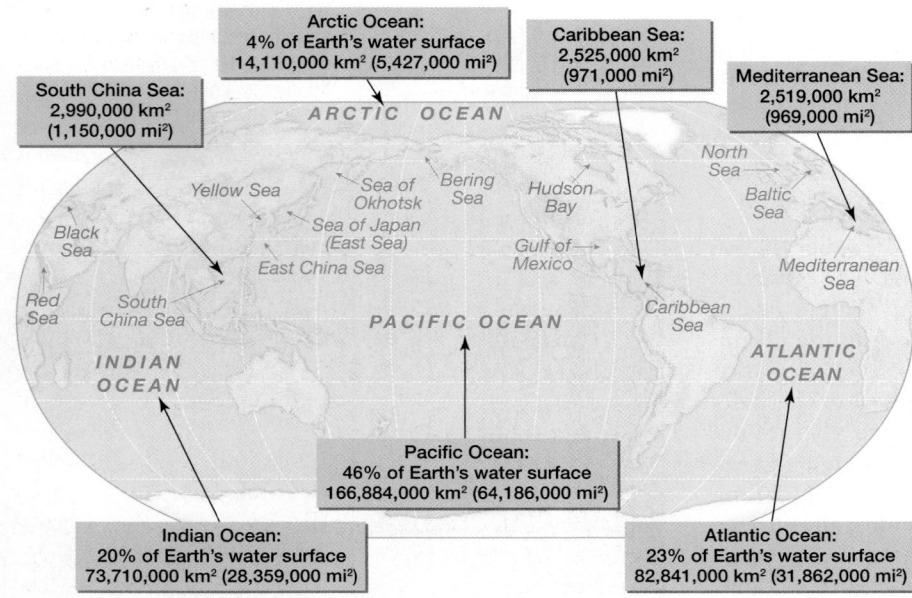

Arctic Ocean: 4% of Earth's water surface 14,110,000 km² (5,427,000 mi²)

Caribbean Sea: 2,525,000 km² (971,000 mi²)

South China Sea: 2,990,000 km² (1,150,000 mi²)

Mediterranean Sea: 2,519,000 km² (969,000 mi²)

ARCTIC OCEAN

North Sea

Yellow Sea · Sea of Okhotsk · Bering Sea · Hudson Bay · Baltic Sea

Black Sea

Sea of Japan (East Sea)

Gulf of Mexico

Mediterranean Sea

Red Sea

South China Sea

East China Sea

PACIFIC OCEAN

Caribbean Sea

ATLANTIC OCEAN

INDIAN OCEAN

Pacific Ocean: 46% of Earth's water surface 166,884,000 km² (64,186,000 mi²)

Indian Ocean: 20% of Earth's water surface 73,710,000 km² (28,359,000 mi²)

Atlantic Ocean: 23% of Earth's water surface 82,841,000 km² (31,862,000 mi²)

◀ **Figure 9-4** The four principal oceans and major seas of the world.

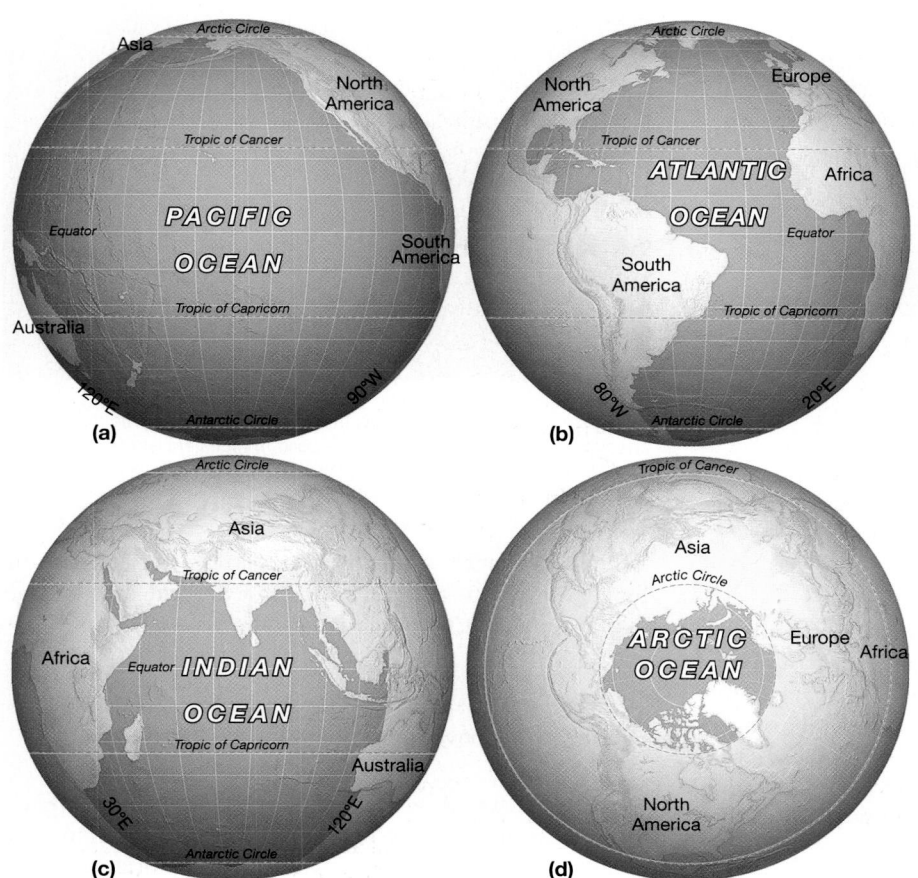

◀ **Figure 9-5** The four major parts of the world ocean: (a) the Pacific Ocean, (b) the Atlantic Ocean, (c) the Indian Ocean, (d) the Arctic Ocean.

belies its tranquil name, for it houses some of the most disastrous of all storms (typhoons) and, as we'll see in Chapter 14, its rim is called the "Ring of Fire" because of its many volcanoes and earthquakes.

- The *Atlantic Ocean* is slightly less than half the size of the Pacific (Figure 9-5b). Its north–south extent is roughly the same as that of the Pacific, but its east–west spread is only about half as great. Its average depth is a little less than that of the Pacific.
- The *Indian Ocean* (Figure 9-5c) is a little smaller than the Atlantic, and its average depth is slightly less than that of the Atlantic. Nine-tenths of its area is south of the equator.
- The *Arctic Ocean* (Figure 9-5d) is much smaller and shallower than the other three and is mostly covered with ice. It is connected to the Pacific by a relatively narrow passageway between Alaska and Siberia, but it has a broad and indefinite connection with the Atlantic between North America and Europe.

Learning Check 9-2 **Why is it difficult to designate distinct boundaries between the oceans of the world?**

Characteristics of Ocean Waters

Wherever they are found, the waters of the world ocean have many similar characteristics, but they also show significant differences from place to place. The differences are particularly notable in the surface layers, down to a depth of about 100 meters (about 350 feet).

Chemical Composition: Almost all known elements are found to some extent in seawater, but by far the most important are sodium (Na) and chlorine (Cl), which form sodium chloride (NaCl)—the common salt we know as "table salt." In the language of chemistry, "salts" are substances that result when a *base* neutralizes an *acid*. For instance, sodium chloride is formed when the base sodium hydroxide (NaOH) neutralizes hydrochloric acid (HCl).

The **salinity** of seawater is a measure of the concentration of dissolved salts, which are mostly sodium chloride but also include salts containing magnesium, sulfur, calcium, and potassium. The average salinity of seawater is about 35 parts per thousand, or 3.5 percent of total mass.

The geographic distribution of surface salinity varies (Figure 9-6). At any given location on the ocean surface, the salinity depends on how much evaporation is taking place and how much freshwater (primarily from rainfall and stream discharge) is being added. Where the evaporation rate is high, so is salinity; where the inflow of freshwater is high, salinity is low.

Typically the lowest salinities are found where rainfall is heavy and near the mouths of major rivers. Salinity is highest in partly landlocked seas in dry, hot regions because here the evaporation rate is high and stream discharge is minimal. As a general pattern, salinity is low

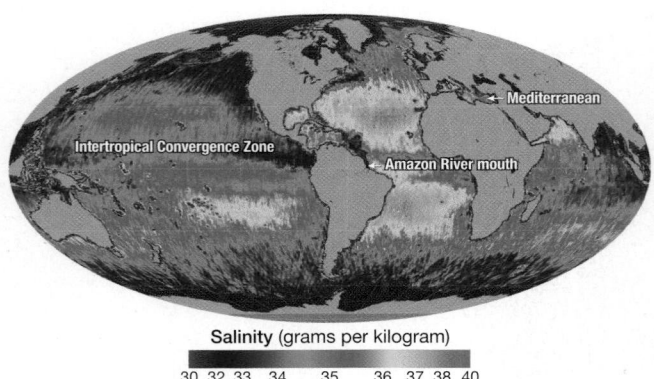

▲ Figure 9-6 Average salinity of oceans from May 27 to June 2, 2012. Lowest salinity (violet and blue areas) is found in areas of freshwater runoff, such as the mouths of rivers, and where rainfall is high (as in the ITCZ); highest salinity (red and yellow) is found where evaporation rates are highest. The data were gathered by NASA's Aquarius instrument onboard Argentina's *Satélite de Aplicaiones Cientificas.*

▲ Figure 9-7 Scanning electron microscope image of *Elphidium crispum,* one of many kinds of single-celled foraminifera whose exoskeletons are made of calcium carbonate, shown here magnified approximately 80 times.

in equatorial regions because of heavy rainfall, cloudiness, and humidity, all of which inhibit evaporation, and also because of considerable river discharge. Salinity rises to a general maximum in the subtropics, where precipitation is low and evaporation extensive, and decreases to a general minimum in the polar regions, where evaporation is minimal and there is considerable inflow of freshwater from rivers and ice caps.

Increasing Acidity: The oceans absorb carbon dioxide from the atmosphere. Perhaps one-third of the excess CO_2 released into the air each year by human activity is absorbed by the oceans. When CO_2 is taken in by the ocean, it forms *carbonic acid* (H_2CO_3), a weak acid. Research now suggests that as a result of the great quantities of CO_2 absorbed since the beginning of the industrial revolution, the ocean is becoming more acidic.

Currently, ocean water is slightly alkaline, with a pH of 8.1 (see "Acid Rain" in Chapter 6 for a description of the pH scale). Although still alkaline, this value is estimated to be about 0.1 lower—in other words more acidic—than it was in the preindustrial era. Given the current rate of fossil fuel use and continued absorption of CO_2 by the oceans, the pH of ocean water could drop to 7.7 by the end of this century.

The consequences of a slightly more acidic ocean are not completely known, but it is likely that it will affect the growth of organisms such as coral polyps and microscopic creatures such as *foraminifera* (Figure 9-7) that build their shells or exoskeletons from calcium carbonate ($CaCO_3$) extracted from seawater. As the oceans become more acidic, there are fewer calcium ions in seawater and so the growth of calcium carbonate shells is inhibited. It is not clear if these creatures will be able to adapt to the changing chemistry of the ocean.

Because foraminifera are at the bottom of the oceanic food web, among the potentially important consequences of a decline in their numbers would be the loss of food for a number of fish, such as mackerel and salmon. If the increased acidity of the oceans reduces the growth of coral polyps, coral reefs—already under stress worldwide from higher temperatures—might possibly degrade even further (a more complete discussion of coral reefs is in Chapter 20).

Learning Check 9-3　How and why does the salinity of seawater vary around the world?

Temperature: As expected, surface seawater temperatures generally decrease with increasing latitude. The temperature often exceeds 26°C (80°F) in equatorial locations and decreases to –2°C (28°F), the average freezing point for seawater, in Arctic and Antarctic seas. (Dissolved salts lower the freezing point of the water from the 0°C [32°F] of pure water.) The western sides of oceans are nearly always warmer than the eastern margins because of the movement of major ocean currents (see Figure 4-26 in Chapter 4). This pattern of warmer western parts is due to the contrasting effects of poleward-moving warm currents on the west side of ocean basins and equatorward-moving cool currents on the east side of ocean basins.

Density: Seawater density varies with temperature, degree of salinity, and depth. High temperature produces low density, and high salinity produces high density. Deep water has high density because of low temperature and because of the pressure of the overlying water.

Surface layers of seawater tend to contract and sink in cold regions, whereas in warmer areas deeper waters tend to rise to the surface. Surface currents also affect this situation, particularly by producing an upwelling of colder, denser water in some localities. As we will see later in this chapter, differences in density are partially responsible for a vast, slow circulation of deep ocean water.

MOVEMENT OF OCEAN WATERS

The liquidity of the ocean permits it to be in continuous motion, and this motion can be grouped under three headings: tides, currents, and waves. The movement of almost anything over the surface—the wind, a boat, a swimmer—can set the water surface into motion, and so the ocean surface is almost always ridged with swells and waves. Disturbances of the ocean floor can also trigger significant movements in the water (see Chapter 20 for a discussion of *tsunami*). Currents may entail considerable displacement of water, particularly horizontally, but also vertically and obliquely. The gravitational attraction of the Moon and Sun causes the greatest movements of all: the tides.

Tides

On the shores of the world ocean, almost everywhere, sea level fluctuates regularly. For about six hours each day, the water rises, and then for about six hours it falls. These rhythmic oscillations have continued unabated, day and night, winter and summer, for eons. **Tides** are essentially bulges in the sea surface in some places that are compensated by lower areas or "sinks" in the surface at other places. Thus, tides are primarily vertical motions of the water. In shallow-water areas around the margins of the oceans, however, the vertical oscillations of the tides may produce significant horizontal water movements as well, when tides cause ocean water to advance and retreat along gently sloping coastal plains.

Animation
Tides

Causes of Tides: Every object in the universe exerts an attractive gravitational force on every other object. Thus, Earth exerts an attractive force on the Moon, and the Moon exerts an attractive force on Earth. The same is true for Earth and the Sun. It is the gravitational attraction between the Moon and Earth, and between the Sun and Earth, that cause tides.

The strength of the force of gravity is inversely proportional to the square of the distance between the two bodies, and so, because the Sun is 150,000,000 kilometers (93,000,000 miles) from Earth and the Moon is 385,000 kilometers (239,000 miles), the Moon produces a greater percentage of Earth's tides than does the Sun. The *lunar tides* are about twice as strong as the *solar tides*. To keep things simple, let us first discuss lunar tides alone, ignoring solar tides for the moment.

Gravitational attraction pulls ocean water toward the Moon. There is more gravitational attraction on the side of Earth facing the Moon (the side closest to the Moon) than on the opposite side of Earth. The difference in force slightly elongates the shape of the global ocean, so that two bulges of ocean water develop—one on the side of Earth facing the Moon and the other on the opposite side of Earth. As Earth rotates, coastlines move into and out of these bulges, producing simultaneous high tides on the opposite sides of Earth and low tides halfway between.

As Earth rotates eastward, the tidal progression appears to move westward. The tides rise and fall twice in the interval between two "rising" Moons, an interval that is about 50 minutes longer than a 24-hour day. The combination of Earth's rotation and the Moon's revolution

around Earth means that Earth makes about 12° more than a full rotation between each rising of the Moon. Thus, two complete tidal cycles have a duration of about 24 hours and 50 minutes. This means that on all oceanic coastlines there are normally two high tides and two low tides about every 25 hours.

The magnitude of tidal fluctuation is quite variable in time and place, but the sequence of the cycle is generally similar everywhere. From its lowest point, the water rises gradually for about 6 hours and 13 minutes, so that there is an actual movement of water toward the coast in what is called a **flood tide**. At the end of the flooding period, the maximum water level, *high tide*, is reached. Soon the water level begins to drop, and for the next 6 hours and 13 minutes there is a gradual movement of water away from the coast, a movement called an **ebb tide**. When the minimum water level (*low tide*) is reached, the cycle begins again.

Monthly Tidal Cycle: The vertical difference in elevation between high and low tide is called the **tidal range**. Changes in the relative positions of Earth, Moon, and Sun induce periodic variations in tidal ranges, as shown in Figure 9-8. The greatest range (in other words, the highest tide) occurs when the three bodies are positioned in a straight line, which usually occurs twice a month near the times of the full and new Moon. When thus aligned, the joint gravitational pull of the Sun and Moon is along the same line, so that the combined pull is at a maximum. This is true both when the Moon is between Earth and the Sun and when Earth is between the Moon and Sun. In either case, this is a time of higher than usual tides, called **spring tides**. (The name has nothing to do with the season; think of water "springing" up to a very high level.)

When the Sun and Moon are located at right angles to one another with respect to Earth, their individual gravitational pulls are diminished because they are now pulling at right angles to each other. This right-angle pulling results in a lower than normal tidal range called a **neap tide**. The Sun–Moon alignment that causes neap tides generally takes place twice a month at about the time of first-quarter and third-quarter moons.

Tidal range is also affected by the Moon's nearness to Earth. The Moon follows an elliptical orbit in its revolution around Earth, the nearest point (called *perigee*) is about 50,000 kilometers (31,200 miles), or 12 percent, closer than the farthest point (*apogee*). During perigee, tidal ranges are greater than during apogee.

> Learning Check 9-4   Describe the positions of the Sun, Moon, and Earth that produce the highest high tides and the lowest low tides.

Global Variations in Tidal Range: Tidal range fluctuates all over the world at the same times of the month. There are, however, enormous variations in range along different coastlines (Figure 9-9). Midocean islands may experience tides of only 1 meter (3 feet) or less, whereas continental seacoasts have greater tidal ranges, because the amplitude is

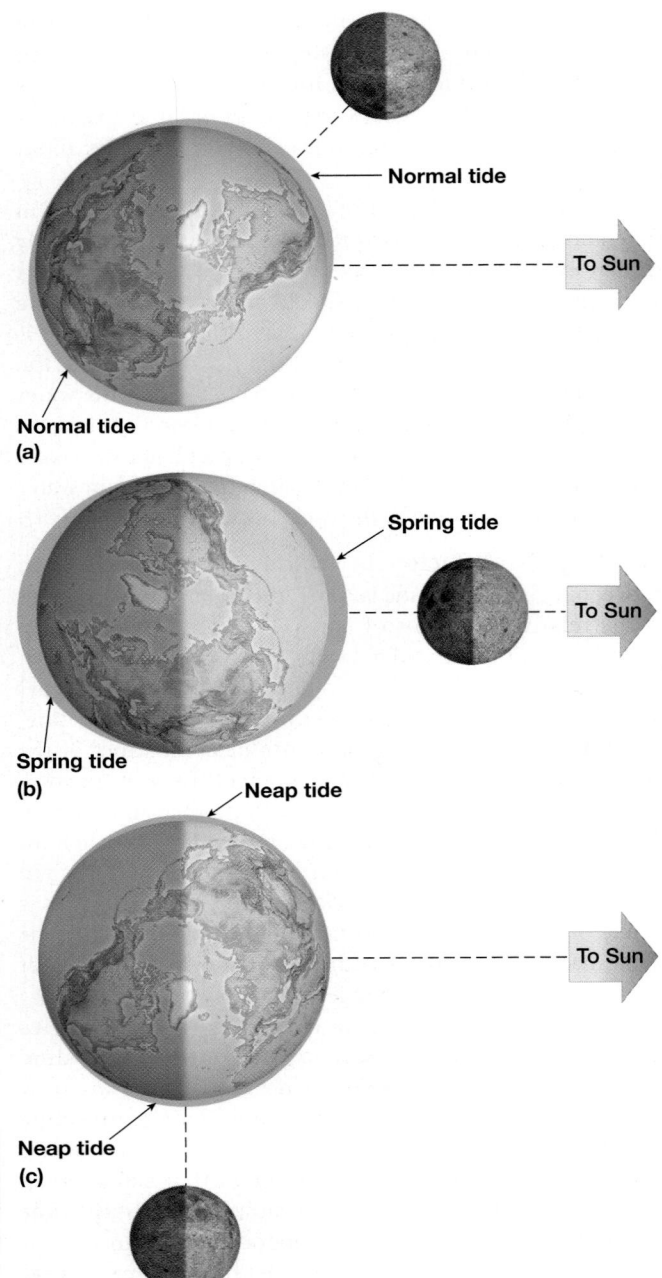

(a) Normal tide — Normal tide — To Sun

(b) Spring tide — Spring tide — To Sun

(c) Neap tide — Neap tide — To Sun

▲ **Figure 9-8** The monthly tidal cycle. The juxtaposition of the Sun, Moon, and Earth accounts for variations in Earth's tidal range. (a) When the Moon and Sun are neither aligned nor at right angles to each other, we have normal levels of high tides on both sides of Earth. (b) When the Sun, Earth, and Moon are positioned along the same line, *spring tides* (the highest high tides) are produced. (c) When the line joining Earth and the Moon forms a right angle with the line joining Earth and the Sun, *neap tides* (the lowest high tides) result.

greatly influenced by the shape of the coastline and the configuration of the sea bottom beneath coastal waters. Along most coasts, there is a moderate tidal range of 1.5 to 3 meters (5 to 10 feet). Some partly landlocked seas, such as the Mediterranean, have almost negligible tides. Other places, such as the northwestern coast of Australia, experience enormous tides of 10 meters (35 feet) or so.

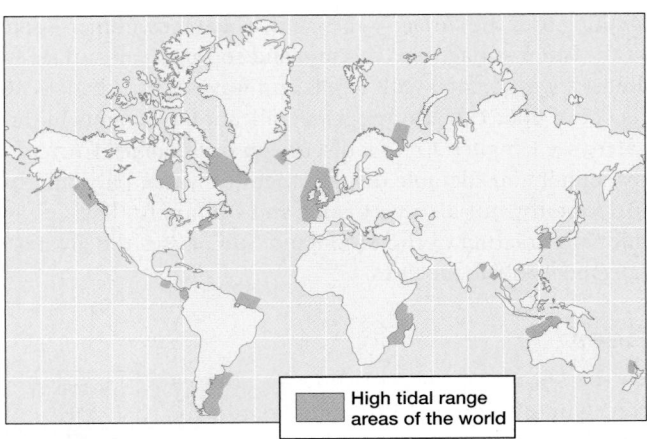

High tidal range areas of the world

▲ **Figure 9-9** Areas with tidal ranges exceeding 4 meters (13 feet). The pattern is not a predictable one because it depends on a variety of unrelated factors, particularly shoreline and sea bottom configuration.

The greatest tidal range in the world is found at the upper end of the Bay of Fundy in eastern Canada (Figure 9-10), where a 15-meter (50-foot) water-level fluctuation twice a day is not uncommon, and a wall of seawater—called a **tidal bore**—several centimeters to more than a meter in height rushes up the Petitcodiac River in New Brunswick for many kilometers.

Tidal variation is exceedingly small in inland bodies of water. Even the largest lakes usually experience a tidal rise and fall of no more than 5 centimeters (2 inches). Effectively, then, tides are important only in the world ocean, and they are normally noticeable only around its shorelines.

Ocean Currents

As we learned in Chapter 4, the world ocean contains a variety of currents that shift vast quantities of water both horizontally and vertically. Surface currents are caused primarily by wind flow, whereas other currents are set in motion by contrasts in temperature and salinity. All currents may be influenced by the size and shape of the particular ocean, the configuration and depth of the sea bottom, and the Coriolis effect. Some currents involve subsidence of surface waters downward; other vertical flows bring an upwelling of deeper water to the surface.

Animation
Ocean
Circulation
Patterns—
Subtropical
Gyres

Geographically speaking, the most prominent currents are the major horizontal flows that make up the general circulation of the various oceans. The dominant surface currents introduced in Chapter 4 are generally referred to as *subtropical gyres* (see Figure 4-26). They are set up by the action of the dominant surface wind systems in the tropics and midlatitudes: the trade winds and the westerlies.

Ocean currents not only can transport floating debris, both natural and human-produced, across large expanses of ocean, but they also can concentrate trash in several

▲ **Figure 9-10** (a) The world's maximum tides are in the Bay of Fundy, where ocean water moves long distances up many of the coastal rivers twice a day. (b) A tidal bore moving up the Petitcodiac River in New Brunswick, Canada.

areas of the Pacific Ocean—see the box, "People and the Environment: The Great Pacific Garbage Patch."

Deep Ocean Circulation: In addition to the major surface ocean currents, there is an important system of deep ocean circulation as well. This circulation of deep ocean water occurs because of differences in water density that arise from differences in salinity and temperature. For this reason, this water movement is sometimes referred to as **thermohaline circulation**. Ocean water will become denser, and thus sink, if its salinity increases or its temperature decreases. This happens predominantly in high-latitude ocean areas where the water is cold and salinity increases when sea ice develops (the dissolved salts are not taken up in the ice when water freezes, so the salinity of the remaining water increases).

The combination of deep ocean water movement through thermohaline circulation, along with influences from surface ocean currents, establishes an overall **global conveyer-belt circulation** pattern (Figure 9-11). Beginning in the North Atlantic, cold, dense water sinks and slowly flows deep below the surface to the south, where it eventually joins the eastward moving deep, cold, high salinity water circulating around Antarctica. Some of this deep water eventually flows north into the Indian and Pacific Oceans, where it rises to

Animation
Ocean
Circulation
Patterns—Global
Conveyer-Belt
Circulation

form a shallow, warm current that flows back to the North Atlantic Ocean, where it sinks and begins its long journey once again. These deep ocean currents might travel only 15 kilometers (9 miles) in a year—thus requiring many centuries to complete a single circuit.

The global conveyer-belt circulation does not have as immediate an effect on weather and climate as do the subtropical gyres and other surface currents discussed in Chapter 4. Nonetheless, this circulation plays a role in energy transfer around the globe—and therefore long-term climate patterns. Recent research suggests that a connection exists between the global conveyer-belt circulation and global climate. For example, if global climate becomes warmer, the freshwater runoff from the melting of Greenland's glaciers could form a pool of lower density water in the North Atlantic; this lower-density surface water could disrupt the downwelling of water in the North Atlantic, altering the redistribution of heat—and so climate—around the world.

Learning Check 9-5 **Explain what causes the movement of water in the global conveyer–belt circulation.**

Waves

To the casual observer, the most conspicuous motion of the ocean is provided by waves. Most of the sea surface is in a

The Great Pacific Garbage Patch

▶ Jennifer Rahn, Samford University, Birmingham, Alabama

Characteristics that make plastic items useful to consumers—their strength and durability—also make them a problem in marine environments. Each year more than 90 billion kilograms (200 billion pounds) of plastic is produced worldwide, and about 10 percent of this ends up in the ocean. The trash tends to accumulate in areas where winds and currents are weak in the center of the ocean current *subtropical gyres* (see Figure 4-26)—especially in the area of the subtropical high (Figure 9-A).

Some of the trash sinks but most of it floats in the upper 10 meters (30 feet) of the ocean (Figure 9-B). Estimates of the size of the floating trash patch now in the Pacific Ocean vary from the size of Texas to twice the size of Texas. It contains approximately 3.2 billion kilograms (3.5 million tons) of trash, and 80 percent of it is plastic. In the last few years, this floating mass of trash has received a vast amount of media attention and is now known as the *Great Pacific Garbage Patch*. A 2012 study based on research by Scripps Institution of Oceanography estimates that the trash accumulating in the patch has increased by 100 times in just the last four decades.

Loction of Pacific Garbage Patch: The Great Pacific Garbage Patch actually consists of two main regions of ever-growing garbage accumulation. The eastern garbage patch—the first to gain attention—floats between Hawai'i and California, generally in the location of the subtropical high. The western garbage patch extends east of Japan to the western archipelago of the Hawaiian Islands, within what is called the *North Pacific Subtropical Convergence Zone*. These patches of garbage and flotsam in the Pacific (and evidently other ocean basins as well) are not new; they have always been there. What is new is that now most of it is nonbiodegradable plastic—formerly it was debris such as wood, glass bottles, and fishing floats.

Hazards to Marine Life: A variety of environmental hazards are associated with the Great Pacific Garbage Patch. Plastic sea trash often floats at the surface and includes bottle caps, bags, and wrappers. Marine animals often mistake the floating plastic for food. To sea turtles or birds, a plastic bag floating in the water looks like a jellyfish—one of their favorite foods. However, they have no way of digesting plastic. Animals that eat too much plastic die because they cannot pass it—it fills their stomachs and they starve to death.

Marine animals can also become entangled in plastic bags or the plastic rings that hold canned drinks; unable to eat, they starve to death. More than 267 marine species have been harmed by the debris, and about 100,000 whales, seals, turtles, birds, dolphins, and other marine animals are killed each year by plastic–induced asphyxiation, strangulation, contamination, and entanglement.

Instead of biodegrading, most plastic slowly breaks up by photodegrading into smaller and smaller pieces. Fish mistakenly consume these small plastic particles, thinking they are plankton, their main food source. In the Great Pacific Garbage Patch there is now six times more plastic than plankton. The small particles of plastic ingested by the small fish have many toxic qualities. In the Great Pacific Garbage Patch toxic chemical levels in fish have been as high as a million times the concentration in the surrounding water. The chemicals in the plastic break down and enter the system of the fish, and these toxins are concentrated in the top of the food chain where they may be consumed by whales, dolphins—and humans. As people eat the large fish (tuna, shark, king mackerel, marlin and swordfish, to name a few), they are receiving concentrated doses of these toxins because the effects of the pollutants increase as they advance up the food chain.

Debris from 2011 Japanese Tsunami: By the spring of 2012, debris washed offshore by the great March 2011 tsunami in Japan (see Chapter 20) was beginning to come ashore on the opposite side of the Pacific—for example, a 20-meter (66-foot) dock arrived on an Oregon beach in June 2012. One computer model suggests that much of the tsunami debris will be incorporated into the Great Pacific Garbage Patch by 2016.

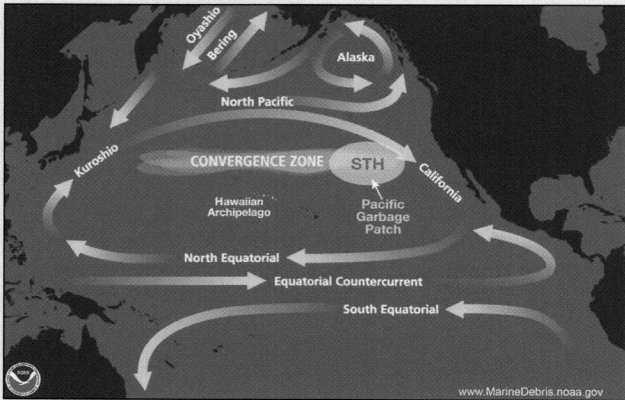

▲ **Figure 9-A** Map showing the location of the Great Pacific Garbage Patch. In addition to the garbage patch generally located in the area of the subtropical high (STH), garbage also accumulates in the western portion of the North Pacific Subtropical Convergence Zone.

▲ **Figure 9-B** Floating debris in the Great Pacific Garbage Patch. Credit: Scripps Institution of Oceanography, UC San Diego

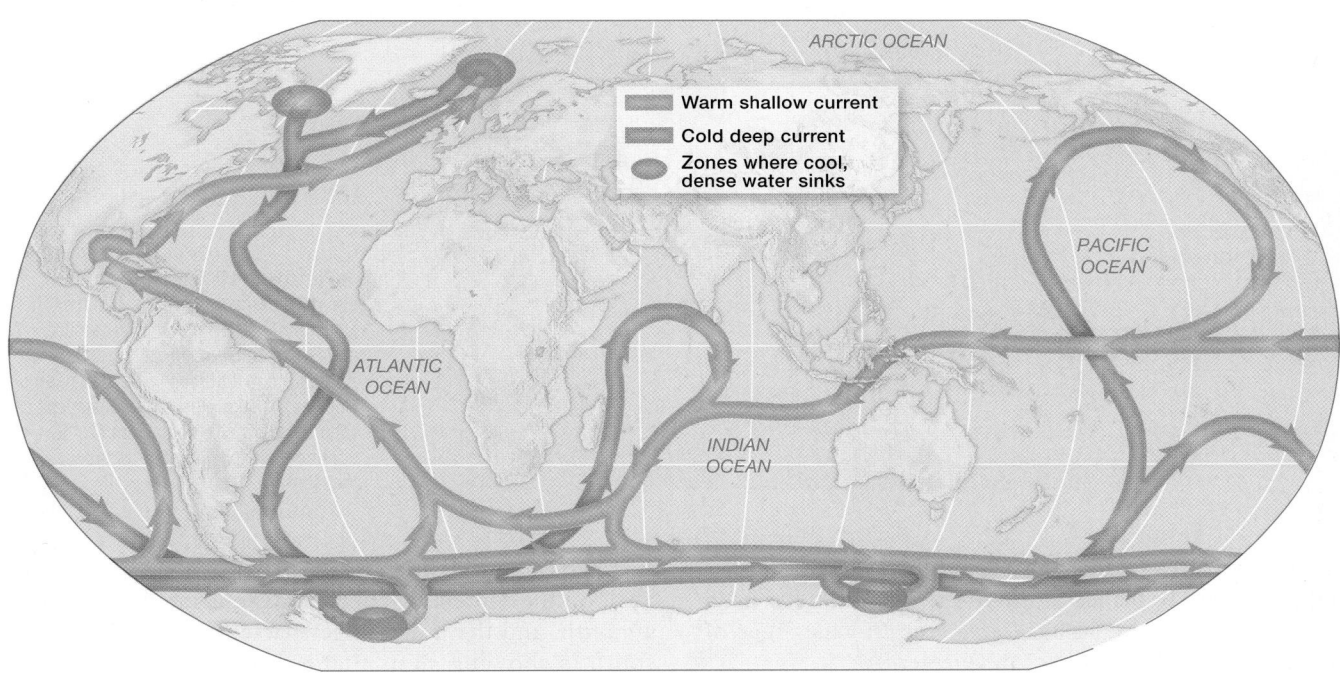

▲ **Figure 9-11** Idealized global conveyor-belt circulation. In the North Atlantic Ocean cool, dense water sinks and moves south as a deep subsurface flow. It joins cold, deep water near Antarctica, eventually moving into the Indian and North Pacific Ocean where the water rises slowly, eventually flowing back into the North Atlantic where it again sinks. The violet ovals show major locations where cool, dense surface water feeds the flow of deep water. One circuit may take many hundreds of years to complete.

state of constant agitation, with wave crests and troughs bobbing up and down most of the time. Moreover, around the margin of the ocean, waves of one size or another lap, break, or pound on the shore in endless procession.

Most of this movement is like "running in place" from the water's point of view, with little forward progress. Waves in the open ocean are mostly just shapes, and the movement of a wave across the sea surface is a movement of form rather than of substance or, to say the same thing another way, of energy rather than matter. Individual water particles make only small oscillating movements. Only when a wave "breaks" does any significant shifting of water take place. Waves are discussed in detail in Chapter 20.

PERMANENT ICE—THE CRYOSPHERE

Second only to the world ocean as a storage reservoir for moisture is the solid portion of the hydrosphere—the ice of the world, or *cryosphere*—as we learn from a glance back at Figure 9-1. Although minuscule in comparison with the amount of water in the oceans, the moisture content of ice at any given time is more than twice as large as the combined total of all other types of storage (groundwater, surface waters, soil moisture, atmospheric moisture, and biological water).

The ice portion of the hydrosphere is divided between ice on land and ice floating in the ocean, with the land portion

being the larger. Ice on land is found as mountain glaciers, ice sheets, and ice caps, all of which are studied in Chapter 19. Approximately 10 percent of the land surface of Earth is covered by ice (Figure 9-12). It is estimated that enough water is locked up in this ice to feed all the rivers of the world at their present rate of flow for nearly 900 years.

Oceanic ice has various names, depending on size:

- **Ice pack:** An extensive and cohesive mass of floating ice.
- **Ice shelf:** A massive portion of a continental ice sheet that projects out over the sea.
- **Ice floe:** A large, flattish mass of ice that breaks off from larger ice bodies and floats independently.
- **Iceberg:** A chunk of floating ice that breaks off from an ice shelf or glacier. Because ice has a lower density than that of liquid water, only about 14 percent of the mass of an iceberg is exposed above the water, with about 86 percent below (the exact ratio varies slightly; Figure 9-13).

Despite the fact that some oceanic ice freezes directly from seawater, all forms of oceanic ice are composed almost entirely of freshwater because the salts present in the seawater in its liquid state are not incorporated into ice crystals when that water freezes.

The largest ice pack covers most of the surface of the Arctic Ocean (Figure 9-14); on the other side of the globe, an ice pack fringes most of the Antarctic continent (Figure 9-15). Both of these packs become greatly enlarged during their respective winters, their areas are essentially

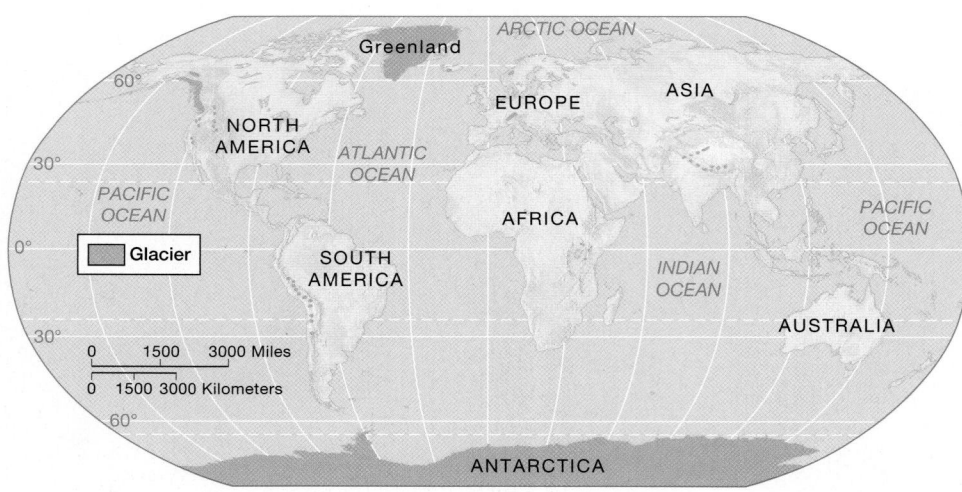

◀ **Figure 9-12** Glacial ice covers about 10 percent of Earth's surface. This ice is confined primarily to Antarctica and Greenland, with small amounts also found at high altitudes in the Canadian Rockies, Andes, Alps, and Himalayas. (The apparent size of glaciers on the continents is exaggerated to show locations.)

doubled by increased freezing around their margins. As we saw in Chapter 8, sea ice in the Arctic especially has been diminishing over the last 35 years (see "Focus: Signs of Climate Change in the Arctic" in Chapter 8).

There are a few small ice shelves in the Arctic, mostly around Greenland, but several gigantic shelves are attached to the Antarctic ice sheet, most notably the Ross Ice Shelf of some 100,000 square kilometers (40,000 square miles). Some Antarctic ice floes are enormous; the largest ever observed was 10 times as large as the state of Rhode Island.

Over the last two decades, because of increasing temperatures, formerly stable ice shelves in Antarctica have broken apart. Since the early 1990s as much as 8000 square kilometers (over 3000 square miles) of Antarctic ice shelves have disintegrated. In 2002, the Larsen-B Ice Shelf on the Antarctic Peninsula disintegrated in less than a month, and the much larger Larsen-C shelf just to the south is showing signs that its mass is being reduced because of increasing water temperatures below it. In 2008, the Wilkins Ice Shelf in Antarctica also began to

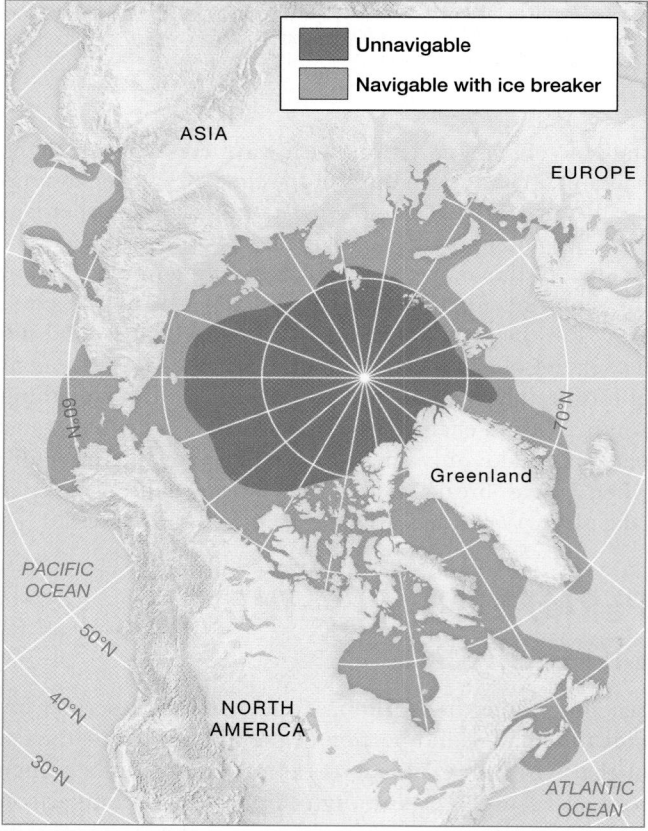

▲ **Figure 9-14** The largest ice pack on Earth covers most of the Arctic Ocean, making that body of water essentially unnavigable. Powerful icebreaker ships allow passage from the Atlantic to the Pacific via this northern route, the fabled "Northwest Passage" of early European explorers. Over the last 35 years the Arctic summer ice pack has diminished by more than 40 percent from its twentieth-century long-term average shown here, and so the Northwest Passage may well become a reality in the future.

▲ **Figure 9-13** Most of an iceberg is underwater, as shown here in the waters of Disko Bay, Greenland.

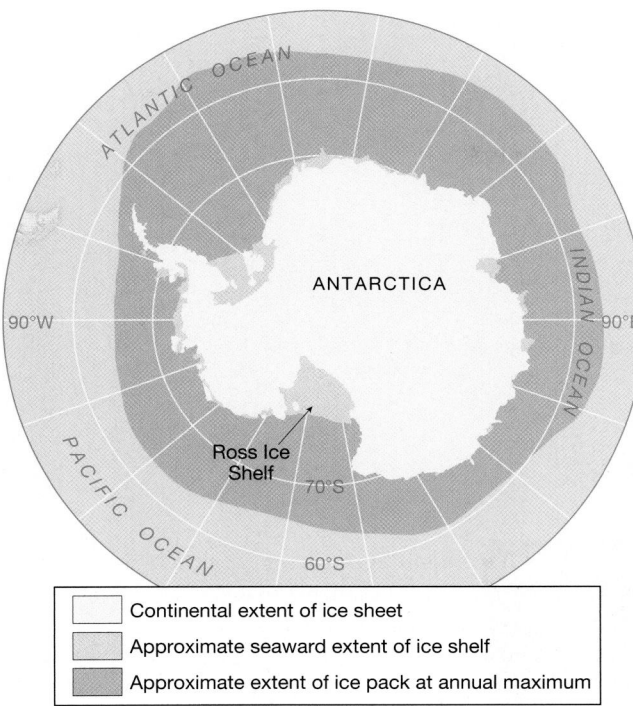

▲ **Figure 9-15** Maximum extent of ice in Antarctica. The ice sheet covers land, and the ice shelf and ice pack are oceanic ice. As is true in the Arctic, over the last three decades the extent of sea ice around Antarctica has diminished from its earlier twentieth-century long-term average shown here.

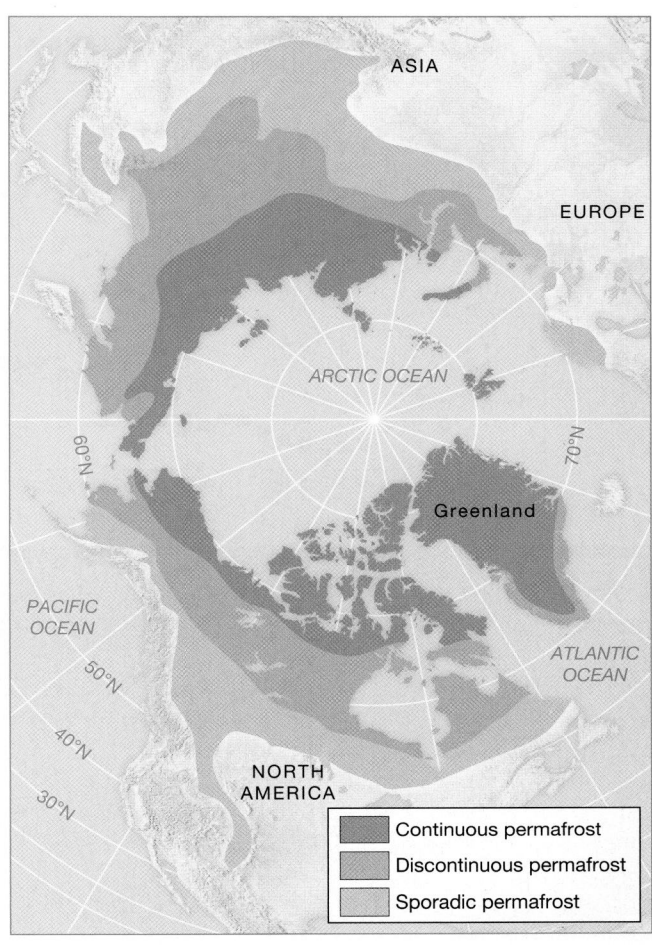

▲ **Figure 9-16** Extent of permafrost in the Northern Hemisphere. All the high-latitude land areas and some of the adjacent midlatitude land areas are underlain by permafrost. Climate change is slowly reducing the extent of permafrost.

disintegrate. (See Chapter 19 for further discussion of changes in glaciers and ice sheets around the world.)

Learning Check 9-6 **Where is most of the ice in the cryosphere found?**

Permafrost

A relatively small proportion of the world's ice occurs beneath the land surface as ground ice. This type of ice occurs only in areas where the temperature is continuously below the freezing point, and so it is restricted to high-latitude and high-elevation regions (Figure 9-16). Most permanent ground ice is **permafrost**, which is permanently frozen subsoil. It is widespread in northern Canada, Alaska, and Siberia and found in small patches in many high mountain areas. Some ground ice is aggregated as veins of frozen water, but most of it develops as ice crystals in the spaces between soil particles.

Thawing of Permafrost: In locations such as the region around the city of Fairbanks in central Alaska, permafrost is widespread just below the surface. During the summer, only the upper 30 to 100 centimeters (12 to 40 inches) of soil thaws in what is called the *active layer*; below that is a layer of permanently frozen ground perhaps 50 meters (165 feet) thick. Much of the permafrost found in the high latitude areas of the world has been frozen for at least the last few thousands of years, but as a response to higher

average temperatures, it is beginning to thaw. In just the last 35 years, a warming trend has been observed, bringing the ground temperature in some areas above the melting point of the permafrost. Deep in the permafrost layer where ground still remains frozen, temperatures are rising also (Figure 9-17).

For people accustomed to living in temperate environments, it might seem that having the ground thaw would not be a problem, but such is not the case. As the ground thaws, buildings, roads, pipelines, and airport runways are increasingly destabilized, and transportation and business are likely to be disrupted as a consequence (Figure 9-18). In areas with poor surface drainage, the degradation of permafrost can lead to what is called *wet thermokarst* conditions, where the surface subsides and the ground becomes oversaturated with water. In some cases, unpaved roads become impassable. In the last three decades, the number of days that the Alaska Department of Natural Resources permits oil exploration activity in areas of tundra has been cut in half due to the increasingly soft ground.

Along the Beaufort Sea, rising temperatures are thawing permafrost in the coastal bluffs and contributing to more

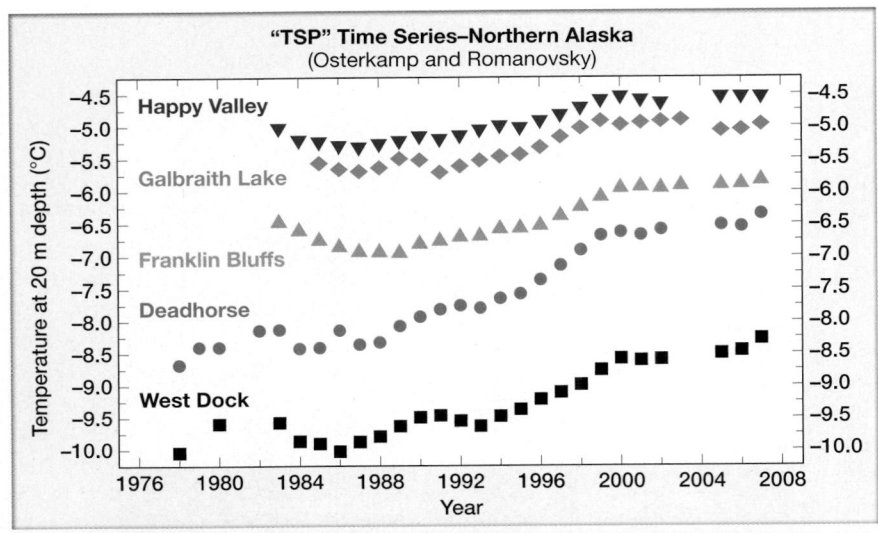

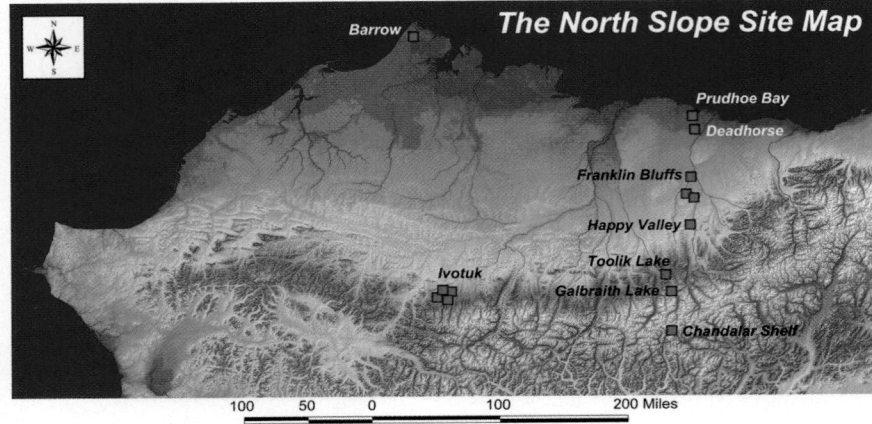

◄ **Figure 9-17** Changes in permafrost temperature at a depth of 20 meters (65 feet) from 1976 to 2008 in Alaska. Sites ranged from the Brooks Range to the North Slope.

rapid erosion of the coastline. From an average rate of erosion of 6 meters (20 feet) per year between the mid-1950s and 1970s, the rate jumped to nearly 14 meters (45 feet) per year between 2002 and 2007 (Figure 9-19).

The thawing of frozen soils will likely lead to an increase in the activity of microorganisms in the soil. This could in turn increase the rate of decomposition of organic matter long sequestered in the frozen ground. As this organic matter is decomposed by microorganisms, carbon dioxide or methane can be released, perhaps contributing to increasing greenhouse gas concentrations in the atmosphere.

Learning Check 9-7 **What are some of the consequences of thawing permafrost around the Arctic?**

▼ **Figure 9-18** House in Alaska collapsed as a result of melting permafrost.

▼ **Figure 9-19** Cabin lost to coastal erosion along the Arctic Ocean in Alaska. The increased erosion here is associated with melting permafrost.

SURFACE WATERS

Surface waters represent only about 0.02 percent of the world's total moisture supply (see Figure 9-1), but from the human viewpoint they are of incalculable value. Lakes, wetlands, swamps, and marshes abound in many parts of the world, and all but the driest parts of the continents are seamed by rivers and streams.

Lakes  FG6

In the simplest terms, a **lake** is a body of water surrounded by land. No minimum or maximum size is attached to this definition, although the word *pond* is often used to designate a very small lake. Well over 90 percent of the nonfrozen surface water of the continents is contained in lakes.

Lake Baykal (often spelled Baikal) in Siberia is by far the world's largest freshwater lake in terms of volume of water, containing considerably more water than the combined contents of all five Great Lakes in central North America. It is also the world's deepest lake—1742 meters (5715 feet) deep.

Saline Lakes: Most of the world's lakes contain freshwater, but some of the largest lakes are saline. Indeed, more than 40 percent of the lake water of the planet is salty, with the lake we call the Caspian Sea containing more than three-quarters of the total volume of the world's nonoceanic saline water. (In contrast, Utah's famous Great Salt Lake contains less than 1/2500 the volume of the Caspian.) Any lake that has no natural drainage outlet, either as a surface stream or as a sustained subsurface flow, will become saline.

Most small salt lakes and some large ones are *ephemeral*, which means that they contain water only sporadically and are dry much of the time because they are in dry regions with insufficient inflow to maintain them on a permanent basis. We will discuss ephemeral lakes in desert regions in greater detail in Chapter 18.

Formation of Lakes: Most lakes are fed and drained by streams, but lake origin is usually due to other factors. Two conditions are necessary for the formation and continued existence of a lake: (1) some sort of natural basin having a restricted outlet, and (2) sufficient inflow of water to keep the basin at least partly filled. The water balance of most lakes is maintained by surface inflow, sometimes combined with springs and seeps below the lake surface. A few lakes are fed entirely by springs. Most freshwater lakes have only one stream that serves as a drainage outlet.

Lakes are distributed very unevenly over the land (Figure 9-20). They are very common in regions that were glaciated in the recent geologic past because glacial erosion and deposition deranged the normal drainage patterns and created innumerable basins (Figure 9-21; also see Figure 19-28 in Chapter 19). Some parts of the world notable for lakes were not glaciated, however. For example, the remarkable series of large lakes in eastern and central Africa was created by faulting as Earth's crust spread apart tectonically (for example, see Figure 14-14 in Chapter 14); and the many thousands of small lakes in Florida were formed by sinkhole collapse when rainwater dissolved calcium carbonate from the limestone bedrock (for example, see Figure 17-9 in Chapter 17).

Most lakes are relatively temporary features of the landscape. Few have been in existence for more than a few thousand years, a time interval that is momentary in the grand scale of geologic time. Inflowing streams bring sediment to fill lakes up; outflowing streams cut channels progressively deeper to drain them; and as the lake becomes shallower, a continuous increase in plant growth accelerates the infilling (a process discussed in Chapter 10). Thus, the destiny of most lakes is to disappear naturally.

Human Alteration of Natural Lakes: Human activity also plays a part in the disappearance of lakes. For example, the diversion of streams flowing into California's Mono Lake (to the east of Yosemite National Park) has reduced its volume by one-half since the 1940s.

More dramatically, the Aral Sea was once the world's fourth-largest lake in terms of surface area, but beginning

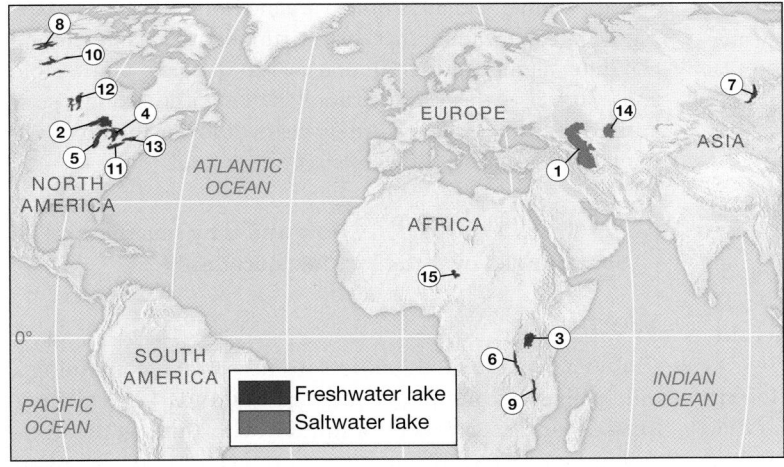

World's Largest Lakes by Surface Area		
	Square km	*Square mi*
(1) Caspian Sea	372,450	143,250
(2) Lake Superior	82,420	31,700
(3) Lake Victoria	69,400	26,700
(4) Lake Huron	59,800	23,000
(5) Lake Michigan	58,000	22,300
(6) Lake Tanganyika	33,000	12,650
(7) Lake Baikal	31,700	12,200
(8) Great Bear Lake	31,500	12,100
(9) Lake Nyasa (L. Malawi)	30,000	11,550
(10) Great Slave Lake	29,400	11,300
(11) Lake Erie	25,700	9900
(12) Lake Winnipeg	23,500	9100
(13) Lake Ontario	19,500	7500
(14) Aral Sea	*	*
(15) Lake Chad	*	*

* Greatly reduced in size from that shown here

▲ **Figure 9-20** The largest lakes of the world, ranked by surface area.

◀ **Figure 9-21** Glaciation is responsible for the formation of Convict Lake in California.

in the 1960s, irrigation projects designed to boost agricultural production in Soviet Central Asia cut off much of the water flowing into the lake. The sea is now only about 10 percent of its original size (Figure 9-22). The once viable commercial fishing industry is gone, and winds now carry away a cloud of choking clay and salt dust lifted from the exposed lake bottom. The sea has split into several pieces. A new dam on the Syr Darya River is allowing the northern remnant of the Aral Sea to recover slightly, but the southern remnants are likely to remain dry.

In some cases, both human and natural changes are responsible for the loss of a lake. Fifty years ago, Lake Chad was one of the largest lakes in Africa, but ongoing drought has reduced it to about 5 percent of its original size (Figure 9-23). Nearly all of the lake's water comes from the Chari River flowing into the lake from the south. The lake is shallow and surrounded by an extensive wetlands area—once the second largest in Africa. Because the lake is shallow, it responds quite quickly to changes in inflow. Although water diversion projects along the Chari River have contributed to the reduction of Lake Chad, climate change in the region is likely responsible for much of its ongoing decline.

Reservoirs: One of the most notable things people have done to alter the natural landscape is to produce artificial lakes, or *reservoirs*. Such lakes have been created largely by the construction of dams, ranging from small earth mounds heaped across a gully to immense concrete structures blocking the world's major rivers (Figure 9-24). Some reservoirs are as large as medium-sized natural lakes.

Reservoirs are constructed for a number of different reasons, including controlling floods, ensuring a stable agricultural or municipal water supply, and for the generation of hydroelectric power—frequently for all of these reasons.

The creation of artificial lakes has had immense ecological and economic consequences, not all of them foreseen at the time of construction (Figure 9-25). In addition to the obvious loss of the land that has been inundated by the waters of the reservoir, downstream ecosystems may be altered by restricted stream flows; and in some locations rapid sedimentation may restrict the useful life of a reservoir. In Chapter 16, we will consider the implications of flood control through the use of dams and river levees.

In the arid southwest of the United States—part of the so-called "Sunbelt" of the country—population growth has been especially rapid over the last two decades (Las Vegas more than doubled in population between 1990 and 2010). The populations here have depended on a network of dams and reservoirs (and, as discussed later in this chapter, groundwater pumping) for drinking water and agriculture. Recall from Chapter 6 that precipitation in regions of low average annual rainfall is quite variable from year to year (see Figure 6-37), meaning that surface runoff into local reservoirs can differ significantly from one year to the next. One visible consequence of this varying runoff is the "bathtub rings" seen around many reservoirs—a few years of lower-than-average rainfall causes a large drawdown in water level.

Learning Check 9-8   How and why has the Aral Sea changed over the last few decades?

Wetlands   FG13

Closely related to lakes but less numerous and containing a much smaller volume of water are **wetlands**—broadly defined as land areas where saturation with water is the overriding factor that influences soil development and plant and animal communities. As we will see in Chapter 11,

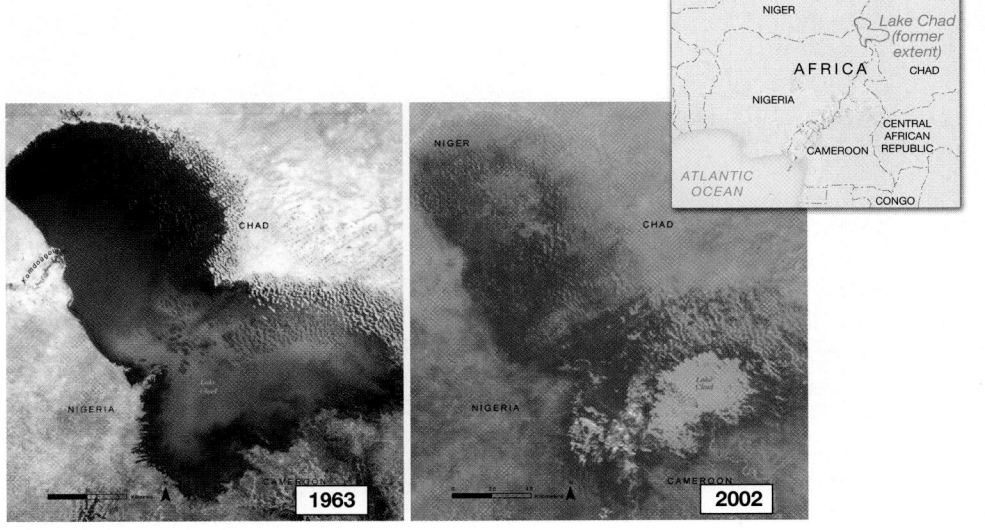

▲ **Figure 9-22** In 1960, the Aral Sea was the world's fourth-largest lake. However, as irrigation needs have forced farmers to drain more and more water from the rivers feeding the Aral, its size has decreased by 90 percent in the last 40 years. (a) The Aral Sea in 1973 (left) and in 2012 (right). (b) Where fish once swam, camels now wander over the floor of the "sea." If present trends continue, the Aral may cease to exist.

wetland areas play important roles in not only local ecosystems as sources of food and nutrients, but are keys to the water quality of many lakes, streams, and coastal waters by acting as "filters" for surface runoff. Further, as we saw in Chapter 7, coastal saltwater wetlands can act as buffers, reducing the immediate impact of hurricane storm surges.

Swamps and Marshes: Swamps and marshes are flattish places that are submerged in water at least part of the time but are shallow enough to permit the growth of water-tolerant plants (Figure 9-26). The conceptual distinction between the terms is that a **swamp** has a plant growth that is dominantly trees, whereas a **marsh** is

◀ **Figure 9-23** Lake Chad in 1963 and 2002.

▲ **Figure 9-24** Hoover Dam and Lake Mead on the Colorado River. The "bathtub ring" around the margin of the reservoir marks the water level when Lake Mead is at full capacity.

vegetated primarily with grasses and rushes. Both are usually associated with coastal plains, broad river valleys, or recently glaciated areas. Sometimes they represent an intermediate stage in the infilling of a lake.

Rivers and Streams

Although containing only a small proportion of the world's water at any given time, rivers and streams are an extremely dynamic component of the hydrologic cycle. (Although the terms are basically interchangeable, in common usage a *stream* is smaller than a *river*; geographers, however, call any flowing water a "stream," no matter what its size.) Streams provide the means by which the land surface drains and by which water, sediment, and dissolved chemicals are moved ever seaward. The occurrence of rivers and streams is closely, but not absolutely, related to precipitation patterns. Humid lands have many rivers and streams, most of which flow year-round; dry lands have fewer, almost all of which are ephemeral (which means they are dry most of the time).

Table 9-2 lists the world's largest rivers by discharge volume and length, while Figure 9-27 shows the world's largest river drainage basins (a *drainage basin* is all the land area drained by a river and its tributaries). A mere two dozen great rivers produce one-half of the total stream discharge of the world. The mighty Amazon yields nearly 20 percent of the world total, more than five times the discharge of the second-ranking river, the Congo River. Indeed, the discharge of the Amazon is three times as great as the total combined discharge of all rivers in the United States. The Mississippi is North America's largest river by far, with a drainage basin that encompasses about 40 percent of the total area of the 48 conterminous states and a flow that amounts to about one-third of the total discharge from all other rivers of the country.

We will explore the ways in which streams shape the landscape of the continents in Chapter 16.

▲ **Figure 9-25** The Three Gorges Dam and reservoir on the Yangtze River in China. The Landsat satellite image on the left was taken in 1987 before the dam was constructed; the image on the right was taken in 2009 after the reservoir behind the 2300-meter-wide dam was nearly full. As many as 1 million people will be displaced by the 600-kilometer-long reservoir.

▲ **Figure 9-26** Marshes are particularly numerous along the poorly drained South Atlantic and Gulf of Mexico coasts of the United States.

GROUNDWATER

Beneath the land surface is another important component of the hydrosphere—underground water. As Figure 9-1 shows, the total amount of underground water is many times that contained in lakes and streams. Moreover, underground water is much more widely distributed than surface water. Whereas lakes and rivers are found only in restricted locations, underground water is almost ubiquitous, occurring beneath the land surface throughout the world. Its quantity is sometimes limited, its quality is sometimes poor, and its occurrence is sometimes at great depth, but almost anywhere on Earth one can dig deep enough and find water. Strictly speaking, the term **groundwater** refers to underground water in the subsurface zone where the pore spaces are completely filled with water (the *zone of saturation*), but the term is often used broadly to refer to all underground water.

More than half of the world's underground water is found within 800 meters (about half a mile) of the surface. Below that depth, the amount of water generally decreases gradually and erratically. Although water has been found at depths below 10 kilometers (6 miles), it is almost immobilized because the pressure exerted by overlying rocks is so great and openings are so few and small.

Movement and Storage of Underground Water

Almost all underground water comes originally from above. Its source is precipitation that either percolates directly into the soil or eventually seeps downward from lakes and streams.

Porosity: Once the moisture gets underground, any one of several things can happen to it depending largely on the nature of the soil and rocks it infiltrates. The quantity of water that can be held in subsurface material (rock or soil) depends on the **porosity** of the material, which is the percentage of the total volume of the material that consists

TABLE 9-2	The World's Largest Rivers by Discharge and Length					
Name	Rank by Discharge Volume	Rank by Length	Approximate Discharge (cubic meters per second)	Approximate Length (kilometers)	Approximate Drainage Area (square kilometers)	Continent
Amazon	1	2	210,000	6400	5,800,000	South America
Congo	2	9	40,000	4700	4,000,000	Africa
Ganges-Brahmaputra	3	23	39,000	2900	1,730,000	Eurasia
Yangtze	4	3	21,000	6300	1,900,000	Eurasia
Paranà-La Plata	5	8	19,000	4900	2,200,000	South America
Yenisey	6	5	17,000	5550	2,600,000	Eurasia
Mississippi-Missouri	7	4	17,000	6000	3,200,000	North America
Orinoco	8	27	17,000	2700	880,000	South America
Nile	25	1	5000	6650	2,870,000	Africa

Note: Estimates of river lengths and discharges are approximate; the relative rankings of some rivers vary from one data source to another.

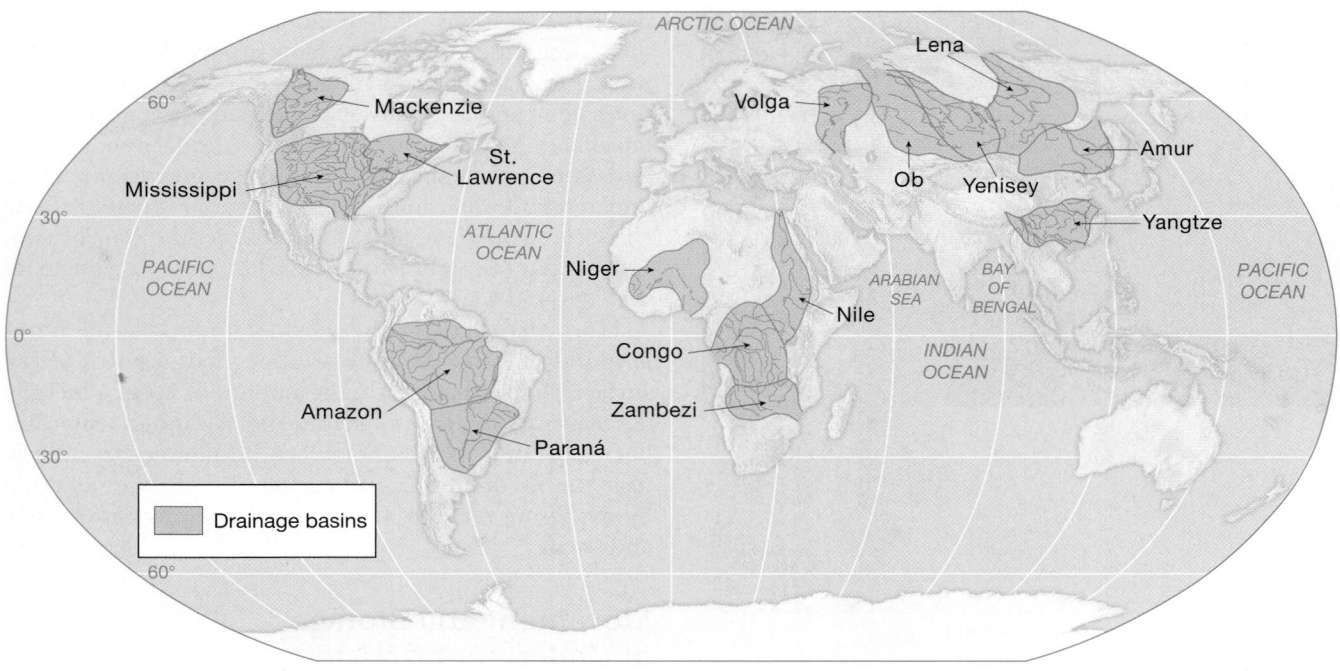

▲ **Figure 9-27** The world's largest drainage basins are scattered over the four largest continents in all latitudes.

of voids (pore spaces or cracks) that can fill with water. The more porous a material is, the greater the amount of open space it contains and the more water it can hold.

Permeability: Porosity is not the only factor affecting underground water flow. If water is to move through rock or soil, the pores must be connected to one another and be large enough for the water to move through them. The ability to transmit underground water (as opposed to just hold it) is termed **permeability**, and this property of subsurface matter is determined by the size of pores and by their degree of interconnectedness. The water moves by twisting and turning through these small, interconnected openings. The smaller and less connected the pore spaces, the less permeable the material and the slower the water moves.

The rate at which water moves through rock depends on both porosity and permeability. For example, clay is usually of high porosity because it has a great many *interstices* (openings) among the minute flakes that make up the clay, but it generally has low permeability because the interstices are so tiny that the force of molecular attraction binds the water to the clay flakes and holds it in place. Thus, clay is typically very porous but relatively impermeable and consequently can trap large amounts of water and keep it from draining.

Aquifers: Underground water is stored in, and moves slowly through, moderately to highly permeable rocks called **aquifers** (from the Latin, *aqua*, "water," and *ferre*, "to bear"). The rate of movement of the water varies with the situation. In some aquifers, the flow rate is only a few centimeters a day; in others, it may be several hundred

meters per day. A "rapid" rate of flow would be 12 to 15 meters (40 to 50 feet) per day.

Impermeable materials composed of components such as clay or very dense unfractured rock, which hinder or prevent water movement, are called **aquicludes** (Figure 9-28).

The general distribution of underground water can probably best be understood by visualizing a vertical subsurface cross section. Usually at least three and often four hydrologic zones are arranged one below another. From top to bottom, these layers are called the *zone of aeration*, the *zone of saturation*, the *zone of confined water*, and the *waterless zone*.

Zone of Aeration

The topmost band, the **zone of aeration**, is a mixture of solids, water, and air. Its depth can be quite variable, from a few centimeters to hundreds of meters. The interstices in this zone are filled partly with water and partly with air. The amount of water fluctuates considerably with time. After a rain, the pore spaces may be saturated with water, but the water may drain away rapidly. Some of the water evaporates, but much is absorbed by plants, which later return it to the atmosphere by transpiration. Water that molecular attraction cannot hold seeps downward into the next zone.

Animation
The Water Table

Learning Check 9-9   **What is an *aquifer*?**

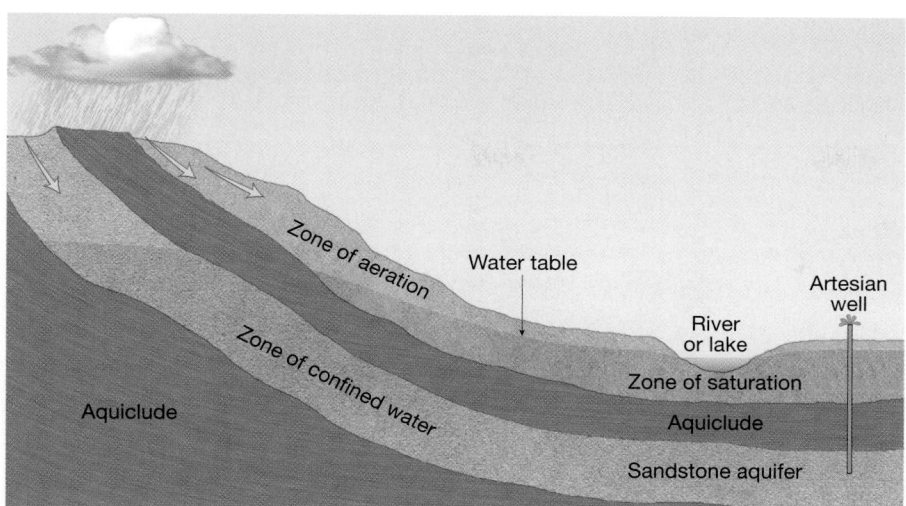

◀ **Figure 9-28** An aquifer is a rock structure that is permeable and/or porous enough to hold water, whereas an aquiclude has a structure that is too dense to allow water to penetrate it.

Zone of Saturation

Immediately below the zone of aeration is the **zone of saturation**, in which all pore spaces in the soil and cracks in the rocks are fully saturated with water. The moisture in this zone is properly called *groundwater*. Groundwater seeps slowly through the ground following the pull of gravity and guided by rock structure.

The top of the saturated zone is referred to as the **water table**. The orientation and slope of the water table usually conform roughly to the slope of the land surface above, nearly always approaching closer to the surface in valley bottoms and being more distant from it beneath a ridge or hill. Where the water table intersects Earth's surface, water flows out, forming a spring. A lake, swamp, marsh, or permanent stream is almost always an indication that the water table reaches the surface there. In humid regions, the water table is higher than in arid regions, which means that the zone of saturation is nearer the surface in humid regions. Some desert areas have no saturated zone at all.

Sometimes a localized zone of saturation develops above an aquiclude, and this configuration forms a *perched water table*.

Cones of Depression: A well dug into the zone of saturation fills with water up to the level of the water table. When water is taken from the well faster than it can flow in from the saturated rock, the water table drops in the immediate vicinity of the well in the approximate shape of an inverted cone. This striking feature is called a **cone of depression** (Figure 9-29). If many wells are withdrawing water faster than it is being replenished naturally, the water table may be significantly depressed over a large area, causing shallower wells to go dry.

Water percolates slowly through the saturated zone. Gravity supplies much of the energy for groundwater

Animation
Groundwater Cone
of Depression

percolation, leading it from areas where the water table is high toward areas where it is lower—that is, toward surface streams or lakes. Percolation flow is not always downward, however. Often the flow follows a curving path and then turns upward (against the force of gravity) to enter the stream or lake from below. This trajectory is possible because saturated-zone water at any given height is under greater pressure beneath a hill than beneath a stream valley. Thus, the water moves toward points where the pressure is least.

The lower limit of the zone of saturation is marked by the absence of pore spaces and therefore the absence of water. This boundary may be a single layer of impermeable rock, or it may simply be that the increasing depth has created so much pressure that no pore spaces exist in any rocks at that level.

Learning Check 9-10   *How does a cone of depression form and how does it affect an aquifer?*

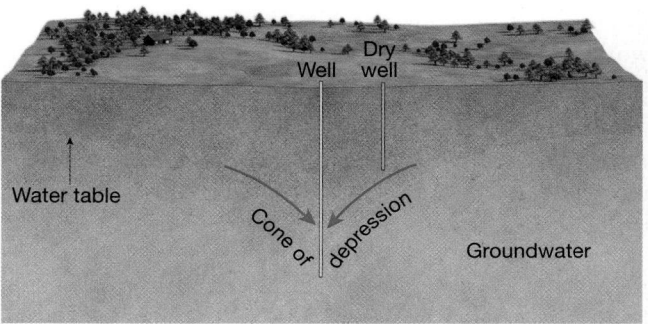

▲ **Figure 9-29** If water is withdrawn from a well faster than it can be replenished, a cone of depression will develop. This can effectively lower the water table over a large area. Nearby shallow wells may run dry because they lie above the lowered water table.

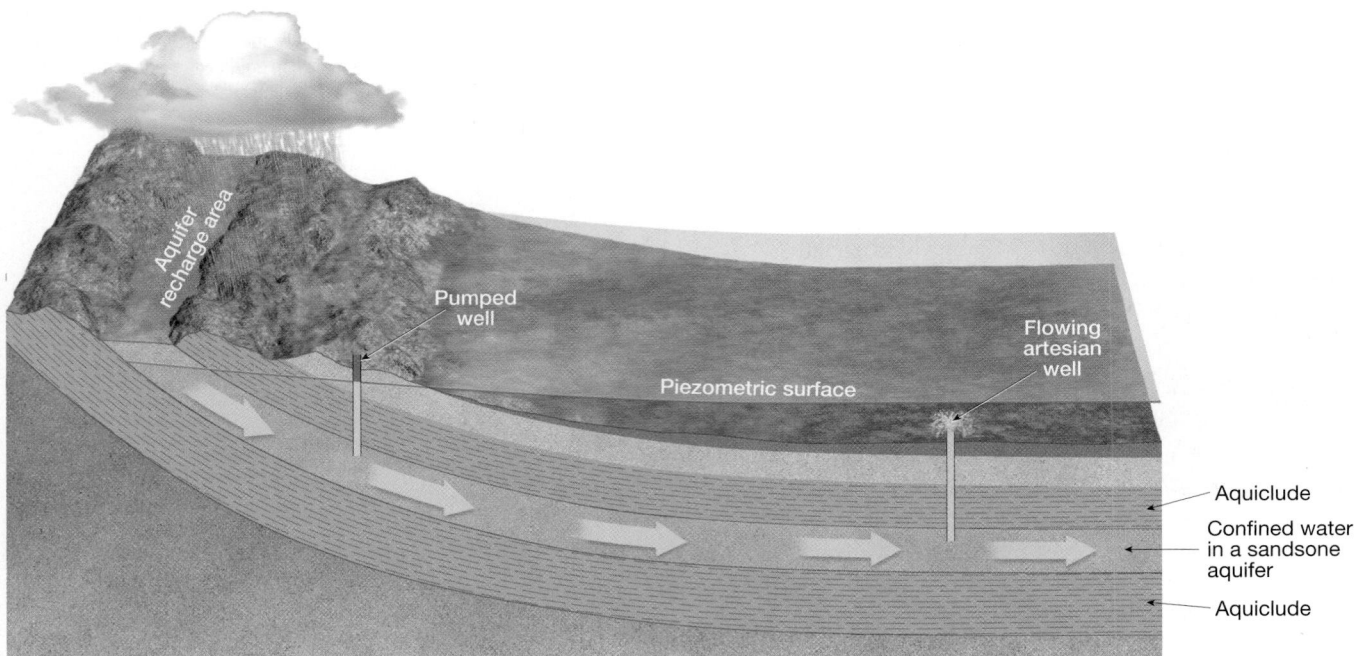

▲ **Figure 9-30** An artesian system. Surface water penetrates the aquifer in the recharge area and infiltrates downward. It is confined to the aquifer by impermeable strata (aquicludes) above and below. If a well is dug through the upper aquiclude into the aquifer, the confining pressure forces the water to rise in the well to the level of the piezometric surface. In an artesian well, the pressure forces the water to the surface; in a subartesian well, the water is forced only part way to the surface and must be pumped the rest of the way.

Zone of Confined Water

In many, but not most, parts of the world, a third hydrologic zone lies beneath the zone of saturation, separated from it by impermeable rock. This **zone of confined water** contains one or more aquifers into which water can infiltrate (Figure 9-30). Sometimes aquifers alternate with impermeable layers (aquicludes). Water cannot penetrate an aquifer in this deep zone by infiltration from above because of the impermeable barrier, and so any water the zone contains must have percolated along the aquifer from a more distant area where no aquiclude interfered. Characteristically, then, an aquifer in the confined water zone is a sloping or dipping layer that reaches to, or almost to, the surface at some location, where it can absorb infiltrating water. The water works its way down the sloping aquifer from the catchment area, building up considerable pressure in its confined situation.

Artesian Wells: If a well is drilled from the surface down into the confined aquifer, which may be at considerable depth, the confining pressure forces water to rise in the well. The elevation to which the water rises is known as the **piezometric surface**. In some cases, the pressure is enough to allow the water to rise above the ground, as shown in Figure 9-31. This free flow of water is called an **artesian well**. If the confining pressure is sufficient to push the water only partway to the surface and it must be pumped the rest of the way, the well is *subartesian*.

Unlike the distribution of groundwater, which is closely related to precipitation, the distribution of confined water is quite erratic over the world. Confined water underlies

▲ **Figure 9-31** An artesian well in Australia's Great Artesian Basin, the largest and most productive source of confined water in the world. This scene shows the Pilliga Bore in northwestern New South Wales.

many arid or semiarid regions that are poor in surface water or groundwater, thus providing a critical resource for these dry lands.

Waterless Zone

At some depth below the surface, the overlying pressure on the rock is so great that there are effectively no pore spaces—and so the rock here cannot hold or transmit groundwater. This *waterless zone* generally begins several kilometers beneath the land surface.

Groundwater Mining

In most parts of the world where groundwater occurs, it has been accumulating for a long time. Rainfall and snowmelt seep and percolate downward into aquifers, where the water may be stored for decades or centuries or millennia. Only in recent years have most of these aquifers been discovered and tapped by humans. They represent valuable sources of water that can supplement surface water resources. Underground water has been particularly utilized by farmers to irrigate in areas that contain insufficient surface water.

The accumulation of underground water is tediously slow. Its use by humans, however, can be distressingly rapid. In many parts of the U.S. Southwest, for example, the recharge (replenishment) rate averages only 0.5 centimeter (0.2 inch) per year, but it is not uncommon for a well to pump 75 centimeters (30 inches) per year. Thus, yearly pumpage is equivalent to 150 years' recharge. This rate of groundwater use can be likened to mining because a finite resource is being removed with no hope of replenishment. For this reason, the water in some aquifers is referred to as "fossil water." Almost everywhere in the world that underground water is being utilized on a large scale, the water table is dropping steadily and often precipitously.

In addition to depleting the water supply, groundwater mining causes a variety of problems. In some places, the compaction of sediments that takes place when groundwater is extracted faster than it is recharged leads to subsidence of the surface. For example, in the southern part of California's Central Valley, groundwater pumping resulted in 8.5 meters (about 29 feet) of subsidence in the mid-twentieth century. During the 1990s, groundwater pumping in the Las Vegas Valley of Nevada produced as much as 20 centimeters (8 inches) of subsidence. Because populations in many parts of the world are becoming more dependent on groundwater, monitoring the state of this vital resource is becoming ever more critical—see the box, "Focus: Monitoring Groundwater Resources from Space."

The Ogallala Aquifer: A classic example of groundwater mining is seen in the southern and central parts of the Great Plains, where the largest U.S. aquifer, the Ogallala or High Plains Aquifer, underlies 585,000 square kilometers (225,000 square miles) of eight states. The Ogallala formation consists of a series of limey and sandy layers that

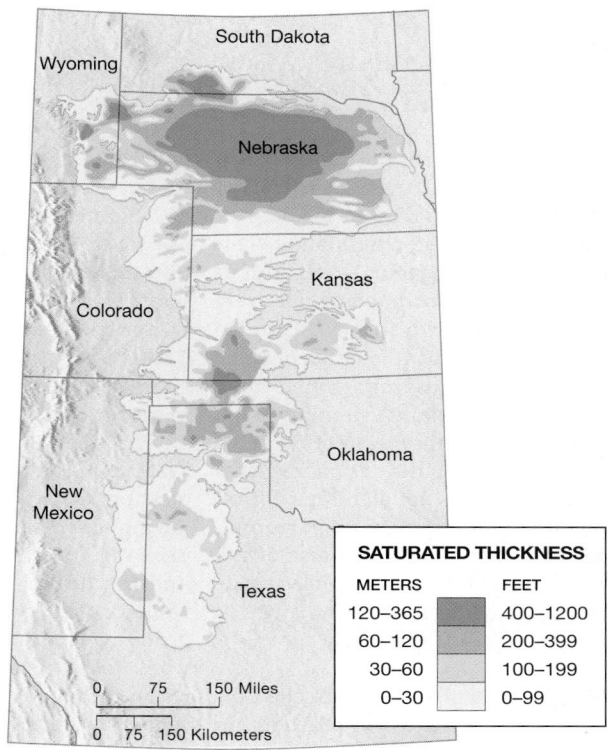

▲ **Figure 9-32** The Ogallala or High Plains Aquifer. Darker areas indicate greater thickness of the water-bearing strata.

function as a gigantic underground reservoir ranging in thickness from a few centimeters in parts of Texas to more than 300 meters (1000 feet) under the Nebraska Sandhills (Figure 9-32). Water has been accumulating in this aquifer for some 30,000 years. At the midpoint of the twentieth century, it was estimated to contain 1.4 billion acre-feet (1.7 quadrillion liters or 456 trillion gallons) of water, an amount roughly equivalent to the volume of one of the larger Great Lakes.

Farmers began to tap the Ogallala in the early 1930s. Before the end of that decade, the water table was already dropping. After World War II, the development of high-capacity pumps, sophisticated sprinklers, and other technological innovations encouraged the rapid expansion of irrigation based on Ogallala water. Water use in the region has almost quintupled since 1950. The results of this accelerated usage have been spectacular. Above ground, there has been a rapid spread of high-yield farming into areas never before cultivated (especially in Nebraska) and a phenomenal increase in irrigated crops in all eight Ogallala states. Beneath the surface, however, the water table is sinking ever deeper—dropping as much as 30 meters (100 feet) over large areas (Figure 9-33). Farmers who once obtained water from 15-meter (50-foot) wells now must bore to 45 or 75 meters (150 or 250 feet), and as the price of energy increases, the cost of pumping increases operating expenses enormously and so extraction has dropped slightly over the last few years. Some 170,000 wells tapped the Ogallala in the 1970s, but thousands of those have now been abandoned.

Monitoring Groundwater Resources from Space

The United Nations Educational, Scientific and Cultural Organization (UNESCO) estimates that 2.5 billion people around the world obtain all of their drinking water from groundwater, including large populations in some relatively poor parts of the world. UNESCO also estimates that about 40 percent of all irrigation water comes from groundwater. The demand for groundwater is so high in many regions that extraction rates currently far exceed the natural recharge rates, leading to depletion of this critical resource. Monitoring changes in groundwater is difficult in many parts of the world. Innovative technology, however, is allowing scientists to monitor changes in the status of groundwater from space.

GRACE Satellites: In 2002, the German Aerospace Center in partnership with NASA launched a pair of polar orbiting satellites that circle the planet about 220 kilometers (137 miles) apart. Called the *Gravity Recovery and Climate Experiment* (GRACE), the satellites measure tiny differences in the distance between them that are caused by slight variations in Earth's gravity field. These local differences in gravity are caused by differences in the mass of Earth below.

The GRACE system is so sensitive that it can detect differences in the mass of water and ice on and within Earth, allowing scientists to track changes in the exchange of water between ice sheets and the ocean, and between groundwater and the surface. The depletion of groundwater and the lowering of the water table of aquifers can result from overpumping as well as from declines that occur during droughts.

For example, data show that between October 2003 and March 2009, aquifers in California's Central Valley, the state's primary agricultural region, lost more than 30 cubic kilometers of water—enough water to nearly fill Lake Mead (Figure 9-C).

GRACE data is also used on an experimental basis to measure short-term differences in soil moisture and groundwater levels caused by weather variations such as droughts. For example, Figure 9-D shows the wetness percentile of groundwater storage in July 2012 relative to the average of wetness from 1948 to 2009; the decline in groundwater associated with the 2011–2012 drought in the southwestern United States and the upper Mississippi basin is clearly shown.

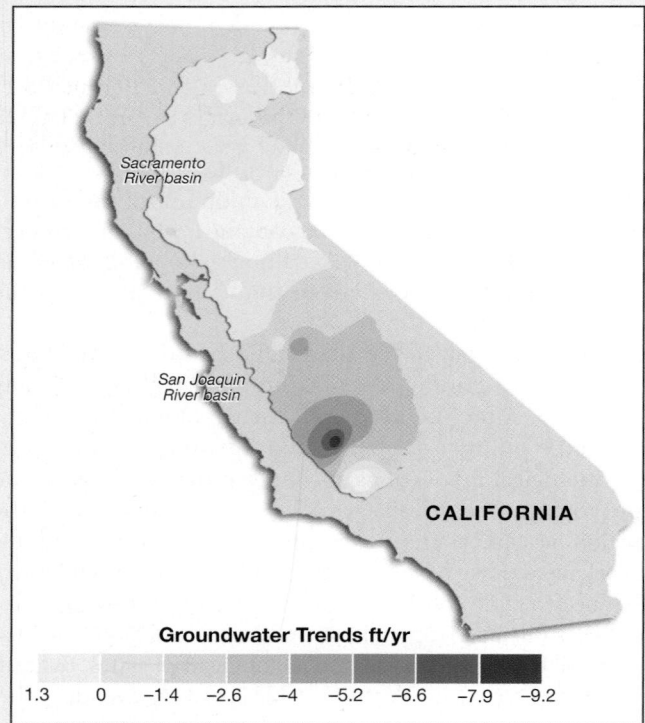

▲ **Figure 9-C** Observed change in groundwater level trend between October 2003 and March 2009 based on GRACE satellite data. Areas shown in dark blue and green experienced water table declines of 0.8 to 2.4 meters (2.7 to 7.9 feet) per year.

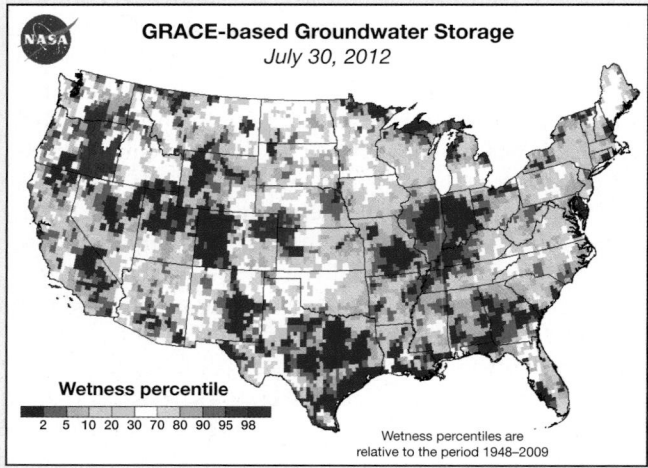

▲ **Figure 9-D** Estimated wetness percentiles of groundwater storage on July 30, 2012, compared with the average moisture content of the ground between 1948 and 2009, based on GRACE satellite data. The dark maroon areas show the extreme dryness of the ground during the 2012 drought.

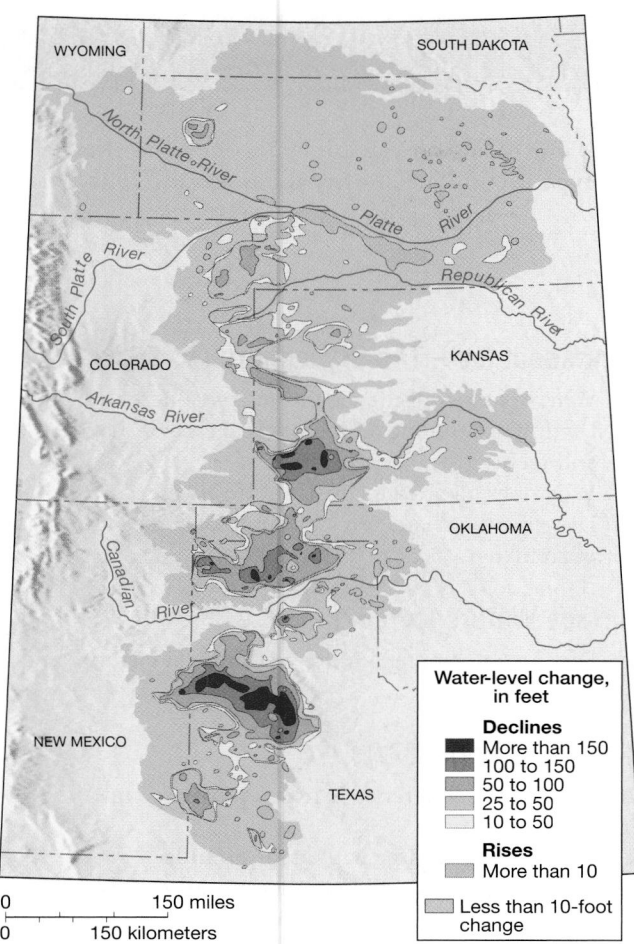

Figure 9-33 Water table change in the Ogallala Aquifer from the early twentieth century through 2009. Increases in the water table occurred in places where surface water irrigation has been extensive.

Some farmers have been shifting to crops that require less water. Others are adopting water- and energy-conserving measures that range from a simple decision to irrigate less frequently to the installation of sophisticated machinery that uses water in the most efficient fashion (Figure 9-34). Many farmers have faced or will soon face the prospect of abandoning irrigation entirely. During the next four decades, it is estimated that 2 million hectares (5 million acres) now irrigated will revert to dry-land production. Other farmers concentrate on high-value crops before it is too late, hoping to make a large profit and then get out of farming.

Learning Check 9-11 **How has groundwater mining affected the Ogallala Aquifer since the 1930s?**

Water conservation is further complicated by the obvious fact that groundwater is no respecter of property boundaries. A farmer who is very conservative in his or her water use must face the reality that less careful neighbors are pumping from the same aquifer and that their recklessness may seriously diminish the water available to everyone.

The situation varies from place to place. The Nebraska Sandhills have the most favorable conditions. The aquifer is deepest there, previous water use was minimal, and there is a relatively rapid recharge rate. Indeed, for the 13-county area that makes up the bulk of the Sandhills, withdrawal averages only about 10 percent of recharge, a remarkable situation. In contrast, the 13 counties of southwestern Kansas have a withdrawal rate more than 20 times the recharge rate—a clearly unsustainable situation.

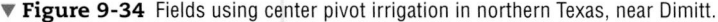

▼ **Figure 9-34** Fields using center pivot irrigation in northern Texas, near Dimitt.

Chapter 9 **LEARNING REVIEW**

After studying this chapter, you should be able to answer the following questions. Key terms from each text section are shown in **bold type**. Definitions for key terms are also found in the glossary at the back of the book.

KEY TERMS AND CONCEPTS

The Hydrologic Cycle (*p. 253*)

1. Where is most of the world's freshwater found?
2. Explain the role of evaporation in the **hydrologic cycle**.
3. What is the relationship between transpiration and evaporation?
4. Describe the roles of advection and **runoff** in the hydrologic cycle.

The Oceans (*p. 256*)

5. Is the Pacific Ocean significantly different from other oceans? Explain.
6. Why does **salinity** vary in different parts of the world ocean?
7. Why are the oceans becoming slightly more acidic?

Movement of Ocean Waters (*p. 258*)

8. Why do most oceanic areas experience two high **tides** and two low tides each day?
9. What is meant by the **tidal range** of a coastal location?
10. Distinguish between **flood tide** and **ebb tide**.
11. Describe and explain **spring tides** and **neap tides**.
12. What is a **tidal bore**?
13. What is **thermohaline circulation**?
14. Explain the **global conveyor–belt circulation**.

Permanent Ice—The Cryosphere (*p. 263*)

15. Where is most of the ice in the cryosphere found?
16. Distinguish among an **ice pack**, **ice shelf**, **ice floe**, and **iceberg**.
17. Why does all sea ice consist of freshwater?
18. Describe the characteristics and global distribution of **permafrost**.

Surface Waters (*p. 267*)

19. Distinguish among a **lake**, **wetlands**, a **swamp**, and a **marsh**.

Groundwater (*p. 271*)

20. What is the difference between **porosity** and **permeability**?
21. Contrast an **aquifer** with an **aquiclude**.
22. Briefly define the following terms: **zone of aeration**, **zone of saturation**, **groundwater**.
23. Explain the concept of a **water table**.
24. Describe and explain the cause of a **cone of depression**.
25. Under what circumstances can a **zone of confined water** develop?
26. What is meant by the **piezometric surface**?
27. Distinguish between an **artesian well** and a subartesian well.

STUDY QUESTIONS

1. In what part of the hydrologic cycle is water most likely to stay for a very short time? A very long time? Why?
2. "How many oceans are there?" Why is this a difficult question to answer?
3. How can an increase in the acidity of ocean water affect corals and other ocean creatures with calcite skeletons?
4. What are some of the consequences of melting permafrost?

5. Explain why and how the Aral Sea has changed in recent decades.
6. Why are most lakes considered to be "temporary" features of the landscape?
7. Why is the water from some aquifers referred to as fossil water?
8. How has groundwater mining affected the Ogallala Aquifer since the 1930s?

EXERCISES

1. If a floating iceberg has a surface area of 100 square meters and is 10 meters high, what is the total volume of ice including both the exposed portion above water and the portion below the water? _____ cubic meters

2. If the natural recharge rate of an aquifer is 1 centimeter per year, but the rate of groundwater pumping is 15 centimeters per year, how far will the water table drop in 10 years? _____ centimeters

3. Assuming a natural recharge rate of 0.5 centimeters per year, if groundwater pumping lowers the water table by 50 centimeters, how many years of "fossil water" have been extracted? _____ years

Seeing Geographically

Look again at the photograph of the waterfall in Iceland at the beginning of the chapter (p. 252). Which components of the hydrologic cycle can you observe here? Find Iceland on a map of the North Atlantic Ocean or the world map on the inside cover of this book. Where do you think is the source of most of the water vapor that condenses and falls as precipitation here? Why do you say that?

MasteringGeography™

Looking for additional review and test prep materials? Visit the Study Area in MasteringGeography™ to enhance your geographic literacy, spatial reasoning skills, and understanding of this chapter's content by accessing a variety of resources, including geoscience animations, MapMaster interactive maps, videos, RSS feeds, flashcards, web links, self-study quizzes, and an eText version of *McKnight's Physical Geography: A Landscape Appreciation*.

Chapter 10 CYCLES AND PATTERNS IN THE BIOSPHERE

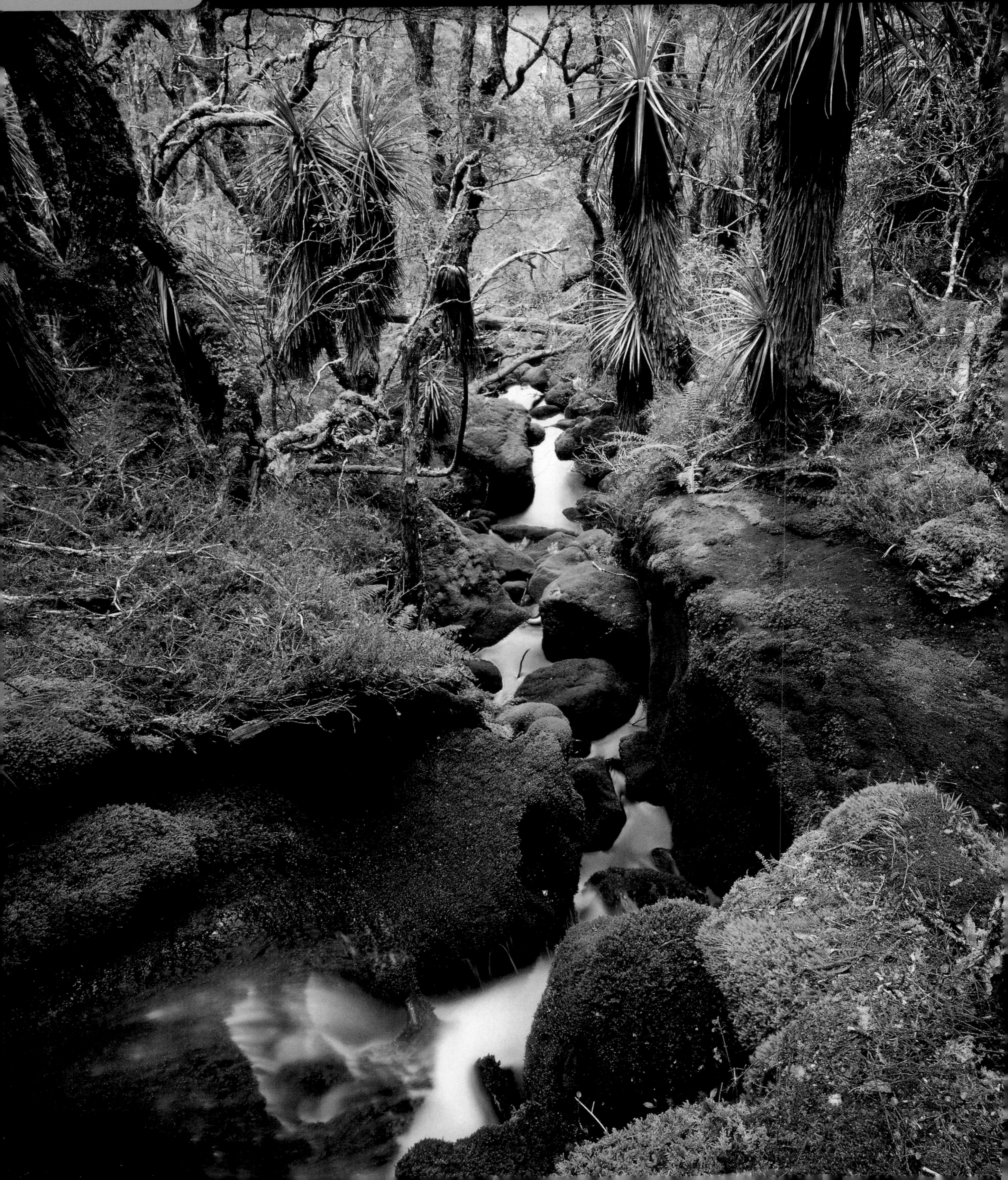

OF THE FOUR PRINCIPAL COMPONENTS OF OUR EARTHLY

environment, the biosphere has the boundaries that are hardest to pin down. The atmosphere consists of the envelope of air that surrounds the planet, the lithosphere is the solid portion, and the hydrosphere encompasses the various forms of water. These three spheres are distinct from one another and easy to visualize. The biosphere, on the other hand, impinges spatially on the other three. It consists of the incredibly numerous and diverse array of organisms that populate our planet—most obviously plants and animals, but also less obvious types of organisms such as bacteria and fungi.[1] Most of these organisms exist at the interface between atmosphere and lithosphere, but some live largely or entirely within the hydrosphere or the lithosphere, and others move relatively freely from one sphere to another.

As we begin our study of the biosphere, look for connections to Earth systems and processes discussed in earlier chapters—for example, the close relationship of Earth's solar radiation budget (presented in Chapter 4) and hydrologic cycle (presented in Chapters 6 and 9) to the *biogeochemical cycles* that will be presented in this chapter. Especially, note the relationship between the distribution patterns of organisms and the distribution of climate we presented in Chapter 8.

As you study this chapter, think about these key questions:

- **How do biogeographers approach the study of the biosphere?**
- **How do water, carbon, oxygen, and nitrogen move through the biosphere and other Earth systems in biogeochemical cycles?**
- **What are food chains, and how can pollution affect them?**
- **What are the major biological factors that influence distribution patterns in the biosphere?**
- **What are the major environmental factors that affect the survival and distribution patterns of plants and animals?**

The Impact of Plants and Animals on the Landscape

More than ten thousand years ago, when Earth was sparsely populated by humans, vegetation grew in profusion wherever the land surface was not too dry or too cold. Today, native plants are still widespread in the sparsely populated parts of the world as Figure 10-1a shows. However, much of the vegetation in populated areas has been removed, and much that persists has been modified by human introduction of crops, weeds, and ornamental plants (Figure 10-1b).

---

[1]Biologists now generally recognize six kingdoms of living organisms: *Plantae, Animalia, Archaea, Eubacteria, Protista,* and *Fungi.* See Appendix VI.

Seeing Geographically

Stream running through the forest in the Walls of Jerusalem National Park, Tasmania. Describe the kinds of plants you see in this photograph. What do you see that suggests the relative amount of moisture available in this location?

▲ **Figure 10-1** (a) Many parts of Earth are still covered with native vegetation, with little or no human impact in evidence. This forested scene is near Blackwater Canyon, West Virginia. (b) A small natural depression of wetland remains, but most of the natural vegetation in this scene has been displaced by crops in this field near Tosterup, Sweden.

(a)

(b)

Native animal life is much less apparent in the landscape than plant life and is often more conspicuous by sound (especially birds and insects) than by sight. Still we should keep in mind that wildlife usually is shy and reclusive, and its absence may be more apparent than real. Moreover, most species of animals are tiny and therefore less noticeable in our normal scale of vision. In addition, both plants and animals interact with other components of the natural landscape (such as soil, landforms, and water) and sometimes become important influences in the development and evolution of these components.

THE GEOGRAPHIC APPROACH TO THE STUDY OF ORGANISMS

Even the simplest living organism is an extraordinarily complex entity. When we set out to learn about an organism—alga or anteater, tulip or turtle—we embark on a complicated quest for knowledge. An organism differs in many ways from other aspects of the environment, but most obviously in that it is alive and its survival depends on an enormously intricate set of life processes. As

beneficial as a complete understanding of the world's organisms might be for us, as with every other feature of the world, the geographer focuses only on certain aspects of the landscape.

Biogeography

As we've seen in earlier chapters, the geographic viewpoint is that of broad understanding, whether we are dealing with plants and animals or with anything else. This does not mean that we ignore the individual organism; rather it means that we seek generalizations and patterns and assess their overall significance. Here, as elsewhere, the geographer is interested in distributions and relationships. The subfield of geography that looks at the biosphere is known as *biogeography*. **Biogeography** is the study of the distribution patterns of living organisms and how these patterns change over time.

Biodiversity: As geographers look for and explain patterns in the biosphere, one of the most significant components of these patterns is *biodiversity*. **Biodiversity** refers to the number of different kinds of organisms present in a location. *High biodiversity* means that there are many different organisms present, whereas *low biodiversity* means that just a few kinds of organisms are present. As we will see, declining biodiversity in a location is often an indication that the overall health of the natural environment is in decline.

Flora and Fauna: Among the life-forms of our planet are perhaps 600,000 species of plants and more than twice that many species of animals. The term **biota** refers to this total complex of plant and animal life. The basic subdivision of biota separates **flora**, or plants, from **fauna**, or animals. In this book, we recognize a further fundamental distinction—between *oceanic biota* and *terrestrial biota* (living on land; *terrenus* is Latin for "earth").

The inhabitants of the oceans are generally divided into three groups—*plankton* (floating plants and animals), *nekton* (animals such as fish and marine mammals that swim freely), and *benthos* (animals and plants that live on or in the ocean bottom). Although these marine life-forms are fascinating, and despite the fact that 70 percent of Earth's surface is oceanic, in this book we pay scant attention to oceanic biota primarily because of constraints of time and space. The terrestrial biota will be our primary focus of interest for most of our study of the biosphere.

> **Learning Check 10-1** **Describe the focus of the science of *biogeography*. (Answer on p. AK-3)**

With such an overwhelming diversity of organisms, how can we study their distributions and relationships in any meaningful manner?

The Search for a Meaningful Classification Scheme

When a geographer studies any phenomena, he or she attempts to classify specific observations in such a way that meaningful broad patterns may be recognized. In some cases, the geographer borrows classification schemes from other disciplines, but sometimes these schemes are not ideally suited for geographic studies.

For example, the most widely used system of biological classification is the *binomial* (two-name) system originally developed by the Swedish botanist Carolus Linnaeus in the eighteenth century. This system focuses primarily on the morphology (structure and form) of organisms and groups them on the basis of structural similarity (see Appendix VI). The Linnaean scheme is generally useful for geographers, but its principal disadvantage for geographic use is that it is based entirely on anatomic similarities, whereas geographers are more interested in distribution patterns and habitat preferences.

Ecosystems and Biomes: Biogeographers are especially interested in the relationships between the different organisms in a location, and in the relationships between those organisms and the surrounding environment. The term *ecosystem* is used to describe all of the organisms in an area and their interactions with the immediate environment. At the global scale, biogeographers recognize broader groupings of plants and animals known as *biomes*—large,

recognizable assemblages of plants and animals living in a functional relationship with the environment.

Both ecosystems and biomes are explored in much greater detail in Chapter 11. In this chapter, we set the stage for that discussion by describing fundamental cycles and relationships in the biosphere. We begin with a look at the broadest patterns and cycles in the biosphere—*biogeochemical cycles*.

BIOGEOCHEMICAL CYCLES

The web of life comprises a great variety of organisms coexisting in a diversity of ecosystems. Organisms survive sustained by flows of energy, water, and nutrients. These flows are different in different parts of the world, in different seasons of the year, and under various local circumstances (Figure 10-2).

It is generally believed that, for the last billion years or so, Earth's atmosphere and hydrosphere have been composed of approximately the same balance of chemical components we live with today. This constancy implies a planetwide condition in which the various chemical elements have been maintained by cyclic passage through the tissues of plants and animals—first absorbed by an organism and then returned to the air/water/soil through decomposition. These grand cycles are collectively called *biogeochemical cycles*.

If the biosphere is to function properly, its chemical substances must be recycled continually through these biogeochemical cycles. In other words, after one organism uses a substance, that substance must be converted, at the expense of some energy, to a reusable form. For some components, this conversion can be accomplished in less than a decade; for others, it may require hundreds of millions of years. In recent years, however, the rapid growth of the human population and the accompanying ever-accelerating rate at which we consume Earth's resources have had a harmful effect on many of these cycles. Not all of the damage is irreparable, but the threat that such disruption will produce irreversible harm to the biosphere is increasing.

▼ **Figure 10-2** Organisms survive in the biosphere through a complex of systemic flows of energy, water, and nutrients. These wildflowers are in Joffre Lakes Provincial Park, British Columbia, Canada.

Although we describe biogeochemical cycles separately in the following subsections, you will see that many of these cycles are closely interrelated. It is appropriate, then, for us to begin with the most fundamental of these cycles—the flow of energy through the biosphere.

The Flow of Energy

The Sun is the basic energy source on which nearly all life ultimately depends (forms of life utilizing geochemical energy from hydrothermal vents on the ocean floor are a well-known exception). Solar energy drives life processes in the biosphere through *photosynthesis*, the production of organic matter by chlorophyll-containing plants and bacteria.

Only about 0.1 percent of the solar energy that reaches Earth is captured for use in photosynthesis. More than half of that total is used immediately in the plant's own *respiration*, and the remainder is temporarily stored. Eventually this remainder enters a *food chain*.

Solar energy is of course fundamental to life on Earth. Although readily absorbed by some substances, this energy is also readily reradiated. Thus, it is difficult to store and easy to lose.

Photosynthesis and Respiration: The biosphere is a temporary recipient of a small fraction of the solar energy that reaches Earth, which is "fixed" (made stable) by green plants through the process of **photosynthesis** (Figure 10-3). The

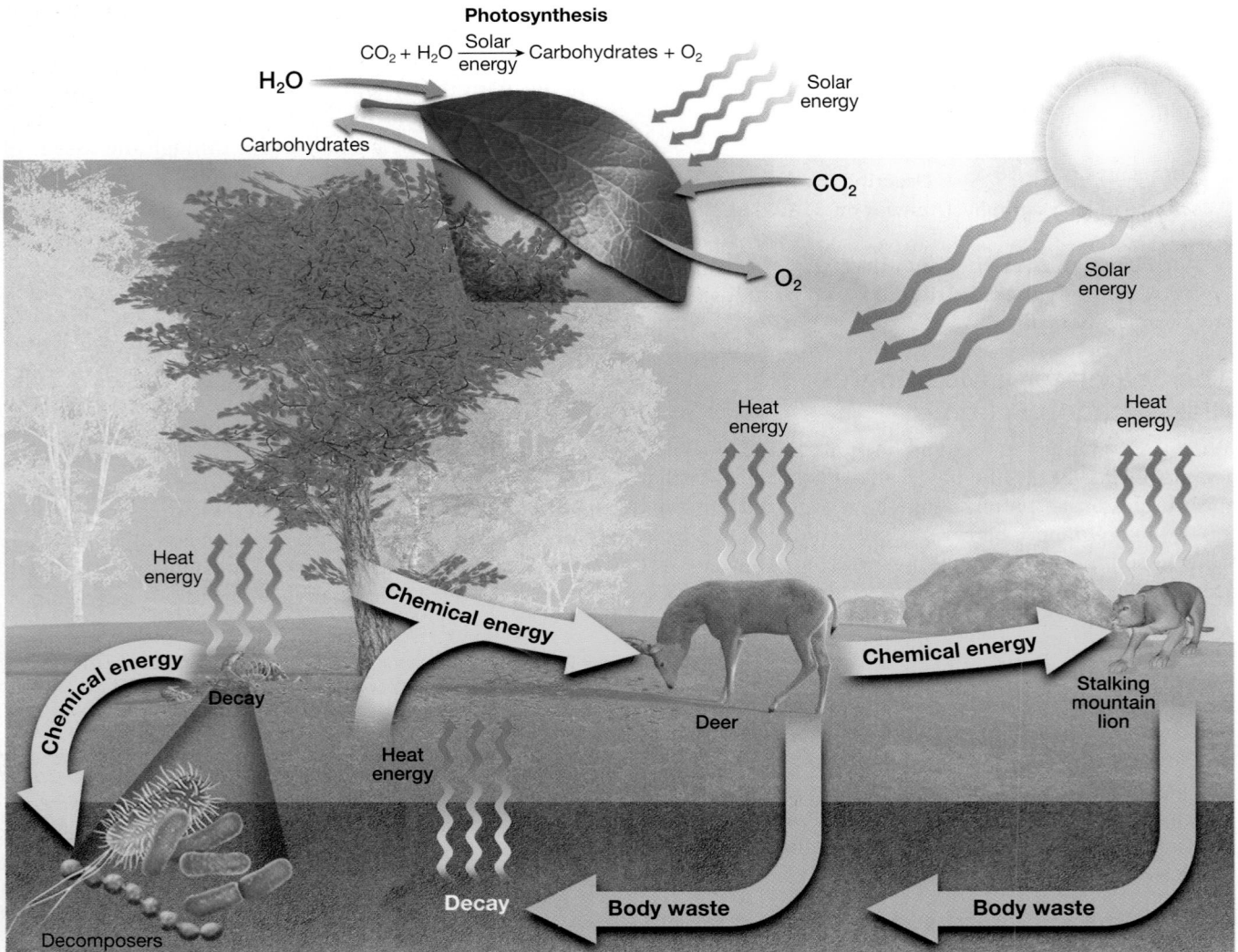

Photosynthesis

$$CO_2 + H_2O \xrightarrow{\text{Solar energy}} \text{Carbohydrates} + O_2$$

▲ **Figure 10-3** Energy flow in the terrestrial biosphere. Plants use solar energy in photosynthesis, storing that energy in the sugar molecules they manufacture. Grazing and browsing animals then acquire that energy when they eat the plants. Other animals eat the grazers/ browsers and thereby acquire some of the energy originally in the plants. Body wastes from all the animals, the bodies of the animals once they die, and dead plant matter that has fallen to the ground all return energy to the soil. As all this waste and dead matter decays, it gives off energy in the form of heat. The arrows represent energy pathways but do not reflect the relative amounts of energy moving along any one pathway.

key to photosynthesis is a light-sensitive pigment known as *chlorophyll* that is found within organelles in leaf cells called *chloroplasts*. Chlorophyll absorbs certain wavelengths of visible light, while prominently reflecting green light (this is why leaves look green).

 Video — Global Carbon Uptake by Plants

In the presence of sunlight and chlorophyll, a photochemical reaction takes carbon dioxide (CO_2) from the air and combines it with water (H_2O) to form the energy-rich *carbohydrate* compounds we know as sugars while also releasing molecular oxygen. In this process, the energy from sunlight is stored as chemical energy in the sugars. In simplified form, the chemical equation for photosynthesis is

$$CO_2 + H_2O \xrightarrow{light} \text{Carbohydrates} + O_2$$

In turn, plants can use simple sugars to build more complex carbohydrates, such as starches. The stored chemical energy in the form of carbohydrates is utilized in the biosphere primarily in two ways. First, some of the stored energy cycles through the biosphere when animals eat either the photosynthesizing plants or other animals that have eaten plants. Second, the other portion of the stored energy in carbohydrates is consumed directly by the plant itself in a process known as **plant respiration**. In the process of respiration, the stored energy in carbohydrates is *oxidized*, releasing water, carbon dioxide, and heat energy. The simplified chemical equation for plant respiration is

 Animation — Net Primary Productivity

$$\text{Carbohydrates} + O_2 \rightarrow CO_2 + H_2O + \text{Energy (heat)}$$

Learning Check 10-2 **Why is *photosynthesis* so critical to the existence of the biosphere?**

Net Primary Productivity: Plant growth depends on a surplus of carbohydrate production. *Net photosynthesis* is the difference between the amount of carbohydrate produced in photosynthesis and that lost in plant respiration. Annual **net primary productivity** describes the net photosynthesis of a plant community over a period of one year, usually measured in the amount of fixed carbon per unit area (grams of carbon per square meter per year). Monthly or seasonal variations in productivity can also be determined by measuring net photosynthesis. Net primary productivity is, in effect, a measure of the amount of chemical energy stored in a plant community and is reflected in the dry weight of organic material, or **biomass**, of that community.

Net primary productivity varies widely from environment to environment around the world. It tends to be highest on land within the tropics where both high precipitation and high insolation are available for plant growth but generally diminishes poleward, especially in extremely arid and extremely cold environments (Figure 10-4). In the oceans, productivity is strongly influenced by the nutrient content of the water (Figure 10-5). For example, off the west coasts of continents in the midlatitudes, the upwelling of cold, nutrient-rich water results in high net primary productivity (upwelling is discussed in Chapter 4).

 Animation — Biological Productivity in Midlatitude Oceans

The carbohydrates incorporated into plant tissue are in turn consumed by animals or decomposed by microorganisms. Plant-eating animals convert some of the consumed carbohydrates back to carbon dioxide and exhale it into the air (animal respiration); the remainder is decomposed by microorganisms after the animal dies. The carbohydrates acted upon by microorganisms are ultimately oxidized into carbon dioxide and returned to the atmosphere (soil respiration).

Because photosynthesis captures and stores solar energy, it is possible for us to utilize this energy reservoir in a number of different ways. Burning wood for cooking or heating, for example, takes advantage of this stored solar energy, as does our use of other kinds of *biofuels*—see the box, "Energy for the 21st Century: Biofuels."

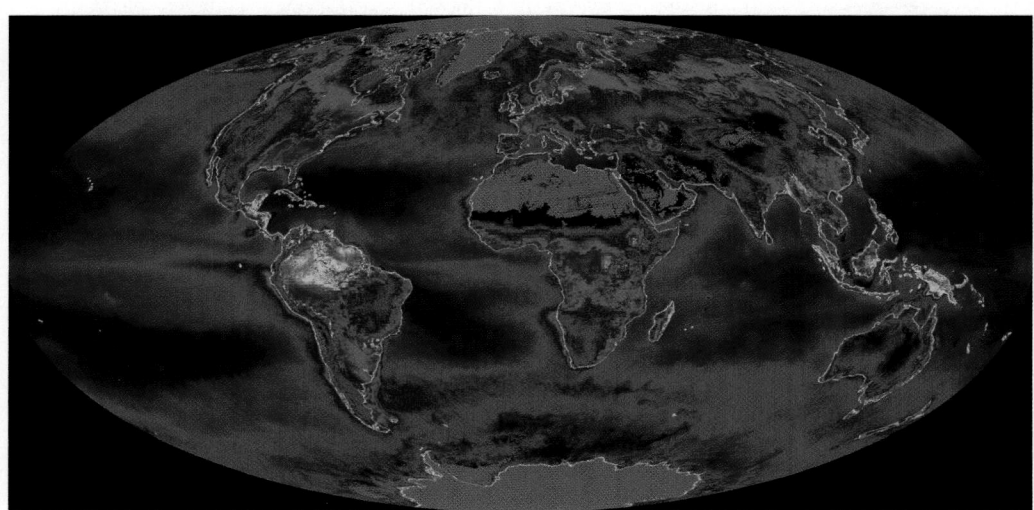

◀ **Figure 10-4** Annual net primary productivity. This composite satellite image shows net primary productivity, based on the rate at which plants absorb carbon dioxide from the air (the mass of carbon absorbed per square meter per year). The areas of highest annual average productivity are shown in yellow and red—most notably in the tropical rainforests of the world; areas of progressively lower productivity are shown in green, blue, and purple.

ENERGY FOR THE 21ST CENTURY

Biofuels

▶ Valerie Sloan, University of Colorado at Boulder, Ph.D.

As concerns about greenhouse gas emissions affecting climate change have come to the forefront, the search for alternatives to burning fossil fuels is under way. Two fuels of interest are ethanol, an alcohol fuel fermented from crops (much like wine or beer), and biodiesel, which is made by chemically processing vegetable oil or animal fat. By the early twentieth century, both Rudolph Diesel and Henry Ford had successfully designed engines that would run on such biofuels, and many modern internal combustion engines are easily converted to biofuel use.

Burning fossil fuels emits carbon dioxide (CO_2) that has been buried for millions of years, whereas burning biofuels emits CO_2 that is taken out of the atmosphere during plant or animal growth and so is not considered a new emission. The hope has been that biofuels would emit less greenhouse gas than gasoline and become a new domestic energy source as global oil reserves are depleted. Biofuels have also gained great political and economic momentum, partly because they offer lucrative new markets for the farming industry and because an increase in their production was mandated by the U.S. government in 2007. Biofuels may not be the cure-all originally hoped for, however.

Ethanol: Studies suggest that corn ethanol, the biggest source of biofuel in the United States, takes more energy to produce than it provides. In fact, converting most crops, such as soybeans, switchgrass, and palm fruit, into fuel consumes more energy than is produced when all aspects of fossil fuel consumption are accounted for, such as fertilizer production.

Currently, about one-third of the corn grown in the United States goes into making ethanol (Figure 10-A), but the 34 billion liters (9 billion gallons) of ethanol per year provides the United States with the energy equivalent of only 1.3 percent of total oil consumption. This is a small return, given the environmental costs of growing corn, including the impacts of pesticides, herbicides, groundwater irrigation, and the contribution

▲ **Figure 10-A** Corn being harvested in Iowa.

of nitrogen fertilizer to creating "dead zones," such as the one recently found in the Gulf of Mexico.

Sugar cane ethanol, however, does have a positive energy balance, providing more energy than it takes to produce. This is the primary crop used to produce ethanol in Brazil, the second largest producer and the largest exporter of biofuel in the world. How sugarcane ethanol production and combustion compare to fossil fuels with respect to greenhouse gas emissions depends on whether land use changes were involved to grow the crops. When mature forests are replaced by biofuel crops, trees storing vast quantities of carbon are lost and huge amounts of CO_2 are released to the atmosphere. Critics disagree about whether Brazil's sugarcane ethanol industry creates a net decrease or increase in greenhouse gas emissions compared to fossil fuels.

Biodiesel: Recently, carbon accounting problems in international cap-and-trade agreements have surfaced: biodiesel is considered carbon-neutral, and yet the effects of land use change and energy used in production are not taken into account. For example, when Indonesians clear tropical hardwood forests or peat swamps to produce palm oil that ends up in European biodiesel, Indonesia does not count the change in land use emissions or production energy, and Europe does not count the carbon coming out of the tailpipe.

Innovators and scientists are turning to other sources for biologically produced energy: yeast, algae, and bacteria. The idea is that fats grown inside algae or cyanobacteria can be released by an added chemical solvent; this fat is then refined into biodiesel (Figure 10-B). The U.S. Department of Energy tried to make biodiesel from algae for 18 years but concluded that it was not economically feasible; however, today, several companies are researching this prospect nationally and globally with interest.

Crops versus Food: The ethics of using land to grow crops for fuel rather than for food is becoming a global concern. According to the Director-General of the United Nations and of the Food and Agriculture Organization, using food crops for fuel is contributing to world hunger, partly because subsistence farmland is replaced by biofuel cash crops. In the United States, the impact is felt through higher food prices, which are estimated to have increased 10 to 20 percent because of the use of food and cattle feed crops for fuel.

▲ **Figure 10-B** Algae growing in research laboratory to make biodiesel.

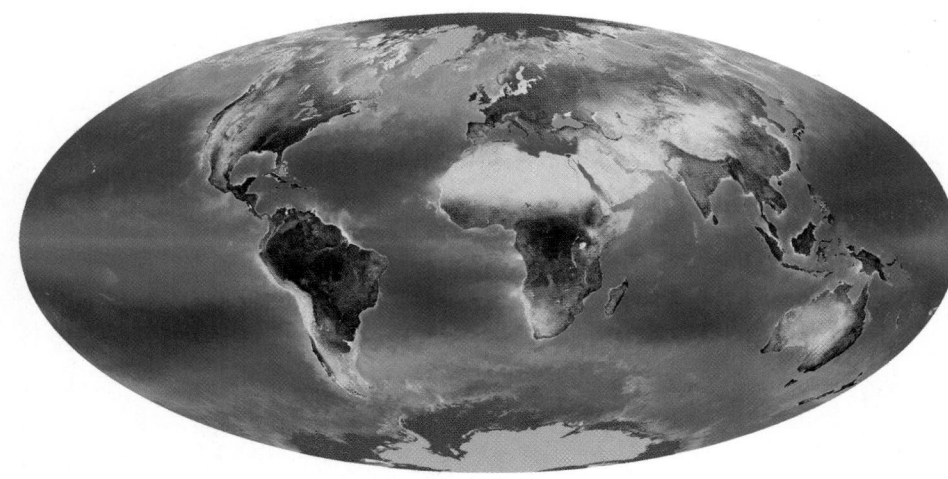

◄ **Figure 10-5** Global vegetation index on land and chlorophyll concentration at the ocean surface for 2008. Relative differences in the amount of vegetation growth on land are depicted with the *vegetation index*: the areas of greatest plant growth are shown in dark green, whereas areas of the least growth are shown in tan. Chlorophyll concentration in the ocean is an indication of net primary productivity. Values range from 0.01 milligrams of chlorophyll per square meter (dark blue color) to 50 mg/m² (yellow). Chlorophyll is generally greatest in areas where phytoplankton is most concentrated, such as in the cold, productive waters of the Arctic and Antarctic, and along coastlines where upwelling brings nutrients to the surface. In the center of ocean basins, away from the continental shelves, productivity is generally low. Data were collected by NOAA satellites and the SeaWiFS satellite.

The Hydrologic Cycle

The most abundant single substance in the biosphere, by far, is water. As we learned in Chapter 9, the movement of water from one sphere to another is called the *hydrologic cycle* (see Figure 9-2). There are two ways in which water is found in the biosphere as part of the hydrologic cycle: (1) *in residence*, with its hydrogen chemically bound into plant and animal tissues; and (2) *in transit*, as part of the transpiration-respiration stream in which water moves back and forth between the environment and living organisms.

All living things require water to carry out their life processes. Water is the medium of life processes and the source of their hydrogen. Watery solutions dissolve nutrients and carry them to all parts of an organism. Through chemical reactions that take place in a watery solution, the organism converts nutrients to energy or to materials it needs to grow or to repair itself. In addition, the organism needs water to carry away waste products.

Most organisms contain considerably more water in their mass than anything else, as Table 10-1 shows. Every living thing depends on keeping its water supply within a narrow range. For example, humans can survive without food for two months or more, but they can live without water for only about a week.

TABLE 10-1	Water Content in Some Plants and Animals	
Organism	**Percentage Water in Body Mass**	
Human	65	
Elephant	70	
Earthworm	80	
Ear of corn	70	
Tomato	95	

The Carbon Cycle

Carbon is one of the basic elements of life and a part of all living things. The biosphere contains a complex mixture of carbon compounds, more than half a million in total. These compounds are in continuous states of creation, transformation, and decomposition.

The main processes of the **carbon cycle** entail the transfer of carbon from carbon dioxide to living matter and then back again to carbon dioxide (Figure 10-6). This conversion is initiated when carbon dioxide from the atmosphere is photosynthesized into carbohydrate compounds (*assimilation*), as shown in the photosynthesis equation we learned earlier. In turn, respiration by plants and soil returns carbon to the atmosphere in the form of carbon dioxide. You can think of the carbon cycle as a complex of interlocking cycles in which carbon moves constantly from the inorganic reservoir to the living system and back again. A similar cycle takes place in the ocean.

The carbon cycle operates relatively rapidly (the time measured in years or centuries), but only a small proportion (thought to be less than 1 percent) of the total quantity of carbon on or near Earth's surface is part of the cycle at any given moment. The overwhelming bulk of near-surface carbon has been concentrated over millions of years in geologic deposits—such as coal, petroleum, and carbonate rocks—composed of dead organic matter that accumulated mostly on sea bottoms and was subsequently buried. Carbon from this reservoir is normally incorporated into the cycle very gradually, mostly by normal rock weathering.

In the last century and a half, however, humans have added considerable carbon dioxide to the atmosphere by extracting and burning fossil fuels (coal, oil, natural gas) containing carbon fixed by photosynthesis many millions of years ago. This rapid acceleration of the rate at which

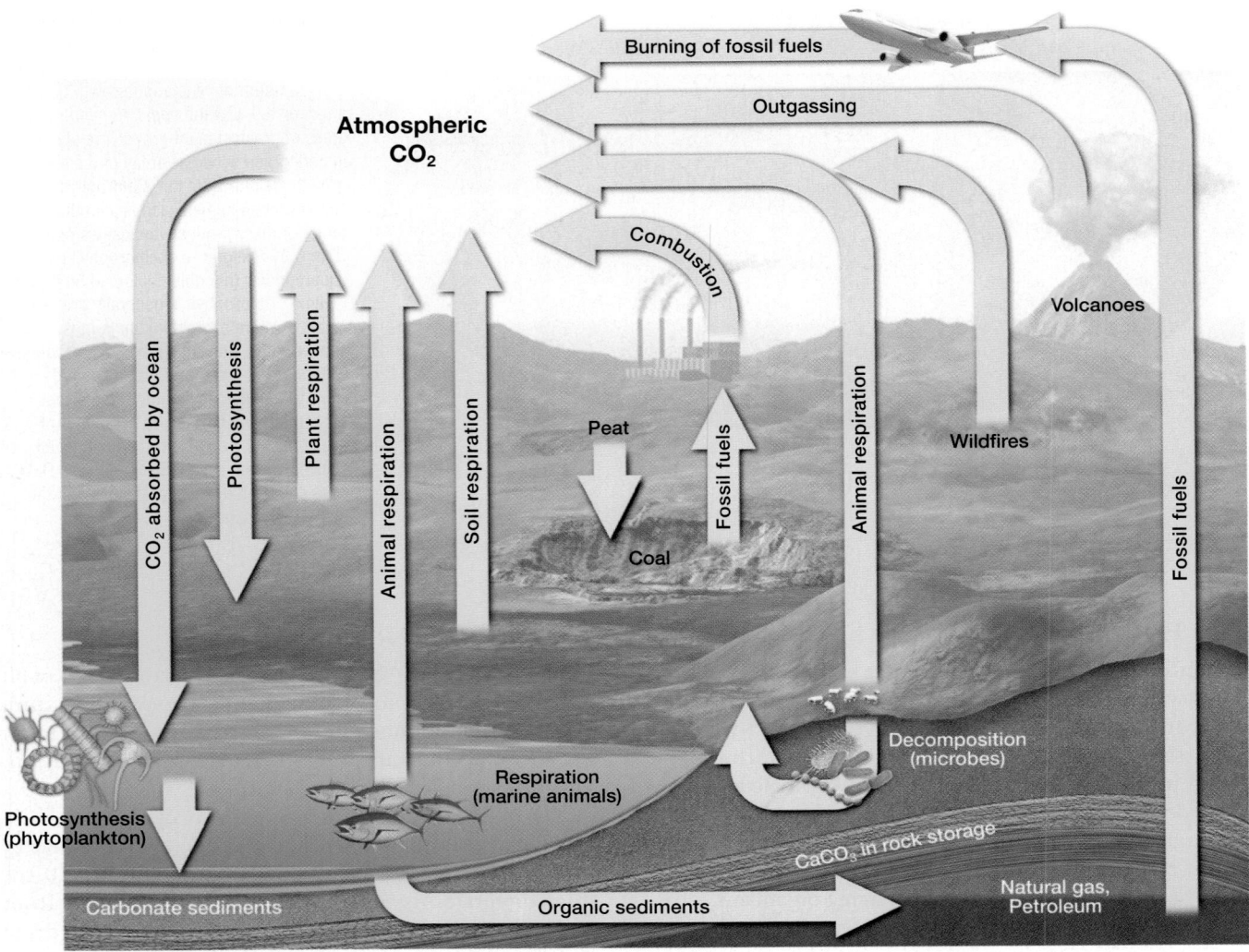

▲ **Figure 10-6** The carbon cycle. Carbon from the carbon dioxide in the atmosphere is used by plants to make the carbon-containing sugars formed during photosynthesis. Some organic compounds are stored in rocks or petroleum. Over time, these compounds are eventually again converted to carbon dioxide and returned to the atmosphere. The arrows represent pathways but do not reflect the relative amounts of carbon moving along any one pathway.

carbon is freed and converted to carbon dioxide is likely to have far-reaching effects on both the biosphere and atmosphere. For example, global warming from increasing concentrations of carbon dioxide in the atmosphere may lead to changes in the natural distribution patterns of both plants and animals.

Learning Check 10-3   **Over long periods of time, how can a molecule of carbon dioxide move from the atmosphere to the biosphere to the lithosphere and back again to the atmosphere?**

The Oxygen Cycle

Oxygen is a building block in most organic molecules and consequently makes up a significant proportion of the atoms in living matter. As part of the **oxygen cycle**, oxygen

released into the atmosphere through photosynthesis can be taken up by living organisms in respiration or react chemically with rocks. However the oxygen cycle (Figure 10-7) is extremely complicated and is summarized only briefly here.

Oxygen occurs in many chemical forms and is released into the atmosphere in a variety of ways. Most of the oxygen in the atmosphere is molecular oxygen (O_2) produced when plants decompose water molecules in photosynthesis. Some atmospheric oxygen is bound up in water molecules that came from evaporation or plant transpiration, and some is bound up in the carbon dioxide released during animal respiration. Much of this carbon dioxide and water is eventually recycled through the biosphere via photosynthesis.

Other sources of oxygen for the oxygen cycle include atmospheric ozone, oxygen involved in the oxidative weathering of rocks, oxygen stored in and sometimes released from carbonate rocks, and various other processes, including some (such as the burning of fossil fuels,

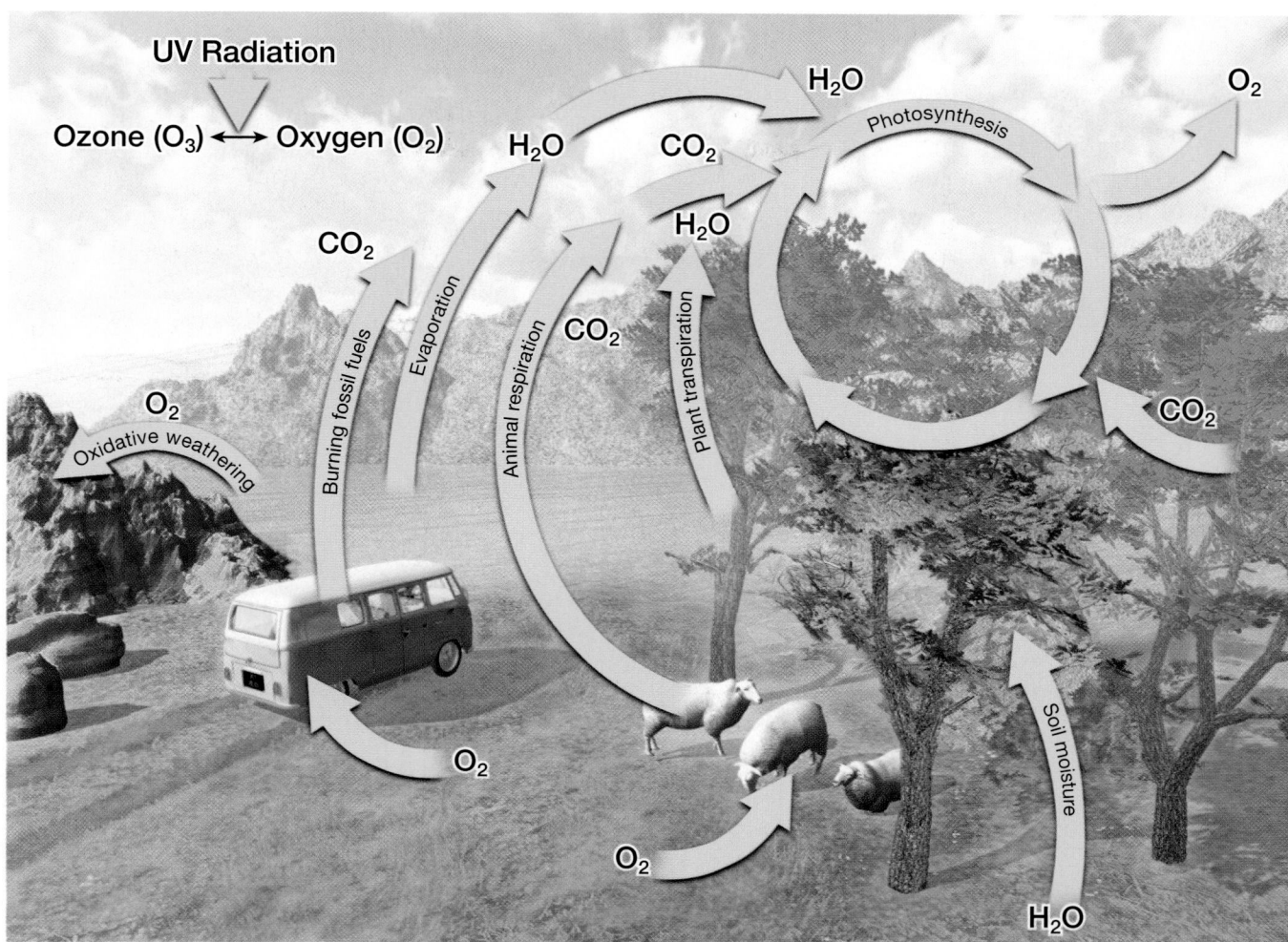

▲ **Figure 10-7** The oxygen cycle. Molecular oxygen is essential for almost all forms of life. It is made available to the air through a variety of processes such as photosynthesis, and is recycled in a variety of ways. The arrows represent pathways but do not reflect the relative amounts of oxygen moving along any one pathway.

in which oxygen is combined with carbon in carbon dioxide) that are human induced.

Although our atmosphere is now rich in oxygen, it was not always so. Earth's earliest atmosphere was oxygen poor; indeed, in the early days of life on this planet, about 3.4 billion years ago, oxygen was poisonous to living cells. Evolving life had to develop mechanisms to neutralize or, better still, exploit its poisonous presence. This exploitation was so successful that most life now cannot function without oxygen. The oxygen now in the atmosphere is largely a byproduct of plant life, as the equation for photosynthesis shows. Thus, once life could sustain itself in the presence of high amounts of oxygen in the air, primitive plants made possible the evolution of higher plants and animals by providing molecular oxygen for their metabolism.

The Nitrogen Cycle

Although nitrogen gas (N_2) is an apparently inexhaustible component of the atmosphere (air is about 78 percent N_2),

only a limited number of organisms can use this essential nutrient in its gaseous form. The movement of nitrogen in and out of the biosphere—from forms of nitrogen that can be used by organisms, and then back again to forms that cannot—is called the **nitrogen cycle**.

For the vast majority of living organisms, atmospheric nitrogen is usable only after it has been converted to nitrogen compounds (*nitrates*) that can be used by plants (Figure 10-8). This conversion process is called **nitrogen fixation**. Some nitrogen is fixed in the atmosphere by lightning and cosmic radiation, and some is fixed in the ocean by marine organisms, but the amount involved in these processes is modest. It is nitrogen-fixing bacteria living in the soil and associated plant root nodules that provides most of the usable nitrogen for Earth's biosphere.

Once atmospheric nitrogen has been fixed into an available form (nitrates), it is assimilated by green plants, some of which are eaten by animals. The animals then excrete nitrogenous wastes in their urine. These wastes, as well as

▲ **Figure 10-8** The nitrogen cycle. Atmospheric nitrogen is fixed into nitrates in various ways, and the nitrates are then assimilated by green plants, some of which are eaten by animals. Dead plant and animal materials, as well as animal wastes, contain various nitrogen compounds, and these compounds are acted on by bacteria so that nitrites are produced. The nitrites are then converted by other bacteria to nitrates, and thus the cycle continues. Still other bacteria denitrify some of the nitrates, releasing free nitrogen into the air again. The arrows represent pathways but do not reflect the relative amounts of nitrogen moving along any one pathway.

the dead animal and plant material, are attacked by bacteria, and *nitrite* compounds are released as a further waste product. Other bacteria convert the nitrites to nitrates, making them available again to green plants. Still other bacteria convert some of the nitrates to nitrogen gas in a process called **denitrification**, and the gas becomes part of the atmosphere. This atmospheric nitrogen is then carried by rain back to Earth, where it enters the soil-plant portion of the cycle once more.

Human activities have produced a major modification in the natural nitrogen cycle. The synthetic manufacture of

nitrogenous fertilizers and widespread introduction of nitrogen-fixing crops (such as alfalfa, clover, and soybeans) have significantly changed the balance between fixation and denitrification. The short-term result has been an excessive accumulation of nitrogen compounds in many lakes and streams. This buildup of nitrogen depletes the oxygen supply of the water and upsets the natural balance.

Learning Check 10-4 **How is nitrogen made available to living organisms through the nitrogen cycle?**

Mineral Cycles

Although carbon, oxygen, and nitrogen—along with hydrogen—are the principal chemical components of the biosphere, many minerals are critical nutrients for plants and animals. Most notable among these trace minerals are phosphorus, sulfur, and calcium, but more than a dozen others are occasionally significant.

Some nutrients are cycled along gaseous pathways, which primarily involve an interchange between biota and the atmosphere-ocean environment, as we just saw in the carbon, oxygen, and nitrogen cycles. Other nutrients follow sedimentary pathways, which involve interchange between biota and the Earth–ocean environment. Elements with sedimentary cycles include calcium, phosphorus, sulfur, copper, and zinc.

In a typical sedimentary cycle, the element is weathered from bedrock into the soil. Some of it is then washed downslope with surface runoff or percolated into the groundwater supply. Much of it reaches the ocean, where it may be deposited in the next round of sedimentary rock formation. Some, however, is ingested by aquatic organisms and later released into the cycle again through waste products and dead organisms.

In general, the amounts of biotic nutrients available on Earth are finite. These nutrients move over and over through cycles that are extremely variable from place to place; increasingly, some of these cycles have either been damaged or modified by human interference.

FOOD CHAINS

The unending flows of energy, water, and nutrients through the biosphere are channeled in significant part by direct passage from one organism to another in pathways referred to as *food chains*. A **food chain** is a simple concept, as Figure 10-9 shows: Organism A is eaten by Organism B, which thereby absorbs A's energy and nutrients; Organism B is eaten by Organism C, with similar results; Organism C is eaten by D; and so on.

In nature, however, the matter of who eats whom may be extraordinarily complex, with a bewildering number of interlaced strands. Therefore, *chain* probably is a misleading word in this context because it implies an orderly linkage of equivalent units. It is more accurate to think of this energy transfer process as a "web" with interconnected parts or links. Each link acts as an energy transformer that ingests some of the energy of the preceding link, uses some of that energy for its own sustenance, and then passes some of the balance on to the next link.

The fundamental units in any food chain are the **producers**—the *autotrophs*, or "self-feeders"—in other words, plants. Plants fix carbon and effectively store solar energy through photosynthesis. The plants may then be eaten by the **consumers**, or *heterotrophs*. Plant-eating animals are called *herbivores* (*herba* is Latin for "plant"; *vorare*, "to devour"), and are referred to as **primary**

▲ **Figure 10-9** A simple food chain.

consumers. The herbivores then become food for other animals, *carnivores* (*carne*, is Latin for "meat"), and are referred to as **secondary consumers** or *predators*. There may be many levels of secondary consumers in a food chain, as Figure 10-9 shows.

Food Pyramids

A food chain can also be conceptualized as a **food pyramid** because the number of energy-storing organisms is much, much larger than the number of primary consumers; the number of primary consumers is larger than the number of secondary consumers; and so on up the pyramid (Figure 10-10). There are usually several levels of carnivorous secondary consumers, each succeeding level consisting of fewer and usually larger animals. The final consumers at the top of the pyramid are usually the largest and most powerful predators in the area (Figure 10-11). We say that organisms share the same *trophic level* when they consume the same general types of food in a food pyramid.

The consumers at the apex of the pyramid do not constitute the final link in the food chain, however. When

▲ **Figure 10-11** A lynx about to pounce on a snowshoe hare in a Montana forest.

they die, they are fed on by scavenging animals and by tiny (mostly microscopic) organisms that function as **decomposers**, returning the nutrients to the soil to be recycled into yet another food pyramid.

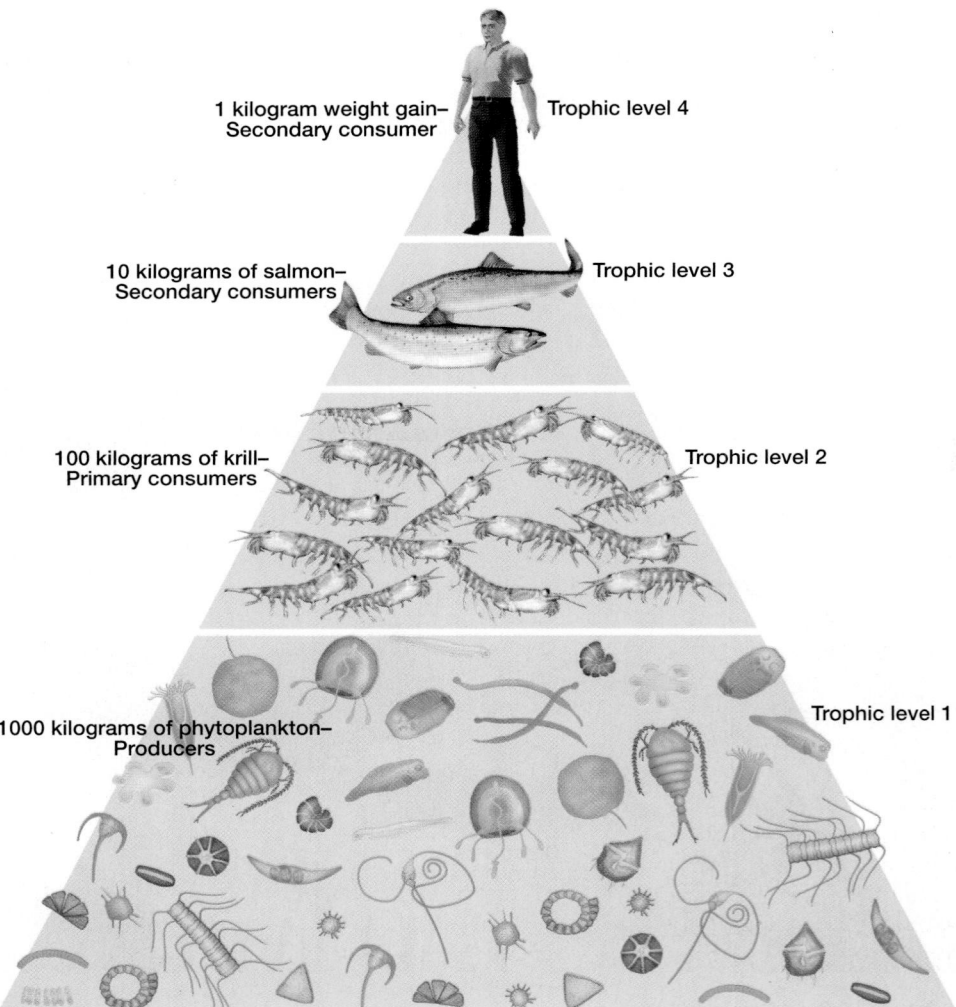

1 kilogram weight gain–
Secondary consumer — Trophic level 4

10 kilograms of salmon–
Secondary consumers — Trophic level 3

100 kilograms of krill–
Primary consumers — Trophic level 2

Trophic level 1

1000 kilograms of phytoplankton–
Producers

▶ **Figure 10-10** A food pyramid. It takes 1000 kilograms (about 1 ton) of phytoplankton (microscopic marine plants) to provide a 1-kilogram (2-pound) weight gain for a human. Notice that only about 10 percent of the stored energy in one tropic level is eventually passed on to the next tropic level.

So why are so many producers needed to support so few top predators in a food pyramid? The answer has to do with the relative inefficiency with which stored energy is transferred from one trophic level to the next. When a primary consumer eats a plant, perhaps only 10 percent of the total energy stored in the plant can be effectively stored by that primary consumer. In turn, when a secondary consumer eats the primary consumer, there is further energy transfer inefficiency. In short, only a portion of the stored energy is transferred from the organisms of one trophic level to those in the next trophic level. (In terms of human diet and food supply, this is why it is much more energy efficient to feed a population directly with grains than with meat from grain-fed animals.)

> **Learning Check 10-5**   **Why does the amount of biomass change at each trophic level of a food pyramid?**

Pollutants in the Food Chain

Although stored energy is not efficiently passed on from one organism to the next in a food chain, some chemical pollutants can be. An increasing concern is evidence that some chemical pollutants can become concentrated within a food chain—a process referred to as *biomagnification*. For example, although some chemical pesticides released into the air, water, or soil degrade relatively quickly into harmless substances, others, such as DDT (dichlorodiphenyltrichloroethane), are quite stable and may become concentrated in the fatty tissues of organisms at higher levels of a food chain. The concentration of chemical pesticides, as well as the concentration of some heavy metals such as mercury and lead, have resulted in harmful effects and even death in the animal (and human) consumers at the top of the food chain (Figure 10-12).

A somewhat similar but unanticipated problem was discovered in 1982 at the Kesterson National Wildlife Refuge amid the farmland of California's southern Central Valley. This artificial wetlands area was created by using runoff from local agricultural irrigation. Minute quantities of natural selenium dissolved in the irrigation water ended up being concentrated through evaporation in the water entering the Wildlife Refuge, resulting in deformities and high mortality for waterfowl using the wetlands. This discovery at Kesterson prompted the U.S. Department of the Interior to create the National Irrigation Water Quality Program to reduce the likelihood of similar problems elsewhere.

The major oil spill in the Gulf of Mexico following the *Deepwater Horizon* accident in 2010 not only resulted in an immediate loss of marine life and birds, but will likely have long-term consequences through the effects of the oil and the chemical dispersants in the food chain—see the box, "People and the Environment: The 2010 Deepwater Horizon Oil Spill."

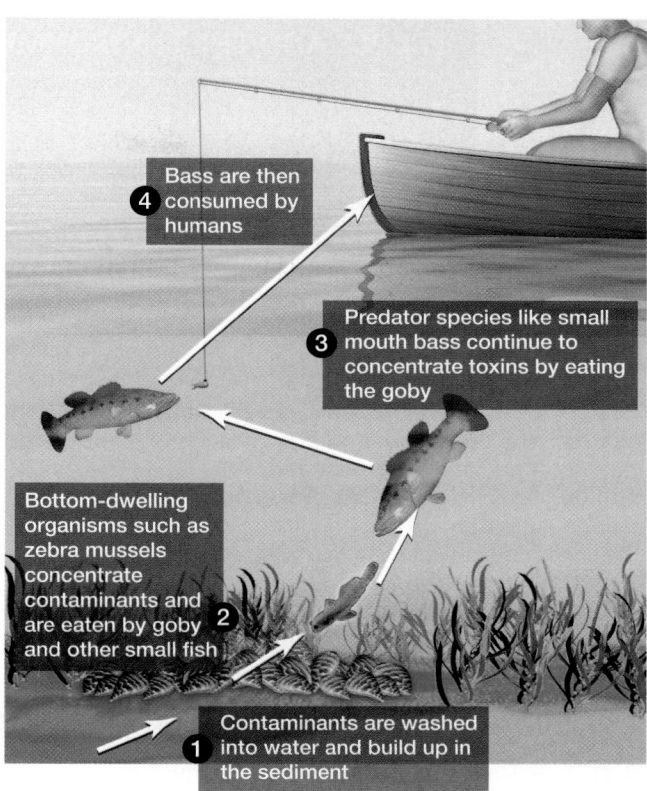

▲ **Figure 10-12** Biomagnification. Toxins such as mercury or some pesticides are washed into a body of water and build up in the sediments. Bottom-dwelling organisms, which are primary consumers, concentrate the toxins in their bodies and are eaten by secondary consumers such as small fish that further concentrate the toxins. Small fish are in turn eaten by larger fish and eventually by humans.

BIOLOGICAL FACTORS AND NATURAL DISTRIBUTIONS
FG10, FG13

The study of biogeochemical cycles and food chains shows how the biosphere is part of the flow of materials through Earth systems. But the most basic studies of organisms by geographers are usually concerned with distribution. Biogeography is concerned with such questions as, "What is the range of a certain species or group of plants/animals?" "What are the reasons behind this distribution pattern?" and "What is the significance of the distribution?"

Here we begin our discussion of factors influencing distribution patterns in the biosphere at the most fundamental level. The natural distribution of any species or group of organisms is determined by several primarily biological factors: evolutionary development, migration and dispersal, reproductive success, population die-off and extinction, and succession.

Evolutionary Development

The Darwinian theory of natural selection, sometimes simplistically referred to as "survival of the fittest," explains the origin of any species as a normal process of descent, with modification, from parent forms. The progeny best

PEOPLE AND THE ENVIRONMENT

The 2010 Deepwater Horizon Oil Spill

▶ Matthew T. Huber, Department of Geography, Syracuse University

On April 20, 2010, an explosion on the Deepwater Horizon drilling platform in the Gulf of Mexico resulted in the worst maritime oil spill in U.S. history (Figure 10-C). The blowout and explosion killed 11 oil workers and injured 17. By the time the damaged wellhead on the ocean floor was capped three months later, approximately 4.9 million barrels (775 million liters; 205 million gallons) of oil were spilled into the environment (Figure 10-D).

Unconventional Oil: The crippled well in the Macondo Prospect far offshore

▲ **Figure 10-C** Fire on the Deepwater Horizon drilling platform in the Gulf of Mexico, on April 22, 2010.

▲ **Figure 10-D** Satellite image taken on April 25, 2010, showing the oil slick caused by the ruptured wellhead of the Deepwater Horizon.

in the Gulf of Mexico dramatically illustrates the changing geography of petroleum production. Offshore oil constitutes nearly 24 percent of U.S. and 30 percent of global oil production. As "easy" conventional oil reserves are depleted, oil companies have embarked upon a new frontier of exploration and development in increasingly inhospitable environments. Similar to heavy tar sand oil in Alberta, Canada, or the hydraulic fracturing of shale gas (see Chapter 13), deep-water oil production in the Gulf of Mexico is just one example of a wider boom in unconventional fossil fuel production across the world. The process of extracting oil in water 1500 meters (5000 feet) deep, with a well 4000 meters (13,000 feet) under the seabed requires technology and engineering of utmost complexity, and it creates inevitable challenges for containing spills.

Regulatory Failure: To some observers, such as historian Tyler Priest, the Deepwater Horizon oil spill demonstrates the U.S. government's inability to effectively monitor and enforce environmental and safety procedures for this increasingly complex industry. Now renamed The Bureau of Ocean Energy Management, Regulation, and Enforcement, The Minerals Management Service was charged with regulating the offshore oil industry. In 2010, the MMS had only 55 inspectors in charge of 3500 production platforms and 90 drilling vessels. The lack of oversight was evident after the spill when it became clear that not only did British Petroleum (BP) have no idea how to contain a blowout in deepwater, neither did anyone in the U.S. government.

Environmental Justice and the Ecology of Oil Spills: The Deepwater Horizon oil spill represented the latest in a series of struggles between communities on the U.S. Gulf Coast and the oil complex of refineries, chemical plants, and oil production platforms concentrated in the region. The term "environmental justice" is used by some analysts when referring to the disproportional exposure of low-income people and communities of color to environmental toxins and pollution.

Contamination from the oil spill devastated the local fishing industry that relies on Gulf Coast wetlands for marine life such as shrimp. In addition, many cleanup workers were not only exposed to the toxic residues of the oil itself, but also to chemical oil dispersants that BP and the Environmental Protection Agency (EPA) said were necessary in the cleanup. Some observers believe that the extensive use of chemical dispersants was a public relations strategy to disperse the visible and extensive oil sheen from the surface of the Gulf into the water below.

Apart from human exposure, the spilled oil floating on the surface of the water—and the large plume of oil that remained out of sight below the surface—had dramatic impacts on Gulf Coast animal and marine life. Most visible were oil-soaked birds and beached dolphins, but it is likely that the most extensive and long-lasting effects of the spill will be the circulation of oil and chemical pollution through marine food webs. Moving forward, it is unclear whether much has been learned from the spill. The U.S. is still by far the largest consumer of oil in the world, and, after a brief drilling moratorium, the Obama administration has approved new drilling projects in the gulf (in addition to the highly inhospitable and increasingly melted waters of the Arctic)

◀ **Figure 10-13** Hundreds of species of acacias grow in semiarid and subhumid portions of the tropics. This scene from central Kenya shows acacias in tree form, although lower shrub forms are more common.

adapted to the struggle for existence survive to produce viable offspring, whereas those less well adapted perish. This long, slow, and essentially endless process accounts for the development of all organisms.

To understand the distribution of any species or *genus* (a closely related group of organisms), therefore, we begin with a consideration of where those species evolved. For example, consider the contrast in apparent origin of two important groups of plants—*acacias* and *eucalyptus* (Figures 10-13 and 10-14). Acacias are an extensive genus of shrubs and low-growing trees represented by numerous species found in low-latitude portions of every continent that extends into the tropics or subtropics. Eucalyptus, on the other hand, is a genus of trees native only to Australia and a few adjacent islands. Acacias apparently evolved prior to the separation of the continents and are now present throughout the Southern Hemisphere, whereas the genus Eucalyptus evolved after the Australian continent was isolated and only occurs naturally in Australia. (We will discuss the changing locations of the continents over

◀ **Figure 10-14** The original forests of Australia were composed almost entirely of species of eucalyptus. This scene is near Kalgoorlie, Western Australia.

geologic time when we introduce the theory of plate tectonics in Chapter 14.)

Migration and Dispersal

Throughout the millennia of Earth's history, organisms have always moved from one place to another. Animals possess active mechanisms for locomotion—legs, wings, fins, and so on—and their possibilities for migration are obvious. Plants are also mobile, however. Although most individual plants become rooted and therefore fixed in location for most of their life, there is much opportunity for passive migration, particularly in the seed stage. Wind, water, and animals are the principal natural mechanisms of seed dispersal.

The contemporary distribution pattern of many organisms is often the result of natural migration or dispersal from an original center of development. Among thousands of examples that could be used to illustrate this process are the following:

Coconut Palms: The coconut palm (*Cocos nucifera*) is believed to have originated in southeastern Asia and adjacent Melanesian islands. It is now extraordinarily widespread along the coasts of tropical continents and islands all over the world. Most of this dispersal apparently has come about because coconuts, the large hard-shelled seeds of the plant, can float in the ocean for months or years without losing their fertility. Thus, they wash up on beaches throughout the world and colonize successfully if environmental conditions are right (Figure 10-15). This natural dispersion

▲ **Figure 10-15** Coconuts have a worldwide distribution in tropical coastal areas, in part because the nut can float long distances and then take root if it finds a favorable environment. This sprouting example is from the island of Vanua Levu in Fiji.

was significantly augmented by human help in the Atlantic region, particularly by the deliberate transport of coconuts from the Indian and Pacific Ocean areas to the West Indies.

Cattle Egrets: The cattle egret (*Bubulcus ibis*) apparently originated in southern Asia, but during the last few centuries has spread to other warm areas of the world, particularly Africa (Figure 10-16). In recent decades, a change in land use in South America has caused a dramatic expansion in the cattle egret's range. At least as early as the nineteenth century, some cattle egrets crossed the Atlantic from West Africa to Brazil, but they were unable to find suitable ecological conditions and thus did not become established. The twentieth-century introduction of extensive cattle raising in tropical South America apparently provided the missing ingredient, and egrets quickly adapted to the newly suitable habitat. Their descendants spread northward throughout the subtropics and are now common inhabitants of the Gulf coastal plain in the southeastern United States, are well-established in California, and occur as far north as southeastern Canada. Also within the twentieth century, cattle egrets dispersed at the other end of their "normal" range to enter northern Australia and spread across that continent.

Learning Check 10-6 **What factors account for the distribution of acacias and cattle egrets?**

Reproductive Success

A key factor in the continued survival of any biotic population is reproductive success. Poor reproductive success can come about for a number of reasons—heavy predation (a fox eats quail eggs from a nest); climatic change (heavy-furred animals perishing in a climate that was once cold but has warmed up for some reason or other); failure of food supply (a string of unusually cold winters keeps plants from setting seed); and so on.

Changing environmental conditions are also likely to favor one group over another, as when warming waters on the fringes of the Arctic Ocean allowed cod to expand their range at the expense of several other types of fishes. Thus, reproductive success is usually the limiting factor that allows one competing population to flourish while another languishes (Figure 10-17).

Population Die-off and Extinction

The range of a species can be diminished by the dying out of some or all of the population. The history of the biosphere is replete with examples of such range diminution, varying from minor adjustments in a small area to extinction over the entire planet. Evolution is a continuing process. No species is likely to be a permanent inhabitant of Earth, and during the period of its ascendancy there is apt to be a great deal of distributional variation within a species, part of which is caused by local die-offs.

Extinction means a species is extinct over the entire world, eliminated forever from the landscape. Extinction has taken place many times in Earth's history. Indeed, it is

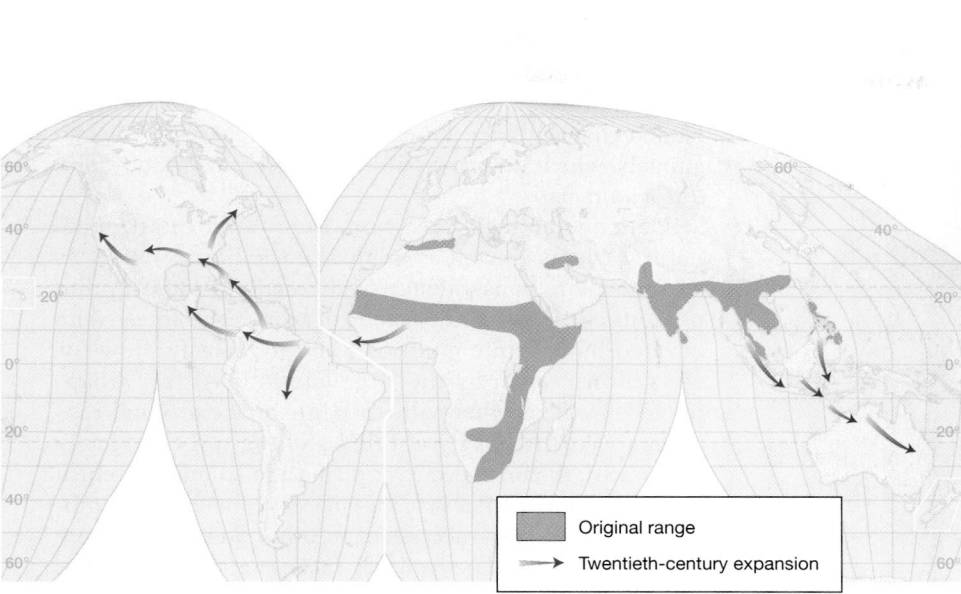

Original range

Twentieth-century expansion

▲ **Figure 10-16** Natural dispersal of an organism. **(a)** During the twentieth century, cattle egrets expanded from their Asian–African range into new habitats in the Americas and Australia. **(b)** Cattle egrets have found a happy home among the cattle herds of Texas.

estimated that half a billion species have become extinct during the several-billion-year life of our planet. Probably the most dramatic example is the disappearance of the dinosaurs about 65 million years ago. For many millions of years, those gigantic reptiles were the dominant terrestrial life-forms of our planet, and yet in a relatively short period of geologic time they were all wiped out. The reasons behind their extermination are imperfectly understood (evidently due in part to the environmental changes associated with massive volcanic eruptions of flood basalt and a catastrophic asteroid impact), but the fact remains that there have been innumerable such natural extinctions of entire species in the history of the world.

As we will discuss in Chapter 11, human activities are currently leading to the extinctions of plant and animal species at an alarming rate, primarily through the destruction of natural habitat.

Plant Succession  FG5, FG12

One of the simplest and most localized examples of species change over time is **plant succession**, in which one type of vegetation is replaced naturally by another. Plant succession is a normal occurrence in a host of situations; a very common one involves the infilling of a lake (Figure 10-18). As the lake gradually fills with sediments and organic debris,

◄ **Figure 10-17** Once nearly exterminated, American bison now occur in large numbers in areas of suitable habitat, as here in Elk Island National Park, Alberta, Canada. Under natural conditions they have a high level of reproductive success.

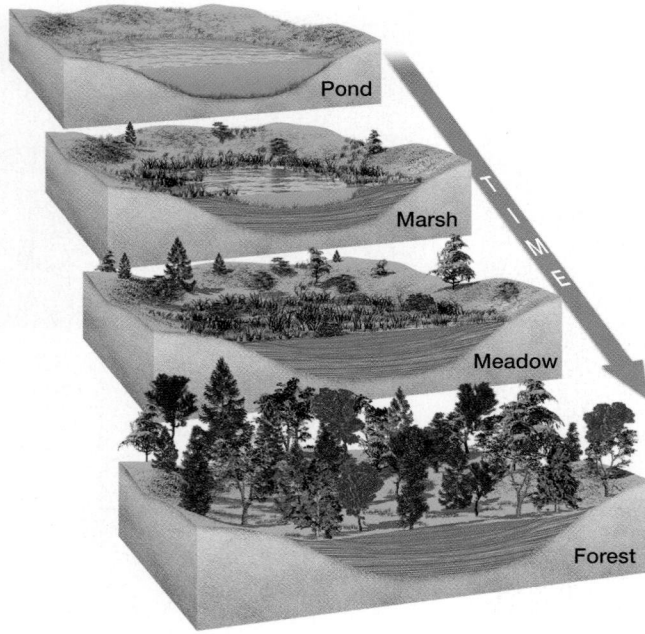

▲ **Figure 10-18** A simple example of plant succession: infilling of a small lake with sediment and organic material. Over time, successional colonization by different kinds of plants changes the area from pond to marsh to meadow to forest.

the aquatic plants at the bottom are slowly choked out while the sedges, reeds, and mosses of the shallow edge waters become more numerous and extensive. Continued infilling further diminishes the aquatic habitat and allows for the increasing encroachment of low-growing land plants such as grasses and shrubs. As the process continues, trees move in to colonize the site, replacing the grasses and shrubs and completing the transition from lake to marsh to meadow to forest.

A similar series of local animal replacements would accompany the plant succession because of the significant habitat changes. Lake animals would be replaced by marsh animals, which in turn would be replaced by meadow and forest animals.

Plant and animal succession occurs after catastrophic natural events as well as gradual ones. For example, as an immediate consequence of the major 1980 eruption of Mount St. Helens, thousands of hectares of forest were covered by volcanic mudflows and pyroclastic flows or were blown down by the large lateral blast (see Chapter 14). In areas where all remnants of the original ecosystem were effectively covered and the soil completely obliterated, the first species of plants and animals to return comprised what is known as a *pioneer community* in a process called *primary succession*. In other areas—and more common in general—*secondary succession* is taking place, in which remnants of the original plant communities and soil become the starting point for a succession sequence (Figure 10-19).

Plant succession is not to be confused with true extinction. Extinction is permanent, but species succession is not. Although a particular plant species may not be growing at a given time in a given location, it may reappear quickly if environmental conditions change and if there is an available seed source.

Learning Check 10-7 **Explain the long-term process of plant succession in an infilling lake.**

◀ **Figure 10-19** The lateral blast from the 1980 eruption of Mount St. Helens in Washington flattened trees many kilometers from the volcano. In this photograph taken 17 years after the eruption, the dead trees are still visible, but a cover of new vegetation has been clearly established.

ENVIRONMENTAL FACTORS

The survival of plants and animals depends on a set of environmental factors, including light, moisture, temperature, wind, soil, topography, and wildfire. The specific influence of these factors, of course, varies from species to species.

Environmental factors can be discussed at various scales of generalization. For example, if we are considering global or continental patterns of biotic distribution, we are concerned primarily with gross generalizations that deal with average conditions, seasonal characteristics, latitudinal extent, zonal winds, and other broad-scale factors. If our interest is instead a small area, such as an individual valley or a single hillside, we are more concerned with such localized environmental factors as degree of slope, direction of exposure, and permeability of topsoil.

Whatever the scale, there are nearly always exceptions to the generalizations, and the larger the area, the more numerous the exceptions. Thus, in a region that is generally humid, there are probably many localized sites that are dry, such as cliffs or sand dunes. In even a very dry desert, there are likely to be several places that are always damp, such as an oasis or a spring.

Limiting Factors: Throughout the following discussion of environmental factors, keep in mind that both *intraspecific competition* (among members of the same species) and *interspecific competition* (among members of different species) are at work. Both plants and animals compete with one another as they seek light, water, nutrients, and shelter in a dynamic environment. The term **limiting factor** is often used to describe the variable that is most important in determining the survival of an organism.

Human activities sometimes may be a factor in encouraging a species—see the box, "Focus: Bark Beetle Killing Forests in Western North America."

The Influence of Climate

At almost any scale, the most prominent environmental constraints on biota are exerted by various climatic factors.

Light: No green plant can survive without light. We have already discussed the basic process—photosynthesis—whereby plants produce stored chemical energy; this process is activated by light. It is essentially for this reason that photosynthetic vegetation is absent from deeper ocean areas, where light does not penetrate.

Light can have a significant effect on plant shape, as Figure 10-20 shows. In places where the amount of light is restricted, such as in a dense forest, trees are likely to be very tall but have limited lateral growth. In areas that have less dense vegetation, more light is available, and as a result trees are likely to be expansive in lateral spread but truncated vertically.

Another important light relationship involves how much light an organism receives during any 24-hour period. This relationship is called **photoperiodism**. Except

▲ **Figure 10-20** In an open stand (left), there is abundant light all around the tree and it responds by broad lateral growth rather than vertical growth. Under crowded conditions (right), less light reaches the tree and it elongates upward rather than spreading laterally.

in the immediate vicinity of the equator, the seasonal variation in the photoperiod becomes greater with increasing latitude. Fluctuation in the photoperiod stimulates seasonal behavior—such as flowering, leaf fall, mating, and migration—in both plants and animals.

Moisture: The broad distribution patterns of the biota are governed more significantly by the availability of moisture than by any other single environmental factor besides light. A prominent trend throughout biotic evolution has been the adaptation of plants and animals to either excesses or deficiencies in moisture availability (Figure 10-21).

Temperature: The temperature of the air and the soil is also important to biotic distribution patterns. Fewer species of both plants and animals can survive in cold regions than in areas of more moderate temperatures. Plants, in particular, have a limited tolerance for low temperatures because they are continuously exposed to the weather, and they experience tissue damage and other physical disruption when their cellular water freezes. Animals in some instances are able to avoid the bitterest cold by moving to seek shelter. Even so, the cold-weather areas of high latitudes and high elevations have a limited variety of animals and plants.

Wind: The influence of wind on biotic distributions is more limited than that of the other climatic factors. Where winds are persistent, however, they often serve as a constraint. The principal negative effect of wind is that it causes excessive drying by increasing evaporation from exposed surfaces, thus causing a moisture deficiency (Figure 10-22). In cold regions, wind escalates the rate at which animals lose body warmth.

The sheer physical force of wind can also be influential: a strong wind can uproot trees, modify plant forms, and increase the heat intensity of wildfires. On the positive side,

FOCUS

Bark Beetle Killing Forests in Western North America

Across western North America, from Canada to New Mexico, millions of acres of pine forest are dead or dying because of an infestation of the mountain pine beetle (*Dendroctonus ponderosae*). Year by year, and acre by acre, green pine forest is being replaced by expanses of brown dead and dying trees (Figure 10-E). By some estimates, the beetles are affecting more than 6 million acres of forest in the United States, and perhaps 34 million acres in British Columbia—and growing rapidly (Figure 10-F). It may well be the largest insect infestation in North American during historic times.

The black mountain pine beetle is about the size of a fingertip. It drills into the wood to lay its eggs, and then injects a fungus that stops the tree from excreting sap—which would kill the beetle larvae. The fungus causes a stain that turns the wood blue. The tree responds to the beetle holes by emitting a waxy resin that can plug the holes and kill the beetles, but usually a tree is ultimately overwhelmed as more beetles arrive and drill still more holes.

Causes of Infestation:
This extensive mountain pine beetle infestation probably has several causes. First, fire suppression over the last century

Mountain pine beetle

Radial Mountain

Radial Mountain

Aftermath of beetle infestation

Before beetle infestation

◀ **Figure 10-F** Landsat satellite images of the area near Grand Lake, Colorado, showing the expansion of the mountain pine beetle infestation (brown areas) from September 2005 to September 2011.

prevented large sections of the western forests—especially the expanses of lodgepole pines—from burning on a regular basis. This means that a large proportion of the trees are just about the same age—old enough to be susceptible to the bark beetle (younger trees are generally not targeted by the beetles). Second, extended drought over the last decade or so has weakened many of the trees, making them more susceptible to the beetle. Finally, climate change in western North America is bringing less frequent severely cold winters, allowing the beetle to extend its range. Today, the absolute winter low temperatures are about 3.5 to 5.5°C (6 to 10°F) higher than 50 years ago. With fewer extremely cold days in winter, more beetle larvae are surviving.

Consequences of Infestation:
All of the consequences of bark beetle infestation are not yet known. Resort towns in the Rocky Mountains are worried about the loss of tourism in areas where forests are dying. Another concern is the threat of rapidly moving "crown fires" that can jump from tree to tree; once many of the needles in a dying tree have dropped to the ground that hazard is greatly reduced. Once the trees die or have burned, nearby watersheds may be

more susceptible to flash floods and debris flows. Finally, falling dead trees are becoming a problem along highways; as such, large strips are being clear cut along highways to prevent closure by tree blow-downs from storms.

Although the mountain pine beetle infestation is seen as an environmental disaster by many, some scientists see things somewhat differently. The mountain pine beetle is not an exotic species. Rather, it is a native insect that has been around for thousands of years, playing its role in western pine forest ecosystems. Lodgepole pines are well adapted to major stand replacement events during which large expanses of old forest are killed by some event such as a fire—or in this case, an insect infestation. The forest then quickly regenerates as nutrients are cycled through the soil; grasses and other low vegetation return first, to be replaced in time by a new forest.

The wild card in this infestation, however, is climate change. With milder winters, there are fewer checks on the beetles and so they are spreading almost as an exotic species would in some places. At the moment, there is nothing to indicate that the infestation will end any time soon, and the prospect of ever larger expanses of dying pine forests is a real one.

▲ **Figure 10-E** Pine forest in Rocky Mountain National Park, Colorado, dying from the infestation of the mountain pine beetle.

◀ **Figure 10-21** Even the most stressful environments often contain distinctive and conspicuous plants, as in this scene from the Sonoran Desert.

▲ **Figure 10-22** Some plants are remarkably adaptable to environmental stress. In this timberline scene from north-central Colorado, there is no question about the prevailing wind direction. Persistent wind from the right has so desiccated this subalpine fir that only branches growing toward the left survive. This preferred growth direction places the trunk of the tree between them and the wind.

wind sometimes aids in the dispersal of biota by carrying pollen, seeds, lightweight organisms, and flying creatures.

Learning Check 10-8 Explain how the climate-related limiting factors of light and wind can influence plant distributions.

Edaphic Influences

Soil characteristics, known as **edaphic factors** (from *edaphos*, Greek for "ground" or "soil"), also influence biotic distributions. These factors are direct and immediate in their effect on flora but usually indirect in their effect on fauna. Soil is a major component of the habitat of any vegetation, of course, and its characteristics significantly affect rooting capabilities and nutrient supply. Especially significant are soil texture, soil structure, humus content, chemical composition, and the relative abundance of soil organisms. Soil is discussed in much greater detail in Chapter 12.

Topographic Influences

In global distribution patterns of plants and animals, general topographic characteristics are the most important factor affecting distribution. For example, the assemblage of plants and animals in a plains region is very different from that in a mountainous region. At a more localized scale, the factors of slope and drainage are likely to be significant, primarily the steepness of the slope, its orientation with regard to sunlight, and the porosity of the soil on the slope.

FG2, FG12

Wildfire

Most environmental factors that affect the distribution of plants and animals are passive, and their influences are slow and gradual. Occasionally, however, abrupt and

◀ **Figure 10-23** Wildfires are commonplace in many parts of the world. This ground fire in the Top End of the Northern Territory of Australia is almost an annual occurrence under natural conditions.

catastrophic events, such as floods, earthquakes, volcanic eruptions, landslides, insect infestations, and droughts, also play a significant role. By far the most important of these is wildfire (Figure 10-23). In almost all portions of the continents, except for the always-wet regions where fire simply cannot start and the always-dry regions where there is an insufficiency of combustible vegetation, uncontrolled natural fires have occurred with surprising frequency. Fires generally result in complete or partial devastation of the plant life and the killing or driving away of all or most of the animals. These results, of course, are only temporary; sooner or later, vegetation sprouts and animals return. At least in the short run, however, the composition of the biota is changed, and if the fires occur with sufficient frequency, the change may be more than temporary.

Wildfire can be very helpful to the seeding or sprouting of certain plants and the maintenance of certain types of forest. For example, the forest fires that burned nearly half of Yellowstone National Park in 1988 triggered the extensive regrowth of understory plants and young trees (Figure 10-24)—the lodgepole pine is especially well adapted to rapid regeneration after "stand-replacement" events such as fire. In some cases, grasslands are sustained by relatively frequent natural fires, which inhibit the encroachment of tree seedlings. Moreover, many plant species, particularly certain trees such as the giant sequoia and the southern yellow pine, scatter their seeds only after the heat of a fire has caused the cones or other types of seedpods to open.

Learning Check 10-9 **How can a wildfire be beneficial to a forest?**

Environmental Correlations: The Example of Selva

One of the most important themes in physical geography is the intertwining relationships of the various components of the environment. Time after time, we note situations in which one aspect of the environment affects another—sometimes conspicuously, sometimes subtly. In terms of broad distribution patterns, climate, vegetation, and soil have a particularly close correlation. Before we discuss some of the details of biogeographical patterns in the following chapter, it may be helpful to provide an example of some of these correlations by examining the distribution of tropical rainforest.

On any map showing the world distribution of major *plant associations* (a grouping of plant species typically found together in a particular environment), one of the conspicuous units is the *selva*, or *tropical rainforest*. A tropical rainforest's plant association consists of many different species of trees and other plants, such as vines and orchids, that grow on the trees.

A vast extent of selva exists in northern South America (primarily within the Amazon River watershed) and central Africa (mostly within the Congo River watershed) with more limited patches in Central America, Colombia, West Africa, Madagascar, Southeast Asia, and northeastern Australia (Figure 10-25).

Climate: A general explanation of the distribution of tropical rainforest is simple. With very limited exceptions, the tropical rainforest occurs wherever relatively abundant precipitation and uniformly warm temperatures occur throughout the year, especially in areas of tropical wet (Af) climate (described in Chapter 8). It is tempting to state that the tropical wet climate "creates" the conditions

(a)

(b)

(c)

◀ **Figure 10-24** Regrowth after the Yellowstone wildfires. (a) Firefighter mopping up some of the last remnants of Yellowstone's fires in 1988. (b) Photograph taken from the same location as (a) five years after the fires showing the regrowth of vegetation on the forest floor. (c) Regrowth near Dunraven Pass 20 years after the fires.

necessary for tropical rainforest, but the cause-and-effect relationship is not that simple—for example, transpiration from the local vegetation is very much a part of the hydrologic cycle in tropical rainforest regions.

Flora: Because of the high temperatures and high humidity, regions with a tropical wet climate are normally covered with natural vegetation that is unexcelled in luxuriance and variety. Tropical rainforest is a broadleaf evergreen forest with numerous tree species. Many of the trees are very tall, and their intertwining tops form an essentially continuous canopy that prohibits sunlight from shining on the forest floor. Often shorter trees form a second and even a third partial canopy at lower elevations. Most of the trees are smooth barked and have no low limbs, although there is a profusion of vines and hanging plants that entangle the trunks and dangle from higher limbs (Figure 10-26). The dimly lit forest floor is relatively clear of growth because lack of sunlight inhibits survival of bushes and shrubs. Where much sunlight reaches the ground, as along the edge of a clearing or banks of a stream, a maze of undergrowth can prosper. This sometimes impenetrable tangle of bushes, shrubs, vines, and small trees is called a *jungle*.

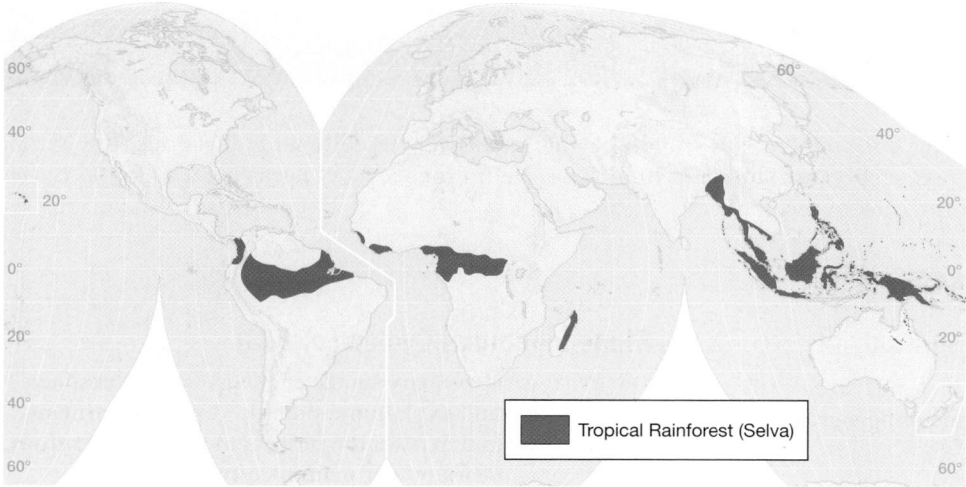

Tropical Rainforest (Selva)

◀ **Figure 10-25** Generalized historical distribution of tropical rainforest, or *selva*.

▲ **Figure 10-26** A tropical rainforest scene in Ecuador.

Fauna: Regions of tropical rainforest are the realm of flyers, crawlers, creepers, and climbers. Larger species, particularly hoofed animals, are not common. Birds and monkeys inhabit the forest canopy often in great quantity and diversity. Snakes and lizards are common both on the forest floor and in the trees. Rodents are sometimes numerous at ground level, but the sparser population of larger mammals is typically secretive and nocturnal. Aquatic life, particularly fish and amphibians, is usually abundant. Invertebrates, especially insects and arthropods, are characteristically superabundant.

Soil: The copious, warm, year-round rains provide an almost continuous infiltration of water downward, with the result that soils are usually deep but highly leached and infertile. Leaves, twigs, flowers, and branches frequently fall from the trees to the ground, where they are rapidly decomposed by the abundant earthworms, ants, bacteria, and microfauna of the soil. The accumulated litter is continuously incorporated into the soil, where some of the nutrients are taken up by plants and the remainder are carried away by the infiltrating water. *Laterization* (rapid weathering of mineral matter and speedy decomposition of organic matter) is the principal soil-forming process; it produces a thin layer of fertile topsoil that is rapidly used by plants and a deep subsoil that is largely an infertile mixture of such insoluble constituents as iron, aluminum, and magnesium compounds. These minerals typically impart a reddish color to the soil. River floodplains tend to develop soils of higher fertility because of flood-time deposition of silt.

Learning Check 10-10   How is it possible for relatively infertile tropical soils to support the huge biomass of a tropical rainforest?

Hydrography: The abundance of runoff water on the surface feeds well-established drainage systems. There is usually a dense network of streams, most of which carry both a great deal of water and a heavy load of sediment. Lakes are not common because there is enough erosion to drain them naturally. Where the land is very flat, swamps sometimes develop through inadequate drainage and the rapid growth of vegetation. In the next chapter, we will explore many other correlations among the patterns in the biosphere, lithosphere, atmosphere, and hydrosphere.

Chapter 10   LEARNING REVIEW

After studying this chapter, you should be able to answer the following questions. Key terms from each text section are shown in **bold type**. Definitions for key terms are also found in the glossary at the back of the book.

KEY TERMS AND CONCEPTS

The Geographic Approach to the Study of Organisms (*p. 282*)

1. Briefly define the following terms: **biogeography**, **biota**, **flora**, **fauna**.
2. What is meant by **biodiversity**?

Biogeochemical Cycles (*p. 283*)

3. What is the primary source of energy for the biosphere?
4. Describe and explain the process of **photosynthesis**.
5. Describe and explain the process of **plant respiration**.
6. What is meant by **net primary productivity**?

7. What is the relationship of **biomass** to net primary productivity?
8. Describe the basic steps in the **carbon cycle**.
9. Briefly describe some of the components of the **oxygen cycle**.
10. Why is it difficult to integrate nitrogen gas from the atmosphere into the **nitrogen cycle** of the biosphere?
11. Explain the differences between **nitrogen fixation** and **denitrification**.

Food Chains (*p. 291*)

12. What is the relationship of a **food chain** to a **food pyramid**?
13. Explain the roles of **producers**, **consumers**, and **decomposers** in the food chain.

14. What is the difference between **primary consumers** and **secondary consumers**?

Biological Factors and Natural Distributions (*p. 293*)

15. Describe one mechanism through which plant seeds can be dispersed over great distances.
16. Explain the concept of **plant succession**.

Environmental Factors (*p. 299*)

17. What is meant by the term **limiting factor**?
18. Explain how both photosynthesis and **photoperiodism** are dependent on sunlight.
19. What is meant by **edaphic factors**?
20. What are the beneficial effects of wildfire?

STUDY QUESTIONS

1. How is solar energy "stored" in the biosphere?
2. Most of the carbon at or near Earth's surface is not involved in any short-term cycling. Explain.
3. What is the primary source of carbon that humans have added to the atmosphere?
4. What is the importance of photosynthesis to the flow of energy, water, oxygen, and carbon through the biosphere?

5. Looking at Figure 10-10, why does it take 1000 kilograms of plankton to produce only 10 kilograms of fish?
6. Explain *biomagnification*.
7. Why are trees in dense forests likely to be tall with narrow tops?

EXERCISES

1. Using the diagram of a food pyramid (Figure 10-10) for reference, estimate the following:
   a. How many kilograms of plankton does it take to produce 25 kilograms of invertebrates? _____ kilograms of plankton
   b. How many kilograms of invertebrates does it take to produce 5 kilograms of fish? _____ kilograms of invertebrates

2. Using the map of tropical rainforest distribution (Figure 10-25), as well as climate maps in Chapter 8, for reference, explain which natural factors likely inhibit the presence of tropical rainforest in:
   a. Equatorial East Africa?
   b. Along the west coast of equatorial South America?

Seeing Geographically

Look again at the photograph of the stream in Walls of Jerusalem National Park at the beginning of the chapter (p. 280). Explain the role of the carbon, nitrogen, and hydrologic cycles in sustaining the forest in the photograph. Which environmental factors are likely most important in supporting the vegetation you see? Why?

MasteringGeography™

Looking for additional review and test prep materials? Visit the Study Area in MasteringGeography™ to enhance your geographic literacy, spatial reasoning skills, and understanding of this chapter's content by accessing a variety of resources, including geoscience animations, MapMaster interactive maps, videos, RSS feeds, flashcards, web links, self-study quizzes, and an eText version of *McKnight's Physical Geography: A Landscape Appreciation*.

HAVING CONSIDERED FUNDAMENTAL PATTERNS AND

processes in the biosphere in the previous chapter, we now turn more specifically to the geographical distribution of plants and animals. Here, the relationships between the biosphere, atmosphere, hydrosphere, and lithosphere are more fully explored.

We begin with some concepts to help us study groups of organisms and then look at the geographical patterns of groups of organisms.

As you study this chapter, think about these key questions:

- **How is a biome different from an ecosystem?**
- **What are some of the major adaptations of plants to local environments?**
- **What are some of the ways animals adapt to harsh environments?**
- **What are Earth's major zoogeographical regions, and what factors help explain the differences in animals among these regions?**
- **What are the characteristics and distribution of Earth's major biomes?**
- **How have humans modified the natural distribution patterns of plants and animals?**

ECOSYSTEMS AND BIOMES

As we first saw in Chapter 10, *biogeography* is the study of the distribution patterns of living organisms and how these patterns change over time, and that in our search for organizing principles to help us comprehend the biosphere, the concepts of *ecosystem* and *biome* are of particular value. We now explore those concepts in greater detail.

Ecosystem: A Concept for All Scales

The term **ecosystem** is a contraction of the phrase *ecological system*. An ecosystem includes all the organisms in a given area, but it is more than simply a community of plants and animals existing together. The ecosystem concept encompasses the totality of interactions among the organisms and between the organisms and the nonliving portion of the environment in the area under consideration. The nonliving portion of the environment includes soil, rocks, water, sunlight, and atmosphere, but it can essentially be considered as nutrients and energy.

An ecosystem, then, is fundamentally an association of plants and animals along with the surrounding nonliving environment and all the interactions in which the organisms take part. The concept is built around the flow of energy among the various components of the ecosystem, which is the essential determinant of how a biological community functions (Figure 11-1).

This functional ecosystem concept is very attractive as an organizing principle for the geographic study of the biosphere. It must be approached with caution, however, because of the various scales at which it can be applied. There is an almost infinite variety in the geographic size of ecosystems we might study. At one extreme of scale, for example, we can conceive of a global ecosystem that encompasses the entire biosphere; at the other end of the scale might be the ecosystem of a fallen log, the underside of a rock, or even a drop of water.

If we are going to identify and understand broad distributional patterns in the biosphere, we must focus only on ecosystems that can be recognized at a useful scale.

Seeing Geographically

Black-browed albatross and chick nest near a sheer cliff on the Falkland Islands in the South Atlantic Ocean. What are the characteristics of the environment in which the albatross nests? Why might an open cliff such as this be a practical nesting area for this bird?

▲ **Figure 11-1** The flow of energy in a simple ecosystem. Energy from the Sun is fixed by the grass during photosynthesis. The grass is then eaten by a rabbit, which is eaten by a hawk, which then dies. The energy originally contained in the photosynthetic products made by the grass passes through stages during which it is bound up in the body molecules of the rabbit and the hawk but ultimately becomes heat energy lost from the live animals and from the decaying dead matter.

Biome: A Scale for All Biogeographers

Among terrestrial ecosystems, the type that provides the most appropriate scale for understanding world distribution patterns is called a **biome**, defined as any large, recognizable assemblage of plants and animals in functional interaction with its environment—in other words, a collection of plants and animals over a large area that have broadly similar adaptations and relationships with the environment and climate. A biome is usually identified and named on the basis of its dominant vegetation, which normally constitutes the bulk of the *biomass* (the total weight of all organisms—plant and animal) in the biome, as well as being the most obvious and conspicuous visible component of the landscape.

There is no universally recognized classification system of the world's terrestrial biomes, but scholars commonly accept 10 major types:

- Tropical rainforest
- Tropical deciduous forest
- Tropical scrub
- Tropical savanna
- Desert
- Mediterranean woodland and shrub
- Midlatitude grassland
- Midlatitude deciduous forest
- Boreal forest
- Tundra (Arctic and alpine)

A biome comprises much more than merely the *plant association*—the grouping of plant species typically found together in a particular environment—that gives it its name. A variety of other kinds of vegetation usually grows among, under, and occasionally over the dominant plants.

Diverse animal species also occupy the area. Often, as we saw in Chapter 10, significant and even predictable relationships exist between the biota (particularly the flora) of a biome and the associated climate and soil types.

On any map showing the major biome types of the world (such as Figure 11-25 later in this chapter), the regional boundaries are somewhat arbitrary. Biomes do not occupy sharply defined areas in nature, no matter how sharp the demarcations may appear on a map. Normally the communities merge more or less imperceptibly with one another through **ecotones**—transition zones of competition in which the typical species of one biome intermingle with those of another (Figure 11-2).

Learning Check 11-1 **What does the name of a biome tell you about the landscapes of that area? (Answer on p. AK-3)**

Before we describe the flora and fauna of the world's terrestrial biomes, we need to say something about plants and animals.

TERRESTRIAL FLORA

The natural vegetation of the land surfaces of Earth is of interest to the geographer for three reasons:

1. Over much of the planet, the terrestrial (land-dwelling) flora is the most significant visual component of the landscape—topography, soils, animal life, and

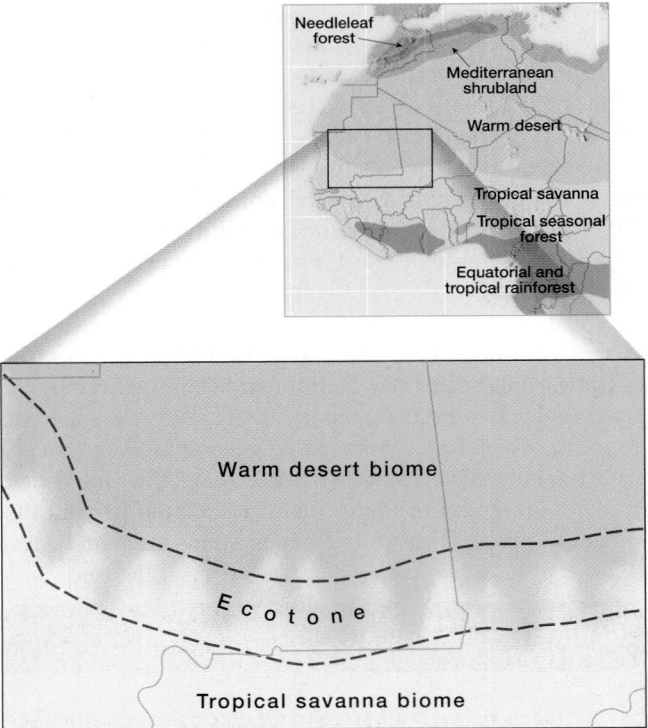

▲ **Figure 11-2** A hypothetical boundary between two biomes of the world. The irregular boundary between the two shows much interfingering, or interdigitation. This transition zone is called an ecotone.

even water surfaces are often obscured or even completely covered by plants. Only in areas of rugged terrain, harsh climate, or significant human activities are plants not likely to dominate the landscape.

2. Vegetation is a sensitive indicator of other environmental attributes, reflecting subtle variations in sunlight, temperature, precipitation, evaporation, drainage, slope, soil conditions, and other natural parameters. Moreover, the influence of vegetation on soil, animal life, and microclimatic characteristics is frequently pervasive.

3. Vegetation often has a prominent and tangible influence on human settlement and activities. In some cases, it is a barrier or hindrance to human endeavor; in other instances, it provides an important resource to be exploited or developed.

Characteristics of Plants

Despite the fragile appearance of many plants, most varieties are remarkably hardy. They survive, and often flourish, in the wettest, driest, hottest, coldest, and windiest places on Earth. Much of their survival potential is based on a subsurface root system that is capable of sustaining life despite whatever may happen to the above-surface portion of the organism.

The survival capability of a species also depends in part on its reproductive mechanism. Plants that endure seasonal climatic fluctuations from year to year are called **perennials**, whereas those that perish during times of climatic stress (such as winter) but leave behind a reservoir of seeds to germinate during the next favorable period are called **annuals**.

Plant life varies remarkably in form, from microscopic algae to gigantic trees. Most plants, however, have common characteristics—roots to gather nutrients and moisture and anchor the plant; stems and/or branches for support and for nutrient transportation from roots to leaves; leaves to absorb and convert solar energy for sustenance and to exchange gases and transpire water; and reproductive organs for regeneration.

> **Learning Check 11-2** **Explain the difference between an *annual* plant and a *perennial* plant.**

Floristic Terminology

To continue our consideration of plants, we need a specialized vocabulary.

First of all, plants can be divided into two categories: those that reproduce through *spores* and those that reproduce through *seeds*. Plants that reproduce through spores include two major groups:

1. *Bryophytes* include the true mosses, peat mosses, and liverworts. Presumably they have never in geologic history been very dominant among plant communities, except in localized situations.

2. *Pteridophytes* are ferns, horsetails, and club mosses (which are not true mosses). During much of geologic history, great forests of tree ferns, giant horsetails, and tall club mosses dominated continental vegetation, but they are less dominant today.

Plants that reproduce by means of seeds are encompassed in two broad groups:

1. The more primitive of the two groups, the **gymnosperms** ("naked seeds"), carry their seeds in cones, and when the cones open, the seeds fall out. For this reason, gymnosperms are sometimes called **conifers**. Gymnosperms were largely dominant in the geologic past; today the only large surviving gymnosperms are cone-bearing trees such as pines.

2. **Angiosperms** ("vessel seeds") are the flowering plants. Their seeds are encased in some sort of protective body, such as a fruit, nut, or pod. Trees, shrubs, grasses, crops, weeds, and garden flowers are angiosperms. Along with a few conifers, they have dominated the vegetation of the planet for the last 50 or 60 million years.

Several other terms are commonly used to describe vegetation, as summarized in Figure 11-3. Their definitions are not always precise, but their meanings generally are clear.

- One fundamental distinction is made on the basis of stem or trunk composition. *Woody plants* have stems composed of hard fibrous material, whereas *herbaceous plants* have soft stems. Woody plants are mostly trees and shrubs; herbaceous plants are mostly grasses, forbs, and lichens.
- With trees, whether or not a plant loses its leaves sometime during the year is an important distinguishing characteristic. An **evergreen tree** is one

Hardwood
Deciduous
Broadleaf
Angiosperm

Softwood
Coniferous
Needleleaf
Gymnosperm

▲ **Figure 11-3** Terminology used in describing plants. Although the terminology is somewhat confusing, there are conspicuous differences between hardwood (angiosperm) and softwood (gymnosperm) trees. The most obvious difference is in general appearance.

that sheds its leaves on a sporadic or successive basis but always appears to be fully leaved. A **deciduous tree** is one that experiences an annual period in which all leaves die and usually fall from the tree, due to either a cold season or a dry season.

- Trees are also often described in terms of leaf shapes. **Broadleaf trees** have leaves that are flat and expansive in shape, whereas **needleleaf trees** are adorned with thin slivers of tough, leathery, waxy needles rather than typical leaves. Almost all needle leaf trees are evergreen, and the great majority of all broadleaf trees are deciduous, except in the rainy tropics, where everything is evergreen.

- *Hardwood* and *softwood* are two of the most unsatisfactory terms in biogeography, but they are widely used in everyday parlance, so we must not ignore them. Hardwoods are angiosperm trees that are usually broad leaved and deciduous. Their wood has a relatively complicated structure, but it is not always hard. Softwoods are gymnosperms; nearly all are needleleaf evergreens. Their wood has a simple cellular structure, but it is not always soft.

> **Learning Check 11-3**   **Contrast *evergreen* trees and *deciduous* trees.**

Environmental Adaptations   FG6, FG9

Despite the hardiness of most plants, there are definite tolerance limits that govern their survival, distribution, and dispersal. During hundreds of millions of years of development, plants have evolved a variety of protective mechanisms to shield against harsh environmental conditions and to enlarge their tolerance limits. Two prominent adaptations to environmental stress are associated with low water availability and high water availability.

Xerophytic Adaptations: The descriptive term for plants that are structurally adapted to withstand protracted dry conditions is *xerophytic* (*xero* is Greek for "dry"; *phyt–* comes from *phuto–*, Greek for "plant"). **Xerophytic adaptations** can be grouped into four general types:

1. Roots are modified in shape or size to enable them to seek widely for moisture. Sometimes *taproots* extend to extraordinary depths to reach subterranean moisture. Also, root modification may involve the growth of a large number of thin hairlike rootlets to penetrate tiny pore spaces in soil (Figure 11-4).

2. Stems are sometimes modified into fleshy, spongy structures that can store moisture. Plants with such fleshy stems are called *succulents*; most cacti are prominent examples.

3. Leaf modification takes many forms; all are designed to decrease transpiration. Sometimes a leaf surface is hard and waxy to inhibit water loss or white and shiny to reflect insolation and thus reduce evaporation. Still more effective is for the plant to have either tiny leaves or no leaves at all. In many types of

▲ **Figure 11-4** Desert plants have evolved various mechanisms for survival in an arid climate. Some plants produce long taproots that penetrate deeply in search of the water table. More common are plants that have no deep roots but rather have myriad small roots and rootlets that seek any moisture available near the surface over a broad area.

dry-land shrubs, leaves have been replaced by spines, from which there is virtually no transpiration (Figure 11-5).

4. Perhaps the most remarkable floristic adaptation to aridity is not structural but involves the plant's reproductive cycle. Many xerophytic plants lie dormant for years without perishing. When rain eventually arrives, these plants promptly initiate and pass through an entire annual cycle of germination, flowering, fruiting, and seed dispersal in only a few days, then lapse into dormancy again if the drought resumes.

▲ **Figure 11-5** Cacti mostly or completely lack leaves, but instead have spines from which there is no water loss through transpiration.

Hygrophytic Adaptations: Plants with **hygrophytic adaptations** are particularly suited to a wet terrestrial environment. A distinction is sometimes made between *hydrophytes* (species living more or less permanently immersed in water, such as the water lilies in Figure 11-6a) and *hygrophytes* (moisture-loving plants that generally require frequent soakings with water, as do many ferns, mosses, and rushes), but both groups are often identified by the latter term.

Hygrophytes are likely to have extensive root systems to anchor them in the soft ground, and hygrophytic trees often develop a widened, flaring trunk near the ground to provide

(a)

(b)

▲ **Figure 11-6** Some types of plants flourish in a totally aqueous environment. (a) These lily pads virtually cover the surface of a bay of Cold Lake, on the Alberta–Saskatchewan border in western Canada. (b) Many hygrophytic trees, such as these cypress in Chicot State Park, Louisiana, have wide, flaring trunks near the ground to provide firmer footing in the wet environment.

better support (Figure 11-6b). Many hygrophytic plants that grow in standing or moving water have weak, pliable stems that can withstand the ebb and flow of currents rather than standing erect against them; the buoyancy of the water, rather than the stem, provides support for the plant.

Learning Check 11-4 **How are *xerophytic* adaptations different from *hygrophytic* adaptations?**

Competition and the Inevitability of Change

As important as climatic, edaphic, and other environmental characteristics are to plant survival, a particular species will not necessarily occupy an area just because all these conditions are favorable. Plants are just as competitive as animals. Of the dozens of plant species that might be suitable for an area, only one or a few are likely to survive. This is not to say that all plants are mutually competitive; indeed, thousands of ecologic niches can be occupied without impinging on one another. However, most plants draw their nutrients from the same soil and their energy from the same Sun, and what one plant obtains cannot be used by another.

The floristic pattern of Earth is impermanent. The plant cover that exists at any given time and place may be in a state of constant change or may be relatively stable for millennia before experiencing significant changes. Sooner or later, however, change is inevitable. Sometimes the change is slow and orderly, as when a lake is filled in, as described in Chapter 10, or when there is a long-term trend toward different climatic conditions over a broad area. On occasion, however, the change is abrupt and chaotic, as in the case of a wildfire.

When a landmass is newly formed, it is unvegetated. Such new land is first occupied by pioneer species and *primary succession* (discussed in Chapter 10) takes place over time, with one plant community giving way to another, and then another. Each succeeding association alters the local environment, making possible the establishment of the next association. The general sequential trend is toward taller plants and greater stability in species composition. The longer plant succession continues, the more slowly change takes place because more advanced associations usually contain species that live a relatively long time.

Eventually a plant association of constant composition may come into being, where each succeeding generation of the association is much like its predecessor. This stable association is generally referred to as the **climax vegetation**, and the various associations leading up to it are called *seral stages*. The implication of the term *climax vegetation* is that the dominant plants of a climax association have demonstrated that, of all possibilities for that particular situation, they can compete the most successfully. Thus, they represent the "optimal" floristic cover for that environmental context.

However, it is important to emphasize that the idealized climax vegetation for a location is rarely realized for long in many environments. Nearly all ecosystems are continually changing—even if subtly—in response to patterns of disturbance and environmental change. When these conditions change, the climax stage is disturbed and another succession sequence is initiated.

> **Learning Check 11-5**   **Explain the concept of climax vegetation.**

Spatial Associations of Plants

The geographer attempting to recognize spatial groupings of plants faces some significant difficulties. Plant associations that are similar in appearance and in environmental relationships can occur in widely separated localities and are likely to contain totally different species. At the other extreme, exceedingly different plant associations can often be detected within a very small area. As the geographer tries to identify patterns and recognize relationships, generalization invariably is needed. This generalization must accommodate gradations, ecotones, and other irregularities. When associations are portrayed on maps, therefore, their boundaries represent approximations in nearly all cases.

Another problem is that in many areas of the world the natural vegetation has been completely removed or replaced through human interference. Forests have been cut, crops planted, pastures seeded, and urban areas paved. Over extensive areas of Earth's surface, therefore, climax vegetation is the exception rather than the rule. Most world maps that purport to show natural vegetation ignore human interference and are actually maps of theoretical natural vegetation, in which the mapmaker makes assumptions about what the natural vegetation would be if it had not been modified by human activity.

The Major Floristic Associations: There are many ways to classify plant associations. For broad geographical purposes, emphasis is usually placed on the structure and appearance of the dominant plants. The major associations generally recognized (Figure 11-7) include the following:

- **Forests** consist of trees growing so close together that their individual leaf canopies generally overlap. This means that the ground is largely in shade, a condition that usually prevents the development of much undergrowth. Forests require considerable annual precipitation but can survive in widely varying temperature zones. Except where moisture is inadequate or the growing season very short, forests are likely to become the climax vegetation association in any area. Trees depend so much on the availability of moisture primarily because, unlike other plants, they must have a mechanism for transporting mineral nutrients a relatively great distance from their roots to their leaves. Such transport can take place only in a dilute solution; therefore, much water is needed by trees throughout the growing season. Other plant forms can flourish in areas of relatively high precipitation, but they rarely become dominant because they are shaded out by trees.
- **Woodlands** are tree-dominated plant associations in which the trees are spaced more widely apart than in forests and do not have interlacing canopies (Figure 11-8). Ground cover may be either dense or sparse, but it is not inhibited by lack of sunlight. Woodland environments are generally drier than forest environments.
- **Shrublands** are plant associations dominated by relatively short woody plants generally called *shrubs* or *bushes*. Shrubs take a variety of forms, but most have several stems branching near the ground and leafy foliage that begins very close to ground level. Trees

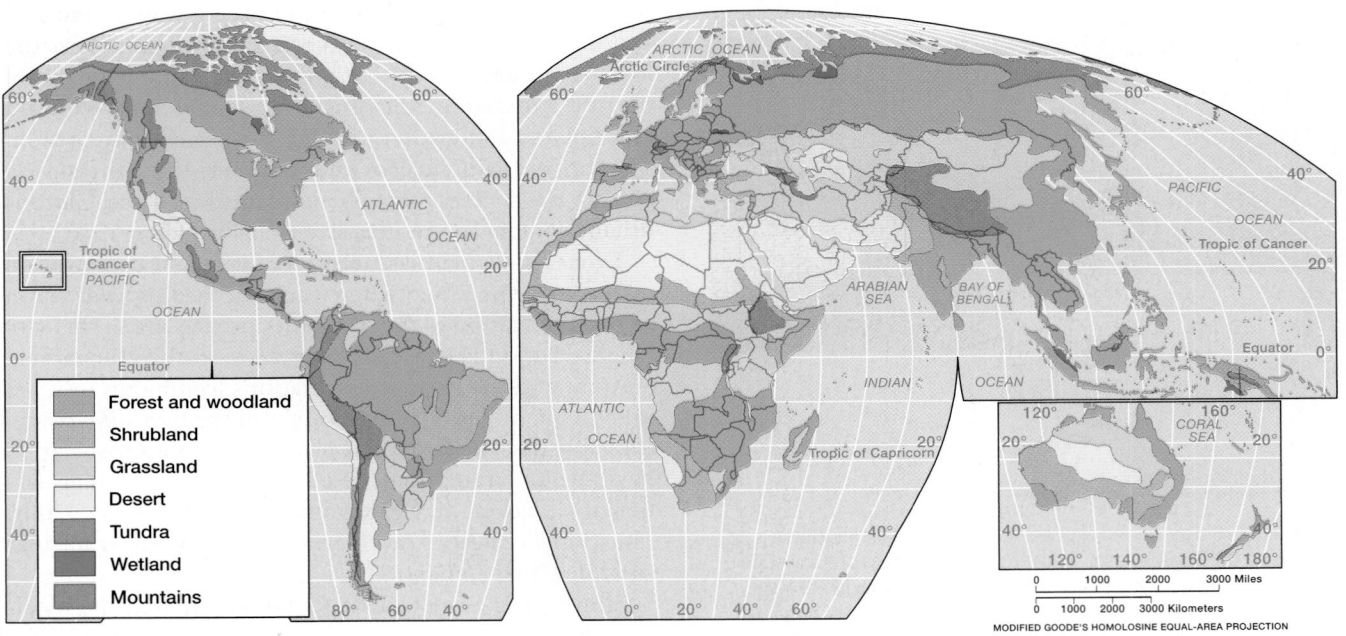

▲ **Figure 11-7** The major natural vegetation associations.

▲ **Figure 11-8** A piñon-juniper woodland scene in northern New Mexico.

and grasses may be interspersed with the shrubs but are less prominent in the landscape. Shrublands have a wide latitudinal range, but they are generally restricted to semiarid or arid locales.

- **Grasslands** may contain scattered trees and shrubs, but the landscape is dominated by grasses and forbs (broadleaf herbaceous plants). Prominent types of grassland include *savanna*, low-latitude grassland characterized by tall grasses; *prairie*, midlatitude grassland characterized by tall grasses; and *steppe*, midlatitude grassland characterized by short grasses and bunchgrasses. Grasslands are associated with semiarid and subhumid climates.
- **Deserts** are typified by widely scattered plants with much bare ground interspersed. Desert is actually a climatic term, and desert areas may have a great variety of vegetation, including grasses, succulent herbs, shrubs, and straggly trees (Figure 11-9). Some

▼ **Figure 11-9** Some deserts contain an abundance of plants, but they are usually spindly and always xerophytic. This scene is from the Tonto National Forest near Phoenix, Arizona.

extensive desert areas comprise loose sand, bare rock, or extensive gravel, with virtually no plant growth.
- **Tundra**, as we noted in Chapter 8, consists of a complex mix of very low plants, including grasses, forbs, dwarf shrubs, mosses, and lichens, but no trees. Tundra occurs only in the perennially cold climates of high latitudes or high altitudes.
- **Wetlands** have a much more limited geographic extent than the associations described above. They are characterized by shallow standing water all or most of the year, with vegetation rising above the water level. The most widely distributed wetlands are swamps (with trees as the dominant plant forms) and marshes (with grasses and other herbaceous plants dominant) (for example, see Figure 11-6).

Vertical Zonation

FG1, FG4

In Figure 8-34 we learned that mountainous areas often have a distinct pattern of **vertical zonation** in vegetation patterns (Figure 11-10). Significant elevational changes in short horizontal distances cause various plant associations to exist in relatively narrow zones on mountain slopes. This zonation is largely due to the effects of elevation on temperature and precipitation (Figure 11-11).

The essential implication is that elevation changes are the counterpart of latitude changes. In other words, to travel from sea level to the top of a tall tropical peak is roughly equivalent environmentally to a horizontal journey from the equator to the Arctic. This elevation–latitude relationship is shown most clearly by how the elevation of the upper **treeline** (the elevation above which trees are unable to survive, especially due to low summer temperatures and moisture availability) varies with latitude (Figure 11-12).

An interesting detail of vertical zonation is that the elevation–latitude graph for the Southern Hemisphere is different from the Northern Hemisphere. For example, between latitudes 35° S and 40° S in Australia and New Zealand, the treeline is below 1800 meters (6000 feet); at comparable latitudes in North America, the treeline is nearly twice as high. The reason for this significant discrepancy is not completely understood.

Treeline variation represents only one facet of the broader design of vertical zonation in vegetation patterns. All vegetation zones are displaced downward with increasing distance from the equator. This principle accounts for the significant vegetational complexity found in all mountainous areas.

Learning Check 11-6   **What environmental factors determine the *treeline* for a location?**

Local Variations

Each major vegetation association extends over a large area of Earth's surface. Within a given association, however, there are also significant local variations caused by a

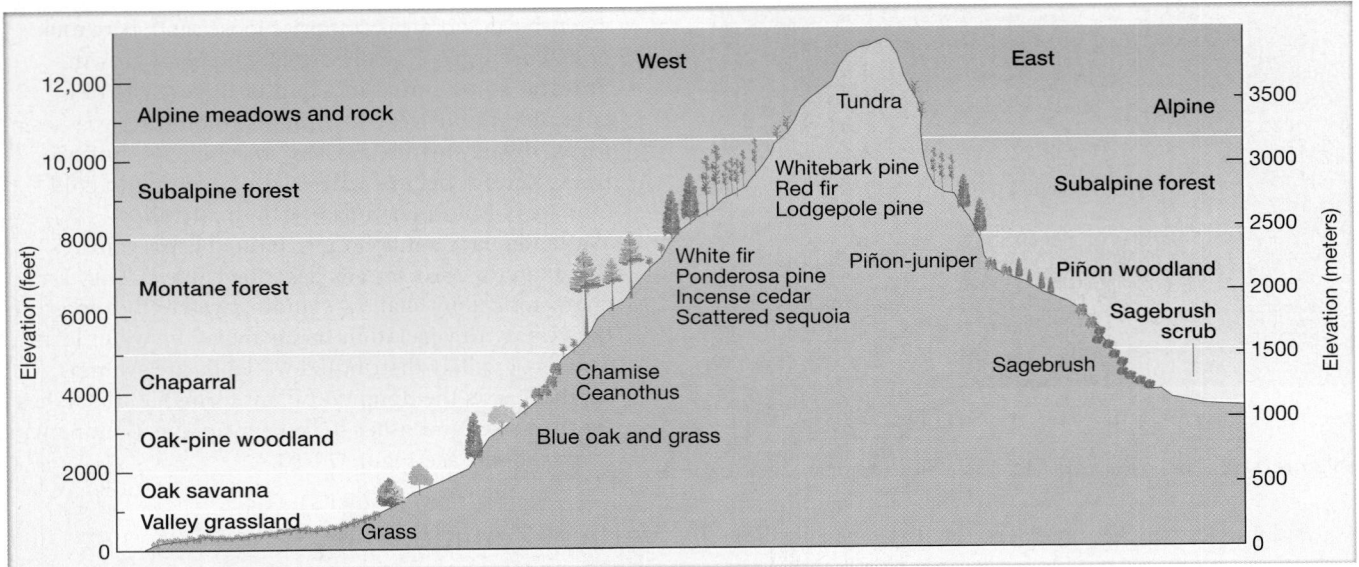

▲ **Figure 11-10** A west–east profile of California's Sierra Nevada, indicating the principal vegetation at different elevations on the western (wet) and eastern (dry) sides of the range. Characteristic plants within each vegetation zone are labeled along the mountain slope.

variety of local environmental conditions, as illustrated by the following two examples:

Exposure to Sunlight: The direction in which a sloped surface faces is often a critical determinant of vegetation composition, as illustrated by Figure 11-13. Exposure has many aspects, but one of the most pervasive is simply the angle at which sunlight strikes the slope. If the Sun's rays arrive at a high angle, they are much more effective in heating the ground and thus in evaporating available moisture. Such a sunny slope, also called an **adret slope**, is hot and dry, and its vegetation is not only sparser and smaller than that on adjacent slopes having a different exposure to sunlight, but is also likely to have a different species composition.

The opposite condition is a shaded slope, called a **ubac slope**, which is oriented so that sunlight strikes it at a low angle and is thus much less effective in heating and evaporating. This cooler condition produces more luxuriant vegetation of a richer diversity.

The difference between adret and ubac slopes decreases with increasing latitude, presumably because the ubac flora becomes impoverished under the cooler conditions that prevail as latitude increases and the relative warmth of the adret surface encourages plant diversity.

Valley-Bottom Location: In mountainous areas where a river runs through a valley, the vegetation associations growing on either side of the river have a composition that

◀ **Figure 11-11** Vertical zonation of vegetation patterns on the east slope of the Sierra Nevada in California. Sagebrush in the lowest elevations (about 1525 m; 5000 ft.) gives way to piñon woodland and pockets of subalpine forest in higher elevations; above the treeline, alpine tundra is found. The high peak in the center is Mount Whitney (4418 m; 14,494 ft.).

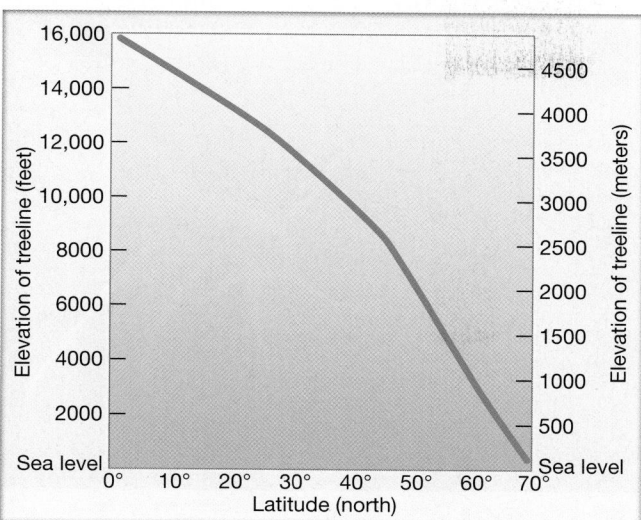

▲ **Figure 11-12** Treeline elevation varies with latitude. This graph for the Northern Hemisphere shows that trees cease to grow at an elevation of about 5000 meters (16,000 feet) in the equatorial Andes of South America but at only 3000 meters (10,000 feet) at 40° N in Colorado. At 70° N in northern Canada, the treeline is at sea level.

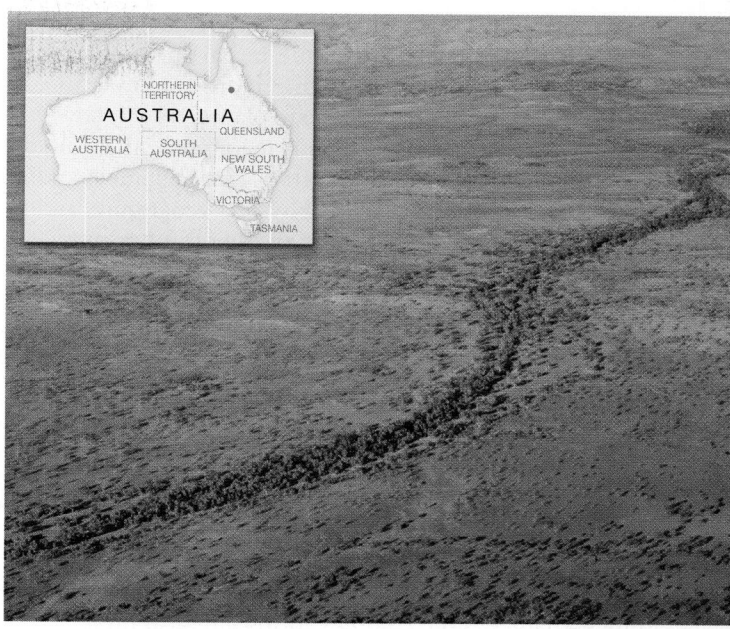

▲ **Figure 11-14** Riparian vegetation is particularly prominent in dry lands. This stream in northern Queensland (Australia) would be inconspicuous in this photograph if it were not for the trees growing along it.

is significantly different from that found higher up on the slopes forming the valley. This floral gradient is sometimes restricted to immediate streamside locations and sometimes extends more broadly over the valley floor.

The difference is primarily a reflection of the perennial availability of subsurface moisture near the stream and is manifested in a more diversified and more luxuriant flora. This vegetative contrast is particularly prominent in dry regions, where streams may be lined with trees even though no other trees are to be found in the landscape. Such streamside growth is called **riparian vegetation** (Figure 11-14).

TERRESTRIAL FAUNA

Animals occur in much greater variety than plants over Earth. As objects of geographical study, however, they have been relegated to a place of lesser prominence for at least two reasons. First, animals are often less prominent than plants in the landscape; apart from extremely localized situations—such as waterfowl flocking on a lake or an insect plague attacking a crop—animals are often secretive and so inconspicuous. Second, environmental

▶ **Figure 11-13** A typical adret–ubac situation. (a) The noon Sun rays strike the adret (sunny) slope at approximately a 90° angle, a condition that results in maximum heating. The same rays strike the ubac (shaded) slope at approximately a 40° angle, with the result that the heating is spread over a large area and is therefore less intense. (b) Vegetation differences on south-facing slopes (left and right) and the cooler north-facing slope (center) in the Blue Mountains of eastern Oregon.

interrelationships are much less clearly evidenced by animals than by plants. This is due in part to the fact that animals are mobile and therefore more able to adjust to environmental variability than are plants.

This is not to say that fauna is inconsequential for students of geography. Under certain circumstances, wildlife is a prominent element of physical geography; and in some regions of the world, it is an important resource for human use and/or a significant hindrance to human activity. Moreover, it is increasingly clear that animals are sometimes more sensitive indicators than plants of the health of a particular ecosystem.

Characteristics of Animals

The diversity of animal life-forms is not realized by most people. We commonly think of animals as being relatively large and conspicuous creatures that run across the land or scurry through the trees, seeking to avoid contact with humankind. Actually, the term *animal* encompasses not only the larger, more complex forms, but also hundreds of thousands of species of smaller and simpler organisms that may be inconspicuous or even invisible.

The variety of animal life is so great that it is difficult to find many unifying characteristics. The contrast, for example, between an enormous elephant and a tiny insect is so extreme as to make their kinship appear ludicrous. Animals really have only two universal characteristics, and even these are so highly modified in some cases as to be almost unrecognizable:

1. Animals are capable of self-generated movement.
2. Animals must eat plants and/or other animals for sustenance. They are incapable of manufacturing their food from air, water, and sunlight, which plants can do.

Kinds of Animals

Although the vast majority of animals are tiny, size is not a valid indicator of their significance for geographic study. Very small and seemingly inconsequential animals sometimes play exaggerated roles in the biosphere—as carriers of disease or as hosts of parasites, sources of infection, or providers of scarce nutrients. For example, no geographic assessment of Africa, however cursory, can afford to ignore the presence and distribution of the small tsetse fly and the tiny protozoan called *Trypanosoma*, which together are responsible for the transmission of trypanosomiasis (sleeping sickness), a widespread and deadly disease for humans and livestock over much of the continent.

Zoological classification is much too detailed to be useful in most geographical studies. Therefore, presented in the paragraphs that follow is a brief summation of the principal kinds of animals that might be recognized in a general study of physical geography.

Invertebrates: Animals without backbones are called **invertebrates**. More than 90 percent of all animal species are encompassed within this broad grouping. Invertebrates

▲ **Figure 11-15** Insects, such as this moth, are arthropods, the largest group of invertebrate animals.

include worms, sponges, mollusks, various marine animals, and a vast host of creatures of microscopic or near-microscopic size. Very prominent among invertebrates are the *arthropods*, a group that includes insects (Figure 11-15), spiders, centipedes, millipedes, and crustaceans (shellfish). With some 300,000 recognized species, beetles are the most numerous of animals, comprising about 40 percent of all insect species and more than one-fourth of all known animals.

Vertebrates: **Vertebrates** are animals that have a backbone that protects the main nerve (or spinal cord). Geographers generally follow biologists in recognizing five principal groups of vertebrates:

1. *Fishes* are the only vertebrates that can breathe under water (a few fish species are also capable of breathing in air). Most fishes inhabit either freshwater or saltwater only, but some species are capable of living in both environments (such as the bull shark, *Carcharhinus leucas*); and several species, most notably salmon, spawn in freshwater streams but live most of their lives in the ocean.
2. *Amphibians* are semiaquatic animals. When first born, they are fully aquatic and breathe through gills; as adults, they are air-breathers by means of lungs and through their glandular skin. Most amphibians are either frogs or salamanders.
3. Most *reptiles* are totally land based. Ninety-five percent of all reptile species are either snakes or lizards. The remainder are mostly turtles and crocodilians.
4. *Birds* are believed to have evolved from reptiles; indeed, they have so many reptilian characteristics that they have been called "feathered reptiles." There are more than 9000 species of birds, all of which reproduce by means of eggs. Birds are so adaptable that some species can live almost anywhere on Earth's surface. They are **endothermic**, which means that, regardless of the temperature of the air or water in

◄ **Figure 11-16** Most large land animals are placental mammals, as exemplified by this moose and her young calf in Algonquin Park, Ontario, Canada.

which they live, they maintain a constant body temperature.

5. *Mammals* are distinguished from all other animals by several internal characteristics as well as by two prominent external features. The external features are that only mammals produce milk with which they feed their young, and only mammals possess true hair. (Some mammals have very little hair, but no creatures other than mammals have any hair.) Mammals are also notable for being endothermic. Thus, the body temperature of mammals and birds stays about the same under any climatic conditions, which enables them to live in almost all parts of the world.

The great majority of all mammals are *placentals*, which means that their young grow and develop in the mother's body, nourished by an organ known as the *placenta*, which forms a vital connecting link with the mother's bloodstream (Figure 11-16). A small group of mammals (about 135 species) are *marsupials*, whose females have pouches in which the young, which are born in a very undeveloped condition, live for several weeks or months after birth (Figure 11-17). The most primitive of all mammals are the *monotremes*, of which only two types exist (Figure 11-18); they are egg-laying mammals.

Learning Check 11-7   **Which major groups of animals are *endothermic*, and what are the advantages of this for a species?**

Environmental Adaptations

As with plants, animals have evolved slowly and diversely through eons of time. Evolution has made it possible for animals to diverge remarkably in adjusting to different environments. Just about every existing environmental extreme has been met by some (or many) evolutionary adaptations that make it feasible for some (or many) animal species to survive and even flourish. Recent climate changes, however, challenge the adaptability of many

▲ **Figure 11-17** A red kangaroo joey (baby) peers out from its mother's pouch. As with other marsupials, baby kangaroos live for a time in their mother's pouch after birth.

(a)

(b)

▲ **Figure 11-18** There are only two kinds of monotremes, or egg-laying mammals, in existence—the echidna and the duckbill platypus. (a) The echidna is found only in Australia and New Guinea. (b) The platypus is primarily aquatic in its lifestyle.

(a)

(b)

▲ **Figure 11-19** (a) An Arctic fox near Cape Churchill in the Canadian province of Manitoba. Its tiny ears are an adaptation to conserve body heat in a cold environment. (b) Desert foxes have large ears, the better to radiate away body heat. This is a bat-eared fox in northern Kenya.

species, as you can see in the box, "Focus: Changing Climate Affects Bird Populations."

Physiological Adaptations: The majority of animal adaptations to environmental diversity have been physiological, which is to say that they are anatomical and/or metabolic changes. A classic example is the size of fox ears. Ears are prime conduits for body heat in furred animals as they provide a relatively bare surface for its loss. Arctic foxes (Figure 11-19a) have unusually small ears, which minimizes heat loss; desert foxes (Figure 11-19b) possess remarkably large ears, which are a great advantage for radiating heat during the blistering desert summers.

There are several hundred species of mammals whose skin is covered with a fine, soft, thick, hairy coat referred to as *fur*. These mammals range in size from tiny mice and moles to the largest bears. An examination of their ranges reveals several generalized habitat preferences. Many fur-bearing species live in high-latitude and/or

high-elevation locations, where winters are long and cold; a number of fur-bearing species live in aquatic environments; the remainder are widely scattered over the continents, occupying a considerable diversity of habitats. We can conclude tentatively that many fur-bearing species, including all those with the heaviest, thickest fur, live in regions where cold temperatures are common, but the climatic correlation in this case is partial because of the many other factors involved.

The catalog of similar adaptations is almost endless: webbing between toes to make swimming easier; broad feet that will not sink in soft snow; increase in size and number of sweat glands to aid in evaporative cooling; and a host of others.

Changing Climate Affects Bird Populations

Bird populations can be especially sensitive indicators of climate change because many species have specific environmental requirements for feeding, nesting, and migration. Further, because birds are generally quite mobile, a bird population may respond fairly quickly to local environmental changes.

Audubon Annual Bird Counts:
Data suggests that higher global temperatures are already affecting some bird populations. The National Audubon Society's annual Christmas Bird Count (CBC) has gathered information about bird populations for more than a century.

Birds and Climate Change, the 2009 National Audubon Society study based on data gathered over the last 40 years in its Christmas Bird Counts, reports that 177 of 305 North American bird species are wintering an average of 56 kilometers (35 miles) farther north than 40 years ago. In addition, the "center of abundance" for more than 60 bird species shifted 160 kilometers (100 miles) or more north. The report concludes that higher temperatures are the most likely cause of these shifts—increasing temperatures in winter make areas that were once too cold now habitable for some bird species.

Shifting Bird Populations in Europe:
A study of European birds and butterflies published in 2012 looked at changes in the average temperature of locations where species were found between 1990 and 2008. The study concluded that the northward shift of bird populations lagged behind the northward shift of average temperature by 212 kilometers (132 miles)—in other words, birds are not adjusting their range as fast as climate changes. In addition, some birds are nesting earlier than in past decades because plants are blooming sooner—which results in an earlier proliferation of insects on which the birds feed. The British Trust for Ornithology reports that 20 out of 65 species of birds studied are laying eggs nine days earlier now than they did just 40 years ago.

Projections of Future Ranges:
Although some bird species may be able to adjust to a warming climate by altering their migration patterns—shifting their ranges north in the Northern Hemisphere, for example—this may not actually occur in some cases. New evidence suggests that forest communities in North America may not simply shift north of their present locations in response to a warmer climate. Instead, individual plant and animal species within a forest community may respond differently to climate change, perhaps leaving a dislocated and altered habitat for birds and other creatures.

One of the earliest studies of the potential effects of climate change on bird populations in North America looked at the bobolink (*Dolichonyx oryzivorus*), a songbird (Figure 11-A). Bobolinks have an extraordinarily long migration—a round-trip of about 20,000 kilometers (12,400 miles). In summer, they nest in meadows and fields from southern Canada, New England, and south of the Great Lakes to Idaho. In the Northern Hemisphere winter, they fly south to the grasslands of northern Argentina, Paraguay, and southwestern Brazil.

A study in the mid-1990s concluded that with the projected climate and vegetation changes associated with a doubling of atmospheric CO_2, the bobolink might not be able to nest south of the Great Lakes—depriving this region of one of its most beloved songbirds. More recently, scientists working with the U.S. Forest Service developed an online *Climate Change Bird Atlas* for 147 eastern U.S. bird species (http://www.nrs.fs.fed.us/atlas/). The computer model assumes a doubling of CO_2 by the end of the century, and it relates projected differences in temperature and precipitation to changes in tree distribution—and in turn relates forest habitat change to changes in bird range. Using their most conservative General Circulation Model projections, the model forecasts a dramatic change in bobolink range (Figure 11-B).

▲ **Figure 11-A** Adult male bobolink, *Dolichonyx oryzivorus*.

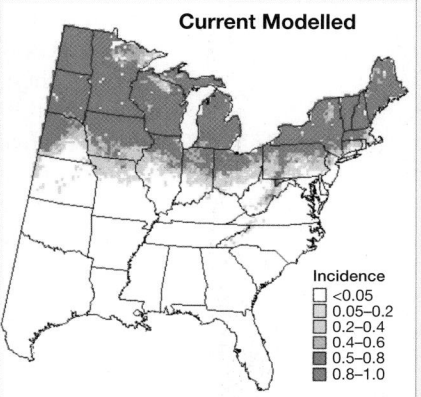

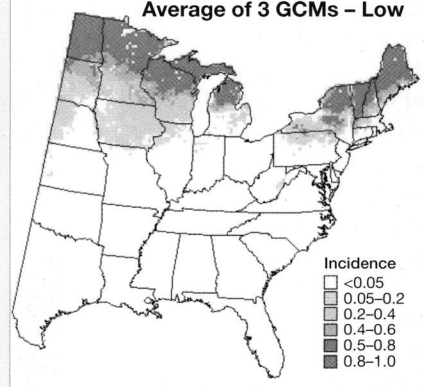

▲ **Figure 11-B** Maps comparing the modeled current incidence of the bobolink in the eastern United States with their projected incidence by the end of the century. The model was based on the average of three conservative General Circulation Models of climate change.

Behavioral Adaptations: An important advantage that animals have over plants, in terms of adjustment to environmental stress, is that the former can move about and therefore modify their behavior to minimize the stress. Animals can seek shelter from heat, cold, flood, or fire; they can travel far in search of relief from drought or famine; and they can shift from daytime (diurnal) to nighttime (nocturnal) activities to minimize water loss during hot seasons. Such techniques as migration (periodic movement from one region to another), *hibernation* (spending winter in a dormant condition), and *estivation* (spending a dry–hot period in an inactive state) are behavioral adaptations employed regularly by many species of animals.

Reproductive Adaptations: Harsh environmental conditions are particularly destructive to the newly born. As partial compensation for this factor, many species have evolved specialized reproductive cycles or have developed modified techniques of baby care. During lengthy periods of bad weather, for example, some species delay mating or postpone nest building. If fertilization has already taken place, some animal reproductive cycles are capable of almost indefinite delay, resulting in a protracted egg or larval stage or even total suspension of embryo development until the weather improves.

If the young have already been born, they sometimes remain longer than usual in the nest, den, or pouch, and the adults may feed them for a longer time. When good weather finally returns, some species are capable of hastened *estrus* (the period of heightened sexual receptivity by the female), nest building, den preparation, and so on, and the progeny produced may be in greater than normal numbers.

> **Learning Check 11-8** **What advantage is there for an animal to hibernate during the winter?**

Example of Animal Adaptations to Desert Life:
The desert is a classic illustration of a stressful environment for biotic life, as well as the many adaptations on the part of animals.

The simplest and most obvious adaptation to life in an arid land is for the animals to remain near a reliable source of water. Thus, the permanent streams and enduring springs of the desert attract a resident faunal population that is often rich and diverse. Even in areas where open water is not available, it is rare for the desert to be uniformly inhospitable.

Often animals follow the rains in nomadic fashion. Many species demonstrate remarkable instincts for knowing where precipitation has occurred and will travel tens or even hundreds of kilometers to take advantage of locally improved conditions. Some African antelopes and Australian kangaroos have been observed to double in numbers almost overnight after a good rain, a feat impossible except by rapid, large-scale movement from one area to another.

(a)

(b)

▲ **Figure 11-20** Desert animals exhibit a number of remarkable adaptations. (a) The Ord kangaroo rat in Arizona can live its entire life without taking a drink, receiving all necessary moisture from the food it eats. (b) Camels are ideal pack animals in arid environments, as here in Sudan.

Many smaller desert creatures spend a great deal of time underground beneath the level of desiccating heat. Most desert rodents and reptiles live in underground burrows, and many lesser creatures do the same. Desert frogs, although not numerous, are noted burrowers; some have been found as deep as 2 meters (6 feet) underground. Freshwater crayfish and crabs often survive long dry spells by burying themselves. Most desert ants and termites live in underground nests. Most desert animals except birds, *ungulates* (hooved mammals), and many flying insects are almost completely nocturnal.

A few species of rodents, most notably kangaroo rats (Figure 11-20a), can exist from birth to death without ever taking a drink, surviving exclusively on moisture ingested with their food.

Of all animals, perhaps the *dromedary* or one-humped camel (*Camelus dromedarius*) has developed the most remarkable series of adjustments to the desert environment (Figure 11-20b). The upper lip of the dromedary is deeply cleft, with a groove that extends to each nostril so that any moisture expelled from the nostrils can be caught in the mouth rather than being wasted. The nostrils consist of horizontal slits that can be closed tightly to keep out blowing dust and sand. The eyes are set beneath shaggy brows, which help to shield them from the Sun's glare; the eyes are further protected from blowing sand by a complex double set of eyelids. Dromedaries can tolerate extreme dehydration without their body temperatures rising to a fatal level: whereas humans and most other large animals have body temperatures that fluctuate by only 1° to 2°C (2° to 4°F) on hot days, the range for dromedaries is 7°C (12°F), meaning that the dromedary sweats little except during the very hottest hours, thereby conserving body water. When drinking water is available, they are capable of completely rehydrating in only a short time.

Perhaps the most astounding of all faunal adaptations to arid conditions is one that is overtly very similar to a vegetational adaptation—the ability to delay reproductive processes over long dry periods until more favorable conditions occur, at which time rapid breeding or birth can allow remarkable population regeneration. Australian desert kangaroos, for example, are capable of "delayed implantation," in which a fertilized *blastocyst* (early stage embryo) can remain in an inactive state of development in the uterus during a period of difficult living and then spontaneously resume normal development after conditions have improved. Desert birds may experience enormous die-offs when waters dry up during a prolonged drought, but when rains finally come, the survivors may begin nest construction within a week and ovulation within a fortnight. Moreover, clutch size (the number of eggs laid) may increase, as may the number of clutches produced.

Invertebrates, too, can take advantage of a favorable weather change to proliferate their numbers extraordinarily. Many of them survive the dry period in an egg or larval stage that is extremely resistant to desiccation; when the drought breaks, the egg hatches or the larva develops into an active stage that may not be at all drought resistant. Development continues with great rapidity until the adult form can breed and more drought-resistant eggs can be laid—this is a commonplace circumstance for brine shrimp, crayfish, grasshoppers, locusts, flies, mosquitoes, and various other desert arthropods. There have been cases in which more than a quarter of a century has passed between successive generations of these tiny creatures, which have an adult cycle that lasts for only a few weeks.

> **Learning Check 11-9** **Describe and explain one kind of adaptation animals have in deserts.**

Competition among Animals

Competition among animals is even more intense than that among plants because the former involves not only indirect competition in the form of rivalry for space and resources but also the direct antagonism of predation. Animals with similar dietary habits compete for food and occasionally for territory. Animals in the same area also sometimes compete for water. And animals of the same species often compete for territory and for mates. In addition to these ecological rivalries, animals are also involved in predator–prey relationships—as one or the other.

Competition among animals is a major part of the general struggle for existence that characterizes natural relationships in the biosphere. Individual animals are concerned either largely or entirely with their own survival (and sometimes with that of their mates) in response to instincts. In some species, this concern is broadened to include their own young, although such maternal (and, much more rarely, paternal) instinct is by no means universal among animals. Still fewer species show individual concern for the group, as represented in colonies of ants or prides of lions. For the most part, however, animal survival is a matter of every creature for itself, with no individual helping another and no individual deliberately destroying another apart from normal predatory activities.

Cooperation among Animals

In spite of the intensity of competition among animals, many kinds of animals also exhibit cooperative behaviors. Many animals live together in social groups of varying sizes, generally referred to as herds, flocks, or colonies. This is a common, but by no means universal, behavioral characteristic among animals of the same species (Figure 11-21), and sometimes a social group encompasses several species in a communal relationship, such as zebras, wildebeest, and impalas living together on an East African savanna. Within such groupings, there may be a certain amount of cooperation among unrelated animals, but

▲ **Figure 11-21** Seals and sea lions are among the most gregarious of mammals. This "hauling-out" beach near Point Año Nuevo on the central coast of California is crowded with elephant seals.

▲ **Figure 11-22** There is often a symbiotic relationship between hoofed animals and insectivorous birds. In this scene from South Africa's Kruger National Park, two red-billed oxpeckers are riding on a zebra, whose back can provide tasty morsels.

competition for both space and resources is likely to be prominent as well.

Symbiosis: Symbiosis is the arrangement in which two dissimilar organisms live together. There are three principal forms:

1. *Mutualism* involves a mutually beneficial relationship between the two organisms, as exemplified by the tickbirds that are constant companions of many African ungulates. The birds aid the mammals by removing ticks and other insects that infest the latter's skin, and the birds benefit by having a readily available supply of food (Figure 11-22).
2. *Commensalism* involves two dissimilar organisms living together with no injury to either, as represented by burrowing owls sharing the underground home of prairie dogs.

3. *Parasitism* involves one organism living on or in another, obtaining nourishment from the host, which is usually weakened and sometimes killed by the actions of the parasite. Mistletoe, for example, is a parasite of forest trees that is widespread in North America and Europe.

Learning Check 11-10 **What is the difference between *mutualism* and *parasitism*?**

ZOOGEOGRAPHIC REGIONS

The distribution of animals over the world is much more complex and irregular than that of plants, primarily because animals are mobile and therefore capable of more rapid dispersal. As with plants, however, the broad distributions of animals are reflective of the general distribution of energy and of food diversity. Thus, the richest faunal assemblages are found in the diverse, energy-rich environment of the humid tropics, and the dry lands and cold lands have the sparsest representations of both species and individuals.

When considering the global patterns of animal geography, most attention is usually paid to the distribution of terrestrial vertebrates, with other animals being given only casual notice. The classical definition of world zoogeographic regions is credited to the nineteenth-century British naturalist A. R. Wallace, whose scheme is based on the work of P. L. Sclater. As shown in Figure 11-23, nine **zoogeographic regions** are generally recognized, but you should understand that this or any other system of faunal regions represents average conditions and cannot portray some common pattern in which different groups of animals fit precisely. It is simply a composite of many diverse distributions of contemporary fauna.

- **Ethiopian Region:** The *Ethiopian Region* is primarily tropical or subtropical and has a rich and diverse fauna. It is separated from other regions by an oceanic barrier on three sides and a broad desert on the fourth. Despite its isolation, however, the Ethiopian Region has many faunal affinities with the Oriental

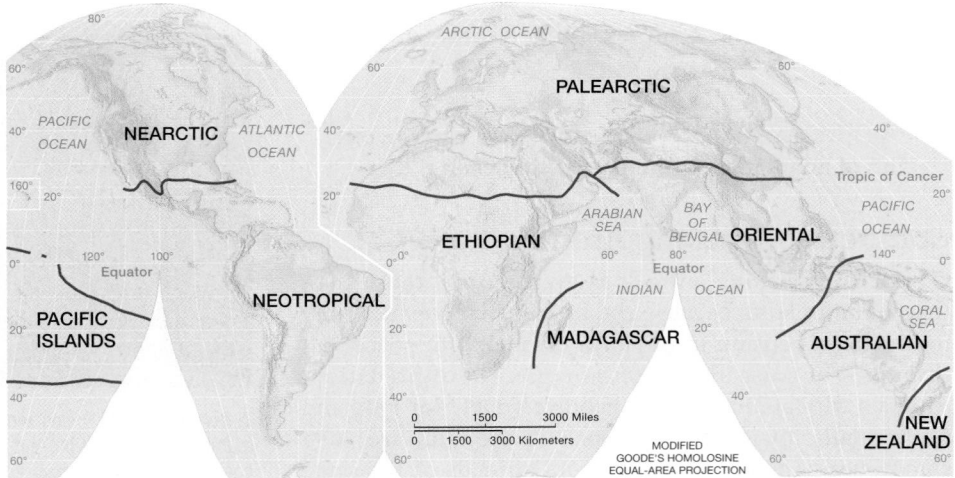

▶ **Figure 11-23** Zoogeographic regions of the world.

and Palearctic regions. Its vertebrate fauna is the most diverse of all the zoogeographic regions and includes the greatest number of mammalian families, many of which have no living relatives outside Africa.

- **Oriental Region:** The *Oriental Region* is separated from the rest of Eurasia by mountains. Its faunal assemblage is generally similar to that of the Ethiopian Region, with somewhat less diversity. The Oriental Region has some **endemic** groups (*endemic* means these groups are found nowhere else) and a few species that are found only in the Oriental, Palearctic, and Australian regions. Many brilliantly colored birds live in the Oriental Region, and reptiles are numerous, with a particularly large number of venomous snakes.

- **Palearctic Region:** The *Palearctic Region* includes the rest of Eurasia, all of Europe, and most of North Africa. Its fauna as a whole is much poorer than that of the two regions previously discussed, which is presumably a function of its location in higher latitudes with a more rigorous climate. This region has many affinities with all three bordering regions, particularly the Nearctic. Indeed, the Palearctic has only two minor mammal families (both rodents) that are endemic, and almost all of its birds belong to families that have a very wide distribution.

- **Nearctic Region:** The *Nearctic Region* consists of the nontropical portions of North America. Its faunal assemblage (apart from reptiles, which are well represented) is relatively poor and is largely a transitional mixture of Palearctic and Neotropical groups. It has few important groups of its own except for freshwater fishes. The considerable similarities between Palearctic and Nearctic fauna have persuaded some zoologists to group them into a single superregion, the *Holarctic*, which had a land connection in the recent geologic past when glaciation lowered global sea level—the Bering land bridge across which considerable faunal dispersal took place (Figure 11-24).

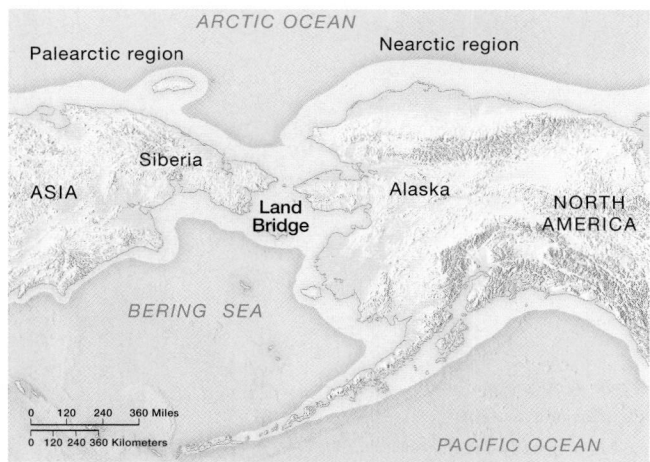

▲ **Figure 11-24** The Bering land bridge facilitated the interchange of animals between the Palearctic and Nearctic regions when sea level was lower during recent glaciations. Most of the dispersal was from Asia (Palearctic) to North America (Nearctic).

- **Neotropical Region:** The *Neotropical Region* encompasses all of South America and the tropical portion of North America. Its fauna is rich and distinctive, which reflects both a variety of habitats and a considerable degree of isolation from other regions. Neotropic faunal evolution often followed a path different from that in other regions. It contains a larger number of endemic mammal families than any other region. Moreover, its bird fauna is exceedingly diverse and conspicuous.

- **Madagascar Region:** The *Madagascar Region*, restricted to the island of that name, has a fauna very different from that of nearby Africa. The Madagascan fauna is dominated by a relic assemblage of unusual forms in which primitive primates (lemurs) are notable.

- **New Zealand Region:** The *New Zealand Region* has a unique fauna dominated by birds, with a remarkable proportion of flightless types. It has almost no terrestrial vertebrates (no mammals; only a few reptiles and amphibians).

- **Pacific Islands Region:** The *Pacific Islands Region* includes a great many far-flung islands, mostly quite small. Its faunal assemblage is very limited.

- **Australian Region:** The *Australian Region* is restricted to the continent of Australia and some adjacent islands, particularly New Guinea. Its fauna is by far the most distinctive of any major region, due primarily to its lengthy isolation from other principal landmasses. The lack of variety of its vertebrate fauna is made up for by uniqueness. There are only nine families of terrestrial mammals, but eight of them are unique to the region. The bird fauna is varied, and both pigeons and parrots reach their greatest diversity here. There is a notable scarcity of freshwater fishes and amphibians. The Australian Region has a moderate amount of reptiles, mostly snakes and lizards, including the largest lizard of all: the Komodo dragon. Within the region, there are many significant differences between the fauna of Australia and that of New Guinea.

So why is the Australian Region so different from the other zoogeographic regions? The answer will become clearer when we discuss plate tectonics in Chapter 14, but for now, a quick explanation.

The Unique Biota of Australia: The unusual faunal and floristic developments of Australia are largely the result of isolation. During long periods of time in the geologic past, while most of the continents were connected, the climate was more equitable, allowing for a vast evolution of plant species. As the continents began to separate about two hundred million years ago, climatic changes occurred requiring new adaptation and continued evolution. Australia became isolated from the rest of the continents, and so evolution continued with little genetic influence from the outside. This has engendered specialized evolutionary development among the isolated flora and fauna of Australia.

The most notable vegetation distinction is that nearly all the native trees in Australia—more than 90 percent of the total—are members of a single genus, *Eucalyptus*. Moreover, the eucalyptus (see Figure 10-14), of which there are more than 400 species, are native to no other continent but Australia. The shrubs and bushes of Australia are also dominated by a single genus, *Acacia*, which encompasses about half of the intermediate level (between grasses and trees) flora of the continent. Australia has several unusual grasses as well, but their distinctiveness is less pronounced.

If the flora of Australia is unusual, the fauna is absolutely unique; its assemblage of terrestrial animal life is completely without parallel in other parts of the world. This, too, is primarily the result of isolation. Through a chain of varied geological events and biological repercussions, the Australian continent functioned for millions of years as a faunal asylum, where rare and vulnerable species were able to flourish in relative isolation from the competitive and predatory pressures that influenced animal evolution in other parts of the world. The results of this isolation are bizarre, especially with regard to the highest forms of animal life—the mammals.

Unlike all other continents, the Australian fauna is dominated by a single primitive mammalian order, the marsupials (see Figure 11-17), an order that has long disappeared from most other parts of the world. Australia also provides the only continental home for an even more primitive group, the monotremes (see Figure 11-18). More remarkable, perhaps, is what is lacking in Australia—placental mammals, so notable elsewhere, are limited and inconspicuous. Australia is completely without native representatives from such common groups as cats, dogs, bears, monkeys, hoofed animals, and many others.

Learning Check 11-11 **Why does the Australian zoogeographic region have so many unique animal species?**

THE MAJOR BIOMES

We now turn to a description of the major biomes of the world (Figure 11-25). As we learned earlier, most biomes are named for their dominant vegetation association, but the biome concept also encompasses fauna as well as interrelationships with soil, climate, and topography.

▶ **Figure 11-25** Major biomes of the world.

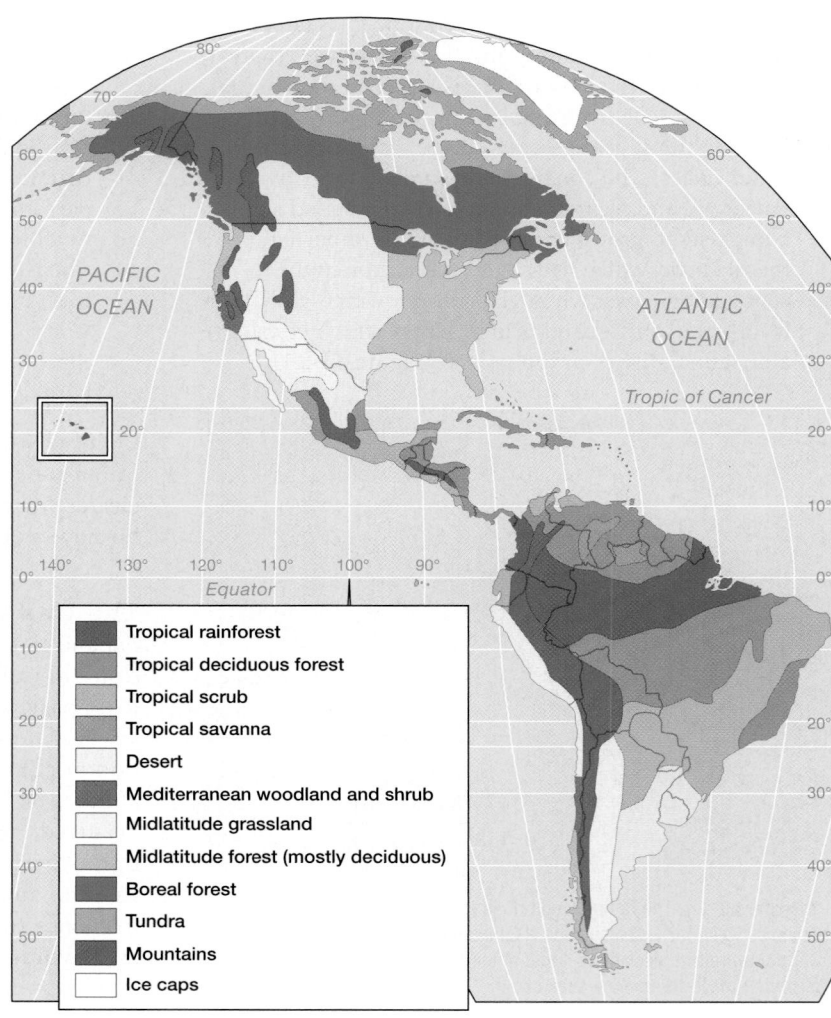

Tropical rainforest
Tropical deciduous forest
Tropical scrub
Tropical savanna
Desert
Mediterranean woodland and shrub
Midlatitude grassland
Midlatitude forest (mostly deciduous)
Boreal forest
Tundra
Mountains
Ice caps

Tropical Rainforest

As we first saw in Chapter 10, the distribution of the **tropical rainforest** or *selva* biome (selva is the Portuguese-Spanish word for "forest") is closely related to climate—consistent rainfall and relatively high temperatures. Thus, there is an obvious correlation with the location of tropical wet (Af) and some tropical monsoon (Am) climatic regions (Figure 11-26).

The rainforest is probably the most complex of all terrestrial ecosystems, and the one with the greatest *biodiversity* (many different species are found in an area, but often relatively few individuals of each species are present). It contains a bewildering variety of trees growing in close conjunction. Most are tall, high-crowned, broadleaf evergreen species that never experience a seasonal leaf fall because seasons are unknown in this environment of continuous warmth and moistness (Figure 11-26a). The selva has a layered structure; the second layer down from the top usually forms a complete canopy of interlaced branches that provides continuous shade to the forest floor. Bursting through the canopy to form the top layer are the forest giants—tall trees that often grow to great heights above the general level. Beneath the canopy is an erratic third layer

of lower trees, palms and tree ferns, able to survive in the shade. Sometimes still more layers of increasingly shade-tolerant trees grow at lower levels.

Undergrowth is relatively sparse in the tropical rainforest because the lack of light precludes the survival of most green plants. Only where there are gaps in the canopy, as alongside a river, does light reach the ground, resulting in the dense undergrowth associated with a jungle. *Epiphytes* like orchids and bromeliads hang from or perch on tree trunks and branches. Vines and lianas often dangle from the arching limbs.

The interior of the rainforest, then, is a region of heavy shade, high humidity, windless air, continuous warmth, and an aroma of mold and decomposition. As plant litter accumulates on the forest floor, it is acted on very rapidly by plant and animal decomposers. The upper layers of the forest are areas of high productivity, and there is a much greater concentration of nutrients in the vegetation than in the soil. Indeed, most selva soil is surprisingly infertile.

Rainforest fauna is largely *arboreal* (tree dwelling) because the principal food sources are in the canopy rather than on the ground. Large animals are generally scarce on

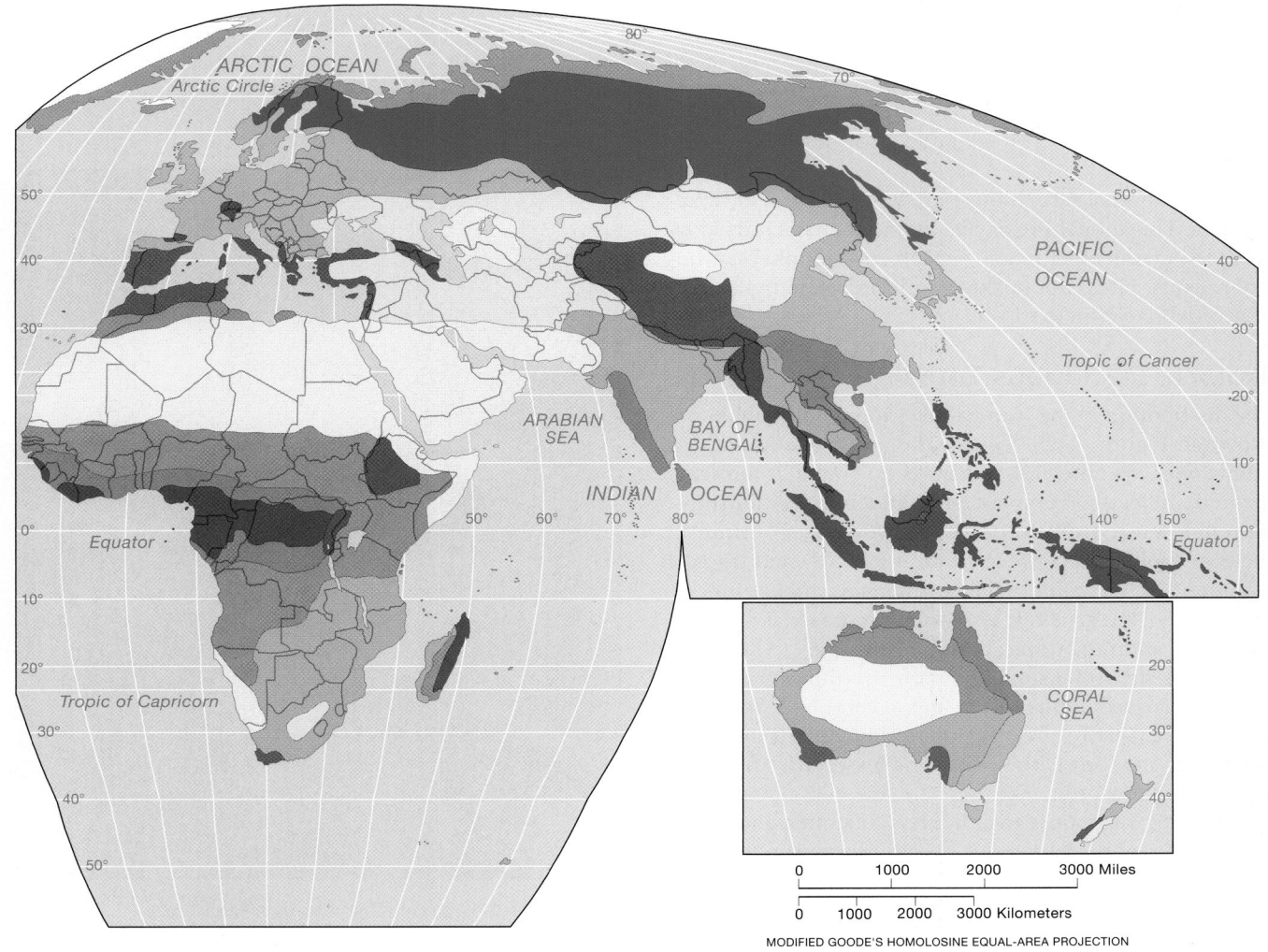

MODIFIED GOODE'S HOMOLOSINE EQUAL-AREA PROJECTION

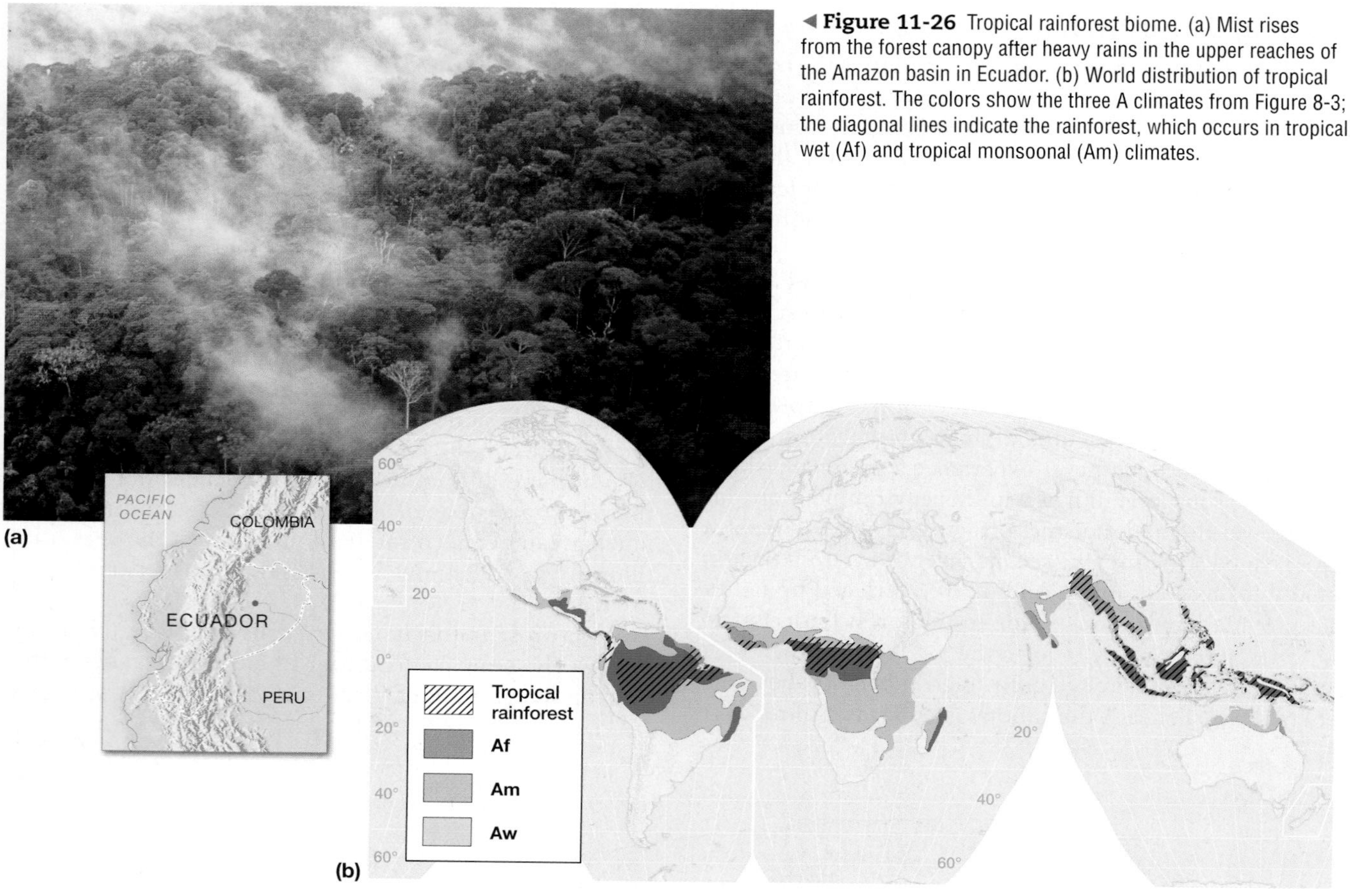

◀ **Figure 11-26** Tropical rainforest biome. (a) Mist rises from the forest canopy after heavy rains in the upper reaches of the Amazon basin in Ecuador. (b) World distribution of tropical rainforest. The colors show the three A climates from Figure 8-3; the diagonal lines indicate the rainforest, which occurs in tropical wet (Af) and tropical monsoonal (Am) climates.

the forest floor, although there are vast numbers of invertebrates. The animal life of this biome is characterized by creepers, crawlers, climbers, and flyers—monkeys, arboreal rodents, birds, tree snakes and lizards, and multitudes of invertebrates (Figure 11-27).

Tropical Deciduous Forest

The distribution of the **tropical deciduous forest** biome is shown in Figure 11-28. The locational correlation of this biome with specific climatic types is irregular and fragmented, indicating complex environmental relationships, although many tropical deciduous forests are found in the transition zone between tropical wet (Af) and tropical savanna (Aw) climates. Such regions have high temperatures all year, but generally less—or more seasonal—rainfall patterns than in the tropical rainforest biome.

There is structural similarity between tropical rainforest and tropical deciduous forest, but several important differences are usually obvious (Figure 11-28a). In the tropical deciduous forest, the canopy is less dense, the trees are somewhat shorter, and there are fewer layers, all these details being a response to either less total precipitation or less periodic precipitation. As a result of a pronounced dry period that lasts for several weeks or months, many of the trees shed their leaves at the same time, allowing light to

▲ **Figure 11-27** A pair of scarlet macaws in Costa Rica.

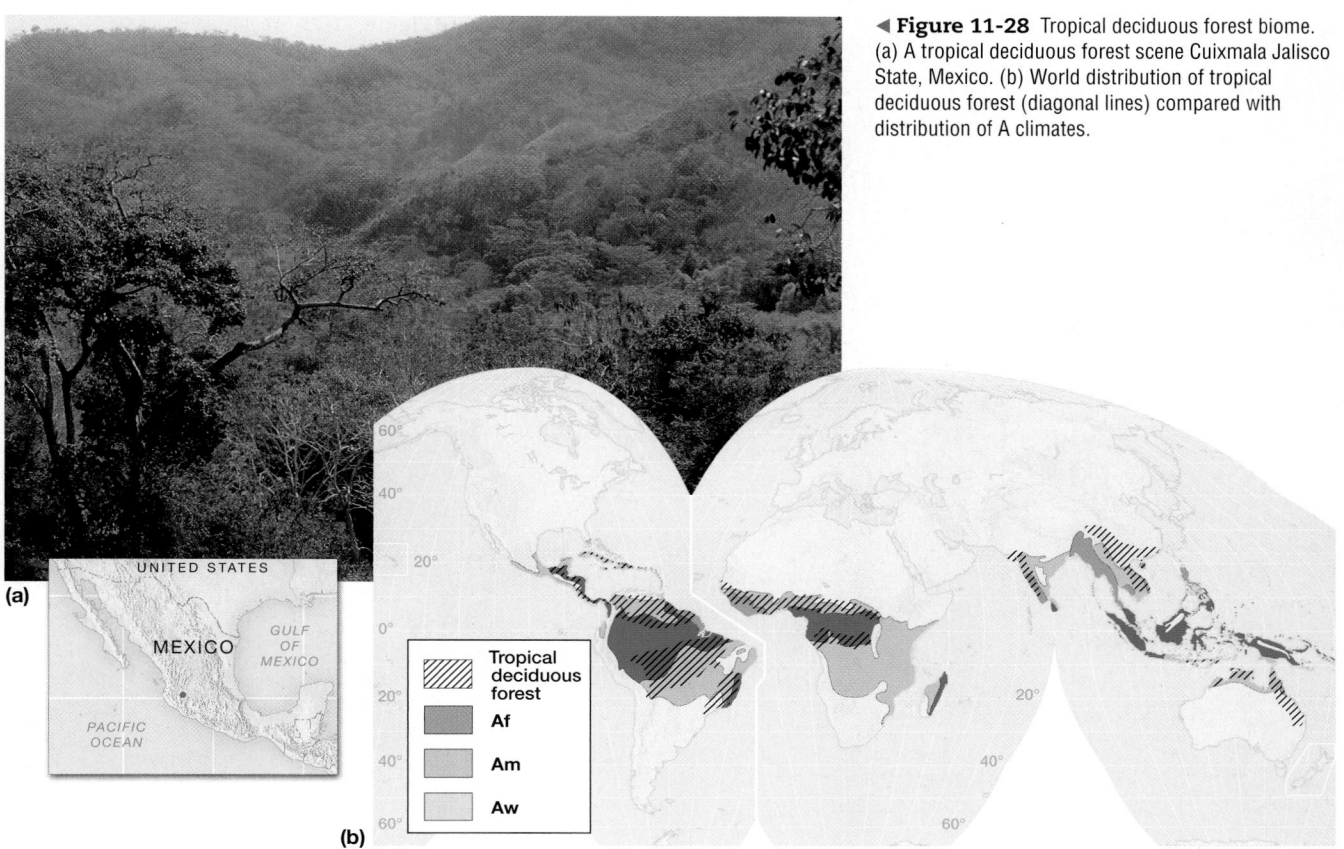

◄ **Figure 11-28** Tropical deciduous forest biome. (a) A tropical deciduous forest scene Cuixmala Jalisco State, Mexico. (b) World distribution of tropical deciduous forest (diagonal lines) compared with distribution of A climates.

penetrate to the forest floor. This light produces an understory of lesser plants that often grows in such density as to produce classic jungle conditions. The diversity of tree species is not as great in this biome as in tropical rainforest, but there is a greater variety of shrubs and other lesser plants.

The faunal assemblage of the tropical deciduous forest is generally similar to that of the rainforest. Although there are more ground-level vertebrates than in the selva, arboreal species such as monkeys, birds, bats, and lizards are particularly conspicuous in both biomes.

Learning Check 11-12 **Explain what it means to say that the tropical rainforest biome typically has high biodiversity.**

Tropical Scrub

The **tropical scrub** biome is widespread in drier portions of tropical savanna (Aw) climate and in some areas of subtropical steppe (BSh) climate (Figure 11-29). It is dominated by low-growing, scraggly trees and tall bushes, usually with an extensive understory of grasses (Figure 11-29a). The trees range from 3 to 9 meters (10 to 30 feet) in height. Their density is quite variable, with the trees sometimes growing in close proximity to one another but often spaced much more openly. Biodiversity is much less than in the tropical

rainforest and tropical deciduous forest biomes; frequently just a few species comprise the bulk of the taller growth over vast areas. In the more tropical and wetter portions of the tropical scrub biome, most of the trees and shrubs are evergreen; elsewhere most species are deciduous. In some areas, a high proportion of the shrubs are thorny.

The fauna of tropical scrub regions is notably different from that of the two biomes previously discussed. There is a moderately rich assemblage of ground-dwelling mammals and reptiles, and of birds and insects.

Tropical Savanna

As Figure 11-30 shows, there is an incomplete correlation between the distribution of the **tropical savanna** biome (also called the *tropical grassland* biome) and that of the tropical savanna (Aw) climate. The correlation tends to be most noticeable where seasonal rainfall contrasts are greatest, a condition particularly associated with the broad-scale annual shifting of the intertropical convergence zone (ITCZ).

Savanna lands are dominated by tall grasses (Figure 11-30a). Sometimes the grasses form a complete ground cover, but sometimes there is bare ground among dispersed tufts of grass in what is called a bunchgrass pattern. The name "savanna" without any modifier usually refers to areas that are virtually without shrubs or trees, but this type of savanna is not the most common. In most cases, a

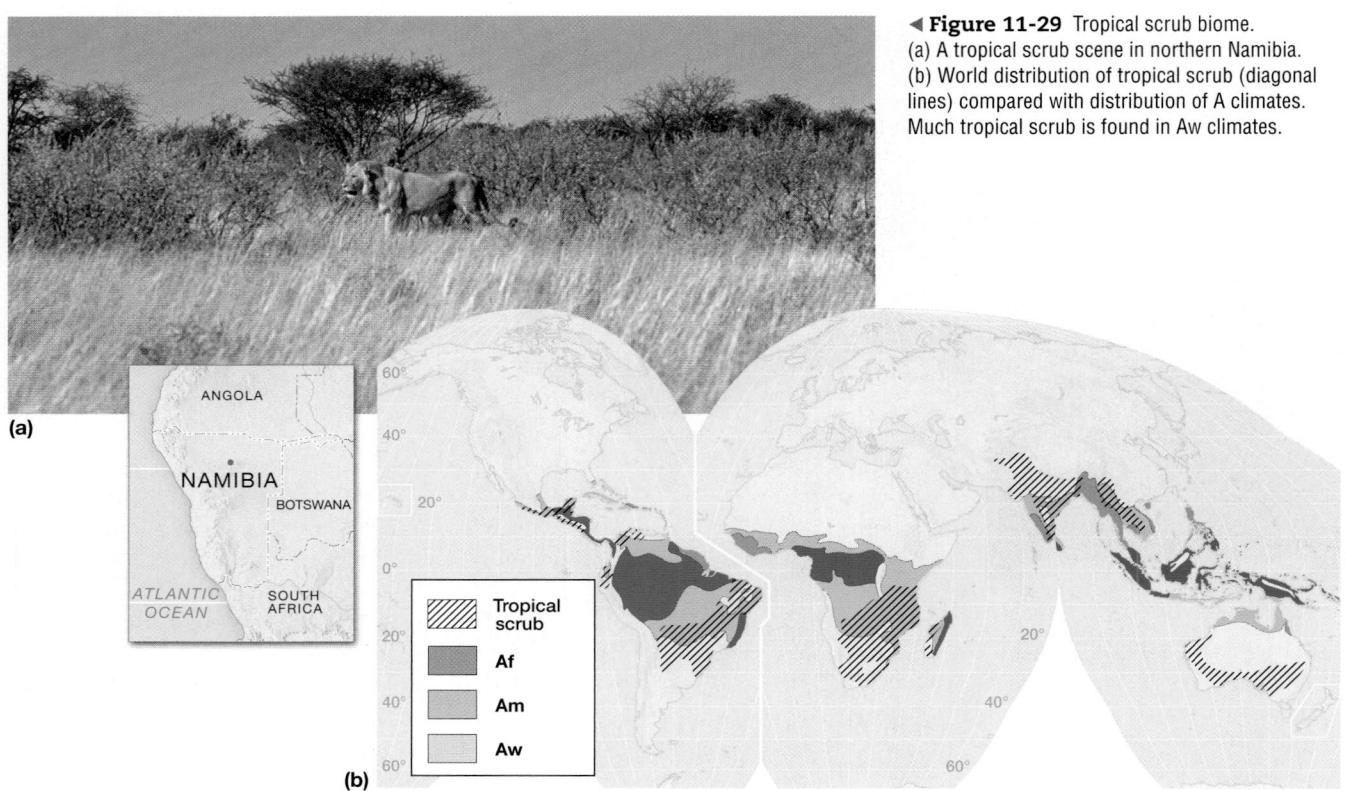

◀ **Figure 11-29** Tropical scrub biome.
(a) A tropical scrub scene in northern Namibia.
(b) World distribution of tropical scrub (diagonal lines) compared with distribution of A climates. Much tropical scrub is found in Aw climates.

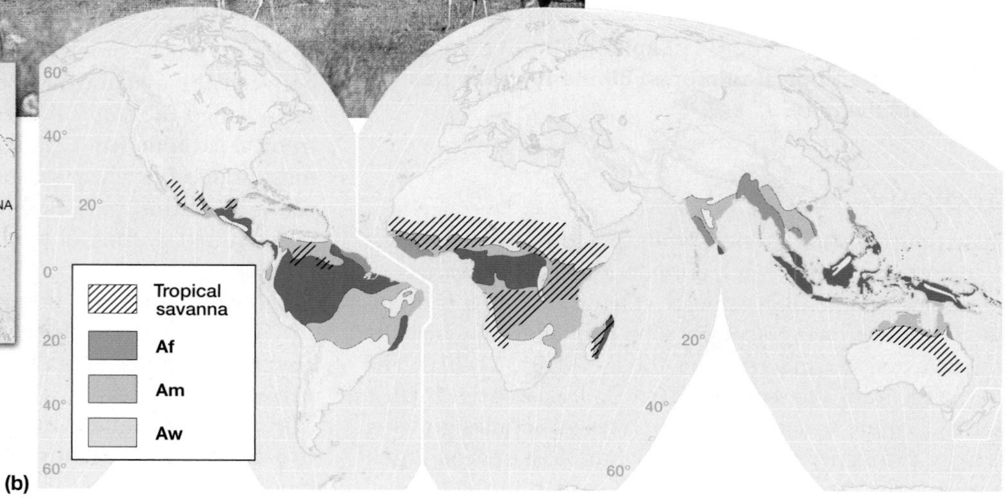

◀ **Figure 11-30** Tropical savanna biome.
(a) A mixed array—zebra, kudu, and springbok—of ungulates surrounds a waterhole in a typical savanna landscape in Namibia's Etosha National Park. (b) World distribution of tropical savanna (diagonal lines) compared with distribution of A climates.

wide scattering of both types dots the grass-covered terrain, and this mixture of plant forms is often referred to as *parkland* or *park savanna*.

In much of the savanna, the vegetation has been altered by human interference with natural processes. A considerable area of tropical deciduous forest and tropical scrub, and perhaps some tropical rainforest, has been converted to savanna over thousands of years through fires set by humans and through the grazing and browsing of domestic animals.

The savanna biome has a very pronounced seasonal rhythm. During the wet season, the grass grows tall, green, and luxuriant. At the onset of the dry season, the grass begins to wither, and before long the above-ground portion is dead and brown. At this time, too, many of the trees and shrubs shed their leaves. The third "season" is the time of wildfires. The accumulation of dry grass provides abundant fuel, and most parts of the savannas experience natural burning every year or so. The recurrent grass fires are stimulating for the ecosystem, as they burn away the unpalatable portion of the grass without causing significant damage to shrubs and trees. When the rains of the next wet season arrive, the grasses spring into growth with renewed vigor.

Savanna fauna varies from continent to continent. The African savannas are the premier "big game" lands of the world, with an unmatched richness of large animals, particularly ungulates and carnivores, but also including a remarkable diversity of other fauna. The Latin American savannas, on the other hand, have only a sparse population of large wildlife, with Asian and Australian areas intermediate between these two extremes.

Learning Check 11-13 **Describe the typical climate in regions of the tropical savanna biome.**

Desert FG9

In previous chapters, we noted a general decrease in precipitation as one moves away from the equator in the low latitudes. This progression is matched by a gradation from the tropical rainforest biome of the equator to the **desert** biome of the subtropics. The desert biome also occurs extensively in midlatitude locations in Eurasia, North America, and South America with a fairly close correlation to subtropical desert (BWh) and midlatitude desert (BWk) climates (Figure 11-31).

◀ **Figure 11-31** Desert biome. (a) Natural vegetation typically is spindly and thorny in deserts, as in this scene from Red Rock Canyon in California's Mojave Desert. (b) World distribution of desert (diagonal lines) compared with distribution of B climates.

(a)

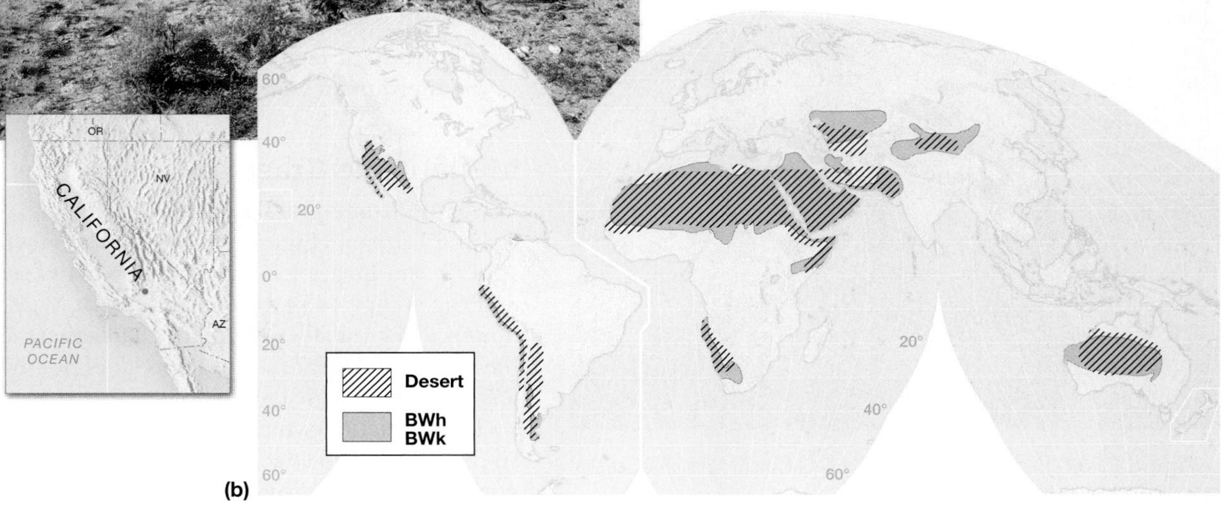

OR

NV

CALIFORNIA

AZ

PACIFIC
OCEAN

60°

40°

20°

0°

20°

40°

60°

20°

40°

60°

20°

40°

Desert

BWh
BWk

(b)

Desert vegetation is surprisingly variable (Figure 11-31a). It consists largely of xerophytic plants such as succulents and other drought-resisting plants with structural modifications that allow them to conserve moisture and drought-evading plants capable of hasty reproduction during brief rainy times. The plant cover is usually sparse, with considerable bare ground dotted by a scattering of individual plants. Typically the plants are shrubs, which occur in considerable variety, each with its own mechanisms to combat the stress of limited moisture. Succulents are common in the drier parts of most desert areas, and many desert plants have either tiny leaves or no leaves at all as a moisture-conserving strategy. Grasses and other herbaceous plants are widespread but sparse in desert areas. Despite the dryness, trees can be found sporadically in the desert, especially in Australia.

Animal life is inconspicuous in most desert areas, leading to the erroneous idea that animals are nonexistent. Actually, most deserts have a moderately diverse faunal assemblage, although the variety of large mammals is limited. A large proportion of desert animals avoid the principal periods of desiccating heat (daylight in general and the hot season in particular) by resting in burrows or crevices during the day and prowling at night (Figure 11-32).

Generally speaking, life in the desert biome is characterized by an appearance of stillness. In favorable times and in favored places (around water holes and oases), however, there is a great increase in biotic activities, and sometimes the total biomass is of remarkable proportions. Favorable times are at night, and particularly after rains. For example, a heavy rain might trigger the germination of wildflower seeds that had remained dormant for decades.

Mediterranean Woodland and Shrub   FG7, FG12

As Figure 11-33 shows, the **mediterranean woodland and shrub** biome is found in six widely scattered and relatively small areas of the midlatitudes, all of which experience the pronounced dry summer–wet winter precipitation typical of mediterranean (Cs) climates. In this biome, the dominant vegetation associations are physically very similar to each other but taxonomically quite varied. The biome is dominated mostly by a dense growth of woody shrubs known as a *chaparral* in North America (Figure 11-33a), but having other names in other areas; chaparral includes many species of *sclerophyllous* plants, adapted to the prominent summer dry season by the presence of small, hard leaves that inhibit moisture loss. A second significant plant association of mediterranean regions is an open grassy woodland, in which the ground is almost completely grass covered but has a considerable scattering of trees as well (Figures 11-33b and 11-33c).

The plant species vary from region to region. Oaks of various kinds are by far the most significant genus in the Northern Hemisphere mediterranean lands, sometimes occurring as prominent medium-sized trees but also appearing as a more stunted, shrubby growth. In all areas, the trees and shrubs are primarily broadleaf evergreens. Their leaves are mostly small and have a leathery texture or waxy coating, which inhibits water loss during the long dry season. Moreover, most plants have deep roots.

Summer is a virtually rainless season in mediterranean climates, and so summer fires are relatively common. Many of the plants are adapted to rapid recovery after a wildfire has swept over the area. Indeed, as noted in Chapter 10, some species have seeds that are released for germination only after the heat of a fire has caused their seedpods to open. Part of the seasonal rhythm of this biome is that winter floods sometimes follow summer fires, as slopes left unprotected by the burning away of grass and lower shrubs are susceptible to abrupt erosive runoff if the winter rains arrive before the vegetation has a chance to resprout.

The fauna of this biome is not particularly distinctive. Seed-eating, burrowing rodents are common, as are some bird and reptile groups. There is a general overlap of animals between this biome and adjacent ones.

Learning Check 11-14   **Which climate characteristic is most closely associated with the mediterranean woodland and shrub biome?**

Midlatitude Grassland   FG13

Vast **midlatitude grasslands** occur widely in North America and Eurasia (Figure 11-34). In the Northern Hemisphere, the locational coincidence between this biome and the steppe (BSh and BSk) climatic type is very pronounced. The smaller Southern Hemisphere areas (mostly the *pampa* of Argentina and the *veldt* of South Africa) have less distinct climatic correlations.

The vegetation typical of a grassland biome is a general response either to a lack of precipitation sufficient to support larger plant forms or to the frequency of fires (both

▲ **Figure 11-32** This fierce-looking thorny devil lizard in Western Australia is just 10 centimeters (4 inches) long.

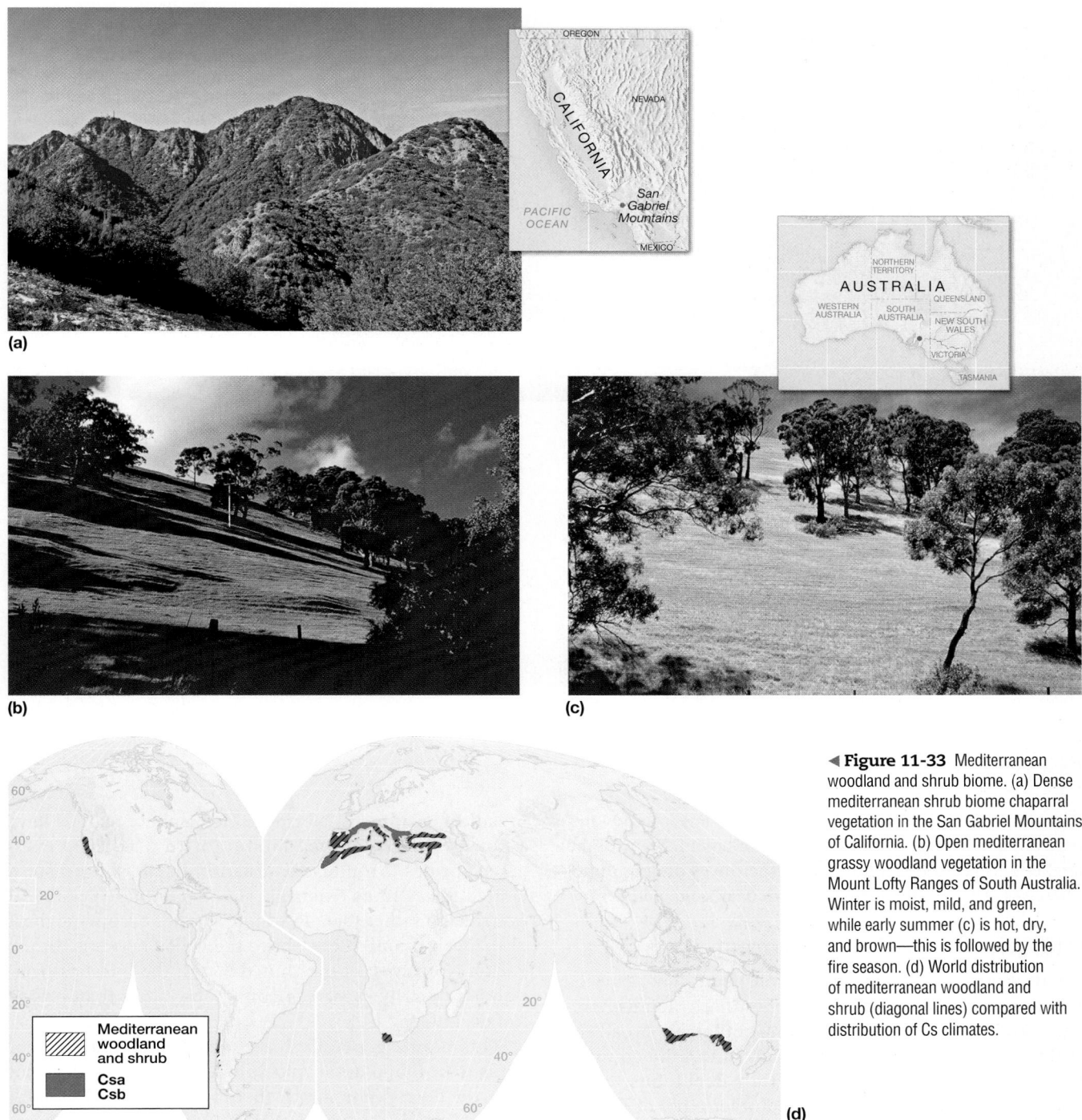

◄ **Figure 11-33** Mediterranean woodland and shrub biome. (a) Dense mediterranean shrub biome chaparral vegetation in the San Gabriel Mountains of California. (b) Open mediterranean grassy woodland vegetation in the Mount Lofty Ranges of South Australia. Winter is moist, mild, and green, while early summer (c) is hot, dry, and brown—this is followed by the fire season. (d) World distribution of mediterranean woodland and shrub (diagonal lines) compared with distribution of Cs climates.

natural and human induced) that prevent the growth of tree or shrub seedlings. In the wetter areas of a grassland biome, the grasses grow tall and the term *prairie* is often applied in North America. In drier regions, the grasses are shorter; such growth is often referred to as *steppe* (Figure 11-34a). Sometimes a continuous ground cover is missing, and the grasses grow in discrete tufts as bunchgrass or tussock grass.

Most of the grass species are perennials, lying dormant during the winter and sprouting anew the following

summer. Trees are mostly restricted to riparian locations, whereas shrubs and bushes occur sporadically on rocky sites. Grass fires are fairly common in summer, which helps to explain the relative scarcity of shrubs. The woody plants cannot tolerate fires and can generally survive only on dry slopes where there is little grass cover to fuel a fire.

Grasslands provide extensive pastures for grazing animals, and before encroachment by humans drastically changed population sizes, the grassland fauna comprised

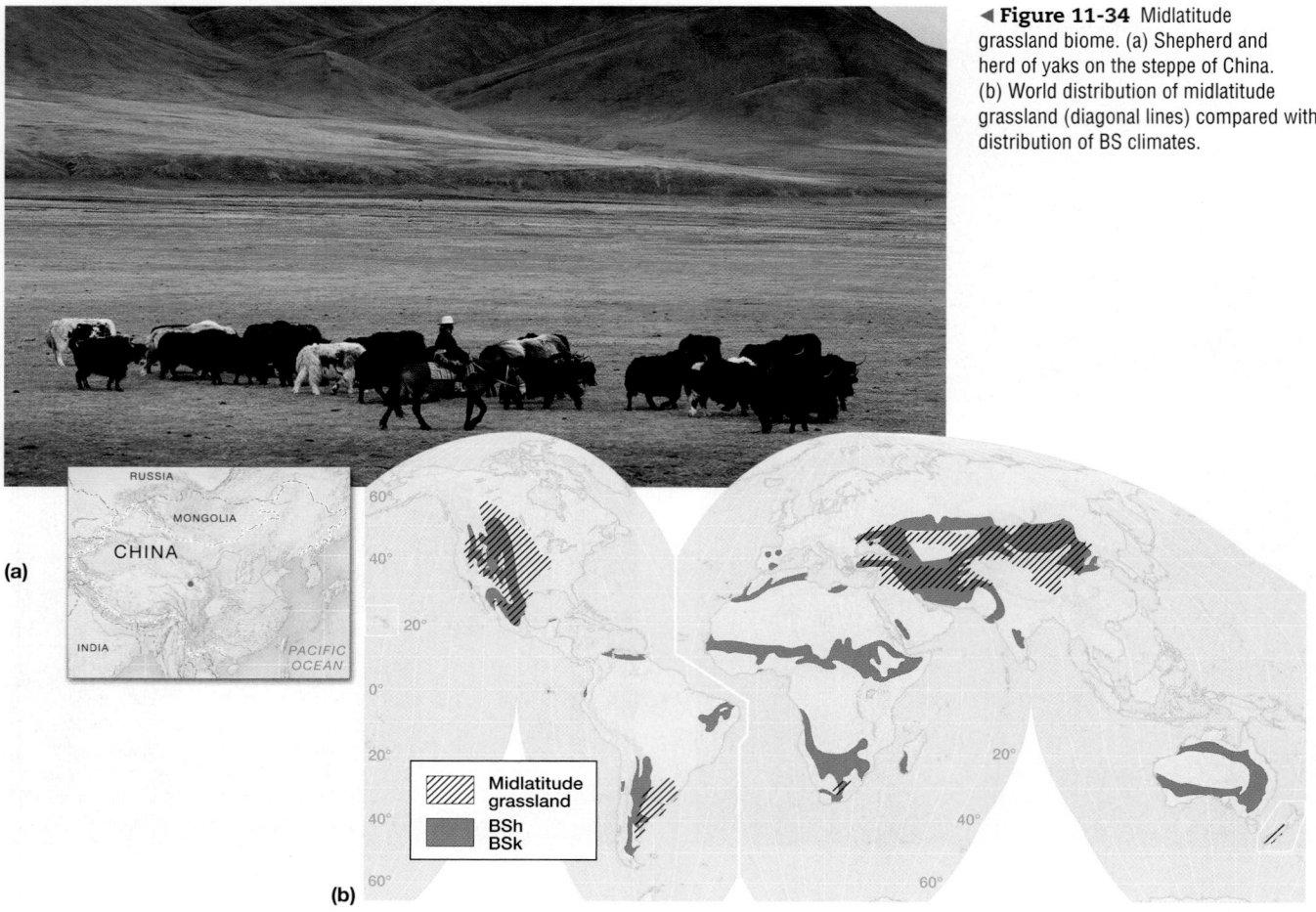

◄ **Figure 11-34** Midlatitude grassland biome. (a) Shepherd and herd of yaks on the steppe of China. (b) World distribution of midlatitude grassland (diagonal lines) compared with distribution of BS climates.

large numbers of relatively few species. The larger herbivores were often migratory prior to human settlement. Many of the smaller animals spend all or part of their lives underground, where they find some protection from heat, cold, and fire.

Midlatitude Deciduous Forest

Extensive areas on all Northern Hemisphere continents, as well as more limited tracts in the Southern Hemisphere, were originally covered with a forest of largely broadleaf deciduous trees (Figure 11-35). Except in hilly country, a large proportion of this **midlatitude deciduous forest** has been cleared for agriculture and other types of human use, so that very little of the original natural vegetation remains.

The forest is characterized by a fairly dense growth of tall broadleaf trees with interwoven branches that provide a complete canopy in summer. Some smaller trees and shrubs exist at lower levels, but for the most part, the forest floor is relatively barren of undergrowth. In winter, the appearance of the forest changes dramatically, owing to the seasonal fall of leaves (Figure 11-35a).

Tree species vary considerably from region to region, although most are broadleaf and deciduous. The principal exception is in eastern Australia, where the forest is composed almost entirely of varieties of eucalyptus, which are

broadleaf evergreens. Northern Hemisphere regions have a northward gradational mixture with needleleaf evergreen species. An unusual situation in the southeastern United States finds extensive stands of pines (needleleaf evergreens) rather than deciduous species occupying most of the well-drained sites above the valley bottoms. In the Pacific Northwest of the United States, the forest association is primarily evergreen coniferous rather than broadleaf deciduous.

This biome generally has the richest assemblage of fauna to be found in the midlatitudes, although it does not have the diversity to match that of most tropical biomes. It has (or had) a considerable variety of birds and mammals, and in some areas reptiles and amphibians are well represented. Summer brings a diverse and active population of insects and other arthropods. All animal life is less numerous (partly due to migrations and hibernation) and less conspicuous in winter.

Boreal Forest

One of the most extensive biomes is the **boreal forest**, sometimes called *taiga* after the Russian word for the northern fringe of the boreal forest in that country (paralleling the way these synonyms are used to describe

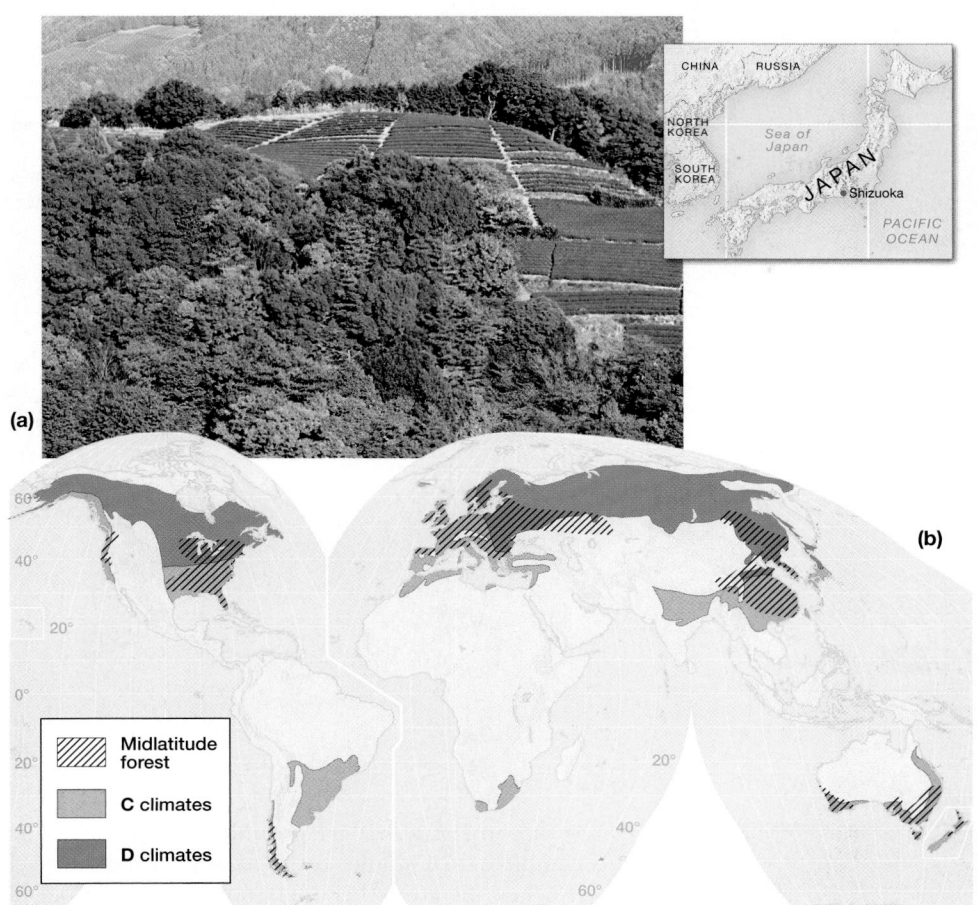

◀ **Figure 11-35** Midlatitude deciduous forest biome. (a) This midlatitude forest scene is in the mountains near Shizuoka, Japan. As is common in some midlatitude locations, the forest here consists of both deciduous and evergreen trees. (b) World distribution of midlatitude forest (diagonal lines) before human activities made significant changes in this biome. The colors indicate distribution of C and D climates.

climates, as mentioned in Chapter 8). The boreal forest occupies a vast expanse of northern North America and Eurasia (Figure 11-36). There is very close correlation between the location of the boreal forest biome and the subarctic (Dfc) climatic type, with a similar correlation between the locations of the tundra climate and the tundra biome.

This great northern forest contains perhaps the simplest assemblage of plants of any biome (Figure 11-36a). Most of the trees are conifers, nearly all needleleaf evergreens, with the important exception of the tamarack or larch which drops its needles in winter. The variety of species is limited to mostly pines, firs, and spruces extending broadly in homogeneous stands. In some places, the coniferous cover is interrupted by areas of deciduous trees. These deciduous stands are also of limited variety (mostly birch, poplar, and aspen) and often represent a seral situation following a forest fire.

The trees grow taller and more densely near the southern margins of this biome, where the summer growing season is longer and warmer. Near the northern margins, the trees are spindly, short, and more openly spaced. Undergrowth is normally not dense beneath the forest canopy, but a layer of deciduous shrubs sometimes grows in profusion. The ground is usually covered with a complete growth of mosses and lichens, with some grasses in the south and a considerable accumulation of decaying needles overall.

Poor drainage is typical in summer, due partially to permanently frozen subsoil, which prevents downward percolation of water, and partially to the derangement of normal surface drainage by the action of glaciers during the recent Pleistocene ice age. Thus, bogs and swamps are numerous, and the ground is generally spongy in summer. During the long winters, of course, all is frozen.

The immensity of the boreal forest gives an impression of biotic productivity, but such is not the case. Harsh climate, floristic homogeneity, and slow plant growth produce only a limited food supply for animals. Faunal species diversity is limited, although the number of individuals of some species is astounding. With relatively few animal species in such a vast biome, populations sometimes fluctuate enormously within the space of only a year or so. Mammals are represented prominently by species that have been traditionally hunted for their fur (Figure 11-37) and by a few species of ungulates. Birds are numerous and fairly diverse in summer, but nearly all migrate to milder latitudes in winter. Insects are totally absent in winter but superabundant during the brief summer.

Learning Check 11-15 **How does the biodiversity of the boreal forest biome differ from that of the tropical rainforest biome?**

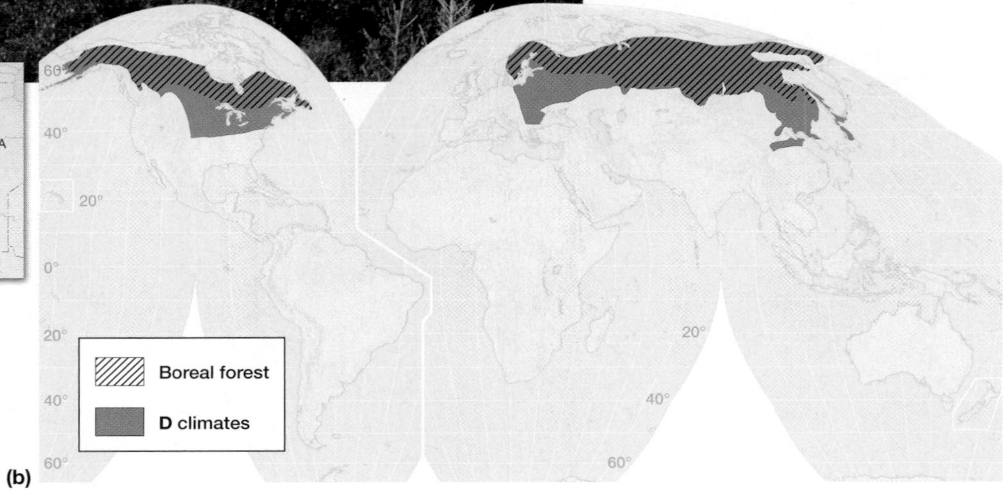

<figure>
◄ **Figure 11-36** Boreal forest biome. (a) The boreal forest contains trees that generally are short, close growing, and of uniform species composition. This spruce forest surrounds Shady Lake near Prince Albert in the Canadian province of Saskatchewan. (b) World distribution of boreal forest (diagonal lines) compared with distribution of D climates.
</figure>

ALBERTA
MANITOBA
SASKATCHEWAN
CANADA
UNITED STATES
(a)

▨ Boreal forest

▨ D climates

(b)

▲ **Figure 11-37** Bears live in diverse habitats, but mostly in cold climates. This grizzly bear inhabits Katmai National Park in Alaska.

Tundra

The **tundra** is essentially a cold desert or grassland in which moisture is scarce and summers so short and cool that trees are unable to survive. This biome is distributed along the northern edge of the Northern Hemisphere continents, correlating closely to the distribution of tundra (ET) climate (Figure 11-38). The plant cover consists of a considerable mixture of species, many of them in dwarf forms (Figure 11-38a). Included are grasses, mosses, lichens, flowering herbs, and a scattering of low shrubs. These plants often occur in a dense, ground-hugging arrangement, although some places have a more sporadic

cover with considerable bare ground interspersed. The plants complete their annual cycles hastily during the brief summer, when the ground is often moist and waterlogged because of inadequate surface drainage and particularly inadequate subsurface drainage—often as a consequence of *permafrost* just below the surface (permafrost was discussed in Chapter 9).

Animal life is dominated by birds and insects during the summer. Extraordinary numbers of birds flock to the tundra for summer nesting, migrating southward as winter approaches. Mosquitoes, flies, and other insects proliferate astoundingly during the short warm season, laying eggs that can survive the bitter winter. Other forms of animal life are scarcer—a few species of mammals and freshwater fishes but almost no reptiles or amphibians.

Alpine Tundra: An alpine version of tundra is found in many high-elevation areas. Many mountain areas above the timberline exhibit areas with a sparse cover of vegetation consisting of herbaceous plants, grasses, and low shrubs (Figure 11-39).

HUMAN MODIFICATION OF NATURAL DISTRIBUTION PATTERNS

Thus far in our discussion of the biosphere, most of our attention has been focused on "natural" conditions, that is, events and processes that take place in nature without the aid or interference of human activities. Such natural processes have been going on for millennia, and their effects

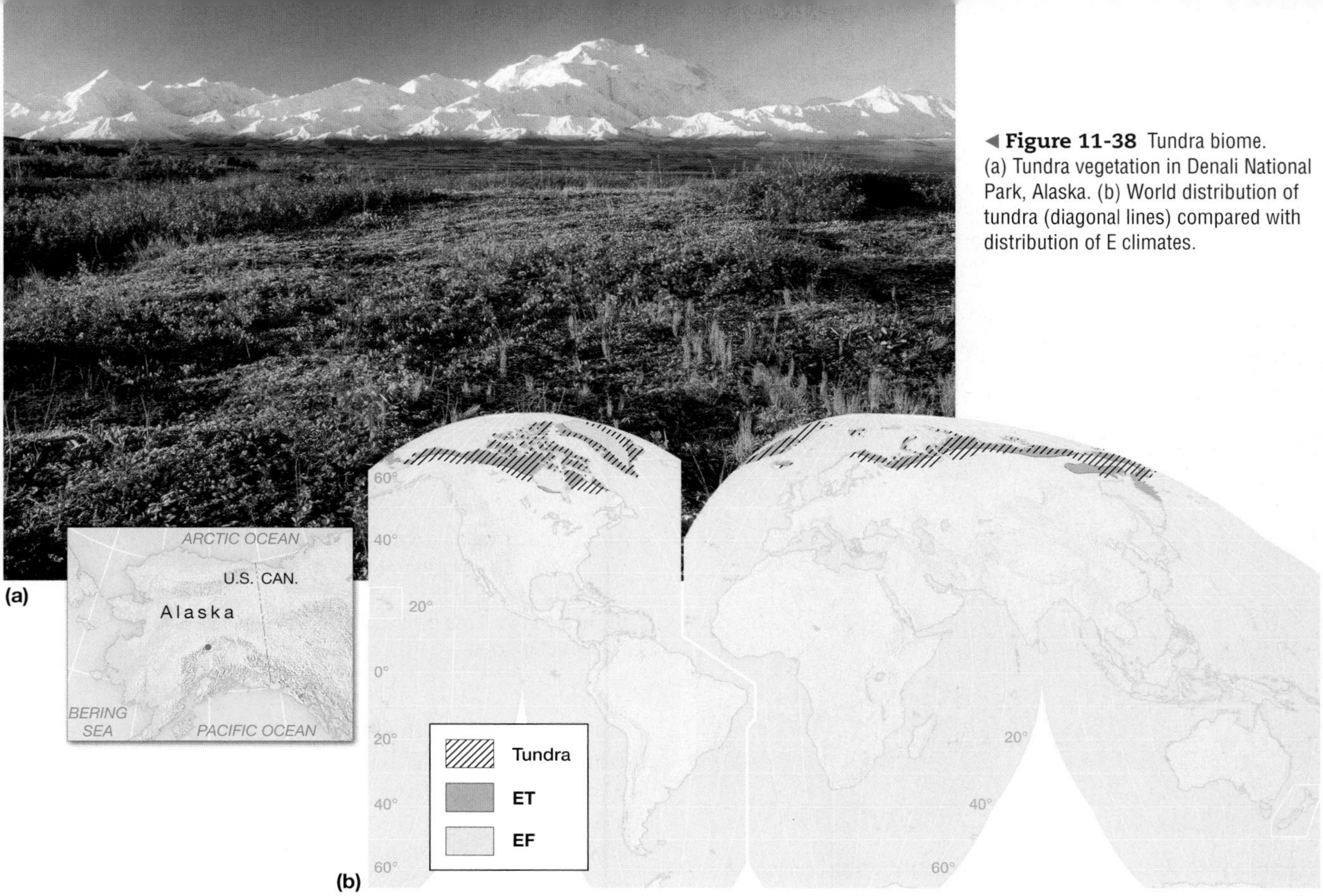

◀ **Figure 11-38** Tundra biome.
(a) Tundra vegetation in Denali National Park, Alaska. (b) World distribution of tundra (diagonal lines) compared with distribution of E climates.

(a)

(b)

on floral and faunal distribution patterns have normally been very slow and gradual. The pristine environment, uninfluenced by humankind, experiences its share of abrupt and dramatic events, to be sure, but environmental changes generally proceed at a gradual pace. When *Homo sapiens* appear, however, the tempo changes dramatically.

People are capable of exerting extraordinary influences on the distribution of plants and animals. Not only is the magnitude of the changes likely to be great, but also the speed with which they are affected is sometimes exceedingly rapid. In broadest perspective, humankind exerts three types of direct influences on biotic distributions: physical removal of organisms, habitat modification, and the introduction of *exotic* species.

Physical Removal of Organisms

One of humankind's most successful skills is in the elimination of other living things. As human population increases and spreads over the globe, there is often a wholesale removal of native plants and animals to make way for the severely modified landscape that is thought necessary for civilization. The natural plant and animal inhabitants are cut down, plowed up, paved over, burned, poisoned, shot, trapped, and otherwise eradicated in actions that have far-reaching effects on overall distribution patterns.

▼ **Figure 11-39** Alpine tundra vegetation high in the Rocky Mountains.

Habitat Modification  FG6, FG8

Habitat modification is another activity in which humankind excels. The soil environment is changed by farming, grazing, engineering, and construction practices (Figure 11-40); the atmospheric environment is degraded by the introduction of impurities of various kinds; the waters of the planet are impounded, diverted, and polluted. All these deeds influence the native plants and animals in the affected areas.

Video
Climate, Crops
and Bees

Among the most dramatic recent human-initiated changes to global habitat have involved the removal of vast areas of tropical rainforest.

▲ **Figure 11-40** An overgrazed range in the Colorado high country illustrates human-induced habitat modification caused by overstocking of livestock in the area to the right of the fence. The locale is near Central City.

Tropical Rainforest Removal:

Throughout much of history, most rainforests of the world were only modestly populated and as a consequence they were affected by human activities in limited ways. Since the twentieth century, however, rainforests have been exploited and devastated at an accelerating pace; and over the past 40 years or so, tropical deforestation has become one of Earth's most serious environmental problems.

The exact rate of deforestation around the world—in both the tropics and temperate forest regions—is not precisely known, but the United Nations Food and Agriculture Organization (FAO) estimates that between 2000 and 2010, about 13 million hectares (32 million acres) of forest were being lost each year. Between 1990 and 2005 about 42 million hectares (104 million acres) of rainforest was cleared in Brazil alone—the greatest total of any country during that time period (Figure 11-41) and an area approximately equal to that of California (see the box, "People and the Environment: Rainforest Loss in Brazil"). Indonesia ranked second with more than 25 million hectares (62 million acres) cleared during those years.

In terms of the total percentage of rainforest cleared in each country, the picture is somewhat different (Figure 11-42). The FAO estimates that between 1990 and 2005, the tiny African island country of Comoros lost almost 60 percent of its rainforest, whereas Burundi in central equatorial Africa ranked second with a loss of about 47 percent. Overall, about half of Africa's original rainforest is now gone, but in some countries, such as Nigeria and Ghana, losses now total more than 80 percent.

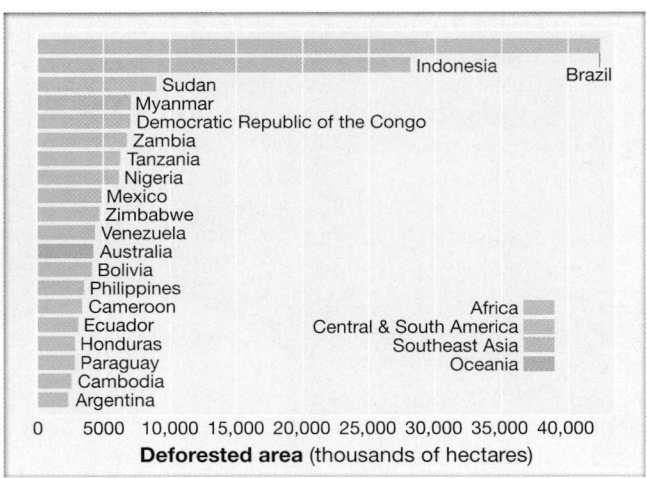

▲ **Figure 11-41** Loss of forest by country between 1990 and 2005 in thousands of hectares.

In South and Southeast Asia, where commercial exploration, especially for teak and mahogany is important, about 45 percent of the original forest no longer exists. Approximately 40 percent of Latin America's rainforest has been cleared. Much of the very rapid deforestation in Central America has been due to expanded cattle ranching. Deforestation of the Amazon region as a percentage of the total area of rainforest has been moderate (perhaps 20 percent of the total has been cleared).

As the forest goes, so goes its habitability for both indigenous peoples and native animal life. In the mid-1980s, it was calculated that tropical deforestation was responsible for the extermination of one species per day; by the mid-1990s, it was estimated that the rate was two species per hour. Moreover, loss of the forests contributes to accelerated soil erosion, drought, flooding, water quality degradation, declining agricultural productivity, and greater poverty for rural inhabitants. In addition, atmospheric carbon dioxide continues to be increased because burning trees as a way of clearing forest releases carbon to the air.

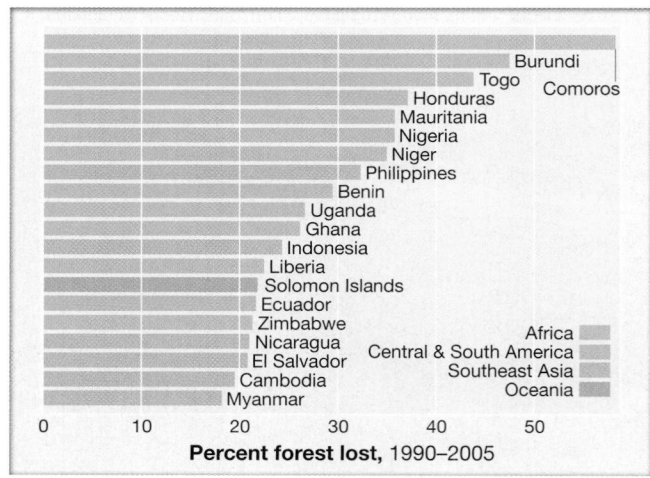

▲ **Figure 11-42** Percentage of forest lost by country between 1990 and 2005.

The irony of tropical deforestation is that the anticipated economic benefits are usually temporary. Much of the forest clearing is in response to the social pressure of overcrowding and poverty in societies where many people are landless. The governments open "new lands" for settlement in the rainforest. The settlers clear the land for crop or livestock. The result is almost always an initial nutrient pulse of high soil productivity, followed in only two or three years by a pronounced fertility decline as the nutrients are quickly leached and cropped out of the soil, weed species rapidly invade, and erosion becomes rampant (Figure 11-43). Ongoing commercial agriculture can generally be expected only with continuous heavy fertilization, a costly procedure, while sustainable land-extensive forms of traditional agriculture are slowly disappearing.

If left alone, forests can regenerate, providing there are seed trees in the vicinity and the soil has not been stripped of all its nutrients—but the increasing fragmentation of tropical rainforest in some regions means that the original species composition may not return. This loss of biodiversity from tropical rainforests is an increasing concern because extinction is irreversible. Valuable potential resources—pharmaceutical products, new food crops, natural insecticides, industrial materials—may disappear before they are even discovered. Wild plants and animals that could be bred with domesticated cousins to impart resistance to disease, insects, parasites, and other environmental stresses may also be lost.

Much concern has been expressed about tropical deforestation, and some concrete steps have been taken. The development of *agroforestry* (planting crops with trees, rather than cutting down the trees and replacing them

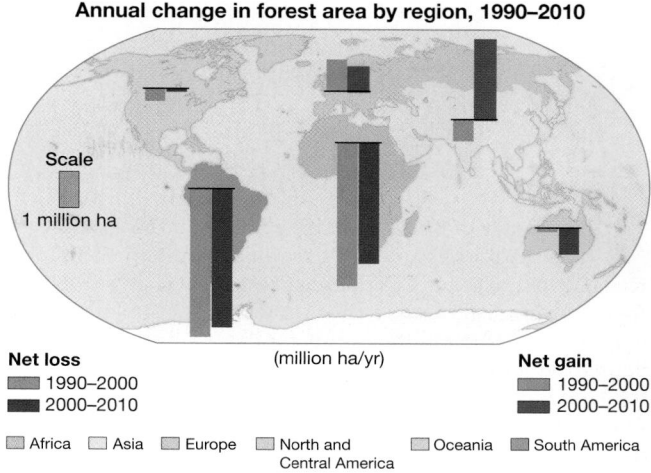

▲ **Figure 11-44** Annual change in forest cover between 1990 and 2010. Although the annual forest loss is still very high in South America and Africa, the rate of forest loss decreased slightly between 2000 and 2010.

with crops) is being fostered in many areas. The United Nations Educational, Scientific, and Cultural Organization (UNESCO) administers the *Man and the Biosphere Programme* that coordinates an international effort to establish and protect biosphere reserves. The goal of this project is to set aside tracts of largely pristine land—including regions of tropical rainforest—to preserve biodiversity before it is lost to development. At present, 580 biosphere reserves have been established in 114 countries.

Although deforestation remains high in many locations, the *rate* of forest loss around the world has slowed over the last decade (Figure 11-44). In addition, efforts around the world to replant cleared forest with new trees are expanding. The FAO estimates that the *net forest loss* (the difference between forest loss and forest expansion through replanting) decreased from an annual loss of 8.3 million hectares between 1990 and 2000 to an annual loss of 5.2 million hectares between 2000 and 2010—and some countries are actually experiencing a net gain in forest cover (Figure 11-45).

▲ **Figure 11-43** When rainforests are cleared for agriculture, the results are often small yields and accelerated soil erosion. This scene is from central Thailand.

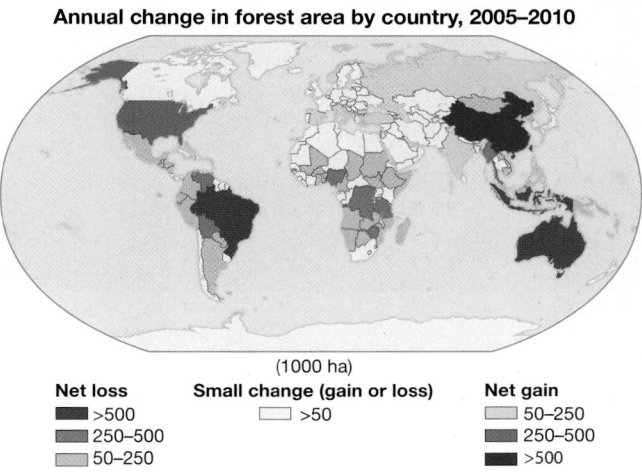

▲ **Figure 11-45** Net forest cover change 2005 to 2010. Because of replanting, some countries experienced a net gain in forest cover.

PEOPLE AND THE ENVIRONMENT

Rainforest Loss in Brazil

The country of Brazil contains about one-third of the world's tropical forest, most of it part of the vast rainforest spreading across the Amazon River basin. Although the rainforest has supported a modest human population for thousands of years, over the last half century large tracts of the forest have been opened up for settlers. As a consequence, the pristine forest is being cleared for settlements, agriculture, ranching, and logging.

Opening Rondônia to Settlers:
The Brazilian government completed construction of the Cuiabá–Port Velho highway across the province of Rondônia in 1960. Although the road opened up the region to immigrants and development, the forest was still relatively unchanged 15 years later (Figure 11-C-a). By the late 1980s, however, the rate of deforestation had increased substantially and the region had taken on a "fishbone" pattern as forest was cleared along an expanding network of roads. By 2012 the extent of deforestation was extraordinary (Figure 11-C-b).

Widespread deforestation is leading to a loss of both habitat and species, and in the end, many of the uses of the cleared land are simply not sustainable. In Rondônia, less than 10 percent of agricultural land use has gone toward potentially sustainable perennial crops such as cacao and coffee; much of the rest is either used for cattle grazing or annual crops—and this land must usually be abandoned in a few years after the generally poor tropical soils are depleted of nutrients. Once abandoned for agriculture, it may be decades before the forest can grow back to near its original density and composition.

Over the last few decades, the area of greatest deforestation has shifted to the east from Rondônia into the Brazilian states of Mato Grosso and Pará, where land is often cleared for large-scale mechanized agriculture. Although about 20 percent of the Amazon rainforest has thus far been cleared, the pace of deforestation in recent years has slowed.

(a) 1975

(b) 2012

▲ **Figure 11-C** Deforestation in Rondônia, Brazil, (a) in 1975 and (b) in 2012. Images taken by Landsat satellites jointly managed by NASA and the U.S. Geological Survey.

It is important to note, however, that both planted forests (which account for about 7 percent of the world forest cover today) and naturally regenerated forests (which account for about 57 percent of the world total) frequently do not contain the same biodiversity as the original forest—and in many parts of the world, replanted forests consists of exotic tree species. Thus, even in areas where forest cover is expanding, the original biodiversity has been lost. Overall, only about one-third of the world's forest cover is *primary forest*—forest with its natural species composition and little signs of human activity.

Learning Check 11-16 Why is tropical rainforest loss a major environmental concern today?

Introduction of Exotic Species FG13

People are capable of elaborate rearrangement of the natural complement of plants and animals in almost every part of the world. This is shown most clearly with domesticated species—crops, livestock, pets. There is now, for example, more corn than native grasses in Iowa, more cattle than native gazelles in Sudan, and more canaries than native thrushes in Detroit. More importantly for our discussion here, humans have also accounted for many introductions of wild plants and animals into "new" habitats; such organisms are called **exotic species** in their new homelands.

In some cases, the introduction of exotic species was deliberate. A few examples among a great many include taking prickly-pear cactus from Arizona to Australia; crested wheat grass from Russia to Kansas; European boar from Germany to Tennessee; pronghorn antelope from Oregon to Hawai'i; and red fox from England to New Zealand. Frequently, however, the introduction of an exotic species was an accidental result of human carelessness. The European flea, for example, has become one of the most widespread creatures on Earth because it has been an unseen accompaniment to human migrations all over the world. Similarly, the English sparrow and European brown rat have inadvertently been introduced to all inhabited continents by traveling as stowaways on ships.

One other type of human-induced introduction of animals involves the deliberate release or accidental escape of livestock to become established as a "wild"—properly termed *feral*—population. This has happened in many parts of the world, most notably in North America and Australia (Figure 11-46).

In many parts of the world, natural biotic distribution patterns have been rearranged through deliberate and accidental human efforts to introduce plants and animals. When an exotic species is released in a new area, the results are usually one of two extremes. Either it dies out in a short time because of environmental hazards and/or competitive-predatory pressures, or the introduced species finds both a benign climate and an unfilled ecologic niche

▲ **Figure 11-46** Burros are prominent feral animals in much of the southwestern desert area of the United States. This group is in the Panamint Range of California.

and is able to flourish extraordinarily—sometimes with disastrous results.

The world abounds with examples—sparrows and starlings, rabbits and pigs, mongooses and mynas, lantana and prickly pear, mesquite and broomweed, Australia and New Zealand, Hawai'i and Mauritius; the list of species and places is virtually endless. An argument could be made, however, that the recent and contemporary biotic history of Florida represents one of the worst examples of all, made all the more frightening because the cumulative impact will almost surely be much worse in the near future than it is already.

Learning Check 11-17 What is an *exotic species*?

The Proliferation of Exotic Species in Florida:

Florida is a very attractive place for human settlement. Particularly in the last four decades, it has experienced one of the highest rates of in-migration of people ever known anywhere in the world. The major inducement is climate. A mild winter more than compensates for a hot summer, particularly when the latter can be ameliorated by artificial air conditioning. Florida's subtropical climate is also very suitable for many plants and animals. The tropical regions of the world contain an incredible variety of biota. Only a small fraction of this total is native to Florida.

In the last few years, Florida has become the major world center for the animal-import industry, and it is almost as important as a focus for plant imports as well. It is inevitable that many of these organisms escape from confinement and try their luck at survival in the wild. Others are deliberately turned loose—by fishers who want new quarry, pet owners who are tired of their pets, gardeners who would like a new shrub in the backyard. Still others are brought in inadvertently, in the holds of freighters or the baggage of travelers. Through these and similar events, which have been accelerating year by year, Florida has become what has been termed a "biological cesspool" of introduced life-forms. More than 50 species of exotic animals, not counting invertebrates, have now taken up residence in Florida, and exotic plants are almost too numerous to count.

Exotics are most likely to prosper in a new environment when the natural ecosystems of the host region are unstable. Florida has experienced massive disruption of its ecosystems in recent years due to the explosive human population increase and the associated accelerated changes in land use. Particularly contributory has been the modification of drainage systems in this flattish state of normally expansive water surfaces (lakes, swamps, marshes, everglades). In contemporary Florida, human interference has destabilized the natural ecosystems, and human-induced introductions provide a large and steady source of exotic plants and animals on a year-round basis.

Dozens of species of exotic plants have become widespread, and almost all of them are continually expanding their ranges. Prominent among them is the *melaleuca* tree from Australia. Seeds from these "paperbark" trees were deliberately sown by airplane in the 1930s in the hope of developing a timber industry in the swamplands of southwestern Florida. The spread of melaleuca has changed swamp to forest, radically altering the entire regional ecosystem, but the lumber potential has turned out to be negligible.

Much more extensive and deleterious in impact has been the spread of exotic aquatic weeds, which now infest more than 200,000 hectares (a half million acres) of Florida's waters. The two most significant are the water hyacinth and the hydrilla.

- The Amazon water hyacinth (*Eichhornia crassipes*) grows incredibly fast. A single plant can double its mass in two weeks under ideal conditions. These plants grow so thickly as to impede boat traffic and shade out other flora, sometimes to the extent that the water receives virtually no oxygen, and biological deserts are created. They are very difficult to cut out, and even when this is done, the decay of displaced portions puts more nutrients into the water, which promotes even lusher growth.
- The hydrilla (*Hydrilla verticillata*) is a native of tropical Africa and Southeast Asia that was brought to Florida as an aquarium plant but has now spread vastly in the wild (Figure 11-47). It has the form of long green tentacles, growing 2.5 centimeters (an inch) a day, which can become intertwined and form dense mats that will stop an outboard motor propeller

▲ **Figure 11-47** Hydrilla-choked canal near Everglades National Park, Florida.

dead. It overwhelms native plants and can even thrive in deep water where there is almost total darkness. Tiny pieces, when broken off, can regenerate into a new plant, so it is easily spread by birds, boat propellers, and other things that move from lake to lake. It has already clogged more than 60,000 hectares (150,000 acres) of waterways in Florida and has become established in almost all other southeastern states.

Exotic animals are less overwhelming in their occurrence, but many species are already well established and some are spreading rapidly. A sampling of nonaquatic species includes Mexican armadillos, Indian rhesus monkeys, Australian parakeets, Cuban lizards, Central American jaguarundi cats, South American giant toads, Great Plains jack rabbits, Amazonian parrots, and, especially in recent years, the Burmese python (*Python molurus bivittatus*) which is decimating populations of some southern Florida native animals (Figure 11-48).

Exotic fish are much more numerous than their terrestrial counterparts and pose even more serious problems, primarily through fierce competition with native species. Most of the drainage systems of Florida are interconnected by numerous irrigation and drainage canals; thus any introduced freshwater species now has access to most of the stream systems of the state. Moreover, Florida has a great abundance of springs that have stable water temperatures throughout the year, providing havens for many tropical fish that would otherwise find winter water temperatures below their tolerance limits.

▲ **Figure 11-48** Burmese python in Florida.

▲ **Figure 11-49** The walking catfish (*Clarias batrachus*) is originally from Southeast Asia, but now is found throughout Florida.

South American *acaras* are already the dominant canal fish throughout southern Florida, and African *tilapias* are the most numerous fish in many lakes in the central part of the state. The greatest present and potential threat, however, is the so-called "walking catfish" (*Clarias batrachus*) from Southeast Asia, which numbers in the millions throughout the state and is considered to be "out of control," with "no practical method of eradication" (Figure 11-49). These catfish eat insect larvae until the insects are gone; then they eat other fish. They are overwhelming rivals of almost all the native fish, eventually reducing the entire freshwater community to a single species—the walking catfish. They are significantly hardier than other fish because if they do not like the local waters, or if the waters dry up, they can simply hike across land, breathing directly from the air, until they find a new lake or stream!

Chapter 11   LEARNING REVIEW

After studying this chapter, you should be able to answer the following questions. Key terms from each text section are shown in **bold type**. Definitions for key terms are also found in the glossary at the back of the book.

KEY TERMS AND CONCEPTS

Ecosystems and Biomes (*p. 307*)

1. Contrast and explain the concepts of **ecosystem** and **biome**.
2. What is an **ecotone**?

Terrestrial Flora (*p. 308*)

3. What is the difference between a **perennial** and an **annual plant**?

4. Explain the difference between a **gymnosperm (conifer)** and an **angiosperm**. Name trees that are examples of each.
5. Explain the difference between a **deciduous tree** and an **evergreen tree**. Name trees that are examples of each.
6. Explain the difference between a **broadleaf tree** and a **needleleaf tree**. Name trees that are examples of each.

7. Describe some typical **xerophytic adaptations** of plants.
8. Describe some typical **hygrophytic adaptations** of plants.
9. Explain the concept of **climax vegetation.**
10. What are the differences among **forest, woodland,** and **shrubland**?
11. What are the similarities and differences among the **grasslands**: savanna, prairie, and steppe?
12. Briefly describe the **desert, tundra,** and **wetlands** plant associations.
13. Explain what is meant by **vertical zonation** of vegetation patterns.
14. Define and explain what causes the **treeline**?
15. What is the difference between an **adret slope** and a **ubac slope**? How and why is vegetation likely to be different on an adret slope and a ubac slope?
16. What is **riparian vegetation**?

Terrestrial Fauna (*p. 315*)

17. What are some basic characteristics that distinguish plants from animals?
18. Contrast **invertebrates** with **vertebrates**. Provide one example of each.
19. Describe the distinguishing characteristics of mammals.
20. What are the advantages for an animal to be **endothermic**?
21. Distinguish among the three ways (physiological, behavioral, reproductive) animals adapt to the environment.
22. What is meant by **symbiosis**?
23. Distinguish between *mutualism* and *parasitism*.

Zoogeographic Regions (*p. 322*)

24. Explain the concept of **zoogeographic regions**.
25. What is an **endemic** plant or animal?

The Major Biomes (*p. 324*)

26. What climate characteristics are most closely associated with the tropical rainforest biome?
27. Contrast the general characteristics of the **tropical rainforest, tropical deciduous forest,** and **tropical scrub** biomes.
28. Describe the seasonal patterns of the **tropical savanna** biome.
29. Describe and explain the global distribution of the **desert** biome.
30. Discuss the general climate characteristics and types of vegetation associated with the **mediterranean woodland and shrub** biome.
31. What are the general differences in climate associated with the tropical savanna and **midlatitude grassland** biomes?
32. What are the general differences in climate associated with the **midlatitude deciduous forest** and **boreal forest** biomes?
33. Contrast the general species diversity in the tropical rainforest and boreal forest biomes.
34. Describe the general vegetation cover found in the **tundra** biome.

Human Modification of Natural Distribution Patterns (*p. 334*)

35. What is an **exotic species**?
36. What is a feral animal population? Provide an example.

STUDY QUESTIONS

1. Why do trees require so much more moisture to survive than grass?
2. In what ways is an increase in altitude similar to an increase in latitude?
3. What generally happens to the elevation of the treeline going from the equator toward the poles? Why?
4. Describe and explain at least one animal adaptation to desert life.
5. Why are the flora and fauna of the Australian Region so distinctive?
6. Why is it usually difficult to maintain productive agriculture year after year in a cleared area of tropical rainforest?
7. Describe and explain one example of an exotic species that has disrupted a region's natural ecosystem.

EXERCISES

1. Using Figure 11-10 for reference and the average lapse rate (discussed in Chapter 4), estimate the typical temperature difference between the near-sea level valley grassland ecosystem on the west side of the Sierra Nevada and the alpine tundra ecosystem near the summit of the range at an elevation of about 3500 meters (11,500 feet): _____ °C (°F)

2. Refer to the climate map (Figure 8-3) and biomes map in the textbook (Figure 11-25). The boreal forest biome generally corresponds to the distribution of which climate type?

3. Given an annual rate of world forest loss of 13 million hectares (32 million acres) per year, how much forest cover was lost around the world between 2000 and 2010? _____ million hectares

Seeing Geographically

Look again at the photograph of the nesting albatross in the Falkland Islands at the beginning of the chapter (p. 306). Based on the location of these islands (54° S) what general climate do you expect is found here? Discuss some physiological and behavioral characteristics that would allow the albatross and its chick to thrive here. In which zoogeographical region are these birds nesting?

MasteringGeography™

Looking for additional review and test prep materials? Visit the Study Area in MasteringGeography™ to enhance your geographic literacy, spatial reasoning skills, and understanding of this chapter's content by accessing a variety of resources, including geoscience animations, MapMaster interactive maps, videos, RSS feeds, flashcards, web links, self-study quizzes, and an eText version of *McKnight's Physical Geography: A Landscape Appreciation.*

THE FINAL MAJOR COMPONENT IN OUR STUDY OF EARTH'S

environment is the lithosphere. This fourth sphere is just as complex as the atmosphere, biosphere, or hydrosphere but contrasts with these other realms in its enormity and particularly in its seeming stability.

It is easy to observe change in the three other spheres—clouds forming, flowers blooming, rivers flowing—but the dynamics of the lithosphere, with a few spectacular exceptions, such as earthquakes and volcanic eruptions, operate with such incredible slowness that Earth's crust often appears changeless. Most laypersons consider the phrase "the everlasting hills" a literal expression aptly describing the permanence of Earth's topography. In reality, the phrase is hyperbole that fails to recognize the remarkable alterations that take place over time, largely unrecognizable by the casual observer.

Our goal in the remaining chapters of this book is to understand the contemporary character of Earth's surface and to explain the processes that have caused it to be as it is. In this chapter, we begin with the aspect of Earth that perhaps most dramatically links the lithosphere, the atmosphere, the hydrosphere, and the biosphere: the thin veneer of soil.

As you study this chapter, think about these key questions:

- **How are soil, regolith, and bedrock related?**
- **What are the five factors involved in soil formation?**
- **What are the components of soil?**
- **What are the main properties of soil?**
- **What are colloids and how do they relate to soil fertility?**
- **How do differences in soil profile develop?**
- **How are the five major soil-forming regimes related to climate?**
- **How are soils classified and mapped?**
- **What factors influence the global distribution of soils?**

SOIL AND REGOLITH

Although the lithosphere encompasses the entire planet, from surface to core,[1] the part that holds our attention here is soil, the topmost layer. Soil is the essential medium in which most terrestrial life is nurtured. Almost all land plants sprout from this precious medium, spread so thinly across the continental surfaces that it has an average worldwide depth of only about 15 centimeters (6 inches).

Despite the implication of the well-known simile "as common as dirt," soil is remarkably diverse. It is a nearly infinitely varying mixture of weathered mineral particles, decaying organic matter, living organisms, gases, and liquid solutions.

---

[1]In this chapter we use the word *lithosphere* as a general term for the solid part of Earth. In Chapter 13 we will see that the term lithosphere has a more limited definition when discussing plate tectonics.

Seeing Geographically

Wheat fields in Saskatchewan, Canada. Describe the general topography of this region. How is the land being used? State two reasons that the land is probably well suited for this purpose.

Preeminently, however, soil is a zone of plant growth. **Soil** is a relatively thin surface layer of mineral matter that normally contains a considerable amount of organic material and is capable of supporting living plants. It occupies that part of the outer skin of Earth that extends from the surface down to the maximum depth to which living organisms penetrate, which means basically the area occupied by plant roots. Soil is characterized by its ability to produce and store plant nutrients, an ability made possible by the interactions of such diverse factors as water, air, sunlight, rocks, plants, and animals.

Although thinly distributed over the land surface, soil functions as a fundamental interface where atmosphere, lithosphere, hydrosphere, and biosphere meet. The bulk of most soil is inorganic material, so soil is usually classified as part of the lithosphere, but it is intimately related to the other three Earth spheres (Figure 12-1).

From Regolith to Soil

Soil development begins with the physical and chemical disintegration of rock exposed to the atmosphere and to the action of water percolating down from the surface. This disintegration is called *weathering*. As we shall learn in Chapter 15, the basic result of weathering is the weakening and breakdown of solid rock, the fragmentation of coherent rock masses, and the making of little rocks from big ones. The principal product is a layer of loose inorganic material called **regolith** ("blanket rock") because it lies like a blanket over the unfragmented rock below (Figure 12-2). Typically then, the regolith consists of material that has weathered

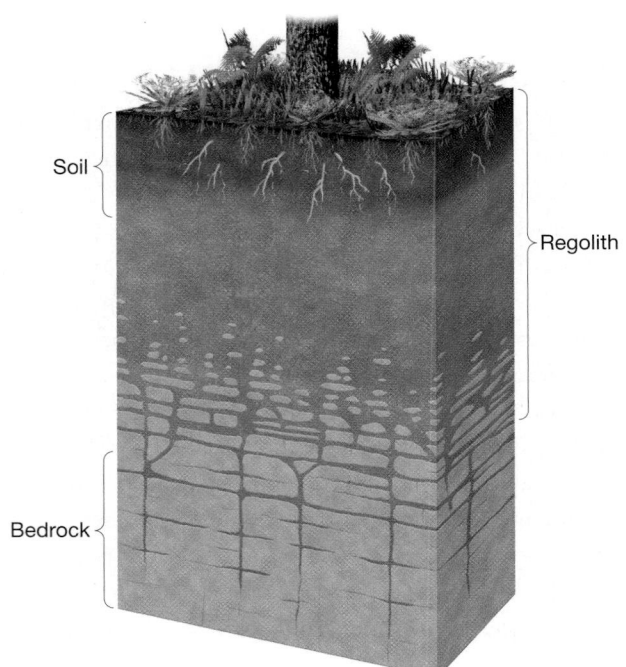

▲ **Figure 12-2** Vertical cross section from surface to bedrock, showing the relationship between soil and regolith.

from the underlying rock and that has a crude gradation of particle sizes, with the largest and least fragmented pieces at the bottom, immediately adjacent to the bedrock. Sometimes, however, the regolith consists of material that was transported from elsewhere by the action of wind, water, or ice. Thus, the regolith may vary significantly in composition from place to place.

The upper half meter or so of the regolith normally differs from the material below in several ways, most notably in the intensity of biological and chemical processes taking place. This upper portion is soil. It is composed largely of finely fragmented mineral particles, and is the ultimate product of weathering. It normally also contains an abundance of living plant roots, dead and rotting plant parts, microscopic plants and animals both living and dead, and a variable amount of air and water. Soil is not the end product of a process, but rather a stage in a never-ending continuum of physical–chemical–biological processes (Figure 12-3).

Soil as a Component of the Landscape

The surface of the lithosphere is usually, but not always, covered by soil. Although extremely pervasive, soil is often an inconspicuous component of the landscape because its presence is normally masked by either vegetation or human-constructed features.

We recognize soil in the landscape mostly by its color, which can often be seen through the filigree of plant life that covers it. A second main aspect of soil—its depth—becomes obvious only where some of its

▲ **Figure 12-1** The soil in which crops grow, as here in Lancaster County, Pennsylvania, is a fundamental interface of the lithosphere, atmosphere, hydrosphere, and biosphere.

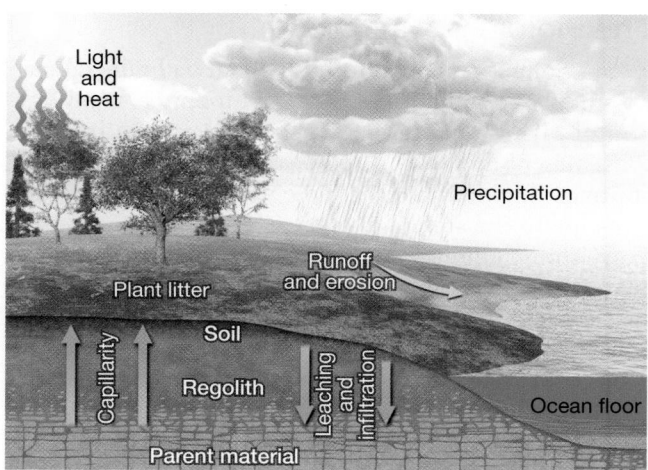

▲ **Figure 12-3** Soil develops through a complex interaction of physical, chemical, and biological processes. Parent-material bedrock weathers to regolith, and then plant litter combines with the regolith to form soil. Some of that soil washes to the ocean floor, where, over the expanse of geologic time, it is transformed to sedimentary rock. Someday that ocean floor may be uplifted above sea level and the exposed sedimentary rock will again be weathered into soil.

vertical dimension is exposed by gully erosion, road cuts, or some other type of excavation.

Learning Check 12-1 Describe the first step in the formation of soil. (Answer on p. AK-3)

SOIL-FORMING FACTORS

Soil is an ever-evolving material. Metaphorically, soil acts like a sponge—taking in inputs and being acted upon by the local environment—changing over time and when the inputs or local environment change. Five principal soil-forming factors are responsible for soil development: geology, climate, topography, biology, and time.

The Geologic Factor

The source of the rock fragments that make up soil is **parent material**, which may be either bedrock or loose sediments transported from elsewhere by water, wind, or ice. Whatever the parent material, it is sooner or later disintegrated and decomposed at and near Earth's surface, providing the raw material for soil formation.

The nature of the parent material often influences the characteristics of the soil that develop from it; this factor sometimes dominates all others, particularly in the early stages of soil formation. The chemical composition of parent material is obviously reflected in the resulting soil, and parent-material physical characteristics may also be influential in soil development, particularly in terms of texture and structure. Bedrock that weathers into large particles (as does sandstone, for example) normally produces a coarse-textured soil, one easily penetrated by

air and water to some depth. Bedrock that weathers into minute particles (shale, for example) yields fine-textured soils with a great number of pores but of very small size, which inhibits air and water from easily penetrating the surface.

Young soils are likely to be very reflective of the rocks or sediments from which they were derived. With the passage of time, however, other soil-forming factors become increasingly important, and the significance of the parent material diminishes. Eventually the influence of the parent material may be completely obliterated, so that it is sometimes impossible to ascertain the nature of the rock from which the soil evolved.

The Climatic Factor

Temperature and moisture are the climatic variables of greatest significance to soil formation. As a basic generalization, both the chemical and biological processes in soil are usually accelerated by high temperatures and abundant moisture and are slowed by low temperatures and lack of moisture. One predictable result is that soils tend to be deepest in warm, humid regions and shallowest in cold, dry regions.

It is difficult to overemphasize the role of moisture moving through the soil. The flow is mostly downward because of the pull of gravity, but it is sometimes sideways in response to drainage opportunities and sometimes, in special circumstances, even upward. Wherever and however water moves, it always carries dissolved chemicals in solution and usually also carries tiny particles of matter in suspension. Thus, moving water is ever engaged in rearranging the chemical and physical components of the soil, as well as contributing to the variety and availability of plant nutrients.

In terms of general soil characteristics, climate is likely to be the most influential factor in the long run. This generalization has many exceptions, however, and when soils are considered on a local scale, climate is likely to be less prominent as a determinant.

The Topographic Factor

Slope and drainage are the two main features of topography that influence soil characteristics. Wherever soil develops, its vertical extent undergoes continuous, if usually very slow, change. This change comes about through a lowering of both the bottom and top of the soil layer (Figure 12-4). The bottom slowly gets deeper as weathering penetrates into the regolith and parent material and as plant roots extend to greater depths. At the same time, the soil surface is being lowered by sporadic removal of its uppermost layer through normal erosion, which is the removal of individual soil particles by running water, wind, and gravity.

Where the land is flat, soil tends to develop at the bottom more rapidly than it is eroded away at the top. This does not mean that the downward development is speedy; rather it means that surface erosion is extraordinarily slow. Thus, the deepest soils are usually on flat land. Where slopes

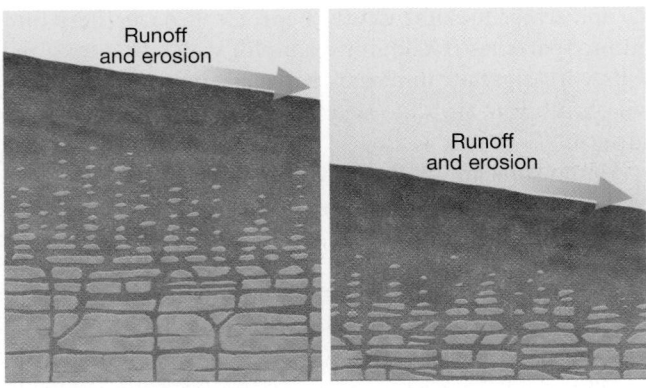

▲ **Figure 12-4** Over time, the extent of soil undergoes slow, continuous change. The bottom of the soil layer is lowered by the breakup of parent material as weathering processes extend deeper into the regolith and bedrock. At the same time, the top of the soil layer can be lowered through erosional processes.

are relatively steep, surface erosion is more rapid than soil deepening, with the result that such soils are nearly always thin and immaturely developed (Figure 12-5).

If soils are well drained, moisture relationships may be relatively unimportant factors in soil development. If soils have poor natural drainage, however, significantly different characteristics may develop. For example, a waterlogged soil tends to contain a high proportion of organic matter, and the biological and chemical processes that require free oxygen are impeded (because air is the source of the needed oxygen and a waterlogged soil contains essentially no air). Most poorly drained soils are in valley bottoms or in some other flat locale because soil drainage is usually related to slope.

In some cases, such subsurface factors as permeability and the presence or absence of impermeable layers are more influential than slope.

Learning Check 12-2 **How is the soil texture that develops from decomposing sandstone likely to be different from soil that develops from shale?**

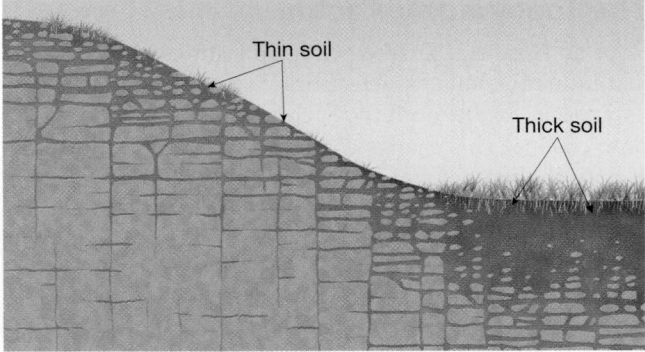

▲ **Figure 12-5** Slope is a critical determinant of soil depth. On flat land, soil normally develops more deeply with the passage of time because there is very little erosion washing away the topmost soil. On a slope, the rate of erosion is equal to or greater than the rate at which soil is formed at the bottom of the soil layer, with the result that the soil remains shallow.

The Biological Factor

From a volume standpoint, soil is about half mineral matter and about half air and water, with only a small fraction of organic matter. However, the organic fraction, consisting of both living and dead plants and animals, is of utmost importance. The biological factor in particular gives life to the soil and makes it more than just "dirt." Every soil contains a quantity (sometimes an enormous quantity) of living organisms, and every soil incorporates some (sometimes a vast amount of) dead and decaying organic matter.

Vegetation of various kinds growing in soil performs certain vital functions. Plant roots, for instance, work their way down and around, providing passageways for drainage and aeration, as well as being the vital link between soil nutrients and the growing plants.

Many kinds of animals contribute to soil development as well. Even such large surface-dwelling creatures as elephants and bison affect soil formation by compaction with their hooves, rolling in the dirt, grazing the vegetation, and dropping excreta. Ants, worms, and all other land animals fertilize the soil with their waste products and contribute their carcasses for eventual decomposition and incorporation into the soil.

Many small animals spend most or all of their lives in the soil layer, tunneling here and there, moving soil particles upward and downward, and providing passageways for water and air (Figure 12-6). Mixing and plowing by soil fauna is sometimes remarkably extensive. Ants and termites, as they build mounds, also transport soil materials from one layer to another. The mixing activities of animals in the soil, generalized under the term *bioturbation*, tend to counteract the tendency of other soil-forming

▲ **Figure 12-6** Like other burrowing animals, these prairie dogs in South Dakota contribute to soil development by bringing subsoil to the surface and providing passageways for air and moisture to get underground.

▲ **Figure 12-7** The common earthworm (*Lumbricus terrestris*) in an underground burrow.

processes to accentuate the vertical differences among soil layers.

The abundance and variety of animal life connected with the soil are quite surprising. Such organisms vary in size from the gigantic to the microscopic, and in numbers from a few per hectare to billions per gram. The organic life of the soil ranges from microscopic protozoans to larger animals that may accidentally alter certain soil characteristics. Of all creatures, however, it is probable that the earthworm is the most important to soil formation and development (Figure 12-7).

Earthworms: The cultivating and mixing activities of earthworms are of great value in improving the structure, increasing the fertility, lessening the danger of accelerated erosion, and deepening the profile of the soil. The distinctive evidence of this value is that the presence of many well-nourished earthworms is almost always a sign of productive, or potentially productive, soil.

The mere presence of earthworms, however, does not guarantee that a soil will be highly productive, as there may be other kinds of inhibiting factors such as a high water table. Nevertheless, an earthworm-rich soil has a higher potential productivity than similar soils lacking earthworms. In various controlled experiments, the addition of earthworms to wormless soil has enhanced plant productivity by several hundred percent.

At least seven beneficial functions have been attributed to earthworms:

1. Their innumerable tunnels facilitate drainage and aeration and the deepening of the soil profile.

2. The continual movement of the creatures beneath the surface tends to bring about the formation of a crumbly structure, which is generally favorable for plant growth.

3. The soil is further mixed by material being carried and washed downward into their holes from the surface. This is notably in the form of leaf litter dragged downward by the worms, which fertilizes the subsoil.

4. The digestive actions and tunneling of earthworms form aggregate soil particles that increase porosity and resist the impact of raindrops, helping to deter erosion.

5. Nutrients in the soil are increased by the addition of *casts* excreted by earthworms (casts are expelled by earthworms and consist of mineral material bound together with decomposed organic material), which have been shown to be 5 times richer in available nitrogen, 7 times richer in available phosphates, and 11 times richer in available potash than the surrounding soil.

6. They rearrange material in the soil, especially by bringing deeper matter to the surface, where it can be weathered more rapidly. Where earthworms are numerous, they may deposit as much as 9000 kg/hectare (25 tons/acre) of casts on the surface in a year.

7. Nitrification is also promoted by the presence of earthworms, due to increased aeration, alkaline fluids in their digestive tracts, and the decomposition of earthworm carcasses.

In many parts of the world, of course, earthworms are lacking. They are, for example almost totally absent from arid and semiarid regions. In these dry lands, some of the earthworm's soil-enhancing functions are carried out by ants and earth-dwelling termites, but much less effectively.

Microorganisms in the Soil: Another important component of the biological factor is microorganisms, both plant and animal, that occur in uncountable billions. An estimated three-quarters of a soil's metabolic activity is generated by microorganisms. These microbes help release nutrients from dead organisms for use by live ones by decomposing organic matter and by converting nutrients to forms usable by plants. Algae, fungi, protozoans, actinomycetes, and other minuscule organisms all play a role in soil development, but bacteria probably make the greatest contribution overall. This is because certain types of bacteria are responsible for the decomposition and decay of dead plant and animal material and the consequent release of nutrients into the soil.

Learning Check 12-3   **What are several ways that earthworms tend to increase the productivity of soil?**

The Time Factor

For soil to develop on a newly exposed land surface requires time, with the length of time needed varying according to the nature of the exposed parent material and the characteristics of the environment. Soil-forming processes are generally very slow, and many centuries may be required for a thin layer of soil to form on a newly exposed surface. A warm, moist environment is conducive to soil development. Normally of much greater importance, however, are the attributes of the parent material. For example, soil develops from sediments relatively quickly and from bedrock relatively slowly.

Soil Erosion: Most soil develops with geologic slowness—so slowly that changes are almost imperceptible within a human life span. It is possible, however, for a soil to be degraded, either through the physical removal associated with accelerated erosion or through depletion of nutrients, in only a few years (Figure 12-8).

Soils that have fine textures—especially those with low rates of rainwater infiltration—tend to be those that are most easily eroded by rainwater runoff and wind; steep slopes and lack of a vegetation cover also increase the likelihood of erosion. In regions where single-crop agriculture ("monoculture") is practiced, fields are often left bare and unplanted for several months each year, increasing the likelihood of erosion.

Estimates of the amount of agricultural land lost to soil erosion vary greatly. In the United States, some researchers estimate that nearly 40 percent of the productive soil in the wheat growing Palouse region of Washington and Idaho, and as much as 50 percent of the topsoil of Iowa, has been lost to erosion over the last 150 years. Globally, perhaps

▲ **Figure 12-8** Accelerated erosion cutting a deep gully in the Coast Ranges of central California.

10 million hectares of cropland are lost each year to soil erosion—a rate that is 10 to 40 times faster than productive soil can develop. It is important to realize that in the grand scale of geologic time, soil can be formed and reformed, but in the dimension of human time, it is a mostly nonrenewable resource.

SOIL COMPONENTS

Soil is made up of a variety of natural components existing together in myriad combinations. All these components can be classified, however, into just a few main groups: inorganics, organics, air, and water.

Inorganic Materials

As mentioned earlier, the bulk of most soils is mineral matter, mostly in the form of small but macroscopic particles. Inorganic material also occurs as microscopic clay particles and as dissolved minerals in solution.

About half the volume of an average soil is small, granular mineral matter called *sand* and *silt*. These particles may consist of a great variety of minerals, depending on the nature of the parent material from which they were derived, and are simply fragments of the wasting rock. Most common are bits of quartz, which are composed of silica (SiO_2) and appear in the soil as very resistant grains of sand. Other prominent minerals making up sand and silt are some of the feldspars and micas.

The smallest particles in the soil are **clay**, which is usually a combination of silica and oxides of aluminum and iron found only in the soil and not in the parent material. Clay has properties significantly different from those of larger (sand and silt) fragments. Most clay particles are *colloidal* in size, which means they are larger than molecules but too small to be seen with the naked eye. They are usually flat platelets, as Figure 12-9 illustrates, and therefore have a relatively large surface area. For this reason, clay has an important influence on chemical activity in the soil because many chemical reactions occur at the surfaces of soil particles. The platelets group together in loose, sheetlike assemblages, and water moves easily between these sheets. Substances dissolved in the water are attracted to and held by the sheets. Since the sheets are negatively charged, they attract positively charged ions called **cations**. Many essential plant nutrients occur in soil solutions as cations, with the result that clay is an important reservoir for plant nutrients, just as it is for soil water. We discuss the role of cations in soils in greater detail later in this chapter.

Organic Matter
FG10

Although organic matter generally constitutes less than 5 percent of total soil volume, it has an enormous influence on soil characteristics and plays a fundamental role in the biochemical processes that make soil an effective medium of plant growth. Some of the organic matter is living

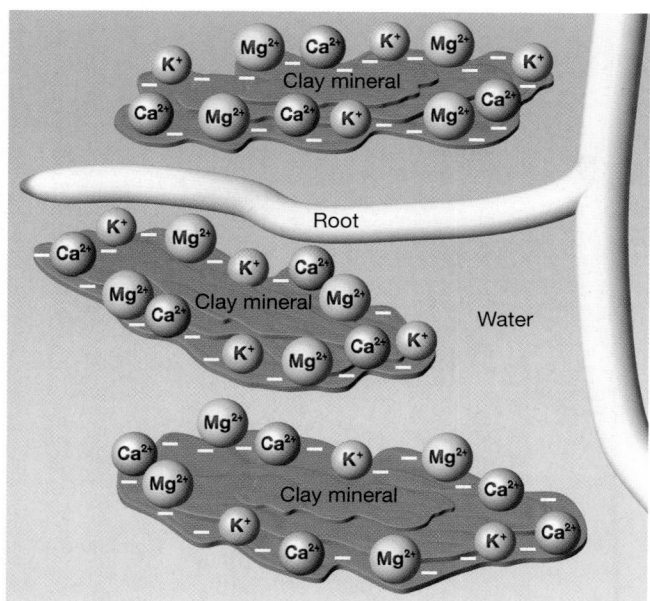

▲ **Figure 12-9** Clay particles offer a large surface area on which substances dissolved in soil water can cling. The particles are negatively charged and therefore attract cations (positively charged ions) from the water. These cations held by the clay are then absorbed by plant roots and become nutrients for the plant.

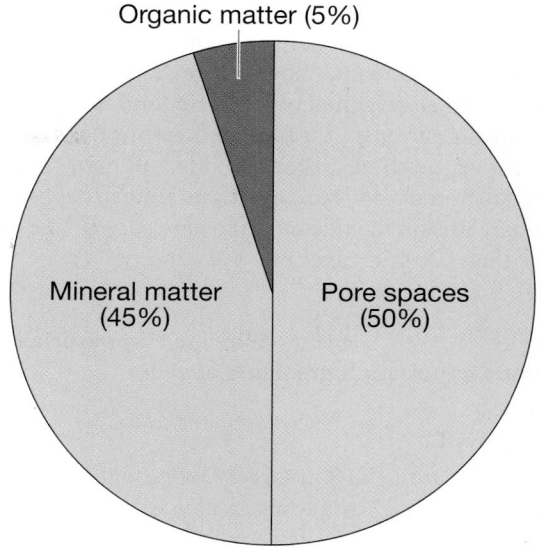

▲ **Figure 12-10** The best soil for plant growth is about half solid material (by volume) and about half pore spaces. Most of the solids are mineral matter, with only a small amount being organic. On average, about half of the pore spaces in an ideal soil are filled with air and the other half are filled with water.

organisms, some is dead but undecomposed plant parts and animal carcasses, some is totally decomposed and so has become *humus*, and some is in an intermediate stage of decomposition.

Apart from plant roots, evidence of the variety and bounty of organisms living in the soil may be inconspicuous or invisible, but most soils are seething with life. A half hectare (about one acre) may contain a million earthworms, and the total number of organisms in 30 grams (about 1 ounce) of soil is likely to exceed 100 trillion. Microorganisms far exceed more complex life-forms, both in total numbers and in cumulative mass. They are active in rearranging and aerating the soil and in yielding waste products that are links in the chain of nutrient cycling. Some make major contributions to the decay and decomposition of dead organic matter, and others make nitrogen available for plant use.

Litter: Leaves, twigs, stalks, and other dead plant parts accumulate at the soil surface, where they are referred to collectively as **litter**. The eventual fate of most litter is decomposition, in which the solid parts are broken down into chemical components, which are then either absorbed into the soil or washed away. In cold, dry areas, litter may remain undecomposed for a very long time; where the climate is warm and moist, however, decomposition may take place almost as rapidly as litter accumulates.

Humus: After most of the residues have been decomposed, a brown or black, gelatinous, chemically stable organic matter remains; this is referred to as **humus**. This "black gold" is of utmost importance to agriculture because it loosens the structure and lessens the density of the soil,

thereby facilitating root development. Moreover, humus, like clay, is a catalyst for chemical reactions and a reservoir for plant nutrients and soil water.

Soil Air

Nearly half the volume of an average soil is made up of pore spaces (Figure 12-10). These spaces provide a labyrinth of interconnecting passageways, called *interstices*, among the soil particles. This labyrinth lets air and water penetrate into the soil. On the average, the pore spaces are about half filled with air and half with water, but at any given time and place, the amounts of air and water are quite variable, the quantity of one varying inversely with that of the other (Figure 12-11).

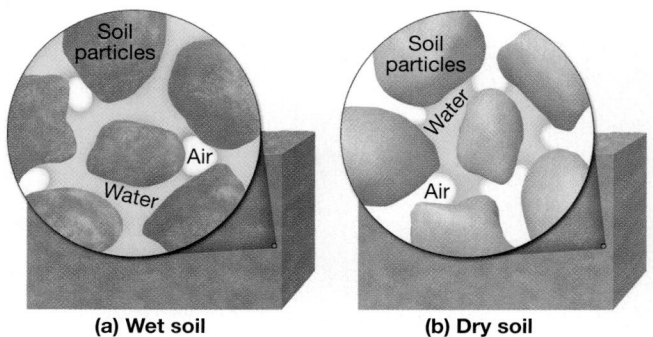

(a) Wet soil   **(b) Dry soil**

▲ **Figure 12-11** The relative amounts of water and air in soil pores vary from place to place and from time to time. (a) The interstices of wet soil contain much water and little air. (b) In dry soil there is much air and little water.

The characteristics of air in the soil are significantly different from those of atmospheric air. Soil air is found in openings generally lined with a film of water, and because this air exists in such close contact with water and is not exposed to moving air currents, it is saturated with water vapor. Soil air is also very rich in carbon dioxide and poor in oxygen because plant roots and soil organisms remove oxygen from, and respire carbon dioxide into, the pore spaces. The carbon dioxide then slowly escapes into the atmosphere.

Learning Check 12-4   Why are clay particles and humus important ingredients of soil?

Soil Water

Water comes into the soil largely by percolation of rainfall and snowmelt, but some is also added from below when groundwater is pulled up above the water table by *capillary action* (Figure 12-12; see Chapter 6 for a discussion of capillarity). Once water has penetrated the soil, it envelops in a film of water each solid particle that it contacts, and it either wholly or partially fills the pore spaces. Water can be lost from the soil by percolation down into the groundwater, by upward capillary movement to the surface followed by evaporation, or by plant use (transpiration).

Four forms of soil moisture have roles in soil processes (Figure 12-13):

1. **Gravitational Water (Free Water):** *Gravitational water* is temporary in that it results from prolonged infiltration from above (usually due to prolonged precipitation) and is pulled downward by gravity, through the interstices toward the groundwater zone. Thus, this water stays in the soil only for a short time and is not very effective in supplying plants because it drains away rapidly once the external supply ceases. Gravitational water accomplishes significant functions

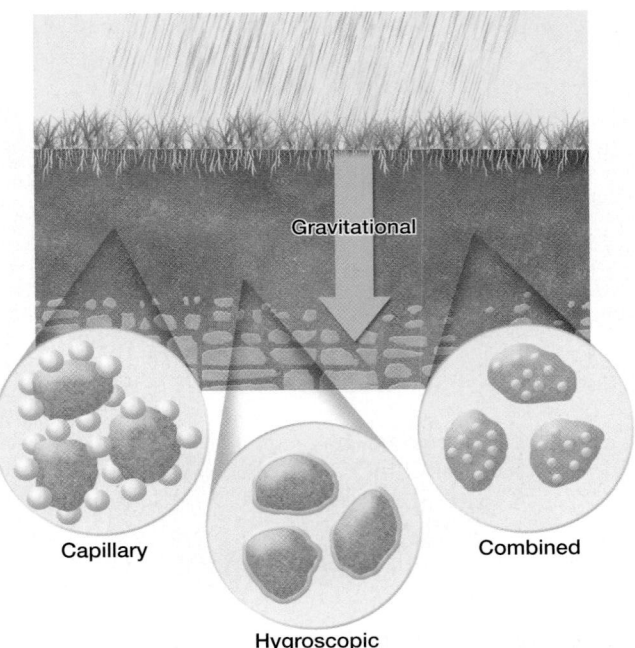

▲ **Figure 12-13** The four forms of soil moisture.

during its passage through the soil, however. It is the principal agent of *eluviation* and *illuviation* (discussed below) and thus makes the top soil coarser and more open textured and the subsoil denser and more compact.

2. **Capillary Water (Water of Cohesion):** *Capillary water*, which remains after gravitational water has drained away, consists of moisture held at the surface of soil particles by *surface tension*, which is the attraction of water molecules to each other (discussed in Chapter 6, this is the same property that causes water to form rounded droplets rather than dispersing in a thin film). Capillary water is by far the principal source of moisture for plants. In this form of soil moisture, the surface-tension forces are stronger than the downward pull of gravity, so this water is free to move about equally well in all directions in response to capillary tension. It tends to move from wetter areas toward drier ones, which accounts for the upward movement of capillary water when no gravitational water is percolating downward.

3. **Hygroscopic Water (Water of Adhesion):** *Hygroscopic water* consists of a microscopically thin film of moisture bound rigidly to all soil particles by *adhesion*, which is the attraction of water molecules to solid surfaces. Hygroscopic water adheres so tightly to the particles that it is normally unavailable to plants.

4. **Combined Water:** *Combined water* is least available of all. It is held in chemical combination with various soil minerals and is freed only if the chemical is altered.

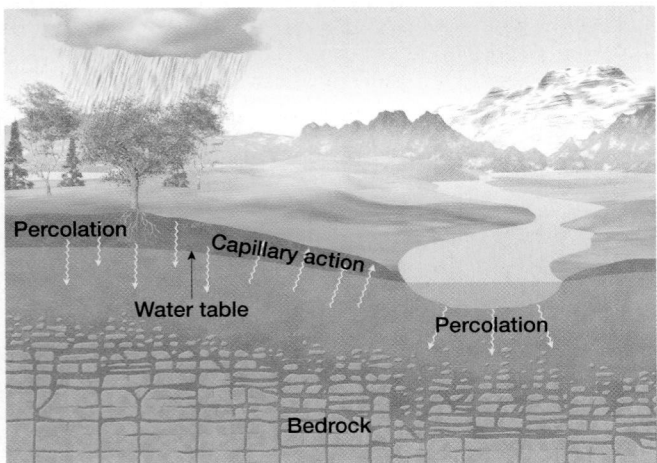

▲ **Figure 12-12** Water is added to the soil layer by the percolation of rainwater and snowmelt from above. Additional moisture enters the soil from below as groundwater is pulled up above the water table by capillary action.

For plants, capillary water is the most important and gravitational water is largely superfluous. After gravitational water has drained away, the remaining volume of water represents the **field capacity** of the soil. If drought conditions prevail and the capillary water is all used up by plants or evaporated, the plants are no longer able to extract moisture from the soil; then, the **wilting point** is reached.

Leaching: Water performs a number of important functions in the soil. It is an effective solvent, dissolving essential soil nutrients and making them available to plant roots. These dissolved nutrients are carried downward in solution, to be partly redeposited at lower levels. This process, called **leaching**, tends to deplete the topsoil of soluble nutrients. Water is also required for many of the chemical reactions of clay and for the actions of the microorganisms that produce humus. In addition, it can have considerable influence on the physical characteristics of soil by moving particles.

Eluviation and Illuviation: Water can have considerable influence on the physical characteristics of soil by moving particles around and depositing them elsewhere in the soil. For example, as water percolates into the soil, it picks up fine particles of mineral matter from the upper layers and carries them downward in a process called **eluviation** (Figure 12-14). These particles are eventually deposited at a lower level, and this deposition process is known as **illuviation**.

> Learning Check 12-5   **Which form of soil moisture is most important for plants?**

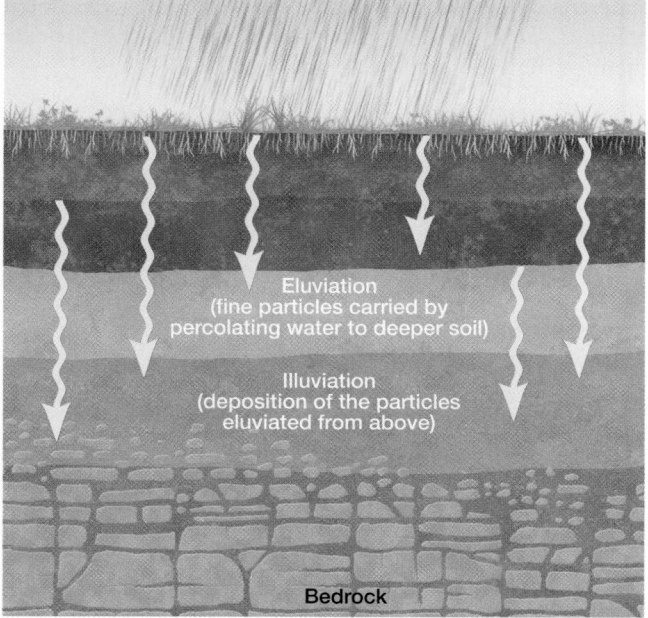

▲ **Figure 12-14** In the process of eluviation, fine particles in upper soil layers are picked up by percolating water and carried deeper into the soil. In the process of illuviation, these particles are deposited in a lower soil layer.

Soil-Water Budget: The moisture added to the soil by percolation of rainfall or snowmelt is diminished largely through evapotranspiration. The dynamic relationship between these two processes is referred to as the **soil–water balance**. It is influenced by a variety of factors, including soil and vegetation characteristics, but it is primarily determined by temperature and humidity.

How much water is available to plants is much more important to an ecosystem than is the amount of precipitation. Much water derived from rainfall or snowmelt becomes unavailable to plants because of evaporation, run-off, deep infiltration, or other processes. At any given time and place, there is likely to be either a surplus or a deficit of water in the soil. Such a condition is only temporary, and it varies in response to changing weather conditions, particularly those related to seasonal changes. Generally speaking, warm weather causes increased evapotranspiration, which diminishes the soil–water supply, and cool weather slows evapotranspiration, allowing more moisture to be retained in the soil.

In a hypothetical Northern Hemisphere midlatitude location, January is a time of surplus water in the soil because low temperatures inhibit evaporation and there is little or no transpiration from plants. The soil is likely to be at or near field capacity at this time, which means that most of the pore spaces are filled with water. With the arrival of spring, temperatures rise and plant growth accelerates, so that both evaporation and transpiration increase. The soil–water balance tips from a water surplus to a water deficit. This deficit builds to a peak in middle or late summer, as temperatures reach their greatest heights and plants need maximum water. Heavy use and diminished precipitation may combine to deplete all the moisture available to plants, and the wilting point is reached. Thus, the amount of soil moisture available for plant use is essentially the difference between field capacity and wilting point.

In late summer and fall, as air temperature decreases and plant growth slackens, evapotranspiration diminishes rapidly. At this time, the soil–water balance shifts once again to a water surplus, which continues through the winter. Then the cycle begins again. Figure 12-15 illustrates the annual sequence just described. Such variation in the soil–water balance through time is called a **soil–water budget**.

SOIL PROPERTIES

As one looks at, feels, smells, tastes, and otherwise examines soils, various physical and chemical characteristics appear useful in describing, differentiating, and classifying them. Some soil properties are easily recognized, but most can be ascertained only by precise measurement.

Color

The most conspicuous property of a soil is usually its color, but color is by no means the most definitive property. Soil

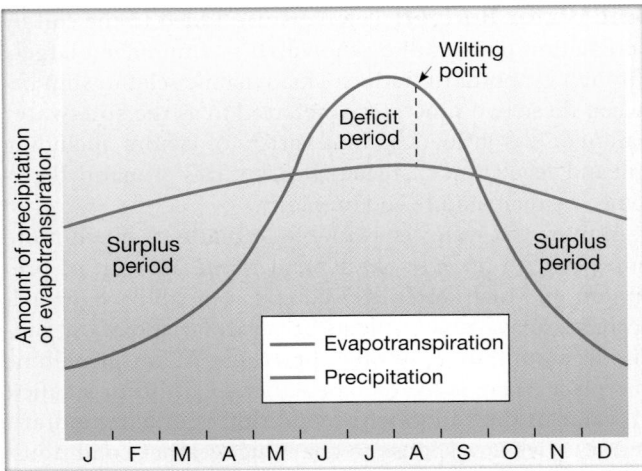

▲ **Figure 12-15** Hypothetical soil–water budget for a Northern Hemisphere midlatitude location. From January through May, there is more precipitation than evapotranspiration, and consequently the soil contains a surplus of water, more than sufficient for any plant needs. From mid-May to mid-September, the evapotranspiration curve rises above the precipitation curve, indicating that more water leaves the soil than enters it. About the first of August, so much water has been removed from the soil that plants begin to wilt. After mid-September, the evapotranspiration curve again dips below the precipitation curve and there is again a surplus of water in the soil.

color can provide clues about the nature and capabilities of the soil, but the clues are sometimes misleading. Soil scientists recognize 175 gradations of color. The standard colors are generally shades of black, brown, red, yellow, gray, and white. Soil color occasionally reflects the color of the unstained mineral grains, but in most cases, color is imparted by stains on the surface of the particles; these stains are caused by either metallic oxides or organic matter.

Black or dark brown usually indicates a considerable humus content; the blacker the soil, the more humus it contains. Color gives a strong hint about fertility, therefore, because humus is an important catalyst in releasing nutrients to plants. Dark color is not invariably a sign of fertility, however, because it may be due to other factors, such as poor drainage or high carbonate content.

Reddish and yellowish colors generally indicate iron oxide stains on the outside of soil particles. These colors are most common in tropical and subtropical regions, where many minerals are leached away by water moving under the pull of gravity, leaving insoluble iron compounds behind. In such situations, a red color bespeaks good drainage, and a yellowish hue suggests imperfect drainage. Red soils are also common in desert and semi-desert environments, where the color is carried over intact from reddish parent materials rather than representing a surface stain (Figure 12-16).

Gray and bluish colors typically indicate poor drainage, whereas mottling indicates saturated conditions for part of the year. In humid areas, a light color implies so much leaching that even the iron has been removed, but in dry climates, it indicates an accumulation of salts. It may also indicate simply a lack of organic matter.

Texture

All soils are composed of myriad particles of various sizes, as Figure 12-17 shows, although smaller particles usually predominate. Rolling a sample of soil between the fingers can provide a feel for the principal particle sizes. Table 12-1 shows the standard classification scheme for particle sizes; in this scheme, the size groups are called **separates**. The gravel, sand, and silt separates are fragments of the weathered parent material and are mostly the grains of minerals found commonly in rocks, especially quartz, feldspars, and micas. These coarser particles are the inert materials of the soil mass, its skeletal framework. As noted previously, only the clay particles take part in the intricate chemical activities that occur in the soil.

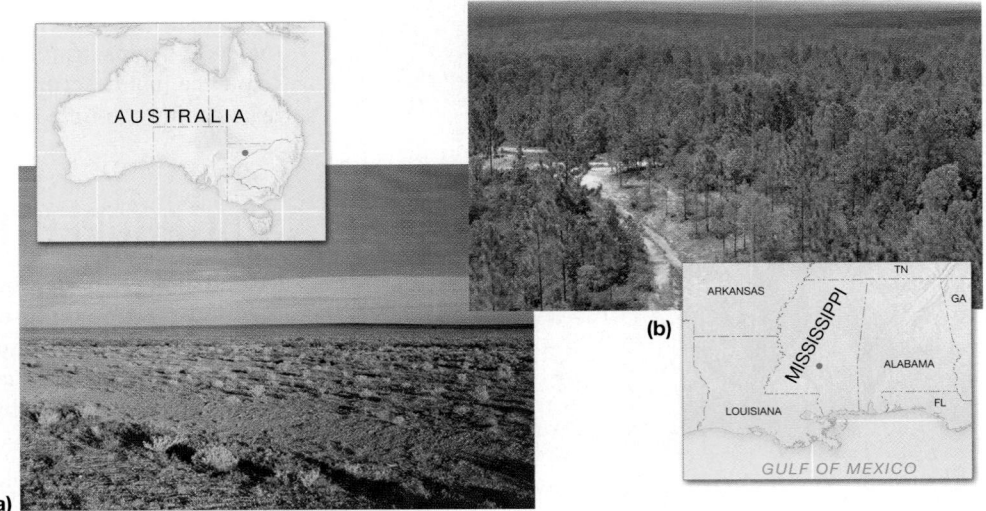

▲ **Figure 12-16** A red soil means different things in different places. (a) In this Mississippi forest, the soluble minerals have been leached away, leaving the insoluble iron to impart its reddish color to the soil. (b) In this Australian desert, the reddish color reflects the iron content of the underlying bedrock.

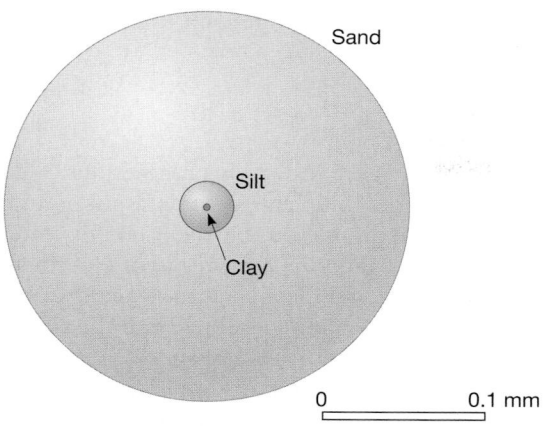

▲ **Figure 12-17** The relative sizes of sand, silt, and clay particles.

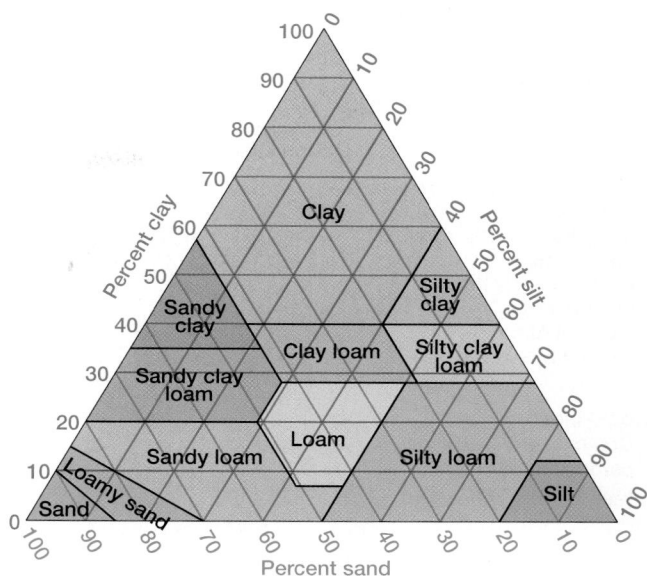

▲ **Figure 12-18** The standard soil-texture triangle. The texture of a soil is determined by the relative proportions of sand, silt, and clay particles.

Because no soil is made up of particles of uniform size, the texture of any soil is determined by the relative amounts of the various separates present. The *texture triangle* (Figure 12-18) shows the standard classification scheme for soil texture; this scheme is based on the percentage of each separate by weight. Near the center of the triangle is **loam**, the name given to a texture in which none of the three principal separates dominates the other two. This fairly even-textured mix is generally the most productive for plants.

Structure

The individual particles of most soils tend to aggregate into clumps called **peds**, and it is these clumps that determine soil structure. The size, shape, and stability of peds have a marked influence on how easily water, air, and organisms (including plant roots) move through the soil, and consequently on soil fertility. Peds are classified on the basis of shape as spheroidal, platy, blocky,

or prismatic, with these four shapes giving rise to seven generally recognized soil structure types (Figure 12-19). Aeration and drainage are usually facilitated by peds of intermediate size; both massive and fine structures tend to inhibit these processes.

Some soils, particularly those composed largely of sand, do not develop a true structure, which is to say that the individual grains do not aggregate into peds. Silt and clay particles readily aggregate in most instances. Other things being equal, aggregation is usually greatest in moist soils and least in dry ones.

Structure is an important determinant of a soil's *porosity* and *permeability*. As we learned in Chapter 9, porosity refers to the amount of pore space between soil particles or between peds. We can define it as

$$\text{porosity} = \frac{\text{volume of voids}}{\text{total volume}}$$

Porosity is usually expressed as a percentage or a decimal fraction. It is a measure of a soil's capacity to hold water and air.

The relationship between porosity and permeability is not simple; that is, the most porous materials are not necessarily the most permeable. Clay, for example, is the most porous separate, but it is the least permeable because the pores are too small for water to easily pass through.

TABLE 12-1	Standard U.S. Classification of Soil Particle Size	
Separate	**Diameter**
Gravel	Greater than 2 mm (0.08 in.)
Very coarse sand	1–2 mm (0.04–0.08 in.)
Coarse sand	0.5–1 mm (0.02–0.04 in.)
Medium sand	0.25–0.5 mm (0.01–0.02 in.)
Fine sand	0.1–0.25 mm (0.004–0.01 in.)
Very fine sand	0.05–0.1 mm (0.002–0.004 in.)
Coarse silt	0.02–0.05 mm (0.0008–0.002 in.)
Medium silt	0.006–0.02 mm (0.00024–0.0008 in.)
Fine silt	0.002–0.006 mm (0.00008–0.00024 in.)
Clay	0.002 mm (less than 0.00008 in.)

Learning Check 12-6   **Distinguish between soil porosity and permeability.**

Spheroidal
Characteristic of surface (A) horizons. Subject to wide and rapid changes.

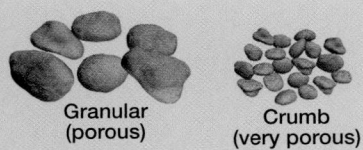

Granular (porous)

Crumb (very porous)

Plate-like
Common in E-horizons, may occur in any part of the profile. Often inherited from parent material of soil, or caused by compaction.

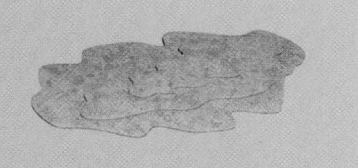

Block-like
Common in B-horizons, particularly in humid regions. May occur in A-horizons.

Angular blocky

Subangular blocky

Prism-like
Usually found in B-horizons. Most common in soils of arid and semiarid regions.

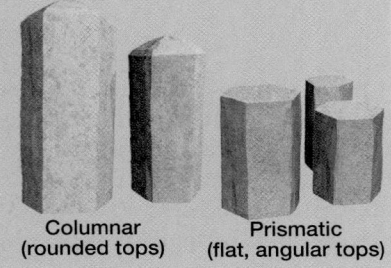

Columnar (rounded tops)

Prismatic (flat, angular tops)

▲ **Figure 12-19** Various structure types of soil particle clumps, or peds, found in mineral soils.

SOIL CHEMISTRY

The effectiveness of soil as a growth medium for plants is based largely on the presence and availability of nutrients, which are determined by an intricate series of chemical reactions. Soil chemistry involves the study of microscopic soil particles and electrically charged atoms or groups of atoms called *ions*.

Colloids

Soil particles smaller than about 0.1 micrometer in diameter are called **colloids**. Inorganic colloids consist of clay in thin, crystalline, platelike forms created by the chemical alteration of larger particles; organic colloids represent decomposed organic matter in the form of humus; and both types are the chemically active soil particles. When mixed with water, colloids remain suspended indefinitely as a homogeneous, murky solution. Some have remarkable storage capacities, and consequently colloids are major determinants of the water-holding capacity of a soil. They function as a virtual sponge, soaking up water, whereas the soil particles that are too large to be classified as colloids can maintain only a surface film of water.

Both inorganic and organic colloids attract and hold great quantities of ions.

Cation Exchange

As we saw earlier, *cations* are positively charged ions. Elements that form them include calcium, potassium, and magnesium, which are all essential for soil fertility and plant growth. Colloids carry mostly negative electrical charges on their surfaces, and these charges attract swarms of nutrient cations that would be leached from the soil if their ions were not retained by the colloids.

The combination of colloid and attached cations is called the *colloidal complex*, and it is a delicate mechanism. If it holds the nutrients strongly, they will not be leached away, yet if the bond is too strong, they cannot be absorbed by plants. Thus, a fertile soil is likely to be one in which the cation–colloid attraction is intricately balanced.

Adding to the complexity of the situation is the fact that some types of cations are bound more tightly than others. Cations that tend to bond strongly in the colloid complex may replace those that bond less strongly. For example, basic ions are fairly easily replaced by metal ions or hydrogen ions, a process called *cation exchange*. The capability of a soil to attract and exchange cations is known as its **cation exchange capacity (CEC)**. As a generalization, the higher the CEC, the more fertile the soil. Soils with a high clay content have a higher CEC than more coarsely grained soils because the former have more colloids. Humus is a particularly rich source of high-CEC activity because humus colloids have a much higher CEC than inorganic clay minerals. The most fertile soils, then, tend to be those with a notable clay and humus content.

> **Learning Check 12-7**   **What is cation exchange capacity and how does it relate to soil fertility?**

Acidity/Alkalinity

Chemical solutions—including those in soil—can be characterized on the basis of acidity or alkalinity. An *acid* is a chemical compound that produces hydrogen ions (H^+) or hydronium ions (H_3O^+) when dissolved in water, whereas a *base* is a chemical compound that produces hydroxide ions (OH^-) when dissolved in water. An acid reacts with a base to form a *salt*. Solutions that contain dissolved acids are described as being *acidic*. Those that contain dissolved bases are called either *basic* or *alkaline* solutions. Any chemical solution can be characterized on the basis of its acidity or alkalinity.

Nearly all nutrients are provided to plants in solution. An overly alkaline soil solution is inefficient in dissolving minerals and releasing their nutrients. However, if the solution is highly acidic, the nutrients are likely to be dissolved and leached away too rapidly for plant roots to absorb them. The optimum situation, then, is for the soil solution to be neutral, neither too alkaline nor too acidic. The acidity/alkalinity of a soil is determined to a large extent by its CEC.

As we first saw in Chapter 6, the chemist's symbol for the measure of the acidity/alkalinity of a solution is pH, which is based on the relative concentration of hydrogen ions (H⁺) in the solution. The scale ranges from 0 to 14. The lower end represents acidic conditions; higher numbers indicate alkaline conditions (Figure 12-20). Neutral conditions are represented by a value of 7, and it is soil having a pH of about 7 that is most suitable for the great majority of plants and microorganisms.

SOIL PROFILES

The development of any soil is expressed in two dimensions: depth and time. There is no straight-line relationship between depth and age, however; some soils deepen and develop much more rapidly than others.

Four processes deepen and age soils: *addition* (ingredients added to the soil), *loss* (ingredients lost from the soil), *translocation* (ingredients moved within the soil), and *transformation* (ingredients altered within the soil; Figure 12-21). The five soil-forming factors discussed earlier—geologic, climatic, topographic, biological, and time—influence the rate of these four processes, the result being the development of various soil *horizons* and the soil *profile*.

Soil Horizons

The vertical variation of soil properties is not random but rather an ordered layering with depth. Soil tends to have

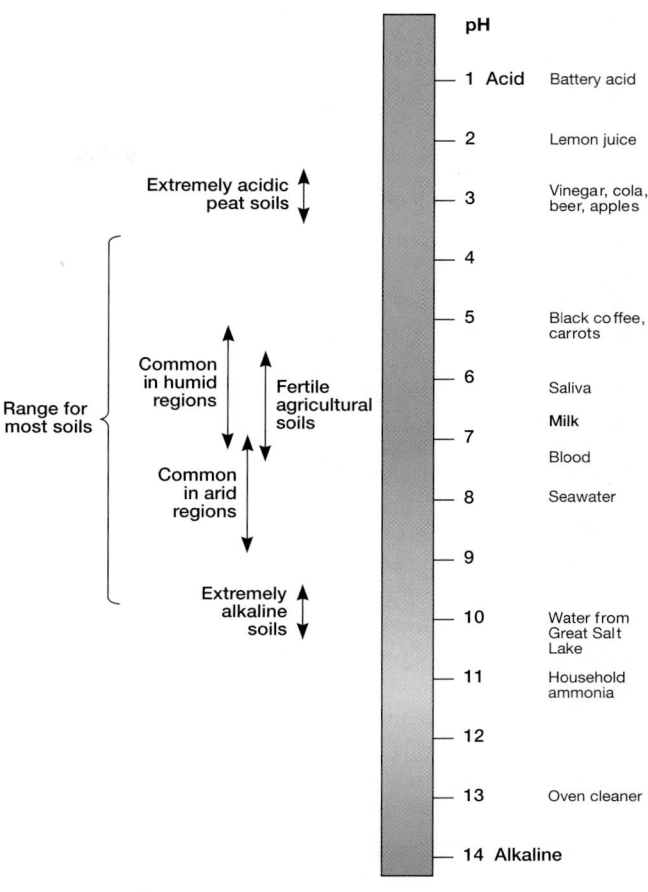

▲ **Figure 12-20** The standard pH scale. The most fertile soils tend to be neither too acidic nor too alkaline.

ADDITION
- Water as precipitation, condensation, and runoff
- Oxygen and carbon dioxide from atmosphere
- Nitrogen, chlorine, and sulfur from atmosphere and precipitation
- Organic matter
- Sediments
- Energy from Sun

LOSS
- Water by evapotranspiration
- Nitrogen by denitrification
- Carbon as carbon dioxide from oxidation of organic matter
- Soil by erosion
- Energy by radiation

TRANSLOCATION
- Clay and organic matter carried by water
- Nutrients circulated by plants
- Soluble salts carried in water
- Soil carried by animals

TRANSFORMATION
- Organic matter converted to humus
- Particles made smaller by weathering
- Structure and concretion formation
- Minerals transformed by weathering
- Clay and organic matter reactions

LOSS
- Water and materials in solution or suspension

◄ **Figure 12-21** The four soil-forming processes: addition, loss, translocation, transformation. Geologic, climatic, topographic, biological, and chronological (time) soil-forming factors influence the rate at which these four processes occur and therefore the rate at which soil is formed.

more or less distinctly recognizable layers, called **horizons**, each with different characteristics. The horizons are positioned approximately parallel with the land surface, one above the other, normally, but not always, separated by a transition zone rather than a sharp line. A vertical cross section (as might be seen in a road cut or the side of a trench dug in a field) from the Earth's surface down through the soil layers and into the parent material is referred to as a **soil profile**. The almost infinite variety of soils in the world are usually grouped and classified on the basis of differences exhibited in their profiles.

Figure 12-22 presents an idealized sketch of a well-developed soil profile, in which six horizons are differentiated:

- The **O horizon** is sometimes the surface layer, and in it organic matter, both fresh and decaying, makes up most of the volume. This horizon results essentially from litter derived from dead plants and animals. It is common in forests and generally absent in grasslands. It is actually more typical for soils not to possess an O horizon; the surface horizon of most soils is the A horizon.
- The **A horizon**, colloquially referred to as *topsoil*, is a mineral horizon that also contains considerable organic matter. It is formed either at the surface or immediately below an O horizon. A horizons generally contain enough partially decomposed organic matter to give the soil a darker color than underlying horizons. They are also normally coarser in texture,

having lost some of the finer materials by erosion and eluviation. Seeds germinate mostly in the A horizon.

- The **E horizon** is normally lighter in color than either the overlying A or the underlying B horizon. It is essentially an eluvial layer from which clay, iron, and aluminum have been removed, leaving a concentration of abrasion-resistant sand or silt particles.
- The **B horizon**, usually called *subsoil*, is a mineral horizon of illuviation where most of the materials removed from above have been deposited. A collecting zone for clay, iron, and aluminum, this horizon is usually of heavier texture, greater density, and relatively greater clay content than the A horizon.
- The **C horizon** is unconsolidated parent material (regolith) beyond the reach of plant roots and most soil-forming processes except weathering. It is lacking in organic matter.
- The **R horizon** is bedrock, with little evidence of weathering.

True soil, which is called **solum**, only extends down through the B horizon.

As we learned earlier in the chapter, time is a critical passive factor in profile development, but the vital active factor is surface water. If there is no surface water, from rainfall or snowmelt or some other source, to infiltrate the soil, there can be no profile development. Descending water carries material from the surface downward, from topsoil into subsoil, by eluviation and leaching. This transported material is mostly deposited a few tens of centimeters (a few feet) below the surface. In the usual pattern, topsoil (A) becomes a somewhat depleted horizon through eluviation and leaching, and subsoil (B) develops as a layer of accumulation due to illuviation.

A profile that contains all horizons is typical of a humid area on well-drained but gentle slopes in an environment that has been undisturbed for a long time. In many parts of the world, however, such idealized conditions do not pertain, and the soil profile may have one horizon particularly well developed, one missing altogether, a *fossil horizon* formed under a different past climate, an accumulation of a hardpan (a very dense and impermeable layer), surface layers removed through accelerated erosion, or some other variation. Moreover, many soils are too young to have evolved a normal profile. A soil containing only an A horizon atop partially altered parent material (C horizon) is said to be *immature*. The formation of an illuvial B horizon is normally an indication of a *mature* soil.

Learning Check 12-8   Describe the soil horizons found in *solum*.

PEDOGENIC REGIMES

Soil-forming factors and processes interact in almost limitless variations to produce soils of all descriptions. Fundamental to an understanding of soil classification and distribution is the realization that only five major **pedogenic regimes**

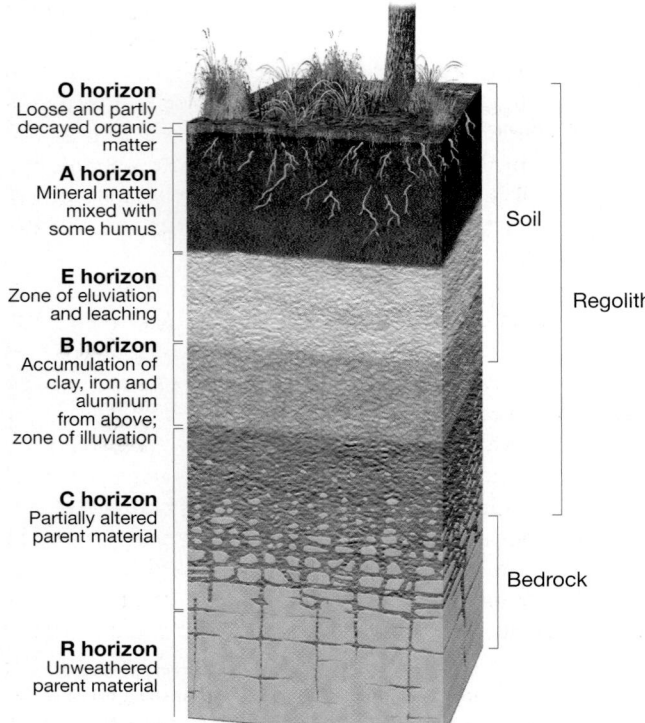

O horizon
Loose and partly decayed organic matter

A horizon
Mineral matter mixed with some humus

E horizon
Zone of eluviation and leaching

B horizon
Accumulation of clay, iron and aluminum from above; zone of illuviation

C horizon
Partially altered parent material

R horizon
Unweathered parent material

Soil

Regolith

Bedrock

▲ **Figure 12-22** Idealized soil profile. The true soil, or solum, consists of the O, A, E, and B horizons.

("soil-forming" regimes) exist: *laterization, podzolization, gleization, calcification,* and *salinization.* These regimes can be thought of as environmental settings in which certain physical–chemical–biological processes prevail.

Laterization

Laterization is named for the brick-red color of the soil it produces (*later*: Latin, "brick"). The processes associated with this regime are typical of the warm, moist regions of the world, and a significant annual moisture surplus is a requisite condition. The soil formed by laterization is most prominent, then, in the tropics and subtropics, in regions dominated by forest, shrub, and savanna vegetation.

A laterization regime is characterized by rapid weathering of parent material, dissolution of nearly all minerals, and speedy decomposition of organic matter. Probably the most distinctive feature of laterization is the leaching away of silica, the most common constituent of most rock and soil and a constituent that is usually highly resistant to being dissolved. That silica is indeed removed during laterization indicates the extreme effectiveness of chemical weathering and leaching under this regime. Most other minerals are also leached out rapidly, leaving behind primarily iron and aluminum oxides and barren grains of quartz sand. This residue normally imparts to the resulting soil the reddish color that gives this regime its name (Figure 12-23). The A horizon is highly eluviated and leached, whereas the B horizon has a considerable concentration of illuviated materials.

▲ **Figure 12-23** In the wet tropics, laterization is the dominant soil-forming regime, and most soils are reddish as a result of the prominence of iron and aluminum compounds. Lateritic soils are exposed in this road cut near Savusavu on the Fijian island of Vanua Levu.

Because plant litter is rapidly decomposed in places where laterization is the predominant regime, little humus is incorporated into the soil. Even so, plant nutrients are not totally removed by leaching because the natural vegetation, particularly in a forest, quickly absorbs many of the nutrients in solution. If the vegetation is relatively undisturbed by human activities, this regime has the most rapid of nutrient cycles, and the soil is not totally impoverished by the speed of mineral decomposition and leaching. Where the forest is cleared for agriculture or some other human purpose, however, most base nutrients are likely to be lost from the cycle because the tree roots that would bring them up are gone. The soil then rapidly becomes impoverished, and hard crusts of iron and aluminum compounds are likely to form.

Latosols: The general term applied to soils produced by laterization is *latosols*. These soils sometimes develop to depths of several meters because of the strong weathering activities and the fact that laterization continues year-round in these benign climates. Most latosols have little to offer as agricultural soils, but laterization often produces such concentrations of iron and aluminum oxides that mining them can be profitable.

Podzolization

Podzolization is another regime named after the color of the soil it produces; in this case, gray (*podzol*: Russian for "like ashes"). It also occurs in regions having a positive moisture balance and involves considerable leaching, but beyond those two characteristics, it bears little similarity to laterization. Podzolization occurs primarily in areas where the vegetation has limited nutrient requirements and where the plant litter is acidic. These conditions are most prominent in mid- and high-latitude locales with a coniferous forest cover. Thus, podzolization is largely a Northern Hemisphere phenomenon because there is not much land in the higher midlatitudes south of the equator. The typical location for podzolization is under a boreal forest in subarctic climates, which is found only in the Northern Hemisphere.

In these cool regions, chemical weathering is slow, but the abundance of acids, plus adequate precipitation, makes leaching very effective. Mechanical weathering from frost action is relatively rapid during the unfrozen part of the year. Moreover, much of the land was "bulldozed" by Pleistocene glaciers, leaving an abundance of broken rock debris at the surface. Bedrock here consists mostly of ancient crystalline rocks rich in quartz and aluminum silicates and poor in the alkaline mineral cations important in plant nutrition. The boreal forests, dominated by conifers, require little in the way of soil nutrients, and their litter returns few nutrient minerals when it decays. The litter is largely needles and twigs, which accumulate on the surface of the soil and decompose slowly. Microorganisms do not thrive in this environment, and so humus production is retarded. Moisture is relatively abundant in summer, so that leaching of whatever nutrient cations are present in the topsoil—along with iron oxides, aluminum oxides, and colloidal clays—is relatively complete.

Podzols: Podzolization, then, produces soils that are shallow and acidic and have a fairly distinctive profile. There is usually an O horizon. The upper part of the A horizon is eluviated to a silty or sandy texture and is so leached as to appear bleached. It is usually the ashy, light gray color that gives this regime its name, a color imparted by its high silica content. The illuviated B horizon is a receptacle for the iron-aluminum oxides and clay minerals leached from above and has a sharply contrasting darker color (sometimes with an orange or yellow tinge). Soil fertility is generally low, and a crumbly structure makes the soil very susceptible to accelerated erosion if the vegetation cover is disturbed, whether by human activities or by such natural agencies as wildfire. Soils produced by podzolization often are referred to collectively as *podzols.*

Learning Check 12-9 **Contrast the processes of laterization and podzolization. What are the characteristics of soils produced by each process?**

Gleization

Gleization is a regime restricted to waterlogged areas, normally in a cool climate. (The name comes from *glej,* Polish for "muddy ground.") Although occasionally widespread, it is generally much more limited in occurrence than laterization and podzolization. The poor drainage that produces a waterlogged environment can be associated with flat land, but it can also result from a topographic depression, a high water table, or various other conditions. In North America, gleization is particularly prominent in areas around the Great Lakes, where recent glacial deposition has interrupted preglacial drainage patterns.

Gley Soils: The general term for soils produced by gleization is *gley soils.* They characteristically have a highly organic A horizon, where decomposition proceeds slowly because bacteria are inhibited by the lack of oxygen in a waterlogged situation. In such *anaerobic* conditions, chemical reduction takes place—notably ferric iron (Fe^{3+}) compounds are reduced to ferrous iron (Fe^{2+}) compounds (*reduction* occurs when a substance gains an electron—the opposite of *oxidation*). Reduced iron is more easily carried away than oxidized iron, and so over time the soil tends to become poor in iron and gray in color.

Gley soils are usually too acidic and oxygen poor to be productive for anything but water-tolerant vegetation. If drained artificially, however, and fertilized with lime to counteract the acid, their fertility can be greatly enhanced.

Calcification

In semiarid and arid climates, where precipitation is less than potential evapotranspiration, leaching is either absent or transitory. Natural vegetation in such areas consists of grasses or shrubs. **Calcification** (so called because many calcium salts are produced in this regime) is the dominant pedogenic process in these regions, as typified by the drier prairies of North America, the steppes of Eurasia, and the savannas and steppes of the subtropics.

Calcic Hardpans: Both eluviation and leaching are restricted by the absence of percolating water, and so materials that would be carried downward in other regimes become concentrated in the soil where calcification is at work. Moreover, there is considerable upward movement of water by capillary action in dry periods. Calcium carbonate ($CaCO_3$) is the most important chemical compound active in a calcification regime. It is carried downward by limited leaching after a rain and is often concentrated in the B horizon to form a dense layer of *hardpan*, then brought upward by capillary water and by grass roots, and finally returned to the soil when the grass dies. Little clay is formed because of the limited amount of chemical weathering. Organic colloidal material, however, is often present in considerable quantity.

Where calcification takes place under undisturbed grassland, the resulting soils are likely to have remarkable agricultural productivity. Humus from decaying grass yields abundant organic colloidal material, imparting a dark color to the soil and contributing to a structure that can retain both nutrients and soil moisture. Grass roots tend to bring calcium up from the B horizon sufficiently to inhibit or delay the formation of calcic hardpans. Where shrubs are the dominant vegetation, roots are fewer but deeper, so that nutrients are brought up from deeper layers, and little accumulates at the surface with less humus incorporated into the soil.

Where a calcification regime is operative in true deserts, the soils tend to be shallower and sandier, calcic hardpans may form near the surface, little organic matter accumulates either on or in the soil, and the soils are not very different from the parent material.

Salinization

In arid and semiarid regions, it is fairly common to find areas with inadequate drainage, particularly in enclosed valleys and basins. Moisture is drawn upward and into the atmosphere by intense evaporation. The evaporating water leaves behind various salts in or on the surface of the soil, sometimes in such quantity as to impart a brilliant white surface color to the land, and the pedogenic regime is called **salinization**. These salts, which are mostly chlorides and sulfates of calcium and sodium, are toxic to most plants and soil organisms, and the resulting soil is able to support very little life apart from a few salt-tolerant grasses and shrubs.

Soils developed in a salinization (*salin:* Latin for "salt") regime can be sometimes made productive through careful water management, but artificial drainage is equally necessary or else salt accumulation will be intensified. Indeed, human-induced salinization has ruined good agricultural land in various parts of the world many times in the past (Figure 12-24).

Learning Check 12-10 **Under what conditions can salinization lead to soils that are unsuitable for agriculture?**

▲ **Figure 12-24** Soil salinization in a vineyard near San Juan, Argentina.

Climate and Pedogenic Regimes

The pedogenic regimes are distinguished primarily on the basis of climate as reflected in temperature and moisture availability (Figure 12-25) and secondarily on the basis of vegetation cover. In regions where there is normally a surplus of moisture—which is to say annual precipitation exceeds annual evapotranspiration—water movement in the soil is predominantly downward and leaching is a prominent process. In such areas where temperatures are relatively high throughout the year, laterization is

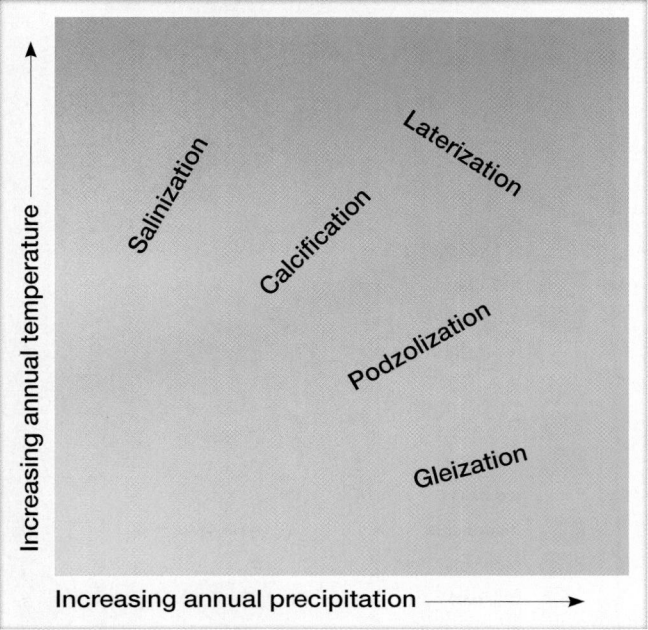

▲ **Figure 12-25** Temperature–moisture relationships for the five principal pedogenic regimes. Where temperature is high but precipitation low, salinization is the main method of soil formation. Where temperature is low but precipitation high, gleization predominates. Laterization occurs where both temperature and precipitation are high. Calcification and podzolization take place in less extreme environments.

the dominant regime; where winters are long and cold, podzolization predominates; and where the soil is saturated most of the time due to poor drainage, gleization is notable. A broadly valid generalization is that gleization can occur in any of the pedogenic regimes, as it is more dependent on local topography than on macroclimate. In regions having a moisture deficit, the principal soil moisture movement is upward (through capillarity) and leaching is limited. Calcification and salinization are the principal pedogenic regimes under these conditions.

Because soils reflect the climate in which they formed, studying a cross-section of the soil enables soil scientists to reconstruct past conditions, as described in the box, "Focus: Using Soil Properties to Decipher Past Environmental Changes."

SOIL CLASSIFICATION

Some of the most significant products of scholarly studies are classification systems. If phenomena can be classified meaningfully, it becomes easier to remember them and to understand the relationships among them. Our consideration thus far has included various classifications (for example, climate and biomes). In no other subdiscipline of physical geography, however, is the matter of classification more complicated than with soil.

The Soil Taxonomy

Over the past century, various soil classifications have been devised in the United States and other countries. As the knowledge of soil characteristics and processes has become greater, so have the efforts at soil classification become more sophisticated. Several different systems have been developed in other countries, particularly in Canada, the United Kingdom, Russia, France, and Australia. Moreover, United Nations agencies have their own classification schemes. The system that is presently in use in the United States is called simply **Soil Taxonomy**.

The basic characteristic that sets Soil Taxonomy apart from previous systems is that it is *generic*, which means it is organized on the basis of observable soil characteristics. The focus is on the existing properties of a soil rather than on the environment, processes of development, or properties it would possess under virgin conditions. The logic of such a generic system is theoretically impeccable: soil has certain properties that can be observed, measured, and at least partly quantified.

Like other logical generic systems, the Soil Taxonomy is a hierarchical system, which means that it has several levels of generalization, with each higher level encompassing several members of the level immediately below it. There are only a few similarities among all the members of the highest level category, but the number of similarities increases with each step downward in the hierarchy, so that in the lowest-level category, all members have mostly the same properties. (See Appendix VII for details.)

TABLE 12-2	Name Derivations of Soil Orders
Order	**Derivation**
Alfisols	"al" for aluminum, "f" for iron (chemical symbol Fe), two prominent elements in these soils
Andisols	andesite, rock formed from type of magma in Andes Mountains volcanoes; soils high in volcanic ash
Aridisols	Latin *aridus*, "dry"; dry soils
Entisols	last three letters in "recent"; these are recently formed soils
Gelisols	Latin *gelatio*, "freezing"; soils in areas of permafrost
Histosols	Greek *histos*, "living tissue"; these soils contain mostly organic matter
Inceptisols	Latin *inceptum*, "beginning"; young soils at the beginning of their "life"
Mollisols	Latin *mollis*, "soft"; soft soils
Oxisols	soils with large amounts of oxygen-containing compounds
Spodosols	Greek *spodos*, "wood ash"; ashy soils
Ultisols	Latin *ultimus*, "last"; soils that have had the last of their nutrient bases leached out
Vertisols	Latin *verto*, "turn"; soils in which material from O and A horizons falls through surface cracks and ends up below deeper horizons; the usual horizon order is inverted

Soil Order: At the highest level of the Soil Taxonomy is **soil order**, of which only 12 are recognized worldwide (Table 12-2). The soil orders, and many of the lower-level categories as well, are distinguished from one another largely on the basis of certain diagnostic properties, which are often expressed in combination to form *diagnostic horizons*. The two basic types of diagnostic horizon are the *epipedon* (based on the Greek word *epi*, meaning "over" or "upon"), which is essentially the A horizon or the combined O/A horizon, and the *subsurface horizon*, which is roughly equivalent to the B horizon. (Note that all A and B horizons are not necessarily diagnostic, and so the terms and concepts are not synonymous.)

Soil orders are subdivided into suborders, of which about 50 are recognized in the United States. The third level consists of *great groups*, which number about 250 in the United States. Successively lower levels in the classification are subgroups, families, and series. About 19,000 soil series have been identified in the United States to date, and the list will undoubtedly be expanded in the future. For the purpose of comprehending general world distribution patterns, however, we need to concern ourselves only with orders (Figure 12-26).

Learning Check 12-11 **What does it mean to say that the Soil Taxonomy is a *generic* system of classification?**

The Mapping Question

Maps are a basic tool of geographic study, and one of the fundamental problems that confronts any geographic inquiry is how the phenomena under study should be mapped. Because the higher levels of the Soil Taxonomy do not represent phenomena that actually exist but rather are generalized abstractions of average or typical conditions over broad areas, the selection of an appropriate mapping technique can significantly influence our understanding of soil distribution.

Most soil maps use the same timeworn technique of areal expression. If one soil type (at whatever level of generalization is being studied) is more common in an area than any other, that area is classified by the prevailing type and colored or shaded appropriately. Such a map is effective in indicating the

▼ **Figure 12-26** Soils of the world.

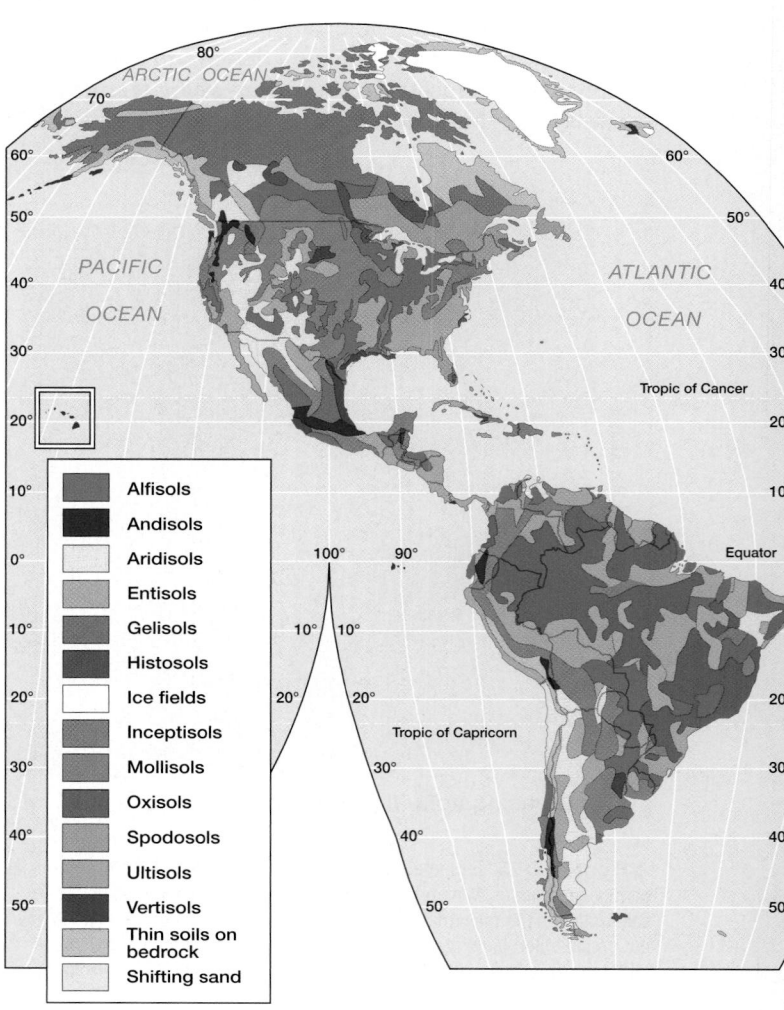

principal type of soil in each region and is useful in portraying the general distribution of the major soil types.

Maps of this type are compiled through generalization of data, and the smaller the scale, the greater the generalization needed. Thus, more intricate patterns can be shown on the larger scale map of the United States (Figure 12-40 on p. 371) than on the smaller scale world map (Figure 12-26). In either case, the map is only as good as its generalizations are meticulous.

GLOBAL DISTRIBUTION OF MAJOR SOILS

 FG13

There are 12 orders of soils, which are distinguished largely on the basis of properties that reflect a major course of development, with considerable emphasis on the presence or absence of notable diagnostic horizons. We consider each of the 12 orders, beginning with those characterized by little profile development and progressing to those with the most highly weathered profiles, as generally represented from top to bottom in Figure 12-27.

Entisols (Very Little Profile Development)

The least well developed of all soils, **Entisols** have experienced little mineral alteration and are virtually without pedogenic horizons. Their undeveloped state is usually a function of time (the very name of the order connotes recency); most Entisols are surface deposits that have not been in place long enough for pedogenetic processes to have had much effect. Some, however, are very old, and in these soils the lack of horizon development is due to a mineral content that does not alter readily, to a very cold climate, or to some other factor totally unrelated to time.

The distribution of Entisols is therefore very widespread and cannot be specifically correlated with particular moisture or temperature conditions or with certain types of vegetation or parent materials (Figure 12-28). In the United States, Entisols are most prominent in the dry lands of the West but are found in most other parts of the country as well. They are commonly thin and/or sandy and have limited productivity, although those developed on recent alluvial deposits tend to be quite fertile.

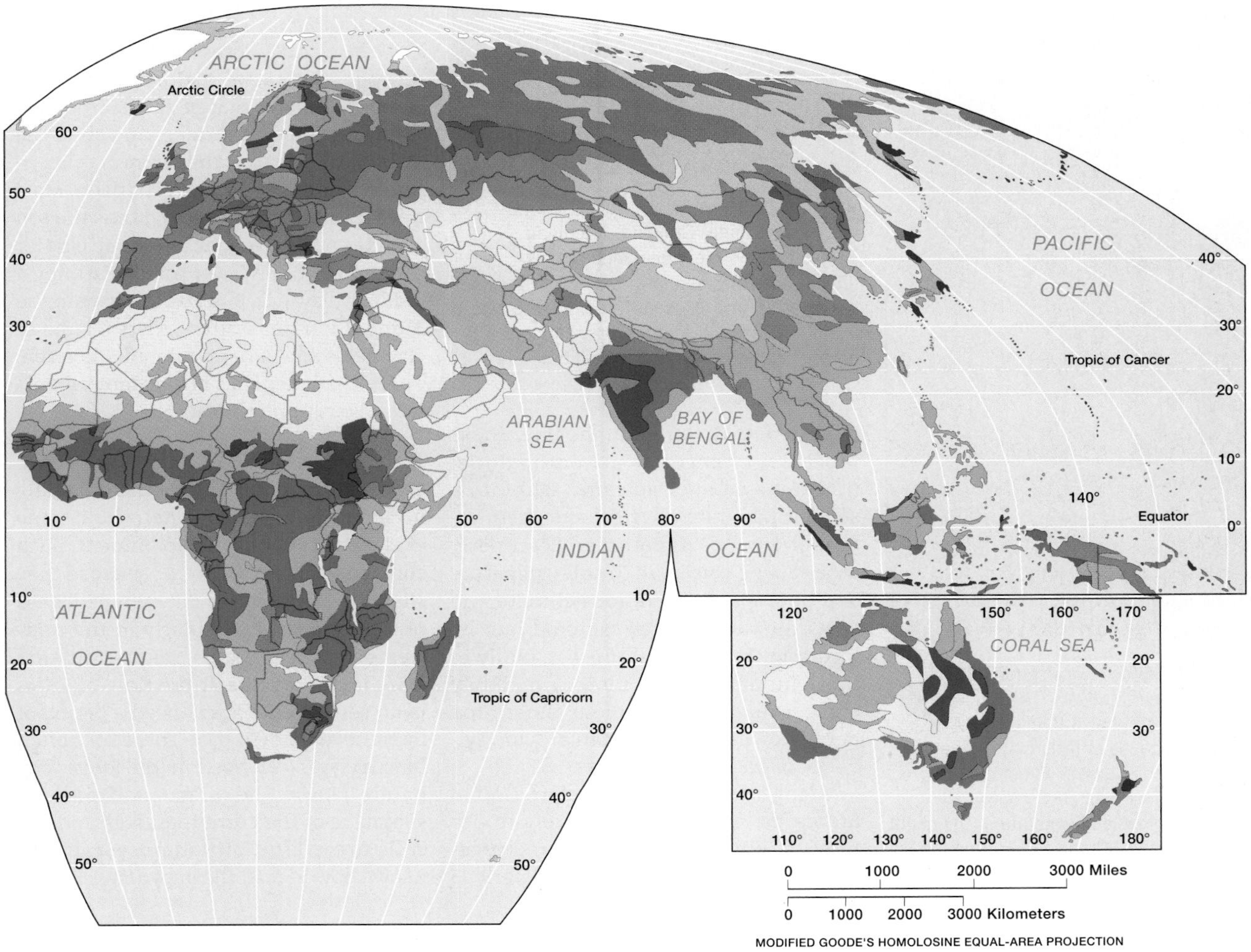

MODIFIED GOODE'S HOMOLOSINE EQUAL-AREA PROJECTION

FOCUS

Using Soil Properties to Decipher Past Environmental Changes

▶ Randall Schaetzl, Michigan State University

In ancient Egypt, papyrus served as the equivalent of paper and could be used and reused many times, forming a *palimpsest*. In a palimpsest, earlier writings on papyrus were never quite completely erased, and so were often still faintly legible. Something similar also happens with soils.

Soils develop their physical characteristics and chemical properties depending on the soil-forming processes that affect them. These processes vary from place to place, and time to time. Climate and vegetation largely govern the types of processes that soils

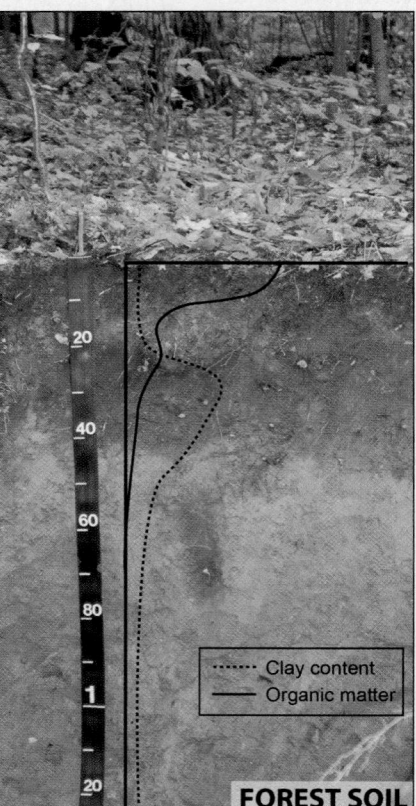

▲ **Figure 12-B** Profile of forest soil in a maple forest near Grayling, Michigan. The soil shows clear evidence of clay illuviation—the reddish-brown B horizon between 20 and 44 centimeters. Note also the thin A horizon and the light-colored E horizon between 12 and 20 centimeters.

experience. Given enough time, these processes change raw parent material (like dune sand or volcanic ash) into a soil with definite physical and chemical properties, or "signatures." If properly trained, one can "read" a soil's signature and determine the various climate and vegetation inputs that factored into its formation. As in a palimpsest, many of these inputs are difficult to completely erase. One such example is illustrated here, showing how soils can provide evidence of past environments.

Many soils in the midwestern United States have developed entirely under forest or entirely under grassland vegetation. Some, however, have had periods

of development under both. The structure and properties of the soils can often help us understand the extent to which each soil was influenced by forest and/or grassland.

Grassland Soils: Under grassland vegetation, as grass roots continually form and decay into humus, soils develop a thick, dark, humus-rich A horizon in the upper part of the soil. Because the grasses biocycle certain base cations (especially Ca^{2+} and Mg^{2+}), the pH of the soil remains high. The high pH inhibits weathering of soil minerals, as well as the movement of clay to the lower profile. Thus, Mollisols like this one often lack a reddish, clay-rich B horizon (Figure 12-A). They have relatively simple profiles: a thick, dark A horizon, a weak B horizon, and a C horizon (parent material). When one sees this kind of "soil writing," it is easy to infer a history of long-term grassland influence.

Forest Soils: Forest soils have a very different formative history. Their main source of organic matter comes from leaf decay on the soil surface, and thus the little organic matter they have is concentrated in a much thinner A horizon. Most trees do not cycle bases, and thus the soil acidifies over time, which frees up clay for movement to the lower profile, forming a reddish, clay-rich B horizon. Between the A and B horizons often exists a zone of clay depletion, a light-colored E horizon. These characteristics are evident in most forest soils (Figure 12-B).

Polygenetic Soils: Soils that have experienced major environmental shifts in climate or vegetation often retain some evidence of that past environment. Such soils are called *polygenetic,* because they show clear evidence of different pathways of soil genesis. Particularly in the midwestern United States, many soils that were under grasses at the time of European settlement experienced a period of forest cover in their past. These soils often have a clay-rich B horizon (the forest "signature") below the thick A horizon—the signature of the current grasses. Indeed, soils are a kind of palimpsest, if one knows how to read the papyrus!

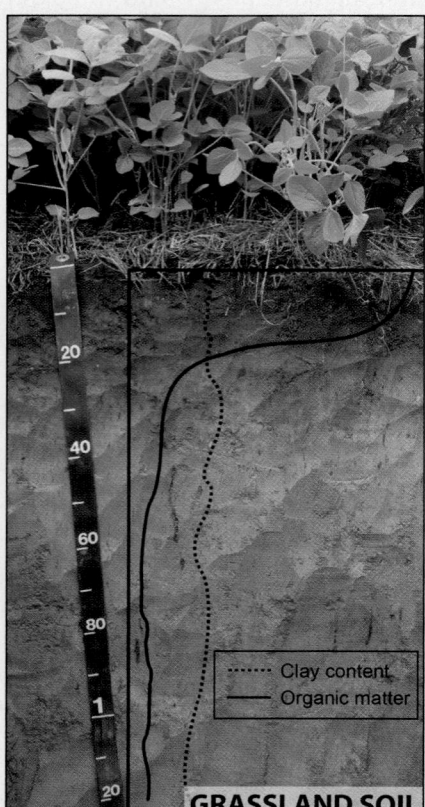

▲ **Figure 12-A** Profile of grassland soil in a soybean field near Markesan, southeastern Wisconsin. The soil has a thick, dark A horizon, but because of little clay illuviation, it lacks a reddish, clay-rich B horizon, probably because it has been continually forming under grassland vegetation (the slight reddening between 60 and 90 centimeters is mainly due to weak, in situ weathering).

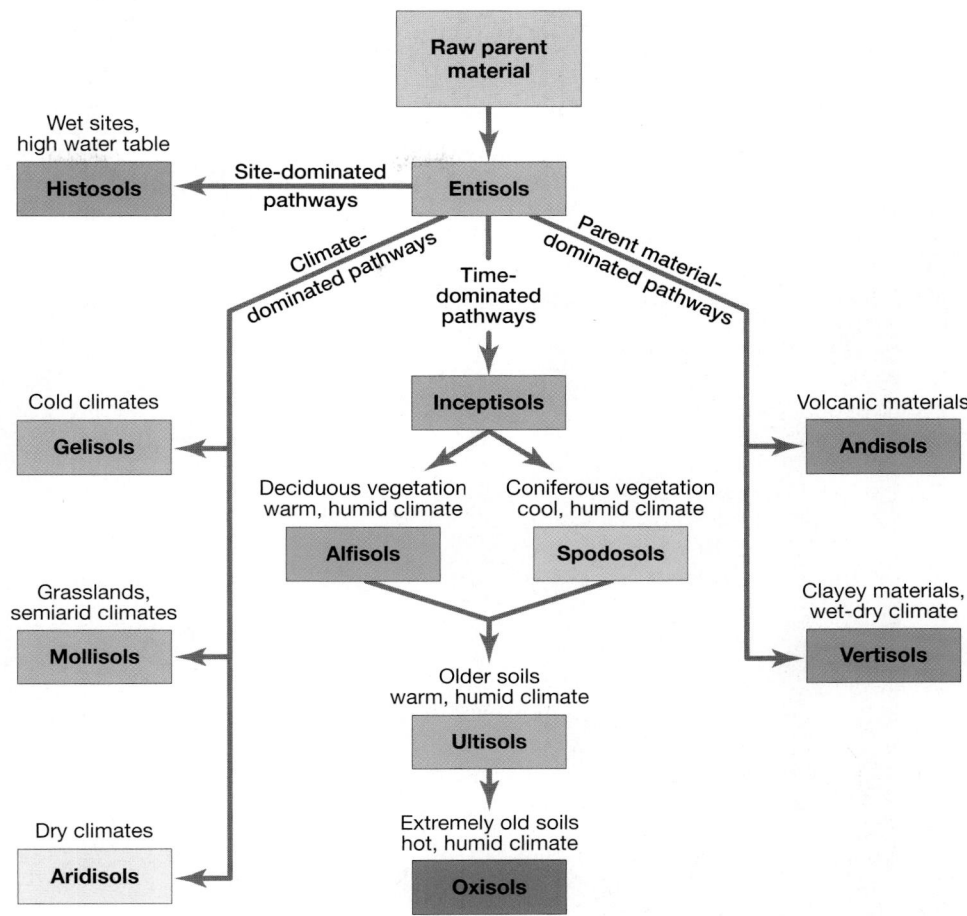

▶ **Figure 12-27** Theoretical soil order development pathways. Soils evolve along "pathways" in which different factors—such as parent material, climate, local site conditions, or length of time—may dominate. (The colors for each soil order match those on the soil distribution maps in this chapter.)

Inceptisols (Few Diagnostic Features)

Another immature order of soils is the **Inceptisols**. Their distinctive characteristics are relatively faint, not yet prominent enough to produce diagnostic horizons (Figure 12-29). If the Entisols can be called "youthful," the Inceptisols might be classified "adolescent." They are primarily eluvial soils and lack illuvial layers.

Like Entisols, Inceptisols are widespread over the world in various environments. Also like Entisols, they include a variety of fairly dissimilar soils whose common characteristic is lack of maturity. They are most common in tundra and mountain areas but are also notable in older valley floodplains. Their world distribution pattern is very irregular. This is also true in the United States, where they are most typical of the Appalachian Mountains, the Pacific Northwest, and the lower Mississippi Valley.

Learning Check 12-12 **Describe and explain the soil horizon development of *entisols*.**

Andisols (Volcanic Ash Soils)

Having developed from volcanic ash, **Andisols** have been deposited in relatively recent geological time. They are not highly weathered, therefore, and there has been little downward translocation of their colloids. There is minimum profile development, and the upper layers are dark (Figure 12-30). Their inherent fertility is relatively high.

Andisols are found primarily in volcanic regions of Japan, Indonesia, and South America, as well as in the very productive wheat lands of Washington, Oregon, and Idaho.

Gelisols (Cold Soils with Permafrost)

Gelisols are young soils with minimal profile development (Figure 12-31). They develop only slowly because of cold temperatures and frozen conditions. These soils typically have a permafrost layer that is a defining characteristic. Also commonly found in Gelisols is *cryoturbation* or frost churning, which is the physical disruption and displacement of soil material by freeze–thaw action in the soil. Most of the soil-forming processes in Gelisols take place above the permafrost in the active layer that thaws every year or so.

Gelisols are the dominant soils of Arctic and subarctic regions. They occur in association with boreal forest and tundra vegetation; thus, they are primarily found in Russia, Canada, and Alaska and are prominent in the Himalaya Mountain country of central Asia. Altogether nearly 9 percent of Earth's land area has a Gelisol soil cover.

Learning Check 12-13 **In which kind of climate are *gelisols* typically found?**

▲ **Figure 12-28** Entisols. (a) World distribution of Entisols. (b) Profile of an Entisol in northern Michigan. This weakly developed soil evolved from sandy parent material in an area with only moderate precipitation.

▲ **Figure 12-29** Inceptisols. (a) World distribution of Inceptisols. (b) Profile of a New Zealand Inceptisol with a distinctive B horizon of white pebbly material. The scale is in meters.

Histosols (Organic Soils on Very Wet Sites)

Least important among the soil orders are the **Histosols**, which occupy only a small fraction of Earth's land surface, a much smaller area than any other order. These are organic rather than mineral soils, and they are invariably saturated with water all or most of the time. They may occur in any waterlogged environment but are most characteristic in mid- and high-latitude regions that experienced Pleistocene glaciation. In the United States, they are most common around the Great Lakes, but they also occur in southern Florida and Louisiana. Nowhere, however, is their occurrence extensive (Figure 12-32).

Some Histosols are composed largely of undecayed or only partly decayed plant material, whereas others consist of a thoroughly decomposed mass of muck. The lack of oxygen in the waterlogged soil slows down the rate of bacterial action, and the soil becomes deeper mostly by growing upward, that is, by more organic material being added from above.

Histosols are usually black, acidic, and fertile only for water-tolerant plants. If drained, they can be very productive agriculturally for a short while. Before long, however, they are likely to dry out, shrink, and oxidize, a series of steps that leads to compaction, susceptibility to wind erosion, and danger of fire.

Aridisols (Soils of Dry Climates)

Nearly one-eighth of Earth's land surface is covered with **Aridisols**, one of the most extensive spreads of any soil order (Figure 12-33). They are preeminently soils of the

▲ **Figure 12-30** Andisols. (a) World distribution of Andisols. (b) Profile of an Andisol in Washington state. The various horizons are very clearly delineated.

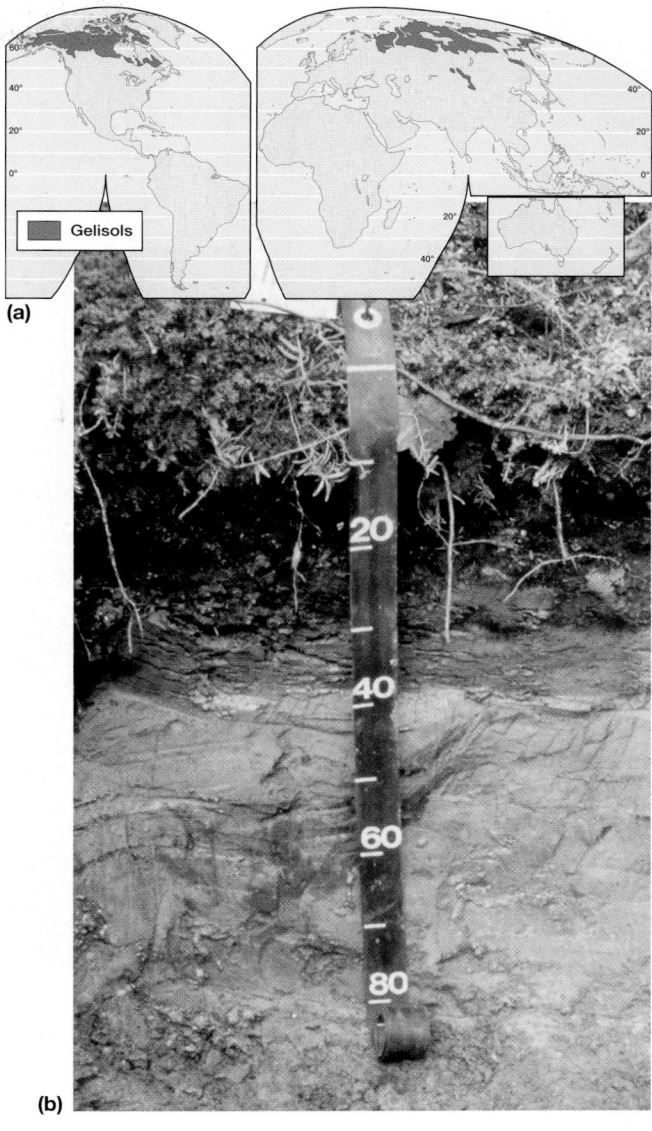

▲ **Figure 12-31** Gelisols. (a) World distribution of Gelisols. (b) Profile of a Gelisol in Alaska. The scale is in centimeters.

dry lands, occupying environments that do not have enough water to remove soluble minerals from the soil. Thus, their distribution pattern is largely correlated with that of desert and semidesert climates.

Aridisols are typified by a thin profile that is sandy and lacking in organic matter, characteristics clearly associated with a dry climate and a scarcity of penetrating moisture. The epipedon is almost invariably light in color. There are various kinds of diagnostic subsurface horizons, nearly all distinctly alkaline. Most Aridisols are unproductive, particularly because of lack of moisture; if irrigated, however, some display remarkable fertility. The threat of salt accumulation is nonetheless ever present.

Learning Check 12-14 **In what kind of environment are *Aridisols* typically found?**

Vertisols (Swelling and Cracking Clays)

Vertisols contain a large quantity of clay that becomes a dominant factor in the soil's development. The clay of Vertisols is described as "swelling" or "cracking" clay. This clay-type soil has an exceptional capacity for absorbing water: when moistened, it swells and expands; as it dries, deep, wide cracks form, sometimes 2.5 centimeters (an inch) wide and as much as 1 meter (3 feet) deep. Some surface material falls into the cracks, and more is washed in when it rains. When the soil is wetted again, more swelling takes place and the cracks close. This alternation of wetting and drying and expansion and contraction produces a churning effect that mixes the soil constituents (the name Vertisol connotes an inverted condition), inhibits the development of horizons, and may even cause minor irregularities in the land surface (Figure 12-34).

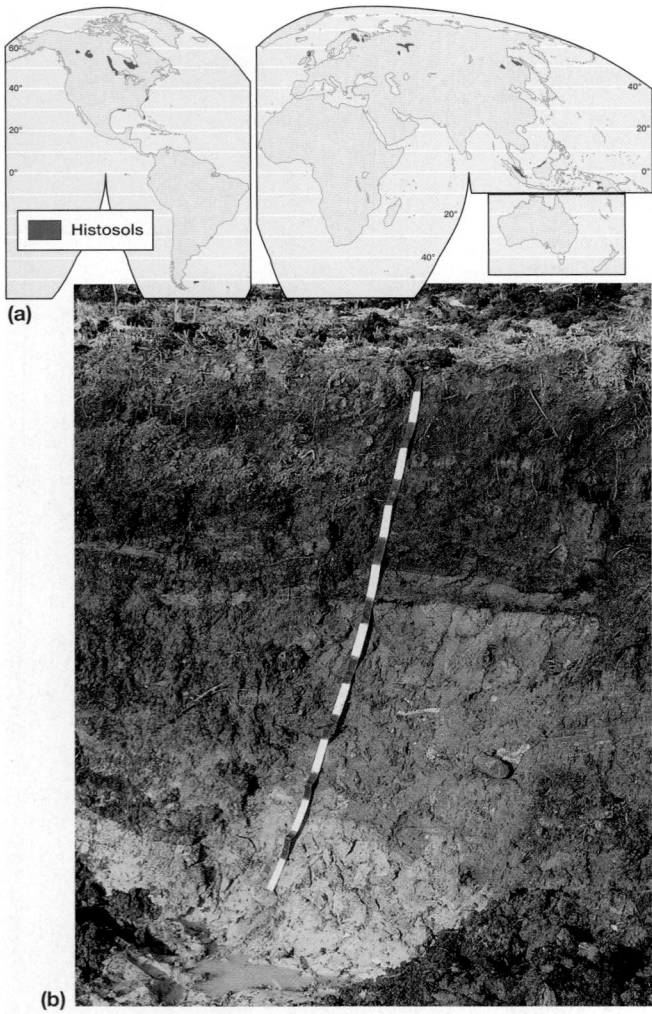

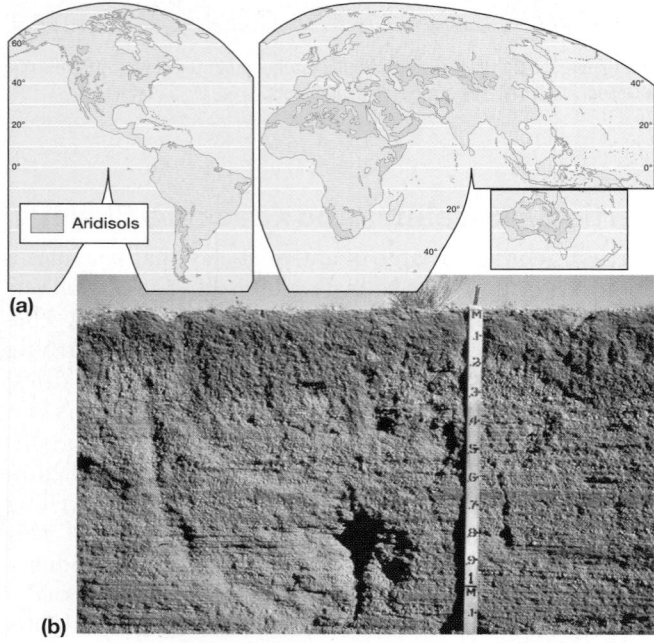

▲ **Figure 12-32** Histosols. (a) World distribution of Histosols. (b) Histosols are characteristically dark in color and composed principally of organic matter.

▲ **Figure 12-33** Aridisols. (a) World distribution of Aridisols. (b) The typical sandy profile of an Aridisol, in this case from New Mexico.

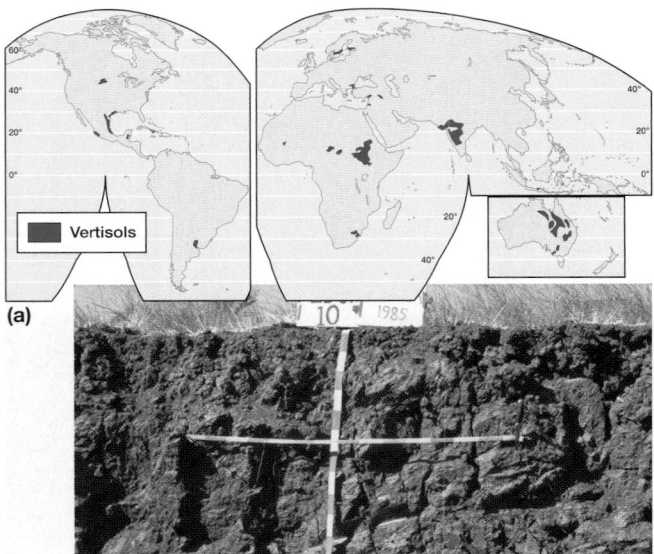

▲ **Figure 12-34** Vertisols. (a) World distribution of Vertisols. (b) A dark Vertisol profile from Zambia. Many cracks are typically found in Vertisols.

An alternating wet and dry climate is needed for Vertisol formation because the sequence of swelling and contraction is necessary. Thus, the wet–dry climate of tropical and subtropical savannas is ideal, but there must also be the proper parent material to yield the clay minerals. Consequently, Vertisols are widespread in distribution but are very limited in extent. The principal occurrences are in eastern Australia, India, and a small part of East Africa. They are uncommon in the United States, although prominent in some parts of Texas and California.

The fertility of Vertisols is relatively high, as they tend to be rich in nutrient bases. They are difficult to till, however, because of their sticky plasticity, and so they are often left uncultivated.

Mollisols (Dark, Soft Soils of Grasslands)

The distinctive characteristic of **Mollisols** is the presence of a mollic epipedon, which is a mineral surface horizon that is dark and thick, contains abundant humus and basic cations, and retains a soft character (rather than becoming hard and crusty) when it dries out (Figure 12-35). Mollisols can be thought of as transition soils that evolve in regions not dominated by either humid or arid conditions. They are typical of the midlatitude grasslands and are thus most common in central Eurasia, the North American Great Plains, and the pampas of Argentina.

The grassland environment generally maintains a rich clay–humus content in a Mollisol soil. The dense, fibrous mass of grass roots permeates uniformly through the epipedon and to a lesser extent into the subsurface layers. There is almost continuous decay of plant parts to produce a nutrient-rich humus for the living grass.

Mollisols on the whole are probably the most productive soil order. They are generally derived from loose parent

▲ **Figure 12-35** Mollisols. (a) World distribution of Mollisols. (b) A Mollisol profile from Nebraska. It has a typical mollic epipedon, a surface horizon that is dark and replete with humus.

▲ **Figure 12-36** Alfisols. (a) World distribution of Alfisols. (b) Profile of an Alfisol in east-central Illinois. The soil has reddened, clay-rich B horizon. It formed under forest vegetation and is heavily cropped with corn and soybeans.

material rather than from bedrock and tend to have favorable structure and texture for cultivation. Because they are not overly leached, nutrients are generally retained within reach of plant roots. Moreover, Mollisols provide a favored habitat for earthworms, which contribute to softening and mixing of the soil.

Alfisols (Clay-Rich B Horizons, High Base Status)

The most wide ranging of the mature soils, **Alfisols** occur extensively in low and middle latitudes, as Figure 12-36 shows. They are found in a variety of temperature and moisture conditions and under diverse vegetation associations. By and large, they tend to be associated with transitional environments and are less characteristic of regions that are particularly hot or cold or wet or dry. Their global distribution is extremely varied. They are also widespread

in the United States, with particular concentrations in the Midwest.

Alfisols are distinguished by a subsurface clay horizon and a medium to generous supply of basic cations, plant nutrients, and water. The epipedon is ochric (light-colored), as Figure 12-36b shows, but beyond that, it has no characteristics that are particularly diagnostic and can be considered an ordinary eluviated horizon. The relatively moderate conditions under which Alfisols develop tend to produce balanced soils that are reasonably fertile. Alfisols rank second only to Mollisols in agricultural productivity.

Learning Check 12-15 **Compare the relative suitability for agriculture of Vertisols, Mollisols, and Alfisols.**

▲ Figure 12-37 Ultisols. (a) World distribution of Ultisols. (b) A tropical Ultisol from Thailand. It is reddish throughout its profile, indicative of much leaching and weathering.

Ultisols (Clay-Rich B Horizons, Low Base Status)

Ultisols are roughly similar to Alfisols except that Ultisols are more thoroughly weathered and more completely leached of nutrient bases. They have experienced greater mineral alteration than any other soil in the midlatitudes, although they also occur in the low latitudes. Many pedologists believe that the ultimate fate of Alfisols is to degenerate into Ultisols.

Typically, Ultisols are reddish as a result of the significant proportion of iron and aluminum in the A horizon. They usually have a fairly distinct layer of subsurface clay accumulation. The principal properties of Ultisols have been imparted by a great deal of weathering and leaching (Figure 12-37). Indeed, the connotation of the name (derived from the Latin *ultimos*) is that these soils

represent the ultimate stage of weathering. The result is a fairly deep soil that is acidic, lacks humus, and has a relatively low fertility due to the lack of bases.

Ultisols have a fairly simple world distribution pattern. They are mostly confined to humid subtropical climates and to some relatively youthful tropical land surfaces. In the United States, they are restricted largely to the southeastern quarter of the country and to a narrow strip along the northern Pacific Coast.

Spodosols (Soils of Cool, Forested Zones)

The key diagnostic feature of a **Spodosol** is a spodic subsurface horizon, an illuvial dark or reddish layer where organic matter, iron, and aluminum accumulate. The upper layers are light-colored and heavily leached (Figure 12-38). At the top of the profile is usually an O

▲ Figure 12-38 Spodosols. (a) World distribution of Spodosols. (b) Profile of a Spodosol in northern Michigan. This weakly developed soil was formed in sandy material under coniferous forest vegetation and contains few nutrients. The scale is in centimeters.

horizon of organic litter. Such a soil is a typical result of podzolization.

Spodosols are notoriously infertile. They have been leached of useful nutrients and are acidic throughout. They do not retain moisture well and are lacking in humus and often in clay. Spodosols are most widespread in areas of coniferous forest where there is a subarctic climate. Alfisols, Histosols, and Inceptisols also occupy these regions, however, and Spodosols are sometimes found in other environments, such as poorly drained portions of Florida.

Oxisols (Highly Weathered and Leached)

The most thoroughly weathered and leached of all soils are the **Oxisols**, which invariably display a high degree of mineral alteration and profile development. They occur mostly on ancient landscapes in the humid tropics, particularly in Brazil and equatorial Africa, and to a lesser extent in Southeast Asia (Figure 12-39). The distribution pattern is often spotty, with Oxisols mixed with less developed Entisols, Vertisols, and Ultisols. Oxisols' are totally absent from the United States, except for Hawai'i, where they are common.

Oxisols are essentially the products of laterization (and in fact were called Latosols in older classification systems). They have evolved in warm, moist climates, although some are now found in drier regions, an indication of climatic change since the soils developed. The diagnostic horizon for Oxisols is a subsurface dominated by oxides of iron and aluminum and with a minimal supply of nutrient bases (this is called an *oxic horizon*). These are deep soils but not inherently fertile. The natural vegetation is efficient in cycling the limited nutrient supply, but if the flora is cleared (to attempt agriculture, for example), the

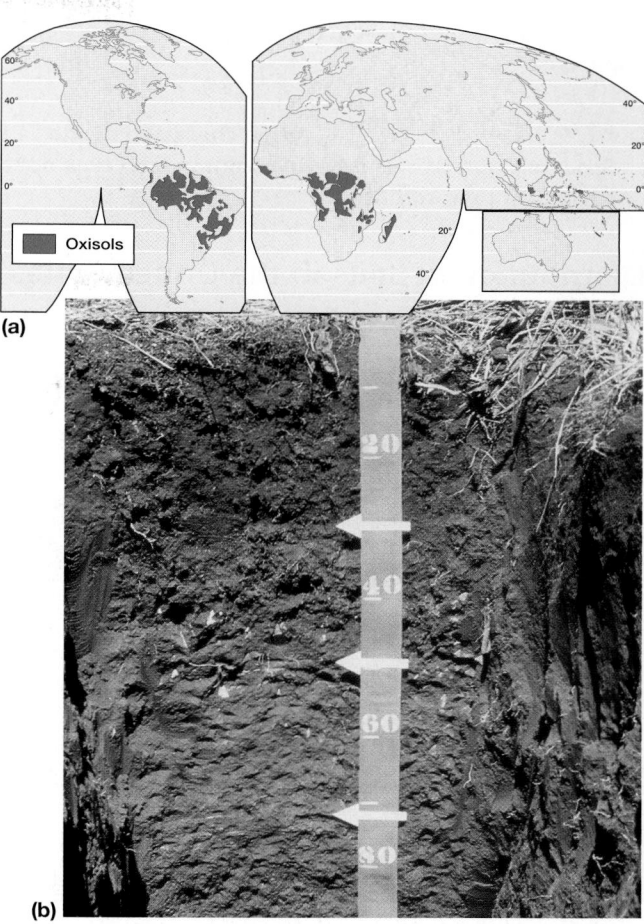

▲ **Figure 12-39** Oxisols. (a) World distribution of Oxisols. (b) Oxisols are impoverished tropical soils that usually are heavily leached. The horizons typically are indistinct. This sample is from Hawai'i. The scale is in centimeters.

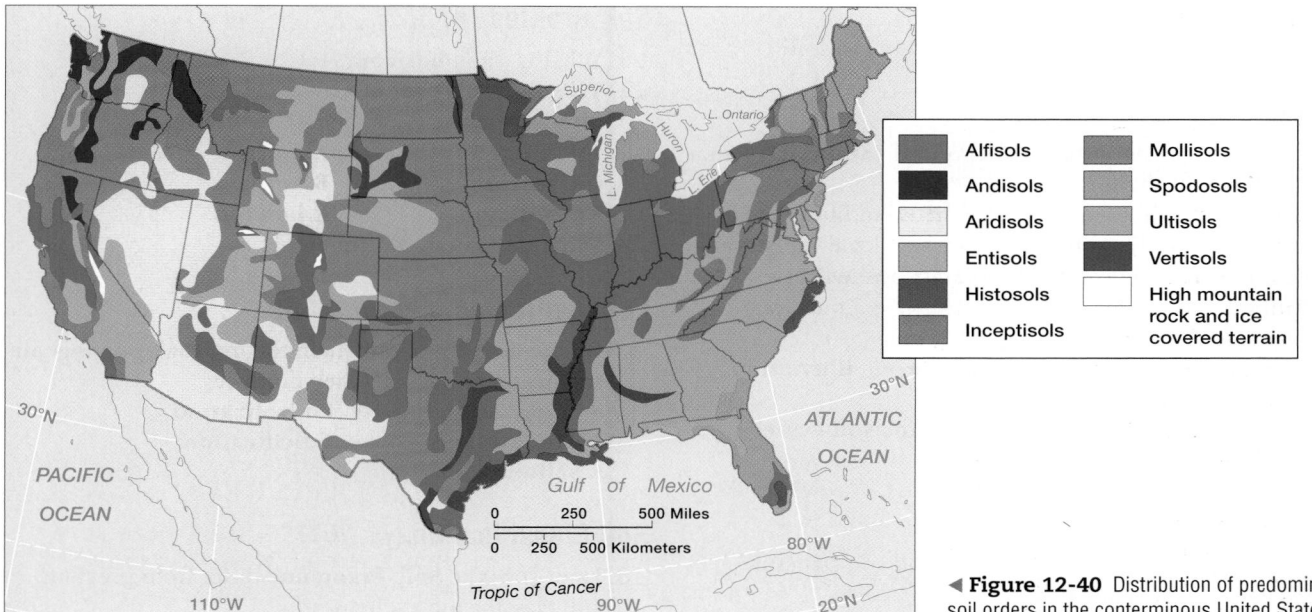

◀ **Figure 12-40** Distribution of predominant soil orders in the conterminous United States.

nutrients are rapidly leached out, and the soil becomes impoverished.

> **Learning Check 12-16** **What characteristic do Spodosols and Oxisols have in common, and how does this affect their fertility?**

Distribution of Soils in the United States

The distribution of the various soils in the United States is quite different from that of the world as a whole. This difference is due to many factors, the most important being that the United States is essentially a midlatitude country, and it lacks significant expanses of area in the low and high latitudes (Figure 12-40).

Mollisols are much more common in the United States than in the world as a whole; they are the most prevalent soil order throughout the Great Plains and in much of the West. Also significantly more abundant in the United States than in other parts of the world are Inceptisols and Ultisols. Aridisols and Entisols are proportionally less extensive. Almost totally lacking are Oxisols.

Chapter 12   **LEARNING REVIEW**

After studying this chapter, you should be able to answer the following questions. Key terms from each text section are shown in **bold type**. Definitions for key terms are also found in the glossary at the back of the book.

KEY TERMS AND CONCEPTS

Soil and Regolith (*p. 345*)

1. What is the relationship between weathering and regolith?
2. What is the difference between **soil** and **regolith**?

Soil-Forming Factors (*p. 347*)

3. Briefly describe the five principal soil-forming factors.
4. Explain the importance of **parent material** to the nature of the overlying soil.
5. What are some of the roles of animals in soil formation?
6. What roles do microorganisms play in the soil?

Soil Components (*p. 350*)

7. What are the importance of **clay** and **cations** to plant nutrients in the soil?
8. What is the difference between **litter** and **humus**?
9. Describe and explain the four forms of soil moisture.
10. Distinguish between **field capacity** and **wilting point**.
11. What is meant by **leaching**?
12. Explain the processes of **eluviation** and **illuviation**.
13. What is the **soil–water balance**?
14. What is the role of temperature in the **soil–water budget**?

Soil Properties (*p. 353*)

15. Distinguish between soil texture and soil structure.
16. What are soil **separates**?
17. What is meant by **loam**?

18. Explain the difference between porosity and permeability.
19. How do **peds** influence soil porosity?

Soil Chemistry (*p. 356*)

20. What is a **colloid**?
21. Explain what is meant by the **cation exchange capacity (CEC)** of a soil.
22. Which soil is more likely to be fertile—acidic soil or neutral soil? Why?

Soil Profiles (*p. 357*)

23. What is a soil **horizon**?
24. What is a **soil profile**?
25. Briefly describe the six possible soil horizons:
    - **0 horizon**
    - **A horizon**
    - **E horizon**
    - **B horizon**
    - **C horizon**
    - **R horizon**
26. What is mean by **solum**?

Pedogenic Regimes (*p. 358*)

27. Briefly describe and explain the five major **pedogenic regimes** and the soils they produce:
    - **Laterization**
    - **Podzolization**
    - **Gleization**
    - **Calcification**
    - **Salinization**

Soil Classification (*p. 361*)

28. How does the **Soil Taxonomy** differ from previous soil classification schemes?
29. What is meant by a **soil order**?

Global Distribution of Major Soils (*p. 363*)

30. Briefly describe the most distinguishing characteristics for each of the 12 soil orders:
    - **Entisols**
    - **Andisols**
    - **Inceptisols**
    - **Gelisols**
    - **Histosols**
    - **Vertisols**
    - **Alfisols**
    - **Spodosols**
    - **Aridisols**
    - **Mollisols**
    - **Ultisols**
    - **Oxisols**

STUDY QUESTIONS

1. Why does soil tend to be deepest on flat land?
2. Why are earthworms generally considered beneficial to humans?
3. Explain the importance of clay as a constituent of soil.
4. What is a colloidal complex and how does it relate to soil fertility?
5. What can you learn about a soil from its color?
6. Why do tropical rainforests usually have poor soils?
7. Why is it so difficult to portray soil distribution with reasonable accuracy on a small-scale map?
8. For each of the following circumstances, indicate which soil order is mostly likely to be found and the reasons for this:
   - Regions of permafrost
   - Areas with coniferous forest
   - Deserts
9. Assuming a warm climate with moderate rainfall, how would a soil developing on a sloping, sandstone surface compare with a soil developing on a flat, shale surface?

EXERCISES

1. Using the map of soil distribution in the United States (Figure 12-40) or the map showing the world distribution of soils (Figure 12-26), choose one of the soil orders that is found nearby your home and describe that order's general distribution and characteristics.

2. Use the soil-texture triangle (Figure 12-18) to determine the soil texture for the following combinations of clay, sand, and silt:
   a. 70% clay; 10% silt; 20% sand: _____
   b. 20% clay; 40% silt; 40% sand: _____
   c. 50% clay; 50% silt; 0% sand: _____

Seeing Geographically

Look again at the photograph of the wheat fields in Saskatchewan at the beginning of the chapter (p. 344). Based on this location (at about 52° N, 105° W) what kind of climate is mostly likely found here? Which of the five principal soil-forming factors are likely to be most important in this area? The least important?

MasteringGeography™

Looking for additional review and test prep materials? Visit the Study Area in MasteringGeography™ to enhance your geographic literacy, spatial reasoning skills, and understanding of this chapter's content by accessing a variety of resources, including geoscience animations, MapMaster interactive maps, videos, RSS feeds, flashcards, web links, self-study quizzes, and an eText version of *McKnight's Physical Geography: A Landscape Appreciation*.

WE NOW TURN OUR ATTENTION MORE DIRECTLY TO THE

study of the solid portion of Earth—an object of study that is a size well beyond our usual scale of living and thinking. Our endeavor is simplified, however, because as geographers we largely focus our attention on the surface. We need to know about Earth's interior primarily because it helps us to comprehend the nature and characteristics of the processes shaping Earth's surface features. In this chapter we introduce basic Earth systems operating within and on the surface of the lithosphere—especially the flow of energy and rock material within Earth, as well as the interaction of the atmosphere and hydrosphere with the lithosphere—that together shape Earth's surface topography.

We begin our task with a description of the structure of Earth as a whole. We then turn to a discussion of rocks—the solid material from which the planet is made. We conclude the chapter by introducing some fundamental concepts that we will use in our study of Earth's surface features.

As you study this chapter, think about these key questions:

- **What is the internal structure of Earth?**
- **What are the three classes of rocks, and how do they differ in their formation?**
- **What is the focus of the study of geomorphology?**
- **How do the concepts of *uniformitarianism* and *geologic time* help us understand how internal and external processes are shaping Earth's surface?**
- **Why is consideration of scale and process important in the study of geomorphology?**

THE STRUCTURE OF EARTH

Our knowledge of the interior of Earth is based largely on indirect evidence. No human activity has explored more than a minute fraction of the vastness beneath the surface. No one has penetrated as much as one-thousandth of the radial distance from the surface to the center of Earth; the deepest existing mine shaft extends a mere 3.8 kilometers (2.4 miles). Nor have probes extended much deeper; the deepest drill holes from which sample cores have been brought up have penetrated only a modest 12 kilometers (8 miles) into Earth. Earth scientists, in the colorful imagery of writer John McPhee, "are like dermatologists: they study, for the most part, the outermost two per cent of the earth. They crawl around like fleas on the world's tough hide, exploring every wrinkle and crease, and try to figure out what makes the animal move."[1]

Even so, a considerable body of inferential knowledge concerning Earth's interior has been amassed by geophysical means, primarily by monitoring patterns of vibrations transmitted through Earth from earthquakes or from humanmade explosions. Such seismic waves change their speed and direction whenever they cross a boundary from one type of material to another. Analysis of these changes, augmented by related data on Earth's magnetism and gravitational attraction, has enabled Earth scientists to develop a model of Earth's internal structure.

---

[1]John McPhee, *Assembling California* (New York: Farrar, Straus and Giroux, 1993), p. 36.

The Grand Canyon from Desert View Point, Grand Canyon National Park, Arizona. Describe the general topography and patterns of rocks in this area. What kind of climate appears to exist in this region? Why do you say that?

Earth's Hot Interior

In general, temperature and pressure increase with depth inside Earth, with the highest temperatures and pressures at the center. The source of this warmth is largely from the release of energy from the decay of radioactive elements (in much the same way as the decay of radioactive material supplies the warmth to power a nuclear power plant). As we will see, it is the transfer of heat from Earth's interior that drives many Earth processes such as plate tectonics and volcanism (discussed in Chapter 14).

Figure 13-1 shows the internal structure of Earth. It has been deduced that Earth has a dense inner core surrounded by three concentric layers of various compositions and density. Starting at the surface and moving inward, these four regions are called the *crust*, the *mantle*, the *outer core*, and the *inner core*.

The Crust

The **crust**, the outermost shell, consists of a broad mixture of rock types. Beneath the oceans the crust has an average thickness of only about 7 kilometers (4 miles), whereas beneath the continents the thickness averages more than five times as much, and in places exceeds 70 kilometers (40 miles). Oceanic crust is thinner but is comprised of denser ("heavier") rocks than continental crust. In general within the crust there is a gradual increase in density with depth. Altogether, the crust makes up less than 1 percent of Earth's volume and about 0.4 percent of Earth's mass.

At the base of the crust there is a significant change in mineral composition. This relatively narrow zone of change is called the **Mohorovičić discontinuity**, or simply the **Moho** for short, named for the Yugoslavian seismologist Andrija Mohorovičić (1857–1936) who discovered it.

The Mantle

Beneath the Moho is the **mantle**, which extends downward to a depth of approximately 2900 kilometers (1800 miles). In terms of volume, the mantle is by far the largest of the four layers. Although its depth is only about one-half the distance from the surface to the center of Earth,

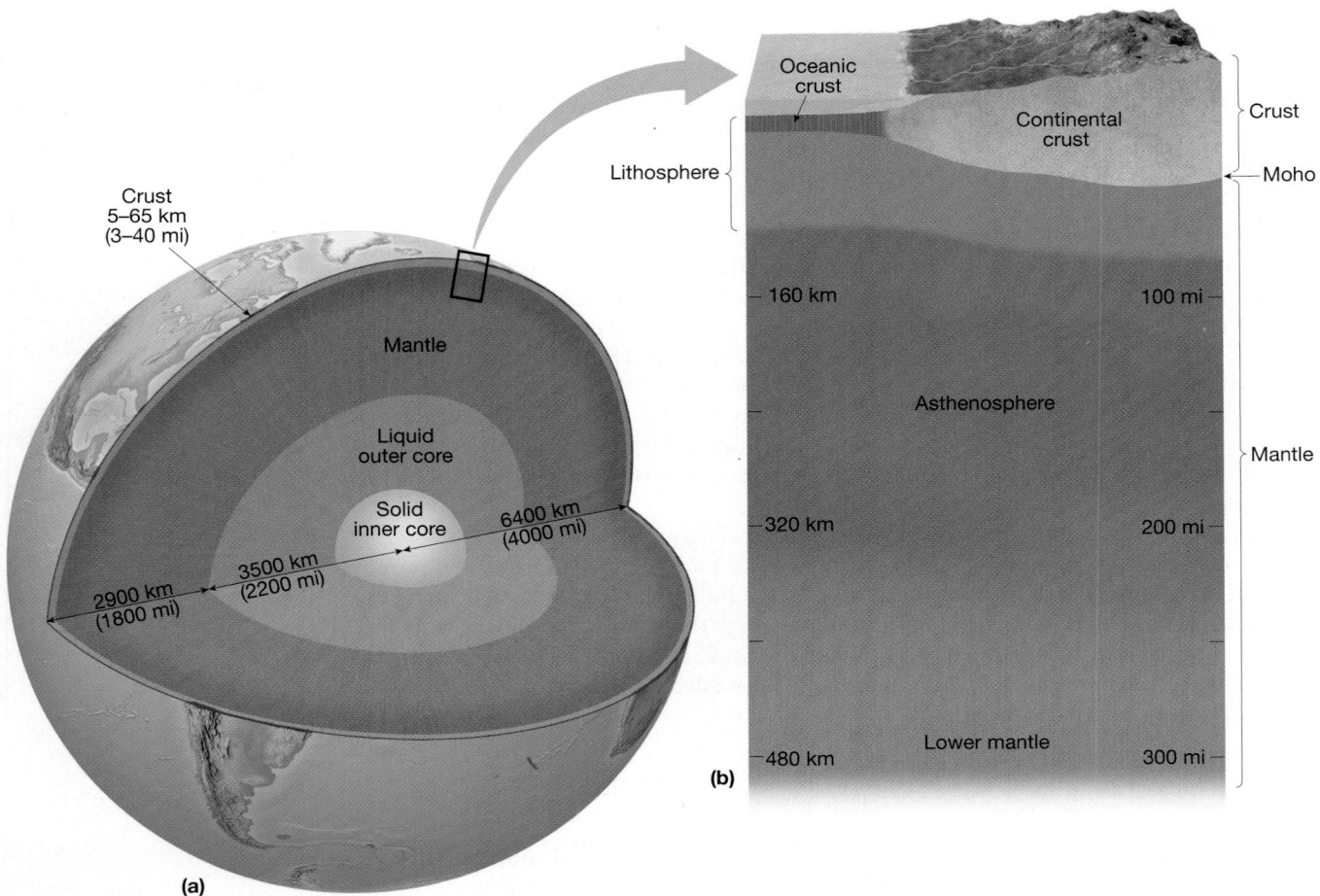

(a)

(b)

▲ **Figure 13-1** The vertical structure of Earth's interior. (a) Below the thin outer crust of Earth is the broad zone of the mantle, and below the mantle are the liquid outer core and the solid inner core. (b) Idealized cross section through Earth's crust and part of the mantle. The crust and uppermost mantle, both rigid zones, are together called the *lithosphere*—the "plates" of plate tectonics. In the asthenosphere, the mantle is hot and therefore weak and easily deformed. In the lower mantle, the rock is generally rigid again.

its location on the periphery of the sphere gives it a vast breadth. It makes up 84 percent of the total volume of Earth and about two-thirds of Earth's total mass.

There are three sublayers within the mantle, as Figure 13-1b shows. The uppermost zone is relatively thin but hard and rigid, extending down to a depth of 65 to 100 kilometers (40 to 60 miles)—somewhat deeper under the continents than under the ocean floors. This uppermost mantle zone together with the overlying oceanic or continental crust is called the **lithosphere**. For the remainder of this book as we study landforms, the term *lithosphere* has a more restricted meaning than earlier when we introduced the Earth "spheres." For our purposes now, "lithosphere" refers specifically to the combination of the crust and upper rigid mantle—and as we'll see shortly, it is large pieces of the lithosphere that are the "plates" of plate tectonics.

Beneath the rigid layer of the lithosphere, and extending downward to a depth of as much as 350 kilometers (200 miles), is a mantle zone in which the rocks are hot enough that they lose much of their strength and become "plastic"—they are easily deformed, somewhat like tar. This is called the **asthenosphere** ("weak sphere"). Below the asthenosphere is the *lower mantle*, where the rocks are very hot, but largely rigid again because of higher pressures.

The Inner and Outer Cores

Beneath the mantle is the **outer core** (Figure 13-1a), thought to be molten (liquid) and extending to a depth of about 5000 kilometers (3100 miles).

The innermost portion of Earth is the **inner core**, an evidently solid (because of extremely high pressure) and very dense mass having a radius of about 1450 kilometers (900 miles). Both the inner and outer cores are thought to be made of iron/nickel or iron/silicate. These two zones together make up about 15 percent of Earth's volume and 32 percent of its mass.

A common misconception is that the liquid outer core of Earth is the source of molten rock ("magma" and "lava") that is expelled by volcanoes, but this is not the case. Instead, the near-surface mantle is the source for magma, while Earth's cores are the source of energy that drives the slow movement of hot rock through the mantle toward the surface (through the process of *convection*). This rising hot rock in the mantle is under so much pressure that it remains essentially solid—only when this rising mantle material is very close to the surface is pressure low enough for it to melt.

Earth's Magnetic Field:
Earth's *magnetic field* is generated in the outer core: convective circulation within the conductive liquid iron and nickel outer core, spiraling in line with Earth's rotational axis, induces the magnetic field of our planet through what is sometimes called a *geodynamo*.[2] Interestingly, the strength and orientation of the

magnetic field changes over time, and the location of the north magnetic pole does not exactly match the true geographic North Pole. The position of the north magnetic pole slowly but continually drifts several tens of kilometers each year—it is currently located at about 86° N, 147° W—but the position of the north magnetic pole can even change significantly during a single day! In addition, for reasons that are not completely understood, at irregular intervals of thousands to millions of years, the polarity of Earth's magnetic field reverses, with the north magnetic pole becoming the south. As we will see in Chapter 14, a record of these magnetic polarity reversals has been recorded in the iron-rich rocks of the ocean floor.

> **Learning Check 13-1**   **Describe the characteristics of Earth's lithosphere and asthenosphere. (Answer on p. AK-4)**

Plate Tectonics and the Structure of Earth

The generalized model of Earth's interior shown in Figure 13-1 is a useful starting point for understanding physical geography. Geophysicists model the interior of Earth using computer methods, high-pressure lab experiments, data from the study of earthquakes, variations in gravity, heat flow maps, and other physical properties of Earth. Much is already known, however, many details of the processes taking place within the interior of Earth are still being worked out.

Our understanding of the interior of Earth was dramatically transformed in the 1960s when the notion of "continental drift," first propounded in the early 1900s but held in disdain by most scientists for the next half-century, was revived and expanded into the present-day theory of *plate tectonics*—a theory that is now accepted by virtually all Earth scientists.

Geological, paleontological, seismic, and magnetic evidence makes it clear that the lithosphere of Earth is broken into large, sometimes continent-sized slabs, commonly called "plates," that are floating on and slowly moving over the hot, soft asthenosphere below. These enormous plates are quite literally pulling apart, colliding, and sliding past each other—driven by the convective heat flow within Earth. Many internal processes, such as faulting, folding, and volcanic activity, are directly linked to the interactions taking place along the boundaries of these plates.

We will explore the dynamics of plate tectonics in much greater detail in Chapter 14. For the remainder of this chapter, however, we set the stage for that discussion by introducing some key concepts in the study of the surface features of Earth, such as rocks, geologic time, and the doctrine of uniformitarianism.

THE COMPOSITION OF EARTH

About 100 natural chemical elements are found in Earth's crust, mantle, and core, occasionally as discrete elements but usually bonded with one or more other elements to

---

[2]Most geophysicists think that for such a geodynamo to work, the presence of an initial weak magnetic field was needed, most likely coming from the Sun.

form compounds. A number of these compounds and elements form what are called *minerals*—the building blocks of *rocks*, which are in turn the building blocks of the landscape itself.

Minerals

For a substance to be considered a **mineral**, it must

- Be solid
- Be naturally found in nature
- Be inorganic
- Have a specific chemical composition that varies only within certain limits
- Contain atoms arranged in a regular pattern to form solid crystals

Only about one-fourth of the elements are involved in the formation of minerals to any significant extent, and just eight elements account for more than 98 percent of the mass of Earth's crust—oxygen and silicon alone make up more than three-quarters of the mass of the crust. Approximately 4400 minerals have been identified, with new types identified almost every year. The majority of known minerals are found in the crust; a more limited number of minerals are found within the mantle or have been identified in extraterrestrial rocks such as meteorites or those brought back from the Moon.

Of the more than 4000 recognized minerals, only a few dozen are of much importance as constituents of the rocks of Earth's crust. Some of the most common rock-forming minerals are listed in Table 13-1. Mineral nomenclature

TABLE 13-1   Some Common Rock-forming Minerals

Group	Mineral	Chemical Composition	Common Characteristics
Ferromagnesian ("dark") Silicate	Olivine	$(Mg, Fe)_2SiO_4$	Green to brown color; glassy luster; gem peridot
	Pyroxene group (Augite)	$(Mg, Fe)SiO_3$	Green to black color; commonly has two cleavage planes at 90°
	Amphibole group (Hornblende)	$Ca_2(Fe, Mg)_5Si_8O_{22}(OH)_2$	Black or dark green color; often appear as elongated rod-shaped crystals
	Biotite mica	$K(Mg, Fe)_3AlSi_3O_{10}(OH)_2$	Black or brown; often appear as hexagonal crystals in thin sheets
Nonferromagnesian ("light") Silicate	Muscovite mica	$KAl_2(AlSi_3O_{10})(OH)_2$	Colorless or brown; splits into thin, translucent sheets
	Potassium feldspar (Orthoclase)	$KAlSi_3O_8$	White to gray or pink color; good cleavage in two planes at 90°
	Plagioclase feldspar	$(Ca, Na)AlSi_3O_8$	White to gray color; striations often appear along cleavage planes
	Quartz	SiO_2	Commonly colorless; forms six-sided elongated crystals
Oxide	Hematite	Fe_2O_3	Red to silver-gray color; type of iron ore
	Magnetite	Fe_3O_4	Black with metallic luster; magnetic
	Corundum	Al_2O_3	Brown or blue color; gems sapphires and rubies
Sulfide	Galena	PbS	Black to silver metallic luster; lead ore
	Pyrite	FeS_2	Brassy or golden yellow color; often seen in well-formed cubes
	Chalcopyrite	$CuFeS_2$	Brassy or yellow metallic luster; copper ore
Sulfate	Gypsum	$CaSO_4 \cdot 2H_2O$	White or transparent; used in plaster and wallboard
Carbonate	Calcite	$CaCO_3$	White or colorless; cleavage in 3 planes forms rhombohedra; fizzes in dilute acid
	Dolomite	$CaMg(CO_3)_2$	White or transparent; cleaves into rhombohedra; powdered form fizzes in dilute acid
Halide	Halite	$NaCl$	Transparent or white; table salt
	Fluorite	CaF_2	Transparent purple, green or yellow color; fluorine ore
Native Elements	Gold	Au	Bright yellow color; highly malleable
	Silver	Ag	Brilliant white metallic luster when polished

◀ **Figure 13-2** Quartz crystal, a common silicate mineral.

▲ **Figure 13-3** Pyrite crystal, a common sulfide mineral.

is very unsystematic. Some names reflect the mineral's chemical composition or a physical property, some names are based on a person or a place, and some appear to have been simply chosen at random!

The rock-forming minerals can be grouped into seven principal categories or "families" based on their chemical properties and internal crystal structure.

Silicates: The largest and most important mineral family consists of the **silicates**. The bulk of the rocks of the crust are composed of silicate minerals, which combine the two most abundant chemical elements in the lithosphere: oxygen (O) and silicon (Si). Most silicates are hard and durable. The major subcategories of this group are *ferromagnesian silicates* (sometimes called the "dark" silicates) and *nonferromagnesian silicates* (sometimes called the "light" silicates), which are distinguished from one another by the presence or absence of iron and magnesium in their composition. Feldspars and quartz (Figure 13-2) are the most abundant of the silicate minerals. Quartz is composed of pure *silica* (SiO_2).

Oxides: An *oxide* is an element combined with oxygen. The most widespread of the oxides are those that combine with iron, particularly hematite, magnetite, and limonite, all three of which are major sources of iron ore as well as being common rock-forming minerals. (Although quartz has the chemical composition of an oxide, it is classified as a silicate because of its internal structure.)

Sulfides: *Sulfides* are composed of reduced sulfur in some combination with one or more other elements. Pyrite (Figure 13-3), for example, is a combination of iron and sulfur (FeS_2). Many of the most important ore minerals— such as galena (lead), sphalerite (zinc), and chalcopyrite (copper)—are sulfides. This group is common in many types of rock and may be massive or abundant in veins.

Sulfates: The *sulfate* group includes minerals such as gypsum that contain sulfur and oxygen in combination with some other element. Calcium is the principal combining element. The sulfate minerals are usually light-colored and are mostly found in sedimentary rocks.

Carbonates: *Carbonates* are also light-colored (or colorless) minerals that are common constituents of sedimentary rocks such as limestone (largely made from calcium carbonate [$CaCO_3$] in its mineral form of *calcite*). Carbonates in general are composed of one or more elements in combination with carbon and oxygen.

Halides: The *halide* group is the least widespread of any. The name is derived from a word meaning "salt." Halide minerals are notably salty—such as halite, or common table salt (NaCl).

Native Elements: A few minerals may occur as discrete elements (not combined chemically with another element) in nature. These are referred to as native elements. Included are such precious metals as gold and silver.

Learning Check **13-2** **Which family of minerals is most abundant in Earth's crust, and what is the common chemical starting point of these minerals?**

Rocks

Rocks are consolidated combinations of mineral material—sometimes just one kind of mineral, but usually several different minerals. Rocks occur in bewildering variety and complexity in the lithosphere, although fewer than 20 minerals account for more than 95 percent of the composition of all continental and oceanic crustal rocks.

Solid rock is sometimes found right at the surface, in which case it is called an **outcrop** (Figure 13-4). Over most of Earth's land area, though, solid rock exists as a buried layer of *bedrock* and covered by a layer of broken rock called *regolith*. Soil, when present, comprises the upper portion of the regolith (see Chapter 12).

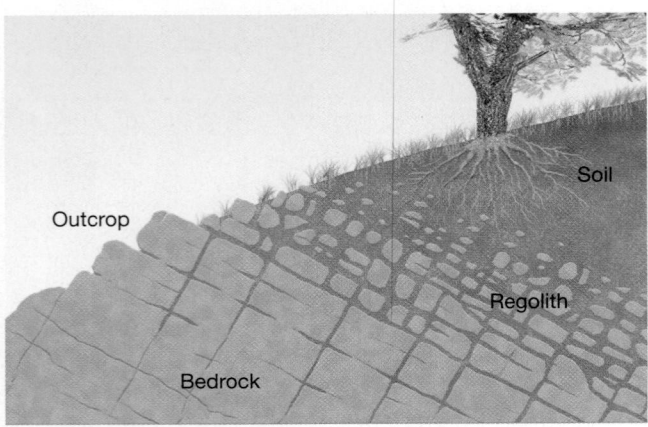

▲ **Figure 13-4** Bedrock is usually buried under a layer of soil and regolith but occasionally appears as an outcrop.

The enormous variety of rocks can be classified systematically. A detailed knowledge of *petrology* (the study of the origin and characteristics of rocks) is unnecessary for our purposes here, however, so we restrict coverage to a survey of the three major rock groups or classes—*igneous*, *sedimentary*, and *metamorphic*—and their basic attributes (Figure 13-5 and Table 13-2).

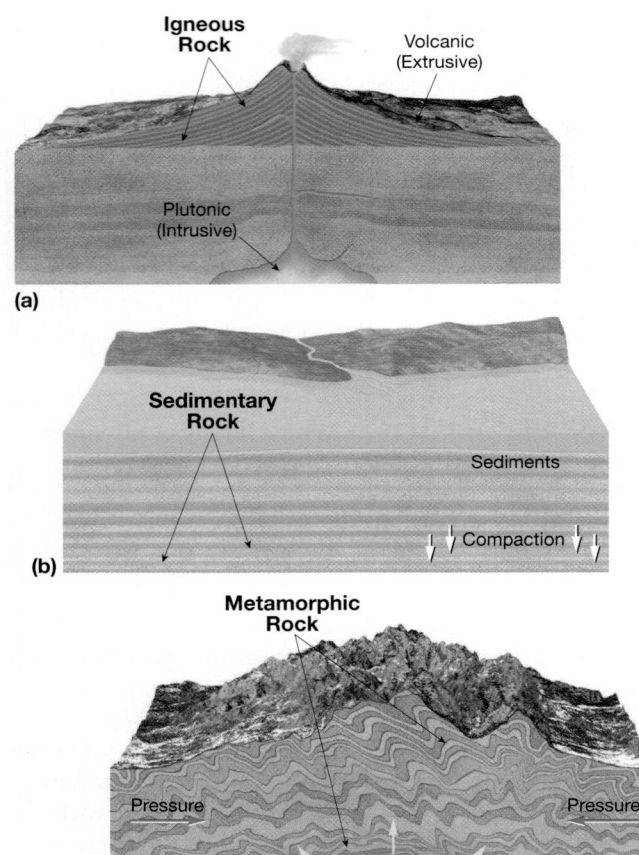

▲ **Figure 13-5** The three rock classes. (a) Igneous rocks are formed when magma or lava cools. (b) Sedimentary rocks result from consolidation of deposited particles. (c) Metamorphic rocks are produced when heat and/or pressure act on existing igneous and sedimentary rocks.

Igneous Rocks

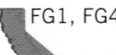 FG1, FG4

The word *igneous* is derived from the Latin, *igneus* ("fire"). **Igneous rocks** are formed by the cooling and solidification of molten rock (Figure 13-5a). **Magma** is a general term for molten rock beneath the surface of Earth, whereas the term **lava** refers to molten rock when it flows out on, or is squeezed up onto, the surface. Most igneous rocks form directly from the cooling of magma or lava; however, some igneous rocks develop from the "welding" of tiny pieces of solid volcanic rock, called **pyroclastics**, that have been explosively ejected out onto the surface by a volcanic eruption.

The classification of igneous rocks is based largely on mineral composition and texture. The mineral composition of an igneous rock is determined by the "chemistry" of the magma—in other words, by the particular combination of molten mineral material in the magma. As we will see in Chapter 14, one of the most important variables of magma composition is the relative amount of *silica* (SiO_2) present. Magmas with relatively large amounts of silica generally cool to form *felsic* igneous rocks that contain large portions of light-colored silicate minerals such as quartz and feldspar. The word *felsic* comes from *fel*dspar and *si*lica (quartz). Felsic minerals tend to have relatively lower densities and lower melting temperatures than *mafic* minerals. Magmas with relatively low amounts of silica generally cool to form mafic igneous rocks that contain large portions of dark-colored, magnesium- and iron-rich silicate minerals such as olivine and pyroxene. "Mafic" comes from *ma*gnesium and *f*errum (Latin for iron).

The texture of an igneous rock is determined primarily by where and how the molten material cools; for example, the slow cooling of magma beneath the surface leads to a coarse-grained texture, whereas the rapid cooling of lava on the surface leads to a fine-grained texture. Thus, one particular kind of magma can produce a number of quite different igneous rocks depending on whether the material cools below the surface, on the surface as a lava flow, or on the surface as an accumulation of pyroclastics.

Igneous rocks are generally subdivided into two main categories based on where the rocks form: **volcanic**, or **extrusive igneous rocks**, form from the cooling of lava or the bonding of pyroclastic materials on the surface, whereas **plutonic**, or **intrusive igneous rocks**, form from the cooling of magma below the surface. Some common plutonic and volcanic rocks are shown in Figure 13-6.

> **Learning Check 13-3**   **How are igneous rocks classified according to their composition and texture?**

Plutonic (Intrusive) Rocks: Plutonic rocks cool and solidify beneath Earth's surface, where surrounding rocks serve as insulation around the intrusion of magma that greatly slows the rate of cooling. Because the magma may require many thousands of years for complete cooling, the individual mineral crystals in a plutonic rock can grow to a relatively large size—large enough to see with the naked eye—giving the rock a very coarse-grained texture.

Class	Subclass	Rock	General Characteristics
Igneous	Plutonic (Intrusive)	Granite	Coarse-grained: "salt & pepper" appearance; from high-silica felsic magma; plutonic equivalent of rhyolite.
		Diorite	Coarse-grained; from intermediate silica magma; plutonic equivalent of andesite.
		Gabbro	Coarse-grained; black or dark gray color; from low-silica mafic magma; plutonic equivalent of basalt.
		Peridotite	Common mantle rock consisting primarily of olivine and/or pyroxene.
	Volcanic (Extrusive)	Rhyolite	Light color; from high-silica felsic magma; volcanic equivalent of granite.
		Andesite	Typically gray in color; from intermediate silica magma; volcanic equivalent of diorite.
		Basalt	Usually black in color; from low-silica mafic magma; volcanic equivalent of gabbro.
		Obsidian	Volcanic glass; typically black in color and rhyolitic in composition.
		Pumice	Volcanic glass with frothy texture; often rhyolitic in composition.
		Tuff	Rock made from volcanic ash or pyroclastic flow deposits.
Sedimentary	Detrital (Clastic)	Shale	Composed of very fine-grained sediments; typically thin bedded.
		Sandstone	Composed of sand-sized sediments.
		Conglomerate	Composed of rounded, pebble-sized sediments in a fine-textured matrix.
		Breccia	Composed of coarse-grained, angular, sediments; typically thin-bedded, poorly sorted fragments.
	Chemical & Organic	Limestone	Composed of calcite; may contain shells or shell fragments.
		Travertine	Limestone deposited in caves or around hot springs; often deposited in banded layers.
		Chert	Common chemical rock composed of microcrystalline quartz.
		Bituminous coal	Composed of compacted plant material.
Metamorphic	Foliated	Slate	Fine-grained; smooth surfaces; typically forms from the low-grade metamorphism of shale.
		Phyllite	Fine-grained; glossy, wavy surfaces.
		Schist	Thin, flaky layers of platy minerals.
		Gneiss	Coarse-grained; granular texture; distinct mineral layers; high-grade metamorphism.
	Nonfoliated	Quartzite	Composed primarily of quartz; often derived from sandstone.
		Marble	Composed principally of calcite; typically derived from limestone.
		Serpentinite	Greenish-black color; slippery feel; from hydrothermal alteration of peridotite.
		Anthracite	High-grade coal often derived from bituminous coal

Although originally buried, plutonic rocks may subsequently become important to topographic development by being pushed upward to the surface or by being exposed by erosion.

The most common and well-known plutonic rock is **granite**, a generally light-colored, coarse-grained igneous rock (Figure 13-7). Granite is made of a combination of light- and dark-colored minerals such as quartz, plagioclase feldspar, potassium feldspar, hornblende, and biotite (granite is a felsic igneous rock; see Figure 13-6).[3] Granite and similar plutonic rocks such as *granodiorite* make up the core of many mountain ranges, such as the Sierra Nevada in California, as well as the deep interior "shield" of many continents.

[3]Sometimes the term *granitic rock* is used broadly to refer to granite, as well as closely related plutonic rocks such as granodiorite and tonalite that have varying amounts of quartz and slightly different combinations of potassium feldspar and plagioclase feldspar from true granite.

Common Igneous Rocks

	Felsic	Intermediate	Mafic
Volcanic (fine-grained)	Rhyolite	Andesite	Basalt
Plutonic (coarse-grained)	Granite	Diorite	Gabbro
Composition	These rocks contain large portions of light-colored silicate minerals such as quartz and feldspar.	These rocks have a mineral composition between that of rhyolite/granite and basalt/gabbro.	These rocks contain large portions of dark-colored silicate minerals such as olivine and pyroxene.

◄ Higher silica content of magma   Lower silica content of magma ►

▲ **Figure 13-6** Common igneous rocks. The chemistry of the magma and the rate of cooling help determine the final igneous rock formed. Felsic magmas contain relatively high amounts of silica and cool to form a plutonic rock such as granite or the volcanic rock rhyolite. Mafic magmas contain relatively low amounts of silica and cool to form a plutonic rock such as gabbro or the volcanic rock basalt. Intermediate composition magmas cool to form a plutonic rock such as diorite or the volcanic rock andesite.

Volcanic (Extrusive) Rocks: Volcanic rocks form on the surface of Earth, either from the cooling of lava or from the accumulation of pyroclastic material such as volcanic ash and cinders. When lava cools rapidly on Earth's surface, the solidification may be complete within hours, and so the mineral crystals in many volcanic rocks are so small as to be invisible without a microscope. On the other hand, volcanic rocks that form from the accumulation of pyroclastics may clearly show tiny fragments of shattered rock that was explosively ejected from a volcano.

Of the many kinds of volcanic rocks, by far the most common is the black or dark gray, fine-grained rock called **basalt** (Figure 13-8). Basalt forms from the cooling of lava and is comprised only of dark-colored minerals such as plagioclase feldspar, pyroxene, and olivine (basalt is a mafic igneous rock; see Figure 13-6). Basalt is the most common volcanic rock in Hawai'i and is widespread in

parts of some continents—such as in the Columbia Plateau of the northwestern United States. Basalt also makes up the bulk of the ocean floor crust.

There are many other well-known volcanic rocks. *Obsidian*—typically black in color—is a type of volcanic "glass" (meaning it has no crystal structure) that forms from extremely rapid cooling of lava. *Pumice* forms from the rapid cooling of frothy, gas-rich molten material (a piece of pumice is sometimes light enough to float on water!). *Tuff* is a volcanic rock consisting of welded pyroclastic fragments (see Figure 13-13b).

In Chapter 14 we will discuss volcanism and some of the topographic features associated with plutonic and volcanic activity.

Learning Check 13-4 **In what ways are granite and basalt different?**

▲ **Figure 13-7** (a) Massive outcrops of granite at Sylvan Lake reservoir in the Black Hills of South Dakota. Granite is a plutonic (intrusive) igneous rock that solidified beneath Earth's surface and was subsequently exposed by erosion. (b) A sample of granite, showing glassy quartz grains and black biotite mica.

Sedimentary Rocks

FG2, FG12

External processes, mechanical and chemical, operating on rocks cause them to disintegrate (such rock "weathering" is discussed in Chapter 15). This disintegration produces fragmented mineral material—called **sediment**—some of which is removed by water, wind, ice, gravity, or a combination of these agents. Much of this material, along with ions of compounds in solution, is transported by water moving in rivers or streams, eventually to be deposited somewhere in a quiet body of water, particularly on the floor of an ocean (Figure 13-5b).

Over a long period of time, sedimentary deposits can build to a remarkable thickness—many thousands of meters. The sheer weight of this massive overburden exerts enormous pressure, which causes individual particles of sediment to adhere to each other and to interlock through compaction. In addition, chemical cementation

▼ **Figure 13-8** (a) Several horizontal layers of basalt are exposed on the wall of the Snake River Canyon south of Boise, Idaho. (b) A porous chunk of black basalt.

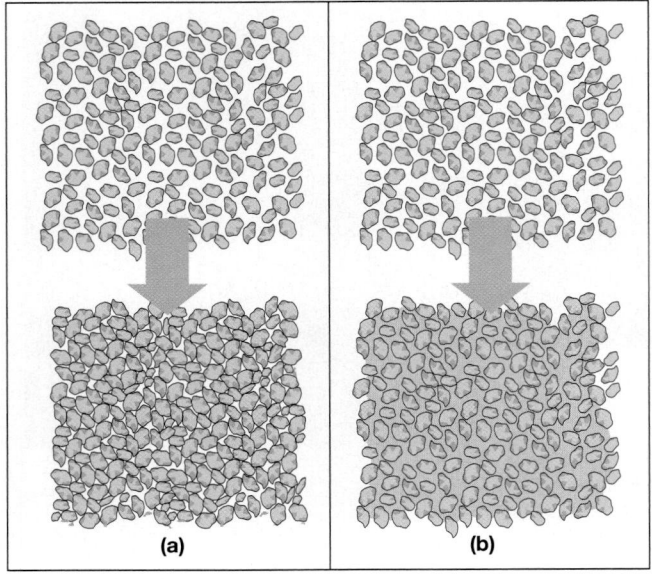

▲ **Figure 13-9** Sedimentary rocks are typically composed of small particles of sediment deposited by water or wind in layers and then consolidated by compaction and/or cementation. (a) Compaction consists of the packing of the particles as a result of the weight of overlying material. (b) Cementation involves infilling pore spaces among the particles by a cementing agent, such as silica, calcium carbonate, or iron oxide.

normally takes place. Various cementing agents—especially silica (SiO_2), calcium carbonate ($CaCO_3$), and iron oxide (Fe_2O_3)—precipitate from the water into the pore spaces between sediment grains (Figure 13-9). This combination of compaction and cementation consolidates and transforms the sediments to **sedimentary rock**.

In some cases, buried organic material—such the remains of plants or algae—accumulate along with inorganic sediments. This organic material may in time also become sedimentary rock.

As we will see in Chapter 16, during transportation and deposition, sediments may be sorted roughly by size and so many sedimentary rocks are comprised of particles of fairly uniform size. Other variations in the composition of the sediments may be due to factors such as different rates of deposition, changes in climatic conditions, patterns of sediment movement in the oceans, or the composition of the original source material. Most sedimentary deposits are built up in more or less distinct horizontal layers called **strata** (Figure 13-10), which vary in thickness and composition (wind-deposited sediments are a notable exception to the horizontal layers of most sedimentary rocks). The resulting parallel structure, or *stratification*, is a characteristic feature of most sedimentary rocks, with some sedimentary rocks exhibiting distinct **bedding planes**—flat surfaces separating one layer from the next. Although originally deposited and formed in horizontal orientation, the strata may later be uplifted, tilted, and deformed by pressures from within Earth (Figure 13-11).

Sedimentary rocks are generally classified into three subcategories based on how they were formed.

Detrital Sedimentary Rocks: Sedimentary rocks composed of fragments of preexisting rocks in the form of cobbles, gravel, sand, silt, or clay are known as *detrital* or *clastic* sedimentary rocks. By far the most common of these rocks are *shale* (or *mudstone*), which is composed of very fine silt and clay particles, and *sandstone*, which is made up of compacted, sand-size grains (Figure 13-12). When the rock is composed of rounded, pebble-size fragments it is called *conglomerate*.

▼ **Figure 13-10** (a) Nearly horizontal strata of limestone and shale in a road cut near Lyons, Colorado. (b) A sample of limestone containing an abundance of small fossil mollusks.

◀ **Figure 13-11** Sedimentary strata (mostly limestone and shale) that have been folded and tilted into an almost vertical orientation on Mount Angeles in the Olympic Mountains of Washington.

Chemical Sedimentary Rocks: Chemically accumulated sedimentary rocks are usually formed by the precipitation of solids from ions in solution, but sometimes by more complicated chemical reactions. Calcium carbonate ($CaCO_3$) is a common component of such rocks, and *limestone* is the most widespread result (see Figure 13-10). Limestone can also form from the accumulated skeletal remains of coral and other lime-secreting sea animals. *Chert* forms in a similar way to limestone but is composed of silica (SiO_2) instead of calcium carbonate. Rock salt is an example of an *evaporite*—rock that forms as water evaporates and leaves behind dissolved minerals such as common table salt (NaCl; see Figure 18-31).

Organic Sedimentary Rocks: Organically accumulated sedimentary rocks, including *lignite* (soft brown coal) and *bituminous coal* (soft, black coal), are formed from the compacted remains of dead plant material.

There is considerable overlap among these formation methods, with the result that, in addition to there being many different kinds of sedimentary rocks, there also are many gradations among them. Taken together, however,

(a)

(b)

▲ **Figure 13-12** (a) The structure of these abrupt sandstone cliffs (nearly flat bedding planes) in southeastern Utah is easy to see. (b) A typical light-colored piece of sandstone.

the vast majority of all sedimentary rocks are shale (45 percent of total), sandstone (32 percent), or limestone (22 percent).

Learning Check 13-5 Describe and explain the formation of *detrital*, *chemical*, and *organic sedimentary rocks*. Give one example of each.

Petroleum and Natural Gas: Although petroleum and natural gas are not rocks, their formation is associated with the accumulation of organic material in sedimentary deposits. The formation processes for petroleum and natural gas are complex, but involve the accrual of hydrocarbons derived from marine organisms, often in association with heat. See the box, "Energy for the 21st Century: Fracking for Natural Gas."

Metamorphic Rocks  FG4, FG12

Originally either igneous or sedimentary, **metamorphic rocks** are those that have been physically, and possibly chemically, altered by heat, pressure and/or chemically active fluids. Metamorphic rocks are associated with conditions in the lithosphere where the pressures and temperatures are greater than those that form sedimentary rocks, but less than those that melt rocks to form magma. The effects of heat and pressure on rocks are complex, being strongly influenced by such things as the amount and composition of fluids in the rocks, as well as

Video
Black Smokers

the length of time the rocks are heated and/or subjected to high pressure. Metamorphism can be an almost dry "baking" process that heats the rock, causing its mineral components to be recrystallized and rearranged (Figure 13-13), or it can be a more active, wet process, like the hydrothermal metamorphism happening at "black smokers" on the ocean floor (Figure 13-14). In any case, the metamorphic result is often quite different from the original rock—metamorphism can alter the original rock's composition, texture, and structure.

Causes of Metamorphism: Metamorphism can take place in a number of different environments. For example, metamorphism can occur beneath the surface of Earth where magma comes in contact with surrounding rocks, altering the surrounding rocks through heat and pressure—because of such **contact metamorphism** it is common to find exposed metamorphic rocks adjacent to plutonic rocks such as granite. **Regional metamorphism** takes place where large volumes of rock deep within the crust are subjected to heat and/or pressure over long periods of time, such as happens in areas of mountain building (see Figure 13-5c) or in *subduction zones* between lithospheric plates. **Hydrothermal metamorphism** occurs when hot, mineral-rich fluids circulate through cracks in rocks. As we will see in Chapter 14, these and other kinds of metamorphism are common along many of the boundaries between lithospheric plates.

In the case of some metamorphic rocks, it is possible to know what the original, unaltered rock was. In other

(a)

(b)

▲ **Figure 13-13** (a) This bedrock exposure in northeastern California, near Alturas, shows a light brown basalt overlying a colorful layer of tuff (a volcanic rock formed by consolidation of volcanic ash). The basalt was extruded onto the tuff in molten form, and its great heat "baked," or metamorphosed, the upper portion of the tuff. Visual evidence of the metamorphosis is seen in the difference in color between the metamorphosed and unmetamorphosed part of the tuff stratum. (b) A representative sample of tuff, which is formed by the consolidation of pyroclastic material.

ENERGY FOR THE 21ST CENTURY

Fracking for Natural Gas
▶ Karl Byrand, University of Wisconsin Colleges

Hydraulic fracturing, or "fracking," is a mining technique designed to remove trapped natural gas from rock and sand formations that lie deep underground. Natural gas that is found in such locations is known as *unconventional gas*. Conventional natural gas is gas that escapes freely from the ground when a wellbore is drilled. Natural gas is chiefly composed of methane and other hydrocarbons. It forms from the decay of organic material that was deposited along with the sediment that formed the rock.

A form of unconventional natural gas, known as *shale gas*, is found in large rock formations known as *plays*. These plays are mostly comprised of shale, a sedimentary rock made up of mud particles that have turned to stone. Shale has high density and poor permeability, allowing few avenues for trapped gas to escape naturally, so technology must be employed in order to free the gas. Aside from shale, natural gas can also be trapped in other rock formations, such as sandstone, as well as highly compacted sand formations at depth.

Fracturing Process:
The fracturing process involves several steps (Figure 13-A). In order to release the natural gas trapped in rock formations, a wellbore is drilled into the rock formation, and then a fluid is pumped under high pressure into the wellbore, fracturing the rock. This fracking fluid is a highly pressurized slurry of water, chemicals, and materials such as sand that aid in keeping the created fractures open. The fractures serve as pathways for the movement of the natural gas to the wellbore and subsequently to the wellhead. Here the gas is collected and then transported to other areas for use. As gas is released by this process, the pressure of the overlying rock causes the fracking fluid to return to the surface where it then has to be captured and contained.

Shale Gas Production:
The shale gas produced from fracking comes from 26 major plays located across the country (Figure 13-B). The most active plays include the Barnett, the Haynesville/Bossier, the Antrium, the Fayetteville, the Marcellus, and the New Albany. Some of these plays are quite extensive. For example, the Marcellus, at 95,000 mi², stretches from upstate New York through Pennsylvania, Ohio, and West Virginia.

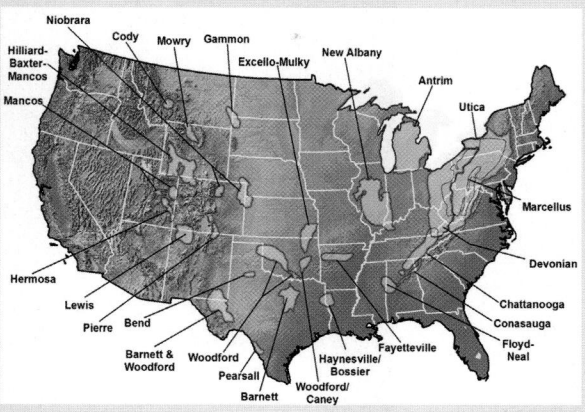

▲ **Figure 13-B** Major shale gas deposits in the conterminous United States.

Once, unconventional gas was too difficult to extract cost effectively. However, improvements in fracking technology have allowed significantly greater amounts to be extracted at lower cost. Within the past decade, this form of unconventional gas production has supplied the country with more of its natural gas needs. In 2007, 8.9 tf³ (trillion cubic feet) of shale gas was produced in the United States. Today, unconventional gas makes up 46 percent of the 21.6 tf³ of total U.S. natural gas production, making it a critical resource for the energy economy.

Environmental Concerns: Even given shale gas's contribution to our country's energy needs, fracking has several serious disadvantages. For example, the fracking fluid uses large volumes of water. This can reduce the local availability of water for other purposes, such as drinking. Likewise, if not properly contained, fracking fluid can leak and pollute areas adjacent to wellheads, and pollutants can migrate via water and air pathways. Because of the numerous chemicals involved in fracking (several hundred in some fracking fluid recipes), the water used cannot be safely reintroduced to the environment, but must be contained. As a means of disposal, sometimes it is injected back into an abandoned wellbore. Furthermore, the high-pressure injection of the fluid, whether during the initial fracking process or later for fracking fluid disposal, may cause small seismic events (earthquakes), referred to as *induced seismicity*. Finally, although wellbores are not large, initially accessing the well site, drilling the wellbore, and creating containment ponds all disturb the land surface. Such disturbances can cause habitat fragmentation, habitat destruction, and overall visual blight on the landscape.

▲ **Figure 13-A** The hydraulic fracturing process involves injecting a pressurized slurry of water, chemicals, and particles into shale beds.

▶ **Figure 13-14** A "black smoker" at the Broken Spur Vent Field at a depth of 3100 meters (10,000 feet) along the Mid-Atlantic Ridge. The release of hot volcanic fluids leads to hydrothermal metamorphism of the nearby rocks, as well as supports the existence of specialized forms of life.

cases, the metamorphosis is so great that it is difficult to know with certainty the nature of the original rock.

Foliated Metamorphic Rocks: If the minerals in a metamorphic rock show a prominent alignment or orientation, we say that the rock is *foliated*. Such rocks may have a platy, wavy, or banded texture. Ranging from the least ("low-grade") metamorphism to the most ("high-grade") metamorphism, some of the most common foliated metamorphic rocks include: fine-grained *slate* (when shale undergoes low-grade metamorphism); narrowly foliated/medium-grained *schist* (Figure 13-15); and broadly banded *gneiss* (Figure 13-16). Dynamic geologic environments, such as the margins of colliding plates, create the directed stresses necessary to produced foliated metamorphic rocks.

Nonfoliated Metamorphic Rocks: If the original rock was dominated by a single mineral (as in some sandstones

Animation
Metamorphic
Rock Foliation

(a)

(b)

▲ **Figure 13-15** (a) The presidents' heads at Mount Rushmore, South Dakota, are carved out of granite. Just below the granite is a much older metamorphic rock, a mica schist, into which the granite-forming magma was intruded. (b) A close-up of a sample of mica schist.

(a)

(b)

▲ **Figure 13-16** (a) An outcrop of banded gneiss in western Greenland. This particular formation is one of the oldest on Earth; its age is 3.8 billion years. (b) A typical piece of gneiss, showing contorted foliation.

or limestones), foliation is less common. When limestone undergoes metamorphism it usually becomes *marble*, whereas sandstone is frequently metamorphozed into *quartzite*. When the organic sedimentary rock bituminous coal undergoes metamorphism, it becomes high-grade *anthracite* coal.

Learning Check 13-6 **Define foliation, and explain under what conditions metamorphic rocks are likely to be foliated.**

The Rock Cycle

As the preceding description suggests, over long periods of time, the minerals in one rock might well end up in a different rock: igneous rocks can be broken down into sediments that might then form a sedimentary rock, which in turn might undergo metamorphism, only to be worn back again into sediments. This ongoing "recycling" of lithospheric material is sometimes referred to as the **rock cycle** (Figure 13-17). For example, as we just saw, the quartz in

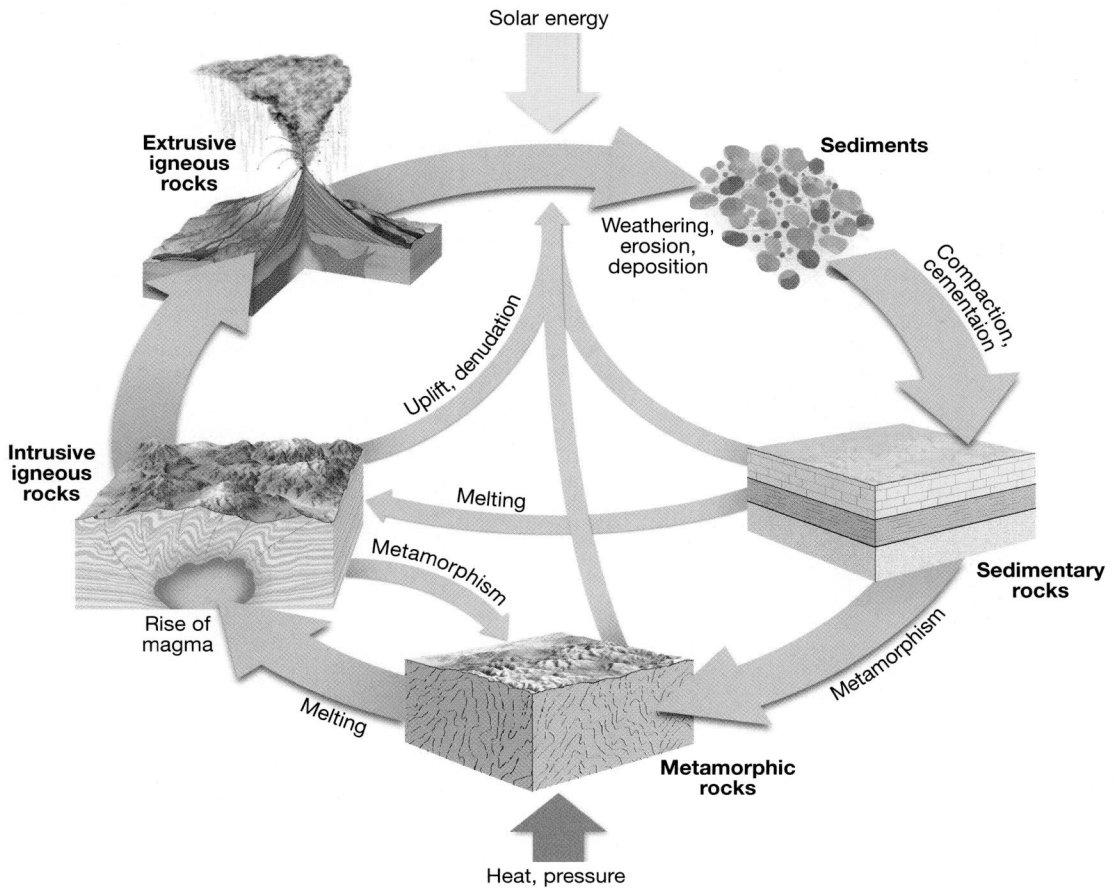

▲ **Figure 13-17** The rock cycle, showing some of the relationships among the three classes of rocks.

a piece of granite might over time be broken down into sediments; grains of quartz sand from the granite might then be formed into sandstone, that in turn might undergo metamorphism to become quartzite.

Continental and Ocean Floor Rocks

The distribution of the three principal rock classes on Earth's surface is uneven and may at first glance appear chaotic. However, this pattern is not random. The distribution of rocks in Earth's crust is a consequence of processes operating on the surface and in the planet's interior.

On the continents, sedimentary rocks compose the most commonly exposed bedrock (perhaps as much as 75 percent) (Figure 13-18). The sedimentary cover is not thick, however, averaging less than 2.5 kilometers (1.5 miles), and sedimentary rocks accordingly constitute only a very small proportion (perhaps 4 percent) of the total volume of the crust. The bulk of the continents consist of granite (along with an unknown proportion of metamorphic rocks such as gneiss and schist). On the other hand, the ocean floor crust is composed almost entirely of basalt and *gabbro* (the plutonic equivalent of basalt), covered by a relatively thin veneer of oceanic sediments.

The distinction between the dominant rocks of the ocean floors and continents is important. Basalt is a denser rock than granite (the density of basalt is about 3.0 g/cm^3, whereas that of granite is about 2.7 g/cm^3), and for this reason, continental lithosphere is less dense than oceanic lithosphere. Continental lithosphere "floats" quite easily on the denser asthenosphere below, whereas oceanic lithosphere is dense enough that it can actually be pushed down, or *subducted*, into the asthenosphere—the consequences of this are discussed at length in the following chapter.

Isostasy

Animation
Isostasy

Related to differences between oceanic crust, continental crust, and the mantle, is the principle of **isostasy**. In simplest terms, the lithosphere is "floating" on the denser, deformable, asthenosphere below. The addition of a significant amount of mass onto a portion of the lithosphere causes it to sink, whereas the removal of a large mass allows the lithosphere to rise.

Isostatic adjustment can have a variety of causes. The surface may be depressed, for example, by deposition of a large amount of sediment on a continental shelf, or by the accumulation of a great mass of glacial ice on a landmass, as illustrated in Figure 13-19, or even by the weight of water trapped behind a large dam. Depressed crust may rebound to a higher elevation as material is eroded away, as an ice sheet melts, or as a large body of water drains. Florida, for example, has experienced recent isostatic uplift because of the mass removed as groundwater dissolved the extensive limestone bedrock underlying the state. In central Canada around Hudson Bay, the region has uplifted more than 300 meters (almost 1000 feet) since the last of the Pleistocene ice sheets melted away 8000 years ago. More recently, parts of southern Alaska have been uplifting at the astonishing rate of as much as 36 mm (1.4 in.) a year—most likely at least in part as a response to the retreat of glaciers over the last century or so.

Learning Check 13-7 **Is oceanic lithosphere or continental lithosphere denser? Why?**

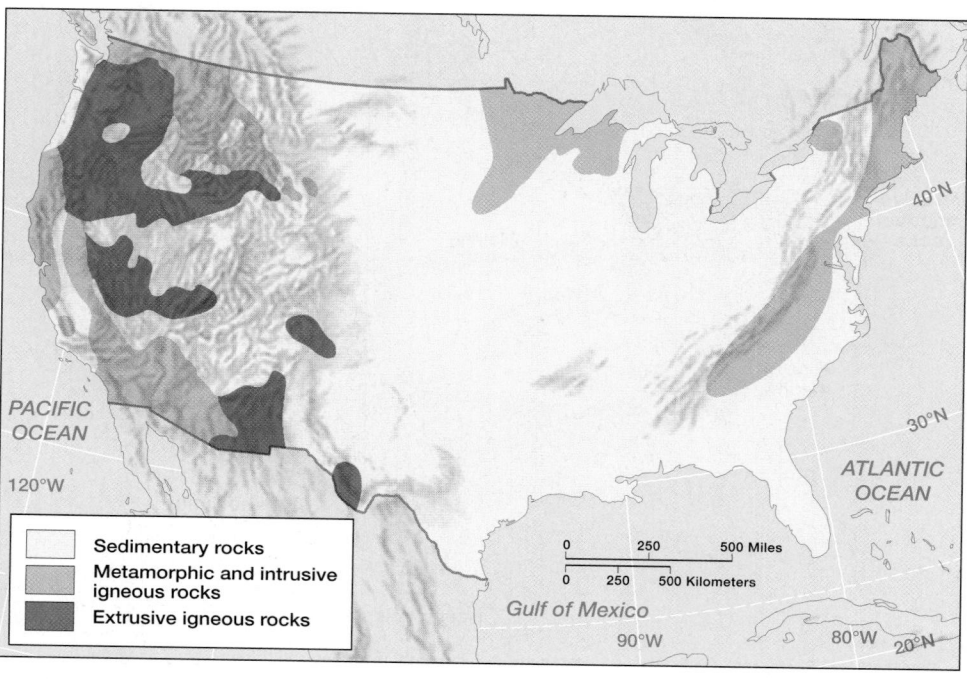

▶ **Figure 13-18** Distribution of rock classes exposed at the surface in the conterminous United States. Sedimentary rocks clearly dominate, as they do in most places around the world. Overall, about 75 percent of exposed continental rocks are sedimentary; however, sedimentary rocks make up only about 4 percent of the total volume of crustal rocks.

PACIFIC OCEAN

120°W

Sedimentary rocks
Metamorphic and intrusive igneous rocks
Extrusive igneous rocks

40°N

30°N

ATLANTIC OCEAN

0   250   500 Miles
0   250   500 Kilometers

Gulf of Mexico

90°W   80°W   20°N

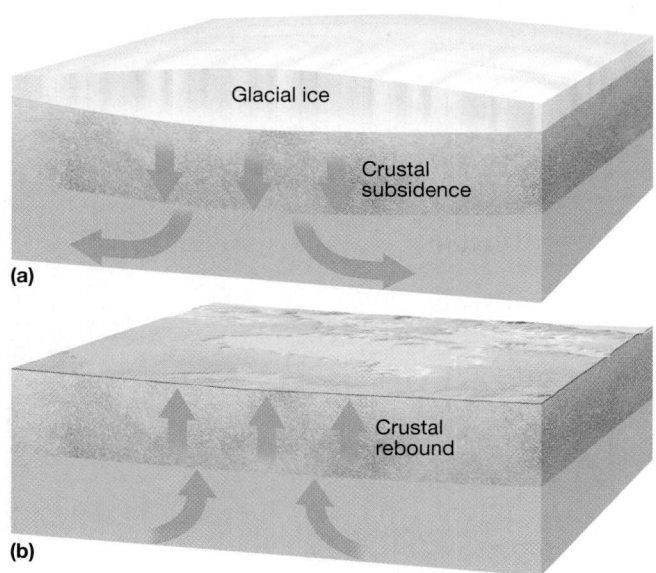

▲ Figure 13-19 Isostatic adjustment. (a) During a glacial period, the heavy weight of accumulated ice depresses the crust. (b) Deglaciation removes the weighty overburden, and as the ice melts, the crust rises or "rebounds."

THE STUDY OF LANDFORMS

Our attention for the remainder of this book is directed primarily to **topography**—the surface configuration of Earth. A **landform** is an individual topographic feature, of any size. Thus, the term could refer to something as minor as a cliff or a sand dune, as well as to something as major as a peninsula or a mountain range. The plural—landforms—is less restrictive and is generally considered synonymous with topography. Our focus on surface features is a field of study known as **geomorphology**—the study of the characteristics and development of landforms.

Although our focus as geographers is primarily Earth's surface, that surface is vast, complex, and often hidden from our direct view. Even without considering the 70 percent of our planet covered by the ocean, Earth includes more than 150 million square kilometers (58 million square miles) of land—the continents and islands of the world. This area encompasses the widest possible latitudinal range and the full diversity of environmental conditions. Moreover, much of the land surface is obscured from view by the presence of vegetation, soil, or the works of people. We must try to penetrate those obstructions, observe the characteristics of the lithospheric surface, and encompass the immensity and diversity of a worldwide landscape. This is far from a simple task.

To organize our thinking for such a complex endeavor, it may be helpful to isolate certain basic elements of the landscape for an analytic approach:

Structure: *Structure* refers to the nature, arrangement, and orientation of the materials making up the landform being studied. Structure is essentially the geologic underpinning of the landform. Is it composed of bedrock or not? If so, what kind of bedrock and in what configuration? If not made of bedrock, what are the nature and orientation of the sediments or other deposits? With a structure as clearly visible as that shown in Figures 13-11 and 13-12, these questions are easily answered, but such is not always the case, of course.

Process: *Process* considers the actions that have combined to produce the landform. A variety of processes—geologic, hydrologic, atmospheric, and biotic—may be at work shaping the features of the lithospheric surface, and their interaction is critical to the formation of the feature(s). For example, a landscape resulting primarily from the processes of *glaciation* is shown in Figure 13-20.

◄ Figure 13-20 The spectacular terrain of Montana's Glacier National Park was produced by a variety of interacting processes including glaciation. This view is across St. Mary Lake, past Citadel Mountain (the steep cliff on the left) toward Fusillade Mountain.

▶ **Figure 13-21** Slope is a conspicuous visual element of some landscapes. The abrupt cliffs of the volcanic backbone of the island of Bora-Bora (in French Polynesia) dominate this scene.

Slope: *Slope* is the fundamental aspect of shape for any landform. The angular relationship between a surface and the surrounding landscape is essentially a reflection of the contemporary balance among the various components of structure and process (Figure 13-21). The inclinations and lengths of the slopes provide details that are important both in describing and analyzing the feature.

Drainage: *Drainage* refers to the movement of water (from rainfall and snowmelt), either over Earth's surface or down into the soil and bedrock. Although moving water is an outstanding force under the "process" heading, the ramifications of slope wash, streamflow, stream patterns, and other aspects of drainage are so significant that the general topic of drainage is considered a basic element in landform analysis (a topic discussed in detail in Chapter 16).

Once these basic elements have been recognized and identified, the geographer is prepared to analyze the topography by answering the fundamental questions at the heart of any geographic inquiry:

- What?   The form of the feature or features
- Where?   The distribution and pattern of the landform assemblage
- Why?   An explanation of origin and development
- So what?   The significance of the topography in relationship to other elements of the environment and to human life and activities

Learning Check 13-8 **Explain what is meant by the "structure" of a landform.**

SOME CRITICAL CONCEPTS

One term used frequently in the following pages is **relief**, which refers to the difference in elevation between the highest and lowest points in an area. The term can be used at any scale. Thus, as we saw in Figure 1-10, the maximum world relief is approximately 20 kilometers (12 miles), which is the difference in elevation between the top of Mount Everest and the bottom of the Mariana Trench. At the other extreme, the local relief in some places like Florida can be a matter of merely a few meters.

Internal and External Geomorphic Processes

The relief we see in a landscape is temporary. It represents the momentary balance of two largely opposing sets of processes that are operating to shape and reshape the surface of Earth: *internal processes* and *external processes* (Figure 13-22). These processes are relatively few in number but extremely varied in nature and operation. The great variety of Earth's topography reflects the complexity of interactions between these processes and the underlying structure of the surface.

Internal Processes: The **internal processes** originate from within Earth, initiated by internal energy that generates forces that apparently operate outside of any surface or atmospheric influences. These processes result in crustal movements through folding, faulting, and volcanic activity of various kinds. In general, they are "constructive," uplifting, building processes that tend to increase the relief of the land surface. These processes are considered in detail in the chapter that follows.

External Processes: In contrast, the **external processes** are largely subaerial (meaning that they operate at the base of the atmosphere) and draw their energy mostly from sources above the lithosphere, either in the atmosphere or in the oceans. The external processes may be thought of generally as "wearing-down" or "destructive" processes—broadly called *denudation*—that eventually tend to diminish

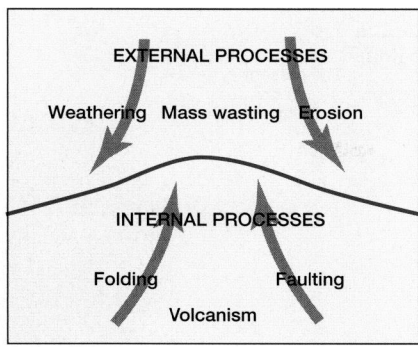

▲ **Figure 13-22** Schematic relationship between external and internal geomorphic processes. Earth's surface is uplifted by internal processes and worn away by external processes.

topographic irregularities and decrease the relief of Earth's surface.

Thus, internal and external processes work in more or less direct opposition to one another—in some landscapes, both operating at the same time; we see the momentary balance between them. Their battleground is Earth's surface, the interface between all of the Earth-system spheres—the lithosphere, hydrosphere, atmosphere, and biosphere—a place shaped by this ongoing struggle that has persisted for billions of years.

In succeeding chapters, we consider these various processes—their nature, dynamics, and effects—in detail, but it is useful here to summarize them so that they can be glimpsed in totality before we treat them one at a time. Table 13-3 presents such an overview. Note, however, that our classification scheme is a great simplification of reality; whereas some items are clearly separate and discrete, others overlap with each other. The table, then, represents a simple, logical way to begin a study of the processes, but is not necessarily the only or ultimate framework.

Learning Check 13-9 Contrast the internal and external processes shaping Earth's surface.

Uniformitarianism

Fundamental to an understanding of internal and external processes and topographic development is familiarity with the doctrine of **uniformitarianism**, which holds that "the present is the key to the past." This concept—first put forth by geologist James Hutton in 1795—means that the processes that are shaping the contemporary landscape are the same processes that formed the topography of the past—and are the same processes that will shape the topography of the future.

In the centuries before Hutton, most scientists accepted the doctrine of *catastrophism*—the idea that Earth's major features such as large canyons and mountain ranges had been produced by sudden upheavals and catastrophic events in the past. Uniformitarianism, instead, says that by understanding the geomorphic processes we see working today—and taking into account long periods of time—we can study a landscape and begin to comprehend the history of its development. The development of landforms is an ongoing process, with the topography at any given time simply representing one moment in a continuum of change.

It is important to understand that uniformitarianism doesn't say that all geomorphic processes have operated at the same rate or in the same balance throughout Earth's history—for example, there have been periods of time in the past when glaciation was more important than it is today. Further, it doesn't mean that landscape change always takes place through slow "grain-by-grain" wearing away of the rock. Change often comes rather episodically and abruptly—such as through an earthquake, a volcanic eruption, a flood, or a landslide.

Overall, however, because many of the internal and external processes operate very slowly by human standards, they may be difficult for us to grasp. For example, the enormous lithospheric plates that we will discuss in Chapter 14 are moving a few centimeters a year, on average, about as fast as your fingernails grow. To understand how sometimes imperceptibly slow processes work to alter the landscape, we must stretch our concept of time.

Geologic Time

Probably the most mind-boggling concept in physical geography is the length of geologic time (Figure 13-23). In our daily lives, we deal with such brief intervals of time as hours, months, years, and sometimes centuries, which does nothing to prepare us for the scale of Earth's history. The sweep of geologic time encompasses epochs of millions and hundreds of millions of years.

The concept of *geologic time* refers to the vast periods of time over which geologic processes operate. For

TABLE 13-3	A Summary of Geomorphic Processes

Internal

Lithospheric Rearrangement (plate tectonics)

Volcanism

    Extrusive

    Intrusive

Tectonism (Diastrophism)

    Folding

    Faulting

External (Denudation)

Weathering

Mass Wasting

Erosion/deposition

    Fluvial (running water)

    Aeolian (wind)

    Glacial (moving ice)

    Solution (ground water)

    Waves and currents (oceans/lakes)

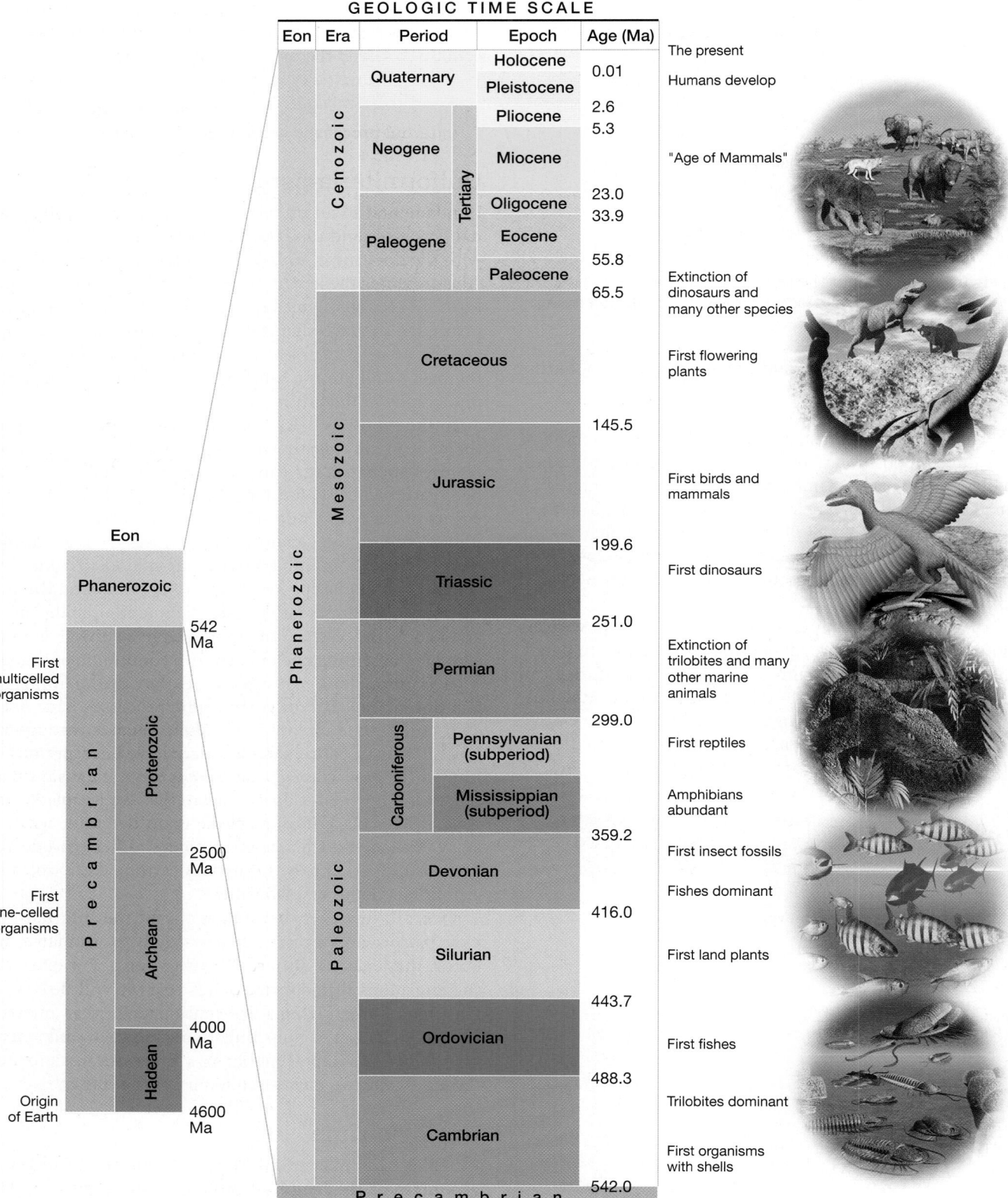

GEOLOGIC TIME SCALE

Eon	Era	Period	Epoch	Age (Ma)	
Phanerozoic	Cenozoic	Quaternary	Holocene	0.01	The present
			Pleistocene		Humans develop
				2.6	
		Neogene (Tertiary)	Pliocene	5.3	
			Miocene		"Age of Mammals"
				23.0	
		Paleogene (Tertiary)	Oligocene	33.9	
			Eocene		
				55.8	
			Paleocene		Extinction of dinosaurs and many other species
				65.5	
	Mesozoic	Cretaceous			First flowering plants
				145.5	
		Jurassic			First birds and mammals
				199.6	
		Triassic			First dinosaurs
				251.0	
	Paleozoic	Permian			Extinction of trilobites and many other marine animals
				299.0	
		Carboniferous	Pennsylvanian (subperiod)		First reptiles
			Mississippian (subperiod)		Amphibians abundant
				359.2	First insect fossils
		Devonian			Fishes dominant
				416.0	
		Silurian			First land plants
				443.7	
		Ordovician			First fishes
				488.3	
		Cambrian			Trilobites dominant
					First organisms with shells
Precambrian				542.0	

Eon

Phanerozoic

542 Ma — First multicelled organisms

Precambrian:
- Proterozoic
- 2500 Ma — First one-celled organisms
- Archean
- 4000 Ma
- Hadean
- 4600 Ma — Origin of Earth

▲ **Figure 13-23** The geologic time scale. The divisions of Earth's history were originally based on relative dating—the sequence of major changes and extinctions seen in the fossil record. The absolute dates, shown as millions of years ago (Ma) were established more recently but are subject to revision, as are some of the time divisions themselves: in 2009 the Neogene Period was designated to include the Miocene and Pliocene but no later epochs, although the older designation of the Tertiary Period is still in use; the designation of the Hadean Eon of the Precambrian has not been formalized.

uniformitarianism to work as a basic premise for interpreting Earth history, that history must have occurred over a span of time vast enough to allow feats of considerable magnitude to be accomplished by the internal and external processes operating at infinitesimally slow rates when measured on a human time scale.

Age of Earth: Scientists estimate that Earth is 4.6 billion years old—a length of time of almost unfathomable scope. It is difficult to grasp such an enormous sweep of geologic time in which the Age of Dinosaurs lasted some 160 million years, or one in which the Rocky Mountains were initially uplifted approximately 65 million years ago. An analogy may help us begin to comprehend the almost incomprehensible length of geologic time:

If we could envision the entire 4.6-billion-year history of Earth compressed into a single calendar year, each day would be equivalent to 12.6 million years, each hour to 525,000 years, each minute to 8750 years, and each second to 146 years. On such a time scale, the planet was lifeless for the first four months, with primal forms of one-celled life not appearing until early May. These primitive algae and bacteria had the world to themselves until early November, when the first multicelled organisms began to evolve. The first vertebrate animals, fishes, appeared about November 21; and before the end of the month, amphibians began establishing themselves as the first terrestrial vertebrates. Vascular plants, mostly tree ferns, club mosses, and horsetails, appeared about November 27, and reptiles began their era of dominance about December 7. Mammals arrived about December 14, with birds on the following day. Flowering plants would first bloom about December 21, and on Christmas Eve would appear both the first grasses and the first primates. The first hominids walked upright in midafternoon on New Year's Eve, and *Homo sapiens* appeared on the scene about an hour before midnight. The age of written history encompassed the last minute of the year—just the last 60 ticks of the clock!

This extraordinary time scale gives credence to the doctrine of uniformitarianism, allowing us to see the Grand Canyon as a "youthful" feature carved by that relatively small river seen deep in its inner gorge and envision how Africa and South America were once joined together and have drifted 3200 kilometers (2000 miles) apart. The geomorphic processes generally operate with slowness, but the vastness of geologic history provides a suitable time frame for their accomplishments.

Geologic Time Scale: The geologic time scale shown in Figure 13-23 is divided into units of time that reflect major events in Earth's history, especially changes in life on Earth. The largest units are called *eons:* the *Phanerozoic* (the time of "visible life") that began about 542 million years ago and the *Precambrian*—the Precambrian includes about 88 percent of Earth's history. The Phanerozoic Eon is divided into three major *eras*—the *Cenozoic* (Age of Recent Life), *Mesozoic* (Age of Middle Life), and *Paleozoic* (Age of Ancient Life). Each era is

divided into *periods*, which are in turn further subdivided into *epochs* (shown here for only the Cenozoic Era).

The absolute dates in the geologic time scale were established in the twentieth century, long after the original divisions were made by geologists back in the nineteenth century using relative dating methods—largely based on the sequence of major transitions (especially mass extinctions) they observed in the fossil record. The absolute dates are subject to periodic revision as new data become available. For example, in 2009 the *International Commission on Stratigraphy* recommended changing the boundary between the Pleistocene and Pliocene Epochs from 1.806 million years ago to 2.588 million years ago.

Because of the enormous impact humans have had on the planet in recent centuries, some scholars now propose that we call the current epoch of geologic time the *Anthropocene*, although this designation has yet to be widely accepted.

> **Learning Check 13-10** **Explain the importance of *geologic time* to the doctrine of *uniformitarianism*.**

SCALE AND PATTERN

Before we proceed with our systematic study of geomorphic processes, several final concepts should be kept in mind—scale and pattern.

An Example of Scale

The question of scale is fundamental in geography. Regardless of the subject of geographic inquiry, recognizable features and associations are likely to vary considerably depending on the scale of observation. This simply means that the aspects of the landscape one observes in a close-up view are different from those observed from a more distant view.

As an example of the complexity and significance of scale, let us focus our attention on a particular place on Earth's surface and view it from different perspectives. The location is north-central Colorado within the boundaries of Rocky Mountain National Park, some 13 kilometers (8 miles) due west of the town of Estes Park. It encompasses a small valley called Horseshoe Park, through which flows a clear mountain stream named Fall River and adjacent to which is the steep slope of Bighorn Mountain (Figure 13-24).

1. To illustrate the largest or closest scale of ordinary human experience, we will hike northward from the center of Horseshoe Park up the side of Bighorn Mountain. At this level of observation we can observe such effects as streamflow and local erosion. The first topographic feature of note is a smooth stretch of Fall River we must cross. We walk over a small sandbar at the south edge of the river, wade for a few steps in the river, and step up a half-meter (20-inch) bank

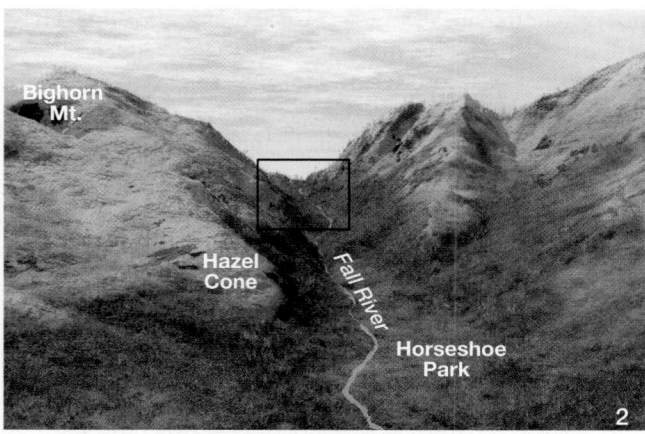

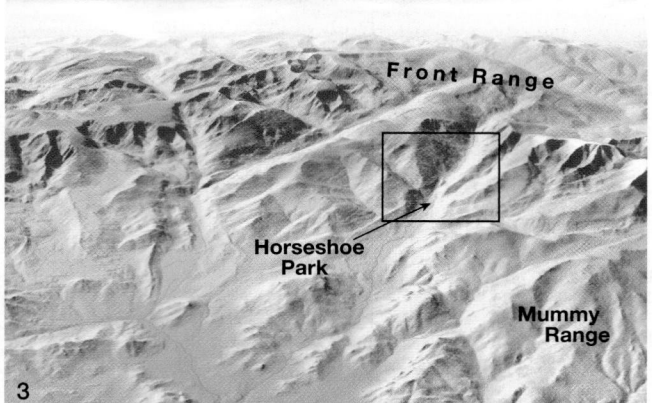

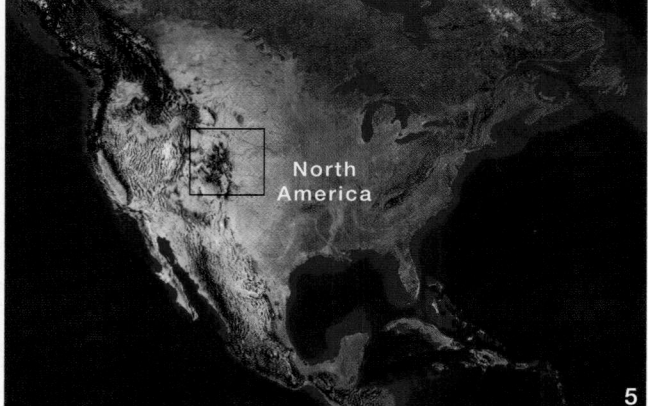

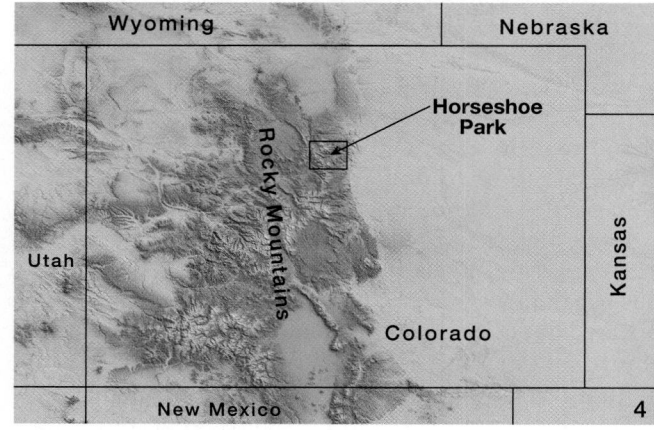

◄ **Figure 13-24** An experience with change of scale: (1) A close view of Horseshoe Park, Colorado, from the west. (2) Looking down on Horseshoe Park from Trail Ridge Road. (3) An aerial view of the Mummy Range and part of the Front Range. (4) A high-altitude look at Colorado. (5) North America as it might be seen from a distant spacecraft.

onto the mountainside, noting the dry bed of a small intermittent pond on our left. After 20 minutes or so of steep uphill scrambling, we reach a rugged granite outcrop (locally called Hazel Cone), which presents us with an almost vertical cliff face to climb.

2. For a significantly different scale of observation, we might travel by car in this same area. The road through Horseshoe Park is part of U.S. Highway 34, which is called the Trail Ridge Road. After 20 minutes, we reach a magnificent viewpoint high on the mountain to the

southwest of Horseshoe Park. From this vantage point, our view of the country through which we have hiked is significantly widened—here we may observe the relationships between rock type, vegetation, and slope. We can no longer recognize the sandbar, the bank, or the dry pond, and even the rugged cliff of Hazel Cone appears as little more than a pimple on the vast slope of Bighorn Mountain. Instead, we see that Fall River is a broadly meandering stream in a flat valley and that Bighorn Mountain is an impressive peak rising high above.

3. Our third observation of this area might take place from an airplane flying at 12 kilometers (39,000 feet) on a run between Omaha and Salt Lake City. From this elevation, Fall River is nearly invisible, and only careful observation reveals Horseshoe Park. Bighorn Mountain is now merged indistinguishably as part of the Mummy Range, which is seen as a minor offshoot of a much larger and more impressive mountain system called the Front Range—here we may be able to discern broader stream patterns and begin to see the connection of Bighorn Mountain to the rest of the local mountain range.

4. A fourth level of observation would be available to us if we could hitch a ride in the International Space Station, orbiting 390 kilometers (240 miles) above Earth. Our brief glimpse of northern Colorado would probably be inadequate to distinguish the Mummy Range, and even the 400-kilometer (250-mile) long Front Range would appear only as a component of the mighty Rocky Mountain cordillera, which extends from New Mexico to northern Canada—from this vantage point we may begin to recognize the relationship of the Front Range to the regional tectonic context of the Rocky Mountains as a whole.

5. At the smallest scale, the final viewpoint possible to humans could come from a spacecraft rocketing away from Earth toward the Moon. Looking back in the direction of Horseshoe Park, one might possibly recognize the Rocky Mountains, but the only conspicuous feature in this small-scale view would be the North American continent—from here, we may be able to place the present-day Rocky Mountains in the context of the sequence of events that "assembled" North America over billions of years.

Learning Check 13-11 **Which level of scale in Figure 13-24 is most suitable for studying an individual landform? The structure of a continent?**

Pattern and Process in Geomorphology

The prime goals of any geographic study are to recognize the distribution pattern of some phenomenon, and to understand the processes that produced that pattern. In previous portions of this book, we saw that there is broad geographic predictability to many patterns of weather, climate, ecosystems, biomes, and soils based on latitude or location on a continent. We now enter into a part of physical geography in which such orderly patterns of distribution are more difficult to discern, as the landform distribution pattern in Figure 13-25 so readily shows.

There are a few aspects of predictability; for example, one can anticipate that in desert areas, certain geomorphic processes are more conspicuous than others and certain landform features are likely to be found (Figure 13-26). Overall, however, the global distribution of topography appears somewhat irregular. Largely for this reason, the geomorphology portion of this book concentrates less on distribution and more on process. Comprehending the processes associated with topographic development are more important to an understanding of systematic physical geography than any amount of detailed study of landform distribution. We begin this study of landform-shaping processes in the chapter that follows.

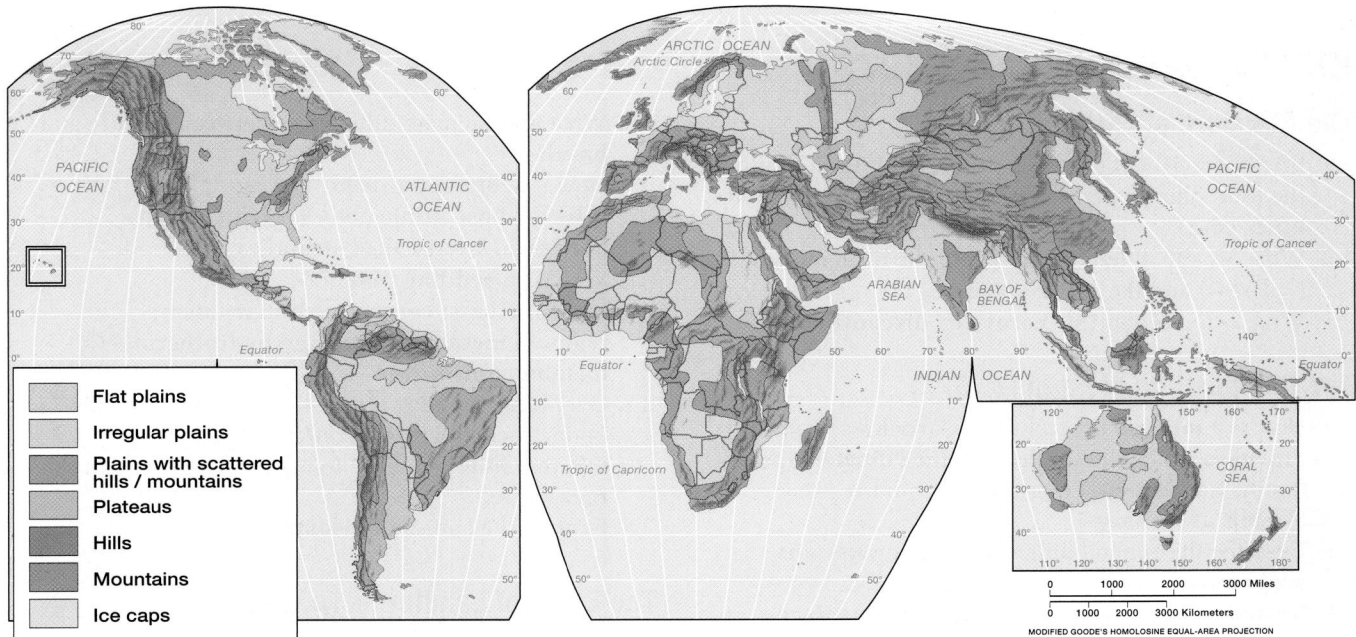

▲ **Figure 13-25** Major landform assemblages of the world.

▶ **Figure 13-26** The development of landforms in the basin-and-range region of North America, as here in the Mojave Desert of southeastern California, is being influenced by a distinct set of desert processes and conditions.

Chapter 13   LEARNING REVIEW

After studying this chapter, you should be able to answer the following questions. Key terms from each text section are shown in **bold type**. Definitions for key terms are also found in the glossary at the back of the book.

KEY TERMS AND CONCEPTS

The Structure of Earth (*p. 375*)

1. Briefly describe the overall structure of Earth, noting the four main layers: **crust**, **mantle**, **outer core**, and **inner core**.
2. What are the differences between the **lithosphere** ("plates") and the **asthenosphere**?
3. What is the **Moho (Mohorovičic' discontinuity)**?

The Composition of Earth (*p. 377*)

4. How is a **mineral** different from a **rock**?
5. Provide a general description of the **silicate** mineral family. Name at least one common silicate mineral.
6. What is an **outcrop**?
7. Describe the general differences among **igneous**, **sedimentary**, and **metamorphic** rocks.
8. Briefly define the following terms: **magma**, **lava**, **pyroclastics**.
9. What is the difference between a **plutonic (intrusive) igneous rock** and a **volcanic (extrusive) igneous rock**?

10. What are the main differences between **granite** and **basalt**?
11. How is **sediment** formed?
12. Why do most sedimentary rocks form in flat, horizontal layers called **strata**?
13. What is a **bedding plane**?
14. Briefly contrast **contact metamorphism, regional metamorphism** and **hydrothermal metamorphism.**
15. Over long periods of time, how can the minerals in one rock end up in a different rock (or in a different kind of rock)? In other words, explain the **rock cycle**.
16. Explain the concept of **isostasy**.

The Study of Landforms (*p. 391*)

17. Briefly define the terms **topography**, **landform**, and **geomorphology**.
18. What is meant by the *structure* of a landform?

Some Critical Concepts (*p. 392*)

19. In the context of geomorphology, what is meant by the term **relief**?
20. Contrast the concepts of **internal processes** and **external processes** in geomorphology.
21. How does the doctrine of **uniformitarianism** help us understand the history of Earth?

22. What is generally meant by the term *geologic time*?

Scale and Pattern (*p. 395*)

23. In the study of geomorphology, why do we primarily concentrate on processes rather than on distribution patterns by latitude?

STUDY QUESTIONS

1. How can one kind of magma (one kind of magma chemistry) produce two or more different kinds of igneous rock?
2. Why are metamorphic rocks often found in contact with plutonic rocks such as granite?
3. Contrast the composition and characteristics of oceanic lithosphere with that of continental lithosphere.

4. Why are sedimentary rocks so common on the surface of the continents?
5. Describe the general structure, slope, drainage, and processes involved in the development of the landscape in Figure 13-20.
6. What is the importance of geologic time to the doctrine of uniformitarianism?

EXERCISES

1. If sediments are deposited in a body of water at a rate of 2 centimeters every 1000 years, how long does it take to accumulate a layer of sediment 10 meters thick? _____ years
2. Using Figure 13-23 for reference, calculate the percentage of Earth's 4.6 billion year history:

a. Fishes have been present (since the beginning of the Ordovician Period): _____ %
b. Dinosaurs were present (throughout the Mesozoic Era): _____ %
c. Humans have been present (since the beginning of the Pleistocene Epoch): _____ %

Seeing Geographically

Look again at the photograph of the Grand Canyon at the beginning of the chapter (p. 374). How would you describe the structure of the rocks that make up the canyon walls? What general class of rocks most likely makes up the bulk of the rocks you see here? Why do you say this? Why might both internal and external processes be responsible for this landscape?

MasteringGeography™

Looking for additional review and test prep materials? Visit the Study Area in MasteringGeography™ to enhance your geographic literacy, spatial reasoning skills, and understanding of this chapter's content by accessing a variety of resources, including geoscience animations, MapMaster interactive maps, videos, RSS feeds, flashcards, web links, self-study quizzes, and an eText version of *McKnight's Physical Geography: A Landscape Appreciation.*

THE GEOMORPHIC PROCESSES ORIGINATING FROM WITHIN

Earth are our starting points for understanding processes shaping the planet's surface features. We begin our study of these internal processes with the theory of plate tectonics and finish by looking more specifically at volcanism, folding, and faulting.

It is in this chapter that we fully develop our discussion of the key Earth system operating within the planet: the processes and consequences of heat flow from the hot interior toward the cooler surface. As we'll see, it is the slow movement of hot—but largely solid—rock through the mantle that drives plate tectonics and is responsible for nearly all other internal processes of volcanism, folding, and faulting. The internal processes we describe and explain here are largely responsible for increasing the relief of the surface of Earth; we will leave it to the chapters that follow to explain how this relief can be worn down.

As you study this chapter, think about these key questions:

- **What was Wegener's *continental drift* hypothesis and why was it rejected by most scientists at the time?**

- **What evidence helps verify the theory of plate tectonics and that the configuration of continents and ocean basins was different in the geologic past?**

- **What are the general features and processes taking place at divergent, convergent, and transform plate boundaries?**

- **How do *hot spots* and *terranes* fit in with the theory of plate tectonics?**

- **How do differences in magma chemistry influence the eruption style, shape, and structure of different kinds of volcanoes?**

- **What are the differences between a *pyroclastic flow* and a *volcanic mudflow*?**

- **What are the differences and similarities of a *batholith* and a *dike*?**

- **What are *synclines* and *anticlines*, and how can they form?**

- **In what ways are normal faults, reverse faults, and strike-slip faults different from each other, and what kind of landforms can develop from each?**

- **How does the nature of the bedrock influence the severity of ground shaking during an earthquake?**

- **How can tectonism help explain how older rocks can end up on top of much younger rocks, as we see in places such as the northern Rocky Mountains?**

The Impact of Internal Processes on the Landscape

In our endeavor to understand the development of Earth's landscape, no pursuit is more rewarding than a consideration of the internal processes, for they are the supreme builders of terrain. Energized by forces within Earth, the internal processes actively reshape the crustal surface. The crust is buckled and bent, land is raised and lowered, rocks are fractured and folded, solid material is melted, and molten material is solidified. These actions have been going on for billions of years and are fundamentally responsible for the gross shape of the lithospheric landscape at any given time. The internal processes do not always act independently and separately from each other, but in this chapter we isolate them in order to simplify our analysis.

Mount Bromo (foreground) and Mount Semeru (in the distance) on the island of Java, Indonesia. Based on this photograph, what can you infer about how the island of Java formed? Does it appear that the low peak in the foreground is composed of resistant rock? Why do you say this? What was the wind direction on the day this photograph was taken? (*Hint*: the photo was taken in early morning). Is that what you would expect based on its latitude (8° S)? Why?

FROM RIGID EARTH TO PLATE TECTONICS

The shapes and positions of the continents may seem fixed at the time scale of human experience, but at the geologic time scale, measured in millions or tens of millions of years, continents are quite mobile. Continents have moved, collided and merged, and then been torn apart again; ocean basins have formed, widened, only to be eventually closed off. These changes on the surface of Earth continue today, so that the contemporary configuration of the ocean basins and continents is by no means the ultimate one. It is only in the last half century, however, that Earth scientists have come to understand how all of this could actually happen.

Until the mid-twentieth century, most Earth scientists assumed that the planet's crust was static, with continents and ocean basins fixed in position and significantly modified only by changes in sea level and periods of mountain building. The uneven shapes and irregular distribution of the continents were puzzling, but it was generally accepted that the present arrangement was emplaced in some ancient age when Earth's crust cooled from its original molten state.

Although not widely accepted, the idea that the continents had changed position over time, or that a single "supercontinent" once existed before separating into large fragments, has been around for a long time. Various naturalists, physicists, astronomers, geologists, botanists, and geographers from a number of countries have been putting forth this idea since the days of geographer Abraham Ortelius in the 1590s and philosopher Francis Bacon in 1620. Until fairly recently, however, the idea was generally unacceptable to the scientific community at large.

Wegener's Continental Drift

During the second and third decades of the twentieth century, the notion of **continental drift** was revived, most notably by the German meteorologist and geophysicist Alfred Wegener. Wegener put together the first comprehensive theory to describe and partially explain the phenomenon, publishing his landmark book *Die Entstehung der Kontinente und Ozeane* (*The Origin of Continents and Oceans*) in 1915. Wegener postulated a massive supercontinent, which he called **Pangaea** (Greek for "whole land"), as existing about 225 million years ago and then breaking apart into several large sections—the present-day continents—that have continued to move away from one another to this day (Figure 14-1).

Wegener's Evidence for Continental Drift: Wegener accumulated a great deal of evidence to support his hypothesis, most notably the remarkable number of close affinities of geologic features on both sides of the Atlantic Ocean. He found the continental margins of the subequatorial portions of Africa and South America fit together with jigsaw-puzzle-like precision (Figure 14-2). He also determined that the petrologic (rock) records on both sides of the Atlantic show many distributions—such as ancient coal deposits—that would be continuous if the ocean did not intervene. Moreover, when the continents are placed back in their Pangaean configuration, mountain belts in Scandinavia and the British Isles match up with the Appalachian Mountains in eastern North America (Figure 14-3).

Supporting evidence came from paleontology: the fossils of some dinosaur and other reptile species, such as the freshwater swimming reptile the *Mesosaurus*, are found on both sides of the southern Atlantic Ocean, but nowhere else in the world (Figure 14-4). Fossilized

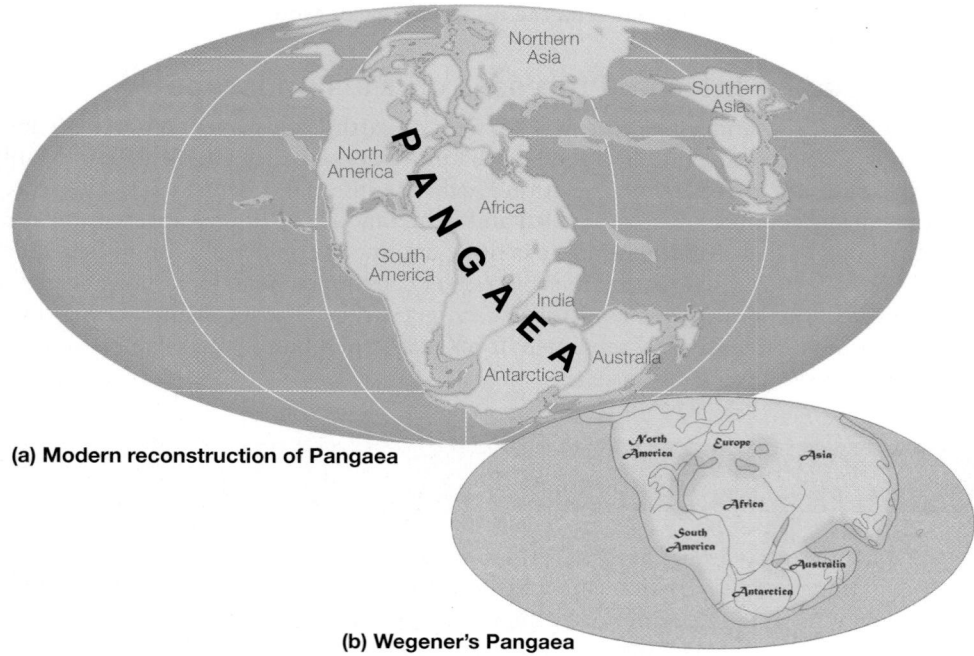

(a) Modern reconstruction of Pangaea

(b) Wegener's Pangaea

▶ **Figure 14-1** The supercontinent Pangaea. (a) Contemporary reconstruction of Pangaea as it probably appeared about 200 million years ago. (b) Wegener's reconstruction from 1915.

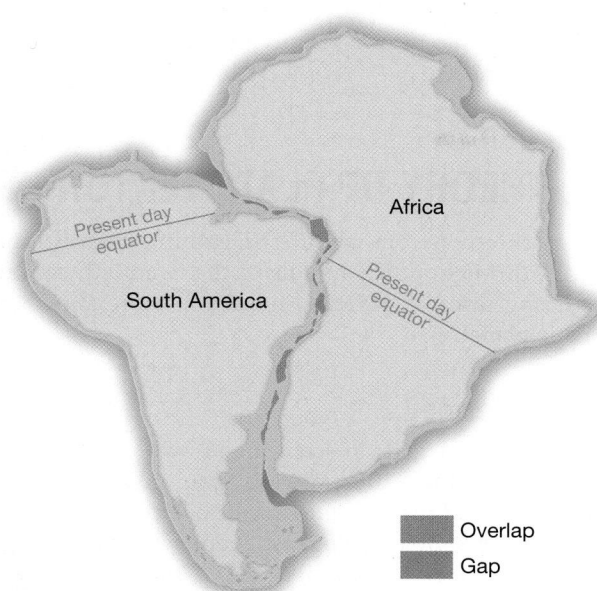

▲ **Figure 14-2** Matching the coastlines of Africa and South America. When the continental shapes are compared at a depth of about 900 meters (500 fathoms) along the continental slope, there are few large gaps or overlaps.

plants, such as the fernlike *Glossopteris*, are found in similar-aged rocks in South America, South Africa, Australia, India, and Antarctica—its seeds too large and heavy to have been carried across the expanse of the present-day oceans by wind.

Wegener worked with climatologist Wladimir Köppen to study the past climate patterns of Earth. For example, they studied glacial deposits that indicated that large portions of the southern continents and India were extensively glaciated about 300 million years ago. The pattern of deposits made sense if the continents had

been together in Pangaea when this glaciation took place (Figure 14-5).

Learning Check 14-1 **How did the shape of continental coastlines and evidence of past glaciation support Wegener's idea of continental drift? (Answer on p. AK-4)**

Rejection of Continental Drift: Wegener's accumulated evidence could be most logically explained by continental drift. His ideas attracted much attention in the 1920s—and generated much controversy. Some Southern Hemisphere geologists, particularly in South Africa, responded with enthusiasm. The general response to Wegener's hypothesis, however, was disbelief. Despite the vast amount of evidence

▲ **Figure 14-4** *Mesosaurus* fossils have been found in southeastern South America and southwestern Africa. These animals were alive at the time that present-day South America and Africa were together as part of a larger landmass in the geologic past.

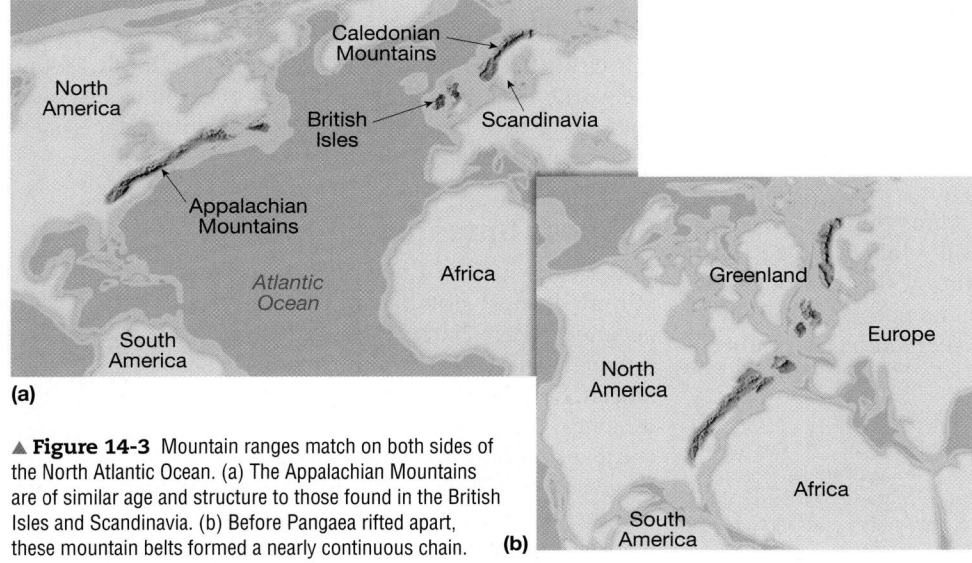

(a)

(b)

▲ **Figure 14-3** Mountain ranges match on both sides of the North Atlantic Ocean. (a) The Appalachian Mountains are of similar age and structure to those found in the British Isles and Scandinavia. (b) Before Pangaea rifted apart, these mountain belts formed a nearly continuous chain.

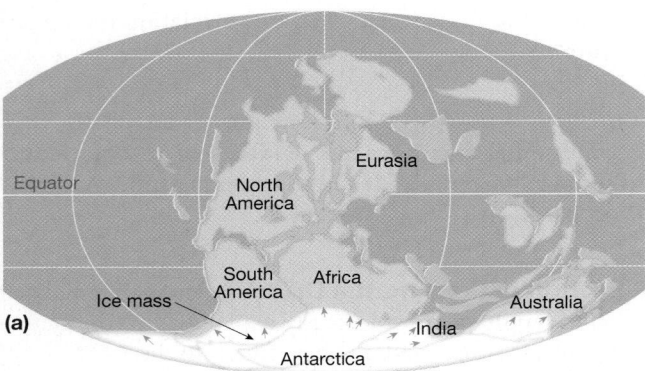

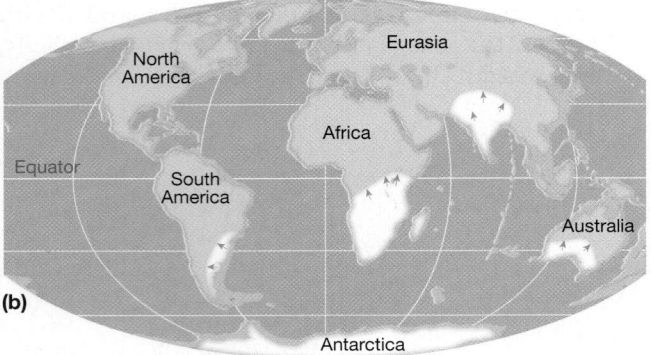

▲ **Figure 14-5** (a) About 300 million years ago extensive areas of Pangaea were glaciated. (b) When the continents are placed back in their former positions, the patterns of ice movement and glacial deposition make sense.

Wegener presented, most scientists felt that two difficulties made the theory improbable if not impossible: (1) Earth's crust was believed to be too rigid to permit such large-scale motions—after all, how could solid rock plow through solid rock? (2) Further, Wegener did not offer a suitable mechanism that could displace such large masses for a long journey. For these reasons, most Earth scientists ignored or even debunked the idea of continental drift for the better part of half a century after Wegener's theory was presented.

Although certainly discouraged that his ideas on continental drift were rejected by most scientists, Wegener continued his other scientific work—most notably in meteorology and polar research, where his contributions are widely acknowledged.[1] In 1930, Wegener was leading a meteorological expedition to the ice cap of Greenland. After delivering supplies to scientists stationed in the remote research outpost of Eismitte in the middle of the ice cap (see Figure 8-31b for a climograph of this station), on November 1 Wegener and a fellow expedition member, Rasmus Villumsen, set out by skis and dogsled to return to their base camp near the coast, but neither arrived. Wegener's body was found six months later buried

---

[1]Before Wegener developed his ideas on continental drift, his 1911 textbook *The Thermodynamics of the Atmosphere* had become a standard in German universities. Swedish meteorologist Tor Bergeron openly acknowledged Wegener's contribution to our understanding of the raindrop formation process known today as the *Bergeron process* (see Chapter 6).

---

in the snow—he died decades before his ideas on continental drift would receive serious attention by the majority of Earth scientists.

THE THEORY OF PLATE TECTONICS

Despite the questions about the validity of continental drift, throughout the middle of the twentieth century continuing research revealed more and more about our dynamic planet.

The Evidence

Among the many gaps in scientific knowledge at the time of Alfred Wegener was an understanding of the dynamics of the ocean floors. By the 1950s, geologists, geophysicists, seismologists, oceanographers, and physicists had accumulated a large body of data about the ocean floor and the underlying crust.

Animation
Plate
Boundaries

One of the most intriguing early findings came when thousands of depth soundings from the oceans of the world were used to construct a detailed map of ocean floor topography (Figure 14-6). The result was remarkable: vast abyssal plains were seen dotted with chains of undersea volcanoes known as *seamounts*. Narrow, deep *oceanic trenches* occurred in many places, often around the margins of the ocean basins. Perhaps most stunning of all was a continuous ridge system running across the floors of all the oceans for 64,000 kilometers (40,000 miles), wrapping around the globe like the stitching on a baseball. The mid-Atlantic segment of this *midocean ridge system* is especially striking, running exactly halfway between—and matching the shape of—the coastlines on both sides, almost as if a giant seam had opened up in the ocean floor between the continents.

By the 1960s a world network of seismographs was able to pinpoint the location of every significant earthquake in the world. When earthquake locations were mapped, it was clear that earthquakes do not occur randomly around the world; instead, most earthquakes occur in bands, often coinciding with the pattern of the midocean ridge system and oceanic trenches (Figure 14-7).

Seafloor Spreading

In the early 1960s, a new theory was propounded, most notably by the American oceanographer Harry Hess and geologist Robert S. Dietz, that could explain the significance of the midocean ridges, the oceanic trenches, the pattern of earthquakes—and could provide a possible mechanism for

Animation
Seafloor
Spreading

Wegener's continental drift. Known as **seafloor spreading**, this theory stated that midocean ridges are formed by currents of magma rising up from the mantle; volcanic eruptions

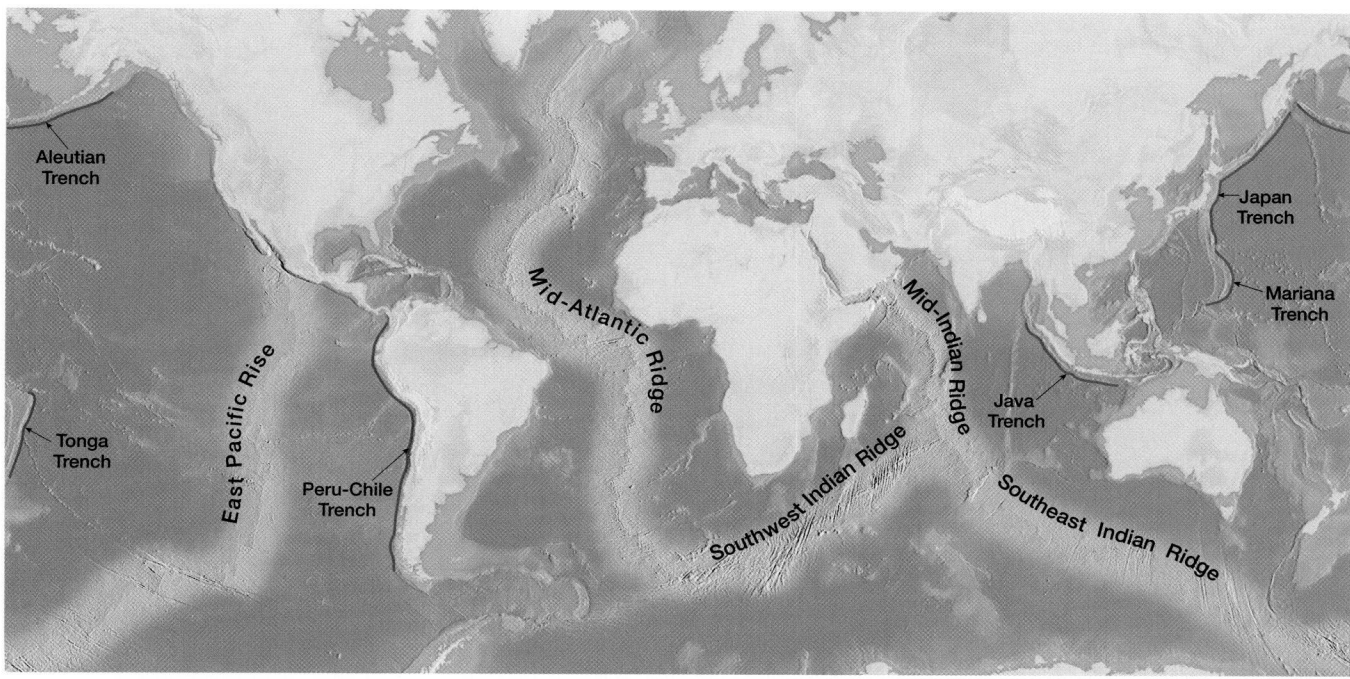

▲ **Figure 14-6** A continuous system of ridges—including the Mid-Atlantic Ridge, the East Pacific Rise, and the Southwest- and Southeast Indian Ridges—runs across the floor of the world ocean. In addition to the ridges, this map also shows the major oceanic trenches.

create new basaltic ocean floor that then spreads away laterally from the ridge (Figure 14-8). Thus, the midocean ridges contain the newest crust formed on the planet. At other places in the ocean basin—at the oceanic trenches—older lithosphere descends into the asthenosphere in a process called **subduction**, where it is ultimately "recycled." The

amount of new seafloor created is compensated for by the amount lost at subduction zones.

Learning Check 14-2 **How do midocean ridges and oceanic trenches fit in with the idea of *seafloor spreading?***

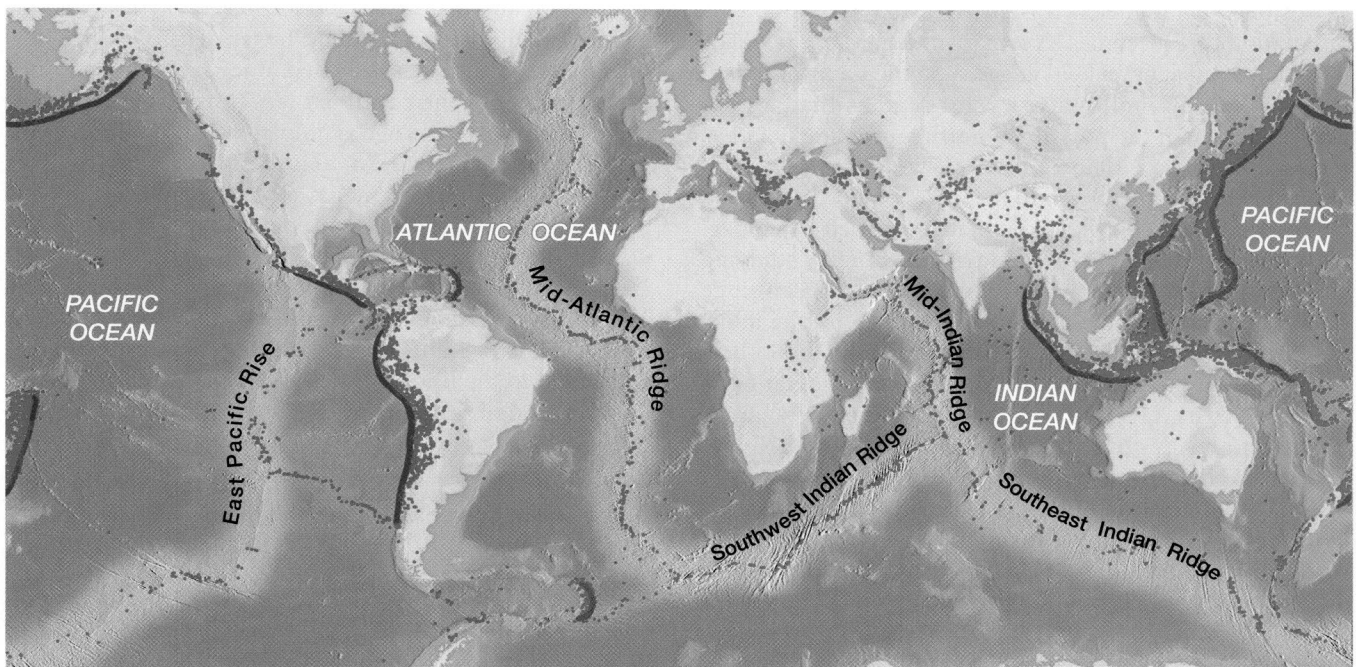

▲ **Figure 14-7** The distributions of epicenters for all earthquakes of at least 5.0 magnitude over a 10-year period. Their relationship to midocean ridges and oceanic trenches is striking.

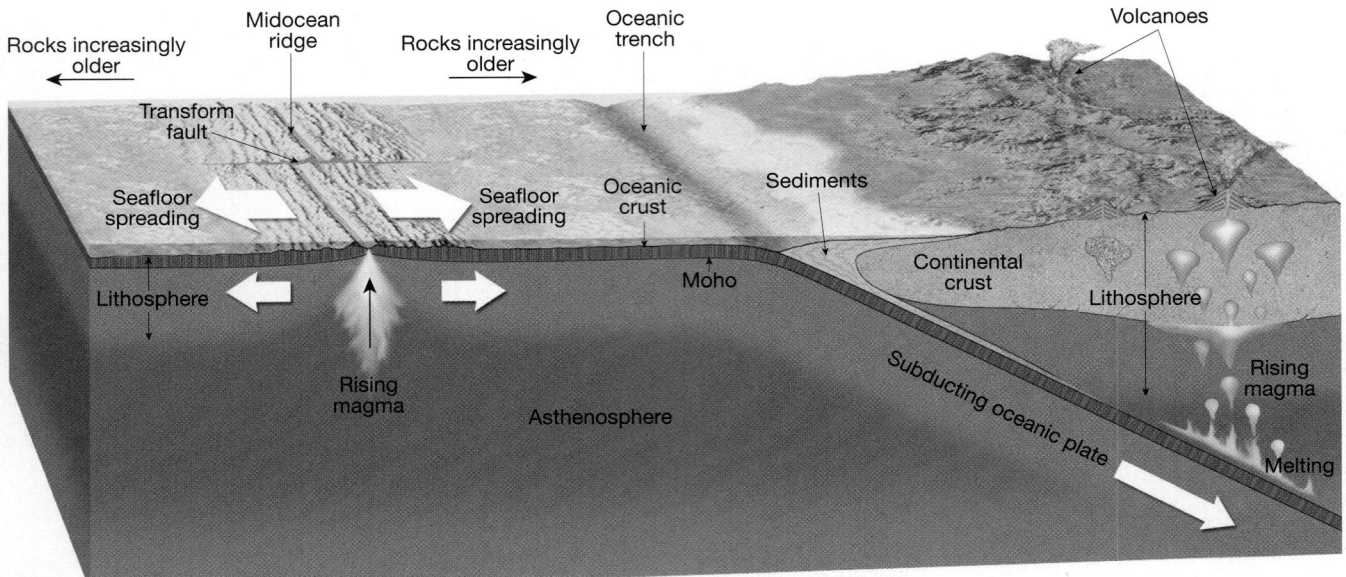

▲ **Figure 14-8** Seafloor spreading. Convection currents bring magma from the asthenosphere up through fissures in the oceanic lithosphere at the midocean ridge. The solidified magma becomes a new portion of ridge along the ocean floor and the two sides of the ridge spread away from each other. Where denser ocean lithosphere converges with less dense continental lithosphere, the oceanic plate slides under the continental plate in a process called *subduction*. Magma produced by this subduction rises to form volcanoes and igneous intrusions.

Verification of Seafloor Spreading:

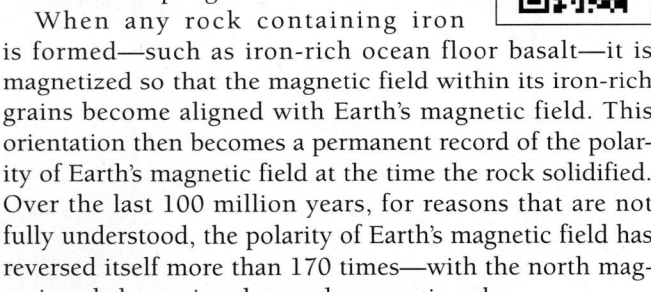

The validity of seafloor spreading was confirmed most notably by two lines of evidence: paleomagnetism and ocean floor core sampling.

When any rock containing iron is formed—such as iron-rich ocean floor basalt—it is magnetized so that the magnetic field within its iron-rich grains become aligned with Earth's magnetic field. This orientation then becomes a permanent record of the polarity of Earth's magnetic field at the time the rock solidified. Over the last 100 million years, for reasons that are not fully understood, the polarity of Earth's magnetic field has reversed itself more than 170 times—with the north magnetic pole becoming the south magnetic pole.

In 1963, Fred Vine and D.H. Matthews used **paleomagnetism** to test the theory of seafloor spreading by studying paleomagnetic data from a portion of the midocean ridge system. If the seafloor has spread laterally by the addition of new crust at the oceanic ridges, there should be a relatively symmetrical pattern of magnetic orientation—normal polarity, reversed polarity, normal polarity, and so on—on both sides of the ridges (Figure 14-9). Such was found to be the case, as Figure 14-10 clearly shows.

Final confirmation of seafloor spreading was obtained from core holes drilled into the ocean floor by the research ship, the *Glomar Challenger* in the late 1960s. Several thousand **ocean floor cores** of sea-bottom sediments were analyzed, and it was evident from this work that, almost invariably, sediment thickness and the age of fossils in the sediment increase with increasing distance from the midocean ridges, indicating that sediments

farthest from the ridges are oldest. At the ridges, ocean floor material is almost all igneous, with little accumulation of sediment—any sediment near the ridges is thin and young.

Thus, the seafloors can be likened to gigantic conveyor belts, moving ever outward from the midocean ridges toward the trenches. Oceanic lithosphere has a relatively short life at Earth's surface. New crust is formed at the oceanic ridges, and within 200 million years is returned to the mantle by subduction. Because lower density continental lithosphere cannot be subducted, once it forms it is virtually permanent. The continual recycling of oceanic crust means that its average age is only about 100 million years, whereas the average age of continental crust is 20 times that. Indeed, some fragments of continental crust have been discovered that are more than 4 billion years old—nearly nine-tenths of the age of Earth!

So, as it turns out, Alfred Wegener was wrong about one important detail in his theory of continental drift: it is not just the continents that are drifting. The continents are embedded in the thicker lithospheric plates, carried along by the action of seafloor spreading.

Learning Check 14-3 **Describe the age pattern of the ocean floors. How does this help verify seafloor spreading?**

Plate Tectonic Theory

By 1968, on the basis of these details and a variety of other evidence, the theory of **plate tectonics**, as it had become known, was being accepted by the scientific community.

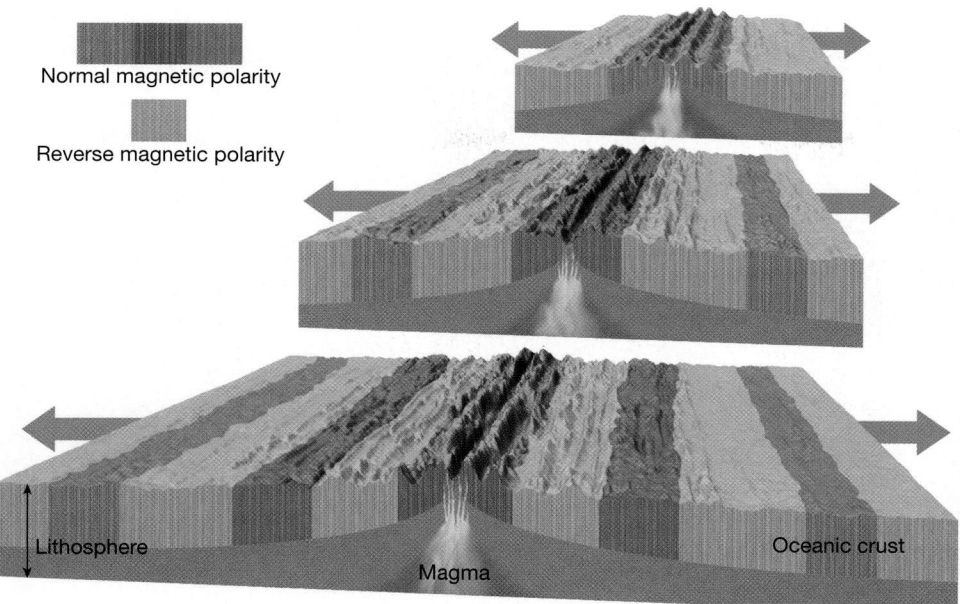

Normal magnetic polarity

Reverse magnetic polarity

Lithosphere

Magma

Oceanic crust

◀ **Figure 14-9** New basaltic ocean floor is magnetized according to the existing magnetic field of the Earth. As ocean floor spreads away from a ridge (shown from top to bottom in the diagram), a symmetrical pattern of normal and reversed magnetic polarity develops on both sides of the spreading center.

Plate tectonics provides a framework with which we can understand and relate a wide range of internal processes and topographic patterns around the world.

The lithosphere is a mosaic of rigid plates floating over the underlying plastic asthenosphere (Figure 14-11).

These lithospheric plates, consisting of the crust together with the upper mantle, vary considerably in area; some are almost hemispheric in size, whereas others are much smaller. The exact number of plates and some of their boundaries are not completely clear. Seven major plates,

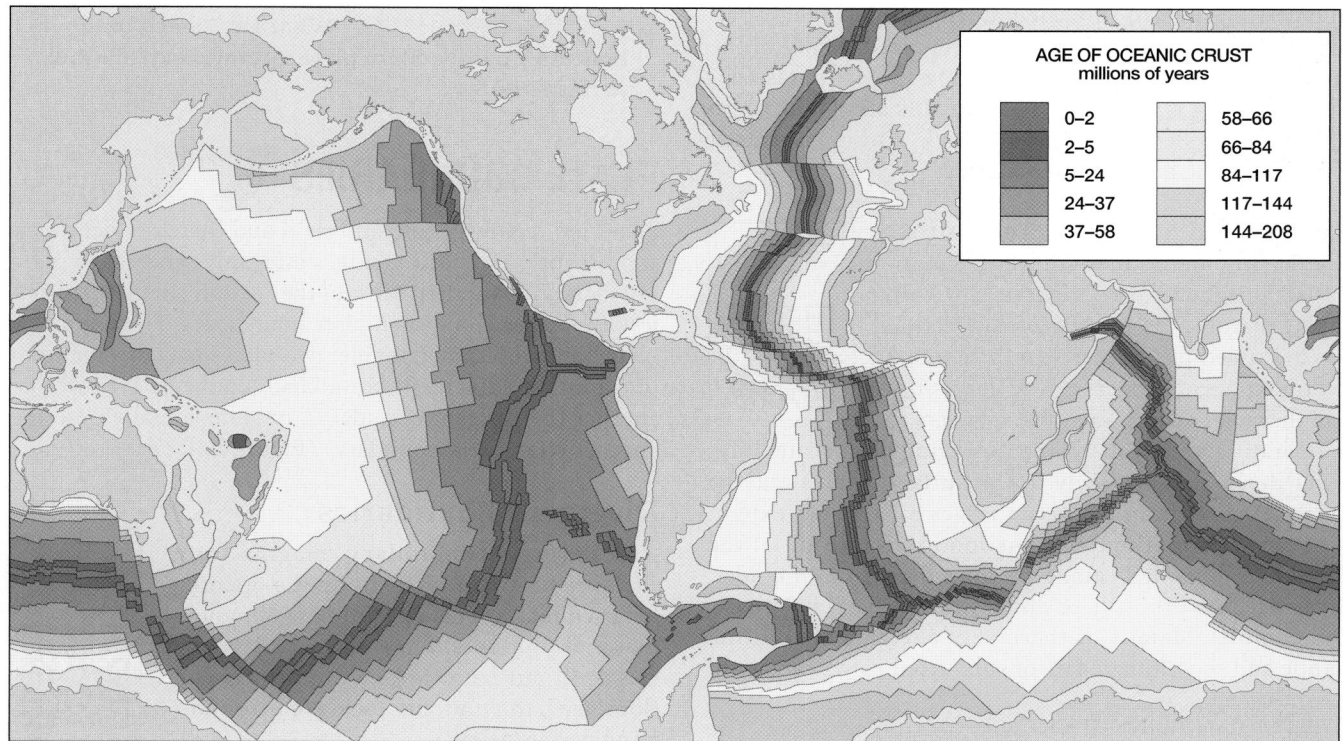

AGE OF OCEANIC CRUST
millions of years

0–2	58–66
2–5	66–84
5–24	84–117
24–37	117–144
37–58	144–208

▲ **Figure 14-10** The age of the ocean floors. The patterns of magnetic reversals recorded in the ocean floor as it spreads away from midocean ridges have helped establish the age of oceanic crust. The youngest ocean floor is found at midocean ridges, whereas ocean floor farther from the ridges is the oldest. (*Note:* The length of time shown is not the same in each age category.)

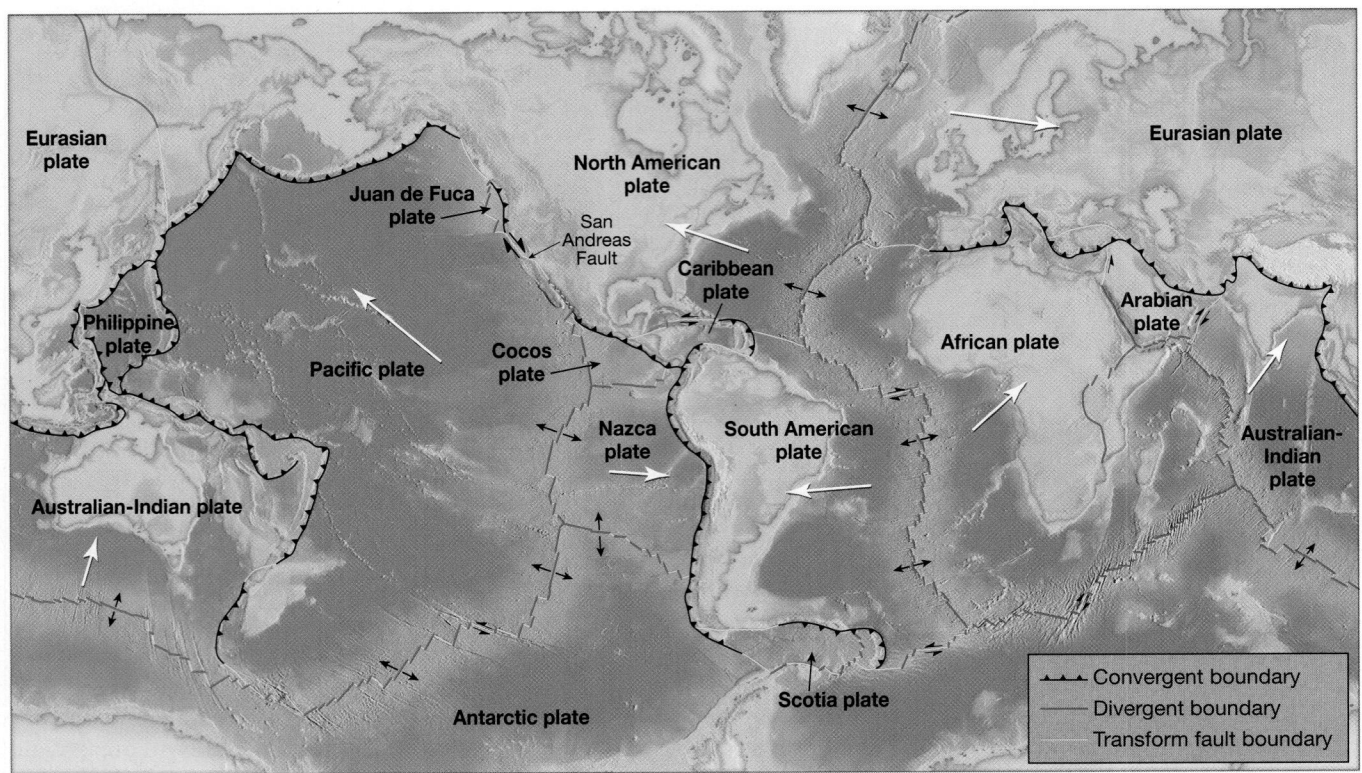

▲ **Figure 14-11** The major contemporary tectonic plates and their generalized direction of movement.

an equal number of intermediate-sized plates, and perhaps a dozen smaller plates, are recognized. Many of the smaller plates are remnants of once-larger plates that are now being subducted. These plates are about 65 to 100 kilometers (40 to 60 miles) thick, and most consist of both oceanic and continental crust.

Mechanism for Plate Tectonics:

Animation
Convection and
Plate Tectonics

The driving mechanism for plate tectonics is thought to be convection within Earth's mantle (the process of convection was discussed in Chapter 4 in the context of atmospheric processes). A very sluggish thermal convection system appears to be operating within the planet, bringing deep-seated hot, lower density rock slowly to the surface. Plates may be "pushed" away from midocean ridges to a certain extent, but it appears that much of the motion is a result of the plates being "pulled" along by the subduction of colder, dense oceanic lithosphere down into the asthenosphere. The complete details of thermal convection within the mantle and the ultimate fate of subducted plates remain to be confirmed.

These plates move slowly over the asthenosphere. The rates of seafloor spreading vary from less than 1 cm (0.4 in.) per year in parts of the Mid-Atlantic Ridge to as much as 10 cm (4 in.) per year in the Pacific–Antarctic Ridge.

Learning Check 14-4 What are "plates" and how does the theory of plate tectonics explain their movement?

PLATE BOUNDARIES  FG1, FG3

Plates are relatively cold and rigid and therefore deformed significantly only at the edges and only where one plate interacts with another. Most of the "action" in plate tectonics takes place along such plate boundaries. Three types of plate boundaries are possible: two plates may diverge from one another (divergent boundary), converge toward one another (convergent boundary), or slide laterally past one another (transform boundary) (Figure 14-12).

Divergent Boundaries

At a **divergent boundary**, magma from the asthenosphere wells up in the opening between plates. This upward flow of molten material produces a line of volcanic vents that spill out basaltic lava onto the ocean floor, with the plutonic rock gabbro solidifying deeper below.

Animation
Divergent
Boundaries

Midocean Ridges: A divergent boundary is usually represented by a **midocean ridge** (Figure 14-13). Most

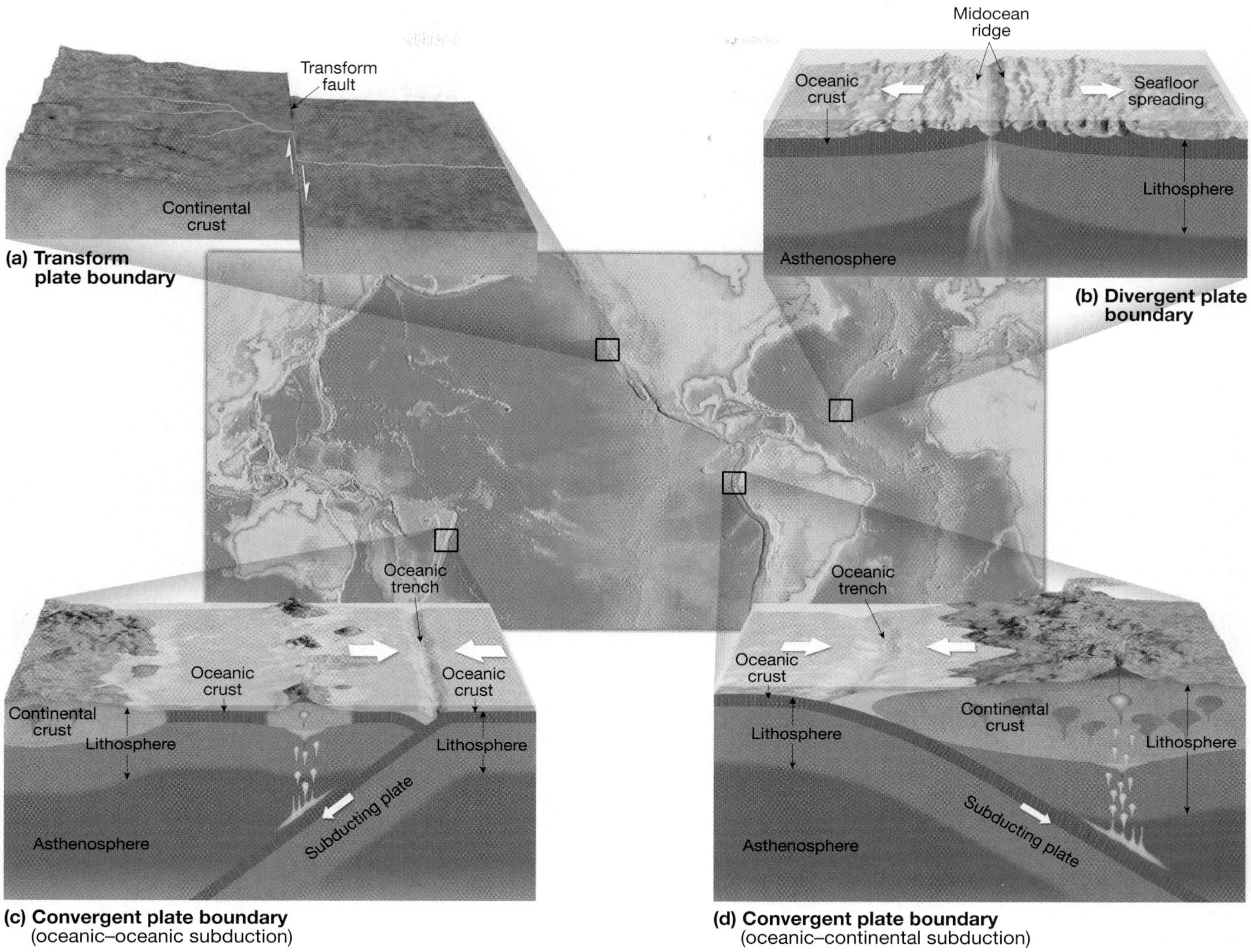

(a) Transform plate boundary

Transform fault

Continental crust

Midocean ridge

Oceanic crust

Seafloor spreading

Lithosphere

Asthenosphere

(b) Divergent plate boundary

Oceanic trench

Oceanic crust

Oceanic crust

Continental crust

Lithosphere

Lithosphere

Asthenosphere

Subducting plate

(c) Convergent plate boundary
(oceanic–oceanic subduction)

Oceanic trench

Oceanic crust

Continental crust

Lithosphere

Lithosphere

Asthenosphere

Subducting plate

(d) Convergent plate boundary
(oceanic–continental subduction)

▲ **Figure 14-12** Three kinds of plate boundaries. The edges of lithospheric plates slide past each other along transform boundaries such as the San Andreas Fault system in California (a); move apart at divergent boundaries such as continental rift valleys and midocean ridges (b); and come together at convergent boundaries such as oceanic-oceanic plate subduction zones (c), oceanic-continental plate subduction zones (d), and continental collision zones.

of the midocean ridges of the world are either active or extinct spreading ridges. Such *spreading centers* are associated with *shallow-focus earthquakes* (meaning that the ruptures that generate the earthquakes are within about 70 kilometers [45 miles] of the surface), volcanic activity, and hydrothermal metamorphism—as well as the presence of remarkable marine life-forms thriving in the hostile environment of hydrothermal vents on the ocean floor. Divergent boundaries are "constructive" because material is being added to the crustal surface at such locations.

Continental Rift Valleys: Divergent boundaries can also develop within a continent (Figure 14-14), resulting in a **continental rift valley** such as the Great East African Rift Valley that extends from Ethiopia southward through

Mozambique. The Red Sea is also the outcome of spreading taking place within a continent—in this case the spreading has been great enough to form a "proto-ocean."

Learning Check 14-5 How are *midocean ridges* and *continental rift valleys* related?

Convergent Boundaries

At a **convergent boundary**, plates collide and as such are sometimes called "destructive" boundaries because they result in removal or compression of the surface crust (Figure 14-15). Convergent plate boundaries are responsible for some of the most massive and spectacular of earthly

Animation
Subduction
Zones

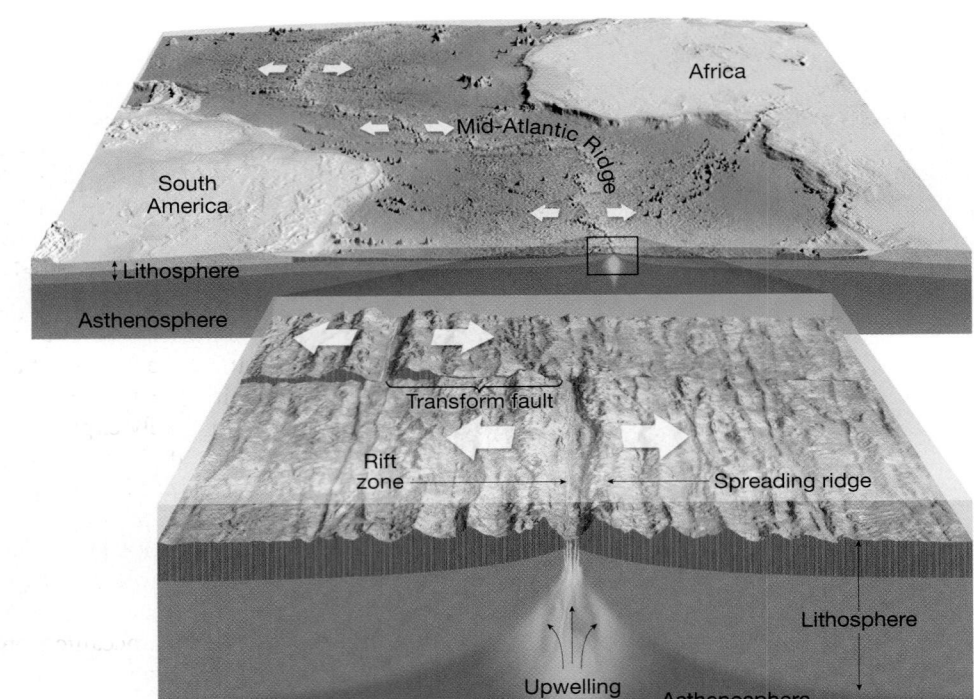

▶ **Figure 14-13** Midocean ridge spreading center. Seafloor spreading involves the rise of magma from within Earth and the lateral movement of new ocean floor away from the zone of upwelling. This gradual process moves the older material farther away from the spreading center as it is replaced by newer material from below. Transform faults are found along the short offsets associated with slight bends in the ridge system.

landforms: major mountain ranges, volcanoes, and oceanic trenches. The three types of convergent boundaries are: *oceanic–continental convergence*, *oceanic–oceanic convergence*, and *continental–continental convergence*.

Oceanic–continental Convergence: Because oceanic lithosphere includes dense basaltic crust, it is denser than

continental lithosphere, and so oceanic lithosphere always underrides continental lithosphere when the two collide (Figure 14-15a). The dense oceanic plate slowly and inexorably sinks into the asthenosphere in the process of **subduction**. The subducting slab pulls on the rest of the plate—such "slab pull" is probably the main cause of most plate movement, pulling the rest of the plate in after itself, as

▼ **Figure 14-14** (a) A continental rift valley develops where divergence takes place within a continent. As spreading proceeds, blocks of crust drop down to form a rift valley. (b) Ol Doinyo Lengai volcano and the East African Rift Valley in Tanzania.

it were. Wherever such an oceanic–continental convergent boundary exists, a mountain range is formed on land (the Andes range of South America is one notable example; the Cascades in northwestern North America is another) and a parallel **oceanic trench** develops as the seafloor is pulled down by the subducting plate.

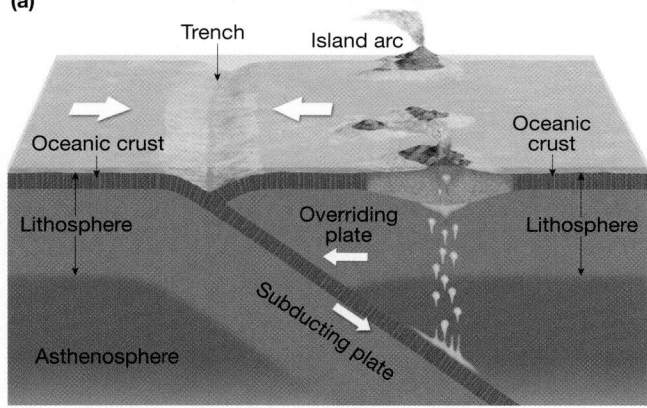

(a)

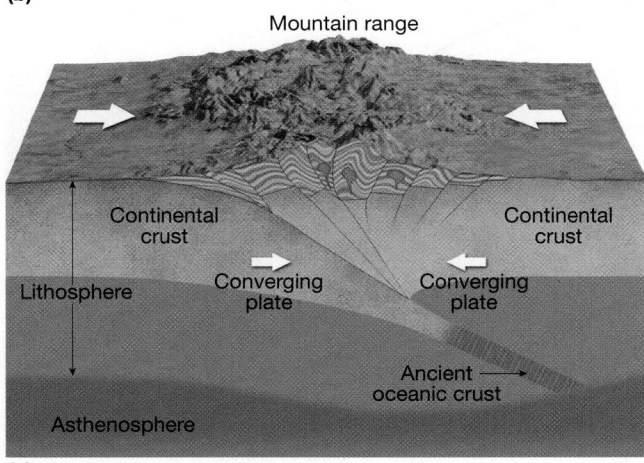

(b)

(c)

▲ **Figure 14-15** Idealized portrayals of three kinds of convergent plate boundaries: (a) Where an oceanic plate converges with a continental plate, the oceanic plate is subducted and an oceanic trench and coastal mountains with volcanoes are usually created. (b) Where an oceanic plate subducts beneath another oceanic plate, an oceanic trench and volcanic island arc result. (c) Where a continental plate collides with a continental plate no subduction takes place, but mountains are generally thrust upward.

Earthquakes take place along the margin of a subducting plate. Shallow-focus earthquakes are common at the trench, but as the subducting plate descends into the asthenosphere, the earthquakes become progressively deeper, with some subduction zones generating earthquakes as deep as 600 kilometers (375 miles) below the surface.

Volcanoes develop from magma generated in the subduction zone. Early researchers thought that a subducted plate would completely melt when pushed down into the hot asthenosphere. However, more recent research indicates that such a result is unlikely. Oceanic crust is relatively cold when it approaches a subduction zone and would take a long time to become hot enough to melt. A more likely explanation is that beginning at a depth of about 100 kilometers (about 60 miles) water is driven off from the oceanic crust as it is subducted, and this water reduces the melting temperature of the mantle rock above, causing it to melt. This magma rises through the overriding plate, producing both extrusive and intrusive igneous rocks. The chain of volcanoes that develops in association with an oceanic–continental plate subduction zone is sometimes referred to as a *continental volcanic arc*. As we will see later in this chapter, such subduction zone volcanoes frequently erupt explosively.

Metamorphic rocks often develop in association with subduction zones. The margin of a subducting oceanic plate is subjected to increasing pressure, although relatively modest heating, as it begins to descend—this can lead to the formation of high-pressure, low-temperature metamorphic rocks, such as *blueschist*. In addition, the magma generated in the subduction zone may cause contact metamorphism as it rises through the overlying continental rocks.

Oceanic–oceanic Convergence: If the convergent boundary is between two oceanic plates, subduction also takes place, as in Figure 14-15b. As one of the oceanic plates subducts beneath the other, an oceanic trench is formed, shallow- and deep-focus earthquakes occur (Figure 14-16), and volcanic activity is initiated with volcanoes forming on the ocean floor. With time, a **volcanic island arc** (such as the Aleutian Islands and Mariana Islands) develops; such an arc may eventually become a more mature island arc system (such as Japan and the islands of Sumatra and Java in Indonesia are today).

Continental–continental Convergence: Where there is a convergent boundary between two continental plates, no subduction takes place because continental crust is too buoyant to subduct. Instead, huge mountain ranges, such as the Alps, are built up (Figure 14-15c).

Animation
Collision of India with Eurasia

The most dramatic present-day example of continental collision has resulted in the formation of the Himalayas (Figure 14-17). The Himalayas began to form more than 45 million years ago, when the subcontinent of India started its collision with the rest of Eurasia. Under the conditions of continental collision, volcanoes are rare, but

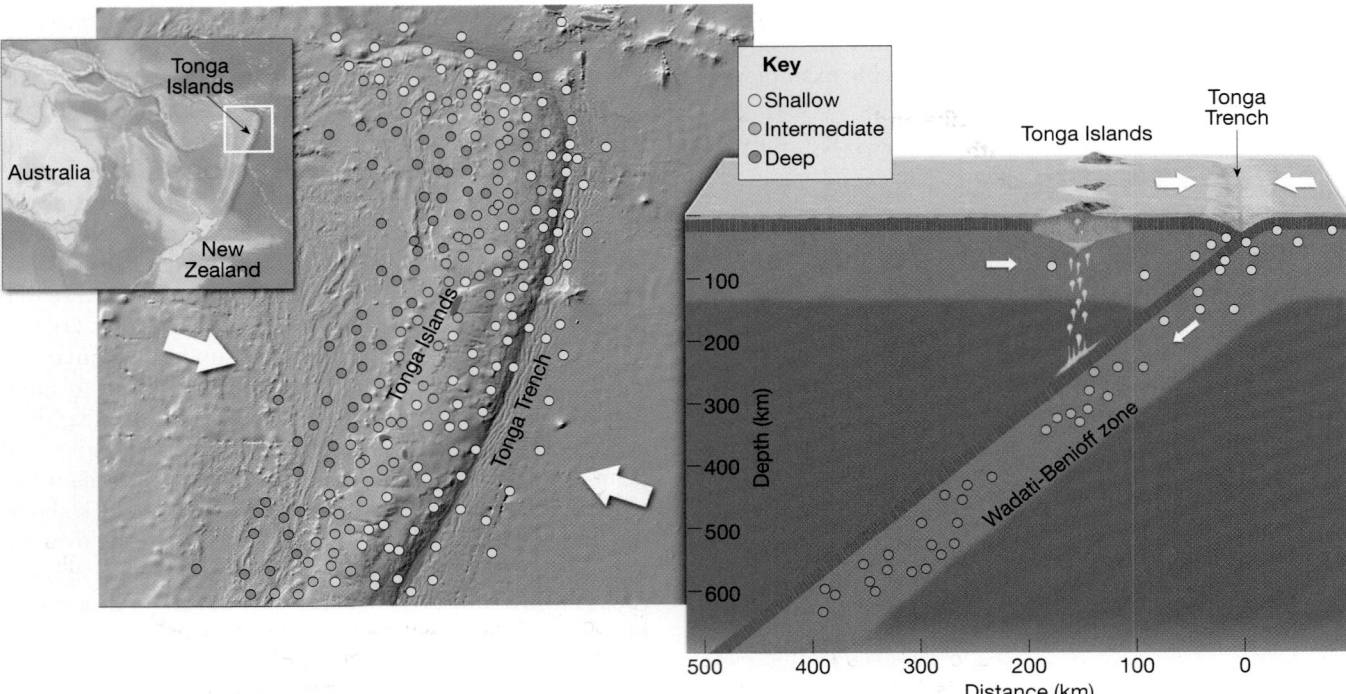

▲ **Figure 14-16** Earthquake patterns associated with the Tonga Trench subduction zone (shown in a map view on the left and a side view on the right). Shallow-focus earthquakes occur where the Pacific Plate begins to subduct at the trench. Intermediate- and deep-focus earthquakes occur as the subducting oceanic plate goes deeper into the asthenosphere below. The *Wadati–Benioff zone* is named for seismologists Kigoo Wadati and Hugo Benioff, who were the first scientists to describe these inclined zones of earthquakes.

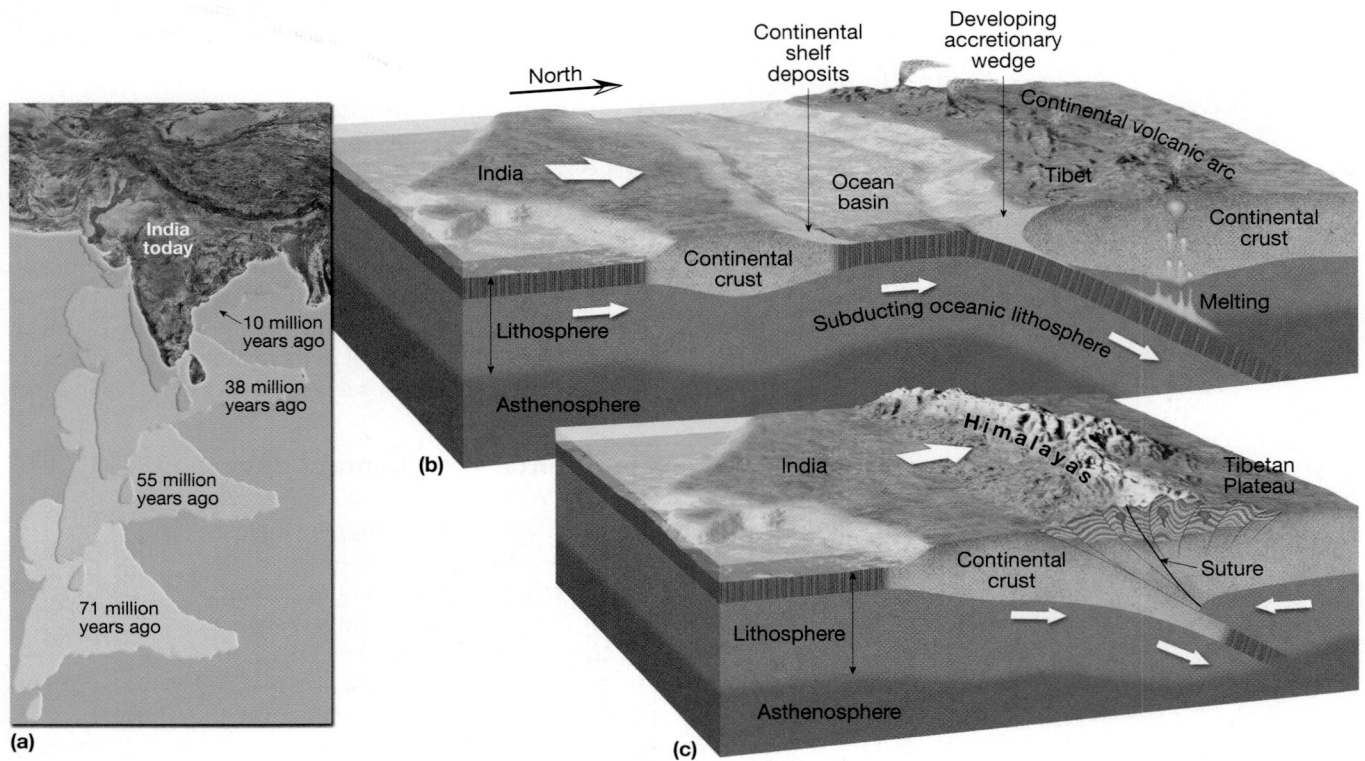

▲ **Figure 14-17** (a) The collision of the subcontinent of India with Eurasia began about 45 million years ago. (b and c) This collision and continental "suture" has uplifted the Himalayas and the Tibetan Plateau.

shallow-focus earthquakes and regional metamorphism are common.

Describe and explain the major features associated with oceanic–continental convergence and oceanic–oceanic convergence.

Transform Boundaries

At a **transform boundary**, two plates slip past one another laterally. This slippage occurs along great vertical fractures called *transform faults* (a type of *strike-slip fault* discussed in more detail later in this chapter). Because the plate movement is basically parallel to a transform boundary, these boundaries neither create new crust nor destroy old. Transform faults are associated with a great deal of seismic activity, commonly producing shallow-focus earthquakes.

Animation
Transform Faults
and Boundaries

Most transform faults are found along the midocean ridge system, where they form short offsets in the ridge perpendicular to the spreading axis (see Figure 14-13). However, in some places, transform faults extend for great distances, occasionally through continental lithosphere. For example, the most famous fault system in the United States, the San Andreas Fault in California, is on a transform boundary between the Pacific and North American plates (Figure 14-18).

Plate Boundaries Over Geologic Time

FG2, FG4

Animation
Assembly and
Breakup of
Pangaea

Plate tectonics provides us with a grand framework for understanding the extensive lithospheric rearrangement that has taken place during the history of Earth. A brief summary of major events in Earth's history might highlight the following:

- Between about 1.1 billion and 800 million years ago—before Pangaea existed—there was an earlier supercontinent, called *Rodinia* by geologists.
- By about 700 million years ago, Rodinia was rifting apart into continental pieces that would eventually "suture" (fuse) back together again—first into a large southern continent called *Gondwana* (which included present-day South America, Africa, India, Australia, and Antarctica), and later into a northern continent called *Laurasia* (comprised of present-day North America and Eurasia). By about 250 million years ago, Gondwana and Laurasia had joined to form Pangaea.

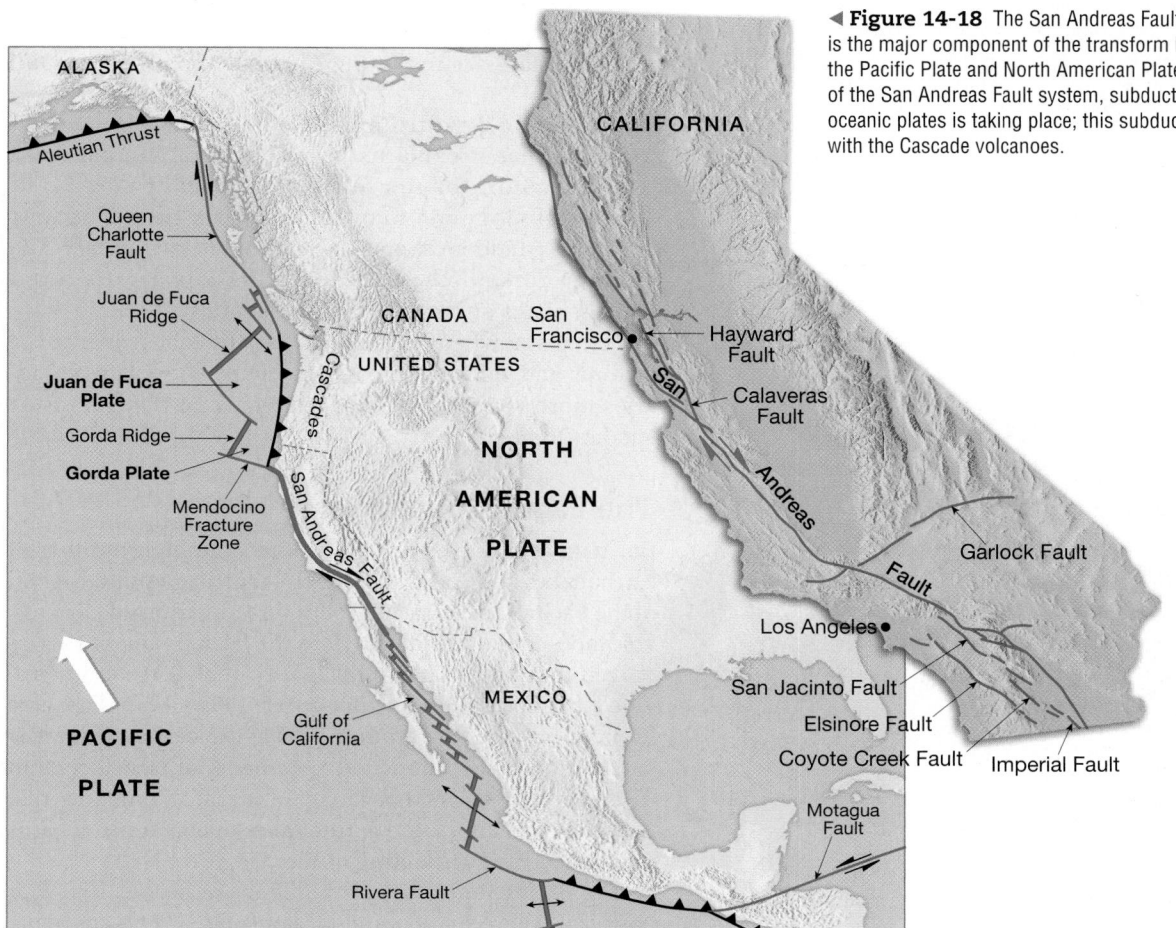

◀ **Figure 14-18** The San Andreas Fault system of California is the major component of the transform boundary between the Pacific Plate and North American Plate. Notice that north of the San Andreas Fault system, subduction of several small oceanic plates is taking place; this subduction is associated with the Cascade volcanoes.

- About 200 million years ago, when Pangaea was beginning to rift apart, there was only one largely uninterrupted ocean (Figure 14-19).
- By 90 million years ago, continental fragmentation was well under way. The North Atlantic Ocean was beginning to open, and the South Atlantic began to separate South America from Africa. Antarctica is the only continent that has remained near its original position.

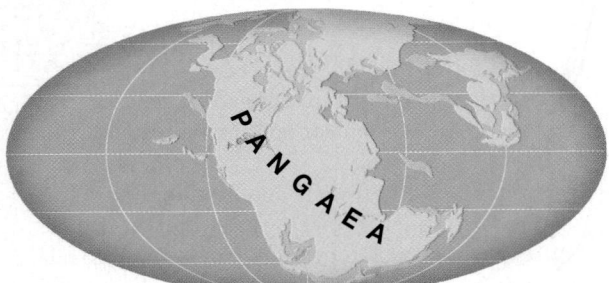

(a) 200 Million Years Ago (Late Triassic Period)

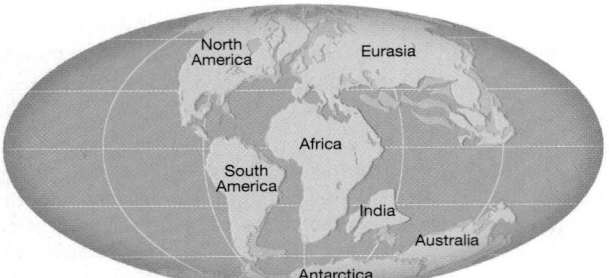

(b) 90 Million Years Ago (Cretaceous Period)

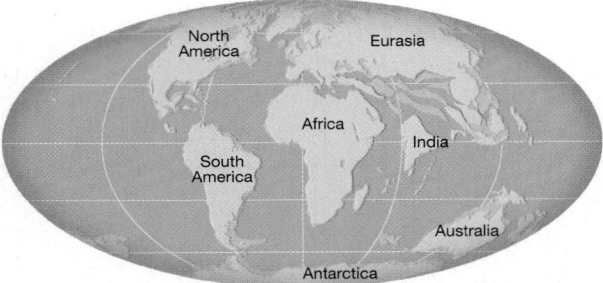

(c) 50 Million Years Ago (Early Tertiary/Paleogene)

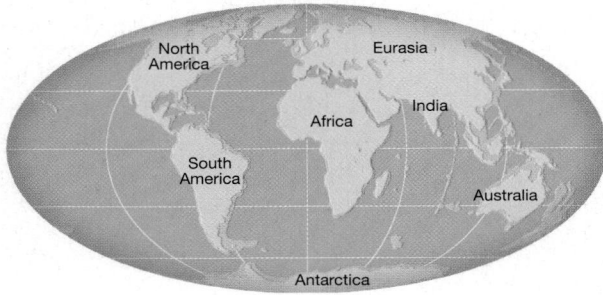

(d) Present

▲ **Figure 14-19** The break-up of Pangaea beginning about 200 million years ago.

- By 50 million years ago, the North and South Atlantic Oceans had both opened, and South America was a new and isolated continent that was rapidly moving westward. The Andes were growing as South America overrode the Pacific Ocean basin; the Rockies and the ancestral Sierra Nevada had risen in North America.
- Today, South America has connected with North America. North America has separated from western Eurasia, Australia has split from Antarctica, and India has collided with Eurasia to thrust up the Himalayas. Africa is splitting along the Great Rift Valley and slowly rotating counterclockwise.

Learning Check 14-7   How does the theory of plate tectonics explain the history of the Atlantic Ocean, the Himalayas, and the Andes Mountains?

Plate Motion into the Future: If current plate movement continues, 50 million years into the future Australia will straddle the equator as a huge tropical island. Africa may pinch shut the Mediterranean, and East Africa may become a new large island like Madagascar. The Atlantic will widen while the Pacific will shrink. Southern California—perhaps along with much of the rest of the state—will slide past the rest of North America en route to its ultimate destiny in the Aleutian Trench in the Gulf of Alaska.

One of the great triumphs of the theory of plate tectonics is that it explains broad topographic patterns. It can account for the formation of many *cordilleras* (groups of mountain ranges), midocean ridges, oceanic trenches, island arcs, and the associated earthquake and volcanic zones. Where these features appear, there are usually plates either colliding or separating.

Perhaps nowhere in the world are the consequences of tectonic and volcanic activity associated with plate boundaries more vividly displayed than around the rim of the Pacific Ocean.

The Pacific Ring of Fire

For many decades, geologists noted the high number of earthquakes and active volcanoes occurring around the rim of the Pacific Ocean basin. About three-quarters of all active volcanoes in the world lie within the Pacific Rim, but it was only in the late 1960s that the theory of plate tectonics provided an explanation for this pattern. Plate boundaries are found all of the way around the Pacific basin—primarily subduction zones, along with segments of transform and divergent boundaries. It is along these plate boundaries that the many volcanoes and earthquakes take place in what is now called the **Pacific Ring of Fire** (Figure 14-20).

The Pacific Rim is home to millions of people. Active or potentially active volcanoes and major faults systems are within

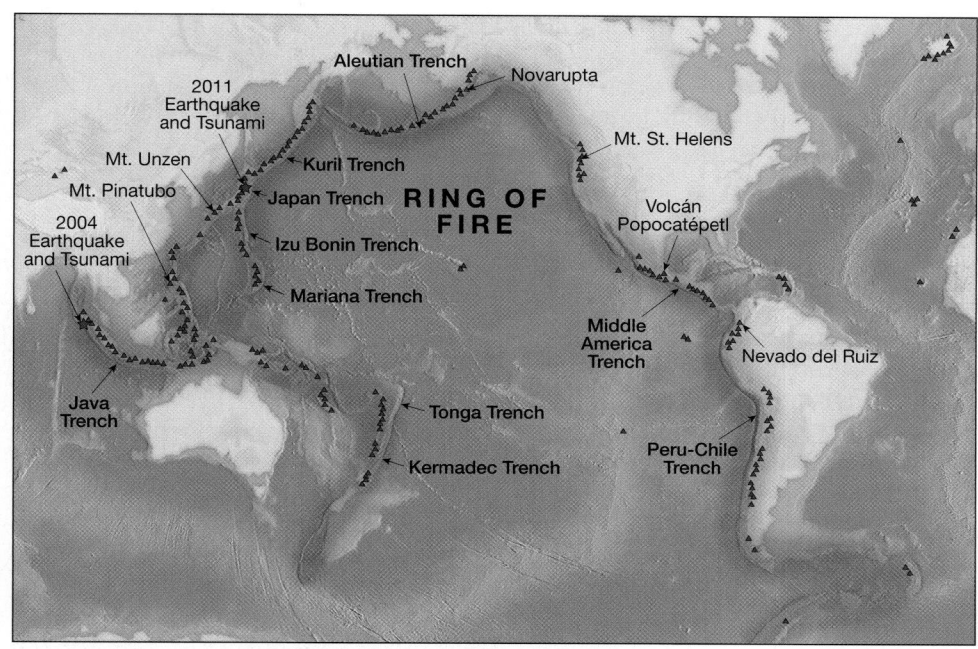

◀ **Figure 14-20** The Pacific Ring of Fire.

sight of some of the largest metropolitan regions in the world, such as Mexico City, Los Angeles, and Tokyo. In recent decades we have had many reminders of the ever-active Ring of Fire: the 1980 Mount St. Helens eruption; the 1985 Nevado del Ruiz volcano tragedy in Colombia; the 1991 eruption of Mount Pinatubo in the Philippines; the 1994 Northridge earthquake in California; the December 2004 Sumatra, Indonesia, earthquake and tsunami that killed more than 227,000 people; and the March 2011 earthquake and tsunami that killed 15,000 people in Japan.

ADDITIONS TO PLATE TECTONIC THEORY

With each passing year, we learn more about plate tectonics. Two examples of important additions to plate tectonic theory are *hot spots* and *accreted terranes*.

Hot Spots and Mantle Plumes

One augmentation to plate tectonic theory was introduced at the same time as the original model. The basic theory of plate tectonics can explain tectonic and volcanic activity along the margins of plates, however, there are many places on Earth where magma rising from the mantle comes either to or almost to the surface at locations that may not be anywhere near a plate boundary. These locations of volcanic activity in the interior of a plate are referred to as **hot spots**—more than 50 have thus far been identified.

Animation
Mantle Plumes

Explaining Hot Spots: To explain the existence of hot spots, the **mantle plume** model was proposed in the late 1960s. This explanation suggests that midplate volcanic activity develops over narrow plumes of heated material rising through the mantle—perhaps originating as deep as the core–mantle boundary (Figure 14-21). Such mantle

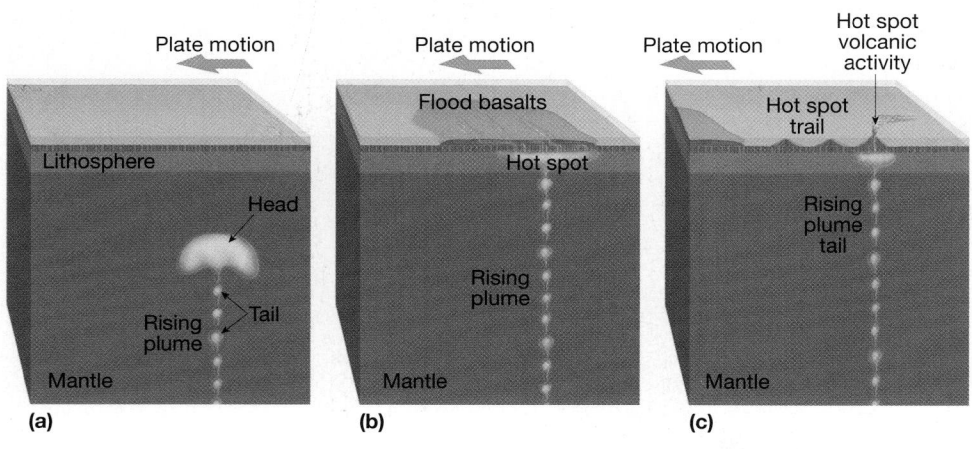

◀ **Figure 14-21** The idealized mantle plume model of hot spot origin. A plume of heated material rises from deep within the mantle. When the large head of the plume reaches the surface, an outpouring of flood basalt results. Plate motion carries the flood basalts off the stationary plume and a new volcano or volcanic island forms. As the moving plate carries each volcano off the hot spot, it becomes extinct, resulting in a straight-line "hot spot trail." As volcanic islands move off the hot spot, the plate cools, becomes denser, and subsides; some islands may eventually sink below the surface to become *seamounts*.

plumes are believed to be relatively stationary over long periods of time (in some cases, as long as tens of millions of years). As the magma rises through the plate above, it creates hot spot volcanoes and/or hydrothermal (hot water) features on the surface—often after an initial large outpouring of lava known as *flood basalt* (discussed later in this chapter).

The plate above the hot spot is moving, so the volcanoes or other hot spot features are eventually carried off the plume and become inactive, while in turn new volcanic features develop over the plume, so generating a straight-line *hot spot trail*. Volcanic islands carried off the hot spot may eventually subside to form underwater *seamounts* as the oceanic lithosphere cools and becomes denser. Because many hot spots seem to be effectively fixed in position for long periods of time, the hot spot trails they produce can indicate both the direction and speed of plate motion with seamounts becoming progressively older in the direction of plate movement.

The Hawaiian Hot Spot: The most dramatic present-day example of a hot spot is associated with the Hawaiian Islands. Although both developed over the same hot spot, the ancient volcanic remnants of Midway Island are now 2500 kilometers (1600 miles) northwest of the presently active volcanoes on the Big Island of Hawai'i, separated in time by more than 27 million years. The volcanoes of the Hawaiian chain are progressively younger from west to east; as the Pacific Plate drifts northwestward, new volcanoes are produced on an "assembly line" moving over the persistent hot spot (Figure 14-22). After the Big Island is carried off the hot spot by the movement of the plate, the next Hawaiian

island will rise in its place—in fact, scientists are already studying the undersea volcano Lō'ihi as it builds up on the ocean floor just southeast of the Big Island (Figure 14-23). Other well-known hot spot locations are Yellowstone National Park, Iceland, and the Galapagos Islands.

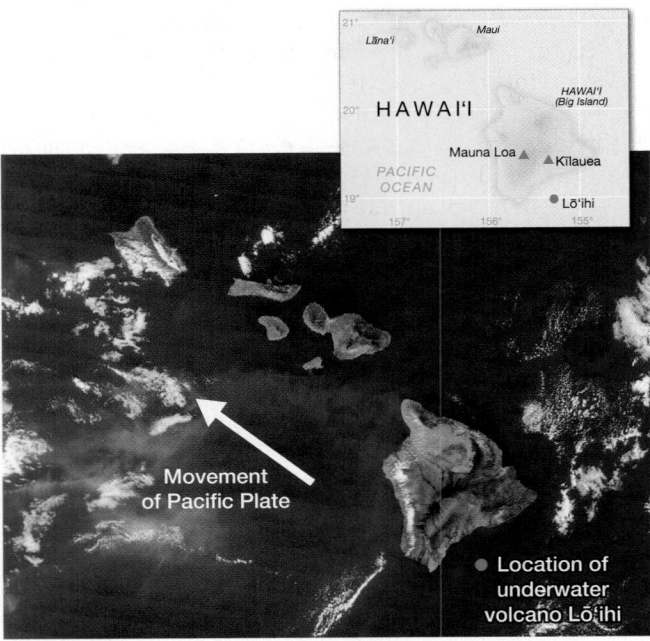

▲ **Figure 14-23** The only recently active volcanoes in the Hawaiian chain are on the Big Island of Hawai'i—Mauna Loa and Kīlauea have been repeatedly active during historic times. Lō'ihi, an underwater volcano southeast of the Big Island, is the next volcanic island being built.

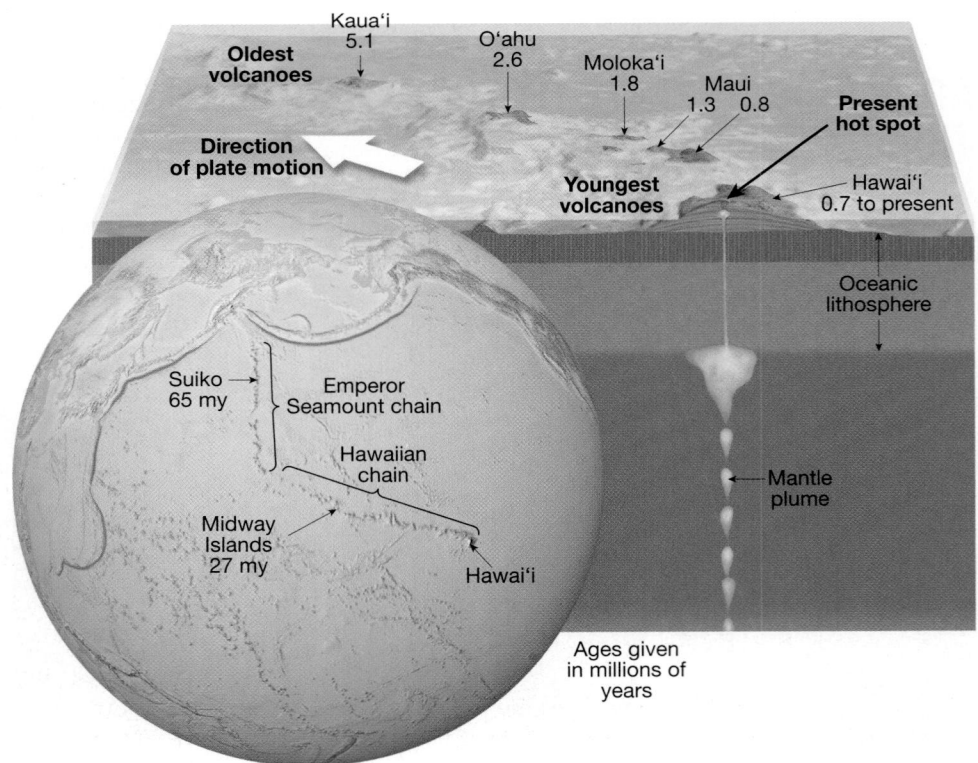

▶ **Figure 14-22** The Hawaiian hot spot. A hot spot has persisted here for many millions of years. As the Pacific Plate moved northwest, a progression of volcanoes was created and then died as their source of magma was shut off. Among the oldest is Midway Island. Later volcanoes developed down the chain. The numbers on the main islands indicate the age of the basalt that formed the volcanoes, in millions of years before the present.

Recent research indicates that the complete explanation of hot spots may turn out to be more complex than the original mantle plume model suggested. *Seismic tomography*—a technique that uses earthquake waves to produce a kind of "ultrasound" of Earth—suggests that the magma source of at least some hot spots is quite shallow, whereas the source for others are mantle plumes originating deep from within the mantle. Further, some researchers cite evidence suggesting that several mantle plumes may have changed location in the geologic past. For example, the Emperor Seamounts—a chain of seamounts to the northwest of Midway Island—are part of the Hawaiian hot spot trail, but they appear to divert quite significantly in direction from the straight line of the rest of the Hawaiian chain (see Figure 14-22). This "bend" in the hot spot trail is due either to a significant change in direction of the Pacific Plate about 43 million years ago or to the migration of the hot spot itself—perhaps both.

As additional information is gathered, a more complete understanding of hot spots, mantle plumes, and midplate volcanic activity will likely emerge.

> **Learning Check 14-8** **How does the *mantle plume* model explain the formation of the Hawaiian Islands?**

Accreted Terranes

 FG2, FG4

A more recent discovery has helped explain the often confusing juxtaposition of different types of rock seen along the margins of some continents. A **terrane** is a small-to-medium mass of lithosphere—bounded on all sides by faults—that may have been carried a long distance by a moving plate,

Animation
Terrane
Formation

eventually to converge with the edge of another plate. The terrane is too buoyant to be subducted in the collision and instead is fused ("accreted") to the other plate, often being fragmented in the process. In some cases, slices of oceanic lithosphere have accreted in terranes (including the accumulated sediment in what is called the *accretionary wedge* of a subduction zone); in other cases, it appears that entire old island arcs have fused with the margin of a continent (Figure 14-24).

Terranes are distinctive geologically because their lithologic complement (types of rock) is generally quite different from that of the plate to which they are accreted. It is generally believed that every continent has grown outward by the accumulation of accreted terranes on one or more of its margins. North America is a prominent example (Figure 14-25): most of Alaska and much of western Canada and the western United States consist of a mosaic of several dozen accreted terranes, some of which have been traced to origins south of the equator.

> **Learning Check 14-9** **How does the idea of a *terrane* help explain the geologic history of western North America?**

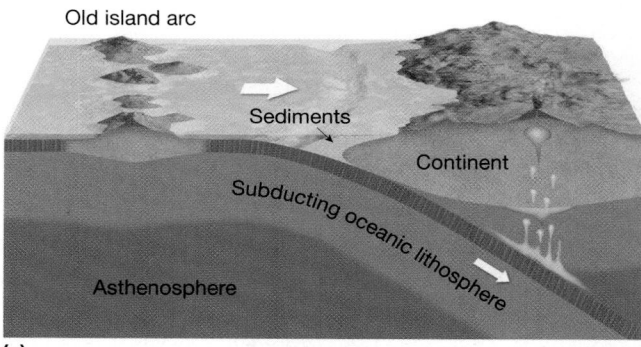
(a)

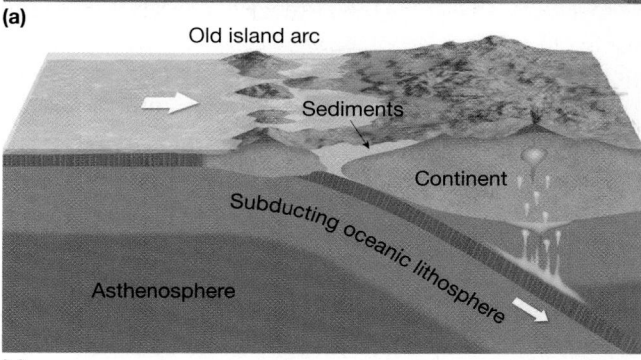
(b)

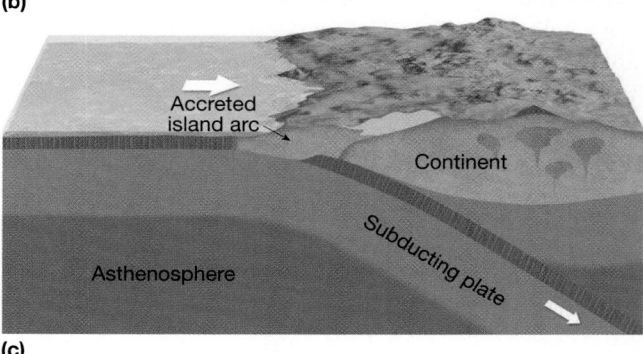
(c)

▲ **Figure 14-24** The origin of an accreted terrane in a convergent boundary. (a) A moving oceanic plate carries along an old island arc. (b) The oceanic plate converges with a continental plate. (c) The oceanic plate begins to subduct under the continental plate, but the island arc is too buoyant for subduction and so is accreted to the continental plate.

Remaining Questions

Plate tectonic theory has advanced our understanding of the internal processes of Earth dramatically. However, a number of questions remain unanswered for the time being. For example, several major mountain ranges in North America and Eurasia are in the middle of plates rather than in boundary zones. Although the genesis of some midplate ranges, such as the Appalachians in North America and the Ural Mountains in Eurasia, can be traced to continental collisions in the geologic past, other midplate mountain ranges or regions of seismic activity are not yet fully understood. Further, although convection of heated material within the mantle provides the general mechanism for plate movement, the details of heat flow within Earth and the possible relationships

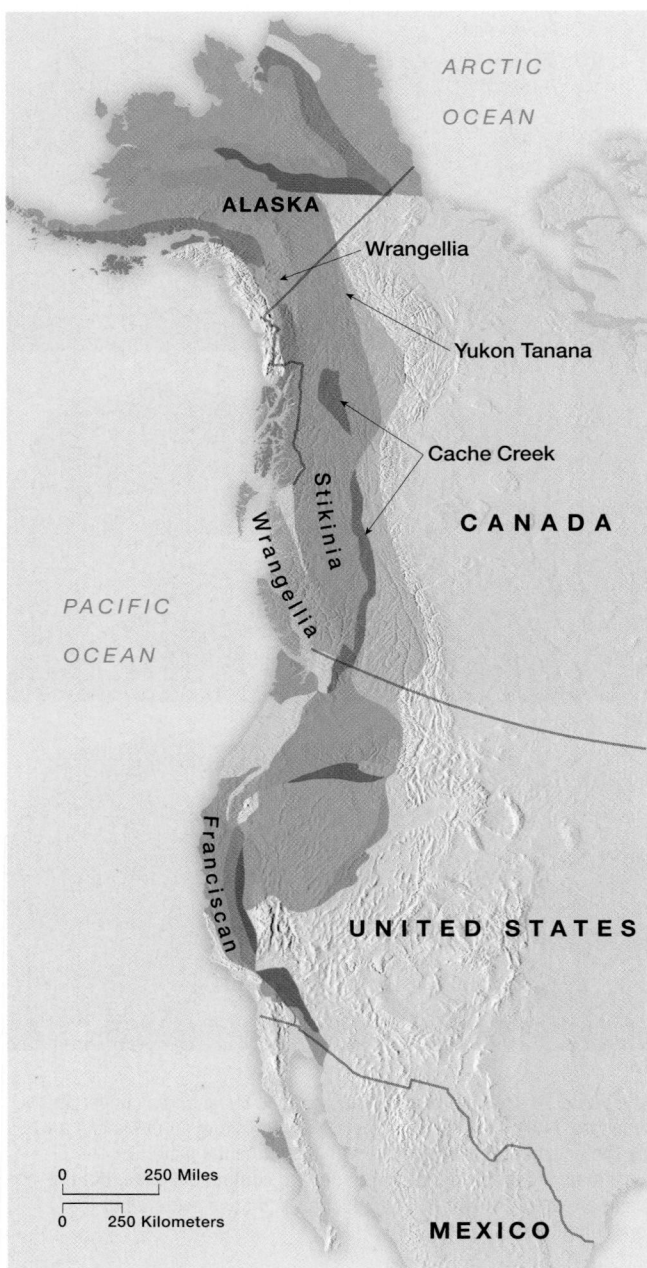

▲ **Figure 14-25** The western part of North America consists of a complicated mixture of terranes that have been accreted to the North American Plate.

of mantle plumes to these overall patterns are still being worked out.

Our present state of knowledge about plate tectonics, however, is ample to provide a firm basis for understanding the patterns of most of the world's major relief features— the size, shape, and distribution of the continents, major mountain ranges, and ocean basins. To understand more localized topographic features, however, we must now turn to less spectacular, but no less fundamental, internal processes that are often directly associated with tectonic movement.

VOLCANISM

Volcanism (or *igneous processes*) is a general term that refers to all the phenomena connected with the origin and movement of molten rock. These phenomena include the well-known explosive volcanic eruptions that are among the most spectacular and terrifying events in all nature, along with much more quiescent events, such as the slow solidification of molten material below the surface.

We noted in Chapter 13 the distinction between *volcanic* (extrusive) and *plutonic* (intrusive) igneous rocks; a similar differentiation is made between extrusive and intrusive volcanism. When magma is expelled onto Earth's surface while still molten, the activity is extrusive and is called *volcanism*; when magma solidifies below the surface it is referred to as *intrusive* or *plutonic activity* and results in intrusive igneous features.

Volcano Distribution

Areas of volcanism are widespread over the world (Figure 14-26), but their distribution is uneven. As we saw earlier in this chapter, volcanic activity is primarily associated with plate boundaries. At a divergent boundary, magma wells up from the interior both by eruption from active volcanoes and by flooding out of fissures. At convergent boundaries where subduction of oceanic lithosphere is taking place, volcanoes are formed in association with the generation of magma. Hot spots are responsible for volcanic and hydrothermal activity in many places such as Yellowstone, Hawai'i, and the Galapagos Islands.

It is apparent from Figure 14-26 that the most notable area of volcanism in the world is around the margin of the Pacific Ocean in the Pacific Ring of Fire (see Figure 14-20)— also called the *Andesite Line* because the volcanoes consist primarily of the volcanic rock andesite. About 75 percent of the world's volcanoes, both active and inactive, are associated with the Pacific Rim.

Volcanic Activity: A volcano is considered active if it has erupted at least once within historical times and is considered likely to do so again. There are about 550 active volcanoes in the world. On average, about 15 of them will erupt this week, 55 this year, and perhaps 160 this decade. Moreover, there will be one or two eruptions per year from volcanoes with no historic activity. In addition to surface eruptions on continents and islands, there is a great deal of underwater volcanic activity; indeed, it is estimated that more than three-fourths of all volcanic activity is undersea activity such as at midocean ridge spreading centers.

Within the conterminous 48 states prior to the 1980 eruption of Mount St. Helens, there was only one volcano classified as active—Lassen Peak in California, which last erupted in 1917 but still occasionally produces gas and steam. A number of other volcanoes, notably California's Mount Shasta and Long Valley Caldera, Washington's Mount Baker and Mount Rainier, and the Yellowstone Caldera show signs of potential activity but have not erupted

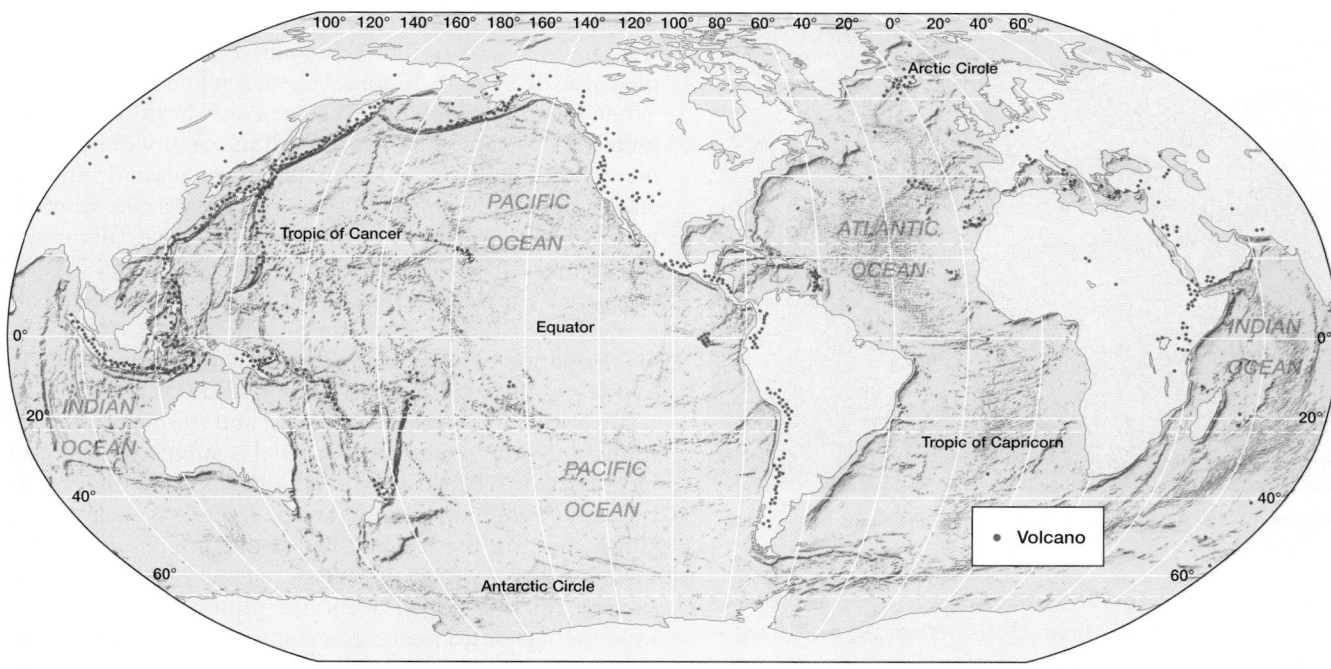

▲ **Figure 14-26** Distribution of volcanoes known to have erupted at some time in the recent geological past. The Pacific Ring of Fire is quite conspicuous.

in recorded time, and there are hundreds of extinct volcanoes, primarily in the West Coast states. Alaska and Hawai'i have many volcanoes, both active and inactive.

Active volcanoes are relatively temporary features of the landscape. Some may have an active life of only a few years, whereas others are sporadically active for thousands of years. At the other end of the scale, new volcanoes are spawned from time to time. Three of the more spectacular recent events were the birth of Surtsey, which rose out of the sea as a new island above a hot spot off the coast of Iceland in 1964, the eruption of an undersea volcano near Tonga in 2009, and a new island appearing in the Red Sea in December 2011 (Figure 14-27).

Despite the destruction they cause, volcanoes do provide vital services to the planet. Much of the water on Earth today was originally released as water vapor during volcanic eruptions during the early history of our planet. Magma also contains elements such as phosphorus, potassium, calcium, magnesium, and sulfur required for plant growth. When this magma is extruded as lava that hardens into rock, the weathering that releases the nutrients into soil may require decades or centuries (Figure 14-28). When the magma is ejected as ash, however, nutrients can be leached into the soil within months. It is no coincidence that Java, one of the most volcanically active parts of the planet, is also one of the world's most fertile areas.

Magma Chemistry and Styles of Eruption

As we saw in the previous chapter, **magma** (molten mineral material below the surface) extruded onto Earth's surface is called **lava** (Figure 14-29). The ejection of lava into

the open air is sometimes volatile and explosive, devastating the area for many kilometers around; in other cases, it is gentle and quiet, affecting the landscape more gradually. All eruptions, however, alter the landscape because they add new material to Earth's surface.

▲ **Figure 14-27** A new volcanic island appeared in the Red Sea in December 2011. The new island is part of the Zubair Group of islands along the Red Sea Rift, just west of Yemen.

▲ **Figure 14-28** Young basalt of the Big Island of Hawai'i.

During an explosive volcanic eruption, solid rock fragments, solidified lava blobs, cinders, and dust—collectively called **pyroclastic** material—as well as gas and steam, may be hurled upward in extraordinary quantities. In some cases, the volcano literally explodes, disintegrating in an enormous self-destructive blast. The supreme

▼ **Figure 14-29** Eruption of Kīlauea Volcano, Hawai'i. Note the streams of very fluid basaltic lava flowing away from the vent toward the left.

example of such self-destruction within historic times was the final eruption of Krakatau, a volcano that occupied a small island in Indonesia between Sumatra and Java. When it exploded in 1883, the noise was heard 2400 kilometers (1500 miles) away in Australia, and 9 cubic kilometers (2.2 cubic miles) of material was blasted into the air. The island disappeared, leaving only open sea where it had been. The *tsunamis* (great seismic sea waves; discussed in Chapter 20) it generated drowned more than 30,000 people, and sunsets in various parts of the world were colored by fine volcanic dust for many months afterward.

The nature of a volcanic eruption is determined largely by the chemistry of the magma that feeds it, although the relative strength of the surface crust and the degree of confining pressure to which the magma is subjected may also be important. The chemical relationships are complex, but the critical component seems to be the relative amount of silica (SiO_2) in the magma. Recall that common magmas include relatively high-silica *felsic* magma (which produces the volcanic rock rhyolite and the plutonic rock granite), intermediate-silica andesitic magma (which produces the volcanic rock andesite and the plutonic rock diorite), and relatively low-silica *mafic* magma (which produces the volcanic rock basalt and the plutonic rock gabbro). See Figure 13-6 in Chapter 13 for a review of igneous rocks resulting from different magma chemistries.

Felsic Magmas: In high-silica felsic magmas, long chains consisting of silicate structures can develop even before crystallization of minerals begins, greatly increasing the *viscosity* (thickness or "stickiness") of the magma. A high silica content also usually indicates cooler magma in which some of the heavier minerals have already crystallized and a considerable amount of gas has already separated. Some of this gas is trapped in pockets in the magma under great pressure. Unlike the more fluid lavas, gas bubbles can rise only slowly through viscous felsic magma. As the magma approaches the surface, the confining pressure is diminished and the pent-up gases are released explosively, generating an eruption in which large quantities of pyroclastic material are ejected from the volcano. Any lava flows are likely to be very thick and slow moving.

Mafic Magmas: On the other hand, mafic magma is likely to be hotter and considerably more fluid because of its lower silica content. Dissolved gases can bubble out of very fluid mafic magma much more easily than from viscous felsic magma. The resulting eruptions usually yield a great outpouring of lava, quietly and without explosions or large quantities of pyroclastic material. (*Quietly* is a descriptive term that is relative and refers to the nonexplosive flow of fluid lava.) The highly active volcanoes of Hawai'i erupt in this fashion.

Intermediate Magmas: Volcanoes with intermediate-silica content andesitic magmas erupt in a style somewhat between that of felsic and mafic magmas: periodically venting fairly fluid andesitic lava flows and periodically having explosive eruptions of pyroclastic material. Many

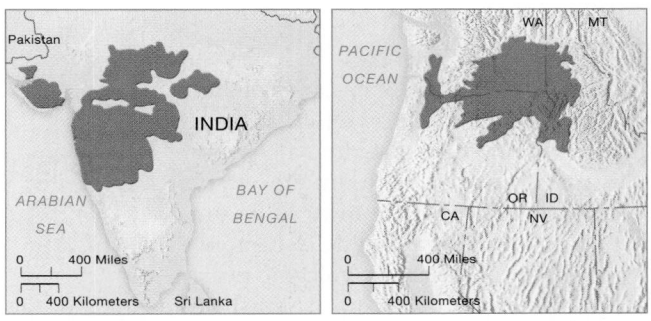

◀ **Figure 14-30** The Giant's Causeway in Northern Ireland. Note the hexagonal columns—a common result when a fluid lava flow cools uniformly.

of the major volcanoes associated with subduction zones are this type.

Learning Check 14-10 **Which factor determines whether a volcano's lava is viscous or fluid, and whether an eruption will be explosive or quiet?**

Lava Flows

Whether originating from a volcanic crater or a crustal fissure, a lava flow spreads outward approximately parallel with the surface over which it is flowing, and this parallelism is maintained as the lava cools and solidifies. Although some viscous flows cling to relatively steep slopes, the vast majority eventually solidify in a horizontal orientation that may resemble the stratification of sedimentary rock, particularly if several flows have accumulated on top of one another.

The topographic expression of a lava flow, then, is often a flat plain or plateau. The strata of sequential flows may be exposed by erosion as streams usually incise very steep-sided gullies into lava flows. The character of the flow surface varies with the nature of the lava and with the extent of erosion, but as a general rule the surface of relatively recent lava flows tends to be extremely irregular and fragmented.

Columnar Basalt: One of the most distinctive of all volcanic landscape features commonly develops from flows of fluid lava such as basalt. When such a lava flow cools uniformly, it contracts and forms a distinctive pattern of vertical *joints* (cracks in the rock), leaving prominent hexagonal columns known as *columnar basalt* (Figure 14-30). Devils Postpile near Yosemite National Park in California, and the Giant's Causeway—or *Clochán an Aifir*—in Northern Ireland are famous examples of columnar basalt.

Flood Basalt: Many of the world's most extensive lava flows were not extruded from volcanic peaks but rather issued from fissures associated with hot spots. The lava that flows out of these vents is nearly always basaltic and frequently comes forth in great volume. As we saw in Figure 14-21, many scientists think that the initial consequence of a large mantle plume reaching the surface can be a huge outpouring of lava. The term **flood basalt** is applied to the vast accumulations of lava that build up, layer upon layer, sometimes covering tens of thousands of square kilometers to depths of many hundreds of meters. A prominent example of flood basalt in the United States is the Columbia Plateau, which covers 130,000 square kilometers (50,000 square miles) in Washington, Oregon, and Idaho (Figure 14-31). Larger outpourings are seen on other continents, most notably the Deccan Traps of India (520,000 square kilometers [200,000 square miles]; *trap* is derived from the Sanskrit word for "step" in reference to the layers of lava flows found here). Over the world as

▲ **Figure 14-31** Two extensive outpourings of flood basalt: the Deccan Traps (also called the Deccan Plateau) in India and the Columbia Plateau in the northwestern United States.

421

TABLE 14-1	Principal Types of Volcanoes			
Volcano Type	Shape and Size	Structure	Magma and Eruption Style	Examples
Shield	Broad, gently sloping mountain; much broader than high; size varies greatly.	Layers of solidified lava flows.	Magma usually basaltic; characterized by quiet eruptions of fluid lava.	Hawaiian Islands; Tahiti
Composite (Stratovolcano)	Steep-sided symmetrical cone; heights to over 3700 m (12,000 ft.).	Layers of lava flows, pyroclastics, and hardened mudflow deposits.	Magma usually intermediate in chemistry, often andesitic; long life span; characterized by both explosive eruptions of pyroclastics and quiet eruptions of lava.	Mt. Fuji, Japan; Mt. Rainier, Washington; Mt. Shasta, California; Mt. Vesuvius, Italy; Mt. St. Helens, Washington
Lava Dome (Plug Dome)	Usually small, typically less than 600 m (2000 ft.) high; sometimes irregular shape.	Solidified lava that was thick and viscous when molten; plug of lava often covered by pyroclastics; frequently occur within the crater of composite volcano.	Magma usually high in silica, often rhyolitic; dome grows by expansion of viscous lava from within; explosive eruptions common.	Lassen Peak, California; Mono Craters, California
Cinder Cone	Small, steep-sided cone; maximum height 500 m (1500 ft.).	Loose pyroclastic material; may be composed of ash or cinder-size pieces.	Chemistry of magma varies, often basaltic; short life span; pyroclastics ejected from central vent; occasionally produce lava flows.	Paricutin, Mexico; Sunset Crater, Arizona

a whole, more lava has issued quietly from fissures than from the combined outpourings of all volcanoes.

Research indicates that the timing of several major flood basalt eruptions in the geologic past correlate with mass extinctions of plants and animals—perhaps caused by the environmental disruption brought by the massive lava flows and "outgassing" (release of volcanic gases) from the eruptions. For example, some scientists now think that the major extinctions about 65 million years ago that ended the reign of the dinosaurs were as much, or more, a consequence of the flood basalt eruptions of the Deccan Traps than of the asteroid impact that occurred at the same time.

Volcanic Peaks  FG1, FG6

Volcanoes are surface expressions of subsurface igneous activity. Often starting small, a volcano may grow into a conspicuous hill or a massive mountain. Many volcanic peaks take the form of a cone that has a symmetrical profile. A common denominator of nearly all volcanic peaks is a crater normally set conspicuously at the apex of the cone. Frequently, smaller subsidiary cones develop around the base or on the side of a principal peak, or even in the crater. Generally, differences in magma, and therefore

Animation
Volcanoes

eruption style, result in different types of volcanic peaks (Table 14-1).

Shield Volcanoes: Basaltic lava tends to flow quite easily over the surrounding surface, forming broad, low-lying **shield volcanoes**, built up of layer upon layer of solidified lava flows with relatively little pyroclastic material. Some shield volcanoes are massive and very high, but they are never steep-sided (Figure 14-32).

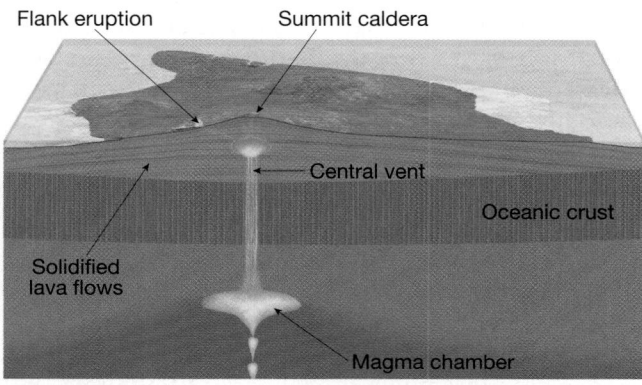

▲ **Figure 14-32** Shield volcanoes, such as those on the Big Island of Hawai'i, have gentle slopes and consist of layer after layer of solidified lava flows with little pyroclastic material.

◀ **Figure 14-33** The gentle slopes of the shield volcano of Mauna Loa on the Big Island of Hawai'i, shown here dusted with snow. The wide, shallow depression at the top of the volcano is known as a *summit caldera*. The shield volcano Mauna Kea is in the distance.

The Hawaiian Islands are composed of numerous shield volcanoes. Produced by the Hawaiian "hot spot," Mauna Loa on the Big Island of Hawai'i is the world's largest volcano (Figure 14-33)—it is more than 9 kilometers (6 miles) high from its base on the floor of the ocean to the top of its summit (Figure 14-34). Kīlauea, currently the most active of the Hawaiian shield volcanoes, is on the southeast flank of Mauna Loa (see Figure 14-29).

Composite Volcanoes: Volcanoes that emit higher silica "intermediate" lavas such as andesite often erupt explosively and tend to develop into symmetrical, steep-sided volcanoes known as **composite volcanoes** or *stratovolcanoes* (Figure 14-35). These mountains build up steep sides by having layers of ejected pyroclastics (ash and cinders) from explosive eruptions alternate with lava flows from nonexplosive eruptions. The pyroclastic material tends to produce the steep slopes, whereas the solidified lava flows hold the pyroclastics together. Famous examples of composite volcanoes include Mt. Fuji in Japan, Mt. Rainier in Washington, and Volcán Popocatépetl near Mexico City (Figure 14-36).

Learning Check 14-11 **Contrast the shape, structure, and formation of *composite volcanoes* and *shield volcanoes*.**

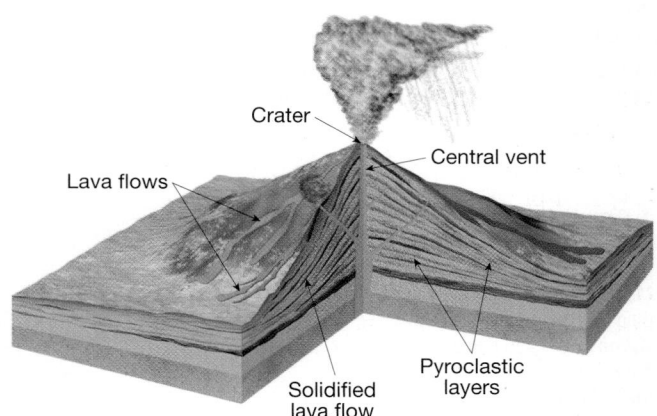

▲ **Figure 14-35** Composite volcanoes consist of layers of pyroclastic material and solidified lava flows.

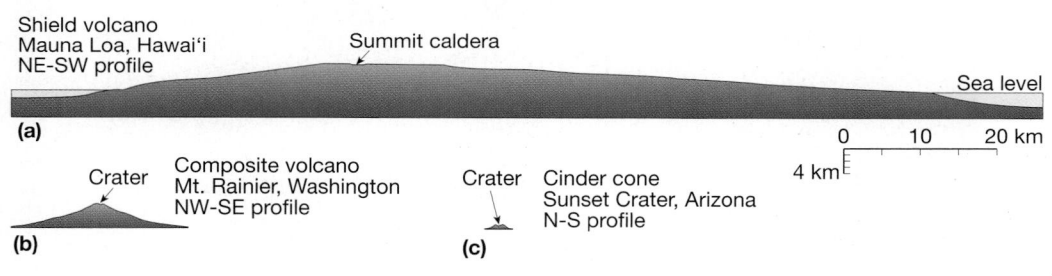

◀ **Figure 14-34** Profiles of volcanoes drawn at identical scales. (a) Mauna Loa, Hawai'i—a shield volcano. (b) Mt. Rainier, Washington—a composite volcano. (c) Sunset Crater, Arizona—a cinder cone.

▶ **Figure 14-36** Volcán Popocatépetl, a composite volcano near Mexico City, erupting in December 2005.

Lava Domes: Lava domes—also called **plug domes**—have masses of very viscous lava such as high-silica rhyolite that are too thick and pasty to flow very far. Instead, lava bulges up from the vent, and the dome grows largely by expansion from below and within (Figure 14-37). The Mono Craters are a chain of young rhyolitic plug domes just to the east of the Sierra Nevada and Yosemite National Park in California—the most recent activity taking place just a few hundred years ago (Figure 14-38).

Lava domes may also develop within the craters of composite volcanoes when viscous lava moves up into the vent. Shortly after the large eruption of Mount St. Helens in 1980, such a lava dome began to develop.

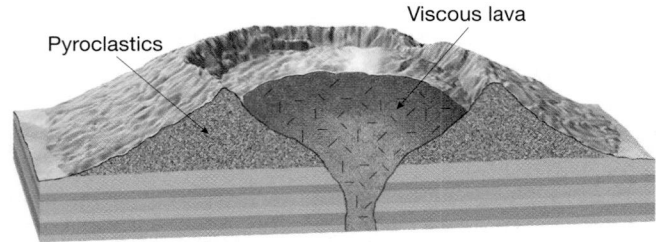

▲ **Figure 14-37** Lava domes (plug domes) develop when viscous lava (commonly rhyolite or dacite) is "squeezed" up into a volcanic vent. The plug of lava may be mantled or surrounded by explosively ejected pyroclastic material.

▶ **Figure 14-38** Crater Mountain is the highest peak in the Mono Craters (also called the Mono Domes) chain of rhyolitic plug domes east of Yosemite National Park and south of Mono Lake in California. Note the irregular summits of these volcanoes, formed by the bulging up of viscous lava.

Cinder Cones: Cinder cones are the smallest of the volcanic peaks. Their magma chemistry varies, but basaltic magma is most common. They are cone-shaped peaks built by the unconsolidated pyroclastic materials that are ejected from the volcanic vent (Figure 14-39). The size of the particles being ejected determines the steepness of the slopes. Tiny particles ("ash") can support slopes as steep as 35 degrees, whereas the larger ejecta ("cinders") will produce slopes up to about 25 degrees. Cinder cones are generally less than 450 meters (1500 feet) high and are often found in association with other volcanoes (Figure 14-40). Lava flows occasionally issue from the same vent that produces a cinder cone.

Calderas: Uncommon in occurrence but spectacular in result is the formation of a **caldera**, which is produced when a volcano explodes, collapses, or does both.

The result is an immense basin-shaped depression, generally circular, that has a diameter many times larger than that of the original volcanic vent or vents. Some calderas are tens of kilometers in diameter.

North America's most famous caldera is Oregon's misnamed Crater Lake (Figure 14-41). Mount Mazama was a composite volcano that reached an estimated elevation of 3660 meters (12,000 feet) above sea level. During a major eruption about 7700 years ago, the walls of Mount Mazama weakened and collapsed as enormous volumes of pyroclastic material were ejected from the volcano (Figure 14-42).

Animation
Formation of
Crater Lake

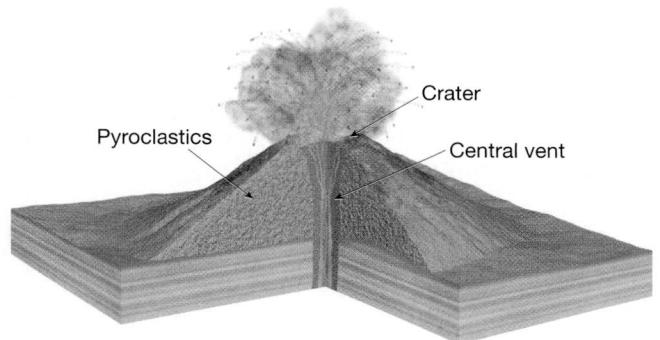

▲ **Figure 14-39** Cinder cones are small volcanoes consisting of pyroclastic material.

▲ **Figure 14-41** Oregon's Crater Lake occupies an immense caldera. Wizard Island represents a more recent subsidiary volcanic cone.

◄ **Figure 14-40** Sunset Crater, in northern Arizona near Flagstaff, is a classic example of a cinder cone volcano.

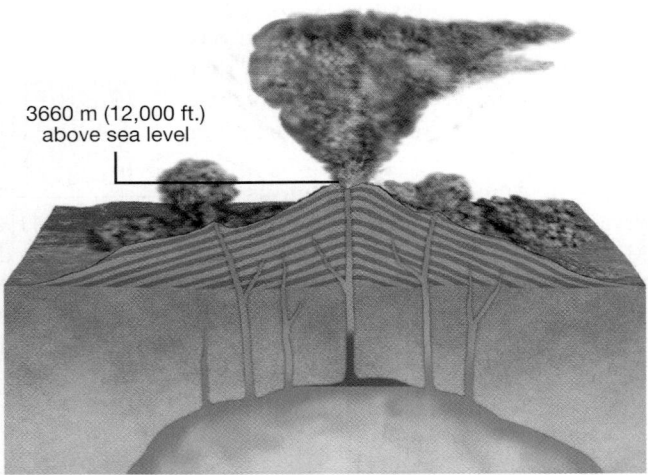

(a) 3660 m (12,000 ft.) above sea level

(b) 2440 m (8000 ft.) above sea level

(c) 1220 m (4000 ft.) above sea level

8 km (5 miles)

Wizard Island

▲ **Figure 14-42** Formation of Crater Lake. (a) Mount Mazama about 7700 years ago. (b) During the cataclysmic eruption, an enormous volume of pyroclastic material erupted from the magma chamber and the volcano collapsed, forming a caldera 1220 meters (4000 feet) deep. (c) The caldera partially filled with water to form a lake; a new fissure formed the volcano known as Wizard Island.

The partial emptying of magma chamber below Mount Mazama may have contributed to this collapse. The final, cataclysmic eruption removed—by explosion and collapse—the upper 1220 meters (4000 feet) of the peak and produced a caldera whose bottom is 1220 meters (4000 feet) below the crest of the remaining rim. Later, half this depth filled with water, creating one of the deepest lakes in North America. A subsidiary volcanic cone has subsequently built up from the bottom of the caldera and now breaks the surface of the lake as Wizard Island (Figure 14-43). Other major calderas in North America

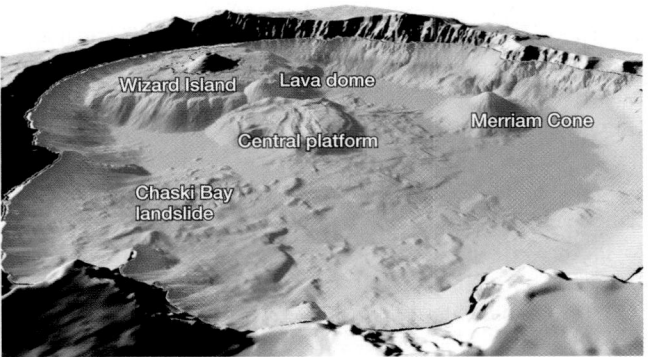

▲ **Figure 14-43** Bathymetry of Crater Lake. This detailed map of the floor of Crater Lake in Oregon shows evidence of postcollapse volcanic activity and massive landslides.

include California's Long Valley Caldera, and the Yellowstone Caldera in Wyoming.

Shield volcanoes may develop *summit calderas* in a different way. When large quantities of fluid lava are vented from rift zones along the sides of a volcano, the magma chamber below the summit can empty and collapse, forming a relatively shallow caldera. Both Mauna Loa and Kīlauea on the Big Island of Hawai'i have calderas that formed in this way (see Figure 14-33).

Learning Check 14-12 How does a *caldera* such as the one now occupied by Crater Lake in Oregon form?

VOLCANIC HAZARDS FG1

Millions of people around the world live in close proximity to active or potentially active volcanoes. In the United States alone, there are more than 50 volcanoes that have erupted within the last 200 years, and others that could well become active in the near geologic future. Some of these volcanoes are located near population centers in Washington, Oregon, California, Alaska, Hawai'i, and the region around Yellowstone National Park. Future eruptions could expose large numbers of people to a wide range of volcanic hazards (Figure 14-44).

Volcanic Gases

A volcano emits large quantities of gas during an eruption. Water vapor makes up the bulk of the gas emitted, but other volcanic gases include carbon dioxide, sulfur dioxide, hydrogen sulfide, and fluorine. The hazards resulting from these gases vary. For example, in 1986 the sudden release of carbon dioxide from a magma chamber beneath Lake Nyos in the country of Cameroon killed 1700 people.

Sulfur dioxide released during an eruption may combine with water in the atmosphere to form a mist of sulfuric acid that falls to the surface as acid rain, harming vegetation and causing corrosion. High in the atmosphere, these same droplets may reflect incoming solar radiation,

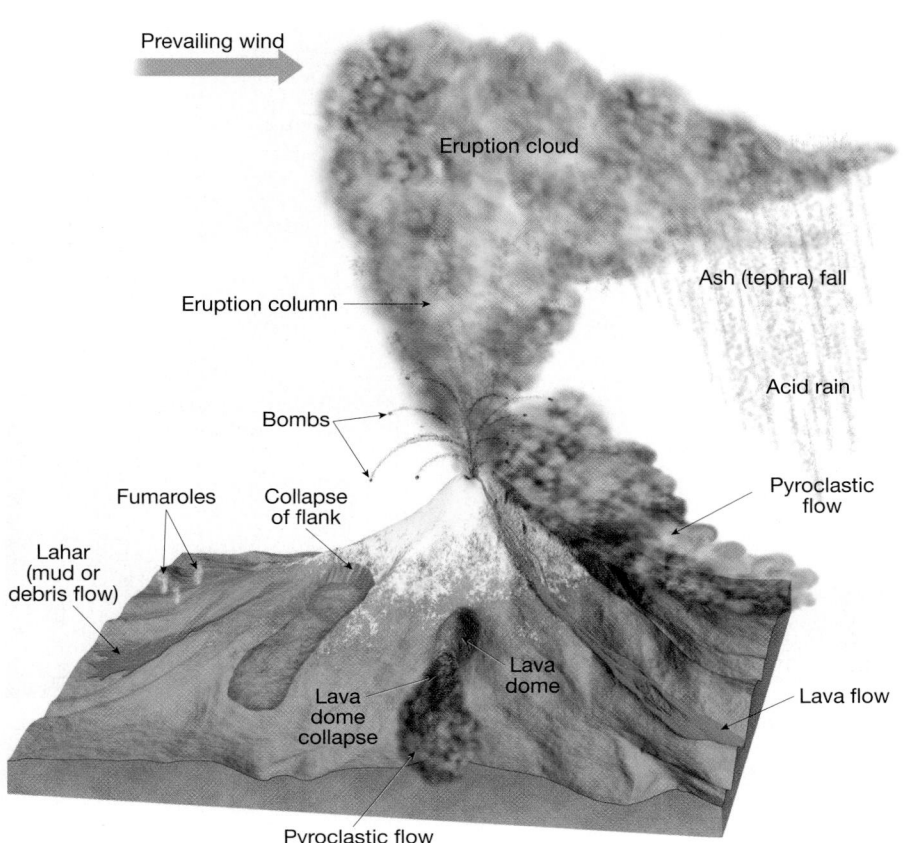

Prevailing wind

Eruption cloud

Eruption column

Ash (tephra) fall

Acid rain

Bombs

Fumaroles

Collapse
of flank

Pyroclastic
flow

Lahar
(mud or
debris flow)

Lava
dome
collapse

Lava
dome

Lava flow

Pyroclastic flow

◀ **Figure 14-44** The hazards associated with a typical composite volcano. Some of these hazards may also occur with other kinds of volcanoes.

altering global weather. As we described in Chapter 8, the large quantities of sulfur dioxide emitted by Mount Pinatubo in the Philippines in 1991 reduced insolation enough to lower global temperatures slightly for more than a year.

Lava Flows

Perhaps surprisingly, lava flows rarely cause loss of life, although they can produce significant property damage. The speed and distance covered by a lava flow depends mostly on its viscosity, which in turn depends on its silica content. Low-silica basaltic lava associated with shield volcanoes, such as those on Hawai'i, tends to be quite fluid and fast moving. Although most basaltic lava flows move more slowly than a person can walk, some flows travel at speeds of over 25 kilometers (15 miles) per hour and cover distances of more than 120 kilometers (75 miles) before congealing. Because the paths taken by lava flows tend to be predictable, they cause few injuries, although many dozens of homes have been destroyed by lava flows from Kīlauea volcano in Hawai'i over the last few decades.

Higher-silica lava, such as the andesitic lava associated with the many composite volcanoes around the rim of the Pacific, tends to be thicker than basaltic lava, usually moving only short distances down the slopes of the volcano. Very viscous rhyolitic lava often does little more than squeeze out of a vent, bulging up to form a lava

dome. Although lava flows from intermediate- and high-silica magmas rarely represent a direct danger to people, the explosive nature of these volcanoes does often produce a number of significant hazards.

Eruption Column and Ash Fall

It is common for composite volcanoes and lava domes to erupt explosively. The violent ejection of pyroclastic material and gases from a volcano can form an *eruption column* reaching altitudes of 16 kilometers (10 miles) or more. Large fragments of solid rock, called volcanic "bombs," drop to the ground immediately around the volcano, whereas smaller fragments of volcanic ash and dust form an enormous *eruption cloud* from which great quantities of ash may fall. A heavy covering of ash can damage crops and even cause the collapse of buildings.

Pyroclastic Flows

The collapse of a lava dome or the rapid subsidence of an eruption column during an explosive eruption of a volcano can lead to a terrifying high-speed avalanche of searing hot gases, ash, and rock fragments known as a **pyroclastic flow**. A pyroclastic flow (sometimes called a *nuée ardente*) can travel down a volcano at speeds of more than 160 kilometers (100 miles) per hour, burning and burying everything in its path (Figure 14-45). Probably the most famous example of a pyroclastic flow took place in 1902 on

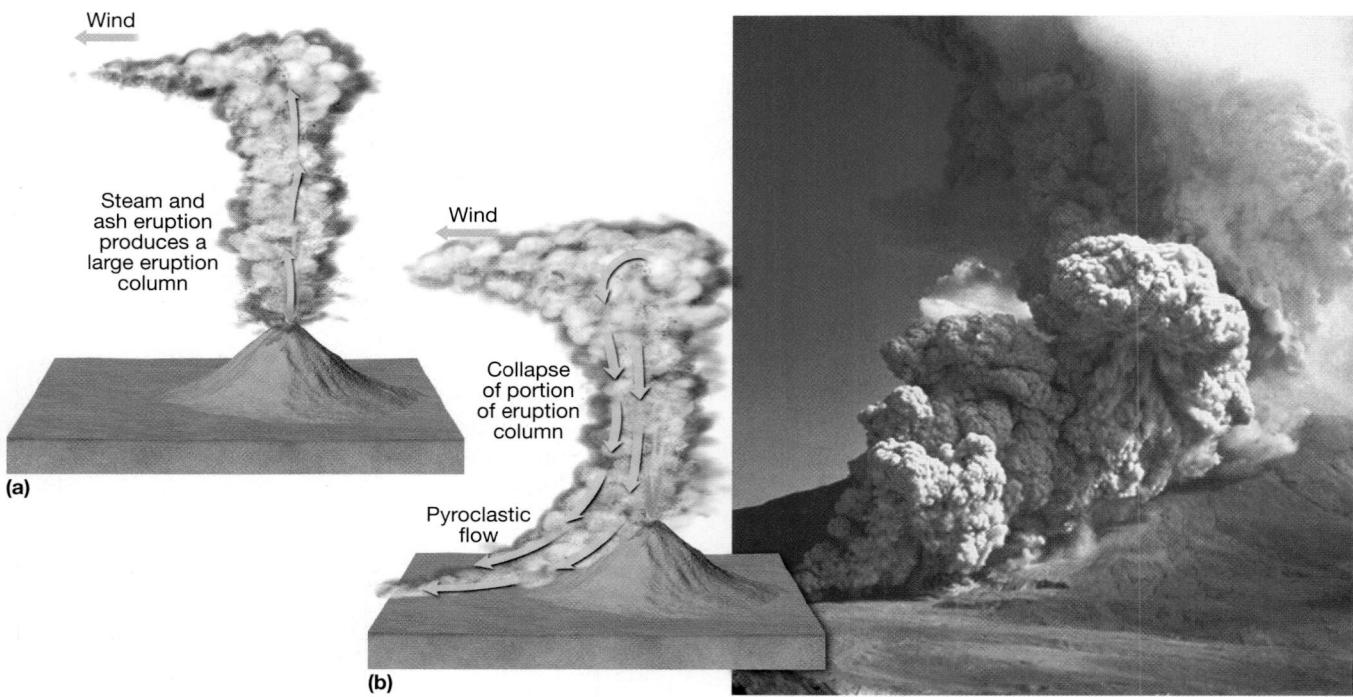

▲ **Figure 14-45** A pyroclastic flow can develop when an eruption column collapses, sending a surge of hot gases and pyroclastic material down the side of a volcano. The photograph shows a pyroclastic flow heading down the flank of Mount St. Helens during an eruption on August 7, 1980.

the Caribbean island of Martinique. An explosive eruption of Mont Pelée sent a massive pyroclastic flow down onto the port city of St. Pierre, destroying the town and killing nearly all of its 28,000 inhabitants in a matter of moments.

More recently, the Unzen volcano complex on the Japanese island of Kyushu began a series of eruptions in 1990. After a period of escalating seismic activity, a lava dome formed in Fugen-dake, a peak adjacent to the large Mayuyama dome. By the spring of 1991, lava blocks were collapsing off the dome, generating hundreds of pyroclastic flows, some of which traveled more than 5 kilometers (3 miles) off the flanks of the volcano. By 1993, pyroclastic flows and volcanic mudflows had destroyed 2000 structures, forced the evacuation of as many as 12,000 local residents, and took the lives of 43 people, including the well-known French filmmakers and volcanologists Maurice and Katia Krafft.

Volcanic Mudflows (Lahars)

One of the most common hazards associated with composite volcanoes are **volcanic mudflows**—also known by their Indonesian name, **lahar**. A loose mantle of ash and pyroclastic flow deposits on the slopes of a volcano can be mobilized easily by heavy rain or by the melting of snow and glaciers during an eruption. The water mixes with unconsolidated pyroclastic material to produce a fast-moving—and sometimes hot—slurry of mud and boulders, flowing with the consistency of wet concrete. Lahars typically flow down stream valleys off the slopes of a volcano, leaving the valley floor buried in thick mud and debris (Figure 14-46). They can reach speeds of over

▼ **Figure 14-46** A lahar from Mount Ruapehu in New Zealand fills the valley of the Whangaehu River in 2007. In 1953, more than 150 people were killed in this same location when the railroad bridge was destroyed by large lahar.

50 kilometers (30 miles) per hour and travel distances of over 80 kilometers (50 miles).

One of the most tragic examples of a lahar took place in 1985 when the Nevado del Ruiz volcano in Colombia produced a mudflow that inundated the town of Armero nearly 50 kilometers (30 miles) away, killing more than 20,000 people.

> **Learning Check 14-13** **Explain the differences between a *pyroclastic flow* and a *volcanic mudflow* (lahar).**

Monitoring Volcanoes

Volcanoes may lie dormant for hundreds of years between major eruptions, and so the volcanic hazards in the surrounding regions are not always evident. In North America, the Cascade Range alone contains more than a dozen potentially active volcanoes, including seven that have exhibited activity since the late 1700s (Figure 14-47). Because of rapidly expanding populations here and elsewhere around the Pacific Rim, increasing numbers of people are now exposed to the same volcanic hazards that have killed thousands in the past.

By the 1970s, a concerted international effort was underway to both assess volcanic hazards and to gain enough knowledge to anticipate the onset of major volcanic eruptions. In the United States, the U.S. Geological Survey and research universities are looking at past historical eruptions as well as evidence from the geological record to map out the most likely paths of pyroclastic flows and lahars from volcanoes such as Mt. Rainier in Washington; Mt. Hood in Oregon; the Yellowstone Caldera; and Mt. Shasta, Lassen Peak, and the Long Valley Caldera in California.

The monitoring of active volcanoes includes measuring slight changes in the slope of a mountain using sensitive "tiltmeters" that can detect swelling of a volcano with magma, measuring variations in gas composition and quantity vented from a volcano that may indicate changes in magma, and monitoring earthquake activity below a volcano—swarms of small earthquakes may indicate the filling of the magma chamber below a volcanic peak. Remote cameras can produce time-lapse movie sequences that document changes to lava domes and other crater features. Especially promising research is pointing toward distinctive seismic patterns that often accompany the onset of major eruptions.

Eruption of Mount St. Helens: In early 1980, Mount St. Helens in Washington, one of the most beautiful volcanic peaks of the Cascades, suddenly came back to life after lying dormant for 123 years and became one of the most studied volcanoes in history. On the morning of May 18, after several months of seismic activity, swelling, and sporadic eruptions of steam and ash, the volcano unleashed a devastating eruption (Figure 14-48).

Animation
The Eruption of Mount St. Helens

With little warning, the entire north slope of the mountain unhinged during an earthquake in an enormous landslide. The landslide depressurized the magma within the volcano, triggering a powerful lateral blast that leveled trees more than 24 kilometers (15 miles) north of the volcano (see Figure 10-19), completely devastating an area of more than 500 square kilometers (200 square miles). At the foot of the volcano, Spirit Lake, once one of the most scenic bodies of water in North America, was instantly laden with debris and dead trees.

Immediately following the lateral blast, a strong vertical explosion of ash and steam began, forming an eruption column that rose to an altitude of 19 kilometers (12 miles) in less than 10 minutes. Over the course of the day, more than 470 billion kilograms (520 million tons) of ash were carried to the east by the prevailing winds. Spokane, Washington, 400 kilometers (250 miles) from the volcano, was in darkness at midday. During the course of the eruption, a series of pyroclastic flows rolled down the mountain, and lahars—some created when the eruption melted snow and

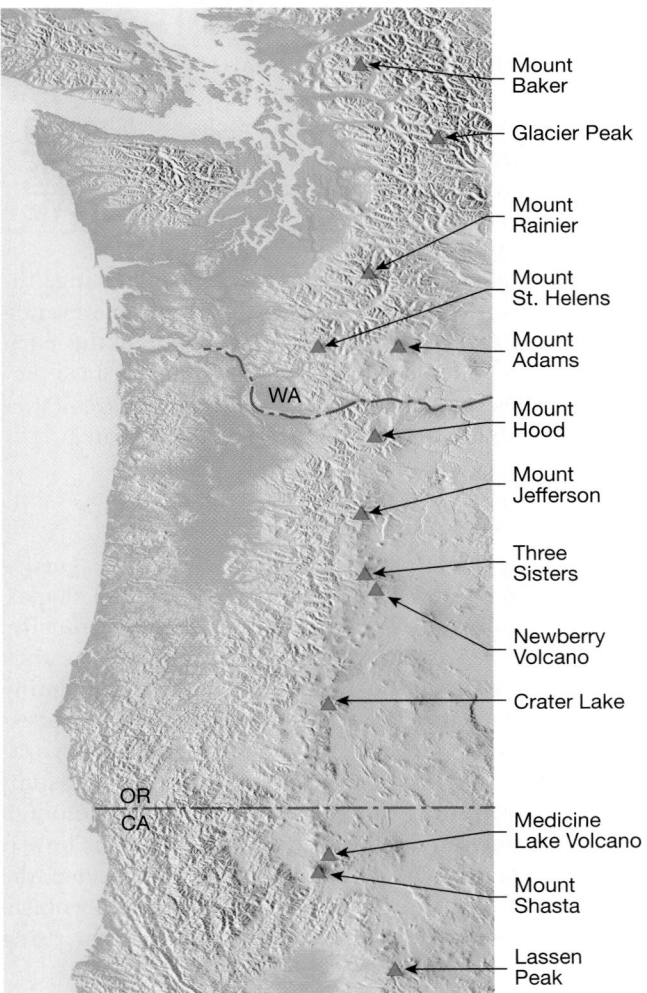

Mount Baker
Glacier Peak
Mount Rainier
Mount St. Helens
Mount Adams
WA
Mount Hood
Mount Jefferson
Three Sisters
Newberry Volcano
Crater Lake
OR
CA
Medicine Lake Volcano
Mount Shasta
Lassen Peak

▲ **Figure 14-47** Prominent volcanoes of the Cascade Range.

▶ **Figure 14-48** (a) Mount St. Helens prior to the 1980 eruption. The peak in the background is Mount Adams. (b) Mount St. Helens after the 1980 eruption. Its posteruption elevation is 400 meters (1300 feet) less than the pre-eruption elevation.

ice that capped the volcano—poured down nearby river valleys. The largest of these lahars carried tons of mud and debris into the Toutle River, where the raging mudflow knocked out every bridge for 48 kilometers (30 miles), overwhelmed the Cowlitz River valley, and clogged the Columbia River shipping channel to less than half of its normal depth of 12 meters (40 feet).

The cataclysmic eruption of May 18, 1980, reduced the elevation of Mount St. Helens by more than 390 meters (1300 feet), removed about 2.8 cubic kilometers (0.67 cubic miles) of rock from the volcano, spread volcanic ash over an area of 56,000 square kilometers (22,000 square miles), caused more than $1 billion in property and economic losses, and killed 57 people.

Now more than 30 years after its last major eruption, Mount St. Helens continues to show activity. In 2004, the volcano had a series of small eruptions, and glaciers inside the crater that had grown back since the 1980 eruption were pushed aside by a bulging new lava dome. In recent years, the volcano has lapsed back into a quiet period. Whether another major eruption comparable to the one in 1980 will occur anytime soon is unclear, although in the long run, Mount St. Helens is quite likely to erupt vigorously again.

It is sobering to realize that the 1980 eruption of Mount St. Helens was not an extraordinarily large volcanic eruption. The 1991 eruption of Mount Pinatubo in the Philippines was more than 10 times larger, and the 1912 eruption of Novarupta in Alaska 30 times larger. It is hoped that the knowledge gained from monitoring Mount St. Helens and other active volcanoes will enable authorities to make informed choices about when and where to evacuate local populations when the next volcano erupts.

INTRUSIVE IGNEOUS FEATURES

FG4, FG5

When magma solidifies below Earth's surface it produces plutonic igneous rock. In general, these types of igneous rocks form structures called **igneous intrusions**. Most such intrusions have no immediate effect on the surface landscape, but sometimes the igneous mass is raised high enough to deform the overlying material and change the shape of the surface. In many cases, the intrusion is eventually exposed at the surface through the action of the external processes, often becoming conspicuous because they are usually resistant to erosion and with the passage of time stand up relatively higher than the surrounding land.

Animation
Igneous Features

Plutons

Pluton is a general term used to refer to intrusive igneous bodies of nearly any size. Intrusions come in all shapes, sizes, and compositions. Moreover, their relationship to overlying or surrounding rock is also quite variable. The intrusive process usually disturbs the preexisting rock. Rising magma makes room for itself by a process called *stoping* (a mining term for ore removal by working upward). The molten, invading magma can assimilate the surrounding or *country rock* or heat it enough to make it flow out of the way, or either split or bow it upward. Adjacent to the area the magma has invaded, the country rock usually experiences contact metamorphism from being exposed to the heat and pressure of the rising intrusion.

Although there is almost infinite variety in the forms assumed by igneous intrusions, most can be broadly

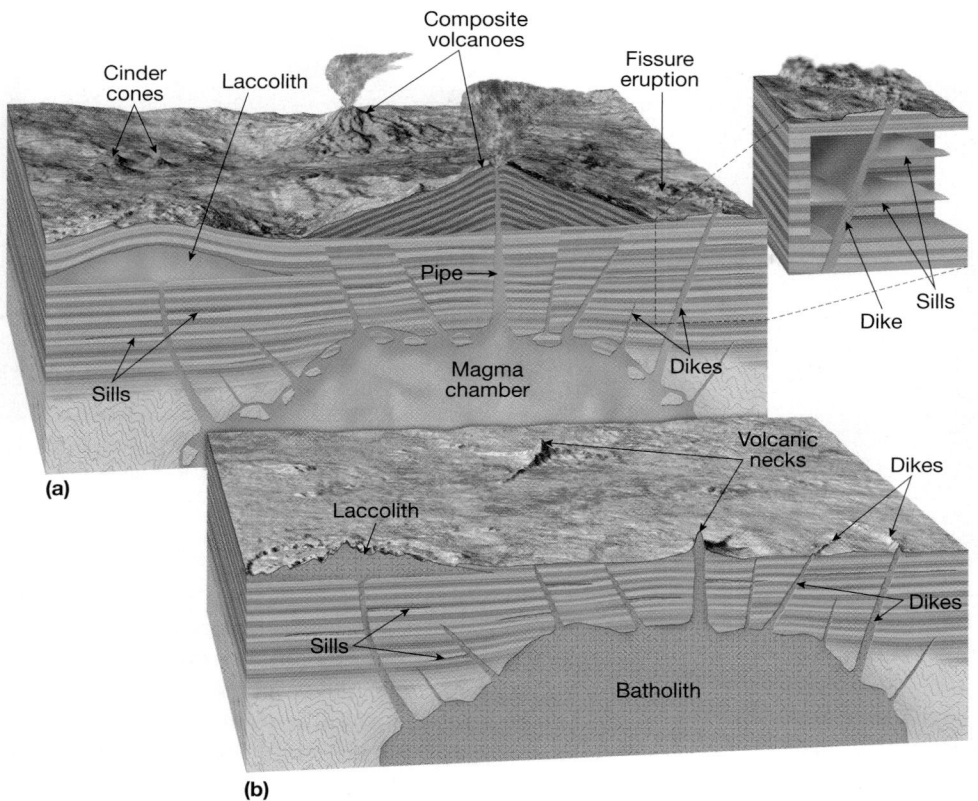

(a)

(b)

◀ **Figure 14-49** The formation of common types of igneous intrusions. (a) Volcanic eruptions and intrusion of magma. (b) After erosion.

classified according to a scheme that contains only a few types (Figure 14-49).

Batholiths: By far the largest and most amorphous intrusion is the **batholith**, which is a subterranean igneous body of enormous size (typically with a surface area of at least 100 square kilometers [40 square miles]) and perhaps of unknown depth. A large batholith may be comprised of dozens of plutons, perhaps emplaced as a series of "pulses" of magma over periods of millions of years. The term *stock* is sometimes used to refer to similar but smaller igneous intrusions of indefinite depth.

Batholiths form the core of many major mountain ranges. Such notable ranges as the Sierra Nevada in California, Idaho's Sawtooth Mountains, and Colorado's Front Range were created at least partially by the uplift of massive batholiths (Figure 14-50). Almost all the plutonic bedrock exposed in these ranges consists of granite or granodiorite (a felsic plutonic rock with a mineral composition between that of granite and diorite see Figure 13-6), now exposed after the extensive overburden of other rocks eroded away.

Volcanic Necks: More limited still but very prominent where it does occur is a *volcanic neck*, a small, sharp spire that rises abruptly above the surrounding land. It represents the pipe, or throat, of an old volcano that filled with solidified lava after its final eruption. Millennia of erosion

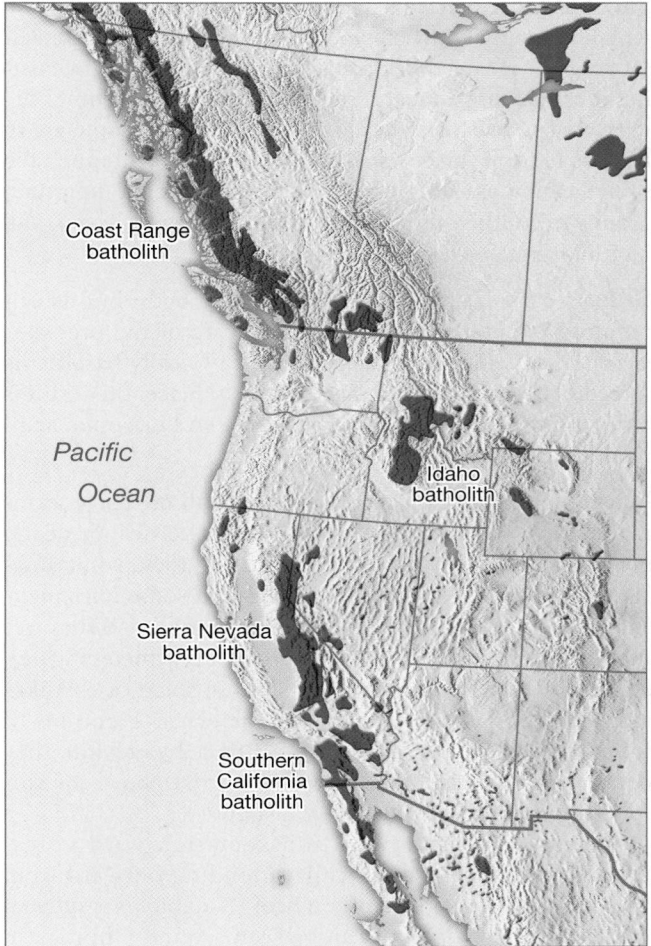

▶ **Figure 14-50** The major batholiths of western North America. These extensive intrusions are mostly associated with a former subduction boundary along the western edge of the North American Plate.

▲ Figure 14-51 Shiprock in northwestern New Mexico is a prime example of a volcanic neck. It rises 490 meters (1600 feet) above the surrounding landscape. A *dike* extends to the left away from Shiprock.

▲ Figure 14-52 The erosion of less resistant surrounding material has left this dike standing as an abrupt natural wall. This scene is in southern Colorado near La Veta.

have removed the less resistant material that made up the cone, leaving the harder, lava-choked neck as a conspicuous remnant (Figure 14-51).

Laccoliths: A specialized form of intrusion is the *laccolith*, which is produced when slow-flowing, usually viscous felsic magma, is forced between horizontal layers of preexisting rock forming a mushroom-shaped mass that domes the overlying strata. Many laccoliths are small, but some are so large as to form the cores of hills or mountains in much the same fashion as batholiths. Several well-known mountain groups in southeastern Utah such as the Henry, Abajo, and La Sal Mountains have laccolithic cores.

Sills: A *sill* is also a long, thin intrusive body, but its orientation is determined by the structure of the preexisting rocks. It is formed when magma, typically basaltic, is forced between strata that are already in place; the result is often a horizontal igneous sheet between horizontal sedimentary layers.

Dikes: One of the most widespread of all intrusive forms is the **dike**, formed by the intrusion of a vertical or nearly vertical sheet of magma into preexisting rock, sometimes forcing its way into vertical fractures and sometimes melting its way upward. Dikes are notable because they are vertical, narrow (a few centimeters to a few meters wide), and usually quite resistant to erosion. In some cases, dikes are quite long, extending for kilometers or even tens of kilometers. When exposed at the surface by erosion, they commonly form sheer-sided walls that rise above the surrounding terrain, as Figure 14-52 shows.

Dikes are often found in association with volcanoes, occurring as radial walls extending outward from the volcano like spokes of a wheel. Notable examples of radial dike development can be seen around Shiprock in

northwestern New Mexico (see Figure 14-51) and around the Spanish Peaks in south-central Colorado.

A special kind of dike complex is found below the layers of basaltic lava on the ocean floor. A sequence of *sheeted dikes*—one vertical dike right next to another—develops in a midocean ridge spreading center as basaltic magma is injected into the ever-spreading gap produced by the diverging plates.

> **Learning Check 14-14** **What are the differences and similarities among a *batholith*, a *laccolith*, and a *dike*?**

Veins: Least prominent among igneous intrusions but widespread in occurrence are thin *veins* of igneous rock that may occur individually or in profusion. They are commonly formed when hydrothermal fluids are forced into small fractures in the preexisting rocks.

FOLDING

Tectonism: Rocks may be bent or broken in a variety of ways in response to great pressure exerted either in the crust or the mantle. *Tectonism* (or *diastrophism*) is a general term that refers to such deformation of Earth's crust.

Sometimes the *stress* (pressure exerted on an object) that results in tectonism is caused by the rise of molten material from below. In some cases the stress is clearly the result of plate movement, but in other cases it may be unrelated directly to plate boundaries. Whatever the causes of tectonism, the results are often conspicuous in the landscape. Tectonic movements are particularly obvious in sedimentary rocks because nearly all sedimentary strata are initially deposited in a horizontal or near-horizontal attitude—so if they now are bent, broken, or tilted, we know that they have clearly experienced tectonism (Figure 14-53).

▲ **Figure 14-53** Folded and faulted sedimentary strata in a road cut near Los Angeles.

In this chapter we describe two types of tectonism—*folding* and *faulting*. We begin with folding.

The Process of Folding

When crustal rocks are subjected to stress, particularly lateral compression, they are often deformed by being bent in a process called **folding**. The notion of folding is sometimes difficult to conceptualize. Our common experience is that rocks are hard and brittle. If subjected to stresses, they might be expected to break—bending is harder to visualize. In nature, however, when great pressure is applied for long periods, particularly in an enclosed, heated, buried, subterranean environment, the result is often a slow plastic deformation that can produce folded structures of incredible complexity. Folding can occur in any kind of rock, but

Animation
Folding

it is often most recognizable when once-flat sedimentary strata have been deformed.

Folding can take place at almost any scale. Some folds can be measured in no more than centimeters, whereas others can develop over such broad areas that crest and trough are tens of kilometers apart.

Types of Folds

Structural geologists recognize many kinds of folds. For introductory physical geography, however, only a few terms are necessary (Figure 14-54). A *monocline* is a one-sided fold—a slope connecting two horizontal or gently inclined strata. A simple symmetrical upfold is an **anticline**, and a simple downfold is a **syncline**. Also relatively common is an upfold that has been pushed so extensively from one side that it becomes oversteepened enough to have a reverse orientation on the other side; such a structure is referred to as an *overturned fold*. If the pressure is enough to break the oversteepened fold and cause a shearing movement, the result is an *overthrust fold*, which causes older rock to ride above younger rock.

Topographic Features Associated with Folding

The simplest relationship between structure and topography, and one that often occurs in nature, finds the upfolded anticlines producing ridges and the downfolded synclines forming valleys. The converse relationship is also possible, however, with valleys developing on the anticlines and ridges on the synclines (Figure 14-55). This inverted topography is most easily explained by the effects of *tension* (pulling apart) and *compression* (pushing together) on the folded strata. Where a layer is arched over an upfold, tension cracks can form and provide easy footholds for erosional processes to remove materials and incise downward into the underlying strata. Conversely, the compression that acts on the downfolded beds increases their density and therefore their resistance to erosion. Thus, over a long period of time, the upfolds may be eroded away faster than

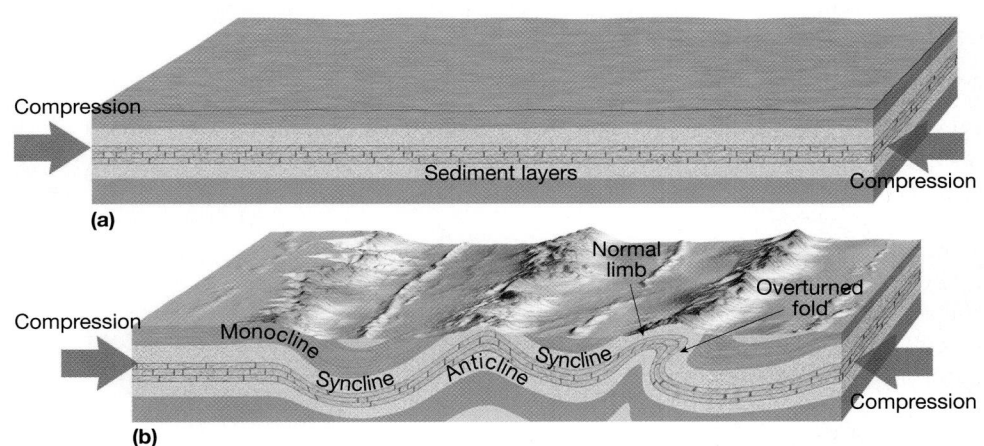

◀ **Figure 14-54** The development of folded structures. (a) Compressive stresses cause sedimentary strata that are initially horizontal to fold. (b) The basic types of folds.

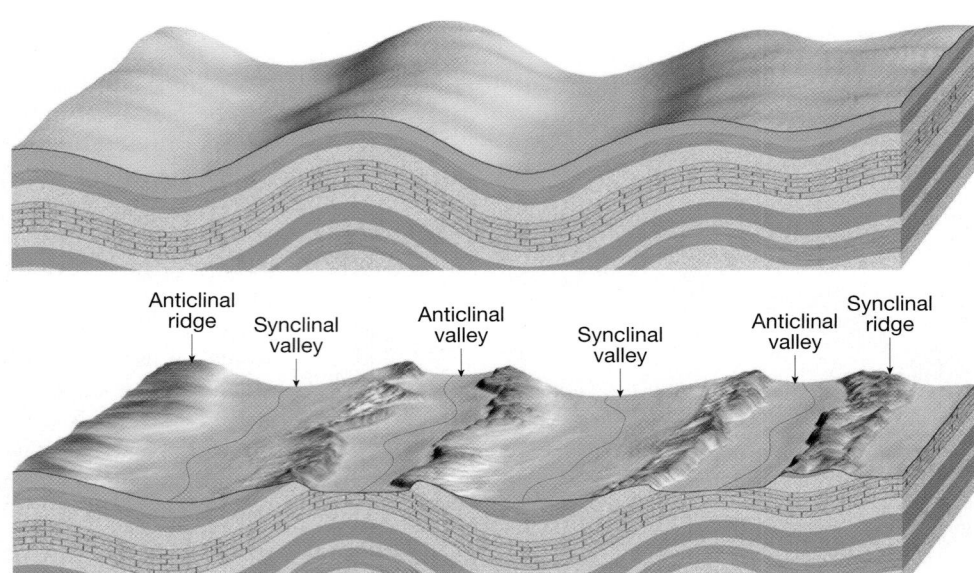

▶ **Figure 14-55** Formation of anticlinal valleys and synclinal ridges.

the downfolds, producing *anticlinal valleys* and *synclinal ridges*.

All these types of folding, as well as many variations, are found in what is called the Ridge-and-Valley section of the Appalachian Mountains, a world-famous area noted for its remarkably parallel sequence of mountains and valleys developed from folds (Figure 14-56). The section extends for about 1600 kilometers (1000 miles) in a northeast-southwest direction across parts of nine states, with a width that varies from 40 to 120 kilometers (25 to 75 miles).

> **Learning Check 14-15** What are *synclines* and *anticlines*, and what kind of topography is associated with them?

▼ **Figure 14-56** The prominently folded Appalachian Mountains are clearly shown in this shaded relief map of south-central Pennsylvania.

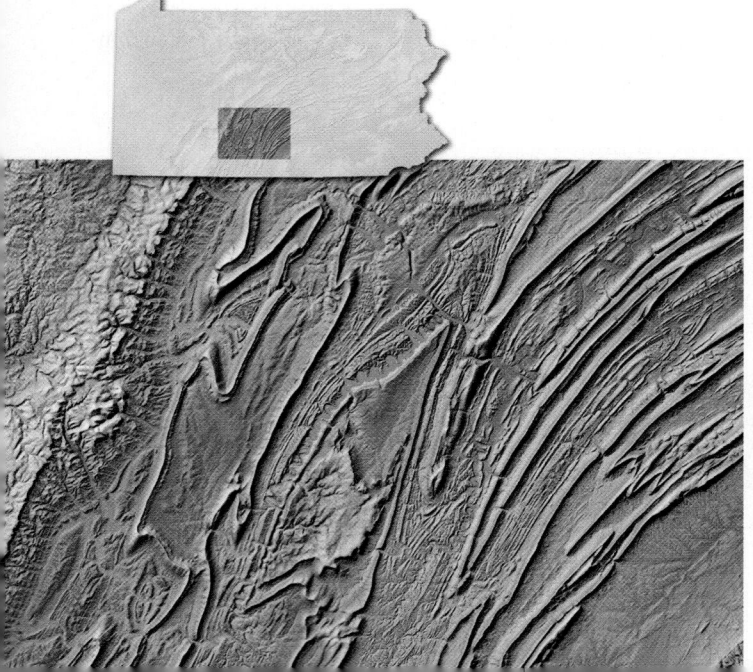

FAULTING  FG3, FG9

Another prominent result of tectonism is the breaking apart of rock structures. When rock is broken with accompanying displacement (movement of the crust on one or both sides of the break), the action is called **faulting** (Figure 14-57). The displacement can be vertical or horizontal or a combination of both. Faulting usually takes place along zones of weakness in the crust; such an area is referred to as a *fault zone*, and the intersection of that zone with Earth's surface is called a *fault line*.

Major faults penetrate many kilometers into Earth's crust. Indeed, the deeper fault zones can serve as conduits to allow both water and magma from inside Earth to approach the surface. Frequently springs are found along fault lines, sometimes with hot water gushing forth. Volcanic activity is also associated with some fault zones as magma forces its way upward in the zone of weakness.

Movement of crust along a fault zone is sometimes very slow, but it commonly occurs as a sudden rupture. A single rupture may result in a displacement of only a few centimeters or so, but in some cases the movement may be as much as 5 or 10 meters (15 or 30 feet). Successive ruptures may be years or even centuries apart, but the cumulative

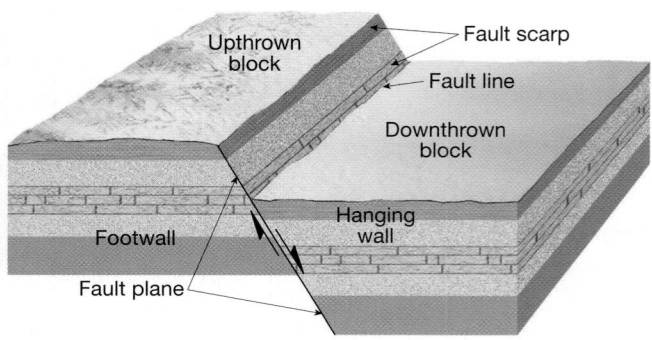

▲ **Figure 14-57** A simple fault structure.

displacement over millions of years could conceivably amount to hundreds of kilometers horizontally and tens of kilometers vertically. It is the sudden rupture and displacement along a fault that cause most large earthquakes, such as the one that devastated Haiti in 2010—see the box, "People and the Environment: The 2010 Haiti Earthquake."

Types of Faults  FG12

Although structural geologists recognize more than a dozen kinds of faults, they can be generalized into four principal types on the basis of direction and angle of movement (Figure 14-58). Two types involve displacement that is mostly

Animation
Faulting

▲ **Figure 14-59** The Calaveras Fault, one of the strike-slip faults in the San Andreas Fault system, runs through the town of Hollister, California. Dramatic evidence of its activity is shown by this offset wall and sidewalk.

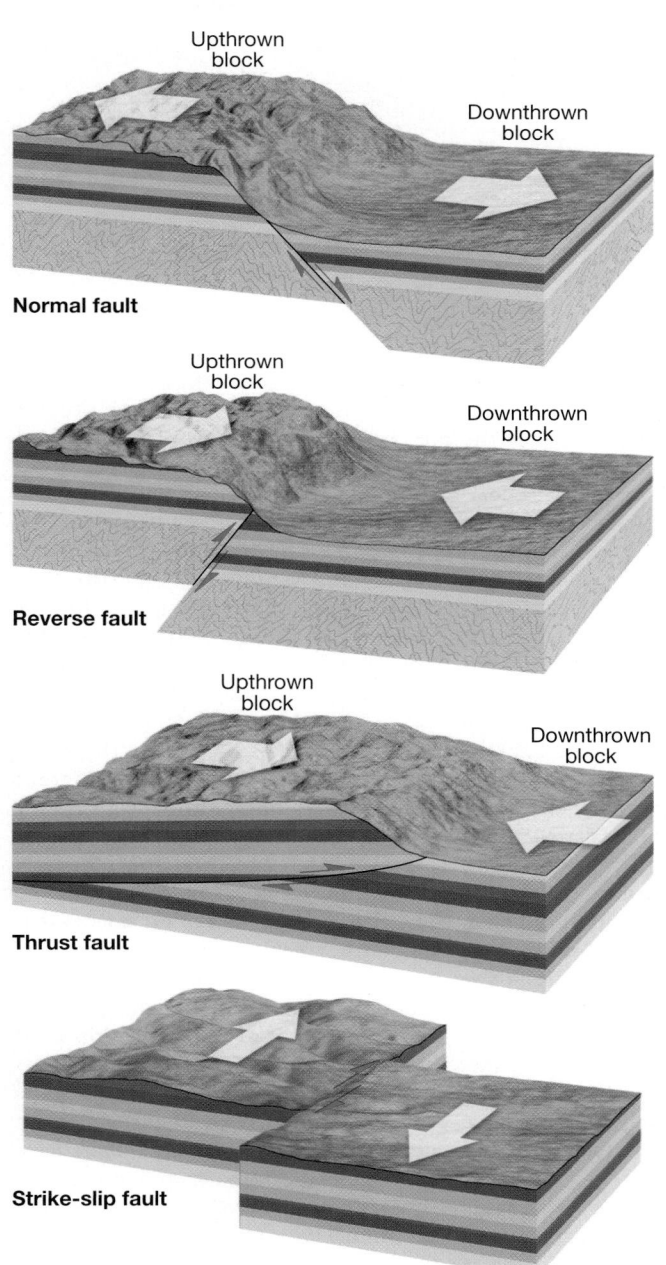

▲ **Figure 14-58** The principal types of faults. The large arrows show the direction of stress.

vertical, a third encompasses only horizontal movement, and the fourth includes both horizontal and vertical offsets:

1. **Normal faults:** A normal fault results from *tension stresses* (pulling apart or extension) in the crust. It produces a very steeply inclined fault zone, where the upper block slides down the fault plane "normal" to the sense of gravity. A prominent *fault scarp* is usually formed.

2. **Reverse faults:** A reverse fault is produced from *compression stresses* (pushing together), where the upper block slides up the incline of the fault plane in "reverse" of the sense of gravity, so that the fault scarp would be severely oversteepened if erosion did not act to smooth the slope somewhat.

3. **Thrust faults:** More complicated in structure and more impressive in their dynamics are **thrust faults** (or *overthrust faults*), in which compression forces the upthrown block to override the downthrown block at a relatively low angle, sometimes for many kilometers. Overthrusting occurs frequently in mountain building, resulting in unusual geologic relationships such as older strata being piled on top of younger rocks. Both thrust faults and reverse faults are commonly associated with subduction zones and continental collision zones.

4. **Strike-slip faults:** In a **strike-slip fault** the movement is horizontal (side-to-side), with the adjacent blocks being displaced laterally relative to each other (Figure 14-59). Strike-slip faults are a consequence of *shear stresses* (stress causing two parallel surfaces to slide past one another). Transform faults described earlier in this chapter are one variety of strike-slip fault.

Learning Check 14-16 Contrast the direction of stress and displacement along *normal, reverse,* and *strike-slip faults.*

The 2010 Haiti Earthquake

On the afternoon of January 12, 2010, a magnitude 7.0 earthquake struck the city of Port-au-Prince, Haiti. The loss of life and damage was staggering. The exact death toll may never be known, but at least 85,000 people were killed, with some Haitian government reports estimating that over 300,000 died. Immediately following the earthquake, 1.5 million people were left homeless, and even two years after the earthquake, perhaps 500,000 people were still living in emergency camps.

Haiti is by most measures the poorest country in the Western Hemisphere and the earthquake crippled its fragile infrastructure. Large sections of the capital Port-au-Prince and nearby cities were leveled or extensively damaged (Figure 14-A). Many government buildings, schools, and public services were in ruin, including every hospital in the capital city. In October 2010, cholera broke out and killed an additional 3000, and to add to the misery of the Haitian people, in November 2010, heavy rain from Hurricane Tomas brought widespread flooding and further damage.

Tectonic Setting: The Caribbean island of Hispaniola—the eastern half of

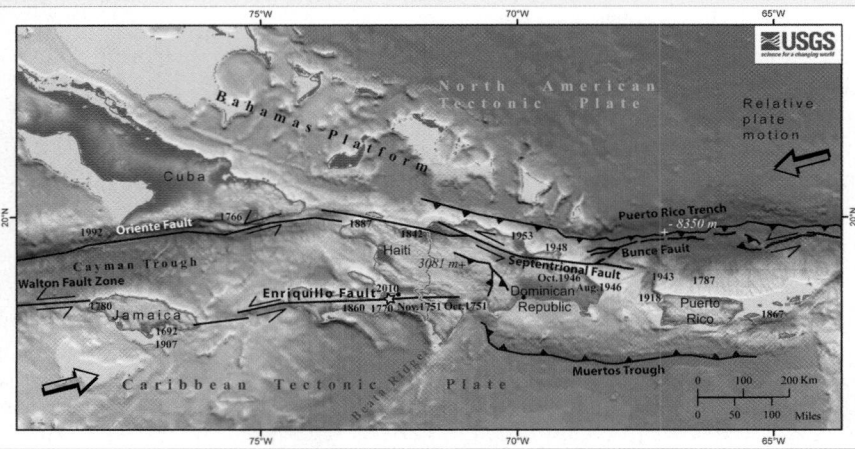

▲ **Figure 14-B** Haiti is bounded by two major strike-slip faults along the transform boundary between the North American Plate and the Caribbean Plate.

▲ **Figure 14-A** Damage in Port-au-Prince, Haiti, following the January 2010 earthquake.

which is the country of the Dominican Republic and the western half the country of Haiti—sits along a portion of the splintered transform boundary between the North American Plate and the Caribbean Plate (Figure 14-B). Here, the Caribbean Plate is moving at an average long-term rate of about 20 millimeters (0.8 inches) per year to the east relative to the North American Plate. On Hispaniola, the accumulated strain from this lateral motion is periodically released by displacement along two roughly parallel strike-slip faults—the Septentrional Fault along the northern coast of the island and the Enriquillo-Plantain Garden Fault along the southern coast. The 2010 earthquake occurred along the southern fault zone that runs just south of Port-au-Prince. This fault was the likely source of large earthquakes in 1751, 1770, and 1860, but no large earthquakes had occurred along this fault in many decades.

Why So Devastating? Although this was a large earthquake, the loss of life and damage was much greater in Haiti than from roughly similar-size earthquakes near large metropolitan areas in places such as California and Japan over the last few decades. The 1971 San Fernando Earthquake killed 65, the 1989 Loma Prieta Earthquake killed 63, and the 1994 Northridge Earthquake killed 57—even the 1995 Kobe Earthquake in Japan that killed more than 6400 people didn't approach the level of damage in Haiti. Although two earthquakes of exactly the same magnitude can produce quite different effects depending on the local geology and depth of fault rupture, the most important differences in damage usually have to do with local building codes.

Seismic engineers often say, "Earthquakes don't kill people, buildings do." Following each major earthquake in California, for example, engineers review the damage and try to determine what changes in building design or construction can prevent building collapse or severe damage in the next quake. In recent decades, tens of millions of dollars have been invested in earthquake retrofitting public buildings and infrastructure in California—an investment that poor countries such as Haiti simply cannot afford.

▼ **Figure 14-60** The western slope of the Sierra Nevada is long and gentle, whereas the eastern slope is short and steep. (a) This gentle-steep combination is the result of enormous block faulting on the eastern side. (b) The steep east side of the Sierra Nevada Mountains in California is a prominent fault scarp.

Fault Scarps: Fault lines are often marked by prominent topographic features. Most obvious perhaps are **fault scarps**—steep cliffs that represent the edge of a vertically displaced block (see Figure 14-57). Although most commonly associated with normal faulting, slight amounts of vertical displacement along strike-slip faults may also leave a scarp. Some fault scarps are as much as 3 kilometers (2 miles) high and extend for more than 150 kilometers (100 miles) in virtually a straight line. The abruptness of their rise, the steepness of their slope, and the linearity of their orientation combine to make some fault scarps extremely spectacular features in the landscape.

Landforms Associated with Normal Faulting FG4, FG6

Under extensional stresses, a surface block may be faulted along one side without any faulting or uplift on the other. When this happens, the block is tilted asymmetrically, producing a steep slope along the fault scarp and a relatively gentle slope on the other side of the block. The classic example of such a **tilted fault-block mountain** range (also simply called a **fault-block mountain**) is California's

Sierra Nevada (Figure 14-60), an immense block nearly 640 kilometers (400 miles) north–south and about 96 kilometers (60 miles) east–west. The spectacular eastern face is a fault scarp that has a vertical relief of about 3 kilometers (about 2 miles) in a horizontal distance of only about 20 kilometers (12 miles). In contrast, the general slope of the western flank of the range, from crest toward its "hinge line" (the line along which the gentle side begins to rise), covers a horizontal distance of more than 80 kilometers (50 miles). The shape of the range has of course been modified by other processes, but its general configuration was determined by block faulting.

Another occurrence is the relative uplift of a block of land between two parallel faults, an action that produces a structure called a **horst** (Figure 14-61). Frequently such horsts are the result of the land on both sides being downthrown rather than the block itself being uplifted. In either case, the horst may take the form of a plateau or a mountain mass with two steep, straight sides.

At the other extreme is a **graben**—a block of land bounded by parallel faults in which the block has been relatively downthrown, producing a distinctive structural valley with straight, steep-sided fault scarps on both sides.

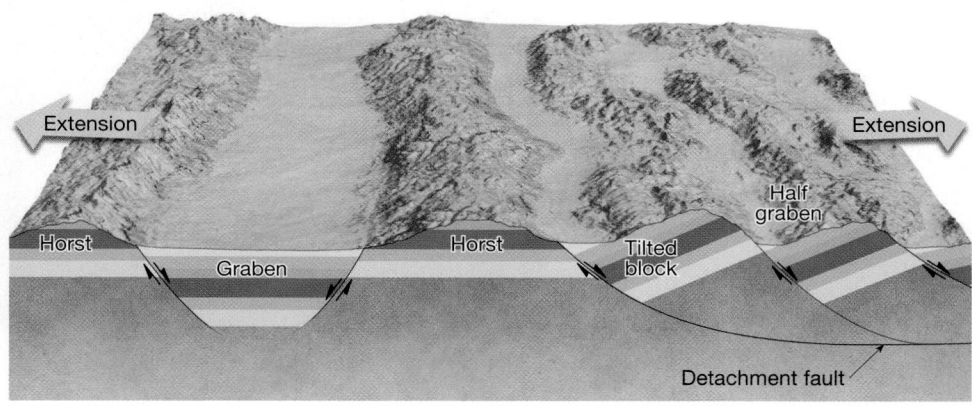

◄ **Figure 14-61** Landforms associated with tensional stresses and normal faulting. Horsts and grabens are bound by faults on both sides, while tilted blocks have been faulted along just one side, forming fault block mountains and "half grabens." Extension may also result in detachment faults, where a steep normal fault ties in with a nearly horizontal fault below.

Tilted fault-block mountains, grabens, and horsts may occur side by side. The basin-and-range region of the western United States (covering most of Nevada and portions of surrounding states; see Figure 18-27) is a vast sequence of tilted fault-block mountains and *half-grabens* (basins formed by blocks tilting down along just one fault), along with a few true grabens and horsts. As the basin-and-range region undergoes sustained extensional faulting, the landscape continues to spread and develop along normal faults and *detachment faults*. Detachment faults form where steeply dipping normal faults tie into low angle (or nearly horizontal) faults below the surface that develop along the boundary between brittle crustal rocks above and more ductile crustal rocks below.

Rift Valleys: Where a divergent plate boundary develops within a continent, the resulting downfaulted grabens occasionally extend for extraordinary distances as linear valleys enclosed between steep fault scarps. Such lengthy troughs are called *rift valleys* (see Figure 14-14), and they comprise some of Earth's most notable structural lineaments, particularly the Great East African Rift Valley.

Landforms Associated with Strike-Slip Faulting  FG3, FG12

A wide variety of landforms can result from strike-slip faulting (Figure 14-62). The surface trace of a large strike-slip fault may be marked by a **linear fault trough** or valley, formed by repeated movement and fracturing of rock within the fault zone. Small depressions known as *sags* develop through the settling of rock within the fault zone, and may become filled with water to form **sag ponds**. Linear ridges and scarps trending parallel to the trace of the fault may develop from slight vertical displacement that may occur along a strike-slip fault.

Perhaps the most conspicuous landform produced by strike-slip faulting is an **offset stream** (see Figure 14-62).

Streams flowing across the fault are displaced by periodic fault movement or diverted when a *shutter ridge* is faulted in front of a drainage channel, closing off a valley.

> **Learning Check 14-17**   **Explain the formation of** *grabens* **and** *offset streams.*

EARTHQUAKES  FG2, FG3

Usually, but not exclusively, associated with faulting is the abrupt shaking of the crust known as an *earthquake*. The movement varies from mild, imperceptible tremors to wild shaking that can persist for several minutes.

An **earthquake** is essentially a vibration in Earth produced by shock waves resulting from a sudden displacement along a fault (earthquakes may also develop from the movement of magma or sudden ground subsidence). The fault movement allows an abrupt release of energy, usually after a long, slow accumulation of strain. Although a fault rupture can take place at the surface, displacement can also take place at considerable depth—as deep as 600 kilometers (375 miles) beneath the surface in the case of subduction zones.

Seismic Waves

The energy released in an earthquake moves through Earth in several different kinds of seismic waves that originate at the center of fault motion, called the *focus* of the earthquake (Figure 14-63). These waves travel outward in widening circles, like the ripples produced when a rock is thrown into a pond, gradually diminishing in amplitude with increasing distance from the focus. The strongest shocks, and greatest crustal vibration, are often felt on the ground directly above the focus, at the location known as the **epicenter** of the earthquake.

Animation
Seismic Waves

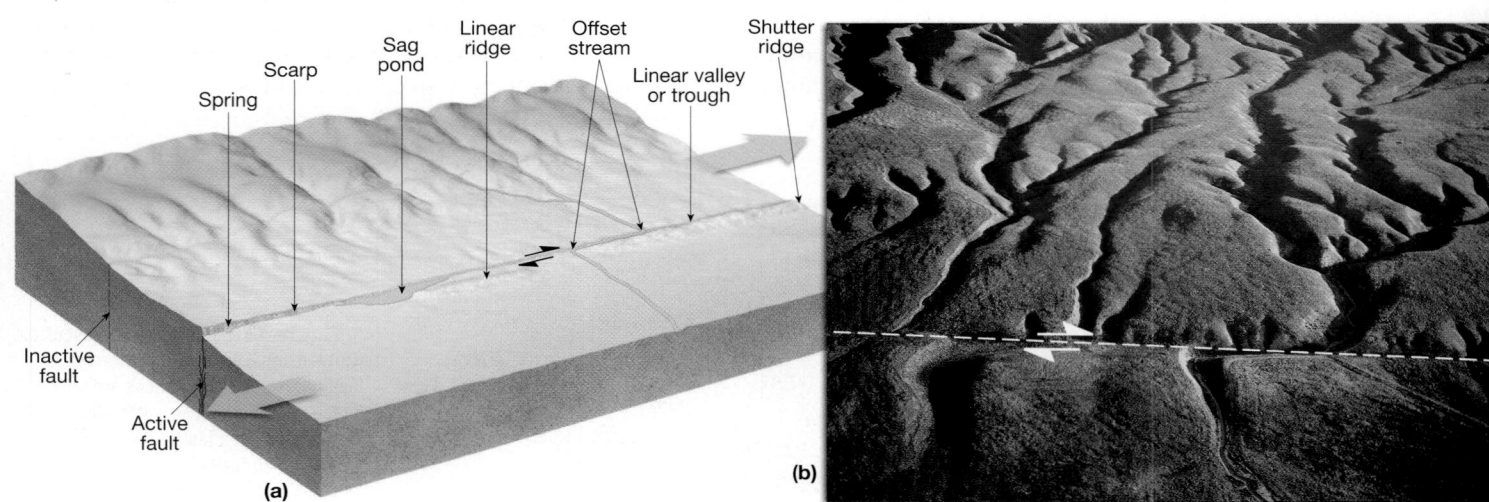

▲ **Figure 14-62** (a) Common landforms produced by strike-slip faulting. (b) Offset stream along the San Andreas Fault in the Temblor Range of California.

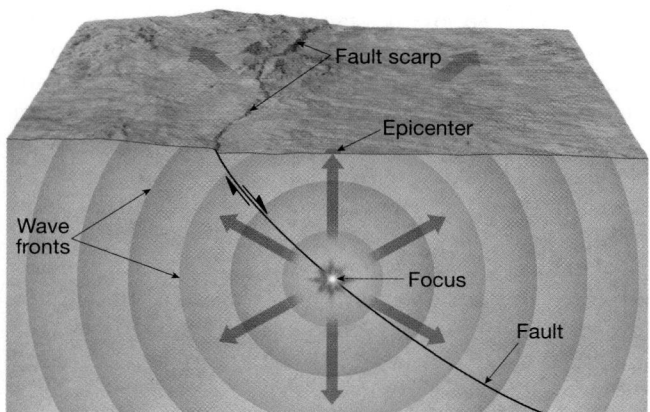

▲ **Figure 14-63** Relationship among focus, epicenter, and seismic waves of an earthquake. The seismic waves are indicated by the concentric circles.

The fastest-moving seismic waves, and the first to be felt during an earthquake, are known as P or *primary waves*. P waves move through Earth in the same fashion as sound waves, by alternately compressing and relaxing the medium through which they are traveling. The initial jolt of the P waves is followed by the strong side-to-side and up-and-down shearing motion of the slower-moving S or *secondary waves*. Both P waves and S waves travel through the body of Earth (so they are also known as *body waves*), whereas the motion of a third type of seismic wave is limited to the surface. These *surface waves* typically arrive immediately after the S waves and produce strong side-to-side movement as well as the up-and-down "rolling" motion often experienced during a large earthquake.

Because P waves and S waves travel at different speeds—at the surface P waves travel through bedrock at about 6 kilometers (3.7 miles) per second, while S waves travel at about 3.5 kilometers (2.2 miles) per second—it is possible to determine the distance to an earthquake's focus. The farther away an earthquake, the greater the time lag between the arrival of the P waves and the S waves. By using a network of *seismographs* (instruments used to record earthquakes) and comparing arrival times of the seismic waves, seismologists can pinpoint the focus of an earthquake with great precision.

Animation
Seismographs

Earthquake Magnitude

Perhaps the most widely mentioned—and most widely misunderstood—aspect of an earthquake is its **magnitude**. Magnitude describes the relative amount of energy released during an earthquake. Magnitudes are calculated on a logarithmic scale, with an energy increase from one magnitude to the next of about 32 times. The difference in size between small earthquakes (magnitudes less than 3) and large earthquakes (magnitude 7 and higher) is enormous. A magnitude 4 earthquake releases about 32 times more energy than a magnitude 3; a magnitude 5 releases 1000 times more energy than a magnitude 3; and

a magnitude 7 releases 1,000,000 times more energy than a magnitude 3.

The most commonly quoted magnitude is the *Richter scale*, devised in 1935 by Charles Richter at the California Institute of Technology in Pasadena. Although the Richter scale magnitude is relatively easy for seismologists to calculate, it is not ideal for comparing the sizes of very large earthquakes (magnitude 7 and higher). The more recently devised *moment magnitude* is now the most commonly used scale to describe the size of large quakes, although the Richter scale (also known as the *local magnitude* scale) and other scales are still in use. Because the method of calculation varies among the magnitude scales, slightly different magnitude numbers are often reported for the same earthquake.

In any given year, tens of thousands of earthquakes occur around the world (Table 14-2). The vast majority of these are too small to be felt by people, but perhaps 60 or 70 are large enough to cause damage or loss of life (commonly magnitude 6 or higher). Great earthquakes—those with magnitude 8 or higher—might occur only once every few years. The two largest earthquakes yet recorded were the 1960 Chile earthquake with a moment magnitude of 9.5, and the 1964 Alaska earthquake with a moment magnitude of 9.2. The great Sumatra earthquake of December 2004 also had a moment magnitude of about 9.2. For comparison, the famous 1906 San Francisco earthquake had a moment magnitude of 7.7, the 1989 Loma Prieta earthquake a moment magnitude of 7.0, and the 1994 Northridge earthquake a moment magnitude of 6.8.

Shaking Intensity

Even though each earthquake can be assigned a single magnitude number to describe its relative size, every earthquake generates a wide range of local ground-shaking intensities—and it is the strength of local ground shaking that directly influences the amount of damage that results from an earthquake. Local variations in the shaking intensity of an earthquake can be quantitatively measured—usually

TABLE 14-2	Worldwide Earthquake Frequency
Magnitude	**Number per Year**
< 3.4	800,000
3.5–4.2	30,000
4.3–4.8	4800
4.9–5.4	1400
5.5–6.1	500
6.2–6.9	100
7.0–7.3	15
7.4–7.9	4
8.0	1 every 1 or 2 years

as the peak horizontal ground acceleration expressed as a percentage of gravity—but the most widely used intensity scale was originally devised in 1902 by Italian geologist Giuseppe Mercalli. Updated by the U.S. Coast and Geodetic Survey, the **modified Mercalli intensity scale** assigns the strength of local shaking to 1 of 12 categories, based on the observed effects and damage (Table 14-3). The modified Mercalli scale is also used by seismologists to describe the anticipated intensity of ground shaking that may occur during future earthquakes in a region.

> **Learning Check 14-18** How is earthquake *magnitude* different from earthquake shaking intensity?

Earthquake Hazards

Most of the damage from an earthquake is due to ground shaking. Generally, the strength of ground shaking decreases with increasing distance from the epicenter of the earthquake, but this pattern can be significantly modified by the local geology. Loose, unstable regolith, sediments, and soil tend to amplify ground shaking—buildings on such "soft" ground will shake much more strongly than those located on bedrock the same distance from the epicenter. In addition, loose, water-saturated sediments, such as coastal landfill, may undergo **liquefaction**—during the shaking of an earthquake, the water-saturated material turns fluid, resulting in subsidence, fracturing, and horizontal sliding of the ground surface. A great deal of the damage in the 1989 Loma Prieta earthquake and in the 1995 Kobe earthquake was due to amplified ground shaking and liquefaction in artificial fill (Figure 14-64).

Landslides are often triggered by earthquakes. During the 1964 Alaska earthquake, for example, dozens of homes in the Turnagain Heights residential area outside of Anchorage were destroyed when a 2.6-kilometer (1.6-mile) wide section of the development moved toward the sea in a series of massive landslides.

Another kind of hazard associated with earthquakes involves water movements in lakes and oceans. Abrupt crustal movement can set great waves (known as *seiches*) in motion in lakes and reservoirs, causing them to overflow shorelines or dams in the same fashion that water can be sloshed out of a dishpan.

Much more significant, however, are great seismic sea waves called *tsunami* (the Japanese term for these large waves), which are sometimes generated by undersea earthquakes or landslides. These waves, often occurring in a sequential train, move quickly across the ocean. They are barely perceptible in deep water, but when they reach shallow coastal waters, they sometimes build up to heights of more than 15 meters (50 feet) and crash onto the shoreline with devastating effects (where they are often incorrectly called "tidal waves"). Most of the deaths from the 1964 Alaska earthquake were the result of tsunami—even as far away as Crescent City, California, 12 people were killed when a 6-meter (19-foot) high tsunami came on shore. In December 2004, about 227,000 people were killed when a tsunami generated by a subduction zone earthquake off the Indonesian island of Sumatra spread through the Indian Ocean. The March 2011 Japan earthquake generated a tsunami as high as 30 meters (100 feet) that killed more than 15,000 people. A detailed description of tsunami formation and the 2011 Japan earthquake and tsunami is found in Chapter 20, where we discuss the dynamics of ocean waves.

TABLE 14-3	Modified Mercalli Intensity Scale
I.	Not felt except by very few people under especially favorable circumstances
II.	Felt only by a few persons at rest, especially on upper floors of buildings
III.	Felt quite noticeably indoors, especially on upper floors of buildings, but many people do not recognize it as an earthquake
IV.	During the day felt indoors by many, outdoors by few; sensation like heavy truck striking building
V.	Felt by nearly everyone, many awakened; disturbances of trees, poles, and other tall objects sometimes noticed
VI.	Felt by all; many frightened and run outdoors; some heavy furniture moved; few instances of fallen plaster or damaged chimneys; damage slight
VII.	Everybody runs outdoors; damage negligible in buildings of good design and construction; slight to moderate in well-built ordinary structures; considerable damage in poorly built or badly designed structures
VIII.	Damage slight in specially designed structures; considerable in ordinary substantial buildings, with partial collapse; great damage in poorly built structures; fall of chimneys, factory stacks, columns, monuments, and other vertical features
IX.	Damage considerable in specially designed structures; buildings shifted off foundations; ground cracked conspicuously
X.	Some well-built wooden structures destroyed; most masonry and frame structures destroyed with foundations; ground badly cracked
XI.	Few, if any, masonry structures remain standing; bridges destroyed; broad fissures in ground
XII.	Damage total; waves seen on ground surfaces; objects thrown upward into the air

(a)

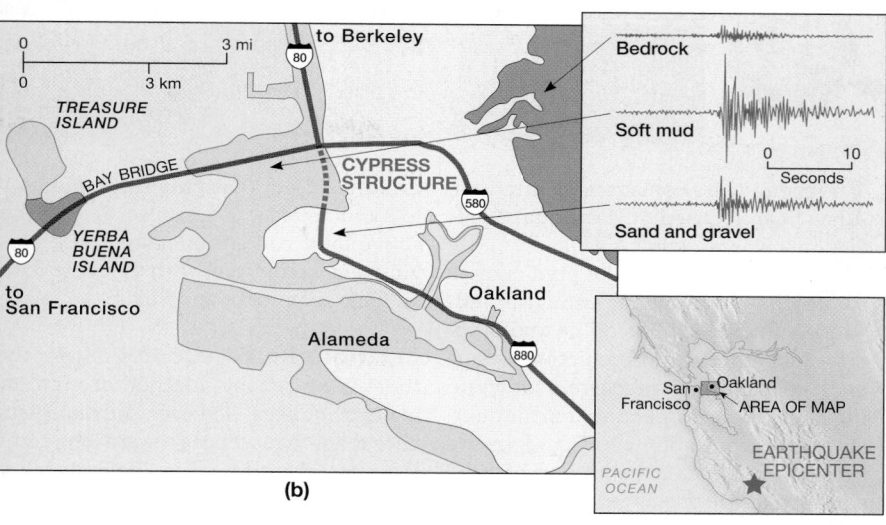

(b)

▲ **Figure 14-64** (a) The portion of the Cypress freeway structure in Oakland, California, that collapsed during the 1989 magnitude 7.0 Loma Prieta earthquake stood on soft mud (b; dashed red line). Adjacent parts of the structure built on firmer ground (solid red line) remained standing. Seismograms in the upper-right show that ground shaking was more severe on the soft mud than on the nearby bedrock.

In the Pacific Ocean, there is a tsunami warning system, made up of buoys and sensors, that can detect a tsunami in midocean and provide advanced warning to endangered coastal populations. Currently, however, this is no technology that can predict an earthquake—see the box, "Focus: Earthquake Prediction."

Learning Check 14-19 **What causes *liquefaction* during an earthquake?**

COMPLEXITIES OF THE INTERNAL PROCESSES—EXAMPLE OF THE NORTHERN ROCKIES

Considering each internal process in turn as we have just done is a helpful way to systematize knowledge. Doing so presents an artificial and misleading picture, however, because in nature these processes are interrelated. To attempt a more balanced assessment, let us consider a highly simplified statement of the origin of the topographic features of a small part of Earth's surface—a mountainous section of northwestern Montana that encompasses the spectacular scenery of Glacier National Park.

This area, now part of the northern Rocky Mountains, was below sea level for many millions of years. Most of the rocks in the region were formed in the Precambrian Era (more than 542 million years ago), when much of the area now occupied by the Rocky Mountain Cordillera consisted of a large, shallow, seawater-filled trough. Silt and sand was washed into this Precambrian sea for millennia, and a vast thickness of sedimentary strata built up. These limestones, shales, and sandstones accumulated

as six distinct formations, each with a conspicuous color variation known collectively as the Belt Series.

Occasionally during this lengthy epoch of sedimentary accumulation, igneous activity added variety. Most notable was a vast outpouring of flood basalt that issued from fissures in the ocean floor and was extruded in the form of a submarine lava flow. Further sediments were then deposited on top of the lava flow.

Igneous intrusions were also injected from time to time, including one large sill and a number of dikes. The igneous rocks—both the flood basalt and the various intrusions—initiated contact metamorphism, whereby the tremendous heat of the igneous material converted some of the adjacent sedimentary rocks into metamorphic rocks (mostly changing limestone to marble and sandstone to quartzite).

After a long gap in the geologic record, during which the Rocky Mountain region was mostly above sea level, the land once again sank below the ocean during the Cretaceous Period (145.5 to 65.5 million years ago) and another thick series of sediments was deposited. This was followed by a period of mountain building so significant that it has been named the Rocky Mountain Revolution. In the Glacier National Park area, the rocks were compressed and uplifted, converting the site of the former sea into a mountainous region.

Along with uplift came extreme lateral pressure from the west (Figure 14-65), convoluting the gently downfolded strata into a prominent anticline. Continuing pressure then overturned the anticline toward the east. This additional strain on the rock and the persistent crustal pressure eventually caused a vast rupture and faulting. The entire block was then pushed eastward by one of the greatest thrust faults known, the *Lewis Overthrust*. This remarkable fault forced the Precambrian sedimentary rocks out over the Cretaceous strata that underlie the plains to the

In recent years considerable attention has been focused on earthquake prediction and forecasting.

The goal of earthquake prediction is to provide warnings far enough in advance to minimize loss of life and property. Such short-term predictions hinge on the existence of "precursors" or warning signs of an impending earthquake. Many such possible warning signs are being studied, including patterns of small earthquakes that sometimes occur before major quakes ("foreshocks"), changes in water-well levels, changes in the amount of dissolved radon gas in groundwater, variations in electrical conductivity of rocks, the bulging of the ground surface, and changes in the behavior of animals.

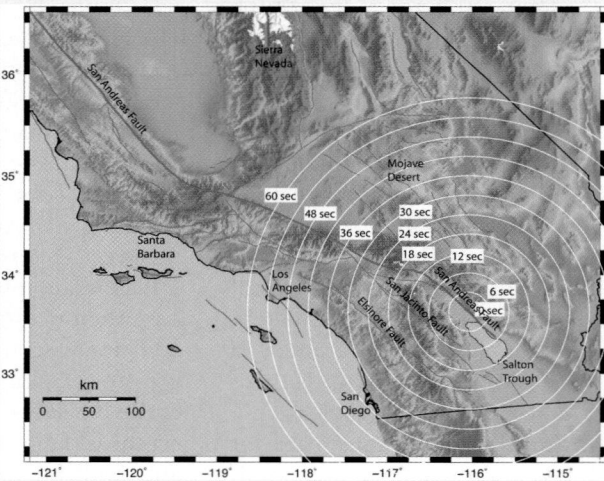

▲ **Figure 14-C** The San Andreas Fault runs through the town of Parkfield, California.

The Parkfield Project: One of the world's most elaborate earthquake precursor research projects began in 1985 in the tiny California town of Parkfield (Figure 14-C), which sits atop the San Andreas Fault in the central part of the state. Since the mid-1800s this segment of the fault has ruptured at fairly regular intervals—1857, 1881, 1901, 1922, 1934, 1966, and, most recently, in 2004—each time producing an earthquake of about magnitude 6. In addition to many kinds of instruments designed to "capture" earthquakes as they happen, Parkfield is also the location of the San Andreas Fault Observatory at Depth—an ambitious

drilling project that puts instruments 2 to 3 kilometers (1.2–1.9 miles) deep in the active fault zone (see Figure 14-C), providing seismologists with valuable data on fault-zone rocks and fluids.

Earthquake Forecasts: Currently, there is no reliable method of predicting earthquakes. However, seismologists have made great strides toward long-term forecasts of earthquakes: the probability of an earthquake occurring along a segment of a fault within a period of several decades. Long-term probabilities are based on the balance of two processes: the loading of strain onto faults, and the slip along the faults (which should, over time, release the strain). For example, the USGS recently concluded that in the San Francisco Bay region, there is a 63 percent probability of at least one magnitude 6.7 or greater earthquake occurring before the year 2036. Long-term forecasts can help local governments, businesses, and the general public to establish priorities for retrofitting structures and for disaster preparation.

Earthquake Early Warning Systems: Although predicting earthquakes remains an elusive possibility, the technology already exists to warn people of the impending arrival of the strong ground shaking from a nearby large earthquake.

The USGS, in cooperation with several research universities, is developing an Earthquake Early Warning (EEW) system for the West Coast of the United States. Such a system can provide between 10 and 60 seconds advance warning of the arrival of destructive seismic waves from a large earthquake (Figure 14-D).

The principal of an EEW system is simple and is based on existing seismic monitoring networks. The damaging high-amplitude S waves radiating away from an earthquake focus travel at about 3.5 kilometers (2.2 miles) per second—the farther away the earthquake origin, the longer it takes the S waves to arrive. When a strong earthquake is detected by a seismic network, within about 10 seconds its location and size can be computed. The EEW system then sends out an automatic alert that can give enough warning for people to move to a safe location; for trains to safely slow down and airports to stop take-offs and landings; for fire stations to open their doors and for emergency generators to be started; and for medical personal to stop delicate surgical procedures.

The amount of warning time depends on the distance to the epicenter. Because seismic waves travel so quickly, locations within about 30 kilometers (20 miles) of an earthquake epicenter will receive effectively no warning. Locations about 65 kilometers (40 miles) will have about a 10-second warning, whereas locations 225 kilometers (140 miles) will have a 60-second warning.

◀ **Figure 14-D** Estimated warning times from an Earthquake Early Warning System in southern California for a major earthquake occurring on the southern San Andreas Fault.

(a)

(b) Fault

(c) Fault

(d) Lewis Overthrust   Chief Mountain

(e)

▲ **Figure 14-65** Sequential development of the Lewis Overthrust. (a) Compression of original sedimentary rocks begins the process of uplift and folding. (b and c) Continued pressure from the west causes overturning of the fold and faulting along the eastern limb of the anticline. (d) Subsequent erosion produces the present topography, with Chief Mountain as a residual outlier to the east of the range. (e) Chief Mountain sits in splendid isolation because of the massive movement associated with the Lewis Overthrust and subsequent erosion.

CANADA

Glacier National Park

MONTANA

IDAHO   WYOMING

east by as much as 30 kilometers (about 20 miles). The plane of the thrust fault was only slightly above the horizontal, nowhere exceeding a dip of 10°. This had the peculiar effect of placing older rock layers on top of much younger strata. The terrain thus produced is referred to as "mountains without roots." Chief Mountain is world famous as a rootless mountain because of its conspicuous location as an erosional outlier east of the main range (Figure 14-65e). Such an erosional outlier is called a *klippe*.

Learning Check 14-20 **Describe how Chief Mountain, Montana, is associated with faulting.**

After studying this chapter, you should be able to answer the following questions. Key terms from each text section are shown in **bold type**. Definitions for key terms are also found in the glossary at the back of the book.

KEY TERMS AND CONCEPTS

From Rigid Earth to Plate Tectonics (*p. 402*)

1. Describe and explain at least two lines of evidence that Alfred Wegener used to support his theory of **continental drift** and the existence of the supercontinent of **Pangaea**.
2. Why was Wegener's theory of continental drift rejected for so long?

The Theory of Plate Tectonics (*p. 404*)

3. What lines of evidence confirm that **seafloor spreading** has been taking place? You should be able to explain evidence from both **paleomagnetism** and **ocean floor cores**.
4. Describe and explain the driving mechanism for **plate tectonics**—in other words, explain why and how lithospheric plates move.

Plate Boundaries (*p. 408*)

5. Describe the fundamental differences among **divergent**, **convergent**, and **transform plate boundaries**.
6. Describe and explain the tectonic activity, volcanic activity, and general topographic features associated with the two kinds of divergent plate boundary: **midocean ridges** and **continental rift valleys**. Mention at least one present-day example of each of these kinds of divergent boundaries.
7. Describe and explain the tectonic activity, volcanic activity, and general topographic features associated with the three kinds of convergent plate boundary: oceanic–continental plate **subduction**, oceanic–oceanic plate subduction, and continental plate collision. Mention at least one present-day example of each of these kinds of convergent boundaries.
8. Describe the differences between an **oceanic trench** and a midocean ridge.
9. How does the San Andreas Fault system fit in with the theory of plate tectonics?
10. Why are volcanoes and earthquakes concentrated around the margin of the Pacific Ocean—the region referred to as the **Pacific Ring of Fire**?

Additions to Plate Tectonic Theory (*p. 415*)

11. What is a **hot spot**? Name at least one present-day example of a hot spot.
12. How is a hot spot trail different from a **volcanic island arc**?

13. How does the **mantle plume** model explain the existence of hot spots?
14. What is a **terrane** and how does one form?

Volcanism (*p. 418*)

15. What is meant by the term **volcanism**?
16. Define and contrast the following: **magma**, **lava**, and **pyroclastics**.
17. Explain the general differences in silica content and style of volcanic eruption (i.e., quiet lava flows versus explosive eruptions of pyroclastics) associated with basaltic magma, andesitic magma, and rhyolitic magma.
18. What is **flood basalt**?
19. Describe and explain the general formation, shape, and structure of the following kinds of volcanic peaks: **shield volcanoes**, **composite volcanoes**, **lava domes (plug domes)**, and **cinder cones**.
20. Explain the formation of a **caldera** such as Crater Lake in Oregon.

Volcanic Hazards (*p. 426*)

21. Describe and explain the origin and characteristics of **pyroclastic flows** and **volcanic mudflows (lahars)**.

Intrusive Igneous Features (*p. 430*)

22. Define the following terms: **igneous intrusion**, **pluton**, **batholith**, and **dike**.

Folding (*p. 432*)

23. How is **folding** different from **faulting**?
24. What is a **syncline**? What is an **anticline**?

Faulting (*p. 434*)

25. Explain the differences in stress direction and displacement among the four basic kinds of faults: **normal faults**, **reverse faults**, **thrust faults**, and **strike-slip faults**.
26. What is a **fault scarp**?
27. Describe and explain the formation of landforms that result from normal faulting (such as **grabens**, **horsts**, and **tilted fault-block mountains**).
28. Describe and explain the formation of landforms that result from strike-slip faulting (such as **linear fault troughs**, **sag ponds**, and **offset streams**).

Earthquakes (*p. 438*)

29. What is an **earthquake**?
30. What is the difference between the focus of an earthquake and the **epicenter** of an earthquake?
31. What is the difference between earthquake **magnitude** and earthquake shaking intensity?
32. What does the **modified Mercalli intensity scale** convey?

33. Briefly describe the differences among the P waves, S waves, and surface waves of an earthquake.
34. Under what conditions does **liquefaction** occur?

Complexities of the Internal Processes—Example of the Northern Rockies (*p. 441*)

35. Explain how faulting can leave older rocks resting over younger rocks.

STUDY QUESTIONS

1. What is the general relationship between global earthquake activity and plate boundaries?
2. Why doesn't subduction take place in a continental plate collision zone?
3. Why are deep-focus earthquakes (those originating many hundreds of kilometers below the surface) associated with subduction zones, but not with divergent boundaries and transform boundaries?
4. In what ways do hot spots not fit in with the basic theory of plate tectonics and plate boundaries?

5. In what ways have hot spots been used to verify that plate motion is taking place?
6. How is it possible for a syncline to be associated with a topographic ridge and for an anticline to be associated with a topographic valley?
7. Why do areas far away from the epicenter sometimes experience greater damage during an earthquake than areas closer to the epicenter? (Consider factors other than differences in building construction.)

EXERCISES

1. If the Mid-Atlantic Ridge continues to spread at the same rate into the future (about 2.5 centimeters [1 inch] per year), how long would it take for the Atlantic Ocean to become 1 kilometer wider? _____ years
2. Assuming that the long-term rate of displacement along the San Andreas Fault (about 3.5 cm/year) remains the same and that the location of the fault remains the same, how long would it take Los Angeles (on the west side of the fault) to move north 620 kilometers (385 miles) to the position of San Francisco (on the east side of the fault)?

3. If a lahar (volcanic mudflow) is traveling down a stream valley from a volcano at a speed of 30 km/hour, how long with it take to reach a town 10 kilometers away?
4. About how much more energy is released during a magnitude 6 earthquake than during a magnitude 5 earthquake?
5. About how much more energy is released during a magnitude 8 earthquake than during a magnitude 5 earthquake?

Seeing Geographically

Look again at the photograph of Mount Bromo and Mount Semeru at the beginning of the chapter (p. 400). What kind of volcano is Mount Semeru? Why do you say this? Plumes emitted by a volcano are often incorrectly called "smoke"—what is the likely actual composition of the plume being ejected from Mount Semeru? What kind of volcanic hazards are likely in this part of Java?

MasteringGeography™

Looking for additional review and test prep materials? Visit the Study Area in MasteringGeography™ to enhance your geographic literacy, spatial reasoning skills, and understanding of this chapter's content by accessing a variety of resources, including geoscience animations, MapMaster interactive maps, videos, RSS feeds, flashcards, web links, self-study quizzes, and an eText version of *McKnight's Physical Geography: A Landscape Appreciation*.

IF THE INTERNAL PROCESSES OF LANDSCAPE FORMATION

are overwhelming, the external processes are inexorable. During all the time that lithospheric plates are moving, the crust is bending and breaking, and volcanoes are erupting and intrusions forming, another suite of natural processes is simultaneously at work. These are the external processes, often mundane and even minute in contrast to those described in the preceding chapter. Yet the cumulative effect of the external processes is awesome; they are capable of wearing down anything the internal processes can erect. No rock is too resistant and no mountain too massive to withstand their unrelenting power. Ultimately, the detailed configuration of peaks, slopes, valleys, and plains is molded by the work of gravity, water, wind, and ice.

As you study this chapter, think about these key questions:

- **How do *weathering*, *mass wasting*, and *erosion* work together to change the landscape?**
- **How do rock openings influence weathering processes?**
- **What are the principal processes of *mechanical weathering* and *chemical weathering*?**
- **What are the four main types of mass wasting and what factors influence each?**

DENUDATION

The overall effect of the disintegration, wearing away, and removal of rock material is generally referred to as **denudation**, a term that implies a lowering of continental surfaces. Denudation is accomplished by the interaction of three types of activities:

- **Weathering** is the breaking down of rock into smaller components by atmospheric and biotic action agencies.
- **Mass wasting** involves the relatively short-distance downslope movement of broken rock material under the direct influence of gravity.
- **Erosion** consists of the removal, transportation, and eventual deposition of fragmented rock material over wider areas and sometimes to greater distances than is the case in mass wasting.

All three processes are illustrated conceptually in Figure 15-1.

The Impact of Weathering and Mass Wasting on the Landscape

The most readily observable landscape effect of weathering is the fragmentation of bedrock—the reduction of large rock units into more numerous and less cohesive smaller units.

Mass wasting always involves the downslope movement of rock material. Its impact on the landscape is normally twofold: an open scar may be left on the surface that was vacated, and an accumulation of debris is deposited somewhere downslope from the scar.

Although weathering and mass wasting are often de-emphasized as processes of landform modification and shaping, the role they play is critical. Take the Grand Canyon of the Colorado River, for example. One of the most impressive landscape features of the world, the canyon is usually attributed only to the erosive powers of the river. However,

Wensu Grand Canyon in Aksu Prefecture, Xingjian, western China. What do you see in the photograph that suggests that this is an arid location? Describe the general trend of the structure in the bedrock here. Does it appear that bedrock has been removed from this landscape? Why do you say this?

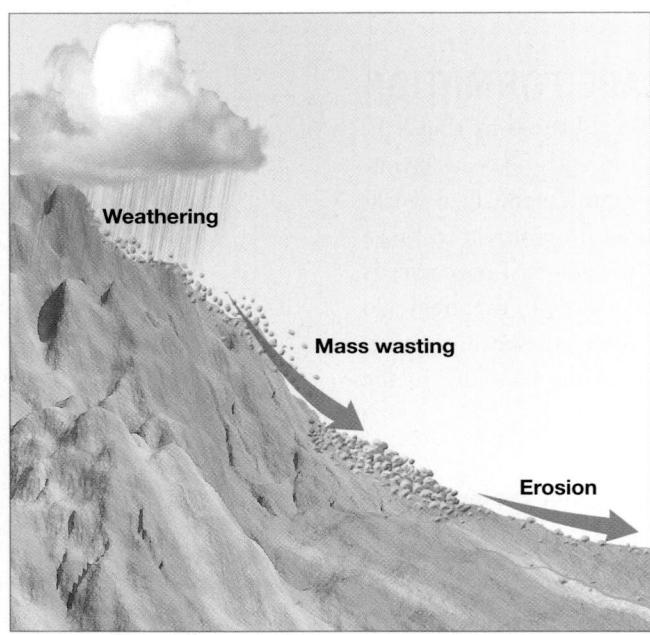

▲ **Figure 15-1** Denudation, the lowering of continental surfaces, is accomplished by a combination of weathering, mass wasting, and erosion.

WEATHERING AND ROCK OPENINGS

The first step in shaping Earth's surface by external processes is *weathering*, the mechanical disintegration and/or chemical decomposition that begins to fragment rock masses into progressively smaller components. Fast or slow, mechanical and chemical weathering occurs wherever the lithosphere and atmosphere meet. It occurs with great subtlety, however, breaking chemical bonds, separating grain from grain, pitting the smooth, and fracturing the solid. It is the aging process of rock surfaces, the process that must precede the other, more active, forms of denudation.

Significance of Rock Openings: Whenever bedrock is exposed, it weathers. Weathered rock often has a different color or texture from neighboring unexposed bedrock. Most significant from a topographic standpoint, exposed bedrock is likely to be looser than the underlying rock. Blocks or chips may be so loose that they can be detached with little effort. Sometimes pieces are so "rotten" that they can be crumbled by finger pressure. Slightly deeper in the bedrock, there is firmer, more solid rock, although along cracks or crevices weathering may extend to considerable depths. In some cases, the weathering may reach as much as several hundred meters beneath the surface. This penetration is made possible by open spaces in the rock bodies and even between the mineral grains. Subsurface weathering is initiated along these openings, which can be penetrated by such weathering agents as water, air, and plant roots. As time passes, the weathering effects spread from the immediate vicinity of the openings into the denser rock beyond (Figure 15-3).

Openings in the surface and near-surface bedrock are frequently microscopic, but they may also be large enough to be conspicuous and are sometimes huge. In any case, they occur in vast numbers and provide avenues along which weathering agents can attack the bedrock and break it apart.

weathering and mass wasting produce most of the forms we see in the Grand Canyon. (Figure 15-2). Besides deepening its channel, the river's main role is to transport the sediment loosened by weathering and pulled into the stream by gravity and mass wasting. The Grand Canyon also exhibits the mark of *differential weathering*: some kinds of rock are easily weathered, whereas others are much more resistant (this important topic will be explored later in this chapter).

> **Learning Check 15-1** **What is the main effect of weathering on the landscape? Of mass wasting? (Answer on p. AK-4)**

◀ **Figure 15-2** The Colorado River in Arizona's Grand Canyon is the principal erosive agent that transports rock out of the canyon, but nearly all of the material removed to form the massive canyon is the result of weathering and mass wasting.

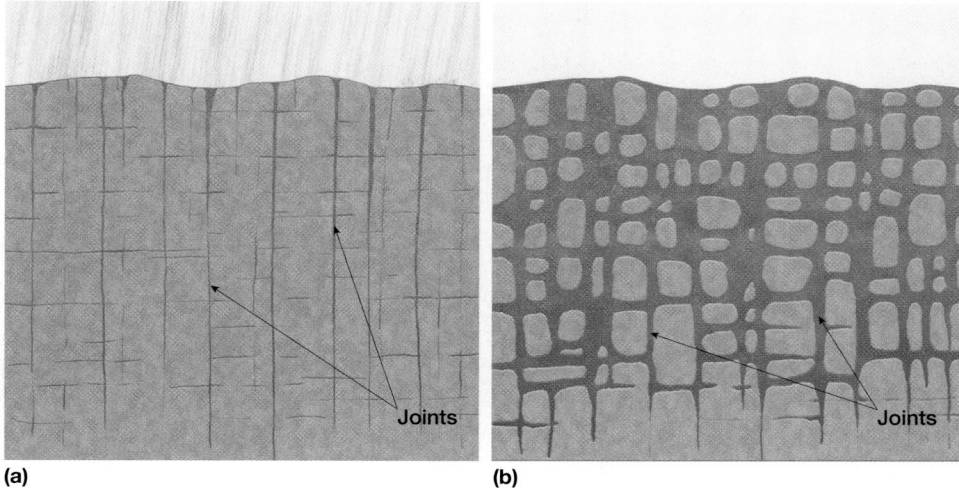

▶ **Figure 15-3** Weathering below the surface can take place in bedrock containing many openings such as joints (a) before weathering; (b) after weathering.

(a)   **(b)**

Joints   Joints

Learning Check 15-2   **Why are rock openings important in weathering processes?**

Types of Rock Openings

Broadly speaking, five types of rock openings are common:

1. **Microscopic openings:** Microscopic openings in the rock surface occur in profusion. Although tiny, they are so numerous that they can be responsible for extensive weathering. They may consist of spaces between crystals of igneous or metamorphic rocks, pores between grains of sedimentary rocks, or minute fractures within or alongside mineral grains in any kind of rock.

2. **Joints:** The most common structural features of the rocks of the lithosphere are **joints**—cracks that develop as a result of stress—but the rocks do not show appreciable displacement along these breaks parallel to the joint walls. Joints are innumerable in most rock masses, dividing them into blocks of various sizes. Because of their ubiquity, joints are the most important of all rock openings in facilitating weathering.

3. **Faults:** As we saw in Chapter 14, *faults* are breaks in bedrock along which there is relative displacement of the walls of the crack (Figure 15-4). Faults are generally individual or occur only in small numbers, whereas joints normally are numerous. A further difference between faults and joints is that faults sometimes appear as major landscape features, extending for tens or even hundreds of kilometers, whereas joints are normally minor structures extending only a few meters. Faults allow easy penetration of weathering agents into subsurface areas because not only fracturing but also displacement is involved.

4. **Lava vesicles:** Lava *vesicles* are holes of various sizes, usually small, that develop in cooling lava when gas is unable to escape as the lava solidifies.

5. **Solution cavities:** *Solution cavities* are holes formed in carbonate rocks (particularly limestone) as the soluble minerals are dissolved and carried away by percolating water. Most solution cavities are small, but sometimes huge holes and even massive caverns are created when large amounts of solubles are removed. (A more lengthy description of solution processes and topography appears in Chapter 17.)

The Importance of Jointing

FG4, FG5

Almost all lithospheric bedrock is jointed, resulting sometimes from the contraction of molten material as it cools, sometimes from contraction of sedimentary strata as they dry, and sometimes from tectonic stresses. At Earth's surface, the separation between blocks on either side of a joint may be conspicuous because weathering emphasizes the fracture. Below the surface, however, the visible separation is minimal.

Joints are relatively common in most rock, but they are clearly more abundant in some places than in others. Where numerous, they are usually arranged in sets, each set comprising a series of approximately parallel fractures. Frequently, two prominent sets intersect almost at right angles; such a combination constitutes a *joint system* (Figure 15-5). A well-developed joint system, particularly in sedimentary rock having prominent natural bedding

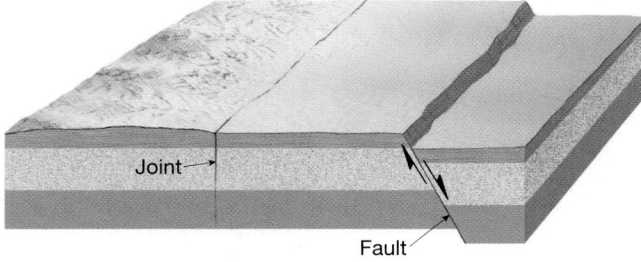

Joint

Fault

▲ **Figure 15-4** The essential difference between joints and faults is that joints exhibit no displacement along either side of the crack.

▶ **Figure 15-5** Jointing. (a) The badlands topography of Bryce Canyon in southern Utah from Inspiration Point. The closely spaced joints and bedding planes contribute to intricate sculpturing by weathering and erosion. (b) In Utah's Zion National Park master joints are widely spaced, allowing for the development of massive blocks and precipitous cliffs.

(a)   (b)

planes, can divide stratified rock into a remarkably regular series of close-fitting blocks. Generally speaking, jointing is more regularly patterned, and the resulting blocks are more sharply defined in fine-grained rocks than in coarse-grained ones.

In some places, large joints or joint sets extend for long distances and through a considerable thickness of rocks; these are termed **master joints** (Figure 15-5b). Master joints play a role in topographic development by functioning as a plane of weakness, a plane more susceptible to weathering and erosion than the rock around it. Thus, the location of large features of the landscape, such as valleys and cliffs, may be influenced by the position of master joints.

Learning Check 15-3   **Describe the difference between a *joint* and a *fault*.**

WEATHERING AGENTS

Most weathering agents are atmospheric in origin. Because it is gaseous, the atmosphere is able to penetrate readily into all cracks and crevices in bedrock. From a chemical standpoint, oxygen, carbon dioxide, and water vapor are the three atmospheric components of greatest importance in rock weathering.

Temperature changes are a second important weathering agent. Most notable, however, is water, which can penetrate downward effectively into openings in the bedrock. Biotic agents also contribute to weathering, in part through the burrowing activities of animals and the rooting effects of plants, but especially through the production of chemical substances that attack and decompose the rock.

The total effect of these agents is complicated and is influenced by a variety of factors: the nature and structure of the bedrock, the abundance and size of openings in it, the surface configuration, prevailing climatic conditions, the vegetative cover, and the variety and abundance of digging animals. For analytical purposes, however, it is convenient to recognize three principal categories of weathering—*mechanical*, *chemical*, and *biotic*. Although we now consider each of them in turn, we should bear in mind that they often act together.

Mechanical Weathering
FG4, FG5

Animation
Mechanical
Weathering

Mechanical weathering (or *physical weathering*) is the physical disintegration of rock material without any change in its chemical composition. In essence, big rocks are mechanically weathered into little ones by various stresses that cause the rock to fracture into smaller and usually angular fragments. Most mechanical weathering occurs at or very near the surface, but under certain conditions it may occur at considerable depth.

Frost Wedging: Probably the most important single agent of mechanical weathering is the freeze-thaw action of water. As we first saw in Chapter 6, when water freezes, it expands by almost 10 percent. Moreover, the upper surface of the water freezes first, which means that the principal force of expansion is exerted against the wall of the confining rock rather than upward. This expanding wedge of ice splits the rock, as shown in Figure 15-6.

Even the strongest rocks cannot withstand frequent alternation of freezing and thawing. Repetition is the key to understanding the inexorable force of **frost wedging**

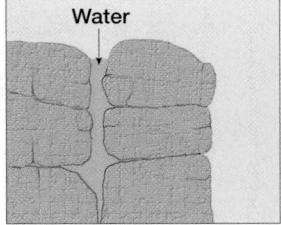
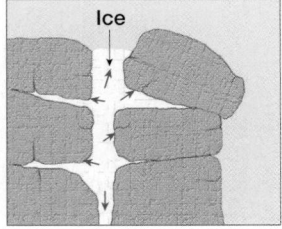

▲ **Figure 15-6** Schematic illustration of frost wedging. When water in a rock crack freezes, the ice expansion exerts a force that can deepen and widen the crack, especially if the process is repeated many times.

◄ **Figure 15-7** Frost wedging is an especially pervasive force on mountaintops above the treeline, as with these rocks near the summit of Glyder Fach mountain in northwestern Wales.

or *frost shattering*. Regardless of its size, if an opening in rock contains water, when the temperature falls below 0°C (32°F) ice forms, wedging its way downward. When the temperature rises above freezing, the ice melts and the water sinks farther into the slightly enlarged cavity. With renewed freezing, the wedging is repeated. Such a freeze–thaw pattern may be repeated millions of times through the eons of Earth history, providing what is literally an irresistible force.

Frost wedging in large openings may produce large boulders, whereas that occurring in small openings may granulate the rock into sand and dust particles, with every size gradation in between. A common form of breakup in coarse-grained crystalline rocks is a shattering caused by frost wedging between grains. This type of shattering produces gravel or coarse sand in a process termed *granular disintegration*.

The physical characteristics of the rock are important determinants of the rate and magnitude of mechanical weathering, as are temperature and moisture variations. The process is most effective where freezing is prolonged and intense—in high latitudes, in midlatitudes during winters, and at high elevations. It is most conspicuous above the treeline of mountainous areas (Figure 15-7), where broken blocks of rock are likely to be found in profusion everywhere except on slopes that are too steep to allow them to lie without sliding downhill.

Salt Wedging: Related to frost wedging but much less significant is **salt wedging**, which happens when salts crystallize out of solution as water evaporates. In areas of dry climate, water is often drawn upward in rock openings by capillary action (*capillarity* was discussed in Chapter 6). This water nearly always carries dissolved salts. When the water evaporates, as it commonly does, the salts are left behind as tiny crystals. With time, the crystals grow, prying apart the rock grain by grain, much in the fashion previously described for freezing water, although less intensely (Figure 15-8).

Along ocean coastlines, salt wedging may also be a weathering factor. Above the tideline, seawater from ocean spray gets between mineral grains; after the water evaporates the growth of salt crystals can slowly pry off mineral grains.

Learning Check 15-4   **Explain the process of *frost wedging*.**

Temperature Changes: Temperature changes not accompanied by freeze–thaw cycles may also weather rock mechanically, but they do so much more gradually than the processes just described. The fluctuation of temperature from day to night and from summer to winter can cause minute changes in the volume of most mineral particles, forcing expansion when heated and contraction when cooled. This volumetric variation weakens the coherence

▲ **Figure 15-8** Salt wedging. This crystalline rock is being shattered by salt wedging near the floor of Death Valley in California.

▶ **Figure 15-9** Two large exfoliation domes in Yosemite National Park, California.

of the mineral grains and tends to break them apart. Millions of repetitions are normally required for much weakening or fracturing to occur. This factor is most significant in arid areas and near mountain summits, where direct solar radiation is intense during the day and radiational cooling is prominent at night.

Probably more important but less widespread than simple solar heating and cooling is heating from forest fires or brushfires. The intense heating of a fire can cause a rock to expand and break apart.

Exfoliation: One of the most striking of all weathering processes is **exfoliation**, in which curved layers peel off bedrock. Curved and concentric sets of joints develop in the bedrock, and parallel shells of rock break away in succession, somewhat analogous to the way layers of an onion separate. The sheets that split off are sometimes only a few centimeters thick; in other cases, however, they may be several meters thick.

The results of exfoliation are conspicuous. If the rock mass is a large one, such as Half Dome or one of the other granitic monoliths overlooking Yosemite Valley, California, its surface consists of imperfect curves punctuated by several partially fractured shells of the surface layers, and the mass is referred to as an **exfoliation dome** (Figure 15-9). Overall, especially in regions of exposed plutonic bedrock, exfoliation tends to gently smooth the landscape.

The dynamics of exfoliation are not fully understood. The most widely accepted explanation of massive exfoliation is that the rock cracks after an overlying weight has been removed, a process called *unloading* or *pressure release* (Figure 15-10). The intrusive bedrock may originally have been deeply buried beneath a heavy overburden—perhaps several kilometers deep. When the overlying material is stripped away by erosion, the release of pressure allows expansion in the rock. The outer layers are unable to contain the expanding mass, and the expansion can be absorbed only by cracking along the sets of *sheeting joints*. Exfoliation occurs mainly in granite and related intrusive rocks, but under certain circumstances it is also seen in sandstone and other sedimentary strata.

▶ **Figure 15-10** When formerly buried rocks such as granite are exposed at the surface, the unloading of confining pressure causes slight expansion of the rock mass. As a consequence, curved layers of rock peel off in the process of exfoliation.

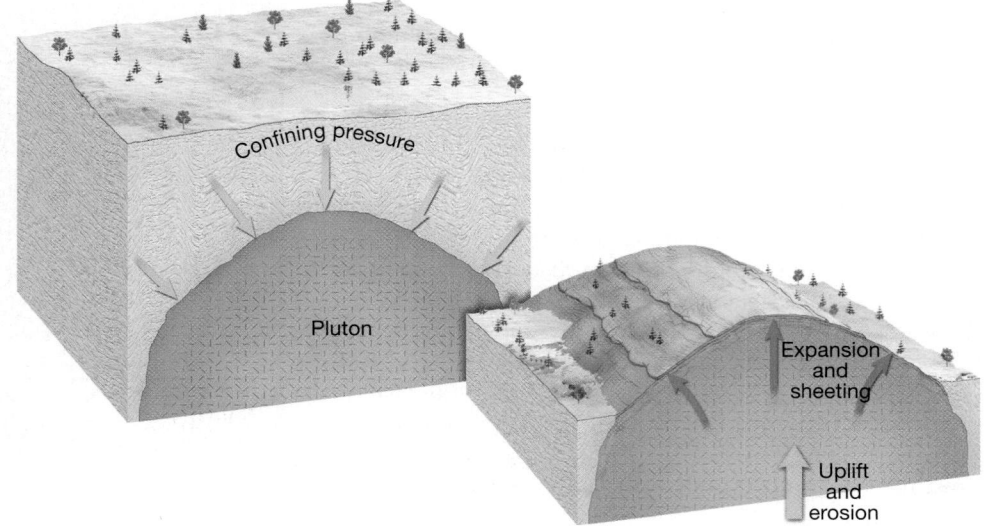

Recent research has suggested an alternative explanation of exfoliation in some locations: it takes place when convex exposures of strong rock (such as granite) are subjected to significant sideways compression. As the rock is compressed, vertical tension within the rock mass is enough to cause joints just below the convex surface to "pop open" parallel to the surface. Further research may clarify if this mechanism is more important than simple unloading of pressure.

The term *exfoliation* is occasionally used to describe the peeling away of very thin rock weathering layers—usually only a few millimeters thick— that is often seen on exposed boulders, gently rounding them over time (Figure 15-11). The term *spheroidal weathering* is also used to describe this process. Processes other than pressure release are likely at work in this case, however. Fracturing resulting from temperature variations may be a component of the mechanism, although this kind of weathering is also found in areas where temperature fluctuations are not marked. Volumetric changes in minerals, which set up strains in the rock, may also be involved. Such changes are most notably produced by *hydration*, in which water molecules become attached to other substances and then the added water causes the original substance to swell without any change in its chemical composition. This swelling weakens the rock mass and is usually sufficient to produce some fracturing.

> **Learning Check 15-5** **Explain the formation of exfoliation domes.**

Other Mechanical Weathering Processes:

Chemical changes (discussed in more detail in the next subsection) may also contribute to mechanical weathering. Various chemical actions can cause an increase in volume of the affected mineral grains. This swelling sets up strain that weakens the coherence of the rock and causes fractures.

▲ **Figure 15-11** A thin layer of rock is peeling, or *exfoliating*, from the surface of this granite boulder in California's Joshua Tree National Park.

Some biotic activities also contribute to mechanical weathering. Most notable is the penetration of growing plant roots into cracks and crevices, which exerts an expansive force that widens the openings. This factor is especially conspicuous where trees grow out of joint or fault planes, with their large roots showing amazing tenacity and persistence as wedging devices (Figure 15-12). Additionally, burrowing animals sometimes are factors in rock disintegration. The total effect of these biotic actions is probably significant, but it is difficult to assess because it is obscured by subsequent chemical weathering.

When acting alone, mechanical weathering breaks up rock masses into ever smaller (and often angular) pieces,

(a)

(b)

▶ **Figure 15-12** Roots can serve as formidable natural tools to enlarge cracks and crevices in bedrock. (a) A small plant growing out of a rock crack in California's Desolation Valley. (b) A full-sized lodgepole pine tree growing out of a joint in the granitic bedrock of Desolation Valley.

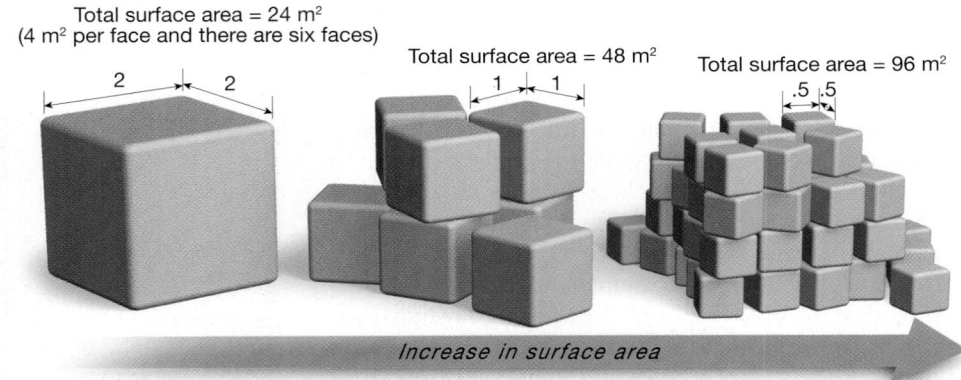

Total surface area = 24 m²
(4 m² per face and there are six faces)

Total surface area = 48 m²

Total surface area = 96 m²

Increase in surface area

▶ **Figure 15-13** As mechanical weathering fragments rock, the amount of surface area exposed to further weathering is increased. Each successive step shown here doubles the surface area of the preceding step.

producing boulders, cobbles, pebbles, sand, silt, and dust. As more and more rock surface area is exposed over time, the process proceeds at an accelerating rate (Figure 15-13).

Chemical Weathering

Mechanical weathering is often, but not always, accompanied by **chemical weathering**, which is the decomposition of rock by the chemical alteration of its minerals. Almost all minerals are subject to chemical alteration when exposed to atmospheric and biotic agents. Some minerals, such as quartz, are extremely resistant to chemical change, but many others are very susceptible. There are very few rocks that cannot be significantly affected by chemical weathering because the alteration of even a single significant mineral constituent can lead to the eventual disintegration of an entire rock mass.

One important effect of mechanical weathering is to expose bedrock to the forces of chemical weathering. The greater the surface area exposed, the more effective the chemical weathering. Thus, finer-grained materials decompose more rapidly than coarser-grained materials of identical composition because in fine-grained materials there is more exposed surface area (see Figure 15-13).

Virtually all chemical weathering requires moisture. Thus, an abundance of water enhances the effectiveness of chemical weathering, and chemical processes operate more rapidly in humid climates than in arid areas. Moreover, chemical reactions are more rapid under high-temperature conditions than in cooler regions. Consequently, chemical weathering is most efficient and conspicuous in warm, moist climates. In cold or dry lands, there is less chemical weathering and so mechanical weathering tends to dominate.

Some of the chemical reactions that affect rocks are very complex, but others are simple and predictable. The principal reacting agents are oxygen, water, and carbon dioxide, and the most significant processes are *oxidation*, *hydrolysis*, and *carbonation*. These processes often take place more or less simultaneously, largely because they all involve water that contains dissolved atmospheric gases. Water percolating

into the ground acts as a weak acid because of the presence of these gases and of decay products from the local vegetation; the presence of these impurities increases the water's capacity to drive chemical reactions.

Learning Check 15-6 **Describe the main difference between *mechanical weathering* and *chemical weathering*.**

Oxidation: When the oxygen dissolved in water comes into contact with certain rock minerals, the minerals undergo **oxidation**, in which the oxygen atoms combine with atoms of various metallic elements making up the minerals in the rock and form new products. The new substances are usually more voluminous, softer, and more easily removed than the original compounds.

When iron-bearing minerals react with oxygen (in other words, become oxidized), *iron oxide* is produced:

$$4Fe \quad + \quad 3O_2 \quad \rightarrow \quad 2Fe_2O_3$$

Iron + Oxygen → Iron Oxide (Hematite)

This reaction, probably the most common oxidation in the lithosphere, is called *rusting*, and the prevalence of rusty red stains on the surface of many rocks attests to its widespread occurrence (Figure 15-14). Similar effects are produced by the oxidation of aluminum. Because iron and aluminum are very common in Earth's crust, a reddish-brown color is seen in many rocks and soils, particularly in tropical areas because there oxidation is the most notable chemical weathering process. Rusting contributes significantly to weathering because oxides are usually softer and more easily removed than the original iron and aluminum compounds from which the oxides were formed.

Hydrolysis: Hydrolysis is the chemical union of water with another substance to produce a new compound that is nearly always softer and weaker than the original. Igneous rocks are particularly susceptible to hydrolysis because

◄ **Figure 15-14** Iron oxide (rust) stains on a sandstone cliff in Capitol Reef National Park in Utah.

their silicate minerals combine readily with water. Hydrolysis invariably increases the volume of the mineral, and this expansion can contribute to mechanical disintegration. In tropical areas, where water frequently percolates to considerable depth, hydrolysis often occurs far below the surface.

Carbonation: When carbon dioxide is dissolved in water *carbonic acid* (H_2CO_3) is formed. In **carbonation**, the carbonic acid reacts with carbonate rocks such as limestone to produce the very soluble product calcium bicarbonate. Calcium bicarbonate is readily removed by runoff or percolation and can also be deposited in crystalline form if the water is evaporated. We will discuss this process in greater detail in Chapter 17.

These and other less common chemical weathering processes are continuously at work at and beneath Earth's surface. Most chemically weathered rocks are changed physically, too. Their coherence is weakened, and the loose particles produced at Earth's surface are quite unlike the parent material. Beneath the surface, the rock holds together—but in a chemically altered condition. The major eventual products of chemical weathering are clays.

Learning Check 15-7 How are oxidation and carbonation similar? How are they different?

Biological Weathering

As already mentioned, plants frequently and animals occasionally contribute to weathering, and such processes involving living organisms are called **biological weathering**. Most notable is the penetration of growing plant roots into cracks and crevices (see Figure 15-12).

Lichens are primitive organisms that consist of algae and fungi living as a single unit. Typically they live on bare rock, bare soil, or tree bark (Figure 15-15). They draw minerals from the rock by ion exchange, and this leaching can weaken the rock. Moreover, expansion and contraction of lichens as they get alternately wet and dry flake off tiny particles of rock.

Burrowing by animals mixes soil effectively and is sometimes a factor in rock disintegration (for example, see Figure 12-6 in Chapter 12).

The total effect of all of these biotic actions is probably significant but difficult to evaluate because it may be obscured by subsequent chemical or mechanical weathering.

Differential Weathering

As we've just seen, all rock does not weather at the same rate or to the same extent—some kinds of rock are relatively weak and easily weathered, whereas other kinds of

▼ **Figure 15-15** Rocks covered with multicolored lichens in the Lake District of England.

rock are strong and more resistant to weathering. This is the simple but crucial concept in geomorphology of **differential weathering**. As we will see in the chapters that follow, differential weathering often leaves a prominent mark in the landscape: exposures of weaker rock are more obviously susceptible to mass wasting and erosion than exposures of stronger rock.

Although the inherent strength of the rock, of course, strongly influences differential weathering, the local environment also plays a role. For example, rock that resists weathering in an arid environment might actually be relatively "weak" in a humid environment, and so climate is one of the key variables influencing weathering.

> **Learning Check 15-8**   **Explain the concept of differential weathering.**

Climate and Weathering

The basic generalization is that weathering, particularly chemical weathering, is enhanced by a combination of high temperatures and abundant precipitation. Of these two factors, the moisture is usually more important than temperature. For example, we will see in Chapter 18 (The Topography of Arid Lands) that in most desert regions, because of a general lack of precipitation, mechanical weathering may be more conspicuous than chemical weathering. As we saw in Chapter 12 (Soils), the climatic regime significantly influences patterns of soil development.

There are many variations in the connection between weathering and climate; Figure 15-16 represents a generalized model of relevant relationships. Notice that, all else being equal, the depth of active weathering tends to be relatively shallow in regions of tundra and desert but relatively deep in regions of tropical rainforest.

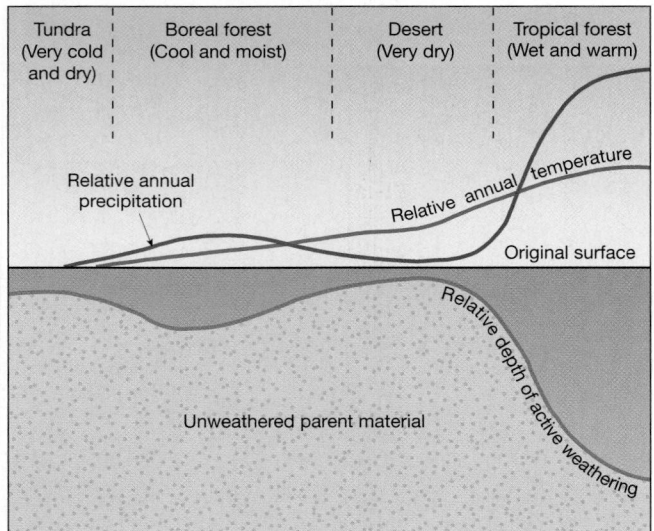

▲ **Figure 15-16** Relationship between important climatic elements and depth of weathering. The extreme effectiveness of weathering in the humid tropics is clearly shown. Humid midlatitude regions are omitted from this diagram because the relationships are more complex there.

MASS WASTING

Animation
Mass
Wasting

As we learned above, the denudation of Earth's surface is accomplished by weathering followed by mass wasting followed by erosion. The ultimate destiny of all weathered material is to be carried away by erosion, a topic we cover in the remaining chapters of this book. The remainder of this chapter is concerned with mass wasting (also called *mass movement*), the process whereby weathered material is moved a relatively short distance downslope under the direct influence of gravity. Although it is sometimes circumvented when erosive agents act on weathered material directly, mass wasting is normally the second step in a three-step denudation process: weathering, mass wasting, and erosion.

Gravity is inescapable; everywhere on the surface it pulls objects toward the center of Earth. Where the land is flat, the influence of gravity on topographic development is minimal. Even on gentle slopes, however, minute effects are likely to be significant in the long run, and on steep slopes the results are often immediate and conspicuous. Any loosened material is impelled downslope by gravity—in some cases falling abruptly or rolling rapidly, in others flowing or creeping with imperceptible gradualness.

The materials involved in these movements are all the varied products of weathering. Gigantic boulders respond to the pull of gravity in much the same fashion as do particles of dust, although the larger the object, the more immediate and pronounced the effect. Of particular importance, however, is the implication of "mass" in mass wasting; the accumulations of material moved—fragmented rock, regolith, and soil—are often extremely large and contain enormous amounts of mass.

Factors Influencing Mass Wasting

A variety of factors determine the characteristics of a mass wasting event, including the slope and the nature of the material involved.

Angle of Repose: All rock materials, from individual fragments to cohesive layers of soil, lie at rest on a slope if undisturbed unless the slope attains a critical steepness. The steepest angle that can be assumed by loose fragments on a slope without downslope movement is called the **angle of repose**. This angle, which varies with the nature and internal cohesion of the material, represents a fine balance between the pull of gravity and the cohesion and friction of the rock material. If additional material accumulates on a debris pile lying on a slope that is near the angle of repose, the newly added material may upset the balance (because the added weight overcomes the friction force that is keeping the pile from sliding) and may cause all or part of the material to slide downward.

Water: If water is added to the rock material through rainfall, snowmelt, or subsurface flow, the mobility is usually increased, particularly if the rock fragments are small. Water is a "lubricating" medium, and it diminishes friction between particles so that they can slide past one another more readily. Water also adds to the buoyancy and weight of the weathered material, which makes for a lower angle of repose and adds momentum once movement is under way. For this reason, mass wasting is particularly likely during and after heavy rains.

Clay: Another facilitator of mass wasting is *clay*. As noted in Chapter 12, clays readily absorb water. This absorbed water, combined with the fine-grained texture of the material, makes clay a very slippery and mobile substance. Any material resting on clay can often be set in motion by rainfall or an earthquake shock, even on very gentle slopes. Indeed, some clay formations are called *quick clays* because they spontaneously change from a relatively solid mass to a near-liquid condition as the result of a sudden disturbance or shock.

Permafrost: In subarctic regions and at high latitudes, mass wasting is often initiated by the heaving action of frozen groundwater. The presence of thawed, water-saturated ground in summer overlying permanently frozen subsoil (*permafrost*) also contributes to mass wasting in such regions. Some geomorphologists assert that, in the subarctic, mass wasting is the single most important means of transport of weathered material.

Although some types of mass wasting are rapid, others are slow and gradual (Figure 15-17). In fact, the rate of movement can be quite variable. Here, as a way of highlighting the key characteristics of movement, we group all kinds of mass wasting into just four categories—*fall, slide, flow,* and *creep*—although in nature the various types often overlap.

Learning Check 15-9 **What is meant by the *angle of repose* of a rock deposit?**

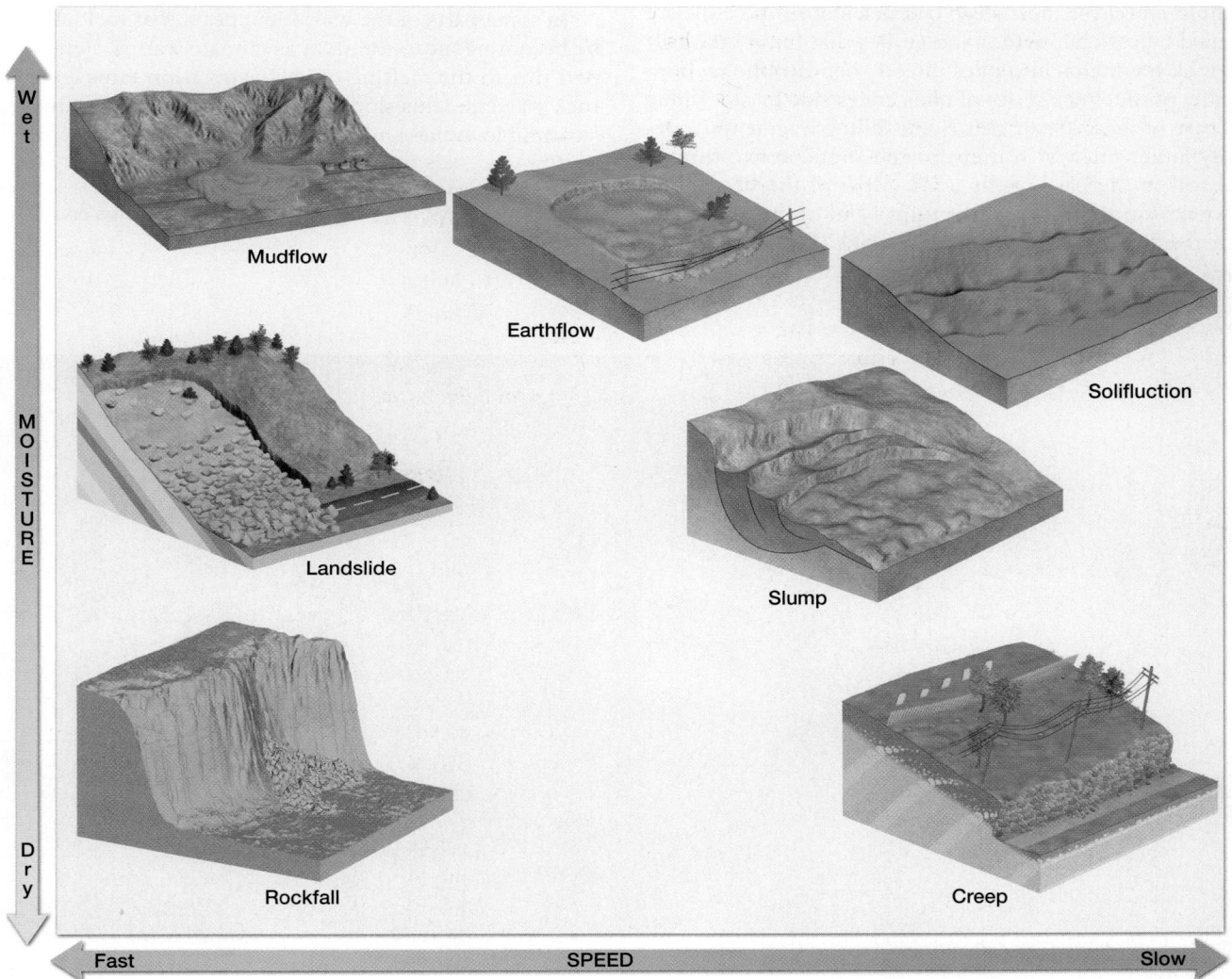

▲ **Figure 15-17** Speed and moisture relationships for the various types of mass wasting. For example, *mudflow* entails the rapid movement of very wet material, whereas *rockfall* is the very rapid movement of dry material.

Fall  FG4, FG5

The simplest and most obvious form of mass wasting is **rockfall**, or simply **fall**, the falling of pieces of rock downslope. When loosened by weathering on a very steep slope, a rock fragment may simply be dislodged and fall, roll, or bounce down to the bottom of that slope. This is a very characteristic event in mountainous areas, particularly as a result of frost wedging. Normally the fragments do not travel far before they become lodged, although the lodging may be unstable and temporary.

Pieces of unsorted, angular rock that fall in this fashion are referred to collectively as **talus** or **scree** (some geomorphologists use the term *talus* when referring to larger blocks and *scree* when the material is smaller, but the terms are often used interchangeably). Sometimes the fragments accumulate relatively uniformly along the base of the slope, in which case the resultant landform is called a *talus slope* or *talus apron*. More characteristically, however, the dislodged rocks collect in sloping, cone-shaped heaps called **talus cones** (Figure 15-18). This cone pattern is commonplace because most steep bedrock slopes and cliffs are seamed by vertical ravines and gullies that funnel the falling rock fragments into piles directly beneath the ravines, usually producing a series of talus cones side by side along the base of the slope or cliff. Some falling fragments, especially larger ones with their greater momentum, tumble and roll to the base of the cone. Most of the new talus, however, comes to rest at the upper end of the cone. The cone thereby grows up the mountainside (Figure 15-18b).

The angle of repose for talus is very high, generally about 35° and sometimes as great as 40°. New material is frequently added to the top of the cone, where the fragments are invariably in delicate equilibrium. Each new piece that falls onto the talus cone may dislodge material, causing rock to tumble down the cone until it again stabilizes at the angle of repose.

Rock Glaciers: In some rugged mountain areas, talus accumulates in great masses, and these masses may move slowly downslope under their own weight. As we shall see in Chapter 19, glaciers move in a somewhat similar way, and for this reason these extremely slow flows of talus are called **rock glaciers**. The flow in rock glaciers is caused primarily by the pull of gravity, aided by freeze–thaw temperature changes and may largely be independent of any lubricating effect of water. Rock glaciers occur primarily in glacial environments; many are found in midlatitude mountains that are relics of periods of glaciation. They are normally found on relatively steep slopes but sometimes extend far down-valley and even out onto an adjacent plain.

In some parts of the world it appears that rockfalls may be becoming more common as climate warms. Perhaps in part due to the melting of ice deep within talus cones or rock glaciers, talus slopes may become more unstable and susceptible to mass movement.

Learning Check 15-10 **How does a *talus cone* form?**

▲ **Figure 15-18** (a) Talus cones at the foot of a steep slope develop as a result of rockfall. (b) An accumulation of talus at the base of a steep slope in Bloody Canyon, near Tioga Pass in the Sierra Nevada of California.

▲ **Figure 15-19** Landslide is a type of slope failure that entails the rapid downslope movement of masses of weathered rock along a flat sliding plane.

Slide FG8

In mountainous terrain, landslides carry large masses of rock and soil downslope abruptly and often catastrophically. A **landslide** is a general term for a type of *slope failure* involving an instantaneous collapse of a slope and movement along a generally flat sliding plane (Figure 15-19). In other words, the sliding material represents a rigid mass that is suddenly displaced without any fluid flow. Landslides do not require the lubricating effects of water or clay, although the presence of water may contribute to the action; many slides are triggered by rains that add weight to already overloaded slopes. Landslides may be activated by other stimuli as well, most notably by earthquakes (Figure 15-20). Slides are also sometimes initiated simply by lateral erosion of a stream that undercuts its bank and thus oversteepens the slope.

Some slides move only regolith, but many large slides also involve masses of bedrock detached along joint planes and fracture zones. The term *rock avalanche* (or *debris avalanche*) is often used to describe slides consisting primarily of rock without large quantities of soil or other fine-grained material.

Animation
The Eruption of
Mount St. Helens

Landslide action is not only abrupt but also rapid. Precise measurement of the rate of movement is obviously impossible, but eyewitness accounts affirm speeds of 160 kilometers (100 miles) per hour. Thunderous noise accompanies the slide, and the blasts of air that the slide creates can strip leaves, twigs, and even branches from nearby trees.

The immediate topographic result of a landslide may be threefold. First, on the hill where the slide originated, there is a deep and extensive *scar*, usually exposing a mixture of bedrock and scattered debris.

Second, because most landslides occur in steep, mountainous terrain, the great mass of material (displaced volume is sometimes measured in cubic kilometers) that roars downslope may choke the valley at the bottom with debris, usually in the form of either a broad ridge or low-lying cone. Its surface consists of a jumble of unsorted material, ranging from immense boulders to fine dust. Moreover, the momentum of the slide may push material several hundred meters up the slope on the other side of the valley.

Finally, in the valley bottom where the slide material comes to rest, a natural dam across the width of the valley may form, blocking the valley-bottom stream and producing a new lake, which becomes larger and larger until it either overtops the dam or cuts a path through it.

Slump: An extremely common form of mass wasting is the type of slide called a **slump**. Slumping involves slope failure in which the rock or regolith moves downward and at the same time rotates outward along a curved slide plane that has its concave side facing upward (for this reason, a slump is sometimes called a *rotational slide*). The upper portion of the moving material tilts down and back, and the lower portion moves upward and outward. The top of the slump is usually marked by a crescent-shaped scarp face, sometimes with a steplike arrangement of smaller scarps and terraces below. The bottom of the slumping block consists of a bulging lobe of saturated debris protruding downslope or into the valley bottom (Figure 15-21).

Learning Check 15-11 **Explain how heavy rainfall can trigger a *landslide* or *slump*.**

▼ **Figure 15-20** An earthquake in July 2007 triggered this landslide that slipped down on a seafront road in Kashiwazaki, northern Japan.

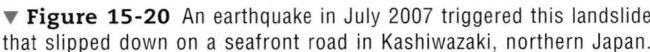

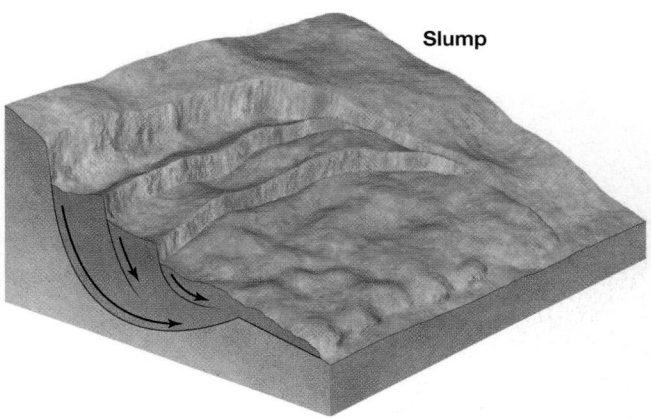

▲ **Figure 15-21** Slump involves movement along a curved sliding plane.

Slump

Flow FG9, FG12

In another form of mass wasting, a section of a slope becomes unstable, owing to the addition of water, and flows downhill. In some cases, the flow is fairly rapid, but it is in others gradual and sluggish. Usually the center of the mass moves more rapidly than the base and sides, which are retarded by friction.

Many flows are relatively small, often encompassing an area of only a few square meters. More characteristically, however, they cover several tens or hundreds of hectares. (A hectare equals about 2.5 acres.) Normally, they are relatively shallow phenomena, including only soil and regolith, but under certain conditions a considerable amount of bedrock may be involved.

As with other forms of mass movement, gravity is the impelling force. Water is an important catalyst to the movement; the surface materials become unstable with the added weight of water, and their cohesion is diminished by waterlogging, so that they are more responsive to the pull of gravity. The presence of clay also promotes flow, as some clay minerals become very slippery when lubricated with any sort of moisture.

Earthflow: The most common flow movement is **earthflow**, in which a portion of a water-saturated slope moves a limited distance downhill, normally during or immediately after a heavy rain. At the place where the flow originates, there is usually a distinct scar in the surface of the slope, either cracks or a prominent oversteepened scarp face (Figure 15-22). An earthflow is most conspicuous in its lower portion, where a bulging lobe of material pushes out onto the valley floor.

This type of slope failure is relatively common on hillsides that are not densely vegetated and often results in blocked transportation lines (roads, railways) in valley bottoms. Property damage is occasionally extensive, but the rate of movement is usually so sluggish that there is no threat to life.

Slope failures such as slides and earthflows often exhibit repeated movement over a period of years or decades. Once a slope has been destabilized, it may move again when the combination of factors is right—especially after heavy rainfall. One example of such repeated mass wasting

events is described in the box, "People and the Environment: The La Conchita Landslides."

> **Learning Check 15-12** In what ways are *landslides* and *earthflows* similar? In what ways are they different?

Mudflow: A mudflow originates in drainage basins in arid and semiarid country when a heavy rain following a long dry spell produces a cascading runoff too voluminous to be absorbed into the soil. Fine debris is picked up from the hillsides by the runoff and concentrated in the valley bottoms, where it flows down-valley with the consistency of wet concrete. The leading edge of the mudflow continues to accumulate load, becoming increasingly stiff and retarding the flow of the more liquid upstream portions, so that the entire mudflow moves haltingly down the valley. When a mudflow reaches the mouth of the valley and abruptly leaves its confining walls, the pent-up liquid behind the glutinous leading edge breaks through with a rush, spreading muddy debris into a wide sheet (Figure 15-23). A *volcanic mudflow* (*lahar*) described in Chapter 14 is a special kind of mudflow that develops on the slopes of volcanoes.

Mudflows often pick up large rocks, including huge boulders, and carry them along as part of their load. In some cases, the large pieces are so numerous that the term **debris flow** is used in preference to mudflow (Figure 15-24).

An important distinction between earthflow and mudflow is that mudflows (and debris flows) move along the surface of a slope and down established drainage channels, whereas earthflow involves a slope failure and has little or no relationship to the drainage network. Moreover, mudflows are normally much more rapid, with a rate of movement intermediate between the sluggish surge of an earthflow and the rapid flow of a stream of water. Mudflows and debris flows are potentially more dangerous to humans than earthflows because of the more rapid movement, the larger quantity of debris involved, and the fact that the mudflow often discharges abruptly across a piedmont zone at the foot of a mountain, which is likely to be a favored area for human settlement and intensive agriculture.

▲ **Figure 15-22** Earthflow takes place on hillsides when wet surface material begins to flow downslope.

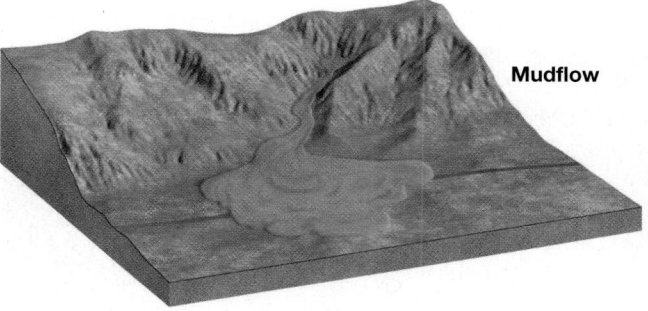

▲ **Figure 15-23** Mudflows entail the rapid movement of very wet material through a canyon or valley. The mud and debris is typically deposited at the mouth of the valley in a fan-shaped deposit.

◀ **Figure 15-24** In January 2011, a large debris flow poured through the streets of Nova Friburgo in Brazil. More than 500 people were killed by floods, mudflows, and landslides in this region.

As we will see in Chapter 18, mudflow and debris flow are especially important mass wasting processes in arid regions. In the mountain areas of deserts, an intense, local thunderstorm can quickly mobilize loose, weathered material; the flow will move rapidly down a desert canyon, depositing the mud and debris at the foot of the mountains.

The media often incorrectly refers to almost all kinds of mass wasting with the rather ambiguous term *mudslide*. As we have just seen, there are significant differences between the various kinds of slides and flows.

Learning Check 15-13 **Describe and explain the differences between an *earthflow* and a *mudflow*.**

Creep

The slowest and least perceptible form of mass wasting, **creep**—or **soil creep**—consists of a very gradual downhill movement of soil and regolith so unobtrusive that it can normally be recognized only by indirect evidence. Generally the entire slope is involved. Creep is such a pervasive phenomenon that it occurs all over the world on sloping land. Although most notable on steep, lightly vegetated slopes, it also occurs on gentle slopes that have a dense plant cover. Wherever weathered materials are available for movement on land that is not flat, creep is a persistent form of mass wasting.

Creep is universal. Infinite numbers of tiny bits of lithospheric material, as well as many larger pieces, march slowly and sporadically downslope from the places where they were produced by weathering or deposited after erosion. When water is present in the surface material, creep is usually accelerated because the lubricating effect allows individual particles to move more easily and because water adds to the weight of the mass.

Causes of Creep: Creep is caused by the interaction of various factors, the most significant being alternation of freeze/thaw or wet/dry conditions. When water in the soil freezes, soil particles tend to be displaced upward and in the direction perpendicular to the ground surface due to ice expansion, as Figure 15-25 shows. After thawing, however, the particles settle downward, not directly into their original position but rather pulled slightly downslope by gravity. With countless repetitions, this process can result in downhill movement of the entire slope.

Many other agents also contribute to creep. Indeed, any activity that disturbs soil and regolith on a sloping surface is a contributor because gravity affects every rearrangement of particles, attracting them downslope. For example, burrowing animals pile most of their excavated material downslope, and subsequent infilling of burrows is mostly by material from the upslope side. As plant roots grow, they also tend to displace particles downslope. Animals that walk on the surface exert a downslope movement as well. Even the shaking of earthquakes or thunder produces disturbances that stimulate creep.

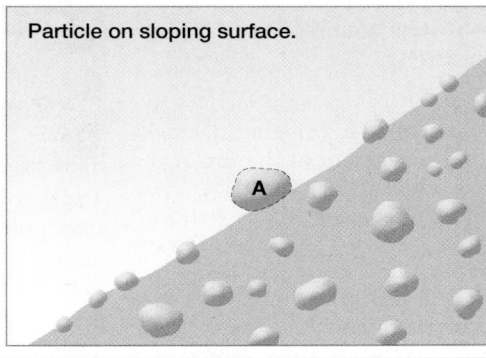

Particle on sloping surface.

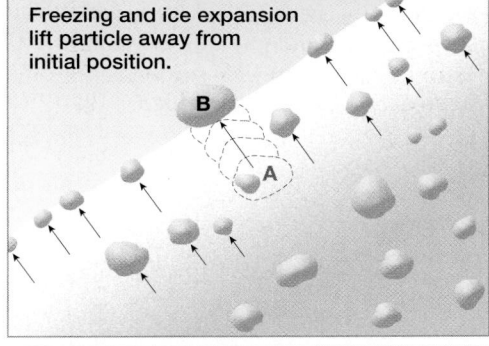

Freezing and ice expansion lift particle away from initial position.

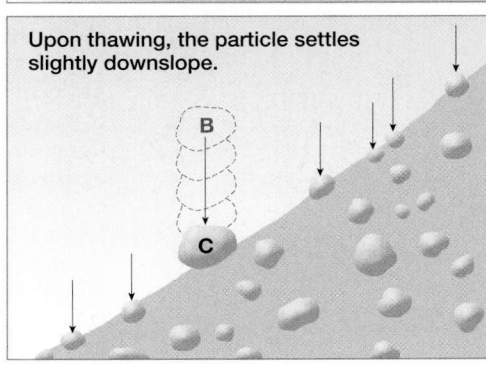

Upon thawing, the particle settles slightly downslope.

▲ **Figure 15-25** The movement of a typical rock particle in a freeze–thaw situation. Freezing and ice expansion lift the particle perpendicular to the slope (from A to B); upon thawing, the particle settles slightly downslope (from B to C).

PEOPLE AND THE ENVIRONMENT

The La Conchita Landslides

Once a landslide has occurred on a hillside, in coming years that slide is quite likely to move again. A good example of the propensity for destabilized slopes to fail multiple times is found in the coastal California community of La Conchita (Figure 15-A).

La Conchita is a small town just southeast of Santa Barbara. Houses here are built on a narrow coastal strip at the foot of a steep bluff about 180 meters (600 feet) high. The bluff is comprised of poorly cemented marine sedimentary rocks and shows evidence of prehistoric landslides. The recent sequence of slope failures at La Conchita began in 1995.

1995 Landslide: Evidence of cracks and slight movement at the top of the bluff was noticeable by December 1994. That winter was exceptionally wet, with the region receiving twice its average amount of rainfall. In January 1995 alone 62.3 centimeters (24.53 inches) of rain fell—more than five times the monthly average. Then, after a dry February, a modest-size storm arrived on March 2 and 3. On the afternoon of March 4, 1995, a 120 meter (400 foot) wide section of the slope above La Conchita failed,

▲ **Figure 15-B** Aerial photograph of the 1995 La Conchita landslide.

moving about 330 meters (1100 feet) downhill as a slump and earthflow, destroying or damaging nine homes (Figure 15-B). Ten days later, a debris flow from a canyon just to the northwest of the town damaged five more homes. The 1995 slide appears to have taken place within the area of a much larger prehistoric slide that involved the entire bluff above the town.

2005 Debris Flow: Ten years later, following a 15-day period that brought record or near-record amounts of rainfall to the region, the La Conchita slide moved again. Between December 27, 2004, and January 10, 2005, the nearby city of Ventura (about 20 kilometers [12 miles] southeast of La Conchita) received 37.8 centimeters (14.9 inches) of rain—the equivalent of nearly

a year's average rainfall. On the afternoon of January 10, 2005, the slope above La Conchita failed again, this time remobilizing a 90 meter (300 foot) wide, 350 meter (1150 foot) long section of the 1995 landslide deposit as a fast-moving debris flow (Figure 15-C). The 2005 event destroyed 13 houses, damaged 23 more, and killed 10 people.

Analysis showed that the 1995 slide entailed fairly deep movement—consistent with deep infiltration of water into the slope, and therefore the long lag time between the heavy rains of January and the slide itself. The 2005 event, on the other hand, was much shallower and much more fluid in its movement than the 1995 slide; this type of movement is consistent with the very short lag time between the heavy rains that occurred in the two weeks prior, and the debris flow that followed.

Will the La Conchita slide move again? The answer is probably yes, and local authorities are being cautious. During a heavy rain event in December 2010, several homes north of the main slide were evacuated when a new small landslide began to develop. What remains uncertain is whether the next large slide event will involve the rapid movement of remobilized material as in 2005, or movement originating deeper within the slope as in 1995.

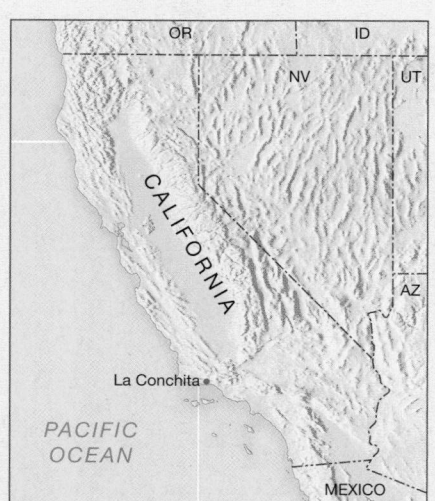

▲ **Figure 15-A** Regional map of La Conchita, California.

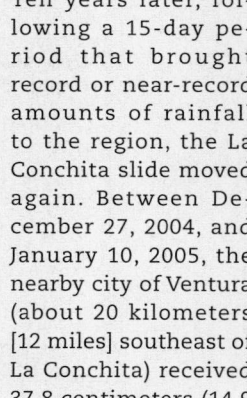

▲ **Figure 15-C** Aerial photograph of the 2005 La Conchita debris flow.

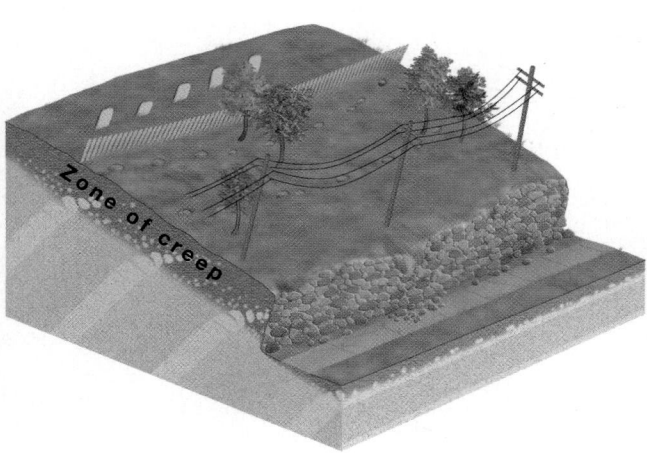

▲ **Figure 15-26** Visual evidence of soil creep: displacement and/or bending of fences, utility poles, and retaining walls.

▲ **Figure 15-27** A hillside laced with terracettes near Palmerston North, on the North Island of New Zealand. Heavy use of the slope by sheep accentuates the ridges.

Whenever it occurs, creep is a very slow process, commonly just a fraction of a centimeter per year. Creep operates faster on steep or water-saturated slopes than on gentle or dry or vegetated slopes.

Whatever the creep rate, it is much too slow for the eye to perceive and the results are all but invisible. Creep is usually recognized only through the displacement of human-built structures—most commonly when fence posts and utility poles are tilted downhill. Retaining walls may be broken or displaced, and even roadbeds may be disturbed (Figure 15-26). Unlike the other forms of mass wasting, creep produces few distinctive landforms. Rather it induces an imperceptible diminishing of slope angles and gradual lowering of hilltops—in other words, a widespread but minute smoothing of the land surface.

Under certain conditions, and usually on steep grassy slopes, grazing animals accentuate soil creep through the formation of a network of hillside ridges known as *terracettes*. Over time, the entire hillside may be covered with a maze of these terracettes (Figure 15-27).

Learning Check 15-14 **What processes are responsible for soil creep?**

Solifluction: A special form of creep that produces a distinctive surface appearance is **solifluction** (meaning "soil flowage"), a process largely restricted to high latitude and high elevation tundra landscapes beyond the treeline (Figure 15-28). During the summer, the near-surface portion of the ground (called the *active layer*) thaws, but the meltwater cannot percolate deeper because of the permafrost below. The spaces between the soil particles become saturated, and the heavy surface material sags slowly downslope. Movement is erratic and irregular, with lobes overlapping one another in a haphazard, fish-scale pattern. The lobes move only a few centimeters per year, but they remain very

▶ **Figure 15-28** Solifluction in the high country of Colorado's Rocky Mountain National Park. The surface has gradually slipped downslope about 60 meters (200 feet). For scale, note the cars on Trail Ridge Road in the upper right.

obvious in the landscape, in part because of the scarcity of vegetation. Where solifluction occurs, drainage channels are usually scarce because water flow during the short summer is mostly lateral through the soil rather than across the surface (Figure 15-29).

▲ **Figure 15-29** Solifluction lobes on a hillside near Breidalfjellet, Troms, Norway.

Chapter 15   LEARNING REVIEW

After studying this chapter, you should be able to answer the following questions. Key terms from each text section are shown in **bold type**. Definitions for key terms are also found in the glossary at the back of the book.

KEY TERMS AND CONCEPTS

Denudation (*p. 447*)

1. What is meant by **denudation**?
2. Distinguish among **weathering**, **mass wasting**, and **erosion**.

Weathering and Rock Openings (*p. 448*)

3. What roles do rock openings play in weathering processes?
4. What is the difference between a **joint** and a fault?
5. What are **master joints**, and how can they influence the topography of a landscape?

Weathering Agents (*p. 450*)

6. What are the general differences between **mechanical weathering** and **chemical weathering**?
7. Explain the mechanics of **frost wedging**.
8. Explain the process of **salt wedging**.
9. Explain the weathering process of **exfoliation** ("unloading") that is responsible for features such as **exfoliation domes**.
10. What is the relationship between **oxidation** and rust?
11. Briefly describe the chemical weathering processes of **hydrolysis** and **carbonation**.

12. Describe and explain one example of **biological weathering**.
13. What is meant by **differential weathering**?

Mass Wasting (*p. 456*)

14. How does the **angle of repose** affect mass wasting?
15. Describe the process of **rockfall (fall)**.
16. Describe the origin and general characteristics of **talus (scree)**.
17. What is a **talus cone**, and where does one typically develop?
18. What is a **rock glacier**?
19. What roles may heavy rain play in triggering a **landslide**?
20. How is a **slump** different from other kinds of landslide?
21. What are the differences between a landslide and a **mudflow**?
22. How is **earthflow** different from mudflow and **debris flow**?
23. Explain the process of **soil creep**.
24. In what kinds of environments is **solifluction** common?

STUDY QUESTIONS

1. Explain how it is possible for weathering to take place beneath the surface of bedrock.
2. Why is chemical weathering more effective in humid climates than in arid climates?
3. What is the relationship between gravity and mass wasting?
4. What is the role of clay in mass wasting?
5. In what ways can rainfall expedite mass wasting?

EXERCISES

1. A large square slab of granite, 1 meter thick and 100 meters to a side, falls off an exfoliation dome. The density of granite is 2.7 grams/cm³. Calculate the total mass of the rock that fell: _____ kilograms
2. Assume that the rate of movement of the solifluction lobe in Figure 15-28 is 5 centimeters per year. How many years did it take for the lobe to travel 60 meters (200 feet) downslope? _____ years
3. The chemical weathering of rocks such as basalt produces a "rind" of altered minerals that increases in thickness the longer the rock has been exposed. Although the rate of weathering varies from location to location (especially due to differences in climate),

the thickness of the weathering rind can offer a rough estimate of how long a rock has been exposed to weathering—the thicker the rind, the longer the rock as been exposed. One study found that the thickness of the weathering rind increased by about 0.007 millimeters for every 1000 years of exposure. Assuming a constant rate of weathering (a simplistic assumption), estimate how long the rocks have been exposed to weathering if the:
   a. Weathering rind is 0.5 mm thick = _____ years of exposure
   b. Weathering rind is 1.5 mm thick = _____ years of exposure

Seeing Geographically

Look again at the photograph of Wensu Grand Canyon in China at the beginning of the chapter (p. 446). What kinds of structures in the bedrock are most likely responsible for the general orientation of the landforms here? Which mass wasting processes are likely responsible for removing weathered material away from the bedrock?

MasteringGeography™

Looking for additional review and test prep materials? Visit the Study Area in MasteringGeography™ to enhance your geographic literacy, spatial reasoning skills, and understanding of this chapter's content by accessing a variety of resources, including geoscience animations, MapMaster interactive maps, videos, RSS feeds, flashcards, web links, self-study quizzes, and an eText version of *McKnight's Physical Geography: A Landscape Appreciation.*

THE LANDSCAPE IS SHAPED BY A VARIETY OF PROCESSES

functioning in concert. In Chapter 14 we considered internal processes, and in Chapter 15 we studied the external processes of weathering and mass wasting. In Chapters 16 through 20, we concentrate on the external land-shaping agents that work by erosion and deposition: running water, subsurface waters, wind, moving ice, and coastal waters. By far the most important of these external agents in transporting and depositing material is running water moving over the land: *fluvial processes*—the topic of this chapter.

Running water probably contributes more to shaping landforms than all other external agents combined. This is true not because running water is more forceful than other agents (moving ice and pounding waves often apply much greater amounts of energy per unit area), but rather because running water is nearly ubiquitous: it exists everywhere except in Antarctica. (Wind is ubiquitous, too, but trivial in its power as a terrain sculptor.) So it is appropriate for us to begin our study of erosional and depositional processes with the work of running water.

As you study this chapter, think about these key questions:

- **What is the difference between streamflow and overland flow, and how do these concepts help define valleys and interfluves?**

- **Why are floods so important in understanding the erosional and depositional work of streams?**

- **Under what circumstances do streams tend to develop sinuous, meandering, and braided channel patterns?**

- **How do stream drainage patterns reflect the underlying structure of a landscape?**

- **Through which processes do streams deepen, widen, and lengthen their valleys?**

- **What are the typical landforms found on a floodplain, and how do they change over time?**

- **What is stream rejuvenation and what landforms can it produce?**

- **How do different theories of landform development explain changes in the fluvial landscape?**

The Impact of Fluvial Processes on the Landscape

Moving water is so widespread and effective as an agent of erosion and deposition that its influence on the landscape is usually the prominent—and in many cases, the dominant—process at work. The shapes of most valleys are strongly influenced by the water that runs through them—especially through the transportation and deposition of sediment (Figure 16-1). Areas above the valleys are less affected by running water, but even there flowing water may significantly influence the shape of the land.

The basic landscape-sculpting effect of running water is to smooth irregularities—in simplest terms, to wear down the topography by erosion and transportation of debris, and fill up the valleys by deposition.

The Green River in western Wyoming. Describe the general relief of this valley and the gradient of the river here. What do you see in this valley that suggests that the river has changed course in the past? Does it appear that more deposition from the river is occurring along the inside bank of a river turn or along the outside bank?

▲ **Figure 16-1** The work of some rivers is very conspicuous. The Green River in northeastern Utah helped carve Whirlpool Canyon through fluvial erosion and by transporting away the rock deposited into the valley bottom by side streams and mass wasting.

STREAMS AND STREAM SYSTEMS

As we learned in Chapter 9, in the study of geomorphology we call any channeled flow of water a **stream**—whether it is a tiny creek or an enormous river. Streams and their valleys dissect the land in a multitude of patterns. However, those patterns exhibit important similarities, and so the study of individual streams can produce additional generalities to aid in our understanding of topographic development. Before we get into the specifics of fluvial processes and their topographic results, we need to introduce a few basic concepts.

Streamflow and Overland Flow

Fluvial processes, defined as those that involve running water, encompass both the unchanneled downslope movement of surface water, called **overland flow**, and the channeled movement of water along a valley bottom, called **streamflow**.

Valleys and Interfluves

All the surfaces of the continents can be considered to consist of two topographic elements: *valleys* and *interfluves*. The distinction between the two is not always obvious in nature, but the conceptual difference is clear. A **valley** is that portion of the terrain in which a drainage system is clearly established (Figure 16-2). It includes the valley bottom that is partially or totally occupied by the channel of a stream, as well as the valley walls that rise above the

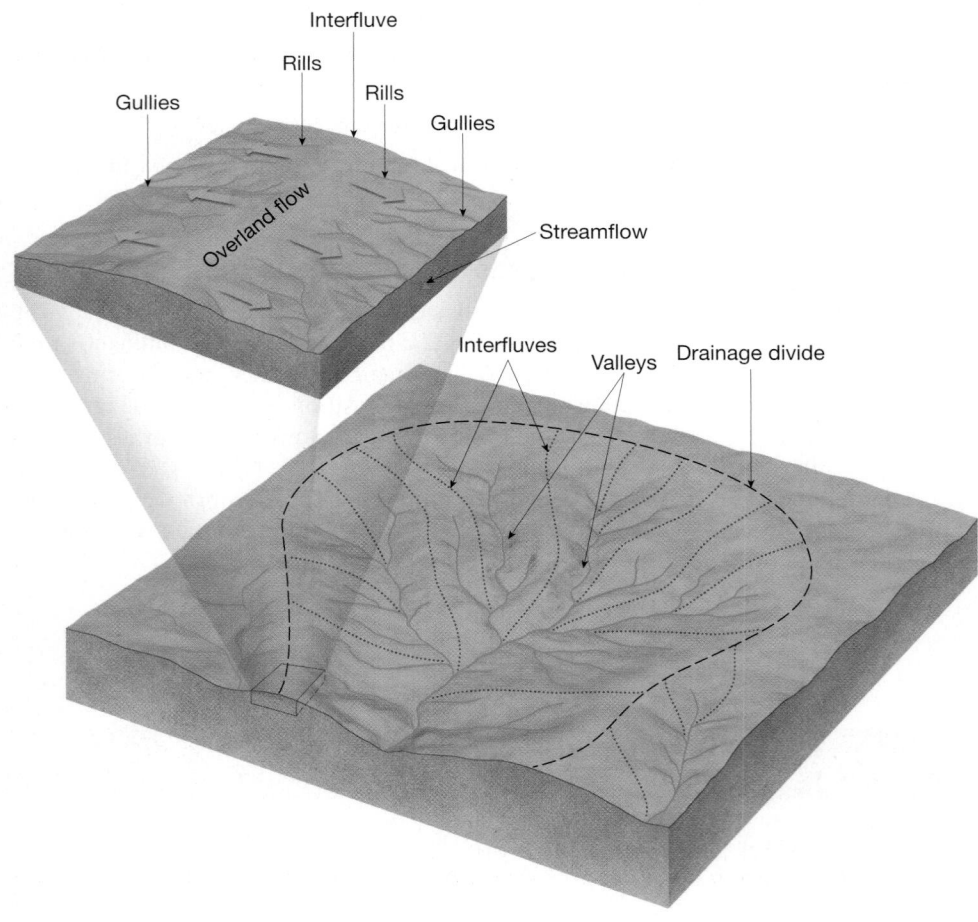

▶ **Figure 16-2** Valleys and interfluves. Valleys normally have clear-cut drainage systems; interfluves do not.

valley bottom on both sides. The upper limit of a valley is not always readily apparent, but it can be clearly conceptualized as a lip or rim at the top of the valley walls above which drainage channels are either absent or indistinct.

An **interfluve** (from Latin, *inter*, meaning "between," and *fluvia*, meaning "rivers") is the higher land above the valley walls that separates adjacent valleys. Some interfluves consist of ridgetops or mountain crests with precipitous slopes, but others are simply broad and flattish divides between drainage systems. Conceptually, all parts of the terrain not in a valley are part of an interfluve. We can envision that, on an interfluve, water will move downslope through unchanneled overland flow until it reaches the lip of the interfluve; there, as the water drops off the lip of the interfluve into the first small gullies of the valley system, streamflow begins.

However, these simplistic definitions are not always applicable in nature. Swamps and marshes, for example, are typically found in sections of valleys where there is not a clearly established drainage system, but may also be found on interfluves.

Drainage Basins

The **drainage basin** or **watershed** of a particular stream is all the area that contributes overland flow, streamflow, and groundwater to that stream. In other words, the drainage basin consists of a stream's valley bottom, valley sides, and those portions of the surrounding interfluves that drain toward the valley. Conceptually, the drainage basin terminates at a **drainage divide**, which is the line of separation between runoff that descends in the direction of one drainage basin and runoff that goes toward an adjacent basin. A drainage divide can be a sharp ridge between drainage basins, or it can be a more subtle separation of basins in the form of an interfluve.

Every stream of any size has its own drainage basin, but for practical purposes the term is often reserved for major streams. The drainage basin of a principal river encompasses the smaller drainage basins of all its tributaries; consequently, larger basins include a hierarchy of smaller tributary basins (Figure 16-3).

Dams are often built to capture the runoff of a drainage basin. The impounded water may serve a variety of purposes, including the generation of electrical power. See the box, "Energy for the 21st Century: Hydropower."

> **Learning Check 16-1** **Explain the relationship of *streamflow* to *interfluves* and *valleys*. (Answer on p. AK-5)**

Stream Orders

In every drainage basin, small streams come together to form successively larger ones, and small valleys join

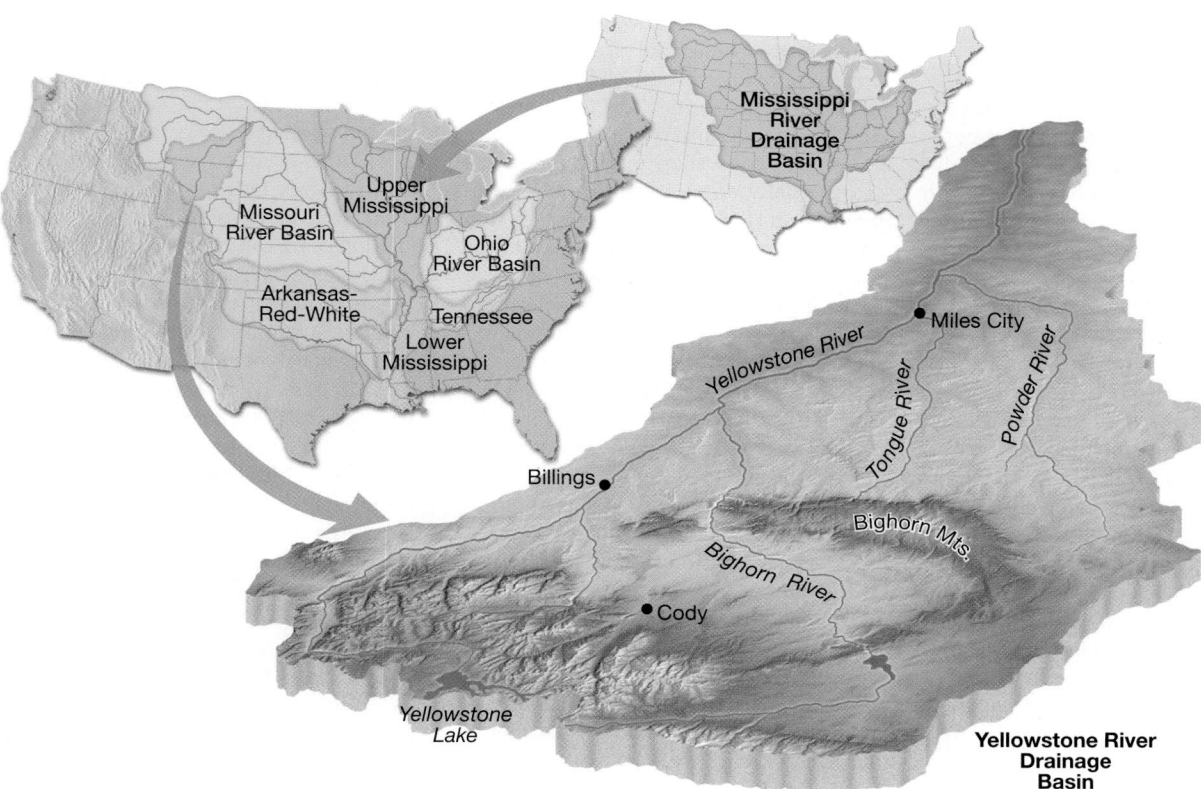

▲ **Figure 16-3** A nested hierarchy of drainage basins. Many sub-basins are found within the overall Mississippi River drainage basin. For example, beginning in the Yellowstone River drainage basin, the Bighorn River flows into the Yellowstone River, which flows into the Missouri River, which flows into the Mississippi River; finally, the Mississippi empties into the Gulf of Mexico.

Hydropower

▶ Nancy Lee Wilkinson, San Francisco State University

Moving water has the power to do work, as people discovered long ago. Water wheels powered the mills and looms of the Industrial Revolution, making "fall line" sites with sufficient volume and velocity of flowing water especially valuable. Hydroelectric generation on a commercial scale began in the United States in the early 1880s and currently provides about 20 percent of the world's electricity, with the largest facilities in China (Figure 16-A), Canada, Brazil, the United States, and Russia.

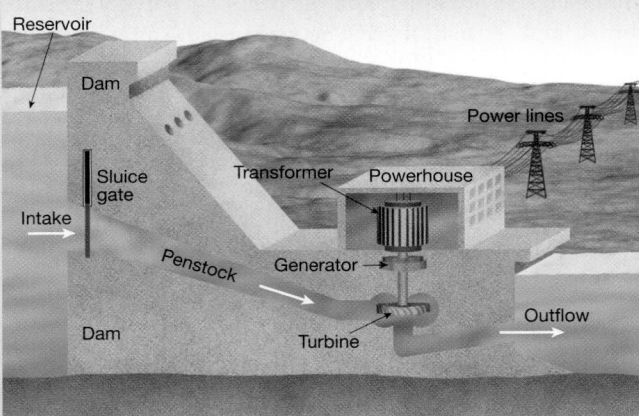

▲ **Figure 16-B** Hydroelectric generator.

▲ **Figure 16-A** Three Gorges Dam in China.

How Hydropower Works:

Hydroelectric plants convert the potential energy of water stored behind a dam into kinetic energy (energy of motion). The dam stores water in a reservoir to increase its volume and depth; the reservoir may also serve other purposes, such as flood control, recreation, and water storage for agriculture or cities. Water exits the reservoir through large pipes (penstocks) near the base of the dam, turning turbines several meters across. The turbines spin giant shafts topped by generators. As the turbines spin, the generator produces electric current (Figure 16-B).

The amount of electricity a hydropower plant generates depends on the volume of water available and the elevation difference between the water supply and the turbine. The best hydropower sites are deep, narrow canyons with solid bedrock where elevation changes rapidly and a tall dam can be built with little material.

Hydropower's Advantages: Hy-

dropower has important advantages. Once built, dams generate minimal air and water pollution, providing an appealing alternative to coal, gas, or nuclear power plants. They require no fuel and only a small labor force to operate, and can be turned on quickly in response to power demand.

Dams built for hydropower production can store water for irrigation or other uses, facilitate navigation, and provide recreational opportunities and flood protection. Revenues from these multiple uses can offset construction and operating costs. Finally, dams are impressive public projects that symbolize progress and permanence and can continue generating electricity for a hundred years or more. For these reasons, hydropower dams are an attractive tool for economic development.

Social and Environmental Impacts of Dams: The social and

environmental impacts of dams are substantial. Dams flood forests, fertile fields, and cities along streams, displacing millions of people worldwide. They block the upstream migration of fish that spawn in freshwater, flood upstream habitats, and dry up wetlands that harbor great biodiversity. They block transport of river sediment, increasing riverbank erosion and starving downstream beaches of sand and gravel. The failure of aging or poorly built dams can also pose a hazard to downstream communities.

The consequences of dam building became apparent as hydroelectric development boomed in the southeastern and western United States during the twentieth century and dams became a major tool in international development. By the year 2000, there were large dams on more than half of Earth's major rivers, and major hydropower projects were under construction in China, Amazonia, Southeast Asia, and Africa. Some of these projects encountered angry resistance. Meanwhile, American environmentalists began calling for dams to be decommissioned if they had outlived their usefulness and for their damaged streams and watersheds to be restored.

Hydropower's Future: Dam building has declined from a peak in the 1970s, but many massive projects are still under construction and more are proposed. China recently completed the world's largest dam at Three Gorges; international interests continue to support dam construction in the Global South.

Hydropower's environmental and social impacts make it difficult to build large dams anywhere in the United States today. Off-stream reservoirs that store water but do not disrupt the stream's flow are one way to reduce the social and environmental costs of hydropower. Alternatively, "small hydro" facilities can utilize stream flows to generate electricity at a smaller scale, without dams.

Although hydropower is often thought of as a "green" energy source, social and environmental impacts suggest that dam projects must be planned and sited carefully to serve long-term interests. Changing precipitation patterns associated with global warming may also call for reassessment of hydroelectricity's role in regional energy production.

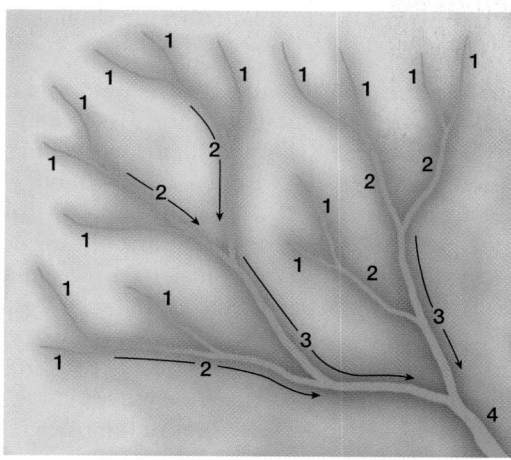

▲ **Figure 16-4** Stream orders. The branching component of a stream and its tributaries can be classified into a hierarchy of segments, ranging from smallest to largest (in this case, from 1 to 4).

more extensive ones. This relationship, although variable in detail, holds true for drainage basins of any size. This systematic characteristic makes it possible to recognize a natural organization within a watershed, and the concept of **stream order** has been devised to describe the arrangement (Figure 16-4).

A *first-order stream*, the smallest unit in the system, is a stream without tributaries. Where two first-order streams unite, a *second-order stream* is formed. At the confluence of two second-order streams, a *third-order stream* begins, and so on through successively higher orders.

Notice in Figure 16-4 that the joining of a lower-order stream with a higher-order stream does not increase the order below that junction. For example, the confluence of a first-order stream and a second-order one does not produce a third-order stream. A third-order stream is formed only by the joining of two second-order streams.

The concept of stream order is more than simply a numbers game because several significant relationships are involved. In a well-developed drainage system, for example, one can predict with some certainty that first-order streams and valleys are more numerous than all others combined and that each succeeding higher order is represented by fewer and fewer streams. More importantly we see that average stream length generally increases with increasing order, average watershed area generally increases with increasing order, and average stream **gradient** (elevation change over a given distance) decreases with increasing order.

FLUVIAL EROSION AND DEPOSITION

All external processes remove fragments of bedrock, regolith, and soil from their original positions (erosion), transport them to another location, and set them down (deposition). The fluvial processes, our concern in this chapter, produce one set of landforms by erosion and another quite different set by deposition.

Erosion by Overland Flow

On the interfluve, fluvial erosion begins when rain starts to fall. Unless the impact of rain is absorbed by vegetation or some other protective covering, the collision of raindrops with the ground is strong enough to blast fine soil particles upward and outward, shifting them a few millimeters laterally. On sloping ground, most particles move downhill by this *splash erosion* (Figure 16-5).

In the first few minutes of a rain, much of the water infiltrates the soil; consequently, there is little runoff. During heavy or continued rain, however, particularly if the land is sloping and has only a sparse vegetative cover, infiltration is greatly diminished and most of the water moves downslope as overland flow. The water flows across the surface as a thin sheet, transporting material already loosened by splash erosion, in a process termed *sheet erosion*. As overland flow moves downslope and its volume increases, the resulting turbulence tends to break up the sheet flow into multitudinous tiny channels called *rills*. This more concentrated flow picks up additional material and scores the slope with numerous parallel seams; this sequence of events is termed *rill erosion*. If the process continues, the rills begin to coalesce into fewer and larger channels called *gullies*, and *gully erosion* becomes recognizable. As the gullies get larger and larger, they tend to become incorporated into the drainage system of the adjacent valley, and the flow changes from overland flow to streamflow (see Figure 16-2).

Erosion by Streamflow

Once surface flow is channeled, its ability to erode and transport material is greatly enhanced by the increased volume and velocity of water. Erosion is accomplished in part by the direct hydraulic power of the moving water, which can excavate and transport material from the bottom and sides of the channel. Channel banks can also be undercut by streamflow, particularly at times of high discharge. Undercutting causes landsides that dump more loose material into the water to be swept downstream.

▲ **Figure 16-5** The impact of a raindrop produces splash erosion.

▲ **Figure 16-6** Rock transported by streams becomes rounded by frequent collisions. These streamworn cobbles are in the bed of the Aluna River in the Southern Highlands of Papua New Guinea.

The erosive capability of streamflow is also increased by the abrasive "tools" it picks up and carries along with it. All sizes of rock fragments, from silt to boulders, chip and grind the stream bed as they travel downstream in the moving water. These rock fragments break off more fragments from the bottom and sides of the channel, and they collide with one another, becoming both smaller and rounder from the wear and tear of the frequent collisions (Figure 16-6).

A certain amount of chemical action also accompanies streamflow, and some chemical weathering processes—particularly solution action and hydrolysis—also help erode the stream channel through *corrosion* (soluble rock being dissolved by water).

The erosive effectiveness of streamflow varies enormously from one situation to another, determined primarily by the speed and turbulence of the flow on the one hand, and by the resistance of the bedrock on the other. Flow speed is governed by the gradient (slope angle) of the streambed (the steeper the gradient, the faster the flow), the shape of the channel (generally the narrower the channel, the faster the flow), and by the volume of flow (more water normally means higher speed). The degree of turbulence is determined in part by the flow speed (faster flows are more turbulent) and in part by the roughness of the stream channel (an irregular channel surface increases turbulence).

Transportation

Any water moving downslope, whether moving as overland flow or as stream-flow, can transport rock material. At any given time and place, the load carried by overland flow is likely to be small in comparison with what a stream can transport. Eventually, most of this material reaches the streams in the valley bottoms, where it is added to the stream-eroded debris and material contributed by mass wasting to constitute the **stream load**.

Animation
Stream
Sediment
Movement

Essentially, the stream load contains three fractions (Figure 16-7):

1. Some minerals, mostly salts, are dissolved in the water and carried in solution as the **dissolved load**.
2. Very fine particles of clay and silt are carried in suspension, moving along with the water without ever touching the streambed. These tiny particles, called the **suspended load**, have a very slow settling speed, even in still water. (Fine clay may require as much as a year to sink 30 meters [100 feet] in perfectly quiet water.)
3. Sand, gravel, and larger rock fragments constitute the **bedload**. The smaller particles are moved along with the general streamflow in a series of jumps or bounces collectively referred to as *saltation*. Coarser pieces are moved by *traction*, which is defined as rolling or sliding along the streambed. The bedload is normally moved spasmodically, especially during floods: debris is transported some distance, dropped, and then picked up later and carried farther.

Competence: Geomorphologists employ two concepts—*competence* and *capacity*—in describing the load a stream can transport. **Stream competence** is a measure of the particle size a stream can transport, expressed by the diameter of the largest particles that can be moved. Competence depends mainly on flow speed, with the power of the water generally increasing by the square of its speed. In other words, if the flow speed is doubled, the size of the largest movable particle is increased fourfold (2^2); if the flow speed triples, the force increases ninefold (3^2)—as stream speed increases even moderately, the largest moveable particle increases significantly. Thus, a stream that normally can transport only sand grains might easily be able to move large boulders during the greater flow of a flood.

Capacity: **Stream capacity** is a measure of the amount of solid material a stream has the potential to transport, normally expressed as the volume of material passing a given point in the stream channel during a given time interval. Capacity may vary tremendously over time, depending

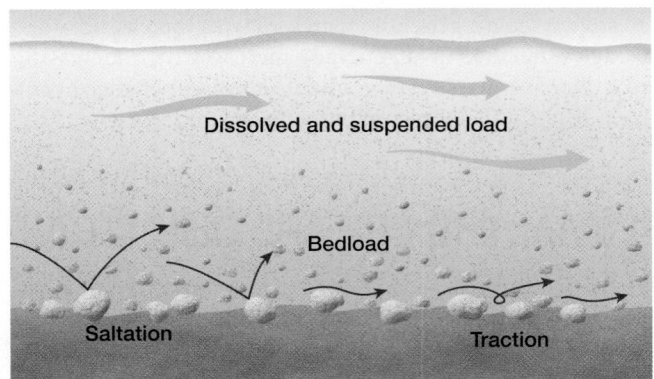

▲ **Figure 16-7** A stream moves its load in three ways. The dissolved and suspended loads are carried in the general water flow. The bedload is moved by traction (dragging) and saltation (bouncing).

mostly on fluctuations in volume and flow speed but also on the characteristics of the load (particularly the mix of coarse and fine sediments). It is difficult to overemphasize the significance of the greatly expanded capacity of a stream to transport material during floods.

▲ **Figure 16-8** Most desert streams are either intermittent or ephemeral, carrying water only rarely. This dry bed is near Wiluna in Western Australia.

Learning Check 16-2 What factor determines the size of rock a stream is able to transport?

Deposition

Whatever is picked up must eventually be set down, which means that erosion is inevitably followed by deposition. Moving water, whether moving as overland flow or as streamflow, carries its load downslope or downvalley toward an ultimate destination—either ocean, lake, or interior drainage basin. A large volume of fast-moving water can carry its debris a great distance, but sooner or later deposition will take place as either flow speed or water volume decreases. Diminished flow is often the result of a change in gradient, but it may also occur when a channel either widens or changes direction. Therefore, stream deposits are found at the mouths of canyons, on floodplains, and along the inside bank of river bends. Eventually, however, much of a stream's load is deposited into quiet water, such as the ocean or a lake.

Alluvium: The general term for stream-deposited sediment is **alluvium**. Deposits of alluvium may include all sizes of rock debris, but smaller particles constitute by far the bulk of the total. Alluvial deposits often—but not always—exhibit one or more of the following characteristics:

1. Alluvial material is typically smooth and round due to the battering the rocks receive from each other as they flow downstream. In addition, over the great distances of many stream systems, this battering and abrasion (along with chemical weathering) eventually reduces larger rocks (boulders, cobbles, and pebbles) to smaller sizes (sand and silt).
2. Alluvial deposits often display distinct *strata* or layers, due to episodes of deposition following periodic floods.
3. Finally, alluvium is often "sorted"—that is, an alluvial deposit is often comprised of rocks of just about the same size. Sorting can occur when the speed of water flow diminishes—as stream competence drops, the heaviest (and therefore largest) rocks are deposited first, while smaller rocks are carried away to be deposited elsewhere.

Learning Check 16-3 Why is *alluvium* often rounded, stratified, and sorted by size?

Perennial and Intermittent Streams

We tend to think of rivers as permanent, but in fact many of the world's streams do not flow year-round. In humid regions, the large rivers and most tributaries are **perennial streams**—that is, permanent. However, in more arid parts of the world, many of the major streams and most tributaries carry water only part of the time, either during the wet season or during and immediately after rains. These impermanent flows are called **intermittent streams** or *seasonal streams* if they flow for only part of the year and **ephemeral streams** if they carry water only during and immediately after a rain, although the term *intermittent* is sometimes applied to both cases (Figure 16-8).

Even in humid regions, many first-order and second-order streams are intermittent. These are generally short streams with relatively steep gradients and small watersheds. If rain is not frequent, or snowmelt not continuously available, these low-order streams simply run out of water. High-order streams in the same regions are likely to have permanent flow because of their larger drainage areas and because previous rainfall or snowmelt that sank into the ground can emerge in the valleys as groundwater runoff long after the rains have ceased.

Floods as Agents of Erosion and Deposition  FG9, FG12

Our discussion of factors associated with effective stream erosion and deposition leads us to an important concept in fluvial geomorphology—the role of floods as agents of erosion and deposition. Most of us have stood on a bridge or on the brink of a canyon looking at a small stream far below and wondered how that meager flow could have carved the enormous gorge we see beneath us. On such occasions, we might be tempted to discount uniformitarianism and consider some brief, catastrophic origin as a more logical linking of what we can see with what we can imagine. Such reasoning, however, is wrong, because uniformitarianism easily accounts for the existence of tiny streams in extensive valleys by invoking three geomorphic principles: (1) the extraordinary length of geologic time, (2) the role of mass wasting in moving weathered rock down into valleys where it can be transported away, and (3) the remarkable effectiveness of floods.

We have already discussed the incredible expanse of time involved in the evolution of topography (Chapter 13). This vast temporal sweep provides the opportunity for countless repetitions of an action, and the repetitive movement of even a tiny flow of water can wear away the strongest rock. In Chapter 15 we discussed the range of processes that can move masses of rock downslope where later it can be picked up and carried away.

Of perhaps equal importance is that the amount of water flowing in a stream varies. Most streams have fairly erratic flow regimes, with great fluctuation in **discharge**, or volume of flow. Many of the world's streams carry a relatively modest amount of water during most of the year but a relatively large volume during flood time. In some streams, flood flow occurs for several weeks or even months each year; however, in the vast majority, the duration of high-water flow is much more restricted. In many cases, the "wet season" may be only one or two days a year. Yet the amount of denudation that can be accomplished during high-water flow is supremely greater than that done during periods of normal discharge. As stream discharge increases during a flood, so does the speed of the stream; recall that as the speed of flow increases, the competence and capacity of the stream increase exponentially. Thus, the epic work of almost all streams—the excavating of great valleys, the forming of vast floodplains—is primarily accomplished during flood flow.

> **Learning Check 16-4** **Why are floods so important in fluvial geomorphology?**

Measuring Streamflow: Each stream system has its own characteristic flow regime, influenced by local factors such as the climate and area of drainage. To understand the flow characteristics of a particular stream, data are gathered from a network of *stream gages*. Some 14,000 such stream gaging stations are operating across the United States and Canada, with many thousands more in operation around the world. On an ongoing basis, stream gages log information about the height of a stream (or "gage height" above a local reference point) and flow velocity from which the discharge of a stream is calculated, commonly measured in cubic feet of water flow per second (cfs) or in cubic meters per second (cms).

By correlating stream discharge and gage height to local weather events, it is possible to estimate when floods will arrive or crest at difference places along the course of a river. The amount of urbanization in a region significantly influences this relationship. For example, in heavily urbanized areas, where there tends to be less infiltration of rain because much of the region is covered with impermeable surfaces such as pavement and buildings, a heavy rain tends to produce greater and faster runoff into local streams than in areas with more permeable surfaces (Figure 16-9).

Flood Recurrence Intervals: Streamflow data gathered for a stream over many decades can also provide information about the relative frequency and size of floods. The probability of a given-size flood occurring is usually described

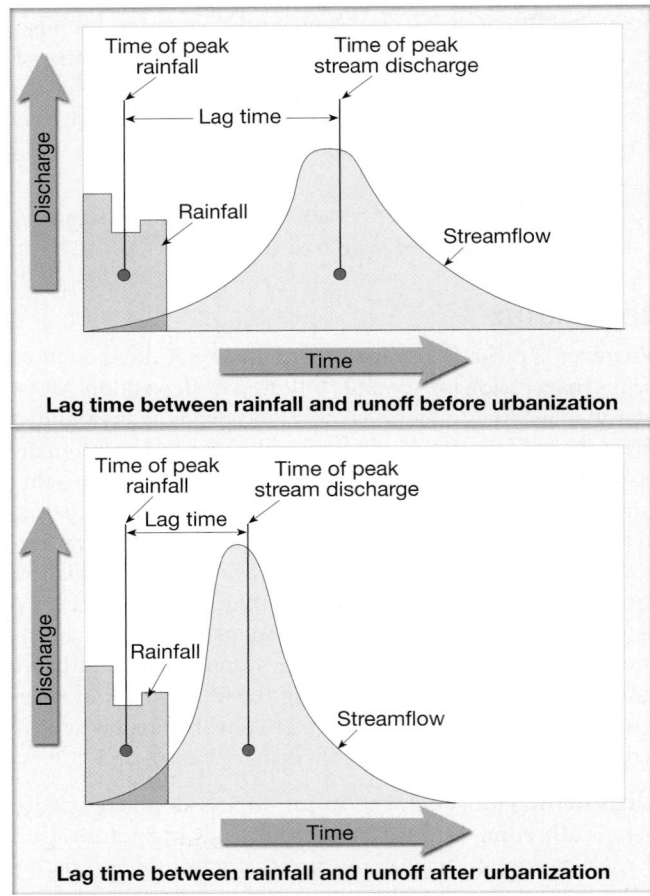

▲ **Figure 16-9** The lag time between the peak of rainfall and peak stream discharge during a flood is usually reduced in urbanized areas where there is less infiltration of runoff.

as a **recurrence interval** (or *return period*). For example, a "100-year flood" refers to stream discharge that has a 1 in 100 (1 percent) probability of being exceeded in any single year. Such terminology is somewhat unfortunate, since it may leave the impression that such a flood is expected only once every 100 years, but this is not the case—it is possible to have more than one 100-year flood each century, or no such floods (Figure 16-10).

Flood recurrence intervals are calculated based on available streamflow data—the longer the record, the more accurate the probabilities. But changing circumstances—such as greater urbanization or climate change—can, of course, alter these probabilities.

STREAM CHANNELS

Overland flow is a relatively simple process. It is affected by such factors as rainfall intensity and duration, vegetative cover, surface characteristics, and slope shape, but its general characteristics are straightforward and easily understood. Streamflow is much more complicated, in part because streams represent not only a process of denudation

▲ **Figure 16-10** Flooding in North Wagga Wagga, Australia, in March 2012

but also an element of the landscape—an active force as well as an object of study.

Channel Flow

A basic characteristic of streamflow, and one that distinguishes it from overland flow, is that it is normally confined to channels, which gives it a three-dimensional nature with scope for considerable complexity. In any channel having even a slight gradient, gravitational pull overcomes friction forces to move the water down-channel. Except under unusual circumstances, however, this movement is not perfectly straight, smooth, and regular. Rather it tends to be somewhat unsystematic and irregular, with many directional components and with different speeds in different parts of the channel.

Channel Cross Section: A principal cause of flow irregularity is the retarding effect of friction along the bottom and sides of the channel, which causes the water to move most slowly there and fastest in the center of the stream (Figure 16-11). The amount of friction is determined by the width and depth of the channel and the roughness of

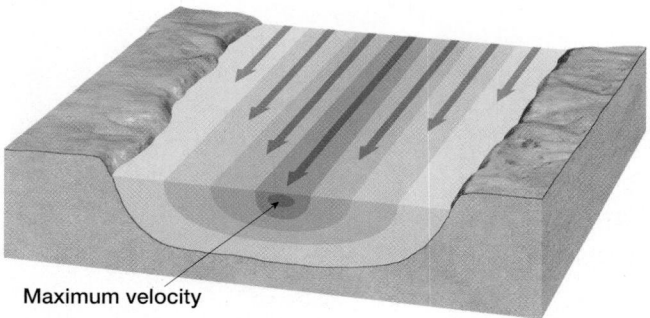

Maximum velocity

▲ **Figure 16-11** Friction between the stream bank and liquid surfaces cause a stream to flow fastest in the middle and at the surface. The arrow lengths indicate that water speed is greatest at the surface, where the water is farthest from any solid surfaces, and least at the bottom, where the water drags along the streambed.

its surface. For example, a shallow channel with a rough bottom has a much greater retarding effect on streamflow than a deep, smooth-bottomed one.

Turbulence: In turbulent flow, the general downstream movement is interrupted by irregularities in the direction and speed of the water. Such irregularities produce momentary currents that can move in any direction, including upward. Turbulence in streamflow is caused partly by friction, partly by internal shearing stresses between currents within the flow, and partly by surface irregularities in the channel. Stream speed also contributes to the development of turbulence, with faster streams more turbulent than slow-moving ones.

Eddies and whirlpools are conspicuous results of turbulence, as is the roiling whitewater of rapids. Even streams that appear very placid and smooth on the surface, however, are often turbulent at lower levels.

Turbulent flow creates a great deal of frictional stress as the numerous internal currents interfere with one another. This stress dissipates much of the stream's energy, decreasing the amount available to erode the channel and transport sediment. On the other hand, turbulence contributes to erosion by creating flow patterns that pry and lift rock materials from the streambed.

Stream Channel Patterns

Irregularities in streamflow are manifested in various ways, but perhaps most conspicuously by variations in channel patterns. If streamflow were smooth and regular, one might expect stream channels to be straight and direct. Few natural stream channels are straight and uniform for any appreciable distance, however. Instead, they curve about to a greater or lesser extent, sometimes developing remarkable sinuosity. In some instances, this winding is a response to the underlying geologic structure, but even in areas of perfectly uniform structure, stream channels are rarely straight.

Stream channel patterns are generally grouped into four categories—straight, sinuous, meandering, and braided—each with variations:

1. Straight channels are short and uncommon, and usually indicative of strong control by the underlying geologic structure. A straight channel does not necessarily mean straight flow, however. A line running in the direction of the water and indicating the deepest parts of the channel, called the *thalweg* (German: *thal*, meaning "valley," and *weg*, meaning "way"), rarely follows a straight path midway between the stream banks; rather it wanders back and forth across the channel, as Figure 16-12 shows. Opposite the place where the thalweg approaches one bank, a deposit of alluvium is likely to be found. Thus, straight channels are likely to have many of the characteristics of sinuous channels.

2. **Sinuous channels** are much more common than straight ones. They are winding channels and are found in almost every type of topographic setting

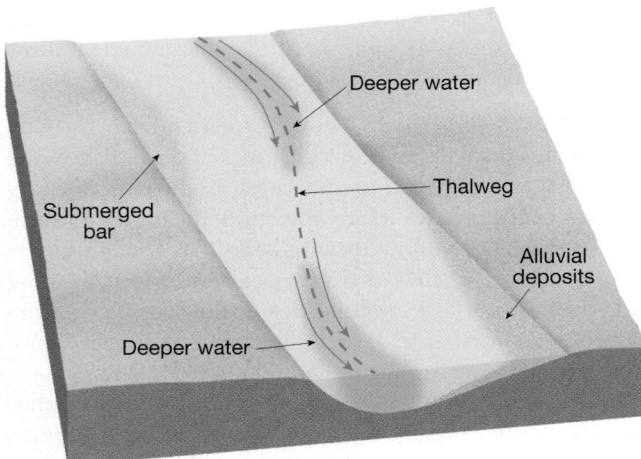

▲ **Figure 16-12** Even in a straight stream channel, the course of the deepest and fastest flow (the *thalweg*) tends to be slightly sinuous.

(Figure 16-13). Their curvature is usually gentle and irregular. Stream channels are likely to be sinuous even when the gradient of the stream is high (in other words, when flowing down a steep slope); where gradients are low (over flatter land), many stream channels will tend to develop greater sinuosity and begin to meander.

3. **Meandering channels** exhibit an extraordinarily intricate pattern of smooth curves in which the

▼ **Figure 16-13** Sinuous channel pattern of a stream in Wrangell-St. Elias National Park, Alaska.

stream follows a serpentine course, twisting and contorting and turning back on itself, forming tightly curved loops and then abandoning them, cutting a new, different, and equally twisting course. Meandering generally occurs when the land is flat and the gradient is low, especially when most of the rock being transported by the stream is fine-grained suspended load (Figure 16-14). A meander shifts its location almost continuously. This is accomplished by erosion on the outside of curves and deposition on the inside. In this fashion, meanders migrate across the floodplain and also tend to shift downvalley, producing rapid and sometimes abrupt changes in the channel. (Landforms that develop along a meandering stream channel will be discussed later in this chapter.)

4. **Braided channels** consist of a multiplicity of interwoven and interconnected channels separated by low bars or islands of sand, gravel, and other loose debris (Figure 16-15). Braiding often takes place when a very flat stream channel has a heavy load of sediment (such as the coarse-grained bedload supplied by glaciers to a meltwater stream) and in regions with prominent dry seasons and periods of low stream discharge (such as is common in arid environments). At any given time, the

▲ **Figure 16-14** The meandering stream channel and floodplain of the Trinity River in Big Thicket National Preserve, Texas.

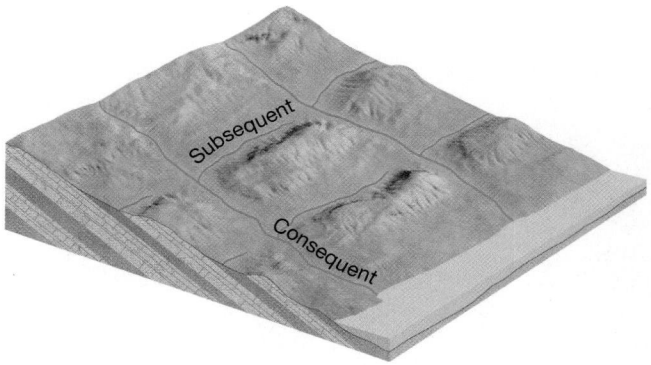

▲ **Figure 16-15** A typical braided stream on the South Island of New Zealand. This is the valley of the Lower Matukituki River.

▲ **Figure 16-16** A consequent stream follows the initial slope of the land, whereas a subsequent stream flows along structural weaknesses.

active channels of a braided stream may cover less than one-tenth of the width of the entire channel system, but in a single year most or all of the surface sediments may be reworked by the flow of the laterally shifting channels.

> **Learning Check 16-5** **Under what conditions does a *meandering channel* pattern commonly develop? A *braided channel* pattern?**

STRUCTURAL RELATIONSHIPS

Many factors affect stream development, and perhaps the most important is the geologic–topographic structure over or through which the stream must make its way and carve its valley. Each stream faces particular structural obstacles as it seeks the path of least resistance in its descending course to the sea. Most streams respond directly and conspicuously to structural controls, which is to say that their courses are guided and shaped by the nature and arrangement of the underlying bedrock.

Although streams change in pattern and flow characteristics, they may persist through eons of time, outlasting mountain ranges and other topographic assemblages that are more temporary occupants of continental surfaces. Thus, sometimes a relationship can be seen between the location of a stream and the contemporary structure of the land over which it flows, although sometimes it is necessary to delve into the geomorphic history of a region before the location of a drainage channel can be comprehended.

Consequent and Subsequent Streams

The simplest and most common relationship between underlying structure and channel development is one

in which the stream follows the initial slope of the land. Such a *consequent stream* is normally the first to develop on newly uplifted land, and many streams remain consequent throughout their evolutionary development (Figure 16-16). Streams that develop along zones of structural weakness are termed *subsequent streams*—they may excavate their channels along an outcrop of weak bedrock, or perhaps follow a fault zone or a master joint. Subsequent streams often trend at right angles to other drainage channels.

Antecedent and Superimposed Streams: Some streams seem to "defy" the structure with courses that cut through ridges or other significant structures. One way this can occur is when an established stream is interrupted by an uplift of land that is so slow that the stream is able to maintain its previously established course by downward erosion, leaving a deep gorge carved through hills or mountains. Because such a stream antedates (predates) the existence of the uplift, it is called an **antecedent stream** (Figure 16-17).

A *superimposed stream* may also seem to ignore the local structure. Such streams originally existed when the landscape was higher; this older, higher landscape has since been entirely or largely eroded away, so that the original drainage pattern becomes incised into an underlying sequence of rocks of quite different structure. The result may be a drainage system that seems to bear no relation at all to the present surface structure.

Stream Drainage Patterns

In addition to the response of individual streams to the underlying structure, entire stream systems often form conspicuous drainage patterns in the landscape. These patterns develop largely in response to the underlying structure and slope of the land surface. Geologic-topographic structure can often be deduced from a stream drainage pattern, and, conversely, drainage patterns often can be predicted from the underlying structure.

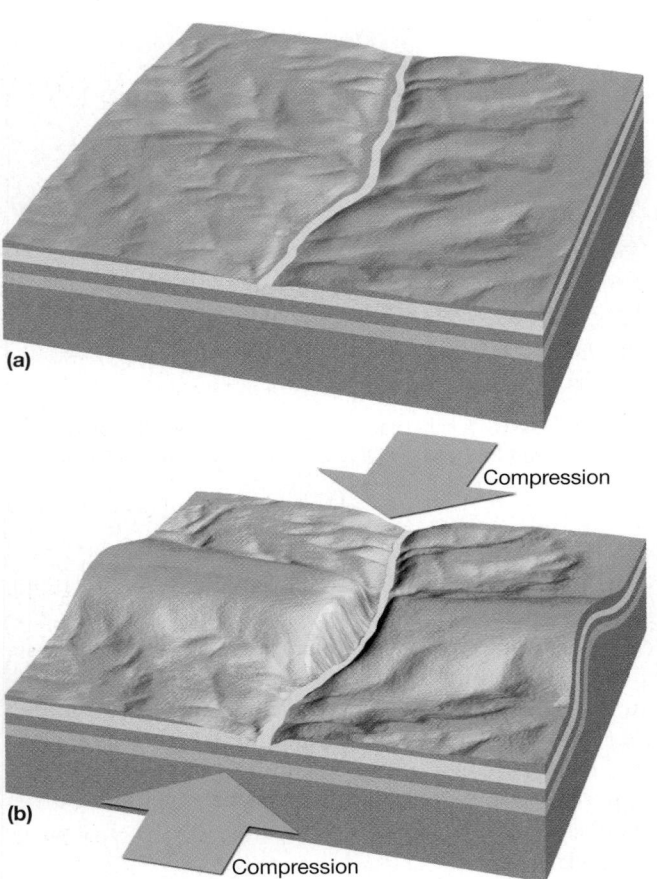

▲ **Figure 16-17** The development of an antecedent stream. (a) Stream course established before uplift begins. (b) Stream maintains its course and erodes through slowly rising anticlinal ridge.

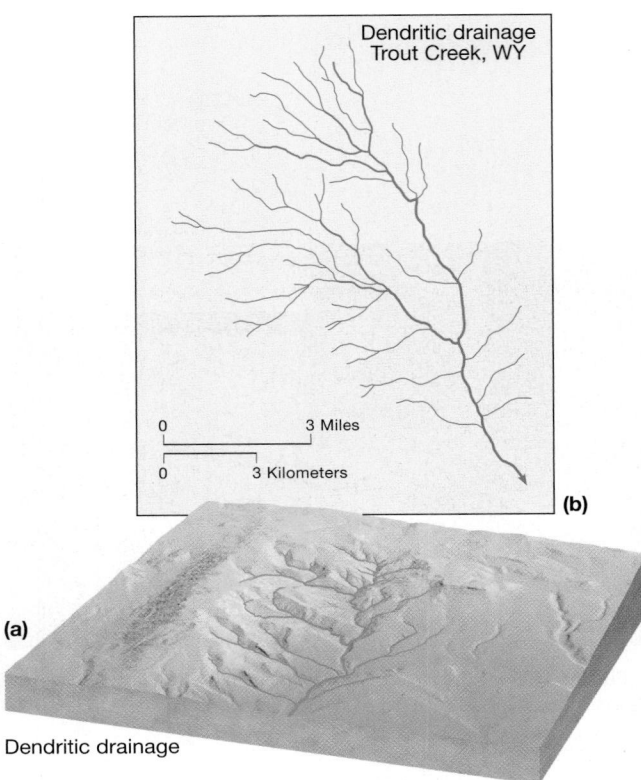

▲ **Figure 16-18** (a) Dendritic drainage pattern. (b) Trout Creek, from the *Pat O'Hara Mountain, Wyoming,* topographic quadrangle.

Dendritic Pattern: The most common drainage pattern over the world is a treelike, branching one called a **dendritic drainage pattern** (Figure 16-18). It consists of a random merging of streams, with tributaries joining larger streams irregularly but always at an angle smaller than 90°. The pattern resembles branches on a tree or veins on a leaf ("dendritic" comes from the Greek word *dendron* for "tree"). With dendritic drainage, the underlying structure does not control the evolution of the drainage pattern—the underlying rocks are more or less equally resistant to erosion. Dendritic patterns are more numerous than all others combined and can be found almost anywhere.

Trellis Pattern: A **trellis drainage pattern** develops as a response to underlying structural control—in this case, alternating bands of tilted hard and soft strata, with long, parallel streams linked by short, right-angled segments (Figure 16-19). Two regions of the United States are particularly noted for their trellis drainage patterns: the ridge-and-valley section of the Appalachian Mountains and the Ouachita Mountains of western Arkansas and southeastern Oklahoma.

In the ridge-and-valley section, which extends northeast–southwest for more than 1280 kilometers (800

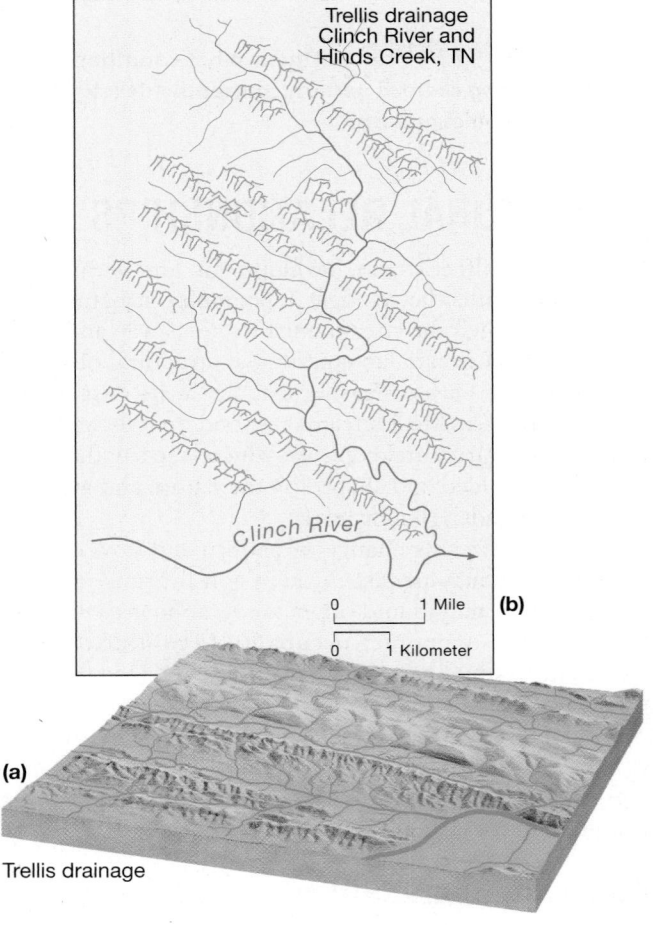

▲ **Figure 16-19** (a) Trellis drainage pattern. (b) Clinch River and Hinds Creek from the *Norris, Tennessee,* topographic quadrangle.

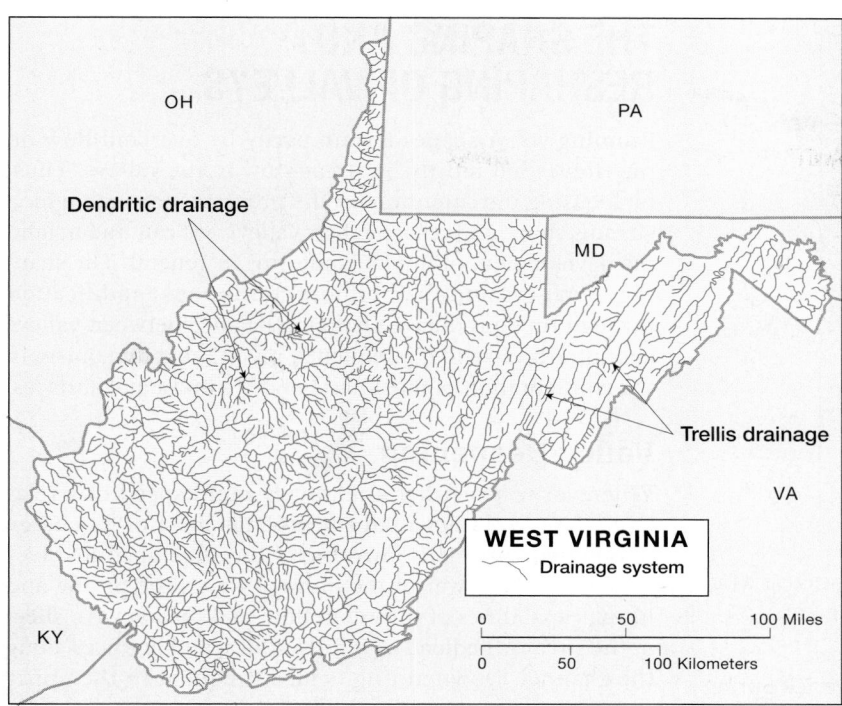

◀ **Figure 16-20** Drainage pattern contrasts in West Virginia. The trellis systems in the east are a response to parallel folding; the dendritic drainages in the west have developed because there are no prominent structural controls.

miles) from New York to Alabama, the drainage pattern developed in response to tightly folded Paleozoic sedimentary strata forming a world-famous series of parallel ridges and valleys (see Figure 14-56). Parallel streams flow in the valleys between the ridges, with short, right-angled connections here and there cutting through the ridges.

The marked contrast between trellis and dendritic patterns is shown dramatically by the principal streams of West Virginia (Figure 16-20). The folded structures of the eastern part of the state produce trellising, whereas the nearly horizontal strata of the rest of the state are characterized by dendritic patterns.

> **Learning Check 16-6** **Contrast the influence of the underlying geologic structure in areas of *dendritic drainage* to that in areas of *trellis drainage*.**

Radial Pattern: A *radial drainage pattern* is usually found when streams descend from some sort of concentric uplift, such as an isolated volcano. Figure 16-21 shows one example: Mount Egmont on the North Island of New Zealand.

Centripetal Pattern: A *centripetal drainage pattern*, essentially the opposite of a radial one, is usually associated with streams converging in a basin. Occasionally, however, centripetal drainage develops on a much grander scale. Shown in Figure 16-22 is the northeastern part of Australia, where rivers from hundreds of kilometers away converge toward the Gulf of Carpentaria, a basin partially inundated by the sea.

Annular Pattern: More complex is an *annular drainage pattern*. This ring-shaped drainage pattern can develop either on a dome or in a basin where dissection has exposed alternating concentric bands of tilted hard and soft rock ("annular" comes from the Latin word *annularis* meaning a "ring"). The principal streams follow curving courses on the softer material, occasionally breaking through the harder

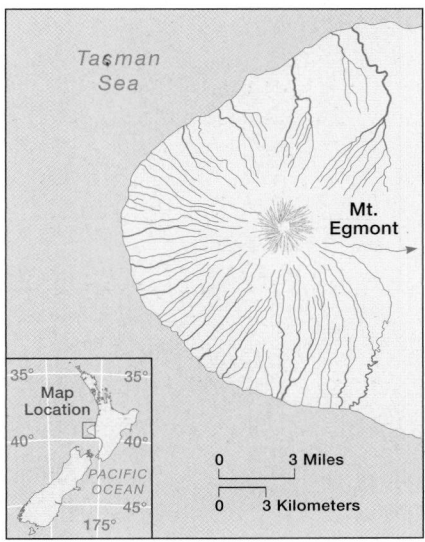

▲ **Figure 16-21** The extraordinary radial drainage pattern of Mount Egmont in New Zealand.

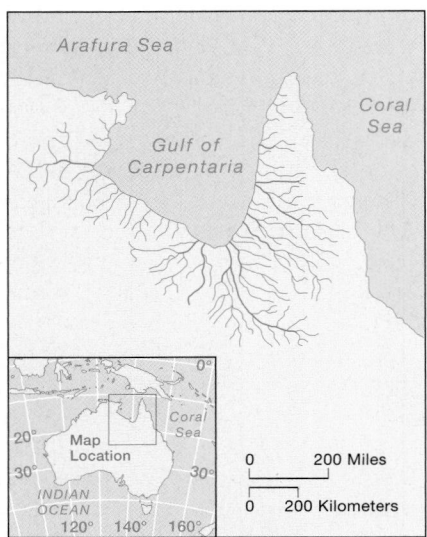

▲ **Figure 16-22** The centripetal drainage pattern of the region around the Gulf of Carpentaria in northeastern Australia.

layers in short, right-angled segments. The Maverick Spring Dome of Wyoming portrays a prominent example of annular drainage (Figure 16-23). This dome of ancient crystalline rocks was pushed up through a sedimentary overlay and has been deeply eroded, thus exposing erosion-resistant crystalline rocks in the higher part of the hills, with upturned concentric sedimentary ridges (called *hogbacks*) around the margin. The streams are mostly incised into the softer sedimentary layers.

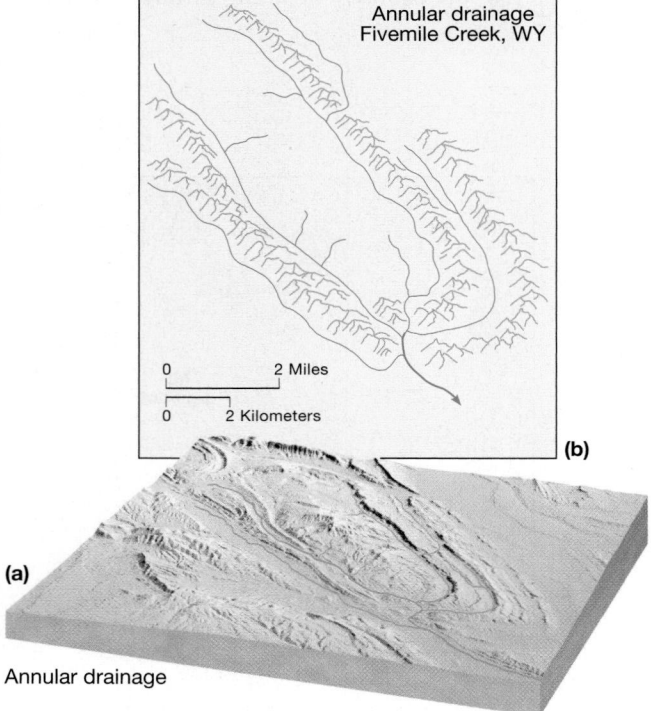

▲ **Figure 16-23** (a) Annular drainage pattern. (b) Fivemile Creek from the *Maverick Spring Dome, Wyoming,* topographic quadrangle.

THE SHAPING AND RESHAPING OF VALLEYS

Running water shapes terrain partly by overland flow on interfluves but mostly by streamflow in the valleys. Thus, by focusing our attention on the processes through which streams shape and reshape their valleys, we can understand the development of fluvial landforms in general. The shaping of valleys and their almost continuous modification through time produce a changing balance between valleys and interfluves and consequently an ongoing dynamism in the configuration of most parts of the continental surfaces.

Valley Deepening  FG5, FG12

Wherever it has either a relatively rapid speed or a relatively large volume, a stream expends most of its energy in **downcutting**. This lowering of the streambed involves the hydraulic power of the moving water, the prying and lifting capabilities of turbulent flow, and the abrasive effect of the stream's bedload as it rolls, slides, and bounces along the channel. Downcutting is most frequent in the upper reaches of a stream, where the gradient is usually steep and the valley narrow. The general effect of downcutting is to produce a deep valley with steep sides and often a V-shaped cross section (Figure 16-24).

Base Level: A stream excavates its valley by eroding the channel bed. If only downcutting were involved, the resulting valley would be a narrow, steep-sided gorge. Such gorges sometimes occur, but usually other factors are at work also and the result is a wider valley. In either case, there is a lower limit to how much downcutting a stream can do, and this limit is called the **base level** of the stream. Base level is an imaginary surface extending underneath the continents from sea level at the coasts (Figure 16-25). This imaginary surface is not simply a horizontal extension of sea level, however; inland it is gently inclined at a gradient that allows streams to maintain some flow. Sea level, then, is the absolute, or *ultimate base lev*el, or lower limit of downcutting for most streams.

As Figure 16-25 shows, there are also local, or temporary, base levels, which are limits to downcutting imposed on particular streams or sections of streams by structural or drainage conditions. For example, no tributary can cut deeper than its level of confluence with the higher-order stream it joins, and so the level of their point of junction is a local base level for the tributary. Similarly, a lake normally serves as the temporary base level for all streams that flow into it.

Some valleys have been downfaulted to elevations below sea level (Death Valley in California is one example), a situation producing a temporary base level lower than the ultimate base level. This can occur because the stream does not reach the ocean but terminates in an inland basin or body of water that is itself below sea level.

> **Learning Check 16-7**   **Under what conditions does a stream typically downcut rapidly?**

▲ **Figure 16-24** The Yellowstone River occupies a conspicuous V-shaped valley, shaped in part through downcutting.

Graded Streams: The longitudinal profile of a stream (the downvalley change in elevation from source to mouth) is ultimately restricted by base level, but the profile at any given time—whether smooth, stepped, or a combination of both—depends on a variety of factors. The long-term tendency is toward a profile in which the amount of sediment entering a stretch of a stream is equal to the amount leaving it. This hypothetical condition is called a *graded stream*, defined as one in which the gradient just allows the stream to transport its load. A graded stream is more theoretical than actual because equilibrium is so difficult to achieve and so easy to upset.

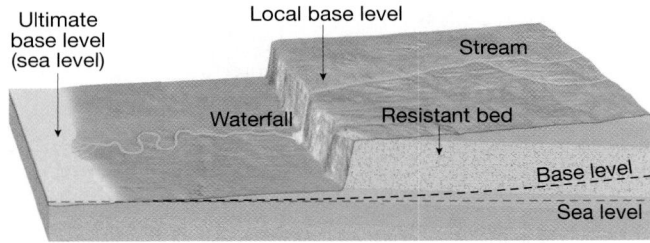

▲ **Figure 16-25** Comparison of sea level, base level, and local base level.

Knickpoint Migration: Waterfalls and rapids are often found in valleys where downcutting is prominent. They occur in steeper sections of the channel, and their faster, more turbulent flow intensifies erosion. These irregularities in the channel are collectively termed **knickpoints** (or *nickpoints*). Knickpoints may originate in various ways but are commonly the result of abrupt changes in bedrock resistance. The more resistant material inhibits downcutting, and as the water plunges over the waterfall or rapids with accelerated vigor, it tends to scour the channel above and along the knickpoint and fill the channel immediately downstream. This intensified action eventually erodes away the harder material, so that the position of the knickpoint migrates upstream with a successively lower profile until it finally disappears and the channel gradient is smoothed (Figure 16-26). Knickpoint migration can be relatively rapid when the bedrock consists of soft sedimentary rocks, but relatively slow when the rock is resistant plutonic or metamorphic rock.

Niagara Falls is a particularly good example of knickpoint migration on a massive scale (Figure 16-27). The Niagara River forms the connecting link between Lake Erie and Lake Ontario. As the contemporary drainage system became established in this area following the last

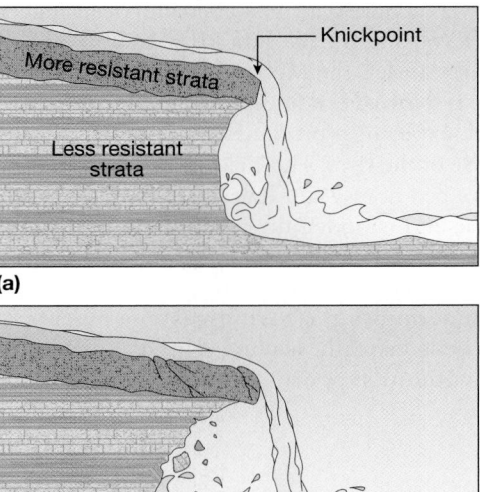

(a)

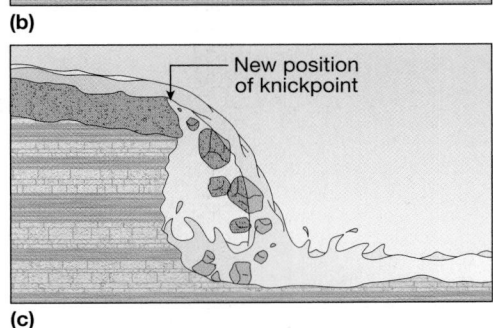

(c)

▲ **Figure 16-26** (a) Knickpoint formed where a stream flows over a resistant layer of rock. (b) The water flow undercuts the lip and (c) causes it to collapse. Position of knickpoint has migrated upstream.

▲ **Figure 16-27** Niagara Falls from the American side. The Niagara River drops about 55 meters (180 feet) over a knickpoint formed by the Niagara Escarpment.

retreat of Pleistocene ice sheets about 12,000 years ago, Lake Ontario was about 50 meters (about 150 feet) higher than its present level, and the Niagara River had no falls. However, an easterly outlet, the Mohawk Valley, developed for Lake Ontario, and the lake drained down to approximately its present level, exposing a prominent escarpment directly across the course of the river. The Niagara Escarpment is formed by a massive bed of resistant limestone that dips gently toward Lake Erie and is underlain by similarly dipping but softer strata of shale, sandstone, and limestone (Figure 16-28).

As the river pours over the escarpment, the swirling water undermines the hard limestone by erosion of the weaker beds beneath, leaving a lip of resistant rock projecting without support. Through the years, the lip has collapsed, with block after block of limestone tumbling into the gorge below. After each collapse, rapid undermining takes place again, leading to further collapse. In this fashion the falls has gradually retreated upstream, moving southward a distance of about 11 kilometers (7 miles) from its original position along the trend of the escarpment, the retreat being marked by a deep gorge.

This principle of **knickpoint migration** is important in understanding fluvial erosion because it illustrates dramatically the manner in which valley shape often develops first in the lower reaches and then proceeds progressively upstream, even though the water obviously flows downstream!

Learning Check 16-8 Why does the position of a waterfall generally shift upstream over time?

Valley Widening

Where a stream gradient is steep and the channel well above the local base level, downcutting is usually the dominant activity; as a result, valley widening is likely to be slow. Even at this stage, however, some widening takes place as the combined action of weathering, mass wasting, and overland flow removes material from the valley sides. Downcutting diminishes with time as the stream reduces its gradient, or wherever the stream course flows down a gentle slope. The stream's energy is then increasingly diverted into a meandering flow pattern. As the stream sways from side to side, **lateral erosion** begins: the main flow of the current swings from one bank to the other, eroding where the water speed is greatest and depositing where it is least. The water moves fastest on the outside of curves (the *cut bank*), and there it undercuts the bank. On the inside of a curve where water is moving most slowly, alluvium is likely to accumulate, forming a *point bar* along the inside bank of the stream (Figure 16-29). The channel shifts position often, so that undercutting

▶ **Figure 16-28** The situation of Niagara Falls. The falls was originally located where the Niagara River crosses the Niagara Escarpment, but it has retreated upstream to its present location.

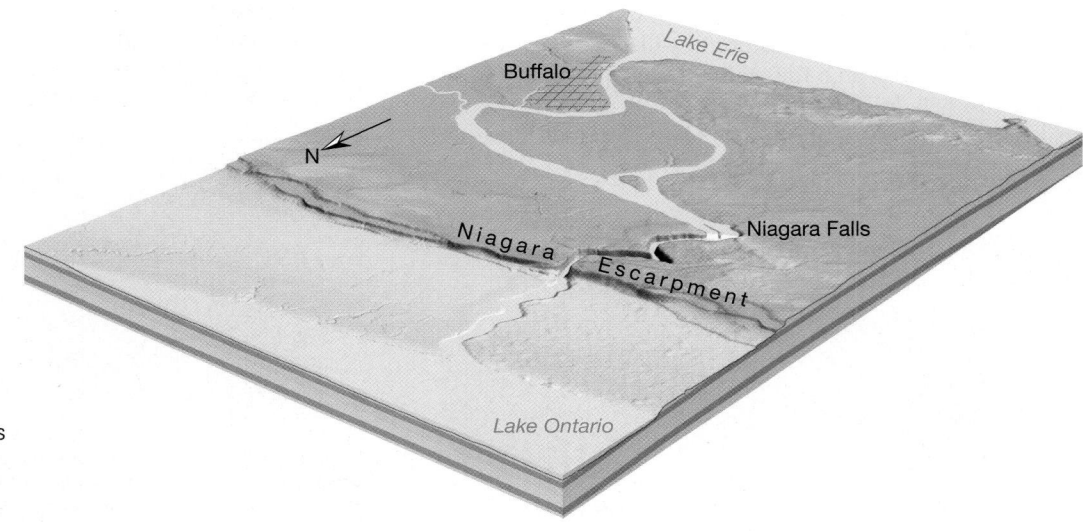

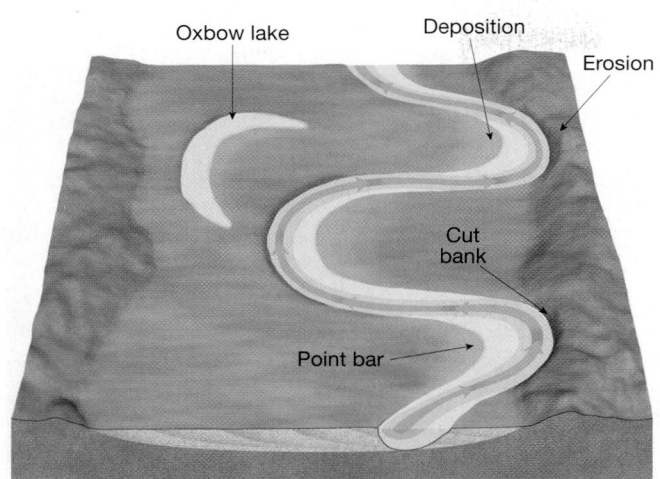

▲ **Figure 16-29** Lateral erosion in a meandering stream. Erosion occurs on the outside of the meander bend where the water flow is fastest, forming a cut bank, whereas deposition of alluvium is common on the inside of a bend, forming a point bar. If the neck of a meander is cut through by the stream, an oxbow lake is formed.

is not concentrated in just a few locations. Rather, over a long period of time, most or all parts of the valley sides are undercut. (Landforms associated with such meandering streams will be described later in this chapter.)

All the while a valley floor is being widened through lateral erosion, mass wasting is usually helping wear back the valley walls—and in some valleys, mass wasting is the dominant process responsible for widening. In addition, similar processes along tributary streams also contribute to the general widening of the main valley.

Valley Lengthening

A stream may lengthen its valley in two quite different ways: by *headward erosion* at the upper end or by *delta formation* at the lower end. For our purposes, understanding the fluvial processes that lead to valley lengthening is more important than the actual distances involved, which may be quite modest.

Headward Erosion: No concept is more fundamental to an understanding of fluvial processes than **headward erosion** because it is the basis of rill, gully, and valley formation and extension. The upper perimeter of a valley is the

line where the gentle slope of an interfluve changes to the steeper slope of a valley side. Overland flow from the interfluve drops abruptly over this slope break, and the fast-moving water tends to undercut the rim of the perimeter, weakening it and often causing a small amount of material to collapse (Figure 16-30).

The result of this action is a decrease in interfluve area and a proportionate increase in valley area. As the overland flow of the interfluve becomes part of the streamflow of the valley, there is a minute but distinct extension of rills and gullies into the drainage divide of the interfluve—in other words, a headward extension of the valley. Although minuscule as an individual event, when multiplied by a thousand gullies and a million years, this action can lengthen a valley by tens of kilometers and the expansion of a drainage basin by hundreds of square kilometers. Thus, the valley lengthens at the expense of the interfluve (Figure 16-31).

Stream Capture: Headward erosion is illustrated dramatically when a portion of the drainage basin of one stream is diverted into the basin of another stream by natural processes. This event, called **stream capture** or **stream piracy**, is relatively uncommon in nature, but evidence that it does sometimes occur is found in many places.

As a hypothetical example, let us consider two streams flowing across a coastal plain, as shown in Figure 16-32. Their valleys are separated by an interfluve, which for this example can be thought of as an undulating area of low relief. Stream A is shorter than stream B but is also more powerful, and A's valley is aligned so that headward extension will project it in the direction of B's valley.

As stream A lengthens its valley through headward erosion, the drainage divide between the two valleys is reduced. As the process continues, the headwaters of stream A eventually extend completely into the valley bottom of stream B and the flow from the upper reaches of B is diverted into A. In the parlance of the geographer, stream A has "captured" part of stream B. Stream A is called the *captor stream*, the lower part of B is the *beheaded stream*, the upper part of B is the *captured stream*, and the abrupt bend in the stream channel where the capture took place is called an *elbow of capture*.

Stream capture on a grand scale can be detected on a map of West Africa. The mighty Niger River has its headwaters

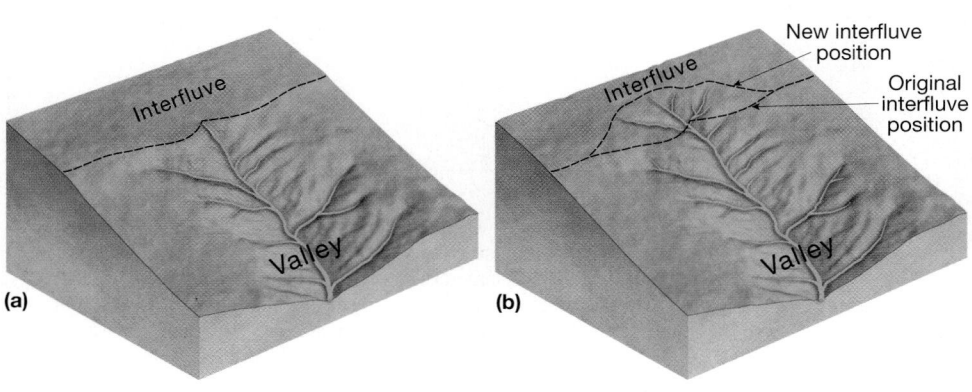

(a)   **(b)**

◀ **Figure 16-30** Headward erosion occurs at the upper end of a stream where overland flow pours off the lip of the interfluve into the valley. (b) The channeled streamflow wears back the lip of the interfluve. Over time, this erosion extends the valley headward at the expense of the interfluve.

► **Figure 16-31** Headward erosion of ephemeral streams into flat-lying sedimentary rock near Holbrook, Arizona.

relatively near the Atlantic Ocean, but it flows inland rather than seaward. After flowing northeast for nearly 1600 kilometers (1000 miles), it makes an abrupt turn to the southeast and then continues in that direction for another 1600 kilometers before finally emptying into the Atlantic. At some time in the past, the upper reaches of what is now the Niger was a separate river, one that did not change course but rather flowed northeast until it reached a great inland lake in what is now the central Sahara (Figure 16-33). This river was beheaded by the ancestral Niger, producing a great elbow of capture and leaving the beheaded stream to wither and dry up as the climate became more arid.

The map of Africa provides us with still another major point of interest concerning stream capture, but in this case the capture has not yet taken place. The Chari River of central Africa flows northwesterly into Lake Chad (see Figure 9-23). Because its lower course has a very low gradient, the stream flows sluggishly without any power for downcutting. West of the Chari is an active and powerfully

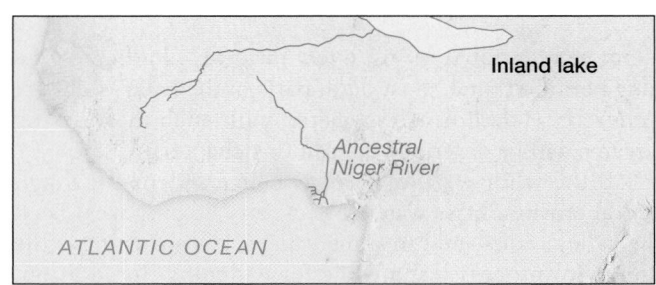

(a)

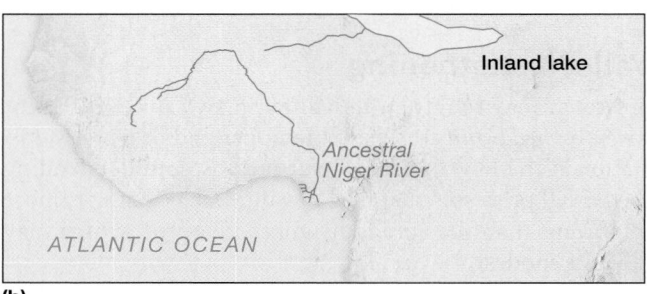

(b)

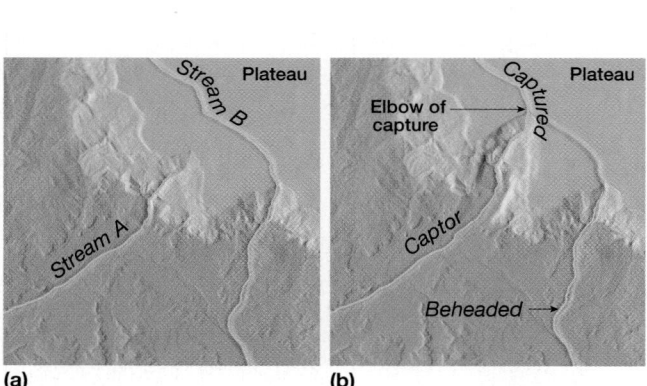

(a)   **(b)**

▲ **Figure 16-32** A hypothetical stream-capture sequence. The valley of stream A is extended by headward erosion until stream A captures and beheads stream B.

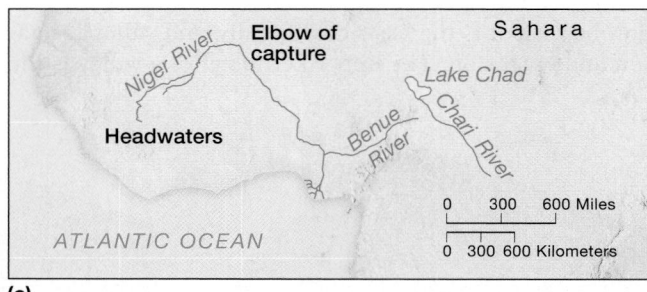

(c)

▲ **Figure 16-33** Stream capture, actual and anticipated in West Africa. (a) The upper course of the Niger River was once part of an unnamed stream that flowed into a large lake in what is now the Sahara. (b) This ancient stream was captured by headward erosion of the ancestral Niger. (c) At present, headward erosion on the Benue River gives promise of capturing the Chari River just a few tens or hundreds of centuries from now.

downcutting river in Nigeria, the Benue, a major tributary of the Niger. Some of the tributary headwaters of the Benue originate in a flat, swampy interfluve only a short distance from the floodplain of the Chari. Since the Benue is more active than the Chari and its alignment is such that headward erosion cuts directly into the Chari drainage, the Benue is likely to behead the Chari before our very eyes, so to speak, provided we can wait a few thousand years.

Learning Check 16-9 Explain the role of *headward erosion* in *stream capture*.

Delta Formation: A valley can also be lengthened at its seaward end—in this case, by deposition. Flowing water slows down whenever it enters the quiet water of a lake or ocean and deposits its load. Most of this debris is dropped right at the mouth of the river in a landform called a **delta**, after a fancied resemblance to the Greek capital letter delta, Δ (Figure 16-34). The classic triangular shape is maintained in some deltas, but it is severely modified in others because of imbalances between the amount of sediment deposited by rivers and the removal of those sediments by ocean waves and currents.

The stream slows down, losing both competence and capacity, and drops much of its load, which partially blocks the channel and forces the stream to seek another path (Figure 16-35). Later this new path is likely to become clogged, and the pattern is repeated. As a result, deltas usually consist of a maze of roughly parallel channels called *distributaries* through which the water flows slowly toward the sea. Continued deposition builds up the surface of the delta so that it is at least partially exposed above sea level. Rich alluvial sediments and an abundance of water favor the establishment of vegetation, which provides a base for further expansion of the delta. In this fashion, the stream valley is extended downstream.

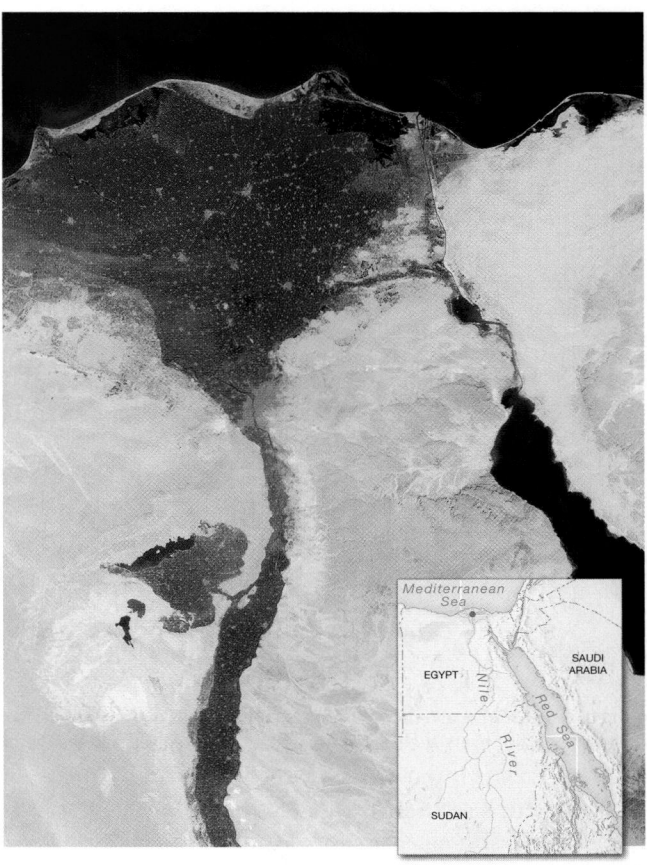

▲ **Figure 16-34** The Nile River delta captured by a NASA satellite using the Multi-angle Imaging Spectroradiometer's (MISR's) nadir camera in January 2001. The view is northward, with the Nile entering from the bottom and the Mediterranean Sea at the top.

At some river mouths, the local coastal currents are so vigorous that no delta is formed—the stream sediment is simply swept away to be deposited elsewhere along the coast or offshore (Figure 16-36). Often, however, a prominent and clear-cut delta does form (Table 16-1).

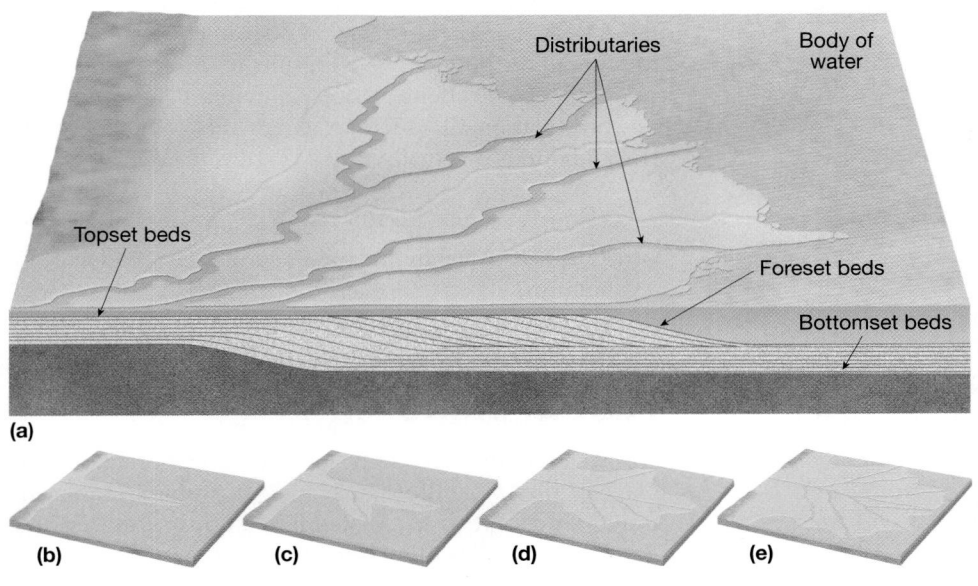

◄ **Figure 16-35** Hypothetical sequence showing the formation of a simple delta in a quiet body of water. (a) *Foreset bed* deposits are comprised of coarser sediments dropped immediately by the stream; *topset beds* are deposited during floods over the foreset beds; *bottomset beds* are composed of fine sediments that settle some distance from the mouth of the stream. (b) to (e) show the sequential process of delta extension.

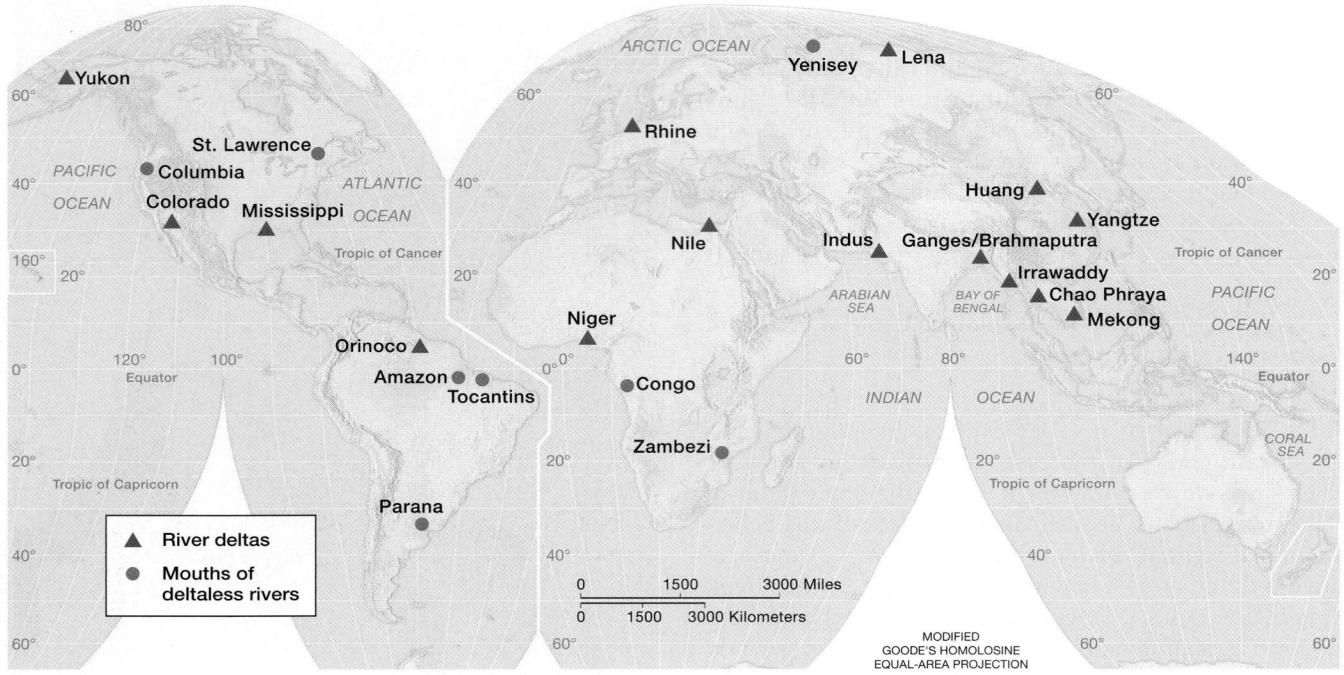

▲ **Figure 16-36** Locations of the world's largest deltas and deltaless rivers. Not all large rivers form deltas. Major rivers such as the Amazon, Congo, Yenisey, and the Paraná do not have deltas.

As we will see later in this chapter when we discuss flood control strategies, many of the world's major deltas, such as the Nile and Mississippi, are becoming smaller as a consequence of direct human manipulation of the rivers that feed them, as well as slowly rising sea levels.

Deposition in Valleys

Thus far, we have emphasized the prominence of the removal and transportation of material in the formation and shaping of valleys, but deposition, too, has a role in these processes.

Nearly every stream continuously rearranges its sediment in response to variations in flow speed and volume. Alluvium can be deposited almost anywhere in a valley bottom any time the stream loses power to transport its load—on the stream bottom, on the sides, in the center, at the base of knickpoints, in overflow areas, and in a variety of other locations. **Aggradation** is a general term that refers to this process of deposition.

During high-water periods, when flow is fast and voluminous, the stream scours its bed by detaching particles from it and shifting most or all sediment downstream. During low-water periods, particularly after a period of flood flow, the flow is slowed and sediment is more likely to settle to the bottom, which results in filling of the channel. Under some circumstances, alluvium may accumulate on the streambed to such an extent that the level of the stream bottom is actually raised (Figure 16-37).

TABLE 16-1	The World's Largest Deltas	
Rank	**River (Country)**	**Area [Km² × 1000]**
1	Indus (Pakistan)	163.0
2	Nile (Egypt)	160.0
3	Hwang Ho (China)	127.0
4	Yangtze (China)	124.0
5	Ganges/Brahmaputra(Bangladesh)	91.0
6	Orinoco (Venezuela)	57.0
7	Yukon (United States)	54.0
8	Mekong (Vietnam)	52.0
9	Irrawaddy (Myanmar)	31.0
10	Lena (Russia)	28.5
11	Mississippi (United States)	28.0
12	Chao Phraya (Thailand)	24.6
13	Rhine (Netherlands)	22.0
14	Colorado (Mexico)	19.8
15	Niger (Nigeria)	19.4

Learning Check 16-10 **Under what conditions will a stream begin to deposit some of its load as alluvium?**

FLOODPLAINS FG13

Special attention needs to be given to an important assemblage of fluvial landforms. The most prominent depositional landscape is the **floodplain**—a low-lying, nearly flat alluvial valley floor that is periodically inundated with floodwaters. Floodplains are frequently formed where

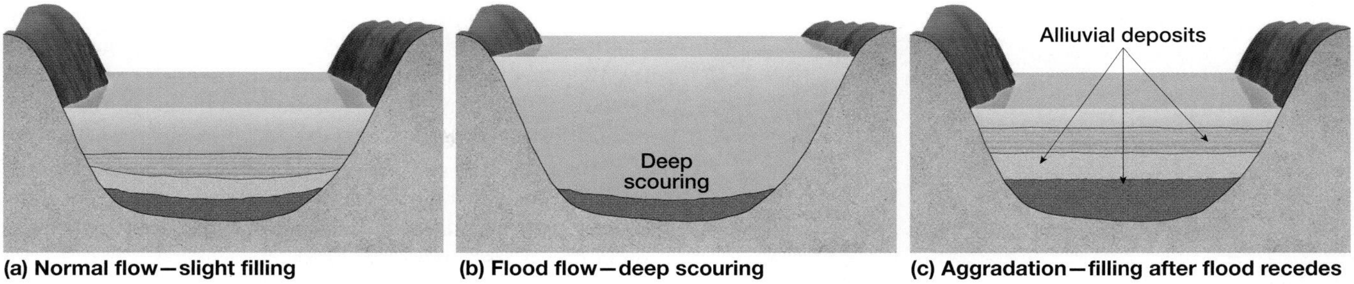

(a) Normal flow—slight filling

(b) Flood flow—deep scouring

Deep
scouring

(c) Aggradation—filling after flood recedes

Alliuvial deposits

▲ **Figure 16-37** Changing channel depth and shape during a flood: (a) Normal flow with slight filling. (b) Flood flow significantly deepens the channel by scouring. (c) As the flood recedes, considerable filling raises the channel bed again.

a meandering stream flows across a wide, nearly level valley floor.

Floodplain Landforms

The frequent shifting of stream meanders produces an increasingly broader, flattish valley floor largely or completely covered with deposits of alluvium left by periodic floods. At any given time, a stream is likely to occupy only a small portion of the flatland, although during periods of flood flow, the entire floor may be flooded. For this reason, the valley bottom is properly termed a *floodplain*.

The outer edges of a floodplain are usually bounded by an increase in slope, sometimes marking the outer limit of lateral erosion and undercutting where the flat terrain abruptly changes to a line of *bluffs*. Valley widening and floodplain development can extend for great distances; the floodplains of many of the world's largest rivers are so broad that a person standing on the bluffs at one side cannot see the bluffs on the other.

Animation
Oxbow Lake
Formation

Cutoff Meanders: The most conspicuous feature of a floodplain is often the meandering channel of its river (Figure 16-38). A meandering river swings back and forth in ever-expanding loops. Eventually, when the radius of a loop reaches about 2.5 times the stream's width, the loop stops growing. Often a meander loop is bypassed as the

CANADA

MINNESOTA

ND

SD

WI

IA

◀ **Figure 16-38** The floodplain of the upper Misssissippi River near Itasca Park, Minnesota. As with other floodplains, the meandering river channel is the most conspicuous feature.

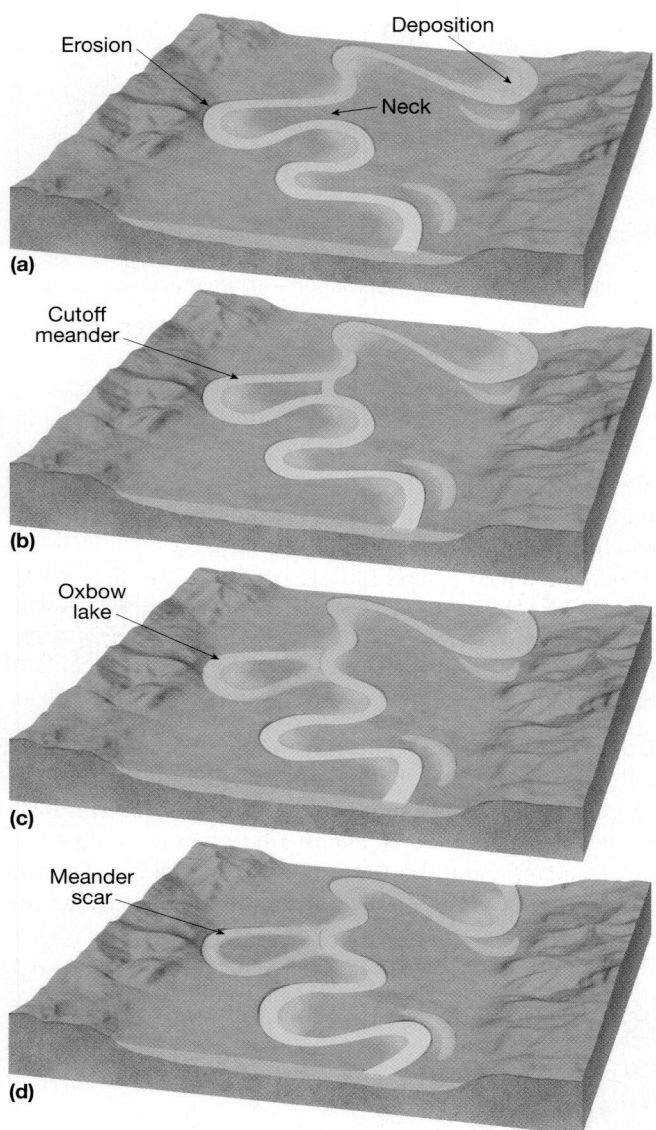

(a)

(b)

(c)

(d)

▲ **Figure 16-39** The formation of a cutoff meander on a floodplain. As the river cuts across the narrow neck of a meander, the river bend becomes an oxbow lake, which becomes an oxbow swamp, which becomes a meander scar.

stream channel shifts through lateral erosion and cuts a new channel across its neck and starts meandering again, leaving the old meander loop as a **cutoff meander**. The cutoff portion of the channel may remain for a period of time as an **oxbow lake**, so named because its rounded shape resembles the bow part of yokes used on teams of oxen. Oxbow lakes gradually fill with sediment and vegetation to become oxbow swamps and eventually retain their identity only as **meander scars** (Figure 16-39).

Natural Levees: A floodplain is slightly higher along the banks of the stream channel. As the stream overflows at flood time, the current, as it leaves the normal channel, is abruptly slowed by friction with the floodplain surface. This slowdown causes the principal deposition to take place along the margins of the main channel, producing **natural levees** (from the Old French word *levée*, meaning "act of raising," derived from the Latin *levare*, meaning "to raise") on each side of the stream (Figure 16-40). The natural levees merge outwardly and almost imperceptibly with the less well-drained and lower portions of the floodplain, generally referred to as *backswamps*.

Sometimes a tributary stream entering a floodplain that has prominent natural levees cannot flow directly into the main channel and so flows down-valley in the backswamp zone, running parallel to the main stream for some distance before finding an entrance. A tributary stream with such a pattern is referred to as a **yazoo stream**, after Mississippi's Yazoo River, which flows parallel to the Mississippi River for about 280 kilometers (175 miles) before joining it.

Animation
Floods and
Natural Levee
Formation

Although the landforms we have just described are most prominently displayed on the floodplains of large streams, nearly identical processes and landforms may also be found where a stream is meandering over a nearly flat surface and down a gentle slope. Thus, examples of

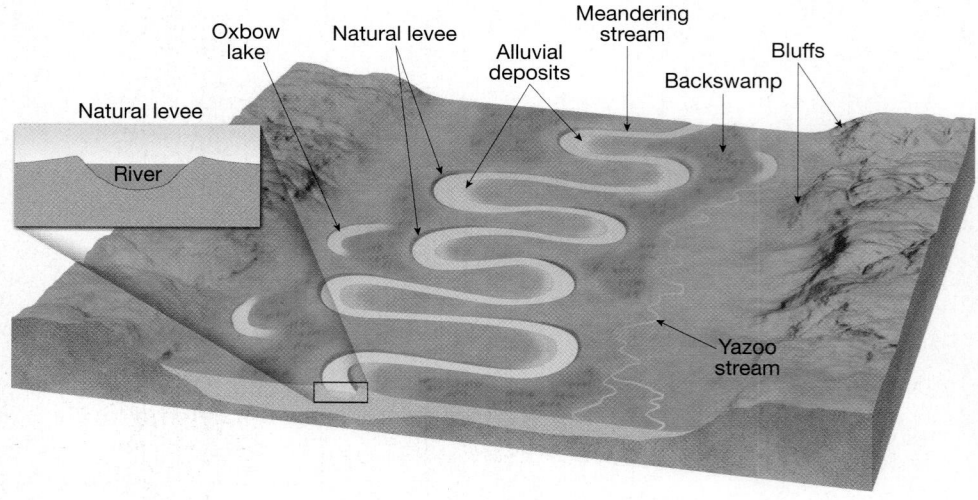

▶ **Figure 16-40** Typical landforms in a floodplain. Natural levees build up from alluvium deposited along the sides of a stream during floods.

cutoff meanders and oxbow lakes might well be seen on the valley floor of a small creek meandering across a flat alpine meadow.

> **Learning Check 16-11**   **How does an oxbow lake form?**

Modifying Rivers for Flood Control

Obvious attributes—flat land, abundant water, productive soils—attract humans to valley bottoms, and therefore such areas are often places of intensive agriculture, transportation routes, and urban development. However, fluvial processes are always ongoing in valley bottoms, with the result that nature and humans coexist in an uneasy juxtaposition shrouded by the specter of flood. We have seen that every stream is subject to at least occasional flooding, and thus the existence of a floodplain—so very attractive for human settlement—is incontrovertible evidence that floods do occur from time to time.

Accordingly, wherever people have settled in large numbers in river valleys, they have gone to extraordinary lengths to mitigate potential flood damage. The principal means for averting disaster are sizable structures in the form of dams, artificial levees, and overflow floodways. As an example of the remarkable efforts that go into such endeavors, we might consider the major river system of North America: the Mississippi.

Flood Control on the Mississippi River

The Mississippi originates in Minnesota and flows more or less directly southward to the Gulf of Mexico below New Orleans (Figure 16-41). It is joined by a number of right-bank tributaries along the way, of which the Missouri is by far the most important. There are also many left-bank tributaries, of which the Ohio, with its tributary the Tennessee, is the most notable. (Tributary streams are designated as "right bank" or "left bank" from the perspective of an observer looking downstream.)

Dams: All four of these rivers have been thoroughly dammed, largely for flood control but also for such other benefits as hydroelectricity production, navigation stabilization, and recreation. On the Mississippi, the Army Corps of Engineers operates and maintains 27 low dams between St. Louis and the head of navigation at Minneapolis, most equipped with hydroelectricity facilities and each with locks to allow barges and other shallow-draft boats to pass (one of the purposes of the dams is to maintain a water depth of at least 2.7 meters [9 ft.] throughout the navigable course of the river). The Missouri has fewer but larger dams, six in all, widely scattered from Montana to Nebraska. They are primarily flood-control dams. The Ohio is punctuated by more than three dozen low dams, whose primary purpose is maintenance of pools deep enough for barge navigation, with flood control as a secondary consideration. Most thoroughly dammed is the Tennessee, whose nine mainstream dams have reduced it to a series of quiet reservoirs for its entire length, apart from the upper headwaters. These are Tennessee Valley Authority (TVA) dams built during the 1930s particularly for flood control and other subsidiary benefits.

Artificial Levees: These four river valleys contain an extensive series of artificial levees designed to protect the local floodplain and move floodwaters downstream. There is a vicious-circle aspect to levee building: anytime a levee is raised in an upstream area, most downstream locales require higher levees to pass the floodwaters on without overflow. These levees are usually the highest parts of the landscape, particularly in the ever-flatter and more extensive floodplains downstream. In addition, although the system of artificial levees may work to contain flooding in most years, if the levees should fail, the results can be catastrophic for the population living on the adjacent floodplain. (Many experienced hydrologists and geologists say, somewhat cynically, that there are only two kinds of flood control levees: "those that have failed, and those that will fail.")

Managing the Lower Mississippi: At the lower end of the Mississippi system, in southern Louisiana, river control is extremely complicated and the results of human efforts are somewhat ambiguous. This region, which receives the full flow of the continent's mightiest river system, is exceedingly flat and thus has poor natural drainage. During the past 5000 years, the lower course of the river has shifted several times, producing at least seven subdeltas that are the principal elements of the present complicated *bird's-foot delta* of the Mississippi—a series of narrow, sediment-lined distributary channels (Figure 16-42). The main flow of the river during the past 600 years or so has been along its present course, southeast from New Orleans. This portion of the

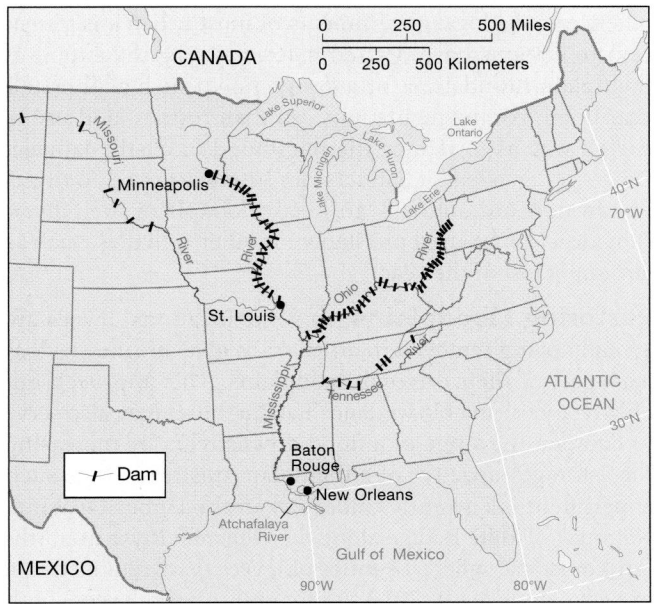

▲ **Figure 16-41** Dams on the Mississippi, Missouri, Ohio, and Tennessee Rivers.

▶ **Figure 16-42** Over the last 5000 years, seven subdeltas were built by the Mississippi River (on the map, "1" is the oldest and "7" is the youngest). The present bird's foot delta ("7") began to form about 600 years ago.

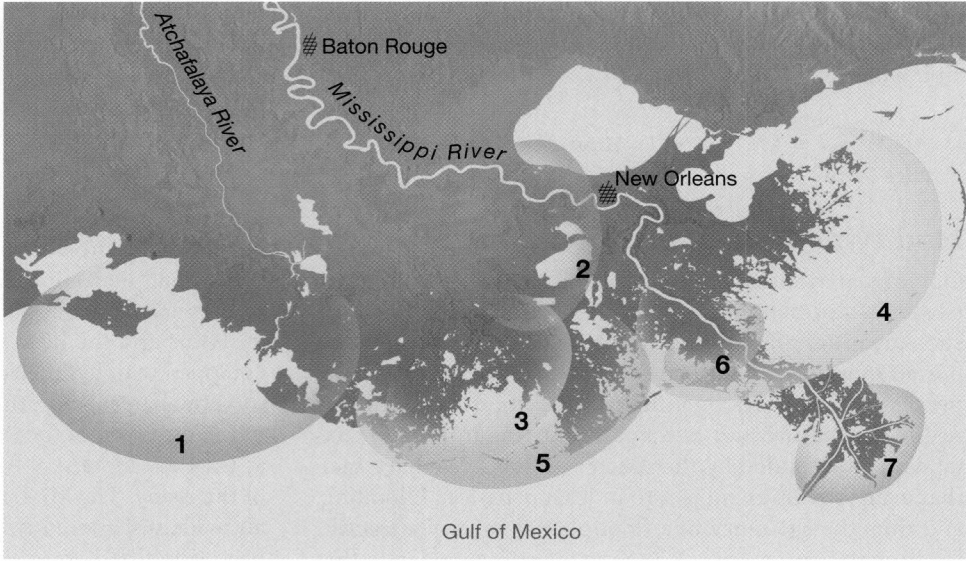

delta was built out into the Gulf of Mexico at a rate of more than 10 kilometers (6 miles) per century in that period.

Under the normal pattern of deltaic fluctuations, the main flow of the river would now be shifting to the shorter and slightly steeper channel of the Atchafalaya River, a prominent distributary of the ancestral delta a few kilometers west of the present main channel of the Mississippi. However, enormous flood-control structures—part of the Old River Control Project—were erected upstream from Baton Rouge in an effort (thus far successful) to prevent the river from abandoning its present channel and delta (Figure 16-43).

▲ **Figure 16-43** Old River Control Project on the Mississippi River near Baton Rouge, Louisiana. Diversion dams keep most of the Mississippi River (in the upper left) from draining into the Atchafalaya River.

In part because of human-built flood control and navigation measures, the natural processes operating on the floodplain and delta of the Mississippi River are changing—the delta is sinking and natural marshlands are retreating—see the boxes "People and the Environment: The Changing Mississippi River Delta" in this chapter, and "People and the Environment: Lessons from Hurricane Katrina" in Chapter 7.

Learning Check 16-12   **How has human activity contributed to changes in the Mississippi River delta?**

Living on the Floodplain: So, can people live on a floodplain without incurring untenable economic and ecological costs? Part of the answer rests in sensible land use practices—the local governments of most urban areas adjacent to streams have drafted maps showing the extent of floodplain inundation for a *design flood*, such as the 100-year flood; zoning regulations can then restrict land use in such a way as to reduce the likelihood of costly damage. Diversion or bypass channels can be constructed to divert floodwaters out onto an "artificial" floodplain; such diversion areas can be used profitably for other activities, such as farming, most of the year.

Restoring Floodplains: In some locations, levees are actually being removed in an effort to give streams back at least part of their original floodplains. This approach not only restores valuable wetlands habitat, but it may also serve to dampen the surge of a flood downstream by increasing the "storage capacity" of a floodplain upstream. One such experiment is currently underway in the Upper Ouachita National Wildlife Refuge along the Ouachita River in northern Louisiana, where 17 miles of levees were removed in a project completed in 2010. A proposal to open levees south of New Orleans is currently under review by state officials in Louisiana.

The Changing Mississippi River Delta

Since the end of the last ice age, the "bird's-foot" delta of the Mississippi River has changed its form many times and occupied different locations along a 320-kilometer (200-mile) stretch of the Gulf coastline (see Figure 16-42). It has been in its current position for about the last 600 years.

The size, shape, and configuration of the delta are the outcome of a number of different processes. The Mississippi River supplies sediment to the delta, deposited when the velocity of the river decreases as it flows into the Gulf of Mexico. At the same time, however, the delta slowly subsides into the gulf. Before dams and other kinds of human manipulation of the Mississippi–Missouri River system began decreasing the sediment load of the river, the delta was growing faster than it was sinking. Today the delta is sinking faster than sediments can replenish it (Figure 16-C).

Increasing Saltwater Encroachment:
The extensive artificial-drainage and river-channeling efforts have restricted the Mississippi and its distributaries to relatively narrow channels, thus keeping both silt and freshwater from getting to the extensive surrounding marshlands. The slight increase in sea level that has occurred over the last century has also led to increased erosion of the delta. As saltwater moves farther into the formerly freshwater marshes of the delta, the marsh vegetation dies, leaving the delta more susceptible to erosion (Figure 16-D).

▲ **Figure 16-D** Freshwater marsh within the Mississippi River delta, Louisiana.

Reduction of Sediment Deposits:
Before the shipping channels were lined with artificial levees as extensively as they are today, floodwaters would regularly deposit sediment into the marshes of the delta. With time, the sediment compacted around the roots of the marsh plants—the delta would subside, but a continuing supply of sediment would replenish the marshes. Once the artificial levees cut off much of the sediment supply to the marshes just outside the shipping channels, the marsh vegetation became discontinuous and much more susceptible to storm damage. Once damaged—as happened in many areas of the delta as a result of Hurricane Katrina—the marshlands degrade even more. A U.S. Geological Survey study estimated that 560 square kilometers (217 square miles) of delta land were at least temporarily lost after Hurricanes Katrina and Rita in 2005.

Delta Restoration:
Scientists and policy makers have been struggling for years to come up with a practical way to restore the wetlands of the delta, but no approach can be agreed upon by all. One promising strategy involves controlled diversions of water into the marshes, but it is too early to tell if that will be enough to restore some of the marshlands—or even stop the ongoing decline.

The health of the delta was stressed further by the Deepwater Horizon oil spill in 2010 (Figure 16-E; see the box, "People and the Environment: The 2010 Deepwater Horizon Oil Spill," in Chapter 10). In September 2012, President Obama signed an executive order establishing the Gulf Coast Ecosystem Restoration Council. The council continues the work of a federal task force assembled to establish goals for ecosystem restoration along the Gulf Coast following the oil spill—projects funded by fines received from the spill—projects that may also help slow the ongoing decline of the delta.

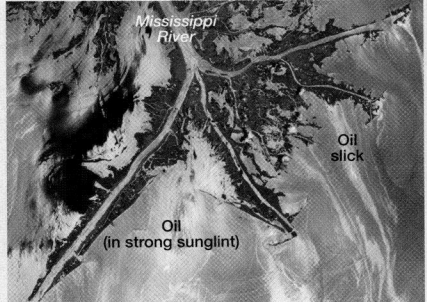

▲ **Figure 16-E** False-color image of the Mississippi River delta taken by NASA's Terra satellite on May 24, 2010, shows the oil slick resulting from the Deepwater Horizon oil spill in the Gulf of Mexico. Water covered with oil is more reflective and so appears brighter than clean water in this image.

▲ **Figure 16-C** Land loss in the Mississippi River delta between 1932 and 2010. Green areas represent land gain; red shows land loss 1932–1973; orange and yellow show land loss 1973–1990; blue shows land loss 1990–2004; lavender shows land loss 2004–2010.

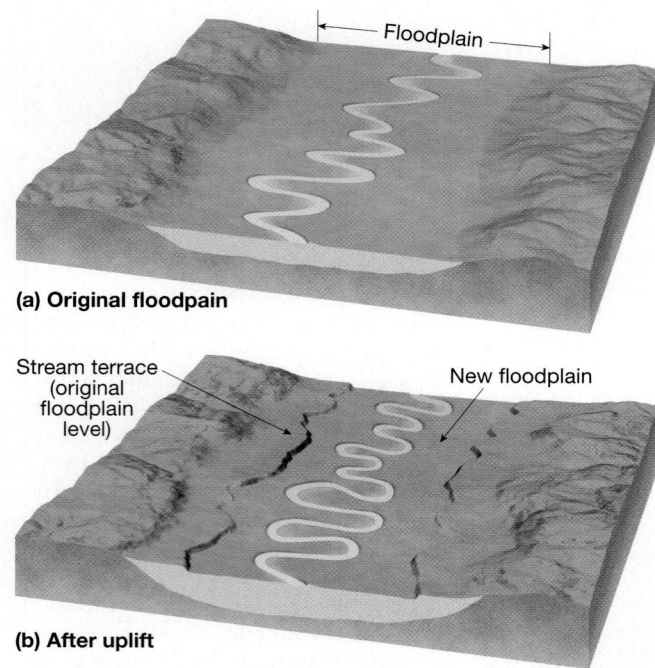

(a) Original floodpain

Stream terrace
(original
floodplain
level)

New floodplain

(b) After uplift

▲ **Figure 16-44** Stream terraces normally represent sequences of uplift and rejuvenation. (a) Before uplift, a river meanders across an alluvial floodplain. (b) After uplift, the stream downcuts and then widens a new floodplain, leaving the remnants of the original floodplain as a pair of stream terraces.

STREAM REJUVENATION

All parts of the continental surfaces experience episodes, sometimes frequent and sometimes rare, when their elevation relative to sea level changes. This change is occasionally caused by a drop in sea level (as occurred around the world during the various ice ages when frozen water accumulated on the land, reducing the amount of water in the oceans), but it is much more commonly the result of tectonic uplift of the land surface. When such uplift occurs, it "rejuvenates" the streams in the area by increasing their gradients. The increased gradient causes the streams to flow faster, which provides renewed energy for downcutting (a dramatic, sustained increase in discharge may also rejuvenate a stream). Vertical incision, which may have long been dormant, is initiated or intensified by such **stream rejuvenation**.

Stream Terraces: If a stream occupied a broad floodplain prior to rejuvenation, renewed downcutting enables the stream to carve a new valley floor (Figure 16-44). This means that the old floodplain can no longer function as an overflow area and instead becomes an abandoned stretch of flat land overlooking the new valley. This remnant of the previous valley floor is called a **stream**

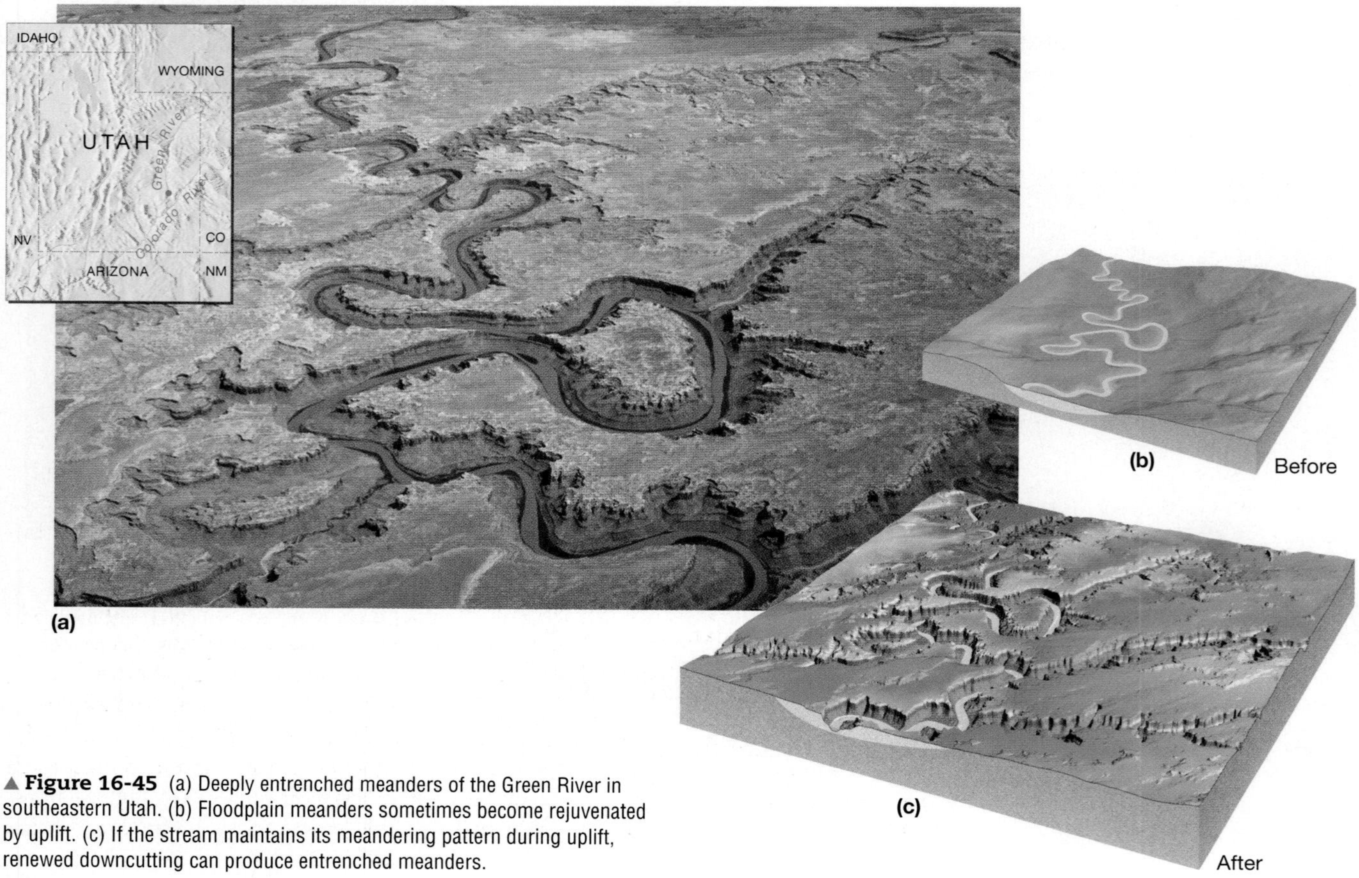

Animation
Stream
Terrace
Formation

▲ **Figure 16-45** (a) Deeply entrenched meanders of the Green River in southeastern Utah. (b) Floodplain meanders sometimes become rejuvenated by uplift. (c) If the stream maintains its meandering pattern during uplift, renewed downcutting can produce entrenched meanders.

(a)

(b) Before

(c)

After

terrace. Terraces often, but not always, occur in pairs, one on either side of the newly incised stream channel.

Entrenched Meanders: Under certain circumstances, uplift and rejuvenation have a different and even more conspicuous topographic effect: **entrenched meanders** (Figure 16-45). These topographic features are formed when an area containing a meandering stream is uplifted slowly and the stream incises downward while still retaining the meandering course—often with the entrenchment extending itself headward upstream. In some cases, such meanders may become entrenched in narrow gorges hundreds of meters deep.

> **Learning Check 16-13** **How do stream terraces develop?**

THEORIES OF LANDFORM DEVELOPMENT

The various internal and external processes operating on Earth's surface produce an infinite variety of landscapes. Systematizing this vast array of facts and relationships into a coherent body of knowledge has been the goal of many geomorphologists. As we finish this chapter describing the often dominant role of running water in all of these processes, it may be helpful to discuss how comprehensive theories of landform development were devised in the past and how they have changed over time.

Davis's Geomorphic Cycle

The first, and in many ways most influential, model of landscape development was propounded by William Morris Davis, an American geographer and geomorphologist active in the 1890s and early 1900s. Sometimes called the *cycle of erosion*, Davis's theory is now usually referred to as the *geomorphic cycle*.

Davis believed that any landscape can be comprehended by analyzing structure, process, and stage. *Structure* refers to the type and arrangement of the underlying rocks and surface materials, *process* is concerned with the internal and external forces that shape the landforms, and *stage* is the length of time during which the processes have been at work.

Davis metaphorically likened the development of landforms to the life cycle of an organism, recognizing stages of development he called "youth," "maturity," and "old age" (Figure 16-46). He envisioned a continuous sequence of terrain evolution in which a relatively flat surface is uplifted rapidly with little erosion taking place until uplift is complete:

Youth: The initial flat surface is dissected by streams which begin to incise deep, narrow, steep-sided, V-shaped valleys separated by flattish interfluves. The streams flow rapidly and have irregular gradients marked by waterfalls and rapids.

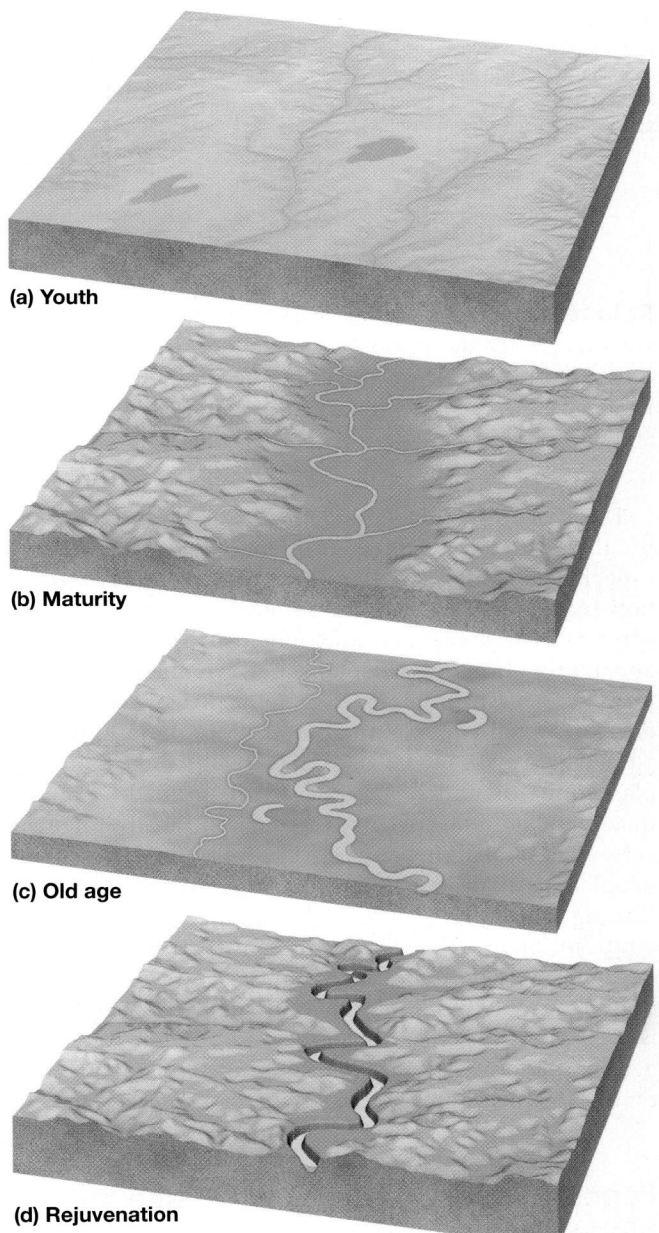

(a) Youth

(b) Maturity

(c) Old age

(d) Rejuvenation

▲ **Figure 16-46** The idealized Davisian geomorphic cycle.

Maturity: The streams approach an equilibrium condition, having worn away the falls and rapids and developed smooth profiles. As stream gradient is reduced, streams begin to meander and floodplains are formed, and the drainage system expands to dissect all of the interfluves.

Old Age: Over time, erosion reduces the entire landscape to near base level, and the entire region is dominated by extensive floodplains over which a few major streams meander broadly and slowly. The end product is a flat, featureless landscape with minimal relief that Davis called a *peneplain* (*paene* is Latin for "almost"; hence, "almost a plain"). He envisioned occasional remnants of exceptionally resistant rock rising slightly above the peneplain surface; such erosional remnants are dubbed *monadnocks* after a mountain of this name in New Hampshire.

▶ **Figure 16-47** Slope retreat in (1) the Davis model and (2) the Penck model. The Davis concept proposes a continually diminishing angle of slope, whereas Penck theorized parallel retreat in which the slope angle remains approximately the same over time.

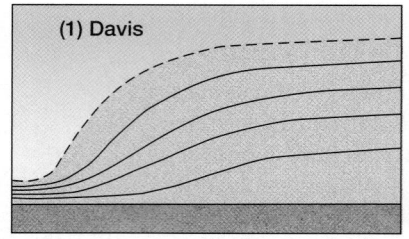
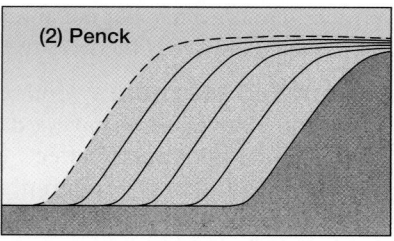

Rejuvenation: Davis's theory also took into account rejuvenation, whereby regional uplift could raise the land and interrupt the cycle at any stage. This tectonic activity would reenergize the system, initiate a new period of downcutting, and restart the cycle.

Davis was a prolific writer and a persuasive teacher, and his theory had a profound influence for many decades, especially in the United States. Even in the early days, however, there were strong dissenters who questioned some of his assumptions and conclusions. For example, apparently no intact peneplains exist; remnants of peneplain surfaces are recognized in some areas, but nowhere does an actual peneplain occur. A more important difficulty with Davis's model is his idea that little erosion takes place while the initial surface is being uplifted—a notion unacceptable to most geomorphologists. Finally, there are serious doubts about sequential development and some people feel that the biological analogy may be more misleading than helpful; although some landscapes appear youthful, mature, or old age, there is little evidence that one stage necessarily precedes another in regular fashion, even in a single valley. For landform analysis, therefore, it is probably better to use the terms *youth, maturity*, and *old age* as descriptive summaries of regional topography rather than as distinct implications of sequential development.

Penck's Theory of Crustal Change and Slope Development

Walther Penck, a young German geomorphologist and a prominent early critic of Davis, pointed out in the 1920s that slopes assume various shapes as they erode. Penck stressed that uplift stimulates erosion immediately and that slope form is significantly influenced by the rate of uplift or other crustal deformation. He argued that

steep slopes, particularly, maintain a constant angle as they erode, retaining their steepness as they diminish in a sort of "parallel retreat" rather than being worn down at a continually lower slope angle—meaning that the shape of many initial surfaces is retained long after they would have been worn away in Davis's concept (Figure 16-47). Many, but not all, of Penck's ideas have been substantiated by subsequent workers, and his ideas have come to be called the *theory of crustal change and slope development*.

Learning Check 16-14 **Explain some of the problems with Davis's *geomorphic cycle* theory.**

Equilibrium Theory

A third model of landform development became known as *equilibrium theory*. In the last 50 years or so, many geomorphologists studied the physics of landform development, emphasizing the delicate balance between form and process in the landscape. Both the influence of crustal movement and the resistance of the underlying rock vary significantly from place to place, and these variations are as significant as differences in process in determining terrain. Equilibrium theory suggests that slopes are adjusted to geomorphic processes so that there is a balance of energy—the energy provided is just adequate for the work to be done. For example, harder rock develops steeper slopes and higher relief, and softer rock has gentler slopes and lower relief. The uniformity inherent in both the Davis and Penck theories is thus called into question.

The application of equilibrium theory can be seen in mountainous areas where the land is being simultaneously uplifted tectonically and eroded fluvially, as is happening in the Alps and the Himalayas today (Figure 16-48). If the slopes are in equilibrium, they are being wasted away by

▶ **Figure 16-48** The dynamic equilibrium concept. This vertical cross section through an area of the Swiss Alps shows that (a) erosion reduces relief just about as rapidly as uplift raises the land, with the result that (b) the elevation and shape of the mountains remains approximately the same because removal and replacement are in balance.

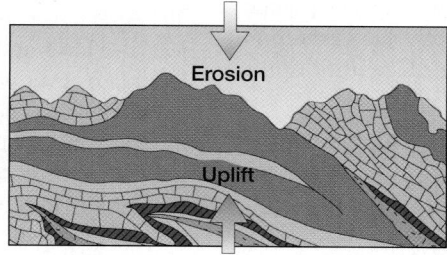
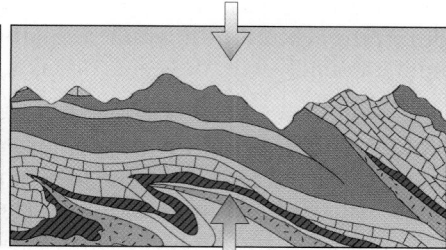

(a) **(b)**

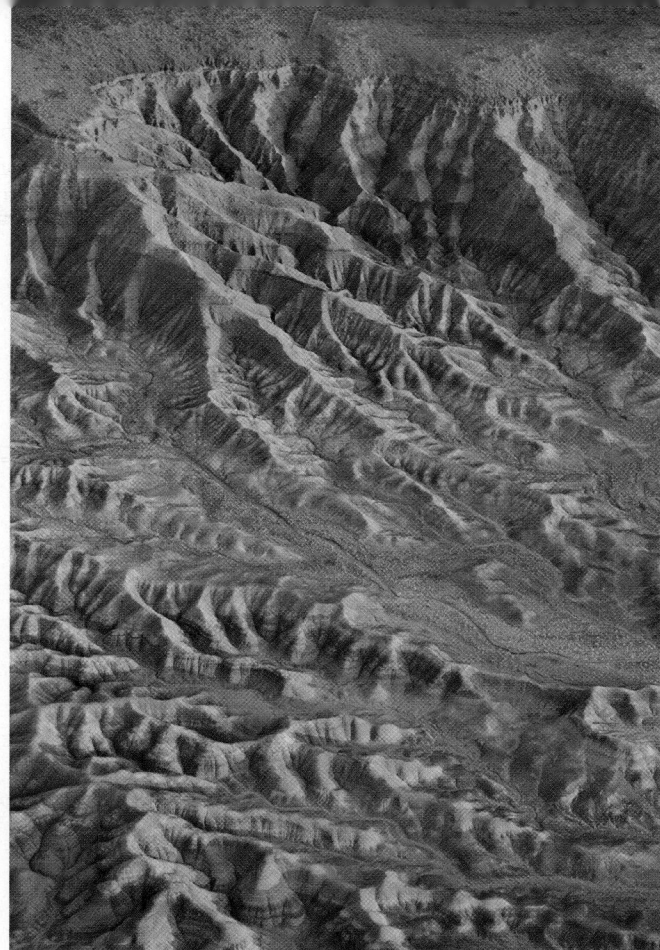

◄ **Figure 16-49** Highly dissected hillsides near the Little Colorado River, just north of Winslow, Arizona.

mass wasting and erosion at the same rate as they are being regenerated by uplift, so the general form of the surface remains largely the same. A change in either the rate of erosion or the rate of uplift forces the landscape through a period of adjustment until the slopes again reach a gradient at which the rate of erosion equals the rate of uplift (Figure 16-49).

Equilibrium theory has serious shortcomings in areas that are tectonically stable or have limited streamflow (deserts, for example). It does, however, focus more precisely than our other two models on the relationship between geomorphic processes and surface forms and for this reason has dominated fluvial geomorphology since the 1960s.

Chapter **16** **LEARNING REVIEW**

After studying this chapter, you should be able to answer the following questions. Key terms from each text section are shown in **bold type**. Definitions for key terms are also found in the glossary at the back of the book.

KEY TERMS AND CONCEPTS

Streams and Stream Systems (*p. 468*)

1. In the study of geomorphology, what is meant by a **stream**?
2. What are **fluvial processes**?
3. Describe the difference between **streamflow** and **overland flow**.
4. What are the differences between an **interfluve** and a **valley**?
5. What is a **drainage basin (watershed)**? A **drainage divide**?
6. Using the concept of **stream order**, explain the difference between a first-order stream and a second-order stream, and the general relationship between stream order and stream **gradient**.

Fluvial Erosion and Deposition (*p. 471*)

7. Describe the different components of **stream load**: **dissolved load**, **suspended load**, and **bedload**.
8. What is the difference between stream **competence** and stream **capacity**?
9. How does a stream sort **alluvium** by size?
10. Contrast **perennial streams** with **intermittent streams** and **ephemeral streams**.
11. What is meant by stream **discharge**?
12. What is meant by a flood **recurrence interval** of 50 years—in other words, what is meant by a 50-year flood?

Stream Channels (*p. 474*)

13. In what way is the pattern of water flow in a straight stream channel likely to be similar to that of a **sinuous channel**?
14. Under what circumstances is a stream likely to have a **meandering channel** pattern?
15. Under what circumstances is a stream likely to have a **braided channel** pattern?

Structural Relationships (*p. 477*)

16. What is an **antecedent stream** and how might one form?
17. Describe and explain the circumstances under which **dendritic drainage patterns** develop, and the conditions under which **trellis drainage patterns** develop.

The Shaping and Reshaping of Valleys (*p. 480*)

18. Explain the process of valley deepening through **downcutting**.
19. What is meant by **base level**?
20. What is a **knickpoint**?
21. Describe and explain the process of **knickpoint migration**.
22. Explain how a meandering stream widens its valley through the process of **lateral erosion**.
23. Describe and explain the process of **headward erosion**.

24. Explain the process of **stream capture (stream piracy)**.
25. Describe the formation of a **delta**.
26. Under what conditions does **aggradation** of a stream channel take place?

Floodplains (*p. 486*)

27. Describe the general characteristics of a **floodplain**.
28. Describe and explain the formation process of a **cutoff meander**.
29. Explain the relationships among a cutoff meander, an **oxbow lake**, and a **meander scar**.
30. What are **natural levees** and how do they form?
31. What explains the presence of a **yazoo stream** on a floodplain?

Stream Rejuvenation (*p. 492*)

32. Explain the circumstances that can lead to **stream rejuvenation**.
33. Describe and explain the formation of **stream terraces**.
34. How is it possible for **entrenched meanders** to form?

Theories of Landform Development (*p. 493*)

35. Describe and explain at least one problem with Davis's geomorphic cycle model of fluvial landform development.
36. How does equilibrium theory differ from earlier theories of topographic development?

STUDY QUESTIONS

1. What factors influence the erosional effectiveness of a stream?
2. What are the abrasive "tools" used by a stream in erosion?
3. What factor determines the competence of a stream?
4. Why are deposits of alluvium often rounded and stratified?
5. Explain how talus from rockfall (Chapter 15) is likely to look different from a deposit of alluvium.
6. Why are floods so important in the development of fluvial landforms?
7. Describe radial drainage patterns and one kind of location where such a drainage pattern might be found.

8. What prevents a stream from downcutting to sea level throughout its entire course?
9. Why would few depositional features be found in most V-shaped stream valleys?
10. Why don't all large rivers form deltas where they enter the ocean?
11. Why might meandering rivers make poor political boundaries?
12. What are some of the negative consequences of using artificial levees for flood control along a major river?

EXERCISES

1. Assume that the rate of knickpoint migration for Niagara Falls has been constant (a simplistic assumption):
   a. If it took 12,000 years for the position of the waterfall to shift 11 kilometers upstream, what is the average annual rate of movement? _____ meters
   b. Assuming the annual rate of knickpoint migration continues into the future (again, a simplistic assumption) how long will it take before the position of the falls migrates the remaining 27 kilometers to Lake Erie? _____ years

2. Assume that the competence of a stream increases with the square of the speed of flow. If a stream can move a 1-kilogram rock with its normal flow, what is the mass of a rock that can be moved if the speed increases by a factor of 3 during a flood? _____ kilograms

3. Using the map of Trout Creek, Wyoming, in Figure 16-18 for reference, what is the stream order where the stream runs off the map? _____ order stream.

Seeing Geographically

Look again at the photograph of the Green River in Wyoming at the beginning of the chapter (p. 466). What kind of floodplain landform is shown by the curved lake in the foreground? How did it form? What will happen to this lake over time? Where do you see other examples of these features on this floodplain? Where do you see point bars along the course of the river? Why do they form in these locations?

MasteringGeography™

Looking for additional review and test prep materials? Visit the Study Area in MasteringGeography™ to enhance your geographic literacy, spatial reasoning skills, and understanding of this chapter's content by accessing a variety of resources, including geoscience animations, MapMaster interactive maps, videos, RSS feeds, flashcards, web links, self-study quizzes, and an eText version of *McKnight's Physical Geography: A Landscape Appreciation.*

Chapter 17

KARST AND HYDROTHERMAL PROCESSES

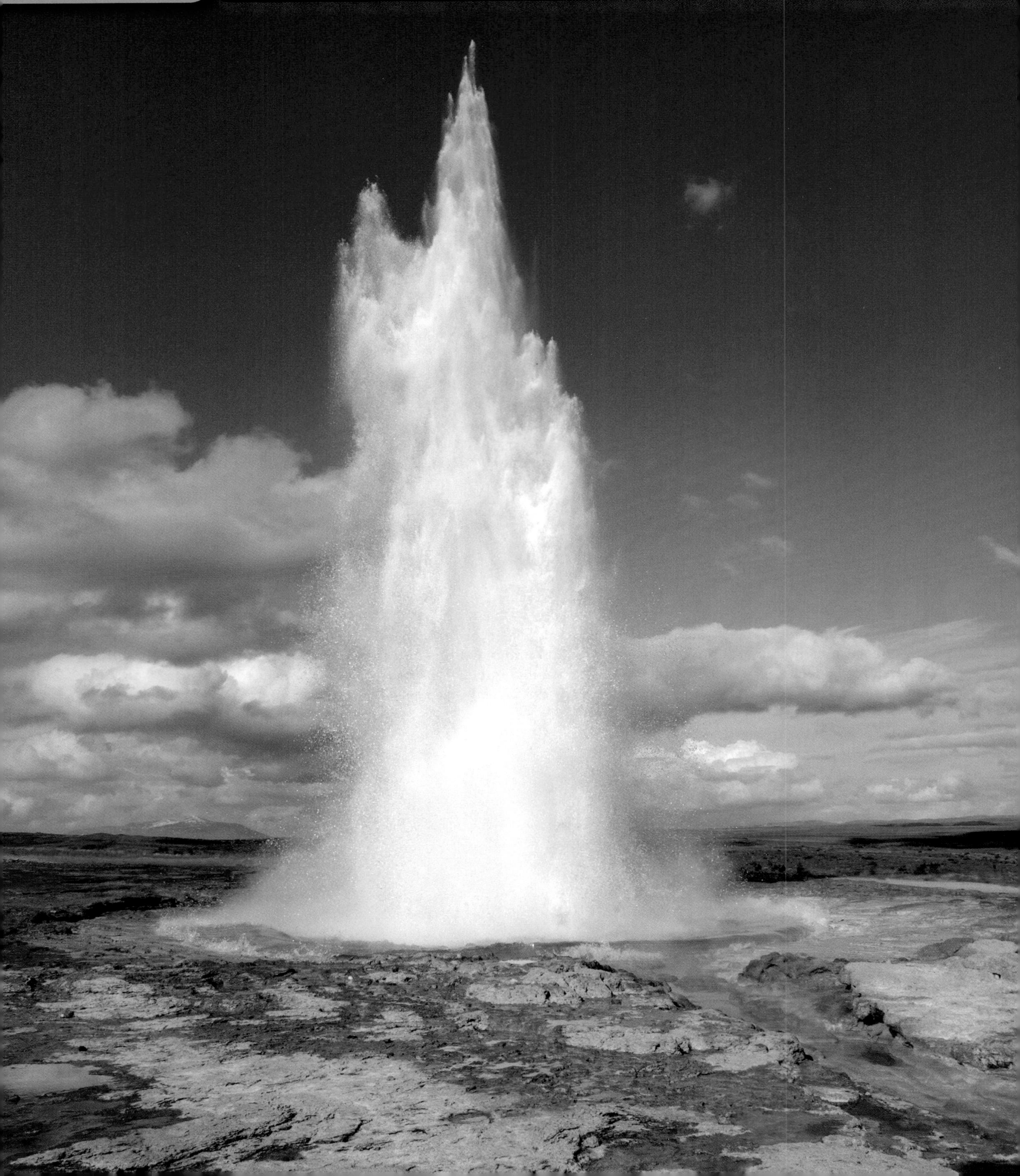

IN STUDYING TOPOGRAPHIC DEVELOPMENT, WE PAY A GREAT

deal of attention to the role of water. We noted that water running across the ground is a significant external shaper of terrain, and we will see that coastal waters produce distinctive landforms around the margins of oceans and lakes. In both cases, the water moves rapidly, and much energy is expended in erosion, transportation, and deposition.

In this brief chapter, we focus on water beneath the surface, which, because it is confined, functions in a much more restricted fashion than surface water. Underground water is largely unchanneled and therefore generally diffused, and it moves very slowly for the most part. Consequently, it is almost totally ineffective in terms of hydraulic power and other kinds of mechanical erosion. However, underground water can leave a distinctive mark on the surface landscape through a variety of solution processes associated with the development of karst and hydrothermal features—the topic of this chapter.

As you study this chapter, think about these key questions:

- **How do dissolution and precipitation processes affect bedrock such as limestone?**
- **How do limestone caverns develop?**
- **How do subsurface processes influence surface landforms in areas of karst topography?**
- **What conditions are necessary for hydrothermal features to develop?**

The Impact of Solution Processes on the Landscape

The mechanical effects of underground water have only a limited influence on topographic development (recall from Chapter 9 that *underground water* refers to any water beneath the surface, whereas the term *groundwater* specifically refers to water below the water table within the zone of saturation). Some subsurface mechanical weathering does take place, but the surface landscape is rarely directly affected by it, although certain forms of mass wasting (such as earthflows and slumps) are facilitated when loose materials are lubricated by underground water.

Through its chemical action, however, underground water is an effective shaper of the topographic landscape. Water is a solvent for certain rock-forming minerals, dissolving them from rock and then carrying them away in solution and depositing them elsewhere. Under some circumstances, the aboveground results of this dissolution are widespread and distinctive.

Underground water also affects surface topography via the creation of such hydrothermal features as hot springs and geysers, formed when hot water from underground is discharged at the ground surface.

SOLUTION AND PRECIPITATION

The chemical reactions involving underground water are relatively simple. Although pure water is a relatively poor solvent, almost all underground water is laced with enough chemical impurities to make it a good solvent for the compounds that make up a few common minerals (Figure 17-1). Basically, underground water is a weak solution of

Stokkur Geyser, in the Haukadalur geothermal area in south-central Iceland. Describe the general topography around the geyser. What suggests that some of the rocks around the geyser have been deposited by minerals originally dissolved in the geyser? What factors do you think determine the distribution of plants visible on this landscape?

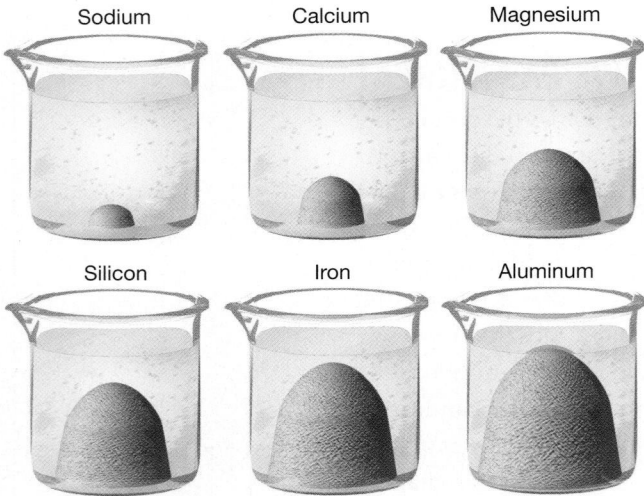

Sodium   Calcium   Magnesium

Silicon   Iron   Aluminum

▲ **Figure 17-1** Relative solubility in water of some common rock-forming elements. The "lumps" in each beaker represent the proportion of the element that remains undissolved in a given amount of water. Sodium and calcium can be almost completely dissolved, for instance, whereas iron and aluminum are essentially insoluble.

carbonic acid (H_2CO_3) because it contains dissolved carbon dioxide gas—as we first saw in Chapter 15, the resulting *carbonation* can lead to the dissolution of bedrock.

Dissolution Processes: Dissolution is the removal of bedrock through the chemical action of water. Dissolution is an important weathering and erosional process for all rocks, but it is particularly effective on carbonate sedimentary rocks, especially limestone. A common sedimentary rock, limestone is composed largely of calcium carbonate ($CaCO_3$), which reacts strongly with carbonic acid solution to yield calcium bicarbonate, a compound that is very soluble in (and thus easily removed by) water. Other carbonate rocks, such as gypsum and even the metamorphic rock marble, undergo similar reactions. Dolomite is a calcium magnesium carbonate rock that dissolves almost as quickly as limestone. In simplified form, the chemical equations for the dissolution of limestone and dolomite are as follows:

$$CaCO_3 \quad + \quad H_2O \quad + \quad CO_2 \rightarrow Ca(HCO_3)_2$$
limestone   water   carbon   calcium
(calcium   dioxide   bicarbonate
carbonate)

$$CaMg(CO_3)_2 + 2H_2O + 2CO_2 \rightarrow Ca(HCO_3)_2 + Mg(HCO_3)_2$$
dolomite   water   carbon   calcium   magnesium
                     dioxide bicarbonate   bicarbonate

These reactions are the most notable dissolution processes. Water percolating down into carbonate bedrock dissolves and carries away a part of the rock mass. Because limestone and related rocks are largely composed of soluble minerals, great volumes of rock are sometimes dissolved and removed, leaving conspicuous voids in the bedrock. This action occurs more rapidly and on a larger scale in humid climates, where abundant precipitation provides plenty of water containing dissolved carbon dioxide necessary for dissolution. In arid

regions, evidence of dissolution action is unusual except for relict features dating from a more humid past.

Although reactions with carbonic acid are the most common processes involved in the dissolution of carbonate rocks, recent studies suggest that in some locations sulfuric acid (H_2SO_4) may also be important. For example, it appears that Lechuguilla Cave in New Mexico was at least in part enlarged through dissolution of limestone by sulfuric acid, formed when hydrogen sulfide (H_2S) from deeper petroleum deposits combined with oxygen in the groundwater.

Role of the Bedrock Structure: Bedrock structure is also a factor in dissolution. A profusion of *joints* and *bedding planes* permits groundwater to penetrate the rock readily. That the water is moving also helps because, as a given volume of water becomes saturated with dissolved calcium bicarbonate, it can drain away and be replaced by fresh unsaturated water that can dissolve more rock. Such drainage is enhanced by some outlet at a lower level, such as a deep subsurface stream.

Most limestone is resistant to mechanical erosion and often produces rugged topography. Thus, its ready solubility contrasts notably with its mechanical durability—a vulnerable interior beneath a durable surface.

Learning Check 17-1   **Why is limestone so susceptible to *dissolution*? (Answer on p. AK-5)**

Precipitation Processes: Complementing the removal of calcium carbonate is its precipitation from solution. Mineralized water may trickle in along a cave roof or wall. The reduced air pressure in the open cave induces precipitation of the minerals the water is carrying.

One other type of precipitation is worth mentioning despite its scarcity because of its dramatic distinctiveness. Hot springs and geysers nearly always provide an accumulation of precipitated minerals, frequently brilliant white but sometimes orange, green, or some other color due to associated algae. Wherever it comes in contact with magma, groundwater becomes heated, and this water sometimes finds its way back to the surface through a natural opening so rapidly that it is still hot when it reaches the open air. Hot water is generally a much better solvent than cold, and so a hot spring or geyser usually contains a significant quantity of dissolved minerals. When exposed to the open air, the hot water precipitates much of its mineral content as its temperature and the pressure on it decrease, and as the dissolved gases that helped keep the minerals in solution dissipate or as algae and other organisms living in it secrete mineral matter. These deposits (such as *travertine, tufa,* and *sinter*) contain a variety of calcareous minerals and take the form of mounds, terraces, walls, and peripheral rims (see Figure 17-17).

It should be noted, however, that the solubility of carbon dioxide *decreases* as water temperature increases. Thus, cool water often is more potent than hot water as a solvent for calcium carbonate.

Learning Check 17-2   **How do rocks such as *travertine* and *tufa* form?**

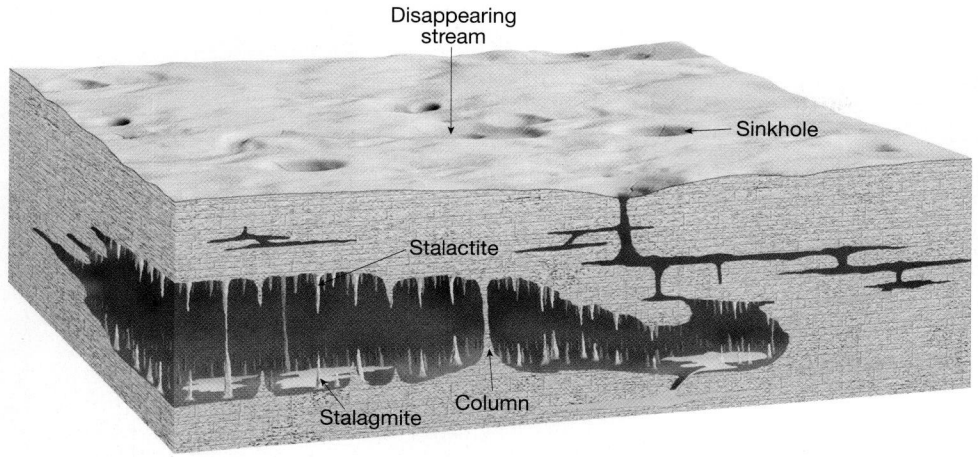

◀ **Figure 17-2** Caverns are formed by solution action of underground water as it trickles along bedding planes and joint systems.

CAVERNS AND RELATED FEATURES

Some of the most spectacular landforms produced by dissolution are not visible at Earth's surface. Solution along joints and bedding planes in limestone beneath the surface often creates large open areas called **caverns**. The largest of these openings are usually more expansive horizontally than vertically, indicating a development along bedding planes. In many cases, however, the cavern pattern has a rectangularity that demonstrates a relationship to the joint system (Figure 17-2).

Caverns are found almost anywhere there is a massive limestone deposit at or near the surface. The state of Missouri, for example, has more than 6000. Caverns often are difficult to find because their connection to the surface may be extremely small and obscure, or nonexistent. Beneath the surface, however, some caverns are very extensive (Mammoth Cave in Kentucky has more than 630 kilometers [390 miles] of known passages), with an elaborate system of galleries and passageways, usually very irregular in shape and sometimes including massive openings ("rooms") scattered here and there along the galleries. A stream may flow along the floor of a large cavern, adding another dimension to erosion and deposition.

Speleothems

There are two principal stages in cavern formation. First there is the initial excavation, wherein percolating water dissolves the carbonate bedrock and leaves voids. This dissolution is followed, often after a drop in the water table, by a "decoration stage" in which ceilings, walls, and floors are decorated with a wondrous variety of **speleothems** (Figure 17-3). These forms are deposited when water

▲ **Figure 17-3** A multitude of stalactites hang from the ceiling of this room in Arizona's Kartchner Caverns. The smooth, gently-rounded surfaces are often referred to as *flowstone*.

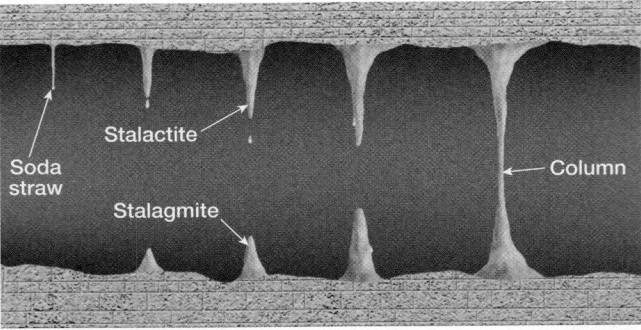

▲ **Figure 17-4** The development of soda straws, stalagmites, stalactites, and columns.

▲ Figure 17-5 Irregular topography and collapsed caves are prominent in the karst region of Primorska in Slovenia

leaves behind the compounds (principally carbon dioxide and calcite) it was carrying in solution. Once out of solution, the carbon dioxide gas diffuses into the cave atmosphere, and calcite is deposited. Much of the deposition occurs on the sides of the cavern, but the most striking features are formed on the roof and floor. Where water drips from the roof, a pendant structure grows slowly downward like an icicle—a **stalactite**. Where the drip hits the floor, a companion feature, a **stalagmite**, grows upward. Stalactites and stalagmites may extend until they meet to form a *column* (Figure 17-4). In some caverns, long, slender *soda straws* hang down from the ceiling; little more than one water drop wide, these delicate hollow tubes may eventually grow into stalactites.

> **Learning Check 17-3**　**Explain the two stages of** *cavern* **development.**

KARST TOPOGRAPHY

In many areas where the bedrock is limestone or similarly soluble rock, dissolution has been so widespread and effective that a distinctive landform assemblage has developed at the surface, in addition to whatever caves may exist underground. The term **karst** (a Germanized form of an ancient Slavic word meaning "barren land") is applied to this topography. The name derives from the Kras or Krš Plateau region of Slovenia (formerly part of Yugoslavia), a rugged hilly area that has been shaped almost entirely by solution action in limestone formations (Figure 17-5).

The term *karst* connotes both a set of processes and an assemblage of landforms. The word is used as the catchall name of a cornerstone concept that describes the special landforms that develop on exceptionally soluble rocks, although there is a broad international vocabulary to refer to specific features in specific regions.

Karst Landforms

Typical landforms in karst regions include sinkholes, disrupted surface drainage, and underground drainage networks that have openings formed from solution action. The openings range in size from enlarged cracks to huge caverns.

Karst landscapes usually evolve where there is massive limestone bedrock. However, karst features may also occur where other highly soluble rocks—dolomite, gypsum, or halite—predominate. Karst landforms are worthy of study not only because of their dramatic appearance but also because of their abundance. It is estimated that about 10 percent of Earth's land area has soluble carbonate rocks at or near the surface; in the conterminous United States, this total rises to 15 percent (Figure 17-6).

Sinkholes: The most common surface features of karst landscapes are **sinkholes** (also called *dolines*), which occur by the hundreds and sometimes by the thousands. Sinkholes are rounded depressions formed by the dissolution of surface carbonate rocks, typically (but by no means always) at joint intersections. The sinkholes erode more rapidly than the surrounding area, forming closed depressions. Their

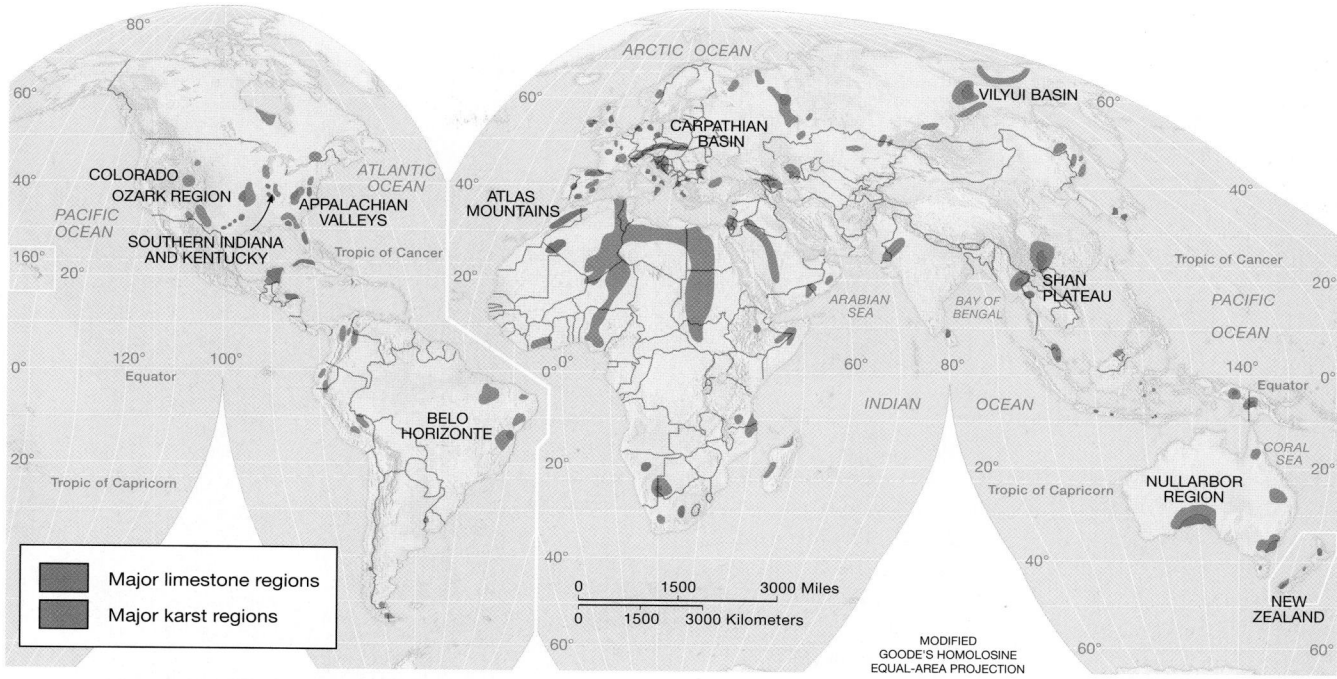

▲ **Figure 17-6** Major limestone and karst regions of the world.

sides generally slope inward at the angle of repose (usually 20° to 30°) of the adjacent material, although some have more gentle side slopes. A sinkhole that results from the collapse of the roof of a subsurface cavern is called a **collapse sinkhole** (or *collapse doline*); these may have vertical walls or even overhanging cliffs (Figure 17-7a/b).

Sinkholes range in size from shallow depressions a few meters in diameter and a few centimeters deep to major features kilometers in diameter and hundreds of meters deep. The largest are associated with tropical regions, where they develop rapidly and where adjacent holes often intersect.

The bottom of a sinkhole may lead into a subterranean passage, down which water pours during a rainstorm. More commonly, however, the subsurface entrance is blocked by rock rubble, soil, or vegetation, and rains form temporary lakes until the water percolates away. Indeed, sinkholes are the karst equivalent of river valleys, in that they are the fundamental unit of both erosion and weathering.

In many karst locations, depressions dominate the landscape. Sinkholes are commonplace in central Florida and parts of the Midwest, particularly Kentucky, Illinois, and Missouri. For example, at the University of Missouri in Columbia, both the football stadium and the basketball fieldhouse are built in sinkholes, and parking lots around them occasionally sink.

Apart from the ubiquity of sinkholes, karst areas show considerable topographic diversity. Where the relief is slight, as in central Florida, sinkholes are the dominant features. Where the relief is greater, however, cliffs and steep slopes alternate with flat-floored, streamless valleys. Limestone bedrock exposed at the surface tends to be pitted, grooved, etched, and fluted with a great intricacy of erosive detail.

Surface Drainage in Karst Areas: Where sinkholes occur in profusion, they often channel surface runoff into the groundwater circulation, leaving networks of dry valleys as relict surface forms. The Serbo-Croatian term **uvala** refers to such a chain of intersecting sinkholes. In many cases, sinkholes evolve into uvala over time.

In many ways, the most notable feature of karst regions is what is missing: surface drainage. Most rainfall and snowmelt seep downward along joints and bedding planes, enlarging them by dissolution. Surface runoff that does become channeled does not usually go far before it disappears into a sinkhole or joint crack—such streams are often termed **disappearing streams** (see Figure 17-7a). The water that collects in sinkholes generally percolates downward, but some sinkholes have distinct openings at their bottom, called **swallow holes**, through which surface drainage can pour directly into an underground channel, often to reappear at the surface through another hole some distance away. Where dissolution has been effective for a long time, there may be a complex underground drainage system that has superseded any sort of surface drainage network. An appropriate generalization concerning surface drainage in karst regions is that valleys are relatively scarce and mostly dry.

Tower Karst: Residual karst features, in the form of very steep-sided hills, dominate some parts of the world (Figure 17-7c). These formations are sometimes referred to as **tower karst** because of their almost vertical sides and conical or hemispheric shapes. Such towers are sometimes riddled with caves. The tower karst of southeastern China, adjacent parts of northern Vietnam, and southern Thailand is world famous for its spectacular scenery (Figure 17-8), as are the *mogotes* (haystack hills) of western Cuba.

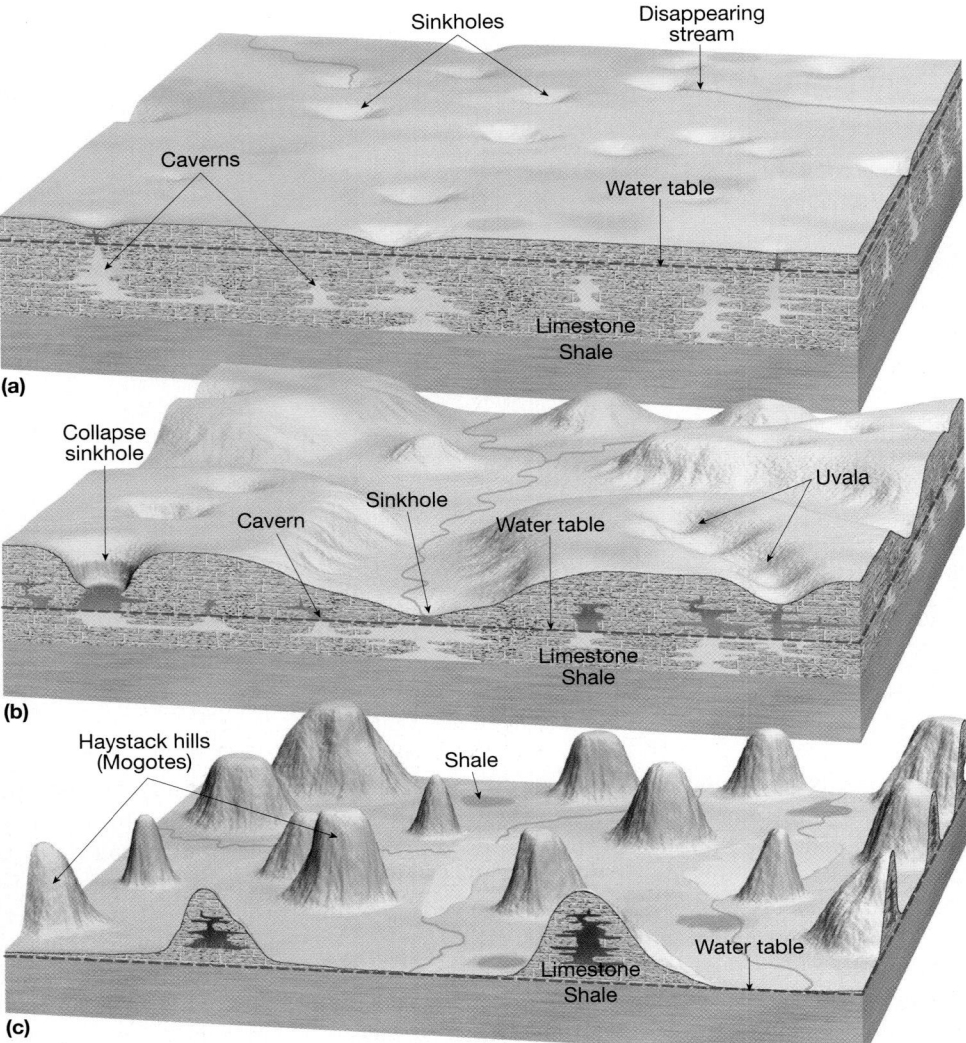

(a)

(b)

(c)

► **Figure 17-7** The development of karst topography. (a) Landscape dominated by sinkholes and disappearing streams. Dissolution of bedrock below the water table may leave openings that develop into caverns. (b) Where underground caverns collapse, a collapse sinkhole forms. Streams may disappear into sinkholes through swallow holes. If the water table drops enough to leave open caverns, speleothems may gradually develop. (c) Tower karst topography consists of residual towers of limestone (haystack hills or mogotes).

▲ **Figure 17-8** Spectacular tower karst hills (mogotes) in Guilin, China.

◀ **Figure 17-9** This sinkhole developed in the front yard of a house in Lake City, Florida, in March 2005.

Learning Check 17-4   **What is a *sinkhole* and how does one form?**

Groundwater Extraction and Sinkhole Formation: Human activities can have direct and immediate consequences in some areas of karst topography. For example, most of central Florida is underlain by massive limestone bedrock, which is particularly susceptible to the formation of sinkholes and collapse sinkholes. This process is accelerated when the water table drops. Sinkholes have been forming in Florida for a long time, with several thousand of them having appeared in the twentieth century. Indeed, most of central Florida's scenic lakes began as sinkholes.

The population growth that Florida has experienced in recent decades put a heavy drain on its underground water supply, causing a drawdown of the water table. As a result, the number and size of Florida sinkholes increased to a disturbing pace, reaching a rate of about one per day in the early 1980s, although the tempo has slowed since then (Figure 17-9).

HYDROTHERMAL FEATURES FG1

In many parts of the world, there are small areas where hot water comes to the surface through natural openings. Such outpouring of hot water, often accompanied by steam, is known as **hydrothermal activity** and usually takes the form of either a hot spring or a geyser.

Hot Springs

The appearance of hot water at Earth's surface usually indicates that the underground water has come in contact with heated rocks or magma and has been forced upward through a fissure by the pressures that develop when water is heated (Figure 17-10). The usual result at the surface is a **hot spring**, with water bubbling out either continuously or intermittently. The hot water invariably contains a large amount of dissolved mineral matter, and a considerable proportion of this load is precipitated out as soon as the

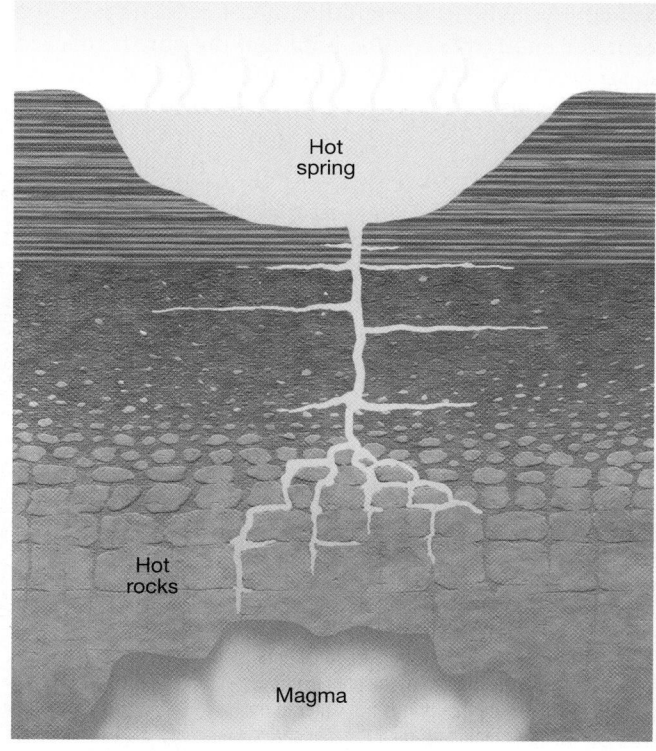

▲ **Figure 17-10** Cross section through a hot spring.

water reaches the surface and its temperature and the pressure on it both decrease.

The deposits around and downslope from hot springs can take many forms. If the opening is on sloping land, terraces are usually formed. Where the springs emerge onto flat land, there may be cones, domes, or irregular concentric deposits. Since calcium carbonate is so readily soluble in water containing carbonic acid, the deposits of most springs are composed largely of massive (*travertine*) or porous (*tufa* or *sinter*) accumulations of calcium carbonate. Various other minerals are also contained in the deposits on occasion, especially silica, but are much less common than calcium compounds.

Sometimes the water bubbling out of a hot spring builds a continually enlarging mound or terrace. As the structure is built higher, the opening through which the hot water comes to the surface also rises, so that the water is always emerging above the highest point. As the water flows down the sides of the structure, more deposition takes place there, thus broadening the structure as well, often with brilliantly colored algae, which add to the striking appearance as well as contribute mineral secretions to the deposit (Figure 17-11).

Geysers

A special form of intermittent hot spring is the **geyser**. Hot water usually issues from a geyser only sporadically, and most or all of the flow is a temporary ejection (called an *eruption*) in which hot water and steam spout upward. Then the geyser subsides into apparent inactivity until the next eruption.

Eruption Mechanisms: The basic principle of geyser activity involves the building up of pressure within a restricted subterranean tube until that pressure is relieved by an eruption. The process begins when underground water seeps into subterranean openings that are connected in a series of narrow caverns and shafts. Heated rocks and/or magma are close enough to these storage reservoirs to provide a constant source of heat. As the water accumulates in the reservoirs, it is heated to 200°C (400°F) or higher, which is much above the boiling point at sea level and normal pressure. (Such superheating is possible because of the high underground water pressure.) At these high temperatures, much of the water becomes steam. The accumulation of steam deep in the tube along with boiling water higher up eventually causes a great upward surge that sends water and steam showering out of the geyser vent. This eruption releases the pressure, and when the eruption subsides, underground water again begins to collect in the reservoirs in preparation for a repetition of the process.

A tremendous supply of heat is essential for geyser activity. Recent studies in Yellowstone Park's Upper Geyser Basin indicate that the heat emanating from that basin is at least 800 times greater than the heat flowing from a nongeyser area of the same size.

Learning Check 17-5   **Describe the conditions that typically lead up to a geyser eruption.**

Eruption Patterns: Some geysers erupt continuously, indicating that they are really hot springs that have a constant supply of water through which steam is escaping. Most geysers are only sporadically active, however, apparently depending on the accumulation of sufficient water to force an eruption. Some eruptions are very brief, whereas others continue for many minutes. The interval between eruptions for most geysers is variable. Most erupt at intervals of a few hours or a few days, but some wait years or even decades between eruptions. The temperature of the erupting water

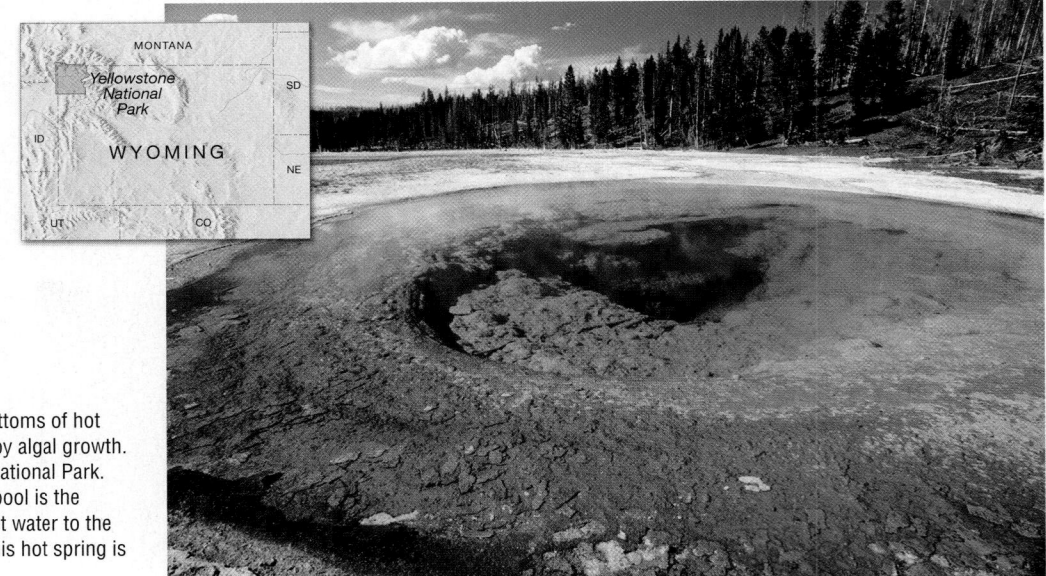

▶**Figure 17-11** The sides and bottoms of hot springs are often brilliantly colored by algal growth. This is Beauty Pool in Yellowstone National Park. The black area at the bottom of the pool is the opening to the fissure that brings hot water to the surface. The water temperature of this hot spring is typically about 77°C (170°F).

generally is near the boiling point for pure water (100°C or 212°F at sea level). In some geysers, the erupting water column goes up only a few centimeters in the air, whereas in others the column rises to more than 45 meters (150 feet).

Geyser comes from the Icelandic word *geysir* ("to gush" or "to rage"), the Great Geysir in southern Iceland being the namesake origin for this term. The most famous of all geysers is Old Faithful in Yellowstone National Park (Figure 17-12). Its reputation is based partly on the force of its eruptions (the column goes more than 30 meters or 100 feet high) but primarily on its regularity. Since first timed by scientists more than a century ago, Old Faithful maintained an average interval of 65 minutes between eruptions (ranging from about 30 minutes to 120 minutes), day and night, winter and summer, year after year throughout most of the twentieth century. In the early 1980s, however, several consecutive earthquakes on the Yellowstone plateau apparently upset the geyser's internal plumbing. Over the last few decades, Old Faithful's average interval between eruptions has been about 90 minutes, typically varying between 44 and 125 minutes. Thus, Old Faithful has become slightly more erratic, which is to say, more like other geysers.

Mineral Deposits: The deposits resulting from geyser activity are usually much less notable than those associated with hot springs. Some geysers erupt from open pools of hot water, throwing tremendous sheets of water and steam into the air but usually producing relatively minor depositional features. Other geysers are of the "nozzle" type and consequently build up a depositional cone and erupt through a small opening in it (Figure 17-13). Most deposits resulting from geyser activity are simply sheets of precipitated mineral matter spread irregularly over the ground.

▲ **Figure 17-12** Yellowstone's Old Faithful geyser in all its eruptive grandeur.

◀ **Figure 17-13** Most geysers erupt from vents or hot pools, but some build up prominent depositional "nozzles" through which water is expelled. This is Castle Geyser in Yellowstone National Park.

▶ **Figure 17-14** A fumarole is like a geyser except that it erupts no liquid water; it sends out only steam. This scene is from near Mývatn Lake, Iceland.

Fumaroles

A third hydrothermal feature is the **fumarole**, a surface crack directly connected to a deep-seated heat source (Figure 17-14). For some reason, very little water drains into the tube of a fumarole. The water that does drain in is instantly converted to steam by the heat, and a cloud of steam is then expelled from the opening—often with an accompanying roaring or hissing sound. Thus, a fumarole is marked by steam issuing either continuously or sporadically from a surface vent; in essence, a fumarole is simply a hot spring that lacks liquid water.

In many places around the world, people have tapped hydrothermal resources as a source of clean energy—see the box "Energy for the 21st century: Geothermal Energy."

Hydrothermal Features in Yellowstone

Hydrothermal features are found in many volcanic areas, being particularly notable in Iceland, New Zealand, Chile, and Siberia's Kamchatka Peninsula. By far the largest concentration, however, occurs in Yellowstone National Park, located mostly in northwestern Wyoming, which contains about 225 of the world's 425 geysers as well as more than half of the world's other hydrothermal phenomena.

Geologic Setting: The Yellowstone area consists of a broad, flattish plateau bordered by extensive mountains (the Absaroka Range) on the east and by more limited highlands (particularly the Gallatin Mountains) on the west. The bedrock surface of the plateau is almost entirely volcanic materials, although no volcanic cones are in evidence. About 640,000 years ago, a catastrophic volcanic eruption here ejected about 1000 cubic kilometers (240 cubic miles) of pyroclastics—about 1000 times more material than the 1980 Mount St. Helens eruption—covering the surrounding region with thick deposits of volcanic ash, and resulting in the formation of a 70 kilometer (43 mile) diameter caldera (Figure 17-15). An even larger

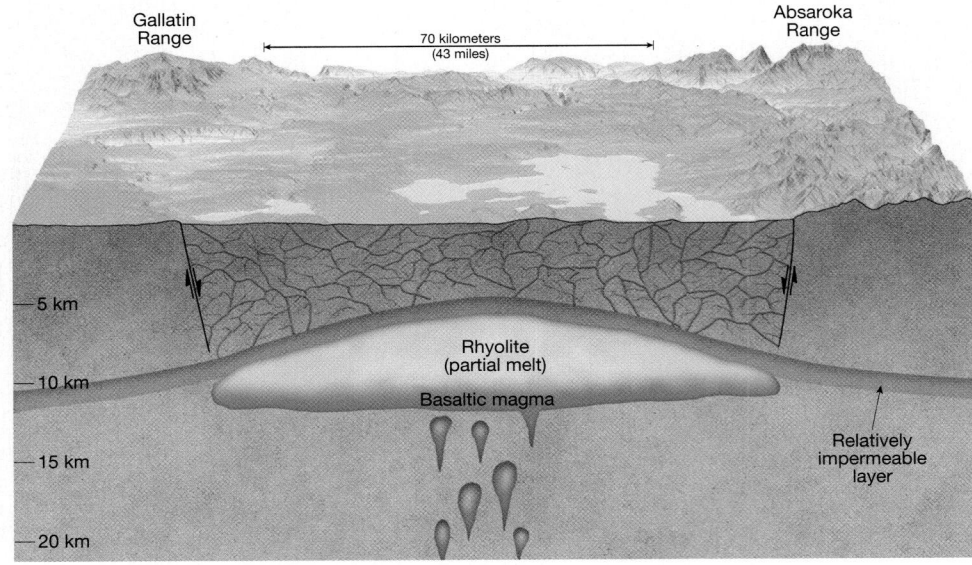

▶ **Figure 17-15** Schematic west–east cross section through the Yellowstone Plateau showing the extent of the Yellowstone Caldera and the magma chamber below.

Geothermal Energy

▶ Karl Byrand, University of Wisconsin Colleges

Geothermal technology harnesses the heat of Earth's interior either to warm buildings directly or to generate electricity. Geothermal heat exists throughout Earth's interior because of the radioactive decay of certain elements, as well as because of the conduction of heat from Earth's core.

Geothermal Technology: Geothermal technology includes geothermal heat pumps that consist of shallow piping systems (around three meters in depth) incorporating a pump that can draw heat from the ground in the winter and return it to the ground in the summer as a way to heat and cool a small structure. In geothermally active regions, steam from the ground can be used directly to heat a structure.

Larger-scale technologies that can harness even more geothermal energy include *dry steam*, *closed-loop*, and *enhanced geothermal systems* (EGS).

- The dry steam process—the most common geothermal technology—directly extracts steam from inside Earth to turn a turbine. Once used, the steam is then condensed and returned to the ground to be reheated naturally and used again.
- A closed loop system uses subterranean pipes filled with fluids such as isobutane and pentafluoropropane, which have a lower boiling point than water, thus requiring less heat to create steam.
- An EGS pumps cold water directly under ground to fragment geothermally active, but dry, rock to create paths of subsurface water flow (Figure 17-A). It is estimated that the energy potential for EGS alone is 200 gigawatts (GW) in the United States and 60 GW in Europe.

Advantages and Disadvantages: Geothermal energy generation provides energy day and night, is self-sustaining, virtually inexhaustible, and free of combustion-based emissions. Although CO_2, a known greenhouse gas, is released from Earth's interior during extraction of steam, the amount is considerably smaller than the amount generated by coal-fired facilities. According to the Department of

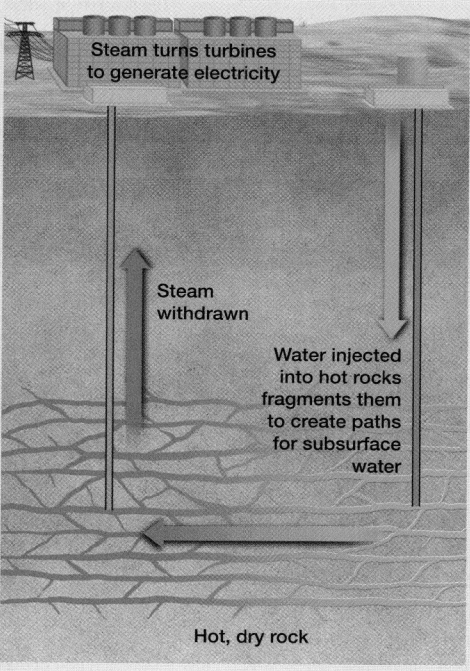

▲ **Figure 17-A** Electrical generation using an enhanced geothermal system. Water is injected into hot, but dry rock. The steam produced is then extracted to power the electrical generator turbines.

Energy, to generate 1 megawatt of electricity, on average a geothermal facility releases 27 to 40 kilograms (60–90 pounds) of CO_2, whereas a coal-fired one creates 900 kilograms (2000 pounds).

Under certain conditions, dry steam systems are not self-sustaining. If a power plant's water or steam extraction rate exceeds the natural recharge rate, a reduction in steam pressure may result. It is estimated that more than 250 geysers worldwide have been depleted for this reason.

The other major disadvantage associated with geothermal energy generation is the possibility of induced seismicity—microearthquakes caused by well drilling, water extraction, and the injection of water into the ground. For instance, in 2006 operations at a geothermal power plant in Basel, Switzerland, were halted after several earthquakes. Because geothermal facilities operate within already seismically active

regions, it can be difficult to distinguish natural seismic activity from induced seismicity. However, in the Basel case, it was relatively clear that the injection of water into the plant's well caused the earthquakes.

The greatest risk of seismic activity is associated with the EGS process. EGS continues to be developed and tested because it can capture geothermal energy in regions without adequate groundwater flow. A study from Australia, which has the world's largest EGS project, and studies at facilities in California, determined that the potential for induced microearthquakes exists, but that the risk is negligible.

Geography of Geothermal Technology: As of 2012, about 70 countries have implemented geothermal energy to produce more than 11,000 MW globally. The United States leads production, with more than 3000 MW of installed capacity (Figure 17-B), whereas in Europe, Italy, Iceland, and Turkey have a collective installed capacity of nearly 1600 MW. Other regions expanding or exploring geothermal technology include Indonesia, Latin American, and the Caribbean nations, and the East Africa Rift Valley.

▲ **Figure 17-B** Geothermal power generation facilities at The Geysers in northern California.

eruption took place about 2.1 million years ago, and geologists think that future eruptions of the Yellowstone volcano are a distinct possibility.

Hydrothermal Conditions: The uniqueness of Yellowstone's geologic setting stems from the presence of a large, shallow magma chamber beneath the plateau—thought to be the result of a hot spot formed by a mantle plume rising up from the mantle. Test boreholes and geophysical studies reveal a high thermal gradient, in which the temperature increases with depth at a rate of about 67°C per 100 meters (36°F per 100 feet), and indicate that the top of the magma chamber is perhaps only 8 kilometers (5 miles) below the surface. Between 2004 and 2010, the ground in the caldera rose by 25 centimeters (10 inches)—most likely as a result of swelling of the magma chamber below; since 2010, the ground has subsided—a cycle of ground movement volcanologists have observed in the past. This shallow magma pool provides the heat source—the most important of the three conditions necessary for the development of hydrothermal features.

The second requisite is an abundance of water that can seep downward and become heated. Yellowstone receives copious summer rain and a deep winter snowpack (averaging more than 250 centimeters or 100 inches).

The third necessity for hydrothermal development is a weak or broken ground surface that allows water to move up and down easily. Here, too, Yellowstone fits the bill, for the ground surface there is very unstable and subject to frequent earthquakes, faulting, and volcanic activity. Consequently, many fractures and weak zones provide easy avenues for vertical water movement.

> **Learning Check 17-6** **Identify three conditions that make Yellowstone ideal for the development of hydrothermal features.**

Geyser Basins: The park contains about 225 geysers, more than 3000 hot springs, and 7000 other thermal features (fumaroles, steam vents, hot-water terraces, hot-mud cauldrons, and so forth). There are five major geyser basins, a half dozen minor ones, and an extensive scattering of individual or small groups of thermal features.

The principal geyser basins are all in the same watershed on the western side of the park (Figure 17-16). The Gibbon River from the north and the Firehole River from the south unite to form the Madison River, which flows westward into Montana, eventually to join two other rivers in forming the Missouri (a 1959 earthquake in the Yellowstone area triggered a major landslide in the Madison River valley just to the west of the park). The Gibbon River drains the Norris and Gibbon geyser basins, whereas the Firehole drains the Upper, Midway, and Lower basins. The Firehole River derives its name from the great quantity of hot water fed into it from the hot springs and geysers along its way. Approximately two-thirds of the hydrothermal features of Yellowstone are in the drainage area of the Firehole River.

All the major geyser basins consist of gently undulating plains or valleys covered mostly with glacial sediments and large expanses of whitish siliceous material called *geyserite*. Each basin contains from a few to several dozen geysers, some of which are inconspicuous holes in the geyserite, but others of which are built-up cones that rise a few meters above the basin. In addition, each basin contains a number of hot springs and fumaroles.

Yellowstone's geysers exhibit an extraordinary range of behavior. Some erupt continually; others have experienced only a single eruption in all history. Most, however, erupt irregularly several times a day or week. Some shoot their hot water only a few centimeters into the air, but the largest (such as Steamboat and Excelsior) erupt to heights of 100 meters (330 feet), with clouds of steam rising much higher.

Mammoth Hot Springs: In the northwestern portion of the park is the most remarkable aggregation of hot-water terraces in the world—the Mammoth Hot Springs Terraces (Figure 17-17). There, groundwater percolates down from surrounding hills into thick layers of limestone. Hot water, carbon dioxide, and other gases rise from the heated magma to mingle with the groundwater and produce a mild carbonic acid solution that rapidly dissolves great quantities of the limestone. Saturated with dissolved minerals, the temporarily carbonated water seeps downslope until it gushes forth near the base of the hills as the Mammoth Hot Springs (Figure 17-18). The carbon dioxide escapes into the air, and the calcium carbonate is precipitated as massive deposits of travertine in the form of flat-topped, steep-sided terraces.

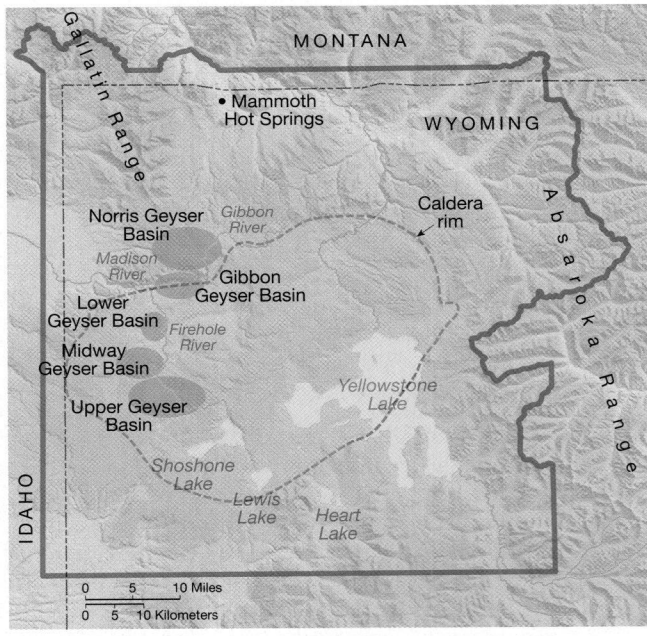

▲ **Figure 17-16** Yellowstone National Park and its major geyser basins. The approximate outline of the Yellowstone Caldera is shown.

(b)

(a)

▲ **Figure 17-17** Yellowstone's Mammoth Hot Springs. (a) Although the white material looks like snow or ice, it is actually travertine. (b) Water from rainfall and snowmelt percolates down into the underlying limestone, where it is heated and flows downslope. Hot water issues onto the surface and precipitates travertine deposits when exposed to the air.

◄ **Figure 17-18** Travertine terraces in Mammoth Hot Springs, Yellowstone National Park.

After studying this chapter, you should be able to answer the following questions. Key terms from each text section are shown in **bold type**. Definitions for key terms are also found in the glossary at the back of the book.

KEY TERMS AND CONCEPTS

Solution and Precipitation (*p. 499*)

1. How does **carbonic acid** form?
2. What is meant by **dissolution**?
3. What kinds of rock are most susceptible to solution processes? Why?

Caverns and Related Features (*p. 501*)

4. What is the importance of jointing and bedding planes to the underground structure of **caverns**?
5. Describe and explain the formation of **speleothems** such as **stalactites**, **stalagmites**, and columns.

Karst Topography (*p. 502*)

6. In what kinds of rocks does **karst** topography usually develop?
7. Explain how a **sinkhole** is formed.

8. Describe the formation of a **collapse sinkhole** and an **uvala**.
9. Describe the characteristics of **tower karst**.
10. What is a **swallow hole**? A **disappearing stream**?
11. Why is there a scarcity of surface drainage in karst areas?

Hydrothermal Features (*p. 505*)

12. What is **hydrothermal activity**?
13. What are the differences among a **hot spring**, a **geyser**, and a **fumarole**? What causes these differences?
14. Briefly explain the eruption sequence of a typical geyser.

STUDY QUESTIONS

1. Which is more important for the weathering action of underground water, mechanical or chemical weathering? Why?
2. How does the underground structure of the bedrock influence the dissolution process?
3. How is it possible for percolating groundwater to both remove mineral material and deposit it?
4. How can groundwater pumping by people lead to sinkhole formation?
5. What three conditions are necessary for hydrothermal features to develop?

6. What is the importance of jointing and bedding planes to the development of hot springs and geysers?
7. Why don't most geysers erupt at regular intervals?
8. The 1912 eruption of Mount Katmai in Alaska buried a nearby river valley beneath a thick layer of volcanic ash. Today the area is called "The Valley of 10,000 Smokes." What do you think this name refers to? Explain.

EXERCISES

1. If a "soda straw" speleothem in a cavern grows at an average rate of 1.7 mm per year, how long does it take to form a soda straw 18 centimeters long?
2. During the morning of August 14, 2011, Old Faithful Geyser in Yellowstone National Park erupted at the

following times (to the nearest minute): 12:07 A.M., 1:42 A.M., 3:05 A.M., 4:41 A.M., 6:07 A.M., 7:37 A.M., 9:08 A.M., and 10:34 A.M. What was the average interval between eruptions on this morning? _____ minutes

Seeing Geographically

Look again at the photograph of Stokkur Geyser in Iceland at the beginning of the chapter (p. 498). Which kinds of rock are most likely found around the base of the geyser? Does the eruption shown in the photograph appear to consist mostly of water or mostly of steam? What is the role of steam in causing a geyser's eruption?

MasteringGeography™

Looking for additional review and test prep materials? Visit the Study Area in MasteringGeography™ to enhance your geographic literacy, spatial reasoning skills, and understanding of this chapter's content by accessing a variety of resources, including geoscience animations, MapMaster interactive maps, videos, RSS feeds, flashcards, web links, self-study quizzes, and an eText version of *McKnight's Physical Geography: A Landscape Appreciation*.

ARID LANDS ARE IN MANY WAYS DISTINCTIVE FROM HUMID

ones, but there are no obvious boundaries to separate the two. In this chapter, we focus on the dry lands of the world without attempting to establish precise definitions or borders. We are concerned not with where such borders lie, but rather with the processes that shape desert landscapes. It should be understood, however, that both the processes and the landforms of desert landscapes occur more widely than the term *desert* might imply, and some of the landforms we describe may even be seen in humid regions.

It also important to understand that some of today's deserts had quite different climates in the geologic past. Parts of today's Sahara Desert, for example, were much wetter just a few thousand years ago than they are today. Thus, in addition to processes operating today, some desert landscapes we see have also been shaped by a different set of processes that were at work in the past.

As you study this chapter, think about these key questions:

- **What special conditions and factors influence landform development in deserts?**
- **What is the role of running water in erosion and deposition in deserts?**
- **What is the role of wind in shaping desert landforms?**
- **What are the characteristics of the three common desert landscape surfaces—the *erg*, the *reg*, and the *hamada*?**
- **Why are landforms such as *playas* and *alluvial fans* so prevalent in the basin-and-range desert region of North America?**
- **How do landforms such as *buttes* and *mesas* develop in the mesa-and-scarp desert region of the United States?**

A SPECIALIZED ENVIRONMENT

As we learned in Chapter 11, desert terrain is usually stark and abrupt, unsoftened by regolith, soil, or vegetation. Despite the great difference in appearance between arid lands and humid, most of the terrain-forming processes active in humid areas are also at work in desert areas. There are, however, special conditions found in deserts that do significantly influence landform development.

Special Conditions in Deserts

Desert landforms are often conspicuously different from those found in wetter locations. These differences are largely the result of a variety of factors and special conditions found in arid regions. The most important of these special conditions include the following:

Weathering: Because moisture is required for nearly all kinds of chemical weathering, in many desert regions mechanical weathering is dominant—although chemical weathering is

Seeing Geographically

Badwater Basin in Death Valley National Park, California. Describe the topography you see in the photograph. What kind of relief is found in the white area at the bottom of the basin? What do you see in the photograph that suggests that this is a very arid environment? What do you see that indicates that at least from time to time running water is active here?

likely to be absent in only the driest of deserts. Mechanical weathering processes such as *salt wedging* are more common in arid regions than in humid ones (see Figure 15-8). This predominance of mechanical weathering results not only in a generally slower rate of total weathering in deserts, but also in the production of more angular particles of weathered rock.

Soil and Regolith: In deserts, the covering of soil and regolith is either thin or absent in most places, a condition that exposes the bedrock to weathering and erosion, and contributes to the stark, rugged, rocky terrain (Figure 18-1).

Soil Creep: Soil creep is a relatively minor phenomenon on most desert slopes. This is due partly to the lack of soil but primarily to the lack of the lubricating effects of water. Creep is a smoothing phenomenon in more humid climates, and its lack in deserts accounts in part for the angularity of desert slopes.

Impermeable Surfaces: A relatively large proportion of the desert surface is impermeable to percolating water, permitting little moisture to seep into the ground. *Caprocks* (resistant bedrock surfaces) and *hardpans* (hardened and generally water-impermeable subsurface soil layers) of various types are widespread, and what soil has formed is usually thoroughly compacted and often does not readily absorb water. Such impermeable surfaces lead to high runoff when it rains.

Sand: Some deserts have an abundance of sand in comparison with other parts of the world. This is not to say, however, that deserts are mostly sand covered. Indeed, the notion that all deserts consist of great seas of sand is incorrect. Nevertheless, the relatively high proportion of sand in some deserts has three important influences on topographic development: (1) A sandy cover allows water to infiltrate the ground and inhibits drainage via streams and overland flow, (2) sand is readily moved by heavy rains, and (3) it can be transported and redeposited by the wind (the development of desert sand dunes is discussed later in this chapter).

Learning Check 18-1 How do impermeable surfaces influence the amount of runoff when it rains in a desert? (Answer on p. AK-5)

Rainfall: Although rainfall is limited in desert areas, much of the rain that does fall comes from intense convective thunderstorms—which result in very high and rapid runoff. Floods, although often brief and covering only a limited area, are the rule rather than the exception in deserts. Thus, fluvial erosion and deposition, however sporadic and rare, are remarkably effective and conspicuous.

Fluvial Deposition: Almost all streams in desert areas are *ephemeral*, flowing only during and immediately after a rain. Such streams are effective agents of erosion, shifting enormous amounts of material in a short time. This is mostly short-distance transportation, however. A large volume of unconsolidated debris is moved to a nearby location, and as the stream dries up, the debris is dumped on slopes or in valleys, where it is readily available for the next rain. As a consequence, depositional features of alluvium are unusually common in desert areas.

Wind: Another fallacy associated with deserts is that their landforms are produced largely by wind action. This is not true, even though high winds are characteristic of most deserts and even though sand and dust particles are easily shifted.

Basins of Interior Drainage: Desert areas contain many watersheds that do not drain ultimately into any ocean. For most continental surfaces, rainfall has the potential of flowing all the way to the sea. In dry lands, however, drainage networks are frequently underdeveloped, and the terminus of a drainage system is often a basin or valley with no external outlet, as Figure 18-2 shows for the United States. Any rain that falls in Nevada, for example, except in the extreme southeastern and northeastern corners of the state, has no chance of flowing in a stream to the sea.

Vegetation: All the previous environmental factors have important effects on topographic development, but perhaps the single most obvious feature of dry lands is the lack of a continuous cover of vegetation. The plant cover consists mostly of widely spaced shrubs or sparse grass, which provide little protection from the force of raindrops and function inadequately to bind the surface material with roots (Figure 18-3).

Learning Check 18-2 How does the sparse cover of soil and vegetation influence weathering and erosion in deserts?

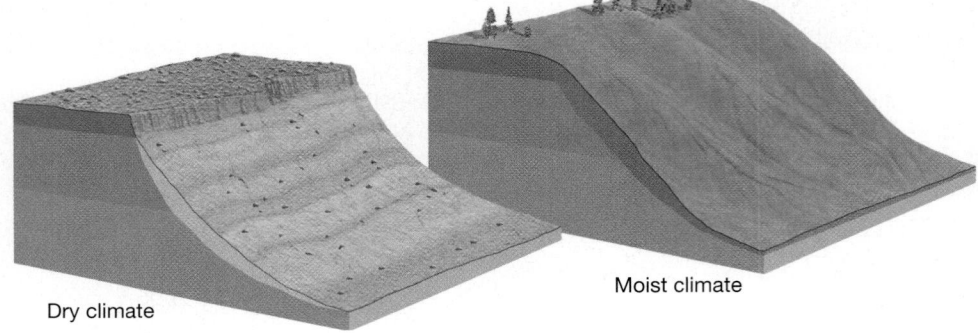

▶ **Figure 18-1** Slope comparisons in dry and moist climates. The steep relief is more easily seen in a dry climate because there is very little obscuring vegetation cover. In a humid climate, the steep faces are to some degree obscured by vegetation.

Dry climate

Moist climate

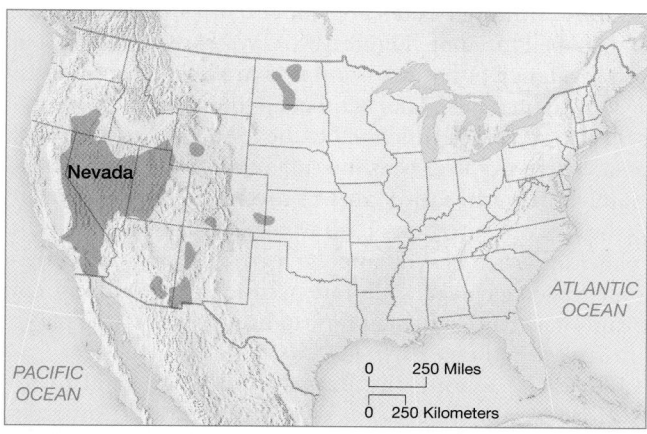

▲ **Figure 18-2** The basins of interior drainage (shown in green) in the conterminous United States are all in the western part of the nation. By far the largest area of interior drainage is in the "Great Basin" centered in Nevada and the adjoining states.

RUNNING WATER IN WATERLESS REGIONS

 FG9

Probably the most fundamental fact of desert geomorphology is that running water is by far the most important external agent of landform development. The erosional and depositional work of running water influences the shape of the terrain surface almost everywhere outside areas of extensive sand accumulation. The lightly vegetated ground is defenseless to whatever rainfall may occur, and erosion by rain splash, sheetwash, rilling, and streamflow is enormously effective. Despite the rarity of precipitation, its intensity and the presence of impermeable surfaces produce abrupt runoff, and great volumes of sediment can be moved in a very short time.

The steeper gradients of mountain streams increase the capacity of these streams for carrying large loads, of course, but the sporadic flow of mountain streams in arid lands results in an unpredictable imbalance between erosion and deposition. At any given time, therefore, much transportable rock debris and alluvium sit at rest in the dry stream bed of a desert mountain, awaiting the next flow. Loose surface material is either thin or absent on the slopes, and bedrock is often clearly exposed, with the more resistant strata standing out as caprocks and cliff faces.

Where slopes are gentle in an arid land, the streams rapidly become choked with sediment as a brief flood subsides. Here stream channels are readily subdivided by braiding, and main channels often break up into distributaries in the basins. Much silt and sand are thus left on the surface for the next flood to move, unless wind moves them first.

Surface Water in the Desert

Surface water in deserts is conspicuous by its absence. These are lands of sandy streams and dusty lakes, in which the presence of surface water is usually episodic and brief.

Exotic Streams: Permanent streams in dry lands are few, far between, and, with scarce exceptions, *exotic*, meaning they are sustained by water that originates outside the desert. This water that feeds **exotic streams** comes from an adjacent wetter area or a higher mountain area in the desert and has sufficient volume to survive passage across the dry lands. The Nile River of North Africa is the classic example of an exotic stream (Figure 18-4). Its water comes from the mountains and lakes of central Africa and Ethiopia in sufficient quantity

◀ **Figure 18-3** In most arid regions, the cover of vegetation is sparse. The creosote bush is the green shrub in this Death Valley, California, scene.

to survive a 3200-kilometer (2000-mile) journey across the desert without benefit of tributaries. In North America, the Colorado River is a prominent example of an exotic stream.

In humid regions, a river becomes larger as it flows downstream, nourished by tributaries and groundwater inflow. In dry lands, however, the flow of exotic rivers diminishes downstream because the water seeps into the riverbed, evaporates—or is diverted for irrigation.

Ephemeral Streams: Although almost every desert has a few prominent exotic rivers, more than 99 percent of all desert streams are **ephemeral streams** (Figure 18-5). The brief periods during which these streams flow are times of intense erosion, transportation, and deposition, however. Most ephemeral desert streamflow eventually dissipates through seepage and evaporation, although sometimes such a stream is able to reach the sea, a lake, or an exotic river.

The normally dry beds of ephemeral streams typically have flat floors, sandy bottoms, and steep sides. In the United States, they are variously referred to as *arroyos, gullies, washes,* or *coulees.* In North Africa and Arabia, the name *wadi* is common; in South Africa, *donga;* in India, *nullah.*

Playas: Although lakes are uncommon in desert areas, dry lake beds are not (Figure 18-6). We have already noted the prevalence of basins of interior drainage in dry lands; most of them have a lake bed occupying their area of lowest elevation, which functions as the local base level for that basin. These dry lake beds are called **playas** (Figure 18-7), although the term **salina** may be used if there is an unusually heavy concentration of salt in the lake-bed sediments. If a playa surface is heavily impregnated with clay, the formation is called a *claypan.* On rare occasions, the intermittent streams may have sufficient flow to bring water to the playa, forming a temporary *playa lake.*

Playas are among the flattest and most level of all landforms—in some cases they are several kilometers across, but with a local relief of only a few centimeters. A playa develops such a flat surface when it is periodically covered with water as a playa lake. The suspended silt in the shallow lake eventually settles out and the water evaporates, leaving a flat layer of dried mud. Through repeated episodes such as this, over the centuries a playa attains its flat surface.

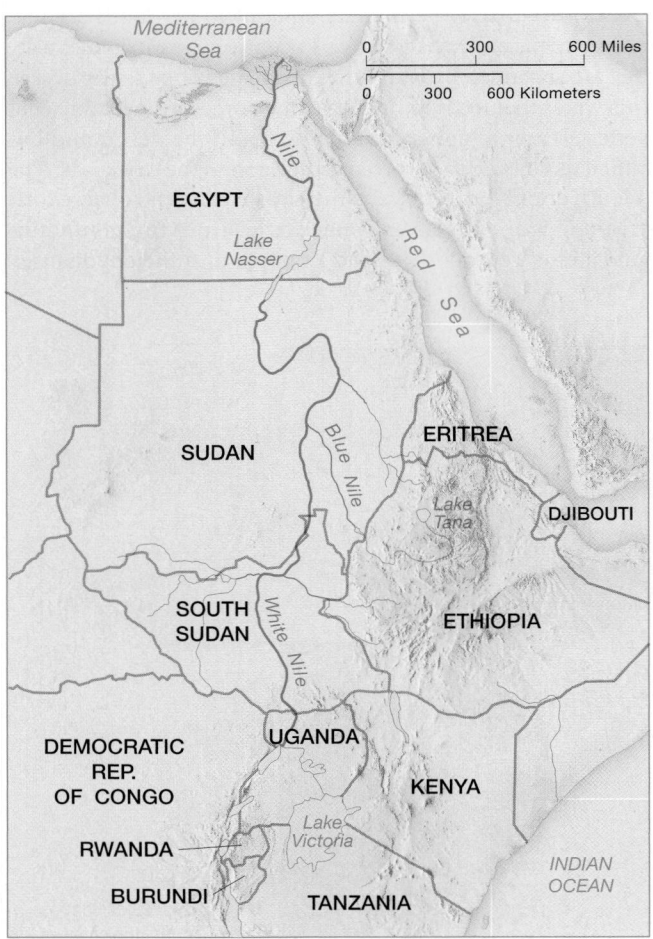

▲ **Figure 18-4** The world's preeminent example of an exotic stream, the Nile River, flows for many hundreds of kilometers without being joined by a tributary.

▲ **Figure 18-5** Ephemeral stream channel in the Mojave Desert near Baker, California.

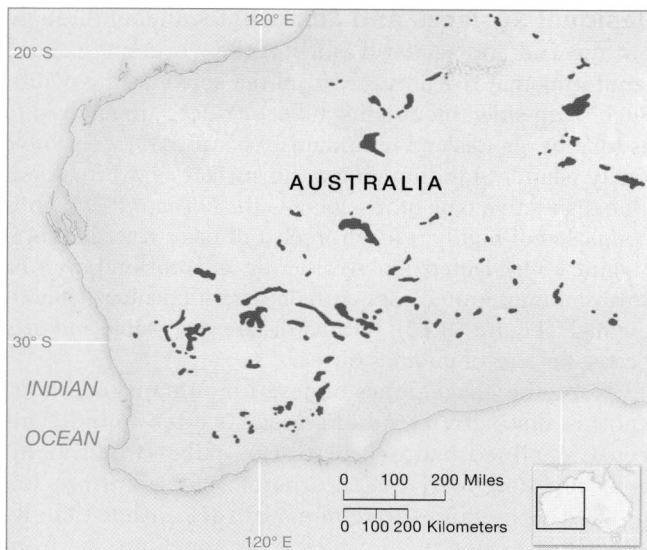

▲ **Figure 18-6** Dry lake beds are often numerous in desert areas. This map shows the principal playas and salinas in western Australia.

Saline Lakes: A few desert lakes are permanent. The smaller ones are nearly always the product of either subsurface structural conditions that provide water from a permanent spring or exotic streams or from streams flowing down from nearby mountains. Many permanent lakes in desert areas are **saline lakes**—high rates of evaporation relative to the inflow and/or basins of interior drainage lead to the accumulation of dissolved salts in such lake waters.

Many of the largest natural desert lakes are remnants of still larger bodies of water that formed in a previously wetter climate. Utah's Great Salt Lake is the outstanding example in the United States. Although in terms of surface area it is the second largest lake wholly in the United States (after Lake Michigan), it is a mere shadow of the former Lake Bonneville, which was formed during the wetter conditions of the Pleistocene Epoch (see Figure 19-6).

Learning Check 18-3 **Distinguish between an *exotic stream* and an *ephemeral stream* in a desert.**

Fluvial Erosion in Arid Lands

Although fluvial erosion takes place in desert areas only during a small portion of each year, it does its work rapidly and effectively, and the results are conspicuous. In desert areas of any significant relief, large expanses of exposed bedrock are common because of the lack of soil and vegetation. During the rare rains, this bedrock is both mechanically weathered and eroded by running water, and the result of the latter process is steep, rugged, rocky surfaces.

A typical circumstance leading to fluvial erosion in a desert might first entail a brief but intense thunderstorm, perhaps over a mountain drainage basin. The localized thunderstorm puts lots of water on the ground, but because the desert surface is either exposed bedrock or some other kind of relatively impermeable surface, most of the water quickly runs off into a nearby dry ephemeral

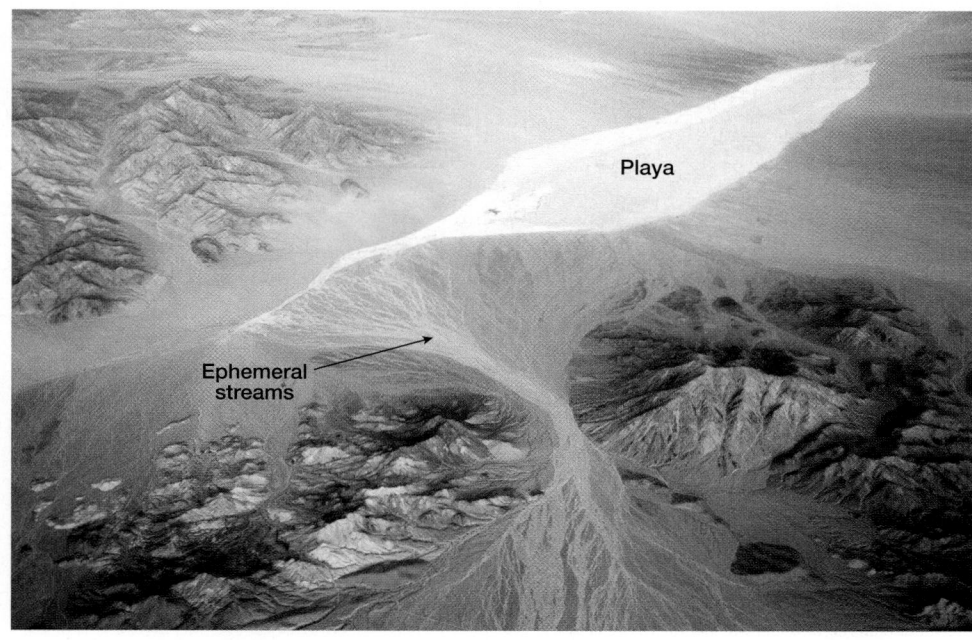

◀ **Figure 18-7** Broadwell Lake in California is a desert playa. Playas are among the flattest of all landforms.

stream channel. This stream channel quickly fills up with water, perhaps developing into a *flash flood* or a debris flow (described in Chapter 15) that travels for many kilometers down out of the desert mountains onto a basin floor. Such flash floods and debris flows can move a remarkable amount of material in just a few minutes. It is through such localized but infrequent events that most change takes place in the desert.

Flash floods and debris flows also pose a significant hazard to humans in arid lands—travelers are cautioned against camping or parking in dry stream washes because such floods can arrive with little local warning.

Differential Weathering and Erosion in Deserts: As we saw in Chapter 15, variations in rock type and structure influence the rate of weathering, and in turn, the ease of erosion. Such **differential weathering and erosion** frequently produces differences in the slope and shape of the resulting landform (Figure 18-8). Because of the generally sparse cover of soil and vegetation in deserts, the mark of differential weathering and erosion is often striking (see Figure 18-1).

In many cases, rocks resistant to weathering and erosion form the cliffs, pinnacles, spires, and other sharp crests, while softer rocks wear away more rapidly to produce gentler slopes. Differential erosion is very common in sedimentary landscapes because there are significant differences in resistance from one stratum to the next; such areas often have vertical *escarpments* (steep, cliff-like slopes) and abrupt changes in slope angle. In areas dominated by igneous or metamorphic bedrock, however, differential weathering and erosion may be less obvious because there is not much difference in resistance from one part of the bedrock to another.

Residual Surfaces and Features: Scattered throughout the arid and semiarid lands of the world are isolated landforms that rise abruptly from the surrounding plains. Such steep-sided mountains, hills, or ridges are referred to as **inselbergs** ("island mountains") because they resemble rocky islands standing above the surface of a broad sea. One distinctive type of inselberg is the *bornhardt*, which is composed of highly resistant rock and has a rounded form (Figure 18-9). Differential weathering and erosion lower the surrounding terrain, leaving the resistant bornhardt standing high (Figure 18-10). Bornhardts are very stable and may persist for tens of millions of years.

Along the lower slopes of desert mountains and hills, another distinctive kind of surface is often found. This gently inclined bedrock platform, called a **pediment**, is a "residual" surface (in other words, a surface left by weathering and the removal of rock rather than by deposition) extending outward from the mountain front (Figure 18-11).

Pediments have a complicated origin that is still incompletely understood. Long thought to develop as desert mountains are worn down and back by weathering and erosion during previous periods of wetter climate, recent analysis suggests that pediments may form in other ways. Some pediments may be the result of deep subsurface weathering during a period of wetter climate—after the overlying weathered material is removed by erosion, a flat or gently sloping bedrock surface remains. Other pediments may have formed as a consequence of *detachment faulting* in areas undergoing tectonic extension (see Figure 14-61), whereby blocks of crust are displaced along nearly horizontal fault planes—the bedrock surface of the pediment representing the fault plane.

▲ **Figure 18-8** The effects of differential weathering and erosion are conspicuous on the Red Cliffs near Gateway in western Colorado. The more resistant layers near the top form an abrupt escarpment, whereas the softer layers below are weathered and eroded into gentler slopes.

▶ **Figure 18-9** Kata Tjuta (the Olgas) is a massive bornhardt in the desert of central Australia.

Pediments can be found in many deserts and are sometimes the dominant terrain feature. They are not easily recognizable, however, because almost invariably they are covered with a veneer of debris deposited by water and wind.

> **Learning Check 18-4** **Explain the significance of flash floods and debris flows in deserts.**

Fluvial Deposition in Arid Lands

Except in hills and mountains, depositional features are more notable than erosional ones in a desert landscape. Depositional features consist mostly of talus accumulations at the foot of steep slopes and deposits of alluvium and other fragmented debris in ephemeral stream channels, the latter representing bedload left behind with the subsidence of the last flood.

Piedmont is a generic term meaning any zone at the foot of a mountain range (the term *pediment* comes from the same Latin root but refers to a specific landform). The **piedmont zone** of a desert mountain range is a prominent area of fluvial deposition. There is normally a pronounced change in slope at the mountain base, with a steep slope giving way abruptly to a gentle one (Figure 18-12). This is an area of significant accumulation of alluvium because the break in slope greatly reduces the speed of any sheetwash, streamflow, or debris flow that travels into the piedmont zone. Moreover, the streams issue more or less abruptly from canyons onto the more open piedmont and so are freed from lateral constraint. The resulting fluvial deposition in the piedmont often reaches depths of hundreds of meters, frequently in the form of an *alluvial fan* (alluvial fans are discussed in detail later in this chapter).

The flatter portions of desert areas also often exhibit a prominent accumulation of alluvium, in part because there is not usually enough streamflow to carry sediments very far from a mountain front—and there is no place to go if it is a basin of interior drainage. Any sheetwash or streamflow that reaches into such low-lying flatlands usually had to travel a considerable distance over low-angle slopes, which means that both flow volume and flow speed are likely to be limited. Consequently, larger rock fragments are rarely transported into the middle of the basins; instead, they are covered with fine particles of sand, silt, and clay, sometimes to a considerable depth.

> **Learning Check 18-5** **Why is the *piedmont zone* an area of fluvial deposition in most deserts?**

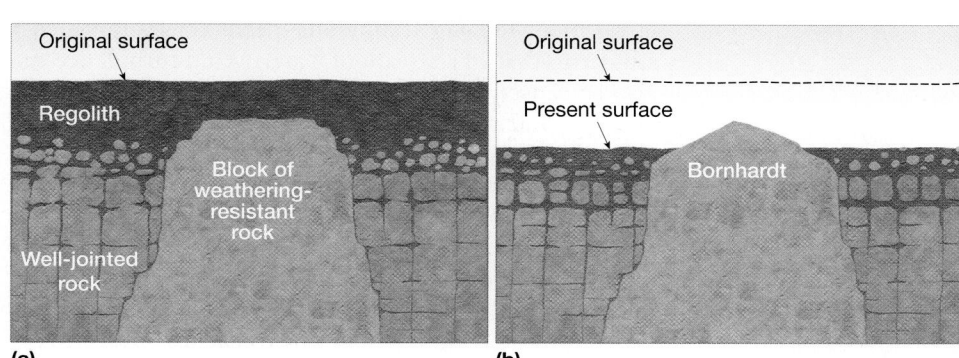

(a) (b)

◀ **Figure 18-10** The development of a bornhardt. (a) The well-jointed rock is more susceptible to weathering and erosion than the resistant block in the center. (b) As a result, the bornhardt remains as a conspicuous result of differential weathering and erosion.

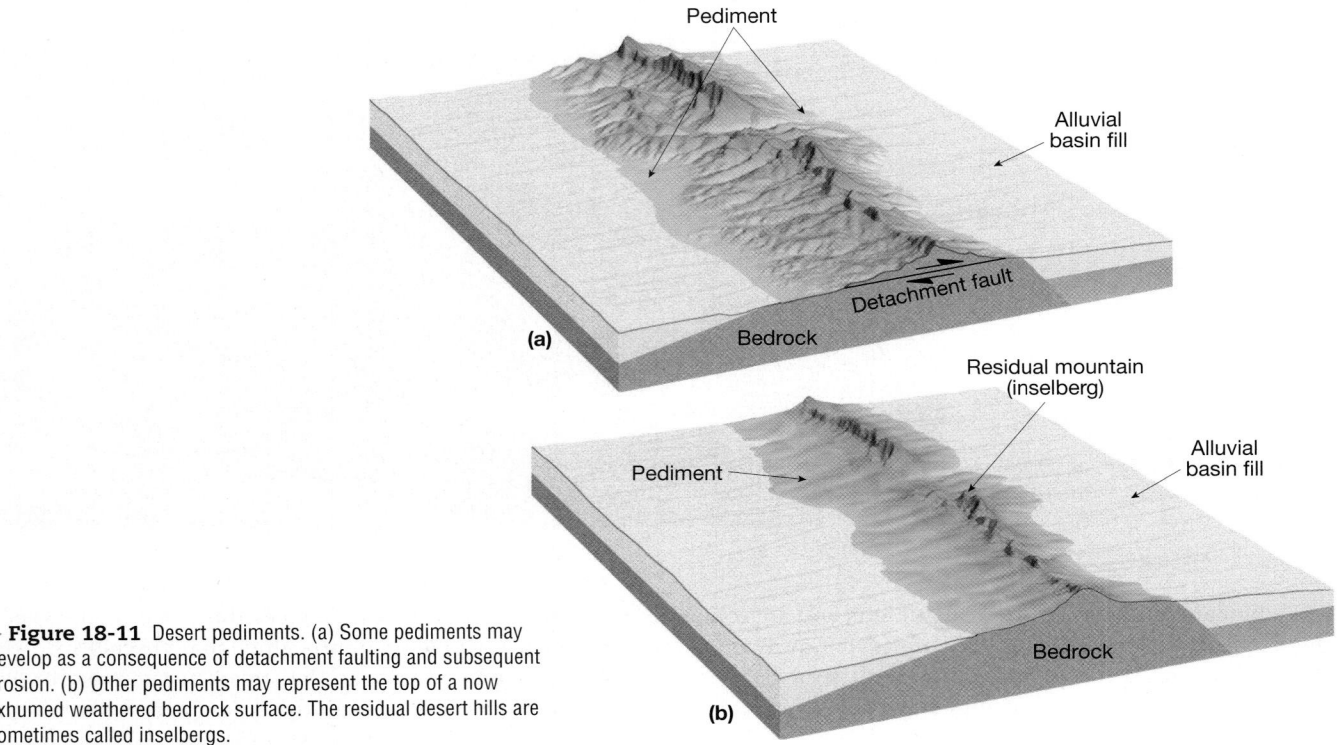

▶ **Figure 18-11** Desert pediments. (a) Some pediments may develop as a consequence of detachment faulting and subsequent erosion. (b) Other pediments may represent the top of a now exhumed weathered bedrock surface. The residual desert hills are sometimes called inselbergs.

Climate Change and Deserts

Recall from Chapter 6 that rainfall in arid regions tends to exhibit high year-to-year variability, and some projections suggest that climate change associated with current global warming may well make rainfall in deserts even more erratic. Of great concern to policy planners are regions of the world—especially in poor developing countries—where desert regions have been expanding in recent decades in a process called *desertification*. Desertification can be brought on by both natural and human-caused reasons—see the box, "People and the Environment: Desertification."

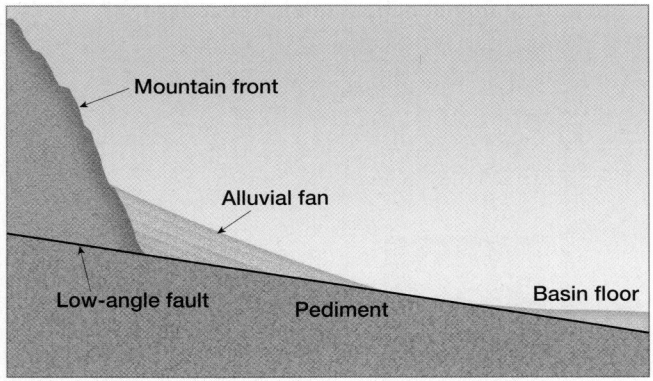

▲ **Figure 18-12** An idealized cross section of a desert piedmont zone. The pediment surface (in this case associated with a low-angle fault) is often covered with alluvial deposits at the mountain front and along the basin floor.

THE WORK OF THE WIND FG9

The irrepressible winds of the desert create spectacular sand and dust storms and continuously reshape minor details of the landscape (Figure 18-13). However, the effect of wind as a sculptor of terrain is very limited, with the important exception of such relatively impermanent features as sand dunes.

The term *wind* is theoretically restricted to horizontal air movement. Some turbulence is nearly always involved, however, so there is usually a vertical component of flow as well. In general, the motion of air passing over the ground is similar to that of water flowing over a streambed, and that similarity is the cause of the turbulence. In a thin layer right at the ground surface, wind speed is zero, just as the speed of the water layer touching the banks and bed of a stream is zero, but wind speed increases with distance above the ground. The shear developed between different layers of air moving at different speeds causes turbulence similar to that in a stream of water. Wind turbulence can also be caused by warming from below, which causes the air to expand and move upward.

Aeolian processes are those related to wind action (Aeolus was the Greek god of the winds). They are most pronounced, widespread, and effective wherever fine-grained unconsolidated sedimentary material is exposed to the atmosphere, without benefit of vegetation, moisture, or some other form of protection—in other words, in deserts and along sandy beaches. Our primary focus here is wind action in desert regions.

◀ **Figure 18-13** The wind is sometimes a prominent force in rearranging loose particles. This scene is near Barrow Creek in the Northern Territory of Australia.

Aeolian Erosion

The erosive effect of wind can be divided into two categories: deflation and abrasion.

Deflation: Deflation is the shifting of loose particles as a result of their being blown either through the air or along the ground. Except under extraordinary circumstances, the wind is not strong enough to move anything more than dust and small sand grains, and therefore no significant landforms are created by deflation. Sometimes a **blowout**, or *deflation hollow*, may be formed (Figure 18-14); this is a shallow depression from which an abundance of fine material has been deflated. Most blowouts are small, but some exceed 1.5 kilometers (1 mile) in diameter. Along with fluvial erosion, deflation is also a factor in the formation of a *reg* surface (discussed later in this chapter).

Abrasion: Aeolian abrasion is analogous to fluvial abrasion, except that the aeolian variety is much less effective. Whereas deflation is accomplished entirely by air currents, abrasion requires "tools" in the form of airborne sand and dust particles. The wind drives these particles against rock and soil surfaces in a form of natural sandblasting. Wind abrasion does not construct or even significantly shape a landform; it merely sculpts those already in existence. The principal results of aeolian abrasion are the pitting, etching, faceting, and polishing of exposed rock surfaces and the further fragmenting of rock fragments. Rocks so faceted by such wind "sandblasting" are called **ventifacts** (Figure 18-15).

▲ **Figure 18-14** A blowout forms where wind deflation removes loose material from the surface, leaving a depression, as here in Nebraska's Sandhills.

▲ **Figure 18-15** A sand-blasted rock, or ventifact. This piece of basalt is in Death Valley, near Badwater.

Desertification

▶ Mike Pease, Central Washington University

Desertification is the process by which a desert encroaches upon nondesert lands. The idea of deserts as growing entities taking over land may sound like a bad science fiction novel. However, it is a major environmental issue in arid and semiarid regions across the globe and may impact food security on several continents. Nearly every continent has experienced instances of desertification over the last century. From the Dust Bowl of the 1930s in the western Great Plains of the United States to the current expansion of the Gobi Desert into central China, desertification has made a series of top

The Sahel in Sub-Saharan Africa is one such region. This 4000-kilometer-wide east–west band of semiarid shrub-lands and savanna found south of the Sahara Desert is a transitional zone that extends through the countries of Mali, Niger, Chad, Sudan, South Sudan, and Ethiopia (Figure 18-A). Annual precipitation varies from less than 100 millimeters (4 in.) in the north on the border of the Sahara to 500 millimeters (20 in.) in the south, and this precipitation is both highly seasonal and highly variable.

Drought is common in the region. Moreover, changes to the seasonal patterns of

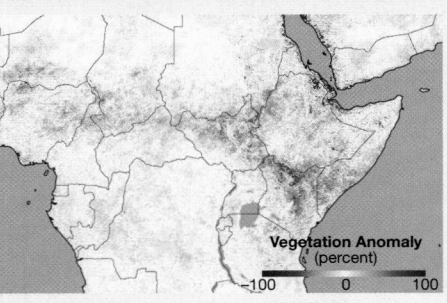

▲ **Figure 18-B** Drought in the southern Sahel region during 2011. Brown areas show less-than-average vegetation growth, whereas green areas show greater-than-average growth. The data were gathered by using the AVHRR instrument aboard the NOAA-18 satellite.

model outputs since 1988. In 2011, the IPCC released a report suggesting that over the next 50 years, most places on Earth will experience an increase in severe weather phenomena, including an increase in the amount of precipitation that falls during high-intensity storms and an increase in extended drought periods. Of particular concern was the suggestion that both the frequency and the severity of drought will increase. Some regional climate models have suggested many semiarid areas and those areas already vulnerable to drought such as the Southwestern United States and central China may experience a higher frequency of drought periods.

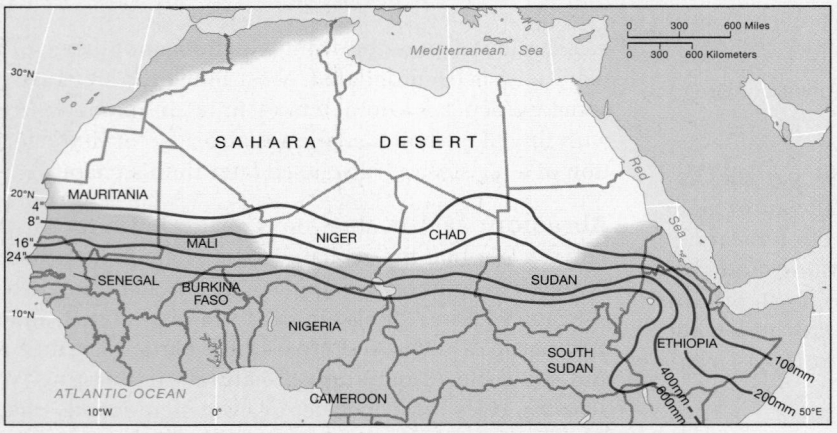

▲ **Figure 18-A** The Sahel Region of Africa. The isolines are isohyets of average annual rainfall. Only the Sahelian countries are labeled.

10 global environmental issue lists. Desertification, and the land use issues surrounding it, are so significant, the United Nations Convention to Combat Desertification (UNCCD) was established in 1994 to "mitigate the effect of drought in affected areas."

How Desertification Occurs:

The peripheral regions surrounding deserts are transition zones and tend to be semi-arid with sparse vegetation. Soils in these regions are vulnerable to degradation. With poor land-use management or periods of drought, soils can quickly lose their remaining vegetation; the soil then becomes less stable and increasingly susceptible to erosion by water and wind. If these conditions persist for several years, these lands can convert or revert to desert environments.

the ITCZ because of global climate change may intensify these normal drought cycles. For the countries in this region, desertification is an issue of national importance and a growing problem (Figure 18-B). Most people in the Sahel engage in subsistence agriculture or pastoral nomadism, and the poverty in the region leaves many ill-equipped to deal with even short-term losses of agricultural productivity. Expansion of the desert into the Sahel comes at the cost of habitat for wildlife, rangeland for livestock, and agricultural lands. Similar concerns about loss of land to desertification exist for central Asia, northern China, and northern and eastern Australia.

The Climate Change–Desertification Nexus: The Intergovernmental Panel on Climate Change (IPCC) has funded and produced a series of climate

Food Production: Unfortunately, one of the causes of accelerated desertification is the excessive cultivation of erosion-vulnerable soils. This trend may intensify. In 2012, the world's population crossed the seven-billion threshold. Over the last two decades, considerable research has focused on the question of how to sustainably feed this growing population. The UNCCD estimates that by 2030, global food demand will increase 50 percent over 2012 levels. At the same time, desertification is leading to the loss of what UNCCD estimates to be 12 million hectares (26.5 million acres) of agricultural land annually. Much of that land will be needed for growing food. Yet a strong argument can be made that the future rate of desertification will likely be determined by our commitment to protecting native vegetation and soil through sustainable farming practices.

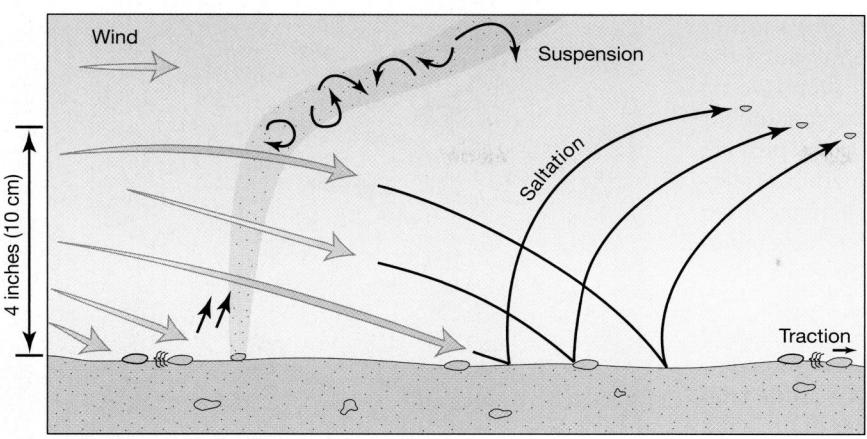

◀ **Figure 18-16** Wind carries tiny dust particles in suspension; larger particles are moved by saltation and traction.

Aeolian Transportation

Rock materials are transported by wind in much the same fashion as they are moved by water, but less effectively. The finest particles are carried in suspension as dust. Strong, turbulent winds can lift and carry thousands of tons of suspended dust. Some dust storms extend for hundreds of meters above Earth's surface and may move material through more than 1600 kilometers (1000 miles) of horizontal distance.

Animation
Wind
Transportation
of Sediment

Particles larger than dust are moved by wind through *saltation* and *traction*, just as in streamflow (Figure 18-16). Wind is unable to lift particles larger than the size of sand grains, and even these are likely to be carried less than one meter above the surface. Indeed, most sand, even when propelled by a strong wind, leaps along in the low, curved trajectory typical of saltation, striking the ground at a low angle and bouncing onward. Larger particles move by traction, being rolled or pushed along the ground by the wind. It is estimated that three-fourths of the total volume of all wind-moved material in dry lands is shifted by saltation and traction, particularly the former. At the same time, the entire surface layer of sand moves slowly downwind as a result of the frequent impact of the saltating grains; this process is called *creep* (but should not be confused with *soil creep*).

Because the wind can lift particles only so high, a true *sandstorm* is a cloud of horizontally moving sand that extends for only a few centimeters or feet above the ground surface. Persons standing in its path have their legs peppered by sand grains, but their heads are most likely above the sand cloud. The abrasive impact of a sandstorm, while having little erosive effect on the terrain, may be quite significant for the works of humans near ground level; unprotected wooden poles and posts can be rapidly cut down by the sandblasting, and cars traveling through a sandstorm are likely to suffer etched windshields and chipped paint.

Learning Check 18-6 **Why is evidence of wind erosion of bedrock usually quite limited?**

Aeolian Deposition

Sand and dust moved by the wind are eventually deposited when the wind dies down. The finer material, which may be carried long distances, is usually laid down as a thin coating of silt and has little or no landform significance. The coarser sand, however, is normally deposited locally. Sometimes it is spread across the landscape as an amorphous sheet called a *sandplain*. The most notable of all aeolian deposits, however, is the **sand dune**, in which loose, wind-blown sand is heaped into a mound or low hill.

Animation
Desert Sand
Dunes

Desert Sand Dunes: In some instances, dunefields are composed entirely of unanchored sand that is mostly uniform grains of quartz (occasionally gypsum, rarely some other minerals) and usually brownish-gray colored, although sometimes a brilliant white. Unanchored dunes are deformable obstructions to airflow. Because they are unanchored, they can move, divide, grow, or shrink. They develop sheltered air pockets on their leeward sides that slow down and baffle the wind, so that deposition is promoted there.

Unanchored dunes are normally moved by local winds. Wind erodes the windward slope of the dune, forcing the sand grains up and over the crest to be deposited on the steeper leeward side, or **slip face** (Figure 18-17). The slip face of a dune typically maintains an angle of 32° to 34°—the *angle of repose* of dry sand. If the wind prevails from one direction for many days, the dune may migrate downwind without changing shape. Such migration is usually slow, but in some cases dunes can move tens of meters in a year.

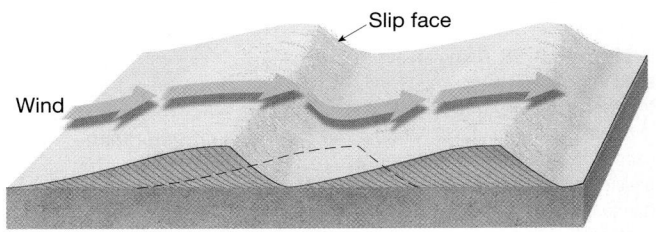

▲ **Figure 18-17** Sand dunes migrate downwind as sand grains move up the gentle windward slope and are deposited on the steep slip face.

Not all dunes are unanchored, however, and another characteristic dunefield arrangement is one in which the dunes are mostly or entirely anchored and therefore no longer shifting with the wind. Various agents can anchor dunes, the primary one being vegetation. Dunes provide little nourishment or moisture for plant growth, but desert vegetation is remarkably hardy and persistent and often able to survive in a dune environment. Where vegetation manages to gain a foothold, it may proliferate and anchor the dunes.

Dune patterns are almost infinite in their variety. Several characteristic dune forms are widespread in the world's deserts, their configuration largely a consequence of the relative amount of sand present and the persistence of the wind direction. Here we consider four of the most common:

1. Best known of all dune forms is the **barchan**, which usually occurs as an individual dune migrating across a nonsandy surface, although barchans may also be found in groups. A barchan is crescent-shaped, with the horns of the crescent pointing downwind (Figures 18-18a and 18-19). Sand movement in a barchan is not only over the crest, from windward side to slip face, but also around the edges of the crescent to extend the horns. Barchans form where strong winds blow consistently from one direction. They tend to be the fastest moving of all dunes and are found in all deserts except those of Australia. They are most widespread in the deserts of central Eurasia (Thar and Takla Makan) and in parts of the Sahara.

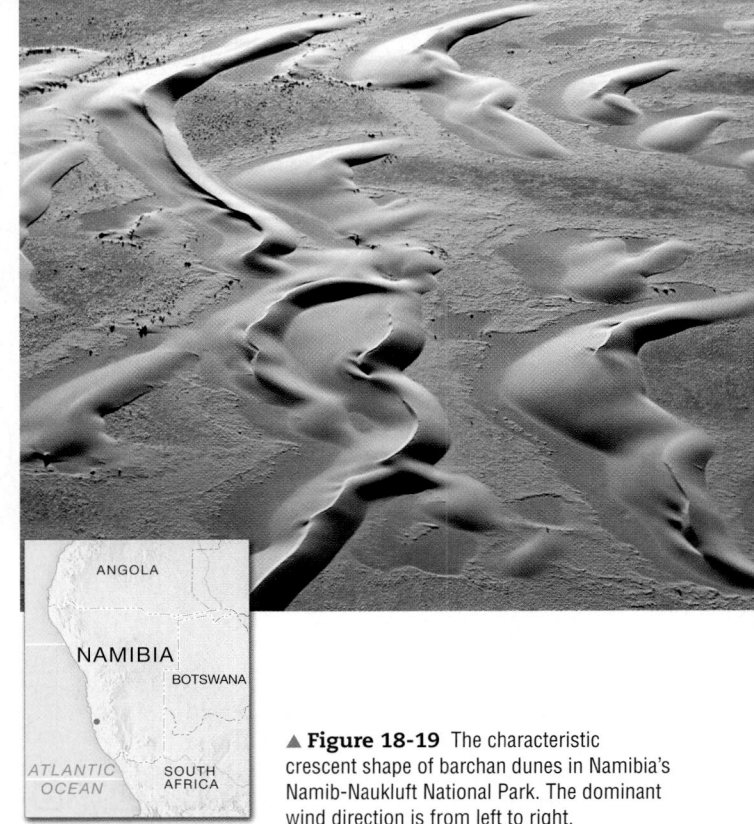

▲ **Figure 18-19** The characteristic crescent shape of barchan dunes in Namibia's Namib-Naukluft National Park. The dominant wind direction is from left to right.

2. **Transverse dunes**, which are also crescent-shaped but less uniformly so than barchans (Figure 18-18b), occur where the supply of sand is much greater than that found in locations that have barchans; normally the entire landscape leading to transverse dune formation

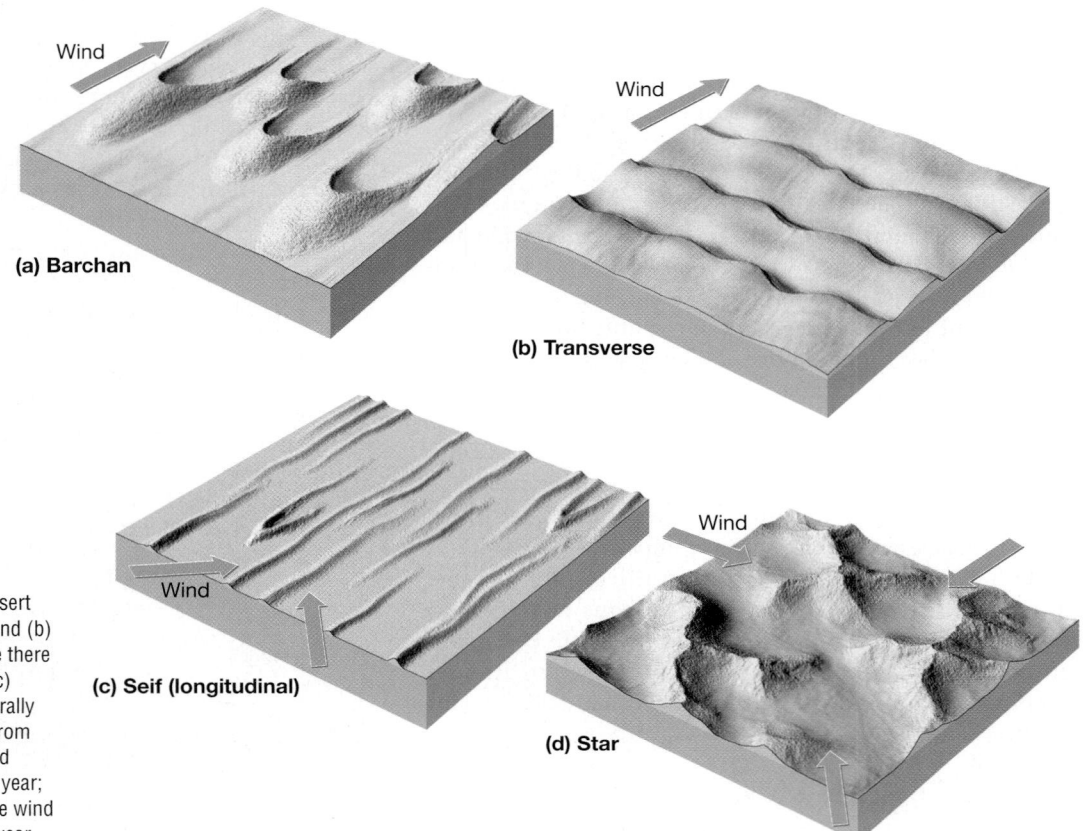

▶ **Figure 18-18** Common desert sand dune types: (a) barchans and (b) transverse dunes develop where there is a consistent wind direction; (c) seifs or longitudinal dunes generally develop where the wind blows from one direction part of the year and another direction the rest of the year; (d) star dunes develop where the wind direction varies throughout the year.

(a) Barchan

(b) Transverse

(c) Seif (longitudinal)

(d) Star

▲ **Figure 18-20** The parallel linearity of seifs is characteristic of many desert areas. This scene is from the Simpson Desert of central Australia.

is sand covered. As with a barchan, the convex side of a transverse dune faces the prevailing wind direction. In a formation of transverse dunes, all the crests are perpendicular to the wind direction, and the dunes are aligned in parallel waves across the land. They migrate downwind just as barchans do, and if the sand supply decreases, they are likely to break up into barchans.

3. **Seifs** are a type of linear or *longitudinal dune*. They are long, narrow dunes that usually occur in multiplicity and in a generally parallel arrangement (Figures 18-18c and 18-20). They are typically a few dozen to a few hundred meters high, a few tens of meters wide, and kilometers or even tens of kilometers long. Their lengthy, parallel orientation apparently represents an intermediate direction between two dominant wind directions—blowing from one direction part of the year, and from another direction the rest of the year. Seifs are rare in American deserts but may be the most common dune forms in other parts of the world.

4. **Star dunes** are large pyramid-shaped dunes with arms radiating out in three or more directions (Figure 18-18d). Star dunes develop in areas where the wind frequently varies in direction (Figure 18-21).

Learning Check 18-7   **Why does the leeward side of a sand dune (the *slip face*) have a steeper slope than the windward side?**

Fossil Sand Dunes: In some locations, what are sometimes called "fossil" sand dunes are found. For example, in some regions of the southwestern United States, vast deposits of sandstone exhibit the characteristic "cross-bedding" of wind-deposited sand, rather than the more typical horizontal strata of sediments accumulated in bodies of water (Figure 18-22).

▲ **Figure 18-21** Star dunes in Namib-Naukluft National Park, Namibia.

▲ **Figure 18-22** Cross-bedded sandstone in "fossil" sand dunes near Zion National Park in Utah.

Cross-bedding in sand dunes develops when wind-blown sand slides down the slip face of a dune, leaving thin layers inclined relative to the ground surface (see Figure 18-17).

Aeolian Processes in Nondesert Regions

Although our discussion thus far has concerned the work of wind in desert areas, two kinds of wind-produced features are frequently found in nondesert areas as well.

Coastal Dunes: Winds are also active in dune formation along many stretches of ocean and lake coasts, whether the climate is dry or not. On almost all flattish coastlines, ocean waves deposit sand along the beach. A prominent onshore wind can blow some of the sand inland, often forming dunes. In areas where vegetation becomes established on the sand, *parabolic dunes* develop—they look much like a barchan dune, but with the "horns" pointing into the wind offshore. Most coastal dune aggregations are small, but they sometimes cover extensive areas. The largest area is probably along the Atlantic coastline of southern France, where dunes extend for 240 kilometers (150 miles) along the shore and reach inland for 3 to 10 kilometers (2 to 6 miles).

Loess: Another form of aeolian deposit not associated with dry lands is **loess**, a wind-deposited silt that is fine grained, calcareous, and usually buff colored. (Pronounced *luhss* to rhyme with "hearse" if one left out the "r"; this is a German word derived from the name of a village in Alsace.) Despite its depositional origin, loess lacks horizontal stratification. Perhaps its most distinctive characteristic is its great vertical durability, which results from its fine grain size, high porosity, and vertical jointlike cleavage planes. The tiny grains have great molecular attraction for one another, making the particles very cohesive. Moreover, the particles are angular, which increases porosity. Thus, loess accepts and holds large amounts of water. Although relatively soft and unconsolidated, loess maintains almost vertical slopes when it is exposed to erosion because of its structural characteristics, as though it were firmly

▲ **Figure 18-23** Loess has a remarkable capability for standing in vertical cliffs, as seen in this road cut near Maryville, Missouri.

cemented rock (Figure 18-23). Prominent bluffs are often produced as erosional surfaces in loess deposits.

The formational history of loess is complex, although much of the silt was produced in association with Pleistocene glaciation (discussed in Chapter 19). During both glacial and interglacial periods, rivers carried large amounts of debris-laden meltwater from the glaciers, producing many broad floodplains. During periods of low water, winds whipped the smaller, dust-sized particles from the floodplains and dropped them in some places in very thick deposits. Some loess also seems to have been generated by deflation of dust from desert areas, especially in central Eurasia.

Most deposits of loess are in the midlatitudes, where some are very extensive, particularly in the United States, Russia, China, and Argentina (Figure 18-24). Indeed, some

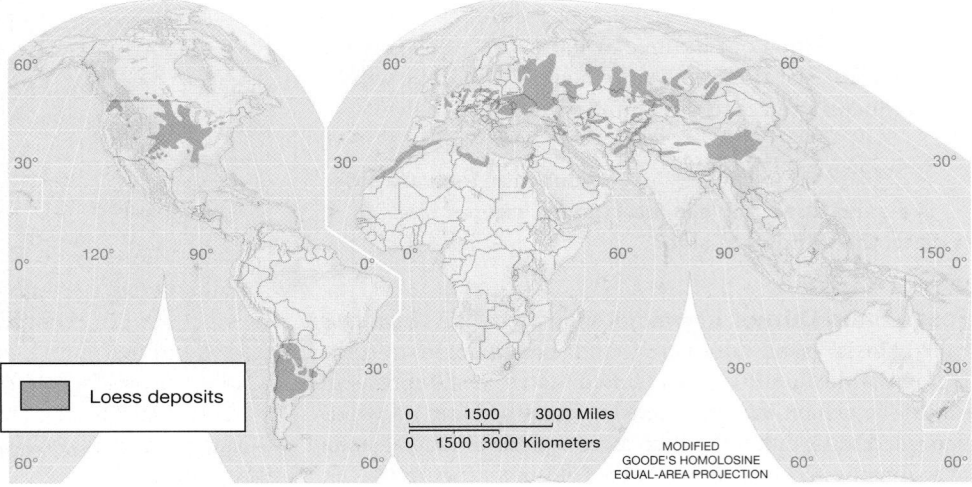

▶ **Figure 18-24** Major loess deposits of the world.

10 percent of Earth's land surface is covered with loess, and in the conterminous United States, the total approaches 30 percent. Loess deposits provide fertile possibilities for agriculture, for they serve as the parent material for some of the world's most productive soils, especially for growing grain.

The loess areas have been particularly significant in China because of their agricultural productivity. The Yellow River (Hwang Ho) received its name from the vast amount of buff-colored sediment it carries, as did its destination, the Yellow Sea. Also, numerous cave dwellings have been excavated in the Chinese loess because of its remarkable capability for standing in vertical walls. Unfortunately, however, this region is also prone to earthquakes, and the cave homes collapse readily when tremors occur; thus, some of the world's greatest earthquake disasters in terms of loss of life have taken place there.

CHARACTERISTIC DESERT LANDSCAPE SURFACES

Surface features vary considerably from one desert to the next, and it is impossible to describe all of the possible landforms found in arid regions. So instead, for the remainder of this chapter we will first describe distinct kinds of landscape surfaces found in many deserts of the world, and then we will offer detailed descriptions of two representative desert landform assemblages found in North America.

Common Desert Surfaces

Over time, the weathering, erosional, and depositional processes at work in deserts produce distinctly different kinds of landscapes. Three common types of landscape surfaces are found only in desert areas: the *erg*, the *reg*, and the *hamada*—Arabic words for these desert landscapes.

Erg—A Sea of Sand

The most notable desert surface is the **erg**, the classic "sea of sand" often associated in the public mind with the term *desert* (Figure 18-25). An erg (Arabic for "sand") is a large area covered with loose sand generally arranged in some sort of dune formation by the wind. The accumulation of the vast amount of sand necessary to produce an erg probably cannot be explained only by processes operating in deserts today—because desert weathering processes are very slow. Rather, much of this sand probably accumulated during a period of more humid climate. After being formed, these products were carried by streams into an area of accumulation. Then the climate became drier, and consequently wind, rather than water, became the principal agent of transportation and deposition of the sand.

Several large ergs occur in the Sahara and Arabian deserts, and smaller ergs are found in most other deserts. The Australian deserts are dominated by large accumulations of sand, including extensive dunefields, but these are not true ergs because most of the sand is anchored by vegetation

▲ **Figure 18-25** Sand dunes in an erg area of the Namib Desert, Sossusvlei National Park, Namibia.

and therefore not free to move with the wind. "Relict" ergs (usually in the form of sand dunes covered with vegetation) are sometimes found in nonarid areas, indicative of a drier climate in the past. Much of western Nebraska has such relict ergs, now stabilized by prairie grasses.

Reg—Stony Deserts

A second type of desert landscape surface is the **reg**, a tight covering of coarse gravel, pebbles, and/or boulders from which all sand and dust have been removed by wind and water. A reg (Arabic for "stone"), then, is a stony desert, although the surface covering of stones may be very thin (in some cases, it is just one pebble deep). The finer material was removed through surface erosion—perhaps aided by sediment movement below the surface through the action of rainwater percolation—so the surface pebbles often fit closely together, sealing whatever material is below from further erosion. For this reason, a reg is often referred to as **desert pavement** or *desert armor* (Figure 18-26). In Australia, where regs are widespread, they are called *gibber plains*. Because it usually takes a long time to form (at least hundreds and often thousands of years), the presence of well-developed desert pavement is an indication of a relatively undisturbed surface.

Desert Varnish: A striking feature of some deserts, one particularly but not exclusively associated with regs, is **desert varnish**. This is a dark, shiny coating, consisting mostly of iron and manganese oxides, that forms on the surface of pebbles, stones, and larger outcrops after long exposure to the desert air (see the larger rocks shown in Figure 18-26). Desert varnish is characterized by a high content of iron and manganese oxides along with wind-delivered clay. The

▲ **Figure 18-26** Desert pavement in California's Panamint Valley. Note the dark brown coating of desert varnish on the larger rocks.

relatively high concentrations of manganese in desert varnish seem to be a consequence of a biochemical process involving bacteria. Desert varnish can be used as a relative dating tool for geomorphologists because the longer a rock surface has been exposed to weathering, the greater is the concentration of the oxide coating and thus the darker the color.

Hamada—Barren Bedrock

A third desert landscape surface is the **hamada** (Arabic for "rock"), a barren surface of consolidated material. A hamada surface usually consists of exposed bedrock, but it is sometimes composed of sedimentary material that has been cemented together by salts evaporated from groundwater. In either case, fragments formed by weathering are quickly swept away by the wind, so that little loose material remains.

> **Learning Check 18-8** **Explain what the presence or absence of *desert pavement* and *desert varnish* can reveal about the likelihood of relatively recent erosion or deposition on a desert surface.**

Ergs, regs, and hamadas are all limited to plains areas. Regs and hamadas are exceedingly flat, whereas ergs are as high as the sand dunes built by the wind. The boundaries of these landscapes are often sharp because of the abrupt change in friction-layer speed as the wind moves from a sandy surface to a nonsandy surface. For example, wind passing from an erg to a reg or hamada is no longer slowed by the drag of loose sand and so can speed up and sweep the hard surface clean. On the other hand, wind moving from a barren reg or hamada to a sandy erg is slowed down perceptibly, and deposition results.

Although the extent of ergs, regs, and hamadas is significant in some desert areas, the majority of the arid land in the world contains only a limited number of these surfaces. For example, only one-third of the Arabian Desert, the sandiest desert of all, is covered with sand, and much of that is not in the form of an erg.

Two Representative Desert Landform Assemblages

We now turn to more detailed examples of landform development in arid lands. Two prominent assemblages of landforms are found in the deserts of North America: basin-and-range terrain and mesa-and-scarp terrain. Their pattern of development is repeated time and again over thousands of square kilometers of the American Southwest (Figure 18-27). Although desert landscapes vary greatly around the world, these two landform assemblages are good examples of the outcome of the special conditions and the external desert landform-shaping processes we describe in this chapter.

BASIN-AND-RANGE LANDFORMS FG9

As Figure 18-27 shows, most of the southwestern interior of the United States is characterized by basin-and-range topography. This is a land largely without external drainage, with only a few exotic rivers (notably the Colorado and Rio Grande) flowing through or out of the region. This region of North America has undergone extensive normal faulting—including movement along low-angle detachment faults—leaving a landscape consisting of numerous fault-block mountain ranges surrounding a series of interior drainage basins, including many down-dropped grabens and down-tilted "half-grabens" (see Figure 14-61).

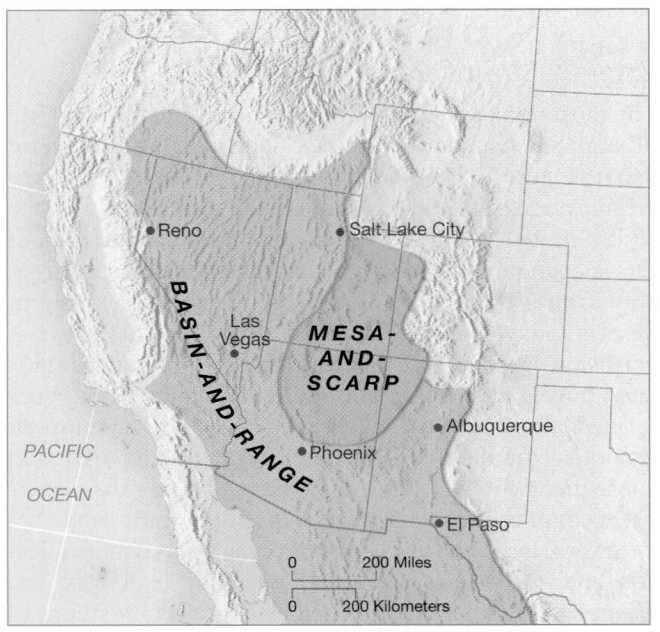

▲ **Figure 18-27** The southwestern interior of the United States contains two principal assemblages of landforms: basin-and-range and mesa-and-scarp.

The aridity of the basin-and-range region is mostly due to rain shadows—especially that of the Sierra Nevada range in eastern California.

Basin-and-range terrain has three principal features: ranges, piedmont zones, and basins (Figure 18-28).

The Ranges

If we stand in the basin of any basin-and-range landscape, the mountain ranges dominate the horizon in all directions. Some of the ranges are high and some quite low, but the prevalence of steep and rocky slopes presents an aura of ruggedness. Although the tectonic origins of these mountains vary (most have been tilted by faulting, but others were formed by folding, by volcanism, or in a more complex fashion), their surface features have been largely shaped by weathering, mass wasting, and fluvial processes.

Ridge crests and peaks are usually sharp, steep cliffs are common, and rocky outcrops protrude at all elevations. The mountain ranges of a basin-and-range formation are usually long, narrow, and parallel to one another. Most of them are seamed by numerous gullies, gorges, and canyons that rarely have flowing streams. These dry drainage channels are usually narrow and steep sided and have a V-shaped cross section. Typically the channel bottoms are filled with sand and other loose debris.

In some areas, the ranges may have been eroding for a long time, but in other places the ranges are just a few million years old, and bare rock outcrops are still prominent. As we saw earlier, if the range stands in isolation and the alluvial plains and basins roundabout are extensive, the term *inselberg* is applied to the mountain remnant (see Figure 18-11).

The Piedmont Zone

At the base of the ranges, there is usually a sharp break in slope that marks the change from range to basin floor (see Figure 18-12). This piedmont zone is a transition area from the steep slopes of the ranges to the near-flatness of the basins.

Much of the piedmont zone may be underlain by a *pediment*, although the pediment is rarely visible. It is normally covered with several meters of unconsolidated sediment because the piedmont zone is an area of fluvial deposition. During the occasional rainfall, flash floods and debris flows come roaring out of the gullies and gorges of the surrounding ranges, heavily laden with sedimentary material. As they burst out of the mouths of the confining canyons onto the piedmont zone, their speed and load capacity drop abruptly. Significant deposition is the result.

Alluvial Fans: One of the most prominent and widespread topographic features to be found in any desert area is the **alluvial fan**, particularly characteristic of the basin-and-range region (although a dominant feature in many deserts, alluvial fans also can develop in humid areas). As a flowing stream leaves the narrow confines of a mountain gorge and emerges onto the open piedmont zone, it slows down and abruptly loses both capacity and competence. The flow breaks into distributary channels that wend their way down the piedmont slope, sometimes cutting shallow new channels in the loose alluvium but frequently depositing more debris atop the old (Figure 18-29). Channels become choked and overflow, developing new ones. In this fashion, a moderately sloping, fan-shaped landform is constructed at the mouth of the canyon. When one part of the fan is built up, the channeled flow shifts to another section and builds that up. This means that the entire fan is eventually covered more or less symmetrically with alluvium. In general, large boulders are dropped near the apex of the fan and finer material accumulates around the margins, with a considerable mixture of particle sizes throughout. As deposition continues, the fan is extended outward across the piedmont zone and onto the basin floor.

Bajadas: As alluvial fans become larger, neighboring ones often overlap. Continued growth and more complete overlap may eventually result in a continuous alluvial surface all across the piedmont zone, in which case it is difficult to distinguish between individual fans. This feature is known as a **bajada** (see Figure 18-28). Near the mountain front, a bajada surface is undulating, with convex sections near the canyon mouths and concave sections in the overlap areas between the canyons. In the portion of the bajada away from the range and out on the basin floor, however, no

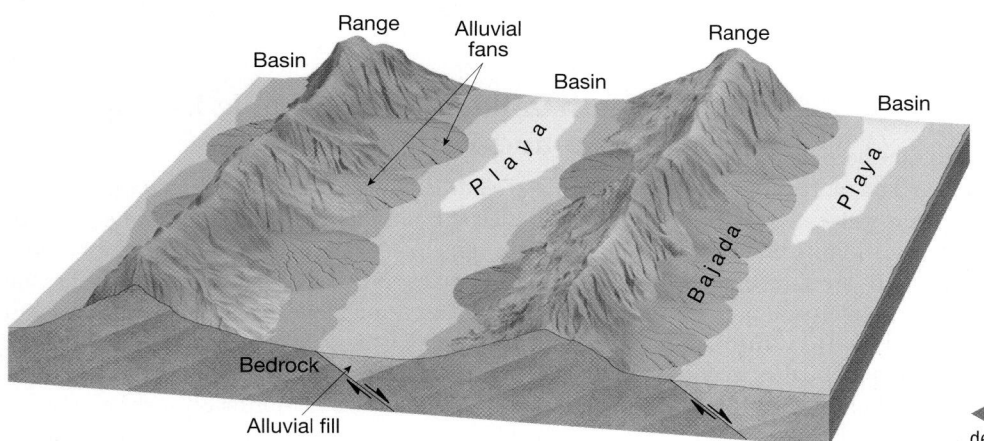

◀ **Figure 18-28** A typical basin-and-range desert landscape.

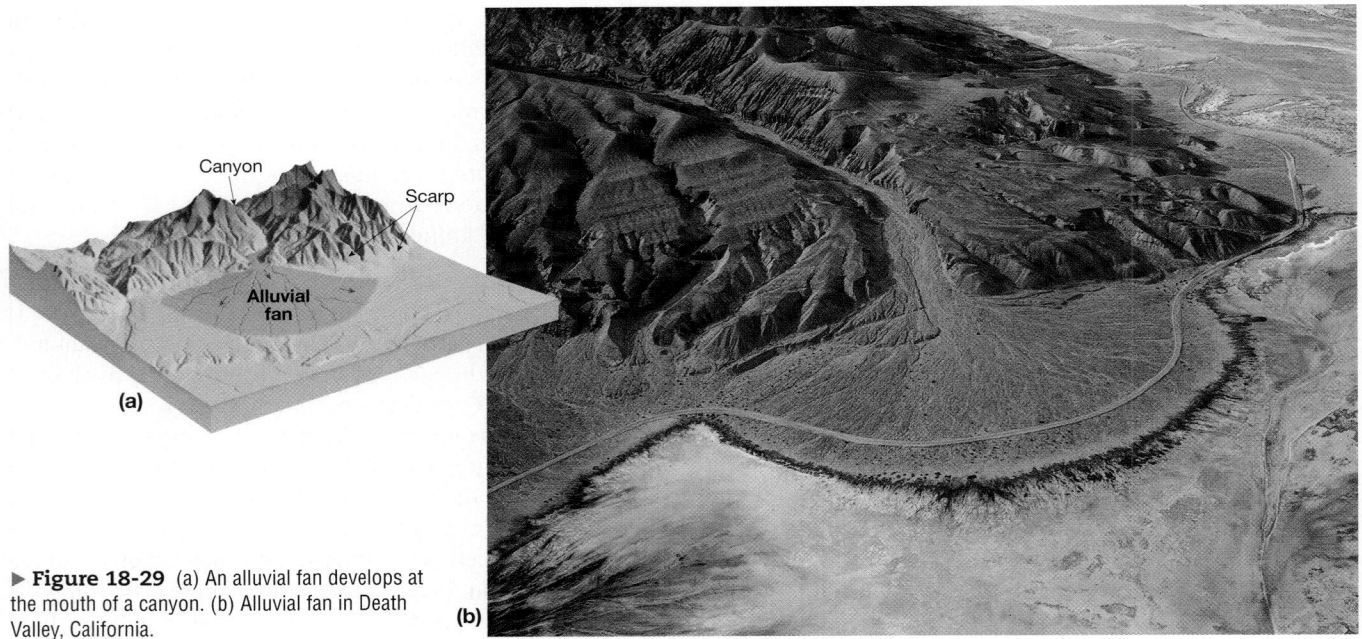

(a)

(b)

▶ **Figure 18-29** (a) An alluvial fan develops at the mouth of a canyon. (b) Alluvial fan in Death Valley, California.

undulations occur because the component fans have coalesced so thoroughly.

Learning Check 18-9   What is an *alluvial fan* and why are they so common in the basin-and-range desert?

The Basins

Beyond the mountain front is the flattish floor of the basin, which has a very gentle slope from all sides toward some low point. A *playa* is usually found in this low point (see Figure 18-7). Drainage channels across the basin floor are sometimes clear cut, but more often shallow and ill defined, frequently disappearing before reaching the low point. This low point thus functions as the drainage terminal for all overland and streamflow from the near sides of the surrounding ranges, but only sometimes does much water reach it. Most is lost by evaporation and seepage long before.

Salt accumulations are commonplace on the playa surrounding the low point of a desert basin because of all the water-soluble minerals washed out of the surrounding watershed. Once out of the mountains and in the basin, the water evaporates or seeps away, but the salts cannot evaporate and are only marginally involved in seepage. There is usually sufficient water to allow flow across the outer rim of the basin floor and into the playa area, however, and so salts become increasingly concentrated in the playa, which is then more properly called a *salina*. The presence of the salt usually gives a brilliant whitish color to the playa or salina surface. Many different salts can be involved, and their accumulations are sometimes large enough to support a prosperous mining enterprise.

In the rare occasions when water does flow into a playa, the formation becomes a playa lake. Such lakes may be extensive, but they are usually very shallow and normally persist for only a few days or weeks. Saline lakes are marked by clear water and a salty froth around the edges, whereas shallow freshwater lakes have muddy water. Why are saline lakes clear? In a process called *flocculation*, saltwater introduces cations that neutralize the often negative charge of silt and clay particles, allowing the particles to clump together and settle, leaving the water clear.

The basin floor is covered with very fine-grained material because the contributory streams are too weak to transport large particles. Silt and sand predominate and sometimes accumulate to remarkable depths. Indeed, the normal denudation processes in basin-and-range country tend to raise the floor of the basins. Debris from the surrounding ranges has nowhere to go but the basin of interior drainage. Thus, as the mountains are being worn down, the basin is gradually filling up. The fine material of basin floors is very susceptible to the wind, with the result that small concentrations of sand dunes are often found in some corner of the basin.

Learning Check 18-10   What is a *playa* and why is one found is almost all basins of the basin-and-range region?

Death Valley: A Remarkable Example of Basin-and-Range Terrain

California's Death Valley is a vast topographic museum—a veritable primer of basin-and-range terrain. Located in east-central California, close to the Nevada border, the "valley" is actually a down-dropped basin—the result of the crustal extension taking place throughout the basin-and range—with extensive and complex fault zones both east and west of the valley floor (Figure 18-30). The trough is about 225 kilometers (140 miles) long, in a general northwest–southeast orientation; its width ranges from 6 to 26 kilometers (4 to 16 miles).

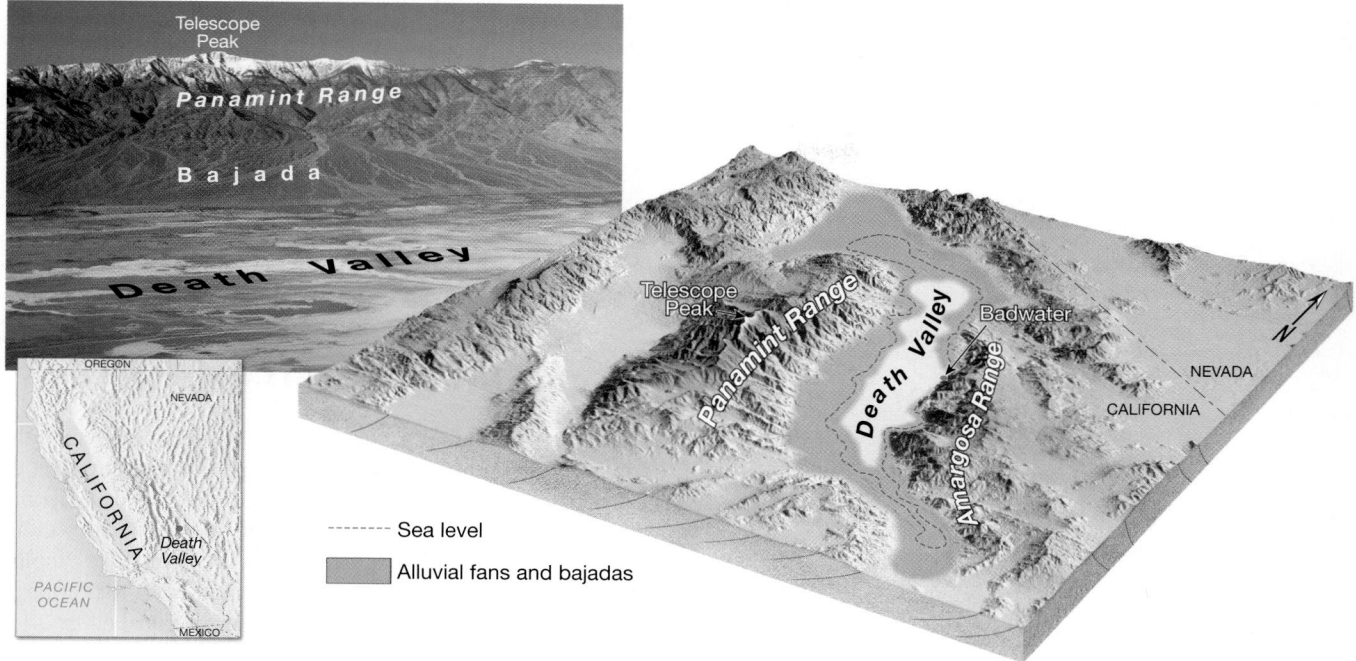

▲ **Figure 18-30** The setting of Death Valley. The mountains and basins are a consequence of extensional faulting. Alluvial fans and bajadas are found all along the mountain fronts.

Not a classic graben, the basin floor of Death Valley has tilted down more along its eastern side than its western side—created at least in part as a "pull-apart" basin, formed where land drops down between two parallel strike-slip faults. The downfaulting has been so pronounced that nearly 1425 square kilometers (550 square miles) of the valley floor is below sea level, reaching a depth of 86 meters below sea level (–282 feet). Lengthy, tilted fault-block mountain ranges border the valley on either side. The Panamint Range on the west is the most prominent; the high point at Telescope Peak 3368 meters or 11,049 feet above sea level is only 29 kilometers (18 miles) due west from the low point of the valley near Badwater. The Amargosa Range on the east is equally steep and rugged, but a bit lower overall. It is the series of high mountain ranges to the west of the basin that generate the rain shadow that makes Death Valley so dry.

Mountains and Wineglass Canyons: The most conspicuous topography associated with Death Valley is the surrounding mountains. The ranges have all the characteristic features of desert mountains, being rugged, rocky, and generally barren. Their erosional slopes are steep and their escarpments steeper. The canyons that seam the ranges are invariably deep, narrow, V-shaped gorges. Many of those in the Amargosa Range and some in the Panamints are *wineglass canyons*. The cup of the glass is the open area of dispersed headwater tributaries high in the range, the stem is the narrow gorge cut through the mountain front, and the base is the fan that opens out onto the piedmont zone.

Alluvial Fans: The piedmont zone at the foot of the Panamints and the Amargosas is almost completely covered with alluvium in one of the most extensive fan complexes imaginable. Every canyon mouth is the apex either of a fan or a fan-shaped debris flow deposit, and most of the fans overlap with neighbors to the north and south. The fans on the western side of the valley (those formed by debris from the Panamints) are much more extensive than those on the eastern side. For the most part, the Panamint fans are thoroughly coalesced into a conspicuous bajada that averages about 8 kilometers (5 miles) wide, with the outer margin of the bajada as much as 610 meters (2000 feet) lower than the canyon mouths.

The Amargosa fans are much smaller, primarily because faulting has tilted down the eastern side basin floor so that the thickest sediments are nestled close to the base of the Amargosa Range. Thus, the west-side fans have been able to extend outward onto the valley floor, whereas tilting has reduced the size of the east-side fans by creating shorter slopes (and therefore, smaller drainage basins to supply sediment), and by facilitating their partial burial by valley-floor deposits. The Amargosa fans, then, are mostly short, steep, and discrete so there is no bajada on the eastern side of Death Valley, although some of the fans do overlap with one another.

Basin Floor: The floor of Death Valley is also of great topographic interest, although its flatness makes the features less easy to see and understand. The valley is filled with an incredible depth of alluvium, most of which has been washed down from the surrounding mountains; in places the fill is estimated to consist of 900 meters (3000 feet) of young alluvium resting atop another 1800 meters (6000 feet) of Tertiary sediment. The surface of the valley floor has little relief and slopes gently toward the low point near Badwater, a permanent saltwater pond. Drainage channels appear irregularly on the valley

▲ **Figure 18-31** The Death Valley "salt pan" here consists mostly of ordinary table salt (NaCl). The polygonal ridges form as salt crystals grow through the evaporation of water from a salty "slush" just below the surface.

floor, trending toward Badwater. In some places, distinct braided channels appear; in other locations, the channels disappear in sand or playa.

There are several extensive crusty-white *salt pans*, particularly in the middle of the valley (Figure 18-31), along with several sand accumulations, with one area of mobile dunes covering 36 square kilometers (14 square miles).

During the most recent ice age, Death Valley was occupied by an immense lake. Lake Manly, as it is now called, was more than 160 kilometers (100 miles) long and 180 meters (600 feet) deep. It was fed by three rivers that flowed into the valley from the west, carrying meltwater from Sierra Nevada glaciers. As the climate became drier

and warmer, the lake eventually disappeared through evaporation and seepage, but traces of its various shoreline levels can still be seen at several places on the lower slopes. Much of the salt accumulated in the valley is due to the evaporating waters of Lake Manly as well as lakes that existed more recently.

Learning Check 18-11　　**How did Death Valley become both below sea level and so arid?**

MESA-AND-SCARP TERRAIN

The other major landform assemblage of the American Southwest is mesa-and-scarp terrain. It is most prominent in Four Corners country—the place where Colorado, Utah, Arizona, and New Mexico come together (Figure 18-32) in the regionally uplifted Colorado Plateau. **Mesa** is Spanish for "table" and implies a flat-topped surface. *Scarp* is short for "escarpment" and refers to the steep, more or less vertical cliffs.

Structure of Mesa-and-Scarp Landforms

Mesa-and-scarp terrain is normally associated with horizontal sedimentary strata—shown off prominently in this arid region because it lacks a continuous cover of trees and vegetation. Such strata invariably offer different degrees of resistance to weathering and erosion, and so abrupt changes in slope angle are characteristic of this terrain. The most resistant layers, typically limestone or sandstone, often play a dual role in the development of a mesa-and-scarp terrain. They form an extensive caprock, which becomes the mesa; and at the eroded edge of the caprock, the hard layer protects underlying strata and produces an escarpment. Thus, it is the resistant layers

◀ **Figure 18-32** The stair-step pattern of mesa-and-scarp terrain is shown on an imposing scale in Arizona's Grand Canyon.

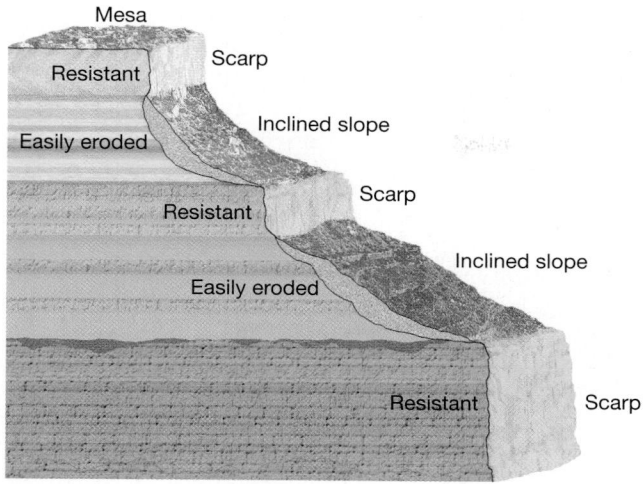

▲ **Figure 18-33** Cross section of a mesa-and-scarp formation. Differential weathering and erosion shows up prominently: The resistant strata weather and erode into mesas or scarps, whereas the more easily eroded strata yield gentler inclined slopes.

that are responsible for both elements of slope (mesa and scarp) that describe this terrain type.

Often mesa-and-scarp topography has a broad and irregular stair-step pattern. Figure 18-33 shows a cross section through a typical formation. An extensive, flat platform (the mesa) in the topmost resistant layer of a sedimentary accumulation terminates in an escarpment (the scarp) that extends downward to the bottom of the resistant layer(s). From here, another slope, steep but not as steep as the escarpment, continues down through softer strata. This inclined slope extends downward as far as the next resistant layer, which forms either another escarpment or another mesa ending in an escarpment.

The top platforms are properly referred to as **plateaus** if they are bounded on one or more sides by a prominent escarpment. If a scarp edge is absent or relatively inconspicuous, the platform is called a *stripped plain*.

Erosion of Escarpment Edge

The escarpment edge is worn back by weathering, mass wasting, and fluvial erosion. The cliffs retreat, maintaining their perpendicular faces, as they are undermined by the more rapid removal of the less resistant strata (often shale) beneath the caprock. Much of the undermining is accomplished by a process called *sapping*, in which groundwater seeps and trickles out of the scarp face, eroding fine

particles and weakening the cohesion of the face. When thus undermined, blocks of the caprock break off, usually along vertical joint lines. Throughout this process, the harder rocks are the cliff-formers, and the less resistant beds develop more gently inclined slopes. Talus often accumulates at the base of the slope.

Although the term mesa is applied generally to many flat surfaces in dry environments, it properly refers to a particular landform: a flat-topped, steep-sided hill with a limited summit area. It is a remnant of a formerly more extensive surface, most of which has been worn away (Figure 18-34). Sometimes it stands in splendid isolation as a final remnant in an area where most of the previous surface has been removed, but more commonly it occurs as an outlying mass not very distant from the retreating escarpment face to which it was once connected. A mesa is invariably capped by some sort of resistant material that helps keep the summit flat even as the bulk of the rock mass is reduced by continuing mass wasting and erosion of its rimming cliffs.

A related but smaller topographic feature is the **butte**, an erosional remnant having a very small surface area and cliffs that rise conspicuously above their surroundings. Some buttes have other origins, but most are formed by the mass wasting of mesas (Figure 18-35). With further denudation, a still smaller residual feature, usually referred to as a **pinnacle** or *pillar*, may be all that is left—a final spire of resistant caprock protecting weaker underlying beds. Buttes, mesas, and pinnacles are typically found not far from some retreating escarpment face (see Figure 18-34).

Learning Check 18-12 **Explain the role of resistant caprock in the formation of mesa-and-scarp terrain.**

Arches and Natural Bridges

Mesa-and-scarp terrain is also famous for numerous minor erosional features, most produced by a combination of weathering, mass wasting, and fluvial erosion. These features are not confined to arid regions, but the mesa-and-scarp region has many examples. An *arch* (Figure 18-36) can form when the lower portions of a narrow "fin" of sedimentary rock—associated with prominent, closely-spaced vertical joints—weaken and collapse, leaving an arch of more resistant rock above. A *natural bridge* can form anytime the rock over which water flows changes from an erosion-resistant type to a less resistant type. One place

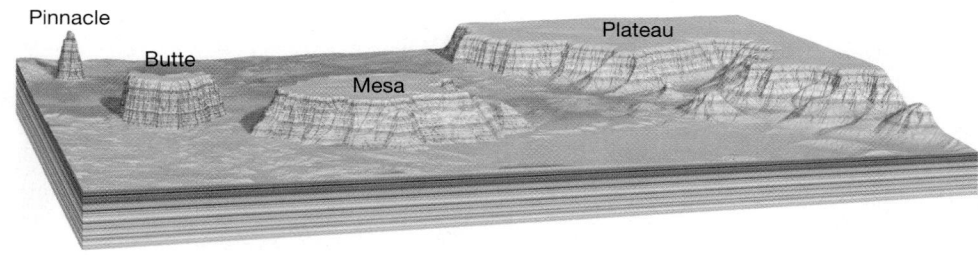

◀ **Figure 18-34** Typical development of residual landforms in horizontal sedimentary strata with a hard caprock. With the passage of time, larger features are eroded into smaller features.

▶ **Figure 18-35** The spectacular starkness of arid-land topography is demonstrated dramatically in the view of the Mitten Buttes in Arizona's Monument Valley.

a natural bridge frequently forms is where an entrenched meander wears away the rock in a narrow neck between meander loops (see Figure 16-45 in Chapter 16).

Pedestals and pillars, sometimes larger at the top than at the bottom, rise abruptly above their surroundings, their caps resistant material but their narrow bases continuously weathered by rainwater trickling down the surface. This water dissolves the cementing material that holds the sand grains together, and the loosened grains are easily blown or washed away.

One other notable characteristic of mesa-and-scarp terrain is vivid colors. The sedimentary outcrops and sandy debris of these regions are often resplendent in various shades of red, brown, yellow, and gray, due mostly to iron compounds.

Badlands

One of the most striking topographic features of arid and semiarid regions is the intricately rilled and barren terrain known as **badlands** (Figure 18-37). In areas underlain by horizontal strata of shale and other clay formations that are poorly consolidated, overland flow after the occasional rains is an extremely effective erosive agent. Innumerable tiny rills that develop over the surface evolve into ravines and gullies that dissect the land in an extraordinarily

▶ **Figure 18-36** Delicate Arch in Utah's Arches National Park.

▲ **Figure 18-37** Badlands are characterized by innumerable ravines and gullies dissecting the land and forming a maze of low but very steep slopes. This scene is from Zabriskie Point, in Death Valley, California.

▲ **Figure 18-38** Badlands National Park in South Dakota exhibits the characteristic terrain of heavily dissected badlands topography.

detailed manner. A maze of short but very steep slopes is etched in a filigree of rills, gullies, and gorges, with a great many ridges, ledges, and other erosional remnants scattered throughout. Erosion is too rapid to permit soil to form or plants to grow, and so badlands are barren, lifeless wastelands of almost impassable terrain. They are found in scattered locations (most of them mercifully small) in every western state, the most famous areas being in Bryce Canyon National Park in southern Utah and in Badlands National Park in western South Dakota (Figure 18-38).

Chapter 18   LEARNING REVIEW

After studying this chapter, you should be able to answer the following questions. Key terms from each text section are shown in **bold type**. Definitions for key terms are also found in the glossary at the back of the book.

KEY TERMS AND CONCEPTS

A Specialized Environment (*p. 515*)

1. List several ways in which topographic development in arid lands is different from humid regions.
2. What is meant by an impermeable surface, and how does such a surface influence the runoff from rainfall in a desert?
3. What is a basin of interior drainage?

Running Water in Waterless Regions (*p. 517*)

4. What is the difference between an **ephemeral stream** and an **exotic stream** in a desert?
5. What is a **playa** and why does one form?
6. What is the difference between a playa and a **salina**?

7. Why is a desert lake in a basin of interior drainage likely to be a **saline lake**?
8. Explain the concept of **differential weathering and erosion**.
9. Describe the formation of an **inselberg**.
10. What is the difference between **pediment** and **piedmont zone**?

The Work of the Wind (*p. 522*)

11. Contrast the **aeolian processes** of **deflation** and abrasion.
12. How does a **blowout** form?
13. What is a **ventifact** and how does one form?

14. Describe and explain the general cross section of an unanchored desert **sand dune**. Be sure to contrast the windward side with the **slip face** of the dune.
15. Explain the general shape and movement of **barchan** sand dunes.
16. How are **transverse dunes** different from **seif** dunes?
17. Under what circumstances do **star dunes** form?
18. Most **loess** is not found in arid regions; why is it discussed in this chapter?

Characteristic Desert Landscape Surfaces (*p. 529*)

19. Distinguish among **erg**, **reg**, and **hamada**.
20. Describe and explain the formation of **desert pavement** and **desert varnish**.

Basin-and-Range Landforms (*p. 530*)

21. What is an **alluvial fan** and why are they so prevalent in the basin-and-range desert area of North America?
22. How is a **bajada** different from an alluvial fan?

Mesa-and-Scarp Terrain (*p. 534*)

23. How does a **plateau** differ from a **mesa**?
24. Describe and explain the processes involved that can change a mesa into a **butte** or **pinnacle**.
25. What is distinctive about **badlands** terrain? How did it become that way?

STUDY QUESTIONS

1. Although there is very little rainfall in deserts, running water is still the most important process of erosion and deposition in arid environments. Describe and explain at least two special conditions in deserts that tend to increase the likelihood of fluvial erosion whenever it does rain.
2. Why are playas so flat and level?
3. Why are depositional features of alluvium so prominent in many desert regions?
4. Overall, how important is wind in the erosion of desert landforms?
5. Why are some playas in the basin-and-range desert so salty?
6. How does an alluvial fan differ from a delta?
7. Why are few deep stream channels cutting across basin floors in the basin-and-range desert?

EXERCISES

1. Assume that the dunes in a field of barchan sand dunes are moving at an average long-term rate of 30 meters (about 100 feet) a year:
   a. How long does it take a dune to move a distance of 500 meters? _____ years
   b. If one of the dunes is 10 meters wide, how many years does it take that dune to completely cross an abandoned 100-meter wide airport runway? _____ years
2. Today, the lowest part of Death Valley is near Badwater, an elevation of 86 meters (282 feet) below sea level. One of the abandoned shorelines, cut by waves when the basin was filled with water as a lake during the Pleistocene, is found at an elevation of 80 meters (262 feet) above sea level.
   a. Estimate the depth of this lake stand during the Pleistocene: _____ meters
   b. What factors might complicate calculating the true depth of the lake that left these shorelines?

Look again at the photograph of Death Valley at the beginning of the chapter (p. 514). What kind of landform is shown at the foot of the mountains in the foreground? How did it form? Why is this landform riddled with tiny stream channels? What kind of landform occupies the white area in the photograph? Its surface mostly consists of table salt (NaCl)—how did the salt come to be deposited in the bottom of Death Valley?

MasteringGeography™

Looking for additional review and test prep materials? Visit the Study Area in MasteringGeography™ to enhance your geographic literacy, spatial reasoning skills, and understanding of this chapter's content by accessing a variety of resources, including geoscience animations, MapMaster interactive maps, videos, RSS feeds, flashcards, web links, self-study quizzes, and an eText version of *McKnight's Physical Geography: A Landscape Appreciation.*

IN THE LONG HISTORY OF OUR PLANET, ICE AGES HAVE

occurred an unknown number of times. The cause or causes of the climate changes that led to these ice ages are still incompletely understood, a topic we discuss further at the end of the chapter. With one outstanding exception, however, much of the evidence of past glacial periods has been eradicated by subsequent geomorphic events, with the result that only the most recent ice age has influenced contemporary topography. Consequently, when referring to the Ice Age, capitalized, we usually mean this most recent ice age, which is the main feature of the geologic epoch known as the *Pleistocene*, a period that began about 2.5 million years ago and ended about 10,000 years ago.

In this chapter, we are concerned with Pleistocene events both because they significantly modified pre-Pleistocene topography and because their results are so thoroughly imprinted on many parts of the continental terrain today. Glacial processes are still at work, to be sure, but their importance is much less now than it was just a few thousand years ago simply because so much less glacial ice is present today.

As has been our approach for much of our study of geomorphology, this chapter largely focuses on processes—in this case, the erosional and depositional work of glacial ice—but unlike some aspects of landform study, here we can broadly generalize about global distribution patterns. The landforms resulting from continental glaciation conform quite closely to the clearly defined limits of continental ice sheets during the Pleistocene, and landforms from mountain glaciation can be found in almost all high mountain areas—even in the tropics.

As we first illustrated in Chapter 1, glaciers are clear-cut examples of open systems with inputs and outputs of both material and energy (see Figure 1-6). Moreover, now that we've discussed climate and many different aspects of the hydrologic cycle, we are in a position to understand the sometimes subtle ways that glaciers fit in with Earth systems—most importantly, how they are influenced by the changing energy balance associated with contemporary climate change.

As you study this chapter, think about these key questions:

- **What are the two main types of glaciers?**
- **How is the extent of glaciers today different from what it was at the peak of the Pleistocene glaciations?**
- **How do glaciers form and move?**
- **How do glaciers erode, transport, and deposit rock?**
- **What landforms are produced by the erosion, deposition, and meltwater of continental ice sheets?**
- **What landforms are produced by the erosion and deposition of mountain glaciers?**
- **How can glacial conditions affect the landscape beyond the margin of the ice?**
- **What are some of the likely causes of the Pleistocene glaciations?**

Seeing Geographically

The Barnard Glacier in Wrangell–St. Elias National Park, Alaska. How many different glaciers have joined to form the main glacier as it flows off the area of the photograph in the foreground? What pattern do you see on the glacier that is a result of tributaries joining the main glacier? What do you see in the photograph that helps you define what a glacier is and explain how a glacier works?

The Impact of Glaciers on the Landscape

Wherever glaciers have developed, they have had a significant impact on the landscape simply because moving ice grinds away almost anything in its path: most soil is carried away, and bedrock is polished, scraped, gouged, plucked, and abraded. Moreover, the rock that is picked up is eventually deposited in a new location, further changing the shape of the terrain. In short, preglacial topography is significantly reshaped.

Perhaps 7 percent of all contemporary erosion and transportation of rock debris on the continents is accomplished by glaciers. This is a small amount in comparison with fluvial erosion, to be sure, but considering how small a land area is covered by glacial ice today, it is clear that glaciers make a significant contribution to continental denudation.

Glaciation modifies flat landscapes greatly, with the result that postglacial slope, drainage, and surficial material are likely to be totally different from what they were before the glacier passed by. In mountainous areas, the metamorphosis of the landscape may be less complete, but the topography is often deepened and steepened, and in many places rounded, by glacial action.

TYPES OF GLACIERS

A glacier is more than a block of ice filling up a mountain valley or resting on a continental plain; it is a finely tuned environmental system with a delicately balanced nourishment budget. Although glacial ice behaves in similar fashion wherever it accumulates, its pattern of movement and its effect on topographic shaping can vary considerably depending on the quantity of ice involved and particularly on the environment. These variations are best understood by first considering the different types of glaciers: *mountain glaciers* and *continental ice sheets*.

Mountain Glaciers

In a few high-mountain areas today, ice accumulates in an unconfined sheet that may cover a few hundred or few thousand square kilometers, submerging all the underlying topography except perhaps for some protruding pinnacles called *nunataks*. Such **highland icefields** are notable in parts of the high country of western Canada and southern Alaska and on various Arctic islands (particularly Iceland). Their outlets are often tongues of ice that travel down valleys in the mountains and so are called **valley glaciers** (Figure 19-1). If the leading edge of a valley glacier reaches a flat area and so escapes from the confines of its valley walls, it is called a *piedmont glacier* (Figure 19-2).

Sometimes the term **alpine glacier** is used to describe glaciers that develop individually, high in the mountains rather than as part of a broad icefield, usually at the heads of valleys. Very small alpine glaciers confined to the basins where they originate are called **cirque glaciers** (because the basin is called a *cirque*, as we shall see later in the chapter). Normally, however, alpine glaciers spill out of their originating basins and flow downvalley as long, narrow valley glaciers. Occasionally they extend to the mouth of the valley and become piedmont glaciers.

Continental Ice Sheets

Glaciers that form in nonmountainous areas of the continents are called **continental ice sheets**. During the Pleistocene these were vast blankets of ice that completely inundated the underlying terrain to depths of hundreds or even thousands of meters. Because of their immense size, ice sheets have been the most significant agents of glaciation across the land surface. Only two exist today,

◄ **Figure 19-1** Mountain glaciers in southeastern Alaska near Skagway. A half-dozen small valley glaciers in the high country have united to form the very large Davidson Glacier, which extends off the bottom of the photo.

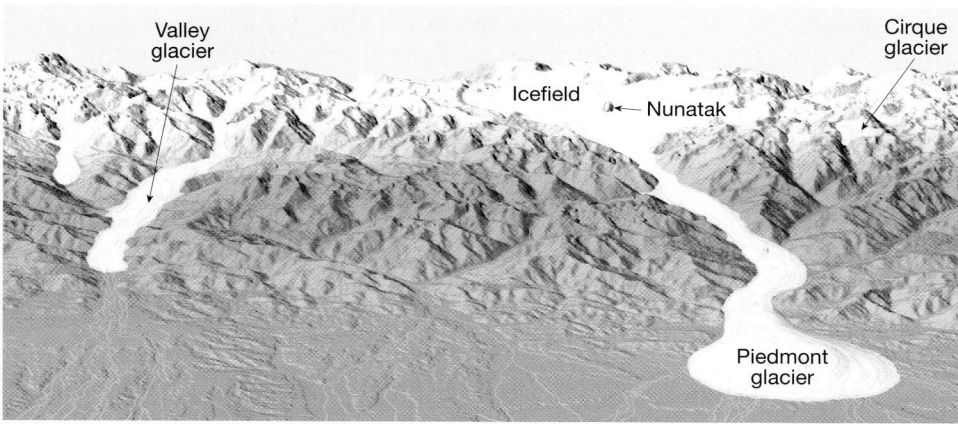

◀ **Figure 19-2** Types of mountain glaciers. Valley and piedmont glaciers can originate in a highland icefield, or when an alpine glacier overflows its cirque and flows downvalley. Nunataks are pinnacles rising above the ice of a highland icefield.

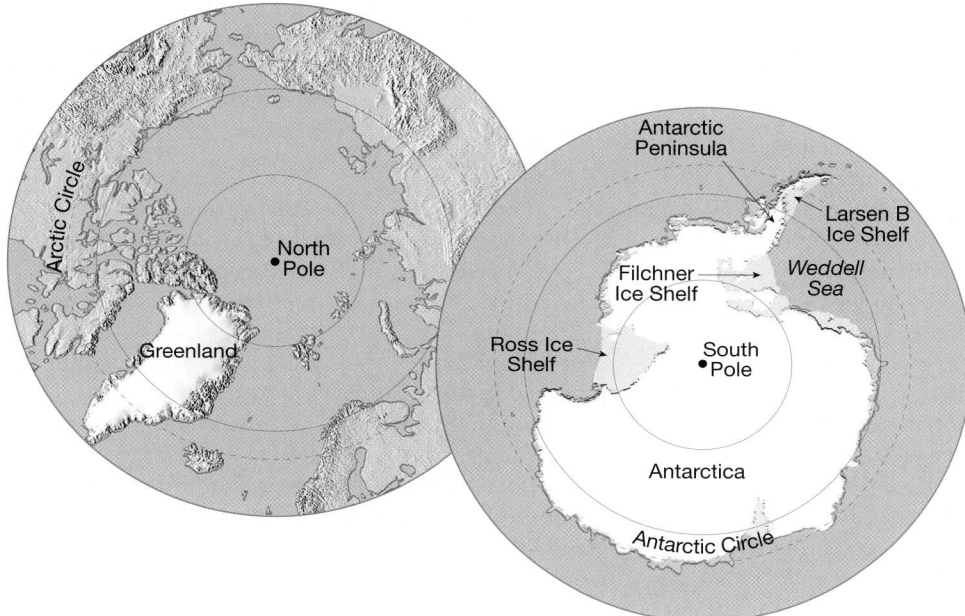

◀ **Figure 19-3** Current continental ice sheets in the Arctic and Antarctic.

in Antarctica and Greenland (Figure 19-3). The ice in an ice sheet accumulates to great depths in the interior of the sheet but is much thinner at the outer edges. Around the margin of the sheet, some long tongues of ice, called *outlet glaciers*, extend between rimming hills to the sea. In other places, the ice reaches the ocean along a massive front, where it sometimes projects out over the sea as an *ice shelf*

(Figure 19-4). As we saw in Chapter 9, great chunks of ice frequently break off, both from the ice shelves and from the ends of outlet glaciers, fall into the sea, and float away. These huge floating ice masses are *icebergs*.

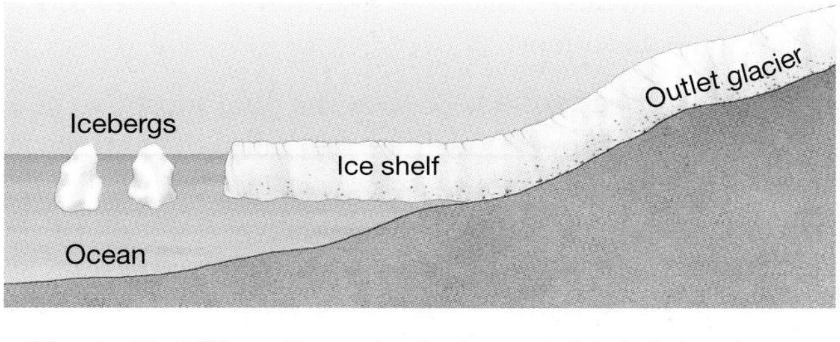

Learning Check 19-1   How are highland ice fields and continental ice sheets similar? How are they different? **(Answer on p. AK-5)**

GLACIATIONS PAST AND PRESENT

The amount of glacial ice on Earth's surface has varied remarkably over the last few million years, with periods of accumulation interspersed with periods of melting and times of ice advance alternating with times of ice retreat. A great deal of secondary evidence was left behind by the moving and melting ice, and scientists have been remarkably insightful in piecing together the chronology of past glaciations. Nevertheless, the record is incomplete and

▲ **Figure 19-4** When either an ice sheet or an outlet glacier reaches the ocean, some of the ice may extend out over the water as an ice shelf. Icebergs form when the hanging ice of the shelf breaks off and floats away, a process called *calving*.

often approximate. As is to be expected, the more recent events are best documented; the further one delves into the past, the murkier the evidence becomes.

Pleistocene Glaciation  FG5, FG6

The dominant environmental characteristic of the Pleistocene was the cooling of high-latitude and high-elevation areas, so that a vast amount of ice accumulated in many places. However, the epoch was by no means universally icy. During several lengthy periods, most or all of the ice melted, only to be followed by intervals of ice accumulation. In broad terms, the Pleistocene consisted of an alternation of *glacial* periods (times of ice accumulation) and *interglacial* periods (times of ice retreat). Current evidence suggests at least 18 or 19 glacial episodes took place during the Pleistocene.

Animation
End of the
Last Ice Age

Dating the Ice Age: The precise timing of the **Pleistocene Epoch** (see Figure 13-23) is still subject to debate. Current estimates define the start of the Pleistocene as 2.59 million years ago, but geochronologists now recognize that the glaciations began even earlier. Evidence suggests, for example, that Antarctica was covered by an ice cap similar in size to today's as long ago as perhaps 10 million years. The most recent findings tell us that by the start of the Pleistocene, the "amplitude" of climate fluctuations—from glacial period to interglacial period—had increased and some parts of the Northern Hemisphere were covered by glaciers.

New evidence has also changed the date of the close of the Pleistocene. Although the end of the Pleistocene is now set at 11,700 years ago, evidence suggests that some of the Pleistocene glaciers were still retreating as recently as 9000 years ago. Even this most recent estimate for the close date cannot be cast in stone, however, because the Ice Age may not yet have ended at all, a possibility we consider later in the chapter. For now, let us just say that, to the best of present knowledge, the Pleistocene Epoch occupied almost all of the most recent two and a half million years of Earth's history.

The end of the Pleistocene Epoch coincided with the conclusion of what is known in North America as the "Wisconsin" glacial stage (known as the "Würm" in the Alps), approximately 11,000 years ago. The period since then is identified as the *Holocene Epoch*. Conceptually, then, the Holocene is either a postglacial epoch or the latest in a series of interglacial interludes.

Extent of Pleistocene Glaciations: At its maximum Pleistocene extent, ice covered one-third of the total land area of Earth—nearly 47,000,000 square kilometers (19 million square miles), as Figure 19-5 shows. Ice thickness varied and can be estimated only roughly, but we do know that in some areas it reached a depth of several thousands of meters.

- The greatest total area of ice-covered land was in North America. The *Laurentide* ice, which covered most of Canada and a considerable portion of the northeastern United States, was the most extensive Pleistocene ice mass; its area was slightly larger than that of the present glacier covering Antarctica. It extended southward into the United States to approximately the present location of Long Island, the Ohio River, and the Missouri River.

Most of western Canada and much of Alaska were covered by an interconnecting network of smaller glaciers. For reasons we do not fully understand, however, a small area in northwestern Canada as well as extensive portions of northern and western Alaska were never glaciated during the Pleistocene. Moreover, a small area (29,000 square kilometers, 11,200 square miles) in southwestern Wisconsin and parts of three adjoining states was also left uncovered, as Figure 19-5b shows. This area, referred to as the *Driftless Area*, was apparently never completely surrounded by ice; rather, ice encroached first on one side during one glacial advance and then on the other side during a different advance.

- More than half of Europe was overlain by ice during the Pleistocene (Figure 19-5c). Asia was less extensively covered, presumably because in much of its subarctic portion there was not enough precipitation for the ice to last. Nevertheless, ice covered much of Siberia, and extensive glaciation occurred in most Eurasian mountain ranges.

- In the Southern Hemisphere, Antarctic ice was only slightly more extensive than it is today, a large ice complex covered southernmost South America, and the South Island of New Zealand was largely covered with ice. Other high mountain areas all over the world—in central Africa, New Guinea, Hawai'i—experienced more limited glaciation.

Learning Check 19-2 **Describe the extent of glaciation during the peak of the Pleistocene glaciations.**

Indirect Effects of Pleistocene Glaciations

The accumulation of ice and the movement and melting of the resulting glaciers had an enormous effect on topography and drainage, a topic we discuss in detail shortly. In addition, however, there were several indirect effects of Pleistocene glaciations:

Periglacial processes: Beyond the outermost extent of ice advance is an area of indefinite size called the **periglacial zone**, which was never touched by glacial ice but where indirect influence of the ice was felt. The most important periglacial processes were the erosion and deposition done by the prodigious amounts of meltwater released as the glaciers melted. Also important were frost weathering caused by the low temperatures in the periglacial zone and the associated *solifluction* of frozen subsoil (see Chapter 15 for a discussion of solifluction). It is estimated that periglacial conditions

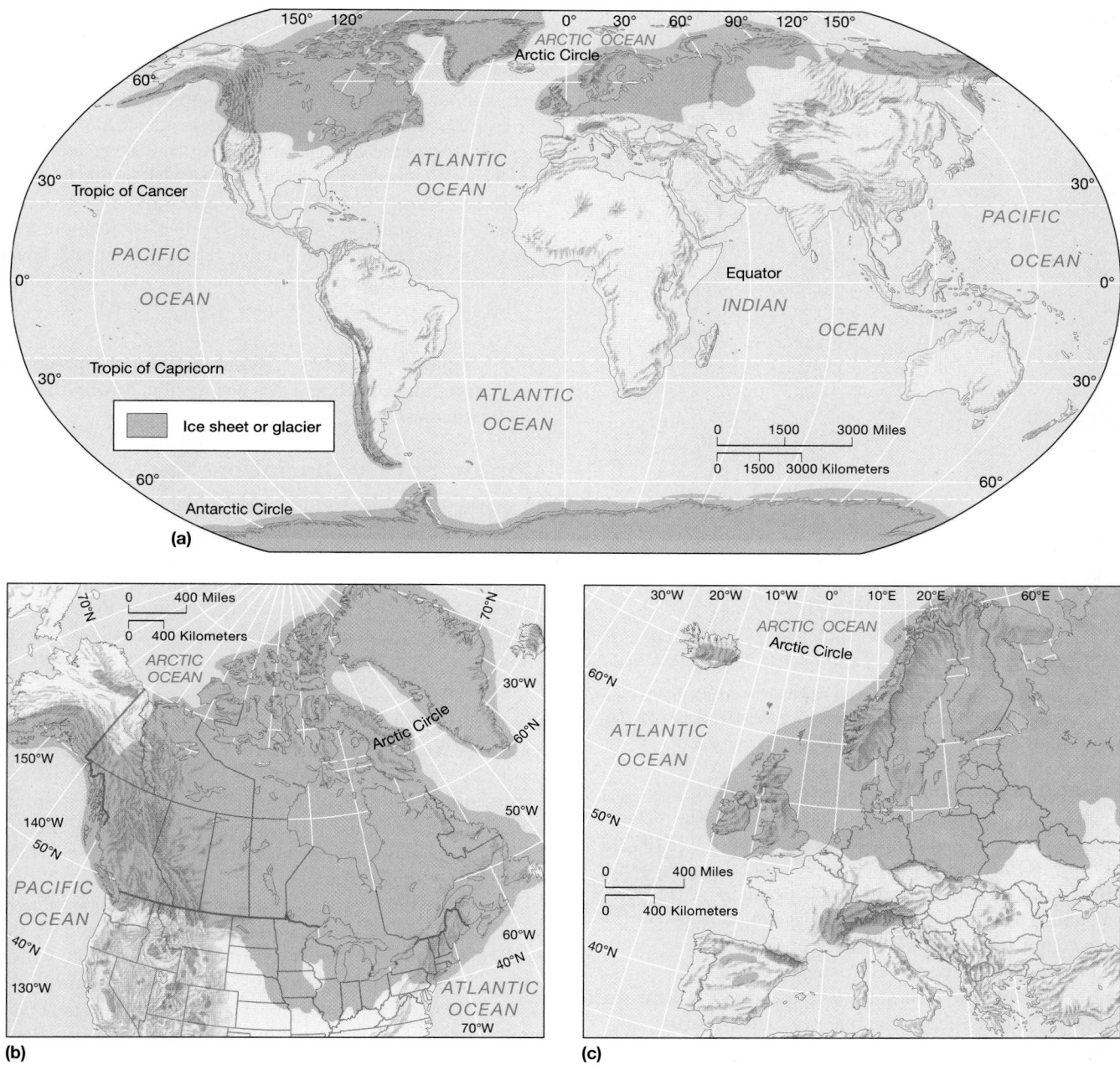

▲ **Figure 19-5** The maximum extent of Pleistocene glaciation: (a) worldwide; (b) in North America; (c) in western Eurasia.

extended over more than 20 percent of Earth's land area. (Periglacial landforms are discussed later in this chapter.)

Sea-level changes: The buildup of ice on the continents meant that less water was available to drain from the continents into the oceans, a condition that resulted in a worldwide lowering of sea level during every episode of glacial advance; when the glaciers retreated, sea level would again rise as meltwater returned to the oceans. At the peak of the Pleistocene glaciations, global sea level was about 130 meters (430 feet) lower than it is today. These fluctuations

in the amount of ocean water caused a significant difference in drainage patterns and topographic development on seashores and coastal plains (the influence of Pleistocene sea level changes on coastal topography will be discussed in Chapter 20). At the peak of the Pleistocene glaciations, the Bering Strait between present-day Alaska and Russia was a dry land bridge, allowing the migration of both animals and humans (see Figure 11-24).

Learning Check 19-3 **Why did sea level fluctuate during the Pleistocene?**

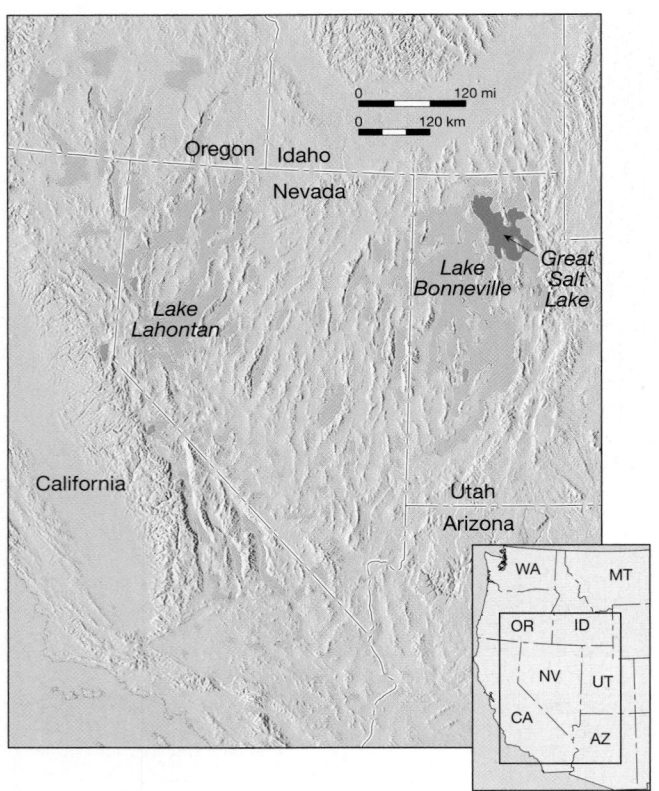

▲ **Figure 19-6** Pleistocene lakes of the intermontane region of the United States. Today's Great Salt Lake (Utah) is shown outlined in blue inside the boundaries of the ancestral Lake Bonneville.

Crustal depression: The enormous weight of accumulated ice on the continents caused portions of Earth's crust to sink, in some cases by as much as 1200 meters (4000 feet). After the ice melted, the crust slowly began to rebound. This *isostatic adjustment* has not yet been completed, and some portions of Canada and northern Europe are still rising as much as 20 centimeters (8 inches) per decade. Isostasy is discussed in detail in Chapter 13 (for example, see Figure 13-19).

Animation
Isostasy

Pluvial (increased rain) developments: During the Pleistocene glaciations, there was, on almost all areas of the continents, a considerable increase in the amount of moisture available. This increase was caused by a combination of meltwater runoff, increased precipitation, and decreased evaporation. A prominent result of these **pluvial effects** was the creation of many lakes in areas where none had previously existed. Most of these lakes have subsequently been drained or significantly reduced in size, but they have left lasting imprints on the landscape. These **Pleistocene lakes** in the western part of the United States are shown in Figure 19-6. The present-day Great Salt Lake in Utah is a tiny remnant of a much larger Pleistocene lake known as Lake Bonneville, and today's Bonneville Salt Flats were once the floor of this enormous lake.

Learning Check 19-4 **What explains the presence of large lakes, such as Lake Bonneville, during the Pleistocene?**

Contemporary Glaciation FG1

In marked contrast to Pleistocene glaciation, the extent of ice covering the continental surfaces today is very limited (Figure 19-7). About 10 percent of Earth's land surface—some 15 million square kilometers (6 million square miles)—is covered with ice today, but more than 96 percent of that total is in Antarctica and Greenland. Something more than two-thirds of all the world's freshwater is at this moment frozen into glacial ice.

Antarctic Ice Sheet: Antarctic ice is by far the most extensive ice sheet on Earth (see Figure 19-3). At present, about 98 percent of its surface is covered with glacial ice, representing almost 90 percent of the world's land–ice total. This ice is more than 4000 meters (13,000 feet) thick in some places and more than 1500 meters (5000 feet) thick over most of the continent.

Physically the continent and its ice sheets can be thought of as consisting of two unequal sections separated by the wide upland belt of the Transantarctic Mountains, which extend for some 4000 kilometers (2500 miles; Figure 19-8). West Antarctica, the smaller of the two sections, is generally mountainous. It contains, however, a few interior valleys that are curiously ice free. The "Dry Valleys" area consists of about 3900 square kilometers (1500 square miles) which,

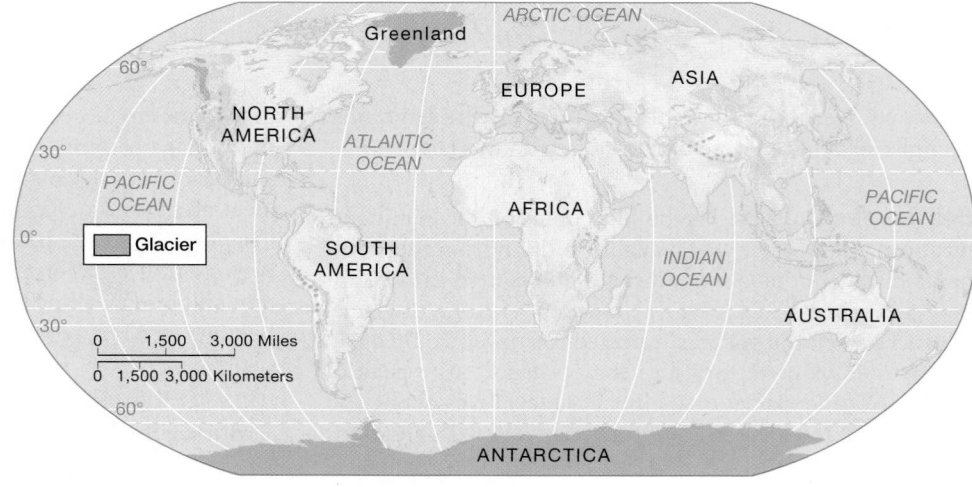

▶ **Figure 19-7** World distribution of glacial ice today.

◀ **Figure 19-8** The Transantarctic Mountains separate the ice sheets of West and East Antarctica.

because winds blast away snow and keep precipitation out, does not build ice. The three major parallel valleys contain several large lakes, a number of ponds, and a river that flows for one or two months each year.

If West Antarctica were to lose its ice, it would appear as a considerable number of scattered islands. East Antarctica is more extensive, and its subglacial relief is less varied, appearing to be largely a broad plateau with scattered mountains. The ice is considerably deeper in West Antarctica, and the surface of the ice is generally at a greater elevation than in the eastern section. Most of the surface of West Antarctica exceeds 2.4 kilometers (8000 feet) above sea level, and a considerable portion is more than 3 kilometers (10,000 feet) in altitude.

Greenland Ice Sheet: Greenland ice is much less extensive—1,740,000 square kilometers (670,000 square miles)—but still of impressive size (see Figure 19-3). Elsewhere, there are only relatively small ice masses on certain islands in the Canadian Arctic, Iceland, and some of the islands north of Europe.

Mountain Glaciers: Other than the two major ice caps, the remainder of the world's present-day glaciers are concentrated in high mountain areas. In the conterminous United States, most glaciers are in the Pacific Northwest, and more than half of these are in the North Cascade Mountains of Washington (Figure 19-9). In Alaska, there are 75,000 square kilometers (29,000 square miles) of glacial ice,

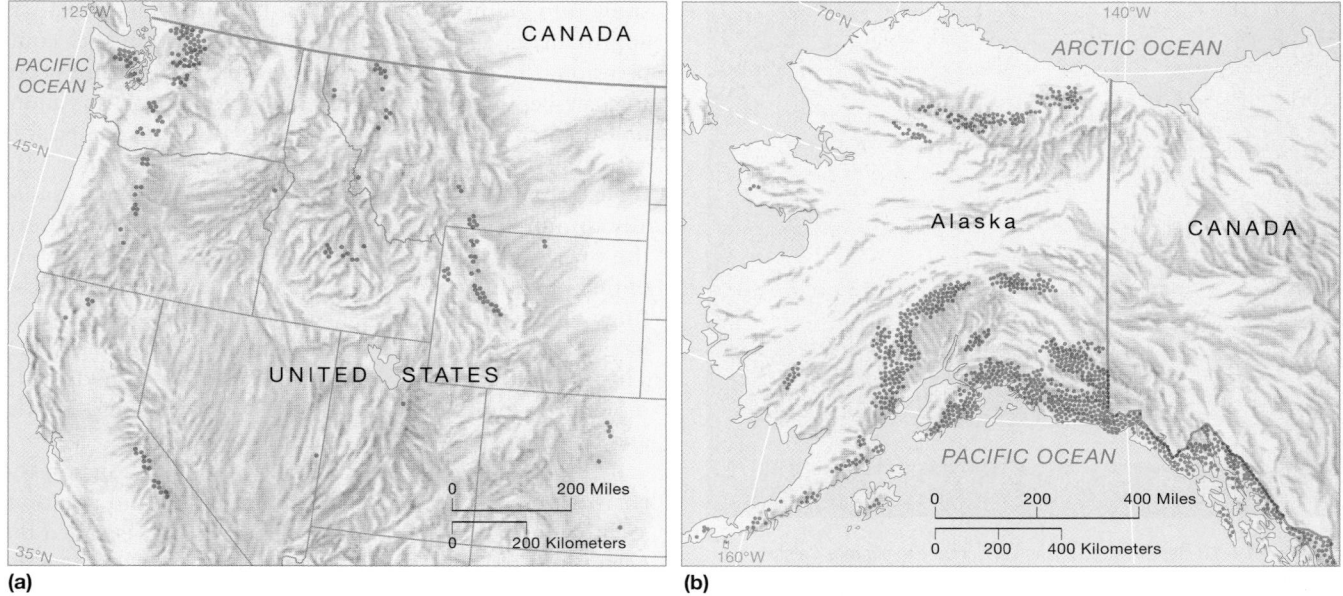

(a)   (b)

▲ **Figure 19-9** The location of contemporary glaciers and perennial snowfields in (a) the conterminous western United States and (b) Alaska. The dots on the map considerably exaggerate the size of each glacier.

amounting to about 5 percent of the total area of the state. The largest Alaskan glacier is the Bering Glacier, near Cordova, which covers 5175 square kilometers (2000 square miles) and is more than twice the size of Rhode Island.

Climate Change and Contemporary Glaciation: As we saw in earlier chapters, global climate change is significantly influencing the extent of contemporary glaciation. The retreat of the Arctic sea ice pack and the loss of mass of Greenland's ice sheets is indicative of the higher temperatures experienced in the high latitudes of the Northern Hemisphere over the last 30 years (for example, see the box, "Focus: Signs of Climate Change in the Arctic" in Chapter 8). As we will see later in this chapter ("Focus: Shrinking Glaciers"), glaciers are sensitive indicators of environmental change—reflecting variations in both temperature and precipitation.

Perhaps nowhere today is the attention of scientists focused more keenly on contemporary ice sheets than in Antarctica. Not only does the Antarctic ice sheet provide invaluable information about Earth's past climate (see Chapter 8), but changes in the ice sheet today are pointing to a contemporary climate shift, as discussed in the box, "People and the Environment: Disintegration of Antarctic Ice Shelves."

A NASA study released in January 2009 showed that Antarctica has been warming at a rate of about 0.12°C (0.22°F) per decade over the last 50 years—much faster than scientists thought even a few years ago. Further, West Antarctica has been warming much faster than the continent as a whole (Figure 19-10). This warming is not only leading to the breakup of Antarctic ice shelves, but to higher flow rates of outlet glaciers as well.

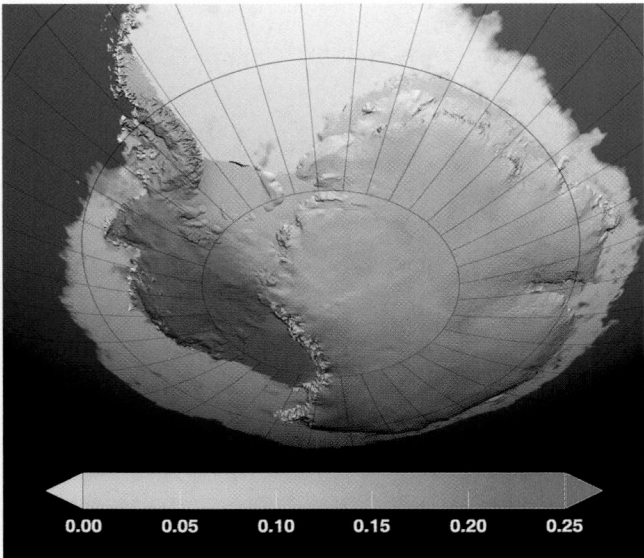

▲ **Figure 19-10** Temperature change per decade in degrees Celsius in Antarctica between 1957 and 2006. West Antarctica, shown in orange, has warmed more than the rest of the continent. The data were acquired from land and satellite measurements, and overlain on a digital elevation model of the continent.

Learning Check 19-5 **How is climate change affecting glaciers today?**

GLACIER FORMATION AND MOVEMENT

Snow falls and ice accumulates in many parts of the world, but glaciers do not always develop from these events. Glaciers require certain circumstances to form and then depend on just the right combination of temperature and moisture to survive. A slight warming or drying trend for a few decades can cause even the most extensive ice sheet to disappear.

A glacier may begin to develop when there is a net year-to-year accumulation of snow—that is, when over a period of years the amount of snow that falls in a winter is greater than the amount that melts the following summer. The snow that falls the next winter weighs down on the old snow and turns it to ice. After many years of such accumulation, the ice mass begins to move under the pull of gravity—and a glacier is formed. The persistence of any glacier depends on the balance between **accumulation** (addition of ice by incorporation of snow) and **ablation** (wastage of ice through melting and sublimation).

Changing Snow to Ice

Snow is not merely frozen water; rather, it is a substance that has crystallized directly from water vapor in the atmosphere and floats to Earth as lacy, hexagonal crystals that are only about one-tenth as dense as liquid water. Sooner or later (within a few hours if the temperature is near freezing, but only over a period of years in very cold situations), crystalline snow is compressed by overlying snow into granular form, and in the process its density is approximately doubled. With more time and further compression, the granules are packed more closely and begin to coalesce, the density increasing steadily until it is about half the density of water (Figure 19-11). This material is called **névé or** *firn*. As time passes, the pore spaces with their trapped air among the whitish névé crystals gradually diminish as the air is squeezed out by the weight of the overlying snow; the density approaches 90 percent of that of liquid water, and the material takes on the bluish tinge of glacial ice (dense glacial ice absorbs most wavelengths of visible light, but reflects and scatters blue light). This ice continues to change, although very slowly, with more air being forced out, the density increasing slightly, and the crystals increasing in size.

Every glacier can be divided into two portions on the basis of the balance between accumulation and ablation, as shown in Figure 19-12. The upper portion is called the **accumulation zone** because here the amount of new ice from snowfall added each year exceeds the amount lost by melting and sublimation. The lower portion is called the **ablation zone** because here the amount of new ice added

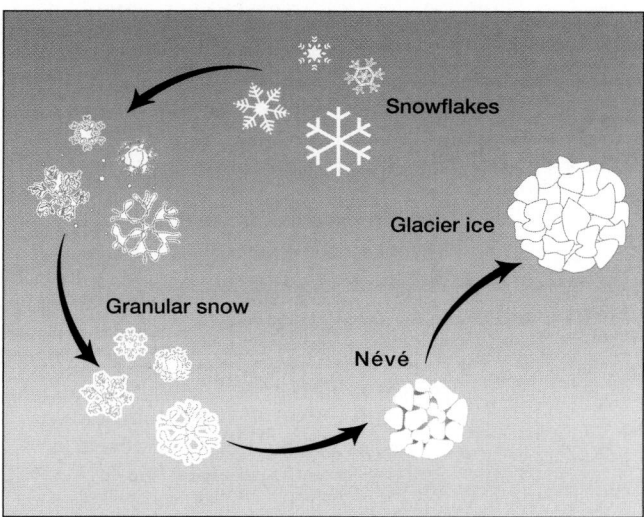

▲ **Figure 19-11** Snow is changed to ice by compression and coalescence, following a sequence from snowflake to granular snow to névé to glacial ice.

each year is less than the amount lost. Separating the two zones is a theoretical **equilibrium line**, along which accumulation exactly balances ablation.

Learning Check 19-6   **Explain what conditions are necessary for a glacier to form.**

Glacier Movement

Despite the fact that glaciers are often likened to rivers of ice, there is little similarity between liquid flow and glacial movement.

Animation
Flow of Ice
within a Glacier

We usually think of ice as being a brittle substance that breaks rather than bends and resists any sort of deformation. This is generally true for surface ice, as evidenced by the cracks and *crevasses* that often appear at the surface of a glacier. However, ice under considerable confining pressure, as below the surface of a glacier, behaves quite differently: it deforms rather than breaks. Moreover, partial melting, due to the stresses within and the pressure at the bottom of the glacier, aids movement because the meltwater sinks to the bottom of the glacier and becomes a slippery layer on which the glacier can slide.

Plastic Flow of Ice: When a mass of ice attains a thickness of about 50 meters (165 feet)—less on steep slopes—the **plastic flow of ice** begins in response to the overlying weight. The entire mass does not move uniformly; rather, there is an oozing outward from around the edge of an ice sheet or downvalley from the toe (the end) of an alpine glacier.

Basal Slip: A second kind of glacier movement is **basal slip** at the bottom of the glacier, in which the entire mass slides over its bed on a lubricating film of water. The glacier

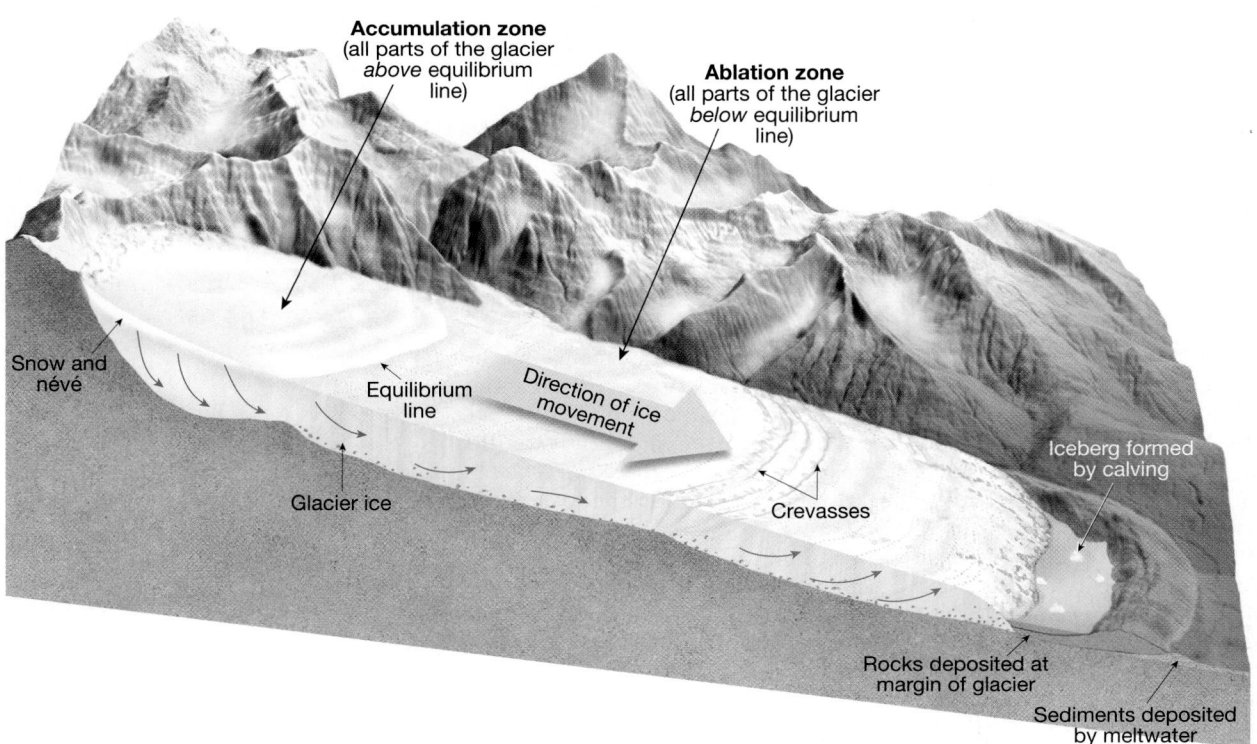

▲ **Figure 19-12** Cross section through an alpine glacier. The upper portion is an area of net ice accumulation. Below the equilibrium line there is more ablation than accumulation.

Disintegration of Antarctic Ice Shelves

Despite its remoteness, Antarctica exerts a prominent influence on the world's environment—global sea level, oceanic temperature, ocean nutrient content, and patterns of atmospheric circulation all are affected by conditions in Antarctica. At the same time, the global environment exerts its own influence on the conditions in Antarctica. Over the last half century, average temperatures in the Antarctic have increased by about 2.5°C (4.5°F)—much more than the average increase in temperature worldwide. As a consequence, Antarctic ice has been undergoing changes.

Although the complete melting of the Antarctic ice cap is unlikely, the long-term equilibrium between accumulation and wastage of the ice does appear to be changing significantly as a response to higher global temperatures. Some of the most dramatic changes are occurring in Antarctica's ice shelves.

Antarctic Ice Shelves: The Antarctic ice sheets flow outward from the interior of the continent in nearly all directions toward the sea, which means that icebergs are being calved (broken off) into the sea more or less continuously around the perimeter of the continent. Some of these icebergs originate through outlet glaciers, but many are broken off from ice shelves. There are several of these great plates of floating ice, particularly in West Antarctica, with the Ross Ice Shelf being the largest (520,000 square kilometers or 200,000 square miles; see Figure 19-3). On the Antarctic Peninsula, a number of smaller ice shelves are found, such as the Larsen Ice Shelves on the eastern side of the peninsula (Figure 19-A).

Over the last few years, large sections of the ice shelves along the Antarctic Peninsula have disintegrated—more than 8000 square kilometers (3100 square miles) of ice shelf have disappeared since 1993. In 1995 the Larsen-A Ice Shelf simply collapsed and disappeared. In 2002, the Larsen-B Ice Shelf collapsed in little more than a month (Figure 19-B). The Wilkins Ice Shelf began to disintegrate in February 2008; and in January 2012, a piece of floating ice the size of Rhode Island broke off the Ronne-Filchner Ice Shelf.

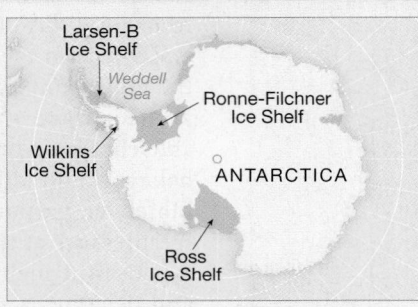

▲ **Figure 19-A** Portions of Antarctic ice shelves, such as the Larsen-B, Wilkins, and Ronne-Filchner, have disintegrated in recent years.

January 31, 2002   March 7, 2002

▲ **Figure 19-B** The Larsen-B Ice Shelf in Antarctica began to collapse in January 2002, as shown in these images taken by NASA's Terra satellite. On January 31, 2002, blue "melt ponds" are seen on top of the ice shelf. By March 7, 2002, the ice shelf had disintegrated. The blue area shows the shattered floating ice from the shelf.

Warm Currents Melting Ice Shelves: A 2012 study showed that many West Antarctica ice shelves are losing mass primarily because warm ocean currents are melting the ice from below—a process known as *basal melt* (Figure 19-C). Using satellite data gathered between 2003 and 2008, researchers measured the loss of ice thickness not associated with variations in natural ice accumulation and compaction, and they concluded that changes in wind and ocean currents are directing warmer water beneath the ice shelves.

Although the loss of ice shelves does not raise global sea level (for the same reason that a floating ice cube does not raise the level of the water in a glass as it melts), changing ice shelves can trigger a change in the flow of land-based ice off the continent. To a certain extent, an intact ice shelf holds back the flow of continental ice into the ocean. Once an ice shelf is gone, the continental ice may flow faster into the ocean, and with land-based ice entering the ocean at a greater rate than before, sea level will rise. For example, since the breakup of the Larsen-B shelf, the flow rate of glaciers feeding it accelerated by as much as six times their previous rate.

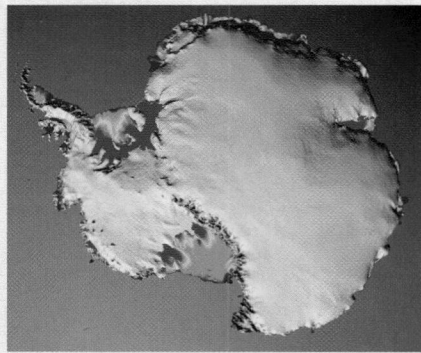

▲ **Figure 19-C** Thinning of Antarctic ice shelves from below by warm ocean currents between 2003 and 2008. Red indicates thicker ice, and blue indicates thinner ice.

more or less molds itself to the shape of the terrain over which it is riding.

Rates of Movement: Glaciers usually move very slowly; indeed, the adjective "glacial" is synonymous with "exceedingly slow." The movement of many glaciers can be measured in a few centimeters per day, although an advance of several meters per day would not be unusual, and extreme examples of nearly 30 meters (100 feet) in a 24-hour period have been recorded. Also, the flow is often erratic, with irregular pulsations and surges over a short span of time.

As might be expected, all parts of a glacier do not move at the same rate. The fastest-moving ice is that at and near the surface, with speed generally decreasing with depth. If the glacier is confined, the way a valley glacier is, for instance, the center of the surface ice moves faster than the sides, which is similar to streamflow patterns.

Glacier Flow versus Glacier Advance

In discussing glacier movement, it is important to distinguish between glacier *flow* and glacier *advance*. As long as a glacier exists, the ice in it is flowing, either laterally outward or downhill. This does not necessarily mean that the outer edge of the ice is advancing, however. The ice in a glacier always moves forward, but the outer margin of the glacier may or may not be advancing, depending on the balance between accumulation and ablation (Figure 19-13). Even in a retreating glacier (one whose outer margin is retracting toward its point of origin due to heavy ablation), the ice is flowing forward.

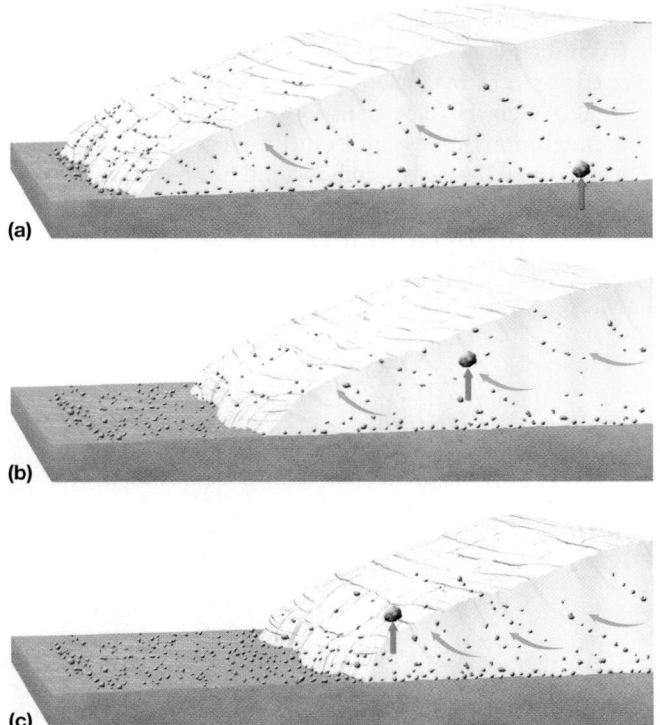

(a)

(b)

(c)

▲ **Figure 19-13** A flowing glacier is not necessarily an advancing glacier. In this sequential illustration, the front of the glacier is clearly retreating, but the ice continues to flow forward. The boulder marked by the red arrow illustrates the principle.

During wetter or cooler periods when there is a great accumulation of ice, a glacier can flow farther before it finally wastes away, and so the outer margin of the glacier advances. During warmer or drier periods when the rate of ablation is increased, the glacier continues to flow, but it wastes away sooner, and so the end or terminus of the glacier retreats.

Learning Check 19-7   **Why can a retreating glacier continue to erode and transport rock?**

THE EFFECTS OF GLACIERS

Animation: Glacial Processes

FG4, FG5

As glaciers move across a landscape, they can reshape the topography through the erosion, transportation, and deposition of rock.

Erosion by Glaciers

The amount of erosion caused by a glacier is roughly proportional to the thickness of the ice and its rate of flow. The depth of the erosion is limited in part by the structure and texture of the bedrock and in part by the relief of the terrain.

Glacial Plucking: The direct erosive power of moving ice is greater than that of flowing water but not remarkably so. As the slowly moving ice scrapes against bedrock, friction between rock and ice causes the lowermost ice to melt, and the layer of water created reduces the pressure on the rock. This water can refreeze around rocky protrusions, however, and the refrozen ice can exert a significant force as it is pushed by the ice behind it. Probably the most significant erosive work of glacial ice is accomplished by this **glacial plucking**. Rock fragments beneath the ice are grasped as meltwater refreezes in bedrock joints and fractures where frost wedging further loosens the rock. As the ice moves along, these particles are plucked out and dragged along. This action is particularly effective on leeward slopes (slopes facing away from the direction of ice movement) and in well-jointed bedrock.

Glacial Abrasion: Glaciers also erode by abrasion, in which the bedrock is worn down by the rock debris being dragged along in the moving ice. Abrasion mostly produces minor features, such as polished surfaces when the bedrock is of highly resistant material and striations (fine parallel indentations) and grooves (indentations deeper and larger than striations) in less resistant bedrock (Figure 19-14). Whereas plucking tends to roughen the underlying surface, abrasion tends to polish it and to dig striations and grooves.

Subglacial Meltwater Erosion: A third process also contributes to glacial erosion: Meltwater streams flowing below the glacier not only transport rock, they can erode smooth grooves and channels into the bedrock (Figure 19-15).

▲ **Figure 19-14** Glacial polish on granite in Yosemite National Park. The glaciers flowed from upper left to lower right.

In plains areas, the topography produced by glacial erosion may be inconspicuous. Prominences are smoothed and small hollows may be excavated, but the general appearance of the terrain changes little. In hilly areas, however, the effects of glacial erosion are much more notable. Mountains and ridges are sharpened, valleys are deepened and steepened and made more linear, and the entire landscape becomes more angular and rugged.

Learning Check 19-8 **Explain the process of glacial plucking.**

Transportation by Glaciers

Glaciers are extremely competent, as well as indiscriminate, in their ability to transport rock debris. They can move immense blocks of rock—the size of houses in some cases—for dozens or even hundreds of kilometers. Most of a glacier's load, however, is not such huge blocks but rather a heterogeneous collection of particles of all sizes, including finely ground rock material known as **glacial flour**.

Most of the material transported by continental glaciers is plucked or abraded from the underlying surface and so is carried along at the base of the ice. Thus, there is a narrow zone at the bottom of the glacier that is likely to be well armored by rock debris frozen into it, with most of the rest of the glacial ice relatively free of rock fragments.

With mountain glaciers, in addition to rock transported within the ice, some of the material is also transported on top of the ice, deposited by rockfall or other forms of mass wasting from the surrounding slopes. With at least some mountain glaciers, mass wasting may supply more rock debris to a glacier than that added by glacial erosion.

A glacier transports its load outward or downvalley at a variable speed. The rate of flow usually increases in summer and slows in winter but also depends on variations in ice accumulation and in the gradient of the underlying slopes.

Melt Streams: Another important aspect of transportation by glaciers is the role of flowing water on, in, and under the ice. During the warmer months, streams of meltwater normally flow along with the moving ice (Figure 19-16). Such streams may run along the surface of the glacier until they find cracks or crevasses into which to plunge—including steep drainage shafts in the ice called *moulins*—continuing their flow as a subglacial stream either within the ice or along the interface between glacier and bedrock. Wherever such streams flow, they transport rock debris, particularly smaller particles and glacial flour, providing an effective mechanism for shifting debris from the ice surface to a position within or at the bottom of the glacier. Further, where subglacial streams encounter finely ground rock along the bottom of a glacier, the lubricating effect can accelerate the flow of ice.

Even if a glacier is retreating, the debris inside it is still carried forward because of the ice flow taking place all through the glacier. The transport function of a glacier persists indefinitely unless and until the ice becomes so thin that subglacial obstacles, such as a hill, prevent further flow.

Deposition by Glaciers

Probably the major role of glaciers in landscape modification is to pick up rock from one area and take it to a

▶ **Figure 19-15** Grooves and striae near Cusco, Peru, caused by meltwater erosion below a glacier.

surface bedrock, leaving a relatively barren, rocky, gently undulating surface dotted with bodies of water. Much of the removed material was taken southward and deposited in the midwestern part of the United States, producing an extensive plains area of remarkably fertile soil. Thus, the legacy of Pleistocene ice sheets for the U.S. Midwest was the evolution of one of the largest areas of productive soils ever known, at the expense of central Canada, which was left impoverished of soil by those same glaciers. (On the other hand, many valuable Canadian mineral deposits were exposed when the glaciers removed soil and regolith.)

The general term for all material moved by glaciers is **drift**, a misnomer coined in the eighteenth century when it was believed that the vast debris deposits of the Northern Hemisphere were leftovers from biblical floods. Despite the erroneous thinking that led to the name, the term is still used today to refer to any material deposited by glaciers and/or their meltwater.

Direct Deposition by Glacial Ice: Rock debris deposited directly by moving or melting ice, with no meltwater redeposition involved, is given the more distinctive name **till** (Figure 19-17). Direct deposition by ice is usually the result of melting around the margin of an ice sheet or near the lower end of a mountain glacier, but it is also accomplished whenever debris is dropped on the ground beneath the ice, especially in the ablation area. In either case, the result is an unsorted and unstratified agglomeration of fragmented rock material. Most of the fragments are angular because they have been held in position while carried in the ice (and so had little opportunity to become rounded by frequent impact the way pebbles in a stream would) or were deposited on top of the ice by mass wasting.

Sometimes outsized boulders are deposited by a retreating glacier. Such enormous fragments, which may be very

▲ **Figure 19-16** Meltwater stream flowing over the surface of Athabasca Glacier in the Canadian Rockies.

distant region, where it is left in a fragmented and vastly changed form. This is clearly displayed in North America, where an extensive portion of central Canada has been glacially scoured of its soil, regolith, and much of its

▶ **Figure 19-17** Unsorted glacial till in a roadcut near Bridgeport, California.

▶ **Figure 19-18** A glacial erratic carried many kilometers before being deposited by a Pleistocene glacier near the Yorkshire Dales, England.

different from the local bedrock, are called **glacial erratics** (Figure 19-18).

Learning Check 19-9 How and why does a deposit of glacial till look different from a deposit of alluvium?

Secondary Deposition by Meltwater: Glacial stream runoff has several peculiarities—peak flows in midsummer, distinct day-and-night differences in volume, large silt content, and occasional floods—that set meltwater streams apart from other kinds of natural waterways. Much of the debris carried by glaciers is eventually deposited or redeposited by meltwater. In some cases, this is accomplished by subglacial streams issuing directly from the ice and carrying sedimentary material washed from positions in, on, or beneath the glacier. Much meltwater deposition, however, involves debris that was originally deposited by ice and subsequently picked up and redeposited by the meltwater well beyond the outer margin of the ice. Such **glaciofluvial deposition** occurs around the margins of all glaciers, as well as far out in some periglacial zones.

CONTINENTAL ICE SHEETS

Apart from the oceans and continents, continental ice sheets are the most extensive features ever to appear on the face of the planet. Their actions during the Pleistocene significantly reshaped both the terrain and the drainage of nearly one-fifth of the total surface area of the continents.

Development and Flow

Pleistocene ice sheets, with the exception of the one covering Antarctica, did not originate in the polar regions. Rather, they developed in subpolar and midlatitude locations and then spread outward in all directions, including poleward. Several (perhaps several dozen) centers of original ice accumulation have been identified. The accumulated snow/névé/ice eventually produced such a heavy weight that the ice began to flow outward from each center of accumulation.

The initial flow was channeled by the preexisting terrain along valleys and other low-lying areas, but in time the ice developed to such depths that it overrode almost all preglacial topography. In many places, it submerged even the highest points under thousands of meters of ice. Eventually the various ice sheets coalesced into only one, two, or three massive sheets on each continent. These vast ice sheets flowed and ebbed as the climate changed, always modifying the landscape with their enormous erosive power and the great masses of debris they deposited. The elaborate result was nothing less than a total reshaping of the land surface and a total rearrangement of the drainage pattern.

Erosion by Ice Sheets

Except in mountainous areas of great initial relief, the principal topography resulting from the erosion caused by an ice sheet is a gently undulating surface. The most conspicuous features are valley bottoms gouged and deepened by the moving ice. Such troughs are deepest where the preglacial valleys were oriented parallel to the direction of ice movement, particularly in areas of softer bedrock. A prime example of such development is the Finger Lakes District of central New York, where a set of parallel stream valleys was accentuated by glaciation into a group of long, narrow, deep lakes (Figure 19-19). Even where the preglacial valley was not oriented parallel to the direction of ice flow, however, glacial gouging and scooping normally produced a large number of shallow excavations that became lakes after the

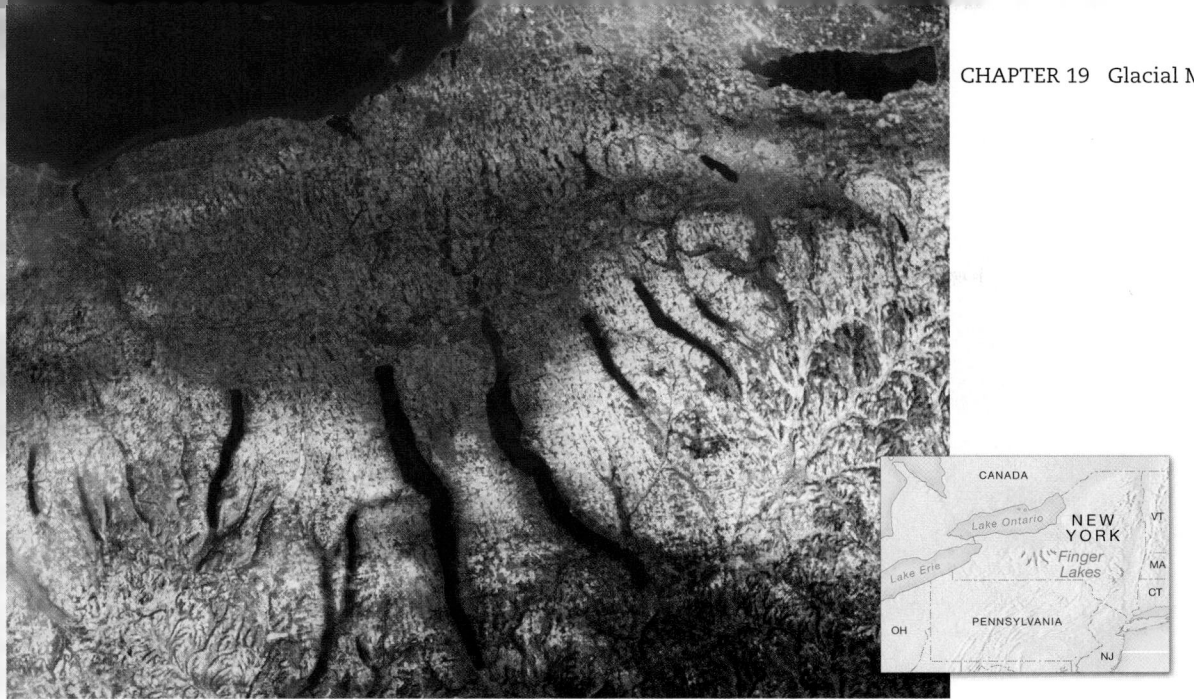

◀ **Figure 19-19** The Finger Lakes of upstate New York occupy glacial valleys that were accentuated by ice sheets moving from north–northwest to south–southeast. The large body of water at upper left is Lake Ontario. This photograph was taken from the International Space Station after a winter storm left a dusting of snow on the hills around the lakes.

ice disappeared. Indeed, the postglacial landscape in areas of ice-sheet erosion is notable for its profusion of lakes.

Roche Moutonnée: Hills are generally sheared off and rounded by the moving ice. A characteristic shape produced by both continental ice sheets and mountain glaciers is the **roche moutonnée**, which is often produced when a bedrock hill is overridden by moving ice (Figure 19-20).[1] The *stoss side* (facing in the direction from which the ice came) of a roche moutonnée is smoothly rounded and streamlined

[1]The origin of the French term *roche moutonnée* is unclear. It is often translated as "sheep's back," but some authorities believe it is based on a fancied resemblance to wavy wigs that were fashionable in France in the late 1700s and were known as *moutonnées* because they were pomaded with mutton tallow.

by grinding abrasion as the ice rides up the slope, but the lee side (facing away from the direction from which the ice came) is shaped largely by plucking, which produces a steeper and more irregular slope.

The postglacial landscape produced by ice sheets is one of relatively low relief but not absolute flatness. The principal terrain elements are ice-scoured rocky knobs and scooped-out depressions. Soil and weathered materials are largely absent, with bare rock and lakes dominating the surface. Stream patterns are erratic and inadequately developed because the preglacial drainage system was deranged by ice erosion. Once eroded by the passing ice sheet, however, most of this landscape was subjected to further modification

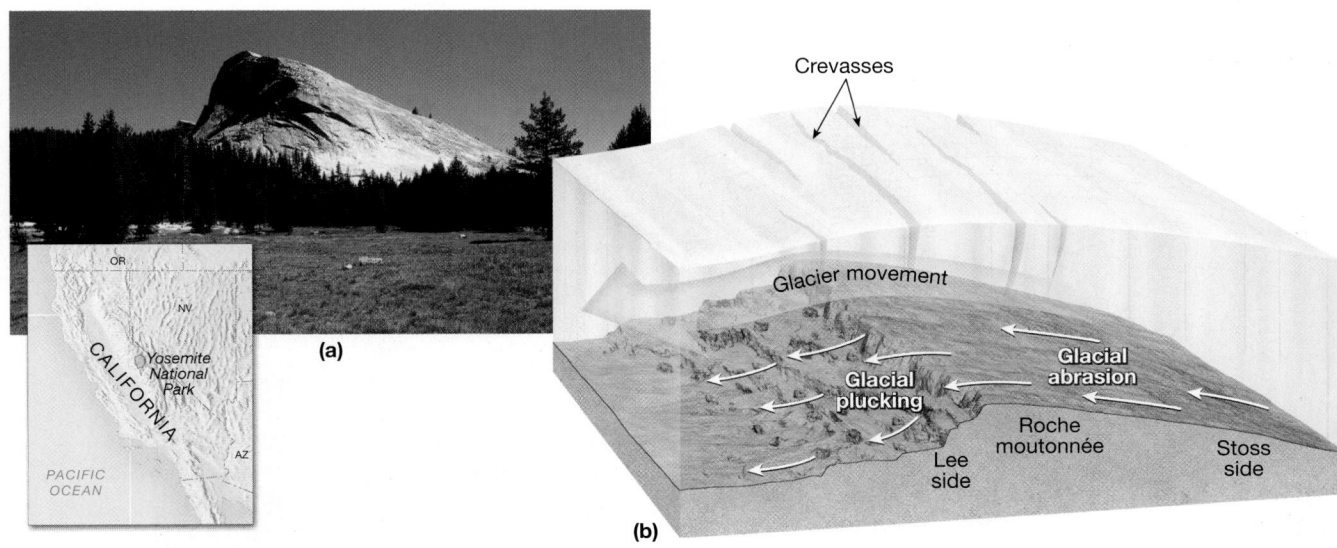

▲ **Figure 19-20** (a) Lembert Dome in Yosemite National Park is an example of a roche moutonnée. The glaciers moved from right to left (from east to west) across this granite dome. (b) The formation of a roche moutonnée. The glacier rides over a resistant bedrock surface, smoothing the stoss side by abrasion and steepening the lee side by plucking. When the ice has melted, an asymmetrical hill is the result.

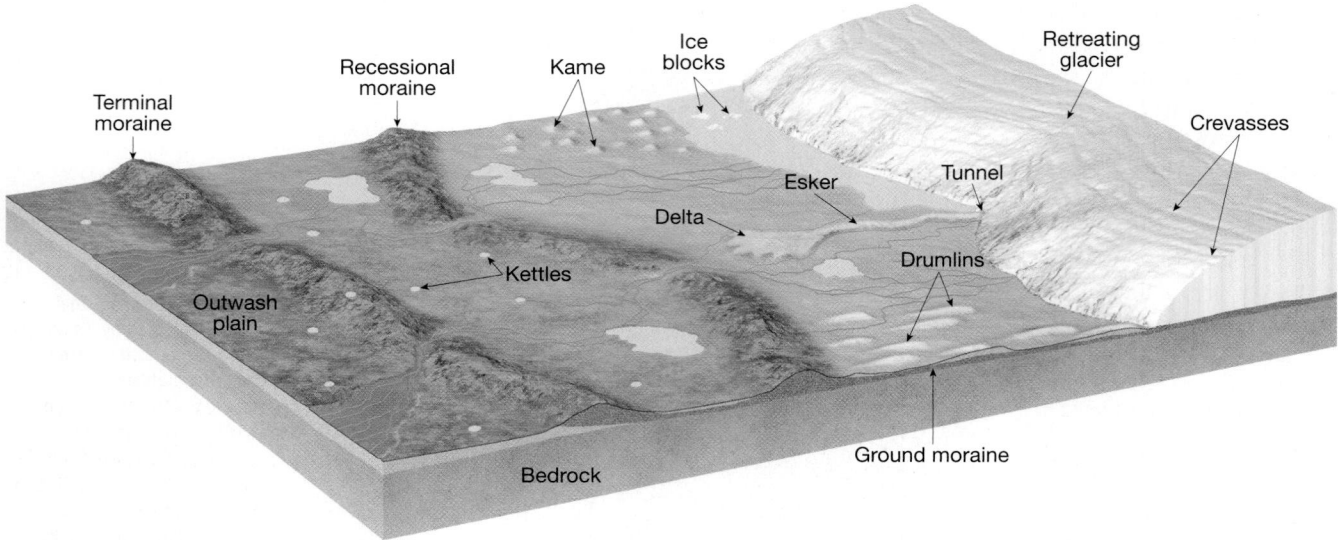

▲ **Figure 19-21** Glacier-deposited and glaciofluvially deposited features of a landscape as a continental ice sheet retreats.

by glacial deposition. Thus, the starkness of the erosional landscape is modified by depositional debris.

> **Learning Check 19-10** **Explain the shape and formation of a *roche moutonnée*.**

Deposition by Ice Sheets

In some cases, the till transported by ice sheets is deposited heterogeneously and extensively, without forming any identifiable topographic features; a veneer of unsorted debris is simply laid down over the preexisting terrain. This veneer is sometimes quite shallow and does not mask the original topography. In other cases, till is deposited to a depth of several hundred meters, completely obliterating the shape of the preglacial landscape. In either case, deposition tends to be uneven, producing an irregularly undulating surface of broad, low rises and shallow depressions. Such a surface is referred to as a *till plain*.

Moraines: In many instances, glacial sediments are laid down in more defined patterns, creating characteristic and identifiable landforms (Figure 19-21). **Moraine** is a general term for glacier-deposited landforms composed entirely or largely of till. They typically consist of irregular rolling topography rising some small height above the surrounding terrain. Moraines are usually much longer than they are wide, although the width can vary from a few tens of meters to as much as several kilometers. Some moraines are distinct ridges, whereas others are much more irregular in shape. Their relief is not great, varying from a few meters to a few hundred meters. When originally formed, moraines tend to

► **Figure 19-22** The maximum advance of the Exit Glacier in Kenai Fjords National Park, Alaska, is marked by a prominent terminal moraine.

have relatively smooth and gentle slopes, which become more uneven with the passage of time, as the blocks of stagnant ice, both large and small, included within the till eventually melt, leading to the collapse of the surface of the moraine.

Three types of moraines are particularly associated with deposition from continental ice sheets, although all three may be produced by mountain glaciers as well. A **terminal moraine** is a ridge of till that marks the outermost limit of glacial advance. It can vary in size from a conspicuous ridge tens of meters high to a low, discontinuous wall of debris (Figure 19-22). A terminal moraine is formed when a glacier reaches its equilibrium point and so is wasting at the same rate that it is being nourished. Although the toe of the glacier is not advancing, the interior continues to flow forward, delivering a supply of till. As the ice melts around the margin, the till is deposited, and the moraine grows (Figure 19-23).

Behind the terminal moraine, **recessional moraines** may develop as the glacier recedes. These are ridges that mark positions where the ice front was temporarily stabilized during the final retreat of the glacier. Both terminal and recessional moraines normally occur in the form of concave arcs that bulge outward in the direction of ice movement, indicating that the ice sheets advanced not along an even line but rather as a connecting series of great tongues of ice, each with a curved front (Figure 19-24).

The third type of moraine is the **ground moraine**, formed when large quantities of till are laid down from underneath the glacier rather than from its edge. A ground moraine usually means gently rolling plains across the landscape. It may be shallow or deep and often consists of low knolls and shallow *kettles*.

Kettles: Depressions known as **kettles** can form when large blocks of ice left by a retreating glacier become surrounded or even covered by glacial drift. After the ice

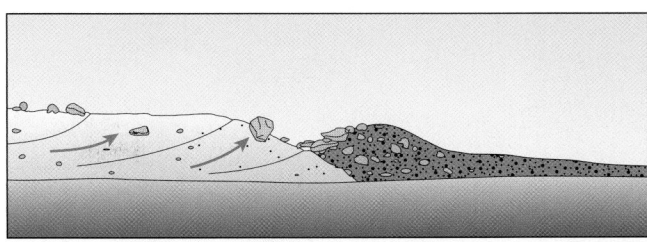
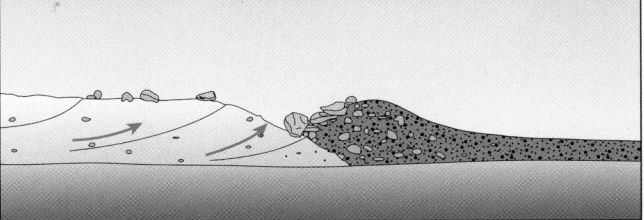
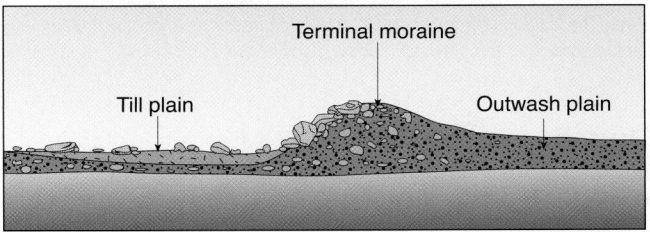

▲ **Figure 19-23** Moraine growth at the terminus of a glacier. Rock is carried within the ice, emerging at the end of the glacier where it is deposited in a moraine. Some debris also moves on top of the ice. The final diagram represents the situation after the ice has melted.

block melts, the morainal surface collapses, leaving an irregular depression (Figure 19-25). Today, many kettles remain filled with water as lakes—the water in the kettles is not the same water that was left by the melting ice; the ice simply left the depression that forms the basin of the lake.

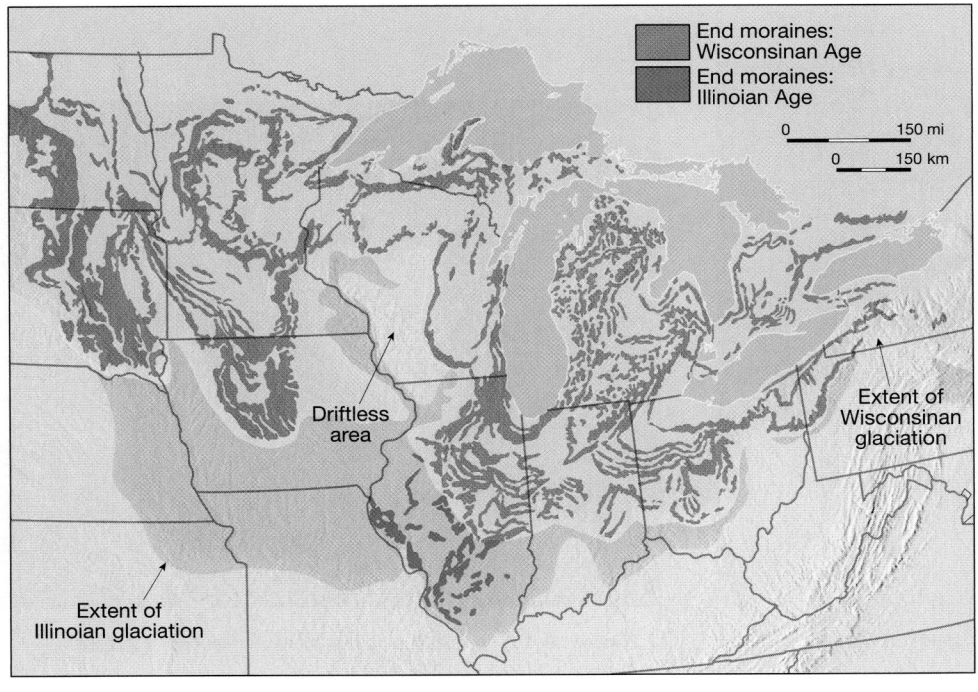

◄ **Figure 19-24** Terminal and recessional moraines (collectively referred to as end moraines) near the Great Lakes in the United States left by the more recent Wisconsin stage glaciations are more prominent than those left by the earlier Illinoian stage glaciations.

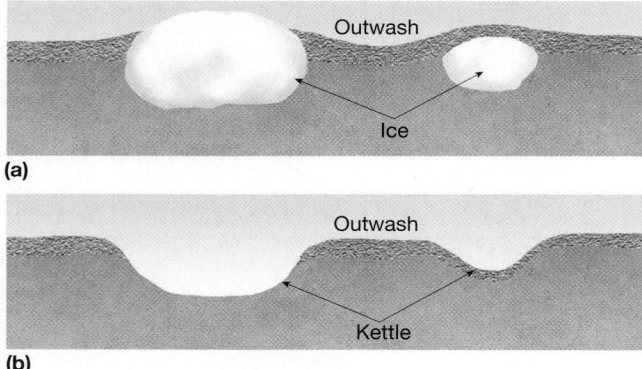

▲ **Figure 19-25** The formation of kettles. During deglaciation, isolated masses of ice are often mixed in with the glacial debris and outwash and melt slowly because of the insulation provided by the surrounding debris. When the ice does eventually melt, sizable depressions known as kettles may pit the surface of the outwash. Today, many kettles contain water as lakes.

Drumlins: Another prominent feature deposited by ice sheets is a low, elongated hill called a **drumlin,** a term that comes from *druim,* an old Irish word for "ridge." Drumlins are much smaller than moraines but composed of similarly unsorted till. The long axis of the drumlin is aligned parallel with the direction of ice movement. The end of the drumlin facing the direction from which the ice came is blunt and slightly steeper than the opposite end. Thus, the configuration is the reverse of that of a roche moutonnée.

The origin of drumlins is complex, but most of them are apparently the result of ice readvance into an area of previous glacial deposition. In other words, they are depositional features subsequently shaped by erosion. Drumlins usually occur in groups, sometimes numbering in the hundreds, with all drumlins in a group oriented parallel to each other (Figure 19-26). The greatest concentrations

of drumlins in the United States are found in central New York and eastern Wisconsin.

Learning Check 19-11   Contrast the formation of a terminal moraine and a recessional moraine.

Glaciofluvial Features

The deposition or redeposition of debris by ice-sheet meltwater produces certain features both where the sheet covered the ground and in the periglacial region. These features are composed of **stratified drift,** deposits that resemble alluvium in that they may appear both layered and sorted to a certain extent because they were carried along by the meltwater. Glaciofluvial features are composed largely or entirely of gravel, sand, and silt because meltwater is rarely capable of moving larger material.

Outwash Plains: The most extensive glaciofluvial features are **outwash plains,** which are smooth, flat alluvial aprons deposited beyond recessional or terminal moraines by streams issuing from the ice (see Figure 19-21). Streams heavily loaded with reworked till or with debris washed directly from the ice, extend from the melting glacier to form a braided pattern of channels across the area beyond the glacial front (see Figure 16-15). As they flow away from the ice, these braided streams, choked with debris, rapidly lose their speed and deposit their load. Such outwash deposits sometimes cover many hundreds of square kilometers. They are occasionally pitted by kettles that often become ponds or small lakes. Beyond the outwash plain, there is sometimes a lengthy deposit of glaciofluvial alluvium confined to a valley bottom; such a deposit is termed a **valley train.**

Eskers: Less common than outwash plains, but more conspicuous, are long sinuous ridges of stratified drift called

▲ **Figure 19-26** Drumlin west of Rochester, New York. The glacier flowed from right to left.

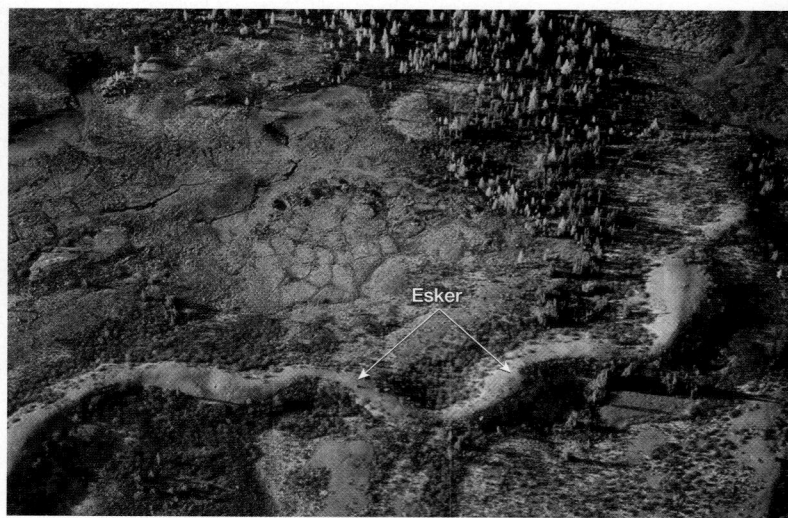

▲ **Figure 19-27** The sinuous ridge of an esker near Whitefish Lake, Northwest Territories, Canada.

eskers, named from *eiscir*, another Irish word for "ridge." These landforms are composed largely of glaciofluvial gravel and are thought to have originated when streams flowing through tunnels in the interior of the ice sheet became clogged during a time in which the ice was neither flowing nor advancing. These streams beneath the stagnating sheet often carry a great deal of debris, and as the ice melts, the streams deposit much of their load in the tunnel. Eskers are this debris exposed once the ice melts away. They are usually a few dozen meters high, a few dozen meters wide, and may be a few dozen kilometers (or up to 160 kilometers [a hundred miles]) long (Figure 19-27).

Kames: Small, steep mounds or conical hills of stratified drift are found sporadically in areas of ice-sheet deposition. These *kames* (the word derives from *comb*, an old Scottish word referring to an elongated steep ridge) appear to be of diverse origin, but they are clearly associated with meltwater deposition in stagnant ice. They are mounds of poorly sorted sand and gravel that probably formed within glacial fissures or between the glacier and the land surface (Figure 19-28). Many seem to have been built as steep fans or deltas against the edge of the ice that later collapsed partially when the ice melted. Morainal surfaces containing a number of mounds and depressions are called *kame-and-kettle topography*.

Lakes: Lakes are very common in areas that were glaciated during the Pleistocene. The old stream systems were

▲ **Figure 19-28** A kame in southeastern Wisconsin, near Dundee.

obliterated or deranged by the ice sheets, and water remains ponded in the many erosional basins and kettles, and behind morainal dams. One has only to compare the northern and southern parts of the United States to recognize this fact (Figure 19-29). Most of Europe and the northern part of Asia demonstrate a similar correlation between past glaciation and present-day lakes.

Learning Check 19-12   **Explain the formation and characteristics of a glacial outwash plain.**

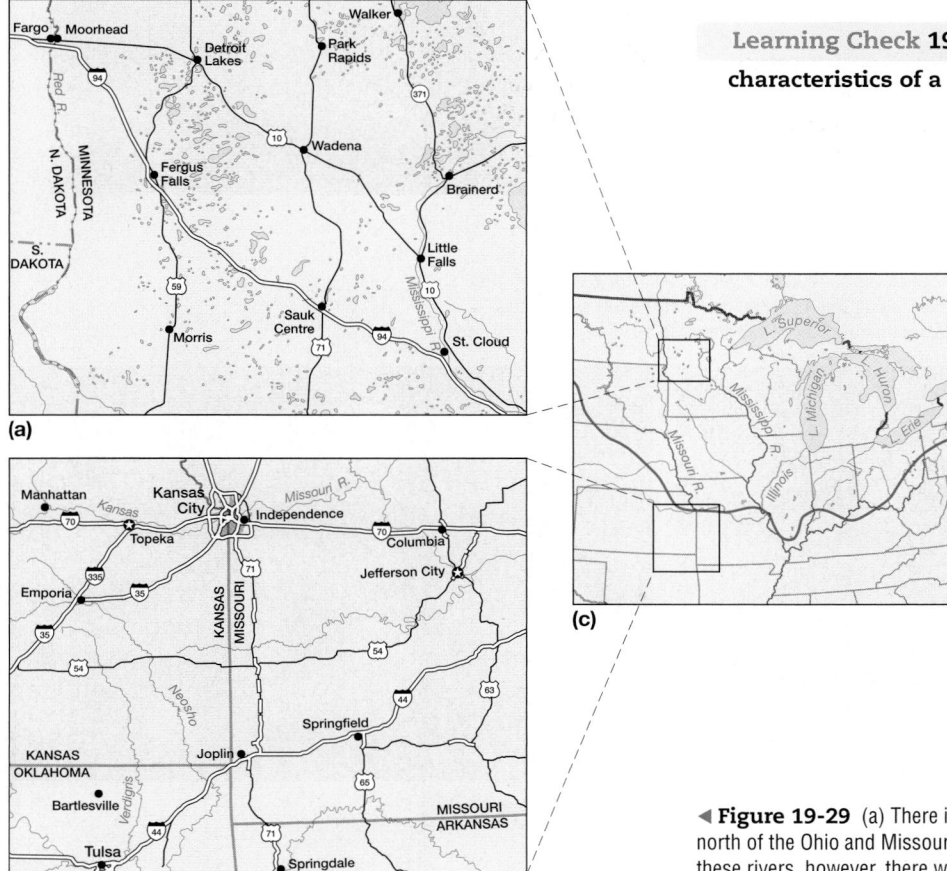

(a)

(b)

(c)

◀ **Figure 19-29** (a) There is an abundance of natural lakes in the region north of the Ohio and Missouri rivers, a result of glacial action. (b) South of these rivers, however, there was no glaciation (c) and consequently natural lakes are almost unknown.

FOCUS

Shrinking Glaciers

Glaciers are sensitive indicators of environmental change. As we have seen, the size of a glacier is a delicate balance between the accumulation of ice and the ablation of ice. A relatively small increase in summer temperature or decrease in winter precipitation for a number of years may lead to the retreat of a glacier. But the relationships are sometimes counterintuitive: a glacier might also advance if slightly higher temperatures lead to an increase in winter precipitation.

Repeat Photography Shows Glacier Retreat: Throughout most of the world, glaciers are retreating, and some of the most striking evidence for this comes not from specialized instruments or satellite measurements, but from old-fashioned photographs. Bruce Molina of the U.S. Geological Survey (USGS) compared photographs of Alaskan glaciers taken from the 1890s to the 1970s with new photographs he has taken from the exact same locations. The contrast between pairs of images taken just decades apart in some cases is remarkable (Figure 19-D). Overall, Molina estimates that since the most recent peak of glacial ice cover in the 1700s, Alaska has lost about 15 percent of its total glacier cover—a loss of perhaps 10,000 square kilometers (3800 square miles) of ice surface area.

Not only have glaciers been shrinking, but the photographs also reveal that vegetation patterns have been changing. In some areas where little vegetation was visible in the past, an extensive plant cover is now obvious.

Satellite Imagery Monitors Glacier Changes: Satellite imagery provides another way to measure changes in glacier size. Around the world, the retreat of glaciers is being documented: in the Alps, the Himalayas, the Cascades, the Andes, and the Sierra Nevada. For example, time-series ground surveys and satellite images show that the Jakobshavn's Isbrae Glacier—Greenland's largest outlet glacier—retreated more than 40 kilometers (25 miles) over the last 150 years, and that the Columbia Glacier in southeastern Alaska retreated more than 20 kilometers (12 miles) between 1986 and 2011 alone (Figure 19-E).

▲ **Figure 19-D** Change in the Muir Glacier and Riggs Glacier in Alaska's Glacier Bay National Park and Preserve. In 1941 (left), the Muir and Riggs Glaciers filled Muir Inlet. By 2004 (right), the Muir Glacier had retreated out of view and lush vegetation is now growing on the hillsides in the foreground. The "trimline" along the mountain front of the left side of the photograph indicates that the Muir Glacier was at least 600 meters (2000 feet) thick in 1941.

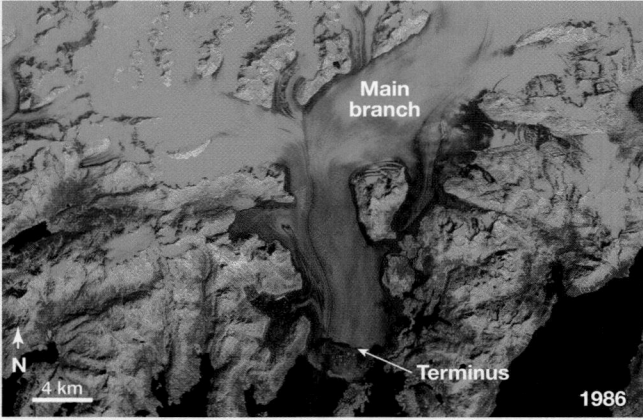
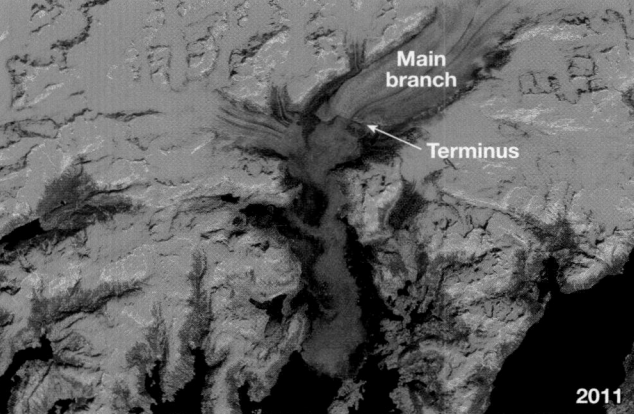

▲ **Figure 19-E** Retreat of the Columbia Glacier in Alaska between 1986 and 2011. The terminus of the Columbia glacier retreated about 20 kilometers over the last 25 years. Images were gathered by Landsat satellites.

COASTLINES ARE AMONG THE MOST VARIED OF ALL LANDSCAPES

on the planet. This diversity of form and appearance is a result of the great variety of local geology, climate, and geomorphic processes at work along the coastlines of the world. In addition to virtually all of the internal and external processes we've discussed so far, coastlines may also be shaped by waves and local ocean currents. The result is that coastal terrain is often quite different from the landscape just a short distance inland from shore.

The coastal environment is usually dynamic, often showing changes in appearance and process from day to day or even hour to hour. Part of this dynamism is a consequence of shorelines acting as an interface of the lithosphere, hydrosphere, and atmosphere—and quite often the cryosphere and biosphere as well. As we saw in the chapters on weather and climate, bodies of water—especially the oceans—are important components of a number of key Earth systems. In addition to the ocean's role of regulating the temperature of Earth, some of the energy received from the Sun ultimately powers wind that creates currents and waves that, as we will see in this chapter, can in turn shape coastal landforms.

As you study this chapter, think about these key questions:

- **In what ways does landform development along ocean coastlines differ from that along lakeshores?**
- **How are waves generated and how do waves affect shorelines?**
- **How do changes in sea level, coastal sediment deposition, and coastal sediment transport influence shorelines?**
- **How can a changing sediment budget affect the size and shape of depositional landforms such as beaches and spits?**
- **What coastal features are seen with shorelines of submergence and emergence?**
- **How do coral features such as fringing reefs, barrier reefs, and atolls develop?**

The Impact of Waves and Currents on the Landscape

Coastal processes affect only a tiny fraction of the total area of Earth's surface, but they create a landscape that is almost totally different from any other on the planet. Generally along shorelines, waves are agents of erosion, and currents are agents of transportation and deposition. The most notable land features created by wave erosion are rocky cliffs and headlands. Depositional features along coastlines are diverse in form, but by far the most common are beaches and sandbars. Beaches along the shorelines of both oceans and lakes are sometimes the most distinctive aspect of coastal landscapes. They develop as a transition from land to water, and are usually impermanent features of the landscape—building up during times of "normal" weather and eroding or completely disappearing during storms.

Seeing Geographically

Big Sur coastline of central California. Describe the pattern the waves make as they approach this irregular coastline. What do you see that suggests that the coastal cliffs are being worn back by the waves? Does the coastline seem to be comprised all of the same resistant material? Why do you say this?

COASTAL PROCESSES  FG2, FG8

The coastlines of the world's oceans and lakes extend for hundreds of thousands of kilometers. Every conceivable variety of structure, relief, and topography can be found somewhere along these coasts. Coastlines are a dynamic and highly energetic environment, primarily because of the restless motions of the waters (Figure 20-1).

The Role of Wind in Coastal Processes

We saw in Chapter 18 that wind can be an important shaper of landforms on the continents—particularly through the deposition of sand. Along coastlines, the wind has an even greater influence on topography. As we discussed in Chapter 5, one manifestation of Earth's unequal warming by the Sun is the global pattern of pressure and wind, and it is primarily wind blowing over the surface of a body of water that generates waves and ocean currents.

The wind is not the only force causing water to move, of course. As we saw in Chapter 9, oceanic coastlines also experience daily tidal fluctuations that often move enormous quantities of water. Tectonic events, particularly earthquakes, contribute to water motion, as does volcanic activity upon occasion. Even more fundamental are long-term variations in sea or lake level caused by tectonic forces and *eustatic sea-level change* (sea-level change due to an increase or decrease in the amount of water in the world ocean). However, from the standpoint of geomorphic effects, wind is the most important cause of water movement.

Coastlines of Oceans and Lakes

The processes that shape the topography of oceanic coastlines are similar to the processes acting on lakeshores, with three important exceptions:

1. Along lakeshores, the range of tides is so small that they are insignificant to landform development.
2. The causes of sea-level fluctuations are quite different from the causes of lake-level fluctuations.
3. Coral reefs are built only in tropical and subtropical oceans, not in lakes.

With these exceptions, the topographic forms produced on seacoasts and lakeshores are generally similar. Even so, the larger the body of water, the greater the effects of the coastal processes. Thus, topographic features developed along seacoasts are normally larger, more conspicuous, and more distinctive than those found along lakeshores, and the focus of this chapter is largely ocean shorelines.

Learning Check 20-1 **In what ways are ocean shoreline-shaping processes different from those shaping lakeshores? (Answer on p. AK-6)**

Many processes contribute to the shaping of coastal features. In addition to the internal and external processes discussed in earlier chapters, a number of processes largely confined to coastal areas may be at work along a shoreline, and of these, by far the most important is the work of waves, our next topic.

▼ **Figure 20-1** A coastline is the place where hydrosphere, lithosphere, and atmosphere meet. It is often an interface of ceaseless movement and energy transfer. Pounding waves do not always erode evenly and smoothly. Sea stacks and cliffs testify to the principle of differential erosion in this scene from Port Campbell National Park, Victoria, Australia.

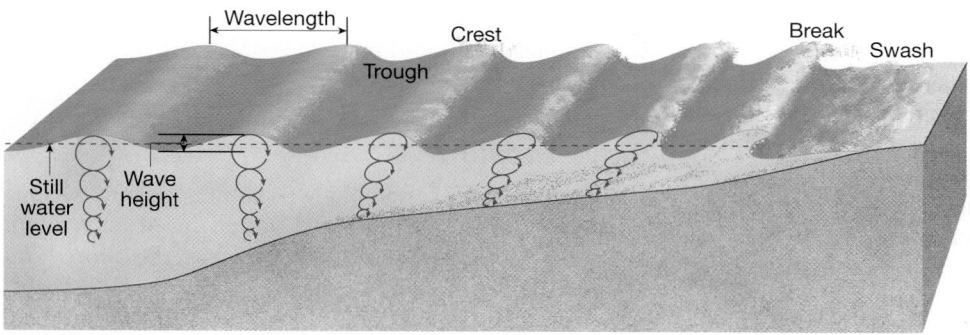

◀ **Figure 20-2** In deep water, the passage of a wave involves almost circular movements of the water. Water movement diminishes rapidly with increasing depth, as shown here by decreasing orbital diameter downward. As the wave moves into shallow water, the revolving orbits of the water become more elliptical, the wavelength becomes shorter, and the wave becomes steeper. Eventually the wave "breaks" and dissipates its remaining energy as it washes up onto the beach.

WAVES

Waves entail the transfer of energy through a cyclical rising and falling motion in a substance. Our interest here is in water waves, which are undulations in the surface layers of a water body.

Wave Motion

Although water waves appear to move water horizontally, this appearance is misleading: in open water, the form of the wave (and therefore its energy) moves along through the water, although the water moves forward only very slightly; as we will see, this motion changes in shallow water, where waves crest and break.

Most water waves are wind generated, set in motion largely by the friction of air blowing across the water. This transfer of energy from wind to water initiates wave motion. Some water waves (called *forced waves*) are generated directly by wind stress on the water surface; they can develop to considerable size if the wind is strong, but these waves usually last for only a limited time and do not travel far. Water waves become **swells** when they travel beyond the location where they were generated by wind, and in so doing can travel enormous distances. A small number of all water waves are generated by something other than the wind, such as a tidal surge, volcanic activity, or undersea tectonic movement (discussed later in this chapter).

Animation
Wave Motion

Waves of Oscillation: As a wave passes a given point on the water surface, the water at that point makes a small circular or oscillatory movement, with very little forward motion (to "oscillate" means to move back and forth over the same space again and again). Waves that cause water to move this way are called **waves of oscillation**. As the wave passes, the water moves upward, producing a *wave crest*, as shown in Figure 20-2. Then crest formation is followed by a sinking of the surface that creates a *wave trough*. The horizontal distance from crest to crest or from trough to trough is called the **wavelength**. The vertical dimension of wave development is determined by the circular orbit of the surface water as the wave form passes; the vertical distance from crest to trough is equivalent to the diameter of this orbit and is called the **wave height**. The height of a wave depends on wind speed, wind duration, water depth, and *fetch* (the area of open water over which the wind blows).

The passage of a wave of oscillation normally moves water only very slightly in the direction of flow. Thus when a wave passes through an object floating on the surface simply bobs up and down without advancing, except as it may be pushed by the wind. The influence of wave movement diminishes rapidly with depth; even very high waves stir the subsurface water to a depth of only a few tens of meters.

Waves of Translation: Waves often travel great distances across deep water with relatively little change in speed or shape. As they roll into shallow water, however, a significant metamorphosis occurs. When the water depth becomes equal to about half the wavelength, the wave motion begins to be affected by frictional drag on the sea bottom. The waves of oscillation then rapidly become changed into **waves of translation**, and the result is significant horizontal movement of the surface water. Friction retards the progress of the waves so that they are slowed and bunch together, marking a decrease in wavelength, while at the same time their height is increased. As the wave moves into still shallower water, frictional drag becomes even greater and the wave becomes higher and steeper, which causes the wave to tilt forward and become more unstable. Soon and abruptly the wave *breaks* (Figure 20-3), collapsing into whitewater surf or plunging forward as a breaker or, if the height is small, perhaps simply surging up the beach without cresting.

When a wave breaks, the motion of the water instantly becomes turbulent, like that of a swift river. The breaking

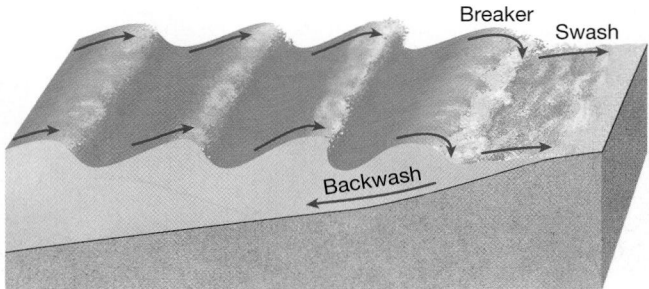

▲ **Figure 20-3** A breaking wave. In shallow water the ocean bottom impedes oscillation, causing the wave to become increasingly steeper until it is so oversteepened that it collapses and tumbles forward as a breaker. The surging water then rushes up the beach as swash, and then drains off the beach below the waves as backwash.

wave rushes toward shore or up the beach as **swash**. This surge can carry sand and rock particles onto the beach, or it can pound onto rocky headlands and sea cliffs with considerable force (Figure 20-4). The momentum of the surging swash is soon overcome by friction and gravity, and a return flow, called **backwash**, drains much of the water seaward again carrying loose material with it, usually to meet the oncoming swash of the next wave.

Learning Check 20-2 **How do waves of oscillation change as they reach shallow water?**

Wave Refraction

Waves often change direction as they approach the shore, a phenomenon known as **wave refraction**. It occurs when a line of waves does not approach exactly parallel to the shore, or where the coastline is uneven or there are irregularities in water depth in the near-shore zone. For one or more of these reasons, one portion of a wave reaches shallow water sooner than other portions and is thus slowed down. This slowing down causes the wave line to bend (*refract*) as it pivots toward the obstructing area, finally breaking roughly parallel to shore. Thus, wave energy tends to be concentrated in the vicinity of an obstruction and diminished in other areas (Figure 20-5).

Animation
Wave
Refraction

The most conspicuous geomorphic result of wave refraction is the focusing of wave action on headlands (Figure 20-6), subjecting them to the direct onslaught of pounding waves, whereas an adjacent bay experiences much gentler, low-energy wave action. Other things being equal (such as the resistance of the bedrock), the differential effect of wave refraction tends to smooth the coastal outline by wearing back the headlands and increasing sediment accumulation in the bays.

Wave Erosion

The most notable erosion along coastlines is accomplished by wave action. The incessant pounding of even small waves is a potent force in wearing away the shore, and the enormous power of storm waves almost defies comprehension—it is often large storm waves that accomplish most of the erosion along a shoreline. Waves break with abrupt and dramatic impact, hurling water, debris, and air in a thunderous crash onto the shore. Spray from breaking waves commonly moves as fast as 115 kilometers (70 miles) per hour, and small jets have been measured at more than twice that speed. This speed, coupled with the sheer mass of the water involved in such hydraulic pounding, is responsible for much coastal erosion, which is made much more effective by the abrasive rock particles carried by the waves.

Wherever the land along a shore is rocks or cliffs rather than sand, there is another dimension to wave erosion: air is forced into cracks in the rock as the wave hits the shore. The resulting compression is abruptly released as the water recedes, allowing instant expansion of the air. This pneumatic action is often very effective in loosening rock particles of various sizes.

Chemical action also plays a part in the erosion of rocks and cliffs because most rocks are to some extent soluble in seawater. In another form of weathering action, salts from seawater crystallize in the crevices and pores of onshore rocks and cliffs, and this deposition is a further mechanism for weakening and breaking up the rock (such *salt wedging* is discussed in Chapter 15).

▶ **Figure 20-4** The continuous pounding of waves can erode even the most resistant coastal rocks. This scene is Cape Kiwanda State Natural Area along the Oregon coast.

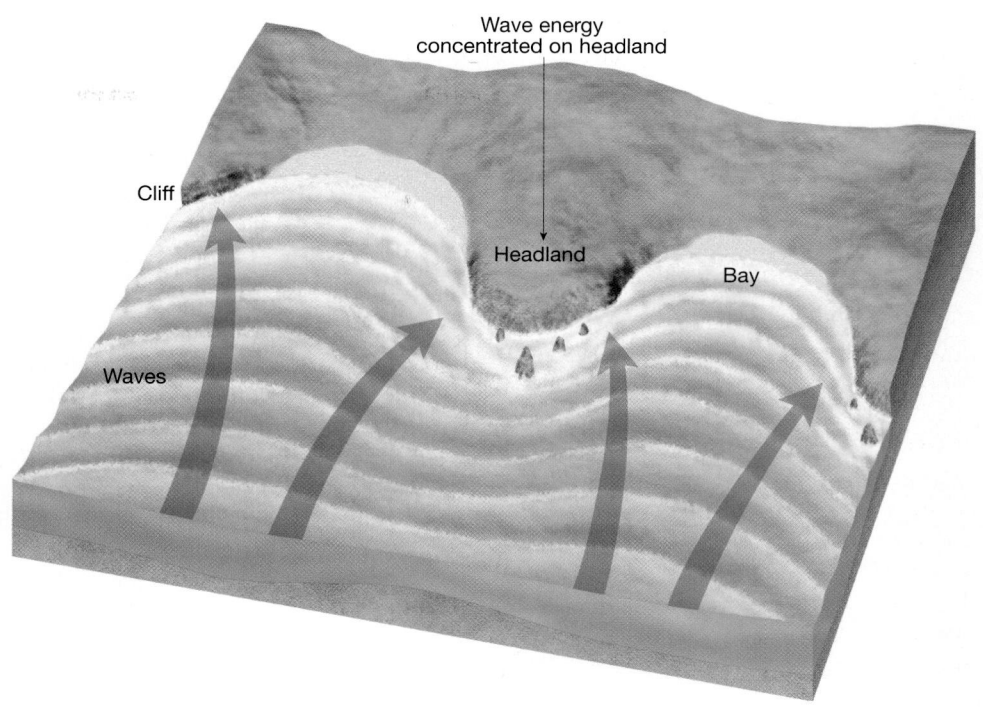

▶ **Figure 20-5** Refraction of waves on an irregular coastline. The waves reach the headland first and then "wrap" around it, breaking nearly parallel to the coastline as a result of wave refraction. Thus, wave energy is concentrated on the headlands and is diminished in the bays.

On shorelines made up of cliffs, the most effective erosion takes place just at or slightly above sea level, so that a notch is cut in the base of the cliff. The cliff face then retreats as the slope above the undercutting collapses (Figure 20-7). The resulting debris is broken, smoothed, and made smaller by further wave action, and eventually most of it is carried seaward.

As we will see later in this chapter, where a shoreline is composed of sand or other unconsolidated material,

currents and tides may also cause rapid erosion. Storms greatly accelerate the erosion of sandy shores; a violent storm can remove an entire beach in just a few hours, cutting it right down to bedrock.

Whether they are awesome storm waves or mild swells, the peculiar contradiction of water waves is that they normally pass harmlessly under such fragile things as boats or swimmers in open water but can wreak

▲ **Figure 20-6** The incessant pounding of waves on this soft-rock headland on the southern coast of the state of Victoria, Australia, produced a double arch that eventually eroded into a single arch. The double-arch photograph was taken in 1985 and the single-arch one in 1992. The view is in Port Campbell National Park.

(a)

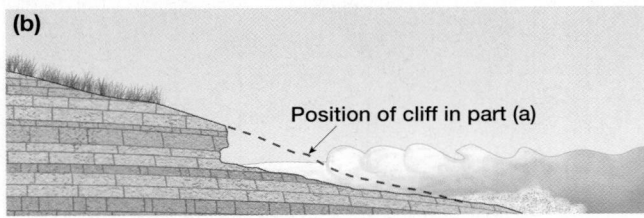

(b)

Position of cliff in part (a)

(c)

▲ **Figure 20-7** (a) Waves pounding an exposed rocky shoreline erode the rock most effectively at water level, with the result that a notch may be cut in the face of the headland. (b) The presence of this notch undermines the higher portion of the headland, which may subsequently collapse, producing a steep cliff. (c) The notching/undercutting/collapse sequence may be repeated many times, causing the cliff face to retreat.

devastation on even the hardest rocks of a shoreline. In other words, a wave of oscillation is a relatively gentle phenomenon, but a wave of translation can be a powerful force of destruction.

Learning Check 20-3 **Why are storm waves so important in coastal erosion?**

Tsunami

Occasionally, major oceanic wave systems are triggered by a sudden disruption of the ocean floor. These waves are called **tsunami** (from the Japanese *tsu* for "harbor" and *nami* for "wave") or *seismic sea waves* (improperly called "tidal waves").

Animation
Tsunami

Tsunami Formation: Most tsunami are a consequence of abrupt movement along an ocean floor fault—especially from the vertical displacement caused by reverse or thrust faulting along a subduction zone. Tsunami may also result from underwater volcanic eruptions and major underwater and coastal landslides.

The great destructive power unleashed by some tsunami comes from the way in which the ocean is disrupted to form such a wave. Recall that with wind-generated waves, only the surface of the ocean exhibits significant movement—the orbital movement of the water only extends down to a depth of about one-half the wavelength of the wave (rarely more than a few tens of meters). On the other hand, when fault rupture on the ocean floor generates a tsunami, the entire water column—from the floor of the ocean to the surface—is disrupted, displacing an enormous volume of water (Figure 20-8).

Out in the open ocean, tsunami are usually quite inconspicuous because they are low and have very long wavelengths (in the open sea a tsunami might have a wave height of only 0.5 meter [1.5 feet] with a wavelength of perhaps 200 kilometers [125 miles]), although they can travel at speeds exceeding 700 kilometers an hour (435 miles per hour). When a tsunami reaches shallow water, however, it changes considerably. As a tsunami approaches a coast, it slows—as do all waves—causing the wavelength to decrease and the wave height to increase.

Effects of Tsunami: When they strike a shoreline, tsunami rarely form towering breaking waves. Instead, most tsunami arrive as a very rapidly advancing surge of water,

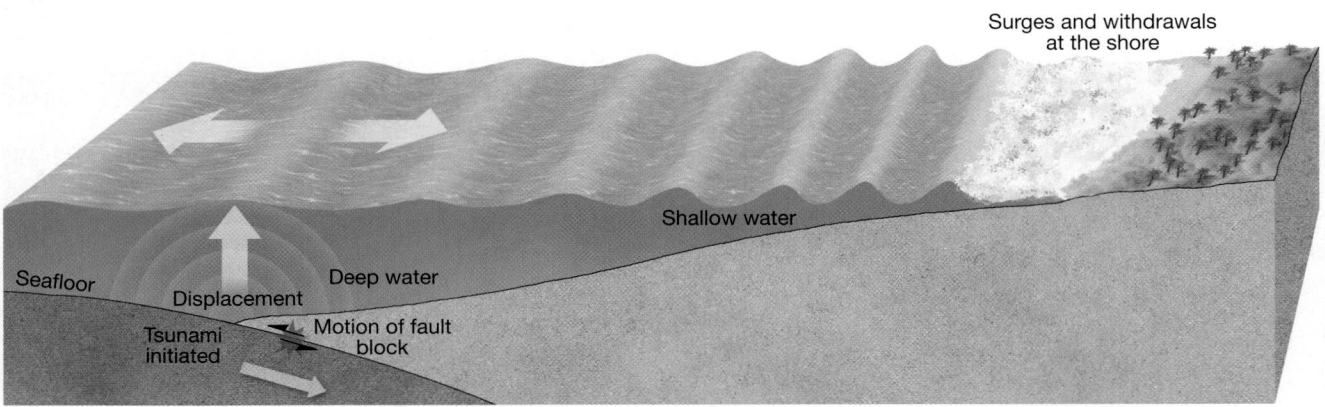

Surges and withdrawals
at the shore

Shallow water

Seafloor

Displacement

Deep water

Tsunami
initiated

Motion of fault
block

▲ **Figure 20-8** The formation of a tsunami. A vertical disruption of the ocean floor, such as from faulting, displaces the entire water column from the ocean floor to the surface. In the open ocean, the tsunami may be almost indistinguishable because of its great wavelength. Once it reaches shallow water, however, wave height increases and the tsunami comes onshore as a series of surges and withdrawals.

sometimes up to 40 meters (130 feet) high. Unlike many large wind-generated waves, however, immediately behind the wave crest of a tsunami is an enormous volume of water that can surge great distances inland before receding. In many cases, before a tsunami arrives, the water withdraws from the coast, appearing like a very sudden, very low tide—this happens when the trough of the tsunami arrives. Unfortunately, people sometimes venture out on the freshly exposed subtidal areas to collect shellfish or stranded fish, only to be caught a few minutes later by the rapid surge of water when the crest of the tsunami comes onshore. Frequently, there is a series of surges and withdrawals, with the largest surge not necessarily the first to arrive.

The Sumatra–Andaman Earthquake and Tsunami of 2004: On December 26, 2004, one of the greatest natural disasters in recent history was triggered after a magnitude 9.2 earthquake shook the northern coast of Sumatra in Indonesia. A 1200 kilometer- (750 mile-) long section of the interplate thrust fault (or "megathrust"), formed where the Indo–Australian Plate is subducting beneath the Burma Plate, ruptured, uplifting the ocean floor by as much as 4.9 meters (16 feet). The sharp movement of the ocean floor generated a tsunami that spread away in all directions.

About 28 minutes after the earthquake struck, a 24-meter- (80-foot-) high wave rushed onshore at the city of Banda Aceh on the northern tip Sumatra, Indonesia, just 100 kilometers (60 miles) from the epicenter of the earthquake (Figure 20-9). The tsunami spread across the Indian Ocean, striking Sri Lanka, the Maldives Islands, and the coast of Somalia in northeast Africa. The exact death toll will likely never be known, but estimates now suggest that nearly 227,000 people died and many tens of thousands

▼ **Figure 20-9** Damage from the December 26, 2004, tsunami in Banda Aceh, Indonesia.

more were seriously injured. In a few locations, entire villages were quite literally washed away.

Learning Check 20-4 Why are tsunami often so much more destructive than even very large storm waves?

Tsunami Warnings: Because most tsunami originate from sudden fault displacement in a subduction zone, the resulting earthquakes are readily detectable by seismographs. For decades, the Pacific Tsunami Warning Center in Hawai'i has used seismographic and other data to detect tsunami heading for coastlines around the Pacific basin. With such information, a tsunami warning can usually be issued long enough in advance to allow time for evacuation of the impact area. However, as the Sumatra tsunami disaster of 2004 revealed, if local warning systems are not in place, there may be no way to get evacuation orders to coastal populations in time. Further, as we saw in Sumatra in 2004 and in Japan in March 2011, if a large tsunami-generating earthquake originates close to a populated coastline, the waves can arrive so quickly that coastal residents may have only a few minutes to evacuate—see the box, "People and the Environment: The 2011 Japan Earthquake and Tsunami."

IMPORTANT SHORELINE-SHAPING PROCESSES

In addition to wind-generated waves and tsunami, a variety of other processes also modify coastlines in ways that range from gradual and subtle, to sudden and spectacular.

Tides

As we learned in Chapter 9, the waters of the world ocean oscillate in a regular and predictable pattern called *tides*, resulting from the gravitational influence of the Sun and Moon (see Figure 9-8). The tides rise and fall in a cycle that takes about 12 hours, producing two high tides and two low tides a day on most (but not all) seacoasts.

Animation
Tides

Despite the enormous amount of water moved by tides and despite the frequency of this movement, the topographic effects are surprisingly small. Tides are significant agents of erosion only in narrow bays, around the margin of shallow seas, and in passages between islands, where they produce currents strong enough to scour the bottom and erode cliffs and shorelines (Figure 20-10). The movement of water through tides is, however, a promising source of power for generating electricity—see the box, "Energy for the 21st Century: Tidal Power."

Changes in Sea Level and Lake Level

Sea-level changes can result either from the uplift or sinking of a landmass (tectonic cause), or from an increase or decrease in the amount of water in the oceans—**eustatic**

The 2011 Japan Earthquake and Tsunami

On the afternoon of March 11, 2011, a magnitude 9.0 earthquake struck the northeast coast of Honshu, the largest island of Japan. The result of the Great Tohoku Earthquake was devastation and loss of life almost unimaginable in a country that is as well prepared for large earthquakes as any in the world.

More than 15,000 people lost their lives, with many hundreds of other victims still missing. Initially, more than 130,000 people were left homeless; more than 300,000 buildings were destroyed; telecommunications, transportation, and water supplies were widely disrupted. Utilities were damaged, most dramatically when several nuclear reactors were damaged near Fukushima.

The Earthquake: The earthquake was caused by the sudden rupture and movement along a thrust fault where the Pacific Plate subducts beneath the Okhotsk "microplate" on which the northern part of Honshu rests (Figure 20-A). (Some geologists consider this part of Honshu to be on either the Eurasian Plate or the North American Plate.)

The severe ground shaking of the earthquake lasted for more than 3 minutes. During that time, a 300-kilometer-long by 150-kilometer-wide (185 mile by 90 mile) segment of the subduction zone slipped as much as 30 meters (100 feet). After the earthquake, the northeastern coast of Japan had jumped about 2.4 meters (8 feet) to the east, and parts of the coastline in Miyagi Prefecture had subsided by more than 1 meter (3.3 feet).

The Tsunami: Although the earthquake caused extensive damage, it was the tsunami that followed that was most deadly and destructive. The ocean floor above the fault rupture was abrupted uplifted, displacing an enormous volume of water. Tsunami warnings were issued in Japan within 10 minutes of the earthquake, but the coastal populations closest to the epicenter had almost no time to evacuate.

As the waves reached shallow water along the Japanese coast, wave height increased dramatically. The height of the tsunami along the coast was typically about 10 meters (33 feet), but in some confined harbors the height was more than 30 meters (100 feet). In low-lying coastal plains, such as in parts of the Sendai region north of Tokyo, the surge of water advanced as much as 10 kilometers (6 miles) inland, leveling buildings, ruining roads, and depositing tons of debris (Figure 20-B).

▲ **Figure 20-B** Tsunami coming onshore in Miyako, Iwate Prefecture, Japan on March 11, 2011.

Global Effects of the Tsunami: The tsunami was so large that it caused damage thousands of kilometers away. The tsunami waves spread out in all directions (Figure 20-C), racing across the Pacific Ocean at 800 kilometers per hour (500 mph). Small tsunami waves caused flooding in Hawai'i, and even damaged boats and harbors as far away as California— where one person was killed when he was swept offshore by the wave.

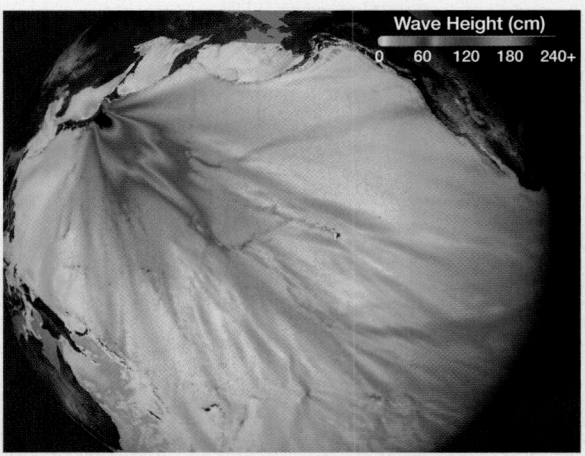

▲ **Figure 20-A** The 2011 Japan earthquake fault rupture zone. The maximum movement along the fault plane was more than 30 meters (100 feet), shown in red.

▲ **Figure 20-C** Map showing the estimated maximum height of the 2011 Japanese tsunami across the Pacific Ocean.

► **Figure 20-10** Under certain circumstances, a large tidal range can influence the shaping of coastal landforms. These gigantic pedestal rocks on the edge of the Bay of Fundy in New Brunswick, Canada, were carved by waves in this region which has the greatest tidal range in the world of up to 15 meters. For scale, the spruce trees on top of the rocks are about 9 meters (30 feet) tall.

sea-level change. During Earth's recent history, there have been many changes in sea level, sometimes worldwide and sometimes only around one or a few continents or islands. The eustatic changes of greatest magnitude and most extensive effect are those associated with seawater volume before, during, and after the Pleistocene glaciations. As we saw in Chapter 19, at the peak of the Pleistocene glaciations, sea level around the world was as much as 130 meters (430 feet) lower than today.

As a result of both tectonic and eustatic sea-level changes, many present-day ocean coastlines have been submerged, with a portion of a previous landscape now underwater, whereas others show emergent characteristics, in which shoreline topography of the past is now situated well above the contemporary sea level (Figure 20-11). We will consider the topographic consequences of these circumstances later in this chapter.

Most water-level changes in lakes are less extensive and less notable than those along ocean shorelines. These changes are usually the result of the total or partial drainage of a lake, and their principal topographic expression is exposed ancestral beach lines and wave-cut cliffs above present lake levels.

Global Warming and Sea-Level Change: In Chapters 4 and 8, we discussed the consequences of global climate change—especially what is commonly called "global warming." We noted that as global climate warms, there is a rise in sea level associated with the thermal expansion

► **Figure 20-11** A tectonically active coastline has helped produce the sharp cliffs in this scene along the north coast of California.

Tidal Power

▶ Jennifer Rahn, Samford University, Birmingham, Alabama

Before large-scale commercial electrical power generation, many civilizations used the force of moving water to power machines such as textile mills and lumber mills. Just as wind turns the blades of a windmill, recent technological advances utilize the inflow and outflow of tidal water during flood tides and ebb tides to turn a turbine in order to generate electricity (Figure 20-D).

Tides are more predictable than solar power and wind energy—tides change

▲ **Figure 20-E** Tidal power turbine in Strangford Lough, Northern Ireland.

▲ **Figure 20-D** Tidal power turbines generate electric power when tidal currents turn underwater propellers that in turn power generators.

twice a day (in some places just once a day) like clockwork—and the higher the tidal range, the greater the potential for tidal energy generation. The ideal locations for tidal power are areas with high flow volumes and/or high tidal ranges (see Figure 9-9).

Existing Tidal Power Installations:
The first tidal power plant was built in 1966 in France, and the first one in North America was installed in the 1980s in an inlet of the Bay of Fundy in eastern Canada. One of the world's largest tidal power installations was completed in 2008 in Strangford Lough in Northern Ireland (Figure 20-E). The first commercial tidal power installation in the United

States became operational in September 2012 off eastern Maine. Tidal power facilities have also been built in China, Russia, and South Korea.

Internationally, new tidal power projects have been proposed in the Philippines, India, New Zealand, and along the River Severn between Wales and England. In the United States, tidal power has been suggested for the Puget Sound in the Pacific Northwest, San Francisco Bay, New York's East River, Alaska, Hawai'i, and off Atlantic City, New Jersey.

Limitations of Tidal Power:
Currently, tidal power is not widely used, in part because a limited number of places in the world have high-flow tidal regimes. Tidal-power projects are also extremely expensive because massive structures must be built in difficult saltwater environments. However, there are many long-term advantages for using this technology. Tidal power is a renewable energy resource with a virtually unlimited supply and no greenhouse gas emissions.

Estimates suggest that tidal power could meet 10 percent of the United States' and 20 percent of the United Kingdom's electricity demand within the next few decades. Globally, in about 10 years tidal energy could supply 10

percent of the world's energy if full commercialization of this technology materializes.

Technical Obstacles:
The technology needed to efficiently and economically turn the tides into electricity is still being developed. Several new models for generating tidal power have been developed in recent years but none are operating commercially. Other problems include damage to the local aquatic environment, mostly with small fish getting caught in the rotors. Many people are hesitant to adopt large-scale tidal power plants because of the unknown harm they could cause the environment. As we are now seeing with dammed rivers, when humans alter the flow of energy and the surrounding environment, many times there are unintended consequences.

The growth of tidal power generation will depend on the public and political desire for governments to make the large investment needed for this type of alternative energy. Also important are the efforts of green energy entrepreneurs to develop better and more cost-effective infrastructure, as well as the ability of scientists to predict the major environmental effects of individual projects ahead of time in order to protect local ecosystems.

of ocean water as well as the increase in volume from the melting of continental glaciers and ice caps. If worldwide temperature continues to warm, we can anticipate an ongoing period of deglaciation, with the ice sheets of Antarctica and Greenland slowly melting. Such a situation would cause a global eustatic rise in sea level that would inundate many islands and coastal plains of the world, and would expose coastal populations to greater risks from storm waves such as those generated by hurricanes.

Should the ice caps of Antarctica and Greenland melt completely (a result not anticipated by most climate scientists, even over the next century or so), global sea level would rise by about 80 meters (260 feet). However, even a modest increase in global sea level will be potentially devastating to populations now living in low-lying coastal areas. Given the anticipated levels of greenhouse gases and the associated temperature rise due to global warming, in 2007 the *Fourth Assessment Report* of the Intergovernmental Panel on Climate Change projected a sea level rise of 0.18 to 0.59 meters (7.1 to 23.2 inches) by the end of this century. More recent studies suggest that the rise could be as much as 1.4 meters (55 inches), with some projections suggesting even more. Such an increase in sea level would cause shorelines around the world to retreat on average more than 30 meters (about 100 feet)—eliminating thousands of square kilometers of coastal land in North America alone. With such an increase in global sea level, some island countries would literally disappear (Figure 20-12).

> **Learning Check 20-5**   **Explain how current climate change may affect the coastlines of oceans.**

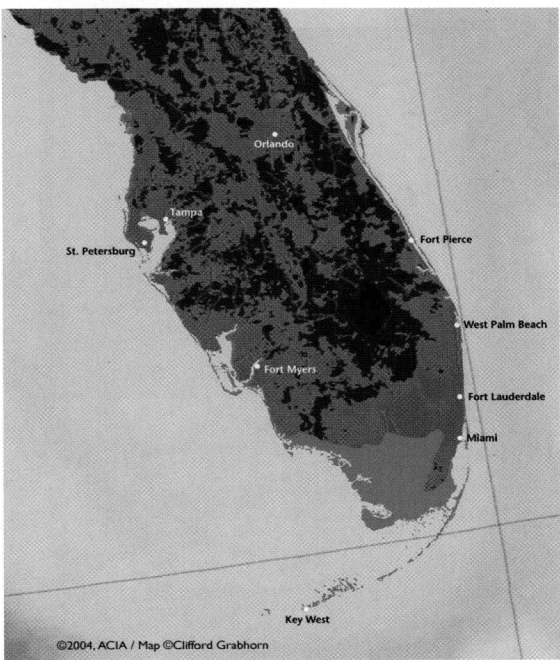

▲ **Figure 20-12** NASA map with red showing the estimated coastal area of southern Florida that will be flooded by a 1-meter rise in sea level.

Ice Push

The shores of bodies of water that freeze over in winter are sometimes significantly affected by *ice push*, which is usually the result of the contraction and expansion that occurs when the water freezes and thaws as the weather changes. As more and more water turns to ice—and therefore expands in volume (recall the discussion of *frost wedging* in Chapter 15)—near-shore ice is shoved onto the land, where it can deform the shoreline by pushing against it, more or less in the fashion of a small glacial advance.

Ice push is usually unimportant on seashores outside the Arctic and Antarctic, but it can be responsible for numerous minor alterations of the shorelines of high-latitude or high-elevation lakes.

Organic Secretions

Several aquatic animals and plants produce solid masses of rocklike material by secreting calcium carbonate. By far the most significant of these organisms is the coral *polyp*, a tiny animal that builds a hard external skeleton of calcium carbonate and then lives inside it. Coral polyps are of many species, and they cluster together in social colonies of uncounted billions of individuals. Under favorable conditions (clear, shallow, salty warm water), the coral can accumulate into enormous masses, forming reefs, platforms, and atolls, all commonplace features in tropical and subtropical oceans. (Coral reef structures will be discussed later in this chapter.)

Stream Outflow

The source of most sediment deposited in shoreline beaches and other depositional features is the outflow from streams, although in some locations all or part of the sediment may come directly from the erosion of coastal rocks. As we saw in Chapter 16, in some cases the sediment carried by streams is deposited as alluvium in a delta. Even in such cases, at least some of the sediment carried by streams into the ocean is further transported and then deposited elsewhere by coastal waters (Figure 20-13).

> **Learning Check 20-6**   **What is the source of most coastal sediment?**

Coastal Sediment Transport

FG8

Animation
Coastal
Sediment
Transport

Many kinds of currents flow in the oceans and lakes of the world, but nearly all transportation of sediment along coastlines is accomplished by wave action and local currents.

Longshore Currents: Coastal topography is affected most by **longshore currents**, in which the water and sediment move roughly parallel to the shoreline. (Think of *longshore* as a contraction for "along the shore.") Longshore currents develop just offshore and are set up by the action of the waves striking the coast at a

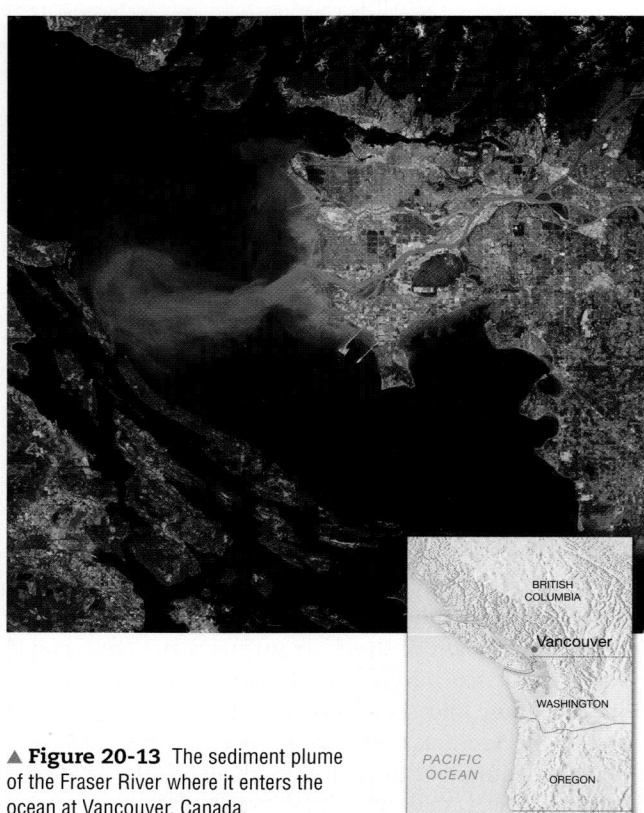

Video
Movement of
Sand in Beach
Compartment

shifting of sand directly onshore by breaking waves and the retreating water from the beach. This movement takes the form of **beach drifting** along a coastline, a zigzag movement of sediment that results in a general downwind displacement parallel to the coast (see Figure 20-14). Nearly all waves approach the coast obliquely rather than at a right angle (Figure 20-15), and therefore the sand and other debris carried onshore by the breaking wave move up the beach at an oblique angle. Some of the water soaks into the beach, but much of it returns seaward directly downslope, which is normally at a right angle to the shoreline. This return flow takes some of the sand with it, much of which is picked up by the next surging wave and carried shoreward again along an oblique path. This infinitely repetitious pattern of movement shifts the debris farther and farther along the coastline. Because wind is the driving force for wave motion, the strength, direction, and duration of the wind are the principal determinants of beach drifting.

Some sediment transport along shorelines is accomplished directly by the wind. Wherever waves have carried or hurled sand and finer-grained particles to positions above the water level, these particles can be picked up by a breeze and moved overland. This type of movement frequently results in dune formation and sometimes moves sand a considerable distance inland (Figure 20-16; see Chapter 18 for a more lengthy discussion of sand dunes).

▲ **Figure 20-13** The sediment plume of the Fraser River where it enters the ocean at Vancouver, Canada.

slight angle (Figure 20-14). Because most waves are generated by wind, the direction of a longshore current typically reflects the local wind direction. Longshore currents are prominent transporters of sand and other sediment along many shorelines.

Beach Drifting: Another significant mechanism of coastal sediment transport involves the short-distance

Learning Check 20-7 **Explain the coastal sediment transport processes of beach drifting and longshore currents.**

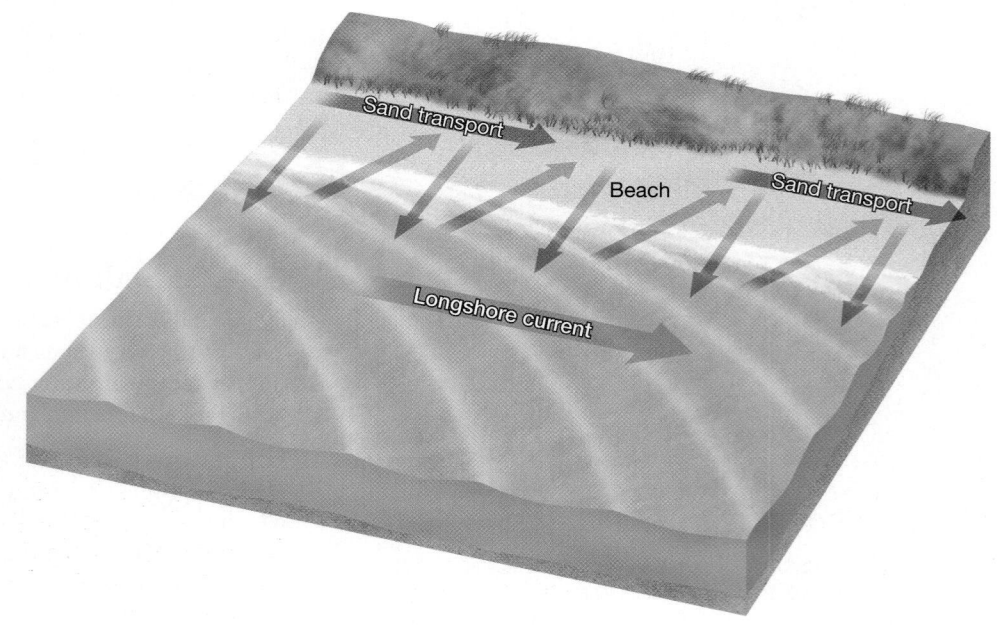

▶ **Figure 20-14** Beach drifting involves a zigzag movement of sand along the coast. Sand is brought obliquely onto the beach by the wave and is then returned seaward by the backwash. Longshore currents develop just offshore and move sediment parallel to the coastline. Because most waves develop in response to the wind, longshore currents and beach drifting typically move sediment in a general downwind direction along a shore.

▲ **Figure 20-15** Here, a series of wave roll in obliquely to the beach at Cape Byron, on the eastern coast of Australia. The direction of beach drifting would be from the bottom of the photograph toward the top.

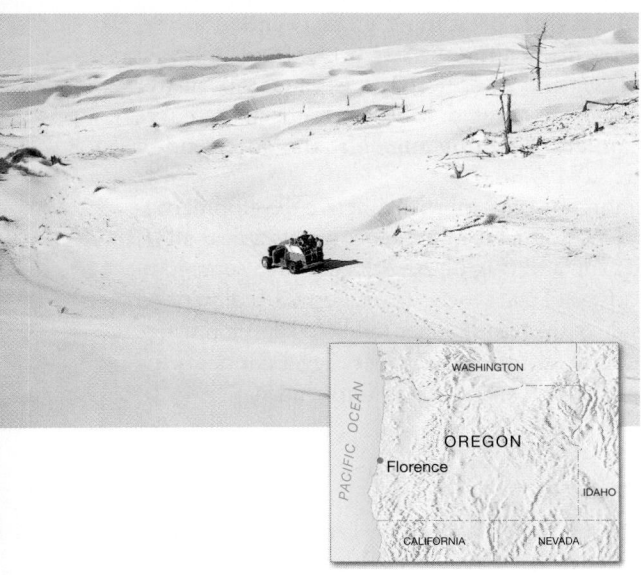

▲ **Figure 20-16** Sand is sometimes heaped into dunes that cover extensive areas. One of the largest sand accumulations in North America is along the central coast of Oregon, near Florence.

COASTAL DEPOSITIONAL LANDFORMS

 FG2, FG8

Although the restless waters of coastal areas accomplish notable erosion and transportation, in many cases the most conspicuous topographic features of a shoreline are formed by the deposition of sediment, especially sand-size sediment. Just as with streamflow on the surface of a continent, coastal deposition occurs wherever the energy of moving water is diminished.

Sediment Budget of Depositional Landforms

Maritime deposits along coastlines tend to be more ephemeral than noncoastal deposits. This is due primarily to the composition of marine deposits, which typically consist of relatively small particles (sand and gravel), and to the fact that the sand is not stabilized by a vegetation cover. Most coastal deposits are under constant onslaught by agitated waters that can rapidly wash away portions of the sediment. Consequently, the **sediment budget** must be in balance if the deposit is to persist; for the budget to be in balance, removal of sand must be offset by addition of sand. Most marine deposits have a continuing sediment flux, with debris arriving in some places and departing in others. During storms, the balance is often upset, with the result that the deposit is either significantly reshaped or totally removed, only to be replaced when calmer conditions prevail.

Beaches

The most widespread marine depositional feature is the **beach**, which is an exposed deposit of loose sediment adjacent to a body of water. Although the sediment can range in size from fine sand to large cobbles, it is usually relatively homogeneous in size on a given section of beach. Beaches composed of smaller particles (which is to say sand, because silt and clay get carried away in suspension and do not form beaches) are normally broad and slope gently seaward, whereas those formed of larger particles (gravel, cobbles) generally slope more steeply.

Beach Profiles: Beaches occupy the transition zone between land and water, sometimes extending well above the normal sea level into elevations reached only by the highest storm

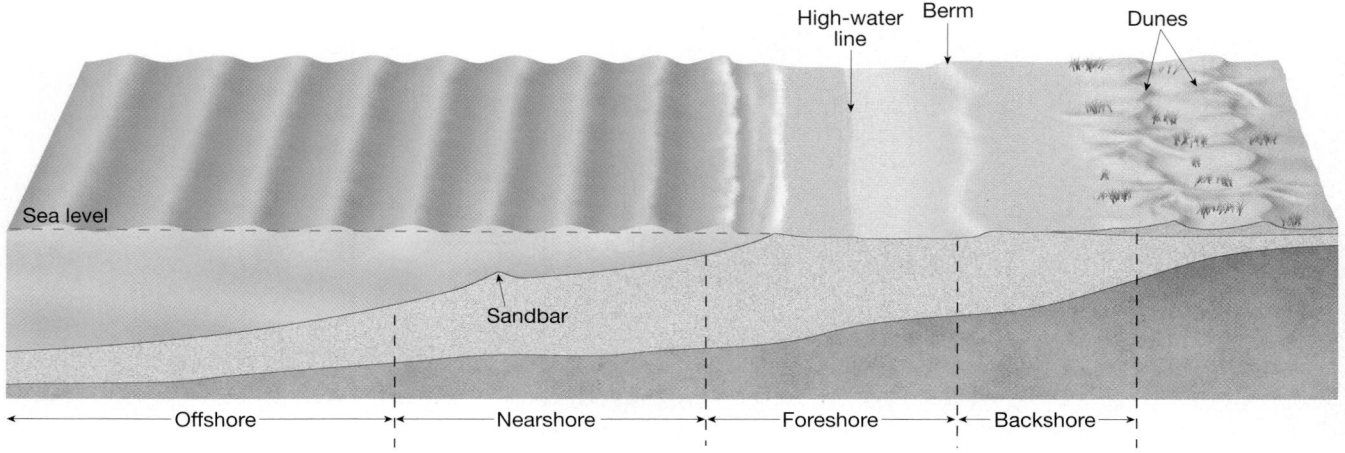

▲ **Figure 20-17** An idealized beach profile.

waves. On the seaward side, they generally extend down to the level of the lowest tides and can often be found at still lower levels, where they merge with muddy bottom deposits. Figure 20-17 portrays an idealized beach profile.

The *backshore* is the upper part of the beach, landward of the high-water line. It is usually dry, being covered by waves only during severe storms. It contains one or more *berms*, which are flattish wave-deposited sediment platforms. The *foreshore* is the zone that is regularly covered and uncovered by the rise and fall of tides. The *nearshore* extends from the low-tide mark, seaward to where the low-tide breakers begin to form—the nearshore is not exposed to the atmosphere, but it is the place where waves break and where surf action is greatest. The *offshore* zone is permanently underwater and deep enough that wave action rarely influences the bottom.

Beaches sometime extend for dozens of kilometers along straight coastlines, particularly if the relief of the land is slight and the bedrock unresistant. Along irregular shorelines, beach development may be restricted largely or entirely to bays, with the bays frequently alternating with rocky headlands.

Beach shape may change greatly from day to day and even from hour to hour—anytime the sediment budget of the beach changes. Normally beaches are built up during quiet weather and removed rapidly during storms. Most midlatitude beaches are longer and wider in summer and greatly worn away by the storminess of winter.

Video Summertime/ Wintertime Beach Conditions

Learning Check 20-8 What is the *sediment budget of a beach, and how can it change?*

Spits

At the mouth of a bay, sediment transported by longshore currents moves into deeper water. There the flow speed is slowed and the sediment is deposited. The growing bank of land guides the current farther into the deep water, where still more material is dropped. Any such linear deposit attached to the land at one end and extending into open water in a downcurrent direction is called a **spit** (Figure 20-18).

Although most spits are straight, sandy peninsulas projecting out into a bay or other coastal indentation, variations in local currents, winds, and waves often give them other configurations. In some cases, the spit becomes extended clear across the mouth of a bay to connect with land on the other side, producing what is called a **baymouth bar** and transforming the bay to a lagoon. Another common modification of spit shape is caused by water movements in the bay that can cause the deposits to curve toward the mainland, forming a *hook* at the outer end of the spit (Figure 20-19).

A less common but even more distinctive development is a **tombolo**—a depositional feature that connects a near-shore island with the mainland (Figure 20-20). Although some tombolos form as a type of spit where waves deposit sediment on the landward side of the island, other tombolos develop where a bedrock structure at, or just below, sea level connects the island with the mainland and serves to trap sand.

Barrier Islands

Another prominent coastal deposition is the **barrier island** (Figure 20-21), a long, narrow sandbar built up in shallow offshore waters, sometimes only a few hundred meters from the coast but often several kilometers at sea. Barrier islands are always oriented approximately parallel to the shore. They are believed to result from the deposition of sediment where large waves (particularly storm waves) begin to break in the shallow waters of continental shelves. However, many larger barrier islands may have more complicated histories linked to the lowered sea level during the Pleistocene.

Barrier islands often become the dominant element of a coastal terrain. Although they usually rise at most only a few meters above sea level and are typically only a few hundred meters wide, they may extend many kilometers in length. Most of the Atlantic and Gulf of Mexico coastline of the United States, for instance, is paralleled by lengthy

Narrow beach
Lagoon
Baymouth bar
Bay
Spit
Tombolo
Longshore current

◄ **Figure 20-18** Common depositional landforms along a coastline include spits, baymouth bars, and tombolos. Note the orientation of the spit to the direction of the longshore current.

barrier islands, several more than 50 kilometers (30 miles) long (Figure 20-22).

Barrier Island Lagoons: An extensive barrier island isolates the water between itself and the mainland, forming a body of quiet salt- or brackish water called a **lagoon**. Over time, a lagoon becomes increasingly filled with water-deposited sediment from coastal streams, wind-deposited sand from the barrier island, and tidal deposits if the lagoon has an opening to the sea. All three of these sources contribute to the buildup of mudflats on the edges of the lagoon. Unless tidal inlets across the barrier island permit vigorous tides or currents to carry lagoon debris seaward, the ultimate destiny of most lagoons is

AUSTRALIA

▲ **Figure 20-20** This tombolo connects the nearshore island of Point Stephens to the mainland in Tomaree National Park, New South Wales, Australia.

170°   180°
Tasman Sea
40°
NEW ZEALAND
PACIFIC OCEAN

▲ **Figure 20-19** Farewell spit on the South Island of New Zealand has developed a slight hook that curves back toward shore.

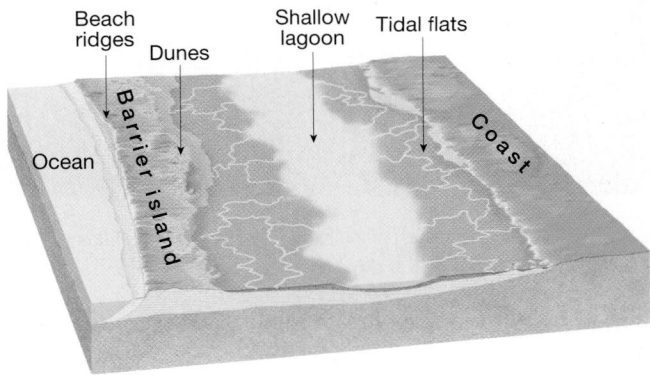

Beach ridges
Dunes
Shallow lagoon
Tidal flats
Ocean
Barrier island
Coast

▲ **Figure 20-21** A typical relationship between ocean, barrier island, and lagoon.

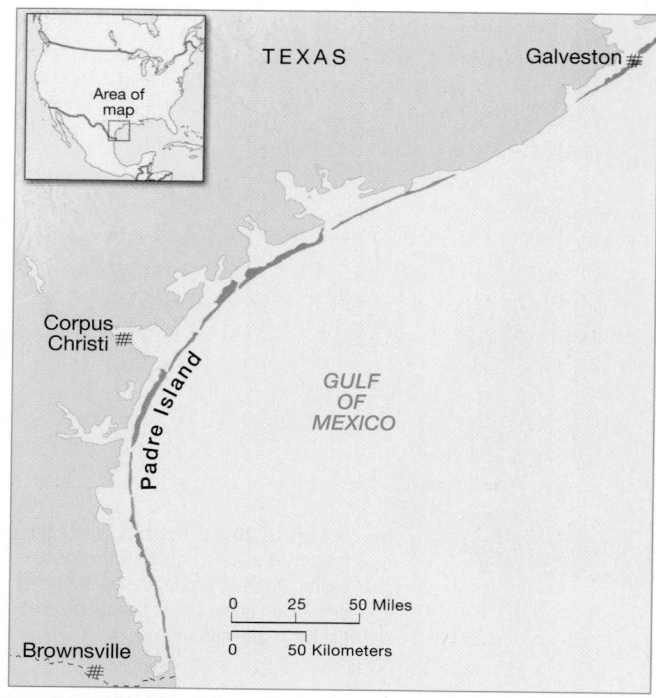

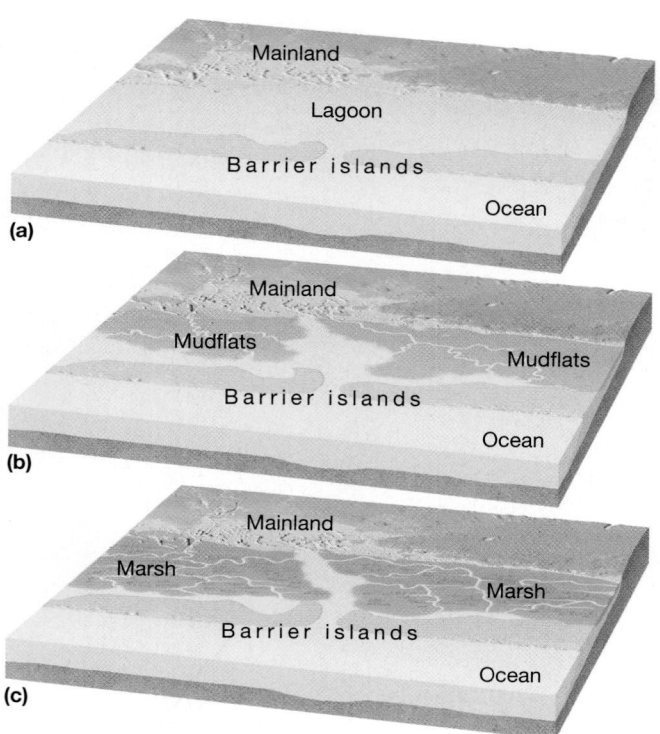

▲ **Figure 20-23** Barrier islands are separated from the mainland by lagoons (a). With the passage of time, the lagoons often become choked with sediment and become converted to mudflats (b) or marshes (c).

▲ **Figure 20-22** The longest of the barrier islands off the Gulf Coast of the United States is Padre Island, Texas.

to be slowly transformed, first to mudflats and then to coastal marshes (Figure 20-23).

In addition to infilling by sediment, another factor contributes to a lagoon's disappearance. After a barrier island becomes a certain size, it often begins to migrate slowly shoreward as waves wear away its seaward shore and sediments accumulate to build up its landward shore. Eventually, if the pattern is not interrupted by such things as changing sea level, the island and the mainland shore will merge.

Animation
Movement of
Barrier Island

Because most barrier islands rise just a few meters above sea level and are largely built up of coastal sediment, they can be quite susceptible to damage from large storms. A number of inhabited barrier islands along the Gulf Coast of the United States experienced severe erosion during hurricanes such as Lili in 2002, Katrina in 2005 (Figure 20-24), Ike in 2008, and Sandy in 2012. With even the slight rise in global sea level anticipated this century by the Intergovernmental Panel on Climate Change, barrier islands will become even more vulnerable to storm waves.

Human Alteration of Coastal Sediment Budgets

Over the last century, human activity has disrupted the sediment budgets of beaches along many shorelines of the world—this has been especially true in many coastal areas of North America. For example, dams built along rivers for flood control or hydroelectric power generation effectively act as sediment traps. With less sediment reaching the mouths of rivers, there

Animation
Coastal
Stabilization
Structures

▲ **Figure 20-24** Dauphin Island south of Mobile, Alabama, experienced extensive erosion from storm waves during Hurricane Katrina in 2005. The top photograph was taken on July 21, 2001, before Katrina. The bottom photograph was taken on August 31, 2005, after the passage of Hurricane Katrina. The oil rig in the foreground was washed onto the island during the storm.

is less sediment to be transported along the shoreline by longshore currents and beach drifting, and so the downcurrent beaches begin to shrink. In addition, artificial structures built by one community to increase or stabilize their beaches may reduce the amount of sediment transported farther down a shoreline, thus causing downcurrent beaches to be reduced in size.

Beach Nourishment: Local communities have taken a number of different approaches to solving the problem of shrinking beaches. One direct, but relatively expensive, approach is to "nourish" a beach by dumping tons of sand just slightly upcurrent of the beach. Unfortunately, since longshore currents and beach drifting will eventually transport the sand away, such nourishment must be undertaken repeatedly in order to maintain the beach at a desired size. Many of the most famous beaches in the world are maintained through such nourishment, including Hawai'i's iconic Waikīkī Beach in Honolulu.

Stabilization Structures: Another approach to maintaining beaches is the use of "hard" stabilization structures. For example, a **groin** is a short wall or dam built out from a beach to impede the longshore current and force sand deposition on the upcurrent side of the structure (Figure 20-25). Although groins do trap sediment on their upcurrent side, erosion tends to take place on their downcurrent side; to reduce this erosion, another groin can be built just downcurrent. In some locations, a series of groins, known as a *groin field*, has been built (Figure 20-26).

Jetties are usually built in pairs on either side of a river or harbor entrance. The idea is to confine the flow of water to a narrow zone, thereby keeping the sand in motion and inhibiting its deposition in the navigation channel. Jetties tend to interfere with longshore currents in the same way as groins, trapping sand on the upcurrent side while causing erosion on the downcurrent side.

Even after undertaking such expensive projects as building groin fields and carrying out regular beach nourishment, some communities are finding that it is a losing proposition—the beaches continue to shrink and there seems to be no clear solution available to them.

Learning Check 20-9 **How do groins and jetties typically influence the beach around them?**

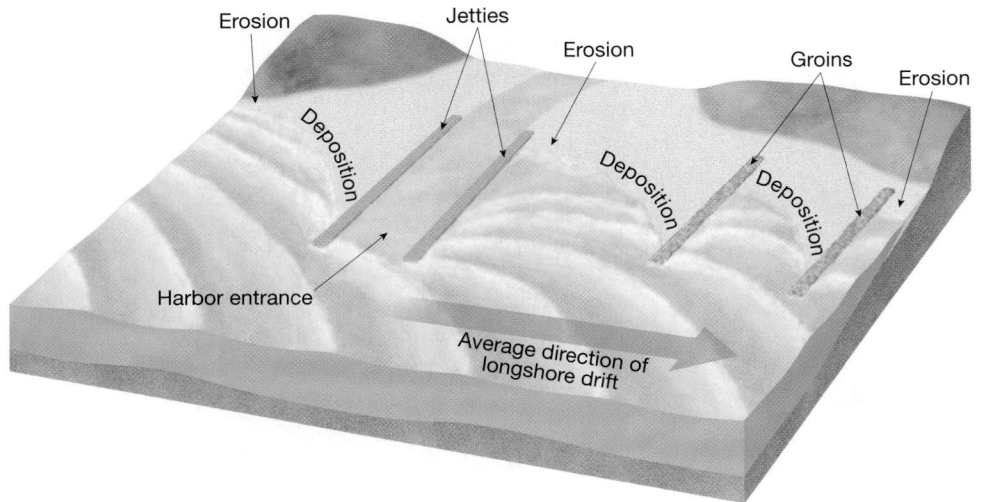

◄ **Figure 20-25** Jetties and groins along a shoreline trap sediment on their upcurrent side, while erosion tends to remove sediment on their downcurrent side.

▲ **Figure 20-26** Groin field along Norderney Island in northern Germany. The dominant direction of the longshore current is from left to right.

SHORELINES OF SUBMERGENCE AND EMERGENCE

One of the most conspicuous changes influencing coastal topography, especially oceanic coastlines, comes from a change in the relative height of the water relative to the coastal land—a relative rise in sea level leading to a *shoreline of submergence*, or a relative rise in the land leading to a *shoreline of emergence*. As we've seen, such changes can occur from either an actual increase or decrease in the amount of ocean water, or when the land is tectonically rising or sinking relative to the ocean.

Coastal Submergence

In the recent geological past, sea level has fluctuated sharply. For example, during a warmer climatic interval in an interglacial period, 125,000 years ago, sea level was about 6 meters (20 feet) higher than it is today. During the last glacial peak (about 20,000 years ago), sea level is estimated to have been about 120 meters (400 feet) lower than it is at present.

Almost all the world's oceanic coastlines show evidence of submergence during the last 15,000 years or so, a result of the melting of the Pleistocene ice sheets. As water from melting glaciers returned to the oceans, rising sea level caused widespread submergence of coastal zones. Further, as contemporary global warming leads to a slight increase in sea level, a slow but gradual expansion of flooded shorelines is expected to continue during this century.

Ria Shorelines: The most prominent result of submergence is the drowning of previous river valleys, which produces *estuaries*, or long fingers of seawater projecting inland. A coast along which there are numerous estuaries is called a **ria shoreline**. A ria (from the Spanish *ría*, meaning "river") is a long, narrow inlet of a river that gradually decreases in depth from mouth to head (Figure 20-27). If a hilly or mountainous coastal area is submerged, numerous offshore islands may indicate the previous location of hilltops and ridge crests.

Fjorded Coasts: Spectacular coastlines often occur where high-relief coastal terrain has undergone extensive glaciation. Troughs once occupied by valley glaciers or by continental ice sheets may be so deep that their bottoms are presently far below sea level—as sea level rose at the end of the Pleistocene the troughs filled with seawater. In some localities these deep, sheer-walled coastal indentations—called **fjords**—are so numerous that they create an extraordinarily irregular coastline, often with long, narrow fingers of saltwater reaching more than 160 kilometers (100 miles) inland.

The most extensive and spectacular fjorded coasts are in Norway, western Canada, Alaska, southern Chile, the South Island of New Zealand, Greenland, and Antarctica (Figure 20-28).

Learning Check 20-10 Why do so many coastlines around the world show signs of submergence?

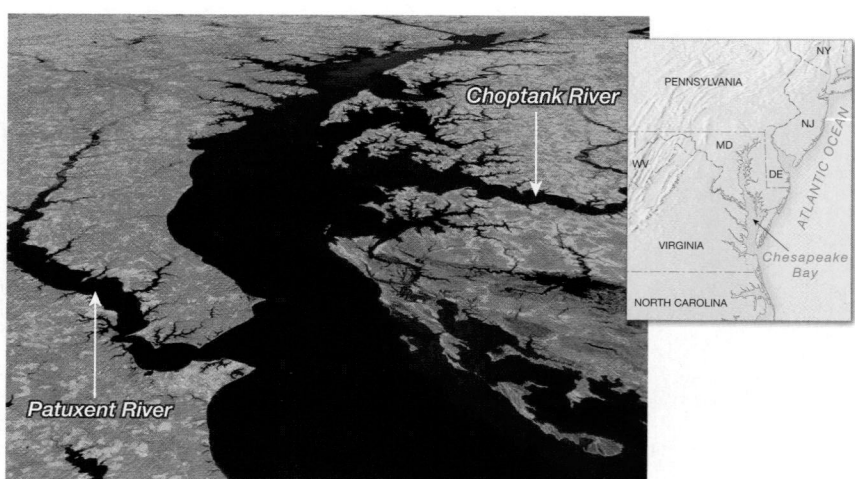

▶ **Figure 20-27** Landsat image of Chesapeake Bay. On the left, the flooded mouth of the Patuxent River can be seen running parallel to the Bay; on the right the flooded mouth of the Choptank River connects with the bay.

NEWFOUNDLAND
AND LABRADOR

QUEBEC

*LABRADOR
SEA*

50°

NEWFOUNDLAND

NOVA SCOTIA
60°

◄ **Figure 20-28** The Grey River Fjord along the southern coast of Newfoundland, Canada.

Coastal Emergence   FG2, FG8

Evidence of previously higher sea levels is sometimes related to ice melting during past interglacial ages but is more often associated with tectonic uplift. The clearest topographic results of coastal emergence are shoreline features raised well above the present water level. Often the emerged portion of a continental shelf appears as a broad, flat coastal plain, with erosion wearing back the land at a cliff dropping down to the sea.

Wave-Cut Cliffs and Platforms: One of the most common coastal landform complexes comprises wave-cut cliffs, sea stacks, and wave-cut platforms (see Figure 20-11). As we discussed earlier, as waves erode away at a rocky headland, steep wave-cut cliffs are formed, and these cliffs receive the greatest pounding at their base, where the power of the waves is concentrated.

A combination of hydraulic pounding, abrasion, pneumatic push, and chemical solution at the cliff base frequently cuts a notch at the high-water level (Figure 20-29a). As the notch is enlarged, the overhang sporadically collapses, and the cliff recedes as the ocean advances. Where wave action cuts through the bottom of a cliff-topped headland, a *sea arch* may be formed (see Figure 20-6), while *sea stacks* develop where wave erosion leaves towers of rock isolated just offshore from the coastal cliff (see Figure 20-1).

Seaward of the cliff face, the pounding and abrasion of the waves create a broad erosional surface called a **wave-cut platform** (or *wave-cut bench*) usually slightly below water level. The combination of wave-cut cliff and wave-cut platform produces a profile that resembles a letter "L," with the steep vertical cliff descending to a notched base and the flat horizontal platform extending seaward.

The debris eroded from cliff and platform is mostly removed by the swirling waters. The larger fragments are battered into smaller and smaller pieces until they are small

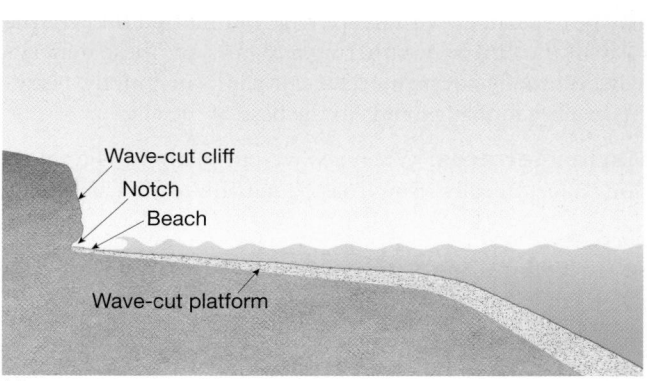

(a)

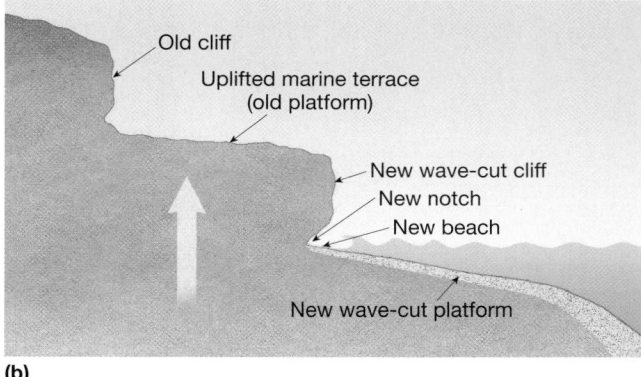

(b)

▲ **Figure 20-29** (a) A wave-cut platform develops where a coastal cliff is worn back by wave erosion. (b) A marine terrace develops when a wave-cut platform is tectonically uplifted above sea level.

591

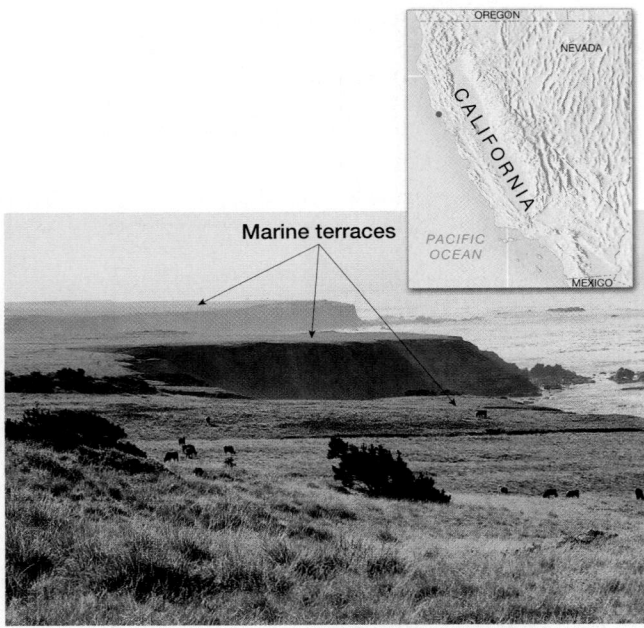

▲ **Figure 20-30** Uplifted marine terraces, well above the present shoreline. This scene is on the north coast of California near Fort Ross.

enough to be transportable. Some of the sand and gravel produced in this fashion may be washed into an adjacent bay to become, at least temporarily, a part of the beach. Much of the debris, however, is shifted directly seaward where it may be deposited. With the passage of time and the wearing away of the cliff by weathering and erosion, these deposits may eventually cover the wave-cut platform entirely, resulting in a beach that extends to the base of the cliff.

Marine Terraces: When a wave-cut platform is uplifted along a tectonically rising coast, a **marine terrace** is formed

(Figure 20-29b). It appears that fluctuations of sea level during the Pleistocene played a part in the formation of at least some marine terraces: when sea level drops during a glacial period, the wave-cut platform is left well above sea level; gradual tectonic uplift during the period of low sea level leaves the terrace high enough to be preserved after sea level rises again during the subsequent interglacial period.

Along some shorelines of the world, a series of marine terraces is present, reflecting several episodes of terrace formation (Figure 20-30).

> **Learning Check 20-11**   **What can you infer about a coastline that has a series of marine terraces?**

CORAL REEF COASTS

In tropical oceans, nearly all continents and islands are fringed with either *coral reefs* or some other type of coralline formation (Figure 20-31). Coralline structures are built by a complicated series of events that involve animals, algae, and various physical and chemical processes.

Coral Polyps

The critical element in the development of coral reefs is a group of anthozoan animals (members of the class *Anthozoa* that are closely related to jellyfish and sea anemones) called *stony corals*. These tiny creatures (most are only a few millimeters long) live in colonies of countless individuals, attaching themselves to one another both with living tissue and with their external skeletons (Figure 20-32). Each individual *coral polyp* extracts calcium carbonate from the seawater and secretes a limy skeleton around the lower half of its body. Most polyps withdraw into their skeletal cups during the day and extend their armlike feeding structures

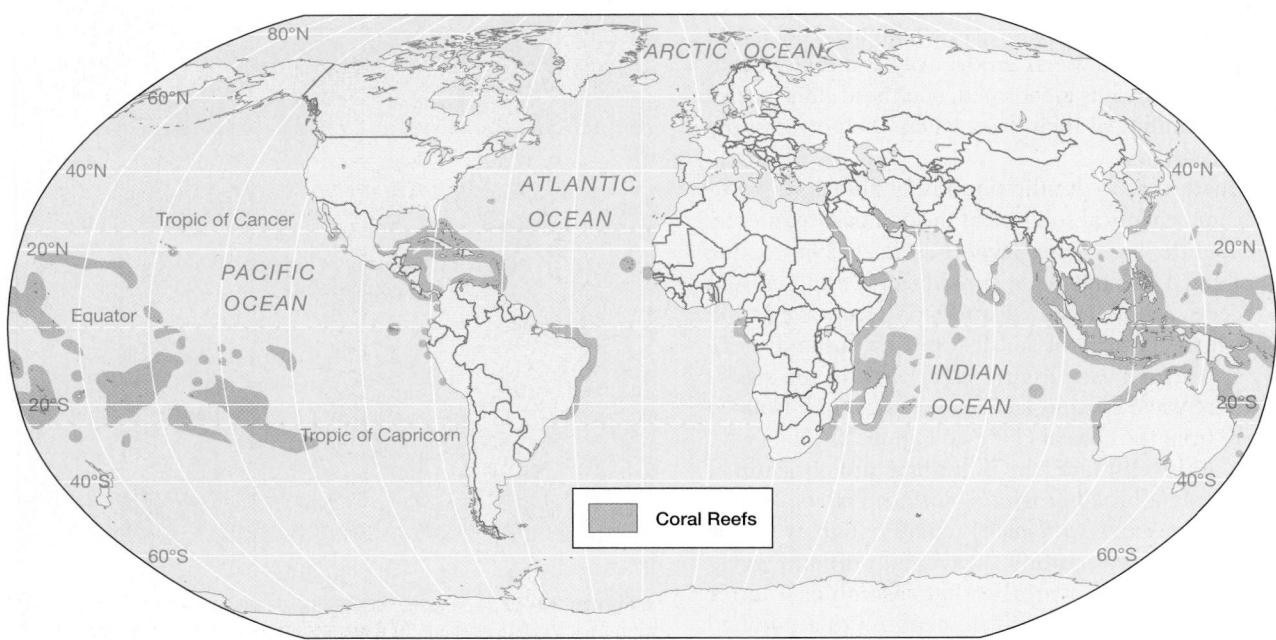

▲ **Figure 20-31** Distribution of coral reefs and other coralline structures in the oceans of the world.

◀ **Figure 20-32** Coral comes in an extraordinary variety of sizes, shapes, forms, and species. This close-up reef scene in the Bahamas shows a "Christmas tree" worm in a colony of coral.

at night. At the top of the body is a mouth surrounded by rings of tentacles, which gives them a blossom-like appearance that for centuries caused biologists to believe that they were plants rather than animals. They feed on minute animal and plant plankton. Although the coral polyp is an animal, reef-building hard corals are hosts to symbiotic algae that provide additional food for the coral polyp through photosynthesis.

The ubiquity of coral reefs in shallow tropical waters is a tribute to the remarkable productiveness of the polyps because they are not actually very hardy creatures. They cannot survive in water that is very cool or very fresh or very dirty. Moreover, they require considerable sunlight, so most cannot live more than a few tens of meters below the surface of the ocean (recently explored *deep-* or *cold-water corals*, found at depths of more than 1000 meters [3200 feet)], are a fascinating exception to this).

Many coral reefs around the world show signs of degradation—from both natural and human-generated causes. For example, see the box, "Focus: Imperiled Coral Reefs."

Coral Reefs

Coral polyps can build coralline formations almost anywhere in shallow tropical waters where a coastline provides a stable foundation. Coral reefs in the shallows off the coasts of Florida, for instance, are built on such stable bases. The famous Great Barrier Reef off the northeastern coast of Australia is an immense shallow-water platform of bedrock largely, but not entirely, covered with coral. Its enormously complex structure includes many individual reefs, irregular coral masses, and a number of islands (Figure 20-33).

One favored location for coral reefs is around a volcanic island in tropical waters; as the volcano forms and then

subsides, a sequence of different kinds of reefs may grow upward: *fringing reefs, barrier reefs,* and *atolls.*

▲ **Figure 20-33** A view of Australia's Great Barrier Reef.

Imperiled Coral Reefs

All species of reef-building coral contain zooxanthellae, a type of algae that lives in a symbiotic relationship with the coral polyp. Through photosynthesis, the algae provide nutrients to the coral—it is also the algae that give coral its beautiful color.

Coral Bleaching: For reasons that are not completely understood, when coral is stressed, it expels the algae, leaving its exoskeleton of calcium carbonate a translucent white color. This phenomenon is known as *coral bleaching* (Figure 20-F). In some cases, bleached corals die within just a few weeks if the zooxanthellae are not replaced.

Bleaching events have been observed for decades, caused by such factors as a sharp decrease in water salinity, sedimentation, pollution, and abrupt changes in temperature; but it became clear to researchers in the 1980s that stress from high water temperature was the most common cause. The warming of coastal waters during the 1982–83 El Niño was observed to cause coral bleaching in Panama; the 1997–98 El Niño was even stronger and caused bleaching in reefs around the world.

In recent years, some researchers have started pointing to higher sea-surface temperatures (SST) associated with climate change warming as at least one of the causes of the rising number of coral bleaching incidents. In 2010, a major bleaching event associated with high SST occurred in the Indian Ocean and the coral reefs of Southeast Asia; scientists at the Australian Research Council reported that it may be the worst coral die-off ever documented.

Monitoring Coral Bleaching: The National Oceanic and Atmospheric Administration (NOAA) monitors stress on coral reefs through its Coral Reef Watch program. NOAA is currently testing a Bleaching Outlook system that issues predictions of bleaching potential for periods of up to three months based on experimental SST forecasts (Figure 20-G).

Acidification of Oceans: In addition to bleaching, coral reefs are being stressed by the slight acidification of the ocean waters caused by the absorption of carbon dioxide (acidification of the oceans is discussed in Chapter 9). In January 2009, an international panel of 155 marine scientists issued the Monaco Declaration, stating that damage from ocean acidification is already detectable, and that with the projected increase in atmospheric carbon dioxide—and the associated increased acidification of the ocean—many regions of the world will become "chemically inhospitable" to coral reefs by midcentury.

Ecosystem Loss: The loss of coral reefs through bleaching and other natural and human-produced causes is alarming many researchers. When coral dies, an entire ecosystem is at risk: the fish and other creatures that depend on coral for survival are stressed, local fisheries can decline, the protection from storm waves offered to low-lying islands fringed with reefs is diminished, and, of course, the loss of species and biodiversity may be irreparable.

▲ **Figure 20-F** Bleached coral in the Great Barrier Reef, Australia.

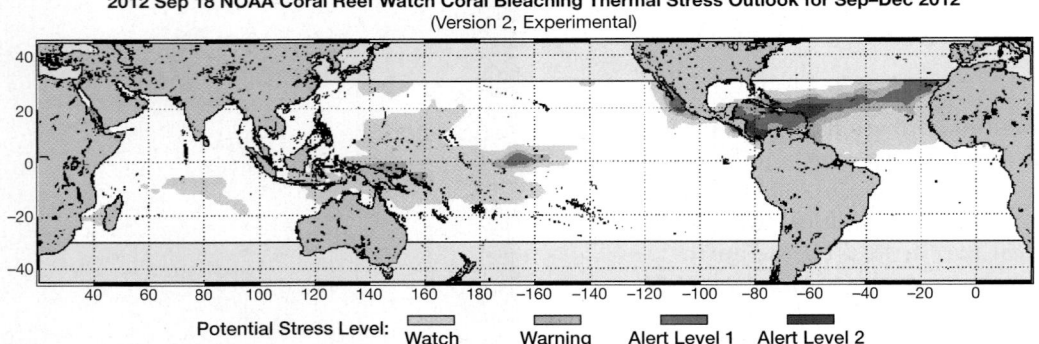

▲ **Figure 20-G** Coral Reef Watch experimental Coral Bleaching Thermal Stress Outlook for fall 2012. The darker the shade of red, the higher the potential for coral bleaching.

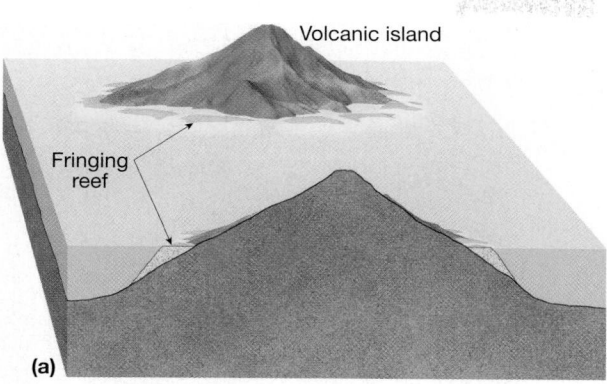

(a)

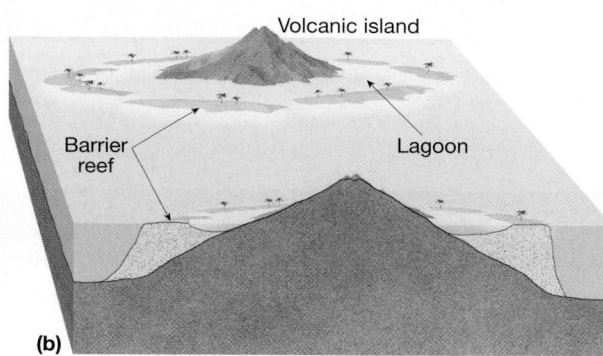

(b)

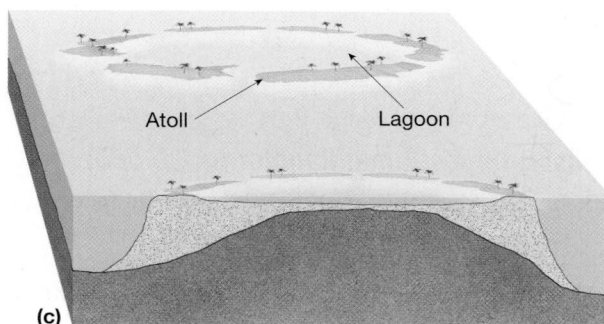

(c)

◄ **Figure 20-34** Coral reef formation around a sinking volcano. (a) Around a newly formed volcano rising above the water of a tropical ocean, secretions from coral polyps living along the shallow-water flanks of the volcano accumulate into a fringing reef attached to the mountain. (b) As the volcano becomes dormant and begins to sink, the coral continues to grow upward over the original base, essentially a cylinder surrounding the mountain. Such a reef separated from its mainland by a lagoon is a barrier reef. (c) Once the volcano is completely submerged, the coral surrounding a landless lagoon is called an atoll reef.

Fringing Reefs: When the volcano first forms, as, for example, over the Hawaiian hot spot described in Chapter 14, coral accumulates on the part of the mountain flank just below sea level because it is in these shallow waters that polyps live. The result is a reef built right onto the volcano, as shown in Figure 20-34a; such an attached reef is called a **fringing reef** (Figure 20-35). As the plate moves off the hot spot it cools and becomes denser, so the volcano begins to sink.

Animation
Seamounts &
Coral Reefs

Barrier Reefs: As new layers are laid down over old, the coral builds upward around the volcano as a cylinder of irregular height. At the same time, the volcano is sinking and pulling the original reef base downward. When the coral has been built up enough and the volcano has sunk enough, the result at the water surface is a coral ring separated by a lagoon from the part of the volcano still above water, as in Figure 20-34b. Called a **barrier reef**, this ring of coral may be a broken circle because of the varying thickness of the coral, appearing to "float" around a central volcanic peak (but, of course, is actually attached to the flanks of the sinking mountain far below the water surface). The surface of a barrier reef is usually right at sea level, with some portions projecting upward into the air.

► **Figure 20-35** A part of the fringing reef on the island of Moorea in French Polynesia.

Atolls: Coral polyps continue to live in the upper, shallow-water portions of a barrier reef, and so the reef continues to grow upward. Once the top of the volcano sinks below the water surface, the reef surrounding a now landless lagoon is called an **atoll** (Figure 20-34c). The term *atoll* implies a ring-shaped structure. In actuality, however, the ring is rarely unbroken; rather it consists of a string of closely spaced coral islets separated by narrow channels of water. Each individual islet is called a *motu*. Because coral cannot live above sea level, much of the coral debris that makes up the above-water portion of an atoll has been deposited there by storm waves (Figure 20-36).

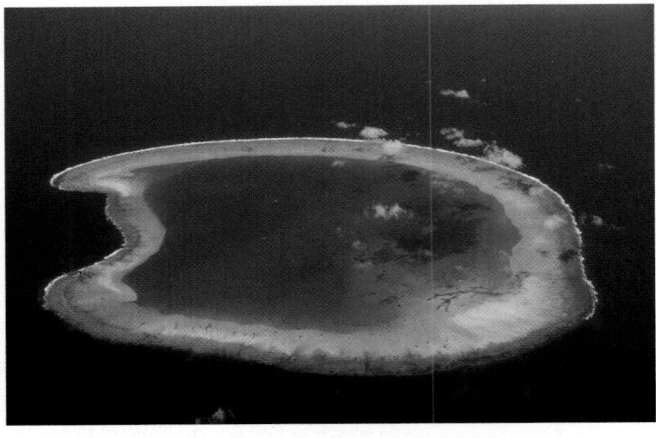

▲ **Figure 20-36** Bassas da India is a coral atoll west of Madagascar.

Learning Check 20-12 **How can an atoll develop from a fringing reef or a barrier reef?**

Chapter 20	**LEARNING REVIEW**

After studying this chapter, you should be able to answer the following questions. Key terms from each text section are shown in **bold type**. Definitions for key terms are also found in the glossary at the back of the book.

KEY TERMS AND CONCEPTS

Coastal Processes (*p. 574*)

1. What are some of the ways that landform development along ocean shorelines is different from that along lakeshores?

Waves (*p. 575*)

2. How are most ocean waves generated?
3. What are **swells** in the ocean?
4. How is a **wave of oscillation** different from a **wave of translation**?
5. Contrast the characteristics of ocean waves in deep water with waves in shallow water, especially note how **wavelength** and **wave height** change as a wave comes onshore.
6. Contrast **swash** and **backwash** on a beach.
7. Describe and explain the process of **wave refraction**.
8. Explain the formation and characteristics of a **tsunami**.

Important Shoreline-Shaping Processes (*p. 579*)

9. Why did **eustatic sea-level changes** take place during the Pleistocene?
10. What is the source of most sediment along the shorelines of the continents?
11. Describe the formation and characteristics of **longshore currents**.
12. Describe the process of **beach drifting**.

Coastal Depositional Landforms (*p. 585*)

13. Explain the concept of the **sediment budget** of a coastal depositional landform such as a beach.
14. What causes a **beach** to change shape and size?
15. Describe and contrast a coastal **spit** and a **baymouth bar**.
16. Under what circumstances does a **tombolo** form?
17. Describe the features of a **barrier island**.
18. What happens to most coastal **lagoons** with the passage of time?
19. How do **groins** and **jetties** typically affect the beaches around them?

Shorelines of Submergence and Emergence (*p. 590*)

20. Explain the formation of **ria shorelines** and **fjords**.
21. Explain how wave-cut cliffs and **wave-cut platforms** develop.
22. Describe the formation of a **marine terrace** along a shoreline of emergence.

Coral Reef Coasts (*p. 592*)

23. Explain how a coral **fringing reef** forms and how it can subsequently become transformed first to a **barrier reef** and then to an **atoll**.

STUDY QUESTIONS

1. What factors influence the erosional power of waves striking a coastline?
2. How does air serve as a tool of erosion in wave action?
3. What will likely happen to a downcurrent beach when a major river flowing into the ocean is dammed? Why?
4. What is beach nourishment, and is it a good investment for a coastal community? Why or why not?
5. Why are shorelines of submergence so common today?
6. How might global warming and other environmental changes caused by human activities affect coral reefs?

EXERCISES

1. The steepness of a wave is described with the ratio of the wave height to wavelength (in other words: wave steepness = wave height ÷ wavelength). When the steepness of a wave is greater than 1/7, the wave breaks.
   a. What is the maximum wave height for a wavelength of 7 meters? _____ meters
   b. What is the maximum wave height for a wavelength of 20 meters? _____ meters
   c. If a breaking wave is 2 meters high, what is the wavelength? _____ meters
2. As a rough generalization, most waves will break when they reach a water depth that is 1.3 times the wave height.
   a. If a breaking wave has a height of 1.5 meters, how deep is the water below? _____ meters
   b. If a breaking wave has a height of 7 meters, how deep is the water below? _____ meters

Seeing Geographically

Look again at the photograph of the Big Sur coastline at the beginning of the chapter (p. 572). What explains the way the waves approach shore? The distance from shore where waves break varies along this stretch of coastline—why? Where along this coastline is wave erosion strongest? Why is this so? Where does it appear that most of the coastal sediment is being deposited? What explains this?

MasteringGeography™

Looking for additional review and test prep materials? Visit the Study Area in MasteringGeography™ to enhance your geographic literacy, spatial reasoning skills, and understanding of this chapter's content by accessing a variety of resources, including geoscience animations, MapMaster interactive maps, videos, RSS feeds, flashcards, web links, self-study quizzes, and an eText version of *McKnight's Physical Geography: A Landscape Appreciation.*

Chapter 1

1-1: *Physical geography* primarily focuses on patterns in the natural environment and on human interaction with the environment; *cultural geography* primarily focuses on patterns of human activity and culture. **1-2:** Many patterns and processes in the natural environment can be influenced by economic activity—such as the consequences of the extraction of resources or the burning of fossil fuels; economic activity in one part of the world can influence the environment in another part of the world. **1-3:** Strictly speaking, science uses evidence to eliminate unsupported ideas or hypotheses; science must always leave open the possibility that new evidence will cause us to come to new conclusions. **1-4:** The *lithosphere* is the solid part of Earth, the *atmosphere* the gases surrounding Earth, the *hydrosphere* the waters of Earth, the *cryosphere* the frozen water of Earth, and the *biosphere* the living organisms on Earth. **1-5:** When the inputs to a system are balanced by the outputs, the conditions within a system remain the same over time. **1-6:** With a *positive feedback loop*, change in one direction tends to reinforce change in that direction; with a *negative feedback loop*, change tends to bring the system back toward equilibrium. **1-7:** Terrestrial planets are relatively small and are composed primarily of mineral material; Jovian planets are larger, less dense, and composed primarily of gases, liquids, and ices. **1-8:** Earth's highest point is Mount Everest (8850 m; 29,035 ft.) and its lowest point is the bottom of the Mariana Trench (–11,033 m; –36,198 ft.)—a difference of about 19,883 m (65, 233 ft.). **1-9:** A *great circle* is the largest circle that can be drawn on a sphere, dividing it into two hemispheres; the equator is a great circle. **1-10:** Because all parallels are parallel to each other—they never cross or touch. **1-11:** North America is west of the prime meridian, so it is described by west longitude. **1-12:** Earth rotates, or "spins," on its axis; Earth revolves, or "orbits," around the Sun. **1-13:** No; the North Pole leans most directly toward the Sun on the June solstice and leans most directly away from the Sun on the December solstice. **1-14:** 23.5° N. **1-15:** Not at all—the equator has virtually 12 hours of daylight every day of the year. **1-16:** On the March equinox and September equinox. **1-17:** 6 months. **1-18:** Crossing from west to east into a new time zone it becomes one hour later. **1-19:** Crossing the IDL going from west to east it becomes the previous day.

Chapter 2

2-1: Because it is impossible to flatten a sphere without distortion. **2-2:** 10,000 centimeters. **2-3:** A system that mathematically transfers the graticule and features of Earth onto the flat surface of a map. **2-4:** An *equivalent (equal area) map* shows correct area (size) relationships over the entire map; a *conformal map* maintains correct angular (shape) relationships over the entire map. **2-5:** No; a *Mercator projection* shows correct shapes, but severely distorts apparent area in the high latitudes, making it unsuitable for studying area distribution patterns. **2-6:** *Goode's interrupted projection* is equivalent, making it suitable for studying area distribution patterns; in addition, Goode's maintains reasonable shape relationships for the continents (although it isn't conformal). **2-7:** A line of equal value on a map; for example, temperature patterns can be mapped with *isotherms* and topography mapped with *elevation contour* lines. **2-8:** An oblique view of the landscape is mathematically constructed from elevation data, using shaded relief, as if the Sun were illuminating the topography from the northwest. **2-9:** Timing signals from at least three satellites are received by the GPS unit; by determining the slight difference in arrival time of the signals, the GPS unit calculates the distance to each satellite, and from that information, triangulates a location. **2-10:** Near infrared images measure short infrared radiation, typically resulting in a "false-color" image that can, for example, be used to detect differences in living vegetation; thermal infrared imagery detects differences in emitted longwave radiation, and so, in effect, measures differences in temperature. **2-11:** Multispectral remote sensing detects radiation in several different bands of radiation simultaneously, such as visible light, near infrared, middle infrared, and thermal infrared. **2-12:** Geographic information systems (GIS) integrate data bases and maps, allowing sophisticated overlay spatial analysis; the Global Positioning System (GPS) determines location precisely.

Chapter 3

3-1: Density of the atmosphere decreases with increasing altitude. **3-2:** Nitrogen; nitrogen gas (N_2) has virtually no effect on weather processes. **3-3:** Temperature generally decreases from the surface up to the *tropopause*; in the *stratosphere* temperature increases with increasing altitude. **3-4:** No; although ozone is not the most abundant gas in the ozone layer, this is where the concentration of ozone is greatest. **3-5:** CFCs (chlorofluorocarbons) and other ozone-depleting chemicals in the ozone layer undergo a photochemical reaction that destroys ozone. **3-6:** A secondary pollutant; *smog* forms from a photochemical reaction of primary pollutants such as nitrogen dioxide. **3-7:** *Weather* refers to the short-run conditions in the atmosphere, whereas *climate* refers to the aggregate of weather conditions over at least 30 years. **3-8:** The *controls of weather and climate* influence or act upon the *elements of weather and climate* to produce variations in atmospheric conditions. **3-9:** As a result of the rotation of Earth, the path of any free-moving object is deflected to the right in the Northern Hemisphere, and to the left in the Southern Hemisphere.

Chapter 4

4-1: *Temperature* is a description of the average kinetic energy of the molecules in a substance; *heat* is the energy that transfers from one object to another because of a difference in temperature. **4-2:** *Shortwave radiation* is emitted by the Sun and includes ultraviolet, visible, and short (near) infrared wavelengths of electromagnetic radiation; *longwave radiation* is emitted by Earth's surface and atmosphere and consists of thermal infrared (far infrared) wavelengths. **4-3:** *Radiation* is the flow (or emission) of electromagnetic energy; *absorption* entails the assimilation of electromagnetic energy by an object; *reflection* occurs when an object repels the electromagnetic waves that strike it. **4-4:** Shortwave radiation from the Sun transmits through the atmosphere and is absorbed by Earth's surface; the surface is warmed and so emits longwave radiation that is absorbed by greenhouse gases (such as water vapor and carbon dioxide), thus delaying the eventual loss of this energy to space. **4-5:** *Conduction* involves the transfer of energy through molecule-to-molecule collision, whereas *convection* involves the transfer of energy through the vertical circulation of a fluid (such as air). **4-6:** Rising air expands and cools adiabatically; descending air compresses and warms adiabatically. **4-7:** The surface of Earth warms the troposphere through conduction and convection, through the emission of longwave radiation and the greenhouse effect, and through the transfer of latent heat that is absorbed during the evaporation of water and released during condensation. **4-8:** When the Sun is high in the sky, the energy from a beam of sunlight will pass through less atmosphere and will be concentrated into a smaller surface area than when the Sun is lower in the sky. **4-9:** Because of its high *specific heat*, water must absorb about five times more energy than land to exhibit a comparable temperature increase. **4-10:** The interior location will usually be warmer in summer than the coast; water only slowly warms in summer, whereas land warms quickly. **4-11:** The ocean current flowing along the west coast of a continent is cool, whereas the current flowing along the east coast is warm. **4-12:** A *temperature inversion* is present when temperature increases with increasing altitude—this is the opposite, or inverse, of the usual situation. **4-13:** Temperature generally decreases, going from the equator toward the poles, because low latitudes receive more total insolation over the year than high latitudes. **4-14:** The tropics and coastal areas have small annual temperatures ranges, whereas high latitudes in the middle of continents experience the greatest temperature ranges. **4-15:** Increasing greenhouse gas emissions, especially carbon dioxide released through the burning of fossil fuels since the mid-1700s, have increased the greenhouse effect in the atmosphere.

Chapter 5

5-1: The density of the atmosphere decreases with altitude, and so pressure decreases. **5-2:** Descending air is most likely associated with high atmospheric pressure at the surface, whereas rising air is more likely to be associated with low pressure. **5-3:** In the lowest 1000 meters of the atmosphere, friction slows the wind, and so the amount of Coriolis effect deflection decreases. **5-4:** Wind converges in a counterclockwise direction in a surface *cyclone* in the Northern Hemisphere. **5-5:** Air descends toward the surface in an *anticyclone*. **5-6:** Warm air rises near the equator; by an altitude of about 15 kilometers, the air spreads north and south and descends toward the surface at about 30° N and S, where it moves back toward the equator to be uplifted again in the *Hadley cells*. **5-7:** *Subtropical highs* are generally located over the ocean, just off the west coasts of continents at about 25° to 30° N and S; weather is generally sunny and dry. **5-8:** The *ITCZ* is generally near the equator; weather is characterized by clouds, thunderstorms and rain. **5-9:** The *trade winds* and *westerlies* diverge from the subtropical highs. **5-10:** *Jet streams* are high-speed currents of air in the upper troposphere; in each hemisphere one jet stream is generally located just poleward of the subtropical highs, and one just equatorward of the polar front. **5-11:** The position of the ITCZ shifts with the seasons, following the location of greatest insolation and surface warming. **5-12:** During the summer *monsoon*, wind blows onshore, off the ocean; during the winter monsoon, wind blows offshore. **5-13:** Warming of land during the day creates relatively lower pressure over land, so the wind blows off the water toward land. **5-14:** During an *El Niño* event the trades weaken or reverse direction. **5-15:** A *teleconnection* is a connection between the weather or the ocean in one part of the world with that in another; for example, during a strong El Niño, the North Atlantic Ocean usually experiences fewer hurricanes.

Chapter 6

6-1: A *hydrogen bond* is the attraction between the negative (oxygen) side of one water molecule, to the positive (hydrogen) side of another. **6-2:** As liquid water freezes into ice, its volume increases. **6-3:** About 5 times as much energy is needed to increase the temperature of water as a comparable mass of soil or rock, slowing water's rate of warming in summer. **6-4:** In order for ice to melt, it must absorb

energy (the *latent heat* of melting) to break bonds and allow a phase change; this energy does not increase the temperature of the water. **6-5:** As air comes close to saturation with water vapor, the rate of evaporation drops off sharply. **6-6:** 10 grams of water as vapor are in each cubic meter of air. **6-7:** 5 g ÷ 20 g = ¼ or 25% *relative humidity*. **6-8:** As temperature decreases, water vapor capacity decreases, so relative humidity increases. **6-9:** Condensation can take place when the air reaches 100% relative humidity if surfaces, such as *condensation nuclei*, are available. **6-10:** Above the *lifting condensation level*, rising air is expanding and cooling adiabatically, but latent heat released during condensation counteracts some of this cooling. **6-11:** The three clouds forms are *cirriform* (wispy clouds), *stratiform* (widespread layered clouds), and *cumuliform* (puffy clouds). **6-12:** A parcel of air will be unstable (will rise without being forced) if it is warmer, and so less dense, than the surrounding air. **6-13:** Highly unstable air is associated with strong updrafts in cumulonimbus clouds; such updrafts are necessary to lift liquid water drops high up into a cloud where they freeze into hail. **6-14:** When air is forced to rise on the windward side of a mountain, adiabatic cooling often leads to cloud formation and precipitation; air on the leeward side of the mountain (in the *rain shadow*) has lost moisture rising up the windward side; if this air descends down the leeward side, it will warm adiabatically, reducing its relative humidity even more. **6-15:** Warm, moist air rising in the ITCZ leads to high rainfall. **6-16:** The descending air of the subtropical highs leads to dry conditions. **6-17:** Deserts will have high precipitation variability from year to year. **6-18:** Sulfur dioxide (SO_2) from power plants and nitrogen oxides (NO_x) from vehicle exhaust are common sources of the chemicals that lead to acid rain.

Chapter 7

7-1: *Air masses* form over uniform surfaces, such as the ocean or tundra, when wind stops for a few days, allowing the surface to impart its characteristics to the air above. **7-2:** *Maritime polar* air masses are moist and cool. **7-3:** A *cold front* forms when a cold air mass advances into the area of a warm air mass; a *warm front* forms when a warm air mass advances into the area of a cold air mass. **7-4:** The convergence of air into the low of a *midlatitude cyclone* brings together two unlike air masses. **7-5:** Precipitation develops where air is rising and cooling adiabatically within a midlatitude cyclone—typically along the cold front, the warm front, and in the center of the low. **7-6:** An *occluded front* forms when the faster moving cold front catches up with the warm front, lifting all of the warm air mass off the surface. **7-7:** A *trough* is found along the surface position of a well-developed cold front; as the front approaches, the trough is getting closer, so pressure falls; as the front moves away, pressure rises because the trough is moving away. **7-8:** Descending air cannot make clouds and rain, and the diverging wind pattern does not bring together

air masses (and so no fronts are formed). **7-9:** An *easterly wave* is a migrating, weak low-pressure disturbance in the tropics that generally produces a band of small thunderstorms. **7-10:** As warm, moist air converges and rises in a *hurricane*, it cools; condensation releases latent heat that increases instability, strengthening the updrafts and low pressure of the storm. **7-11:** Warm ocean currents are found along the east coasts of continents; the cool currents along the west coast quickly weaken a hurricane. **7-12:** The strong winds of a hurricane generate high waves (and the very low pressure allows sea level to rise slightly); when the storm reaches a coastline, this bulge of ocean water is pushed onshore. **7-13:** Initially, updrafts dominate and the cumulonimbus cloud grows; when mature, falling precipitation initiates downdrafts that eventually lead to storm dissipation. **7-14:** Slower winds near the surface, with faster winds above, generate air spinning along a horizontal axis; strong thunderstorm updrafts lift this spinning air into a rotating *mesocyclone*, from which a tornado may form.

Chapter 8

8-1: The *Köppen climate classification system* is based on the average monthly temperature and precipitation for a location. **8-2:** A *climograph* plots the average monthly temperature for a location with a solid line, and average monthly precipitation with bars coming up from the bottom of the chart. **8-3:** Areas of Af climate are generally under the influence of the ITCZ all year, whereas areas of Aw climate come under the influence the ITCZ when it migrates into the area during summer. **8-4:** Most deserts are caused by the atmospheric stability associated with cool ocean currents and the presence of the subtropical high all year, or are in the rain shadows of mountains or deep in a continent, far from sources of moisture. **8-5:** BWh climates have hot summers and mild winters, whereas BWk climates are found in the midlatitudes, and so have warm summers but cold winters. **8-6:** Areas of both Cs and Cfa climate receive rain in the winter from midlatitude cyclones traveling in the westerlies; during summer, Cfa climates receive rain from thunderstorms and tropical cyclones; however, along the west coasts, where Cs climates are found, the subtropical highs migrate poleward in summer, bringing stable conditions and dry weather. **8-7:** The prevailing westerlies bring cold, continental air masses all of the way to the eastern side of the continent. **8-8:** The very cold air has almost no water vapor capacity, so little precipitation is possible. **8-9:** As elevation increases, temperature general decreases—roughly similar to what happens to temperature with increasing latitude. **8-10:** Water molecules containing the lighter isotope of oxygen (^{16}O) evaporate more easily than those with the heavier isotope of oxygen (^{18}O); therefore, when climate is cold, more water molecules with ^{16}O than ^{18}O will evaporate and can fall as snow; by comparing the ratio of ^{18}O to ^{16}O in ice, we can infer if that layer of glacial ice accumulated during a colder period or a warmer period.

8-11: Tiny air bubbles frozen in the glacial ice retain the atmospheric gas mixture present at the time the snow fell. **8-12:** For example, high concentrations of volcanic ash in the atmosphere can block incoming solar radiation, lowering global temperatures for a period of time. **8-13:** *Milankovitch cycles* are long-term but predictable variations in Earth–Sun relations taking place over periods of thousands of years; these cycles combine to influence the onset and end of glacial periods. **8-14:** For example, higher temperatures will lead to reduced ice and snow cover; the resulting lower albedo will increase absorption of solar radiation by the surface, and so lead to higher temperatures. **8-15:** *Temperature anomaly* refers to a difference from the long-term average temperature; over the last century, both land and ocean temperatures have increased. **8-16:** In addition to a continued increase in average global temperature, the IPCC projects that sea level will rise slightly, polar sea ice will diminish, and the frequency of extreme weather events will increase.

Chapter 9

9-1: No; more water falls on the continents as precipitation than is added to the air above through evapotranspiration—the "extra" precipitation falling on the continents comes from water evaporated from the oceans. **9-2:** The oceans of the world are interconnected—no ocean basin is completely blocked off by land from an adjacent basin. **9-3:** Salinity is generally highest in subtropical areas where evaporation is high; salinity is generally lowest near the mouths of major rivers, near the equator where rainfall is high, and in polar areas where evaporation is low and meltwater from glaciers enters the ocean. **9-4:** The highest high tides (*spring tides*) occur around the time of the new moon and full moon, when the Sun, Earth, and moon are in a line; the lowest high tides (*neap tides*) occur when the moon and Sun are at right angles to each other. **9-5:** It is associated with *thermohaline circulation*, in which cold, dense, relatively salty ocean water sinks in high-latitude ocean areas; this cold, dense water slowly flows along the bottom of the ocean, eventually to rise into warmer, shallow currents. **9-6:** Most ice is locked in continental ice sheets in Antarctica and Greenland. **9-7:** With thawing *permafrost*, buildings and roads may be damaged by subsidence, coastal areas may erode more quickly, and greenhouse gases may be released from decomposing, newly thawed organic matter. **9-8:** The Aral Sea has shrunk significantly, mainly because dams and irrigation projects diverted much of the water that once flowed into the lake. **9-9:** An *aquifer* is a layer of permeable rock into which groundwater can infiltrate. **9-10:** When a well pumps groundwater faster than it recharges, the *water table* drops around the well, forming an inverted cone pattern. **9-11:** Because withdrawal has exceeded recharge, the water table of the Ogallala Aquifer has dropped significantly (more than 30 m/100 ft.) in some places.

Chapter 10

10-1: *Biogeography* is the study of the patterns of distribution and change of living organisms. **10-2:** *Photosynthesis* is the pathway through which most solar energy enters the biosphere. **10-3:** Photosynthesis converts CO_2 into *carbohydrates*; sediments derived from this organic material can be stored in carbonate rocks or coal, later to be released into the atmosphere as CO_2 through rock weathering or the burning of fossil fuels. **10-4:** Nitrogen becomes usable to plants after it has been "fixed" into *nitrates*, primarily by nitrogen-fixing bacteria in the soil. **10-5:** Typically only about 10% of the energy stored in the *biomass* of one organism can be passed on and stored by an organism that consumes it. **10-6:** Acacias evolved before the continents began to rift apart millions of years ago, and so are found widely in the Southern Hemisphere; the range of cattle egrets increased recently, following the expansion of cattle ranching around the world. **10-7:** Over time, the pond will first develop marsh vegetation around its edges; as sediment continues to fill the pond, it will eventually become a meadow, and finally a forest. **10-8:** All plants require light for photosynthesis, and so in dense groves, trees are likely to be tall and slender in order to gain access to light; wind especially has a drying effect on plants, favoring growth on protected sides of branches. **10-9:** Wildfire improves the health of some ecosystems by clearing away old vegetation; the seedpods or cones of some trees are opened by the heat of a fire. **10-10:** Nutrients cycle very quickly through the tropical rainforest; in effect, most of the nutrients are held in the living vegetation.

Chapter 11

11-1: *Biome* names highlight the dominant kind of vegetation present. **11-2:** *Annual plants* die off during the winter or dry season, leave seeds, and then germinate when the conditions are favorable again; *perennial plants* live through weather and environmental fluctuations on an ongoing basis. **11-3:** *Evergreen trees* are fully leaved at all times, whereas *deciduous trees* lose their leaves each year during the cold or dry season. **11-4:** *Xerophytic adaptations* allow plants to survive dry conditions, whereas *hygrophytic adaptations* allow plants to survive in wet, terrestrial environments. **11-5:** *Climax vegetation* refers to a stable association of plants that tends to change little over time—such plants can be thought of as representing the "optimal" vegetation for that environment. **11-6:** The upper *treeline* for a location is generally determined by a limiting low summer temperature and to a lesser extent the availability of moisture. **11-7:** Mammals and birds are *endothermic*; this allows them to maintain a constant body temperature, even in harshly cold environments. **11-8:** *Hibernation* during the winter allows animals to survive a harsh winter without the need to find food. **11-9:** Many desert animals are nocturnal, sparing them the need to be out during the hottest part of the day; some desert animals can delay reproduction until conditions are favorable. **11-10:** *Mutualism* is a mutually beneficial relationship between organisms, whereas *parasitism* entails one organism obtaining nourishment from another, weakening the host organism. **11-11:** The Australian continent was isolated from other continents quite early in geologic terms, so species here adapted and evolved with little influence from the outside. **11-12:** The *tropical rainforest* biome is characterized by a great many different species of plants and animals—although in any given area, there might be only a few individuals of each species. **11-13:** The *tropical savanna* biome is associated with a marked rainfall seasonality—often the tropical savanna (Aw) climate, caused by the season shift of the ITCZ. **11-14:** The *mediterranean woodland and shrub* biome is most closely associated with the winter wet/summer dry mediterranean (Cs) climate. **11-15:** The *boreal forest* biome has much lower biodiversity than the tropical rainforest biome—typically just a few species of trees that dominate the forest. **11-16:** Tropical rainforest loss not only results in the extinction of many species, but once the forest cover is removed, the soil quickly loses fertility and becomes susceptible to rapid erosion from the high rainfall in these areas. **11-17:** An *exotic species* is a nonnative plant or animal that becomes established in a new environment—introduced sometimes unintentionally by human activities.

Chapter 12

12-1: Soil formation generally begins with the weathering of bedrock. **12-2:** Soils derived from sandstone will tend to be coarse-textured and will more easily allow the deep transfer of water and air than will the fine-textured soils derived from weathered shale. **12-3:** Earthworms aerate the soil and facilitate drainage; the organic material in earthworm *casts* increases the fertility of most soils. **12-4:** Many plant nutrients are held to clay particles; *humus* is a source of organic material that can increase soil fertility. **12-5:** *Capillary water*—held on the surface of soil particles by surface tension—is the most important source of moisture for plants. **12-6:** *Porosity* refers to the amount of open space between soil particles (influencing the amount of water a soil can hold), whereas *permeability* refers to the interconnectedness of the pore spaces (influencing how easily water can move through a soil). **12-7:** *Cation exchange capacity* is the ability of a soil to attract and exchange cations, and so the nutrients associated with them. **12-8:** From top to bottom, *solum* includes: a thin *O horizon* of organic material at the surface; an *A horizon* ("topsoil") with a mixture of mineral material and humus; an *E horizon* where *eluviation* removes clay, iron and aluminum; and a *B horizon* where *illuviation* deposits clay, iron, and aluminum from above. **12-9:** *Laterization* takes place in warm, wet climates, and entails the rapid decomposition of organic material and the leaching away of most minerals (including silica)—leaving relatively infertile, brick-red soils with high concentrations of iron- and aluminum oxides; *podsolization* takes place in the cool, moist, boreal forests of subarctic regions—leaving acidic, sandy, leached soils of low fertility. **12-10:** *Salinization* takes place in areas of high evaporation; as water is drawn up toward the surface, it evaporates and leaves salts deposited in the soil. **12-11:** *Soil Taxonomy* is based on observable characteristics of the soil, not on the local environment or processes of formation. **12-12:** *Entisols* are typically very immature and so show little soil profile development. **12-13:** *Gelisols* are found in the Arctic and subarctic, where permafrost is present. **12-14:** *Aridisols* are generally found in areas of desert climate. **12-15:** *Vertisols* are often good agricultural soils (although sometimes difficult to plow because of their high clay content); *Mollisols* are grassland soils that are highly productive for agriculture; *Alfisols* are typically fertile soils and only second to Mollisols in terms of agricultural productivity. **12-16:** Both *Spodosols* and *Oxisols* are highly leached and so are generally quite infertile.

Chapter 13

13-1: The *lithosphere* (the "plates") consist of the crust and upper, rigid mantle; the *asthenosphere* is the dense, warm, plastic (deformable) layer the mantle over which the lithosphere moves. **13-2:** *Silicate family* minerals are the most abundant; the chemical starting point of these minerals is silica (SiO_2), often in combination with other elements. **13-3:** *Felsic* rocks contain large portions of light-colored silicate minerals (such as quartz and feldspar), whereas *mafic* rocks include large portions of dark-colored minerals (such as olivine and pyroxene); fine-grained igneous rocks form from the rapid cooling of lava, whereas coarse-grained igneous rocks develop from the slow cooling of magma below the surface. **13-4:** *Granite* forms from the slow-cooling of felsic magma below the surface (and so it has a coarse-grained texture with both light- and dark-colored minerals); *basalt* forms from the rapid cooling of mafic lava (and so it has a fine-grained texture of only dark-colored minerals). **13-5:** *Detrital sedimentary rocks*, such as sandstone, form from the accumulated fragments of weathered rock; *chemical sedimentary rocks*, such as limestone, develop from the precipitation of dissolved compounds (such as calcium carbonate); *organic sedimentary rocks*, such as bituminous coal, consist of compacted dead plant material. **13-6:** *Foliation* develops when directed stress is applied to rocks during metamorphism, leaving the minerals oriented with a distinctly platy or banded texture. **13-7:** Because oceanic lithosphere includes basaltic crust, it is denser than continental lithosphere; the dominant crustal rocks of the continents, such as granite, are less dense than basalt, the dominant crustal rock of the ocean floors. **13-8:** *Structure* refers to the nature and orientation of the rocks in a landform. **13-9:** *Internal processes* originate within Earth, and include the lithospheric rearrangement associated with plate tectonics,

as well as volcanism, folding, and faulting—such processes can increase the relief of the landscape; the *external processes* of weathering, mass wasting and erosion operate on, or just below, the surface of Earth and have the ability to wear down the landscape and diminish relief. **13-10:** In order for the incrementally slow internal and external processes to operate and make a significant difference in the landscape, very long periods of time (by human standards) are required. **13-11:** An individual landform is best studied at the local scale (frame 1 in Figure 13-24); continental structure is best studied from a more distant perspective (as in frame 5).

Chapter 14

14-1: Continental coastlines (especially across the Atlantic Ocean) match up like the pieces of a jigsaw puzzle; patterns of ancient glaciation also align if the continents are put back into their positions in Pangaea, where they were when this glaciation took place. **14-2:** Ocean floor is created and spreads away in both directions from a *midocean ridge*; ocean floor is "recycled" through the process of *subduction* at *oceanic trenches*. **14-3:** The ocean floor is youngest at midocean ridges, and becomes progressively older in both directions away from the ridge—showing that the ocean floor is indeed spreading away from the ridges. **14-4:** Plates are large slabs of lithosphere (the crust and upper mantle) that are moving over the dense, warm asthenosphere below, put in motion by the slow convection of heated rock within the mantle. **14-5:** Both *midocean ridges* and *continental rift valleys* are types of *divergent plate boundary* where two plates are spreading away from each other. **14-6:** Both are subduction zones, and so are associated with both shallow- and deep-focus earthquakes; oceanic-continental subduction produces a deep oceanic trench and a chain of volcanoes just inland from the continental coastline; oceanic-oceanic convergence also produces a deep oceanic trench along with a *volcanic island arc* parallel to the trench. **14-7:** The Atlantic Ocean is the result of the divergence of the continents away from the Mid-Atlantic Ridge; the Himalayas are being uplifted by the continental collision of India with the Eurasia; the volcanoes of the Andes are a result of the subduction of the Nazca Plate beneath the South American Plate. **14-8:** The chain of islands is being formed as the Pacific Plate moves over a stationary plume of magma rising from the mantle. **14-9:** The western edge of North America has grown through the accretion of material—especially lithosphere that was too buoyant to subduct. **14-10:** The relative amount of silica in the lava; high-silica (rhyolitic) lava tends to be viscous and often explosive, whereas lower-silica (basaltic) lava tends to be fluid and less explosive during an eruption. **14-11:** *Composite volcanoes* are steep-sided cones, comprised of alternating layers of *pyroclastics* from explosive eruptions and *lava flows* from more quiet eruptions; *shield volcanoes* are wide, gently sloped volcanoes, consisting of layer after layer of solidified lava

flows. **14-12:** *Calderas* develop when a volcano expels an enormous quality of pyroclastic material during an explosive eruption; the weakened volcano collapses, leaving a wide, low depression. **14-13:** A *pyroclastic flow* is a dense, rapidly moving avalanche of pyroclastics and searing-hot gases; a *volcanic mudflow* is a fast-moving mixture of water and pyroclastics, flowing down a volcano with the consistency of wet concrete. **14-14:** All *igneous intrusions* formed by magma solidifying below the surface; a *batholith* is the largest kind of intrusion; a *laccolith* develops when magma is forced between horizontal layers of strata, bulging up the overlying rock; a *dike* forms when a sheet of magma is injected into a vertical fracture. **14-15:** A *syncline* is a simple structural downfold, whereas an *anticline* is a simple upfold; sometimes a syncline is associated with a topographic valley and an anticline with a topographic ridge. **14-16:** *Normal faults* are caused by tension (extension) and result in vertical displacement along the fault plane; *reverse faults* are cause by compression and also result in vertical displacement; *strike-slip faults* are associated with shearing, in which one side of the fault moves sideways past the other. **14-17:** A *graben* develops when a block of crust drops down between two parallel faults (most commonly normal faults); an *offset stream* develops when the course of a stream is displaced by lateral movement along a strike-slip fault. **14-18:** *Magnitude* describes the relative "size" or amount of energy released in an earthquake; *earthquake intensity* describes how violently the local ground is shaking during an earthquake. **14-19:** *Liquefaction* occurs when water-saturated sediments lose strength and liquefy during the moments of earthquake ground shaking. **14-20:** Chief Mountain is older rock that has been moved over younger rock along a *thrust fault*.

Chapter 15

15-1: *Weathering* fragments the bedrock into smaller pieces that can be moved away; *mass wasting* moves this weathered rock a relatively short distance down slope. **15-2:** Rock openings allow moisture and atmospheric gases to penetrate the bedrock, increasing the surface area of the rock exposed to weathering processes. **15-3:** Both are breaks in the rock structure; along a *fault* there has been displacement, whereas along a *joint* there has not. **15-4:** Liquid water seeps into a joint or crack in the rock; when the water freezes, the ice expands and pries open the crack. **15-5:** When formerly buried rock (such as granite) is exposed at the surface, the unloading of pressure allows the outer part of the rock to expand, and layer after layer of rock breaks off along curved *sheeting joints*, much like the skin of an onion. **15-6:** *Mechanical weathering* entails the physical breakup of rock through stress; chemical *weathering* entails chemical reactions that decompose the minerals in a rock. **15-7:** Both are chemical weathering processes that require water; *oxidation* involves the combination of metallic elements and oxygen to produce softer oxides (such as rust); *carbonation* involves a weak acid (*carbonic acid*) that is especially effective in weathering carbonate rocks such as limestone. **15-8:** Some rock is strong and resistant to weathering, whereas other rock is weak, and easily weathered. **15-9:** The *angle of repose* is the steepest angle that can be maintained by loose material before it begins to move downslope. **15-10:** *Talus cones* at the foot of steep slopes develop from the accumulation of material deposited by *rockfall*. **15-11:** Rain can soak in and add weight to weathered rock on a slope, making it more susceptible to sliding. **15-12:** Both landslides and earthflows are slope failures that occur on hillsides; *earthflows* involve more water and the flow of material down a slope, whereas *landslides* involve material moving down a slide plane and can be completely dry. **15-13:** Both involve quite a bit of water; *earthflows* are slope failures that occur on hillsides, whereas *mudflows* entail more water and flow down valleys. **15-14:** The freeze-thaw cycle aides in slowly moving soil particles downslope (as ice forms, the soil expands slightly outward; with melting, soil particles drop slightly downslope), as does the slight swelling and contraction of soil through simple wetting and drying.

Chapter 16

16-1: Channeled *streamflow* is found in *valleys*, whereas unchanneled *overland flow* is found on *interfluves*. **16-2:** The speed of flow determines the largest size of rock that can be moved by a stream (known as stream *competence*). **16-3:** *Alluvium* is often rounded because as rocks are tumbled along in a stream, rough edges are worn off; stratification is often visible because alluvium will be deposited after a periodic flood; sorting may occur because as stream speed drops, rocks of the same weight are deposited at the same time. **16-4:** Because stream *competence* and *capacity* increase significantly during periods of floods when a stream has its fastest flow and greatest volume, most streams accomplish most of their erosion (and eventual deposition of alluvium) during floods. **16-5:** *Meandering channel* patterns typically develop when a stream is flowing down a gentle slope (especially streams with large *suspended loads*); *braided channel* patterns typically develop when a stream has a large *bed load* (especially larger-size rocks), but doesn't have enough flow to keep this material moving. **16-6:** *Dendritic* drainage patterns tend to develop in areas where the underlying structure does not significantly influence erosion; *trellis* drainage patterns develop in response to structural control, especially in regions of parallel ridges and valleys. **16-7:** *Downcutting* typically occurs when a stream is flowing down a steep slope (or has especially high speed and large volume). **16-8:** Undercutting and erosion of the lip of the waterfall leads to collapse of the *knickpoint*, and so the location of the waterfall gradually shifts upstream as it is worn away. **16-9:** *Headward erosion* may allow one stream to extend its valley into the course of another

stream, and so capture the other stream's water. **16-10:** Deposition of alluvium will occur any time and any place a stream loses power, such as when flow speed diminishes after a flood, on the inside bank of a meander, or where the stream enters a quiet body of water. **16-11:** An *oxbow lake* develops when one bend of a meander turn cuts into an adjacent bend, forming a *cutoff meander*—leaving an old portion of the stream channel filled with water but isolated from the rest of the stream. **16-12:** Dams have trapped sediment, reducing the amount of alluvium that would have been deposited in the delta; artificial levees and other structures have prevented the river from naturally changing course, and so from depositing material in different parts of the delta. **16-13:** *Stream terraces* develop when a stream flowing across a *floodplain* is rejuvenated (gains downcutting ability due to regional uplift or higher discharge); the stream downcuts into its old floodplain, leaving remnants of its original floodplain as terraces on both sides of the new stream level. **16-14:** Davis's theory assumed that little erosion occurred during the initial uplift of a landscape (very unlikely); no *peneplains* are found anywhere.

Chapter 17

17-1: Limestone (and other carbonate rocks) readily undergo *dissolution* (chemical weathering) when exposed to *carbonic acid*—and most surface water and underground water contains at least some dissolved carbon dioxide, and so is slightly acidic. **17-2:** Travertine and tufa are carbonate rocks that form from the precipitation of calcium carbonate when carbon dioxide leaves solution, such as inside the openings of a cave, or around a surface opening of a hot spring. **17-3:** The first stage of *cavern* formation entails the removal of carbonate rocks by percolating underground water; the second "decoration" stage involves the precipitation of calcium carbonate *speleothems* into the voids left by the excavation stage. **17-4:** *Sinkholes* are depressions that develop from the dissolution of rock, often at the intersection of a joint. **17-5:** Pressure builds up in an underground opening where steam and superheated water (liquid water well above the boiling temperature were it at surface pressure) accumulate; finally, pressure is great enough to expel the water and steam in a surge out of the *geyser*. **17-6:** Yellowstone has magma and hot rocks close to the surface, lots of water to seep down into the rock to be heated, and highly fractured rocks that allow water to move up and down easily,

Chapter 18

18-1: Because impermeable surfaces don't readily absorb water, whenever it rains, most of the water will run off into the nearest dry stream channel. **18-2:** With little soil and vegetation covering it, the bedrock in deserts is directly exposed to weathering and erosional processes. **18-3:** An *exotic stream* gets its water from a humid area, but flows across a

desert; an *ephemeral stream* is dry most of the time (perhaps for many years), but fills up with water whenever there is a local rainstorm. **18-4:** Most fluvial transportation of material in deserts occurs through infrequent events such as flash floods and debris flows—in effect, in a desert the streams are either dry or are flooding. **18-5:** In regions with little rainfall, a flash flood or debris flow out of a mountain canyon will transport material until it reaches the gentle slopes of the piedmont zone; as flow speed decreases, deposition of alluvium will occur at the foot of the mountain. **18-6:** Under all but extremely rare circumstances, wind is simply not capable of exerting enough force to move any material larger than sand, and so erosion of bedrock is limited to abrasion from "sandblasting." **18-7:** Wind blows sand grains up the gentle windward side of a dune (through the bouncing action of *saltation*); at the top of the dune crest, sand drops down the leeside *slip face* of the dune, typically remaining at the *angle of repose* for dry sand (about 33°). **18-8:** Both *desert pavement* and *desert varnish* require many centuries to develop, but can be disturbed or covered by erosion or deposition; so, we can infer that a surface with well-developed pavement and/or varnish has been unaffected by significant erosion or deposition for many years. **18-9:** An *alluvial fan* is a gently sloping, fan-shaped accumulation of flash flood and debris flow deposits (alluvium) at the mouth of a canyon; they are common in the basin-and-range region because most of the fault-produced mountains here have abrupt slope changes in the *piedmont zone* (and so fluvial deposition will occur here); in addition, in this desert environment there isn't enough streamflow to move this alluvium much beyond the piedmont zone. **18-10:** A *playa* is a nearly level, dry lake bed comprised of fine-grained, dried mud; playas are found throughout the basin-and-range region because most of the basins here have interior drainage—ephemeral streamflow will occasionally fill the bottom of the basin with water (forming a playa lake); once the water evaporates and the silt settles out, the playa remains. **18-11:** Faulting has lowered the floor of Death Valley well below sea level; the dryness of Death Valley is due to its location in a multiple-mountain range *rain shadow*, cut off from moisture coming from the Pacific Ocean. **18-12:** The caprock of resistant horizontal sedimentary rock maintains the steep scarp below; the scarp retreats as this resistant caprock is undercut by weathering and erosion of the weaker rock below (which forms a gently sloping surface).

Chapter 19

19-1: Both *highland ice fields* and *continental ice sheets* are continuous covers of glacial ice; highland ice fields are found only in high-elevation mountain areas, and are much smaller in area than continental ice sheets. **19-2:** During the *Pleistocene*, glaciers covered about one-third of the continents, including all of Antarctica, much of the mid- and high latitude portions of North America and Eurasia, and high mountain areas. **19-3:** Sea level dropped during glacial advances because water evaporated from the ocean was locked up as ice on the continents; during interglacial periods this water flowed back into the oceans. **19-4:** *Pleistocene lakes* developed in basins away from the ice sheets due to increased rainfall and lower evaporation. **19-5:** Warmer global temperatures are causing the retreat or thinning of most mountain glaciers and continental ice sheets today. **19-6:** Snow left over at the end of summer is covered by new winter snow; as this continues for a number of years, the old snow is increasingly compacted and recrystallized into glacial ice; once this ice begins to move, a glacier has formed. **19-7:** Glaciers are always flowing or moving downslope; even when a glacier is getting smaller because *ablation* is greater than *accumulation* of ice, the glacier continues to move (and so transport rock)—it can't flow as far before wasting away, so its terminus retreats. **19-8:** Meltwater seeps down into cracks below a glacier and refreezes; *frost wedging* shatters the rock below, and when the glacier moves on, this shattered rock is incorporated into the glacier. **19-9:** Because it is melted out of a glacier at its terminus or edges, glacial *till* is typically unsorted, unstratified, and often angular; *alluvium* is moved by water, and so it is often sorted by size, deposited in distinct strata, and rounded by tumbling in a stream. **19-10:** A *roche moutonnée* has a gentle *stoss side* smoothed by glacial abrasion on the way up; the steep, irregular lee side is due to glacial plucking as the glacier pulls away. **19-11:** A *terminal moraine* is the ridge of till that marks the maximum advance of a glacier; a *recessional moraine* forms as the glacier retreats and

stagnates for a period of time, leaving another ridge of till. **19-12:** Meltwater streams from a glacier carry glacial *drift* out beyond the area directly glaciated, leaving deposits of *stratified drift*, typically in a gently undulating *outwash plain* of low relief. **19-13:** A *cirque* is a bowl-shaped glacial valley head, eroded out of bedrock primarily through glacial plucking and frost wedging of the headwall. **19-14:** Glaciers may slightly straighten a stream valley, and typically deepen and steepen the valley into a U-shaped *glacial trough*; often irregular *glacial steps* are left in the downvalley profile. **19-15:** *Lateral moraines* are ridges of till that accumulate along the sides of a valley glacier, especially near the mouth of the glacial valley. **19-16:** Washington's channeled scablands are the result of a series of major floods during the Pleistocene, caused when large lakes impounded behind a lobe of a continental ice sheet abruptly drained. **19-17:** The timing of all of the advances and retreats of Pleistocene ice sheets do not correlate with *Milankovitch cycles*.

Chapter 20

20-1: Along ocean coastlines, tides are significant, and coral reefs can develop in tropical areas; the causes of sea-level changes are different from those that lead to lake-level changes. **20-2:** As a *wave of oscillation* reaches shallow water, it is slowed by friction with the bottom; as the wave slows, wavelength decreases and wave height increases, until the wave falls forward and breaks, forming a *wave of translation*. **20-3:** Storm waves are larger than normal waves; when they break on a shoreline, their higher speed and greater volume of water are capable of rapid erosion. **20-4:** Because the entire water column, from the ocean floor to the surface, is displaced

when a *tsunami* forms, the volume of water that comes onshore with even a modest-size tsunami is much greater that of a comparable-height storm wave. **20-5:** With a warming climate, the melting of glaciers is increasing global sea level slightly, leading to the gradual flooding of low-lying coastal areas. **20-6:** Most coastal sediment is deposited into the ocean through the outflow of streams. **20-7:** *Beach drifting* moves sand down a beach in a zigzag fashion—waves push sand up on a beach at an angle, but this sand drains straight back down off the beach; longshore currents are set up by the action of waves striking a coastline at an angle—water offshore transports sediment down the coast, parallel to shore. **20-8:** The size of a beach is the result of the balance between the amount of sediment coming in to that beach, and the amount of sediment being carried away; if for a period of time more sand is carried away than is deposited, a beach will grow smaller. **20-9:** The upcurrent side of a *groin* or *jetty* will tend to trap sand, expanding the width of the beach; however, more sand will be eroded on the downcurrent side of these structures, so the beach will tend to become narrower there. **20-10:** At the end of the Pleistocene glaciations about 10,000 years ago, water flowed back into the ocean, raising sea level and submerging most coastlines. **20-11:** The presence of *marine terraces* usually indicates that the coastline has been rising tectonically, lifting former *wave-cut platforms* above sea level. **20-12:** A *fringing reef* develops along the shore of a tropical volcanic island (such as those formed by a *hot spot*); as the plate carries the island off the hot spot, the plate cools, becomes denser, and so the island slowly begins to sink; coral continues to build up toward the surface, but as the volcanic island sinks, the ring of coral may become a *barrier reef*, or even an *atoll* if the island sinks completely below sea level.

THE INTERNATIONAL SYSTEM OF UNITS (SI)

With the major exception of the United States, the system of weights and measures used worldwide both in scientific work and in everyday life is the International System, usually abbreviated SI from its French name, *Système Internationale*. The system has seven base units and supplementary units for angles (Table I-1). The beauty of the system lies in its reliance on multiples of the number 10, with the prefixes shown in Table I-2 being used to cover a magnitude range from the astronomically large to the infinitesimally small. Table I-3 lists the most frequently used conversion factors.

TABLE I-1	SI Units	
Quantity	**Unit**	**Symbol**
Base Units		
Length	Meter	m
Mass	Kilogram	kg
Time	Second	s
Electric current	Ampere	A
Temperature	Kelvin	K
Amount of substance	Mole	mol
Luminous intensity	Candela	Cd
Supplementary Units		
Plane angle	Radian	rad
Solid angle	Steradian	Sr

TABLE I-2	Common Multiples and SI Prefixes		
Multiple	**Value**	**Prefix**	**Symbol**
1 000 000 000 000	10^{12}	tera	T
1 000 000 000	10^{9}	giga	G
1 000 000	10^{6}	mega	M
1000	10^{3}	kilo	k
100	10^{2}	hecto	h
10	10^{1}	deka	da
0.1	10^{-1}	deci	d
0.01	10^{-2}	centi	c
0.001	10^{-3}	milli	m
0.000001	10^{-6}	micro	μ
0.000000001	10^{-9}	nano	n
0.000000000001	10^{-12}	pico	P

TABLE I-3	SI-English Conversion Units	
Multiply	**By**	**To Get**
Length		
Inches	2.540	Centimeters
Foot	0.3048	Meters
Yards	0.9144	Meters
Miles	1.6093	Kilometers
Millimeters	0.039	Inches
Centimeters	0.3937	Inches
Meters	3.2808	Foot
Kilometers	0.6214	Miles

TABLE I-3 SI-English Conversion Units (Continued)

Multiply	By	To Get
Area		
Square inches	6.452	Square centimeters
Square feet	0.0929	Square meters
Square yards	0.8361	Square meters
Square miles	2.590	Square kilometers
Acres	0.4047	Hectares
Square centimeters	0.155	Square inches
Square meters	10.764	Square feet
Square meters	1.196	Square yards
Square kilometers	0.3861	Square miles
Hectares	2.471	Acres
Volume		
Cubic inches	16.387	Cubic centimeters
Cubic feet	0.028	Cubic meters
Cubic yards	0.7646	Cubic meters
Fluid ounces	29.57	Milliliters
Pints	0.47	Liters
Quarts	0.946	Liters
Gallons	3.785	Liters
Cubic centimeters	0.061	Cubic inches
Cubic meters	35.3	Cubic feet
Cubic meters	1.3079	Cubic yards
Milliliters	0.034	Fluid ounces
Liters	1.0567	Quarts
Liters	0.264	Gallons
Mass (Weight)		
Ounces	28.3495	Grams
Pounds	0.4536	Kilograms
Tons (2000 lb)	907.18	Kilograms
Tons (2000 lb)	0.90718	Tonnes
Grams	0.03527	Ounces
Kilograms	2.2046	Pounds
Kilograms	0.0011	Tons (2000 lb)
Tonnes	1.1023	Tons (2000 lb)

U.S. GEOLOGICAL SURVEY TOPOGRAPHIC MAPS

The U.S. Geological Survey (USGS) is one of the world's largest mapping agencies and is primarily responsible for the country's National Mapping Program. The USGS produces a broad assortment of maps, but its topographic "quadrangles" are among the most widely used by geographers. The quadrangles come in various sizes and scales (from 1:24,000 to 1:1,000,000), but all are rectangles bordered by parallels and meridians rather than by political boundaries. For many years the quadrangles were produced by surveys on the ground. Today, however, they are created from aerial photographs, satellite imagery, and computer rectification.

Topographic maps convey both human-built features such as roads and buildings and natural features such as rivers, glaciers, and areas of forest cover. Topographic maps also depict the topography of a landscape with *elevation contour lines* (Figure II-1). From these two-dimensional maps, it is possible to envision the three-dimensional topography, making "topo" maps especially useful when studying landform patterns.

The USGS has produced more than 55,000 different printed topographic quadrangles, as well as about 220,000 digital orthorectified aerial images. In 2001, the USGS began an ambitious multiyear plan to develop a seamless, continuously maintained, nationally consistent set of online, public-domain, geographic-based information for the United States known as *The National Map*. The National Map incorporates topographic maps, aerial and satellite imagery, along with a wide range of other map layers, and is available online at http://nationalmap.gov.

ELEVATION CONTOUR LINES

USGS topographic maps use elevation contour lines to portray the shape, slope, elevation, and relief (the difference in elevation between the highest and lowest locations) of a landscape (Figure II-2). The following guidelines are followed when interpreting contour lines:

1. A contour line connects points of equal elevation.
2. The difference in elevation between two contour lines is called the *contour interval*.
3. Usually every fourth or fifth contour line is a darker *index contour*.
4. Elevations on one side of a contour line are higher than on the other side.

5. Contour lines never touch or cross one another (except at some cliffs).
6. Contour lines have no beginning or end—every line closes on itself, either on or off the map.
7. Uniformly spaced contours indicate a uniform slope.
8. If spaced far apart, contour lines indicate a relatively gentle slope; if spaced close together, they represent a steep slope.
9. Contour lines bend upstream in a "V" shape when crossing a stream valley, gully, or "draw" (the "V" points uphill).
10. Along a spur or ridge running down a hillside, a contour line forms a "V" pointing downhill.
11. A contour line that closes within the limits of the map represents a hill or rise. The land inside that contour is higher than the elevation of the closed contour itself.
12. A depression may be represented by a closed contour that is hachured on the side leading into the depression—the elevation of such a *depression contour* is the same as that of the adjacent lower regular contour (unless otherwise marked).

TOPOGRAPHIC MAP SYMBOLS

Topographic quadrangles also portray a variety of other features using symbols and colors. Standard colors are used to distinguish various kinds of map features:

- **Brown:** contour lines and other topographic features
- **Blue:** hydrographic (water) features
- **Black:** features constructed or designated by humans, such as buildings, roads, boundary lines, and names
- **Green:** areas of vegetation, such as woodlands, forests, orchards, and vineyards
- **Red:** important roads and lines of the public land survey system
- **Gray or red tint:** urban areas
- **Purple:** features added from aerial photos during map revision

The principal standard symbols used on USGS topographic maps are shown in Figure II-3. Note that in a few cases more than one kind of symbol is used to show the same kind of feature.

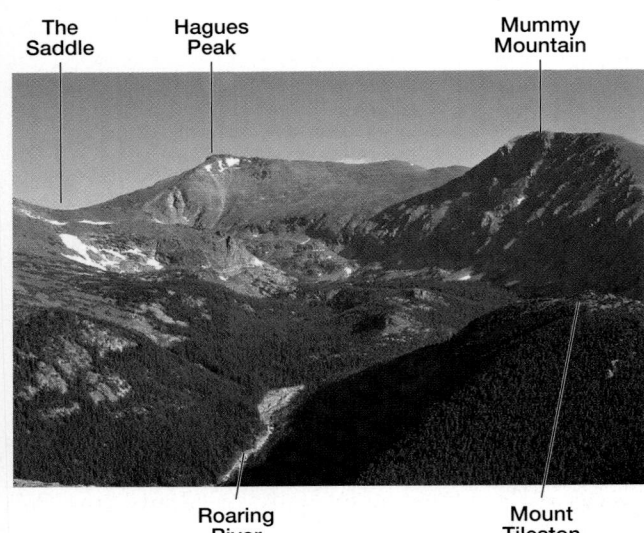

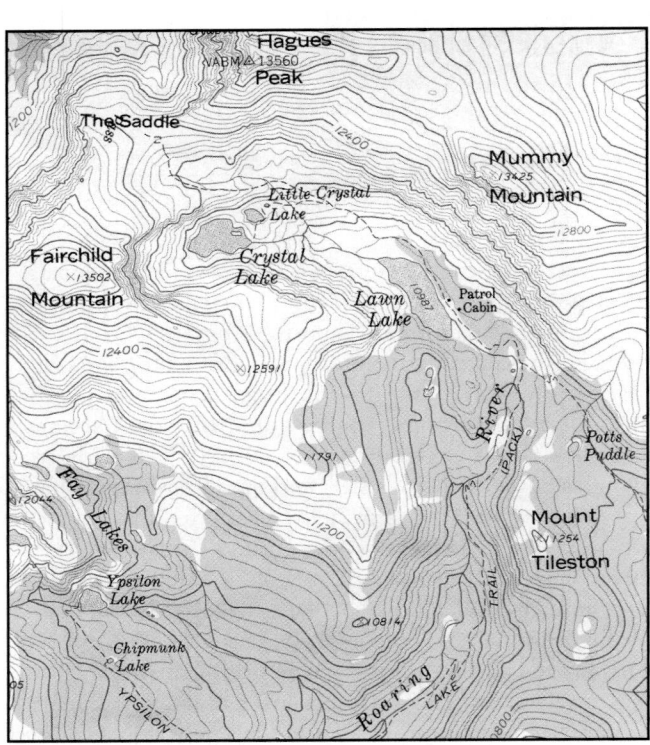

▶ **Figure II-1** Portrayal of terrain by means of elevation contour lines. Here is a photo of Hagues Peak and Mummy Mountain in Colorado's Rocky Mountain National Park, along with a standard topographic map of the same area. (Original map scale 1:125,000; contour interval is 80 feet [27 meters].)

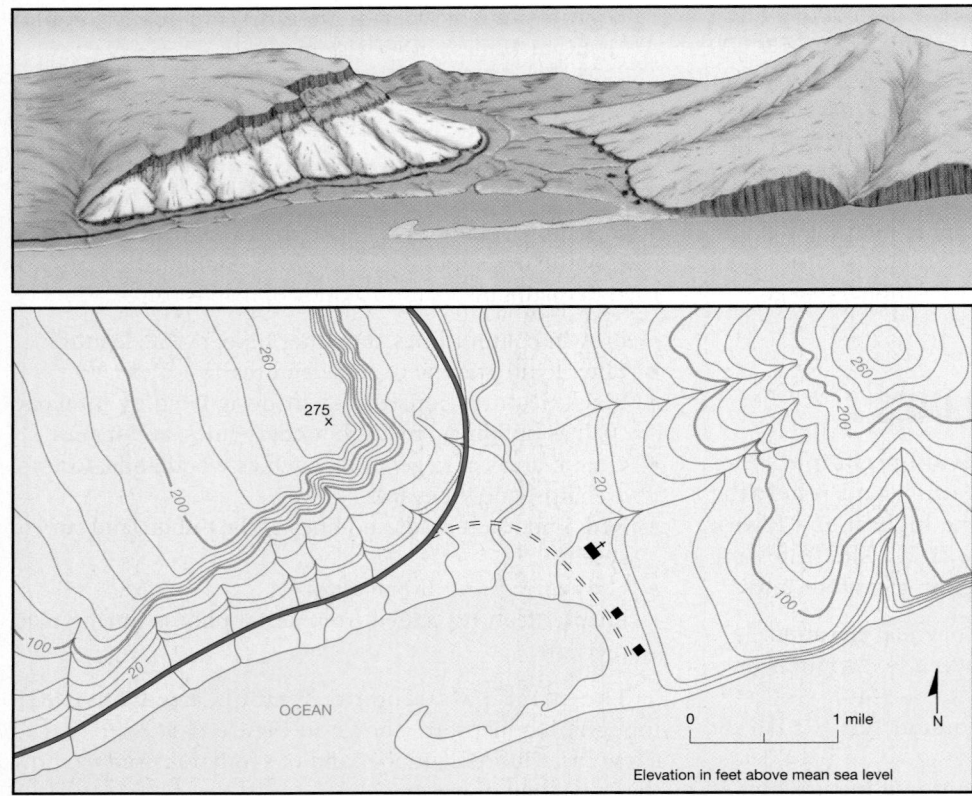

▲ **Figure II-2** A fictitious landscape and a contour line map of the same area. Where the contours are close together, the slope is steep; where the lines are far apart, the slope is gentle.

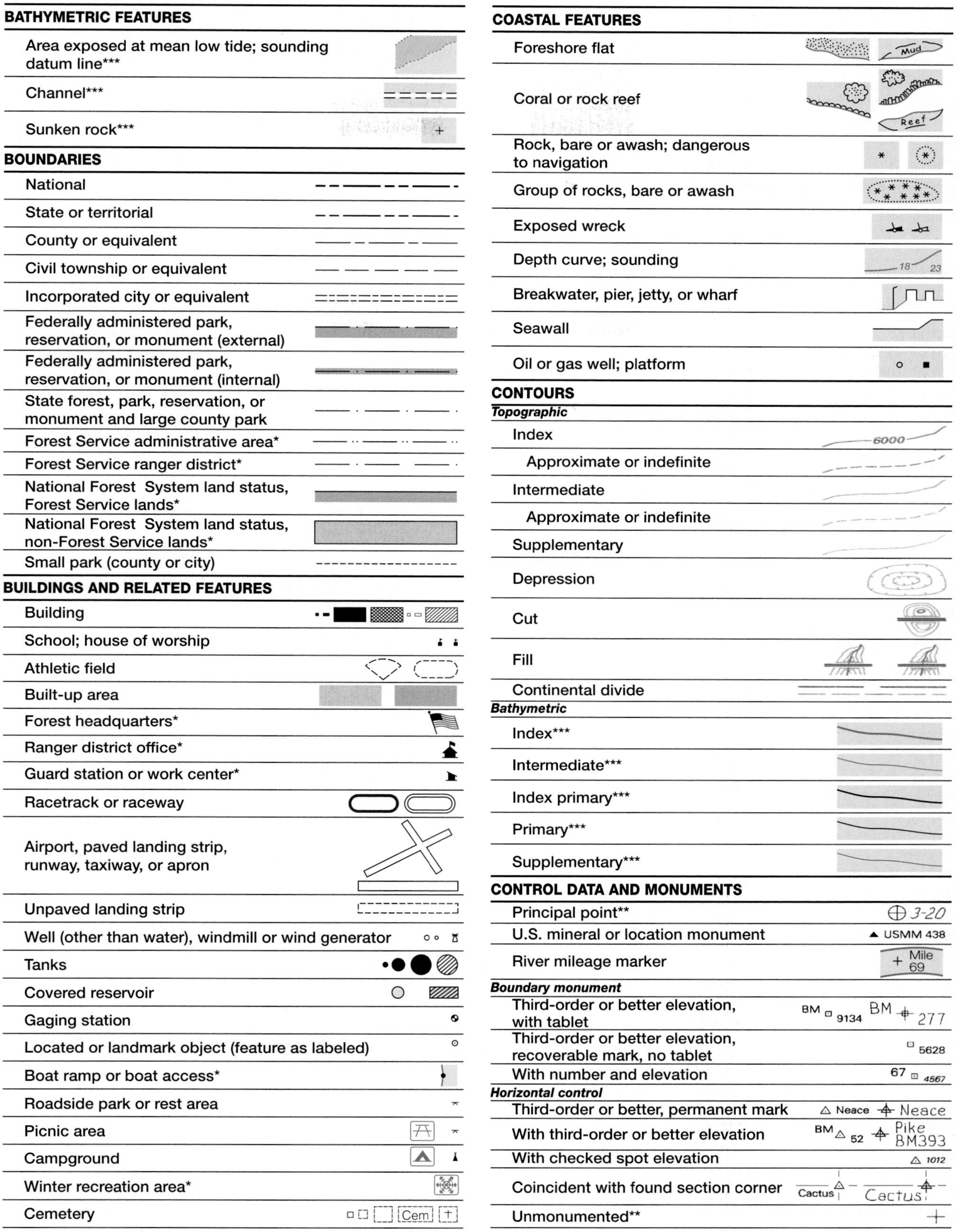

BATHYMETRIC FEATURES

Area exposed at mean low tide; sounding datum line***	
Channel***	
Sunken rock***	

BOUNDARIES

National	
State or territorial	
County or equivalent	
Civil township or equivalent	
Incorporated city or equivalent	
Federally administered park, reservation, or monument (external)	
Federally administered park, reservation, or monument (internal)	
State forest, park, reservation, or monument and large county park	
Forest Service administrative area*	
Forest Service ranger district*	
National Forest System land status, Forest Service lands*	
National Forest System land status, non-Forest Service lands*	
Small park (county or city)	

BUILDINGS AND RELATED FEATURES

Building	
School; house of worship	
Athletic field	
Built-up area	
Forest headquarters*	
Ranger district office*	
Guard station or work center*	
Racetrack or raceway	
Airport, paved landing strip, runway, taxiway, or apron	
Unpaved landing strip	
Well (other than water), windmill or wind generator	
Tanks	
Covered reservoir	
Gaging station	
Located or landmark object (feature as labeled)	
Boat ramp or boat access*	
Roadside park or rest area	
Picnic area	
Campground	
Winter recreation area*	
Cemetery	

COASTAL FEATURES

Foreshore flat	
Coral or rock reef	
Rock, bare or awash; dangerous to navigation	
Group of rocks, bare or awash	
Exposed wreck	
Depth curve; sounding	
Breakwater, pier, jetty, or wharf	
Seawall	
Oil or gas well; platform	

CONTOURS

Topographic

Index	
Approximate or indefinite	
Intermediate	
Approximate or indefinite	
Supplementary	
Depression	
Cut	
Fill	
Continental divide	

Bathymetric

Index***	
Intermediate***	
Index primary***	
Primary***	
Supplementary***	

CONTROL DATA AND MONUMENTS

Principal point**	⊕ 3-20
U.S. mineral or location monument	▲ USMM 438
River mileage marker	+ Mile 69

Boundary monument

Third-order or better elevation, with tablet	BM □ 9134 BM ⊹ 277
Third-order or better elevation, recoverable mark, no tablet	□ 5628
With number and elevation	67 □ 4567

Horizontal control

Third-order or better, permanent mark	△ Neace ⊹ Neace
With third-order or better elevation	BM △ 52 ⊹ Pike BM393
With checked spot elevation	△ 1012
Coincident with found section corner	Cactus Cactus
Unmonumented**	+

▲ **Figure II-3** Topographic map symbols used on USGS quadrangles.

CONTROL DATE AND MONUMENTS — *continued*

Vertical control

Third-order or better elevation, with tablet	BM × 5280
Third-order or better elevation, recoverable mark, no tablet	× 528
Bench mark coincident with found section corner	BM + 5280
Spot elevation	×7523

GLACIERS AND PERMANENT SNOWFIELDS

Contours and limits	
Formlines	
Glacial advance	
Glacial retreat	

LAND SURVEYS

Public land survey system

Range or Township line	
Location approximate	
Location doubtful	
Protracted	
Protracted (AK 1:63,360-scale)	
Range or Township labels	R1E T2N R3W T4S
Section line	
Location approximate	
Location doubtful	
Protracted	
Protracted (AK 1:63,360-scale)	
Section numbers	1 - 36 1 - 36
Found section corner	
Found closing corner	
Witness corner	WC
Meander corner	MC
Weak corner*	

Other land surveys

Range or Township line	
Section line	
Land grant, mining claim, donation land claim, or tract	
Land grant, homestead, mineral, or other special survey monument	□
Fence or field lines	

MARINE SHORELINES

Shoreline	
Apparent (edge of vegetation)***	
Indefinite or unsurveyed	

MINES AND CAVES

Quarry or open pit mine	⚒
Gravel, sand, clay, or borrow pit	×
Mine tunnel or cave entrance	⊸
Mine shaft	◼
Prospect	X
Tailings	(Tailings)
Mine dump	
Former disposal site or mine	

PROJECTION AND GRIDS

Neatline	3915 ′ 9037 30 ″
Graticule tick	55′
Graticule intersection	
Datum shift tick	

State plane coordinate systems

Primary zone tick	640 000 FEET
Secondary zone tick	247 500 METERS
Tertiary zone tick	260 000 FEET
Quaternary zone tick	98 500 METERS
Quintary zone tick	320 000 FEET

Universal transverse metcator grid

UTM grid (full grid)	273
UTM grid ticks*	269

RAILROADS AND RELATED FEATURES

Standard guage railroad, single track	
Standard guage railroad, multiple track	
Narrow guage railroad, single track	
Narrow guage railroad, multiple track	
Railroad siding	
Railroad in highway	
Railroad in road	
Railroad in light duty road*	
Railroad underpass; overpass	
Railroad bridge; drawbridge	
Railroad tunnel	
Railroad yard	
Railroad turntable; roundhouse	

RIVERS, LAKES, AND CANALS

Perennial stream	
Perennial river	
Intermittent stream	
Intermittent river	
Disappearing stream	
Falls, small	
Falls, large	
Rapids, small	
Rapids, large	
Masonry dam	
Dam with lock	
Dam carrying load	

▲ Figure II-3 (continued)

RIVERS, LAKES, AND CANALS — *continued*

Perennial lake/pond	
Intermittent lake/pond	
Dry lake/pond	Dry Lake
Narrow wash	
Wide wash	Wash
Canal, flume, or aqueduct with lock	
Elevated aqueduct, flume, or mud pot	
Aqueduct tunnel	
Water well, geyser, fumarole, or mud pot	
Spring or creep	

ROADS AND RELATED FEATURES

Please note: Roads on Provisional-edition maps are not classified as primary, secondary, or light duty. These roads are all classified as improved roads and are symbolized the same as light duty roads.

Primary highway	
Secondary highway	
Light duty road	
Light duty road, paved*	
Light duty road, gravel*	
Light duty road, dirt*	
Light duty road, unspecified*	
Unimproved road	
Unimproved road*	
4WD road	
4WD road*	
Trail	
Highway or road with median strip	
Highway or road under construction	Under Const
Highway or road underpass; overpass	
Highway or road bridge; drawbridge	
Highway or road tunnel	
Road block, berm, or barrier*	
Gate on road*	
Trailhead*	TH

* USGS-USDA Forest Service Single-Edition.
** Provisional-Edition maps only.
*** Topographic Bathymetric maps only.

▲ Figure II-3 (continued)

SUBMERGED AREAS AND BOGS

Marsh or swamp	
Submerged marsh or swamp	
Wooded marsh or swamp	
Submerged wooded marsh or swamp	
Land subject to inundation	Max Pool 431

SURFACE FEATURES

Levee	Levee
Sand or mud	Sand
Disturbed surface	
Gravel beach or glacial moraine	Gravel
Tailings pond	Tailings Pond

TRANSMISSION LINES AND PIPELINES

Power transmission line; pole, tower	
Telephone line	Telephone
Aboveground pipeline	
Underground pipeline	Pipeline

VEGETATION

Woodland	
Shrubland	
Orchard	
Vineyard	
Mangrove	Mangrove

METEOROLOGICAL TABLES

DETERMINING RELATIVE HUMIDITY

A *psychrometer* is an instrument used for measuring relative humidity. It consists of two thermometers mounted side by side. One of these is an ordinary thermometer (called a *dry bulb*), which simply measures air temperature. The other thermometer (called a *wet bulb*) has its bulb encased in a covering of muslin or gauze which is saturated with distilled water prior to use. The two thermometers are then thoroughly ventilated either by being whirled around (this instrument has a handle around which the thermometers can be whirled and is referred to as a *sling psychrometer*) or by fanning air past them. This ventilation encourages evaporation of water from the covering of the wet bulb at a rate that is directly related to the humidity of the surrounding air. Evaporation is a cooling process, and the temperature of the wet bulb drops. In dry air there is more evaporation, and therefore more cooling, than in moist air. The difference between the resulting wet-bulb and dry-bulb temperatures (called the *depression of the wet bulb*) is an expression of the relative saturation of the surrounding air. A large difference indicates low relative humidity; a small difference means that the air is near saturation. If the air is completely saturated, no net evaporation will take place; thus the two thermometers would have identical readings.

To determine relative humidity, measure the wet-bulb and dry-bulb temperatures using a sling psychrometer. Then use these two values to read the relative humidity from Table III-1 (for degrees Celsius) or Table III-2 (for degrees Fahrenheit).

TABLE III-1	Relative Humidity Psychrometer Tables (°C)

Air Temp °C	\multicolumn{22}{Depression of Wet-Bulb Thermometer (°C)}
	1	2	3	4	5	6	7	8	9	10	11	12	13	14	15	16	17	18	19	20	21	22
−4	77	54	32	11																		
−2	79	58	37	20	1																	
0	81	63	45	28	11																	
2	83	67	51	36	20	6																
4	85	70	56	42	27	14																
6	86	72	59	46	35	22	10	0														
8	87	74	62	51	39	28	17	6														
10	88	76	65	54	43	33	24	13	4													
12	88	78	67	57	48	38	28	19	10	2												
14	89	79	69	60	50	41	33	25	16	8	1											
16	90	80	71	62	54	45	37	29	21	14	7	1										
18	91	81	72	64	56	48	40	33	26	19	12	6	0									
20	91	82	74	66	58	51	44	36	30	23	17	11	5									
22	92	83	75	68	60	53	46	40	33	27	21	15	10	4	0							
24	92	84	76	69	62	55	49	42	36	30	25	20	14	9	4	0						
26	92	85	77	70	64	57	51	45	39	34	28	23	18	13	9	5						
28	93	86	78	71	65	59	53	45	42	36	31	26	21	17	12	8	4					
30	93	86	79	72	66	61	55	49	44	39	34	29	25	20	16	12	8	4				
32	93	86	80	73	68	62	56	51	46	41	36	32	27	22	19	14	11	8	4			
34	93	86	81	74	69	63	58	52	48	43	38	34	30	26	22	18	14	11	8	5		
36	94	87	81	75	69	64	59	54	50	44	40	36	32	28	24	21	17	13	10	7	4	
38	94	87	82	76	70	66	60	55	51	46	42	38	34	30	26	23	20	16	13	10	7	5

Relative Humidity (%)

TABLE III-2	**Relative Humidity Psychrometer Tables (°F)**

Air temp °F / Depression of Wet-Bulb Thermometer °F

Air temp °F	1	2	3	4	5	6	7	8	9	10	11	12	13	14	15	16	17	18	19	20	21	22	23	24	25	26	27	28	29	30
0	67	33	1																											
5	73	46	20																											
10	78	56	34	13	15																									
15	82	64	46	29	11																									
20	85	70	55	40	26	12																								
25	87	74	62	49	37	25	13	1																						
30	89	78	67	56	46	36	26	16	6																					
35	91	81	72	63	54	45	36	27	19	10	2																			
40	92	83	75	68	60	52	45	37	29	22	15	7																		
45	93	86	78	71	64	57	51	44	38	31	25	18	12	6																
50	93	87	74	67	61	55	49	43	38	32	27	21	16	10	5															
55	94	88	82	76	70	65	59	54	49	43	38	33	28	23	19	11	9	5												
60	94	89	83	78	73	68	63	58	53	48	43	39	34	30	26	21	17	13	9	5	1									
65	95	90	85	80	75	70	66	61	56	52	48	44	39	35	31	27	24	20	16	12	9	5	2							
70	95	90	86	81	77	72	68	64	59	55	51	48	44	40	36	33	29	25	22	19	15	12	9	6	3					
75	96	91	86	82	78	74	70	66	62	58	54	51	47	44	40	37	34	30	27	24	21	18	15	12	9	7	4	1		
80	96	91	87	83	79	75	72	68	64	61	57	54	50	47	44	41	38	35	32	29	26	23	20	18	15	12	10	7	5	3
85	96	92	88	84	81	77	73	70	66	63	59	57	53	50	47	44	41	38	36	33	30	27	25	22	20	17	15	13	10	8
90	96	92	89	85	81	78	74	71	68	65	61	58	55	52	49	47	44	41	39	36	34	31	29	26	24	22	19	17	15	13
95	96	93	89	86	82	79	76	73	69	66	63	61	58	55	52	50	47	44	42	39	37	34	32	30	28	25	23	21	19	17
100	96	93	89	86	83	80	77	73	70	68	65	62	59	56	54	51	49	46	44	41	39	37	35	33	30	28	26	24	22	21
105	97	93	90	87	84	81	78	75	72	69	66	64	61	58	56	53	51	49	46	44	42	40	38	36	34	32	30	28	26	24

Relative Humidity (%)

For example, if the dry-bulb temperature is 20°C and the wet-bulb temperature is 14°C, the depression of the wet bulb is 6°C. In Table III-1, find 20°C in the "Air Temperature" column; move across to the 6° column under "Depression of the Wet-Bulb Thermometer," and at the point of intersection, read the relative humidity, 51 percent.

THE BEAUFORT SCALE OF WIND SPEED

Early in the nineteenth century Admiral Beaufort of the British Navy developed a scale of wind speed widely used in the English-speaking world. It has been modified through the years, but the essentials have not changed. The scale is shown in Table III-3.

WIND CHILL

Wind chill is the popular name used to describe what cold weather feels like at various combinations of low temperature and high wind. On a cold, windless day, one's body heat is conducted sluggishly to a thin layer of atmospheric molecules near the skin. These heated molecules diffuse away slowly, to be replaced by other, cooler molecules. One's body thus comes into contact with a relatively small number of cool molecules, and one's body heat dissipates slowly.

With an increase in wind speed, however, body heat dissipates much more rapidly, as the protective layer of warmer molecules is speedily removed and supplanted by a continually renewing supply of cold air molecules against the skin. Up to a certain speed, the greater the wind velocity, the greater the cooling effect on one's body. Wind

TABLE III-3 | Beaufort Scale

	Speed			
Beaufort Force	Kilometers per Hour	Miles per Hour	Knots	Description
0	<1	<1	<1	Calm
1	1–5	1–3	1–3	Light air
2	6–11	4–7	4–6	Light breeze
3	12–19	8–12	7–10	Gentle breeze
4	20–29	13–18	11–16	Moderate breeze
5	30–38	19–24	17–21	Fresh breeze
6	39–49	25–31	22–27	Strong breeze
7	50–61	32–38	28–33	Near gale
8	62–74	39–46	34–40	Gale
9	75–87	47–54	41–47	Strong gale
10	88–101	55–63	48–55	Storm
11	102–116	64–72	56–63	Violent storm
12	117–132	73–82	64–71	Hurricane
13	133–148	83–92	72–80	Hurricane
14	149–166	93–103	81–89	Hurricane
15	167–183	104–114	90–99	Hurricane
16	184–201	115–125	100–108	Hurricane
17	202–219	126–136	109–118	Hurricane

chill affects only organisms that generate heat; inanimate objects have no such heat to lose, so their temperatures are not affected at all by wind movement.

The term *wind chill* was apparently first used in 1939 by Paul Siple, a geographer and polar explorer. Meteorologists from the National Weather Service of the United States and from the Meteorological Services of Canada have refined the calculations several times, most recently in 2002. The revised wind-chill index currently in use accounts for the wind effects at face level (the "old" system relied on observed winds 10 meters [33 feet] above the ground) and is a better calculation for body heat loss.

The updated index also includes a new frostbite chart, which shows how long skin can safely be exposed to the air given varying temperatures and wind (Tables III-4 and III-5).

THE HEAT INDEX

Sensible temperatures may be significantly influenced by humidity, which can make the weather seem either colder or warmer than it actually is—although humidity is more likely to impinge on our lives in hot weather. Quite simply, high humidity makes hot weather seem hotter.

The National Weather Service has developed a *heat index* that combines temperature and relative humidity to produce an "apparent temperature" that quantifies how hot the air feels to one's skin. A sample heat index chart is given in Table III-6.

To this index has been added a general heat stress index to indicate heat-related dangers at various apparent temperatures, as shown in Table III-7.

Table III-4 Wind Chill (°C)

Actual Air Temperature °C

	Calm	5	0	−5	−10	−15	−20	−25	−30	−35	−40
Wind Speed (kilometers per hour) 5		4	−2	−7	−13	−19	−24	−30	−36	−41	−47
10		3	−3	−9	−15	−21	−27	−33	−39	−45	−51
15		2	−4	−11	−17	−23	−29	−35	−41	−48	−54
20		1	−5	−12	−18	−24	−31	−37	−43	−49	−56
25		1	−6	−12	−19	−25	−32	−38	−45	−51	−57
30		0	−7	−13	−20	−26	−33	−39	−46	−52	−59
35		0	−7	−14	−20	−27	−33	−40	−47	−53	−60
40		−1	−7	−14	−21	−27	−34	−41	−48	−54	−61
45		−1	−8	−15	−21	−28	−35	−42	−48	−55	−62
50		−1	−8	−15	−22	−29	−35	−42	−49	−56	−63
55		−2	−9	−15	−22	−29	−36	−43	−50	−57	−63
60		−2	−9	−16	−23	−30	−37	−43	−50	−57	−64
65		−2	−9	−16	−23	−30	−37	−44	−51	−58	−65
70		−2	−9	−16	−23	−30	−37	−44	−51	−59	−66
75		−3	−10	−17	−24	−31	−38	−45	−52	−59	−66
80		−3	−10	−17	−24	−31	−38	−45	−52	−60	−67

Frostbite within 30 minutes   Frostbite within 10 minutes   Frostbite within 5 minutes

Table III-5 Wind Chill (°F)

Actual Air Temperature °F

	Calm	40	35	30	25	20	15	10	5	0	−5	−10	−15	−20	−25	−30	−35	−40
Wind Speed (miles per hour) 5		36	31	25	19	13	7	1	−5	−11	−16	−22	−28	−34	−40	−46	−52	−57
10		34	27	21	15	9	3	−4	−10	−16	−22	−28	−35	−41	−47	−53	−59	−66
15		32	25	19	13	6	0	−7	−13	−19	−26	−32	−39	−45	−51	−58	−64	−71
20		30	24	17	11	4	−2	−9	−15	−22	−29	−35	−42	−48	−55	−61	−68	−74
25		29	23	16	9	3	−4	−11	−17	−24	−31	−37	−44	−51	−58	−64	−71	−78
30		28	22	15	8	1	−5	−12	−19	−26	−33	−39	−46	−53	−60	−67	−73	−80
35		28	21	14	7	0	−7	−14	−21	−27	−34	−41	−48	−55	−62	−69	−76	−82
40		27	20	13	6	−1	−8	−15	−22	−29	−36	−43	−50	−57	−64	−71	−78	−84
45		26	19	12	5	−2	−9	−16	−23	−30	−37	−44	−51	−58	−65	−72	−79	−86
50		26	19	12	4	−3	−10	−17	−24	−31	−38	−45	−52	−60	−67	−74	−81	−88
55		25	18	11	4	−3	−11	−18	−25	−32	−39	−45	−54	−61	−68	−75	−82	−89
60		25	17	10	3	−4	−11	−19	−26	−33	−40	−48	−55	−62	−69	−76	−84	−91

Frostbite within 30 minutes   Frostbite within 10 minutes   Frostbite within 5 minutes

Table III-6　Heat Index (Apparent Temperature)

Relative Humidity

Temperature	10%	20%	30%	40%	50%	60%	70%	80%	90%
46°C	44°C	49°C	57°C	66°C					
115°F	111°F	120°F	135°F	151°F	*	*	*	*	*
43°C	41°C	44°C	51°C	58°C	66°C				
110°F	105°F	112°F	123°F	137°F	150°F	*	*	*	*
41°C	38°C	41°C	45°C	51°C	57°C	65°C			
105°F	100°F	105°F	113°F	123°F	135°F	149°F	*	*	*
38°C	35°C	37°C	40°C	43°C	49°C	56°C	62°C		
100°F	95°F	99°F	104°F	110°F	120°F	132°F	144°F	*	*
35°C	32°C	34°C	36°C	38°C	42°C	46°C	51°C	58°C	
95°F	90°F	93°F	96°F	101°F	107°F	114°F	124°F	136°F	*
32°C	29°C	31°C	32°C	34°C	36°C	38°C	41°C	45°C	50°C
90°F	85°F	87°F	90°F	93°F	96°F	100°F	106°F	113°F	122°F
29°C	27°C	28°C	29°C	30°C	31°C	32°C	34°C	36°C	39°C
85°F	80°F	82°F	84°F	86°F	88°F	90°F	93°F	97°F	102°F
27°C	24°C	25°C	26°C	26°C	27°C	28°C	29°C	30°C	31°C
80°F	75°F	77°F	78°F	79°F	81°F	82°F	85°F	86°F	88°F

*Temperature–relative humidity conditions rarely observed in the atmosphere.

Table III-7　General Heat Stress Index

Danger Category	Heat Index	Heat Syndrome
IV. Extreme Danger	Above 54°C (130°F)	Heat/sunstroke highly likely with continued exposure.
III. Danger	40–54°C (105–130°F)	Sunstroke, heat cramps, or heat exhaustion likely; heatstroke possible with prolonged exposure and/or physical activity.
II. Extreme Caution	32–40°C (90–105°F)	Sunstroke, heat cramps, or heat exhaustion possible with prolonged exposure and/or physical activity.
I. Caution	27–32°C (80–90°F)	Fatigue possible with prolonged exposure and/or physical activity.

THE WEATHER STATION MODEL

Weather data are recorded at regular intervals for a great many locations on Earth, each location being called a *weather station*. These data are then plotted on weather maps according to a standard format and code. The format for a standard *station model* is shown in Figure IV-1, along with an explanation of the code. Figure IV-2 shows the same model but with the codes replaced by sample data, and Figures IV-3 and IV-4 list some of the codes and symbols used by meteorologists. Tables IV-1 through IV-3 give additional codes and symbols, and Figure IV-5 is a sample weather map.

The wind symbol (Table IV-3) gives two pieces of information. Wind direction is indicated by an arrow shaft entering the station circle from the direction in which the wind is blowing, as at the one-o'clock position in Figure IV-2, and wind speed is indicated by the number of "feathers" and half-feathers protruding from the shaft; each half-feather represents a 5-knot increase in speed (a knot is one nautical mile per hour, which is the same as 1.15 statute miles per hour or 1.85 kilometers per hour); each full feather represents a 10-knot increase; a triangular pendant represents a 50-knot increase.

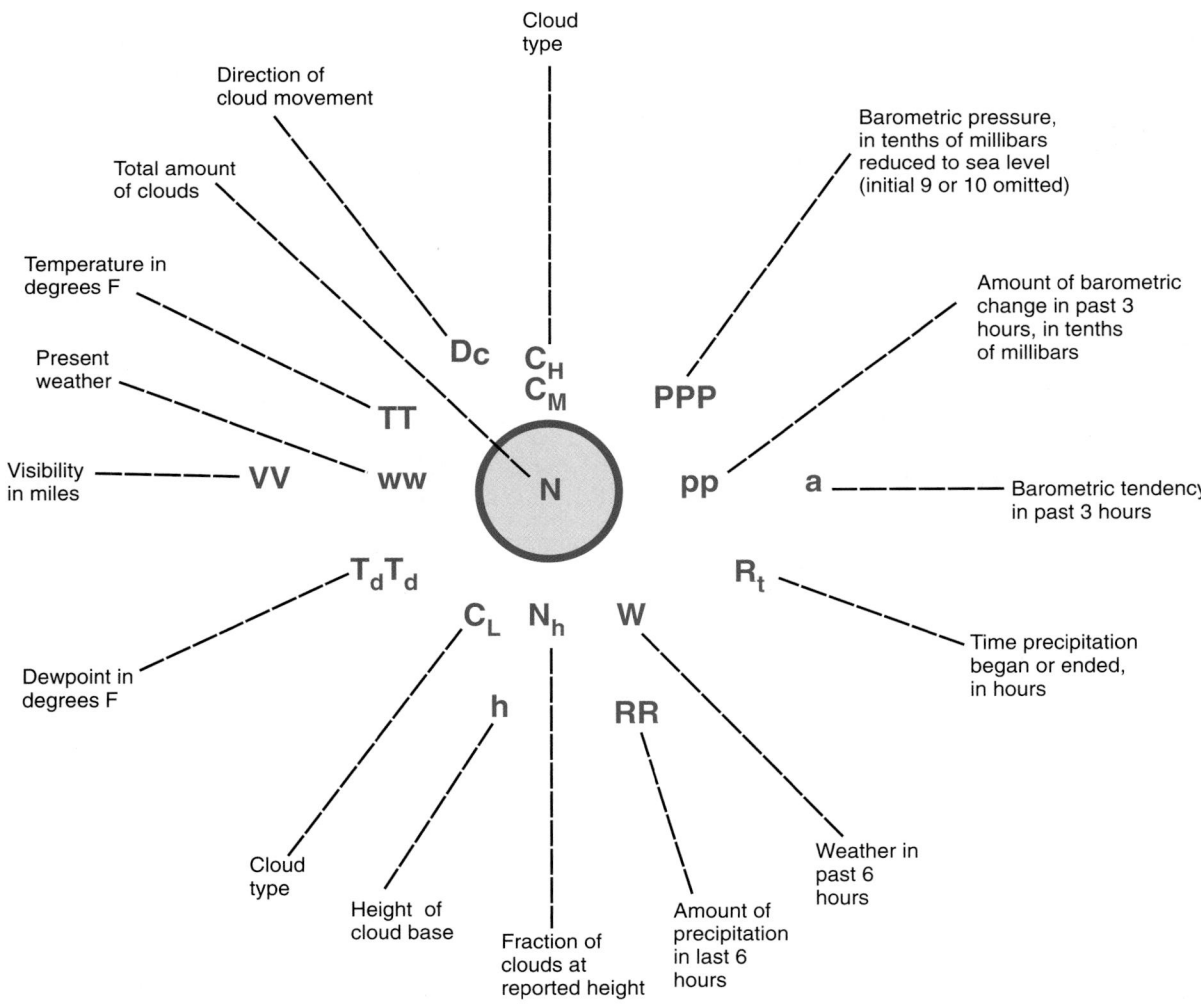

▲ **Figure IV-1** A standard weather station model. (No symbol for wind speed and direction is shown here because there is no one assigned place for this symbol; instead, its position on the model depends on wind direction.)

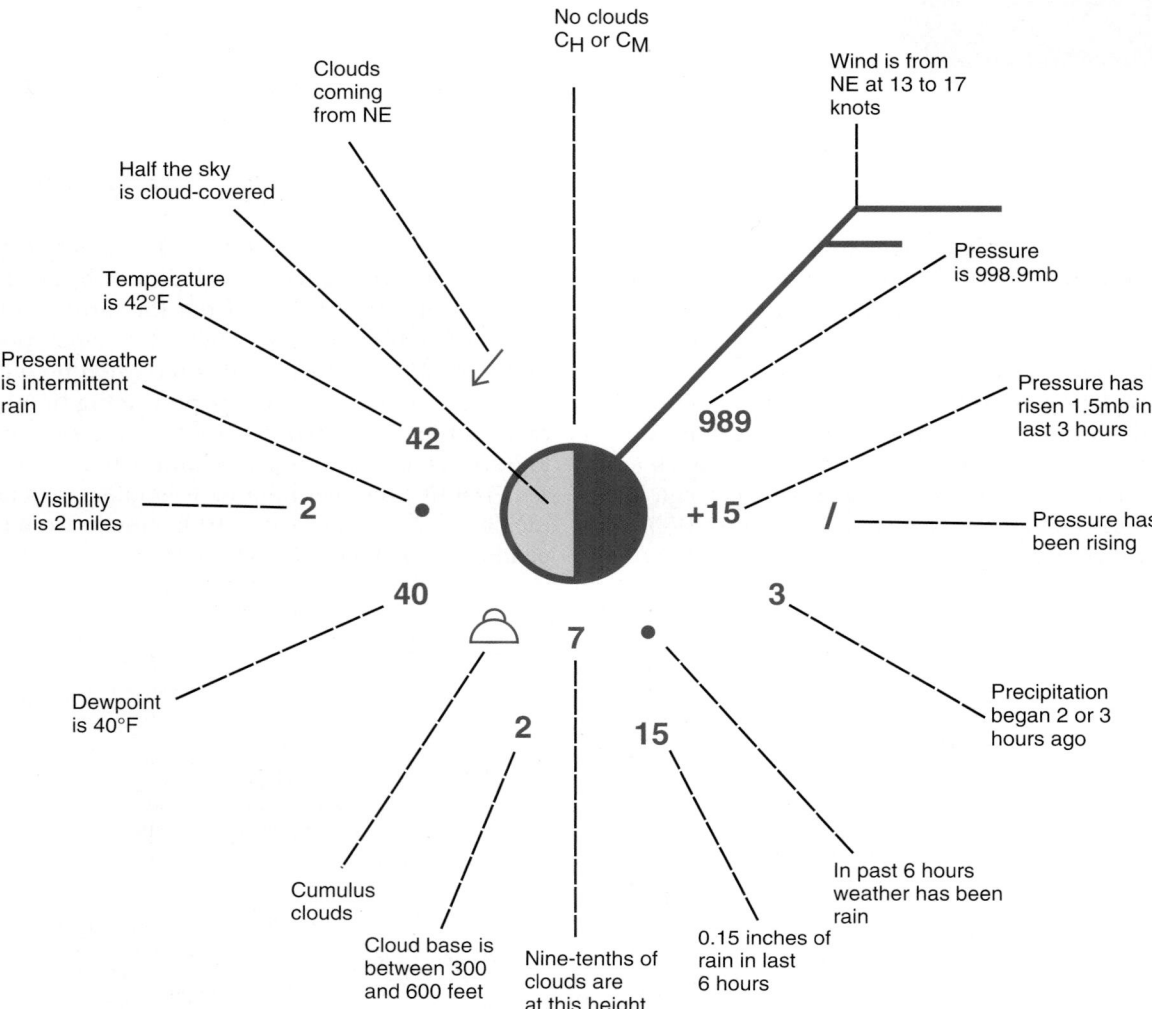

No clouds
C_H or C_M

Clouds
coming
from NE

Wind is from
NE at 13 to 17
knots

Half the sky
is cloud-covered

Temperature
is 42°F

Pressure
is 998.9mb

Present weather
is intermittent
rain

Pressure has
risen 1.5mb in
last 3 hours

42

989

Visibility
is 2 miles

2

+15

/

Pressure has
been rising

40

3

Dewpoint
is 40°F

7

15

Precipitation
began 2 or 3
hours ago

2

Cumulus
clouds

In past 6 hours
weather has been
rain

Cloud base is
between 300
and 600 feet

Nine-tenths of
clouds are
at this height

0.15 inches of
rain in last
6 hours

▲ **Figure IV-2** A standard weather station model with the codes replaced by sample data.

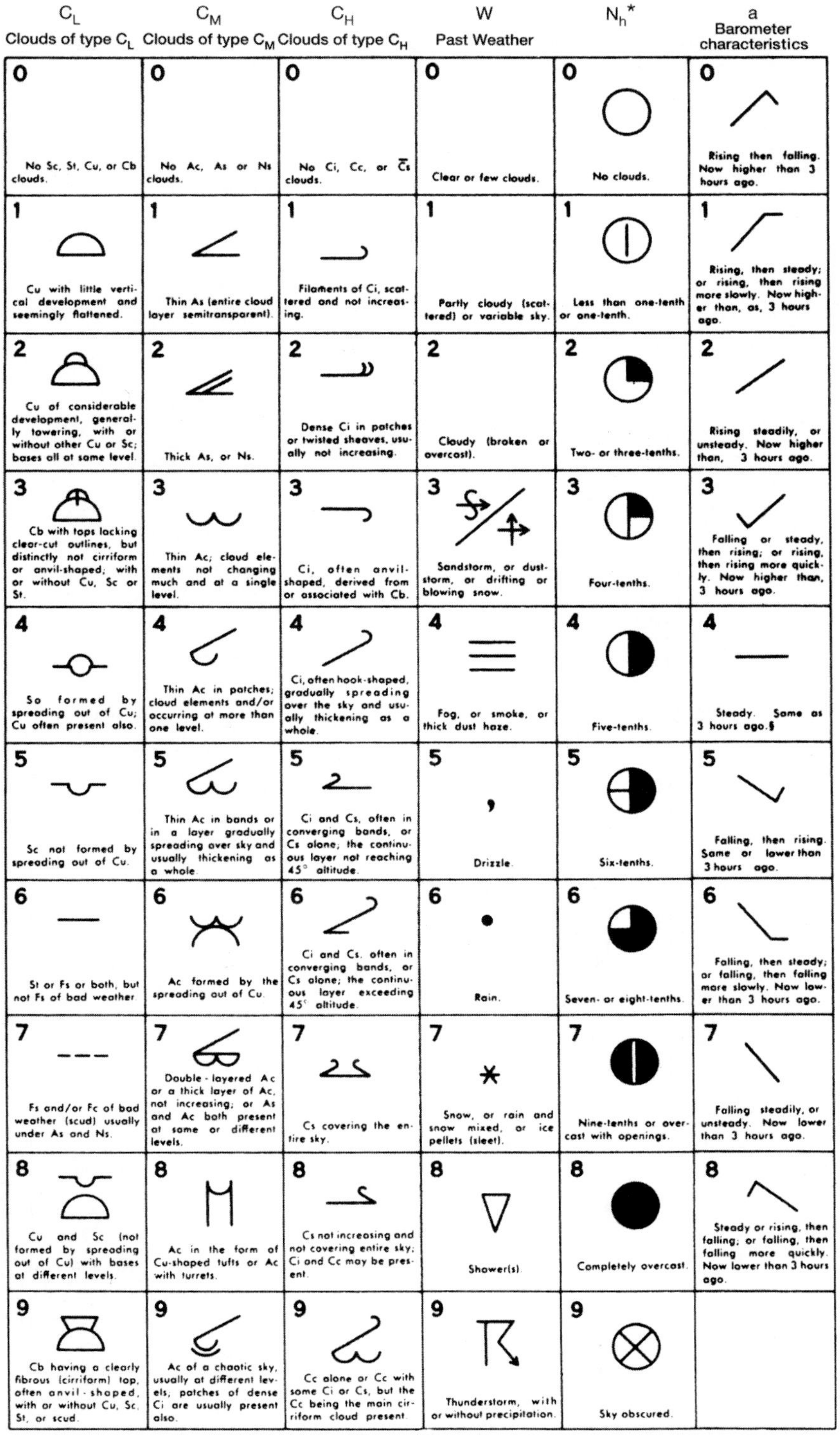

C_L Clouds of type C_L	C_M Clouds of type C_M	C_H Clouds of type C_H	W Past Weather	N_h*	a Barometer characteristics
0 No Sc, St, Cu, or Cb clouds.	**0** No Ac, As or Ns clouds.	**0** No Ci, Cc, or $\overline{C}s$ clouds.	**0** Clear or few clouds.	**0** No clouds.	**0** Rising then falling. Now higher than 3 hours ago.
1 Cu with little vertical development and seemingly flattened.	**1** Thin As (entire cloud layer semitransparent).	**1** Filaments of Ci, scattered and not increasing.	**1** Partly cloudy (scattered) or variable sky.	**1** Less than one-tenth or one-tenth.	**1** Rising, then steady; or rising, then rising more slowly. Now higher than, as, 3 hours ago.
2 Cu of considerable development, generally towering, with or without other Cu or Sc; bases all at same level.	**2** Thick As, or Ns.	**2** Dense Ci in patches or twisted sheaves, usually not increasing.	**2** Cloudy (broken or overcast).	**2** Two- or three-tenths.	**2** Rising steadily, or unsteady. Now higher than, 3 hours ago.
3 Cb with tops lacking clear-cut outlines, but distinctly not cirriform or anvil-shaped; with or without Cu, Sc or St.	**3** Thin Ac; cloud elements not changing much and at a single level.	**3** Ci, often anvil-shaped, derived from or associated with Cb.	**3** Sandstorm, or duststorm, or drifting or blowing snow.	**3** Four-tenths.	**3** Falling or steady, then rising; or rising, then rising more quickly. Now higher than, 3 hours ago.
4 So formed by spreading out of Cu; Cu often present also.	**4** Thin Ac in patches; cloud elements and/or occurring at more than one level.	**4** Ci, often hook-shaped, gradually spreading over the sky and usually thickening as a whole.	**4** Fog, or smoke, or thick dust haze.	**4** Five-tenths.	**4** Steady. Same as 3 hours ago.§
5 Sc not formed by spreading out of Cu.	**5** Thin Ac in bands or in a layer gradually spreading over sky and usually thickening as a whole.	**5** Ci and Cs, often in converging bands, or Cs alone, the continuous layer not reaching 45° altitude.	**5** Drizzle.	**5** Six-tenths.	**5** Falling, then rising. Same or lower than 3 hours ago.
6 St or Fs or both, but not Fs of bad weather.	**6** Ac formed by the spreading out of Cu.	**6** Ci and Cs, often in converging bands, or Cs alone, the continuous layer exceeding 45° altitude.	**6** Rain.	**6** Seven- or eight-tenths.	**6** Falling, then steady; or falling, then falling more slowly. Now lower than 3 hours ago.
7 Fs and/or Fc of bad weather (scud) usually under As and Ns.	**7** Double-layered Ac or a thick layer of Ac, not increasing; or As and Ac both present at some or different levels.	**7** Cs covering the entire sky.	**7** Snow, or rain and snow mixed, or ice pellets (sleet).	**7** Nine-tenths or overcast with openings.	**7** Falling steadily, or unsteady. Now lower than 3 hours ago.
8 Cu and Sc (not formed by spreading out of Cu) with bases at different levels.	**8** Ac in the form of Cu-shaped tufts or Ac with turrets.	**8** Cs not increasing and not covering entire sky; Ci and Cc may be present.	**8** Shower(s).	**8** Completely overcast.	**8** Steady or rising, then falling; or falling, then falling more quickly. Now lower than 3 hours ago.
9 Cb having a clearly fibrous (cirriform) top, often anvil-shaped, with or without Cu, Sc, St, or scud.	**9** Ac of a chaotic sky, usually at different levels, patches of dense Ci are usually present also.	**9** Cc alone or Cc with some Ci or Cs, but the Cc being the main cirriform cloud present.	**9** Thunderstorm, with or without precipitation.	**9** Sky obscured.	

*Fraction representing how much of the total cloud cover is at the reported base height.

▲ **Figure IV-3** Standard symbols used to indicate cloud conditions, past weather, and barometer characteristics. The numbers in the upper-left-hand corner of the cells are used in a standard model and the icons are used on weather maps.

W W
Present weather

00 Cloud development NOT observed or NOT observable during past hour.§	**01** Clouds generally dissolving or becoming less developed during past hour.§	**02** State of sky on the whole unchanged during past hour.§
03 Clouds generally forming or developing during past hour.§	**04** Visibility reduced by smoke.	**05** Dry haze.
06 Widespread dust in suspension in the air, NOT raised by wind, at time of observation.	**07** Dust or sand raised by wind, at time of ob.	**08** Well developed dust devil(s) within past hr.
09 Duststorm or sandstorm within sight of or at station during past hour.		

10 Light fog.	**11** Patches of shallow fog at station, NOT deeper than 6 feet on land.
12 More or less continuous shallow fog at station, NOT deeper than 6 feet on land.	**13** Lightning visible, no thunder heard.
14 Precipitation within sight, but NOT reaching the ground or station.	**15** Precipitation within sight, reaching the ground, but distant from station.
16 Precipitation within sight, reaching the ground, near to but NOT at station.	**17** Thunder heard, but no precipitation at the station.
18 Squall(s) within sight during past hour.	**19** Funnel cloud(s) within sight during past hr.

20 Drizzle (NOT freezing and NOT falling as showers) during past hour, but NOT at time of ob.	**21** Rain (NOT freezing and NOT falling as showers) during past hr., but NOT at time of ob.
22 Snow (NOT falling as showers) during past hr., but NOT at time of ob.	**23** Rain and snow (NOT falling as showers) during past hour, but NOT at time of observation.
24 Freezing drizzle or freezing rain (NOT falling as showers) during past hour, but NOT at time of observation.	**25** Showers of rain during past hour, but NOT at time of observation.
26 Showers of snow, or of rain and snow, during past hour, but NOT at time of observation.	**27** Showers of hail, or of hail and rain, during past hour, but NOT at time of observation.
28 Fog during past hour, but NOT at time of ob.	**29** Thunderstorm (with or without precipitation) during past hour, but NOT at time of ob.

30 Slight or moderate duststorm or sandstorm, has decreased during past hour.	**31** Slight or moderate duststorm or sandstorm, no appreciable change during past hour.
32 Slight or moderate duststorm or sandstorm, has increased during past hour.	**33** Severe duststorm or sandstorm, has decreased during past hr.
34 Severe duststorm or sandstorm, no appreciable change during past hour.	**35** Severe duststorm or sandstorm, has increased during past hr.
36 Slight or moderate drifting snow, generally low.	**37** Heavy drifting snow, generally low.
38 Slight or moderate drifting snow, generally high.	**39** Heavy drifting snow, generally high.

40 Fog at distance at time of ob., but NOT at station during past hour.	**41** Fog in patches.
42 Fog, sky discernible, has become thinner during past hour.	**43** Fog, sky NOT discernible, has become thinner during past hour.
44 Fog, sky discernible, no appreciable change during past hour.	**45** Fog, sky NOT discernible, no appreciable change during past hr.
46 Fog, sky discernible, has begun or become thicker during past hr.	**47** Fog, sky NOT discernible, has begun or become thicker during past hour.
48 Fog, depositing rime, sky discernible.	**49** Fog, depositing rime, sky NOT discernible.

50 Intermittent drizzle (NOT freezing) slight at time of observation.	**51** Continuous drizzle (NOT freezing) slight at time of observation.
52 Intermittent drizzle (NOT freezing) moderate at time of ob.	**53** Intermittent drizzle (NOT freezing), moderate at time of ob.
54 Intermittent drizzle (NOT freezing), thick at time of observation.	**55** Continuous drizzle (NOT freezing), thick at time of observation.
56 Slight freezing drizzle.	**57** Moderate or thick freezing drizzle.
58 Drizzle and rain slight.	**59** Drizzle and rain, moderate or heavy.

60 Intermittent rain (NOT freezing), slight at time of observation.	**61** Continuous rain (NOT freezing), slight at time of observation.
62 Intermittent rain (NOT freezing), moderate at time of ob.	**63** Continuous rain (NOT freezing), moderate at time of observation.
64 Intermittent rain (NOT freezing), heavy at time of observation.	**65** Continuous rain (NOT freezing), heavy at time of observation.
66 Slight freezing rain.	**67** Moderate or heavy freezing rain.
68 Rain or drizzle and snow, slight.	**69** Rain or drizzle and snow, mod. or heavy.

70 Intermittent fall of snow flakes, slight at time of observation.	**71** Continuous fall of snowflakes, slight at time of observation.
72 Intermittent fall of snow flakes, moderate at time of observation.	**73** Continuous fall of snow flakes, moderate at time of observation.
74 Intermittent fall of snow flakes, heavy at time of observation.	**75** Continuous fall of snowflakes, heavy at time of observation.
76 Ice needles (with or without fog).	**77** Granular snow (with or without fog).
78 Isolated starlike snow crystals (with or without fog).	**79** Ice pellets (sleet, U.S. definition).

80 Slight rain shower(s).	**81** Moderate or heavy rain shower(s).
82 Violent rain shower(s).	**83** Slight shower(s) of rain and snow mixed.
84 Moderate or heavy shower(s) of rain and snow mixed.	**85** Slight snow shower(s).
86 Moderate or heavy snow shower(s).	**87** Slight shower(s) of soft or small hail with or without rain or rain and snow mixed.
88 Moderate or heavy shower(s) of soft or small hail with or without rain or rain and snow mixed.	**89** Slight shower(s) of hail††, with or without rain or rain and snow mixed, not associated with thunder.

90 Moderate or heavy shower(s) of hail††, with or without rain or rain and snow mixed, not associated with thunder.	**91** Slight rain at time of ob.; thunderstorm during past hour, but NOT at time of observation.
92 Moderate or heavy rain at time of ob.; thunderstorm during past hour, but NOT at time of observation.	**93** Slight snow or rain and snow mixed or hail† at time of ob.; thunderstorm during past hour, but not at time of ob.
94 Mad. or heavy snow, or rain and snow mixed or hail† at time of ob.; thunderstorm during past hour, but NOT at time of observation.	**95** Slight or mod. thunderstorm without hail†, but with rain and or snow at time of observation.
96 Slight or mod. thunderstorm with hail† at time of observation.	**97** Heavy thunderstorm without hail†, but with rain and or snow at time of ob.
98 Thunderstorm combined with duststorm or sandstorm at time of ob.	**99** Heavy thunderstorm with hail† at time of observation.

§ The symbol is not plotted for "ww" when "00" is reported. When "01, 02, or 03" is reported for "ww," the symbol is plotted on the station circle. Symbols are not plotted for "a" when "3 or 8" is reported.

† Refers to "hail" only.

†† Refers to "soft hail," "small hail," and "hail."

▲ **Figure IV-4** Standard weather map symbols used to indicate present weather.

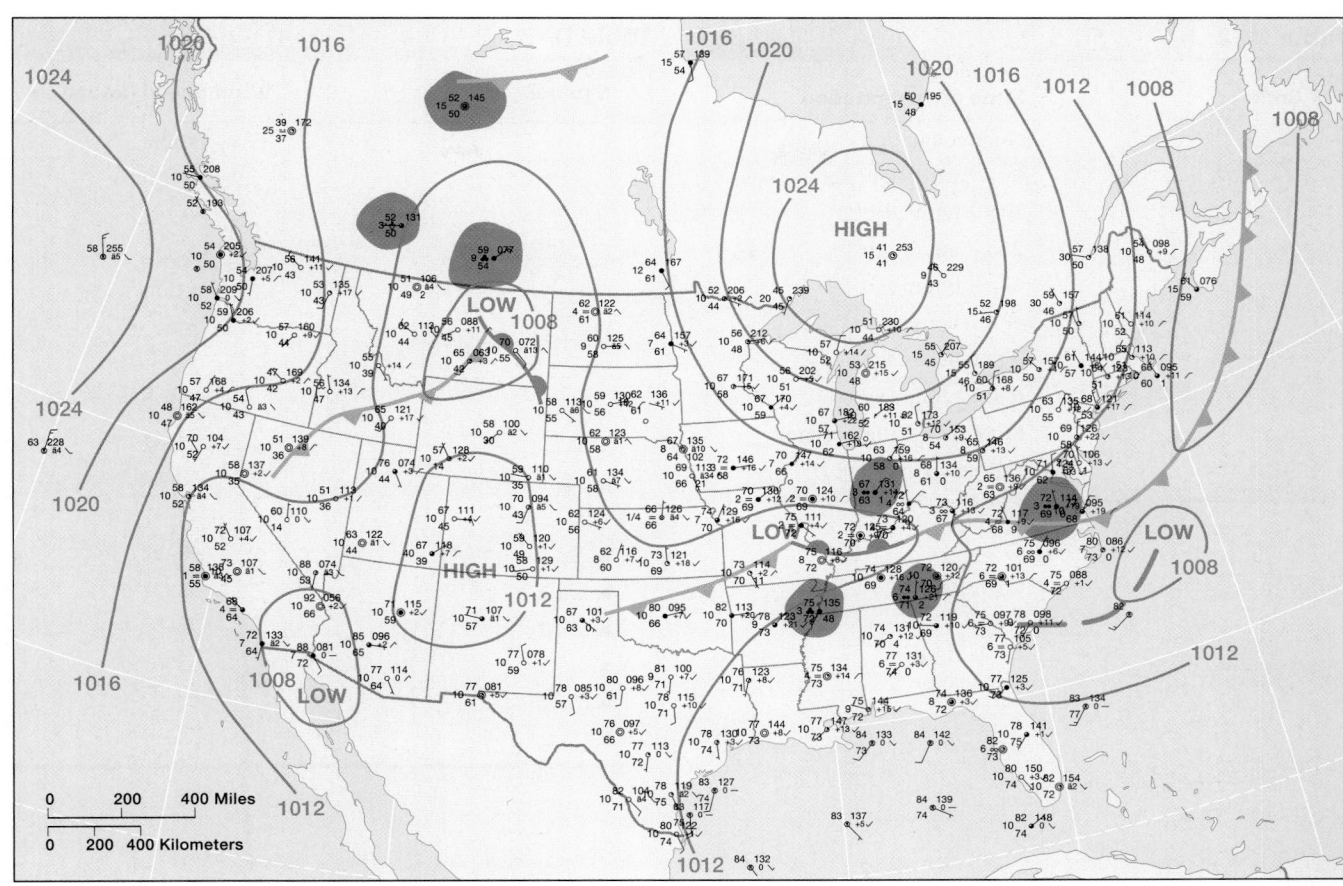

▲ **Figure IV-5** A sample weather map.

Table IV-1 Standard Cloud Height Codes

h (height of cloud base)	Approximate Cloud Height	
	Meters	Feet
0	0–49	0–149
1	50–99	150–299
2	100–199	300–599
3	200–299	600–999
4	300–599	1000–1999
5	600–999	2000–3499
6	1000–1499	3500–4999
7	1500–1999	5000–4699
8	2000–2499	6500–7999
9	> 2500 or no clouds	> 8000 or no clouds

Table IV-2	Standard Precipitation Codes

R_t Code	Time of Precipitation
0	No precipitation
1	Less than 1 hour ago
2	1 to 2 hours ago
3	2 to 3 hours ago
4	3 to 4 hours ago
5	4 to 5 hours ago
6	5 to 6 hours ago
7	6 to 12 hours ago
8	More than 12 hours ago
9	Unknown

Table IV-3	Wind Speed/Direction Symbols

Symbol	Wind Speed (knots)
◎	Calm
	1–2
	3–7
	8–12
	13–17
	18–22
	23–27
	28–32
	33–37
	38–42
	43–47
	48–52
	53–57
	58–62
	63–67
	68–72
	73–77

KÖPPEN CLIMATE CLASSIFICATION

Table V-1 provides the definitions of the code letters used in the modified Köppen climate classification system. The exact classification of a climate using the Köppen system may require additional calculations, and so the definitions of each letter given here may be approximate. For more detailed directions for classifying climates with the Köppen system, see the *Physical Geography Laboratory Manual* for *McKnight's Physical Geography: A Landscape Appreciation,* 11th edition, by Darrel Hess.

TABLE V-1 Code Letters of the Modified Köppen Classification System

1st	2nd	3rd	Description	Definitions
A			Low-latitude humid climates	Average temperature of each month above 18°C (64°F)
	f		No dry season [German: *feucht* ("moist")]	Average rainfall of each month at least 6 cm (2.4 in.)
	m		Monsoon; short dry season compensated by heavy rains in other months	1 to 3 months with average rainfall less than 6 cm (2.4 in.)
	w		Winter dry season (low-Sun season)	3 to 6 months with average rainfall less than 6 cm (2.4 in.)
B			Dry climates	Evaporation exceeds precipitation
	W		Desert [German: *wüste* ("desert")]	Average annual precipitation generally less than 38 cm (15 in.) in low latitudes; 25 cm (10 in.) in midlatitudes
	S		Steppe (semiarid)	Average annual precipitation generally between 38 cm (15 in.) and 76 cm (30 in.) in low latitudes; between about 25 cm (10 in.) and 64 cm (25 in.) in midlatitudes; without pronounced seasonal concentration
		h	Low-latitude (subtropical) dry climate [German: *heiss* ("hot")]	Average annual temperature more than 18°C (64°F)
		k	Midlatitude dry climate [German: *kalt* ("cold")]	Average annual temperature less than 18°C (64°F)
C			Mild midlatitude climates	Average temperature of coldest month between 18°C (64°F) and −3°C (27°F) average temperature of warmest month above 10°C (50°F)
	s		Summer dry season	Wettest winter month has at least 3× precipitation of driest summer month
	w		Winter dry season	Wettest summer month has at least 10× precipitation of driest winter month
	f		No dry season [German: *feucht* ("moist")]	Does not fit either s or w above
		a	Hot summers	Average temperature of warmest month more than 22°C (72°F)
		b	Warm summers	Average temperature of warmest month below 22°C (72°F) at least 4 months with average temperature above 10°C (50°F)
		c	Cool summers	Average temperature of warmest month below 22°C (72°F) less than 4 months with average temperature above 10°C (50°F) coldest month above −38°C (−36°F)
D			Humid midlatitude climates with severe winters (2nd and 3rd letters same as in C climates)	Warmest month above 10°C (50°F) coldest month below −3°C (27°F)
		d	Very cold winters	Average temperature of coldest month less than −38°C (−36°F)

TABLE V-1	Code Letters of the Modified Köppen Classification System (*Continued*)

Letters			**Description**	**Definitions**
1st	**2nd**	**3rd**		
E			Polar climates; no true summer	No month with average temperature more than 10°C (50°F)
	T		Tundra climates	At least one month with average temperature more than 0°C (32°F) but less than 10°C (50°F)
	F		Ice cap climates ("frost")	No month with average temperature more than 0°C (32°F)
H			Highland climates	Significant climatic changes within short horizontal distances due to altitudinal variations

BIOLOGICAL TAXONOMY

Taxonomy is the science of classification. As a term, it was originally applied to the classification of plants and animals, although its meaning has been broadened to encompass any sort of systematic classification. Our concern here is only with biological taxonomy. People have attempted to devise meaningful classifications of plants and animals for thousands of years. One of the most useful of the early classifications was designed by Aristotle 2300 years ago, and this system was in general use for nearly 20 centuries. In the late 1700s, the Aristotelian classification was finally replaced by a much more comprehensive and systematic one developed by the Swedish naturalist Carolus Linnaeus. Linnaeus made use of ideas from other biologists, but the system is largely his own work.

The Linnaean System: The *Linnaean system of classification* is generic, hierarchical, comprehensive, and binomial. *Generic* means that it is based on observable characteristics of the organisms it classifies, primarily their anatomy, structures, and details of reproduction. *Hierarchical* means that the organisms are grouped on the basis of similar characteristics, with each lower level of grouping having a larger number of similar characteristics and therefore containing fewer individuals in the group. *Comprehensive* means that all plants and animals, existing and extinct, can be encompassed within the system. *Binomial* means that every kind of plant and animal is identified by two names.

Binomial Names: The binomial naming of organisms is highly systematized. Each type of living thing has a name with two parts. The first part, in which the first letter is capitalized, designates the *genus*, or group; the second part, which is not capitalized, indicates the *species*, or specific kind of organism. The combination of genus and species is referred to as the *scientific name*; it is always in Latin, although many of the words have Greek derivations.

Each type of organism, then, has a scientific name that distinguishes it from all other organisms. Although the popular name may be variable, or even indefinite, the scientific name is unvarying. Thus, in different parts of the Western Hemisphere, the large native cat may be called a mountain lion, cougar, puma, panther, painter, or leon, but its scientific name is always *Felis concolor*.

The intellectual beauty of the Linnaean system is twofold: (1) every organism that has ever existed can be fitted into the scheme in a logical and orderly manner for the system is capable of indefinite expansion, and (2) the various hierarchical levels in the system provide a conceptual framework for understanding the relationships among different organisms or groups of organisms. This is not to say the system is perfect. Linnaeus believed that species were unchanging entities, and his original system had no provision for variations. The concept of subspecies was a major modification of the system that was introduced subsequently to accommodate observed conditions of evolution.

Nor is the system even completely objective. Whereas its concept and general organization are accepted by scientists throughout the world, details of the classification depend on judgments and opinions made by biologists. These judgments and opinions are based on careful measurements and observations of plant and animal specimens, but there is often room for differing interpretations of the relevant data. Consequently, some details of biological taxonomy are disputed and even controversial. Despite confusion about some of the details, the generally accepted Linnaean system provides a magnificent framework for biological classification.

Levels of Classification: The seven main levels of the system, in order from largest to smallest, are (1) kingdom, (2) phylum, (3) class, (4) order, (5) family, (6) genus, and (7) species.

Kingdom is the broadest category and contains the largest number of organisms. Until recently, the system recognized only two kingdoms: one encompassing all plants and the other including all animals. Increasingly, however, taxonomists encountered difficulty in accommodating the many varieties of one-celled and other simple microscopic organisms into such a two-kingdom system. It is now widely, but by no means universally, accepted that six kingdoms exist at the highest level of taxonomic distinction.[1]

1. *Archaea* are simple organisms that live in harsh environments such as underwater hydrothermal vents, hot sulfur springs, and hypersaline water. Some may also live in the open ocean and can be either autotrophs or heterotrophs.
2. *Eubacteria* are true, one-celled bacteria.
3. *Protista* consist of other one-celled organisms and some simple multicelled algae, most of which were formerly classified as plants.
4. *Fungi* were also previously classified as plants, but it is now recognized that they differ in origin, direction of evolution, and primary nutrition from plants and therefore deserve separation.

---

[1]Until a few years ago only five kingdoms were recognized: *Monera, Protista, Fungi, Plantae,* and *Animalia.* The new six-kingdom classification is not recognized by all biologists.

5. *Plantae* include the multicelled green plants and higher algae.
6. *Animalia* consist of the multicelled animals.

Phylum is the second major level of the system. Of the two or three dozen phyla within the animal kingdom, one, *Chordata*, includes all animals with backbones, which means almost every animal more than a few centimeters in length (Figure VI-1). In the plant kingdom, the term *division* is often used in place of phylum. Most large plants belong to the division *Tracheophyta*, or vascular plants, which have efficient internal systems for transporting water and sugars and a complex differentiation of organs into leaves, stem, and roots.

The third principal level is *class*. Among the several dozen animal classes, the most important are *Mammalia* (mammals), *Aves* (birds), *Reptilia* (reptiles), *Amphibia* (amphibians), and two classes that encompass fishes. There are somewhat fewer classes of plants, of which the most notable is *Angiospermae*, the flowering plants (Figure VI-2).

The fourth level of the classification is called *order*, and the three lower levels are *family*, *genus*, and *species*. As in all levels of the hierarchy, each succeeding lower level contains organisms that are increasingly alike. Species is the basic unit of the classification. In theory, only members of the same species are capable of breeding with one another. In practice, however, interbreeding is possible among just a few species (always within the same genus), although the offspring of such interspecific breeding are nearly always infertile (i.e., totally incapable of reproducing). In some cases, species are further subdivided into subspecies, also called *varieties* or *races*.

The relative diversity of living and extinct species is worthy of note. About 1,500,000 species of living organisms have been identified and described. From 3 to 10 million additional species, mostly microscopic in size, may not yet be identified. An estimated 500 million species have become extinct in Earth's history. Thus, more than 95 percent of all evolutionary lines have already completely disappeared.

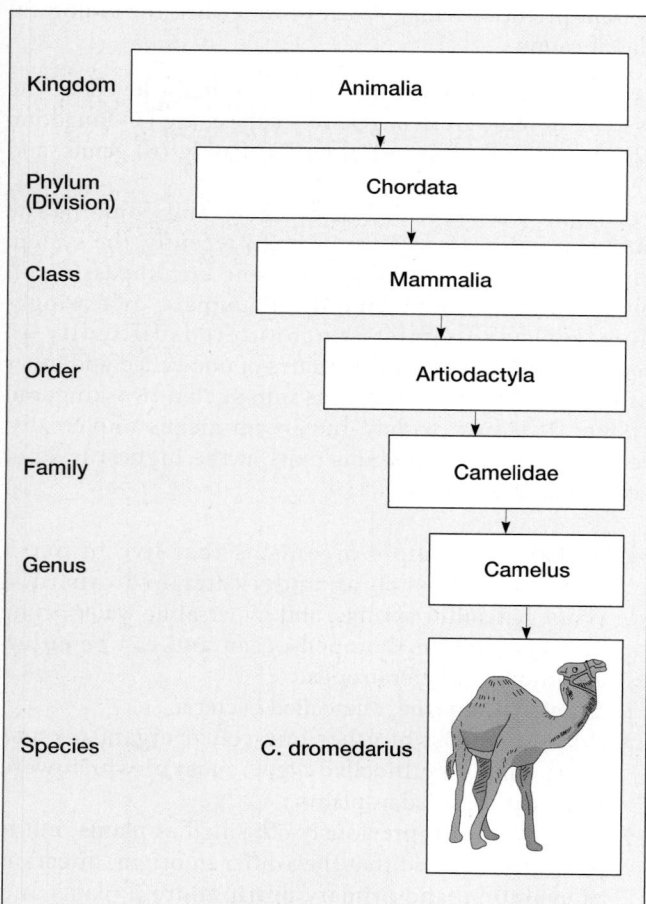

▲ **Figure VI-1** The taxonomic classification of an animal, as illustrated by the Arabian camel, or dromedary.

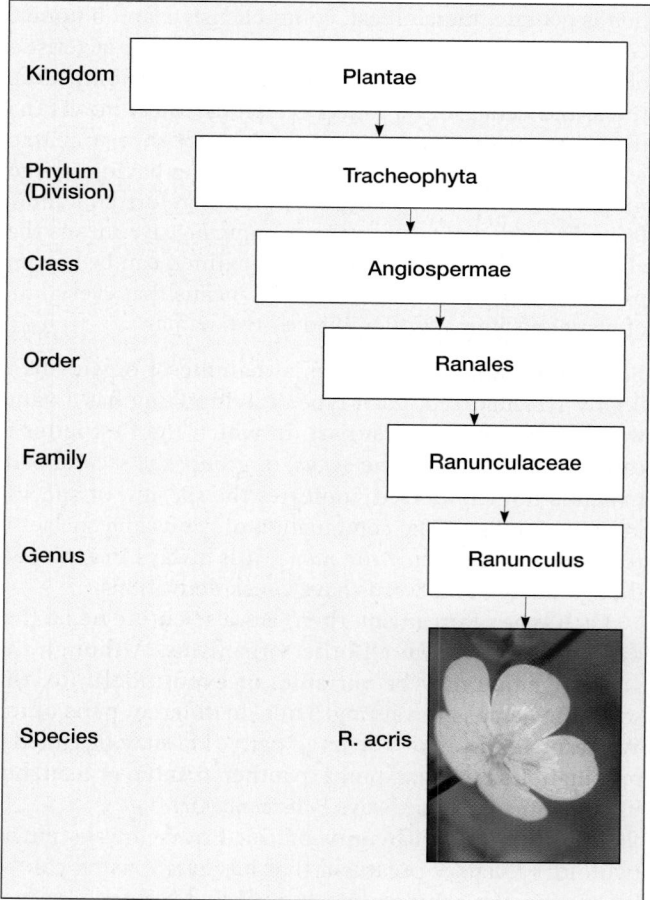

▲ **Figure VI-2** The taxonomic classification of a plant, as illustrated by the buttercup.

THE SOIL TAXONOMY

The Soil Taxonomy, described in Chapter 12, utilizes a nomenclature "invented" for the purpose. This nomenclature consists of "synthetic" names, which means that syllables from existing words are rearranged and combined to produce new words for the names of the various soil types. The beauty of the system is that each newly coined name is highly descriptive of the soil it represents.

The awkwardness of the nomenclature is threefold:

1. Most of the terms are new and have never before appeared in print or in conversation. Thus they look strange, and the words do not easily roll off the tongue. It is almost a new language.
2. Many of the words are difficult to write, and great care must be taken in the spelling of seemingly bizarre combinations of letters.
3. Many of the syllables sound so much alike that differences in pronunciation are often slight, although enunciating these slight differences is essential if the new nomenclature is to serve its purpose.

Nevertheless, the Soil Taxonomy has a sound theoretical base, and once the user is familiar with the vocabulary, every syllable of every word gives important information about a soil. Almost all the syllables are derived from Greek or Latin roots, in contrast to the English and Russian terms used in previous systems. In some cases, the appropriateness of the classical derivatives may be open to question, but the uniformity and logic of the terminology extend throughout the system.

THE HIERARCHY

The top level in the Soil Taxonomy hierarchy is *soil order*. The names of orders are made up of three or four syllables, the last of which is always *sol* (from the Latin word *solum*, "soil"). The next-to-last syllable consists of a single linking vowel, either *i* or *o*. The syllable (or two) that begins the word contains the formative element of the name and gives information regarding some distinctive characteristic of the order. Thus, each of the 12 soil order names contains a distinctive syllable that (1) identifies the formative element of that soil order and (2) appears in all the names in the next three levels of the hierarchy for that soil order.

Suborder is the second level in the hierarchy. All suborder names contain two syllables: the first indicates some distinctive characteristic of the suborder; the second identifies the order to which the suborder belongs. For example, *aqu* is derived from the Latin word for "water,"
and so *Aquent* is the suborder of wet soils of the order Entisols. The names of the four dozen suborders are constructed from the two dozen root elements shown in Table VII-1.

The third level of the hierarchy contains *great groups*, the names of which are constructed by grafting one or more syllables to the beginning of a suborder name. Hence, a *Cryaquent* is a cold soil that is a member of the Aquent suborder of the Entisol order (*cry* comes from the Greek word for "coldness"). The formative prefixes for the great group names are derived from about 50 root words, samples of which are presented in Table VII-2.

The next level is called *subgroup*, and there are more than 1000 subgroups recognized in the United States. Each subgroup name consists of two words: the first derived from a formative element higher up in the hierarchy (with a few exceptions), the second the same as that of the relevant great group. Thus, a *Sphagnic Cryaquent* is of the order Entisol, the suborder Aquent, the great group *Cryaquent*, and it contains sphagnum moss (derived from the Greek word *sphagnos*, "bog").

The *family* is the penultimate level in the hierarchy. It is not given a proper name but is simply described by one or more lowercase adjectives, as "a skeletal, mixed, acidic family."

Finally, the lowest level of the hierarchy is the *series*, named for geographic location. Table VII-3 gives a typical naming sequence.

SUMMARY OF SOIL SUBORDERS

Alfisols

Alfisols have five suborders. *Aqualfs* have characteristics associated with wetness. *Boralfs* are associated with cold boreal forests. *Udalfs* are brownish or reddish soils of moist midlatitude regions. *Ustalfs* are similar to Udalfs in color but subtropical in location and usually have a hard surface layer in the dry season. *Xeralfs* are found in mediterranean climates and are characterized by a thick, hard surface horizon in the dry season.

Andisols

Seven suborders are recognized in the Andisols, five of which are distinguished by moisture content. *Aquands* have abundant moisture, often with poor drainage. *Torrands* are associated with a hot, dry regime. *Udands* are found in humid climates; *Ustands* in dry climates with hot summers. *Xerands* have a pronounced annual dry season.

TABLE VII-1   Name Derivations of Soil Suborders

Root	Derivation	Connotation	Example of Suborder Name
alb	Latin *albus*, "white"	Presence of bleached eluvial horizon	Alboll
and	Japanese *ando*, a volcanic soil	Derived from pyroclastic material	Andept
aqu	Latin *aqua*, "water"	Associated with wetness	Aquent
ar	Latin *arare*, "to plow"	Horizons are mixed	Arent
arg	Latin *argilla*, "white clay"	Presence of a horizon containing illuvial clay	Argid
bor	Greek *boreas*, "northern"	Associated with cool conditions	Boroll
ferr	Latin *ferrum*, "iron"	Presence of iron	Ferrod
fibr	Latin *fibra*, "fiber"	Presence of undecomposed organic matter	Fibrist
fluv	Latin *fluvius*, "river"	Associated with floodplains	Fluvent
fol	Latin *folia*, "leaf"	Mass of leaves	Folist
hem	Greek *hemi*, "half"	Intermediate stage of decomposition	Hemist
hum	Latin *humus*, "earth"	Presence of organic matter	Humult
ochr	Greek *ochros*, "pale"	Presence of a light-colored surface horizon	Ochrept
orth	Greek *orthos*, "true"	Most common or typical group	Orthent
plag	German *plaggen*, "sod"	Presence of a human-induced surface horizon	Plaggept
psamm	Greek *psammos*, "sand"	Sandy texture	Psamment
rend	Polish *rendzino*, a type of soil	Significant calcareous content	Rendoll
sapr	Greek *sapros*, "rotten"	Most decomposed stage	Saprist
torr	Latin *torridus*, "hot and dry"	Usually dry	Torrox
trop	Greek *tropikos*, "of the solstice"	Continuously warm	Tropept
ud	Latin *udud*, "humid"	Of humid climates	Udoll
umbr	Latin *umbro*, "shade"	Presence of a dark surface horizon	Umbrept
ust	Latin *ustus*, "burnt"	Of dry climates	Ustert
xer	Greek *xeros*, "dry"	Annual dry season	Xeralf

TABLE VII-2   Name Derivations for Great Groups

Root	Derivation	Connotation	Example of Great Group Name
calc	Latin *calcis*, "lime"	Presence of calcic horizon	Calciorthid
ferr	Latin *ferrum*, "iron"	Presence of iron	Ferrudalf
natr	Latin *natrium*, "sodium"	Presence of a natric horizon	Natraboll
pale	Greek *paleos*, "old"	An old development	Paleargid
plinth	Greek *plinthos*, "brick"	Presence of plinthite	Plenthoxeralf
quartz	The German name	High quartz content	Quartzipsamment
verm	Latin *vermes*, "worm"	Notable presence of worms	Vermudoll

TABLE VII-3 | A Typical Soil Taxonomy Naming Sequence

Order	Entisol
Suborder	Aquent
Great group	Cryaquent
Subgroup	Sphagnic Cryaquent
Family	Skeletal, mixed, acidic, Sphagnic Cryaquent
Series	Aberdeen

In addition, *Cryands* are found in cold climates, and *Vitrands* are distinguished by the presence of glass.

Aridisols

Two suborders are generally recognized on the basis of degree of weathering. *Argids* have a distinctive subsurface horizon with clay accumulation, whereas *Orthids* do not.

Entisols

There are five suborders of Entisols. *Aquents* occupy wet environments where the soil is more or less continuously saturated with water; they may be found in any temperature regime. *Arents* lack horizons because of human interference, particularly that involving large agricultural or engineering machinery. *Fluvents* form on recent water-deposited sediments that have satisfactory drainage. *Orthents* develop on recent erosional surfaces. *Psamments* occur in sandy situations, where the sand is either shifting or stabilized by vegetation.

Gelisols

The three suborders of Gelisols—*Histels*, *Orthels*, and *Turbels*—are distinguished largely on the basis of quantity and distribution of organic material.

Histosols

The four suborders of Histosols—*Fibrists*, *Folists*, *Hemists*, and *Saprists*—are differentiated on the basis of degree of plant-material decomposition.

Inceptisols

The six suborders of Inceptisols—*Andepts*, *Aquepts*, *Ochrepts*, *Plaggepts*, *Tropepts*, and *Umbrepts*—have relatively complicated distinguishing characteristics.

Mollisols

The seven suborders of Mollisols—*Albolls*, *Aquolls*, *Borolls*, *Rendolls*, *Udolls*, *Ustolls*, and *Xerolls*—are distinguished largely, but not entirely, on the basis of relative wetness/dryness.

Oxisols

The five suborders of Oxisols—*Aquox*, *Humox*, *Orthox*, *Torrox*, and *Ustox*—are distinguished from one another primarily by what effect varying amounts and seasonality of rainfall have on the profile.

Spodosols

Of the four suborders of Spodosols, most widespread are the *Orthods*, which represent the typical Spodosols. *Aquods*, *Ferrods*, and *Humods* are differentiated on the basis of the amount of iron in the spodic horizon.

Ultisols

Five suborders of Ultisols—*Aquults*, *Humults*, *Udults*, *Ustults*, and *Xerults*—are recognized. The distinction among them is largely on the basis of temperature and moisture conditions and on how these parameters influence the epipedon.

Vertisols

The four principal suborders of Vertisols are distinguished largely on the frequency of "cracking," which is a function of climate. *Torrerts* are found in arid regions, and the cracks in these soils remain open most of the time. *Uderts* are found in humid areas, and in these soils cracking is irregular. *Usterts* are associated with monsoon climates and have a relatively complicated cracking pattern. *Xererts* occur in mediterranean climates and have cracks that open and close regularly once each year.

GLOSSARY

A

ablation Wastage of glacial ice through melting and sublimation.

ablation zone The lower portion of a glacier where there is a net annual loss of ice due to melting and sublimation.

absolute humidity One measure of the actual water vapor content of air, expressed as the mass of water vapor in a given volume of air, usually as grams of water per cubic meter of air.

absorption The ability of an object to assimilate energy from electromagnetic waves that strike it.

accumulation (glacial ice accumulation) Addition of ice into a glacier by incorporation of snow.

accumulation zone The upper portion of a glacier where there is a greater annual accumulation of ice than there is wastage.

acid rain Precipitation with a pH less than 5.6. It may involve dry deposition without moisture.

adiabatic cooling Cooling by expansion, such as in rising air.

adiabatic warming Warming by compression, such as in descending air.

adret slope A slope oriented so that the Sun's rays arrive at a relatively high angle. Such a slope tends to be relatively warm and dry.

advection Horizontal transfer of energy, such as through the movement of wind across Earth's surface.

aeolian processes Processes related to wind action that are most pronounced, widespread, and effective in dry lands.

aerosols Solid or liquid particles suspended in the atmosphere; also called *particulates*.

aggradation The process in which a stream bed is raised as a result of the deposition of sediment.

A horizon Upper soil layer in which humus and other organic materials are mixed with mineral particles.

air mass An extensive body of air that has relatively uniform properties in the horizontal dimension and moves as an entity.

albedo The reflectivity of a surface. The fraction of total solar radiation that is reflected back, unchanged, into space.

Alfisol A widely distributed soil order distinguished by a subsurface clay horizon and a medium-to-generous supply of plant nutrients and water.

alluvial fan A fan-shaped depositional feature of alluvium laid down by a stream issuing from a mountain canyon.

alluvium Any stream-deposited sedimentary material.

alpine glacier Individual glacier that develops near a mountain crest line and normally moves down-valley for some distance.

Andisol Soil order derived from volcanic ash.

angiosperms Plants that have seeds encased in some sort of protective body, such as a fruit, a nut, or a seedpod.

angle of incidence The angle at which the Sun's rays strike Earth's surface.

angle of repose Steepest angle that can be assumed by loose fragments on a slope without downslope movement.

annual plants (annuals) Plants that perish during times of environmental stress but leave behind a reservoir of seeds to germinate during the next favorable period.

Antarctic Circle The parallel of 66.5° south latitude.

antecedent stream Stream that predates the existence of the hill or mountain through which it flows.

anticline A simple symmetrical upfold in the rock structure.

anticyclone A high-pressure center.

antitrade winds Tropical upper-atmosphere westerly winds at the top of the Hadley cells that blow toward the northeast in the Northern Hemisphere and toward the southeast in the Southern Hemisphere.

aphelion The point in Earth's elliptical orbit at which Earth is farthest from the Sun (about 152,100,000 kilometers or 94,500,000 miles).

aquiclude An impermeable rock layer that is so dense as to exclude water.

aquifer A permeable subsurface rock layer that can store, transmit, and supply water.

Arctic Circle The parallel of 66.5° north latitude.

arête A narrow, jagged, serrated spine of rock; remainder of a ridge crest after several glacial cirques have been cut back into an interfluve from opposite sides of a divide.

Aridisol A soil order occupying dry environments that do not have enough water to remove soluble minerals from the soil; typified by a thin profile that is sandy and lacking in organic matter.

artesian well The free flow that results when a well is drilled from the surface down into the aquifer and the confining pressure is sufficient to force the water to the surface without artificial pumping.

asthenosphere Plastic layer of the upper mantle that underlies the lithosphere. Its rock is dense, but very hot and therefore weak and easily deformed.

atmosphere The gaseous envelope surrounding Earth.

atmospheric pressure The force exerted by the atmosphere on a surface.

atoll Coral reef in the general shape of a ring or partial ring that encloses a lagoon.

average annual temperature range Difference in temperature between the average temperature of the hottest and coldest months for a location.

average lapse rate The average rate of temperature decrease with height in the troposphere—about 6.5° C per 1000 meters (3.6° F per 1000 feet).

B

backwash Water moving seaward after the momentum of the wave swash is overcome by gravity and friction.

badlands Intricately rilled and barren terrain of arid and semiarid regions, characterized by a multiplicity of short, steep slopes.

bajada A continual alluvial surface that extends across the piedmont zone, slanting from the range toward the basin, in which it is difficult to distinguish between individual alluvial fans.

barchan dune A crescent-shaped sand dune with cusps of the crescent pointing downwind.

barometer Instrument used to measure atmospheric pressure.

barrier island Narrow offshore island composed of sediment; generally oriented parallel to shore.

barrier reef A prominent ridge of coral that roughly parallels the coastline but lies offshore, with a shallow lagoon between the reefs and the coast.

basal slip The term used to describe the sliding of the bottom of a glacier over its bed on a lubricating film of water.

basalt Fine-grained, dark (usually black) volcanic rock; forms from mafic (relatively low silica content) lava.

base level An imaginary surface extending underneath the continents from sea level at the coasts and indicating the lowest level to which land can be eroded.

batholith The largest and most amorphous of igneous intrusions.

baymouth bar A spit that extends entirely across the mouth of a bay, transforming the bay into a lagoon.

beach An exposed deposit of loose sediment, normally composed of sand and/or gravel, and occupying the coastal transition zone between land and water.

beach drifting The zigzag movement of sediment caused by waves washing particles onto a beach at a slight angle; the net result is the movement of sediment along the coast in a general downwind direction.

bedding plane Flat surfaces separating one sedimentary layer from the next.

bedload Sand, gravel, and larger rock fragments moving in a stream by saltation and traction.

B horizon Mineral soil horizon located beneath the A horizon.

biodiversity The number of different kinds of organisms present in a location.

biogeography The study of the distribution patterns of plants and animals, and how these patterns change over time.

biological weathering Rock weathering processes involving the action of plants or animals.

biomass The total mass (or weight) of all living organisms in an ecosystem or per unit area.

biome A large, recognizable assemblage of plants and animals in functional interaction with its environment.

biosphere The living organisms of Earth.

biota The total complex of plant and animal life.

blowout (deflation hollow) A shallow depression from which an abundance of fine material has been deflated by wind.

boreal forest (taiga) An extensive needleleaf forest in the subarctic regions of North America and Eurasia.

braided channel pattern (braided stream) A stream that consists of a multiplicity of interwoven and interconnected shallow channels separated by low islands of sand, gravel, and other loose debris.

broadleaf trees Trees that have flat and expansive leaves.

butte An erosional remnant of very small surface area and clifflike sides that rises conspicuously above the surroundings.

C

calcification One of the dominant pedogenic regimes in areas where the principal soil moisture movement is upward because of a moisture deficit. This regime is characterized by a concentration of calcium carbonate ($CaCO_3$) in the B horizon, forming a hardpan.

caldera Large, steep-sided, roughly circular depression resulting from the explosion and/or collapse of a large volcano.

capacity (stream capacity) The maximum load that a stream can transport under given conditions.

capacity (water vapor capacity) Maximum amount of water vapor that can be present in the air at a given temperature.

capillarity The action by which water can climb upward in restricted confinement as a result of its high surface tension, and thus the ability of its molecules to stick closely together.

carbonation A process in which carbon dioxide in water reacts with carbonate rocks to produce a very soluble product (calcium bicarbonate), which can readily be removed by runoff or percolation, and which can also be deposited in crystalline form if the water is evaporated.

carbon cycle The change from carbon dioxide to living matter and back to carbon dioxide.

carbon dioxide CO_2; minor gas in the atmosphere; one of the greenhouse gases; by-product of combustion and respiration.

carbonic acid Mild acid formed when carbon dioxide dissolves in water; H_2CO_3.

cation An atom or group of atoms with a positive electrical charge.

cation exchange capacity (CEC) Capability of soil to attract and exchange cations.

cavern Large opening or cave, especially in limestone; often decorated with *speleothems*.

chemical weathering The chemical decomposition of rock by the alteration of rock-forming minerals.

chinook A localized downslope wind of relatively dry and warm air, which is further warmed adiabatically as it moves down the leeward slope of the Rocky Mountains.

chlorofluorocarbons (CFCs) Synthetic chemicals commonly used as refrigerants and in aerosol spray cans; destroy ozone in the upper atmosphere.

C horizon Lower soil layer composed of weathered parent material that has not been significantly affected by translocation or leaching.

cinder cone Small, common volcano that is composed primarily of pyroclastic material blasted out from a vent in small but intense explosions. The structure of the volcano is usually a conical hill of loose material.

circle of illumination The edge of the sunlit hemisphere that is a great circle separating Earth into a light half and a dark half.

cirque A broad amphitheater hollowed out at the head of a glacial valley by glacial erosion and frost wedging.

cirque glacier A small glacier confined to its cirque and not moving down-valley.

cirrus cloud High cirriform clouds of feathery appearance.

clay Very small inorganic particles produced by chemical alteration of silicate minerals.

climate An aggregate of day-to-day weather conditions and weather extremes over a long period of time, usually at least 30 years.

climax vegetation A stable plant association of relatively constant composition that develops at the end of a long succession of changes.

climograph (climatic diagram) Chart showing the average monthly temperature and precipitation for a weather station.

cloud Visible accumulation of tiny liquid water droplets or ice crystals suspended in the atmosphere.

col A pass or saddle through a ridge produced when two adjacent glacial *cirques* on opposite sides of a divide are cut back enough to remove part of the *arête* between them.

cold front The leading edge of a cool air mass actively displacing warm air.

collapse sinkhole A sinkhole produced by the collapse of the roof of a subsurface cavern; a collapse doline.

colloids Organic and inorganic microscopic particles of soil that represent the chemically active portion of particles in the soil.

competence (stream competence) The size of the largest particle that can be transported by a stream.

composite volcano Volcanoes with the classic symmetrical, cone-shaped peak, produced by a mixture of lava outpouring and pyroclastic explosion; also *stratovolcano*.

compromise map projection A map projection that is neither conformal or equivalent, but a balance of those, or other, map properties.

condensation Process by which water vapor is converted to liquid water; a warming process because latent heat is released.

condensation nuclei Tiny atmospheric particles of dust, bacteria, smoke, and salt that serve as collection centers for water molecules.

conduction The movement of energy from one molecule to another without changing the relative positions of the molecules. It enables the transfer of heat between different parts of a stationary body.

cone of depression The phenomenon whereby the water table has sunk into the approximate shape of an inverted cone in the immediate vicinity of a well as the result of the removal of a considerable amount of groundwater.

conformal map projection A projection that maintains proper angular relationships over the entire map; over limited areas shows the correct shapes of features shown on a map.

conic projection A family of maps in which one or more cones is set tangent to, or intersecting, a portion of the globe and the geographic grid is projected onto the cone(s).

conifer See *gymnosperm*.

consumer Animal that consumes plants or other animals; heterotrophs.

contact metamorphism Metamorphism of surrounding rocks by contact with magma.

continental drift Theory that proposed that the present continents were originally connected as one or two large landmasses that have broken up and drifted apart over the last several hundred million years.

continental ice sheet Large ice sheet covering a portion of a continental area.

continental rift valley Fault-produced valley resulting from spreading or rifting of continent.

controls of weather and climate The most important influences acting upon the elements of weather and climate.

convection Energy transfer through the vertical circulation and movement of fluids, such as air, due to density differences.

convection cell Closed pattern of convective circulation.

convective lifting Air lifting with showery precipitation resulting from convection.

convergent [plate] boundary Location where two lithospheric plates collide.

convergent lifting Air lifting as a result of wind convergence.

Coriolis effect (Coriolis force) The apparent deflection of free-moving objects to the right in the Northern Hemisphere and to the left in the Southern Hemisphere, in response to the rotation of Earth.

creep (soil creep) The slowest and least perceptible form of mass wasting, which consists of a very gradual downhill movement of soil and regolith.

crust The outermost solid layer of Earth.

cryosphere Subsphere of the hydrosphere that encompasses water frozen as snow or ice.

cultural geography The study of the human and/or cultural elements of geography.

cumulonimbus cloud Tall cumulus cloud associated with rain, thunderstorms, and other kinds of severe weather such as tornadoes and hurricanes.

cumulus cloud Puffy white cloud that forms from rising columns of air.

cutoff meander A portion of an old meandering stream course left isolated from the present stream channel because the narrow meander neck has been cut through by stream erosion.

cyclone Low-pressure center.

cylindrical projection A family of maps derived from the concept of projection onto a paper cylinder that is tangential to, or intersecting with, a globe.

D

daylight-saving time Shifting of clocks forward one hour.

debris flow Stream-like flow of dense, muddy water heavily laden with sediments of various sizes; a *mudflow* containing large boulders.

December solstice Day of the year when the vertical rays of the Sun strike the Tropic of Capricorn; on or about December 21; winter solstice in the Northern Hemisphere.

deciduous tree A tree that experiences an annual period in which all leaves die and usually fall from the tree, due either to a cold season or a dry season.

decomposers Mainly microscopic organisms such as bacteria that decompose dead plant and animal matter.

deflation The shifting of loose particles by wind blowing them into the air or rolling them along the ground.

delta A landform comprised of alluvium at the mouth of a river produced by the sudden reduction of a stream's velocity and the resulting deposition of the stream's load.

dendritic drainage pattern A treelike, branching pattern that consists of a random merging of streams, with tributaries joining larger streams irregularly, but always at acute angles; generally develops in regions where the underlying structure does not significantly control the drainage pattern.

dendrochronology Study of past events and past climate through the analysis of tree rings.

denitrification The conversion of nitrates into free nitrogen in the air.

denudation The total effect of all actions (weathering, mass wasting, and erosion) that lower the surface of the continents.

desert Climate, landscape, or biome associated with extremely arid conditions.

desert pavement Hard and relatively impermeable desert surface of tightly packed small rocks.

desert varnish A dark shiny coating of iron and manganese oxides that forms on rock surfaces exposed to desert air for a long time.

dew The condensation of beads of water on relatively cold surfaces.

dew point temperature (dew point) The critical air temperature at which water vapor saturation is reached.

differential weathering and erosion The process whereby different rocks or parts of the same rock weather and/or erode at different rates.

digital elevation model (DEM) Computer-generated shaded-relief image of a landscape derived from a database of precise elevation measurements.

dike A vertical or nearly vertical sheet of magma that is thrust upward into preexisting rock.

disappearing stream Stream that abruptly disappears from the surface where it flows into an underground cavity; common in karst regions.

discharge Volume of flow of a stream.

dissolution Removal of bedrock through chemical action of water; includes removal of subsurface rock through action of groundwater.

dissolved load The minerals, largely salts, that are dissolved in water and carried invisibly in solution.

divergent [plate] boundary Location where two lithospheric plates spread apart.

doldrums Belt of calm air associated with the region between the trade winds of the Northern and Southern hemispheres, generally in the vicinity of the equator. The region of the intertropical convergence zone (ITCZ).

downcutting Action of stream to erode a deeper channel; occurs when stream is flowing swiftly and/or flowing down a steep slope.

drainage basin An area that contributes overland flow and groundwater to a specific stream (also called a *watershed* or *catchment*).

drainage divide The line of separation between runoff that descends into two different drainage basins.

drift (glacial drift) All material carried and deposited by glaciers.

drumlin A low, elongated hill formed by ice-sheet deposition and erosion. The long axis is aligned parallel with the direction of ice movements, with the blunt, steeper end facing the direction from which the ice came.

dry adiabatic rate (dry adiabatic lapse rate) The rate at which a parcel of unsaturated air cools as it rises ($10°C$ per 1000 meters [$5.5°F$ per 1000 feet]).

dynamic high High-pressure cell associated with prominently descending air.

dynamic low Low-pressure cell associated with prominently rising air.

E

earthflow Mass wasting process in which a portion of a water-saturated slope moves a short distance downhill.

earthquake Vibrations generated by abrupt movement of Earth's crust.

easterly wave A long but weak migratory low-pressure trough in the tropics.

ebb tide A periodic falling of sea level during a tidal cycle.

ecosystem The totality of interactions among organisms and the environment in the area of consideration.

ecotone The transition zone between biotic communities in which the typical species of one community intermingle with those of another.

edaphic factors Having to do with soil.

E horizon A light-colored, eluvial layer that usually occurs between the A and B horizons.

electromagnetic radiation Flow of energy in the form of electromagnetic waves; radiant energy.

electromagnetic spectrum Electromagnetic radiation, arranged according to wavelength.

elements of weather and climate The basic ingredients of weather and climate—temperature, pressure, wind, and moisture.

elevation contour line (contour line) A line on a map joining points of equal elevation.

El Niño Periodic atmospheric and oceanic phenomenon of the tropical Pacific that typically involves the weakening or reversal of the trade winds and the warming of surface water off the west coast of South America.

eluviation The process by which gravitational water picks up fine particles of soil from the upper layers and carries them downward.

emission See *radiation*.

endemic Organism found only in a particular area.

endothermic [animal] Warm-blooded animal.

energy The ability to do work; anything that has the ability to change the state or condition of matter.

Enhanced Fujita Scale Classification scale of tornado strength, with EF-0 being the weakest tornadoes and EF-5 being the most powerful.

ENSO (El Niño/Southern Oscillation) Linked atmospheric and oceanic phenomenon of pressure and water temperature. *Southern Oscillation* refers to a periodic seesaw of atmospheric pressure in the tropical southern Pacific Ocean basin. Also see *El Niño*.

Entisol The least developed of all soil orders, with little mineral alteration and no pedogenic horizons.

entrenched meanders A winding, sinuous stream valley with abrupt sides; possible outcome of the rejuvenation of a meandering stream.

environmental lapse rate The observed vertical temperature gradient of the troposphere.

ephemeral stream A stream that carries water only during the "wet season" or during and immediately after rains.

epicenter Location on the surface directly above the center of fault rupture during an earthquake.

equal area projection See *equivalent map projection*.

equator The parallel of 0° latitude.

equilibrium line A theoretical line separating the ablation zone and accumulation zone of a glacier along which accumulation exactly balances ablation.

equivalent map projection A projection that maintains constant area (size) relationships over the entire map; also called an *equal area projection*.

erg "Sea of sand." A large area covered with loose sand, generally arranged in some sort of dune formation by the wind.

erosion Detachment, removal and transportation of fragmented rock material.

esker Long, sinuous ridge of stratified glacial drift composed largely of glaciofluvial gravel and formed by the choking of subglacial streams during a time of glacial stagnation.

eustatic sea-level change Change in sea level due to an increase or decrease in the amount of water in the world ocean; also known as *eustasy*.

evaporation Process by which liquid water is converted to gaseous water vapor; a cooling process because latent heat is stored.

evapotranspiration The transfer of moisture to the atmosphere by transpiration from plants and evaporation from soil and plants.

evergreen tree A tree or shrub that sheds its leaves on a sporadic or successive basis but at any given time appears to be fully leaved.

exfoliation Weathering process in which curved layers peel off bedrock in sheets. This process commonly occurs in granite and related intrusive rocks after overlying rock has been removed, allowing the body to expand slightly. Also referred to as *unloading*.

exfoliation dome A large rock mass with a surface configuration that consists of imperfect curves punctuated by several partially fractured shells of the surface layers; result of exfoliation.

exotic species (exotics) Organisms that are introduced into "new" habitats in which they did not naturally occur.

exotic stream A stream that flows into a dry region, bringing its water from somewhere else.

external [geomorphic] processes Destructive processes that serve to denude or wear down the landscape. Includes weathering, mass wasting, and erosion.

extrusive igneous rock Igneous rock formed on the surface of Earth; also called *volcanic rock*.

eye (eye of tropical cyclone) The nonstormy center of a tropical cyclone, which has a diameter of 16 to 40 kilometers (10 to 25 miles) and is a singular area of calmness in the maelstrom that whirls around it.

F

fall Mass wasting process in which pieces of weathered rock fragments fall to the bottom of a cliff or steep slope; also called *rockfall*.

fault A fracture or zone of fracture where the rock structure is forcefully broken and one side is displaced relative to the other. The movement can be horizontal or vertical, or a combination of both.

fault-block mountain (tilted-fault-block mountain) A mountain formed where a surface block is faulted and relatively upthrown on one side without any faulting or uplift on the other side. The block is tilted asymmetrically, producing a steep slope along the fault scarp and a relatively gentle slope on the other side of the block.

faulting See *fault*.

fault scarp Cliff formed by faulting.

fauna Animals.

field capacity The maximum amount of water that can be retained in the soil after the gravitational water has drained away.

fjord A glacial trough that has been partly drowned by the sea.

flood basalt A large-scale outpouring of basaltic lava that may cover an extensive area of Earth's surface.

floodplain A flattish valley floor covered with stream-deposited sediments (alluvium) and subject to periodic or episodic inundation by overflow from the stream.

flood tide The movement of ocean water toward the coast in a tidal cycle—from the ocean's lowest surface level the water rises gradually for about 6 hours and 13 minutes.

flora Plants.

fluvial processes Processes involving the work of running water on the surface of Earth.

foehn See *chinook*. The word *foehn* is used particularly in Europe.

fog A cloud whose base is at or very near ground level.

folding The bending of crustal rocks by compression and/or uplift.

food chain Sequential predation in which organisms feed upon one another, with organisms at one level providing food for organisms at the next level, and so on. Energy is thus transferred through the ecosystem.

food pyramid A conceptualization of energy transfer through the ecosystem from large numbers of "lower" forms of life through succeedingly smaller numbers of "higher" forms, as the organisms at one level are eaten by the organisms at the next higher level. Also see *food chain*.

forest An assemblage of trees growing closely together so that their individual leaf canopies generally overlap.

fractional scale (fractional map scale) Ratio of distance measured on a map and the actual distance that represents on Earth's surface, expressed as a ratio or fraction; assumes that the same units of measure are used on the map and on Earth's surface.

friction layer Zone of the atmosphere, between Earth's surface and an altitude of about 1000 meters (3300 feet), where most frictional resistance to air flow is found.

fringing reef A coral reef built out laterally from the shore, forming a broad bench that is only slightly below sea level, often with the tops of individual coral "heads" exposed to the open air at low tide.

front A sharp zone of discontinuity between unlike air masses.

frontal lifting The forced lifting of air along a front.

frost wedging Fragmentation of rock due to expansion of water that freezes into ice within rock openings.

fumarole A hydrothermal feature consisting of a surface crack that is directly connected with a deep-seated source of heat. The little water that drains into this tube is instantly converted to steam by heat and gases, and a cloud of steam is then expelled from the opening.

funnel cloud Funnel-shaped cloud extending down from a cumulonimbus cloud; a tornado is formed when the funnel cloud touches the surface.

G

Gelisol Soil order that develops in areas of permafrost.

geographic information systems (GIS) Computerized systems for the capture, storage, retrieval, analysis, and display of spatial (geographic) data.

geomorphology The study of the characteristics, origin, and development of landforms.

geostrophic wind A wind that moves parallel to the isobars as a result of the balance between the pressure gradient force and the Coriolis effect.

geyser A specialized form of intermittent hot spring with water issuing only sporadically as a temporary ejection, in which hot water and steam are spouted upward for some distance.

glacial erratic Outsize boulder included in the glacial till, which may be very different from the local bedrock.

glacial flour Rock material that has been ground to the texture of very fine talcum powder by glacial action.

glacial plucking Action in which rock fragments beneath the ice are loosened and grasped by the freezing of meltwater in joints and fractures, and then pried out and dragged along in the general flow of a glacier. Also called *glacial quarrying*.

glacial steps Series of level or gently sloping bedrock benches alternating with steep drops in the down-valley profile of a glacial trough.

glacial trough A valley reshaped by an alpine glacier, usually U-shaped.

glaciofluvial deposition The action whereby rock debris that is carried along by glaciers is eventually deposited or redeposited by glacial meltwater.

gleization The dominant pedogenic regime in areas where the soil is saturated with water most of the time due to poor drainage.

global conveyer-belt circulation Slowly moving circulation of deep ocean water that forms a continuous loop from the North Atlantic to the Antarctic, into the Indian and Pacific Oceans, and back into the North Atlantic.

Global Positioning System (GPS) A satellite-based system for determining accurate positions on or near Earth's surface.

global warming Popular name given to the recent warming of Earth's climate due to human-released greenhouse gases.

graben A block of land bounded by parallel faults in which the block has been downthrown, producing a distinctive structural valley with a straight, steep-sided fault scarp on either side.

gradient Elevation change of a stream over a given distance.

granite The most common and well-known plutonic (intrusive) rock; coarse-grained rock consisting of both dark- and light-colored minerals; forms from felsic (relatively high silica content) magma.

graphic scale (graphic map scale) The use of a line marked off in graduated distances as a map scale.

grassland Plant association dominated by grasses and forbs.

great circle Circle on a globe formed by the intersection of Earth's surface with any plane that passes through Earth's center.

greenhouse effect The warming in the lower troposphere because of differential transmissivity for shortwave and longwave radiation through the *greenhouse gases* in the atmosphere; the atmosphere easily transmits *shortwave radiation* from the Sun but inhibits the transmission of *longwave radiation* from the surface.

greenhouse gases Gases with the ability to transmit incoming shortwave radiation from the Sun but absorb outgoing longwave terrestrial radiation. The most important natural greenhouse gases are water vapor and carbon dioxide.

Greenwich Mean Time (GMT) Time in the Greenwich time zone. Today more commonly called *UTC* or *Universal Time Coordinated*.

groin A short wall built perpendicularly from the beach into the shore zone to interrupt the longshore current and trap sand.

ground moraine A moraine consisting of glacial till deposited widely over a land surface beneath an ice sheet.

groundwater Water found underground in the zone of saturation.

gymnosperms Seed-reproducing plants that carry their seeds in cones; "naked seeds."

H

Hadley cells Two complete vertical convective circulation cells between the equator, where warm air rises in the *ITCZ*, and 25° to 30° of latitude, where much of the air subsides into the *subtropical highs*.

hail Rounded or irregular pellets or lumps of ice produced in cumulonimbus clouds as a result of active turbulence and vertical air currents. Small ice particles grow by collecting moisture from supercooled cloud droplets.

hamada A barren desert surface of consolidated material that usually consists of exposed bedrock but is sometimes composed of sedimentary material that has been cemented together by salts evaporated from groundwater.

hanging valley (hanging trough) A tributary glacial trough, the bottom of which is considerably higher than the bottom of the principal trough that it joins.

headward erosion Erosion that cuts into the interfluve at the upper end of a gully or valley.

heat Energy that transfers from one object or substance to another because of a difference in temperature. Sometimes the term *thermal energy* is used interchangeably with the term heat.

high [pressure cell] Area of relatively high atmospheric pressure.

highland climate High mountain climate where altitude is dominant control. Designated H in Köppen system.

highland ice field Largely unconfined ice sheet in high mountain area.

Histosol A soil order characterized by organic, rather than mineral, soils, which is invariably saturated with water all or most of the time.

horizon (soil horizon) The more or less distinctly recognizable layer of soil, distinguished from one another by differing characteristics and forming a vertical zonation of the soil.

horn A steep-sided, pyramidal rock pinnacle formed by expansive glacial plucking and frost wedging of the headwalls where three or more cirques intersect.

horse latitudes Areas in the *subtropical highs* characterized by warm sunshine and an absence of wind.

horst A relatively uplifted block of land between two parallel faults.

hot spot An area of volcanic activity within the interior of a lithospheric plate associated with magma rising up from the mantle below.

hot spring Hot water at Earth's surface that has been forced upward through fissures or cracks by the pressures that develop when underground water has come in contact with heated rocks or magma beneath the surface.

humid continental climate Severe midlatitude climate characterized by hot summers, cold winters, and precipitation throughout the year.

humid subtropical climate Mild midlatitude climate characterized by hot summers and precipitation throughout the year.

humus A dark-colored, gelatinous, chemically stable fraction of organic matter on or in the soil.

hurricane A tropical cyclone with wind speeds of 119 km/hr (74 mph; 64 knots) or greater affecting North or Central America.

hydrogen bond Attraction between water molecules in which the negatively charged oxygen side of one water molecule is attracted to the positively charged hydrogen side of another water molecule.

hydrologic cycle A series of storage areas interconnected by various transfer processes, in which there is a ceaseless interchange of moisture in terms of its geographical location and its physical state.

hydrolysis A chemical union of water with another substance to produce a new compound that is nearly always softer and weaker than the original.

hydrophytic adaptations Terrestrial plants adapted to living in very wet environments.

hydrosphere Total water realm of Earth, including the oceans, surface waters of the lands, groundwater, and water held in the atmosphere.

hydrothermal activity The outpouring or ejection of hot water, often accompanied by steam, which usually takes the form of either a hot spring or a geyser.

hydrothermal metamorphism Metamorphism associated with hot, mineral-rich solutions circulating around preexisting rock.

I

iceberg A great chunk of floating ice that breaks off an ice shelf or the end of an outlet glacier.

ice cap climate Polar climate characterized by temperatures below freezing throughout the year.

ice floe A mass of ice that breaks off from larger ice bodies (ice sheets, glaciers, ice packs, and ice shelves) and floats independently in the sea. This term is generally used with large, flattish, tabular masses.

ice pack The extensive and cohesive mass of floating ice that is found in the Arctic and Antarctic oceans.

ice shelf A massive portion of an ice sheet that projects out over the sea.

igneous intrusion Features formed by the emplacement and cooling of magma below the surface.

igneous rock Rock formed by solidification of molten magma.

illuviation The process by which fine particles of soil from the upper layers are deposited at a lower level.

Inceptisol An immature order of soils that has relatively faint characteristics; not yet prominent enough to produce diagnostic horizons.

inclination [of Earth's axis] The tilt of Earth's rotational axis relative to its orbital plane (the *plane of the ecliptic*).

infrared [radiation] Electromagnetic radiation in the wavelength range of about 0.7 to 1000 micrometers; wavelengths just longer than visible light.

inner core The solid, dense, innermost portion of Earth, believed to consist largely of iron and nickel.

inselberg "Island mountain"; isolated summit rising abruptly from a low-relief surface.

insolation Incoming solar radiation.

interfluve The higher land or ridge above the valley sides that separates adjacent valleys; drained by overland flow.

intermittent stream A stream that carries water only part of the time, during the "wet season" or during and immediately after rains.

internal [geomorphic] processes Geomorphic processes originating below the surface; include volcanism, folding, and faulting.

International Date Line The line marking a time difference of an entire day from one side of the line to the other. Generally, this line falls on the 180th meridian except where it deviates to avoid separating an island group.

International System of measurement (SI) Popularly known as the "metric system" of measurement.

intertropical convergence zone (ITCZ) The region near or on the equator where the northeast trades and the southeast trades converge; associated with rising air of the Hadley cells and frequent thunderstorms.

intrusive igneous rock Igneous rock formed below ground from the cooling and solidification of magma; also called *plutonic rock*.

invertebrates Animals without backbones.

island arc See *volcanic island arc*.

isobar A line joining points of equal atmospheric pressure.

isohyet A line joining points of equal numerical value of precipitation.

isoline A line on a map connecting points that have the same quality or intensity of a given phenomenon.

isostasy Maintenance of the hydrostatic equilibrium of Earth's crust; the sinking of the crust as weight is applied and the rising of crust as weight is removed.

isotherm A line joining points of equal temperature.

ITCZ See *intertropical convergence zone*.

J

jet stream A rapidly moving current of wind in the upper troposphere; jet streams can be thought of as the high-speed "cores" of the high altitude westerly wind flow that frequently meander in a north-south direction over the midlatitudes.

jetty A wall built into the ocean at the entrance of a river or harbor to protect against sediment deposition, storm waves, and currents.

joints Cracks that develop in bedrock due to stress, but in which there is no appreciable movement parallel to the walls of the joint.

June solstice Day of the year when the vertical rays of the Sun strike the Tropic of Cancer; on or about June 21; summer solstice in the Northern Hemisphere.

K

karst Topography developed as a consequence of subsurface solution.

katabatic wind A wind that originates in cold upland areas and cascades toward lower elevations under the influence of gravity.

kettle An irregular depression in a morainal surface created when blocks of stagnant ice eventually melt.

kinetic energy The energy of movement.

knickpoint A sharp irregularity (such as a waterfall, rapid, or cascade) in a stream-channel profile; also known as a *nickpoint*.

knickpoint migration Upstream shift in location of a knickpoint due to erosion.

Köppen climate classification system A climatic classification of the world devised by Wladimir Köppen.

L

lagoon A body of quiet salt or brackish water in an area between a barrier island or a barrier reef and the mainland.

lahar Volcanic mudflow; a fast-moving muddy flow of volcanic ash and rock fragments.

lake A body of water surrounded by land.

land breeze Local wind blowing from land to water, usually at night.

landform An individual topographic feature, of any size; the term *landforms* refers to topography.

landslide An abrupt and often catastrophic event in which a large mass of rock and/or soil slides bodily downslope in only a few seconds or minutes. An instantaneous collapse of a slope.

La Niña Atmospheric and oceanic phenomenon associated with cooler than usual water off the west coast of South America. Sometimes described as the opposite of *El Niño*.

large-scale map A map with a scale that is a relatively large representative fraction and therefore portrays only a small portion of Earth's surface, but in considerable detail.

latent heat Energy stored or released when a substance changes state. For example, evaporation is a cooling process because latent heat is stored and condensation is a warming process because latent heat is released.

latent heat of condensation Heat released when water vapor condenses back to liquid form.

latent heat of evaporation Energy stored when liquid water evaporates to form water vapor.

lateral erosion Erosion that occurs when the principal current of a stream swings laterally from one bank to the other, eroding where the velocity is greatest on the outside bank and depositing alluvium where it is least on the inside bank.

lateral moraine Well-defined ridge of unsorted debris (till) built up along the sides of valley glaciers, parallel to the valley walls.

laterization The dominant pedogenic regime in areas where temperatures are relatively high throughout the year and which is characterized by rapid weathering of parent material, dissolution of nearly all minerals, and the speedy decomposition of organic matter.

latitude Location described as an angle measured north and south of the equator.

lava Molten magma that is extruded onto the surface of Earth, where it cools and solidifies.

lava dome (plug dome) Dome or bulge formed by the pushing up of viscous magma in a volcanic vent.

leaching Process in which dissolved nutrients are transported down in solution and deposited deeper in a soil.

lifting condensation level (LCL) The altitude at which rising air cools sufficiently to reach 100 percent relative humidity at the dew point temperature, and condensation begins.

lightning A luminous electric discharge in the atmosphere caused by the separation of positive and negative charges associated with cumulonimbus clouds.

limiting factor Variable that is important or most important in determining the survival of an organism.

linear fault trough Straight-line valley that marks the surface position of a fault, especially a strike-slip fault; formed by the erosion or settling of crushed rock along the trace of a fault.

liquefaction Phenomenon observed during an earthquake when water-saturated soil or sediments become soft or even fluid during the time of strong ground shaking.

lithosphere Tectonic plates consisting of the crust and upper rigid mantle. Also used as a general term for the entire solid Earth (one of the Earth "spheres").

litter The collection of dead plant parts that accumulate at the surface of the soil.

loam A soil texture in which none of the three principal soil separates—sand, silt, and clay—dominates the other two.

loess A fine-grained, wind-deposited silt. Loess lacks horizontal stratification, and its most distinctive characteristic is its ability to stand in vertical cliffs.

longitude Location described as an angle measured (in degrees, minutes, and seconds) east and west from the prime meridian on Earth's surface.

longshore current A current in which water moves roughly parallel to the shoreline in a generally downwind direction; also called a *littoral current*.

longwave radiation Wavelengths of thermal infrared radiation emitted by Earth and the atmosphere; also referred to as *terrestrial radiation*.

low [pressure cell] Area of relatively low atmospheric pressure.

loxodrome (rhumb line) A true compass heading; a line of constant compass direction.

M

magma Molten material below Earth's surface.

magnitude [of an earthquake] Scale used to describe the relative amount of energy released during an earthquake. Several different magnitude scales are in current use, such as the *moment magnitude* and the *Richter scale*.

mantle The portion of Earth beneath the crust and surrounding the core.

mantle plume A plume of mantle magma that rises to, or almost to, Earth's surface; not directly associated with most lithospheric plate boundaries, but associated with many *hot spots*.

map A flat representation of Earth at a reduced scale, showing only selected detail.

map projection A systematic representation of all or part of the three-dimensional Earth surface on a two-dimensional flat surface.

map scale Relationship between distance measured on a map and the actual distance on Earth's surface.

March equinox One of two days of the year when the vertical rays of the Sun strike the equator; every location on Earth has equal day and night; occurs on or about March 20 each year.

marine west coast climate Mild midlatitude climate characterized by mild temperatures and precipitation throughout the year.

marine terrace A platform formed by marine erosion that has been uplifted above sea level.

marsh Flattish surface area that is submerged in water at least part of the time but is shallow enough to permit the growth of water-tolerant plants, primarily grasses and sedges.

mass wasting The short-distance downslope movement of weathered rock under the direct influence of gravity; also called *mass movement*.

master joints Major joints that run for great distances through a bedrock structure.

meandering channel pattern (meandering stream channel) Highly twisting or looped stream channel pattern.

meander scar A dry former stream channel meander through which the stream no longer flows.

mechanical weathering The physical disintegration of rock material without any change in its chemical composition; also called *physical weathering*.

medial moraine A dark band of rocky debris down the middle of a glacier created by the union of the *lateral moraines* of two adjacent glaciers.

mediterranean climate Mild midlatitude climate characterized by dry summers and wet winters.

mediterranean woodland and shrub Woodland and shrub plant association found in regions of mediterranean climate.

Mercator projection A cylindrical projection mathematically adjusted to attain complete conformality which has a rapidly increasing scale with increasing latitude; straight lines on a Mercator projection are lines of constant compass heading (loxodromes).

meridian An imaginary line of longitude extending from pole to pole, crossing all parallels at right angles, and being aligned in true north–south directions.

mesa A flat-topped, steep-sided hill with a limited summit area.

mesocyclone Cyclonic circulation of air within a severe thunderstorm; diameter of about 10 kilometers (6 miles).

metamorphic rock Rock that was originally something else but has been drastically changed by massive forces of heat, pressure, and/or hydrothermal fluids working on it from within Earth.

midlatitude anticyclone An extensive migratory high-pressure cell of the midlatitudes that moves generally with the westerlies.

midlatitude cyclone Large migratory low-pressure system that occurs within the midlatitudes and moves generally with the westerlies. Also called *extratropical cyclone* and *wave cyclone*.

midlatitude deciduous forest Broadleaf forest plant assemblage comprised of mostly deciduous trees.

midlatitude desert climate Desert climate characterized by warm summers but cold winters.

midlatitude grassland Grassland plant assemblage in semiarid regions of the midlatitudes; regionally called *steppe*, *prairie*, *pampa*, and *veldt*.

midocean ridge A lengthy system of deep-sea mountain ranges, generally located at some distance from any continent; formed by divergent plate boundaries on the ocean floor.

Milankovitch cycles Combination of long-term astronomical cycles involving Earth's inclination, precession, and eccentricity of orbit; believed at least partially responsible for major periods of glaciation and deglaciation. Named for Milutin Milankovitch, an early twentieth-century Yugoslavian astronomer, who studied these cycles.

millibar A measure of pressure, consisting of one-thousandth part of a bar, or 1000 dynes per square centimeter (1 dyne is the force needed to accelerate 1 gram of mass 1 centimeter per second per second).

mineral A naturally formed solid inorganic substance that has a specified chemical composition and crystal structure.

modified Mercalli intensity scale Qualitative scale from I to XII used to describe the relative strength of ground shaking during an earthquake.

Mohorovičić discontinuity The boundary between Earth's crust and mantle. Also known simply as the *Moho*.

Mollisol A soil order characterized by the presence of a mollic epipedon, which is a mineral surface horizon that is dark, thick, contains abundant humus and base nutrients, and retains a soft character when it dries out.

monsoon A seasonal reversal of winds; a general onshore movement in summer and a general offshore flow in winter, with a very distinctive seasonal precipitation regime.

moraine The largest and generally most conspicuous landform feature produced by glacial deposition of *till*, which consists of irregular rolling topography that rises somewhat above the level of the surrounding terrain.

mountain breeze Downslope breeze from a mountain due to chilling of air on its slopes at night.

mudflow Rapid, downslope movement of a dense mixture of weathered rock and water through or within a valley.

multispectral [remote sensing] A remote sensing instrument that collects multiple digital images simultaneously in different electromagnetic wavelength bands.

N

natural levee An embankment of slightly higher ground fringing a stream channel in a floodplain; formed by deposition during floodtime.

neap tides The lower-than-normal tidal variations that occur twice a month as the result of the alignment of the Sun and Moon at a right angle to one another.

needleleaf trees Trees adorned with thin slivers of tough, leathery, waxy needles rather than typical leaves.

net primary productivity The net photosynthesis of a plant community over a period of one year, usually measured in the amount of fixed carbon per unit area (kilograms of carbon per square meter per year).

névé Snow granules that have become packed and begin to coalesce due to compression, achieving a density about half as great as that of water; also called *firn*.

nitrogen cycle An endless series of processes in which nitrogen moves through the environment.

nitrogen fixation Conversion of gaseous nitrogen into forms that can be used by plant life.

normal fault The result of tension (extension) producing a steeply inclined fault plane, with the block of land on one side being pushed up, or upthrown, in relation to the block on the other side, which is downthrown.

North Pole Latitude of 90° north.

O

occluded front A complex front formed when a cold front overtakes a warm front, lifting all of the warm air mass off the ground.

occlusion Process of cold front overtaking a warm front to form an occluded front.

ocean floor core samples Rock and sediment samples removed from ocean floor.

oceanic trench (deep oceanic trench) Deep linear depression in the ocean floor where subduction is taking place.

offset stream A stream course displaced by lateral movement along a fault.

O horizon The immediate surface layer of a soil profile, consisting mostly of organic material.

orographic lifting Uplift that occurs when air is forced to rise over topographic barriers.

outcrop Surface exposure of bedrock.

outer core The liquid (molten) shell beneath the mantle that encloses Earth's inner core.

outwash plain Extensive glaciofluvial feature that is a relatively smooth, flattish alluvial apron deposited beyond recessional or terminal moraines by streams issuing from ice.

overland flow The general movement of unchanneled surface water down the slope of the land surface.

oxbow lake A cutoff meander that initially holds water.

oxidation The chemical union of oxygen atoms with atoms from various metallic elements to form new products, which are usually more voluminous, softer, and more easily eroded than the original compounds.

Oxisol The most thoroughly weathered and leached of all soils. This soil order invariably displays a high degree of mineral alteration and profile development.

oxygen cycle The movement of oxygen by various processes through the environment.

oxygen isotope analysis Using the ratio of ^{16}O (oxygen 16) and ^{18}O (oxygen 18) isotopes in compounds such as water and calcium carbonate to infer temperature and other conditions in the past.

ozone A gas composed of molecules consisting of three atoms of oxygen, O_3.

ozone layer The layer in the atmosphere between 16 and 40 kilometers (10 and 25 miles) high, where the concentration of ozone is greatest; the ozone layer absorbs much of the incoming ultraviolet solar radiation.

P

Pacific ring of fire Name given to the rim of the Pacific Ocean basin due to widespread volcanic and seismic activity; associated with lithospheric plate boundaries.

paleoclimatology The study of past climates.

paleomagnetism Past magnetic orientation.

Pangaea The massive supercontinent that Alfred Wegener first postulated to have existed about 200 million years ago. Pangaea broke apart into several large sections that have continually moved away from one another and that now comprise the present continents.

parallel A line connecting all points of equal latitude; such a line is parallel to all other parallels.

parallelism See *polarity*.

parent material The source of the weathered fragments of rock from which soil is made; solid bedrock or loose sediments that have been transported from elsewhere by the action of water, wind, or ice.

particulate Composed of distinct tiny particles or droplets suspended in the atmosphere; also known as *aerosols*.

paternoster lakes A sequence of small lakes found in the shallow excavated depressions or steps within a glacial trough.

patterned ground Polygonal patterns in the ground that develop in areas of seasonally frozen soil and permafrost.

pediment A gently inclined bedrock platform that extends outward from a mountain front, usually in an arid region.

pedogenic regimes Soil-forming regimes that can be thought of as environmental settings in which certain physical/chemical/biological processes prevail.

ped A larger mass or clump that individual soil particles tend to aggregate into and that determines the structure of the soil.

perennial plants (perennials) Plants that can live more than a single year despite seasonal environmental variations.

perennial stream A permanent stream that contains water the year-round.

periglacial zone An area of indefinite size beyond the outermost extent of ice advance that was indirectly influenced by glaciation.

perihelion The point in its orbit where Earth is nearest to the Sun (about 147,100,000 kilometers or 91,400,000 miles).

permafrost Permanent ground ice or permanently frozen subsoil.

permeability A soil or rock characteristic in which there are interconnected pore spaces through which water can move.

photochemical smog Form of secondary air pollution caused by the reaction of nitrogen compounds and hydrocarbons to ultraviolet radiation in strong sunlight.

photoperiodism The response of an organism to the length of exposure to light in a 24-hour period.

photosynthesis The basic process whereby plants produce stored chemical energy from water and carbon dioxide and which is activated by sunlight.

physical geography Study of the physical elements of geography.

piedmont zone Zone at the "foot of the mountains."

piezometric surface The elevation to which groundwater will rise under natural confining pressure in a well.

pinnacle An erosional remnant in the form of a steep-sided spire that has a resistant caprock; normally found in an arid or semiarid environment; also speleothem column.

planar projection (plane projection) A family of maps derived by the perspective extension of the geographic grid from a globe to a plane that is tangent to the globe at some point.

plane of the ecliptic The imaginary plane that passes through the Sun and through Earth at every position in its orbit around the Sun; the orbital plane of Earth.

plant respiration Stored energy in carbohydrates consumed directly by the plant itself; carbohydrates are oxidized, releasing water, carbon dioxide, and heat energy.

plant succession The process whereby one type of vegetation is replaced naturally by another.

plastic flow [of glacial ice] Slow, nonbrittle flow and movement of ice under pressure.

plateau Flattish erosional platform bounded on at least one side by a prominent escarpment.

plate tectonics A coherent theory of massive lithospheric rearrangement based on the movement of continent-sized plates.

playa Dry lake bed in a basin of interior drainage.

Pleistocene Epoch An epoch of the Cenozoic era between the Pliocene and the Holocene; from about 2.6 million to about 11,700 years ago.

Pleistocene lakes Large freshwater lakes that formed in basins of interior drainage because of higher rainfall and/or lower evaporation during the Pleistocene.

plucking See *glacial plucking*.

plug dome Volcano dome or bulge formed by the pushing up of viscous magma in a volcanic vent; also *lava dome*.

pluton A large, intrusive igneous body.

plutonic rock Igneous rock formed below ground from the cooling and solidification of magma; also called *intrusive rock*.

pluvial (pluvial effects) Pertaining to rain; often used in connection with a past rainy period.

podzolization The dominant pedogenic regime in areas where winters are long and cold, and which is characterized by slow chemical weathering of soils and rapid mechanical weathering from frost action, resulting in soils that are shallow, acidic, and with a fairly distinctive profile.

polar easterlies A global wind system that occupies most of the area between the *polar highs* and about 60° of latitude. The winds move generally from east to west and are typically cold and dry.

polar front The contact between unlike air masses in the subpolar low-pressure zone at about 60° N and S.

polar high A high-pressure cell situated over either polar region.

polarity [of Earth's rotation axis] A characteristic of Earth's axis wherein it always points toward Polaris (the North Star) at every position in Earth's orbit around the Sun. Also called *parallelism*.

porosity The amount of pore space between the soil particles and between the *peds*, which is a measure of the capacity of the soil to hold water and air.

precipitation Drops of liquid or solid water falling from clouds.

precipitation variability Expected departure from average annual precipitation in any given year.

pressure gradient Change in atmospheric pressure over some horizontal distance.

primary consumer Animals that eat plants as the first stage in a food pyramid or chain.

primary pollutants Contaminants released directly into the air.

prime meridian The meridian passing through the Royal Observatory at Greenwich (England), just east of central London, and from which longitude is measured.

producers Organisms that produce their own food through photosynthesis; plants.

proglacial lake A lake formed when ice flows across or against the general slope of the land and the natural drainage is impeded or completely blocked so that meltwater from the ice becomes impounded against the ice front.

pseudocylindrical projection (elliptical projection) A family of map projections in which the entire world is displayed in an oval shape.

pyroclastic flow High-speed avalanche of hot gases, ash, and rock fragments emitted from a volcano during an explosive eruption; also known as a *nuée ardente*.

pyroclastics (pyroclastic material) Solid rock fragments thrown into the air by volcanic explosions.

R

radar Radio detection and ranging.

radiant energy See *electromagnetic radiation*.

radiation The process in which electromagnetic energy is emitted from a body; the flow of energy in the form of electromagnetic waves.

rain The most common and widespread form of precipitation, consisting of drops of liquid water.

rain shadow Area of low rainfall on the leeward side of a mountain range or topographic barrier.

recessional moraine A glacial deposit of till formed during a pause in the retreat of the ice margin.

recurrence interval [of a flood] The probability of a given-size flood occurring in a year; also called the *return period*.

reflection The ability of an object to repel waves without altering either the object or the waves.

reg A desert surface of coarse material from which all sand and dust have been removed by wind and water erosion. Often referred to as *desert pavement* or *desert armor*.

regional metamorphism Widespread subsurface metamorphism of rock as a result of prolonged exposure to heat and high pressure, such as in areas of plate collision or subduction.

regolith A layer of broken and partly decomposed rock particles that covers bedrock.

relative humidity An expression of the amount of water vapor in the air (the water vapor content) in comparison with the maximum amount that could be there if the air were saturated (the *capacity*). This is a ratio that is expressed as a percentage.

relief The difference in elevation between the highest and lowest points in an area; the vertical variation from mountaintop to valley bottom.

remote sensing Measurement or acquisition of information by a recording device that is not in physical contact with the object under study; instruments used commonly include cameras and satellites.

reverse fault A fault produced from compression, with the upthrown block rising steeply above the downthrown block.

revolution [around the Sun] The orbital movement of Earth around the Sun over the year.

R horizon The consolidated bedrock at the base of a soil profile.

ria shoreline An embayed coast with numerous estuaries; formed by the flooding of stream valleys by the sea.

ridge [of atmospheric pressure] Linear or elongated area of relatively high atmospheric pressure.

rift valley See *continental rift valley*.

riparian vegetation Streamside growth, particularly prominent in relatively dry regions, where stream courses may be lined with trees, although no other trees are to be found in the landscape.

roche moutonnée A characteristic glacial landform produced when a bedrock hill or knob is overridden by moving ice. The *stoss* side is smoothly rounded and streamlined by grinding abrasion as the ice rides up the slope, but the lee side is shaped largely by plucking, which produces a steeper and more irregular slope.

rock Solid material composed of aggregated mineral material.

rock cycle Term given to the long-term "recycling" of mineral material from one kind of rock to another.

rockfall (fall) Mass wasting process in which weathered rock drops to the foot of a cliff or steep slope.

rock glacier An accumulated *talus* mass that moves slowly but distinctly downslope under its own weight.

Rossby wave A very large north–south undulation of the upper-air westerlies and jet stream.

rotation [of Earth] The spinning of Earth around its imaginary north–south axis.

runoff Flow of water from land to oceans by overland flow, streamflow, and groundwater flow.

S

Saffir-Simpson Hurricane Scale Classification system of hurricane strength with category 1 the weakest and category 5 the strongest.

sag pond A pond caused by the collection of water from springs and/or runoff into sunken ground, resulting from the crushing of rock in an area of fault movement.

salina Dry lake bed that contains an unusually heavy concentration of salt in the lake-bed sediment.

saline lake Salt lake; commonly caused by interior stream drainage in an arid environment.

salinity A measure of the concentration of dissolved salts.

salinization One of the dominant pedogenic regimes in areas where principal soil moisture movement is upward because of a moisture deficit.

salt wedging Rock disintegration caused by the crystallization of salts from evaporating water.

sand dune A mound, ridge, or low hill of loose, windblown sand.

Santa Ana winds Name given to dry, usually warm, and often very strong winds blowing offshore in southern California region.

saturated adiabatic rate (saturated adiabatic lapse rate) The diminished rate of cooling, averaging about 6°C per 1000 meters (3.3°F per 1000 feet) of rising air above the lifting condensation level; a result of the latent heat of condensation counteracting some of the adiabatic cooling of rising air.

saturation vapor pressure The maximum pressure that can be exerted by water vapor at a given temperature; the pressure exerted by water vapor when the air is saturated.

scattering The deflection of light waves in random directions by gas molecules and particulates in the atmosphere; shorter wavelengths of visible light are more easily scattered than longer wavelengths.

scree Pieces of weathered rock, especially small pieces, that fall directly downslope; also called *talus*.

sea breeze A wind that blows from the sea toward the land, usually during the day.

seafloor spreading The pulling apart of lithospheric plates to permit the rise of deep-seated magma to Earth's surface in midocean ridges.

secondary consumer Animals that eat other animals, as the second and further stages in a food pyramid or chain.

secondary pollutant Pollutants formed in the atmosphere as a consequence of chemical reactions or other processes; for example see *photochemical smog*.

sediment Small particles of rock debris or organic material deposited by water, wind, or ice.

sediment budget [of a beach] The balance between the sediment being deposited on a beach and the sediment that is being transported away from a beach.

sedimentary rock Rock formed of sediment that is consolidated by the combination of pressure and cementation.

seif (longitudinal) dune Long, narrow desert dunes that usually occur in multiplicity and in parallel arrangement.

sensible temperature The relative apparent temperature that is sensed by a person's body.

separates The size groups within the standard classification of soil particle sizes.

September equinox One of two days of the year when the vertical rays of the Sun strike the equator; every location on Earth has equal day and night; occurs on or about September 22 each year.

shield volcanoes Volcanoes built up in a lengthy outpouring of very fluid basaltic lava. Shield volcanoes are broad mountains with gentle slopes.

shortwave radiation Wavelengths of radiation emitted by the Sun, especially ultraviolet, visible, and short infrared radiation.

shrubland Plant association dominated by relatively short woody plants.

silicate mineral (silicates) A category of minerals composed of silicon and oxygen combined with another element or elements.

sinkhole (doline) A small, rounded depression that is formed by the dissolution of surface limestone, typically at joint intersections.

sinuous channel pattern (sinuous stream channel) Gently curving or winding stream channel pattern.

slip face [of sand dune] Steeper leeward side of a sand dune.

slump A slope collapse slide with rotation along a curved sliding plane.

small-scale map A map whose scale is a relatively small representative fraction and therefore shows a large portion of Earth's surface in limited detail.

snow Solid precipitation in the form of ice crystals, small pellets, or flakes, which is formed by the direct conversion of water vapor into ice.

soil An infinitely varying mixture of weathered mineral particles, decaying organic matter, living organisms, gases, and liquid solutions. Soil is that part of the outer "skin" of Earth occupied by plant roots.

soil order The highest (most general) level of soil classification in the *Soil Taxonomy*.

soil profile A vertical cross section from Earth's surface down through the soil layers into the parent material beneath.

Soil Taxonomy The system of soil classification currently in use in the United States. It is genetic in nature and focuses on the existing properties of the soil rather than on environment, genesis, or the properties it would possess under virgin conditions.

soil–water balance The relationship between gain, loss, and storage of soil water.

soil–water budget An accounting that demonstrates the variation of the soil–water balance over a period of time.

solar altitude Angle of the Sun above the horizon.

solifluction A special form of soil creep in tundra areas; associated with summer thawing of the near-surface portion of permafrost, causing the wet, heavy surface material to sag slowly downslope.

solum The true soil that includes only the top four horizons: O, the organic surface layer; A, the topsoil; E, the eluvial layer; and B, the subsoil.

sonar Sound navigation and ranging.

Southern Oscillation Periodic "seesaw" of high and low atmospheric pressure between northern Australia and Tahiti; first recognized by Gilbert Walking in the early twentieth century.

South Pole Latitude of 90° south.

specific heat The amount of energy required to raise the temperature of 1 gram of a substance by 1°C. Also called *specific heat capacity*.

specific humidity A direct measure of water-vapor content expressed as the mass of water vapor in a given mass of air (grams of vapor/kilograms of air).

speleothem A feature formed by precipitated deposits of minerals on the wall, floor, or roof of a cave.

spit A linear deposit of marine sediment that is attached to the land at one or both ends.

Spodosol A soil order characterized by the occurrence of a spodic subsurface horizon, which is an illuvial layer where organic matter and aluminum accumulate, and which has a dark, sometimes reddish, color.

spring tide A time of maximum tide that occurs as a result of the alignment of Sun, Moon, and Earth.

stable [air] Air that rises only if forced.

stalactite A pendant structure hanging downward from a cavern's roof.

stalagmite A projecting structure growing upward from a cavern's floor.

star dune Pyramid-shaped sand dune with arms radiating out in three or more directions.

stationary front The common boundary between two air masses in a situation in which neither air mass displaces the other.

storm surge A surge of wind-driven water as much as 8 meters (25 feet) above normal tide level, which occurs when a hurricane advances onto a shoreline.

storm warning Weather advisory issued when a severe thunderstorm or tornado has been observed in an area; people should seek safety immediately.

storm watch Weather advisory issued when conditions are favorable for strong thunderstorms or tornadoes.

strata Distinct layers of sediment or layers in sedimentary rock.

stratified drift Drift that was sorted as it was carried along by the flowing glacial meltwater.

stratosphere Atmospheric layer directly above the troposphere.

stratus clouds Layered, horizontal clouds, often below altitudes of 2 kilometers (6500 feet), which sometimes occur as individual clouds but more often appear as a general overcast.

stream Channeled flow of water, regardless of size.

stream capacity The maximum load that a stream can transport under given conditions.

stream capture (stream piracy) An event where a portion of the flow of one stream is diverted into that of another by natural processes.

stream competence The size of the largest particle that can be transported by a stream.

streamflow Channeled movement of water along a valley bottom.

stream load Solid matter carried by a stream.

stream order Concept that describes the hierarchy of a drainage network.

stream piracy See *stream capture*.

stream rejuvenation When a stream gains downcutting ability, usually through regional tectonic uplift.

stream terrace Remnant of a previous valley floodplain of a rejuvenated stream.

strike-slip fault A fault produced by shearing, with adjacent blocks being displaced laterally with respect to one another. The movement is mostly or entirely horizontal.

subarctic climate Severe midlatitude climate found in high latitude continental interiors, characterized by very cold winters and an extreme annual temperature range.

subduction Descent of the edge of an oceanic lithospheric plate under the edge of an adjoining plate.

sublimation The process by which water vapor is converted directly to ice, or vice versa.

subpolar low A zone of low pressure that is situated at about 50° to 60° of latitude in both Northern and Southern Hemispheres (also referred to as the *polar front*).

subtropical gyres The closed-loop pattern of surface ocean currents around the margins of the major ocean basins; the flow is clockwise in the Northern Hemisphere and counterclockwise in the Southern Hemisphere.

subtropical desert climate A hot desert climate; generally found in subtropical latitudes, especially on the western sides of continents.

subtropical high (STH) Large, semipermanent, high-pressure cells centered at about 30° N and S over the oceans, which have average diameters of 3200 kilometers (2000 miles) and are usually elongated east–west.

supercooled water Water that persists in liquid form at temperatures below freezing.

supersaturated [air] Air in which the relative humidity is greater than 100 percent but condensation is not taking place.

surface tension Because of electrical polarity, liquid water molecules tend to stick together—a thin "skin" of molecules forms on the surface of liquid water causing it to "bead."

suspended load The very fine particles of clay and silt that are in suspension and move along with the flow of water without ever touching the streambed.

swallow hole The distinct opening at the bottom of some sinkholes through which surface drainage can pour directly into an underground channel.

swamp A flattish surface area that is submerged in water at least part of the time but is shallow enough to permit the growth of water-tolerant plants—predominantly trees.

swash The cascading forward motion of a breaking wave that rushes up the beach.

swell An ocean wave, usually produced by stormy conditions, that can travel enormous distances away from the source of the disturbance.

symbiosis A mutually beneficial relationship between two organisms.

syncline A simple downfold in the rock structure.

T

talus Pieces of weathered rock, of various sizes, that fall directly downslope; also called *scree*.

talus cone Sloping, cone-shaped heaps of dislodged talus.

tarn Small lake in the shallow excavated depression of a glacial cirque.

teleconnection The coupling or relationship of weather and/or oceanic events in one part of the world with those in another.

temperature Description of the average kinetic energy of the molecules in a substance; the more vigorous the "jiggling" of the molecules (and therefore the greater the internal kinetic energy), the higher the temperature of a substance; in popular terms, a measure of the degree of hotness or coldness of a substance.

temperature inversion A situation in which temperature increases with higher altitude and so the normal condition is inverted.

terminal moraine A glacial deposit of till that builds up at the outermost extent of ice advance.

terrane A mass of lithosphere, bounded on all sides by faults, that has become accreted to a lithospheric plate margin with different lithologic characteristics from those of the terrane; often comprised of lithosphere that is too buoyant to subduct; also *accreted terrane*.

terrestrial radiation Longwave radiation emitted by Earth's surface or atmosphere.

thermal high High-pressure cell associated with cold surface conditions.

thermal infrared radiation (thermal IR) The middle and far infrared part of the electromagnetic spectrum.

thermal low Low pressure cell associated with warm surface conditions.

thermohaline circulation Slow circulation of deep ocean water because of differences in water density that arise from differences in salinity and temperature.

thrust fault A fault created by compression forcing the upthrown block to override the downthrown block at a relatively low angle; also called an *overthrust fault*.

thunder The sound that results from the shock wave produced by the instantaneous expansion of air that is abruptly heated by a lightning bolt.

thunderstorm A relatively violent convective storm accompanied by thunder and lightning.

tidal bore A wall of seawater several centimeters to more than a meter in height that rushes up a river as the result of enormous tidal inflow.

tidal range The vertical difference in elevation between high and low tide.

tides The rise and fall of the coastal water levels caused by the alternate increasing and decreasing gravitational pull of the Moon and the Sun on varying parts of Earth's surface.

till Rock debris that is deposited directly by moving or melting ice, with no meltwater flow or redeposition involved.

tilted fault block mountain See *fault-block mountain*.

time zone Region on Earth (generally a north–south band defined by longitude) within which the agreed-upon local time is the same.

tombolo A spit formed by sand deposition that connects an island to the mainland.

topography Surface configuration of Earth.

tornado A localized cyclonic low-pressure cell surrounded by a whirling cylinder of violent wind; characterized by a funnel cloud extending below a cumulonimbus cloud.

tower karst Tall, steep-sided hills in an area of karst topography.

trade winds The major easterly wind system of the tropics, issuing from the equatorward sides of the subtropical highs and diverging toward the west and toward the equator.

transform [plate] boundary Two plates slipping past one another laterally.

transmission The ability of a medium to allow electromagnetic waves to pass through it.

transverse dune Crescent-shaped sand dune ridges that have convex sides facing the prevailing direction of wind and which occur where the supply of sand is great. The crest is perpendicular to the wind direction vector and aligned in parallel waves across the land.

treeline The elevation above (or below) which trees do not grow.

trellis drainage pattern A drainage pattern that is usually developed on alternating bands of hard and soft strata, with long parallel subsequent streams linked by short, right-angled segments and joined by short tributaries.

tropical cyclone A storm most significantly affecting the tropics and subtropics; an intense low-pressure center that is essentially circular in shape. When wind speed reaches 119 km/hr (74 mph; 64 knots), they are called *hurricanes* in North America and the Caribbean.

tropical deciduous forest Tropical forest found in regions with a pronounced dry period during which many of the trees shed their leaves.

tropical depression By international agreement, an incipient tropical cyclone with winds not exceeding 33 knots.

tropical monsoon climate Tropical humid climate with a pronounced winter dry season and a very wet summer rainy season; associated with monsoon wind pattern.

tropical rainforest A distinctive assemblage of tropical vegetation that is dominated by a great variety of tall, high-crowned trees; also called *selva*.

tropical savanna A tropical grassland dominated by tall grasses.

tropical savanna climate Tropical humid climate with a dry winter season and a moderately wet summer season; associated with the seasonal migration of the ITCZ.

tropical scrub A widespread tropical assemblage of low trees and bushes.

tropical storm By international agreement, an incipient tropical cyclone with winds between 34 and 63 knots.

tropical wet climate Tropical humid climate that is wet all year; usually under the influence of the ITCZ all year.

Tropic of Cancer The parallel of 23.5° N latitude, which marks the northernmost location reached by the vertical rays of the Sun in the annual cycle of Earth's revolution.

Tropic of Capricorn The parallel of 23.5° S latitude, which marks the southernmost location reached by the vertical rays of the Sun in the annual cycle of Earth's revolution.

troposphere The lowest thermal layer of the atmosphere, in which temperature decreases with height; the layer of the atmosphere in contact with Earth's surface.

trough [of atmospheric pressure] Linear or elongated band of relatively low atmospheric pressure.

tsunami Very long wavelength oceanic wave generated by submarine earthquake, landslide, or volcanic eruption; also called *seismic sea wave*.

tundra A complex mix of very low-growing plants, including grasses, forbs, dwarf shrubs, mosses, and lichens, but no trees. Tundra occurs only in the perennially cold climates of high latitudes or high altitudes.

tundra climate Polar climate in which no month of the year has an average temperature above 10°C (50°F).

U

ubac slope A slope oriented so that sunlight strikes it at a low angle and hence is much less effective in heating and evaporating than on the *adret slope*, thus producing more luxuriant vegetation of a richer diversity.

Ultisol A soil order similar to Alfisols, but more thoroughly weathered and more completely leached of bases.

ultraviolet (UV) radiation Electromagnetic radiation in the wavelength range of 0.1 to 0.4 micrometers.

uniformitarianism The concept that the "present is the key to the past" in geomorphic processes. The processes now operating have also operated in the past.

Universal Time Coordinated (UTC) or Coordinated Universal Time The world time standard reference; previously known as *Greenwich mean time (GMT)*.

unstable [air] Air that rises without being forced.

upwelling Cold, deep ocean water that rises to the surface where wind patterns deflect surface water away from the coast; especially common along the west coasts of continents in the subtropics and midlatitudes.

urban heat island (UHI) effect Observed higher temperatures measured in urban area compared with the surrounding rural area.

uvala A compound sinkhole (doline) or chain of intersecting sinkholes.

V

valley That portion of the total terrain in which a stream drainage system is clearly established.

valley breeze Upslope breeze up a mountain due to heating of air on its slopes during the day.

valley glacier A long, narrow feature resembling a river of ice, which spills out of its originating basins and flows down-valley.

valley train A lengthy deposit of glaciofluvial alluvium confined to a valley bottom beyond the outwash plain.

vapor pressure The pressure exerted by water vapor in the atmosphere.

ventifact Rock that has been sandblasted by the wind.

verbal map scale Scale of a map stated in words; also called a *word scale*.

vertebrates Animals that have a backbone that protects their spinal cord—fishes, amphibians, reptiles, birds, and mammals.

vertical zonation The horizontal layering of different plant associations on a mountainside or hillside.

Vertisol A soil order comprising a specialized type of soil that contains a large quantity of clay and has an exceptional capacity for absorbing water. An alternation of wetting and drying, expansion and contraction, produces a churning effect that mixes the soil constituents, inhibits the development of horizons, and may even cause minor irregularities in the surface of the land.

visible light Waves in the electromagnetic spectrum in the narrow band between about 0.4 and 0.7 micrometers in length; wavelengths of electromagnetic radiation to which the human eye is sensitive.

volcanic island arc Chain of volcanic islands associated with an oceanic plate–oceanic plate subduction zone; also simply *island arc*.

volcanic mudflow A fast-moving, muddy flow of volcanic ash and rock fragments; also called a *lahar*.

volcanic rock Igneous rock formed on the surface of Earth; also called *extrusive rock*.

volcanism General term that refers to movement of magma from the interior of Earth to or near the surface.

W

Walker Circulation General circuit of air flow in the southern tropical Pacific Ocean; warm air rises in the western side of the basin (in the updrafts of the ITCZ), flows aloft to the east where it descends into the subtropical high off the west coast of South America; the air then flows back to the west in the surface trade winds. Named for the British meteorologist Gilbert Walker (1868–1958) who first described this circumstance.

warm front The leading edge of an advancing warm air mass.

waterspout A funnel cloud in contact with the ocean or a large lake; similar to a weak tornado over water.

watershed See *drainage basin*.

water table The top of the saturated zone within the ground.

water vapor Water in the form of a gas.

wave-cut platform Gently sloping, wave-eroded bedrock platform that develops just below sea level; common where coastal cliff is being worn back by wave action; also called *wave-cut bench*.

wave height The vertical distance from wave crest to trough.

wavelength The horizontal distance from wave crest to crest or from trough to trough.

wave of oscillation Motion of wave in which the individual particles of the medium (such as water) make a circular orbit as the wave form passes through.

wave of translation The horizontal motion produced when a wave reaches shallow water and finally "breaks" on the shore.

wave refraction Phenomenon whereby waves change their directional trend as they approach a shoreline; results in ocean waves generally breaking parallel with the shoreline.

weather The short-term atmospheric conditions for a given time and a specific area.

weathering The physical and chemical disintegration of rock that is exposed to the atmosphere.

westerlies The great wind system of the midlatitudes that flows basically from west to east around the world in the latitudinal zone between about 30° and 60° both north and south of the equator.

wetland Landscape characterized by shallow, standing water all or most of the year, with vegetation rising above the water level.

wilting point The point at which plants are no longer able to extract moisture from the soil because the capillary water is all used up or evaporated.

wind Horizontal air movement.

wind shear (vertical wind shear) Significant change in wind direction or speed in the vertical dimension.

woodland Tree-dominated plant association in which the trees are spaced more widely apart than those of forests and do not have interlacing canopies.

X

xerophytic adaptations Plants that are structurally adapted to withstand protracted dry conditions.

Y

yazoo stream A tributary unable to enter the main stream because of natural levees along the main stream.

Z

zone of aeration (vadose zone) The topmost hydrologic zone within the ground, which contains a fluctuating amount of moisture (soil water) in the pore spaces of the soil (or soil and rock).

zone of confined water The third hydrologic zone below the surface of the ground, which contains one or more permeable rock layers (*aquifers*) into which water can infiltrate and is separated from the zone of saturation by impermeable layers.

zone of saturation (phreatic zone) The second hydrologic zone below the surface of the ground, whose uppermost boundary is the water table. The pore spaces and cracks in the bedrock and the regolith of this zone are fully saturated.

zoogeographic regions Division of land areas of the world into major realms with characteristic fauna.

PHOTO CREDITS

Chapter 1
p.2: NASA; p.4: NASA; p.6: Fletcher & Baylis/Photo Researchers, Inc.; p.15: Jon Arnold/Alamy Images; p.16: Tom L. McKnight; p.24: Shutterstock.

Chapter 2
p.30: NASA Earth Observing System; p.32: NASA/Goddard Space Flight Center; p.33: Shutterstock; p.43: Landov; p.47: NASA Earth Observing System; p.48: Robert Simmon; p.48: NASA Earth Observing System; p.49: NASA Earth Observing System; p.51: NASA/Goddard Space Flight Center; p.51: NASA Earth Observing System, USGS.

Chapter 3
p.54: NASA; p.56: NASA Earth Observing System; p.58: Tom L. McKnight; p.62: Getty Images Royalty Free; p.64: NASA Earth Observing System; p.64: ; p.66: Alexander Chaikin/Shutterstock; p.71: Tom L. McKnight; p.71: European Space Agency/SPL/Photo Researchers, Inc.; p.73: NASA Earth Observing System.

Chapter 4
p.76: Randy Wells/Getty Images; p.78: Larry Lilac/Alamy; p.82: Paul Mayall/age fotostock; p.85: Darrel Hess; p.92: Getty Images, Inc - Liaison; p.97: Johns Hopkins University Applied Physics Laboratory; p.99: Tom L. McKnight; p.103: NASA; p.103: NASA; p.103: NASA; p.81: Martin Shields/Photo Researchers, Inc.

Chapter 5
p.108: Jim Reed/Photo Researchers, Inc.; p.110: Darrel Hess; p.112: Tom L. McKnight; p.123: Naval Research Laboratory; p.124: NASA; p.127: ANDREW BIRAJ/Reuters/Newscom; p.133: U.S. Geological Survey, Denver; p.117: Angus Mobsby/Alamy.

Chapter 6
p.140: Jeff Foott/Getty Images; p.144: Fedorov Oleksiy/Shutterstock; p.152: Fedorov Oleksiy/Shutterstock; p.154: zebra0209 /Shutterstock; p.154: Steven J. Kazlowski/Alamy Images; p.154: Pavelk/Shutterstock; p.154: Wallace Garrison/Alamy; p.154: Michelle Marsan/Shutterstock; p.154: Julius Kielaitis/Shutterstock; p.156: Tom L. McKnight; p.157: Christopher Ewing /Shutterstock; p.157: Tom L. McKnight; p.161: Homer Sykes/Alamy; p.163: Georg Gerster/Photo Researchers, Inc.; p.163: Nicole Gordon, UCAR; p.173: Photofusion Picture Library/Alamy; p.158: Jacques Descloitres, MODIS Rapid Response Team, NASA/GSFC.

Chapter 7
p.176: Reed Timmer/Photo Researchers, Inc.; p.183: NASA/Goddard Space Flight Center; p.190: NASA Earth Observing System; p.195: NASA Earth Observing System; p.195: NASA Earth Observing System; p.196: AP Wide World Photos; p.197: ABACA/Newscom; p.199: Universal Images Group/SuperStock; p.199: Eric Nguyen/Photo Researchers, Inc.; p.195: NASA Earth Observing System; p.195: Vincent Laforet/EPA/Newscom; p.201: J.B. Forbes/St. Louis Post-Dispatch/MCT/Newscom; p.203: Douglas Pulsipher/Alamy.

Chapter 8
p.208: Sylvain/hem/AGE fotostock; p.215: Juan Carlos Munoz/AGE Fotostock; p.217: Renee Lynn/Corbis RF; p.218: AP Photo/Biswaranjan Rout; p.221: Tom L. McKnight; p.223: N Mrtgh/Shutterstock; p.226: Tom L. McKnight; p.228: Clint Farlinger/Alamy; p.229: Chris Cheadle/Glow Images; p.231: Tom L. McKnight; p.232: Bill Brooks/Alamy; p.235: Thomas Sbampato/Alamy; p.236: Maria Stenzel/National Geographic Stock; p.238: Tom L. McKnight; p.241: Matthijs Wetterauw/Shutterstock; p.241: Chris Gilbert/British Antarctic Survey; p.243: Kyodo/AP Images; p.246: Kristin Piljay; p.234: NASA; p.234: NASA; p.251: Image Source/Alamy.

Chapter 9
p.254: McPHOTO/AGE Fotostock America, Inc.; p.257: David Gn/AGE Fotostock America, Inc.; p.260: Andrew Syred/Photo Researchers, Inc.;

p.263: J. Robinson/Getty Images; p.266: Paul Souders/Getty Images; p.268: Ashley Cooper/Alamy Images; p.268: Tom L. McKnight; p.270: Sasha Buzko/Shutterstock; p.271: NASA; p.271: NASA; p.271: Gerd Ludwig/National Geographic Stock; p.271: NASA; p.271: NASA; p.272: Bryan Mullennix/Alamy; p.272: EROS Data Center, U.S. Geological Survey; p.272: EROS Data Center, U.S. Geological Survey; p.273: M. Timothy O'Keefe/Alamy; p.276: Tom L. McKnight; p.279: Jim Wark/AGE fotostock; p.264: Scripps Institution of Oceanography, UC San Diego.

Chapter 10
p.280: Rob Blakers/Getty Images; p.282: Robert Finken/AGE Fotostock; p.282: Roine Magnusson/AGE Fotostock; p.283: Michael Wheatley/SuperStock; p.285: NASA; p.292: Alan Carey/Photo Researchers, Inc.; p.295: Tom L. McKnight; p.295: Bill Bachman/Alamy; p.296: Tom L. McKnight; p.297: Alan D. Carey/Photo Researchers, Inc.; p.297: Robert McGouey/Alamy; p.298: Darrel Hess; p.301: vlynder/iStockphoto.com; p.301: Tom L. McKnight; p.302: Tom L. McKnight; p.303: Tom L. McKnight; p.303: H. Mark Weidman Photography/Alamy; p.304: Darrel Hess; p.286: AgStock Images, Inc./Alamy; p.286: Global Warming Images/Alamy; p.294: EPA/US COAST GUARD/Newscom; p.294: NASA; p.300: Jack Thomas/Alamy; p.300: NASA; p.300: Jim West/Alamy.

Chapter 11
p.306: Enrique R. Aguirre/AGE fotostock; p.310: Darrel Hess; p.311: Tom L. McKnight; p.311: Goss Images/Alamy; p.313: Dennis Tasa; p.313: Niebrugge Images/Alamy; p.314: Darrel Hess; p.315: Kevin Ebi/Alamy; p.315: Tom L. McKnight; p.316: Darrel Hess; p.317: Doug Hamilton/AGE fotostock; p.317: Juniors Bildarchiv/Alamy Images; p.318: Tom L. McKnight; p.318: Dave Watts/Alamy; p.318: Barrett & MacKay/Glow Images; p.318: Joe Austin/Alamy; p.319: National Audubon Society; p.319: Jim Zipp/Photo Researchers, Inc.; p.320: Rick & Nora Bowers/Alamy; p.320: John Serafin; p.321: Darrel Hess; p.322: Tom L. McKnight; p.326: Dr. Morley Read/SPL/Photo Researchers, Inc.; p.326: Worldswildlife Wonders/Shutterstock; p.327: Terry Whittaker/Alamy; p.328: Tom L. McKnight; p.328: Tom L. McKnight; p.329: Darrel Hess; p.330: Darrel Hess; p.331: Design Pics/Alamy; p.331: Tom L. McKnight; p.331: Tom L. McKnight; p.332: Aldo Pavan/AGE fotostock; p.333: Darrel Hess; p.334: Tom L. McKnight; p.334: Darrel Hess; p.335: Cornforth Images/Alamy; p.335: Darrel Hess; p.336: Tom L. McKnight; p.337: Nigel Cattlin/Holt Studios International/Photo Researchers, Inc.; p.339: Tom L. McKnight; p.340: William F. Campbell/Time Life Pictures/Getty Images; p.341: Mark Conlin/Alamy; p.341: Bob Gossington/Photoshot; p.338: NASA Earth Observing System; p.338: NASA Earth Observing System.

Chapter 12
p.344: Russ Heinl/AGE fotostock; p.346: SuperStock, Inc.; p.348: Tom McHugh/Photo Researchers, Inc.; p.349: Stephen Dalton/naturepl.com; p.350: Richard R. Hansen/Photo Researchers, Inc.; p.354: Tom L. McKnight; p.354: Tom L. McKnight; p.359: Tom L. McKnight; p.361: Eduardo Pucheta/Alamy; p.364: Randall J. Schaetzl; p.364: Randall J. Schaetzl; p.366: Randall J. Schaetzl; p.366: U.S. Department of Agriculture; p.367: USDA National Soil Survey Center; p.367: USDA National Soil Survey Center; p.368: Randall J. Schaetzl; p.368: U.S. Department of Agriculture; p.368: U.S. Department of Agriculture; p.369: USDA National Soil Survey Center; p.369: Randall J. Schaetzl; p.370: U.S. Department of Agriculture; p.370: Randall J. Schaetzl; p.371: Randall J. Schaetzl.

Chapter 13
p.374: Alan Majchrowicz/AGE Fotostock; p.379: G. Tompkinson/Photo Researchers, Inc.; p.379: Dennis Tasa; p.382: Dennis Tasa; p.382: Dennis Tasa; p.382: Tyler Boyes/Shutterstock; p.382: Dennis Tasa; p.382: Dennis Tasa; p.383: Tom L. McKnight; p.383: Michael Szoenyi/Photo Researchers, Inc.; p.383: David R. Frazier Photolibrary, Inc./Alamy; p.383: Donna Tucker; p.384: Tom L. McKnight; p.384: Andreas Einsiedel/Dorling Kindersley Media Library; p.385: Tom L. McKnight; p.385: Tom L. McKnight; p.385: Harry Taylor/Dorling Kindersley Media Library; p.386: Tom L. McKnight; p.386: Dennis Tasa; p.388: B. Murton/

Southampton Oceanography Centre/Photo Researchers, Inc.; p.388: Darrel Hess; p.388: Doug Martin/Photo Researchers, Inc.; p.389: Kevin Schafer/Corbis; p.389: Tyler Boyes/Shutterstock; p.391: Dennis MacDonald/AGE Fotostock; p.392: Tom L. McKnight; p.398: Michael Collier.

Chapter 14

p.400: Michele Falzone/Alamy; p.410: Ulrich Doering/Alamy; p.419: Jesse Allen/NASA Earth Observatory; p.420: DANA STEPHENSON/Getty Images; p.420: Darrel Hess; p.421: Chris Hill/National Geographic Stock/Superstock; p.423: D.W. Peterson, USGS; p.424: Ronaldo Schemidt/Getty Images; p.424: Michael Collier; p.425: Michael Collier; p.425: Greg Vaughn/Alamy; p.428: Peter W. Lipman/USGS; p.428: AP Photo/NZPA, Stephen Barker; p.430: Tom L. McKnight; p.430: Tom L. McKnight; p.432: Dennis Tasa; p.432: Tom L. McKnight; p.433: Tom L. McKnight; p.434: Biological Resources Division, U.S. Geological Survey; p.435: Tom L. McKnight; p.436: EFE/Orlando Barría/Newscom; p.436: U.S. Geological Survey, Denver; p.437: Darrel Hess; p.438: Michael Collier; p.441: Peter Menzel/Photo Researchers, Inc.; p.443: David Cobb/Alamy; p.442: NASA/Jet Propulsion Laboratory.

Chapter 15

p.446: TAO IMAGES/AGE Fotostock; p.448: DOUGLAS PEEBLES/Alamy; p.450: Tom L. McKnight; p.450: Tom L. McKnight; p.451: Jason Friend/Loop Images Ltd / Alamy; p.451: Darrel Hess; p.452: MICHAEL RUNKEL/SuperStock; p.453: Tetra Images/AGE Fotostock; p.453: Darrel Hess; p.453: Darrel Hess; p.455: Charlie Ott/Photo Researchers, Inc.; p.455: Martin Bond/Science Photo Library/Photo Researchers, Inc.; p.458: Darrel Hess; p.459: REUTERS/Japan Coast Guard; p.461: JOSE PATRICIO/AGENCIA ESTADO/ZUMA/Newscom; p.463: Tom L. McKnight; p.463: Tom L. McKnight; p.464: H Baesemann/AGE Fotostock; p.462: USGS; p.462: Mark Reid/USGS.

Chapter 16

p.466: Michael Collier; p.468: Tom L. McKnight; p.471: U.S. Department of Agriculture; p.472: Tom L. McKnight; p.473: Tom L. McKnight; p.475: Andrew Meares/AFP/Getty Images/Newscom; p.476: Frans Lanting/Mint Images/Getty Images; p.476: Michael Collier; p.477: Bill Bachman/Photo Researchers, Inc.; p.481: Zoonar/Charles L Bol/AGE Fotostock; p.482: Nathan Blaney/Getty Images; p.484: Michael Collier; p.485: NASA Earth Observing System; p.487: Hemis.fr/SuperStock; p.490: MICHAEL MAPLES/U.S. Army Corps of Engineers, Detroit District; p.492: Tom L. McKnight; p.495: Michael Collier; p.470: MIVA Stock/SuperStock; p.491: RIGOULET Gilles/hemis.fr/Getty Images; p.491: NASA.

Chapter 17

p.498: PicturePress/Glow Images; p.501: AP Photo/John Miller; p.502: David Robertson/Alamy; p.504: iStockphoto.com; p.505: AP Photo/The Florida Times-Union, Jon M. Fletcher; p.506: Darrel Hess; p.507:

Tom L. McKnight; p.507: Darrel Hess; p.508: Iñaki Caperochipi/AGE Fotostock; p.511: Tom L. McKnight; p.511: Caitlin Mirra/Shutterstock; p.509: TOM BRAKEFIELD/Getty Images Royalty Free.

Chapter 18

p.514: Michael Collier; p.517: Darrel Hess; p.518: Darrel Hess; p.519: Michael Collier; p.520: Tom L. McKnight; p.521: Tom L. McKnight; p.523: Tom L. McKnight; p.523: Robert and Jean Pollock/Photo Researchers, Inc; p.523: Darrel Hess; p.526: Frantisek Staud/Alamy; p.527: Tom L. McKnight; p.527: Hauke Dressler/LOOK Die Bildagentur der Fotografen GmbH/Alamy; p.527: Darrel Hess; p.528: Tom L. McKnight; p.529: Mlenny/iStockphoto.com; p.530: Darrel Hess; p.532: Michael Collier; p.533: Dennis Tasa; p.534: Darrel Hess; p.534: A Hartl/AGE Fotostock; p.536: Tom L. McKnight; p.536: Darrel Hess; p.537: Darrel Hess; p.537: iofoto/AGE Fotostock.

Chapter 19

p.540: Frans Lanting/Mint Images/Getty Images; p.542: Tom L. McKnight; p.547: John Goodge, University of Minnesota; field research sponsored by the US National Science Foundation; p.552: Darrel Hess; p.552: Toño Labra/AGE Fotostock; p.553: Heather Elton/AGE Fotostock; p.553: Tom L. McKnight; p.554: chris joint/Alamy; p.555: NASA; p.555: Darrel Hess; p.556: Michael Collier; p.558: Ward's Natural Science Establishment; p.558: Grambo Photography/All Canada Photos/SuperStock; p.559: Tom L. McKnight; p.561: Darrel Hess; p.561: Tom L. McKnight; p.562: Marli Miller; p.563: Tom L. McKnight; p.563: Jon Arnold Images Ltd/Alamy; p.564: Tom L. McKnight; p.564: Leslie Garland Picture Library/Alamy; p.565: Darrel Hess; p.566: Tom L. McKnight; p.566: Darrel Hess; p.567: Tom L. McKnight; p.567: Steven J. Kazlowski/Alamy Images; p.568: Michael Collier; p.569: Wayne Lynch/Glow Images; p.550: Courtesy of Rapid Response Team, NASA; p.560: W.O. Field, U.S. Geological Survey, Denver; p.560: Bruce Molnia, U.S. Geological Survey, Denver.

Chapter 20

p.572: Dale Jorgenson/SuperStock; p.574: Martin Zwick/AGE Fotostock; p.576: Sascha Burkard/Shutterstock; p.577: Tom L. McKnight; p.577: Tom L. McKnight; p.579: Choo Youn-Kong/Agence France Presse/Getty Images; p.581: Tom L. McKnight; p.581: Darrel Hess; p.584: NASA; p.585: Tom L. McKnight; p.585: Tom L. McKnight; p.587: David Wall/Danita Delimont/Newscom; p.587: David Wall/Alamy; p.588: Michael Collier; p.589: USGS; p.590: LOOK Die Bildagentur der Fotografen GmbH/Alamy; p.590: NASA/Goddard Space Flight Center; p.591: Russ Heinl/All Canada Photos/SuperStock; p.592: Darrel Hess; p.593: Darrel Hess; p.593: Tony Roberts/Sportshot/Photo Researchers, Inc.; p.595: Jack Fields/Photo Researchers, Inc.; p.596: A & J Visage/Alamy; p.580: JIJI PRESS/AFP/Getty Images; p.582: MARINE CURRENT TURBINES TM LTD/AF/Getty Images/Newscom; p.582: Paul Lindsay/Alamy; p.594: Greenpeace/ZUMA Press/Newscom.

ILLUSTRATION AND TEXT CREDITS

Chapter 1
Figure 1.3: From the NASA Earth Observatory website; Table 1-3: Source: Smithsonian Meteorological Tables.

Chapter 2
Figure 2.1: © 2012 Google; Figure 2.3: Map from NG MAPS / NATIONAL GEOGRAPHIC STOCK. Copyright © by National Geographic Society. Reprinted with permission; Figure 2.13: Source: 2009 WORLD ALMANAC; Figure 2.14: Source: U.S. Geological Survey; Figure 2.27: Maps from "Cape Cod: Land Cover and Ecology" by Thomas Stone, from Woods Hole Research Center website. Copyright © 2012 by Woods Hole Research Center. Reprinted with permission.

Chapter 3
p.62: From the United States Global Change Research Program; Figure 3.13: From the NASA Earth Observatory website; p.67: Source: TIME ENOUGH FOR LOVE by Robert Heinlein. Ace Books, 1987; Figure 3-A: Source: United States Environmental Protection Agency website; Table 3-A: Source: Based on "UV Index Scale" from United States Environmental Protection Agency website; Figure 3-C: "2011 Key World Energy Statistics" from the International Energy Agency website. Copyright © 2010 OECD/IEA. Reprinted with permission; p.68: Reprinted with permission of Matthew T. Huber.

Chapter 4
Table 4-1: THE ATMOSPHERE: AN INTRODUCTION TO METEOROLOGY, 11th Edition, by Frederick K. Lutgens, Edward J. Tarbuck, and Dennis Tasa. Copyright © 2010 by Pearson Education, Inc. Reprinted and Electronically reproduced by permission of Pearson Education, Inc. Upper Saddle River, New Jersey; Figure 4.36: From the NOAA National Climate Data Center website; Figure 4.37: Figure from FLOODS, DROUGHTS, AND CLIMATE CHANGE by Michael Collier and Robert H. Webb. Copyright © 2002 by The Arizona Board of Regents. Reprinted with permission of the University of Arizona Press; p.105: From "Contribution of Working Group I to the Fourth Assessment Report of the Intergovernmental Panel on Climate Change, 2007" by S. Solomon, D. Quin, M. Manning, Z. Chen, M. Marquis, K.B. Averyt, M. Tignor and H.L. Miller. Copyright © 2007 by Cambridge University Press. Figure 4.38: Figure from "Climate Change 2007: The Physical Science Basis." Contribution of Working Groups I, II and III to the Fourth Assessment Report of the Intergovernmental Panel on Climate Change. Copyright © 2007 by Cambridge University Press. Reprinted with permission; p.105: From Climate Change 2007: Working Group I: The Physical Science Basis: http://ipcc.ch/publications_and_data/ar4/wg1/en/spmsspm-understanding-and.html. Reprinted with permission; p.81: Reprinted with permission of Karl Byrand; Figure 4-C: Source: Map from "Radiation Budget Products," from Office of Satellite and Product Operations website. National Oceanic and Atmospheric Administration; Figure 4-D: Source: Map from "Radiation Budget Products," from Office of Satellite and Product Operations website. National Oceanic and Atmospheric Administration; Figure 4-E: Source: Map from "Radiation Budget Products," from Office of Satellite and Product Operations website. National Oceanic and Atmospheric Administration. 4-35a, b & c: From the NASA Earth Observations website.

Chapter 5
5-42: "College of the Environment" from University of Washington website, January, 2000. Reprinted with permission; Figure 5.43: From the NOAA Climate Services website; p.117: Reprinted with permission of Stephen Stadler; Figure 5-B: Courtesy of Michael Larson, Coordinator, OSU Cartography Services; Figure 5-C: Source: Map from Pacific Marine Environment Laboratory website. National Oceanic and Atmospheric Administration; Figure 5-C: Source: "El Niño Conditions," from El Niño Theme Page website. National Oceanic and Atmospheric Administration; Figure 5-C: Source: Map from "NASA/NOAA Study Finds El Niños Growing Stonger," from Physical Oceanography Distributed Active Archive Center website, August 25, 2010. National Oceanic and Atmospheric Administration.

Chapter 6
Figure 6.2a & b: Figure from ESSENTIALS OF OCEANOGRAPHY, 8th Edition, by Alan P. Trujillo and Harold V. Thurman. Copyright © by Pearson Education, Inc. Printed and Electronically reproduced by permission of Pearson Education, Inc., Upper Saddle River, New Jersey; Figure 6.8: UNDERSTANDING WEATHER AND CLIMATE by Edward Aguado and James E. Burt, 4th Ed. Copyright © 2007 by Pearson Education, Inc. Reprinted and Electronically reproduced by permission of Pearson Education, Inc., Upper Saddle River, New Jersey; Figure 6.10, 22: Figure from EARTH SCIENCE, 12th Edition, by Edward J. Tarbuck, Frederick K. Lutgens and Dennis Tasa. Copyright © 2009 by Pearson Education, Inc. Printed and Electronically reproduced by permission of Pearson Education, Inc., Upper Saddle River, New Jersey.

Chapter 7
7-20: Figure from "Tropical Cyclone Report" Hurricane Katrina 23-30 August 2005 by Richard D. Knabb, Jamie R. Rhome and Daniel P. Brown, from the NATIONAL HURRICANE CENTER, December 20, 2005. Copyright © by the National Oceanic and Atmospheric Administration; Figure 7.22: THE ATMOSPHERE by Edward J. Tarbuck, Frederick K. Lutgens and Dennis Tasa, 12th Ed. Copyright © 2011 by Pearson Education, Inc. Reprinted and Electronically reproduced by permission of Pearson Education, Inc., Upper Saddle River, New Jersey; 7-25: Source: Map by National Weather Service, Hydrometeorological Prediction Center. National Oceanic and Atmospheric Administration; p.187: Reprinted with permission of Ted Eckmann. p.201: Reprinted with permission of Ted Eckmann; Figure 7-E: Map data from the National Weather Service website. Copyright © 2012 by Google, INEGI; p.203: Reprinted with permission of Stephen Stadler; Figures 7-H & 7-I: From the Oklahoma Mesonetwork.

Chapter 8
p.246: "AGU Position Statement" from the American Geographical Union website. Copyright © 2012 by the American Geophysical Union. Reprinted with permission. Figure 8.38: Figure from UNDERSTANDING WEATHER AND CLIMATE by Edward Aguado and James E. Burt, 4th Edition. Copyright © 2007 by Pearson Education, Inc. Reprinted and Electronically reproduced by permission of Pearson Education, Inc., Upper Saddle River, New Jersey; Figure 8.42: SOURCE: From the NASA Earth Observatory website; Figure 8.46a: From "GISS Surface Temperature Analysis" on the NASA Goddard Institute for Space Studies website; Figure 8.46a: Item by James Hansen, from PROCEEDINGS OF THE NATIONAL ACADEMY OF SCIENCES, July 2006, Volume 103. Copyright © 2006 by the National Academy of Sciences. Reprinted with permission; Figure 8.46b: Source: "Global Maps from GHCN v3 Data" from Goddard Institute for Space Studies website. National Aeronautics and Space Administration (NASA); Figure 8-B: Source: Maps by Jesse Allen from "Satellites Observe Widespread Melting Event on Greenland," from NASA Earth Observatory website, July 25, 2012. NASA.

Chapter 9
Figure 9.6: Source: By Norman Kuring from Earth Observatory website. National Aeronautics and Space Administration (NASA); Figure 9.9: GEOGRAPHICAL VARIATIONS IN COASTAL DEVELOPMENT by John Lloyd Davies and K. M. Clayton, 1st Ed. Copyright © 1930. Reprinted and Electronically reproduced by permission of Pearson Education, Inc., Upper Saddle River, New Jersey; Figure 9.11: ESSENTIALS OF OCEANOGRAPHY by Alan P. Trujillo and Harold V. Thurman, 9th Ed. Copyright © 2008 by Pearson Education, Inc. Reprinted and Electronically reproduced by permission of Pearson Education, Inc., Upper Saddle River, New Jersey. Figure 9.17: Source: "'TSP' Time Series - Northern Alaska" from "Artcic Report Card: Update for 2010," from Arctic Theme Page website. National Oceanic and Atmospheric Administration; Figure 9.17: From "Thermal State of Permafrost in Alaska During the Fourth Quarter of the Twentieth Century" by T. E. Osterkamp, from PROCEEDINGS OF THE NINTH INTERNATIONAL CONFERENCE ON PERMAFROST, 2010,

Volume 2. Copyright © 2010 by T. E. Osterkamp, University of Alaska Fairbanks Library. Reprinted with permission; Figure 9.17: Source: "The North Slope Site Map" from "Artcic Report Card: Update for 2010," Arctic Theme Page website. National Oceanic and Atmospheric Administration; Figure 9.33: Source: Adaptation of Figure 1 from "Changes in Water Levels and Storage in the High Plains Aquifer, Predevelopment to 2009" by V. L. Miller, Fact Sheet 2011-3069, December 2011. United States Geological Survey; p.262: Reprinted with permission of Jennifer Rahn; Figure 9-A: Source: Map from Marine Debris website, July 19, 2012. National Oceanic and Atmospheric Administration; Figure 9-C: Figure based on "GRACE Observed Trends in Sacramento and San Joaquin Basins, Oct. 2003 to March 2009." Copyright © by University of California Center for Hydrologic Modeling. Reprinted with permission; Figure 9-D: Source: "GRACE-based Ground Water Storage" from the National Drought Mitigation Center website, July 30, 2012. NASA.

Chapter 10

Figure 10.12: Source: Figure 23 from "Water Quality in the Lake Erie-Lake Saint Clair Drainages: Michigan, Ohio, Indiana, New York, and Pennsylvania, 1996–98" by Donna N. Myers, et al., U.S. Geological Survey Circular 1203. United States Geological Survey; p.286: Reprinted with permission of Valerie Sloan; p.294: Reprinted with permission of Matthew T. Huber; Figure 10-F: Source: Based on maps by Robert Simmons from "Tiny Beetles Take a Large Bite Out of the Forest," from NASA Earth Observatory website, July 28, 2012.

Chapter 11

Figure 11.44: Figure from Food and Agriculture Organization website. Copyright © by the Food and Agriculture Organization of the United Nation. Reprinted with permission. Figure 11.45: Figure from Food and Agriculture Organization website. Copyright © by the Food and Agriculture Organization of the United Nation. Reprinted with permission. Figure 11-B: Source: Maps from "A Climate Change Atlas for 147 Bird Species of the Eastern United States" by Steve N. Matthews, et al., from USDA Forest Service website, March, 29, 2012; Figure 11-C: Source: Maps of Rondônia, Brazil, 1975 and 2012 by the Landsat team, from NASA Earth Observatory website.

Chapter 12

Figure 12.19: THE NATURE AND PROPERTIES OF SOILS by Nyle C. Brady and Ray R. Weil, 12th Ed. Copyright © 1999 by Pearson Education. Reprinted and Electronically reproduced by permission of Pearson Education, Inc., Upper Saddle River, New Jersey; p.364: Reprinted with permission of Randall Schaetzl.

Chapter 13

p.375: Source: ASSEMBLING CALIFORNIA by John McPhee. Farrar, Straus & Giroux, 1993; p.387: Reprinted with permission of Karl Byrand; Figure 13-A: Figure by Al Granberg, from "What is Hydraulic Fracturing," from the ProPublica website. Copyright © 2012 by ProPublica Inc. Reprinted with permission; Figure 13-B: Exhibit from MODERN SHALE GAS DEVELOPMENT IN THE UNITED STATES: A PRIMER. Copyright © 2009 by All Consulting, LLC. Reprinted with permission; Figure 13-B: From MODERN SHALE GAS DEVELOPMENT IN THE UNITED STATES: A PRIMER. Copyright © 2009 by ALL Consulting, LLC and the Ground Water Protection Council, Inc. Reprinted with permission.

Chapter 14

14-9: Figure from THE BEDROCK GEOLOGY OF THE WORLD by Roger L. Larson and Walter C. Pitman III. Copyright © 1985 by Roger L. Larson and Walter C. Pitman III; 14-10: Adaptation from THE BEDROCK GEOLOGY OF THE WORLD by Roger L. Larson and Walter C. Pitman III. Copyright © 1985 by Roger L. Larson and Walter C. Pitman III; 14-56: Source: United States Geological Survey; 14-63: Data from the U.S. Geological Survey; Figure 14-A: Source: Map from "Caribbean Tsunami and Earthquake Hazards Studies: Introduction," from Woods Hole Science Center website, February 23, 2010. United States Geological Survey; Figure 14-C: Source: Figure from "San Andreas Fault Observatory at Depth," from Unites States Geological Survey website, July 23, 2012; Figure 14-D: Figure courtesy of Egill Hauksson, Caltech, Pasadena, CA in "Earthquake Early Warning: Is California Ready?" by Doug Given, from PUBLIC LECTURE SERIES AT PASADENA CITY COLLEGE, 2009-2010. Copyright © by Egill Hauksson. Reprinted with permission.

Chapter 16

p.470: Reprinted with permission of Nancy Lee Wilkinson; Figure 16-B: From the Environment Canada website. Copyright © by Environment Canada; Figure 16-C: SOURCE: Figure from "Land Area Change in Coastal Louisiana from 1932 to 2010" by Brady R. Couvillion, John A. Barras, Gregory D. Steyer, William Sleavin, Michelle Fischer, Holly Beck, Nadine Trahan, Brad Griffin, and David Heckman, from the U.S. GEOLOGICAL SURVEY SCIENTIFIC INVESTIGATIONS MAP 3164, scale 1: 265,000, 12 p. pamphlet.

Chapter 17

p.509: Reprinted with permission of Karl Byrand; Figure 17-A: SOURCE: From the Earth Science Division of the Lawrence Berkeley National Laboratory and the U. S. Department of Energy website.

Chapter 18

18-18: ESSENTIALS OF GEOLOGY by Frederick K. Lutgens, Edward J. Tarbuck and Dennis Tasa, 10th Ed. Copyright © 2009 by Pearson Education, Inc. Reprinted and Electronically reproduced by permission of Pearson Education, Inc., Upper Saddle River, New Jersey; p.524: Reprinted with permission of Mike Pease; Figure 18-B: Source: Map by Jesse Allen from "Severe Drought Causes Famine in East Africa," from NASA Earth Observatory website, June 30, 2011.

Chapter 19

19-3: ESSENTIALS OF GEOLOGY by Frederick K. Lutgens, Edward J. Tarbuck and Dennis Tasa, 10th Ed. Copyright © 2009 by Pearson Education, Inc. Reprinted and Electronically reproduced by permission of Pearson Education, Inc., Upper Saddle River, New Jersey; 19-6: ESSENTIALS OF GEOLOGY by Frederick K. Lutgens, Edward J. Tarbuck and Dennis Tasa, 10th Ed. Copyright © 2009 by Pearson Education, Inc. Reprinted and Electronically reproduced by permission of Pearson Education, Inc., Upper Saddle River, New Jersey; Figure 19.10: Map by NASA/GSFC Scientific Visualization Studio NASA, from "Satellites Confirm Half-Century of West Antarctic Warming" by Kathryn Hansen, from NASA website, January 21, 2009; 19-24: ESSENTIALS OF GEOLOGY by Frederick K. Lutgens, Edward J. Tarbuck and Dennis Tasa, 10th Ed. Copyright © 2009 by Pearson Education, Inc. Reprinted and Electronically reproduced by permission of Pearson Education, Inc., Upper Saddle River, New Jersey; 19-39: Source: Based on GEOLOGIC HISTORY OF THE YOSEMITE VALLEY (Geological Survey Professional Paper 160) by Francois E. Matthes. United States Geological Survey, 1930; 19-47: UNDERSTANDING WEATHER AND CLIMATE by Edward Aguado and James E. Burt, 5th Ed. Copyright © 2010 by Pearson Education, Inc. Reprinted and Electronically reproduced by permission of Pearson Education, Inc., Upper Saddle River, New Jersey.

Chapter 20

20-12: Source: NASA; 20-A: Figure by Mark Simons from "Caltech Researchers Release First Large Observational Study of 9.0 Tohoku-Oki Earthquake" by Katie Neith from the California Institute of Technology website, May 18, 2011. Copyright © 2011 by the California Institute of Technology. Reprinted with permission; p.592: Reprinted with permission of Jennifer Rahn; Figure 20-G: Source: Coral Reef Watch website, September 18, 2012. National Oceanic and Atmospheric Administration.

Appendices

Figure II-3: From the U. S. Geological Survey website; Figure IV-3: Based on METEOROLOGY by William L. Donn, 4th Ed. Copyright © 1975 by McGraw Hill Book Company, New York; Figure IV-4: Based on METEOROLOGY by William L. Donn, 4th Ed. Copyright © 1975 by McGraw Hill Book Company, New York.

California Field Guides

For the Third California Edition of *McKnight's Physical Geography*

Edited by Darrel Hess
City College of San Francisco

Field Guide Locations

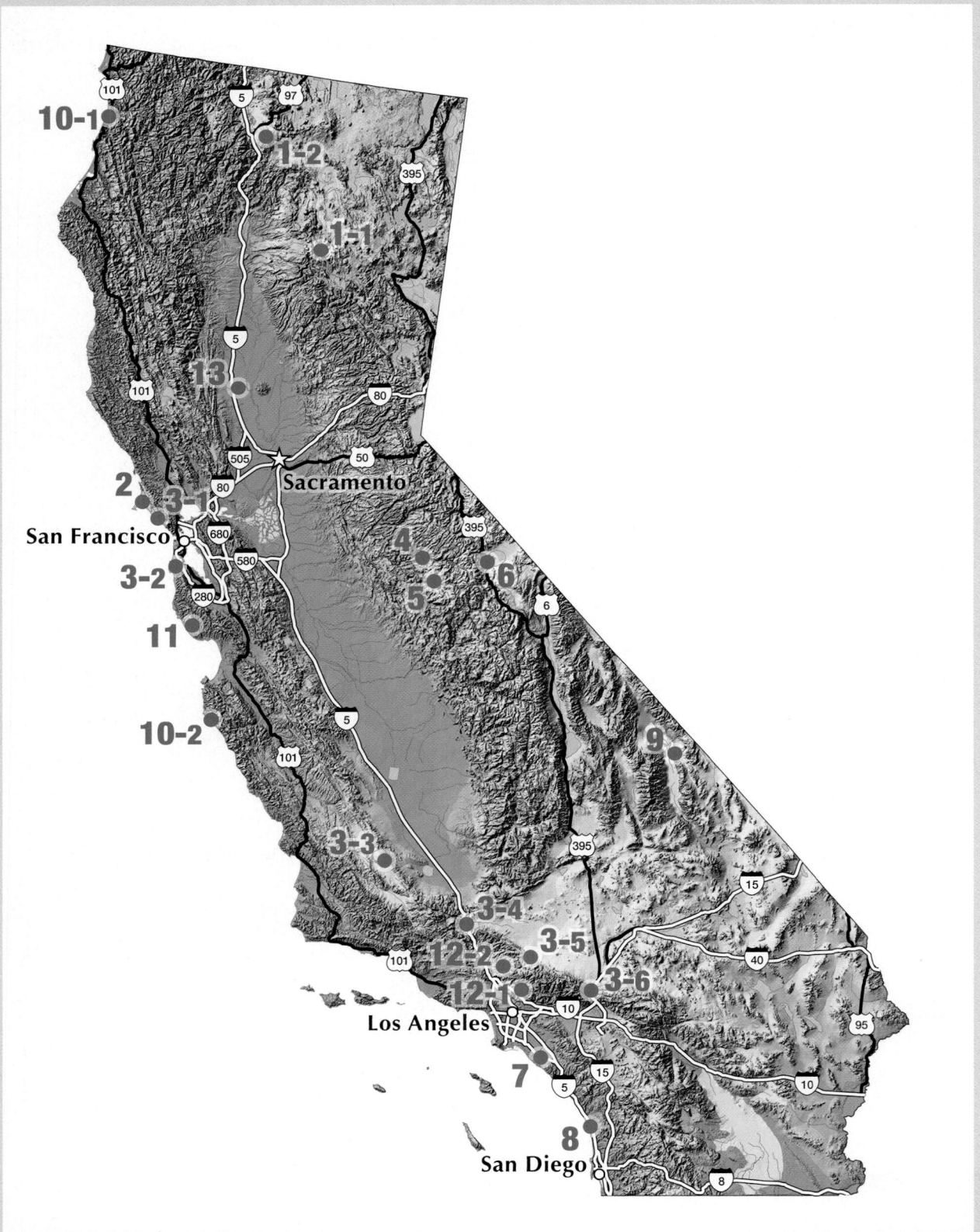

Field Guide #1

The California Cascades: Lassen Volcanic National Park and Mount Shasta

Les Rowntree, University of California, Berkeley

Introduction

The Cascade Range is composed of volcanic landforms stretching from southern British Columbia to northern California and is part of the **Pacific Ring of Fire** circumscribing the Pacific Basin. At least six North American Cascade Range volcanoes are considered active because of eruptions during historical time and only a few are characterized as geologically extinct. While the 1980 Mount St. Helens eruption in southern Washington State is the most recent, major Cascade volcanoes such as Mount Baker, Mount Rainier and Mount Shasta are active enough to be considered hazardous, and therefore are monitored constantly for a possible eruption.

Tectonically, the Cascade Range is linked to the **convergent boundary** between the North American, Gorda, and Juan de Fuca Plates just offshore from northern California, Oregon, Washington, and British Columbia (see textbook Figure 14-18).

In northern California the Cascade geologic province is expressed in a wide variety of volcanic landforms, ranging from undulating lava flows and small cinder cones to the major composite volcano of Mount Shasta and the lava dome of Lassen Peak. California's Cascade Range can be experienced readily in a two- or, better, three-day field trip to the area.

Location

Both Lassen Volcanic National Park and Mount Shasta are accessed from Interstate 5 (I-5) in northern California. The Shasta area, for example, is 220 miles north of Sacramento, or a bit over three hours driving time. Count on just over four hours of driving time from the San Francisco Bay Area.

Campgrounds abound in Lassen Park itself, along California Highway 89 to the north, and even in the Shasta area. Beds and other creature comforts are available in the numerous motels and cafes of Mt. Shasta City, a picturesque small town nestled at the western flanks of the mountain with its own unique social geography.

Visiting this area is best done in late spring, summer, or early autumn since Highway 89 through Lassen Park closes with the first significant snowfall, which can come in late October, and remains closed until snowplows clear the road in May or early June.

Background

Formation of Lassen Peak: The foundation for Lassen Peak was laid down half a million years ago with the formation of Mount Tehama, an 11,000-foot (3,350 m) high **composite volcano** (or *stratovolcano*; see textbook Figure 14-35). Later, around 350,000 years ago, following a series of violent eruptions, Mount Tehama collapsed into itself, forming a large **caldera** (see textbook Figure 14-42). Brokeoff Mountain, the second highest peak in the area at 9,235 feet (2,815 m), is one of the best preserved remnants of ancient Mount Tehama.

Then, roughly 27,000 years ago, a **lava dome** (or **plug dome;** see textbook Figure 14-37) with an active vent pushed its way through the northeastern portion of the caldera to become the current 10,457-foot

Figure FG1-1 Lassen Peak from Lake Helen near field guide Site 1, Stop 2. Eagle Peak is the low peak on the left. *(Darrel Hess photo.)*

(3,187 m) high Lassen Peak (Figure FG1-1). This new mountain was subsequently modified by late **Pleistocene** glaciation. Today, though, unlike on Mount Shasta, there are no living glaciers on the mountain.

Volcanic activity has continued into the present with smaller lava domes (such as Chaos Crags) appearing in the last eleven hundred years. Cinder Cone in the northeast corner of the Park reportedly appeared only in the mid-eighteenth century. More recently, Lassen Peak itself erupted in 1914 and remained active for several years. This activity was punctuated by violent eruptions on May 19 and 22, 1915, which created a new crater on the peak and also sent a superheated **volcanic mudflow (lahar)** and **pyroclastic flow** down the northern flank of the mountain to create the Devastated Area.

Formation of Mount Shasta: Mount Shasta, a composite volcano, like Lassen Peak was built upon the remnants of a collapsed (yet unnamed) predecessor dating back 600,000 years. The modern mountain has been formed within the past 200,000 years from four separate volcanic vents. Lava and **pyroclastic** material from numerous eruptions have coalesced to form the present day 14,160-foot (4,316 m) high Mount Shasta.

Remnants of these four vents can be seen near the mountain's summit. The Sargents Ridge cone, southeast of the summit, and dated to 200,000 years ago, is the oldest. Part of its crater forms Thumb Rock, a prominent feature at the top of Avalanche Gulch (see Bunny Flat, Site 2, Stop 3). The Misery Hill cone is next oldest, dating back to 30,000 to 50,000 years ago, and makes up a large part of the upper mountain. The Shastina cone actually forms a separate peak of 12,330 feet (3,758 m) attached to the western flank of Mount Shasta, and volcanologists date its origin back 9,000 years. The fourth and most recent vent

is Hotlum on the northeastern side of the mountain, and the dome that fills its crater forms the current summit of Mount Shasta. Although the Hotlum vent originated at the same time as Shastina, most of the cone has grown within the last 6,000 years. Even more recently, the Hotlum cone was responsible for an explosion about 200 years ago when it exhaled an ash cloud that covered the northern flanks of the mountain.

Mount Shasta's Growing Glaciers: There are at least seven living glaciers on Mount Shasta's flanks, with three more small ice fields whose status is debated. For our purposes we'll stick with those glaciers recognized by the U.S. Geological Survey in their 1986 mapping of the mountain. Most of the glaciers are on the colder, more shadowed north side of the mountain, and on a topographic map are, from west to east: Whitney—the longest glacier; Bolam; Hotlum—the largest in terms of area and volume; Wintun; Watkins; Konwakiton; and Mud Creek.

Scientists believe the larger Pleistocene glaciers that shaped so much of Mount Shasta's landscape melted away completely during the early Holocene (10,000 years ago to present) warming, and that the current glaciers formed during the *Little Ice Age* (~1550-1850 AD), when global climates cooled for several centuries.

Interestingly enough, Mount Shasta's five main glaciers have grown during the last several decades, unlike most of the world's glaciers, which have retreated as the global climate has warmed. Several explanations are offered to account for the growth of Mount Shasta's glaciers, including the fact that the mountain makes is own weather because of its isolation from other mountain ranges; a northward shift of Pacific storm tracks, bringing more snow to Mount Shasta; the warming of the Pacific Ocean, which adds more moisture to the storms visiting northern California—or a combination of all or some of those various factors.

Site Descriptions

Approaching the area from the south on Interstate 5, a loop trip to see Lassen Peak and Mount Shasta can be made by taking California Highway 36 east from Red Bluff to California Highway 89, which then enters Lassen Volcanic National Park at the southwest entrance, traverses the park close to Lassen Peak, then exits at the northern Park boundary near Manzanita Lake. Continuing northwest on Highway 89 for 106 miles (170 km) brings one to Mt. Shasta City at the foot of this spectacular volcano.

Site 1—Lassen Volcanic National Park

Driving California Highway 89 through Lassen Volcanic National Park is an extraordinary introduction to an array of volcanic processes and landforms and will occupy at least one full day (Figure FG1-2). As at all National Parks, there is an entrance fee, so be prepared. A number of the trails, exhibits and campgrounds in the Park are wheelchair accessible—check the Park Web site on page F-8 for details.

When entering the Park at the southwestern entrance, your first stop should be at the new Kohm Yah-mah-nee Visitor Center that opened in October 2008; the Center's name comes from the local Native American tribe's name for "snow mountain." There, visitors can see displays about the physical and cultural geography of the region, watch films and videos, and buy books and maps that will guide one through the Park.

Here are just a few highlights of the Highway 89 drive across the Park:

Stop 1—Sulphur Works (40°26′55″N, 121°32′08″W):
The Sulfur Works are 1.1 miles from the southwest entrance to the Park. A one-quarter-mile self-guided nature trail leads through this active hydrothermal area. Because it's one of the most visited areas in the Park, try for an early morning or early evening visit. Boardwalks provide safe passage around hydrothermal features thought to be remains of the central vent of ancient Mount Tehama. **Fumaroles,** boiling **hot springs** (see textbook Figure 17-10), and mudpots abound.

Stop 2—Bumpass Hell Trailhead (40°27′57″N, 121°30′52″W):
About 5.7 miles from the southwest Park entrance is the parking area for Bumpass Hell. This is the largest of the Park's hydrothermal areas and in sixteen acres one will find an array of steaming fumaroles, gurgling mud pots, and boiling hot springs. Again, the crowds can be thick and the parking lot packed, so try for an early or late visit. The main hydrothermal area is 1.4 miles from the trailhead. Bumpass Hell is the result of fissures that connect to volcanic heat three miles (4.8 km) deep.

Stop 3—Lassen Peak Trailhead (40°28′27″N, 121°30′20″W):
The trailhead for Lassen Peak is 6.9 miles from the southwest entrance to the Park. The 2.5-mile trail begins at 8,500 feet (2,590 m), and zigzags to the 10,457-foot summit of Lassen Peak. This is another popular trail, so don't expect to be alone, although because of altitude and steepness many hikers drop by the wayside before the halfway point. At about 9,200 feet (2,800 m), you pass the last of the dwarf Mountain Hemlocks (Tsuga mertensiana) and enter into the alpine zone.

From the summit one can better visualize ancient Mount Tehama, whose summit once stood about two miles south-southwest. Only parts of Tehama's flanks can be seen, primarily Brokeoff Mountain about four miles southwest and Mount Diller, the long sloping ridge just north of Brokeoff.

Stop 4—Devastated Area Interpretive Trail (40°30′56″N, 121°27′55″W):
This 0.4-mile wheelchair-accessible trail loop begins 18.7 miles from the Park's southwest entrance.

On May 19, 1915, hot **lava** spilled over the crater rim of Lassen Peak onto a thick snowfield layered with volcanic ash from previous minor eruptions, creating a slow-moving mudflow or lahar down the northeast slope of the mountain. Three days later, a massive eruption sent a blast of superheated air and ash (pyroclastic flow) down the same path, leveling a swath of forest one mile wide and three miles long. Thousands of downed evergreen trees were blown over like matchsticks, all pointing away from the source of the blast. Although the Devastated Area has been healing for almost a century, this is still a vivid portrait of nature's power of destruction (Figure FG1-3).

▲ **Figure FG1-2**   Regional map of Lassen Volcanic National Park showing Site 1 field guide stops.

▲ **Figure FG1-3**   The northeastern side of Lassen Peak showing the mature forest in the foreground before the eruptions of 1915 (left). The Devastated Area after the eruptions of May 1915 (right). The large boulder in the foreground can still be seen on the Devastated Area Interpretive Trail at Site 1, Stop 4. *(Photographs courtesy of the National Park Service.)*

Site 2—Mount Shasta

To reach the Mount Shasta area, take the Mt. Shasta City central exit off I-5 and head east on West Lake Street into Mt. Shasta City (Figure FG1-4). Continue east toward Mount Shasta itself, passing through several stoplights; after crossing North Mt. Shasta Boulevard—the town's main street—West Lake Street changes to East Lake Street. Continue several blocks until East Lake Street dead-ends into North Washington Drive; turn left and head north, passing Mt. Shasta High School on your right. At this point North Washington Drive turns into the Everitt Memorial Highway, also signed Siskiyou County Route A-10.

This 15.2-mile highway goes up the southern flank of Mount Shasta, taking you from 3,500 feet (1,065 m) to almost 8,000 feet (2,440 m). Not only does it provide a spectacular close-up of Mount Shasta itself, but it also provides a fascinating look at the biogeography of the mountain as one travels from dry chaparral scrub lands at the lower elevations, into coniferous forests between 4,000 and 7,000 feet (1,220–2,130 m), then terminating at the **treeline** with alpine meadows at 8,000 feet above sea level.

Stop 1 (rolling stop)—The Everitt Memorial Highway from Mt. Shasta City (41°19′33″N, 122°18′23″W): Going up the mountain, look for small U.S. Forest Service signs on the right-hand side that provide elevation and mileage information.

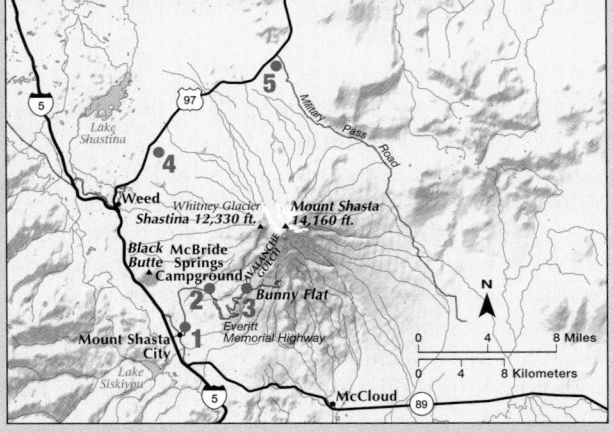

▲ **Figure FG1-4**   Regional map of Mount Shasta area showing Site 2 field guide stops.

Before going too far up the road, pull over to the right shoulder and stop to ponder the landscape (Figure FG1-5). Most impressive, of course, is snow-covered Mount Shasta itself, rising before you to 14,162 feet, with Shastina, the more recent volcanic cone, to the left. On the north flank of Mount Shasta, in the gap between it and Shastina, you can see the head of Whitney Glacier. Note also, on the summit of Mount Shasta, the several promontories that compose the four different volcanic vents from past eruptions. These will become even more prominent as you travel up the highway and get different views of the summit area.

▲ **Figure FG1-5** View of Mount Shasta from Mt. Shasta City at Site 2, Stop 1. *(Les Rowntree photo.)*

▲ **Figure FG1-6** Avalanche Gulch on Mount Shasta from Bunny Flat at Site 2, Stop 3. *(Les Rowntree photo.)*

Stop 2—McBride Springs Campground

(41°21'07"N, 122°17'13"W): McBride Springs Campground is about four miles up the highway, on your left, at an elevation of 4,880 feet (1,487 m). This is a good place to get acquainted with the different **coniferous trees** found on Mount Shasta. Between the town of Mt. Shasta and the campground you've passed through an extensive second-growth Ponderosa Pine forest (*Pinus ponderosa;* see Figure FG4-2 in *Field Guide #4* and Figure FG5-3 in *Field Guide #5*). The original old growth was cut for timber in the early part of the twentieth century. Once the forest was gone, different chaparral species expanded into the area. But in 1957, the U.S. Forest Service began planting rows and rows of Ponderosa Pine— note that the trees are in fairly straight lines, giving clue to their heritage as planted seedlings.

But at McBride Springs Campground you'll be leaving the Ponderosa Pine belt and entering into the zone of fir trees, which will continue unbroken to near the treeline when the Whitebark Pine (*Pinus albicaulis*) appears around 7,500 feet (2,300 m). If you have the time and inclination, and are equipped with a good tree identification book, you'll be able to identify the different kinds of firs—Red Fir (*Abies magnifica*), White Fir (*Abies concolor*), and the endemic Shasta Fir (*Abies magnifica var. shastensis*)— as well as the Whitebark Pine.

As you proceed up the mountain, pull over frequently to admire the view beyond Mount Shasta. To the southwest, the jagged rocks of the Castle Crags State Park remind you that you're on the border between the volcanic Cascade Range and the metamorphic rock of the Klamath Massive to the west. Looking to the south you'll see snowcapped Lassen Peak and Mount Brokeoff. Additionally, as you drive higher on Mount Shasta, notice the volcanic ash and pyroclastic material in the roadcuts.

Stop 3—Bunny Flat (41°21'14"N, 122° 14'00"W):

Twelve miles up Everitt Memorial Highway at an elevation of 6,900 feet (2,100 m) is Bunny Flat, the trailhead for hikers and climbers going up the mountain. Even if you're not interested in hiking, the view up Avalanche Gulch to the summit is definitely worth the stop. The Bunny Flat parking area is hard to miss, so find an empty space and park.

From Bunny Flat you look across a small alpine meadow and then up Avalanche Gulch to a glacial **cirque.** Running laterally across the upper cirque are the Red Banks, an outcrop of reddish tephra that separates the cirque from the summit plateau at 12,000 feet (3,660 m). To the right of Red Banks is Thumb Rock, a remnant of the Sargents Ridge cone. The summit itself is barely visible above the left side of Red Banks (Figure FG1-6).

Avalanche Gulch itself was originally carved into the soft volcanic material by a Pleistocene glacier that has long since melted. As noted earlier, today Mount Shasta's largest glaciers are all on the colder north side of the mountain, protected somewhat from the Sun's direct rays.

A short 1.7-mile hike from Bunny Flat will take you up a thousand feet to Horse Camp, the Sierra Club stone shelter, a spring, and solar-composting toilets; this area serves as base camp for climbers and hikers. This hike shouldn't take more than an hour and offers a closer look at the treeline environment of forest and meadows.

From Bunny Flat the road continues for another two miles past Panther Meadows to an old ski area that was wiped out by a huge avalanche in 1978. Although the U.S. Forest Service removed the debris in the 1980s, traces of the avalanche pathway can still be seen in the hundreds of downed and uprooted mature trees; young seedlings that have grown up since 1978 fill the pathway, with older forests on either side.

Stop 4—North Side of Mount Shasta

(41°29′45″N, 122°19′51″W): Mount Shasta's glaciers are best seen by driving around to the north
side of the mountain where one can ponder the
mountain from a distance on a paved state highway.
Get even closer by driving on an unimproved dirt
road, or, for the truly adventurous, hike to the foot
of several glaciers from remote trailheads.

To get to the north side of the mountain, return
to Interstate 5 and drive north (passing close to Black
Butte on the route) eight miles to the Central Weed
exit. Take this exit through town to U.S. Highway
97, noting your mileage, then drive northeast a couple of miles until you find a safe place to pull off,
park, and view Mount Shasta (Figure FG1-7).

From any vantage point along Highway 97 at
least three of Shasta's seven glaciers can be seen.
From Shastina going east, one sees first, Whitney
glacier (the mountain's longest glacier); Bolum glacier; and then Hotlum glacier.

Stop 5 (rolling stop)—An Off-road Adventure: Military Pass Road

(41°
33′32″N, 122°12′33″W): For those driving a high-
clearance vehicle (preferably 4WD) and carrying a
good supply of food and drink, as well as a good
map of the area (namely the *Shasta-Trinity National
Forest* map), a closer view of Mount Shasta and its
glaciers can be had by turning off Highway 97 onto
an unimproved Forest Service dirt road, the Military
Pass Road, signed U.S. Forest Service road 43N19.
Driving east on Highway 97, this road is about thirteen miles from Weed, and is marked by a small sign
on the right.

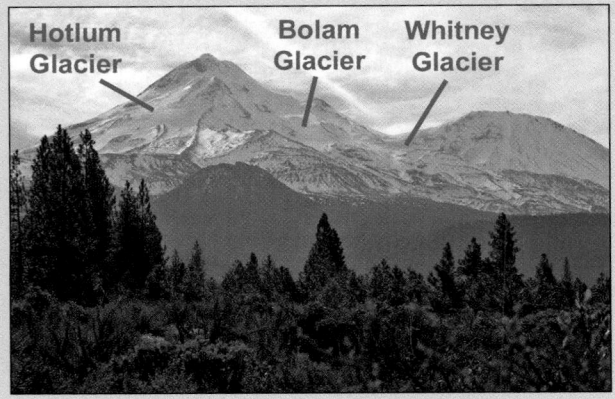

▲ **Figure FG1-7**   North side of Mount Shasta at Site 2,
between Stops 4 and 5, showing glaciers. *(Les Rowntree
photo.)*

Since there are dozens of small dirt roads intersecting 43N19, pay close attention to all signs so that
you don't end up on a dead-end logging road. And
even though the first several miles of Military Pass
Road are relatively smooth, later on there are many
areas where deep ruts and protruding boulders will
require you to creep along at a snail's pace.

But by the time you're four miles in from
Highway 97, the views of Shasta and its glaciers will
be absolutely spectacular as you get closer and closer
to the mountain. Hotlum glacier dominates the view
early on, with Wintum glacier becoming visible after
eight miles from the paved highway.

For the truly adventurous (and well prepared),
turn off Military Pass Road to either the North Gate
or Brewer Creek trailheads, then hike to the foot of
either glacier. A trail guide is strongly recommended
in both cases.

Additional Resources

Textbook:
Hess, Darrel. *McKnight's Physical Geography: A
Landscape Appreciation*, 11th ed. Upper Saddle
River, NJ: Pearson, 2014. Chapters 6, 11, 14, 17
and 19.

Further Reading:
Alt, David, and Donald W. Hyndman. *Roadside Geology of Northern and Central California*. Missoula, MT: Mountain Press, 2000.
Selters, Andy, and Michael Zanger. *The Mt. Shasta
Book*, 3rd ed. Berkeley, CA: Wilderness Press,
2006.

White, Mike. *Lassen Volcanic National Park: A
Complete Hiker's Guide*, 4th ed. Berkeley, CA:
Wilderness Press, 2008.

Web Sites:
Lassen Volcanic National Park
http://www.nps.gov/lavo/

Mount Shasta Companion, College of the Siskiyous
http://www.siskiyous.edu/shasta/index.htm

Textbook Page References for Key Terms

caldera *(p. 425)*

cirque *(p. 561)*

composite volcano (stratovolcano) *(p. 423)*

coniferous trees (conifers) *(p. 309)*

convergent boundary *(p. 409)*

fumaroles *(p. 508)*

hot spring *(p. 505)*

lava *(p. 419)*

lava dome (plug dome) *(p. 424)*

Pacific Ring of Fire *(p. 414)*

Pleistocene Epoch *(p. 544)*

pyroclastic flow *(p. 427)*

pyroclastic [material] *(p. 420)*

treeline *(p. 313)*

volcanic mudflow (lahar) *(p. 428)*

Field Guide #2

Point Reyes National Seashore

Barbara A. Holzman, San Francisco State University

Introduction

The Point Reyes National Seashore (PRNS) reaches out into the Pacific Ocean, greeting the Gray Whales that pass by on their annual migration between December and April. The geography of the Peninsula's mysterious fog-drenched landscape is characterized by the critical role of geologic time, moving tectonic plates, mild mediterranean climate, and human impact on the land. The Peninsula is defined by its distinct geographic boundaries, most notably the San Andreas Fault and Inverness Ridge that run along its eastern flank. Situated approximately at latitude 38° N, it comprises over 100 square miles of biologically rich diversity not found in the rest of Marin County.

Location

Point Reyes National Seashore is located 35 miles north of San Francisco in Marin County, along the west coast of California. PRNS is located just west of the Coast Highway (California Highway 1). The easiest way to get there from San Francisco is to take U.S. Highway 101 north across the Golden Gate Bridge to the Sir Frances Drake Boulevard exit and head west through several Marin County towns until you reach Highway 1 at Olema (Figure FG2-1). Turn right on Highway 1 and then left onto Bear Valley Road to the Bear Valley Visitor Center. A more winding approach is to drive across the Golden Gate Bridge and take the

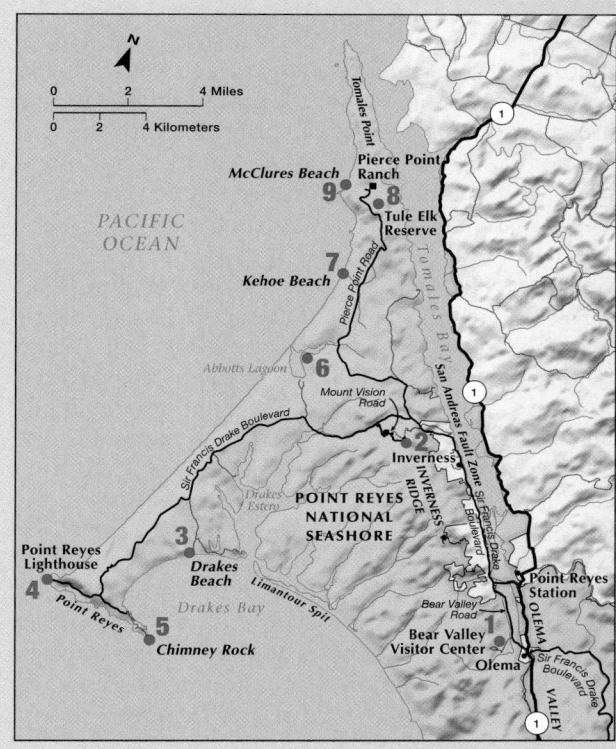

▲ **Figure FG2-1** Regional map of Point Reyes National Seashore showing field guide stops.

exit to Highway 1 and Stinson Beach. From there travel along Highway 1 until you reach Olema and PRNS. The views from this road are fantastic on a clear day, but the road is only two lanes and very winding.

Parts of the PRNS may also be reached by public transportation with Golden Gate Transit and West Marin Stagecoach—see *Additional Resources* on F-17.

Park hours are sunrise to sunset. The Bear Valley Visitor Center is open 9 AM to 5 PM on weekdays and 8 AM to 5 PM on weekends and holidays. The lighthouse and its Visitor Center are open 10 AM to 4:30 PM, Thursday through Monday, but closed during high winds. There is no car camping inside the park, and only a few walk-in camps. If you want to camp at PRNS you must go to the Visitor Center to check in and get your camping permit. Reservations are advised, as camping is very limited and fills quickly. Many exhibits and trails in Point Reyes National Seashore are wheelchair accessible—check the PRNS Web site on F-17 for details.

Background

Point Reyes National Seashore is well known in the San Francisco Bay Area as a place to view coastal forests, a great diversity of spring wildflowers and native plants, and Gray Whales on their migration north and south. What underlies these wonders is as interesting as what lies above them.

Geologic History: The exact origin of the Point Reyes Peninsula is still unclear. It is a geologic anomaly compared to its neighboring inland landscape. Beneath the spiny, tree-covered Inverness Ridge and gradually sloping rangelands lies a very distinct geology that separates the Peninsula from the rest of the nearby California coastline. Like coastal Santa Barbara County to the south and Bodega Head to the north, the Point Reyes Peninsula is a geologic "island." It is part of the northwesterly moving Pacific Plate and separated from the rest of California by the San Andreas Fault system. The fault cuts through Tomales Bay, Olema Valley, and Bolinas Lagoon, passes into the Pacific Ocean, and then returns east and inland just south of San Francisco.

The rest of California and the United States are part of the slower, westerly-moving North American Plate (see textbook Figure 14-18). These plate movements result in periodic seismic activity along the San Andreas Fault. On average, the Pacific Plate moves in a northwesterly direction about 2 inches (5 cm) per year. The San Andreas Fault, running alongside the east border of Point Reyes (along Highway 1) is an example of a **strike-slip fault,** and is the main component of the **transform boundary** between the Pacific and North American Plates. The Pacific Plate and North American Plate glide past each other in fits and starts, causing earthquakes.

The epicenter of the famous 1906 San Francisco earthquake was located along this fault, and Olema Valley, just outside the park boundary, was the site of maximum observed displacement.

The most notable geologic difference between the Point Reyes Peninsula and the remainder of the California coast is the presence of *Salinian* **granite** basement rock and the absence of the *Franciscan Complex* (graywacke [sandstone], shale, greenstone [metamorphosed basalt], and chert) commonly found east of the San Andreas Fault. The Peninsula's granite is overlain with marine deposits thought to be from the late Jurassic and Cretaceous Periods (about 65 to 150 million years ago). However, the granite probably originated from much deeper in Earth and several hundred miles south of its current location. Some other widespread geologic formations found on top of the granitic basement rock include Laird Sandstone, Monterey Shale, and the Purisima Formation (Figure FG2-2). With the exception of the granite, most of the Peninsula's geologic formations are from the Tertiary Period (2.6 to 65.5 million years ago)—younger than many other formations found along the California coast.

Weather and Climate: The Point Reyes Peninsula, similar to the rest of California, is characterized by winter rains and summer drought. The temperature varies little between seasons (average ranges from 50°–55°F [10–13°C]). Rainfall varies dramatically on the Peninsula. The interior Olema Valley receives approximately 40 inches (102 cm) of rain per year, while during the same period, the Point Reyes Headlands may receive only 20 inches (51 cm). The weather at Point Reyes can get very windy and cold along the coast. Often fog will envelop the whole coast. It is best to check weather forecasts before traveling here.

▲ **Figure FG2-2**   The cliffs along Drakes Beach near Stop 3 consist of sedimentary rocks of the Purisima Formation. *(Darrel Hess photo.)*

Site Descriptions

Most of these sites can be reached by automobile. Several sites require a short hike, and they will be noted below. Many of these sites can be reached in one day, but it is more advisable to take only one of the options and spend the entire day in that area, returning to PRNS on another day to visit the other sites. There are two general routes described below. Both start at the Bear Valley Visitor Center. *Option 1* heads to the most western point, the headlands and the Point Reyes Lighthouse, and *Option 2* to the farthest northern point, Pierce Point Ranch.

Stop 1—Bear Valley Visitor Center and Earthquake Trail (38°02'29"N, 122°48'01"W):
The Bear Valley Visitor Center and Park Headquarters are located near the town of Olema. It is the best place to start your Point Reyes adventure. The center provides brochures, maps, and books for sale, as well as an exhibit about the area's ecosystems, wildlife, and cultural history.

The Visitor Center is located near the above-ground rupture of the San Andreas Fault caused by the famous 1906 earthquake. The National Seashore maintains a short Earthquake Loop Trail to the 1906 fault rupture zone. The wheelchair-accessible Earthquake Trail starts at the Visitor Center parking lot. There are signs and displays along the trail that provide information on plate tectonics, earthquakes, and the San Andreas Fault. As you walk along the half-mile loop trail, the **fault scarp** is clearly visible. Along the trail, a historic fence offset caused by the 1906 earthquake was reconstructed. The original offset was about 18 feet (5.5 m). Along with the fence, blue posts trace the surface rupture of the 1906 earthquake. There is a longer, four-mile Rift Zone Trail from the Visitor Center south to the trailhead at Five Brooks in Olema, which follows the trace of the 1906 rupture. (For additional information see *Field Guide #3—The San Andreas Fault.*)

Option 1—Western Point Reyes:
From the Visitor Center, continue along Bear Valley Road until it intersects Sir Francis Drake Boulevard; continue north along Sir Francis Drake, turning left before you reach the bridge that leads to Point Reyes Station. Continue north on Sir Francis Drake Boulevard into the park and stay to your left following signs to the lighthouse. It is about 20 miles to the lighthouse.

Stop 2—Mount Vision, Inverness Ridge, and the 1995 Mount Vision Fire (38°06'03"N, 122°53'08"W):
Your first stop is the Bishop Pine forest and Inverness Ridge. Turn left off the main road onto Mount Vision Road. Mount Vision Road winds uphill for four miles along the crest of Inverness Ridge. This narrow, winding road leads through mature Bishop Pine forests and into the fire area. Bishop Pine *(Pinus muricata)* is a closed-cone pine that needs fire or heat to release seeds from its resinous cones.

On October 3, 1995, the Mount Vision fire was started by an improperly extinguished illegal campfire on State Park lands adjacent to the National Seashore. The fire swept through the area, at a rate of up to 3,100 acres per hour. It burned over 12,000 acres, mostly inside the PRNS boundary. It took two weeks to bring the fire under control, and 45 homes along Inverness Ridge were destroyed. The fire consumed a majority of the Bishop Pine forest, along with Douglas Fir forests and coastal strand communities. It traveled from the top of the ridge to the Pacific Ocean. On a clear day, Mount Vision Road provides spectacular views of Point Reyes and the extent of the fire. The road ends in a parking lot, next to a fire road that is closed to vehicles. Walk along the fire road to see a new Bishop Pine forest developing. The stand of new trees is dense and difficult to walk through. Additional trees that either stump-sprouted or germinated after the fire include Madrone, California Bay, and Coast Live Oak, and these, as well as many native shrubs like *Ceanothus* ("California Lilac"), California Coffeeberry, Huckleberry, and Sticky Monkey Flower, have returned. Unlike the mature forest you passed on the way up, the new forest has little understory vegetation due to the dense cover of young Bishop Pine trees. As the forest naturally thins out, more light will become available for understory species.

From the fire site, take Mount Vision Road back to Sir Francis Drake Boulevard and continue toward the lighthouse. As you can see, the area you are passing through is largely used for cattle grazing. These ranches were here prior to PRNS and have been allowed to continue ranching. Grass covers about 50 percent of Point Reyes, and, like much of California's grasslands, many native perennial grasses have been replaced with non-native annuals (see *Field Guide #13—The Central Valley*). The gullying and erosion you see on the rolling hills are examples of some of the effects of heavy grazing in these grasslands.

Stop 3—Drakes Bay and Beach (38°01'40"N, 122°57'45"W):
Drakes Bay is accessed along a road left off Sir Francis Drake Boulevard,

▲ **Figure FG2-3**   Walking along Drakes Beach at Stop 3. The cliffs are exposed porcellanite, mudstones, sandstones, and siltstones of the Purisima Formation. *(Barbara Holzman photo.)*

▲ **Figure FG2-4**   Point Reyes Conglomerate from Stop 4 at the lighthouse. *(Barbara Holzman photo.)*

5.8 miles north of the lighthouse. From the beach, you can see exposed white cliffs of *porcellanite* (an impure chert with an appearance similar to unglazed porcelain) and *glauconitic* mudstones, silt-stones, and sandstones, which include fossils of Miocene age (5.3 to 23.0 million years ago; Figure FG2-3). These sedimentary rocks formed from mate-rial deposited under the sea while the landmass was submerged offshore as the Pacific Plate moved northward. These cliffs are part of the Santa Margarita Sandstone and Purisima Formation that can also be seen along the Santa Cruz coast and the San Francisco peninsula. The exposed cliffs near the east end of Drakes Bay unveil a **syncline** and adja-cent **anticline** (see textbook Figure 14-54). As you walk along the beach, you can examine marine beds, sea cliffs, and a **wave-cut platform** (*wave-cut bench;* see textbook Figure 20-29) near the Visitor Center.

Return to Sir Francis Drake Boulevard and follow signs to the lighthouse. On winter weekends buses shuttle visitors from Drakes Beach to the lighthouse.

Stop 4—The Point Reyes Lighthouse

(37°59'44"N, 123°01'23"W): From the lighthouse parking lot, a stairway of 300 steps takes you to the lighthouse, Visitor Center, and museum. Along the stairway and above the Visitor Center are examples of Point Reyes Conglomerate (Figure FG2-4). These outcrops have been dated from the Paleocene and Eocene (33.9 to 65.5 million years ago). The con-glomerates are colorful, and consist of white and black granodiorite clasts, purple and black por-phyritic volcanic clasts, light-colored quartzite peb-bles, red chert, and green pebbles, most of volcanic origin. This area consists of both conglomerates and sandstones deposited as *turbidites* (deposits from underwater sand flows) and debris flows in deep water. These beds were deposited in a submarine channel that was cut into the underlying granodi-orite. It is the oldest marine sediment found atop the granitic bedrock.

The lighthouse projects about ten miles into the Pacific Ocean, providing great views of the entire peninsula, and making the headlands of the Point Reyes Peninsula a great spot to view Gray Whales *(Eschrictius robustus)*. The Gray Whales pass Point Reyes during their winter migration (November and December) to the southern waters of Baja California, and return along the same route in March and April on their journey back to Alaska. It is possible to see mothers and calves close to shore during the spring migration. While there are many potential locations for whale watching in the Point Reyes area, the light-house is considered one of the best.

Stop 5—Chimney Rock (37°59'42"N, 122°

58'47"W): The Chimney Rock and Sea Lion Overlook trails start at the Chimney Rock parking lot east of the lighthouse. The trail to the Chimney Rock overlook is about one mile. From the overlook, you can see several sea *stacks;* the one that looks like a chimney is the namesake of the area (Figure FG2-5). There is also a sea arch in view from the overlook. These are made from Salinian granite. A short loop trail leads over the bluffs and provides great views of the ocean as well as the beaches below, where Elephant Seals and Harbor Seals often haul out.

▲ **Figure FG2-5** Chimney Rock from Stop 5. The cliffs and sea stacks are granite. *(Barbara Holzman photo.)*

Continuing on the trail, you will see more sea stacks and a sea arch on the eastern side. Be very careful near the cliffs as they are in a constant state of erosion. The Chimney Rock area resembles a mesa. It is capped by a gravel-covered **marine terrace** (see textbook Figures 20-29 and 20-30). The gravel is overlain by sand and a thin layer of rich organic soil, which provides the perfect habitat for a coastal prairie type ecosystem with a grand showing of native wildflowers in the spring.

Another trail, heading north from the parking lot, leads you to the Sea Lion Overlook where you can see the white cliffs that surround Drakes Bay mentioned at the last stop. From the overlook you can also see a cobble-strewn beach where Northern Elephant Seals *(Mirounga angustirostris;* see textbook Figure 11-21) and Harbor Seals *(Phoca vitulina)* frequently haul out and give birth in the protected bay. The beach has no public access.

Returning along Sir Francis Drake Boulevard, visit North or South Beach and watch the wave action of the Pacific. These areas have several types of sand dunes; some are dominated by non-native species introduced to stabilize dunes, such as European Beachgrass *(Ammophila arenaria)* and Ice Plant *(Caprobrotus species)*. Prior to these introductions, this dune community was dominated by American Dune Grass *(Leymus mollis)* and coastal plants like Dune Lupine *(Lupinus chamissonis)*, and Sand Verbena *(Abronia umbellata)*. This coastal beach and dune area is characterized by stretches of loose, windswept, sandy dunes that vary in width from a few to several hundred feet. If you hike on the dunes, you will find examples of continually shifting foredunes (nearest the shore), sparsely vegetated central dunes, and stable and densely vegetated hind dunes.

Option 2—Northern Point Reyes: Another way to explore Point Reyes National Seashore geography is to take a more northern route, along Pierce Point Road to Abbotts Lagoon, Kehoe Beach, and the Tule Elk Reserve ending at Pierce Point Ranch and McClures Beach. After starting at the Bear Valley Visitor Center, continue north along Bear Valley Road until it intersects Sir Francis Drake Boulevard, continue north along Sir Francis Drake, then turn left before you reach the bridge that leads to Point Reyes Station. Continue to follow Sir Francis Drake Boulevard into the Park and stay to your right, turning onto Pierce Point Road.

At the intersection of Sir Francis Drake and Pierce Point Road, Bishop Pine and Douglas Fir forests dominate the landscape on the more exposed granitic basement rock. Farther north, there are several cattle and dairy farms along the road, taking advantage of the hilly grasslands. These areas represent a change in geology to Laird Sandstone, a medium- to coarse-grained rock of Middle Miocene origin (about 12 million years ago), deposited by the sea. Also visible is the Monterey Formation capped by Santa Margarita Sandstone. The Monterey Formation is made up of sandstone, chert, and organic shales, and the outcrops turn white when bleached by the Sun. These changes in lithology are represented by changes in vegetation.

Stop 6—Abbotts Lagoon (38°07′09″N, 122°57′04″W): Three and one-half miles from the Pierce Point Road intersection lies Abbotts Lagoon. From the dirt parking lot, a two-mile trail winds around a 200-acre brackish lagoon that is connected by a spillway to two freshwater ponds. Alternatively, a short, wheelchair-accessible trail leads to an overlook of the lagoon.

This is a submerged valley blocked by coastal dunes and beaches. A hilly escarpment of Monterey Formation capped by Santa Margarita Sandstone can be seen along the south side of lagoon (Figure FG2-6).

▲ **Figure FG2-6** Abbotts Lagoon at Stop 6. The cliff consists of Monterey Shale capped with Santa Margarita Sandstone. *(Barbara Holzman photo.)*

Beyond the ponds are green cattle pastures, endless huge drifting sand dunes, and the ocean. Keep a lookout for the abundant wildlife that inhabits the area, such as Grey Fox, Striped Skunk, Badger, Mule Deer, and a wide variety of bird species including California Quail and Northern Harrier. Herons and grebes can be seen in the ponds and lagoon, and Brown and White Pelicans are common closer to the ocean. It is rare to find both pelican species together, but Abbotts Lagoon and the ponds attract them.

Stop 7—Kehoe Beach (38°09'10"N, 122°56'21"W): About two miles north of Abbotts Lagoon is Kehoe Beach. Kehoe Beach provides an opportunity to see several geomorphic features. From the parking lot, a 1.5-mile trail along a freshwater marsh leads to the beach. Monterey Formation underlies the pasture lands of the area, and the formation is exposed in the cliffs on the beach. Further north, cliffs of Laird Sandstone meet Salinian granitic rocks. The sandstone formation and the granitic lower layer are visible from the beach. Sea stacks can be seen from the beach. The exposed rock is a mix of several types, including quartz diorite, schist, and gneiss among others. The cliffs are heavily fractured, displaying incidents of ancient and historic faulting. These rocks are highly erodible due to wave action and should not be climbed upon.

Stop 8 (rolling stop)—Tule Elk Reserve (38°10'50"N, 122°56'48"W): As you continue north along Pierce Point Road, about two miles from Kehoe Beach you will cross several cattle guards and enter the Tule Elk Reserve. Tule Elk (*Cervus elaphus*

nannodes) were reintroduced to Point Reyes National Seashore in 1978. They have grown from ten animals to over 550, making it one of the largest populations in California. There are two separate herds of Tule Elk at Point Reyes: A small group recently transferred to the southern grasslands, and this larger herd at Tomales Point, a 2,600-acre fenced reserve at the north end of the PRNS. The elk are easy to see from the road as they graze freely on the grassy hills of the reserve.

Stop 9—McClures Beach and Tomales Point (38°11'19"N, 122°57'28"W): Continue through the Elk Reserve to the end of the road and Upper Pierce Point Ranch. McClures Beach is reached by a 0.5-mile trail to the west. The Salinian basement rock discussed previously is well exposed at the beach. Towards the end of the trail, there is a clear demarcation between that ancient granite and the overlying dune deposits from the Quaternary Period (less than about 2.6 million years ago) that accumulated in what appears to have been a valley. These dunes are heavily eroded due to wave action from rising sea level that followed the last glaciation.

From upper Pierce Point Ranch, a four-mile trail (one way) leads to Tomales Point with great views of the granitic headlands on the Pacific side. The trail is very cold and windy in the winter, but the spring brings views of wildflowers as well as whales offshore.

There are other routes and many other geographic features to explore throughout Point Reyes. You are encouraged to come back to PRNS many times, in different seasons. Each time you are sure to discover something new and fascinating.

Additional Resources

Textbook:
Hess, Darrel. *McKnight's Physical Geography: A Landscape Appreciation*, 11th ed. Upper Saddle River, NJ: Pearson, 2014. Chapters 11, 14 and 20.

Further Reading:
Brown, M., and Barbara Holzman. *Point Reyes Peninsula and Vicinity Ecosystem Field Trip.* Online, 1997. http://online.sfsu.edu/bholzman/ptreyes/
Evens, Jules, G. *Natural History of the Point Reyes Peninsula.* Berkeley, CA: University of California Press, 2008.
McConnaughey, Bayard H., and Evelyn McConnaughey. *The Audubon Society Nature Guides:*

Pacific Coast. New York, New York: Alfred A. Knopf, Inc., 1985.
Stoffer, Phillip. "Geology at Point Reyes National Seashore and Vicinity, California: A Guide to San Andreas Fault Zone and the Point Reyes Peninsula," in *The San Andreas Fault in the San Francisco Bay Area, California: A Geology Fieldtrip Guidebook to Selected Stops on Public Lands.* U.S. Geological Survey: Open-File Report 2005-1127, 2005. Online. http://pubs.usgs.gov/of/2005/1127/chapter9.pdf
Whitnah, Dorothy L. *Point Reyes: A Guide to the Trails, Roads, Beaches, Campgrounds, Lakes Trees, Flowers, and Rocks of Point Reyes National Seashore.* Berkeley, CA: Wilderness Press, 1985.

Web Sites:
Golden Gate Transit Bus & Ferry Service
http://goldengatetransit.org/

West Marin Stagecoach
http://www.marintransit.org/stage.html

Point Reyes National Seashore
http://www.nps.gov/pore/

Textbook Page References for Key Terms

anticline *(p. 433)*

fault scarp *(p. 437)*

granite *(p. 381)*

marine terrace *(p. 592)*

syncline *(p. 433)*

strike-slip fault *(p. 435)*

transform boundary *(p. 413)*

wave-cut platform *(p. 591)*

Field Guide #3

The
San Andreas Fault

Darrel Hess, City College of San Francisco

Introduction

The San Andreas Fault is probably the world's most famous fault. It cuts through California for a distance of 800 miles (1,300 km), from the Gulf of California in the south to Cape Mendocino in the north. It has generated many large earthquakes, including the 1906 San Francisco and 1989 Loma Prieta Earthquakes. Movement along the San Andreas and related faults continues to shape the topography of coastal California—and rattle the nerves of Californians. This field guide describes six locations along the San Andreas Fault where its features may easily be seen.

Location

The six sites in this field guide will likely be visited at different times, although Sites 1 and 2—the Point Reyes Peninsula and the San Francisco Peninsula—in the northern part of the state may be visited in one day. Sites 4, 5 and 6—Tejon Pass, Palmdale and Cajon Pass—in the southern part of the state, although spread over a distance of about 100 miles (160 km), may also be visited within one day. Site 3 in the southern Coast Range's Carrizo Plain National Monument deserves special mention. It is the most remote—although perhaps most interesting—location described in this field guide. There are few services in the vicinity, so be sure top off your gas tank and fill up your water bottles before leaving the major freeways for the Carrizo Plain.

Background

Plate Tectonics and the San Andreas Fault: Although the San Andreas Fault is sometimes called the "plate boundary" between the North American Plate and the Pacific Plate (see textbook Figure 14-18), this is somewhat simplistic. The San Andreas Fault itself is the most important component of this **transform plate boundary** that includes many other faults in the San Andreas system such as the Hayward and Calaveras Faults in northern California, and the San Jacinto and Elsinore Faults in southern California. Overall, about 60% of the 2.2 inches (5.6 cm) per year of relative motion between the North American and Pacific Plates is released along the San Andreas Fault. Most of this plate motion is released during fault rupture events that unload many decades of accumulated strain in a matter of seconds—and generate large earthquakes as a result.

The San Andreas Fault is a **strike-slip fault** (see textbook Figure 14-58), so the predominant displacement is lateral (although a slight amount of "dip-slip" or vertical displacement is not uncommon as well). The San Andreas, and nearly all of the other mostly parallel faults in the system, are *right-lateral strike-slip faults*—this means that looking across the fault, the displacement of features on the other side is to the right. (The Garlock Fault, which splinters off of the San Andreas near Site 4 at Tejon Pass, is an example of a left-lateral strike-slip fault.)

Origin: The origin of the San Andreas Fault is associated with a significant change in the plate boundary along the west coast of North America beginning about 30 million years ago. For many tens of millions of years before that time, a **mid-ocean ridge** was present to the west of what is today California. Out of this spreading center, the ancestral Pacific Plate moved to the northwest (as it continues to do today) while a southeast-moving oceanic plate, called the Farallon Plate, subducted beneath the west-moving North American Plate. Much of the magma generated in this **subduction zone** cooled below the surface to form the granites of the Sierra Nevada batholith (see *Field Guide #4—Sierra Nevada via Tioga Pass*).

By about 30 million years ago, the Farallon Plate was almost entirely "consumed" by subduction, and the North American Plate began to override the midocean ridge to the west. At that point, a transform boundary developed between the North American Plate and the Pacific Plate, forming the ancestral San Andreas Fault (Figure FG3-1). By 20 million years ago, the San Andreas Fault was growing in length as the two "triple junctions" between the North American Plate, Pacific Plate, and the old Farallon Plate migrated north and south.

Today, remnants of the Farallon Plate are still subducting beneath the North American Plate: North of the Mendocino Triple Junction, subduction of the Juan de Fuca and Gorda Plates is associated with the Cascade volcanoes; south of the Rivera Triple Junction near Baja, subduction of the Cocos Plate is associated with the volcanoes of central Mexico.

Earthquakes: Most of the relative motion between the Pacific Plate and the North American Plate is released episodically through abrupt fault ruptures along the San Andreas Fault system—each time, the Pacific Plate side of the fault system (which includes Los Angeles, Monterey Bay and Point Reyes) jumps a little closer to the subduction zone of the Aleutian Islands. In a very simplistic sense, the size of an earthquake is determined by the length of fault rupture and amount of offset, which in turn are generally related to how many years that fault segment remained "locked" and strain accumulated before the rupture.

In the last 150 years or so, there have been two "great" earthquakes along the San Andreas Fault. The January 9, 1857, Great Fort Tejon Earthquake was a rupture of the southern section of the San Andreas Fault—from roughly Parkfield in the north to Cajon Pass in the south—a distance of more than 200 miles (320 km), with a maximum offset of about 30 feet (9.5 m) in the area of the Carrizo Plain. The April 18, 1906, San Francisco Earthquake was a rup-

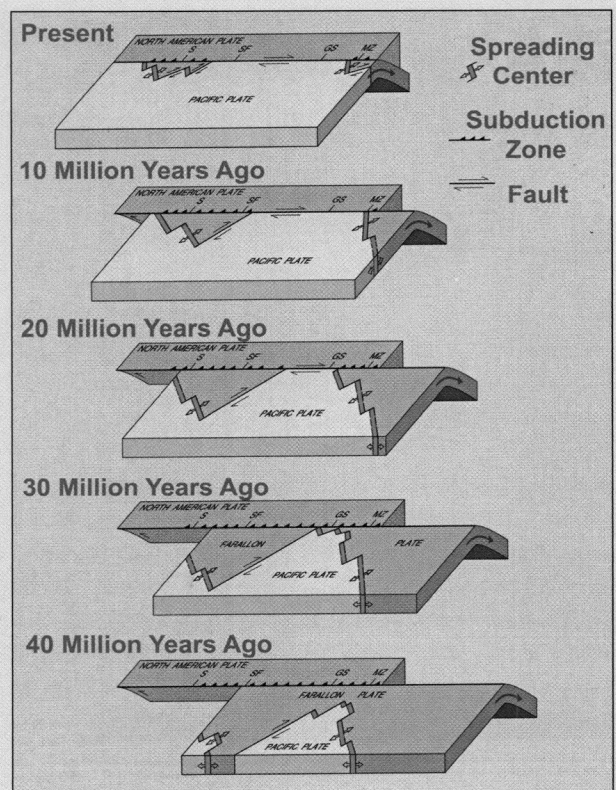

▲ **Figure FG3-1** Development of the San Andreas Fault system as the North American Plate overrode the spreading center of the Pacific and Farallon Plates. *(Adapted from U.S. Geological Survey Professional Paper 1515.)*

ture of the northern segment of the fault—from Cape Mendocino in the north to San Juan Bautista in the south—a distance of about 270 miles (430 km), with a maximum observed offset of about 20 feet (6 m) in the area of Point Reyes. Both earthquakes had **magnitudes** of about 8 (roughly one magnitude, or 32 times larger, than the 1989 Loma Prieta and 1994 Northridge earthquakes). Contemporary estimates put the *moment magnitude* of the 1857 earthquake at 7.8 and the 1906 earthquake at 7.7.

Topographic Features: The location of a strike-slip fault such as the San Andreas Fault is often revealed by linear features in the landscape (see textbook Figure 14-62). For example, the surface location of a strike-slip fault is often marked by a narrow *linear fault trough* or valley that forms in the zone of crushed rock along the fault plane. In some places—such as along the San Francisco Peninsula and the Point Reyes Peninsula (Sites 1 and 2 described below)—a wide fault zone is present. In such places multiple breaks of the fault are found, and a wide valley—in some cases more than a half-mile across—has developed.

Where small depressions form in the fault zone, sags or **sag ponds** may be formed. Linear ridges and *fault scarps* may develop parallel to the fault from either compression or slight vertical displacement. A hill may be displaced by fault movement to close off a valley with a *shutter ridge*. Perhaps the most conspicuous feature formed by a strike-slip fault is an **offset stream,** formed when repeated movement along the fault displaces the course of a stream flowing across it.

Site Descriptions

Unlike the site descriptions found in most of the other field guides in this collection, the six sites for the San Andreas Fault are separated by great distances. The following sites are described from north to south in the state, and they may be visited in any order. Each site includes two or more local stops (or "rolling stops" where features may be observed from the road).

Site 1—Point Reyes Peninsula

It was in the vicinity of the Point Reyes Peninsula—especially within the Olema Valley—that the significance of the San Andreas Fault to the 1906 San Francisco earthquake was realized and studied extensively. Because much of the region is part of the Point Reyes National Seashore, large areas within the fault zone remain undeveloped, and so many fault features can be easily observed here.

There are a number of ways to reach the Point Reyes National Seashore (Figure FG3-2). If traveling north from San Francisco on U.S. 101, after crossing the Golden Gate Bridge take the Stinson Beach exit just past Sausalito and follow California Highway 1 for sixteen winding, but very scenic, miles to Stinson Beach. Alternatively, you can take Sir Francis Drake Boulevard the 21 miles from U.S. 101 at San Rafael to the town of Olema. Parts of the Point Reyes National Seashore may also be reached by public transportation with Golden Gate Transit and West Marin Stagecoach—see *Additional Resources* on F-28.

The stops described below take you from Stinson Beach in the south, to Tomales Bay in the north.

Stop 1—Stinson Beach (37°53'48"N, 122°38'26"W): From one of the roadside turnouts on Highway 1 just above the town of Stinson Beach, or from the beach parking area (where there are public restrooms), you can observe the San Andreas Fault zone where it comes onshore after leaving land at Mussel Rock south of San Francisco. Bolinas Lagoon itself formed in the zone of crushed rock along the fault.

Stinson Beach is a **spit** (see textbook Figure 20-18) that nearly closes off the lagoon from Bolinas Bay. The 1906 trace of the San Andreas Fault cuts through the spit near its western end (Figure FG3-3), although all evidence of the rupture quickly disappeared.

Traveling north from Stinson Beach on Highway 1, for the next 4.5 miles you drive along Bolinas Lagoon. The main trace of the San Andreas Fault runs along, or just offshore of, the western side of the lagoon. North of Bolinas Lagoon you enter the Olema Valley—a linear trough produced by repeated displacement along the San Andreas Fault.

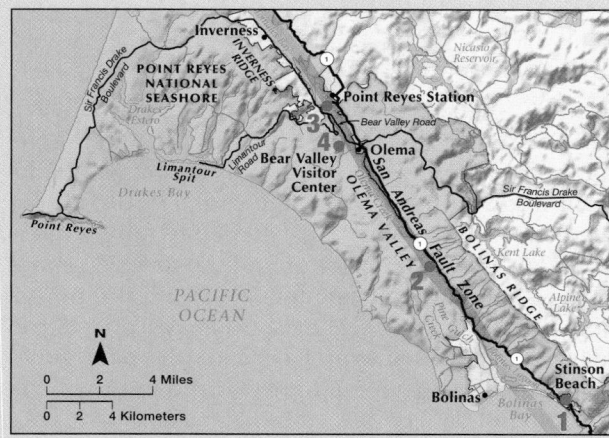

▲ **Figure FG3-2** Regional map of the Point Reyes Peninsula, showing Site 1 field guide stops.

▲ **Figure FG3-3** View northwest across Bolinas Bay showing Stinson Beach and the location of the San Andreas Fault (SAF) at Site 1, Stop 1. *(Darrel Hess photo.)*

Although little direct evidence of the 1906 rupture remains, traveling through Olema Valley toward Point Reyes Station you can see many examples of shutter ridges, fault scarps and seasonal sag ponds. Use caution when driving or cycling along the highway here—the road is narrow and twisting.

Stop 2 (rolling stop)—Olema Valley

(37°58'37"N, 122°44'01"W): About 7.5 miles north of Stinson Beach, you pass a prominent linear ridge running down the middle of the valley. Drainage patterns in the fault zone have been so disrupted that Olema Creek, which runs next to the highway, flows to the north, while Pine Gulch Creek only 1,200 feet (165 m) away on the other side of the ridge flows to the south.

Stop 3 (rolling stop)—1906 Road Offset Location (38°03'47"N, 122°48'45"W):

About fifteen miles north of Stinson Beach, you pass through the town of Olema. Two miles beyond Olema at Point Reyes Station, turn left (west) onto Sir Francis Drake Boulevard. About 0.3 miles down this stretch of road you'll pass over the fault where the maximum offset of 20 feet (6 m) from the 1906 earthquake was observed (the road has since been repaired). To your right (north) is Tomales Bay—a flooded portion of the San Andreas Fault zone.

Continue a short distance to Bear Valley Road and turn left (south).

Stop 4—Bear Valley Visitor Center and Earthquake Trail (38°02'29"N, 122°48'01"W): About two miles south of Sir Francis Drake Boulevard, turn right onto the road leading to the Bear Valley Visitor Center of the Point Reyes National Seashore. At the Visitor Center you can see natural history displays and purchase maps and other publications.

A short distance south of the Visitor Center is a sign directing you to the Earthquake Trail. This short, wheelchair-accessible, self-guided interpretive trail takes you past the location where a fence was offset by 18 feet (5.5 m) during the 1906 earthquake (38°02'28"N, 122°47'46"W). The fence has since been reconstructed, but a series of blue posts clearly marks the location of the 1906 surface rupture along the fault scarp here.

From the Bear Valley Visitor Center, you can expand your exploration of the Point Reyes area with *Field Guide #2—Point Reyes National Seashore.*

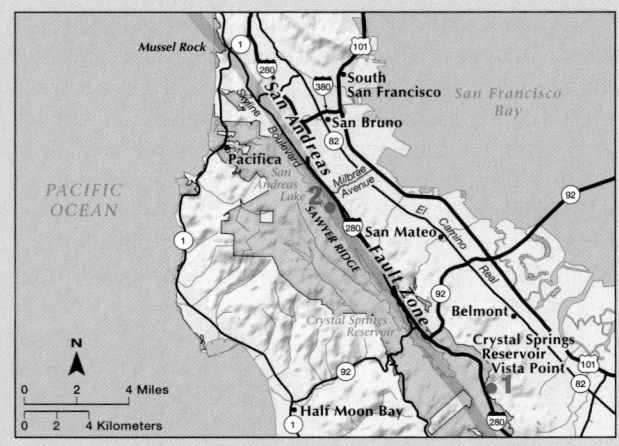

▲ **Figure FG3-4**   Regional map of the San Francisco Peninsula, showing Site 2 field guide stops.

Site 2—San Francisco Peninsula

Along the peninsula south of San Francisco the San Andreas Fault has produced one of its largest and most prominent features anywhere in the state: a wide, linear fault trough, made all the more obvious by the presence of two long reservoirs that flood portions of this valley (Figure FG3-4). The fault valley of the San Andreas is so large here that it may be difficult to recognize from ground level—but it is often easily seen from the air by passengers flying in or out of San Francisco International Airport.

It is along the San Francisco Peninsula, too, that the San Andreas Fault passes closest to a major metropolitan area. Over the last century, housing development, transportation networks and urban water delivery projects have all expanded within, or adjacent to, the fault zone.

Stop 1—Crystal Springs Reservoir Vista Point (37°28'42"N, 122°17'50"W): Interstate 280 runs along or within the fault zone of the San Andreas from roughly Woodside in the south, to South San Francisco in the north. A convenient vantage point to observe the fault zone is the Vista Point off northbound Interstate 280 about three miles south of the Interstate 280/California 92 junction (if you're traveling southbound on I-280, to reach this Vista Point you'll need to drive a few miles south to the Edgewood Road exit and return northbound on I-280).

The broad fault zone of the San Andreas is clearly seen here. Sawyer Ridge (on the far side of the reservoir) runs parallel to both the San Andreas Fault and the Pilarcitos Fault (on the western side of Sawyer Ridge). Looking across the fault zone at Sawyer Ridge, notice that many of the stream valleys have had their courses deflected slightly to the south by periodic fault movement.

The earliest development of Crystal Springs Reservoir area dates back to the 1860s when the Spring Valley Water Company began delivering water from the watersheds here to San Francisco. The dam at the south end of the reservoir was first constructed in 1888, but was enlarged in 1890 and 1911 to its present height of 149 feet. By 1934 both Crystal Springs Reservoir and San Andreas Lake farther north, had been incorporated into San Francisco's Hetch Hetchy Aqueduct water delivery system (see *Field Guide #4—Sierra Nevada via Tioga Pass* for additional information). The 1906 rupture of the San Andreas Fault ran though the reservoir close to the far (western) shore, but didn't damage the dam itself.

A causeway for California Highway 92 separates Crystal Springs into Lower and Upper reservoirs. The 1906 earthquake offset the original road embankment there by 8 feet (2.4 m), but the dam at Lower Crystal Springs was undamaged.

Stop 2—San Andreas Lake (37°34′49″N, 122°24′39″W):
Traveling north on Interstate 280, drive about 6.8 miles north of the I-280/CA-92 junction, then take the Millbrae Avenue/Hillcrest Boulevard exit. Continue straight for 0.3 miles, and then turn left on Hillcrest Boulevard. (If you're traveling southbound on I-280, take the Hillcrest Boulevard exit and turn left at the bottom of the offramp.) You may park below the freeway. Just to the west is the trailhead for the Sawyer Camp Trail along San Andreas Lake, and if you have time to visit only one place along the San Francisco Peninsula, this is a good choice.

From the fenced area at the trailhead (37°35′19″N, 122°24′47″W), walk south along the paved but moderately steep and twisting Sawyer Camp Trail for about one mile until you reach the dam at the southeast end of San Andreas Lake.

The San Andreas Fault was named after this lake in 1895 by geologist Andrew C. Lawson, who recognized the fault in the San Francisco Peninsula— although the full extent of the fault was not realized until after the 1906 earthquake. Originally a large sag pond in the fault zone, San Andreas Lake was enlarged in 1868 with a dam. During the 1906 earthquake, the dam was damaged but did not fail. The trace of the 1906 rupture was through the eastern

▲ **Figure FG3-5** View northwest across San Andreas Lake showing the location of the San Andreas Fault (SAF) at Site 2, Stop 2. *(Darrel Hess photo.)*

side of the dam (where it is marked with a stone monument) and along the eastern shore of the lake (Figure FG3-5). From near the center of the dam, you can look south and see Upper Crystal Springs Reservoir. The wooded valley below the dam is typical of the wide and remarkably straight fault zone in this area.

After leaving San Andreas Lake, if you continue north on Interstate 280 and then on Skyline Boulevard toward Pacifica, for the next few miles you're traveling in or next to the San Andreas Fault zone. The **epicenter** of the 1906 earthquake was offshore of San Francisco, a few miles northeast of Mussel Rock—the San Andreas Fault actually never crosses San Francisco itself.

Site 3—Carrizo Plain

The Carrizo Plain is the most dramatic place in California to see features of the San Andreas Fault. Here the fault has a fairly simple configuration: Rather than a wide fault zone, in many places the fault here has a single active trace with a clear topographic expression that is easily recognized from ground level. Although it isn't possible to straddle the San Andreas Fault and really have one foot on the North American Plate and one foot on the Pacific Plate, the Carrizo Plain comes closest to letting you do that. Since the Carrizo Plain is undeveloped and fairly dry, many subtle strike-slip fault features are visible here that are obscured in urbanized regions or in areas with denser vegetation.

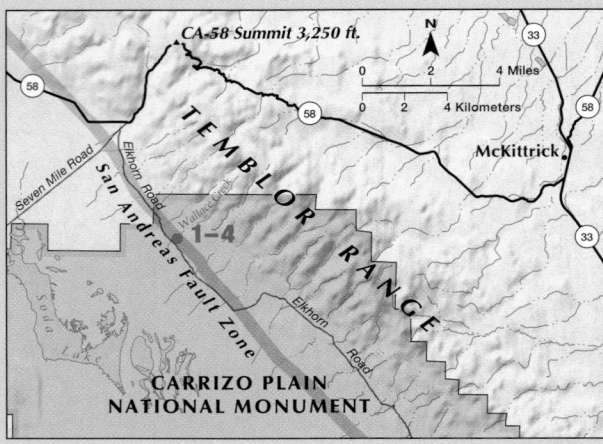

▲ **Figure FG3-6**   Regional map of the Carrizo Plain, showing Site 3 field guide stops.

▲ **Figure FG3-7**   View southeast across Wallace Creek, showing the location of the San Andreas Fault (SAF) at Site 3, Stop 1. *(Darrel Hess photo.)*

To reach Carrizo Plain National Monument, travel west on California Highway 58 from Interstate 5 at Buttonwillow, through the town of McKittrick and its surrounding oil fields, and over the Temblor Range on a steep and windy road to the Carrizo Plain (Figure FG3-6). About 35 miles west of Interstate 5 (about 55 miles east of Santa Margarita if you're coming from U.S. 101) you'll come to the foot of the Temblor Range where Highway 58 turns sharply to the west (to the right, if you're coming from I-5). At the bend in the highway continue straight, leaving Highway 58 and going on to Seven Mile Road. After 0.3 miles turn left (southwest) onto Elkhorn Road.

Elkhorn Road is a graded dirt road that is easily driven with ordinary passenger vehicles in dry weather but becomes impassible during rainy weather (in some cases even to four-wheel drive vehicles). The road follows the foot of the Temblor Range, and in places runs exactly along the trace of the fault. From Seven Mile Road, proceed for 4.2 miles along Elkhorn Road until you see a sign and small parking area for Wallace Creek. The "walking" stops at Wallace Creek are visited on a round-trip hike of about three miles. Wear sturdy shoes and be alert to the possibility that you might surprise a rattlesnake.

Stop 1—Wallace Creek (35°16′16″N, 119°49′38″W): A hike of about one-quarter mile along a well-worn dirt trail takes you up the hillside to an overlook of Wallace Creek—probably the most famous (and most studied) offset stream in the world (Figure FG3-7).

Named for the U.S. Geological Survey geologist Robert E. Wallace, who spent decades studying the San Andreas Fault in this area, Wallace Creek is an **ephemeral stream** that has been offset 430 feet (130 m) by movement along the San Andreas Fault. Wallace and others determined that this offset occurred over a period of approximately 3,700 years, meaning that the average long-term rate of displacement along the fault in this area is about 1.4 inches (34 mm) per year. However, movement along this part of the San Andreas Fault occurs only intermittently: When the fault ruptures, it produces many feet of offset as decades of accumulated stress is suddenly released during an earthquake.

The last major earthquake along this segment of the San Andreas Fault was the 1857 Great Fort Tejon Earthquake. Lateral offset of about 31 feet (9.5 m) from this earthquake was measured here on the Carrizo Plain.

There is a short self-guiding nature trail at Wallace Creek with several signs pointing out features of the fault. Visit the five "Posts" along the trail in the area of Wallace Creek. As you walk along the trail south of Wallace Creek, notice the steep scarp produced by vertical displacement along the fault. Notice also that there are many small gullies that run down this scarp that stop abruptly at the bottom. If you look carefully, you may be able to find the offset continuations of some of these gully channels below the fault (for example, at Post 4; 35°16′09″N, 119°49′30″W).

If you do match the gullies on the scarp with their offset continuations, you'll see that the smallest amount of displacement for any of these offset streams is about 30 feet. This suggests that there hasn't been any movement along this part of the

San Andreas since the 1857 earthquake. In fact, most channels you see here (and those farther south along the fault trace) have been offset for distances that are roughly multiples of 30 feet—suggesting that this part of the San Andreas tends to produce fault rupture displacements of about the same length each time.

Once you reach Post 5, if you're up for a longer walk, continue south along the fault for another mile or so. There is no trail, but it's easy to find the way. Do, however, watch your step on the uneven ground.

Stop 2 (walking stop)—Shutter Ridge

(35°15'45"N, 119°49'06"W): About 0.8 miles south of Wallace Creek, you come to a long, low shutter ridge, with deposits of alluvium dammed behind it. A short distance farther, you come to a prominent "beheaded" stream channel, cutoff by displacement along the fault (35°15'40"N, 119°48'59"W).

Stop 3 (walking stop)—Offset Streams

(35°15'33"N, 119°48'53"W): A short distance beyond the beheaded stream, you cross two prominent offset ephemeral stream channels. The second one (the larger of the two) is offset about 65 feet (20 m)—the total offset of this stream is a combination of displacement from the Great Fort Tejon Earthquake and the prehistoric large earthquake that preceded it.

Stop 4 (walking stop)—Sag (35°15'25"N, 119°48'45"W): Finally, about 1.5 miles south of Wallace Creek, you come to a "sag" along the fault trace. Here the surface probably dropped down between to parallel segments of the fault, forming a miniature version of what is known as a *pull-apart basin* (see Figure FG9-2 in *Field Guide #9—Death Valley* for a diagram showing how pull-apart basins form). In wet years, a temporary sag pond forms in this depression.

Site 4—Tejon Pass

Tejon Pass is one of the few places in California where the San Andreas Fault is easily seen along a commonly-traveled major freeway (Figure FG3-8). At the southwestern end of the Tehachapi Mountains, Tejon Pass is located along what is called the "Big Bend" segment of the San Andreas Fault.

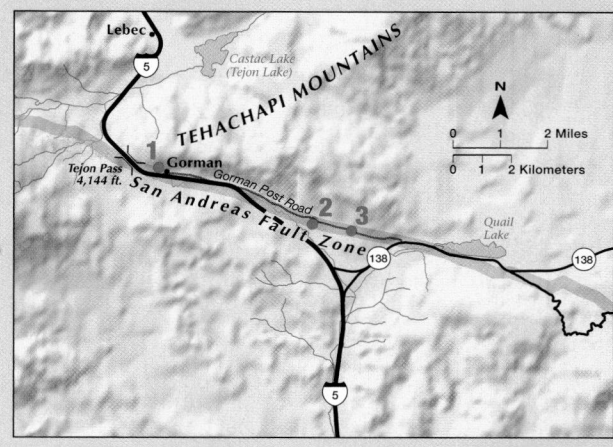

▲ **Figure FG3-8**   Regional map of Tejon Pass, showing Site 4 field guide stops.

In this part of the state the fault takes a decidedly east-west turn, deviating from its generally northwest-southeasterly trend south and north of here. In the most basic sense, the uplift of the Transverse Ranges (such as the San Gabriel Mountains and San Bernardino Mountains) is a result of compression along this bend where southern California southwest of the fault converges into the land northeast of the fault. The last major fault rupture here occurred during the Great Fort Tejon Earthquake of 1857.

Tejon Pass is reached on Interstate 5, just south of the "Grapevine" section of the freeway where it climbs steeply out of the Central Valley into the mountains; snow occasionally closes the freeway in winter. The San Andreas Fault crosses Interstate 5 almost exactly at the small freeway sign marking Tejon Pass (4,144 feet; 1,263 m), but there is no safe place to pull off the freeway and little to see here. Whether you are traveling north or south on I-5, take the Gorman exit (about 1.5 miles south of Tejon Pass) and drive north one block to the cluster of gas stations and other buildings along the Gorman Post Road (if you've been traveling northbound on I-5, turn right after exiting the freeway; if you've been traveling southbound, turn left and drive under the freeway).

Stop 1—Gorman (34°47'49"N, 118°51'46"W):

Turn left on Gorman Post Road and drive northwest until it dead-ends in a turnaround about 0.6 miles from the freeway exit. Look back toward the tiny town of Gorman. The steep hillside here (with the water tank that says "Gorman") is a scarp produced by the San Andreas Fault (Figure FG3-9). In the distance, about four miles to the southeast,

▲ **Figure FG3-9**   View southeast to Gorman and Interstate 5 near Tejon Pass, showing the location of the San Andreas Fault (SAF) at Site 4, Stop 1. *(Darrel Hess photo.)*

▲ **Figure FG3-10**   Regional map of Palmdale, showing Site 5 field guide stops.

you see a notch in the mountains where Gorman Post Road and Interstate 5 begin to run parallel to each other toward you—both are following the trace of the San Andreas Fault.

Stop 2 (rolling stop)—Sag Ponds

(34°46'57"N, 118°48'24"W): Retrace your path to the southeast along Gorman Post Road, continuing past the Gorman freeway exit. For the next few miles, Gorman Post Road parallels the freeway, running along the path of the San Andreas Fault. About 2.6 miles from Gorman you pass a small sag pond, and 0.2 miles beyond this, you come to a much larger sag pond.

Stop 3—Fault Valley (34°46'44"N, 118° 47'32"W): Continuing 0.9 miles from the large sag pond (3.7 miles from the Gorman freeway exit) is a turnout on the left (north) side of the road where you can park. From this parking area, walk a short distance north to the top of the small rise and look back in the direction of Gorman. The San Andreas Fault runs through the valley below toward you, marked roughly by the series of "notches" in the hills in the distance.

From here you can return to Gorman and Interstate 5. If you continue east, Gorman Post Road soon merges with California Highway 138 (one of the ways to reach *Site 5—Palmdale*), which in turn passes Quail Lake—one of the reservoirs in the State Water Project (see *Field Guide #13*)—impounded in the fault trough of the San Andreas and a likely location of an old natural sag pond.

Site 5—Palmdale

The city of Palmdale is located at the northern foot of the San Gabriel Mountains at the edge of the Mojave Desert, about 60 miles (95 km) north of downtown Los Angeles (Figure FG3-10). Palmdale is a great place to see major topographic features of the San Andreas Fault, and it has a spectacular road-cut exposing severely deformed rocks in the fault zone.

To reach Palmdale, travel north on California Highway 14 (the Antelope Valley Freeway) from San Fernando, or south from the nearby desert city of Lancaster. A good first stop is the Lamont Odett Vista Point, about one mile south of Palmdale (about two miles north of Soledad Pass) along Highway 14. The Vista Point can be reached only when traveling northbound on Highway 14; if traveling southbound from Lancaster you'll need to drive past the Vista Point on the other side of the freeway, then travel several miles to an exit where you can return on the freeway toward Palmdale.

Stop 1—Lamont Odett Vista Point

(34°32'27"N, 118°07'22"W): The Lamont Odett Vista Point offers a panoramic view of Palmdale, the California Aqueduct, and the fault zone below you. The lake you see is Lake Palmdale—an old sag pond that has been extensively modified for human use. The active trace of the San Andreas Fault runs just along the northern (far) shore of the lake. Extending both northwest and southeast (to the right and left) of Lake Palmdale—and generally aligned with the north shore of the lake—is a low, linear ridge. This ridge is the fault scarp of the San Andreas. Just west (left) of the lake, where the freeway cuts through this ridge, is your next stop.

Stop 2—Roadcut in California Highway 14 (34°33'29"N, 118°08'03"W): Continue north from the Vista Point on Highway 14 for 1.2 miles to the Avenue S exit in Palmdale. Turn left (west) on Avenue S, driving under the freeway, and then park in a dirt pullout just west of the freeway. Walk up the hill west of the freeway about one-quarter mile, for a view of perhaps the most famous roadcut in California (Figure FG3-11).

The short, steep slope you first encounter when walking to the top of the roadcut is the fault scarp of the San Andreas. When you reach the middle of the roadcut (34°33'45"N, 118°08'00"W), you have a great view across Highway 14 to the east wall of the roadcut. Most of the exposure consists of interbedded layers of sandstone and shale, severely folded by compression in the San Andreas Fault zone. Although you can see a number of minor faults in the roadcut, the main trace of the San Andreas itself is at the far southern end of the roadcut—at the steep scarp at the end of the roadcut.

Use caution when walking along the roadcut and don't stand too close to its edge. The slope of the roadcut is somewhat unstable, especially beyond the halfway point.

Site 6—Cajon Pass

Cajon Pass is a major gap in the Transverse Ranges between the San Gabriel and San Bernardino Mountains, and is a good location to see features associated with the San Andreas Fault (Figure FG3-12).

From the San Bernardino area, take either Interstate 15 or 215 north toward Cajon Pass. The San Andreas Fault crosses I-15 about four miles north of the I-15/I-215 junction—where the topography opens dramatically into the "Cajon amphitheater" and Lone Pine Canyon to the northwest. There isn't a safe place to pull off the freeway, so continue to the Cleghorn Road exit (about one mile south of the I-15/CA-138 junction). Turn left (west) and then immediately left again (south) onto Cajon Boulevard (an old stretch of Route 66); after 1.8 miles turn right onto Swarthout Canyon Road, following the road for about a mile—over a creek, past roadcuts exposing steeply tilted and deformed rock layers, over two sets of railroad tracks (beyond which the pavement ends), and then up Lone Pine Canyon to the

▲ **Figure FG3-11**   View southeast across California Highway 14 in Palmdale, showing the location of the San Andreas Fault (SAF) at Site 5, Stop 2. *(Darrel Hess photo.)*

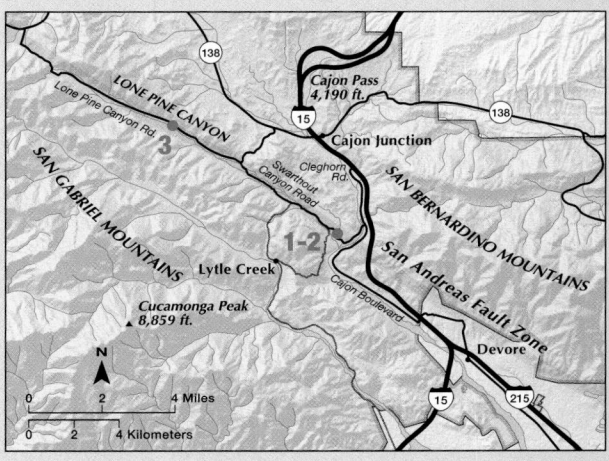

▲ **Figure FG3-12**   Regional map of Cajon Pass, showing Site 6 field guide stops.

parking area to the right for Lost Lake. Swarthout Canyon Road here is a steep, graded dirt road that is drivable with normal-clearance passenger vehicles in dry weather, but may be impassible after heavy rain.

Stop 1—Lost Lake (34°16'20"N, 117°27'57"W): To park at Lost Lake, you need to pay a nominal fee for a Forest Adventure Pass available at most gas stations at the I-15/CA-138 junction, or online through the U.S. Forest Service (see *Additional Resources* below). A short hike from the parking area takes you to Lost Lake—a sag pond along the San Andreas Fault (Figure FG3-13). The active trace of the fault runs along the southwest side of Lost Lake, close to where you're standing.

Figure FG3-13 View north across Lost Lake near Cajon Pass, showing the location of the San Andreas Fault (SAF) at Site 6, Stop 1. *(Darrel Hess photo.)*

is the Pelona Schist, formed through the metamorphism of sedimentary rock. Notice that many of these rocks are slightly rounded, having been brought down Lone Pine Canyon by periodic flash-floods.

Stop 3 (rolling stop)—Lone Pine Canyon (34°18'05"N, 117°30'41"W): From Lost Lake continue driving up Swarthout Canyon Road for 3.5 miles, then turn left (northwest) off the dirt road onto Lone Pine Canyon Road. The nearly straight path of Lone Pine Canyon here is controlled by the San Andreas Fault. The active trace of the fault runs along the foot of the hills to your left (along the southwest side of the canyon) where you can see examples of deflected drainage channels. After driving up the canyon for about a mile, pull over and look back down Lone Pine Canyon—you can trace the path of the fault across Interstate 15 and through a notch in the San Bernardino Mountains in the distance.

To return to I-15, reverse direction but stay on Lone Pine Canyon Road where it turns northeast away from the fault. When you reach the steeply tilted sandstone "Mormon Rocks," turn right on to California 138; I-15 is about 1.3 miles to the southeast.

Stop 2 (walking stop)—Offset Stream (34°16'16"N, 117°27'47"W): Follow one of the informal trails southeast from the lake to a dirt road that goes past a large power line tower about 0.2 miles from Lost Lake. Just southeast of the tower is a vantage point where you can look down at a prominent offset stream. This deeply incised ephemeral creek has been offset by about 600 feet (180 m) by movement along the fault. On the ground around you are many shiny foliated rocks—this rock

Additional Resources

Textbook:

Hess, Darrel. *McKnight's Physical Geography: A Landscape Appreciation*, 11th ed. Upper Saddle River, NJ: Pearson, 2014. Chapter 14.

Further Reading:

Hough, Susan Elizabeth. *Finding Fault in California: An Earthquake Tourist's Guide*. Missoula: Mountain Press Publishing Company, 2004.

Wallace, Robert E., editor. *The San Andreas Fault System, California*. U.S. Geological Survey Professional Paper 1515. Washington, D.C.: U.S. Government Printing Office, 1990.

Web Sites:

Carrizo Plain National Monument
http://www.blm.gov/ca/st/en/fo/bakersfield/Programs/carrizo.html

Golden Gate Transit Bus & Ferry Service
http://goldengatetransit.org/

Point Reyes National Seashore
http://www.nps.gov/pore/

San Bernardino National Forest Adventure Pass Information
http://www.fs.fed.us/r5/sanbernadino/ap/welcome.shtml

West Marin Stagecoach
http://www.marintransit.org/stage.html

U.S. Geological Survey, Recent California Earthquakes
http://quake.usgs.gov/recenteqs/

Textbook Page References for Key Terms

ephemeral stream *(p. 518)*
epicenter *(p. 438)*
magnitude (of an earthquake)
    (p. 439)

midocean ridge *(p. 408)*
offset stream *(p. 438)*
sag pond *(p. 438)*
spit *(p. 586)*

strike-slip fault *(p. 435)*
subduction zone (subduction)
    (p. 410)
transform plate boundary *(p. 413)*

Field Guide #4

Sierra Nevada via Tioga Pass

Darrel Hess, City College of San Francisco

Introduction

The Sierra Nevada is one of the most stunning mountain ranges in North America. Four hundred miles (650 km) long from north to south, it rises from near sea level along its foothills at the Central Valley to an elevation of over 14,000 feet (4,300 m) at its crest less than 70 miles (110 km) to the east. Travelers crossing the Sierra see dramatic examples of the work of faulting, volcanoes, streams, and glaciers, and pass through a wide range of habitats that include oak savanna, montane forest, subalpine forest, piñon-juniper woodland and sagebrush scrub.

This field guide highlights features you can see traveling across the Sierra along California Highway 120 from the foothills at the edge of the Central Valley, across the high country of Yosemite National Park to Tioga Pass, and down into the Mono Lake basin.

Location

If you're traveling out of the Central Valley, take California Highway 120 east from California Highway 99 near the town of Manteca. The highway winds through the communities of Escalon and Oakdale before climbing up into the foothills of the Sierra along the south bank of the Stanislaus River (Figure FG4-1). If you're traveling from Mono Lake, take California 120 west toward Tioga Pass from U.S. Highway 395 at the town of Lee Vining.

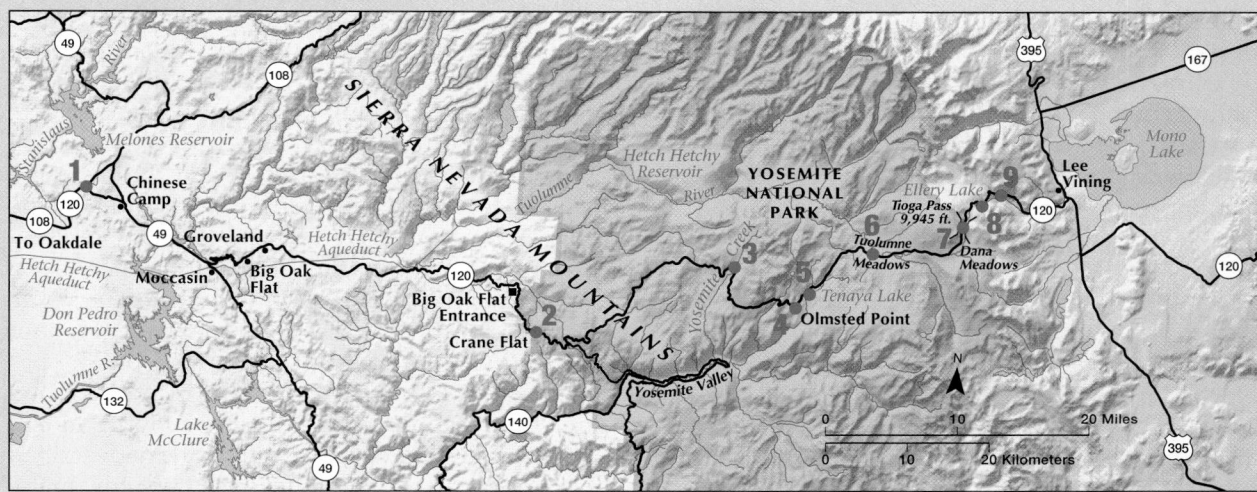

▲ **Figure FG4-1** Regional map of Sierra Nevada showing California Highway 120 and field guide stops.

Gasoline and supplies are available in most towns in the Central Valley's western foothills and in Lee Vining; however, facilities are limited once you enter Yosemite National Park and begin your drive along the 59-mile (95-km) "Tioga Pass Road" portion of the highway. At the western side of the Park, gasoline is available in Crane Flat (about eight miles east of the Big Oak Flat Entrance to Yosemite National Park), and at Tuolumne Meadows, but nowhere else along the Tioga Pass Road. The speed limit through much of the Park is 45 mph—but lower in areas with many pedestrians.

During the summer, bus service is available from Yosemite Valley to Tuolumne Meadows and Lee Vining via the Tioga Pass Road with the Yosemite Area Regional Transportation System—see *Additional Resources* on F-36.

Most of the Forest Service campgrounds outside the Park do not take reservations, but if you arrive early, especially in the middle of the week, you should be able to find a campsite. However, reservations are recommended if you want to stay in the Park at either the Crane Flat or Tuolumne Meadows campgrounds.

A number of exhibits, campgrounds and trails within Yosemite National Park are wheelchair accessible—see the Park Web site on F-36 for details.

Although Yosemite National Park remains open all year, the Tioga Pass Road usually closes with the first heavy snow of the season, and doesn't open again until summer (typically by early June, but in some heavy snow years the pass remains closed until late June).

Summer temperatures are likely to be hot in the Central Valley (often over 100°F [38°C]), but mild in the high country. However, because of the high elevations (Tioga Pass is at 9,945 feet [3,030 m]), nighttime temperatures can drop below freezing any time of year. In late summer, be aware of thunderstorms when hiking in exposed high country areas, especially above the timberline. Because of the thinner atmosphere, in higher elevations everyone should take precautions against sunburn by wearing a hat and applying sun cream.

Background

Geologic History: The geologic history of the Sierra Nevada is complex, but the long-held view goes something like this: About 200 million years ago—around the time that the supercontinent of *Pangaea* was beginning to break apart—the plate boundary of western North America was quite different from today. Rather than the **transform boundary** of the San Andreas Fault system, a **midocean ridge** was west of the continent, and an oceanic plate (called the Farallon Plate) was subducting beneath the west coast of ancestral North America (see textbook Figure 14-8). The coastline, however, was much farther east than it is now, perhaps near the location of the present foothills of the Sierra. Magma generated in this subduction zone rose to form a series of volcanoes, much like the present-day Cascade Range north of the Sierra (see *Field Guide #1—The California Cascades*). Much of this magma, however, cooled deep below the surface, forming the plutonic rocks such as granite (see textbook Figure 13-6) that we see exposed in the Sierra today. By about 80 million years ago the intrusion of granitic plutons into the Sierra Nevada **batholith** stopped, leaving an ancestral Sierra Nevada mountain range that was perhaps a bit lower than the present range.

The subduction zone would occasionally "jam" as slices of unsubducted lithosphere were added to the margin of California. As ancestral California grew through the accretion of such **terranes** (see textbook Figure 14-24), the coastline increasingly shifted westward to its present location.

By about 65 million years ago, erosion had removed enough overlying rock to begin to expose the granites of the batholith and to reduce the ancestral Sierra to a gently rolling highland. Today, some of the rocks that existed before the Sierran granites formed remain as **metamorphic rocks**. The western metamorphic belt runs along the western foothills of the range, and includes the famous *Mother Lode* region; the eastern metamorphic belt is found near the crest of the Sierra.

By about 30 million years ago, the Farallon Plate was largely "consumed" by subduction, and the North American Plate began to override the mid-ocean ridge to the west—this eventually resulted in the development of the present-day transform boundary of the San Andreas Fault system (see *Field Guide #3—The San Andreas Fault* for additional information). The change of plate boundary also changed the direction of stress; the western part of the continent began to stretch, and the resulting faulting (especially *normal faulting*) initiated the uplift of the modern Sierra as well as the faulting throughout the Basin-and-Range province to the east. The uplift of the Sierra along its eastern side continues today, at a long-term rate of about 1½ inches (3.8 cm) per 100 years. This faulting has left one of the world's best examples of a **tilted fault-block mountain** (see textbook Figure 14-60).

Although the evolution of the Sierra described above has been generally accepted for many decades, some current research calls into question the "recent" uplift of the Sierra over the last few million years. A growing number of geologists and geo-

| Gray Pine | Valley Oak | Douglas Fir | Ponderosa Pine | Incense Cedar | Black Oak | Jeffrey Pine | Lodgepole Pine | White Fir | Red Fir |

Foothills   **Montane Forest**   **Upper Montane and Subalpine Forest**

▲ **Figure FG4-2** Characteristic silhouettes of common Sierra Nevada foothills trees, montane forest trees, and upper montane/subalpine forest trees. *(Adapted from P.V. Peterson and P.V. Peterson, Jr., Native Trees of the Sierra Nevada. California Natural History Guide #36. Berkeley: University of California Press, 1975.)*

morphologists think that the uplift of the Sierra was essentially complete by about 65 million years ago. Since then, extensional faulting east of the Sierra has mostly "lowered" the Basin-and-Range province rather than uplifted the Sierra itself. Further research may clarify which view is correct.

Between about 15 and 5 million years ago, extensive volcanic eruptions, especially in the northern Sierra, covered large areas with lava flows, *volcanic mudflows (lahars)* and pyroclastics such as volcanic ash.

Glaciation: With the onset of the **Pleistocene Epoch** about 2.6 million years ago, the Sierra underwent a series of extensive glaciations, at their peak covering the Sierra with a highland icefield 100 miles (160 km) long. Today, the mark of glacial erosion and deposition is found throughout the Sierra (see *Field Guide #5—Yosemite Valley* for additional information about glaciation in the Sierra).

Weather and Climate: The great mountain barrier of the Sierra Nevada dramatically influences the climate, and so the entire biogeography, of the region. Westerly winds encounter the range and are forced to rise, yielding high rainfall and snowfall in winter. The slow melting of the winter snow pack provides much of California with its water supply. By removing much of the moisture of the westerlies on its west side, the Sierra creates a **rain shadow** east of the range, leaving the Mono Basin, Owens Valley and most of Nevada with a *desert* or *steppe* climate.

Plant Communities: Traveling from west to east over the range, you pass through a sequence of vegetation zones, beginning in the foothills with the valley grassland and oak savanna; with increasing elevation you move into the montane forests of Ponderosa Pine and Incense Cedar, and finally into the subalpine forests of Lodgepole Pine, Red Fir and Whitebark Pine as you approach Tioga Pass. Dropping down from the crest to the east side of the Sierra, you pass through the piñon-juniper woodland, and finally down into the arid zone of sagebrush scrub (see textbook Figure 11-10).

Site Descriptions

The following stops describe major features along California 120 traveling across the Sierra from west to east from Oakdale in the Central Valley to Lee Vining in the Mono Basin. (The approximate mileage between each stop is provided to make following the field guide easier if you're traveling from east to west.) The total distance is about 135 miles (217 km), so it is possible to visit all of these sites in one day, but more time is needed if you wish to explore some of the other locations you'll pass along the way.

After leaving Oakdale, you begin to see large, isolated Valley Oaks (*Quercus lobata*; Figure FG4-2) in the grassy fields. About 22 miles east of Oakdale, notice the thin slabs of rock that are standing up on end in the grassy hills among the oak trees—these are known as the "tombstone" rocks. They are meta-morphosed 140-million-year-old ocean floor volcanic and sedimentary rocks, and although they look like they're rising out of the ground, the opposite is actually true: the softer rock that once surrounded them has since eroded away—an example of **differential weathering and erosion.**

Stop 1—Table Mountain (37°53'26"N, 120°29'21"W):

About 24 miles east of Oakdale pull off the road where California 120 splits to the right (southeast) from California 108 and temporarily joins California Highway 49.

About nine million years ago, a volcano near the crest of the ancestral Sierra in the area of Sonora Pass erupted, sending lava flowing for 60 miles (95 km) down a channel of an ancestral river. The lava cooled and solidified into the resistant rock *latite* (a volcanic rock similar to basalt). Over time, the softer rock that once surrounded the river channel eroded away, leaving the dark-colored volcanic rock as a ridge. This is known as the Stanislaus Table Mountain (Figure FG4-3), and it is one of the world's best examples of "inverted topography" (what was once the lowest part of the landscape is now the highest part of the landscape). Table Mountain is best preserved here in the foothills, but remnants can be seen well up the western slope of the Sierra along California Highway 108.

Continue east on California 120/49 through Chinese Camp. At its peak in the early 1850s, about 5,000 Chinese mine workers—many of them indentured servants—lived in this community. Thirteen miles from Table Mountain you reach Moccasin, where water from the Tuolumne River drops in penstocks to a powerhouse before continuing along in the 167-mile-long Hetch Hetchy Aqueduct system to San Francisco. At this elevation,

Gray Pines *(Pinus sabiniana)*, recognized by their long, sparse needles and forked trunks, increasingly replace the oaks of the lower foothills.

At Moccasin, Highway 120 turns sharply uphill, climbing up the steep Priest Grade where you pass a sequence of roadcuts exposing dark brown rocks of the western metamorphic belt. A short distance from here you pass through the southern section of the Mother Lode—a 120-mile-long band of gold-bearing quartz that runs along the foothills of the Sierra (California Highway 49 roughly follows the Mother Lode north to south). More than 100 million years ago, hydrothermal fluids containing gold and other elements circulated into the cracks of the hard metamorphic rocks next to the cooling Sierra batholith, leaving veins of quartz with concentrations of gold.

Three miles beyond the top of Priest Grade, you pass through the old gold rush town of Groveland. As you continue east on Highway 120 toward Buck Meadows, you've gained enough elevation to begin to move into the montane forest zone of Douglas Fir *(Pseudotsuga menziesii)*, Incense Cedar *(Calocedrus decurrens)*, and Ponderosa Pine *(Pinus ponderosa;* see Figure FG4-2 and Figure FG5-3 in *Field Guide #5).*

About 36 miles east of Table Mountain you begin passing roadcuts of granite. The granite here was not glaciated, and it is slowly weathering into coarse sand called *grus.* About 43 miles from Table Mountain (1.2 miles west of the entrance to Yosemite National Park), you pass the turnoff for the winding, seventeen-mile Evergreen Road through Mather to the Hetch Hetchy Reservoir—the source of much of San Francisco's drinking water.

Forty-five miles east of Table Mountain is the Big Oak Flat Entrance to Yosemite National Park (37°48'02"N, 119°52'29"W). In addition to the ranger station where you'll need to pay the Park entrance fee, there are restrooms and other visitor facilities here.

Stop 2—Crane Flat, Yosemite National Park (37°45'12"N, 119°47'50"W):

About 53 miles east of Table Mountain on California 120 (7.7 miles from the Big Oak Flat Entrance to Yosemite National Park) you arrive at Crane Flat. There is a campground here (reservations are required), as well as gasoline and basic groceries.

At the intersection just beyond the campground entrance, turn left (north) onto the Tioga Pass Road segment of California 120. You may want to reset your trip odometer to zero in order to read the field guide mileage to stops along the Tioga Pass Road. (If you continue straight on the Big Oak Flat Road for another ten miles, you reach Yosemite Valley [*Field Guide #5—Yosemite Valley*].)

▲ **Figure FG4-3** Stanislaus Table Mountain near Stop 1. *(Darrel Hess photo.)*

About 0.6 miles from Crane Flat along the Tioga Pass Road you pass the parking area for the Tuolumne Grove. A one-mile hike (with an elevation drop of about 500 feet), takes you to the Tuolumne Grove of Big Trees—the Giant Sequoia (*Sequoiadendron giganteum*)—where there is a short, self-guided nature trail.

Stop 3 (rolling stop)—Yosemite Creek

(37°51′08″N, 119°34′34″W): About twenty miles from Crane Flat, you pass over Yosemite Creek. Seven miles south of here the creek drops 2,425 feet (739 m) out of a **hanging valley** to the floor of Yosemite Valley—the highest waterfall in the park (see Hike C in *Field Guide #5—Yosemite Valley*).

Stop 4—Olmsted Point (37°48′42″N, 119°29′08″W):

Twenty-nine miles from Crane Flat (ten miles from Yosemite Creek), take the right (south) pullout to the parking lot for Olmsted Point. This is one of the best stops anywhere along the Tioga Pass Road. There is a great view of Half Dome and other features from the wheelchair-accessible exhibits near the parking area, but it's worth the effort to hike the quarter-mile-long trail out to Olmsted Point itself—a gently sloping exposure of granite with a wonderful view of Tenaya Canyon (Figure FG4-4).

The granitic bedrock here is the Half Dome Granodiorite, one of the last plutons to be emplaced in the Yosemite area, about 87 million years ago. Notice that the granite here contains many small *inclusions* of darker rock. Some of this dark rock was derived from preexisting rock that dropped down in to the magma, while some probably was derived from globs of darker magma that chilled before the lighter rock around it solidified.

At the peak of the Pleistocene glaciations, this area was thoroughly scoured by ice. As you walk over the granite here, you see fine examples of glacial polish and striations. Glacial polish is sometimes incorrectly pointed out as a demonstration of the erosional power of glaciers, but the opposite is actually true—it indicates that the rock was quite resistant to erosion. Much of the rock removed by glaciers is from *plucking.* The amount of plucking is in part dependent upon *jointing* and other fractures in the rock within which *frost wedging* can loosen material (see textbook Figure 15-6). Notice that the granodiorite in this area is relatively free of joints, and so offered great resistance to the ice. Notice also that much of the glacial polish is now peeling off as *weathering* proceeds. In a short time geologically, this polish will disappear.

Glacial **erratics** are all around you at Olmsted Point. These large boulders were left behind as the Pleistocene glaciers retreated (Figure FG4-5). Erratics are sometimes different from the rock on which they rest, making it possible in some cases to trace their origin back up-valley to their source.

Olmsted Point is a great location to see examples of **exfoliation,** in which curved layers of rock are peeling off like the layers of an onion. Exfoliation is thought to be the consequence of the unloading of pressure from formerly buried rocks such as granite. As the overlying rock is removed, the release of pressure causes the rock to expand slightly, and so joints develop roughly parallel to the surface. Exposed knobs of granite tend to become rounded over time, forming *exfoliation domes* (see textbook Figure 15-10). In a similar way, valley walls also tend to be smoothed by exfoliation.

Down Tenaya Canyon toward Yosemite Valley is perhaps the most distinctive landmark in the Park, Half Dome—a granite monolith rising 4,748 feet (1,447 m) above the valley floor (the elevation of the

▲ **Figure FG4-4** Tenaya Canyon and Half Dome from Olmsted Point at Stop 4. *(Darrel Hess photo.)*

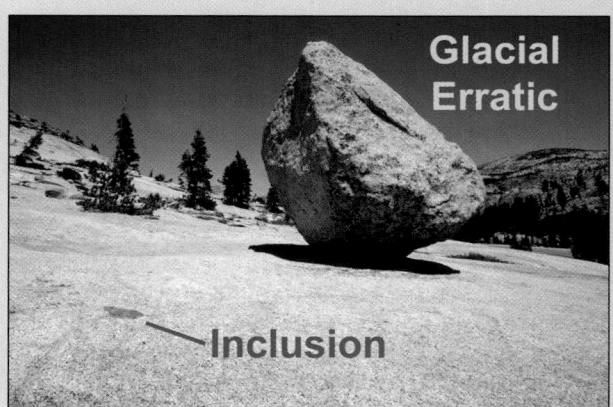

▲ **Figure FG4-5** Glacial erratic near Olmsted Point at Stop 4. Note the inclusion of darker plutonic rock in the granite. *(Darrel Hess photo.)*

summit is 8,842 feet [2,695 m]). The shape of Half Dome is due to jointing and exfoliation: The 2,000-foot (600 m) vertical cliff face is associated with a prominent set of vertical joints that cut through the batholith here, roughly aligned with Tenaya Canyon; the rounded back side of Half Dome is due to exfoliation. Glaciers did skirt Half Dome, carrying away the *talus* that would have accumulated below the vertical face, but the ice probably didn't get much higher than about 700 feet (210 m) below the top of the dome.

Clouds Rest is another example of exfoliation in granitic rock that is undergoing pressure release. The gently undulating surface illustrates the general tendency of the sheet joints of exfoliation to align parallel to the exposed surface of rock.

Return to the Olmsted Point parking lot and continue east on the Tioga Pass Road. As you gain elevation, you move through the mixed coniferous and upper montane forest of Jeffrey Pine (*Pinus jeffreyi*) and White Fir (*Abies concolor*), and eventually into the subalpine forest of Red Fir (*Abies magnifica*), and Lodgepole Pine (*Pinus contorta*; see Figure FG4-2).

Stop 5 (rolling stop)—Tenaya Lake

(37°49'55"N, 119°28'01"W): About 31 miles from Crane Flat (1.8 miles from Olmsted Point) is Tenaya Lake. The lake rests in a basin scoured by the series of Pleistocene glaciers that flowed from near Tioga Pass, past Half Dome, and into the Yosemite Valley. Notice that Tenaya Canyon here has the characteristic broad U-shape of many glacial troughs (see textbook Figure 19-32). Tenaya Lake and Tenaya Canyon were named for Chief Tenaya of the Yosemite Indians. In June of 1851, Captain John Boling led a surprise attack here with the Mariposa Battalion of the U.S. Army, capturing the band of Indians led by Chief Tenaya. Chief Tenaya himself wasn't captured until a month later.

Stop 6—Tuolumne Meadows (37°52'53"N, 119°23'59"W): Thirty-seven miles from Crane Flat (6.1 miles from Tenaya Lake) you arrive at the western end of Tuolumne Meadows. At an elevation of 8,600 feet (2,620 m) it is the largest meadow in the High Sierra. There are many places to stop and explore here. Gasoline and groceries are available in the summer months in the visitor area near the eastern end of the meadow.

During the Pleistocene, this entire area was buried beneath the enormous Tuolumne Icefield. A large glacier flowed out of this region to the northwest about fifteen miles to help carve the "Grand Canyon of the Tuolumne" and the Hetch Hetchy Valley—the "sister"

valley to Yosemite. Hetch Hetchy Valley was blocked by O'Shaughnessy Dam in 1938 to form Hetch Hetchy Reservoir—the penstocks at Moccasin (between Stops 1 and 2) are part of the aqueduct system that transports this drinking water to San Francisco.

Other glaciers extended down from this area into Yosemite Valley—one glacier down Tenaya Canyon, and another down "Little Yosemite Valley"—the canyon of the upper Merced River; these two glaciers then joined to flow through Yosemite Valley. At the height of the Pleistocene glaciations only the highest peaks in the area stood above the ice. After the Pleistocene, a succession of shallow lakes remained in the area of present-day Tuolumne Meadows, slowly filling with sand and gravel transported by streams.

Two prominent granite domes are found at Tuolumne Meadows on the north side of the road—one on the western end, and the other on the eastern end. The western dome is Pothole Dome (37°52'53"N, 119°23'59"W). Pothole Dome is a **roche moutonnée,** formed when a glacier flows over a resistant hill of bedrock. Ice flows up the "stoss" side, smoothing and polishing the rock through glacial abrasion, leaving a gentle slope. As the glacier pulls away from the lee side of the hill, glacial plucking leaves a steeper, blocky slope (see textbook Figure 19-20). The orientation of Pothole Dome clearly shows that the ice flowed from east to west.

The larger, eastern dome at Tuolumne Meadows is Lembert Dome (37°52'39"N, 119°21'12"W)—it is also a roche moutonnée (Figure FG4-6).

Both domes make nice day hikes—Lembert Dome offers a wonderful view of Tuolumne Meadows and the surrounding area, while the western side of Pothole Dome has a series of "potholes" carved and polished by meltwater streams that flowed below the glacial ice.

Figure FG4-6 Lembert Dome is a roche moutonnée at the eastern end of Tuolumne Meadows at Stop 6. The glaciers moved from right to left (east to west) through this area. *(Darrel Hess photo.)*

Stop 7—Tioga Pass and Dana Meadows

(37°54'40"N, 119°15'29"W): Forty-seven miles east of Crane Flat (6.9 miles from Lembert Dome at the eastern end of Tuolumne Meadows) you reach Tioga Pass. At 9,945 feet (3,030 m) this is the highest highway pass in the Sierra. There is a parking area just west of the Tioga Pass Entrance Station to Yosemite National Park (where you'll pay the Park entrance fee if you're arriving from the east). Many of the trees you see here are the five-needled Whitebark Pine (Pinus albicaulis).

Dana Meadows is the gently rolling grassy meadow south of the road. The little lakes and depressions you see on the meadow are **kettles**—depressions left by melting blocks of ice from the retreating glaciers (see textbook Figure 19-25).

Across Dana Meadows to the southeast is the northern shoulder of Mt. Dana (13,053 feet; 3,979 m). The western slope of Mt. Dana and the Dana Plateau to the east were not glaciated during the Pleistocene—these are thought to be "residual" surfaces, remnants of the original landscape surface before it was uplifted into the modern Sierra.

From Tioga Pass, the highway begins its drop of about 3,400 feet (1,000 m) down to the Mono Lake basin to the east. The original trail from Mono Lake to Tioga Pass was the Indian trail up through Bloody Canyon and Mono Pass, about five miles south of here. (On the east side of the Sierra you have a nice view of Bloody Canyon from Stop 2 in *Field Guide #6—Mono Lake*.) The first modern road up Lee Vining Canyon from Mono Lake was completed in 1911; the present highway was completed in 1963.

Stop 8—Ellery Lake (37°56'11"N, 119°14'05"W):

As you continue east from Tioga Pass, you first pass Tioga Lake, and then, about three miles east of Tioga Pass (50 miles east of Crane Flat), you come to Ellery Lake. There are several automobile pull-outs on the south side of the road along the lake. Ellery Lake sits in a basin carved by Pleistocene glaciers that flowed from the Conness Icefield that existed north of here, and then down Lee Vining Canyon to the east.

Look across the lake to the large slope of talus along the southern side of the lake. Notice that the color of the rocks to the left (east) is light gray—this is granite. The rocks to the right (west) are reddish brown. These reddish brown rocks are part of the eastern metamorphic belt, and are probably at least 250 million years old. This is one of the most distinctive contacts between the relatively younger plutonic rocks of the Sierra Nevada batholith, and the older metamorphic rocks into which the granitic magma intruded. Much of the metamorphic rock here is called *hornfels*—a catch-all term for fine-grained metamorphic rocks that formed from the recrystalization of sedimentary or volcanic rocks. The old geologic term *roof pendants* is still used to describe these metamorphic rocks that appear to "hang down" into the younger granite.

Continue down Tioga Pass toward the Mono Lake basin. Once past Ellery Lake, Lee Vining Canyon takes a steep drop down. This is an example of a **glacial step**—an abrupt drop in the floor of a glacial valley (see textbook Figure 19-39). Water from Ellery Lake falls 1,640 feet (500 m) through a penstock to power turbines in the powerhouse below.

Stop 9—Lee Vining Canyon (37°56'59"N, 119°12'27"W):

As you continue down the canyon, the road becomes steeper. This is typical of the east-side passes of the Sierra. The steep eastern face is the eroded *fault plane* along which the Sierra was uplifted. There are several turnouts on the way down where you can safely stop and look at the topography (for example, there is one about 3 miles from Ellery Lake; 53 miles from Crane Flat).

Looking toward the south wall of Lee Vining Canyon you see several short hanging valleys that originate in **cirques** eroded into the Dana Plateau (Figure FG4-7). During the Pleistocene, small tributary glaciers entered the main Lee Vining glacier from these valleys, but were unable to erode as deeply as the main glacier (see textbook Figure 19-32). Notice also the large **talus cones** along the south wall of the canyon. This debris has accumulated since the glaciations ended about 10,000 years ago.

▲ **Figure FG4-7**   Seen from Stop 9, a hanging valley along the south side of Lee Vining Canyon originates in a cirque eroded into the Dana Plateau. A talus cone has developed below the hanging valley. *(Darrel Hess photo.)*

As you continue down Lee Vining Canyon, notice that some of the roadcuts expose glacial **till** deposited by Pleistocene glaciers. Near the bottom of the canyon, especially along the south wall, you see large **lateral moraines** left by the glaciers (see textbook Figure 19-41). The glaciers that flowed down this canyon were the largest in this part of the eastern Sierra, more than 700 feet (210 m) thick. The highest lateral moraine ridge was left by the "Tahoe" stage glaciation, about 70,000 years ago. Inside and below this rim is another smaller ridge of till from the "Tioga" stage glaciation, about 20,000 years ago (see *Field Guide #5—Yosemite Valley,* for more information about stages of glaciation during the Pleistocene). Near the bottom of the canyon, the lat-eral moraines begin to converge together—these are the eroded remnants of *recessional moraines* left by the terminus of the glaciers as they receded at the end of a glacial advance.

By the time you've reached the lower parts of Lee Vining Canyon, notice that the vegetation has changed considerably from just a few miles higher—here the piñon-juniper woodland becomes visible, with the sagebrush scrub dominating the lower parts of the arid Mono Basin in the distance.

This field guide ends at the junction of the Tioga Pass Road (California 120) and U.S. Highway 395, near the town of Lee Vining. *Field Guide #6—Mono Lake* describes this region of California.

Additional Resources

Textbook:

Hess, Darrel. *McKnight's Physical Geography: A Landscape Appreciation,* 11th ed. Upper Saddle River, NJ: Pearson, 2014. Chapters 14 and 19.

Further Reading:

Ditton, Richard P., and Donald E. McHenry. *Yosemite Road Guide.* Yosemite National Park, CA: Yosemite Association, 1989.

Glazner, Allen F., and Greg M. Stock. *Geology Underfoot in Yosemite National Park.* Missoula, MT: Mountain Press Publishing Company, 2010.

Hill, Mary. *Geology of the Sierra Nevada,* revised edition. California Natural History Guide, 80. Berkeley: University of California Press, 2006.

Huber, N. King. *The Geologic Story of Yosemite National Park.* U.S. Geological Survey Bulletin 1595, 1987.

Web Sites:

Yosemite Area Regional Transportation System
http://www.yarts.com

Yosemite National Park
http://www.nps.gov/yose

Textbook Page References for Key Terms

batholith *(p. 431)*
cirque *(p. 561)*
differential weathering and erosion *(p. 456)*
erratic (glacial erratic) *(p. 554)*
exfoliation *(p. 452)*
glacial steps *(p. 564)*

hanging valley *(p. 565)*
kettle *(p. 557)*
lateral moraine *(p. 566)*
metamorphic rock *(p. 386)*
midocean ridge *(p. 408)*
Pleistocene Epoch *(p. 544)*
rain shadow *(p. 166)*

roche moutonnée *(p. 555)*
talus cone *(p. 458)*
terrane *(p. 417)*
till *(p. 553)*
tilted fault-block mountain *(p. 437)*
transform boundary *(p. 413)*

Field Guide #5

Yosemite Valley

Darrel Hess, City College of San Francisco

Introduction

In the words of naturalist John Muir, Yosemite is the "Incomparable Valley." It has sheer granite cliffs, towering waterfalls, cascading streams, quiet meadows and lush forest. Within the valley you can see evidence of the remarkable sequence of events and processes that shaped the region. This field guide describes many of the most popular sights within Yosemite Valley. All of these sites can be visited in one day; however, you'll be rewarded by taking the extra time to explore some of the less-crowded locations and trails within the valley as well.

▲ **Figure FG5-1** Regional map of Yosemite Valley, showing California Highway 140 and field guide stops. Letters indicate locations of "Hikes" within the valley.

Location

This field guide starts in Yosemite Valley about seven miles east of the Arch Rock entrance to Yosemite National Park. The valley is reached by following California Highway 140 east from the Central Valley town of Merced for 75 miles (120 km; Figure FG5-1). You may also reach Yosemite Valley from Crane Flat to the north via the New Big Oak Flat Road (see *Field Guide #4—Sierra Nevada via Tioga Pass*), or from the south via California Highway 41/ Wawona Road.

Yosemite Valley may also be reached with Amtrak train/motorcoach service, and locally with the Yosemite Area Regional Transportation System—see *Additional Resources* on F-44.

Yosemite Valley is one of the most popular tourist destinations in the country, and so expect large crowds during the peak summer tourist season. Reservations for lodging and campsites within the valley should be made well in advance. Yosemite Village is the service center for the valley—restaurants, groceries and other visitor services are found here.

Parking is limited or restricted in most parts of the valley—the Park Service encourages visitors to leave their vehicles in day-use parking lots, and then if possible walk, ride bicycles, or take the free Yosemite Valley Shuttle Bus—especially in the crowded east end of the valley. Many exhibits, campgrounds, and trails in Yosemite Valley are wheelchair accessible, as are the Yosemite Valley Shuttle Buses—check the Park Web site on F-44 for details.

Yosemite Valley is open throughout the year. Summer is the most popular season, although smaller crowds make visits during the other seasons of the year especially satisfying. Summers are usually warm during the day, but cool—or even cold—at night (the elevation of the valley floor is 4,000 feet [1,220 m]). Fall and spring are generally mild, but occasionally wet, while winter is cold with frequent heavy snow. Tire chains for snow may be required as early as October.

Observe all Park Service guidelines regarding bears. Bears are strong, fast and smart. They will exert remarkable effort to get inside your car, tent or backpack if they see or smell anything that even resembles food (including non-food items such as sun cream and insect repellant), as well ice chests and empty food containers or soft drink cans.

Background

Geologic History: Yosemite Valley is sometimes described as a "classic" glacial valley, but this really isn't the case. In some regards it is an "extreme" example of a glacial trough—the valley walls are steeper, the valley floor flatter, and the hanging valleys and waterfalls much higher than those of most glacial valleys. The reasons for these differences include the characteristics of the rocks and the geologic history of the valley.

Yosemite Valley is made of granite (see textbook Figure 13-6) and similar plutonic rocks such as granodiorite, ranging in age from about 80 million years to 140 million years. This granite was emplaced deep below the surface through series of "pulses" of magma that cooled into the collection of *plutons* that comprise the Sierra Nevada **batholith.**

By perhaps as early as 80 million years ago—and certainly by about 25 million years ago—the Sierra had been uplifted. As extensional faulting took place along its eastern side, it became one of the world's best examples of a *tilted fault-block mountain range* (see textbook Figure 14-60). Over millions of years, erosion removed the overlying volcanic and metamorphic rock, exposing the granitic batholith below. Streams, such as the ancestral Merced River, cut deep valleys into the gentle western slope of the mountain range. (For a more detailed description of the early geologic history of the Sierra, see *Field Guide #4—Sierra Nevada via Tioga Pass*).

Glaciation: During the **Pleistocene Epoch,** from about 2.6 million years ago to 11,700 years ago, glaciers formed in the higher parts of the Sierra. The glaciers flowed down the western and eastern sides of the range, largely following the paths of

existing stream valleys. At the peak of the Pleistocene glaciations, however, a highland ice-field 100 miles (160 km) long covered the High Sierra, in some areas to depths of hundreds of feet, with ice more than 3,000 feet (900 m) deep in some valleys. The last large glaciers in the Sierra had retreated by about 10,000 years ago.

The Pleistocene glaciers reshaped the old stream valleys through which they flowed. Glaciers tend to deepen, steepen and widen an existing valley, often transforming a V-shaped stream valley into a U-shaped glacial trough. Glaciers also often leave irregular *glacial steps* in the down-valley profile (see textbook Figure 19-39).

Yosemite Valley underwent multiple glaciations. The names and time periods for each of these glaciations have been subject to vigorous debate and revision by geologists in recent years—and may well be revised again as new evidence is deciphered. The most extensive of the Pleistocene glaciations in the Yosemite area took place roughly 800,000 years ago and is known as the Sherwin glaciation (the Sherwin and earlier glaciations are often collectively referred to as "pre-Tahoe" glaciations). During the Sherwin glaciation, glaciers completely filled Yosemite Valley to a depth of more than 2,000 feet (600 m) in places, flowing as far west as El Portal (Figure FG5-2). During the multiple advances and retreats of the more recent Tahoe and Tioga glaciations (the Tahoe glaciations took place between roughly 60,000 and 140,000 years ago, and the Tioga glaciations between roughly 14,000 and 30,000 years ago), glaciers in the valley advanced only as far as El Capitan. Following the retreat of the Tioga glaciers, it's likely that a marsh occupied the valley floor, before filling up with sediment and turning into a meadow and later a forest.

Weather and Climate: The present-day climate of Yosemite Valley is largely the consequence of two important factors. (1) The influence of the seasonal migration of the *subtropical high:* As with the coastal *mediterranean climate* to the west, the summer influence of the subtropical high leads to stability and generally dry conditions in the Yosemite area. During the winter, the subtropical high migrates equatorward, allowing the *westerlies* to bring in *mid-latitude cyclones.* In the Sierra as a whole, winter is the wet season, although summer thunderstorms also bring some rain. (2) The role of altitude: Because of the greater cooling of air that results when storms are given an *orographic* lift up the west slope of the Sierra, much of the precipitation during the winter falls as snow. The winter snow pack melts in the spring and summer, draining into reservoirs (such as into the Hetch Hetchy Valley to the north of Yosemite) providing the water supply for much of California.

▲ **Figure FG5-2**   Artist's depiction of glaciation in Yosemite Valley. **(A)** Pre-Tahoe glaciation about 1,000,000 years ago. **(B)** Tioga glaciation about 20,000 years ago. **(C)** A marsh occupied the floor of Yosemite Valley after retreat of Tioga glaciers, eventually filling with sediment. *(Adapted from U.S. Geological Survey Bulletin 1595.)*

Plant Communities: The high elevation generally leads to cooler summers than in lower areas—which in turn influences the patterns of vegetation in the Sierra (see textbook Figure 11-10). Vegetation changes from the valley grassland and oak savanna in the western foothills into the montane forests of Ponderosa Pine *(Pinus ponderosa)* and Incense Cedar *(Calocedrus decurrens)* on the floor of Yosemite Valley. In the higher areas above the rim of the valley, the vegetation transitions into subalpine forests of Lodgepole Pine *(Pinus contorta)* and Red Fir *(Abies magnifica)*.

A number of common Sierra Nevada trees can be identified by looking for the distinctive pattern of bark on the trunks of mature trees (Figure FG5-3), making it possible to quickly identify them even when driving by. Three Sierra trees are particularly easy to identify, especially in combination with their often characteristic "silhouettes" (see Figure FG4-2 in *Field Guide #4*): the Ponderosa Pine has large deep furrows in the yellow bark, giving it a "jig-saw puzzle" appearance; in contrast, the subalpine Lodgepole Pine has tiny, scaly-looking yellow-orange bark; the Incense Cedar has fibrous dark reddish-brown bark.

Site Descriptions

If you're traveling east from Merced along Highway 140, notice that for much of the way, the Merced River Canyon is generally "V" shaped—in this case, cut primarily through stream erosion, not glaciation. Once in Yosemite Valley, however, the walls become much steeper and the valley floor flatter and wider—indication that processes other than simple stream erosion have been at work. About 69 miles east of Merced you reach the Arch Rock Entrance Station to Yosemite National Park, where you'll need to pay the Park entrance fee. About five miles beyond the Park entrance, you enter Yosemite Valley itself.

Once in the valley, you'll generally loop around the valley floor in a counterclockwise direction (following the one-way-road loop). Because many of the sites in the valley are reached by short walks, once you've reached the Visitor Center (Stop 5), sites are described through a series of "Hikes." These hikes, of course, may be taken in any order.

Once you enter the far western end of Yosemite Valley, road signs direct you to turn right (southeast) onto a one-way road that curves east into the valley's Southside Drive. Less than a mile after the turnoff (about 6.7 miles east of the Arch Rock Entrance Station), follow the signs and make a sharp right turn (heading west) onto the Wawona Road that climbs out of the valley. In 1.6 miles pull off at the parking lot at the Yosemite Valley Overlook (often simply called the Wawona "Tunnel View").

Ponderosa Pine   Lodgepole Pine   Incense Cedar

▲ **Figure FG5-3**   The trunks of three common Sierra trees: Ponderosa Pine, Lodgepole Pine, and Incense Cedar. *(Darrel Hess photos.)*

▲ **Figure FG5-4**   Yosemite Valley from Wawona Tunnel View at Stop 1. *(Darrel Hess photo.)*

Stop 1—Wawona Tunnel View (37° 42'56"N, 119°40'37"W): This is one of the best views of Yosemite Valley, and a great starting point to see many features of the valley you'll visit at other stops (Figure FG5-4).

The exposed rock of the valley walls consists of the plutonic rocks granite and granodiorite. The valley was originally deepened by the ancestral Merced River. During the Pleistocene, glaciers reshaped the stream valley through a series of advances and retreats.

Many glacial valleys (or more correctly, glacial troughs) are U-shaped—having been widened, deepened and steepened somewhat by glacial abrasion and glacial *plucking* along the sides and bottom of the glacier. Notice that Yosemite Valley isn't really U-shaped—it has a flat floor and nearly vertical walls.

The vertical walls are due primarily to **jointing** in the granite. Prominent, widely-spaced vertical *master joints* in otherwise unjointed, resistant rock influenced where weathering, mass wasting, and erosion could easily remove rock. Yosemite's enormous granite monoliths such as El Capitan and Half Dome remain as nearly vertical cliffs because they are largely unjointed, and so resist erosion. On the other hand, more closely-jointed rock, such as the source of **talus** that makes up the Rockslides just to the west of El Capitan, is much more susceptible to weathering and mass wasting. **Rockfall** is a continuing process within Yosemite Valley. In October of 2008, two rockfalls forced the permanent closure of about one-third of the guest accommodations at Curry Village at the far eastern end of the valley.

The floor of Yosemite Valley is unusually flat for a glacial valley. The bottom of the valley has been filled with as much as 2,000 feet (600 m) of sediment. Following the last glaciation, deposition of alluvium leveled the valley floor, which was eventually covered with meadow and forest.

In the far distance, you see Half Dome. The flat face of Half Dome is due to a prominent vertical joint that runs through the pluton in this area (see textbook Figure 19-37). Contrary to popular misconception, Half Dome was not cut in half by glaciers. Glaciers flowed down Tenaya Canyon past Half Dome, removing rock that broke off its face along the vertical jointing plane. The rounded top and back side of Half Dome—as well and the gently undulating surface of Clouds Rest farther up canyon—is due to **exfoliation** (also see Figure FG4-4 in Field Guide #4). The unloading of pressure on these formerly buried rocks caused the rock to crack along curved joints parallel to the surface (see textbook Figures 15-9 and 15-10). Over time, layer after layer of rock peeled off, gently rounding and smoothing exposed granite into domes and valley walls.

A short distance from Wawona Tunnel View along the south side of the valley is Bridalveil Fall, dropping from one of the world's most spectacular examples of a **hanging valley** (see textbook Figure 19-32). During the peak of the Pleistocene glaciations, tributary glaciers entered the main glacier flowing down Yosemite Valley. These smaller tributary glaciers didn't deepen their valleys very much, so today these tributary valleys enter high up on the main valley walls. Because the walls of Yosemite Valley are nearly vertical, streams flowing out of these hanging valleys form many of the most beautiful waterfalls in the Park, such as Bridalveil Fall (Stop 2) and Yosemite Falls (Hike C).

There are relatively few areas in the valley where glacial **till** remains. Unlike the eastern side of the Sierra Nevada, only poorly developed **moraines** are found in Yosemite Valley, probably because the amount of meltwater was so great that debris melted out of the glaciers was immediately transported by streams down into the Central Valley.

Although Yosemite Valley has certainly undergone extensive glaciation, some geologists and geomorphologists question if Yosemite Valley was significantly widened or deepened by glacial erosion. In this view, earlier stream erosion, as well as ongoing rockfall and exfoliation of the resistant granitic bedrock, are more responsible for the shape of the valley than glacial erosion during the Pleistocene. Further research may help determine which interpretation is correct.

Stop 2—Bridalveil Fall (37°42'59"N, 119° 39'05"W): Retrace your route back down the Wawona Road toward the valley floor. Near where the Wawona Road intersects Southside Drive is the

parking lot and trailhead for Bridalveil Fall. A trail from the east end of the parking lot takes you 0.2 miles to an observation area near the bottom of the fall.

Bridalveil Fall forms where Bridalveil Creek drops 620 feet (189 m) out of a hanging valley (see textbook Figure 19-40). The fall has its peak flow during the late spring and early summer, but has water all year. The steep spire to the right (west) of Bridalveil Fall is the Leaning Tower, and the three peaks just to the left (east) are the Cathedral Rocks.

Stop 3—El Capitan View (37°43'15"N, 119°38'53"W):
From the Bridalveil Fall parking lot, continue east on Southside Drive for 0.5 miles where there are long pullouts on both sides of the road (with a wooden post labeled "V14"). From here, there are great views of Bridalveil Fall to the south and El Capitan across the valley to the north.

El Capitan, "The Chief," is a sheer granite wall rising 3,000 feet (910 m) above the valley floor—perhaps the highest uninterrupted cliff face in the world. It is made from nearly unjointed granite which resisted both stream and glacial erosion, and constricted the valley width here. The Cathedral Rocks on the opposite side of the valley are made of the same resistant granite, and similarly resisted erosion.

About halfway down the eastern side of El Capitan (and better seen from vantage points farther east of here) is a patch of the darker plutonic rock called diorite, which was intruded as a **dike** into the El Capitan granite. This dark patch reminds some people of a map of North America.

About 0.2 miles beyond the eastern end of this parking area, you cross a ridge of glacial till. This till is part of a recessional moraine left by the last glacier in Yosemite Valley. This moraine may have helped dam the valley floor, allowing it to fill with alluvium following the Pleistocene.

Stop 4—Three Brothers View (37° 43'18"N, 119°37'28"W):
About 1.3 miles farther east on the Southside Drive, you reach a small pullout (designated by a wooden post labeled "V16"). This spot provides a good view of the Three Brothers on the opposite side of the valley. The tallest, Eagle Peak, rises more than 3,800 feet (1,160 m) above the valley floor and is the highest peak along the north rim of Yosemite Valley (Figure FG5-5). Notice that these three dramatic peaks share the same geometry: All three formed along a prominent set of parallel diagonal joints in the granite, and each ends with a parallel vertical cliff. On the south side of the valley, opposite the Three Brothers, you may be able to recognize rocks with similar jointing patterns.

Stop 5—Visitor Center at Yosemite Village (37°44'55"N, 119°35'17"W):
Continue east on Southside Drive, past the Yosemite Chapel, until you come to the day-use parking area at Yosemite Village. To reach the Visitor Center or

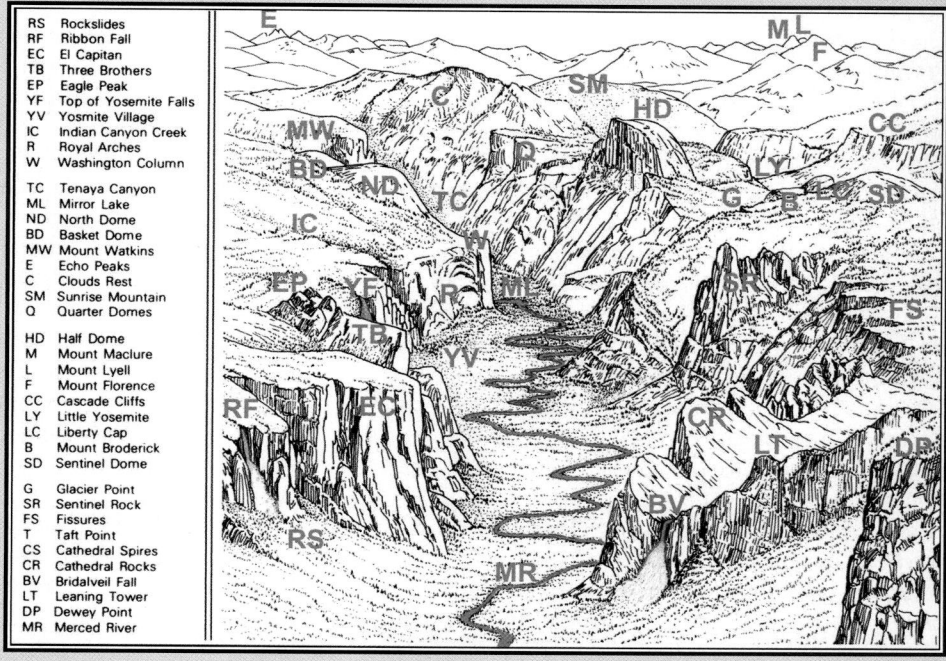

RS	Rockslides
RF	Ribbon Fall
EC	El Capitan
TB	Three Brothers
EP	Eagle Peak
YF	Top of Yosemite Falls
YV	Yosemite Village
IC	Indian Canyon Creek
R	Royal Arches
W	Washington Column
TC	Tenaya Canyon
ML	Mirror Lake
ND	North Dome
BD	Basket Dome
MW	Mount Watkins
E	Echo Peaks
C	Clouds Rest
SM	Sunrise Mountain
Q	Quarter Domes
HD	Half Dome
M	Mount Maclure
L	Mount Lyell
F	Mount Florence
CC	Cascade Cliffs
LY	Little Yosemite
LC	Liberty Cap
B	Mount Broderick
SD	Sentinel Dome
G	Glacier Point
SR	Sentinel Rock
FS	Fissures
T	Taft Point
CS	Cathedral Spires
CR	Cathedral Rocks
BV	Bridalveil Fall
LT	Leaning Tower
DP	Dewey Point
MR	Merced River

▶ **Figure FG5-5** Bird's-eye view of features around Yosemite Valley. *(Adapted from U.S. Geological Survey Bulletin 1595.)*

other sites in the often congested eastern part of the valley, you may walk, bicycle or take the free Yosemite Valley Shuttle Bus that loops around the valley floor from Yosemite Lodge in the west to Curry Village and Happy Isles in the east. Many day hikes are possible from this part of the valley, ranging from short and easy to long and strenuous. The following are among the most popular and interesting easy hikes:

Hike A—Vernal Fall Footbridge (37° 43'34"N, 119°33'06"W):
From Shuttle Bus Stop #16 at Happy Isles, hike 0.8 miles along the cascading Merced River to the footbridge near the bottom of Vernal Fall. A short distance along the Merced River after leaving the Bus Stop, you pass the U.S. Geological Survey Happy Isles Bridge Stream Gage Station. Data on the flow of the Merced River—unaltered by human action upstream from here—has been gathered continuously since 1915 (view near-real time streamflow data from the Web site listed on F-44).

From the stream gage station, the paved but steep trail climbs along a talus slope at the foot of the north side of the Merced River Canyon. In most places trees are growing among the large moss-covered boulders. Many of the trees here are oaks, along with smaller willows—which thrive in wet areas such as this. Notice, however, that in a few places along the trail there are no trees among the rocks—these are areas of relatively recent rockfall and trees haven't had a chance to become established.

After an elevation gain of about 400 feet (120 m), you reach a footbridge crossing the Merced River. From this location, Vernal Fall can be seen upstream in the distance. Vernal Fall forms where the Merced River drops 317 feet (97 m) off one of the glacial steps in Merced Canyon. Glaciers deepen their valleys (primarily through glacial plucking) where the bedrock is weaker or more closely jointed, but leave flatter benches or "steps" in areas where the rock is stronger (see textbook Figure 19-39).

From the footbridge you may continue up the "Mist Trail" an additional 0.7 miles, climbing more than 600 steps along the south wall of the canyon to the top of Vernal Fall. About 1.3 miles beyond Vernal Fall, you reach Nevada Fall where it drops 594 feet (181 m) off the lip of another glacial step in Merced Canyon. *Use great caution when hiking up the Mist Trail—in addition to getting hikers quite wet from the windblown spray, the trail can be extremely slippery. Also, be careful at the top of Vernal Fall where strong currents have swept hikers off the rocks.*

If you walk or take the Shuttle Bus from the start of the Vernal Fall trail (Shuttle Bus Stop #16) to

Figure FG5-6   Half Dome above Mirror Lake on Hike B. *(Darrel Hess photo.)*

Shuttle Bus Stop #17 (Hike B to Mirror Lake) you'll pass over a gentle rise in the road—you can see in the small roadcut that this rise consists of till. Although sometimes called "Medial Moraine," it is more likely a **lateral moraine** or **recessional moraine** left by the last glacier that flowed down Tenaya Canyon into Yosemite Valley.

Hike B—Mirror Lake (37°44'47"N, 119° 33'03"W):
Take the Shuttle Bus to the trailhead for Mirror Lake at Shuttle Bus Stop #17. From there, it's a one-mile hike up a paved trail to Mirror Lake at the foot of Half Dome (Figure FG5-6). Visitors with Accessibility Placards may drive to Mirror Lake. Named for the beautiful reflections of the surrounding valley walls, Mirror Lake is slowly disappearing. The low rock dam built by visitors in the late 1800s to try to preserve the lake divides Mirror Lake into upper and lower pools. During the fall and winter, sand builds up in the lower pool, but this sand is scoured away by the spring floods. By early autumn, Mirror Lake is usually nearly dry. Although some hydrologists hypothesize that Mirror Lake will remain a seasonal pool in Tenaya Creek, others expect that silt deposited by Tenaya Creek will gradually fill the shallow lake, eventually turning it into a meadow.

Half Dome rises 4,748 feet (1,447 m) from the valley floor above you to the southeast. The 2,000 foot (600 m) vertical face of Half Dome was accentuated when Pleistocene glaciers carried away slabs of rock that broke off along the master joint in the granite here, while the rounded summit and back side is due to exfoliation. Glaciers themselves never went higher than about 700 feet (210 m) below its summit, and it's doubtful there ever was a "full dome" exposed.

If you want a slightly longer hike, instead of a round-trip to Shuttle Bus Stop #17, about halfway back you can follow the bike trail west to Yosemite Village. This will give you a closer view of the Royal Arches along the north wall of the Valley—these great arcs in the granite were formed by exfoliation.

Hike C—Lower Yosemite Falls (37° 45′00″N, 119°35′43″W):

Just west of the Visitor Center, at Shuttle Bus Stop #6, is an easy half-mile hike along a well-maintained loop trail to a bridge near the foot of Yosemite Falls. The eastern part of the loop is wheelchair accessible. Yosemite Falls is one of the highest waterfalls in the world, dropping a total of 2,425 feet (739 m) from the hanging valley of Yosemite Creek to the valley floor below (see *Field Guide #4—Sierra Nevada via Tioga Pass,* Stop 3, for a description of Yosemite Creek along the Tioga Pass Road). Yosemite Falls is at its most spectacular in the late spring and early summer, and will often go dry by early autumn.

The Upper Fall drops 1,430 feet (436 m) down a near-vertical wall of granite until it strikes a narrow rock ledge marked by a line of trees (Figure FG5-7). This ledge forms along a joint that runs through the pluton here. The Middle Cascade drops 675 feet (206 m) through a narrow gorge to another wooded ledge, again formed by a horizontal joint in the granite. After the final 320-foot (98 m) drop of the Lower Fall, Yosemite Creek empties into the Merced River.

▲ **Figure FG5-7**   Yosemite Falls on Hike C. *(Darrel Hess photo.)*

Hike D—Cook's Meadow and Merced River (37°44′36″N, 119°35′36″W):

From Shuttle Bus Stop #6 ("Yosemite Falls"), cross the road to the south along a trail and boardwalk that take you across Cook's Meadow to the Merced River. In the late 1800s, Cook's Hotel was established near here, and cattle grazed in this meadow until the 1920s.

First, follow the path across the meadow to the footbridge crossing the Merced River. The river is fed by the snow pack along the crest of the High Sierra, nearly 20 miles (30 km) to the east. Although it is tempting to swim in the Merced River during a hot summer day, use extreme caution: The water is very cold and the current is much stronger than it first appears.

From the footbridge, backtrack a short distance to where the boardwalk forks and you can turn east out into the open area of Cook's Meadow. In order to improve hunting and gathering conditions, the Miwok Indians used fire to keep the valley floor

meadows open. Since that time, forest has increasingly encroached on the meadows, although the Park Service does undertake prescribed burns to keep the ecosystem healthy. Common trees on the valley floor include the deciduous California Black Oak *(Quercus kelloggii)*, Ponderosa Pine, and Incense Cedar (see Figure FG4-2 in *Field Guide #4*). In late spring and early summer, you may see the blossoms of the Western Azalea *(Rhododendron occidentale)* in places along the banks of the Merced River.

About midway along the path across Cook's Meadow, notice the elongated, low grassy depression—this is an abandoned channel of the Merced River. During the spring floods, this channel has flowing water, but for most of the rest of the year, only a shallow pond contains water.

If you continue along the boardwalk to the eastern end of the meadow, you come to a parking area and Shuttle Bus Stop #11. From here it is a short walk to Sentinel Bridge—a stone bridge across the Merced River that offers a wonderful view of Half Dome in the distance.

Additional Resources

Textbook:
Hess, Darrel. *McKnight's Physical Geography: A Landscape Appreciation*, 11th ed. Upper Saddle River, NJ: Pearson, 2014. Chapters 14 and 19.

Further Reading:
Ditton, Richard P., and Donald E. McHenry. *Yosemite Road Guide*. Yosemite National Park, CA: Yosemite Association, 1989.

Glazner, Allen F., and Greg M. Stock. *Geology Underfoot in Yosemite National Park*. Missoula, MT: Mountain Press Publishing Company, 2010.

Guyton, Bill. *Glaciers of California*. California Natural History Guide, 59. Berkeley: University of California Press, 1998.

Huber, N. King. *The Geologic Story of Yosemite National Park*. U.S. Geological Survey Bulletin 1595. Washington, D.C.: United States Government Printing Office, 1987.

Web Sites:
Amtrak Train and Motorcoach Service
http://www.amtrak.com

Merced River Stream Gage, Happy Isles
http://waterdata.usgs.gov/nwis/uv?11264500

Yosemite Area Regional Transportation System
http://www.yarts.com

Yosemite National Park
http://www.nps.gov/yose

Textbook Page References for Key Terms

batholith *(p. 431)*
dike *(p. 432)*
exfoliation *(p. 452)*
hanging valley *(p. 565)*

joint *(p. 449)*
lateral moraine *(p. 566)*
moraine *(p. 556)*
Pleistocene Epoch *(p. 544)*

recessional moraine *(p. 557)*
rockfall *(p. 458)*
talus *(p. 458)*
till *(p. 553)*

Field Guide #6

Mono Lake

Darrel Hess, City College of San Francisco

Introduction

The Mono Basin offers some of the most varied and fascinating natural history of any place in California. It includes Mono Lake itself—a salt lake with a specialized ecosystem and dramatic tufa towers—as well as a chain of young volcanoes and steep glacial canyons carved into the spectacular eastern face of the Sierra Nevada.

This field guide highlights features you can easily see in one day around Mono Lake.

Location

Lee Vining, the largest town in the Mono Basin, is reached via U.S. Highway 395 or California Highway 120 (Figure FG6-1). (*Field Guide #4—Sierra Nevada via Tioga Pass* describes the trip across the Sierra to Lee Vining along California Highway 120.)

During the summer, bus service is available from Yosemite Valley to Tuolumne Meadows and Lee Vining via the Tioga Pass Road with the Yosemite Area Regional Transportation System— see *Additional Resources* on F-50.

Gasoline, groceries, restaurants and lodging are available in Lee Vining. Several small campgrounds are located a few miles away off California 120 in the lower portion of Lee Vining Canyon. The Mono Basin Scenic Area Visitor Center is about one mile north of Lee Vining off U.S. 395. The Visitor Center is wheelchair accessible and includes a natural history museum, a ranger information counter, and a museum store where you can purchase maps and

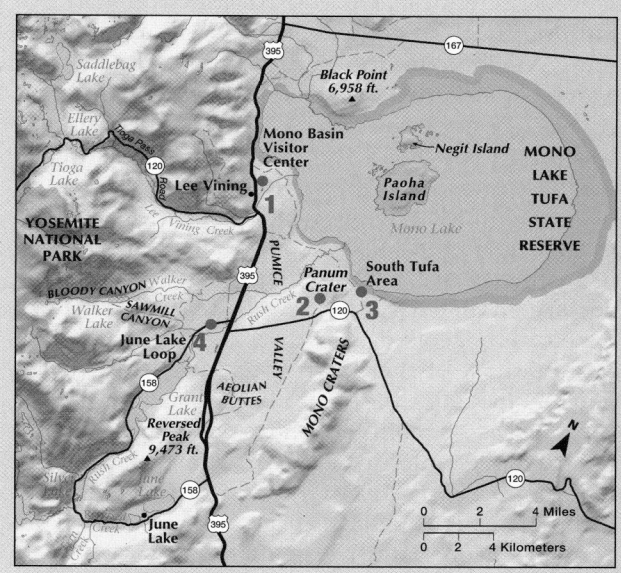

▲ **Figure FG6-1** Regional map of Mono Lake area showing field guide stops.

additional guide books for the region. The Visitor Center is closed during winter months.

Winters here are cold and often snowy. Tioga Pass usually remains closed until June, but sections of U.S. 395 may also close during snowstorms, so check road conditions before traveling here in winter months. The summers are warm and pleasant, but often punctuated by thunderstorms. Because of the relatively high elevation of Mono Lake (6,382 feet; 1,945 m) take precautions against sunburn in summer by wearing a hat and sun cream, and be sure to drink plenty of water to avoid dehydration.

Background

Geologic History: Mono Lake is found at the western edge of the Basin-and-Range province of North America. The down-dropped Mono Basin was formed through the same processes of crustal extension and faulting that uplifted the Sierra Nevada (see *Field Guide #4—Sierra Nevada via Tioga Pass*) and down-dropped Death Valley (see *Field Guide #9— Death Valley*). The eastern face of the Sierra Nevada was uplifted and the Mono Basin down-dropped along a series of high-angle faults (see textbook Figure 14-60). The basin itself is structurally much deeper than it appears, having been filled in some places with more than 3,000 feet (900 m) of sediments deposited by glacial streams and ash ejected from nearby volcanoes.

This region has experienced geologically-recent volcanic activity, at least in part associated with the faulting and crustal extension in the Basin-and-Range region over the last few million years. The Mono Craters are a young chain of **plug dome** volcanoes (see textbook Figure 14-37), some erupting less than 1,000 years ago. Just south of the Mono Basin, a catastrophic eruption 760,000 years ago blanketed much of western North America with volcanic ash and formed the Long Valley **Caldera.** It is likely that *magma* remains just a few miles below the surface in the region, and future eruptions are expected by geologists.

Like most of the down-dropped basins in the Basin-and-Range, the Mono Basin is a *basin of interior drainage*—streams here have no natural outlet to the sea. Water enters Mono Lake from streams flowing from the east slope of the Sierra, but leaves only through evaporation. Because of this, over time the waters of Mono Lake became naturally salty.

Hydrology: Mono Lake is one of the oldest lakes in North America, formed at least 700,000 years ago. During the **Pleistocene Epoch,** a wetter and cooler climate allowed the formation of large glaciers in the Sierra Nevada; it also allowed the formation of many large lakes in basins of interior drainage. At the peak of the Pleistocene glaciations, Mono Lake— known to geologists as Lake Russell—was about 800 feet (240 m) deeper than today. Lake Russell filled the Mono Basin, then overflowed into the Owens Valley to the south, which also filled as a lake and overflowed into the Searles Basin and Panamint Valley farther south—which in turn overflowed into Death Valley to form Pleistocene Lake Manly (see *Field Guide #9—Death Valley*). When the Sun is right, you can still see the marks of the wave-cut shorelines of Pleistocene Lake Russell on the mountain face of the Sierra to the west.

Water Diversion: Mono Lake shrank naturally after the end of Pleistocene about 10,000 years ago, but the white alkali "bathtub ring" you see around the lake today was exposed more recently. In 1913, the Los Angeles Aqueduct began transporting water from Owens Valley south of here to Los Angeles, 233 miles (370 km) away. By the mid-1930s, Los Angeles was purchasing water rights in the Mono Basin as well, and by the early 1940s water was diverted from four streams entering Mono Lake.

As soon as the water diversion from the Mono Basin began, the level of Mono Lake began to drop, threatening the delicate ecosystem of the lake. In 1978 the Mono Lake Committee was formed to help protect Mono Lake. Through a legal ruling in 1994, the Los Angeles Department of Water and Power was mandated to reduce diversions and let the lake level rise and stabilize at an elevation of 6,392 feet (1,948 m)—about 20 feet (6 m) higher than its lowest diversion-era level of 6,372 feet (1,942 m), but lower than its original pre-diversion level that fluctuated between 6,400 and 6,425 feet (1,951 m and 1,958 m).

Weather and Climate: The arid climate of the Mono Basin is due to the Sierra Nevada to the west. The moist westerlies (often carrying midlatitude cyclones in winter) are lifted **orographically** along the windward west slope of the Sierra. The forced lifting results in high precipitation (especially winter snowfall) on the west slope of the Sierra, while a **rain shadow** develops on the leeward side (see textbook Figure 6-33b).

Plant Communities: The dominant types of vegetation in the Mono Basin reflect the generally arid conditions here, although vertical zonation patterns reveal surprising diversity. High on the eastern slope of the Sierra subalpine forest is found, while piñon-juniper woodland typically covers the lower elevations along the mountain front. In the lowest parts of the basin, sagebrush scrub dominates the landscape (see textbook Figure 11-10), with salt-tolerant alkali sink scrub vegetation found along the shore of Mono Lake itself.

Site Descriptions

These stops can be visited in any order, but the Mono Basin Visitor Center is a good starting point. In addition to its exhibits, it has an overlook of Mono Lake where you can view the entire basin before heading off to the other stops. Stops 2 and 3 are reached via graded dirt roads that are passable in dry weather with ordinary passenger automobiles.

Stop 1—Mono Basin Visitor Center

(37°57'59"N, 119°07'15"W): About one mile north of Lee Vining on U.S. 395, turn right (east) into the Mono Basin Scenic Area Visitor Center. From the outside overlook you can see many features around the lake.

On the hills above Lee Vining you see piñon-juniper woodland. This plant community is dominated by the Piñon Pine (*Pinus monophylla*) recognized by its single needles, along with the Utah Juniper (*Juniperus osteosperma*) with its scaly needles and small, blue cones.

The large island in the middle of Mono Lake is Paoha Island, and the smaller one in the north is Negit Island. Both of the islands are the result of volcanic eruptions—as is Black Point along the northern shore (which originally formed from an underwater volcanic eruption). Negit Island is an andesitic volcano that last erupted only 270 years ago. Although Paoha Island had volcanic eruptions along its north shore (and still has active steam vents), it largely originated from lake bed deposits that were uplifted along faults.

The islands were named by geologist Israel Russell in the 1870s (for whom Pleistocene Lake Russell is named). He used words from the language of the Paiute Indians for the islands. "Negit" is the Paiute word for gull—quite appropriate considering the large number of gulls often found nesting there. "Paoha" refers to spirits with wavy long hair thought to rise in the vapor from hot springs, such as those found on the island.

Because of water diversion to southern California, by 1979 the level of Mono Lake had dropped so much that a land bridge developed between the mainland and Negit Island. The California National Guard in cooperation with California Fish and Game used dynamite to blast a channel between island and the mainland, but eventually coyotes crossed over and killed thousands of nesting birds.

Directly south of the lake you see the northern end of the Mono Craters volcanoes (described at Stop 2). The highest peak in the chain is Crater Mountain (see textbook Figure 14-38), with an elevation of 9,172 feet (2,796 m). In several places along the shore of the lake, you can see the famous white towers of tufa (which you'll visit at Stop 3).

Return to U.S. 395, turn left (south), and drive back through Lee Vining.

Stop 2—Panum Crater (37°55'32"N, 119° 02'56"W):

Drive south from Lee Vining on U.S. 395. About 4.7 miles south of the turnoff for Tioga Pass, turn left (east) onto California 120 East. After 3.1 miles, turn left (north) on to a graded gravel road, following the signs 0.9 miles to the parking area at Panum Crater.

The plant community around you here is sagebrush scrub. The most common plant you see is the pale green, upward branching, fragrant Big Sagebrush (*Artemisia tridentata*), probably North America's most abundant shrub (although it smells similar, it is not in the same genus as sage used for cooking). Other common shrubs are the woody Bitterbrush (*Purshia tridentata*), recognized by the three little "teeth" on its leaves, and Rabbitbrush (*Chrysothamnus viscidiflorus*), with narrow and pointed, twisted leaves, and yellow flowers in late summer.

Panum is the youngest and the northern-most volcano of the Mono Craters chain (although the volcanic islands in Mono Lake also appear related). The term "craters" is a bit of a misnomer, since the chain is really a series of plug domes, lava flows and explosion pits that began forming perhaps only 35,000 years ago. Roughly twenty domes make up the Mono Craters-Inyo Craters volcanic chain that extends in a gentle arc south into the Mammoth Lake basin. These volcanoes are composed of solidified **lava** and explosively ejected **pyroclastics** such as pumice. The composition of the lava is mostly rhyolite and dacite—volcanic rocks that have the same mineral composition as the plutonic rocks granite and granodiorite respectively.

From the parking lot, hike the short distance up to the outer rim of the volcano. Panum erupted as recently as 640 years ago, and is quite typical of rhyolitic plug domes. You see that Panum consists of two parts: an outer ring of pumice that was exploded out of the volcano, and an inner plug of solidified lava (Figure FG6-2).

The first stage in the life of a volcano like Panum is a series of explosive events that produce the

▲ **Figure FG6-2** Panum Crater at Stop 2 showing inner plug of solidified rhyolitic lava and the outer ring of pyroclastics. *(Darrel Hess photo.)*

outer ring of light-colored pumice. Pumice is a type of volcanic glass that forms when molten material cools so quickly there is no crystalline mineral structure—the molecules simply "freeze" in place. Because this magma was thick and frothy with gases, pumice is full of tiny open spaces—often a piece of pumice is light enough to float on water. A layer of pumice several feet thick blankets the region around the Mono Craters (an area appropriately named Pumice Valley).

After its explosive phase, Panum went into another phase of formation. A plug of viscous, pasty rhyolitic lava—molten rock with the consistency of toothpaste—slowly pushed up into the throat of the volcano, where it cooled. The inner plug of Panum consists of the volcanic rock rhyolite as well as rhyolitic obsidian—another kind of volcanic glass that forms from the rapid solidification of lava that isn't frothy with gas.

If you hike a short distance around the rim of Panum toward the east, you can get a good view of the other Mono Craters volcanoes to the south. During the eruption of the plug dome just south of you, rhyolitic lava poured over the edge of the crater, leaving a thick flow of rhyolitic obsidian called a "coulee." Coulees are very rugged, steep and blocky since the surface hardens while the interior of the flow is still molten, pushing out at the edges of the flow.

Walk back along the rim of Panum a short distance to where you have a good view of the Sierra. Looking west you may be able to see the Farrington Siphon along the hills near Lee Vining. This pipe takes water from Lee Vining Creek, down to Grant Lake in the south; an aqueduct then takes the water in a tunnel beneath the Mono Craters into Long Valley to the south.

A short distance farther to the south along the crest of the Sierra, you see Mono Pass and Bloody Canyon—the location of the old Mono Trail up into the Sierra (described in *Field Guide #4—Sierra Nevada via Tioga Pass*, Stop 7). Two pairs of large **lateral moraines** are found at the bottom of Bloody Canyon (Figure FG6-3), each formed by a different glacial advance during the Pleistocene (see *Field Guide #5—Yosemite Valley* for additional information about glaciation in the Sierra).

The earliest advance roughly 100,000 to 120,000 years ago (probably during the beginning of the Tahoe-stage glaciations or what is sometimes called the "Mono Basin" glaciation) left the pair of moraines to the left (south), forming Sawmill Canyon. The second, larger advance came perhaps 60,000 to 80,000 years ago (probably toward the end of the Tahoe-stage glaciations, although some studies suggest these moraines are only slightly younger than the Sawmill moraines)—this time, the glacier turned north at the bottom of the canyon, cutting off

▲ **Figure FG6-3** Bloody Canyon and Sawmill Canyon lateral moraines seen from Stop 2. *(Darrel Hess photo.)*

the Sawmill Canyon moraines. Out of sight behind the lateral moraines of the larger advance, more recent glacial advances (Tioga-stage glaciations and a slightly older stage locally called the "Tenaya" glaciation) left smaller moraines that created the natural dam impounding Walker Lake.

From Panum Crater, return to California 120 and turn left (east).

Stop 3—South Tufa Area (37°56'20"N, 119°01'38"W):
About 1.6 miles east of the road to Panum Crater (4.7 miles east of U.S. 395), turn left onto a graded gravel road, following the signs about one mile to the South Tufa Area parking lot. Here you can pay a nominal entrance fee and take a short walk along a self-guided partially accessible boardwalk and nature trail that loops through tufa towers to the lake, and then back again to the parking lot. Please remember that tufa is quite fragile, so please do not climb on any of the towers—and no collecting of any kind is allowed.

Because Mono Lake has no natural outlet, its waters have become salty. All streams carry very small concentrations of dissolved salts and minerals. These substances are naturally concentrated in the lake as freshwater evaporates. If you were to taste the water of Mono Lake, you would find it both salty and bitter. The salty taste is mostly from sodium chloride (NaCl)—common table salt. The bitter taste is from carbonates—such as sodium carbonate (Na_2CO_3), which is similar to baking soda—and other natural alkaline chemicals that give the water its "slippery" feel. The lake also contains relatively large amounts of sulfates such as sodium sulfate (Na_2SO_4). Mono Lake is about three times as salty as the ocean, and 80 times as alkaline.

If you look closely at the water, you may see some glistening or "oily" looking patches of water just offshore. These are the upwellings from freshwater springs that come out of the lake bottom. The fresh-water doesn't mix immediately with the saltwater of the lake, producing the "shiny" looking water.

The most famous features of Mono Lake are the towers of tufa you see all around you at the lake shore (Figure FG6-4). The tufa towers are made of calcium carbonate ($CaCO_3$)—the chemical from which lime-stone is made. Tufa forms beneath the lake surface where freshwater springs enter the water. The fresh-water contains dissolved calcium compounds, which combine with the carbonate-rich lake water to form calcium carbonate. It also appears that algae play at least a minor role in the form and texture of the tufa. These limestone towers build up as calcium carbon-ate precipitates out around the springs. In the quiet waters below the surface of the lake, the towers grad-ually extend themselves higher and higher.

Most of the tufa towers you see here at the South Tufa Area were not visible until the level of Mono Lake began dropping as a result of water diversions in the 1940s. Some of the tufa towers are 30 feet (9 m) high, visual evidence of the lake's former level. The towers exposed here are probably less than 500 years old. Much older tufa formations are found along the ancient shorelines of the lake—especially along the north shore—some dating back as much as 13,000 years.

Although the waters of Mono Lake may at first seem rather lifeless, a fascinating ecosystem exists here. At the bottom of the food chain are micro-scopic, single-celled algae that live in the lake. The algae support two animal species: brine shrimp and brine flies. The shrimp and flies reproduce in extraordinary numbers, providing food for the many species of migratory water birds that visit the lake—some estimates suggest that as many as 900,000 birds stop or nest at Mono Lake each year.

The brine shrimp (*Artemia monica*) thrive during the summer months. After laying their eggs in September, the adults die. A new generation of brine shrimp hatches in the spring. During the winter, the lake water turns green because shrimp aren't pres-ent to eat the algae. In summer, when the numbers of brine shrimp are at their peak, the lake waters are usually quite clear.

The brine flies (*Ephydra hians*) around the lake shore are harmless. They were gathered for food by the Kuzedika Paiute people of the Mono Basin. You may also notice how birds catch large numbers of the flies: by running into a swarm along the shore with their mouths open.

Stop 4 (rolling stop)—June Lake Loop

(37°53'32"N, 119°05'34"W): Retrace your route to U.S. 395 and turn right (north) toward Lee Vining; after 0.5 miles turn left (west) onto California Highway 158—the June Lake Loop—one of the most scenic highways of the eastern Sierra.

After turning onto California 158, you'll have a closer view of the lateral moraines of Bloody Canyon and Sawmill Canyon; in the distance to your left are the irregular peaks of the Mono Craters. The small, pine tree-lined stream running along the left (east) side of the road is Rush Creek—once the largest stream feeding Mono Lake.

The highway ascends glacial deposits, reaching the crest of the large terminal moraine that impounds Grant Lake about 2.5 miles from U.S. 395 (37°51'45"N, 119°06'34"W). The original natural lake was made deeper by the construction of a series of progressively higher dams beginning in 1915. The highway along Grant Lake hugs the slope of a large lateral moraine—during the Pleistocene, this entire valley was filled with ice up to the crest of this moraine (Figure FG6-5). Straight ahead is Reversed Peak. A Pleistocene glacier flowed down from the crest of the Sierra where it was split by Reversed

▲ **Figure FG6-4** Tufa towers in South Tufa Area at Stop 3. *(Darrel Hess photo.)*

▲ **Figure FG6-5** Looking south over Grant Lake along the June Lake Loop, showing Reversed Peak and large lateral moraines. *(Darrel Hess photo.)*

Peak—part of the glacier moved toward you into the valley of Grant Lake; the other part flowed to the east of the peak into the valley occupied by June Lake (a few miles ahead).

At Grant Lake Marina, 4.9 miles from U.S. 395, you cross over one of several recessional moraines that cut across Grant Lake. Most of the vegetation along the highway is sagebrush, but in a few places where small streams come off the slope, small stands of Quaking Aspen (*Populus tremuloides*) thrive. At the south end of Grant Lake, 6.4 miles from U.S. 395, you enter a narrow valley with high walls and steep talus slopes leading down from Reversed Peak. About 2.5 miles later, the valley opens into beautiful Silver Lake—a popular fishing spot. Straight ahead is the hanging valley of Fern Creek, and to the right you see a cascade of water where Rush Creek drops out of its hanging valley.

About 10.1 miles from U.S. 395 you come to the Southern California Edison Rush Creek Power Plant (37°46′00″N, 119°07′20″W). A hydroelectric power plant was first built here by the Pacific Power Corporation in 1917; the current 8.4 Megawatt facility was built after 1941 when the City of Los Angeles began water diversion from Mono Lake. Water from Rush Creek is stored in Silver Lake and Grant Lake, and then channeled through a tunnel below the Mono Craters south into Long Valley where it feeds the Los Angeles Aqueduct. Rush Creek—now with greatly reduced discharge—continues into Mono Lake.

Immediately after passing over Rush Creek, the road turns northeast and begins to climb through dense forest. Now you're climbing up the canyon of Reversed Creek—one of the few streams that flows back *toward* the foot of the Sierra, instead of away from it. During the Pleistocene, the glacier split by Reversed Peak encountered such resistant rock that it was pushed *uphill* toward June Lake. For the next few miles the road winds up the steep floor of Reversed Creek valley, passing over several moraines, past Gull Lake, and then finally into the resort community of June Lake 13 miles from U.S. 395. At the far northern end of town, next to the June Lake Fire Department, you see a famous "perched" *erratic*—a large boulder left by a receding Pleistocene glacier (37°46′59″N, 119°04′23″W). After crossing the large terminal moraine at the northern end of June Lake the road drops steeply, reaching U.S. 395 again at June Lake Junction, 16 miles from our start.

Turn left (north) onto U.S. 395 and head back toward Lee Vining. In about 3.2 miles you pass by the gently rounded pink hills of Aeolian Buttes. The volcanic rock covering these hills is the 760,000-year-old Bishop Tuff, a volcanic rock made from "welded" pyroclastic material ejected during an enormous volcanic eruption of the Long Valley Caldera to the south. This eruption buried the area with as much as 600 feet of hot ash; winds carried some of this volcanic ash as far east as Nebraska. Continue on U.S. 395 for another 8 miles and you're back in Lee Vining.

Additional Resources

Textbook:
Hess, Darrel. *McKnight's Physical Geography: A Landscape Appreciation*, 11th ed. Upper Saddle River, NJ: Pearson, 2014. Chapters 14, 18 & 19.

Further Reading:
Glazner, Allen F., and Greg M. Stock. *Geology Underfoot in Yosemite National Park*. Missoula, MT: Mountain Press Publishing Company, 2010.
Hill, Mary. *Geology of the Sierra Nevada,* revised edition. California Natural History Guide, 80. Berkeley: University of California Press, 2006.

Teirney, Timothy. *Geology of the Mono Basin*. Lee Vining, CA: Kutsavi Press, 2011.

Web Sites:
Inyo National Forest
http://www.fs.fed.us/r5/inyo

Mono Lake Committee
http://www.monolake.org

Yosemite Area Regional Transportation System
http://www.yarts.com

Textbook Page References for Key Terms

caldera *(p. 425)*
granite *(p. 381)*
lateral moraine *(p. 566)*

lava *(p. 419)*
orographic lifting *(p. 166)*
Pleistocene Epoch *(p. 544)*

plug dome *(p. 424)*
pyroclastic *(p. 420)*
rain shadow *(p. 166)*

Field Guide #7

Santa Ana Winds

Edward Aguado, San Diego State University

Introduction

The coastal areas of southern California generally avoid extreme temperatures; summers don't usually get extremely hot and subfreezing temperatures are rare at the lower elevations. But temperatures can become surprisingly high during the fall and winter months due to a phenomenon known as Santa Ana winds. People from other parts of the United States might envy reports of 85°F (29°C) temperatures in January, but the winds sometimes have catastrophic consequences in the way of massive wildfires. This field guide departs from the format of most others in this collection; rather than describing a particular region, it will explain how one of the most important weather conditions arises in southern California.

Location

While Santa Anas are associated with southern California, similar warm, dry winds can occur elsewhere. For example, **foehn winds** (locally called *Chinooks*) often bring hot and dry conditions in the plains east of the Rocky Mountains, causing rapid snowmelt and extremely rapid changes in temperature. And northern California can get descending, warm winds out of the east. But the term *Santa Ana* is primarily associated with southern California.

Background

Across the California coast there is a tendency for winds, especially in the afternoon, to blow from west to east. This is due to a combination of the state's position in the westerly wind belt and the classic **sea and land breeze** system. Santa Ana winds bring a major departure from this pattern, bringing winds out of the northeast rather than the west.

Santa Ana winds develop as part of a larger-scale pattern wherein a large **anticyclone** (high pressure cell) migrates from the Pacific into the Great Basin. Surface-level winds in the Northern Hemisphere rotate clockwise out of high pressure cells toward areas of low pressure. If low pressure occurs offshore near southern California, winds can move from the interior states, across southern California, and even into the eastern Pacific.

To understand the high temperatures associated with Santa Anas, we need to consider the topography of the western United States and the idea of **adiabatic warming.** Nevada, Utah, and western Colorado occupy a large part of the Great Basin, whose elevation is mostly above 4,000 feet (1,200 m). As air flows southwestward out of the region to the southern California coastal area, it descends as it moves across the lowering surface. This is extremely important because sinking air undergoes compression, and this compression in turn causes the air's temperature to increase. (If you find this hard to imagine, take a hand pump and hold the base of it while you inflate a ball or bicycle tire—the base of the pump will feel warm because of the air's compression.)

If unsaturated air sinks, it warms at the **dry adiabatic rate** of 5.5°F per thousand feet (10°C/1,000 m). So if air starts out at an elevation of 6,000 feet with a temperature of 40°F, its temperature will rise 33 degrees by the time it reaches the Los Angeles or San Diego coast. This air is not only cool before it leaves the Great Basin, it is also dry, and as its temperature increases its **relative humidity** automatically decreases. Thus the air approaches southern California both warm and dry.

The local topography of southern California also plays a major role in the behavior of the Santa Anas. The region is bounded by several high mountain chains that have numerous lower-elevation passes. The Santa Ana winds funnel into these passes, and in so doing undergo major increases in wind speed—often with greater than 50 miles per hour (80 kph) sustained winds and even faster gusts.

Coastal southern California has a climate typical of west-coast areas with latitudes of about 30 to 40 degrees north and south, known as a **mediterranean climate.** This climate, named for the Mediterranean region of southern Europe and north Africa, is marked by generally mild winter and summer temperatures, moderate levels of humidity, and dry summers that can give way to sometimes very rainy winters. Such a climate favors natural vegetation that can tolerate the annual summer drought by having dry, waxy leaves and short, scrubby stems and branches that retard water loss. This type of vegetation, known as *chaparral* (Figure FG7-1), not only tolerates the dry season but has also adapted to withstand the natural fires that can sweep through these regions. But while these fires may leave no permanent mark on the vegetation, they can be catastrophic to the people who live in these areas.

Typical Santa Ana Airflow Patterns: Figure FG7-2 shows the weather pattern over the western United States at the peak of a Santa Ana wind event on October 23, 2007. The high pressure over southern Idaho, Utah and Nevada is very well developed and lower pressure is found off the southern California coast. This event generated very strong winds over the entire southern California region.

Figure FG7-3 shows the local wind flow pattern brought on during a different Santa Ana event. Notice that air enters the Los Angeles basin from the north and northeast through several canyons and, most notably, through Cajon Pass, which separates the San Gabriel Mountains from the San Bernardino Mountains. The winds not only flow from the northeast over much of the Los Angeles basin but even extend some distance offshore.

Residents of southern California have no trouble discerning Santa Ana winds from the normal wind patterns that otherwise dominate the region. The usual wind pattern over the area is dominated by the classic sea breeze and land breeze complex (see textbook Figure 5-34). Sea breezes form during the late morning in response to the low pressure inland generated by solar heating. This surface warming causes air to rise and spread out at higher altitudes, reducing the amount of air over the local area and creating a low pressure system. The offshore waters do

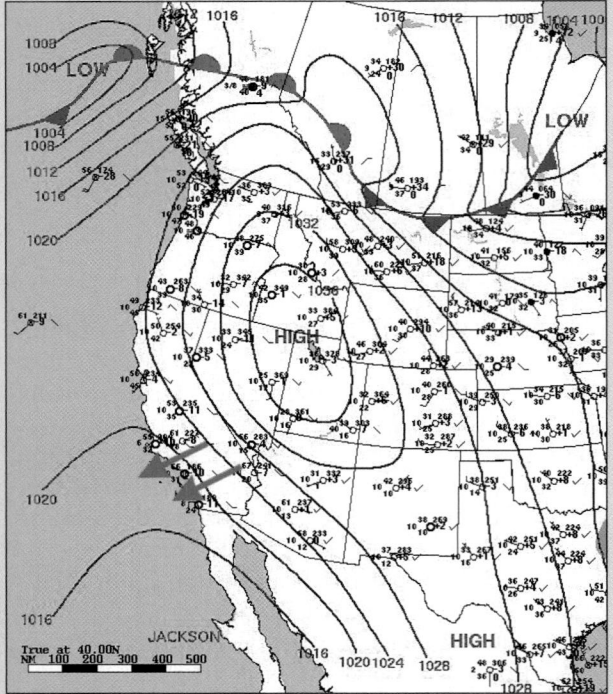

▲ **Figure FG7-2** Weather map during peak of the October 23, 2007 Santa Ana wind event. *(Adapted from National Weather Service.)*

▲ **Figure FG7-1** Chaparral vegetation in coastal southern California. *(Edward Aguado photo.)*

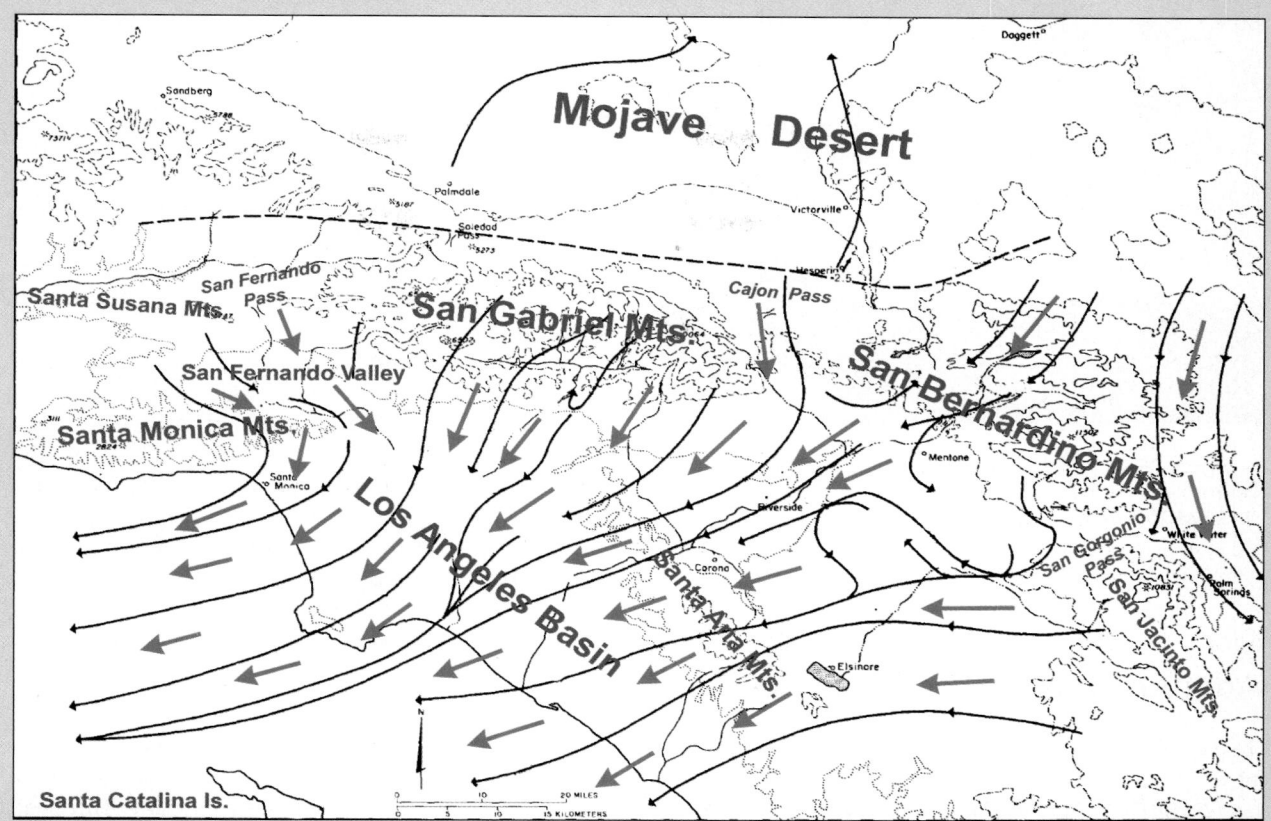

▲ **Figure FG7-3** Typical wind flow pattern in southern California during a Santa Ana wind event. *(Adapted from M.A. Fosberg, C.A. O'Dell, and M.J. Schroeder,* Some Characteristics of the Three-Dimensional Structure of Santa Ana Winds. *U.S. Forest Service Research Paper PSW—30. Forest Service, U.S. Department of Agriculture, 1966.)*

not undergo such warming, so the air stays cooler and more dense. The result is a greater air pressure offshore and a west-to-east wind. Because the sea breeze originates over cool waters, it tends to bring moderate temperatures and humidities—a far cry from the dry northeasterly Santa Ana winds.

Frequency and Timing of Santa Ana Winds: Almost all Santa Ana winds occur between the months of September through April, and they are infrequent during the summer months. While Santa Ana wind conditions represent a departure from the normal wind conditions in southern California, they cannot be considered rarities. A recent study analyzing the weather over a 33-year period has found that an average of 20 Santa Ana events occur each year, each typically lasting several days.

December is the month having the greatest average number of Santa Anas, closely followed by November and January. But Santa Anas are almost as frequent in October and are often far more significant. This is partly because Santa Ana events in the late fall and winter normally don't bring the intensely hot conditions that their October coun-

terparts do. But October Santa Anas also follow the normally dry summer months associated with mediterranean climates. Thus they can bring hot, dry conditions to an area dominated by dry vegetation. The combination of intense temperature and humidity conditions, dry vegetation, and strong winds provides the perfect situation for catastrophic wildfires. Such was the case in the Octobers of 2003 and 2007.

Impacts of Santa Ana Winds: The October 2007 weather map shown in Figure FG7-2 was selected because the Santa Ana event triggered an outbreak of major wildfires across San Diego County. The fires burned about 560 square miles of land (Figure FG7-4), taking with them some 1,600 homes and forcing the evacuation of a half million people. The conflagration had one other noteworthy aspect: It followed an even worse outbreak only four years earlier. In that event, several major fires burned large portions of southern California, especially in San Diego and San Bernardino counties. Those fires caused the destruction of over 3,500 homes and the loss of 40 lives.

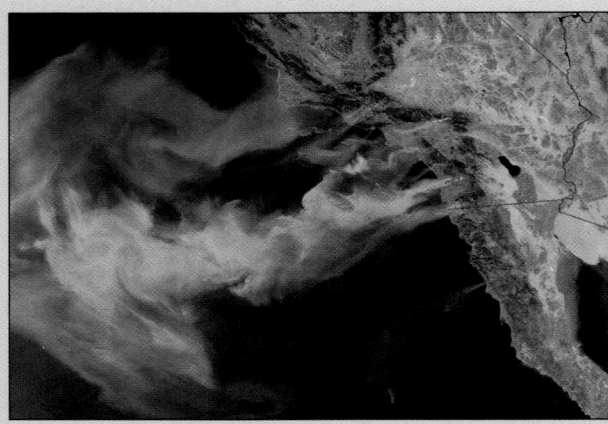

Figure FG7-4 Satellite image showing southern California fires on October 23, 2007. *(Image courtesy of NASA/MODIS Rapid Response.)*

Fire ecology specialists have had a long debate about the role of fire suppression's impact on the spread of uncontrollable wildfires in chaparral regions. Some have argued that when humans extinguish relatively small wildfires, they allow the amount of chaparral to grow so much that it provides a greater amount of fuel for subsequent fires. The subsequent fires, they believe, can become unmanageable and destined to destroy huge areas. Other experts argue that chaparral fuel builds up to these levels very quickly and that fire suppression therefore has little effect on the development of huge burns such as those of 2003 and 2007.

It should be noted that much of the area burned in 2007 had already been burned in 2003. Thus the vegetation that had been part of the huge 2007 fires had regenerated in only four years. This lends support to the notion that fire suppression is not a major factor in the threat of major conflagrations.

Additional Resources

Textbook:

Hess, Darrel. *McKnight's Physical Geography: A Landscape Appreciation*, 11th ed. Upper Saddle River, NJ: Pearson, 2014. Chapters 5 and 6.

Further Reading:

Aguado, Edward, and James E. Burt. *Understanding Weather & Climate*, 6th edition. Upper Saddle River, NJ: Pearson, 2013.

Raphael, M.N. "The Santa Ana Winds of California" in *Earth Interactions*, v. 7, issue 8, 2003, pp. 1–13 (Available online through the American Meteorological Society: *http://www.ametsoc.org/*).

Web Sites:

NASA Web page of 2007 Fires
http://www.nasa.gov/vision/earth/lookingatearth/socal_wildfires_oct07.html

Textbook Page References for Key Terms

adiabatic warming *(p. 88)*
anticyclone *(p. 115)*
dry adiabatic rate *(p. 152)*

Foehn/chinook winds *(p. 131)*
mediterranean climate *(p. 222)*

relative humidity *(p. 149)*
sea/land breeze *(p. 129)*

Field Guide #8

Southern Coast:
Dana Point to La Jolla

Patricia Deen, Palomar College

Introduction

The coast of southern California from Dana Point to La Jolla provides an opportunity to explore a variety of coastal processes, landforms, and ecosystems. Changes in sea level from repeated ice ages and active uplift along faults have resulted in an extraordinary cliffed coastline with intervening stream valleys and coastal lagoons.

Urbanization has taken its toll on the coastal zone. Construction of dams and coastal structures such as seawalls and jetties has decreased sand supply and increased rates of bluff erosion. Construction of highways and railroads across lagoons has decreased tidal flow, degrading the health of wetland ecosystems. However, several recent projects have been initiated to minimize some of these human impacts. This field guide surveys natural processes that have shaped this coastline, the impacts of urbanization, and the ongoing battle to restore the quality of this coastal region.

Location

Dana Point is located in Orange County, California, about halfway between Los Angeles and San Diego. Figure FG8-1 shows the general location of field guide stops. Specific directions with mileages are provided; the total distance is about 65 miles (104 km). All seven stops can be visited in one day; however, you may find it more enjoyable to linger on the beach or at the tide pools, making a two-day trip optimal.

The mild climate makes this field trip possible at any time of the year; however, warm summer weather brings large crowds and parking problems to beach areas. Note that beach access and tide pools are best at low tide, so check a tide table before you go (see *Additional Resources* on F-60).

Background

Beach Compartments: Beaches are deposits of wave-worked sediment along the coast. In southern California, beaches are divided into *beach compartments*. The rocky headland at Dana Point is the beginning of the Oceanside Beach Compartment (see Figure FG8-1). Sand is delivered to the coast by streams and erosion of coastal bluffs. Wave energy generates **longshore currents** that transport sand southward along the coast (see textbook Figure 20-14). The Oceanside Beach Compartment ends 50 miles (80 km) down the coast where sand is drained off the beach through La Jolla Submarine Canyon, which extends to a depth of over 3,000 feet (1,000 meters).

Sandy beaches are valuable not only for their recreational use but also for the protection they provide to coastal bluffs. Construction of harbors and jetties diverts sand from the coastal **sediment budget,** leaving downstream beaches and coastal cliffs prone to erosion.

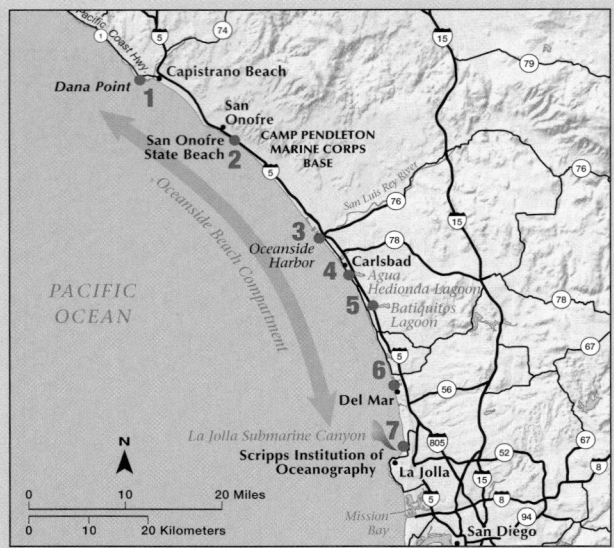

▲ **Figure FG8-1** Regional map of the southern California Coast from Dana Point to San Diego, showing field guide stops and the Oceanside Beach Compartment.

Site Descriptions

To reach Stop 1 from Interstate 5 (I-5) take Exit #79 (California Highway 1—the Pacific Coast Highway or PCH) near the town of Capistrano Beach. Turn left onto Dana Point Harbor Drive and continue 1.3 miles to where the road dead-ends into the parking lot of the Ocean Institute.

Stop 1—Ocean Institute at Dana Point

(33°27'42"N, 117°42'23"W): In 1835, Richard Henry Dana, Jr. described the tall cliffs, rocky shore, and dangerous landing at Dana Point in his epic tale *Two Years Before the Mast*. In the 1960s, Dana Cove became legendary to surfers for **wave refraction** around the point (see textbook Figure 20-5), building into the surf break known as "Killer Dana." In 1968, a breakwater was built to provide safe harbor for recreational boats, spelling the end of the "Killer Dana" surf break. Today, Dana Point Harbor is the home of the Ocean Institute, a wheelchair-accessible facility which offers a variety of public programs including whale-watching trips aboard its research vessel R/V *Sea Explorer*. A reproduction of the brig *Pilgrim*, which carried Dana on his voyage, helps to transport visitors back in time to the days of early California. Check the Ocean Institute's Web site for a schedule of activities. If the tide is low, investigate the tide pools below the rocky point.

Tourist attractions aside, Dana Point marks a significant place along the southern California coastline; its rock promontory or *headland* marks the

beginning of the Oceanside Beach Compartment. Just south of the harbor, San Juan Creek delivers sand to Doheny State Beach. Sand is carried by longshore currents down the coast where it will eventually drain out of the beach system through La Jolla Submarine Canyon.

Stop 2—San Onofre State Beach

(33°21'43"N, 117°32'26"W): From the Ocean Institute, travel east on Dana Point Harbor Drive for 1.2 miles. Turn right onto PCH/Highway 1, and after one mile enter southbound Interstate 5. After 7.6 miles take Exit 71 (Basilone Road) and turn right at the end of the offramp. Continue for 3.2 miles to the San Onofre State Beach entrance station; stop and pay the entrance fee. Park in the lot for *Beach Trail #1*.

Beach Trail #1 leads to a spectacular overlook. (For a wheelchair-accessible path, instead of parking next to Beach Trail #1, continue 100 yards and park by the entrance to a gravel access road—from there it is about 50 yards to the overlook.). The flat surface along the top of the bluffs is a **marine terrace,** eroded by waves 125,000 years ago and then uplifted by faulting (see textbook Figure 20-29). Looking north, you can see the San Onofre Nuclear Generating Station (SONGS). SONGS uses seawater as part of its cooling system. Seawater that is drawn into the power plant contains large numbers of small fish and microscopic plants and animals. The destruction of these organisms has been linked to the decline of fisheries along the coast. Legislation mandates that coastal users mitigate the negative effects of their activities. As a result, SONGS helped pay for projects including lagoon restoration and fish stock enhancement. In order to combat the negative effects of its warm water outfall on kelp growth, an artificial kelp reef was constructed to the north of the plant. In January 2012, the SONGS nuclear reactors were shut down for repairs and it is unclear when both reactors will be operational again.

The amphitheater-shaped scarps in the bluff are from **landslide** activity. Nearly 80% of the bluffs between SONGS and Marine Corps Base Camp Pendleton to the south are fronted by landslides. To see the reason for this, follow the trail downhill and walk north along the beach about 0.25 miles. Note the change from contorted landslide deposits to a light-colored vertical sandstone cliff (Figure FG8-2). This marks the location of the Christianitos Fault. The Christianitos Fault is a normal fault (see textbook Figure 14-58) that brings erosion-resistant sandstone into contact with landslide-prone mudstones. Although there has been no recent movement on the fault, it is still considered active. As such, its proximity to SONGS has caused some concern.

▲ **Figure FG8-2**   View looking north along San Onofre State Beach at Stop 2. *(Patricia Deen photo.)*

▲ **Figure FG8-3**   Oceanside Harbor area at Stop 3. *(Image adapted from Google Earth™.)*

The beach here can be difficult to walk along. Although sand dominates the beach in summer, winter waves uncover cobbles composed of an amazing assortment of igneous and metamorphic rocks. The variety of colors and crystals in these rocks will certainly catch your eye.

Stop 3—Oceanside Harbor (33°12'11"N, 117°23'31'''W):

From the San Onofre State Beach entrance, return to Interstate 5 and continue south. After 16.5 miles take Exit 54C (Harbor Drive) and turn right at the end of the offramp. Turn left onto Harbor Drive South (a "T" intersection) and left again at the "Y" to stay on Harbor Drive South. Continue for about 0.5 miles past restaurants and shops until you reach Parking Lot #10 where there is two-hour free parking

Oceanside Harbor is located between Marine Corps Base Camp Pendleton to the north and a chain of coastal cities to the south (Figure FG8- 3). The **jetty** was built in 1942 to protect Del Mar Boat Basin, which was used for amphibious training exercises during World War II. A civilian small-craft marina was added in 1958. The Santa Margarita River, located just north of the harbor, delivers huge volumes of sand to the coast. Longshore currents pile up sand against the north side of the jetty (see textbook Figure 20-25) providing Camp Pendleton with one of the widest beaches in the region. Sand is transported around the jetty and deposited in the harbor entrance where it must be dredged regularly. Sand is pumped from the harbor entrance back into the longshore current system south of the harbor. In addition, the jetty deflects a large quantity of sand offshore. Ever since its construction, Oceanside Harbor has severely impeded coastal sand transport and has resulted in less sand on beaches down the coast.

The long rock wall structure along the south side of Parking Lot #10 marks the north bank of the San Luis Rey River. This river is a major source of sand for beaches south of Oceanside Harbor. However, due to the region's dry climate and upstream development, sand rarely reaches the coast from its large inland watershed. It is only during exceptionally wet years that floods deliver a significant volume of sand to the beaches. The newly constructed Pacific Street Bridge is a testament to flooding of the San Luis Rey River; the City of Oceanside will no longer have to periodically rebuild Pacific Street, which was once laid over the sand at the river's mouth.

Stop 4—Agua Hedionda Lagoon (33°08'30"N, 117°20'28"W):

Return to Interstate 5 via Harbor Drive South and continue south on I-5. After 5.0 miles, take Exit 49 (Tamarack Avenue) and turn right at the end of the offramp. Turn left onto Carlsbad Boulevard and go 0.5 miles. Park along the street near lifeguard tower #32.

Agua Hedionda Lagoon is one of several coastal **lagoons** in San Diego County; its development and successful multi-use history is unique to the region. This relatively deep-water lagoon stretches inland 1.5 miles (2.4 km); it is divided into three sections by Interstate 5 and the railroad. The eastern section contains a small boat launch and dock for recreational users. The central section is home to a YMCA youth aquatics camp.

From your position, you can see the activities in the western basin. The rows of barrel-shaped floats suspend mussels and oysters grown commercially by Carlsbad Aquafarms. Carlsbad Aquafarms has recently partnered with Scripps Institution of Oceanography scientists to culture abalone, a highly prized yet severely depleted resource along our coast. On the north shore of the lagoon is a low building with green circles; this is the Leon Raymond Hubbard Marine Fish Hatchery, which is operated by the Hubbs-SeaWorld Research Institute. Inside the building, wild adult White Seabass *(Astractoscion nobilis)* are spawned to produce eggs. Eggs are then raised into juvenile seabass, which are then released into the ocean. The goal of this program is to increase the population of White Seabass, whose numbers have decreased substantially due to overfishing. So far, the hatchery has released more than 1.4 million juvenile White Seabass along the southern California coast.

All of these activities are made possible by the Encina Power Plant. The deepened lagoon is the result of dredging to accommodate sufficient circulation of seawater for use in the plant's cooling system. Two pairs of jetties allow water to flow through the lagoon. Seawater flows into the lagoon through the north pair of jetties; the inflow captures sand, which must be dredged regularly and placed back on the beach. The south pair of jetties is locally known as "warm-water jetties" due to the outflow of warm seawater from the power plant.

The Encina Power Plant is also the future site of the Poseidon Resources Carlsbad Desalination Project. Upon completion in 2016, 50 million gallons of fresh drinking water will be produced daily, which constitutes 9% of San Diego's freshwater needs. Currently, over 95% of the county's freshwater is imported.

Stop 5—Batiquitos Lagoon and Nature Center (33°05'37"N, 117°18'05"W): From Agua Hedionda Lagoon continue south on Carlsbad Boulevard. After 0.6 miles turn south onto Cannon Road, and then after 0.4 miles turn right onto southbound Interstate 5. After 2.1 miles take Exit 45 (Poinsettia Lane) and turn left at the end of the offramp; after 0.6 miles turn right onto Batiquitos Drive, and after 0.5 miles turn right onto Gabbiano Lane. Drive about 0.3 miles and park at the end of Gabbiano Lane. This is a residential area.

Batiquitos Lagoon is the site of the first major lagoon restoration project on the West Coast. Tidal flow had been severely restricted by the construction of Pacific Coast Highway, the railroad, and Interstate 5. The lagoon had also been sectioned off for salt evaporation ponds, and, up until the 1970s, used for sewage discharge. By 1980, the lagoon was an odorous, mosquito-ridden mudflat that posed a health risk to humans. The City of Carlsbad, in cooperation with other government agencies, developed a plan to restore tidal flushing and enhance wildlife

habitat. The Batiquitos Lagoon Enhancement Plan was put into action with mitigation funds largely from the Port of Los Angeles and was completed in 1996. Since then, biological monitoring has shown a marked increase in the number of marine fish and bird species. Nesting of endangered bird species, including the Least Tern (Sterna antillarum) and Snowy Plover *(Charadrius alexandrinus)*, has also proven a success.

The Batiquitos Lagoon Foundation operates a wheelchair-accessible nature center where you can learn more about the restoration project, lagoon ecology, and the hundreds of species of birds that can be seen at Batiquitos Lagoon throughout the year. Pick up a lagoon trail guide and take a leisurely stroll to experience a healthy coastal lagoon environment.

Stop 6—Del Mar Shores (32°58'51"N, 117°16'14"W): Retrace your route back to I-5 via Gabbiano Lane, Batiquitos Drive, and Poinsettia Lane, then turn left onto southbound Interstate 5. After 9.0 miles take Exit 36 (Via de la Valle) and turn right at the end of the offramp. About 1.2 miles after exiting the freeway, continue straight across S-21/Old Highway 101 (the street name becomes Border Avenue). After 0.1 mile turn right onto Sierra Avenue, then immediately left onto Del Mar Shores Terrace. Park along the street.

From the "Coastal Access" sign next to the Del Mar Shores condominium complex, follow the alleyway to the stairs overlooking the beach. This section of coastal cliffs is composed of fractured sandstone overlain by poorly cemented sandy terrace deposits. The lack of beach sand makes access difficult except at low tide. At high tide, waves undermine the base of the cliffs, accelerating their retreat. Heed the warning signs to keep your distance from the base of the cliffs!

Walk along the beach to the north and south to observe erosional features such as sea caves, small landslides, and gullies from runoff erosion. Also note the remnants of staircases that have been destroyed by storms. A variety of methods have been used to protect the base of the cliffs from wave erosion (Figure FG8-4); these include seawalls, riprap, and concrete plugs that fill sea caves. Crib walls and plaster coatings, called *gunite,* have also been installed to hold the upper portion of the bluff in place. One homeowner has piled decades of yard waste in an attempt to protect the upper portion of the bluff!

Armoring coastal bluffs against wave attack is very controversial. Opponents note that structures

▲ **Figure FG8-4**   Structures armoring bluffs in Solana Beach near Stop 6. *(Patricia Deen photo.)*

take up large sections of public beach and are visually unappealing. In addition, scientists have recently determined that up to 50% of beach sand in the Oceanside Beach Compartment is derived from bluff erosion; armoring the cliffs therefore accelerates disappearing beaches. Current legislation mandates that new construction must be properly set back from the edge of a cliff. However, structures built in the coastal zone before passage of the California Coastal Act in 1976 can be granted a permit to build a seawall.

A new approach to prevent bluff erosion is the addition of sand to the beach in a process called "beach nourishment." In 2001, the San Diego Regional Beach Sand Project spent $17 million to add two million cubic yards of sand onto twelve sections of San Diego County beaches. The project utilized sand from former river channels and offshore beach deposits and transported the sand via barge to the beach. The newly widened beaches lasted about two years; the longshore current system has long since carried the sand down the coast. However, the value of sand to promote tourism and protect coastal bluffs has made beach nourishment a viable policy option. The latest large-scale beach nourishment project was completed in 2012.

Stop 7—Scripps Institution of Oceanography and the Birch Aquarium (32° 51'58"N, 117°15'11"W): From Del Mar Shores turn left onto Sierra Avenue and then left again onto Border Avenue. In 0.2 miles turn right onto Old Highway 101 and drive south through the city of

Del Mar (the street name becomes Camino del Mar). Continue past Torrey Pines State Reserve (the street name becomes North Torrey Pines Road). After about 6.5 miles turn right to continue on North Torrey Pines Road. In 1.4 miles turn right onto Expedition Way; note the sign for the Birch Aquarium. After 0.5 miles turn left into the Birch Aquarium parking lot. Parking is free for three hours.

The Birch Aquarium at Scripps provides an opportunity to explore marine ecosystems from the Pacific Northwest, southern California, Mexico, and the tropical Pacific. Displays also highlight oceanographic research at Scripps Institution of Oceanography (SIO). The aquarium is well worth a visit and is wheelchair accessible. However, begin by walking downhill along Downwind Way toward Scripps pier and the beach. Use the pedestrian bridge to cross La Jolla Shores Drive; you can then use a series of elevators or stairs to walk through the campus towards the pier.

The platform next to the pier provides a beautiful place from which to view La Jolla Cove and the surrounding area. To the south, Mount Soledad rises 822 feet (250 meters) along the Rose Canyon Fault, which is part of an active fault system that parallels the coast northward into Los Angeles. La Jolla Submarine Canyon follows the fault out into the bay and marks the end of the Oceanside Beach Compartment. Sand that enters the Oceanside Beach Compartment is drained off here through La Jolla Submarine Canyon.

As you look out on the bay, you will probably notice large areas of Giant Kelp (*Macrocystis pyrifera*) offshore. La Jolla Cove and the area around Point La Jolla have a robust forest of kelp due to cold, nutrient-rich water rises to the surface. Under ideal conditions, Giant Kelp can grow up to two feet (0.6 meters) per day! Giant Kelp is the foundation for a biologically rich ecosystem that stretches all along the California coast. In 2005, La Jolla Cove was designated the La Jolla State Marine Conservation Area, part of a state-wide network of reserves created to protect critical marine habitats.

If the tide is low, you can walk down to the beach and north of the pier for some good tide pooling. The 200-foot (60-meter) cliffs provide a look at channeled conglomerates and contorted mudstones that are similar to those being deposited beyond La Jolla Submarine Canyon today. Further north, you can see the tall cliffs of Torrey Pines, which are subject to massive landslides.

Additional Resources

Textbook:

Hess, Darrel. *McKnight's Physical Geography: A Landscape Appreciation*, 11th ed. Upper Saddle River, NJ: Pearson, 2014. Chapter 20.

Further Reading:

Dana, Richard Henry Jr. *Two Years Before the Mast: A Personal Narrative of Life at Sea*, introduction by Gary Kinder. New York: Modern Library Paperback Edition, 2001.

Griggs, Gary, Kiki Patsch, and Lauret Savoy. *Living With the Changing California Coast*. Berkeley: University of California Press, 2005.

Sheldon, Ian. *Seashore of Southern California*. Auburn, WA: Lone Pine Publishing International Inc., 2007.

Web Sites:

Batiquitos Lagoon Foundation
http://www.batiquitosfoundation.org

Birch Aquarium
http://aquarium.ucsd.edu

Carlsbad Desalination Project
http://www.carlsbad-desal.com

Hubbs SeaWorld Research Institute
http://www.hswri.org

Ocean Institute
http://www.ocean-institute.org

Tidelines Online
http://www.tidelines.com

Textbook Page References for Key Terms

beach *(p. 585)*

jetty *(p. 589)*

lagoon *(p. 587)*

landslide *(p. 459)*

longshore current *(p. 583)*

marine terrace *(p. 592)*

normal fault *(p. 435)*

sediment budget *(p. 585)*

wave refraction *(p. 576)*

Field Guide #9

Death Valley

Darrel Hess, City College of San Francisco

Introduction

Death Valley offers some of the most spectacular examples of desert processes and landforms in the world. It is the driest and hottest location in the United States, with an average annual rainfall of less than 2.0 inches (5.1 cm) and summertime high temperatures that regularly exceed 120°F (49°C). Death Valley's July 10, 1913 temperature of 134°F (56.7°C) is the highest temperature ever recorded in the world.

Death Valley National Park encompasses not only Death Valley itself, but also portions of surrounding desert valleys, including Saline Valley, Eureka Valley, and northern Panamint Valley. This field guide describes a number of easily-reached sites within the Park that provide a wide sampling of Basin-and-Range desert features such as alluvial fans, sand dunes, a fascinating display of evaporative salt and mineral deposits, evidence of recent tectonic activity, and remarkable examples of plant and animal adaptations to the desert environment.

▲ **Figure FG9-1** Regional map of Death Valley showing field guide stops.

Location

The main Visitor Center for Death Valley National Park is at Furnace Creek (36°27'39"N, 116°52'01"W), reached by traveling east on California Highway 190 from U.S. 395 or traveling west on Highway 190 from California Highway 127 (Figure FG9-1). In addition to the Visitor Center where you can pay the Park entrance fee, the Furnace Creek area has several campgrounds (during the spring, reserve your campsite ahead of time or you're likely to end up in the "overflow" Sunset campground that doesn't have picnic tables or fire rings). Gasoline, groceries, restaurants, and water are available near the campgrounds and Visitor Center. Lodging is available in the two private resorts in the area—Furnace Creek Ranch and Furnace Creek Inn—as well as in Stovepipe Wells to the north.

The Furnace Creek Visitor Center and many campgrounds in the Park are wheelchair accessible. However, a limited number of trails in Death Valley are fully accessible—check the Park Web site below for details.

Spring is the most popular time to visit Death Valley. The weather is warm, but not oppressively hot—and you may be lucky enough to see a wildflower bloom (see *Additional Resources*). Be prepared for cool nights (or even snow in the surrounding mountains), and expect that at least a few of the days will be very windy.

There are three important cautions for travelers in Death Valley: (1) Even if temperatures are not especially high, because of the extremely dry air you can quickly lose a great deal of fluid through perspiration without realizing it. To avoid dehydration be sure to drink lots of water. (2) Flash floods and debris flows can be hazards any time of year. Watch the sky for growing thunderstorms and avoid narrow canyons if you see storm clouds developing over the surrounding mountains—a flash flood or debris flow can fill up a dry canyon in a matter of seconds with almost no warning. (3) Nearly every year visitors are injured in single-vehicle accidents that occur when a quickly-moving vehicle's passenger-side tires veer off the pavement onto the lower "soft shoulder." If this happens to you, *do not* brake hard or turn sharply to get back up on the pavement—this may cause your car to overturn. Instead, gradually slow down before reentering the road.

Background

Geology and Landforms: Death Valley is part of the Basin-and-Range province of North America (see textbook Figure 18-27). Although called a "valley," Death Valley was not produced by stream erosion—this region of the continent has been undergoing tectonic extension for several million years, resulting in a series of down-tilted **grabens** and relatively uplifted **tilted-fault block mountains** and **horsts** (see textbook Figures 14-61 and 18-28). Although much of the structure of Death Valley is due to such **normal faulting**, at least part of the valley is thought to be a *pull-apart basin*, formed where land drops between two parallel **strike-slip faults** (Figure FG9-2).

Death Valley itself is the deepest of the desert grabens in North America, with more than 500 square miles (1,300 square kilometers) of the basin floor below sea level (see textbook Figure 18-30). Like most basins in the region, Death Valley is a *basin of interior drainage*, with no stream outlet to the sea. Ongoing deposition from the surrounding mountains has filled the basin with great thickness of sediment, and active

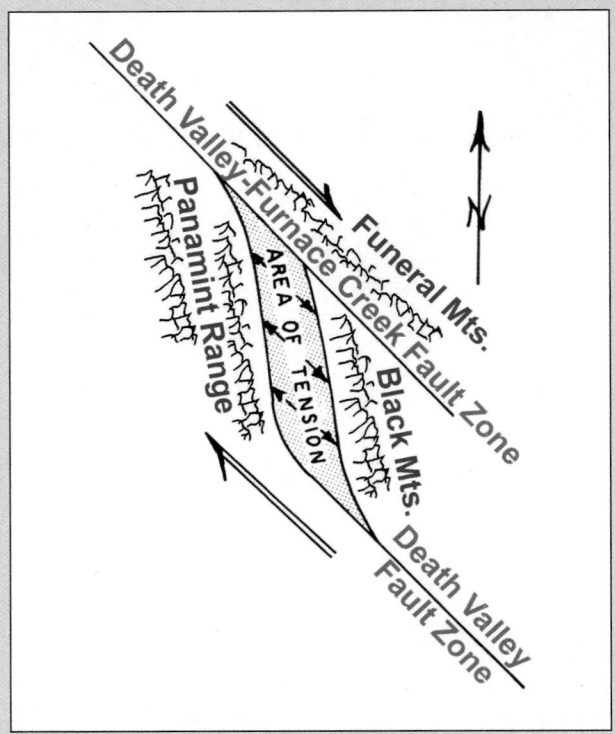

▲ **Figure FG9-2** Extension is taking place between two parallel strike-slip faults in Death Valley, forming a pull-apart basin. *(Adapted from California Division of Mines and Geology, Special Report 106.)*

alluvial fans are found at the mouths of nearly every canyon (see textbook Figure 18-29). Rather than the more typical desert **playa**, the lowest part of Death Valley has a *salt pan*—an expanse of dry salt deposits.

While the basin itself is relatively young geologically—and is still undergoing faulting—the rocks in Death Valley vary enormously in age. In the salt pan *evaporite* rocks are still forming, while in other parts of the Park rocks as old as 1.7 billion years are exposed.

Weather and Climate: The dryness of Death Valley is primarily a result of its position in a "quadruple" **rain shadow** formed by the mountain ranges to the west—especially the Sierra Nevada. By the time the moist air of the westerlies coming off Pacific Ocean reaches the valley, it's been forced to rise and cool several times by mountain ranges, condensing out almost all of the moisture. Over the last 95 years, Death Valley rainfall has averaged less than 2.0 inches (5.1 cm) per year, although over the last 30 years rainfall has increased to 2.5 inches (6.4 cm) per year.

When it does rain in Death Valley, it often comes in the form of a localized thunderstorm, which in turn may trigger a flash flood or **debris flow**. It is through such episodic events that most change takes

Figure FG9-3 The Creosote Bush is one of the most common shrubs in Death Valley. Desert Holly is found in some of the driest locations in the Park. *(Darrel Hess photos.)*

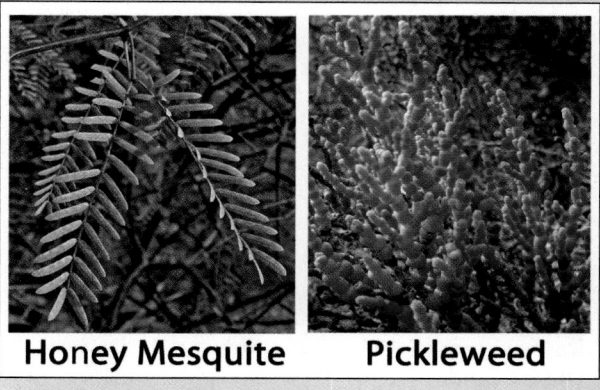

Figure FG9-4 Honey Mesquite thrives in areas where groundwater is close to the surface. Pickleweed survives in salty soil. *(Darrel Hess photos.)*

place in desert areas such as this. It may seem paradoxical in such an arid location, but evidence of both fluvial erosion and fluvial deposition are common sights in Death Valley.

The high summer temperatures are due to the lack of moderating water bodies nearby, and to the great total *insolation* produced by the high Sun and clear skies. It also appears that convection within the deep valley circulates warm air back down to the basin floor, without much cooling.

Plant Communities: A great variety of shrubs and wildflowers grows in Death Valley. Nearly all are *xerophytic* (adapted to dry conditions), but salt tolerance also influences distribution patterns.

The most common large, multi-stemmed shrub seen on the slopes of alluvial fans is the dark, glossy green-leaved Creosote Bush (*Larrea tridentata*; Figure FG9-3), named for the strong smell of its leaves. This plant depends on rainwater percolating down into the groundwater *zone of aeration* (see textbook Figure 9-28); competition for this infrequent and transitory water supply causes Creosote Bushes to distance themselves from each other. Creosote can reproduce through cloning—asexual reproduction from an existing plant. Overtime, clones tend to spread away from the original plant, forming a large ring. Some clone colonies are thought to be more than 10,000 years old.

Mixed in with Creosote in many locations—and by themselves in drier locations along the bottom edges of alluvial fans leading down to the basin floor—you see the light-green, sharp-leaved Desert Holly (*Atriplex hymenelytra*).

In places where groundwater is found fairly close to the surface, such as along major ephemeral stream channels at the bottom of large alluvial fans (as in the area of Furnace Creek), stands of Honey Mesquite (*Prosopis glandulosa*) often thrive (Figure FG9-4). These shrubs have long *taproots* that extend down as much as 50 feet (15 m) to reach the groundwater *zone of saturation* (see textbook Figure 11-4).

In the saltiest locations, such as around Badwater and Salt Creek, Pickleweed (*Allenrolfea occidentalis*) is found. Pickleweed is easily recognized by its distinctive "beaded" appearance.

If you travel to Death Valley in the spring, you may be treated to a display of wildflowers. The magnitude of the wildflower display depends mostly on the amount and timing of winter rains. Some wildflower seeds remain dormant for years (or even decades) until just the right combination of rain and temperature triggers a bloom. A relatively wet winter in Death Valley usually leads to a wildflower bloom in the spring, but in even the driest years at least a few wildflowers are found up in the canyons. The Death Valley National Park Web site has a link that provides a seasonal wildflower update (see *Additional Resources*).

One of the most common valley floor wildflowers is the Desert Gold (*Geraea canescens*). This bright yellow, tall sunflower is seen along the roadsides and up on the alluvial fans (Figure FG9-5). During a large wildflower bloom, stands of Desert Gold form a stunning blanket of yellow across the usually barren Death Valley landscape.

The Gravel Ghost (*Atrichoseris platyphylla*) is a tall, thin-stemmed, multi-petaled white flower with leaves that lie flat on the ground; from a distance the flowers almost disappear against the background of rocks on an alluvial fan.

In most years, up in the narrow canyons leading down to the basin floor, you may find the distinctive Desert Five Spot (*Eremalche rotundifolia*). This lovely small, bowl-shaped lavender flower is easily recognized by the large dark red spots on the inside of its petals.

▲ **Figure FG9-5** Desert Gold (left); Gravel Ghost (top right); Desert Five Spot (lower right). *(Darrel Hess photos.)*

▲ **Figure FG9-6** View northwest across Death Valley from Dantes View at Stop 1. *(Darrel Hess photo.)*

Site Descriptions

The following stops can be reached easily by ordinary automobiles. Although it is possible to visit all of these sites in one day, it's best to spend at least a couple of days in the Park, perhaps going to sites east and south of Furnace Creek on the first day (Stops 1 through 6), and sites north and west on the second day (Stops 7 through 9). Along the way, you'll find many other interesting spots to explore.

Stop 1—Dantes View (36°13'15"N, 116°43'36"W):

A good starting point for first-time visitors to the Park is the high mountain overlook of Dantes View. Drive southeast from Furnace Creek on California 190, climbing up off the valley floor along the dry Furnace Creek Wash. About eleven miles from Furnace Creek, a sign directs you to turn right (south) onto a road that will take you the final thirteen miles up to Dantes View (the last few miles of the road are very steep). This 5,475-foot (1,669 m) high vantage point in the Black Mountains offers spectacular views of the valley and surrounding mountains (Figure FG9-6). It is typically very windy at Dantes View, and usually more than 20°F (12°C) cooler than at Badwater 5,700 feet below you—recall that the **average lapse rate** is about 3.6°F/1000 feet (6.5°C/1000 m).

Directly below you at the foot of the Black Mountains are Badwater (Stop 5) and the Badwater alluvial fan (Stop 6). The Death Valley salt pan stretches across valley floor to the enormous **bajada** running along the foot of the Panamint Range to the

west. Telescope Peak (11,049 feet; 3,368 m) is the high point in the Panamints 21 miles across the valley.

Several times during the **Pleistocene Epoch**, Death Valley was filled with water as a freshwater lake (called Lake Manly) as much as 600 feet (180 m) deep (see textbook Figure 19-6 and *Field Guide #6—Mono Lake* for more information about Pleistocene lakes). If the season has been especially wet, the salt pan may be temporarily covered with a shallow salty lake that can take weeks to completely evaporate.

Stop 2—Zabriskie Point (36°25'15"N, 116°48'44"W):

As you retrace your path back down to the valley floor, about four miles before Furnace Creek, you'll come to a turnout for Zabriskie Point. This is a great location to see **badlands** topography (see textbook Figure 18-37). Here, three- to nine-million-year-old lake bed deposits have been heavily dissected by ephemeral streams into this stark landscape. The dark-colored material was derived mostly from lava flows and volcanic ash, while the lighter tan and yellow material was derived mostly from weathered iron-rich deposits. Zabriskie Point is a popular spot to view the sunset.

Stop 3—Fault Scarp (36°26'12"N, 116°51'05"W):

Continue west on Highway 190. Just past the Furnace Creek Inn turn left (south) onto the Badwater Road—the main road along the east side of the valley. After traveling south about 0.7 miles, pull off the road and look to the left (east). Notice the six-foot (two m) high fault scarp running parallel to the road along the front of the Black Mountains (Figure FG9-7).

This fault scarp was produced by a prehistoric fault rupture along the east side of the valley (per-

Figure FG9-7 Fault scarp along Badwater Road at Stop 3. *(Darrel Hess photo.)*

haps 2,000 years ago). During the large earthquake produced by this fault rupture, the basin floor dropped down more than six feet relative to the Black Mountains—indication of geologically-recent tectonic activity in Death Valley. As you continue south on the Badwater Road, you'll see evidence of this and similar fault scarps cutting through the tops of some of the alluvial fans.

Stop 4—Ventifacts (36°19'48"N, 116°49'48"W): Continue south on the Badwater Road for about 7.8 miles until you see the turn-off for Artists Drive (Artists Drive and Golden Canyon, which you passed north of here, are very popular destinations in the Park). However, instead of turning left (east) onto Artists Drive, pull off the road and walk right (to the west) up along a low ridge that extends toward the valley floor. The large rocks you see are mostly **basalt**. As you approach the crest of the ridge, notice that most of the rocks have been fluted through sandblasting by the wind (see textbook Figure 18-15). Although wind is not generally a very powerful process of erosion, these rocks, known as "ventifacts," are the most conspicuous evidence of the wind erosion of rock in the valley. (Recall that sand dunes, which you'll visit at Stop 8, are primarily the consequence of wind deposition, not wind erosion.)

Stop 5—Badwater and the Death Valley Salt Pan (36°13'48"N, 116°46'01"W): Continue south on the Badwater Road another eight miles until you reach the parking lot at Badwater. The elevation here is about 280 feet (85 m) below sea level. The official weather station for Death Valley is at Furnace Creek, but summer temperatures here at Badwater typically run one or two degrees hotter. In fact, some researchers suggest that during the summer Badwater may be the hottest place on Earth.

If you look back to the Black Mountains just north of Badwater, you will see the gently rounded, convex surface of the Badwater *turtleback* extending slightly away from the generally straight mountain front. This turtleback (and two others just south of here) have been studied and debated for decades by geologists (they're called turtlebacks because they resemble the shape of a turtle shell). Turtlebacks along the Black Mountains consist of very old rock (probably more than one billion years old), exposed relatively recently by faulting along curved fault planes.

The salty pond that gives Badwater its name originates from freshwater issuing out of the Black Mountains into the salty valley floor. The water isn't poisonous—just salty.

Walk along the path out onto the salt pan. Out in the middle of the valley floor, a few miles to the northwest of you, is the lowest spot in North America: 282 feet (86 m) below sea level. However, the structural floor of the valley is as much as 8,000 feet (2,500 m) below the present elevation of the salt pan, having been filled with sediments washed down from the surrounding mountains.

Although the lowest part of most desert basins contains a playa consisting of dried mud, because of great volumes of water that have occupied the floor of Death Valley from time to time, a "salt pan" is found here—a layer of salt averaging two to three feet (60 to 90 cm) thick. Some of the salt in the salt pan accumulated from the evaporation of Pleistocene Lake Manly; however, most of the salt here was left by the evaporation of more recent lakes on the basin floor.

The streams that flow into Death Valley contain a variety of dissolved salts. As this water evaporates, the salts crystallize out in a sequence that reflects their solubility. From the center to near its edges (including where you're standing now) the salt pan consists of nearly pure table salt (NaCl). However, around the outer edge of the salt pan a discontinuous ring of deposits of less soluble sulfates are found. In some places, deposits of even less soluble carbonates are seen. Near Furnace Creek to the north, in the Cottonball Basin, deposits of borate minerals derived from volcanic sediments are found—these borate deposits were mined beginning in the 1880s and transported out of the valley by the famous twenty-mule teams.

The polygonal ridges you see on the salt pan form as salt crystals grow through the evaporation of water from a salty slush just below the surface (textbook Figure 18-31). If you visit the Devils Golf Course on the way back to Furnace Creek, you can see other examples of the formation and expansion of salt crystals on the basin floor. On a hot day, you may be able to hear the hard salt crust crack as it expands.

Stop 6—Alluvial Fan (36°13'30"N, 116° 46'15"W):

While parked at Badwater, you may want to walk south across the road onto the alluvial fan at the foot of the Black Mountains. This is a typical isolated alluvial fan, built up from deposits left by periodic mudflows, debris flows and flash floods (see textbook Figure 15-23). As you hike up the fan toward its mouth at the mountain front, notice the gravels and cobbles that make up the fan. There is almost no **desert varnish** or **desert pavement** on this fan (see textbook Figure 18-26), indicating that this fan is quite active—recall that it takes hundreds, if not thousands, of years for desert varnish and desert pavement to develop. If you travel across the valley to the large fans and bajada at the foot of the Panamint Range, you'll find much more varnish and desert pavement. The gravel and cobbles on the Badwater alluvial fan are somewhat angular—this alluvium simply hasn't traveled far enough to become smooth and rounded. Also notice the abrupt low fault scarp along the top of the fan—this scarp is associated with the same faulting that you saw at Stop 3.

If you continue to hike up to the top the fan, you come to the mouth of a narrow canyon at the foot of the Black Mountains. You can hike into in the steep-walled canyon for a short distance until it dead-ends at a dry waterfall (remember to watch the sky above for potential thunderstorms). In the springtime, be sure to look for tiny "belly" flowers as you walk up the fan and into the canyon—often the only wildflowers you'll find in Death Valley are those you need to get down on your belly to see.

Return to Furnace Creek.

On the second day, travel north from Furnace Creek on Highway 190 toward the settlement of Stovepipe Wells, about 28 miles from Furnace Creek. There are guest facilities there, a Park ranger station, and a campground.

Stop 7—Salt Creek (36°35'27"N, 116° 59'26"W):

About thirteen miles north of Furnace Creek, take the turnoff to the left (west) for Salt Creek. From the parking area, follow the wheelchair-accessible boardwalk with its self-guided nature trail. Salt Creek is one of several streams originating at the foot of the Panamint Mountains to the west. Along the edges of the creek and in the surrounding flat valley bottom you see a crust of salts built up through the ongoing evaporation of creek water. The water in Salt Creek is about as salty as in the ocean, and a creature that lives here is one of the most intriguing in Death Valley. At the end of the Pleistocene, as freshwater Lake Manly dried up and became saltier, only a few organisms were able to

▲ **Figure FG9-8**   Large dunes in the Mesquite Flat sand dune field near Stovepipe Wells at Stop 8. *(Darrel Hess photo.)*

adapt to the changing environment. The Salt Creek Pupfish *(Cyprinodon salinus)* is a tiny fish found nowhere else in the world (several different species of pupfish are found in other parts of the desert Southwest). In spring and early summer, you'll see the tiny bright blue male pupfish defending their territories in the shallow water, trying to attract spawning females.

Stop 8—Sand Dunes (36°36'22"N, 117° 06'53"W):

About 26 miles from Furnace Creek (about 1.2 miles before Stovepipe Wells) you come to the pull-out parking area for the Mesquite Flat sand dunes. This extensive field of sand dunes is the most accessible and popular in the Park (Figure FG9-8). Morning is a nice time to visit the dunes—you can make the first footprints on the dunes, wiped smooth by the wind the night before. Distances are deceiving here—the tallest dunes in the distance are about a mile from the road, so be sure to take plenty of water.

Most of the lower dunes are configured in short, irregular transverse ridges. Between many dunes you'll see dried fine-grain mud, deposited by periodic mudflows coming out of the nearby mountains and now partially covered by the shifting sand. You'll also see Mesquite and Creosote Bushes among the dunes.

You can usually tell the most recent persistent wind direction by comparing the steepness of the dune slopes—the gentler slope tends to develop on the windward side, where sand bounces up until it reaches the crest of the dune. On the leeward or *slip face* of the dune, the sand falls down, leaving a slope that is at the *angle of repose* for dry sand (about 32–34°; see textbook Figure 18-17). As you hike up and over the dunes, you'll find that the slip face is much harder to climb than the windward side, since the slip face is steeper and consists of less compacted sand.

The largest sand dunes here are a type of dune known as **star dunes**. Star dunes develop in areas where the wind comes from several directions during the year. The configuration of the smaller **transverse dune** ridges (as well as isolated *barchan* dunes such as are found in other desert areas) generally reflects the most recent dominant wind direction (see textbook Figure 18-18).

Stop 9—Mosaic Canyon (36°34′24″N, 117°08′37″W):

Return to Highway 190 and continue west to Stovepipe Wells. About 0.2 miles beyond Stovepipe Wells, turn left (south) following the sign to the Mosaic Canyon parking area, 2.4 miles up an alluvial fan on a well-graded gravel road. Mosaic Canyon is one of the most scenic and interesting short day hikes in Death Valley.

From the parking area, walk up the flat floor of the canyon's wash toward the mouth of Mosaic Canyon. Notice the cliffs cut from alluvium brought down by flash floods and debris flows. The gravel layers in which most of the stones are well sorted by size—or in which the small platy stones are mostly lined up parallel with each other—were left by running water such as a flash flood. However, the gravel layers in which the larger stones came to rest at all angles, especially deposits in which the large rocks came to rest without touching each other, were left by debris flows—water with a large amount of sand-size material and large rocks flowing with the consistency of wet concrete. You can find evidence of deposits left by both running water and debris flows in Mosaic Canyon itself.

As you walk up the narrow canyon, you'll begin to see the nearly vertical walls of the Noonday Dolomite and the Noonday Dolomite *breccia*—a sedimentary rock formed from the cemented angular fragments of 700-million-year-old marine carbonate deposits—scoured and polished by periodic floods and debris flows (Figure FG9-9). As you walk up the canyon, you'll see patches of this breccia, plastered and cemented onto the canyon walls, indicating that Mosaic Canyon has undergone repeated episodes of both cutting and filling.

The lowest half-mile of Mosaic Canyon is the most spectacular, but you may want to continue your hike farther up where the walls begin to open into a wider valley floor. Even in the driest years, you're likely to see spring wildflowers blooming in some of the small side canyons.

Further Explorations:

If time permits, before returning to Furnace Creek you may want to explore

▲ **Figure FG9-9**   The narrow polished walls of lower Mosaic Canyon at Stop 9. *(Darrel Hess photo.)*

sites in the northern part of the Park. Popular destinations include: Titus Canyon, a spectacular 26-mile, one-way drive through a remote region of the Grapevine Mountains (a high-clearance vehicle is needed; a short hike up into the lower canyon "narrows" is a great alternative to the drive); Scotty's Castle, the desert mansion of millionaire Albert Johnson built in the 1920s at the encouragement of his eccentric and flamboyant friend Walter "Death Valley Scotty" Scott (reservations and additional entry fee required); Ubehebe Crater, part of a small field of volcanic features that includes craters formed by steam explosions caused by magma coming in contact with groundwater; and The Racetrack, a remarkable, isolated high-mountain playa across which strong winds periodically push rocks (a high-clearance vehicle is needed for the 30-mile drive up the rough jeep-road; disturbing or collecting these famous "sliding rocks" is, of course, forbidden).

The jumping off point for all four of these sites is the junction of California 190 and Scotty's Castle Road—about 7.4 miles east of Stovepipe Wells. You should check road conditions at the Park Visitor Center before attempting the drive through Titus Canyon or up to The Racetrack.

Additional Resources

Textbook:

Hess, Darrel. *McKnight's Physical Geography: A Landscape Appreciation*, 11th ed. Upper Saddle River, NJ: Pearson, 2014. Chapters 14 and 18.

Further Reading:

Decker, Robert, and Barbara Decker. *Road Guide to Death Valley National Park*, 4th ed. Mariposa, CA: Double Decker Press, 2004.

Hunt, Charles B. *Death Valley: Geology, Ecology, Archaeology*. Berkeley: University of California Press, 1975.

Sharp, Robert P., and Allen F. Glazner. *Geology Underfoot in Death Valley and Owens Valley*. Missoula, MT: Mountain Press Publishing Company, 1997.

Web Sites:
Death Valley National Park
http://www.nps.gov/deva

DesertUSA Wildflower Report
http://www.desertusa.com/wildflo/ca_dv.html

Textbook Page References for Key Terms

alluvial fan *(p. 531)*
average lapse rate *(p. 99)*
badlands *(p. 536)*
bajada *(p. 531)*
basalt *(p. 382)*
debris flow *(p. 460)*

desert pavement *(p. 529)*
desert varnish *(p. 529)*
graben *(p. 437)*
horst *(p. 437)*
normal fault *(p. 435)*
playa *(p. 518)*

Pleistocene Epoch *(p. 544)*
rain shadow *(p. 166)*
star dunes *(p. 527)*
strike-slip fault *(p. 435)*
tilted-fault block mountain *(p. 437)*
transverse dune *(p. 526)*

Field Guide #10

Redwood Forests

Darrel Hess, City College of San Francisco

Introduction

The coastal mountains of northern California are home to one of the most distinctive trees in North America—the Coast Redwood (*Sequoia sempervirens*). The redwood is both the tallest and one of the longest-living trees in the world. Some redwoods reach heights of more than 350 feet (100 meters) and live more than 2,000 years.

In this field guide we introduce the redwood forest ecosystem that can be visited in many different locations, and provide brief descriptions of two representative redwood forest sites.

Location

Groves of Coast Redwoods are found in many locations in coastal northern California (Figure FG10-1). Generally limited to coastal areas with moderate temperatures and high rainfall, they are found along a narrow 450-mile-long strip of coastal central and northern California. Redwoods thrive in areas with winter rains of about 40 inches (100 cm) or more per year (some locations may receive as much as 100 inches [250 cm] a year), as well as summer **fog** which condenses on the needles and drips down to the forest floor (see *Field Guide #11—Coastal Fog*). These trees cannot tolerate high amounts of salt spray from the ocean, nor freezing winters. The ideal locations tend to be just beyond the first ridge of coastal hills, especially in valleys where summer *advection fog* is funneled inland and where winter frontal precipitation is increased through **orographic lifting**.

▲ **Figure FG10-1** Locations of redwood forests in California (green), with Field Guide sites shown. *(Adapted from Verna R. Johnston,* California Forests and Woodlands: A Natural History, *California Natural History Guide #58, Berkeley: University of California Press, 1994.)*

Among the many popular spots to visit old-growth redwood groves are Redwood National and State Parks in Humboldt County, Muir Woods National Monument in Marin County, Armstrong Redwoods State Park in Sonoma County, and Pfeiffer Big Sur State Park in Monterey County, although redwood groves are found in many other locations.

Background

The Coast Redwood is an easy tree to identify. The bark is usually rusty red in color, thick and fibrous. As is typical with **conifers**, rather than leaves, the redwood tree has thin needles. Given the enormous size of mature trees, the cones of the Coast Redwood are remarkably small—only about 3/4 of an inch (2 cm) long (Figure FG10-2).

Reproduction: Once you enter a redwood grove, you will notice that there are usually few tiny red-wood tree seedlings on the forest floor. Every year the Coast Redwood produces thousands of seeds, but few of these germinate. The forest floor is typi-cally covered with 6 to 8 inches (15 to 20 cm) of **litter** called "duff"—a layer of decomposing vegetation and needles that prevents seeds from reaching the soil and sprouting. When the forest floor is dis-turbed, however, such as from a flood or from the uprooting of a large tree, seeds may have a chance to sprout.

If you are in a climax forest in which the ecosys-tem has reached a kind of equilibrium after perhaps several hundred years without a major disturbance, most of the reproduction of redwoods will be through sprouting from an existing root system or trunk. The ecological benefit of this is that new trees can take advantage of an established root system. In many groves you will see rings of redwood trees—these "fairy rings" develop where new trees sprout around the remnants of an older tree that has since disappeared.

Sprouts typically start in the growing layer of the tree as a small bud. However, rather than extending into a branch, these buds can remain dormant for many years until some stress—perhaps a fire or bro-ken trunk—stimulates its growth. When buds begin to grow and divide, they form a lump on the side of the tree known as a *burl*. Most burls develop below ground level at the crown of the root system where a new tree could sprout, although some develop along the trunk where they can develop into a new branch.

Adaptation to Fire: The Coast Redwood is well adapted to fire. Redwoods lack the kind of sap and resins that allow most conifers to burn easily, and their thick, fibrous bark insulates the heart of the tree from fire (the tannins in the bark also make the redwood resistant to insect pests). You may see examples of trees in which a fire has burned through the bark and killed part of the heartwood, but the tree itself has survived.

Natural fires are a regular event in the redwood forest. Fire clears the layer of duff and allows seeds to germinate. The burn also helps maintain the health of the ecosystem by recycling nutrients.

Floods and Wind: Many of the largest redwood trees are found in river valleys where periodic floods bring in nutrients in the freshly-deposited **alluvium**. Because redwoods can sprout from their trunks, if a mature tree is damaged or buried with flood debris, a new root system can quickly develop out of the trunk just below the new ground level.

Protected valleys also shelter redwoods from wind. Although well adapted to fire and flood, red-woods are not as well adapted to strong winds. They have relatively shallow roots—a 200-foot (60 m) high, 10-foot (3 m) diameter redwood tree might have a root system that extends down to a depth of only 6 feet (1.8 m) and spreads out to a diameter of only 150 feet (45 m). In redwood groves, the root sys-tems of adjacent trees may interlock, giving the trees greater support.

The Redwood Forest Ecosystem: The redwood for-est is a relatively simple **ecosystem** (Figure FG10-3). Unlike the high species diversity found in tropical rainforests, the redwood forest ecosystem is com-prised of relatively few species. In additional to the Coast Redwood, it is common to find Douglas Fir (*Pseudotsuga menziesii*; see Figure FG4-2 in *Field Guide #4—Sierra Nevada via Tioga Pass*)—one of the most important trees for commercial lumber in the Pacific Northwest. You are also likely to see the evergreen Tanbark Oak (*Lithocarpus densiflora*) growing as a large shrub in the shaded forest, recognized by its sharp spines on its leaf edges that have a smooth top and velvety underside.

On the deeply shaded forest floor, you'll likely see the Redwood Sorrell (*Oxalis oregana*) which looks

▲ **Figure FG10-2** The needles and cones of the Coast Redwood. *(Adapted from John D. Stuart and John O. Sawyer,* Trees and Shrubs of California, *California Natural History Guide #62, Berkeley: University of California Press, 2001.)*

Figure FG10-3 Redwood forest understory with Sword Ferns in Muir Woods National Monument, Marin County. *(Darrel Hess photo.)*

much like a large clover with pink flowers, as well as the Bracken Fern (*Pteridium aquilinum*) with multiple fronds on each stem, and groups of Sword Fern (*Polystichum munitum*) with long, single blades extending as much as 5 feet.

Site Descriptions

Two popular parks in coastal California offer great opportunities to see the redwood forest ecosystem: Redwood National and State Parks in Humboldt County, and Pfeiffer Big Sur State Park in Monterey County.

Site 1—Redwood National and State Parks

Redwood National and State Parks (RNSP) protect about 40,000 acres of old growth redwood forest—including the tallest trees in the world—along a 40-mile stretch of northern California coast. In 1994 the National Park Service and California State Parks began cooperatively managing three existing state parks and one national park; collectively RNSP was

designated a *United Nations World Heritage Site* and an *International Biosphere Reserve* in 1980. Although many outstanding sites and hikes are found in RNSP, several of the nicest are in the southern part of the Park.

About 50 miles north of Eureka on U.S. Highway 101 you enter Prairie Creek State Park. Turn onto the Newton B. Drury Scenic Parkway—a 10-mile-long road through some of the most beautiful old-growth redwood forest in the region. After traveling 1.1 miles north on the Parkway, turn left (west) into the Prairie Creek Visitor Center (41°21′49″N, 124°01′24″W), where you can pick up park maps; it's also one of the places you're likely to see the magnificent Roosevelt Elk (*Cervus elaphus roosevelti*). About 0.8 miles farther north on the Parkway, turn right (east) into the Big Tree Wayside parking area (41°22′22″N, 124°00′50″W).

Of the many easy short hikes you can take in the area, one of the best is along the Cathedral Trees Trail. About 100 yards up the trail from the parking area you reach "Big Tree"—a 304-foot (92.6 m) tall, 21.6-foot (6.6 m) diameter redwood. The trail then takes you across a ridge through a redwood grove that includes some of the tallest trees in the Park. After about 0.8 miles, you reach a trail junction where you see two great examples of fairy rings.

Continue on the Cathedral Trees Trail along Boyes Creek—in this segment of the trail, redwoods are replaced by stands of Bigleaf Maple (*Acer macrophyllum*), Red Alder (*Alnus rubra*), and Sitka Spruce (*Picea sitchensis*). After a total of 1.4 miles, cross the Parkway toward the Visitor Center and then take the Prairie Creek Trail back to the parking area—this mostly level, wheelchair-accessible trail follows crystal-clear Prairie Creek through the redwood forest (Figure FG10-4). After about 1.2 miles, follow the signs to a short trail back to the Parkway and the Wayside parking area.

Figure FG10-4 Old-growth redwoods along the Prairie Creek Trail in Prairie Creek State Park, Redwood National and State Parks. *(Darrel Hess photo.)*

Continuing north from the Big Tree Wayside parking area on the Parkway for another 0.5 miles, you reach a left-side (west) pullout. Take the short trail down to the "Corkscrew Tree"—a large fairy ring of tall, twisted redwoods.

If time permits, also visit Fern Canyon (41°24′03″N, 124°03′56″W)—a shaded, steep-walled coastal stream valley draped with many varieties of fern.

Site 2—Pfeiffer Big Sur State Park

Pfeiffer Big Sur State Park is located about 30 miles south of Monterey along California's spectacular central coast. Access to the park is from California Highway 1—one of the most scenic stretches of coastal highway anywhere in the country. Known for its high bridge crossings and breathtaking views overlooking the rocky Pacific Ocean shoreline, California 1 passes in and out of small groves of Coast Redwood, pine, and coastal chaparral on the way to Big Sur.

The Big Sur region marks the southern end of the Coast Redwood range. Unlike the large expanses of redwoods in the northern part of the state, here redwoods are found in discontinuous groves in narrow valleys, intermixed in places with willows and Bigleaf Maple. On the higher ridges above the redwoods, low coastal chaparral shrub with manzanita, ceanothus and chamise is dominant. Poison Oak (*Toxicodendron diversilobum*) is found throughout the Park, recognized by its lobed, shiny green or reddish-green leaves in groups of three—avoid contact with either leaves or stems (remember, "Leaves of three, let them be!").

Some of the best stands of redwoods in the Park are near Big Sur Lodge (36°15′03″N, 121°47′10″W), about 0.2 miles from the park entrance. The easy 0.3-mile-long Nature Trail starts just east of the Lodge and takes you through both redwood and oak woodlands.

The more strenuous Valley View Trail starts 0.2 miles north of the Lodge in a dense grove of redwoods with a thick carpet of Redwood Sorrel below. The trail climbs steeply for about 0.6 miles through oak woodlands to Valley View Overlook (36°15′31″N, 121°47′07″W), where you can look down on Big Sur River Valley—a nearly straight erosional valley following the trend of the Sur Fault to Point Sur, 6 miles to the northwest. As you backtrack down the trail, take the 0.5 mile detour down to Pfeiffer Falls—a 60-foot high waterfall on Pfeiffer Redwood Creek (36°15′24″N, 121°46′53″W).

Additional Resources

Textbook:

Hess, Darrel. *McKnight's Physical Geography: A Landscape Appreciation*, 11th ed. Upper Saddle River, NJ: Pearson, 2014. Chapters 10 and 11.

Further Reading:

Johnston, Verna R. *California Forests and Woodlands: A Natural History.* Berkeley: University of California Press, 1994.

Web Sites:

Muir Woods National Monument: *http://www.nps.gov/muwo/*

Pfeiffer Big Sur State Park: *http://www.parks.ca.gov/?page_id=570*

Redwood National Park: *http://www.nps.gov/redw/*

Textbook Page References for Key Terms

alluvium *(p. 473)*
conifer *(p. 309)*

ecosystem *(p. 307)*
fog *(p. 156)*

litter *(p. 351)*
orographic lifting *(p. 166)*

Field Guide #11

Coastal Fog

Darrel Hess, City College of San Francisco

Introduction

Of all the features of coastal California's natural environment, its summer fog may seem most distinctive to visitors and residents alike. In places such as San Francisco, the fog acts as summer "air conditioning," keeping temperatures mild—or even cold—while the rest of the state may be roasting in the heat. Although San Francisco is famous for its fog, the summer fog bank—or "marine layer" as it's locally known—is an important component of the weather for much of coastal California, and much of what is discussed in this field guide applies to most coastal areas in the state.

Location

Unlike most others in this collection, this field guide doesn't describe specific sites for you to visit. Rather, it describes regional patterns you can observe in the San Francisco Bay Area and other parts of coastal California. These fog patterns may also be observed by viewing weather satellite images available on the Internet. Several recommended Web sites are noted below (for a review of interpreting weather satellite images, see textbook *Focus: GOES Weather Satellites* in Chapter 6).

Background

The general weather and climate of coastal California is largely controlled by two major factors:

(1) A location next to the ocean, which moderates temperatures throughout the year. (2) The seasonal migration of the **subtropical high**—locally known as the Pacific High or Hawaiian High—which strongly influences seasonal precipitation patterns.

Microclimates of Coastal California: Most of coastal California has a **mediterranean climate**—*Köppen climate classification* designations *Csa* and *Csb* (see textbook Figures 8-3 and 8-20 for maps showing the global distribution of mediterranean climates). Mediterranean climates are characterized by a moderate annual temperature range and a summer dry season (representative climographs for mediterranean climates are shown in textbook Figure 8-21). Within the regions of mediterranean climate, however, there are great local variations in temperature and precipitation. These "microclimates" are dramatically exhibited in San Francisco, especially during the summer, where one neighborhood might be wrapped in fog, while at that same moment another neighborhood, just a few blocks away but protected by the hills, might be in sunshine.

San Francisco Bay lies between two of the sets of ridges in the Coast Ranges. As you travel inland from the coast over each ridge, the climate becomes increasingly continental and less maritime—especially with regard to temperature. However, this general pattern is modified by the water of San Francisco Bay, as well as by the major gaps in the Coast Ranges that allow marine influence to selectively enter some areas (Figure FG11-1). The end result is a mosaic of local variations in temperature, rainfall, and fog.

▲ **Figure FG11-1** Gaps and passes in the San Francisco Bay Area. (*Adapted from: Gilliam, Harold.* Weather of the San Francisco Bay Region, *2nd edition.* California Natural History Guide, *63. Berkeley: University of California Press, 2002.*)

▲ **Figure FG11-2** Advection fog along north coast of California, near Fort Ross. (*Darrel Hess photo.*)

Advection Fog: The summer coastal fog of California is known as *advection fog*. It forms when moist air passes over a cool surface, chilling the air to its **dew point** and forming fog (see textbook Figure 6-18b). Recall that fog is essentially a **stratus cloud** that is in contact with the surface.

The seasonal summer coastal fog pattern typically begins to develop during the spring. Week by week as the Northern Hemisphere moves into summer, the latitude of the greatest solar heating shifts northward and the Pacific High shifts closer to the latitude of central California (see textbook Figure 5-15). By early summer, the Pacific High brings stable atmospheric conditions and effectively blocks most **midlatitude cyclones** that might be traveling in the **westerlies**, producing coastal California's summer dry season. Because of the relatively high latitude of the Pacific High in summer, the westerlies, which diverge clockwise from the California side of this **anticyclone**, generally blow from the northwest— blowing down the coast, in some cases nearly parallel to shore (which runs northwest-southeast in central California).

As the westerlies blow over the ocean, the surface water is pushed along by the wind—this moving surface water then deflects to the right as a consequence of the **Coriolis effect**. As the surface water deflects to the right, it veers away from the coast and is replaced by cold, nutrient-rich water from below in the process of **upwelling** (see text-

book Figure 4-28). This upwelling lowers the temperature of the already cool California Current flowing equatorward down the coast (see textbook Figure 4-26). During the summer, when the upwelling pattern is usually most prominent, the sea surface temperature off the coast of central California can be less than 50°F (10°C).

The streak of upwelled cold ocean water along the coast chills the moist winds passing over it, forming advection fog just above the water surface. This fog bank, however, remains over the ocean along the coast unless something acts to bring it inland (Figure FG11-2). In the summer, as California's Central Valley warms during the day, a **thermal low** develops inland. The thermal low, aided by the "push" of the Pacific High, draws the fog inland from the coast. So, perhaps counter-intuitively, the cooling fog is most likely to be drawn in over San Francisco when the Central Valley—just a short distance away—is at its warmest.

Because of the configuration of the coastline, upwelling tends to take place farther offshore in southern California. So while advection fog also forms in this region, it is less commonly pulled onshore into the communities around Los Angeles.

Fog Gaps and Seasonal Patterns: The low fog bank is typically held back by the coastal mountains and so can only move inland easily through the lowest gaps and passes in the Coast Ranges. The Golden Gate of San Francisco Bay is the only sea level opening through the Coast Ranges into the Central Valley—and so often the first place fog is drawn into the Bay Area is through the Golden Gate, sending a finger of fog across the bay toward the cities of Berkeley and Oakland (Figure FG11-3).

The amount of fog experienced in any particular location along the coast is generally determined by its relationship to the coast and to fog gaps. Some

▲ **Figure FG11-3**   Fog moving through Golden Gate. *(Darrel Hess photo.)*

▲ **Figure FG11-4**   Visible light satellite image showing winter tule fog in the Central Valley and advection fog along the coast. *(Image courtesy of Naval Research Laboratory, Marine Meteorology Division.)*

coastal locations in summer may remain covered with fog night and day for many days at a time, while many interior communities will see the fog arrive in the afternoon, remain all night, then "burn off" the next morning.

By the middle of summer, the fog bank tends to lift a short distance off the water, becoming "high fog"—especially as it moves inland and the lowest part of the fog bank is warmed slightly by the surface. The lowest fog—where the fog passes below the 230-foot (70 m) high deck of the Golden Gate Bridge—usually occurs in the spring and fall. High fog is more common in the mid-summer months.

"Fog drip" is usually the only kind of measurable precipitation that comes to the central and southern coast of California during the summer dry season. The wettest fogs often form far out to sea, and so the droplets have had the opportunity to increase in size before reaching the coast. Groves of California's Coastal Redwood (*Sequoia sempervirens*) are generally confined to the moist coastal valleys where fog provides enough moisture for these trees to survive the summer dry season (see *Field Guide #10—Redwood Forests*).

The summer fog pattern begins to break down in the fall. The Pacific High shifts with the heating of the Sun and migrates closer to the equator, and so the upwelling begins to diminish. The fog bank may be present off the coast any time of year, but during winter the Central Valley generally isn't warm enough to create the thermal pull needed to bring the fog onshore (see textbook Figure 4-11; this photograph was taken during the winter—notice the fog bank beyond the Golden Gate Bridge).

Tule Fog: California exhibits another kind of fog that is prevalent in the winter months. Locally called "tule fog," it is technically known as *radiation fog*. After a winter storm passes, lots of moisture may be on the ground. In the cold, clear weather commonly experienced after the passing of a midlatitude cyclone, with little cloud cover to inhibit the loss of **longwave radiation** from the surface, the air immediately above the ground is chilled enough to form fog (see textbook Figure 6-18a). Tule fog is much more common in inland valleys than along the coast where the moderating effect of the ocean tends to reduce nighttime cooling.

Tule fog often forms as a dense, but typically not very thick, layer of ground fog. In the Central Valley tule fog tends to develop in the lowest areas where cold air pools at night (Figure FG11-4). Almost every year there are chain reaction traffic accidents along Interstate 5 or California Highway 99 when the tule fog reduces driving visibility to just a few car lengths.

If you view a satellite movie loop of the Central Valley during the winter when tule fog is developed, you may notice that the fog develops at night when the air is coldest. The fog will disappear after the Sun rises in the morning and the temperature increases enough to evaporate the fog.

Additional Resources

Textbook:
Hess, Darrel. *McKnight's Physical Geography: A Landscape Appreciation*, 11th ed. Upper Saddle River, NJ: Pearson, 2014. Chapters 6 and 8.

Further Reading:
Aguado, Edward, and James E. Burt. *Understanding Weather & Climate*, 6th edition. Upper Saddle River, NJ: Pearson, 2013.

Gilliam, Harold. *Weather of the San Francisco Bay Region*, 2nd edition. California Natural History Guide, 63. Berkeley: University of California Press, 2002.

Web Sites:
Geostationary Satellite Server:
http://www.goes.noaa.gov/
Naval Research Laboratory, Satellite Images:
http://www.nrimry.navy.mil/sat_products.html

Textbook Page References for Key Terms

anticyclone *(p. 115)*
Coriolis effect *(p. 71)*
dew point *(p. 150)*
longwave radiation *(p. 83)*

mediterranean climate *(p. 222)*
midlatitude cyclones *(p. 182)*
stratus cloud *(p. 154)*
subtropical high *(p. 119)*

thermal low *(p. 112)*
upwelling *(p. 98)*
westerlies *(p. 122)*

Field Guide #12

San Gabriel Mountains

Darrel Hess, City College of San Francisco

Introduction

The San Gabriel Mountains of southern California are one of the most remarkable mountain ranges in North America. They are being uplifted—and at the same time being worn down—about as quickly as any mountain range on the continent. The San Gabriels form the abrupt northern boundary—as well as a spectacular backdrop—to one of the largest metropolitan areas in the world. Because of the steep terrain and dense chaparral vegetation, in some places you can enter virtual wilderness just a few hundred yards from the nearest houses or roads.

These mountains are also a source of hazard for the residents of Los Angeles County through wildfires and through periodic debris flows that can transport tons of mud and large boulders down to the mountain front. In the words of author John McPhee in his book *The Control of Nature*, these mountains "are not kidding with this city."

This field guide highlights features you can see on two one-day driving trips through the San Gabriel Mountains from the Los Angeles area. Site 1 is a loop through the central San Gabriels, from near Pasadena to the San Fernando Valley. Site 2 is a trip over the northwestern flank of the range, from the northern San Fernando Valley toward Palmdale and the Mojave Desert.

Location

You can travel through the San Gabriels any time of year although winter storms can lead to road clo-

sures, so check conditions ahead of time if the weather has been poor. In places you'll be traveling along steep, winding and narrow roads. Use extreme caution and don't attempt to drive and sightsee at the same time—if something catches your eye between field guide stops, find a place to safely pull off the road before you take a look. Also, keep an eye out for bicycle riders negotiating these same roads, especially on weekends when the weather is nice.

In order to park alongside the road in some places in Angeles National Forest, you need to pay a nominal fee for a *Forest Adventure Pass* available at many local gas stations, Forest Stations, or online through the U.S. Forest Service (see *Additional Resources* below). A single Forest Adventure Pass can be used in both the Angeles National Forest (the area described in this field guide) and in the San Bernardino National Forest (*Field Guide #3—The San Andreas Fault*, Site 6—Cajon Pass).

Much of the route described in Site 2 can be reached via the Antelope Valley Line of the Metro Link commuter light rail system. See *Additional Resources* below for information.

In August and September 2009, one of the largest wildfires in California history burned a vast expanse of chaparral in the central San Gabriel Mountains. Known as the Station Fire, this arson-started fire burned 161,000 acres and took the lives of two firefighters. Much of the route described in Site 1 winds through the burn area of the Station Fire. Because of damage to roads, unstable slopes, and increased danger from debris flows, over the next few years segments of roads described here may be closed temporarily—especially during winter—so be sure to check for road closures before proceeding into Angeles National Forest. Although the aftermath of the Station Fire adds an element of uncertainty to traveling in the central San Gabriels, it also provides a remarkable opportunity to observe changes in the landscape as the recovery progresses in coming years.

Background

Geologic History: To characterize the geologic history of the San Gabriel Mountains as "complex" is an understatement. The San Gabriel Mountains are part of the Transverse Ranges, the generally east-west trending mountains that include the Santa Ynez and Topatopa Mountains to the west, and the San Bernardino and Little San Bernardino Mountains to the east.

In general, the San Gabriels (and the other Transverse Ranges) have been uplifted as a result of compression from the south in association with the "Big Bend" segment of the San Andreas Fault system (see textbook Figure 14-18 and *Field Guide #3— The San Andreas Fault*). Here, the part of California immediately south of the San Andreas Fault has been pushing into the part immediately north of the fault. As a result, much of the uplift—especially along the southern flank of the San Gabriels—has been along **reverse faults** (see textbook Figure 14-58) such as the Sierra Madre Fault. However, this compression has been accompanied by substantial lateral displacement along **strike-slip faults**— especially along the San Andreas Fault on the northern side of the range and the San Gabriel Fault on the southern side. This faulting has significantly controlled the orientation of most of the mountain ridges and many of the stream valleys within the San Gabriels.

While the mountains in the western Transverse Ranges are comprised largely of **sedimentary rocks**, the bulk of the San Gabriels is composed of igneous and **metamorphic rocks**—including some of the oldest rocks in California—covered in places with very young stream- and debris flow deposits.

In the central San Gabriel Mountains there are several major rock units. The oldest is the Mendenhall Gneiss—rock metamorphosed nearly 1.7 billion years ago. About 1.2 billion years ago this gneiss was intruded by a rock called *anorthosite*—one of the most interesting rocks in California. Rarely exposed on Earth, rocks found in some areas of the Moon are anorthosite. Anorthosite is a very light-colored **plutonic rock** composed mostly of calcium-rich, plagioclase feldspar along with small amounts of

minerals such as olivine and pyroxene. In places, feldspar crystals several inches across can be found—including beautiful lavender crystals of *labrodorite* feldspar. Locally, the anorthosite is cut by dikes of gabbro (the plutonic equivalent of basalt).

Intruding much later than the anorthosite are younger plutonic rock units, including the Mount Lowe Granodiorite (roughly 225 million years ago), the Wilson Diorite (about 80 to 90 million years ago) and the Mount Josephine Granodiorite (also about 80 million years ago).

Together, these rock units are part of what is sometimes referred to as the San Gabriel Terrane— a fault-bounded **terrane** located roughly between the San Gabriel and San Andreas Faults. In many places in the San Gabriels the rocks are deeply weathered, highly sheared and crumbling, and often exposed on steep slopes at or near the **angle of repose**.

Weather and Climate: The Los Angeles area of southern California has an archetypical **mediterranean climate** (see textbook Figure 8-21): mild and wet winters, along with dry and sunny summers. The poleward migration of the subtropical high in summer brings dry conditions, while migrating midlatitude cyclones in winter provide most of the area's rainfall.

Downtown Los Angeles receives an average of about 15 inches (38 cm) of rainfall a year, although as is the case throughout most of southern California, the rainfall in any given year can deviate greatly from this average. Up in the San Gabriel Mountains, the extra **orographic lifting** of air along the southern mountain front—especially when wind is "funneled" up into steep canyons—can yield astonishing single storm rainfall totals. During a 1943 storm, 26 inches of rain fell in one 24-hour period; in 1978 almost 1.5 inches of rain fell in less than 30 minutes. These rare, intense rainfall events are one factor associated with producing large debris flows in the San Gabriel Mountains.

Plant Communities: Dense *chaparral* vegetation dominates the slopes of the San Gabriel Mountains. This **mediterranean shrub** ecosystem is characterized by plants well-adapted to the long summer dry season as well as frequent droughts. Most of the plants are evergreens, with stiff and woody branches, small, often waxy-feeling leaves to reduce moisture loss to transpiration, and deep root systems to tap moisture well below the surface.

Although as many as 100 different species of shrubs are found in the chaparrals of southern

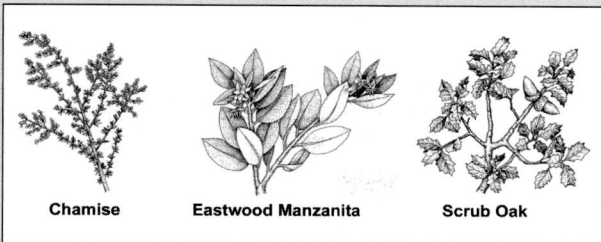

▲ **Figure FG12-1** Common chaparral plants of the San Gabriel Mountains include Chamise, Eastwood Manzanita, and Scrub Oak. *(Adapted from Stuart, John D., and John O. Sawyer.* Trees and Shrubs of California. *California Natural History Guide #62. Berkeley: University of California Press, 2001.)*

California, just a few dominate in some areas. Especially in dry areas such as sunny, south-facing slopes, Chamise (*Adenostoma fasciculatum*) may cover vast areas—this shrub is recognized by its peeling bark and small needle-shaped leaves; in spring small white flowers cover the tips of its branches (Figure FG12-1).

In slightly less arid areas, such as on north-facing slopes, a greater variety of shrubs is found forming "mixed" chaparral. Common species include the Scrub Oak (*Quercus berberidifolia*), with its shiny, flat and spine-toothed leaves, and the Eastwood Manzanita (*Arcostaphylos glandulosa*), with its leathery leaves, red bark and small red berries (see Figure FG12-1), along with the nitrogen-fixing Greenbark Ceanothus (*Ceanothus spinosus*), recognized by its single-veined leaves, flexible spine-tipped branches and green bark.

On higher slopes White Thorn (*Ceanothus leucodermis*) with rigid, spiny branches and leaves thinly coated with a white powder, replaces the Greenbark Ceanothus. In the higher elevations of the San Gabriels, conifers such as the Coulter Pine (*Pinus coulteri*) are found, recognized by its long needles in bunches of three and its very large pine cones. In moister stream valleys, varieties of cottonwood and willow are found, along with Canyon Live Oak (*Quercus chrysolepis*) on valley slopes.

Chaparral vegetation is well adapted to fire. Many shrubs have burls or thick root tops just below the surface, and so are protected from fire—such plants resprout quickly after a burn. Many species of ceanothus and manzanita are killed by fire, but heat from the burn triggers their seeds in the soil to germinate. Fires may also cause a spectacular springtime bloom of wildflowers whose seeds may have been lying dormant in the soil for years, prompted to germinate by the flush of nitrogen compounds released from the ash.

Chaparral fires can be among the hottest of all wildfires—and they can be remarkably fast moving, especially when fanned by Santa Ana Winds (see *Field Guide #7—Santa Ana Winds*). Because of the usually dry conditions, dead vegetation rots slowly, accumulating in a layer of fuel below the living chaparral vegetation. Many chaparral plant leaves burn easily—the resin-coated or oily leaf surfaces retain moisture, but also ignite quickly. Fire also tends to make chaparral soil especially impermeable to rainfall—leading to high runoff when rain does fall.

Debris Flows and Flood Control: The three-part combination of steep slopes with lots of loose weathered rock, a chaparral fire to clear vegetation and make the soil less permeable to rainfall, and an intense rainfall event in a mountain drainage area, form the ideal conditions to generate a **debris flow**. Periodically these fast-moving mixtures of sand, water and boulders come rushing down the canyons of the San Gabriels, emptying out at the mountain front, forming an apron of overlapping **alluvial fans** that is now largely covered with houses.

In the early twentieth century, the City of Los Angeles and other municipalities began their battle with the infrequent, but sometimes catastrophic floods and debris flows. Most of the major streams flowing out of the San Gabriels—such as the Los Angeles River, the San Gabriel River, Arroyo Seco, and Big Tujunga Creek—contain relatively little water most of the time. However, when the conditions are right, these streams become torrents for a few days. Although rare, such events may lead to extensive property damage and occasional loss of life through flooding, debris flows and the resulting alluvial deposits of sand, cobbles, and boulders.

To reduce property damage and loss of life, an extensive network of flood control channels and debris basins has been constructed throughout southern California. Virtually every surface stream is "channeled" with concrete or gunite; nearly every large canyon has a debris dam with an empty basin behind it to "catch" debris flows before they can move through mountain-front neighborhoods; and several enormous flood controls basins (such as the Hansen and Santa Fe Flood Control Basins)—each several square miles in area—have been constructed beyond the mountain front to act as a final line of defense. Even with these protective measures, from time to time debris flows and floods still damage homes and wash out roads.

Site Descriptions

Site 1—Central San Gabriels

The Site 1 field guide route begins near Pasadena just north of downtown Los Angeles on Interstate 210 (the Foothill Freeway), loops through the central San Gabriels on the Angeles Crest Highway, Angeles Forest Highway, Big Tujunga Canyon Road, and ends back on I-210 near the community of San Fernando (Figure FG12-2).

From Interstate 210 take the exit for the Angeles Crest Highway (California Highway 2) at La Cañada Flintridge. Proceed up the hill toward the mountain front. As you drive up this steep slope, you're traveling over an alluvial fan, built up from thousands of years of flood and debris flow deposits. Where the road makes a sharp turn to the right, you're passing over the Sierra Madre Fault zone—it is along faults such as this that the southern side of the San Gabriels is being uplifted. Soon you begin to pass roadcuts exposing the Wilson Diorite—found here weathered and sliced by light-colored dikes in places, this rock is the plutonic equivalent of the volcanic rock andesite.

Stop 1—Arroyo Seco Overlook Turnout (34°13'43"N, 118°10'59"W): About 2.7 miles from I-210 pull off the road to the right and park at the large turnout. Here you can look down the steep, winding canyon cut by Arroyo Seco, a perennial stream. Toward the mouth of the canyon and just above the narrow wooded valley floor of Arroyo Seco, you can see gently sloping stream ter-

races—these are remnants of old valley floors, left after uplift of the mountains caused Arroyo Seco to incise down into its old valley floor.

Continue up the Angeles Crest Highway. One-half mile from Stop 1 (3.3 miles from I-210) you pass the Angeles Crest Forest Station. From here, you begin to pass roadcuts exposing plutonic rock as well as both light pink and darker rocks of the 1.67-billion-year-old Mendenhall Gneiss. About 4.8 miles from the Forest Station, you pass a steep landslide scar on the left.

Stop 2—Angeles Forest Clear Creek Vista (34°16'12"N, 118°10'06"W): About 5.7 miles from Stop 1 (8.4 miles from I-210), pull off to the left into the parking area for the Angeles Forest Clear Creek Vista. A low retaining wall keeps talus back from the steep slope in front of the parking area—the rocks here are part of the 225-million-year-old Mount Lowe Granodiorite. Ahead of you to the north is the deep canyon of Clear Creek with Josephine Peak (5,558 ft.; 1,694 m) rising steeply above (Figure FG12-3).

The road you see across the canyon is the Angeles Forest Highway (on which you'll be traveling shortly). The brownish roadcuts along the highway include exposures of the Mendenhall Gneiss, while the light-colored rock exposed above is the Mount Josephine Granodiorite—1.5 billion years younger.

The ridge you're standing on is known as Georges Gap. It forms the drainage divide between Arroyo Seco behind you to the south, and Clear Creek—a major tributary of Big Tujunga Creek—to the west and north. Notice that the canyon of Clear Creek is nearly straight. Here, its path has been influenced by the zone of erosional weakness along a

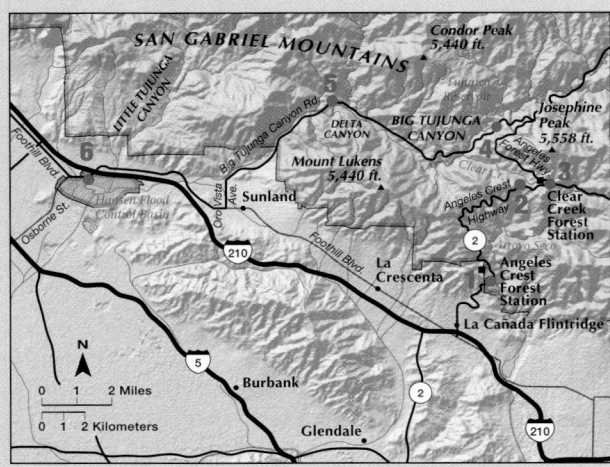

▲ **Figure FG12-2** Regional map of the central San Gabriel Mountains showing Site 1 field guide stops.

▲ **Figure FG12-3** View from Clear Creek Vista at Site 1, Stop 2. *(Darrel Hess photo.)*

branch of the San Gabriel Fault—as has the canyon of the West Fork of the San Gabriel River out of view to the east. Although this segment of San Gabriel Fault may not be currently active (it is perhaps a former component of the San Andreas Fault system), in the past this branch of the fault produced 14 miles (23 km) of right-lateral offset.

Continue up the Angeles Crest Highway. Immediately after leaving the Vista parking area, notice the roadcut to the right—here dark dikes of gabbro cut through the much lighter Mount Lowe Granodiorite.

Stop 3—Clear Creek Forest Station

(34°16′12″N, 118°09′12″W): About 1 mile from Stop 2 (9.4 miles from I-210) you come to the Clear Creek Forest Station. There are restrooms here, and on weekends Forest Adventure Passes may be purchased. Look to the east up Clear Creek Canyon toward Red Box Gap—the drainage divide between the upper reaches of Arroyo Seco and the West Fork of the San Gabriel River which flows east from there for 15 miles before turning sharply south and leaving the San Gabriel Mountains at Azusa.

After you leave the ranger station, turn left (west) on the Angeles Forest Highway (County Highway N-3). For the next few miles you're driving along a branch of the San Gabriel Fault toward Big Tujunga Canyon, passing roadcuts of Mendenhall Gneiss and Mount Josephine Granodiorite.

About 3.9 miles from the Clear Creek Forest Station (13.3 miles from I-210), you take a left turn off the Angeles Forest Highway onto Big Tujunga Canyon Road toward Sunland. You are now traveling down the canyon of Big Tujunga Creek. Big Tujunga Creek flows through a very narrow, steep V-shaped valley here, in this case a consequence of rapid downcutting associated with tectonic uplift.

Stop 4—Big Tujunga Dam Overlook

(34°17′40″N, 118°10′49″W): About 1.6 miles after turning onto Big Tujunga Canyon Road (14.9 miles from I-210) turn right into the Big Tujunga Dam Overlook parking area (Figure FG12-4). This 200-foot high concrete gravity arch dam was constructed for purposes of flood control in 1931; it underwent extensive seismic retrofit work in 2009. The shape of Tujunga Reservoir behind the dam shows off the steep, deep and sinuous canyon cut by Big Tujunga Creek through this part of the San Gabriels.

Continue down Big Tujunga Canyon Road. A mile after the dam overlook, notice the large cobbles in the roadcuts—these are young stream terrace deposits left after tectonic uplift caused Big Tujunga Creek to downcut. Clear Creek, which we saw back

▲ **Figure FG12-4**   View of Big Tujunga Reservoir at Site 1, Stop 4. *(Darrel Hess photo.)*

at Stop 2, enters Big Tujunga Creek shortly after this. Over the next three miles or so, the canyon follows a trace of the San Gabriel Fault, and you see other examples of stream terrace deposits and numerous landslides along the roadside.

Stop 5—Delta Flats Overlook (34° 18′19″N, 118°15′46″W): About 6.4 miles from the Big Tujunga Dam Overlook (21.3 miles from I-210), find a pullout where you can safely park. Walk across the road and look at Big Tujunga Canyon. This is called Delta Flats, however, the namesake of this area is not a delta but rather a spectacular alluvial fan at the mouth of steep-walled Delta Canyon (Figure FG12-5).

As you continue down Big Tujunga Canyon, for the next mile or so you travel alongside the cobble-strewn stream bed. About 4.3 miles from Delta Flats (25.6 miles from I-210) the road turns left and

▲ **Figure FG12-5**   Alluvial fan at the mouth of Delta Canyon along Big Tujunga Creek at Site 1, Stop 5. *(Darrel Hess photo.)*

becomes Oro Vista Avenue. Notice the concrete wall designed to keep Big Tujunga Creek in its channel during floods. About one-half mile later, turn right onto Foothill Boulevard in the community of Sunland. Continue straight for about one mile (Foothill Boulevard feeds straight into Sunland Boulevard), following the signs to Interstate 210. Take Interstate 210 west.

Stop 6—Hansen Dam Recreation Area

(34°16'19"N, 118°23'06"W): After traveling west on I-210 for about one mile you pass over Big Tujunga Wash. Two miles later you pass over Little Tujunga Wash. Although likely to be nearly dry when you see them, these wide washes are filled with the cobbles and boulders carried down these creeks by floods and debris flows.

About three miles west of Sunland, take the Osborne Street exit off I-210. At the bottom of the offramp, turn left onto Foothill Boulevard. After 0.2 miles, turn left into the Hansen Dam Recreation Area. Head to the far right portion of this parking area (on weekends, parking here can be very limited). Walk a short distance to the southwest away from the parking area for an overlook of Hansen Dam.

Built in 1940 by the Army Corps of Engineers, Hansen Dam is one of the major flood control dams built along the foot of the San Gabriel Mountains, in this case primarily designed to contain flood water coming out of Big Tujunga and Little Tujunga Canyons. In most years most of the area behind the dam is dry (with the exception of tiny Hansen Lake), and this area is used for picnicking and other recreational activities. However, the size of the empty basin behind the dam where you are now gives some sense of the potential volume of floods and debris flows that can come out of the San Gabriel Mountains.

Site 2—Northwestern San Gabriels

Here we explore the northwestern slopes of the San Gabriel Mountains, following the Santa Clara River from Santa Clarita up Soledad Canyon to Acton (Figure FG12-6).

Traveling north on Interstate 5 from the San Fernando Valley, take the Palmdale-Lancaster exit onto eastbound California 14 (the Antelope Valley Freeway). As you pass the first large roadcut on CA-14, notice the steeply tilted layers of sedimen-

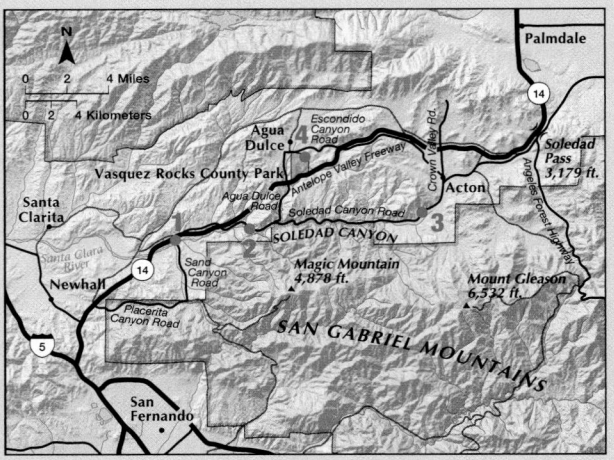

▲ **Figure FG12-6**   Regional map of the northwestern San Gabriel Mountains showing Site 2 field guide stops.

tary rock. The rocks here are 5 to 8-million-year-old marine sandstones, shales, and conglomerates.

About 3.2 miles from I-5, you pass the Placerita Canyon exit. Placerita Canyon is named for the placer (stream deposit) gold that was discovered here by the Spanish in 1842. Notice the many oil wells (some still working; some not) on the hills to the north. The Placerita oil field was exploited beginning in 1948 and remains modestly productive today. In the lower, unurbanized grassy slopes to the south, oak trees can be seen, while dense chaparral covers the steeper high slopes.

About 1.7 miles beyond Placerita Canyon (4.9 miles from I-5) you reach the crest of a rise in the highway. The San Gabriel Fault (which we saw near Site 1, Stop 2) crosses the freeway near here. Notice the roadcuts—the weak, tilted sedimentary rocks are deeply gullied and terracing must be used on the slopes to make them stable enough for building.

From here, you drop down into the wide Santa Clara River Valley. This basin has been filled with several thousand feet of sediment—much of it derived from the northwestern side of the San Gabriel Mountains. In recent years, the basin has been filling with houses—the city of Santa Clarita. As the freeway passes over the Santa Clara River (about 7.4 miles from I-5), notice the wide, cobble-filled bed of the river—although nearly dry much of the time, periodically the Santa Clara River carries enormous volumes of water and sediment.

Stop 1—Sand Canyon Overpass Unconformity (34°25'30"N, 118°25'26"W):

About 8.6 miles from I-5 you come to the Sand Canyon Road freeway exit. Although you can catch

▲ **Figure FG12-7**   The angular unconformity with Pleistocene gravel and cobbles on top of the tilted Mint Canyon Formation sandstone viewed from Site 2, Stop 1. *(Darrel Hess photo.)*

▲ **Figure FG12-8**   View across the dry channel of the Santa Clara River, looking south into the narrow mouth of Soledad Canyon. *(Darrel Hess photo.)*

a quick glimpse of this feature driving past, it is better to exit the freeway and park (there are fast-food restaurants, gas stations, or stores on all corners at the top of the offramp). Take the pedestrian sidewalk out to the center of the west side of the freeway overpass and look at the roadcut on the north side of the highway. Here you see what is called an *angular unconformity*—an abrupt boundary between two different rock units. The gently tilted rocks on the bottom are part of the Mint Canyon Formation, a collection of 6 to 10-million-year-old sandstone and conglomerate beds. After erosion removed a portion of these rocks, much younger **Pleistocene** gravels and cobbles were deposited in nearly level beds on top of them (Figure FG12-7).

Return to eastbound CA-14 and take the Soledad Canyon Road exit (about 2.3 miles from Stop 1; 10.9 miles from I-5). At the bottom of the offramp, turn right onto Soledad Canyon Road. Over the next half-mile or so you are paralleling the freeway heading northeast, passing by several tall roadcuts of Pleistocene sand, gravel, and cobbles—in places quite rusted through **chemical weathering**. The road drops down to the right and crosses the Santa Clara River where you see an extensive quarrying operation. The road then climbs into a narrow portion of Soledad Canyon (Figure FG12-8).

Stop 2—Soledad Canyon Narrows Overlook (34°26′00″N, 118°21′40″W): As soon as you enter the canyon narrows, about 4.4 miles from Stop 1 (13.0 miles from I-5), the road turns left. Stop and park in the first pullout to the right. To your right (south) you can look down into a narrow, slightly sinuous stretch of Soledad Canyon with the Santa Clara River at its bottom and railroad tracks (along which the Metro Link trains travel) partway up the slope. Although the vegetation on the slopes above is typical chaparral, the greater moisture here in the bottom of the canyon supports a mixture of

trees including cottonwoods; you also might glimpse a Fan Palm (*Washingtonia filifera*)—the only type of palm tree native to California—here perhaps planted intentionally.

The roadcut behind you (north of the road) exposes the 1.2-billion-year-old San Gabriel Anorthosite Complex. The white rock is anorthosite, a plutonic rock composed mostly of plagioclase feldspar, here cut through by dark dikes of metamorphic rock (Figure FG12-9). You'll be seeing many exposures of this anorthosite as you continue up Soledad Canyon.

Continue traveling east on Soledad Canyon Road. Shortly after passing through a tunnel, you cross the Santa Clara River again and continue up Soledad Canyon. For the next few miles you'll be traveling up a long, straight stretch of Soledad Canyon, in part following the trace of the Soledad Fault. Although the fault itself didn't directly produce Soledad Canyon, the fault weakened the rock along its trace, making it easier to erode. While chaparral vegetation

▲ **Figure FG12-9**   Roadcut showing light-colored anorthosite cut by dark dikes at Site 2, Stop 2. *(Darrel Hess photo.)*

dominates the higher slopes, along the river bottom you see many trees such as cottonwood and Coast Live Oak.

Most of the roadcuts you're passing are anorthosite although in a few places you can see much younger deposits of sand, gravel, and cobbles. Across the river to the northeast, you can catch glimpses of the reddish sandstones of the Vasquez Formation (which we'll see close up at Stop 4).

About 3.4 miles from Stop 2 you pass a Wildlife Viewing Area on the left—there are restrooms here and a few interpretive signs describing the riparian ecosystem of the Santa Clara River here in its upper reaches. About 7 miles from Stop 2 you pass a high fence on the left (north) side of the road. This is Shambala, a sanctuary for large exotic felines.

About 7.3 miles from Stop 2 (20.3 miles from I-5) you pass over the Santa Clara River once again. You immediately pass through two roadcuts exposing dark, 30-million-year-old basalt—part of the Vasquez Formation. From this point on, you'll see that Soledad Canyon has become much wider than before—probably reflecting the highly fractured, less resistant rock in this area. Looking to the north you can see a few mine shafts and tailings—gold, copper, and titanium were all mined here beginning in the late 1800s.

Stop 3—Upper Soledad Canyon Overlook (34°26'43"N, 118°12'51"W): About 9.6 miles from Stop 2 (22.6 miles from I-5)—shortly after the river makes a turn to the north—you come to the first of several roadcuts exposing a pink-looking, weathered rock. Park in the pullout to the right, just beyond the first roadcut. The rock exposed here (and for the next few miles) is the 220-million-year-old Mount Lowe Granodiorite (the same rock unit you see at Site 1, Stop 2)—in places it is shot through with darker dikes. Notice how easily this rock breaks apart.

Looking across Soledad Canyon to the south, the high peak in the distance is Mount Gleason (6,532 ft.; 1,991 m); it is comprised largely of Lowe Granodiorite. Across the river to the southeast, you see a gently-sloping terrace consisting of alluvial deposits—now dissected by streams.

Continuing up the canyon you reach the small town of Acton about 2 miles from Stop 3 (24.6 miles from I-5). Acton was first established in 1887 by workers of the famous Red Rover gold mine (a few miles north of here); Acton later became a stop along the Southern Pacific Railroad. Acton rests in a valley in the upper reaches of the Santa Clara River drainage. Although the crest of the mountains (and Antelope Valley and the desert beyond) is just a few

miles to the northeast of here, all of the drainage in this area still flows west toward the Santa Clarita Valley—the Santa Clara River itself enters the Pacific Ocean near Ventura, 60 miles away.

At the stop sign in Acton, turn left onto Crown Valley Road. In about 0.4 miles, turn left onto Syracuse Avenue/Escondido Canyon Road. As you drive among the many ranches here, notice that the vegetation has changed significantly from Soledad Canyon—here it is dominated by juniper and yucca. In a few places, you can see mines in the hills to the south.

About 6.3 miles from Acton, you cross over CA-14 and enter the community of Agua Dulce ("sweet water"). Some of the roadcuts you're passing expose consolidated stream cobbles, as well as darker volcanic rock.

Stop 4—Vasquez Rocks County Park

(34°29'10"N, 118°18'52"W): About 2.4 miles after crossing over CA-14 (33.7 miles from I-5), turn left into Vasquez Rocks County Park. Drive for about 0.5 miles along the graded dirt road to the main parking area.

The spectacular tilted reddish rocks here—called *hogbacks*—are part of the Vasquez Formation (Figure FG12-10). These rocks consist of 30-million-year-old sandstone and fanglomerate (consolidated alluvial fan deposits); deeper down, this formation also includes thick layers of dark lava flows (those you passed by earlier). Although it appears that the hogbacks are sticking up out of the ground, they are actually the result of **differential weathering and erosion**—the less resistant rocks that once covered them have since been removed.

▲ **Figure FG12-10** The tilted sandstone hogbacks at Vasquez Rocks County Park at Site 2, Stop 4. *(Darrel Hess photo.)*

The trees here are mostly California Juniper (*Juniperus californica*), along with yucca and Scrub Oak.

The rocks are named for the bandit Tiburcio Vasquez, who is said to have used the rocks and caves here to hide from the law in the mid 1800s. The rocks also formed the backdrop for many movies and television shows—including some episodes of the original Star Trek TV series in the 1960s.

From Vasquez Rocks County Park, turn left (west) back on Escondido Canyon Road, which becomes Agua Dulce Road before it turns sharply left (south) back to CA-14 about 2.2 miles from the Park. From there, you can either head west back toward Los Angeles, or east toward Palmdale (*Field Guide #3—The San Andreas Fault, Site 5—Palmdale*).

Additional Resources

Textbook:
Hess, Darrel. *McKnight's Physical Geography: A Landscape Appreciation*, 11th ed. Upper Saddle River, NJ: Pearson, 2014. Chapters 11, 14, and 15.

Further Reading:
McPhee, John. "Los Angeles Against the Mountains" in *The Control of Nature*. New York: Farrar, Straus and Giroux, 1989.

Rundel, Philip W., and Robert Gustafson. *Introduction to the Plant Life of Southern California*. California Natural History Guide, 85. Berkeley: University of California Press, 2005.

Sharp, Robert P. *A Field Guide to Southern California*, 3rd edition. Dubuque, Iowa: Kendall/Hunt Publishing Company, 1994.

Web Sites:
Angeles National Forest: *http://www.fs.fed.us/r5/angeles/*

Metro Link Transit Information: *http://www.metrolinktrains.com*

Textbook Page References for Key Terms

alluvial fan (*p. 531*)
angle of repose (*p. 456*)
chemical weathering (*p. 454*)
debris flow (*p. 460*)
differential weathering and erosion (*p. 520*)

mediterranean climate (*p. 222*)
mediterranean woodland and shrub (*p. 330*)
metamorphic rocks (*p. 386*)
orographic lifting (*p. 166*)
Pleistocene Epoch (*p. 544*)

plutonic rock (*p. 380*)
reverse fault (*p. 435*)
sedimentary rock (*p. 384*)
strike-slip fault (*p. 435*)
terrane (*p. 417*)

Field Guide #13

The Central Valley

Darrel Hess, City College of San Francisco

Introduction

The Central Valley—or "Great Valley"—is one of the most distinctive topographic features of California. It runs for more than 400 miles (640 km) from north to south down the center of the state, bounded by the Sierra Nevada on the east and the Coast Ranges on the west. It is one of the flattest landscapes in California (see the map of California on page F-2)—there are few places in the entire country where the topography has such comparably low relief over such a great distance.

For more than a century the Central Valley has been one of the most productive agricultural regions in the world, and even though urban sprawl has encroached on many areas of fine farmland in recent decades, the valley remains predominately rural. However, the Central Valley is one of the most intensely human-altered rural landscapes in the state.

This field guide highlights features you can see on a one-day driving trip in the Central Valley north of Sacramento. Locations with similar features—with the exception of the Sutter Buttes volcanoes—can be found throughout the Central Valley.

Location

The Central Valley actually consists of two valleys: the Sacramento Valley in the north and the San Joaquin Valley in the south. The two valleys join where the Sacramento River from the north and the San Joaquin River from the south come together in a network of channels that makes up the inland delta of California. From the delta, the water from both rivers flows into San Francisco Bay.

Several major highways serve the Central Valley. Interstate 80 cuts across the valley west-to-east, from the San Francisco Bay Area to Sacramento, and then up and across the Sierra. The major north-south arteries are Interstate 5, running along the western edge of the valley, and California 99, running up the eastern side of the valley from Bakersfield in the south, to Red Bluff in the north where it joins I-5.

Gasoline, groceries, restaurants and lodging are available in small towns throughout the valley. Although few public campgrounds are located in the valley itself, many are found in the foothills of the Sierra to the east and in the Coast Ranges to the west.

Travel in the Central Valley is pleasant almost any time of year, although summers are hot, and dense fog can make driving hazardous in the winter. If you are interested in viewing the vast flocks of migrating birds that pass through the Central Valley, late fall is the best time to visit.

Background

Geologic History: Long before the present-day *transform plate boundary* associated with the San Andreas Fault system began to operate about 25 million years ago (see *Field Guide #3—The San Andreas Fault*), a **subduction zone** was located along the western margin of North America. For tens of millions of years, the Farallon Plate subducted beneath the North American Plate. This subduction generated magma that eventually cooled to form the granites now uplifted and exposed in the Sierra Nevada (see *Field Guide #4—Sierra Nevada via Tioga Pass*).

It is likely that the ancestral Central Valley began forming at around the same time that the Farallon Plate/North American Plate subduction zone and its associated trench were located in the position of the present-day Coast Ranges (Figure FG13-1). By about 150 million years ago, a slice of ocean floor, known as the *Coast Range Ophiolite*, had been scraped off the subducting plate and added to the edge of the continent. An *ophiolite* is a sequence of oceanic-plate rocks that forms at a *midocean ridge.* From top to bottom, the sequence of rocks in an ophiolite includes: deep-ocean sedimentary rocks such as *chert* or *limestone; pillow basalt* formed when an underwater lava flow is quickly chilled into pillow-shaped blobs; vertical sheeted dikes of *diabase* formed where magma is injected from below into a spreading center; *gabbro* where basaltic magma cools slowly in the magma chamber below the spreading center; and finally, *peridotite* or *serpentinite*—mantle rock from the bottom of the plate.

To the west of the Coast Range Ophiolite are the rocks of the *Franciscan Complex*—the last of the **terranes** added to this part of ancestral North America. The Franciscan Complex consists of a jumble of ophiolite rocks, along with sandstones derived from continental sediments (*graywacke*), and metamorphic rocks (such as *blueschist*), some of which formed in

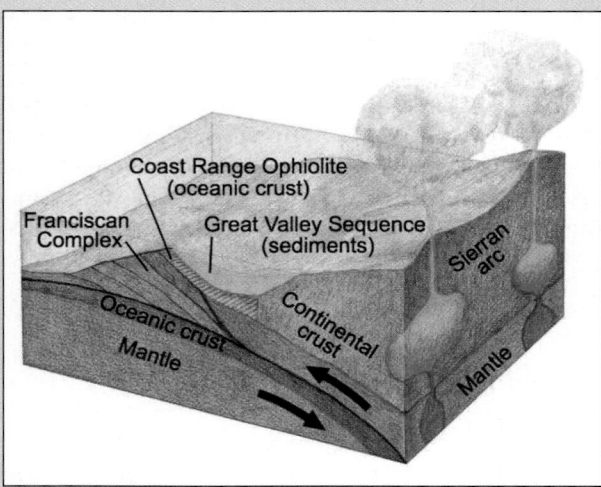

▲ **Figure FG13-1** Origin of the Great Valley Sequence, the Coast Range Ophiolite, and the Franciscan Complex about 150 million years ago. *(From William P. Elder, Geology of the Golden Gate Headlands, in Geology and Natural History of the San Francisco Bay Area: A Field Trip Guidebook. U.S. Geological Survey Bulletin 2188, 2001.)*

the subduction zone before being uplifted into today's Coast Ranges.

At first, the ancient Central Valley was a shallow marine trough—a gently down-warped *forearc basin* east of the Franciscan subduction zone. Today, sandstones and shales derived from sediments deposited in this trough—a collection of rocks called the *Great Valley Sequence*—are exposed in steeply-tilted strata along the eastern and western edges of the Central Valley.

For millions of years, this shallow marine basin slowly filled with sediment from the continent—as much as 6 miles (10 kilometers) thick in places. Organic matter in the sediments was "cooked" over time into petroleum, much of it remaining trapped under structures of impermeable shale in the San Joaquin Valley, where both oil and natural gas are extracted today. Natural gas, but not oil, is found in the Sacramento Valley—perhaps because the temperature of the sediments here was never high enough to form petroleum.

Extensive deposition has left a nearly level valley floor today, gently sloping down from an elevation of about 400 feet (120 m) above sea level in the far northern and southern parts of the valley, to about sea level (or even slightly below sea level) in the delta. The remarkable flatness of the Central Valley is broken in few places. Other than the tilted ridges along the edges of the valley, the only significant break in topography in the Central Valley is Sutter Buttes in the Sacramento Valley (described later in this Field Guide).

Soil type varies within the valley, but large areas consist of highly productive *Alfisols,* including the *San Joaquin Soil*—a sandy *loam* with a cemented hardpan found along the eastern side of the valley (designated the California State Soil). Clay-rich and poorly drained *Vertisols* are found in some areas now under rice cultivation in the Sacramento Valley, and dark, peat-rich *Histosols* are found in the wetlands of the delta.

Weather and Climate: The climate of the Central Valley is predominately **mediterranean** (Csa), with its classic wet winter/dry summer precipitation pattern. Precipitation generally decreases from north to south in the valley. In the north at Redding, the average annual precipitation is about 38 inches (97 cm), in Sacramento, 18 inches (46 cm), and in the far south of the San Joaquin Valley the climate transitions into a steppe climate, and even a desert climate in some locations—Bakersfield receives just 6 inches (15 cm) of rain a year. As would be expected because of its inland location, the Central Valley is generally hotter in summer and colder in winter than coastal areas just a short distance to the west.

Although summer coastal *advection fog* rarely moves farther inland than the delta, the Central Valley is a location of frequent, and often dense, winter *radiation fog* (see *Field Guide #11—Coastal Fog*). Locally called *tule fog*, in the cold clear nights of winter, the lowest parts of the valley fill with dense fog, sometimes for several days at a time. When driving in winter, especially at night, be aware that a slight dip in elevation can bring you down into "pea soup" so thick that safe driving may be impossible.

Plant Communities: Before the changes brought by Europeans in the early 1800s, the Central Valley was the equivalent of California's prairie. The valley was dominated by vast expanses of grassland, along with large areas of freshwater marshes and riparian woodland corridors along the stream channels. Today, 99 percent of the native grassland is gone, along with more than 90 percent of the original freshwater marshes and nearly the same proportion of riparian woodlands.

The transformation of the valley's ecosystems began slowly during the Spanish colonial era, and accelerated with Anglo-American settlement—especially with the California Gold Rush that was underway by 1849. Cattle ranching expanded, as did grain production. The ecological transformation of the valley took place through the intentional tilling of the soil, the planting of crops, and the manipulation of water, as well as through the unintentional introduction of **exotic species** of plants and animals.

The original grasslands of the Central Valley were dominated by perennial *bunchgrasses*—tufts of grass that produce new growth every spring. The most widespread native bunchgrass was probably Purple Needlegrass (*Stipa pulchra*; Figure FG13-2), today found in few locations. Over time, the native bunchgrasses were replaced by exotic grasses brought inadvertently as seeds in the digestive tracts and on the coats of domesticated livestock. Especially during dry years, livestock would overgraze on the bunchgrasses, eating the grass stems down to the ground, killing the root crown. The seeds from exotic annual grasses, on the other hand, could survive these dry years—quickly sprouting when the rains returned, growing in the bare places between the dead bunchgrasses. Thus, decade by decade the bunchgrasses were replaced by exotic annual grasses, such as Ripgut Brome (*Bromus diandrus*) and Wild Oats (*Avena fatua*)—both are now widespread in open fields in the Central Valley, as well as in vacant urban lots (see Figure FG13-2).

Water Diversion: The transformation of the Central Valley's waterscape over the last two centuries has been as complete as the transformation of its plant life. In the late 1800s, three lakes occupied the southern end of the San Joaquin Valley: farthest south were Kern and Buena Vista Lakes, with Tulare Lake just to the north—Tulare Lake had a greater surface area than Lake Tahoe. The Sacramento and San Joaquin Rivers meandered across wide floodplains in the valley. About 5 million acres of wetlands were found on the valley floor—much of it flooded each year by the winter rains and spring runoff from the Sierra. In addition, *vernal pools* were found throughout the valley—small depressions in areas with impermeable hardpans that collected water during winter; after the winter rains, the vernal pools would come to life in the spring with shrimp, insects and plants, only to become dormant again as the pools dried out by the end of summer. Today, the lakes are gone, the rivers are confined by artificial levees, and only remnants of the original wetlands and vernal pools survive in the valley.

The waterscape of the Central Valley—and much of the rest of California as well—was "reengineered" because the location of the water supply does not match the location of the greatest demand: roughly three-quarters of the supply of water is north of Sacramento, whereas three-quarters of the demand for water is south of Sacramento.

Although local irrigation districts played a part in altering the waterscape of the Central Valley, it was large-scale projects that truly transformed the geography of water in California (Figure FG13-3). Four of the six major aqueduct systems in the

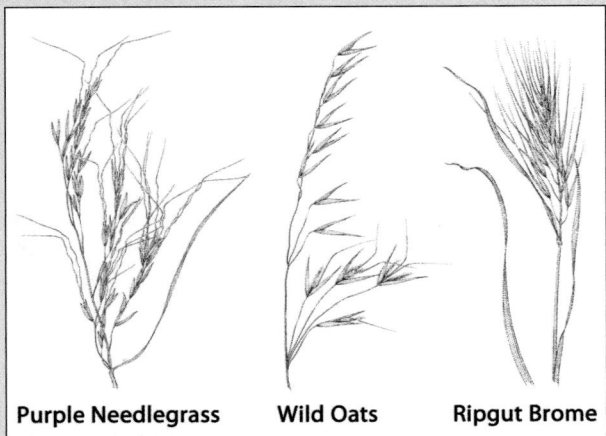

Purple Needlegrass   Wild Oats   Ripgut Brome

▲ **Figure FG13-2** Purple Needlegrass, Ripgut Brome, and Wild Oats. *(Adapted from Paul Henson and Donald J. Usner, The Natural History of Big Sur. California Natural History Guide #57. Berkeley: University of California Press, 1993.)*

▲ **Figure FG13-3** Generalized map of major rivers and water projects in California. *(Adapted from Bureau of Reclamation, U.S. Department of the Interior.)*

state cross the Central Valley: The Hetch Hetchy Aqueduct (described in *Field Guide #4—Sierra Nevada via Tioga Pass*) and the Mokelumne Aqueduct bring water from the Sierra across the valley to Bay Area cities; the State Water Project and the Central Valley Project transfer water from north to south through the Central Valley. The other two major aqueducts are the Los Angeles Aqueduct from Mono Lake and Owens Valley to Los Angeles (described in *Field Guide #6—Mono Lake*), and the Colorado River Aqueduct to southern California.

The State Water Project (SWP) diverts some of the water from the Sacramento River—including Feather River water initially impounded behind 770-foot (235 m) high Oroville Dam (the tallest dam in the United States)—into the 444-mile (715 km) long California Aqueduct that flows south from the delta. The California Aqueduct largely parallels Interstate 5 down the west side of the San Joaquin Valley; at the southern end of the valley it is pumped up 1926 feet (587 m) to cross over the Tehachapi Mountains, eventually to arrive in southern California. Through its branching distribution network, about 70 percent of the SWP deliveries are for urban and industrial use—with nearly half going to the Metropolitan Water District of Southern California.

The federally funded Central Valley Project (CVP) is even larger in scale than the SWP. Initiated in the

1930s primarily for agriculture, the CVP impounds, then diverts, water from several large rivers, including the Sacramento (behind Shasta Dam), the American (behind Folsom Dam), and the Stanislaus (behind New Melones Dam). Some CVP water in the Sacramento Valley is channeled into the Tehama-Colusa Canal; another portion of the water that flows south in the Sacramento River to the delta is pumped into the Delta-Mendota Canal at Tracy (near where the California Aqueduct begins heading south). Water in the CVP is transferred as far south as Bakersfield. The CVP water delivery obligations within the Central Valley are so high that enough water is diverted from the San Joaquin River that a section of the river goes dry almost every year.

Wildlife: The transformation of the Central Valley's natural vegetation and waterscape transformed its animal life as well. The large herds of Mule Deer (*Odocoileus hemionus*), Pronghorn (*Antilocapra americana*) and Tule Elk (*Cervus elaphus nannodes*) that once occupied the valley are gone, although small herds of Tule Elk have been reintroduced into refuges after having their numbers decline to a few dozen individuals by the early 1900s.

In spite of the loss of natural wetlands, the Central Valley—especially the Sacramento Valley— remains one of the most important wintering stops for millions of water birds migrating along the Pacific Flyway each year from as far north as the Arctic. In an attempt to reduce crop loss from feeding migratory birds displaced from diminished natural wetlands—as well as the efforts of hunters to provide habitat for game birds—managed wildlife refuges were established in the valley by the early 1900s. Today, an extensive network of refuges exists throughout the Central Valley. Although little natural wetland area remains in these wildlife refuges, these managed habitats support the great annual bird migrations of the Pacific Flyway.

The list of birds that pass through or winter in the valley's wetland refuges is long. During the peak period of November to March, you are likely to see large numbers of Canada Geese (*Branta canadensis*), Snow Geese (*Chen caerulescens*), Greater White-fronted Geese (*Anser albifrons*), Northern Pintails (*Anas acuta*), Northern Shovelers (*Anas clypeata*; Figure FG13-4)—and dozens of other birds. Even in the dry summer months, you'll see year-round residents, such as Mallards (*Anas platyrhynchos*), as well as Great Blue Herons (*Ardea herodias*; see Figure FG13-4) and Great Egrets (*Ardea alba*) wading through the marshes and nearby rice fields. You're also likely to see Red-tailed Hawks (*Buteo jamaicensis*) and Turkey Vultures (*Cathartes aura*) circling overhead. A good bird identification book will

Figure FG13-4 Great Blue Heron, Mallard, and Northern Shoveler. *(Adapted from Howard L. Cogswell,* Water Birds of California. *California Natural History Guide #40. Berkeley: University of California Press, 1977.)*

Figure FG13-5 Regional map of the Sacramento Valley showing field guide stops.

enhance your enjoyment of the refuges in the Central Valley (see *Additional Resources*).

Seeing the flocks of tens of thousands of water birds arriving in the Central Valley each fall and departing each spring is one of the great sights in all of California.

Site Descriptions

These stops can be visited in any order, but our site description begins at the small Sacramento Valley town of Williams—about 60 miles north of Sacramento on Interstate 5. The stops take you across the Central Valley, from the edge of the Coast Ranges, through wetlands habitat, along the Sacramento River, and finally to the volcanic landscape of Sutter Buttes (Figure FG13-5).

Stop 1 (rolling stop)—Tehama-Colusa Canal (39°07′39″N, 122°16′59″W): Drive west from Williams on California Highway 20. As you travel across the level valley floor toward the Coast Ranges, you pass by fields of rice and other crops such as corn, sunflowers, grapes, and almonds. Notice the natural vegetation on the approaching sharp ridges—the dryer, sunnier south sides have fewer trees than the shaded north sides (see textbook Figure 11-13).

About 8.4 miles from Williams you pass over the Tehama-Colusa Canal, a component of the Central Valley Project. This south-flowing canal brings irrigation water to the western side of the Sacramento Valley, as well as supplies water to some of the valley's wildlife refuges.

Stop 2—Cortina Ridge (39°06′15″N, 122°19′41″W): Continuing west on CA 20, the road winds steeply through manzanita, oak, and pine trees up into a narrow gap in Cortina Ridge, the eastern-most ridge of the Coast Ranges. About 3.1 miles from Stop 1 (11.5 miles from Williams), you come to a pullout on the right (north) side of the road; another paved left pullout is about 0.1 miles farther ahead. The tree-lined stream to the south is Salt Creek. Look at the roadcut opposite the paved pullout. Here you see steeply tilted layers of marine sandstone and shale of the Great Valley Sequence. These rocks dip down to the east, disappearing under the alluvial fill of the Central Valley.

Retrace your route back to Williams along CA 20.

Stop 3—Sacramento National Wildlife Refuge (39°25′46″N, 122°11′14″W): From Williams, travel north on Interstate 5, past rice fields and large rice-processing plants. About 17.3 miles from Williams, take the Road 68 exit (Exit 595). At

▲ **Figure FG13-6** Wetlands and flocks of water birds at the Sacramento National Wildlife Refuge at Stop 3. *(Darrel Hess photo.)*

the bottom of the offramp, turn right and then immediately left (north) onto Old Highway 99W. In 1.6 miles, turn right (east) into the Sacramento National Wildlife Refuge (NWR). Stop and pay the entrance fee, then proceed about 0.2 miles to the Visitor Center parking lot. The Visitor Center is open on weekdays year-round, and seven days a week November through February.

The Sacramento NWR was established in 1937, and is now part of a six-refuge complex in the Sacramento Valley managed by the U.S. Fish and Wildlife Service to provide habitat for migratory birds. The wetlands in the Sacramento NWR and the five other components of the NWR Complex are almost completely artificial—most of the original wetlands in this part of the Central Valley had disappeared by the early twentieth century. The habitat in the Refuge is managed through periodic flooding, mowing, overturning, and burning—all designed to replicate as closely as possible the lost marsh and pond environments for birds and other wildlife (Figure FG13-6).

The best times of year to visit the Sacramento NWR are fall and winter when the ponds and marshes are occupied by migratory birds. Even if your time in the Refuge is short, take the Wetlands Walk Trail that starts near the Visitor Center. This level, 2-mile-long trail takes you past marshes, ponds, vernal pools, grasslands and creek habitat, where in addition to birds, you may see Western Pond Turtles (*Clemmys marmorata*), Black-tailed Jack Rabbits (*Lepus californicus*), California Ground Squirrels (*Spermophilus beecheyi*), as well as the most common wetlands plants such as the Bulrush or "tule" (the tall, green stalks with squishy stems; *Scirpus acutus*), Cattails (with their distinctive fuzzy, brown spikes; *Typha latifolia*), and Black Willow trees (*Salix gooddingii*).

Especially during the late fall and winter months, to see the greatest concentrations of birds, take the 6-mile auto route. This one-way, graded gravel road takes you deep into the Refuge. In order to protect nesting and feeding waterfowl, you must stay in your car throughout most of the route, but there are several designated places where you may get out and view wildlife, including a large, raised viewing platform with spotting scopes located half-way around the loop (39°25'20"N, 122°08'51"W).

From the Sacramento National Wildlife Refuge turn right (north) back onto Old Highway 99W. After 2.4 miles turn right (east) onto Road 60, which eventually merges into Road 61. For the next 9.9 miles you drive past rice fields—this is one of the main rice-growing regions in the state. In the distance to the east, you'll soon see a dense line of trees running north to south—these trees mark the course of the Sacramento River.

Stop 4 (rolling stop)—Packer Lake

(39°26'36"N, 122°00'51"W): Turn right (south) off of Road 61 onto California 45. This road parallels the west bank of the Sacramento River all of the way to the town of Colusa—part of the way on top of one of the artificial levees that now confines the river.

After 1.0 miles, you pass Packer Lake on your left—an **oxbow lake** remaining in an abandoned *cut-off meander* of the Sacramento River (see textbook Figure 16-39). (If you would like to stop to get a closer look at the lake, turn right at Road 64 and park at the foot of the levee.) Notice that vegetation is encroaching over the water from the shores of this gently curved lake (Figure FG13-7). Over time, the lake will silt up with alluvium and disappear, leaving only a *meander scar*.

▲ **Figure FG13-7** Packer Lake is an oxbow lake along the Sacramento River, seen here at Stop 4. *(Darrel Hess photo.)*

Figure FG13-8   The Sacramento River from Stop 6 in Colusa. *(Darrel Hess photo.)*

Stop 5 (rolling stop)—Sacramento River at Princeton (39°25′03″N, 122°00′39″W):

Continue south on CA 45. About 1.8 miles from Packer Lake, the Sacramento River itself comes into view. Here the outside bank of a meander butts up against the artificial levee. On the opposite side of the river, you can see a *point bar* of alluvium extending away from the inside bank of the meander bend (see textbook Figure 16-29).

About 0.4 miles farther south, you can see the rusting barge of the abandoned Princeton Ferry that once shuttled cars across the river here. After passing through the small town of Princeton, the road drops down off the levee and for the next few miles you're crossing the nearly level, old **floodplain** of the Sacramento River.

Stop 6—Sacramento River at Colusa (39°12′54″N, 122°00′00″W):

About 14 miles south of Stop 5 (about 17 miles after turning onto CA 45) the road turns left (east) as you enter the town of Colusa. In about one mile, the road comes to a "T" intersection; turn left onto Bridge Street and cross over the river. Immediately after crossing the river, turn right onto Butte Slough Road. Pull off and park in the dirt pullout, and walk back up on the sidewalk on the bridge crossing the Sacramento River.

From this location you have an excellent view of the *artificial levees* that now bound the Sacramento River (Figure FG13-8). Notice how steep and high the levees are. These artificial levees were built on top of the river's original **natural levees**—which were much lower, and gradually sloped away from the river banks (see textbook Figure 16-40).

The artificial levees are designed to keep the river from flooding; they also effectively prevent the river from changing course naturally. Dams of the Central Valley Project and California Water Project control the amount of water entering the Sacramento River—reducing its potential discharge during peak periods of winter and spring runoff, while increasing its discharge during the dry summer by releasing water from reservoirs.

The dams and artificial levees are somewhat of a mixed blessing. They help prevent floods that once regularly inundated the Central Valley—because of urbanization in the valley, such floods today would cause a great deal of property damage. However, it was the annual flooding that replenished the Central Valley's fertile soils—that source of fertile alluvium is now cutoff from the valley.

Continue southeast along Butte Slough Road. This narrow, windy road follows the artificial levee along the east bank of the Sacramento River (drive carefully!). Notice that the level of the Sacramento River is just about the same as the farmland to the east—should this artificial levee fail, enormous areas will be flooded.

In the distance to the east you'll see the jagged peaks of Sutter Buttes—our next stop. After following Butte Slough Road for 6.0 miles, the road comes to a stop sign where you turn left (east) onto Pass Road. In about one mile, the road rises up over a levee marking the western side of the Sutter Bypass—a flood control channel that empties into the Sacramento River a few miles to the south of here. Notice the old abandoned Mawson Bridge roadway crossing the bypass just to the south of you.

Stop 7—Sutter Buttes (39°11′16″N, 121°51′47″W):

About 3.1 miles after turning on to Pass Road, you drive through the intersection for southbound West Butte Road. Continue on Pass Road for another 0.8 miles or so and pull off the side of the road. Here you have a great view of the Sutter Buttes, an out-of-place volcano complex that rises more than 2,000 feet above the valley floor (Figure FG13-9). Although some of the land here is designated to become part of the State Park system, there is no public access into Sutter Buttes and almost all

Figure FG13-9   Sutter Buttes from Stop 7 along Pass Road. The high peak is South Butte. *(Darrel Hess photo.)*

of the land remains in private ownership—do not trespass without permission. However, the view of Sutter Buttes from here at Stop 7 is by far the best from any public road.

The formation and structure of Sutter Buttes is complex. Thought by some (but not all) geologists to represent the southernmost volcano of the Cascade Range, Sutter Buttes is a volcanic dome complex that formed about 1.5 million years ago when a series of andesite and rhyolite **lava domes** (see textbook Figure 14-37) pushed up through layers of older sedimentary rocks on the valley floor. Surrounding the resistant spires of the domes that make up the core of the volcano—such as South Butte, the high peak with the radio towers you see to the northeast—is a ring of upturned sedimentary rocks seen at the foot of the buttes just north of you. After the central domes formed, a series of explosive eruptions ejected volumes of pyroclas-

tic material, today seen in the gently sloping low ring surrounding the buttes (behind you to the south)—evidently this material was deposited by both *pyroclastic flows* and *lahars*.

Notice also the many gas wells in the area. Natural gas was discovered here in the 1860s, and commercially exploited beginning in the 1930s.

Retrace your route west on Pass Road 0.8 miles and turn left (south) on West Butte Road. To your left (northeast) are the gentle, boulder-covered slopes of volcanic deposits of Sutter Buttes; to your right, you see the wide overflow area of the Sutter Bypass—another wildlife refuge. After 4.6 miles turn right (west) onto CA 20. In 12 miles you reach Colusa again, and in another 10 miles you're back at I-5 and Williams. You pass by the Colusa NWR along the way, another great spot to observe birds.

Additional Resources

Textbook:

Hess, Darrel. *McKnight's Physical Geography: A Landscape Appreciation*, 11th ed. Upper Saddle River, NJ: Pearson, 2014. Chapters 11, 14, and 16.

Further Reading:

Carle, David. *Introduction to Water in California.* California Natural History Guide, 76. Berkeley: University of California Press, 2004.

Dunn, Jon L., and Jonathan Alderfer, eds. *National Geographic Field Guide to the Birds of Western*

North America. Washington D.C.: National Geographic, 2008.

McPhee, John. *Assembling California.* New York: Farrar, Straus and Giroux, 1993.

Web Sites:

Sacramento National Wildlife Refuge: *http://www.fws.gov/sacramentovalleyrefuges/*

Sutter Buttes Regional Land Trust: *http://www.middlemountain.org*

Textbook Page References for Key Terms

exotic species *(p. 339)*	mediterranean climate *(p.222)*	subduction zone *(p. 410)*
floodplain *(p. 486)*	natural levee *(p. 488)*	terrane *(p. 417)*
lava dome (plug dome) *(p. 424)*	oxbow lake *(p. 488)*	

World – Political

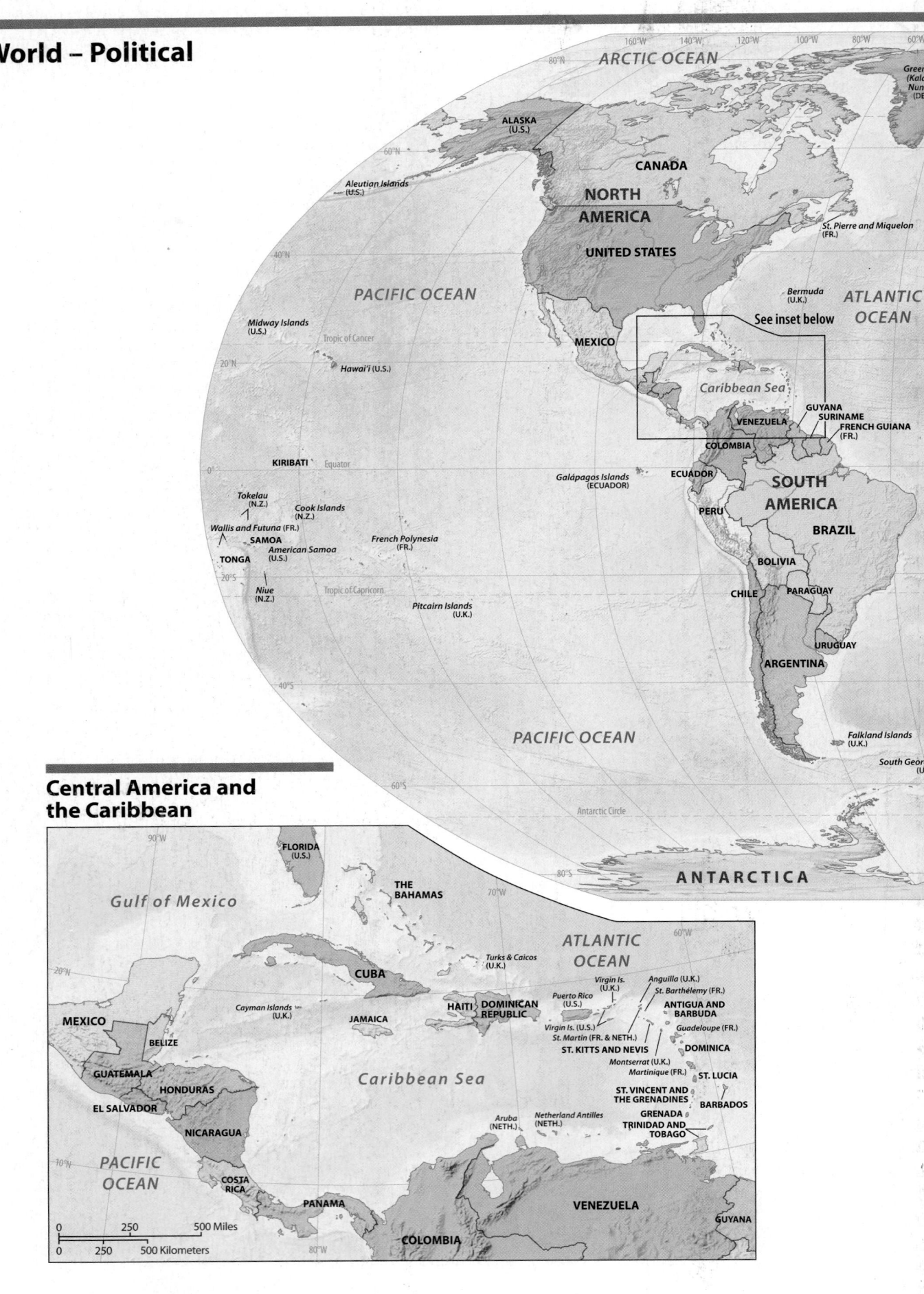

ARCTIC OCEAN

Greenland
(Kalaallit
Nunaat)
(DEN.)

ALASKA
(U.S.)

CANADA

NORTH
AMERICA

Aleutian Islands
(U.S.)

UNITED STATES

St. Pierre and Miquelon
(FR.)

PACIFIC OCEAN

Bermuda
(U.K.)

ATLANTIC
OCEAN

See inset below

Midway Islands
(U.S.)

Tropic of Cancer

MEXICO

Hawai'i (U.S.)

Caribbean Sea

GUYANA
SURINAME
FRENCH GUIANA
(FR.)

VENEZUELA

COLOMBIA

KIRIBATI

Equator

Galápagos Islands
(ECUADOR)

ECUADOR

SOUTH
AMERICA

Tokelau
(N.Z.)

Cook Islands
(N.Z.)

PERU

BRAZIL

Wallis and Futuna (FR.)

SAMOA

French Polynesia
(FR.)

TONGA

American Samoa
(U.S.)

BOLIVIA

Niue
(N.Z.)

Tropic of Capricorn

CHILE

PARAGUAY

Pitcairn Islands
(U.K.)

URUGUAY

ARGENTINA

PACIFIC OCEAN

Falkland Islands
(U.K.)

South Georgia
(U.K.)

Antarctic Circle

ANTARCTICA

Central America and the Caribbean

FLORIDA
(U.S.)

Gulf of Mexico

THE
BAHAMAS

ATLANTIC
OCEAN

Turks & Caicos
(U.K.)

CUBA

Virgin Is.
(U.K.)

Anguilla (U.K.)
St. Barthélemy (FR.)

MEXICO

Cayman Islands
(U.K.)

JAMAICA

HAITI

DOMINICAN
REPUBLIC

Puerto Rico
(U.S.)

ANTIGUA AND
BARBUDA

Virgin Is. (U.S.)
St. Martin (FR. & NETH.)

Guadeloupe (FR.)

BELIZE

ST. KITTS AND NEVIS

DOMINICA

GUATEMALA

Montserrat (U.K.)
Martinique (FR.)

ST. LUCIA

HONDURAS

Caribbean Sea

EL SALVADOR

ST. VINCENT AND
THE GRENADINES

BARBADOS

NICARAGUA

Aruba
(NETH.)

Netherland Antilles
(NETH.)

GRENADA

TRINIDAD AND
TOBAGO

PACIFIC
OCEAN

COSTA
RICA

PANAMA

VENEZUELA

GUYANA

COLOMBIA

0	250	500 Miles
0	250	500 Kilometers